The Longman Anthology
of British Literature

Compact Edition

David Damrosch

General Editor

VOLUME B

THE ROMANTICS AND
THEIR CONTEMPORARIES
Susan Wolfson *and* Peter Manning

THE VICTORIAN AGE
Heather Henderson *and* William Sharpe

THE TWENTIETH CENTURY
Kevin Dettmar *and* Jennifer Wicke

LONGMAN

An imprint of Addison Wesley Longman, Inc.

New York • Reading, Massachusetts • Menlo Park, California • Harlow, England
Don Mills, Ontario • Sydney • Mexico City • Madrid • Amsterdam

Editorial Director: *Richard Wohl*
Development Editor: *Mark Getlein*
Senior Marketing Manager: *Melanie Goulet*
Supplements Editor: *Donna Campion*
Senior Production Manager: *Valerie Zaborski*
Project Coordination: *Dora Rizzuto*
Electronic Page Makeup: *Sarah Johnson* and *Heather A. Peres*
Senior Cover Design Manager: *Nancy Danahy*
Cover Designer: *Kay Petronio*
On the Cover: *George Gordon Byron, 6th Baron Byron* (1813) by Thomas Phillips, 1770–1845,
   National Portrait Gallery, London
Photo Researcher: *Julie Tesser*
Publishing Services Manager: *Al Dorsey*
Senior Print Buyer: *Hugh Crawford*
Printer and Binder: *World Color Book Services*
Cover Printer: *The Lehigh Press, Inc.*

For permission to use copyrighted material, grateful acknowledgment is made to the copyright holders on pages 2645–2647, which are hereby made part of this copyright page.

Library of Congress Cataloging-in-Publication Data

The Longman anthology of British literature: compact edition / David Damrosch, general
   editor.
        p.   cm.
   Includes bibliographical references and indexes.
   Contents: v. A. The Middle Ages / Christopher Baswell and Anne Howland
Schotter. The early modern period / Constance Jordan and Clare
Carroll. The Restoration and the 18th century / Stuart Sherman —
v. B. The romantics and their contemporaries / Susan Wolfson and Peter
Manning. The Victorian age / Heather Henderson and William Sharpe.
The twentieth century / Kevin Dettmar and Jennifer Wicke.
   1. English literature.   2. Great Britain—Literary collections.
I. Damrosch, David.

ISBN 0-321-07670-2 (Single Volume Edition)
ISBN 0-321-07672-9 (Volume A)
ISBN 0-321-07673-7 (Volume B)

2 3 4 5 6 7 8 9 0–QWT–0201

CONTENTS

The Victorian Age   1783

The Twentieth Century   2165

PREFACE

This is an exciting time to be reading British literature. Literary studies are experiencing a time of transformation, involving lively debate about the nature of literature itself, its relations to the wider culture, and the best ways to read and understand it. These questions have been sharpened by the "culture wars" of recent years, in which traditionalists have debated advocates of fundamental reform, close readers have come up against cultural theorists who may seem more interested in politics than in aesthetic questions, and lovers of canonical texts have found themselves sharing the stage with multiculturalists who typically focus on ethnic and minority literatures, usually contemporary and often popular in nature, rather than on earlier and more elite literary productions.

The goal of this anthology is to present the wealth of British literature, old and new, classic and newly current, in ways that will respond creatively to these debates. We have constructed this anthology in the firm belief that it is important to attend both to aesthetic and to cultural questions as we study literature, and to continue to read the great classics even as we discover or rediscover new or neglected works. Admittedly, it is difficult to do all this at once, especially within the pages of a single anthology or the time constraints of a survey course. To work toward these goals, it has been necessary to rethink the very form of an anthology. This preface can serve as a kind of road map to the many pages that follow.

A NEW LITERARY GEOGRAPHY

Let us begin by defining our basic terms: What is "British" literature? What is literature itself? And just what is the function of an anthology at the present time? The term "British" can mean many things, some of them contradictory, some of them even offensive to people on whom the name has been imposed. If the term has no ultimate essence, it does have a history. The first British were Celtic people who inhabited the British Isles and the northern coast of France (still called Brittany), before various Germanic tribes of Angles and Saxons moved onto the islands in the fifth and sixth centuries. Gradually the Angles and Saxons amalgamated into the Anglo-Saxon culture that became dominant in the southern and eastern regions of Britain and then spread outward; the old British people were pushed west, toward what became known as Cornwall, Wales, and Ireland, which remained independent kingdoms for centuries, as did Celtic Scotland to the north. By an ironic twist of linguistic fate, the Anglo-Saxons began to appropriate the term British from the Britons they had displaced, and they took as a national hero the legendary Welsh King Arthur. By the seventeenth century, English monarchs had extended their sway over Wales, Ireland, and Scotland, and they began to refer to their holdings as "Great Britain." Today, Great Britain includes England, Wales, Scotland, and Northern Ireland, but does not include the Republic of Ireland, which has been independent from England since 1922.

This anthology uses "British" in a broad sense, as a geographical term encompassing the whole of the British Isles. For all its fraught history, it seems a more satisfactory term than to speak simply of "English" literature, for two reasons. First: most speakers of English live in countries that are not the focus of this anthology; second, while the English language and its literature have long been dominant in the British Isles, other cultures in the region have always used other languages and have produced great literature in these languages. Important works by Irish, Welsh, and Scots writers appear regularly in the body of this anthology, some of them written directly in their languages and presented here in translation, others written in an English inflected by the rhythms, habits of thought, and modes of expression characteristic of these other languages and the people who use them. Important works, moreover, have often been written in the British Isles by recent arrivals, from Marie de France in the twelfth century to T. S. Eliot and Salman Rushdie in the twentieth; in a very real sense, their writings too are part of British literary production.

We use the term "literature" itself in a similarly capacious sense, to refer to a range of artistically shaped works written in a charged language, appealing to the imagination at least as much as to discursive reasoning. It is only relatively recently that creative writers have been able to make a living composing poems, plays, and novels purely "for art's sake," and only in the past hundred years or so have "belles lettres" or works of high literary art been thought of as sharply separate from other sorts of writing that the same authors would regularly produce. Sometimes, Romantic poets wrote sonnets to explore the deepest mysteries of individual perception and memory; at other times, they wrote sonnets the way a person might now write an Op-Ed piece, and such a sonnet would be published and read along with parliamentary debates and letters to the editor on the most pressing contemporary issues.

Great literature is double in nature: it is deeply rooted in its cultural moment, and yet it transcends this moment as well, speaking to new readers in distant times and places, long after the immediate circumstances of its production have been forgotten. The challenge today is to restore our awareness of cultural contexts without trapping our texts within them. Great writers create imaginative worlds that have their own compelling internal logic, built around the stories they tell using formal patterns of genre, literary reference, imagery, and style. At the same time, as Virginia Woolf says in A Room of One's Own, the gossamer threads of the artist's web are joined to reality "with bands of steel." To understand where a writer is taking us imaginatively, it is helpful to know where we are supposed to be starting from in reality: any writer assumes a common body of current knowledge, which this anthology attempts to fill in by means of detailed period introductions, full introductions to the individual authors, and notes and glosses to each text. Many of the greatest works of literature, moreover, have been written in response to the most sharply contested issues of the authors' own times. This anthology presents and groups selections in such a way as to suggest the literary and cultural contexts in which, and for which, they were created.

WOMEN'S WRITING, AND MEN'S

Literary culture has always involved an interplay between central and marginal regions, groups, and individuals. At a given time, some will seem dominant; in retrospect, some will remain so and others will be eclipsed, for a time or permanently, while formerly neglected writers may achieve a new currency. A major emphasis in literary study in recent years has been the recovery of writing by a range of women writers, some of them little read until recently, others major figures in their time and now again fascinating to read. Attending to the voices of such compelling writers as Katherine Philips, Aphra Behn, Mary Wollstonecraft, and Elizabeth Bowen often involves a shift in our understanding of the literary landscape, giving a new and lively perspective on much-read works. On a larger scale, the first third of the nineteenth century can be defined more broadly than as a "Romantic Age" dominated by six male poets; looking closely at women's writing as well as men's, and at prose writing as well as poetry, we can deepen our understanding of the period as a whole—including the specific achievements of Blake, William Wordsworth, Coleridge, Keats, Percy Shelley, and Byron, all of whom continue to have a major presence in these pages as most of them did during the nineteenth century.

HISTORICAL PERIODS IN PERSPECTIVE

Overall, we have sought to give a varied presentation of the major periods of literary history, as customarily construed by scholars today: the Middle Ages (punctuated by the Norman Conquest in 1066); the early modern period or Renaissance; the Restoration and the eighteenth century; the era of the Romantics and their contemporaries; the Victorian age; and the twentieth century. These names mix chronology, politics, and literary movements: each period is of course a mixture of all of these elements and many others. Further, the boundaries of all these periods are fluid. Milton, for instance, should be thought of in the context of Restoration politics as well as of early modern humanism. In general, one of the great pleasures of a survey of centuries of British literary production is the opportunity to see the ways texts speak to one another both across periods and within them, and indeed several layers of time may coexist within a single era: many writers consciously or unconsciously hearken back to earlier values (there were medievalists in the nineteenth century), while other writers cast "shadows of futurity" before them, in Percy Shelley's phrase.

Within periods, we have sought a variety of means to suggest the many linkages that make up a rich literary culture, which is something more than a sequence of individual writers all producing their separate bodies of work. In this anthology, each period includes several groupings called "Perspectives," with texts that address an important literary or social issue of the time. These Perspective sections typically illuminate underlying issues in a variety of the major works of their time, as with a section on Arthurian myth that relates broadly to Marie de France, to *Gawain and the Green Knight*, and to Malory's *Morte Darthur*. Most of the writers included in Perspective sections are important period figures, less well known today, who might be neglected if they were listed on their own with just a few pages each; grouping them together should be useful pedagogically as well as intellectually. Perspective sections may also include writing by a major author whose primary listing appears elsewhere in the period (Wordsworth on slavery, Dickens on industry), so as to give a rounded presentation of the issues in ways that can inform the reading of those authors in their individual sections.

WORKS IN CONTEXT

Periodically throughout the anthology we also present major works "In Context," to show the terms of a specific debate to which an author is responding. Thus Sir Philip Sidney's great *Apology for Poetry* is accompanied by a context section to show the controversy that was raging at the time concerning the nature and value of poetry. Additionally, we include "Companion Readings" to present specific prior texts to which a work is responding: when Sir Thomas Wyatt creates a beautiful poem, *The Long Love, That in My Thought Doth Harbor*, by making a free translation of a Petrarch sonnet, we include Petrarch's original (and a more literal translation) as a companion reading. For Conrad's *Heart of Darkness*, companion texts include Conrad's diary of the Congo journey on which he based his novella, and a bizarre lecture by Sir Henry Morton Stanley, the explorer-adventurer whose travel writings Conrad parodies.

ILLUSTRATING VISUAL CULTURE

Literature has always been a product of cultures that are visual as well as verbal. We include many illustrations in the body of the anthology, presenting artistic and cultural images that figured importantly for literary creation. Sometimes, a poem refers to a specific painting, or more generally emulates qualities of a school of visual art. At other times, photographs, advertisements, or political cartoons can set the stage for literary works. In some cases, visual and literary creation have merged, as in Hogarth's series *A Rake's Progress*, or Blake's engravings of his *Songs of Innocence and Experience*.

Our cover illustration gives a good example of a striking and culturally rich image: a portrait of *George Gordon Byron, 6th Baron Byron* (1813) by the fashionable painter Thomas Phillips. While most portraits of male poets favor a pensive, even otherworldly figure, Byron was a creature of the world, with a high sense of theatrical flair. By 1814, still in his mid-twenties, he was already a celebrity, thanks in part to his exotic "Eastern Tales." One of these, *The Corsair*, had just sold ten thousand copies on the day it was published. Byron poured his own personality into the heros of these tales, who were becoming known generically as "the Byronic hero"—at once aloof, transgressive, and passionate—and the writer's own portraits had begun to trade on the image of the hero named after him. Byron acquired the costume he wears in this portrait while visiting Albania in 1809 as guest of the Ali Pacha, the most powerful ruler in the region, "a remorseless tyrant, guilty of the most horrible cruelties," Byron reported in a letter to his mother, adding that the Pacha "said he was certain I was a man of birth, because I had small ears, curling hair, and little white hands, and expressed himself pleased with my appearance and garb." Charmed in turn by the gold-embroidered outfits he saw in Albania—"the only expensive articles in this country"—Byron bought several for fifty guineas each, at that time an entire year's subsistence for a modest household. Well aware of the appeal of this portrait, Byron's publisher Murray had it engraved and sold for readers to put in their copies of the works.

AIDS TO UNDERSTANDING

We have tried to contextualize our selections in a suggestive rather than an exhaustive way, wishing to enhance rather than overwhelm the experience of reading the texts themselves. Our introductions to periods and authors are intended to open up ways of reading rather than dictating a particular interpretation, and the suggestions presented here should always be seen as points of departure rather than definitive pronouncements. We have striven for clarity and ease of use in our editorial matter. Thus, when difficult or archaic words need defining in poems, we use glosses in the margins, in all periods, so as to disrupt the reader's eye as little as possible; footnotes are intended to be concise and informative, rather than massive or interpretive. Spelling and punctuation are modernized through the eighteenth century, except when older forms are important for meter or rhyme, and with general exceptions for certain major writers, like Chaucer and Spenser, whose specific usages are crucial to their understanding. Important literary and social terms are defined when they are used. For further reading, carefully selected bibliographies for each period and for each author can be found at the end of the volume.

VARIETIES OF LITERARY EXPERIENCE

Above all, we have striven to give as full a presentation as possible within the boundaries of a compact edition to the varieties of great literature produced over the centuries in the British Isles, by women as well as by men, in outlying regions as well as in the metropolitan center of London, and in prose, drama, and verse alike. In making our selections for this compact edition from the six thousand pages of the full *Longman Anthology*, we have chosen the best-loved and most often taught works of the classic major authors, together with a range of the most compelling newly-recovered writing we know. We have striven to show the wealth and the variety of the literary culture of the British Isles over the centuries, from medieval works like *Beowulf* and the lyrics of the trenchantly witty Dafydd ap Gwilym to the powerful contemporary voices of Philip Larkin, Seamus Heaney, Nuala Ní Dhomhnaill, and Derek Walcott—himself a product of colonial British education, heir of Shakespeare and James Joyce, who closes the anthology with poems about Englishness abroad and foreignness in Britain.

As topical as these contemporary writers are, we hope that this anthology will show that the great works of earlier centuries can also speak to us compellingly today, their value only increased by the resistance they offer to our views of ourselves and our world. To read and reread the full sweep of this literature is to be struck anew by the degree to which the most radically new works are rooted in centuries of prior innovation. Even this preface can close in no better way than by quoting the words written eighteen hundred years ago by Apuleius—both a consummate artist and a kind of anthologist of extraordinary tales—when he concluded the prologue to his masterpiece *The Golden Ass*: Attend, reader, and pleasure is yours.

David Damrosch

ACKNOWLEDGMENTS

In preparing this new version of our anthology, the editors have benefited enormously from advice and support of many kinds. Our first debt is to Rich Wohl, Editorial Director at Longman's College Division, who has given the project unfailing and indeed ebullient support, seconded by that of Roth Wilkofsky, the head of the division. Our editors Janice Wiggins Clarke, at the start of the process, and Laura McKenna more recently, have helped us refine our work, and as with the original anthology, we benefited greatly from the advice, and the art-historical knowledge, of our developmental editor, Mark Getlein. Melanie Goulet and her associates have been working creatively and effectively to bring both versions of the anthology to our audience.

In producing the volume, Stephanie Argeros-Magean oversaw copyediting with her characteristic lucidity and good judgment. Val Zaborski, Dora Rizzuto, and their associates handled thousands of pages of marked-up text, and a very challenging production schedule, with sunny good humor and exceptional care. Robert Ravas and his associates cleared our hundreds of permissions requests, and Julie Tesser secured our illustrations.

The present volume continues to bear the mark of the excellent advice we received from many colleagues as we prepared the full anthology from which this edition is drawn. In deciding which works to select for this compact edition, we were guided by the thoughtful advice of colleagues both in the United States and in Canada, who often took time to give us very detailed responses to our draft table of contents. We owe hearty thanks to Rosemary Allen (Georgetown College), Matthew C. Brennen (Indiana State University), Gregory Chaplin (University of Texas, Austin), Robert Christopher (Ramapo University), Michael Delahoyde (Washington State University), Laura Fascik (Moorhead State University), Joan Haahr (Yeshiva University), Tony Harrison (North Carolina State University), Nelson Hilton (University of Georgia, Athens), Glenn Hopp (Howard Payne University), Stewart Justman (University of Montana, Missoula), Maurine Magliocco (Western Illinois University), Jean LeDre Metcalfe (Wilfrid Laurier University), Doris Miller (McMurry University), Lanier R. Parks, Jr. (Radford University), Elizabeth Sauer (Brock University), Daniel R. Schwarz (Cornell University), Richard C. Taylor (East Carolina University), Rob Watson (Grand Valley State University), and Carlson Yost (Shawnee State University).

Other colleages brought our developing book into the classroom, teaching from portions of the work-in-progress while it was still in page proof. Our thanks for classroom testing to Lisa Abney (Northwestern State University), Charles Lynn Batten (University of California, Los Angeles), Brenda Riffe Brown (College of the Mainland, Texas), John Brugaletta (California State University, Fullerton), Dan Butcher (Southeastern Louisiana University), Lynn Byrd (Southern University at New Orleans), David Cowles (Brigham Young University), Sheila Drain (John Carroll University), Lawrence Frank (University of Oklahoma), Leigh Garrison (Virginia Polytechnic Institute), David Griffin (New York University), Rita Harkness (Virginia Commonwealth University), Linda Kissler (Westmoreland County Community College, Pennsylvania), Brenda Lewis (Motlow State Community College, Tennessee), Paul Lizotte (River College), Wayne Luckman (Green River Community College, Washington), Arnold Markely (Pennsylvania State University, Delaware County), James McKusick (University of Maryland, Baltimore), Eva McManus (Ohio Northern University), Manuel Moyrao (Old Dominion University), Kate Palguta (Shawnee State University, Ohio), Paul Puccio (University of Central Florida), Sarah Polito (Cape Cod Community College), Meredith Poole (Virginia Western Community College), Tracy Seeley (University of San Francisco), Clare Simmons (Ohio State University), and Paul Yoder (University of Arkansas, Little Rock).

As if all this help weren't enough, the editors also drew directly on friends and colleagues in many ways, for advice, for information, sometimes for outright contributions to headnotes and footnotes, even (in a pinch) for aid in proofreading. In particular, we wish to thank James Cain, Michael Coyle, Pat Denison, Andrew Fleck, Laurie Glover, Lisa Gordis, Joy Hayton, Jean Howard, David Kastan, Stanislas Kemper, Ron Levao, Carol Levin, David Lipscomb, Denise MacNeil, Jackie Maslowski, Richard Matlak, Anne Mellor, James McKusick, Michael North, David Paroissien, Stephen M. Parrish, Peter Platt, Cary Plotkin, Gina Renee, Alan Richardson, Esther Schor, Catherine Siemann, Glenn Simshaw, David Tresilian, Shasta Turner, Nicholas Watson, Michael Winckleman, and Gillen Wood for all their guidance and assistance.

The pages on the Restoration and the eighteenth century are the work of many collaborators, diligent and generous. Michael F. Suarez, S. J. (Campion Hall, Oxford) edited the Swift and Pope sections; Steven N. Zwicker (Washington University) co-wrote the period introduction and the headnotes for the Dryden section. Bruce Redford (Boston University) crafted the footnotes for Dryden, Johnson, and Boswell. Susan Brown, Christine Coch, and Paige Reynolds helped with texts, footnotes, and other matters throughout; William Pritchard gathered texts, wrote notes, and prepared bibliography. To all, abiding thanks.

It has been a pleasure to work with all of these colleagues, and this is, after all, only the beginning of what we hope will be a long-term collaboration with those who use this anthology, as teachers, students, and general readers. This book exists for its readers, whose reactions and suggestions we warmly welcome, as these will in turn reshape this book for later users in the years to come.

Thomas Phillips. *Lord Byron,* 1814.

The Romantics and Their Contemporaries

LITERATURE AND THE AGE: "NOUGHT WAS LASTING"

Reviewing Mary Shelley's *Frankenstein* in 1818, *The Edinburgh Magazine* remarked that "never was a wilder story imagined." Even so, the reviewer went on, "like most of the fictions of this age, it has an air of reality attached to it, by being connected with the favourite projects and passions of the times. The real events of the world have, in our day, too, been of so wondrous and gigantic a kind,—the shiftings of the scenes in our stupendous drama have been so rapid and various, that Shakespeare himself, in his wildest flights, has been completely distanced by the eccentricities of actual existence." The turbulent world and whirl of real events shaped the years of the "Romantic" period. It was marked on the one end by the revolutions in America and France, and on the other, by the reform of Parliament to extend the vote and reconfigure representation, by the emergence of the modern industrial state, and by the abolition of slavery in British colonies. In the early 1820s, Lord Byron protested:

> Talk not of seventy years as age; in seven
>   I have seen more changes, down from monarchs to
> The humblest individual under heaven,
>   Than might suffice a moderate century through.
> I knew that nought was lasting, but now even
>   Change grows too changeable without being new:
> Nought's permanent among the human race . . . (*Don Juan* 11.81)

As the nod toward monarchs indicates, the French Revolution of the 1790s cast a long shadow across British consciousness. Its events had announced a radical break in historical continuity—a sudden, cataclysmic overthrow of a monarchy surrounded by high culture, and the eruption of new social order that no one knew how to "read." New, challenging, and often contradictory energies reverberated across Britain and Europe. Enthusiasts heralded the fall of an oppressive aristocracy and the birth of democratic and egalitarian ideals, a new era, shaped by "the rights of man" rather than the entailments of wealth and privilege, while skeptics and reactionaries rued the end of chivalry, lamented the erosion of order, and foresaw the decline of civilization.

Yet whatever side one took, the upheaval bore a stark realization: politically, socially, economically, and philosophically, an irrevocable tide of new ideas had risen against seemingly entrenched structures. "It was now known," as historian E. J. Hobsbawm puts it, "that revolution in a single country could be a European phenomenon, that its doctrines could spread across the frontiers. . . . It was now known that social revolution was possible, that nations existed as something independent of states, peoples as something independent of their rulers, and even that the poor existed as something independent of the ruling classes." Other challenges appeared, framed in the rhetoric of the Revolution debate and animated by appeals to moral law and natural principle. There were arguments for and against the rights of women (not for the vote, but for better principles of education and improved social attitudes); debates over the abolition of Britain's slave trade and of slavery in its colonies (a moral blight but also a source of enormous and widespread commercial profit); movements for social and political remedies for the poor (versus the traditional spiritual consolations); and a newly emergent class consciousness among discontented workers in Britain's fields, mines, factories, and mills.

Polemical essays and pamphlets helped shape the controversies, and so did various forms of literary writing: sonnets and songs, ballads and poetic epistles, tales and plays, the sensationally turned narrative and the didactic novel. Even literature not forged in the social and political turbulence was caught by a sense of revolution. The first generation of writers (those who made their marks in the 1790s and the first decade of the new century) included William Blake, William Wordsworth, Samuel Taylor Coleridge, and Walter Scott, as well as several remarkable women: Anna Barbauld, Hannah More, Mary Wollstonecraft, Ann Radcliffe, Joanna Baillie, and Mary Robinson. The second generation (emerging before 1820) adds the younger voices and visions of Percy Shelley, Mary Shelley, John Keats, Lord Byron, John Clare. It also witnesses the emergence of international literary celebrity, first and foremost in the charismatic figure of Lord Byron, then extending in the 1820s to the adored Felicia Hemans and at last to venerable Wordsworth, who would become a beloved Poet Laureate in 1843. All these writers were invigorated by a sense of participating in the modern world, of defining its values, and of claiming a place for writers as its instructors, prophets, critics, and inspirers. In 1792 Wollstonecraft urged "a REVOLUTION in female manners," and at the end of the decade, Wordsworth's Preface to the second edition of *Lyrical Ballads* announced his break with "known habits of association" in the genre of poetry—a program, as his collaborator Coleridge later said, of "awakening the mind's attention from the lethargy of custom" (*Biographia Literaria*, 1817). The post-Revolutionary poet "strips the veil of familiarity from the world," declared Shelley in *A Defence of Poetry*, a document he concluded by designating poets the "unacknowledged legislators of the world." This enthusiasm inspired innovations in content and literary form. Lyric, epic, and autobiography became radically subjective, spiraling inward to psychological dramas of mind and memory, or projecting outward into prophecies and visions of new worlds formed by new values. Other hybrid forms, such as political ballads and polemical narrative, emerged to address pressing issues of the day, while novelists were producing new kinds of female heroines and new narrative structures to represent family and social life. Still other writers developed forms such as the personal essay, the travelogue, or the journal, to join the personal and the political, the social and the domestic, the world of feeling to the world of thought, and both to the world of action.

ROMANCE, ROMANTICISM, AND THE POWERS OF THE IMAGINATION

In this vibrant culture of new imaginative possibilities, "Imagination" itself became a subject of reflection, and often debate. Eighteenth-century philosophy and science had put a rigorous emphasis on objective, verifiable truth and the common basis of our experience in a world of concrete, measurable physical realities. Over the century, however, there emerged a competing interest in individual variations, subjective filterings, and the mind's independence of physical realities, or even creative transformation of them: not just a recorder or mirror, the mind was an active, synthetic, dynamic, even visionary power—of particular importance to poets. Poets tended to define "Imagination" against what it was not, even categorically the opposite of: thus, imagination vs. reality; imagination vs. reason; vs. science; vs. the understanding (especially its "fixities" and "certainties"); vs. mere "fancy"; even vs. religious truth. Blake declared its priority: "What is now proved was once, only imagin'd" (*The Marriage of Heaven and Hell*); it is imagination that can "see a World in a Grain of Sand / And a Heaven in a Wild Flower" (*Auguries of Innocence*). Deeming Wordsworth too wedded to observation and description, he scribbled in the margin of Wordsworth's 1815 *Poems*, "One Power alone makes a Poet.—Imagination The Divine Vision." Yet Wordsworth had moods in which he shared Blake's sense of imagination as most potent when severed from ordinary senses and experiences: "Imagination—here the Power so called / Through sad incompetence of human speech, / That awful Power rose from the mind's abyss / Like an unfathered vapour" (1850 *Prelude* Book 6), he writes at a pivotal moment in a work that is the story of imagination, celebrated in his conclusion as the ultimate synthesizing power: "Imagination . . . in truth, / Is but another name for absolute strength / And clearest insight, and amplitude of mind, / And reason in her most exalted mood" (1805 *Prelude* 13.167–70).

Coleridge defined "Primary Imagination" as "the living Power and prime Agent of all human Perception," analogous to but a lesser power than divine creation. Poetry is written by the "secondary Imagination," an "echo" of the Primary "coexisting with conscious will": it dissolves and diffuses the materials of perception "in order to recreate," and thus shows itself "in the balance or reconciliation of opposite or discordant qualities," among these, the general and the individual, the new and the familiar, emotion and order, judgment and enthusiasm, rationality and passion, the artificial and the natural (*Biographia Literaria* chs. 13, 14). Percy Shelley, who also liked binaries, contrasted "Imagination" to "Reason" in the first paragraph of his *Defence of Poetry*, and following Coleridge, coordinated their powers: "Reason is to imagination as the instrument to the agent, as the body to the spirit, as the shadow to the substance." Byron, when he wasn't dramatizing the torments of imagination, was inclined to look wryly: "Imagination droops her pinion, / And the sad truth which hovers o'er my desk / Turns what was once romantic to burlesque" (*Don Juan* 4.3); "And as for other love, the illusion's o'er; / And money, that most pure imagination, / Gleams only through the dawn of its creation" (12.2). Keats proposed the imagination as a link to the ideal world at the dawn of creation: "The Imagination may be compared to Adam's dream—he awoke and found it truth," he suggested, referring to the dream of Eve. But he was ultimately more interested in the way imagination operates on real perception: "probably every mental pursuit takes its reality and worth from the ardour of the pursuer—being in itself a nothing." And like his contemporaries, he was drawn by the involvement of imagination with disease, deviance, delusion, egotism, escapism.

As Keats's analogy of Adam's dream suggests, male imagination often projects an eroticized female or feminized object. How did women writers participate in the discussion? Though not always, they tended to a more skeptical view, accenting dangers, a corruption of rational capacity and moral judgment, an alliance with destructive (rather than creative) passion. This impulse was not just resistance to male schemes of gender; it was also fueled by a discourse of rational education and intellectual dissent that included both men and women. "The imagination should not be allowed to debauch the understanding before it has gained strength, or vanity will become the forerunner of vice," cautioned Wollstonecraft in *A Vindication of the Rights of Woman*; the best books are those "which exercise the understanding and regulate the imagination." When Jane Austen describes Emma's vain, egotistical illusions, she pointedly terms her an "imaginist . . . on fire with speculation and foresight!—especially with such a ground-work of anticipation as her mind had already made" (*Emma*, vol. 3, ch. 3).

In her widely read *Plays on the Passions* Joanna Baillie summons the word to name trouble and torment: "strange imaginations," "dark imaginations . . . frightful . . . / The haunt of damned spirits," "the worst imagination" of a "madden'd brain," "a wild imagination / Which has o'erreach'd . . . judgment." Mary Robinson recognized how, Hamlet-wise, "pall'd imagination, sick'ning, spurns / The sanity of reason!" (*The Sicilian Lover*, 15.23–24). When Mary Shelley recalls, "My imagination, unbidden, possessed and guided me, gifting the successive images that arose in my mind with a vividness far beyond the usual bounds of reverie," the gift was *Frankenstein*. Men often wrote about these dangers, but usually in a pattern of alternation with enthusiastic, idealizing, visionary projections.

Imagination was a heady romance—an inspiring force, a dangerous seduction. Not coincidentally, the issues often took shape in the language of romance. The rapid changes, new demands, and confusions of the age often pressed writers into imagining worlds elsewhere, an impulse summed in the prestige of the mode from which the "Romantic" era gets its name: the "Romance." In 1755 Samuel Johnson's great *Dictionary* defined it thus: "A military fable of the middle ages; a tale of wild adventures in war and love." Under this appeal, the subtitle "A Romance" graced a host of titles in the Romantic era. Radcliffe perfected the gothic romance novel; Scott elaborated the poetic romance and virtually defined the historical romance, while Byron made his name and fame in exotic quest romance: his first success, *Childe Harold's Pilgrimage* (1812), was subtitled "A Romaunt" (an old "romance" spelling), confirming the aura of the main title. In a variety of genres—ballad, narrative poem, novel—Romance turned to other places and times, or shaped timeless, ahistorical tales of quest and desire, love and adventure. A medieval idiom, which flourished into a "gothic" vogue, supplied vivid language for Radcliffe's novels, Coleridge's *Christabel* and *The Rime of the Ancyent Marinere* (in the patently antiqued version of 1798), Scott's *Lay of the Last Minstrel* (1805), Byron's *Childe Harold*, Keats's *La Belle Dame Sans Mercy* and *The Eve of St. Agnes* (1820), and Hemans's many poems of the age of the Crusades. Romance could inhabit the even more distant pasts of Anglo-Saxon legend or classical mythology. Percy Shelley and Keats turned to the landscapes and myths of ancient Greece as resources of imagination before the age of Christian "truth." As the settings of many of these works indicate, Romance is also fascinated with foreign worlds. *Childe Harold*, Coleridge's *Kubla Khan*, and Hemans's *Tales, and Historic Scenes* testify to the vogue of Eastern materials. Byron intrigued readers with a lexicon of "jelicks" and "baracans," "giaours" and "viziers" (*Don Juan*). "Queen of far-away!" Keats hailed "Romance" itself.

In its various forms and stories, Romances shared a feature that Victorians would take as exemplary of the literary (if not the polemical) imagination of the age: a turn, even an escape, from the tumultuous and confusing here-and-now of England. The appeal lay not only in exotic settings and remote ages themselves but also in the freedom these licensed to explore superstitions and customs that had been dismissed by Enlightenment thinkers who championed faith in "Reason," progress, and universal truths. These historically distant worlds were often sites for prophecy of renewed worlds and alternative values. Defined against "neoclassical" values of proportion, rational order, balanced harmony, and a reverence for the traditions that conveyed these values, the adjective "romantic" had long stood for a recurrent impulse in the history of the arts: a passion for the wild, the unfamiliar, the irregular, the irrational, even anti-rational. Johnson's *Dictionary* offered a suggestive cluster for "romantick": "1) resembling the tales of romances; wild. 2) Improbable; false. 3) Fanciful; full of wild scenery." All these senses infuse one powerful model for the male Romantic poet: the enraptured, entranced "bard." Descended from the Old Testament prophet, Englished by Milton and elaborated in the eighteenth-century ode, the bard emerged in the Romantic era as an electrically visionary poet and prophet for the age. Poets as various and as different from one another as Blake, Wordsworth, Coleridge, Shelley, and Keats assume a bardic stance to credit their dreams, hopes, and visions, even as socially oriented reformists, such as Wollstonecraft advocating "the rights of woman" or Wilberforce arguing for the abolition of slavery, adopt bardic tones to project a better, more moral world.

There was another landscape in the Romantic age that overlapped with these exotic worlds: the psychic terrain of imagination. And here a second definition Johnson supplies for "romance"—"A lie; a fiction"—casts its shadow. Romance is not only the genre of enchanted dreams and inspired visions, but also of superstitions and spells, delusions and nightmares. Coleridge said that the poetry he wrote for *Lyrical Ballads* was devoted to "persons and characters supernatural, or at least romantic"; hence the nightmare worlds and sensations of demonic possession in *The Rime of the Ancyent Marinere* and *Christabel*. Infused with sensations of supernatural power, or fed by opiated fantasies, the magical mystery tours of supernatural romance may hold the keys to paradise or the passage to hell, or both by turns—as they do in Thomas De Quincey's bizarrely romantic autobiography, *Confessions of an English Opium Eater*. The genre of romance fairly bristles with complexities. Acutely aware of the chaos of their historical moment, writers often make the attraction to another world a critical theme: "magic casements," said Keats, "opening on the foam / Of perilous seas, in faery lands forlorn" (*Ode to a Nightingale*). The dubiously magic casements, moreover, may turn into mirrors: Romances often reflect, and reflect on, the world seemingly escaped or effaced from consciousness. The most celebrated romancers were hardly uncritical practitioners of the genre. Byron casts *Childe Harold* as a quest romance, but its path turns repeatedly to modern life, in particular the Napoleonic wars that were ravaging Europe.

At the same time, the prestige of "romance" and "romanticism" posed problems for women writers. Keats suggests one of these when he portrays "Romance" itself as a dangerous seductress (a "Queen of far-away," a "Fair plumed Syren") and opposes her allure to the demands of epic and tragedy (by which male poets claimed their fame). The critique of "Romance" could be tinged with sexism—an irony, since many women writers were inclined to criticize the genre, too. Clara Reeve, Wollstonecraft, Barbauld, and Hannah More—whose opinions divided, often sharply, on a variety of political and social issues—found common ground on the dangers of "Romance." Especially in the popular form of the novel, they felt it encouraged too much

John Martin. *The Bard,*
1817. "Ruin seize thee,
ruthless King!" According
to the legend retold in
Thomas Gray's 1757 ode
The Bard, in the thir-
teenth century Edward I
attempted to stamp out
Welsh resistance to Eng-
lish power by ordering
the court poets or bards
put to death. John Mar-
tin's large canvas cap-
tures the sublime
moment at which the last
bard denounced the
invading monarch before
leaping into the river
Conway below.

"sensibility"—the cultivation of emotional refinement over rational intellect—and
fed an appetite for fantasy over sound judgment. Insofar as "Romances" deal in "the
wild and extravagant," worried Reeve in *The Progress of Romance* (1785), they are
"dangerous" for young readers: "they create and encourage the wildest excursions of
imagination." "Novels . . . tend to make women the creatures of sensation," warned
Wollstonecraft's *Rights of Woman* (1792); "their character is thus formed in the
mould of folly." The genre enfeebled reason and stimulated illusions about "romantic
love" that held perilous social consequences. By 1810, Barbauld was willing to argue
that good novels could teach good values, but she was still cautious about the power
of "romances . . . to impress false ideas on the mind." Urging women to cultivate the
Enlightenment values of "Reason" and intellectual strength, these female critics also
challenged romance stereotypes proffered as universal truth: the ideals of "feminine"
silence, self-sacrifice, passivity, and unquestioning obedience; the ideology of female
life contained in the domestic sphere.

There were still more ways that Romance exoticism intersected with the socially
immediate world. Encounters with outcasts of all kinds—refugees, the poor, abandoned and fallen women, discharged soldiers, sailors, vagrants, peasants, north-country shepherds and smallholders, abject slaves—supplied the unusual and unexpected,

and at the same time provoked social self-reflection. Foreign cultures might be close to home, as in the ballads enthusiastically collected by Scott in *Minstrelsy of the Scottish Border* (1802–1803) and his subsequent use of Highland materials in the series of novels begun with *Waverley*. Scots poet Robert Burns packaged himself as a primitive bard: the son of a tenant-farmer and tenant-farmer himself, a heavy-drinking, illegitimate-child-siring, native genius whose dialect verse and egalitarian sentiments seemed to make him the very voice of the people. William Wordsworth produced incidents from rural life in *Lyrical Ballads*, and his sister Dorothy Wordsworth captured the dialects in her journal. John Clare wrote of rural life in a rural idiom and himself embodied the figure of the peasant poet. Meanwhile, the "wild scenery" of Johnson's definition was caught in new travel books and records of "tours," while "tourists"—a word that emerged around 1800—began to delight in locales ignored by previous generations, or thought unpleasantly rough. Once-isolated Wales became so flooded by tourists that by 1833 a Welsh grammar carried an appendix of useful phrases: "I long to see the monastery"; "Is there a waterfall in this neighbourhood?"

This romance of novelty interplays with a powerful sense of a past that might be renewed. Writers created hybrid forms, building on models anywhere from the middle ages through the eighteenth century. Byron remained loyal to neoclassic poets such as Pope and Dryden, even as he gave their forms new vibrancy and reveled in contemporary political satire. Literary tradition was a cherished, if daunting, national heritage. Many admired Chaucer's tale-telling and descriptive detail; others worked variations on Spenser's allegorical epic, *The Faerie Queene*. Hazlitt honored Spenser as "the poet of our waking dreams," and the Spenserian stanza that conveyed these dreams shaped more than a few new "romances"—among them, Byron's *Childe Harold*, Hemans's *Forest Sanctuary*, Keats's *Eve of St. Agnes*, Shelley's *Revolt of Islam* and his homage to Keats, *Adonais*. Shakespeare and Milton were the great progenitors. Shakespeare was admired for the intensity of his imagery, his spectacular versatility, his unparalleled characterizations, as well as his mastery of "organic" (as opposed to "mechanical") aesthetic form, a concept elaborated in the criticism of Coleridge. He was an early inspiration for Coleridge's lectures and poetry; Wordsworth, Byron, and Hemans could hardly write without alluding to him; Keats named him his "Presider," and De Quincey wrote vivid essays about him. For this generation of writers, Milton's revolutionary politics provided an example of anti-monarchal courage, and *Paradise Lost* was indisputably the most important poem in English literature. Milton's Eve focuses the feminist grievances of Wollstonecraft's *Rights of Woman*, while for poets, as Byron declares in *Don Juan*, "the word 'Miltonic' mean[s] 'sublime,'" stimulating epic ambitions in works as diverse as Blake's *Milton* and *Jerusalem*, Charlotte Smith's *Emigrants*, Wordsworth's *Prelude*, Percy Shelley's *Prometheus Unbound*, Keats's *Hyperion*, and Byron's *Don Juan*. Milton's Satan, an epitome of the "sublime," is echoed and doubled everywhere, and along with Milton's God and Adam, casts his shadow across the fable of masculine ambition and heroic alienation that Wollstonecraft's daughter Mary Shelley creates for *Frankenstein*.

At the same time (as the protagonist of *Frankenstein* demonstrates), Romantic creativity also defined itself—often defiantly—against tradition, experimenting with new forms and genres. Blake writes visionary epics; Wordsworth spends half a century on his poetic autobiography, "a thing unprecedented in Literary history," he said. Mary Shelley fuses several myths into a complex, interlocking structure of tales and tellers to form *Frankenstein*. Byron interplays stand-up patter with a tale of adventure to shape his burlesque *Don Juan*, "a poem totally of its own species . . . at once the stamp of originality and a defiance of imitation," Percy Shelley exclaimed to him. Individual experience, simultaneously the most exotic and most common region of all, led to excavations of the depths of the single self—which is to say, the unfolding of a self conceived as having depths and mysterious recesses. Reading Wordsworth's *Tintern Abbey*, Keats found "Genius" in its "dark Passages." In the Prospectus to *The Recluse* (1814), Wordsworth himself proclaimed

> Not Chaos, not
> The darkest pit of lowest Erebus,
> Nor aught of blinder vacancy—scooped out
> By help of dreams, can breed such fear and awe
> As fall upon us often when we look
> Into our Minds, into the Mind of Man,
> My haunt, and the main region of my Song.

Byron jibed that Keats's *Sleep and Poetry* was "an ominous title," but when Wordsworth named "the Mind" as his subject, Keats understood completely, and even women poets participated. This post-Enlightenment, bourgeois Protestant individualism moved beyond the rhetorical first-person of eighteenth-century poetry to produce the "I" as an individual authority, for whom the mind, in all its creative powers and passionate testimony of deeply registered sensations, became a compelling focus. The "I" could sponsor extravagant self-display (Robinson and Byron), prophetic self-elevation (Blake and Shelley), poignant song (Hemans), internal debate (Keats), or what Keats, thinking of Wordsworth, called the "egotistical sublime." Many of its forms defined a radical or alienated subjectivity. Wollstonecraft wrote as a nonconformist, Cowper and Hemans were famous for the melancholy autobiography that haunts their poetry, while poets such as Byron, Coleridge, and Shelley cultivated the "I" as antihero: the exile, the damned visionary, the alienated idealist, the outcast, whose affiliates were Cain, Satan, even the paradoxical figure of Napoleon—all joined by the passion of mind and the torments of imagination.

Whether cast as experiment and innovation or allied with liberty and revolution, these new expressive forms were sharpened by a sense of modernity, with their writers often viewing old forms and traditions as tyranny or, at the very least, as the strictures of custom and habit. Revoking the neoclassical argument of Dryden (in the seventeenth century) that the poet is responsible for "putting bounds to a wilde overflowing Fancy," Wordsworth asserted in the Preface to *Lyrical Ballads* (1800) that poetry should be a "spontaneous overflow of powerful feelings," and explained, in a later version, that in his poems "the feeling . . . gives importance to the action and situation, and not the action and situation to the feeling." Framing "incidents of common life," he made the agents of feeling such socially disenfranchised figures as children, bereft mothers, impoverished shepherds, beggars, veterans, and the rural destitute. In a lecture "On the Living Poets" (1818), William Hazlitt sneered at this "mixed rabble of . . . convicts, female vagrants, gipsies, . . . ideot boys and mad mothers . . . peasants, pedlars," but Wordsworth's revolution was to treat them all as vehicles of worthy imagination and passion. Hazlitt had no trouble linking this program to "the sentiments and opinions which produced the French revolution" as well as its "principles and events":

> The change in the belles-lettres was as complete, and . . . as startling, as the change in politics, with which it went hand in hand. . . . According to the prevailing notions, all was to be natural and new. Nothing that was established was to be tolerated. . . . Kings

and queens were dethroned from their rank and station in legitimate tragedy or epic poetry, as they were decapitated elsewhere; rhyme was looked upon as a relic of the feudal system, and regular metre was abolished along with regular government.

THE FRENCH REVOLUTION AND ITS REVERBERATIONS

In the 1780s, the American Revolution was a recent memory for the British, at once an inspiration to political progressives, an embarrassment for the prestige of the Empire, and a worry to a conservative ruling class concerned about the arrival of democratic ideas on British shores. When the next Revolution exploded in France only twelve miles across the Channel, rather than a hemisphere away, the press of radical, violent, and inevitable change seemed imminent. With the fall of the Bastille prison, a symbol of royal tyranny, on July 14, 1789, and the *Declaration of the Rights of Man* that soon followed, British consciousness was dominated by French events. Conservatives were alarmed, while liberals welcomed the early phase as a repetition of England's "Glorious Revolution" of 1688, an overdue end to feudal abuse and the inauguration of constitutional government. Radicals hoped for a more thorough-going renovation: "Bliss was it in that dawn to be alive, / But to be young was very heaven!" Wordsworth said in retrospect, in a passage from his poetic autobiography that he published in 1809, and again in 1815 under the title *French Revolution as it Appeared to Enthusiasts at its Commencement*. Everything was infused with "the attraction of a country in Romance!" He was not the only one in rapture. Southey recalled how "a visionary world seemed to open. . . . Old things seemed passing away, and nothing was dreamt of but the regeneration of the human race." Burns was certain that "man to man the world o'er / Shall be brithers for a' that." In their own idioms, Wollstonecraft, Blake, and Charles Lamb joined the chorus, and in subsequent generations, Byron and Percy Shelley continued to hope that what was started in France could be continued elsewhere with better consequences.

Better consequences, because millenarian dreams were soon undermined by harsh developments: the overthrow of the French monarchy in August 1792 and in the next month, the massacre of more than a thousand prisoners by a Paris mob. When extremist Jacobins prevailed over moderate Girondins, the French Revolution fragmented into the Reign of Terror. Louis XVI was guillotined in January 1793, Queen Marie Antoinette in October. In February 1793, France declared war on Britain and Britain reciprocated, throwing the political ideals of Wordsworth and his generation into sharp conflict with their love of country. Except for the brief interlude of the deceptive Peace of Amiens (1802–1803: "Peace in a week, war in a month," a British diplomat commented), Britain was at war with France until the final defeat of Napoleon at Waterloo in 1815. The shock of these events lasted for decades, and lent retroactive credit to the conservative polemic of Edmund Burke's *Reflections on the Revolution in France*, published in 1790, after the arrest and imprisonment of the royal family. In 1790 Burke seemed a sentimental hysteric to political opponents and was quickly subject to sarcastic challenge in Wollstonecraft's *Vindication of the Rights of Men* (1790) and Tom Paine's *Rights of Man* (1791). In 1793 radical philosopher William Godwin's *Political Justice*, though not directly about the Revolution, offered a vision of a society governed by individual reason, without the oppression of social institutions or private property. But the course of the Revolution confirmed Burke's alarm.

Under the systematic Terror of Robespierre (1793–1794), thousands of aristocrats, their employees, the clergy, and ostensible opponents of the Revolution were guillotined, the violence swallowing up Robespierre himself in 1794. British unease

THE CONTRAST
1792

BRITISH LIBERTY.   FRENCH LIBERTY

RELIGION.   MORALITY.
LOYALTY OBEDIENCE TO THE LAWS
INDEPENDANCE PERSONAL SECURITY
JUSTICE INHERITANCE PROTECTION
PROPERTY. INDUSTRY. NATIONAL PROSPERITY
HAPPINESS

ATHEISM   PERJURY
REBELLION.TREASON. ANARCHY.MURDER
EQUALITY.MADNESS.CRUELTY. INJUSTICE
TREACHERY INGRATITUDE IDLENESS
FAMINE NATIONAL & PRIVATE RUIN.
MISERY

WHICH IS BEST

Thomas Rowlandson, after a drawing by Lord George Murray. *The Contrast, 1792.*

increased when France offered to support all revolutions abroad, and then invaded the Netherlands and the German states in 1794, Italy in 1796, and republican Switzerland in 1798. Now "Oppressors in their turn," Wordsworth wrote, "Frenchmen had changed a war of self-defense / For one of conquest, losing sight of all / Which they had struggled for" (1805 *Prelude* 10: 791–794). In 1799 Napoleon, a general who consolidated his power in the Italian and Swiss campaigns, staged a coup d'etat and was named First Consul for life. The Revolution had evolved into a military dictatorship, its despotism confirmed when Napoleon crowned himself Emperor in 1804. A complex personality—a nightmare to entrenched monarchies; a charismatic military genius; a ruthless, egotistical imperialist—he generated nearly two decades of war that ravaged the Continent. Although war barely reached Britain, it was a constant threat, cost thousands of British lives and sent its economy into turmoil.

When Napoleon invaded the Iberian Peninsula in 1807, British support for the spontaneous resistance of the Portuguese and Spanish peoples enabled former radicals to return to the patriotic fold, to see their country as the champion of liberty against French imperialism. Napoleon's actions, claimed Coleridge, produced a "national unanimity unexampled in our history since the reign of Elizabeth . . . and made us all once more Englishmen." English self-definition was energized, the contest with France drawing on historical antagonisms that went back for centuries. Unlike the English, the French rejected their monarchy; if France could thus claim to be the first modern nation in the old world, Britain could feel superior to a country defined by the Terror and then Napoleon. National self-definition had strong literary manifestations. Hemans began her career with patriotic anthems celebrating Britain's support for the "noble" (and highly "romantic") Spanish resistance, and across these decades she published *Welsh Melodies, Greek Songs, Songs of Spain, National Lyrics,* and even the canonical American anthem, "The Landing of the Pilgrim Fathers" (our "Thanksgiving" hymn). Thomas Moore wrote *Irish Melodies* (1807–1834) and championed the grievances of Ireland. Byron wrote *Hebrew Melodies* (1815), got involved with Italian liberation movements, and in his last real-life romance, died in Greece where he had gone to aid the revolution against the Ottoman Empire.

Yet even as this literature tamed class differences into a general culture of songs for the salon, or made nationalism itself a vivid "romance," continuing disturbances pointed to those excluded from Coleridge's idealized whole of "us all . . . Englishmen." Its fears heightened by the threat of invasion, the government clamped down on any form of political expression that hinted at French ideas. Efforts to reform Parliament begun in the 1780s were stifled, as was the movement to abolish the slave trade, and even moderates were silenced by accusations of "Jacobinism" (sympathy with Revolutionary extremists). In 1791 authorities in Birmingham connived at three days of riots by a loyal "Church and King" mob against Dissenters who had held a dinner to commemorate the Fall of the Bastille. When his house and laboratory were sacked, the eminent chemist and nonconformist Joseph Priestley fled to London and then emigrated to America. In 1792 Paine fled to France; he was tried and convicted in absentia of sedition for writing *The Rights of Man,* and his publishers and booksellers were regularly prosecuted. In 1794, twelve London radicals were arrested, including a novelist and playwright, Thomas Holcroft, and Horne Tooke, a philologist whose publications seemed a dangerous attempt to democratize language. Charged with high treason, they were defended by Godwin and acquitted, but the trial was a harbinger of repression to come.

In 1794 the government suspended the long-established right of habeas corpus, which required the state to show cause for imprisonment and to conduct trials in a timely fashion; now anyone suspected of a crime could be jailed indefinitely. The Gagging Acts of 1795 targeted radical lecturers and societies, defining any criticism of the monarchy as treason and squelching political organization by limiting the size of meetings called to discuss reform. The Combination Act of 1799 forbade workmen, under penalty of conspiracy charges, to unionize or even to associate for purposes of collective bargaining. All these laws were enforced by government spies. Coleridge and Wordsworth, walking and conversing on the coastal hills of the Bristol Channel and plotting nothing more revolutionary than poems for *Lyrical Ballads,* looked suspicious enough to warrant tailing by a government informer. Coleridge was amused that their talk of the philosopher Spinoza was reported as references to "Spy Nozy," but actual radicals suffered severer consequences, for the government was also deploying *agents provocateurs* to incite them into capital offences. These infiltrators played a major role in plotting the Pentridge Rising of 1817 and the Cato Street Conspiracy of 1820, a scheme to murder cabinet ministers (a prime minister had been assassinated in 1812) and stage a coup d'état. "Cato Street" was "exposed" and its radical conspirators hanged or sent to prison in Australia, but the ultimate conspirator had been the government. Policy was still more severe outside England: in Edinburgh, delegates to the first British Convention of reformers were arrested for sedition and doomed to sentences in Australia; in Ireland, where Britain had more troops than on the Continent, a peasants' rebellion was crushed in a bloodbath (1798). Rather than international "fraternity," it was repression at home and wars abroad that defined the legacy of the French Revolution. When Napoleon was finally defeated in 1815 and the Bourbons were restored to the throne of France, the result was to reinforce reactionary measures and despotic monarchies all over Europe.

In the England of 1815, a further affliction was visited on the poor, among whom were many veterans, by Parliament's passage of the Corn Laws. Because importing grain had been impossible during the war years, prices for native grain soared; the Corn Laws now restricted imports in order to sustain the artificially high prices, a boon for landlords and a disaster for the poor, for whom bread was a chief article of diet. Bad harvests further raised costs. For the first time, in the estimate of the *Morning Chronicle*, protests and petitions erupted from "a majority of the adult male population of England," igniting food riots across the country. Under the unreformed electoral system, petitions to Parliament were the only recourse for those without representatives. In 1800 only males, and only five percent of them, were allowed to vote; only Anglicans, members of the state Church, could serve in the House of Lords. Workers did not have a vote, or even a representative in Parliament. The worker-populated cities of Leeds, Manchester, Birmingham, and Sheffield did not have a vote, whereas depopulated "rotten boroughs," consisting of one or two houses owned by a single landlord, enjoyed one or even two representatives in Parliament. As the Prince Regent returned from the opening of Parliament in January 1817, he found his carriage surrounded by a hostile crowd and stoned.

Workers were also being displaced by new machinery; they sometimes retaliated with attacks on the machines themselves, actions punishable by death (Byron's first speech in the House of Lords was against such a measure, the Frame-breaking Bill provoked by weavers' riots). Throughout the 1820s, farmworkers, angry at their degraded conditions, erupted into sporadic violence, culminating in a great uprising in 1830, in which barns burned across the countryside, and laborers again attacked machinery. The unemployed starved to death. Men scrambled for employment, while women and children, because they were deemed tractable and obedient, found it at pitiful wages. Prevailing attitudes and institutions were inadequate to ameliorate the misery and consequent disruptions. Since Elizabethan times, England had relied on a network of parishes and justices of the peace: local notables, serving in a largely volunteer capacity that enhanced their status, who kept records, assisted the needy, and administered everyday justice. Indigent newcomers to the cities could not easily be returned to their home parishes for support; they were needed as workers. And the parish system left out many: Irish Catholic immigrants, members of dissenting sects, and those lapsed from an Anglicanism that had failed to build churches for the new populations and at worst seemed remote from their concerns. When Lord John Manners declared that "the only means of Christianizing Manchester" was to revive the monasteries, he made clear the inadequacy of the current state Church to supply moral authority, social structure, and needed assistance.

No wonder that it was in Manchester that the modern vocabulary of class struggle emerged. The eighteenth-century ideal of stable social "orders" and "ranks" was challenged by a growing antagonism between successful capitalist entrepreneurs and their workers. In August 1819, nearly a hundred thousand mill-workers and their families gathered at nearby St. Peter's Field for a peaceful demonstration with banners and parades, capped by an address by the radical "Orator" Hunt calling for Parliamentary reform. Alarmed by the spectacle, the local ruling class sent their drunken, sabre-wielding militia to charge the rally and arrest Hunt. Hunt offered no resistance, but the militia struck out at the jeering though unarmed crowd and, backed by mounted Hussars, in ten minutes left an official toll of eleven dead, including one trampled child, and more than four hundred injured, many from sabre wounds. Unreported injuries and later deaths from injury undoubtedly added to the official toll. This pivotal event in nineteenth-century economic and political strife was immediately dubbed "Peterloo" by the left press—a sardonic echo of the celebrated British triumph over Napoleon at Waterloo, four years before. Parliament did not reform, but instead consolidated the repressive measures of previous decades into the notorious Six Acts at the end of 1819. These Acts outlawed demonstrations, empowered magistrates to enter private houses in search of arms, prohibited meetings of more than fifty unless all participants were residents of the parish in which the meeting was held, increased the prosecution of blasphemous or seditious libel (defined as language "tending to bring into hatred or contempt" the monarchy or government), and raised the newspaper tax, thus constricting the circulation of William Cobbett's radical *Political Register* by tripling its price.

THE MONARCHY

Outraged by the situation summed by "Peterloo," Percy Shelley mordantly surveyed *England in 1819*, the title of a sonnet whose language rendered it unpublishable, even in a radical newspaper such as his friend Leigh Hunt's *Examiner*. It began:

> An old, mad, blind, despised, and dying King,
> Princes, the dregs of their dull race, who flow
> Through public scorn,—mud from a muddy spring,—
> Rulers who neither see, nor feel, nor know . . .

The Lear-like king who inspired this contempt was George III, Washington's antagonist in the American Revolution. He had had an episode of mental instability in 1765 and another in 1788: he talked incessantly and rarely slept, and once his eldest son tried to throttle him. The episode at once epitomized their antagonism and reflected the political conflicts of the late Georgian era. The King lived a domestic life and his successive administrations were firmly Tory—that is, socially and politically "conservative," committed to the constitutional power of the monarchy and the Church, and opposed to concessions of greater religious and political liberties. The Prince lived extravagantly at taxpayers' expense, with a devout Roman Catholic mistress whom he secretly and unconstitutionally married. In 1787 he obtained an extra £10,000 from the King, a relief from Parliament of £100,000 to pay his debts, and an additional £60,000 to build his residence, Carlton House—a total equivalent to almost seven million dollars today. But because his comparative political flexibility held out the hope of some reforms, he was backed by the opposition party, the liberal Whigs. He expected the crown in 1788, but the King unexpectedly recovered, hanging on until November 1810, when he relapsed and became permanently mad. In January 1811 the Prince was appointed "Regent."

In this new position of power, he focused all the contradictions and tensions of the time. In 1812, the *Morning Post* addressed him in the loyalist hyperbole that earned it the nickname of the "Fawning Post": "You are the glory of the People . . . You breathe eloquence, you inspire the Graces—You are an Adonis in loveliness." Leigh and John Hunt replied in *The Examiner*, denouncing "this Adonis in Loveliness" as "a corpulent gentlemen of fifty . . . a man who had just closed half a century without one single claim on the gratitude of his country or the respect of posterity."

Thomas Lawrence. *Coronation Portrait of the Prince Regent (George IV), 1820.*

Their scathing rejoinder earned them two-year sentences for libel and fines of £500 each, but Leigh continued to edit *The Examiner* from his prison cell, which he transformed into a gentleman's parlor, where he was visited as a hero by Byron, Moore, Keats, and Lamb.

Meanwhile, the Prince Regent was transforming the face of London. He and his architects recreated Regent's Park in the north and St. James Park in the south, linking them by extending Regent Street, built Trafalgar Square, elevated Buckingham House into Buckingham Palace, and erected the Hyde Park arch. The "metropolitan improvements" bespoke impressive city planning, but also deliberately demarcated the boundaries between rich and poor. The Gothic/Chinese/Indian fantasy of his beloved retreat, the Brighton Pavilion, spoke even more loudly of his distance from the everyday life of his subjects. By 1815, when a mere £150 a year provided a comfortable living for many, he was £339,000 in debt, an extravagance that brought contempt on the monarchy. The pathos of George III attracted sympathy, whereas the son's conduct alienated the nation. On his accession to power, he abandoned his Whig friends, separated his estranged Queen Caroline from their daughter Charlotte, and was absent from Charlotte when she died in childbirth in 1817. In 1820, when George III died and he at last became King, he attempted to divorce Caroline by initiating a sordid investigation of her escapades abroad. The scandal rebounded on a man excoriated, in the Hunts' words, as "a libertine over head and heels in debt and disgrace, a despiser of domestic ties," and provided yet another handle for attacks upon him. The personal elegance that had made him "the first gentleman of Europe" had dissipated; already in 1813, Beau Brummell, an aristocratic "dandy" whose impeccable style and social assurance made him a paragon of the era, responded to a slight by the Regent by loudly inquiring of a fellow dandy, "who's your fat friend?" The Prince was too fat to mount his horse by 1816; by 1818 it was reported that "Prinny has let loose his belly which now reaches his knees." Of his official Coronation portrait, Moore acidly noted that it was "disgraceful both to the King & the painter—a lie upon canvas." It was inevitable that satiric sketches would compete for fame.

INDUSTRIAL ENGLAND AND "NEVER-RESTING LABOUR"

In the decades of this royal extravagance, the general population was rapidly expanding, accompanied by grim social misery. By 1750, the population of England and Wales was around five-and-a-half million; at the turn of the century, when the first census was taken, it was about eight million, with most of the increase in the last two decades. Scotland registered another million and a half, Ireland more than five million. Traditionally viewed as an index to a nation's wealth, population now loomed as a danger, inspiring the dire prophecy of Thomas Malthus's *On the Principle of Population As It Affects the Future Improvement of Society* (1798): "population, when unchecked, increases in a geometrical ratio. Subsistence increases only in an arithmetical ratio. A slight acquaintance with numbers will show the immensity of the first power in comparison of the second." The increase continued: by 1831 the population of Great Britain neared fourteen million.

The numbers do not tell the whole story. Ever since the end of the eighteenth century and then with postwar acceleration, the economic base of England had begun to shift from agriculture, controlled by wealthy aristocrats (the landlords), to manufacture, controlled by new-money industrialists. The war against France fueled a surge: "A race of merchants and manufacturers and bankers and loan jobbers and contractors" was born, remarked William Cobbett in 1802. Factories and mills invaded the countryside, pumped small towns into burgeoning cities, and cities into teeming metropolises. In 1800 only London—with about ten percent of the entire population of England and Wales—had more than a hundred thousand people. By 1837, when Victoria was crowned, there were five such cities, and London was growing by as much as twenty percent a decade. Even more staggering was the growth of the new industrial cities of the north. Manchester's population increased fivefold in fifty years, to 142,000 in 1831. Cobbett denounced these developments as "infernal," and many of his contemporaries, alarmed by the new concentrations of people and their demands for wages, food, and housing, feared a repetition at home of the mob violence of France.

This unprecedented concentration was the result of several converging factors. The 1790s had been racked by poor harvests, and harvests were bad again in 1815. Scarcities were aggravated by the Corn Laws and an increase of "Enclosure acts"—

the consolidation and privatization of the old common fields into larger and more efficient farms. The modernizing did improve agricultural yield and animal husbandry, thus offsetting in some measure Malthus's prediction of an inadequate food supply, but it also produced widespread dislocation and misery. The pattern of country landholding changed. Smallholders, whether independent but modest farmers or proprietors of estates up to a thousand acres, fell away, while the great estates prospered in size and number: "the big bull frog grasps all," Cobbett pungently remarked. Meanwhile, the farmers and herdsmen whom the enclosure acts rendered landless had to settle for meager subsistence wages in the country or migrate to the cities. The census of 1811 revealed for the first time that a majority of families were engaged in nonagricultural employment. The yeomen who had represented the mythic heart of sturdy English freedom became day laborers, while others sank into poverty. The reform of the farms eroded centuries-old social structures. Sending the Whig leader in Parliament a copy of *Lyrical Ballads* that he hoped might call attention to the plight of the rural poor, Wordsworth lamented that without a "little tract of land" as "a kind of permanent rallying point" in their hardships, "the bonds of domestic feeling . . . have been weakened, and in innumerable instances entirely destroyed."

Uprooted families were pulled by hopes of employment to the new factory towns. Cotton made modern Manchester. By 1802 there were more than fifty spinning mills, and the once-provincial city had become one of the commercial capitals of Europe. Textiles produced in vast quantities by power looms eliminated skilled hand-weavers, and extinguished the traditional supplement to the income of the cottager. The city did not incorporate until 1838, and no regulations controlled manufacture, sanitation, or housing; the unchecked boom enriched the few master manufacturers and immiserated the workers. The factories required a workforce disciplined to the constant output of the machines they tended; families accustomed to the ebb and flow of agricultural rhythms found themselves plunged into a world of industrial clock-time. Twelve-to-fifteen-hour shifts, strict discipline, capricious firings, dangerous and unsanitary conditions, injuries, and ruined health were the rule of the day. Children were the preferred staff for the mills, and youngsters of five worked in the mines, their little bodies ideal for hauling coal in the narrow shafts. Workers were often further victimized by debts to their employers for housing and food. There was no philosophy of government restraint and regulation of these practices; all was "laissez-faire," the doctrine associated with Adam Smith's enormously influential *Wealth of Nations* (1777) that national wealth would flourish if businesses were left to operate with unfettered self-interest. By the 1780s there was a measurable gulf between rich and poor, ever more apparent in Manchester in the contrast between the homes of the wealthy in the suburbs and the slums by the polluted city river. "The town is abominably filthy," declared a visitor in 1808, "the Steam Engine is pestiferous, the Dyehouses noisome and offensive, and the water of the river as black as ink or the Stygian lake."

The twin agricultural and industrial revolutions recast both the town and the country and altered the relationship between them. To obtain the waterpower to drive them, early mills and factories were set by rivers, thereby converting peaceful valleys into sites of production. Gas lighting, first used in such buildings, made possible twenty-four-hour operation, and the resulting spectacle affected contemporaries as a weird and ominous splendor. In regions that were once the "assured domain of calm simplicity / And pensive quiet," wrote Wordsworth in *The Excursion* (1814):

> an unnatural light,
> Prepared for never-resting Labour's eyes,
> Breaks from a many-windowed Fabric huge;
> And at the appointed hour a Bell is heard—
> Of harsher import than the Curfew-knoll
> That spake the Norman Conqueror's stern behest,
> A local summons to unceasing toil!
> Disgorged are now the Ministers of day;
> And, as they issue from the illumined Pile,
> A fresh Band meets them, at the crowded door,—
> And in the Courts—and where the rumbling Stream,
> That turns the multitude of dizzy wheels,
> Glares, like a troubled Spirit, in its bed
> Among the rocks below. Men, Maidens, Youths,
> Mother and little Children, Boys and Girls,
> Enter, and each the wonted task resumes
> Within this Temple—where is offered up
> To Gain—the Master Idol of the Realm,
> Perpetual sacrifice.   (8. 169–187)

Industry invaded the most picturesque quarters of the British Isles. A center of tourism, Wales was also home to oppressive slate mines. Richard Pennant of North Wales epitomised the fortunes made in the trade in slaves and new-world commodities. Using the profits from his family's Jamaican sugar plantations, Pennant developed and mechanized the slate quarries on his estates. Elected to Parliament from Liverpool in 1783, he led the planters' defense of the slave trade while boosting the market for slate at home. Slate was an ideal roofing material, and the spread of education created a need for slate blackboards; at Port Penrhyn, the town Pennant established to ship slate, a hundred thousand writing slates were manufactured each year. In the eighteenth century, the quarries employed six hundred and the manufactory thirty more; by 1820 the workforce was a thousand, and it expanded rapidly over the next two decades. The concurrent discovery on the estate of minerals useful to the manufacture of Herculaneum pottery in Liverpool generated still more income. The profits underwrote Penryhn Castle, a lush Norman fantasy constructed (from 1821) by Pennant's heir.

The rhetoric of an 1832 history of Wales obscures the dislocations entailed by the progress it lauds: "About forty years ago, this part of the country bore a most wild, barren, and uncultivated appearance, but it is now covered with handsome villas, well built farm houses, neat cottages, rich meadows, well-cultivated fields, and flourishing plantations; bridges have been built, new roads made, bogs and swampy grounds drained and cultivated, neat fences raised, and barren rocks covered with woods." At Portmadoc, about twelve miles south of the sublime scenery of Mount Snowdon in Wales, William Madocks was performing one of the celebrated technological feats of the day, building a massive embankment (1808–1811), draining the tidal estuary behind it, enlarging the harbor, and founding a model village named after himself, Tremadoc—a project on which Percy Shelley enthusiastically collaborated, until he and his household fled from Wales in 1813 in the wake of a murderous attack. Popular biography ascribed the incident to Shelley's propensity to hallucination, but underlying it were genuine conflicts between idealist radicalism, paternalistic planning, local privilege, and labor unrest.

If Romantic poetry is famous for celebrating "Nature," this affection coincides with the peril to actual nature by modern industry. "Our feeling for nature," wrote Friedrich Schiller in the 1790s, "is like the feeling of an invalid for health." Industry scarred previously rural communities. Visiting Scotland in 1803 with her brother, Dorothy Wordsworth noted of one village: "a pretty place it once has been, but a manufactory is established there; and a townish bustle and ugly stone houses are fast taking the place of the brown-roofed thatched cottages." Of the famous Carron Ironworks, "seen at a distance," she noted, "the sky above them was red with a fiery light." Industry ringed even their beloved Lake District, and on its coast the shafts of the coal mines owned by the employer of Wordsworth's father, Sir James Lowther, ran ever deeper and longer, until they extended under the sea and even caused the collapse of houses in Whitehaven, the planned port city from which the coal was shipped.

The need to bring coal and iron into conjunction spurred improvements in transport. In 1759 the Duke of Bridgewater cut an eleven-mile canal between his colliery at Worsley and Manchester; two years later an extension linked Manchester to the sea. Soon canals transected the country; in 1790–1794 alone, eighty-one Acts for the construction of canals were passed. The cost of carriage was drastically cut, and the interior of England opened for commerce. By 1811 there were steamboats on the rivers; by 1812 locomotives were hauling coal. Large-scale road-building followed, including arteries between Shrewsbury and Holyhead (the port of departure for Ireland) and another between Carlisle and Glasgow in Scotland. During these years, a Scotsman, John Macadam, developed the road surface that bears his name. Across the country, distant regions were joined by a web of new roads and the Royal Mail coaches that ran along them on regular schedules. Decades later, remembering coach travel as it was in 1812, De Quincey recalled the new sensation of speed: "we saw it, we felt it as a thrilling; and this speed was not the product of blind insensate agencies, that had no sympathy to give, but was incarnated in the fiery eyeballs of an animal, in his dilated nostril, spasmodic muscles, and echoing hoofs" (*The English Mail-Coach, or the Glory of Motion* [1849]).

In this age of acceleration, the British Empire was expanding, too. Economically and politically, it had become the preeminent world power. The American colonies had been lost, but Canada and the West Indies remained, and Australia, New Zealand, and India marked a global reach. British forces subjugated natives, defeated rival French ambitions, and held the Turks and Russians in check, while the East India Company, originally a trading organization, gradually assumed administrative control of the subcontinent, even to the point of collecting taxes to protect British interests. The Company penetrated every aspect of British life: Warren Hastings, the first governor-general of India, was tried for cruelty and corruption, having amassed a fortune of over £400,000 in India. His trial, lasting from 1788 to 1795, was a *cause célèbre*, establishing the fame of the prosecutors even though he was acquitted. While his profits were exceptional, they marked a trend of great numbers of younger sons seeking fortunes in India. In a pattern common to north-country boys with the right connections, Wordsworth's family destined his younger brother John for service with the East India Company. "I will work for you," he said to William, "and you shall attempt to do something for the world." Although John lost his life in 1805 in the wreck of a tradeship, so widespread was the phenomenon of English fortunes based on Indian gain that "nabob," Hindi for "vicegerent" or "governor," entered the vernacular as a synonym for a wealthy man.

CONSUMERS AND COMMODITIES

Even more remarkable was the role of the East India Company as the prototype for later colonial rule. At a time when Oxford and Cambridge graduates were preparing for clerical orders, the Company college at Haileybury trained its students for their foreign service. Malthus taught there; both James Mill and son John Stuart Mill worked for the Company; Lamb was a clerk in the home office in London. And thousands more indirectly derived livelihoods or pleasures from the Company's activities. Napoleon sneered at Britain as "a nation of shopkeepers," taking this phrase from Smith's *Wealth of Nations*: "To found a great empire for the sole purpose of raising up a people of customers, may at first sight appear a project fit only for a nation of shopkeepers." But Smith's mercantile empire was a perspicuous forecast, confirmed in 1823 by Byron when he named England's pride as its "haughty shopkeepers, who sternly dealt / Their goods and edicts out from pole to pole, / And made the very billows pay them toll" (*Don Juan* 10:65).

Cotton and tea were major goods. So was opium, and behind the dreams of Coleridge's *Kubla Khan*, Keats's *Ode to a Nightingale* (whose poet compares his state of sensation to intoxication by "some dull opiate"), and De Quincey's *Confessions of an English Opium Eater* were grim realities. Laudanum, opium dissolved in alcohol, was widely prescribed for a variety of complaints; it was the chief ingredient in a host of sedatives for children, especially of the poor, whose families had to leave them at home while they worked. It was also a cheap intoxicant. When Marx said that "religion was the opium of the masses," he was not using a random metaphor. Opium virtually defined foreign profiteering. De Quincey's uncle was a colonel in Bengal, in the military service of the East India Company, which reaped enormous profits from producing opium and smuggling it into China against the prohibition of the Chinese government. A Member of Parliament remarked: "If the Chinese are to be poisoned by opium, I would rather they were poisoned for the benefit of our Indian subjects than for the benefit of any other Exchequer." But the profits accrued less to Indian subjects than to the ruling British, even as the Opium Wars served the larger purpose of opening China to Lancashire cotton, as India had been opened earlier: the Wars concluded with the annexation of Hong Kong, and the opening of five treaty ports to British commerce. Meanwhile, the persistence of slave labor in British colonial plantations (not abolished until 1833) continued to raise ethical questions about the traffic in their commodities. International affairs inescapably cast their shadow on national life: "By foreign wealth are British morals chang'd," charged Barbauld in 1791, "And Afric's sons, and India's, smile aveng'd."

As morals adjusted in relation to economic opportunities, the empire also fed a growing appetite for the exotic among those shut up in urban squalor, or merely in an increasingly routinized commercial life. For those who had the wherewithal, the era proffered a new world of objects, which had begun to proliferate in the late eighteenth century. An exemplary instance of the success of marketing joined to new technological advance is Josiah Wedgwood (1730–1795), whose cream-colored earthenware became known as "Queen's ware" because of Queen Charlotte's patronage in 1765, and, aided by that éclat, soon enjoyed a worldwide sale. In the 1770s he discovered how quickly high art could be transformed into status commodity, and began to produce imitation Greek vases, in vogue because of recent excavations at Herculaneum and Pompeii. The Wedgwood fortune enabled Josiah's sons to offer Coleridge an annuity of £150 so that he could devote himself to literature.

Alfred Bird, inventor of "Bird's Custard," pinned up in his Birmingham shop a telling motto mixing morality and the new imperatives of trade: "Early to bed. Early to rise / Stick to your work . . . And Advertise." From the late eighteenth century on, fashion magazines with colored plates advertised to provincial residents the latest styles of the capital. Even as she denounced the enslavement of women by "the perpetual fluctuation of fashion," Mary Hays conceded that "this constant variation of mode is serviceable to commerce, and promotes a brisk circulation of money" (*Letters and Essays*, 1793). This stimulus reached its acme with the arrival of *The Forget Me Not, a Christmas and New Year's Present for 1823*. More than sixty annuals emerged to capitalize on this pioneering venture, bearing such titles as *The Book of Beauty*. Partly because they targeted female readers, they were hospitable to female authors, including Shelley and Hemans. And becuase they paid so well, they also attracted male writers: Wordsworth, Coleridge, Southey, Lamb, and Scott published in them, even though literary contributions were subordinated to the engravings that were their most compelling feature. The elegantly produced annuals were best-sellers (*The Literary Souvenir* attained a circulation of fifteen thousand); copies were shipped across the empire months in advance.

Not only women and city-dwellers were seduced by the lure of shop windows, magazines, and circulating catalogues. Cobbett hurled jeremiads at the prosperous farmers who aspired to a gentility that set them apart from the workers they had once fed as part of the family:

> Everything about this farm-house was formerly the scene of *plain manners* and *plentiful living*. . . . But all appeared to be in a state of decay and nearly of disuse. There appeared to have been hardly any *family* in that house, where formerly there were, in all probability, from ten to fifteen men, boys, and maids: and, which was the worst of all, there was a *parlour*. Aye, and a *carpet* and a *bell-pull* too! . . . And, there were the decanters, the glasses, the "dinner-set" of crockery-ware, and all just in the true stock-jobber style. And I dare say it has been 'Squire Charington and the *Miss* Charingtons; and not plain Master Charington, and his son Hodge, and his daughter Betty Charington, all of whom this accursed system has, in all likelihood, transmuted into a species of mock gentlefolks, while it has ground the labourers down into real slaves. (*Rural Rides*, 20 October 1825)

This revolution in manners and family structure reduced "family" to its biological nucleus, replacing the economic unit that enfolded laborers, servants, and dependents. This was but one manifestation of the "acceleration" and "agitation" that, in De Quincey's words, characterized the period well before the French Revolution.

AUTHORSHIP, AUTHORITY, AND "ROMANTICISM"

In this fast-moving world, the fortunes of writers, too, began to rise and fall with new speed. Writing in *The Edinburgh Review* in 1829, the critic Francis Jeffrey meditated on "the perishable nature of modern literary fame":

> Since the beginning of our critical career, we have seen a vast deal of beautiful poetry pass into oblivion, in spite of our feeble efforts to recall or retain it in remembrance. The tuneful quartos of Southey are already little better than lumber:—And the rich melodies of Keats and Shelley,—and the fantastical emphasis of Wordsworth,—and the plebeian pathos of Crabbe, are melting fast from the fields of our vision. The novels of Scott have put out his poetry. Even the splendid strains of Moore are fading into distance and dimness, except where they have been married to immortal music; and the blazing star of Byron himself is receding from its place of pride. . . . The two who have the longest withstood this rapid withering of the laurel, and with the least marks of decay on their branches, are Rogers and Campbell; neither of them, it may be remarked, voluminous writers, and both distinguished rather for the fine taste and consummate elegance of their writ-

ings, than for the fiery passion, and disdainful vehemence, which seemed for a time to be so much more in favour with the public. . . . If taste and elegance, however, be titles to enduring fame, we might venture securely to promise that rich boon to the author before us.

The author before Jeffrey as he wrote was Felicia Hemans, a poet widely admired on both sides of the Atlantic but by the end of the century forgotten, except for a few anthology favorites. Meanwhile, with nearly three decades of reviewing experience, Jeffrey was unable to predict the durable fame of some of the writers who by the century's end would be deemed quintessential "romantics": Byron, Wordsworth, Keats, and Shelley. And he misguessed about Rogers and Campbell, though it is clear he would have attributed their demise to degraded public taste rather than intrinsic faults. What Jeffrey helps us see is that naming a literary canon is a matter of selection from a wide field, motivated by personal values. Other than Hemans, for instance, he thinks of English literary tradition as defined by men—even though Jane Austen and Mary Shelley proved to have as much durability as anyone in his census (Austen's novels and Shelley's *Frankenstein* have never been out of print). He also prefers literature of "fine taste" and "elegance" to the fiery passion and disdainful vehemence that other readers would admire in Byron and Shelley.

It was the conservative Jeffrey who first attempted to assess the "new poets," in the inaugural issue of the *Edinburgh* (1802). Here he castigates Southey as a member of a heretical "sect of poets, that has established itself in this country within these ten or twelve years, and is looked upon, we believe, as one of its chief champions and apostles." His polemical intent was to brand with all the excesses of the French Revolution a group he called "the Lakers" (from their residence in the Lake District): Southey, Wordsworth, and Coleridge. Well before Hazlitt, Jeffrey was blaming "the revolution in our literature" on "the agitations of the French revolution, and the discussion as well as the hopes and terrors to which it gave occasion." "A splenetic and idle discontent with the existing institutions of society, seems to be at the bottom of all their serious and peculiar sentiments"; "the ambition of Mr. Southey and some of his associates" is not "of that regulated and manageable sort which usually grows up in old established commonwealths," but "of a more undisciplined and revolutionary character which looks, we think with a jealous and contemptuous eye on the old aristocracy of the literary world."

By the Regency, the revolutionary "Lake School" was joined by the upstart "Cockney School," a term of insult fixed on Londoners Hazlitt, Hunt, and Keats, by the Scotsman John Gibson Lockhart, writing in *Blackwood's* in 1817, partly in response to Hunt's celebration of a vigorous school of "Young Poets" in essays he was writing for *The Examiner*. Hunt was a radical; Lockhart despised his politics. In 1821 ex-Laker and now Poet Laureate Southey identified still a third school. His youthful radicalism well behind him, he denounced the men "of diseased hearts and depraved imaginations" who formed "the Satanic School, . . . characterized by a Satanic spirit of pride and audacious impiety." Provoked by the allusion to himself and Percy Shelley, Byron responded with satiric attacks against both Southey personally and the establishment politics he had come to espouse. All these classifications were politically motivated—in most cases sneers at innovators and nonconformists or class-inflected put-downs. The designation of a "Romantic School" was not a product of the age itself, but was applied much later in the century—by literary historians with their own Victorian motivations and nostalgia.

With no sense of a monolithic movement that could be called "Romanticism," the polemical terms of the age itself mark a field animated by differences of location, class, gender, politics, and audience. The boundaries that appear rigid at one moment re-form when the perspective shifts: to Lockhart, Lakers (whom he respected) and

Cockneys were distinct; to Byron, a champion of Pope, Keats was both "a tadpole of the Lakes" and a Cockney brat who "abused Pope and Swift." And except for Hunt and Scott, most of these men bonded across class and political lines in their contempt of "Blue Stockings" (intellectual women) and female writers, even as these women were defining themselves for and against the stigmatized precedent of Wollstonecraft. Liberals, conservatives, and radicals; Byron and Shelley, self-exiled aristocrats in Italy; Wordsworth, Coleridge, and Southey praising domesticity in the Lakes; Keats, Hazlitt, and Hunt, an apprentice surgeon and working journalists, all precariously middle-class Londoners; women novelists, poets, and essayists, Blue Stockings and Wollstonecraftians, moralizers and rebels: the array is diverse and engaged in a contest for attention too keen to call debate or conversation.

The difficulty of specifying the term "Romantic" arises in part because it hovers between chronological and conceptual references. Its literature emerges in the social and literary ferment of the 1780s, a benchmark being the publication of Blake's *Songs of Innocence* in the climactic year of 1789. The period's close is usually seen in the 1830s—the decade in which George IV died, as did several writers who defined the age: Scott, Lamb, Coleridge, Hemans. By this time, too, Keats, Byron, and Percy Shelley, Austen, and most of the first generation were dead. In the same decade, Alfred Lord Tennyson's poetic career began, and Victoria was crowned Queen. Yet the temporal boundaries are fluid: "Romantic" Keats and "Victorian" Thomas Carlyle were born the same year, 1795, and Wordsworth's major poem, *The Prelude*, though he worked on it for a half century beginning in 1797 or so, was not published until the year of his death, 1850, the same year that Tennyson's quintessentially Victorian *In Memoriam* appeared. Much of Keats's poetry appeared for the first time after 1848, reviving interest in him among a new generation of readers.

Yet even with these ambiguous boundaries, the "Romantic" movement, from its first description in the nineteenth century until the mid-1980s, was characterized by men's writing. This was also a dominant spirit of the age, during which the powers of literary production—publishers, booksellers, reviews, and the press—were men's domains and not always open to female authors, and the culture as a whole was not receptive to female authority. Wollstonecraft's *Rights of Woman* (1792) was one of the first analyses to define "women" as an oppressed class that cut across national distinctions and historical differences—oppressed by lack of education, by lack of legal rights and access to gainful employment, as well as by a "prevailing opinion" about their character: that women were made to feel and be felt, rather than to think; their duty was to bear children and be domestic drudges, to obey their fathers and their husbands without complaint. Women writers faced more than a few challenges. One was the pervasive cultural attitude that a woman who presumed to authority, published her views, and even aspired to make a living as an author was grossly immodest, decidedly "unfeminine," and probably a truant from her domestic calling. Many women published anonymously, under male pseudonyms, with the proper title "Mrs." or, as in Austen's case, under an anonymous and socially modest signature, "by a Lady" (not one of Austen's novels bore her name). They also maintained propriety by hewing to subjects and genres deemed "feminine"—not political polemic, epic poetry, science or philosophy but children's books, conduct literature, travel writing (if it was clear they had proper escorts), household hints, cookbooks, novels of manners, and poems of sentiment and home, of patriotism and religious piety. Women who transgressed provoked harsh discipline. When Barbauld ventured an anti-imperialist poem, *Eighteen Hundred and Eleven*, the Tory *Quarterly Review* exercised reproof precisely in terms of the gender-genre transgression:

> Mrs. Barbauld turned satirist! . . . We had hoped, indeed, that the empire might have
> been saved without the intervention of a lady-author. . . . Her former works have been of
> some utility; her "Lessons for Children," her "Hymns in Prose," her "Selections from the
> Spectator," . . . but we must take the liberty of warning her to desist from satire . . . writ-
> ing any more pamphlets in verse. (June 1812)

Barbauld took this advice to heart, and published no more. About fifteen years earlier,
Anglican arbiter Richard Polwhele viciously listed a whole set of contemporary female
writers in his poem *The Unsex'd Females*, with virulent animosity to Wollstonecraft.
They are "unsex'd" by their public stance, parading what "ne'er our fathers saw."

   The Tory *British Critic*, on the occasion of praising Hemans's excellence "in
painting the strength and the weaknesses of her own lovely sex" and the "womanly
nature throughout all her thoughts and her aspirations," kept up the surveillance,
taking the opportunity to despise anything that advertised the intellectual and critical authority of women. It opened its review of Hemans (1823) not with a discussion
of the work at hand but with an assault on the world that was changing before its
eyes, against which it invokes every counterauthority, from divine creation, to modern science, to Shakespeare, to the language of ridicule and disgust:

> We heartily abjure Blue Stockings. We make no compromise with any variation of the colour,
> from sky-blue to Prussian blue, blue stockings are an outrage upon the eternal fitness of things.
> It is a principle with us to regard an Academicienne of this Society, with the same charity that
> a cat regards a vagabond mouse. We are inexorable to special justifications. We would fain
> make a fire in Charing-Cross, of all the bas bleus in the kingdom, and albums, and common-
> place books, as accessaries [sic] before or after the fact, should perish in the conflagration.
>   Our forefathers never heard of such a thing as a Blue Stocking, except upon their sons'
> legs; the writers of Natural History make no mention of the name. . . . Shakspeare, who paint-
> ed all sorts and degrees of persons and things, who compounded or created thousands, which,
> perhaps, never existed, except in his own prolific mind, even he, in the wildest excursion of
> his fancy never dreamed of such an extraordinary combination as a Blue Stocking! No!

The extraordinary combination, however, was there to stay, and even with all these
constraints, women writers thrived. More, Barbauld, Mary Robinson, Charlotte Smith,
and Maria Edgeworth stand out among those who earned both reputation and a living through poetry, novels, and tracts on education and politics, freely crossing the
borders between public and private spheres, male and female realms.

POPULAR PROSE

When *The Edinburgh Review* was founded in 1802 as an organ of liberal political opinion, it raised the status of periodical writing. "To be an Edinburgh Reviewer," opined
William Hazlitt, who freelanced in the journal, "is, I suspect, the highest rank in modern
literary society." By the end of the decade, the rival Tory *Quarterly Review* arrived on
the scene. The quarterlies favored an authoritative, anonymous voice, while new
monthly magazines revived the lighter manner of the eighteenth-century "familiar
essay." *Blackwood's* (founded 1817) printed raffish conversations set in a nearby tavern,
and the *London* (founded 1820) hosted Lamb's essays and De Quincey's *Confessions of
an English Opium Eater*. Whether the topic was imaginative literature, social observation, science, or political commentary, the personality of the essayist and the literary
performance—by turns meditative, autobiographical, analytical, whimsical, terse and
expansive—were what commanded attention. "All the great geniuses of the day are
Periodical," declared John Wilson, writing in *Blackwood's* in 1829—a self-interested
judgment, but true insofar as it acknowledges the new importance of the periodical

essay. Meanwhile, beneath the realm of the respectable journals, though not out of their anxious sight, thrived William Cobbett, who published a weekly newspaper, the *Political Register* (founded 1802), its price low enough to evade the stamp tax (thus becoming known as "The Two-Penny Trash"). It reached a circulation of forty or fifty thousand and helped make him the most widely read writer of his era, and surely the most prolific, with an output estimated at more than twenty million words.

If later decades tended to represent "Romanticism" largely as an age of poetry, in the age itself, poetry, traditionally the genre of prestige, had to compete with prose, and not just the engaging new essay form, but also, and quite emphatically, the once-disreputable novel. The novel had begun to command new attention after the success of Godwin's political romance from the 1790s, *Caleb Williams*, and new respect after the critical and popular success of Scott's *Waverley* (1814). With dozens of works of narrative fiction over the next two decades, Scott perfected the genre of historical "romance"—"the interest of which turns upon marvelous and uncommon incidents," he said in a review of Austen. As the occasion indicates, the novel was also a genre in which women achieved considerable success—perhaps why, in addition to its status as a "low" form, Sir Walter kept his authorship of the *Waverley* novels anonymous. In *Waverley*, Scott spoofed the gothic devices that animated Ann Radcliffe's sensational "gothic" novels. But Radcliffe was remarkably popular; the genre that she perfected in the 1790s caught everyone's attention, including publishers'. She received the unheard of sum of £500 for *The Mysteries of Udolpho* (1794), topped by £600 for *The Italian* (1797), and achieved unprecedented fame for a novelist of any sex. Edgeworth's regional-historical novels, their career launched in 1800 with *Castle Rackrent* and extending over a quarter century, also caught the attention of Scott, who dubbed her "the great Maria" both out of admiration for a genre that shaped his own ventures and in recognition of her considerable financial success. Hannah More's only novel, *Coelebs in Search of a Wife* (1808), ran through twelve editions in its first year, and before her death in 1833 had sold thirty thousand copies in America alone. Shelley produced a durable masterpiece with *Frankenstein* (1818 and 1831), while Austen's novels caught public interest with their sharp social observation and stories of heroines coming of age in a world of finely calibrated social codes and financial pressures. With Scott, she would be deemed one of the major figures in the genre.

Throughout the years, social turmoil and technological change fostered a proliferation of writing. In the Preface to *Lyrical Ballads* (1800) Wordsworth deplored the "multitude of causes unknown to former times . . . now acting with a combined force to blunt the discriminating powers of the mind," and diagnosed the most virulent as "the great national events which are daily taking place, and the encreasing accumulation of men in cities, where the uniformity of their occupations produces a craving for extraordinary incident which the rapid communication of intelligence hourly gratifies." Newspapers, daily and Sunday, multiplied to meet this craving. In 1814 the London *Times* converted to a steam press, and doubled circulation. Newspaper sales reached thirty million, with yet more readers in the coffee-houses and subscription reading-rooms that took papers that taxes rendered too expensive for individual purchase. Parliamentary commissions and boards of review collected information and compiled statistics and summaries as never before on every aspect of the nation's economy and policies, and the press disseminated them. Cobbett ceaselessly lambasted the fundholders who profited from the debts incurred by the war, even as those who had fought suffered from the postwar depression; John Wade investigated sinecures, aristocratic incomes, pluralism in the Church, corruption in Parliament, and the expenditures of the civil list, and published his findings in the sensational *Black Book* (1820), available in sixpenny installments that sold ten thousand copies each.

THE PRESS, invented much about the same time with the *Reformation*, hath done more mischief to the discipline of our Church, than all the doctrine can make amends for. 'Twas an happy time, when all learning was in manuscript, and some little officer did keep the keys of the library! Now, since PRINTING came into the world, such is the mischief, that a man cannot write a book but presently he is answered! There have been ways found out to *fine* not the people, but even the grounds and fields where they assembled! but so art yet could prevent these SEDITIOUS MEETINGS OF LETTERS! Two or three brawny fellows in a corner, with meer ink and elbow-grease, do more harm than an *hundred systematic divines*. Their ugly printing *letters*, that look but like so many rotten teeth, how oft have they been pulled out by the public tooth-drawers! And yet these rascally operators of the press have got a trick to fasten them again in a few minutes, that they grow as firm a set, and as biting and talkative as ever! O PRINTING! how hast thou *disturbed the peace?* Lead, when moulded into bullets, is not so mortal as when founded into *letters!* There was a mistake sure in the story of Cadmus; and the *serpent's teeth* which he sowed, were nothing else but the *letters* which he invented.

                                    Marvell's Rehearsal transprosed, 4to, 1672.

Being marked only with *four and twenty letters,*—*variously transposed* by the help of a PRINTING PRESS,—PAPER works miracles. The Devil dares no more come near a *Stationer's* heap, or a *Printer's Office,* than *Rats* dare put their noses into a Cheesemonger's Shop.   *A Whip for the Devil,* 1669. p. 92.

George Cruikshank. *The Press,* from the satirical pamphlet *The Political Showman—at Home!* by William Hone, 1821.

The explosion of readers at once liberated authors from patronage and exposed them to the turbulent and precarious world of the literary marketplace. In 1812 Jeffrey reckoned that among "the higher classes" there were twenty thousand readers, but at least "two hundred thousand who read for amusement and instruction, among the middling classes of society," defining "middling" as those "who do not aim at distinction or notoriety beyond the circle of their equals in fortune or station." Faced with an audience fissured along class lines, he thought that it was "easy to see" which group an author should please. But others looked to the growing number of literate poor who lacked traditional education, vast numbers whose allegiance was fought over by radicals like Cobbett and Paine and conservatives such as More, whose *Cheap Repository Tracts* (1795–1799) were circulated by the millions.

    Such journalism diffused and intensified troubled perceptions of the functioning of society and one's place in it. "The beginning of Inquiry is Disease," intoned Carlyle; he inveighed against "the diseased self-conscious state of Literature" but this self-consciousness was its character. Uncertain of the audience(s) by whom they would be read, writers resorted to an ironic wavering that sought to forestall being pinned down to a position and dismissed, or devised various strategies to seduce assent: the development of the authorial "I" whom readers might come to trust as an authentic percipient, personae that insiders would be able to penetrate, and codings that would deepen a sense of solidarity among a constituency. Wordsworth had made his name with the highly personal, but culturally resonant, lyric outpouring of "Lines, Composed a few miles above Tintern Abbey, On Revisiting the Banks of they Wye during a Tour, July 13, 1798" (*Lyrical Ballads,* 1798); he celebrated his return from France in 1802 with a sonnet "Composed in the Valley, near Dover, On the Day of Landing," rejoicing in familiar sights of rivers and boys at play: "All, all are English." In a neighboring sonnet in the same collection, though, he complained, "The world is too much with us," running our lives with "getting and spending" and alienating our hearts from "Nature."

Wordsworth remained ambivalent about developing a voice and a literature that would gain popular reception, and continued to resent those, such as Scott, who were more successful in these terms. But the new world and the new literatures were finding remarkable sympathy in many quarters. Scott's first romance, *The Lay of the Last Minstrel* (1805), sold well over 2,000 copies within a year of publication, and nearly 10,000 more by 1807. His publisher offered him 1,000 guineas, sight unseen, for his next poetic romance, *Marmion* (1808). Scott said the sum "made men's hair stand on end," but the bargain was a good one on both sides: by 1811 it had sold 28,000 copies. These figures were topped by Byron, who, Scott good-naturedly conceded, drove him from the field of poetry, while his own *Waverley* novels proved still more popular. Over his lifetime, Scott made about £80,000 from his writing. That Byron's *Corsair* (1814) could sell 10,000 copies on the day of publication testifies to the mechanisms of production, publicity, and sales the book trade commanded. Byron was not embarrassed to seek £2600 for *Childe Harold IV* (1818). It must have galled Wordsworth that his publisher gave Thomas Moore 3,000 guineas for *Lalla Rookh*, more than had ever been offered for a single poem. Yet along with these stunning successes, other careers were more modestly compensated, and poets, at least, did not often enjoy the degree of prosperity that the novelists did.

The volatility of the market and of public taste points to salient qualities of the period: a heightened awareness of differences and boundaries, and of the energies generated along their unstable edges, and even more, a heightened awareness of time and history, public and cultural as well as personal. "Romanticism" denotes less a unified concept, or even a congeries of ideas, than an era and a literature of clashing systems, each plausibly claiming allegiance, in a world of rapid change.

Anna Laetitia Barbauld
1743–1825

Barbauld's long career exemplifies that of the professional woman of letters: a respected poet (and not only on conventionally feminine themes), a writer on radical causes throughout the 1790s, an early welcomer of Coleridge (who presented her with a prepublication copy of *Lyrical Ballads*), and a friend of Priestley, Hannah More, and Joanna Baillie. The daughter of John Aikin, master of Warrington Academy, a celebrated institution of English Dissenting culture where she lived between the ages of fifteen and thirty, Anna Laetitia Aikin is said to have learned to read English by the age of three, Italian and French not long afterwards, and Greek and Latin while still a child. Her first volume of *Poems* (1773) went through five editions in four years; in the same year, she published *Miscellaneous Pieces in Prose* with her brother John, later editor of the *Monthly Magazine*, an influential radical journal. In 1774 she married Rochemont Barbauld, a Dissenting clergyman, with whom she ran a school. Samuel Johnson derided the activity as the waste of a fine education, but it led to her often reprinted *Lessons for Children* (1778) and *Hymns in Prose for Children* (1781). After the increasing mental instability of her husband led to the closing of their school, she undertook ambitious editorial projects. In 1794 she produced an edition of Akenside, one of Collins in 1797, and in 1804 a six-volume edition of the *Correspondence of Samuel Richardson*, followed by a fifty-volume set of *The British Novelists* (1810), with biographical introductions and a sophisticated preface arguing for the instructive value of a genre derided as mere entertainment, as well as a popular anthology for young women, *The Female Speaker* (1811). Like Wollstonecraft, she believed that young women should be educated to become wives and mothers. Her lively domestic realism is shown in her poem *Washing-Day* (1797), which moves from mock-epic to personal recollection to its concluding instance of a recent scientific advance, the Montgolfier brothers' balloon ascent, effortlessly crossing the conventional boundaries of private and public, feminine and masculine, realms; *The First Fire* likewise surprisingly joins a celebration of the domestic hearth to a vista of geological process. Barbauld thus consistently opens up traditional themes and poetic forms in the service of a powerful social and poetic vision.

The Mouse's Petition to Dr. Priestley[1]

> O hear a pensive prisoner's prayer,
>   For liberty that sighs;
> And never let thine heart be shut
>   Against the wretch's cries!
>
> 5 For here forlorn and sad I sit,
>   Within the wiry grate;
> And tremble at the approaching morn,
>   Which brings impending fate.
>
> If e'er thy breast with freedom glowed,
> 10   And spurned a tyrant's chain,
> Let not thy strong oppressive force
>   A free-born mouse detain!

---

1. The full title in early editions is *The Mouse's Petition, Found in the trap where he had been confined all night*, accompanied by a motto from Virgil's *Aeneid* (6.853): "Parcere subjectis & debellare superbos" [To spare the conquered, and subdue the proud]. Joseph Priestley (1733–1804), political radical and eminent chemist who discovered oxygen, had been testing the properties of gases on captured household mice. Tradition has it that Barbauld's petition succeeded, and this mouse was released.

O do not stain with guiltless blood
    Thy hospitable hearth;
15 Nor triumph that thy wiles betrayed
    A prize so little worth.

The scattered gleanings of a feast
    My frugal meals supply;
But if thine unrelenting heart
20   That slender boon deny,—

The cheerful light, the vital air,
    Are blessings widely given;
Let nature's commoners enjoy
    The common gifts of heaven.

25 The well-taught philosophic mind
    To all compassion gives:
Casts round the world an equal eye,
    And feels for all that lives.

If mind,—as ancient sages taught,—
30   A never-dying flame,
Still shifts through matter's varying forms,
    In every form the same;

Beware, lest in the worm you crush
    A brother's soul you find;
35 And tremble lest thy luckless hand
    Dislodge a kindred mind.

Or, if this transient gleam of day
    Be *all* of life we share,
Let pity plead within thy breast
40   That little *all* to spare.

So may thy hospitable board
    With wealth and peace be crowned;
And every charm of heartfelt ease
    Beneath thy roof be found.

45 So when destruction lurks unseen,
    Which men, like mice, may share,
May some kind angel clear thy path,
    And break the hidden snare.

1771   1773

On a Lady's Writing

Her even lines her steady temper show,
Neat as her dress, and polished as her brow;
Strong as her judgment, easy as her air;
Correct though free, and regular though fair:
And the same graces o'er her pen preside,
That form her manners and her footsteps guide.

                                                 1773

Inscription for an Ice-House[1]

Stranger, approach! within this iron door
Thrice locked and bolted, this rude arch beneath
That vaults with ponderous stone the cell; confined
By man, the great magician, who controuls
5   Fire, earth and air, and genii of the storm,
And bends the most remote and opposite things
To do him service and perform his will,—
A giant sits; stern Winter; here he piles,
While summer glows around, and southern gales
10   Dissolve the fainting world, his treasured snows°   *sherberts*
Within the rugged cave.—Stranger, approach!
He will not cramp thy limbs with sudden age,
Nor wither with his touch the coyest flower
That decks thy scented hair. Indignant here,
15   Like fettered Sampson[2] when his might was spent
In puny feats to glad the festive halls
Of Gaza's wealthy sons; or he who sat
Midst laughing girls submiss, and patient twirled
The slender spindle in his sinewy grasp;[3]
20   The rugged power, fair Pleasure's minister,
Exerts his art to deck the genial board;
Congeals the melting peach, the nectarine smooth,
Burnished and glowing from the sunny wall:
Darts sudden frost into the crimson veins
25   Of the moist berry; moulds the sugared hail:
Cools with his icy breath our flowing cups;
Or gives to the fresh dairy's nectared bowls
A quicker zest. Sullen he plies his task,
And on his shaking fingers counts the weeks
30   Of lingering Summer, mindful of his hour
To rush in whirlwinds forth, and rule the year.

c. 1793   1825

To a Little Invisible Being
Who Is Expected Soon to Become Visible

Germ of new life, whose powers expanding slow
For many a moon their full perfection wait,—
Haste, precious pledge of happy love, to go
Auspicious borne through life's mysterious gate.

5   What powers lie folded in thy curious frame,—
Senses from objects locked, and mind from thought!
How little canst thou guess thy lofty claim
To grasp at all the worlds the Almighty wrought!

---

1. The ice-house, where blocks of ice were kept cold in the warmer months, was the commonest form of refrigeration before the twentieth century.
2. Judges 16 relates the imprisonment of the blinded Samson in Gaza, forced to make "sport" for the Philistines; the story forms the subject of Milton's tragedy, *Samson Agonistes* (1671).
3. Hercules, who served a term as slave to Queen Omphale, during which time he performed women's tasks.

And see, the genial season's warmth to share,
10 Fresh younglings shoot, and opening roses glow!
Swarms of new life exulting fill the air,—
Haste, infant bud of being, haste to blow!°   *bloom*

For thee the nurse prepares her lulling songs,
The eager matrons count the lingering day;
15 But far the most thy anxious parent longs
On thy soft cheek a mother's kiss to lay.

She only asks to lay her burden down,
That her glad arms that burden may resume;
And nature's sharpest pangs her wishes crown,
20 That free thee living from thy living tomb.

She longs to fold to her maternal breast
Part of herself, yet to herself unknown;
To see and to salute the stranger guest,
Fed with her life through many a tedious moon.

25 Come, reap thy rich inheritance of love!
Bask in the fondness of a Mother's eye!
Nor wit nor eloquence her heart shall move
Like the first accents of thy feeble cry.

Haste, little captive, burst thy prison doors!
30 Launch on the living world, and spring to light!
Nature for thee displays her various stores,
Opens her thousand inlets of delight.

If charmed verse of muttered prayers had power,
With favouring spells to speed thee on thy way,
35 Anxious I'd bid my beads° each passing hour,   *tell my rosary*
Till thy wished smile thy mother's pangs o'erpay.

c. 1795   1825

To the Poor[1]

Child of distress, who meet'st the bitter scorn
Of fellow men to happier prospects born,
Doomed art and nature's various stores to see
Flow in full cups of joy,—and not for thee,
5 Who seest the rich, to heaven and fate resign'd,
Bear *thy* afflictions with a patient mind;
Whose bursting heart disdains unjust controll,
Who feel'st oppression's iron in thy soul,
Who drag'st the load of faint and feeble years,
10 Whose bread is anguish and whose water tears—
Bear, bear thy wrongs, fulfil thy destined hour,
Bend thy meek neck beneath the foot of power!

---

1. Barbauld wrote that this poem was "inspired by indignation on hearing sermons in which the poor are addressed in a manner which evidently shows the design of making religion an engine of government."

But when thou feel'st the great deliverer nigh,
And thy freed spirit mounting seeks the sky,
15   Let no vain fears thy parting hour molest,
No whispered terrors shake thy quiet breast,
Think not their threats can work thy future woe,
Nor deem the Lord above, like Lords below.
Safe in the bosom of that love repose
20   By whom the sun gives light, the ocean flows,
Prepare to meet a father undismayed,
Nor fear the God whom priests and kings have made.

1795   1825

Washing-Day

". . . And their voice,
Turning again towards childish treble, pipes
And whistles in its sound."[1]

The Muses are turned gossips; they have lost
The buskined° step, and clear, high-sounding phrase,   *tragic*
Language of gods. Come, then, domestic Muse,
In slipshod measure° loosely prattling on   *loose metres*
5   Of farm or orchard, pleasant curds and cream,
Or drowning flies, or shoe lost in the mire
By little whimpering boy, with rueful face;
Come, Muse, and sing the dreaded Washing-day.
Ye who beneath the yoke of wedlock bend,
10   With bowed soul, full well ye ken the day
Which week, smooth sliding after week, brings on
Too soon;—for to that day nor peace belongs,
Nor comfort; ere the first gray streak of dawn,
The red-armed washers come and chase repose.
15   Nor pleasant smile, nor quaint device of mirth,
E'er visited that day: the very cat,
From the wet kitchen's scared and reeking° hearth,   *smoking*
Visits the parlor,—an unwonted guest.
The silent breakfast-meal is soon despatched;
20   Uninterrupted, save by anxious looks
Cast at the lowering° sky, if sky should lower.   *threatening*
From that last evil, O preserve us, heavens!
For should the skies pour down, adieu to all
Remains of quiet: then expect to hear
25   Of sad disasters,—dirt and gravel stains
Hard to efface, and loaded lines at once
Snapped short,—and linen-horse° by dog thrown down,   *drying rack for sheets*
And all the petty miseries of life.
Saints have been calm while stretched upon the rack,
30   And Guatimozin[2] smiled on burning coals;

---

1. Shakespeare, loosely quoted from *As You Like It* (2.7   2. Cuauhtemoc, the last Aztec emperor of Mexico, tor-
161–63), Jaques's speech on the seven ages of man.   tured and executed by Cortés in 1525.

But never yet did housewife notable°   *efficient*
Greet with a smile a rainy washing-day.
But grant the welkin° fair, require not thou   *the heavens*
Who call'st thyself perchance the master there,
35   Or study swept, or nicely dusted coat,
Or usual 'tendance,—ask not, indiscreet,
Thy stockings mended, though the yawning rents
Gape wide as Erebus;[3] nor hope to find
Some snug recess impervious: shouldst thou try
40   The 'customed garden-walks, thine eyes shall rue
The budding fragrance of thy tender shrubs,
Myrtle or rose, all crushed beneath the weight
Of coarse checked apron,—with impatient hand
Twitched off when showers impend: or crossing lines
45   Shall mar thy musings, as the wet, cold sheet
Flaps in thy face abrupt. Woe to the friend
Whose evil stars have urged him forth to claim
On such a day the hospitable rites!
Looks, blank at best, and stinted courtesy,
50   Shall he receive. Vainly he feeds his hopes
With dinner of roast chicken, savory pie,
Or tart, or pudding:—pudding he nor tart
That day shall eat; nor, though the husband try,
Mending what can't be helped, to kindle mirth
55   From cheer deficient, shall his consort's brow
Clear up propitious: the unlucky guest
In silence dines, and early slinks away.
I well remember, when a child, the awe
This day struck into me; for then the maids,
60   I scarce knew why, looked cross, and drove me from them:
Nor soft caress could I obtain; nor hope
Usual indulgences; jelly or creams,
Relic of costly suppers, and set by
For me their petted one, or buttered toast,
65   When butter was forbid; or thrilling tale
Of ghost or witch or murder,—so I went
And sheltered me beside the parlor fire:
There my dear grandmother, eldest of forms,
Tended the little ones, and watched from harm,
70   Anxiously fond, though oft her spectacles
With elfin cunning hid, and oft the pins
Drawn from her ravelled stockings, might have soured
One less indulgent.—
At intervals my mother's voice was heard,
75   Urging despatch: briskly the work went on,
All hands employed to wash, to rinse, to wring,
To fold, and starch, and clap, and iron, and plait.
Then would I sit me down, and ponder much

3. In Greek mythology, the dark passage through which souls enter Hades.

Why washings were. Sometimes through hollow bowl
80   Of pipe amused we blew, and sent aloft
The floating bubbles; little dreaming then
To see, Montgolfier,[4] thy silken ball
Ride buoyant through the clouds,—so near approach
The sports of children and the toils of men.
85   Earth, air, and sky, and ocean hath its bubbles,
And verse is one of them,—this most of all.

1797

The First Fire

October 1st, 1815

Ha, old acquaintance! many a month has past
Since last I viewed thy ruddy face; and I,
Shame on me! had mean time well nigh forgot
That such a friend existed. Welcome now!—
5   When summer suns ride high, and tepid airs
Dissolve in pleasing langour; then indeed
We think thee needless, and in wanton pride
Mock at thy grim attire and sooty jaws,
And breath sulphureous, generating spleen,—
10   As Frenchmen say; Frenchmen, who never knew
The sober comforts of a good coal fire.
—Let me imbibe thy warmth, and spread myself
Before thy shrine adoring:—magnet thou
Of strong attraction, daily gathering in
15   Friends, brethren, kinsmen, variously dispersed,
All the dear charities of social life,
To thy close circle. Here a man might stand,
And say, This is my world! Who would not bleed
Rather than see thy violated hearth
20   Prest by a hostile foot? The winds sing shrill;
Heap on the fuel! Not the costly board,
Nor sparkling glass, nor wit, nor music, cheer
Without thy aid. If thrifty thou dispense
Thy gladdening influence, in the chill saloon
25   The silent shrug declares th' unpleased guest.
—How grateful to belated traveller
Homeward returning, to behold the blaze
From cottage window, rendering visible
The cheerful scene within! There sits the sire,
30   Whose wicker chair, in sunniest nook enshrined,
His age's privilege,—a privilege for which
Age gladly yields up all precedence else
In gay and bustling scenes,—supports his limbs.
Cherished by thee, he feels the grateful warmth
35   Creep through his feeble frame and thaw the ice

4. In 1783, in France, the Montgolfier brothers launched the first hot-air balloon.

Of fourscore years, and thoughts of youth arise.
—Nor less the young ones press within, to see
Thy face delighted, and with husk of nuts,
Or crackling holly, or the gummy pine,
40   Feed thy immortal hunger: cheaply pleased
They gaze delighted, while the leaping flames
Dart like an adder's tongue upon their prey;
Or touch with lighted reed thy wreaths of smoke;
Or listen, while the matron sage remarks
45   Thy bright blue scorching flame and aspect clear,
Denoting frosty skies. Thus pass the hours,
While Winter spends without his idle rage.

—Companion of the solitary man,
From gayer scenes withheld! With thee he sits,
50   Converses, moralizes; musing asks
How many eras of uncounted time
Have rolled away since thy black unctuous° food   oily
Was green with vegetative life, and what
This planet then: or marks, in sprightlier mood,
55   Thy flickering smiles play round the illumined room,
And fancies gay discourse, life, motion, mirth,
And half forgets he is a lonely creature.

—Nor less the bashful poet loves to sit
Snug, at the midnight hour, with only thee
60   Of his lone musings conscious. Oft he writes,
And blots, and writes again; and oft, by fits,
Gazes intent with eyes of vacancy
On thy bright face; and still at intervals,
Dreading the critic's scorn, to thee commits,
65   Sole confidant and safe, his fancies crude.

—O wretched he, with bolts and massy bars
In narrow cell immured, whose green, damp walls,
That weep unwholesome dews, have never felt
Thy purifying influence! Sad he sits
70   Day after day till in his youthful limbs
Life stagnates, and the hue of hope is fled
From his wan cheek. And scarce less wretched he,—
When wintry winds blow loud and frosts bite keen,—
The dweller of the clay-built tenement,
75   Poverty-struck, who, heart[h]less, strives to raise
From sullen turf, or stick plucked from the hedge,
The short-lived blaze; while chill around him spreads
The dreary fen, and Ague, sallow-faced,
Stares through the broken pane;—assist him, ye
80   On whose warm roofs the sun of plenty shines,
And feel a glow beyond material fire!

1815   1825

The Rights of Man and
the Revolution Controversy

"The Revolution in France," wrote Percy Shelley, "overthrew the hierarchy, the aristocracy, and the monarchy, and the whole of that peculiarly insolent and oppressive system on which they were based." Celebrated international center of high culture and progressive philosophy, eighteenth-century France was also a country of profound social inequalities and oppression. Dissatisfaction had been growing against the corrupt and inefficient aristocracy, who relentlessly taxed the lower classes (the "Third Estate": peasants, serfs, yeomen, industrial workers and economically independent bourgeoisie) without granting them political power. Tensions mounted in the 1780s as the government went bankrupt and tried to hold on with more taxation and the imprisonment of dissidents, without trial, in the Bastille prison in Paris. Open rebellion broke out with the storming of the Bastille in 1789 and radiated into a series of cataclysmic events watched from across the English Channel, and witnessed by some English visitors to France, with a mixture of interest, sympathy, and horror.

Support for the Revolution was a coterie enthusiasm in England rather than widespread, but it was still of concern to the government and allied institutions. Following the American Revolution, and close to the centenary of Britain's "Glorious Revolution" of 1688, this latest upheaval underscored to European monarchies the insecurity of long-standing alliances of church, state, and aristocracy, and seemed to herald an inevitable movement of "the spirit of the age" toward liberalism and democracy. Political idealists took fire, enchanted by the bold reformation of French life, including not only a new government but also new street names, a new calendar (Year I beginning 21 September 1792) with new month names, new deities (the goddesses Reason, Liberty), and new national festivals to replace the old religious holidays. "Bliss was it in that dawn to be alive!" exclaimed William Wordsworth in a retrospect published in 1809 (cf. *Prelude* 10.689). But the dream proved short-lived as the French Republic descended into factionalism, extremist purges, internal violence, terrorism, and imperialist war-mongering: the monarchy was overthrown in August 1792, thousands of artistocrats and suspected sympathizers were massacred in September, Louis XVI was guillotined in January 1793, and Queen Marie Antoinette in October. Wordsworth and others fell into disenchantment and despair ("The scenes that I witnessed during the earlier years of the French Revolution when I was resident in France," he wrote in 1835, "come back on me with appalling violence"). Conservatives sounded the alarm and, citing the likelihood of a French invasion, the British government enacted a series of repressive measures in the 1790s—suspending civil rights, spying on and harassing political groups, outlawing and vigorously prosecuting some kinds of assembly and publication. France and Britain declared war, and the countries remained on hostile terms, often at war, through the 1790s and the rise of Napoleon, who was finally defeated by the British at Waterloo in 1815. The Revolution and its sequels had such a profound effect on British political life that in 1823 Samuel Taylor Coleridge could say, "We are not yet aware of the consequences of that event. We are too near it."

Helen Maria Williams
1762–1827

When Helen Maria Williams died in Paris in 1827, the *Gentleman's Magazine* in England remembered her as "pre-eminent among the violent female devotees of the Revolution." Of

Scots and Welsh descent, Williams made her appearance in London literary circles with the publication of *Edwin and Eltruda* (1782). Subsequent works fixed her reputation as a poet of liberal opinions, among them *Peru* (1784), a critique of imperialism, and *A Poem on the Bill lately passed for regulating the Slave Trade* (1788). A poem on the Bastille in her only novel, *Julia* (1790), signaled her enthusiasm for the Revolution. She visited Paris in 1790, returned in 1791, and settled there in 1792. A close friend of the moderate Girondins, she was imprisoned in 1793, but her support for the principles of the Revolution never wavered. The salon she ran until 1816 was a magnet for many expatriates, including Paine and Wollstonecraft; Wordsworth bore a letter of introduction to her from Charlotte Smith when he arrived in 1791. Her *Letters Written in France in the Summer of 1790* were followed by further volumes of *Letters from France* (1792–1796), and *A Tour in Switzerland* (1798), which recorded the impact of the Revolution on the Swiss republic. Her admiration for Napoleon dimmed only when he crowned himself Emperor in 1804. Her disillusion can be seen in two later works, published in 1815 and 1819, which carry her account of French life through to the restoration of Louis XVIII, but by then her public identification with radicalism was set. Such sentiments, when joined with her enduring affair with the Unitarian radical John Hurford Stone, tarnished her standing at home, provoking Horace Walpole to call her "a scribbling trollop." But Williams's devotion had produced an unparalleled eyewitness narrative of more than twenty-five turbulent years; perhaps no English subject knew so many of those who shaped the course of the Revolution.

from Letters Written in France, in the Summer of 1790,
to a Friend in England, Containing Various Anecdotes
Relative to the French Revolution[1]

[ARRIVAL IN PARIS]

I arrived at Paris, by a very rapid journey, the day before the federation;[2] and when I am disposed to murmur at the evils of my destiny, I shall henceforth put this piece of good fortune into the opposite scale, and reflect how many disappointments it ought to counterbalance. Had the packet which conveyed me from Brighton to Dieppe failed a few hours later; had the wind been contrary; in short, had I not reached Paris at the moment I did reach it, I should have missed the most sublime spectacle which, perhaps, was ever represented on the theatre of this earth.

[A DEPICTION OF A FEDERATION]

I promised to send you a description of the federation: but it is not to be described! One must have been present, to form any judgment of a scene, the sublimity of which depended much less on its external magnificence than on the effect it produced on the minds of the spectators. "The people, sure, the people were the sight!" I may tell you of pavilions, of triumphal arches, of altars on which incense was burnt, of two hundred thousand men walking in procession; but how am I to give you an adequate idea of the behaviour of the spectators? How am I to paint the impetuous feelings of that immense, that exulting multitude? Half a million people assembled at a spectacle, which furnished every image that can elevate the mind of man; which connected the enthusiasm of moral sentiment with the solemn pomp of religious ceremonies; which addressed itself at once to the imagination, the understanding, and the heart!

The Champ de Mars[3] was formed into an immense amphitheatre, round which were erected forty rows of seats, raised one above another with earth, on which

---

1. The selections here are drawn from volume 1, letters 1, 2, 4, and 5.
2. The Festival of the Federation was held in Paris on 14 July 1790, to celebrate the anniversary of the fall of the

Bastille and the new constitution.
3. "The Field of Mars," the former military parade ground on the left bank of the Seine.

wooden forms were placed. Twenty days' labour, animated by the enthusiasm of the people, accomplished what seemed to require the toil of years. Already in the Champ de Mars the distinctions of rank were forgotten; and, inspired by the same spirit, the highest and lowest orders of citizens gloried in taking up the spade, and assisting the persons employed in a work on which the common welfare of the state depended. Ladies took the instruments of labour in their hands, and removed a little of the earth, that they might be able to boast that they also had assisted in the preparations at the Champ de Mars; and a number of old soldiers were seen voluntarily bestowing on their country the last remains of their strength. A young Abbé of my acquaintance told me, that the people beat a drum at the door of the convent where he lived, and obliged the Superior to let all the Monks come out and work in the Champ de Mars. The Superior with great reluctance acquiesced, "Quant à moi," said the young Abbé, "je ne demandois pas mieux" ["As for me, I desired nothing better"].[4]

At the upper end of the amphitheatre a pavilion was built for the reception of the King, the Queen, their attendants, and the National Assembly,[5] covered with striped tent-cloth of the national colours, and decorated with streamers of the same beloved tints, and fleur de lys. The white flag was displayed above the spot where the King was seated. In the middle of the Champ de Mars L'Autel de la Patrie[6] was placed, on which incense was burnt by priests dressed in long white robes, with sashes of national ribbon. Several inscriptions were written on the altar, but the words visible at the greatest distance were, La Nation, la Loi, et le Roi [The Nation, the Law, and the King].

At the lower end of the amphitheatre, opposite to the pavilion, three triumphal arches were erected, adorned with emblems and allegorical figures.

The procession marched to the Champ de Mars, through the central streets of Paris. At La Place de Louis Quinze, the escorts, who carried the colours, received under their banners, ranged in two lines, the National Assembly, who came from the Tuilleries. When the procession passed the street where Henry the Fourth was assassinated,[7] every man paused as if by general consent: the cries of joy were suspended, and succeeded by a solemn silence. This tribute of regret, paid from the sudden impulse of feeling at such a moment, was perhaps the most honourable testimony to the virtues of that amiable Prince which his memory has yet received.

In the streets, at the windows, and on the roofs of the houses, the people, transported with joy, shouted and wept as the procession passed. Old men were seen kneeling in the streets, blessing God that they had lived to witness that happy moment. The people ran to the doors of their houses loaded with refreshments, which they offered to the troops; and crouds of women surrounded the soldiers, and holding up their infants in their arms, and melting into tears, promised to make their children imbibe, from their earliest age, an inviolable attachment to the principles of the new constitution.

[A Visit to the Bastille Prison]

Before I suffered my friends at Paris to conduct me through the usual routine of convents, churches, and palaces, I requested to visit the Bastille; feeling a much stronger desire to contemplate the ruins of that building than the most perfect edifices in

4. The translations of French phrases in the letters are by Williams herself, who wanted her work to reach as broad an audience as possible.
5. The legislative assembly made up of the third estate, or commons, that by declaring itself the governing body of

the nation had precipitated the revolution in 1789.
6. The Altar of the Fatherland.
7. The king of France known for his love of his people, assassinated in 1610.

Paris. When we got into the carriage, our French servant called to the coachman, with an air of triumph, "A la Bastille—mais nous n'y resterons pas" ["To the Bastille,—but we shall not remain there"]. We drove under that porch which so many wretches have entered never to repass, and alighting from the carriage descended with difficulty into the dungeons, which were too low to admit of our standing upright, and so dark that we were obliged at noon-day to visit them with the light of a candle. We saw the hooks of those chains by which the prisoners were fastened round the neck, to the walls of their cells; many of which being below the level of the water, are in a constant state of humidity; and a noxious vapour issued from them, which more than once extinguished the candle, and was so insufferable that it required a strong spirit of curiosity to tempt one to enter. Good God! and to these regions of horror were human creatures dragged at the caprice of despotic power. What a melancholy consideration, that

> ————Man! proud man,
> Drest in a little brief authority,
> Plays such fantastic tricks before high heaven,
> As make the angels weep.[8]————

There appears to be a greater number of these dungeons than one could have imagined the hard heart of tyranny itself would contrive; for, since the destruction of the building, many subterraneous cells have been discovered underneath a piece of ground which was inclosed within the walls of the Bastille, but which seemed a bank of solid earth before the horrid secrets of this prison-house were disclosed. Some skeletons were found in these recesses, with irons still fastened on their decaying bones.

After having visited the Bastille, we may indeed be surprized, that a nation so enlightened as the French, submitted so long to the oppressions of their government; but we must cease to wonder that their indignant spirits at length shook off the galling yoke.

Those who have contemplated the dungeons of the Bastille, without rejoicing in the French revolution, may, for aught I know, be very respectable persons, and very agreeable companions in the hours of prosperity; but, if my heart were sinking with anguish, I should not fly to those persons for consolation. Sterne[9] says, that a man is incapable of loving one woman as he ought, who has not a sort of an affection for the whole sex; and as little should I look for particular sympathy from those who have no feelings of general philanthropy. If the splendour of a despotic throne can only shine like the radiance of lightning, while all around is involved in gloom and horror, in the name of heaven let its baleful lustre be extinguished for ever. May no such strong contrast of light and shade again exist in the political system of France! but may the beams of liberty, like the beams of day, shed their benign influence on the cottage of the peasant, as well as on the palace of the monarch! May liberty, which for so many ages past has taken pleasure in softening the evils of the bleak and rugged climates of the north, in fertilizing a barren soil, in clearing the swamp, in lifting mounds against the inundations of the tempest, diffuse her blessings also on the genial land of France, and bid the husbandman rejoice under the shade of the olive and the vine!

---

8. Isabella's tirade against the tyranny of Angelo, the agent of the Duke, in Shakespeare's *Measure for Measure* 2.2.117–123.

9. Laurence Sterne, author of *Tristram Shandy* (1759–1767) and *A Sentimental Journey* (1768).

from **Letters from France**[1]
[THE EXECUTION OF THE KING]

Paris, Feb. 10, 1793

The faction of the anarchists desired that the French king should be put to death without the tedious forms of a trial. This opinion, however, was confined to the summit of the Mountain,[2] that elevated region, where aloof from all the ordinary feelings of our nature, no one is diverted from his purpose by the weakness of humanity, or the compunction of remorse; where urbanity is considered as an aristocratical infringement of les grands principes, and mercy as a crime de leze-nation [treason].

The trial of the king was decreed by the National Convention, and the eleventh of December was fixed upon for that purpose. Lewis the sixteenth had supported his long imprisonment with fortitude; and, when he heard that the day for his trial was fixed, he said with great calmness, "Eh bien! qu'on me guillotine si on veut; je suis preparé" ["Well! let them *guillotine* me if they will; I am prepared"].

A short time after the taking of the Bastille the king was observed reading the history of Charles the first.[3] "Why, sire," said an attendant, "do you read that history? it will make you melancholy." "Je me mets dans l'esprit," replied the king, "qu'un jour je finirai comme lui" ["I feel an impression on my mind, that one day I shall end like him"]. It appears that the French queen has also chosen a model for her behaviour, in the last scene of life, from the English annals; for since her imprisonment she has been employed in reading the history of Mary queen of Scots.[4] Marie Antoinette, however, is in no danger of sharing the same fate: if she were, her haughty indignant spirit, which preferred the chance of losing empire and life to the certainty of retaining any thing less than absolute dominion, would probably meet death with becoming dignity, feeling, that "to be weak is to be miserable, doing or suffering."[5]

* * * History will, indeed, condemn Lewis the sixteenth. The evidence of his guilt is clear; and the historian will fulfil his duty in passing sentence upon his memory; for the historian has not, like the judge, the prerogative to pardon. But Lewis the sixteenth will not stand alone at the bar of posterity. His judges also must appear at that tribunal; on them, also, the historian will pass sentence. He will behold the same men acting at once as accusers, party, and judge; he will behold the unfortunate monarch deprived, not only of his inviolability as a king, but of his rights as a citizen; and perhaps the irrevocable decree of posterity may reverse that of the National Convention.

The detail of the interrogation which the French king underwent at the bar of the National Convention is too well known to need repetition.—He was conducted back to the Temple about six in the evening: the night was dark; but the town was illuminated; and those objects which appeared only half formed, and were seen indistinctly, imagination finished and filled up, as best suited the gloomy impressions of the moment. By the way, since the second of September, when the whole town was

1. The selections here are from the second edition (1796), volume 4, letters 1 and 5.
2. Term for the radical Jacobin deputies, who sat on the high benches in the left of the National Convention.
3. The civil war between Charles I, king of Great Britain from 1625, and the Parliamentary forces under Oliver Cromwell, culminated in his execution on 30 January 1649.

4. Daughter of James V of Scotland, Mary became queen as an infant; in 1558 she married the Dauphin of France; a romantic figure, for the next three decades, she was the Roman Catholic threat to Elizabeth for the throne of Britain. Imprisoned from 1569 and tried for treason in 1586, she was beheaded in 1587.
5. Paraphrasing Milton's Satan, *Paradise Lost* 1.156–57.

lighted up for security, an illumination at Paris appears no gaudy pageant, which beams the symbol of public festivity; but is considered as the harbinger of danger—the signal of alarm—the tocsin of night. A considerable number of horse as well as foot-guards formed the escort of the king; and the trampling of the horses' feet—the hoarse sounds of the collected multitude—the beating of drums—the frequent report of fire-arms—all conspired to excite the most solemn emotions. The long page of human history rushed upon the mind—age after age arose to memory, in sad succession, like the line of Ban-quo;[6] and each seemed disfigured by crimes or darkened by calamity. The past was cloud-ed with horror—a great experiment was about to be made for the future; but it was impossible to reflect, without trembling anxiety, that the stake was human happiness, and that the issue was doubtful, while all that could be calculated with certainty was, that millions must perish in the trial. It is asserted that the philosophers of France pro-duced the revolution; I believe this to be an error. They, indeed, have disseminated the principles which form the basis of the new fabric of French government; but the ancient system was overthrown, not because it was unphilosophical, but because it could be upheld no longer. The revolution was the effect of imperious necessity; for, whatever permanent good may result from a change of government, the temporary evil is so cer-tain, that every age is disposed to leave that work to a succeeding generation. The instinct of the people teaches them, that in framing a new government they can only hope, like Moses, to see the promised land, but not to enter it. They may plant the seeds of general prosperity, sown with toil and trouble, and bathed in blood; but the blooming vegetation and the golden fruit belong to another race of men.

The defence of Lewis the sixteenth * * * though it failed to prove his innocence, at least interested the humane part of the audience in behalf of his misfortunes: and such of that audience as reflected, that he who now stood an arraigned criminal at the bar of the Convention, had, four years ago, the destiny of twenty-five millions of people at the disposal of his will, felt that, whatever were his sins against the nation, he was already punished enough. * * * The attention of all Europe was fixed in anx-ious suspense on the issue of this important trial; and the situation of Lewis the six-teenth excited universal sympathy. But at Paris it cast a peculiar horror—a sort of local gloom over the whole city; it seemed as if the National Convention had chosen the very means most proper to re-kindle the dying flame of loyalty. We remembered that the king had betrayed his people, till, by the rigour of their resentment, they made us lose the sense of his guilt in the greatness of his calamities. They wished us to feel indignation at his offence, and they compelled us to weep for his misfortunes. They called on our abhorrence of the ungenerous use he had made of the power with which he was entrusted, and we saw how little magnanimous was the use which they made of theirs. Their decision seemed at once so cruel and so impolitic, that it is not surprising if, instead of appearing to foreign nations in the light of a painful sacrifice made to public security, it bore the aspect of public security sacrificed to inhumanity and vengeance. It were, however, an error to believe, either that Lewis the sixteenth fell the victim of that barbarous thirst for his blood displayed by the chiefs of the Mountain, or that he was devoted to death by the pusillanimity of those who were influenced by considerations of their own personal safety. No; while we admire the heroic courage of such as, in defiance of the popular outcry, pleased with pathetic eloquence the cause of mercy; while we love the humanity of Brissot, the philosophy of Condorcet, we must admit, that amongst those who voted for the death of Lewis

6. See Shakespeare, *Macbeth*, 4.1.112–24.

the sixteenth are found men equally incapable of being actuated by fear or by vengeance; men, who, considering the king's death as essential to security of the republic, pronounced the fatal sentence in the bitterness of their souls, and as the performance of a cruel duty which their country imperiously required.

The proposition of an appeal to the departments was rejected, because it was apprehended, that such an appeal might lead to civil war. * * * The French king received the intelligence of his approaching fate without dismay. He displayed far more firmness upon the scaffold than he had done upon the throne, and atoned for the weakness and inconsistency of his conduct in life, by the calmness and fortitude of his behaviour in death. The evening before his execution, his family, from whom he had been separated since the commencement of his trial, were conducted to the tower of the Temple, and allowed the sad indulgence of a last interview, unmolested by the presence of his guards. * * * Ah, surely, amidst the agonies of final separation from those to whom we are bound by the strongest ties of nature and affection! surely when we cling to those we love, in the unutterable pang of a last embrace—in such moments the monarch must forget his crown, and the regrets of disappointed ambition must be unfelt amidst the anguish which overwhelms the broken heart. * * *

The king had sufficient firmness to avoid seeing his family on the morning of his execution! He desired the queen might be told that he was unable to bear the sight of her and his children in those last moments! he took a ring off his finger, which contained some of his own hair, of the queen's, and of his two children, and desired it might be given to the queen. He called the municipal officers round him, and told them, it was his dying request, that Clery, his valet-de-chambre, might remain with his son. He then said to Santerre, "Marchons" ["Let us go"]; and after crossing, with a hurried pace, the inner court of the Temple, he got into the mayor's carriage, which was in waiting, and was attended by his confessor.

It is certain that many of those acts of illegal power, which brought the unhappy monarch to the scaffold, were dictated by the fanatical and discontented clergy which swarmed about his palace; by non-juring bishops and archbishops; men who, having lost their wealth and their influence by the revolution, prompted the king to run all risks in order to gratify their own resentment. * * *

The calmness which Lewis the sixteenth displayed on this great trial of human fortitude, is attributed not only to the support his mind received from religious faith, but also to the hope which it is said he cherished, even till his last moment, that the people, whom he meant to address from the scaffold, would demand that his life might be spared. And his confessor, from motives of compassion, had encouraged him in this hope. After ascending the scaffold with a firm step, twice the unhappy monarch attempted to speak, and twice Santerre prevented him from being heard, by ordering the drums to beat immediately. * * * Then it was that despair seized upon the mind of the unfortunate monarch—his countenance assumed a look of horror—twice with agony he repeated, "Je suis perdu! je suis perdu!" ["I am undone! I am undone!"] His confessor mean time called to him from the foot of the scaffold, "Louis, fils de St. Louis, montez au ciel" ["Son of St. Louis, ascend to heaven!"]; and in one moment he was delivered from the evils of mortality.

The executioner held up the bleeding head, and the guards cried "Vive la Republique!" ["Long live the Republic!"] Some dipt their handkerchiefs in the blood—but the greater number, chilled with horror at what had passed, desired the commandant would lead them instantly from the spot. The hair was sold in separate tresses at the foot of the scaffold.

["WHAT THEN IS THE CONCLUSION OF THE WHOLE MATTER?"]

Paris, March 1793

* * * The destruction of the monarchy in France on the 10th of August—the horrors of the massacre of the 2d of September,[7] and then the death of the king, finally alienated the minds of Englishmen from the French revolution; rendered popular a war, which otherwise no minister would have dared to undertake; disgusted all wise, and shocked all humane men; and left to us, and all who had espoused the cause, no hope but that Heaven, which knows how to bring good out of evil, would watch over an event so interesting to the welfare of mankind as the French revolution; nor suffer the folly and vice of the agents concerned in it, to spoil the greatest and noblest enterprise ever undertaken by a nation.

A variety of secondary causes operated, in conjunction with these primary ones, to alienate the minds of our countrymen from the French revolution. It is curious, and may be useful to trace a few of them.

Those who have long held the first rank in any society are always reluctant to yield up their place, or suffer others, who were below, to be raised above them. Accustomed to regard their own constitution as the perfection of civil polity, the English found a new source of disapprobation of the French institution: they forgot that their dearest privileges, trial by jury, the liberty of the press, and other advantages, had once been regarded by foreign nations as audacious novelties; and had scandalized the despots of Europe and their degraded subjects, as much as the new experiments of the French did at present. It was a common saying in France, under the old system, that "Le roi d'Angleterre / Regne dans l'enfer" ["The king of England reigns in hell"] and the freedom of speech, and of writing on public affairs, the dearest rights of Englishmen, were constantly represented as absurd and noxious privileges, that occasioned eternal commotion in the state, and *disturbed the peace of government*. In spite of these facts, when circumstances arose that hurt their national vanity, by exalting a rival people, many of our countrymen appear to have forgotten the ancient history of England—the nations seemed to have changed sides, and Englishmen talked of France as Frenchmen were wont to talk of England. But truth changes not with the fashions of the times. It was not to be forgotten, that the English had been the first *bold experimenters* in the science of government in modern Europe—the first who carried into practical execution the calumniated principle of EQUALITY—the first people who formally brought a monarch to the scaffold—the first asserters of the neglected *rights of man*. In the common law of England, and the commentaries of the older lawyers on it, I have found all the fundamental principles of the French declaration des droits de l'homme [of the rights of man].

But, said some, we made our revolution without bloodshed, and theirs has been a continued scene of confusion and murder. It is true, the revolution of 1688 was accomplished with little trouble; but it produced the wars of 1715 and 1745, in the last of which the metropolis very nearly fell into the hands of the enemy; a circumstance that would have placed a popish despot on the throne, and annihilated the liberties of England. And it is to be observed, that the revolution of 1688 was but one of many events that formed the English constitution. That system was the fruit of the labours of ages of struggle and confusion. The establishment of our liberties cost us

---

7. Between 2 and 6 September 1792, more than a thousand prisoners, aristocrats, priests, and purported sympathizers were seized from the Paris jails and summarily executed.

many wars—and amidst the civil dissensions caused by the contest of principles against ancient error, our history records a sad catalogue of crimes and cruelties committed on all sides. Whoever, Madam, will examine these annals, will soon be convinced, that we have not much ground to reproach our neighbours. In France, indeed, a greater number of events have been crowded into a shorter space of time; and the enormities in France have been committed at a period, when, by means of the facility of communication, all public events are more widely and rapidly circulated than in former ages; circumstances that alter the appearance, but not the reality, of the case. We now enjoy the blessings of freedom, and have forgotten the price it cost our ancestors to obtain it. But no people ever travelled to the temple of Liberty by a path strewed with roses; nor has established tyranny ever yielded to reason and justice, till after a severe struggle. I do not pretend to justify the French, but I do not see much right that we at least have to condemn them. We cannot even reproach them with the fate of Louis the sixteenth, without calling up to remembrance that of Charles the first. * * *

If the destruction of the monarchy was absolutely necessary, certainly the death of the king was not; and France might have struck surrounding nations with reverence at her sublime clemency, in place of shocking all Europe by a condemnation, the justice of which was at best doubtful, and which the generality of them at present consider as an atrocious crime. * * * However much indisposed our countrymen were to the French from preceding reasons, it is certain that the death of the king alone prepared their minds for war, and completed the triumph of the enemies of France in England. * * *

Whether France will finally be able to extricate herself from an intestine, as well as external war, which now assail her at once—whether she will be able to support her republic; or, fatigued with anarchy, repose herself in limited monarchy; or finally, overwhelmed by her foes, be forced to accept that constitution which they choose to give her, are points that surpass my powers to decide. Were I to conjecture, I would say, that she will succeed in maintaining her own freedom, but not in communicating it to her neighbours. But should she even be overpowered by her enemies, and should continental despots wish to load her with the most galling chains, I cannot forget, Madam, that Britain is concerned in this transaction! And this recollection cheers my mind; for a free and generous people cannot condemn twenty-five millions of men to be slaves! No: the severest sentence that England can suffer to be pronounced, even on her rival, would be, "Let France be delivered from the dominion of a ferocious mob—let her be delivered from anarchy, and restored to reason and lawful sway!" Thus terminate how it will, I trust the French revolution will promote the good of France, and this prospect consoles me amidst the present evils. * * *

When I said that the French revolution began in wisdom, I admitted that it came afterwards into the hands of fools. But *the foundation was laid in wisdom*. I must intreat you to mark that circumstance; for if even the superstructure should fall, the foundation would remain. The BASTILLE, though honoured by Mr. Burke with the title of the *king's castle* (a shocking satire on every humane and just prince), will never be rebuilt in France; and the declaration of the rights of man will remain eternal, as the truths it contains. In the early ages of the world, the revolutions of the states, and the incursions of barbarians, often overwhelmed knowledge, and occasioned *the loss of principles:* but since the invention of printing has diffused science over Europe, and accumulated the means of extending and preserving truth, PRINCIPLES can no more be lost. Like vigorous seeds committed to the bosom of the fertile earth, accidental circumstances may prevent their vegetation for a time, but they will remain alive, and ready to spring up at the first favourable moment.

What then is the conclusion of the whole matter? This, surely, that PRINCIPLES are never to be abandoned, however unsuccessful may be the attempt to carry them into *practice*. We in England, however, have had practical experience of the good effects of right principles: our maxims of liberty have proved their intrinsic worth, by counteracting even the natural defects of our country. They have made, as Addison happily expresses, "our bleak rocks and barren mountains smile"; and on the careful preservation of these maxims depends the continuance of the blessings they have procured us. But I must conclude:

> O Liberty! expand thy vital ray,
> O'er the dark globe diffuse celestial day;
> Glad distant regions by thy blissful voice,
> Till India's wilds and Afric's sands rejoice;
> Thy spirit breathe, wide as creation's space;
> Exalt, illume, inspire the human race;
> As heaven's own æther thro' expansion whirl'd,
> Attracts, sublimes, and animates the world.[8]

Thus wishes a worthy member of the British Senate, and such are your wishes and mine.

ADIEU

◆◆◆

Edmund Burke
1729–1797

A political writer and Irish member of Parliament for nearly thirty years, famous for electrifying oratory, Edmund Burke embodied the debates of his century. Although he was allied with the Whigs and not the Tories, and with them often advocated liberal and reform clauses, his politics were never of a piece. The son of a Protestant minister and a Catholic mother, he castigated Britain's handling of Ireland, urging the emancipation of Irish trade, the Irish Parliament, and Irish Catholics. He endorsed William Wilberforce's movement for the abolition of the slave trade, worked for the reform of the East India Company's abuses in India, and argued for better treatment of and greater autonomy for the American colonies. Yet he also supported Britain's right to tax the colonies and was a celebrated opponent of the French Revolution, denouncing it as an unparalleled disaster in modern history.

"Burke never shows his powers, except he is in a passion. The French Revolution was alone a subject fit for him," remarked Samuel Taylor Coleridge. Burke's best known work is *Reflections on the Revolution in France*, published in 1790, after the arrest and imprisonment of Louis XVI and Marie Antoinette but before the Terror and their execution. (Wordsworth, who as a young man saw the Revolution heralding a new golden age in human history, was horrified by the Terror and later praised the "Genius of Burke.") Selling quickly and widely (5,500 copies in seventeen days and 30,000 in the next few years), *Reflections* provoked strong

---

8. Attributed by Williams to John Courtenay (1738–1816), dissenter, abolitionist, supporter of the French Revolution. The prior reference is to Joseph Addison (1672–1719), poet, Whig statesman, and essayist.

James Gillray. *Smelling out a Rat,* 1790.

reactions, pro and con. It was championed throughout Europe for a principled conservatism that revered an idealized past and historical continuity, and on this basis defended the moral authority of a nation's institutions: the monarchy, the aristocracy, the church, and the constitution that guaranteed their power. A famous passage dramatized the arrest and imprisonment of the royal family, with a dignified queen as tragic heroine. Sympathizers with the Revolution immediately produced rebuttals, among the first, Mary Wollstonecraft's *Vindication of the Rights of Men*, and the most influential, Tom Paine's *Rights of Man*.

from Reflections on the Revolution in France
["THIS STRANGE CHAOS"]

All circumstances taken together, the French Revolution is the most astonishing that has hitherto happened in the world. The most wonderful things are brought about in many instances by means the most absurd and ridiculous; in the most ridiculous modes; and, apparently, by the most contemptible instruments. Everything seems out of nature in this strange chaos of levity and ferocity, and of all sorts of crimes jumbled together with all sorts of follies. In viewing this monstrous tragicomic scene, the most opposite passions necessarily succeed, and sometimes mix with each other in the mind; alternate contempt and indignation; alternate laughter and tears; alternate scorn and horror.

It cannot however be denied, that to some this strange scene appeared in quite another point of view. Into them it inspired no other sentiments than those of exultation and rapture. They saw nothing in what has been done in France, but a firm and temperate exertion of freedom; so consistent, on the whole, with morals and with piety as to make it deserving not only of the secular applause of dashing Machiavelian politicians,[1] but to render it a fit theme for all the devout effusions of sacred eloquence.

[THE CONSTITUENT PARTS OF A STATE]

The constituent parts of a state are obliged to hold their public faith with each other, and with all those who derive any serious interest under their engagements, as much as the whole state is bound to keep its faith with separate communities. Otherwise competence and power would soon be confounded, and no law be left but the will of a prevailing force. On this principle the succession of the crown has always been what it now is, an hereditary succession by law: in the old line it was a succession by the common law; in the new by the statute law, operating on the principles of the common law, not changing the substance, but regulating the mode, and describing the persons. Both these descriptions of law are of the same force, and are derived from an equal authority, emanating from the common agreement and original compact of the state, *communi sponsione reipublicae*,[2] and as such are equally binding on king and people too, as long as the terms are observed, and they continue the same body politic.

[LEVELLERS CAN NEVER EQUALISE]

Your present confusion, like a palsy, has attacked the fountain of life itself. Every person in your country, in a situation to be actuated by a principle of honour, is disgraced and degraded, and can entertain no sensation of life, except in a mortified and humiliated indignation. But this generation will quickly pass away. The next generation of the nobility will resemble the artificers and clowns, and money-jobbers, usurers, and Jews, who will be always their fellows, sometimes their masters. Believe me, Sir, those who attempt to level,[3] never equalise. In all societies, consisting of various descriptions of citizens, some description must be uppermost. The levellers therefore only change and pervert the natural order of things.

[THE REAL RIGHTS OF MEN]

Far am I from denying in theory, full as far is my heart from withholding in practice, (if I were of power to give or to withhold,) the *real* rights of men.[4] In denying their false claims of right, I do not mean to injure those which are real, and are such as their pretended rights would totally destroy. If civil society be made for the advantage of man, all the advantages for which it is made become his right. It is an institution of beneficence; and law itself is only beneficence acting by a rule. Men have a right to live by that rule; they have a right to do justice, as between their fellows,

---

1. Niccolo Machiavelli (1469–1527), Florentine statesman, was famous for *The Prince*, a handbook on power; "Machiavelian" came to refer to a cynical politics of cunning, manipulation, and duplicity.
2. Burke summons the Latin phrase "common compact of the state" to give classical Roman republican authority to the principle of rule based on mutual agreement.
3. An allusion to the Levellers, the radical republicans of

the English Civil War period of the 1640s, who advocated principles that were to shape democratic movements in Burke's day: universal suffrage for men, a written constitution, proportional representation in a single governing body, and abolition of the monarchy and class privileges.
4. An allusion to the French Revolutionary Assembly's Declaration of the Rights of Man.

whether their fellows are in public function or in ordinary occupation. They have a right to the fruits of their industry; and to the means of making their industry fruitful. They have a right to the acquisitions of their parents; to the nourishment and improvement of their offspring; to instruction in life, and to consolation in death. Whatever each man can separately do, without trespassing upon others, he has a right to do for himself; and he has a right to a fair portion of all which society, with all its combinations of skill and force, can do in his favour. In this partnership all men have equal rights; but not to equal things. He that has but five shillings in the partnership, has as good a right to it, as he that has five hundred pounds has to his larger proportion. But he has not a right to an equal dividend in the product of the joint stock; and as to the share of power, authority, and direction which each individual ought to have in the management of the state, that I must deny to be amongst the direct original rights of man in civil society.

[THE ARREST AND IMPRISONMENT OF THE KING AND QUEEN]

History will record, that on the morning of the 6th of October, 1789, the king and queen of France, after a day of confusion, alarm, dismay, and slaughter, lay down, under the pledged security of public faith, to indulge nature in a few hours of respite, and troubled, melancholy repose. From this sleep the queen was first startled by the voice of the sentinel at her door, who cried out to her to save herself by flight—that this was the last proof of fidelity he could give—that they were upon him, and he was dead. Instantly he was cut down. A band of cruel ruffians and assassins, reeking with his blood, rushed into the chamber of the queen, and pierced with a hundred strokes of bayonets and poniards the bed, from whence this persecuted woman had but just time to fly almost naked, and, through ways unknown to the murderers, had escaped to seek refuge at the feet of a king and husband, not secure of his own life for a moment.

This king, to say no more of him, and this queen, and their infant children, (who once would have been the pride and hope of a great and generous people,) were then forced to abandon the sanctuary of the most splendid palace in the world, which they left swimming in blood, polluted by massacre, and strewed with scattered limbs and mutilated carcases. Thence they were conducted into the capital of their kingdom. Two had been selected from the unprovoked, unresisted, promiscuous slaughter, which was made of the gentlemen of birth and family who composed the king's body guard. These two gentlemen, with all the parade of an execution of justice, were cruelly and publicly dragged to the block, and beheaded in the great court of the palace. Their heads were stuck upon spears, and led the procession; whilst the royal captives who followed in the train were slowly moved along, amidst the horrid yells, and shrilling screams, and frantic dances, and infamous contumelies, and all the unutterable abominations of the furies of hell, in the abused shape of the vilest of women. After they had been made to taste, drop by drop, more than the bitterness of death, in the slow torture of a journey of twelve miles, protracted to six hours, they were, under a guard, composed of those very soldiers who had thus conducted them through this famous triumph, lodged in one of the old palaces of Paris, now converted into a bastile for kings.

Is this a triumph to be consecrated at altars? to be commemorated with grateful thanksgiving? to be offered to the divine humanity with fervent prayer and enthusiastic ejaculation? * * *

Such treatment of any human creatures must be shocking to any but those who are made for accomplishing revolutions. But I cannot stop here. Influenced by the inborn feelings of my nature, and not being illuminated by a single ray of this new sprung modern light, I confess to you, Sir,[5] that the exalted rank of the persons suffering, and particularly the sex, the beauty, and the amiable qualities of the descendant of so many kings and emperors, with the tender age of royal infants, insensible only through infancy and innocence of the cruel outrages to which their parents were exposed, instead of being a subject of exultation, adds not a little to my sensibility on that most melancholy occasion.

I hear that the august person,[6] who was the principal object of our preacher's triumph, though he supported himself, felt much on that shameful occasion. As a man, it became him to feel for his wife and his children, and the faithful guards of his person, that were massacred in cold blood about him; as a prince, it became him to feel for the strange and frightful transformation of his civilized subjects, and to be more grieved for them than solicitous for himself. It derogates little from his fortitude, while it adds infinitely to the honour of his humanity. I am very sorry to say it, very sorry indeed, that such personages are in a situation in which it is not becoming in us to praise the virtues of the great.

I hear, and I rejoice to hear, that the great lady[7] the other object of the triumph, has borne that day, (one is interested that beings made for suffering should suffer well,) and that she bears all the succeeding days, that she bears the imprisonment of her husband, and her own captivity, and the exile of her friends, and the insulting adulation of addresses, and the whole weight of her accumulated wrongs, with a serene patience, in a manner suited to her rank and race, and becoming the offspring of a sovereign distinguished for her piety and her courage: that, like her, she has lofty sentiments; that she feels with the dignity of a Roman matron;[8] that in the last extremity she will save herself from the last disgrace; and that, if she must fall, she will fall by no ignoble hand.[9]

It is now sixteen or seventeen years since I saw the queen of France, then the dauphiness [princess], at Versailles;[1] and surely never lighted on this orb, which she hardly seemed to touch, a more delightful vision. I saw her just above the horizon, decorating and cheering the elevated sphere she just began to move in,—glittering like the morning-star, full of life, and splendour, and joy. Oh! what a revolution! and what a heart must I have to contemplate without emotion that elevation and that fall! Little did I dream when she added titles of veneration to those of enthusiastic, distant, respectful love, that she should ever be obliged to carry the sharp antidote against disgrace concealed in that bosom; little did I dream that I should have lived to see such disasters fallen upon her in a nation of gallant men, in a nation of men of honour, and of cavaliers. I thought ten thousand swords must have leaped from their

5. *Reflections* is framed as a letter to a "gentleman in Paris."
6. King Louis XVI. The preacher is Richard Price (1723–1791), to whose *Discourse on the Love of our Country* Burke is replying.
7. Queen Marie Antoinette.
8. The women of ancient Rome were famous for dignified self-possession in the face of adversity; Marie Antoinette was the daughter of the Empress of Austria, Maria Theresa.

9. The ancient Roman course of action in defeat was to take one's own life (cf. below: "the sharp antidote to disgrace concealed in that bosom"—a small knife or poison). Such hope was not realized for Marie Antoinette, who was beheaded in a noisy public event in 1793 (three years after the publication of *Reflections*).
1. The royal palace outside Paris from 1682 until the ejection of the royal family here described.

scabbards to avenge even a look that threatened her with insult. But the age of chivalry is gone. That of sophisters, economists, and calculators, has succeeded; and the glory of Europe is extinguished for ever. Never, never more shall we behold that generous loyalty to rank and sex, that proud submission, that dignified obedience, that subordination of the heart, which kept alive, even in servitude itself, the spirit of an exalted freedom. The unbought grace of life, the cheap defence of nations, the nurse of manly sentiment and heroic enterprise, is gone! It is gone, that sensibility of principle, that chastity of honour, which felt a stain like a wound, which inspired courage whilst it mitigated ferocity, which ennobled whatever it touched, and under which vice itself lost half its evil, by losing all its grossness.

This mixed system of opinion and sentiment had its origin in the ancient chivalry; and the principle, though varied in its appearance by the varying state of human affairs, subsisted and influenced through a long succession of generations, even to the time we live in. If it should ever be totally extinguished, the loss I fear will be great. It is this which has given its character to modern Europe. It is this which has distinguished it under all its forms of government, and distinguished it to its advantage, from the states of Asia, and possibly from those states which flourished in the most brilliant periods of the antique world. It was this, which, without confounding ranks, had produced a noble equality, and handed it down through all the gradations of social life. It was this opinion which mitigated kings into companions, and raised private men to be fellows with kings. Without force or opposition, it subdued the fierceness of pride and power; it obliged sovereigns to submit to the soft collar of social esteem, compelled stern authority to submit to elegance, and gave a dominating vanquisher of laws to be subdued by manners.

But now all is to be changed. All the pleasing illusions, which made power gentle and obedience liberal, which harmonized the different shades of life, and which, by a bland assimilation, incorporated into politics the sentiments which beautify and soften private society, are to be dissolved by this new conquering empire of light and reason.[2] All the decent drapery of life is to be rudely torn off. All the super-added ideas, furnished from the wardrobe of a moral imagination, which the heart owns, and the understanding ratifies, as necessary to cover the defects of our naked, shivering nature, and to raise it to dignity in our own estimation, are to be exploded as a ridiculous, absurd, and antiquated fashion.

On this scheme of things, a king is but a man, a queen is but a woman; a woman is but an animal, and an animal not of the highest order. All homage paid to the sex[3] in general as such, and without distinct views, is to be regarded as romance and folly. Regicide, and parricide, and sacrilege, are but fictions of superstition, corrupting jurisprudence by destroying its simplicity. The murder of a king, or a queen, or a bishop, or a father, are only common homicide; and if the people are by any chance, or in any way, gainers by it, a sort of homicide much the most pardonable, and into which we ought not to make too severe a scrutiny.

On the scheme of this barbarous philosophy, which is the offspring of cold hearts and muddy understandings, and which is as void of solid wisdom as it is destitute of all taste and elegance, laws are to be supported only by their own terrors,

---

2. A sarcastic reference to the Enlightenment ideology of Reason championed by political reformers and revolutionaries alike.

3. Women; a common usage.

and by the concern which each individual may find in them from his own private speculations, or can spare to them from his own private interests. In the groves of *their* academy,[4] at the end of every vista, you see nothing but the gallows. Nothing is left which engages the affections on the part of the commonwealth. On the principles of this mechanic philosophy, our institutions can never be embodied, if I may use the expression, in persons; so as to create in us love, veneration, admiration, or attachment. But that sort of reason which banishes the affections is incapable of filling their place. These public affections, combined with manners, are required sometimes as supplements, sometimes as correctives, always as aids to law. The precept given by a wise man, as well as a great critic, for the construction of poems, is equally true as to states:—*Non satis est pulchra esse poemata, dulcia sunto.*[5] There ought to be a system of manners in every nation, which a well-formed mind would be disposed to relish. To make us love our country, our country ought to be lovely.

But power, of some kind or other, will survive the shock in which manners and opinions perish; and it will find other and worse means for its support. The usurpation which, in order to subvert ancient institutions, has destroyed ancient principles, will hold power by arts similar to those by which it has acquired it. When the old feudal and chivalrous spirit of *fealty*,[6] which, by freeing kings from fear, freed both kings and subjects from the precautions of tyranny, shall be extinct in the minds of men, plots and assassinations will be anticipated by preventive murder and preventive confiscation, and that long roll of grim and bloody maxims, which form the political code of all power, not standing on its own honour, and the honour of those who are to obey it. Kings will be tyrants from policy, when subjects are rebels from principle.

When ancient opinions and rules of life are taken away, the loss cannot possibly be estimated. From that moment we have no compass to govern us; nor can we know distinctly to what port we steer. Europe, undoubtedly, taken in a mass, was in a flourishing condition the day on which your revolution was completed. How much of that prosperous state was owing to the spirit of our old manners and opinions is not easy to say; but as such causes cannot be indifferent in their operation, we must presume, that, on the whole, their operation was beneficial.

We are but too apt to consider things in the state in which we find them, without sufficiently adverting to the causes by which they have been produced, and possibly may be upheld. Nothing is more certain, than that our manners, our civilization, and all the good things which are connected with manners and with civilization, have, in this European world of ours, depended for ages upon two principles; and were indeed the result of both combined; I mean the spirit of a gentleman, and the spirit of religion. The nobility and the clergy, the one by profession, the other by patronage, kept learning in existence, even in the midst of arms and confusions, and whilst governments were rather in their causes, than formed. Learning paid back what it received to nobility and to priesthood; and paid it with usury,[7] by enlarging their ideas, and by furnishing their minds. Happy if they had all continued to know their indissoluble union, and their proper place! Happy if learning, not debauched by

---

4. In ancient Greece, philosophers and students met outside under the shade of the trees.

5. "It is not enough that poems be beautiful, they must be sweet [tender, touching]" (Horace, *Ars Poetica*).

6. Medieval ideal of a vassal's obligation of fidelity to his lord; by extension, the faithful allegiance that secures social order both from fear of violent revolt and from preventive lordly tyranny.

7. Interest; a positive term.

ambition, had been satisfied to continue the instructor, and not aspired to be the master! Along with its natural protectors and guardians, learning will be cast into the mire, and trodden down under the hoofs of a swinish multitude.[8]

["THIS GREAT DRAMA"]

[W]hen kings are hurled from their thrones by the Supreme Director[9] of this great drama, and become the objects of insult to the base, and of pity to the good, we behold such disasters in the moral, as we should behold a miracle in the physical, order of things. We are alarmed into reflection; our minds (as it has long since been observed) are purified by terror and pity;[1] our weak, unthinking pride is humbled under the dispensations of a mysterious wisdom. Some tears might be drawn from me, if such a spectacle were exhibited on the stage. I should be truly ashamed of finding in myself that superficial, theatric sense of painted distress, whilst I could exult over it in real life. With such a perverted mind, I could never venture to show my face at a tragedy. People would think the tears that Garrick formerly, or that Siddons not long since, have extorted from me, were the tears of hypocrisy;[2] I should know them to be the tears of folly.

Indeed the theatre is a better school of moral sentiments than churches, where the feelings of humanity are thus outraged. Poets who have to deal with an audience not yet graduated in the school of the rights of men, and who must apply themselves to the moral constitution of the heart, would not dare to produce such a triumph as a matter of exultation. There, where men follow their natural impulses, they would not bear the odious maxims of a Machiavelian policy, whether applied to the attainment of monarchical or democratic tyranny. They would reject them on the modern, as they once did on the ancient stage, where they could not bear even the hypothetical proposition of such wickedness in the mouth of a personated tyrant, though suitable to the character he sustained. No theatric audience in Athens would bear what has been borne, in the midst of the real tragedy of this triumphal day; a principal actor weighing, as it were in scales hung in a shop of horrors,—so much actual crime against so much contingent advantage,—and after putting in and out weights, declaring that the balance was on the side of the advantages. They would not bear to see the crimes of new democracy posted as in a ledger against the crimes of old despotism, and the book-keepers of politics finding democracy still in debt, but by no means unable or unwilling to pay the balance. In the theatre, the first intuitive glance, without any elaborate process of reasoning, will show, that this method of political computation would justify every extent of crime. They would see, that on these principles, even where the very worst acts were not perpetrated, it was owing rather to the fortune of the conspirators, than to their parsimony in the expenditure of treachery and blood. They would soon see, that criminal means once tolerated are soon preferred. They present a shorter cut to the object than through the highway of the moral virtues. Justifying perfidy and murder for public benefit, public benefit would soon become the pretext, and perfidy and murder the end;

8. Among the several rebuttals provoked by *Reflections* was *The Reply of the Swinish Multitude to Mr. Burke.*
9. God.
1. In his extended metaphor of the "great drama," Burke refers to Aristotle's argument in *Poetics* for the salutary effect of drama in its controlled release of sensations of pity and fear.
2. David Garrick (1717–1779) and Sarah Siddons (1755–1831) were two of the leading actors of the age, both celebrated for their performances in Shakespeare's tragedies; "hypocrisy" is in the same metaphor system, derived from a Greek word for "stage-acting."

until rapacity, malice, revenge, and fear more dreadful than revenge, could satiate their insatiable appetites. Such must be the consequences of losing, in the splendour of these triumphs of the rights of men, all natural sense of wrong and right.

[THE CONTRACT OF SOCIETY]

To avoid therefore the evils of inconstancy and versatility, ten thousand times worse than those of obstinacy and the blindest prejudice, we have consecrated the state, that no man should approach to look into its defects or corruptions but with due caution; that he should never dream of beginning its reformation by its subversion; that he should approach to the faults of the state as to the wounds of a father, with pious awe and trembling solicitude. By this wise prejudice we are taught to look with horror on those children of their country, who are prompt rashly to hack that aged parent in pieces, and put him into the kettle of magicians, in hopes that by their poisonous weeds, and wild incantations, they may regenerate the paternal constitution, and renovate their father's life.[3]

Society is indeed a contract. Subordinate contracts for objects of mere occasional interest may be dissolved at pleasure—but the state ought not to be considered as nothing better than a partnership agreement in a trade of pepper and coffee, calico or tobacco, or some other such low concern, to be taken up for a little temporary interest, and to be dissolved by the fancy of the parties. It is to be looked on with other reverence; because it is not a partnership in things subservient only to the gross animal existence of a temporary and perishable nature. It is a partnership in all science; a partnership in all art; a partnership in every virtue, and in all perfection. As the ends of such a partnership cannot be obtained in many generations, it becomes a partnership not only between those who are living, but between those who are living, those who are dead, and those who are to be born. Each contract of each particular state is but a clause in the great primæval contract of eternal society, linking the lower with the higher natures, connecting the visible and invisible world, according to a fixed compact sanctioned by the inviolable oath which holds all physical and all moral natures, each in their appointed place. This law is not subject to the will of those, who by an obligation above them, and infinitely superior, are bound to submit their will to that law. The municipal corporations of that universal kingdom are not morally at liberty at their pleasure, and on their speculations of a contingent improvement, wholly to separate and tear asunder the bands of their subordinate community, and to dissolve it into an unsocial, uncivil, unconnected chaos of elementary principles. It is the first and supreme necessity only, a necessity that is not chosen, but chooses, a necessity paramount to deliberation, that admits no discussion, and demands no evidence, which alone can justify a resort to anarchy. This necessity is no exception to the rule; because this necessity itself is a part too of that moral and physical disposition of things, to which man must be obedient by consent or force: but if that which is only submission to necessity should be made the object of choice, the law is broken, nature is disobeyed, and the rebellious are outlawed, cast forth, and exiled, from this world of reason, and order, and peace, and virtue, and fruitful penitence, into the antagonist world of madness, discord, vice, confusion, and unavailing sorrow.

3. Manipulated by the sorceress Medea, the daughters of Pelias, King of Thessaly, took this course of action, not realizing that Medea was in league with Pelias's dispossessed half-nephew, Jason.

+·+ 〓◆〓 ·+

Mary Wollstonecraft
1759–1797

Wollstonecraft was living on her own in London on Bastille Day, 14 July 1789, writing for and serving on the staff of the *Analytical Review*, enjoying a lively circle of artists, writers, and intellectuals gathered around Joseph Johnson, its politically radical publisher. *A Vindication of the Rights of Men* (published by Johnson) appeared anonymously, in two printings in rapid succession in late 1790, leading a flood of responses to Burke's *Reflections on the Revolution in France*, which had appeared only weeks earlier. Her title refers to the Declaration of the Rights of Man voted by the French Constituent Assembly in August 1789. Caustic, trenchant, and frequently sarcastic, *Rights of Men* made her reputation when the second edition bore her name in 1791. Concerned chiefly to refute Burke's arguments for the hereditary succession of the crown, the inviolability of a national constitution, and the necessary alliance of church and state, Wollstonecraft also drew notice for her collateral arguments about the property of the poor, and for her bitter critiques of naval impressment, antipoaching laws, slavery, and Burke's attitudes about women and gender, which had already irritated her in his widely influential *Inquiry into the Origin of Our Ideas of the Sublime and Beautiful* (1757), where the feminine was equated with the qualities of "beautiful"—proportion, smoothness, delicacy, and smallness.

For more about Wollstonecraft, see her principal listing, page 1469.

from A Vindication of the Rights of Men
in a Letter to the Right Honourable Edmund Burke;
Occasioned by his Reflections on the Revolution in France

Mr. Burke's Reflections on the French Revolution first engaged my attention as the transient topic of the day. ✳ ✳ ✳ My indignation was roused by the sophistical arguments, that every moment crossed me, in the questionable shape[1] of natural feelings and common sense. ✳ ✳ ✳ I have confined my strictures, in a great measure, to the grand principles at which he has levelled many ingenious arguments in a very specious garb.

[SENSIBILITY]

Sensibility is the *manie* of the day,[2] and compassion the virtue which is to cover a multitude of vices, whilst justice is left to mourn in sullen silence, and balance truth in vain.

In life, an honest man with a confined understanding is frequently the slave of his habits and the dupe of his feelings, whilst the man with a clearer head and colder heart makes the passions of others bend to his interest; but truly sublime is the character that acts from principle. ✳ ✳ ✳ All your pretty flights arise from your pampered sensibility; and that, vain of this fancied pre-eminence of organs, you foster every

---

1. A sardonic allusion to Hamlet's first address to his father's ghost: "Angels and ministers of grace defend us! / Be thou a spirit of health or goblin damned, / Bring with thee airs from heaven or blasts from hell, / Be thy intents wicked or charitable, / Thou com'st in such a questionable shape / That I will speak to thee" (*Hamlet* 1.4.39–44).

2. A reference to the "Cult of Sensibility," the elevation of feelings over rationality, particularly by poets and sentimental novelists of both sexes, but with a general sense that such culture is primarily the province of women and men of "feminine" character. *Manie*, a quasi-medical term, combines the senses of emotional hyperactivity and mania, a cultural craze.

emotion till the fumes, mounting to your brain, dispel the sober suggestions of reason. It is not in this view surprising, that when you should argue you become impassioned, and that reflection inflames your imagination, instead of enlightening your understanding.

Quitting now the flowers of rhetoric, let us, Sir, reason together.[3] * * *

The birthright of man, to give you, Sir, a short definition of this disputed right, is such a degree of liberty, civil and religious, as is compatible with the liberty of every other individual with whom he is united in a social compact, and the continued existence of that compact.[4]

Liberty, in this simple, unsophisticated sense, I acknowledge, is a fair idea that has never yet received a form in the various governments that have been established on our bounteous globe; the demon of property has ever been at hand to encroach on the sacred rights of men, and to fence round with awful pomp laws that war with justice. * * * If there is any thing like argument, or first principles, in your wild declamation, behold the result:—that we are to reverence the rust of antiquity, and term the unnatural customs, which ignorance and mistaken self-interest have consolidated, the sage fruit of experience: nay, that, if we do discover some errors, our *feelings* should lead us to excuse, with blind love, or unprincipled filial affection, the venerable vestiges of ancient days. These are gothic notions of beauty[5]—the ivy is beautiful, but, when it insidiously destroys the trunk from which it receives support, who would not grub it up? * * *

The civilization which has taken place in Europe has been very partial, and, like every custom that an arbitrary point of honour has established, refines the manners at the expence of morals, by making sentiments and opinions current in conversation that have no root in the heart, or weight in the cooler resolves of the mind.—And what has stopped its progress?—hereditary property—hereditary honours. The man has been changed into an artificial monster by the station in which he was born, and the consequent homage that benumbed his faculties like the torpedo's touch;[6]—or a being, with a capacity of reasoning, would not have failed to discover, as his faculties unfolded, that true happiness arose from the friendship and intimacy which can only be enjoyed by equals; and that charity is not a condescending distribution of alms, but an intercourse of good offices and mutual benefits, founded on respect for justice and humanity.

[AUTHORITY, SLAVERY, AND NATURAL RIGHTS]

Are we to seek for the rights of men in the ages when a few marks were the only penalty imposed for the life of a man, and death for death when the property of the rich was touched? when—I blush to discover the depravity of our nature—when a

---

3. A parody of Isaiah: "Come now, and let us reason together, saith the Lord: though your sins be as scarlet, they shall be as white as snow" (1.18). Rhetoric, the ornamental art of language, may displace or distort reason; cf. Wollstonecraft's remarks on her style in Introduction to *Rights of Woman*, page 1473.
4. An allusion to the notion of "social compact" in political philosophy. John Locke's *Two Treatises on Government* (1690) defines the "*original Compact*," whereby every man "with others incorporates into *one Society*": "by consenting with others to make one Body Politick under one Government, [he] puts himself under an obligation to every one of that Society, to submit to the determination of the *majority*, and to be concluded by it"

(2.97). Jean-Jacques Rousseau's *Social Contract* (1762) similarly argues that a free acceptance of this contract involves the surrender of the individual to the State, their reciprocal obligations, and their legal equality. Although Rousseau distrusted democracy and preferred monarchy, this work would be cited as the philosophical basis for the "democratic despotism" fostered by the French Revolution.
5. A reference to the "gothic" aesthetic of the 18th century, which admired the gloomy, wild, and untamed, and adored ivy-covered ruins (preferably of medieval gothic architecture); ivy is a parasite.
6. The numbing electric discharges of the torpedo, a ray fish; *torpedo* in Latin means *numbness*.

deer was killed![7] Are these the laws that it is natural to love, and sacrilegious to invade?—Were the rights of men understood when the law authorized or tolerated murder?—or is power and right the same in your creed? * * *

It is necessary emphatically to repeat, that there are rights which men inherit at their birth, as rational creatures, who were raised above the brute creation by their improvable faculties; and that, in receiving these, not from their forefathers but, from God, prescription can never undermine natural rights.

A father may dissipate his property without his child having any right to complain;—but should he attempt to sell him for a slave, or fetter him with laws contrary to reason; nature, in enabling him to discern good from evil, teaches him to break the ignoble chain, and not to believe that bread becomes flesh, and wine blood, because his parents swallowed the Eucharist[8] with this blind persuasion.

There is no end to this implicit submission to authority—some where it must stop, or we return to barbarism; and the capacity of improvement, which gives us a natural sceptre on earth, is a cheat, an ignis-fatuus,[9] that leads us from inviting meadows into bogs and dunghills. And if it be allowed that many of the precautions, with which any alteration was made, in our government, were prudent, it rather proves its weakness that substantiates an opinion of the soundness of the stamina, or the excellence of the constitution.

But on what principle Mr. Burke could defend American independence, I cannot conceive;[1] for the whole tenor of his plausible arguments settles slavery on an everlasting foundation. Allowing his servile reverence for antiquity, and prudent attention to self-interest, to have the force which he insists on, the slave trade ought never to be abolished;[2] and, because our ignorant forefathers, not understanding the native dignity of man, sanctioned a traffic that outrages every suggestion of reason and religion, we are to submit to the inhuman custom, and term an atrocious insult to humanity the love of our country, and a proper submission to the laws by which our property is secured.—Security of property! Behold, in a few words, the definition of English liberty. And to this selfish principle every nobler one is sacrificed.—The Briton takes place of the man, and the image of God is lost in the citizen! But it is not that enthusiastic flame which in Greece and Rome consumed every sordid passion: no, self is the focus; and the disparting rays rise not above our foggy atmosphere. But softly—it is only the property of the rich that is secure; the man who lives by the sweat of his brow has no asylum from oppression. * * * It is a farce to pretend that a man fights *for his country, his hearth, or his altars,* when he has neither liberty nor property.—His property is in his nervous arms—and they are compelled to pull a strange rope at the surly command of a tyrannic boy, who probably obtained his rank on account of his family connections, or the prostituted vote of his father, whose interest in a borough, or voice as a senator, was acceptable to the minister.[3] * * *

7. From 1389 to 1831, British law restricted the right to kill game to wealthy landlords and leaseholders; poaching, a theft of game often motivated by desperate hunger, was punishable by death.
8. Catholic theology stressed that the communion bread and wine are inwardly transformed into Christ's body and blood. Wollstonecraft was religious; her contempt issues from a general English disdain of Roman Catholicism as well as from her Enlightenment deism, which distrusted the institutional authority of an established Church.
9. Latin for false/foolish fire; the name for nighttime lights over marshlands supposedly caused by spontaneous combustion of gases released by the decay of organic material; by extension, a deceptive guiding light, an illusory ideal.
1. Burke's *Speech on Conciliation with America* (22 March 1775) defended the American Revolution on principles of traditional British liberties (e.g., taxation by consent and representation).
2. The institution of slavery in ancient Greece and Rome poses a contradiction to Burke's support in the 1780s of the parliamentary movement to abolish the slave trade.
3. A reference to impressment, the conscription of men into naval service; men of means could buy their way out or pay for a substitute; "nervous" means "well strung, vigorous."

Misery, to reach your heart, I perceive, must have its cap and bells;[4] your tears are reserved, very *naturally* considering your character, for the declamation of the theatre, or for the downfall of queens, whose rank alters the nature of folly, and throws a graceful veil over vices that degrade humanity; whilst the distress of many industrious mothers, whose *helpmates* have been torn from them, and the hungry cry of helpless babes, were vulgar sorrows that could not move your commiseration, though they might extort an alms. * * *

A brutal attachment to children has appeared most conspicuous in parents who have treated them like slaves, and demanded due homage for all the property they transferred to them, during their lives. It has led them to force their children to break the most sacred ties; to do violence to a natural impulse, and run into legal prostitution to increase wealth or shun poverty.[5] * * * It appears to be a natural suggestion of reason, that a man should be freed from implicit obedience to parents and private punishments, when he is of an age to be subject to the jurisdiction of the laws of his country; and that the barbarous cruelty of allowing parents to imprison their children, to prevent their contaminating their noble blood by following the dictates of nature when they chose to marry, or for any misdemeanor that does not come under the cognizance of public justice, is one of the most arbitrary violations of liberty.[6]

Who can recount all the unnatural crimes which the *laudable, interesting* desire of perpetuating a name has produced? The younger children have been sacrificed to the eldest son; sent into exile, or confined in convents, that they might not encroach on what was called, with shameful falsehood, the *family* estate.[7] Will Mr Burke call this parental affection reasonable or virtuous?—No; it is the spurious offspring of over-weening, mistaken pride—and not that first source of civilization, natural parental affection, that makes no difference between child and child, but what reason justifies by pointing out superior merit.

Another pernicious consequence which unavoidably arises from this artificial affection is, the insuperable bar which it puts in the way of early marriages. It would be difficult to determine whether the minds or bodies of our youth are most injured by this impediment. Our young men become selfish coxcombs. * * *

The same system has an equally pernicious effect on female morals.—Girls are sacrificed to family convenience, or else marry to settle themselves in a superior rank, and coquet, without restraint, with the fine gentleman whom I have already described.

[ROMANCE AND CHIVALRY]

Whether the glory of Europe is set, I shall not now enquire; but probably the spirit of romance and chivalry is in the wane; and reason will gain by its extinction.

From observing several cold romantic characters I have been led to confine the term romantic to one definition—false, or rather artificial, feelings. Works of genius

---

4. A court-jester's bell-tipped hat; hence, any device of foolish entertainment.
5. Marriage for financial reasons rather than mutual love, affection, and esteem—a frequent term in Wollstonecraft's *Rights of Woman*, used earlier by Daniel Defoe in *Conjugal Lewdness: or, Matrimonial Whoredom* (1727).
6. In her *Letters Written in France in the Summer of 1790*, Helen Maria Williams tells the story of one family that suffered such injustice (chs. 16–22); until 1791, it was

possible for a French citizen to imprison another without trial by using a "lettre de cachet" signed by the king. Wordsworth tells a story based on Williams of French parental tyranny against young lovers at the end of Book 9 of the 1805 *Prelude* (556–935).
7. A reference to primogeniture, a system to preserve the family estate by restricting inheritance to the first-born son, abolished in the French Revolution.

are read with a prepossession in their favour, and sentiments imitated, because they were fashionable and pretty, and not because they were forcibly felt.

In modern poetry the understanding and memory often fabricate the pretended effusions of the heart, and romance destroys all simplicity; which, in works of taste, is but a synonymous word for truth. This romantic spirit has extended to our prose, and scattered artificial flowers over the most barren heath; or a mixture of verse and prose producing the strangest incongruities. The turgid bombast of some of your periods[8] fully proves these assertions; for when the heart speaks we are seldom shocked by hyperbole, or dry raptures. * * * I am led very often to doubt your sincerity, and to suppose that you have said many things merely for the sake of saying them well. * * * The mock dignity and haughty stalk, only reminds me of the ass in the lion's skin.

A sentiment of this kind glanced across my mind when I read the following exclamation. "Whilst the royal captives, who followed in the train, were slowly moved along, amidst the horrid yells, and shrilling screams, and frantic dances, and infamous contumelies, and all the unutterable abominations of the furies of hell, in the abused shape of the vilest of women."[9] Probably you mean women who gained a livelihood by selling vegetables or fish, who never had any advantages of education; or their vices might have lost part of their abominable deformity, by losing part of their grossness.[1] The queen of France—the great and small vulgar, claim our pity; they have almost insuperable obstacles to surmount in their progress towards true dignity of character; still I have such a plain downright understanding that I do not like to make a distinction without a difference. But it is not very extraordinary that *you* should, for throughout your letter you frequently advert to a sentimental jargon, which has long been current in conversation, and even in books of morals, though it never received the *regal* stamp of reason. A kind of mysterious instinct is *supposed* to reside in the soul, that instantaneously discerns truth, without the tedious labour of ratiocination. This instinct, for I know not what other name to give it, has been termed *common sense*, and more frequently *sensibility*, and, by a kind of *indefeasible* right, it has been *supposed*, for rights of this kind are not easily proved, to reign paramount over the other faculties of the mind, and to be an authority from which there is no appeal. * * * It is to this instinct, without doubt, that you allude, when you talk of the "moral constitution of the heart."

In the name of the people of England, you say, " * * * In England we have not yet been completely emboweled of our natural entrails; we still feel within us, and we cherish and cultivate those inbred sentiments which are the faithful guardians, the active monitors of our duty, the true supporters of all liberal and manly morals."— What do you mean by inbred sentiments? From whence do they come? How were they bred? Are they the brood of folly, which swarms like the insects on the banks of the Nile, when mud and putrefaction have enriched the languid soil? Were these *inbred* sentiments faithful guardians of our duty when the church was an asylum for murderers, and men worshipped bread as a God? when slavery was authorized by law to fasten her fangs on human flesh, and the iron eat into the very soul? If these sentiments are not acquired, if our passive dispositions do not expand into virtuous affections and passions, why are not the Tartars in the first rude horde endued with sentiments white and *elegant* as the driven snow? Why is passion or heroism the child of reflection, the consequence of dwelling with intent contemplation on one object?

8. Sentences.
9. See Burke's *Reflections*, page 1359.

1. Echoing Burke's *Reflections*, page 1360.

The appetites are the only perfect inbred powers that I can discern; and they like instincts have a certain aim, they can be satisfied—but improveable reason has not yet discovered the perfection it may arrive at—God forbid!

[BURKE'S VIEW OF WOMEN]

Where is the dignity, the infallibility of sensibility, in the fair ladies, whom, if the voice of rumour is to be credited, the captive negroes curse in all the agony of bodily pain, for the unheard of tortures they invent? It is probable that some of them, after the sight of a flagellation, compose their ruffled spirits and exercise their tender feelings by the perusal of the last imported novel.—How true these tears are to nature, I leave you to determine. But these ladies may have read your Enquiry concerning the origin of our ideas of the Sublime and Beautiful, and, convinced by your arguments, may have laboured to be pretty, by counterfeiting weakness.[2]

You may have convinced them that *littleness* and *weakness* are the very essence of beauty; and that the Supreme Being, in giving women beauty in the most supereminent degree, seemed to command them, by the powerful voice of Nature, not to cultivate the moral virtues that might chance to excite respect, and interfere with the pleasing sensations they were created to inspire. Thus confining truth, fortitude, and humanity, within the rigid pale of manly morals, they might justly argue, that to be loved, woman's high end and great distinction! they should "learn to lisp, to totter in their walk, and nickname God's creatures."[3] Never, they might repeat after you, was any man, much less a woman, rendered amiable by the force of those exalted qualities, fortitude, justice, wisdom, and truth; and thus forewarned of the sacrifice they must make to those austere, unnatural virtues, they would be authorized to turn all their attention to their persons, systematically neglecting morals to secure beauty. * * * You have clearly proved that one half of the human species, at least, have not souls; and that Nature, by making women *little, smooth, delicate, fair* creatures, never designed that they should exercise their reason to acquire the virtues that produce opposite, if not contradictory, feelings. The affection they excite, to be uniform and perfect, should not be tinctured with the respect which moral virtues inspire, lest pain should be blended with pleasure, and admiration disturb the soft intimacy of love. This laxity of morals in the female world is certainly more captivating to a libertine[4] imagination than the cold arguments of reason, that give no sex to virtue. If beautiful weakness be interwoven in a woman's frame, if the chief business of her life be (as you insinuate) to inspire love, and Nature has made an eternal distinction between the qualities that dignify a rational being and this animal perfection, her duty and happiness in this life must clash with any preparation for a more exalted state. So that Plato and Milton were grossly mistaken in asserting that human love led to heavenly, and was only an exaltation of the same affection.[5]

---

2. In his influential treatise on aesthetics, A Philosophical Enquiry into the Origin of Our Ideas of the Sublime and Beautiful (1757), Burke genders these categories, with the sublime, characterized by sensations of pain, danger, and terror, as masculine; and the beautiful, characterized by qualities evoking heterosexual love—smallness, delicacy to the point of fragility, smoothness, proportion, softness—as feminine; see ch. 3.9 and 14. Wollstonecraft's sneer at "fair ladies" aims at both class status ("ladies" are aristocrats) and the "delicacy" that can abide the violent abuse of the slaves whose labor enables their luxury.
3. The traditional notion that reason is a male capacity allows women to excuse their immoral conduct on

grounds of not knowing any better and to claim that their only responsibility is to make themselves attractive objects for men's love. The phrase in quotation is from Hamlet's misogynist diatribe at Ophelia, whom he suspects of treachery (3.1.145–50), also quoted by Burke in Sublime and Beautiful ch.3.9.
4. Unconstrained, sensual.
5. See Plato (5th–4th c. B.C.), Symposium (Diotima's lesson, 201d ff., esp. 210–11), and Raphael's lesson to Adam in Milton's Paradise Lost: "Love refines / The thoughts, and heart enlarges, . . . is the scale / By which to heav'nly Love thou may'st ascend" (8.589–592). Wollstonecraft elaborates the arguments of this section in Rights of Woman (1792).

[THE RICH AND THE POOR]

The rich and weak, a numerous train, will certainly applaud your system, and loudly celebrate your pious reverence for authority and establishments—they find it pleasanter to enjoy than to think; to justify oppression than correct abuses.—*The rights of men* are grating sounds that set their teeth on edge; the impertinent enquiry of philosophic meddling innovation. If the poor are in distress, they will make some *benevolent* exertions to assist them; they will confer obligations, but not do justice. Benevolence is a very amiable specious quality; yet the aversion which men feel to accept a right as a favour, should rather be extolled as a vestige of native dignity, than stigmatized as the odious offspring of ingratitude. The poor consider the rich as their lawful prey; but we ought not too severely to animadvert on[6] their ingratitude. When they receive an alms they are commonly grateful at the moment; but old habits quickly return, and cunning has ever been a substitute for force. * * *

Among all your plausible arguments, and witty illustrations, your contempt for the poor always appears conspicuous, and rouses my indignation. The following paragraph in particular struck me, as breathing the most tyrannic spirit, and displaying the most factitious feelings. "Good order is the foundation of all good things. To be enabled to acquire, the people, without being servile, must be tractable and obedient. The magistrate must have his reverence, the laws their authority. The body of the people must not find the principles of natural subordination by art rooted out of their minds. They *must* respect that property of which they *cannot* partake. *They must labour to obtain what by labour can be obtained; and when they find, as they commonly do, the success disproportioned to the endeavour, they must be taught their consolation in the final proportions of eternal justice.* Of this consolation, whoever deprives them, deadens their industry, and strikes at the root of all acquisition as of all conservation. He that does this, is the cruel oppressor, the merciless enemy, of the poor and wretched; at the same time that, by his wicked speculations, he exposes the fruits of successful industry, and the accumulations of fortune, (ah! there's the rub)[7] to the plunder of the negligent, the disappointed, and the unprosperous."

This is contemptible hard-hearted sophistry, in the specious form of humility, and submission to the will of Heaven.—It is, Sir, *possible* to render the poor happier in this world, without depriving them of the consolation which you gratuitously grant them in the next. They have a right to more comfort than they at present enjoy; and more comfort might be afforded them, without encroaching on the pleasures of the rich: not now waiting to enquire whether the rich have any right to exclusive pleasures. What do I say?—encroaching! No; if an intercourse were established between them, it would impart the only true pleasure that can be snatched in this land of shadows, this hard school of moral discipline.

I know, indeed, that there is often something disgusting in the distresses of poverty, at which the imagination revolts, and starts back to exercise itself in the more attractive Arcadia of fiction.[8] The rich man builds a house, art and taste give it the highest finish. His gardens are planted, and the trees grow to recreate the fancy of the planter, though the temperature of the climate may rather force him to avoid the dangerous damps they exhale, than seek the umbrageous retreat. Every thing on the estate is cherished but man;—yet, to contribute to the happiness of man, is the most sublime of all enjoyments. But if, instead of sweeping pleasure-grounds, obelisks, temples, and elegant cottages, as

---

6. Censure.
7. The flaw in the argument; the phrase is from *Hamlet* 3.1.65, referring to the way the attraction of suicide is

thwarted by fear of the afterlife.
8. In ancient Greece, a region of pastoral simplicity, beauty, and harmony.

objects for the eye,[9] the heart was allowed to beat true to nature, decent farms would be scattered over the estate, and plenty smile around. Instead of the poor being subject to the griping hand of an avaricious steward, they would be watched over with fatherly solicitude, by the man whose duty and pleasure it was to guard their happiness, and shield from rapacity the beings who, by the sweat of their brow, exalted him above his fellows.

I could almost imagine I see a man thus gathering blessings as he mounted the hill of life; or consolation, in those days when the spirits lag, and the tired heart finds no pleasure in them. It is not by squandering alms that the poor can be relieved, or improved—it is the fostering sun of kindness, the wisdom that finds them employments calculated to give them habits of virtue, that meliorates their condition. * * *

Why cannot large estates be divided into small farms? these dwellings would indeed grace our land. Why are huge forests still allowed to stretch out with idle pomp and all the indolence of Eastern [Asian] grandeur? Why does the brown waste meet the traveller's view, when men want work? But commons cannot be enclosed without *acts of parliament* to increase the property of the rich![1] Why might not the industrious peasant be allowed to steal a farm from the heath? This sight I have seen;—the cow that supported the children grazed near the hut, and the cheerful poultry were fed by the chubby babes, who breathed a bracing air, far from the diseases and the vices of cities. Domination blasts all these prospects; virtue can only flourish amongst equals, and the man who submits to a fellow-creature, because it promotes his worldly interest, and he who relieves only because it is his duty to lay up a treasure in heaven,[2] are much on a par, for both are radically degraded by the habits of their life.

In this great city, that proudly rears its head, and boasts of its population and commerce, how much misery lurks in pestilential corners, whilst idle mendicants assail, on every side, the man who hates to encourage impostors, or repress, with angry frown, the plaints of the poor! How many mechanics, by a flux of trade or fashion, lose their employment; whom misfortunes, not to be warded off, lead to the idleness that vitiates their character and renders them afterwards averse to honest labour! Where is the eye that marks these evils, more gigantic than any of the infringements of property, which you piously deprecate? Are these remediless evils? And is the humane heart satisfied with turning the poor over to *another* world, to receive the blessings this could afford? * * *

What were the outrages of a day[3] to these continual miseries? Let those sorrows hide their diminished head before the tremendous mountain of woe that thus defaces our globe![4] Man preys on man; and you mourn * * * for the empty pageant of a name, when slavery flaps her wing, and the sick heart retires to die in lonely wilds, far from the abodes of men. Did the pangs you felt for insulted nobility, the anguish that rent your heart when the gorgeous robes were torn off the idol human weakness had set up [Queen Marie Antoinette], deserve to be compared with the long-drawn sigh of melancholy reflection, when misery and vice are thus seen to haunt our steps, and swim on the top of

9. A reference to the 18th-century vogue of landscaping on aristocratic estates, which frequently involved vast rearrangements of topography and the addition of picturesque enhancements such as pillars, classical temples, instant ruins, quaint cottages.
1. "Brown waste" is arable but untilled land; Wollstonecraft may also be alluding to Lancelot "Capability" Brown, a famous landscaper of aristocratic estates, who devised, among other "improvements," idle, though picturesque, stretches of forests and plains. In the 18th century, Parliament enacted a series of extreme "enclosure" acts, deeding to private ownership formerly public lands (the "commons" being the least arable of these), on

which the poor lived, grew crops, and pastured livestock.
2. See Jesus' instruction to "lay up for yourselves treasures in heaven, where neither moth nor rust doth corrupt, and where thieves do not break through nor steal" (Matthew 6.20). Wollstonecraft is referring to charity motivated by self-interest, the belief that such acts will count in one's favor in the judgment of Heaven.
3. The 6th of October (1789) [Wollstonecraft's note]; see Burke, *Reflections*, page 61.
4. In *Paradise Lost*, Satan notes how "all the Stars / Hide thir diminisht heads" at the sight of the noonday sun, "that with surpassing Glory crown'd, / Look'st from [its] sole dominion like the God / Of this new World" (4.32–35).

every cheering prospect? Why is our fancy to be appalled by terrific perspective of a hell beyond the grave?—Hell stalks abroad;—the lash resounds on the slave's naked sides; and the sick wretch, who can no longer earn the sour bread of unremitting labour, steals to a ditch to bid the world a long good night—or, neglected in some ostentatious hospital, breathes his last amidst the laugh of mercenary attendants.

Such misery demands more than tears—I pause to recollect myself; and smother the contempt I feel rising for your rhetorical flourishes and infantine sensibility.

Thomas Paine
1737–1809

"These are the times that try men's souls," declared Thomas Paine in a pamphlet that was read to George Washington's suffering and discouraged troops before the battle of Trenton. Paine was already famous for *Common Sense* (1776), urging the colonies to revolt from Britain; selling briskly, more than 100,000 copies in three months, it was a critical inspiration for the Declaration of Independence and the American Revolution. Born in England, and with only a grammar-school education, Paine wandered through various unsatisfactory jobs until he met Benjamin Franklin in London. At thirty-seven, with letters of introduction from Franklin, he sailed to America, where he launched his career as a writer with articles on women's rights and the abolition of slavery. After he returned to England in 1787, he shuttled back and forth to France, and when Edmund Burke's *Reflections on the Revolution in France* appeared in 1790, he quickly began his rebuttal, *The Rights of Man*, published early the next year. Burke wrote eloquent prose for the educated elite; Paine's simple, electric style was framed for the common reader, and his tract, priced cheaply, was an immediate and widespread success, selling 200,000 copies by 1793—but not without cost. Paine's incitement to revolution over reform and his attack on monarchies sent his bookseller to jail and led to his own indictment for treason. Fleeing to France in 1792 (just after the September Massacres), he was warmly received, elected to the National Assembly and given honorary citizenship. But he soon got into trouble for criticizing the execution of Louis XVI. Imprisoned by the Jacobins, he only narrowly escaped the guillotine himself through the intercession of James Monroe, then American ambassador to France. Convicted in absentia in England, he could not return without imprisonment, so he went back to America. There he completed *The Age of Reason* (1792–1795), a case for Deism begun during his imprisonment in France. Its strident denunciation of institutionalized Christianity and the Bible cost Paine sympathetic readers, however, and his reputation fell further in 1796 when he attacked Washington and federalism. He died in 1809, impoverished, angry, and ostracized. Denounced as an atheist, he was denied a consecrated burial, but in 1819, William Cobbett, a sympathetic English radical, exhumed his remains and took them to England.

from The Rights of Man
Being an answer to Mr. Burke's attack on the French Revolution
["MAN HAS NO PROPERTY IN MAN"]

There never did, there never will, and there never can, exist a Parliament, or any description of men, or any generation of men, in any country, possessed of the right or the power of binding and controuling posterity to the *"end of time."* * * * Every age and generation must be as free to act for itself *in all cases* as the ages and generations which preceded it. The vanity and presumption of governing beyond the grave is the most ridiculous and insolent of all tyrannies. Man has no property in man; neither has any generation a property in the generations which are to follow. The Parliament or the people of 1688,[1] or of any other period, had no more right to dispose of the people of the present day, or to bind or to controul them *in any shape whatever*, than the Parliament or the people of the present day have to dispose of, bind or controul those who are to live a hundred or a thousand years hence. Every generation is, and must be, competent to all the purposes which its occasions require. It is the living, and not the dead, that are to be accommodated. When man ceases to be, his power and his wants cease with him; and having no longer any participation in the concerns of this world, he has no longer any authority in directing who shall be its governors, or how its Government shall be organised, or how administered.

I am not contending for nor against any form of Government, nor for nor against any party, here or elsewhere. That which a whole Nation chooses to do, it has a right to do. Mr. Burke says, No. Where, then does the right exist? I am contending for the rights of the *living*, and against their being willed away, and controuled and contracted for, by the manuscript assumed authority of the dead; and Mr. Burke is contending for the authority of the dead over the rights and freedom of the living. There was a time when Kings disposed of their Crowns by will upon their death-beds, and consigned the people, like beasts of the field, to whatever successor they appointed. This is now so exploded as scarcely to be remembered, and so monstrous as hardly to be believed; but the Parliamentary clauses upon which Mr. Burke builds his political church are of the same nature.

The laws of every country must be analogous to some common principle. In England no parent or master, nor all the authority of Parliament, omnipotent as it has called itself, can bind or controul the personal freedom even of an individual beyond the age of twenty-one years. On what ground of right, then, could the Parliament of 1688, or any other Parliament, bind all posterity for ever?

Those who have quitted the world, and those who are not yet arrived at it, are as remote from each other as the utmost stretch of mortal imagination can conceive. What possible obligation, then, can exist between them; what rule or principle can be laid down that of two non-entities, the one out of existence and the other not in, and who never can meet in this world, the one should controul the other to the end of time? * * * It is the nature of man to die, and he will continue to die as long as he continues to be born. But Mr. Burke has set up a sort of political Adam, in whom all posterity are bound for ever; he must, therefore, prove that his Adam possessed such a power, or such a right. * * * It requires but a very small glance of thought to perceive that altho' laws made in one generation often continue in force through succeeding generations, yet that they continue to derive their force from the consent of the living. A law not repealed continues in force, not because it *cannot* be repealed, but because it *is not* repealed; and the non-repealing passes for consent.

[PRINCIPLES, NOT PERSONS]

Mr. Burke shows that he is ignorant of the springs and principles of the French Revolution. It was not against Louis XVI., but against the despotic principles of the government, that the Nation revolted. These principles had not their origin in him, but in the original establishment, many centuries back; and they were become too deeply rooted to be removed, and the Augean stable of parasites and plunderers too abom-

---

1. In the Glorious Revolution of 1688 (so named by the Whigs), Parliament deposed James II and installed William and Mary in the monarchy, along with a bill of rights that shifted the balance of power from the monarchy to Parliament.

inably filthy to be cleansed,[2] by anything short of a complete and universal Revolution. When it becomes necessary to do a thing, the whole heart and soul should go into the measure, or not attempt it. That crisis was then arrived, and there remained no choice but to act with determined vigour, or not to act at all. The King was known to be the friend of the Nation, and this circumstance was favourable to the enterprise.[3] Perhaps no man bred up in the style of an absolute King, ever possessed a heart so little disposed to the exercise of that species of power as the present King of France. But the principles of the Government itself still remained the same. The Monarch and the Monarchy were distinct and separate things; and it was against the established despotism of the latter, and not against the person or principles of the former, that the revolt commenced, and the Revolution has been carried.

Mr. Burke does not attend to the distinction between *men* and *principles*; and, therefore, he does not see that a revolt may take place against the despotism of the latter, while there lies no charge of despotism against the former.

The natural moderation of Louis XVI contributed nothing to alter the hereditary despotism of the Monarchy. All the tyrannies of former reigns, acted under that hereditary despotism, were still liable to be revived in the hands of a successor. It was not the respite of a reign that would satisfy France, enlightened as she then was become. A casual discontinuance of the *practice* of despotism, is not a discontinuance of its *principles*; the former depends on the virtue of the individual who is in immediate possession of the power; the latter, on the virtue and fortitude of the nation. In the case of Charles I and James II of England, the revolt was against the personal despotism of the men;[4] whereas in France, it was against the hereditary despotism of the established government. But men who can consign over the rights of posterity for ever on the authority of a mouldy parchment, like Mr. Burke, are not qualified to judge of this Revolution. It takes in a field too vast for their views to explore, and proceeds with a mightiness of reason they cannot keep pace with.

But there are many points of view in which this Revolution may be considered. When despotism has established itself for ages in a country, as in France, it is not in the person of the King only that it resides. It has the appearance of being so in show, and in nominal authority; but it is not so in practice and in fact. It has its standard everywhere. Every office and department has its despotism, founded upon custom and usage. Every place has its Bastille, and every Bastille its despot.[5] The original hereditary despotism resident in the person of the King, divides and subdivides itself into a thousand shapes and forms, till at last the whole of it is acted by deputation. This was the case in France; and against this species of despotism, proceeding on

2. One of Hercules' labors was to purge the notoriously filthy stables of King Augeas—hence, a place of entrenched corruption.
3. In the 1770s and 1780s, Louis XVI tried unsuccessfully to initiate some reforms, including moderate taxation of the nobility. After the fall of the Bastille in July 1789, he withdrew his troops, reinstated his reform-minded director of the treasury (ousted by reactionary factions), and outwardly accepted the Revolution.
4. Charles I, son of James I (successor of Elizabeth I), was unpopular for imposing exorbitant taxes, suspending Parliament, and harshly oppressing religious dissent; defeated in the 1640s Civil War with Parliament, he was beheaded for "high treason and other high crimes" in 1649. The monarchy was restored in 1660, and his

Roman Catholic son James II became king in 1685, but was soon forced from office for his attempt to restore absolute monarchy and Catholicism as the state religion. Seven powerful nobles, with the consent of Parliament, invited William III of Orange (grandson of Charles I) to invade England to protect its liberties and become joint monarch with Charles's Protestant daughter, Mary; William advanced bloodlessly to London with 15,000 troops, and Parliament proclaimed him and Mary monarchs in 1689.
5. The Bastille was France's infamous prison, holding many political prisoners, mostly without trial; it was the icon of the abuse of power that fomented the Revolution, which began with the storming of the Bastille and the liberation of its prisoners on 14 July 1789.

through an endless labyrinth of office till the source of it is scarcely perceptible, there is no mode of redress. It strengthens itself by assuming the appearance of duty, and tyrannises under the pretence of obeying.

When a man reflects on the condition which France was in from the nature of her Government, he will see other causes for revolt than those which immediately connect themselves with the person or character of Louis XVI. There were, if I may so express it, a thousand despotisms to be reformed in France, which had grown up under the hereditary despotism of the monarchy, and became so rooted as to be in great measure independent of it. Between the Monarchy, the Parliament, and the Church, there was a *rivalship* of despotism; besides the feudal despotism operating locally, and the ministerial despotism operating everywhere. But Mr. Burke, by considering the King as the only possible object of a revolt, speaks as if France was a village, in which everything that passed must be known to its commanding officer, and no oppression could be acted but what he could immediately controul. Mr. Burke might have been in the Bastille his whole life, as well under Louis XVI as Louis XIV,[6] and neither the one nor the other have known that such a man as Mr. Burke existed. The despotic principles of the Government were the same in both reigns, though the dispositions of the men were as remote as tyranny and benevolence.

What Mr. Burke considers as a reproach to the French Revolution (that of bringing it forward under a reign more mild than the preceding ones) is one of its highest honours. The Revolutions that have taken place in other European countries, have been excited by personal hatred. The rage was against the man, and he became the victim. But, in the instance of France we see a revolution generated in the rational contemplation of the rights of man, and distinguishing from the beginning between persons and principles.

But Mr. Burke appears to have no idea of principles when he is contemplating Governments. "Ten years ago," says he, "I could have felicitated France on her having a Government, without inquiring what the nature of that Government was, or how it was administered." Is this the language of a rational man? Is it the language of a heart feeling as it ought to feel for the rights and happiness of the human race? On this ground, Mr. Burke must compliment all the Governments in the world, while the victims who suffer under them, whether sold into slavery, or tortured out of existence, are wholly forgotten. It is power, and not principles, that Mr. Burke venerates.

* * *

As to the tragic paintings by which Mr. Burke has outraged his own imagination, and seeks to work upon that of his readers, they are very well calculated for theatrical representation, where facts are manufactured for the sake of show, and accommodated to produce, through the weakness of sympathy, a weeping effect. But Mr. Burke should recollect that he is writing history, and not *plays*, and that his readers will expect truth, and not the spouting rant of high-toned exclamation.

When we see a man dramatically lamenting in a publication intended to be believed that "*The age of chivalry is gone! that The glory of Europe is extinguished for ever! that the unbought grace of life* (if any one knows what it is), *the cheap defence of nations, the nurse of manly sentiment and heroic enterprise is gone!*" and all this

---

6. Louis XVI's ancestor (1638–1715), known as the Sun King, a notorious spendthrift, advocate of the divine right of kings, and patron of the arts.

because the Quixote age of chivalry nonsense is gone, what opinion can we form of his judgment, or what regard can we pay to his facts?[7] In the rhapsody of his imagination he has discovered a world of windmills, and his sorrows are that there are no Quixotes to attack them. But if the age of Aristocracy, like that of Chivalry, should fall (and they had originally some connection), Mr. Burke, the trumpeter of the order, may continue his parody to the end, and finish with exclaiming: "*Othello's occupation's gone!*"[8]

Notwithstanding Mr. Burke's horrid paintings, when the French Revolution is compared with the Revolutions of other countries, the astonishment will be that it is marked with so few sacrifices; but this astonishment will cease when we reflect that *principles*, and not *persons*, were the meditated objects of destruction. The mind of the nation was acted upon by a higher stimulus than what the consideration of persons could inspire, and sought a higher conquest than could be produced by the downfall of an enemy. Among the few who fell there do not appear to be any that were intentionally singled out. They all of them had their fate in the circumstances of the moment. * * * From his violence and his grief, his silence on some points and his excess on others, it is difficult not to believe that Mr. Burke is sorry, extremely sorry, that arbitrary power, the power of the Pope[9] and the Bastille, are pulled down.

Not one glance of compassion, not one commiserating reflection that I can find throughout his book, has he bestowed on those who lingered out the most wretched of lives, a life without hope in the most miserable of prisons. It is painful to behold a man employing his talents to corrupt himself. Nature has been kinder to Mr. Burke than he is to her. He is not affected by the reality of distress touching his heart, but by the showy resemblance of it striking his imagination. He pities the plumage, but forgets the dying bird.[1] Accustomed to kiss the aristocratical hand that hath purloined him from himself, he degenerates into a composition of art, and the genuine soul of nature forsakes him. His hero or his heroine must be a tragedy-victim expiring in show, and not the real prisoner of misery, sliding into death in the silence of a dungeon.

[THE DOCTRINE OF EQUAL RIGHTS]

If the mere name of antiquity is to govern in the affairs of life, the people who are to live an hundred or a thousand years hence, may as well take us for a precedent, as we make a precedent of those who lived an hundred or a thousand years ago. The fact is, that portions of antiquity, by proving everything, establish nothing. It is authority against authority all the way, till we come to the divine origin of the rights of man at the creation. Here our inquiries find a resting-place, and our reason finds a home. If a dispute about the rights of man had arisen at the distance of an hundred years from the creation, it is to this source of authority they must have referred, and it is to this same source of authority that we must now refer.

---

7. Paine is quoting Burke's *Reflections*, page 1361, and alluding to Cervantes' *Don Quixote*, a country gentleman who, overfed on chivalric romances, sets out in search of knightly adventure and winds up tilting at windmills in lieu of real opponents.
8. Othello utters this cry, when, falsely convinced of his wife's infidelity, he feels he has nothing more to live for (*Othello* 3.3.354).

9. Pre-Revolutionary France was Catholic (like Burke's Ireland), and so answerable to the Pope, at least in theory.
1. Perhaps the most famous sentence in this tract. Royalty frequently ornamented itself with elaborate plumage (feathers); Paine's point is that Burke is so wrapped up in the disgrace of the royal family that he neglects the misery of the state that sustains it, and which itself is dying from poverty and corruption.

Though I mean not to touch upon any sectarian principle of religion, yet it may be worth observing, that the genealogy of Christ is traced to Adam. Why then not trace the rights of man to the creation of man? I will answer the question. Because there have been upstart Governments, thrusting themselves between and presumptuously working to *un-make* man.

If any generation of men ever possessed the right of dictating the mode by which the world should be governed for ever, it was the first generation that existed; and if that generation did it not, no succeeding generation can show any authority for doing it, nor can set any up. The illuminating and divine principle of the equal rights of man (for it has its origin from the Maker of man) relates, not only to the living individuals, but to generations of men succeeding each other. Every generation is equal in rights to the generations which preceded it, by the same rule that every individual is born equal in rights with his contemporary.

Every history of the creation, and every traditionary account, whether from the lettered or unlettered world, however they may vary in their opinion or belief of certain particulars, all agree in establishing one point, *the unity of man*; by which I mean that men are all of *one degree*, and consequently that all men are born equal, and with equal natural rights, in the same manner as if posterity had been continued by *creation* instead of *generation*, the latter being only the mode by which the former is carried forward; and consequently every child born into the world must be considered as deriving its existence from God. The world is as new to him as it was to the first man that existed, and his natural right in it is of the same kind.

The Mosaic account of the creation,[2] whether taken as divine authority or merely historical, is fully up to this point, *the unity or equality of man*. The expressions admit of no controversy. "And God said, Let us make man in our own image. In the image of God created he him; male and female created he them." The distinction of sexes is pointed out, but no other distinction is even implied. If this be not divine authority, it is at least historical authority, and shows that the equality of man, so far from being a modern doctrine, is the oldest upon record. * * *

It is not among the least of the evils of the present existing Governments in all parts of Europe that man, considered as man, is thrown back to a vast distance from his Maker, and the artificial chasm filled up by a succession of barriers, or sort of turnpike gates, through which he has to pass. I will quote Mr. Burke's catalogue of barriers that he has set up between Man and his Maker. Putting himself in the character of a herald, he says: *We fear God—we look with* AWE *to kings—with affection to Parliaments—with duty to magistrates—with reverence to priests, and with respect to nobility.* Mr. Burke has forgotten to put in "*chivalry*." He has also forgotten to put in Peter.[3]

The duty of man is not a wilderness of turnpike gates, through which he is to pass by tickets from one to the other. It is plain and simple, and consists but of two points. His duty to God, which every man must feel; and with respect to his neighbour, to do as he would be done by. If those to whom power is delegated do well, they will be respected; if not, they will be despised; and with regard to those to whom no power is delegated, but who assume it, the rational world can know nothing of them.

---

2. Moses (adj. Mosaic) was traditionally thought to be the author of Genesis. Paine's ensuing quotation is patched from Genesis 1.26–27; in Genesis 2, which Milton follows

in *Paradise Lost*, God creates man first, and woman second.
3. In popular Christian lore, St. Peter keeps the gates to Heaven, deciding whom to admit.

[THE REPUBLICAN SYSTEM]

When we survey the wretched condition of Man, under the monarchical and heredi-tary systems of Government, dragged from his home by one power, or driven by another, and impoverished by taxes more than by enemies, it becomes evident that those systems are bad, and that a general Revolution in the principle and construc-tion of Governments is necessary.

What is Government more than the management of the affairs of a Nation? It is not, and from its nature cannot be, the property of any particular man or family, but of the whole community, at whose expence it is supported; and though by force and contrivance it has been usurped into an inheritance, the usurpation cannot alter the right of things. Sovereignty, as a matter of right, appertains to the Nation only, and not to any individual; and a Nation has at all times an inherent, indefeasible right to abolish any form of Government it finds inconvenient, and to establish such as accords with its interest, disposition, and happiness. The romantic and barbarous dis-tinction of men into Kings and subjects, though it may suit the conditions of courtiers, cannot that of citizens; and is exploded by the principle upon which Gov-ernments are now founded. Every citizen is a member of the sovereignty, and, as such, can acknowledge no personal subjection: and his obedience can be only to the laws.

* * * In this view of Government, the Republican system, as established by Ameri-ca and France, operates to embrace the whole of a Nation. * * * What we formerly called Revolutions, were little more than a change of persons, or an alteration of local circumstances. They rose and fell like things of course, and had nothing in their exis-tence or their fate that could influence beyond the spot that produced them. But what we now see in the world, from the Revolutions of America and France, are a renovation of the natural order of things, a system of principles as universal as truth and the exis-tence of man, and combining moral with political happiness and national prosperity.

William Godwin
1756–1836

Husband of Mary Wollstonecraft and father of Mary Wollstonecraft Shelley, William Godwin has his own claim to fame as the author of *An Enquiry Concerning Political Justice*, an intellec-tually if not politically influential work published in the wake of the execution of Louis XVI of France. The son of a dissenting minister, Godwin entered this profession in 1778, but under the influence of Enlightenment philosophy, he was beset by religious doubts, and in 1782 he left the calling for political writing. *Political Justice*, begun in 1791 and published in 1793, is one of the most emphatic English statements of "anarchist" political philosophy: the disdain of governmental institutions and their legal apparatus as the source of manifold evils and corrup-tions. In a kind of radical Protestantism, Godwin placed faith in the capacity of man to be guided by private judgment, arguing that rational men, pursuing common good, would cease to need government, law, and religion. He went so far as to abolish marriage and private proper-ty. This work appalled conservatives but for a time had a strong following, including William Wordsworth, Samuel Taylor Coleridge, Lord Byron, and Percy Shelley. "No work in our time gave such a blow to the philosophical mind of the country," wrote William Hazlitt in *The Spir-it of the Age* (1825); "Tom Paine was considered for the time as Tom Fool to him; . . . Edmund Burke a flashy sophist." For Wordsworth's account of his romance and disillusionment with Godwinian philosophy, see *The Prelude* 10:805–865. *Political Justice* was revised and expanded in 1796 and saw a third edition in 1798, in an atmosphere of increasing censorship of "seditious" writing. Excerpts here are from the first edition, the one that blazed on the scene of English debate in the wake of the Terror.

from An Enquiry Concerning Political Justice and Its Influence on General Virtue and Happiness
from *Of Justice*

If justice have any meaning, it is just that I should contribute every thing in my power to the benefit of the whole. * * * Justice is a rule of conduct originating in the connection of one percipient being with another. A comprehensive maxim which has been laid down upon the subject is, "that we should love our neighbour as ourselves."[1] But this maxim, though possessing considerable merit as a popular principle, is not modelled with the strictness of philosophical accuracy.

In a loose and general view I and my neighbour are both of us men; and of consequence entitled to equal attention. But in reality it is probable that one of us is a being of more worth and importance than the other. A man is of more worth than a beast; because, being possessed of higher faculties, he is capable of a more refined and genuine happiness. In the same manner the illustrious archbishop of Cambray was of more worth than his chambermaid, and there are few of us that would hesitate to pronounce, if his palace were in flames, and the life of only one of them could be preserved, which of the two ought to be preferred.[2]

But there is another ground of preference, beside the private consideration of one of them being farther removed from the state of a mere animal. We are not connected with one or two percipient beings, but with a society, a nation, and in some sense with the whole family of mankind. Of consequence that life ought to be preferred which will be most conducive to the general good. In saving the life of Fenelon, suppose at the moment when he was conceiving the project of his immortal Telemachus, I should be promoting the benefit of thousands, who have been cured by the perusal of it of some error, vice and consequent unhappiness. Nay, my benefit would extend farther than this, for every individual thus cured has become a better member of society, and has contributed in his turn to the happiness, the information and improvement of others.

Supposing I had been myself the chambermaid, I ought to have chosen to die, rather than that Fenelon should have died. The life of Fenelon was really preferable to that of the chambermaid. But understanding is the faculty that perceives the truth of this and similar propositions; and justice is the principle that regulates my conduct accordingly. It would have been just in the chambermaid to have preferred the archbishop to herself. To have done otherwise would have been a breach of justice.

Supposing the chambermaid had been my wife, my mother or my benefactor. This would not alter the truth of the proposition. The life of Fenelon would still be more valuable than that of the chambermaid; and justice, pure, unadulterated justice,

---

1. The second of the great Commandments, according to Jesus (Mark 12.31).
2. In a later edition, Godwin changed "chambermaid" to "valet" (a male personal attendant). Archbishop of Cambrai; François Fénelon lost favor in the court of Louis XIV upon the publication of *Télémaque* (1699), a didactic romance that indirectly criticized the king's policies by urging humane internationalism and stressing the king's obligations to the welfare of his subjects.

would still have preferred that which was most valuable. Justice would have taught me to save the life of Fenelon at the expence of the other. What magic is there in the pronoun "my," to overturn the decisions of everlasting truth? My wife or my mother may be a fool or a prostitute, malicious, lying or dishonest. If they be, of what consequence is it that they are mine?

   "But my mother endured for me the pains of child bearing, and nourished me in the helplessness of infancy." When she first subjected herself to the necessity of these cares, she was probably influenced by no particular motives of benevolence to her future offspring. Every voluntary benefit however entitles the bestower to some kindness and retribution. But why so? Because a voluntary benefit is an evidence of benevolent intention, that is, of virtue. It is the disposition of the mind, not the external action, that entitles to respect. But the merit of this disposition is equal, whether the benefit was conferred upon me or upon another. I and another man cannot both be right in preferring our own individual benefactor, for no man can be at the same time both better and worse than his neighbour. My benefactor ought to be esteemed, not because he bestowed a benefit upon me, but because he bestowed it upon a human being. His desert will be in exact proportion to the degree, in which that human being was worthy of the distinction conferred. Thus every view of the subject brings us back to the consideration of my neighbour's moral worth and his importance to the general weal, as the only standard to determine the treatment to which he is entitled. Gratitude therefore, a principle which has so often been the theme of the moralist and the poet, is no part either of justice or virtue. * * *

   Now the same justice, that binds me to any individual of my fellow men, binds me to the whole. If, while I confer a benefit upon one man, it appear, in striking an equitable balance, that I am injuring the whole, my action ceases to be right and becomes absolutely wrong. But how much am I bound to do for the general weal, that is, for the benefit of the individuals of whom the whole is composed? Every thing in my power. What to the neglect of the means of my own existence? No; for I am myself a part of the whole. Beside, it will rarely happen but that the project of doing for others every thing in my power, will demand for its execution the preservation of my own existence; or in other words, it will rarely happen but that I can do more good in twenty years than in one. If the extraordinary case should occur in which I can promote the general good by my death, more than by my life, justice requires that I should be content to die. * * * I hold my person as a trust in behalf of mankind. I am bound to employ my talents, my understanding, my strength and my time for the production of the greatest quantity of general good. Such are the declarations of justice, so great is the extent of my duty.

   But justice is reciprocal. If it be just that I should confer a benefit, it is just that another man should receive it, and, if I withhold from him that to which he is entitled, he may justly complain. My neighbour is in want of ten pounds that I can spare. There is no law of political institution that has been made to reach this case, and to transfer this property from me to him. But in the eye of simple justice, unless it can be shewn that the money can be more beneficially employed, his claim is as complete, as if he had my bond in his possession, or had supplied me with goods to the amount. * * *

   Society is nothing more than an aggregation of individuals. Its claims and its duties must be the aggregate of their claims and duties, the one no more precarious and arbitrary than the other. What has the society a right to require from me? The question is already answered: every thing that it is my duty to do. * * * What is it that the society is bound to do for its members? Every thing that can contribute to their welfare. But the nature of their welfare is defined by the nature of mind. That will most contribute to it, which enlarges the understanding, supplies incitements to virtue, fills us with a generous consciousness of our independence, and carefully removes whatever can impede our exertions.

Should it be affirmed, "that it is not in the power of any political system to secure to us these advantages," the conclusion I am drawing will still be incontrovertible. * * * There is one thing that political institutions can assuredly do, they can avoid positively counteracting the true interests of their subjects.

from *Of Revolutions*

No question can be more important than that which respects the best mode of effecting revolutions. Before we enter upon it however, it may be proper to remove a difficulty which has suggested itself to the minds of some men, how far we ought generally speaking to be the friends of revolution; or, in other words, whether it be justifiable in a man to be the enemy of the constitution of his country.

"We live," it will be said, "under the protection of this constitution; and protection, being a benefit conferred, obliges us to a reciprocation of support in return."

To this it may be answered, first, that this protection is a very equivocal thing; and, till it can be shown that the vices, from the effects of which it protects us, are not for the most part the produce of that constitution, we shall never sufficiently understand the quantity of benefit it includes. * * * Affection to my countrymen will be much better proved, by my exertions to procure them a substantial benefit, than by my supporting a system which I believe to be fraught with injurious consequences.

He who calls upon me to support the constitution must found his requisition upon one of two principles. It has a claim upon my support either because it is good, or because it is British. * * * He that desires a revolution for its own sake is to be regarded as a madman. He that desires it from a thorough conviction of its usefulness and necessity has a claim upon us for candour and respect. As to the demand upon me for support to the English constitution, because it is English, there is little plausibility in this argument. It is of the same nature as the demand upon me to be a Christian, because I am a Briton, or a Mahometan, because I am a native of Turkey. * * * If men reason and reflect, it must necessarily happen that either the Englishman or the Turk will find his government to be odious and his religion false. For what purpose employ his reason, if he must for ever conceal the conclusions to which it leads him? How would man have arrived at his present attainments, if he had always been contented with the state of society in which he happened to be born? In a word, either reason is the curse of our species, and human nature is to be regarded with horror; or it becomes us to employ our understanding and to act upon it, and to follow truth wherever it may lead us. It cannot lead us to mischief, since utility, as it regards percipient beings, is the only basis of moral and political truth.

* * * The true instruments for changing the opinions of men are argument and persuasion. The best security for an advantageous life is free and unrestricted discussion. In that field truth must always prove the successful champion. If then we would improve the social institutions of mankind, we must write, we must argue, we must converse. To this business there is no close; in this pursuit there should be no pause. Every method should be employed,—not so much positively to allure the attention of mankind, or persuasively to invite them to the adoption of our opinions—as to

remove every restraint upon thought, and to throw open the temple of science and the field of enquiry to all the world. * * * The phalanx of reason is invulnerable; it advances with deliberate and determined pace; and nothing is able to resist it. But when we lay down our arguments, and take up our swords, the case is altered. Amidst the barbarous pomp of war and the clamorous din of civil brawls, who can tell whether the event[1] shall be prosperous or miserable?

We must therefore carefully distinguish between informing the people and inflaming them. Indignation, resentment and fury are to be deprecated; and all we should ask is sober thought, clear discernment and intrepid discussion. Why were the revolutions of America and France a general concert of all orders and descriptions of men, without so much (if we bear in mind the multitudes concerned) as almost a dissentient voice; while the resistance against our Charles the first divided the nation into two equal parts?[2] Because the latter was the affair of the seventeenth century, and the former happened in the close of the eighteenth. Because in the case of America and France philosophy had already developed some of the great principles of political truth, and Sydney and Locke and Montesquieu and Rousseau had convinced a majority of reflecting and powerful minds of the evils of usurpation.[3] If these revolutions had happened still later, not one drop of the blood of one citizen would have been shed by the hands of another, nor would the event have been marked so much perhaps as with one solitary instance of violence and confiscation.

There are two principles therefore which the man who desires the regeneration of his species ought ever to bear in mind, to regard the improvement of every hour as essential in the discovery and dissemination of truth, and willingly to suffer the lapse of years before he urges the reducing his theory into actual execution. With all his caution it is possible that the impetuous multitude will run before the still and quiet progress of reason. * * * But, if his caution be firmly exerted, there is no doubt that he will supersede many abortive attempts, and considerably prolong the general tranquility.

from *Of the Enjoyment of Liberty*

["EVILS OF COHABITATION—AND MARRIAGE"]

Cohabitation is not only an evil as it checks the independent progress of mind; it is also inconsistent with the imperfections and propensities of man. It is absurd to expect that the inclinations and wishes of two human beings should coincide through any long period of time. To oblige them to act and to live together, is to subject them to some inevitable portion of thwarting, bickering, and unhappiness. This cannot be otherwise, so long as man has failed to reach the standard of absolute perfection. The supposition that I must have a companion for life, is the result of a complication of vices. It is the dictates of cowardice, and not of fortitude. It flows from the desire of being loved and esteemed for something that is not desert.

---

1. Outcome.
2. A reference to the parliamentary resistance, and then English Civil Wars of the 1640s, concluding in the execution of Charles I.
3. Algernon Sydney, English politician who took Parliament's side in the English Civil Wars. After the Restoration, he joined the opposition to Charles II; he was executed in 1683. In 1698, his influential liberal *Discourses Concerning Government* was published. John Locke's *Two Treatises on Civil Government* (1690), in part a justification of the Glorious Revolution of 1688, set forth the qualified rights of revolution, of property, the rights to the products of one's labor, and a system of governmental checks and balances. Influenced by Locke, Charles Montesquieu wrote *The Spirit of the Laws* (1748), an analysis of three types of government—monarchy, republic, despotism—also advocating a separation and balance of powers. The political philosophy of Rousseau is best known from *The Social Contract* (1762), an argument for the voluntary submission of social subjects to a common good, determined by rational reflection.

But the evil of marriage as it is practised in European countries lies deeper than this. The habit is, for a thoughtless and romantic youth of each sex to come together, to see each other for a few times and under circumstances full of delusion, and then to vow to each other eternal attachment. What is the consequence of this? In almost every instance they find themselves deceived. They are reduced to make the best of an irretrievable mistake. They are presented with the strongest imaginable temptation to become the dupes of falsehood. They are led to conceive it their wisest policy to shut their eyes upon realities, happy if by any perversion of intellect they can persuade themselves that they were right in their first crude opinion of their companion. The institution of marriage is a system of fraud; and men who carefully mislead their judgments in the daily affair of their life, must always have a crippled judgment in every other concern. We ought to dismiss our mistake as soon as it is detected; but we are taught to cherish it. We ought to be incessant in our search after virtue and worth; but we are taught to check our enquiry, and shut our eyes upon the most attractive and admirable objects. Marriage is law, and the worst of all laws. Whatever our understandings may tell us of the person from whose connexion we should derive the greatest improvement, of the worth of one woman and the demerits of another, we are obliged to consider what is law, and not what is justice.

Add to this, that marriage is an affair of property, and the worst of all properties. So long as two human beings are forbidden by positive institution to follow the dictates of their own mind, prejudice is alive and vigorous. So long as I seek to engross one woman to myself, and to prohibit my neighbor from proving his superior desert and reaping the fruits of it, I am guilty of the most odious of all monopolies. Over this imaginary prize men watch with perpetual jealousy, and one man will find his desires and his capacity to circumvent as much excited, as the other is exited to traverse his projects and frustrate his hopes. As long as this state of society continues, philanthropy will be crossed and checked in a thousand ways, and the still augmenting stream of abuse will continue to flow.

The abolition of marriage will be attended with no evils. We are apt to represent it to ourselves as the harbinger of brutal lust and depravity. But it really happens in this as in other cases, that the positive laws which are made to restrain our vices, irritate and multiply them. Not to say, that the same sentiments of justice and happiness which in a state of equal property would destroy the relish for luxury, would decrease our inordinate appetites of every kind, and lead us universally to prefer the pleasures of intellect to the pleasures of sense.

The intercourse[1] of the sexes will in such a state fall under the same system as any other species of friendship. Exclusively of all groundless and obstinate attachments, it will be impossible for me to live in the world without finding one man of worth superior to that of any other whom I have an opportunity of observing. To this man I shall feel a kindness in exact proportion to my appreciation of his worth. The case will be precisely the same with respect to the female sex. I shall assiduously cultivate the intercourse of that woman whose accomplishments shall strike me in the most powerful manner. "But it may happen that other men will feel for her the same preference that I do." This will create no difficulty. We may all enjoy her conversation; and we shall all be wise enough to consider the sensual intercourse as a very trivial object. This, like every other affair in which two persons are concerned, must be regulated in each successive instance by the unforced consent of either party. It is a mark of the extreme depravity of our present habits, that we are inclined to suppose

---

1. Social interaction.

the sensual intercourse [of] any wife material to the advantages arising from the purest affection. Reasonable men now eat and drink, not from the love of pleasure, but because eating and drinking are essential to our healthful existence. Reasonable men then will propagate their species, not because a certain sensible pleasure is annexed to this action, but because it is right the species should be propagated; and the manner in which they exercise this function will be regulated by the dictates of reason and duty.

Such are some of the considerations that will probably regulate the commerce of the sexes. It cannot be definitively affirmed whether it will be known in such a state of society who is the father of each individual child. But is may be affirmed that such knowledge will be of no importance. It is aristocracy, self love and family pride that teach us to set a value upon it at present. I ought to prefer no human being to another, because that being is my father, my wife, or my son, but because, for reasons which equally appeal to all understandings, that being is entitled to preference. One among the measures which will successively be dictated by the spirit of democracy, and that probably at no great distance, is the abolition of surnames.

The Anti-Jacobin

In thirty-six numbers between November 1797 and July 1798 *The Anti-Jacobin*, or *Weekly Examiner*, under the editorship of William Gifford, defended Pitt's government by brilliantly lampooning any and all signs of radical opposition. Avowedly devoted to combating the spread of subversive ideas, George Ellis, John Hookham Frere, George Canning, and their fellows deployed a wit as pointed as it was exuberant against political figures and at writers such as Wordsworth and Charles Lamb suspected of dangerous sympathies. Robert Southey's *The Widow* (1796) offered an irresistible target: Frere and Canning derided its classical Sapphic meter as an "absurdity" in true English verse, even as they denounced Southey's "new topics of invective against the pride of property"—a characteristic juxtaposition of abstract republican philanthropy with Jacobin conduct, whether real or imagined. Their burlesque, *The Friend of Humanity and the Knife-Grinder*, appeared in *The Anti-Jacobin* on November 27, 1797. It was illustrated by the leading caricaturist of the day, James Gillray, with an instantly recognizable portrait of James Tierney, Member of Parliament and of the reformist society, The Friends of the People. The piece caused a sensation. As late as 1890, an editor could say of it: "perhaps no lines in the English language have been more effective, or oftener quoted." They endure as a vivid index of the charged climate in which the poems of the Romantics emerged.

from The Anti-Jacobin
[THE FRIEND OF HUMANITY AND THE KNIFE-GRINDER]

In the specimen of JACOBIN POETRY which we gave in our last number was developed a principle, perhaps one of the most universally recognised in the Jacobin creed; namely, "that the animadversion of *human law* upon *human actions* is for the most part nothing but *gross oppression*; and that, in all cases of the administration of *criminal justice*, the truly benevolent mind will consider only the *severity of the punishment*, without any reference to the *malignity of the crime*." This principle has of late years been laboured with extraordinary industry, and brought forward in a variety of shapes, for the edification of the public. It has been inculcated in bulky quartos, and illustrated in popular novels. It remained only to fit it with a poetical dress, which had been attempted in the INSCRIPTION for CHEPSTOW CASTLE, and which (we flatter ourselves) was accomplished in that for MRS. BROWNRIGG'S CELL.[1]

Another principle, no less devoutly entertained, and no less sedulously disseminated, is the *natural and eternal warfare of the POOR and the RICH*. In those orders and gradations of society, which are the natural result of the original difference of talents and of industry among mankind, the Jacobin sees nothing but a graduated scale of violence and cruelty. He considers every rich man as an oppressor, and every person in a lower situation as the victim of avarice, and the slave of aristocratical insolence and contempt. These truths he declares loudly, not to excite compassion, or to soften the consciousness of superiority in the higher, but for the purpose of aggravating discontent in the inferior orders.

A human being, in the lowest state of penury and distress, is a treasure to the reasoner of this cast. He contemplates, he examines, he turns him in every possible light, with a view of extracting from the variety of his wretchedness new topics of invective against the pride of property. He, indeed (if he is a true Jacobin), refrains from *relieving* the object of his compassionate contemplation; as well knowing that every diminution from the general mass of human misery must proportionably diminish the force of his argument.

This principle is treated at large by many authors. It is versified in sonnets and elegies without end. We trace it particularly in a poem by the same author [Southey] from whom we borrowed our former illustration of the Jacobin doctrine of crimes and punishments. In this poem, the pathos of the matter is not a little relieved by the absurdity of the metre. * * * The learned reader will perceive that the metre is SAPPHIC, and affords a fine opportunity for his *scanning* and *proving*, if he has not forgotten them.

The Widow

Sapphics

Cold was the night wind; drifting fast the snows fell;
Wide were the downs, and shelterless and naked;
When a poor wand'rer struggled on her journey,
    Weary and way-sore.

5   Drear were the downs, more dreary her reflections;
Cold was the night wind, colder was her bosom:
She had no home, the world was all before her,[2]
    She had no shelter.

Fast o'er the heath a chariot rattled by her:
10   "Pity me!" feebly cried the poor night wanderer.
"Pity me, strangers! lest with cold and hunger
    Here I should perish.

Once I had friends—but they have all forsook me!
Once I had parents—they are now in heaven!
15   I had a home once—I had once a husband—
    Pity me, strangers!

1. The first issue of the *Anti-Jacobin*, 20 November 1797, had parodied Robert Southey's sympathetic "Inscription for the Apartment in Chepstow Castle, where Henry Marten, the Regicide, was imprisoned thirty years" with an "Inscription for the Door of the Cell in Newgate, where Mrs. Brownrigg, the 'Prentice-cide,' was confined previous to her Execution." Henry Marten was a republican who signed the death warrant of Charles I; he was imprisoned at the Restoration in 1660.
2. See Milton, *Paradise Lost* 12.646–47, page 903.

I had a home once—I had once a husband—
I am a widow, poor and broken-hearted!"
Loud blew the wind, unheard was her complaining;
20   On drove the chariot.

Then on the snow she laid her down to rest her;
She heard a horseman: "Pity me!" she groaned out.
Loud was the wind, unheard was her complaining;
            On went the horseman.

25 Worn out with anguish, toil, and cold and hunger,
Down sunk the wanderer; sleep had seized her senses:
There did the traveller find her in the morning—
            God had released her.

                            —*Robert Southey* [1796]

We proceed to give our IMITATION, which is of the *Amoeboean* or *Collocutory* kind.[3]

Sapphics
The Friend of Humanity and the Knife-Grinder

Friend of Humanity:

"Needy Knife-grinder! whither are you going?
Rough is the road, your wheel is out of order—
Bleak blows the blast; your hat has got a hole in't,
            So have your breeches!

5 Weary Knife-grinder! little think the proud ones,
Who in their coaches roll along the turnpike-
-road, what hard work 'tis crying all day 'Knives and
            Scissars to grind O!'

Tell me, Knife-grinder, how you came to grind knives?
10 Did some rich man tyrannically use you?
Was it the squire? or parson of the parish?
            Or the attorney?

Was it the squire, for killing of his game? or
Covetous parson, for his tithes° distraining?   *Church tax*
15 Or roguish lawyer, made you lose your little
            All in a lawsuit?

(Have you not read the Rights of Man, by Tom Paine?)
Drops of compassion tremble on my eyelids,
Ready to fall, as soon as you have told your
20   Pitiful story."

Knife-Grinder:

"Story! God bless you! I have none to tell, sir,
Only last night a-drinking at the Chequers,
This poor old hat and breeches, as you see, were
            Torn in a scuffle.

---

3. A poem composed in strophes with alternating speakers; a dialogue.

James Gillray. Illustration to *The Friend of Humanity and the Knife Grinder*, 1797.

25   Constables came up for to take me into
       Custody; they took me before the justice;
       Justice Oldmixon put me in the parish-
                              -Stocks for a vagrant.

       I should be glad to drink your Honour's health in
30   A pot of beer, if you will give me sixpence;
       But for my part, I never love to meddle
                              With politics, sir."

Friend of Humanity:

       "*I give* thee sixpence! I will see thee damned first—
       Wretch! whom no sense of wrongs can rouse to vengeance—
35   Sordid, unfeeling, reprobate, degraded,
       Spiritless outcast!"
       [*Kicks the Knife-grinder, overturns his wheel, and exit in a transport
           of Republican enthusiasm and universal philanthropy.*]

William Blake
1757–1827

It was from Blake's *Marriage of Heaven and Hell* that a sensationally transgressive rock band of the 1960s, the Doors, took their name:

> If the doors of perception were cleansed
> every thing would appear to man as it is: In-
> -finite.

But unlike the Doors, Blake needed no pharmaceutical assistance in cleansing his vision. His eccentricity and imaginative intensity, which seemed like madness to more than a few contemporaries, emerged from a childhood punctuated by such events as beholding God's face pressed against his window, seeing angels among the haystacks, and being visited by the Old Testament prophet Ezekiel. When his favorite brother died in 1787, Blake claimed that he saw his "released spirit ascend heavenwards, clapping its hand for joy." Soon after, he reports, this spirit visited him with a critical revelation of the method of "Illuminated Printing" that he would use in his major poetical works.

Rebellious, unconventional, fiercely idealistic, Blake became a celebrity in modern counterculture—Allen Ginsberg and many of the Beat poets of the 1950s and 1960s cited him as a major influence. But for a good part of the nineteenth century, he was known only to a coterie. He did not support himself as a poet but got by on patronage and commissions for engraving and painting. His projects included the Book of Job and other scenes from the Bible; Chaucer's Canterbury Pilgrims; characters in Spenser's *Faerie Queene*; Milton's *L'Allegro, Il Penseroso, Paradise Lost,* and *Paradise Regained*; Gray's *The Bard*; Young's *Night Thoughts*; and Blair's *The Grave*. His obscurity as a poet was due in part to the difficulty of his work after the mid-1790s but chiefly to the very limited issue of his books, a consequence of the painstaking and time-consuming process of "Illuminated Printing." He hoped to reach a wider audience with a private exhibition of his illustrations in 1809, but his adventurous originality, coupled with his cantankerous and combative personality, left him ignored, except by one of the radical journals, *The Examiner,* which called him a lunatic in a vicious review. At the time of his death, he was impoverished and almost entirely unknown except to a small group of younger painters. Only in 1863 did interest begin to grow, thanks to Alexander Gilchrist's biography, *The Life of William Blake: Pictor Ignotus*, its second volume a selection of poems edited by Dante Gabriel Rossetti. The revival was fanned by the enthusiasm of the Pre-Raphaelite circle and subsequent essays by Algernon Charles Swinburne, William Michael Rossetti (Dante Gabriel's brother), and William Butler Yeats.

Although Blake had no formal education, he was an avid reader, immersing himself in English poetry, the Bible, and works of mysticism and philosophy, as well as a study of Greek, Latin, and Hebrew. With precocious talent as a sketcher, he hoped to become a painter, but his father could not afford the tuition, and so apprenticed him at age fourteen as an engraver. During this seven-year term, Blake found time to write the poems gathered into his first publication, *Poetical Sketches* (1783), his only unilluminated volume. The later illuminated books, by contrast, were not products of the letter-press, but of a process of hand-etching designs onto copper plates, using these plates to ink-print pages that were then individually hand-colored and hand-bound into volumes. So labor-intensive a method was not adaptable to any production of quantity: there are, for instance, only twenty-seven known copies of *Songs of Innocence and of Experience* and only nine of *The Marriage of Heaven and Hell*. Yet Blake was committed to the product. By involving his verbal text with pictures and pictorial embellishments, he created books of extraordinary beauty and an innovative "composite art" of word and image.

In this art, the script is visually meaningful—flowing versus starkly blocked letters, for instance—and the pictorial elements play a significant role, sometimes illustrating, sometimes adding another perspective or an ironic comment on the verbal text, sometimes even presenting contradictory information. We hope to suggest the value of this composite art with several black-and-white plates, and our transcriptions follow their linear arrangements. We urge you to consult the illuminated editions as well, for a vitally important dimension abides in Blake's total designs.

Blake's popularity is based chiefly on his earlier and most accessible works from the 1790s. *Songs of Innocence and of Experience* (1789–1794) was much admired in his own day by Samuel Taylor Coleridge, Charles Lamb, and William Wordsworth (even though Blake deemed him too enamored of "Natural Piety"—faith in the natural world as spiritual and poetic resource: "I see in Wordsworth the Natural man rising up against the Spiritual Man Continually, & then he is No Poet but a heathen Philosopher at Enmity against all true Poetry or Inspiration"). *Songs* is notable not only for a concern with the different ways children and adults see and understand their world (a theme that would occupy Wordsworth, too) but also for its acid critiques of social evils, political injustice, and their agents, the triumvirate of "God & his Priest & King" (in the voice of a too-experienced chimney sweeper). Reflecting Blake's familiarity with the range of freethinking contemporary biblical commentary that became the "Higher Criticism," *The Marriage of Heaven and Hell* (1790) brings visionary energy and poetic extravagance to a trenchant argument for imaginative freedom over psychological inhibition, conventional morality, and institutionalized authority. It is also one of the first Romantic-era appropriations of Milton's *Paradise Lost*, the archetypal story of right and wrong, sin and punishment. Blake takes as an important effect a common reaction (including even Alexander Pope): that Satan and the scenes in Hell provide far more exciting and imaginatively powerful reading than the Angels and God's court in Heaven. "The reason Milton wrote in fetters when / he wrote of Angels & God, and at liberty when of / Devils & Hell," proposes Blake's "Voice of the Devil," is "because he was a true Poet and / of the Devils party without knowing it." Unfettering himself from Milton's moral machinery with this outrageously subversive commentary, Blake presents devils who are a lot more fun than his angels. Indeed, the *Proverbs of Hell* offer their wisdom with a kind of transgressive glee, sarcastic levity, and diabolical wit that anticipates the sly aphorisms of Oscar Wilde and the exuberance of American Beat poetry.

Visions of the Daughters of Albion (1793), a potent commentary on the tyranny of rape and sexual possession, reflects Blake's admiration for Mary Wollstonecraft, whose *Vindication of the Rights of Woman* had been published to controversial reception the year before. These works and others of this decade emerge from Blake's involvement with the London circle gathered around bookseller Joseph Johnson, including Wollstonecraft, William Godwin, Tom Paine, and Dr. Joseph Priestley—a radical political group of artists and religious dissenters joined by their sociopolitical criticism and a general support of the French Revolution. Like many of this group, Blake read the revolutions in America and France as heralds of a new millennium, and thus inspired, he produced a sequence of (sometimes abstruse) visionary works celebrating the overthrow of tyranny: *The French Revolution* (1791), *America: A Prophecy* (1793), *Europe: A Prophecy* (1794), and *The Book of Urizen* (1794). His later "prophetic" works—*Milton* (1804) and *Jerusalem* (1804–1820)—develop some of these themes with an increasingly esoteric vocabulary and elaborate personal mythology, and are notoriously difficult to read, although they contain passages of impressive energy and imagination.

An emblematic episode from 1803 suggests the real-life consequences of Blake's uncompromising visions. When a drunken dragoon trespassed onto his cottage garden and refused to leave, Blake vigorously ejected him. In consequence, he was arrested on a spiteful accusation of seditious threats against the crown; with England at war with France, this was a capital offense for which the penalty could have been death. Blake's trial ended in an acquittal loudly applauded by the spectators, but the ordeal exacerbated his memory of having been arrested in 1780 under the suspicion of being a

spy for France while on a riverboat sketching excursion, and it crystallized his anger at state authority. Energizing all Blake's works is his commitment to imagination and the potency of visionary idealism, sharpened by resistance to psychological, ideological, institutional, and political tyrannies.

[Plate 1]

The voice of one crying in the
Wilderness[1]

[Plate 2]

All Religions Are One[2]

[Plate 3]

The Argument
As the true meth-
-od of knowledge
is experiment,
the true faculty
of knowing must
be the faculty which
experiences. This
faculty I treat of.

[Plate 4]

PRINCIPLE 1st
That the Poetic Genius is
the true Man, and that
the body or outward form
of Man is derived from the
Poetic Genius. Likewise
that the forms of all things
are derived from their
Genius, which by the
Ancients was calld an
Angel & Spirit & Demon.

[Plate 5]

PRINCIPLE 2d
As all men are alike in
outward form, So (and
with the same infinite
variety) all are alike in
the Poetic Genius

[Plate 6]

PRINCIPLE 3d
No man can think
write or speak from his
heart, but he must intend
truth. Thus all sects of
Philosophy are from the
Poetic Genius, adapted
to the weaknesses of
every individual.

---

1. The prophecy of Isaiah 40.3, which Matthew 3.3 takes to
refer to John the Baptist; Blake places himself in this line of
visionary authority.
2. Blake asserts that religious sects are only various forms of a

central truth, divined by the poet's imagination. He did not
subscribe his name to the potentially heretical *All Religions
Are One* but presents its argument and principles as if from
the voice of a biblical prophet speaking to the modern age.

[Plate 7]

PRINCIPLE 4th

As none by trave
ling over known
lands can find out
the unknown, So,
from already ac
quired knowledge,
Man could not ac
quire more; there
fore an universal
Poetic Genius exists.

[Plate 8]

PRINCIPLE 5th

The Religions of all Nat-
-ions are derived from each
Nations different reception
of the Poetic Genius which
is every where call'd the Spi
rit of Prophecy

[Plate 9]

PRINCIPLE 6th

The Jewish & Chris-
tian Testaments are
An original derivati-
-on from the Poetic Ge-
nius: this is necessary
from the confined natu
re of bodily sensation

[Plate 10]

PRINCIPLE 7th

As all men are alike
(tho' infinitely vari
ous) So all Religions:
& as all similars have
one source,
   The true Man is the
source, he being the
Poetic Genius

SONGS OF INNOCENCE AND OF EXPERIENCE

Blake's most popular work appeared in two phases. In 1789 he published *Songs of Innocence*; five years later he bound these poems with a set of new poems in a volume titled *Songs of Innocence and of Experience Shewing the two contrary States of the Human Soul.* "Innocence" and "Experience" are definitions of consciousness that rethink Milton's existential-mythic states of "Paradise" and the "Fall." Blake's categories are modes of perception that tend to coordinate with a chronological story that would become standard in Romanticism: childhood is a time and a state of protected "innocence," but it is a qualified innocence, not immune to the fallen world and its institutions. This world sometimes impinges on childhood itself, and in any event becomes known through "experience," a state of being marked by the loss of childhood vitality, by fear and inhibition, by social and political corruption, and by the manifold oppression of Church, State, and the ruling classes. The volume's "Contrary States" are sometimes signaled by patently repeated or contrasted titles: in *Innocence, Infant Joy,* in *Experience, Infant Sorrow;* in *Innocence, The Lamb,* in *Experience, The Fly* and *The Tyger.*

These contraries are not constructed as simple oppositions, however. Unlike Milton's narrative of the Fall from Paradise, Blake shows either state of soul possible at any moment. Some children, even infants, have already lost their innocence through a soiling contact with the world; some adults, particularly joyously visionary poets, seem able to retain a kind of innocent vitality even as they enter the world of experience. Moreover, the values of "Innocence" and "Experience" are themselves complex. At times, the innocent state of soul reflects a primary, untainted vitality of imagination; but at other times, Blake, like Mary Wollstonecraft, implicates innocence with dangerous ignorance and vulnerability to oppression. Thus, in their rhetorical structure, the poems may present an innocent speaker against dark ironies that a more experienced reader, alert to social and political evil, will grasp. But just as trickily, experience can also define an imagination self-darkened by its own "mind-forg'd manacles." Blake's point is not that children are pure and adults fallen, or that children are naive and adults perspicacious. The contrary possibilities coexist, with different plays and shades of emphasis in different poems. And these values are often further complicated by the ambiguous significance of the illustrations that accompany and often frame the poems' texts. Sometimes these illustrations sustain the speaker's tone and point of view (e.g., *The Lamb*), and sometimes (e.g., *The Little Black Boy*) they offer an ironic counter-commentary.

FROM **Songs of Innocence and of Experience**

Shewing the Two Contrary States of the Human Soul

from *Songs of Innocence*

Introduction

Piping down the valleys wild
Piping songs of pleasant glee
On a cloud I saw a child
And he laughing said to me.

5   Pipe a song about a Lamb:
So I piped with merry chear,
Piper, pipe that song again—
So I piped, he wept to hear.

Drop thy pipe thy happy pipe
10   Sing thy songs of happy chear,
So I sang the same again
While he wept with joy to hear

Piper sit thee down and write
In a book that all may read—
15   So he vanish'd from my sight
And I pluck'd a hollow reed

And I made a rural pen,
And I stain'd the water clear,
And I wrote my happy songs,
20   Every child may joy to hear

The Ecchoing Green

The Sun does arise,
And make happy the skies.
The merry bells ring
To welcome the Spring.
5 The sky-lark and thrush,
The birds of the bush,
Sing louder around,
To the bells chearful sound
While our sports shall be seen
10 On the Ecchoing Green.

Old John with white hair
Does laugh away care,
Sitting under the oak,
Among the old folk,
15 They laugh at our play,
And soon they all say,
Such such were the joys
When we all girls & boys,
In our youth time were seen,
20 On the Ecchoing Green.

Till the little ones weary
No more can be merry
The sun does descend,
And our sports have an end:
25 Round the laps of their mothers
Many sisters and brothers,
Like birds in their nest,
Are ready for rest:
And sport no more seen,
30 On the darkening Green.

The Lamb

Little Lamb who made thee
Dost thou know who made thee
Gave thee life & bid thee feed,
By the stream & o'er the mead;
5 Gave thee clothing of delight,
Softest clothing wooly bright;
Gave thee such a tender voice,
Making all the vales rejoice:
Little Lamb who made thee
10 Dost thou know who made thee

Little Lamb, I'll tell thee.
Little Lamb, I'll tell thee;
He is called by thy name
For he calls himself a Lamb:
15 He is meek & he is mild,

William Blake. *The Lamb*, from *Songs of Innocence*.

He became a little child:
I a child & thou a lamb,
We are called by his name.
   Little Lamb God bless thee
20   Little Lamb God bless thee

The Little Black Boy

My mother bore me in the southern wild,
And I am black, but O! my soul is white
White as an angel is the English child:
But I am black as if bereav'd of light.

5   My mother taught me underneath a tree
And sitting down before the heat of day,
She took me on her lap and kissed me,
And, pointing to the east, began to say.

Look on the rising sun: there God does live
10 And gives his light and gives his heat away.
And flowers and trees and beasts and men recieve
Comfort in morning joy in the noon day.

William Blake. *The Little Black Boy*, from *Songs of Innocence*. In some copies, Blake tints the black boy's skin as light as the English boy's; in others, he colors them differently. While the heavenly scene (right) shows both boys sheltered by the tree and welcomed by Christ, it also puts the black boy outside the inner circle formed by the curve of Christ's body and the praying English boy. He is not part of this configuration of prayer, but rather a witness to it, stroking the hair of the English boy who has no regard for him.

> And we are put on earth a little space
> That we may learn to bear the beams of love.
> 15   And these black bodies and this sun-burnt face
> Is but a cloud, and like a shady grove.
>
> For when our souls have learn'd the heat to bear
> The cloud will vanish we shall hear his voice
> Saying: come out from the grove, my love & care,
> 20   And round my golden tent like lambs rejoice.
>
> Thus did my mother say, and kissed me.
> And thus I say to little English boy.
> When I from black and he from white cloud free,
> And round the tent of God like lambs we joy:
>
> 25   Ill shade him from the heat till he can bear,
> To lean in joy upon our fathers knee
> And then Ill stand and stroke his silver hair,
> And be like him and he will then love me.

The Chimney Sweeper[1]

When my mother died I was very young
And my father sold me while yet my tongue
Could scarcely cry weep weep weep weep.[2]
So your chimneys I sweep & in soot I sleep.

5   Theres little Tom Dacre, who cried when his head
That curl'd like a lambs back, was shav'd, so I said:
Hush Tom never mind it, for when your head's bare
You know that the soot cannot spoil your white hair

And so he was quiet, & that very night,
10   As Tom was a sleeping he had such a sight,
That thousands of sweepers Dick, Joe, Ned & Jack
Were all of them lock'd up in coffins of black,

And by came an Angel who had a bright key,
And he open'd the coffins & set them all free.
15   Then down a green plain leaping laughing they run
And wash in a river and shine in the Sun.

Then naked & white, all their bags left behind,
They rise upon clouds, and sport in the wind
And the Angel told Tom if he'd be a good boy,
20   He'd have God for his father & never want joy

And so Tom awoke and we rose in the dark
And got with our bags & our brushes to work.
Tho' the morning was cold, Tom was happy & warm
So if all do their duty they need not fear harm.[3]

The Divine Image

To Mercy Pity Peace and Love,
All pray in their distress:
And to these virtues of delight
Return their thankfulness.

5   For Mercy Pity Peace and Love
Is God our father dear:
And Mercy Pity Peace and Love,
Is Man his child and care.

For Mercy has a human heart
10   Pity, a human face:

---

1. Chimney-sweeps were young children, mostly boys, whose impoverished parents sold them into the business, or who were orphans, outcasts, or illegitimate children with no other means of living. It was filthy, health-ruining labor, aggravated by overwork and inadequate clothing, food, and shelter. Among the hazards were burns, permanently blackened skin, deformed legs, black lung disease, and cancer of the scrotum. Protective legislation passed in 1788 was never enforced. Blake's outrage at this exploitation also sounds in "London." Admiring the poem, Charles Lamb sent it to James Montgomery (a topical poet and radical-press editor) for inclusion in *The Chimney-Sweeper's Friend, and Climbing Boy's Album* (1824), which he was assembling for the Society for Ameliorating the Condition of Infant Chimney-Sweepers.
2. With a relevant pun, the child's lisping street cry advertising his trade, "sweep! sweep!"
3. A typical conduct homily.

And Love, the human form divine,
And Peace, the human dress.

Then every man, of every clime
That prays in his distress,
15   Prays to the human form divine
Love Mercy Pity Peace.

And all must love the human form,
In heathen, turk or jew.
Where Mercy, Love & Pity dwell,
20   There God is dwelling too.

HOLY THURSDAY[1]

Twas on a Holy Thursday their innocent faces clean
The children walking two & two in red & blue & green[2]
Grey headed beadles[3] walkd before with wands as white as snow
Till into the high dome of Pauls they like Thames waters flow

5   O what a multitude they seemd these flowers of London town
Seated in companies they sit with radiance all their own
The hum of multitudes was there but multitudes of lambs
Thousands of little boys & girls raising their innocent hands

Now like a mighty wind they raise to heaven the voice of song
10   Or like harmonious thunderings the seats of heaven among
Beneath them sit the aged men wise guardians of the poor
Then cherish pity lest you drive an angel from your door[4]

COMPANION READING

Charles Lamb: from *The Praise of Chimney-Sweepers*[1]

I like to meet a sweep; understand me,—not a grown sweeper, (old chimney-sweepers are by no means attractive,) but one of those tender novices, blooming through their first nigritude, the maternal washings not quite effaced from the

---

1. One of the poems with a marked companion in *Experience* (see page 1402). Holy Thursday in the calendar of England's official state religion celebrated the Ascension; it was customary to conduct the children in London's charity schools, many of them orphans, to services at St. Paul's, the chief Anglican cathedral.

2. The colors denote different school uniforms.

3. Minor officials charged with ushering and preserving order at services.

4. A conduct homily, perhaps echoing Hebrews 13.1–2: "Let brotherly love continue. Be not forgetful to entertain strangers: for thereby some have entertained angels unawares."

1. Published in *London Magazine*, May 1822, under pseudonym "Elia." Charles Lamb (1775–1834) was born in London, the son of a legal clerk; his brother John and sister Mary, his literary collaborator and companion, were more than a decade older. At seven he entered Christ's Hospital, a charity school where he become a lifelong friend of Coleridge, to whose *Poems on Various Subjects* he con-

tributed in 1796–1797. Unlike Coleridge, Lamb, a stammerer, did not distinguish himself academically or go on to university. Shortly after leaving school he joined his brother briefly as a clerk at the South Sea House, moving in 1792 to the East India House, where he remained until his retirement in 1825. His early writings had little success, but Lamb persevered with a self-mocking resilience. In 1796, in a fit of the insanity that ran through the family, Mary fatally stabbed their mother and wounded their father. To prevent her from being committed to an asylum, Charles assumed responsibility for her care. Though her derangements periodically recurred, the weekly suppers that they hosted gathered a diverse group of London artists and intellectuals. Radicals such as Godwin, Hazlitt, and Leigh Hunt mixed with Wordsworth, Coleridge, and Southey, as Charles moved among them, smoking, drinking, and making outrageous puns. Such evenings concentrated the delights of city life that Lamb celebrated in his essays and letters. For more by Lamb, see the Companion Readings under William Wordsworth (page 1558).

cheek: such as come forth with the dawn, or somewhat earlier, with their little professional notes sounding like the *peep peep* of a young sparrow; or liker to the matin lark should I pronounce them, in their aërial ascents not seldom anticipating the sun-rise?

I have a kindly yearning toward these dim specks—poor blots—innocent blacknesses.

I reverence these young Africans of our own growth,—these almost clergy imps, who sport their cloth without assumption; and from their little pulpits, (the tops of chimneys,) in the nipping air of a December morning, preach a lesson of patience to mankind.

When a child, what a mysterious pleasure it was to witness their operation! to see a chit no bigger than one's-self, enter, one knew not by what process, into what seemed the *fauces Averni*,[2]—to pursue him in imagination, as he went sounding on through so many dark stifling caverns, horrid shades!—to shudder with the idea that "now, surely, he must be lost for ever!"—to revive at hearing his feeble shout of discovered day-light—and then (O fulness of delight!) running out of doors, to come just in time to see the sable phenomenon emerge in safety, the brandished weapon of his art victorious like some flag waved over a conquered citadel! I seem to remember having been told that a bad sweep was once left in a stack with his brush, to indicate which way the wind blew. It was an awful spectacle certainly; not much unlike the old stage direction in Macbeth, where the "Apparition of a child crowned, with a tree in his hand, rises."[3]

Reader, if thou meetest one of these small gentry in thy early rambles, it is good to give him a penny. It is better to give him twopence. If it be starving weather, and to the proper troubles of his hard occupation a pair of kibed[4] heels (no unusual accompaniment) be superadded, the demand on thy humanity will surely rise to a tester.[5] * * *

In one of the state-beds at Arundel Castle,[6] a few years since, under a ducal canopy, (that seat of the Howards is an object of curiosity to visitors, chiefly for its beds, in which the late duke was especially a connoisseur,) encircled with curtains of delicatest crimson, with starry coronets inwoven, folded between a pair of sheets whiter and softer than the lap where Venus lulled Ascanius,[7] was discovered by chance, after all methods of search had failed, at noon-day, fast asleep, a lost chimney-sweeper. The little creature, having somehow confounded his passage among the intricacies of those lordly chimneys, by some unknown aperture had alighted upon this magnificent chamber; and, tired with his tedious explorations, was unable to resist the delicious invitement to repose, which he there saw exhibited; so creeping between the sheets very quietly, laid his black head upon the pillow, and slept like a young Howard.

Such is the account given to the visitors at the Castle. But I cannot help seeming to perceive a confirmation of what I had just hinted at in this story. A high instinct was at work in the case, or I am mistaken. Is it probable that a poor child of that description, with whatever weariness he might be visited, would

---

2. The Jaws of Avernus (a phrase from Vergil's *Aeneid*, 6.201); Lake Avernus, near Naples, was thought to lead to the underworld.

3. Cf. *Macbeth* Act 4.1; the crowned child is a sign that a line other than childless Macbeth's will become Scotland's kings.

4. Ulcerated and inflamed from exposure to the cold.

5. Sixpence.

6. Home of the Howard family, Dukes of Norfolk.

7. Aeneas's young son (*Aeneid* bk. 1) who, protected by Venus, escaped with his father from burning Troy.

have ventured, under such a penalty as he would be taught to expect, to uncover the sheets of a Duke's bed, and deliberately to lay himself down between them, when the rug, or the carpet, presented an obvious couch still far above his pretensions? Is this probable, I would ask, if the great power of nature, which I contend for, had not been manifested within him, prompting to the adventure? Doubtless this young nobleman (for such my mind misgives me that he must be) was allured by some memory, not amounting to full consciousness, of his condition in infancy, when he was used to be lapped by his mother, or his nurse, in just such sheets as he there found, into which he was now but creeping back as into his proper *incunabula* [cradle clothes] and resting-place. By no other theory than by this sentiment of a pre-existent state (as I may call it), can I explain a deed so venturous, and indeed upon any other system, so indecorous, in this tender but unseasonable sleeper.

My pleasant friend Jem White[8] was so impressed with a belief of metamorphoses like this frequently taking place, that in some sort to reverse the wrongs of fortune in these poor changelings, he instituted an annual feast of chimney-sweepers, at which it was his pleasure to officiate as host and waiter. * * * O it was a pleasure to see the sable younkers lick in the unctuous meat, with *his* more unctuous sayings— how he would fit the tit-bits to the puny mouths, reserving the lengthier links for the seniors—how he would intercept a morsel even in the jaws of some young desperado, declaring it "must to the pan again to be browned, for it was not fit for a gentleman's eating"—how he would recommend this slice of white bread, or that piece of kissing-crust,[9] to a tender juvenile, advising them all to have a care of cracking their teeth, which were their best patrimony,—how genteelly he would deal about the small ale, as if it were wine, naming the brewer, and protesting, if it were not good, he should lose their custom; with a special recommendation to wipe the lip before drinking. Then we had our toasts—"The King,"—"the Cloth,"— which, whether they understood or not, was equally diverting and flattering;—and for a crowning sentiment, which never failed, "May the Brush supersede the Laurel!" All these, and fifty other fancies, which were rather felt than comprehended by his guests, would he utter, standing upon tables, and prefacing every sentiment with—"Gentlemen, give me leave to propose so and so," which was a prodigious comfort to those young orphans; every now and then stuffing into his mouth (for it did not do to be squeamish on these occasions) indiscriminate pieces of those reeking sausages, which pleased them mightily, and was the savouriest part, you may believe, of the entertainment.

> Golden lads and lasses must,
> As chimney-sweepers, come to dust.[1]

James White is extinct, and with him these suppers have long ceased. He carried away with him half the fun of the world when he died—of my world at least. His old clients look for him among the pens; and missing him, reproach the altered feast of St. Bartholomew, and the glory of Smithfield departed for ever.

---

8. James White, Lamb's schoolmate at Christ's Hospital, a London school for orphans and poor children, also attended by Coleridge and Leigh Hunt.
9. Overhanging crust that touches, or kisses, the crust of another loaf of bread during baking.

1. A couplet from a song in Shakespeare's *Cymbeline* (4.2.262–63); "dust" is both literal for the chimney-sweepers' soot and metaphorical for the return of the body after death to elemental earth.

William Blake. *The Fly*, from *Songs of Experience*.

from *Songs of Experience*
The Fly[1]

Little Fly
Thy summer's play,
My thoughtless hand
Has brush'd away.[3]

5   Am not I
A fly like thee?
Or art not thou
A man like me?

For I dance
10   And drink & sing:
Till some blind hand
Shall brush my wing.

If thought is life
And strength & breath:[2]
15   And the want
Of thought is death;

Then am I
A happy fly,
If I live,
20   Or if I die.

---

1. Blake's plate arranges two columns of verse, with stanzas 1–3 in the left, and stanzas 5 and 6 in the right, placed opposite 1 and 2, respectively; this arrangement allows a reading of the stanzas in an alternative order of left to right: 1-4-2-5-3.

2. Cf. Descartes' famous statement: "I think, therefore I am."
3. Cf. the blinded Gloucester's bitterly rueful comment in *King Lear*: "As flies to wanton boys, are we to th' gods, / They kill us for their sport" (4.1.36–37).

The CLOD & the PEBBLE

Love seeketh not Itself to please,
Nor for itself hath any care;
But for another gives its ease,
And builds a Heaven in Hells despair.[1]

5   So sung a little Clod of Clay
        Trodden with the cattles feet:
        But a Pebble of the brook,
        Warbled out these metres meet.

Love seeketh only Self to please
10   To bind another to Its delight:
        Joys in anothers loss of ease,
        And builds a Hell in Heavens despite.[2]

HOLY THURSDAY[1]

Is this a holy thing to see,
In a rich and fruitful land
Babes reducd to misery
Fed with cold and usurous hand?

5   Is that trembling cry a song?
        Can it be a song of joy?
        And so many children poor?
        It is a land of poverty!

And their sun does never shine,
10   And their fields are bleak & bare,
        And their ways are fill'd with thorns
        It is eternal winter there.

For where-e'er the sun does shine,
And where-e'er the rain does fall:
15   Babe can never hunger there,
        Nor poverty the mind appall.

The Tyger

Tyger Tyger, burning bright,
In the forests of the night;[1]
What immortal hand or eye,
Could frame thy fearful symmetry?

---

1. Cf. I Corinthians 13.4: "Charity suffereth long, and is kind; charity envieth not; charity vaunteth not itself, is not puffed up."
2. Cf. Satan's rebellious declaration in *Paradise Lost*: "The mind is its own place, and in itself / Can make a Heaven of Hell, a Hell of Heaven" (1. 254–55).
1. See *Holy Thursday* in *Songs of Innocence*, page 1398.
1. Not just a time of day but a metaphysical location, characterized by forest mazes—the terrain that conducts to Hell in Dante's *Inferno*. Cf. "midnight streets" in *London*, line 13.

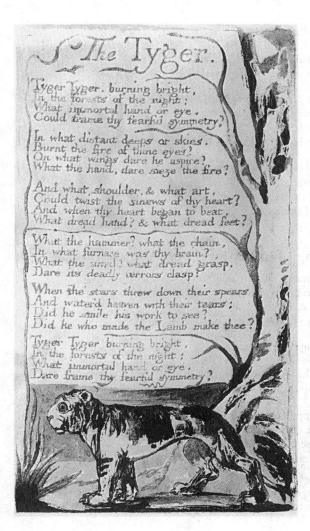

William Blake. *The Tyger,* from *Songs of Experience.* In some copies, Blake colors the tiger in lurid tones; in others, the tiger is colored in pastels.

5   In what distant deeps or skies,
       Burnt the fire of thine eyes?
       On what wings dare he aspire?[2]
       What the hand dare sieze the fire?

       And what shoulder & what art,
10   Could twist the sinews of thy heart?
       And when thy heart began to beat,
       What dread hand? & what dread feet?[3]

2. An allusion to Icarus, who, with his father Dedalus, fashioned wings of feathers and wax to escape from prison. Icarus became enchanted with flight and, ignoring his father's cautions, soared too close to the sun; the wax melted and he fell to his death in the sea.
3. One engraving has, "What dread hand Formd thy dread feet?"

What the hammer? what the chain,
In what furnace was thy brain?
15   What the anvil? what dread grasp,
Dare its deadly terrors clasp!

When the stars threw down their spears
And water'd heaven with their tears:[4]
Did he smile his work to see?[5]
20   Did he who made the Lamb make thee?[6]

Tyger Tyger burning bright,
In the forests of the night:
What immortal hand or eye,
Dare frame thy fearful symmetry?

The Chimney Sweeper[1]

A little black thing among the snow:
Crying weep, weep, in notes of woe!
Where are thy father & mother? say?
They are both gone up to the church to pray.

5   Because I was happy upon the heath
And smil'd among the winters snow:
They clothed me in the clothes of death,
And taught me to sing the notes of woe.

And because I am happy & dance & sing,
10   They think they have done me no injury:
And are gone to praise God & his Priest & King
Who make up a heaven of our misery.[2]

The SICK ROSE

O Rose thou art sick.
The invisible worm,
That flies in the night
In the howling storm:

5   Has found out thy bed
Of crimson joy:
And his dark secret love
Does thy life destroy.

4. In the war in Heaven, *Paradise Lost* (bk. 6), Satan, rebelling against God's authority, is defeated by the Son and driven down to Hell. Blake's verb leaves it undecidable whether the stars "threw down their spears" in desperate surrender or in defiance.
5. In a notebook draft, Blake wrote "did he laugh his work to see."
6. An allusion to Jesus, "The Lamb of God" (John 1.29 and 1.36) and, indirectly, to the poem in *Songs of Innocence*, with Blake as the maker.
1. See *The Chimney Sweeper* in *Songs of Innocence*, page 1397.
2. In both senses: construct their happiness from the elements of our misery; create an illusion of heavenly will in our misery.

AH! SUN-FLOWER[1]

Ah Sun-flower! weary of time,
Who countest the steps of the Sun:
Seeking after that sweet golden clime
Where the travellers journey is done

5   Where the Youth pined away with desire,
And the pale Virgin shrouded in snow:
Arise from their graves and aspire
Where my Sun-flower wishes to go.

The GARDEN of LOVE

I went to the Garden of Love.
And saw what I never had seen:
A Chapel was built in the midst,
Where I used to play on the green.

5   And the gates of this Chapel were shut,
And Thou shalt not, writ over the door;[1]
So I turnd to the Garden of Love,
That so many sweet flowers bore.

And I saw it was filled with graves,
10   And tomb-stones where flowers should be:
And Priests in black gowns, were walking their rounds,
And binding with briars, my joys & desires.[2]

LONDON

I wander thro' each charter'd street,[1]
Near where the charter'd Thames does flow
And mark in every face I meet
Marks of weakness, marks of woe.

5   In every cry of every Man,
In every Infants cry of fear,
In every voice; in every ban,[2]
The mind-forg'd manacles I hear[3]

How the Chimney-sweepers cry
10   Every blackning Church appalls.[4]

---

1. In Ovid's *Metamorphosis* (4.192), a nymph spurned by Apollo, the sun god, so pined for him that she turned into a sunflower. Blake personifies the sunflower as a heliotrope—a plant that turns to follow the sun.
1. An ironic parody of the syntax of the Ten Commandments.
2. An allusion to the crown of thorns that was part of Jesus' torture.
1. A charter is a grant of liberty or privilege, as in Magna Carta (1215). A charter is exclusive: granted to some, it thereby forbids others. Whether rights were chartered or natural was contested in the 1790s.
2. Several meanings are involved: political prohibition, public condemnation, curse, announcement of marriage.

3. The forgers of these fetters are both the authorities of Church and state (Blake originally wrote "german forged," referring to the German descent of King George III) and the individual selves who internalize this oppression with fetters of fear or compliance. Between this "hear" and its rhyming repetition at the end of line 13, note the acrostic of the first letters of the third stanza.
4. The capital C makes it clear that this is the institutional Church of England. Blake's adjective involves the literal blackening of soot with the imagery of moral evil; "appalls" continues the indictment, by drawing into the sense of "dismay" (to which the Church is immune) the literal meaning, "make pale"—that is, clean the soot out of; this color-moral extends into the next stanza's "blasts" and "blights."

And the hapless Soldiers sigh
Runs in blood down Palace walls

But most thro' midnight streets I hear
How the youthful Harlots curse[5]
15   Blasts the new-born Infants tear
And blights with plagues the Marriage hearse[6]

The Human Abstract

Pity would be no more,
If we did not make somebody Poor:
And Mercy no more could be,
If all were as happy as we:

5   And mutual fear brings peace:
Till the selfish loves increase.
Then Cruelty knits a snare,
And spreads his baits with care.

He sits down with holy fears,
10   And waters the ground with tears:
Then Humility takes its root
Underneath his foot.

Soon spreads the dismal shade
Of Mystery over his head;
15   And the Catterpiller and Fly,
Feed on the Mystery.

And it bears the fruit of Deceit,
Ruddy and sweet to eat:
And the Raven his nest has made
20   In its thickest shade.

The Gods of the earth and sea,
Sought thro' Nature to find this Tree
But their search was all in vain:
There grows one in the Human Brain

A POISON TREE[1]

I was angry with my friend:
I told my wrath, my wrath did end.
I was angry with my foe:
I told it not, my wrath did grow.

5   And I waterd it in fears,
Night & morning with my tears:
And I sunned it with smiles.
And with soft deceitful wiles.

And it grew both day and night.
10   Till it bore an apple bright.

5. Many of the prostitutes in London were desperately poor girls barely out of childhood, abandoned or disowned by their families.

6. An allusion to prenatal blindness caused by sexually transmitted diseases.
1. Originally titled "Christian Forbearance."

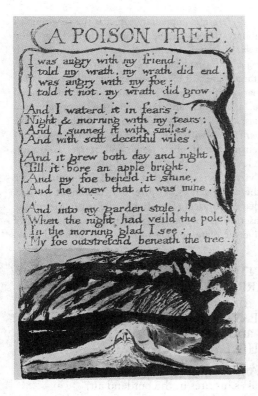

William Blake. *A Poison Tree*, from *Songs of Experience*.

And my foe beheld it shine.
And he knew that it was mine.

And into my garden stole.
When the night had veild the pole.
15   In the morning glad I see.
My foe outstretchd beneath the tree.

A DIVINE IMAGE

Cruelty has a Human Heart
And Jealousy a Human Face
Terror, the Human Form Divine
And Secrecy, the Human Dress

5   The Human Dress, is forged in Iron
The Human Form, a fiery Forge.
The Human Face, a Furnace seal'd
The Human Heart, its hungry Gorge.

THE MARRIAGE OF HEAVEN AND HELL

The Marriage of Heaven and Hell is Blake's first, though hardly systematic, attempt to present a philosophical vision. His aim is to challenge, even outrage, conventional ideologies of good and evil and the moral rewards of Heaven and Hell. His immediate target is the teachings of Emanuel Swedenborg (1688–1772), a visionary theologian he initially admired but then found fault with: it is Swedenborg's *Memorable Relations,* solemn reports of encounters with angels and devils in his *Treatise Concerning Heaven and Hell* (1778), that are satirized in Blake's *Memorable Fancies.* Most of Blake's targets are still recognizable: scientific materialists like Locke who value reason and the information of the senses over imagination; pious moral philosophies that regard the body and soul as distinct, antithetical entities; conventional strictures, keyed to such philosophies, that shame the body and sexuality. Although Blake assails orthodox Christian pieties, his argument is not with religion per se: he is intensely spiritual, believing in visionary prophecy, presenting the prophets Isaiah and Ezekiel as inspirational allies and fellow poets, and admiring Jesus, not as the enforcer of the Ten Commandments but as a compassionate rebel whose "virtue" is precisely that he "acted from im-/-pulse and not from rules." Blake's poem wields the allied genres of satire, enlightenment treatise, and prophecy (of spiritual revolution, signaled by political revolution). The verse lines in the text below vary from standard editorial transcriptions by following the linear arrangement of Blake's plates. Square brackets to the left give the plate number in Blake's illuminated book.

[Plate 1]

THE
MARRIAGE
of
HEAVEN
and
HELL

[Plate 2]

The Argument.[1]

Rintrah[2] roars & shakes his fires in the burdend air;
Hungry clouds swag° on the deep   *sink; lie heavily*

    Once meek, and in a perilous path,
    The just man[3] kept his course along
5   The vale of death.
    Roses are planted where thorns grow.
    And on the barren heath
    Sing the honey bees.

    Then the perilous path was planted:
10   And a river, and a spring
    On every cliff and tomb;
    And on the bleached bones[4]
    Red clay brought forth.[5]

1. An "Argument" is normally a prose summary of a verse passage to follow; Blake deploys the term both inversely and deceptively: he is using poetry to summarize the prose that follows and not really providing a simplified summary at all.
2. A Blake-name for a wrathful poet-prophet of the Old-Testament type and herald (like John the Baptist) of a new messianic era, this figure is Blake's persona for rebuking the present aridity of society and predicting restorative revolution.
3. An allegorical figure for the spiritual pilgrim and prophet, the original inhabitant of Paradise trying to keep faith after the Fall, helped by Christ (who plants the perilous paths) and thwarted by the villains of the Christian Church.
4. See Ezekiel 37, an account of the resurrection of life

from a valley of bones ("can these bones live?").
5. A literal translation of "Adam"; also a reference to the blood of revolutionary violence, and thus its role in redemption (Christ is sometimes called the second Adam). Isaiah 5 prophesies assault by devouring fire and a "roaring" army (30), and chapters 34–35, to which Blake refers on plate 3, prophesy "the day of the Lord's vengeance" on Edom—the destruction of the armies, the dominion of wild beasts, and a land reduced to deserts and thorns and then restored to fertility and the rebirth of faith: "the desert shall . . . blossom as the rose . . . in the wilderness shall waters break out . . . And an highway shall be there . . . called The way of holiness."

Till the villain left the paths of ease,
15 To walk in perilous paths, and drive
The just man into barren climes.

Now the sneaking serpent walks
In mild humility.
And the just man rages in the wilds[6]
20 Where lions roam.

Rintrah roars & shakes his fires in the
burdend air;
Hungry clouds swag on the deep.

[Plate 3]   As a new heaven is begun, and it is now thir-
-ty-three years since its advent:[7] the Eternal Hell[8]
revives. And lo! Swedenborg is the Angel sitting
at the tomb: his writings are the linen clothes folded
up.[9] Now is the dominion of Edom,[1] & the return of
Adam into Paradise; see Isaiah XXXIV & XXXV Chap:[2]
    Without Contraries is no progression. Attraction
and Repulsion, Reason and Energy, Love and
Hate, are necessary to Human existence.
    From these contraries spring what the religious call
Good & Evil. Good is the passive that obeys Reason
Evil is the active springing from Energy.
    Good is Heaven. Evil is Hell.

[Plate 4]   The voice of the
                              Devil[3]
    All   Bibles   or   sacred   codes,   have   been
the causes of the following Errors.
    1. That Man has two real existing princi-
ples Viz: a Body & a Soul.
    2. That Energy, calld Evil, is alone from the
Body, & that Reason, calld Good, is alone from
the Soul.

6. Compare to epigraph for *All Religions Are One*. The voice from the wilderness is prophesied in Isaiah 40.3 and taken by Matthew (3.3) to refer to John the Baptist.
7. In 1757, 33 years before he began this poem in 1790, Blake was born and Swedenborg claimed to have witnessed the Last Judgment and the advent of "New Heaven." At age 33, Christ was crucified and resurrected—hence Blake's sly reference to himself in 1790 in the role of Christ-like prophet.
8. As various sects prophesy new heavens, Hell remains eternal. Blake is also referring to his anti-Swedenborgian writing as the countercreation of his own "Bible of Hell" (see plate 24).
9. See John 20.4–14 for the discovery of Christ's empty sepulchre, the empty burial linens folded and two angels sitting where the body was, and then the appearance of the resurrected body of Christ. Blake puts Swedenborg in the comically ironic situation of announcing his teachings as no longer useful, cast off.
1. See Genesis 27.40: "Edom" is another name for Esau, the honest brother duped out of his inheritance by the

trickery of Jacob; their father Isaac assures Esau that "it shall come to pass when thou shalt have the dominion, that thou shalt break [Jacob's] yoke from off thy neck." Isaiah 63 presents the allegory of an Edomite (Esau's descendant) "red in apparel"—bloodspattered from a vengeful trampling down of the rebellious Israelites. "Edom," like "Adam," means "red earth," a literal pun that in the early 1790s would evoke the blood of political revolution that precedes (in Blake's myth) Adam's return to Paradise.
2. In addition to the chapters and verses named (see Argument), Blake is also, defiantly, recalling Isaiah 5.20, which records the warning "Woe unto them that call evil good and good evil."
3. Not necessarily Blake's own voice, but an antidote to conventionally "sacred codes"—"what the religious call Good & Evil." In such codes, Good is restraint, obedience, prohibition, and rationality, and "Evil" is its judgment on principles of pleasure, bodily desire, imagination, and rebellion. The diabolic voice argues that Good is only a synonym for sterility unto death and that Evil is energy, freedom, and life.

3. That God will torment Man in Eternity for following his Energies.

But the following Contraries to these are True

1. Man has no Body distinct from his Soul for that calld Body is a portion of Soul discernd by the five Senses, the chief inlets of Soul in this age.

2. Energy is the only life and is from the Body and Reason is the bound or outward circumference of Energy.

3. Energy is Eternal Delight

[Plate 5]   Those who restrain desire, do so because theirs is weak enough to be restrained; and the restrainer or reason usurps its place & governs the unwilling.

And being restraind it by degrees becomes passive till it is only the shadow of desire.

The history of this is written in Paradise Lost. & the Governor or Reason is call'd Messiah.[4]

And the original Archangel or possessor of the command of the heavenly host is call'd the Devil or Satan and his children are call'd Sin & Death[5]

But in the Book of Job Miltons Messiah is call'd Satan.[6]

For this history has been adopted by both parties

It indeed appear'd to Reason as if Desire was cast out, but the Devil's account is, that the Messi-

[Plate 6]   ah fell. & formed a heaven of what he stole from the Abyss

This is shewn in the Gospel, where he prays to the Father to send the comforter or Desire that Reason may have Ideas to build on,[7] the Jehovah of the Bible being no other than he   who dwells in flaming fire.

Know that after Christs death, he became Jehovah.

But in Milton; the Father is Destiny, the Son, a Ratio of the five senses.[8] & the Holy-ghost, Vacuum![9]

Note. The reason Milton wrote in fetters when he wrote of Angels & God, and at liberty when of

---

4. Blake is referring to the value of "Reason" in *Paradise Lost*, the highest mental capacity, through which man knows God, and thus the agency by which "lower" faculties such as passion and appetite are disciplined.

5. A reference to Satan's status as Archangel Lucifer before his fall from Heaven along with the rebel faction he commanded in the war against God (see *Paradise Lost* 6:824ff.). In Bk. 2.746–814, Milton provides a lurid account of the birth of Satan's children: first his daughter Sin, and then their incestuous son, Death.

6. In the Book of Job, God tests Job's faith by allowing Satan to torment him.

7. An ironic twist on Christ's assurance that after his earthly death he will send the Holy Ghost as comforter; see John 14.16–17.

8. Blake puns on the Latin meanings of "sum" and "Reason." He argues that philosophical and theological exaltations of reason demote the creative power of imagination.

9. Milton was skeptical of the Trinitarian completion of divinity by the Holy Ghost, but Blake here satirizes what he sees as imaginative emptiness.

Devils & Hell, is because he was a true Poet and of the Devils party[1] without knowing it

A Memorable Fancy

As I was walking among the fires of hell, de-lighted with the enjoyments of Genius; which to An--gels look like torment and insanity. I collected some of their Proverbs: thinking that as the sayings used in a nation, mark its character, so the Proverbs of Hell, shew the nature of Infernal wisdom better than any description of buildings or garments

When I came home, on the abyss of the five sen--ses, where a flat sided steep frowns over the pre--sent world. I saw a mighty Devil folded in black clouds hovering on the sides of the rock, with cor-

[Plate 7]   -roding fires[2] he wrote the following sentence now per--cieved by the minds of men, & read by them on earth.

How do you know but ev'ry Bird that cuts the airy way, Is an immense world of delight, clos'd by your senses five?[3]

Proverbs of Hell.[4]

In seed time learn, in harvest teach, in winter enjoy.
Drive your cart and your plow over the bones of the dead.
The road of excess leads to the palace of wisdom.
Prudence is a rich ugly old maid courted by Incapacity.
He who desires but acts not, breeds pestilence.
The cut worm forgives the plow.
Dip him in the river who loves water.
A fool sees not the same tree that a wise man sees.
He whose face gives no light, shall never become a star.
Eternity is in love with the productions of time.
The busy bee has no time for sorrow.
The hours of folly are measur'd by the clock, but of wis-
      -dom: no clock can measure.
All wholsom food is caught without a net or a trap.
Bring out number weight & measure in a year of dearth

1. Both the Devil's point of view and the political faction he led against the authority of God. This "Note" is a famous example of what was later called "Romantic Satanism" and its reading Paradise Lost against Milton's avowed "Argu-ment."

2. Casting himself and other poets as Devils, Blake refers to his process of book production, whereby he etched his designs on copper plates with an acid-resistant fluid, then washed the plate in acid so that the designs emerged in relief. Hand-colored, this relief plate was then used to print the pages. See plate 14 for a reference to the sym-bolic value of this method.

3. These lines allude to verses by Thomas Chatterton: "How dydd I know that eve'ry darte, / That cutte the Airie waie, / Myghte nott find passage toe my harte, / And close myne eyes for aie?" (Bristowe Tragedie). At age 17, Chatterton committed suicide in despair of success and thereby won celebrity in the Romantic era as a mar-tyred genius (see, e.g., William Wordsworth's Resolution and Independence, 43–50).

4. Blake's diabolic version of the Old Testament's Book of Proverbs as well as his satire on the Aphorisms of Kas-par Lavater (1788), a Swiss moralist and friend of Henry Fuseli, an artist who was also Blake's friend.

No bird soars too high. if he soars with his own wings.
A dead body. revenges not injuries.
The most sublime act is to set another before you.
If the fool would persist in his folly he would become
Folly is the cloke of knavery.   [wise
Shame is Prides cloke.

[Plate 8]   Proverbs of Hell
Prisons are built with stones of Law, Brothels with
      bricks of Religion.
The pride of the peacock is the glory of God.
5   The lust of the goat is the bounty of God.
The wrath of the lion is the wisdom of God.
The nakedness of woman is the work of God.
Excess of sorrow laughs. Excess of joy weeps.
The roaring of lions, the howling of wolves the raging
10   of the stormy sea, and the destructive sword, are
      portions of eternity too great for the eye of man.
The fox condemns the trap. not himself.
Joys impregnate. Sorrows bring forth.
Let man wear the fell of the lion. woman the fleece of
15   the sheep.
The bird a nest, the spider a web, man friendship.
The selfish smiling fool. & the sullen frowning fool. shall
      be both thought wise, that they may be a rod.
What is now proved was once, only imagin'd.
20   The rat, the mouse, the fox, the rabbet; watch the roots,
      the lion, the tyger, the horse, the elephant, watch
      the fruits.
The cistern contains: the fountain overflows
One thought. fills immensity.
25   Always be ready to speak your mind, and a base man
      will avoid you.
Every thing possible to be believ'd is an image of truth.
The eagle never lost so much time. as when he submit-
    -ted to learn of the crow.

[Plate 9]   Proverbs of Hell
The fox provides for himself. but God provides for the lion.
Think in the morning. Act in the noon, Eat in the even-
    -ing, Sleep in the night.
5   He who has sufferd you to impose on him knows you.
As the plow follows words, so God rewards prayers.
The tygers of wrath are wiser than the horses of in-
Expect poison from the standing water.   [-struction
You never know what is enough unless you know what is
10   more than enough.
Listen to the fools reproach! it is a kingly title!
The eyes of fire, the nostrils of air, the mouth of water,
      the beard of earth.
The weak in courage is strong in cunning.

15   The apple tree never asks the beech how he shall grow,
         nor the lion, the horse, how he shall take his prey.
      The thankful reciever bears a plentiful harvest.
      If others had not been foolish. we should be so.
      The soul of sweet delight. can never be defil'd,
20   When thou seest an Eagle, thou seest a portion of Ge
         -nius. lift up thy head!
      As the catterpiller chooses the fairest leaves to lay
         her eggs on, so the priest lays his curse on
         the fairest joys.
25   To create a little flower is the labour of ages.
      Damn, braces: Bless relaxes.
      The best wine is the oldest. the best water the newest
      Prayers plow not! Praises reap not!
      Joys laugh not! Sorrows weep not!

[Plate 10]   Proverbs of Hell
      The head Sublime, the heart Pathos, the genitals Beauty
         the hands & feet Proportion.
      As the air to a bird or the sea to a fish, so is contempt
         to the contemptible.
      The crow wish'd every thing was black, the owl, that eve-
         -ry thing was white.
      Exuberance is Beauty.
      If the lion was advised by the fox. he would be cunning.
10   Improvent makes strait roads, but the crooked roads
         without Improvement. are roads of Genius.
      Sooner murder an Infant in its cradle than nurse unact
         -ed desires
      Where man is not nature is barren.
15   Truth can never be told so as to be understood and
         not be believd.
                    Enough! or Too much

[Plate 11]   The ancient Poets animated all sensible objects
      with Gods or Geniuses, calling them by the names and
      adorning them with the properties of woods, rivers,
      mountains, lakes, cities, nations, and whatever their
      enlarged & numerous senses could percieve.
         And particularly they studied the genius of each
      city & country. placing it under its mental deity.
         Till a system was formed, which some took ad-
      vantage of & enslav'd the vulgar by attempting to
      realize or abstract the mental deities from their
      objects: thus began Priesthood.
         Choosing forms of worship from poetic tales.
         And at length they pronouncd that the Gods
      had orderd such things.
         Thus men forgot that All deities reside
      in the human breast.

[Plate 12]   A Memorable Fancy.

The Prophets Isaiah and Ezekiel dined with me, and I asked them how they dared so roundly to assert. that God spake to them; and whether they did not think at the time, that they would be mis--understood, & so be the cause of imposition.

Isaiah answer'd. I saw no God, nor heard any, in a finite organical perception; but my sen--ses discover'd the infinite in every thing, and as I was then perswaded, & remain confirmd; that the voice of honest indignation is the voice of God, I cared not for consequences but wrote.

Then I asked: does a firm perswasion that a thing is so, make it so?

He replied. All poets believe that it does. & in ages of imagination this firm perswasion remo ved mountains; but many are not capable of a firm perswasion of any thing.

Then Ezekiel said. The philosophy of the east taught the first principles of human perception some nations held one principle for the origin & some another; we of Israel taught that the Poetic Genius (as you now call it) was the first principle and all the others merely derivative, which was the cause of our despising the Priests & Philosophers of other countries. and prophecying that all Gods

[Plate 13]   would at last be proved to originate in ours & to be the tributaries of the Poetic Genius, it was this. that our great poet King David desired so fervently & invokes so patheticly, saying by this he conquers enemies & governs kingdoms; and we so loved our God. that we cursed in his name all the deities of surrounding nations, and asserted that they had rebelled; from these opinions the vulgar came to think that all nati--ons would at last be subject to the jews.

This said he, like all firm perswasions, is come to pass, for all nations believe the jews code and wor--ship the jews god, and what greater subjection can be

I heard this with some wonder. & must confess my own conviction. After dinner I ask'd Isaiah to fa-vour the world with his lost works, he said none of equal value was lost. Ezekiel said the same of his.

I also asked Isaiah what made him go naked and barefoot three years?[5] he answerd, the same that made our friend Diogenes the Grecian.

---

5. See Isaiah 20.2; the Lord instructs Isaiah to walk "naked and barefoot."

I then asked Ezekiel. why he eat dung, & lay so long on his right & left side?[6] he answerd, the desire of raising other men into a perception of the infinite this the North American tribes practise. & is he honest who resists his genius or conscience. only for the sake of present ease or gratification?

[Plate 14]   The ancient tradition that the world will be con-sumed in fire at the end of six thousand years[7] is true. as I have heard from Hell.

For the cherub with his flaming sword is hereby commanded to leave his guard at tree of life,[8] and when he does, the whole creation will be consumed and appear infinite. and holy whereas it now appears finite & corrupt.

This will come to pass by an improvement of sensual enjoyment.

But first the notion that man has a body distinct from his soul, is to be expunged; this I shall do, by printing in the infernal method, by corrosives, which in Hell are salutary and me-dicinal, melting apparent surfaces away, and displaying the infinite which was hid.

If the doors of perception were cleansed every thing would appear to man as it is: In-finite.

For man has closed himself up, till he sees all things thro' narrow chinks of his cavern.[9]

[Plate 15]   A Memorable Fancy[1]
I was in a Printing house in Hell & saw the method in which knowledge is transmitted from generation to generation.

6. See Ezekiel 4. Ezekiel is instructed to act out with his body the siege of Jerusalem by lying on his left side for 390 days to represent the years of Israel's iniquity and for 40 days on his right side for the years of the iniquity of the house of Judah; he is also ordered to eat barley cakes mixed with dung. Diogenes, famous for searching in daylight with a lantern for one honest man, was a 4th-century Greek Cynic philosopher who led a severely ascetic life. Blake alludes to these extraordinary actions to reflect the eccentricity often associated with visionary prophets.
7. This prophetic tradition is represented in the Book of Revelation and based on the translation of the six days of creation into six millennia (see 2 Peter 3.8); Blake relates this symbolism to his own era of the American and French revolutions.
8. See Genesis 3.24. After evicting Adam and Eve from Eden, God "placed at the east of the garden of Eden cherubims, and a flaming sword which turned every way, to keep the way of the tree of life" (this is one of the last images in Book 12 of *Paradise Lost*). Blake in turn imagines the expulsion of this angelic policeman and the restoration of Adam to the garden, free from sexual shame.
9. A reference to Plato's allegory of the Cave (*Republic* 7),
which compares the human mind to a cavern where men sit with their backs to the aperture of daylight, apprehending only shadows cast by firelight on the wall. A more immediate reference for Blake is Locke's description in his *Essay Concerning Human Understanding* (1690–1700) of "external and internal sensation" as "the only passages . . . of knowledge to the understanding . . . the windows by which light is let into [the] dark room" of the mind: "understanding is not much unlike a closet wholly shut from light, with only some little openings left, to let in external visible resemblances, or ideas of things without" (2.11.17).
1. The caverns continue the imagery of plate 14. The allegory is cryptic but seems to refer to Blake's creative process: in the first cavern, a figure of diabolic energy is clearing away the rubbish of wasted systems; the second chamber is undergoing artistic restoration; the third is being made into a place for liberated imagination; in the fourth and fifth chambers, the metal plates for Blake's book-making processes are being formed; in the sixth, men take possession of these books, imaging the decline from energy to system.

In the first chamber was a Dragon-Man, clear-
-ing away the rubbish from a caves mouth; within, a
number of Dragons were hollowing the cave.

In the second chamber was a Viper folding round
the rock & the cave, and others adorning it with gold
silver and precious stones.

In the third chamber was an Eagle, with wings
and feathers of air, he caused the inside of the cave
to be infinite, around were numbers of Eagle like
men, who built palaces in the immense cliffs.

In the fourth chamber were Lions of flaming fire
raging around & melting the metals into living fluids.

In the fifth chamber were Unnam'd forms, which
cast the metals into the expanse.

There they were reciev'd by Men who occupied
the sixth chamber, and took the forms of books &
were arranged in libraries.

[Plate 16]   The Giants who formed this world into its
sensual existence and now seem to live in it
in chains; are in truth. the causes of its life
& the sources of all activity, but the chains
are, the cunning of weak and tame minds which
have power to resist energy. according to the pro-
-verb, the weak in courage is strong in cunning.

Thus one portion of being, is the Prolific. the
other, the Devouring: to the devourer it seems as
if the producer was in his chains, but it is not so;
he only takes portions of existence and fancies
that the whole.

But the Prolific would cease to be Prolific
unless the Devourer as a sea recieved the excess
of his delights.

Some will say, Is not God alone the Prolific?
I answer. God only Acts & Is, in existing beings
or Men.

These two classes of men are always upon
earth. & they should be enemies: whoever tries

[Plate 17]   to reconcile them seeks to destroy existence.

Religion is an endeavour to reconcile the two.

Note. Jesus Christ did not wish to unite
but to separate them, as in the Parable of sheep and
goats! & he says I came not to send Peace but a
Sword.²

Messiah or Satan or Tempter was formerly
thought to be one of the Antediluvians³ who are our
Energies.

---

2. The Prolific (diabolical creators) and the Devourers
(sterile pious reasoners) accord with the parable of the
sheep and goats (Matthew 25.32–33): Jesus, the Shepherd, separates the sheep on his right hand, admitting
them to his kingdom, and the goats on his left, condemning them to the punishment of everlasting fire—having
cautioned, "think not that I am come to send peace on
earth: I came not to send peace, but a sword" (10.34).
3. Inhabitants of the earth "before the flood" survived by
Noah.

A Memorable Fancy[4]

An Angel came to me and said. O pitiable foolish young man! O horrible! O dreadful state! consider the hot burning dungeon thou art preparing for thyself to all eternity, to which thou art going in such career.

I said. perhaps you will be willing to shew me my eternal lot & we will contemplate together upon it and see whether your lot or mine is most desirable.

So he took me thro' a stable & thro' a church & down into the church vault at the end of which was a mill: thro' the mill we went, and came to a cave. down the winding cavern we groped our tedi-ous way till a void boundless as a nether sky ap-peard beneath us & we held by the roots of trees and hung over this immensity: but I said, if you please we will commit ourselves to this void, and see whether providence is here also, if you will not I will? but he answerd, do not presume O young-man but as we here remain behold thy lot which will soon appear when the darkness passes away

So I remaind with him sitting in the twisted

[Plate 18]

root of an oak; he was suspended in a fungus which hung with the head downward into the deep:

By degrees we beheld the infinite Abyss, fiery as the smoke of a burning city; beneath us at an immense distance was the sun, black but shining round it were fiery tracks on which revolv'd vast spiders, crawling after their prey; which flew or rather swum in the infinite deep, in the most ter-rific shapes of animals sprung from corruption. & the air was full of them, & seemd composed of them; these are Devils. and are called Powers of the air. I now asked my companion which was my eternal lot? he said, between the black & white spiders

But now, from between the black & white spiders a cloud and fire burst and rolled thro the deep blackning all beneath, so that the nether deep grew black as a sea & rolled with a terrible noise: be-neath us was nothing now to be seen but a black tempest, till looking east between the clouds & the waves, we saw a cataract of blood mixed with fire and not many stones throw from us appeard and sunk again the scaly fold of a monstrous serpent. at last to the east, distant about three degrees[5] ap-peard a fiery crest above the waves slowly it rear-ed like a ridge of golden rocks till we discoverd two globes of crimson fire, from which the sea

---

4. In this Memorable Fancy, a kind of dream allegory, Blake wages an elaborately comic argument with a pious Swedenborgian Angel, the voice of conventional moral-ity and religion. The geography of their fantastic tour images the decline of Christianity, beginning in the sta-ble of Christ's birth and the church founded in His name, and descending into the vault, the cave, the mill, and the abyss—into the rigidity of institutional religion.
5. The longitudinal position of Paris, heart of the French Revolution, relative to London.

fled away in clouds of smoke, and now we saw, it was the head of Leviathan.[6] his forehead was divided into streaks of green & purple like those on a tygers forehead: soon we saw his mouth & red gills hang just above the raging foam, tinging the black deep with beams of blood, advancing toward

[Plate 19]   us with all the fury of a spiritual exsitence.

My friend the Angel climb'd up from his station into the mill; I remain'd alone, & then this appearance was no more, but I found myself sitting on a pleasant bank beside a river by moon light hearing a harper who sung to the harp. & his theme was, The man who never alters his opinion is like standing water, & breeds reptiles of the mind.

But I arose, and sought for the mill & there I found my Angel, who surprised asked me, how I escaped?

I answerd. All that we saw was owing to your metaphysics: for when you ran away, I found myself on a bank by moonlight hearing a harper, But now we have seen my eternal lot, shall I shew you yours? he laughd at my proposal; but I by force suddenly caught him in my arms, & flew westerly thro' the night, till we were elevated above the earths shadow: then I flung myself with him directly into the body of the sun, here I clothed myself in white,[7] & taking in my hand Swedenborgs volumes sunk from the glorious clime, and passed all the planets till we came to saturn, here I staid to rest & then leap'd into the void, between saturn & the fixed stars.

Here said I! is your lot, in this space, if space it may be calld. Soon we saw the stable and the church, & I took him to the altar and open'd the Bible, and lo! it was a deep pit, into which I de--scended driving the Angel before me, soon we saw seven houses of brick,[8] one we enterd; in it were a

[Plate 20]   number of monkeys, baboons, & all of that species chaind by the middle, grinning and snatching at one another, but witheld by the shortness of their chains:[9] however I saw that they sometimes grew nu merous, and then the weak were caught by the strong and with a grinning aspect first coupled with & then devourd, by plucking off first one limb & then ano-

6. A beast described in the Bible (Job 41.1, Isaiah 27.1, Psalms 104.26), and alluded to by Thomas Hobbes (1588–1679) in his famous treatise on government, *Leviathan, or the Matter, Form, and Power of a Commonwealth, Ecclesiastical and Civil* (1651), written during the commonwealth and defending a secular monarchy; Hobbes argues that appetitive self-interest must be controlled only by the laws and institutions of government, whose authority is agreed upon by common contract. In Blake's view, this vision of the state is monstrous.
7. In Revelation 7.9, those who have been redeemed appear before the throne of Christ in white robes.
8. The seven churches to whom John addresses the Book of Revelation (1.4).
9. Blake's satire of theological dispute.

-ther till the body was left a helpless trunk. this after grinning & kissing it with seeming fondness they de--vourd too; and here & there I saw one savourily pic--king the flesh off of his own tail; as the stench ter--ribly annoyd us both we went into the mill, & I in my hand brought the skeleton of a body, which in the mill was Aristotles Analytics.[1]

So the Angel said: thy phantasy has imposed upon me & thou oughtest to be ashamed.

I answerd: we impose upon one another. & it is but lost time to converse with you whose works are only Analytics

Opposition is true Friendship[2]

[Plate 21]   I have always found that Angels have the vani--ty to speak of themselves as the only wise; this they do with a confident insolence sprouting from systema--tic reasoning:

Thus Swedenborg boasts that what he writes is new: tho' it is only the Contents or Index of already publish'd books

A man carried a monkey about for a shew, & be--cause he was a little wiser than the monkey, grew vain, and conciev'd himself as much wiser than se--ven men. It is so with Swedenborg: he shews the folly of churches & exposes hypocrites, till he im--agines that all are religious, & himself the single

[Plate 22]   one on earth that ever broke a net.

Now hear a plain fact: Swedenborg has not writ--ten one new truth: Now hear another: he has written all the old falshoods.

And now hear the reason. He conversed with Angels who are all religious. & conversed not with Devils who all hate religion for he was incapable thro' his conceited notions.

Thus Swedenborgs writings are a recapitulation of all superficial opinions, and an analysis of the more sublime. but no further.

Have now another plain fact: Any man of mechani--cal talents may from the writings of Paracelsus or Ja--cob Behmen,[3] produce ten thousand volumes of equal value with Swedenborg's, and from those of Dante or Shakespear, an infinite number.

But when he has done this, let him not say that he knows better than his master, for he only holds a can--dle in sunshine.

---

1. A "skeleton" both in the sense of an abstract summary and as a symbolic comment on the lifeless form of knowl-edge represented by Aristotle's treatise on logic as the highest kind of mental discipline. Compare the reference to "bleached bones" in the Argument.
2. This motto appears in only three of the nine known

copies of the poem.
3. Paracelsus (1493–1541) was a Swiss physician, occultist, and alchemist; Behmen is Jakob Boehme (1575–1624), a German mystic, who believed that God was knowable from the unity of the natural world.

A Memorable Fancy

Once I saw a Devil in a flame of fire, who arose be
fore an Angel that sat on a cloud, and the Devil ut-
-terd these words.

The worship of God is. Honouring his gifts in other
men each according to his genius. and loving the

[Plate 23]

greatest men best, those who envy or calumniate
great men hate God, for there is no other God.

The Angel hearing this became almost blue
but mastering himself he grew yellow, & at last
white pink & smiling. and then replied,

Thou Idolater, is not God One? & is not he
visible in Jesus Christ? and has not Jesus Christ
given his sanction to the law of ten commandments
and are not all other men fools sinners & nothings?

The Devil answer'd; bray a fool in a morter with
wheat yet shall not his folly be beaten out of him[4]
if Jesus Christ is the greatest man, you ought to
love him in the greatest degree; now hear how he
has given his sanction to the law of ten command
-ments: did he not mock at the sabbath, and so
mock the sabbaths God? murder those who were
murderd because of him? turn away the law from
the woman taken in adultery? steal the labor of
others to support him? bear false witness when
he omitted making a defence before Pilate? covet
when he pray'd for his disciples, and when he bid
them shake off the dust of their feet against such
as refused to lodge them? I tell you, no virtue
can exist without breaking these ten commandments: Jesus was all virtue, and acted from im-

[Plate 24]

-pulse: not from rules.[5]

When he had so spoken, I beheld the Angel who
stretched out his arms embracing the flame of fire
& he was consumed and arose as Elijah.[6]

Note. This Angel, who is now become a Devil, is
my particular friend: we often read the Bible to-
-gether in its infernal or diabolical sense which
the world shall have if they behave well.

I have also: **The Bible of Hell**:[7] which the world
shall have whether they will or no.

One Law for the Lion & Ox is Oppression

1790–1793   1793–1825

---

4. See Proverbs 27.22: "Though thou shouldest bray
[crush] a fool in a mortar among wheat with a pestle, yet
will not his foolishness depart from him."
5. For Jesus' breaking of Jewish law, see John 8.2–11, and
Matthew 9.14–17, 12.1–8, and 27.11–14.

6. See 2 Kings 2.11: "there appeared a chariot of fire, and
horses of fire, and . . . Elijah went up by a whirlwind into
heaven."
7. Blake's own scripture—that is, his illuminated poems.

VISIONS OF THE DAUGHTERS OF ALBION

Although "Albion," a mythical name for England, gives this poem the aura of a fable, its immediate context is Wollstonecraft's *Rights of Woman* (1792). Blake presents a chorus comprised of the Daughters of Albion (oppressed Englishwomen) and three characters: Oothoon, "the soft soul of America," that is, freedom and new hope; Theotormon ("God-Tormented"), her lover; and Bromion, who rapes her. Theotormon, paralyzed by jealousy (sexual possessiveness), binds Bromion and Oothoon back-to-back in his cave, and sits at the entry weeping. The remainder of the poem consists of the monologues of the three characters in this unchanging situation. Bromion expresses a tyrant's ideology of violent oppression and terror; Theotormon laments the debilitating effects of religious strictures; Oothoon inveighs against egotism and envisions love free from sexual and economic oppression. Like Wollstonecraft, Blake means to shock the sons of Albion by linking sexual tyranny and oppression to slavery, including the ravages of colonialism and the exploitation of children. The poem concludes with the Daughters of Albion echoing Oothoon's woe, but its subtitle, "The Eye sees more than the Heart knows," invites a regard of Oothoon's long soliloquy not only as a potent detailing of the oppression her heart knows well but also as a visionary hymn to unfettered love infused with a passionate hope for transformation. Square brackets at the front of lines indicate the plate number in Blake's illuminated book.

VISIONS
of
the Daughters of
Albion

[Plate ii]   The Eye sees more than the Heart knows.

[Plate iii]   The Argument[1]
                     I loved Theotormon
                     And I was not ashamed
                     I trembled in my virgin fears
5   And I hid in Leutha's vale![2]

                     I plucked Leutha's flower,[3]
                     And I rose up from the vale;
                     But the terrible thunders tore
                     My virgin mantle in twain.

[Plate 1]   **Visions**
ENSLAV'D,[4] the Daughters of Albion weep: a trembling lamentation
Upon their mountains; in their valleys. sighs toward America.[5]

For the soft soul of America, Oothoon[6] wanderd in woe,
5   Along the vales of Leutha seeking flowers to comfort her;
And thus she spoke to the bright Marygold of Leutha's vale

        Art thou a flower! art thou a nymph! I see thee now a flower:
        Now a nymph! I dare not pluck thee from thy dewy bed!

        The Golden nymph replied; pluck thou my flower Oothoon the mild
10   Another flower shall spring, because the soul of sweet delight
        Can never pass away. she ceas'd & closd her golden shrine.

---

1. Oothoon's description of herself before being raped.
2. A world of sexual shyness and sexual desire.
3. Traditional image for sexual initiation.
4. Blake's inscription of this word with large letters advertises the affinity of sexual slavery and chattel slavery, a recurrent theme in Wollstonecraft's *Rights of Woman*

(1792) and Thompson and Wheeler's *Appeal* (1825).
5. A country that has already revolted against tyranny.
6. An evocation of Oi-thona, the name of the "virgin of the waves" in James Macpherson's *Ossian*, who is kidnapped and raped by a rejected suitor.

Then Oothoon pluck'd the flower saying, I pluck thee from thy bed,
Sweet flower, and put thee here to glow between my breasts
And thus I turn my face to where my whole soul seeks.

15   Over the waves she went in wing'd exulting swift delight;
And over Theotormons reign, took her impetuous course.

Bromion rent her with his thunders.[7] on his stormy bed
Lay the faint maid, and soon her woes appalld his thunders hoarse

Bromion spake. behold this harlot[8] here on Bromions bed
20   And let the jealous dolphins sport around the lovely maid:
Thy soft American plains are mine, and mine thy north & south:
Stampt with my signet are the swarthy children of the sun:[9]
They are obedient, they resist not, they obey the scourge:
Their daughters worship terrors and obey the violent:[1]

[Plate 2]   Now thou maist marry Bromions harlot, and protect the child
Of Bromions rage, that Oothoon shall put forth in nine moons
                                                                [time
Then storms rent Theotormons limbs; he rolled his waves around.
5   And folded his black jealous waters round the adulterate pair
Bound back to back in Bromions caves[2] Terror & meekness dwell
At entrance Theotormon sits wearing the threshold hard
With secret tears; beneath him sound like waves on a desart shore
The voice of slaves beneath the sun, and children bought with money,
10   That shiver in religious caves beneath the burning fires
Of lust, that belch incessant from the summits of the earth

Oothoon weeps not: she cannot weep! her tears are locked up;
But she can howl incessant, writhing her soft snowy limbs.
And calling Theotormons Eagles to prey upon her flesh.

15   I call with holy voice! kings of the sounding air,
Rend away this defiled bosom that I may reflect.
The image of Theotormon on my pure transparent breast.

The Eagles at her call descend & rend their bleeding prey;
Theotormon severely smiles. her soul reflects the smile;
20   As the clear spring mudded with feet of beasts grows pure & smiles

The Daughters of Albion hear her woes, & eccho back her sighs.

Why does my Theotormon sit weeping upon the threshold;
And Oothoon hovers by his side, perswading him in vain:
I cry arise O Theotormon for the village dog

7. The imagery conveys both his wrath and the physical violence of rape.
8. "Harlot" reflects the common prejudice that despises the rape victim as fallen, soiled, blamable. In *Rights of Woman*, Wollstonecraft observes that rape, or even seduction out of wedlock, was often a prelude to prostitution: "A woman who has lost her honour, imagines that she cannot fall lower, and as for recovering her former station, it is impossible; no exertion can wash this stain away. Losing thus every spur, and having no other means of support, prostitution becomes her only refuge."
9. Referring to the branding of African slaves.
1. A tyrant's ideology: the victims of tyranny actually crave such treatment.
2. As in *The Marriage of Heaven and Hell*, these caves image the imprisoned mind—a prison evident in Theotormon's jealous regard of the rapist and his victim as "the adulterate pair" and his susceptibility to Bromion's taunting presentation of Oothoon to him for marriage, pregnant by Bromion.

25   Barks at the breaking day, the nightingale has done lamenting,
      The lark does rustle in the ripe corn, and the Eagle returns
      From nightly prey, and lifts his golden beak to the pure east;
      Shaking the dust from his immortal pinions to awake
      The sun that sleeps too long. Arise my Theotormon I am pure.
30   Because the night is gone that clos'd me in its deadly black.
      They told me that the night & day were all that I could see;
      They told me that I had five senses to inclose me up.
      And they inclos'd my infinite brain into a narrow circle.
      And sunk my heart into the Abyss, a red round globe hot burning
35   Instead of morn arises a bright shadow, like an eye
      In the eastern cloud; instead of night a sickly charnel house;
      That Theotormon hears me not! to him the night and morn
      Are both alike: a night of sighs, a morning of fresh tears;

[Plate 3]   And none but Bromion can hear my lamentations.

      With what sense is it that the chicken shuns the ravenous hawk
      With what sense does the tame pigeon measure out the expanse?
      With what sense does the bee form cells? have not the mouse & frog
5   Eyes and ears and sense of touch? yet are their habitations,
      And, their pursuits, as different as their forms and as their joys:
      Ask the wild ass why he refuses burdens: and the meek camel
      Why he loves man: is it because of eye ear mouth or skin
      Or breathing nostrils? No, for these the wolf and tyger have.
10   Ask the blind worm the secrets of the grave, and why her spires
      Love to curl round the bones of death! and ask the rav'nous snake
      Where she gets poison: & the wing'd eagle why he loves the sun
      And then tell me the thoughts of man, that have been hid of old.

      Silent I hover all the night, and all day could be silent.
15   If Theotormon once would turn his loved eyes upon me;
      How can I be defild when I reflect thy image pure?
      Sweetest the fruit that the worm feeds on. & the soul prey'd on by woe
      The new wash'd lamb ting'd with the village smoke & the bright swan
      By the red earth[3] of our immortal river: I bathe my wings.
20   And I am white and pure to hover round Theotormons breast.

      Then Theotormon broke his silence. and he answered.

      Tell me what is the night or day to one oerflowd with woe?
      Tell me what is a thought? & of what substance is it made?
      Tell me what is a joy? & in what gardens do joys grow?
25   And in what rivers swim the sorrows? and upon what mountains
[Plate 4]   Wave shadows of discontent? and in what houses dwell the wretched
      Drunken with woe forgotten, and shut up from cold despair.

      Tell me where dwell the thoughts forgotten till thou call them forth
      Tell me where dwell the joys of old? & where the ancient loves?

---

3. An evocation of Adam, whose name means literally "red earth."

5　And when will they renew again & the night of oblivion past?
　　That I might traverse times & spaces far remote and bring
　　Comforts into a present sorrow and a night of pain
　　Where goest thou O thought? to what remote land is thy flight?
　　If thou returnest to the present moment of affliction
10　Wilt thou bring comforts on thy wings. and dews and honey and balm;
　　Or poison From the desart wilds, from the eyes of the envier.

　　Then Bromion said: and shook the cavern with his lamentation

　　Thou knowest that the ancient trees seen by thine eyes have fruit;
　　But knowest thou that trees and fruits flourish upon the earth
15　To gratify senses unknown? trees beasts and birds unknown:
　　Unknown, not unpercievd, spread in the infinite microscope,
　　In places yet unvisited by the voyager, and in worlds
　　Over another kind of seas, and in atmospheres unknown?
　　Ah! are there other wars, beside the wars of sword and fire!
20　And are there other sorrows, beside the sorrows of poverty?
　　And are there other joys, besides the joys of riches and ease?
　　And is there not one law for both the lion and the ox?[4]
　　And is there not eternal fire, and eternal chains?
　　To bind the phantoms of existence from eternal life?

25　Then Oothoon waited silent all the day, and all the night,
[Plate 5]　But when the morn arose, her lamentation renewd.
　　The Daughters of Albion hear her woes, & eccho back her sighs.

　　O Urizen! Creator of men! mistaken Demon of heaven:[5]
　　Thy joys are tears! thy labour vain, to form men to thine image.
5　How can one joy absorb another? are not different joys
　　Holy, eternal, infinite! and each joy is a Love.

　　Does not the great mouth laugh at a gift? & the narrow eyelids mock
　　At the labour that is above payment, and wilt thou take the ape
　　For thy councellor? or the dog for a schoolmaster to thy children?
10　Does he who contemns poverty, and he who turns with abhorrence
　　From usury: feel the same passion or are they moved alike?
　　How can the giver of gifts experience the delights of the merchant?
　　How the industrious citizen the pains of the husbandman.
　　How different far the fat fed hireling with hollow drum;
15　Who buys whole corn fields into wastes, and sings upon the heath:
　　How different their eye and ear! how different the world to them!
　　What are his nets & gins & traps, & how does he surround him
　　With cold floods of abstraction, and with forests of solitude,
　　To build him castles and high spires, where kings & priests may dwell.

---

4. See the last line of *The Marriage of Heaven and Hell*.
5. Oothoon wonders if the limitations of both Bromion and Theotormon are the work of Urizen, a creator of men in his own image: his name sounds like "your reason" (and so evokes the constraints of sterile rationality) as well as "horizon" (derived from the Greek word for outward limit, or boundary circle).

20 Till she who burns with youth and knows no fixed lot; is bound
    In spells of law to one she loaths: and must she drag the chain
    Of life, in weary lust! must chilling murderous thoughts, obscure
    The clear heaven of her eternal spring! to bear the wintry rage
    Of a harsh terror driv'n to madness, bound to hold a rod
25 Over her shrinking shoulders all the day; & all the night
    To turn the wheel of false desire: and longings that wake her womb
    To the abhorred birth of cherubs in the human form
    That live a pestilence & die a meteor & are no more.
    Till the child dwell with one he hates, and do the deed he loaths
30 And the impure scourge force his seed into its unripe birth
    E'er yet his eyelids can behold the arrows of the day.

    Does the whale worship at thy footsteps as the hungry dog?
    Or does he scent the mountain prey, because his nostrils wide
    Draw in the ocean? does his eye discern the flying cloud
35 As the ravens eye? or does he measure the expanse like the vulture?
    Does the still spider view the cliffs where eagles hide their young?
    Or does the fly rejoice, because the harvest is brought in?
    Does not the eagle scorn the earth & despise the treasures beneath?
    But the mole knoweth what is there, & the worm shall tell it thee.
40 Does not the worm erect a pillar in the mouldering church yard?
[Plate 6]   And a palace of eternity in the jaws of the hungry grave
    Over his porch these words are written. Take thy bliss O Man!
    And sweet shall be thy taste, & sweet thy infant joys renew!

    Infancy, fearless, lustful, happy! nestling for delight
5   In laps f pleasure; Innocence! honest, open, seeking
    The vigorous joys of morning light; open to virgin bliss.
    Who taught thee modesty, subtil modesty! child of night & sleep
    When thou awakest. wilt thou dissemble all thy secret joys
    Or wert thou not awake when all this mystery was disclos'd!
10 Then comst thou forth a modest virgin knowing to dissemble
    With nets found under thy night pillow, to catch virgin joy,
    And brand it with the name of whore: & sell it in the night,
    In silence, ev'n without a whisper, and in seeming sleep:
    Religious dreams and holy vespers, light thy smoky fires:
15 Once were thy fires lighted by the eyes of honest morn
    And does my Theotormon seek this hypocrite modesty!
    This knowing, artful, secret, fearful, cautious, trembling hypocrite.
    Then is Oothoon a whore indeed! and all the virgin joys
    Of life are harlots: and Theotormon is a sick mans dream
20 And Oothoon is the crafty slave of selfish holiness.

    But Oothoon is not so, a virgin fill'd with virgin fancies
    Open to joy and to delight where ever beauty appears
    If in the morning sun I find it: there my eyes are fix'd
[Plate 7]   In happy copulation; if in evening mild wearied with work,
    Sit on a bank and draw the pleasures of this free born joy.

        The moment of desire! the moment of desire! The virgin
        That pines for man; shall awaken her womb to enormous joys
5   In the secret shadows of her chamber; the youth shut up from
        The lustful joy, shall forget to generate. & create an amorous image
        In the shadows of his curtains and in the folds of his silent pillow.
        Are not these the places of religion? the rewards of continence?
        The self enjoyings of self denial? Why dost thou seek religion?
10   Is it because acts are not lovely, that thou seekest solitude,
        Where the horrible darkness is impressed with reflections of desire.

        Father of Jealousy,[6] be thou accursed from the earth!
        Why hast thou taught my Theotormon this accursed thing?
        Till beauty fades from off my shoulders, darken'd and cast out,
15   A solitary shadow wailing on the margin of non-entity.

        I cry, Love! Love! Love! happy happy Love! free as the mountain wind!
        Can that be Love, that drinks another as a sponge drinks water?
        That clouds with jealousy his nights, with weepings all the day:
        To spin a web of age around him, grey and hoary! dark!
20   Till his eyes sicken at the fruit that hangs before his sight.
        Such is self-love that envies all! a creeping skeleton
        With lamplike eyes watching around the frozen marriage bed.

        But silken nets and traps of adamant will Oothoon spread,
        And catch for thee girls of mild silver, or of furious gold:
25   I'll lie beside thee on a bank & view their wanton play
        In lovely copulation bliss on bliss with Theotormon:
        Red as the rosy morning, lustful as the first born beam,
        Oothoon shall view his dear delight, nor e'er with jealous cloud
        Come in the heaven of generous love; nor selfish blightings bring.

30   Does the sun walk in glorious raiment. on the secret floor
[Plate 8] Where the cold miser spreads his gold? or does the bright cloud drop
        On his stone threshold? does his eye behold the beam that brings
        Expansion to the eye of pity? or will he bind himself
        Beside the ox to thy hard furrow? does not that mild beam blot
5   The bat, the owl, the glowing tyger, and the king of night.
        The sea fowl takes the wintry blast, for a cov'ring to her limbs:
        And the wild snake, the pestilence to adorn him with gems & gold.
        And trees & birds, & beasts, & men, behold their eternal joy.
        Arise you little glancing wings. and sing your infant joy!
10   Arise and drink your bliss, for every thing that lives is holy![7]

        Thus every morning wails Oothoon. but Theotormon sits
        Upon the margind ocean conversing with shadows dire.

        The Daughters of Albion hear her woes, & eccho back her sighs.

            The End

                            1793

6. Urizen, who creates men with this passion; as in *Oth-ello*, "jealousy" refers specifically to sexual possessiveness.

7. In some editions of *The Marriage of Heaven and Hell*, Blake appended "A Song of Liberty," of which this declaration is the concluding line.

Letters
To Dr. John Trusler[1]

23 August 1799

Rev'd Sir,

I really am sorry that you are fall'n out with the Spiritual World, Especially if I should have to answer for it. I feel very sorry that your Ideas & Mine on Moral Painting differ so much as to have made you angry with my method of Study. If I am wrong, I am wrong in good company. I had hoped your plan comprehended All Species of this Art, & Especially that you would not regret that Species which gives Existence to Every other, namely, Visions of Eternity. You say that I want somebody to Elucidate my Ideas. But you ought to know that What is Grand is necessarily obscure to Weak men. That which can be made Explicit to the Idiot is not worth my care. The wisest of the Ancients considered what is not too Explicit as the fittest for Instruction, because it rouses the faculties to act. I name Moses, Solomon, Esop, Homer, Plato.

But as you have favor'd me with your remarks on my Design, permit me in return to defend it against a mistaken one, which is, That I have supposed Malevolence without a Cause.[2] Is not Merit in one a Cause of Envy in another, & Serenity & Happiness & Beauty a Cause of Malevolence? But Want of Money & the Distress of A Thief can never be alleged as the Cause of his Thieving, for many honest people endure greater hardships with Fortitude. We must therefore seek the Cause elsewhere than in want of Money, for that is the Miser's passion, not the Thief's.

I have therefore proved your Reasonings Ill-proportion'd, which you can never prove my figures to be; they are those of Michael Angelo, Rafael & the Antique, & of the best living Models. I perceive that your Eye is perverted by Caricature Prints, which ought not to abound so much as they do. Fun I love, but too much Fun is of all things the most loathsome. Mirth is better than Fun, & Happiness is better than Mirth. I feel that a Man may be happy in This World. And I know that This World Is a World of IMAGINATION & Vision. I see Every thing I paint In This World, but Everybody does not see alike. To the Eyes of a Miser a Guinea is more beautiful than the Sun, & a bag worn with the use of Money has more beautiful proportions than a Vine filled with Grapes. The tree which moves some to tears of joy is in the Eyes of others only a Green thing that stands in the way. Some See Nature all Ridicule & Deformity, & by these I shall not regulate my proportions; & Some Scarce see Nature at all. But to the Eyes of the Man of Imagination, Nature is Imagination itself. As a man is, So he Sees. As the Eye is formed, such are its Powers. You certainly Mistake, when you say that the Visions of Fancy are not to be found in This World. To Me This World is all One continued Vision of Fancy or Imagination & I feel Flattered when I am told so. What is it sets Homer, Virgil & Milton in so high a rank of Art. Why is the Bible more Entertaining & Instructive than any other book? Is it not because they are addressed to the Imagination, which is Spiritual Sensation, & but mediately to the Understanding or Reason? Such is True Painting and such <was> alone valued by the Greeks & the best modern Artists. Consider what Lord Bacon

---

1. Rev. Dr. John Trusler (1735–1820), clergyman and minor man of letters, was interested in Blake as an illustrator for his books, but the two proved incompatible, Trusler deeming Blake's designs too much "in the other world, or the World of Spirits, which accords not with my Intentions, which, whilst living in This World, Wish to follow *the Nature of it*."

2. A reference to one of the illustrations Blake submitted to Trusler.

says: "Sense sends over to Imagination before Reason have judged, & Reason sends over to Imagination before the Decree can be acted." See Advancem[ent] of Learning Part 2, P. 47 of first Edition.[3]

But I am happy to find a Great Majority of Fellow Mortals who can Elucidate My Visions & Particularly they have been Elucidated by Children, who have taken a greater delight in contemplating my Pictures than I even hoped. Neither Youth nor Childhood is Folly or Incapacity. Some Children are Fools & so are some Old Men. But There is a vast Majority on the side of Imagination or Spiritual Sensation.

To Engrave after another Painter is infinitely more laborious than to Engrave ones own Inventions. And of the Size you require my price has been Thirty Guineas & I cannot afford to do it for less. I had Twelve for the Head I sent you as a Specimen, but after my own designs I could do at least Six times the quantity of labour in the same time which will account for the difference of price as also that Chalk Engraving is at least six times as laborious as Aqua tinta. I have no objection to Engraving after another Artist. Engraving is the profession I was apprenticed to, & should never had attempted to live by any thing else, If orders had not come in for my Designs & Paintings, which I have the pleasure to tell you are Increasing Every Day. Thus If I am a Painter it is not to be attributed to Seeking after. But I am contented whether I live by painting or Engraving.

I am Revd Sir, Your very obedient servant,

WILLIAM BLAKE

To Thomas Butts[1]

22 November 1802

Dear Sir,

* * * I will bore you more with some Verses which My Wife desires me to Copy out & send you with her kind love & Respect; they were Composed above a twelve-month ago, while walking from Felpham to Lavant to meet my Sister:

> With happiness stretch'd across the hills
> In a cloud that dewy sweetness distills,
> With a blue sky spread over with wings
> And a mild Sun that mounts & sings,
> 5　With trees & fields full of Fairy elves
> And little devils who fight for themselves,
> Rememb'ring the Verses that Hayley sung[2]
> When my heart knock'd against the root of my tongue,
> With Angels planted in Hawthorn bowers
> 10　And God himself in the passing hours,
> With Silver Angels across my way

3. Referring to Francis Bacon's *Advancement of Learning* (1605). Although Blake seems to agree with Bacon here, he despised Bacon's commitment to patronage, scientific reason, and the monarchy. In his later works, "Bacon & Newton & Locke" are an infernal trinity of materialism.
1. Thomas Butts (1757–1845), a government worker and real estate entrepreneur, was a lifelong friend and patron of Blake. Blake produced 80 biblical illustrations for him from 1800 to 1805, and twenty-one watercolors of the Book of Job from 1805 to 1810. Altogether, Butts purchased about two hundred pictures and ten illuminated

books, a collection so voluminous that it spilled out of his home and into his greenhouse.
2. William Hayley (1745–1820), minor poet and patron of art, was Blake's patron and neighbor in Felpham (on the English channel) from 1800 to 1803. He commissioned him to illustrate his *Life of Cowper* (another poet) and his *Essay on Sculpture*. He disapproved of Blake's visionary bent and urged him toward more conventional modes. As with Trusler, the relationship proved uncongenial, and the two had a falling out. When, however, Blake was arrested for treason (the cottage garden episode), Hayley contributed to his defense.

And Golden Demons that none can stay,
With my Father hovering upon the wind
And my Brother Robert just behind

15   And my Brother John the evil one
In a black cloud making his moan;[3]
Tho' dead, they appear upon my path,
Notwithstanding my terrible wrath;
They beg, they intreat, they drop their tears,

20   Fill'd full of hopes, fill'd full of fears;
With a thousand Angels upon the Wind
Pouring disconsolate from behind
To drive them off, & before my way
A frowning Thistle implores my stay.

25   What to others a trifle appears
Fills me full of smiles or tears;
For double the vision my Eyes do see,
And a double vision is always with me.[4]
With my inward Eye 'tis an old Man grey;

30   With my outward, a Thistle across my way.
"If thou goest back," the thistle said,
"Thou art to endless woe betray'd;
For here does Theotormon lower,°   brood
And here is Enitharmon's bower,

35   And Los the terrible thus hath sworn,[5]
Because thou backward dost return,
Poverty, Envy, old age & fear
Shall bring thy Wife upon a bier;
And Butts shall give what Fuseli gave,[6]

40   A dark black Rock & a gloomy Cave."

I struck the Thistle with my foot,
And broke him up from his delving root.
"Must the duties of life each other cross?
Must every joy be dung & dross?

45   Must my dear Butts feel cold neglect
Because I give Hayley his due respect?
Must Flaxman look upon me as wild,
And all my friends be with doubts beguil'd?[7]
Must my Wife live in my Sister's bane,[8]

3. The spirits of Blake's father (d. 1784); his favorite brother Robert (1767–1787); and brother John (b. 1760), who had enlisted in the army, was once apprenticed to a gingerbread maker, but fell into poverty and alcoholism, and died young.

4. "Single vision" (see 1.88) is mere sense perception or "Newton's sleep"—the sleep of imagination in the domain of mathematical reason; "double [or twofold] vision" is perception infused with individual imagination.

5. Theotormon is one of the four sons of Enitharmon and Los, both figures in Blake's later poetry. Enitharmon, the spirit of Beauty, is the twin and consort of Los, the spirit of poetry and imagination. In this letter, this Blakean trinity emerges to support his fidelity to poetic genius.

6. Henry Fuseli, a neoclassical painter and lifelong friend; he frequently employed Blake as an engraver of his own

paintings, and like almost everyone else, had a falling out with him over matters of artistic vision, in consequence of which he ceased to employ him by 1802—hence the snippiness here and the worry that Butts will turn out the same way, as someone who would push Blake into a gloomy Cave devoid of imagination.

7. John Flaxman (1755–1826), one of England's major sculptors, was a close friend and supporter of Blake in his early career, subsidizing the printing of his first, unillustrated, volume, Poetical Sketches, in 1783. Like Hayley, he urged Blake to devote himself to drawing and engraving and to forgo his grand visionary paintings and prophetic illuminated poems.

8. Blake's sister was living with him and his wife at Felpham while he worked for Hayley, and did not get along with his wife.

50   Or my Sister survive on my Love's pain?
     The curses of Los, the terrible shade,
     And his dismal terrors make me afraid."

     So I spoke & struck in my wrath
     The old man weltering upon my path.
55   Then Los appeared in all his power;
     In the Sun he appear'd, descending before
     My face in fierce flames; in my double Sight[9]
     'Twas outward a Sun, inward Los in his might.

     "My hands are labour'd day and night,
60   And Ease comes never in my sight.
     My Wife has no indulgence given
     Except what comes to her from Heaven.
     We eat little, we drink less;
     This Earth breeds not our happiness.
65   Another Sun feeds our life's streams,
     We are not warmed with thy beams;
     Thou measurest not the Time to me,
     Nor yet the Space that I do see;
     My Mind is not with thy light array'd.
70   Thy terrors shall not make me afraid."

     When I had my Defiance given,
     The Sun stood trembling in heaven;
     The Moon that glowed remote below,
     Became leprous & white as snow;
75   And every soul of men on the Earth
     Felt affliction & sorrow & sickness & dearth.
     Los flam'd in my path, & the Sun was hot
     With the bows of my Mind & the Arrows of Thought.
     My bowstring fierce with Ardour breathes;
80   My arrows glow in their golden sheaves;
     My brothers & father march before;
     The heavens drop with human gore.

     Now I a fourfold vision see,
     And a fourfold vision is given to me;
85   'Tis fourfold in my supreme delight
     And threefold in soft Beulah's night
     And twofold Always. May God us keep
     From Single vision & Newton's sleep![1]

---

9. See "double vision," n. 4 to line 28.

1. In Blake's hierarchy, fourfold vision is pure visionary inspiration, with no reliance on the physical senses and the material world; threefold vision is the deep source of poetic vision: the subconscious, the world of dreams, figuratively "Beulah's night." Beulah, which means "married," is an important spiritual location in Blake's later poetry. In the Bible, it is the name given to Zion in Isaiah 62.4 when it is restored to God's favor. In John Bunyan's dream allegory, *Pilgrim's Progress from This World to That Which Is to Come* (1678–1684), the country of Beulah is the Earthly Paradise, which wayfaring Christians gain after a long journey of toils and challenges, and where they abide until they cross the River of Death into the Celestial City. For "twofold" and "Single," see note 4 to line 28. "Newton's sleep" is the dormancy of imagination in the scientific (empirical) mind, referring to Isaac Newton (1642–1727), discoverer of the law of gravity and formulator of the laws of modern physics.

I also enclose you some Ballads by Mr. Hayley,[2] with prints to them by Your H^{mble} Servt. I should have sent them before now but could not get any thing done for You to please myself; for I do assure you that I have truly studied the two little pictures I now send, & do not repent of the time I have spent upon them.

God bless you.

Yours,

W. B.

P.S. I have taken the liberty to trouble you with a letter to my Brother, which you will be so kind as to send or give him, & oblige yours, W. B.

PERSPECTIVES

The Abolition of Slavery and the Slave Trade

Slavery and the slave trade provoked sharp controversy in the age of Romanticism, and literary writing played a major role in shaping public opinion. From 1783 to 1793 more than 300,000 slaves were sold in the British colonies, at a value of over £15,000,000. A "triangular trade" flourished, whereby British merchants financed expeditions to the African Gold Coast to buy or kidnap human cargo, to be shipped (the "Middle Passage") under brutal conditions to markets in the West Indies and South America. About 13 percent of this cargo died, while the survivors suffered heat, cramped quarters, fettering, physical abuse, poor sanitation, and disease. In *Thoughts Upon the African Slave Trade* (1788), John Newton guessed that on the voyages he captained, one-fourth of the slave-cargo was lost, not counting those who died right after capture. With the profits, which usually exceeded a hundred percent of the initial investment, traders filled their ships with exotic colonial goods—tobacco, sugar, molasses, rum, spices, cotton—which they sold in Europe, also at tremendous profits. Moral opposition to this trade, spearheaded by the Quakers and Evangelical Christian sects, was invigorated by Lord Mansfield's ruling in 1772 declaring the absence of any legal basis for slavery in England. Over the 1770s, several abolitionist tracts appeared, and by the end of the decade, bills were being introduced in Parliament to regulate the trade. National attention was galvanized by the scandal of the slave ship *Zong* (1781) whose captain ordered 133 weak and diseased slaves ejected into shark-infested waters in order to collect on a policy that held the insurer liable for cargo jettisoned in order to salvage the remainder.

In the 1780s the Quakers continued to petition Parliament and distribute pamphlets, while other abolitionists wrote tracts challenging the scriptural as well as economic justifications for slavery, and reformed slave-traders published memoirs detailing the horrors of the trade. By the end of the decade, William Wilberforce was heading a Parliamentary investigation and the former slave Olaudah Equiano's *Interesting Narrative* quickly became a best-seller. But the advent of the French Revolution in 1789 increased fear of slave-revolts, and Wilberforce's first bill for abolition was defeated in 1791.

Yet the abolition movement persisted. In 1792 Edmund Burke's *Sketch of a Negro Code* gave a plan for orderly abolition and emancipation, and in 1793 Wilberforce's second bill for abolition at least won in the House of Commons. By the end of the decade, the British treasury

---

2. *Designs to a Series of Ballads written by William Hayley* (1802), for which Blake did 14 engravings.

was reeling under the cost of regulating the trade and defending the plantation owners. The abolition movement achieved its first major success in 1807, when Parliament ended British participation in the trade. Wilberforce's stirring *Letter on the Abolition of the Slave Trade* (1807) commemorated the moral importance of the event and helped sustain the movement for abolishing slavery itself (still legal in the colonies)—as did Thomas Clarkson's gripping *History of the Abolition of the African Slave-Trade by the British Parliament* (1808), which detailed the horrors of the trade both for the slaves and the seamen. By the 1820s, the movement was benefiting from the increasing involvement of women, who were horrified by the often violent and sexually abusive treatment of female slaves. In 1823 Clarkson and Wilberforce founded the influential *Anti-Slavery Monthly Reporter*, which relentlessly publicized all the horrors, and Parliament seriously addressed the issue, with Foreign Secretary George Canning arguing that "the spirit of the Christian religion is hostile to slavery." The year 1831 was a critical one, marked not only by a massive slave rebellion in Jamaica, with severe reprisals against slaves and sympathetic missionaries, but also by the publication of former slave Mary Prince's autobiography, with searing reports of atrocities, especially to female slaves. The Reform Parliament of 1832 proved hospitable to emancipation, and in 1833 it passed the Emancipation Bill, liberating 800,000 slaves in British colonies and compensating the owners with more than £20,000,000.

It was the planters and the merchants in Bristol and Liverpool, who were enjoying immense profits, who opposed abolition. Supported by their Standing Committee in Parliament, they justified slavery by arguing that Africans had already enslaved each other on their own continent; that they were mental and moral primitives, animals and heathens, to whom plantation life brought a work-ethic, civilized behavior, and the grace of Christian religion; and finally, that British abolition would not end the trade, only leave the profits to other nations. Their literary propaganda tended toward the genre of "romance," pastoral stories with happy endings in which slaves are grateful and planters benevolent. Their appeals to social stability were amplified by alarm at the French Revolution, and in 1791 a massive slave revolt in Santo Domingo made it possible to link abolitionism to Jacobinism and to embarrass at least the Evangelical abolitionists, who tended to be critical of the Revolution.

Abolitionists came from differing, often opposed political groups: Tory, Evangelical, Quaker, Unitarian, Dissenter, Nonconformist, radical. Some, such as Anna Barbauld, Mary Wollstonecraft, and Tom Paine, energized abolitionism with related commitments to social reform and the new philosophies of "the rights of man" and "the rights of woman." Wordsworth's excoriation of slavery in *The Prelude* powerfully sounds this note. But others, including the Parliamentarians Burke and Wilberforce and most Evangelical Christians, were politically conservative, often wealthy; wanting to avoid the revolutionary cast of "rights of man" arguments, the Evangelicals instead condemned slavery as a moral blight on a Christian nation and advocated Parliamentary reform. They refuted the planters' claims of kind treatment on slave-ships and plantations, and vividly purveyed what amounts to a pornography of atrocities, even as the moral stress was on common humanity and Christian values. With their own version of African primitivism, their fables evoked sympathy for the slaves' childlike simplicity and the pathos of their destroyed families, their physical tortures and suffering. In these narratives, redemption for the slaves appears not through rebellion, but through the salvational processes of Christian conversion, forbearance, and an appeal to enlightened authority.

Many well-known writers produced abolitionist literature, rallying support by using vivid individual stories to exemplify the broad social and ethical issues involved. The texts that follow show the range of literary resources, and the range of viewpoints, employed by writers who composed poems, essays, and stories as part of the protracted struggle over abolition.

---- ≍✦≍ ----

Olaudah Equiano
c. 1745–1797

In the Parliamentary inquiry into the condition of the slave trade in 1788–1789, evidence came almost exclusively from the traders. Olaudah Equiano's *Interesting Narrative* was crucial for presenting dramatic evidence from the slaves' harrowing experiences. Born to a high-ranking, prosperous, slave-owning family of the Ebo tribe, in the region of modern Nigeria, Equiano was kidnapped by freelance slavers at age ten, shipped first to Barbados, then North America. The disorienting effects of this brutal experience are reflected in the series of names he was given by successive owners: on the slave-ship he was "Michael," then named "Jacob" by a Virginia plantation owner, and then dubbed "Gustavus Vassa," after a sixteenth-century Swedish hero, when he was purchased by Lieutenant Michael Pascal of the British navy. Pascal took him to England in 1757, and then to Canada where he fought in the Seven Years' war in 1758; he was baptized in 1759, and worked for the British navy in the Mediterranean as a servant and gunner's mate. Pascal then sold him to an American Quaker merchant, Robert King, on whose trading ships he worked. With profits from private trade conducted by his own initiative and entrepreneurial skill, he earned enough from the system he abhorred to purchase his freedom, for £70, in 1766. Subsequent adventures took him on a Grand Tour of the Mediterranean, to the Caribbean, and even on an expedition to the Arctic in 1773 (seeking a polar route to India), where a shipmate was young Horatio Nelson (later, one of England's celebrated naval heroes). At various times, Equiano managed a plantation in Central America, earned a living as a hairdresser in London, and worked for the Sierra Leone project (a planned colony for freed slaves in Africa), until he protested against financial mismanagement and was dismissed.

Once settled in England, he renewed his commitment to Christianity and worked with the Evangelicals, campaigned tirelessly for abolition, and became an acquaintance of the founder of the radical working-class London Corresponding Society. In 1792 Equiano married an English woman with whom he had two daughters, and was well enough off at his death in 1797 to leave his one surviving daughter an inheritance of £950 on her twenty-first birthday in 1816. Equiano's *Interesting Narrative* witnesses the cruelty of the Middle Passage, the violence of slavery, and the uncertain status of even the free black; at the same time, it is a vivid picaresque adventure, a religious conversion narrative, and a document of surprising social mobility. A story of triumph as well as oppression, the *Narrative* has a complexity the more compelling for its seeming artlessness. It was an immediate sensation, selling 5,000 copies the first year, and going through thirty-six editions over the next half century. Published as far afield as Germany and Russia, it was influential in promoting abolition, a cause that Equiano continued to serve as a devoted public speaker until the end of his life.

From The Interesting Narrative of the Life of Olaudah Equiano
or Gustavus Vassa, the African
[THE SLAVE SHIP AND ITS CARGO]

The first object that saluted my eyes when I arrived on the coast was the sea, and a slave ship, which was then riding at anchor, and waiting for its cargo.[1] These filled me with astonishment, that was soon converted into terror, which I am yet at a loss to describe, and much more the then feelings of my mind when I was carried on board. I was immediately handled and tossed up to see if I was sound, by some of the

---

1. Captured by slavers along with his sister, Equiano was soon separated from her and sold to different masters over a period of several months before reaching the African coast for shipment to Barbados.

crew; and I was now persuaded that I had got into a world of bad spirits, and that they were going to kill me. Their complexions too, differing so much from ours, their long hair, and the language they spoke, which was very different from any I had ever heard, united to confirm me in this belief. Indeed such were the horrors of my views and fears at the moment, that if ten thousand worlds had been my own, I would have freely parted with them all to have exchanged my condition with the meanest slave in my own country. When I looked round the ship too, and saw a large furnace or copper boiling and a multitude of black people, of every description, chained together, every one of their countenances expressing dejection and sorrow, I no longer doubted of my fate; and, quite overpowered with horror and anguish, I fell motionless on the deck, and fainted. When I recovered a little, I found some black people about me, who I believed were some of those who brought me on board, and had been receiving their pay: they talked to me in order to cheer me, but all in vain. I asked them if we were not to be eaten by those white men with horrible looks, red faces, and long hair. They told me I was not: and one of the crew brought me a small portion of spirituous liquor in a wine glass; but, being afraid of him, I would not take it out of his hand. One of the blacks therefore took it from him and gave it to me, and I took a little down my palate, which, instead of reviving me, as they thought it would, threw me into the greatest consternation at the strange feeling it produced, having never tasted any such liquor before.

Soon after this the blacks who brought me on board went off, and left me abandoned to despair. I now saw myself deprived of all chance of returning to my native country, or even the least glimpse of gaining the shore, which I now considered as friendly; and I even wished for my former slavery, in preference to my present situation, which was filled with horrors of every kind, still heightened by my ignorance of what I was to undergo. I was not long suffered to indulge my grief. I was soon put down under the decks, and there I received such a salutation in my nostrils as I had never experienced in my life: so that, with the loathsomeness of the stench, and with my crying together, I became so sick and low that I was not able to eat, nor had I the least desire to taste any thing. I now wished for the last friend, death, to relieve me; but soon, to my grief, two of the white men offered me eatables; and, on my refusing to eat, one of them held me fast by the hands, and laid me across, I think, the windlass, and tied my feet, while the other flogged me severely. I had never experienced any thing of this kind before, and although, not being used to the water, I naturally feared that element the first time I saw it, yet nevertheless, could I have got over the nettings, I would have jumped over the side, but I could not; and besides the crew used to watch us very closely, who were not chained down to the decks, lest we should leap into the water. I have seen some of these poor African prisoners most severely cut for attempting to do so, and hourly whipped for not eating. This indeed was often the case with myself. In a little time after, amongst the poor chained men, I found some of my own nation, which in a small degree gave ease to my mind. I inquired of these what was to be done with us. They gave me to understand we were to be carried to these white people's country to work for them. I was then a little revived, and thought if it were no worse than working, my situation was not so desperate. But still I feared I should be put to death, the white people looked and acted, as I thought, in so savage a manner; for I had never seen among any people such instances of brutal cruelty: and this is not only shewn towards us blacks, but also to some of the whites themselves. One white man in particular I saw, when we were permitted to be on deck, flogged so unmercifully with a large rope near the foremast, that he died in consequence of it; and they tossed him over the side as they would have done a brute. This made me fear these people the more; and I expected nothing less than to be treated in the same manner. I could not help expressing my fearful apprehensions to some of my countrymen; I asked them if these people had no country, but lived in this hollow place, the ship. They told me they did not, but came from a distant one. "Then," said I, "how comes it, that in all our country we never heard of them?" They told me, because they lived so very far off. I then asked, where their women were: had they any like themselves. I was told they had. "And why," said I, "do we not see them?" They answered, because they were left behind. I asked how the vessel could go. They told me they could not tell; but that there was cloth put upon the masts by the help of the ropes I saw, and then the vessel went on; and the white men had some spell or magic they put in the water, when they liked, in order to stop the vessel. I was exceedingly amazed at this account, and really thought they were spirits. I therefore wished much to be from amongst them, for I expected they would sacrifice me; but my wishes were in vain, for we were so quartered that it was impossible for any of us to make our escape.

[EQUIANO, AGE 12, REACHES ENGLAND]

One morning, when I got upon deck, I perceived it covered over with the snow that fell overnight. As I had never seen any thing of the kind before, I thought it was salt; so I immediately ran down to the mate and desired him, as well as I could, to come and see how somebody in the night had thrown salt all over the deck. He, knowing what it was, desired me to bring some of it down to him; accordingly I took up a handful of it, which I found very cold indeed; and when I brought it to him he desired me to taste it. I did so, and was surprised above measure. I then asked him what it was; he told me it was snow; but I could not by any means understand him. He asked me if we had no such thing in our country; and I told him "No." I then asked him the use of it, and who made it; he told me a great man in the heavens, called God: but here again I was to all intents and purposes at a loss to understand him; and the more so, when a little after I saw the air filled with it, in a heavy shower, which fell down on the same day.

After this I went to church; and having never been at such a place before, I was again amazed at seeing and hearing the service. I asked all I could about it; and they gave me to understand it was "worshiping God, who made us and all things." I was still at a loss, and soon got into an endless field of inquiries, as well as I was able to speak and ask about things. However, my dear little friend Dick[2] used to be my best interpreter; for I could make free with him and he always instructed me with pleasure. And from what I could understand by him of this God, and in seeing that these white people did not sell one another as we did, I was much pleased: and in this I thought they were much happier than we Africans. I was astonished at the wisdom of the white people in all things which I beheld; but I was greatly amazed at their not sacrificing, not making any offerings, and at their eating with unwashen hands, and touching of the dead. I also could not help remarking the particular slenderness of their women, which I did not at first like, and I thought them not so modest and shamefaced as the African women.

I had often seen my master Dick employed in reading; and I had a great curiosity to talk to the books, as I thought they did; and so to learn how all things had a beginning. For that purpose I have often taken up a book and talked to it, and then put my ears to it, when alone, in hopes it would answer me; and I have been very much concerned when I found it remaining silent.

---

2. Richard Baker, an American boy four or five years older than Equiano.

[EMPLOYMENT IN THE WEST INDIES]

I had the good fortune to please my master in every department in which he employed me; and there was scarcely any part of his business, or household affairs, in which I was not occasionally engaged. I often supplied the place of a clerk, in receiving and delivering cargoes to the ships, in tending stores, and delivering goods; and, besides this, I used to shave and dress my master, when convenient, and take care of his horse; and when it was necessary, which was very often, I worked likewise on board of his different vessels. By these means I became very useful to my master, and saved him, as he used to acknowledge, above a hundred pounds a year. Nor did he scruple to say I was of more advantage to him than any of his clerks; tho' their usual wages in the West-Indies are from sixty to a hundred pounds current a year.

I have sometimes heard it asserted that a negro cannot earn his master the first cost; but nothing can be further from the truth. I suppose nine tenths of the mechanics throughout the West-Indies are negro slaves; and I well know the coopers[3] among them earn two dollars a-day; the carpenters the same, and oftentimes more; also the masons, smiths, and fishermen, &c. and I have known many slaves whose masters would not take a thousand pounds current for them. But surely this assertion refutes itself: for, if it be true, why do the planters and merchants pay such a price for slaves? And, above all, why do those, who make this assertion, exclaim the most loudly against the abolition of the slave trade? So much are men blinded, and to such inconsistent arguments are they driven by mistaken interest! I grant, indeed, that slaves are sometimes, by half-feeding, half-clothing, over-working, and stripes,[4] reduced so low, that they are turned out as unfit for service, and left to perish in the woods, or to expire on a dunghill.

My master was several times offered by different gentlemen one hundred guineas[5] for me; but he always told them he would not sell me, to my great joy: and I used to double my diligence and care for fear of getting into the hands of these men, who did not allow a valuable slave the common support of life. Many of them used to find fault with my master for feeding his slaves so well as he did; although I often went hungry, and an Englishman might think my fare very indifferent: but he used to tell them he always would do it, because the slaves thereby looked better and did more work.

While I was thus employed by my master, I was often a witness to cruelties of every kind, which were exercised on my unhappy fellowslaves. I used frequently to have different cargoes of new negroes in my care for sale; and it was almost a constant practice with our clerks, and other whites, to commit violent depredations on the chastity of the female slaves; and to these atrocities I was, though with reluctance, obliged to submit at all times, being unable to help them. When we have had some of these slaves on board my master's vessels to carry them to other islands, or to America, I have known our mates commit these acts most shamefully, to the disgrace not of christians only, but of men. I have even known them gratify their brutal passion with females not ten years old; and these abominations some of them practised to such a scandalous excess, that one of our captains discharged the mate and others on that account. And yet in Montserrat[6] I have seen a negro-man staked to the ground, and cut most shockingly, and then his ears cut off, bit by bit, because he had been con-

---

3. Barrel-makers.
4. Lashings and the welts they leave.
5. The guinea coin, first struck in 1663 by a company of merchants chartered by the British crown to obtain slaves

from the Guinea coast of Africa (hence the name), was worth 21 shillings; made of gold, it often traded for more than its face value and connoted a certain prestige.
6. Island in the British West Indies.

nected with a white woman, who was a common prostitute! As if it were no crime in the whites to rob an innocent African girl of her virtue; but most heinous in a black man only to gratify a passion of nature, where the temptation was offered by one of a different colour, though the most abandoned woman of her species.

[THE PERILS OF BEING A FREEMAN]

I have since often seen in Jamaica and other islands, free men, whom I have known in America, thus villainously trepanned[7] and kept in bondage. I have heard of two similar practices even in Philadelphia: and were it not for the benevolence of the Quakers in that city, many of the sable race, who now breathe the air of liberty, would, I believe, be groaning under some planter's chains. These things opened my mind to a new scene of horror, to which I had been before a stranger. Hitherto I had thought only slavery dreadful; but the state of a free negro appeared to me now equally so at least, and in some respects even worse; for they live in constant alarm for their liberty, which is but nominal; and they are universally insulted and plundered without the possibility of redress; such being the equity of the West-Indian laws, that no free negro's evidence will be admitted in their courts of justice. * * *

I determined to make every exertion to obtain my freedom, and to return to Old England. For this purpose I thought a knowledge of Navigation might be of use to me; for, though I did not intend to run away unless I should be ill used, yet, in such a case, if I understood navigation, I might attempt my escape in our sloop, which was one of the swiftest sailing vessels in the West-Indies, and I could be at no loss for hands to join me. Had I made this attempt, I had intended to go in her to England; but this, as I said, was only to be in the event of my meeting with any ill usage. I therefore employed the mate of our vessel to teach me Navigation, for which I agreed to give him twenty-four dollars, and actually paid him part of the money down; though when the captain, some time after, came to know that the mate was to have such a sum for teaching me, he rebuked him, and said it was a shame for him to take any money from me. However, my progress in this useful art was much retarded by the constancy of our work.

Had I wished to run away I did not want opportunities, which frequently presented themselves; and particularly at one time, soon after this. When we were at the island of Guadaloupe there was a large fleet of merchantmen bound for Old France; and seamen then being very scarce, they gave from fifteen to twenty pounds a man for the run. Our mate and all the white sailors left our vessel on this account, and went aboard of the French ships. They would have had me also to go with them, for they regarded me, and swore to protect me, if I would go: and, as the fleet was to sail the next day, I really believe I could have got safe to Europe at that time. However, as my master was kind, I would not attempt to leave him; still remembering the old maxim, that *honesty is the best policy*, I suffered them to go without me. Indeed my captain was much afraid of my leaving him and the vessel at that time, as I had so fair an opportunity: but, I thank God, this fidelity of mine turned out much to my advantage hereafter, when I did not in the least think of it; and made me so much in favour with the captain, that he used now and then to teach me some parts of Navigation himself. But some of our passengers, and others, seeing this, found much fault with him for it, saying it was a very dangerous thing to let a negro know Navigation; and thus I was hindered again in my pursuits.

---

7. Betrayed.

[MANUMISSION]

When we had unladen the vessel, and I had sold my venture,[8] finding myself master of about forty-seven pounds, I consulted my true friend, the Captain, how I should proceed in offering my master the money for my freedom.[9] He told me to come on a certain morning, when he and my master would be at breakfast together. Accordingly, on that morning I went, and met the Captain there, as he had appointed. When I went in I made my obeisance to my master, and with my money in my hand, and many fears in my heart, I prayed him to be as good as his offer to me, when he was pleased to promise me my freedom as soon as I could purchase it. This speech seemed to confound him; he began to recoil; and my heart that instant sunk within me. "What," said he, "give you your freedom? Why, where did you get the money? Have you got forty pounds sterling?" "Yes, sir," I answered. "How did you get it?" replied he. I told him, "very honestly." The Captain then said he knew I got the money very honestly and with much industry, and that I was particularly careful. On which my master replied, I got money much faster than he did; and said he would not have made me the promise which he did, had he thought I should have got the money so soon. "Come, come," said my worthy Captain, clapping my master on the back, "Come, Robert, (which was his name) I think you must let him have his freedom. You have laid your money out very well; you have received good interest for it all this time, and here is now the principal at last. I know GUSTAVUS has earned you more than a hundred a year, and he will still save you money, as he will not leave you. Come, Robert, take the money." My master then said, he would not be worse than his promise; and, taking the money, told me to go to the Secretary at the Register Office, and get my manumission[1] drawn up.

These words of my master were like a voice from heaven to me: in an instant all my trepidation was turned into unutterable bliss, and I most reverently bowed myself with gratitude, unable to express my feelings, but by the overflowing of my eyes, and a heart replete with thanks to God; while my true and worthy friend, the Captain, congratulated us both with a peculiar degree of heartfelt pleasure. As soon as the first transports of my joy were over, and that I had expressed my thanks to these my worthy friends in the best manner I was able, I rose with a heart full of affection and reverence, and left the room, in order to obey my master's joyful mandate of going to the Register Office. As I was leaving the house I called to mind the words of the Psalmist, in the 126th Psalm, and like him, "I glorified God in my heart, in whom I trusted."[2] These words had been impressed on my mind from the very day I was forced from Deptford[3] to the present hour, and I now saw them, as I thought, fulfilled and verified.

My imagination was all rapture as I flew to the Register Office; and in this respect, like the apostle Peter (whose deliverance from prison was so sudden and extraordinary, that he thought he was in a vision)[4] I could scarcely believe I was awake. Heavens! who could do justice to my feelings at this moment? Not conquering heroes themselves, in the midst of a triumph—Not the tender mother who has just regained her long-lost infant, and presses it to her heart—Not the weary, hungry

---

8. The stock he was permitted to trade for himself.
9. In 1763 Equaino was sold to Robert King, a Quaker merchant, and thereafter served in the West Indies in one of his ships under Captain Thomas Farmer.
1. The formal liberation of a slave.
2. Psalm 126 celebrates release from captivity; the phrase

Equiano quotes does not appear there, though it echoes several other psalms (28, 33, 86, 125).
3. A borough southeast of London, where in 1762 Captain Michael Henry Pascal sold Equiano back into slavery, after several years' service.
4. Acts 12.9 [Equiano's note].

mariner, at the sight of the desired friendly port—Not the lover, when he once more embraces his beloved mistress, after she has been ravished from his arms!—All within my breast was tumult, wildness, and delirium! My feet scarcely touched the ground; for they were winged with joy, and, like Elijah, as he rose to Heaven, they "were with lightning sped as I went on."[5] Every one I met I told of my happiness, and blazed about the virtue of my amiable master and Captain. * * *

In short, the fair as well as black people immediately styled me by a new appellation,—to me the most desirable in the world,—which was "Freeman," and, at the dances I gave, my Georgia superfine blue clothes made no indifferent appearance, as I thought. Some of the sable females, who formerly stood aloof, now began to relax and appear less coy; but my heart was still fixed on London, where I hoped to be ere long. So that my worthy Captain, and his owner, my late master, finding that the bent of my mind was towards London, said to me, "We hope you won't leave us, but that you will still be with the vessels." Here gratitude bowed me down; and none but the generous mind can judge of my feelings, struggling between inclination and duty. However, notwithstanding my wish to be in London, I obediently answered my benefactors that I would go in the vessel, and not leave them; and from that day I was entered on board as an able-bodied seaman, at thirty-six shillings per month, besides what perquisites I could make.[6] My intention was to make a voyage or two, entirely to please these my honoured patrons; but I determined that the year following, if it pleased God, I would see Old England once more, and surprise my old master, Captain Pascal, who was hourly in my mind: for I still loved him, notwithstanding his usage to me, and I pleased myself with thinking of what he would say when he saw what the Lord had done for me in so short a time, instead of being, as he might perhaps suppose, under the cruel yoke of some planter.

+•+ ⚏ +•+

Mary Prince
c. 1788–after 1833

The History of Mary Prince, a West Indian Slave, Related by Herself is the earliest known slave narrative by a woman. Sponsored by the Anti-Slavery Society to galvanize support for abolition, especially from Britain's women, its saga of overwork, abuse, and sexual violence was chronicled in unprecedented depth and detail. Prince's *History* was a sensation, reaching a third edition the year it was published, 1831.

Prince was born a slave on a farm in Bermuda, a British colony whose major industries were shipbuilding and salting, and whose population was half slave. In her childhood, she was treated with relative kindness, but things changed dramatically when she was twelve. She was sold to sadistic, sexually abusive new owners. After several years of brutality, she was sold to an even more ghastly situation in the "cruel, horrible" salt ponds of Turks Island, about 200 miles northeast of Bermuda, where her labor left her legs covered with boils and eventually crippled her with rheumatism. Perpetually beaten, and sexually assaulted by an "indecent master," she requested to be sold to a merchant from Antigua, who was impressed by her reputation as a good worker. Overworked and exhausted, she began to rebel at her status there, and suffered imprisonment and repeated beatings and floggings. In 1827, with the help of abolitionist sympathizers, she escapted from these owners, when they took her to London. There Thomas

5. In 2 Kings (2.11), Elijah has a vision of a chariot of fire and is carried to Heaven in a whirlwind.

6. Equiano has the right to trade for himself and to receive tips.

Pringle, a Methodist and secretary of the Anti-Slavery Society, employed her as a domestic servant. He also edited her *History* as publicity for the movement; it sparked a national controversy when attacked in *Blackwood's Edinburgh Magazine* and *The Glasgow Courier* as fraudulent propaganda by a loose-moraled liar. Libel suits erupted, Prince's owner suing Pringle, and Pringle suing *Blackwood's*. *Blackwood's* declined to cross-examine her, letting her statement stand, but Pringle lost the other case because he couldn't produce witnesses from the West Indies to substantiate the allegations of *The History*. Even so, *The History* commanded wide readership, influencing the cause not only in its representation of general atrocities, but also in its image of Prince's individual resilience and determination. "All slaves want to be free," she declared in the final paragraph; "to be free is very sweet. . . . I can tell by myself what other slaves feel, and by what they have told me. The man that says slaves be quite happy in slavery—that they don't want to be free—that man is either ignorant or a lying person. I never heard a slave say so."

from The History of Mary Prince, a West Indian Slave
Related by Herself

It was night when I reached my new home. The house was large, and built at the bottom of a very high hill; but I could not see much of it that night. I saw too much of it afterwards. The stones and the timber were the best things in it; they were not so hard as the hearts of the owners.[1]

Before I entered the house, two slave women, hired from another owner, who were at work in the yard, spoke to me, and asked who I belonged to? I replied, "I am come to live here." "Poor child, poor child!" they both said; "you must keep a good heart, if you are to live here."—When I went in, I stood up crying in a corner. Mrs. I—— came and took off my hat, a little black silk hat Miss Pruden[2] made for me, and said in a rough voice, "You are not come here to stand up in corners and cry, you are come here to work." She then put a child into my arms, and, tired as I was, I was forced instantly to take up my old occupation of a nurse.—I could not bear to look at my mistress, her countenance was so stern. She was a stout tall woman with a very dark complexion, and her brows were always drawn together into a frown. I thought of the words of the two slave women when I saw Mrs. I——, and heard the harsh sound of her voice.

The person I took the most notice of that night was a French Black called Hetty, whom my master took in privateering[3] from another vessel, and made his slave. She was the most active woman I ever saw, and she was tasked to her utmost. A few minutes after my arrival she came in from milking the cows, and put the sweet-potatoes on for supper. She then fetched home the sheep, and penned them in the fold; drove home the cattle, and staked them about the pond side;[4] fed and rubbed down my master's horse, and gave the hog and the fed cow[5] their suppers; prepared the beds, and undressed the children, and laid them to sleep. I liked to look at her and watch all her doings, for hers was the only friendly face I had as yet seen, and I felt glad that she was there. She gave me my supper of potatoes and milk, and a blanket to sleep upon, which she spread for me in the passage before the door of Mrs. I——'s chamber.

1. These strong expressions, and all of a similar character in this little narrative, are given verbatim as uttered by Mary Prince [Thomas Pringle's note].
2. Prince's first owner, Mrs. Williams, had fallen on hard times and hired her out at age 12 to Mrs. Pruden; with Mrs. Williams's death, she was sold to "Captain I—."

3. Sanctioned raiding of enemy ships by armed private vessels.
4. The cattle on a small plantation in Bermuda are, it seems, often thus staked or tethered, both night and day, in situations where grass abounds. [Pringle's note].
5. A cow fed for slaughter. [Pringle's note].

I got a sad fright, that night. I was just going to sleep, when I heard a noise in my mistress's room; and she presently called out to inquire if some work was finished that she had ordered Hetty to do. "No, Ma'am, not yet," was Hetty's answer from below. On hearing this, my master started up from his bed, and just as he was, in his shirt, ran down stairs with a long cow-skin in his hand.[6] I heard immediately after, the cracking of the thong, and the house rang to the shrieks of poor Hetty, who kept crying out, "Oh, Massa! Massa! me dead. Massa! have mercy upon me—don't kill me outright."—This was a sad beginning for me. I sat up upon my blanket, trembling with terror, like a frightened hound, and thinking that my turn would come next. At length the house became still, and I forgot for a little while all my sorrows by falling fast asleep.

The next morning my mistress set about instructing me in my tasks. She taught me to do all sorts of household work; to wash and bake, pick cotton and wool, and wash floors, and cook. And she taught me (how can I ever forget it!) more things than these; she caused me to know the exact difference between the smart of the rope, the cart-whip, and the cow-skin, when applied to my naked body by her own cruel hand. And there was scarcely any punishment more dreadful than the blows I received on my face and head from her hard heavy fist. She was a fearful woman, and a savage mistress to her slaves.

There were two little slave boys in the house, on whom she vented her bad temper in a special manner. One of these children was a mulatto,[7] called Cyrus, who had been bought while an infant in his mother's arms; the other, Jack, was an African from the coast of Guinea, whom a sailor had given or sold to my master. Seldom a day passed without these boys receiving the most severe treatment, and often for no fault at all. Both my master and mistress seemed to think that they had a right to ill-use them at their pleasure; and very often accompanied their commands with blows, whether the children were behaving well or ill. I have seen their flesh ragged and raw with licks.—Lick—lick—they were never secure one moment from a blow, and their lives were passed in continual fear. My mistress was not contented with using the whip, but often pinched their cheeks and arms in the most cruel manner. My pity for these poor boys was soon transferred to myself; for I was licked, and flogged, and pinched by her pitiless fingers in the neck and arms, exactly as they were. To strip me naked—to hang me up by the wrists and lay my flesh open with the cow-skin, was an ordinary punishment for even a slight offence. My mistress often robbed me too of the hours that belong to sleep. She used to sit up very late, frequently even until morning; and I had then to stand at a bench and wash during the greater part of the night, or pick wool and cotton; and often I have dropped down overcome by sleep and fatigue, till roused from a state of stupor by the whip, and forced to start up to my tasks.

Poor Hetty, my fellow slave, was very kind to me, and I used to call her my Aunt; but she led a most miserable life, and her death was hastened (at least the slaves all believed and said so), by the dreadful chastisement she received from my master during her pregnancy. It happened as follows. One of the cows had dragged the rope away from the stake to which Hetty had fastened it, and got loose. My master flew into a terrible passion, and ordered the poor creature to be stripped quite naked, notwithstanding her pregnancy, and to be tied up to a tree in the yard. He then flogged her as hard as he could lick, both with the whip and cow-skin, till she was all

---

6. A thong of hard twisted hide, known by this name in the West Indies [Pringle's note].

7. A person of mixed African and Caucasion descent.

over streaming with blood. He rested, and then beat her again and again. Her shrieks were terrible. The consequence was that poor Hetty was brought to bed before her time, and was delivered after severe labour of a dead child. She appeared to recover after her confinement, so far that she was repeatedly flogged by both master and mistress afterwards; but her former strength never returned to her. Ere long her body and limbs swelled to a great size; and she lay on a mat in the kitchen, till the water burst out of her body and she died. All the slaves said that death was a good thing for poor Hetty; but I cried very much for her death. The manner of it filled me with horror. I could not bear to think about it; yet it was always present to my mind for many a day.

After Hetty died all her labours fell upon me, in addition to my own. I had now to milk eleven cows every morning before sunrise, sitting among the damp weeds; to take care of the cattle as well as the children; and to do the work of the house. There was no end to my toils—no end to my blows. I lay down at night and rose up in the morning in fear and sorrow; and often wished that like poor Hetty I could escape from this cruel bondage and be at rest in the grave. But the hand of God whom then I knew not, was stretched over me; and I was mercifully preserved for better things. It was then, however, my heavy lot to weep, weep, weep, and that for years; to pass from one misery to another, and from one cruel master to a worse. But I must go on with the thread of my story.

One day a heavy squall of wind and rain came on suddenly, and my mistress sent me round the corner of the house to empty a large earthen jar. The jar was already cracked with an old deep crack that divided it in the middle, and in turning it upside down to empty it, it parted in my hand. I could not help the accident, but I was dreadfully frightened, looking forward to a severe punishment. I ran crying to my mistress, "O mistress, the jar has come in two." "You have broken it, have you?" she replied; "come directly here to me." I came trembling; she stripped and flogged me long and severely with the cow-skin; as long as she had strength to use the lash, for she did not give over till she was quite tired.—When my master came home at night, she told him of my fault; and oh, frightful! how he fell a swearing. After abusing me with every ill name he could think of, (too, too bad to speak in England,) and giving me several heavy blows with his hand, he said, "I shall come home to-morrow morning at twelve, on purpose to give you a round hundred." He kept his word—Oh sad for me! I cannot easily forget it. He tied me up upon a ladder, and gave me a hundred lashes with his own hand, and master Benjy[8] stood by to count them for him. When he had licked me for some time he sat down to take breath; then after resting, he beat me again and again, until he was quite wearied, and so hot (for the weather was very sultry), that he sank back in his chair, almost like to faint. While my mistress went to bring him drink, there was a dreadful earthquake.[9] Part of the roof fell down, and every thing in the house went—clatter, clatter, clatter. Oh I thought the end of all things near at hand; and I was so sore with the flogging, that I scarcely cared whether I lived or died. The earth was groaning and shaking; every thing tumbling about; and my mistress and the slaves were shrieking and crying out, "The earthquake! the earthquake!" It was an awful day for us all. * * *

Some little time after this, one of the cows got loose from the stake, and eat one of the sweet-potatoe slips.[1] I was milking when my master found it out. He came to me, and without any more ado, stooped down, and taking off his heavy boot, he struck

---

8. Captain I—'s son, about Prince's age.   1. A cutting, rooted and planted.
9. An earthquake shook Bermuda on 19 February 1801.

me such a severe blow in the small of my back, that I shrieked with agony, and thought I was killed; and I feel a weakness in that part to this day. The cow was frightened at his violence, and kicked down the pail and spilt the milk all about. My master knew that this accident was his own fault, but he was so enraged that he seemed glad of an excuse to go on with his ill usage. I cannot remember how many licks he gave me then, but he beat me till I was unable to stand, and till he himself was weary.

After this I ran away and went to my mother, who was living with Mr. Richard Darrel.[2] My poor mother was both grieved and glad to see me; grieved because I had been so ill used, and glad because she had not seen me for a long, long while. She dared not receive me into the house, but she hid me up in a hole in the rocks near, and brought me food at night, after every body was asleep. My father, who lived at Crow-Lane, over the salt-water channel, at last heard of my being hid up in the cavern, and he came and took me back to my master. Oh I was loth, loth to go back; but as there was no remedy, I was obliged to submit.

When we got home, my poor father said to Cap. I——, "Sir, I am sorry that my child should be forced to run away from her owner; but the treatment she has received is enough to break her heart. The sight of her wounds has nearly broke mine.—I entreat you, for the love of God, to forgive her for running away, and that you will be a kind master to her in future." Capt. I—— said I was used as well as I deserved, and that I ought to be punished for running away. I then took courage and said that I could stand the floggings no longer; that I was weary of my life, and therefore I had run away to my mother; but mothers could only weep and mourn over their children, they could not save them from cruel masters—from the whip, the rope, and the cow-skin. He told me to hold my tongue and go about my work, or he would find a way to settle me. He did not, however, flog me that day.

━━◆☰◆━━

Thomas Bellamy
1745–1800

Thomas Bellamy had various careers, as a hosier, a bookseller's clerk, magazine publisher, writer, and proprietor of a circulating library. In 1789 he wrote *The Benevolent Planters* in support of the anti-abolitionist West Indian lobby. Staged at the Theatre Royal, Haymarket, with some of the leading actors of the day, his playlet presents a world of kindly paternal masters whose slaves proclaim their happiness and gratitude.

The Benevolent Planters
A Dramatic Piece

Scene, Jamaica

Characters
Planters: GOODWIN, STEADY, HEARTFREE
Slaves: ORAN, SELIMA
Archers, &c. &c.

---

2. Captain Darrell had purchased Prince and her mother, and then gave Prince to his daughter-in-law, Mrs. Williams.

Prologue (By a Friend)[1]

AN AFRICAN SAILOR   To Afric's torrid clime, where every day
                    The sun oppresses with his scorching ray,
                    My birth I owe; and here for many a year,
                    I tasted pleasure free from every care.
5   There 'twas my happy fortune long to prove
                    The fond endearments of parental love.
                    'Twas there my Adela, my favourite maid,
                    Return'd my passion, love with love repaid.
                    Oft on the banks where golden rivers flow,
10   And aromatic woods enchanting grow,
                    With my lov'd Adela I pass'd the day,
                    While suns on suns roll'd unperceiv'd away.
                    But ah! this happiness was not to last,
                    Clouds now the brightness of my fate o'ercast;
15   For the white savage fierce upon me sprung,
                    Wrath in his eye, and fury on his tongue,
                    And dragg'd me to a loathsome vessel near,
                    Dragg'd me from every thing I held most dear,
                    And plung'd me in the horrors of despair.
20   Insensible to all that pass'd around,
                    Till, in a foreign clime, myself I found,
                    And sold to slavery!—There with constant toil,
                    Condemn'd in burning suns to turn the soil.
                    Oh! if I told you what I suffer'd there,
25   From cruel masters, and the lash severe,
                    Eyes most unus'd to melt, would drop the tear.
                    But fortune soon a kinder master gave,
                    Who made me soon forget I was a slave,
                    And brought me to this land, this generous land,°   Jamaica
30   Where, they inform me, that an hallow'd band,
                    Impelled by soft humanity's kind laws,
                    Take up with fervent zeal the Negroe's cause,
                    And at this very moment, anxious try,
                    To stop the widespread woes of slavery.
35   But of this hallow'd band a part appears,
                    Exult my heart, and flow my grateful tears.
                    Oh sons of mercy! whose extensive mind
                    Takes in at once the whole of human kind,
                    Who know the various nations of the earth,
40   To whatsoever clime they owe their birth,
                    Or of whatever colour they appear,
                    All children of one gracious Parent are.
                    And thus united by paternal love,
                    To all mankind, of all the friend you prove.
45   With fervent zeal pursue your godlike plan,
                    And man deliver from the tyrant man!
                    What tho' at first you miss the wish'd-for end,

1. Spoken by John Philip Kemble, a leading tragic actor, as "An African Sailor." In the play Kemble performed Olah, whose beloved, Selima, was performed by his wife.

Success at last your labours will attend.
Then shall your worth, extoll'd in grateful strains,
50   Resound through Gambia's and Angola's plains.[2]
Nations unborn your righteous zeal shall bless,
To them the source of peace and happiness.
Oh mighty Kannoah, thou most holy power,
Whom humbly we thy sable race adore!
55   Prosper the great design—thy children free
From the oppressor's hand, and give them liberty!

Scene 1

A Room in Goodwin's House; Enter Goodwin, meeting Steady and Heartfree.

GOODWIN Good morrow, neighbours, friend Steady,[3] is your jetty tribe ready for the diversions?

STEADY My tribe is prepared and ready to meet thine, and my heart exults on beholding so many happy countenances. But an added joy is come home to my bosom. This English friend, who, some time since, came to settle among us, in order that he might exhibit to his brother Planters, the happy effects of humanity, in the treatment of those who, in the course of human chance, are destined to the bonds of slavery, has honoured my dwelling with his presence, and gladdened my heart with his friendship.

HEARTFREE A cause like the present, makes brothers of us all, and may heaven increase the brothers of humanity—Friend Steady informs me, that we are to preside as directors of the different diversions.

GOODWIN It is our wish to prevent a repetition of disorders, that last year disturbed the general happiness. They were occasioned by the admission of one of those games, which, but too often, begin in sport, and end in passion. The offenders, however, were soon made sensible of the folly of attacking each other without provocation, and with no other view than to shew their superior skill, in an art, which white men have introduced among them.[4]

HEARTFREE If that art was only made use of as a defence against the attacks of an unprincipled and vulgar violence, no man could with propriety form a wish of checking its progress. But while it opens another field where the gambler fills his pocket at the expence of the credulous and unsuspecting, whose families too often mourn in poverty and distress the effects of their folly; every member of society will hold up his hand against it, if his heart feels as it ought. I am sorry likewise to add, that too many recent instances of its fatal effects among my own countrymen, have convinced me of the guilt and folly of venturing *a life* to display *a skill*.

GOODWIN We are happy to find our union strengthened by corresponding sentiments.

HEARTFREE The sports, I find, are to continue six days; repeat your design, respecting the successful archers.

STEADY The archers, friend, to the number of twelve, consist of selected slaves, whose honest industry and attachment have rendered them deserving of reward. They are to advance in pairs, and the youth who speeds the arrow surest, is to be proclaimed victor.

2. Gambia: northwest African country, with a strong British colonial presence. Angola: Portuguese colony on the southwest coast.
3. "Friend" evokes the Quaker term of address; Bellamy may be trying to suggest that not all Quakers were adamant abolitionists.
4. Perhaps boxing or duelling.

HEARTFREE And what is his reward?

STEADY A portion of land for himself, and his posterity—freedom for his life, and the maiden of his heart.

HEARTFREE Generous men! humanity confers dignity upon authority. The grateful Africans have hearts as large as ours, and shame on the degrading lash, when it can be spared—Reasonable obedience is what we expect, and let those who look for more, feel and severely feel the sting of disappointment.

STEADY Will your poor fellow attend the festival?

HEARTFREE He will. I respect your feelings for the sorrows of the worthy Oran.

GOODWIN Oran, did you say? What know you of him; pardon my abruptness, but relate his story, it may prove a task of pleasure.

HEARTFREE By the fate of war,[5] Oran had been torn from his beloved Selima. The conquerors were on the point of setting fire to the consuming pile to which he was bound, while the partner of his heart, who was devoted[6] to the arms of the chief of the adverse party, was rending the air with her cries; at this instant a troop of Europeans broke in upon them, and bore away a considerable party to their ships; among the rest was the rescued Oran, who was happily brought to our mart, where I had the good fortune to become his master—he has since served me well and affectionately. But sorrow for his Selima is so deeply rooted in his feeling bosom, that I fear I shall soon lose an excellent domestic and as valuable a friend, whose only consolation springs from a sense of dying in the possession of Christian principles, from whence he acknowledges to have drawn comforts inexpressible.

GOODWIN And comfort he shall still draw from a worldly as well as a heavenly source. For know, I can produce the Selima he mourns. She has told me her story, which is indeed a tale of woe. Inward grief has preyed upon her mind, and like her faithful Oran, she is bending to her grave. But happiness, love, and liberty shall again restore them.

HEARTFREE When the mind has made itself up to misery—discoveries admitting of more than hope, ought ever to be made with caution. But you have a heart to feel for the distress of another, and conduct to guide you in giving relief to sorrow; leave me to my poor fellow, and do you prepare his disconsolate partner.

GOODWIN I'll see her immediately, and when we take our seats on the plain of sports, we will communicate to each other the result of our considerations.

STEADY Till then, my worthy associates, farewell. [*Exeunt*]

Scene II

Another Apartment in Goodwin's house. Enter Goodwin and Selima.

GOODWIN Come, my poor disconsolate, be composed, and prepare to meet your friends on those plains, where you never shall experience sorrow; but on the contrary, enjoy every happiness within the power of thy grateful master to bestow; you once told me, Selima, that my participation of your griefs abated their force; will you then indulge me with that pleasing tho' mournful Song you have made, on the loss of him, who, perhaps, may one day be restored?

SELIMA Good and generous Master! ever consoling me with hope, can I deny you who have given me mind, taught me your language, comforted me with the

---

5. Tribal warfare in Africa.   6. Destined.

knowledge of books, and made me every thing I am? Prepared too, my soul for joys, which you say are to succeed the patient bearing of human misery. Oh, Sir, with what inward satisfaction do I answer a request in every way grateful to my feelings!

SONG. SET TO MUSIC BY MR. REEVE[7]

How vain to me the hours of ease,
　　When every daily toil is o'er;
In my sad heart no hope I find,
　　For Oran is, alas! no more.

Not sunny Africa could please,
　　Nor friends upon my native shore,
To me the dreary world's a cave,
　　For Oran is, alas! no more.

In bowers of bliss beyond the moon,
　　The white man says, his sorrow's o'er,
And comforts me with soothing hope,
　　Tho' Oran is, alas, no more.

O come then, messenger of death,
　　Convey me to yon starry shore,
Where I may meet with my true love,
　　And never part with Oran more.

GOODWIN There's my kind Selima! and now attend to a discovery, on which depends your future happiness; not only liberty, but love awaits you.
SELIMA The first I want not—the last can never be! for where shall I find another Oran?
GOODWIN O my good girl, your song of sorrow shall be changed into that of gladness. For know—the hours of anguish are gone by, your Oran lives, and lives but to bless his faithful Selima.
SELIMA [after a pause] To that invisible Being who has sustained my suffering heart, I kneel, overwhelmed with an awful[8] sense of his protecting power. But how?
GOODWIN As we walk on, I will explain every thing. You soon will embrace your faithful Oran, and his beloved Selima shall mourn no more. [Exeunt.]

Scene III

An open Plain.
　　[On one side a range of men-slaves; on the other a range of women-slaves—at some distance, seated on decorated chairs, Heartfree, Goodwin, and Steady—twelve archers close the line on the men-side, meeting the audience with Oran at their head, distinguished from the rest by a rich dress—Oran, advancing to the front of the stage, stands in a dejected posture.]

HEARTFREE Now let the air echo to the sound of the enlivening instruments, and beat the ground to their tuneful melody; while myself and my two worthy friends,

7. William Reeve (1757–1815), actor and composer.　　8. Awe-filled.

who since our last festival have reaped the benefit of your honest labours, in full goblets drink to your happiness.

[*Flourish of music, and a dance.*]

HEARTFREE Now let the archers advance in pairs, and again, in replenished cups, health and domestic peace to those who surest speed the arrow.

[*Flourish. Here the archers advance in pairs to the middle of the Stage, and discharge their arrows through the side wings—the victor is saluted by two female slaves, who present to him the maiden of his choice—then a flourish of music, and the parties fall back to the side. After the ceremony has been repeated five times to as many pair of archers, and Oran and Almaboe only remain to advance as the sixth pair, Oran appears absorbed in grief, which is observed with evident concern by Heartfree.*]

HEARTFREE Why Oran, with looks divided between earth and heaven, dost thou appear an alien among those who are encompassed with joy and gladness? Though your beloved Selima is torn from your widowed arms, yet it is a duty you owe yourself, as a man, an obligation due to me, as your friend, to take to your bosom one whom I have provided for you. A contest with Almaboe is needless; he has fixed on his partner, to whom, according to your request, he is now presented. [*A flourish of music—two female slaves advance with a third, who is presented to Almaboe—the parties embrace.*] It remains, therefore, for you to comply with the wishes of those who honour your virtues, and have respected your sorrows.

ORAN Kind and benevolent masters; I indeed came hither unwillingly, to draw the bow, with a heart already pierced with the arrow of hopeless anguish. You have done generously by my friend, to whom I meant to have relinquished the victor's right, had the chance been mine. For alas, Sirs! Selima was my first and only love; and when I lost her, joy fled from a bosom it will never again revisit. The short date of my existence is therefore devoted alone to that Power whom you have taught me to revere. Sacred to gratitude, and sacred to her whose beckoning spirit seems at this moment to call on me from yonder sky—

GOODWIN What say you, Oran, if I should produce a maiden whose virtues will bring you comfort, and whose affection you will find as strong as hers, whose loss you so feelingly deplore?

ORAN O Sirs! had you but known my Selima, you would not attempt to produce her equal! Poor lost excellence! Yes, thy spirit, released from all its sufferings, is now looking down upon its Oran! But let not imagination too far transport me: perhaps she yet lives, a prey to brutal lust. [*Turns to Almaboe.*] Brother of my choice, and friend of my adverse hour, long may your Coanzi be happy in the endearments of her faithful Almaboe. And O my friend! when thy poor Oran is no more, if [it] chance that Selima yet lives, if blessed Providence *should* lead her to these happy shores, if she should escape the cruel enemy, and be brought hither with honour unsullied;[9] tell her how much she owes to these generous men; comfort her afflicted spirit, and teach her to adore the God of truth and mercy.

---

9. Not sexually compromised either by rape or forced consent.

ALMABOE Oran must himself endeavour to live for that day, and not by encouraging despair, sink self-devoted to the grave.[1] The same Providence, my friend, which has turned the terrors of slavery into willing bondage, may yet restore thy Selima.

ORAN The words of Almaboe come charged with the force of truth, and erring Oran bends to offended Heaven! Yet erring Oran must still feel his loss, and erring Oran must for ever lament it.

GOODWIN It is true, Oran, our arguments to urge thee to be happy, have hitherto proved fruitless. But know, thou man of sorrow, we are possessed of the means which will restore thee to thyself and to thy friends. Hear, then, the important secret, and know, that thy Selima yet lives!

ORAN [after a pause] Yet lives! Selima yet lives! what my Selima! my own dear angel! O speak again, your words have visited my heart, and it is lost in rapture.

HEARTFREE Nay, Oran, but be calm.

ORAN I am calm—Heaven will permit me to support my joy, but do you relieve me from suspence.

GOODWIN Let the instruments breathe forth the most pleasing strains—Advance, my happy virgins, with your charge, and restore to Oran his long-lost Selima. You receive her pure as when you parted, with a mind released from the errors of darkness, and refined by its afflictions.

[Soft music—Selima comes down the stage, attended by six virgins in fancied dresses, who present her to Oran—the lovers embrace—flourish of music, and a shout.]

ORAN Lost in admiration, gratitude, and love, Oran has no words, but can only in silence own the hand of Heaven; while to his beating heart he clasps his restored treasure. And O my masters! for such, though free, suffer me still to call you; let my restored partner and myself bend to such exalted worth; while for ourselves, and for our surrounding brethren, we declare, that you have proved yourselves *The Benevolent Planters*, and that under subjection like yours,

SLAVERY IS BUT A NAME

SONG. TO THE TUNE OF *RULE BRITANNIA*.[2]

In honour of this happy day,
    Let Afric's sable sons rejoice;
To mercy we devote the lay,
    To heaven-born mercy raise the voice.
Long may she reign, and call each heart her own,
And nations guard her sacred throne.

Fair child of heaven, our rites approve,
    With smiles attend the votive song,
Inspire with universal love,
    For joy and peace to thee belong.
Long may'st thou reign, and call each heart thy own,
While nations guard thy sacred throne.

---

1. By suicide; "devoted" means "doomed."

2. A famous song, written by James Thomson in 1740, with music by Thomas Arne.

⊢ ⋈ ⊣

William Cowper
1731–1800

The son of a rector and a mother who traced her descent to Henry III and John Donne, Cowper was beset through his life with manic, sometimes suicidal depressions, aggravated by his attraction to sects emphasizing man's original sin. He studied law but found poetry more congenial, and with the Evangelical minister and abolitionist John Newton published a volume of hymns in 1779, including Newton's great hymn *Amazing Grace*. He followed with a series of moral satires in the early 1780s, and his most famous poem, *The Task* (1785), whose second book opens with a strong critique of slavery. Feeling deeply the moral blight of slavery as an institution sustained only by greed, Cowper responded to Wilberforce's call for popular abolitionist literature with four ballads in 1788 that were widely reprinted. The poet of *The Morning Dream* envisions the goddess Britannia sailing west to a "slave-cultured island" to confront the cruel "Demon" of slave-ownership, who sickens and dies at her sight; the balladeer of *Pity for Poor Africans*, insisting that he is "shock'd at the purchase of slaves," justifies his participation by arguing that foreigners will not give up the trade: "He shar'd in the plunder, but he pitied the man." *Sweet Meat Has Sour Sauce: or, The Slave-Trader in the Dumps*, printed here, is the ditty of a trader lamenting the inevitable abolition of his business and trying to unload his gear. And *The Negro's Complaint*, the most popular of the group in part because of its stark wood-cut illustrations, doubly refutes the view of slaves as subhuman: its slave-speaker not only expresses his own profound humanity but also exposes the inhumanity of the "iron-hearted" masters, whom he calls "slaves of gold." Cowper grew so depressed with his involvement in the slavery issue that eventually he had to stop writing about it. His last poem, written shortly before his death, is the beautifully melancholy *The Castaway* (see page 1242).

Sweet Meat Has Sour Sauce
or, The Slave-Trader in the Dumps

> A trader I am to the African shore,
> But since that my trading is like to be o'er,
> I'll sing you a song that you ne'er heard before,
>   Which nobody can deny, deny,
> 5   Which nobody can deny.
>
> When I first heard the news it gave me a shock,
> Much like what they call an electrical knock,
> And now I am going to sell off my stock,
>   Which nobody can deny.
>
> 10   'Tis a curious assortment of dainty regales,°   *choice pieces*
> To tickle the Negroes with when the ship sails—
> Fine chains for the neck, and a cat with nine tails,[1]
>   Which nobody can deny.
>
> Here's supple-jack plenty, and store of rat-tan,[2]
> 15   That will wind itself round the sides of a man,
> As close as a hoop round a bucket or can,
>   Which nobody can deny.

1. Cat-o'-nine-tails: a whip made with nine knotted lashes.

2. Both supple-jack (a woody vine) and rattan (a climbing palm) were used to make whips, canes, and ropes.

Here's padlocks and bolts, and screws for the thumbs,
That squeeze them so lovingly till the blood comes;
20 They sweeten the temper like comfits or plums,
        Which nobody can deny.

When a Negro his head from his victuals withdraws,
And clenches his teeth and thrusts out his paws,
Here's a notable engine to open his jaws,[3]
25   Which nobody can deny.

Thus going to market, we kindly prepare
A pretty black cargo of African ware,
For what they must meet with when they get there,
        Which nobody can deny.

30 'Twould do your heart good to see 'em below
Lie flat on their backs all the way as we go,[4]
Like sprats on a gridiron, scores in a row,[5]
        Which nobody can deny.

But ah! if in vain I have studied an art
35 So gainful to me, all boasting apart,
I think it will break my compassionate heart,
        Which nobody can deny.

For oh! how it enters my soul like an awl!
This pity, which some people self-pity call,
40 Is sure the most heart-piercing pity of all,
        Which nobody can deny.

So this is my song, as I told you before;
Come, buy off my stock, for I must no more
Carry Caesars and Pompeys to Sugar-cane shore,[6]
45   Which nobody can deny, deny,
        Which nobody can deny.

Hannah More
1745–1833

Poet and essayist More published 114 Cheap Repository Tracts between 1795 and 1798. With simple language cast into stories, ballads, poems, dialogues, sermons, prayers, parables, and moral tales, she strove, with an Evangelical view, "to improve the habits, and raise the principles of the common people . . . not only to counteract vice and profligacy on the one hand, but error, discontent, and false religion on the other." Among her concerns were quelling political discontent and class antagonisms and shaping public opinion in favor of abolition. Priced at a halfpenny, and marketed not only in shops but also at fairs and on street corners, the Tracts sold quickly and

---

3. Force-feeding of a slave meaning to starve to death.
4. A reference to the tortuous tight-packing of slave-cargo; see illustration, page 1462.
5. Sprats are herrings (metaphorically, insignificant people); a gridiron is a griddle—an image of slaves cooking

in hot cargo-holds.
6. Caesar and Pompey were famous ancient Romans (many slaves were royalty in their African cultures); "Sugar-cane shore" is the West Indies.

widely, over two million in the first year alone. They were purchased in bulk by preachers for their congregations, landlords for their tenants and laborers, and missionaries for their work in Africa and India, and disseminated in hospitals, prisons, the armed forces, and the workhouses.

More had first treated the issue in *Slavery: A Poem* (1788), a 356-line polemical oration aimed at creating support for Wilberforce in Parliament. Eager to involve a popular audience, she devoted four of her Tracts to slavery. The most popular and most frequently reprinted were *The Sorrows of Yamba* (More's authorship is debated) and *The Black Prince*, perhaps coauthored by More and her mentor John Newton, whose own *Authentic Narrative* (1764) vividly recounted his conversion from slave-trading to Evangelical Christianity and abolition. The Tracts repeat such a conversion in the lives of the slaves. When the tortured slavewoman Yamba attempts suicide, she is prevented by a missionary who converts her to Christianity, teaching her patient endurance and ultimate salvation.

An additional work by More is included in A "Vindication" in Context: The Wollstonecraft Controversy and the Rights of Women, page 1497.

The Sorrows of Yamba
or, The Negro Woman's Lamentation

In St. Lucia's distant isle,[1]
   Still with Afric's love I burn;
Parted many a thousand mile,
   Never, never to return.

5 Come, kind death! and give me rest;
   Yamba has no friend but thee;
Thou canst ease my throbbing breast;
   Thou canst set the Prisoner free.

Down my cheeks the tears are dripping,
10   Broken is my heart with grief;
Mangled my poor flesh with whipping,
   Come, kind death, and bring relief.

Born on Afric's golden coast,[2]
   Once I was as blest as you;
15 Parents tender I could boast,
   Husband dear, and children too.

Whity man he came from far,
   Sailing o'er the briny flood;
Who with help of British Tar,°   *seaman*
20   Buys up human flesh and blood.

With the baby at my breast
   (Other too were sleeping by)
In my hut I sat at rest,
   With no thought of danger nigh.

25 From the brush at even-tide,
   Rush'd the fierce man-stealing crew;
Seiz'd the children by my side,
   Seiz'd the wretched Yamba too.

---

1. In the British West Indies.
2. An evocation of an idyllic world (golden age) and iron-

ically a naming of "Gold Coast," a British West African colony (now Ghana) trading chiefly in gold and slaves.

Then for love of filthy gold,
30   Strait they bore me to the sea,
Cramm'd me down a slave-ship's hold,
      Where were hundreds stow'd like me.

Naked on the platform lying,
      Now we cross the tumbling wave;
35 Shrieking, sickening, fainting, dying;
      Deed of shame for Britons brave!

At the savage Captain's beck,
      Now, like brutes, they make us prance;
Smack the cat° about the deck,   *whip*
40   And in scorn they make us dance.

Nauseous horse-beans they bring nigh,
      Sick and sad we cannot eat;
Cat must cure the sulks, they cry,
      Down their throats we'll force the meat.[3]

45 I, in groaning pass'd the night,
      And did roll my aching head;
At the break of morning light
      My poor child was cold and dead.

Happy, happy, there she lies;
50   Thou shalt feel the lash no more;
Thus full many a Negro dies,
      Ere we reach the destin'd shore.

Thee, sweet infant, none shall sell;
      Thou hast gain'd a wat'ry grave;
55 Clean escap'd the tyrants fell,°   *fierce*
      While thy mother lives a slave.

Driven like cattle to a fair,
      See, they sell us, young and old;
Child from mother too they tear,
60   All for love of filthy gold.

I was sold to Massa° hard,   Master
      Some have Massas kind and good:
And again my back was scarr'd,
      Bad and stinted was my food.

65 Poor and wounded, faint and sick,
      All expos'd to burning sky,
Massa bids me grass to pick,
      And I now am near to die.

What, and if to death he send me,
70   Savage murder tho' it be,
British laws shall not befriend me,
      They protect not slaves like me.

---

3. Forced feeding; horse-beans are food for horses.

Mourning thus my wretched state
   (Ne'er may I forget the day)
75   Once in dusk of evening late,
   Far from home I dar'd to stray.

Dar'd, alas! with impious haste,
   Tow'rds the roaring sea to fly;
Death itself I longed to taste,
80   Long'd to cast me in and die.

There I met upon the Strand,
   English missionary good;
He had Bible book in hand;
   Which poor me no understand.

85   Led by pity from afar,
   He had left his native ground;
Thus, if some inflict a scar,
   Others fly to cure the wound.

Strait he pull'd me from the shore,
90   Bid me no self-murder do;
Talk'd of state when life is o'er,
   All from Bible good and true.

Then he led me to his cot,°   cottage
   Sooth'd and pity'd all my woe;
95   Told me 'twas the Christian's lot
   Much to suffer here below.

Told me then of God's dear Son
   (Strange and wondrous is the Story)
What sad wrong to him was done,
100   Tho' he was the Lord of Glory.

Told me too, like one who knew him
   (Can such love as this be true?)
How he died for them that slew him,
   Died for wretched Yamba too.

105   Freely he his mercy proffer'd
   And to Sinners he was sent;
E'en to Massa pardon's offered;
   O, if Massa would repent!

Wicked deed full many a time,
110   Sinful Yamba too hath done;
But she wails to God her crime,
   But she trusts his only Son.

O, ye slaves whom Massas beat,
   Ye are stain'd with guilt within;
115   As ye hope for Mercy sweet,
   So forgive your Massas' sin.
           * * *

125 Now I'll bless my cruel capture
  (Hence I've known a Saviour's name)
 Till my grief is turn'd to rapture,
  And I half forget the blame.

 But tho' here a convert rare
130 Thanks her God for Grace divine;
 Let not man the glory share:
  Sinner still the guilt is thine.

 Here an injur'd Slave forgives,
  There a host for vengeance cry;
135 Here a single Yamba lives,
  There a thousand droop and die.

 Only now baptiz'd am I,
  By good Missionary man:
 Lord, my nature purify,
140 As no outward water can!
   * * *
 But tho' death this hour may find me,
  Still with Afric's love I burn;
155 (There I've left a spouse behind me)
  Still to native land I turn.

 And when Yamba sinks in death,
  This my latest prayer shall be,
 While I yield my parting breath,
160 *O, that Afric might be free!*

 Cease, ye British sons of murder!
  Cease from forging Afric's chain:
 Mock your Saviour's name no further,
  Cease your savage lust of gain.

165 Ye that boast *"Ye rule the waves,"*
  Bid no Slave-ship soil the sea;
 Ye, that *"never will be slaves,"*
  Bid poor Afric's land be free.[4]

 Where ye gave to war its birth,
170 Where your traders fix'd their den,
 There go publish *"Peace on Earth,"*
  Go, proclaim *"good will to men."*[5]

 Where ye once have carried slaughter,
  Vice, and slavery, and sin;
175 Seiz'd on Husband, Wife, and Daughter,
  Let the Gospel enter in.

 Thus, where Yamba's native home,
  Humble hut of rushes stood;
 Oh, if there should chance to roam
180 Some dear Missionary good;

---

4. The quotations are from the British imperialist hymn, *Rule Britannia*. See also page 1449.

5. Quoting the angels' proclamation of the birth of Jesus in Luke (2.14).

Tho' in Afric's distant land,
 Still shalt see the man I love;
Join him to the Christian band,
 Guide his soul to the realms above.

185 There no fiend again shall sever
 Those whom God hath join'd and blest:
There they dwell with him for ever,
 There *"the weary are at rest."*[6]

✦ ✦ ✦

Thomas Clarkson
1760–1846

"The grand mover of the main efforts for the abolition of the Slave Trade," in Dorothy Wordsworth's phrase, Thomas Clarkson was the hero of the movement. In 1785, while a student at Cambridge University, he wrote a prize-winning essay, *On the Slavery and Commerce of the Human Species,* its moral arguments supported with a litany of atrocities documented in the West Indies. When it was published in 1786, one slave owner protested, "I declare to God, I do not believe that a series of more abominable falsehoods ever blotted a page in the wide history of human depravity!" The next year, Clarkson joined with the English Quakers' Anti-Slavery Society, and at its behest began an arduous investigation of atrocities, centering his research in Bristol and Liverpool, whose merchants were financing and thriving on the trade. Often at great personal risk, Clarkson gathered detailed information, from the devastating effects on the seamen impressed into the brutal service, to the abuse of the slaves and the conditions aboard ship, to the conduct of the slave-markets. This labor supplied William Wilberforce with critical material for his Parliamentary campaign. In the 1790s, Clarkson traveled to France to urge the Revolutionary government to abolish its slave trade and colonial slavery, agitated in England for a boycott of West Indian sugar and tea, and continued to document the atrocities that the planters' lobby continued to deny and excoriate as falsehoods, working himself into physical collapse in 1794. His most famous work, the *History of . . . the Abolition of the African Slave-Trade* (1808), helped fuel the movement for the abolition of slavery itself, a cause in which Clarkson remained active.

from The History of the Rise, Progress, & Accomplishment of the Abolition of the African Slave-Trade by the British Parliament
["THE NATURE OF THE EVIL"]

This may be seen by examining it in three points of view: First, As it has been proved to arise on the continent of Africa in the course of reducing the inhabitants of it to slavery; Secondly, In the course of conveying them from thence to the lands or colonies of other nations; And, Thirdly, In continuing them there as slaves.

To see it as it has been shown to arise in the first case, let us suppose ourselves on the Continent just mentioned. Well then: We are landed; we are already upon our travels; we have just passed through one forest; we are now come to a more open place, which indicates an approach to habitations. And what object is that, which first obtrudes itself upon our sight? Who is that wretched woman, whom we discover under that noble tree, wringing her hands, and beating her breast, as if in the agonies

---

6. Job, tormented by Satan on a mission from God as a test of his faith, longs for death, where "the wicked cease from troubling; and . . . the weary be at rest" (3.17).

of despair? Three days has she been there at intervals to look and to watch, and this is the fourth morning, and no tidings of her children yet. Beneath its spreading boughs they were accustomed to play: But alas! the savage man-stealer interrupted their playful mirth, and has taken them for ever from her sight.

But let us leave the cries of this unfortunate woman, and hasten into another district: And what do we first see here? Who is he that just now started across the narrow pathway, as if afraid of a human face? What is that sudden rustling among the leaves? Why are those persons flying from our approach, and hiding themselves in yon darkest thicket? Behold, as we get into the plain, a deserted village! The rice-field has been just trodden down around it. An aged man, venerable by his silver beard, lies wounded and dying near the threshold of his hut. War, suddenly instigated by avarice, has just visited the dwellings which we see. The old have been butchered, because unfit for slavery, and the young have been carried off, except such as have fallen in the conflict, or have escaped among the woods behind us. * * *

Let us examine the state of the unhappy Africans, reduced to slavery in this manner, while on board the vessels, which are to convey them across the ocean to other lands. And here I must observe at once, that, as far as this part of the evil is concerned, I am at a loss to describe it. Where shall I find words to express properly their sorrow, as arising from the reflection of being parted for ever from their friends, their relatives, and their country? Where shall I find language to paint in appropriate colours the horror of mind brought on by thoughts of their future unknown destination, of which they can augur nothing but misery from all that they have yet seen? How shall I make known their situation, while labouring under painful disease, or while struggling in the suffocating holds of their prisons, like animals inclosed in an exhausted receiver?[1] How shall I describe their feelings as exposed to all the personal indignities, which lawless appetite or brutal passion may suggest? How shall I exhibit their sufferings as determining to refuse sustenance and die, or as resolving to break their chains, and, disdaining to live as slaves, to punish their oppressors? How shall I give an idea of their agony, when under various punishments and tortures for their reputed crimes? Indeed every part of this subject defies my powers, and I must therefore satisfy myself and the reader with a general representation, or in the words of a celebrated member of Parliament [Wilberforce], that "Never was so much human suffering condensed in so small a space."

I come now to the evil, as it has been proved to arise in the third case; or to consider the situation of the unhappy victims of the trade, when their painful voyages are over, or after they have been landed upon their destined shores. And here we are to view them first under the degrading light of cattle.[2] We are to see them examined, handled, selected, separated, and sold. Alas! relatives are separated from relatives, as if, like cattle, they had no rational intellect, no power of feeling the nearness of relationship, nor sense of the duties belonging to the ties of life! We are next to see them labouring, and this for the benefit of those, to whom they are under no obligation, by any law either natural or divine, to obey. We are to see them, if refusing the commands of their purchasers, however weary, or feeble, or indisposed, subject to corporal punishments, and, if forcibly resisting them, to death. We are to see them in a state of general degradation and misery. The knowledge, which their oppressors have of their own crime in having violated the rights of nature, and of the disposition of

1. Emptied tank.
2. Clarkson's analogy to cattle evokes "chattel," a syn-   onym for "slave" that shares an etymology with "cattle" and "capital."

the injured to seek all opportunities of revenge, produces a fear which dictates to them the necessity of a system of treatment by which they shall keep up a wide distinction between the two, and by which the noble feelings of the latter shall be kept down, and their spirits broken. We are to see them again subject to individual persecution, as anger, or malice, or any bad passion may suggest. Hence the whip; the chain; the iron-collar. Hence the various modes of private torture, of which so many accounts have been truly given. Nor can such horrible cruelties be discovered so as to be made punishable, while the testimony of any number of the oppressed is invalid against the oppressors, however they may be offences against the laws. And, lastly, we are to see their innocent offspring, against whose personal liberty the shadow of an argument cannot be advanced, inheriting all the miseries of their parents' lot.

* * * While the miseries endured by the unfortunate Africans excite our pity on the one hand, the vices, which are connected with them, provoke our indignation and abhorrence on the other. The Slave-trade, in this point of view, must strike us as an immense mass of evil on account of the criminality attached to it. * * * Is not that man made morally worse, who is induced to become a tyger to his species, or who, instigated by avarice, lies in wait in the thicket to get possession of his fellow-man? Is no injustice manifest in the land, where the prince, unfaithful to his duty, seizes his innocent subjects, and sells them for slaves? Are no moral evils produced among those communities, which make war upon other communities for the sake of plunder, and without any previous provocation or offence?

* * * The counterpart of the evil is to be seen in the conduct of those, who purchase the miserable natives in their own country, and convey them to distant lands. And here questions, similar to the former, may be asked. Do they experience no corruption of their nature, or become chargeable with no violation of right, who, when they go with their ships to this continent, know the enormities which their visits there will occasion, who buy their fellow-creature man, and this, knowing the way in which he comes into their hands, and who chain, and imprison, and scourge him? Do the moral feelings of those persons escape without injury, whose hearts are hardened? And can the hearts of those be otherwise than hardened, who are familiar with the tears and groans of innocent strangers forcibly torn away from every thing that is dear to them in life, who are accustomed to see them on board their vessels in a state of suffocation and in the agonies of despair, and who are themselves in the habits of the cruel use of arbitrary power?

The counterpart of the evil in its third branch is to be seen in the conduct of those, who, when these miserable people have been landed, purchase and carry them to their respective homes. And let us see whether a mass of wickedness is not generated also in the present case. Can those have nothing to answer for, who separate the faithful ties which nature and religion have created? Can their feelings be otherwise than corrupted, who consider their fellow-creatures as brutes, or treat those as cattle, who may become the temples of the Holy Spirit, and in whom the Divinity disdains not himself to dwell? Is there no injustice in forcing men to labour without wages? Is there no breach of duty, when we are commanded to clothe the naked, and feed the hungry, and visit the sick and in prison, in exposing them to want, in torturing them by cruel punishment, and in grinding them down by hard labour, so as to shorten their days? Is there no crime in adopting a system, which keeps down all the noble faculties of their souls, and which positively debases and corrupts their nature? Is there no crime in perpetuating these evils among their innocent offspring? And finally, besides all these crimes, is there not naturally in the familiar sight of the exercise, but more especially in the exercise itself, of uncontroulled power, that which vitiates the internal man? In seeing misery stalk daily over the land, do not all become insensibly hardened? By giving birth to that misery themselves, do they not become abandoned? In what state of society are the corrupt appetites so easily, so quickly, and so frequently indulged, and where else, by means of frequent indulgence, do these experience such a monstrous growth? Where else is the temper subject to such frequent irritation, or passion to such little controul? Yes; if the unhappy slave is in an unfortunate situation, so is the tyrant who holds him. ＊ ＊ ＊

＊ ＊ ＊ If we were to take the vast extent of space occupied by these crimes and sufferings from the heart of Africa to its shores, and that which they filled on the continent of America and the islands adjacent, and were to join the crimes and sufferings in one to those in the other by the crimes and sufferings which took place in the track of the vessels successively crossing the Atlantic, we should behold a vast belt as it were of physical and moral evil, reaching through land and ocean to the length of nearly half the circle of the globe.

[THE RECRUITMENT OF SEAMEN FOR THE SLAVE-SHIPS]

The young mariner if a stranger to the port [of Bristol] and unacquainted with the nature of the Slave-trade, was sure to be picked up. The novelty of the voyages, the superiority of the wages in this over any other trades, and the privileges of various kinds, were set before him. Gulled in this manner he was frequently enticed to the boat, which was waiting to carry him away. If these prospects did not attract him, he was plied with liquor till he became intoxicated, when a bargain was made over him between the landlord and the mate. After this his senses were kept in such a constant state of stupefaction by the liquor, that in time the former might do with him what he pleased. Seamen also were boarded in these houses, who, when the slave-ships were going out, but at no other time, were encouraged to spend more than they had money to pay for; and to these, when they had thus exceeded, but one alternative was given, namely, a slave-vessel, or a jail. These distressing scenes I found myself obliged frequently to witness, for I was no less than nineteen times occupied in making these hateful rounds. And I can say from my own experience, and all the information I could collect from Thompson and others, that no such practices were in use to obtain seamen for other trades.

The treatment of the seamen employed in the Slave-trade had so deeply interested me, and now the manner of procuring them, that I was determined to make myself acquainted with their whole history; for I found by report, that they were not only personally ill-treated, ＊ ＊ ＊ but that they were robbed by artifice of those wages, which had been held up to them as so superior in this service. ＊ ＊ ＊ On whatever branch of the system I turned my eyes, I found it equally barbarous. The trade was, in short, one mass of iniquity from the beginning to the end. ＊ ＊ ＊

In pursuing another object, which was that of going on board the slave-ships, and learning their construction and dimensions, I was greatly struck, and indeed affected, by the appearance of two little sloops, which were fitting out for Africa, the one of only twenty-five tons, which was said to be destined to carry seventy; and the other of only eleven, which was said to be destined to carry thirty slaves. I was told also that which was more affecting, namely, that these were not to act as tenders on the coast, by going up and down the rivers, and receiving three or four slaves at a time, and then carrying them to a large ship, which was to take them to the West

Indies, but that it was actually intended, that they should transport their own slaves themselves. * * * In the vessel of twenty-five tons, the length of the upper part of the hold, or roof, of the room, where the seventy slaves were to be stowed, was but little better than ten yards, or thirty-one feet. The greatest breadth of the bottom, or floor, was ten feet four inches, and the least five. Hence, a grown person must sit down all the voyage, and contract his limbs within the narrow limits of three square feet. In the vessel of eleven tons, the length of the room for the thirty slaves was twenty-two feet. The greatest breadth of the floor was eight, and the least four. The whole height from the keel to the beam was but five feet eight inches, three feet of which were occupied by ballast, cargo, and provisions, so that two feet eight inches remained only as the height between the decks. Hence, each slave would have only four square feet to sit in, and, when in this posture, his head, if he were a full-grown person, would touch the ceiling, or upper deck.

[CLARKSON'S NIGHTMARES]

At Bristol my feelings had been harassed by the cruel treatment of the seamen, which had come to my knowledge there: but now I was doomed to see this treatment over again in many other melancholy instances; and additionally to take in the various sufferings of the unhappy slaves. These accounts I could seldom get time to read till late in the evening, and sometimes not till midnight, when the letters containing them were to be answered. The effect of these accounts was in some instances to overwhelm me for a time in tears, and in others to produce a vivid indignation, which affected my whole frame. Recovering from these, I walked up and down the room. I felt fresh vigour, and made new determinations of perpetual warfare against this impious trade. I implored strength that I might proceed. I then sat down, and continued my work as long as my wearied eyes would permit me to see. Having been agitated in this manner, I went to bed: but my rest was frequently broken by the visions which floated before me. When I awoke, these renewed themselves to me, and they flitted about with me for the remainder of the day. Thus I was kept continually harassed: my mind was confined to one gloomy and heart-breaking subject for months. It had no respite, and my health began now materially to suffer.

[THE DEFENSE OF THE TRADE IN PARLIAMENT]

The public papers began to be filled with such statements as were thought most likely to influence the members of the house of commons, previously to the discussion of the question [bill for abolition].

The first impression attempted to be made upon them was with respect to the slaves themselves. It was contended, and attempted to be shown by the revival of the old argument of human sacrifices in Africa, that these were better off in the islands than in their own country. It was contended also, that they were people of very inferior capacities, and but little removed from the brute creation; whence an inference was drawn, that their treatment, against which so much clamour had arisen, was adapted to their intellect and feelings.

The next attempt was to degrade the abolitionists in the opinion of the house, by showing the wildness and absurdity of their schemes. It was again insisted upon that emancipation was the real object of the former; so that thousands of slaves would be let loose in the islands to rob or perish, and who could never be brought back again into habits of useful industry.

An attempt was then made to excite their pity in behalf of the planters. The abolition, it was said, would produce insurrections among the slaves. But insurrections would produce the massacre of their masters; and, if any of these should happily escape from butchery, they would be reserved only for ruin.

An appeal was then made to them on the ground of their own interest and of that of the people, whom they represented. It was stated that the ruin of the islands would be the ruin of themselves and of the country. Its revenue would be half annihilated. Its naval strength would decay. Merchants, manufacturers and others would come to beggary. But in this deplorable situation they would expect to be indemnified for their losses. Compensation indeed must follow. It could not be withheld. But what would be the amount of it? The country would have no less than from eighty to a hundred millions to pay the sufferers; and it would be driven to such distress in paying this sum as it had never before experienced.

The last attempt was to show them that a regulation of the trade was all that was now wanted. While this would remedy the evils complained of, it would prevent the mischief which would assuredly follow the abolition. The planters had already done their part. The assemblies of the different islands had most of them made wholesome laws upon the subject. The very bills passed for this purpose in Jamaica and Grenada had arrived in England, and might be seen by the public: the great grievances had been redressed: no slave could now be mutilated or wantonly killed by his owner; one man could not now maltreat, or bruise, or wound the slave of another; the aged could not now be turned off to perish by hunger. There were laws also relative to the better feeding and clothing of the slaves. It remained only that the trade to Africa should be put under as wise and humane regulations as the slavery in the islands had undergone.

[COUNTER-TESTIMONY FROM A SLAVE-SHIP INVESTIGATOR]

Having said thus much on the subject of procuring slaves in Africa, he would now go to that of the transportation of them. * * * This was the most wretched part of the whole subject. He was incapable of impressing the house with what he felt upon it. A description of their conveyance was impossible. So much misery condensed in so little room was more than the human imagination had ever before conceived. Think only of six hundred persons linked together, trying to get rid of each other, crammed in a close vessel with every object that was nauseous and disgusting, diseased, and struggling with all the varieties of wretchedness. It seemed impossible to add any thing more to human misery. Yet shocking as this description must be felt to be by every man, the transportation had been described by several witnesses from Liverpool to be a comfortable conveyance. Mr. Norris had painted the accommodations on board a slaveship in the most glowing colours. He had represented them in a manner which would have exceeded his attempts at praise of the most luxurious scenes. Their apartments, he said, were fitted up as advantageously for them as circumstances could possibly admit: they had several meals a day; some, of their own country provisions, with the best sauces of African cookery; and, by way of variety, another meal of pulse, according to the European taste. After breakfast they had water to wash themselves, while their apartments were perfumed with frankincense and lime-juice. Before dinner they were amused after the manner of their country: instruments of music were introduced: the song and the dance were promoted: games of chance were furnished them: the men played and sang, while the women

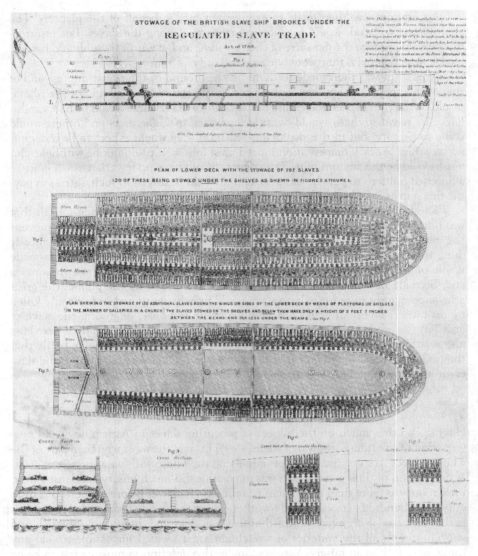

Packing methods on a slave ship. Illustration to *The History of the Rise, Progress, & Accomplishment of the Abolition of the African Slave-Trade by the British Parliament*, by Thomas Clarkson, 1808.

and girls made fanciful ornaments from beads, with which they were plentifully supplied. They were indulged in all their little fancies, and kept in sprightly humour. Another of them had said, when the sailors were flogged, it was out of the hearing of the Africans, lest it should depress their spirits. He by no means wished to say that such descriptions were wilful misrepresentations. If they were not, it proved that interest or prejudice was capable of spreading a film over the eyes thick enough to occasion total blindness.

Others, however, and these men of the greatest veracity, had given a different account. What would the house think, when by the concurring testimony of these the true history was laid open? The slaves who had been described as rejoicing in their captivity, were so wrung with misery at leaving their country, that it was the constant practice to set sail in the night, lest they should know the moment of their departure. With respect to their accommodation, the right ancle of one was fastened to the left ancle of another by an iron fetter; and if they were turbulent, by another on the wrists. Instead of the apartments described, they were placed in niches, and along the decks, in such a manner, that it was impossible for any one to pass among them, however careful he might be, without treading upon them. Sir George Yonge had testified, that in a slave-ship, on board of which he went, and which had not completed her cargo by two hundred and fifty, instead of the scent of frankincense being perceptible to the nostrils, the stench was intolerable. The allowance of water was so deficient, that the slaves were frequently found gasping for life, and almost suffocated. The pulse with which they had been said to be favoured, were absolutely English horse-beans. The legislature of Jamaica had stated the scantiness both of water and provisions, as a subject which called for the interference of parliament. As Mr. Norris had said, the song and the dance were promoted, he could not pass over these expressions without telling the house what they meant. It would have been much more fair if he himself had explained the word *promoted*. The truth was, that, for the sake of exercise, these miserable wretches, loaded with chains and oppressed with disease, were forced to dance by the terror of the lash, and sometimes by the actual use of it. "I," said one of the evidences, "was employed to dance the men, while another person danced the women." Such then was the meaning of the word *promoted*; and it might also be observed with respect to food, that instruments were sometimes carried out, in order to force them to eat; which was the same sort of proof, how much they enjoyed themselves in this instance also. With respect to their singing, it consisted of songs of lamentation for the loss of their country. While they sung they were in tears: so that one of the captains, more humane probably than the rest, threatened a woman with a flogging because the mournfulness of her song was too painful for his feelings. Perhaps he could not give a better proof of the sufferings of these injured people during their passage, than by stating the mortality which accompanied it. This was a species of evidence which was infallible on this occasion. Death was a witness which could not deceive them; and the proportion of deaths would not only confirm, but, if possible, even aggravate our suspicion of the misery of the transit. It would be found, upon an average of all the ships, upon which evidence had been given, that, exclusively of such as perished before they sailed from Africa, not less than twelve and a half per cent. died on their passage: besides these, the Jamaica report stated that four and a half per cent. died while in the harbours, or on shore before the day of sale, which was only about the space of twelve or fourteen days after their arrival there; and one third more died in the seasoning:[3] and this in a climate exactly similar to their own, and where, as some of the witnesses pretended, they were healthy and happy. Thus, out of every lot of one hundred, shipped from Africa, seventeen died in about nine weeks, and not more than fifty lived to become effective labourers in our islands.

["REFLECTIONS ON THIS GREAT EVENT"]

With respect to the end obtained by this contest, or the great measure of the abolition of the Slave-trade as it has now passed, I know not how to appreciate its impor-

3. Breaking-in.

tance. To our own country, indeed, it is invaluable. We have lived, in consequence of it, to see the day, when it has been recorded as a principle in our legislation, that commerce itself shall have its moral boundaries. We have lived to see the day, when we are likely to be delivered from the contagion of the most barbarous opinions.

 * * * though nature shrinks from pain, and compassion is engendered in us when we see it become the portion of others, yet what is physical suffering compared with moral guilt? The misery of the oppressed is, in the first place, not contagious like the crime of the oppressor. Nor is the mischief, which it generates, either so frightful or so pernicious. The body, though under affliction, may retain its shape; and, if it even perish, what is the loss of it but of worthless dust? But when the moral springs of the mind are poisoned, we lose the most excellent part of the constitution of our nature, and the divine image is no longer perceptible in us. Nor are the two evils of similar duration. By a decree of Providence, for which we cannot be too thankful, we are made mortal. Hence the torments of the oppressor are but temporary; whereas the immortal part of us, when once corrupted, may carry its pollutions with it into another world.

But independently of the quantity of physical suffering and the innumerable avenues to vice in more than a quarter of the globe, which this great measure will cut off, there are yet blessings, which we have reason to consider as likely to flow from it. Among these we cannot overlook the great probability, that Africa, now freed from the vicious and barbarous effects of this traffic, may be in a better state to comprehend and receive the sublime truths of the Christian religion. Nor can we overlook the probability, that, a new system of treatment necessarily springing up in our islands, the same bright sun of consolation may visit her children there. But here a new hope rises to our view. Who knows but that emancipation, like a beautiful plant, may, in its due season, rise out of the ashes of the abolition of the Slave-trade, and that, when its own intrinsic value shall be known, the seed of it may be planted in other lands? And looking at the subject in this point of view, we cannot but be struck with the wonderful concurrence of events as previously necessary for this purpose, namely, that two nations, England and America, the mother and the child, should, in the same month of the same year, have abolished this impious traffic; nations, which at this moment have more than a million of subjects within their jurisdiction to partake of the blessing; and one of which, on account of her local situation and increasing power, is likely in time to give, if not law, at least a tone to the manners and customs of the great continent, on which she is situated.

Reader! Thou art now acquainted with the history of this contest! Rejoice in the manner of its termination! And, if thou feelest grateful for the event, retire within thy closet,[4] and pour out thy thanksgivings to the Almighty for this his unspeakable act of mercy to thy oppressed fellow-creatures.

+—+ ≡◆≡ +—+

William Wordsworth
1770–1850

When they were all living in the Lake District of England, the Wordsworths and Coleridge became close friends with Thomas Clarkson and his wife, and were inspired by Clarkson's intense commitment to abolition. William Wordsworth's sonnet *To Thomas Clarkson*, pub-

---

4. Private sitting room. This is the closing paragraph of the *History*.

lished in 1807, honors his heroic persistence in behalf of the Abolition Bill. *To Toussaint L'Ouverture* honors François Dominique Toussaint (1743?–1803), a self-educated slave freed shortly before the 1791 revolt in San Domingo, who became a leader of the revolutionaries (dubbed "L'Ouverture" for his skill in "opening" gaps in enemy ranks, he adopted this as a surname). In 1801, he conquered San Domingo and became governor of the whole island. When, in 1802, he resisted Napoleon's attempt to re-establish French rule and slavery, he was arrested and dungeoned in the French Alps, where he died in April 1803, after ten months of cold and hunger. Wordsworth published his sonnet in *The Morning Post* in February 1803, and then in *Poems* of 1807 under "Sonnets Dedicated to Liberty." *Humanity*—written decades later, in 1829, before colonial emancipation, and published soon after, in 1835—demonstrates his unwavering moral revulsion at slavery and contempt for the economic justifications for it. But in a letter of 1833, he joined the now Tory Poet Laureate Southey in declining to contribute to a volume of antislavery poetry, expressing qualified sympathy for the planters, who, he suggests, have been too one-sidedly villainized.

For more about Wordsworth, see the principal listing on page 1520.

To Toussaint L'Ouverture

Toussaint, the most unhappy man of men!
Whether the whistling Rustic tend his plough
Within thy hearing, or thy head be now
Pillowed in some deep dungeon's earless den;—
5   O miserable Chieftain! where and when
Wilt thou find patience? Yet die not; do thou
Wear rather in thy bonds a cheerful brow:
Though fallen thyself, never to rise again,
Live, and take comfort. Thou hast left behind
10   Powers that will work for thee; air, earth, and skies;
There's not a breathing of the common wind
That will forget thee; thou hast great allies;
Thy friends are exultations, agonies,
And love, and man's unconquerable mind.

1802   1807

To Thomas Clarkson

On the Final Passing of the Bill for the Abolition of the Slave Trade, March, 1807

Clarkson! it was an obstinate Hill to climb;
How toilsome—nay, how dire—it was, by Thee
Is known,—by none, perhaps, so feelingly:
But Thou, who, starting in thy fervent prime,
5   Didst first lead forth this pilgrimage sublime,
Hast heard the constant Voice its charge repeat,
Which, out of thy young heart's oracular seat,
First roused thee.—O true yoke-fellow of Time,
With unabating effort, see, the palm
10   Is won, and by all Nations shall be worn!
The bloody Writing is forever torn;
And Thou henceforth shalt have a good Man's calm,
A great Man's happiness; thy zeal shall find
Repose at length, firm Friend of human kind!

1807   1807

Letter to Mary Ann Rawson[1]

Dear Madam,

Your letter which I lose no time in replying to, has placed me under some embarrassment, as I happen to possess some Mss verses of my own upon the subject to which you solicit my attention. But I frankly own to you, that neither with respect to this subject nor to the kindred one, the Slavery of the children in the Factories,[2] which is adverted to in the same Poem, am I prepared to add to the excitement already existing in the public mind upon these, and so many other points of legislation and government. Poetry, if good for any thing, must appeal forcibly to the Imagination and the feelings; but what at this period we want above every thing, is patient examination and sober judgement. It can scarcely be necessary to add that my mind revolts as strongly as any one's can, from the law that permits one human being to sell another. It is in principle monstrous, but it is not the worst thing in human nature. Let precipitate advocates for its destruction bear this in mind. But I will not enter farther into the question than to say, that there are three parties—the Slave—the Slave owner—and the imperial Parliament, or rather the people of the British Islands, acting through that Organ. Surely the course at present pursued is hasty, intemperate, and likely to lead to gross injustice. Who in fact are most to blame? the people—who, by their legislation, have sanctioned not to say encouraged, slavery. But now we are turning round at once upon the planters, and heaping upon them indignation without measure, as if we wished that the Slaves should believe that their Masters alone were culpable—and they alone fit objects of complaint and resentment.

Excuse haste and believe me Dear Madam
respectfully yours,
Wm Wordsworth

❧ ❦ ❧

The Edinburgh Review

One of the most influential quarterly journals of the day, *The Edinburgh* Review was edited by its co-founder Francis Jeffrey (1773–1850) from its inception in 1802 until 1829. Although Jeffrey tended to conservative standards as a literary critic (famously attacking the Lake school for presenting peasants sympathetically), the *Edinburgh* was an important organ for liberal political opinion and was committed to supporting the Whigs in their parliamentary campaign for reform. Among its other co-founders, Henry Brougham (1778–1868) was a leader in the abolitionist movement, and Sydney Smith (1771–1845) excoriated the slave trade as an "enormous wickedness." Although England had abolished the trade in 1807, other countries, including France and the United States, remained involved, and slavery was still legal in Eng-

---

1. Wordsworth wrote this letter about May 1833 to Mary Ann Rawson, an original member of the Sheffield Female anti-Slavery Society, founded in 1825; in 1826 she began collecting pieces for an anthology of antislavery prose and poetry, *The Bow in the Cloud,* which she published in 1834, after colonial Emancipation, in a small edition of 500 copies.

2. A Parliamentary commission issued a shocking report in 1832 about child labor in the factories that led to the "Act of 1833," which prevented those under 9 from such labor and limited those under 13 to 48 hours a week, with no more than 9 hours in any one day; it also required these children to receive at least two hours of schooling a day. It failed in its goal to secure a 10-hour day for teenagers.

land's colonies. Reports such as the one below (October 1821) kept public attention focused on the atrocities.

from Abstract of the Information laid on the Table of the House of Commons, on the Subject of the Slave Trade

The French ship Le Rodeur, of two hundred tons burden, sailed from the port of Havre for the river Calabar on the coast of Africa, where she arrived after a prosperous voyage, and anchored at Bonny on the fourteenth of March. Her crew, of twenty-two men, had enjoyed perfect health; and this continued during her stay of three weeks, while she received on board one hundred and sixty negroes, with whom she set sail for Guadaloupe[1] on the sixth of April. No traces of any epidemy had been perceived among the natives; the cargo (as it is called), no more than the crew, exhibited any symptoms of disease; and the first fortnight of the voyage to the West Indies promised a continuance of all the success which had seemed to attend the earlier stages of the expedition. The vessel had now approached the line,[2] when a frightful malady broke out. At first the symptoms were slight, little more than a redness of the eyes; and this being confined to the negroes, was ascribed to the want of air in the hold, and the narrow space between the decks, into which so large a number of those unhappy beings were crowded; something, too, was imagined to arise from the scarcity of water, which had thus early begun to be felt, and pressed chiefly upon the slaves; for they were allowed only eight ounces, which was soon reduced to half a wine glass per day. By the surgeon's advice, therefore, they were suffered, for the first time, to breathe the purer air upon the deck, where they were brought in succession; but many of these poor creatures being affected with that mighty desire of returning to their native country, which is so strong as to form a disease, termed *Nostalgia* by the physicians, no sooner found they were at liberty, than they threw themselves into the sea, locked in each other's arms, in the vain hope, known to prevail among them, of thus being swiftly transported again to their homes. With the view of counteracting this propensity, the Captain ordered several who were stopt in the attempt, to be shot or hanged in the sight of their companions; but this terrible example was unavailing to deter them; and it became necessary, once more, to confine them entirely to the hold.

The disease proved to be a virulent ophthalmia, and it now spread with irresistible rapidity among the Africans, all of whom were seized; but it soon attacked the crew; and its ravages were attended, perhaps its violence exasperated, by a dysentery, which the use of rain-water was found to have produced. A sailor who slept near the hatch communicating with the hold, was the first who caught it; next day a landsman was taken ill; and in three days more, the Captain and almost all the rest of the crew were infected. The resources of medicine were tried in vain; the sufferings of the people, and the number of the blind, were daily increasing; and they were in constant expectation that the negroes, taking advantage of their numbers, would rise and destroy them. From this danger they were only saved by the mutual hatred of the tribes to which these unfortunate beings belonged, and which was so fierce and inextinguishable, that, even under the load of chains and sickness, they were ready every instant, in their fury, to tear one another in pieces. * * *

The consternation now became general and horrid; but it did not preclude calculation; for, thirty-six of the negroes having become quite blind, were *thrown into the*

---

1. In the Caribbean.   2. Equator.

sea and drowned, in order to save the expense of supporting slaves rendered unsaleable, and to obtain grounds for a claim against the under-writers.[3] * * *

The reader may think that we have been going back to the times when the slave-trade flourished under the protection of the law in England and France; and that we have been citing from the writings of some political author, some advocate for the abolition. Not so. All these horrors darken the history of the year 1819; and the tale is almost all told incidentally by the scientific compilers of a Medical Journal. Yes—in 1819 * * * twelve years after England had forbidden the traffic—eight years after she had declared it a crime—and four years after France, first by law, and then by solemn treaty, had become a party to its positive, unqualified, immediate abolition.

Dreadful as are the scenes disclosed in the case of the Rodeur, there are even worse horrors in the Parliamentary Papers of which the abstract lies before us. In March 1820, the Tartar, commanded by Sir George Collier, boarded a French vessel, called La Jeune Estelle of Martinique, after a long chase. The captain admitted that he had been engaged in the slave-trade, but denied that he had any slaves on board, declaring that he had been plundered of his cargo. The English officers, however, observed that all the French seamen appeared agitated and alarmed; and this led to an examination of the hold. Nothing, however, was found; and they would have departed with the belief that the captain's story was a true one, had not a sailor happened to strike a cask, and hear, or fancy he heard, a faint voice issue from within. The cask was opened, and two negro girls were found crammed into it, and in the last stage of suffocation. Being brought upon the deck of the Tartar, they were recognised by a person who had before seen them in the possession of an American who had died on the coast. An investigation now took place; and it was ascertained that they formed part of a cargo of fourteen slaves, whom the French captain had carried off by an attack which he and his crew made on the American's property after his decease. This led to a new search of the slave-ship for the other twelve, whom he was thus proved to have obtained by the robbery; when a platform was discovered, on which the negroes must have been laid in a space twenty-three inches in height, and beneath it a negro was found, not, however, one of the twelve, jammed into the crevice between two water casks. Still there were no traces of those twelve slaves; and the French captain persisted in his story, that he had been plundered by a Spanish pirate. But suddenly a most horrible idea darted across the minds of the English officers and men; they recollected that, when the chase began, they had seen several casks floating past them, which, at the time, they could not account for; but now, after the examination of the one which remained on board the Jeune Estelle, little doubt could be entertained that those casks contained the wretched slaves, whom the infernal monster had thus thrown overboard, to prevent the detection that would have ensued, either upon their being found in his ship, or by their bodies floating exposed on the sea. * * *

May we not then appeal to the body of our most enlightened European neighbours, and call upon them to stimulate their rulers not only to follow the example set by England and America in classing the slave-trade among heinous crimes, but to join them in that measure which, if those three great maritime powers adopt it, must speedily become the law of all nations? That the French people at large are prepared for such a step, there can be little reason to doubt. All their ablest statesmen have the most sound views upon

---

3. The notorious precedent was the case of the slave ship Zong (1781), whose captain ordered 133 weak and diseased slaves ejected into shark-infested waters in order to collect on a policy that held the insurer liable for cargo jettisoned in order to salvage the remainder. The insurance trial (not about the captain's criminal liability but the underwriter's financial liability) was presided over by Mansfield, who ruled in favor of the captain.

this important question; and the remains of prejudice with respect to the means, when so generous an anxiety is entertained for the attainment of the object, must soon give way to the enlightened genius of the age; and certainly, what has passed in America, is calculated to assist in dispelling those prejudices beyond any thing we can conceive.

Our attention has, in this article, been confined to the portion of the Parliamentary Papers which treats of the French slave-trade, as out of all comparison the most important in every point of view. Much to lament and to amend is, however, contained in the correspondence with Spain, Portugal, and the Netherlands; and it is to be hoped that our Government, acting under the control of the almost unanimous opinion upon this subject entertained both by Parliament and the country, will be enabled, before long, to obtain some more satisfactory arrangements with those three powers. The late Revolutions, and the establishment of a popular constitution in Portugal and Spain, afford additional grounds for such expectations.

[END OF PERSPECTIVES: THE ABOLITION OF SLAVERY AND THE SLAVE TRADE]

⬩—◄═◊═►—⬩

Mary Wollstonecraft
1759–1797

It is hard to imagine how anyone advocating the education of young women, the virtues of sense over sensibility, chastity for men as well as women, school uniforms, and regular physical exercise, could be reviled as a radical revolutionary, an atheist, a slut, and a pathologically castrating threat to masculine authority. But Mary Wollstonecraft suffered all these abuses. The attacks were provoked, in part, by her principled, frequently caustic refutation in *A Vindication of the Rights of Men* of Edmund Burke's *Reflections on the Revolution in France*. She went further in her *Vindication of the Rights of Woman*, a trenchant critique of the ideologies of gender in such culturally revered works as Milton's *Paradise Lost* and the admired "conduct" literature of the day—advice to young women on how to be attractive to men and cultivate the Christian virtues of submission, obedience, and service. It was not only Wollstonecraft's publications that provoked censure; it was also her private life, taken to be the basis of her ideas. The litany included helping a sister run away from an abusive husband (an assault on the social institution and religious sacrament of marriage); her financial independence and career as a professional writer (very unfeminine); her enamored pursuit of Swiss artist Henry Fuseli in the early 1790s (most immodest) and the outright sinfulness of her tempestuous affair with American adventurer Gilbert Imlay a few years later; her out-of-wedlock daughter by Imlay; the two attempts at suicide provoked by Imlay's infidelities; her affair with William Godwin and a premarital pregnancy. When she died from complications in childbirth, her detractors intuited divine judgment.

A brilliant thinker and conversationalist, a prolific polemical writer, a commanding social presence, Wollstonecraft led a life of passionate commitments, and was one of the most impressive figures of the radical circle in England in the 1790s. Born in 1759, she spent a childhood suffering the consequences of her father's failures at various enterprises, as he squandered a large inheritance and sought refuge in drink; more than once she defended her mother from his drunken rages. To escape, she became a lady's companion in Bath but returned after two years to nurse her mother. After her mother's death, she left home for good, supporting herself with eye-straining work as a seamstress and then as a schoolmistress in North London with a friend and another sister. When the school failed, Wollstonecraft wrote to pay off her debts, publishing *Thoughts on the Education of Daughters* in 1786; she worked for a year as a governess in an Irish aristocratic family, during which time she wrote her first novel, *Mary, A Fiction*.

Determined to make a living as a writer, she returned to London where she met Joseph Johnson, a radical bookseller, who in 1788, published *Mary* and her book for children, *Original Stories from Real Life*, and in 1789, her anthology, *The Female Reader* (under a male pen name). He also hired her to work for and write articles for *The Analytic Review* and to produce translations of German and French moral philosophers. In London Wollstonecraft became part of Johnson's lively circle of artists, writers, liberal political thinkers, progressive philosophers, and religious Dissenters—among them, Anna Laetitia Barbauld, Thomas Paine, William Blake, Joel Barlow, Joseph Priestley, Fuseli, and her future husband, Godwin. Blake and Robert Southey were completely enamored of her, though Godwin was at first put off by her forwardness in conversation. In 1790 Johnson published *A Vindication of the Rights of Men*, written quickly to respond to Edmund Burke's *Reflections on the Revolution in France*; this was anonymous, and when Wollstonecraft signed her name to the second edition in 1791, her fame was established.

She began *Rights of Woman* the same year and early in 1792 spent time with Talleyrand, the French minister of education, on his visit to London; she dedicated *Rights of Woman* to him when its second edition was published later that year. Her reasonable, modest proposals for the improved education and social development of young women were etched with acid comparisons of the state of women to that of plantation and harem slaves, equally oppressed, tyrannized, and brutalized by morally illegitimate masters. Wollstonecraft called for a "revolution in female manners," arguing that no agenda for "the rights of man" could claim moral authority if it entailed the unchanged degradation of women. At the end of 1792, she left on her own for Paris, partly to wean herself from her crush on Fuseli and partly to witness Revolutionary France. Here she met Helen Maria Williams, and within a few months, Imlay, dashing veteran of the American Revolution. Paris in 1793 was a dangerous world, still reeling from the September massacres of 1792 and the arrest and trial of Louis XVI, who was beheaded in January 1793. Over the course of this year, the Reign of Terror beheaded thousands more, including Wollstonecraft's friend Madame Roland and Queen Marie Antoinette in October. Wollstonecraft left Paris to seek safety in the suburbs, but returned to register as Imlay's wife at the American embassy in order to gain protection as an American citizen, France being at war with England. Early in 1794, she and Imlay went to Le Havre, where their daughter Fanny was born. They all returned to Paris; then Imlay went to London, leaving wife and daughter behind.

Wollstonecraft's *Historical and Moral View of the Origin and Progress of the French Revolution* was published later that year. On returning to London, she was devastated to discover Imlay living with an actress. He prevented her attempted suicide, and to distance himself from her, sent her (with Fanny and a French nurse) on a business trip to Scandinavia during the summer of 1795. She returned in October to find him living with yet another actress and again attempted suicide, jumping off a bridge into the Thames. Imlay left for Paris with his new amour in November, and Wollstonecraft, ever resourceful, decided to publish her letters to him recording her experiences in Scandinavia. When *Letters Written during a Short Residence in Sweden, Norway, and Denmark* appeared the following year, Godwin exclaimed, "If ever there was a book calculated to make a man in love with its author, this appears to me to be the book." They renewed their friendship in January 1796 and by the summer, "friendship melting into love," they became lovers. When she became pregnant at the end of the year, they set aside principle and decided to marry. They were wed in March, but insisted on keeping separate residences. Mary Wollstonecraft Godwin—the future Mary Shelley—was born in August; in ten days, her mother, having suffered agonizing pain from poisoning by an incompletely expelled placenta, was dead, at age thirty-seven.

When Godwin published a *Memoir* of her and her unfinished novel, *The Wrongs of Woman, or Maria* in 1798, both works fed anti-Jacobin attacks on her ideas and moral character. His grief clouded his judgment about what he could recount without offending propriety, and the *Memoir* proved a scandal, embarrassing even those who had welcomed *Rights of*

Woman. An anonymous *Defence of the Character and Conduct of the Late Mary Wollstonecraft Godwin* (often credited to Mary Hays, her friend and fellow feminist), appeared in 1803, but the defense could hardly rest. Hays did not feel safe including her in her *Female Biography, or Memoirs of Illustrious and Celebrated Women of all Ages and Countries* (also 1803), even though she found space for the Lesbian Sappho and Marat's assassin Charlotte Corday. Decades later, in 1869, John Stuart Mill forgot to mention *Rights of Woman* in his *Subjection of Women*. Attacks on Wollstonecraft's character and conduct persisted well into the 1970s, not only stig- matizing the arguments of her writing but providing anti-feminists with fuel to impugn any advocacy of women's rights. Yet there always persisted a community of admiration for her courage and intelligence, including (for better or worse) Percy Shelley, and over ensuing decades, such women of intellect as George Eliot, Emma Goldman, and Virginia Woolf.

Selections from *A Vindication of the Rights of Men* are included in Perspectives: The Rights of Man and the Revolution Controversy, page 1365.

A VINDICATION OF THE RIGHTS OF WOMAN

With the French Revolutionary Assembly's Declaration of the Rights of Man granting partici- patory citizenship only to men, Wollstonecraft's "second *Vindication*" responds to a concern of many progressive women, namely, that the vibrant declarations of the "Rights of Man" were all too serious about the *fraternity* of "liberty, fraternity, equality." Bluntly comparing marriage to slavery and tyrannical oppression, Wollstonecraft boldly challenges the ideology that sustains and frequently idealizes this subjection: the view of women's subordination as a universal fact of nature, human history, rational philosophy, and divine ordination. She proceeds first to identi- fy this view as a sociocultural text, a "prevailing opinion," and then to subject it to a sharp crit- ical reading. This textual critique is embedded in the overt literary criticism that fills her pages, incisive and often sarcastic examinations of the attitudes about gender in long-standing misog- ynist myths (Pandora) and in the most influential works of her day: John Milton's *Paradise Lost* (and its informing biblical stories), Alexander Pope's second *Moral Essay*, "Of the Characters of Women" (1735), Samuel Richardson's *Clarissa* (1747–1748), Jean-Jacques Rousseau's influen- tial education novel, *Émile* (1762) and *Julie, ou la Nouvelle Héloïse* (1791), Dr. John Gregory's *A Father's Legacy to His Daughters* (1774), Dr. James Fordyce's *Sermons to Young Women* (1765). Her literary criticism extends to an unforgiving focus on a set of interlocked key terms used to flatter women into subjection—"innocent," "delicate," "feminine," "beautiful"—embellished with praise for their "fair defects" of character (an oxymoron she despises) and reverence for them as "angels" or "girls," rather than rationally capable, intelligent, mature adults.

Wollstonecraft's argument for a gender-neutral capacity of "reason" simultaneously draws on eighteenth-century rationalist philosophy and democratizes the Miltonic value of "Reason" as the highest mental capacity. For Milton, this capacity is located in men only; Woll- stonecraft argues that this hierarchical arrangement is not a divine but a social formation. She counters that if God is Reason, He surely would not have created women without this capaci- ty, the source of both virtuous conduct and spiritual salvation—a religious argument Woll- stonecraft uses not only to refute appeals to divine ordination, but also to invest her social polemic with what she hopes will be an unimpeachable moral foundation. Alongside this moral argument, her *Vindication* wields the discourse of tyranny and revolution that already had currency with her male colleagues, allowing her to point out the reactionary attitudes about women that may be tolerated, even supported, by progressive political thinkers.

from A Vindication of the Rights of Woman
Introduction

After considering the historic page, and viewing the living world with anxious solici- tude, the most melancholy emotions of sorrowful indignation have depressed my spirits, and I have sighed when obliged to confess, that either nature has made a great difference between man and man, or that the civilization which has hitherto taken place in the world has been very partial. I have turned over various books written on the subject of education, and patiently observed the conduct of parents and the management of schools; but what has been the result?—a profound conviction that the neglected education of my fellow-creatures is the grand source of the misery I deplore; and that women, in particular, are rendered weak and wretched by a variety of concurring causes, originating from one hasty conclusion. The conduct and manners of women, in fact, evidently prove that their minds are not in a healthy state; for, like the flowers which are planted in too rich a soil, strength and usefulness are sacrificed to beauty; and the flaunting leaves, after having pleased a fastidious eye, fade, disregarded on the stalk, long before the season when they ought to have arrived at maturity.—One cause of this barren blooming I attribute to a false system of education, gathered from the books written on this subject by men who, considering females rather as women than human creatures, have been more anxious to make them alluring mistresses than affectionate wives and rational mothers; and the understanding of the sex has been so bubbled[1] by this specious homage, that the civilized women of the present century, with a few exceptions, are only anxious to inspire love, when they ought to cherish a nobler ambition, and by their abilities and virtues exact respect.

In a treatise, therefore, on female rights and manners, the works which have been particularly written for their improvement must not be overlooked; especially when it is asserted, in direct terms, that the minds of women are enfeebled by false refinement; that the books of instruction, written by men of genius, have had the same tendency as more frivolous productions; and that, in the true style of Mahometanism, they are treated as a kind of subordinate beings, and not as a part of the human species,[2] when improveable reason is allowed to be the dignified distinction which raises men above the brute creation, and puts a natural sceptre in a feeble hand.

Yet, because I am a woman, I would not lead my readers to suppose that I mean violently to agitate the contested question respecting the equality or inferiority of the sex; but as the subject lies in my way, and I cannot pass it over without subjecting the main tendency of my reasoning to misconstruction, I shall stop a moment to deliver, in a few words, my opinion.—In the government of the physical world it is observable that the female in point of strength is, in general, inferior to the male. This is the law of nature; and it does not appear to be suspended or abrogated in favour of woman. A degree of physical superiority cannot, therefore, be denied—and it is a noble prerogative! But not content with this natural pre-eminence, men endeavour to sink us still lower, merely to render us alluring objects for a moment; and women, intoxicated by the adoration which men, under the influence of their senses, pay them, do not seek to obtain a durable interest in their hearts, or to become the friends of the fellow creatures who find amusement in their society.

I am aware of an obvious inference:—from every quarter have I heard exclamations against masculine women; but where are they to be found? If by this appellation men mean to inveigh against their ardour in hunting, shooting, and gaming, I shall most cordially join in the cry; but if it be against the imitation of manly virtues, or, more properly speaking, the attainment of those talents and virtues, the exercise of

---

1. Gas-filled; deluded.
2. A Western misconception that the sacred texts of

Islam stated that women lack souls and therefore have no afterlife in Heaven.

which ennobles the human character, and which raise females in the scale of animal being, when they are comprehensively termed mankind;—all those who view them with a philosophic eye must, I should think, wish with me, that they may every day grow more and more masculine.

This discussion naturally divides the subject. I shall first consider women in the grand light of human creatures, who, in common with men, are placed on this earth to unfold their faculties; and afterwards I shall more particularly point out their peculiar designation.

I wish also to steer clear of an error which many respectable writers have fallen into; for the instruction which has hitherto been addressed to women, has rather been applicable to *ladies*, if the little indirect advice, that is scattered through Sandford and Merton, be excepted;[3] but, addressing my sex in a firmer tone, I pay particular attention to those in the middle class, because they appear to be in the most natural state.[4] Perhaps the seeds of false-refinement, immorality, and vanity, have ever been shed by the great. Weak, artificial beings, raised above the common wants and affections of their race, in a premature unnatural manner, undermine the very foundation of virtue, and spread corruption through the whole mass of society! As a class of mankind they have the strongest claim to pity; the education of the rich tends to render them vain and helpless, and the unfolding mind is not strengthened by the practice of those duties which dignify the human character.—They only live to amuse themselves, and by the same law which in nature invariably produces certain effects, they soon only afford barren amusement.

But as I purpose taking a separate view of the different ranks of society, and of the moral character of women, in each, this hint is, for the present, sufficient; and I have only alluded to the subject, because it appears to me to be the very essence of an introduction to give a cursory account of the contents of the work it introduces.

My own sex, I hope, will excuse me, if I treat them like rational creatures, instead of flattering their *fascinating* graces, and viewing them as if they were in a state of perpetual childhood, unable to stand alone. I earnestly wish to point out in what true dignity and human happiness consists—I wish to persuade women to endeavour to acquire strength, both of mind and body, and to convince them that the soft phrases, susceptibility of heart, delicacy of sentiment, and refinement of taste, are almost synonymous with epithets of weakness, and that those beings who are only the objects of pity and that kind of love, which has been termed its sister, will soon become objects of contempt.

Dismissing then those pretty feminine phrases, which the men condescendingly use to soften our slavish dependence, and despising that weak elegancy of mind, exquisite sensibility, and sweet docility of manners, supposed to be the sexual characteristics of the weaker vessel, I wish to shew that elegance is inferior to virtue, that the first object of laudable ambition is to obtain a character as a human being, regardless of the distinction of sex; and that secondary views should be brought to this simple touchstone.

This is a rough sketch of my plan; and should I express my conviction with the energetic emotions that I feel whenever I think of the subject, the dictates of experience and reflection will be felt by some of my readers. Animated by this important

---

3. The tutor in Thomas Day's popular children's story, *The History of Sandford and Merton* (1786–1789), influenced by Rousseau's *Émile*), tells several moral tales.

4. "Ladies" are upper-class; Wollstonecraft suggests that the middle class is the most "natural" state because it has not been corrupted by extremes of wealth or poverty.

object, I shall disdain to cull my phrases or polish my style;—I aim at being useful, and sincerity will render me unaffected; for, wishing rather to persuade by the force of my arguments, than dazzle by the elegance of my language, I shall not waste my time in rounding periods,[5] or in fabricating the turgid bombast of artificial feelings, which, coming from the head, never reach the heart.—I shall be employed about things, not words!—and, anxious to render my sex more respectable members of society, I shall try to avoid that flowery diction which has slided from essays into novels, and from novels into familiar letters and conversation.

These pretty superlatives, dropping glibly from the tongue, vitiate the taste, and create a kind of sickly delicacy that turns away from simple unadorned truth; and a deluge of false sentiments and over-stretched feelings, stifling the natural emotions of the heart, render the domestic pleasures insipid, that ought to sweeten the exercise of those severe duties, which educate a rational and immortal being for a nobler field of action.

The education of women has, of late, been more attended to than formerly; yet they are still reckoned a frivolous sex, and ridiculed or pitied by the writers who endeavour by satire or instruction to improve them. It is acknowledged that they spend many of the first years of their lives in acquiring a smattering of accomplishments; meanwhile strength of body and mind are sacrificed to libertine notions of beauty, to the desire of establishing themselves,—the only way women can rise in the world,—by marriage. And this desire making mere animals of them, when they marry they act as such children may be expected to act:—they dress; they paint, and nickname God's creatures.[6]—Surely these weak beings are only fit for a seraglio![7]— Can they be expected to govern a family with judgment, or take care of the poor babes whom they bring into the world?

If then it can be fairly deduced from the present conduct of the sex,[8] from the prevalent fondness for pleasure which takes place of ambition and those nobler passions that open and enlarge the soul; that the instruction which women have hitherto received has only tended, with the constitution of civil society, to render them insignificant objects of desire—mere propagators of fools!—if it can be proved that in aiming to accomplish them, without cultivating their understandings, they are taken out of their sphere of duties, and made ridiculous and useless when the short-lived bloom of beauty is over,[9] I presume that *rational* men will excuse me for endeavouring to persuade them to become more masculine and respectable.

Indeed the word masculine is only a bugbear: there is little reason to fear that women will acquire too much courage or fortitude; for their apparent inferiority with respect to bodily strength, must render them, in some degree, dependent on men in the various relations of life; but why should it be increased by prejudices that give a sex to virtue,[1] and confound simple truths with sensual reveries?

Women are, in fact, so much degraded by mistaken notions of female excellence, that I do not mean to add a paradox when I assert, that this artificial weakness produces a propensity to tyrannize, and gives birth to cunning, the natural opponent of strength, which leads them to play off those contemptible infantine airs that undermine esteem even whilst they excite desire. Let men become more chaste and mod-

---

5. Crafting elaborate sentences—the oratorical style for which Burke was famous.
6. A reference to Hamlet's misogynist diatribe at Ophelia, whom he suspects of treachery: "God hath given you one face, and you make yourselves another. You jig and amble, and you lisp; you nickname God's creatures and make your wantonness [seem] your ignorance" (*Hamlet*

3.1.145–48). Cf. *Rights of Men*, page 1370, n.3.
7. Harem.
8. The female sex, a common usage.
9. A lively writer . . . asks what business women turned of forty have to do in the world? [Wollstonecraft's note.]
1. The prevailing opinion that only men have the rational and hence moral capacity for virtuous behavior.

est, and if women do not grow wiser in the same ratio, it will be clear that they have weaker understandings. It seems scarcely necessary to say, that I now speak of the sex in general. Many individuals have more sense than their male relatives; and, as nothing preponderates where there is a constant struggle for an equilibrium, without it has naturally more gravity, some women govern their husbands without degrading themselves, because intellect will always govern.

from *Chapter 1. The Rights and Involved Duties of Mankind Considered*

In the present state of society it appears necessary to go back to first principles in search of the most simple truths, and to dispute with some prevailing prejudice every inch of ground. To clear my way, I must be allowed to ask some plain questions, and the answers will probably appear as unequivocal as the axioms on which reasoning is built; though, when entangled with various motives of action, they are formally contradicted, either by the words or conduct of men.

In what does man's pre-eminence over the brute creation consist? The answer is as clear as that a half is less than the whole; in Reason.

What acquirement exalts one being above another? Virtue; we spontaneously reply.

For what purpose were the passions implanted? That man by struggling with them might attain a degree of knowledge denied to the brutes; whispers Experience.

Consequently the perfection of our nature and capability of happiness, must be estimated by the degree of reason, virtue, and knowledge, that distinguish the individual, and direct the laws which bind society: and that from the exercise of reason, knowledge and virtue naturally flow, is equally undeniable, if mankind be viewed collectively.

The rights and duties of man thus simplified, it seems almost impertinent to attempt to illustrate truths that appear so incontrovertible; yet such deeply rooted prejudices have clouded reason, and such spurious qualities have assumed the name of virtues, that it is necessary to pursue the course of reason as it has been perplexed and involved in error, by various adventitious circumstances, comparing the simple axiom with casual deviations.

Men, in general, seem to employ their reason to justify prejudices, which they have imbibed, they can scarcely trace how, rather than to root them out. The mind must be strong that resolutely forms its own principles; for a kind of intellectual cowardice prevails which makes many men shrink from the task, or only do it by halves. Yet the imperfect conclusions thus drawn, are frequently very plausible, because they are built on partial experience, on just, though narrow, views. * * *

The civilization of the bulk of the people of Europe is very partial; nay, it may be made a question, whether they have acquired any virtues in exchange for innocence, equivalent to the misery produced by the vices that have been plastered over unsightly ignorance, and the freedom which has been bartered for splendid slavery. The desire of dazzling by riches, the most certain pre-eminence that man can obtain, the pleasure of commanding flattering sycophants, and many other complicated low calculations of doting self-love, have all contributed to overwhelm the mass of mankind, and make liberty a convenient handle for mock patriotism. For whilst rank and titles are held of the utmost importance, before which Genius "must hide its diminished head,"[1] it is, with a few exceptions, very unfortunate for a nation when a

---

1. A sardonic reference to Satan's noting how "all the Stars / Hide thir diminisht heads" at the sight of the noonday sun "that with surpassing Glory crown'd, / Look'st from [its] sole dominion like the God / Of this new World" (*Paradise Lost* 4.32–35). Wollstonecraft also quotes this phrase in *Rights of Men*; see page 1372.

man of abilities, without rank or property, pushes himself forward to notice.—Alas! what unheard of misery have thousands suffered to purchase a cardinal's hat for an intriguing obscure adventurer, who longed to be ranked with princes, or lord it over them by seizing the triple crown![2] * * *

Nothing can set the regal character in a more contemptible point of view, than the various crimes that have elevated men to the supreme dignity.—Vile intrigues, unnatural crimes, and every vice that degrades our nature, have been the steps to this distinguished eminence; yet millions of men have supinely allowed the nerveless limbs of the posterity of such rapacious prowlers to rest quietly on their ensanguined thrones.[3]

What but a pestilential vapour can hover over society when its chief director is only instructed in the invention of crimes, or the stupid routine of childish ceremonies? Will men never be wise?—will they never cease to expect corn from tares, and figs from thistles?[4]

It is impossible for any man, when the most favourable circumstances concur, to acquire sufficient knowledge and strength of mind to discharge the duties of a king, entrusted with uncontrouled power; how then must they be violated when his very elevation is an insuperable bar to the attainment of either wisdom or virtue; when all the feelings of a man are stifled by flattery, and reflection shut out by pleasure! Surely it is madness to make the fate of thousands depend on the caprice of a weak fellow creature, whose very station sinks him *necessarily* below the meanest of his subjects! But one power should not be thrown down to exalt another—for all power inebriates weak man; and its abuse proves that the more equality there is established among men, the more virtue and happiness will reign in society. But this and any similar maxim deduced from simple reason, raises an outcry—the church or the state is in danger, if faith in the wisdom of antiquity is not implicit; and they who, roused by the sight of human calamity, dare to attack human authority, are reviled as despisers of God, and enemies of man. These are bitter calumnies, yet they reached one of the best of men,[5] whose ashes still preach peace, and whose memory demands a respectful pause, when subjects are discussed that lay so near his heart.—

After attacking the sacred majesty of Kings, I shall scarcely excite surprise by adding my firm persuasion that every profession, in which great subordination of rank constitutes its power, is highly injurious to morality.

A standing army, for instance, is incompatible with freedom; because subordination and rigour are the very sinews of military discipline; and despotism is necessary to give vigour to enterprizes that one will directs. A spirit inspired by romantic notions of honour, a kind of morality founded on the fashion of the age, can only be felt by a few officers, whilst the main body must be moved by command, like the waves of the sea; for the strong wind of authority pushes the crowd of subalterns forward, they scarcely know or care why, with headlong fury.

2. Papal crown.
3. "Could there be a greater insult offered to the rights of man than the beds of justice in France, when an infant was made the organ of the detestable Dubois!" [Wollstonecraft's note.] Guillaume Dubois (1656–1723) was foreign affairs advisor to Philippe II, Duc d'Orleans, the appointed regent (acting ruler) of France during the minority of Louis XV (1710–1774), who became king at age five (Louis XVI, king in 1792, was his grandson and successor).
4. See Jesus' Sermon on the Mount: "Beware of false prophets. . . . Ye shall know them by their fruits. Do men gather . . . figs of thistles? (Matthew 7.15–16); tares: weeds. See also Shakespeare, *Hamlet* (2.2.310).
5. Dr. Price [Wollstonecraft's note]. "Calumnies" are maliciously false charges. Wollstonecraft's friend Richard Price, dissenting minister and radical political writer, championed the American and French Revolutions. His lecture to the Revolution Society in 1789, *A Discourse on the Love of our Country*, provoked sharp criticism in Burke's *Reflections on the Revolution in France* and spirited defense in Wollstonecraft's *Vindication of the Rights of Men*.

Besides, nothing can be so prejudicial to the morals of the inhabitants of country towns as the occasional residence of a set of idle superficial young men, whose only occupation is gallantry, and whose polished manners render vice more dangerous, by concealing its deformity under gay ornamental drapery. An air of fashion, which is but a badge of slavery, and proves that the soul has not a strong individual character, awes simple country people into an imitation of the vices, when they cannot catch the slippery graces, of politeness. Every corps is a chain of despots, who, submitting and tyrannizing without exercising their reason, become dead weights of vice and folly on the community. A man of rank or fortune, sure of rising by interest, has nothing to do but to pursue some extravagant freak; whilst the needy *gentleman*, who is to rise, as the phrase turns, by his merit, becomes a servile parasite or vile pander.

Sailors, the naval gentlemen, come under the same description, only their vices assume a different and a grosser cast. They are more positively indolent, when not discharging the ceremonials of their station; whilst the insignificant fluttering of soldiers may be termed active idleness. More confined to the society of men, the former acquire a fondness for humour and mischievous tricks; whilst the latter, mixing frequently with well-bred women, catch a sentimental cant.—But mind is equally out of the question, whether they indulge the horse-laugh, or polite simper.

May I be allowed to extend the comparison to a profession where more mind is certainly to be found; for the clergy have superior opportunities of improvement, though subordination almost equally cramps their faculties? The blind submission imposed at college to forms of belief serves as a novitiate to the curate, who must obsequiously respect the opinion of his rector or patron, if he mean to rise in his profession. Perhaps there cannot be a more forcible contrast than between the servile dependent gait of a poor curate and the courtly mien of a bishop. And the respect and contempt they inspire render the discharge of their separate functions equally useless.

It is of great importance to observe that the character of every man is, in some degree, formed by his profession. A man of sense may only have a cast of countenance that wears off as you trace his individuality, whilst the weak, common man has scarcely ever any character, but what belongs to the body; at least, all his opinions have been so steeped in the vat consecrated by authority, that the faint spirit which the grape of his own vine yields cannot be distinguished.

Society, therefore, as it becomes more enlightened, should be very careful not to establish bodies of men who must necessarily be made foolish or vicious by the very constitution of their profession.

from *Chapter 2. The Prevailing Opinion of a Sexual Character Discussed*

To account for, and excuse the tyranny of man, many ingenious arguments have been brought forward to prove, that the two sexes, in the acquirement of virtue, ought to aim at attaining a very different character: or, to speak explicitly, women are not allowed to have sufficient strength of mind to acquire what really deserves the name of virtue. Yet it should seem, allowing them to have souls, that there is but one way appointed by Providence to lead *mankind* to either virtue or happiness.

If then women are not a swarm of ephemeron[1] triflers, why should they be kept in ignorance under the specious name of innocence? Men complain, and with reason,

1. Flying insect that lives for only a day.

of the follies and caprices of our sex, when they do not keenly satirize our headstrong passions and groveling vices.—Behold, I should answer, the natural effect of ignorance! The mind will ever be unstable that has only prejudices to rest on, and the current will run with destructive fury when there are no barriers to break its force. Women are told from their infancy, and taught by the example of their mothers, that a little knowledge of human weakness, justly termed cunning, softness of temper, *outward* obedience, and a scrupulous attention to a puerile kind of propriety, will obtain for them the protection of man; and should they be beautiful, every thing else is needless, for, at least, twenty years of their lives.

Thus Milton describes our first frail mother; though when he tells us that women are formed for softness and sweet attractive grace,[2] I cannot comprehend his meaning, unless, in the true Mahometan strain, he meant to deprive us of souls, and insinuate that we were beings only designed by sweet attractive grace, and docile blind obedience, to gratify the senses of man when he can no longer soar on the wing of contemplation.

How grossly do they insult us who thus advise us only to render ourselves gentle, domestic brutes! For instance, the winning softness so warmly, and frequently, recommended, that governs by obeying. What childish expressions, and how insignificant is the being—can it be an immortal one? who will condescend to govern by such sinister methods! "Certainly," says Lord Bacon, "man is of kin to the beasts by his body; and if he be not of kin to God by his spirit, he is a base and ignoble creature!"[3] Men, indeed, appear to me to act in a very unphilosophical manner when they try to secure the good conduct of women by attempting to keep them always in a state of childhood. Rousseau was more consistent when he wished to stop the progress of reason in both sexes, for if men eat of the tree of knowledge, women will come in for a taste; but, from the imperfect cultivation which their understandings now receive, they only attain a knowledge of evil.[4]

Children, I grant, should be innocent; but when the epithet is applied to men, or women, it is but a civil term for weakness. For if it be allowed that women were destined by Providence to acquire human virtues, and by the exercise of their understandings, that stability of character which is the firmest ground to rest our future hopes upon, they must be permitted to turn to the fountain of light, and not forced to shape their course by the twinkling of a mere satellite. Milton, I grant, was of a very different opinion; for he only bends to the indefeasible right of beauty, though it would be difficult to render two passages which I now mean to contrast, consistent. But into similar inconsistencies are great men often led by their senses.

> To whom thus Eve with *perfect beauty* adorn'd.
> "My Author and Disposer, what thou bidst
> *Unargued* I obey; So God ordains;
> God is *thy law, thou mine:* to know no more
> Is Woman's *happiest* knowledge and her *praise*."[5]

These are exactly the arguments that I have used to children; but I have added, your reason is now gaining strength, and, till it arrives at some degree of maturity, you must look up to me for advice—then you ought to *think*, and only rely on God.

---

2. See Satan's first view of Adam and Eve in *Paradise Lost:* "Not equal, as thir sex not equal seem'd; / For contemplation hee and valor form'd, / For softness shee and sweet attractive Grace, / He for God only, shee for God in him" (4.296–99). Fordyce quotes these lines in *Sermons to Young Women*, ch. 13.

3. Francis Bacon , *Essay* (1606) 16: "Of Atheism."

4. See Rousseau's *Émile* (1.1): "Only reason teaches us good from evil."

5. *Paradise Lost* 4.634–38; Wollstonecraft's emphases.

Yet in the following lines Milton seems to coincide with me; when he makes Adam thus expostulate with his Maker.

> Hast thou not made me here thy substitute,
> And these inferior far beneath me set?
> Among *unequals* what society
> Can sort, what harmony or true delight?
> Which must be mutual, in proportion due
> Giv'n and receiv'd; but in *disparity*
> The one intense, the other still remiss
> Cannot well suit with either, but soon prove
> Tedious alike: of *fellowship* I speak
> Such as I seek, fit to participate
> All rational delight[6]—

In treating, therefore, of the manners of women, let us, disregarding sensual arguments, trace what we should endeavour to make them in order to co-operate, if the expression be not too bold, with the supreme Being.

By individual education, I mean, for the sense of the word is not precisely defined, such an attention to a child as will slowly sharpen the senses, form the temper, regulate the passions as they begin to ferment, and set the understanding to work before the body arrives at maturity; so that the man may only have to proceed, not to begin, the important task of learning to think and reason. * * *

In fact, it is a farce to call any being virtuous whose virtues do not result from the exercise of its own reason. This was Rousseau's opinion respecting men: I extend it to women, and confidently assert that they have been drawn out of their sphere by false refinement, and not by an endeavour to acquire masculine qualities. Still the regal homage which they receive is so intoxicating, that till the manners of the times are changed, and formed on more reasonable principles, it may be impossible to convince them that the illegitimate power, which they obtain, by degrading themselves, is a curse, and that they must return to nature and equality, if they wish to secure the placid satisfaction that unsophisticated affections impart. But for this epoch we must wait—wait, perhaps, till kings and nobles, enlightened by reason, and, preferring the real dignity of man to childish state, throw off their gaudy hereditary trappings: and if then women do not resign the arbitrary power of beauty—they will prove that they have *less* mind than man.

I may be accused of arrogance; still I must declare what I firmly believe, that all the writers who have written on the subject of female education and manners from Rousseau to Dr. Gregory, have contributed to render women more artificial, weak characters, than they would otherwise have been; and, consequently, more useless members of society.[7] * * * My objection extends to the whole purport of those books, which tend, in my opinion, to degrade one half of the human species, and render women pleasing at the expense of every solid virtue.

Though, to reason on Rousseau's ground, if man did attain a degree of perfection of mind when his body arrived at maturity, it might be proper, in order to make a

---

6. *Paradise Lost* 8.381–91; Wollstonecraft's emphases.
7. In *Émile*, ch. 5, "Sophy or Woman," Rousseau advises that a "woman's education must . . . be planned in relation to man. To be pleasing in his sight, to win his respect and love, to train him in childhood, to tend him in manhood, to counsel and console, to make his life pleasant and happy"; at any state of life, she "will always be in subjection to a man, or to man's judgment, and she will never be free to set her own opinion above his." Dr. John Gregory (1724–1773) wrote a popular English conduct book, *A Father's Legacy to His Daughters* (1774).

man and his wife *one*, that she should rely entirely on his understanding; and the graceful ivy, clasping the oak that supported it, would form a whole in which strength and beauty would be equally conspicuous. But, alas! husbands, as well as their help-mates, are often only overgrown children; nay, thanks to early debauchery, scarcely men in their outward form—and if the blind lead the blind, one need not come from heaven to tell us the consequence.[8] * * *

Probably the prevailing opinion, that woman was created for man, may have taken its rise from Moses's poetical story;[9] yet, as very few, it is presumed, who have bestowed any serious thought on the subject, ever supposed that Eve was, literally speaking, one of Adam's ribs, the deduction must be allowed to fall to the ground; or, only be so far admitted as it proves that man, from the remotest antiquity, found it convenient to exert his strength to subjugate his companion, and his invention to shew that she ought to have her neck bent under the yoke, because the whole creation was only created for his convenience or pleasure.

Let it not be concluded that I wish to invert the order of things; I have already granted, that, from the constitution of their bodies, men seem to be designed by Providence to attain a greater degree of virtue. I speak collectively of the whole sex; but I see not the shadow of a reason to conclude that their virtues should differ in respect to their nature. In fact, how can they, if virtue has only one eternal standard? I must therefore, if I reason consequentially, as strenuously maintain that they have the same simple direction, as that there is a God.

It follows then that cunning should not be opposed to wisdom, little cares to great exertions, or insipid softness, varnished over with the name of gentleness, to that fortitude which grand views alone can inspire.

I shall be told that woman would then lose many of her peculiar graces, and the opinion of a well known poet might be quoted to refute my unqualified assertion. For Pope has said, in the name of the whole male sex,

> Yet ne'er so sure our passion to create,
> As when she touch'd the brink of all we hate.

In what light this sally[1] places men and women, I shall leave to the judicious to determine; meanwhile I shall content myself with observing, that I cannot discover why, unless they are mortal, females should always be degraded by being made sub-servient to love or lust.

To speak disrespectfully of love is, I know, high treason against sentiment and fine feelings; but I wish to speak the simple language of truth, and rather to address the head than the heart. To endeavour to reason love out of the world, would be to out Quixote Cervantes, and equally offend against common sense;[2] but an endeavour to restrain this tumultuous passion, and to prove that it should not be allowed to dethrone superior powers, or to usurp the sceptre which the understanding should ever coolly wield, appears less wild.

Youth is the season for love in both sexes; but in those days of thoughtless enjoy-ment provision should be made for the more important years of life, when reflection

---

8. See Jesus' admonition, "if the blind lead the blind, both shall fall into the ditch" (Matthew 15.14). "Rousseau's ground" is given in *Émile*, ch. 5.
9. The first five books of the Old Testament are tradi-tionally attributed to Moses; Genesis gives two versions of the creation of woman: in 1:27, God creates man and woman simultaneously; in 2:21–23, the one followed by

Milton, God creates Eve out of Adam's rib.
1. The "sally" (an attack by besieged troops; an outburst of wit) is from Pope's *Epistle II, to a Lady*, "Of the Charac-ters of Women" (1735), 51–52.
2. To outdo Cervantes' comic hero Don Quixote in inef-fectual idealism, including the ideals of courtly love.

takes place of sensation. But Rousseau, and most of the male writers who have followed his steps, have warmly inculcated that the whole tendency of female education ought to be directed to one point:—to render them pleasing.[3]

Let me reason with the supporters of this opinion who have any knowledge of human nature, do they imagine that marriage can eradicate the habitude of life? The woman who has only been taught to please will soon find that her charms are oblique sunbeams, and that they cannot have much effect on her husband's heart when they are seen every day, when the summer is passed and gone. Will she then have sufficient native energy to look into herself for comfort, and cultivate her dormant faculties? or, is it not more rational to expect that she will try to please other men; and, in the emotions raised by the expectation of new conquests, endeavour to forget the mortification her love or pride has received? When the husband ceases to be a lover—and the time will inevitably come, her desire of pleasing will then grow languid, or become a spring of bitterness; and love, perhaps, the most evanescent of all passions, gives place to jealousy or vanity.

I now speak of women who are restrained by principle or prejudice; such women, though they would shrink from an intrigue with real abhorrence, yet, nevertheless, wish to be convinced by the homage of gallantry that they are cruelly neglected by their husbands; or, days and weeks are spent in dreaming of the happiness enjoyed by congenial souls till their health is undermined and their spirits broken by discontent. How then can the great art of pleasing be such a necessary study? it is only useful to a mistress; the chaste wife, and serious mother, should only consider her power to please as the polish of her virtues, and the affection of her husband as one of the comforts that render her task less difficult and her life happier.—But, whether she be loved or neglected, her first wish should be to make herself respectable, and not to rely for all her happiness on a being subject to like infirmities with herself. * * *

Women ought to endeavour to purify their heart; but can they do so when their uncultivated understandings make them entirely dependent on their senses for employment and amusement, when no noble pursuit sets them above the little vanities of the day, or enables them to curb the wild emotions that agitate a reed over which every passing breeze has power? To gain the affections of a virtuous man is affectation necessary? Nature has given woman a weaker frame than man; but, to ensure her husband's affections, must a wife, who by the exercise of her mind and body whilst she was discharging the duties of a daughter, wife, and mother, has allowed her constitution to retain its natural strength, and her nerves a healthy tone, is she, I say, to condescend to use art and feign a sickly delicacy in order to secure her husband's affection? Weakness may excite tenderness, and gratify the arrogant pride of man; but the lordly caresses of a protector will not gratify a noble mind that pants for, and deserves to be respected. Fondness is a poor substitute for friendship!

In a seraglio, I grant, that all these arts are necessary; the epicure must have his palate tickled, or he will sink into apathy; but have women so little ambition as to be satisfied with such a condition? Can they supinely dream life away in the lap of pleasure, or the languor of weariness, rather than assert their claim to pursue reasonable pleasures and render themselves conspicuous by practising the virtues which dignify mankind? Surely she has not an immortal soul who can loiter life away merely employed to adorn her person, that she may amuse the languid hours, and soften the

---

3. See *Émile*, ch. 5.

cares of a fellow-creature who is willing to be enlivened by her smiles and tricks, when the serious business of life is over.

Besides, the woman who strengthens her body and exercises her mind will, by managing her family and practising various virtues, become the friend, and not the humble dependent of her husband; and if she, by possessing such substantial qualities, merit his regard, she will not find it necessary to conceal her affection, nor to pretend to an unnatural coldness of constitution to excite her husband's passions. In fact, if we revert to history, we shall find that the women who have distinguished themselves have neither been the most beautiful nor the most gentle of their sex. * * *

I own it frequently happens that women who have fostered a romantic unnatural delicacy of feeling,[4] waste their lives in *imagining* how happy they should have been with a husband who could love them with a fervid increasing affection every day, and all day. But they might as well pine married as single—and would not be a jot more unhappy with a bad husband than longing for a good one. That a proper education; or, to speak with more precision, a well stored mind, would enable a woman to support a single life with dignity, I grant; but that she should avoid cultivating her taste, lest her husband should occasionally shock it, is quitting a substance for a shadow. To say the truth, I do not know of what use is an improved taste, if the individual be not rendered more independent of the casualties of life; if new sources of enjoyment, only dependent on the solitary operations of the mind, are not opened. People of taste, married or single, without distinction, will ever be disgusted by various things that touch not less observing minds. On this conclusion the argument must not be allowed to hinge; but in the whole sum of enjoyment is taste to be denominated a blessing? * * *

But to view the subject in another point of view. Do passive indolent women make the best wives? Confining our discussion to the present moment of existence, let us see how such weak creatures perform their part? Do the women who, by the attainment of a few superficial accomplishments, have strengthened the prevailing prejudice, merely contribute to the happiness of their husbands? Do they display their charms merely to amuse them? And have women, who have early imbibed notions of passive obedience, sufficient character to manage a family or educate children? So far from it, that, after surveying the history of woman, I cannot help, agreeing with the severest satirist, considering the sex as the weakest as well as the most oppressed half of the species. What does history disclose but marks of inferiority, and how few women have emancipated themselves from the galling yoke of sovereign man?—So few, that the exceptions remind me of an ingenious conjecture respecting Newton: that he was probably a being of a superior order, accidentally caged in a human body.[5] Following the same train of thinking, I have been led to imagine that the few extraordinary women who have rushed in eccentrical directions out of the orbit prescribed to their sex, were *male* spirits, confined by mistake in female frames. But if it be not philosophical to think of sex when the soul is mentioned, the inferiority must depend on the organs; or the heavenly fire, which is to ferment the clay, is not given in equal portions.[6] * * *

4. For example, the herd of novelists [Wollstonecraft's note, attacking the influence of popular sentimental fiction].

5. Isaac Newton (1642–1727), brilliant physicist and mathematician.

6. In the 18th century, the question whether the soul was marked by a sexual character, like the body, was widely debated. "Clay" is a familiar figure for the body.

from *Chapter 3. The Same Subject Continued*

If it be granted that woman was not created merely to gratify the appetite of man, or to be the upper servant, who provides his meals and takes care of his linen, it must follow, that the first care of those mothers or fathers, who really attend to the education of females, should be, if not to strengthen the body, at least, not to destroy the constitution by mistaken notions of beauty and female excellence; nor should girls ever be allowed to imbibe the pernicious notion that a defect can, by any chemical process of reasoning, become an excellence. In this respect, I am happy to find, that the author of one of the most instructive books, that our country has produced for children, coincides with me in opinion; I shall quote his pertinent remarks to give the force of his respectable authority to reason.[1]

But should it be proved that woman is naturally weaker than man, whence does it follow that it is natural for her to labour to become still weaker than nature intended her to be? Arguments of this cast are an insult to common sense, and savour of passion. The *divine right* of husbands, like the divine right of kings, may, it is to be hoped, in this enlightened age, be contested without danger, and, though conviction may not silence many boisterous disputants, yet, when any prevailing prejudice is attacked, the wise will consider, and leave the narrow-minded to rail with thoughtless vehemence at innovation.

The mother, who wishes to give true dignity of character to her daughter, must, regardless of the sneers of ignorance, proceed on a plan diametrically opposite to that which Rousseau has recommended with all the deluding charms of eloquence and philosophical sophistry: for his eloquence renders absurdities plausible, and his dogmatic conclusions puzzle, without convincing, those who have not ability to refute them.

Throughout the whole animal kingdom every young creature requires almost continual exercise, and the infancy of children, conformable to this intimation, should be passed in harmless gambols, that exercise the feet and hands, without requiring very minute direction from the head, or the constant attention of a nurse. In fact, the care necessary for self-preservation is the first natural exercise of the understanding, as little inventions to amuse the present moment unfold the imagination. But these wise designs of nature are counteracted by mistaken fondness or blind zeal. The child is not left a moment to its own direction, particularly a girl, and thus rendered dependent—dependence is called natural.

To preserve personal beauty, woman's glory! the limbs and faculties are cramped with worse than Chinese bands,[2] and the sedentary life which they are

1. "If women are in general feeble both in body and mind, it arises less from nature than from education. We encourage a vicious indolence and inactivity, which we falsely call delicacy; instead of hardening their minds by the severer principles of reason and philosophy, we breed them to useless arts, which terminate in vanity and sensuality. In most of the countries which I had visited, they are taught nothing of an higher nature than a few modulations of the voice, or useless postures of the body; their time is consumed in sloth or trifles, and trifles become the only pursuits capable of interesting them. We seem to forget, that it is upon the qualities of the female sex that our own domestic comforts and the education of our children must depend. And what are the comforts or the education which a race of beings, corrupted from their infancy, and unacquainted with all the duties of life, are fitted to bestow? To touch a musical instrument with useless skill, to exhibit their natural or affected graces to the eyes of indolent and debauched young men, to dissipate their husband's patrimony [his inheritance as well as his children's] in riotous and unneccessary [sic] expences, these are the only arts cultivated by women in most of the polished nations I had seen. And the consequences are uniformly such as may be expected to proceed from such polluted sources, private misery and public servitude . . . ." Mr. [Thomas] Day's *Sandford and Merton*, Vol III [Wollstonecraft's note].

2. The Chinese practice of binding girls' feet to keep them delicately small often left them crippled for life, reinforcing dependency.

condemned to live, whilst boys frolic in the open air, weakens the muscles and relaxes the nerves.—As for Rousseau's remarks, which have since been echoed by several writers, that they have naturally, that is from their birth, independent of education, a fondness for dolls, dressing, and talking[3]—they are so puerile as not to merit a serious refutation. That a girl, condemned to sit for hours together listening to the idle chat of weak nurses, or to attend at her mother's toilet,[4] will endeavour to join the conversation, is, indeed, very natural; and that she will imitate her mother or aunts, and amuse herself by adorning her lifeless doll, as they do in dressing her, poor innocent babe! is undoubtedly a most natural consequence. For men of the greatest abilities have seldom had sufficient strength to rise above the surrounding atmosphere; and, if the page of genius have always been blurred by the prejudices of the age, some allowance should be made for a sex, who, like kings, always see things through a false medium.

Pursuing these reflections, the fondness for dress, conspicuous in women, may be easily accounted for, without supposing it the result of a desire to please the sex on which they are dependent. The absurdity, in short, of supposing that a girl is naturally a coquette, and that a desire connected with the impulse of nature to propagate the species, should appear even before an improper education has, by heating the imagination, called it forth prematurely, is so unphilosophical, that such a sagacious observer as Rousseau would not have adopted it, if he had not been accustomed to make reason give way to his desire of singularity, and truth to a favorite paradox.[5] * * *

I have, probably, had an opportunity of observing more girls in their infancy than J. J. Rousseau[6]—I can recollect my own feelings, and I have looked steadily around me; yet, so far from coinciding with him in opinion respecting the first dawn of the female character, I will venture to affirm, that a girl, whose spirits have not been damped by inactivity, or innocence tainted by false shame, will always be a romp, and the doll will never excite attention unless confinement allows her no alternative. Girls and boys, in short, would play harmlessly together, if the distinction of sex was not inculcated long before nature makes any difference.—I will go further, and affirm, as an indisputable fact, that most of the women, in the circle of my observation, who have acted like rational creatures, or shewn any vigour of intellect, have accidentally been allowed to run wild—as some of the elegant formers of the fair sex would insinuate. * * *

I once knew a weak woman of fashion, who was more than commonly proud of her delicacy and sensibility. She thought a distinguishing taste and puny appetite the height of all human perfection, and acted accordingly.—I have seen this weak sophisticated being neglect all the duties of life, yet recline with self-complacency on a sofa, and boast of her want of appetite as a proof of delicacy that extended to, or, perhaps, arose from, her exquisite sensibility: for it is difficult to render intelligible such ridiculous jargon.—Yet, at the moment, I have seen her insult a worthy old gentlewoman, whom unexpected misfortunes had made dependent on her ostentatious bounty, and who, in better days, had claims on her gratitude. Is it possible that a human creature could have become such a weak and depraved being, if, like the Sybarites,[7] dissolved in luxury, every thing like virtue had not been worn away, or

3. See *Émile*, ch. 5.
4. Grooming and dressing.
5. See *Émile*, ch. 5.
6. Wollstonecraft was the eldest sister in a family with

three girls and had also worked as a governess.
7. The inhabitants of a 5th-century Greek colony in Italy famed for luxurious decadence.

never impressed by precept, a poor substitute, it is true, for cultivation of mind, though it serves as a fence against vice?

Such a woman is not a more irrational monster than some of the Roman emperors, who were depraved by lawless power. Yet, since kings have been more under the restraint of law, and the curb, however weak, of honour, the records of history are not filled with such unnatural instances of folly and cruelty, nor does the despotism that kills virtue and genius in the bud, hover over Europe with that destructive blast which desolates Turkey, and renders the men, as well as the soil, unfruitful.[8] * * *

It is time to effect a revolution in female manners—time to restore to them their lost dignity—and make them, as a part of the human species, labour by reforming themselves to reform the world. It is time to separate unchangeable morals from local manners.—If men be demi-gods—why let us serve them! And if the dignity of the female soul be as disputable as that of animals—if their reason does not afford sufficient light to direct their conduct whilst unerring instinct is denied—they are surely of all creatures the most miserable! and, bent beneath the iron hand of destiny, must submit to be a *fair defect* in creation. But to justify the ways of Providence respecting them, by pointing out some irrefragable reason for thus making such a large portion of mankind accountable and not accountable, would puzzle the subtilest casuist.[9] * * *

I must relieve myself by drawing a different picture.

Let fancy now present a woman with a tolerable understanding, for I do not wish to leave the line of mediocrity, whose constitution, strengthened by exercise, has allowed her body to acquire its full vigour; her mind, at the same time, gradually expanding itself to comprehend the moral duties of life, and in what human virtue and dignity consist.

Formed thus by the discharge of the relative duties of her station, she marries from affection, without losing sight of prudence, and looking beyond matrimonial felicity, she secures her husband's respect before it is necessary to exert mean arts to please him and feed a dying flame, which nature doomed to expire when the object became familiar, when friendship and forbearance take place of a more ardent affection.—This is the natural death of love, and domestic peace is not destroyed by struggles to prevent its extinction. I also suppose the husband to be virtuous; or she is still more in want of independent principles.

Fate, however, breaks this tie.—She is left a widow, perhaps, without a sufficient provision; but she is not desolate! The pang of nature is felt; but after time has softened sorrow into melancholy resignation, her heart turns to her children with redoubled fondness, and anxious to provide for them, affection gives a sacred heroic cast to her maternal duties. She thinks that not only the eye sees her virtuous efforts from whom all her comfort now must flow, and whose approbation is life; but her imagination, a little abstracted and exalted by grief, dwells on the fond hope that the eyes which her trembling hand closed, may still see how she subdues every wayward passion to fulfil the double duty of being the father as well as the mother of her children. Raised to heroism by misfortunes, she represses the first faint dawning of a natural inclination, before it ripens into love, and in the bloom of life forgets her sex—forgets the pleasure of an awakening passion, which might again have been inspired and returned. She no longer thinks of pleasing, and conscious dignity prevents her from priding herself on account of the praise which her conduct demands. Her children have her love, and her brightest hopes are beyond the grave, where her imagination often strays.

8. Both the hot, dusty winds from the deserts to the south and the infamously despotic Ottoman Empire.
9. For "fair defect," see *Paradise Lost* 8.891–92; Milton begins his epic invoking divine inspiration to "justify the ways of God to men" (1.26); a casuist is one who debates ethical questions with overtones of dishonesty.

I think I see her surrounded by her children, reaping the reward of her care. The intelligent eye meets hers, whilst health and innocence smile on their chubby cheeks, and as they grow up the cares of life are lessened by their grateful attention. She lives to see the virtues which she endeavoured to plant on principles, fixed into habits, to see her children attain a strength of character sufficient to enable them to endure adversity without forgetting their mother's example.

The task of life thus fulfilled, she calmly waits for the sleep of death, and rising from the grave, may say—Behold, thou gavest me a talent—and here are five talents.[1]

I wish to sum up what I have said in a few words, for I here throw down my gauntlet, and deny the existence of sexual virtues, not excepting modesty.[2] For man and woman, truth, if I understand the meaning of the word, must be the same; yet the fanciful female character, so prettily drawn by poets and novelists, demanding the sacrifice of truth and sincerity, virtue becomes a relative idea, having no other foundation than utility, and of that utility men pretend arbitrarily to judge, shaping it to their own convenience.

Women, I allow, may have different duties to fulfil; but they are *human* duties, and the principles that should regulate the discharge of them, I sturdily maintain, must be the same. * * *

from Chapter 13. Some Instances of the Folly Which the Ignorance of Women Generates; with Concluding Reflections on the Moral Improvement That a Revolution in Female Manners Might Naturally Be Expected to Produce

[CONCLUDING REFLECTIONS]

That women at present are by ignorance rendered foolish or vicious, is, I think, not to be disputed; and, that the most salutary effects tending to improve mankind might be expected from a REVOLUTION in female manners, appears, at least, with a face of probability, to rise out of the observation. For as marriage has been termed the parent of those endearing charities which draw man from the brutal herd, the corrupting intercourse that wealth, idleness, and folly, produce between the sexes, is more universally injurious to morality than all the other vices of mankind collectively considered. To adulterous lust the most sacred duties are sacrificed, because before marriage, men, by a promiscuous intimacy with women, learned to consider love as a selfish gratification—learned to separate it not only from esteem, but from the affection merely built on habit, which mixes a little humanity with it. Justice and friendship are also set at defiance, and that purity of taste is vitiated which would naturally lead a man to relish an artless display of affection rather than affected airs. But that noble simplicity of affection, which dares to appear unadorned, has few attractions for the libertine, though it be the charm, which by cementing the matrimonial tie, secures to the pledges of a warmer passion the necessary parental attention; for children will never

---

1. An extravagant rewriting of Jesus' parable of the talents (Matthew 25.15–28), on the duty to make good use of God's gifts. A master, having given one servant five talents (a talent is a silver coin worth about $1,000 today), another two, and another only one, is pleased to learn that first two have doubled their money; but he is so enraged at the timidity of the third servant, who has only buried his talent, that he takes the money away from him and gives it to the first servant.

2. Wollstonecraft is using an image of male warfare: to throw down one's gauntlet, the glove of combat armor, is a challenge to combat. By "sexual virtues," she means sex-specific; "modesty" (usually regarded as a "feminine" characteristic) refers to the general moral discipline of self-restraint and respect for others desirable in both sexes.

be properly educated till friendship subsists between parents. Virtue flies from a house divided against itself—and a whole legion of devils take up their residence there.[1]

The affection of husbands and wives cannot be pure when they have so few sentiments in common, and when so little confidence is established at home, as must be the case when their pursuits are so different. That intimacy from which tenderness should flow, will not, cannot subsist between the vicious.

Contending, therefore, that the sexual distinction which men have so warmly insisted upon, is arbitrary, I have dwelt on an observation, that several sensible men, with whom I have conversed on the subject, allowed to be well founded; and it is simply this, that the little chastity to be found amongst men, and consequent disregard of modesty, tend to degrade both sexes; and further, that the modesty of women, characterized as such, will often be only the artful veil of wantonness instead of being the natural reflection of purity, till modesty be universally respected.[2]

From the tyranny of man, I firmly believe, the greater number of female follies proceed; and the cunning, which I allow makes at present a part of their character, I likewise have repeatedly endeavoured to prove, is produced by oppression.

Were not dissenters,[3] for instance, a class of people, with strict truth, characterized as cunning? And may I not lay some stress on this fact to prove, that when any power but reason curbs the free spirit of man, dissimulation is practised, and the various shifts of art are naturally called forth? Great attention to decorum, which was carried to a degree of scrupulosity, and all that puerile bustle about trifles and consequential solemnity, which Butler's caricature of a dissenter, brings before the imagination, shaped their persons as well as their minds in the mould of prim littleness.[4] I speak collectively, for I know how many ornaments to human nature have been enrolled amongst sectaries; yet, I assert, that the same narrow prejudice for their sect, which women have for their families, prevailed in the dissenting part of the community, however worthy in other respects; and also that the same timid prudence, or headstrong efforts, often disgraced the exertions of both. Oppression thus formed many of the features of their character perfectly to coincide with that of the oppressed half of mankind; or is it not notorious that dissenters were, like women, fond of deliberating together, and asking advice of each other, till by a complication of little contrivances, some little end was brought about? A similar attention to preserve their reputation was conspicuous in the dissenting and female world, and was produced by a similar cause.

Asserting the rights which women in common with men ought to contend for, I have not attempted to extenuate their faults; but to prove them to be the natural consequence of their education and station in society. If so, it is reasonable to suppose that they will change their character, and correct their vices and follies, when they are allowed to be free in a physical, moral, and civil sense.[5]

1. An allusion to Jesus' lesson that "if a house be divided against itself, that house cannot stand" (Mark 3.25).
2. By chastity and modesty, Wollstonecraft means sexual self-control and self-discipline; male chastity entails fidelity, not sexual self-denial, in marriage.
3. Those who dissented from the established Church of England to form independent religious sects; many of Wollstonecraft's friends were dissenters.
4. Samuel Butler's mock-heroic, satirical poem Hudibras (1663–1678) takes aim at Puritans (dissenters who formed the commonwealth government after the execution of Charles I); Sir Hudibras, pedant and hypocrite, is a country justice who sets out to reform England of various popular entertainments.
5. I had further enlarged on the advantages which might reasonably be expected to result from an improvement in female manners, towards the general reformation of society; but it appeared to me that such reflections would more properly close the last volume. [Wollstonecraft's note; no further volumes were published].

Let woman share the rights and she will emulate the virtues of man; for she must grow more perfect when emancipated, or justify the authority that chains such a weak being to her duty.—If the latter, it will be expedient to open a fresh trade with Russia for whips; a present which a father should always make to his son-in-law on his wedding day, that a husband may keep his whole family in order by the same means; and without any violation of justice reign, wielding this sceptre, sole master of his house, because he is the only being in it who has reason:—the divine, indefeasible earthly sovereignty breathed into man by the Master of the universe. Allowing this position, women have not any inherent rights to claim; and, by the same rule, their duties vanish, for rights and duties are inseparable.

Be just then, O ye men of understanding! and mark not more severely what women do amiss, than the vicious tricks of the horse or the ass for whom ye provide provender—and allow her the privileges of ignorance, to whom ye deny the rights of reason, or ye will be worse than Egyptian task-masters, expecting virtue where nature has not given understanding!

A "VINDICATION" IN CONTEXT
The Wollstonecraft Controversy and the Rights of Women

Wollstonecraft's *Vindication of the Rights of Woman* challenged an age when women had no legal standing as daughters or wives, being under the coverture (legal identity) of their fathers and husbands. They could not own property, form contracts, or conduct business. "Obedience" was expected behavior, sanctioned by religion, law, and custom; a rebellious daughter (one, for instance, refusing her father's choice of her husband) could be disowned; divorce was granted only by husbands, who retained custody of all property (including dowry) as well as the children (a prime reason many women remained in abusive marriages). Female suffrage was so outrageous a notion that it could not be debated for another century or so. Far from having any power to change the law by vote, women did not even have legal status, or any representatives for their concerns in Parliament. It was not until 1870 that The Married Woman's Property Act was passed, allowing such women to keep their earnings, and not until 1882 that it was amended to allow them to keep the property, including personal property, that they brought to the marriage (dowry) or acquired during it; this act also gave a woman the right to enter legal contracts and to sue in courts, as well as a legally distinct identity from her husband.

England was not alone in the 1790s in resisting change: even in France the case for women's rights fared so poorly with the Revolutionary government that its champions were sent to the guillotine. French women did not secure the vote until 1944, nearly a century after American feminists presented the Declaration of Sentiments and Resolutions at Seneca Falls. The way was paved for these changes by the constant debate from the 1790s onward over systems of female education, women's rights, and social policy—a debate that even among women involved ideologically disparate, even opposed, commitments. When Maria Edgeworth proposed to Anna Barbauld that they coedit a periodical featuring "the literary ladies of the present day," Barbauld declined on the question of common cause: "There is no bond of union among literary women, any more than among literary men; different sentiments and different connections separate them much more than the joint interest of their sex would unite them. Mrs. Hannah More would not write along with you or me, and we should probably hesitate at joining Miss Hays, or if she were living, Mrs. Godwin" [Wollstonecraft]. Our selections from this tremendous body of literature show the wide range of concerns in this debate and the wide range of responses it involved, in particular to Wollstonecraft—a lightning rod in this charged atmosphere.

Catherine Macaulay
1731–1791

The daughter of a wealthy landowner in Kent and an heiress of a London banker, Macaulay grew up in comfort, and was left well off at the death of her husband, an eminent London obstetrician, in 1776. Her major work is the controversial eight-volume *History of England from the Accession of James I to that of the Brunswick Line* (the current monarchy), published over twenty years (1763–1783). Its defense of Cromwell's regicidal government and its generally antimonarchal Whig sympathies endeared her to Wollstonecraft, poet Thomas Gray, and even Prime Minister William Pitt, even as it earned Edmund Burke's contempt of her as a "republican Virago." Not surprisingly, her political writings were more popular in France and America than in England. In 1785, she visited George and Martha Washington at Mount Vernon and later corresponded with them, as well as with John Adams and Benjamin Franklin. But as with Wollstonecraft, her politics produced enemies and vicious misogynist attacks on her private life, attacks gleefully sharpened by her marriage in 1779, at the age of fifty-seven, to a twenty-one-year-old William Graham.

Letters on Education, published in 1790, deeply influenced Wollstonecraft, who called Macaulay "the woman of the greatest abilities, undoubtedly, that this country has ever produced." She did not live to see the publication of *Rights of Woman*, in which Wollstonecraft praises her "strong and clear" intellect and echoes many of her polemics: the attack on the gender ideologies proffered by Rousseau and Pope and on the cultural systems that educate women into "a state of slavery"; a disdain of "coquetry" (the female art of manipulating men through their passions); a scathing critique of the language of female compliments; and advocacy of coeducation and a gender-neutral standard of "rational" conduct.

from Letters on Education
from Letter 22. No Characteristic Difference in Sex

The great difference that is observable in the characters of the sexes, Hortensia,[1] as they display themselves in the scenes of social life, has given rise to much false speculation on the natural qualities of the female mind.—For though the doctrine of innate ideas, and innate affections, are in a great measure exploded by the learned, yet few persons reason so closely and so accurately on abstract subjects as, through a long chain of deductions, to bring forth a conclusion which in no respect militates with their premises.

It is a long time before the crowd give up opinions they have been taught to look upon with respect. * * * It is from such causes that the notion of a sexual difference in the human character has, with very few exceptions, universally prevailed from the

---

1. The fictitious recipient of the letter.

earliest times, and the pride of one sex, and the ignorance and vanity of the other, have helped to support an opinion which a close observation of Nature, and a more accurate way of reasoning, would disprove.

It must be confessed, that the virtues of the males among the human species, though mixed and blended with a variety of vices and errors, have displayed a bolder and a more consistent picture of excellence than female nature has hitherto done. It is on these reasons that, when we compliment the appearance of a more than ordinary energy in the female mind, we call it masculine; and hence it is, that Pope has elegantly said *a perfect woman's but a softer man*.[2] And if we take in the consideration, that there can be but one rule of moral excellence for beings made of the same materials, organized after the same manner, and subjected to similar laws of Nature, we must either agree with Mr. Pope, or we must reverse the proposition, and say, that *a perfect man is a woman formed after a coarser mold*. The difference that actually does subsist between the sexes, is too flattering for men to be willingly imputed to accident; for what accident occasions, wisdom might correct; and it is better, says Pride, to give up the advantages we might derive from the perfection of our fellow associates, than to own that Nature has been just in the equal distribution of her favours. These are the sentiments of the men: but mark how readily they are yielded to by the women; not from humility I assure you, but merely to preserve with character those fond vanities on which they set their hearts. No; suffer them to idolize their persons, to throw away their life in the pursuit of trifles, and to indulge in the gratification of the meaner passions, and they will heartily join in the sentence of their degradation.

Among the most strenuous asserters of a sexual difference in character, Rousseau is the most conspicuous, both on account of that warmth of sentiment which distinguishes all his writings, and the eloquence of his compositions: but never did enthusiasm and the love of paradox, those enemies to philosophical disquisition, appear in more strong opposition to plain sense than in Rousseau's definition of this difference.[3] He sets out with a supposition, that Nature intended the subjection of the one sex to the other; that consequently there must be an inferiority of intellect in the subjected party; but as man is a very imperfect being, and apt to play the capricious tyrant, Nature, to bring things nearer to an equality, bestowed on the woman such attractive graces, and such an insinuating address, as to turn the balance on the other scale. Thus Nature, in a giddy mood, recedes from her purposes, and subjects prerogative to an influence which must produce confusion and disorder in the system of human affairs. Rousseau saw this objection; and in order to obviate it, he has made up a moral person of the union of the two sexes, which, for contradiction and absurdity, outdoes every metaphysical riddle that was ever formed in the schools. In short, it is not reason, it is not wit; it is pride and sensuality that speak in Rousseau, and, in this instance, has lowered the man of genius to the licentious pedant. * * * for so little did a wise and just Providence intend to make the condition of slavery an unalterable law of female nature, that in the same proportion as the male sex have consulted the interest of their own happiness, they have relaxed in their tyranny over women; and such is

---

2. A slight misquotation of *Epistle II*, "Of the Characters of Women": "Heaven, when it strives to polish all it can / Its last best work, but forms a softer man" (271–272).

3. Referring to Rousseau's arguments throughout *Émile*, especially ch. 5 ("Sophy").

their use in the system of mundane creation, and such their natural influence over the male mind, that were these advantages properly exerted, they might carry every point of any importance to their honour and happiness. However, till that period arrives in which women will act wisely, we will amuse ourselves in talking of their follies.

The situation and education of women, Hortensia, is precisely that which must necessarily tend to corrupt and debilitate both the powers of mind and body. From a false notion of beauty and delicacy, their system of nerves is depraved before they come out of their nursery; and this kind of depravity has more influence over the mind, and consequently over morals, than is commonly apprehended. But it would be well if such causes only acted towards the debasement of the sex; their moral education is, if possible, more absurd than their physical. The principles and nature of virtue, which is never properly explained to boys, is kept quite a mystery to girls. They are told indeed, that they must abstain from those vices which are contrary to their personal happiness, or they will be regarded as criminals, both by God and man; but all the higher parts of rectitude, every thing that ennobles our being, and that renders us both innoxious and useful, is either not taught, or is taught in such a manner as to leave no proper impression on the mind. This is so obvious a truth, that the defects of female education have ever been a fruitful topic of declamation for the moralist; but not one of this class of writers have laid down any judicious rules for amendment. Whilst we still retain the absurd notion of a sexual excellence, it will mitigate against the perfecting a plan of education for either sex. The judicious Addison animadverts on the absurdity of bringing a young lady up with no higher idea of the end of education than to make her agreeable to a husband, and confining the necessary excellence for this happy acquisition to the mere graces of person.[4]

Every parent and tutor may not express himself in the same manner as is marked out by Addison; yet certain it is, that the admiration of the other sex is held out to women as the highest honour they can attain; and whilst this is considered as their *summum bonum* [highest good] and the beauty of their persons the chief *desideratum* [thing wanted] of men, Vanity, and its companion Envy, must taint, in their characters, every native and every acquired excellence. Nor can you, Hortensia, deny, that these qualities, when united to ignorance, are fully equal to the engendering and riveting all those vices and foibles which are peculiar to the female sex; vices and foibles which have caused them to be considered, in ancient times, as beneath cultivation, and in modern days have subjected them to the censure and ridicule of writers of all descriptions, from the deep thinking philosopher to the man of ton[5] and gallantry, who, by the bye, sometimes distinguishes himself by qualities which are not greatly superior to those he despises in women. Nor can I better illustrate the truth of this observation than by the following picture, to be found in the polite and gallant Chesterfield. "Women," says his Lordship, "are only children of a larger growth. They have an entertaining tattle, sometimes wit; but for solid reasoning, and good sense, I never in my life knew one that had it, or who acted or reasoned in consequence of it for four and twenty hours together. A man of sense only trifles with them, plays with

---

4. Joseph Addison (1672–1719), essayist and poet. Macaulay wrongly attributes to Addison an unsigned essay on this subject in *The Spectator* by his collaborator,

Richard Steele. Animadverts: criticizes.
5. Fashion.

them, humours and flatters them, as he does an engaging child; but he neither consults them, nor trusts them in serious matters." 6

⊷ ⥇◆⥇ ⥱

Richard Polwhele
1760–1838

Reverend Polwhele was educated at Oxford, first training for the law. He wrote poetry, histories, journalism, theological tracts, and translations of Greek literature, and was a frequent contributor to some leading conservative journals of his day, including the *Anti-Jacobin*. Among his mother's friends were two outspoken writers about the situation of women, Hannah More and Catherine Macaulay, whom he met in 1777. He participated in an elaborate birthday celebration for Macaulay, writing an ode for her that he included in his first volume of poetry, published in 1777. *The Unsex'd Females* appeared in 1798, at the end of a decade of vigorous debate about women's rights inaugurated by Macaulay's *Letters on Education* (1790) and Wollstonecraft's *Rights of Woman* (1792).

By 1798, both Macaulay and Wollstonecraft were dead, and a reactionary political climate as well as the scandal of Wollstonecraft's life had dealt "rights of woman" a serious setback. The only voices to command popular sympathy were calls for female education in modest, virtuous intelligence, trained to the values of piety, obedience, and domestic duty, and devoted to the formation of Christian daughters, wives, and mothers. Fresh from reading Godwin's memoir of Wollstonecraft, Polwhele, with tones tipping from nasty to horrified, castigated its revelations in a review for the *European Magazine* and in *The Unsex'd Females*. With an explicit political agenda, the poem casts radicals such as Wollstonecraft as "unnatural," "licentious," anti-Christian revolutionaries, driven by the ideology of godless "Reason." Yet the animosities extend to a strange sorority. In addition to Wollstonecraft and her allies, Helen Maria Williams and Mary Hays, its indictment includes women of quite different views, having in common with the radicals only a public voice: poet and novelist Charlotte Smith, initially a sympathizer with the French Revolution, but famous by 1793 for *The Emigrants* (a long poem expressing her outrage at the massacre of French aristocrats and her sympathy for those forced to flee) and by the decade's end, an outspoken reactionary; Anna Barbauld, an abolitionist, but no revolutionary, no fan of Wollstonecraft, and very qualified on women's rights; Mary Robinson, advocate of abolition but not primarily a political writer; Anne Yearsley, advocate for the poor and an abolitionist but also a voice of anti-Revolution sympathies in *Reflections on the Death of Louis XVI* (1793) and *An Elegy on Marie Antoinette* (1795). So as not to seem flatly misogynist, Polwhele ends his poem celebrating conservative eighteenth-century bluestocking women, a "kindred train" who "influence" through "modest virtue," and allied with such conservatives as Horace Walpole, Joshua Reynolds, Samuel Johnson, and Edmund Burke: the "Queen of the Blues" Elizabeth Montagu (1720–1800), scholar and poet Elizabeth Carter (1717–1806), poet and educational theorist Hester Chapone (1727–1801), poet Anna Seward (1743–1809), woman of letters Hester Thrale Piozzi (1741–1821), novelists Frances Burney (1752–1840) and Anne Radcliffe (1764–1823). He ventriloquizes his praise through the voice of their disciple Hannah More, whose views on the "natural" differences of the sexes and their separate spheres he warmly endorses. Polwhele's numerous footnotes, which nearly overwhelm his poem, are not supplementary but an important part of his polemic. Some of these notes, especially ones on the question of women's rights and ones relevant to other writers in this volume, are included in the excerpt here.

---

6. *Letters to His Son* no. 294 (16 Nov. 1752), also cited in *Rights of Woman*, ch. 4. Philip Chesterfield (1694–1773), statesman, author, and wit, wrote letters of advice to his illegitimate son from age five until his own death; published in 1774, these became famous (or infamous) for their comments on sexual behavior and rituals.

from The Unsex'd Females

Thou, who with all the poet's genuine rage,
Thy "fine eye rolling" o'er "this aweful age,"[1]
Where polish'd life unfolds its various views,
Hast mark'd the magic influence of the muse;
5　Sever'd, with nice precision, from her beam
Of genial power, her false and feeble gleam;
Expos'd the Sciolist's[2] vain-glorious claim,
And boldly thwarted Innovation's aim,
Where witlings wildly think, or madly dare,[3]
10　With Honor, Virtue, Truth, announcing war;
Survey with me, what ne'er our fathers saw,
A female band despising NATURE's law,[4]
As "proud defiance"[5] flashes from their arms,
And vengeance smothers all their softer charms.
15　　*I* shudder at the new unpictur'd scene,
Where unsex'd woman vaunts the imperious mien;
Where girls, affecting to dismiss the heart,
Invoke the Proteus of petrific art;[6]
With equal ease, in body or in mind,
20　To Gallic freaks or Gallic faith[7] resign'd,
The crane-like neck, as Fashion bids, lay bare,
Or frizzle, bold in front, their borrow'd hair;°　　　　　　　*wigs*
Scarce by a gossamery film carest,
Sport, in full view, the meretricious breast;[8]
25　Loose the chaste cincture,[9] where the graces shone,
And languish'd all the Loves, the ambrosial zone;

1. The addressee is another Tory conservative scourge, Thomas James Mathias, whose long satirical poem *The Pursuits of Literature* (1794–1797), also encased in footnotes, inspired Polwhele's. In his Preface to the 4th dialogue of this popular poem (16 editions), Mathias lamented that "our *unsexed* female writers now instruct, or confuse, us and themselves in the labyrinth of politics, or turn us wild with Gallic frenzy"—French-inspired ideas and fashions. He begins representing himself "not unconscious of this awful age" (1.7), echoing Milton's representation of himself and other visionary poets as chastisers of their own age, "fall'n on evil days" (*Paradise Lost* 7.25). Theseus in *A Midsummer Night's Dream* describes "the poet's eye, in a fine frenzy rolling" (5.1.12).
2. Displayer of superficial learning.
3. "Greatly think, or nobly die." Pope [Polwhele's note, slightly misquoting l.10 of *Elegy to the Memory of an Unfortunate Lady*, about a woman whom seems to have committed suicide in despair of love].
4. Nature is the grand basis of all laws human and divine: and the woman, who has no regard to nature, either in the decoration of her person, or the culture of her mind, will soon "walk after the flesh, in the lust of uncleanness, and despise government" [Polwhele's note, quoting 2 Peter 2:10; Rousseau and other defenders of sexual inequality routinely invoke "Natural" or "Nature's" law].
5. "A troop came next, who crowns and armour wore, / And proud defiance in their looks they bore." Pope. The Amazonian band—the female Quixotes of the new philosophy, are, here, too justly characterised [Polwhele's

note]. The quotation is from *The Temple of Fame* (1711, ll.342–343), the troop answering "the direful trump of Slander." The Amazons, legendary race of warrior women from Scythia, near the Black Sea, frequently assailed the Greeks; they were fabled to have burnt off the right breast (*a*, without; *mazos*, breast) to facilitate use of bow or javelin; the term is used, not always disparagingly, for any "masculine" woman, or, disparagingly, as a synonym for virago. Quixotes (from Cervantes' hero) are impractical idealists.
6. Proteus: god able to change shapes at will; petrific: able to turn to stone, as if a Medusa, an unfeeling woman.
7. French fashions and the new French (Godless) religion.
8. To "sport a face," is a cant phrase in one of our Universities, by which is meant an impudent obtrusion of a man's person in company. It is not inapplicable, perhaps, to the open bosom—a fashion which we have never invited or sanctioned. The fashions of France, which have been always imitated by the English, were, heretofore, unexceptionable in a moral point of view; since, however ridiculous or absurd, they were innocent. But they have now their source among prostitutes—among women of the most abandoned character. [Polwhele's note]. Meretricious: whorish. An 18th-century French aristocratic fashion was a fancy-gown neckline plunged below the bosom, displaying it bare.
9. A wide belt surrounding the waist and sometimes the bosom, as a girdle; it is "chaste" for concealing breasts and hips.

As lordly domes inspire dramatic rage,
Court prurient Fancy to the private stage;
With bliss botanic[1] as their bosoms heave,
30   Still pluck forbidden fruit, with mother Eve,
For puberty in sighing florets pant,
Or point the prostitution of a plant;
Dissect[2] its organ of unhallow'd lust,
And fondly gaze the titillating[3] dust;
35   With liberty's sublimer views expand,
And o'er the wreck of kingdoms[4] sternly stand;
And, frantic, midst the democratic storm,
Pursue, Philosophy! thy phantom-form.
　　　Far other is the female shape and mind,
40   By modest luxury heighten'd and refin'd;
Those limbs, that figure, tho' by Fashion grac'd,
By Beauty polish'd, and adorn'd by Taste;
That soul, whose harmony perennial flows,
In Music trembles, and in Color glows;
45   Which bids sweet Poesy reclaim the praise
With faery light to gild fastidious days,
From sullen clouds relieve domestic care,
And melt in smiles the withering frown of war.
Ah! once the female Muse, to NATURE true,
50   The unvalued store from FANCY, FEELING drew;
Won, from the grasp of woe, the roseate hours,
Cheer'd life's dim vale, and strew'd the grave with flowers.
　　　But lo! where, pale amidst the wild,[5] she draws

1. Botany has lately become a fashionable amusement with the ladies. But how the study of the sexual system of plants can accord with female modesty, I am not able to comprehend. I had first written: "More eager for illicit knowlege [sic] pant, / With lustful boys anatomize a plant; / The virtues of its dust prolific speak, / Or point its pistill with unblushing cheek." I have, several times, seen boys and girls botanizing together [Polwhele's note]. Such judgment of the immodesty of botanizing was probably fueled by Erasmus Darwin, whose popular poem, *The Botanic Garden*, especially Part II, *The Loves of the Plants* (1789; 1791), is explicit about sexual organs and activity. 2. Miss Wollstonecraft does not blush to say, in an introduction to a book designed for the use of young ladies, that, "in order to lay the axe at the root of corruption, it would be proper to familiarize the sexes to an unreserved discussion of those topics, which are generally avoided in conversation from a principle of false delicacy; and that it would be right to speak of the organs of generation as freely as we mention our eyes or our hands." To such language our botanizing girls are doubtless familiarized: and, they are in a fair way of becoming worthy disciples of Miss W. If they do not take heed to their ways, they will soon exchange the blush of modesty for the bronze of impudence [Polwhele's note, alluding to Luke 3.9]. He misrepresents Wollstonecraft's statement in "Introductory Address to Parents," *Elements of Morality, For the Use of Children* (1792): concerned with masturbation and other "impure" practices, she contends that "the most efficacious method to root out this dreadful evil, which poisons the source of human happiness, would be to speak to children of the organs of generation as freely as we speak of the other parts of the body, and explain to them the noble use which they were designed for, and how they may be injured." In *Rights of Woman* (ch. 7: "Modesty") she refutes as "absurd" the "gross idea" that botany is inconsistent with female modesty, and lists it among the subjects that boys and girls might study together (ch. 12: "On National Education").
3. "Each pungent grain of titillating dust." Pope; "The prolific dust"—of the botanist [Polwhele's note, alluding to the "Charge of *Snuff*"—"The pungent Grains of titillating Dust"—Belinda hurls at her adversary in *The Rape of the Lock* (5.84)].
4. The female advocates of Democracy in this country, though they have had no opportunity of imitating the French ladies, in their atrocious acts of cruelty; have yet assumed a stern serenity in the contemplation of those savage excesses. "To express their abhorrence of royalty, they (the French ladies) threw away the character of their sex, and bit the amputated limbs of their murdered countrymen.—I say this on the authority of a young gentleman who saw it.—I am sorry to add, that the relation, accompanied with looks of horror and disgust, only provoked a contemptuous smile from an illuminated British fair-one." See Robinson [Polwhele's note, quoting *Proofs of a Conspiracy*].
5. "A wild, where flowers and weeds promiscuous shoot; / A garden tempting with forbidden fruit." Pope [Polwhele's note, quoting *Essay on Man* (1733): Epistle I, 7–8].

Each precept cold from sceptic Reason's[6] vase;
55   Pours with rash arm the turbid stream along,
And in the foaming torrent whelms the throng.[7]
       Alas! her pride sophistic° flings a gloom,   *specious*
To chase, sweet Innocence! thy vernal bloom,
Of each light joy to damp the genial glow,
60   And with new terrors clothe the groupe of woe,
Quench the pure daystar° in oblivion deep,   *sun*
And, Death! restore thy "long, unbroken sleep."[8]
       See Wollstonecraft, whom no decorum checks,
Arise, the intrepid champion of her sex;
65   O'er humbled man assert the sovereign claim,
And slight the timid blush[9] of virgin fame.
       "Go, go (she cries) ye tribes of melting maids,
Go, screen your softness in sequester'd shades;
With plaintive whispers woo the unconscious grove,
70   And feebly perish, as depis'd ye love.
What tho' the fine Romances of Rousseau
Bid the frame flutter, and the bosom glow;
Tho' the rapt Bard, your empire fond to own,
Fall prostrate and adore your living throne,
75   The living throne his hands presum'd to rear,
Its seat a simper, and its base a tear;[1]
Soon shall the sex disdain the illusive sway,
And wield the sceptre in yon blaze of day;
Ere long, each little artifice discard,
80   No more by weakness[2] winning fond regard;
Nor eyes, that sparkle from their blushes, roll,
Nor catch the languors of the sick'ning soul,
Nor the quick flutter, nor the coy reserve,
But nobly boast the firm gymnastic nerve;[3]
85   Nor more affect with Delicacy's fan
To hide the emotion from congenial man;
To the bold heights where glory beams, aspire,
Blend mental energy with Passion's fire,
Surpass their rivals in the powers of mind

6. A troubled stream only, can proceed from the vase of scepticism [Polwhele's note, alluding to the Revolutionaries' (Godless) ideology of "Reason"].

7. "Raging waves, foaming out their own shame"—St. Jude. Such were those infamous publications of Paine and others, which, like the torrents of December, threatened to sweep all before them—to overwhelm the multitude [Polwhele's note].

8. "We, the great, the valiant and the wise, / When once the seal of death hath clos'd our eyes, / Shut in the hollow tomb obscure and deep, / Slumber, to wake no more, one long unbroken sleep." Moschus [Polwhele's note; Moschus: 2nd-century B.C. Greek pastoral poet, whom he translated in a well-received publication of 1786].

9. That Miss Wollstonecraft was a sworn enemy to blushes, I need not remark. But many of my readers, perhaps, will be astonished to hear, that at several of our boarding-schools for young ladies, a blush incurs a penalty [Polwhele's note].

1. According to Rousseau, the empire of women is the empire of softness—of address: their commands, are caresses; their menaces, are tears. [Polwhele's note, referring to Rousseau's views on women in *La Nouvelle Heloise* (1760) and *Émile* (1762), both criticized by Wollstonecraft in *Rights of Woman*.]

2. "Like monarchs, we have been flattered into imbecillity, by those who wish to take advantage of our weakness," says Mary Hays (*Essays and Letters*, p. 92). But, whether flattered or not, women were always weak: and female weakness hath accomplished, what the force of arms could not effect [Polwhele's note, quoting her passionate endorsement of Wollstonecraft's *Rights of Woman*]. Hays's feminist *Appeal to the Men of Great Britain on Behalf of Women* appeared anonymously in 1798.

3. Miss Wollstonecraft seriously laments the neglect of all muscular exercises, at our female Boarding-schools [Polwhele's note].

90   And vindicate *the Rights of womankind."*
               She spoke: and veteran BARBAULD[4] caught the strain,
            And deem'd her songs of Love, her Lyrics vain;
            And ROBINSON[5] to Gaul her Fancy gave,
            And trac'd the picture of a Deist's grave!
95   And charming SMITH[6] resign'd her power to please,
            Poetic feeling and poetic ease;
            And HELEN,[7] fir'd by Freedom, bade adieu
            To all the broken visions of Peru.
            And YEARSELEY,[8] who had warbled, Nature's child,
100   Midst twilight dews, her minstrel ditties wild,

4. Here . . . I have formed a groupe of female Writers; whose productions have been appreciated by the public as works of learning or genius—though not praised with that extravagance of panegyric, which was once a customary tribute to the literary compositions of women. In this country, a female author was formerly esteemed a Phenomenon in Literature: and she was sure of a favourable reception among the critics, in consideration of her sex. This species of gallantry, however, conveyed no compliment to her understanding. It implied such an inferiority of woman in the scale of intellect as was justly humiliating: and critical forbearance was mortifying to female vanity. At the present day, indeed, our literary women are so numerous, that their judges, wa[i]ving all complimentary civilities, decide upon their merits with the same rigid impartiality as it seems right to exercise towards the men. The tribunal of criticism is no longer charmed into complacence by the blushes of modest apprehension. It no longer imagines the pleading eye of feminine diffidence that speaks a consciousness of comparative imbecillity, or a fearfulness of having offended by intrusion. Experience hath drawn aside the flimsy veil of affected timidity, that only served to hide the smile of complacency; the glow of self-gratulation. Yet, alas! the crimsoning blush of modesty, will be always more attractive, than the sparkle of confident intelligence.—Mrs. Barbauld stands the most conspicuous figure in the groupe. She is a veteran in Literature . . . Her poetry . . . is certainly, chaste and elegant. . . . I was sorry to find Mrs. B. . . . classed with such females as a Wollstonecraft. . . . But though Mrs. B. has lately published several political tracts, which if not discreditable to her talents and virtues, can by no means add to her reputation, yet, I am sure, she must reprobate, with me, the alarming eccentricities of Miss Wollstonecraft [Polwhele's note].
5. In Mrs. Robinson's Poetry, there is a peculiar delicacy: but her Novels, as literary compositions, have no great claim to approbation—As containing the doctrines of Philosophism, they merit the severest censure. Would that, for the sake of herself and her beautiful daughter (whose personal charms are only equalled by the elegance of her mind) would, that, for the sake of the public morality, Mrs. Robinson were persuaded to dismiss the gloomy phantom of annihilation; to think seriously of a future retribution; and to communicate to the world, a recantation of errors that originated in levity, and have been nursed by pleasure! I have seen her, "glittering like the morning-star, full of life, and splendor and joy!" Such, and more glorious, may I meet her again, when the just "shall shine forth as the brightness of the firmament, and as the stars for ever and ever!" [Polwhele, quoting Burke's famous description of his first sight of princess Marie Antoinette; see *Reflections*, pages 62–63.] "Philosophism" refers to the Enlightenment ideology of progress and human perfectibility through reason.
6. The Sonnets of Charlotte Smith, have a pensiveness peculiarly their own. It is not the monotonous plaintiveness of Shenstone, the gloomy melancholy of Gray, or the meek subdued spirit of Collins. It is a strain of wild, yet softened sorrow, that breathes a romantic air, without losing, for a moment, its mellowness. Her images, often original, are drawn from nature: the most familiar, have a new and charming aspect. Sweetly picturesque, she creates with the pencil of a Gilpin, and infuses her own soul into the landscape. There is so uncommon a variety in her expression, that I could read a thousand of such sonnets without lassitude. In general, a very few Sonnets fatigue attention, partly owing to the sameness of their construction. Petrarch, indeed, I can relish for a considerable time: but Spenser and Milton soon produce somnolence. . . . But why does she suffer her mind to be infected with the Gallic mania? [Polwhele's note]. For Smith's sonnets, see the Companion Readings to Wordsworth, page 1562. Other references are to the 18th-century poets William Shenstone, Thomas Gray, and William Collins, and to William Gilpin (1724–1804), author of illustrated picturesque tours of Britain.
7. Miss Helen Williams is, doubtless, a true poet. But is it not extraordinary, that such a genius, a female and so young, should have become a politician—that the fair Helen, whose notes of love have charmed the moonlight vallies, should stand forward, an intemperate advocate for Gallic licentiousness—that such a woman should import with her, a blast more pestilential than that of Avernus, though she has so often delighted us with melodies, soft as the sighs of the Zephyr, delicious as the airs of Paradise? [Polwhele's note]. See Williams's *Letters from France* (1792–1796), page 1347; her long political poem condemning imperial conquest, *Peru,* was published in 1784. Avernus is a lake in Italy thought to be the gate to the underworld; zephyr is the spring breeze.
8. Mrs. Yearseley's [sic] Poems, as the product of an untutored milk-woman, certainly entitled her to patronage: and patronage she received, from Miss H. More, liberal beyond example. Yet, such is the depravity of the human heart, that this milk-woman had no sooner her hut cheered by the warmth of benevolence, than she spurned her benefactor from her door. . . . My business, however, with Mrs. Y. is to recall her, if possible, from her Gallic wanderings—if an appeal to native ingenuousness be not too late; if the fatal example of the Arch-priestess of female Libertinism, have any influence on a mind once stored with the finest moral sentiment [Polwhele's note]. The "fatal example" is Wollstonecraft.

(Tho' soon a wanderer from her meads and milk,
  She long'd to rustle, like her sex, in silk)
  Now stole that modish grin, the sapient sneer,
  And flippant HAYS[9] assum'd a cynic leer * * *

1798

✦

Hannah More
1745–1833

More came from a High Church–Tory family, and though she would turn Evangelical and become a vigorous abolitionist, her politics never swung left. In *Village Politics* (1792), she criticized the French Revolution and the "Rights of Man," hewing to the Evangelical line that the lot of the poor was to be improved by philanthropy and faith in ultimate salvation. "Rights of women! We shall be hearing of the Rights of Children next!" she scoffed on hearing of Wollstonecraft's *Rights of Woman*. Yet she shared many of its principles: the value of rationality, modesty, chastity, and "practical education" over trivial "accomplishments" like needlework, painting, dancing, and musical performance. Her life, moreover, was not conducted in the traditional "female sphere" of hearth and home. As a child, she learned Latin (a man's language) and mathematics from a father who wanted his daughters to be capable of self-sufficiency as teachers. She later learned French, Italian, and Spanish from her elder sisters. As a young woman, she came to London and entered a lively literary world, becoming friends with Samuel Johnson, actor David Garrick, and Horace Walpole, as well as the women of the Bluestocking Club, celebrated in her long poem *The Bas Bleu* (1786). She was a successful writer even before she gained an annuity of £200 in compensation for a reneged engagement; with this income she was able to live independently, never marrying, and devoting herself to philanthropy and writing, the latter with considerable financial success.

First published in 1799, *Strictures on Female Education* went through thirteen editions and was in demand for decades, selling 19,000 copies. Even more popular (eight editions in its first two months) was her didactic "conduct" novel of 1809, *Coelebs in Search of a Wife*—an easy target for Byron (see *Don Juan* 1.16, page 1688). Like Wollstonecraft, More was willing to condescend to this genre for propaganda. An ideal and idealist young man in quest of an ideal wife, Coelebs auditions several near and not so near Misses until he finds perfection in quiet, proper, prudent Lucilla, blessed with skills in household management and given to compassionate visits to the poor to read to them from the Bible. *Strictures* sets the didactic curriculum, arguing for rational education, Christian virtue, the "separate spheres" of male and female life, and the subordination of women to men.

Another work by More appears in Perspectives: The Abolition of Slavery and the Slave Trade, page 1452.

9. Mary Hays from her "Letters and Essays" . . . is evidently a Wollstonecraftian. "I cannot mention (says she) the admirable advocate for the rights of women, without pausing to pay a tribute of grateful respect, in the name of my sex, to the virtue and talents of a writer, who with equal courage and ability, hath endeavoured to rescue the female mind from those prejudices which have been the canker of genuine virtue. . . . The rights of woman and the name of Wollstonecraft, will go down to posterity with reverence." Mary Hays ridicules "the good lady who studied her Bible, and obliged her children to say their prayers, and go statedly to church." Her expressions respecting the European Governments are, in a high degree, inflammatory [Polwhele's note]. The attacks on

Wollstonecraft continue in subsequent notes, recounting her infatuation with the married Fuseli, her affair with Imlay, her suicide attempts despite a young daughter, her premarital affair with Godwin, and her lack of church attendance or death-bed conversion. "I cannot but think, that the Hand of Providence is visible, in her life, her death and in [Godwin's] Memoirs. . . . As she was given up to her 'heart's lusts,' and let 'to follow her own imaginations,' that the fallacy of and the effects of an irreligious conduct, might be manifested to the world; and as she died a death that strongly marked the distinction of the sexes, by pointing out the destiny of women and the diseases to which they are liable."

from **Strictures on the Modern System of Female Education;**
*with a View of the Principles and Conduct Prevalent
among Women of Rank and Fortune*

from *Introduction*

It is a singular injustice which is often exercised towards women, first to give them a very defective education, and then to expect from them the most undeviating purity of conduct;—to train them in such a manner as shall lay them open to the most dangerous faults, and then to censure them for not proving faultless. Is it not unreasonable and unjust, to express disappointment if our daughters should, in their subsequent lives, turn out precisely that very kind of character for which it would be evident to an unprejudiced by-stander that the whole scope and tenour of their instruction had been systematically preparing them?

Some reflections on the present erroneous system are here with great deference submitted to public consideration. The author is apprehensive that she shall be accused of betraying the interests of her sex by laying open their defects; but surely an earnest wish to turn their attention to objects calculated to promote their true dignity, is not the office of an enemy. So to expose the weakness of the land, as to suggest the necessity of internal improvement, and to point out the means of effectual defence, is not treachery, but patriotism. * * *

Let it not be suspected that the author arrogantly conceives *herself* to be exempt from that natural corruption of the heart which it is one chief object of this slight work to exhibit; that she superciliously erects herself into the impeccable censor of her sex and of the world; as if from the critic's chair she were coldly pointing out the faults and errors of another order of beings, in whose welfare she had not that lively interest which can only flow from the tender and intimate participation of fellow-feeling.

Bath, March 14, 1799

from *Chapter 8. On Female Study*

Will it not be ascribed to a captious singularity, if I venture to remark that real knowledge and real piety, though they may have gained in many instances, have suffered in others from that profusion of little, amusing, sentimental books with which the youthful library overflows? Abundance has its dangers as well as scarcity. In the first place, may not the multiplicity of these alluring little works increase the natural reluctance to those more dry and uninteresting studies, of which, after all, the rudiments of every part of learning *must* consist? And, secondly, is there not some danger (though there are many honourable exceptions) that some of those engaging narratives may serve to infuse into the youthful heart a sort of spurious goodness, a confidence of virtue, a parade of charity? And that the benevolent actions with the recital of which they abound, when they are not made to flow from any source but *feeling*, may tend to inspire a self-complacency, a self-gratulation, a "stand by, for I am holier than thou?" May not the success with which the good deeds of the little heroes are uniformly crowned; the invariable reward which is made the instant concomitant of well-doing, furnish the young reader with false views of the condition of life, and the nature of the divine dealings with men? May they not help to suggest a false standard of morals, to infuse a love of popularity and an anxiety for praise, in the place of that simple and unostentatious rule of doing whatever good we do, *because it is the will of*

God? The universal substitution of this principle would tend to purify the worldly morality of many a popular little story. And there are few dangers which good parents will more carefully guard against than that of giving their children a mere political piety; that sort of religion which just goes to make people more respectable, and to stand well with the world; a religion which is to save appearances without inculcating realities; a religion which affects to "preach peace and good will to men," but which forgets to give "glory to God in the highest."[1]

There is a certain precocity of mind which is much helped on by these superficial modes of instruction; for frivolous reading will produce its correspondent effect, in much less time than books of solid instruction; the imagination being liable to be worked upon, and the feelings to be set a going, much faster than the understanding can be opened and the judgment enlightened. A talent for conversation should be the result of instruction, not its precursor: it is a golden fruit when suffered to ripen gradually on the tree of knowledge; but if forced in the hot-bed of a circulating library,[2] it will turn out worthless and vapid in proportion as it was artificial and premature. Girls who have been accustomed to devour a multitude of frivolous books, will converse and write with a far greater appearance of skill, as to style and sentiment, at twelve or fourteen years old, than those of a more advanced age, who are under the discipline of severer studies; but the former having early attained to that low standard which had been held out to them, become stationary; while the latter, quietly progressive, are passing through just gradations to a higher strain of mind; and those who early begin with talking and writing like women, commonly end with thinking and acting like children.

I would not, however, prohibit such works of imagination as suit this early period. When moderately used, they serve to stretch the faculties and expand the mind; but I should prefer works of vigorous genius and pure unmixed fable to many of those tame and more affected moral stories, which are not grounded on Christian principle. I should suggest the use, on the one hand, of original and acknowledged fictions; and, on the other, of accurate and simple facts; so that truth and fable may ever be kept separate and distinct in the mind. * * *

This suggestion is, however, by no means intended to exclude works of taste and imagination, which must always make the ornamental part, and of course a very considerable part of female studies. It is only intimated, that they should not form them entirely and exclusively. For what is called dry tough reading, independent of the knowledge it conveys, is useful as a habit, and wholesome as an exercise. Serious study serves to harden the mind for more trying conflicts; it lifts the reader from sensation to intellect; it abstracts her from the world and its vanities; it fixes a wandering spirit and fortifies a weak one; it divorces her from matter; it corrects that spirit of trifling which she naturally contracts from the frivolous turn of female conversation and the petty nature of female employments. * * *

Far be it from me to desire to make scholastic ladies or female dialecticians; but there is little fear that the kind of books here recommended, if thoroughly studied, and not superficially skimmed, will make them pedants, or induce conceit; for by showing them the possible powers of the human mind, you will bring them to see the

1. An ingenious (and in many respects useful) French Treatise on Education has too much encouraged this political piety [More's note; her quotations are from Luke 2.14].

2. Lending libraries that flourished from the 1790s carried stores of popular fiction, much of it written by and for women.

littleness of their own: and surely to get acquainted with the mind, to regulate, to inform it; to show it its own ignorance and its own weakness, does not seem the way to puff it up. But let her who is disposed to be elated with her literary acquisitions check the rising vanity by calling to mind the just remark of Swift, "that after all her boasted acquirements, a woman will, generally speaking, be found to possess less of what is called learning than a common school-boy."[3]

Neither is there any fear that this sort of reading will convert ladies into authors. The direct contrary effect will be likely to be produced by the perusal of writers who throw the generality of readers at such an unapproachable distance as to check presumption, instead of exciting it. Who are those ever-multiplying authors, that with unparalleled fecundity are overstocking the world with their quick-succeeding progeny? They are NOVEL-WRITERS: the easiness of whose productions is at once the cause of their own fruitfulness, and of the almost infinitely numerous race of imitators to whom they give birth. Such is the frightful facility of this species of composition, that every raw girl, while she reads, is tempted to fancy that she can also write. And as Alexander, on perusing the Iliad, found by congenial sympathy the image of Achilles stamped on his own ardent soul, and felt himself the hero he was studying; and as Corregio, on first beholding a picture which exhibited the perfection of the graphic art, prophetically felt all his own future greatness, and cried out in rapture, "And I, too, am a painter!" so a thorough-paced novel-reading Miss, at the close of every tissue of hackneyed adventures, feels within herself the stirring impulse of corresponding genius, and triumphantly exclaims, "And I, too, am an author!" The glutted imagination soon overflows with the redundance of cheap sentiment and plentiful incident, and by a sort of arithmetical proportion, is enabled by the perusal of any three novels, to produce a fourth; till every fresh production, like the prolific progeny of Banquo, is followed by "Another, and another, and another!"[4] Is a lady, however destitute of talents, education, or knowledge of the world, whose studies have been completed by a circulating library, in any distress of mind? the writing a novel suggests itself as the best soother of her sorrows! Does she labour under any depression of circumstances? writing a novel occurs as the readiest receipt for mending them! and she solaces her imagination with the conviction that the subscription which has been extorted by her importunity, or given to her necessities, has been offered as a homage to her genius; and this confidence instantly levies a fresh contribution for a succeeding work. Capacity and cultivation are so little taken into the account, that writing a book seems to be now considered as the only sure resource which the idle and the illiterate have always in their power.

May the Author be indulged in a short digression, while she remarks, though rather out of its place, that the corruption occasioned by these books has spread so wide, and descended so low, as to have become one of the most universal, as well as most pernicious, sources of corruption among us. Not only among milliners, mantua-makers, and other trades where numbers work together, the labour of one girl is frequently sacrificed that she may be spared to read those mischievous books to the others; but she has been assured by clergymen who have witnessed the fact, that they are

3. From *Letter to a Young Lady* (1727) by Jonathan Swift: "Those who are commonly called Learned Women have lost all manner of Credit by their impertinent Talkativeness and Conceit of themselves; but there is an easy remedy for this, if you once consider, that after all the pains you may be at, you can never arrive in point of learning to the perfection of a School-boy."

4. References are to the famous anecdote of Alexander the Great's sympathy with the Greek hero Achilles in Homer's epic of the Trojan War; the Italian Renaissance painter; and to the vision of Banquo's royal heirs that frustrates Macbeth (4.1).

procured and greedily read in the wards of our hospitals! an awful hint, that those who teach the poor to read, should not only take care to furnish them with principles which will lead them to abhor corrupt books, but that they should also furnish them with such books as shall strengthen and confirm their principles.[5]

from *Chapter 14. The Practical Use of Female Knowledge, with a Sketch of the Female Character, and a Comparative View of the Sexes*

The chief end to be proposed, in cultivating the understandings of women is to qualify them for the practical purposes of life. Their knowledge is not often, like the learning of men, to be reproduced in some literary composition, and never in any learned profession; but it is to come out in conduct: it is to be exhibited in life and manners. A lady studies, not that she may qualify herself to become an orator or a pleader; not that she may learn to debate, but to act. She is to read the best books, not so much to enable her to talk to them, as to bring the improvement which they furnish to the rectification of her principles and the formation of her habits. The great uses of study to a woman are to enable her to regulate her own mind, and to be instrumental to the good of others. * * *

But there is one *human* consideration which would perhaps more effectually tend to damp in an aspiring woman the ardours of literary vanity—I speak not of real genius, though there the remark often applies—than any which she will derive from motives of humility, or propriety, or religion; which is, that in the judgment passed on her performances, she will have to encounter the mortifying circumstance of having her sex always taken into account, and her highest exertions will probably be received with the qualified approbation *that it is really extraordinary for a woman*. Men of learning, who are naturally disposed to estimate works in proportion as they appear to be the result of art, study, and institution, are inclined to consider even the happier performances of the other sex as the spontaneous productions of a fruitful but shallow soil, and to give them the same kind of praise which we bestow on certain salads, which often draw from us a sort of wondering commendation, not, indeed, as being worth much in themselves, but because, by the lightness of the earth, and a happy knack of the gardener, these indifferent cresses spring up in a night, and therefore we are ready to wonder they are no worse.

As to men of sense, however, they need be the less hostile to the improvement of the other sex, as they themselves will be sure to be gainers by it; the enlargement of the female understanding being the most likely means to put an end to those petty and absurd contentions for equality which female smatterers so anxiously maintain. I say smatterers, for between the first class of both sexes the question is much more rarely and always more temperately agitated. Cooperation, and not competition, is, indeed, the clear principle we wish to see reciprocally adopted by those higher minds in each sex which really approximate the nearest to each other. The more a woman's understanding is improved, the more obviously she will discern that there can be no happiness in any society where there is a perpetual struggle for power; and the more her judgment is rectified, the more accurate views will she take of the station she was born to fill, and the more readily will she accommodate herself to it. * * *

5. The above facts furnish no argument on the side of those who would keep the poor in ignorance. Those who cannot *read* can *hear*, and are likely to hear to worse purpose than those who have been better taught. And that ignorance furnishes no security for integrity either in morals or politics, the late revolts in more than one country, remarkable for the ignorance of the poor, fully illustrate. It is earnestly hoped that the above facts may tend to impress ladies with the importance of superintending the instruction of the poor, and of making it an indispensable part of their charity to give them moral and religious books [More's note].

There is this singular difference between a woman vain of her wit, and a woman vain of her beauty; * * * she who is vain of her genius, more liberal at least in her vanity, is jealous for the honour of her whole sex, and contends for the equality of their pretensions as a body, in which she feels that her own are involved as an individual. The beauty vindicates her own rights, the wit the rights of women; * * * and while the more selfish though more moderate beauty "would but be Queen for life," the public-spirited wit struggles to abrogate the Salique law of intellect, and to enthrone "a whole sex of Queens."[1]

At the revival of letters in the sixteenth and the following century, the controversy about this equality was agitated with more warmth than wisdom; and the process was instituted and carried on, on the part of the female complainant, with that sort of acrimony which always raises a suspicion of the justice of any cause; for violence commonly implies doubt, and invective indicates weakness rather than strength. * * * Among the innovations of this innovating period, the imposing term of *rights* has been produced to sanctify the claim of our female pretenders,[2] with a view not only to rekindle in the minds of women a presumptuous vanity, dishonourable to their sex, but produced with a view to excite in their hearts an impious discontent with the post which God has assigned them in this world.[3]

But *they* little understand the true interests of woman who would lift her from the important duties of her allotted station, to fill, with fantastic dignity, a loftier but less appropriate niche. Nor do they understand her true happiness, who seek to annihilate distinctions from which she derives advantages, and to attempt innovations which would depreciate her real value. Each sex has its proper excellences, which would be lost were they melted down into the common character by the fusion of the new philosophy. Why should we do away distinctions which increase the mutual benefits and enhance the satisfactions of life? Whence, but by carefully preserving the original marks of difference, stamped by the hand of the Creator, would be derived the superior advantage of mixed society? Is either sex so abounding in perfection, as to be independent on the other for improvement? Have men no need to have their rough angles filed off, and their harshnesses and asperities smoothed and polished by assimilating with beings of more softness and refinement? Are the ideas of women naturally so *very* judicious, are their principles so *invincibly* firm, are their views so *perfectly* correct, are their judgments so *completely* exact, that there is occasion for no additional weight, no superadded strength, no increased clearness, none of that enlargement of mind, none of that additional invigoration, which may be derived from the aids of the stronger sex? What identity could advantageously supersede such an enlivening opposition, such an interesting variety of character? * * *

Natural propensities best mark the designations of Providence as to their application. The fin was not more clearly bestowed on the fish that he should swim, nor the wing given to the bird that he should fly, than superior strength of body and a firmer texture of mind were given to man, that he might preside in the deep and daring scenes of action and of council; in the complicated arts of government, in the contention of arms, in the intricacies and depths of science, in the bustle of commerce, and in those professions which demand a higher reach and a

---

1. Pope's *Epistle II*, "of the Characters of Women," assumes that "ev'ry Lady would be Queen for life" and shudders at the thought of "a whole Sex of Queens! / Pow'r all their end" (218–220). Salique (Salic) law, deriving from old French law, excludes females from the line of succession to a throne.

2. False claimants, especially to a throne; More is also suggesting "fantasizers" and dissemblers.
3. This was written soon after the publication of a work intitled "The Rights of Woman" [More's note, referring to Wollstonecraft's *Vindication*].

wider range of powers. The true value of woman is not diminished by the imputation of inferiority in those talents which do not belong to her, of those qualities in which her claim to excellence does not consist. She has other requisites, better adapted to answer the end and purposes of her being, from "Him who does all things well;" who suits the agent to the action; who accommodates the instrument to the work.

Let not, then, aspiring, because ill-judging, woman view with pining envy the keen satirist, hunting vice through all the doublings and windings of the heart; the sagacious politician, leading senates, and directing the fate of empires; the acute lawyer, detecting the obliquities of fraud; and the skilful dramatist, exposing the pretensions of folly; but let her ambition be consoled by reflecting, that those who thus excel, to all that Nature bestows and books can teach, must add besides that consummate knowledge of the world to which a delicate woman has no fair avenues, and which, even if she could attain, she would never be supposed to have come honestly by.

In almost all that comes under the description of polite letters, in all that captivates by vivid imagery or warms by just and affecting sentiment, women are excellent. They possess in a high degree that delicacy and quickness of perception, and that nice discernment between the beautiful and defective which comes under the denomination of taste. Both in composition and in action they excel in details; but they do not so much generalise their ideas as men, nor do their minds seize a great subject with so large a grasp. They are acute observers, and accurate judges of life and manners, as far as their own sphere of observation extends, but they describe a smaller circle. A woman sees the world, as it were, from a little elevation in her own garden, whence she makes an exact survey of home scenes, but takes not in that wider range of distant prospects which he who stands on a loftier eminence commands.

⊷⊷ ⊰⊹⊱ ⊶⊶

William Thompson and Anna Wheeler
1775–1833   1785–post-1848?

Karl Marx's *Manifesto of the Communist Party*, published in London in 1848, assured proletarians that they "have nothing to lose but their chains" and closed with the call, "Working Men of All Countries, Unite!" In these ringing phrases, English socialists heard a striking echo of the "Address to Women" that concluded William Thompson and Anna Wheeler's *Appeal:* "Women of England! women, in whatever country ye breathe—wherever ye breathe, degraded—awake! . . . O wretched slaves of such wretched masters! Awake, arise, shake off these fetters!" The work of two leading socialists of the 1820s, *Appeal* is the most important English feminist document between Wollstonecraft's *Rights of Woman* (1792) and John Stuart Mill's *Subjection of Women* (1869).

Born into Protestant Irish gentry, Thompson came of age during the tumultuous era of the French Revolution. At his father's death in 1814, he inherited the family's thousand-acre estate and prosperous businesses, including a fleet of trading vessels. He did not fall into step with Protestant capitalism, however, but agitated for Catholic Emancipation, denounced the division between laborers and "idle classes," and experimented with socialist alternatives, including organizing the 700 vagrants on the family estate into a highly successful experimental community. He then went to London, where he befriended leading social theorists John Stuart Mill, Jeremy Bentham, and Robert Owen. He published books on labor and wealth, including *An Inquiry into the Principles of the Distribution of Wealth Most Conducive to Human Happiness, Applied to the Newly Proposed System of Voluntary Equality of Wealth* (1824). Another London friend was Anna Wheeler, whose family, like his, was Irish gentry. A "reigning beauty" in her youth, she married a pampered Irish nobleman at age 15, bore six children (only two surviving infancy), and still found time to read widely, especially in philosophy and social theory. Increasingly disaffected from her idle, heavily drinking husband, she left him in 1812, eventually heading for London and France, where she met leading socialists and feminists. A dynamic figure in the movement for women's rights, she struck Benjamin Disraeli as "very clever, but awefully revolutionary."

Thompson and Wheeler were deeply concerned over the indifference of some of their socialist friends to women's rights. Some were even opposed—for instance, Bentham's disciple, James Mill, whose *Article on Government* for the 1824 *Encyclopedia Britannica* (a separate pamphlet in 1825) argued against political representation for women, contending that their interests were "involved" and "included" with their fathers or their husbands and had no separate claim. Thompson and Wheeler immediately began a refutation, publishing it in 1825. He was the author named on the title page of this *Appeal,* but his introduction credits Wheeler as co-author: he is the scribe of their "feelings, sentiments, and reasonings" and the work is their "joint property." Patently allied with Wollstonecraft's *Rights of Woman, Appeal* expands her social analysis into a critique of the underlying economic system. As the full title suggests, it also expands Wollstonecraft's discourse of female slavery. The blunt comparisons of English women to Turkish harem-slaves and the plantation slaves of the new world ally the polemic with the moral consensus fueling the expanding movement for the abolition of colonial slavery.

APPEAL of One Half the Human Race, WOMEN, Against the Pretensions of the Other Half, MEN, To Retain Them in Political, and Thence in CIVIL AND DOMESTIC SLAVERY

"'Tis all stern duty on the female side;
On man's, mere sensual gust and surly pride."[1]

from *Introductory Letter to Mrs. Wheeler*

The days of dedication and patronage are gone by. It is *not* with the view of obtaining the support of your name or your influence to the cause of truth and humanity that these lines are addressed to you. * * * I address you then simply to perform towards you a debt of justice. * * * Anxious that you should take up the cause of your proscribed sex, and state to the world in writing, in your own name, what you have so often and so well stated in conversation, and under feigned names in such of the periodical publications of the day as would tolerate such a theme, I long hesitated to arrange our common ideas, even upon a branch of the subject like the present. Anxious that the hand of a woman should have the honor of raising from the dust that neglected banner which a woman's hand nearly thirty years ago unfolded boldly, in face of the prejudices of thousands of years, and for which a woman's heart bled, and her life was all but the sacrifice—I hesitated to write. Were courage the quality wanting, you would have shown, what every day's experience proves, that women have more fortitude in endurance than men. Were comprehensiveness of mind, above the narrow views which too often marred Mary Wolstonecroft's [sic] pages and narrowed their usefulness, the quality wanting,—above the timidity and impotence of conclu-

---

1. A slight misquotation of Dryden's *Palamon and Arcite; or, The Knight's Tale, From Chaucer* (3.230–31) in *Fables Ancient and Modern; Translated into Verse* (1700); the virgin Emily begs the goddess Cynthia to accept her as a votress, pleading, "Like Death, thou know'st, I loath the Nuptial state, / And Man, the Tyrant of our Sex, I hate, / A lowly Servant, but a lofty Mate. / Where Love is Duty, on the Female side; / On theirs meer sensual Gust, and sought with surly Pride" (227–32); "Gust" is appetite. In *Rights of Woman*, ch. 6, Wollstonecraft quotes 230–31 correctly, using these lines to gloss the lack of "satisfaction" that any woman of delicate affections would confront "in a union with such a man."

sion accompanying the gentle eloquence of Mary Hays, addressed, about the same time that Mary Wolstonecroft wrote, in the shape of an *"Appeal"* to the then closed ears of unreasoning men;[2] yours was the eye which no prejudice obscured, open to the rays of truth from whatever quarter they might emanate. But leisure and resolution to undertake the drudgery of the task were wanting. A few only therefore of the following pages are the exclusive produce of your mind and pen, and written with your own hand. The remainder are our joint property, I being your interpreter and the scribe of your sentiments. * * *

You look forward, as I do, to a state of society very different from that which now exists, in which the effort of all is to out wit, supplant, and snatch from each other; where interest is systematically opposed to duty; where the so-called system of morals is little more than a mass of hypocrisy preached by knaves, unpractised by them, to keep their slaves, male as well as female, in blind uninquiring obedience; and where the whole motley fabric is kept together by fear and blood. You look forward to a better aspect of society, where the principle of benevolence shall supersede that of fear; where restless and anxious individual competition shall give place to mutual co-operation and joint possession; where individuals in large numbers, male and female, forming voluntary associations, shall become a mutual guarantee to each other for the supply of all useful wants, and form an unsalaried and uninsolvent insurance company against all insurable casualties; where perfect freedom of opinion and perfect equality will reign amongst the co-operators; and where the children of all will be equally educated and provided for by the whole, even these children longer the slaves of individual caprice.

In truth, under the present arrangements of society, the principle of individual competition remaining, as it is, the master-key and moving principle of the whole social organization, *individual* wealth the great object sought after by all, and the quantum of happiness of each individual (other things being equal) depending on the quantum of wealth, the means of happiness, possessed by each; it seems impossible—even were all unequal legal and unequal moral restraints removed, and were no secret current of force or influence exerted to baffle new regulations of equal justice—that women should attain to equal happiness with men. Two circumstances—permanent inferiority of strength, and occasional loss of time in gestation and rearing infants—must eternally render the average exertions of women in the race of the competition for wealth less successful than those of men. The pleasant compensation that men now affect to give for these two natural sources of inferior accumulation of wealth on the part of women (aggravated a thousand degrees by their exclusions from knowledge and almost all means of useful exertions, (the very lowest only excepted)), is the existing system of marriage; under which, for the mere faculty of eating, breathing and living, in whatever degree of comfort husbands may think fit, women are reduced to domestic slavery, without will of their own, or power of locomotion, otherwise than as permitted by their respective masters. * * *

With you I would equally elevate both sexes. Really enlightened women, disdaining equally the submissive tricks of the slave and the caprices of the despot,

---

2. Mary Hays, disciple and friend of Wollstonecraft, published her feminist polemic, *Appeal to the Men of Great Britain in Behalf of Women* anonymously in 1798, by which time Wollstonecraft was a scandal and the English political climate increasingly conservative as it confronted growing social unrest at home and the emergence of Napoleon abroad. Despite her numerous defenses of Wollstonecraft, Hays felt it unwise to include her in her *Female Biography, or Memoirs of Illustrious and Celebrated Women of all Ages and Countries* (1803).

breathing freely only in the air of the esteem of equals, and of mutual, *unbought, uncommanded,* affection, would find it difficult to meet with associates worthy of them in men as now formed, full of ignorance and vanity, priding themselves on a *sexual* superiority, entirely independent of any merit, any superior qualities, or pretensions to them, claiming respect from the strength of their arm and the lordly faculty of producing beards attached by nature to their chins! No: unworthy of, as incapable of appreciating, the delight of the society of such women, are the great majority of the existing race of men. The pleasures of mere animal appetite, the pleasures of commanding (the prettier and more helpless the slave, the greater these pleasures of the brute), are the only pleasures which the majority of men seek for from women, are the only pleasures which their education and the hypocritical system of morals with which they have been necessarily imbued, permit them to expect. * * *

Even under the present arrangements of society, founded as they all are on the basis of individual competition, nothing could be more easy than to put the *rights* of women, political and civil, on a perfect equality with those of men. It is only to abolish all prohibitory and exclusive laws,—statute or what are called "common,"—the remnants of the barbarous customs of our ignorant ancestors; particularly the horrible and odious inequality and indissolubility of that disgrace of civilization, the present marriage code. Women then might exert in a free career with men their faculties of mind and body, to whatever degree developed, in pursuit of happiness by means of exertion, as men do. But this would not raise women to an equality of happiness with men: their rights might be equal, but not their happiness, because unequal powers under free competition must produce unequal effects.

In truth, the system of the most enlightened of the school of those reformers called political economists, is still founded on exclusions. Its basis is too narrow for human happiness. A more comprehensive system, founded on equal benevolence, on the true development of the principle of Utility, is wanting.[3] Let the *competitive* political economists be satisfied with the praise of causing the removal of some of the rubbish of ignorant restrictions, under the name of laws, impeding the development of human exertion in the production of wealth. To build up a new fabric of social happiness, comprehending equally the interests of all existing human beings, has never been contemplated by them, and is altogether beyond the scope of their little theories; aiming at the utmost at increasing the number of what they style the happy middling orders, but leaving the great bulk of human beings to eternal ignorance and toil, requited by the mere means of prolonging from day to day an unhealthy and precarious existence. To a new science, the *social science,* or the science of promoting human happiness, that of political economy, or the mere science of producing wealth by individual competition, must give way.

from *Part 2*
[ON DAUGHTERS]

Business, professions, political concerns, local affairs, the whole field of sciences and arts, are open to the united and mutually sympathizing efforts of the males. To their mutual judgments and speculations, the disposal of the family income and capital are

---

3. The philosophy of utilitarianism, formulated by contemporaries Jeremy Bentham and James Mill, that there is no inherent right and wrong; the only issue is consequence, whether an action contributes to "the happiness of man."

intrusted. From all these commanding sources of intellectual and muscular activity, the daughters, like the little children, are excluded, previous care having been taken, by shutting them out from all means of intellectual culture, and from the view of and participation in the real incidents of active life, to render them as unfit for, as unambitious of, such high occupations. Confined, like other domestic animals, to the house and its little details, their "sober wishes" are never permitted "to stray" into the enlarged plains of general speculation and action. The dull routine of domestic incidents is the world to them. * * *

So much more completely is the interest of the sons involved than that of the daughters in the interest of fathers, that as soon as the daughters become adult, they, necessarily operated upon by the system under which they live, look out of their artificial cages of restraint and imbecility, to catch glances at the world with the hope of freedom from parental control, by leaving behind them the very name of their fathers, and vainly hoping for happiness without independence, in the gratification of one passion, love, round which their absurd training for blind male sensuality, has caused all their little anxieties to centre. The adult sons go in and out of the father's house when they choose: they are frequently treated with liberality as visitors or equals. But the adult daughters are, for the most part, under as much restraint as little children: they must ask leave to open the door or take a walk: not one of their actions that does not depend on the will of another: they are never permitted, like the sons, to regulate their conduct by their own notions of propriety and prudence and to restrain them where necessary, like rational beings, from a regard to their consequences: every thing is prescribed to them: their reason and foresight are not cultivated like those of the sons; and the despotism which creates their imbecility, adduces its own work as a justification of its unrelenting pressure and of its eternal duration. To marriage therefore, as the only means allowed them of emerging from paternal control; as the only means of gratifying one passion, to which all their thoughts have been exclusively directed, but which they are at the same time told it is highly improper they should wish to enjoy; as the only means of obtaining, through cunning and blandishment, that direction of their own voluntary actions, which all rational beings ought to possess, and which is the sure and only basis of intelligence and morals; to marriage, as the fancied haven of pleasure and freedom—the freedom of the slave to-be-sure, to be acquired not by right but by coaxing, by the influence of passions inapplicable to the cold despotism of the fathers—daughters look forward. No sooner adult, than their home and their name are daughters anxious to get rid of, because the retaining of them is made incompatible with the only views of happiness presented to them.

[ON WIVES]

By way of distinguishing and honoring this class of the proscribed half of the human race, man condescends to enter into what he calls a *contract* with certain women, for certain purposes, the most important of which is, the producing and rearing of children to maturity. Each man yokes a woman to his establishment, and calls it a *contract*. Audacious falsehood! A contract! where are any of the attributes of contracts, of equal and just contracts, to be found in this transaction? A contract implies the voluntary assent of both the contracting parties. Can even both the parties, man and woman, by agreement alter the terms, as to *indissolubility* and *inequality*, of this pretended contract? No. Can any individual man divest himself, were he even so inclined, of his power of despotic control? He cannot. Have women been consulted as to the terms of this pretended contract? A contract, all of whose enjoyments—wherever nature has not imposed a physical bar on the depravity of selfishness—are on one side, while all of its pains and privations are on the other! A contract, giving all power, arbitrary will and unbridled enjoyment to the one side; to the other, unqualified obedience, and enjoyments meted out or withheld at the caprice of the ruling and enjoying party. Such a contract, as the owners of *slaves* in the West Indies and every other slave-polluted soil, enter into with their slaves—the law of the stronger imposed on the weaker, *in contempt* of the interests and wishes of the weaker. * * *

As soon as adult daughters become wives, their civil rights disappear; they fall back again, and remain all their lives—should their owners and directors live so long—into the state of children or idiots, the passive property of their owners; protected by the law in some few respects only, like other slaves, from the excessive abuse of despotic power.

Woman is then compelled, in marriage, by the possession of superior strength on the part of men, by the want of knowledge, skill and wealth, by the positive, cruel, partial, and cowardly enactments of law, by the terrors of superstition, by the mockery of a pretended vow of obedience, and to crown all, and as the result of all, by the force of an unrelenting, unreasoning, unfeeling, public opinion, to be the literal unequivocal *slave* of the man who may be styled her husband. I say emphatically the slave; for a slave is a person whose actions and earnings, instead of being, under his own control, liable only to equal laws, to public opinion, and to his own calculations, under these, of his own interest, are under the arbitrary control of any other human being, by whatever name called. This is the essence of slavery, and what distinguishes it from freedom. A domestic, a civil, a political slave, in the plain unsophisticated sense of the word—in no metaphorical sense—is every married woman. No matter with what wealth she may be surrounded, with what dainties she may be fed, with what splendor of trappings adorned, with what voluptuousness her corporeal, mental, or moral sweets may be gathered; that high prerogative of human nature, the faculty of self-government, the basis of intellectual development, without which no moral conduct can exist, is to her wanting. * * * Till laws afford married women the same protection against the restraints and violence of the men to whom they are married, that they affect to afford them against all other individuals; till they afford them the same protection against the restraints and violence of their husbands, that their husbands enjoy against their caprices and violence, the social condition of the civilized wife will remain more completely slavish than that of the female slave of the West Indies.

[EXHORTATION TO MEN]

Be consistent, men! Ye stronger half of the race, be at length rational! Three or four thousand years have worn threadbare your vile cloak of hypocrisy. Even women, your poor, weak, contented slaves, at whose impotence of penetration, the result of your vile exclusions, you have been accustomed to laugh, begin to see through it and to shudder at the loathsomeness beneath. Cast aside this tattered cloak before it leaves you naked and exposed. Clothe yourselves with the new garments of sincerity. Be rational human beings, not mere male sexual creatures. Cast aside the ferocious brute of your nature: give up the pleasures of the brute, those of mere lust and command, for the pleasures of the rational being. So shall you enjoy the love of your *equals*, enlightened, benevolent, graceful, like yourselves, founded on an appreciation of your real merits: so shall you be happy. For the intercourse of the *bought* prostitute, or of the *commanded* household slave, you shall have full and equal participation in the compounded and associated pleasures of sense, intellect and benevolence. To the highest enjoyments of which your nature is susceptible, there is no shorter road than the simple road of equal justice.

[WHAT DO WOMEN WANT?]

The simple and modest request is, that they may be permitted equal enjoyments with men, *provided they can by the free and equal development and exercise of their faculties procure for themselves such enjoyments*. They ask the same means that men possess of acquiring every species of knowledge, of unfolding every one of their faculties of mind and body that can be made tributary to their happiness. They ask every facility of access to every art, occupation, profession, from the highest to the lowest, without one exception, to which their inclination and talents may direct and may fit them to occupy. They ask the removal of *all* restraints and exclusions not applicable to men of equal capacities. They ask for perfectly equal political, civil and domestic rights. They ask for equal obligations and equal punishments from the law with men in case of infraction of the same law by either party. They ask for an equal system of morals, founded on utility instead of caprice and unreasoning despotism, in which the same action attended with the same consequences, whether done by man or woman, should be attended with the same portion of approbation or disapprobation; in which every pleasure, accompanied or followed by no preponderant evil, should be equally permitted to women and to men; in which every pleasure accompanied or followed by preponderant evil should be equally censured in women and in men.

* * *

Women of England! women, in whatever country ye breathe—wherever ye breathe, degraded—awake! Awake to the contemplation of the happiness that awaits you when all your faculties of mind and body shall be fully cultivated and developed; when every path in which ye can exercise those improved faculties shall be laid open and rendered delightful to you, even as to them who now ignorantly enslave and degrade you. If degradation from long habitude have lost its sting, if the iron have penetrated so deeply into your frame that it has been gradually taken up into the system and mingles unperceived amidst the fluids of your life; if the prostration of reason and the eradication of feeling have kept pace within you, so that you are insensible alike to what you suffer and to what you might enjoy,—your case were all but hopeless. Nothing less, then, than the sight presented before your eyes, of the superior happiness enjoyed by other women, under arrangements of perfect equality with men, could arouse you. Such a sight, even under such circumstances, would excite your envy and kindle up all your extinct desires. But you are not so degraded. The unvaried despotism of so many thousand years, has not so entirely degraded you, has not been able to extinguish within you the feelings of nature, the love of happiness and of equal justice. The united exertions of law, superstition, and pretended morals of past ages of ignorance, have not entirely succeeded. * * *

Nor will your fellow-creatures, men, long resist the change. They are too deeply concerned to continue long to oppose what palpably tends to their happiness: they are too deeply concerned not to be compelled to re-consider the barbarous systems of law and morals under which they have been brought up. In justice, in pity to them, submit no longer; no longer *willingly* submit to their caprices. Though your bodies may be a little longer kept in servitude, degrade not yourselves by the repetition of superfluous vows of obedience: cease to kiss the rod: let your *minds* be henceforth free. The morn of loosening your physical chains will not be far distant.

O woman, from your auspicious hands may the new destiny of your species proceed! The collective voices of your sex raised against oppression will ultimately make men themselves your advocates and debtors. Reflect then seriously on your miserable and degraded position—your youth, your beauty, your feelings, your opinions, your actions, your time, your few years' fever of meritricious life—all made tributary to the appetites and passions of men. Whatever pleasures you enjoy, are permitted you for man's sake. Nothing is your own; protection of person and of property are alike withheld from you. Nothing is yours, but secret pangs, the bitter burning tears of regret, the stifled sobs of outraged nature thrown back upon your own hearts, where the vital principle itself stands checked, or is agitated with malignant passions, until body and mind become the frequent prey to overwhelming disease; now finding vent in sudden phrensy, now plunged in pining melancholy, or bursting the weak tenement of reason, seeking relief in self-destruction.

How many thousand of your sex *daily* perish thus unpitied and unknown; often victims of pressing want, always of privation and the arbitrary laws of heartless custom; condemned to cheerless solitude, or an idiot round of idle fashionable pursuits; your morning of life perhaps passed by, and with it the lingering darling hope of sympathy expired—puppets once of doting ignorant parents, whose tenderness for you outlived not your first youth; who, careless of your future fate, "launched you into life without an oar," indigent and ignorant, to eat the tear-steeped bread of dependence as wives, sisters, hired mistresses or unpitied prostitutes! This is the fate of the many, nay, of all your sex, subject only to those shades of difference arising from very peculiar circumstances or the accident of independent fortune; though even here the general want of knowledge, withheld from your sex, keeps even those individuals who are favored by fortune bowed to the relentless yoke which man's laws, his superstitions, and hypocritical morality, have prepared for you.

For once then instruct man in what is good, wash out the foul stain, equally disgraceful to both sexes—that your sex has unbounded influence in making men to do evil, but cannot induce them to do good.

How many Thaises are there, who, vain of the empire they hold over the passions of men, exercise at all risks this contemptible and pernicious influence—the only influence permitted them—in stimulating these masters of the world to destroy cities; and, regardless of the whispers of conscience and humanity, often shake men's tardy resolutions to repair the evils they have caused![1]—Shall none be found with sufficient knowledge and elevation of mind to persuade men to do good, to make the most certain step towards the regeneration of degraded humanity, by opening a free course for justice and benevolence, for intellectual and social enjoyments, by no colour, by no sex to be restrained? As your bondage has chained down man to the ignorance and vices of despotism, so will your liberation reward him with knowledge, with freedom and with happiness.[2]

[END OF PERSPECTIVES: THE WOLLSTONECRAFT CONTROVERSY
AND THE RIGHTS OF WOMEN]

1. Probably the 4th-century B.C. Athenian courtesan, patronized by Alexander the Great and then by the King of Egypt; she was said to have accompanied Alexander on his conquests. Another Thais was a 1st-century Alexandrian, famous for her beauty, wealth, and sexual indulgences, who repented and converted to Christianity and a life of piety.
2. The last paragraph of *Appeal*.

Joanna Baillie

1762–1851

In 1824, Blackwood's *Edinburgh Magazine* observed the influence of Baillie's plays on Lord Byron: "the dark shadows of his Lordship's imagination have received a deeper gloom from his early acquaintance with those wild and midnight forests, in which the passion of De Monfort [*De Monfort*, 1798] consummated its dreadful purpose, and the dim aisles in which it met its retribution." The influence is also reflected in his Lordship's nervous admiration. In 1813, Byron insisted that Baillie could not have "a more enthusiastic admirer than myself," and he was eager to meet her; in 1817, in the throes of rewriting his gothic closet drama *Manfred*, he mulled over Voltaire's reply to a question about "why no woman has ever written even a tolerable tragedy": "Ah (said the Patriarch) the composition of a tragedy requires *testicles*." "If this be true," Byron comments to his publisher, "Lord knows what Joanna Baillie does—I suppose she borrows them." Byron's regard for Baillie's potency was shared (without the regendering speculation) by many of her contemporaries, including William Wordsworth, who called her "the bold enchantress," Anna Laetitia Barbauld, Maria Edgeworth, Robert Southey, Samuel Taylor Coleridge, Felicia Hemans, who dedicated *Records of Woman* to her, and Sir Walter Scott, who deemed her the finest English dramatist since Shakespeare.

Born in 1762 in Scotland, Baillie traced her ancestry to the famously brave-hearted patriot William Wallace. She never married and lived her adult life with her unmarried sister. Her first literary efforts were poetry, published anonymously in 1790 as *Poems: Wherein it is Attempted to Describe Certain Views of Nature and Rustic Manners*. This was unsuccessful, and she turned to drama, with *Plays on the Passions*, as it is commonly known; the full title was *A Series of Plays in Which it is Attempted to Delineate the Stronger Passions of the Mind*. This appeared in three installments from 1798 to 1812. The first one was anonymous, and a curious public speculated about the identity of the author, believing it to be a man; Samuel Rogers, writing for *The Monthly Review*, insisted that the "Introductory Discourse" could have been written only by a man, and ascribed it to Baillie's brother. The program Baillie gave of "unveiling the human mind under the dominion of . . . strong and fixed passions" was echoed two years later by Wordsworth in his Preface to *Lyrical Ballads* (1800), which announces his similar devotion to tracing "the essential passions of the heart" in states of excitement. Although *De Monfort* attracted the leading actors of the day, including Sarah Siddons, John Philip Kemble, and Edmund Kean, the psychological emphases and philosophical introspectiveness of Baillie's plays were ill-suited to popular theater, and however much they impressed other poets, they were not successful on the stage. Baillie continued to write and publish plays over the next three decades, conceiving them as dramas for "the mental theatre of the reader," in Byron's words, taking a cue from Charles Lamb's essay on the unsuitability of Shakespeare's tragedies for stage representation (1811). In 1821, she published *Metrical Legends of Exalted Characters*, including "chronicles" of her ancestors Wallace and Lady Griselda Baillie, and she put out an expanded edition of her poems in 1840 under the title *Fugitive Verses*. Some of these pieces show her skill at the poetry in Scots dialect that Robert Burns popularized, while others follow the program of her dramas, voicing passion, sometimes in stormy moods, but often in quieter and more domestic scenes.

London

It is a goodly sight through the clear air,
From Hampstead's heathy height[1] to see at once

---

1. Hampstead heath, to the north, offers a view of London.

England's vast capital in fair expanse,
Towers, belfries,° lengthen'd streets, and structures fair.   *bell-towers*
5   St. Paul's high dome[2] amidst the vassal bands
Of neighb'ring spires, a regal chieftain stands,
And over fields of ridgy roofs appear,
With distance softly tinted, side by side,
In kindred grace, like twain of sisters dear,
10   The Towers of Westminster, her Abbey's pride;[3]
While, far beyond, the hills of Surrey shine[4]
Through thin soft haze, and show their wavy line.
View'd thus, a goodly sight! but when survey'd
Through denser air when moisten'd winds prevail,
15   In her grand panoply° of smoke array'd,   *armor*
While clouds aloft in heavy volumes sail,
She is sublime.——She seems a curtain'd gloom
Connecting heaven and earth,—a threat'ning sign of doom.
With more than natural height, rear'd in the sky
20   'Tis then St. Paul's arrests the wondering eye;
The lower parts in swathing mist conceal'd,
The higher through some half spent shower reveal'd,
So far from earth removed, that well, I trow,°   *believe*
Did not its form man's artful structure show,
25   It might some lofty alpine peak be deem'd,
The eagle's haunt, with cave and crevice seam'd.
Stretch'd wide on either hand, a rugged screen,
In lurid dimness, nearer streets are seen
Like shoreward billows of a troubled main,°   *open sea*
30   Arrested in their rage. Through drizzly rain,
Cataracts of tawny sheen pour from the skies,
Of furnace smoke black curling columns rise,
And many tinted vapours, slowly pass
O'er the wide draping of that pictured mass.

35   So shows by day this grand imperial town,
And, when o'er all the night's black stole is thrown,
The distant traveller doth with wonder mark
Her luminous canopy athwart the dark,
Cast up, from myriads of lamps that shine
40   Along her streets in many a starry line:—
He wondering looks from his yet distant road,
And thinks the northern streamers° are abroad.   *northern lights*
"What hollow sound is that?" approaching near,
The roar of many wheels breaks on his ear.
45   It is the flood of human life in motion!
It is the voice of a tempestuous ocean!

---

2. London's chief Anglican cathedral.
3. Westminster, a city within London, is the seat of government, the location of Westminster Palace (Parliament), Buckingham Palace (the royal family home), and Westminster Abbey, an imposing gothic church.
4. County southwest of London.

With sad but pleasing awe his soul is fill'd,
Scarce heaves his breast, and all within is still'd,
As many thoughts and feelings cross his mind,—
50   Thoughts, mingled, melancholy, undefined,
Of restless, reckless man, and years gone by,
And Time fast wending to Eternity.

1790, 1840

Thunder

Spirit of strength! to whom in wrath 'tis given,
To mar the earth and shake its vasty dome,
Behold the sombre robes whose gathering folds,
Thy secret majesty conceal. Their skirts
5   Spread on mid air move slow and silently,
O'er noon-day's beam thy sultry shroud is cast,
Advancing clouds from every point of heaven,
Like hosts° of gathering foes in pitchy volumes,   *armies*
Grandly dilated, clothe the fields of air,
10   And brood° aloft o'er the empurpled earth.   *hover*
Spirit of strength! it is thy awful hour;
The wind of every hill is laid to rest,
And far o'er sea and land deep silence reigns.

Wild creatures of the forest homeward hie,
15   And in their dens with fear unwonted° cower;   *unaccustomed*
Pride in the lordly palace is put down,
While in his humble cot° the poor man sits   *cottage*
With all his family round him hush'd and still,
In awful expectation. On his way
20   The traveller stands aghast and looks to heaven.
On the horizon's verge thy lightning gleams,
And the first utterance of thy deep voice
Is heard in reverence and holy fear.

From nearer clouds bright burst more vivid gleams,
25   As instantly in closing darkness lost;
Pale sheeted flashes cross the wide expanse
While over boggy moor or swampy plain,
A streaming cataract of flame appears,
To meet a nether fire from earth cast up,
30   Commingling terribly; appalling gloom
Succeeds, and lo! the rifted° centre pours   *fissured*
A general blaze, and from the war of clouds,
Red, writhing falls the embodied bolt of heaven.
Then swells the rolling peal, full, deep'ning, grand,
35   And in its strength lifts the tremendous roar,
With mingled discord, rattling, hissing, growling;
Crashing like rocky fragments downward hurl'd,
Like the upbreaking of a ruined world,

In awful majesty the explosion bursts
40   Wide and astounding o'er the trembling land.
Mountain, and cliff, repeat the dread turmoil,
And all, to man's distinctive senses known,
Is lost in the immensity of sound.
Peal after peal succeeds with waning strength,
45   And hush'd and deep each solemn pause between.

Upon the lofty mountain's side
The kindled forest blazes wide;
Huge fragments of the rugged steep
Are tumbled to the lashing deep;
50   Firm rooted in his cloven rock,
Crashing falls the stubborn oak.
The lightning keen in wasteful ire
Darts fiercely on the pointed spire,
Rending in twain the iron-knit stone,
55   And stately towers to earth are thrown.
No human strength may brave the storm,
Nor shelter screen the shrinking form,
Nor castle wall its fury stay,
Nor massy gate impede its way:
60   It visits those of low estate,°   *the poor*
It shakes the dwellings of the great,
It looks athwart the vaulted tomb,
And glares upon the prison's gloom.
Then dungeons black in unknown light,
65   Flash hideous on the wretches' sight,
And strangely groans the downward cell,
Where silence deep is wont to dwell.

Now eyes, to heaven up-cast, adore,
Knees bend that never bent before,
70   The stoutest hearts begin to fail,
And many a manly face is pale;
Benumbing fear awhile up-binds,
The palsied action of their minds,
Till waked to dreadful sense they lift their eyes,
75   And round the stricken corse° shrill shrieks of horror rise.   *corpse*

Now rattling hailstones, bounding as they fall
To earth, spread motley winter o'er the plain;
Receding peals sound fainter on the ear,
And roll their distant grumbling far away:
80   The lightning doth in paler flashes gleam,
And through the rent cloud, silvered with his rays,
The sun on all this wild affray° looks down,   *tumult, quarrel*
As, high enthroned above all mortal ken,°   *understanding*
A higher Power beholds the strife of men.

1790, 1840

Robert Burns
1759–1796

A "striking example of native genius bursting through the obscurity of poverty and the obstructions of laborious life" exclaimed the *Edinburgh Magazine* when Burns's *Poems, Chiefly in the Scottish Dialect* appeared from provincial Kilmarnock in 1786. Yet the reality of the "heaven-taught plow-man" was more complex. A tenant farmer like his father, Burns planned to accept a position on a Jamaican plantation until the success of his poetry provided another means of escape from a hard existence. Though poor, Burns was well read; his poems, if "chiefly" in dialect, were never exclusively so: the accents and forms of folk culture play against a range of polite English genres. Fame brought Burns to Edinburgh, where he enlarged and reprinted his book. On the profits, Burns returned to farming and married Jean Armour, who had borne him children in 1786 and 1788.

The farm failed, as had its three predecessors, and Burns moved his family to Dumfries, where he obtained the post of exciseman, or tax-inspector. Government employment might seem anomalous for one who championed the American and French Revolutions, who believed in the goodness of man against the tenets of the Scots church, which he repeatedly satirized, and flamboyantly defied in his many erotic escapades, but Burns fulfilled his duties responsibly. An invitation in 1787 to contribute to *The Scots Musical Museum* intensified his sense of his Scots identity: for the next six years Burns became "absolutely crazed," as he put it, with collecting and editing traditional songs for the successive volumes, and wrote more than two hundred himself, new or adapted. When the fourth volume was finished in 1792, Burns agreed to participate in a *Select Collection of Scottish Airs*, a far more genteelly refining version of Scottish poetry. The more earthy energies of Burns's poetry appear in the posthumously published *Merry Muses of Caledonia* (1799–1800), a collection printed at least partly from Burns's papers following his early death from heart disease at the age of thirty-seven. The second version of *Comin' Thro' the Rye* and *The Fornicator* appeared in this work.

To a Mouse
On Turning Her Up in Her Nest with the Plough, November, 1785

Wee, sleekit,° cowrin, tim'rous beastie,	*sleek*
O, what a panic's in thy breastie!	
Thou need na start awa sae° hasty	*so*
Wi' bickering brattle!°	*scurry*
5 I wad be laith° to rin an' chase thee,	*loath*
Wi' murdering pattle!°	*plough-scraper*
I'm truly sorry man's dominion	
Has broken Nature's social union,	
An' justifies that ill opinion	
10 Which makes thee startle	
At me, thy poor, earth-born companion	
An' fellow mortal!	
I doubt na, whyles,° but thou may thieve;	*sometimes*
What then? poor beastie, thou maun° live!	*must*
15 A daimen icker in a thrave°	*odd ear in 24 sheaves*
'S a sma' request;	

I'll get a blessin wi' the lave,°   *rest*
    An' never miss 't!

Thy wee-bit housie, too, in ruin!
20   Its silly wa's° the win's are strewin!   *feeble walls*
    An' naething, now, to big° a new ane,   *build*
        O' foggage° green!   *coarse grass*
    An' bleak December's win's ensuin,
        Baith snell° an' keen!   *bitter*

25   Thou saw the fields laid bare an' waste,
    An' weary winter comin fast,
    An' cozie here, beneath the blast,
        Thou thought to dwell,
    Till crash! the cruel coulter° past   *plow-blade*
30   Out thro' thy cell.

    That wee bit heap o' leaves an' stibble,°   *stubble*
    Has cost thee monie a weary nibble!
    Now thou's turned out, for a' thy trouble,
        But° house or hald,°   *without/goods*
35   To thole° the winter's sleety dribble,   *endure*
        An' cranreuch° cauld!   *hoarfrost*

    But Mousie, thou art no thy lane,°   *not alone*
    In proving foresight may be vain:
    The best-laid schemes o' mice an' men
40   Gang aft agley,°   *go oft awry*
    An' lea'e us nought but grief an' pain,
        For promis'd joy!

Still thou art blest, compared wi' me!
The present only toucheth thee:
45   But och! I backward cast my e'e,
        On prospects drear!
    An' forward, tho' I canna see,
        I guess an' fear!

1785   1786

Comin' Thro' the Rye (1)[1]

CHORUS
O, Jenny's a' weet, poor body,
    Jenny's seldom dry:
She draigl't° a' her petticoatie,   *bedraggled*
    Comin thro' the rye!

5   Comin thro' the rye, poor body,
        Comin thro' the rye,
    She draigl't a' her petticoatie,
        Comin thro' the rye!

---

1. A revision and expansion of an old song, also popular in various bawdy versions, as in the second version which follows, with obscenities tactfully hyphenated by the 1800 publisher.

Gin° a body meet a body   *if*
10   Comin thro' the rye,
Gin a body kiss a body,
Need a body cry?

Gin a body meet a body
Comin thro' the glen,
15   Gin a body kiss a body,
Need the warld ken?°   *know*

<small>CHORUS</small>

1796

Comin' Thro' the Rye (2)

<small>CHORUS</small>

O gin a body meet a body,
Comin throu the rye;
Gin a body f—k a body,
Need a body cry.

5   Comin' thro' the rye, my jo,°   *sweetheart*
An' comin' thro' the rye;
She fand a staun° o' staunin' graith,°   *stand/tools*
Comin' thro' the rye.

Gin a body meet a body,
10   Comin' thro' the glen;
Gin a body f—k a body,
Need the warld ken.

Gin a body meet a body,
Comin' thro' the grain;
15   Gin a body f—k a body,
C—t's a body's ain.°   *own*

Gin a body meet a body,
By a body's sel,
What na body f—s a body,
20   Wad a body tell.

Mony a body meets a body,
They dare na weel avow;
Mony a body f—s a body,
Ye wadna think it true.

1799–1800

A Red, Red Rose[1]

O, my luve is like a red, red rose,
That's newly sprung in June.
O, my luve is like the melodie,
That's sweetly play'd in tune.

---

1. This poem incorporates elements of several old ballads and folk songs, a common practice of amalgamation at which Burns had great success.

5 As fair art thou, my bonie lass,
   So deep in luve am I,
And I will luve thee still, my dear,
   Till a' the seas gang° dry.   *go*

Till a' the seas gang dry, my dear,
10   And the rocks melt wi' the sun!
And I will luve thee still, my dear,
   While the sands o' life shall run.

And fare thee weel, my only luve,
   And fare thee weel a while!
15 And I will come again, my luve,
   Tho' it were ten thousand mile!

1794   1796

Auld Lang Syne

Should auld acquaintance be forgot,
   And never brought to mind?
Should auld acquaintance be forgot,
   And auld lang syne!°   *long ago times*

                     CHORUS
5   For auld lang syne, my dear,
            For auld lang syne,
       We'll tak a cup o' kindness yet
           For auld lang syne!

And surely ye'll be° your pint-stowp,°   *buy/pint-cup*
10   And surely I'll be mine,
And we'll tak a cup o' kindness yet
   For auld lang syne!

                     CHORUS
We twa hae run about the braes,°   *slopes*
   And pou'd° the gowans° fine,   *pulled/daisies*
15 But we've wander'd monie a weary fit°   *foot*
   Sin'° auld lang syne.   *since*

                     CHORUS
We twa hae paidl'd in the burn[1]
   Frae morning sun till dine,°   *dinner (noon)*
But seas between us braid° hae roar'd   *broad*
20   Sin' auld lang syne.

                     CHORUS
And there's a hand, my trusty fiere,°   *friend*
   And gie's a hand o' thine,
And we'll tak a right guid-willie waught°   *good-will swig*
   For auld lang syne!

                     CHORUS
25   For auld lang syne, my dear,
            For auld lang syne,
       We'll tak a cup o' kindness yet
           For auld lang syne!

1788   1796

1. Stream; waters used for brewing. "Burns" would especially appreciate the double sense.

The Fornicator. A New Song
Tune, Clout the Caldron

Ye jovial boys who love the joys
    The blissful joys of lovers;
Yet dare avow with dauntless brow,
    When the bony lass discovers:[1]
5   I pray draw near and lend an ear,
        And welcome in a Frater,°   *brother*
For I've lately been on quarantine,
    A proven Fornicator.

Before the Congregation wide
10   I pass'd the muster fairly,[2]
My handsome Betsey by my side,[3]
    We gat° our ditty° rarely;   *received/reproof*
But my downcast eye by chance did spy
    What made my lips to water,
15   Those limbs so clean where I, between
    Commenc'd a Fornicator.

With rueful face and signs of grace
    I pay'd the buttock-hire,[4]
The night was dark and thro the park
20   I could not but convoy her;
A parting kiss, what could I less,
    My vows began to scatter,
My Betsey fell—lal de dal lal lal,
    I am a Fornicator.

25   But for her sake this vow I make,
    And solemnly I swear it,
That while I own a single crown,
    She's welcome for to share it;
And my roguish boy his Mother's joy,
30   And the darling of his Pater,°   *father*
For him I boast my pains and cost,
    Although a Fornicator.

Ye wenching blades whose hireling jades[5]
    Have tipt you off blue-boram,[6]
35   I tell you plain, I do disdain
    To rank you in the Quorum;
But a bony lass upon the grass
    To teache her esse Mater,°   *to be a mother*
And no reward but for regard,
40   O that's a Fornicator.

Your warlike kings and heroes bold,
    Great Captains and Commanders;

1. Reveals her pregnancy.
2. In the Scottish Church those found guilty of fornication were required to sit, clothed in black, for three successive Sundays on a raised "stool of repentance."
3. Usually taken as Elizabeth Paton, with whom Burns had an illegitimate child.
4. There was a six-pound fine for fornication.
5. Worn-out horses, a contemptuous term for women.
6. Infected you with syphilis. The term probably derives from the notorious Blue Boar Tavern in London.

Your mighty Cèsars fam'd of old,
        And Conquering Alexanders;
45   In fields they fought and laurels bought
        And bulwarks strong did batter,
But still they grac'd our noble list
        And ranked Fornicator!!!

1784–1785   1799

<hr>

William Wordsworth
1770–1850

Meeting Wordsworth in 1815, Byron told his wife that he had "but one feeling . . . reverence!" The exemplar of "plain living and high thinking," Wordsworth provided an image of poetry and "the Poet" as at once humble and exalted, domestic and severely moral. By the end of his life he had become a cultural institution, respected even by those who opposed his politics. Admirers made pilgrimages to his home at Rydal Mount in the Lake District. His beginnings were less auspicious. Born in the Lake District, Wordsworth was the son of the steward of Lord Lonsdale, the dominant landowner of the beautiful but isolated region. The death of Wordsworth's mother when he was eight years old broke a stable middle-class family life; William and his three brothers were sent to Hawkshead to school, and his sister Dorothy sent to live with various distant relatives. His father died five years later, at which point Lord Lonsdale resisted paying the monies owed to him; the children did not receive their inheritance until 1802, when a new Lord Lowther, who became Wordsworth's patron, succeeded to the title. "The props of my affection were removed, / And yet the building stood," Wordsworth exclaimed in a passage of the *Prelude* that readers have taken to refer obliquely to these early losses and separations; "taught to feel, perhaps too much, / The self-sufficing power of Solitude," Wordsworth developed a potent myth of himself as a "favoured being" shaped by the severe but mysteriously benevolent ministry of Nature.

In 1787 Wordsworth entered St. John's College, Cambridge, taking his degree in 1791 without distinction. As his autobiographical poem *The Prelude* testifies, his travels left deeper impressions than his studies: a summer walking tour in 1790 that brought him to France a year after the fall of the Bastille, then a trip through North Wales in 1791, and a year-long stay in France (1791–1792). There he became an active partisan in the heady early phase of the Revolution. "Bliss was it in that dawn to be alive, / But to be young was very Heaven!" as he wrote in *The Prelude*. The millenarian hopes of a new era were suffused with personal attachments: he had a love affair with Annette Vallon, who bore their daughter in December 1792. By then, lack of funds had forced him back to England, and the English declaration of war against France precluded his return until 1802. In him as in many of his generation, the war produced a crisis of loyalties, aggravated by the increasing violence of revolutionary France. "Sick, wearied out with contrarieties," Wordsworth recovered "a saving intercourse with [his] true self" only through the struggles that his poetry records.

A turning point came in 1795, when a small legacy of £900 from a friend enabled Wordsworth to devote himself to poetry. He reunited with Dorothy, and met Coleridge; in 1797 brother and sister moved to Alfoxden, to be near Coleridge at Nether Stowey. "[B]uoyant spirits / . . . were our daily portion when we first / Together wantoned in wild poesy," Wordsworth later wrote; comfortably housed, free to wander the countryside, Wordsworth and Coleridge collaborated on the poems that became *Lyrical Ballads*, published anonymously in

1798 to mixed reviews. The strangeness of *The Rime of the Ancyent Marinere* disconcerted some readers, and the audacious simplicity of Wordsworth's subjects and style offended more. But others felt the "power and pathos" of the poetry, even (in Hazlitt's words) "the sense of a new style and a new spirit." In 1800 Wordsworth published a second edition under his own name, adding a volume containing *Michael* and the "Lucy" poems and others written during the cold and lonely winter that he and Dorothy had passed in Germany in 1798–1799. A new Preface, defending his principles and repudiating the expectations of his readers, set the terms of his reception and continued to govern the charges against him by critics such as Francis Jeffrey for decades afterwards.

In late 1799 William and Dorothy returned to the Lakes and settled in the beautiful Grasmere valley, where they remained together for the rest of their lives: first at Dove Cottage, then, after 1813, at the more spacious Rydal Mount. In 1802 their household had expanded when Wordsworth married a childhood friend, and the tenor of their life was steady thereafter, though the years were marred by grave losses—his brother John drowned in 1805, when the ship he captained went down in a storm, two of his five children died in 1812, and a rift with Coleridge was not patched up until the 1820s. Harsh reviews of *Poems, in Two Volumes* (1807) and *The Excursion* (1814) paradoxically attested to Wordsworth's emerging centrality, and the publication of his revised and reordered *Poems* in 1815 asserted his claim to enter the canon of English poetry. Wordsworth continued to write and publish almost to the end of his long life. Though his increasingly conservative politics led some of the next generation to regard him as having betrayed his republican youth, and put him in opposition to the democratic and commercializing spirit of post-Reform Bill England, his reputation grew steadily, and in 1843 he was appointed Poet Laureate.

The Prelude, the poem that has most compelled modern readers, was published posthumously. Wordsworth had held back the work ("Title not yet fixed upon") that he had referred to variously as "the poem to Coleridge," "the poem on the growth of my own mind," and "the poem on my own poetical education," in part because he thought it "unprecedented" that an author should talk so much about himself, in part so as to bequeath its copyright as a legacy to his family. Reserving his most intimate and ambitious poem while revising it across four decades must have affected his often touchy attitude to his critics; by the time *The Prelude* appeared in 1850, the same year as Tennyson's *In Memoriam*, not even the "jacobinical" strain that Thomas Macaulay detected could much alter the image of him. For the Victorians, Wordsworth was the poet of nature, whose writings made the Lake District a tourist spot (much to his disgruntlement) and provided a moral philosophy of life, of childhood and "joy in widest commonalty spread," and above all, of memory and consolation. It was chiefly Wordsworth's "healing power" that led Matthew Arnold to declare in 1879 that Wordsworth stood third only to Milton and Shakespeare in English poetry since the Renaissance. Twentieth-century readers have been captivated by the visionary power of his language, those transient moments when "forms and substances . . . through the turnings intricate of verse, / Present themselves as objects recognized, / In flashes, and with a glory scarce their own." In Wordsworth's sustained effort in *The Prelude* to trace the growth of his mind while attending to experiences lying beyond and beneath the rational mind's grasp—"Points have we all of us within our souls / Where all stand single; this I feel, and make / Breathings for incommunicable powers"—some critics have discerned the beginnings of modern subjectivity. For Geoffrey Hartman, Wordsworth is "the most isolated figure among the great English poets." Other readers, though, have found in the tensions and ambivalences of Wordsworth's project a particularly rich embodiment of the strains of the pivotal decades in which he wrote, and he remains a crucial focus for understanding the vivid and contradictory currents of his age.

Other writing by Wordsworth appears in Perspectives: The Abolition of Slavery and the Slave Trade, page 1465.

LYRICAL BALLADS

In spring 1798 the young Wordsworth and Coleridge had been near neighbors in Somerset for almost a year. In the fall of 1797, they had decided to pay for a brief walking tour by collaborating on a poem to be sold to the *Monthly Magazine*. Uncompleted at the time, *The Rime of the Ancyent Marinere* became the opening poem of a more substantial enterprise: *Lyrical Ballads, with a few other poems*, the joint collection they published anonymously in October 1798. The exchange that nourished the project had been so close that Coleridge said that the two poets regarded the volume as "one work, in kind, though not in degree, as an ode is one work; and that our different poems are stanzas, good, relatively rather than absolutely," though of the twenty-three poems he wrote only four. A friend, the Bristol bookseller Joseph Cottle, agreed to pay the poets £30 for the copyright; before the book appeared they had departed for Germany, Coleridge to study philosophy at Göttingen and Wordsworth to learn German at Goslar, in hopes of later earning money as a translator. Priced at five shillings, the volume sold steadily and earned favorable reviews, but the simplicity of style, the focus on rural life and language, and the obscurity of the *Ancyent Marinere* provoked memorably sharp criticism. The volume had been prefixed by an Advertisement describing the majority of the poems as "experiments" to "ascertain how far the language of conversation in the middle and lower classes of society is adapted to the purposes of poetic pleasure." Attacking "the gaudiness and inane phraseology of many modern writers," and anticipating that "readers of superior judgment" would find that many of the poems would not "suit their taste," the Advertisement deliberately positioned the volume as an affront to "pre-established codes of decision," and thereby claimed for its authors the status of innovators.

Returned from Germany in 1800 and living in the Lake District, Wordsworth planned a second edition, which he sold to Longman, an established London publisher. He now dominated the project: the whole collection was published under his name alone, and Wordsworth replaced the Advertisement with an extended Preface vindicating his principles. A new second volume was made up entirely of his poems; the archaisms of the *Ancyent Marinere* were trimmed, and the poem, retitled *The Ancient Mariner: A Poet's Reverie*, was moved from the head of the first volume to the twenty-third position, accompanied by a condescending note ("The Poem of my Friend has indeed great defects"). The expanded collection sold quickly, and by 1802 a revised third edition appeared, with a significant addition to the Preface, "What is a poet?" The harsh critique by Francis Jeffrey in the newly founded *Edinburgh Review* (page 1555) may be seen as sealing the notoriety that Wordsworth had been courting; it surely helped propel the final edition of *Lyrical Ballads* in 1805, after which the contents were dispersed among the author's separate publications. Years later, in 1843, Wordsworth dictated notes on the circumstances of the poems' composition; these notes, recorded by Isabella Fenwick, are indicated as "[I.F.]."

FROM LYRICAL BALLADS (1798)
Simon Lee[1]
The Old Huntsman, with an incident in which he was concerned.

> In the sweet shire of Cardigan,
> Not far from pleasant Ivor-hall,
> An old man dwells, a little man,
> I've heard he once was tall.

---

1. "This old man had been huntsman to the squires of Alfoxden. . . . The old man's cottage stood upon the common, a little way from the entrance to Alfoxden Park. . . . I have, after an interval of 45 years, the image of the old man as fresh before my eyes as if I had seen him yesterday [I.F.]. Wordsworth has relocated the poem from Somersetshire, where he and his sister Dorothy lived from 1797–1798, to Cardiganshire, a former county of southwest Wales. A huntsman manages the hunt and has charge of the hounds. In the Preface of 1800, Wordsworth said he wrote the poem to provoke his readers' feelings "from ordinary moral sensations."

5   Of years he has upon his back,
    No doubt, a burthen weighty;
    He says he is three score and ten,°   *seventy years old*
    But others say he's eighty.

    A long blue livery-coat° has he,   *servant's uniform*
10 That's fair behind, and fair before;
    Yet, meet him where you will, you see
    At once that he is poor.
    Full five and twenty years he lived
    A running huntsman merry;
15 And, though he has but one eye left,
    His cheek is like a cherry.

    No man like him the horn could sound,
    And no man was so full of glee;
    To say the least, four counties round
20 Had heard of Simon Lee;
    His master's dead, and no one now
    Dwells in the hall of Ivor;
    Men, dogs, and horses, all are dead;
    He is the sole survivor.

25 His hunting feats have him bereft
    Of his right eye, as you may see:
    And then, what limbs those feats have left
    To poor old Simon Lee!
    He has no son, he has no child,
30 His wife, an aged woman,
    Lives with him, near the waterfall,
    Upon the village common.[2]

    And he is lean and he is sick,
    His little body's half awry
35 His ancles they are swoln and thick;
    His legs are thin and dry.
    When he was young he little knew
    Of husbandry or tillage;
    And now he's forced to work, though weak,
40 —The weakest in the village.

    He all the country could outrun,
    Could leave both man and horse behind;
    And often, ere the race was done,
    He reeled and was stone-blind.
45 And still there's something in the world
    At which his heart rejoices;
    For when the chiming hounds are out,
    He dearly loves their voices![3]

---

2. Common lands were progressively being enclosed as private property. Wordsworth successfully fought the enclosure of Grasmere's commons.

3. The expression when the hounds were out, "I dearly love their voices," was word for word from his own lips [I.F.].

Old Ruth works out of doors with him,
50   And does what Simon cannot do;
      For she, not over stout° of limb,   *hardy*
      Is stouter of the two.
      And though you with your utmost skill
      From labour could not wean them,
55   Alas! 'tis very little, all
      Which they can do between them.

      Beside their moss-grown hut of clay,
      Not twenty paces from the door,
      A scrap of land they have, but they
60   Are poorest of the poor.
      This scrap of land he from the heath
      Enclosed when he was stronger;
      But what avails the land to them,
      Which they can till no longer?

65   Few months of life has he in store,
      As he to you will tell,
      For still, the more he works, the more
      His poor old ancles swell.
      My gentle reader, I perceive
70   How patiently you've waited,
      And I'm afraid that you expect
      Some tale will be related.

      O reader! had you in your mind
      Such stores as silent thought can bring,
75   O gentle° reader! you would find   *kind, well-born*
      A tale in every thing.
      What more I have to say is short,
      I hope you'll kindly take it;
      It is no tale; but should you think,
80   Perhaps a tale you'll make it.

      One summer-day I chanced to see
      This old man doing all he could
      About the root of an old tree,
      A stump of rotten wood.
85   The mattock° totter'd in his hand;   *pick-ax*
      So vain was his endeavour
      That at the root of the old tree
      He might have worked for ever.

      "You're overtasked, good Simon Lee,
90   Give me your tool" to him I said;
      And at the word right gladly he
      Received my proffer'd aid.
      I struck, and with a single blow
      The tangled root I sever'd,
95   At which the poor old man so long
      And vainly had endeavour'd.

The tears into his eyes were brought,
And thanks and praises seemed to run
So fast out of his heart, I thought
100   They never would have done.
—I've heard of hearts unkind, kind deeds
With coldness still returning.
Alas! the gratitude of men
Has oftner left me mourning.

1798   1798

We Are Seven[1]

A simple child, dear brother Jim,
That lightly draws its breath,
And feels its life in every limb,
What should it know of death?

5   I met a little cottage girl,
She was eight years old, she said;
Her hair was thick with many a curl
That cluster'd round her head.

She had a rustic, woodland air,
10   And she was wildly clad;
Her eyes were fair, and very fair,
—Her beauty made me glad.

"Sisters and brothers, little maid,
How many may you be?"
15   "How many? seven in all," she said,
And wondering looked at me.

"And where are they, I pray you tell?"
She answered, "Seven are we,
And two of us at Conway° dwell,   Welsh seaport
20   And two are gone to sea.

"Two of us in the church-yard lie,
My sister and my brother,
And in the church-yard cottage, I
Dwell near them with my mother."

25   "You say that two at Conway dwell,
And two are gone to sea,
Yet you are seven; I pray you tell
Sweet Maid, how this may be?"

Then did the little Maid reply,
30   "Seven boys and girls are we;

---

1. The little girl who is the heroine I met within the area of Goodrich Castle in the year 1793. . . . I composed it while walking in the grove at Alfoxden. My friends will not deem it too trifling to relate that while walking to and fro I composed the last stanza first having begun with the last line [I.F.]. Coleridge wrote the first stanza. Wordsworth's own mother died when he was turning eight, the age of the girl in the poem.

Two of us in the church-yard lie,
Beneath the church-yard tree."

"You run about, my little Maid,
Your limbs they are alive;
35   If two are in the church-yard laid,
Then ye are only five."

"Their graves are green, they may be seen,"
The little Maid replied,
"Twelve steps or more from my mother's door,
40   And they are side by side.

"My stockings there I often knit,
My 'kerchief there I hem;
And there upon the ground I sit—
I sit and sing to them.

45   "And often after sunset, Sir,
When it is light and fair,
I take my little porringer,°   porridge-bowl
And eat my supper there.

"The first that died was little Jane;
50   In bed she moaning lay,
Till God released her of her pain,
And then she went away.

"So in the church-yard was she laid;
And all the summer dry,
55   Together round her grave we played,
My brother John and I.

"And when the ground was white with snow,
And I could run and slide,
My brother John was forced to go,
60   And he lies by her side."

"How many are you then," said I,
"If they two are in Heaven?"
The little Maiden did reply,
"O Master! we are seven."

65   "But they are dead; those two are dead!
Their spirits are in heaven!"
'Twas throwing words away; for still
The little Maid would have her will,
And said, "Nay, we are seven!"

1798   1798

Lines Written in Early Spring

I heard a thousand blended notes,
While in a grove I sate reclined,
In that sweet mood when pleasant thoughts
Bring sad thoughts to the mind.

5   To her fair works did nature link
       The human soul that through me ran;
       And much it griev'd my heart to think
       What man has made of man.

       Through primrose-tufts, in that sweet bower,
10   The periwinkle trail'd its wreathes;
       And 'tis my faith that every flower
       Enjoys the air it breathes.

       The birds around me hopp'd and play'd:
       Their thoughts I cannot measure,°   *assess, put in meters*
15   But the least motion which they made,
       It seem'd a thrill of pleasure.

       The budding twigs spread out their fan,
       To catch the breezy air;
       And I must think, do all I can,
20   That there was pleasure there.

       If I these thoughts may not prevent,
       If such be of my creed the plan,
       Have I not reason to lament
       What man has made of man?

1798   1798

Expostulation and Reply[1]

       "Why William, on that old grey stone,
       Thus for the length of half a day,
       Why William, sit you thus alone,
       And dream your time away?

5   "Where are your books? that light bequeath'd
       To beings else forlorn and blind!
       Up! Up! and drink the spirit breath'd
       From dead men to their kind.

       You look round on your mother earth,
10   As if she for no purpose bore you;
       As if you were her first-born birth,
       And none had lived before you!"

       One morning thus, by Esthwaite lake,[2]
       When life was sweet I knew not why,
15   To me my good friend Matthew spake,
       And thus I made reply.

       "The eye it cannot chuse but see,
       We cannot bid the ear be still;

---

1. This and the following poem opened the second edition of *Lyrical Ballads*. They are companion pieces that Wordsworth claimed "arose out of a conversation with a friend who was somewhat unreasonably attached to modern books of Moral Philosophy" ("Advertisement," 1798)— probably William Hazlitt, who visited him in 1798 and argued about metaphysics. Wordsworth later noted the poem's popularity among Quakers, whose worship is typically informal and spontaneous.
2. At Hawkshead, where Wordsworth went to school.

20   Our bodies feel, where'er they be,
Against, or with our will.

"Nor less I deem that there are powers,
Which of themselves our minds impress,
That we can feed this mind of ours,
In a wise passiveness.

25   "Think you, mid all this mighty sum
Of things for ever speaking,
That nothing of itself will come,
But we must still be seeking?

"—Then ask not wherefore, here, alone,
30   Conversing as I may,
I sit upon this old grey stone,
And dream my time away."

1798   1798

The Tables Turned
An Evening Scene, on the Same Subject

Up! up! my friend, and clear your looks,
Why all this toil and trouble?[1]
Up! up! my friend, and quit your books,
Or surely you'll grow double.°   *doubled over*

5   The sun above the mountain's head,
A freshening lustre mellow,
Through all the long green fields has spread,
His first sweet evening yellow.

Books! 'tis a dull and endless strife,
10   Come, hear the woodland linnet,°   *finch*
How sweet his music; on my life
There's more of wisdom in it.

And hark! how blithe the throstle° sings!   *thrush*
And he is no mean preacher;
15   Come forth into the light of things,
Let Nature be your teacher.

She has a world of ready wealth,
Our minds and hearts to bless—
Spontaneous wisdom breathed by health,
20   Truth breathed by chearfulness.

One impulse from a vernal wood
May teach you more of man;
Of moral evil and of good,
Than all the sages can.

25   Sweet is the lore which nature brings;
Our meddling intellect

---

1. A joking reference to the witches' incantation in *Macbeth* (4.1.10).

Misshapes the beauteous forms of things;
—We murder to dissect.

Enough of science and of art;°   *liberal arts*
30   Close up these barren leaves;°   *pages*
Come forth, and bring with you a heart
That watches and receives.

1798   1798

Old Man Travelling
Animal Tranquility and Decay[1]

A SKETCH

The little hedge-row birds,
That peck along the road, regard him not.
He travels on, and in his face, his step,
His gait, is one expression; every limb,
5   His look and bending figure, all bespeak
A man who does not move with pain, but moves
With thought—He is insensibly subdued
To settled quiet: he is one by whom
All effort seems forgotten, one to whom
10   Long patience has such mild composure given,
That patience now doth seem a thing, of which
He hath no need. He is by nature led
To peace so perfect, that the young behold
With envy, what the old man hardly feels.[2]
15   —I asked him whither he was bound, and what
The object of his journey; he replied
"Sir! I am going many miles to take
A last leave of my son, a mariner,
Who from a sea-fight has been brought to Falmouth,[3]
20   And there is dying in an hospital."

1798   1798

Tintern Abbey

"No poem of mine was composed under circumstances more pleasant for me to remember than this. I began it upon leaving Tintern, after crossing the Wye, and concluded it just as I was entering Bristol in the evening, after a ramble of 4 or 5 days, with my sister. Not a line of it was altered, and not any part of it written down till I reached Bristol." So Wordsworth recalled in 1843, but he had been practicing the gestures of the poem for some time: a manuscript fragment of 1796–1797 underlies the seemingly spontaneous opening and one of its central formulations: "Yet once again do I behold the forms / Of these huge mountains, and yet once again, / Standing beneath these elms, I hear thy voice, / Beloved Derwent, that peculiar voice / Heard in the stillness of the evening air, / Half-heard and half-created." Wordsworth first visited the

---

1. In 1800 the main title was discarded. "Animal" involves two nearly antithetical senses: mere physical existences; spiritually "animated" life.
2. Lines 15–20 were dropped in 1815 and after. The sub-title "A Sketch" was dropped in 1845.
3. On the south coast of Cornwall. The journey is more than 120 miles.

Wye valley in August 1793, on a solo walking tour; the return with his sister in July 1798 prompted this spacious meditation on time and memory, in which the ruined Abbey, a famous picturesque destination, does not appear. Instead, it is replaced by the inward "fluxes and refluxes of the mind" that shape the poem, which concludes the 1798 *Lyrical Ballads*. In 1800 Wordsworth added a note on the elevated manner: "I have not ventured to call this Poem an Ode; but it was written with a hope that in the transitions, and the impassioned music of the versification, would be found the principal requisites of that species of composition."

Lines Written a Few Miles above Tintern Abbey
On Revisiting the Banks of the Wye during a Tour, July 13, 1798

Five years have passed; five summers, with the length
Of five long winters! and again I hear
These waters, rolling from their mountain-springs
With a sweet inland murmur.[1]—Once again
5   Do I behold these steep and lofty cliffs,
Which on a wild secluded scene impress
Thoughts of more deep seclusion; and connect
The landscape with the quiet of the sky.
The day is come when I again repose
10   Here, under this dark sycamore, and view
These plots of cottage-ground, these orchard-tufts,
Which, at this season, with their unripe fruits,
Among the woods and copses lose themselves,
Nor, with their green and simple hue, disturb
15   The wild green landscape. Once again I see
These hedge-rows, hardly hedge-rows, little lines
Of sportive wood run wild; these pastoral farms
Green to the very door; and wreathes of smoke
Sent up, in silence, from among the trees,
20   With some uncertain notice, as might seem,
Of vagrant dwellers in the houseless woods,
Or of some hermit's cave, where by his fire
The hermit° sits alone.   *religious recluse*

Though absent long,
These forms of beauty have not been to me,
25   As is a landscape to a blind man's eye:
But oft, in lonely rooms, and mid the din
Of towns and cities, I have owed to them,
In hours of weariness, sensations sweet,
Felt in the blood, and felt along the heart,
30   And passing even into my purer mind
With tranquil restoration:—feelings too
Of unremembered pleasure; such, perhaps,
As may have had no trivial influence
On that best portion of a good man's life;
35   His little, nameless, unremembered acts
Of kindness and of love. Nor less, I trust,
To them I may have owed another gift,

---

1. The river is not affected by the tides a few miles above Tintern [Wordsworth's note, 1798].

Of aspect more sublime; that blessed mood,
In which the burthen° of the mystery,[2]   *burden*
40   In which the heavy and the weary weight
Of all this unintelligible world
Is lighten'd:—that serene and blessed mood,
In which the affections gently lead us on,
Until, the breath of this corporeal frame,
45   And even the motion of our human blood
Almost suspended, we are laid asleep
In body, and become a living soul:
While with an eye made quiet by the power
Of harmony, and the deep power of joy,
50   We see into the life of things.

If this
Be but a vain belief, yet, oh! how oft,
In darkness, and amid the many shapes
Of joyless day-light; when the fretful stir
Unprofitable, and the fever of the world,
55   Have hung upon the beatings of my heart,[3]
How oft, in spirit, have I turned to thee
O sylvan Wye! Thou wanderer through the wood
How often has my spirit turned to thee!

And now, with gleams of half-extinguish'd thought.
60   With many recognitions dim and faint,
And somewhat of a sad perplexity,
The picture of the mind revives again:
While here I stand, not only with the sense
Of present pleasure, but with pleasing thoughts
65   That in this moment there is life and food
For future years. And so I dare to hope
Though changed, no doubt, from what I was, when first
I came among these hills; when like a roe
I bounded o'er the mountains, by the sides
70   Of the deep rivers, and the lonely streams,
Wherever nature led; more like a man
Flying from something that he dreads, than one
Who sought the thing he loved. For nature then
(The coarser pleasures of my boyish days,
75   And their glad animal movements all gone by,)
To me was all in all.—I cannot paint
What then I was. The sounding cataract
Haunted me like a passion: the tall rock,
The mountain, and the deep and gloomy wood,
80   Their colours and their forms, were then to me
An appetite: a feeling and a love,
That had no need of a remoter charm,

2. Keats thought this phrase the core of Wordsworth's "genius." See his letter of 3 May 1818 (page 1774).
3. Echoing Macbeth's sense of life's fitful fever (3.2.23)

and Hamlet's view of life as "weary, stale, flat, and unprofitable" (1.2.133).

By thought supplied, or any interest
Unborrowed from the eye.—That time is past,
85   And all its aching joys are now no more,
And all its dizzy raptures. Not for this
Faint° I, nor mourn nor murmur: other gifts   lose heart
Have followed, for such loss, I would believe,
Abundant recompence. For I have learned
90   To look on nature, not as in the hour
Of thoughtless youth, but hearing oftentimes
The still, sad music of humanity,
Not harsh nor grating, though of ample power
To chasten and subdue. And I have felt
95   A presence that disturbs me with the joy
Of elevated thoughts; a sense sublime
Of something far more deeply interfused,
Whose dwelling is the light of setting suns,
And the round ocean, and the living air,
100   And the blue sky, and in the mind of man,
A motion and a spirit, that impels
All thinking things, all objects of all thought,
And rolls through all things. Therefore am I still
A lover of the meadows and the woods,
105   And mountains; and of all that we behold
From this green earth; of all the mighty world
Of eye and ear, both what they half-create,[4]
And what perceive; well pleased to recognize
In nature and the language of the sense,
110   The anchor of my purest thoughts, the nurse,
The guide, the guardian of my heart, and soul
Of all my moral being.

               Nor, perchance,
If I were not thus taught, should I the more
Suffer my genial° spirits to decay: creative
115   For thou art with me, here, upon the banks
Of this fair river; thou, my dearest Friend,[5]
My dear, dear Friend, and in thy voice I catch°   sense, arrest
The language of my former heart, and read
My former pleasures in the shooting lights
120   Of thy wild eyes. Oh! yet a little while
May I behold in thee what I was once,
My dear, dear Sister! And this prayer I make,
Knowing that Nature never did betray
The heart that loved her; 'tis her privilege,
125   Through all the years of this our life, to lead
From joy to joy: for she can so inform
The mind that is within us, so impress

---

4. This line has a close resemblance to an admirable line of Young, the exact expression of which I cannot recollect [Wordsworth's note]. He is thinking of Edward Young's "half create the wondrous world they see" (The *Complaint or Night Thoughts* [1744], 6.427).

5. His sister Dorothy. The language echoes Psalm 23: "Yea, though I walk through the valley of the shadow of death, I will fear no evil: for thou art with me."

With quietness and beauty, and so feed
With lofty thoughts, that neither evil tongues,[6]
130   Rash judgments, nor the sneers of selfish men,
Nor greetings where no kindness is, nor all
The dreary intercourse of daily life,
Shall e'er prevail against us, or disturb
Our chearful faith that all which we behold
135   Is full of blessings. Therefore let the moon
Shine on thee in thy solitary walk;
And let the misty mountain winds be free
To blow against thee: and in after years,
When these wild ecstasies shall be matured
140   Into a sober pleasure, when thy mind
Shall be a mansion for all lovely forms,
Thy memory be as a dwelling-place
For all sweet sounds and harmonies; Oh! then,
If solitude, or fear, or pain, or grief,
145   Should be thy portion,° with what healing thoughts   *dowry, bequest*
Of tender joy wilt thou remember me,
And these my exhortations! Nor, perchance,
If I should be, where I no more can hear
Thy voice, nor catch from thy wild eyes these gleams
150   Of past existence, wilt thou then forget
That on the banks of this delightful stream
We stood together; and that I, so long
A worshipper of Nature, hither came,
Unwearied in that service: rather say
155   With warmer love, oh! with far deeper zeal
Of holier love. Nor wilt thou then forget,
That after many wanderings, many years
Of absence, these steep woods and lofty cliffs,
And this green pastoral landscape, were to me
160   More dear, both for themselves, and for thy sake.
1798   1798

FROM LYRICAL BALLADS (1800, 1802)
from Preface[1]

The First Volume of these Poems has already been submitted to general perusal.[2] It was published, as an experiment which, I hoped, might be of some use to ascertain how far, by fitting to metrical arrangement a selection of the real language of men in a state of vivid sensation, that sort of pleasure and that quantity of pleasure may be imparted, which a Poet may rationally endeavor to impart. * * *

They who have been accustomed to the gaudiness and inane phraseology of many modern writers, if they persist in reading this book to its conclusion, will, no doubt, frequently have to struggle with feelings of strangeness and aukwardness: they

---

6. An echo of Milton's claim to "Sing with mortal voice, unchang'd / To hoarse or mute, though fall'n on evil days, / . . . and evil tongues" (*Paradise Lost* 7.24–26).
1. The Preface first appeared in the edition of 1800. The

text given here is the revised preface of 1802.
2. That is, *Lyrical Ballads,* 1798, which formed the first volume in the two-volume edition of 1800.

will look round for poetry, and will be induced to inquire by what species of courtesy these attempts can be permitted to assume that title. * * * I hope, therefore, the Reader will not censure me, if I attempt to state what I have proposed to myself to perform.

[THE PRINCIPAL OBJECT OF THE POEMS. HUMBLE AND RUSTIC LIFE]

The principal object, then, proposed in these poems was to chuse incidents and situations from common life, and to relate or describe them, throughout, as far as was possible, in a selection of language really used by men, and, at the same time, to throw over them a certain colouring of imagination, whereby ordinary things should be presented to the mind in an unusual way; and further, and above all, to make these incidents and situations interesting by tracing in them, truly though not ostentatiously, the primary laws of our nature: chiefly as far as regards the manner in which we associate ideas in a state of excitement. Low and rustic life was generally chosen, because in that condition the essential passions of the heart find a better soil in which they can attain their maturity, are less under restraint, and speak a plainer and more emphatic language; because in that condition of life our elementary feelings coexist in a state of greater simplicity and consequently may be more accurately contemplated and more forcibly communicated; because the manners of rural life germinate from those elementary feelings; and from the necessary character of rural occupations, are more easily comprehended, and are more durable; and, lastly, because in that condition the passions of men are incorporated with the beautiful and permanent forms of nature. The language, too, of these men has been adopted (purified indeed from what appear to be its real defects, from all lasting and rational causes of dislike or disgust) because such men hourly communicate with the best objects from which the best part of language is originally derived; and because, from their rank in society and the sameness and narrow circle of their intercourse, being less under the influence of social vanity they convey their feelings and notions in simple and unelaborated expressions. Accordingly, such a language, arising out of repeated experience and regular feelings, is a more permanent, and a far more philosophical language, than that which is frequently substituted for it by Poets, who think that they are conferring honour upon themselves and their art, in proportion as they separate themselves from the sympathies of men, and indulge in arbitrary and capricious habits of expression, in order to furnish food for fickle tastes, and fickle appetites of their own creation.[3]

["THE SPONTANEOUS OVERFLOW OF POWERFUL FEELINGS"]

[A]ll good poetry is the spontaneous overflow of powerful feelings: but though this be true, Poems to which any value can be attached, were never produced on any variety of subjects but by a man who, being possessed of more than usual organic sensibility, had also thought long and deeply. For our continued influxes of feeling are modified and directed by our thoughts, which are indeed the representatives of all our past feelings; and, as by contemplating the relation of these general representatives to each other we discover what is really important to men, so, by the repetition and continuance of this act, our feelings will be connected with important subjects, till at length, if we be originally possessed of much sensibility,

---

3. It is worth while here to observe that the affecting parts of Chaucer are almost always expressed in language pure and universally intelligible even to this day [Wordsworth's note].

such habits of mind will be produced that, by obeying blindly and mechanically the impulses of those habits, we shall describe objects, and utter sentiments, of such a nature, and in such connection with each other, that the understanding of the reader must necessarily be in some degree enlightened, and his affections ameliorated.

I have said that each of these poems has a purpose. * * * I should mention one other circumstance which distinguishes these Poems from the popular Poetry of the day; it is this, that the feeling therein developed gives importance to the action and situation, and not the action and situation to the feeling. * * * I will not suffer a sense of false modesty to prevent me from asserting, that I point my Reader's attention to this mark of distinction, far less for the sake of these particular Poems than from the general importance of the subject. The subject is indeed important! For the human mind is capable of being excited without the application of gross and violent stimulants; and he must have a very faint perception of its beauty and dignity who does not know this, and who does not further know, that one being is elevated above another in proportion as he possesses this capability. It has therefore appeared to me, that to endeavor to produce or enlarge this capability is one of the best services in which, at any period, a Writer can be engaged; but this service, excellent at all times, is especially so at the present day. For a multitude of causes, unknown to former times, are now acting with a combined force to blunt the discriminating powers of the mind, and, unfitting it for all voluntary exertion to reduce it to a state of almost savage torpor. The most effective of these causes are the great national events which are daily taking place, and the encreasing accumulation of men in cities, where the uniformity of their occupations produces a craving for extraordinary incident, which the rapid communication of intelligence hourly gratifies.[4] To this tendency of life and manners the literature and theatrical exhibitions of the country have conformed themselves. The invaluable works of our elder writers, I had almost said the works of Shakespear and Milton, are driven into neglect by frantic novels, sickly and stupid German Tragedies, and deluges of idle and extravagant stories in verse.[5]—When I think upon this degrading thirst after outrageous stimulation, I am almost ashamed to have spoken of the feeble effort with which I have endeavoured to counteract it; and, reflecting upon the magnitude of the general evil, I should be oppressed with no dishonorable melancholy, had I not a deep impression of certain inherent and indestructible qualities of the human mind, and likewise of certain powers in the great and permanent objects that act upon it which are equally inherent and indestructible; and did I not further add to this impression a belief, that the time is approaching when the evil will be systematically opposed, by men of greater powers, and with far more distinguished success.

[THE LANGUAGE OF POETRY]

Having dwelt thus long on the subjects and aim of these Poems, I shall request the Reader's permission to apprize him of a few circumstances relating to their *style*, in order, among other reasons, that he may not censure me for not having performed what I never attempted. The reader will find that personifications of abstract ideas rarely occur in these volumes; and, I hope, are utterly rejected as an ordinary device

---

4. That is, the rapid increase in daily newspaper production at this time. The "events" include the war with France, the Irish rebellion, and the sedition trials at home.

5. For example, sentimental melodramas and the popular Gothic novels of Ann Radcliffe and "Monk" Lewis.

to elevate the style, and raise it above prose. I have proposed to myself to imitate, and, as far as is possible, to adopt the very language of men; and assuredly such personifications do not make any natural or regular part of that language. They are, indeed, a figure of speech occasionally prompted by passion, and I have made use of them as such; but have endeavoured utterly to reject them as a mechanical device of style, or as a family language which Writers in metre seem to lay claim to by prescription. I have wished to keep my Reader in the company of flesh and blood, persuaded that by so doing I shall interest him. Others who pursue a different track will interest him likewise; I do not interfere with their claim, I only wish to prefer a claim of my own. There will also be found in these volumes little of what is usually called poetic diction; as much pains has been taken to avoid it as others ordinarily take to produce it; this I have done for the reason already alleged, to bring my language near to the language of men, and further, because the pleasure which I have proposed to myself to impart is of a kind very different from that which is supposed by many persons to be the proper object of poetry. I do not know how without being culpably particular I can give my Reader a more exact notion of the style in which I wished these poems to be written, than by informing him that I have at all times endeavoured to look steadily at my subject; consequently, I hope that there is in these Poems little falsehood of description, and my ideas are expressed in language fitted to their respective importance. Something I must have gained by this practice, as it is friendly to one property of all good poetry, namely, good sense; but it has necessarily cut me off from a large portion of phrases and figures of speech which from father to son have long been regarded as the common inheritance of Poets. * * *

To illustrate the subject in a general manner, I will here adduce a short composition of Gray,[1] who was at the head of those who, by their reasonings, have attempted to widen the space of separation betwixt Prose and Metrical composition, and was more than any other man curiously elaborate in the structure of his own poetic diction.

> In vain to me the smiling mornings shine,
> And reddening Phœbus° lifts his golden fire: *sun god*
> The birds in vain their amorous descant° join,   *song*
> Or chearful fields resume their green attire:
> These ears alas! for other notes repine;°   *languish*
> A *different object do these eyes require;*
> My *lonely anguish melts no heart but mine;*
> And *in my breast the imperfect joys expire;*
> Yet Morning smiles the busy race to cheer,
> And new-born pleasure brings to happier men;
> The fields to all their wonted tribute bear;
> To warm their little loves the birds complain.
> I *fruitless mourn to him that cannot hear*
> And *weep the more because I weep in vain.*

It will easily be perceived, that the only part of this Sonnet which is of any value is the lines printed in Italics; it is equally obvious, that, except in the rhyme, and in

---

1. Thomas Gray (1716–1771) is best known for *Elegy Written in a Country Church-Yard* (page 1245). The poem Wordsworth quotes (adding italics) is *Sonnet On the Death of Richard West* (1775). Grey had said to West that "the language of the age is never the language of poetry."

the use of the single word "fruitless" for fruitlessly, which is so far a defect, the language of these lines does in no respect differ from that of prose.

By the foregoing quotation I have shewn that the language of Prose may yet be well adapted to Poetry; and I have previously asserted that a large portion of the language of every good poem can in no respect differ from that of good Prose. I will go further. I do not doubt that it may be safely affirmed, that there neither is, nor can be, any essential difference between the language of prose and metrical composition.[2]

[WHAT IS A POET?]

What is a Poet? To whom does he address himself? And what language is to be expected from him? He is a man speaking to men: a man, it is true, endued with more lively sensibility, more enthusiasm and tenderness, who has a greater knowledge of human nature, and a more comprehensive soul, than are supposed to be common among mankind; a man pleased with his own passions and volitions, and who rejoices more than other men in the spirit of life that is in him; delighting to contemplate similar volitions and passions as manifested in the goings-on of the Universe, and habitually impelled to create them where he does not find them. To these qualities he has added a disposition to be affected more than other men by absent things as if they were present; an ability of conjuring up in himself passions, which are indeed far from being the same as those produced by real events, yet (especially in those parts of the general sympathy which are pleasing and delightful) do more nearly resemble the passions produced by real events, than anything which, from the motions of their own minds merely, other men are accustomed to feel in themselves; whence, and from practice, he has acquired a greater readiness and power in expressing what he thinks and feels, and especially those thoughts and feelings which, by his own choice, or from the structure of his own mind, arise in him without immediate external excitement.

But, whatever portion of this faculty we may suppose even the greatest Poet to possess, there cannot be a doubt that the language which it will suggest to him, must in liveliness and truth, fall far short of that which is uttered by men in real life, under the actual pressure of those passions, certain shadows of which the Poet thus produces, or feels to be produced, in himself. However exalted a notion we would wish to cherish of the character of a Poet, it is obvious, that while he describes and imitates passions, his situation is altogether slavish and mechanical, compared with the freedom and power of real and substantial action and suffering. So that it will be the wish of the Poet to bring his feelings near to those of the persons whose feelings he describes, nay, for short spaces of time perhaps, to let himself slip into an entire delusion, and even confound and identify his own feelings with theirs; modifying only the language which is thus suggested to him, by a consideration that he describes for a particular purpose, that of giving pleasure. Here, then, he will apply the principle on which I have so much insisted, namely, that of selection; on this he will depend for removing what would otherwise be painful or disgusting in the passion; he will feel that there is no necessity to trick out or to elevate nature: and, the more industriously he applies this principle, the deeper will be his faith that no words which his fancy or imagination can suggest, will be to be compared with those which are the emanations of reality and truth.

2. Wordsworth's footnote says that he means "Poetry" as opposed to "Prose, and synonymous with metrical composition"; he concedes that "much confusion has been introduced into criticism by this contradistinction of Poetry and Prose, instead of the more philosophical one of Poetry and Matter of fact, or Science. The only strict antithesis to Prose is Metre; nor is this, in truth, a *strict* antithesis; because lines and passages of metre so naturally occur in writing prose, that it would be scarcely possible to avoid them, even were it desirable."

["Emotion Recollected in Tranquillity"]

I have said that Poetry is the spontaneous overflow of powerful feelings; it takes its origin from emotion recollected in tranquillity: the emotion is contemplated till, by a species of reaction, the tranquillity gradually disappears, and an emotion, kindred to that which was before the subject of contemplation, is gradually produced, and does itself actually exist in the mind. In this mood successful composition generally begins.

There was a Boy[1]

There was a Boy; ye knew him well, ye Cliffs
And Islands of Winander![2] many a time,
At evening, when the earliest stars had just begun
To move along the edges of the hills,
5   Rising or setting, would he stand alone,
Beneath the trees, or by the glimmering lake,
And there, with fingers interwoven, both hands
Press'd closely palm to palm and to his mouth
Uplifted, he, as through an instrument,
10   Blew mimic hootings to the silent owls
That they might answer him. And they would shout
Across the wat'ry vale and shout again
Responsive to his call, with quivering peals,
And long halloos, and screams, and echoes loud
15   Redoubled and redoubled, a wild scene
Of mirth and jocund din! And, when it chanced
That pauses of deep silence mock'd his skill,
Then, sometimes, in that silence, while he hung
Listening, a gentle shock of mild surprize
20   Has carried far into his heart the voice
Of mountain-torrents; or the visible scene
Would enter unawares into his mind
With all its solemn imagery, its rocks,
Its woods, and that uncertain heaven receiv'd
25   Into the bosom of the steady lake.
    Fair are the woods, and beauteous is the spot,
The vale where he was born: the Church-yard hangs
Upon a slope above the village school;[3]
And there along that bank where I have pass'd
30   At evening, I believe, that near his grave
A full half-hour together I have stood,
Mute—for he died when he was ten years old.

1797–1798   1800

1. First drafted in Germany in 1798 in the first person, these lines were later assimilated to *The Prelude* Book 5 as an example of education by "Nature." In his collection of 1815, Wordsworth had this poem lead off the subsection "Poems of the Imagination," commenting in his Preface that it displayed "one of the earliest processes of Nature in the development of this faculty. Guided by one of my own primary consciousnesses, I have presented a commu-tation and transfer of internal feelings, co-operating with external accidents, to plant, for immortality, images of sound and sight, in the celestial soil of the Imagination."
2. Windermere, in the Lake District.
3. Hawkshead Grammar School, which Wordsworth attended as a child in the Lake district village of Esth-waite.

Strange fits of passion have I known[1]

Strange fits of passion have I known,
And I will dare to tell,
But in the lover's ear alone,
What once to me befel.

5 When she I lov'd, was strong and gay
And like a rose in June,
I to her cottage bent my way,
Beneath the evening moon.

Upon the moon I fix'd my eye,
10 All over the wide lea;
My horse trudg'd on, and we drew nigh
Those paths so dear to me.

And now we reach'd the orchard plot,
And, as we climb'd the hill,
15 Towards the roof of Lucy's cot°   cottage
The moon descended still.

In one of those sweet dreams I slept,
Kind Nature's gentlest boon!
And, all the while, my eyes I kept
20 On the descending moon.

My horse mov'd on; hoof after hoof
He rais'd, and never stopp'd:
When down behind the cottage roof
At once the planet dropp'd.

25 What fond and wayward thoughts will slide
Into a Lover's head—
"O mercy!" to myself I cried,
"If Lucy should be dead!"[2]

1798–1799   1800

Song (She dwelt among th' untrodden ways)

She dwelt among th' untrodden ways
    Beside the springs of Dove,[1]
A Maid whom there were none to praise
    And very few to love:

A Violet by a mossy stone
5   Half-hidden from the Eye![2]
—Fair, as a star when only one
    Is shining in the sky!

1. This and the three following lyrics, all written during a lonely winter that William and Dorothy spent in Germany, compose four of five lyrics traditionally called the "Lucy Poems." Lucy has not been conclusively identified. The name "Lucy" comes from the Latin "lux" (light); "Lucina" is an old name for the goddess of the moon.
2. A manuscript from 1799 shows a final stanza later deleted: "I told her this: her laughter light / Is ringing in my ears: / And when I think upon that night / My eyes are dim with tears."
1. A river in England.
2. See Gray's *Elegy in a Country Churchyard*, page 1246: "Full many a flower is born to blush unseen" (55).

She *liv'd* unknown, and few could know
10   When Lucy ceas'd to be;
But she is in her Grave, and Oh!
      The difference to me!

Three years she grew in sun and shower

Three years she grew in sun and shower,
Then Nature said, "A lovelier flower
On earth was never sown;
This Child I to myself will take
5   She shall be mine, and I will make
A Lady of my own.

"Myself will to my darling be
Both law and impulse, and with me
The Girl in rock and plain,
10   In earth and heaven, in glade and bower,
Shall feel an overseeing power
To kindle or restrain.

"She shall be sportive as the fawn
That wild with glee across the lawn
15   Or up the mountain springs,
And hers shall be the breathing balm,
And hers the silence and the calm
Of mute insensate things.

"The floating clouds their state shall lend
20   To her; for her the willow bend,
Nor shall she fail to see
Even in the motions of the storm
Grace that shall mould the Maiden's form
By silent sympathy.

25   "The stars of midnight shall be dear
To her, and she shall lean her ear
In many a secret place
Where rivulets dance their wayward round,
And beauty born of murmuring sound
30   Shall pass into her face.

"And vital feelings of delight
Shall rear her form to stately height,
Her virgin bosom swell,
Such thoughts to Lucy I will give
35   While she and I together live
Here in this happy dell."

Thus Nature spake—The work was done —
How soon my Lucy's race was run!
She died, and left to me
40   This heath, this calm and quiet scene,
The memory of what has been,
And never more will be.

Song (A slumber did my spirit seal)[1]

A slumber did my spirit seal;
   I had no human fears:
She seem'd a thing that could not feel
   The touch of earthly years.

5   No motion has she now, no force
   She neither hears nor sees
Roll'd round in earth's diurnal° course,   *daily*
   With rocks, and stones, and trees.

1798–1799   1800

Lucy Gray[1]

Oft I had heard of Lucy Gray,
And when I cross'd the Wild,
I chanc'd to see at break of day
The solitary Child.

5   No Mate, no comrade Lucy knew;
She dwelt on a wild Moor,
The sweetest Thing that ever grew
Beside a human door!

You yet may spy the Fawn at play,
10   The Hare upon the Green;
But the sweet face of Lucy Gray
Will never more be seen.

"To-night will be a stormy night,
You to the Town must go,
15 And take a lantern, Child, to light
Your Mother thro' the snow."

"That, Father! will I gladly do;
'Tis scarcely afternoon—
The Minster°-clock has struck two,   *church*
20 And yonder is the Moon."[2]

At this the Father rais'd his hook
And snapp'd a faggot-band;°   *bundle of firewood*
He plied his work; and Lucy took
The lantern in her hand.

25 Not blither is the mountain roe,
With many a wanton° stroke   *frolicsome*
Her feet disperse the powd'ry snow
That rises up like smoke.

---

1. Coleridge wrote to a friend, "Some months ago Wordsworth transmitted to me a most sublime Epitaph. Whether it had any reality, I cannot say. Most probably, in some gloomier moment he had fancied the moment in which his Sister might die."

1. Founded on a circumstance told me by my Sister, of a little girl who, not far from Halifax in Yorkshire, was bewildered in a snow-storm. . . . Her footsteps were traced by her parents to the middle of the lock of a canal, and no other vestige of her, backward or forward, could be traced. The body, however, was found in the canal. The way in which the incident was treated & the spiritualizing of the character might furnish hints for contrasting the imaginative influences which I have endeavoured to throw over common life with Crabbe's matter of fact style of treating subjects of the same kind. [I.F., referring to poet George Crabbe.] In 1815, Wordsworth changed the title to *Lucy Gray, or Solitude*.

2. Wordsworth remarked that "the day-moon" is something "no town or village girl would ever notice" (1816).

The storm came on before its time,
30   She wander'd up and down,
And many a hill did Lucy climb
But never reach'd the Town.

The wretched Parents all that night
Went shouting far and wide;
35   But there was neither sound nor sight
To serve them for a guide.

At day-break on a hill they stood
That overlook'd the Moor;
And thence they saw the Bridge of Wood,
40   A furlong° from their door.   *220 yards*

And now they homeward turn'd, and cry'd
"In Heaven we all shall meet!"
When in the snow the Mother spied
The print of Lucy's feet.

45   Then downward from the steep hill's edge
They track'd the footmarks small;
And through the broken hawthorn-hedge,
And by the long stone-wall;

And then an open field they cross'd,
50   The marks were still the same;
They track'd them on, nor ever lost,
And to the Bridge they came.

They follow'd from the snowy bank
Those footmarks, one by one,
55   Into the middle of the plank,
And further there were none.

Yet some maintain that to this day
She is a living Child,
That you may see sweet Lucy Gray
60   Upon the lonesome Wild.

O'er rough and smooth she trips along,
And never looks behind;
And sings a solitary song
That whistles in the wind.

1798–1799   1800

Poor Susan[1]

At the corner of Wood-Street, when day-light appears,
There's a Thrush that sings loud, it has sung for three years:
Poor Susan has pass'd by the spot, and has heard
In the silence of morning the song of the bird.

---

1. The title was changed to *The Reverie of Poor Susan* in 1815. The poem is set in London's mercantile district.

5   'Tis a note of enchantment; what ails her? She sees
      A mountain ascending, a vision of trees;
      Bright volumes of vapour through Lothbury glide,
      And a river flows on through the vale of Cheapside.

      Green pastures she views in the midst of the dale,
10   Down which she so often has tripp'd with her pail,
      And a single small cottage, a nest like a dove's,
      The one only dwelling on earth that she loves.

      She looks, and her heart is in Heaven, but they fade,
      The mist and the river, the hill and the shade;
15   The stream will not flow, and the hill will not rise,
      And the colours have all pass'd away from her eyes.

      Poor Outcast! return—to receive thee once more
      The house of thy Father will open its door,
      And thou once again, in thy plain russet gown,
20   May'st hear the thrush sing from a tree of its own.[2]

1798   1800

Nutting[1]

                It seems a day
      (I speak of one from many singled out)
      One of those heavenly days that cannot die;
      When forth I walked from our cottage-door,[2]
5   And with a wallet o'er my shoulder slung,
      A nutting-crook in hand; and turn'd my steps
      Towards the distant wood, a Figure quaint,
      Trick'd out in proud disguise of Beggar's weeds°   *clothing*
      Put on for the occasion, by advice
10   And exhortation of my frugal Dame.
      Motley accoutrement! of power to smile
      At thorns, and brakes, and brambles, and, in truth,
      More ragged than need was. Among the woods,
      And o'er the pathless rocks, I forc'd my way
15   Until, at length, I came to one dear nook
      Unvisited, where not a broken bough
      Droop'd with its wither'd leaves, ungracious sign
      Of devastation, but the hazels rose
      Tall and erect, with milk-white clusters hung,
20   A virgin scene![3]—A little while I stood,
      Breathing with such suppression of the heart
      As joy delights in; and with wise restraint

2. Charles Lamb felt this last stanza "threw a kind of dubiety upon Susan's moral conduct"; it was dropped after 1800.

1. Intended as part of a poem on my own life, but struck out as not being wanted there. Like most of my schoolfellows I was an impassioned nutter. For this pleasure, the vale of Esthwaite, abounding in coppice-wood, furnished a very wide range. The verses arose out of the remembrance of feelings I had when a boy [I.F.].

2. The house at which I boarded during the time I was at School [Wordsworth's note]; supervised by Ann Tyson, the Dame of line 10.

3. The moral terrain of the bower entails two precedents: Spenser's "Bower of Blisse" in *The Faerie Queene*, a dangerously seductive pleasure garden, and the Garden of Eden in Milton's *Paradise Lost*, which Satan invades to ravage Eve.

Voluptuous, fearless of a rival, eyed
The banquet; or beneath the trees I sate
25   Among the flowers, and with the flowers I play'd;
A temper known to those, who, after long
And weary expectation, have been bless'd
With sudden happiness beyond all hope.—
—Perhaps it was a bower beneath whose leaves
30   The violets of five seasons re-appear
And fade, unseen by any human eye,
Where fairy water-breaks[4] do murmur on
For ever, and I saw the sparkling foam,
And with my cheek on one of those green stones
35   That, fleec'd with moss, beneath the shady trees,
Lay round me, scatter'd like a flock of sheep,
I heard the murmur and the murmuring sound,
In that sweet mood when pleasure loves to pay
Tribute to ease, and, of its joy secure
40   The heart luxuriates with indifferent things,
Wasting its kindliness on stocks° and stones,   *tree stumps*
And on the vacant air. Then up I rose,
And dragg'd to earth both branch and bough, with crash
And merciless ravage: and the shady nook
45   Of hazels, and the green and mossy bower
Deform'd and sullied, patiently gave up
Their quiet being: and unless I now
Confound my present feelings with the past,
Even then, when from[5] the bower I turn'd away,
50   Exulting, rich beyond the wealth of kings
I felt a sense of pain when I beheld
The silent trees, and saw the intruding sky.—

Then, dearest Maiden![6] move along these shades°   *shadows, spirits*
In gentleness of heart; with gentle hand
55   Touch,—for there is a Spirit in the woods.
1798–1799   1800

Michael

Sending a copy of the 1800 *Lyrical Ballads* to Charles James Fox, leader of the Whig opposition in Parliament, Wordsworth drew attention to *Michael*: "I have attempted to draw a picture of the domestic affections . . . amongst a class of men who are now almost confined to the North of England. They are small independent *proprietors* of land here called statesmen, men of respectable education who daily labour on their own little properties. The domestic affections will always be strong amongst men who live in a country not crowded with population, if these men are placed above poverty. But if they are proprietors of small estates, which have descended to them from their ancestors, the power which these affections will acquire . . . is inconceivable by those who have only had an opportunity of observing hired labourers, farmers, and the manufacturing Poor.

---

4. Wordsworth's coinage for "little rapids."
5. Later revised to "ere from," making the "sense of pain" precede rather than coincide with "exulting."
6. In a much longer manuscript draft, Wordsworth pre-

ceded this poem with the story of a "Lucy" who had been ravaging a bower—her ungentle, unmaidenly action provoking her companion to recount this episode from his past, seemingly to admonish her with his remorse.

Their little tract of land serves as a kind of permanent rallying point for their domestic feelings, as a tablet upon which they are written which makes them objects of memory in a thousand instances when they would otherwise be forgotten"; *Michael* shows "that men who do not wear fine cloaths can feel deeply." Later that year Wordsworth wrote to a friend, "I have attempted to give a picture of a man, of strong mind and lively sensibility, agitated by two of the most powerful affections of the human heart; the parental affection, and the love of property, *landed* property, including the feelings of inheritance, home, and personal and family independence." Wordsworth drew on two local tales, one of "the son of an old couple having become dissolute and run away from his parents" (who once owned Dove Cottage, Wordsworth's home at the time); and one of "an old shepherd having been seven years in building up a sheepfold in a solitary valley." The austere biblical aura of the "covenant" between Michael and his son evokes Old Testament prototypes, and Luke is the Gospel that contains the parable of the Prodigal Son (15.11–32). In focusing on contemporary conditions and refusing to provide any relief except in Michael's "comfort in the strength of love," Wordsworth significantly revises the genre of pastoral.

Michael

A Pastoral Poem

If from the public way you turn your steps
Up the tumultuous brook of Green-head Gill,[1]
You will suppose that with an upright path
Your feet must struggle; in such bold ascent
5   The pastoral Mountains front you, face to face.
But, courage! for around that boisterous Brook
The mountains have all open'd out themselves,
And made a hidden valley of their own.
No habitation can be seen; but such
10   As journey thither find themselves alone
With a few sheep, with rocks and stones, and kites°   *hawks*
That overhead are sailing in the sky.

It is in truth an utter solitude;
Nor should I have made mention of this Dell
15   But for one object which you might pass by,
Might see and notice not. Beside the brook
There is a straggling heap of unhewn stones!
And to that place a story appertains,
Which, though it be ungarnish'd with events,
20   Is not unfit, I deem, for the fire-side,
Or for the summer shade. It was the first,
The earliest of those tales that spake to me
Of Shepherds, dwellers in the valleys, men
Whom I already lov'd; not verily
25   For their own sakes, but for the fields and hills
Where was their occupation and abode.
And hence this Tale, while I was yet a boy
Careless of books, yet having felt the power
Of Nature, by the gentle agency
30   Of natural objects, led me on to feel
For passions that were not my own, and think

1. Green-head Gill (valley) and the poem's other settings are near Wordsworth's cottage at Grasmere.

At random and imperfectly indeed
On man; the heart of man, and human life.
Therefore, although it be a history
35   Homely and rude, I will relate the same
For the delight of a few natural hearts,
And with yet fonder feeling, for the sake
Of youthful Poets, who among these Hills
Will be my second self when I am gone.

40   Upon the Forest-side in Grasmere Vale
There dwelt a Shepherd, Michael was his name,
An old man, stout of heart, and strong of limb.
His bodily frame had been from youth to age
Of an unusual strength; his mind was keen
45   Intense and frugal, apt for all affairs,
And in his Shepherd's calling he was prompt
And watchful more than ordinary men.
Hence had he learn'd the meaning of all winds,
Of blasts of every tone, and often-times,
50   When others heeded not, He heard the South°   south wind
Make subterraneous music, like the noise
Of Bagpipers on distant Highland hills;
The Shepherd, at such warning, of his flock
Bethought him, and he to himself would say
55   The winds are now devising work for me!
And truly at all times the storm, that drives
The Traveller to a shelter, summon'd him
Up to the mountains: he had been alone
Amid the heart of many thousand mists
60   That came to him, and left him, on the heights.
So liv'd he till his eightieth year was pass'd.

And grossly that man errs, who should suppose
That the green Valleys, and the Streams and Rocks
Were things indifferent to the Shepherd's thoughts.
65   Fields, where with chearful spirits he had breath'd
The common air; the hills, which he so oft
Had climb'd, with vigorous steps; which had impress'd
So many incidents upon his mind
Of hardship, skill or courage, joy or fear;
70   Which, like a book, preserv'd the memory
Of the dumb animals, whom he had sav'd,
Had fed or shelter'd, linking to such acts,
So grateful in themselves, the certainty
Of honourable gains; these fields, these hills
75   Which were his living Being, even more
Than his own Blood—what could they less? had laid
Strong hold on his affections, were to him
A pleasurable feeling of blind love,
The pleasure which there is in life itself.

80   He had not passed his days in singleness.
He had a Wife, a comely Matron, old

Though younger than himself full twenty years.
She was a woman of a stirring life
Whose heart was in her house: two wheels she had
85 Of antique form; this large, for spinning wool,
That small for flax; and if one wheel had rest,
It was because the other was at work.
The Pair had but one Inmate° in their house,   resident
An only Child, who had been born to them
90 When Michael telling° o'er his years began   counting
To deem that he was old, in Shepherd's phrase,
With one foot in the grave. This only son,
With two brave sheep dogs tried° in many a storm,   tested
The one of an inestimable worth,
95 Made all their Household. I may truly say,
That they were as a proverb in the vale
For endless industry. When day was gone,
And from their occupations out of doors
The Son and Father were come home, even then
100 Their labour did not cease, unless when all
Turn'd to the cleanly supper-board, and there
Each with a mess of pottage° and skimm'd milk,   stew
Sate round the basket pil'd with oaten cakes,
And their plain home-made cheese. Yet when their meal
105 Was ended, LUKE (for so the Son was nam'd)
And his old Father, both betook themselves
To such convenient work as might employ
Their hands by the fire-side; perhaps to card°   comb out
Wool for the House-wife's spindle, or repair
110 Some injury done to sickle, flail, or scythe,
Or other implement of house or field.

Down from the ceiling, by the chimney's edge,
That in our ancient uncouth country style
Did with a huge projection overbrow
115 Large space beneath, as duly as the light
Of day grew dim, the House-wife hung a lamp;
An aged utensil, which had perform'd
Service beyond all others of its kind.
Early at evening did it burn and late,
120 Surviving Comrade of uncounted Hours
Which going by from year to year had found
And left the Couple neither gay perhaps
Nor chearful, yet with objects and with hopes
Living a life of eager industry.
125 And now, when LUKE was in his eighteenth year,
There by the light of this old lamp they sate,
Father and Son, while late into the night
The House-wife plied her own peculiar work,
Making the cottage thro' the silent hours
130 Murmur as with the sound of summer flies.
Not with a waste of words, but for the sake
Of pleasure, which I know that I shall give

To many living now, I of this Lamp
Speak thus minutely: for there are no few
135   Whose memories will bear witness to my tale.
This Light was famous in its neighbourhood,
And was a public Symbol of the life,
That thrifty Pair had liv'd. For, as it chanc'd,
Their Cottage on a plot of rising ground
140   Stood single, with large prospect North and South,
High into Easedale, up to Dunmal-Raise,
And Westward to the village near the Lake;
And from this constant light so regular
And so far seen, the House itself by all
145   Who dwelt within the limits of the vale,
Both old and young, was nam'd The Evening Star.

Thus living on through such a length of years,
The Shepherd, if he lov'd himself, must needs
Have lov'd his Help-mate; but to Michael's heart
150   This Son of his old age was yet more dear—
Effect which might perhaps have been produc'd
By that instinctive tenderness, the same
Blind Spirit, which is in the blood of all,
Or that a child, more than all other gifts,
155   Brings hope with it, and forward-looking thoughts,
And stirrings of inquietude, when they
By tendency of nature needs must fail.
From such, and other causes, to the thoughts
Of the old Man his only Son was now
160   The dearest object that he knew on earth.
Exceeding was the love he bare to him,
His Heart and his Heart's joy! For oftentimes
Old Michael, while he was a babe in arms,
Had done him female service, not alone
165   For dalliance and delight, as is the use
Of Fathers, but with patient mind enforc'd
To acts of tenderness; and he had rock'd
His cradle, as with a woman's gentle hand.

And in a later time, ere yet the Boy
170   Had put on Boy's attire, did Michael love,
Albeit of a stern unbending mind,
To have the young one in his sight, when he
Had work by his own door, or when he sate
With sheep before him on his Shepherd's stool,
175   Beneath that large old Oak, which near their door
Stood, and from its enormous breadth of shade
Chosen for the Shearer's covert from the sun,
Thence in our rustic dialect was call'd
The CLIPPING TREE,[2] a name which yet it bears.
180   There, while they two were sitting in the shade,

---

2. Clipping is the word used in the North of England for shearing [Wordsworth's note].

With others round them, earnest all and blithe,
Would Michael exercise his heart with looks
Of fond correction and reproof bestow'd
Upon the child, if he disturb'd the sheep
185 By catching at their legs, or with his shouts
Scar'd them, while they lay still beneath the shears.

And when by Heaven's good grace the Boy grew up
A healthy Lad, and carried in his cheek
Two steady roses that were five years old,
190 Then Michael from a winter coppice° cut   *grove of small trees*
With his own hand a sapling, which he hoop'd
With iron, making it throughout in all
Due requisites a perfect Shepherd's Staff,
And gave it to the Boy; wherewith equipp'd
195 He as a Watchman oftentimes was plac'd
At gate or gap, to stem or turn the flock,
And to his office prematurely call'd
There stood the urchin, as you will divine,
Something between a hindrance and a help,
200 And for this cause not always, I believe,
Receiving from his Father hire of praise.
Though nought was left undone which staff or voice,
Or looks, or threatening gestures, could perform.
But soon as Luke, full ten years old, could stand
205 Against the mountain blasts, and to the heights,
Not fearing toil, nor length of weary ways,
He with his Father daily went, and they
Were as companions, why should I relate
That objects which the Shepherd loved before
210 Were dearer now? that from the Boy there came
Feelings and emanations, things which were
Light to the sun and music to the wind;
And that the Old Man's heart seemed born again.
Thus in his Father's sight the Boy grew up:
215 And now, when he had reached his eighteenth year,
He was his comfort and his daily hope.

While this good household thus were living on
From day to day, to Michael's ear there came
Distressful tidings. Long before the time
220 Of which I speak, the Shepherd had been bound
In surety° for his Brother's Son, a man   *guaranteed a loan*
Of an industrious life, and ample means;
But unforeseen misfortunes suddenly
Had press'd upon him, and old Michael now
225 Was summon'd to discharge the forfeiture,°   *collateral*
A grievous penalty, but little less
Than half his substance. This un-look'd for claim,
At the first hearing, for a moment took
More hope out of his life than he supposed
230 That any old man ever could have lost.

As soon as he had gather'd so much strength
That he could look his trouble in the face,
It seem'd that his sole refuge was to sell
A portion of his patrimonial fields.
235   Such was his first resolve; he thought again,
And his heart fail'd him. "Isabel," said he,
Two evenings after he had heard the news,
"I have been toiling more than seventy years,
And in the open sun-shine of God's love
240   Have we all liv'd; yet if these fields of ours
Should pass into a Stranger's hand, I think
That I could not lie quiet in my grave.
Our lot is a hard lot; the Sun itself
Has scarcely been more diligent than I,
245   And I have liv'd to be a fool at last
To my own family. An evil Man
That was, and made an evil choice, if he
Were false to us; and if he were not false,
There are ten thousand to whom loss like this
250   Had been no sorrow. I forgive him—but
'Twere better to be dumb than to talk thus.
When I began, my purpose was to speak
Of remedies and of a chearful hope.
Our Luke shall leave us, Isabel; the land
255   Shall not go from us, and it shall be free;°   *not mortgaged*
He° shall possess it, free as is the wind   *Luke*
That passes over it. We have, thou knowest,
Another Kinsman, he will be our friend
In this distress. He is a prosperous man,
260   Thriving in trade, and Luke to him shall go,
And with his Kinsman's help and his own thrift,
He quickly will repair this loss, and then
May come again to us. If here he stay,
What can be done? Where every one is poor
265   What can be gained?" At this the old Man paus'd,
And Isabel sate silent, for her mind
Was busy, looking back into past times.
There's Richard Bateman, thought she to herself,[3]
He was a parish-boy° at the church-door   *on welfare*
270   They made a gathering for him, shillings, pence,
And halfpennies, wherewith the Neighbours bought
A Basket, which they fill'd with Pedlar's wares,
And with this Basket on his arm, the Lad
Went up to London, found a Master° there,   *employer*
275   Who out of many chose the trusty Boy
To go and overlook his merchandise
Beyond the seas, where he grew wond'rous rich,
And left estates and monies to the poor,
And at his birth-place, built a Chapel, floor'd

3. The story alluded to here is well known in the country [Wordsworth's note, 1802].

280 With Marble, which he sent from foreign lands.
    These thoughts, and many others of like sort,
    Pass'd quickly thro' the mind of Isabel,
    And her face brighten'd. The old Man was glad,
    And thus resum'd. "Well! Isabel, this scheme
285 These two days, has been meat and drink to me.
    Far more than we have lost is left us yet.
    —We have enough—I wish indeed that I
    Were younger, but this hope is a good hope.
    —Make ready Luke's best garments, of the best
290 Buy for him more, and let us send him forth
    To-morrow, or the next day, or to-night:
    —If he could go, the Boy should go to-night."

    Here Michael ceas'd, and to the fields went forth
    With a light heart. The House-wife for five days
295 Was restless° morn and night, and all day long   *without rest*
    Wrought on with her best fingers to prepare
    Things needful for the journey of her Son.
    But Isabel was glad when Sunday came
    To stop her in her work; for, when she lay
300 By Michael's side, she through the last two nights
    Heard him, how he was troubled in his sleep:
    And when they rose at morning she could see
    That all his hopes were gone. That day at noon
    She said to Luke, while they two by themselves
305 Were sitting at the door, "Thou must not go,
    We have no other Child but thee to lose,
    None to remember—do not go away,
    For if thou leave thy Father he will die."[4]
    The Lad made answer with a jocund voice,
310 And Isabel, when she had told her fears,
    Recover'd heart. That evening her best fare
    Did she bring forth, and all together sate
    Like happy people round a Christmas fire.

    Next morning Isabel resum'd her work,
315 And all the ensuing week the house appear'd
    As chearful as a grove in Spring: at length
    The expected letter from their Kinsman came,
    With kind assurances that he would do
    His utmost for the welfare of the Boy,
320 To which requests were added, that forthwith
    He might be sent to him. Ten times or more
    The letter was read over; Isabel
    Went forth to shew it to the neighbours round:
    Nor was there at that time on English Land
325 A prouder heart than Luke's. When Isabel
    Had to her house return'd, the Old Man said,

---

4. Echoing the story of Joseph in Genesis 44.22: "The lad cannot leave his father: for if he should leave his father, his father would die."

"He shall depart to-morrow." To this word
The House-wife answered, talking much of things
Which, if at such short notice he should go,
330   Would surely be forgotten. But at length
She gave consent, and Michael was at ease.

Near the tumultuous brook of Green-head Gill,
In that deep Valley, Michael had design'd
To build a Sheep-fold;[5] and, before he heard
335   The tidings of his melancholy loss,
For this same purpose he had gathered up
A heap of stones, which close to the brook side
Lay thrown together, ready for the work.
With Luke that evening thitherward he walk'd;
340   And soon as they had reach'd the place he stopp'd,
And thus the Old Man spake to him. "My Son,
To-morrow thou wilt leave me; with full heart
I look upon thee, for thou art the same
That wert a promise to me ere thy birth,
345   And all thy life hast been my daily joy.
I will relate to thee some little part
Of our two histories; 'twill do thee good
When thou art from me, even if I should speak
On things thou canst not know of.—After thou
350   First cam'st into the world—as oft befalls
To new-born infants, thou didst sleep away
Two days, and blessings from thy Father's tongue
Then fell upon thee. Day by day pass'd on,
And still I lov'd thee with encreasing love.
355   Never to living ear came sweeter sounds
Than when I heard thee by our own fire-side
First uttering without words a natural tune,
While thou, a feeding babe, didst in thy joy
Sing at thy Mother's breast. Month followed month,
360   And in the open fields my life was pass'd
And on the mountains, else I think that thou
Hadst been brought up upon thy father's knees.
—But we were playmates, Luke; among these hills,
As well thou know'st, in us the old and young
365   Have play'd together, nor with me didst thou
Lack any pleasure which a boy can know."

Luke had a manly heart; but at these words
He sobb'd aloud. The Old Man grasp'd his hand,
And said, "Nay do not take it so—I see
370   That these are things of which I need not speak.
—Even to the utmost I have been to thee
A kind and a good Father: and herein
I but repay a gift which I myself

5. A sheepfold in these mountains is an unroofed building of stone walls, with different divisions. It is generally placed by the side of a brook [Wordsworth's note, 1802]. "The Sheepfold . . . remains, or rather ruins of it," Wordsworth remarked in 1843.

Receiv'd at others' hands, for, though now old
375   Beyond the common life of man, I still
Remember them who lov'd me in my youth.
Both of them sleep together: here they liv'd,
As all their Forefathers had done, and when
At length their time was come, they were not loth
380   To give their bodies to the family mold.
I wish'd that thou should'st live the life they liv'd.
But 'tis a long time to look back, my Son,
And see so little gain from sixty years.
These fields were burthen'd° when they came to me;   mortgaged
385   'Till I was forty years of age, not more
Than half of my inheritance was mine.
I toil'd and toil'd; God bless'd me in my work,
And 'till these three weeks past the land was free.
—It looks as if it never could endure
390   Another Master. Heaven forgive me, Luke,
If I judge ill for thee, but it seems good
That thou should'st go." At this the Old Man paus'd;
Then, pointing to the Stones near which they stood,
Thus, after a short silence, he resum'd:
395   "This was a work for us, and now, my Son,
It is a work for me. But, lay one Stone—
Here, lay it for me, Luke, with thine own hands.
I for the purpose brought thee to this place.
Nay, Boy, be of good hope:—we both may live
400   To see a better day. At eighty-four
I still am strong and stout;°—do thou thy part;   hardy
I will do mine[6]—I will begin again
With many tasks that were resign'd to thee;
Up to the heights, and in among the storms,
405   Will I without thee go again, and do
All works which I was wont to do alone,
Before I knew thy face.—Heaven bless thee, Boy!
Thy heart these two weeks has been beating fast
With many hopes—it should be so—yes—yes—
410   I knew that thou could'st never have a wish
To leave me, Luke, thou hast been bound to me
Only by links of love, when thou art gone
What will be left to us!—But, I forget
My purposes. Lay now the corner-stone,
415   As I requested, and hereafter, Luke,
When thou art gone away, should evil men
Be thy companions, let this sheep-fold be
Thy anchor and thy shield; amid all fear
And all temptation, let it be to thee
420   An emblem of the life thy Fathers liv'd,
Who, being innocent, did for that cause

6. "Nature . . . hath done her part; / Do thou but thine," Raphael instructs Adam about his responsibility for Eve (*Paradise Lost* 8.561–62); "God toward thee hath done his part, do thine," Adam cautions Eve, before she goes off alone in Eden, the prelude to her Fall (9.375).

Bestir them in good deeds. Now, fare thee well—
When thou return'st, thou in this place wilt see
A work which is not here, a covenant
425 'Twill be between us—but, whatever fate
Befall thee, I shall love thee to the last,
And bear thy memory with me to the grave."

The Shepherd ended here; and Luke stoop'd down,
And as his Father had requested, laid
430 The first stone of the Sheep-fold; at the sight
The Old Man's grief broke from him, to his heart
He press'd his Son, he kissed him and wept;
And to the House together they return'd.

Next morning, as had been resolv'd, the Boy
435 Began his journey, and when he had reach'd
The public Way, he put on a bold face;
And all the Neighbours, as he pass'd their doors
Came forth with wishes and with farewell pray'rs,
That follow'd him 'till he was out of sight.

440 A good report did from their Kinsman come,
Of Luke and his well-doing; and the Boy
Wrote loving letters, full of wond'rous news,
Which, as the House-wife phrased it, were throughout
The prettiest letters that were ever seen.
445 Both parents read them with rejoicing hearts.
So, many months pass'd on: and once again
The Shepherd went about his daily work
With confident and chearful thoughts; and now
Sometimes when he could find a leisure hour
450 He to that valley took his way, and there
Wrought at the Sheep-fold. Meantime Luke began
To slacken in his duty; and, at length
He in the dissolute city gave himself
To evil courses: ignominy and shame
455 Fell on him, so that he was driven at last
To seek a hiding-place beyond the seas.

There is a comfort in the strength of love;
'Twill make a thing endurable, which else
Would break the heart:—Old Michael found it so.
460 I have convers'd with more than one who well
Remember the Old Man, and what he was
Years after he had heard this heavy news.
His bodily frame had been from youth to age
Of an unusual strength. Among the rocks
465 He went, and still look'd up upon the sun,
And listen'd to the wind; and as before
Perform'd all kinds of labour for his Sheep,
And for the land, his small inheritance.
And to that hollow Dell from time to time
470 Did he repair, to build the Fold of which

His flock had need. 'Tis not forgotten yet
The pity which was then in every heart
For the Old Man—and 'tis believed by all
That many and many a day he thither went,
475   And never lifted up a single stone.

There, by the Sheep-fold, sometimes was he seen
Sitting alone, with that his faithful Dog,
Then old, beside him, lying at his feet.
The length of full seven years from time to time
480   He at the building of this Sheep-fold wrought,
And left the work unfinished when he died.

Three years, or little more, did Isabel,
Survive her Husband: at her death the estate
Was sold, and went into a Stranger's hand.
485   The Cottage which was nam'd The Evening Star
Is gone, the ploughshare has been through the ground
On which it stood;[7] great changes have been wrought
In all the neighbourhood, yet the Oak is left
That grew beside their Door; and the remains
490   Of the unfinished Sheep-fold may be seen
Beside the boisterous brook of Green-head Gill.

1800   1800

COMPANION READINGS

Francis Jeffrey: from *A Review of Robert Southey's* Thalaba[1]

Poetry has this much, at least, in common with religion, that its standards were fixed long ago, by certain inspired writers, whose authority it is no longer lawful to call in question; and that many profess to be entirely devoted to it, who have no *good works* to produce in support of their pretensions. * * * The author who is now before us, belongs to a *sect* of poets, that has established itself in this country within these ten or twelve years, and is looked upon, we believe, as one of its chief champions and apostles. The peculiar doctrines of this sect, it would not, perhaps, be very easy to explain; but, that they are *dissenters* from the established systems in poetry and criticism, is admitted, and proved indeed, by the whole tenor of their compositions. Though they lay claim, we believe, to a creed and a revelation of their own, there can be little doubt, that their doctrines are of *German* origin, and have been derived from some of the great modern reformers in that country. Some of their leading principles, indeed, are probably of an earlier date, and seem to have been borrowed from the great apostle of Geneva.[2] * * *

The disciples of this school boast much of its originality, and seem to value themselves very highly, for having broken loose from the bondage of ancient authority,

---

7. The grazing fields have been enclosed for agriculture; also evoking the strife between the herdsman Abel and his farming brother Cain.
1. Francis Jeffrey (1773–1850) was editor and chief literary critic for *The Edinburgh Review*, one of the most influential liberal journals of the age. Jeffrey's literary tastes were more neoclassical than modern, and his attacks on Wordsworth's principles persisted for decades.

Wordsworth's fellow "Lake Poet" Robert Southey was committed to political reform in his youth. His *Thalaba, the Destroyer* (1801) is a verse romance set in the East, involving magic, vengeance, and vampires.
2. Referring chiefly to Goethe and to German poets of sensational verse narrative. The apostle of Geneva is Rousseau.

and re-asserted the independence of genius. Originality, however, we are persuaded, is rarer than mere alteration; and a man may change a good master for a bad one, without finding himself at all nearer to independence. * * * The productions of this school, we conceive, are so far from being entitled to the praise of originality, that they cannot be better characterised, than by an enumeration of the sources from which their materials have been derived. The greater part of them, we apprehend, will be found to be composed of the following elements: 1. The antisocial principles, and distempered sensibility of Rousseau—his discontent with the present constitution of society—his paradoxical morality, and his perpetual hankerings after some unattainable state of voluptuous virtue and perfection. 2. The simplicity and energy (*horresco referens* [I dread to say it]) of Kotzebue and Schiller. 3. The homeliness and harshness of some of Cowper's language and versification, interchanged occasionally with the *innocence* of Ambrose Philips, or the quaintness of Quarles and Dr Donne.[3] * * *

The authors, of whom we are now speaking [Southey, Wordsworth, and Coleridge], have, among them, unquestionably, a very considerable portion of poetical talent, and have, consequently, been enabled to seduce many into an admiration of the false taste (as it appears to us) in which most of their productions are composed. They constitute, at present, the most formidable conspiracy that has lately been formed against sound judgment in matters poetical; and are entitled to a larger share of our censorial notice, than could be spared for an individual delinquent. * * *

Their most distinguishing symbol, is undoubtedly an affection of great simplicity and familiarity of language. They disdain to make use of the common poetical phraseology, or to ennoble their diction by a selection of fine or dignified expressions. There would be too much *art* in this, for that great love of nature with which they are all of them inspired; and their sentiments, they are determined shall be indebted, for their effect, to nothing but their intrinsic tenderness or elevation. There is something very noble and conscientious, we will confess, in this plan of composition; but the misfortune is, that there are passages in all poems, that can neither be pathetic nor sublime; and that, on these occasions, a neglect of the embellishments of language is very apt to produce absolute meanness and insipidity. * * * It is in such passages, accordingly, that we are most frequently offended with low and inelegant expressions; and that the language, which was intended to be simple and natural, is found oftenest to degenerate into mere slovenliness and vulgarity. * * *

One of their own authors, indeed, has very ingeniously set forth, (in a kind of manifesto that preceded one of their most flagrant acts of hostility), that it was their capital object "to adapt to the uses of poetry, the ordinary language of conversation among the middling and lower orders of the people." What advantages are to be gained by the success of this project, we confess ourselves unable to conjecture. The language of the higher and more cultivated orders may fairly be presumed to be better than that of their inferiors: at any rate, it has all those associations in its favour, by means of which, a style can ever appear beautiful or exalted, and is adapted to the purposes of poetry, by having been long consecrated to its use. The language of the vulgar, on the other hand, has all the opposite associations to contend with; and must seem unfit for poetry, (if there were no other reason), merely because it has scarcely ever been employed in it. A great genius may indeed overcome these disad-

---

3. August von Kotzebue was famed for his sentimental plays. Ambrose Phillips (1675–1749) was admired and ridiculed for his sweet verses; Francie Quarles was best known for *Emblems* (1635), a book of devotional poems with quaint illustrations. John Donne (1572–1631) wrote boldly experimental poetry known for its passion, its rough meters, and extravagant wit.

vantages; but we can scarcely conceive that he should court them. We may excuse a certain homeliness of language in the productions of a ploughman or a milkwoman;[4] but we cannot bring ourselves to admire it in an author, who has had occasion to indite odes to his college bell, and inscribe hymns to the Penates.[5]

But the mischief of this new system is not confined to the depravation of language only; it extends to the sentiments and emotions, and leads to the debasement of all those feelings which poetry is designed to communicate. It is absurd to suppose, that an author should make use of the language of the vulgar, to express the sentiments of the refined. His professed object, in employing that language, is to bring his compositions nearer to the true standard of nature; and his intention to copy the sentiments of the lower orders, is implied in his resolution to make use of their style. Now, the different classes of society have each of them a distinct character, as well as a separate idiom; and the names of the various passions to which they are subject respectively, have a signification that varies essentially, according to the condition of the persons to whom they are applied. The love, or grief, or indignation of an enlightened and refined character, is not only expressed in a different language, but is in itself a different emotion from the love, or grief, or anger, of a clown,[6] a tradesman, or a market-wench. The things themselves are radically and obviously distinct; and the representation of them is calculated to convey a very different train of sympathies and sensations to the mind. The question, therefore, comes simply to be—which of them is the most proper object for poetical imitation? It is needless for us to answer a question, which the practice of all the world has long ago decided irrevocably. The poor and vulgar may interest us, in poetry, by their *situation*; but never, we apprehend, by any sentiments that are peculiar to their condition, and still less by any language that is characteristic of it. The truth is, that is impossible to copy their diction or their sentiments correctly, in a serious composition; and this, not merely because poverty makes men ridiculous, but because just taste and refined sentiment are rarely to be met with among the uncultivated part of mankind; and a language, fitted for their expression, can still more rarely form any part of their "ordinary conversation."

* * * It has been argued, indeed, (for men will argue in support of what they do not venture to practice), that as the middling and lower orders of society constitute by far the greater part of mankind, so, their feelings and expressions should interest more extensively, and may be taken, more fairly than any other, for the standards of what is natural and true. To this, it seems obvious to answer, that the arts that aim at exciting admiration and delight, do not take their models from what is ordinary, but from what is excellent; and that our interest in the representation of any event, does not depend upon our familiarity with the original, but on its intrinsic importance, and the celebrity of the parties it concerns. The sculptor employs his art in delineating the graces of Antinous or Apollo, and not in the representation of those ordinary forms that belong to the crowd of his admirers. When a chieftain perishes in battle, his followers mourn more for him, than for thousands of their equals that may have fallen around him. * * *

The qualities of style and imagery, however, form but a small part of the characteristics by which a literary faction is to be distinguished. The subject and object of their compositions, and the principles and opinions they are calculated to support, constitute a far more important criterion, and one to which it is usually altogether

---

4. Alluding to the popularity of Robert Burns, Scots farmer poet (see page 1515) and Anne Yearsley, "the poetical milkwoman."
5. A sarcastic reference to Southey's mock ode *The*

Chapel-Bell (1793) and his long *Hymn to the Penates* (1796); penates were Roman household deities.
6. A peasant.

easy to refer. Some poets are sufficiently described as the flatterers of greatness and power, and others as the champions of independence. One set of writers is known by its antipathy to decency and religion; another, by its methodistical cant and intolerance. Our new school of poetry has a moral character also; though it may not be possible, perhaps, to delineate it quite so concisely.

A splenetic and idle discontent with the existing institutions of society, seems to be at the bottom of all their serious and peculiar sentiments. Instead of contemplating the wonders and the pleasures which civilization has created for mankind, they are perpetually brooding over the disorders by which its progress has been attended. They are filled with horror and compassion at the sight of poor men spending their blood in the quarrels of princes, and brutifying their sublime capabilities in the drudgery of unremitting labour. For all sorts of vice and profligacy in the lower orders of society, they have the same virtuous horror, and the same tender compassion. While the existence of these offences overpowers them with grief and confusion, they never permit themselves to feel the smallest indignation or dislike towards the offenders. The present vicious constitution of society alone is responsible for all these enormities: the poor sinners are but the helpless victims or instruments of its disorders, and could not possibly have avoided the errors into which they have been betrayed. Though they can bear with crimes, therefore, they cannot reconcile themselves to punishments; and have an unconquerable antipathy to prisons, gibbets, and houses of correction, as engines of oppression, and instruments of atrocious injustice. While the plea of moral necessity is thus artfully brought forward to convert all the excesses of the poor into innocent misfortunes, no sort of indulgence is shown to the offences of the powerful and rich. Their oppressions, and seductions, and debaucheries, are the theme of many an angry verse; and the indignation and abhorrence of the reader is relentlessly conjured up against those perturbators of society, and scourges of mankind.

It is not easy to say, whether the fundamental absurdity of this doctrine, or the partiality of its application, be entitled to the severest reprehension.

1802

Charles Lamb: from *Letter to William Wordsworth*[1]

[Jan. 30, 1801]

Thanks for your Letter and Present. I had already borrowed your second volume.[2] What most please me are, the Song of Lucy. * * * *Simon's sickly daughter* in the Sexton made me *cry*.[3] * * * I will mention one more: the delicate and curious feeling in the wish for the Cumberland Beggar, that he may have about him the melody of Birds, altho' he hear them not. Here the mind knowingly passes a fiction upon herself, first substituting her own feelings for the Beggar's, and, in the same breath detecting the fallacy, will not part with the wish.— * * * I will just add that it appears to me a fault in the Beggar, that the instructions conveyed in it are too direct and like a lecture:[4] they don't slide into the mind of the reader, while he is imagining no such matter. An intelligent reader

1. For Lamb, see page 1398. At the time of these letters, Lamb was an old friend of Coleridge and a newer acquaintance of the Wordsworths; he had published a novel and some verses, but his major career as an essayist was still to come.
2. Wordsworth had sent the two-volume *Lyrical Ballads* (1800) to Lamb, who knew the poems in the first volume from the 1798 edition. The poems he discusses are newly published in volume 2.
3. Referring to *Song* (*She dwelt among th'untrodden ways*) and *To a Sexton*, where the charnel house worker is chastised for disturbing the bones of the dead, including Simon's daughter.
4. The poem includes a polemic by Wordsworth against forcing beggars into miserable workhouses (lines 177–178).

finds a sort of insult in being told, I will teach you how to think upon this subject. * * * There is implied an unwritten compact between Author and reader; I will tell you a story, and I suppose you will understand it. * * * —I am sorry that Coleridge has christened his Ancient Marinere "a poet's Reverie"—it is as bad as Bottom the Weaver's declaration that he is not a Lion but only the scenical representation of a Lion.[5] What new idea is gained by this Title, but one subversive of all credit, which the tale should force upon us, of its truth? For me, I was never so affected with any human Tale. After first reading it, I was totally possessed with it for many days.—I dislike all the miraculous part of it, but the feelings of the man under the operation of such scenery dragged me along like Tom Piper's magic whistle. I totally differ from your idea that the Marinere should have had a character and profession. This is a Beauty in Gulliver's Travels, where the mind is kept in a placid state of little wonderments; but the Ancient Marinere undergoes such Trials, as overwhelm and bury all individuality or memory of what he was, like the state of a man in a Bad dream, one terrible peculiarity of which is: that all consciousness of personality is gone. Your other observation is I think as well a little unfounded: the Marinere from being conversant in supernatural events *has* acquired a supernatural and strange cast of *phrase*, eye, appearance, &c. which frighten the wedding guest. You will excuse my remarks, because I am hurt and vexed that you should think it necessary, with a prose apology,[6] to open the eyes of dead men that cannot see. To sum up a general opinion of the second vol.—I do not feel any one poem in it so forcibly as the Ancient Marinere, the Mad Mother, and the Lines at Tintern Abbey in the first.—I could, too, have wished the Critical preface had appeared in a separate treatise. All its dogmas are true and just, and most of them new, *as* criticism. But they associate a *diminishing* idea with the Poems which follow, as having been written for *Experiment* on the public taste, more than having sprung (as they must have done) from living and daily circumstances.—I am prolix, because I am gratifyed in the opportunity of writing to you, and I don't well know when to leave off. I ought before this to have reply'd to your very kind invitation into Cumberland.[7] With you and your Sister I could gang any where. But I am afraid whether I shall ever be able to afford so desperate a Journey. Separate from the pleasure of your company, I don't much care if I never see a mountain in my life. I have passed all my days in London, until I have formed as many and intense local attachments, as any of you mountaineers can have done with dead nature. The Lighted shops of the Strand and Fleet Street, the innumerable trades, tradesmen and customers, coaches, waggons, playhouses, all the bustle and wickedness round about Covent Garden, the very women of the Town, the Watchmen, drunken scenes, rattles,—life awake, if you awake, at all hours of the night, the impossibility of being dull in Fleet Street, the crowds, the very dirt & mud, the Sun shining upon houses and pavements, the print shops, the old book stalls, parsons cheap'ning books, coffee houses, steams of soups from kitchens, the pantomimes, London itself a pantomime and a masquerade,—all these things work themselves into my mind and feed me, without a power of satiating me. The wonder of these sights impells me into night-walks about her crowded streets, and I often shed tears in the motley Strand from fulness of joy at so much Life.—All these emotions must be strange to you. So are your rural emotions to me. But consider, what must I have been doing all my life, not to have lent great portions of my heart with usury to such scenes?———

---

5. In 1800, the poem was subtitled "A Poet's Reverie." In Shakespeare's *Midsummer Night's Dream* (5.1), Snug the Joiner says this, on Bottom's fervent recommendation, fearing that the ladies in the audience will take him for a real lion (5.1.220 ff; cf. Bottom, 3.1.35–45).
6. The Preface of 1800.
7. In the Lake District.

Charles Lamb: from Letter to Thomas Manning[1]

[Feb. 15, 1801]

I had need be cautious henceforward what opinion I give of the "Lyrical Ballads." All the North of England are in a turmoil. Cumberland and Westmoreland have already declared a state of war.[2] I lately received from Wordsworth a copy of the second volume, accompanied by an acknowledgement of having received from me many months since a copy of a certain Tragedy,[3] with excuses for not having made any acknowledgement sooner, it being owing to an "almost insurmountable aversion from Letter-writing." This letter I answered in due form and time, and enumerated several of the passages which had most affected me, adding, unfortunately, that no single piece had moved me so forcibly as the "Ancient Mariner," "The Mad Mother," or the "Lines at Tintern Abbey." The Post did not sleep a moment. I received almost instantaneously a long letter of four sweating pages from my Reluctant Letter-Writer, the purport of which was, that he was sorry his 2d vol. had not given me more pleasure (Devil a hint did I give that it had *not pleased me*), and "was compelled to wish that my range of sensibility was more extended, being obliged to believe that I should receive large influxes of happiness and happy Thoughts" (I suppose from the L. B.)—With a deal of stuff about a certain Union of Tenderness and Imagination, which in the sense he used Imagination was not the characteristic of Shakspeare, but which Milton possessed in a degree far exceeding other Poets: which Union, as the highest species of Poetry, and chiefly deserving that name, "He was most proud to aspire to;" then illustrating the said Union by two quotations from his own 2d vol. (which I had been so unfortunate as to miss) [quotes *Michael* 349–53]. These lines [52–53] were thus undermarked, and then followed "This Passage, as combining in an extraordinary degree that Union of Imagination and Tenderness which I am speaking of, I consider as one of the Best I ever wrote!" * * * good Poetry: but after one has been reading Shakspeare twenty of the best years of one's life, to have a fellow start up, and prate about some unknown quality, which Shakspeare possessed in a degree inferior to Milton and *somebody else!!* This was not to be *all* my castigation. Coleridge, who had not written to me some months before, starts up from his bed of sickness to reprove me for my hardy presumption: four long pages, equally sweaty and more tedious, came from him; assuring me that, when the works of a man of true genius such as W. undoubtedly was, do not please me at first sight, I should suspect the fault to lie "in me and not in them," etc. etc. etc. etc. etc. What am I to do with such people? I certainly shall write them a very merry Letter. Writing to *you,* I may say that the 2d vol. has no such pieces. * * * It is full of original thinking and an observing mind, but it does not often make you laugh or cry.—It too artfully aims at simplicity of expression. And you sometimes doubt if Simplicity be not a cover for Poverty. The best Piece in it I will send you, being *short.* I have grievously offended my friends in the North by declaring my undue preference; but I need not fear you:— [quotes *Song (She dwelt among th'untrodden ways)*]. This is choice and genuine, and so are many, many more. But one does not like to have 'em rammed down one's throat. "Pray, take it—it's very good—let me help you—eat faster."

---

1. One of Lamb's closest friends, Manning (1772–1840), mathematician and traveler, was considered the first scholar of Chinese literature in Europe; he was the first and, for many years, only Englishman to enter the holy city of Lhasa, Tibet.
2. Coleridge was living in Cumberland county, the Wordsworths in Westmoreland.
3. By Lamb.

SONNETS, 1802–1807[1]
Prefatory Sonnet

Nuns fret not at their Convent's narrow room;[2]
And Hermits are contented with their Cells;
And Students with their pensive Citadels;
Maids at the Wheel, the Weaver at his Loom,
5 Sit blithe and happy; Bees that soar for bloom,
High as the highest Peak of Furness-fells,°   *mountains*
Will murmur by the hour in Foxglove bells:
In truth, the prison, into which we doom
Ourselves, no prison is: and hence for me,
10 In sundry moods, 'twas pastime to be bound
Within the Sonnet's scanty plot of ground:
Pleas'd if some Souls (for such there needs must be)
Who have felt the weight of too much liberty,
Should find brief solace there, as I have found.

The world is too much with us

The world is too much with us; late and soon,
Getting and spending, we lay waste our powers:
Little we see in nature that is ours;
We have given our hearts away, a sordid boon!
5 The Sea that bares her bosom to the moon;
The Winds that will be howling at all hours
And are up-gathered now like sleeping flowers;
For this, for everything, we are out of tune;
It moves us not. Great God! I'd rather be
10 A Pagan° suckled in a creed outworn;   *pre-Christian*
So might I, standing on this pleasant lea,
Have glimpses that would make me less forlorn;
Have sight of Proteus rising from the sea;
Or hear old Triton blow his wreathed horn.[1]

Composed upon Westminster Bridge, Sept. 3, 1802[1]

Earth has not anything to shew more fair:
Dull would he be of soul who could pass by

---

1. William Bowles and Charlotte Smith had revived sonnet writing at the end of the 18th century. Wordsworth's first publication was his sonnet *On seeing Miss Helen Maria Williams Weep at a Tale of Distress* (1787) and he was impressed by this revival as well as by Milton's political sonnets. He composed may of the sonnets in this section in 1802, when he briefly visited France during the Peace of Amiens to settle affairs with Annette Vallon, prior to his marriage. Other sonnets from this period are included in Perspectives: The Abolition of Slavery and the Slave Trade, page 1465.
2. In 1802 Wordsworth praised Milton's sonnets for their "energetic and varied flow of sound crowding into narrow room more of the combined effect of rhyme and blank verse than can be done by any other kind of verse that I know of." He particulary liked Milton's stanzaic and linear enjambments (see his own wit about this device in

line 10 where *bound* is thus unbound). For another sonnet on sonnet writing, see Keats's *Incipet altera sonneta*, page 1764.
1. Proteus is the shape-changing herdsman of the sea; Triton, usually depicted blowing a conch shell, is a sea deity. Cf. the personified "Sea" in line 5.
1. Composed on the roof of a coach, on my way to France [Wordsworth's note, 1843]. For a description of the circumstances, see Dorothy Wordsworth's *Grasmere Journals*, July 1802, page 1628. Wordsworth misremembered the date as September (the time of his return, not his departure), and gave the year as 1803 (corrected to 1802 in the edition of 1838). His evasiveness about the date may have had to do with his anxiety about his reunion with—and final departure from—Annette Vallon and their daughter Caroline.

A sight so touching in its majesty:
This City now doth like a garment wear
5   The beauty of the morning; silent, bare,
Ships, towers, domes, theatres, and temples lie
Open unto the fields, and to the sky;
All bright and glittering in the smokeless air.
Never did sun more beautifully steep
10   In his first splendour, valley, rock, or hill;
Ne'er saw I, never felt, a calm so deep!
The river glideth at his own sweet will:
Dear God! the very houses seem asleep;
And all that mighty heart is lying still!

It is a beauteous Evening[1]

It is a beauteous Evening, calm and free;
The holy time is quiet as a Nun
Breathless with adoration; the broad sun
Is sinking down in its tranquillity;
5   The gentleness of heaven is on the Sea:[2]
Listen! the mighty Being is awake
And doth with his eternal motion make
A sound like thunder—everlastingly.
Dear Child! dear Girl! that walkest with me here,[3]
10   If thou appear'st untouch'd by solemn thought,
Thy nature is not therefore less divine:
Thou liest in Abraham's bosom[4] all the year;
And worshipp'st at the Temple's inner shrine,
God being with thee when we know it not.

<hr>

COMPANION READINGS

Charlotte Smith: from *Elegiac Sonnets*[1]

To Melancholy. Written on the Banks of the Arun, October, 1785

When latest Autumn spreads her evening veil
    And the grey mists from these dim waves arise,
    I love to listen to the hollow sighs,
Thro' the half leafless wood that breathes the gale.
5   For at such hours the shadowy phantom pale,
    Oft seems to fleet before the poet's eyes;

1. This was composed on the beach near Calais, in the autumn of 1802 [Wordsworth's note, 1843].
2. In 1836 Wordsworth changed "is on" to "broods o'er."
3. Wordsworth's daughter Caroline.
4. Christ's description of the resting place for heaven-bound souls (Luke 16.22).
1. Charlotte Smith was born in 1749; a disastrous marriage when she was sixteen culminated in her spendthrift husband's imprisonment for debt in 1783. Pregnant with her twelfth child, Smith was left to support herself and her family by her pen. The successful first edition of *Ele-*

giac Sonnets (1784) led to eight more, ever-expanding editions by 1800. Though the ten novels she produced in those years were far more lucrative, poetry was the more exalted genre, and she was admired for the sonnets, her substantial blank-verse poem *The Emigrants* (1793), and her final work, *Beachy-Head,* published in 1807, the year of her death. Coleridge acknowledged Bowles and Smith as "they who first made the Sonnet popular in English," and Wordsworth was reading her sonnets in 1802 as he worked on his own sonnet sequence.

Strange sounds are heard, and mournful melodies,
  As of night wanderers, who their woes bewail!
Here, by his native stream, at such an hour,
10   Pity's own Otway,[2] I methinks could meet,
    And hear his deep sighs swell the sadden'd wind!
Oh Melancholy!—such thy magic power,
   That to the soul these dreams are often sweet,
    And soothe the pensive visionary mind!

                   1789

Far on the Sands

Far on the sands, the low, retiring tide,
  In distant murmurs hardly seems to flow,
And o'er the world of waters, blue and wide,
  The sighing summer-wind, forgets to blow.
5 As sinks the day star in the rosy West,
   The silent wave, with rich reflection glows;
Alas! can tranquil nature give *me* rest,
   Or scenes of beauty, soothe me to repose?
Can the soft lustre of the sleeping main,
10   Yon radiant heaven, or all creation's charms,
"Erase the written troubles of the brain,"[1]
   Which Memory tortures, and which Guilt alarms?
Or bid a bosom transient quiet prove,
That bleeds with vain remorse, and unextinguish'd love!

                   1800

To Tranquillity

In this tumultuous sphere, for thee unfit,
  How seldom art thou found—Tranquillity!
  Unless 'tis when with mild and downcast eye
By the low cradles, thou delight'st to sit,
5 Of sleeping infants—watching the soft breath,
  And bidding the sweet slumberers easy lie;
Or sometimes hanging o'er the bed of death,
  Where the poor languid sufferer—hopes to die.
Oh! beauteous sister of the halcyon peace![1]
10 I sure shall find thee in that heavenly scene
   Where care and anguish shall their power resign;
Where hope alike, and vain regret shall cease;
  And Memory—lost in happiness serene,
Repeat no more—that misery has been mine!

                   1789

2. Thomas Otway (1652–1685), author of the dramas *The Orphan* and *Venice Preserved,* was known for the pathos of his work.
1. Macbeth asks his wife's doctor, "Canst thou not minister to a mind diseased, / Pluck from the memory of a rooted sorrow, / Raze out the written troubles of the brain?" He replies, "Therein the patient / Must minister to himself"
(5.3.39–46).
1. When her husband perished in a shipwreck, Halcyone threw herself into the sea; in pity the gods changed the pair into kingfishers and calmed the sea for a brief interval each year so they could mate. A halcyon peace is a blessed interval of calm amid adversity.

Written in the Church Yard at Middleton in Sussex

Press'd by the Moon, mute arbitress of tides,
    While the loud equinox its power combines,
    The sea no more its swelling surge confines,
But o'er the shrinking land sublimely rides.
5 The wild blast, rising from the Western cave,
    Drives the huge billows from their heaving bed;
    Tears from their grassy tombs the village dead,
And breaks the silent sabbath of the grave![1]
With shells and sea-weed mingled, on the shore
10   Lo! their bones whiten in the frequent wave;
    But vain to them the winds and waters rave;
They hear the warring elements no more:
While I am doom'd—by life's long storm opprest,
To gaze with envy, on their gloomy rest.

                                  1789

On being cautioned against walking on an headland overlooking the sea, because it was frequented by a lunatic

Is there a solitary wretch who hies
    To the tall cliff, with starting pace or slow,
And, measuring, views with wild and hollow eyes
    Its distance from the waves that chide below;
5 Who, as the sea-born gale with frequent sighs
    Chills his cold bed upon the mountain turf,
    With hoarse, half-utter'd lamentation, lies
    Murmuring responses to the dashing surf?
In moody sadness, on the giddy brink,
10 I see him more with envy than with fear;
He has no *nice felicities* that shrink[1]
    From giant horrors; wildly wandering here,
He seems (uncursed with reason) not to know
The depth or the duration of his woe.

                                  1800

THE PRELUDE

Now regarded as Wordsworth's major work, *The Prelude* was unknown in his lifetime except to a small circle of family and friends. Though the poem was largely complete by 1805, Wordsworth continued to rework and polish the poem for the remaining forty-five years of his life, in an ongoing and intense self-inquiry into his childhood and youth. Published posthu-

---

1. Middleton is a village on the margin of the sea. . . . There were formerly several acres of ground between its small church and the sea, which now, by its continual encroachments, approaches within a few feet of this half-ruined and humble edifice. The wall, which once surrounded the church-yard, is entirely swept away, many of the graves broken up, and the remains of bodies interred washed into the sea; whence human bones are found among the sand and shingles on the shore [Smith's note, 1800].

1. "'Tis delicate felicity that shrinks / When rocking winds are loud." Walpole [Smith's note, 1800]; compare Milton's *Il Penseroso:* "while rocking winds are piping loud" (line 126); Smith's reference to Walpole is uncertain.

mously in 1850, *The Prelude* incorporates passages first written in the late 1790s. In a poignant passage of Book 4 (1805), Wordsworth compared his enterprise, "Incumbent o'er the surface of past time," to that of a man "who hangs down-bending from the side / Of a slow-moving Boat," incapable of distinguishing what resides below from what is reflected from above, and repeatedly "cross'd by gleam / Of his own image" (4.247–264). On first reading, *The Prelude* appears a paean to the recovery of the past; on closer acquaintance it is a great and self-conscious testimony to the construction of the past out of the urgent needs of the present. To compose the poem was also to compose the poet, to create Wordsworth as The Poet, a meditative and resolute figure who had struggled through years of family disruption and revolutionary turmoil to a position of authority.

    The Prelude evolved in three principal versions. Isolated in Germany in the coldest winter of the century in 1798–1799, Wordsworth wrote several passages drawing on his childhood experiences in nature, sketches for *The Recluse,* a philosophic poem that Coleridge had urged him to write. By the time he and his sister Dorothy had settled in Grasmere, he had completed the text now known as *The Two-Part Prelude* of 1799, almost a thousand lines of blank verse narrating his life from schooldays through the age of seventeen.

    In 1801 Wordsworth began to revise his poem, though it was not until 1804 that he set to work in earnest. An initial plan to write it in five books quickly gave way to a greater expansion into thirteen books, allowing Wordsworth to include an account of his experiences in France and the crisis that followed the failure of his hopes for the French Revolution. The full version finished in 1805 combines earlier and later material, not always in chronological order, suggesting that the sequence of Wordsworth's life is less important than the imperatives shaping its argument. Further revised over the years, the poem was finally published by Wordsworth's widow in 1850. This was the only known text until 1926, when Ernest de Selincourt published that of 1805, the version printed here.

    Part confession, a crisis-autobiography descended from Saint Augustine's exemplary *Confessions, The Prelude* is also a consciously English document. Exceptionally personal, it is also a representative story of one seduced by youthful radicalism from his native heritage and returning from his errors to become a national poet. To that degree, *The Prelude* stands as a rejoinder to Rousseau's notorious *Confessions,* but its chief parallel is Milton's *Paradise Lost,* with which it regularly challenges comparison. *The Prelude* turns epic inward even as it claims the growth of the poet's mind as an exalted subject. But *The Prelude* is not everywhere epic and prophetic: it is also an epistle to Coleridge, intimate and domestic, a record of friendship. The result is a shifting interplay between high genre and familiar, between the adult poet looking back and trying to explain and the child from whose sense of the mysterious the poem derives its originating power. "So wide appears / The vacancy between me and those days," Wordsworth wrote of his childhood, "Which yet have such self-presence in my mind / That, sometimes, when I think of them, I seem / Two consciousnesses, conscious of myself / And of some other Being" (2.28–33). As he tries to close the gap in the act of writing, the ungraspable, elusive vacancies generate a structure that circles back in its large patterns, animated throughout by countermovements that uncannily create the effect of authenticity:

> As oftentimes a River, it might seem,
> Yielding in part to old remembrances,
> Part sway'd by fear to tread an onward road
> That leads direct to the devouring sea,
> Turns and will measure back his course, far back
> Towards the very regions which he cross'd
> In his first outset; so have we long time
> Made motions retrograde, in like pursuit
> Detain'd.   (9.1–9)

FROM THE PRELUDE, OR GROWTH OF A POET'S MIND
Book First. Introduction, Childhood, and School time

Oh there is blessing in this gentle breeze[1]
That blows from the green fields and from the clouds
And from the sky: it beats against my cheek
And seems half conscious of the joy it gives.
5 O welcome Messenger! O welcome Friend!
A Captive greets thee, coming from a house
Of bondage,[2] from yon City's walls set free,
A prison where he hath been long immured.
Now I am free, enfranchis'd and at large,
10 May fix my habitation where I will.
What dwelling shall receive me? In what Vale
Shall be my harbour? Underneath what grove
Shall I take up my home, and what sweet stream
Shall with its murmurs lull me to my rest?
15 The earth is all before me:[3] with a heart
Joyous, nor scar'd at its own liberty
I look about, and should the guide I chuse
Be nothing better than a wandering cloud
I cannot miss my way. I breathe again;
20 Trances of thought and mountings of the mind
Come fast upon me: it is shaken off,
As by miraculous gift 'tis shaken off,
That burthen of my own unnatural self,
The heavy weight of many a weary day
25 Not mine, and such as were not made for me.
Long months of peace (if such bold word accord
With any promises of human life)
Long months of ease and undisturb'd delight
Are mine in prospect: whither shall I turn
30 By road or pathway or through open field,
Or shall a twig or any floating thing
Upon the river, point me out my course?
    Enough that I am free; for months to come
May dedicate myself to chosen tasks;
35 May quit the tiresome sea, and dwell on shore,
If not a settler on the soil, at least
To drink wild water, and to pluck green herbs,
And gather fruits fresh from their native bough.
Nay more, if I may trust myself, this hour
40 Hath brought a gift that consecrates my joy;
For I, methought, while the sweet breath of Heaven
Was blowing on my body, felt within
A corresponding mild creative breeze,

---

1. Lines 1–54, which Wordsworth later called his "glad preamble" (7.4), were composed in late 1799 or 1800. Nature itself is his inspiring Muse or spirit ("spiritus" in Latin means both "spirit" and "breeze").
2. Cf. Exodus 13.14: "the Lord brought us out from Egypt, from the house of bondage."
3. Compare the ending of *Paradise Lost*, when Adam and Eve leave Eden: "the world was all before them" (12.646ff, page 903).

A vital breeze which travell'd gently on
45 O'er things which it had made, and is become
A tempest, a redundant° energy   *abounding*
Vexing its own creation. 'Tis a power
That does not come unrecognis'd, a storm,
Which, breaking up a long continued frost
50 Brings with it vernal° promises, the hope   *springtime*
Of active days, of dignity and thought,
Of prowess in an honorable field,
Pure passions, virtue, knowledge, and delight,
The holy life of music and of verse.
55   Thus far, O Friend! did I, not used to make
A present joy the matter of my Song,[4]
Pour out, that day, my soul in measur'd strains,
Even in the very words which I have here
Recorded: to the open fields I told
60 A prophecy: poetic numbers° came   *verses*
Spontaneously, and cloth'd in priestly robe
My spirit, thus singled out, as it might seem,
For holy services: great hopes were mine;
My own voice chear'd me, and, far more, the mind's
65 Internal echo of the imperfect sound:
To both I listen'd, drawing from them both
A chearful confidence in things to come.
        Whereat, being not unwilling now to give
A respite to this passion, I paced on
70 Gently, with careless steps, and came erelong
To a green shady place where down I sate
Beneath a tree, slackening my thoughts by choice
And settling into gentler happiness.
'Twas Autumn, and a calm and placid day,
75 With warmth as much as needed from a sun
Two hours declin'd towards the west, a day
With silver clouds, and sunshine on the grass
And, in the shelter'd grove where I was couch'd,
A perfect stillness. On the ground I lay
80 Passing through many thoughts, yet mainly such
As to myself pertain'd. I made a choice
Of one sweet Vale° whither my steps should turn   *Grasmere*
And saw, methought, the very house and fields
Present before my eyes: nor did I fail
85 To add, meanwhile, assurance of some work
Of glory, there forthwith to be begun,[5]
Perhaps, too, there perform'd. Thus, long I lay
Chear'd by the genial pillow of the earth
Beneath my head, sooth'd by a sense of touch
90 From the warm ground, that balanced me, though lost
Entirely, seeing nought, nought hearing, save

4. The poem is addressed to Coleridge; in the Preface to *Lyrical Ballads*, Wordsworth describes poetic creation as "emotion recollected in tranquillity." 5. *The Recluse* (never finished).

When here and there, about the grove of Oaks
Where was my bed, an acorn from the trees
Fell audibly, and with a startling sound.

95   Thus occupied in mind, I linger'd here
Contented, nor rose up until the sun
Had almost touch'd the horizon; bidding then
A farewell to the City° left behind,   *Goslar, Germany*
Even on the strong temptation of that hour

100   And with its chance equipment, I resolved
To journey towards the Vale which I had chosen.
It was a splendid evening: and my soul
Did once again make trial of her strength
Restored to her afresh; nor did she want

105   Eolian visitations; but the harp[6]
Was soon defrauded, and the banded host
Of harmony dispers'd in straggling sounds
And, lastly, utter silence. "Be it so,
It is an injury," said I, "to this day

110   To think of any thing but present joy."
So like a Peasant I pursued my road
Beneath the evening sun; nor had one wish
Again to bend the sabbath of that time
To a servile yoke. What need of many words?

115   A pleasant loitering journey, through two days
Continued, brought me to my hermitage.°   *secluded dwelling*
     I spare to speak, my Friend, of what ensued,
The admiration and the love, the life
In common things; the endless store of things

120   Rare, or at least so seeming, every day
Found all about me in one neighbourhood,
The self-congratulation,° the complete   *rejoicing*
Composure, and the happiness entire.
But speedily a longing in me rose

125   To brace myself to some determin'd aim,
Reading or thinking, either to lay up
New stores, or rescue from decay the old
By timely interference, I had hopes
Still higher, that with a frame of outward life,

130   I might endue,° might fix in a visible home   *endow*
Some portion of those phantoms of conceit°   *mental images*
That had been floating loose about so long,
And to such Beings temperately deal forth
The many feelings that oppress'd my heart.

135   But I have been discouraged: gleams of light
Flash often from the East, then disappear
And mock me with a sky that ripens not
Into a steady morning: if my mind,
Remembering the sweet promise of the past,

140   Would gladly grapple with some noble theme,

6. The Aeolian harp, named for Aeolus, mythic god of the winds, resounds at the wind's touch.

Vain is her wish; where'er she turns she finds
Impediments from day to day renew'd.
    And now it would content me to yield up
Those lofty hopes a while for present gifts
145   Of humbler industry. But, O dear Friend!
The Poet, gentle creature as he is,
Hath, like the Lover, his unruly times;
His fits when he is neither sick nor well,
Though no distress be near him but his own
150   Unmanageable thoughts. The mind itself,
The meditative mind, best pleased, perhaps,
While she, as duteous as the Mother Dove,
Sits brooding,[7] lives not always to that end
But hath less quiet instincts, goadings-on
155   That drive her, as in trouble, through the groves.
With me is now such passion, which I blame
No otherwise than as it lasts too long.
    When, as becomes a man who would prepare
For such a glorious work, I through myself
160   Make rigorous inquisition, the report
Is often chearing; for I neither seem
To lack, that first great gift! the vital soul,
Nor general truths which are themselves a sort
Of Elements and Agents, Under-Powers,
165   Subordinate helpers of the living mind.
Nor am I naked in external things,
Forms, images; nor numerous other aids
Of less regard, though won perhaps with toil,
And needful to build up a Poet's praise.
170   Time, place, and manners;° these I seek, and these   *customs*
I find in plenteous store; but nowhere such
As may be singled out with steady choice;
No little Band of yet remember'd names
Whom I, in perfect confidence, might hope
175   To summon back from lonesome banishment
And make them inmates in the hearts of men
Now living, or to live in times to come.
Sometimes, mistaking vainly, as I fear,
Proud spring-tide swellings for a regular sea
180   I settle on some British theme, some old
Romantic tale, by Milton left unsung:[8]
More often, resting at some gentle place
Within the groves of Chivalry, I pipe
Among the Shepherds, with reposing Knights
185   Sit by a Fountain-side, and hear their tales.
Sometimes, more sternly mov'd, I would relate
How vanquish'd Mithridates northward pass'd,

---

7. In *Paradise Lost*, the epic narrator asks for inspiration from the Holy Spirit who, at Creation, "Dove-like satst brooding on the vast Abyss / And mad'st it pregnant" (1.21–2).

8. Milton considered writing an epic about Arthurian knights before settling on his biblical theme; a "Romantic" tale is a story of knightly adventure.

And, hidden in the cloud of years, became
That Odin, Father of a Race by whom
190   Perish'd the Roman Empire:[9] how the Friends
And Followers of Sertorius, out of Spain
Flying, found shelter in the Fortunate Isles;[1]
And left their usages, their arts, and laws
To disappear by a slow gradual death;
195   To dwindle and to perish one by one
Starved in those narrow bounds: but not the Soul
Of Liberty, which fifteen hundred years
Surviv'd, and when the European° came   *Spanish conquerors*
With skill and power that could not be withstood,
200   Did like a pestilence maintain its hold,
And wasted down by glorious death that Race
Of natural Heroes: or I would record
How in tyrannic times some unknown Man,
Unheard of in the Chronicles of Kings,
205   Suffer'd in silence for the love of truth:
How that one Frenchman,[2] through continued force
Of meditation on the inhuman deeds
Of the first Conquerors of the Indian Isles,
Went single in his ministry across
210   The Ocean, not to comfort the Oppress'd,
But, like a thirsty wind, to roam about,
Withering the Oppressor: how Gustavus found
Help at his need in Dalecarlia's Mines;[3]
How Wallace fought for Scotland,[4] left the name
215   Of Wallace to be found like a wild flower,
All over his dear Country, left the deeds
Of Wallace, like a Family of Ghosts,
To people the steep rocks and river banks,
Her natural sanctuaries, with a local soul
220   Of independence and stern liberty.
Sometimes it suits me better to shape out
Some Tale from my own heart, more near akin
To my own passions and habitual thoughts,
Some variegated story, in the main
225   Lofty, with interchange of gentler things;
But deadening admonitions will succeed,
And the whole beauteous Fabric seems to lack
Foundation, and, withal, appears throughout
Shadowy and unsubstantial. Then, last wish,
230   My last and favorite aspiration! then

9. In his *Decline and Fall of the Roman Empire* (1776–1788), Edward Gibbon had proposed that the Norse god Odin had originally been a tribal chieftain who had attacked Rome, his story taking on elements from the historical figure of King Mithridates, a Near Eastern king defeated by the Romans in the 1st century B.C.
1. The Canary Islands. Sertorius was a Roman general and ally of Mithridates, slain in 72 B.C.

2. In the 1560s Dominique de Gourges avenged Spanish cruelties to his countrymen in Florida.
3. Gustavus I of Sweden (1496–1530) planned his country's liberation from Danish rule, while hiding in the Dalecarlia mines of Sweden.
4. William Wallace was a Scottish hero who fought for the liberty of his country; he was executed by the British in 1305.

I yearn towards some philosophic Song
Of Truth that cherishes° our daily life;   *holds dear*
With meditations passionate from deep
Recesses in man's heart, immortal verse
235   Thoughtfully fitted to the Orphean lyre;[5]
But from this awful° burthen I full soon   *solemn*
Take refuge, and beguile myself with trust
That mellower years will bring a riper mind
And clearer insight. Thus from day to day
240   I live, a mockery of the brotherhood
Of vice and virtue, with no skill to part
Vague longing that is bred by want of power
From paramount impulse not to be withstood,
A timorous capacity from prudence;
245   From circumspection infinite delay.
Humility and modest awe themselves
Betray me, serving often for a cloak
To a more subtle selfishness, that now
Doth lock my functions up in blank reserve,°   *inertia*
250   Now dupes me by an over anxious eye
That with a false activity beats off
Simplicity and self-presented truth.
—Ah! better far than this, to stray about
Voluptuously° through fields and rural walks,   *luxuriantly*
255   And ask no record of the hours, given up
To vacant musing, unreprov'd neglect
Of all things, and deliberate holiday:
Far better never to have heard the name
Of zeal and just ambition, than to live
260   Thus baffled by a mind that every hour
Turns recreant to her task, takes heart again
Then feels immediately some hollow thought
Hang like an interdict upon her hopes.
This is my lot; for either still I find
265   Some imperfection in the chosen theme;
Or see of absolute accomplishment
Much wanting, so much wanting in myself,
That I recoil and droop, and seek repose
In indolence from vain perplexity,
270   Unprofitably travelling towards the grave,
Like a false Steward who hath much receiv'd
And renders nothing back.[6]—Was it for this
That one, the fairest of all Rivers,[7] lov'd
To blend his murmurs with my Nurse's song
275   And from his alder shades and rocky falls,
And from his fords and shallows sent a voice

5. In Greek myth, Orpheus singing and playing on his lyre could enthrall the natural world as well as people. Coleridge later praised *The Prelude* as "an Orphic Tale indeed."
6. An allusion to the parable of the steward who fails to

use his talents (literally a coin, metaphorically, God-given abilities), Matthew 25.14–30.
7. The Derwent, which flows behind Wordsworth's childhood residence in Cockermouth, Cumberland.

That flow'd along my dreams? For this didst Thou,
O Derwent! travelling over the green Plains
Near my sweet birth-place,[8] didst thou, beauteous Stream,
280   Make ceaseless music through the night and day
Which with its steady cadence tempering
Our human waywardness, composed my thoughts
To more than infant softness, giving me,
Among the fretful dwellings of mankind,
285   A knowledge, a dim earnest of the calm
Which Nature breathes among the hills and groves.
    When, having left his Mountains, to the Towers
Of Cockermouth that beauteous River came,
Behind my Father's House he pass'd, close by,
290   Along the margin of our Terrace Walk.
He was a Playmate whom we dearly lov'd.
Oh! many a time have I, a five years' Child,
A naked Boy, in one delightful Rill,
A little Mill-race sever'd from his stream,
295   Made one long bathing of a summer's day,
Bask'd in the sun, and plunged, and bask'd again,
Alternate all a summer's day, or cours'd
Over the sandy fields, leaping through groves
Of yellow grunsel,° or when crag and hill,   *ragweed*
300   The woods, and distant Skiddaw's[9] lofty height,
Were bronz'd with a deep radiance, stood alone
Beneath the sky, as if I had been born
On Indian Plains,° and from my Mother's hut   *in America*
Had run abroad in wantonness, to sport,
305   A naked Savage, in the thunder shower.
    Fair seed-time had my soul, and I grew up
Foster'd alike by beauty and by fear;
Much favor'd in my birth-place, and no less
In that beloved Vale[1] to which, erelong,
310   I was transplanted. Well I call to mind,
('Twas at an early age, ere I had seen
Nine summers) when upon the mountain slope
The frost, and breath of frosty wind had snapp'd
The last autumnal crocus, 'twas my joy
315   To wander half the night among the Cliffs
And the smooth Hollows, where the woodcocks ran
Along the open turf. In thought and wish,
That time, my shoulder all with springes° hung,   *bird-traps*
I was a fell destroyer. On the heights
320   Scudding away from snare to snare, I plied
My anxious visitation, hurrying on,
Still hurrying, hurrying onward: moon and stars
Were shining o'er my head; I was alone

---

8. Quoting Coleridge's *Frost at Midnight* (28).
9. At 3053 feet, the fourth-highest peak of the Lake District, nine miles east of Cockermouth.

1. Esthwaite, location of the village of Hawkshead, where Wordsworth went to school, 35 miles from Cockermouth.

And seem'd to be a trouble to the peace
325   That was among them. Sometimes it befel
In these night-wanderings, that a strong desire
O'erpower'd my better reason, and the bird
Which was the captive of another's toils°   *labors, snares*
Became my prey; and, when the deed was done,
330   I heard among the solitary hills
Low breathings coming after me, and sounds
Of undistinguishable motion, steps
Almost as silent as the turf they trod.
    Nor less in spring-time when on southern banks
335   The shining sun had from her knot of leaves
Decoy'd the primrose flower, and when the Vales
And woods were warm, was I a plunderer then
In the high places, on the lonesome peaks
Where'er, among the mountains and the winds,
340   The Mother Bird had built her lodge. Though mean
My object, and inglorious, yet the end
Was not ignoble. Oh! when I have hung
Above the raven's nest, by knots of grass,
And half-inch fissures in the slippery rock
345   But ill sustain'd, and almost, as it seem'd,
Suspended by the blast which blew amain,
Shouldering the naked crag; Oh! at that time,
While on the perilous ridge I hung alone,
With what strange utterance did the loud dry wind
350   Blow through my ears! the sky seem'd not a sky
Of earth, and with what motion mov'd the clouds!
    The mind of man is framed even like the breath
And harmony of music. There is a dark
Invisible workmanship that reconciles
355   Discordant elements, and makes them move
In one society. Ah me! that all
The terrors, all the early miseries,
Regrets, vexations, lassitudes, that all
The thoughts and feelings which have been infus'd
360   Into my mind should ever have made up
The calm existence that is mine when I
Am worthy of myself. Praise to the end!
Thanks likewise for the means! But I believe
That Nature, oftentimes, when she would frame
365   A favor'd Being, from his earliest dawn
Of infancy doth open out the clouds,
As at the touch of lightning, seeking him
With gentlest visitation: not the less,
Though haply° aiming at the self-same end,   *perhaps*
370   Does it delight her sometimes to employ
Severer interventions, ministry
More palpable, and so she dealt with me.
    One evening (surely I was led by her)
I went alone into a Shepherd's Boat,

375 A Skiff that to a Willow tree was tied
Within a rocky Cave, its usual home.
'Twas by the Shores of Patterdale, a Vale
Wherein I was a Stranger, thither come,
A School-boy Traveller, at the Holidays.
380 Forth rambled from the Village Inn alone
No sooner had I sight of this small Skiff,
Discover'd thus by unexpected chance,
Than I unloos'd her tether and embark'd.
The moon was up, the Lake was shining clear
385 Among the hoary mountains: from the Shore
I push'd, and struck the oars and struck again
In cadence, and my little Boat mov'd on
Even like a Man who walks with stately step
Though bent on speed. It was an act of stealth
390 And troubled pleasure: nor without the voice
Of mountain echoes did my Boat move on,
Leaving behind her still on either side
Small circles glittering idly in the moon
Until they melted all into one track
395 Of sparkling light. A rocky steep uprose
Above the Cavern of the Willow tree
And now, as suited one who proudly row'd
With his best skill, I fix'd a steady view
Upon the top of that same craggy ridge,
400 The bound of the horizon, for behind
Was nothing but the stars and the grey sky.
She was an elfin Pinnace;° lustily   *a small boat*
I dipp'd my oars into the silent Lake,
And, as I rose upon the stroke, my Boat
405 Went heaving through the water, like a Swan,
When from behind that craggy Steep, till then
The bound of the horizon, a huge Cliff,
As if with voluntary power instinct,°   *endowed*
Uprear'd its head: I struck, and struck again,
410 And, growing still in stature, the huge Cliff
Rose up between me and the stars, and still,
With measur'd motion, like a living thing,
Strode after me. With trembling hands I turn'd,
And through the silent water stole my way
415 Back to the Cavern of the Willow tree.
There, in her mooring-place, I left my Bark
And, through the meadows homeward went with grave
And serious thoughts: and after I had seen
That spectacle, for many days my brain
420 Work'd with a dim and undetermin'd sense
Of unknown modes of being: in my thoughts
There was a darkness, call it solitude,
Or blank desertion, no familiar shapes
Of hourly objects, images of trees,
425 Of sea, or sky, no colours of green fields;

But huge and mighty Forms that do not live
Like living men mov'd slowly through my mind
By day and were the trouble of my dreams.
    Wisdom and Spirit of the Universe!
430   Thou Soul that art the Eternity of Thought!
And giv'st to forms and images a breath
And everlasting motion! not in vain,
By day or starlight thus from my first dawn
Of Childhood didst Thou intertwine for me
435   The passions that build up our human Soul,
Not with the mean and vulgar° works of Man,   *lowly and ordinary*
But with high objects, with enduring things,
With life and nature, purifying thus
The elements of feeling and of thought,
440   And sanctifying by such discipline
Both pain and fear until we recognise
A grandeur in the beatings of the heart.
    Nor was this fellowship vouchsaf'd to me
With stinted kindness. In November days
445   When vapours, rolling down the valleys, made
A lonely scene more lonesome; among woods
At noon, and 'mid the calm of summer nights,
When by the margin of the trembling Lake
Beneath the gloomy hills I homeward went
450   In solitude, such intercourse was mine;
'Twas mine among the fields both day and night,
And by the waters all the summer long.
—And in the frosty season, when the sun
Was set, and, visible for many a mile,
455   The cottage windows through the twilight blaz'd,
I heeded not the summons:—happy time
It was indeed for all of us; to me
It was a time of rapture: clear and loud
The village clock toll'd six; I wheel'd about,
460   Proud and exulting, like an untired horse,
That cares not for its home.—All shod with steel
We hiss'd along the polish'd ice, in games
Confederate, imitative of the chace,
And woodland pleasures, the resounding horn,
465   The Pack, loud bellowing, and the hunted hare.
So through the darkness and the cold we flew,
And not a voice was idle: with the din,
Meanwhile, the precipices rang aloud,
The leafless trees, and every icy crag
470   Tinkled like iron, while the distant hills
Into the tumult sent an alien sound
Of melancholy, not unnoticed, while the stars,
Eastward, were sparkling clear, and in the west,
The orange sky of evening died away.
475   Not seldom from the uproar I retired
Into a silent bay, or sportively

Glanced sideway, leaving the tumultuous throng,
To cut across the image of a star
That gleam'd upon the ice: and oftentimes,
480   When we had given our bodies to the wind,
And all the shadowy banks, on either side,
Came sweeping through the darkness, spinning still
The rapid line of motion; then at once
Have I, reclining back upon my heels,
485   Stopp'd short, yet still the solitary Cliffs
Wheel'd by me, even as if the earth had roll'd
With visible motion her diurnal° round;   *daily*
Behind me did they stretch in solemn train
Feebler and feebler, and I stood and watch'd
490   Till all was tranquil as [   ]²
    Ye Presences of Nature, in the sky
Or on the earth! Ye Visions of the hills!
And Souls of lonely places! can I think
A vulgar hope was yours when Ye employ'd
495   Such ministry, when Ye through many a year
Haunting me thus among my boyish sports,
On caves and trees, upon the woods and hills,
Impress'd upon all forms the characters°   *marks, signs*
Of danger or desire, and thus did make
500   The surface of the universal earth
With triumph, and delight, and hope, and fear
Work like a sea.
                Not uselessly employ'd,
I might pursue this theme through every change
Of exercise and play, to which the year
505   Did summon us in its delightful round.
    —We were a noisy crew; the sun in heaven
Beheld not vales more beautiful than ours
Nor saw a race, in happiness and joy
More worthy of the fields where they were sown.
510   I would record with no reluctant voice
The woods of autumn and their hazel bowers
With milk-white clusters hung; the rod and line,
True symbol of the foolishness of hope,
Which with its strong enchantment led us on
515   By rocks and pools, shut out from every star
All the green summer, to forlorn cascades
Among the windings of the mountain-brooks.
    —Unfading recollections! at this hour
The heart is almost mine with which I felt
520   From some hill-top, on sunny afternoons,
The Kite high up among the fleecy clouds
Pull at its rein, like an impatient Courser,°   *race-horse*
Or, from the meadows sent on gusty days
Beheld her breast the wind, then suddenly
525   Dash'd headlong; and rejected by the storm.

2. Wordsworth left the end of this line blank in 1805. In 1809, it was completed as "a dreamless sleep."

Ye lowly Cottages in which we dwelt,
A ministration of your own was yours,
A sanctity, a safeguard, and a love!
Can I forget you, being as ye were
530 So beautiful among the pleasant fields
In which ye stood? Or can I here forget
The plain and seemly countenance with which
Ye dealt out your plain comforts? Yet had ye
Delights and exultations of your own.
535 Eager and never weary we pursued
Our home amusements by the warm peat fire
At evening; when with pencil and with slate,
In square divisions parcell'd out, and all
With crosses and with cyphers scribbled o'er,°   *tic-tac-toe*
540 We schemed and puzzled, head opposed to head,
In strife too humble to be named in Verse;
Or round the naked Table, snow-white deal,°   *pine*
Cherry, or maple, sate in close array,
And to the combat, Lu or Whist,° led on   *card games*
545 A thick-ribb'd Army, not as in the world
Neglected and ungratefully thrown by
Even for the very service they had wrought,
But husbanded through many a long campaign.
Uncouth assemblage was it, where no few
550 Had changed their functions, some, plebean cards,
Which Fate beyond the promise of their birth
Had glorified, and call'd to represent
The persons of departed Potentates.
Oh! with what echoes on the Board they fell!
555 Ironic Diamonds; Clubs, Hearts, Diamonds, Spades,
A congregation piteously akin;
Cheap matter did they give to boyish wit,
Those sooty Knaves, precipitated down
With scoffs and taunts, like Vulcan out of Heaven,
560 The paramount Ace, a moon in her eclipse,
Queens, gleaming through their splendour's last decay,
And Monarchs, surly at the wrongs sustain'd
By royal visages. Meanwhile, abroad
The heavy rain was falling, or the frost
565 Raged bitterly, with keen and silent tooth,
And, interrupting the impassion'd game,
From Esthwaite's neighbouring Lake the splitting ice,
While it sank down towards the water, sent,
Among the meadows and the hills, its long
570 And dismal yellings, like the noise of wolves
When they are howling round the Bothnic Main.°   *Baltic sea*
Nor, sedulous[3] as I have been to trace
How Nature by extrinsic passion first
Peopled my mind with beauteous forms or grand,
575 And made me love them, may I well forget

3. Diligent; revising Milton's claim that he is "Not sedulous by Nature" to treat epic themes (*Paradise Lost* 9.27).

How other pleasures have been mine, and joys
Of subtler origin; how I have felt
Not seldom, even in that tempestuous time,
Those hallow'd and pure motions of the sense
580 Which seem, in their simplicity, to own
An intellectual charm, that calm delight
Which, if I err not, surely must belong
To those first-born affinities that fit
Our new existence to existing things
585 And, in our dawn of being, constitute
The bond of union betwixt life and joy.
　　　Yes, I remember, when the changeful earth,
And twice five seasons on my mind had stamp'd
The faces of the moving year, even then,
590 A Child, I held unconscious intercourse
With the eternal Beauty, drinking in
A pure organic pleasure from the lines
Of curling mist, or from the level plain
Of waters colour'd by the steady clouds.
595 　　The Sands of Westmoreland, the Creeks and Bays
Of Cumbria's[4] rocky limits, they can tell
How when the Sea threw off his evening shade
And to the Shepherd's hut beneath the crags
Did send sweet notice of the rising moon,
600 How I have stood to fancies such as these,
Engrafted in the tenderness of thought,
A stranger, linking with the spectacle
No conscious memory of a kindred sight,
And bringing with me no peculiar sense
605 Of quietness or peace, yet have I stood,
Even while mine eye has mov'd o'er three long leagues
Of shining water, gathering, as it seem'd,
Through every hair-breadth of that field of light,
New pleasure, like a bee among the flowers.
610 　　Thus, often in those fits of vulgar° joy   *ordinary*
Which through all seasons, on a child's pursuits
Are prompt attendants, 'mid that giddy bliss
Which, like a tempest, works along the blood
And is forgotten; even then I felt
615 Gleams like the flashing of a shield: the earth
And common face of Nature spake to me
Rememberable things: sometimes, 'tis true,
By chance collisions, and quaint accidents
Like those ill-sorted unions, work suppos'd
620 Of evil-minded fairies, yet not vain,
Nor profitless, if haply they impress'd
Collateral° objects and appearances,   *subordinate*
Albeit lifeless then, and doom'd to sleep
Until maturer seasons call'd them forth

4. Lake District counties.

625   To impregnate and to elevate the mind.
    And if the vulgar joy by its own weight
    Wearied itself out of the memory
    The scenes which were a witness of that joy
    Remained, in their substantial lineaments
630   Depicted on the brain, and to the eye
    Were visible, a daily sight: and thus,
    By the impressive discipline of fear,
    By pleasure, and repeated happiness,
    So frequently repeated, and by force
635   Of obscure feelings representative
    Of joys that were forgotten, these same scenes,
    So beauteous and majestic in themselves,
    Though yet the day was distant, did at length
    Become habitually dear; and all
640   Their hues and forms were by invisible links
    Allied to the affections.
                    I began
    My Story early, feeling as I fear,
    The weakness of a human love, for days
    Disown'd by memory, ere the birth of spring
645   Planting my snow-drops among winter snows.
    Nor will it seem to thee, my Friend! so prompt
    In sympathy, that I have lengthen'd out,
    With fond and feeble tongue, a tedious tale.
    Meanwhile, my hope has been that I might fetch
650   Invigorating thoughts from former years,
    Might fix the wavering balance of my mind,
    And haply meet reproaches, too, whose power
    May spur me on, in manhood now mature,
    To honorable toil. Yet should these hopes
655   Be vain, and thus should neither I be taught
    To understand myself, nor thou to know
    With better knowledge how the heart was fram'd
    Of him thou lovest, need I dread from thee
    Harsh judgments, if I am so loth to quit
660   Those recollected hours that have the charm
    Of visionary things, and lovely forms,
    And sweet sensations that throw back our life
    And almost make our Infancy itself
    A visible scene on which the sun is shining.
665   One end hereby, at least, hath been attain'd—
    My mind hath been reviv'd, and if this mood
    Desert me not, I will forthwith bring down,
    Through later years, the story of my life.
    The road lies plain before me; 'tis a theme
670   Single, and of determin'd bounds; and hence
    I chuse it rather, at this time, than work
    Of ampler or more varied argument.[5]

---

5. Wordsworth wrote this last paragraph in 1804, further explaining why he is not following Coleridge's advice to write a major philosophical epic.

from **Book Second. School time continued**

[Two Consciousnesses]

Thus far, O Friend! have we, though leaving much
Unvisited, endeavour'd to retrace
My life through its first years, and measur'd back
The way I travell'd when I first began
5   To love the woods and fields: the passion yet
Was in its birth, sustain'd, as might befal,
By nourishment that came unsought; for still,
From week to week, from month to month we liv'd
A round of tumult: duly were our games
10   Prolong'd in summer till the daylight fail'd;
No chair remain'd before the doors, the bench
And threshold steps were empty; fast asleep
The Labourer, and the Old Man who had sate,
A later lingerer, yet the revelry
15   Continued, and the loud uproar: at last,
When all the ground was dark, and the huge clouds
Were edged with twinkling stars, to bed we went
With weary joints, and with a beating mind.
Ah! is there one who ever has been young,
20   And needs a monitory voice to tame
The pride of virtue, and of intellect?
And is there one, the wisest and the best
Of all mankind, who does not sometimes wish
For things which cannot be, who would not give,
25   If so he might, to duty and to truth
The eagerness of infantine desire?
A tranquillizing spirit presses now
On my corporeal frame: so wide appears
The vacancy between me and those days,
30   Which yet have such self-presence in my mind
That, sometimes, when I think of them, I seem
Two consciousnesses, conscious of myself
And of some other Being.

[Blessed Infant Babe]

Bless'd the infant Babe,[1]
(For with my best conjectures I would trace
The progress of our being) blest the Babe,
240   Nurs'd in his Mother's arms, the Babe who sleeps
Upon his Mother's breast, who, when his soul
Claims manifest kindred with an earthly soul,
Doth gather passion from his Mother's eye!
Such feelings pass into his torpid life
245   Like an awakening breeze, and hence his mind

---

1. Wordsworth has been discussing how hard it is "to analyse a soul" when no clear beginning can be found for one's habits and desires, or even for any "obvious and particular thought." He then moves on to this general speculation in psychobiography.

Even [in the first trial of its powers,][2]
Is prompt and watchful, eager to combine
In one appearance, all the elements
And parts of the same object, else detach'd
250 And loth to coalesce. Thus, day by day,
Subjected to the discipline of love,
His organs and recipient faculties
Are quicken'd, are more vigorous, his mind spreads,
Tenacious of the forms which it receives.
255 In one beloved presence, nay and more,
In that most apprehensive habitude°   *capacity to assimilate*
And those sensations which have been deriv'd
From this beloved Presence, there exists
A virtue which irradiates and exalts
260 All objects through all intercourse of sense.
No outcast he, bewilder'd and depress'd:
Along his infant veins are interfus'd
The gravitation and the filial bond
Of nature, that connect him with the world.
265 Emphatically such a Being lives,
An inmate of this *active* universe;
From nature largely he receives; nor so
Is satisfied, but largely gives again,
For feeling has to him imparted strength,
270 And powerful in all sentiments of grief,
Of exultation, fear, and joy, his mind,
Even as an agent of the one great mind,
Creates, creator and receiver both,
Working but in alliance with the works
275 Which it beholds.——Such, verily, is the first
Poetic spirit of our human life;
By uniform controul of after years
In most abated and suppress'd, in some,
Through every change of growth or of decay,
280 Pre-eminent till death.
                        From early days,
Beginning not long after that first time
In which, a Babe, by intercourse of touch,
I held mute dialogues with my Mother's heart,
I have endeavour'd to display the means
285 Whereby the infant sensibility,
Great birth-right of our Being, was in me
Augmented and sustain'd. Yet is a path
More difficult before me, and I fear
That in its broken windings we shall need
290 The chamois'° sinews, and the eagle's wing: *mountain antelope*
For now a trouble came into my mind
From unknown causes. I was left alone,
Seeking the visible world, nor knowing why.

2. This line was completed decades later.

295 The props of my affections were remov'd,
And yet the building stood, as if sustain'd
By its own spirit![3] All that I beheld
Was dear to me, and from this cause it came,
That now to Nature's finer influxes°   *influences, impressions*
My mind lay open, to that more exact
300 And intimate communion which our hearts
Maintain with the minuter properties
Of objects which already are belov'd,
And of those only.

from Book Sixth. Cambridge, and the Alps

[TRAVELLING IN THE ALPS. SIMPLON PASS]

Yet still in me, mingling with these delights°   *of travel*
Was something of stern mood, an under thirst
490 Of vigour, never utterly asleep.
Far different dejection once was mine,
A deep and genuine sadness then I felt:
The circumstances I will here relate
Even as they were. Upturning with a Band
495 Of Travellers, from the Valais we had clomb
Along the road that leads to Italy;
A length of hours, making of these our guides
Did we advance, and having reach'd an Inn
Among the mountains, we together ate
500 Our noon's repast, from which the Travellers rose,
Leaving us at the Board. Erelong we follow'd,
Descending by the beaten road that led
Right to a rivulet's edge, and there broke off.
The only track now visible was one
505 Upon the further side, right opposite,
And up a lofty Mountain. This we took
After a little scruple,° and short pause,   *hesitation*
And climb'd with eagerness, though not, at length,
Without surprize and some anxiety
510 On finding that we did not overtake
Our Comrades gone before. By fortunate chance,
While every moment now encreas'd our doubts,
A Peasant met us and from him we learn'd
That to the place which had perplex'd us first
515 We must descend, and there should find the road
Which in the stony channel of the Stream
Lay a few steps, and then along its Banks,
And, further, that thenceforward all our course
Was downwards, with the current of that Stream.
520 Hard of belief we questioned him again,
And all the answers which the Man return'd

---

3. Perhaps an oblique reference to the death of Wordsworth's mother when he was almost eight years old.

To our inquiries, in their sense and substance,
Translated by the feelings which we had,
Ended in this, that we had cross'd the Alps.
525   Imagination! lifting up itself
Before the eye and progress of my Song
Like an unfather'd vapour; here that Power,
In all the might of its endowments, came
Athwart me; I was lost as in a cloud,
530   Halted without a struggle to break through,
And now[1] recovering to my Soul I say
I recognize thy glory; in such strength
Of usurpation, in such visitings
Of awful° promise, when the light of sense   awe-filled
535   Goes out in flashes that have shewn to us
The invisible world, doth Greatness make abode,
There harbours whether we be young or old.
Our destiny, our nature, and our home
Is with infinitude, and only there;
540   With hope it is, hope that can never die,
Effort, and expectation, and desire,
And something evermore about to be.
The mind beneath such banners militant
Thinks not of spoils, trophies nor of aught
545   That may attest its prowess, blest in thoughts
That are their own perfection and reward,
Strong in itself, and in the access of joy
Which hides it like the overflowing Nile.
         The dull and heavy slackening which ensu'd
550   Upon those tidings by the Peasant given
Was soon dislodg'd; downwards we hurried fast,
And enter'd with the road which we had miss'd
Into a narrow chasm: the brook and road
Were fellow-travellers in this gloomy Pass,
555   And with them did we journey several hours
At a slow step. The immeasurable height
Of woods decaying, never to be decay'd,
The stationary blasts of waterfalls,
And every where along the hollow rent
560   Winds thwarting winds, bewilder'd and forlorn,
The torrents shooting from the clear blue sky,
The rocks that mutter'd close upon our ears,
Black drizzling crags that spake by the way-side
As if a voice were in them, the sick sight
565   And giddy prospect of the raving stream,
The unfetter'd clouds, and region of the heavens,
Tumult and peace, the darkness and the light
Were all like workings of one mind, the features
Of the same face, blossoms upon one tree,
570   Characters° of the great Apocalyps,   signs, letters

---

1. This apostrophe was written in 1804, fourteen years after the disappointment of the missed climax.

The types and symbols of Eternity,
Of first and last, and midst, and without end.[2]
    That night our lodging was an Alpine House,
An Inn or Hospital, as they are named,
575   Standing in that same valley by itself
And close upon the confluence of two streams,
A dreary Mansion, large beyond all need,
With high and spacious rooms, deafen'd and stunn'd
By noise of waters, making innocent Sleep
580   Lie melancholy among weary bones.
    Uprisen betimes, our journey we renew'd
Led by the Stream, ere noon-day magnified
Into a lordly River, broad and deep,
Dimpling along in silent majesty,
585   With mountains for its neighbours, and in view
Of distant mountains and their snowy tops,
And thus proceeding to Locarno's Lake,
Fit resting-place for such a Visitant.
——Locarno, spreading out in width like Heaven,
590   And Como, thou a treasure by the earth
Kept to itself, a darling bosom'd up
In Abyssinian[3] privacy, I spake
Of thee, thy chesnut woods, and garden plots
Of Indian corn tended by dark-eyed Maids,
595   Thy lofty steeps, and path-ways roof'd with vines
Winding from house to house, from town to town,
Sole link that binds them to each other, walks
League after league, and cloistral avenues
Where silence is, if music be not there:
600   While yet a Youth, undisciplined in Verse,
Through fond ambition of my heart, I told
Your praises; nor can I approach you now,
Ungreeted by a more melodious Song,
Where tones of learned Art and Nature mix'd
605   May frame enduring language. Like a breeze
Or sunbeam over your domain I pass'd
In motion without pause; but Ye have left
Your beauty with me, an impassion'd sight
Of colours and of forms, whose power is sweet
610   And gracious, almost might I dare to say,
As virtue is, or goodness, sweet as love
Or the remembrance of a noble deed,
Or gentlest visitations of pure thought
When God, the Giver of all joy, is thank'd
615   Religiously, in silent blessedness,
Sweet as this last itself, for such it is.

2. Milton's terms for God (*Paradise Lost* 5.165), echoing God's description of himself in the book of Revelation (the Apocalypse) as "Alpha and Omega, the beginning and the ending"—the first and last letters of the Greek alphabet. "Types" are people or events that foreshadow God's future works.

3. Abyssinia was a legendary location for Paradise.

Through those delightful pathways we advanced
Two days, and still in presence of the Lake,
Which, winding up among the Alps, now changed
620 Slowly its lovely countenance, and put on
A sterner character. The second night,
In eagerness, and by report misled
Of those Italian Clocks that speak the time
In fashion different from ours, we rose
625 By moonshine, doubting not that day was near,
And that, meanwhile, coasting the Water's edge,
As hitherto, and with as plain a track
To be our guide, we might behold the scene
In its most deep repose.—We left the Town
630 Of Gravedona with this hope; but soon
Were lost, bewilder'd among woods immense,
Where, having wander'd for a while, we stopp'd
And on a rock sate down, to wait for day.
An open place it was, and overlook'd
635 From high the sullen water underneath,
On which a dull red image of the moon
Lay bedded, changing oftentimes its form
Like an uneasy snake: long time we sate,
For scarcely more than one hour of the night,
640 Such was our error, had been gone, when we
Renew'd our journey. On the rock we lay,
And wish'd to sleep but could not for the stings
Of insects, which with noise like that of noon
Fill'd all the woods: the cry of unknown birds,
645 The mountains, more by darkness visible[4]
And their own size than any outward light,
The breathless wilderness of clouds, the clock
That told with unintelligible voice
The widely-parted hours, the noise of streams
650 And sometimes rustling motions nigh at hand
Which did not leave us free from personal fear,
And lastly the withdrawing Moon, that set
Before us while she yet was high in heaven,
These were our food; and such a summer night
655 Did to that pair of golden days succeed,
With now and then a doze and snatch of sleep,
On Como's Banks, the same delicious Lake.

from Book Tenth. Residence in France and French Revolution

[THE REIGN OF TERROR. CONFUSION. RETURN TO ENGLAND]

It was a beautiful and silent day
That overspread the countenance of earth,
Then fading, with unusual quietness

---

4. Recalling Milton's description of Hell (*Paradise Lost* 1.61ff., page 787), which resonates throughout this passage.

When from the Loire I parted, and through scenes
5   Of vineyard, orchard, meadow-ground and tilth,
Calm waters, gleams of sun, and breathless trees
Towards the fierce Metropolis turn'd my steps
Their homeward way to England. From his Throne
The King had fallen;[1] the congregated Host,
10   Dire cloud upon the front of which was written
The tender mercies of the dismal wind
That bore it, on the Plains of Liberty
Had burst innocuously:—say more, the swarm
That came elate and jocund, like a Band
15   Of Eastern Hunters, to enfold in ring
Narrowing itself by moments and reduce
To the last punctual° spot of their despair   *precise*
A race of victims, so they deem'd, themselves
Had shrunk from sight of their own task, and fled
20   In terror; desolation and dismay
Remain'd for them whose fancies had grown rank
With evil expectations, confidence
And perfect triumph to the better cause.
The State, as if to stamp the final seal
25   On her security, and to the world
Shew what she was, a high and fearless soul,
Or rather in a spirit of thanks to those
Who had stirr'd up her slackening faculties
To new transition, had assumed with joy
30   The body and the venerable name
Of a Republic: lamentable crimes
'Tis true had gone before this hour, the work
Of massacre in which the senseless sword
Was pray'd to as a judge; but these were past,
35   Earth free from them for ever, as was thought,
Ephemeral monsters, to be seen but once,
Things that could only shew themselves and die.
     This was the time in which enflam'd with hope,
To Paris I return'd. Again I rang'd,
40   More eagerly than I had done before,
Through the wide City and in progress pass'd
The Prison where the unhappy Monarch lay
Associate with his Children and his Wife
In bondage; and the Palace lately storm'd
45   With roar of canon, and a numerous Host.
I cross'd, (a blank and empty area then)
The Square of the Carousel, few weeks back
Heap'd up with dead and dying,[2] upon these
And other sights looking as doth a man
50   Upon a volume whose contents he knows

1. Louis XVI had been imprisoned in August 1792, and the invading armies of Austria and Prussia had been defeated by the French at Valmy on 20 September 1792, a month before Wordsworth returned from Orleans to Paris.

2. The royal palace had been stormed by a mob in August, with over a thousand lives lost; their bodies were cremated in the square in front of the palace.

Are memorable, but from him lock'd up,
Being written in a tongue he cannot read;
So that he questions the mute leaves with pain
And half upbraids their silence. But that night
55 When on my bed I lay I was most mov'd
And felt most deeply in what world I was;
My room was high and lonely, near the roof
Of a large Mansion or Hotel, a spot
That would have pleas'd me in more quiet times
60 Nor was it wholly without pleasure then.
With unextinguish'd taper I kept watch,
Reading at intervals; the fear gone by
Press'd on me almost like a fear to come;
I thought of those September Massacres,
65 Divided from me by a little month,[3]
And felt and touch'd them, a substantial dread;
The rest was conjured up from tragic fictions
And mournful Calendars° of true history,   records
Remembrances and dim admonishments.
70 "The horse is taught his manage° and the wind   paces
Of heaven wheels round and treads in his own steps,[4]
Year follows year, the tide returns again,
Day follows day, all things have second birth;
The earthquake is not satisfied at once."
75 And in such way I wrought upon myself
Until I seem'd to hear a voice that cried
To the whole City, "Sleep no more."[5] To this
Add comments of a calmer mind, from which
I could not gather full security,
80 But at the best it seemed a place of fear,
Unfit for the repose of night,
Defenceless as a wood where tigers roam.
        Betimes next morning to the Palace Walk
Of Orleans I repair'd and entering there
85 Was greeted, among divers° other notes,   various
By voices of the Hawkers in the crowd
Bawling, *Denunciation of the crimes*
Of Maximilian Robespierre: the speech
Which in their hands they carried was the same
90 Which had been recently pronounced the day
When Robespierre, well-knowing for what mark
Some words of indirect reproof had been
Intended, rose in hardihood and dared
The Man who had an ill surmise of him
95 To bring his charge in openness: whereat
When a dead pause ensued and no one stirr'd,
In silence of all present, from his seat

3. Between September 2 and 7, a newly powerful radical
faction of the Republican government organized massacres in which 3,000 prisoners were executed.
4. The National Convention of France now met at a former riding school near the Tuileries.
5. The quotation recalls Macbeth's guilty fantasy after he
has murdered his king: "Methought I heard a voice cry
'Sleep no more!'" (*Macbeth* 2.2.35).

Louvet walked singly through the avenue
And took his station in the Tribune,° saying   rostrum
100   "I, Robespierre, accuse thee"! 'Tis well known
What was the issue of that charge, and how
Louvet was left alone without support
Of his irresolute Friends:[6] but these are things
Of which I speak only as they were storm
105   Or sunshine to my individual mind,
No further. Let me then relate that now
In some sort seeing with my proper° eyes   own
That Liberty, and Life and Death would soon
To the remotest corners of the Land
110   Lie in the arbitriment° of those who ruled   government
The capital City, what was struggled for,
And by what combatants victory must be won,
The indecision on their° part whose aim   Girondin moderates
Seem'd best, and the straight-forward path of those
115   Who in attack or in defense alike
Were strong through their impiety,° greatly I   the Jacobin radicals
Was agitated; yea I could almost
Have pray'd that throughout earth upon all souls
Worthy of liberty, upon every soul
120   Matured to live in plainness and in truth
The gift of tongues might fall,[7] and men arrive
From the four quarters of the winds to do
For France what without help she could not do,
A work of honour: think not that to this
125   I added work of safety; from such thought
And the least fear about the end of things
I was as far as Angels are from guilt.
      Yet did I grieve, nor only grieved, but thought
Of opposition and of remedies,
130   An insignificant Stranger, and obscure,
Mean° as I was, and little graced with powers   humble
Of eloquence even in my native speech,
And all unfit for tumult and intrigue,
Yet would I willingly have taken up
135   A service at this time for cause so great,
However dangerous. Inly I revolved
How much the destiny of man had still°   always
Hung upon single persons, that there was,
Transcendant to all local patrimony,
140   One Nature, as there is one Sun in heaven,
That objects, even as they are great, thereby
Do come within the reach of humblest eyes,
That Man was only weak through his mistrust
And want of hope, where evidence divine

---

6. In the National Convention, on 29 October 1792, the moderate Girondist J. B. Louvet de Couvray accused Robespierre of dictatorial behavior and aspirations. The phrase "walked singly" in line 98 evokes the solitary resis-tance of archangel Abdiel to Satan's revolt against God (*Paradise Lost* 5.877ff).

7. Apostles began to speak in tongues at Pentacost, miracu-lously understood by foreigners of many languages (Acts 2).

145   Proclaim'd to him that hope should be most sure,
      That, with desires heroic and firm sense,
      A Spirit thoroughly faithful to itself,
      Unquenchable, unsleeping, undismay'd,[8]
      Was as an instinct among men, a stream
150   That gather'd up each petty straggling rill
      And vein of water, glad to be roll'd on
      In safe obedience, that a mind whose rest
      Was where it ought to be, in self-restraint,
      In circumspection and simplicity,
155   Fell rarely in entire discomfiture
      Below its aim, or met with from without
      A treachery that defeated it, or foil'd.
      —On the other side I call'd to mind those truths
      Which are the common-places of the Schools,
160   A theme° for Boys, too trite even to be felt,   *essay subject*
      Yet with a revelation's liveliness
      In all their comprehensive bearings known
      And visible to Philosophers of old,
      Men who, to business of the world untrain'd,
165   Liv'd in the Shade, and to Harmodius known
      And his Compeer Aristogiton, known
      To Brutus,[9] that tyrannic Power is weak,
      Hath neither gratitude, nor faith, nor love,
      Nor the support of good or evil men
170   To trust in, that the Godhead which is ours
      Can never utterly be charm'd° or still'd,   *expelled*
      That nothing hath a natural right to last
      But equity and reason, that all else
      Meets foes irreconcilable, and at best
175   Doth live but by variety of disease.
          Well might my wishes be intense, my thoughts
      Strong and perturb'd, not doubting at that time,
      Creed which ten shameful years have not annull'd,
      But that the virtue of one paramount mind
180   Would have abash'd those impious crests, have quell'd
      Outrage and bloody power, and in despite
      Of what the People were through ignorance
      And immaturity, and, in the teeth
      Of desperate opposition from without,
185   Have clear'd a passage for just government,
      And left a solid birth-right to the State,
      Redeem'd according to example given
      By ancient Lawgivers.
                        In this frame of mind
      Reluctantly to England I return'd,[1]
190   Compell'd by nothing less than absolute want

8. Again evoking Abdiel's faithful heroism (*Paradise Lost* 5.897–99).
9. Harmodius and Aristogiton were killed when they tried to overthrow the tyrant Hippias in 514 B.C. in Athens. Brutus was the idealistic assassin of Julius Caesar, who seemed ready in 44 B.C. to name himself emperor.
1. Wordsworth returned to England late in 1792.

Of funds for my support, else, well assured
That I both was and must be of small worth,
No better than an alien in the Land,
I doubtless should have made a common cause
195   With some who perish'd, haply° perish'd too,²   *perhaps*
A poor mistaken and bewilder'd offering,
Should to the breast of Nature have gone back
With all my resolutions, all my hopes,
A Poet only to myself, to Men
200   Useless, and even, beloved Friend, a soul
To thee unknown.³

[FURTHER EVENTS IN FRANCE]

In France, the Men who for their desperate ends
Had pluck'd up mercy by the roots were glad
Of this new enemy. Tyrants, strong before
310   In devilish pleas were ten times stronger now,⁴
And thus beset with Foes on every side
The goaded Land wax'd mad; the crimes of few
Spread into madness of the many, blasts
From hell came sanctified like airs from heaven;⁵
315   The sternness of the Just,⁶ the faith of those
Who doubted not that Providence had times
Of anger and vengeance, theirs who throned
The human understanding paramount
And made of that their God,⁷ the hopes of those
320   Who were content to barter short-lived pangs
For a paradise of ages, the blind rage
Of insolent tempers, the light vanity
Of intermeddlers, steady purposes
Of the suspicious, slips of the indiscreet,
325   And all the accidents of life were press'd
Into one service, busy with one work;
The Senate was heart-stricken, not a voice
Uplifted, none to oppose or mitigate:
Domestic carnage now fill'd all the year
330   With Feast-days; the Old Man from the chimney-nook,
The Maiden from the bosom of her Love,
The Mother from the Cradle of her Babe,
The Warrior from the Field, all perish'd,
Friends, enemies, of all parties, ages, ranks,
335   Head after head, and never heads enough

2. Wordsworth's revolutionary sympathies were with the moderate Girondins, almost all of whom were executed or committed suicide following Robespierre's rise to power.
3. Wordsworth met Coleridge in 1795.
4. After France declared war on England in February 1793, England joined the coalition against France led by Austria and Prussia. Except for a brief peace in 1802, England would be at war with France until 1815.

5. Echoing Hamlet's uncertainty about whether his murdered father's ghost brings "airs from heaven or blasts from hell" (*Hamlet* 1.4.41).
6. Referring obliquely to Robespierre's associate Louis St. Just, a leader of the Terror.
7. "La Raison" (Reason) was embodied as a symbolic goddess of the Republic, and churches were turned into Temples of Reason.

For those who bade them fall: they found their joy,
They made it, ever thirsty.—As a Child,
(If light desires of innocent little Ones
May with such heinous appetites be match'd)
340 Having a toy, a windmill, though the air
Do of itself blow fresh, and makes the vane
Spin in his eyesight, he is not content,
But with the play-thing at arm's length, he sets
His front against the blast, and runs amain°   *full force*
345 To make it whirl the faster.
          In the depth
Of these enormities, even thinking minds
Forgot at seasons whence they had their being,
Forgot that such a sound was ever heard
As Liberty, upon earth; yet all beneath
350 Her innocent authority was wrought,
Nor could have been without her blessed name.
The illustrious Wife of Roland, in the hour
Of her composure, felt that agony
And gave it vent in her last words.[8] O Friend!
355 It was a lamentable time for man
Whether a hope had e'er been his or not,
A woful time for them whose hopes did still
Outlast the shock, most woful for those few—
They had the deepest feeling of the grief—
360 Who still were flatter'd,° and had trust in man.   *deluded*
Meanwhile, the Invaders fared as they deserv'd;
The Herculean Commonwealth had put forth her arms
And throttled with an infant Godhead's might
The snakes about her cradle:[9] that was well
365 And as it should be, yet no cure for those
Whose souls were sick with pain of what would be
Hereafter brought in charge against mankind;
Most melancholy at that time, O Friend!
Were my day thoughts, my dreams were miserable;
370 Through months, through years, long after the last beat
Of those atrocities (I speak bare truth,
As if to thee alone in private talk)
I scarcely had one night of quiet sleep,
Such ghastly visions had I of despair
375 And tyranny and implements of death,
And long orations which in dreams I pleaded
Before unjust Tribunals, with a voice
Labouring, a brain confounded, and a sense
Of treachery and desertion in the place
380 The holiest that I knew of, my own soul.

8. Madame Roland, an important supporter of the Girondins, was guillotined in November 1793. Her famous last words were: "O Liberté, que des crimes l'on commet en ton nom!" ("O Liberty, what crimes are committed in your name!").

9. As an infant in his cradle, Hercules strangled the two serpents sent by Hera to destroy him, just as the infant Republic had repelled foreign invasions.

[The Death of Robespierre and Renewed Optimism][1]

　　　　　the scene appear'd
So gay and chearful, when a Traveller
Chancing to pass, I carelessly inquired
If any news were stirring: he replied
In the familiar language of the day
535　That "*Robespierre was dead.*" Nor was a doubt,
On further question, left within my mind
But that the tidings were substantial truth,
That he and his supporters all were fallen.
　　　Great was my glee of spirit, great my joy
540　In vengeance, and eternal justice, thus
Made manifest. "Come now ye golden times,"
Said I, forth-breathing on those open Sands
A Hymn of triumph, "as the morning comes
Out of the bosom of the night, come Ye:
545　Thus far our trust is verified; behold!
They who with clumsy desperation brought
A river of blood, and preach'd that nothing else
Could cleanse the Augean Stable,[2] by the might
Of their own helper have been swept away;
550　Their madness is declared and visible,
Elsewhere will safety now be sought,[3] and Earth
March firmly towards righteousness and peace."
Then schemes I framed more calmly, when and how
The madding Factions might be tranquillised,
555　And though through hardships manifold and long,
The mighty renovation would proceed:
Thus, interrupted by uneasy bursts
Of exultation, I pursued my way
Along that very Shore which I had skimm'd
560　In former times, when, spurring from the Vale
Of Nightshade and St Mary's mouldering Fane°　　　　　　*shrine*
And the Stone Abbot, after circuit made
In wantonness of heart, a joyous Crew
Of School-boys, hastening to their distant home,
565　Along the margin of the moonlight Sea,
We beat with thundering hoofs the level Sand.
　　　　　　　* * *
　　O pleasant exercise of hope and joy![4]
690　For great were the auxiliars° which then stood　　　　　　*allies*
Upon our side, we who were strong in love;

1. Wordsworth is back in England, spending the summer on the coast near Peele Castle. On 28 July 1794, Robespierre and 21 of his associates were guillotined. Wordsworth is walking near the shore when he learns of Robespierre's death.
2. In one of his 12 labors, Hercules cleaned the filthy stable of King Augeus, by diverting two rivers through the stable.
3. Instead of with Robespierre's Committee of Public Safety, which had instigated the Terror.
4. Wordsworth's renewed faith in the French Republic extended to hope for peaceful reforms in England. Here he recalls his first enthusiasm for the Revolution; he published this passage in Coleridge's journal *The Friend* in 1809 and again in his *Poems* of 1815, as "French Revolution as It Appeared to Enthusiasts at Its Commencement," classing it with "Poems of the Imagination."

Bliss was it in that dawn to be alive,
But to be young was very heaven: O times,
In which the meagre, stale, forbidding ways
695   Of custom, law and statute took at once
The attraction of a Country in Romance;
When Reason seem'd the most to assert her rights
When most intent on making of herself
A prime Enchanter to assist the work
700   Which then was going forwards in her name:
Not favor'd spots alone, but the whole earth
The beauty wore of promise, that which sets,
To take an image which was felt, no doubt,
Among the bowers of paradise itself,
705   The budding rose above the rose full blown.
What temper° at the prospect did not wake   *temperament*
To happiness unthought-of? The inert
Were rouz'd, and lively natures rapt° away.   *carried, enraptured*
They who had fed their childhood upon dreams,
710   The Play-fellows of Fancy, who had made
All powers of swiftness, subtlety, and strength
Their ministers, used to stir in lordly wise
Among the grandest objects of the sense
And deal with whatsoever they found there
715   As if they had within some lurking right
To wield it:—they too, who, of gentle mood,
Had watch'd all gentle motions, and to these
Had fitted their own thoughts, schemers more mild,
And in the region of their peaceful selves—
720   Did now find helpers to their heart's desire,
And stuff at hand, plastic° as they could wish,   *malleable*
Were call'd upon to exercise their skill,
Not in Utopia, subterraneous fields,
Or some secreted Island Heaven knows where;
725   But in the very world which is the world
Of all of us, the place on which in the end
We find our happiness, or not at all.

[BRITAIN DECLARES WAR ON FRANCE.
THE RISE OF NAPOLEON AND IMPERIALIST FRANCE]

In the main outline, such, it might be said
Was my condition, till with open war
Britain opposed the Liberties of France:[5]
760   This threw me first out of the pale° of love,   *boundary*
Sour'd, and corrupted upwards to the source
My sentiments, was° not, as hitherto,   *this was*
A swallowing up of lesser things in great;
But change of them into their opposites,
765   And thus a way was open'd for mistakes

---

5. France declared war on Holland and England on 1 February 1793. Ten days later, England reciprocated.

And false conclusions of the intellect
As gross in their degree and in their kind
Far, far more dangerous. What had been a pride
Was now a shame; my likings and my loves
770   Ran in new channels, leaving old ones dry,
And thus a blow which in maturer age
Would but have touch'd the judgement struck more deep
Into sensations near the heart: meantime,
As from the first, wild theories were afloat
775   Unto the subtleties of which at least
I had but lent a careless ear, assured
Of this, that time would soon set all things right,
Prove that the multitude had been oppress'd,
And would be so no more.
                                        But when events
780   Brought less encouragement, and unto these
The immediate proof of principles no more
Could be entrusted, while the events themselves,
Worn out in greatness and in novelty,
Less occupied the mind and sentiments,
785   Could through my understanding's natural growth
No longer justify themselves through faith
Of inward consciousness, and hope that laid
Its hand upon its object; evidence
Safer, of universal application, such
790   As could not be impeach'd was sought elsewhere.
      And now, become Oppressors in their turn,
Frenchmen had changed a war of self-defense
For one of conquest, losing sight of all
Which they had struggled for; and mounted up
795   Openly in the view of earth and heaven
The scale of Liberty.[6] I read her doom,
Vex'd inly somewhat, it is true, and sore,
But not dismay'd, nor taking to the shame
Of a false Prophet; but, rouz'd up, I stuck
800   More firmly to old tenets, and to prove
Their temper,° strain'd them more, and thus in heat   *test their strength*
Of contest did opinions every day
Grow into consequence till round my mind
They clung, as if they were the life of it.
805   This was the time when all things tended fast
To depravation; the Philosophy
That promised to abstract the hopes of man
Out of his feelings, to be fix'd thenceforth
For ever in a purer element
810   Found ready welcome.[7] Tempting region that
For Zeal to enter and refresh herself

---

6. Initially fighting only in self-defense, by late 1794 France was clearly the aggressor in wars on several foreign fronts.

7. A reference to William Godwin's *Political Justice* (1793), which argued for the power of individual rational judgment to bring about reform.

Where passions had the privilege to work,
And never hear the sound of their own names:
But, speaking more in charity, the dream
815 Was flattering° to the young ingenuous mind,   *seductive*
Pleas'd with extremes, and not the least with that
Which makes the human Reason's naked self
The object of its fervour: what delight!
How glorious! in self-knowledge and self-rule
820 To look through all the frailties of the world
And, with a resolute mastery shaking off
The accidents of nature, time, and place
That make up the weak being of the past,
Build social freedom on its only basis,
825 The freedom of the individual mind,
Which, to the blind restraint of general laws
Superior, magisterially adopts
One guide, the light of circumstances, flash'd
Upon an independent intellect.
830   For, howsoe'er unsettled, never once
Had I thought ill of human kind, or been
Indifferent to its welfare; but, enflamed
With thirst of a secure intelligence
And sick of other passion, I pursued
835 A higher nature, wish'd that man should start
Out of the worm-like° state in which he is,   *caterpillar-like*
And spread abroad the wings of Liberty,
Lord of himself in indisturb'd delight—
A noble aspiration, yet° I feel   *even now*
840 The aspiration, but with other thoughts
And happier; for I was perplex'd and sought
To accomplish the transition by such means
As did not lie in nature, sacrificed
The exactness of a comprehensive mind
845 To scrupulous and microscopic views
That furnish'd out materials for a work
Of false imagination, placed beyond
The limits of experience and of truth.
    Enough, no doubt, the advocates themselves
850 Of ancient institutions had performed
To bring disgrace upon their° very names,   *the institutions'*
Disgrace of which custom and written law
And sundry moral sentiments, as props
And emanations of these institutes,
855 Too justly bore a part. A veil had been
Uplifted; why deceive ourselves? 'Twas so,
'Twas even so, and sorrow for the man,
Who either had not eyes wherewith to see,
Or seeing hath forgotten. Let this pass;
860 Suffice it that a shock had then been given
To old opinions; and the minds of all men
Had felt it; that my mind was both let loose,

Let loose and goaded. After what hath been
Already said of patriotic love,
865   And hinted at in other sentiments
We need not linger long upon this theme.
This only may be said, that from the first
Having two natures in me, joy the one
The other melancholy, and withal
870   A happy man, and therefore bold to look
On painful things, slow somewhat too and stern
In temperament, I took the knife in hand
And stopping not at parts less sensitive,
Endeavour'd with my best of skill to probe
875   The living body of society
Even to the heart: I push'd without remorse
My speculations forward; yea, set foot
On Nature's holiest places. Time may come
When some dramatic Story may afford
880   Shapes livelier to convey to thee, my Friend,
What then I learn'd, or think I learn'd of truth
And the errors into which I was betray'd
By present objects, and by reasonings false
From the beginning, inasmuch as drawn
885   Out of a heart which had been turn'd aside
From nature by external accidents,
And which was thus confounded more and more,
Misguiding and misguided. Thus I fared,
Dragging all passions, notions, shapes of faith
890   Like culprits to the bar,° suspiciously   *courtroom*
Calling the mind to establish in plain day
Her titles and her honours, now believing,
Now disbelieving, endlessly perplex'd
With impulse, motive, right and wrong, the ground
895   Of moral obligation, what the rule
And what the sanction, till, demanding proof
And seeking it in every thing, I lost
All feeling of conviction, and in fine°   *in the end*
Sick, wearied out with contrarieties,
900   Yielded up moral questions in despair,
And for my future studies, as the sole
Employment of the inquiring faculty,
Turn'd towards mathematics, and their clear
And solid evidence.—Ah! then it was
905   That Thou, most precious Friend! about this time
First known to me, didst lend a living help
To regulate my soul, and then it was,
That the beloved Woman,[8] in whose sight
Those days were pass'd, now speaking in a voice
910   Of sudden admonition like a brook

---

8. After a long separation, Dorothy Wordsworth and her brother were able to realize their dream of sharing a household in September 1795; Coleridge lived nearby.

That does but cross a lonely road, and now
Seen, heard, and felt, and caught at every turn,
Companion never lost through many a league,
Maintain'd for me a saving intercourse°   *communion*
915   With my true self: for, though impair'd and changed,
Much, as it seem'd, I was no further changed
Than as a clouded, not a waning moon.
She in the midst of all preserv'd me still
A Poet, made me seek beneath that name
920   My office upon earth, and nowhere else,
And lastly, Nature's self, by human love
Assisted, through the weary labyrinth
Conducted me again to open day,
Revived the feelings of my earlier life,
925   Gave me that strength, and knowledge full of peace,
Enlarged, and never more to be disturb'd,
Which through the steps of our degeneracy,
All degradation of this age, hath still
Upheld me, and upholds me at this day°   *1804*
930   In the catastrophe (for so they dream,
And nothing less) when finally, to close
And rivet up the gains of France, a Pope
Is summon'd in, to crown an Emperor;
This last opprobrium° when we see the dog   *disgrace*
935   Returning to his vomit,[9] when the sun
That rose in splendour, was alive, and moved
In exultation among living clouds
Hath put his function and his glory off,
And, turn'd into a gewgaw, a machine,°   *stage machine*
940   Sets like an opera phantom. * * *

COMPANION READING

William Wordsworth: from *The Prelude (1850)*

[APOSTROPHE TO EDMUND BURKE][1]

Genius of Burke! forgive the pen seduced
By specious wonders, and too slow to tell
Of what the ingenuous, what bewildered men,
515   Beginning to mistrust their boastful guides,
And wise men, willing to grow wiser, caught,
Rapt auditors! from thy most eloquent tongue—
Now mute, for ever mute in the cold grave.
I see him,—old, but vigorous in age,—
520   Stand like an oak whose stag-horn branches start

---

9. In November 1804 Pope Pius VII attended Napoleon's coronation as Emperor; as Pius was about to crown him, Napoleon snatched the crown and put it on himself. Wordsworth alludes to 2 Peter 2.22: the persistently evil man is like a dog "turned to his own vomit again."

1. This passage, composed in 1832, appears in Book 7 of the 1850 *Prelude*, as Wordsworth pauses before Parliament and remembers Burke's parliamentary career and his anti-revolutionary *Reflections on the Revolution in France* (see page 1357).

Out of its leafy brow, the more to awe
The younger brethren of the grove. But some—
While he forewarns, denounces, launches forth,
Against all systems built on abstract rights,
525   Keen ridicule; the majesty proclaims
Of Institutes and Laws, hallowed by time;
Declares the vital power of social ties
Endeared by Custom; and with high disdain,
Exploding upstart Theory, insists
530   Upon the allegiance to which men are born—
Some—say at once a froward° multitude—   *willful*
Murmur (for truth is hated, where not loved)
As the winds fret within the Aeolian cave,
Gall'd by their monarch's chain.[2] The times were big
535   With ominous change, which, night by night, provoked
Keen struggles, and black clouds of passion raised;
But memorable moments intervened,
When Wisdom, like the Goddess° from Jove's brain,   *Athena*
Broke forth in armour of resplendent words,
540   Startling the Synod.° Could a youth, and one   *Parliament*
In ancient story versed, whose breast had heaved
Under the weight of classic eloquence,
Sit, see, and hear, unthankful, uninspired?

---

from Book Eleventh. Imagination, How Impaired and Restored

[IMAGINATION RESTORED BY NATURE]

Long time hath Man's unhappiness and guilt
Detain'd us; with what dismal sights beset
For the outward view, and inwardly oppress'd
With sorrow, disappointment, vexing thoughts,
5   Confusion of the judgement, zeal decay'd
And lastly, utter loss of hope itself,
And things to hope for. Not with these began
Our Song; and not with these our Song must end:
Ye motions of delight that through the fields
10   Stir gently, breezes and soft airs that breathe
The breath of paradise, and find your way
To the recesses of the soul! Ye Brooks
Muttering along the stones, a busy noise
By day, a quiet one in silent night,
15   And you, Ye Groves, whose ministry it is
To interpose the covert of your shades,
Even as a sleep, betwixt the heart of man
And the uneasy world, 'twixt man himself,
Not seldom, and his own unquiet heart,
20   Oh! that I had a music and a voice,
Harmonious as your own, that I might tell

---

2. The wind god Aeolus kept the winds chained in a cave.

What ye have done for me. The morning shines,
Nor heedeth Man's perverseness; Spring returns,
I saw the Spring return when I was dead
25 To deeper hope, yet had I joy for her,
And welcomed her benevolence, rejoiced
In common with the Children of her Love,
Plants, insects, beast in field, and bird in bower.
So neither were complacency° nor peace   *satisfaction*
30 Nor tender yearnings wanting° for my good   *lacking*
Through those distracted times; in Nature still
Glorying, I found a counterpoise in her,
Which, when the spirit of evil was at height
Maintain'd for me a secret happiness;
35 Her I resorted to, and lov'd so much
I seem'd to love as much as heretofore;
And yet this passion, fervent as it was,
Had suffer'd change; how could there fail to be
Some change, if merely hence, that years of life
40 Were going on, and with them loss or gain
Inevitable, sure alternative.
     This History, my Friend, hath chiefly told
Of intellectual° power, from stage to stage   *mental and spiritual*
Advancing, hand in hand with love and joy,
45 And of imagination teaching truth
Until that natural graciousness of mind
Gave way to over-pressure of the times
And their disastrous issues. What avail'd,
When Spells forbade the Voyager to land,
50 The fragrance which did ever and anon
Give notice° of the Shore, from arbours breathed   *reports*
Of blessed sentiment and fearless love?
What did such sweet remembrances avail,
Perfidious then, as seem'd, what serv'd they then?
55 My business was upon the barren seas,
My errand was to sail to other coasts:
Shall I avow that I had hope to see,
I mean that future times would surely see
The man to come parted as by a gulph
60 From him who had been, that I could no more
Trust the elevation which had made me one
With the great Family that here and there
Is scatter'd through the abyss of ages past,
Sage, Patriot, Lover, Hero; for it seem'd
65 That their best virtues were not free from taint
Of something false and weak which could not stand
The open eye of Reason. Then I said,
Go to the Poets; they will speak to thee
More perfectly of purer creatures, yet
70 If Reason be nobility in man
Can aught be more ignoble than the man
Whom they describe, would fasten if they may

Upon our love by sympathies of truth.
　　Thus strangely did I war against myself.

["SPOTS OF TIME." TWO MEMORIES FROM CHILDHOOD AND LATER REFLECTIONS] [1]

In truth, this degradation, howsoe'er
Induced, effect in whatsoe'er degree
245　Of custom, that prepares such wantonness
As makes the greatest things give way to least,
Of any other cause which hath been named,
Or, lastly, aggravated by the times,
Which with their passionate sounds might often make
250　The milder minstrelsies of rural scenes
Inaudible, was transient; I had felt
Too forcibly, too early in my life
Visitings of imaginative power,
For this to last: I shook the habit off
255　Entirely and for ever, and again
In Nature's presence stood, as I stand now,
A sensitive and a creative Soul.
　　There are in our existence spots of time,
Which with distinct preeminence retain
260　A renovating Virtue,° whence, depress'd　　　　　　　　power
By false opinion and contentious thought,
Or aught of heavier or more deadly weight
In trivial occupations, and the round
Of ordinary intercourse, our minds
265　Are nourish'd, and invisibly repair'd,
A virtue by which pleasure is enhanced
That penetrates, enables us to mount
When high, more high, and lifts us up when fallen.
This efficacious spirit chiefly lurks
270　Among those passages of life in which
We have had deepest feeling that the mind
Is lord and master, and that outward sense
Is but the obedient servant of her will.
Such moments, worthy of all gratitude,
275　Are scatter'd every where, taking their date
From our first childhood; in our childhood even
Perhaps are most conspicuous. Life with me
As far as memory can look back, is full
Of this beneficent influence. At a time
280　When scarcely (I was then not six years old)
My hand could hold a bridle, with proud hopes
I mounted, and we rode towards the hills:
We were a pair of Horsemen; honest James [2]

---

1. This sequence, which concludes Book 11, was drafted in 1799. Originally placed early in Book 1 of the *Two-Part Prelude*, the discussion of "spots of time" explores the way memories can have a restorative power on the imagination. By transferring these early memories to this late point in his autobiography, Wordsworth empowers them to enact what they describe—the revivification of poetic powers through recollection.
2. Later identified as "an ancient servant of my father's house."

285 Was with me, my encourager and guide.
     We had not travell'd long ere some mischance
     Disjoin'd me from my Comrade, and through fear
     Dismounting, down the rough and stony Moor
     I led my Horse, and, stumbling on, at length
     Came to a bottom,° where in former times   *dell*
290 A Murderer had been hung in iron chains.
     The Gibbet mast was moulder'd down, the bones
     And iron case were gone; but on the turf
     Hard by, soon after that fell deed was wrought
     Some unknown hand had carved the Murderer's name.
295 The monumental writing was engraven
     In times long past, and still, from year to year,
     By superstition of the neighbourhood
     The grass is clear'd away; and to this hour
     The letters are all fresh and visible.
300 Faltering, and ignorant where I was, at length
     I chanced to espy those characters inscribed
     On the green sod: forthwith I left the spot
     And, reascending the bare Common,° saw   *field*
     A naked Pool that lay beneath the hills,
305 The Beacon on the summit, and more near
     A Girl who bore a Pitcher on her head
     And seem'd with difficult steps to force her way
     Against the blowing wind. It was, in truth,
     An ordinary sight; but I should need
310 Colours and words that are unknown to man
     To paint the visionary dreariness
     Which, while I look'd all round for my lost Guide,
     Did at that time invest the naked Pool,
     The Beacon on the lonely Eminence,
315 The Woman, and her garments vex'd and toss'd
     By the strong wind. When in a blessed season
     With those two dear Ones,[3] to my heart so dear,
     When in the blessed time of early love,
     Long afterwards, I roam'd about
320 In daily presence of this very scene;
     Upon the naked pool and dreary crags,
     And on the melancholy Beacon, fell
     The spirit of pleasure, and youth's golden gleam;
     And think ye not with radiance more divine
325 From these remembrances, and from the power
     They left behind? So feeling comes in aid
     Of feeling, and diversity of strength
     Attends us, if but once we have been strong.
     Oh! mystery of Man, from what a depth
330 Proceed thy honours! I am lost, but see
     In simple childhood something of the base
     On which thy greatness stands, but this I feel,

---

3. His sister and Mary Hutchinson, whom he would marry in 1802.

That from thyself it is that thou must give,
Else never canst receive. The days gone by
335   Come back upon me from the dawn almost
Of life: the hiding-places of my power
Seem open; I approach, and then they close;[4]
I see by glimpses now; when age comes on
May scarcely see at all, and I would give,
340   While yet we may, as far as words can give,
A substance and a life to what I feel:
I would enshrine the spirit of the past
For future restoration. Yet another
Of these to me affecting incidents
With which we will conclude.
345   One Christmas-time,
The day before the Holidays began,
Feverish, and tired, and restless, I went forth
Into the fields, impatient for the sight
Of those two Horses which should bear us home,
350   My Brothers and myself.[5] There was a Crag,
An Eminence, which from the meeting point
Of two high-ways ascending, overlook'd
At least a long half-mile of those two roads,
By each of which the expected Steeds might come,
355   The choice uncertain. Thither I repair'd,
Up to the highest summit: 'twas a day
Stormy, and rough and wild, and on the grass
I sate, half shelter'd by a naked wall:
Upon my right hand was a single sheep,
360   A whistling hawthorn on my left, and there
With those Companions at my side, I watch'd,
Straining my eyes intensely, as the mist
Gave intermitting prospect of the wood
And plain beneath. Ere I to School return'd
365   That dreary time, ere I had been ten days
A Dweller in my Father's House, he died
And I and my two Brothers, Orphans then,
Followed his Body to the Grave.[6] The event
With all the sorrow which it brought appear'd
370   A chastisement; and when I call'd to mind
That day so lately pass'd, when from the crag
I look'd in such anxiety of hope,
With trite reflections of morality,
Yet in the deepest passion, I bow'd low
375   To God, who thus corrected my desires;
And afterwards, the wind and sleety rain
And all the business of the elements,
The single sheep, and the one blasted tree,

4. In the 1850 text, this line became "I would approach them, but they close" (12.280).
5. December 1783; William and his two brothers were away from home at Hawkshead Grammar School.
6. Wordsworth's father died on 30 December 1783; his mother had died five years earlier.

And the bleak music of that old stone wall,
380 The noise of wood and water, and the mist
Which on the line of each of those two Roads
Advanced in such indisputable shapes,[7]
All these were spectacles and sounds to which
I often would repair, and thence would drink
385 As at a fountain: and I do not doubt
That in this later time, when storm and rain
Beat on my roof at midnight, or by day
When I am in the woods, unknown to me
The workings of my spirit thence are brought.
390   Thou wilt not languish here, O Friend! for whom
I travel in these dim uncertain ways;
Thou wilt assist me as a pilgrim gone
In quest of highest truth. Behold me then
Once more in Nature's presence, thus restored
395 Or otherwise, and strengthen'd once again
(With memory left of what had been escaped)
To habits of devoutest sympathy.

from Book Thirteenth. Conclusion

[CLIMBING MOUNT SNOWDON. MOONLIT VISTA. MEDITATION ON "MIND,"
"SELF," "IMAGINATION," "FEAR," AND "LOVE"]

In one of these excursions, travelling then
Through Wales, on foot, and with a youthful Friend,[1]
I left Bethkelet's huts at couching-time,°   *bedtime*
And westward took my way to see the sun
5 Rise from the top of Snowdon. Having reach'd
The Cottage at the Mountain's foot, we there
Rouz'd up the Shepherd, who by ancient right
Of office is the Stranger's usual Guide,
And after short refreshment sallied forth.
10 —It was a Summer's night, a close warm night,
Wan, dull and glaring,° with a dripping mist   *clammy*
Low-hung and thick that cover'd all the sky,
Half-threatening storm and rain: but on we went
Uncheck'd, being full of heart and having faith
15 In our tried Pilot. Little could we see,
Hemm'd round on every side with fog and damp,
And, after ordinary Traveller's chat
With our Conductor, silently we sunk
Each into commerce with his private thoughts:
20 Thus did we breast the ascent, and by myself
Was nothing either seen or heard the while
Which took me from my musings, save that once

---

7. An echo of Hamlet's cry to his father's ghost: "Thou
com'st in such a questionable shape / That I will speak to
thee" (*Hamlet* 1.4.43–44).
1. Robert Jones, the friend with whom Wordsworth had

toured Europe in 1790. During a walking tour of North
Wales in the summer of 1791, they climbed Mount
Snowdon, the highest peak in Wales, starting from the
village of Beddgelert, four miles away.

The Shepherd's Cur did to his own great joy
Unearth a hedge-hog in the mountain crags
25   Round which he made a barking turbulent.
This small adventure, (for even such it seem'd
In that wild place and at the dead of night)
Being over and forgotten, on we wound
In silence as before. With forehead bent
30   Earthward, as if in opposition set
Against an enemy, I panted up
With eager pace, and no less eager thoughts.
Thus might we wear perhaps an hour away,
Ascending at loose distance each from each,
35   And I, as chanced, the foremost of the Band,
When at my feet the ground appear'd to brighten,
And with a step or two seem'd brighter still,
Nor had I time to ask the cause of this,
For instantly a Light upon the turf
40   Fell like a flash: I look'd about, and lo!
The Moon stood naked in the Heavens, at height
Immense above my head, and on the shore
I found myself of a huge sea of mist,
Which meek and silent, rested at my feet:
45   A hundred hills their dusky backs upheaved
All over this still Ocean,[2] and beyond,
Far, far beyond, the vapours shot themselves,
In headlands, tongues, and promontory shapes
Into the Sea, the real Sea,° that seem'd   *the Irish Sea*
50   To dwindle and give up its majesty,
Usurp'd upon as far as sight could reach.
Meanwhile the Moon look'd down upon this shew
In single glory, and we stood, the mist
Touching our very feet: and from the shore
55   At distance not the third part of a mile
Was a blue chasm, a fracture in the vapour,
A deep and gloomy breathing-place thro' which
Mounted the roar of waters, torrents, streams
Innumerable, roaring with one voice.
60   The universal spectacle throughout
Was shaped for admiration and delight,
Grand in itself alone, but in that breach
Through which the homeless voice of waters rose,
That dark deep thorough-fare had Nature lodg'd
65   The Soul, the Imagination of the whole.
      A meditation rose in me that night
Upon the lonely Mountain when the scene
Had pass'd away, and it appear'd to me
The perfect image of a mighty Mind,
70   Of one that feeds upon infinity,

---

2. Echoing Milton's description of God's creation of land from the sea (*Paradise Lost* 7.285–877).

That is exalted by an underpresence,
The sense of God, or whatsoe'er is dim
Or vast in its own being; above all
One function of such mind had Nature there
75 Exhibited by putting forth, in midst
Of circumstance most awful° and sublime,   *awe-inspiring*
That domination which she oftentimes
Exerts upon the outward face of things,
So molds them and endues, abstracts, combines
80 Or by abrupt and unhabitual influence
Doth make one object so impress itself
Upon all others, and pervade them so
That even the grossest minds must see and hear
And cannot chuse but feel. The Power which these
85 Acknowledge when thus moved, which Nature thus
Thrusts forth upon the senses, is the express
Resemblance, in the fullness of its strength
Made visible, a genuine Counterpart
And Brother of the glorious faculty
90 Which higher minds bear with them as their own;
This is the very spirit in which they deal
With all the objects of the universe.
They from their native selves can send abroad
Like transformation, for themselves create
95 A like existence, and whene'er it is
Created for them catch it by an instinct;
Them the enduring and the transient both
Serve to exalt; they build up greatest things
From least suggestions; ever on the watch,
100 Willing to work and to be wrought upon,
They need not extraordinary calls
To rouze them, in a world of life they live
By sensible impressions not enthrall'd,
But quicken'd, rouz'd, and made thereby more fit
105 To hold communion with the invisible world.
Such minds are truly from the Deity;
For they are Powers; and hence the highest bliss
That can be known is theirs, the consciousness
Of whom they are habitually infused
110 Through every image, and through every thought,
And all impressions: hence religion, faith,
And endless occupation for the soul
Whether discursive or intuitive,
Hence sovereignty within and peace at will,
115 Emotion which best foresight need not fear,
Most worthy then of trust when most intense:
Hence chearfulness in every act of life,
Hence truth in moral judgements and delight
That fails not in the external universe.
120   Oh! who is he that hath his whole life long
Preserved, enlarged this freedom in himself!

For this alone is genuine Liberty.
Witness, ye Solitudes! where I received
My earliest visitations, careless then
125 Of what was given me, and which now I roam
A meditative, oft a suffering Man,
And yet, I trust, with undiminish'd powers,
Witness, whatever falls my better mind,
Revolving with the accidents of life,
130 May have sustain'd, that, howsoe'er misled,
I never, in the quest of right and wrong,
Did tamper with myself° from private aims;   *my conscience*
Nor was in any of my hopes the dupe
Of selfish passions; nor did wilfully
135 Yield ever to mean cares and low pursuits;
But rather did with jealousy° shrink back   *vigilance*
From every combination that might aid
The tendency, too potent in itself,
Of habit to enslave the mind, I mean
140 Oppress it by the laws of vulgar° sense,   *mere*
And substitute a universe of death,
The falsest of all worlds, in place of that
Which is divine and true. To fear and love,
To love, as first and chief, for there fear ends,
145 Be this ascribed; to early intercourse,
In presence of sublime and lovely Forms,
With the adverse principles of pain and joy,
Evil, as one° is rashly named by those   *i.e., pain*
Who know not what they say. From love, for here
150 Do we begin and end, all grandeur comes,
All truth and beauty, from pervading love,
That gone, we are as dust. Behold the fields
In balmy spring-time, full of rising flowers
And blissful Creatures: see that Pair, the Lamb
155 And the Lamb's Mother, and their tender ways
Shall touch thee to the heart: in some green bower
Rest, and be not alone, but have thou there
The One who is thy choice of all the world;
There linger, lull'd, and lost, and rapt away,
160 Be happy to thy fill: thou call'st this love,
And so it is; but there is higher love
Than this, a love that comes into the heart
With awe and a diffusive° sentiment;   *bountiful*
Thy love is human merely; this proceeds
165 More from the brooding Soul, and is divine.
    This love more intellectual° cannot be   *spiritual*
Without Imagination, which in truth
Is but another name for absolute strength
And clearest insight, amplitude of mind,
170 And reason in her most exalted mood.
This faculty hath been the moving soul
Of our long labour: we have traced the stream

From darkness, and the very place of birth
In its blind cavern, whence is faintly heard
175 The sound of waters, follow'd it to light
And open day, accompanied its course
Among the ways of Nature; afterwards
Lost sight of it, bewilder'd and engulph'd,
Then given it greeting, as it rose once more
180 With strength, reflecting in its solemn breast
The works of man and face of human life,
And lastly, from its progress have we drawn
The feeling of life endless, the one thought
By which we live, Infinity and God.
185 Imagination having been our theme,
So also hath that intellectual love,
For they are each in each, and cannot stand
Dividually.°—Here must thou be, O Man!   *separately*
Strength to thyself; no Helper hast thou here;
190 Here keepest thou thy individual state:
No other can divide with thee this work,
No secondary hand can intervene
To fashion this ability; 'tis thine,
The prime and vital principle is thine
195 In the recesses of thy nature, far
From any reach of outward fellowship,
Else 'tis not thine at all.—But joy to him,
O joy to him who here hath sown, hath laid
Here the foundations of his future years!
200 For all that friendship, all that love can do,
All that a darling countenance can look
Or dear voice utter to complete the man,
Perfect him, made imperfect in himself,
All shall be his: and he whose soul hath risen
205 Up to the height of feeling intellect
Shall want no humbler tenderness, his heart
Be tender as a nursing Mother's heart,
Of female softness shall his life be full,
Of little loves and delicate desires,
210 Mild interests and gentlest sympathies.

[CONCLUDING RETROSPECT AND PROPHECY]

Having now
Told what best merits mention, further pains
Our present labour seems not to require
370 And I have other tasks. Call back to mind
The mood in which this Poem was begun,
O Friend! the termination of my course
Is nearer now, much nearer; yet even then
In that distraction and intense desire
375 I said unto the life which I had lived,
Where art thou? Hear I not a voice from thee

Which 'tis reproach to hear?[3] Anon I rose
As if on wings, and saw beneath me stretch'd
Vast prospect of the world which I had been
380 And was; and hence this Song which like a lark
I have protracted, in the unwearied Heavens
Singing, and often with more plaintive voice
Attemper'd to the sorrows of the earth;
Yet centring all in love, and in the end
385 All gratulant° if rightly understood.   *expressing joy*
    Whether to me shall be allotted life,
And with life power to accomplish aught of worth
Sufficient to excuse me in men's sight
For having given this Record of myself
390 Is all uncertain: but, beloved Friend,
When, looking back, thou seest in clearer view
Than any sweetest sight of yesterday
That summer when on Quantock's grassy Hills[4]
Far ranging, and among the sylvan Coombs°   *small valleys*
395 Thou in delicious words with happy heart
Didst speak the Vision of that Ancient Man,
The bright-eyed Mariner, and rueful woes
Didst utter of the Lady Christabel
And I, associate in such labour, walk'd
400 Murmuring of him who, joyous hap! was found,
After the perils of his moonlight ride
Near the loud Waterfall; or her who sate
In misery near the miserable Thorn;[5]
When thou dost to that summer turn thy thoughts,
405 And hast before thee all which then we were,
To thee, in memory of that happiness
It will be known, by thee at least, my Friend,
Felt, that the history of a Poet's mind
Is labour not unworthy of regard.
410 To thee the work shall justify itself.
    The last, and later portions of this Gift
Which I for Thee design have been prepared
In times which have from those wherein we first
Together wanton'd in wild Poesy,
415 Differ'd thus far, that they have been, O Friend,
Times of much sorrow, of a private grief
Keen and enduring,[6] which the frame of mind
That in this meditative History
Hath been described, more deeply makes me feel;
420 Yet likewise hath enabled me to bear
More firmly; and a comfort now, a hope,
One of the dearest which this life can give,

3. Recalling Coleridge's urging that he should undertake a major philosophical epic, Book 1.625–72.
4. The Wordsworths lived near Coleridge in the Quantock Hills above Alfoxden, in Somerset, from 1797–1798.

5. Referring to the lyrical ballads Wordsworth wrote at that time, and to Coleridge's *Rime of the Ancyent Mariner* and *Christabel.*
6. Wordsworth's younger brother John drowned on a shipwreck on 5 February 1805.

Is mine; that Thou art near and wilt be soon
Restored to us in renovated health:[7]
425 When, after the first mingling of our tears,
'Mong other consolations we may find
Some pleasure from this Offering of my love.
     Oh! yet a few short years of useful life,
And all will be complete, thy race be run,
430 Thy monument of glory will be raised;
Then, though, too weak to tread the ways of truth,
This Age fall back to old idolatry,
Though men return to servitude as fast
As the tide ebbs, to ignominy and shame
435 By Nations° sink together, we shall still   *nation by nation*
Find solace in the knowledge which we have,
Bless'd with true happiness if we may be
United helpers forward of a day
Of firmer trust, joint-labourers in the work,
440 (Should Providence such grace to us vouchsafe)
Of their redemption, surely yet to come.
Prophets of Nature, we to them will speak
A lasting inspiration, sanctified
By reason and by truth: what we have loved
445 Others will love; and we may teach them how,
Instruct them how the mind of man becomes
A thousand times more beautiful than the earth
On which he dwells, above this Frame of things
(Which 'mid all revolutions in the hopes
450 And fears of men doth still remain unchanged)
In beauty exalted, as it is itself
Of substance and of fabric more divine.

I wandered lonely as a cloud[1]

I wandered lonely as a cloud
That floats on high o'er vales and hills,
When all at once I saw a crowd,
A host, of golden daffodils;
5 Beside the lake, beneath the trees,
Fluttering and dancing in the breeze.

Continuous as the stars that shine
And twinkle on the milky way,
They stretched in never-ending line
10 Along the margin of a bay:
Ten thousand saw I at a glance,
Tossing their heads in sprightly dance.

The waves beside them danced; but they
Outdid the sparkling waves in glee:—

---

7. Coleridge had gone to the Mediterranean island of Malta for his health.

1. Compare Dorothy Wordsworth's *Grasmere Journal*, 15 April 1802, page 1627.

15   A Poet could not but be gay,
        In such a jocund company:
        I gazed—and gazed—but little thought
        What wealth the show to me had brought:

        For oft when on my couch I lie
20   In vacant or in pensive mood,
        They flash upon that inward eye
        Which is the bliss of solitude;[2]
        And then my heart with pleasure fills,
        And dances with the daffodils.

1804/1815   1807/1815

My heart leaps up

        My heart leaps up when I behold
          A Rainbow in the sky:
        So was it when my life began;
        So is it now I am a Man;
5   So be it when I shall grow old,
          Or let me die!
        The Child is Father of the Man;
        And I could wish my days to be
        Bound each to each by natural piety.

1802   1807

Ode: Intimations of Immortality[1]

In a letter from 1814, Wordsworth remarks, "The poem rests entirely on two recollections of childhood, one that of a splendour in the objects of sense which is passed away, and the other an indisposition to bend to the law of death as applying to our particular case. A Reader who has not a vivid recollection of these feelings having existed in his mind cannot understand that Poem." In 1843 he recalled, "Two years at least passed between the writing of the four first stanzas and the remaining part. To the attentive and competent reader the whole sufficiently explains itself; but there may be no harm in adverting here to particular feelings or *experiences* of my own mind on which the structure of the poem partly rests. Nothing was more difficult for me in childhood than to admit the notion of death as a state applicable to my own being. I have said elsewhere—

        A simple child,
     That lightly draws its breath,
     And feels its life in every limb,
     What should it know of death!— [*We Are Seven*, 1–4]

But it was not so much from feelings of animal vivacity that *my* difficulty came as from a sense of the indomitableness of the Spirit within me. I used to brood over the stories of Enoch and Elijah, and almost to persuade myself that, whatever might become of others, I should be translated, in something of the same way, to heaven.[2] With a feeling congenial to this, I was often unable to think of external things as having external existence, and I communed with all that I saw as something not apart from, but inherent in, my own immaterial nature. Many times while going to school have I grasped at a wall or tree to recall myself from this abyss of idealism

---

2. Lines 21–22 were composed by Wordsworth's wife. He thought them the "two best lines," though Coleridge called them "mental bombast."
1. A version published in 1807 was titled simply *Ode*, with an epigraph from Virgil's *Fourth* (*Messianic*) *Eclogue*: *Paulò majora canamus* (Let us sing of somewhat higher

things). The long title and epigraph from *My heart leaps up* were added in 1815, and the Latin phrase was dropped.
2. Old Testament prophets: Enoch did not die, but was taken directly to heaven (Genesis 5.24) and Elijah was carried to heaven in a chariot of fire (2 Kings 2.11).

to the reality. At that time I was afraid of such processes. In later periods of life I have deplored, as we have all reason to do, a subjugation of an opposite character, and have rejoiced over the remembrances, as is expressed in the lines—

> Obstinate questionings
> Of sense and outward things,
> Fallings from us, vanishings; etc. [141–43]

To that dream-like vividness and splendour which invest objects of sight in childhood, every one, I believe, if he would look back, could bear testimony, and I need not dwell upon it here: but having in the poem regarded it as presumptive evidence of a prior state of existence, I think it right to protest against a conclusion, which has given pain to some good and pious persons, that I meant to inculcate such a belief. It is far too shadowy a notion to be recommended to faith, as more than an element in our instincts of immortality. But let us bear in mind that, though the idea is not advanced in revelation, there is nothing there to contradict it, and the fall of Man presents an analogy in its favour. Accordingly, a pre-existent state has entered into the popular creeds of many nations; and, among all persons acquainted with classic literature, is known as an ingredient in Platonic philosophy. Archimedes said that he could move the world if he had a point whereon to rest his machine. Who has not felt the same aspirations as regards the world of his own mind? Having to wield some of its elements when I was impelled to write this poem on the 'Immortality of the Soul,' I took hold of the notion of pre-existence as having sufficient foundation in humanity for authorising me to make for my purpose the best use of it I could as a Poet." [I. F.]

Ode
Intimations of Immortality from Recollections of Early Childhood

> The Child is Father of the Man;
> And I could wish my days to be
> Bound each to each by natural piety.

1

There was a time when meadow, grove, and stream,
The earth, and every common sight,
    To me did seem
    Apparelled in celestial light,
5   The glory and the freshness of a dream.
It is not now as it hath been of yore;—
    Turn wheresoe'er I may,
      By night or day,
The things which I have seen I now can see no more.

2

10   The Rainbow comes and goes,
    And lovely is the Rose,
    The Moon doth with delight
Look round her when the heavens are bare,
    Waters on a starry night
15   Are beautiful and fair;
    The sunshine is a glorious birth;
    But yet I know, where'er I go,
That there hath past away a glory from the earth.

3

Now, while the birds thus sing a joyous song,
20   And while the young lambs bound

As to the tabor's° sound,   *small drum*
To me alone there came a thought of grief:
A timely utterance gave that thought relief,
    And I again am strong:
25   The cataracts blow their trumpets from the steep;
No more shall grief of mine the season wrong;
I hear the Echoes through the mountains throng,
The Winds come to me from the fields of sleep,
    And all the earth is gay;
30   Land and sea
    Give themselves up to jollity,
    And with the heart of May
Doth every Beast keep holiday;—
    Thou Child of Joy,
35   Shout round me, let me hear thy shouts, thou happy Shepherd-boy!

4

Ye blessèd Creatures, I have heard the call
    Ye to each other make; I see
The heavens laugh with you in your jubilee;
    My heart is at your festival,
40   My head hath its coronal,°   *flower wreath*
The fulness of your bliss, I feel—I feel it all.
    Oh evil day! if I were sullen
    While Earth herself is adorning,
        This sweet May-morning,
45   And the Children are culling
        On every side,
    In a thousand valleys far and wide,
    Fresh flowers; while the sun shines warm,
And the Babe leaps up on his Mother's arm:—
50   I hear, I hear, with joy I hear!
    —But there's a Tree, of many, one,
A single Field which I have looked upon,
Both of them speak of something that is gone:
    The Pansy³ at my feet
55   Doth the same tale repeat:
Whither is fled the visionary gleam?
Where is it now, the glory and the dream?⁴

5

Our birth is but a sleep and a forgetting:
The Soul that rises with us, our life's Star,°   *the sun*
60   Hath had elsewhere its setting,
        And cometh from afar:
    Not in entire forgetfulness,
    And not in utter nakedness,
But trailing clouds of glory do we come⁵
65   From God, who is our home:
Heaven lies about us in our infancy!

---

3. From the French *pensée*, "thought," this flower is its emblem.

4. A sounding of the "Ubi sunt" trope of elegiac literary tradition. In 1802, Wordsworth stopped writing the ode

at this point and did not resume for two years.

5. Revising a famous line in Thomas Gray's *Elegy Written in a Country Churchyard* (1751): "The paths of glory lead but to the grave."

Shades of the prison-house begin to close
    Upon the growing Boy,
But He beholds the light, and whence it flows,
70   He sees it in his joy;
The Youth, who daily farther from the east
    Must travel, still is Nature's Priest,
    And by the vision splendid
    Is on his way attended;
75 At length the Man perceives it die away,
And fade into the light of common day.

6

Earth fills her lap with pleasures of her own;
Yearnings she hath in her own natural kind,
And, even with something of a Mother's mind,
80   And no unworthy aim,
    The homely° Nurse doth all she can   *simple*
To make her Foster-child, her Inmate° Man,   *resident*
    Forget the glories he hath known,
And that imperial palace whence he came.

7

85 Behold the Child among his new-born blisses,
A six years' Darling of a pigmy size!
See, where 'mid work of his own hand he lies,
Fretted by sallies of his mother's kisses,
With light upon him from his father's eyes!
90 See, at his feet, some little plan or chart,
Some fragment from his dream of human life,
Shaped by himself with newly-learned art;
    A wedding or a festival,
    A mourning or a funeral;
95   And this hath now his heart,
    And unto this he frames his song:
      Then will he fit his tongue
To dialogues of business, love, or strife;
    But it will not be long
100   Ere this be thrown aside,
    And with new joy and pride
The little Actor cons another part;
Filling from time to time his "humorous stage"[6]
With all the Persons, down to palsied Age,
105 That Life brings with her in her equipage;
    As if his whole vocation
    Were endless imitation.

8

Thou, whose exterior semblance doth belie
    Thy Soul's immensity;
110 Thou best Philosopher, who yet dost keep
Thy heritage, thou Eye among the blind,
That, deaf and silent, read'st the eternal deep,
Haunted for ever by the eternal mind,—

6. A phrase from the dedicatory sonnet for Samuel Daniel's *Musophilus* (1599), referring to the different character types of Renaissance drama, defined by their "humors" (natural temperaments).

Mighty Prophet! Seer blest!
115   On whom those truths do rest,
Which we are toiling all our lives to find,
In darkness lost, the darkness of the grave;
Thou, over whom thy Immortality
Broods like the Day, a Master o'er a Slave,
120   A Presence which is not to be put by;
Thou little Child, yet glorious in the might
Of heaven-born freedom on thy being's height,
Why with such earnest pains dost thou provoke
The years to bring the inevitable yoke,
125   Thus blindly with thy blessedness at strife?
Full soon thy Soul shall have her earthly freight,
And custom lie upon thee with a weight,
Heavy as frost, and deep almost as life!

                    9

            O joy! that in our embers
130   Is something that doth live,
            That Nature yet remembers
            What was so fugitive!
The thought of our past years in me doth breed
Perpetual benediction: not indeed
135   For that which is most worthy to be blest—
Delight and liberty, the simple creed
Of Childhood, whether busy or at rest,
With new-fledged hope still fluttering in his breast:—
            Not for these I raise
140   The song of thanks and praise;
        But for those obstinate questionings
        Of sense and outward things,
        Fallings from us, vanishings;
        Blank misgivings of a Creature
145   Moving about in worlds not realised,°   *seeming unreal*
High instincts before which our mortal nature
Did tremble like a guilty Thing surprised:
            But for those first affections,
            Those shadowy recollections,
150   Which, be they what they may,
Are yet the fountain light of all our day,
Are yet a master light of all our seeing;
        Uphold us, cherish, and have power to make
Our noisy years seem moments in the being
155   Of the eternal Silence: truths that wake,
            To perish never;
Which neither listlessness, nor mad endeavour,
            Nor Man nor Boy,
Nor all that is at enmity with joy,
160   Can utterly abolish or destroy!
            Hence in a season of calm weather
            Though inland far we be,
Our Souls have sight of that immortal sea
            Which brought us hither,

165   Can in a moment travel thither,
And see the Children sport upon the shore,
And hear the mighty waters rolling evermore.

10

Then sing, ye Birds, sing, sing a joyous song!
   And let the young Lambs bound
170   As to the tabor's sound!
We in thought will join your throng,
   Ye that pipe and ye that play,
   Ye that through your hearts to-day
   Feel the gladness of the May!
175 What though the radiance which was once so bright
Be now for ever taken from my sight,
   Though nothing can bring back the hour
Of splendour in the grass, of glory in the flower;
   We will grieve not, rather find
180   Strength in what remains behind;
   In the primal sympathy
   Which having been must ever be;
   In the soothing thoughts that spring
   Out of human suffering;
185   In the faith that looks through death,
In years that bring the philosophic mind.

11

And O, ye Fountains, Meadows, Hills, and Groves,
Forebode not any severing of our loves!
Yet in my heart of hearts I feel your might;
190 I only have relinquished one delight
To live beneath your more habitual sway.
I love the Brooks which down their channels fret,
Even more than when I tripped lightly as they;
The innocent brightness of a new-born Day
195   Is lovely yet;
The Clouds that gather round the setting sun
Do take a sober colouring from an eye
That hath kept watch o'er man's mortality;
Another race hath been, and other palms° are won.   *prizes*
200 Thanks to the human heart by which we live,
Thanks to its tenderness, its joys, and fears,
To me the meanest° flower that blows can give   *humblest*
Thoughts that do often lie too deep for tears.

1802–1804/1815   1807/1815

The Solitary Reaper[1]

Behold her, single in the field,
Yon solitary Highland Lass!
Reaping and singing by herself;

---

1. Suggested by Wordsworth's reading in manuscript of "a beautiful sentence" in Thomas Wilkinson's *Tours to the British Mountains* (1824): "Passed a female who was reaping alone: she sung in Erse [Scottish Gaelic] as she bended over her sickle; the sweetest human voice I ever heard: her strains were tenderly melancholy, and felt delicious, long after they were heard no more."

Stop here, or gently pass!
5 Alone she cuts, and binds the grain,
And sings a melancholy strain;
O listen! for the Vale profound
Is overflowing with the sound.

No Nightingale did ever chaunt
10 More welcome notes to weary bands
Of Travellers in some shady haunt,
Among Arabian Sands:
No sweeter voice was ever heard[2]
In spring-time from the Cuckoo-bird,
15 Breaking the silence of the seas
Among the farthest Hebrides.°   *Scottish islands*

Will no one tell me what she sings?—
Perhaps the plaintive numbers flow
For old, unhappy, far-off things,
20 And battles long ago:
Or is it some more humble lay,
Familiar matter of today?
Some natural sorrow, loss, or pain,
That has been, and may be again!

25 Whate'er the theme, the Maiden sang
As if her song could have no ending;
I saw her singing at her work,
And o'er the sickle bending;—
I listen'd till I had my fill.[3]
30 And, as I mounted up the hill,
The music in my heart I bore,
Long after it was heard no more.

1805   1807

Surprized by joy

Surprized by joy—impatient as the Wind
I turned to share the transport—Oh! with whom
But thee, long buried in the silent Tomb,
That spot which no vicissitude can find?[1]
5 Love, faithful love, recalled thee to my mind—
But how could I forget thee? Through what power,
Even for the least division of an hour,
Have I been so beguiled as to be blind
To my most grievous loss!—That thought's return
10 Was the worst pang that sorrow ever bore,
Save one, one only, when I stood forlorn,
Knowing my heart's best treasure was no more;
That neither present time, nor years unborn
Could to my sight that heavenly face restore.

1812–1815   1815

---

2. In 1836 this line became "A voice so thrilling ne'er was heard."
3. In 1820 this became "I listened, motionless and still."

1. The Wordsworths' daughter Catherine, who died in 1812 at age 3.

Dorothy Wordsworth
1771–1855

Dorothy Wordsworth would probably be surprised at her presence in this anthology, for unlike just about everyone else in our pages, she did not think of herself primarily as a writer, and she did not aspire to publication. Her brother William Wordsworth did put a few of her poems in his volumes (including *Address to a Child* and *Floating Island*), specifying them as "By my Sister"—an apt credit, for this was Dorothy's own chief self-identification. When friends urged her to publish her remarkable account of her community's response to a local tragedy (*George and Sarah Green*, 1808), she protested that she had written it only at her brother's urging and only as a local record; "I should detest the idea of setting myself as an Author," she said. Similar encouragement for her journals of her tours of Scotland and Europe was similarly rebuffed, Dorothy insisting that she had written only for the amusement of family and friends. When she began her Grasmere journal, she told herself that she was writing to give William "pleasure."

Born in the Lake District of England in 1771, Dorothy Wordsworth lived happily there with her four brothers until 1778, when their mother died. Their father, who was often absent on business, felt unable to sustain the household and sent the boys away to school and Dorothy to live with a series of distant relatives, in situations ranging from happy to bleak. She saw her brothers rarely and especially missed William, with whom she was closest, less than two years his junior. As soon as they were reunited in 1787, they longed to have a home together, and in 1795, with the advantage of William's legacy from a college friend, they were able to realize this dream. They first lived in southwest England, in Dorset, as a quasi-family with a friend's young son as their ward. Moving to Alfoxden in 1797 to be near Samuel Taylor Coleridge, they became acquainted with Charles and Mary Lamb and Robert Southey. During their summer tour of the Wye valley in 1798, William wrote *Tintern Abbey* with its homage to Dorothy's companionship and her continuing inspiration to him. They spent the next winter miserably in Goslar, Germany (following Coleridge there on a scheme to learn the language); after they returned to England, they settled at the end of 1799 in Grasmere, in their beloved native Lake District, where they remained together for the rest of their lives.

Dorothy began her Grasmere journal in May 1800, just as William was beginning to court their childhood friend, Mary Hutchinson, and she left off at the beginning of 1803, a few months after Mary and William returned from their honeymoon. There was never any question about her remaining in the household: Mary married *them*. A beloved aunt to their children, Dorothy was really more a third parent. She not only shared the domestic labors but functioned for William as companion, encourager, sounding board, secretary, and (along with Mary) perpetual transcriber of his drafts into fair-copy. In 1829 she was stricken by the first in a series of devastating illnesses, with relapses and new afflictions occurring over the next six years, each event wracking her with pain and leaving her further debilitated. By 1835 it was clear that her temperament and mental acuity were also afflicted, a pre-senile dementia akin to Alzheimer's disease. Cared for with affection by her family, she lived a kind of invalid half-life, with lucid intervals, for the next twenty years, surviving her brother by five.

This demise is especially poignant, given the intelligence, sensitivity, and physical vitality with which she had impressed everyone. It was not until the end of the nineteenth century that her poems and journals were collected and published, and for a long time the journals were treated as subordinate documents, read chiefly for information about Coleridge, William, and the circumstances of the poems he wrote between 1798 and 1802. Placed alongside these poems, however, some of Dorothy's passages suggest that William may have been inspired as much by her language as by events and appearances in the external world; and recently,

Dorothy Wordsworth has come to light as a writer in her own right. Her Grasmere journal is a fascinating chronicle of early nineteenth-century life in the Lake District—full of brilliantly detailed descriptions of nature (admired by Virginia Woolf), accounts of domestic life and household labors, precise observations of the people, the social textures and economic distresses of rural England. In the cast of characters that cross her pages—children, neighbors, local laborers, tinkers and itinerants, beggars and vagrants, abandoned wives and mothers, a leech-gatherer, discharged and often injured soldiers, sailors, and veterans—Dorothy Wordsworth captures, as much as her brother hoped his poetry would, the "language really used by men" (and women). In addition to journals, records of tours, numerous letters, and ceaseless secretarial work and manuscript transcription for William, Dorothy wrote about thirty poems. Composed sporadically from 1805 to 1840, these often allude to or converse with her brother's poetry, sometimes marking different investments of imagination, giving alternative views of the world they share, or showing a different sensibility—one less solitary and more social in orientation, less visionary than domestic in idiom, and more self-effacing and self-discrediting in character, especially about the vocation and practice of writing poetry.

Address to a Child

During a boisterous Winter Evening in a high wind[1]

What way does the wind come? what way does he go?
He rides over the water and over the snow,
Through wood, and through vale; and o'er rocky height
Which the goat cannot climb takes his sounding flight.[2]
5   He tosses about in every bare tree,
As, if you look up you plainly may see
But how he will come, and whither he goes
There's never a Scholar in England knows.

He will suddenly stop in a cunning nook
10   And rings a sharp larum:°—but if you should look   *call to arms*
There's nothing to see but a cushion of snow,
Round as a pillow and whiter than milk
And softer than if it were cover'd with silk.

Sometimes he'll hide in the cave of a rock;
15   Then whistle as shrill as the buzzard cock;
—Yet seek him and what shall you find in his place
Nothing but silence and empty space
Save in a corner a heap of dry leaves
That he's left for a bed for beggars or thieves.

20   As soon as 'tis daylight tomorrow with me
You shall go to the orchard & then you will see
That he has been there, & made a great rout,°   *debacle*
And cracked the branches, & strew'd them about:
Heaven grant that he spare but that one upright twig

---

1. Written 1806 for nephew Johnny (see letter to Lady Beaumont, page 1630); in late 1805 she commented to Lady Beaumont: "what a fearful thing a windy night is now at our house! I am too often haunted with dreadful images of Shipwrecks and the Sea when I am in bed and hear a stormy wind"—evoking the loss of her beloved brother John in a shipwreck in 1805. Published unsigned in William's *Poems*, 1815; our text follows this version, with significant variants from the ms. ("An address to a Child in a high wind") indicated in footnotes.

2. In the manuscript, these lines read: "Through the valley, and over the hill / And roars as loud as a thundering Mill" (waterfall where a mill is located).

25   That look'd up at the sky so proud & so big
      All last summer, as well you know
      Studded with apples, a beautiful shew!

      Hark! over the roof he makes a pause
      And growls as if he would fix his claws
30   Right in the slates, and with a huge rattle
      Drive them down like men in a battle.
      —But let him range round; he does us no harm
      We build up the fire; we're snug and warm,
      Untouch'd by his breath see the candle shines bright,
35   And burns with a clear and steady light;
      Books have we to read,—hush! that half-stifled knell,
      Methinks 'tis the sound of the eight o'clock bell.[3]

      Come, now we'll to bed, and when we are there
      He may work his own will, & what shall we care.
40   He may knock at the door—we'll not let him in
      May drive at the windows—we'll laugh at his din
      Let him seek his own home wherever it be
      Here's a cozy warm house for Edward and me.[4]

1806   1815

Irregular Verses[1]

      Ah Julia! ask a Christmas rhyme
      Of *me* who in the golden time
      Of careless, hopeful, happy youth
      Ne'er strove to decorate the truth,
5   Contented to lay bare my heart
      To one dear Friend, who had her part
      In all the love and all the care
      And every joy that harboured there.
      —To her I told in simple prose
10   Each girlish vision, as it rose
      Before an active busy brain
      That needed neither spur nor rein,
      That still enjoyed the present hour
      Yet for the *future* raised a tower
15   Of bliss more exquisite and pure
      Bliss that (so deemed we) should endure
      Maxims of caution, prudent fears
      Vexed not the projects of those years
      Simplicity our steadfast theme,
20   No works of Art adorned our scheme.—
      A cottage in a verdant dell,

3. In the manuscript, lines 34–37 read: "Old Madam has brought us plenty of coals / And the Glazier has closed up all the holes / In every window that Johnny broke / And the walls are tighter than Molly's new cloak."
4. In the manuscript, the synonym *canny* is used instead of *cozy*; and Johnny's name was used (the pseudonym

protects his privacy).
1. Written in 1829 as Christmas-verses to her 20-year-old goddaughter, daughter of her childhood friend Jane Pollard, later Mrs. Marshall. Dorothy Wordsworth encouraged Julia Marshall's efforts to write poetry. "Irregular" means not metrically regular.

A foaming stream, a crystall Well,
A garden stored with fruit and flowers
And sunny seats and shady bowers,
25   A file of hives for humming bees
Under a row of stately trees
And, sheltering all this faery ground,
A belt of hills must wrap it round,
Not stern or mountainous, or bare,
30   Nor lacking herbs to scent the air;
Nor ancient trees, nor scattered rocks,
And pastured by the blameless flocks
That print their green tracks to invite
Our wanderings to the topmost height.

35   Such was the spot I fondly framed
When life was new, and hope untamed:[2]
There with my one dear Friend would dwell,
Nor wish for aught beyond the dell.
Alas! the cottage fled in air,
40   The streamlet never flowed:
—Yet did those visions pass away[3]
So gently that they seemed to stay,
Though in our riper years we each pursued a different way.

—We parted, sorrowful; by duty led;
45   My Friend, ere long a happy Wife
Was seen with dignity to tread
The paths of usefulness, in active life;
And such her course through later days;
The same her honour and her praise;
50   As thou canst witness, thou dear Maid,
One of the Darlings of her care;[4]
Thy *Mother* was that Friend who still repaid
Frank confidence with unshaken truth:
This was the glory of her youth,
55   A brighter gem than shines in prince's diadem.

You ask why in that jocund time
Why did I not in jingling rhyme
Display those pleasant guileless dreams
That furnished still exhaustless themes?
60   —I *reverenced* the Poet's skill,
And *might have* nursed a mounting Will
To imitate the tender Lays°   songs
Of them who sang in Nature's praise;
But bashfulness, a struggling shame
65   A fear that elder heads might blame
—Or something worse—a lurking pride
Whispering my playmates would deride

2. Cf. W. Wordsworth's, *Elegiac Stanzas* (1806): "Such, in the fond illusion of my heart, / Such Picture would I at that time have made" (29–30).
3. Cf. W. Wordsworth's *Poor Susan* (page 1543): "The stream will not flow, and the hill will not rise, / And the colours have all passed away from her eyes!" (15–16).
4. Jane Marshall bore eleven children.

Stifled ambition, checked the aim
If e'er by chance "the numbers came"[5]
70 —Nay even the mild maternal smile,
That oft-times would repress, beguile
The over-confidence of youth,
Even that dear smile, to own the truth,
Was dreaded by a fond self-love;
75 "'Twill glance on me—and to reprove
Or," (sorest wrong in childhood's school)
"Will *point* the sting of ridicule."[6]

And now, dear Girl, I hear you ask
Is this your lightsome, chearful task?
80 You tell us tales of forty years,
Of hopes extinct, of childish fears,
Why cast among us thoughts of sadness
When we are seeking mirth and gladness?[7]
Nay, ill those words befit the Maid
85 Who pleaded for my Christmas rhyme
Mirthful she is; but placid—staid—
Her heart beats to no giddy chime
Though it with Chearfulness keep time
For Chearfulness, a willing guest,
90 Finds ever in her tranquil breast
A fostering home, a welcome rest.
And well she knows that, casting *thought* away,
We lose the best part of our day;
That joys of youth remembered when our youth is past
95 Are joys that to the end of life will last;[8]

And if this poor memorial strain,
Breathed from the depth of years gone by,
Should touch her Mother's heart with tender pain,
Or call a tear into her loving eye,
100 She will not check the tear or still the rising sigh.
—The happiest heart is given to sadness;
The saddest heart feels deepest gladness.

Thou dost not ask, thou dost not need
A verse from me; nor wilt thou heed
105 A greeting masked in laboured rhyme
From one whose heart has still kept time
With every pulse of thine

1829

5. From Pope's *Epistle To Dr. Arbuthnot* (1735): "Why did I write? what sin to me unknown / Dipt me in Ink, my Parents', or my own? / As yet a Child, nor yet a Fool to Fame, / I lisp'd in Numbers, for the Numbers came" (125–128). Also involved are W. Wordsworth's recollection of his promise as a poet at the beginning of *The Prelude*: "To the open fields I told / A prophesy; poetic numbers came / Spontaneously, and clothed in priestly robe / My spirit, thus singled out, as it might seem, / For holy services" (1.59–63), itself alluding to Milton's claim to "feed on thoughts, that voluntary move / Harmonious numbers" (*Paradise Lost* 3.36–37), blessed by a "Celestial Patroness" who "inspires / Easy . . . unpremeditated Verse" (9.21–24).
6. An imaginary reproof; her mother died when she was seven, before the era of friendship with Jane recounted here.
7. Along with ll.101–102, compare to W. Wordsworth's *Resolution and Independence*: "We Poets in our youth begin in gladness; / But thereof come in the end despondency and madness" (48–49) and Shelley's similar sentiment in *To a Sky-Lark* (88–90), along with the same, probably allusive, rhyme (101–103).
8. A hope frequently voiced in W. Wordsworth's poetry, e.g., *Tintern Abbey*, 64–65: "in this moment there is life and food / For future years" (page 1531).

Thoughts on My Sick-bed[1]

And has the remnant of my life
Been pilfered of this sunny Spring?
And have its own prelusive sounds
Touched in my heart no echoing string?

5   Ah! say not so—the hidden life
Couchant° within this feeble frame   *lying down*
Hath been enriched by kindred gifts,
That, undesired, unsought-for, came

With joyful heart in youthful days
10   When fresh each season in its Round
I welcomed the earliest Celandine[2]
Glittering upon the mossy ground;

With busy eyes I pierced the lane
In quest of known and *un*known things,
15   —The primrose a lamp on its fortress rock,
The silent butterfly spreading its wings,

The violet betrayed by its noiseless breath,
The daffodil dancing in the breeze,
The carolling thrush, on his naked perch,
20   Towering above the budding trees.[3]

Our cottage-hearth no longer our home,
Companions of Nature were we,
The Stirring, the Still, the Loquacious, the Mute—
To all we gave our sympathy.

25   Yet never in those careless days
When spring-time in rock, field, or bower
Was but a fountain of earthly hope
A promise of fruits & the *splendid* flower.[4]

No! then I never felt a bliss
30   That might with *that* compare
Which, piercing to my couch of rest,
Came on the vernal air.

When loving Friends an offering brought,
The first flowers of the year,
35   Culled from the precincts of our home,
From nooks to Memory dear.[5]

---

1. Written in spring 1832, by which time Dorothy was being stricken with a series of debilitating illnesses.
2. A resilient flower, addressed by William in *The Small Celandine* (1804; 1807) as an emblem of inevitable old age.
3. A bouquet of loaded references to William's poems: *The Primrose of the Rock* (c. 1831, about a flower on the Grasmere-Rydal road); *To a Butterfly* ("Stay near me") and *To a Butterfly* ("I've watched you") (both 1802; 1807); *Song* ("*She dwelt among th'untrodden ways*") (page 1539: "a violet by a mossy stone, half hidden from the eye"); *I wandered lonely as a cloud* (page 1609: "golden daffodils . . . dancing in the breeze").
4. W. Wordsworth's "Intimations" *Ode* (page 1615): "Though nothing can bring back the hour / Of splendour in the grass, of glory in the flower; / We will grieve not, rather find / Strength in what remains behind" (177–80).
5. "Intimations" *Ode*: "The fulness of your bliss, I feel—I feel it all. / O evil day! if I were sullen / While Earth herself is adorning, / This sweet May-morning, / And the Children are culling / On every side, / In a thousand valleys far and wide, / Fresh flowers" (41–48); page 1612.

With some sad thoughts the work was done,[6]
Unprompted and unbidden,
But joy it brought to my *hidden* life,
40   To consciousness no longer hidden.

I felt a Power unfelt before,
Controlling weakness, languor, pain;
It bore me to the Terrace walk
I trod the Hills again;—

45   No prisoner in this lonely room,
I *saw* the green Banks of the Wye,
Recalling thy prophetic words,
Bard, Brother, Friend from infancy![7]

No need of motion, or of strength,[8]
50   Or even the breathing air:
—I thought of Nature's loveliest scenes;
And with Memory I was there.

1832

When Shall I Tread Your Garden Path?[1]

When shall I tread your garden path?
Or climb your sheltering hill?
When shall I wander, free as air,
And track the foaming rill?

5   A prisoner on my pillowed couch
Five years in feebleness I've lain,
Oh! shall I e'er with vigorous step
Travel the hills again?
                    To Mr Carter DW
                    Novr 11—1835

Lines Written (Rather Say *Begun*) on the Morning of Sunday April 6th
The Third Approach of Spring-Time Since My Illness Began.
It Was a Morning of Surpassing Beauty.

The worship of this sabbath morn,
How sweetly it begins!
With the full choral hymn of birds
Mingles no sad lament for sins.

5   The air is clear, the sunshine bright.
The dew-drops glitter on the trees;
My eye beholds a perfect Rest,
I hardly hear a stirring breeze.

A robe of quiet overspreads
10   The living lake and verdant field;

---

6. W. Wordsworth's *Lines Written in Early Spring* (page 1526: "I sate reclined, / In that sweet mood when pleasant thoughts / Bring sad thoughts to the mind") and *Three Years She Grew* (page 1540: "Thus nature spake— / The work was done— / How soon my Lucy's race was run! / She died").

7. See *Tintern Abbey* (pages 1530ff.), especially 111ff.
8. W. Wordsworth's *A slumber did my spirit seal* (page 1541: "No motion has she now, no force").
1. Addressed to John Carter, William's assistant in the stamp office and their handyman for more than 40 years.

The very earth seems sanctified,
Protected by a holy shield.

The steed, now vagrant on the hill,
Rejoices in this sacred day,
15 Forgetful of the plough—the goad—
And, though subdued, is happy as the gay.

A chastened call of bleating lambs
Drops steadily from that lofty Steep;
—I could believe this sabbath peace
20 Was felt even by the mother sheep.[1]

Conscious that they are safe from man
On this glad day of punctual rest,
By God himself—his work being done—
Pronounced the holiest and the best

25 'Tis but a fancy, a fond thought,
To which a waking dream gave birth,
Yet heavenly, in this brilliant Calm,
—Yea *heavenly* is the spirit of earth—

Nature attunes the pious heart
30 To gratitude and fervent love
By visible stillne[ss] the chearful voice
Of living things in budding trees & in the air above.

Fit prelude are these lingering hours
To man's appointed, holy task
35 Of prayer and social gratitude:
They prompt our hearts in faith to ask,

Ask humbly for the precious boon
Of pious hope and fixed content
And pardon, sought through trust in Him
40 Who died to save the Penitent.

And now the chapel bell invites
The Old, the Middle-aged, and Young
To meet beneath those sacred walls,
And give to pious thought a tongue

45 That simple bell of jingling tone
To careless ears unmusical,
Speaks to the Serious in a strain
That might their wisest hours recal.

Alas! my feet no more may join
50 The chearful sabbath train;
But if I inwardly lament
Soon may a will subdued all grief restrain.[2]

---

1. In another copy, Dorothy replaces all the subsequent
stanzas with this last one: "Thus have ye passed one glad-
some hour / But [earnest?] youth exhausts its power / The
weary limbs, the panting breast / The throbbing head /
Plead piteously for rest."
2. In yet another copy, Dorothy writes *resigned* instead of
subdued.

No prisoner am I on this couch
My mind is free to roam,
55   And leisure, peace, and loving Friends
Are the best treasures of an earthly home.

Such gifts are mine: then why deplore
The body's gentle slow decay,
A warning mercifully sent
60   To fix my hopes upon a surer stay?

from The Grasmere Journals
[HOME ALONE]

May 14 1800 [Wednesday]. Wm and John set off into Yorkshire[1] after dinner at 1/2
past 2 o'clock—cold pork in their pockets. I left them at the turning of the Low-
wood bay under the trees. My heart was so full that I could hardly speak to W when I
gave him a farewell kiss. I sate a long time upon a stone at the margin of the lake, &
after a flood of tears my heart was easier. The lake looked to me I knew not why dull
and melancholy, the weltering on the shores seemed a heavy sound. I walked as long
as I could amongst the stones of the shore. The wood rich in flowers. A beautiful yellow, palish yellow flower, that looked thick round & double, and smelt very sweet—
I supposed it was a ranunculus—Crowfoot, the grassy-leaved Rabbit-toothed white
flower, strawberries, Geranium—scentless violet, anemones two kinds, orchises,
primroses. The heckberry very beautiful. * * * Met a blind man, driving a very large
beautiful Bull & a cow—he walked with two sticks. Came home by Clappersgate.
The valley very green, many sweet views up to Rydale head when I could juggle away
the fine houses, but they disturbed me even more than when I have been happier—
one beautiful view of the Bridge, without Sir Michaels.[2] Sate down very often, tho' it
was cold. I resolved to write a journal of the time till W & J return, and I set about
keeping my resolve because I will not quarrel with myself, & because I shall give Wm
Pleasure by it when he comes home again. At Rydale a woman of the village, stout
& well dressed, begged a halfpenny—she had never she said done it before, but these
hard times—Arrived at home with a bad head-ach, set some slips of privett. The
evening cold had a fire—my face now flame-coloured. It is nine o'clock. I shall soon
go to bed. A young woman begged at the door—she had come from Manchester on
Sunday morn with two shillings & a slip of paper which she supposed a Bank note—
it was a cheat. She had buried her husband & three children within a year & a
half—all in one grave—burying very dear—paupers all put in one place—20
shillings paid for as much ground as will bury a man—a stone to be put over it or the
right will be lost—11/6 each time the ground is opened.[3] Oh! that I had a letter from
William!

Sunday [18th.] Went to church, slight showers, a cold air. The mountains from this
window look much greener & I think the valley is more green than ever. The corn

---

1. William and younger brother John, who lived with
them at Dove Cottage in 1800; the trip through Yorkshire was to visit childhood friend Mary Hutchinson,
whom William would marry in October 1802.
2. Rydal Hall, the home of Sir Michael le Fleming; in
1813, the Wordsworth household would move to Rydal

Mount, the substantial residence next door, where they
lived the rest of their lives.
3. Eleven shillings, 6 pence; dear: expensive. William and
Dorothy lived modestly but comfortably on £130–140 a
year.

begins to shew itself. The ashes are still bare. ✳ ✳ ✳ A little girl from Coniston came to beg. She had lain out all night—her step-mother had turned her out of doors.

[THE GRASMERE MAILMAN]

Monday Morning 8th February 1802. It was very windy & rained very hard all the morning. William worked at his poem & I read a little in Lessing and the Grammar.[4] A chaise came past to fetch Ellis the Carrier who had hurt his head. After dinner (i.e. we set off at about 1/2 past 4) we went towards Rydale[5] for letters. It was a cold *"Cauld Clash"*—the Rain had been so cold that it hardly melted the snow. We stopped at Park's to get some straw in William's shoes. The young mother was sitting by a bright wood fire with her youngest child upon her lap & the other two sate on each side of the chimney. The light of the fire made them a beautiful sight, with their innocent countenances, their rosy cheeks & glossy curling hair. We sate & talked about poor Ellis, and our journey over the Hawes. It had been reported that we came over in the night. Willy told us of 3 men who were once lost in crossing that way in the night, they had carried a lantern with them—the lantern went out at the Tarn[6] & they all perished. Willy had seen their cloaks drying at the public house in Patterdale[7] the day before their funeral. We walked on very wet through the clashy cold roads in bad spirits at the idea of having to go as far as Rydale, but before we had come again to the shore of the Lake, we met our patient, bow-bent Friend with his little wooden box at his Back. "Where are you going?" said he. "To Rydale for letters.—I have two for you in my Box." We lifted up the lid & there they lay. Poor Fellow, he straddled & pushed on with all his might but we soon outstripped him far away when we had turned back with our letters. We were very thankful that we had not to go on, for we should have been sadly tired. In thinking of this I could not help comparing lots with him! He goes at that slow pace every morning, & after having wrought a hard days work returns at night, however weary he may be, takes it all quietly, & though perhaps he neither feels thankfulness, nor pleasure when he eats his supper, & has no luxury to look forward to but falling asleep in bed, yet I daresay he neither murmurs nor thinks it hard. He seems mechanized to labour.

[A VISION OF THE MOON]

[18 March 1802] ✳ ✳ ✳ As we came along Ambleside vale in the twilight—it was a grave evening—there was something in the air that compelled me to serious thought—the hills were large, closed in by the sky. It was nearly dark ✳ ✳ ✳ night was come on & the moon was overcast. But as I climbed Moss the moon came out from behind a Mountain Mass of Black clouds—O the unutterable darkness of the sky & the Earth below the Moon! & the glorious brightness of the moon itself! There was a vivid sparkling streak of light at this end of Rydale water but the rest was very dark & Loughrigg fell and Silver How were white & bright as if they were covered with hoar frost.[8] The moon retired again & appeared & disappeared several times before I reached home. Once there was no moonlight to be seen but upon the Island house &

---

4. William's poem is *The Pedlar*, abandoned as an independent piece and later incorporated into the first part of Book 1 of his long poem, *The Excursion* (1814). Lessing (1729–1781) is a German dramatist, art theorist, and critic; "the Grammar" is most likely a German grammar (Dorothy had learned German in Germany).
5. About a mile away.

6. Mountain lake.
7. An inn in the village several miles away, reached by treacherous pass over the high mountains.
8. The places mentioned are White Moss Common, Rydale water (a lake nearby Grasmere Lake and the Common), and two peaks to the south of these lakes, Loughrigg and Silver How.

the promontory of the Island where it stands, "That needs must be a holy place" &c—&c.[9] I had many many exquisite feelings and when I saw this lowly Building in the waters among the dark & lofty hills, with that bright soft light upon it—it made me more than half a poet. I was tired when I reached home. I could not sit down to reading & tried to write verses but alas! I gave up expecting William & went soon to bed. Fletcher's carts came home late.[1]

[A FIELD OF DAFFODILS]

Thursday 15th. [*April 1802*] * * * When we were in the woods beyond Gowbarrow[2] park we saw a few daffodils close to the water side, we fancied that the lake had float-ed the seeds ashore & that the little colony had so sprung up—But as we went along there were more & yet more & at last under the boughs of the trees, we saw that there was a long belt of them along the shore, about the breadth of a country turn-pike road.[3] I never saw daffodils so beautiful they grew among the mossy stones about & about them, some rested their heads upon these stones as on a pillow for weariness & the rest tossed & reeled & danced & seemed as if they verily laughed with the wind that blew upon them over the Lake, they looked so gay ever glancing ever changing. This wind blew directly over the lake to them. There was here & there a little knot & a few stragglers a few yards higher up but they were so few as not to dis-turb the simplicity & unity & life of that one busy highway. We rested again & again. The Bays were stormy, & we heard the waves at different distances and in the middle of the water like the Sea.

[A BEGGAR WOMAN FROM COCKERMOUTH[4]]

Tuesday 4th May [*1802*]. William had slept pretty well & though he went to bed ner-vous & jaded in the extreme he rose refreshed. I wrote the Leech Gatherer[5] for him which he had begun the night before & of which he wrote several stanzas in bed this Monday morning. It was very hot, we called at Mr Simpson's door as we passed but did not go in. We rested several times by the way, read & repeated the Leech Gath-erer. We were almost melted before we were at the top of the hill. * * * William & I ate a Luncheon, then went on towards the Waterfall. It is a glorious wild solitude under that lofty purple crag. It stood upright by itself. Its own self and its shadow below, one mass—all else was sunshine. We went on further. A Bird at the top of the crags was flying round & round & looked in thinness & transparency, shape & motion, like a moth. We climbed the hill but looked in vain for a shade except at the foot of the great waterfall, & there we did not like to stay on account of the loose stones above our heads. We came down & rested upon a moss covered Rock, rising out of the bed of the River. There we lay ate our dinner & stayed there till about 4 o clock or later. Wm & C[6] repeated & read verses. I drank a little Brandy & water & was in Heaven. The Stags horn is very beautiful & fresh springing upon the fells. Mountain ashes, green. * * * On the Rays we met a woman with 2 little girls one in

9. Perhaps recalling an early draft of Coleridge's *Kubla Khan*, line 14 (see page 1657), or William's feeling in *Home at Grasmere* that "dwellers in this holy place / Must need themselves be hallow'd" (lines 366–67).
1. William's ride, via the mail carrier.
2. Several miles away in another part of the Lake district, near Patterdale on Ullswater.
3. Dorothy erased the next words, "the end we did not see." Cf. W. Wordsworth's poem, *I wandered lonely as a*

cloud (page 1609): "They stretched in never-ending line."
4. The town where Dorothy and her brothers were born and spent their childhood before the break-up of the household.
5. The early, working title for *Resolution and Independence*.
6. Coleridge, whom they met up with on their excursion.

her arms the other about 4 years old walking by her side, a pretty little thing, but half starved. She had on a pair of slippers that had belonged to some gentlemans child, down at the heels it was not easy to keep them on but, poor thing! young as she was, she walked carefully with them. Alas too young for such cares & such travels. The Mother when we accosted her told us that her husband had left her & gone off with another woman & how she "*pursued*" them. Then her fury kindled & her eyes rolled about. She changed again to tears. She was a Cockermouth woman 30 years of age—a child at Cockermouth when I was. I was moved & gave her a shilling—I believe 6^d more than I ought to have given.[7] We had the crescent moon with the "auld moon in her arms."[8] We rested often— always upon the Bridges. Reached home at about 10 o clock.

[THE CIRCUMSTANCES OF "COMPOSED UPON WESTMINISTER BRIDGE"[9]]

[*27 July 1802*] * * * After various troubles & disasters we left London on Saturday morning at 1/2 past 5 or 6. * * * we mounted the Dover Coach at Charing Cross. It was a beautiful morning. The City, St Pauls, with the River & a multitude of little Boats, made a most beautiful sight as we crossed Westminster Bridge. The houses were not overhung by their cloud of smoke & they were spread out endlessly, yet the sun shone so brightly with such a pure light that there was even something like the purity of one of nature's own grand Spectacles.

[THE CIRCUMSTANCES OF "IT IS A BEAUTEOUS EVENING"[1]]

[*1 August 1802*] * * * We walked by the sea-shore almost every Evening with Annette & Caroline or Wm & I alone.[2] * * * there was always light, & life, & joy upon the Sea.—One night, though, I shall never forget. The day had been very hot, & William & I walked alone together upon the pier—the sea was gloomy for there was a blackness over all the sky except when it was overspread with lightning which often revealed to us a distant vessel. Near us the waves roared & broke against the pier, & as they broke & as they travelled towards us, they were interfused with greenish fiery light. The more distant sea always black & gloomy. It was also beautiful on the calm hot night to see the little Boats row out of harbour with wings of fire & the sail boats with the fiery track which they cut as they went along & which closed up after them with a hundred thousand sparkles balls shootings, & streams of glowworm light. Caroline was delighted.

[THE HOUSEHOLD IN WINTER, WITH WILLIAM'S NEW WIFE. GINGERBREAD]

[*25 December 1802*] * * * It is today Christmas-day Saturday 25th December 1802. I am 31 years of age.—It is a dull frosty day. * * *

   Tuesday January 11th [*1803*] A very cold day. Wm promised me he would rise as soon as I had carried him his Breakfast but he lay in bed till between 12 & one. We

---

7. Six pence; Dorothy inserted "30 years of age—a child at Cockermouth when I was" to explain the generosity.
8. A line from *Sir Patrick Spence*, also quoted by Coleridge in his epigraph for *Dejection: An Ode*.
9. See page 1561; William and Dorothy are on their way to Calais, France, sailing from Dover, to settle affairs with Annette Vallon and her daughter by William, Caroline,

prior to William's marriage to Mary Hutchinson in October. The City is Westminster, a district of London where Parliament, Westminster Abbey, and Buckingham Palace are located; St. Paul's is the chief Anglican church. Westminster Bridge crosses the Thames river.
1. See William's sonnet, page 1562.
2. Without Annette, that is.

talked of walking, but the blackness of the Cold made us slow to put forward & we did not walk at all. Mary read the Prologue to Chaucer's tales to me, in the morning William was working at his poem to C.[3] Letter from Keswick & from Taylor on Wm's marriage. C poorly, in bad spirits. Canaries.[4] Before tea I sate 2 hours in the parlour—read part of The Knight's Tale with exquisite delight. Since Tea Mary has been down stairs copying out Italian poems for Stuart. Wm has been working beside me, & here ends this imperfect summary. I will take a nice Calais Book[5] *& will* for the future write regularly &, if I can legibly, so much for this my resolution on Tuesday night, January 11th 1803. Now I am going to take Tapioca for my supper, & Mary an Egg. William some cold mutton—his poor chest is tired.

Wednesday 12th. Very cold, & cold all the week.

Sunday the 16th. Intensely cold. Wm had a fancy for some ginger-bread I put on Molly's Cloak & my Spenser,[6] and we walked towards Matthew Newtons.[7] I went into the house. The blind Man & his Wife & Sister were sitting by the fire, all dressed very clean in their Sunday's Clothes, the sister reading. They took their little stock of gingerbread out of the cubboard & I bought 6 pennyworth. They were so grateful when I paid them for it that I could not find it in my heart to tell them we were going to make Gingerbread ourselves. I had asked them if they had no thick "No" answered Matthew "there was none on Friday but we'll *endeavour* to get some." The next Day the woman came just when we were baking & we bought 2 pennyworth.

LETTERS
To Jane Pollard[1]
[A SCHEME OF HAPPINESS]

16 Feb. 1793

* * * [William] is steady and sincere in his attachments, has both these Virtues in an eminent degree; and a sort of violence of Affection if I may so Term it which demonstrates itself every moment of the Day when the Objects of his affection are present with him, in a thousand almost imperceptible attentions to their wishes, in a sort of restless watchfulness which I know not how to describe, a Tenderness that never sleeps, and at the same Time such a Delicacy of Manners as I have observed in few Men. I hope you will one day be much better acquainted with him than you are at present, much as I have talked to you about him. I look forward with full confidence to the Happiness of receiving you in my little Parsonage,[2] I hope you will spend at least a year with me. I have laid the particular scheme of happiness for each Season. When I think of Winter I hasten to furnish our little Parlour, I close the Shutters, set out the Tea-table, brighten the Fire. When our Refreshment is ended I produce our Work, and William brings his book to our Table and contributes at once to our Instruction and amusement, and at Intervals we lay aside the Book and each hazard

---

3. *The Prelude,* known during William's lifetime as *Poem to Coleridge,* his addressee; *The Knight's Tale* is one of Chaucer's *Canterbury Tales.*
4. Canary Islands, where Coleridge was hoping to go for his health.
5. A blank notebook purchased in Calais; Dorothy did not continue her journal.
6. Heavy overcoat.

7. A gingerbread shop in Grasmere.
1. Jane Pollard (1771–1847), later Mrs. John Marshall, close childhood friend.
2. Dorothy imagines that she will keep house for William, who planned a career in the Church before receiving the bequest in 1795 that enabled him to attempt a career as a poet.

our observations upon what has been read without the fear of Ridicule or Censure. We talk over past days, we do not sigh for any Pleasures beyond our humble Habitation "The central point of all our joys."[3] Oh Jane! with such romantic dreams as these I amuse my fancy during many an hour which would otherwise pass heavily along, for kind as are my Uncle and Aunt,[4] much as I love my sweet little Cousins, I cannot help heaving many a Sigh at the Reflection that I have passed one and twenty years of my Life, and that the first six years only of this Time was spent in the Enjoyment of the same Pleasures that were enjoyed by my Brothers, and that I was then too young to be sensible of the Blessing. We have been endeared to each other by early misfortune. We in the same moment lost a father, a mother, a home, we have been equally deprived of our patrimony by the cruel Hand of lordly Tyranny.[5] These afflictions have all contributed to unite us closer by the Bonds of affection notwithstanding we have been compelled to spend our youth far asunder. "We drag at each remove a lengthening Chain"[6] this Idea often strikes me very forcibly. Neither absence nor Distance nor Time can ever break the Chain that links me to my Brothers. * * *

To Lady Beaumont

[HER POETRY, WILLIAM'S POETRY]

Grasmere. Saturday afternoon 4 o'clock. April 20th [1806]

* * * I am truly glad that my Brother's manuscript poems give you so much pleasure—I was sure that you would be deeply impressed by the Ode.[7] The last time I read it over, I said: "Lady Beaumont will like this." I long to know your opinion and Sir George's of Benjamin, the Waggoner;[8] I *think* you will be pleased with it, but cannot be so sure of this—And you would persuade *me* that I am capable of writing poems that might give pleasure to others besides my own particular friends!! indeed, indeed you do not know me thoroughly; you think far better of me than I deserve—I must tell you the history of those two little things which William in his fondness read to you.[9] I happened to be writing a letter one evening when he and my Sister were last at Park house, I laid down the pen and thinking of little Johnny (then in bed in the next room) I muttered a few lines of that address to him about the Wind, and having paper before me, wrote them down, and went on till I had finished. The other lines I wrote in the same way, and as William knows every thing that I do, I shewed them to him when he came home, and he was very much pleased; but this I attributed to his partiality; yet because they gave him pleasure and for the sake of the children I ventured to hope that I might do something more at some time or other. Do not think that I was ever bold enough to hope to compose verses for the pleasure of grown persons. Descriptions, Sentiments, or little stories for children was all I could be ambitious of doing, and I did try one story,[1] but failed so sadly that I was completely discouraged. Believe me, since I received your let-

---

3. Quoted from William's *Descriptive Sketches* (1793), l.571.
4. She had been living with her uncle William Cookson and his wife in Norfolk, in northeast England, since 1788.
5. Their mother died in 1778, their father in 1783; she had been separated from her brothers since 1778. Their inheritance was tied up in legal wrangling for several years, complicated by a debt owed by Lord Lowther, whose family did not settle it until 1803.
6. Oliver Goldsmith, *The Traveller, or A Prospect of Soci-*

ety (1755–1764): "Where'er I roam, whatever realms to see, / My heart untravelled fondly returns to thee; / Still to my brother turns with ceaseless pain, / And drags at each remove a lengthening chain" (7–10).
7. *Ode: Intimations of Immortality* (see page 1610), written 1802 and 1804, pub. as *Ode* in 1807.
8. Published 1819.
9 *An Address to a Child* (page 1618) and *To My Niece Dorothy, a Sleepless Baby.*
1. *Mary Jones and Her Pet Lamb.*

ter I have made several attempts (could I do less as you requested that I would *for your sake?*) and have been obliged to give it up in despair; and looking into my mind I find nothing there, even if I had the gift of language and numbers,[2] that I could have the vanity to suppose could be of any use beyond our own fireside, or to please, as in your case, a few partial friends; but I have no command of language, no power of expressing my ideas, and no one was ever more inapt at molding words into regular metre. I have often tried when I have been walking alone (muttering to myself as is my Brother's custom) to express my feelings in verse; feelings, and *ideas* such as they were, I have never wanted at those times; but prose and rhyme and blank verse were jumbled together and nothing ever came of it. As to those two little things which I did write, I was very unwilling to place them beside my Brother's poems, but he insisted upon it, and I was obliged to submit; and though you have been pleased with them I cannot but think that it was chiefly owing to the spirit which William gave them in the reading and to your kindness for me. I have said far more than enough on this subject * * *

Believe me affectionately yours, D. Wordsworth.

My Brother has a copy of my Journal of our Scotch Tour[3] which I have desired him to leave with you when it comes from the Bookbinders, but perhaps you may be too much engaged to find time to read it. My Sister begs her kind remembrances. Excuse blunders and scrawling and this torn paper. I have a very inconvenient desk to write upon * * *

To Mrs Thomas Clarkson[4]

[HOUSEHOLD LABORS]

Thursday Evening December 8 [1808]

* * * I will not attempt to detail the height and depth and number of our sorrows in connection with the smoky chimneys. They are in short so very bad that if they cannot be mended we must leave the house,[5] beautiful as everything will soon be out of doors, dear as is the vale where we have so long lived. The labour of the house is literally doubled. Dishes are washed, and no sooner set into the pantry than they are covered with smoke.—Chairs—carpets—the painted ledges of the rooms, all are ready for the reception of soot and smoke, requiring endless cleaning, and are never clean. This is not certainly the worst part of the business, but the smarting of the eyes etc. etc. you may guess at, and I speak of these other discomforts as more immediately connected with myself. In fact we have seldom an hour's leisure (either Mary or I) till after 7 o'clock (when the children go to bed), for all the time that we have for sitting still in the course of the day we are obliged to employ in scouring (and many of our evenings also). We are regularly thirteen in family, and on Saturdays and Sundays 15 (for when Saturday morning is not very stormy Hartley and Derwent[6] come). I include the servants in the number, but as you may judge, in the most convenient house there would be work enough for two maids and a little Girl. In ours there is far too much. We keep a cow—the stable is two short field lengths from the house, and the cook has both to fodder, and clean after the cow. We have also two pigs, bake all our bread at home and though we do not *wash all* our clothes, yet we wash a part

---

2. Metrical verse.
3. With William and Coleridge in late summer 1803.
4. Catherine Clarkson (1772–1856), wife of Thomas

Clarkson, the abolitionist.
5. New, more spacious family quarters in Grasmere.
6. Coleridge's sons, both at school nearby.

every week, and mangle or iron the whole. This is a tedious tale and I should not have troubled you with it but to let you see plainly that idleness has nothing to do with my putting off to write to you. * * * William and Mary (alas! all involved in smoke) in William's study, where she is writing for him (he dictating). He is engaged in a work which occupies all his thoughts. It will be a pamphlet of considerable length, entitled The Convention of Cintra brought to the Test of Principles and the People of England justified from the Charge of Prejudging, or something to that effect.[7] I believe it will first appear in the *Courier* in different sections. Mr De Quincey,[8] whom you would love dearly, as I am sure I do, is beside me, quietly turning over the leaves of a Greek book—and God be praised *we* are breathing a clear air, for the night is calm, and this room (the Dining-room) only smokes very much in a high wind. Mr De Q. will stay with us, we hope, at least till the Spring. We feel often as if he were one of the Family—he is loving, gentle, and happy—a very good scholar, and an acute Logician—so much for his mind and manners. His person is *unfortunately* diminutive, but there is a sweetness in his looks, especially about the eyes, which soon overcomes the oddness of your first feeling at the sight of so very little a Man. John[9] sleeps with him and is passionately fond of him. * * *

Believe me evermore your affectionate D. W.

To Mrs Thomas Clarkson
[A PROSPECT OF PUBLISHING]

Kendal,[1] Sunday 9 Dec. 1810

My dear Friend, * * * I cannot express what pain I feel in refusing to grant any request of yours, and above all one in which dear Mr Clarkson joins so earnestly, but indeed I cannot have that narrative[2] published. My reasons are entirely disconnected with myself, much as I should detest the idea of setting myself up as an Author. I should not object on that score as if it had been an invention of my own it might have been published without a name, and nobody would have thought of me. But on account of the Family of the Greens I cannot consent. Their story was only represented to the world in that narrative which was drawn up for the collecting of the subscription, so far as might tend to produce the end desired, but by publishing this narrative of mine I should bring the children forward to notice as Individuals, and we know not what injurious effect this might have upon them. Besides it appears to me that the events are too recent to be published in delicacy to others as well as to the children. I should be the more hurt at having to return such an answer to your request, if I could believe that the story would be of that service to the work which Mr Clarkson imagines. I cannot believe that it would do much for it. Thirty or forty years hence when the Characters of the children are formed and they can be no longer objects of curiosity,

---

7. William's pamphlet was one of many criticisms of the British agreement of August 1808, by which Napoleon's imperialist army, halted by Spanish resistance and British forces, was given safe passage home from Spain with their booty, in British ships. Many Britons sympathized with the "noble Spaniards."
8. Thomas De Quincey was helping William with the Cintra pamphlet.
9. Her nephew Johnny.
1. A town about 20 miles from Grasmere.
2. A *Narrative concerning George and Sarah Green of the*

Parish of Grasmere (1808). George and Sarah Green perished in a snowstorm, leaving behind six children. The *Narrative* was written to raise funds for the orphans beyond the minimal parish allotment; the hope was to place them with local families and secure them an education. The narrative circulated to several prominent people, including Scott, Southey, Baillie, DeQuincey, and several of the aristocracy. William did publish a poem on the death of George and Sarah, and De Quincey gave his version of the events some decades later in a magazine article and again in *Recollections of the Lakes*.

if it should be thought that any service would be done, it is my present wish that it should then be published whether I am alive or dead. * * *

> yours affectionately D. W.
> I am called to dinner.

To William Johnson[3]
[MOUNTAIN-CLIMBING WITH A WOMAN]

October 21st, 1818.

* * * we all dined together in the romantic Vale of Borrowdale, at the house of a female friend, an unmarried Lady, who, bewitched with the charms of the rocks, and streams, and mountains of that secluded spot, has there built herself a house, and though she is admirably fitted for society, and has as much enjoyment when surrounded by her friends as any one *can* have, her chearfulness has never flagged, though she has lived more than the year round alone in Borrowdale, at six miles distance from Keswick, with bad roads between.[4] You will guess that she has resources within herself; such indeed she has. She is a painter and labours hard in depicting the beauties of her favorite Vale; she is also found of music and of reading, and has a reflecting mind; besides (though before she lived in Borrowdale she was no great walker) she is become an active climber of the hills, and I must tell you of a feat that she and I performed on Wednesday the 7th of this month. * * * Miss Barker proposed that * * * she and I should go to Seathwaite beyond the Black lead mines at the head of Borrowdale, and thence up a mountain called at the top *Ash Course* * * * At the top of Ash Course Miss Barker had promised that I should see a magnificent prospect; but we had some miles to travel to the foot of the mountain, and accordingly went thither in a cart—Miss Barker, her maid, and myself. We departed before nine o'clock, the sun shone; the sky was clear and blue; and light and shade fell in masses upon the mountains; the fields below *glittered* with the dew, where the beams of the sun could reach them; and every little stream tumbling down the hills seemed to add to the chearfulness of the scene.

We left our cart at Seathwaite and proceeded, with a man to carry our provisions, and a kind neighbour of Miss Barker's, a statesman shepherd of the vale, as our companion and guide. We found ourselves at the top of Ash Course without a weary limb, having had the fresh air of autumn to help us up by its invigorating power, and the sweet warmth of the unclouded sun to tempt us to sit and rest by the way. From the top of Ash Course we beheld a prospect which would indeed have amply repaid us for a *toilsome* journey, if such it had been; and a sense of thankfulness for the continuance of that vigour of body, which enabled me to climb the high mountain, as in the days of my youth, inspiring me with fresh chearfulness, added a delight, a charm to the contemplation of the magnificent scenes before me, which I cannot describe.

* * * We had attained the object of our journey; but our ambition mounted higher. We saw the summit of Scaw Fell, as it seemed, very near to us; we were indeed, three parts up that mountain, and thither we determined to go. We found the distance greater than it had appeared to us, but our courage did not fail; however, when we came nearer we perceived that in order to attain that summit we must make a

---

3. Rev. William Johnson (1784–1864), schoolmaster in Grasmere and later London.

4. Borrowdale and Keswick are at opposite ends of Derwentwater in the Lake District.

great dip, and that the ascent afterwards would be exceedingly steep and difficult, so that we might have been benighted if we had attempted it; therefore, unwillingly, we gave it up, and resolved, instead, to ascend another point of the same mountain, called the Pikes, and which, I have since found, the measurers of the mountains estimate as higher than the larger summit which bears the name of Scaw Fell, and where the Stone Man is built which we, at the time, considered as the point of highest honour. The sun had never once been overshadowed by a cloud during the whole of our progress from the centre of Borrowdale; at the summit of the Pike there was not a breath of air to stir even the papers which we spread out containing our food. There we ate our dinner in summer warmth; and the stillness seemed to be not of this world. We paused, and kept silence to listen, and not a sound of any kind was to be heard. We were far above the reach of the cataracts of Scaw Fell; and not an insect was there to hum in the air. The Vales before described lay in view, and side by side with Eskdale, we now saw the sister Vale of Donnerdale terminated by the Duddon Sands. But the majesty of the mountains below and close to us, is not to be conceived. We now beheld the whole mass of Great Gavel from its base, the Den of Wasdale at our feet, the gulph immeasurable, Grasmere and the other mountains of Crummock, Ennerdale and its mountains, and the sea beyond.

While we were looking round after dinner our Guide said that we must not linger long, for we should have a storm. We looked in vain to espy the traces of it; for mountains, vales, and the sea were all touched with the clear light of the sun. "It is there," he said, pointing to the sea beyond Whitehaven, and, sure enough, we there perceived a light cloud, or mist, unnoticeable but by a shepherd, accustomed to watch all mountain bodings. We gazed around again and yet again, fearful to lose the remembrance of what lay before us in that lofty solitude; and then prepared to depart. Meanwhile the air changed to cold, and we saw the tiny vapour swelled into mighty masses of cloud which came boiling over the mountains. Great Gavel, Helvellyn, and Skiddaw were wrapped in storm; yet Langdale and the mountains in that quarter were all bright with sunshine. Soon the storm reached us; we sheltered under a crag, and almost as rapidly as it had come, it passed away, and left us free to observe the goings-on of storm and sunshine in other quarters—Langdale had now its share, and the Pikes were decorated by two splendid rainbows; Skiddaw also had its own rainbows, but we were glad to see them and the clouds disappear from that mountain. * * * we, indeed, were hardly at all wetted; and before we found ourselves again upon that part of the mountain called Ash Course every cloud had vanished from every summit.

Do not think we here gave up our spirit of enterprise. No! I had heard much of the grandeur of the view of Wasdale from Stye Head, the point from which Wasdale is first seen in coming by the road from Borrowdale; but though I had been in Wasdale I had never entered the dale by that road, and had often lamented that I had not seen what was so much talked of by travellers. Down to that Pass (for we were yet far above it) we bent our course by the side of Ruddle Gill, a very deep red chasm in the mountains which begins at a spring—that spring forms a stream, which must, at times, be a mighty torrent, as is evident from the channel which it has wrought out—thence by Sprinkling Tarn to Stye Head; and there we sate and looked down into Wasdale. We were now upon Great Gavel which rose high above us. Opposite was Scaw Fell and we heard the roaring of the stream from one of the ravines of that mountain, which, though the bending of Wasdale Head lay between us and Scaw Fell, we could look into, as it were, and the depth of the ravine appeared tremendous; it was black and the crags were awful.

We now proceeded homewards by Stye head Tarn along the road into Borrow-dale. Before we reached Stonethwaite a few stars had appeared, and we travelled home in our cart by moonlight.

I ought to have described the last part of our ascent to Scaw Fell Pike. There, not a blade of grass was to be seen—hardly a cushion of moss, and that was parched and brown; and only growing rarely between the huge blocks and stones which cover the summit and lie in heaps all round to a great distance, like skeletons or bones of the earth not wanted at the creation, and there left to be covered with never-dying lichens, which the clouds and dews nourish; and adorn with colours of the most vivid and exquisite beauty, and endless in variety. No gems or flowers can surpass in colour-ing the beauty of some of these masses of stone which no human eye beholds except the shepherd led thither by chance or traveller by curiosity; and how seldom must this happen! The other eminence is that which is visited by the adventurous traveller, and the shepherd has no temptation to go thither in quest of his sheep; for on the Pike there is no food to tempt them. We certainly were singularly fortunate in the day; for when we were seated on the summit our Guide, turning his eyes thoughtfully round, said to us, "I do not know that in my whole life I was ever at any season of the year so high up on the mountains on so calm a day." Afterwards, you know, we had the storm which exhibited to us the grandeur of earth and heaven commingled, yet without terror; for we knew that the storm would pass away; for so our prophetic guide assured us. I forget to tell you that I espied a ship upon the glittering sea while we were looking over Eskdale. "Is it a ship?" replied the Guide. "A ship, yes, it can be nothing else, don't you see the shape of it?" Miss Barker interposed, "It is a ship, of that I am certain. I cannot be mistaken, I am so accustomed to the appearance of ships at sea." The Guide dropped the argument; but a moment was scarce gone when he quietly said, "Now look at your ship, it is now a horse." So indeed it was—a horse with a gal-lant neck and head. We laughed heartily, and, I hope when again inclined to posi-tiveness, I may remember the ship and the horse upon the glittering sea; and the calm confidence, yet submissiveness, of our wise Man of the Mountains, who certainly had more knowledge of clouds than we, whatever might be our knowledge of ships. To add to our uncommon performance on that day Miss Barker and I each wrote a letter from the top of the Pike to our far distant friend in S. Wales, Miss Hutchinson. I believe that you are not much acquainted with the Scenery of this Country, except in the Neighbourhood of Grasmere, your duties when you were a resident here, having confined you so much to that one Vale; I hope, however, that my long story will not be very dull; and even I am not without a further hope, that it may awaken in you a desire to spend a long holiday among the mountains, and explore their recesses.

Samuel Taylor Coleridge
1772–1834

"Come back into memory, like as thou wert in the dayspring of thy fancies, with hope like a fiery column before thee—the dark pillar not yet turned—Samuel Taylor Coleridge—Logi-cian, Metaphysician, Bard!—How have I seen the casual passer through the cloisters stand still, entranced with admiration . . . while the walls of the old Grey Friars re-echoed to the accents of the *inspired charity-boy!*" When Charles Lamb thus memorialized his former schoolfellow, Coleridge had more than a decade yet to live, but he had already made himself into the mythic Romantic figure of promise and failure whom Lamb salutes.

Born in 1772, the last child of the vicar of Ottery St. Mary's in Devon, Coleridge developed a reputation for precocity even before the death of his father led to his enrollment at Christ's Hospital, a London boarding school for the sons of distressed families, where Lamb met him. A brilliant career at Jesus College, Cambridge, ended in an unhappy attempt to enlist in the army under an assumed name, and he left without a degree in 1794. With Robert Southey, a fellow Oxford enthusiast for poetry and radical politics, he planned an ideal democratic community on the banks of the Susquehanna in Pennsylvania, to be named "Pantisocracy," or equal rule by all. The project collapsed over a dispute whether they would have servants, but not before Coleridge had cemented the social bonds by becoming engaged to Sara Fricker, the sister of Southey's fiancée; the marriage proved unhappy. Coleridge later minimized his youthful "squeaking baby-trumpet of sedition," but he founded a short-lived antigovernment periodical, *The Watchman* (1796); to earn a living, he was pointing in the unorthodox direction of the Unitarian ministry until he was relieved by a moderate annuity of £150 from the Wedgwoods, of the famous pottery firm. In 1796 he published *Poems on Various Subjects*, containing the poem later titled *The Eolian Harp*, and in 1797 he began the collaboration with Wordsworth that produced *Lyrical Ballads* (1798), headed by *The Rime of the Ancyent Marinere*, as the poem was called in its archaizing first version. Before the volume was published, Coleridge and the Wordsworths departed for Germany, where Coleridge studied philosophy at Göttingen. Charges of plagiarism have swirled ever since around the readings of Kant, Schiller, Schelling, and Fichte that animated his lifelong effort to combat what he regarded as the spiritless mechanical world of eighteenth-century British empiricism.

In 1800 Coleridge followed the Wordsworths to the Lake District, where his love for Sara Hutchinson, sister of Wordsworth's future wife, sharpened his estrangement from his own wife. He became addicted to laudanum (opium dissolved in alcohol), a standard medical remedy for the rheumatic pains he suffered, but the stomach disorders it produced increased his dependency. The physiology of addiction was not understood in his day, and what was a widespread social phenomenon Coleridge regarded as an individual moral flaw. His inability to break the habit produced a spiral of depression: guilt, a paralytic doubt of his strength of will, the fear that he was unworthy of love. By 1802, in *Dejection: An Ode*, he declared the failure of his "genial spirits" and "shaping spirit of Imagination," but he carried on an active public career. An important political commentator in the newspapers, he also undertook another periodical, *The Friend* (1809–1810), saw his play *Remorse* succeed at Drury Lane (1813), and gave a series of brilliant lectures on Shakespeare, Milton, poetry, drama, and philosophy (1808–1818). That these enterprises often fell short of the triumphant fullness he forecast for them fixed the myth of promise unfulfilled, even as his accomplishments won increasing influence. From 1816 on, he lived in a London suburb under the care of a young doctor, James Gillman, and he flourished in this stable environment. The fabled talk of the "Sage of Highgate," as Carlyle called him, "had a charm much more than literary, a charm almost religious and prophetic." If the "practical intellects of the world did not much heed him," Carlyle continued, "to the rising spirits of the young generation he had this dusky sublime character; and sat there as a kind of *Magus*." Coleridge became, in the judgment of John Stuart Mill, one of the two seminal minds of the nineteenth century, the idealist, Christian, philosopher of organic unity around whose work the opposition to Benthamite utilitarianism crystalized.

In the final decades of his life, Coleridge joined new work and the gathering of old into a substantial body of publication. *Christabel*, long known by reputation, appeared with Byron's enthusiastic sponsorship, in 1816, together with *Kubla Khan*; 1817 brought *Sibylline Leaves*, Coleridge's collected poems, including the marginal-gloss version of the lyrical ballad now titled *The Rime of the Ancient Mariner*, and *Biographia Literaria*, the account of his "literary life and opinions" that has provided the starting-point for much twentieth-century literary criticism. In a series of works, Coleridge advocated a network of conservative principles continuous with but far evolved from the Jacobin associations that had led him to urge anonymous publication of the *Lyrical Ballads* because "Wordsworth's name is nothing, and mine stinks": two *Lay Sermons* (1816–1817), articulating his views in the debate over reform, *The Friend*, expanded in 1818 into a three-volume collection of essays on "politics, morals, and religion," *Aids to Reflection* (1825), emphasizing Christianity as "personal revelation," and *On the Constitution of Church and State* (1830), which outlined conceptions of national culture (and the "clerisy" responsible for preserving it) that resonate throughout the Victorian period. *Table Talk* (1836) posthumously captured the echoes of his voice, but Coleridge has enjoyed a resurrection in our own day. As new scholarly editions bring more of Coleridge's writings to light, they deepen the fascination of a man who was the author of some of the most suggestive poems in the language and an erudite philosopher, a poet who in the *Biographia Literaria* transformed the role of the critic, a theorist of the unifying imagination whose works and life are marked by fragments and discontinuities, a believer in the unity of all whose own method has been aptly described as marginal glosses on the works of others, and an idealist engaged with the daily politics of a turbulent era.

The Eolian Harp[1]

Composed at Clevedon, Somersetshire.

My pensive Sara![2] thy soft cheek reclined
Thus on mine arm, most soothing sweet it is
To sit beside our cot,° our cot o'ergrown   *cottage*
With white-flowered jasmin, and the broad-leaved myrtle,
5   (Meet emblems they of Innocence and Love!)
And watch the clouds, that late were rich with light,
Slow saddening round, and mark the star of eve
Serenely brilliant (such should wisdom be)
Shine opposite! How exquisite the scents
10   Snatched from yon bean-field! and the world so hushed!
The stilly murmur of the distant sea
Tells us of silence.
              And that simplest lute,
Placed length-ways in the clasping casement, hark!
How by the desultory breeze caressed,
15   Like some coy maid half yielding to her lover,
It pours such sweet upbraiding,° as must needs   *reproach*
Tempt to repeat the wrong! And now, its strings
Boldlier swept, the long sequacious° notes   *rhythmic, flowing*
Over delicious surges sink and rise,
20   Such a soft floating witchery of sound
As twilight Elfins make, when they at eve
Voyage on gentle gales from Fairy-Land,
Where Melodies round honey-dropping flowers,
Footless and wild, like birds of Paradise,[3]

---

1. Named after Aeolus, the Greek god of winds, the harp consisted of a guitarlike box, set in an open window where the breeze would cause its strings to sound. Originally titled *Effusium xxxv Composed August 20th, at Clevedon, Sumersetshire.*

2. Sara Fricker, Coleridge's new bride. This poem was written during Coleridge's honeymoon.
3. Birds of the New Guinea islands famed for their colorful plumage.

25 Nor pause, nor perch, hovering on untamed wing!
O the one life within us and abroad,
Which meets all motion and becomes its soul,
A light in sound, a sound-like power in light
Rhythm in all thought, and joyance everywhere—
30 Methinks, it should have been impossible
Not to love all things in a world so filled;
Where the breeze warbles, and the mute still air
Is Music slumbering on her instrument.[4]

And thus, my love! as on the midway slope
35 Of yonder hill I stretch my limbs at noon,
Whilst through my half-closed eyelids I behold
The sunbeams dance, like diamonds, on the main,
And tranquil muse upon tranquillity;
Full many a thought uncalled and undetained,
40 And many idle flitting phantasies,
Traverse my indolent and passive brain,
As wild and various as the random gales
That swell and flutter on this subject lute!

And what if all of animated nature
45 Be but organic harps diversely framed,
That tremble into thought, as o'er them sweeps
Plastic and vast, one intellectual breeze,
At once the Soul of each, and God of All?

But thy more serious eye a mild reproof
50 Darts, O beloved woman! nor such thoughts
Dim and unhallowed dost thou not reject,
And biddest me walk humbly with my God.
Meek daughter in the family of Christ!
Well hast thou said and holily dispraised
55 These shapings of the unregenerate mind;
Bubbles that glitter as they rise and break
On vain Philosophy's aye-babbling spring.
For never guiltless may I speak of him,
The Incomprehensible! save when with awe
60 I praise him, and with Faith that inly feels;
Who with his saving mercies healed me,
A sinful and most miserable man,
Wildered and dark, and gave me to possess
Peace, and this cot, and thee, heart-honored Maid!

1795–1817   1796, 1817

This Lime-Tree Bower My Prison

In the June of 1797, some long-expected Friends[1] paid a visit to the author's cottage; and on the morning of their arrival, he met with an accident, which disabled him

---

4. The eight lines beginning "O the one life" were added to the poem in 1817.

1. Among them was Charles Lamb, to whom the poem is addressed.

from walking during the whole time of their stay. One evening, when they had left him for a few hours, he composed the following lines in the garden-bower.

Well, they are gone, and here must I remain,
This lime-tree bower my prison! I have lost
Beauties and feelings, such as would have been
Most sweet to my remembrance even when age
5   Had dimmed mine eyes to blindness! They, meanwhile,
Friends, whom I never more may meet again,
On springy heath, along the hill-top edge,
Wander in gladness, and wind down, perchance,
To that still roaring dell,° of which I told;   *deep hollow*
10 The roaring dell, o'erwooded, narrow, deep,
And only speckled by the mid-day sun;
Where its slim trunk the ash from rock to rock
Flings arching like a bridge;—that branchless ash,
Unsunned and damp, whose few poor yellow leaves
15 Ne'er tremble in the gale, yet tremble still,
Fanned by the waterfall! and there my friends
Behold the dark green file of long lank weeds,
That all at once (a most fantastic sight!)
Still nod and drip beneath the dripping edge
20 Of the blue clay-stone.

        Now, my friends emerge
Beneath the wide wide Heaven—and view again
The many-steepled tract magnificent
Of hilly fields and meadows, and the sea,
With some fair bark,° perhaps, whose sails light up   *small boat*
25 The slip of smooth clear blue betwixt two Isles
Of purple shadow! Yes! they wander on
In gladness all; but thou, methinks, most glad,
My gentle-hearted Charles! for thou hast pined
And hungered after Nature, many a year,
30 In the great City pent, winning thy way
With sad yet patient soul, through evil and pain
And strange calamity![2] Ah! slowly sink
Behind the western ridge, thou glorious sun!
Shine in the slant beams of the sinking orb,
35 Ye purple heath-flowers! richlier burn, ye clouds!
Live in the yellow light, ye distant groves!
And kindle, thou blue ocean! So my Friend
Struck with deep joy may stand, as I have stood,
Silent with swimming sense; yea, gazing round
40 On the wide landscape, gaze till all doth seem
Less gross than bodily; and of such hues
As veil the Almighty Spirit, when yet he makes
Spirits perceive his presence.

---

2. The fit of insanity in which Mary Lamb, Charles's sister, had killed their mother the year before.

                              A delight
        Comes sudden on my heart, and I am glad
45   As I myself were there! Nor in this bower,
        This little lime-tree bower, have I not marked
        Much that has soothed me. Pale beneath the blaze
        Hung the transparent foliage; and I watched
        Some broad and sunny leaf, and loved to see
50   The shadow of the leaf and stem above
        Dappling its sunshine! And that walnut-tree
        Was richly tinged, and a deep radiance lay
        Full on the ancient ivy, which usurps
        Those fronting elms, and now, with blackest mass
55   Makes their dark branches gleam a lighter hue
        Through the late twilight: and though now the bat
        Wheels silent by, and not a swallow twitters,
        Yet still the solitary humble bee
        Sings in the bean-flower! Henceforth I shall know
60   That Nature ne'er deserts the wise and pure;
        No plot so narrow, be but Nature there,
        No waste so vacant, but may well employ
        Each faculty of sense, and keep the heart
        Awake to Love and Beauty! and sometimes
65   'Tis well to be bereft of promised good,
        That we may lift the Soul, and contemplate
        With lively joy the joys we can not share.
        My gentle-hearted Charles! when the last rook
        Beat its straight path along the dusky air
70   Homewards, I blest it! deeming, its black wing
        (Now a dim speck, now vanishing in light)
        Had crossed the mighty orb's dilated glory,
        While thou stood'st gazing; or when all was still,
        Flew creeking o'er thy head, and had a charm
75   For thee, my gentle-hearted Charles, to whom
        No sound is dissonant which tells of Life.

1797   1800

The Rime of the Ancient Mariner[1]

In Seven Parts

        Facile credo, plures esse Naturas invisibiles quam visibiles
        in rerum universitate. Sed horum omnium familiam quis
        nobis enarrabit, et gradus et cognationes et discrimina et
        singulorum munera? Quid agunt? quae loca habitant?
        Harum rerum notitiam semper ambivit ingenium hu-
        manum, nunquam attigit. Juvat, interea, non diffiteor,
        quandoque in animo, tanquam in Tabulâ, majoris et me-
        lioris mundi imaginem contemplari: ne mens assuefacta

---

1. When he finally published *The Rime* under his own name in 1817, Coleridge added the extensive glosses printed in
the left margins, as well as the Latin epigraph.

hodiernae vitae minutiis se contrahat nimis, et tota subsi-
dat in pusillas cogitationes. Sed veritati interea invigilan-
dum est, modusque servandus, ut certa ab incertis, diem a
nocte, distinguamus.[2]

T. Burnet. Archaeol. Phil. p. 68.

Part 1

An ancient Mariner meeteth three gallants bidden to a wedding feast, and detaineth one.	It is an ancient Mariner,

It is an ancient Mariner,
And he stoppeth one of three.
"By thy long gray beard and glittering eye,
Now wherefore stopp'st thou me?

"The Bridegroom's doors are opened wide,   5
And I am next of kin;
The guests are met, the feast is set:
May'st hear the merry din."

He holds him with his skinny hand,
"There was a ship," quoth he.   10
"Hold off! unhand me, graybeard loon!"
Eftsoons° his hand dropt he.   *immediately*

The wedding-guest is spellbound by the eye of the old sea-faring man, and constrained to hear his tale.

He holds him with his glittering eye—
The wedding-guest stood still,
And listens like a three years' child: 15
The Mariner hath his will.

The wedding-guest sat on a stone:
He can not choose but hear;
And thus spake on that ancient man,
The bright-eyed Mariner.   20

The ship was cheered, the harbor cleared,
Merrily did we drop
Below the kirk,° below the hill.   *church*
Below the light-house top.

The Mariner tells how the ship sailed southward with a good wind and fair weather, till it reached the line.

The sun came up upon the left,   25
Out of the sea came he!
And he shone bright, and on the right
Went down into the sea.

Higher and higher every day,
Till over the mast at noon—   30

2. From the English theologian Thomas Burnet's *Archaeologiae Philosophicae* (1692): "I can easily believe that there are more invisible creatures in the universe than visible ones. But who will tell us to what family each belongs, their ranks and relationships, and what their distinguishing characteristics may be? What do they do? Where do they live? The human mind has always circled around these matters without finding satisfaction. But I do not doubt that it is beneficial sometimes to contemplate in the mind, as in a picture, the image of a grander and better world; for if the mind becomes used to the trival things of everyday life, it may limit itself too much and decline completely into worthless thinking. Meanwhile, however, we must be on the lookout for the truth, keeping a sense of proportion so that we can distinguish what is sure from what is uncertain, and day from night."

The Wedding-Guest here beat his breast,
For he heard the loud bassoon.

The bride hath paced into the hall,
Red as a rose is she;
Nodding their heads before her goes   35
The merry minstrelsy.

The Wedding-Guest he beat his breast,
Yet he can not choose but hear;
And thus spake on that ancient man,
The bright-eyed Mariner.   40

And now the storm-blast came, and he
Was tyrannous and strong:
He struck with his o'ertaking wings,
And chased us south along.

With sloping masts and dipping prow,   45
As who pursued with yell and blow
Still treads the shadow of his foe,
And forward bends his head,
The ship drove fast, loud roared the blast,
And southward aye we fled.   50

And now there came both mist and snow,
And it grew wondrous cold:
And ice, mast-high, came floating by,
As green as emerald.

And through the drifts the snowy clifts   55
Did send a dismal sheen:
Nor shapes of men nor beast we ken°—   saw
The ice was all between.

The ice was here, the ice was there,
The ice was all around: 60
It cracked and growled, and roared and howled,
Like noises in a swound!°   swoon

At length did cross an Albatross,
Through the fog it came;
As if it had been a Christian soul,   65
We hailed it in God's name.

It ate the food it ne'er had eat,
And round and round it flew.
The ice did split with a thunder-fit;
The helmsman steered us through!   70

And a good south wind sprung up behind;
The Albatross did follow,
And every day, for food or play,
Came to the mariner's hollo!

In mist or cloud, on mast or shroud,°   *supporting rope*   75
It perched for vespers nine;
Whiles all the night, through fog-smoke white,
Glimmered the white moon-shine.

"God save thee, ancient Mariner!
From the fiends, that plague thee thus!—   80
Why look'st thou so?"—With my cross-bow
I shot the Albatross.

Part 2

The Sun now rose upon the right:
Out of the sea came he,
Still hid in mist, and on the left   85
Went down into the sea.

And the good south wind still blew behind,
But no sweet bird did follow,
Nor any day for food or play
Came to the mariners' hollo!   90

And I had done a hellish thing,
And it would work 'em woe:
For all averred, I had killed the bird
That made the breeze to blow.
Ah wretch! said they, the bird to slay,   95
That made the breeze to blow!

Nor dim nor red, like God's own head,
The glorious Sun uprist:
Then all averred, I had killed the bird
That brought the fog and mist.   100
'Twas right, said they, such birds to slay,
That bring the fog and mist.

The fair breeze blew, the white foam flew
The furrow followed free;
We were the first that ever burst   105
Into that silent sea.

Down dropt the breeze, the sails dropt down,
'Twas sad as sad could be;
And we did speak only to break
The silence of the sea!   110

All in a hot and copper sky,
The bloody Sun, at noon,
Right up above the mast did stand,
No bigger than the Moon.

Day after day, day after day,   115
We stuck, nor breath nor motion;

As idle as a painted ship
Upon a painted ocean.

And the Albatross begins to be avenged.

Water, water, everywhere,
And all the boards did shrink;   120
Water, water, everywhere,
Nor any drop to drink.

A spirit had followed them; one of the invisible inhabitants of this planet, neither departed souls nor angels; concerning whom the learned Jew, Josephus, and the Platonic Constantino-politan, Michael Psellus, may be consulted. They are very numerous, and there is no climate or element without one or more.

The very deep did rot: O Christ!
That ever this should be!
Yea, slimy things did crawl with legs   125
Upon the slimy sea.

About, about, in reel and rout
The death-fires° danced at night;   *phosphorescent plankton*
The water, like a witch's oils,
Burnt green, and blue and white.   130

And some in dreams assured were
Of the spirit that plagued us so;
Nine fathoms deep he had followed us
From the land of mist and snow.

And every tongue, through utter drought,   135
Was withered at the root;
We could not speak, no more than if
We had been choked with soot.

The ship-mates, in their sore distress, would fain throw the whole guilt on the ancient Mariner; in sign whereof they hang the dead sea-bird round his neck.

Ah! well a-day! what evil looks
Had I from old and young!   140
Instead of the cross, the Albatross
About my neck was hung.

Part 3

There passed a weary time. Each throat
Was parched, and glazed each eye.
A weary time! a weary time!   145
How glazed each weary eye,

The ancient Mariner beholdeth a sign in the element afar off.

When looking westward, I beheld
A something in the sky.

At first it seemed a little speck,
And then it seemed a mist;   150
It moved and moved, and took at last
A certain shape, I wist.°   *knew*

A speck, a mist, a shape, I wist!
And still it neared and neared:
As if it dodged a water-sprite,   155
It plunged and tacked and veered.

At its nearer approach, it seemeth him to be a ship; and at a dear ransom he freeth his speech from the bonds of thirst.

With throats unslaked, with black lips baked,
We could not laugh nor wail;
Through utter drought all dumb we stood!

I bit my arm, I sucked the blood,   160
And cried, A sail! A sail!

With throats unslaked, with black lips baked,
Agape they heard me call:
A flash of joy;   Gramercy!° they for joy did grin,   *many thanks*
And all at once their breath drew in,   165
As they were drinking all.

And horror follows.   See! see! (I cried) she tacks no more!
For can it be a ship   Hither to work us weal;°   *benefit*
that comes onward   Without a breeze, without a tide,
without wind or tide?   She steadies with upright keel!   170

The western wave was all a-flame.
The day was well nigh done!
Almost upon the western wave
Rested the broad bright Sun;
When that strange shape drove suddenly   175
Betwixt us and the Sun.

It seemeth him but the   And straight the sun was flecked with bars,
skeleton of a ship.   (Heaven's Mother send us grace!)
As if through a dungeon-grate he peered
With broad and burning face.   180

And its ribs are seen as   Alas! (thought I, and my heart beat loud)
bars on the face of the   How fast she nears and nears!
setting Sun.   Are those her sails that glance in the Sun,
Like restless gossameres?°   *cobwebs*

The spectre-woman   Are those her ribs through which the Sun   185
and her death-mate,   Did peer, as through a grate?
and no other on board   And is that Woman all her crew?
the skeleton-ship.   Is that a DEATH? and are there two?
Is DEATH that woman's mate?

Like vessel, like crew!   Her lips were red, her looks were free,   190
Her locks were yellow as gold:
Her skin was as white as leprosy,
The Night-Mair LIFE-IN-DEATH was she,
Who thicks man's blood with cold.

DEATH and LIFE-IN-   The naked hulk alongside came,   195
DEATH have diced for   And the twain were casting dice;
the ship's crew, and she "The game is done! I've, I've won!"
(the latter) winneth   Quoth she, and whistles thrice.
the ancient Mariner.

No twilight within the   The Sun's rim dips; the stars rush out:
courts of the Sun.   At one stride comes the dark;   200
With far-heard whisper, o'er the sea,
Off shot the spectre-bark.

At the rising of the   We listened and looked sideways up!
Moon.   Fear at my heart, as at a cup,
My life-blood seemed to sip!   205

The stars were dim, and thick the night,
The steersman's face by his lamp gleamed white;
From the sails the dew did drip—
Till clomb above the eastern bar
The horned Moon, with one bright star   210
Within the nether tip.

One after another,

One after one, by the star-dogged Moon,
Too quick for groan or sigh,
Each turned his face with a ghastly pang,
And cursed me with his eye.   215

His ship-mates drop
down dead.

Four times fifty living men
(And I heard nor sigh nor groan),
With heavy thump, a lifeless lump,
They dropped down one by one.

But LIFE-IN-DEATH
begins her work on the
ancient Mariner.

The souls did from their bodies fly,—   220
They fled to bliss or woe!
And every soul, it passed me by,
Like the whizz of my cross-bow!

Part 4

The wedding-guest
feareth that a spirit is
talking to him.

"I fear thee, ancient Mariner!
I fear thy skinny hand!   225
And thou art long, and lank, and brown,
As is the ribbed sea-sand.

I fear thee and thy glittering eye,
And thy skinny hand, so brown."—

But the ancient
Mariner assureth him
of his bodily life, and
proceedeth to relate
his horrible penance.

Fear not, fear not, thou wedding-guest!   230
This body dropt not down.

Alone, alone, all, all alone,
Alone on a wide wide sea!
And never a saint took pity on
My soul in agony.   235

He despiseth the
creatures of the calm.

The many men, so beautiful!
And they all dead did lie:
And a thousand thousand slimy things
Lived on; and so did I.

And envieth that they
should live, and so
many lie dead.

I looked upon the rotting sea,   240
And drew my eyes away;
I looked upon the rotting deck,
And there the dead men lay.

I looked to heaven, and tried to pray;
But or ever a prayer had gusht,   245
A wicked whisper came, and made
My heart as dry as dust.

I closed my lids, and kept them close,
And the balls like pulses beat;
For the sky and the sea, and the sea and the sky 250

Lay like a load on my weary eye,
And the dead were at my feet.

The cold sweat melted from their limbs,
Nor rot nor reek did they:
The look with which they looked on me   255
Had never passed away.

An orphan's curse would drag to hell
A spirit from on high;
But oh! more horrible than that
Is the curse in a dead man's eye!   260
Seven days, seven nights, I saw that curse,
And yet I could not die.

The moving Moon went up the sky,
And nowhere did abide:
Softly she was going up,   265
And a star or two beside—

Her beams bemocked the sultry main°   *open sea*
Like April hoar-frost spread;
But where the ship's huge shadow lay,
The charmed water burnt alway   270
A still and awful red.

Beyond the shadow of the ship,
I watched the water-snakes:
They moved in tracks of shining white,
And when they reared, the elfish light   275
Fell off in hoary° flakes.   *frosty*

Within the shadow of the ship
I watched their rich attire:
Blue, glossy green, and velvet black,
They coiled and swam; and every track   280
Was a flash of golden fire.

O happy living things! no tongue
Their beauty might declare:
A spring of love gushed from my heart,
And I blessed them unaware: 285
Sure my kind saint took pity on me,
And I blessed them unaware.

The selfsame moment I could pray;
And from my neck so free
The Albatross fell off, and sank   290
Like lead into the sea.

Part 5

Oh sleep! it is a gentle thing,
Beloved from pole to pole!
To Mary Queen the praise be given!
She sent the gentle sleep from Heaven,   295
That slid into my soul.

Marginal glosses:

But the curse liveth for him in the eye of the dead men.

In his loneliness and fixedness he yearneth towards the journeying Moon, and the stars that still sojourn, yet still move onward; and everywhere the blue sky belongs to them, and is their appointed rest, and their native country and their own natural homes, which they enter unannounced, as lords that are certainly expected, and yet there is a silent joy at their arrival.

By the light of the Moon he beholdeth God's creatures of the great calm.

Their beauty and their happiness.

He blesseth them in his heart.

The spell begins to break.

By grace of the holy Mother, the ancient Mariner is refreshed with rain.

The silly° buckets on the deck,   *simple*
That had so long remained,
I dreamt that they were filled with dew;
And when I awoke, it rained.   300

My lips were wet, my throat was cold,
My garments all were dank;
Sure I had drunken in my dreams,
And still my body drank.

I moved, and could not feel my limbs: 305
I was so light—almost
I thought that I had died in sleep,
And was a blessed ghost.

He heareth sounds and   And soon I heard a roaring wind:
seeth strange sights   It did not come anear;   310
and commotions in the   But with its sound it shook the sails,
sky and the element.   That were so thin and sere.°   *withered*

The upper air burst into life!
And a hundred fire-flags sheen,°   *gleamed*
To and fro they were hurried about!   315
And to and fro, and in and out,
The wan stars danced between.

And the coming wind did roar more loud,
And the sails did sigh like sedge;°   *rush-like grass*
And the rain poured down from one black cloud;   320
The Moon was at its edge.

The thick black cloud was cleft, and still
The Moon was at its side:
Like waters shot from some high crag,
The lightning fell with never a jag,   325
A river steep and wide.

The bodies of the   The loud wind never reached the ship,
ship's crew are   Yet now the ship moved on!
inspired, and the ship   Beneath the lightning and the moon
moves on.   The dead men gave a groan.   330

They groaned, they stirred, they all uprose,
Nor spake, nor moved their eyes;
It had been strange, even in a dream,
To have seen those dead men rise.

The helmsman steered, the ship moved on;   335
Yet never a breeze up blew;
The mariners all 'gan work the ropes,
Where they were wont to do;
They raised their limbs like lifeless tools—
We were a ghastly crew.   340

The body of my brother's son
Stood by me, knee to knee:

The body and I pulled at one rope,
But he said naught to me.

But not by the souls of
the men, nor by
daemons of earth or
middle air, but by a
blessed troop of angelic
spirits, sent down by
the invocation of the
guardian saint.

"I fear thee, ancient Mariner!"   345
Be calm, thou Wedding-Guest!
'Twas not those souls that fled in pain,
Which to their corses came again,
But a troop of spirits blest:

For when it dawned—they dropped their arms,   350
And clustered round the mast;
Sweet sounds rose slowly through their mouths,
And from their bodies passed.

Around, around, flew each sweet sound
Then darted to the Sun;   355
Slowly the sounds came back again,
Now mixed, now one by one.

Sometimes a-dropping from the sky
I heard the sky-lark sing;
Sometimes all little birds that are,   360
How they seemed to fill the sea and air
With their sweet jargoning!°   *warbling*

And now 'twas like all instruments,
Now like a lonely flute;
And now it is an angel's song,   365
That makes the heavens be mute.
It ceased; yet still the sails made on

A pleasant noise till noon,
A noise like of a hidden brook
In the leafy mouth of June,   370
That to the sleeping woods all night
Singeth a quiet tune.

Till noon we quietly sailed on,
Yet never a breeze did breathe:
Slowly and smoothly went the ship,   375
Moved onward from beneath.

The lonesome spirit
from the South Pole
carries on the ship as
far as the line, in
obedience to the
angelic troop, but still
requireth vengeance.

Under the keel nine fathom deep,
From the land of mist and snow,
The spirit slid: and it was he
That made the ship to go.   380
The sails at noon left off their tune,
And the ship stood still also.

The Sun, right up above the mast,
Had fixed her to the ocean:
But in a minute she 'gan stir,   385
With a short uneasy motion—
Backwards and forwards half her length
With a short uneasy motion.

Then like a pawing horse let go,
She made a sudden bound: 390
It flung the blood into my head,
And I fell down in a swound.

The Polar Spirit's fellow daemons, the invisible inhabitants of the element, take part in his wrong; and two of them relate, one to the other, that penance long and heavy for the ancient Mariner hath been accorded to the Polar Spirit, who returneth southward.

How long in that same fit I lay,
I have not to declare;
But ere my living life returned,   395
I heard, and in my soul discerned
Two voices in the air.

"Is it he?" quoth one, "Is this the man?
By him who died on cross,
With his cruel bow he laid full low   400
The harmless Albatross.

"The spirit who bideth by himself
In the land of mist and snow,
He loved the bird that loved the man
Who shot him with his bow."   405

The other was a softer voice,
As soft as honeydew.
Quoth he, "The man hath penance done,
And penance more will do."

Part 6

First voice.
"But tell me, tell me! speak again,   410
Thy soft response renewing—
What makes that ship drive on so fast?
What is the ocean doing?"

Second voice.
"Still as a slave before his lord,
The ocean hath no blast;   415
His great bright eye most silently
Up to the Moon is cast—

If he may know which way to go:
For she guides him smooth or grim.
See, brother, see! how graciously   420
She looketh down on him."

First voice.
"But why drives on that ship so fast,
Without or wave or wind?"

Second voice.
"The air is cut away before,
And closes from behind.   425

The Mariner hath been cast into a trance; for the angelic power causeth the vessel to drive northward faster than human life could endure.

Fly, brother, fly! more high, more high!
Or we shall be belated:
For slow and slow that ship will go,
When the Mariner's trance is abated."

The supernatural motion is retarded; the Mariner awakes, and his penance begins anew.

I woke, and we were sailing on   430
As in a gentle weather:
'Twas night, calm night, the moon was high;
The dead men stood together.

All stood together on the deck,
For a charnel-dungeon fitter: 435
All fixed on me their stony eyes,
That in the Moon did glitter.

The pang, the curse, with which they died,
Had never passed away:
I could not draw my eyes from theirs,   440
Nor turn them up to pray.

The curse is finally expiated.

And now this spell was snapped: once more
I viewed the ocean green,
And looked far forth, yet little saw
Of what had else been seen—   445

Like one, that on a lonesome road
Doth walk in fear and dread,
And having once turned round walks on,
And turns no more his head;
Because he knows, a frightful fiend   450
Doth close behind him tread.

But soon there breathed a wind on me,
Nor sound nor motion made:
Its path was not upon the sea,
In ripple or in shade.   455

It raised my hair, it fanned my cheek
Like a meadow-gale of spring—
It mingled strangely with my fears,
Yet it felt like a welcoming.

Swiftly, swiftly flew the ship,   460
Yet she sailed softly too:
Sweetly, sweetly blew the breeze—
On me alone it blew.

And the ancient Mariner beholdeth his native country.

Oh! dream of joy! is this indeed
The light-house top I see?   465
Is this the hill? is this the kirk?
Is this mine own countree?

We drifted o'er the harbor-bar,
And I with sobs did pray—
O let me be awake, my God!   470
Or let me sleep alway.

The harbor-bay was clear as glass,
So smoothly it was strewn!
And on the bay the moonlight lay,
And the shadow of the moon.   475

The rock shone bright, the kirk no less,
That stands above the rock:
The moonlight steeped in silentness
The steady weathercock.

And the bay was white with silent light,   480
Till rising from the same,
Full many shapes, that shadows were,
In crimson colors came.

The angelic spirits leave the dead bodies,

A little distance from the prow
Those crimson shadows were: 485
I turned my eyes upon the deck—
Oh, Christ! what saw I there!

And appear in their own forms of light.

Each corse lay flat, lifeless and flat,
And, by the holy rood!°   *cross*
A man all light, a seraph-man,°   *angel* 490
On every corse there stood.

This seraph-band, each waved his hand:
It was a heavenly sight!
They stood as signals to the land,
Each one a lovely light;   495

This seraph-band, each waved his hand,
No voice did they impart—
No voice; but oh! the silence sank
Like music on my heart.

But soon I heard the dash of oars,   500
I heard the Pilot's cheer;
My head was turned perforce away,
And I saw a boat appear.

The Pilot and the Pilot's boy,
I heard them coming fast: 505
Dear Lord in Heaven! it was a joy
The dead men could not blast.

I saw a third—I heard his voice:
It is the Hermit good!
He singeth loud his godly hymns   510
That he makes in the wood.
He'll shrieve° my soul, he'll wash away   *absolve*
The Albatross's blood.

Part 7

The Hermit of the wood,

This Hermit good lives in that wood
Which slopes down to the sea.   515
How loudly his sweet voice he rears!
He loves to talk with mariners
That come from a far countree.

He kneels at morn, and noon, and eve
He hath a cushion plump: 520

It is the moss that wholly hides
The rotted old oak-stump.

The skiff-boat neared: I heard them talk,
"Why, this is strange, I trow!
Where are those lights so many and fair,   525
That signal made but now?"

Approacheth the ship
with wonder.
"Strange, by my faith!" the Hermit said—
"And they answered not our cheer!
The planks looked warped! and see those sails,
How thin they are and sere!   530
I never saw aught like to them,
Unless perchance it were

"Brown skeletons of leaves that lag
My forest-brook along;
When the ivy-tod° is heavy with snow,   *bush*   535
And the owlet whoops to the wolf below,
That eats the she-wolf's young."

"Dear Lord! it hath a fiendish look—
(The Pilot made reply)
I am a-feared"—"Push on, push on!"   540
Said the Hermit cheerily.

The boat came closer to the ship,
But I nor spake nor stirred;
The boat came close beneath the ship,
And straight a sound was heard.   545

The ship suddenly
sinketh.
Under the water it rumbled on,
Still louder and more dread:
It reached the ship, it split the bay;
The ship went down like lead.

The ancient Mariner is
saved in the Pilot's
boat.
Stunned by that loud and dreadful sound,   550
Which sky and ocean smote,
Like one that hath been seven days drowned
My body lay afloat;
But swift as dreams, myself I found
Within the Pilot's boat.   555

Upon the whirl, where sank the ship,
The boat spun round and round;
And all was still, save that the hill
Was telling of the sound.

I moved my lips—the Pilot shrieked   560
And fell down in a fit;
The holy Hermit raised his eyes,
And prayed where he did sit.

I took the oars: the Pilot's boy,
Who now doth crazy go,   565
Laughed loud and long, and all the while

His eyes went to and fro.
"Ha! ha!" quoth he, "full plain I see,
The Devil knows how to row."

And now, all in my own countree,   570
I stood on the firm land!
The Hermit stepped forth from the boat,
And scarcely he could stand.

"O shrieve me, shrieve me,[6] holy man!"
The Hermit crossed his brow.   575
"Say quick," quoth he, "I bid thee say—
What manner of man art thou?"

Forthwith this frame of mine was wrenched
With a woful agony,
Which forced me to begin my tale;   580
And then it left me free.

Since then, at an uncertain hour,
That agony returns:
And till my ghastly tale is told,
This heart within me burns.   585

I pass, like night, from land to land;
I have strange power of speech;
That moment that his face I see,
I know the man that must hear me:
To him my tale I teach.   590

What loud uproar bursts from that door!
The wedding-guests are there:
But in the garden-bower the bride
And bride-maids singing are:
And hark the little vesper-bell,   595
Which biddeth me to prayer!

O Wedding-Guest! this soul hath been
Alone on a wide wide sea:
So lonely 'twas, that God himself
Scarce seemed there to be.   600

O sweeter than the marriage-feast,
'Tis sweeter far to me,
To walk together to the kirk
With a goodly company!—

To walk together to the kirk,   605
And all together pray,
While each to his great Father bends,
Old men, and babes, and loving friends,
And youths and maidens gay!

6. Hear confession and give absolution.

And to teach, by his own example, love and reverence to all things that God made and loveth.

Farewell, farewell! but this I tell   610
To thee, thou Wedding-Guest!
He prayeth well who loveth well
Both man and bird and beast.

He prayeth best, who loveth best
All things both great and small;   615
For the dear God who loveth us,
He made and loveth all.

The Mariner, whose eye is bright,
Whose beard with age is hoar,
Is gone: and now the Wedding-Guest   620
Turned from the bridegroom's door.

He went like one that hath been stunned,
And is of sense forlorn:
A sadder and a wiser man,
He rose the morrow morn.   625

1797/1817   1817

COMPANION READING

Samuel Taylor Coleridge: from *Table Talk*

May 31, 1830. Mrs. Barbauld once told me that she admired the Ancient Mariner very much, but that there were two faults in it, it was improbable, and had no moral. As for the probability, I owned that that might admit some question; but as to the want of a moral, I told her that in my own judgment the poem had too much; and that the only, or chief fault, if I might say so, was the obtrusion of the moral sentiment so openly on the reader as a principle or cause of action in a work of such pure imagination. It ought to have had no more moral than the Arabian Nights' tale of the merchant's sitting down to eat dates by the side of a well, and throwing the shells aside, and lo! a genie starts up, and says he *must* kill the aforesaid merchant, *because* one of the date shells had, it seems, put out the eye of the genie's son.

Kubla Khan[1]

Or, A Vision in a Dream. A Fragment.

The following fragment is here published at the request of a poet of great and deserving celebrity,[2] and, as far as the author's own opinions are concerned, rather as a psychological curiosity, than on the ground of any supposed *poetic* merits.

    In the summer of the year 1797, the Author, then in ill health, had retired to a lonely farm-house between Porlock and Linton, on the Exmoor confines of Somerset and Devonshire. In consequence of a slight indisposition, an anodyne[3] had been prescribed, from the effect of which he fell asleep in his chair at the moment that he was reading the following sentence, or words of the same substance, in "Purchas's Pilgrimage":[4] "Here the Khan Kubla commanded a palace to be built,

---

1. Kubla Khan was the grandson of Genghis Khan and Emperor of China in the 13th century.
2. Byron.
3. A painkiller, probably laudanum.

4. A collection of often fantastical accounts of foreign lands compiled by Samuel Purchas (1613). As a boy, Coleridge was an avid reader of such literature.

and a stately garden thereunto: and thus ten miles of fertile ground were inclosed with a wall." The author continued for about three hours in a profound sleep, at least of the external senses, during which time he has the most vivid confidence, that he could not have composed less than from two to three hundred lines; if that indeed can be called composition in which all the images rose up before him as things, with a parallel production of the correspondent expressions, without any sensation or consciousness of effort. On awaking he appeared to himself to have a distinct recollection of the whole, and taking his pen, ink, and paper, instantly and eagerly wrote down the lines that are here preserved. At this moment he was unfortunately called out by a person on business from Porlock, and detained by him above an hour, and on his return to his room, found, to his no small surprise and mortification, that though he still retained some vague and dim recollection of the general purport of the vision, yet, with the exception of some eight or ten scattered lines and images, all the rest had passed away like the images on the surface of a stream into which a stone had been cast, but, alas! without the after restoration of the latter:

> Then all the charm
> Is broken—all that phantom-world so fair
> Vanishes, and a thousand circlets spread,
> And each mis-shape[s] the other. Stay awhile,
> Poor youth! who scarcely dar'st lift up thine eyes—
> The stream will soon renew its smoothness, soon
> The visions will return! And lo! he stays,
> And soon the fragments dim of lovely forms
> Come trembling back, unite, and now once more
> The pool becomes a mirror.[5]

Yet from the still surviving recollections in his mind, the Author has frequently purposed to finish for himself what had been originally, as it were, given to him. Σαμερον αδιον ασω:[6] but the to-morrow is yet to come.

As a contrast to this vision, I have annexed a fragment of a very different character, describing with equal fidelity the dream of pain and disease.[7]

(1816)

Kubla Khan

> In Xanadu did Kubla Khan
> A stately pleasure-dome decree:
> Where Alph, the sacred river, ran
> Through caverns measureless to man
> 5   Down to a sunless sea.
> So twice five miles of fertile ground
> With walls and towers were girdled round:
> And there were gardens bright with sinuous rills,
> Where blossomed many an incense-bearing tree;
> 10   And here were forests ancient as the hills,
> Enfolding sunny spots of greenery.

5. From Coleridge's *The Picture* (lines 91–100).
6. From Theocritus, *Idylls*, line 145: "I'll sing a sweeter   song tomorrow."
7. *The Pains of Sleep*.

But oh! that deep romantic chasm which slanted
Down the green hill athwart a cedarn cover!
A savage place! as holy and enchanted
15   As e'er beneath a waning moon was haunted
By woman wailing for her demon-lover!
And from this chasm, with ceaseless turmoil seething,
As if this earth in fast thick pants were breathing,
A mighty fountain momently was forced:
20   Amid whose swift half-intermitted burst
Huge fragments vaulted like rebounding hail,
Or chaffy grain beneath the thresher's flail:
And mid these dancing rocks at once and ever
It flung up momently the sacred river.
25   Five miles meandering with a mazy motion
Through wood and dale the sacred river ran,
Then reached the caverns measureless to man,
And sank in tumult to a lifeless ocean:
And 'mid this tumult Kubla heard from far
30   Ancestral voices prophesying war!
        The shadow of the dome of pleasure
        Floated midway on the waves;
        Where was heard the mingled measure
        From the fountain and the caves.
35   It was a miracle of rare device,
A sunny pleasure-dome with caves of ice!

    A damsel with a dulcimer
        In a vision once I saw:
        It was an Abyssinian maid,
40   And on her dulcimer she played,
        Singing of Mount Abora.
        Could I revive within me
        Her symphony and song,
        To such a deep delight 'twould win me,
45   That with music loud and long,
I would build that dome in air,
That sunny dome! those caves of ice!
And all who heard should see them there,
And all should cry, Beware! Beware!
50   His flashing eyes, his floating hair!
Weave a circle round him thrice,
And close your eyes with holy dread,
For he on honey-dew hath fed,
And drunk the milk of Paradise.

1797–1798   1816

Frost at Midnight

The Frost performs its secret ministry,
Unhelped by any wind. The owlet's cry
Came loud—and hark, again! loud as before.

The inmates of my cottage, all at rest,
5   Have left me to that solitude, which suits
Abstruser musings: save that at my side
My cradled infant slumbers peacefully.
'Tis calm indeed! so calm, that it disturbs
And vexes meditation with its strange
10 And extreme silentness. Sea, hill, and wood
This populous village! Sea, and hill, and wood,
With all the numberless goings on of life,
Inaudible as dreams! the thin blue flame
Lies on my low burnt fire, and quivers not;
15 Only that film,[1] which fluttered on the grate,
Still flutters there, the sole unquiet thing.
Methinks, its motion in this hush of nature
Gives it dim sympathies with me who live,
Making it a companionable form,
20 Whose puny flaps and freaks the idling Spirit
By its own moods interprets, everywhere
Echo or mirror seeking of itself,
And makes a toy of Thought.

                        But O! how oft,
How oft, at school, with most believing mind,
25 Presageful, have I gazed upon the bars,
To watch that fluttering stranger! and as oft
With unclosed lids, already had I dreamt
Of my sweet birth-place, and the old church-tower,
Whose bells, the poor man's only music, rang
30 From morn to evening, all the hot fair-day,
So sweetly, that they stirred and haunted me
With a wild pleasure, falling on mine ear
Most like articulate sounds of things to come!
So gazed I, till the soothing things I dreamt
35 Lulled me to sleep, and sleep prolonged my dreams!
And so I brooded all the following morn,
Awed by the stern preceptor's° face, mine eye   *teacher's*
Fixed with mock study on my swimming book:
Save if the door half opened, and I snatched
40 A hasty glance, and still my heart leaped up,
For still I hoped to see the stranger's face,
Townsman, or aunt, or sister more beloved,
My playmate when we both were clothed alike![2]

    Dear Babe, that sleepest cradled by my side,
45 Whose gentle breathings, heard in this deep calm,
Fill up the interspersed vacancies
And momentary pauses of the thought!
My babe so beautiful! it thrills my heart

---

1. A piece of soot. "In all parts of the kingdom these films are called *strangers* and supposed to portend the arrival of some absent friend" (Coleridge's note).
2. Boys and girls wore the same clothes until age 5.

With tender gladness, thus to look at thee,
50   And think that thou shalt learn far other lore
And in far other scenes! For I was reared
In the great city, pent 'mid cloisters dim,
And saw naught lovely but the sky and stars.
But *thou*, my babe! shalt wander like a breeze
55   By lakes and sandy shores, beneath the crags
Of ancient mountain, and beneath the clouds,
Which image in their bulk both lakes and shores
And mountain crags: so shalt thou see and hear
The lovely shapes and sounds intelligible
60   Of that eternal language, which thy God
Utters, who from eternity doth teach
Himself in all, and all things in himself.
Great universal Teacher! he shall mould
Thy spirit, and by giving make it ask.

65   Therefore all seasons shall be sweet to thee,
Whether the summer clothe the general earth
With greenness, or the redbreast sit and sing
Betwixt the tufts of snow on the bare branch
Of mossy apple-tree, while the nigh thatch
70   Smokes in the sun-thaw; whether the eave-drops fall
Heard only in the trances of the blast,
Or if the secret ministry of frost
Shall hang them up in silent icicles,
Quietly shining to the quiet Moon.
February 1798   1798

Dejection: An Ode[1]

Late, late yestreen I saw the new Moon,
   With the old Moon in her arms;
And I fear, I fear, my Master dear!
   We shall have a deadly storm.

Ballad of Sir Patrick Spence[2]

1

Well! If the Bard was weather-wise, who made
   The grand old ballad of Sir Patrick Spence,
      This night, so tranquil now, will not go hence
Unroused by winds, that ply a busier trade
5   Than those which mould yon cloud in lazy flakes,
Or the dull sobbing draft, that moans and rakes
      Upon the strings of this Aeolian lute,[3]

---

1. *Dejection* evolved from a long verse-letter that Coleridge wrote to Sara Hutchinson in April 1802, after hearing the opening stanzas of Wordsworth's *Ode: Intimations of Immortality* (see page 1610). Cutting the verse letter by half, Coleridge published it on October 4, 1802, Wordsworth's wedding day and the seventh anniversary of his own unhappy marriage.
2. A traditional ballad printed in Thomas Percy's *Reliques of Ancient Poetry* (1765), which profoundly influenced both Coleridge and Wordsworth.
3. An instrument named after Aeolus, the Greek god of winds; see *The Eolian Harp*, page 1637.

Which better far were mute.
For lo! the New-moon winter-bright!
10 And overspread with phantom light,
(With swimming phantom light o'erspread
But rimmed and circled by a silver thread)
I see the old Moon in her lap, foretelling
The coming on of rain and squally blast.
15 And oh! that even now the gust were swelling,
And the slant night-shower driving loud and fast!
Those sounds which oft have raised me, whilst they awed,
And sent my soul abroad,
Might now, perhaps, their wonted impulse give,
20 Might startle this dull pain, and make it move and live!

2

A grief without a pang, void, dark, and drear,
A stifled, drowsy, unimpassioned grief,
Which finds no natural outlet, no relief,
In word, or sigh, or tear—
25 O Lady! in this wan and heartless mood,
To other thoughts by yonder throstle° woo'd,   *thrush*
All this long eve, so balmy and serene,
Have I been gazing on the western sky,
And its peculiar tint of yellow green:
30 And still I gaze—and with how blank an eye!
And those thin clouds above, in flakes and bars,
That give away their motion to the stars;
Those stars, that glide behind them or between,
Now sparkling, now bedimmed, but always seen:
35 Yon crescent Moon, as fixed as if it grew
In its own cloudless, starless lake of blue;
I see them all so excellently fair,
I see, not feel how beautiful they are!

3

My genial° spirits fail;   *creative*
40 And what can these avail
To lift the smothering weight from off my breast?
It were a vain endeavor,
Though I should gaze forever
On that green light that lingers in the west:
45 I may not hope from outward forms to win
The passion and the life, whose fountains are within.

4

O Lady! we receive but what we give,
And in our life alone does Nature live:
Ours is her wedding-garment, ours her shroud!
50 And would we aught behold, of higher worth,
Than that inanimate° cold world allowed   *soulless*
To the poor loveless ever-anxious crowd,
Ah! from the soul itself must issue forth,
A light, a glory, a fair luminous cloud
55 Enveloping the Earth—
And from the soul itself must there be sent

A sweet and potent voice, of its own birth,
Of all sweet sounds the life and element!

5

O pure of heart; thou need'st not ask of me
60   What this strong music in the soul may be!
What, and wherein it doth exist,
This light, this glory, this fair luminous mist,
This beautiful and beauty-making power.
   Joy, virtuous Lady! Joy that ne'er was given,
65   Save to the pure, and in their purest hour,
Life, and Life's effluence, cloud at once and shower
Joy, Lady! is the spirit and the power
Which wedding Nature to us gives in dower,
   A new Earth and new Heaven,
70   Undreamt of by the sensual and the proud—
Joy is the sweet voice, Joy the luminous cloud—
     We in ourselves rejoice!
And thence flows all that charms or ear or sight,
   All melodies the echoes of that voice,
75   All colors a suffusion from that light.

6

There was a time when, though my path was rough,
   This joy within me dallied with distress,
And all misfortunes were but as the stuff
   Whence Fancy made me dreams of happiness:
80   For hope grew round me, like the twining vine,
And fruits, and foliage, not my own, seemed mine.
But now afflictions bow me down to earth:
Nor care I that they rob me of my mirth,
    But oh! each visitation
85   Suspends what nature gave me at my birth,
   My shaping spirit of Imagination.
For not to think of what I needs must feel,
   But to be still and patient, all I can;
And haply by abstruse research to steal
90   From my own nature all the natural man—
   This was my sole resource, my only plan:
Till that which suits a part infects the whole,
And now is almost grown the habit of my soul.

7

Hence, viper thoughts, that coil around my mind,
95   Reality's dark dream!
I turn from you, and listen to the wind,
   Which long has raved unnoticed. What a scream
Of agony by torture lengthened out
That lute sent forth! Thou Wind, that ravest without,
100 Bare craig, or mountain-tairn,° or blasted tree,   *pond*
Or pine-grove whither woodman never clomb,
Or lonely house, long held the witches' home,
   Methinks were fitter instruments for thee,
Mad Lutanist! who in this month of showers,
105 Of dark-brown gardens, and of peeping flowers,

Mak'st Devils' yule,° with worse than wintry song,   *Christmas*
The blossoms, buds, and timorous leaves among.
    Thou Actor, perfect in all tragic sounds!
Thou mighty Poet, e'en to frenzy bold!
110   What tell'st thou now about?
      'Tis of the rushing of a host in rout,
    With groans of trampled men, with smarting wounds—
At once they groan with pain, and shudder with the cold!
But hush! there is a pause of deepest silence!
115   And all that noise, as of a rushing crowd,
With groans and tremulous shudderings—all is over—
    It tells another tale, with sounds less deep and loud!
        A tale of less affright,
        And tempered with delight,
120   As Otway's self had framed the tender lay,[4]
        'Tis of a little child,
        Upon a lonesome wild,
Not far from home, but she hath lost her way:
And now moans low in bitter grief and fear,
125   And now screams loud, and hopes to make her mother hear.

        8

'Tis midnight, but small thoughts have I of sleep;
Full seldom may my friend such vigils keep!
Visit her, gentle Sleep! with wings of healing,
    And may this storm be but a mountain-birth,°   *short-lived*
130   May all the stars hang bright above her dwelling,
    Silent as though they watched the sleeping Earth!
        With light heart may she rise,
        Gay fancy, cheerful eyes,
    Joy lift her spirit, joy attune her voice;
135   To her may all things live, from pole to pole,
Their life the eddying of her living soul!
    O simple spirit, guided from above,
Dear Lady! friend devoutest of my choice,
Thus mayest thou ever, evermore rejoice.

1802   1802

Work Without Hope

Lines Composed 21st February, 1825

All Nature seems at work. Slugs leave their lair—
The bees are stirring—birds are on the wing—
And Winter slumbering in the open air,
Wears on his smiling face a dream of Spring!
5   And I, the while, the sole unbusy thing,
Nor honey make, nor pair, nor build, nor sing.

Yet well I ken° the banks where amaranths° blow,   *know / fadeless flowers*
Have traced the fount whence streams of nectar flow.

---

4. Thomas Otway, author of *The Orphan* (1680) and other tragedies noted for their pathos. In earlier versions the reference is to "William," probably alluding to Wordsworth's *Lucy Gray* (see page 1541).

Bloom, O ye amaranths! bloom for whom ye may,
10   For me ye bloom not! Glide, rich streams, away!
With lips unbrightened, wreathless brow, I stroll:
And would you learn the spells that drowse my soul?
Work without Hope draws nectar in a sieve,
And Hope without an object cannot live.

1825   1828

Constancy to an Ideal Object

Since all that beat about in Nature's range,
Or° veer or vanish; why shouldst thou remain   *either*
The only constant in a world of change,
O yearning Thought! that liv'st but in the brain?
5   Call to the Hours, that in the distance play,
The faery people of the future day—
Fond Thought! not one of all that shining swarm
Will breathe on thee with life-enkindling breath,
Till when, like strangers shelt'ring from a storm,
10   Hope and Despair meet in the porch of Death!
Yet still thou haunt'st me; and though well I see,
She is not thou, and only thou art she,
Still, still as though some dear embodied Good,
Some living Love before my eyes there stood
15   With answering look a ready ear to lend,
I mourn to thee and say—"Ah! loveliest friend!
That this the meed of all my toils might be,
To have a home, an English home, and thee!"
Vain repetition! Home and Thou are one.
20   The peacefull'st cot,° the moon shall shine upon,   *cottage*
Lulled by the thrush, and wakened by the lark,
Without thee were but a becalmed bark,°   *boat*
Whose Helmsman on an ocean waste and wide
Sits mute and pale his mouldering helm beside.

25   And art thou nothing? Such thou art, as when
The woodman winding westward up the glen
At wintry dawn, where o'er the sheep-track's maze
The viewless° snow-mist weaves a glist'ning haze,   *invisible*
Sees full before him, gliding without tread,
30   An image with a glory round its head;[1]
The enamored rustic worships its fair hues,
Nor knows he makes the shadow, he pursues!

1828

Epitaph

Stop, Christian Passer-by—Stop, child of God,
And read with gentle breast. Beneath this sod
A poet lies, or that which once seem'd he—

---

1. Coleridge refers to the phenomenon in which a walker in the mountains, the sun behind him, casts a magnified self-image onto the mists before him. See *Dejection: An Ode*, line 54.

O lift one thought in prayer for S. T. C.;
5   That he who many a year with toil of breath
Found death in life, may here find life in death!
Mercy for° praise—to be forgiven for° fame   *instead of*
He ask'd, and hoped, through Christ. Do thou the same!

1833   1834

---

from **Biographia Literaria**
or, **Biographical Sketches of My Literary Life and Opinions**[1]

from *Chapter 13*

[IMAGINATION AND FANCY]

Thus far had the work been transcribed for the press, when I received the following letter from a friend,[2] whose practical judgement I have had ample reason to estimate and revere, and whose taste and sensibility preclude all the excuses which my self-love might possibly have prompted me to set up in plea against the decision of advisers of equal good sense, but with less tact and feeling.

Dear C.

You ask my opinion concerning your Chapter on the Imagination, both as to the impressions it made on myself, and as to those which I think it will make on the PUBLIC, *i.e. that part of the public, who from the title of the work and from its forming a sort of introduction to a volume of poems, are likely to constitute the great majority of your readers.*

As to myself, and stating in the first place the effect on my understanding, your opinions and method of argument were not only so new to me, but so directly the reverse of all I had ever been accustomed to consider as truth, that even if I had comprehended your premises sufficiently to have admitted them, and had seen the necessity of your conclusions, I should still have been in that state of mind, which in your note, p. 75, 76, you have so ingeniously evolved, as the antithesis to that in which a man is, when he makes a bull.[3] In your own words, I should have felt as if I had been standing on my head.

The effect on my feelings, on the other hand, I cannot better represent, than by supposing myself to have known only our light airy modern chapels of ease, and then for the first time to have been placed, and left alone, in one of our largest Gothic cathedrals in a gusty moonlight night of autumn. "Now in glimmer, and now in gloom;"[4] often in palpable darkness not without a chilly sensation of terror; then suddenly emerging into broad yet visionary

---

1. In 1803 Coleridge contemplated writing "my metaphysical works *as my life,* & *in* my life—intermixed with all the other events of history of the mind and fortunes of S.T. Coleridge." Nothing came of this characteristically Romantic interfusion of personal experience and philosophical generalization until 1815, when Coleridge decided to prefix to a collected edition of his poems "a general preface . . . on the principles" of criticism. Wordsworth's *Poems* (1815), with an extensive essay supplementary to the *Lyrical Ballads* Preface of 1800–1802, further prompted Coleridge to clarify his theoretical divergences from his former collaborator. The resulting *Biographia Literaria,* grown from preface to an independent two-volume work, is an extraordinary text: a revisionary autobiography, in which Coleridge minimizes his youthful radicalism; a philosophical argument to establish the freedom of the will, yet so enmeshed in the material exigencies of book production that publication was delayed for two years; a meditation on original genius heavily indebted to recent German thought; and, in Chapter 13, a comic masquerade that has proved one of the seminal passages for subsequent literary studies. In his sustained, probing commentary on Wordsworth, unprecedented in discussions of modern literature, Coleridge confirmed Wordsworth's stature and, at the same time, by claiming to understand Wordsworth better than he did himself, institutionalized the role of the critic as the reader who completes the poet's task.

2. Coleridge wrote the letter himself.

3. That is, when he unwittingly contradicts himself, thereby leaving himself open to ridicule.

4. From his poem *Christabel,* line 169.

lights with coloured shadows, of fantastic shapes yet all decked with holy insignia and mystic symbols; and ever and anon coming out full upon pictures and stone-work images of great men, with whose names I was familiar, but which looked upon me with countenances and an expression, the most dissimilar to all I had been in the habit of connecting with those names. Those whom I had been taught to venerate as almost super-human in magnitude of intellect, I found perched in little fret-work niches, as grotesque dwarfs; while the grotesques, in my hitherto belief, stood guarding the high altar with all the characters of Apotheosis.[5] *In short, what I had supposed substances were thinned away into shadows, while every where shadows were deepened into substances:*

> If substance may be call'd what shadow seem'd,
> For each seem'd either!

Milton[6]

Yet after all, I could not but repeat the lines which you had quoted from a MS. poem of your own in the FRIEND,[7] *and applied to a work of Mr. Wordsworth's though with a few of the words altered:*

> —————An orphic tale indeed,
> A tale obscure of high and passionate thoughts
> To a strange music chaunted![8]

Be assured, however, that I look forward anxiously to your great book on the CON-STRUCTIVE PHILOSOPHY,[9] *which you have promised and announced: and that I will do my best to understand it. Only I will not promise to descend into the dark cave of Trophonius*[1] *with you, there to rub my own eyes, in order to make the sparks and figured flashes, which I am required to see.*

So much for myself. But as for the PUBLIC, *I do not hesitate a moment in advising and urging you to withdraw the Chapter from the present work, and to reserve it for your announced treatises on the Logos or communicative intellect in Man and Deity.*[2] *First, because imperfectly as I understand the present Chapter, I see clearly that you have done too much, and yet not enough. You have been obliged to omit so many links, from the necessity of compression, that what remains, looks (if I may recur to my former illustration) like the fragments of the winding steps of an old ruined tower. Secondly, a still stronger argument (at least one that I am sure will be more forcible with you) is, that your readers will have both right and reason to complain of you. This Chapter, which cannot, when it is printed, amount to so little as an hundred pages, will of necessity greatly increase the expense of the work; and every reader who, like myself, is neither prepared or perhaps calculated for the study of so abstruse a subject so abstrusely treated, will, as I have before hinted, be almost entitled to accuse you of a sort of imposition on him. For who, he might truly observe, could from your title-page, viz.* "My Literary Life and Opinions," *published too as introductory to a volume of miscellaneous poems, have anticipated, or even conjectured, a long treatise on ideal Realism, which holds the same relation in abstruseness to Plotinus, as Plotinus does to*

---

5. Divinity.
6. *Paradise Lost*, 2.669–70, misquoted.
7. A journal produced by Coleridge in the years 1809–1810.
8. *To William Wordsworth*, lines 45–47 (variant), referring to the 1805 *Prelude*.
9. Perhaps the *Logic* or *Opus Maximum*, perhaps a more general reference to Coleridge's Kantian model of systematic philosophy.

1. Legendary architect of the temple of Apollo at Delphi. After his death an oracle was consecrated to him; visitors were dragged into a cave filled with strange sounds and glaring lights, where they received the oracle's messages.
2. The Word of God, associated with the incarnation of Jesus Christ. Coleridge announced a study of the Gospel of John as part of a work that never appeared, the *Logosophia*.

Plato.[3] It will be well, if already you have not too much of metaphysical disquisition in your work, though as the larger part of the disquisition is historical, it will doubtless be both interesting and instructive to many to whose unprepared minds your speculations on the esemplastic power[4] would be utterly unintelligible. Be assured, if you do publish this Chapter in the present work, you will be reminded of Bishop Berkley's Siris,[5] announced as an Essay on Tar-water, which beginning with Tar ends with the Trinity, the omne scibile [everything knowable] forming the interspace. I say in the present work. In that greater work to which you have devoted so many years, and study so intense and various, it will be in its proper place. Your prospectus will have described and announced both its contents and their nature; and if any persons purchase it, who feel no interest in the subjects of which it treats, they will have themselves only to blame.

I could add to these arguments one derived from pecuniary[6] motives, and particularly from the probable effects on the sale of your present publication; but they would weigh little with you compared with the preceding. Besides, I have long observed, that arguments drawn from your own personal interests more often act on you as narcotics than as stimulants, and that in money concerns you have some small portion of pignature in your moral idiosyncracy, and like these amiable creatures, must occasionally be pulled backward from the boat in order to make you enter it. All success attend you, for if hard thinking and hard reading are merits, you have deserved it.

Your affectionate, &c.

In consequence of this very judicious letter, which produced complete conviction on my mind, I shall content myself for the present with stating the main result of the Chapter, which I have reserved for that future publication, a detailed prospectus of which the reader will find at the close of the second volume.

The IMAGINATION then I consider either as primary, or secondary. The primary IMAGINATION I hold to be the living Power and prime Agent of all human Perception, and as a repetition in the finite mind of the eternal act of creation in the infinite I AM. The secondary I consider as an echo of the former, co-existing with the conscious will, yet still as identical with the primary in the *kind* of its agency, and differing only in *degree*, and in the *mode* of its operation. It dissolves, diffuses, dissipates, in order to re-create; or where this process is rendered impossible, yet still at all events it struggles to idealize and to unify. It is essentially *vital*, even as all objects (*as* objects) are essentially fixed and dead.

FANCY, on the contrary, has no other counters to play with, but fixities and definites. The Fancy is indeed no other than a mode of Memory emancipated from the order of time and space; and blended with, and modified by that empirical phenomenon of the will, which we express by the word CHOICE. But equally with the ordinary memory it must receive all its materials ready made from the law of association.

Whatever more than this, I shall think it fit to declare concerning the powers and privileges of the imagination in the present work, will be found in the critical

---

3. Coleridge saw himself as an "ideal realist," rejecting the Platonic distinction between the essence and appearance of things, for an idea of the world intuited whole by the indwelling human spirit, a position derived from Plato's inheritor Plotinus. The perceptions of that Spirit are thus both ideal and real at once.

4. A term of Coleridge's own invention; "esemplastic" means unifying or synthesizing.

5. George Berkeley (1685–1753), Irish bishop and philosopher. *Siris* (1744) begins with a chemical description of the medicinal advantages of tar and proceeds from there to reflections on theology. It impressed Coleridge as an example of philosophy tied to the empirical truths of the natural sciences.

6. Financial.

essay on the uses of the Supernatural in poetry and the principles that regulate its introduction: which the reader will find prefixed to the poem of 𝔗𝔥𝔢 𝔄𝔫𝔠𝔦𝔢𝔫𝔱 𝔐𝔞𝔯𝔦𝔫𝔢𝔯.

from *Chapter 14*

[OCCASION OF THE *LYRICAL BALLADS*—PREFACE TO THE SECOND EDITION—
THE ENSUING CONTROVERSY]

During the first year that Mr. Wordsworth and I were neighbours, our conversations turned frequently on the two cardinal points of poetry, the power of exciting the sympathy of the reader by a faithful adherence to the truth of nature, and the power of giving the interest of novelty by the modifying colours of imagination. The sudden charm, which accidents of light and shade, which moon-light or sun-set diffused over a known and familiar landscape, appeared to represent the practicability of combining both. These are the poetry of nature. The thought suggested itself (to which of us I do not recollect) that a series of poems might be composed of two sorts. In the one, the incidents and agents were to be, in part at least, supernatural; and the excellence aimed at was to consist in the interesting of the affections by the dramatic truth of such emotions, as would naturally accompany such situations, supposing them real. And real in *this* sense they have been to every human being who, from whatever source of delusion, has at any time believed himself under supernatural agency. For the second class, subjects were to be chosen from ordinary life; the characters and incidents were to be such, as will be found in every village and its vicinity, where there is a meditative and feeling mind to seek after them, or to notice them, when they present themselves.

In this idea originated the plan of the "Lyrical Ballads"; in which it was agreed, that my endeavours should be directed to persons and characters supernatural, or at least romantic; yet so as to transfer from our inward nature a human interest and a semblance of truth sufficient to procure for these shadows of imagination that willing suspension of disbelief for the moment, which constitutes poetic faith. Mr. Wordsworth, on the other hand, was to propose to himself as his object, to give the charm of novelty to things of every day, and to excite a feeling analogous to the supernatural, by awakening the mind's attention from the lethargy of custom, and directing it to the loveliness and the wonders of the world before us; an inexhaustible treasure, but for which in consequence of the film of familiarity and selfish solicitude we have eyes, yet see not, ears that hear not, and hearts that neither feel nor understand.

With this view I wrote the "Ancient Mariner," and was preparing among other poems, the "Dark Ladie," and the "Christabel," in which I should have more nearly realized my ideal, than I had done in my first attempt. But Mr. Wordsworth's industry had proved so much more successful, and the number of his poems so much greater, that my compositions, instead of forming a balance, appeared rather an interpolation of heterogeneous matter. Mr. Wordsworth added two or three poems written in his own character, in the impassioned, lofty, and sustained diction, which is characteristic of his genius. In this form the *Lyrical Ballads* were published; and were presented by him, as an *experiment*,[1] whether subjects, which from their nature rejected the usual ornaments and extra-colloquial style of poems in general, might not be so managed in the language of ordinary life as to produce the pleasurable interest, which it is the peculiar business of poetry to impart. To the second edition he added a preface of

---

1. "Experiments" is Wordsworth's term in the Advertisement to the 1798 *Lyrical Ballads*.

considerable length; in which notwithstanding some passages of apparently a contrary import, he was understood to contend for the extension of this style to poetry of all kinds, and to reject as vicious and indefensible all phrases and forms of style that were not included in what he (unfortunately, I think, adopting an equivocal expression) called the language of *real life*. From this preface, prefixed to poems in which it was impossible to deny the presence of original genius, however mistaken its direction might be deemed, arose the whole long continued controversy. For from the conjunction of perceived power with supposed heresy I explain the inveteracy[2] and in some instances, I grieve to say, the acrimonious passions, with which the controversy has been conducted by the assailants.

Had Mr. Wordsworth's poems been the silly, the childish things, which they were for a long time described as being; had they been really distinguished from the compositions of other poets merely by meanness of language and inanity of thought; had they indeed contained nothing more than what is found in the parodies and pretended imitations of them; they must have sunk at once, a dead weight, into the slough of oblivion, and have dragged the preface along with them. But year after year increased the number of Mr. Wordworth's admirers. They were found too not in the lower classes of the reading public, but chiefly among young men of strong sensibility and meditative minds; and their admiration (inflamed perhaps in some degree by opposition) was distinguished by its intensity, I might almost say, by its *religious* fervour. These facts, and the intellectual energy of the author, which was more or less consciously felt, where it was outwardly and even boisterously denied, meeting with sentiments of aversion to his opinions, and of alarm at their consequences, produced an eddy of criticism, which would of itself have borne up the poems by the violence, with which it whirled them round and round. With many parts of this preface in the sense attributed to them and which the words undoubtedly seem to authorise, I never concurred; but on the contrary objected to them as erroneous in principle, and as contradictory (in appearance at least) both to other parts of the same preface, and to the author's own practice in the greater number of the poems themselves. Mr. Wordsworth in his recent collection has, I find, degraded this prefatory disquisition to the end of his second volume, to be read or not at the reader's choice.[3] But he has not, as far as I can discover, announced any change in his poetic creed. [At] all events, considering it as the source of a controversy, in which I have been honored more, than I deserve, by the frequent conjunction of my name with his, I think it expedient to declare once for all, in what points I coincide with his opinions, and in what points I altogether differ. But in order to render myself intelligible I must previously, in as few words as possible, explain my ideas, first, of a POEM; and secondly, of POETRY itself, in *kind*, and in *essence*.

[PHILOSOPHIC DEFINITIONS OF A POEM AND POETRY]

A poem is that species of composition, which is opposed to works of science, by proposing for its *immediate* object pleasure, not truth; and from all other species (having *this* object in common with it) it is discriminated by proposing to itself such delight from the *whole*, as is compatible with a distinct gratification from each component *part*. * * *

But if this should be admitted as a satisfactory character of a poem, we have still to seek for a definition of poetry. The writings of PLATO, and Bishop TAYLOR, and the

---

2. Deep-seated prejudice.

3. *Poems* (1815), the edition in which Wordsworth represented his works.

Theoria Sacra of BURNET,[4] furnish undeniable proofs that poetry of the highest kind may exist without metre, and even without the contra-distinguishing objects of a poem. The first chapter of Isaiah (indeed a very large proportion of the whole book) is poetry in the most emphatic sense; yet it would be not less irrational than strange to assert, that pleasure, and not truth, was the immediate object of the prophet. In short, whatever *specific* import we attach to the word, poetry, there will be found involved in it, as a necessary consequence, that a poem of any length neither can be, or ought to be, all poetry. * * *

What is poetry? is so nearly the same question with, what is a poet? that the answer to the one is involved in the solution of the other. For it is a distinction resulting from the poetic genius itself, which sustains and modifies the images, thoughts, and emotions of the poet's own mind. The poet, described in ideal perfection, brings the whole soul of man into activity, with the subordination of its faculties to each other, according to their relative worth and dignity. He diffuses a tone, and spirit of unity, that blends, and (as it were) *fuses*, each into each, by that synthetic and magical power, to which we have exclusively appropriated the name of imagination. This power, first put in action by the will and understanding, and retained under their irremissive, though gentle and unnoticed, controul (*laxis effertur habenis* [guided by loose reins]) reveals itself in the balance or reconciliation of opposite or discordant qualities: of sameness, with difference; of the general, with the concrete; the idea, with the image; the individual, with the representative; the sense of novelty and freshness, with old and familiar objects; a more than usual state of emotion, with more than usual order; judgement ever awake and steady self-possession, with enthusiasm and feeling profound or vehement; and while it blends and harmonizes the natural and the artificial, still subordinates art to nature; the manner to the matter; and our admiration of the poet to our sympathy with the poetry. * * *

Finally, GOOD SENSE is the BODY of poetic genius, FANCY its DRAPERY, MOTION its LIFE, and IMAGINATION the SOUL that is every where, and in each; and forms all into one graceful and intelligent whole.

from *Chapter 17*

[EXAMINATION OF THE TENETS PECULIAR TO MR. WORDSWORTH. RUSTIC LIFE AND POETIC LANGUAGE]

As far then as Mr. Wordsworth in his preface contended, and most ably contended, for a reformation in our poetic diction, as far as he has evinced the truth of passion, and the *dramatic* propriety of those figures and metaphors in the original poets, which stript of their justifying reasons, and converted into mere artifices of connection or ornament, constitute the characteristic falsity in the poetic style of the moderns; and as far as he has, with equal acuteness and clearness, pointed out the process in which this change was effected, and the resemblances between that state into which the reader's mind is thrown by the pleasureable confusion of thought from an unaccustomed train of words and images; and that state which is induced by the natural language of empassioned feeling; he undertook a useful task, and deserves all praise, both for the attempt and for the execution. * * *

---

4. The Greek philosopher Plato, Jeremy Taylor, author of *Holy Living* and *Holy Dying* (1650–51), and the 17th-century theologian Thomas Burnet are singled out for the poetical quality of their prose writing.

My own differences from certain supposed parts of Mr. Wordsworth's theory ground themselves on the assumption, that his words had been rightly interpreted, as purporting that the proper diction for poetry in general consists altogether in a language taken, with due exceptions, from the mouths of men in real life, a language which actually constitutes the natural conversation of men under the influence of natural feelings. * * * The poet informs his reader, that he had generally chosen *low and rustic* life; but not *as* low and rustic, or in order to repeat that pleasure of doubtful moral effect, which persons of elevated rank and of superior refinement oftentimes derive from a happy *imitation* of the rude unpolished manners and discourse of their inferiors. * * * He chose low and rustic life, "because in that condition the essential passions of the heart find a better soil, in which they can attain their maturity, are less under restraint, and speak a plainer and more emphatic language; because in that condition of life our elementary feelings coexist in a state of greater simplicity, and consequently may be more accurately contemplated, and more forcibly communicated; because the manners of rural life germinate from those elementary feelings; and from the necessary character of rural occupations are more easily comprehended, and are more durable; and lastly, because in that condition the passions of men are incorporated with the beautiful and permanent forms of nature."

Now it is clear to me, that in the most interesting of the poems, in which the author is more or less dramatic, as the "Brothers," "Michael," "Ruth," the "Mad Mother," &c. the persons introduced are by no means taken *from low or rustic life* in the common acceptation of those words; and it is not less clear, that the sentiments and language, as far as they can be conceived to have been really transferred from the minds and conversation of such persons, are attributable to causes and circumstances not necessarily connected with "their occupations and abode." The thoughts, feelings, language, and manners of the shepherd-farmers in the vales of Cumberland and Westmoreland,[1] as far as they are actually adopted in those poems, may be accounted for from causes, which will and do produce the same results in *every* state of life, whether in town or country. As the two principal I rank that INDEPENDENCE, which raises a man above servitude, or daily toil for the profit of others, yet not above the necessity of industry and a frugal simplicity of domestic life; and the accompanying unambitious, but solid and religious EDUCATION, which has rendered few books familiar, but the bible, and the liturgy or hymn book. * * *

I am convinced, that for the human soul to prosper in rustic life, a certain vantage-ground is pre-requisite. It is not every man, that is likely to be improved by a country life or by country labours. Education, or original sensibility, or both, must pre-exist, if the changes, forms, and incidents of nature are to prove a sufficient stimulant. And where these are not sufficient, the mind contracts and hardens by want of stimulants; and the man becomes selfish, sensual, gross, and hard-hearted. * * *

I adopt with full faith the principle of Aristotle,[2] that poetry as poetry is essentially *ideal*, that it avoids and excludes all *accident*; that its apparent individualities of rank, character, or occupation must be *representative* of a class; and that the *persons* of poetry must be clothed with *generic* attributes, with the *common* attributes of the class; not with such as one gifted individual might *possibly* possess, but such as from his situation it is most probable before-hand, that he *would* possess. If my premises are

---

1. Counties in the northwest of England known together as the Lake District.

2. Author of the earliest known treatise on the theory of poetry (5th century B.C.), the *Poetics*.

right, and my deductions legitimate, it follows that there can be no *poetic* medium between the swains of Theocritus[3] and those of an imaginary golden age.

The characters of the vicar and the shepherd-mariner in the poem of the BROTHERS, those of the shepherd of Green-head Gill in the "MICHAEL," have all the verisimilitude and representative quality, that the purposes of poetry can require. They are persons of a known and abiding class, and their manners and sentiments the natural product of circumstances common to the class. * * *

On the other hand, in the poems which are pitched at a lower note, as the "Harry Gill," "Idiot Boy," &c. the *feelings* are those of human nature in general; though the poet has judiciously laid the *scene* in the country, in order to place *himself* in the vicinity of interesting images, without the necessity of ascribing a sentimental perception of their beauty to the persons of his drama. * * *

In the "Thorn," the poet himself acknowledges in a note the necessity of an introductory poem, in which he should have pourtrayed the character of the person from whom the words of the poem are supposed to proceed: a superstitious man moderately imaginative, of slow faculties and deep feelings, "a captain of a small trading vessel, for example, who being past the middle age of life, had retired upon an annuity, or small independent income, to some village or country town of which he was not a native, or in which he had not been accustomed to live. Such men having nothing to do become credulous and talkative from indolence." But in a poem, still more in a lyric poem (and the NURSE in Shakspeare's Romeo and Juliet alone prevents me from extending the remark even to dramatic *poetry*, if indeed the Nurse itself can be deemed altogether a case in point) it is not possible to imitate truly a dull and garrulous discourser, without repeating the effects of dulness and garrulity. * * *

Still more must I hesitate in my assent to the sentence which immediately follows the former citation[:] * * * "The language too of these men is adopted (purified indeed from what appears to be its real defects, from all lasting and rational causes of dislike or disgust) because such men hourly communicate with the best objects from which the best part of language is originally derived; and because, from their rank in society, and the sameness and narrow circle of their intercourse, being less under the action of social vanity, they convey their feelings and notions in simple and unelaborated expressions." To this I reply; that a rustic's language, purified from all provincialism and grossness, and so far re-constructed as to be made consistent with the rules of grammar (which are in essence no other than the laws of universal logic, applied to Psychological materials) will not differ from the language of any other man of common-sense, however learned or refined he may be, except as far as the notions, which the rustic has to convey, are fewer and more indiscriminate. This will become still clearer, if we add the consideration (equally important though less obvious) that the rustic, from the more imperfect development of his faculties, and from the lower state of their cultivation, aims almost solely to convey *insulated facts*, either those of his scanty experience or his traditional belief; while the educated man chiefly seeks to discover and express those *connections* of things, or those relative *bearings* of fact to fact, from which some more or less general law is deducible. For *facts* are valuable to a wise man, chiefly as they lead to the discovery of the in-dwelling *law*, which is the true *being* of things, the sole solution of their modes of existence, and in the knowledge of which consists our dignity and our power.

3. Greek poet, 3rd century B.C. His *Idylls* are the origin of the Western pastoral tradition.

As little can I agree with the assertion, that from the objects with which the rustic hourly communicates, the best part of language is formed. For first, if to communicate with an object implies such an acquaintance with it, as renders it capable of being discriminately reflected on; the distinct knowledge of an uneducated rustic would furnish a very scanty vocabulary. The few things, and modes of action, requisite for his bodily conveniences, would alone be individualized; while all the rest of nature would be expressed by a small number of confused, general terms. Secondly, I deny that the words and combinations of words derived from the objects, with which the rustic is familiar, whether with distinct or confused knowledge, can be justly said to form the best part of language. It is more than probable, that many classes of the brute creation possess discriminating sounds, by which they can convey to each other notices of such objects as concern their food, shelter, or safety. Yet we hesitate to call the aggregate of such sounds a language, otherwise than metaphorically. The best part of human language, properly so called, is derived from reflection on the acts of the mind itself. It is formed by a voluntary appropriation of fixed symbols to internal acts, to processes and results of imagination, the greater part of which have no place in the consciousness of uneducated man; though in civilized society, by imitation and passive remembrance of what they hear from their religious instructors and other superiors, the most uneducated share in the harvest which they neither sowed or reaped. * * *

The positions, which I controvert, are contained in the sentences—"*a selection of the* REAL *language of men;*"—"*the language of these men* (i.e. men in low and rustic life) *I propose to myself to imitate, and as far as possible, to adopt the very language of men.*" "*Between the language of prose and that of metrical composition, there neither is, nor can be any essential difference.*" It is against these exclusively, that my opposition is directed.

I object, in the very first instance, to an equivocation in the use of the word "real." Every man's language varies, according to the extent of his knowledge, the activity of his faculties, and the depth or quickness of his feelings. Every man's language has, first, its *individualities;* secondly, the common properties of the *class* to which he belongs; and thirdly, words and phrases of *universal* use. The language of Hooker, Bacon, Bishop Taylor, and Burke, differ from the common language of the learned class only by the superior number and novelty of the thoughts and relations which they had to convey. The language of Algernon Sidney[4] differs not at all from that, which every well educated gentleman would wish to write, and (with due allowances for the undeliberateness, and less connected train, of thinking natural and proper to conversation) such as he would wish to talk. Neither one or the other differ half as much from the general language of cultivated society, as the language of Mr. Wordsworth's homeliest composition differs from that of a common peasant. For "real" therefore, we must substitute *ordinary*, or *lingua communis* [common language]. And this, we have proved, is no more to be found in the phraseology of low and rustic life, than in that of any other class. Omit the peculiarities of each, and the result of course must be common to all. * * *

Neither is the case rendered at all more tenable by the addition of the words, "*in a state of excitement.*" For the nature of a man's words, when he is strongly affected by joy, grief, or anger, must necessarily depend on the number and quality of the general truths, conceptions and images, and of the words expressing them, with which his mind had been previously stored. For the property of passion is not to *create;* but to

---

4. Richard Hooker (1554–1600) wrote *The Laws of Ecclesiastical Polity;* he and Bishop Taylor were both known for their style as well as their ideas, as were the philosophers Francis Bacon (1561–1626) and Edmund Burke. The republican Algernon Sidney was executed for his supposed complicity in the so-called Rye House Plot to assassinate Charles II in 1683. Coleridge refers to his *Discourses on Government* (1698).

set in increased activity. At least, whatever new connections of thoughts or images, or (which is equally, if not more than equally, the appropriate effect of strong excitement) whatever generalizations of truth or experience, the heat of passion may produce; yet the terms of their conveyance must have pre-existed in his former conversations, and are only collected and crowded together by the unusual stimulation. It is indeed very possible to adopt in a poem the unmeaning repetitions, habitual phrases, and other blank counters, which an unfurnished or confused understanding interposes at short intervals, in order to keep hold of his subject which is still slipping from him, and to give him time for recollection; or in mere aid of vacancy, as in the scanty companies of a country stage the same player pops backwards and forwards, in order to prevent the appearance of empty spaces, in the procession of Macbeth, or Henry VIIIth. But what assistance to the poet, or ornament to the poem, these can supply, I am at a loss to conjecture. Nothing assuredly can differ either in origin or in mode more widely from the *apparent* tautologies[5] of intense and turbulent feeling, in which the passion is greater and of longer endurance, than to be exhausted or satisfied by a single representation of the image or incident exciting it. Such repetitions I admit to be a beauty of the highest kind; as illustrated by Mr. Wordsworth himself from the song of Deborah [Judges 5.27]. *"At her feet he bowed, he fell, he lay down; at her feet he bowed, he fell; where he bowed, there he fell down dead."*
1815   1817

⊶ ✦ ⊷

George Gordon, Lord Byron
1788–1824

"Mad—bad—and dangerous to know," pronounced Lady Caroline Lamb, before becoming his lover; a "splendid and imperishable excellence of sincerity and strength," declared Matthew Arnold: the fascination that made Byron the archetypal Romantic, in Europe even more than in Britain, grew from both judgments. He was born in London in 1788, the son of Captain John "Mad Jack" Byron and his second wife, Catherine Gordon, a Scots heiress. The Captain quickly ran through her fortune and departed; Byron and his mother withdrew to Aberdeen in 1789. He passed the next ten years in straitened circumstances, sensitive to the clubfoot with which he had been born, left with a mother who displaced resentment against her absconded husband onto him, and tended by a Calvinist nurse whom he later said had early awakened his sexuality. In 1798 his great-uncle the fifth Baron Byron, "the wicked Lord," died childless, and just after his tenth birthday Byron unexpectedly inherited his title. He asked his mother "whether she perceived any difference in him since he had been made a lord, as he perceived none himself," but the difference shaped the poet.

Byron and his mother returned to England and moved into Newstead Abbey, near Nottingham, the now debt-ridden estate presented to the Byrons by Henry VIII; to the lonely boy, the Gothic hall embodied his tempestuous family heritage. In 1801 Byron was sent to school at Harrow; in the same year he probably met his half-sister Augusta. He entered Trinity College, Cambridge, in 1805, living extravagantly and entangling himself with moneylenders, but also making enduring friendships.

Byron's first published volume, *Hours of Idleness*, appeared in 1807, when he was nineteen; the lofty pose he struck in announcing himself as "Lord Byron: A Minor" provoked a savage notice from the *Edinburgh Review*, to which he retaliated in 1809 with a satire in Popean

5. Pointless repetitions.

couplets, *English Bards and Scotch Reviewers*. "Written when I was very young and very angry," Byron later confessed to Coleridge, the poem "has been a thorn in my side ever since; more particularly as almost all the Persons animadverted upon became subsequently my acquaintances, and some of them my friends." He suppressed the fifth edition, but so memorable were its attacks on Coleridge, Southey, Wordsworth, Scott, and others that pirated editions continued to appear. Byron took his seat in the House of Lords that same year, and then departed on a grand tour shaped by the Napoleonic wars, which barred much of Europe. He sailed to Lisbon, crossed Spain, and proceeded to Greece and Albania, through country little known to Western Europeans. There he began *Childe Harold's Pilgrimage*. In March 1810 he sailed for Constantinople, visited the site of Troy and swam the Hellespont in imitation of the mythical Greek lover, Leander. In the East, Byron found a world in which the love of an older aristocrat for a beautiful boy was accepted, and he also developed a political identity as the Western hero who would liberate Greece from the Turks.

Byron returned to London in July 1811, but too late to see his mother before she died. In February 1812 he made his first speech in the House of Lords, denouncing the death penalty proposed for weavers who had smashed the machines they blamed for their loss of work. Byron's parliamentary activity was superseded the next month when the first two cantos of *Childe Harold's Pilgrimage* appeared and he "woke to find himself famous." The poem joined the immediacy of a travelogue to the disillusionment of a speaker who voiced the melancholy of a generation wearied by prolonged war. Despite Byron's claim that Harold was a fiction designed merely to connect a picaresque narrative, readers took him as the mouthpiece of an author speaking passionately of his own concerns. The magnetism of this personality offset the cynicism the poem displayed: the handsome, aristocratic poet, returned from exotic travels, himself became a figure of force. Byron followed this success with a series of "Eastern" tales that added to his aura: one of them, *The Corsair* (1814), written in ten days, sold ten thousand copies on the day of publication. *Hebrew Melodies* (1815) contains some of Byron's most famous lyrics (*She walks in beauty*) and accorded with the vogue for nationalist themes. Byron was both a sensational commercial success and a noble who gave away his copyrights because aristocrats do not write for money. Like all myths, "Byron" embodied contradictions more than he resolved them.

This literary celebrity was enhanced by Byron's lionizing in Whig society. Liaisons with Lady Caroline Lamb and the "autumnal" Lady Oxford magnified his notoriety, but it was his relationship with his half-sister Augusta, now married, that gave rise to most scandal; her daughter Medora, born in 1814 and given the name of the heroine of *The Corsair*, was widely thought to be Byron's, and probably was. Seeking to escape these agitating affairs, and also to repair his debts, Byron proposed to Annabella Milbanke. They married in January 1815; their daughter Augusta Ada was born at the end of the year, but a few weeks later Annabella left Byron to live with her parents, amid rumors of insanity, incest, and sodomy. Pirated editions of Byron's poems on the separation made marital discord into public scandal.

In April 1816 Byron quit England, bearing the pageant of his bleeding heart, in Matthew Arnold's famous phrase, across Europe. He settled in Geneva, near Percy Bysshe Shelley and Mary Godwin, who had eloped two years before. They had been joined by Mary's stepsister, Claire Clairmont, with whom Byron resumed an affair he had begun in England. Poetry was as much in the air as romance: Byron reported that Shelley "dosed him with Wordsworth physic even to nausea"; the influence and resistance the phrase shows are both evident in the third canto of *Childe Harold* (1816). He wrote *The Prisoner of Chillon* at this time and began the closet-drama *Manfred* (1817). At the end of the summer the Shelley party left for England, where Claire gave birth to Byron's illegitimate daughter Allegra; in October Byron departed for Venice, where he rented a palazzo on the Grand Canal.

Byron described his Venetian life in brilliant letters, some of which were meant for circulation in the circle of his publisher John Murray. To a ceaseless round of sexual activity, he joined substantial literary productivity. He studied Armenian, completed *Manfred*, and visited Rome, gathering materials for a fourth canto of *Childe Harold* (1818). The canto was his longest and most sublime, and its invocation of Freedom's torn banner streaming "*against* the wind" fixed his revolutionary reputation. Yet Byron began to feel trapped by the modes that had won him popularity; determining to "repel charges of monotony and mannerism," he wrote *Beppo*, a comic verse tale of a Venetian *ménage-à-trois* (1818). In its colloquial, digressive ease, Byron was testing the form of his greatest poem, *Don Juan*, at once fictional autobiography, picaresque narrative, literary burlesque, and exposure of social, sexual, and religious hypocrisies. The first two cantos were published in 1819 in an expensive edition meant to forestall charges of blasphemy and bearing neither the author's nor the publisher's name. The authorship was nonetheless known: *Blackwood's Magazine* criticized Byron for "a filthy and impious" attack on his wife, and the second canto, which turns to shipwreck and cannibalism, redoubled charges of nihilism. Shocking the proprieties of one audience, Byron moved toward another; the poem sold well in increasingly cheap editions.

In April 1819 Byron met his "last attachment," Countess Teresa Gamba Guiccioli, nineteen years old and married to a man nearly three times her age. Through her family, Byron was initiated into the Carbonari, a clandestine revolutionary organization devoted to achieving Italian independence from Austria. While continuing *Don Juan*, he wrote *Marino Faliero*, *Sardanapalus*, and *The Two Foscari* (all 1821), historical dramas exploring the relationship between the powerful individual and the postrevolutionary state. To the same year belongs *Cain*, a "mystery" drama refused copyright for its unorthodoxy and immediately pirated by radicals.

When Teresa's father and brother were exiled for their part in an abortive uprising, she followed them, and Byron reluctantly went with her to Pisa. There he reunited with Percy Shelley, with whom he planned a radical journal, *The Liberal*. The first number contained *The Vision of Judgment*, a devastating rebuttal to a eulogy of George III by Robert Southey, in the preface to which the poet laureate had alluded to Byron as the head of a "Satanic School."

Restive in the domesticity of life with Teresa, Byron agreed to act as agent of a London committee aiding the Greeks in their struggle for independence. In July 1823 he left for Cephalonia, an island in western Greece. Clear of debt and now attentive to his literary income, Byron devoted his fortune to the cause. Philhellenic idealism was soon confronted by motley reality, but Byron founded, paid, and trained a brigade of soldiers. A serious illness in February 1824, followed by the usual remedy of bleeding, weakened him; in April he contracted a fever, treated by further bleeding, from which he died on 19 April at the age of thirty-six. Deeply mourned, he became a Greek national hero, and throughout Europe his name became synonymous with Romanticism. In England, the stunned reaction of the young Tennyson spoke for many: on hearing the news, he sadly wrote on a rock "Byron is dead." As Arnold later recalled, in placing Byron with Wordsworth as the great English poets of the century, he had "subjugated" his readers, and his influence was immense and lasting.

She walks in beauty[1]

1

She walks in beauty, like the night
   Of cloudless climes and starry skies;
And all that's best of dark and bright
   Meet in her aspect and her eyes:
5   Thus mellow'd to that tender light
   Which heaven to gaudy day denies.

2

One shade the more, one ray the less,
   Had half impair'd the nameless grace
Which waves in every raven tress,

---

1. The first poem in *Hebrew Melodies*, a collection initiated by the Jewish composer Isaac Nathan, and published with his music. The subject is Anne Wilmot, the wife of Byron's cousin, whom he had seen at a party wearing "mourning, with dark spangles on her dress."

10   Or softly lightens o'er her face;
        Where thoughts serenely sweet express
        How pure, how dear their dwelling-place.

                        3

        And on that cheek, and o'er that brow,
        So soft, so calm, yet eloquent,
15   The smiles that win, the tints that glow,
        But tell of days in goodness spent,
        A mind at peace with all below,
        A heart whose love is innocent!

1814   1815

So, we'll go no more a–roving

                        1

        So, we'll go no more a–roving[1]
        So late into the night,
        Though the heart be still as loving,
        And the moon be still as bright.

                        2

5   For the sword outwears its sheath,
        And the soul wears out the breast,
        And the heart must pause to breathe,
        And love itself have rest.

                        3

        Though the night was made for loving,
10   And the day returns too soon,
        Yet we'll go no more a roving
        By the light of the moon.

1817   1830

FROM CHILDE HAROLD'S PILGRIMAGE
from Canto 3[1]
[THUNDERSTORM IN SWITZERLAND][2]

                        92

860   Thy sky is changed!—and such a change! Oh night,
        And storm, and darkness, ye are wondrous strong,

---

1. The poem first appeared in a letter Byron wrote from Venice to Thomas Moore: "The Carnival—that is, the latter part of it—and sitting up late o'nights, had knocked me up a little. But it is over—and it is now Lent . . . though I did not dissipate much upon the whole, yet I find 'the sword wearing out the scabbard,' though I have but just turned the corner of twenty-nine."
1. The first two cantos of Childe Harold's Pilgrimage appeared in 1812. As their subtitle "A Romaunt" indicated, Byron had adopted the form of romance for his unnervingly contemporary poem. The Spenserian stanzas and mock-archaisms—a "childe" is a youth of noble birth—played discordantly against the account of his travels in 1809–1811 through Spain (and his acerbic commentary on the Peninsular War; see Introduction, pages 1322–1323) and then on into parts of Greece unfrequented by Westerners. The overwhelming success of the poem

ensured that Byron would be identified with Childe Harold. Byron protested, but the connection is reinforced by the manuscripts themselves, which disclose that Childe Harold was once Childe Burun, an ancient form of his family name. Canto 3, published in 1816, is independent, though the continuity reflects the degree to which protagonist and poet had come to figure each other. Byron left England on 25 April 1816, and wrote the opening stanzas while crossing the Channel.
2. "The thunder-storms to which these lines refer occurred on the thirteenth of June, 1816, at midnight. I have seen among the Acroceraunian mountains of Chimari several more terrible, but none more beautiful" [Byron's note]. Byron had settled in the Villa Diodati on 10 June, near the Shelley party; a few days after these storms Mary Shelley began Frankenstein in Byron's new residence.

Yet lovely in your strength, as is the light
Of a dark eye in woman! Far along,
From peak to peak, the rattling crags among
865 Leaps the live thunder! Not from one lone cloud,
But every mountain now hath found a tongue,
And Jura answers, through her misty shroud,
Back to the joyous Alps, who call to her aloud![3]

93

And this is in the night:—Most glorious night!
870 Thou wert not sent for slumber! let me be
A sharer in thy fierce and far delight,—
A portion of the tempest and of thee!
How the lit lake shines, a phosphoric sea,
And the big rain comes dancing to the earth!
875 And now again 'tis black,—and now, the glee
Of the loud hills shakes with its mountain-mirth,
As if they did rejoice o'er a young earthquake's birth.

94

Now, where the swift Rhone cleaves his way between
Heights which appear as lovers who have parted
880 In hate, whose mining depths so intervene,
That they can meet no more, though broken-hearted!
Though in their souls, which thus each other thwarted,
Love was the very root of the fond rage
Which blighted their life's bloom, and then departed:
885 Itself expired, but leaving them an age
Of years all winters,—war within themselves to wage.[4]

95

Now, where the quick Rhone thus hath cleft his way,
The mightiest of the storms hath ta'en his stand:
For here, not one, but many, make their play,
890 And fling their thunder-bolts from hand to hand,
Flashing and cast around: of all the band,
The brightest through these parted hills hath fork'd
His lightnings, as if he did understand,
That in such gaps as desolation work'd,
895 There the hot shaft should blast whatever therein lurk'd.

96

Sky, mountains, river, winds, lake, lightnings! ye!
With night, and clouds, and thunder, and a soul
To make these felt and feeling, well may be
Things that have made me watchful; the far roll
900 Of your departing voices, is the knoll
Of what in me is sleepless,—if I rest.
But where of ye, oh tempests! is the goal?
Are ye like those within the human breast?
Or do ye find, at length, like eagles, some high nest?

3. The Jura mountains, to the north and west of Geneva, form the boundary between Switzerland and France; the Alps run to the east and south.
4. This description of the landscape in terms of lovers who have parted in hate obliquely recalls Byron's separation from his wife and illustrates his tendency to turn nature into sublime self-projection.

97

905   Could I embody and unbosom now
    That which is most within me,—could I wreak
    My thoughts upon expression, and thus throw
    Soul, heart, mind, passions, feelings, strong or weak,
    All that I would have sought, and all I seek,
910   Bear, know, feel, and yet breathe—into *one* word,
    And that one word were Lightning, I would speak;
    But as it is, I live and die unheard,
With a most voiceless thought, sheathing it as a sword.

from Canto 4[1]

[THE COLOSSEUM. THE DYING GLADIATOR]

139

    And here the buzz of eager nations ran,
    In murmur'd pity, or loud-roar'd applause,
1245   As man was slaughter'd by his fellow man.[2]
    And wherefore slaughter'd? wherefore, but because
    Such were the bloody Circus' genial laws,
    And the imperial pleasure. Wherefore not?
    What matters where we fall to fill the maws°   stomachs
1250   Of worms—on battle-plains or listed spot?
Both are but theatres where the chief actors rot.

140

    I see before me the Gladiator lie:
    He leans upon his hand—his manly brow
    Consents to death, but conquers agony,
1255   And his droop'd head sinks gradually low—
    And through his side the last drops, ebbing slow
    From the red gash, fall heavy, one by one,
    Like the first of a thunder-shower; and now
    The arena swims around him—he is gone,
1260   Ere ceased the inhuman shout which hail'd the wretch who won.

141

    He heard it, but he heeded not—his eyes
    Were with his heart, and that was far away:
    He reck'd not of the life he lost nor prize,
    But where his rude hut by the Danube lay,
1265   *There* were his young barbarians all at play,
    There was their Dacian mother[3]—he, their sire,
    Butcher'd to make a Roman holiday—

All this rush'd with his blood—Shall he expire
And unavenged?—Arise! ye Goths, and glut your ire![4]

142

1270   But here, where Murder breathed her bloody steam;
And here, where buzzing nations choked the ways,
And roar'd or murmur'd like a mountain stream
Dashing or winding as its torrent strays;
Here, where the Roman millions' blame or praise
1275   Was death or life, the playthings of a crowd,
My voice sounds much—and fall the stars' faint rays
On the arena void—seats crush'd—walls bow'd—
And galleries, where my steps seem echoes strangely loud.

143

A ruin—yet what ruin! from its mass
1280   Walls, palaces, half-cities, have been rear'd;
Yet oft the enormous skeleton ye pass,
And marvel where the spoil could have appear'd.
Hath it indeed been plunder'd, or but clear'd?
Alas! developed,° opens the decay,   *disclosed*
1285   When the colossal fabric's form is near'd:
It will not bear the brightness of the day,
Which streams too much on all years, man, have reft° away.   *ravaged*

144

But when the rising moon begins to climb
Its topmost arch, and gently pauses there;
1290   When the stars twinkle through the loops of time,
And the low night-breeze waves along the air
The garland forest, which the gray walls wear,
Like laurels on the bald first Caesar's head;[5]
When the light shines serene but doth not glare,
1295   Then in this magic circle raise the dead:
Heroes have trod this spot—'tis on their dust ye tread.

145

"While stands the Coliseum, Rome shall stand;
When falls the Coliseum, Rome shall fall;
And when Rome falls—the World."[6] From our own land
1300   Thus spake the pilgrims o'er this mighty wall
In Saxon times, which we are wont to call
Ancient;[7] and these three mortal things are still
On their foundations, and unalter'd all;

4. The Goths were Germanic tribes who overran the Roman Empire in the 5th century A.D. The vivid stanza was inspired by the statue of a dying Gaul in the Capitoline Museum, in Byron's day thought to represent a dying gladiator.

5. The Roman historian Suetonius records that Julius Caesar (102–44 B.C.) was particularly gratified by a decree of the Roman Senate that permitted him to wear a laurel wreath, the traditional symbol of victory, at all times, because it hid his baldness.

6. A note directs the reader to chapter 71 of *The Decline and Fall of the Roman Empire*, by Edward Gibbon (1737–1794), a work Byron had known since adolescence: "Reduced to its naked majesty, the Flavian amphitheatre was contemplated with awe and admiration by the pilgrims of the North: and their rude enthusiasm broke forth in a sublime proverbial expression, which is recorded in the eighth century in the fragments of the venerable Bede."

7. The Anglo-Saxon kingdoms in Britain, established following the withdrawal of the Romans in the 4th century A.D., consolidated into one Saxon kingdom that existed until the Norman Conquest of 1066.

Rome and her Ruin past Redemption's skill,
1305   The World, the same wide den—of thieves, or what ye will.

Don Juan

"Give me a poem," Byron's publisher John Murray wrote him in January 1817, "a good Venetian tale describing manners formerly from the story itself, and now from your own observations." The response was *Beppo*, which Byron based on an anecdote that he had heard from the husband of his mistress, turning it into a seemingly effortless comparison of Italian and British manners. Its success led Murray to ask in July 1818: "Have you not another lively tale like *Beppo*? Or will you not give me some prose in three volumes?—all the adventures that you have undergone, seen, heard of, or imagined, with your reflections on life and manners." In the same week Byron had begun *Don Juan*; his own inclination consorted with the publisher's sketch of a suitable "work to open [his] campaign" for fall sales.

For a work of which he remarked "I *have* no plan—I *had* no plan—but I had or have materials," Byron found an ideal model in the seriocomic Italian romances of the fifteenth and sixteenth centuries by Pulci, Berni, and Ariosto. Their episodic, digressive mode, flexible enough to incorporate a wide range of moods and stylistic levels, enabled Byron to stage aspects of himself that had not appeared in the titanism of his Eastern tales and the loftiness of *Childe Harold's Pilgrimage*. He sought to treat public issues with the conversational fluency of a skeptical intelligence engaged with the ordinary materiality of the world: brand names and ship's pumps, indigestion and thinning hair, literary rivalries and reviewers. Byron regarded the story as a "hinge" on which to mount his reflections, and as the poem proceeds its title character retreats before the ceaseless inventions of the narrator, who both is and is not Byron. "If people contradict themselves," he wrote, "can I / Help contradicting them, and everybody, / Even my veracious self?" Truth's streams, he continued, "cut through such canals of contradiction, / That she must often navigate o'er fiction" (15.88). Such teasing of the borders between fiction and fact intrigued readers, and enhanced the allure of the figure of "Byron" the words create. *Don Juan* is a seemingly inexhaustible improvisatory monologue—sixteen cantos were published between 1819 and 1823, with a fragmentary seventeenth left uncompleted at Byron's death. Through a range of voices, by allusion and quotation, and in the number of perspectives entertained or denounced by the narrator, the poem generates a sense of dialogue and exchange. As the critic Jerome McGann has argued, the poem superimposes three historical levels: Juan's own story is set in the late eighteenth century and was planned to end in the French Revolution; the narrator's reminiscences arise from Byron's years of fame in Regency London (1812–1816); lastly, the narrator's commentary engages the post-Napoleonic moment of the actual writing (1818–1823). As it proceeds, *Don Juan* depicts Greek pirates and Turkish harems, Russian armies and Spanish families, British highwaymen and British aristocrats, story and commentary together building a critical portrait of the Europe of Byron's era, torn by revolution and now subsiding into the conservative restoration the poet condemns. Though he might have begun the poem intending only "to giggle and make giggle," Byron's purposes deepened as he advanced against the opposition of his friends and publisher.

Byron intensifies the sense that he is speaking in *Don Juan*—forms of the first-person pronoun occur almost two thousand times—and he repeatedly reminds the reader of his capricious playing with form, but the poem is personal in a more specific way as well. Readers familiar with Byron's life—and his celebrity had assured that many were—could perceive in Juan's mother, Donna Inez, a caricature of Byron's estranged wife Annabella, Lady Byron. The account of Juan's youth with Inez also draws on Byron's childhood, "an only son left with an only mother" (1.37). Like Wordsworth's *Prelude*, *Don Juan* is autobiography—but in the form of oblique and theatricalized fiction. It is also picaresque adventure, satire, and mock-Homeric epic, whose hero belies the legacy of his name, seduced more often than seducing, kind-hearted rather than ruthless and conniving. Byron's genre-crossing revision of literary tradition made "something wholly new & relative to the age," as Shelley recognized.

Much of the poem's power arises from Byron's fluent handling of ottava rima, the eight-line stanza form rhyming *abababcc*. He credited *The Monks and the Giants* (1817) by his friend John Hookham Frere with having shown him its possibilities, but Frere's work shows little of Byron's deftness. Byron employed a fantastic wealth of rhymes ("Plato" with "potato," "intellectual" with "hen-peck'd you all"), often emphasizing the snap of the concluding couplet for comic surprise, but he could also downplay the rhymes and enjamb lines to yield a rhythm like blank verse. "The most readable poem of its length ever written," Virginia Woolf observed of *Don Juan*, because its "method is a discovery by itself . . . an elastic shape which will hold whatever you choose to put in it." "Like all free and easy things," she added, "only the skilled and mature really bring them off successfully. But Byron was full of ideas—a quality that gives his verse a toughness." The rare combination of ease and power to which both Shelley and Woolf point keeps *Don Juan* subversively fresh today.

FROM DON JUAN
Dedication[1]

1

Bob Southey! You're a poet, Poet-laureate,[2]
   And representative of all the race,
Although 'tis true that you turn'd out a Tory at
   Last,—yours has lately been a common case,—
5   And now, my Epic Renegade! what are ye at?
     With all the Lakers,[3] in and out of place?
A nest of tuneful persons, to my eye
Like "four and twenty Blackbirds in a pye;[4]

2

"Which pye being open'd they began to sing"
10   (This old song and new simile holds good),
"A dainty dish to set before the King,"
   Or Regent, who admires such kind of food;—
And Coleridge, too, has lately taken wing,
     But like a hawk encumber'd with his hood,—
15   Explaining metaphysics to the nation—
I wish he would explain his Explanation.[5]

3

You, Bob! are rather insolent, you know,
   At being disappointed in your wish
To supersede all warblers here below,

---

1. Byron sent the Dedication to his publisher in November 1818 with Canto 1 of *Don Juan*. When Cantos 1-2 were published together, anonymously, in 1819 Byron removed the Dedication because he did not want "to attack the dog [Southey] so fiercely without putting my name." It appeared for the first time in the 1832–1833 edition of Byron's works.
2. Robert Southey became Poet Laureate in 1813. He earned Byron's contempt for having abandoned his early republican principles and for his malicious gossip in 1816 about Byron, Shelley, Claire Clairmont, and Mary Shelley: "The Son of a Bitch . . . said that Shelley and I 'had formed a League of Incest and practiced our precepts

with &c'." The phrase "Epic Renegade" (line 5) glances both at Southey's political reversal and his series of epic poems such as *Thalaba* (1801) and *The Curse of Kehama* (1810).
3. The collective term applied by *The Edinburgh Review* to Coleridge, Southey, and Wordsworth, from their common residence in the Lake District.
4. Henry James Pye (1745–1813) was the Poet Laureate before Southey; his very first official ode had provoked the nursery-rhyme parody Byron repeats here.
5. Referring to Coleridge's *The Statesman's Manual* (1816) and *Biographia Literaria* (1817).

20   And be the only Blackbird in the dish;
      And then you overstrain yourself, or so,
          And tumble downward like the flying fish
      Gasping on deck, because you soar too high, Bob,
      And fall, for lack of moisture quite a-dry, Bob![6]

                              4

25   And Wordsworth, in a rather long "Excursion"[7]
          (I think the quarto holds five hundred pages),
      Has given a sample from the vasty version
          Of his new system to perplex the sages;
      'Tis poetry—at least by his assertion,
30   And may appear so when the dog-star rages—
      And he who understands it would be able
      To add a story to the Tower of Babel.[8]

                              5

      You—Gentlemen! by dint of long seclusion
          From better company, have kept your own
35   At Keswick,[9] and, through still continued fusion
          Of one another's minds, at last have grown
      To deem as a most logical conclusion,
          That Poesy has wreaths for you alone:
      There is a narrowness in such a notion,
40   Which makes me wish you'd change your lakes for ocean.

                              6

      I would not imitate the petty thought,
          Nor coin my self-love to so base a vice,
      For all the glory your conversion brought,
          Since gold alone should not have been its price.
45   You have your salary; was't for that you wrought?
          And Wordsworth has his place in the Excise.[1]
      You're shabby fellows—true—but poets still,
      And duly seated on the immortal hill.°   *Parnassus*

                              7

      Your bays° may hide the baldness of your brows—   *laurel wreaths*
50   Perhaps some virtuous blushes;—let them go—
      To you I envy neither fruit nor boughs—
          And for the fame you would engross below,
      The field is universal, and allows
          Scope to all such as feel the inherent glow:
55   Scott, Rogers, Campbell, Moore, and Crabbe,[2] will try
      'Gainst you the question with posterity.

6. A "dry bob" was slang for sex without ejaculation.
7. Wordsworth's nine-book poem *The Excursion* had appeared in 1814.
8. To punish human presumption, God destroys the Tower of Babel and institutes the multiplicity of languages (Genesis 11.1–9); note the pun on "story."
9. The town where Southey lived, to which Coleridge and his family moved in 1800; Wordsworth lived nearby in Grasmere.
1. In March 1813 Wordsworth obtained a sinecure as distributor of tax stamps for Westmoreland through the aid of his patron, the Earl of Lonsdale, to whom he dedicated

The Excursion.
2. In ranking the living poets in an 1813 journal, Byron declared Walter Scott the "Monarch of Parnassus," Samuel Rogers (1763–1855) next, Thomas Moore (1779–1852) and Thomas Campbell (1777–1844) third, "Southey-Wordsworth-Coleridge" below these. George Crabbe (1754–1832) he elsewhere praised for being "free" of the "wrong revolutionary poetical system" that he and his contemporaries exemplified: "and if I had to begin again—I would model myself accordingly—Crabbe's the man."

8

For me, who, wandering with pedestrian Muses,[3]
   Contend not with you on the winged steed,
I wish your fate may yield ye, when she chooses,
60   The fame you envy, and the skill you need;
And recollect a poet nothing loses
   In giving to his brethren their full meed°   *reward*
Of merit, and complaint of present days
Is not the certain path to future praise.

9

65 He that reserves his laurels for posterity
   (Who does not often claim the bright reversion)
Has generally no great crop to spare it, he
   Being only injured by his own assertion;
And although here and there some glorious rarity
70   Arise like Titan from the sea's immersion,
The major part of such appellants go
To—God knows where—for no one else can know.

10

If, fallen in evil days on evil tongues,
   Milton appeal'd to the Avenger, Time,[4]
75 If Time, the Avenger, execrates his wrongs,
   And makes the word "Miltonic" mean *"sublime,"*
He deign'd not to belie his soul in songs,
   Nor turn his very talent to a crime;
He did not loathe the Sire to laud the Son,
80 But closed the tyrant-hater he begun.[5]

11

Think'st thou, could he—the blind Old Man—arise
   Like Samuel from the grave, to freeze once more
The blood of monarchs with his prophecies,[6]
   Or be alive again—again all hoar
85 With time and trials, and those helpless eyes,
   And heartless daughters[7]—worn—and pale—and poor;
Would *he* adore a sultan? *he* obey
The intellectual eunuch Castlereagh?[8]

12

Cold-blooded, smooth-faced, placid miscreant!
90 Dabbling its sleek young hands in Erin's° gore,   *Ireland's*
   And thus for wider carnage taught to pant,
     Transferr'd to gorge upon a sister shore,

---

3. The "musa pedestris" of the Latin poet Horace (65–8 B.C.) signals a humble, as opposed to exalted or epic, style (*Satires* 2.6.17).
4. Recalling the invocation to Book 7 of *Paradise Lost:* "On evil days though fall'n, and evil tongues" (26).
5. Milton, who had supported the Commonwealth party that overthrew Charles I in 1649, remained loyal to principle and did not praise Charles II after the Restoration in 1660.
6. King Saul, attacked by the Philistines, raises the ghost of the prophet Samuel to ask advice, only to learn that he has disobeyed the Lord and will be delivered to the ene-

my (1 Samuel 28).
7. "Milton's two elder daughters are said to have robbed him of his books, besides cheating and plaguing him in the economy of his house" [Byron's note].
8. The Irish nobleman Robert Stewart, Marquis of Londonderry and Viscount Castlereagh, as chief secretary for Ireland (1799–1801) suppressed the Irish rebellion and secured the Act of Union with England that ended the Irish Parliament; he became Foreign Secretary of Britain (1812–1822). He was instrumental in arranging the balance of power in post-Napoleonic Europe, for which he was detested by Byron and the liberals.

The vulgarest tool that Tyranny could want,
   With just enough of talent, and no more,
95   To lengthen fetters by another fix'd,
   And offer poison long already mix'd.[9]

13

An orator of such set trash of phrase
   Ineffably—legitimately vile,[1]
That even its grossest flatterers dare not praise,
100   Nor foes—all nations—condescend to smile,—
Not even a sprightly blunder's spark can blaze
   From that Ixion grindstone's ceaseless toil,[2]
That turns and turns to give the world a notion
Of endless torments and perpetual motion.

14

105 A bungler even in its disgusting trade,
   And botching, patching, leaving still behind
Something of which its masters are afraid,
   States to be curb'd, and thoughts to be confined,
Conspiracy or Congress to be made—[3]
110   Cobbling at manacles for all mankind—
A tinkering slave-maker, who mends old chains,
With God and man's abhorrence for its gains.

15

If we may judge of matter by the mind,
   Emasculated to the marrow *It*
115 Hath but two objects, how to serve, and bind,
   Deeming the chain it wears even men may fit,
Eutropius[4] of its many masters,—blind
   To worth as freedom, wisdom as to wit,
Fearless—because *no* feeling dwells in ice,
120 Its very courage stagnates to a vice.

16

Where shall I turn me not to *view* its bonds,
   For I will never *feel* them;—Italy!
Thy late reviving Roman soul desponds
   Beneath the lie this State-thing breathed o'er thee—
125 Thy clanking chain, and Erin's yet green wounds,
   Have voices—tongues to cry aloud for me.
Europe has slaves—allies—kings—armies still,
And Southey lives to sing them very ill.

---

9. His opponents regarded Castlereagh as the pawn of the Austrian foreign minister, Prince Metternich.
1. Castlereagh's poor speaking was notorious: "It is the first time indeed since the Normans," Byron wrote in the Preface to Cantos 6–8, "that England has been insulted by a *Minister* (at least) who could not speak English, and that Parliament permitted itself to be dictated to in the language of Mrs. Malaprop" [the character from R. B. Sheridan's *The Rivals* (1773) who has given her name to verbal slips].
2. In Greek mythology Ixion is punished in Hades by being chained to a perpetually rolling wheel.
3. In 1814 Austria, Russia, Prussia, and England formed

the Quadruple Alliance; after the fall of Napoleon, Castlereagh and Metternich reestablished the "legitimate" governments of Europe at the Congress of Vienna (1815), restoring the Bourbons in France and acknowledging Ferdinand VII in Spain.
4. The career of Eutropius, a eunuch who became a magistrate and general in the Eastern Roman Empire (395–408), is narrated by Gibbon, *Decline and Fall* (ch. 32). Byron's denunciation of Castlereagh as a "eunuch" and an "It" may hint private knowledge. Castlereagh's suicide in 1822, officially attributed to overwork, was preceded by an attempt to blackmail him on the grounds of homosexuality: sodomy was a capital crime.

17

Meantime—Sir Laureate—I proceed to dedicate,
130   In honest simple verse, this song to you.
And, if in flattering strains I do not predicate,
    'Tis that I still retain my "buff and blue";[5]
My politics as yet are all to educate:
    Apostasy's so fashionable, too,
135 To keep *one* creed's a task grown quite Herculean;
Is it not so, my Tory, ultra-Julian?[6]

from Canto 1

1

I want a hero: an uncommon want,
    When every year and month sends forth a new one,
Till, after cloying the gazettes with cant,
    The age discovers he is not the true one;
5   Of such as these I should not care to vaunt,
    I'll therefore take our ancient friend Don Juan—
We all have seen him, in the pantomime,
Sent to the devil somewhat ere his time.[1]

2

Vernon, the butcher Cumberland, Wolfe, Hawke,
10 Prince Ferdinand, Granby, Burgoyne, Keppel, Howe,[2]
Evil and good, have had their tithe of talk,
    And fill'd their sign-posts then, like Wellesley now;[3]
Each in their turn like Banquo's monarchs stalk,
    Followers of fame, "nine farrow" of that sow:[4]
15 France, too, had Buonaparté and Dumourier
Recorded in the Moniteur and Courier.[5]

3

Barnave, Brissot, Condorcet, Mirabeau,
    Petion, Clootz, Danton, Marat, La Fayette,[6]
Were French, and famous people, as we know;
20   And there were others, scarce forgotten yet,
Joubert, Hoche, Marceau, Lannes, Desaix, Moreau,

5. Buff and blue were the colors adopted by the Whigs and by the *Edinburgh Review*.
6. Julian was raised as a Christian, but on becoming Roman emperor in 361 he revived the worship of the pagan gods. He was killed in battle in 363. See Gibbon, *Decline and Fall* (ch. 23).
1. Popular melodrama portrayed Don Juan as a seducer who ends in hell; Byron plays against his own reputation as notorious lover by presenting Juan as an innocent boy overwhelmed by women. His attention may have been drawn to the figure by Coleridge's discussion in *Biographia Literaria* (ch. 23). Note that the pronunciation of "Juan" is Anglicized into two syllables, as the rhymes with "true one" and "new one" indicate. "Inez" rhymes with "fine as" and "Jóse" with "nosey."
2. A roll call of recent military heroes. The Duke of Cumberland commanded the forces that defeated the Stuart army at Culloden in 1745; he earned the title "Butcher" for his subsequent suppression of Jacobitism in Scotland.
3. Arthur Wellesley, Duke of Wellington, born in Ireland, the most celebrated British general of his time. Granted a peerage for his victory over the French at Talavera (1808), he commanded the British forces at Waterloo.
4. In Shakespeare's *Macbeth* (4.1), the witches show Macbeth a vision of future Scots kings descended from the murdered Banquo, establishing the triumph of his line and the frustration of Macbeth's ambitions.
5. Charles Dumouriez was a French general and Girondist; suspected by the Jacobins in 1793, he fled to the Austrians whom he had defeated the year before. He settled in England in 1804, and advised the British in their war against Buonaparte. The *Moniteur* and *Courier* were French newspapers.
6. All figures of the French Revolution. Jean Baptiste, Baron von Cloots, a zealot, dropped his title and took the pseudonym Anacharsis; elected to the Convention in 1792, he voted for the King's death and was himself executed in 1794. Byron wrote that he meant Juan "to finish as *Anacharsis Cloots*—in the French Revolution."

  With many of the military set,
  Exceedingly remarkable at times,
  But not at all adapted to my rhymes.

4

25 Nelson was once Britannia's god of war,
   And still should be so, but the tide is turn'd;
  There's no more to be said of Trafalgar,
   'Tis with our hero quietly inurn'd;[7]
  Because the army's grown more popular,
30   At which the naval people are concern'd;
  Besides, the prince is all for the land-service,
  Forgetting Duncan, Nelson, Howe, and Jervis.[8]

5

  Brave men were living before Agamemnon[9]
   And since, exceeding valorous and sage,
35 A good deal like him too, though quite the same none;
   But then they shone not on the poet's page,
  And so have been forgotten:—I condemn none,
   But can't find any in the present age
  Fit for my poem (that is, for my new one);
40 So, as I said, I'll take my friend Don Juan.

6

  Most epic poets plunge "in medias res"
   (Horace makes this the heroic turnpike road),[1]
  And then your hero tells, whene'er you please,
   What went before—by way of episode,
45 While seated after dinner at his ease,
   Beside his mistress in some soft abode,
  Palace, or garden, paradise, or cavern,
  Which serves the happy couple for a tavern.

7

  That is the usual method, but not mine—
50   —My way is to begin with the beginning;
  The regularity of my design
   Forbids all wandering as the worst of sinning,
  And therefore I shall open with a line
   (Although it cost me half an hour in spinning)
55 Narrating somewhat of Don Juan's father,
  And also of his mother, if you'd rather.

8

  In Seville was he born, a pleasant city,
   Famous for oranges and women—he
  Who has not seen it will be much to pity,
60   So says the proverb—and I quite agree;
  Of all the Spanish towns is none more pretty,

---

7. Horatio Nelson, admiral and viscount, died in the Battle of Trafalgar (1805) at which he defeated the French fleet.
8. Byron plays the four distinguished British admirals against the Regent's support of the army.
9. An adaptation of Horace (*Odes* 4.9.25–28): "Many heroes lived before Agamemnon; but all are overwhelmed in unending night, unwept, unknown, because they lacked a sacred bard" (trans. by C. E. Bennett).
1. In his *Ars Poetica* Horace recommends that the epic poet begin dramatically, like Homer, by taking the audience directly "into the midst of things."

Cadiz perhaps—but that you soon may see:—
Don Juan's parents lived beside the river,
A noble stream, and call'd the Guadalquivir.

9

65   His father's name was Jóse—*Don*, of course,
       A true Hidalgo,° free from every stain   *nobleman*
Of Moor or Hebrew blood, he traced his source
       Through the most Gothic gentlemen of Spain;
A better cavalier ne'er mounted horse,
70   Or, being mounted, e'er got down again,
Than Jóse, who begot our hero, who
Begot—but that's to come————Well, to renew:

10

His mother was a learned lady, famed
       For every branch of every science known—
75   In every Christian language ever named,
       With virtues equall'd by her wit alone,
She made the cleverest people quite ashamed,
       And even the good with inward envy groan,
Finding themselves so very much exceeded
80   In their own way by all the things that she did.

11

Her memory was a mine: she knew by heart
       All Calderon and greater part of Lopé,[2]
So that if any actor miss'd his part
       She could have served him for the prompter's copy;
85   For her Feinagle's were an useless art,[3]
       And he himself obliged to shut up shop—he
Could never make a memory so fine as
That which adorn'd the brain of Donna Inez.

12

Her favourite science was the mathematical,
90   Her noblest virtue was her magnanimity,
Her wit (she sometimes tried at wit) was Attic° all,   *refined*
       Her serious sayings darken'd to sublimity;
In short, in all things she was fairly what I call
       A prodigy—her morning dress was dimity,°   *plain cotton*
95   Her evening silk, or, in the summer, muslin,
And other stuffs, with which I won't stay puzzling.

13

She knew the Latin—that is, "the Lord's prayer,"
       And Greek—the alphabet—I'm nearly sure;
She read some French romances here and there,
100   Although her mode of speaking was not pure;
For native Spanish she had no great care,
       At least her conversation was obscure;
Her thoughts were theorems, her words a problem,
As if she deem'd that mystery would ennoble 'em.

2. Pedro Calderón de la Barca (1600–1681) and Lopé de   3. Gregor von Feinagle (1765–1819) lectured on
Vega (1562–1635), Spanish dramatists.   mnemonics.

14

105   She liked the English and the Hebrew tongue,
           And said there was analogy between 'em;
       She proved it somehow out of sacred song,
           But I must leave the proofs to those who've seen 'em,
       But this I heard her say, and can't be wrong,
110   And all may think which way their judgments lean 'em,
       "'Tis strange—the Hebrew noun which means 'I am,'[4]
       The English always use to govern d—n."

15

       Some women use their tongues—she *look'd* a lecture,
           Each eye a sermon, and her brow a homily,
115   An all-in-all-sufficient self-director,
           Like the lamented late Sir Samuel Romilly,
       The Law's expounder, and the State's corrector,
           Whose suicide was almost an anomaly—[5]
       One sad example more, that "All is vanity,"—
120   (The jury brought their verdict in "Insanity.")

16

       In short, she was a walking calculation,
           Miss Edgeworth's novels stepping from their covers,
       Or Mrs. Trimmer's books on education,
           Or "Coelebs' Wife" set out in quest of lovers,[6]
125   Morality's prim personification,
           In which not Envy's self a flaw discovers;
       To others' share let "female errors fall,"[7]
       For she had not even one—the worst of all.

17

       Oh! she was perfect past all parallel—
130   Of any modern female saint's comparison;
       So far above the cunning powers of hell,
           Her guardian angel had given up his garrison;
       Even her minutest motions went as well
           As those of the best time-piece made by Harrison:[8]
135   In virtues nothing earthly could surpass her,
       Save thine "incomparable oil," Macassar![9]

18

       Perfect she was, but as perfection is
           Insipid in this naughty world of ours,
       Where our first parents never learn'd to kiss

4. "God," *Yahweh* in Hebrew, which Moses renders to as "I AM THAT I AM" (Exodus 3.14).
5. Romilly (1757–1818), a liberal member of Parliament, accepted a retainer to represent Byron in the separation proceedings but then switched to Lady Byron. The stanza shows that even his suicide did not soften Byron's resentment; Murray refused to print it in the first edition.
6. Maria Edgeworth was a popular Irish novelist and educational writer; Sarah Trimmer (1741–1810) was a popular writer on education and of children's books. *Coelebs in Search of a Wife* (1809)—its title deliberately misquoted by Byron—was the only novel of Hannah More, for whom see page 1498.
7. Alexander Pope, *The Rape of the Lock* (1714), 2.17.
8. In 1762 the English clockmaker John Harrison claimed the government prize of £20,000 for a chronometer accurate enough to determine longitude.
9. Byron cites the advertisements of the firm A. Rowland and Son for this widely used hair-oil.

140   Till they were exiled from their earlier bowers,
        Where all was peace, and innocence, and bliss
            (I wonder how they got through the twelve hours)
        Don Jóse, like a lineal son of Eve,
        Went plucking various fruit without her leave.

                                    19

145   He was a mortal of the careless kind,
            With no great love for learning, or the learn'd,
        Who chose to go where'er he had a mind,
            And never dream'd his lady was concern'd;
        The world, as usual, wickedly inclined
150   To see a kingdom or a house o'erturn'd,
        Whisper'd he had a mistress, some said *two*,
        But for domestic quarrels *one* will do.

                                    20

        Now Donna Inez had, with all her merit,
            A great opinion of her own good qualities;
155   Neglect, indeed, requires a saint to bear it,
            And such, indeed, she was in her moralities;
        But then she had a devil of a spirit,
            And sometimes mix'd up fancies with realities,
        And let few opportunities escape
160   Of getting her liege lord into a scrape.

                                    21

        This was an easy matter with a man
            Oft in the wrong, and never on his guard;
        And even the wisest, do the best they can,
            Have moments, hours, and days, so unprepared,
165   That you might "brain them with their lady's fan";[1]
            And sometimes ladies hit exceeding hard,
        And fans turn into falchions° in fair hands,   *swords*
        And why and wherefore no one understands.

                                    22

        'Tis pity learned virgins ever wed
170   With persons of no sort of education,
        Or gentlemen, who, though well born and bred,
            Grow tired of scientific conversation:
        I don't choose to say much upon this head,
            I'm a plain man, and in a single station,
175   But—Oh! ye lords of ladies intellectual,
        Inform us truly, have they not hen-peck'd you all?

                                    23

        Don Jóse and his lady quarrell'd—*why*,
            Not any of the many could divine,
        Though several thousand people chose to try,
180   'Twas surely no concern of theirs nor mine;
        I loathe that low vice—curiosity;

---

1. Shakespeare, *1 Henry IV*, 2.3.23.

But if there's any thing in which I shine,
   'Tis in arranging all my friends' affairs,
Not having, of my own, domestic cares.

24

185 And so I interfered, and with the best
   Intentions, but their treatment was not kind;
I think the foolish people were possess'd,
   For neither of them could I ever find,
Although their porter afterwards confess'd—
190   But that's no matter, and the worst's behind,
For little Juan o'er me threw, down stairs,
A pail of housemaid's water unawares.

25

A little curly-headed, good-for-nothing,
   And mischief-making monkey from his birth;
195 His parents ne'er agreed except in doting
   Upon the most unquiet imp on earth;
Instead of quarrelling, had they been but both in
   Their senses, they'd have sent young master forth
To school, or had him soundly whipp'd at home,
200 To teach him manners for the time to come.

26

Don Jóse and the Donna Inez led
   For some time an unhappy sort of life,
Wishing each other, not divorced, but dead;
   They lived respectably as man and wife,
205 Their conduct was exceedingly well-bred,
   And gave no outward signs of inward strife,
Until at length the smother'd fire broke out,
And put the business past all kind of doubt.

27

For Inez call'd some druggists, and physicians,
210   And tried to prove her loving lord was *mad*,[2]
But as he had some lucid intermissions,
   She next decided he was only *bad*;
Yet when they ask'd her for her depositions,
   No sort of explanation could be had,
215 Save that her duty both to man and God
Required this conduct—which seem'd very odd.

28

She kept a journal, where his faults were noted,
   And open'd certain trunks of books and letters,
All which might, if occasion served, be quoted;
220   And then she had all Seville for abettors,
Besides her good old grandmother (who doted);
   The hearers of her case became repeaters,
Then advocates, inquisitors, and judges,
Some for amusement, others for old grudges.

---

2. As Byron believed Lady Byron had tried to do; stanzas 27 and 28 replay details of their separation.

29

225 And then this best and meekest woman bore
  With such serenity her husband's woes,
Just as the Spartan ladies did of yore,
  Who saw their spouses kill'd, and nobly chose
Never to say a word about them more—
230   Calmly she heard each calumny that rose,
And saw *his* agonies with such sublimity,
That all the world exclaim'd, "What magnanimity!"

30

No doubt this patience, when the world is damning us,
  Is philosophic in our former friends;
235 'Tis also pleasant to be deem'd magnanimous,
  The more so in obtaining our own ends;
And what the lawyers call a "*malus animus*"°   *ill will*
  Conduct like this by no means comprehends:
Revenge in person's certainly no virtue,
240 But then 'tis not *my* fault, if *others* hurt you.

31

And if our quarrels should rip up old stories,
  And help them with a lie or two additional,
I'm not to blame, as you well know—no more is
  Any one else—they were become traditional;
245 Besides, their resurrection aids our glories
  By contrast, which is what we just were wishing all:
And science profits by this resurrection—
Dead scandals form good subjects for dissection.

32

Their friends had tried at reconciliation,
250   Then their relations, who made matters worse.
('Twere hard to tell upon a like occasion
  To whom it may be best to have recourse—
I can't say much for friend or yet relation):
  The lawyers did their utmost for divorce,
255 But scarce a fee was paid on either side
Before, unluckily, Don Jóse died.

33

He died: and most unluckily, because,
  According to all hints I could collect
From counsel learned in those kinds of laws,
260   (Although their talk's obscure and circumspect)
His death contrived to spoil a charming cause;
  A thousand pities also with respect
To public feeling, which on this occasion
Was manifested in a great sensation.

34

265 But ah! he died; and buried with him lay
  The public feeling and the lawyers' fees:
His house was sold, his servants sent away,
  A Jew took one of his two mistresses,
A priest the other—at least so they say:
270   I ask'd the doctors after his disease—

He died of the slow fever call'd the tertian,°   *malaria*
And left his widow to her own aversion.

35

Yet Jóse was an honourable man,
    That I must say, who knew him very well;
275   Therefore his frailties I'll no further scan,
    Indeed there were not many more to tell:
And if his passions now and then outran
    Discretion, and were not so peaceable
As Numa's (who was also named Pompilius),[3]
280   He had been ill brought up, and was born bilious.

36

Whate'er might be his worthlessness or worth,
    Poor fellow! he had many things to wound him.
Let's own—since it can do no good on earth—
    It was a trying moment that which found him
285   Standing alone beside his desolate hearth,
    Where all his household gods lay shiver'd round him
No choice was left his feelings or his pride,
    Save death or Doctors' Commons[4]—so he died.

37

Dying intestate,° Juan was sole heir   *without a will*
290   To a chancery suit, and messuages,° and lands,   *houses*
Which, with a long minority and care,
    Promised to turn out well in proper hands:
Inez became sole guardian, which was fair,
    And answer'd but to nature's just demands;
295   An only son left with an only mother
Is brought up much more wisely than another.

38

Sagest of women, even of widows, she
    Resolved that Juan should be quite a paragon,
And worthy of the noblest pedigree:
300   (His sire was of Castile, his dam from Aragon.)
Then for accomplishments of chivalry,
    In case our lord the king should go to war again,
He learn'd the arts of riding, fencing, gunnery,
    And how to scale a fortress—or a nunnery.

39

305   But that which Donna Inez most desired,
    And saw into herself each day before all
The learned tutors whom for him she hired,
    Was, that his breeding should be strictly moral:
Much into all his studies she enquired,
310   And so they were submitted first to her, all,
Arts, sciences, no branch was made a mystery
To Juan's eyes, excepting natural history.

---

3. The second king of Rome, renowned for his piety.   4. The court that presided over divorces.

40

315

The languages, especially the dead,
　　The sciences, and most of all the abstruse,
The arts, at least all such as could be said
　　To be the most remote from common use,
In all these he was much and deeply read;
　　But not a page of any thing that's loose,
Or hints continuation of the species,

320

Was ever suffer'd, lest he should grow vicious.

41

His classic studies made a little puzzle,
　　Because of filthy loves of gods and goddesses,
Who in the earlier ages raised a bustle,
　　But never put on pantaloons or bodices;

325

His reverend tutors had at times a tussle,
　　And for their Aeneids, Iliads, and Odysseys,
Were forced to make an odd sort of apology,
For Donna Inez dreaded the Mythology.

42

Ovid's a rake, as half his verses show him,
　　Anacreon's morals are a still worse sample,

330

Catullus scarcely has a decent poem,
　　I don't think Sappho's Ode a good example,
Although Longinus tells us there is no hymn
　　Where the sublime soars forth on wings more ample;

335

But Virgil's songs are pure, except that horrid one
Beginning with "Formosum Pastor Corydon."[5]

43

Lucretius' irreligion is too strong
　　For early stomachs, to prove wholesome food;
I can't help thinking Juvenal was wrong,

340

　　Although no doubt his real intent was good,
For speaking out so plainly in his song,
　　So much indeed as to be downright rude;
And then what proper person can be partial
To all those nauseous epigrams of Martial?[6]

44

345

Juan was taught from out the best edition,
　　Expurgated by learned men, who place,
Judiciously, from out the schoolboy's vision,
　　The grosser parts; but fearful to deface

5. Byron rehearses the classical erotic poets: the Roman Ovid (43 B.C.–A.D. 18), author of the *Amores* and *The Art of Love*; Anacreon, 6th-century B.C.; the lyric poet Catullus (c. 84–54 B.C.); Sappho, the 7th-century B.C. Greek poet called "the Tenth Muse" by Plato, whose ode beginning "To me he seems like a god / as he sits facing you" (trans. by Willis Barnstone) was praised by Longinus in his essay *On the Sublime* (1st century B.C.). The final reference is to the second Eclogue of Virgil (70–19 B.C.), a homoerotic text beginning: "Corydon the shepherd burned for lovely Alexis, / His master's beloved."
6. *De Rerum Natura* ("On the Nature of Things"), by the 1st century B.C. Roman poet Lucretius, argues a materialistic view of the world; the 16 satires of Juvenal (c. A.D. 60–130) sternly denounce Roman society; the epigrams of Martial (A.D. 40–104) are witty but often blunt.

Too much their modest bard by this omission,
350   And pitying sore his mutilated case,
They only add them all in an appendix,
Which saves, in fact, the trouble of an index;[7]

45

For there we have them all "at one fell swoop,"
        Instead of being scatter'd through the pages;
355   They stand forth marshall'd in a handsome troop,
        To meet the ingenuous youth of future ages,
Till some less rigid editor shall stoop
        To call them back into their separate cages,
Instead of standing staring altogether,
360   Like garden gods—and not so decent either.

46

The Missal too (it was the family Missal)
        Was ornamented in a sort of way
Which ancient mass-books often are, and this all
        Kinds of grotesques illumined; and how they,
365   Who saw those figures on the margin kiss all,
        Could turn their optics to the text and pray,
Is more than I know—but Don Juan's mother
Kept this herself, and gave her son another.

47

Sermons he read, and lectures he endured,
370   And homilies, and lives of all the saints;
To Jerome and to Chrysostom inured,[8]
        He did not take such studies for restraints;
But how faith is acquired, and then ensured,
        So well not one of the aforesaid paints
375   As Saint Augustine in his fine Confessions,
Which make the reader envy his transgressions.[9]

48

This, too, was a seal'd book to little Juan—
        I can't but say that his mamma was right,
If such an education was the true one.
380   She scarcely trusted him from out her sight;
Her maids were old, and if she took a new one,
        You might be sure she was a perfect fright,
She did this during even her husband's life—
I recommend as much to every wife.

49

385   Young Juan wax'd in goodliness and grace;
        At six a charming child, and at eleven

---

7. "Fact. There is, or was, such an edition, with all the
obnoxious epigrams of Martial placed by themselves at
the end" [Byron's note].
8. St. Jerome (340–420), translator of the Vulgate, and
St. John Chrysostom (c. 345–407) were both known for
their asceticism.
9. In his Confessions (397–398) Augustine describes his
life in Carthage, "a hissing cauldron of lust," before his
conversion to Christianity.

With all the promise of as fine a face
    As e'er to man's maturer growth was given:
He studied steadily, and grew apace,
390   And seem'd, at least, in the right road to heaven,
For half his days were pass'd at church, the other
Between his tutors, confessor, and mother.

50

At six, I said, he was a charming child,
    At twelve he was a fine, but quiet boy;
395 Although in infancy a little wild,
    They tamed him down amongst them: to destroy
His natural spirit not in vain they toil'd.
    At least it seem'd so; and his mother's joy
Was to declare how sage, and still, and steady,
400 Her young philosopher was grown already.

51

I had my doubts, perhaps I have them still,
    But what I say is neither here nor there:
I knew his father well, and have some skill
    In character—but it would not be fair
405 From sire to son to augur good or ill:
    He and his wife were an ill-sorted pair—
But scandal's my aversion—I protest
Against all evil speaking, even in jest.

52

For my part I say nothing—nothing—but
410   *This* I will say—my reasons are my own—
That if I had an only son to put
    To school (as God be praised that I have none),
'Tis not with Donna Inez I would shut
    Him up to learn his catechism alone,
415 No—no—I'd send him out betimes to college,
For there it was I pick'd up my own knowledge.

53

For there one learns—'tis not for me to boast,
    Though I acquired—but I pass over *that*,
As well as all the Greek I since have lost:
420   I say that there's the place—but *"Verbum sat,"*[1]
I think I pick'd up too, as well as most,
    Knowledge of matters—but no matter *what*—
I never married—but, I think, I know
That sons should not be educated so.

54

425 Young Juan now was sixteen years of age,
    Tall, handsome, slender, but well knit: he seem'd
Active, though not so sprightly, as a page;
    And every body but his mother deem'd

---

1. Proverbial: "A word to the wise suffices."

Him almost man; but she flew in a rage
430   And bit her lips (for else she might have scream'd)
If any said so, for to be precocious
Was in her eyes a thing the most atrocious.

                   55

Amongst her numerous acquaintance, all
    Selected for discretion and devotion,
435 There was the Donna Julia, whom to call
    Pretty were but to give a feeble notion
Of many charms in her as natural
    As sweetness to the flower, or salt to ocean,
Her zone to Venus,[2] or his bow to Cupid,
440 (But this last simile is trite and stupid.)

                   56

The darkness of her Oriental eye
    Accorded with her Moorish origin;
(Her blood was not all Spanish, by the by;
    In Spain, you know, this is a sort of sin.)
445 When proud Granada fell, and, forced to fly,
    Boabdil[3] wept, of Donna Julia's kin
Some went to Africa, some stay'd in Spain,
Her great great grandmamma chose to remain.

                   57

She married (I forget the pedigree)
450   With an Hidalgo, who transmitted down
His blood less noble than such blood should be;
    At such alliances his sires would frown,
In that point so precise in each degree
    That they bred *in and in*, as might be shown,
455 Marrying their cousins—nay, their aunts, and nieces,
Which always spoils the breed, if it increases.

                   58

This heathenish cross restored the breed again,
    Ruin'd its blood, but much improved its flesh;
For from a root the ugliest in Old Spain
460   Sprung up a branch as beautiful as fresh;
The sons no more were short, the daughters plain:
    But there's a rumour which I fain would hush,
'Tis said that Donna Julia's grandmamma
Produced her Don more heirs at love than law.

                   59

465 However this might be, the race went on
    Improving still through every generation,
Until it centred in an only son,
    Who left an only daughter; my narration
May have suggested that this single one
470   Could be but Julia (whom on this occasion

---

2. The belt ("zone") of Venus made its wearer sexually attractive.

3. Mohammed XI, the last Moorish king of Granada, expelled by Ferdinand and Isabella in 1492.

I shall have much to speak about), and she
   Was married, charming, chaste, and twenty-three.
60

Her eye (I'm very fond of handsome eyes)
   Was large and dark, suppressing half its fire
475   Until she spoke, then through its soft disguise
   Flash'd an expression more of pride than ire,
And love than either; and there would arise
   A something in them which was not desire,
But would have been, perhaps, but for the soul
480   Which struggled through and chasten'd down the whole.
61

Her glossy hair was cluster'd o'er a brow
   Bright with intelligence, and fair, and smooth;
Her eyebrow's shape was like th' aërial bow,
   Her cheek all purple with the beam of youth,
485   Mounting, at times, to a transparent glow,
   As if her veins ran lightning; she, in sooth,
Possess'd an air and grace by no means common:
Her stature tall—I hate a dumpy woman.
62

Wedded she was some years, and to a man
490   Of fifty, and such husbands are in plenty;
And yet, I think, instead of such a ONE
   'Twere better to have TWO of five-and-twenty,
Especially in countries near the sun:
   And now I think on't, "mi vien in mente,"°   *it comes to mind*
495   Ladies even of the most uneasy virtue
Prefer a spouse whose age is short of thirty.
63

'Tis a sad thing, I cannot choose but say,
   And all the fault of that indecent sun,
Who cannot leave alone our helpless clay,
500   But will keep baking, broiling, burning on,
That howsoever people fast and pray,
   The flesh is frail, and so the soul undone:
What men call gallantry, and gods adultery,
Is much more common where the climate's sultry.
64

505   Happy the nations of the moral North!
   Where all is virtue, and the winter season
Sends sin, without a rag on, shivering forth
   ('Twas snow that brought St. Anthony to reason);[4]
Where juries cast up what a wife is worth,
510   By laying whate'er sum, in mulct,° they please on   *penalty*
The lover, who must pay a handsome price,
Because it is a marketable vice.

---

4. As Byron realized in correcting proofs, it was St. Francis of Assisi (1181?–1226) who cast himself into ditches full of snow to quell his desires.

from **Canto 11**[1]

[JUAN IN ENGLAND][2]

21

Through Groves, so call'd as being void of trees,
    (Like *lucus* from *no* light);[3] through prospects named
Mount Pleasant, as containing nought to please,
    Nor much to climb; through little boxes framed
165   Of bricks, to let the dust in at your ease,
    With "To be let,"° upon their doors proclaim'd;   *rented*
Through "Rows" most modestly call'd "Paradise,"
Which Eve might quit without much sacrifice;—

22

Through coaches, drays, choked turnpikes, and a whirl
170   Of wheels, and roar of voices, and confusion;
Here taverns wooing to a pint of "purl,"°   *gin and beer*
    There mails° fast flying off like a delusion;   *mail-coaches*
There barbers' blocks with periwigs in curl
    In windows; here the lamplighter's infusion
175   Slowly distill'd into the glimmering glass
    (For in those days we had not got to gas—);[4]

23

Through this, and much, and more, is the approach
    Of travellers to mighty Babylon:
Whether they come by horse, or chaise, or coach,
180   With slight exceptions, all the ways seem one.
I could say more, but do not choose to encroach
    Upon the Guide-book's privilege. The sun
Had set some time, and night was on the ridge
Of twilight, as the party cross'd the bridge.

24

185   That's rather fine, the gentle sound of Thamis°—   *River Thames*
    Who vindicates a moment, too, his stream—
Though hardly heard through multifarious "damme's."
    The lamps of Westminster's more regular gleam,
The breadth of pavement, and yon shrine[5] where fame is
190   A spectral resident—whose pallid beam
In shape of moonshine hovers o'er the pile—
Make this a sacred part of Albion's isle.

25

The Druids' groves are gone—so much the better:
    Stone-Henge[6] is not—but what the devil is it?—
195   But Bedlam still exists with its sage fetter,

---

1. Byron composed Canto 11 in October 1822. John Hunt published Cantos 9–11 together in August 1823, again anonymously.
2. Having distinguished himself at Ismail, Juan is sent to St. Petersburg, where he becomes the favorite of the Empress Catherine the Great, whose sexual appetite was notorious. Amply rewarded but exhausted, Juan is sent on a diplomatic mission to England to restore his declining health. Juan's journey across Europe enabled Byron lightly to revisit the materials of *Childe Harold's Pilgrimage*, and his arrival in England returns the poem, in a vivid act

of memory, to the Regency England in which Byron had shined. Here Juan is approaching London.
3. In a famous ancient false etymology, it was speculated that the Latin word for "grove," *lucus*, derived from the lack of light (*lux*) under the trees.
4. Gas came into use in London in 1812.
5. Westminster Abbey, filled with monuments to the famous.
6. Interest in the ancient Celtic Druids, to whom the oak was sacred, and Stonehenge, the Druid stone circle on Salisbury Plain, had grown in the 18th century.

That madmen may not bite you on a visit;
The Bench too seats or suits full many a debtor;
    The Mansion House too (though some people quiz it)
To me appears a stiff yet grand erection;
200   But then the Abbey's worth the whole collection.[7]

26

The line of lights too up to Charing Cross,
    Pall Mall,[8] and so forth, have a coruscation°   *sparkle*
Like gold as in comparison to dross,
    Match'd with the Continent's illumination,
205   Whose cities Night by no means deigns to gloss.
    The French were not yet a lamp-lighting nation,
And when they grew so—on their new-found lantern,
Instead of wicks, they made a wicked man turn.[9]

27

A row of gentlemen along the streets
210   Suspended, may illuminate mankind,
As also bonfires made of country seats;
    But the old way is best for the purblind:
The other looks like phosphorus on sheets,
    A sort of ignis fatuus° to the mind,   *will o' the wisp*
215   Which, though 'tis certain to perplex and frighten,
Must burn more mildly ere it can enlighten.

28

But London's so well lit, that if Diogenes
    Could recommence to hunt his *honest man*,[1]
And found him not amidst the various progenies
220   Of this enormous city's spreading spawn,
'Twere not for want of lamps to aid his dodging his
    Yet undiscover'd treasure. What *I* can,
I've done to find the same throughout life's journey,
But see the world is only one attorney.

* * *

65[2]

His morns he pass'd in business—which dissected,
    Was like all business, a laborious nothing,
That leads to lassitude, the most infected
    And Centaur Nessus garb of mortal clothing,[3]
And on our sofas makes us lie dejected,
    And talk in tender horrors of our loathing
All kinds of toil, save for our country's good—.
520   Which grows no better, though 'tis time it should.

66

His afternoons he pass'd in visits, luncheons,
    Lounging, and boxing; and the twilight hour

7. London sites: Bedlam, a corruption of Bethlehem Hospital for the insane; the Bench, the Court of Common Pleas; the Mansion House, the residence of the Lord Mayor.
8. Juan is proceeding to the fashionable West End.
9. A punning capsule history, from the rationalism of the Enlightenment to the hanging of offending persons from lampposts during the French Revolution.
1. The Greek philosopher Diogenes the Cynic (c.

423–323 B.C.) took a lantern in broad daylight to search for an honest man.
2. The intervening stanzas record Juan's enthusiastic reception by high society.
3. When her husband Hercules was unfaithful, Deianira sent him the tunic of the Centaur Nessus, whom he had killed, believing it to be a love charm. Instead Hercules died in agony.

In riding round those vegetable puncheons
   Call'd "Parks," where there is neither fruit nor flower
525 Enough to gratify a bee's slight munchings;
   But after all it is the only "bower,"
(In Moore's phrase) where the fashionable fair
Can form a slight acquaintance with fresh air.

67

Then dress, then dinner, then awakes the world!
530   Then glare the lamps, then whirl the wheels, then roar
Through street and square fast flashing chariots hurl'd
   Like harness'd meteors; then along the floor
Chalk mimics painting; then festoons are twirl'd;
   Then roll the brazen thunders of the door,
535 Which opens to the thousand happy few
An earthly Paradise of "Or Molu."[4]

* * *

74

585 Our hero, as a hero, young and handsome,
   Noble, rich, celebrated, and a stranger,
Like other slaves of course must pay his ransom
   Before he can escape from so much danger
As will environ a conspicuous man.[5] Some
590   Talk about poetry, and "rack and manger,"°   *rack and ruin*
And ugliness, disease, as toil and trouble;—
I wish they knew the life of a young noble.

75

They are young, but know not youth—it is anticipated;
   Handsome but wasted, rich without a sou;
595 Their vigour in a thousand arms is dissipated;
   Their cash comes *from*, their wealth goes to a Jew;
Both senates see their nightly votes participated
   Between the tyrant's and the tribunes' crew;[6]
And having voted, dined, drank, gamed, and whored,
600 The family vault receives another lord.

Stanzas[1]

When a man hath no freedom to fight for at home,
   Let him combat for that of his neighbours;
Let him think of the glories of Greece and of Rome,
   And get knock'd on the head for his labours.

5 To do good to mankind is the chivalrous plan,
   And is always as nobly requited;
Then battle for freedom wherever you can,
   And, if not shot or hang'd, you'll get knighted.

1820   1830

---

4. Gilded bronze, an ornamental material popular in the Regency.
5. Echoing Samuel Butler's satiric poem, *Hudibras* (1663–1678), "Ah me! what perils do environ / The man who meddles with cold iron" (pt. 1, ch. 3).
6. The tyrants are the Tories, in power; the tribunes, rep-resentatives of the people, are the opposition Whigs and radicals.
1. Sent to Thomas Moore in a letter of 5 November 1820, the poem reflects—with his usual irony—Byron's involvement with the Carbonari, rebels against Austrian domination of Italy.

On This Day I Complete My Thirty-Sixth Year
Missolonghi, Jan. 22. 1824[1]

'Tis time this heart should be unmoved,
   Since others it hath ceased to move:
Yet, though I cannot be beloved,
   Still let me love!

5   My days are in the yellow leaf;[2]
     The flowers and fruits of love are gone;
The worm, the canker, and the grief
     Are mine alone!

The fire that on my bosom preys
10   Is lone as some volcanic isle;
No torch is kindled at its blaze—
     A funeral pile!

The hope, the fear, the jealous care,
     The exalted portion of the pain
15   And power of love, I cannot share,
     But wear the chain.

But 'tis not *thus*—and 'tis not *here*—
     Such thoughts should shake my soul, nor *now*,
Where glory decks the hero's bier,
20   Or binds his brow.

The sword, the banner, and the field,
     Glory and Greece, around me see!
The Spartan, borne upon his shield,[3]
     Was not more free.

25   Awake! (not Greece—she *is* awake!)
     Awake, my spirit! Think through *whom*
Thy life-blood tracks its parent lake,
     And then strike home!

Tread those reviving passions down,
30   Unworthy manhood!—unto thee
Indifferent should the smile or frown
     Of beauty be.

If thou regret'st thy youth, *why live?*
     The land of honourable death
35   Is here:—up to the field, and give
     Away thy breath!

Seek out—less often sought than found—
     A soldier's grave, for thee the best;
Then look around, and choose thy ground,
40   And take thy rest.

1824   1824

---

1. Two weeks earlier, Byron had arrived in Missolonghi, a marshy town in western Greece, to support the Greeks in their war against Turkish rule. The poem is the final entry in his Missolonghi journal; he died from a fever and the ignorant medical practice of the day on April 19. The poem reflects Byron's feelings for his 15-year-old page, Loukas Chalandritsanos.

2. Echoing Shakespeare, *Macbeth*, 5.3.22.

3. Spartan warriors were exhorted not to drop their shields and flee battle but to return either with their shields or carried, dead, upon them.

Percy Bysshe Shelley
1792–1822

One of the most radically visionary of the Romantics, Percy Shelley has always had counter-cultural prestige. In the nineteenth century, Karl Marx and Friedrich Engels praised his "prophetic genius," and in the twentieth century, Paul Foot, head of England's Socialist Workers Party, edited an inexpensive volume of his political writing both to answer "the enthusiasm of the members of the SWP for Shelley's revolutionary writings" and to give socialists a means to disseminate their views not "with dogmatic propaganda but with the poetry which carries revolutionary ideas through the centuries." With William Blake he was a celebrity in the youth culture of the 1960s.

Shelley's esteem in these disparate countercultures emerges from a selective reading of his work and life, whose full range complicates and challenges partisan evaluation. Variously described as a selflessly devoted, often misunderstood idealist and as appallingly selfish, Shelley was always a risk-taker, and could be careless about the consequences. As an Oxford undergraduate, he collaborated with a friend on *The Necessity of Atheism*, a pamphlet that got them promptly expelled after they sent it to every university professor and administrative official, as well as every bishop in the United Kingdom. His first long poem, *Queen Mab*, included a vitriolic attack on "Priestcraft" and "Kingcraft" that earned him celebrity in the radical press and infamy in the conservative press; well into the nineteenth century, these atheist and revolutionary passages were expurgated. This censorship was part of the refashioning of Shelley in the Victorian period. In a well-orchestrated campaign by his grieving widow and devoted disciples of his poetry, he was made safe for parlors, refurbished from a dangerous thinker into an impossibly delicate visionary given to chanting at sky-larks, "Hail to thee, blithe Spirit!"

Shelley's life is marked by idealism, scandal, and passionate but shifting emotional commitments, especially to women. Grandson of a wealthy landowner and son of a member of Parliament, he was born into conservative aristocracy. Expected to continue in this world, he was sent to the best schools. But he began to rebel early. At Eton (1804–1810), he challenged the tyrannical system of "fagging," whereby upperclassmen had the privilege of abusing their juniors. He no sooner enrolled in Oxford, in 1810, than he got himself expelled for that pamphlet on atheism, an event that at once surprised him and enraged his father. He took off for London, where he met Harriet Westbrook and, believing her oppressed by her father, convinced her to elope with him in August 1811 (he was eighteen, she sixteen). The next year, he was in Ireland irritating its Protestant aristocracy by distributing pamphlets urging Catholic emancipation and improved conditions for its large population of the poor. Eager to meet William Godwin, author of *Political Justice*, he returned to London, and began *Queen Mab*, a Godwinian dream vision. In 1813 Harriet bore a daughter, and he published *Mab* at his own expense. At once celebrated (and pirated) by the radical press and denounced by the Tory press, this poem would be linked to Shelley for the rest of his life, its infamy persisting even into his obituaries.

In the heat of his Godwinian enthusiasms and mindful of Godwin's disdain of the institution of marriage, Shelley allowed himself to tire of Harriet and become enamored of Godwin and Wollstonecraft's beautiful, intelligent daughter Mary. In July 1814, he and Mary eloped to France, accompanied by her stepsister Claire Clairmont. After a six-week tour of Europe, marveling at the Alps and dismayed by the ravages of the Napoleonic wars, they returned to England and the scandal of their elopement. In December Harriet bore her second child by Percy but declined his invitation to join their menage as a platonic sister. When Shelley's grandfather died at the beginning of 1815, he gained a modest fortune of £1000 per year, one-fifth of which was paid directly to Harriet and a good portion of which he would always spend on philanthropy and loans to friends. Mary's first child, a daughter, was born prematurely in February, and died within a few weeks, an event that devastated her. During this year, they experimented with an "open" relationship, in which Percy had a romance with Claire and she with his college friend T. J. Hogg (collaborator on the pamphlet on atheism). Still at odds with their fathers, Mary and Percy were further strained by debts and a constant shift of residences to avoid their creditors and the bailiffs. Percy wrote *Alastor*, a somewhat equivocally framed story of a young visionary poet alienated by life in the world who seeks visionary fulfillment, finding this ultimately in death. Their second child, William, was born early in 1816.

They left for Switzerland in May 1816 with Claire to meet Lord Byron, now Claire's lover. During this summer, Mary wrote *Frankenstein*, and Percy wrote *Hymn to Intellectual Beauty* and *Mont Blanc*, and toured the lakes with Byron. At the summer's end, the Shelley party returned to England and several catastrophes. Mary's half-sister Fanny Imlay committed suicide in October on discovering that Godwin was not her father, and in November, Harriet, pregnant by a new lover and in despair over rejection by him as well as her husband, drowned herself. Percy and Mary were now able to marry, but the scandal of his life and political writings cost him custody of his children by Harriet—an extraordinary ruling in an age when fathers automatically had custody. He was shocked by this judgment, which deepened his self-mythology as an idealist persecuted by social and political injustice and despised by a world unable to appreciate his "beautiful idealisms of moral excellence" (as he would phrase it in the Preface to *Prometheus Unbound*).

Over the course of 1817, Shelley consoled himself with new political writing and his friendship with Leigh Hunt, minor poet and editor of the radical newspaper *The Examiner*; through Hunt he met John Keats. Mary was pregnant again, and Clara was born in September. In 1818 they moved to Europe. Eager to spend as much time as possible with Byron, now in Italy, Percy subjected his family to much arduous travel during an oppressively hot summer. Clara did not fare well and died in September. The year 1819 was a productive one for Shelley's writing. He finished *Prometheus Unbound*, an epic "closet-drama" begun the year before about the Titan's war with his oppressor; he wrote *The Cenci*, a Jacobean political tragedy of incestuous rape, parricide, and persecution; several other political poems, including *The Mask of Anarchy*, in reaction to the infamous "Peterloo Massacre" of a peaceful workers' rally; a long proto-Marxist political pamphlet, *A Philosophical View of Reform*; and a witty satire of Wordsworth (*Peter Bell the Third*), energized by dismay at the middle-aged poet's didacticism and swing to the political right. He also composed one of his most famous poems, *Ode to the West Wind*, an impassioned cry for spiritual transformation rendered in the astonishingly intricate, overflowing verse of terza-rima sonnet-stanzas. The death of William in June, at age three and a half, wrenched the Shelleys with a grief only partly allayed by the birth, five months later, of a second son, Percy Florence—the only one of their children to survive.

Shelley continued to write poetry over the next two years, including *To a Sky-Lark*, and *Adonais*, an elegy for Keats, representing him as a martyr to vicious, politically motivated reviews. Increasingly identifying with this myth himself, and despairing of his bid for poetic fame, in 1821 he began his *Defence of Poetry* (published posthumously by Mary in 1840), in which he set forth his views on the relation of poets both to their immediate social and historical circumstances and to the "Eternity" that authorized their visions and would vindicate their merits. He was also becoming infatuated with Jane Williams, who with her common-law husband Edward had joined their circle in Pisa, Italy. The Williamses and the Shelleys decided to live together on the Bay of Spezia in the summer of 1822. More and more alienated from Mary, who was understandably moody (pregnant for the fifth time in six years and still grieving for her first three children), Percy frequently left her behind to enjoy excursions with the Williamses or Jane alone. He was charmed by their company, jealous of their relationship, and in love with Jane, to whom he addressed a set of beautiful lyrics interwoven with his affection for her, his resentment of Edward, and his withdrawal from Mary. Mary suffered a nearly fatal miscarriage in June. In July, Percy and Edward sailed to Leghorn to greet Leigh Hunt, who was joining Shelley and Byron in Italy to establish *The Liberal*, a journal of opinion and the arts.

On the sail back, Percy and Edward were caught in a sudden storm, and both drowned. Byron wrote to his publisher, sponsor of the most influential Tory periodical of the day, *The Quarterly Review* (which had savaged Shelley): "You are all brutally mistaken about Shelley who was without exception—the *best* and least selfish man I ever knew.—I never knew one who was not a beast in comparison." Whether or not one shares this judgment of the man, Shelley's accomplishment as an artist has always compelled admiration. Wordsworth, who thought him too fantastic by half and who was famously sparing in praise of other poets, judged Shelley "one of the best *artists* of us all . . . in workmanship of style."

Mont Blanc
Lines Written in the Vale of Chamouni[1]

1

    The everlasting universe of things
Flows through the mind, and rolls its rapid waves,
Now dark—now glittering—now reflecting gloom—
Now lending splendour, where from secret springs
5 The source of human thought its tribute brings
Of waters,—with a sound but half its own.
Such as a feeble brook will oft assume
In the wild woods, among the mountains lone,
Where waterfalls around it leap for ever,
10 Where woods and winds contend, and a vast river
Over its rocks ceaselessly bursts and raves.[2]

2

    Thus thou, Ravine of Arve—dark, deep Ravine—
Thou many-coloured, many-voiced vale,
Over whose pines and crags and caverns sail
15 Fast cloud-shadows and sunbeams: awful° scene,   *awesome*
Where Power in likeness of the Arve comes down
From the ice gulfs that gird his secret throne,
Bursting through these dark mountains like the flame
Of lightning through the tempest;—thou dost lie,—
20 Thy giant brood of pines around thee clinging,
Children of elder° time, in whose devotion   *older and earlier*
The chainless winds still come and ever came
To drink their odours, and their mighty swinging
To hear, an old and solemn harmony;

---

1. At nearly 16,000 ft. in the French Alps, Mont Blanc is the highest peak in Europe, a must-see on everyone's Grand Tour as the epitome of "the sublime"—a vast scene at once exciting and defeating adequate perception and representation; its summit had been attained only a few times by 1816. In Mary's *History of a Six Weeks' Tour*, Percy said the poem "was composed under the immediate impression of the deep and powerful feelings excited by the objects which it attempts to describe; and, as an undisciplined overflowing of the soul, rests its claim to approbation on an attempt to imitate the untamable wildness and inaccessible solemnity from which those feelings sprang." The "imitation" involves a dizzying play of imagery and language: wildly dilated and piled-up syntaxes, dazzling verbal transformations and a welter of sublime negatives (e.g. *unknown, infinite, unearthly, unfathomable, viewless*).

Amid this drama, Shelley poses questions of the mind's ability to perceive and comprehend transcendent power, and ultimately its existence. He portrays the perceiving "mind" with metaphors drawn from the landscape before him, as he stands on a bridge over the River Arve, a deep ravine, and the valley below, the mountain and glacier above. Echoing with a difference Wordsworth's love for "all the mighty world / Of eye, and ear,—both what they half create, / And what perceive; well pleased to recognise / In nature and the language of the sense / The anchor of my purest thoughts" (*Tintern Abbey* 105-109, page 1532), Shelley's poetry alludes to and contests this philosophy of "Nature."
2. Coleridge's *Kubla Khan* (pub. 1816) 17–21, page 1655; the landscape of this poem also appears at 122.

25 Thine earthly rainbows stretched across the sweep
Of the etherial waterfall, whose veil
Robes some unsculptured image;[3] the strange sleep
Which, when the voices of the desart fail,
Wraps all in its own deep eternity;—
30 Thy caverns echoing to the Arve's commotion,
A loud, lone sound no other sound can tame;
Thou art pervaded with that ceaseless motion
Thou art the path of that unresting sound—
Dizzy Ravine! and when I gaze on thee,
35 I seem, as in a trance sublime and strange
To muse on my own separate phantasy,°   *fantasy, delusion*
My own, my human Mind, which passively
Now renders and receives fast influencings,
Holding an unremitting interchange
40 With the clear universe of things around;
One legion of wild thoughts, whose wandering wings
Now float above thy darkness, and now rest
Where that° or thou° art no unbidden guest,   thy *darkness / ravine*
In the still cave of the witch Poesy,
45 Seeking among the shadows that pass by,
Ghosts of all things that are, some shade of thee,
Some phantom, some faint image; till the breast
From which they fled recalls them, thou art there![4]

3

Some say that gleams of a remoter world
50 Visit the soul in sleep,[5]—that death is slumber,
And that its shapes the busy thoughts outnumber
Of those who wake and live.—I look on high;
Has some unknown omnipotence unfurled
The veil of life and death?[6] or do I lie
55 In dream, and does the mightier world of sleep
Spread far around and inaccessibly
Its circles? For the very spirit fails,
Driven like a homeless cloud from steep to steep
That vanishes among the viewless° gales!   *unseeing, invisible*
60 Far, far above, piercing the infinite sky,
Mont Blanc appears, still, snowy, and serene—
Its subject mountains their unearthly forms
Pile around it, ice and rock; broad vales between
Of frozen floods, unfathomable deeps,
65 Blue as the overhanging heaven, that spread
And wind among the accumulated steeps;

3. Rocks behind the waterfall in shapes not sculpted by human artistry.
4. An allusion to Plato's allegory in *Republic* 7, which compares the mind to a cave in which our sense of reality consists of the shadows cast by firelight on its walls, ignorant of the light of "Reality" outside. Shelley's difficult syntax blurs the distinction of inner and outer, human mind and Ravine.

5. Inverting Wordsworth's philosophy of Platonic amnesia in stanza 5 of the "Intimations" *Ode* (see pages 1612–1613), Shelley entertains the idea that this spiritual reality is not forgotten but visits the soul in sleep.
6. The screen of phenomena separating physical from spiritual reality (lifted in sleep, in daydreams and visions).

A desert peopled by the storms alone,
Save° when the eagle brings some hunter's bone,   *except*
And the wolf tracts° her there—how hideously   *tracks, traces*
70   Its shapes are heaped around: rude, bare, and high,
Ghastly, and scarred, and riven!°—Is this the scene   *split*
Where the old Earthquake-daemon taught her young
Ruin?[7] Were these their toys? or did a sea
Of fire envelop once this silent snow?
75   None can reply—all seems eternal now.
The wilderness has a mysterious tongue
Which teaches awful doubt,°—or faith so mild,   *awe-filled questioning*
So solemn, so serene, that man may be,
But for such faith, with nature reconciled.[8]
80   Thou hast a voice, great Mountain, to repeal
Large codes of fraud and woe; not understood
By all, but which the wise and great and good
Interpret, or make felt, or deeply feel.

4

The fields, the lakes, the forests, and the streams,
85   Ocean, and all the living things that dwell
Within the daedal earth,[9] lightning and rain,
Earthquake and fiery flood, and hurricane,
The torpor of the year when feeble dreams
Visit the hidden buds, or dreamless sleep
90   Holds every future leaf and flower; the bound
With which from that detested trance they leap;
The works and ways of man, their death and birth,
And that of him, and all that his may be;
All things that move and breathe with toil and sound
95   Are born and die; revolve, subside, and swell.
Power dwells apart in its tranquillity,
Remote, serene, and inaccessible:
And *this*, the naked countenance of earth,
On which I gaze, even these primaeval mountains
100   Teach the adverting mind. The glaciers creep
Like snakes that watch their prey, from their far fountains,
Slow rolling on; there, many a precipice,
Frost and the sun in scorn of mortal power
Have piled: dome, pyramid, and pinnacle,
105   A city of death, distinct with many a tower
And wall impregnable of beaming ice.
Yet not a city, but a flood of ruin
Is there, that from the boundary of the sky

7. In Greek mythology daemons are (often playful) spirits, usually personifications of natural forces.

8. Shelley first wrote "In such wise faith with Nature reconciled," then revised to "But for such faith" and lowercased "nature." The sense is ambiguous: "But for" may indicate "Only by means of" faith in Nature over the "Large codes of fraud and woe" promulgated by institutional religions (81). Or it may mean "Except for": man might be reconciled to the mysteries of nature's violent power, did it not require a bland faith in a nature that is unknowable and perhaps indifferent to human needs and values.

9. The adjective derives from Daedalus, architect of the famous labyrinth in Crete, and of wings for flight that he crafted with feathers and wax; hence, a wonderfully wrought, inspired creation.

Rolls its perpetual stream; vast pines are strewing
110 Its destined path, or in the mangled soil
Branchless and shattered stand: the rocks, drawn down
From yon remotest waste, have overthrown
The limits of the dead and living world,
Never to be reclaimed. The dwelling-place
115 Of insects, beasts, and birds, becomes its spoil;
Their food and their retreat for ever gone,
So much of life and joy is lost. The race
Of man flies far in dread; his work and dwelling
Vanish, like smoke before the tempest's stream,
120 And their place is not known.[1] Below, vast caves
Shine in the rushing torrents' restless gleam,
Which from those secret chasms in tumult welling
Meet in the vale; and one majestic River,
The breath and blood of distant lands, for ever
125 Rolls its loud waters to the ocean-waves,
Breathes its swift vapours to the circling air.

5

Mont Blanc yet gleams on high:—the power is there,
The still and solemn power, of many sights,
And many sounds, and much of life and death.
130 In the calm darkness of the moonless nights,
In the lone glare of day, the snows descend
Upon that Mountain; none beholds them there,
Nor when the flakes burn in the sinking sun,
Or the star-beams dart through them:—Winds contend
135 Silently there, and heap the snow, with breath
Rapid and strong, but silently! Its home
The voiceless lightning in these solitudes
Keeps innocently, and like vapour broods
Over the snow. The secret strength of things
140 Which governs thought, and to the infinite dome
Of heaven is as a law, inhabits thee!
And what were thou,° and earth, and stars, and sea,   *Mont Blanc*
If to the human mind's imaginings
Silence and solitude were vacancy?

23 July 1816   1817

Hymn to Intellectual Beauty[1]

1

The awful shadow of some unseen Power
Floats, though unseen, amongst us, visiting

---

1. Echoing Psalm 103: "As for man, his days are as grass . . . For the wind passeth over it, and it is gone; and the place thereof shall know it no more" (15–16).

1. Composed the same summer as *Mont Blanc* (1816), *Hymn* shares its metaphysics. "Intellectual" refers to the ideal Platonic spirit apprehended by the mind, over the faint and fleeting information of the senses; Shelley may have taken this term from Wollstonecraft's lament in *Rights of Woman* over the low cultural esteem of women's "intellectual beauty" (ch. 3). As in *Mont Blanc*, "unseen Power" is evoked by a rhetoric of negation, unanswered questions, and merely proximate similes.

This various world with as inconstant wing
As summer winds that creep from flower to flower.—
5   Like moonbeams that behind some piny mountain shower,°   (verb)
        It visits with inconstant glance
        Each human heart and countenance;
    Like hues and harmonies of evening,—
        Like clouds in starlight widely spread,—
10   Like memory of music fled,—
        Like aught that for its grace may be
    Dear, and yet dearer for its mystery.

2

    Spirit of BEAUTY, that dost consecrate
        With thine own hues all thou dost shine upon
15   Of human thought or form,—where art thou gone?
    Why dost thou pass away, and leave our state,
    This dim vast vale of tears, vacant and desolate?—
        Ask why the sunlight not for ever
        Weaves rainbows o'er yon mountain river;
20   Why aught should fail and fade that once is shown;
        Why fear and dream and death and birth
        Cast on the daylight of this earth
        Such gloom,—why man has such a scope
    For love and hate, despondency and hope?

3

25   No voice from some sublimer world hath ever
        To sage or poet these responses given—
        Therefore the names of God and ghost and Heaven,
    Remain the records of their° vain endeavour,   sages and poets
    Frail spells—whose uttered charm might not avail to sever
30   From all we hear and all we see,
        Doubt, chance, and mutability.[2]
    Thy light alone like mist o'er mountains driven,
        Or music by the night wind sent
        Through strings of some still instrument,[3]
35   Or moonlight on a midnight stream,
    Gives grace and truth to life's unquiet dream.

4

    Love, Hope, and Self-esteem, like clouds depart
        And come, for some uncertain moments lent.
        Man were° immortal, and omnipotent,   would be
40   Didst thou,° unknown and awful as thou art,   if thou didst
    Keep with thy glorious train firm state within his heart.
        Thou messenger of sympathies
        That wax and wane in lovers' eyes—
    Thou, that to human thought art nourishment,

---

2. Although some "responses" have been given to the
questions in stanza 2, even the potent vocabulary of
institutional religions has been unable to allay all doubts
and fears.
3. An aeolian or "wind" harp; see Coleridge's *The Eolian
Harp*, page 1637.

45   Like darkness to a dying flame!⁴
          Depart not—as thy shadow came:
          Depart not, lest the grave should be,
    Like life and fear, a dark reality!

               5

    While yet a boy, I sought for ghosts, and sped
50   Through many a listening chamber, cave and ruin,
        And starlight wood, with fearful steps pursuing
    Hopes of high talk with the departed dead.⁵
    I called on poisonous names with which our youth is fed.⁶
          I was not heard—I saw them not—
55   When musing deeply on the lot
    Of life at that sweet time when winds are wooing
         All vital things that wake to bring
         News of birds and blossoming,—
         Sudden, thy shadow fell on me;
60   I shrieked, and clasped my hands in exstasy!

               6

    I vowed that I would dedicate my powers
         To thee and thine—have I not kept the vow?
         With beating heart and streaming eyes, even now
    I call the phantoms of a thousand hours
65   Each from his voiceless grave: they have in visioned bowers
         Of studious zeal or love's delight
         Outwatched with me the envious night—
    They know that never joy illumed my brow
         Unlinked with hope that thou wouldst free
70   This world from its dark slavery,
         That thou, O awful LOVELINESS,
    Wouldst give whate'er these words cannot express.

               7

    The day becomes more solemn and serene
         When noon is past—there is a harmony
75   In autumn, and a lustre in its sky,
    Which through the summer is not heard or seen,
    As if it could not be, as if it had not been!
         Thus let thy power, which like the truth
         Of Nature on my passive youth
80   Descended, to my onward life supply
         Its calm—to one who worships thee,
         And every form containing thee,
         Whom, SPIRIT fair, thy spells did bind
    To fear° himself, and love all humankind.   *revere, fear for*

1816   1817

---

4. Darkness aesthetically nourishes a flame by offsetting its glow, even as the flame ultimately dies into darkness; thus Intellectual Beauty nourishes frail human intellect.
5. An alignment of his childhood with Wordsworth's shadowy recollection in the "Intimations" *Ode* of a boy-

hood sense of a spiritual reality behind the veil of phenomena; see especially lines 141–147 (page 1614).
6. The vocabulary for divinity in institutional religions; see line 27. Shelley is referring to boyhood experiments in conjuration.

Ozymandias[1]

I met a traveller from an antique land
Who said: "Two vast and trunkless° legs of stone   *lacking a torso*
Stand in the desert. . . . Near them on the sand,
Half sunk, a shattered visage° lies, whose frown,   *face*
5   And wrinkled lip, and sneer of cold command,
Tell that its sculptor well those passions read
Which yet survive, stamped on these lifeless things,
The hand that mocked them, and the heart that fed.[2]
And on the pedestal, these words appear:
10   "My name is Ozymandias, King of Kings:
Look on my works, ye Mighty, and despair!"[3]
Nothing beside remains. Round the decay
Of that colossal[4] Wreck, boundless and bare,
The lone and level sands stretch far away."

1817   1818

The Mask of Anarchy

On 16 August 1819, nearly 100,000 millworkers and their families gathered at Saint Peter's Field outside Manchester for a peaceful demonstration, capped by an address by radical Henry "Orator" Hunt calling for parliamentary reform, especially greater representation for the working classes. Alarmed by the spectacle, the local ruling class sent their drunken, sabre-wielding militia to charge the rally and to arrest Hunt; they brutally wounded hundreds, a dozen fatally. It is unclear whether the Home Office (internal security) collaborated in advance with the Manchester elite to suppress the reform movement, or whether, along with the Prince Regent (later George IV), it merely offered congratulations after the fact. The opposition press, notably *The Examiner* (published by Shelley's friends Leigh and John Hunt, no relation to Orator), fueled public outrage with a relentless flow of reports, beginning with eyewitness accounts of what came to be dubbed the "Peterloo Massacre" in sardonic parody of the celebrated English victory at Waterloo, and continuing through Hunt's triumphant entry and subsequent trial in London (he was convicted and sent to prison for two years).

    An expatriate in Italy at the time, Shelley was inspired by a self-described "torrent of indignation" to write *The Mask of Anarchy*, which he sent to Leigh Hunt on September 23, 1819, hoping for publication in *The Examiner*. Hunt was already immersed in a series of articles defending Shelley from defamations in the Tory press provoked by *The Revolt of Islam* (another political poem); he backed off from *The Mask* as too risky, notwithstanding its politics of nonviolent resistance. To print a popular ballad advocating the rights of the poor and envisioning the overthrow of a corrupt and tyrannical government would guarantee prosecution, fines, imprisonment, perhaps even exile to Australia; the Hunts had already been jailed and

---

1. Ozymandias (the Greek name for Ramses II) reigned from 1292–1225 B.C.; he is thought to be the pharaoh of Exodus whom Moses challenged. The story of the statue and its inscription is taken from the Greek historian Diodorus Siculus, 1st century B.C.
2. The sculptor read well those passions that survive his hand (that mocked them) and the tyrant's heart (that fed them); "mocked": "imitated," with a sense of caricature or derision. The passions survive both on the images of the stone fragments and in the hearts of modern tyrants; Shelley published this sonnet in 1818 in Leigh Hunt's

radical journal, *The Examiner*.
3. According to Diodorus, this is the actual boast; by Shelley's time, its language echoes ironically against the subsequent application of this title to Christ.
4. An adjective derived from "colossus," the term in antiquity for any large statue; there were several such of 50–60 feet in ancient Egypt. Shelley is also recalling the depiction of Julius Caesar by one of the conspirators in his assassination: "he doth bestride the narrow world / Like a Colossus" (*Julius Caesar* 1.2.135–136).

heavily fined for prior "libels," and here was Shelley likening "Murder" to the Tory Foreign Secretary Castlereagh (also reviled by Byron in the unpublishable Dedication of *Don Juan*, see pages 1683–1684), "Hypocrisy" to Sidmouth the Home Secretary, and "Fraud" to Lord Chancellor Eldon (who had deprived Shelley of his children by Harriet). Leigh Hunt waited to print the poem until 1832, ten years after Shelley's death and just after the passage of the Reform Bill, when Shelley's hotter rhetoric could be viewed with historical distance and its cooler advice admired as prophetic of the nonviolent persuasion by which reform had been won. By this time, too, the notoriety of "Peterloo" was undisputed as a breach of the right of peaceful assembly. Even so, Hunt felt it best to cancel the names Eldon and Sidmouth, as well as the subtitle. Shelley's main title ironically echoes Eldon's condemnation of the rally as "an overt act of treason" posing a "shocking choice between military government and anarchy"; he turns the word back on the government itself, to name its tyranny. "Mask" builds on *The Examiner*'s reference to the government's "Brazen Masks of power" (22 August) and also puns on the literary-theatrical genre of the "masque" (Shelley called the poem *Masque of Anarchy* in a letter to Hunt, who used this title in 1832). Thus he describes government officials as parading in a "ghastly masquerade" (27), a spectacle that travesties the court-masques of the early seventeenth century, performances for the court and the aristocracy that typically celebrated the structures of order and authority that defined their power.

The Mask of Anarchy
Written on the Occasion of the Massacre at Manchester

As I lay asleep in Italy
There came a voice from over the Sea
And with great power it forth led me
To walk in the visions of Poesy.

5   I met Murder on the way—
He had a mask like Castlereagh—
Very smooth he looked, yet grim;
Seven bloodhounds followed him.[1]

All were fat; and well they might
10   Be in admirable plight,
For one by one, and two by two,
He tossed them human hearts to chew
Which from his wide cloak he drew.

Next came Fraud, and he had on,
15   Like Eldon, an ermined gown;
His big tears, for he wept well,
Turned to mill-stones as they fell:[2]

And the little children, who
Round his feet played to and fro,
20   Thinking every tear a gem,
Had their brains knocked out by them.

1. Castlereagh, Tory Foreign Secretary and leader in the House of the Commons, was known for his violent suppression of political unrest in Ireland and his support of the reactionary Holy Alliance in Europe and of Austria's domination of Italy. In 1815 he secured England's support for the postponement of the abolition of the slave trade by seven European nations; the pro-war faction in Parliament was known as "bloodhounds" (cf. "hawks").
2. Eldon was Lord Chancellor (an office identified by its ermine gown) and famous for his public shedding of tears.

Clothed with the Bible, as with light,
And the shadows of the night,
Like Sidmouth, next, Hypocrisy
25   On a crocodile rode by.[3]

And many more Destructions played
In this ghastly masquerade,
All disguised, even to the eyes,
Like Bishops, lawyers, peers, or spies.

30   Last came Anarchy: he rode
On a white horse splashed with blood;
He was pale even to the lips,
Like Death in the Apocalypse.[4]

And he wore a kingly crown,
35   And in his grasp a sceptre° shone;   royal staff
On his brow this mark I saw—
"I AM GOD, AND KING, AND LAW!"

With a pace stately and fast
Over English land he passed,
40   Trampling to a mire of blood
The adoring multitude.

And a mighty troop around
With their trampling shook the ground,
Waving each a bloody sword,
45   For the service of their Lord.

And with glorious triumph, they
Rode through England proud and gay
Drunk as with intoxication
Of the wine of desolation.

50   O'er fields and towns, from sea to sea,
Passed the Pageant swift and free,
Tearing up and trampling down,
Till they came to London town.

And each dweller, panic-stricken,
55   Felt his heart with terror sicken,
Hearing the tempestuous cry
Of the triumph of Anarchy.

For with pomp to meet him came,
Clothed in arms like blood and flame,
60   The hired Murderers who did sing
"Thou art God, and Law, and King!

3. Sidmouth was Home Secretary (officer of internal security). The crocodile, fabled to weep as it devours its prey, symbolizes hypocrisy; Sidmouth had used provocateurs to incite illegal action among discontented workers (who were then arrested, jailed, deported, or executed); he also spent millions to build churches to teach spiritual patience to the starving poor rather than improve their material conditions.

4. See St. John the Divine's vision of the fourth horseman of the Apocalypse: "behold a pale horse: and his name that sat on him was Death" (Revelation 6.8). Shelley is also evoking Benjamin West's famous painting, *Death on a Pale Horse* (which he may have seen in London in late 1817 or read about in the press), depicting a crowd trampled by crowned Death and his sword-wielding army.

We have waited, weak and lone,
For thy coming, Mighty One!
Our purses are empty, our swords are cold,
65   Give us glory, and blood, and gold."

Lawyers and priests, a motley° crowd,   *ragtag*
To the earth their pale brows bowed;
Like a bad prayer not over loud,
Whispering—"Thou art Law and God!"

70   Then all cried with one accord,
"Thou art King, and God, and Lord;
Anarchy, to Thee we bow,
Be thy name made holy now!"

And Anarchy the Skeleton
75   Bowed and grinned to every one,
As well as if his education
Had cost ten millions to the Nation.

For he knew the Palaces
Of our Kings were rightly his;
80   His the sceptre, crown, and globe,°   *royal emblems*
And the gold-inwoven robe.

So he sent his slaves before
To seize upon the Bank and Tower,[5]
And was proceeding with intent
85   To meet his pensioned Parliament,

When one fled past, a maniac maid,
And her name was Hope, she said,
But she looked more like Despair,
And she cried out in the air:

90   "My father Time is weak and grey
With waiting for a better day;
See how idiot-like he stands,
Fumbling with his palsied hands![6]

He has had child after child
95   And the dust of death is piled
Over every one but me—
Misery! oh Misery!"

Then she lay down in the street,
Right before the horses' feet,
100   Expecting, with a patient eye,
Murder, Fraud, and Anarchy—

When between her and her foes
A mist, a light, an image rose,
Small at first, and weak, and frail
105   Like the vapour of a vale:

5. The Bank of England is the national treasury; the Tower of London houses the crown jewels. Parliament had been bought off with bribes and other lucrative corruption.
6. A dig at George III.

Till as clouds grow on the blast,
Like tower-crowned giants striding fast,
And glare with lightnings as they fly,
And speak in thunder to the sky,

110 It grew—a Shape arrayed in mail°   *suit of armor*
Brighter than the Viper's scale,
And upborne on wings whose grain°   *pattern*
Was as the light of sunny rain.

On its helm, seen far away,
115 A planet, like the Morning's,° lay;   *Venus as morning star*
And those plumes its light rained through,
Like a shower of crimson dew.

With step as soft as wind it passed
O'er the heads of men—so fast
120 That they knew the presence there,
And looked,—but all was empty air.

As flowers beneath May's footstep waken
As stars from Night's loose hair are shaken
As waves arise when loud winds call
125 Thoughts sprung where'er that step did fall.

And the prostrate multitude
Looked—and ankle-deep in blood,
Hope, that maiden most serene,
Was walking with a quiet mien;°   *appearance*

130 And Anarchy, the ghastly birth,
Lay dead earth upon the earth
The Horse of Death tameless as wind
Fled, and with his hoofs did grind
To dust the murderers thronged behind.

135 A rushing light of clouds and splendour,
A sense awakening and yet tender,
Was heard and felt—and at its close
These words of joy and fear arose

As if their Own indignant Earth,
140 Which gave the sons of England birth,
Had felt their blood upon her brow,
And shuddering with a mother's throe

Had turned every drop of blood
By which her face had been bedewed
145 To an accent unwithstood,—
As if her heart had cried aloud:

"Men of England, heirs of Glory,
Heroes of unwritten story,
Nurslings of one mighty Mother,
150 Hopes of her and one another!

Rise, like Lions after slumber
In unvanquishable number!
Shake your chains to Earth, like dew
Which in sleep had fallen on you—
155   Ye are many, they are few.

What is Freedom? ye can tell
That which Slavery is, too well—
For its very name has grown
To an echo of your own.

160   'Tis to work and have such pay
As just keeps life from day to day
In your limbs, as in a cell
For the tyrants' use to dwell:

So that ye for them are made
165   Loom and plough and sword and spade;
With or without your own will, bent
To their defence and nourishment.

'Tis to see your children weak
With their mothers pine° and peak°   *long / waste away*
170   When the winter winds are bleak,—
They are dying whilst I speak.

'Tis to hunger for such diet
As the rich man in his riot
Casts to the fat dogs that lie
175   Surfeiting beneath his eye.

'Tis to let the Ghost of Gold⁷
Take from Toil a thousand fold
More than e'er its substance could
In the tyrannies of old.

180   Paper coin—that forgery
Of the title deeds which ye
Hold to something of the worth
Of the inheritance of Earth.

'Tis to be a slave in soul,
185   And to hold no strong control
Over your own wills, but be
All that others make of ye.

And, at length when ye complain
With a murmur weak and vain,
190   'Tis to see the Tyrant's crew
Ride over your wives and you—
Blood is on the grass like dew!

---

7. Debased paper money; though standard legal tender today, in Shelley's day its use as wages was controversial and devastating. Paper could be issued without adequate backing and thus subject to inflation. The doubly evil effect was to
depress the cost of labor to employers and the purchasing worth of the workers' wages.

Then it is to feel revenge,
Fiercely thirsting to exchange
195   Blood for blood—and wrong for wrong—
Do not thus when ye are strong!

Birds find rest in narrow nest,
When weary of their winged quest;
Beasts find fare in woody lair
200   When storm and snow are in the air;

Horses, oxen, have a home
When from daily toil they come;
Household dogs, when the wind roars,
Find a home within warm doors;[8]

205   Asses, swine, have litter spread,
And with fitting food are fed;
All things have a home but one—
Thou, O Englishman, hast none![9]

This is Slavery!—savage men,
210   Or wild beasts within a den,
Would endure not as ye do—
But such ills they never knew.

What art thou, Freedom? O! could slaves
Answer from their living graves
215   This demand, tyrants would flee
Like a dream's dim imagery;

Thou art not, as impostors say,
A shadow soon to pass away,
A superstition, and a name
220   Echoing from the cave of Fame.°   *Rumor*

For the labourer, thou art bread
And a comely table spread,
From his daily labour come
To a neat and happy home.

225   Thou art clothes, and fire, and food
For the trampled multitude—
No—in countries that are free
Such starvation cannot be
As in England now we see!

230   To the rich thou art a check;
When his foot is on the neck
Of his victim, thou dost make
That he treads upon a snake.[1]

---

8. This stanza is only in *The Masque of Anarchy* (1832).
9. Ironically echoing Jesus' cautions to a scribe who wants
to join his ministry: "The foxes have holes, and the birds
of the air have nests; but the Son of man hath no where
to lay his head" (Matthew 8.20).
1. A famous image from the American Revolutionary
flag, whose motto was "Don't Tread on Me!"

Thou art Justice—ne'er for gold
235   May thy righteous laws be sold
As laws are in England—thou
Shield'st alike the high and low.

Thou art Wisdom: Freemen never
Dream that God will damn for ever
240   All who think those things untrue
Of which Priests make such ado.

Thou art Peace—never by thee
Would blood and treasure wasted be
As tyrants wasted them, when all
245   Leagued to quench thy flame in Gaul.°   *Revolutionary France*

What if English toil and blood
Was poured forth, even as a flood?
It availed, Oh, Liberty!
To dim but not extinguish thee.

250   Thou art Love—the rich have kissed
Thy feet, and, like him following Christ,
Give their substance to the free
And through the rough world follow thee,[2]

Or turn their wealth to arms, and make
255   War for thy beloved sake
On wealth and war and fraud—whence they
Drew the power which is their prey.

Science, Poetry, and Thought,
Are thy lamps; they make the lot
260   Of the dwellers in a cot°   *cottage*
So serene, they curse it not.

Spirit, Patience, gentleness,
All that can adorn and bless
Art thou—let deeds, not words, express
265   Thine exceeding loveliness.

Let a great Assembly be
Of the fearless and the free
On some spot of English ground
Where the plains stretch wide around.

270   Let the blue sky overhead,
The green earth on which ye tread,
All that must eternal be,
Witness the solemnity.

From the corners uttermost
275   Of the bounds of English coast,
From every hut, village, and town

2. An allusion to Jesus' counsel to a rich young man, who rejects it: "If thou wilt be perfect go and sell that thou hast, and give to the poor, and thou shalt have treasure in heaven: and come and follow me" (Matthew 19.21).

Where those who live and suffer moan
For others' misery or their own;

From the workhouse[3] and the prison
280   Where, pale as corpses newly risen,
Women, children, young and old,
Groan for pain, and weep for cold—

From the haunts of daily life
Where is waged the daily strife
285   With common wants and common cares
Which sows the human heart with tares[4]

Lastly, from the palaces
Where the murmur of distress
Echoes, like the distant sound
290   Of a wind alive around

Those prison halls of wealth and fashion,
Where some few feel such compassion
For those who groan and toil and wail
As must make their brethren pale—

295   Ye who suffer woes untold
Or° to feel, or to behold   *either*
Your lost country bought and sold
With a price of blood and gold—

Let a vast assembly be,
300   And with great solemnity
Declare with measured words that ye
Are, as God has made ye, free!

Be your strong and simple words
Keen to wound as sharpened swords,
305   And wide as targes° let them be,   *shields*
With their shade to cover ye.

Let the tyrants pour around
With a quick and startling sound,
Like the loosening of a sea
310   Troops of armed emblazonry.

Let the charged artillery drive
Till the dead air seems alive
With the clash of clanging wheels,
And the tramp of horses' heels.

315   Let the fixed bayonet
Gleam with sharp desire to wet
Its bright point in English blood,
Looking keen as one for food.

---

3. In a system to replace begging and alms-giving, the poor were forced into workhouses where they labored for meager wages in miserable conditions, often with families separated.

4. See Jesus' parable of the tares (weeds) in the wheat field, Matthew 13.24–30.

Let the horsemen's scimitars°   *curved Turkish swords*
320   Wheel and flash, like sphereless stars°   *lacking an orbit*
Thirsting to eclipse their burning
In a sea of death and mourning.

Stand ye calm and resolute,
Like a forest close and mute,
325   With folded arms, and looks which are
Weapons of an unvanquished war,

And let Panic, who outspeeds
The career of armed steeds
Pass, a disregarded shade
330   Through your phalanx° undismayed.   *arrayed troops*

Let the Laws of your own land,
Good or ill, between ye stand,
Hand to hand, and foot to foot,
Arbiters of the dispute,

335   The old laws of England—they
Whose reverend heads with age are grey,
Children of a wiser day;
And whose solemn voice must be
Thine own echo—Liberty!

340   On those who first should violate
Such sacred heralds in their state
Rest the blood that must ensue,
And it will not rest on you.

And, if then the tyrants dare,
345   Let them ride among you there,
Slash and stab and maim and hew,—
What they like, that let them do.

With folded arms and steady eyes,
And little fear and less surprise,
350   Look upon them as they slay
Till their rage has died away.

Then they will return with shame
To the place from which they came,
And the blood thus shed will speak
355   In hot blushes on their cheek.

Every woman in the land
Will point at them as they stand—
They will hardly dare to greet
Their acquaintance in the street.

360   And the bold, true warriors
Who have hugged Danger in wars
Will turn to those who would be free,
Ashamed of such base company.

And that slaughter to the Nation
365 Shall steam up like inspiration,
Eloquent, oracular,
A volcano heard afar;

And these words shall then become
Like Oppression's thundered doom
370 Ringing through each heart and brain
Heard again—again—again!

Rise like lions after slumber,
In unvanquishable number!
Shake your chains to earth like dew
375 Which in sleep had fallen on you—
Ye are many—they are few."

1819   1832

Ode to the West Wind[1]

1

O wild West Wind, thou breath of Autumn's being,
Thou from whose unseen presence the leaves dead
Are driven like ghosts from an enchanter fleeing,

Yellow, and black, and pale, and hectic° red,   *feverish*
5 Pestilence-stricken multitudes![2] O Thou
Who chariotest to their dark wintry bed

The winged seeds, where they lie cold and low,
Each like a corpse within its grave, until
Thine azure sister of the Spring° shall blow   *spring wind*

10 Her clarion° o'er the dreaming earth, and fill   *shrill trumpet*
(Driving sweet buds like flocks to feed in air)
With living hues and odours plain and hill:

Wild Spirit, which art moving everywhere;
Destroyer and Preserver;[3] hear, O hear!

2

15 Thou on whose stream, mid the steep sky's commotion,
Loose clouds like earth's decaying leaves are shed,
Shook from the tangled boughs of heaven and ocean,[4]

Angels° of rain and lightning! there are spread   *messengers*
On the blue surface of thine airy surge,
20 Like the bright hair uplifted from the head

---

1. There is a long tradition, as old as the Bible, of wind as metaphor of life and inspiration—particularly the West Wind, as bearer of new weather, the harbinger of future seasons, events, and transformations, not only in the natural weather, but by symbolic extension, in emotional, spiritual, and political life. The Latin word for "wind," *spiritus*, also means "breath" (1) and soul or spirit (13.61–62), as well as being the root-word for "inspiration" (a taking-in of energy).

2. An allusion to a traditional epic simile (Milton, Dante, Virgil) comparing the dead to wind-driven fallen leaves.
3. Titles for major Hindu gods, Siva the Destroyer and Vishnu the Preserver.
4. Blending the imagery of leaves with that of ocean tumult, the "tangled boughs of Heaven and Ocean" suggest both waterspouts and huge clouds formed of heaven's winds and ocean vapors.

Of some fierce Maenad, even from the dim verge
Of the horizon to the zenith's height,
The locks of the approaching storm.[5] Thou dirge°   *funeral chant*

Of the dying year, to which this closing night
25 Will be the dome of a vast sepulchre,
Vaulted with all thy congregated might

Of vapours, from whose solid atmosphere
Black rain, and fire, and hail, will burst: Oh hear!

3

Thou who didst waken from his summer dreams
30 The blue Mediterranean, where he lay,
Lulled by the coil of his crystalline streams,

Beside a pumice° isle in Baiae's bay,   *volcanic*
And saw in sleep old palaces and towers
Quivering within the wave's intenser day,

35 All overgrown with azure moss, and flowers
So sweet, the sense faints picturing them![6] Thou
For whose path the Atlantic's level powers

Cleave themselves into chasms, while far below
The sea-blooms and the oozy woods which wear
40 The sapless foliage of the ocean, know

Thy voice, and suddenly grow grey with fear,
And tremble and despoil themselves:[7] O hear!

4

If I were a dead leaf thou mightest bear;
If I were a swift cloud to fly with thee;
45 A wave to pant beneath thy power, and share

The impulse of thy strength, only less free
Than thou, O uncontrollable! if even
I were as in my boyhood, and could be

The comrade of thy wanderings over heaven,
50 As then, when to outstrip thy skiey speed
Scarce seemed a vision,—I would ne'er have striven

As thus with thee in prayer in my sore need.
Oh lift me as a wave, a leaf, a cloud!
I fall upon the thorns of life![8] I bleed!

55 A heavy weight of hours has chained and bowed
One too like thee—tameless, and swift, and proud.

---

5. The Greek god of wine Bacchus was attended by Maenads, female votaries who danced in wild worship. Viewing a sculpture of them in Florence, Shelley commented: "The tremendous spirit of superstition aided by drunkenness . . . seems to have caught them in its whirlwinds, and to bear them over the earth as the rapid volutions of a tempest have the ever-changing trunk of a water-spout. . . . Their hair, loose and floating, seems caught in tempest of their own tumultuous motion." Associated in general with vegetation, Bacchus was fabled to die in the autumn and be reborn in the spring.

6. Ruins of imperial Roman villas in the Bay of Baiae, west of Naples.

7. In a note, Shelley says he is alluding to the seasonal change (despoiling) of seaweed, a process he imagines as instigated by the autumn wind.

8. A risky self-comparison to Jesus' torture by a crown of thorns; compare to *Adonais* 305–306.

5

Make me thy lyre,[9] even as the forest is:
What if my leaves are falling like its own?
The tumult of thy mighty harmonies

60   Will take from both a deep autumnal tone,
Sweet though in sadness. Be thou, Spirit fierce,
My spirit! Be thou me, impetuous one![1]

Drive my dead thoughts over the universe,
Like withered leaves, to quicken a new birth;
65   And, by the incantation of this verse,

Scatter, as from an unextinguished hearth
Ashes and sparks, my words among mankind!
Be through my lips to unawakened earth

The trumpet of a prophecy! O Wind,
70   If Winter comes, can Spring be far behind?
1819   1820

To a Sky-Lark

Hail to thee, blithe Spirit!
    Bird thou never wert—
That from Heaven or near it
    Pourest thy full heart
5   In profuse strains of unpremeditated art.[1]

Higher still and higher
    From the earth thou springest,
Like a cloud of fire;
    The blue deep thou wingest,
10   And singing still dost soar, and soaring ever singest.

In the golden lightning
    Of the sunken sun,
O'er which clouds are bright'ning,
    Thou dost float and run,
15   Like an unbodied joy whose race is just begun.

The pale purple even°   evening
    Melts around thy flight;
Like a star of Heaven,
    In the broad daylight
20   Thou art unseen, but yet I hear thy shrill delight—

Keen as are the arrows
    Of that silver sphere°   morning star
Whose intense lamp narrows
    In the white dawn clear
25   Until we hardly see—we feel, that it is there.

---

9. A wind-harp, an image used again in *A Defence* (page 1726), and in Coleridge's *The Eolian Harp* (see page 1637).
1. Shelley hazards the ungrammatical objective case ("me" instead of "I") not only to chime with "Be" but also to represent himself as an object.
1. The skylark sings only in flight; Shelley evokes Milton's thanks to his "Celestial patroness," who "inspires / Easy [his] unpremeditated Verse" (*Paradise Lost* 9.21–24).

All the earth and air
  With thy voice is loud,
As, when night is bare,
  From one lonely cloud

30 The moon rains out her beams, and Heaven is overflowed.

  What thou art we know not;
    What is most like thee?
  From rainbow clouds there flow not
    Drops so bright to see

35 As from thy presence showers a rain of melody:—

  Like a Poet hidden
    In the light of thought,
  Singing hymns unbidden,
    Till the world is wrought

40 To sympathy with hopes and fears it heeded not:

  Like a high-born maiden
    In a palace tower,
  Soothing her love-laden
    Soul in secret hour

45 With music sweet as love which overflows her bower:

  Like a glow-worm golden
    In a dell of dew,
  Scattering unbeholden
    Its aerial hue

50 Among the flowers and grass which screen it from the view:

  Like a rose embowered
    In its own green leaves,
  By warm winds deflowered,
    Till the scent it gives

55 Makes faint with too much sweet these heavy-winged thieves:

  Sound of vernal° showers   *springtime*
    On the twinkling grass,
  Rain-awakened flowers,
    All that ever was,

60 Joyous and clear and fresh,—thy music doth surpass.

  Teach us, Sprite° or Bird,   *spirit, fairy*
    What sweet thoughts are thine:
  I have never heard
    Praise of love or wine

65 That panted forth a flood of rapture so divine.

  Chorus Hymeneal°   *wedding song*
    Or triumphal° chaunt,   *military*
  Matched with thine, would be all
    But an empty vaunt—

70 A thing wherein we feel there is some hidden want.

  What objects are the fountains
    Of thy happy strain?
  What fields, or waves, or mountains?

What shapes of sky or plain?
75   What love of thine own kind? what ignorance of pain?

With thy clear keen joyance
　　Languor cannot be:
Shadow of annoyance
　　Never came near thee:
80   Thou lovest—but ne'er knew love's sad satiety.°　　　　(over)fullness

Waking or asleep,
　　Thou of death must deem
Things more true and deep
　　Than we mortals dream,
85   Or how could thy notes flow in such a crystal stream?

We look before and after,[2]
　　And pine for what is not:
Our sincerest laughter
　　With some pain is fraught;
90   Our sweetest songs are those that tell of saddest thought.

Yet if we could scorn
　　Hate and pride and fear,
If we were things born
　　Not to shed a tear,
95   I know not how thy joy we ever should come near.

Better than all measures
　　Of delightful sound,
Better than all treasures
　　That in books are found,
100   Thy skill to poet were, thou scorner of the ground!

Teach me half the gladness
　　That thy brain must know,
Such harmonious madness
　　From my lips would flow
105   The world should listen then—as I am listening now.[3]
1820   1820

A Defence of Poetry

Shelley was called to the *Defence* by an extravagant essay published in 1820 by his friend Thomas Love Peacock. Peacock described a fall from the grandeur of former ages into a modern poetry marked by triviality, vulgarity, and a studious ignorance "of history, society, and human nature": Wordsworth gives us "the phantastical parturition of the moods of his own mind"; "Scott digs up the poachers and cattle-stealers of the ancient border. Lord Byron cruizes

2. Echoing Hamlet's comment on the human capability of "looking before and after" (4.4.34), as well as alluding to Wordsworth's use of this phrase in Preface to *Lyrical Ballads* (1802 addition), just after declaring that "the Poet, singing a song in which all human beings join with him, rejoices in the presence of truth as our visible friend and hourly companion."

3. Alluding to Wordsworth's rhyme in *Resolution and Independence*: "We Poets in our youth begin in gladness; / But thereof come in the end despondency and madness" (48–49). See also the last lines of Coleridge's *Kubla Khan*, page 1657.

for thieves and pirates," and Coleridge "superadds the dreams of crazy theologians and the mysticisms of German metaphysics." Replete with "obsolete customs, and exploded superstitions . . . the whining of exaggerated feeling, and the cant of factitious sentiment," such poetry, Peacock argued, lacks relevance to modern civilization, which is being shaped by the intellectual power of "mathematicians, astronomers, chemists, moralists, metaphysicians, historians, politicians, and political economists." Even as Shelley recognized the playful taunting of Peacock's essay, he also knew that such views had currency in contemporary Utilitarian philosophies. He began his *Defence* early the next year, but put it aside in the distraction of other projects and a tumultuous personal life. Left unfinished at his death, the fragment did not appear until Mary Shelley published it in 1840.

"Poets are the unacknowledged legislators of the world," Shelley famously concluded, releasing the poet from having to defend his vocation and anointing him as visionary legislator in his own right. Yet what makes *A Defence* so compelling is not any skillful, coherent legal argumentation toward this verdict, but its welter of impassioned, often conflicting arguments and its evocative, often contradictory images for poetic authority and value. On the one hand, a radical dualism invests all truth in "the eternal, the infinite, and the one"—a transcendent realm to which the poet's imagination has visionary access. This is a theme elaborated throughout Shelley's career. Shelley concedes the frustration of any artist who would convey his visions: "the mind in creation is as a fading coal. . . . when composition begins, inspiration is already on the decline, and the most glorious poetry that has ever been communicated to the world is probably a feeble shadow of the original conception." On the other hand, this inevitability has not thwarted poets, Shelley among them, from laboring to make beautiful poems in order to awaken readers' minds to higher values—a precondition for effective political action. In this other line of defense, poetry is not just weak communication of truths beyond the reach of words but is a force of revelation and vital creation in itself. It is not surprising to discover that many of the *Defence*'s sentences, including the celebration of the "electric life" of inspired words and of poets as "unacknowledged legislators," were ones Shelley first drafted for his political pamphlet (also unfinished) *A Philosophical Review of Reform*.

from A Defence of Poetry
or Remarks Suggested by an Essay Entitled "The Four Ages of Poetry"

According to one mode of regarding those two classes of mental action which are called reason and imagination, the former may be considered as mind contemplating the relations borne by one thought to another, however produced; and the latter as mind acting upon those thoughts so as to color them with its own light, and composing from them, as from elements, other thoughts, each containing within itself the principle of its own integrity. The one is the τὸ ποιεῖν,[1] or the principle of synthesis, and has for its object those forms which are common to universal nature and existence itself; the other is the τὸ λογίζειν,[2] or principle of analysis, and its action regards the relations of things simply as relations; considering thoughts not in their integral unity, but as the algebraical representations which conduct to certain general results. Reason is the enumeration of quantities already known; imagination is the perception of the value of those quantities, both separately and as a whole. Reason respects the differences, and imagination the similitudes of things. Reason is to imagination as the instrument to the agent, as the body to the spirit, as the shadow to the substance.

---

1. "Making something," the derivation of "poet." Sir Philip Sidney refers to the poet as "maker" in his late 16th-century *Defense of Poesie*.

2. The logic or reason.

Poetry, in a general sense, may be defined to be "the expression of the imagination"; and poetry is connate with the origin of man. Man is an instrument over which a series of external and internal impressions are driven, like the alternations of an ever-changing wind over an Aeolian lyre,[3] which move it by their motion to ever-changing melody. But there is a principle within the human being (and perhaps within all sentient beings) which acts otherwise than in lyre, and produces not melody alone, but harmony, by an internal adjustment of the sounds and motions thus excited to the impressions which excite them. It is as if the lyre could accommodate its chords to the motions of that which strikes them, in a determined proportion of sound—even as the musician can accommodate his voice to the sound of the lyre. A child at play by itself will express its delight by its voice and motions, and every inflection of tone and every gesture will bear exact relation to a corresponding antitype in the pleasurable impressions which awakened it. It will be the reflected image of that impression; and as the lyre trembles and sounds after the wind has died away, so the child seeks, by prolonging in its voice and motions the duration of the effect, to prolong also a consciousness of the cause. In relation to the objects which delight a child, these expressions are what poetry is to higher objects.

The savage (for the savage is to ages what the child is to years) expresses the emotions produced in him by surrounding objects in a similar manner; and language and gesture, together with plastic[4] or pictorial imitation, become the image of the combined effect of those objects and his apprehension of them. Man in society, with all his passions and his pleasures, next becomes the object of the passions and pleasures of man; an additional class of emotions produces an augmented treasure of expression; and language, gesture, and the imitative arts become at once the representation and the medium, the pencil and the picture, the chisel and the statue, the chord and the harmony. The social sympathies, or those laws from which, as from its elements, society results, begin to develop themselves from the moment that two human beings coexist; the future is contained within the present as the plant within the seed; and equality, diversity, unity, contrast, mutual dependence, become the principles alone capable of affording the motives according to which the will of a social being is determined to action (inasmuch as he is social), and constitute pleasure in sensation, virtue in sentiment, beauty in art, truth in reasoning, and love in the intercourse of kind. Hence men, even in the infancy of society, observe a certain order in their words and actions distinct from that of the objects and the impressions represented by them, all expression being subject to the laws of that from which it proceeds.

But let us dismiss those more general considerations which might involve an inquiry into the principles of society itself, and restrict our view to the manner in which the imagination is expressed upon its forms.

In the youth of the world, men dance and sing and imitate natural objects, observing[5] in these actions (as in all others) a certain rhythm or order. And, although all men observe a similar, they observe not the same order in the motions of the dance, in the melody of the song, in the combinations of language, in the series of their imitations of natural objects. For there is a certain order or rhythm belonging to each of these classes of mimetic representation, from which the hear-

---

3. Wind harp.   5. Seeing and following, obeying.
4. Shaping.

er and the spectator receive an intenser and purer pleasure than from any other. The sense of an approximation to this order has been called taste by modern writers. Every man in the infancy of art observes an order which approximates more or less closely to that from which this highest delight results. But the diversity is not sufficiently marked as that its gradations should be sensible, except in those instances where the predominance of this faculty of approximation to the beautiful (for so we may be permitted to name the relation between this highest pleasure and its cause) is very great. Those in whom it exists to excess are poets, in the most universal sense of the word; and the pleasure resulting from the manner in which they express the influence of society or nature upon their own minds, communicates itself to others, and gathers a sort of reduplication from the community. Their language is vitally metaphorical; that is, it marks the before unapprehended relations of things, and perpetuates their apprehension, until words which represent them, become through time signs for portions or classes of thought instead of pictures of integral thoughts; and then, if no new poets should arise to create afresh the associations which have been thus disorganized, language will be dead to all the nobler purposes of human intercourse.

These similitudes or relations are finely said by Lord Bacon to be "the same footsteps of nature impressed upon the various subjects of the world"—and he considers the faculty which perceives them as the storehouse of axioms common to all knowledge.[6] In the infancy of society every author is necessarily a poet, because language itself is poetry; and to be a poet is to apprehend the true and the beautiful, in a word, the good which exists in the relation subsisting, first between existence and perception, and secondly between perception and expression. Every original language near to its source is in itself the chaos of a cyclic poem:[7] the copiousness of lexicography and the distinctions of grammar are the works of a later age, and are merely the catalogue and the form of the creations of poetry.

But Poets, or those who imagine and express this indestructible order, are not only the authors of language and of music, of the dance and architecture and statuary and painting; they are the institutors of laws, and the founders of civil society, and the inventors of the arts of life, and the teachers who draw into a certain propinquity with the beautiful and the true that partial apprehension of the agencies of the invisible world which is called religion. Hence all original religions are allegorical, or susceptible of allegory, and like Janus have a double face of false and true. Poets, according to the circumstances of the age and nation in which they appeared, were called in the earlier epochs of the world, legislators or prophets. A poet essentially comprises and unites both these characters. For he not only beholds intensely the present as it is, and discovers those laws according to which present things ought to be ordered, but he beholds the future in the present, and his thoughts are the germs of the flower and the fruit of latest time. Not that I assert poets to be prophets in the gross sense of the word, or that they can foretell the form as surely as they foreknow the spirit of events; such is the pretence of superstition, which would make poetry an attribute of prophecy, rather than prophecy an attribute of poetry.[8]

6. In a note, Shelley cites Francis Bacon's *Of the Advancement of Learning* (1605) Book 3, ch. 1.
7. An extended set of poems, not necessarily by the same author, dealing with a common subject, event, or character. The term *cyclic poets* (which Shelley uses in *A Defence*) was first applied to a series of Greek epic poems supplementing Homer's *Iliad*; the most famous example of the genre in British literature is "the Arthurian Cycle," dealing with the court of King Arthur.
8. Sidney's *Defence* observes that the Roman word for poet, *vates*, means "prophet" or "oracle."

A Poet participates in the eternal, the infinite, and the one; as far as relates to his conceptions, time and place and number are not. The grammatical forms which express the moods of time, and the difference of persons and the distinction of place are convertible with respect to the highest poetry without injuring it as poetry and the choruses of Aeschylus, and the Book of Job, and Dante's Paradise would afford, more than any other writings, examples of this fact, if the limits of this essay did not forbid citation.[9] The creations of sculpture, painting, and music, are illustrations still more decisive.

Language, colour, form, and religious and civil habits of action are all the instruments and materials of poetry; they may be called poetry[1] by that figure of speech which considers the effect as a synonym of the cause. But poetry in a more restricted sense expresses those arrangements of language, and especially metrical language, which are created by that imperial faculty whose throne is curtained within the invisible nature of man. And this springs from the nature itself of language, which is a more direct representation of the actions and passions of our internal being, and is susceptible of more various and delicate combinations, than colour, form, or motion, and is more plastic and obedient to the control of that faculty of which it is the creation. For language is arbitrarily produced by the imagination, and has relation to thoughts alone; but all other materials, instruments and conditions of art have relations among each other which limit and interpose between conception and expression. The former is as a mirror which reflects, the latter as a cloud which enfeebles, the light of which both are mediums of communication. Hence the fame of sculptors, painters and musicians (although the intrinsic powers of the great masters of these arts may yield in no degree to that of those who have employed language as the hieroglyphic of their thoughts) has never equalled that of poets in the restricted sense of the term, as two performers of equal skill will produce unequal effects from a guitar and a harp. The fame of legislators and founders of religions (so long as their institutions last) alone seems to exceed that of poets in the restricted sense; but it can scarcely be a question whether, if we deduct the celebrity which their flattery of the gross opinions of the vulgar usually conciliates, together with that which belonged to them in their higher character of poets, any excess will remain. * * *

Poetry is ever accompanied with pleasure: all spirits on which it falls, open themselves to receive the wisdom which is mingled with its delight. * * * it acts in a divine and unapprehended manner, beyond and above consciousness; and it is reserved for future generations to contemplate and measure the mighty cause and effect in all the strength and splendour of their union. * * * no living poet ever arrived at the fulness of his fame; the jury which sits in judgement upon a poet, belonging as he does to all time, must be composed of his peers: it must be impanelled by Time from the selectest of the wise of many generations. A Poet is a nightingale, who sits in darkness and sings to cheer its own solitude with sweet sound; his auditors are as men entranced by the melody of an unseen musician, who feel that they are moved and softened, yet know not whence or why[2]. * * *

---

9. In addition to Job, referring to the Greek tragedian (525–456 B.C.), and *Paradiso*, the third and final part of Dante's epic *Divina Commedia* (completed 1321).
1. In the general sense of creative imagination and creative arts.
2. Compare *To a Sky-Lark*, especially 36–40 and 101–105 (pages 1723 and 1724).

The whole objection * * * of the immorality of poetry rests upon a misconception of the manner in which poetry acts to produce the moral improvement of man.[3] Ethical science[4] arranges the elements which poetry has created, and propounds schemes and proposes examples of civil and domestic life. Nor is it for want of admirable doctrines that men hate, and despise, and censure, and deceive, and subjugate one another. But poetry acts in another and diviner manner. It awakens and enlarges the mind itself by rendering it the receptacle of a thousand unapprehended combinations of thought. Poetry lifts the veil from the hidden beauty of the world, and makes familiar objects be as if they were not familiar; it re-produces all that it represents, and the impersonations clothed in its Elysian light[5] stand thenceforward in the minds of those who have once contemplated them as memorials of that gentle and exalted content[6] which extends itself over all thoughts and actions with which it co-exists. The great secret of morals is love, or a going out of our own[7] nature, and an identification of ourselves with the beautiful which exists in thought, action, or person, not our own. A man, to be greatly good, must imagine intensely and comprehensively; he must put himself in the place of another and of many others; the pains and pleasures of his species must become his own. The great instrument of moral good is the imagination; and poetry administers to the effect by acting upon the cause.

Poetry enlarges the circumference of the imagination by replenishing it with thoughts of ever new delight, which have the power of attracting and assimilating to their own nature all other thoughts, and which form new intervals and interstices whose void forever craves fresh food. Poetry strengthens the faculty which is the organ of the moral nature of man, in the same manner as exercise strengthens a limb. A poet therefore would do ill to embody his own conceptions of right and wrong (which are usually those of his place and time) in his poetical creations (which participate in neither). By this assumption of the inferior office of interpreting the effect, in which perhaps after all he might acquit himself but imperfectly, he would resign a glory in the participation of the cause. There was little danger that Homer, or any of the eternal poets, should have so far misunderstood themselves as to have abdicated this throne of their widest dominion. Those in whom the poetical faculty, though great, is less intense (as Euripides, Lucan, Tasso, Spenser) have frequently affected[8] a moral aim, and the effect of their poetry is diminished in exact proportion to the degree in which they compel us to advert to this purpose.[9] * * *

We have more moral, political and historical wisdom than we know how to reduce into practice; we have more scientific and economical knowledge than can be accommodated to the just distribution of the produce which it multiplies. The poetry in these systems of thought is concealed by the accumulation of facts and calculating processes. There is no want of knowledge respecting what is wisest and best in morals, government, and political economy, or at least what is wiser and better

3. In the previous paragraph, Shelley defended poetry from the charge of immorality (leveled famously by Plato in *The Republic*, renewed by the English Puritans of the 17th century and the Evangelicals of Shelley's own age) for depicting characters "remote from moral perfection" and thus offering no "edifying pattern for general imitation" by their readers. Throughout, *A Defence* also counters Plato's other charge, that all art is only representation, and thus a diminishment of Ideal Truth.
4. Moral philosophy.
5. In Greek myth, Elysium is the abode of the blessed after death.
6. Noun: both "content" and "contentment."

7. In the argument of Plato's *Symposium*, a key sentence reads, "Love, therefore, and every thing else that desires anything, desires that which is absent and beyond his reach, that which it has not, that which is not itself, that which it wants" (Shelley's translation); "wants" means both "desires" and "lacks."
8. Adopted.
9. Euripides: Greek tragedian, 5th century B.C.; Lucan: Roman epic poet, A.D. 1st century; Torquato Tasso: Italian epic poet, 16th century; Edmund Spenser: 16th-century English poet, best known for the romance epic, *The Faerie Queene*.

than what men now practise and endure. But we let "*I dare not* wait upon *I would*, like the poor cat i'the adage."[1] We want the creative faculty to imagine that which we know; we want the generous impulse to act that which we imagine; we want the poetry of life:[2] our calculations have outrun conception; we have eaten more than we can digest. The cultivation of those sciences which have enlarged the limits of the empire of man over the external world, has, for want of the poetical faculty, proportionally circumscribed those of the internal world; and man, having enslaved the elements, remains himself a slave. To what but a cultivation of the mechanical arts in a degree disproportioned to the presence of the creative faculty (which is the basis of all knowledge) is to be attributed the abuse of all invention for abridging and combining labour, to the exasperation of the inequality of mankind? From what other cause has it arisen that these inventions, which should have lightened, have added a weight to the curse imposed on Adam?[3] Poetry, and the principle of Self (of which money is the visible incarnation) are the God and Mammon of the world.[4]

The functions of the poetical faculty are twofold: by one it creates new materials of knowledge and power and pleasure; by the other it engenders in the mind a desire to reproduce and arrange them according to a certain rhythm and order which may be called the beautiful and the good. The cultivation of poetry is never more to be desired than in periods when, from an excess of the selfish and calculating principle, the accumulation of the materials of external life exceed the quantity of the power of assimilating them to the internal laws of human nature. The body has then become too unwieldy for that which animates it.

Poetry is indeed something divine. It is at once the centre and circumference of knowledge;[5] it is that which comprehends all science, and that to which all science must be referred. It is at the same time the root and blossom of all other systems of thought. It is that from which all spring, and that which adorns all; and that which, if blighted, denies the fruit and the seed, and withholds from the barren world the nourishment and the succession of the scions of the tree of life. It is the perfect and consummate surface and bloom of all things; it is as the odour and the colour of the rose to the texture of the elements which compose it, as the form and splendour of unfaded beauty to the secrets of anatomy and corruption. What were [would be] Virtue, Love, Patriotism, Friendship, etc., what were the scenery of this beautiful Universe which we inhabit; what were our consolations on this side of the grave, and what were our aspirations beyond it,—if Poetry did not ascend to bring light and fire from those eternal regions where the owl-winged faculty of calculation dare not ever soar? Poetry is not like reasoning, a power to be exerted according to the determination of the will. A man cannot say, "I will compose poetry." The greatest poet even cannot say it: for the mind in creation is as a fading coal which some invisible influence, like an inconstant wind, awakens to transitory brightness. This power arises

---

1. *Macbeth* 1.7.44–45.
2. In these declarations, "want" means "lack" and "need," shaded by a sense of "desire," "wish for."
3. The Lord says to Adam, in punishment for his sin, "cursed is the ground for thy sake; in sorrow shalt thou eat of it all the days of thy life; thorns also and thistles shall it bring forth. . . . In the sweat of thy face shalt thou eat bread, till thou return unto the ground; . . . dust thou art, and unto dust shalt thou return" (Genesis 3.17–19).
4. Mammon is the false idol of money and worldly goods, against whom Jesus cautions, "Ye cannot serve God and

mammon" (Luke 16.13). Keats told Shelley the year before he wrote his *Defence*, "A modern work it is said must have a purpose, which may be the God—*an artist* must serve Mammon—he must have 'self concentration' selfishness perhaps. You I am sure will forgive me for sincerely remarking that you might curb your magnanimity and be more of an artist" (see page 1779).
5. Shelley is evoking the description of God, often attributed to St. Augustine (A.D. 4th–5th century), as the circle whose center is everywhere and circumference nowhere.

from within, like the colour of a flower which fades and changes as it is developed, and the conscious portions of our natures are unprophetic either of its approach or its departure. Could this influence be durable in its original purity and force, it is impossible to predict the greatness of the results; but when composition begins, inspiration is already on the decline, and the most glorious poetry that has ever been communicated to the world is probably a feeble shadow of the original conceptions of the poet. I appeal to the greatest poets of the present day whether it is not an error to assert that the finest passages of poetry are produced by labour and study. The toil and the delay recommended by critics can be justly interpreted to mean no more than a careful observation of the inspired moments, and an artificial connection of the spaces between their suggestions by the intertexture of conventional expressions—a necessity only imposed by a limitedness of the poetical faculty itself. For Milton conceived the Paradise Lost as a whole before he executed it in portions. We have his own authority also for the muse having "dictated" to him the "unpremeditated song."[6] And let this be an answer to those who would allege the fifty-six various readings of the first line of the Orlando Furioso.[7] Compositions so produced are to poetry what mosaic is to painting. The instinct and intuition of the poetical faculty is still more observable in the plastic and pictorial arts: a great statue or picture grows under the power of the artist as a child in the mother's womb, and the very mind which directs the hands in formation is incapable of accounting to itself for the origin, the gradations, or the media of the process.

Poetry is the record of the best and happiest moments of the happiest and best minds. We are aware of evanescent visitations of thought and feeling sometimes associated with place or person, sometimes regarding our own mind alone, and always arising unforeseen and departing unbidden, but elevating and delightful beyond all expression; so that even in the desire and the regret they leave, there cannot but be pleasure, participating as it does in the nature of its object. It is, as it were, the interpenetration of a diviner nature through our own, but its footsteps are like those of a wind over sea, which the morning calm erases, and whose traces remain only as on the wrinkled sand which paves it. These and corresponding conditions of being are experienced principally by those of the most delicate sensibility and the most enlarged imagination; and the state of mind produced by them is at war with every base desire. The enthusiasm of virtue, love, patriotism, and friendship is essentially linked with emotions; and whilst they last, self appears as what it is, an atom to a Universe. Poets are not only subject to these experiences as spirits of the most refined organization, but they can colour all that they combine with the evanescent hues of this etherial world; a word or a trait in the representation of a scene or a passion will touch the enchanted chord, and reanimate, in those who have ever experienced these emotions, the sleeping, the cold, the buried image of the past. Poetry thus makes immortal all that is best and most beautiful in the world; it arrests the vanishing apparitions which haunt the interlunations[8] of life, and veiling them or [either] in language or in form, sends them forth among mankind, bearing sweet news of kindred joy to those with whom their sisters abide—abide, because there is no portal of expression from the caverns of the spirit

6. In *Paradise Lost*, Milton says that his celestial muse "dictates to me slumb'ring, or inspires / Easy my unpremeditated verse" (9.23–24); compare *To a Sky-* *Lark*, 5 (page 1722).
7. Epic poem by Italian poet Ariosto (1632).
8. The dark intervals between the old and new moons.

which they inhabit into the universe of things.[9] Poetry redeems from decay the visitations of the divinity in man.

Poetry turns all things to loveliness: it exalts the beauty of that which is most beautiful, and it adds beauty to that which is most deformed; it marries exultation and horror, grief and pleasure, eternity and change; it subdues to union under its light yoke all irreconcilable things.[1] It transmutes all that it touches, and every form moving within the radiance of its presence is changed by wondrous sympathy to an incarnation of the spirit which it breathes; its secret alchemy turns to potable gold the poisonous waters which flow from death through life; it strips the veil of familiarity from the world, and lays bare the naked and sleeping beauty which is the spirit of its forms.

All things exist as they are perceived: at least in relation to the percipient. "The mind is its own place, and of itself can make a heaven of hell, a hell of heaven."[2] But poetry defeats the curse which binds us to be subjected to the accident of surrounding impressions. And whether it spreads its own figured curtain or withdraws life's dark veil from before the scene of things, it equally creates for us a being within our being.[3] It makes us the inhabitant of a world to which the familiar world is a chaos. It reproduces the common universe of which we are portions and percipients, and it purges from our inward sight the film of familiarity which obscures from us the wonder of our being. It compels us to feel that which we perceive, and to imagine that which we know. It creates anew the universe after it has been annihilated in our minds by the recurrence of impressions blunted by reiteration. It justifies that bold and true word of Tasso: *Non merita nome di creatore, se non Iddio ed il Poeta.*[4]

A Poet, as he is the author to others of the highest wisdom, pleasure, virtue, and glory, so he ought personally to be the happiest, the best, the wisest, and the most illustrious of men. As to his glory, let time be challenged to declare whether the fame of any other institutor of human life be comparable to that of a poet. That he is the wisest, the happiest, and the best, inasmuch as he is a poet, is equally incontrovertible: the greatest poets have been men of the most spotless virtue, of the most consummate prudence, and (if we would look into the interior of their lives) the most fortunate of men. And the exceptions, as they regard those who possessed the poetic faculty in a high yet inferior degree, will be found on consideration to confirm rather than destroy the rule. Let us for a moment stoop to the arbitration of popular breath, and usurping and uniting in our own persons the incompatible characters of accuser, witness, judge and executioner, let us decide without trial, testimony, or form, that certain motives of those who are "there sitting where we dare not soar,"[5] are reprehensible. Let us assume that Homer was a drunkard, that Virgil was a flatterer, that Horace was a cow-

---

9. Poetry is valuable because it articulates not only what the poet apprehends—those "vanishing apparitions"—but also their "sisters" in the spiritual selves of ordinary mankind, who would lack connection to what is "best and most beautiful in the world" and "the universe of things," were it not for poetry. In his *Defense*, Sidney calls the inner potential for understanding the "fore-conceit," and grants poets similar power.

1. Coleridge's description of imagination, *Biographia Literaria* (1817), the end of ch. 14 (see page 1669).

2. A small but significant misquotation of Satan's boast in Hell, *Paradise Lost* 1.254–55; Milton wrote "in itself" (not "of"), in order to set up, along with the second half of the chiasmus that Shelley goes on to deflect, the horri-

bly ironic return of this boast of mind over place when Satan beholds Eve and Eden in the morning (9.467–70).

3. For these possibilities, recall *Mont Blanc* 53–54 (page 1705).

4. *None merits the name of creator except God and the Poet*; from Serassi's *Life of Torquato Tasso* (1785). Sidney's *Apology* refers to God as the "Maker of [the] maker" (punning on the Greek word root for "poet").

5. "Those" are the poets whose reprehensible motives Shelley is willing to concede for the sake of argument. His quotation adapts Satan's sneering reminder to his former peers of his former state in Heaven: "ye knew me once no mate / For you, there sitting where ye durst not soar" (*Paradise Lost* 4.428–29).

ard, that Tasso was a madman, that Lord Bacon was a peculator, that Raphael was a libertine, that Spenser was a Poet Laureate.[6] It is inconsistent with this division of our subject to cite living poets, but posterity has done ample justice to the great names now referred to. Their errors have been weighed and found to have been dust in the balance; if their sins "were as scarlet, they are now white as snow"; they have been washed in the blood of the mediator and redeemer, Time.[7] Observe in what a ludicrous chaos the imputations of real or fictitious crime have been confused in the contemporary calumnies against poetry and poets; consider how little is as it appears—or appears as it is; look to your own motives, and judge not, lest ye be judged.[8]

Poetry, as has been said, differs in this respect from logic: that it is not subject to the controul of the active power of the mind, and that its birth and recurrence has no necessary connection with the consciousness or will. It is presumptuous to determine that these are the necessary conditions of all mental causation, when mental effects are experienced insusceptible of being referred to them.[9] The frequent recurrence of the poetical power, it is obvious to suppose, may produce in the mind a habit of order and harmony correlative with its own nature and with its effects upon other minds. But in the intervals of inspiration (and they may be frequent without being durable) a poet becomes a man, and is abandoned to the sudden reflux of the influences under which others habitually live. But as he is more delicately organized than other men, and sensible to pain and pleasure (both his own and that of others), in a degree unknown to them,[1] he will avoid the one [pain] and pursue the other [pleasure] with an ardor proportioned to this difference. And he renders himself obnoxious to calumny, when he neglects to observe the circumstances under which these objects of universal pursuit and flight have disguised themselves in one another's garments.

But there is nothing necessarily evil in this error, and thus cruelty, envy, revenge, avarice, and the passions purely evil, have never formed any portion of the popular imputations on the lives of poets.

I have thought it most favourable to the cause of truth to set down these remarks according to the order in which they were suggested to my mind by a consideration of the subject itself, instead of following that of the treatise that excited me to make them public. Thus although devoid of the formality of a polemical reply, if the views which they contain be just, they will be found to involve a refutation of the doctrines

6. All charges that have been made against these poets. Homer: epic poet of ancient Greece; Horace: Roman lyric poet and satirist, 1st century B.C.; Virgil: Roman pastoral and epic poet, 1st century B.C., sometimes accused of being an apologist for Roman imperialism; Bacon: English Renaissance philosopher, essayist, statesman, and scientist, whose public career was ruined by his conviction for accepting bribes (a peculator is an embezzler); Raphael: 16th century Italian painter (a libertine is given to immoral sensual indulgence); for Tasso and Spenser, see n. 9, page 1729. The first Poet Laureate, a royally bestowed office and honor, was Dryden (1670–1689), but because the position is associated with royal patronage and often the defense or celebration of the monarchy, other court poets, including Spenser, have been retroactively accorded the title. Shelley uses the charge against Spenser to sneer at one particular "living poet," the current Laureate, Robert Southey (cf. Byron's Dedication to Don Juan, page 1681).
7. See Isaiah: "Come now, and let us reason together,

saith the Lord: though your sins be as scarlet, they shall be as white as snow" (1.18); and Revelation: those in white robes at the throne of God "came out of great tribulation, and have washed their robes, and made them white in the blood of the Lamb" (i.e., Christ; 7.14).
8. See Christ's admonition, "Judge not, that ye be not judged. For with what judgment ye judge, ye shall be judged" (Matthew 7.1–2); by "contemporary calumnies," slanders and lies intended to ruin reputations, Shelley is referring to attacks on himself and others in Tory journals, especially The Quarterly. In the Preface of his panegyric on the death of King George III (1820), Poet Laureate Southey described Shelley's circle in Italy, which included Byron, as a "League of Incest," and their poetry as the work of "the Satanic School."
9. The plural pronouns refer to "consciousness and will" in the previous sentence.
1. An echo of Wordsworth's Preface to Lyrical Ballads; see page 1537.

of "The Four Ages of Poetry" so far at least as regards the first division of the subject. I can readily conjecture what should have moved the gall of the learned and intelligent author of that paper; I confess myself like him unwilling to be stunned by the *Theseids* of the hoarse Codri of the day. Bavius and Maevius undoubtedly are, as they ever were, insufferable persons. But it belongs to a philosophical critic to distinguish rather than confound.[2]

The first part of these remarks has related to poetry in its elements and principles; and it has been shown, as well as the narrow limits assigned them would permit, that what is called poetry in a restricted sense has a common source with all other forms of order and of beauty according to which the materials of human life are susceptible of being arranged, and which is poetry in a universal sense.

The second part will have for its object an application of these principles to the present state of the cultivation of poetry, and a defense of the attempt to idealize the modern forms of manners and opinions, and compel them into a subordination to the imaginative and creative faculty.[3] For the literature of England, an energetic development of which has ever preceded or accompanied a great and free development of the national will, has arisen, as it were, from a new birth. In spite of the low-thoughted envy which would undervalue contemporary merit, our own will be a memorable age in intellectual achievements, and we live among such philosophers and poets as surpass beyond comparison any who have appeared since the last national struggle for civil and religious liberty.[4] The most unfailing herald, companion, and follower of the awakening of a great people to work a beneficial change in opinion or institution, is poetry. At such periods there is an accumulation of the power of communicating and receiving intense and impassioned conceptions respecting man and nature. The persons in whom this power resides may often (as far as regards many portions of their nature) have little apparent correspondence with that spirit of good of which they are the ministers. But even whilst they deny and abjure, they are yet compelled to serve the power which is seated on the throne of their own soul. It is impossible to read the compositions of the most celebrated writers of the present day without being startled with the electric life which burns within their words.[5] They measure the circumference and sound the depths of human nature with a comprehensive and all-penetrating spirit, and they are themselves perhaps the most sincerely astonished at its manifestations, for it is less their spirit than the spirit of the age. Poets are the hierophants[6] of an unapprehended inspiration, the mirrors of the gigantic shadows which futurity casts upon the present, the words which express what they understand not; the trumpets which sing to battle, and feel not what they inspire; the influence which is moved not, but moves.[7] Poets are the unacknowledged legislators of the world.

---

2. Theseids are epic poems about Theseus, hero of ancient Greek legend; one of the worst and longest, by Roman poet Codrus (*Codri*, the plural, names poems of this type), was savaged by Juvenal and other satirists. Two other inferior Roman poets, Bavius and Maevius, were satirized by Virgil and Horace; the names became bywords for bad poetry. In the 1790s William Gifford (who would go on to edit *The Anti-Jacobin* and *The Quarterly*) gave the titles *The Baviad* and *The Maeviad* to his devastating mock-heroic satires of the sentimental-aesthetic poetry of the day.

3. Never drafted.
4. The Civil Wars of the 1640s, concluding in the execution of Charles I, and the Glorious Revolution of the late 1680s, unseating James II. Among "philosophers and poets," Shelley has Byron and himself in mind.
5. Again, himself and Byron.
6. Ancient priests who interpret sacred mysteries; oracles of revelation.
7. Aristotle (Greek philosopher, 4th century B.C.) described God as the "Unmoved Mover" of the universe.

Felicia Hemans
1793–1835

A best-selling poet in England and America through most of the nineteenth century, Felicia Hemans (née Browne) was a prolific writer. In addition to numerous publications in magazines and gift-books, she produced nineteen volumes of poems and plays between 1808 and 1834. Lord Byron, with whom she shared the publisher John Murray, was sensitive to the competition. In letters to Murray, he tags her "your feminine *He-Man*" or "Mrs. Hewoman's," his punning turning her commercial prowess into a monstrous mockery of sexual identity. Byron preferred women in their place, not his. "I do not despise Mrs. Heman—but if [she] knit blue stockings instead of wearing them it would be better," he declared to Murray, referring to the "blue-stockings," a derisive term for learned women.

Born in Liverpool in 1793, the year of the Terror in France and the execution of its king and queen, Felicia Hemans was raised in the distant calms of North Wales. Under the devoted tutelage of her mother, she became a child prodigy, learning Latin, German, French, and Italian, devouring Shakespeare, and quickly developing a talent for writing; when she was fourteen, her parents underwrote the publication of her first volume. Learning of her talents and beauty, Percy Shelley ventured a correspondence, but (fortunately for young Felicia Browne) her mother intervened and nothing came of his overture. The romance that did blossom was with Captain Alfred Hemans, a veteran of the Peninsular Campaign in Spain in which her brothers also served. They married in 1812, the year of her nineteenth birthday and third volume, *The Domestic Affections*. By 1818, she had produced three more volumes to favorable reviews, as well as five sons. Just before the birth of the last, the Captain left for Italy for reasons unclear; the story was ill health. In any event, they never saw each other again, the breach mirroring her father's desertion of his wife and children in 1810, for a fresh start in Canada. The collapse of her own and her mother's marriages haunts the idealism of home for which "Mrs. Hemans" was becoming famous, shadowing it with repeated stories of men's unreliability or treachery and the necessity of maternal responsibility.

Determined to support herself and her sons with her writing, Hemans returned to her mother's home in Wales. With no wifely obligations or husband to "obey," and with sisters, mother, and brothers to help care for her boys and run the home, Hemans had considerable time to read, study, write, and publish. There was a related cultural advantage. As a daughter under "the maternal wing" and an "affectionate, tender, and vigilant mother" herself (as prefaces to her works later in the century put it), the professional writer was immunized against the stigma of "unfeminine" independence. The death of her mother in 1827 was a deep and devastating grief, aggravated by the disintegration of her home as sons grew up and brothers and sisters married or moved away. Her health suffered, and after a long decline, she died in Dublin in 1835, a few months before her forty-second birthday. William Wordsworth warmly honored her in the memorial verses of his *Extempore Effusion*, even as he indicated his discomfort with her ignorance of household skills and her affectation of being a "literary lady."

Among Hemans's most successful volumes, both critically and commercially, were *Tales, and Historic Scenes* (1819), *The Forest Sanctuary* (1825), *Records of Woman* (1828), which she dedicated to Joanna Baillie, and *Songs of the Affections* (1830). She was popular well into the Victorian age, especially among women. By the middle of our century, she was remembered only by a few favorite poems, including *The Homes of England, The Landing of the Pilgrim Fathers* ("The breaking waves dashed high, / On a stern and rockbound coast") and *Casabianca* ("The boy stood on the burning deck")—this last a parlor-recitation and school-assembly favorite, as well as the subject of multiple parodies. By the 1980s, she was virtually forgotten.

In the recent recovery of the "lost" women writers of the Romantic era, however, her work has received fresh attention, especially for its reflection of many of the key social, psychological, and emotional concerns for women in her day. These involve not only woman's culturally celebrated roles as a patient, devoted, and often long-suffering lover, wife, and mother, but also persistent tensions within these definitions. Some readers still read her poetry as celebrating traditional gender values: women's place at home and her value in upholding "domestic affections," religious faith, and patriotic sentiment. But to others this same poetry seems only tenuously conservative and far from replete—haunted by sensations of the futility and vulnerability of the very ideals it celebrates, invaded by sadness, melancholy, betrayal, suffering, and violence, and repeatedly staging women's heroism in scenes of defeat and death. Hemans's imagination was particularly tuned to conflicts besetting women who achieve fame in nontraditional roles, especially as artists, typically at great cost in personal happiness.

FROM TALES AND HISTORIC SCENES, IN VERSE
The Wife of Asdrubal

"This governor, who had braved death when it was at a distance, and protested that the sun should never see him survive Carthage,[1] this fierce Asdrubal, was so mean-spirited, as to come alone, and privately throw himself at the conqueror's feet. The general, pleased to see his proud rival humbled, granted his life, and kept him to grace his triumph. The Carthaginians in the citadel no sooner understood that their commander had abandoned the place, than they threw open the gates, and put the proconsul in possession of Byrsa. The Romans had now no enemy to contend with but the nine hundred deserters, who, being reduced to despair, retired into the temple of Esculapius, which was a second citadel within the first: there the proconsul attacked them; and these unhappy wretches, finding there was no way to escape, set fire to the temple. As the flames spread, they retreated from one part to another, till they got to the roof of the building: there Asdrubal's wife appeared in her best apparel, as if the day of her death had been a day of triumph; and after having uttered the most bitter imprecations against her husband, whom she saw standing below with Emilianus,[2]—'Base coward!' said she, 'the mean things thou hast done to save thy life shall not avail thee; thou shalt die this instant, at least in thy two children.' Having thus spoken, she drew out a dagger, stabbed them both, and while they were yet struggling for life, threw them from the top of the temple, and leaped down after them into the flames."

Ancient Universal History. [London, 1736–1744]

> The sun sets brightly—but a ruddier glow
> O'er Afric's heaven the flames of Carthage throw;
> Her walls have sunk, and pyramids of fire
> In lurid splendor from her domes aspire;
> 5   Sway'd by the wind, they wave—while glares the sky
> As when the desert's red Simoom° is nigh;   *desert wind*
> The sculptured altar, and the pillar'd hall,
> Shine out in dreadful brightness ere they fall;
> Far o'er the seas the light of ruin streams,
> 10   Rock, wave, and isle, are crimson'd by its beams;

1. Carthage was a powerful city-state on Africa's northern coast; its control of the western Mediterranean was challenged by the Roman empire, which finally destroyed it in the Third Punic War (149–46 B.C.).

2. Scipio Africanus Minor, the Roman general (son of Aemilius Paullus). The surviving Carthaginians were sold into slavery, and Asdrubal lived comfortably as a state prisoner in Italy.

While captive thousands, bound in Roman chains,
Gaze in mute horror on their burning fanes;°   *temples*
And shouts of triumph, echoing far around,
Swell from the victor's tents with ivy crown'd.³

15   But mark! from yon fair temple's loftiest height
What towering form bursts wildly on the sight,
All regal in magnificent attire,
And sternly beauteous in terrific ire?
She might be deem'd a Pythia⁴ in the hour
20   Of dread communion and delirious power;
A being more than earthly, in whose eye
There dwells a strange and fierce ascendancy.
The flames are gathering round—intensely bright,
Full on her features glares their meteor-light,
25   But a wild courage sits triumphant there,
The stormy grandeur of a proud despair;
A daring spirit, in its woes elate,
Mightier than death, untameable by fate.
The dark profusion of her locks unbound,
30   Waves like a warrior's floating plumage round;
Flush'd is her cheek, inspired her haughty mien,
She seems th' avenging goddess of the scene.

Are those *her* infants, that with suppliant-cry
Cling round her, shrinking as the flame draws nigh,
35   Clasp with their feeble hands her gorgeous vest,
And fain would rush for shelter to her breast?
Is that a mother's glance, where stern disdain,
And passion awfully vindictive, reign?

Fix'd is her eye on Asdrubal, who stands,
40   Ignobly safe, amidst the conquering bands;
On him, who left her to that burning tomb,
Alone to share her children's martyrdom;
Who when his country perish'd, fled the strife,
And knelt to win the worthless boon of life.
45   "Live, traitor, live!" she cries, "since dear to thee,
E'en in thy fetters, can existence be!
Scorn'd and dishonour'd, live!—with blasted name,
The Roman's triumph° not to grace, but shame.   *victory parade*
O slave in spirit! bitter be thy chain
50   With tenfold anguish to avenge my pain!
Still may the manès° of thy children rise   *avenging spirits*
To chase calm slumber from thy wearied eyes;
Still may their voices on the haunted air
In fearful whispers tell thee to despair,
55   Till vain remorse thy wither'd heart consume,
Scourged by relentless shadows of the tomb!

3. It was a Roman custom to adorn the tents of victors with ivy [Hemans's note].
4. Priestess and medium of Apollo at the oracle of Delphi, whose entranced, frenzied communications required interpretation by male priests.

E'en now my sons shall die—and thou, their sire,
In bondage safe, shalt yet in them expire.
Think'st thou I love them not?—'Twas thine to fly—
60   'Tis mine with these to suffer and to die.
Behold their fate!—the arms that cannot save
Have been their cradle, and shall be their grave."

Bright in her hand the lifted dagger gleams,
Swift from her children's hearts the life-blood streams;
65   With frantic laugh she clasps them to the breast
Whose woes and passions soon shall be at rest;
Lifts one appealing, frenzied glance on high,
Then deep midst rolling flames is lost to mortal eye.

1819

Evening Prayer, at a Girls' School[1]

"Now in thy youth, beseech of Him
    Who giveth, upbraiding not,
That his light in thy heart becomes not dim,
    And his love be unforgot;
And thy God, in the darkest of days, will be
Greenness, and beauty, and strength to thee."
            —*Bernard Barton*[2]

Hush! 'tis a holy hour—the quiet room
    Seems like a temple, while yon soft lamp sheds
A faint and starry radiance, through the gloom
    And the sweet stillness, down on fair young heads,
5   With all their clustering locks, untouched by care,
    And bowed, as flowers are bowed in night, in prayer.

Gaze on—'tis lovely! Childhood's lip and cheek,
    Mantling° beneath its earnest brow of thought—   *blushing*
Gaze—yet what seest thou in those fair, and meek,
10   And fragile things, as but for sunshine wrought?—
Thou seest what grief must nurture for the sky,
What Death must fashion for Eternity!

Oh! joyous creatures! that will sink to rest,
    Lightly, when those pure orisons° are done,   *prayers*
15   As birds with slumber's honey-dew opprest,
        Midst the dim folded leaves, at set of sun—
Lift up your hearts! though yet no sorrow lies
Dark in the summer-heaven of those clear eyes.

Though fresh within your breasts the untroubled springs
20   Of hope make melody where'er ye tread,
And o'er your sleep bright shadows, from the wings
        Of spirits visiting but youth, be spread—
Yet in those flute-like voices, mingling low,

---

1. First published in a gift-book annual, this poem was
frequently anthologized in the 19th century.
2. From *The Ivy, Addressed to a Young Friend*. Barton,

"the Quaker poet," first sponsored by Quakers, would
later secure a pension after he dedicated *Household
Verses* (1845) to Queen Victoria.

Is woman's tenderness—how soon her wo!

25   Her lot° is on you—silent tears to weep,   *fate*
        And patient smiles to wear through suffering's hour,
    And sumless riches, from affection's deep,
        To pour on broken reeds—a wasted shower!
    And to make idols, and to find them clay,
30   And to bewail that worship.[3]—Therefore pray!

    Her lot is on you—to be found untir'd,
        Watching the stars out by the bed of pain,
    With a pale cheek, and yet a brow inspir'd,
        And a true heart of hope, though hope be vain;
35   Meekly to bear with wrong, to cheer decay,
    And, oh! to love through all things—therefore pray!

    And take the thought of this calm vesper° time,   *evening prayer*
        With its low murmuring sounds and silvery light,
    On through the dark days fading from their prime,
40   As a sweet dew to keep your souls from blight!
    Earth will forsake—oh! happy to have given
    Th'unbroken heart's first fragrance unto Heaven.

1826   1829

FROM **RECORDS OF WOMAN**[1]

Indian Woman's Death-Song

An Indian woman, driven to despair by her husband's desertion of her for another wife, entered a canoe with her children, and rowed it down the Mississippi towards a cataract. Her voice was heard from the shore singing a mournful death-song, until overpowered by the sound of the waters in which she perished. The tale is related in Long's "Expedition to the source of St Peter's River."[2]

    Non, je ne puis vivre avec un coeur brisé. Il faut que je
    retrouve la joie, et que je m'unisse aux esprits libres de l'air.

        Bride of Messina, Translated by Madame de Staël[3]

Let not my child be a girl, for very sad is the life of a woman.

                                                                                        The Prairie[4]

    Down a broad river of the western wilds,
    Piercing thick forest glooms, a light canoe
    Swept with the current: fearful was the speed

---

3. These metaphors were clichés in Hemans's day; "suffering's hour" is any affliction and particularly childbirth; "broken reeds" are children who die young; "idols" of "clay" are those (probably husbands) who prove unworthy of the worship they court.

1. Hemans's most popular volume was first published in 1828, with a dedication to Baillie; as in Wollstonecraft, "Woman" identifies a universal category. Along with the *Records of Woman*, there was a section of *Miscellaneous Poems* that included *The Graves of a Household* and *The Homes of England*.

2. William Hippolytus Keating, *Narrative of an Expedition to the Source of St. Peter's River* (1824) which includes notes from Stephen Long's narrative of his explorations in the American plains states in the 1820s.

3. In *De L'Allemagne* (1810); "No, I cannot live with a broken heart. I must regain joy and join the free spirits of the air."

4. From ch. 26 of *The Prairie* (1827), novel by American James Fenimore Cooper; spoken by the third wife of a Sioux Chief, who has proposed a fourth marriage to a "white" Mexican woman captured by his tribe, promising her status as favorite. The third wife never fully recovers from this betrayal and her sense of inferiority to the white woman.

Of the frail bark, as by a tempest's wing
5   Borne leaf-like on to where the mist of spray
Rose with the cataract's thunder.—Yet within,
Proudly, and dauntlessly, and all alone,
Save that a babe lay sleeping at her breast,
A woman stood: upon her Indian brow
10   Sat a strange gladness, and her dark hair wav'd
As if triumphantly. She press'd her child,
In its bright slumber, to her beating heart,
And lifted her sweet voice, that rose awhile
Above the sound of waters, high and clear,
15   Wafting a wild proud strain, her song of death.

Roll swiftly to the Spirit's land, thou mighty stream and free!
Father of ancient waters,[5] roll! and bear our lives with thee!
The weary bird that storms have toss'd, would seek the sunshine's calm,
And the deer that hath the arrow's hurt, flies to the woods of balm.

20   Roll on!—my warrior's eye hath look'd upon another's face,
And mine hath faded from his soul, as fades a moonbeam's trace;
My shadow comes not o'er his path, my whisper to his dream,
He flings away the broken reed—roll swifter yet, thou stream!

The voice that spoke of other days is hush'd within *his* breast,
25   But *mine* its lonely music haunts, and will not let me rest;
It sings a low and mournful song of gladness that is gone,
I cannot live without that light—Father of waves! roll on!

Will he not miss the bounding step that met him from the chase?°   *hunt*
The heart of love that made his home an ever sunny place?
30   The hand that spread the hunter's board, and deck'd his couch of yore?—
He will not!—roll, dark foaming stream, on to the better shore!

Some blessed fount amidst the woods of that bright land must flow,
Whose waters from my soul may lave the memory of this wo;
Some gentle wind must whisper there, whose breath may waft away
35   The burden of the heavy night, the sadness of the day.

And thou, my babe! tho' born, like me, for woman's weary lot,
Smile!—to that wasting of the heart, my own! I leave thee not;
Too bright a thing art *thou* to pine in aching love away,
Thy mother bears thee far, young Fawn! from sorrow and decay.

40   She bears thee to the glorious bowers where none are heard to weep,
And where th' unkind one hath no power again to trouble sleep;
And where the soul shall find its youth, as wakening from a dream,—
One moment, and that realm is ours—On, on, dark rolling stream!

Joan of Arc, in Rheims

Jeanne d'Arc avait eu la joie de voir à Chalons quelques amis de son enfance. Une joie plus ineffable encore l'attendait à Rheims, au sein de son triomphe: Jacques d'Arc, son père y se trouva, aussitot que de troupes de Charles VII y furent entreés; et

---

5. "Father of waters," the Indian name for the Mississippi [Hemans's note].

comme les deux frères de notre Héroine l'avaient accompagnés, elle se vit, pour un instant au milieu de sa famille, dans les bras d'un père vertueux. *Vie de Jeanne d'Arc.*[1]

> Thou hast a charmed cup, O Fame!
>   A draught that mantles° high,   *expands*
> And seems to lift this earth-born frame
>   Above mortality:
> Away! to me—a woman—bring
> Sweet waters from affection's spring.[2]

That was a joyous day in Rheims of old,
When peal on peal of mighty music roll'd
Forth from her throng'd cathedral; while around,
A multitude, whose billows made no sound,
5   Chain'd to a hush of wonder, tho' elate
With victory, listen'd at their temple's gate.
And what was done within?—within, the light
    Thro' the rich gloom of pictured windows flowing,
Tinged with soft awfulness a stately sight,
10   The chivalry of France, their proud heads bowing
In martial vassalage!—while midst that ring,
And shadow'd by ancestral tombs, a king
Receiv'd his birthright's crown. For this, the hymn
    Swell'd out like rushing waters, and the day
15   With the sweet censer's misty breath grew dim,
        As thro' long aisles it floated o'er th' array
Of arms and sweeping stoles. But who, alone
And unapproach'd, beside the altar-stone,
With the white banner, forth like sunshine streaming,
20   And the gold helm, thro' clouds of fragrance gleaming,
Silent and radiant stood?—the helm was rais'd,
And the fair face reveal'd, that upward gaz'd,
    Intensely worshipping:—a still, clear face,
Youthful, but brightly solemn!—Woman's cheek
25   And brow were there, in deep devotion meek,
        Yet glorified with inspiration's trace
On its pure paleness; while, enthron'd above,
The pictur'd virgin, with her smile of love,
Seem'd bending o'er her votaress.—That slight form!
30   Was that the leader thro' the battle storm?
Had the soft light in that adoring eye,

---

1. "Joan of Arc had the pleasure of seeing at Chalons some childhood friends. A still more exquisite pleasure awaited her at Rheims in the scene of her triumph: Jacques d'Arc, her father, arrived there just as the troops of Charles VII made their entry; and as the two brothers of our Heroine had accompanied him, she found herself for a moment, in the midst of her family, in the arms of a good father" [Jean Masson, *Life of Joan of Arc* (1712)]. French national heroine and later saint, Jeanne d'Arc (1412–1431), inspired by what she took to be holy voices, encouraged the Dauphin (prince and claimant to the throne) to throw off the English claim to France. She led

his troops against the siege of Orleans and conducted him to the cathedral at Rheims, where he was crowned Charles VII and she received acclaim. She continued to lead the war against the English, but suffered defeats and was taken prisoner in 1430; with Charles's cowardly acquiescence, she was turned over to the French ecclesiastical court, which tried her for witchcraft, blasphemy, and dressing in male armor; uneasy about punishing so popular a heroine, however, they handed her over to the English, who burned her at the stake in the marketplace at Rouen.

2. The first stanza of *Woman and Fame*, page 1745.

Guided the warrior where the swords flash'd high?
'Twas so, even so!—and thou, the shepherd's child,
Joanne,[3] the lowly dreamer of the wild!
35 Never before, and never since that hour,
Hath woman, mantled° with victorious power,   *flushed, covered*
Stood forth as *thou* beside the shrine didst stand,
Holy amidst the knighthood of the land;
And beautiful with joy and with renown,
40 Lift thy white banner o'er the olden crown,
Ransom'd for France by thee!

                    The rites are done.
Now let the dome with trumpet-notes be shaken,
And bid the echoes of the tombs awaken,
    And come thou forth, that Heaven's rejoicing sun
45 May give thee welcome from thine own blue skies,
    Daughter of victory!—A triumphant strain,
A proud rich stream of warlike melodies,
    Gush'd thro' the portals of the antique fane,°   *temple*
And forth she came.—Then rose a nation's sound—
50 Oh! what a power to bid the quick heart bound,
The wind bears onward with the stormy cheer
Man gives to glory on her high career!
Is there indeed such power?—far deeper dwells
In one kind household voice, to reach the cells
55 Whence happiness flows forth!—The shouts that fill'd
The hollow heaven tempestuously, were still'd
One moment; and in that brief pause, the tone,
As of a breeze that o'er her home had blown,
Sank on the bright maid's heart.—"Joanne!"—Who spoke
60   Like those whose childhood with *her* childhood grew
Under one roof?—"Joanne!"—*that* murmur broke
    With sounds of weeping forth!—She turn'd—she knew
Beside her, mark'd from all the thousands there,
In the calm beauty of his silver hair,
65 The stately shepherd; and the youth, whose joy
From his dark eye flash'd proudly; and the boy,
The youngest-born, that ever lov'd her best:
"Father! and ye, my brothers!"—On the breast
Of that grey sire she sank—and swiftly back,
70 Ev'n in an instant, to their native track
Her free thoughts flowed.—She saw the pomp no more—
The plumes, the banners:—to her cabin-door,
And to the Fairy's fountain in the glade,[4]
Where her young sisters by her side had play'd,
75 And to her hamlet's chapel, where it rose
Hallowing the forest unto deep repose,
Her spirit turn'd.—The very wood-note, sung

3. Hemans's hybrid of the French "Jeanne" and the English "Joan."
4. A beautiful fountain near Domremi, believed to be
haunted by fairies, and a favourite resort of Jeanne d'Arc
in her childhood [Hemans's note].

In early spring-time by the bird, which dwelt
Where o'er her father's roof the beech-leaves hung,
80   Was in her heart; a music heard and felt,
Winning her back to nature.[5]—She unbound
      The helm of many battles from her head,
And, with her bright locks bow'd to sweep the ground,
      Lifting her voice up, wept for joy, and said,—
85   "Bless me, my father, bless me! and with thee,
To the still cabin and the beechen-tree,
Let me return!"[6]
                Oh! never did thine eye
Thro' the green haunts of happy infancy
Wander again, Joanne!—too much of fame
90   Had shed its radiance on thy peasant-name;
And bought alone by gifts beyond all price,[7]
The trusting heart's repose, the paradise
Of home with all its loves, doth fate allow
The crown of glory unto woman's brow.[8]

1826   1828

The Graves of a Household

They grew in beauty, side by side,
    They filled one home with glee;—
Their graves are sever'd far and wide,
    By mount, and stream, and sea.[1]

5   The same fond mother bent at night
    O'er each fair sleeping brow;
She had each folded flower in sight,—
    Where are those dreamers now?

One, midst the forest of the west,
10   By a dark stream is laid—
The Indian knows his place of rest,
    Far in the cedar shade.

The sea, the blue lone sea, hath one,
    He lies where pearls lie deep;
15   *He* was the lov'd of all, yet none
    O'er his low bed may weep.

One sleeps where southern vines are drest
    Above the noble slain:
He wrapt his colours round his breast
20   On a blood-red field of Spain.[2]

---

5. The world of nature and also her deepest female "nature" as daughterly maid, before her days of fame.
6. Compare to Jesus' parable of the prodigal son, Luke 15.11–32.
7. Salvation through Christ is a promise "great beyond price" (2 Peter).
8. "Thou never from that hour in Paradise / Found'st either sweet repast, or sound repose," Milton writes of Eve as she leaves Adam's side (*Paradise Lost* 9.406–407).
1. Hemans's younger brother died in Canada in 1821.
2. Hemans's brothers and husband had served in the war in Spain against Napoleon; her first long poem was *England and Spain, or Valour and Patriotism* (1808).

And one—o'er *her* the myrtle showers
　　Its leaves, by soft winds fann'd;
She faded midst Italian flowers,—
　　The last of that bright band.

25　　And parted thus they rest, who play'd
　　Beneath the same green tree;
Whose voices mingled as they pray'd
　　Around one parent knee!

They that with smiles lit up the hall,
30　　And cheer'd with song the hearth,—
Alas, for love! if *thou* wert all,
　　And naught beyond, oh, earth!

1825　　　　　　　　　　　　　　　　　　　　　　　　1828

Corinne at the Capitol[1]

"Les femmes doivent penser qu'il est dans cette carrière bien
peu de sorts qui puissent valoir la plus obscure vie d'une
femme aimée et d'une mère heureuse."

—*Madame de Staël*[2]

Daughter of th' Italian heaven!
Thou, to whom its fires are given,
Joyously thy car hath roll'd
Where the conqueror's pass'd of old;
5　And the festal sun that shone,
O'er three hundred triumphs gone,[3]
Makes thy day of glory bright,
With a shower of golden light.

Now thou tread'st th' ascending road,
10　Freedom's foot so proudly trode;
While, from tombs of heroes borne,
From the dust of empire shorn,
Flowers upon thy graceful head,

1. Hemans's title comes from Book II of Madame de Staël's *Corinne, ou l'Italie* (1807); quickly translated into English, this novel was immensely popular, especially with women, not only Hemans, but also Jane Austen and Mary Godwin (Shelley), Elizabeth Barrett (Browning), George Eliot, and Harriet Beecher (Stowe). It was read as the definitive story of female "genius"—as an inspirational and cautionary tale about creative achievement at the cost of domestic happiness. De Staël was famous for her intellect, her social charm, her essays, her forthright conversation (including blunt criticism of Napoleon), and her salons, which were attended by political and literary celebrities. Her heroine, Corinne, half English and half Italian, is a famous performing poet living in Italy, where she meets the English Lord Nelvil. With him, we see her for the first time, at the Roman Capitol, celebrated in all her glorious genius. De Staël elaborates her triumphant perfor-

mance, transcribing "Corinne's Improvisation at the Capitol," and concluding in a female apotheosis: "No longer a fearful woman, she was an inspired priestess, joyously devoting herself to the cult of genius." Corinne and Nelvil fall in love, but she declines his proposal of marriage, fearing a too-constrained life as an English wife. He returns to England and marries her half sister, a fully proper English maid. When Corinne learns of this, she dies of grief.
2. From *De L'influence des Passions* (1796): "Women should consider that in this career there are very few destinies equal in worth to the most obscure life of a beloved wife and a happy mother."
3. The trebly hundred triumphs.—Byron [Hemans's note, referring to *Childe Harold's Pilgrimage*, 4.731, a comment on the number of triumphs (victory parades), in ancient Rome.]

Chaplets° of all hues, are shed,   *head-wreaths*
15   In a soft and rosy rain,
Touch'd with many a gemlike stain.

Thou hast gain'd the summit now!
Music hails thee from below;—
Music, whose rich notes might stir
20   Ashes of the sepulchre;
Shaking with victorious notes
All the bright air as it floats.
Well may woman's heart beat high
Unto that proud harmony!

25   Now afar it rolls—it dies—
And thy voice is heard to rise
With a low and lovely tone
In its thrilling power alone;
And thy lyre's deep silvery string,
30   Touch'd as by a breeze's wing,
Murmurs tremblingly at first,
Ere the tide of rapture burst.

All the spirit of thy sky
Now hath lit thy large dark eye,
35   And thy cheek a flush hath caught
From the joy of kindled thought;
And the burning words of song
From thy lip flow fast and strong,
With a rushing stream's delight
40   In the freedom of its might.

Radiant daughter of the sun!
Now thy living wreath is won.
Crown'd of Rome!—Oh! art thou not
Happy in that glorious lot?—
45   Happier, happier far than thou,
With the laurel on thy brow,[4]
She that makes the humblest hearth
Lovely but to one on earth!

1830

Woman and Fame

Happy—happier far than thou,
With the laurel on thy brow;
She that makes the humblest hearth
Lovely but to one on earth.[1]

Thou hast a charmed cup, O Fame!
A draught° that mantles° high,   *drink/blushes*

---

4. The laurel wreath is a public honor for glorious accomplishment; laurel is the badge of Apollo, classical god of poetry (whence "Poet Laureate").

1. The final lines of Hemans's *Corinne at the Capitol*.

And seems to lift this earthly frame
    Above mortality.
5   Away! to me—a woman—bring
Sweet waters from affection's spring.[2]

Thou hast green laurel-leaves that twine
    Into so proud a wreath;[3]
For that resplendent gift of thine,
10   Heroes have smiled in death.
Give *me* from some kind hand a flower,
The record of one happy hour!

Thou hast a voice, whose thrilling tone
    Can bid each life-pulse beat,
15   As when a trumpet's note hath blown,
    Calling the brave to meet:
But mine, let mine—a woman's breast,
By words of home-born love be bless'd.

A hollow sound is in thy song,
20   A mockery in thine eye,
To the sick heart that doth but long
    For aid, for sympathy;
For kindly looks to cheer it on,
For tender accents that are gone.

25   Fame, Fame! thou canst not be the stay
    Unto the drooping reed,
The cool fresh fountain, in the day
    Of the soul's feverish need;
Where must the lone one turn or flee?—
30   Not unto thee, oh! not to thee!

1827–1829   1829

John Clare
1793–1864

The horizon of John Clare's world was defined by the village of Helpston, Northamptonshire, in which he was born, the son of a barely literate farmhand and an illiterate mother. His formal education was sparse, though his poetry shows his knowledge of Milton and Thomson and he read Wordsworth, Coleridge, Keats, and Byron (two late long poems are entitled *Childe Harold* and *Don Juan*). By the "indefatigable savings of a penny and a halfpenny," the young Clare purchased fairy tales from hawkers, recalling that "I firmly believed every page I read and considerd I possessd in these the chief learning and literature of the country." His own writing was produced swiftly and with few revisions in time seized from agricultural labor, then hid "with all secresy possible" in "an old unused cubbard" or hole in the wall.

2. These lines provide the epigraph for *Joan of Arc, in Rheims*.

3. See n. 4 to *Corinne at the Capitol.*

Clare's condition placed him in the line of those "natural geniuses" eagerly sought by eighteenth-century primitivism: Stephen Duck "The Thresher Poet" (1705–1756), Robert Bloomfield (*The Farmer's Boy*, 1800), Ann Yearsley "The Milkmaid Poet" (1752–1806) and Robert Burns (1759–1796) had all been fit into the stereotype of the peasant poet. In 1817 Keats's publisher John Taylor saw Clare's proposal to publish a volume of poetry by subscription; in 1820 his firm brought out *Poems Descriptive of Rural Life and Scenery*, marketing it as the work of a young "Northamptonshire Peasant," a description that fixed Clare's regional and class identity. The book enjoyed both critical and popular success, going through four editions in a year. The vogue that brought Clare attention quickly came to constrain him: his Evangelical patron disapproved of his social criticism and "vulgar" manner, and Taylor sought to broaden his appeal by standardizing his language and cutting his poems. Clare's pungent dialect usages—which illustrate by contrast how thoroughly Wordsworth "purified" the "language really used by men" in *Lyrical Ballads*—and belief "that what ever is intellig[i]ble to others is grammer and what ever is commonsense is not far from correctness" offended the norms of polite literature. "Grammer in learning," Clare adamantly insisted to Taylor in a phrase that by linking style and politics makes clear the twin offenses he posed to the urban book-buying public, "is like Tyranny in government—confound the bitch Ill never be her slave." Taylor found himself in the awkward position of intermediary between an audience for poetry increasingly represented by genteel women and a prickly lower-class male writer: "*false delicasy* damn it I hate it beyond every thing those primpt up misses brought up in those seminaries of mysterious wickedness (Boarding Schools) what will please 'em? why we well know—but while their heart & soul loves to extravagance (what we dare not mention) false delicasy's seriousness muscles [muzzles] up the mouth & condemns it." If that explosion reminds one of the "rodomontade" with which Keats defended his sexually more explicit revisions to *The Eve of St. Agnes,* the distance between the literariness of Keats, whom Clare admired, and Clare's plainness is manifest in his objection that Keats "keeps up a constant alusion or illusion to the grecian mythology & there I cannot follow . . . the frequency of such classical accompaniment makes it wearisome to the reader where behind every rose bush he looks for a Venus & under every laurel a thrumming Appollo."

New editions of Clare's writings have freed his texts from the emendations of their first publication and have brought unpublished materials to view, winning him the audience he missed in his own time. As illustration, we print two versions of *Written in November*, the first from the manuscripts edited by Eric Robinson and David Powell, the source of our texts, the second as the poem appeared in *The Village Minstrel* (1821).

Written in November (1)

Autumn I love thy latter end to view
In cold novembers day so bleak & bare
When like lifes dwindled thread worn nearly thro
Wi lingering pottering° pace & head bleached bare   *dawdling, uncertain*
5   Thou like an old man bids the world adieu
I love thee well & often when a child
Have roamd the bare brown heath a flower to find
& in the moss clad vale & wood bank wild
Have cropt the little bell flowers paley blue
10   That trembling peept the sheltering bush behind
When winnowing north winds cold & blealy° blew   *coldly, bleakly*
How have I joyd wi dithering° hands to find   *shivering*
Each fading flower & still how sweet the blast
Would bleak novembers hour Restore the joy thats past

Written in November (2)

Autumn, I love thy parting look to view
    In cold November's day, so bleak and bare,
When, thy life's dwindled thread worn nearly thro',
    With ling'ring pott'ring pace, and head bleach'd bare,
5   Thou, like an old man, bidd'st the world adieu.
    I love thee well: and often, when a child,
Have roam'd the bare brown heath a flower to find;
    And in the moss-clad vale, and wood-bank wild
Have cropt the little bell-flowers, pearly blue,
10   That trembling peep the shelt'ring bush behind.
When winnowing north-winds cold and bleaky blew,
    How have I joy'd, with dithering hands, to find
Each fading flower; and still how sweet the blast,
Would bleak November's hour restore the joy that's past.

c. 1812   1821

Clock a Clay°   *lady-bug*

In the cowslips peeps° I lye[1]   *primrose blossoms*
Hidden from the buzzing fly
While green grass beneath me lies
Pearled wi' dew like fishes eyes
5   Here I lye a Clock a clay
Waiting for the time o' day[2]

While grassy forests quake surprise
And the wild wind sobs and sighs
My gold home rocks as like to fall
10   On its pillars green and tall
When the pattering rain drives bye
Clock a Clay keeps warm and dry

Day by day and night by night
All the week I hide from sight
15   In the cowslips peeps I lye
In rain and dew still warm and dry
Day and night and night and day
Red black spotted clock a clay

My home it shakes in wind and showers
20   Pale green pillar top't wi' flowers
Bending at the wild winds breath
Till I touch the grass beneath
Here still I live lone clock a clay
Watching for the time of day

c. 1848   1873

1. Cf. Ariel's song in Shakespeare, *The Tempest*, 5.1.89: "In a cowslip's bell I lie."   2. Refers to the children's game of counting the taps needed to make the lady-bug fly away home.

"I Am"

I am—yet what I am, none cares or knows;
    My friends forsake me like a memory lost:—
I am the self-consumer of my woes;—
    They rise and vanish in oblivion's host,
5   Like shadows in love's frenzied stifled throes:—
And yet I am, and live—like vapours tost

Into the nothingness of scorn and noise,—
    Into the living sea of waking dreams,
Where there is neither sense of life or joys,
10   But the vast shipwreck of my lifes esteems;
Even the dearest, that I love the best
Are strange—nay, rather stranger than the rest.

I long for scenes, where man hath never trod
    A place where woman never smiled or wept
15   There to abide with my Creator, God;
And sleep as I in childhood, sweetly slept,
Untroubling, and untroubled where I lie,
The grass below—above the vaulted sky.

c. 1842   1848

John Keats
1795–1821

"A thing of beauty is a joy for ever"; "tender is the night"; "Beauty is truth; truth Beauty"— these phrases are so well known that we may forget that they once sprung from the imagination of John Keats. Keats's brief career ran only from 1814, when he wrote his first poem, to 1820, when he revised his sonnet *Bright Star* on board a ship to Italy. "Oh, for ten years, that I may overwhelm / Myself in poesy," he said in 1816. Not even getting this decade, his active life as a writer stopped around his twenty-fourth birthday. At age twenty-four, Chaucer had yet to write anything, and if Shakespeare had died at twenty-four, he would be known only (if at all) by a few early works. What if Keats had lived until 1881, like that Victorian sage Thomas Carlyle, also born in 1795?

The drama of Keats is not just the poignancy of genius cut off in youth but also his humble origins—a focus of ridicule during and after his lifetime by class-conscious reviewers and aristocratic poets. Son of a livery-stable keeper who had married the owner's daughter and inherited the suburban London business, Keats was sent to the progressive Enfield School. Here he was tutored and befriended by Charles Cowden Clark, the headmaster's son, who introduced him to literature, music, the theater. When Keats was nine years old, his father died in a riding accident and his mother remarried immediately; her commitment to her children was as erratic as it was doting, and her presence at home was inconstant. Keats was deeply attached to her and devastated when she disappeared for four years, leaving them all with his grandmother. When she returned sick and consumptive, he nursed her, and she died when he was fourteen; the welter of emotions she left in him is reflected in the series of adored, inconstant women around which so much of his poetry revolves. The children were remanded to the guardianship of a practical businessman whose chief concern was to apprentice the boys to some viable trade. Unimaginative himself and unsympathetic to any passion for learning and poetry, he apprenticed Keats to a London hospital surgeon in the grim days before anesthesia. Keats stayed with this training long enough to be licensed as an apothecary (more a general practitioner than a druggist), but he frequently took time off to read and to write poetry. When he came of age in 1817, he gave up medicine and set out to make a living as a poet.

Keats was already enjoying the society of Clarke and his circle of politically progressive thinkers, artists, poets, journalists, and publishers, many of whom became close friends— among them Leigh Hunt, also a poet as well as a radical journalist. Hunt launched Keats's career, publishing him in his weekly paper, *The Examiner*, and advertising him as one of the rising young poets. It was through Hunt that Keats met some of the chief nonestablishment writers of the day—William Wordsworth, William Hazlitt, Charles Lamb, Percy Shelley—and the controversial painter Benjamin Robert Haydon. His inaugural volume, published in 1817, included twenty sonnets, a favorite form for him, as well as Spenserian stanzas, odes, verse epistles, romance fragments, and meditative long poems on the subject of poetry itself. The writers that mattered most to him were Spenser (his first poem, written in 1814, was a deft "Imitation of Spenser" in Spenserian stanzas), Shakespeare, and ambivalently, Milton, and among his contemporaries, Wordsworth and Byron, though again with intelligent ambivalence. Keats warmly dedicated the 1817 *Poems* to Hunt and in a long concluding piece (*Sleep and Poetry*) voiced sharp criticism of what he saw as the arid formalism of eighteenth-century neoclassical poetry, which still had prestige with conservative or aristocratic writers, Byron among the latter. Byron never forgave Keats for this tirade, and it immediately provoked the Tory journalists, who were only too eager to jab at their political enemy Hunt through his protégé. Published in a year when civil rights were weakened and the radical publisher William Hone brought to trial, *Poems* was viciously ridiculed in reviews marked by social snobbery and political prejudice and Keats was indelibly tagged "the Cockney Poet"—one of Hunt's suburban radicals. He was stung, but determined to prove himself with his next effort, *Endymion*, initiated as part of a contest with Hunt and Shelley to see who could write a 4,000-line poem by the end of 1817. The only one to complete the challenge, Keats set off with a sense that it would be "a test" or "trial" of his talents. "A thing of beauty is a joy for ever" begins this tale of a shepherd-prince who dreams of a goddess, and on waking is profoundly alienated from ordinary life in the world. Book I narrates this episode; over the course of the next three books, Endymion dreams of her again, loses her, searches high (more dreams) and low (underground to the Bower of Venus and Adonis and several other labyrinthine terrains), and finally gives up, falling for a maid he finds abandoned in the woods. She turns out to be his goddess in disguise, and his dream comes true. This is the last time in Keats's poetry that dreams are so happily realized.

During 1818 Keats nursed his beloved brother Tom, dying of tuberculosis, the disease that had killed their mother and that would kill Keats himself three years later (already he was suffering from a chronically sore throat). Tom died at the end of 1818, and Keats sought relief in his poetry. In a burst of inspiration that lasted well into the fall of 1819 (when he revised *Hyperion*), he produced the work that established his fame: *The Eve of St. Agnes* (a part serious, part ironic romance), *La Belle Dame sans Merci* (a romance with a vengeance), *Lamia* (a wickedly satirical, bitter romance), all the Great Odes, and a clutch of brilliant sonnets, including *Bright Star*. Although (unlike most of his contemporaries) he wrote no prefaces, defenses, self-promoting polemics, or theoretical essays, his letters display a critical intelligence as brilliant as the poetic talent. A number of their off-the-cuff formulations—the "finer tone" of repetition, "negative capability," "the camelion Poet," "the egotistical sublime," truth "proved upon our pulses"—have become standard terms in literary criticism and theory, and from their first publication, after his death, his letters have been admired for their generosity and playfulness, their insight, their candor, and their critical penetration.

His health worsening over the course of 1819, Keats suffered a major lung hemorrhage early in 1820; with the accuracy of his medical training, he read his "death warrant" and was devastated. For despite the shaky reception of *Poems* and *Endymion*, he was optimistic about his forthcoming volume and full of enthusiasm for new writing (journalism or plays); he was also deeply in love with the girl next door, Fanny Brawne, whom he secretly betrothed and hoped to marry once he was financially capable. He sailed to Italy in September, seeking health in a warmer climate, but died at the end of the next February, four months after his twenty-fifth birthday—far from Fanny and his friends and in such despair of fame that he asked his tombstone to be inscribed "Here lies one whose name was writ in water." Yet he did live long enough to see some favorable reviews of his 1820 volume. Shelley's fable of Keats killed by hostile reviewers in *Adonais,* though often retold as truth, could not have been more out of tune with Keats's own resilience. "This is a mere matter of the moment," he assured his brother George, adding, "I think I shall be among the English Poets after my death."

On First Looking into Chapman's Homer[1]

> Much have I travell'd in the realms of gold,
>   And many goodly states and kingdoms seen;
>   Round many western islands have I been
> Which bards in fealty to Apollo° hold.   God of poetry
> 5 Oft of one wide expanse had I been told
>   That deep-brow'd Homer ruled as his demesne;°   realm
>   Yet did I never breathe its pure serene°   clear sky
> Till I heard Chapman speak out loud and bold:
> Then felt I like some watcher of the skies
> 10   When a new planet swims into his ken;[2]
> Or like stout Cortez when with eagle eyes
>   He star'd at the Pacific—and all his men
> Look'd at each other with a wild surmise—
>   Silent, upon a peak in Darien.[3]

1816   1816, 1817

COMPANION READINGS

Alexander Pope: Homer's Iliad[1]
from *Book 5*
[THE ARMOR OF DIOMEDES, A GREEK WARRIOR]

> High on his helm celestial lightnings play,
> His beamy shield emits a living ray;
> Th' unwearied blaze incessant streams supplies,
> Like the red star that fires th' autumnal skies,

---

1. Written the morning after Keats had stayed up all night with Clarke reading George Chapman's vibrant translation (c. 1611–1614) of Homer at a time when Pope's rendering in polished heroic couplets was the standard. Keats describes his reading as a Homeric voyage through the Greek isles where classical literature had its golden age. In *The Apology for Poetry* (1595), Sidney wrote that poets "deliver a golden" world from the "brazen" world of nature. Keats extends the language of traveling in "realms of gold" to Renaissance-era voyages of discovery to the New World in quest of gold by adventurers such as the conquistador of Mexico, Cortez.
2. Uranus was discovered in 1781; ken: range of apprehension.
3. Mountain range in eastern Panama.
1. When Books 1–4 of Pope's *Iliad* were published in 1715 (book 5 in 1716), he was acclaimed the greatest poet of the age; the successful sale inaugurated the first poetic career in England able to sustain itself independent of political or aristocratic patronage.

5   When fresh he rears his radiant orb to sight,
    And bath'd in Ocean, shoots a keener light.
    Such glories Pallas[2] on the chief bestow'd,
    Such, from his arms, the fierce effulgence flow'd:
    Onward she drives him, furious to engage,
10   Where the fight burns, and where the thickest rage.

George Chapman: Homer's Iliad[1]
from Book 5

    From his bright helme and shield did burne a most unwearied fire,
    Like rich Autumnus' golden lampe, whose brightnesse men admire
    Past all the other host of starres, when, with his cheaerfull face
    Fresh washt in loftir ocean waves he doth the skies enchase.
5   To let whose glory lose no sight, still Pallas made him turne
    Where tumult most expresst his powre, and where the fight did burne.

On Seeing the Elgin Marbles[1]

    My spirit is too weak—mortality
        Weighs heavily on me like unwilling sleep,
        And each imagined pinnacle and steep
    Of godlike hardship, tells me I must die
5   Like a sick eagle looking at the sky.
        Yet 'tis a gentle luxury to weep
        That I have not the cloudy winds to keep
    Fresh for the opening of the morning's eye.
    Such dim-conceived glories of the brain
10   Bring round the heart an undescribable feud;
    So do these wonders a most dizzy pain
        That mingles Grecian grandeur with the rude
    Wasting of old time—with a billowy main°   *sea*
    A sun—a shadow of a magnitude.

1817   1817, 1818

Sonnet: When I have fears

    When I have fears that I may cease to be[1]
        Before my pen has glean'd my teeming brain,
        Before high piled books in charact'ry°   *written symbols*

---

2. Pallas Athene, an epithet of Athena, Greek Goddess of War (and later, wisdom).

1. Chapman uses the fourteener, an iambic seven-beat line, most common in ballad verse (as two lines of four and three beats). Although both Pope and Chapman turn Homer's unrhymed lines into couplets, Keats preferred Chapman's rougher, less balanced lines and direct language.

1. Keats viewed these sculptural fragments from the Athenian Parthenon with Haydon, a champion of Lord Elgin's purchase of them in 1806 from the Turks, then occupying Greece. Elgin (hard *g*) was motivated both by admiration for their powerful beauty and a desire to preserve them from erosion and the further peril of supply-

ing mortar and target practice for Turkish soldiers. Their aesthetic value was debated (some found them crude and even inauthentic), and their purchase by the British government in 1816 for deposit in the British Museum (they are still there) was (and still is) controversial. Keats's sonnet appeared in *The Examiner* in 1817 (the text used here) and in Haydon's *Annals of the Fine Arts* in 1818.

1. Keats's sonnet plays several allusive echoes: Shakespeare's "When I do count the clock that tells the time"; Wordsworth's "few could know / When Lucy ceased to be" (*She dwelt among th'untrodden ways*; see page 1539); Milton's sonnet, "When I consider how my light is spent / Ere half my days, in this dark world and wide . . ."

Hold like rich garners the full-ripened grain;
5   When I behold upon the night's starred face,
     Huge cloudy symbols of a high romance,
And think that I may never live to trace
     Their shadows with the magic hand of chance;
And when I feel, fair creature of an hour,
10   That I shall never look upon thee more,
Never have relish in the fairy power
     Of unreflecting love—then on the shore
Of the wide world I stand alone and think,
     Till love and fame to nothingness do sink.

January 1818

The Eve of St. Agnes

Keats began this poem in the early winter months of 1819, setting it on St. Agnes' Eve, when, according to legend, a young virgin who has performed certain rituals may dream of her future husband. Agnes is the patron saint of virgins, but her story is rather more violent. A thirteen-year-old Christian martyr in early fourth-century Rome, she was condemned to a night of rape in the brothels before her execution. This first stage of the sentence was prevented by a miraculous storm of thunder and lightning, a climate that Keats writes into the end of his poem. Working in the intricate form of Spenserian stanzas, repopularized by Byron's *Childe Harold's Pilgrimage* (1812–1818), Keats spins an ironic romance—at once indulging the traditional pleasures of the genre (love, imagination, gorgeous sensuality with a spiritual aura) and bringing a playful, sometimes satiric, sometimes darkly shaded perspective to its illusions. With *Romeo and Juliet* in mind, Keats at first portrayed the sexual desire of his hero and heroine, but his publishers, worried about indecency, forced him to revise. Though he complied with angry reluctance, the imagery of stars and flowers in stanza 36 shows his skill in retaining some of the original pulsation.

The Eve of St. Agnes

1

St. Agnes' Eve—Ah, bitter chill it was!
The owl, for all his feathers, was a-cold;
The hare limp'd trembling through the frozen grass,
And silent was the flock in woolly fold:
5   Numb were the Beadsman's fingers, while he told
His rosary,[1] and while his frosted breath,
Like pious incense from a censer old,
Seem'd taking flight for heaven, without a death,
Past the sweet Virgin's picture, while his prayer he saith.

2

10   His prayer he saith, this patient, holy man;
Then takes his lamp, and riseth from his knees,
And back returneth, meagre, barefoot, wan,
Along the chapel aisle by slow degrees:
The sculptur'd dead, on each side, seem to freeze,
15   Emprison'd in black, purgatorial rails:
Knights, ladies, praying in dumb orat'ries,°   *chapels*

---

1. A pensioner paid to say prayers, this beadsman is saying a rosary in the estate's cold chapel for the salvation of the aristocrats partying indoors.

He passeth by; and his weak spirit fails
To think how they may ache in icy hoods and mails.

3

Northward he turneth through a little door,
20   And scarce three steps, ere Music's golden tongue
Flatter'd to tears this aged man and poor;
But no—already had his deathbell rung;
The joys of all his life were said and sung:
His was harsh penance on St. Agnes' Eve:
25   Another way he went, and soon among
Rough ashes sat he for his soul's reprieve,
And all night kept awake, for sinners' sake to grieve.

4

That ancient Beadsman heard the prelude soft;
And so it chanc'd, for many a door was wide,
30   From hurry to and fro. Soon, up aloft,
The silver, snarling trumpets 'gan to chide:
The level chambers, ready with their pride,
Were glowing to receive a thousand guests:
The carved angels, ever eager-eyed,
35   Star'd, where upon their heads the cornice rests,
With hair blown back, and wings put cross-wise on their breasts.

5

At length burst in the argent° revelry,   *silvery*
With plume, tiara, and all rich array,
Numerous as shadows haunting fairily
40   The brain, new stuff'd, in youth with triumphs gay
Of old romance.[2] These let us wish away,
And turn, sole-thoughted, to one Lady there,
Whose heart had brooded, all that wintry day,
On love, and wing'd St. Agnes' saintly care,
45   As she had heard old dames full many times declare.

6

They told her how, upon St. Agnes' Eve,
Young virgins might have visions of delight,
And soft adorings from their loves receive
Upon the honey'd middle of the night,
50   If ceremonies due they did aright;
As, supperless to bed they must retire,
And couch supine their beauties, lily white;
Nor look behind, nor sideways, but require°   *beseech*
Of Heaven with upward eyes for all that they desire.[3]

7

55   Full of this whim was thoughtful Madeline:[4]
The music, yearning like a God in pain

---

2. The literary genre.
3. Keats's publishers forced him to cancel as too explicitly erotic a stanza that followed this one, recounting the fable of a maid's "future lord" appearing in her dreams, bringing "delicious food even to her lips": "Viands, and wine, and fruit, and sugared cream, / To touch her palate with the fine extreme / Of relish; the soft music heard;

and then / More pleasures followed in a dizzy stream, / Palpable almost; then to wake again / Warm in the virgin morn, no weeping Magdalen"—i.e., Mary Magdalen, the prostitute befriended by Jesus; in Keats's day hospitals for unwed mothers were called Magdalens.
4. A name derived from Magdalen.

She scarcely heard: her maiden eyes divine,
Fix'd on the floor, saw many a sweeping train°   *long skirt*
Pass by—she heeded not at all: in vain
60   Came many a tiptoe, amorous cavalier,
And back retir'd; not cool'd by high disdain,
But she saw not: her heart was otherwhere:
She sigh'd for Agnes' dreams, the sweetest of the year.

8

She danc'd along with vague, regardless eyes,
65   Anxious her lips, her breathing quick and short:[5]
The hallow'd hour was near at hand: she sighs
Amid the timbrels,° and the throng'd resort   *tambourines*
Of whisperers in anger, or in sport;
'Mid looks of love, defiance, hate, and scorn,
70   Hoodwink'd° with faery fancy; all amort,°   *blinded / dead*
Save to St. Agnes and her lambs unshorn,
And all the bliss to be before to-morrow morn.[6]

9

So, purposing each moment to retire,
She linger'd still. Meantime, across the moors,
75   Had come young Porphyro,[7] with heart on fire
For Madeline. Beside the portal doors,
Buttress'd from moonlight,[8] stands he, and implores
All saints to give him sight of Madeline,
But for one moment in the tedious hours,
80   That he might gaze and worship all unseen:
Perchance speak, kneel, touch, kiss—in sooth such things have been.

10

He ventures in: let no buzz'd whisper tell:
All eyes be muffled, or a hundred swords
Will storm his heart,[9] Love's fev'rous citadel:
85   For him, those chambers held barbarian hordes,
Hyena foemen, and hot-blooded lords,
Whose very dogs would execrations howl
Against his lineage: not one breast affords
Him any mercy, in that mansion foul,
90   Save one old beldame,[1] weak in body and in soul.

11

Ah, happy chance! the aged creature came,
Shuffling along with ivory-headed wand,°   *staff*
To where he stood, hid from the torch's flame,
Behind a broad hall-pillar, far beyond

---

5. Originally: "Her anxious mouth full pulped with rosy thoughts."
6. It was a custom at St. Agnes' Day mass, during the singing of Agnus Dei (Lamb of God), to bless two white unshorn lambs, whose wool nuns then spun and wove.
7. From porphyra, "purple," a precious dye for garments of the nobility; "purple blood" signifies royalty and nobility; a porphyre is a purple-colored serpent. Moreover, Porphyry (3rd c. A.D.), famous antagonist of Christianity, instituted Neoplatonism throughout the Roman Empire a few decades before the martyrdom of St. Agnes.

8. Hidden in the shadow of a buttress (the external architecture that supports the castle walls).
9. Keats echoes Burke's famous account of the arrest of Marie Antoinette: "A band of cruel ruffians and assassins . . . rushed into the chamber of the queen, and pierced with an hundred strokes of bayonets and poniards the bed, from whence this persecuted woman had but just time to fly almost naked" (see *Reflections*, page 1359).
1. Grandmother or old nurse; Keats's Angela evokes Juliet's nurse Angelica in *Romeo and Juliet*, also go-between for the lovers.

95   The sound of merriment and chorus bland:°   *soft*
        He startled her; but soon she knew his face,
        And grasp'd his fingers in her palsied hand,
        Saying, "Mercy, Porphyro! hie thee from this place;
        They are all here to-night, the whole blood-thirsty race!

                                12
100   "Get hence! get hence! there's dwarfish Hildebrand;
        He had a fever late, and in the fit
        He cursed thee and thine, both house and land:
        Then there's that old Lord Maurice, not a whit
        More tame for his grey hairs—Alas me! flit!
105   Flit like a ghost away."—"Ah, Gossip° dear,   *confidant*
        We're safe enough; here in this arm-chair sit,
        And tell me how"—"Good Saints! not here, not here;
        Follow me, child, or else these stones will be thy bier."°   *coffin-platform*

                                13
        He follow'd through a lowly arched way,
110   Brushing the cobwebs with his lofty plume,
        And as she mutter'd "Well-a—well-a-day!"
        He found him in a little moonlight room,
        Pale, lattic'd, chill, and silent as a tomb.
        "Now tell me where is Madeline," said he,
115   "O tell me, Angela, by the holy loom
        Which none but secret sisterhood may see,
        When they St. Agnes' wool are weaving piously."

                                14
        "St. Agnes! Ah! it is St. Agnes' Eve—
        Yet men will murder upon holy days:
120   Thou must hold water in a witch's sieve,
        And be liege-lord of all the Elves and Fays,°   *fairies*
        To venture so: it fills me with amaze
        To see thee, Porphyro!—St. Agnes' Eve!
        God's help! my lady fair the conjuror plays
125   This very night: good angels her deceive!
        But let me laugh awhile, I've mickle° time to grieve."   *much*

                                15
        Feebly she laugheth in the languid moon,
        While Porphyro upon her face doth look,
        Like puzzled urchin on an aged crone
130   Who keepeth clos'd a wond'rous riddle-book,
        As spectacled she sits in chimney nook.
        But soon his eyes grew brilliant, when she told
        His lady's purpose; and he scarce could brook°   *hold back*
        Tears, at the thought of those enchantments cold,
135   And Madeline asleep in lap of legends old.

                                16
        Sudden a thought came like a full-blown rose,
        Flushing his brow, and in his pained heart
        Made purple riot: then doth he propose
        A stratagem, that makes the beldame start:
140   "A cruel man and impious thou art:

Sweet lady, let her pray, and sleep, and dream
Alone with her good angels, far apart
From wicked men like thee. Go, go!—I deem
Thou canst not surely be the same that thou didst seem.”

17

145   “I will not harm her, by all saints I swear,”
Quoth Porphyro: “O may I ne’er find grace
When my weak voice shall whisper its last prayer,
If one of her soft ringlets I displace.
Or look with ruffian passion in her face:
150   Good Angela, believe me by these tears;
Or I will, even in a moment’s space,
Awake, with horrid shout, my foemen’s ears,
And beard° them, though they be more fang’d than wolves and bears.”   *defy*

18

“Ah! why wilt thou affright a feeble soul?
155   A poor, weak, palsy-stricken, churchyard thing,
Whose passing-bell° may ere the midnight toll;   *death-knell*
Whose prayers for thee, each morn and evening,
Were never miss’d.”—Thus plaining,° doth she bring   *lamenting*
A gentler speech from burning Porphyro;
160   So woeful, and of such deep sorrowing,
That Angela gives promise she will do
Whatever he shall wish, betide her weal or woe.

19

Which was, to lead him, in close secrecy,
Even to Madeline’s chamber, and there hide
165   Him in a closet,° of such privacy   *private room*
That he might see her beauty unespied,
And win perhaps that night a peerless bride,
While legion’d fairies pac’d the coverlet,
And pale enchantment held her sleepy-eyed.
170   Never on such a night have lovers met,
Since Merlin paid his Demon all the monstrous debt.[2]

20

“It shall be as thou wishest,” said the Dame:
“All cates° and dainties shall be stored there   *delicacies*
Quickly on this feast-night: by the tambour frame[3]
175   Her own lute thou wilt see: no time to spare,
For I am slow and feeble, and scarce dare
On such a catering trust my dizzy head.
Wait here, my child, with patience; kneel in prayer
The while: Ah! thou must needs the lady wed,
180   Or may I never leave my grave among the dead.”

21

So saying, she hobbled off with busy fear.
The lover’s endless minutes slowly pass’d;

2. In Arthurian legend, the magician Merlin had his powers turned against him by the enchantress Vivien, who
treacherously repaid his love by imprisoning him in a
cave, where he died.
3. Frame for needlework embroidery, shaped like a tam-
bourine.

The dame return'd, and whisper'd in his ear
To follow her; with aged eyes aghast
185   From fright of dim espial.[4] Safe at last,
Through many a dusky gallery, they gain
The maiden's chamber, silken, hush'd, and chaste;
Where Porphyro took covert, pleas'd amain.°   *fully*
His poor guide hurried back with agues° in her brain.   *trembling*

22

190   Her falt'ring hand upon the balustrade,°   *bannister*
Old Angela was feeling for the stair,
When Madeline, St. Agnes' charmed maid,
Rose, like a mission'd spirit,[5] unaware:
With silver taper's° light, and pious care,   *candle's*
195   She turn'd, and down the aged gossip led
To a safe level matting. Now prepare,
Young Porphyro, for gazing on that bed;
She comes, she comes again, like ring-dove fray'd° and fled.   *frightened*

23

Out went the taper° as she hurried in;   *candle*
200   Its little smoke, in pallid moonshine, died:
She clos'd the door, she panted, all akin
To spirits of the air, and visions wide:
No utter'd syllable, or, woe betide!
But to her heart, her heart was voluble,°   *beating audibly*
205   Paining with eloquence her balmy side;
As though a tongueless nightingale should swell
Her throat in vain, and die, heart-stifled, in her dell.[6]

24

A casement° high and triple-arch'd there was,   *window*
All garlanded with carven imag'ries
210   Of fruits, and flowers, and bunches of knot-grass,
And diamonded with panes of quaint device,
Innumerable of stains and splendid dyes,
As are the tiger-moth's deep-damask'd wings;
And in the midst, 'mong thousand heraldries,°   *genealogical emblems*
215   And twilight saints, and dim emblazonings,
A shielded scutcheon blush'd with blood of queens and kings.[7]

25

Full on this casement shone the wintry moon,
And threw warm gules° on Madeline's fair breast,   *red*
As down she knelt for heaven's grace and boon;°   *favor*
220   Rose-bloom fell on her hands, together prest,
And on her silver cross soft amethyst,
And on her hair a glory,° like a saint: *halo*

---

4. Being espied, even in dim light.
5. Commissioned, as if an angel-messenger.
6. In a story in Ovid's *Metamorphoses*, Tereus, after raping his wife's sister Philomela, cut out her tongue to prevent her reporting the crime; but she wove its imagery into a robe that her sister understood, and was so enraged that she butchered her and Tereus's son and fed him a dinner made from the flesh. With Tereus on the verge of violent revenge, all three were turned into birds, Philomela into a nightingale; her name means "lover of honey, sweetness, song."
7. Scutcheon: shield; although "blood" aptly evokes bloodshed, here it refers to Madeline's royal bloodline.

She seem'd a splendid angel, newly drest,
Save wings, for heaven:—Porphyro grew faint:
225   She knelt, so pure a thing, so free from mortal taint.

26

Anon his heart revives: her vespers done,
Of all its wreathed pearls her hair she frees;
Unclasps her warmed jewels one by one;
Loosens her fragrant bodice;[8] by degrees
230   Her rich attire creeps rustling to her knees:
Half-hidden, like a mermaid in sea-weed,
Pensive awhile she dreams awake, and sees,
In fancy, fair St. Agnes in her bed,
But dares not look behind, or all the charm is fled.[9]

27

235   Soon, trembling in her soft and chilly nest,
In sort of wakeful swoon, perplex'd she lay,
Until the poppied° warmth of sleep oppress'd   *fragrant, narcotic*
Her soothed limbs, and soul fatigued away;
Flown, like a thought, until the morrow-day;
240   Blissfully haven'd both from joy and pain;
Clasp'd like a missal where swart Paynims pray;[1]
Blinded alike from sunshine and from rain,
As though a rose should shut, and be a bud again.

28

Stol'n to this paradise,[2] and so entranced,
245   Porphyro gazed upon her empty dress,
And listen'd to her breathing, if it chanced
To wake into a slumberous tenderness;
Which when he heard, that minute did he bless,
And breath'd himself: then from the closet crept,
250   Noiseless as fear in a wide wilderness,
And over the hush'd carpet, silent, stept,
And 'tween the curtains peep'd, where, lo!—how fast she slept.

29

Then by the bed-side, where the faded moon
Made a dim, silver twilight, soft he set
255   A table, and, half anguish'd, threw thereon
A cloth of woven crimson, gold, and jet:—
O for some drowsy Morphean amulet![3]
The boisterous, midnight, festive clarion,
The kettle-drum, and far-heard clarionet,
260   Affray° his ears, though but in dying tone:—   *frighten*
The hall door shuts again, and all the noise is gone.

---

8. Keats tested some even more erotic phrasing: "bursting boddice"; "her boddice and her bosom bare."
9. Evoking the myth of Orpheus and Eurydice, with Madeline in the male role of the lover who wins the opportunity to lead his dead beloved back to life from Hades, on the condition that he not look back at her until they reach the upper world. Orpheus violated this injunction and lost Eurydice forever.

1. Clasped shut and held like a prayer-book concealed from the sight of hostile, dark-skinned pagans (Muslims); "clasped" also suggests "arrested," with "pray" punning as "prey" (on), or persecute.
2. Alluding to Satan's entry into the Garden of Eden to corrupt Eve.
3. Sleep-inducing charm; Morpheus is the divine agent of sleep.

30

And still she slept an azure-lidded sleep,
In blanched linen, smooth, and lavender'd,
While he from forth the closet brought a heap
265   Of candied apple, quince, and plum, and gourd;°   *melon*
With jellies soother⁴ than the creamy curd,
And lucent syrops, tinct° with cinnamon;   *clear syrups, tinged*
Manna° and dates, in argosy° transferr'd   *rare food/merchant fleet*
From Fez; and spiced dainties, every one,
270   From silken Samarcand to cedar'd Lebanon.⁵

31

These delicates he heap'd with glowing hand
On golden dishes and in baskets bright
Of wreathed silver: sumptuous they stand
In the retired quiet of the night,
275   Filling the chilly room with perfume light.—
"And now, my love, my seraph° fair, awake!   *angel*
Thou art my heaven, and I thine eremite:°   *hermit*
Open thine eyes, for meek St. Agnes' sake,
Or I shall drowse beside thee, so my soul doth ache."

32

280   Thus whispering, his warm, unnerved° arm   *weak, unmanned*
Sank in her pillow. Shaded was her dream
By the dusk curtains:—'twas a midnight charm
Impossible to melt as iced stream:
The lustrous salvers° in the moonlight gleam: *trays*
285   Broad golden fringe upon the carpet lies:
It seem'd he never, never could redeem
From such a steadfast spell his lady's eyes;
So mus'd awhile, entoil'd in woofed° phantasies.   *woven*

33

Awakening up, he took her hollow lute,—
290   Tumultuous,—and, in chords that tenderest be,
He play'd an ancient ditty, long since mute,
In Provence call'd, "La belle dame sans mercy":⁶
Close to her ear touching the melody;—
Wherewith disturb'd, she utter'd a soft moan:
295   He ceased—she panted quick—and suddenly
Her blue affrayed° eyes wide open shone: *frayed, afraid*
Upon his knees he sank, pale as smooth-sculptured stone.

34

Her eyes were open, but she still beheld,
Now wide awake, the vision of her sleep:
300   There was a painful change, that nigh expell'd
The blisses of her dream so pure and deep
At which fair Madeline began to weep,

4. A Keats-coinage: smoother and more soothing.
5. All major places in the British trade in exotic goods, the luxuries of the feudal aristocracy: Fez in northern Morocco was a source of sugar; the ancient Persian city of Samarkand was famous for its silk markets, and Lebanon renowned for its fine cedar timber.

6. Provence is a region of southern France famed for troubadours; in the poem by Alain Chartier (1424; translated by Chaucer), a lady earns this title for her determined refusal of a suitor. In a few months, Keats would write his own ballad of a lady "sans mercy"/"sans merci": see n. 1 to *La Belle Dame sans Mercy* (page 1762).

And moan forth witless° words with many a sigh;   *uncomprehending*
While still her gaze on Porphyro would keep;
305   Who knelt, with joined hands and piteous eye,
Fearing to move or speak, she look'd so dreamingly.

35

"Ah, Porphyro!" said she, "but even now
Thy voice was at sweet tremble in mine ear,
Made tuneable with every sweetest vow;
310   And those sad eyes were spiritual and clear:
How chang'd thou art! how pallid, chill, and drear!
Give me that voice again, my Porphyro,
Those looks immortal, those complainings° dear!   *laments*
Oh leave me not in this eternal woe,
315   For if thou diest, my Love, I know not where to go."

36

Beyond a mortal man impassion'd far
At these voluptuous accents, he arose,
Ethereal, flush'd, and like a throbbing star
Seen mid the sapphire heaven's deep repose;
320   Into her dream he melted, as the rose
Blendeth its odour with the violet,—⁷
Solution° sweet: meantime the frost-wind blows   *fusion*
Like Love's alarum,° pattering the sharp sleet   *Cupid's warning*
Against the window-panes; St. Agnes' moon hath set.

37

325   'Tis dark: quick pattereth the flaw-blown° sleet: *storm-driven*
"This is no dream, my bride, my Madeline!"
'Tis dark: the iced gusts still rave and beat:
"No dream, alas! alas! and woe is mine!
Porphyro will leave me here to fade and pine.—
330   Cruel! what traitor could thee hither bring?
I curse not, for my heart is lost in thine,
Though thou forsakest a deceived thing;—
A dove forlorn and lost with sick unpruned° wing."   *bedraggled*

38

"My Madeline! sweet dreamer! lovely bride!
335   Say, may I be for aye° thy vassal blest?⁸   *ever*
Thy beauty's shield, heart-shaped and vermeil° dyed?   *vermillion*
Ah, silver shrine, here will I take my rest
After so many hours of toil and quest,
A famish'd pilgrim,—saved by miracle.
340   Though I have found, I will not rob thy nest
Saving of thy sweet self; if thou think'st well
To trust, fair Madeline, to no rude infidel.°   *unbeliever*

39

"Hark! 'tis an elfin-storm from faery land,
Of haggard° seeming, but a boon indeed: *wild, bewitched*

7. Keats's publishers refused his revision of 314–322, in which Porphyro's "arms encroaching slow . . . zon'd her, heart to heart" as he spoke into "her burning ear," and then "with her wild dream . . . mingled as a rose / Marry-eth its odour to a violet."
8. Keats would tell Fanny Brawne (25 July 1819): "the very first week I knew you I wrote myself your vassal" (page 1778). Vassal: devoted servant.

345   Arise—arise! the morning is at hand;—
       The bloated wassaillers will never heed:—
       Let us away, my love, with happy speed;
       There are no ears to hear, or eyes to see,—
       Drown'd all in Rhenish and the sleepy mead:°   *sweet wine*
350   Awake! arise! my love, and fearless be,
       For o'er the southern moors I have a home for thee."

                                    40
       She hurried at his words, beset with fears,
       For there were sleeping dragons all around,
       At glaring watch, perhaps, with ready spears—
355   Down the wide stairs a darkling° way they found.—   *dark, in the dark*
       In all the house was heard no human sound.
       A chain-droop'd lamp was flickering by each door;
       The arras,° rich with horseman, hawk, and hound,   *tapestry*
       Flutter'd in the besieging wind's uproar;
360   And the long carpets rose along the gusty floor.

                                    41
       They glide, like phantoms, into the wide hall;
       Like phantoms to the iron porch they glide;
       Where lay the Porter,° in uneasy sprawl,   *gate-keeper*
       With a huge empty flagon by his side:
365   The wakeful bloodhound rose, and shook his hide,
       But his sagacious eye an inmate owns:⁹
       By one, and one, the bolts full easy slide:—
       The chains lie silent on the footworn stones;—
       The key turns, and the door upon its hinges groans.

                                    42
370   And they are gone: ay, ages long ago
       These lovers fled away into the storm.
       That night the Baron dreamt of many a woe,
       And all his warrior-guests, with shade and form
       Of witch, and demon, and large coffin-worm,
375   Were long be-nightmar'd. Angela the old
       Died palsy-twitch'd, with meagre face deform;
       The Beadsman, after thousand aves told,¹
       For aye unsought for slept among his ashes cold.
1819   1820

La Belle Dame sans Mercy¹

       Ah, what can ail thee, wretched wight,°   *fellow*
       Alone and palely loitering;

9. Recognizes one of the usual dwellers (i.e., Madeline).
1. "Ave Maria" ("Hail Mary") prayers, part of the rosary ritual.
1. Published in Hunt's aesthetic (as opposed to political) journal, *The Indicator*; a version in a letter of April 1819, with slight differences in title, "La Belle Dame sans Merci," some words and stanza ordering, became, after it was first published in 1848, the preferred version, in part because it was shorn of association with Hunt. Our text is the version published in the Romantic era. The letter text, its French title taken from a medieval poem (see *Eve*

of St. Agnes 292, page 1760), gives the lady both more agency and more remorse. "La Belle Dame" means "the beautiful lady"; "Merci" suggests "Mercy" but carries a sense of gracious obligation. Both words derive from the medieval French *merces*, price paid or wages, suggesting the economy of exchange (the granting of sexual favor in exchange for gifts and service) that courted women are expected to honor. Keats situates the "Belle Dame" of his literary ballad in a long literary tradition of "femmes fatales," temptresses whose seduction proves fatal.

The sedge° is wither'd from the lake,   *marsh grass*
    And no birds sing.

5   Ah, what can ail thee wretched wight,
    So haggard and so woe-begone?
The squirrel's granary is full,
    And the harvest's done.

I see a lily on thy brow,
10   With anguish moist and fever dew;
And on thy cheeks a fading rose
    Fast withereth too.[2]

I met a Lady in the meads°[3]   *meadows*
    Full beautiful, a fairy's child;
15 Her hair was long, her foot was light,
    And her eyes were wild.

I set her on my pacing steed,[4]
    And nothing else saw all day long;
For sideways would she lean, and sing
20   A fairy's song.

I made a garland for her head,
    And bracelets too, and fragrant zone;°   *belt*
She look'd at me as° she did love,   *while, as if*
    And made sweet moan.

25 She found me roots of relish sweet,
    And honey wild, and manna dew;[5]
And sure in language strange she said,
    I love thee true.

She took me to her elfin grot,°   *grotto*
30   And there she gaz'd and sighèd deep,
And there I shut her wild sad eyes—
    So kiss'd to sleep.

And there she slumber'd on the moss,
    And there I dream'd, ah woe betide,
35 The latest° dream I ever dream'd   *last, most recent*
    On the cold hill side

I saw pale kings, and princes too,
    Pale warriors, death-pale were they all;
Who cry'd—"La belle Dame sans mercy
40   Hath thee in thrall!"°   *enslaved, enthralled*

I saw their starv'd lips in the gloom
    With horrid warning gapèd wide,
And I awoke, and found me here
    On the cold hill side.

2. Traditional emblems: the lily, death; the rose, love.
3. This stanza seems to begin the wretched wight's reply to his questioner, but the initial questioner may be continuing with his own story.
4. In the letter text, this stanza was transposed with the next.

5. In Exodus 16, God feeds the Israelites in the wilderness with a miraculous dew that hardens into food called manna; the context here may recall lines Keats marked in *Paradise Lost* describing fallen angel Belial's sophistry: "all was false and hollow, though his Tongue / Dropt Manna" (2.112–113).

45   And this is why I sojourn here
        Alone and palely loitering,
      Though the sedge is wither'd from the lake,
          And no birds sing.

1819   1820

Incipit Altera Sonneta[1]

I have been endeavouring to discover a better sonnet stanza than we have. The legitimate does not suit the language over-well from the pouncing rhymes—the other kind appears too elegaiac[2]—and the couplet at the end of it has seldom a pleasing effect—I do not pretend to have succeeded—it will explain itself—

      If by dull rhymes our English° must be chain'd,   *English language*
      And, like Andromeda,[3] the Sonnet sweet
      Fetter'd in spite of pained loveliness;
      Let us find out, if we must be constrain'd,
5   Sandals more interwoven & complete
      To fit the naked foot of Poesy;[4]
      Let us inspect the Lyre[5], & weigh the stress
      Of every chord & see what may be gain'd
      By ear industrious & attention meet;°   *appropriate*
10   Misers of sound & syllable, no less
      Than Midas of his coinage,[6] let us be
      Jealous of dead leaves in the bay wreath Crown;[7]
      So if we may not let the Muse be free,
      She will be bound with Garlands of her own.

1819   1836; 1848

THE ODES OF 1819

In Keats's career of ode-writing (from *Ode to Apollo*, 1814, to *Ode to Fanny*, 1820), there is a remarkable group composed in a burst of inspiration between April and September 1819 that is often regarded as his highest achievement. Except for *Ode on Indolence*, first published in 1848, all appeared, though not as a sequence, in Keats's 1820 volume. The order of composition is not known, beyond the fact that *Ode to Psyche* was written in April, the others probably in May, and *To Autumn* the last, in September. They reflect personal, cultural, and political contexts of 1819, having to do with everything from the Elgin Marbles controversy, to the widespread use of opium as a painkiller, to social misery and political unrest, to Keats's grief

---

1. Latin: "Here begins another Sonnet"; Keats's heading for this poem in a letter, to his brothers (30 April 1819), in which this sonnet appears. Although every sonnet implicitly comments on sonnet tradition, Keats's *Incipit*, like Wordsworth's *Nuns fret not* (page 1561), is an explicit reading of the tradition and his relation to it. Keats had written more than 60 sonnets by this point (not counting ones embedded in longer poems), but he would write only a few more after. Several allusions to Ovid's *Metamorphoses* reflect his concern with formal transformation.
2. The Petrarchan ("legitimate") sonnet opens with "pouncing rhymes": abbaabba; the "other" kind, the Shakespearean sonnet, deploys three "elegiac" stanzas (quatrains rhymed abab; cdcd; efef).

3. In Ovid's fable, beautiful Andromeda was fettered to a rock to be ravaged by a sea serpent; she was rescued by Perseus on his winged horse, Pegasus, an emblem of poetic inspiration.
4. Alluding to "poetic feet"—that is, meter.
5. The instrument of Apollo, god of poetry.
6. When Ovid's miserly king got his wish that everything he touched would turn to gold, he found he was unable to eat.
7. A head-wreath of bay laurel, first bestowed on military victors, then on poets (hence, "poet laureate"); in *Metamorphoses*, when the nymph Daphne escapes Apollo's amorous pursuit by turning into a laurel, he takes the laurel as his emblem.

over one brother's death and the other's emigration to America, to his nagging sensation that he was doomed to die young. Their language is enriched by literary allusion, as dense as it is casual, ranging through the Bible, Keats's earlier poetry and the hostile reviews of it, and favorite writers: Spenser, Shakespeare, Milton, Thomson, Collins, Chatterton, Coleridge, and Wordsworth. Even so, the odes also have an independent appeal that has made them, like Shakespeare's sonnets, general primers of the pleasure of reading poetry—of discovering how verbal nuance and reverberation, and complex interplays of imagery, shape a dynamic process of thought. Nineteenth-century readers admired the beautiful phrases and sensuous language—the tactile, auditory, visual qualities, even sensations of smell and taste. Readers in our century have added an enthusiasm for the intellectual complexity and mental drama, variously described as a poetry of "internal debate," a structure of "paradox" and "contradiction," a "rhetoric of irony" or a poetics of "indeterminacy."

Keats once suggested that "a question is the best beacon toward a little speculation," and that knowledge was less a matter of "resting places and seeming sure points of Reasoning" than of "question and answer—a little pro and con." The key questions in his odes—"Was it a vision, or a waking dream?"; "What leaf-fringed legend haunts about thy shape . . . ?"; "Where are the songs of spring?"—are met less with answers than with pro and con: a poet's mind as a "rosy sanctuary" and a place of mere "shadowy thought"; a bird-song that evokes "full-throated ease" and "easeful death"; a world of art in which human figures are both "for ever young" and a "cold pastoral"; an intensity of "Beauty" that is always a "Beauty that must die"; a sensuous "indolence" that cannot stay "sheltered from annoy" of busy thoughts; an autumn that is inextricably a season of ripe fruition and of death.

Ode to a Nightingale[1]

1

   My heart aches, and a drowsy numbness pains
     My sense, as though of hemlock I had drunk,
   Or emptied some dull opiate to the drains
     One minute past, and Lethe-wards had sunk:[2]
5   'Tis not through envy of thy happy lot,
     But being too happy in thine happiness,—
       That thou, light-winged Dryad° of the trees,   *wood-nymph*
       In some melodious plot
   Of beechen green, and shadows numberless,
10   Singest of summer in full-throated ease.

2

   O, for a draught of vintage!° that hath been   *wine*
     Cool'd a long age in the deep-delved earth,
   Tasting of Flora and the country green,
     Dance, and Provençal song, and sunburnt mirth![3]
15   O for a beaker full of the warm South,

1. First published in *Annals of the Fine Arts*, 1819. Keats's stanza incorporates sonnet elements: a Shakespearean quatrain (abab) followed by a Petrarchan sestet (cdecde), also the form of the odes on "Melancholy" and "Indolence." The nightingale in literary tradition (including Milton, Charlotte Smith, Wordsworth, Coleridge) often evokes Ovid's story of Philomela, who had been raped by her brother-in-law Tereus, who cut out her tongue to ensure her silence. After she revealed the crime by weaving the story into a robe, the gods changed her into a nightingale. Keats was also inspired by an actual nightingale's song at the house where he was living.
2. In small doses hemlock is a sedative; in large doses, such as Socrates', it is fatal; an opiate is any sense-duller, particularly opium, widely used as a painkiller; Lethe is the mythic river of the underworld whose waters produce forgetfulness of previous life.
3. *Deep-delved* alludes to the magician Merlin's dwelling "in a deep delve, farre from the view of day, / That of no living wight he mote be found" (*Faerie Queene* 3.3.7). Flora: Roman goddess of flowers. Provençal: region in southern France famed for troubadours.

Full of the true, the blushful Hippocrene,[4]
    With beaded bubbles winking at the brim,
        And purple-stained mouth;
That I might drink, and leave the world unseen,[5]
20   And with thee fade away into the forest dim:

3

Fade far away, dissolve, and quite forget
    What thou among the leaves hast never known,
The weariness, the fever, and the fret
    Here, where men sit and hear each other groan;
25   Where palsy shakes a few, sad, last gray hairs,
        Where youth grows pale, and spectre-thin, and dies;[6]
        Where but to think is to be full of sorrow
          And leaden-eyed despairs,
    Where Beauty cannot keep her lustrous eyes,
30   Or new Love pine at them beyond to-morrow.

4

Away! away! for I will fly to thee,
    Not charioted by Bacchus and his pards,[7]
But on the viewless wings of Poesy,
    Though the dull brain perplexes and retards:
35   Already with thee! tender is the night,
    And haply° the Queen-Moon is on her throne,   *happily, perhaps*
        Cluster'd around by all her starry Fays;°   *fairies*
        But here there is no light,
    Save what from heaven is with the breezes blown
40   Through verdurous glooms and winding mossy ways.

5

I cannot see what flowers are at my feet,
    Nor what soft incense hangs upon the boughs,
But, in embalmed darkness, guess each sweet
    Wherewith the seasonable month endows
45   The grass, the thicket, and the fruit-tree wild;
      White hawthorn, and the pastoral eglantine;
      Fast fading violets cover'd up in leaves;
        And mid-May's eldest child,
    The coming musk-rose, full of dewy wine,
50   The murmurous haunt of flies on summer eves.[8]

6

Darkling° I listen; and, for many a time   *in the dark*
    I have been half in love with easeful Death,

---

4. Hippocrene: the fountain of the muses on Mount Helicon.

5. "Unseen" can modify both "I" and "world."

6. An echo of Wordsworth's memory in *Tintern Abbey* of himself in "darkness, and amid the many shapes / Of joyless day-light; when the fretful stir / Unprofitable, and the fever of the world, / Have hung upon the beatings of my heart" (52–55); see page 1531, and Keats's remarks on *Tintern Abbey* in the letter of 3 May 1818 (pages 1774–1776). Both poets recall Macbeth's envy of Duncan "in his grave; / After life's fitful fever he sleeps well"

(*Macbeth* 3.322–323). Also echoed is Wordsworth's image of an ideal life "from diminution safe and weakening age; / While man grows old, and dwindles, and decays" (*Excursion* 4.759–760).

7. Bacchus, god of wine and revelry, whose chariot is drawn by leopards.

8. This guessing of flowers echoes Oberon's description in *A Midsummer Night's Dream* of a verdant bank where one may find a snake-skin whose juices make a sleeper fall in love with whatever is first seen on waking (2.1.249–58).

Call'd him soft names in many a mused rhyme,
　　To take into the air my quiet breath;
55　Now more than ever seems it rich to die,
　　To cease upon the midnight with no pain,
　　　While thou art pouring forth thy soul abroad
　　　In such an ecstasy!
　　Still wouldst thou sing, and I have ears in vain—
60　　To thy high requiem° become a sod.　　　　　　*funeral mass*

7

Thou wast not born for death, immortal Bird!
　　No hungry generations tread thee down;
　　The voice I hear this passing night was heard
　　In ancient days by emperor and clown:°　　　　*rustic, peasant*
65　Perhaps the self-same song that found a path
　　　Through the sad heart of Ruth, when, sick for home,
　　　　She stood in tears amid the alien corn;[9]
　　　　The same that oft-times hath
　　Charm'd magic casements, opening on the foam
70　　Of perilous seas, in faery lands forlorn.

8

Forlorn! the very word is like a bell
　　To toll me back from thee to my sole self!
　　Adieu! the fancy cannot cheat so well[1]
　　As she is fam'd to do, deceiving elf.
75　Adieu! adieu! thy plaintive anthem fades
　　　Past the near meadows, over the still stream,
　　　　Up the hill-side; and now 'tis buried deep
　　　　In the next valley-glades:
　　Was it a vision, or a waking dream?
　　Fled is that music:—Do I wake or sleep?

Ode on a Grecian Urn[1]

1

Thou still unravish'd bride of quietness,
　　Thou foster-child of silence and slow time,
Sylvan° historian, who canst thus express　　　　*woodland*
　　A flowery tale more sweetly than our rhyme:
5　What leaf-fring'd legend haunts about thy shape
　　Of deities or mortals, or of both,

---

9. See Ruth 1–2: compelled by famine to leave her home, Ruth eked out a living as a gleaner in far-away fields.
1. The adieu echoes the opening line of Charlotte Smith's *On the Departure of the Nightingale* (1784), "Sweet poet of the woods!—a long adieu!" The closing question bears several echoes: *Psyche* 5–6; the opening of Spenser's *Amoretti* 77: "Was it a dreame, or did I see it playne?"; Hazlitt's remark that "Spenser was the poet of our waking dreams," his "music . . . lulling the senses into a deep oblivion of the jarring noises of the world from which we have no wish ever to be recalled" (*On Chaucer and Spenser*, 1818); a spellbound lover's confusion in *Midsummer Night's Dream*: "Are you sure / That

we are awake? It seems to me / That yet we sleep, we dream" (4.1.194–96); Wordsworth's lament in the "Intimations" Ode, "Whither is fled the visionary gleam? / Where is it now, the glory and the dream?" (56–57), and his phrase "waking dream" in *Yarrow Visited* (pub. 1815).
1. First published in *Annals of the Fine Arts.* Keats is not describing any particular urn but three scenes on a representative one. The first is an image of revelry and sexual pursuit; the second (stanzas 2–3) is either a detail of this or another: a piper, and a lover in pursuit of a fair maid; in both, the story of Pan is implied. The third (stanza 4) is a sacrificial ritual, perhaps inspired by one of the Elgin Marble friezes.

In Tempe or the dales of Arcady?[2]
What men or gods are these? What maidens loth?
What mad pursuit? What struggle to escape?
10   What pipes and timbrels?° What wild ecstasy?   *tambourines*

2

Heard melodies are sweet, but those unheard
Are sweeter; therefore, ye soft pipes, play on;
Not to the sensual° ear, but, more endear'd,   *physical*
Pipe to the spirit ditties of no tone:
15   Fair youth, beneath the trees, thou canst not leave
Thy song, nor ever can those trees be bare;
    Bold Lover, never, never canst thou kiss,
Though winning near the goal—yet, do not grieve;
    She cannot fade, though thou hast not thy bliss,
20   For ever wilt thou love, and she be fair!

3

Ah, happy, happy° boughs! that cannot shed   *joyous, fortunate*
Your leaves, nor ever bid the Spring adieu;
And, happy melodist, unwearied,
For ever piping songs for ever new;
25   More happy love! more happy, happy love!
    For ever warm and still to be enjoy'd,
      For ever panting, and for ever young;
All breathing human passion far above,
    That leaves a heart high-sorrowful and cloy'd,
30   A burning forehead, and a parching tongue.

4

Who are these coming to the sacrifice?
To what green altar, O mysterious priest,[3]
Lead'st thou that heifer lowing at the skies,
    And all her silken flanks with garlands drest?
35   What little town by river or sea shore,
    Or mountain-built with peaceful citadel,°   *fortress*
      Is emptied of this folk, this pious morn?
And, little town, thy streets for evermore
    Will silent be; and not a soul to tell
40   Why thou art desolate, can e'er return.

5

O Attic shape! Fair attitude!° with brede°   *pose / intricate design*
    Of marble men and maidens overwrought,[4]
With forest branches and the trodden weed;
    Thou, silent form, dost tease us out of thought
45   As doth eternity: Cold Pastoral!
    When old age shall this generation waste,

---

2. A design of leaves frames a "legend" or caption on some vases; Tempe and Arcadia are districts of ancient Greece famed for beauty and serenity, where the gods often recreated.

3. That is, "unknown"; also denoting religious "mysteries" or rites.

4. The urn, made in Attica (where Athens is located), is "overwrought" (overlaid) with its design; Keats may be implying "over-elaborated," with a hint of psychological or emotional anguish in the frozen figures; thus "brede" puns on what cannot happen, "breed."

Thou shalt remain, in midst of other woe
Than ours, a friend to man, to whom thou say'st,
Beauty is truth, truth beauty,—that is all
50   Ye know on earth, and all ye need to know.[5]

Ode on Melancholy[1]

1

No, no, go not to Lethe,° neither twist   *river of forgetfulness*
   Wolf's-bane, tight-rooted, for its poisonous wine;
Nor suffer thy pale forehead to be kiss'd
   By nightshade, ruby grape of Proserpine;[2]
5 Make not your rosary of yew-berries,[3]
     Nor let the beetle, nor the death-moth be
      Your mournful Psyche,[4] nor the downy owl
A partner in your sorrow's mysteries;°   *secret rites*
   For shade to shade will come too drowsily,
10   And drown the wakeful anguish of the soul.

2

But when the melancholy fit shall fall
   Sudden from heaven like a weeping cloud,
That fosters the droop-headed flowers all,
   And hides the green hill in an April shroud;
15 Then glut thy sorrow on a morning rose,
     Or on the rainbow of the salt sand-wave,
      Or on the wealth of globed peonies;
Or if thy mistress some rich anger shows,
   Emprison her soft hand, and let her rave,
20   And feed deep, deep upon her peerless eyes.

3

She[5] dwells with Beauty—Beauty that must die;
   And Joy, whose hand is ever at his lips

---

5. In the 1820 volume, but in no other draft, quotation marks are placed around "Beauty is truth, truth beauty." Keats ponders the relation between "beauty" and "truth" throughout his career.

1. In May 1819, Keats paraphrased a couplet from Wordsworth's "Intimations" Ode: "Nothing can bring back the hour / Of splendour in the grass and glory in the flower" (cf. 177–178; page 1615), commenting, "I once thought this a Melancholist's dream." "Melancholy" is a traditional term for "the blues," or even "black" moods; Hamlet is famously "The Melancholy Dane." Robert Burton's treatise, *Anatomy of Melancholy* (1621), which Keats studied, offers an elaborate medical analysis of melancholy as well as an anthology of notable remarks. Taking a stock subject for poets in the 18th century (Charlotte Smith's sonnet *To Melancholy* among them; see page 1562), Keats prizes melancholy as a sensibility that accepts, even relishes, the evanescence of joy, pleasure, and beauty—their imminent flux into their opposites rendering such sensations all the more exquisite. He originally began the ode with a macabre, mock-heroic stanza about the quest for the goddess Melancholy: "Though you should build a bark of dead men's bones, / And rear a phantom gibbet for a mast, / Stitch creeds together for a sail, with groans / To fill it out, bloodstained and aghast; / Although your rudder be a Dragon's tail, / Long sever'd, yet still hard with agony, / Your cordage large uprootings from the skull / Of bald Medusa: certes you would fail / To find the Melancholy, whether she / Dreameth in any isle of Lethe dull . . ."

2. Wolf's-bane and nightshade are poisons; Proserpine (or Persephone) was abducted to the underworld by its ruler, Hades, but an appeal by her mother Ceres (goddess of grain) allowed her an annual sojourn in the upper world from spring to fall—a fable of seasonal flux relevant to the aesthetic of Melancholy.

3. The yew-tree is an emblem of death; rosary: prayer beads.

4. In Greek, "Psyche" means both "soul" and "butterfly" (its emblem); the markings on the death's-head moth resemble a human skull; the beetle may be the scarab, a jewel-bug placed in tombs by the ancient Egyptians as a portent of resurrection.

5. A double reference, to the mistress and to the goddess Melancholy.

Bidding adieu; and aching Pleasure nigh,
   Turning to poison while the bee-mouth sips:
25 Ay, in the very temple of Delight
   Veil'd Melancholy has her sovran shrine,
     Though seen of none save him whose strenuous tongue
Can burst Joy's grape against his palate fine;°   *sensitive, refined*
   His soul shall taste the sadness of her might,
30   And be among her cloudy trophies hung.

To Autumn[1]

1

Season of mists and mellow fruitfulness,
   Close bosom-friend of the maturing sun;
Conspiring with him how to load and bless
   With fruit the vines that round the thatch-eaves[2] run;
5 To bend with apples the moss'd cottage-trees,
   And fill all fruit with ripeness to the core;
     To swell the gourd, and plump the hazel shells
With a sweet kernel; to set budding more,
   And still more, later flowers for the bees,
10   Until they think warm days will never cease,
     For Summer has o'er-brimm'd their clammy cells.

2

Who hath not seen thee oft amid thy store?
   Sometimes whoever seeks abroad may find
Thee sitting careless on a granary floor,
15   Thy hair soft-lifted by the winnowing wind;
Or on a half-reap'd furrow sound asleep,
   Drowsed with the fume of poppies, while thy hook°   *scythe*
     Spares the next swath and all its twined flowers:
And sometimes like a gleaner thou dost keep
20   Steady thy laden head across a brook;
   Or by a cider-press, with patient look,
     Thou watchest the last oozings hours by hours.

3

Where are the songs of Spring? Ay, where are they?[3]
   Think not of them, thou hast thy music too,—
25 While barred clouds bloom the soft-dying day,

1. Composed 19–21 September 1819 in Winchester, a tranquil village in southern England, from which Keats wrote to a friend: "How beautiful the season is now— How fine the air. A temperate sharpness about it. . . . I never lik'd stubble fields so much as now—Aye better than the chilly green of the spring. Somehow a stubble plain looks warm—in the same way that some pictures look warm—this struck me so much in my sunday's walk that I composed upon it." The ode evokes two competing but related senses of autumn: the social context of harvest bounty; and the symbolic association with death—the reaper as grim reaper, autumn as the presage of winter (see Shakespeare's sonnet, "That time of year thou may'st in me behold"). Among other poems echoed are Thomson's *Autumn* in *The Seasons* (1740) and the last stanza of Coleridge's *Frost at Midnight.*
2. The eaves of thatched cottage roofs.
3. A self-conscious sounding of the "Ubi sunt" trope ("where are they now?"), which traditionally prefaces a nostalgic lament for lost worlds, the implied answer being "gone"; cf. Wordsworth's version at the end of stanza 4 of *Ode: Intimations* (page 1612).

And touch the stubble-plains with rosy hue;
Then in a wailful choir the small gnats mourn
    Among the river sallows,[4] borne aloft
      Or sinking as the light wind lives or dies;
30   And full-grown lambs loud bleat from hilly bourn;°   *boundary, region*
    Hedge-crickets sing; and now with treble soft°   *faint high pitch*
      The red-breast whistles from a garden-croft;°   *enclosure*
      And gathering swallows twitter in the skies.

This living hand[1]

This living hand, now warm and capable
Of earnest grasping, would, if it were cold
and in the icy silence of the tomb,
So haunt thy days and chill thy dreaming nights
5 That thou would wish thine own hea[r]t[2] dry of blood
So in my veins red life might stream again,
and thou be conscience-calm'd—see here it is—
I hold it towards you—

c. 1819   1898

Bright Star[1]

Bright Star, would I were stedfast as thou art—
    Not in lone splendor hung aloft the night,
And watching, with eternal lids apart,
    Like nature's patient, sleepless Eremite,°   *hermit*
5 The moving waters at their priestlike task
    Of pure ablution° round earth's human shores,   *ritual washing*
Or gazing on the new soft-fallen masque[2]
    Of snow upon the mountains and the moors—
No—yet still stedfast, still unchangeable
10   Pillow'd upon my fair love's ripening breast,
To feel for ever its soft swell and fall.
    Awake for ever in a sweet unrest,
Still, still to hear her tender-taken breath,
And so live ever—or else swoon to death—

1820   1838

---

4. Willows (an emblem of death).
1. A mysterious fragment, context unknown; "hand" is also a term for the character of one's "handwriting."
2. Keats inserted "heat" as superscript between "thine" and "own"; his characteristic dropping of "r" in handwriting makes it possible that he meant "heart," which best fits the context (although "heat" is relevant).
1. In summer 1818, Keats remarked that the scenery of the lake country "refine[s] one's sensual vision into a sort of north star which can never cease to be open lidded and stedfast over the wonders of the great Power"; sometime before summer 1819, he drafted this sonnet, then wrote this revised version in early autumn 1820 into the volume of Shakespeare's poems he took to Italy; perhaps the last poetry he wrote, its title in 19th-century editions was "Keats's last sonnet." The opening recalls the heroic self-description of Julius Caesar: "I could be well moved . . . but I am constant as the Northern Star, / Of whose true-fixed and resting quality / There is no fellow in the firmament" (*Julius Caesar* 3.1.58–62).
2. Punning on "mask," the word used in the 1819 draft.

LETTERS[1]
To George and Thomas Keats[2]
["INTENSITY" AND "NEGATIVE CAPABILITY"]

December 1818

My dear Brothers

[21 Dec.] * * * I saw Kean return to the public in Richard III,[3] & finely he did it. * * * Hone the publisher's trial, you must find very amusing; & as Englishmen very encouraging—his <u>Not Guilty</u> is a thing, which not to have been, would have dulled still more Liberty's Emblazoning—Lord Ellenborough has been paid in his own coin—Wooler & Hone have done us an essential service[4]—I spent Friday evening with Wells & went the next morning to see <u>Death on the Pale horse.</u>[5] It is a wonderful picture, when West's age is considered; But there is nothing to be intense upon; no women one feels mad to kiss; no face swelling into reality. the excellence of every Art is its intensity, capable of making all disagreeables evaporate, from their being in close relationship with Beauty & Truth—Examine King Lear[6] & you will find this examplified throughout; but in this picture we have unpleasantness without any momentous depth of speculation excited, in which to bury its repulsiveness. * * *

[?27 Dec.] * * * I had not a dispute but a disquisition with Dilke, on various subjects;[7] several things dovetailed in my mind, & at once it struck me, what quality went to form a Man of Achievement especially in Literature & which Shakespeare posessed so enormously—I mean <u>Negative Capability</u>, that is when man is capable of being in uncertainties, Mysteries, doubts, without any irritable reaching after fact & reason[8]—Coleridge, for instance, would let go by a fine isolated verisimilitude caught from the Penetralium of mystery, from being incapable of remaining content with half knowledge.[9] This pursued through Volumes would

1. In order to convey the character of Keats's letter-writing, idiosyncrasies of spelling, punctuation, and capitalization are for the most part preserved. Our insertions for clarity appear in square brackets [ ]; words or letters canceled by Keats that still seem interesting are inside angled brackets < >.
2. The brothers had lived together since 1816; George (1797–1841) had taken Tom to Teignmouth, Devonshire for his health.
3. Edmund Kean (1787–1833), charismatic and scandal-ridden actor who revolutionized the Shakespearean stage with his passionate performances. Richard III was one of his celebrated roles; Keats had just published an article on him in The Champion.
4. Referring to two notorious prosecutions. William Hone had just been found not guilty on three counts of blasphemous libel for his parodies of the liturgy, of which nearly 100,000 copies had sold. A conservative Lord Chief Justice Ellenborough, who had earlier sentenced John and Leigh Hunt for libel, presided at the loudly applauded verdict. Thomas Wooler, politician, journalist, and editor of the radical weekly The Black Dwarf, was acquitted on similar charges the previous June. The trials were well attended and

extremely amusing because the "offenses" had to be read into the record, thus gaining audience not only in the courtroom but also in reports in the "legitimate" press.
5. Wells was a schoolmate of Tom; Death on a Pale Horse, by American painter Benjamin West, is based on the image in Revelation of the fourth horseman of the Apocalypse.
6. West's painting of the storm scene in the play, not the play itself.
7. Disquisition: legalese for formal inquiry. Charles Dilke (1789–1864), government worker and amateur scholar, was a new friend.
8. "Negative Capability," Keats's most famous formulation, is a self-conscious oxymoron, wittily defined by its refrain from positing certainties of "fact & reason"; compare Keats's antipathy to egotistical assertions of "certain philosophy," "resting places and seeming sure points of Reasoning" (letters to Reynolds, 3 Feb. and 3 May 1818).
9. In 1817, Coleridge published Biographia Literaria and a volume of poems (Sibylline Leaves), in which The Rime of the Ancient Mariner appears with an explanatory marginal gloss. "Penetralium" is Keats's faux-Latin singular of "penetralia," the inmost chamber of a temple.

perhaps take us no further than this, that with a great poet the sense of Beauty overcomes every other consideration, or rather obliterates all consideration.

Shelley's poem is out & there are words about its being objected too, as much as Queen Mab was. Poor Shelley I think he has his Quota of good qualities, in sooth la!!¹ Write soon to your most sincere friend & affectionate Brother

John

To John Hamilton Reynolds²
[WORDSWORTH AND "THE WHIMS OF AN EGOTIST"]

3 February 1818

My dear Reynolds,

* * * It may be said that we ought to read our Contemporaries. that Wordsworth &c should have their due from us. but for the sake of a few fine imaginative or domestic passages, are we to be bullied into a certain Philosophy engendered in the whims of an Egotist—Every man has his speculations, but every man does not brood and peacock over³ them till he makes a false coinage and deceives himself— Many a man can travel to the very bourne of Heaven,⁴ and yet want confidence to put down his halfseeing. Sancho⁵ will invent a Journey heavenward as well as any body. We hate poetry that has a palpable design upon us—and if we do not agree, seems to put its hand in its breeches pocket.⁶ Poetry should be great & unobtrusive, a thing which enters into one's soul, and does not startle it or amaze it with itself but with its subject.—How beautiful are the retired flowers! how would they lose their beauty were they to throng into the highway crying out, "admire me I am a violet! dote upon me I am a primrose!["] * * * I will cut all this—I will have no more of Wordsworth or Hunt in particular. * * * I don't mean to deny Wordsworth's grandeur & Hunt's merit, but I mean to say we need not be teazed with grandeur & merit—when we can have them uncontaminated & unobtrusive. Let us have the old Poets, & robin Hood Your letter and its sonnets gave me more pleasure than will the 4th Book of Childe Harold & the whole of any body's life & opinions.⁷ * * *

Yr sincere friend and Coscribbler
John Keats.

1. Shelley was forced to withdraw *Laon and Cythna* (1817), an epic featuring the incestuous love of its sibling hero and heroine; the outcry was as heated as that against *Queen Mab* (1813), a visionary political epic attacking "Kingcraft, Priestcraft, and Statecraft." Keats's "sooth la!" ("the truth!") echoes the voice of Cleopatra as she tries, ineptly, to help Antony put on his armor after their night of debauchery (*Antony and Cleopatra* 4.4.8).
2. John Hamilton Reynolds (1794–1852), lawyer and poet, became one of Keats's closest friends; he introduced him to many others who would become friends, and to the publishers, Taylor and Hessey, who published *Endymion* and the 1820 volume.
3. To strut about ostentatiously; the OED credits Keats's usage here as the first instance of this verbal sense.
4. Alluding to Hamlet's description of the afterlife as the "undiscovered country, from whose bourn / No traveler returns" (*Hamlet* 3.1. 79–80); bourn: region.
5. Down-to-earth squire to the idealistic hero of Cervantes' *Don Quixote.*
6. Put away one's fist and refuse to fight.
7. Reynolds had just sent Keats some sonnets on Robin Hood; in response, Keats wrote *Robin Hood* and *Lines on the Mermaid Tavern*. The 4th canto of Byron's sensationally popular serial epic *Childe Harold's Pilgrimage* would be published in April.

To John Hamilton Reynolds

[WORDSWORTH, MILTON, AND "DARK PASSAGES"]

3 May 1818

My dear Reynolds.

What I complain of is that I have been in so an uneasy a state of Mind as not to be fit to write to an invalid. I cannot write to any length under a dis-guised feeling. I should have loaded you with an addition of gloom, which I am sure you do not want. I am now thank God in a humour to give you a good groats worth—for Tom, after a Night without a Wink of sleep, and overburdened with fever, has got up after a refreshing day sleep and is better than he has been for a long time. * * * Were I to study physic or rather Medicine again,—I feel it would not make the least difference in my Poetry; when the Mind is in its infancy a Bias is in reality a Bias, but when we have acquired more strength, a Bias becomes no Bias. Every department of knowledge we see excellent and calculated towards a great whole. I am so convinced of this, that I am glad at not having given away my medical Books, which I shall again look over to keep alive the little I know thitherwards. * * * An extensive knowledge is needful to thinking people—it takes away the heat and fever; and helps, by widening speculation, to ease the Burden of the Mystery:[8] a thing I begin to understand a little, and which weighed upon you in the most gloomy and true sentence in your Letter. The difference of high Sensations with and without knowledge appears to me this—in the latter case we are falling continually ten thousand fathoms deep and being blown up again without wings and with all [the] horror of a <bare> shouldered Creature—in the former case, our shoulders are fledge<d>, and we go thro' the same <air> and space without fear.[9] This is running one's rigs[1] on the score of abstracted benefit—when we come to human Life and the affections it is impossible how a parallel of breast and head can be drawn—(you will forgive me for thus privately heading <treading> out my depth and take it for treading as schoolboys head <tread> the water<s>)—it is impossible to know how far knowledge will console [us] for the death of a friend and the ill "that flesh is heir [to"][2] * * *

You seem by that to have been going through with a more painful and acute <test> zest the same labyrinth that I have—I have come to the same conclusion thus far. My Branchings out therefrom have been numerous: one of them is the consideration of Wordsworth's genius and as a help, in the manner of gold being the meridian Line of worldly wealth,—how he differs from Milton.[3]—And here I have nothing but surmises, from an uncertainty whether Miltons apparently less anxiety for Humanity proceeds from his seeing further or no than Wordsworth: And whether Wordsworth has in truth epic passion<s>, and martyrs himself to the human heart, the main region of his song[4]—In regard to his genius alone—we find

---

8. An allusion to Wordsworth's recollection in *Tintern Abbey* of that "blessed mood / In which the burthen of the mystery, / In which the heavy and the weary weight / Of all this unintelligible world, / Is lightened" (37–41).
9. Milton describes the angels in *Paradise Lost* as having "Shoulders fledge with wings" (3.627); even so, Satan is blown about in Chaos: "Flutt'ring his pennons vain plumb down he drops / Ten thousand fadom deep," then propelled "As many miles aloft" (2.933–38).
1. On a ship, running one's rigs means going at top speed; Keats's next image of treading water suggests a shipwreck

on this abstract value.
2. Alluding to Hamlet's longing for death as a way to "end / The heartache, and the thousand natural shocks / That flesh is heir to!" (*Hamlet* 3.1.61–63).
3. Keats treats Milton as the gold standard for assessing wealth, or the meridian line of longitude used by sailors to take their bearings.
4. In the "Prospectus" to *The Excursion*, Wordsworth aligned his epic with *Paradise Lost*, but declared "the Mind of Man" as the "haunt, and the main region of [his] song" (40–41).

what he says true as far as we have experienced and we can judge no further but by larger experience—for axioms in philosophy are not axioms until they are proved upon our pulses: We read fine—things but never feel them to [the] full until we have gone the same steps as the Author.—I know this is not plain; you will know exactly my meaning when I say, that now I shall relish Hamlet more than I ever have done—Or, better—You are sensible no man can set down Venery[5] as a bestial or joyless thing until he is sick of it and therefore all philosophizing on it would be mere wording. Until we are sick, we understand not;—in fine, as Byron says, "Knowledge is Sorrow"; and I go on to say that "Sorrow is Wisdom"—and further for aught we can know for certainty! "Wisdom is folly"[6]—So you see how I have run away from Wordsworth, and Milton. * * * I will return to Wordsworth—whether or no he has an extended vision or a circumscribed grandeur—whether he is an eagle in his nest, or on the wing—And to be more explicit and to show you how tall I stand by the giant, I will put down a simile of human life as far as I now perceive it; that is, to the point to which I say we both have arrived at—Well—I compare human life to a large Mansion of Many Apartments, two of which I can only describe, the doors of the rest being as yet shut upon me—The first we step into we call the infant or thoughtless Chamber, in which we remain as long as we do not think—We remain there a long while, and notwithstanding the doors of the second Chamber remain wide open, showing a bright appearance, we care not to hasten to it; but are at length imperceptibly impelled by the awakening of the thinking principle—within us—we no sooner get into the second Chamber, which I shall call the Chamber of Maiden-Thought, than we become intoxicated with the light and the atmosphere, we see nothing but pleasant wonders, and think of delaying there for ever in delight: However among the effects this breathing is father of is that tremendous one of sharpening one's vision into the <head> heart and nature of Man—of convincing ones nerves that the World is full of Misery and Heartbreak, Pain, Sickness and oppression—whereby This Chamber of Maiden Thought becomes gradually darken'd and at the same time on all sides of it many doors are set open—but all dark—all leading to dark passages—We see not the ballance of good and evil.[7] We are in a Mist—We are now in that state—We feel the "burden of the Mystery," To this point was Wordsworth come, as far as I can conceive when he wrote "Tintern Abbey" and it seems to me that his Genius is explorative of those dark Passages. Now if we live, and go on thinking, we too shall explore them. he is a Genius and superior [to] us, in so far as he can, more than we, make discoveries, and shed a light in them—Here I must think Wordsworth is deeper than Milton—though I think it has depended more upon the general and gregarious advance of intellect, than individual greatness of Mind—From the Paradise Lost and the other Works of Milton, I hope it is not too presuming, even between ourselves to say, his Philosophy, human and divine, may be tolerably understood by one not much advanced in years, In his time englishmen were just

---

5. Venery: sexual debauchery; Keats may have indulged himself thus when he visited Bailey at Oxford.

6. A mismemory or deliberate reversing of the complaint of Byron's tormented scholar-magician Manfred: "Sorrow is knowledge: they who know the most / Must mourn the deepest o'er the fatal truth, / The tree of knowledge is not that of life" (Manfred 1.1.10). Where Manfred alludes to Adam and Eve's gain of knowledge in tandem with a

death sentence, Keats blends the phrase to echo the famous conclusion of Thomas Gray's Ode on a Distant Prospect of Eton College (1747): "where ignorance is bliss, / 'Tis folly to be wise."

7. In the "Prospectus" to The Excursion Wordsworth stated his Miltonic "intent / To weigh the good and evil of our mortal state".

emancipated from a great superstition—and Men had got hold of certain points and resting places in reasoning which were too newly born to be doubted, and too much <oppressed> opposed by the Mass of Europe not to be thought etherial and authentically divine—who could gainsay his ideas on virtue, vice, and Chastity in Comus, just at the time of the dismissal of Cod-pieces and a hundred other disgraces?[8] who would not rest satisfied with his hintings at good and evil in the Paradise Lost, when just free from the inquisition and burrning in Smithfield?[9] The Reformation produced such immediate and great benefits, that Protestantism was considered under the immediate eye of heaven, and its own remaining Dogmas and superstitions, then, as it were, regenerated, constituted those resting places and seeming sure points of Reasoning—from that I have mentioned, Milton, whatever he may have thought in the sequel, appears to have been content with these by his writings[1]—He did not think into the human heart, as Wordsworth has done—Yet Milton as a Philosop[h]er, had sure as great powers as Wordsworth—What is then to be inferr'd? O many things—It proves there is really a grand march of intellect—, It proves that a mighty providence subdues the mightiest Minds to the service of the time being, whether it be in human Knowledge or Religion—Tom has spit a leetle blood this afternoon, and that is rather a damper—but I know—the truth is there is something real in the World Your third Chamber of Life shall be a lucky and a gentle one—stored with the wine of love—and the Bread of Friendship[2] * * *

Your affectionate friend
John Keats.

To Richard Woodhouse[3]

[THE "CAMELION POET" VS. THE "EGOTISTICAL SUBLIME"]

27 October 1818

My dear Woodhouse,

Your Letter gave me a great satisfaction; more on account of its friendliness, than any relish of that matter in it which is accounted so acceptable in the 'genus irritabile'[4] The best answer I can give you is in a clerklike manner to make some observations on two principle points, which seem to point like indices into the midst of the whole pro and con, about genius, and views and achievements and ambition and coetera. 1st As to the poetical Character itself, (I mean that sort of which, if I am any thing, I am a

---

8. The "superstition" was the old theory, enforced by the Catholic Church, of the earth as the center of the universe. In Milton's lifetime, Protestant scientists such as Copernicus overturned this theory, even as society abandoned such archaic fashions in clothing as codpieces. *Comus* (1634) depicts the temptation of a lady's virtue by the enchanter Comus.

9. The medieval Church established the Inquisition to seek out heretics, who were often burned at the stake. Smithfield, northwest of London, was a notorious site of public executions in the 16th and 17th centuries, especially under the reign of Catholic Queen Mary.

1. The "sequel" is the later writings; the Reformation was

a series of religious revolutions in the 16th century that resulted, often with violent warfare, in a variety of Protestant sects, including the Anglican Church.

2. A consciously secular application of the emblems of the Christian Eucharist.

3. Legal and literary adviser to Keats's second publishers, Woodhouse was a great admirer of Keats and assiduously preserved or transcribed his letters, manuscripts, and proof-sheets, as well as collected anecdotes. This is one of Keats's most famous letters, written after he had weathered a summer of negative reviews in highly visible journals.

4. Horace's term for poets, "the irritable tribe" (*Epistles* 2.2.102).

Member; that sort distinguished from the wordsworthian or egotistical sublime;[5] which is a thing per se and stands alone[6] it is not itself—it has no self—it is every thing and nothing—It has no character—it enjoys light and shade; it lives in gusto, be it foul or fair, high or low, rich or poor, mean or elevated—It has as much delight in conceiving an Iago as an Imogen.[7] What shocks the virtuous philosop[h]er, delights the camelion[8] Poet. It does no harm from its relish of the dark side of things any more than from its taste for the bright one; because they both end in speculation. A Poet is the most unpoetical of any thing in existence; because he has no Identity— he is continually in for[ming?]—and filling some other Body—The Sun, the Moon, the Sea and Men and Women who are creatures of impulse are poetical and have about them an unchangeable attribute—the poet has none; no identity—he is cer- tainly the most unpoetical of all God's Creatures. If then he has no self, and if I am a Poet, where is the Wonder that I should say I would <right> write no more? Might I not at that very instant [have] been cogitating on the Characters of saturn and Ops?[9] It is a wretched thing to confess; but is a very fact that not one word I ever utter can be taken for granted as an opinion growing out of my identical nature—how can it, when I have no nature? When I am in a room with People if I ever am free from speculating on creations of my own brain, then not myself goes home to myself: but the identity of every one in the room begins to press upon me that, I am in a very lit- tle time an[ni]hilated—not only among Men; it would be the same in a Nursery of children: I know not whether I make myself wholly understood: I hope enough so to let you see that no dependence is to be placed on what I said that day.

In the second place I will speak of my views, and of the life I purpose to myself— I am ambitious of doing the world some good: if I should be spared that may be the work of maturer years—in the interval I will assay to reach to as high a summit in Poetry as the nerve bestowed upon me will suffer. The faint conceptions I have of Poems to come brings the blood frequently into my forehead—All I hope is that I may not lose all interest in human affairs—that the solitary indifference I feel for applause even from the finest Spirits, will not blunt any acuteness of vision I may have. I do not think it will—I feel assured I should write from the mere yearning and fondness I have for the Beautiful even if my night's labours should be burnt every morning and no eye ever shine upon them. But even now I am perhaps not speaking from myself; but from some character in whose soul I now live. I am sure however that this next sentence is from myself. I feel your anxiety, good opinion and friendli- ness in the highest degree, and am

Your's most sincerely
John Keats

5. By "Character" Keats means not only the poet's per- sonality but also the degree to which a poet's identity, biases, philosophy, etc. are visible in his work. In Keats's day, Shakespeare was admired, by Coleridge and others, for the invisibility of this "character"; in an influential lecture of 1818 (attended by Keats), Hazlitt called Shake- speare "the least of an egotist that it was possible to be. He was nothing in himself; but . . . all that others were." Milton and Wordsworth were typically summoned for contrast, as poets of egotism.
6. A foolish soldier in Shakespeare's *Troilus and Cressida* is described as "a very man per se" who "stands alone" (1.2.15–16).

7. William Hazlitt's *On Gusto* begins, "Gusto in art is power or passion defining any object." Iago is the schem- ing villain of *Othello;* Imogen is the virtuous heroine of *Cymbeline*.
8. Chameleon, a creature able to change color according to circumstance.
9. Keats had remarked to Woodhouse that he felt pre- empted by the great poets of the past. In Greek mytholo- gy, Saturn is the king of the Titan gods and Ops a harvest goddess; cast out of heaven by the revolt of their chil- dren, the fallen Titans focus the major part of the poem Keats was working on during these months, *Hyperion*.

To Fanny Brawne[1]

["YOU TAKE POSSESSION OF ME"]

25 July 1819 Sunday Night.

My sweet Girl,

I hope you did not blame me much for not obeying your request of a Letter on Saturday: we have had four in our small room playing at cards night and morning leaving me no undisturb'd opportunity to write. * * * Brown to my sorrow confirms the account you give of your ill health. You cannot conceive how I ache to be with you: how I would die for one hour—for what is in the world? I say you cannot conceive; it is impossible you should look with such eyes upon me as I have upon you: it cannot be. Forgive me if I wander a little this evening, for I have been all day employ'd in a very abstr[a]ct Poem[2] and I am in deep love with you—two things which must excuse me. I have, believe me, not been an age in letting you take possession of me; the very first week I knew you I wrote myself your vassal; but burnt the Letter as the very next time I saw you I thought you manifested some dislike to me. If you should ever feel for Man at the first sight what I did for you, I am lost. Yet I should not quarrel with you, but hate myself if such a thing were to happen—only I should burst if the thing were not as fine as a Man as you are as a Woman. Perhaps I am too vehement, then fancy me on my knees, especially when I mention a part of you Letter which hurt me; you say speaking of Mr Severn[3] "but you must be satisfied in knowing that I admired you much more than your friend." My dear love, I cannot believe there ever was or ever could be any thing to admire in me especially as far as sight goes—I cannot be admired, I am not a thing to be admired. You are, I love you; all I can bring you is a swooning admiration of your Beauty. I hold that place among Men which snubnos'd brunettes with meeting eyebrows do among women— they are trash to me—unless I should find one among them with a fire in her heart like the one that burns in mine. You absorb me in spite of myself—you alone: for I look not forward with any pleasure to what is call'd being settled in the world; I tremble at domestic cares—yet for you I would meet them, though if it would leave you the happier I would rather die than do so. I have two luxuries to brood over in my walks, your Loveliness and the hour of my death. O that I could have possession of them both in the same minute.[4] I hate the world: it batters too much the wings of my self-will, and would I could take a sweet poison from your lips to send me out of it. From no others would I take it. I am indeed astonish'd to find myself so careless of all cha[r]ms but yours—remembering as I do the time when even a bit of ribband was a matter of interest with me. What softer words can I find for you after this—

1. When Keats met Fanny Brawne (1800–1865) in the summer 1818, he was charmed and vexed by her almost at once. They fell in love within a few months and became engaged at the end of the year, but kept it secret pending Keats's financial ability to make a formal offer. His first letters to her were written from a working vacation with Brown on the Isle of Wight in the summer of 1819. As a tenant in Brown's apartment in Hampstead, Keats lived next door to the Brawnes from October 1819 to May 1820, and they cared for him in their own quarters later that summer. He saw Fanny Brawne for the last time on 13 September 1820, just before he left for Italy. Her identity became public in 1878 when his surviving letters to her were first published, a sensational event that damaged both their reputations.
2. The remodeling of *Hyperion* into *The Fall of Hyperion*.
3. Joseph Severn (1793–1879), an artist; he went with Keats to Rome, and Keats died in his arms.
4. Compare *Bright Star*, page 1771.

what it is I will not read. Nor will I say more here, but in a Postscript answer any thing else you may have mentioned in your Letter in so many words—for I am distracted with a thousand thoughts. I will imagine you Venus tonight and pray, pray, pray to your star like a Hethen.

Your's ever, fair Star,
John Keats.

To Percy Bysshe Shelley
["An Artist Must Serve Mammon"]

16 August 1820

My dear Shelley,

I am very much gratified that you, in a foreign country, and with a mind almost over occupied, should write to me in the strain of the Letter beside me. If I do not take advantage of your invitation it will be prevented by a circumstance I have very much at heart to prophesy.[5] There is no doubt that an english winter would put an end to me, and do so in a lingering hateful manner, therefore I must either voyage or journey to Italy as a soldier marches up to a battery. My nerves at present are the worst part of me, yet they feel soothed when I think that come what extreme may, I shall not be destined to remain in one spot long enough to take a hatred of any four particular bed-posts. I am glad you take any pleasure in my poor Poem;[6]—which I would willingly take the trouble to unwrite, if possible, did I care so much as I have done about Reputation. I received a copy of the Cenci, as from yourself from Hunt. There is only one part of it I am judge of; the Poetry, and dramatic effect, which by many spirits now a days is considered the mammon.[7] A modern work it is said must have a purpose, which may be the God—an artist must serve Mammon—he must have "self concentration" selfishness perhaps. You I am sure will forgive me for sincerely remarking that you might curb your magnanimity and be more of an artist, and "load every rift" of your subject with ore.[8] The thought of such discipline must fall like cold chains upon you, who perhaps never sat with your wings furl'd for six Months together. And is not this extraordina[r]y talk for the writer of Endymion? whose mind was like a pack of scattered cards—I am pick'd up and sorted to a pip.[9] My Imagination is a Monastry and I am its Monk—you must explain my [metaphysics] to yourself. I am in expectation of Prometheus[1] every day. Could I have my own wish for its interest effected you would have it still in manuscript—or be but now putting an end to the second act.

5. Learning of Keats's grave ill health from Hunt, Shelley offered him hospitality in the warmer climate of Italy; Keats accepted the invitation, first going to Rome, where he died.
6. Sympathetic to the sting of negative reviews, Shelley had written some encouraging remarks about *Endymion*.
7. The false idol of money and worldly goods, against whom Jesus cautions, "Ye cannot serve God and mammon" (Matthew 6.24). In the Preface of *The Cenci*

(1820), a tragedy of incestuous rape, tyranny, and parricide, Shelley proffered a moral judgment of its heroine Beatrice Cenci.
8. From the ceiling of the Palace of Mammon in Spenser's *Faerie Queene* hang stalactites "Embost with massy gold of glorious gift, / And with rich metall loaded every rift, / That heavy ruine they did seeme to threat" (2.7.28).
9. Arranged in order; pips are marks on playing cards.
1. Shelley's epic, *Prometheus Unbound,* just published.

I remember you advising me not to publish my first-blights, on Hampstead heath[2]—I am returning advice upon your hands. Most of the Poems in the volume I send you have been written above two years, and would never have been publish'd but from a hope of gain;[3] so you see I am inclined enough to take your advice now. I must exp[r]ess once more my deep sense of your kindness, adding my sincere thanks and respects for M[rs] Shelley. In the hope of soon seeing you I remain

most sincerely yours,
John Keats—

To Charles Brown

[KEATS'S LAST LETTER][4]

Rome. 30 November 1820.

My dear Brown,

'Tis the most difficult thing in the world to me to write a letter. My stomach continues so bad, that I feel it worse on opening any book,—yet I am much better than I was in Quarantine.[5] Then I am afraid to encounter the proing and conning of any thing interesting to me in England. I have a habitual feeling of my real life having past, and that I am leading a posthumous existence. God knows how it would have been—but it appears to me—however, I will not speak of that subject. I must have been at Bedhampton nearly at the time you were writing to me from Chichester— how unfortunate—and to pass on the river too![6] There was my star predominant! I cannot answer any thing in your letter, which followed me from Naples to Rome, because I am afraid to look it over again. I am so weak (in mind) that I cannot bear the sight of any hand writing of a friend I love so much as I do you. Yet I ride the little horse,[7]—and, at my worst, even in Quarantine, summoned up more puns, in a sort of desperation, in one week than in any year of my life. There is one thought enough to kill me—I have been well, healthy, alert &c, walking with her[8]—and now—the knowledge of contrast, feeling for light and shade, all that information (primitive sense) necessary for a poem are great enemies to the recovery of the stomach. There, you rogue, I put you to the torture,—but you must bring your philosophy to bear—as I do mine, really—or how should I be able to live? Dr Clarke is very attentive to me; he says, there is very little the matter with my lungs, but my stomach, he says, is very bad. I am well disappointed in hearing good news from George,—for it runs in my head we shall all die young.[9] I have not written to x x x x x yet, which he must think

2. Many of the pieces in Keats's 1817 *Poems* took inspiration from the landscape of Hampstead Heath; Keats met Shelley through Hunt, who lived there.
3. The 1820 volume; Keats was eager for financial "gain" as a requisite for marriage to Fanny Brawne.
4. Charles Brown (1787–1842), a man of various literary and amorous pursuits, was a close friend, traveling companion, and housemate. He cared assiduously for Keats after his first major hemorrhage in February 1820, but left for his usual summer vacation in May. When Keats realized that he had to go to Italy for his health, his earnest wish was that

Brown would accompany him, but he could not be located.
5. The ship on which Keats sailed was held for quarantine outside Naples, in oppressive summer weather.
6. The towns are near Portsmouth harbor, from which Keats would sail.
7. Recommended by Keats's doctor in Rome as exercise.
8. Fanny Brawne; Brown deleted her name, as well as those of Keats's friends, when he included the letter in a biography of Keats.
9. Tom died at 19, George lived to his mid-40s, and the youngest, Fanny, lived into her 80s.

very neglectful; being anxious to send him a good account of my health, I have delayed it from week to week. If I recover, I will do all in my power to correct the mistakes made during sickness; and if I should not, all my faults will be forgiven. I shall write to x x x to-morrow, or next day. I will write to x x x x x in the middle of next week. Severn is very well, though he leads so dull a life with me. Remember me to all friends, and tell x x x x I should not have left London without taking leave of him, but from being so low in body and mind. Write to George as soon as you receive this, and tell him how I am, as far as you can guess;—and also a note to my sister—who walks about my imagination like a ghost—she is so like Tom. I can scarcely bid you good bye even in a letter. I always made an awkward bow.

God bless you!
John Keats.

Gustave Doré. *Ludgate Hill,* from *London: A Pilgrimage,* 1872.

The Victorian Age

1832–1901

> Never since the beginning of Time was there, that we hear or read
> of, so intensely self-conscious a Society. Our whole relations to the
> Universe and to our fellow-man have become an Inquiry, a Doubt.
>
> —*Thomas Carlyle, 1831*

Nothing characterizes Victorian society so much as its quest for self-definition. The sixty-three years of Victoria's reign were marked by momentous and intimidating social changes, startling inventions, prodigious energies; the rapid succession of events produced wild prosperity and unthinkable poverty, humane reforms and flagrant exploitation, immense ambitions and devastating doubts. Between 1800 and 1850 the population doubled from nine to eighteen million, and Britain became the richest country on earth, the first urban, industrial society in history. For some, it was a period of great achievement, deep faith, indisputable progress. For others, it was "an age of destruction," religious collapse, vicious profiteering. To almost everyone it was apparent that, as Sir Henry Holland put it in 1858, "we are living in *an age of transition.*"

But what Matthew Arnold called the "multitudinousness" of British culture overwhelmed all efforts to give the era a collective identity or a clear sense of purpose. Dazzled and dazed by their steam-powered printing presses, their railways and telegraphs, journalism and junk mail, Victorians suffered from both future shock and the information explosion. For the first time a nation had become self-consciously modern: people were sure only of their differences from previous generations, certain only that traditional ways of life were fast being transformed into something perilously unstable and astonishingly new. As the novelist William Makepeace Thackeray noted, "We are of the time of chivalry. . . . We are of the age of steam."

VICTORIA AND THE VICTORIANS

In an unpredictable, tumultuous era, the stern, staid figure of Queen Victoria came to represent stability and continuity. The adjective "Victorian" was first used in 1851 to celebrate the nation's mounting pride in its institutions and commercial success. That year, the global predominance of British industry had emerged incontestably at the original "world's fair" in London, the "Great Exhibition of the Works of Industry of All Nations," which Prince Albert helped organize. Arrayed for the world to see in a vast "Crystal Palace" of iron and glass, the marvels of British manufacture achieved a regal stature of their own and cast their allure upon the monarchy in turn. In the congratulatory rhetoric that surrounded the event, the conservative, retiring queen emerged as the durable symbol of her dynamic, aggressively businesslike realm.

Sunlight Soap advertisement commemorating the 1897 Jubilee of Victoria's reign.

In succeeding decades, the official portraits of Queen Victoria, gradually aging, reflected her country's sense of its own maturation as a society and world power. Etched by conflict with her prime ministers, the birth of nine children, and the early death of her beloved Prince Albert, Victoria's once pretty face became deeply lined and heavily jowled. Represented as a fairytale teenaged queen at her coronation in 1837, she radiated a youthful enthusiasm that corresponded to the optimism of the earlier 1830s. It seemed a decade of new beginnings. Settling into the role of fertile matron-monarch, she offered a domestic image to match the booming productivity of the 1850s. Reclusive after Albert died in 1861, she eventually took on the austere role of the black-satined Empress of India, projecting a world-weary glumness that lent gravity to the imperial heyday of the 1870s. Finally, as the aged, venerated Widow of Windsor, she became a universal icon, prompting the nostalgic worldwide spectacles of the Golden and Diamond Jubilees in 1887 and 1897. When Victoria died in 1901, after the longest reign in English history, a newspaper wrote: "Few of us, perhaps, have realized till now how large a part she had in the life of everyone of us; how the thread of her life [bound] the warp of the nation's progress."

During the seven decades of her rule, Victoria's calm profile, stamped on currency and displayed in offices and outposts from London to Bombay, presided over the expansion of Britain into the world's greatest empire. Economically and politically, Britannia ruled not only the waves but more than a quarter of the globe's landmass. Among its domains were Canada, Australia, New Zealand, South Africa, the Indian subcontinent and Ceylon, Malaya, Hong Kong, Singapore, Burma, Jamaica, Trinidad,

British Guiana, Bermuda, the Bahamas, Rhodesia, Kenya, Uganda, and Nigeria. By the 1890s one out of every four people on earth was a "subject" of Queen Victoria.

Victoria stood not only for England and Empire, but also for Duty, Family, and, especially, Propriety. "We have come to regard the Crown as the head of our morality" wrote the historian Walter Bagehot. As a description of behavior, "Victorian" signifies social conduct governed by strict rules, formal manners, and rigidly defined gender roles. Relations between the sexes were hedged about with sexual prudery and an intense concern for maintaining the appearance of propriety in public, whatever the private facts. But although she was presented as the ultimate role model, Victoria herself could not escape the contradictions of her era. The most powerful woman on earth, she denounced "this mad, wicked folly of Women's Rights." Her quiet reserve restored the dignity of the monarchy after the rakish ways of George IV, but she allowed advertisers to trade shamelessly on her image and product endorsements. Her face was universally known, featured on everything from postage stamps to tea trays, yet after Albert's death she lived in seclusion, rarely seeing either her ministers or the public. An icon of motherhood, she detested pregnancy, childbirth, and babies. As an emblem of Britain's greatness, Queen Victoria gave her subjects the public identity and purpose that privately they—and she, in her diaries—recognized as an unfulfilled ideal.

The Victorians have left us a contradictory picture of themselves. On the one hand, they were phenomenally energetic, dedicated to the Gospel of Work and driven by a solemn sense of duty to the Public Good. Popular authors like Dickens and Trollope churned out three-volume novels, engaged in numerous philanthropic projects, devoured twelve-course dinners, took twenty-mile walks, and produced a voluminous correspondence. Explorers and missionaries such as Burton, Speke, Stanley, and Livingston took enormous risks to map uncharted territory or spread Christianity "in darkest Africa." Although an invalid, Florence Nightingale revamped the entire British military medical and supply system from her bedroom office. All this activity was sustained by belief in its implicit moral benefit. In matters of character Victorians prized respectability, earnestness, a sense of duty and public service; most would have regarded an industrious, pious conventionality as the best road not only to material recompense but to heavenly rewards as well.

Yet the fabled self-confidence of this overachieving society often rings hollow. Their literature conveys an uneasy sense that their obsession with work was in part a deliberate distraction, as if Victorians were discharging public responsibilities in order to ease nagging doubts about their religious faith, about changing gender roles, about the moral quandaries of class privilege and imperial rule. Much of the era's social conservatism, such as its resistance to women's rights and to class mobility, may be traced to the fear of change. They struggled to dominate the present moment in order to keep an uncertain future at bay. Few questioned that tremendous advances were taking place in science, public health, transportation, and the general standard of living, but each new idea or discovery seemed to have unexpected, distressing repercussions.

The critic J. A. Froude remarked in 1841 that "the very truths which have come forth have produced doubts . . . . this dazzle has too often ended in darkness." Discoveries in geology, biology, and textual scholarship shattered belief in the literal truth of the Bible. The Industrial Revolution shifted power from the landed aristocracy toward an insecure, expanding middle class of businessmen and professionals, impoverishing millions of once-rural laborers along the way. Strident, riotous campaigns to extend voting rights to males of the middle and working classes produced fears of armed insurrection. Coupled with the agitations for and against trade unions, women's equality, socialism, and the separation of church and state, the fitful transformation of Britain's political and economic structure often teetered on the brink of open class warfare. In the national clamor for reform, every sector of the population fought for its privileges and feared for its rights. The following pages introduce the Victorian period by looking at several key issues: the era's energy and invention, its doubts about religion and industrialism, its far-reaching social reforms, its conflicted fascination with Empire, the commercialization and expansion of the reading public, and the period's vigorous self-scrutiny in the mirror of literature.

THE AGE OF ENERGY AND INVENTION

The most salient characteristic of life in this latter portion of the 19th century is its SPEED.

—W. R. Greg, Life at High Pressure, 1875

The "newness" of Victorian society—its speed, progress, and triumphant ingenuity—was epitomized by the coming of the railway. Until the 1830s, the fastest ways to travel or transport goods were still the most ancient ones, by sail or horse. But on seeing the first train pass through the Rugby countryside in 1839, Thomas Arnold astutely remarked: "Feudality is gone forever." The earliest passenger railway line opened in 1830 between Liverpool and Manchester; by 1855, eight thousand miles of track had been laid. Speeds of fifty miles per hour were soon routine; the journey from London to Edinburgh that had taken two weeks in 1800 now took less than a day.

Carrying passengers, freight, newspapers, and mail, the railways helped create a national consciousness by linking once-remote parts of the country into a single economy and culture. Networks of information, distribution, and services moved news, goods, and people from one end of Britain to the other to the rhythm of the railway timetable. The accelerating pace of life that railways introduced became one of the defining features of the age.

Moreover, the railway irrevocably altered the face of the landscape. Its bridges, tunnels, cuttings, crossings, viaducts, and embankments permanently scarred a rural landscape whose fields, hedgerows, and highways were rooted deep in history. In the cities, engineers and entrepreneurs carved room for vast railyards and stations by demolishing populous districts. Discharging commodities and crowds, the railways transformed town centers everywhere, bolstering local economies and stimulating construction as they arrived, but depriving once-thriving coaching inns and former mail routes of traffic and trade. Underground trains restructured the experience of travel within the city as well: the world's first subway line opened in 1863 in London; a complete inner London system was operating by 1884. Finally, railway-sponsored mass tourism eroded the regional distinctiveness and insularity of individual places. The inventor of the organized excursion, Thomas Cook, saw his advertising slogan, "RAILWAYS FOR THE MILLIONS," turned into a simple statement of fact.

Optimistic social prophets envisioned all classes reaping the fruits of the Industrial Revolution. The widespread Victorian belief in Progress was sustained by many factors, including rising incomes, the greater availability of goods, the perception of surplus production, and the leading role of Britain in world affairs. Many people were

Robert Howlett. *Portrait of Isambard Kingdom Brunel and Launching Chains of the Great Eastern*, 1857. Howlett's interest in contemporary subjects, ranging from steamships and Crimean War heroes to telescopic views of the moon, exemplified the belief that as a new medium itself, photography was supremely suited to capture "progress" in all its manifestations. In his portrait of Brunel, the audacious engineer who designed the Great Western Railway and the world's largest steamship, *The Great Eastern*, Howlett evoked both industrial might and Victorian self-confidence; the man of genius dominates the chains that dwarf him.

awed by the sheer size of industrial achievement: the heaviest ships, the longest tunnels, the biggest warehouses, the most massive factory outputs ever known all contributed to a sublimity of scale that staggered the public's imagination.

Every decade brought impressive innovations that transformed the rhythms of everyday life. The first regular Atlantic steamship crossings began in 1838, flouting the age-old dependence on wind and tide, importing tea from China, cotton from India or Alabama, beef from Australia, and exporting to world markets finished goods ranging from Sheffield cutlery and Manchester textiles to Pear's Soap and the latest Dickens novel.

Equally momentous in its own way was Henry Fox Talbot's discovery between 1839 and 1841 of how to produce and print a photographic negative. The technology of his "sun-pictures" revolutionized the entire visual culture and changed the human relationship to the past. A moment in time could now be "fixed" forever. Thus, more than a century later, we have photographic records of many subsequent innovations: the construction of the London sewer system; the laying of the transatlantic cable in 1865, putting London and New York in almost instantaneous contact via telegraph; the popularity in the 1890s of bicycles, gramophones, electric trams, and the first regular motion picture shows; and in the year of Victoria's death, 1901, Marconi's first transatlantic wireless radio message.

Capturing the public mood, Disraeli wrote in 1862: "It is a privilege to live in this age of rapid and brilliant events. What an error to consider it a utilitarian age. It is one of infinite romance." For the growing middle class there was an Aladdin-like sense of wonderment at the astounding abundance of *things*: an incredible hodge-podge of inventions, gimmicks, and gadgets began to make up the familiar parapher-nalia of modern life, including chain stores, washing and sewing machines, postage stamps, canned foods, toothpaste, sidewalk newsstands, illustrated magazines and newspapers, typewriters, breakfast cereal, slide projectors, skin creams, diet pills, shampoo, ready-to-wear clothes, sneakers (called "plimsolls"), and even a cumber-some prototype computer, designed by Charles Babbage.

Victorian architecture, interior design, and clothing embodied the obsession with plenitude, presenting a bewildering variety of prefabricated, highly ornamented styles. A house might feature Gothic revival, neoclassical, Egyptian, Moorish, baronial, or Arts-and-Crafts motifs, every inch of its interior covered with wallpapers, etchings, draperies, carvings, lacework, and knickknacks. Though fashions varied, men and women were usually as well upholstered as their furniture, tightly buttoned from top to toe in sturdy fabrics, their clothes complexly layered on the outside (men's waistcoats, jackets, cravats, and watches) and inside (women's crinolines, petticoats, bustles, corsets, and drawers).

In a Protestant culture that linked industriousness with godliness, both capitalism and consumerism were fueled by prevailing religious attitudes. For Thomas Carlyle, work itself had a divine sanction: "Produce! Produce!" he wrote in *Sartor Resartus*: "Were it but the pitifullest infinitesimal fraction of a Product, produce it in God's name!" His compatriots obliged: by 1848 Britain's output of cotton cloth and iron was more than half of the world total, and the coal output two-thirds of world production. At the Great Exhibition of 1851, when Britain was dubbed "the workshop of the world," the display struck the Reverend Charles Kingsley as triumphant evidence of God's will: "If these forefathers of ours could rise from their graves this day they would be inclined to see in our hospitals, in our railroads, in the achievements of our physical science . . . proofs of the kingdom of God . . . vaster than any of which they had dreamed."

But for Karl Marx, laboring to write *Das Kapital* (1867) at a desk in the British Museum Reading Room, it was not enough to find God in the material world. He saw that through the hoopla of the marketplace, products had acquired a "mystical char-acter" and "theological niceties" of their own. Yet Marx did not regard commodities as proof of God's existence; instead, he argued that they functioned as deities in their own right. An ignored subversive stationed at the heart of the empire, Marx per-ceived how status-filled objects seemed to take on lives that defined human social relations, even as they degraded the workers that produced them. Looking around at the wonders of British industry, Marx decided that people had become, finally, less important than things. For him, it was the Age of Commodity Fetishism.

THE AGE OF DOUBT

> It was the age of science, new knowledge, searching criticism, fol-
> lowed by multiplied doubts and shaken beliefs.
>
> —*John Morley*

Despite their reverence for material accomplishment and the tenets of organized reli-gion, the Victorians were deeply conflicted in their beliefs and intentions. In retro-spect, the forces that shook the foundations of Victorian society might be summed up in two names, Marx and Darwin: though he was virtually unknown at the time, Marx's radical critique of unbridled free enterprise brought to the most acute level contemporary analyses of economic injustice and the class system. Darwin's staggering evolutionary theories implied that biblical accounts of creation could not be literally true. But well before either had published a word, British thought was in crisis: "The Old has passed away," wrote Carlyle in 1831, "but, alas, the New appears not in its stead." In his 1851 novel *Yeast*, Charles Kingsley described how deluged the Victorians felt by challenges to their faith and social order: "The various stereotyped systems . . . received by tradition [are] breaking up under them like ice in a thaw," he wrote; "a thousand facts and notions, which they know not how to classify, [are] pouring in on them like a flood."

The Crisis of Faith

In the midst of this tumult, the Victorians were troubled by Time. On the one hand, there was not enough of it: the accelerated pace of change kept people too busy to assimilate the torrent of new ideas and technologies. In the 1880s the essayist F. R. Harrison contended that Victorians were experiencing "a life lived so full . . . that we have no time to reflect where we have been and whither we intend to go." On the other hand, there was too much time: well before Darwin, scientists were showing that vast eons of geological and cosmic development had preceded human history, itself suddenly lengthening due to such discoveries as the Neanderthal skeletons found in 1856.

Their sense of worth diminished by both time clocks and time lines, Victorians felt they had little opportunity for reflection and often took scant comfort in it. Matthew Arnold complained of "this strange disease of modern life with its sick hurry, its divided aims." Yet this climate of anxious uncertainty provoked intense religious fervor, and debates about church doctrine and the proper forms of Christian worship occupied the national consciousness throughout the century. "This is the age of experiment," wrote the historian E. P. Hood in 1850, regarding the constant testing of belief, "but the cheerful fact is, that almost all men are yearning after a faith."

The most influential group were the "Evangelicals," a term which covers not only "dissenting" or "nonconformist" Protestant sects outside the Church of England (such as Methodists, Presbyterians, Congregationalists, and Baptists), but also the Evangelical party or "Low Church" faction within the Church of England. Anti-Catholic, Bible-oriented, concerned with humanitarian issues, and focused on the salvation of individual souls within a rigid framework of Christian conduct, Evangelicalism dominated the religious and often the social life of working- and middle-class Britons. Evangelicals practiced self-denial and frugality; they rejected most forms of entertainment as sinful or frivolous, and regarded any but the simplest church service as a "popish" throwback to Catholicism, which they abhorred on nationalistic as well as religious grounds. It was Evangelicalism that was largely responsible for the freeing of slaves in the British colonies in 1833, for the strictness of Victorian morality at home, and for British missionary zeal abroad.

At the other end of the spectrum were the Anglo-Catholics of the Tractarian or Oxford Movement, which flourished in the 1830s and 1840s. Through an appeal to early church history, they sought to revitalize the power and spiritual intensity of the Church of England, insisting on the authority of the Church hierarchy, and reaffirming the Church's traditional position as a grace-granting intermediary between

Christians and their God. The movement collapsed when its leader, John Henry Newman, converted to Roman Catholicism in 1845. But the antirational, romantic spirit of this small group left a substantial legacy in the renewed ritualism of "High Church" practices. Gothic revival architecture, the burning of altar candles and incense, the resplendent vestments of the clergy—all these were aspects of a religious apprehension of sensuous beauty and mysticism that had not been seen in England since before the Reformation. This "High Church" aestheticism came into direct and ongoing conflict with "Low Church" sobriety.

The crisis of religious doubt occasioned by biblical scholarship and scientific discoveries hit Christian belief hard. But it prompted an array of coping strategies and new ideas about the position of human beings in the universe that remain significant to this day. Most Victorian authors and intellectuals found a way to reassert religious ideas. Thus George Eliot, for instance, maintained that an Evangelical sense of duty and ethics was essential as a social "glue" to prevent the disintegration of society in the absence of religious authority. That it was still an era which *wanted* to believe is evident from the huge success of Tennyson's *In Memoriam* (1850), in which the poet's hard-won religious faith finally triumphs over science-induced despair. Extending evolutionary theory to spiritual advantage, Tennyson hoped man might transcend animality by encouraging his divine soul to "Move upward, working out the beast, / And let the ape and tiger die." Even Darwin's defender Thomas Huxley, who coined the word "agnostic," also celebrated Auguste Comte's positivism and "the Religion of Humanity." Huxley spoke for many who had renounced organized religion but not spiritual impulses when he said that Carlyle's *Sartor Resartus* "led me to know that a deep sense of religion was compatible with the entire absence of theology." Finally, some artists and writers used Christian icons as an avant-garde protest against the secular direction of modern life. "The more materialistic science becomes," said the artist Edward Burne-Jones, "the more angels shall I paint."

The Industrial Catastrophe

In principle, the Victorian crisis of faith should at least have pleased the Utilitarians. The creed of these atheistic, rationalist followers of Jeremy Bentham was strictly practical: measure all human endeavor by its ability to produce "the greatest happiness for the greatest number." Sharing a committed, "can do" philosophy of social reform, Utilitarianism and Evangelicalism were the two dominant ideologies shaping early and mid-Victorian life. But despite the significant changes they effected in government and education during the 1820s and 1830s, even the Utilitarians ran out of self-assurance and moral steam in the morass of mid-Victorian cultural ferment.

A few energetic idealists dreamed of leveling age-old inequalities. "Glory to Man in the highest!" wrote Swinburne in 1869, "for Man is the master of things." But here too a form of evolutionary theory was undercutting the conventional pieties of social discourse. "Love thy neighbor" had no more moral authority for the "Social Darwinist" than it had historical accuracy for the textual scholar. Summed up in the phrase "survival of the fittest"—coined by the philosopher Herbert Spencer in 1852, seven years before *The Origin of Species* appeared—Social Darwinism viewed as dangerous any attempt to regulate the supposedly immutable laws of society. Evolutionary forces decreed that only the fittest should survive in capitalist competition as well as in nature. Applied to nations and races as well as individuals, this theory supported the apparent destiny of England to prosper and rule the world.

Social Darwinism was a brutal offshoot of the influential economic theory of laissez-faire capitalism. Drawing on Adam Smith's *The Wealth of Nations* (1776), businessmen argued that the unfettered pursuit of self-interest, in the form of unrestricted competition in a free market, would be best for society. This was an idea that Utilitarians and many Evangelicals rejected in favor of legislative regulation, since their view of the imperfections of humanity indicated that one person's self-interest was likely to mean another's exploitation. The desperate need to protect the poor and disadvantaged, and the difficulty of doing so, was cause for much soul-searching, particularly among those who had made a religion of social reform.

Concern about the fairness and efficacy of the social structure was exacerbated by the unprecedented rate of urbanization. "Our age is preeminently the age of great cities" declared historian Robert Vaughan in 1843. At the beginning of the nineteenth century only one-fifth of the British population lived in cities; by the end of the century, more than three-quarters did. Such vast numbers of people crowding into the cities created hideous problems of housing, sanitation, and disease. For the poor, living and working conditions were appalling, particularly in the 1830s and 1840s when neither housing nor factories were regulated. Industrial workers labored six days a week, for as many as fourteen or sixteen hours a day, in stifling, deafening, dangerous workshops, then went home to unheated rooms they often shared with other families, six or seven people to a bed of rags. Drinking water often came from rivers filled with industrial pollution and human waste. Without job security, health-care, or pensions, the injured, the sick, and the aged fell by the wayside. In manufacturing cities the competition for survival was indeed intense: the life expectancy among working people in Manchester in 1841 was about twenty years.

Joseph Paxton. The Crystal Palace, site of the Great Exhibition of 1851, after its re-erection at Sydenham, c. 1855.

Foreign visitors in particular were struck with wonder and horror at the conjunction of so much misery and so much wealth. "From this filthy sewer pure gold flows," marveled the French historian Alexis de Tocqueville: "From this foul drain the greatest stream of human industry flows out to fertilize the whole world." Friedrich Engels spent a year in Manchester, producing the most detailed and shocking firsthand account of Victorian industrial life, *The Condition of the Working Class in England in 1844*. Karl Marx, who lived in England for thirty-four years, worked his observations into his famous theory of "surplus labor value." Under the current system, he said, wretched factory hands would never receive adequate payment for the wealth they created by transforming raw materials into precious commodities. Like many people at the time, both liberal and conservative, Marx expected that violent class warfare was imminent.

On average real wages went up and prices went down in Victoria's reign, with per capita income doubling between 1800 and 1860. But the boom-and-bust cycles of free trade made for unsteady wages, seesaw prices, sudden layoffs, and volatile labor relations, as Britain made a lurching transition to an industrial and commercial economy. There were serious depressions or slowdowns almost every decade, but the worst took place during "the Hungry Forties." Scarce food, widespread unemployment, and general despair provoked riots and fears of revolution. The statesman Charles Greville noted in his diary in 1842, "There is an immense and continually increasing population, no adequate demand for labor . . . no confidence, but a universal alarm, disquietude, and discontent." An American observer of the industrial scene named Henry Coleman remarked, "Every day that I live I thank Heaven that I am not a poor man with a family in England." When the economy recovered, many fled. Between the years 1850 and 1880, three million emigrants left Britain, two-thirds for the United States.

THE AGE OF REFORM

> The whole meaning of Victorian England is lost if it is thought of as a country of stuffy complacency and black top-hatted moral priggery. Its frowsty crinolines and dingy hansom cabs, its gas-lit houses and over-ornate draperies, concealed a people engaged in a tremendously exciting adventure—the daring experiment of fitting industrial man into a democratic society.
>
> —*Historian David Thompson, 1950*

Despite crushing problems and the threat of social breakdown, the Victorian period can justly be called an age of reform. Each of the issues that threatened to bring the country into open conflict or destroy the social fabric was in the course of the century addressed peacefully through legislation: voting rights were extended, working conditions improved, and women's rights began to gain ground, without the bloody revolutions or insurrections that struck France in 1838, 1848, and 1870, and Germany in 1848. As fears of revolution receded, the subtler worries of Mill and Arnold, based on their observation of American democracy, seemed more to the point. How could liberty of thought be preserved in a mass culture dedicated to majority rule? How could the best ideas elevate, rather than succumb to, the lowest common denominator?

Politics and Class

The key to the century's relatively peaceful progress was the passage of legislation for political and social reform. The start of the Victorian era is often dated 1832, five years before Victoria's coronation, because in that year the First Reform Bill was enacted. It gave representation to the new industrial towns, such as Manchester, Birmingham, and Leeds, all cities of over 100,000 inhabitants that had lacked a single seat in Parliament. It also enlarged the electorate by about 50 percent, granting the vote to some propertied portions of the middle class. Still, only one in six adult males could vote, and the aristocracy retained parliamentary control. Agitation for reform continued, especially in the Chartist movement of 1838–1848. Taking its name from the People's Charter of 1838, it was a loose alliance of artisans and factory workers that called for sweeping reforms, including universal male suffrage, the secret ballot, equal electoral districts, and annual elections. Chartism was the world's first independent working-class movement, its membership swelling into the millions during the depressions of the 1840s. The Chartists presented giant petitions, signed by one to five million people, to Parliament in 1839, 1842, and 1848. But each time they were rejected, and the movement collapsed after a government show of force effectively defused the demonstrations accompanying the petition of 1848.

The lot of workers was to improve piecemeal, not through the grand political reorganization envisioned by Chartism, as Parliament grudgingly passed acts regulating food, factories, and the right to unionize. An important breakthrough came with the repeal of the Corn Laws in 1846. The laws levied tariffs on the importation of foreign grain; they were sponsored by the landed aristocracy to protect the high price of their home-grown grains (called "corn" in Britain). Therefore, as the poet Thomas Hood wrote in 1842, "bread was dear and flesh and blood were cheap." The new urban business interests fought the protectionist tariffs in the name of "Free Trade." They preferred a stable, better-fed workforce to one that rioted or starved in times of scarcity, but they also wanted cheap bread to keep their workers' wages down. Later, the Public Health acts of 1848 and 1869 improved the availability of tea, sugar, and beer. In the 1870s the importation of wheat from the United States and refrigerated beef and fruit from Australia and New Zealand meant that the new custom of having large bacon-and-egg breakfasts could be observed even by the working classes.

Beginning in 1833, a crucial series of Factory Acts slowly curtailed the horrors of industrial labor. The 1833 Act provided for safety inspections of machinery, prohibited the employment of children under nine, and limited the work week to forty-eight hours for children under twelve. Though the law was poorly enforced, a trend had begun. The Ten Hours Act of 1847 limited the time women and children could work daily in textile factories, and ensuing acts gradually regulated safety and working conditions in other industries. Workers' political power increased when the Second Reform Bill (1867) doubled the electorate, including all male urban householders. During this period employers also felt increasing pressure from extra-legal trade union movements, including miners, textile workers, and women garment workers. An uncomprehending middle class (including Dickens and Gaskell) often regarded unionists as anarchists and murderers. But trade unions were finally legalized in 1871, and the first working-class Members of Parliament were unionist miners elected in 1874. By the 1890s there were 1.5 million trade union members, many of them part of the growing Socialist movement, and the foundations of the modern Labour Party had been laid.

Thus the high hopes of Chartism had in a sense succeeded, many of its supposedly dangerous demands eventually met. As Engels noted, these changes also benefited the middle class who resisted them, as people realized the value—social as well as economic—of reduced hostilities and improved cooperation between classes. Everyone also gained from related reforms that reflected weakening class barriers and increasing social mobility. In 1870 the Education Act initiated nationally funded public education in England and Wales. In the 1880s, middle-class investigators and social workers spearheaded the "discovery of poverty" in London's East End, one of a range of efforts that brought better housing, nutrition, and education to the poor. Finally, the nation as a whole benefited from what historian Asa Briggs has called "the one great political invention in Victorian England"—a civil service staffed through open examinations rather than patronage.

By the last decades of the century, Britain had become a more democratic and pluralistic society; it enjoyed greater freedom in matters of religion, political views, and intellectual life than any other country. Overall, the middle class were the chief generators and beneficiaries of social change. Outsiders before 1832, they became key players in the Victorian period. Though they never dominated politics, which remained largely an aristocratic preserve, they set the tone and agenda for the era's socioeconomic evolution.

"The Woman Question"

Still, one group found almost all doors closed against it. Throughout much of Victoria's reign, women had few opportunities for higher education or satisfying employment: from scullery maids to governesses, female workers of all ranks were severely exploited, and prior to the 1870s married women had no legal rights. What contemporaries called "the Woman Question" was hotly debated in every decade, but only at the end of the century were the first women allowed to vote in local elections. Full female suffrage came only after World War I. Despite articulate champions such as Harriet Martineau and John Stuart Mill, and the examples of successful women such as George Eliot, the Brontës, Florence Nightingale, and the Queen herself, proponents of women's rights made slow headway against prevailing norms. Victorians were quick to note that theirs was the first era in which women writers achieved literary prominence, producing works widely recognized to be equal in stature to those by men. But many regarded this "brain-work" as a serious aberration that unfitted women for motherhood. The medical establishment backed the conventional view that women were physically and intellectually inferior, a "weaker sex" that would buckle under the weight of strong passion, serious thought, or vigorous exercise. Only in their much-vaunted "femininity" did women have an edge, as nurturers of children and men's better instincts.

The ideal Victorian woman was supposed to be domestic and pure, selflessly motivated by the desire to serve others rather than fulfill her own needs. In particular, her duty was to soothe the savage beast her husband might become as he fought in the jungle of free trade. Her role prescribed by Coventry Patmore's wildly popular poem, *The Angel in the House* (1854–1862), the model woman would provide her family with an uplifting refuge from the moral squalor of the working world. Only small portion of the nation's women could afford to remain at home, but the constant celebration of home and hearth by politicians, the press, and respected authors made conspicuous domesticity the expected role for well-born and well-married women. Many upper- and middle-class women spent their days paying social calls or acquiring "female accomplishments" such as needlework, sketching, or flower-arranging. Though this leisure played an important part in generating new literary markets targeted at women, it provoked devastating satires of time-wasting females by Elizabeth Barrett Browning, Charles Dickens, and Florence Nightingale, among others. By the 1860s, with the birth of the department store and modern advertising, leisured women were also for the first time wooed as consumers and portrayed as smart shoppers.

Though their contribution was minimized, women were in fact heavily involved in the labor force, making up one-third of all workers, and 90 percent of the nation's largest labor category, household servants. For so-called "redundant" women who could not find husbands or work, the situation was especially grim. Low wages and unemployment drove tens of thousands of girls and women into prostitution, which, due to the growth of the military and repressive Victorian sexual mores, became one more "boom industry" whose workers reaped few rewards.

If a woman's life was economically precarious outside marriage, her existence was legally terminated within that bond. A woman lost the few civil rights she had as she became "one body" with her husband. Married women had, at the start of the era, no legal right to custody of their own children or to own property. The Divorce and Matrimonial Causes Act of 1857 established a civil divorce court in London, and subsequent acts created protection against assault, desertion, and cruelty, but only a wealthy few could afford legal proceedings. The Married Women's Property Acts of 1870 and 1882, however, gave women the right to possess wages they earned after marriage, as well as any property they owned before it.

Gradually, with the aid of male allies, women created educational opportunities for themselves. The first women's college opened in London in 1848, and the first women's colleges opened at Cambridge in 1869 and at Oxford in 1879—though women were not allowed to take Oxbridge degrees. Elizabeth Blackwell, the first woman M.D., became an accredited physician both in Britain and the United States in 1859; by 1895 there were 264 women doctors. In the 1890s, the much-parodied image of the liberated "New Woman" began circulating in the press. By then many young women were braving a conservative backlash to take new positions in office work, the civil service, nursing, and teaching. They also enjoyed the social freedom that accompanied their expanding role in the economy. The novelist Walter Besant wrote admiringly in 1897 of the "personal independence that is the keynote of the situation. . . . The girls go off by themselves on their bicycles; they go about as they please. . . . For the first time in man's history it is regarded as a right and proper thing to trust a girl as a boy insists on being trusted."

The uphill battle that feminists faced is conveyed in the cautious motto of a national-market periodical for women. Published from 1890 to 1912, *Woman* magazine declared its mission: "Forward, but not too fast." Antisuffragists of both sexes found willing allies among those who regarded women as weak and unworldly, better equipped for housekeeping than speechmaking. As the nineteenth century waned, many women and most men would still have endorsed Dickens's parodic view of the public woman, Mrs Jellyby in *Bleak House:* she is so focused on missionary work in Africa that she cannot see the lamentable state of her family in the very next room.

THE AGE OF EMPIRE

I contend that we are the first race in the world, and the more of
the world we inhabit, the better it is for the human race.

—*Cecil Rhodes*

With the prime meridian conveniently located at Greenwich, just southeast of London, Victorians could measure all the world in relation to a British focal point, culturally as well as geographically. Abroad, as at home, it was an Englishman's duty to rule
whatever childlike or womanly peoples he came across, for their own good. For Queen
Victoria, the mission of empire was obvious: "to protect the poor natives and advance
civilization." The conviction of innate superiority was reinforced by the implacable
desire of British business to dominate world markets. The vast size of Britain's naval
and commercial fleets and its head start in industrial production helped the cause,
and Britain's military and commercial might was unsurpassed. Victorian advertising
reveals the global realities and hopes of the emerging merchant empires. Tetley's tea
ads depicted their plantations in Ceylon, as well as the ships, trains, and turbanned
laborers that secured "the largest sale in the world." Pear's Soap advertising campaigns
kept up with British expeditionary forces worldwide, finding potential customers in
temporary adversaries such as the "Fuzzy-Wuzzies" of the Sudanese wars, or the Boers
of South Africa. One advertiser even challenged convention by speaking of "Brightest Africa"—because of the continent's vast market potential.

Yet the empire was hard to assemble and expensive—monetarily and morally—
to maintain. Slavery was abolished in British dominions in 1833, but many fortunes
still depended on the cheap production of sugar at West Indian plantations, as well as
slave-produced cotton from the United States. Thus British implication in the slave
trade remained a volatile issue. All Britain took sides in the Governor Eyre scandal of
1865, when the acting governor of Jamaica imposed severe martial law to put down a
rebellion by plantation workers. Carlyle, Dickens, and Ruskin supported the executions and floggings, while John Stuart Mill sought to have Eyre tried for murder.

Closer to home, the perennial "Irish Question" resurfaced urgently during the
potato famine of 1845–1847. Through the British government's callousness and
ineptitude, a million and a half Irish died of starvation and disease and an equal number emigrated. In the wake of this disaster, the Irish engaged in rebellions, uprisings,
and massive political efforts to gain parliamentary "Home Rule" for Ireland. But concern about the unity of the Empire, the safety of Protestants in the north of Ireland,
and the supposed inability of the Irish to govern themselves led Parliament to defeat
all efforts at Irish autonomy during Victoria's reign.

The Asian empire captured the popular imagination for the first time through
the so-called "Indian Mutiny" of 1857–1859, a broad-based rebellion against the East
India Company, the commercial entity that ruled most of India. The gory details of
Indian atrocities, followed by equally bloody and more extensive British reprisals,
filled the press and inflamed the public. The crown now took possession, and henceforth British policy was much more guarded, attempting to respect local institutions
and practices. Later, as Rudyard Kipling recorded in his novel *Kim* (1901), India
became an important setting for the "Great Game" of espionage to prevent foreign
destabilization of British interests worldwide.

THE FORMULA OF BRITISH CONQUEST

PEARS' SOAP IS THE BEST

REG⁰ COPYRIGHT

PEARS' SOAP IN THE SOUDAN.
"Even if our invasion of the Soudan has done nothing else it has at any rate left the Arab something to puzzle his fuzzy head over, for the legend
PEARS' SOAP IS THE BEST,
inscribed in huge white characters on the rock which marks the farthest point of our advance towards Berber,
will tax all the wits of the Dervishes of the Desert to translate."—Phil Robinson, *War Correspondent (in the Soudan) of the Daily Telegraph in London,* 1884.

"The Formula of British Conquest." Pears' Soap advertisement from *Illustrated London News,* 27 August 1887. *Source:* Harvard College Library.

In the second half of the century, frequent and often bungled conflicts riveted public attention. The Crimean War of 1854–1856, in which Britain fought on the side of Turkey to prevent Russian expansion in the Middle East, cost 21,000 British lives but made little change in the European balance of power. "Some one had blunder'd," as Tennyson wrote in *The Charge of the Light Brigade.* The newspapers' exposure of the gross mismanagement of the war effort, however, led to improved supply systems, medical care, and weapons, and the rebuilding of the armed forces, all of which served Britain in ensuing colonial wars. A veteran of the Crimea, General George Gordon, rose to fame in 1860, capturing Peking and protecting far-flung Britons in the Second Opium War. But in 1884 he and several thousand others were massacred at Khartoum in the Sudan after a year's siege by religiously inspired rebels. Governmental dithering caused the British relief force to arrive two days too late. On another front, the Boer War of 1899–1902 stimulated war mania at home but tarnished Britain's image throughout the world. In pursuit of freer access to South African gold and diamond mines, the world's greatest military power bogged down in a guerilla war that ended only when British forces herded Afrikaner civilians into concentration camps, where 20,000 died.

Many viewed these conflicts as part of "the White Man's burden," as Kipling phrased it: the duty to spread British order and culture throughout the world. Yet imperialism had many opponents. In 1877 the Liberal leader William Gladstone argued that the Empire was a drain on the economy and population, serving only "to compromise British character in the judgment of the impartial world." Even Queen Victoria complained of the "overbearing and offensive behavior" of the Indian Civil Service for "trying to trample on the people and continually reminding them and making them feel that they are a conquered people." Like the growth of Victorian cities, the unplanned agglomeration of British colonies involved such a haphazard mixture of economic expansion, high-minded sentiment, crass exploitation, political expediency, and blatant racism that it apparently had no clear rationale. "We seem," said Cambridge historian J. R. Seeley in 1883, "to have conquered and peopled half the world in a fit of absence of mind."

Victorians did not only go to the ends of the earth; they saw the world's abundance come home to them. Britain and especially London became a magnet for all manner of people and things, a world within a world. There were many distinguished foreign sojourners at the center of empire. Among the artists, exiles, and expatriots who visited or stayed were the deposed French emperor Louis Napoleon, the painters Vincent Van Gogh and James McNeill Whistler, and the writers Arthur Rimbaud, Paul Verlaine, and Stephen Crane. Many of the era's great images and cultural moments came from outsiders: London was memorably painted by Claude Monet, anatomized by Henry James, serenaded by Frédéric Chopin and Franz Liszt, and entertained by Buffalo Bill. It received possibly its most searching critique from Karl Marx and Friedrich Engels, who drafted the *Communist Manifesto* there in 1847. Not only the country's prosperity and cultural prestige attracted people, but also its tolerance and democracy. Despite the wage slavery and imperialist ideology that he saw only too clearly, Engels was forced to admit: "England is unquestionably the freest—that is, the least unfree—country in the world, North America not excepted."

THE AGE OF READING

Even idleness is eager now,—eager for amusement; prone to excursion-trains, art-museums, periodical literature, and exciting novels.

—*George Eliot*

Publishing became a major industry in the Victorian period. Magazines, newspapers, novels, poetry, histories, travel narratives, sporting news, scandal sheets, and penny cyclopedias kept people entertained and informed as never before. A thriving commercial literary culture was built on rising literacy rates, with as many as 97 percent of both sexes able to read by 1900. The expansion of the reading public went hand-in-hand with new print technologies, including steam-powered presses, the introduction of cheaper wood-pulp (instead of rag-based) paper, and, eventually, mechanized typesetting. Illustrations were widely used, notably in serialized fiction, where they helped unpracticed readers to follow the story. After 1875 wood engravings gave way to photogravure, and in the 1880s halftone printing enabled photographs to replace hand-drawn works as the primary means of visual communication. Colored illustrations were hand-tinted at first, often by poor women and children working at home; later chromolithography made colored reproductions of artwork possible. British publishing gradually transformed itself into a modern industry with worldwide distribution and influence. Copies of *The Times* circulated in uncharted Africa; illustrations torn from magazines adorned bushmen's huts in the Great Karoo.

Readers' tastes varied according to class, income, and education. The well-educated but unintellectual upper class formed only a small portion of the Victorian reading public. As the historian Walter Bagehot noted at the time, "A great part of the 'best' English people keep their minds in a state of decorous dullness." At the other end of the social scale, working-class literacy rates were far below the general standard but increased as working hours diminished, housing improved, and public libraries spread. The appetite for cheap literature steadily grew, feeding on a diet of religious tracts, self-help manuals, reprints of classics, penny newspapers, and the expanding range of sensational entertainment: "penny dreadfuls and shilling shockers," serials, bawdy ballads, and police reports of lurid crimes.

It was the burgeoning middle class, however, that formed the largest audience for new prose and poetry, and produced the authors to meet an increasing demand for books that would edify, instruct, and entertain. This was the golden age of the English novel, but poetry and serious nonfiction also did a brisk trade, as did "improving" works on religion, science, philosophy, and economics. But new books, especially fiction, were still a luxury in the earlier Victorian period. Publishers inflated prices so that readers would rent novels and narrative poems—just as people rent videos today—from commercial circulating libraries, which provided a larger and steadier income than individual sales. The collaboration between publishers and libraries required authors to produce "three deckers," long novels packaged in three separate volumes that thereby tripled rental fees and allowed three readers to peruse a single novel at one time. An economical alternative was to buy the successive "numbers" of a book as they appeared in individual, illustrated monthly installments. This form of publication became common with the tremendous success of Dickens's first novel *Pickwick Papers,* which came out in parts in 1836 and 1837. By the 1860s most novels were serialized in weekly or monthly magazines, giving the reader a wealth of additional material for about the same price.

The serialization of novels had a significant impact on literary form. Most of the major novelists, including Dickens, Thackeray, Collins, Gaskell, Trollope, and Eliot, had to organize their work into enticing, coherent morsels that kept characters and story lines clear from month to month, and left readers eager to buy the next installment. Authors felt pressure to keep ahead of deadlines, often not knowing which turn a story might take. But they also enjoyed the opportunity to stay in the public eye, to weave in references to current events, or to make adjustments based on sales and reviews. For their part, readers experienced literature as an ongoing part of their lives. They had time to absorb and interpret their reading, and even to influence the outcome of literary events: throughout his career, Dickens was badgered by readers who wanted to see more of one character, less of another, or prevent the demise of a third.

The close relationship authors shared with their public had its drawbacks: writers had to censor their content to meet the prim standards of "circulating library morality." In keeping with the Evangelical temper of the times, middle-class Victorian recreation centered on the home, where one of the most sacred institutions was

A NOVEL FACT.

Old-fashioned Party (with old-fashioned prejudices). "Ah! very Clever, I dare say. But I see it's Written by a Lady, an'
I want a Book that my Daughters may read. Give me Something else!"

Cartoon from *Punch* magazine, 1867.

the family reading circle. Usually wives or daughters read aloud to the rest of the
household. Any hint of impropriety, anything that might bring "a blush to the cheek
of the Young Person"—as Dickens warily satirized the trend—was aggressively ferreted out by publishers and libraries. Even revered poets such as Tennyson and Barrett
Browning found themselves edited by squeamish publishers.

A better testimony to the intelligence and perceptiveness of the Victorian reading
public is the fact that so many of today's classics were bestsellers then, including the novels of the Brontës, Dickens, and George Eliot; the poetry of Tennyson, Elizabeth and
Robert Browning, and Christina Rossetti; and the essays of Carlyle, Ruskin, and Arnold.
These works were addressed to readers who had an impressive level of literary and general culture, kept up to snuff by the same magazines and reviews in which the best fiction,
poetry, and prose appeared. Educated Victorians had an insatiable appetite for "serious"
literature on religious issues, socioeconomic theory, scientific developments, and general information of all sorts. It was an era of outstanding, influential periodicals that combined entertaining writing with intellectual substance: politically oriented quarterlies
such as the Whig *Edinburgh Review* and the Benthamite *Westminster Review;* more varied
monthlies such as *Fraser's Magazine,* where Carlyle's *Sartor Resartus* first appeared, and
Cornhill, which published works by Ruskin, Thackeray, Eliot, Trollope, and Hardy; the
satirical weekly *Punch,* still published today; and Dickens's low-priced weeklies *Household Words* and *All the Year Round* for a more general readership. As a rule, the public had
faith in the press, regarding it as a forum essential to the progress and management of
democracy. At the same time, as political and cultural power broadened, the press took
seriously its new role as creator, shaper, and transmitter of public opinion.

Celebrated authors were hailed as heroes, regarded as public property, and respected as sages; they inspired a passionate adulation. Robert Browning first approached Elizabeth Barrett by writing her a fan letter. The public sought instruction and guidance from authors, who were alternately flattered and dismayed by the responsibilities thrust upon them. The critic Walter Houghton points out that "every writer had his congregation of devoted or would-be devoted disciples who read his work in much the spirit they had once read the Bible." Robert Browning lived to see an international proliferation of Browning Societies, dedicated to expounding his supposed moral teachings. Hero worship was yet another Victorian invention.

THE AGE OF SELF-SCRUTINY

The energy of Victorian literature is its most striking trait, and self-exploration is its favorite theme. Victorians produced a staggeringly large body of literature, renowned for its variety and plenitude. Their writing is distinguished by its particularity, eccentricity, long-windedness, earnestness, ornateness, fantasy, humor, experimentation, and self-consciousness. As befits a scientific age, most authors exhibited a willingness to experiment with new forms of representation, coupled with a penchant for realism, a love of closely observed detail: Tennyson was famous for his myopic descriptions of flowers; Browning transcribed tics of speech like a clinical psychologist; Eliot compared her scenes to Dutch genre paintings; and Dickens indignantly defended the accuracy of his characterization and the plausibility of his plots. Sustained labor was as important as keen observation: "lyric" poems ran to hundreds of lines, novels spanned a thousand pages, essayists constructed lengthy paragraphs with three or four generous sentences. One single book, alternately discredited and revered, underpinned the whole literary enterprise. The King James Version of the Bible shaped the cadences, supplied the imagery, and proposed the structures through which Victorians apprehended the universe; knowledge of it immensely deepens one's appreciation of the time.

Like the photographic close-ups invented by Julia Margaret Cameron, much Victorian literature tries to get at what Matthew Arnold called "the buried life" of individuals struggling for identity in a commercial, technocratic society. In the 1830s Carlyle was already alluding to "these autobiographical times of ours." Autobiography rapidly assumed new importance as a literary form, driven by the apparent necessity of each person working out a personal approach to the universe and a position within the culture. As Matthew Arnold announced in 1853, "the dialogue of the mind with itself has commenced."

Often written under intense emotional pressure, nonfiction prose on social or aesthetic issues turned into an art form as personal as lyric poetry, expressing the writers' interior lives as well as their ideas. Yet the very variety of disguised or semiautobiographical forms (such as the dramatic monologue) suggests that introspection produced its own moral perplexities. In a culture that stressed action, production, civic duty, and family responsibility, such apparently self-indulgent self-scrutiny might well seem unworthy: "I sometimes hold it half a sin / To put in words the grief I feel" said Tennyson about the loss of his best friend. Thus the guilty confessional impulse was forced underground to reemerge almost everywhere: in first-person narratives, devotional poems, travelogues, novels of religious or emotional crisis, intimate essays, dramatic lyrics, fictionalized memoirs, and recollections of famous people and places.

The Major Genres

Victorian literature is remarkable in that there were three great literary genres: non-fiction prose emerged as the artistic equal of poetry and fiction. Topical and influential in their day, the criticism and essays of such writers as Carlyle, Mill, Newman, Ruskin, Darwin, Arnold, Nightingale, Pater, and Wilde achieved classic status by virtue of their distinctive styles and force of intellect. In richly varied rhythms they record the process of original minds seeking to understand the relation of individuals to nature and culture in the new industrial world. Though their works might be categorized as religion, politics, aesthetics, or science, all these authors wrote revealingly of their intellectual development, and all explored the literary resources of the language, from simile and metaphor to fable and fantasy. Oscar Wilde argued for the supreme creativity of the autobiographical critic-as-artist: "That is what the highest criticism really is, the record of one's own soul." His teacher Walter Pater remarked simply that prose is "the special and opportune art of the modern world."

Poets struggled to refute this sentiment. Poetry commanded more respect than prose as a literary genre, but despite the immense success of Tennyson, it gradually lost ground in popularity. Whether this occurred because of, or in spite of, poetry's deliberate cultivation of a mass audience is difficult to say. But whereas Romantic poets were greeted as visionaries, praised for opening dazzling new vistas onto the self and nature, Victorian poets were encouraged to keep their ideas down to earth, to offer practical advice about managing the vicissitudes of heart and soul in a workaday world. The Romantic emphasis on self-expression gave way to more qualified soul-searching with an eye toward moral content that the public could grasp and apply. Carlyle's famous admonition in *Sartor Resartus* set the tone for the period: "Close thy *Byron*; open thy *Goethe*." In other words, forget the self-indulgent quest for happiness or self-knowledge associated with Byronic heroes; strive instead to improve society and practice greater artistic control; know your work and do it.

Whether they felt guilty, inspired, infuriated, or amused over their audience's thirst for instruction, Victorian poets took advantage of it to expand the resources of poetry in English. Though there are obvious lines of influence from the Romantics—Keats to Tennyson, Shelley to Browning, Wordsworth to Arnold—the innovations are perhaps even more striking. Eclectic poets introduced their readers to a bewildering variety of rhythms, stanzas, topics, words, and ideas that had not been seen in poetry before. Contemporary social concerns vied with—and sometimes merged into—Greek mythology and Arthurian legend as subject matter. Swinburne and Hopkins engaged in verbal pyrotechnics that produced new meters amid an ecstasy of sound; Elizabeth Barrett Browning unleashed stormy feminist lyrics marked by a dazzling intellect; Arnold captured readers with his startling emotional honesty; Christina Rossetti whittled her lines down to a thought-teasing purity; Arthur Symons and William Ernest Henley adapted French *vers libre* to create modern "free verse."

Perhaps the most important development was the rise of the dramatic monologue. Almost every poet found occasion to speak through characters apparently quite foreign in time, place, or social situation. Tennyson's liquid vowel sounds and Browning's clotted consonant clusters are trademarks of very different styles, but both poets use their distinctive music to probe the psychology of the speakers in their dramatic poems. Adapting the sound of their lines to fit the rhythms of their speakers' thoughts, poets acquired a more conversational tone and expanded the psychological range of their craft. While Browning was preoccupied with extreme psychological states, many poets shared his desire to represent a person or event from multiple perspectives, through shifting voices and unreliable narrators. These relativistic approaches also encouraged poets to experiment with new angles of vision suggested by the initially disorienting array of developments in visual culture. Photography, panoramas, stereopticons, impressionist painting, illustrated newspapers, and the mass reproduction of art images all left their mark on poetic practice. The ultimate effect was to engender poems whose ability to please or even communicate depended on the active participation of the reader.

Though nonfiction prose and poetry flourished, the Victorian era is still considered the great age of British fiction. Novelists strove to embody the character and genius of the time. The novel's triumphant adaptation of practically any material into "realistic" narrative and detail fueled an obsession with storytelling that spilled over into anecdotal painting, program music, and fictive or autobiographical frames for essays and histories. The novels themselves generally explored the relation between individuals and their society through the mechanism of a central love plot, around which almost any subject could be investigated, including the quest for self-knowledge, religious crises, industrialism, education, women's roles, crime and punishment, or the definition of gentlemanliness.

Convoluted by later standards, Victorian novels received their most famous assessment from Henry James, who regarded them as "loose baggy monsters." The English novel, he said, is "a treasure house of detail, but an indifferent whole." Shrewd as the observation was, it overlooks the thematic density that unifies Dickens's sprawling three-deckers; the moral consciousness that registers every nuance of thought in George Eliot's rural panoramas; the intricate narrative structures and ardent self-questioning that propel the tormented romances of the Brontës. Their novels work within an established social frame, focusing on the characters' freedom to act within fairly narrow moral codes in an unpredictable universe; they deal with questions of social responsibility and personal choice, the impulses of passion and the dictates of conscience. Yet even as they portrayed familiar details of contemporary social life, novelists challenged the confines of "realist" fiction, experimenting with multiple perspectives, unreliable narrators, stories within stories, direct appeals to the reader, and strange extremes of behavior.

The Role of Art in Society

"The past for poets, the present for pigs." This polemical statement by the painter Samuel Palmer sums up much of the period's literary debate. Because Victorian times seemed so thoroughly to break from the past, "modern" became a common but often prejudicial word. Was there anything of lasting artistic value to be found in ordinary everyday life? Many writers felt there was not; they preferred to indulge instead in what Tennyson called the "passion of the past." Most poetry shunned the details of contemporary urban existence, and even the great novelists like Dickens, Eliot, and Thackeray situated much of their work in the pre-Victorian world of their parents. Some of this writing was escapist, but many authors saw in earlier times a more ethically and aesthetically coherent world that could serve as a model for Victorian social reform. The Pre-Raphaelite painters and their literary allies sought out medieval models, while Matthew Arnold returned to the Greco-Roman classics: "They, at any rate, knew what they wanted in art, and we do not."

But another group vigorously disagreed; they stressed the importance of creating an up-to-date art that would validate or at least grapple with the uniqueness of Victorian life. In *Aurora Leigh* Elizabeth Barrett Browning contended that "this live throbbing age" should take precedence over all other topics: "if there's room for poets in this world," she said, "Their sole work is to represent the age / Their age, not Charlemagne's." In 1850 the critic F. G. Stephens argued that poets should emphasize "the poetry of the things about us; our railways, factories, mines, roaring cities, steam vessels, and the endless novelties and wonders produced every day." As the century wore on, there was a broadening in social scope: the life of the working classes became a serious literary topic, and in the 1870s and 1880s "naturalist" writers probed the structures of everyday life at near-subsistence level. Thomas Hardy wrote searching studies of rural life; George Gissing, whose first wife was a prostitute, documented in harsh detail "the nether world" of backstreet London.

Whether they favored the past or present as a literary landscape, whether they criticized or lauded the times they lived in, most Victorian writers felt at home in their era. Though they had their own interests, they did not act as alienated outcasts but addressed social needs and responded to the public desire for instruction and reassurance. They recognized the force of John Stuart Mill's remark: "Whatever we may think or affect to think of the present age, we cannot get out of it; we must suffer with its sufferings, and enjoy with its enjoyments; we must share in its lot."

Amid all this energetic literary production, a substantial portion of readers demanded to know if literature had any value at all. Utilitarians regarded art as a waste of time and energy, while Evangelicals were suspicious of art's appeal to the senses and emotions rather than the soul and the conscience. "All poetry is misrepresentation," said the founder of Utilitarianism, Jeremy Bentham, who could not see how fanciful words might be of service to humanity. Such was the temper of the time that writers strove mightily to prove that audiences could derive moral and religious benefit from impractical things like circuses or watercolors. Even secular critics sought to legitimize art's role in society by contending that if religion failed, literature would take its place as a guiding light. "Literature is but a branch of Religion," said Carlyle; "in our time, it is the only branch that still shows any greenness." "More and more," said Arnold, "mankind will discover that we have to turn to poetry to interpret life for us, to console us, to sustain us."

The great expectations most Victorians had for their literature inevitably produced reactions against such moral earnestness. In the theater, a huge variety of comedies, melodramas, pantomimes, and music-hall skits amused all classes; 150,000 people a day went to theaters in London during the 1860s. Yet in comparison to other literary forms, little of lasting value remains. Though leading authors such as Browning, Tennyson, and Henry James tried their hand at writing for the stage, it was not until the 1890s, with the sophisticated wit of Oscar Wilde, the subtle social inquiry of Arthur Wing Pinero, and the provocative "problem plays" of Bernard Shaw, that British theater offered more than light entertainment for the masses. The way for serious drama had been prepared by the wonderfully clever musicals of W. S. Gilbert and Arthur Sullivan, which satirized such topics as Aestheticism (*Patience,*

1881), the House of Lords (*Iolanthe*, 1882), and the struggle for sexual equality (*Princess Ida*, 1884). Victorian social drama came into its own late in the era, when it began directly to explore its own relevance, dissecting social and theatrical conventions even as it questioned whether art could—or should—teach anything at all.

Doubts about the mission of art to improve society culminated in the Aesthetic Movement of the 1880s and 1890s, whose writers sought to show, in Oscar Wilde's words, that "there is no such thing as a moral or an immoral book. Books are well written or badly written. That is all." In an era of practicality, art declared its freedom by positing its sheer uselessness. Wilde argued that it is "through Art, and through Art only, that we can shield ourselves from the sordid perils of actual existence." Thus many authors at the end of the Victorian period renounced the values that characterize the age as a whole.

And yet the Aesthetes were still quintessentially Victorian in feeling that, as writers, they had to expose their inner being, whether uplifting or shocking, to the public gaze. In their thoughts and deeds, but especially in their words, writers were expected to harness their autobiographical impulses to society's need for guidance and amusement—or even outrage. "I never travel without my diary," one of Wilde's characters remarks: "One should always have something sensational to read in the train."

Every generalization about the Victorians comes with a ready-made contradiction: they were materialist but religious, self-confident but insecure, monstrous exploiters who devoted themselves to humane reforms; they were given to blanket pronouncements about the essential nature of sexes and races, the social order, and the Christian universe, but they relentlessly probed the foundations of their thought; they demanded a moral literature and thrilled to mindless page-turners. Yet in all these matters they were constantly concerned with rules, codes of duty and behavior, their places in a complex and often frustrating social order. Even the alienated rebels of the 1890s cared intensely (a favorite word) what people thought and how shocking their calculated transgressions might make them.

For a few decades after World War I, the Victorians' obsession with the tightly buttoned structures of everyday life seemed their only legacy, offering an easy target for Modernists who sought to declare their own free-thinking independence. "Queen Victoria was like a great paper-weight," wrote H. G. Wells, "that for half a century sat upon men's minds, and when she was removed their ideas began to blow about all over the place haphazardly." But the end of the Victorian period is now almost a century past, and the winds of change have blown many Victorian ideas back into favor. More and more readers delight to discover beneath the stiff manners and elaborate conventions of a bygone era an anxious, humorous, dynamic people very much like ourselves.

Thomas Carlyle

1795–1881

Thomas Carlyle was a difficult and cranky character whose imaginative, eccentric works of history and social criticism had an immense influence on his fellow Victorians. Mill, Tennyson, Browning, Dickens, Ruskin, and many others idolized him. George Eliot believed that even if all Carlyle's books were burnt, "it would be only like cutting down an oak after its acorns have sown a forest. For there is hardly a superior or active mind of this generation that has not been modified by Carlyle's writings; there has hardly been an English book written for the last ten or twelve years that would not have been different if Carlyle had not lived."

Carlyle was born in the small village of Ecclefechan in Scotland, the eldest son of a stonemason and his wife who gave their numerous children a strict Calvinist upbringing. From his devout and self-disciplined parents, Carlyle learned early the value of hard work, and he later preached the Gospel of Work to his generation. His parents recognized his exceptional abilities and sent him to the University of Edinburgh to study for the ministry.

Religious doubts, however, prevented him from seeking ordination; at nineteen he wrote, "I am growing daily and hourly more lukewarm about this preaching business." He tried schoolteaching instead, but hated it, and feared that his youth was "hurrying darkly and uselessly away." Tormented by ill health and his lack of a vocation, Carlyle gradually turned to a literary career. Inspired by German literature and philosophy, he began reviewing and translating.

In 1821 Carlyle met Jane Welsh. Middle-class, well-educated, and with literary aspirations of her own, Jane did not at first take Carlyle seriously as a suitor, but he was determined to marry her. Prophetically, he wrote to a friend that he expected their marriage to be "the most turbulent, incongruous thing on earth—a mixture of honey and wormwood" with "thunder and lightning and furious storms—all mingled together into the same season—and the sunshine always in the *smallest* quantity!" Despite this gloomy forecast, they married in 1826, embarking on one of the century's most famous, and most speculated about, marriages. Jane was sharp-tongued and high-strung, Thomas was perpetually irritable, depressed, and complaining, yet they stayed together for nearly forty years. Samuel Butler rather nastily remarked that "it was very good of God to let Carlyle and Mrs. Carlyle marry one another and so make only two people miserable instead of four, besides being very amusing."

In 1828 they left the social and intellectual pleasures of Edinburgh for six years of self-imposed exile in Craigenputtoch, a bleak, remote sheep farm. Here Carlyle wrote the essays that would begin to make his name, *Signs of the Times, On History,* and *Characteristics,* as well as his first book, *Sartor Resartus* (1833–1834), a symbolic autobiography that records Carlyle's struggle to find meaning in life after his loss of faith. In 1834 the Carlyles moved to London, to a house in Chelsea where they spent the rest of their lives. The bustling city was a great contrast to the lonely farm, providing more access to stimulating books and friendships, but Carlyle continued to struggle with poverty, poor health, and insomnia. He set to work on his chronicle of *The French Revolution* (1837), the most dramatic and apocalyptic event in recent European history. In impassioned and impressionistic prose, he traced the downfall of an aristocracy of corrupt impostors, who had to be swept away to allow for the rebirth of a healthy society. In their destruction he read a warning for England, whose leaders seemed to be abandoning the country to democracy and laissez-faire capitalism.

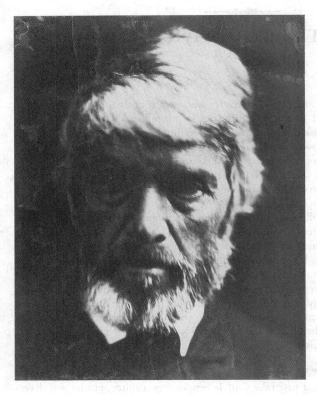

Julia Margaret Cameron. *Thomas Carlyle*, 1867. The greatest of Victorian portrait photographers, Cameron lived near Tennyson on the Isle of Wight, and by virtue of her irrepressible personality managed to get his many distinguished visitors to sit through grueling photo sessions in her drafty greenhouse. Tennyson once brought the American poet Longfellow to her, saying "You will have to do whatever she tells you. I will come back soon and see what is left of you." Cameron's portrait of Carlyle conveys not only his stern prophetic power but also her own sense of photography's ability to discover a transcendent energy in simple human features: "My mortal but yet divine! Art of photography."

After completing the first of three volumes, Carlyle suffered a catastrophic setback: he lent the manuscript to his friend John Stuart Mill, whose housemaid accidentally burned it in the fireplace. Carlyle was devastated, but he forced himself to begin again. Rewriting was torture: Carlyle called *The French Revolution* "a wild savage Book" that "has come out of my own soul; born in blackness, whirl-wind and sorrow."

Yet, to his own surprise, this was the book that finally brought him widespread public recognition and some relief from financial strain. He enjoyed the admiration, and savored his new role as Sage and Prophet—though he complained that nobody listened when he addressed his contemporaries on a variety of social issues. Invited to give a series of lectures, later published as *On Heroes and Hero-Worship* (1841), Carlyle offered historical examples of what he considered true leadership. Then, in *Past and Present* (1843), he contrasted the coherent social and religious fabric of life in the Middle Ages with the chaos of the modern world. Democracy, to Carlyle, meant the breakdown of political order, the "despair of finding any heroes to govern you." He urged the "Captains of Industry" to become modern heroes, as feudal lords had been in an idealized medieval past, and to reestablish a sense of human community in mechanized England.

Carlyle believed that strong leaders were the only hope for social reform. Turning to history once again for examples, he wrote about *Oliver Cromwell* (1845) and *Frederick the Great* (1858–1865). Six volumes long, *Frederick* was hailed as Carlyle's masterpiece, and Carlyle was elected Rector of Edinburgh University. While he was in Scotland delivering his inaugural speech in 1866, Jane Welsh Carlyle died. In his grief, Carlyle wrote a moving memoir of his wife, to which he added others, including portraits of his friend Edward Irving, and Wordsworth; these were published after his death as *Reminiscences* (1881).

Although Carlyle continued to have public honors heaped upon him in old age, a reaction against his authoritarianism had begun as early as 1850, when he published the *Latter-Day Pamphlets*, a jeremiad against democracy, and *Shooting Niagara, and After?* (1867), an attack on the Second Reform Bill. While he remained an important figure, admired and respected, he was frustrated at feeling, as the critic G. B. Tennyson has put it, "everywhere honored and nowhere heeded." Carlyle's lifelong insistence on divine purpose at work in the universe was deeply attractive to a society in the grip of social unrest and religious malaise—but few were willing to accept the tasks that Carlyle claimed God had set for them. Carlyle's reputation rests on his vigorous denunciation of a materialist society and his rousing calls for social reform. Like a biblical prophet, Carlyle exhorts his followers to mend their ways. In powerfully idiosyncratic language, he condemns laziness and greed, alienation and mechanization, and urges the necessity for spiritual rebirth.

from Past and Present[1]

Midas[2]

[THE CONDITION OF ENGLAND]

The condition of England, on which many pamphlets are now in the course of publication, and many thoughts unpublished are going on in every reflective head, is justly regarded as one of the most ominous, and withal one of the strangest, ever seen in this world. England is full of wealth, of multifarious produce, supply for human want in every kind; yet England is dying of inanition. With unabated bounty the land of England blooms and grows; waving with yellow harvests; thick-studded with workshops, industrial implements, with fifteen millions of workers, understood to be the strongest, the cunningest and the willingest our Earth ever had; these men are here; the work they have done, the fruit they have realised is here, abundant, exuberant on every hand of us: and behold, some baleful fiat as of Enchantment has gone forth, saying, "Touch it not, ye workers, ye master-workers, ye master-idlers; none of you can touch it, no man of you shall be the better for it; this is enchanted fruit!" On the poor workers such fiat falls first, in its rudest shape; but on the rich master-workers too it falls; neither can the rich master-idlers, nor any richest or highest man escape, but all are like to be brought low with it, and made "poor" enough, in the money sense or a far fataler one.

Of these successful skilful workers some two millions, it is now counted, sit in Workhouses, Poor-law Prisons;[3] or have "out-door relief"[4] flung over the wall to them,—the workhouse Bastille being filled to bursting, and the strong Poor-law bro-

---

1. *Past and Present* (1843) was Carlyle's response to the crisis of poverty and class estrangement during the Hungry 'Forties. Unemployment among industrial workers, combined with appalling conditions for the relief of the poor, had led to violent rioting. Even the Chartist movement's more peaceful attempts to address social and economic injustices through political reform aroused fears of revolution. Carlyle called for strong leaders to take charge. He contrasted the selfish indifference of laissez-faire industrialists and privileged aristocrats to the responsible paternalism of feudal lords and medieval monks. Medieval inequality and lack of personal freedom, he argued, were preferable to the modern "liberty to starve."
2. From Book 1, ch. 1. Midas was a legendary king who was granted his wish that everything he touched might

turn to gold; belatedly he realized he could not eat, for food became gold in his mouth.
3. Under the Poor Law Amendment Act of 1834, workhouses were established to provide relief to the poor. To deter loafers, the workhouses were made as unpleasant as possible: the standard of living was deliberately rendered worse than that of the lowest paid worker, and the inmates were expected to perform prison labor, such as picking oakum or breaking stones. Men and women were housed separately so that families were broken up.
4. Under the system of "outdoor relief," which existed prior to the Poor Law Amendment Act of 1834, each parish provided for its own poor through minimum allowances.

ken asunder by a stronger. They sit there, these many months now; their hope of deliverance as yet small. In workhouses, pleasantly so-named, because work cannot be done in them. Twelve-hundred-thousand workers in England alone; their cunning right-hand lamed, lying idle in their sorrowful bosom; their hopes, outlooks, share of this fair world, shut-in by narrow walls. They sit there, pent up, as in a kind of horrid enchantment; glad to be imprisoned and enchanted, that they may not perish starved. The picturesque Tourist, in a sunny autumn day, through this bounteous realm of England, descries the Union Workhouse on his path. "Passing by the Work-house of St. Ives in Huntingdonshire, on a bright day last autumn," says the pic-turesque Tourist, "I saw sitting on wooden benches, in front of their Bastille and within their ring-wall and its railings, some half-hundred or more of these men. Tall robust figures, young mostly or of middle age; of honest countenance, many of them thoughtful and even intelligent-looking men. They sat there, near by one another; but in a kind of torpor, especially in a silence, which was very striking. In silence: for, alas, what word was to be said? An Earth all lying round, crying, Come and till me, come and reap me;—yet we here sit enchanted! In the eyes and brows of these men hung the gloomiest expression, not of anger, but of grief and shame and manifold inarticulate distress and weariness; they returned my glance with a glance that seemed to say, "Do not look at us. We sit enchanted here, we know not why. The Sun shines and the Earth calls; and, by the governing Powers and Impotences of this Eng-land, we are forbidden to obey. It is impossible, they tell us!" There was something that reminded me of Dante's Hell in the look of all this; and I rode swiftly away."

So many hundred thousands sit in workhouses: and other hundred thousands have not yet got even workhouses; and in thrifty Scotland itself, in Glasgow or Edin-burgh City, in their dark lanes, hidden from all but the eye of God, and of rare Benevolence the minister of God, there are scenes of woe and destitution and desola-tion, such as, one may hope, the Sun never saw before in the most barbarous regions where men dwelt. Competent witnesses, the brave and humane Dr. Alison,[5] who speaks what he knows, whose noble Healing Art in his charitable hands becomes once more a truly sacred one, report these things for us: these things are not of this year, or of last year, have no reference to our present state of commercial stagnation, but only to the common state. Not in sharp fever-fits, but in chronic gangrene of this kind is Scotland suffering. A Poor-law, any and every Poor-law, it may be observed, is but a temporary measure; an anodyne, not a remedy: Rich and Poor, when once the naked facts of their condition have come into collision, cannot long subsist together on a mere Poor-law. True enough:—and yet, human beings cannot be left to die! Scotland too, till something better come, must have a Poor-law, if Scotland is not to be a byword among the nations. O, what a waste is there; of noble and thrice-noble national virtues; peasant Stoicisms, Heroisms; valiant manful habits, soul of a Nation's worth,—which all the metal of Potosi[6] cannot purchase back; to which the metal of Potosi, and all you can buy with it, is dross and dust!

Why dwell on this aspect of the matter? It is too indisputable, not doubtful now to any one. Descend where you will into the lower class, in Town or Country, by what avenue you will, by Factory Inquiries, Agricultural Inquiries, by Revenue Returns, by Mining-Labourer Committees, by opening your own eyes and looking,

5. William Pulteney Alison, Scottish physician and author of *Observations on the Management of the Poor in Scotland* (1840).

6. Bolivian city noted for its silver, tin, lead, and copper mines.

the same sorrowful result discloses itself: you have to admit that the working body of this rich English Nation has sunk or is fast sinking into a state, to which, all sides of it considered, there was literally never any parallel. At Stockport Assizes,—and this too has no reference to the present state of trade, being of date prior to that,—a Mother and a Father are arraigned and found guilty of poisoning three of their children, to defraud a "burial-society" of some 3*l*.8*s*. due on the death of each child: they are arraigned, found guilty; and the official authorities, it is whispered, hint that perhaps the case is not solitary, that perhaps you had better not probe farther into that department of things. This is in the autumn of 1841; the crime itself is of the previous year or season. "Brutal savages, degraded Irish," mutters the idle reader of Newspapers; hardly lingering on this incident. Yet it is an incident worth lingering on; the depravity, savagery and degraded Irishism being never so well admitted. In the British land, a human Mother and Father, of white skin and professing the Christian religion, had done this thing; they, with their Irishism and necessity and savagery, had been driven to do it. Such instances are like the highest mountain apex emerged into view; under which lies a whole mountain region and land, not yet emerged. A human Mother and Father had said to themselves, What shall we do to escape starvation? We are deep sunk here, in our dark cellar; and help is far.—Yes, in the Ugolino Hunger-tower stern things happen; best-loved little Gaddo fallen dead on his Father's knees![7]—The Stockport Mother and Father think and hint: Our poor little starveling Tom, who cries all day for victuals, who will see only evil and not good in this world: if he were out of misery at once; he well dead, and the rest of us perhaps kept alive? It is thought, and hinted; at last it is done. And now Tom being killed, and all spent and eaten, Is it poor little starveling Jack that must go, or poor little starveling Will?—What a committee of ways and means!

In starved sieged cities, in the uttermost doomed ruin of old Jerusalem fallen under the wrath of God, it was prophesied and said, "The hands of the pitiful women have sodden their own children."[8] The stern Hebrew imagination could conceive no blacker gulf of wretchedness; that was the ultimatum of degraded god-punished man. And we here, in modern England, exuberant with supply of all kinds, besieged by nothing if it be not by invisible Enchantments, are we reaching that?——How come these things? Wherefore are they, wherefore should they be?

Nor are they of the St. Ives workhouses, of the Glasgow lanes, and Stockport cellars, the only unblessed among us. This successful industry of England, with its plethoric wealth, has as yet made nobody rich; it is an enchanted wealth, and belongs yet to nobody. We might ask, Which of us has it enriched? We can spend thousands where we once spent hundreds; but can purchase nothing good with them. In Poor and Rich, instead of noble thrift and plenty, there is idle luxury alternating with mean scarcity and inability. We have sumptuous garnitures for our Life, but have forgotten to *live* in the middle of them. It is an enchanted wealth; no man of us can yet touch it. The class of men who feel that they are truly better off by means of it, let them give us their name!

Many men eat finer cookery, drink dearer liquors,—with what advantage they can report, and their Doctors can: but in the heart of them, if we go out of the dyspeptic stomach, what increase of blessedness is there? Are they better, beautifuler,

---

7. Count Ugolino and his sons and grandsons were starved to death in a tower by his political opponents; in Canto 33 of the *Inferno* Dante implies that Ugolino, out of starvation and desperation, cannibalized his children's corpses.
8. Cf. Lamentations 4.10.

stronger, braver? Are they even what they call "happier"? Do they look with satisfaction on more things and human faces in this God's-Earth; do more things and human faces look with satisfaction on them? Not so. Human faces gloom discordantly, disloyally on one another. Things, if it be not mere cotton and iron things, are growing disobedient to man. The Master Worker is enchanted, for the present, like his Workhouse Workman; clamours, in vain hitherto, for a very simple sort of "Liberty": the liberty "to buy where he finds it cheapest, to sell where he finds it dearest." With guineas jingling in every pocket, he was no whit richer; but now, the very guineas threatening to vanish, he feels that he is poor indeed. Poor Master Worker! And the Master Unworker, is not he in a still fataler situation? Pausing amid his game-preserves, with awful eye,—as he well may! Coercing fifty-pound tenants;[9] coercing, bribing, cajoling; "doing what he likes with his own." His mouth full of loud futilities, and arguments to prove the excellence of his Corn–law;[1] and in his heart the blackest misgiving, a desperate half-consciousness that his excellent Corn-law is indefensible, that his loud arguments for it are of a kind to strike men too literally *dumb*.

To whom, then, is this wealth of England wealth? Who is it that it blesses; makes happier, wiser, beautifuler, in any way better? Who has got hold of it, to make it fetch and carry for him, like a true servant, not like a false mock-servant; to do him any real service whatsoever? As yet no one. We have more riches than any Nation ever had before; we have less good of them than any Nation ever had before. Our successful industry is hitherto unsuccessful; a strange success, if we stop here! In the midst of plethoric plenty, the people perish; with gold walls, and full barns, no man feels himself safe or satisfied. Workers, Master Workers, Unworkers, all men, come to a pause; stand fixed, and cannot farther. Fatal paralysis spreading inwards, from the extremities, in St. Ives workhouses, in Stockport cellars, through all limbs, as if towards the heart itself. Have we actually got enchanted, then; accursed by some god?—

Midas longed for gold, and insulted the Olympians. He got gold, so that whatsoever he touched became gold,—and he, with his long ears, was little the better for it. Midas had misjudged the celestial music-tones; Midas had insulted Apollo and the gods: the gods gave him his wish, and a pair of long ears, which also were a good appendage to it. What a truth in these old Fables!

from *Gospel of Mammonism*[1]
[THE IRISH WIDOW]

One of Dr. Alison's Scotch facts struck us much. A poor Irish Widow, her husband having died in one of the Lanes of Edinburgh, went forth with her three children, bare of all resource, to solicit help from the Charitable Establishments of that City. At this Charitable Establishment and then at that she was refused; referred from one to the other, helped by none;—till she had exhausted them all; till her strength and heart failed her: she sank down in typhus-fever; died, and infected her Lane with fever, so that "seventeen other persons" died of fever there in consequence. The humane Physician asks thereupon, as with a heart too full for speaking, Would it not have been *economy* to help this poor Widow? She took typhus-fever, and killed seventeen of you!—Very curious. The forlorn Irish Widow applies to her fellow-crea-

---

9. The Reform Bill of 1832 enfranchised tenants who paid 50 pounds or more in annual rent.
1. The Corn Laws regulated the import of grain into Eng-

land. Intended to protect domestic agriculture, they also limited food supplies and raised food prices.
1. From Book 3, ch. 2.

tures, as if saying, "Behold I am sinking, bare of help: ye must help me! I am your sister, bone of your bone; one God made us: ye must help me!" They answer, "No, impossible; thou art no sister of ours." But she proves her sisterhood; her typhus-fever kills *them:* they actually were her brothers, though denying it! Had human creature ever to go lower for a proof?

For, as indeed was very natural in such case, all government of the Poor by the Rich has long ago been given over to Supply-and-demand, Laissez-faire and such-like,[2] and universally declared to be "impossible." "You are no sister of ours; what shadow of proof is there? Here are our parchments, our padlocks, proving indisputably our money-safes to be *ours,* and you to have no business with them. Depart! It is impossible!"—Nay, what wouldst thou thyself have us do? cry indignant readers. Nothing, my friends,—till you have got a soul for yourselves again. Till then all things are "impossible." Till then I cannot even bid you buy, as the old Spartans would have done, two-pence worth of powder and lead, and compendiously shoot to death this poor Irish Widow: even that is "impossible" for you. Nothing is left but that she prove her sisterhood by dying, and infecting you with typhus. Seventeen of you lying dead will not deny such proof that she *was* flesh of your flesh; and perhaps some of the living may lay it to heart.

from *Labour*[1]
[KNOW THY WORK]

For there is a perennial nobleness, and even sacredness, in Work. Were he never so benighted, forgetful of his high calling, there is always hope in a man that actually and earnestly works: in Idleness alone is there perpetual despair. Work, never so Mammonish,[2] mean, *is* in communication with Nature; the real desire to get Work done will itself lead one more and more to truth, to Nature's appointments and regulations, which are truth.

The latest Gospel in this world is, Know thy work and do it. "Know thyself": long enough has that poor "self" of thine tormented thee; thou wilt never get to "know" it, I believe! Think it not thy business, this of knowing thyself; thou art an unknowable individual: know what thou canst work at; and work at it, like a Hercules![3] That will be thy better plan.

It has been written, "an endless significance lies in Work"; a man perfects himself by working. Foul jungles are cleared away, fair seedfields rise instead, and stately cities; and withal the man himself first ceases to be a jungle and foul unwholesome desert thereby. Consider how, even in the meanest sorts of Labour, the whole soul of a man is composed into a kind of real harmony, the instant he sets himself to work! Doubt, Desire, Sorrow, Remorse, Indignation, Despair itself, all these like helldogs lie beleaguering the soul of the poor dayworker, as of every man: but he bends himself with free valour against his task, and all these are stilled, all these shrink murmuring far off into their caves. The man is now a man. The blessed glow of Labour in him, is it not as purifying fire, wherein all poison is burnt up, and of sour smoke itself there is made bright blessed flame!

---

2. The free trade philosophy of British industrialists who believed in the market's ability to regulate itself, and in the right to do business unhampered by government regulation.

1. From Book 3, ch. 9.
2. Mammon is the personification of material wealth. "Ye cannot serve God and mammon" (Matthew 7.24).
3. Hercules had to perform twelve labors.

Destiny, on the whole, has no other way of cultivating us. A formless Chaos, once set it *revolving*, grows round and ever rounder; ranges itself, by mere force of gravity, into strata, spherical courses; is no longer a Chaos, but a round compacted World. What would become of the Earth, did she cease to revolve? In the poor old Earth, so long as she revolves, all inequalities, irregularities disperse themselves; all irregularities are incessantly becoming regular. Hast thou looked on the Potter's wheel,—one of the venerablest objects; old as the Prophet Ezechiel and far older? Rude lumps of clay, how they spin themselves up, by mere quick whirling, into beautiful circular dishes. And fancy the most assiduous Potter, but without his wheel; reduced to make dishes, or rather amorphous botches, by mere kneading and baking! Even such a Potter were Destiny, with a human soul that would rest and lie at ease, that would not work and spin! Of an idle unrevolving man the kindest Destiny, like the most assiduous Potter without wheel, can bake and knead nothing other than a botch; let her spend on him what expensive colouring, what gilding and enamelling she will, he is but a botch. Not a dish; no, a bulging, kneaded, crooked, shambling, squint-cornered, amorphous botch,—a mere enamelled vessel of dishonour! Let the idle think of this.

Blessed is he who has found his work; let him ask no other blessedness. He has a work, a life-purpose; he has found it, and will follow it! How, as a free-flowing channel, dug and torn by noble force through the sour mud-swamp of one's existence, like an ever-deepening river there, it runs and flows;—draining-off the sour festering water, gradually from the root of the remotest grass-blade; making, instead of pestilential swamp, a green fruitful meadow with its clear-flowing stream. How blessed for the meadow itself, let the stream and *its* value be great or small! Labour is Life: from the inmost heart of the Worker rises his god-given Force, the sacred celestial Life-essence breathed into him by Almighty God; from his inmost heart awakens him to all nobleness,—to all knowledge, "self-knowledge" and much else, so soon as Work fitly begins. Knowledge? The knowledge that will hold good in working, cleave thou to that; for Nature herself accredits that, says Yea to that. Properly thou hast no other knowledge but what thou hast got by working: the rest is yet all a hypothesis of knowledge; a thing to be argued of in schools, a thing floating in the clouds, in endless logic-vortices, till we try it and fix it. "Doubt, of whatever kind, can be ended by Action alone."

Captains of Industry[1]

If I believed that Mammonism with its adjuncts was to continue henceforth the one serious principle of our existence, I should reckon it idle to solicit remedial measures from any Government, the disease being insusceptible of remedy. Government can do much, but it can in nowise do all. Government, as the most conspicuous object in Society, is called upon to give signal of what shall be done; and, in many ways, to preside over, further, and command the doing of it. But the Government cannot do, by all its signaling and commanding, what the Society is radically indisposed to do. In the long-run every Government is the exact symbol of its People, with their wisdom and unwisdom; we have to say, Like People like Government.—The main substance of this immense Problem of Organising Labour, and first of all of Managing the Working Classes, will, it is very clear, have to be solved by those who stand practically in the middle of

1. From Book 4, ch. 4.

it; by those who themselves work and preside over work. Of all that can be enacted by any Parliament in regard to it, the germs must already lie potentially extant in those two Classes, who are to obey such enactment. A Human Chaos *in* which there is no light, you vainly attempt to irradiate by light shed *on* it: order never can arise there.

But it is my firm conviction that the "Hell of England" will *cease* to be that of "not making money"; that we shall get a nobler Hell and a nobler Heaven! I anticipate light *in* the Human Chaos, glimmering, shining more and more; under manifold true signals from without That light shall shine. Our deity no longer being Mammon,—O Heavens, each man will then say to himself: "Why such deadly haste to make money? I shall not go to Hell, even if I do not make money! There is another Hell, I am told!" Competition, at railway-speed, in all branches of commerce and work will then abate:—good felt-hats for the head, in every sense, instead of seven-feet lath-and-plaster hats on wheels, will then be discoverable! Bubble-periods,[2] with their panics and commercial crises, will again become infrequent; steady modest industry will take the place of gambling speculation. To be a noble Master, among noble Workers, will again be the first ambition with some few; to be a rich Master only the second. How the Inventive Genius of England, with the whirr of its bobbins and billy-rollers[3] shoved somewhat into the backgrounds of the brain, will contrive and devise, not cheaper produce exclusively, but fairer distribution of the produce at its present cheapness! By degrees, we shall again have a Society with something of Heroism in it, something of Heaven's Blessing on it; we shall again have, as my German friend[4] asserts, "instead of Mammon-Feudalism with unsold cotton-shirts and Preservation of the Game, noble just Industrialism and Government by the Wisest!"

It is with the hope of awakening here and there a British man to know himself for a man and divine soul, that a few words of parting admonition, to all persons to whom the Heavenly Powers have lent power of any kind in this land, may now be addressed. And first to those same Master-Workers, Leaders of Industry; who stand nearest and in fact powerfulest, though not most prominent, being as yet in too many senses a Virtuality rather than an Actuality.

The Leaders of Industry, if Industry is ever to be led, are virtually the Captains of the World! if there be no nobleness in them, there will never be an Aristocracy more. But let the Captains of Industry consider: once again, are they born of other clay than the old Captains of Slaughter; doomed forever to be no Chivalry, but a mere gold-plated *Doggery*,—what the French well name *Canaille*, "Doggery" with more or less gold carrion at its disposal? Captains of Industry are the true Fighters, henceforth recognisable as the only true ones: Fighters against Chaos, Necessity and the Devils and Jötuns;[5] and lead on Mankind in that great, and alone true, and universal warfare; the stars in their courses fighting for them, and all Heaven and all Earth saying audibly, Well done! Let the Captains of Industry retire into their own hearts, and ask solemnly, If there is nothing but vulturous hunger, for fine wines, valet reputation and gilt carriages, discoverable there? Of hearts made by the Almighty God I will not believe such a thing. Deep-hidden under wretchedest god-forgetting Cants, Epicurisms, Dead-Sea Apisms;[6] forgotten as under foulest fat Lethe

---

2. Ups and downs in the stock market.
3. Machines that prepare cotton or wool for spinning.
4. Teufelsdröckh, the central character in *Sartor Resartus*.
5. Giants in Norse mythology.

6. An Islamic myth held that a tribe living near the Dead Sea were turned into apes because they refused to heed the prophecies of Moses.

mud and weeds, there is yet, in all hearts born into this God's-World, a spark of the Godlike slumbering. Awake, O nightmare sleepers; awake, arise, or be forever fallen! This is not playhouse poetry; it is sober fact. Our England, our world cannot live as it is. It will connect itself with a God again, or go down with nameless throes and fire-consummation to the Devils. Thou who feelest aught of such a Godlike stirring in thee, any faintest intimation of it as through heavy-laden dreams, follow *it,* I conjure thee. Arise, save thyself, be one of those that save thy country.

Bucaniers, Chactaw Indians, whose supreme aim in fighting is that they may get the scalps, the money, that they may amass scalps and money: out of such came no Chivalry, and never will! Out of such came only gore and wreck, infernal rage and misery; desperation quenched in annihilation. Behold it, I bid thee, behold there, and consider! What is it that thou have a hundred thousand-pound bills laid-up in thy strong-room, a hundred scalps hung-up in thy wigwam? I value not them or thee. Thy scalps and thy thousand-pound bills are as yet nothing, if no nobleness from within irradiate them; if no Chivalry, in action, or in embryo ever struggling towards birth and action, be there.

Love of men cannot be bought by cash-payment; and without love men cannot endure to be together. You cannot lead a Fighting World without having it regiment-ed, chivalried: the thing, in a day, becomes impossible; all men in it, the highest at first, the very lowest at last, discern consciously, or by a noble instinct, this necessity. And can you any more continue to lead a Working World unregimented, anarchic? I answer, and the Heavens and Earth are now answering, No! The thing becomes not "in a day" impossible; but in some two generations it does. Yes, when fathers and mothers, in Stockport hunger-cellars, begin to eat their children, and Irish widows have to prove their relationship by dying of typhus-fever; and amid Governing "Cor-porations of the Best and Bravest," busy to preserve their game by "bushing," dark millions of God's human creatures start up in mad Chartisms, impracticable Sacred-Months, and Manchester Insurrections;[7]—and there is a virtual Industrial Aristocra-cy as yet only half-alive, spell-bound amid money-bags and ledgers; and an actual Idle Aristocracy seemingly near dead in somnolent delusions, in trespasses and double-barrels; "sliding," as on inclined-planes, which every new year they *soap* with new Hansard's-jargon[8] under God's sky, and so are "sliding," ever faster, towards a "scale" and balance-scale whereon is written *Thou art found Wanting:*—in such days, after a generation or two, I say, it does become, even to the low and simple, very palpably impossible! No Working World, any more than a Fighting World, can be led on without a noble Chivalry of Work, and laws and fixed rules which follow out of that,—far nobler than any Chivalry of Fighting was. As an anarchic multitude on mere Supply-and-demand, it is becoming inevitable that we dwindle in horrid suici-dal convulsion and self-abrasion, frightful to the imagination, into *Chactaw* Workers. With wigwams and scalps,—with palaces and thousand-pound bills; with savagery, depopulation, chaotic desolation! Good Heavens, will not one French Revolution and Reign of Terror suffice us, but must there be two? There will be two if needed; there will be twenty if needed; there will be precisely as many as are needed. The Laws of Nature will have themselves fulfilled. That is a thing certain to me.

Your gallant battle-hosts and work-hosts, as the others did, will need to be made loyally yours; they must and will be regulated, methodically secured in their just share

7. Manchester was the site of Chartist agitation in 1838–1839; in 1819, charging cavalry had killed a dozen people at an outdoor workers' meeting.
8. *Hansard* is the official record of Parliamentary debate.

of conquest under you;—joined with you in veritable brotherhood, sonhood, by quite other and deeper ties than those of temporary day's wages! How would mere red-coated regiments, to say nothing of chivalries, fight for you, if you could discharge them on the evening of the battle, on payment of the stipulated shillings,—and they discharge you on the morning of it! Chelsea Hospitals,[9] pensions, promotions, rigor-ous lasting covenant on the one side and on the other, are indispensable even for a hired fighter. The Feudal Baron, much more,—how could he subsist with mere tem-porary mercenaries round him, at sixpence a day; ready to go over to the other side, if sevenpence were offered? He could not have subsisted;—and his noble instinct saved him from the necessity of even trying! The Feudal Baron had a Man's Soul in him; to which anarchy, mutiny, and the other fruits of temporary mercenaries, were intolera-ble: he had never been a Baron otherwise, but had continued a Chactaw and Bucanier. He felt it precious, and at last it became habitual, and his fruitful enlarged existence included it as a necessity, to have men round him who in heart loved him; whose life he watched over with rigour yet with love; who were prepared to give their life for him, if need came. It was beautiful; it was human! Man lives not otherwise, nor can live contented, anywhere or anywhen. Isolation is the sum-total of wretched-ness to man. To be cut off, to be left solitary: to have a world alien, not your world; all a hostile camp for you; not a home at all, of hearts and faces who are yours, whose you are! It is the frightfulest enchantment; too truly a work of the Evil One. To have neither superior, nor inferior, nor equal, united manlike to you. Without father, without child, without brother. Man knows no sadder destiny. "How is each of us," exclaims Jean Paul,[1] "so lonely in the wide bosom of the All!" Encased each as in his transparent "ice-palace"; our brother visible in his, making signals and gesticulations to us;—visible, but forever unattainable: on his bosom we shall never rest, nor he on ours. It was not a God that did this; no!

Awake, ye noble Workers, warriors in the one true war: all this must be remedied. It is you who are already half-alive, whom I will welcome into life; whom I will con-jure, in God's name, to shake off your enchanted sleep, and live wholly! Cease to count scalps, gold-purses; not in these lies your or our salvation. Even these, if you count only these, will not long be left. Let bucaniering be put far from you; alter, speedily abrogate all laws of the bucaniers, if you would gain any victory that shall endure. Let God's justice, let pity, nobleness and manly valour, with more gold-purses or with fewer, testify themselves in this your brief Life-transit to all the Eternities, the Gods and Silences. It is to you I call; for ye are not dead, ye are already half-alive: there is in you a sleepless dauntless energy, the prime-matter of all nobleness in man. Hon-our to you in your kind. It is to you I call: ye know at least this, That the mandate of God to His creature man is: Work! The future Epic of the World rests not with those that are near dead, but with those that are alive, and those that are coming into life.

Look around you. Your world-hosts are all in mutiny, in confusion, destitution; on the eve of fiery wreck and madness! They will not march farther for you, on the sixpence a day and supply-and-demand principle: they will not; nor ought they, nor can they. Ye shall reduce them to order, begin reducing them. To order, to just subor-dination; noble loyalty in return for noble guidance. Their souls are driven nigh mad; let yours be sane and ever saner. Not as a bewildered bewildering mob; but as a firm regimented mass, with real captains over them, will these men march any more. All human interests, combined human endeavours, and social growths in this world,

---

9. A home and hospital for disabled soldiers.   1. Jean Paul Richter (1763–1825), German writer.

have, at a certain stage of their development, required organising: and Work, the grandest of human interests, does now require it.

God knows, the task will be hard: but no noble task was ever easy. This task will wear away your lives, and the lives of your sons and grandsons: but for what purpose, if not for tasks like this, were lives given to men? Ye shall cease to count your thousand-pound scalps, the noble of you shall cease! Nay the very scalps, as I say, will not long be left if you count only these. Ye shall cease wholly to be barbarous vulturous Chactaws, and become noble European Nineteenth-Century Men. Ye shall know that Mammon, in never such gigs[2] and flunky "respectabilities," is not the alone God; that of himself he is but a Devil, and even a Brute-god.

Difficult? Yes, it will be difficult. The short-fibre cotton; that too was difficult. The waste cotton-shrub, long useless, disobedient, as the thistle by the wayside,—have ye not conquered it: made it into beautiful bandana webs; white woven shirts for men; bright-tinted air-garments wherein flit goddesses? Ye have shivered mountains asunder, made the hard iron pliant to you as soft putty: the Forest-giants, Marsh-jötuns bear sheaves of golden-grain; Aegir the Sea-demon himself stretches his back for a sleek highway to you, and on Firehorses and Windhorses ye career. Ye are most strong. Thor red-bearded, with his blue sun-eyes, with his cheery heart and strong thunder-hammer, he and you have prevailed. Ye are most strong, ye Sons of the icy North, of the far East,—far marching from your rugged Eastern Wildernesses, hitherward from the gray Dawn of Time! Ye are Sons of the *Jötun*-land; the land of Difficulties Conquered. Difficult? You must try this thing. Once try it with the understanding that it will and shall have to be done. Try it as ye try the paltrier thing, making of money! I will bet on you once more, against all Jötuns, Tailor-gods, Double-barrelled Law-wards, and Denizens of Chaos whatsoever!

1843   1843

The Industrial Landscape

"The most fundamental transformation of human life in the history of the world"—this is how the historian Eric Hobsbawm describes the Industrial Revolution. In economic terms, the arrival of the "Machine Age" was a huge success: thanks to its technological preeminence, Britain's wealth and prosperity increased enormously. This increase, coupled with pride in the improvements themselves, created a sense of excitement, of living in stirring times, and bolstered the optimistic conviction that further progress was certain. But the rapidity with which industrialization took place was also profoundly disorienting. Overnight, it seemed, the world had been transformed.

The first wave of the Industrial Revolution took place in the cotton industry. During the eighteenth century, new inventions had changed the technique of spinning and speeded up production of thread. This in turn had created a demand for more weavers. But with the development of steam-powered looms in the 1820s, weaving began to be done in factories rather than at home, and handloom weavers became obsolete. Large numbers of people found themselves without a job. Rural workers flocked to the cities to find work, and the population burgeoned in northern cities such as Manchester, Liverpool, Leeds, Birmingham, Sheffield, and Glasgow.

Britain grew richer, but it was not the poor who benefited from this revolution. In the early decades of the century, before legislation was passed to address some of the worst evils of the factory system, workers—including children—toiled for up to sixteen hours a day, six days a week, under inhuman conditions: deafening noise, poor ventilation, dangerous machinery,

2. A two-wheeled, one-horse carriage.

John Leech. *Horseman pursued by a train engine named "Time."*

demanding overseers, and no insurance or benefits to protect them in the event of an accident or illness. Periodic economic depressions resulted in massive unemployment: being "in work" was bad enough, but being out of work could mean actual starvation.

The factory system disrupted not only traditional patterns of work but also family life. As more and more women and children were employed in factories, mills, and mines, there was an inevitable loss of paternal authority. Women had always worked, but never before had their labor been so visible. The "factory girl" became a focus for fears about promiscuity and the undermining of the family structure.

The overcrowded conditions in the cities created urban slums of unimaginable wretchedness. Whole families—sometimes several families—might live in a single room. Tens of thousands of people lived in damp cellars. Because of the lack of sanitation, raw sewage overflowed everywhere, and fresh water was often impossible to obtain. When typhoid and cholera broke out, epidemics spread rampantly among the inhabitants of these foul dens; contagion was impossible to avoid.

Industrial pollution was another byproduct of the machine age. Factories spewed smoke into the air, and cities dumped sewage directly into the rivers. The outlying areas of Birmingham came to be known as "The Black Country." In *Contrasts* (1836) A. W. N. Pugin vividly depicted the sheer ugliness of a landscape dominated by smokestacks. In *The Storm-Cloud of the Nineteenth Century* (1884) John Ruskin denounced the devastation wrought by industrialism: "Blanched Sun,—blighted grass,—blinded man."

The second phase of the Industrial Revolution was brought about by the railway boom of the 1840s. The spreading network of rails linked the cities, and allowed the iron and coal industries to flourish. The railroad transfigured the landscape in ways that were terribly disruptive but also immensely thrilling. More than any other technological innovation, it symbolized the dizzying speed with which Britain was changing.

Psychologically, it was hard to assimilate such a rapidly altering environment. Many people felt that the world of their childhood had been obliterated. In 1860 the novelist William Makepeace Thackeray voiced this sense of bewilderment:

It was only yesterday; but what a gulf between now and then! *Then* was the old world. Stage-coaches, more or less swift, riding-horses, pack-horses, highwaymen, knights in armour, Norman invaders, Roman legions, Druids, Ancient Britons painted blue, and so forth—all these belong to the old period. . . . But your railroad starts the new era. . . . We who lived before railways, and survive out of the ancient world, are like Father Noah and his family out of the Ark.

Writers throughout the nineteenth century shared Thackeray's wistful longing for a romanticized past. Pugin, Carlyle, Tennyson, Morris, and many others used their vision of an idealized medieval England, aesthetically pleasing and socially harmonious, as a device to castigate the evils of industrialization.

This harking back to the past was not mere nostalgia: it reflected the trauma of the experience of industrialization. The transformation from a rural agrarian economy to a machine-dominated system of factories, mines, and railroads meant a very real shift in ancient patterns of life. The clock rather than the natural rhythms of the seasons now dictated working-class existence, and the laissez-faire pursuit of profit changed the relations between masters and men. Despite the huge accumulation of national wealth, the gulf between rich and poor had never been wider. In 1844 Friedrich Engels observed that "class warfare is so open and shameless that it has to be seen to be believed." Hunger, misery, and hopelessness found expression in strikes and trade union activity. The Chartist movement, in which the workers hoped for some relief from their distress by presenting a list of demands to Parliament, fizzled. Far from gaining middle-class compassion, it aroused hostility, and even fears of a revolution in Britain.

Among the key literary responses to the "condition of England" question were Carlyle's *Past and Present* (1843), Elizabeth Gaskell's *Mary Barton* (1848) and *North and South* (1855), and Dickens's *Hard Times* (1854). Their writing helped to focus attention on the human costs of the Industrial Revolution. In an effort to prick the consciences of their readers, they dramatized the sufferings of factory workers, and tried to put a human face on the inflammatory figure of the Chartist; they warned of the dangers of selfish individualism, and urged sympathy, communication, and benevolent leadership as remedies for class alienation.

The Steam Loom Weaver

In traditional bawdy ballads, the lovers meet under a hedge or by a stream, and their agrarian pursuits—herding sheep, milking cows, grinding corn, weaving cotton by hand—provide the pastoral setting and imagery for a sexual encounter. But the Industrial Revolution sent tens of thousands of rural people to live and work in cities. This humorous working-class ballad takes its imagery from the new industrial occupations of the factories, where steam engines powered the weavers' looms in cotton mills. Broadside ballads like this one were printed on flimsy paper and sold in the street for a penny or less; in the early nineteenth century, they were the most common form of reading matter for the urban poor.

The Steam Loom Weaver

> One morning in summer I did ramble,
> In the pleasant month of June,
> The birds did sing the lambkins play,
> Two lovers walking in their bloom,
> 5   The lassie was a steam loom weaver,
> The lad an engine driver keen,
> All their discourse was about weaving.
> And the getting up of steam.
>
> She said my loom is out of fettle,
> 10   Can you right it yes or no,
> You say you are an engine driver,

Which makes the steam so rapid flow;
My lambs and jacks[1] are out of order,
My laith in motion has not been,
15 So work away without delay,
And quickly muster up the steam.

I said fair maid you seem determined,
No longer for to idle be,
Your healds and laith[2] I'll put in motion,
20 Then work you can without delay,
She said young man a pair of pickers,[3]
A shuttle too I want you ween,
Without these three I cannot weave,
So useless would be the steam.

25 Dear lass these things I will provide,
But when to labour will you begin
As soon my lad as things are ready
My loom shop you can enter in.
A shuttle true and pickers too,
30 This young man did provide amain.
And soon her loom was put in tune
So well it supplied with steam.

Her loom worked well the shuttle flew,
His nickers play'd the tune nick-nack,
35 Her laith did move with rapid motion,
Her temples, healds, long-lambs and jacks,
Her cloth beam rolled the cloth up tight,
The yarn beam emptied soon its seam,
The young man cried your loom works, light
40 And quickly then off shot the steam.

She said young man another web,
Upon the beam let's get don't strike,
But work away while yet it's day,
This steam loom weaving well I like.
45 He said good lass I cannot stay,
But if a fresh warp you will beam
If ready when I come this way,
I'd strive for to get up the steam.

c. 1830

Fanny Kemble
1809–1893

The Liverpool and Manchester Railway, opened in 1830, was Britain's first passenger railway, built despite powerful opposition. During the debates in Parliament it had been argued that cows would cease to give milk, hens would be prevented from laying, and horses would become extinct

---

1. Jacks are levers that raise the harness supporting the warp threads; lambs are foot pedals that operate the jacks.
2. Healds are loops through which the warp threads pass;
the laith is the supporting stand of the loom.
3. Pickers are attachments to the picking stick which propels the shuttle through the warp threads.

if this monstrosity were allowed to deface the countryside. Fanny Kemble, a popular young actress, was the first woman to ride on the steam locomotive. She was accompanied by George Stephenson himself, the engineer who had designed the railroad. Her vivid description captures the startling newness of the experience, and the sense of traveling at astonishing speeds.

from Record of a Girlhood

[FIRST RIDE ON A STEAM ENGINE]

Liverpool, August 26th

My dear H————,

A common sheet of paper is enough for love, but a foolscap extra[1] can alone contain a railroad and my ecstasies. * * * We were introduced to the little engine which was to drag us along the rails. She (for they make these curious little fire-horses all mares) consisted of a boiler, a stove, a small platform, a bench, and behind the bench a barrel containing enough water to prevent her being thirsty for fifteen miles,—the whole machine not bigger than a common fire-engine. She goes upon two wheels, which are her feet, and are moved by bright steel legs called pistons; these are propelled by steam, and in proportion as more steam is applied to the upper extremities (the hip-joints, I suppose) of these pistons, the faster they move the wheels; and when it is desirable to diminish the speed, the steam, which unless suffered to escape would burst the boiler, evaporates through a safety-valve into the air. The reins, bit, and bridle of this wonderful beast—a small steel handle, which applies or withdraws the steam from its legs or pistons, so that a child might manage it. The coals, which are its oats, were under the bench, and there was a small glass tube affixed to the boiler, with water in it, which indicates by its fulness or emptiness when the creature wants water, which is immediately conveyed to it from its reservoirs. There is a chimney to the stove, but as they burn coke there is none of the dreadful black smoke which accompanies the progress of a steam-vessel. This snorting little animal, which I felt rather inclined to pat, was then harnessed to our carriage, and, Mr. Stephenson having taken me on the bench of the engine with him, we started at about ten miles an hour. * * * You can't imagine how strange it seemed to be journeying on thus, without any visible cause of progress other than the magical machine, with its flying white breath and rhythmical, unvarying pace, between these rocky walls, which are already clothed with moss and ferns and grasses; and when I reflected that these great masses of stone had been cut asunder to allow our passage thus far below the surface of the earth, I felt as if no fairy tale was ever half so wonderful as what I saw. * * *
* * * He explained to me the whole construction of the steam-engine, and said he could soon make a famous engineer of me, which, considering the wonderful things he *has* achieved, I dare not say is impossible. * * * The engine having received its supply of water * * * set off at its utmost speed, thirty-five miles an hour, swifter than a bird flies (for they tried the experiment with a snipe). You cannot conceive what that sensation of cutting the air was; the motion is as smooth as possible, too. I could either have read or written. * * * When I closed my eyes this sensation of flying was quite delightful, and strange beyond description; yet, strange as it was, I had a perfect sense of security, and not the slightest fear * * * [as] this brave little she-dragon of ours flew on.

1830   1878

1. An extra-long sheet of writing paper.

Thomas Babington Macaulay
1800–1859

Not everyone deplored the high human cost of rapid industrialization: the historian Thomas Babington Macaulay saw it as evidence of social progress. He was a firm believer in "the natural tendency of society to improvement," and he took great pride in the material achievements of his age. He expressed his views forcefully in reviewing Robert Southey, whose *Colloquies on the Progress and Prospects of Society* (1829) had criticized industrialism and urged a return to a romanticized rural past. In reply, Macaulay argued that in the nineteenth century "people live longer because they are better fed, better lodged, better clothed, and better attended in sickness, and that these improvements are owing to that increase of national wealth which the manufacturing system has produced."

from A Review of Southey's Colloquies
[THE NATURAL PROGRESS OF SOCIETY]

History is full of the signs of this natural progress of society. We see in almost every part of the annals of mankind how the industry of individuals, struggling up against wars, taxes, famines, conflagrations, mischievous prohibitions, and more mischievous protections, creates faster than governments can squander, and repairs whatever invaders can destroy. We see the wealth of nations increasing, and all the arts of life approaching nearer and nearer to perfection, in spite of the grossest corruption and the wildest profusion on the part of rulers.

The present moment is one of great distress. But how small will that distress appear when we think over the history of the last forty years; a war, compared with which all other wars sink into insignificance;[1] taxation, such as the most heavily taxed people of former times could not have conceived; a debt larger than all the public debts that ever existed in the world added together; the food of the people studiously rendered dear; the currency imprudently debased, and imprudently restored. Yet is the country poorer than in 1790? We firmly believe that, in spite of all the misgovernment of her rulers, she has been almost constantly becoming richer and richer. Now and then there has been a stoppage, now and then a short retrogression; but as to the general tendency there can be no doubt. A single breaker may recede; but the tide is evidently coming in.

If we were to prophesy that in the year 1930 a population of fifty millions, better fed, clad, and lodged than the English of our time, will cover these islands, that Sussex and Huntingdonshire will be wealthier than the wealthiest parts of the West Riding of Yorkshire now are, that cultivation, rich as that of a flower garden, will be carried up to the very tops of Ben Nevis and Helvelyn,[2] that machines constructed on principles yet undiscovered will be in every house, that there will be no highways but railroads, no traveling but by steam, that our debt, vast as it seems to us, will appear to our great-grandchildren a trifling encumbrance, which might easily be paid off in a year or two, many people would think us insane. We prophesy nothing; but this we say: If any person had told the Parliament which met in perplexity and terror after the crash in 1720 that in 1830 the wealth of England would surpass all their wildest

---

1. The Napoleonic Wars, which took place from 1792 until 1815.

2. Mountains in Scotland and the Lake District of England.

dreams, that the annual revenue would equal the principal of that debt which they considered as an intolerable burden, that for one man of ten thousand pounds then living there would be five men of fifty thousand pounds, that London would be twice as large and twice as populous, and that nevertheless the rate of mortality would have diminished to one-half of what it then was, that the post office would bring more into the exchequer than the excise and customs had brought in together under Charles the Second,[3] that stage coaches would run from London to York in twenty-four hours, that men would be in the habit of sailing without wind, and would be beginning to ride without horses, our ancestors would have given as much credit to the prediction as they gave to *Gulliver's Travels*. Yet the prediction would have been true; and they would have perceived that it was not altogether absurd, if they had considered that the country was then raising every year a sum which would have purchased the fee-simple[4] of the revenue of the Plantagenets, ten times what supported the Government of Elizabeth, three times what, in the time of Cromwell,[5] had been thought intolerably oppressive. To almost all men the state of things under which they have been used to live seems to be the necessary state of things. We have heard it said that five per cent is the natural interest of money, that twelve is the natural number of a jury, that forty shillings is the natural qualification of a county voter. Hence it is that, though in every age everybody knows that up to his own time progressive improvement has been taking place, nobody seems to reckon on any improvement during the next generation. We cannot absolutely prove that those are in error who tell us that society has reached a turning point, that we have seen our best days. But so said all who came before us, and with just as much apparent reason. "A million a year will beggar us," said the patriots of 1640. "Two millions a year will grind the country to powder," was the cry in 1660. "Six millions a year, and a debt of fifty millions!" exclaimed Swift, "the high allies have been the ruin of us." "A hundred and forty millions of debt!" said Junius;[6] "well may we say that we owe Lord Chatham more than we shall ever pay, if we owe him such a load as this." "Two hundred and forty millions of debt!" cried all the statesmen of 1783 in chorus; "what abilities, or what economy on the part of a minister, can save a country so burdened?" We know that if, since 1783, no fresh debt had been incurred, the increased resources of the country would have enabled us to defray that debt at which Pitt, Fox, and Burke[7] stood aghast, nay, to defray it over and over again, and that with much lighter taxation than what we have actually borne. On what principle is it that, when we see nothing but improvement behind us, we are to expect nothing but deterioration before us?

It is not by the intermeddling of Mr Southey's idol, the omniscient and omnipotent State, but by the prudence and energy of the people, that England has hitherto been carried forward in civilization; and it is to the same prudence and the same energy that we now look with comfort and good hope. Our rulers will best promote the improvement of the nation by strictly confining themselves to their own legitimate duties, by leaving capital to find its most lucrative course, commodities their fair price, industry and intelligence their natural reward, idleness and folly their nat-

---

3. Reigned 1660–1685.
4. Complete ownership of their estates. The Plantagenets ruled England from 1154 to 1399.
5. Elizabeth reigned from 1558 to 1603. Oliver Cromwell was Lord Protector from 1653 to 1658.

6. Pseudonym of a political commentator (active from 1769 to 1772) who supported William Pitt, Earl of Chatham. Pitt led the costly war against France.
7. William Pitt, Charles James Fox, and Edmund Burke were 18th-century statesmen.

ural punishment, by maintaining peace, by defending property, by diminishing the price of law, and by observing strict economy in every department of the State. Let the Government do this: the People will assuredly do the rest.

1830

◆━❖━◆

Parliamentary Papers ("Blue Books")

Factories, mills, and mines all employed women and children as cheap labor. They often worked grueling hours under appalling conditions, for wages that barely enabled them to subsist. Their misery attracted the attention of various official fact-finding commissions, whose horrifying reports, known as the "Blue Books," revealed that five-year-old children slaved in pitch-dark mines for twelve hours a day, and that pregnant and half-naked women crawled through mineshafts hauling heavy loads of coal. Such investigations helped bring about the 1833 and 1842 Factory Acts that prohibited the employment of children under nine, and limited those under twelve to forty-eight hours of work per week. In the following passages young girls testify before Parliamentary commissions about the circumstances of their lives.

Testimony of Hannah Goode, a Child Textile Worker

I work at Mr. Wilson's mill. I attend the drawing-head.[1] I get 5s. 9d. It is four or five years since we worked double hours. We only worked an hour over then. We got a penny for that. We went in the morning at six o'clock by the mill clock. It is about half past five by our clock at home when we go in, and we are about a quarter too fast by Nottingham. We come out at seven by the mill. The clock is in the engine-house. It goes like other clocks. I think the youngest child is about seven. There are only two males in the mill. I dare say there are twenty under nine years. They go in when we do and come out when we do. The smallest children work at the cards,[2] and doffing the spinning bobbins.[3] I work in that room. We never stop to take our meals, except at dinner. It has gone on so this six years and more. It is called an hour for dinner from coming out to going in. We have a full hour. Some stop in, if they have a mind. The men stop half an hour at dinner-time to clean the wheels. The children stop to clean their own work; that may take them five or ten minutes or so. That is taken out of the dinner-time. William Crookes is overlooker in our room; he is cross-tempered sometimes. He does not beat me; he beats the little children if they do not do their work right. They want beating now and then. He has a strap; he never beats them with any thing else, except his hand. The children are in a middling way as to goodness. I have sometimes seen the little children drop asleep or so, but not lately. If they are catched asleep they get the strap. They are always very tired at night. I have weakened[4] them sometimes to prevent Crookes seeing them; not very often, because they don't often go to sleep. Sometimes they play about the street when they come out; sometimes they go home. The girls often go home and sew. I sit up often till nine or ten o'clock at

---

1. The drawing-frame, a machine which drew out, or lengthened, the wool after it had been carded.
2. Work at the carding machine, which consisted of rollers studded with wires to comb the wool and remove debris.

3. Removing the full bobbins or spindles of wool, and taking them to other machines to be made into thread.
4. Wakened.

home, picking the spinners waste. I get 2½d. a pound for that. I can pick about half a pound a night, working very hard. I have known the people complain of their children getting beat. There is no rule about not beating the children. When the engine stops, all stops except the reeling. The reelers are all grown up. I can read a little; I can't write. I used to go to school before I went to the mill; I have [not] since. I am sixteen. We have heard nothing in our mill about not working so long.

1833

Testimony of Ann and Elizabeth Eggley, Child Mineworkers

Ann Eggley, eighteen years old.————I'm sure I don't know how to spell my name. We go at four in the morning, and sometimes at half-past four. We begin to work as soon as we get down. We get out after four, sometimes at five, in the evening. We work the whole time except an hour for dinner, and sometimes we haven't time to eat. I hurry[1] by myself, and have done so for long. I know the corves are very heavy they are the biggest corves anywhere about. The work is far too hard for me; the sweat runs off me all over sometimes. I am very tired at night. Sometimes when we get home at night we have not power to wash us, and then we go to bed. Sometimes we fall asleep in the chair. Father said last night it was both a shame and a disgrace for girls to work as we do, but there was nought else for us to do. I have tried to get winding[2] to do, but could not. I begun to hurry when I was seven and I have been hurrying ever since. I have been 11 years in the pit. The girls are always tired. I was poorly twice this winter; it was with headache. I hurry for Robert Wiggins; he is not akin to me. I riddle[3] for him. We all riddle for them except the littlest when there is two. We don't always get enough to eat and drink, but we get a good supper. I have known my father go at two in the morning to work when we worked at Twibell's, where there is a day-hole to the pit, and he didn't come out till four. I am quite sure that we work constantly 12 hours except on Saturdays. We wear trousers and our shifts[4] in the pit, and great big shoes clinkered and nailed. The girls never work naked to the waist in our pit. The men don't insult us in the pit. The conduct of the girls in the pit is good enough sometimes, and sometimes bad enough. I never went to a day-school. I went a little to a Sunday-school, but I soon gave it over. I thought it too bad to be confined both Sundays and week-days. I walk about and get the fresh air on Sundays. I have not learnt to read. I don't know my letters. I never learnt nought. I never go to church or chapel; there is no church or chapel at Gawber, there is none nearer than a mile. If I was married I would not go to the pits, but I know some married women that do. The men do not insult the girls with us, but I think they do in some. I have never heard that a good man came into the world who was God's Son to save sinners. I never heard of Christ at all. Nobody has ever told me about him, nor have my father and mother ever taught me to pray. I know no prayer: I never pray. I have been taught nothing about such things.

   Elizabeth Eggley, sixteen years old.————I am sister to the last witness. I hurry in the same pit, and work for my father. I find my work very much too hard for me. I hurry alone. It tires me in my arms and back most. We go to work between four and five in the morning. If we are not there by half past five we are not allowed to

---

1. A hurrier pushed carriages loaded with ore through the mineshafts. These handtrucks, called corves, weighed as much as 800 pounds.

2. Helping to hoist the coal up the shaft to the surface.
3. Sift the coal through a sieve.
4. Loose-fitting undergarments.

go down at all. We come out at four, five, or six at night as it happens. We stop in generally 12 hours, and sometimes longer. We have to hurry only from the bank-face down to the horse-gate and back. I am sure it is very hard work and tires us very much; it is too hard for girls to do. We sometimes go to sleep before we get to bed. We haven't a very good house; we have but two rooms for all the family. I have never been to school except four times, and then I gave over because I could not get things to go in.[5] I cannot read: I do not know my letters. I don't know who Jesus Christ was. I never heard of Adam either. I never heard about them at all. I have often been obliged to stop in bed all Sunday to rest myself. I never go to church or chapel.

1842

Charles Dickens
1812–1870

The most popular novelist of his century, Dickens combined dramatic plots and brilliantly comic characters to explore themes of all kinds, including the human costs of industrialism and materialism. Two of his portrayals of the new industrial landscape are given here. During the "railway mania" of the 1840s, nearly nine thousand miles of new track were laid across Britain. In 1842 the young Queen Victoria took her first railway journey, and was "quite charmed by it"—though she was also criticized for having risked her life. The railroads were a visible symbol of progress, but as Dickens dramatizes in his novel *Dombey and Son*, their construction brought about a vast demolition of neighborhoods and upheaval of the landscape. In the later novel *Hard Times*, Dickens portrays industrial Manchester as "Coketown" because of the coal residue that blackened the city. He emphasizes the dreary regimentation and the loss of personal identity produced by the mechanization of labor. The workers who tended the machines were called "hands," a term that aptly symbolized their dehumanization. But, as Dickens insists throughout *Hard Times*, oppressive working conditions were only part of the problem; the factory system also fostered alienation and hostility between classes, and the masters were apparently content for their workers to be deprived of education, religion, and even entertainment.

from Dombey and Son
[THE COMING OF THE RAILWAY]

The first shock of a great earthquake had, just at that period, rent the whole neighbourhood to its centre.[1] Traces of its course were visible on every side. Houses were knocked down; streets broken through and stopped; deep pits and trenches dug in the ground; enormous heaps of earth and clay thrown up; buildings that were undermined and shaking, propped by great beams of wood. Here, a chaos of carts, overthrown and jumbled together, lay topsy-turvy at the bottom of a steep unnatural hill; there, confused treasures of iron soaked and rusted in something that had accidentally become a pond. Everywhere were bridges that led nowhere; thoroughfares that were wholly impassable; Babel towers[2] of chimneys, wanting half their height; temporary wooden

---

5. I.e., proper clothing.
1. Dickens is describing the construction of the London-Birmingham railway, which demolished many buildings in Camden Town, an area in London he knew as a boy. The

line opened in 1838.
2. The tower of Babel was supposed to have been built high enough to reach heaven (Genesis 11).

houses and enclosures, in the most unlikely situations; carcases of ragged tenements, and fragments of unfinished walls and arches, and piles of scaffolding, and wilderness-es of bricks, and giant forms of cranes, and tripods straddling above nothing. There were a hundred thousand shapes and substances of incompleteness, wildly mingled out of their places, upside down, burrowing in the earth, aspiring in the air, moulder-ing in the water, and unintelligible as any dream. Hot springs and fiery eruptions, the usual attendants upon earthquakes, lent their contributions of confusion to the scene. Boiling water hissed and heaved within dilapidated walls; whence, also, the glare and roar of flames came issuing forth; and mounds of ashes blocked up rights of way, and wholly changed the law and custom of the neighbourhood.

In short, the yet unfinished and unopened Railroad was in progress; and, from the very core of all this dire disorder, trailed smoothly away, upon its mighty course of civilisation and improvement.

But as yet, the neighbourhood was shy to own the Railroad. One or two bold speculators had projected streets; and one had built a little, but had stopped among the mud and ashes to consider farther of it. A bran-new Tavern, redolent of fresh mortar and size, and fronting nothing at all, had taken for its sign The Railway Arms; but that might be rash enterprise—and then it hoped to sell drink to the workmen. So, the Excavators' House of Call had sprung up from a beer-shop; and the old-estab-lished Ham and Beef Shop had become the Railway Eating House, with a roast leg of pork daily, through interested motives of a similar immediate and popular descrip-tion. Lodging-house keepers were favourable in like manner; and for the like reasons were not to be trusted. The general belief was very slow. There were frowzy fields, and cow-houses, and dunghills, and dustheaps, and ditches, and gardens, and sum-mer-houses, and carpet-beating grounds, at the very door of the Railway. Little tumuli[3] of oyster shells in the oyster season, and of lobster shells in the lobster season, and of broken crockery and faded cabbage leaves in all seasons, encroached upon its high places. Posts, and rails, and old cautions to trespassers, and backs of mean hous-es, and patches of wretched vegetation, stared it out of countenance. Nothing was the better for it, or thought of being so. If the miserable waste ground lying near it could have laughed, it would have laughed it to scorn, like many of the miserable neighbours.

1846

from **Hard Times**

[COKETOWN]

Coketown, to which Messrs Bounderby and Gradgrind[1] now walked, was a triumph of fact; it had no greater taint of fancy in it than Mrs Gradgrind herself. Let us strike the key-note, Coketown, before pursuing our tune.

It was a town of red brick, or of brick that would have been red if the smoke and ashes had allowed it; but, as matters stood it was a town of unnatural red and black like the painted face of a savage. It was a town of machinery and tall chimneys, out of which interminable serpents of smoke trailed themselves for ever and ever, and

---

3. Artificial mounds. Oysters, a luxury today, were popular with poor people in Dickens's day; in *Pickwick Papers* Sam Weller says: "Poverty and oysters always seem to go together."

1. Bounderby is a mill owner; Gradgrind runs a school on Utilitarian principles.

never got uncoiled. It had a black canal in it, and a river that ran purple with ill-smelling dye, and vast piles of building full of windows where there was a rattling and a trembling all day long, and where the piston of the steam-engine worked monotonously up and down, like the head of an elephant in a state of melancholy madness. It contained several large streets all very like one another, and many small streets still more like one another, inhabited by people equally like one another, who all went in and out at the same hours, with the same sound upon the same pavements, to do the same work, and to whom every day was the same as yesterday and tomorrow, and every year the counterpart of the last and the next.

These attributes of Coketown were in the main inseparable from the work by which it was sustained; against them were to be set off, comforts of life which found their way all over the world, and elegancies of life which made, we will not ask how much of the fine lady, who could scarcely bear to hear the place mentioned. The rest of its features were voluntary, and they were these.

You saw nothing in Coketown but what was severely workful. If the members of a religious persuasion built a chapel there—as the members of eighteen religious persuasions had done—they made it a pious warehouse of red brick, with sometimes (but this only in highly ornamented examples) a bell in a bird-cage on the top of it. The solitary exception was the New Church; a stuccoed edifice with a square steeple over the door, terminating in four short pinnacles like florid wooden legs. All the public inscriptions in the town were painted alike, in severe characters of black and white. The jail might have been the infirmary, the infirmary might have been the jail, the town-hall might have been either, or both, or anything else, for anything that appeared to the contrary in the graces of their construction. Fact, fact, fact, everywhere in the material aspect of the town; fact, fact, fact, everywhere in the immaterial. The M'Choakumchild school was all fact, and the school of design was all fact, and the relations between master and man were all fact, and everything was fact between the lying-in hospital and the cemetery, and what you couldn't state in figures, or show to be purchaseable in the cheapest market and saleable in the dearest, was not, and never should be, world without end, Amen.[2]

A town so sacred to fact, and so triumphant in its assertion, of course got on well? Why no, not quite well. No? Dear me!

No. Coketown did not come out of its own furnaces, in all respects like gold that had stood the fire. First, the perplexing mystery of the place was, Who belonged to the eighteen denominations? Because, whoever did, the labouring people did not. It was very strange to walk through the streets on a Sunday morning, and note how few of *them* the barbarous jangling of bells that was driving the sick and nervous mad, called away from their own quarter, from their own close rooms, from the corners of their own streets, where they lounged listlessly, gazing at all the church and chapel going, as at a thing with which they had no manner of concern. Nor was it merely the stranger who noticed this, because there was a native organization in Coketown itself, whose members were to be heard of in the House of Commons every session, indignantly petitioning for acts of parliament that should make these people religious by main force. Then, came the Teetotal Society, who complained that these same people *would* get drunk, and showed in tabular statements that they did get drunk, and proved at tea parties that no inducement, human or Divine (except a medal),

2. The conclusion of the Anglican form of the Lord's Prayer.

would induce them to forego their custom of getting drunk. Then, came the chemist and druggist, with other tabular statements, showing that when they didn't get drunk, they took opium. Then, came the experienced chaplain of the jail, with more tabular statements, outdoing all the previous tabular statements, and showing that the same people *would* resort to low haunts, hidden from the public eye, where they heard low singing and saw low dancing, and mayhap joined in it; and where A. B., aged twenty-four next birthday, and committed for eighteen months' solitary, had himself said (not that he had ever shown himself particularly worthy of belief) his ruin began, as he was perfectly sure and confident that otherwise he would have been a tip-top moral specimen. Then, came Mr Gradgrind and Mr Bounderby, the two gentlemen at this present moment walking through Coketown, and both eminently practical, who could, on occasion, furnish more tabular statements derived from their own personal experience, and illustrated by cases they had known and seen, from which it clearly appeared—in short it was the only clear thing in the case—that these same people were a bad lot altogether, gentlemen; that do what you would for them they were never thankful for it, gentlemen; that they were restless, gentlemen; that they never knew what they wanted; that they lived upon the best, and bought fresh butter, and insisted on Mocha coffee, and rejected all but prime parts of meat, and yet were eternally dissatisfied and unmanageable.

1854

+—+ ≡♦≡ +—+

Benjamin Disraeli
1804–1881

The subtitle of Benjamin Disraeli's novel *Sybil*, "The Two Nations," encapsulates the Victorians' uneasy sense of being a divided society. The Hungry Forties were a time of unprecedented economic distress: Britain was the world's wealthiest nation, yet people were starving in the streets, and many feared that a revolution was in the offing. Thomas Carlyle had argued in *Past and Present* that "isolation is the sum-total of wretchedness to man." Here, Disraeli echoes his call for cooperation and benevolent paternalism to forge new relations between classes. Disraeli went on to become a Conservative Prime Minister, noted both for his nostalgic vision of aristocratic leadership, and for the domestic social reforms that took place during his administration.

from Sybil
[THE TWO NATIONS]

"It is a community of purpose that constitutes society," continued the younger stranger; "without that, men may be drawn into contiguity, but they still continue virtually isolated."

"And is that their condition in cities?"

"It is their condition everywhere; but in cities that condition is aggravated. A density of population implies a severer struggle for existence, and a consequent repulsion of elements brought into too close contact. In great cities men are brought together by the desire of gain. They are not in a state of co-operation, but of isolation, as to the making of fortunes; and for all the rest they are careless of neighbours. Christianity teaches us to love our neighbour as ourself; modern society acknowledges no neighbour."

"Well, we live in strange times," said Egremont, struck by the observation of his companion, and relieving a perplexed spirit by an ordinary exclamation, which often denotes that the mind is more stirred than it cares to acknowledge, or at the moment is able to express.

"When the infant begins to walk, it also thinks that it lives in strange times," said his companion.

"Your inference?" asked Egremont.

"That society, still in its infancy, is beginning to feel its way."

"This is a new reign," said Egremont, "perhaps it is a new era."

"I think so," said the younger stranger.

"I hope so," said the elder one.

"Well, society may be in its infancy," said Egremont, slightly smiling; "but, say what you like, our Queen reigns over the greatest nation that ever existed."

"Which nation?" asked the younger stranger, "for she reigns over two."

The stranger paused; Egremont was silent, but looked inquiringly.

"Yes," resumed the younger stranger after a moment's interval. "Two nations; between whom there is no intercourse and no sympathy; who are as ignorant of each other's habits, thoughts, and feelings, as if they were dwellers in different zones, or inhabitants of different planets; who are formed by a different breeding, are fed by a different food, are ordered by different manners, and are not governed by the same laws."

"You speak of—" said Egremont, hesitatingly.

"The Rich and the Poor."

1845

Friedrich Engels
1820–1895

In the manufacturing city of Manchester, whose size had increased more than tenfold between 1760 and 1830, the average life expectancy of working people in 1841 was only twenty years. Friedrich Engels, a German who had come to Manchester to study the cotton trade, was so appalled by his observations of the urban poor that he wrote an exposé of their degradation, stressing the "hypocritical town planning" that insulated the middle class from the sight of squalor and suffering. Engels's book was published in German in 1845; it became a socialist classic, and laid the groundwork for Engels's collaboration with Karl Marx. Lenin called the book "a terrible indictment of capitalism and of the middle classes." It was finally translated into English in 1892.

from The Condition of the Working Class in England in 1844
from *The Great Towns*

London is unique, because it is a city in which one can roam for hours without leaving the built-up area and without seeing the slightest sign of the approach of open country. This enormous agglomeration of population on a single spot has multiplied a hundred-fold the economic strength of the two and a half million inhabitants concentrated there. This great population has made London the commercial capital of the world and has created the gigantic docks in which are assembled the thousands of ships which always cover the River Thames. I know nothing more imposing than the view one obtains of the river when sailing from the sea up to London Bridge. Especially above Woolwich the houses and docks are packed tightly together on both banks of the river. The further one goes up the river the thicker becomes the concentration of ships lying at anchor, so that eventually only a narrow shipping lane is left free in mid-stream. Here hundreds of steamships dart rapidly to and fro. All this is so magnificent and impressive that one is lost in admiration. The traveller has good reason to marvel at England's greatness even before he steps on English soil.

It is only later that the traveller appreciates the human suffering which has made all this possible. He can only realise the price that has been paid for all this magnificence after he has tramped the pavements of the main streets of London for some days and has tired himself out by jostling his way through the crowds and by dodging the endless stream of coaches and carts which fills the streets. It is only when he has visited the slums of this great city that it dawns upon him that the inhabitants of modern London have had to sacrifice so much that is best in human nature in order to create those wonders of civilisation with which their city teems. The vast majority of Londoners have had to let so many of their potential creative faculties lie dormant, stunted and unused in order that a small, closely-knit group of their fellow citizens could develop to the full the qualities with which nature has endowed them. The restless and noisy activity of the crowded streets is highly distasteful, and it is surely abhorrent to human nature itself. Hundreds of thousands of men and women drawn from all classes and ranks of society pack the streets of London. Are they not all human beings with the same innate characteristics and potentialities? Are they not all equally interested in the pursuit of happiness? And do they not all aim at happiness by following similar methods? Yet they rush past each other as if they had nothing in common. They are tacitly agreed on one thing only—that everyone should keep to the right of the pavement so as not to collide with the stream of people moving in the opposite direction. No one even thinks of sparing a glance for his neighbour in the streets. The more that Londoners are packed into a tiny space, the more repulsive and disgraceful becomes the brutal indifference with which they ignore their neighbours and selfishly concentrate upon their private affairs. We know well enough that this isolation of the individual—this narrow-minded egotism—is everywhere the fundamental principle of modern society. But nowhere is this selfish egotism so blatantly evident as in the frantic bustle of the great city. The disintegration of society into individuals, each guided by his private principles and each pursuing his own aims has been pushed to its furthest limits in London. Here indeed human society has been split into its component atoms.

From this it follows that the social conflict—the war of all against all—is fought in the open. * * * Here men regard their fellows not as human beings, but as pawns in the struggle for existence. Everyone exploits his neighbour with the result that the stronger tramples the weaker under foot. The strongest of all, a tiny group of capitalists, monopolise everything, while the weakest, who are in the vast majority, succumb to the most abject poverty.

What is true of London, is true also of all the great towns, such as Manchester, Birmingham and Leeds. Everywhere one finds on the one hand the most barbarous indifference and selfish egotism and on the other the most distressing scenes of misery and poverty. Signs of social conflict are to be found everywhere. Everyone turns his house into a fortress to defend himself—under the protection of the law—from the depredations of his neighbours. Class warfare is so open and shameless that it has to be seen to be believed. The observer of such an appalling state of affairs must shudder at the consequences of such feverish activity and can only marvel that so crazy a social and economic structure should survive at all.

Capital is the all-important weapon in the class war. Power lies in the hands of those who own, directly or indirectly, foodstuffs and the means of production. The poor, having no capital, inevitably bear the consequences of defeat in the struggle. Nobody troubles about the poor as they struggle helplessly in the whirlpool of modern industrial life. The working man may be lucky enough to find employment, if by his labour he can enrich some member of the middle classes. But his wages are so low that they hardly keep body and soul together. If he cannot find work, he can steal, unless he is afraid of the police; or he can go hungry and then the police will see to it that he will die of hunger in such a way as not to disturb the equanimity of the middle classes. While I was in England at least twenty or thirty people died of hunger under the most scandalous circumstances, and yet when an inquest was held the jury seldom had the courage to bring in a verdict in accordance with the facts. However clear and unequivocal the evidence, the middle classes, from whom the juries were drawn, always found a loophole which enabled them to avoid a verdict of "death from starvation." In such circumstances the middle classes dare not tell the truth, because if they did so, they would be condemning themselves out of their own mouths. * * *

Every great town has one or more slum areas into which the working classes are packed. Sometimes, of course, poverty is to be found hidden away in alleys close to the stately homes of the wealthy. Generally, however, the workers are segregated in separate districts where they struggle through life as best they can out of sight of the more fortunate classes of society. The slums of the English towns have much in common—the worst houses in a town being found in the worst districts. They are generally unplanned wildernesses of one- or two-storied terrace houses built of brick. Wherever possible these have cellars which are also used as dwellings. These little houses of three or four rooms and a kitchen are called cottages, and throughout England, except for some parts of London, are where the working classes normally live. The streets themselves are usually unpaved and full of holes. They are filthy and strewn with animal and vegetable refuse. Since they have neither gutters nor drains the refuse accumulates in stagnant, stinking puddles. Ventilation in the slums is inadequate owing to the hopelessly unplanned nature of these areas. A great many people live huddled together in a very small area, and so it is easy to imagine the nature of the air in these workers' quarters. However, in fine weather the streets are used for the drying of washing and clothes lines are stretched across the streets from house to house and wet garments are hung out on them.

We propose to describe some of these slums in detail. In London there is the well-known "rookery"[1] of St. Giles. * * * St. Giles is situated in the most densely-populated part of London and is surrounded by splendid wide streets which are used by the fashionable world. It is close to Oxford Street, Trafalgar Square and the Strand. It is a confused

---

1. An overcrowded and deteriorating district of tenement dwellings.

conglomeration of tall houses of three or four stories. The narrow, dirty streets are just as crowded as the main thoroughfares, but in St. Giles one sees only members of the working classes. The narrowness of the roads is accentuated by the presence of streetmarkets in which baskets of rotting and virtually uneatable vegetables and fruit are exposed for sale. The smell from these and from the butchers' stalls is appalling. The houses are packed from cellar to attic and they are as dirty inside as outside. No human being would willingly inhabit such dens. Yet even worse conditions are to be found in the houses which lie off the main road down narrow alleys leading to the courts. These dwellings are approached by covered passages between the houses. The extent to which these filthy passages are falling into decay beggars all description. There is hardly an unbroken windowpane to be seen, the walls are crumbling, the door posts and window frames are loose and rotten. The doors, where they exist, are made of old boards nailed together. Indeed in this nest of thieves doors are superfluous, because there is nothing worth stealing. Piles of refuse and ashes lie all over the place and the slops thrown out into the street collect in pools which emit a foul stench. Here live the poorest of the poor. Here the worst-paid workers rub shoulders with thieves, rogues and prostitutes. Most of them have come from Ireland or are of Irish extraction. Those who have not yet been entirely engulfed in the morass of iniquity by which they are surrounded are daily losing the power to resist the demoralising influences of poverty, dirt and low environment. * * *

However wretched may be the dwellings of some of the workers—who do at least have a roof over their heads—the situation of the homeless is even more tragic. Every morning fifty thousand Londoners wake up not knowing where they are going to sleep at night. The most fortunate are those who have a few pence in their pocket in the evening and can afford to go to one of the many lodging houses which exist in all the big cities. But these establishments only provide the most miserable accommodation. They are crammed full of beds from top to bottom—four, five and even six beds in a room—until there is no room for more. Each bed is filled to capacity and may contain as many as four, five or even six lodgers. The lodging house keeper allocates his accommodation to all his customers in rotation as they arrive. No attempt is made to segregate the sick and the healthy, the old and the young, the men and the women, the drunk and the sober. If these ill-assorted bed-fellows do not agree there are quarrels and fights which often lead to injuries. But if they do agree among themselves, it is even worse, for they are either planning burglaries or are engaged in practices of so bestial a nature that no words exist in a modern civilised tongue to describe them. Those who cannot afford a bed in a lodging house sleep where they can, in passages, arcades or any corner where the police and the owners are unlikely to disturb their slumbers. * * *

If we cross Blackstone Edge on foot or take the train we reach Manchester, the regional capital of South Lancashire, and enter the classic home of English industry. This is the masterpiece of the Industrial Revolution and at the same time the mainspring of all the workers' movements. Once more we are in a beautiful hilly countryside. The land slopes gently down towards the Irish Sea, intersected by the charming green valleys of the Ribble, the Irwell, the Mersey and their tributaries. A hundred years ago this region was to a great extent thinly populated marsh-land. Now it is covered with towns and villages and is the most densely-populated part of England. In Lancashire—particularly in Manchester—is to be found not only the origin but the heart of the industry of the United Kingdom. Manchester Exchange is the thermometer which records all the fluctuations of industrial and commercial activity. The evolution of the modern system of manufacture has reached its climax in Manchester. It was in the South Lancashire cotton industry that water and steam power first replaced hand machines. It was here that such machines as the power-loom and the self-acting mule replaced the old hand-loom and spinning wheel. It is here that the division of labour has been pushed to its furthest limits. These three factors are the essence of modern industry. In all three of them the cotton industry was the pioneer and remains ahead in all branches of industry. In the circumstances it is to be expected that it is in this region that the inevitable consequences of industrialisation in so far as they affect the working classes are most strikingly evident. Nowhere else can the life and conditions of the industrial proletariat be studied in all their aspects as in South Lancashire. Here can be seen most clearly the degradation into which the worker sinks owing to the introduction of steam power, machinery and the division of labour. Here, too, can be seen most the strenuous efforts of the proletariat to raise themselves from their degraded situation. I propose to examine conditions in Manchester in greater detail for two reasons. In the first place, Manchester is the classic type of modern industrial town. Secondly, I know Manchester as well as I know my native town and I know more about it than most of its inhabitants. * * *

* * * Owing to the curious lay-out of the town it is quite possible for someone to live for years in Manchester and to travel daily to and from his work without ever seeing a working-class quarter or coming into contact with an artisan. He who visits Manchester simply on business or for pleasure need never see the slums, mainly because the working-class districts and the middle-class districts are quite distinct. This division is due partly to deliberate policy and partly to instinctive and tacit agreement between the two social groups. In those areas where the two social groups happen to come into contact with each other the middle classes sanctimoniously ignore the existence of their less fortunate neighbours. In the centre of Manchester there is a fairly large commercial district, which is about half a mile long and half a mile broad. This district is almost entirely given over to offices and warehouses. Nearly the whole of this district has no permanent residents and is deserted at night, when only policemen patrol its dark, narrow thoroughfares with their bull's eye lanterns. This district is intersected by certain main streets which carry an enormous volume of traffic. The lower floors of the buildings are occupied by shops of dazzling splendour. A few of the upper stories on these premises are used as dwellings and the streets present a relatively busy appearance until late in the evening. Around this commercial quarter there is a belt of built up areas on the average one and a half miles in width, which is occupied entirely by working-class dwellings. This area of workers' houses includes all Manchester proper, except the centre. * * * The upper classes enjoy healthy country air and live in luxurious and comfortable dwellings which are linked to the centre of Manchester by omnibuses which run every fifteen or thirty minutes. To such an extent has the convenience of the rich been considered in the planning of Manchester that these plutocrats can travel from their houses to their places of business in the centre of the town by the shortest routes, which run entirely through working-class districts, without even realising how close they are to the misery and filth which lie on both sides of the road. This is because the main streets which run from the Exchange in all

directions out of the town are occupied almost uninterruptedly on both sides by shops, which are kept by members of the lower middle classes. In their own interests these shopkeepers should keep the outsides of their shops in a clean and respectable condition, and in fact they do so. These shops have naturally been greatly influenced by the character of the population in the area which lies behind them. Those shops which are situated in the vicinity of commercial or middle class residential districts are more elegant than those which serve as a facade for the workers' grimy cottages. Nevertheless, even the less pretentious shops adequately serve their purpose of hiding from the eyes of wealthy ladies and gentlemen with strong stomachs and weak nerves the misery and squalor which are part and parcel of their own riches and luxury. * * *

I am quite aware of the fact that this hypocritical town-planning device is more or less common to all big cities. * * * But in my opinion Manchester is unique in the systematic way in which the working classes have been barred from the main streets. Nowhere else has such care been taken to avoid offending the tender susceptibilities of the eyes and the nerves of the middle classes. Yet Manchester is the very town in which building has taken place in a haphazard manner with little or no planning or interference from the authorities. When the middle classes zealously proclaim that all is well with the working classes, I cannot help feeling that the politically "progressive" industrialists, the Manchester "bigwigs," are not quite so innocent of this shameful piece of town planning as they pretend.

* * * I will now give a description of the working-class districts of Manchester. The first of them is the Old Town, which lies between the northern limit of the commercial quarter and the River Irk. * * * Here one is really and truly in a district which is quite obviously given over entirely to the working classes, because even the shopkeepers and the publicans[2] of Long Millgate make no effort to give their establishments a semblance of cleanliness. The condition of this street may be deplorable, but it is by no means as bad as the alleys and courts which lie behind it, and which can be approached only by covered passages so narrow that two people cannot pass. Anyone who has never visited these courts and alleys can have no idea of the fantastic way in which the houses have been packed together in disorderly confusion in impudent defiance of all reasonable principles of town planning. And the fault lies not merely in the survival of old property from earlier periods in Manchester's history. Only in quite modern times has the policy of cramming as many houses as possible on to such space as was not utilised in earlier periods reached its climax. The result is that today not an inch of space remains between the houses and any further building is now physically impossible. * * *

* * * To the right and left a number of covered passages from Long Millgate give access to several courts. On reaching them one meets with a degree of dirt and revolting filth, the like of which is not to be found elsewhere. The worst courts are those leading down to the Irk, which contain unquestionably the most dreadful dwellings I have ever seen. In one of these courts, just at the entrance where the cov-

2. Pub-keepers.

ered passage ends there is a privy without a door. This privy is so dirty that the inhabitants of the court can only enter or leave the court if they are prepared to wade through puddles of stale urine and excrement.

*** *Enough of this! All along the Irk slums of this type abound. There is an unplanned and chaotic conglomeration of houses, most of which are more or less unhabitable. The dirtiness of the interiors of these premises is fully in keeping with the filth that surrounds them. How can people dwelling in such places keep clean! There are not even adequate facilities for satisfying the most natural daily needs. There are so few privies that they are either filled up every day or are too far away for those who need to use them. How can these people wash when all that is available is the dirty water of the Irk? Pumps and piped water are to be found only in the better-class districts of the town. Indeed no one can blame these helots[5] of modern civilisation if their homes are no cleaner than the occasional pigsties which are a feature of these slums. * * *

This, then, is the Old Town of Manchester. On re-reading my description of the Old Town I must admit that, far from having exaggerated anything, I have not written vividly enough to impress the reader with the filth and dilapidation of a district which is quite unfit for human habitation. The shameful lay-out of the Old Town has made it impossible for the wretched inhabitants to enjoy cleanliness, fresh air, and good health. And such a district of at least twenty to thirty thousand inhabitants lies in the very centre of the second city in England, the most important factory town in the world. It is here that one can see how little space human beings need to move about in, how little air—and what air!—they need to breathe in order to exist, and how few of the decencies of civilisation are really necessary in order to survive. It is true that this is the *Old Town* and Manchester people stress this when their attention is drawn to the revolting character of this hell upon earth. But that is no defence. Everything in this district that arouses our disgust and just indignation is of relatively recent origin and belongs to the industrial age. The two or three hundred houses which survive from the earlier period of Manchester's history have long ago been deserted by their original inhabitants. It is only industry which has crammed them full of the hordes of workers who now live there. It is only the modern industrial age which has built over every scrap of ground between these old houses to provide accommodation for the masses who have migrated from the country districts and from Ireland. It is only the industrial age that has made it possible for the owners of these shacks, fit only for the accommodation of cattle, to let them at high rents for human habitations. It is only modern industry which permits these owners to take advantage of the poverty of the workers, to undermine the health of thousands to enrich themselves. Only industry has made it possible for workers who have barely emerged from a state of serfdom to be again treated as chattels and not as human beings. The workers have been caged in dwellings which are so wretched that no one else will live in them, and they actually pay good money for the privilege of seeing these dilapidated hovels fall to pieces about their ears. Industry alone has been responsible for all this and yet this same industry could not flourish except by degrading and exploiting the workers.

1845

Henry Mayhew
1812–1887

In London, the most visible occupations of children were in the streets. They earned a precarious living hawking goods, begging, performing, and providing various services, from running errands to prostitution. Mayhew interviewed hundreds of street people, gathering four volumes of testimony about the lives of this exploited and neglected underclass. With an extraordinary ear for slang and oddities of speech, he shaped each narrative into a kind of dramatic monologue. By publishing "the history of a people, from the lips of the people themselves . . . in their own 'unvarnished' language," Mayhew gave voice to a multitude of forgotten workers. The critic John D. Rosenberg has described Mayhew's image of London as "a vast, ingeniously balanced mechanism in which each class subsists on the drippings and droppings of the stratum above, all the way from the rich, whom we scarcely glimpse, down to the deformed and starving, whom we see groping for bits of salvageable bone or decaying vegetables in the markets."

from London Labour and the London Poor
Watercress Girl

The little watercress girl who gave me the following statement, although only eight years of age, had entirely lost all childish ways, and was, indeed, in thoughts and manner, a woman. There was something cruelly pathetic in hearing this infant, so young that her features had scarcely formed themselves, talking of the bitterest struggles of life, with the calm earnestness of one who had endured them all. I did not know how to talk with her. At first I treated her as a child, speaking on childish subjects; so that I might, by being familiar with her, remove all shyness, and get her to narrate her life freely. I asked her about her toys and her games with her companions; but the look of amazement that answered me soon put an end to any attempt at fun on my part. I then talked to her about the parks, and whether she ever went to them. "The parks!" she replied in wonder, "where are they?" I explained to her, telling her that they were large open places with green grass and tall trees, where beautiful carriages drove about, and people walked for pleasure, and children played. Her eyes brightened up a little as I spoke; and she asked, half doubtingly, "Would they let such as me go there—just to look?" All her knowledge seemed to begin and end with water-cresses,[1] and what they fetched. She knew no more of London than that part she had seen on her rounds, and believed that no quarter of the town was handsomer or pleasanter than it was at Farringdon-market or at Clerkenwell, where she lived. Her little face, pale and thin with privation, was wrinkled where the dimples ought to have been, and she would sigh frequently. When some hot dinner was offered to her, she would not touch it, because, if she eat too much, "it made her sick," she said; "and she wasn't used to meat, only on a Sunday."

The poor child, although the weather was severe, was dressed in a thin cotton gown, with a threadbare shawl wrapped round her shoulders. She wore no covering

---

1. An herb whose leaves are used in salads and as garnishes.

to her head, and the long rusty hair stood out in all directions. When she walked she shuffled along, for fear that the large carpet slippers that served her for shoes should slip off her feet.

"I go about the streets with water-creases, crying, 'Four bunches a penny, water-creases.' I am just eight years old—that's all, and I've a big sister, and a brother and a sister younger than I am. On and off, I've been very near a twelve-month in the streets. Before that, I had to take care of a baby for my aunt. No, it wasn't heavy—it was only two months old; but I minded it for ever such a time—till it could walk. It was a very nice little baby, not a very pretty one; but, if I touched it under the chin, it would laugh. Before I had the baby, I used to help mother, who was in the fur trade; and, if there was any slits in the fur, I'd sew them up. My mother learned me to needle-work and to knit when I was about five. I used to go to school, too; but I wasn't there long. I've forgot all about it now, it's such a time ago; and mother took me away because the master whacked me, though the missus use'n't to never touch me. I didn't like him at all. What do you think? he hit me three times, ever so hard, across the face with his cane, and made me go dancing down stairs; and when mother saw the marks on my cheek, she went to blow him up,[2] but she couldn't see him—he was afraid. That's why I left school.

"The creases is so bad now, that I haven't been out with 'em for three days. They're so cold, people won't buy 'em; for when I goes up to them, they say, 'They'll freeze our bellies.' Besides, in the market, they won't sell a ha'penny handful now—they're ris to[3] a penny and tuppence. In summer there's lots, and 'most as cheap as dirt; but I have to be down at Farringdon-market between four and five, or else I can't get any creases, because everyone almost—especially the Irish—is selling them, and they're picked up so quick. Some of the saleswomen—we never calls 'em ladies—is very kind to us children, and some of them altogether spiteful. The good one will give you a bunch for nothing, when they're cheap; but the others, cruel ones, if you try to bate them a farden less[4] than they ask you, will say, 'Go along with you, you're no good.' I used to go down to market along with another girl, as must be about fourteen, 'cos she does her back hair up. When we've bought a lot, we sits down on a door-step, and ties up the bunches. We never goes home to breakfast till we've sold out; but, if it's very late, then I buys a penn'orth of pudden, which is very nice with gravy. I don't know hardly one of the people, as goes to Farringdon, to talk to; they never speaks to me, so I don't speak to them. We children never play down there, 'cos we're thinking of our living. No; people never pities me in the street—excepting one gentleman, and he says, says he, 'What do you do out so soon in the morning?' but he gave me nothink—he only walked away.

"It's very cold before winter comes on reg'lar—specially getting up of a morning. I gets up in the dark by the light of the lamp in the court. When the snow is on the ground, there's no creases. I bears the cold—you must; so I puts my hands under my shawl, though it hurts 'em to take hold of the creases, especially when we

---

2. Scold him
3. Their price has risen to.

4. Give them a farthing (a quarter of a penny) less.

takes 'em to the pump to wash 'em. No; I never see any children crying—it's no use.

"Sometimes I make a great deal of money. One day I took 1s. 6d., and the creases cost 6d.; but it isn't often I get such luck as that. I oftener makes 3d. or 4d. than 1s.; and then I'm at work, crying, 'Creases, four bunches a penny, creases!' from six in the morning to about ten. What do you mean by mechanics?—I don't know what they are. The shops buys most of me. Some of 'em says, 'Oh! I ain't a-goin' to give a penny for these;' and they want 'em at the same price as I buys 'em at.

"I always give mother my money, she's so very good to me. She don't often beat me; but, when she do, she don't play with me. She's very poor, and goes out cleaning rooms sometimes, now she don't work at the fur. I ain't got no father, he's a father-in-law. No; mother ain't married again—he's a father-in-law. He grinds scissors, and he's very good to me. No; I dont mean by that that he says kind things to me, for he never hardly speaks. When I gets home, after selling creases, I stops at home. I puts the room to rights: mother don't make me do it, I does it myself. I cleans the chairs, though there's only two to clean. I takes a tub and scrubbing-brush and flannel, and scrubs the floor—that's what I do three or four times a week.

"I don't have no dinner. Mother gives me two slices of bread-and-butter and a cup of tea for breakfast, and then I go till tea, and has the same. We has meat of a Sunday, and, of course, I should like to have it every day. Mother has just the same to eat as we has, but she takes more tea—three cups, sometimes. No; I never has no sweet-stuff; I never buy none—I don't like it. Sometimes we has a game of 'honey-pots' with the girls in the court, but not often. Me and Carry H— carries the little 'uns. We plays, too, at 'kiss-in-the-ring.' I knows a good many games, but I don't play at 'em, 'cos going out with creases tires me. On a Friday night, too, I goes to a Jew's house till eleven o'clock on Saturday night. All I has to do is to snuff the candles and poke the fire. You see they keep their Sabbath then, and they won't touch anything; so they gives me my wittals[5] and 1½d., and I does it for 'em. I have a reg'lar good lot to eat. Supper of Friday night, and tea after that, and fried fish of a Saturday morning, and meat for dinner, and tea, and supper, and I like it very well.

"Oh, yes; I've got some toys at home. I've a fire-place, and a box of toys, and a knife and fork, and two little chairs. The Jews gave 'em to me where I go to on a Friday, and that's why I said they was very kind to me. I never had no doll; but I misses little sister—she's only two years old. We don't sleep in the same room; for father and mother sleeps with little sister in the one pair, and me and brother and other sister sleeps in the top room. I always goes to bed at seven, 'cos I has to be up so early.

"I am a capital hand at bargaining—but only at buying watercreases. They can't take me in. If the woman tries to give me a small handful of creases, I says, 'I ain't a goin' to have that for a ha'porth,' and I go to the next basket, and so on, all round. I know the quantities very well. For a penny I ought to have a full market hand, or as much as I could carry in my arms at one time, without spilling. For 3d. I has a lap full, enough to earn about a shilling; and for 6d. I gets as many as crams my basket. I can't read or write, but I knows how many pennies goes to a shilling, why, twelve, of

5. Victuals, food.

course, but I don't know how many ha'pence there is, though there's two to a penny. When I've bought 3*d*. of creases, I ties 'em up into as many little bundles as I can. They must look biggish, or the people won't buy them, some puffs them out as much as they'll go. All my money I earns I puts in a club and draws it out to buy clothes with. It's better than spending it in sweet-stuff, for them as has a living to earn. Besides it's like a child to care for sugar-sticks, and not like one who's got a living and vittals to earn. I ain't a child, and I shan't be a woman till I'm twenty, but I'm past eight, I am. I don't know nothing about what I earns during the year, I only know how many pennies goes to a shilling, and two ha'pence goes to a penny, and four far-dens goes to a penny. I knows, too, how many fardens goes to tuppence—eight. That's as much as I wants to know for the markets."

[*A Boy Crossing-Sweeper*]

I found the lad who first gave me an insight into the proceedings of the associated crossing-sweepers crouched on the stone steps of a door in Adelaide-street, Strand; and when I spoke to him he was preparing to settle down in a corner and go to sleep—his legs and body being curled round almost as closely as those of a cat on a hearth.

The Boy Crossing-Sweepers. After a daguerrotype by Richard Beard, from Henry Mayhew's *London Labour and the London Poor,* 1851.

The moment he heard my voice he was upon his feet, asking me to "give a half-penny to poor little Jack."

He was a good-looking lad, with a pair of large mild eyes, which he took good care to turn up with an expression of supplication as he moaned for his halfpenny.

A cap, or more properly a stuff bag, covered a crop of hair which had matted itself into the form of so many paint-brushes, while his face, from its roundness of feature and the complexion of dirt, had an almost Indian look about it; the colour of his hands, too, was such that you could imagine he had been shelling walnuts.

He ran before me, treading cautiously with his naked feet, until I reached a convenient spot to take down his statement, which was as follows:—

"I've got no mother or father; mother has been dead for two years, and father's been gone more than that—more nigh five years—he died at Ipswich, in Suffolk.
* * *

* * * "I used, when I was with mother, to go to school in the morning, and go at nine and come home at twelve to dinner, then go again at two and leave off at half-past four,—that is, if I behaved myself and did all my lessons right; for if I did not I was kept back till I *did* them so. Mother used to pay one shilling a-week, and extra for the copy-books and things. I can read and write—oh, yes, I mean read and write well—read anything, even old English; and I write pretty fair,—though I don't get much reading now, unless it's a penny paper—I've got one in my pocket now—it's the *London Journal*—there's a tale in it now about two brothers, and one of them steals the child away and puts another in his place, and then he gets found out, and all that, and he's just been falling off a bridge now.* * *

"After mother died, sister still kept on making nets,[1] and I lived with her for some time, until she told me she couldn't afford to keep me no longer, though she seemed to have a pretty good lot to do; but she would never let me go with her to the shops, though I could crochet, which she'd learned me, and used to run and get her all her silks and things what she wanted. But she was keeping company with a young man, and one day they went out, and came back and said they'd been and got married. It was him as got rid of me.

"He was kind to me for the first two or three months, while he was keeping her company; but before he was married he got a little cross, and after he was married he begun to get more cross, and used to send me to play in the streets, and tell me not to come home again till night. One day he hit me, and I said I wouldn't be hit about by him, and then at tea that night sister gave me three shillings, and told me I must go and get my own living. So I bought a box and brushes (they cost me just the money) and went cleaning boots, and I done pretty well with them, till my box was stole from me by a boy where I was lodging. He's in prison now—got six calendar for picking pockets.

"Sister kept all my clothes. When I asked her for 'em, she said they was disposed of along with all mother's goods; but she gave me some shirts and stockings, and such-like, and I had very good clothes, only they was all worn out. I saw sister after I left her, many times. I asked her many times to take me back, but she used to say, 'It

---

1. Hair-nets, which she sold to hair-dressers.

was not her likes, but her husband's, or she'd have had me back;' and I think it was true, for until he came she was a kind-hearted girl; but he said he'd enough to do to look after his own living; he was a fancy-baker by trade.

"I was fifteen the 24th of last May, sir, and I've been sweeping crossings now near upon two years. There's a party of six of us, and we have the crossings from St. Martin's Church as far as Pall Mall. I always go along with them as lodges in the same place as I do. In the daytime, if it's dry, we do anythink what we can—open cabs, or anythink; but if it's wet, we separate, and I and another gets a crossing—those who gets on it first, keeps it,—and we stand on each side and take our chance.

"We do it in this way:—if I was to see two gentlemen coming, I should cry out, 'Two toffs!' and then they are mine; and whether they give me anythink or not they are mine, and my mate is bound not to follow them; for if he did he would get a hiding from the whole lot of us. If we both cry out together, then we share. If it's a lady and gentleman, then we cries, 'A toff and a doll!' Sometimes we are caught out in this way. Perhaps it is a lady and gentleman and a child; and if I was to see them, and only say, 'A toff and a doll,' and leave out the child, then my mate can add the child; and as he is right and I wrong, then it's his party.

"If there's a policeman close at hand we mustn't ask for money; but we are always on the look-out for the policemen, and if we see one, then we calls out 'Phillup!' for that's our signal. One of the policemen at St. Martin's Church—Bandy, we calls him—knows what Phillup means, for he's up to us; so we had to change the word. (At the request of the young crossing-sweeper the present signal is omitted.)

"Yesterday on the crossing I got threepence halfpenny, but when it's dry like to-day I do nothink, for I haven't got a penny yet. We never carries no pockets, for if the policemen find us we generally pass the money to our mates, for if money's found on us we have fourteen days in prison. * * *

"When we see the rain we say together, 'Oh! there's a jolly good rain! we'll have a good day to-morrow.' If a shower comes on, and we are at our room, which we general are about three o'clock, to get somethink to eat—besides, we general go there to see how much each other's taken in the day—why, out we run with our brooms. * * *

"When we gets home at half-past three in the morning, whoever cries out 'first wash' has it. First of all we washes our feet, and we all uses the same water. Then we washes our faces and hands, and necks, and whoever fetches the fresh water up has first wash; and if the second don't like to go and get fresh, why he uses the dirty. Whenever we come in the landlady makes us wash our feet. Very often the stones cuts our feet and makes them bleed; then we bind a bit of rag round them. * * *

"When there's snow on the ground we puts our money together, and goes and buys an old shovel, and then, about seven o'clock in the morning, we goes to the shops and asks them if we shall scrape the snow away. We general gets twopence every house, but some gives sixpence, for it's very hard to clean the snow away, particular when it's been on the ground some time. It's awful cold, and gives us chilblains on our feet; but we don't mind it when we're working, for we soon gets hot then.

1849–1850   1861–1862

[END OF PERSPECTIVES: THE INDUSTRIAL LANDSCAPE]

John Stuart Mill

1806–1873

The name John Stuart Mill has become synonymous with genius. But for the Victorians it was also associated with outrageously radical views: Mill advocated sexual equality, the right to divorce, universal suffrage, free speech, and proportional representation. He first gained public attention as a social reformer, promoting the rationalist ideas of his godfather, Jeremy Bentham, founder of Utilitarianism. Mill went on to become the era's leading philosopher and political theorist, an outspoken member of Parliament, and Britain's most prestigious proponent of women's rights.

Mill's education is legendary: the Victorians were fond of social experiments, but few were stranger and more disturbing than James Mill's efforts to prove that a child could learn so much so early in life. He began teaching his son Greek at the age of three, making him memorize long lists of Greek words and their English translations. He also "home-schooled" his son in history, languages, calculus, logic, political economy, geography, psychology, and rhetoric. The boy's responsibilities included tutoring his younger siblings—eventually, eight of them—in these subjects. All this went on while his father, busy writing his multivolume *History of British India*, surveyed his children from the other end of the dining-room table.

As Mill's *Autobiography* shows, the human cost of the experiment was high. In an early draft he wrote that "I . . . grew up in the absence of love & in the presence of fear." His stern father denied Mill both pleasures and playmates, and so dominated the boy's mother that he interpreted her submissiveness as indifference to his existence. At fourteen, when his father declared his education finished, Mill had, by his own account, the knowledge of a man of forty—but he still could not brush his own hair.

Undaunted by such trivia, Mill decided he wanted to be "a reformer of the world." When he was seventeen, he founded the Utilitarian Society, which vigorously debated how to achieve the Utilitarian goal of bringing the greatest happiness to the greatest number of people. But at twenty he was plunged into depression when he realized that achieving all his goals would not satisfy him: "I seemed to have nothing left to live for." Overwork and the utter neglect of human emotion in his otherwise comprehensive education led Mill to a nervous breakdown in 1826.

Discovering that "the habit of analysis has a tendency to wear away the feelings," Mill gradually recovered by reading poetry, especially that of Wordsworth. The poet aroused his interest in "the common feelings and common destiny of human beings." Despite his assessment of himself as an "unpoetical nature," Mill became one of the most astute critics of his generation, recognizing before anyone else the unusual strengths and psychological motivations of both Tennyson and Browning. His essay *What is Poetry?* (1833) argues that true poetry expresses the passionate, solitary meditations of the author; it is not so much heard as "*overheard.*"

In 1823 Mill followed in his father's footsteps by taking a clerkship in the Examiner's Office of the East India Company, the commercial enterprise that, in effect, governed British India. He eventually headed the department, as his father had before him. The center of his professional life, however, was his own writing and political activism. His position allowed him time to become an energetic propagandist for radical causes and legal reform—he was even arrested at age seventeen, a few weeks after the job began, for distributing information on birth control. He also edited the *London and Westminster Review* (1836–1840), while writing important essays on Coleridge and Jeremy Bentham. His *System of Logic* (1843) and *Principles of Political Economy* (1848) immediately became standard works in the field; he followed these with influential books on philosophy, politics, and economics, including *Thoughts on Parliamentary Reform* (1859), *Utilitarianism* (1861), *Representative Government* (1861), and *Auguste Comte and Positivism* (1865).

The most significant event of Mill's adult life was meeting the brilliant and beautiful Harriet Taylor in 1830. She shared his radical views on women's rights, and they soon formed an intimate friendship. But she was married and the mother of three children, a fact which lent piquancy to their efforts to establish the legal right of divorce. They finally married in 1851, after the death of her husband. Mill claimed that she deserved equal credit for his works, calling them "joint productions" of their intellectual life together. "When two persons have their thoughts and speculations completely in common," he wrote in his *Autobiography*, "it is of little consequence . . . which of them holds the pen." After Harriet Taylor died in 1858, her daughter Helen became Mill's companion; she carried on their work in woman's rights into the twentieth century.

Mill retired from the East India Company in 1858 when the British government took over the company's affairs. Although he refused to seek votes or curry favor with any constituency, Mill was elected Member of Parliament for Westminster from 1865 to 1868, making memorable speeches on behalf of political reform, Irish freedom, and women's voting rights. A century ahead of mainstream Anglo-American lawmakers, he demanded nonsexist language for legislation, including a proposal that the Second Reform Bill (1867) be rewritten to replace the word "man" with the word "person." After his defeat in the election of 1868, Mill spent most of his remaining years in Avignon, France, where he died in 1873.

In the twentieth century, Mill's reputation has been sustained by the continuing relevance of his work. *On Liberty* (1859) has become the classic defense of the individual's right, in a modern society dominated by bureaucracy and mass culture, to resist the constraints of both government and public opinion. *The Subjection of Women* (1869) insists that men should grant "perfect equality" to women, demonstrating that "what is now called the nature of women is an eminently artificial thing—the result of forced repression in some directions, unnatural stimulation in others." These works also embody Mill's distinctive qualities as a writer and thinker: his arguments unfold with exceptional clarity, anticipating objections and providing interesting examples to prove his points; he makes his appeals to the reader on the basis of reason, no matter how emotionally charged the topic may be; and he displays an underlying concern for what is good for the public at large. Never content merely to assert human rights or display moral outrage, Mill dedicated himself to convincing others that freedom of thought and action—for women as well as for men—is not simply right but beneficial to society as a whole.

from On Liberty
from *Chapter 2. Of the Liberty of Thought and Discussion*

The time, it is to be hoped, is gone by, when any defence would be necessary of the "liberty of the press" as one of the securities against corrupt or tyrannical government. * * * If all mankind minus one, were of one opinion, and only one person were of the contrary opinion, mankind would be no more justified in silencing that one person, than he, if he had the power, would be justified in silencing mankind. Were an opinion a personal possession of no value except to the owner; if to be obstructed in the enjoyment of it were simply a private injury, it would make some difference whether the injury was inflicted only on a few persons or on many. But the peculiar evil of silencing the expression of an opinion is, that it is robbing the human race; posterity as well as the existing generation; those who dissent from the opinion, still more than those who hold it. If the opinion is right, they are deprived of the opportunity of exchanging error for truth: if wrong, they lose, what is almost as great a benefit, the clearer perception and livelier impression of truth, produced by its collision with error.

* * * The majority of the eminent men of every past generation held many opinions now known to be erroneous, and did or approved numerous things which no one will now justify. Why is it, then, that there is on the whole a preponderance among mankind of rational opinions and rational conduct? If there really is this preponderance—which there must be unless human affairs are, and have always been, in an almost desperate state—it is owing to a quality of the human mind, the source of everything respectable in man either as an intellectual or as a moral being, namely, that his errors are corrigible. He is capable of rectifying his mistakes, by discussion and experience. Not by experience alone. There must be discussion, to show how experience is to be interpreted. Wrong opinions and practices gradually yield to fact and argument: but facts and arguments, to produce any effect on the mind, must be brought before it. Very few facts are able to tell their own story, without comments to bring out their meaning. The whole strength and value, then, of human judgment, depending on the one property, that it can be set right when it is wrong, reliance can be placed on it only when the means of setting it right are kept constantly at hand. In the case of any person whose judgment is really deserving of confidence, how has it become so? Because he has kept his mind open to criticism of his opinions and conduct. Because it has been his practice to listen to all that could be said against him; to profit by as much of it as was just, and expound to himself, and upon occasion to others, the fallacy of what was fallacious. Because he has felt, that the only way in which a human being can make some approach to knowing the whole of a subject, is by hearing what can be said about it by persons of every variety of opinion, and studying all modes in which it can be looked at by every character of mind. No wise man ever acquired his wisdom in any mode but this. * * *

In the present age—which has been described as "destitute of faith, but terrified at scepticism"[1]—in which people feel sure, not so much that their opinions are true, as that they should not know what to do without them—the claims of an opinion to be protected from public attack are rested not so much on its truth, as on its importance to society. There are, it is alleged, certain beliefs, so useful, not to say indispensable to well-being, that it is as much the duty of governments to uphold those beliefs, as to protect any other of the interests of society. In a case of such necessity, and so directly in the line of their duty, something less than infallibility may, it is maintained, warrant, and even bind, governments, to act on their own opinion, confirmed by the general opinion of mankind. It is also often argued, and still oftener thought, that none but bad men would desire to weaken these salutary beliefs; and there can be nothing wrong, it is thought, in restraining bad men, and prohibiting what only such men would wish to practise. This mode of thinking makes the justification of restraints on discussion not a question of the truth of doctrines, but of their usefulness; and flatters itself by that means to escape the responsibility of claiming to be an infallible judge of opinions. But those who thus satisfy themselves, do not perceive that the assumption of infallibility is merely shifted from one point to another. The usefulness of an opinion is itself matter of opinion: as disputable, as open to discussion, and requiring discussion as much, as the opinion itself. There is the same need of an infallible judge of opinions to decide an opinion to be noxious, as to decide it to be false, unless the

1. By Thomas Carlyle in *Memoirs of the Life of Scott* (1838).

opinion condemned has full opportunity of defending itself. And it will not do to say that the heretic may be allowed to maintain the utility or harmlessness of his opinion, though forbidden to maintain its truth. The truth of an opinion is part of its utility. If we would know whether or not it is desirable that a proposition should be believed, is it possible to exclude the consideration of whether or not it is true? * * *

We have now recognised the necessity to the mental well-being of mankind (on which all their other well-being depends) of freedom of opinion, and freedom of the expression of opinion, on four distinct grounds; which we will now briefly recapitulate.

First, if any opinion is compelled to silence, that opinion may, for aught we can certainly know, be true. To deny this is to assume our own infallibility.

Secondly, though the silenced opinion be an error, it may, and very commonly does, contain a portion of truth; and since the general or prevailing opinion on any subject is rarely or never the whole truth, it is only by the collision of adverse opinions that the remainder of the truth has any chance of being supplied.

Thirdly, even if the received opinion be not only true, but the whole truth; unless it is suffered to be, and actually is, vigorously and earnestly contested, it will, by most of those who receive it, be held in the manner of a prejudice, with little comprehension or feeling of its rational grounds. And not only this, but, fourthly, the meaning of the doctrine itself will be in danger of being lost, or enfeebled, and deprived of its vital effect on the character and conduct: the dogma becoming a mere formal profession, inefficacious for good, but cumbering the ground, and preventing the growth of any real and heartfelt conviction, from reason or personal experience.

from *Chapter 3. Of Individuality, as One of the Elements of Well-Being*

* * * The majority, being satisfied with the ways of mankind as they now are (for it is they who make them what they are), cannot comprehend why those ways should not be good enough for everybody; and what is more, spontaneity forms no part of the ideal of the majority of moral and social reformers, but is rather looked on with jealousy, as a troublesome and perhaps rebellious obstruction to the general acceptance of what these reformers, in their own judgment, think would be best for mankind. Few persons, out of Germany, even comprehend the meaning of the doctrine which Wilhelm Von Humboldt, so eminent both as a *savant* and as a politician, made the text of a treatise—that "the end of man, or that which is prescribed by the eternal or immutable dictates of reason, and not suggested by vague and transient desires, is the highest and most harmonious development of his powers to a complete and consistent whole;" that, therefore, the object "towards which every human being must ceaselessly direct his efforts, and on which especially those who design to influence their fellow-men must ever keep their eyes, is the individuality of power and development;" that for this there are two requisites, "freedom, and variety of situations;" and that from the union of these arise "individual vigour and manifold diversity," which combine themselves in "originality."[1]

Little, however, as people are accustomed to a doctrine like that of Von Humboldt, and surprising as it may be to them to find so high a value attached to individuality, the question, one must nevertheless think, can only be one of degree. No one's idea of excellence in conduct is that people should do absolutely nothing but

1. From *The Sphere and Duties of Government* by Baron Wilhelm von Humboldt. Although written in 1791, this treatise was not published until 1852; it was translated into English in 1854.

copy one another. No one would assert that people ought not to put into their mode of life, and into the conduct of their concerns, any impress whatever of their own judgment, or of their own individual character. On the other hand, it would be absurd to pretend that people ought to live as if nothing whatever had been known in the world before they came into it; as if experience had as yet done nothing towards showing that one mode of existence, or of conduct, is preferable to another. Nobody denies that people should be so taught and trained in youth, as to know and benefit by the ascertained results of human experience. But it is the privilege and proper condition of a human being, arrived at the maturity of his faculties, to use and interpret experience in his own way. It is for him to find out what part of recorded experience is properly applicable to his own circumstances and character. * * *

He who lets the world, or his own portion of it, choose his plan of life for him, has no need of any other faculty than the ape-like one of imitation. He who chooses his plan for himself, employs all his faculties.

* * * A person whose desires and impulses are his own—are the expression of his own nature, as it has been developed and modified by his own culture—is said to have a character. One whose desires and impulses are not his own, has no character, no more than a steam-engine has a character. If, in addition to being his own, his impulses are strong, and are under the government of a strong will, he has an energetic character. Whoever thinks that individuality of desires and impulses should not be encouraged to unfold itself, must maintain that society has no need of strong natures—is not the better for containing many persons who have much character—and that a high general average of energy is not desirable.

In some early states of society, these forces might be, and were, too much ahead of the power which society then possessed of disciplining and controlling them. There has been a time when the element of spontaneity and individuality was in excess, and the social principle had a hard struggle with it. The difficulty then was, to induce men of strong bodies or minds to pay obedience to any rules which required them to control their impulses. To overcome this difficulty, law and discipline, like the Popes struggling against the Emperors, asserted a power over the whole man, claiming to control all his life in order to control his character—which society had not found any other sufficient means of binding. But society has now fairly got the better of individuality; and the danger which threatens human nature is not the excess, but the deficiency, of personal impulses and preferences. Things are vastly changed, since the passions of those who were strong by station or by personal endowment were in a state of habitual rebellion against laws and ordinances, and required to be rigorously chained up to enable the persons within their reach to enjoy any particle of security. In our times, from the highest class of society down to the lowest, every one lives as under the eye of a hostile and dreaded censorship. Not only in what concerns others, but in what concerns only themselves, the individual or the family do not ask themselves—what do I prefer? or, what would suit my character and disposition? or, what would allow the best and highest in me to have fair play, and enable it to grow and thrive? They ask themselves, what is suitable to my position? what is usually done by persons of my station and pecuniary circumstances? or (worse still) what is usually done by persons of a station and circumstances superior to mine? I do not mean that they choose what is customary, in preference to what suits their own inclination. It does not occur to them to have any inclination, except for what is customary. Thus the mind itself is bowed to the yoke: even in what people do for pleasure, conformity is the first thing thought of; they like in crowds; they exercise choice only among things commonly done: peculiarity of taste, eccentricity of conduct, are shunned equally with crimes: until by dint of not following their own nature, they have no nature to follow: their human capacities are withered and starved: they become incapable of any strong wishes or native pleasures, and are generally without either opinions or feelings of home growth, or properly their own. Now is this, or is it not, the desirable condition of human nature?* * *

Having said that Individuality is the same thing with development, and that it is only the cultivation of individuality which produces, or can produce, well-developed human beings, I might here close the argument: for what more or better can be said of any condition of human affairs, than that it brings human beings themselves nearer to the best thing they can be? or what worse can be said of any obstruction to good, than that it prevents this? Doubtless, however, these considerations will not suffice to convince those who most need convincing; and it is necessary further to show, that these developed human beings are of some use to the undeveloped—to point out to those who do not desire liberty, and would not avail themselves of it, that they may be in some intelligible manner rewarded for allowing other people to make use of it without hindrance.

In the first place, then, I would suggest that they might possibly learn something from them. It will not be denied by anybody, that originality is a valuable element in human affairs. There is always need of persons not only to discover new truths, and point out when what were once truths are true no longer, but also to commence new practices, and set the example of more enlightened conduct, and better taste and sense in human life. * * * Persons of genius, it is true, are, and are always likely to be, a small minority; but in order to have them, it is necessary to preserve the soil in which they grow. Genius can only breathe freely in an *atmosphere* of freedom. Persons of genius are, *ex vi termini* [by definition], *more* individual than any other people—less capable, consequently, of fitting themselves, without hurtful compression, into any of the small number of moulds which society provides in order to save its members the trouble of forming their own character. If from timidity they consent to be forced into one of these moulds, and to let all that part of themselves which cannot expand under the pressure remain unexpanded, society will be little the better for their genius. If they are of a strong character, and break their fetters, they become a mark for the society which has not succeeded in reducing them to commonplace, to point at with solemn warning as "wild," "erratic," and the like; much as if one should complain of the Niagara river for not flowing smoothly between its banks like a Dutch canal.* * *

In sober truth, whatever homage may be professed, or even paid, to real or supposed mental superiority, the general tendency of things throughout the world is to render mediocrity the ascendant power among mankind. In ancient history, in the middle ages, and in a diminishing degree through the long transition from feudality to the present time, the individual was a power in himself; and if he had either great talents or a high social position, he was a considerable power. At present individuals are lost in the crowd. In politics it is almost a triviality to say that public opinion now rules the world. The only power deserving the name is that of masses, and of governments while they make themselves the organ of the tendencies and instincts of masses. This is as true in the moral and social relations of private life as in public transactions. Those whose opinions go by the name of public opinion, are not always the same sort of public: in America they are the whole white population; in England, chiefly the middle class. But they are always a mass, that is to say, collective mediocrity. And what is a still greater novelty, the mass do not now take their opinions from dignitaries in Church or State, from ostensible leaders, or from books. Their thinking is done for them by men much like themselves, addressing them or speaking in their name, on the spur of the moment, through the newspapers. I am not complaining of all this. I do not assert that anything better is compatible, as a general rule, with the present low state of the human mind. But that does not hinder the government of mediocrity from being mediocre government. No government by a democracy or a numerous aristocracy, either in its political acts or in the opinions, qualities, and tone of mind which it fosters, ever did or could rise above mediocrity, except in so far as the sovereign Many have let themselves be guided (which in their best times they always have done) by the counsels and influence of a more highly gifted and instruct-ed One or Few. The initiation of all wise or noble things, comes and must come from individuals; generally at first from some one individual. The honour and glory of the average man is that he is capable of following that initiative; that he can respond internally to wise and noble things, and be led to them with his eyes open. I am not countenancing the sort of "hero-worship" which applauds the strong man of genius for forcibly seizing on the government of the world and making it do his bidding in spite of itself.[2] All he can claim is, freedom to point out the way. The power of com-pelling others into it, is not only inconsistent with the freedom and development of all the rest, but corrupting to the strong man himself. It does seem, however, that when the opinions of masses of merely average men are everywhere become or becoming the dominant power, the counterpoise and corrective to that tendency would be, the more and more pronounced individuality of those who stand on the higher eminences of thought. It is in these circumstances most especially, that excep-tional individuals, instead of being deterred, should be encouraged in acting differ-ently from the mass. In other times there was no advantage in their doing so, unless they acted not only differently, but better. In this age, the mere example of noncon-formity, the mere refusal to bend the knee to custom, is itself a service. Precisely because the tyranny of opinion is such as to make eccentricity a reproach, it is desir-able, in order to break through that tyranny, that people should be eccentric. Eccen-tricity has always abounded when and where strength of character has abounded; and the amount of eccentricity in a society has generally been proportional to the amount of genius, mental vigour, and moral courage which it contained. That so few now dare to be eccentric, marks the chief danger of the time. * * *

* * * We have discarded the fixed costumes of our forefathers; every one must still dress like other people, but the fashion may change once or twice a year. We thus take care that when there is change it shall be for change's sake, and not from any idea of beauty or convenience; for the same idea of beauty or convenience would not strike all the world at the same moment, and be simultaneously thrown aside by all at another moment. But we are progressive as well as changeable: we continually make new inven-tions in mechanical things, and keep them until they are again superseded by better; we are eager for improvement in politics, in education, even in morals, though in this last our idea of improvement chiefly consists in persuading or forcing other people to be as good as ourselves. It is not progress that we object to; on the contrary, we flatter our-selves that we are the most progressive people who ever lived. It is individuality that we war against: we should think we had done wonders if we had made ourselves all alike;

2. Cf. Thomas Carlyle, *On Heroes and Hero-Worship* (1841).

forgetting that the unlikeness of one person to another is generally the first thing which draws the attention of either to the imperfection of his own type, and the superiority of another, or the possibility, by combining the advantages of both, of producing something better than either. We have a warning example in China—a nation of much talent, and, in some respects, even wisdom, owing to the rare good fortune of having been provided at an early period with a particularly good set of customs, the work, in some measure, of men to whom even the most enlightened European must accord, under certain limitations, the title of sages and philosophers. They are remarkable, too, in the excellence of their apparatus for impressing, as far as possible, the best wisdom they possess upon every mind in the community, and securing that those who have appropriated most of it shall occupy the posts of honour and power. Surely the people who did this have discovered the secret of human progressiveness, and must have kept themselves steadily at the head of the movement of the world. On the contrary, they have become stationary—have remained so for thousands of years; and if they are ever to be farther improved, it must be by foreigners. They have succeeded beyond all hope in what English philanthropists are so industriously working at—in making a people all alike, all governing their thoughts and conduct by the same maxims and rules; and these are the fruits. The modern *régime* of public opinion is, in an unorganized form, what the Chinese educational and political systems are in an organized; and unless individuality shall be able successfully to assert itself against this yoke, Europe, notwithstanding its noble antecedents and its professed Christianity, will tend to become another China.

1859

from The Subjection of Women
from *Chapter 1*

The object of this essay is to explain as clearly as I am able, the grounds of an opinion which I have held from the very earliest period when I had formed any opinions at all on social or political matters, and which, instead of being weakened or modified, has been constantly growing stronger by the progress of reflection and the experience of life: That the principle which regulates the existing social relations between the two sexes—the legal subordination of one sex to the other—is wrong in itself, and now one of the chief hindrances to human improvement; and that it ought to be replaced by a principle of perfect equality, admitting no power or privilege on the one side, nor disability on the other. * * *

* * * If the authority of men over women, when first established, had been the result of a conscientious comparison between different modes of constituting the government of society; if, after trying various other modes of social organization—the government of women over men, equality between the two, and such mixed and divided modes of government as might be invented—it had been decided, on the testimony of experience, that the mode in which women are wholly under the rule of men, having no share at all in public concerns, and each in private being under the legal obligation of obedience to the man with whom she has associated her destiny, was the arrangement most conducive to the happiness and well being of both; its general adoption might then be fairly thought to be some evidence that, at the time when it was adopted, it was the best: though even then the considerations which recommended it may, like so many other primeval social facts of the greatest impor-

tance, have subsequently, in the course of ages, ceased to exist. But the state of the case is in every respect the reverse of this. In the first place, the opinion in favour of the present system, which entirely subordinates the weaker sex to the stronger, rests upon theory only; for there never has been trial made of any other: so that experience, in the sense in which it is vulgarly opposed to theory, cannot be pretended to have pronounced any verdict. And in the second place, the adoption of this system of inequality never was the result of deliberation, or forethought, or any social ideas, or any notion whatever of what conduced to the benefit of humanity or the good order of society. It arose simply from the fact that from the very earliest twilight of human society, every woman (owing to the value attached to her by men, combined with her inferiority in muscular strength) was found in a state of bondage to some man. * * *

Some will object, that a comparison cannot fairly be made between the government of the male sex and the forms of unjust power which I have adduced in illustration of it,[1] since these are arbitrary, and the effect of mere usurpation, while it on the contrary is natural. But was there ever any domination which did not appear natural to those who possessed it? There was a time when the division of mankind into two classes, a small one of masters and a numerous one of slaves, appeared, even to the most cultivated minds, to be a natural, and the only natural, condition of the human race. No less an intellect, and one which contributed no less to the progress of human thought, than Aristotle, held this opinion without doubt or misgiving; and rested it on the same premises on which the same assertion in regard to the dominion of men over women is usually based, namely that there are different natures among mankind, free natures, and slave natures; that the Greeks were of a free nature, the barbarian races of Thracians and Asiatics of a slave nature.[2] But why need I go back to Aristotle? Did not the slaveowners of the Southern United States maintain the same doctrine, with all the fanaticism with which men cling to the theories that justify their passions and legitimate their personal interests? Did they not call heaven and earth to witness that the dominion of the white man over the black is natural, that the black race is by nature incapable of freedom, and marked out for slavery? some even going so far as to say that the freedom of manual labourers is an unnatural order of things anywhere. * * * The subjection of women to men being a universal custom, any departure from it quite naturally appears unnatural. But how entirely, even in this case, the feeling is dependent on custom, appears by ample experience. Nothing so much astonishes the people of distant parts of the world, when they first learn anything about England, as to be told that it is under a queen: the thing seems to them so unnatural as to be almost incredible. To Englishmen this does not seem in the least degree unnatural, because they are used to it; but they do feel it unnatural that women should be soldiers or members of Parliament. In the feudal ages, on the contrary, war and politics were not thought unnatural to women, because not unusual; it seemed natural that women of the privileged classes should be of manly character, inferior in nothing but bodily strength to their husbands and fathers. The independence of women seemed rather less unnatural to the Greeks than to other ancients, on account of the fabulous Amazons (whom they believed to be historical), and the partial example afforded by the Spartan women; who, though no less subordinate by law than in other Greek states, were more free in fact, and being trained to

1. Mill has been describing slave owners' power over slaves, or tyrants' power over their subjects.
2. In *Politics* Aristotle asserts that it is as natural for free men to rule over slaves as for men to rule over women (sec. 1260a2–14).

bodily exercises in the same manner with men, gave ample proof that they were not naturally disqualified for them. There can be little doubt that Spartan experience suggested to Plato, among many other of his doctrines, that of the social and political equality of the two sexes.[3]

But, it will be said, the rule of men over women differs from all these others in not being a rule of force: it is accepted voluntarily; women make no complaint, and are consenting parties to it. In the first place, a great number of women do not accept it. Ever since there have been women able to make their sentiments known by their writings (the only mode of publicity which society permits to them), an increasing number of them have recorded protests against their present social condition: and recently many thousands of them, headed by the most eminent women known to the public, have petitioned Parliament for their admission to the Parliamentary Suffrage.[4] The claim of women to be educated as solidly, and in the same branches of knowledge, as men, is urged with growing intensity, and with a great prospect of success; while the demand for their admission into professions and occupations hitherto closed against them, becomes every year more urgent. Though there are not in this country, as there are in the United States, periodical Conventions and an organized party to agitate for the Rights of Women, there is a numerous and active Society organized and managed by women, for the more limited object of obtaining the political franchise. * * *

All causes, social and natural, combine to make it unlikely that women should be collectively rebellious to the power of men. They are so far in a position different from all other subject classes, that their masters require something more from them than actual service. Men do not want solely the obedience of women, they want their sentiments. All men, except the most brutish, desire to have, in the woman most nearly connected with them, not a forced slave but a willing one, not a slave merely, but a favourite. They have therefore put everything in practice to enslave their minds. The masters of all other slaves rely, for maintaining obedience, on fear; either fear of themselves, or religious fears. The masters of women wanted more than simple obedience, and they turned the whole force of education to effect their purpose. All women are brought up from the very earliest years in the belief that their ideal of character is the very opposite to that of men; not self-will, and government by self-control, but submission, and yielding to the control of others. All the moralities tell them that it is the duty of women, and all the current sentimentalities that it is their nature, to live for others; to make complete abnegation of themselves, and to have no life but in their affections. And by their affections are meant the only ones they are allowed to have—those to the men with whom they are connected, or to the children who constitute an additional and indefeasible tie between them and a man. When we put together three things—first, the natural attraction between opposite sexes; secondly, the wife's entire dependence on the husband, every privilege or pleasure she has being either his gift, or depending entirely on his will; and lastly, that the principal object of human pursuit, consideration, and all objects of social ambition, can in general be sought or obtained by her only through him—it would be a miracle if the object of being attractive to men had not become the polar star of feminine education and formation of character. * * *

* * *But I may go farther, and maintain that the course of history, and the tendencies of progressive human society, afford not only no presumption in favour of

3. See *The Republic*, 5: "Then, if we are to set women to the same tasks as men, we must teach them the same things. They must have the same two branches of training for mind and body and also be taught the art of war, and they must receive the same treatment" (trans. by F. M. Cornford).
4. This petition was presented in the House of Commons in 1866 by Mill himself; he was the first member of Parliament to advocate women's suffrage.

this system of inequality of rights, but a strong one against it; and that, so far as the whole course of human improvement up to this time, the whole stream of modern tendencies, warrants any inference on the subject, it is, that this relic of the past is discordant with the future, and must necessarily disappear.

For, what is the peculiar character of the modern world—the difference which chiefly distinguishes modern institutions, modern social ideas, modern life itself, from those of times long past? It is, that human beings are no longer born to their place in life, and chained down by an inexorable bond to the place they are born to, but are free to employ their faculties, and such favourable chances as offer, to achieve the lot which may appear to them most desirable. * * *

The social subordination of women thus stands out an isolated fact in modern social institutions; a solitary breach of what has become their fundamental law; a single relic of an old world of thought and practice exploded in everything else, but retained in the one thing of most universal interest; as if a gigantic dolmen,[5] or a vast temple of Jupiter Olympius, occupied the site of St. Paul's and received daily worship, while the surrounding Christian churches were only resorted to on fasts and festivals. * * *

Neither does it avail anything to say that the *nature* of the two sexes adapts them to their present functions and position, and renders these appropriate to them. Standing on the ground of common sense and the constitution of the human mind, I deny that any one knows, or can know, the nature of the two sexes, as long as they have only been seen in their present relation to one another. If men had ever been found in society without women, or women without men, or if there had been a society of men and women in which the women were not under the control of the men, something might have been positively known about the mental and moral differences which may be inherent in the nature of each. What is now called the nature of women is an eminently artificial thing—the result of forced repression in some directions, unnatural stimulation in others. It may be asserted without scruple, that no other class of dependents have had their character so entirely distorted from its natural proportions by their relation with their masters; for, if conquered and slave races have been, in some respects, more forcibly repressed, whatever in them has not been crushed down by an iron heel has generally been let alone, and if left with any liberty of development, it has developed itself according to its own laws; but in the case of women, a hot-house and stove cultivation has always been carried on of some of the capabilities of their nature, for the benefit and pleasure of their masters. * * *

Even the preliminary knowledge, what the differences between the sexes now are, apart from all question as to how they are made what they are, is still in the crudest and most incomplete state. Medical practitioners and physiologists have ascertained, to some extent, the differences in bodily constitution; and this is an important element to the psychologist: but hardly any medical practitioner is a psychologist. Respecting the mental characteristics of women; their observations are of no more worth than those of common men. It is a subject on which nothing final can be known, so long as those who alone can really know it, women themselves, have given but little testimony, and that little, mostly suborned. It is easy to know stupid women. Stupidity is much the same all the world over. A stupid person's notions and feelings may confidently be inferred from those which prevail in the circle by which the person is surrounded. Not so with those whose opinions and feelings are an emanation from their own nature and faculties. It is only a man here and there

5. Prehistoric monument of standing stones, associated with pagan religious rites.

who has any tolerable knowledge of the character even of the women of his own family. I do not mean, of their capabilities; these nobody knows, not even themselves, because most of them have never been called out. I mean their actually existing thoughts and feelings. Many a man thinks he perfectly understands women, because he has had amatory relations with several, perhaps with many of them. If he is a good observer, and his experience extends to quality as well as quantity, he may have learnt something of one narrow department of their nature—an important department, no doubt. But of all the rest of it, few persons are generally more ignorant, because there are few from whom it is so carefully hidden. The most favourable case which a man can generally have for studying the character of a woman, is that of his own wife: for the opportunities are greater, and the cases of complete sympathy not so unspeakably rare. And in fact, this is the source from which any knowledge worth having on the subject has, I believe, generally come. But most men have not had the opportunity of studying in this way more than a single case: accordingly one can, to an almost laughable degree, infer what a man's wife is like, from his opinions about women in general. To make even this one case yield any result, the woman must be worth knowing, and the man not only a competent judge, but of a character so sympathetic in itself, and so well adapted to hers, that he can either read her mind by sympathetic intuition, or has nothing in himself which makes her shy of disclosing it. Hardly anything, I believe, can be more rare than this conjunction. It often happens that there is the most complete unity of feeling and community of interests as to all external things, yet the one has as little admission into the internal life of the other as if they were common acquaintance. Even with true affection, authority on the one side and subordination on the other prevent perfect confidence. Though nothing may be intentionally withheld, much is not shown. * * * When we further consider that to understand one woman is not necessarily to understand any other woman; that even if he could study many women of one rank, or of one country, he would not thereby understand women of other ranks or countries; and even if he did, they are still only the women of a single period of history; we may safely assert that the knowledge which men can acquire of women, even as they have been and are, without reference to what they might be, is wretchedly imperfect and superficial, and always will be so, until women themselves have told all that they have to tell.

And this time has not come; nor will it come otherwise than gradually. It is but of yesterday that women have either been qualified by literary accomplishments, or permitted by society, to tell anything to the general public. As yet very few of them dare tell anything, which men, on whom their literary success depends, are unwilling to hear. Let us remember in what manner, up to a very recent time, the expression, even by a male author, of uncustomary opinions, or what are deemed eccentric feelings, usually was, and in some degree still is, received; and we may form some faint conception under what impediments a woman, who is brought up to think custom and opinion her sovereign rule, attempts to express in books anything drawn from the depths of her own nature. * * * Literary women are becoming more freespoken, and more willing to express their real sentiments. Unfortunately, in this country especially, they are themselves such artificial products, that their sentiments are compounded of a small element of individual observation and consciousness, and a very large one of acquired associations. This will be less and less the case, but it will remain true to a great extent, as long as social institutions do not admit the same free development of originality in women which is possible to men. When that time comes, and not before, we shall see, and not merely hear, as much as it is necessary to know of the nature of women, and the adaptation of other things to it. * * *

One thing we may be certain of—that what is contrary to women's nature to do, they never will be made to do by simply giving their nature free play. The anxiety of mankind to interfere in behalf of nature, for fear lest nature should not succeed in effecting its purpose, is an altogether unnecessary solicitude. What women by nature cannot do, it is quite superfluous to forbid them from doing. What they can do, but not so well as the men who are their competitors, competition suffices to exclude them from; since nobody asks for protective duties and bounties in favour of women; it is only asked that the present bounties and protective duties in favour of men should be recalled. If women have a greater natural inclination for some things than for others, there is no need of laws or social inculcation to make the majority of them do the former in preference to the latter. Whatever women's services are most wanted for, the free play of competition will hold out the strongest inducements to them to undertake. And, as the words imply, they are most wanted for the things for which they are most fit; by the apportionment of which to them, the collective faculties of the two sexes can be applied on the whole with the greatest sum of valuable result.

The general opinion of men is supposed to be, that the natural vocation of a woman is that of a wife and mother. I say, is supposed to be, because, judging from acts—from the whole of the present constitution of society—one might infer that their opinion was the direct contrary. They might be supposed to think that the alleged natural vocation of women was of all things the most repugnant to their nature; insomuch that if they are free to do anything else—if any other means of living, or occupation of their time and faculties, is open, which has any chance of appearing desirable to them—there will not be enough of them who will be willing to accept the condition said to be natural to them. If this is the real opinion of men in general, it would be well that it should be spoken out. I should like to hear somebody openly enunciating the doctrine (it is already implied in much that is written on the subject)—"It is necessary to society that women should marry and produce children. They will not do so unless they are compelled. Therefore it is necessary to compel them." The merits of the case would then be clearly defined. It would be exactly that of the slaveholders of South Carolina and Louisiana. "It is necessary that cotton and sugar should be grown. White men cannot produce them. Negroes will not, for any wages which we choose to give. *Ergo* they must be compelled." An illustration still closer to the point is that of impressment.[6] Sailors must absolutely be had to defend the country. It often happens that they will not voluntarily enlist. Therefore there must be the power of forcing them. How often has this logic been used! and, but for one flaw in it, without doubt it would have been successful up to this day. But it is open to the retort—First pay the sailors the honest value of their labour. When you have made it as well worth their while to serve you, as to work for other employers, you will have no more difficulty than others have in obtaining their services. To this there is no logical answer except "I will not": and as people are now not only ashamed, but are not desirous, to rob the labourer of his hire,[7] impressment is no longer advocated. Those who attempt to force women into marriage by closing all other doors against them, lay themselves open to a similar retort. If they mean what they say, their opinion must evidently be, that men do not render the married condition so desirable to women, as to induce them to accept it for its own recommendations. It is not a sign of one's thinking the boon one offers very attractive, when one allows only Hobson's choice, "that or

6. The practice of seizing men and forcing them to serve   7. Luke 10.7.
as sailors in the navy.

none." And here, I believe, is the clue to the feelings of those men, who have a real antipathy to the equal freedom of women. I believe they are afraid, not lest women should be unwilling to marry, for I do not think that any one in reality has that apprehension; but lest they should insist that marriage should be on equal conditions; lest all women of spirit and capacity should prefer doing almost anything else, not in their own eyes degrading, rather than marry, when marrying is giving themselves a master, and a master too of all their earthly possessions. And truly, if this consequence were necessarily incident to marriage, I think that the apprehension would be very well founded. I agree in thinking it probable that few women, capable of anything else, would, unless under an irresistible *entrainement* [enchantment], rendering them for the time insensible to anything but itself, choose such a lot, when any other means were open to them of filling a conventionally honourable place in life: and if men are determined that the law of marriage shall be a law of despotism, they are quite right, in point of mere policy, in leaving to women only Hobson's choice. But, in that case, all that has been done in the modern world to relax the chain on the minds of women, has been a mistake. They never should have been allowed to receive a literary education. Women who read, much more women who write, are, in the existing constitution of things, a contradiction and a disturbing element: and it was wrong to bring women up with any acquirements but those of an odalisque,[8] or of a domestic servant.
1860   1869

Statement Repudiating the Rights of Husbands[1]

6th March 1851

Being about, if I am so happy as to obtain her consent, to enter into the marriage relation with the only woman I have ever known, with whom I would have entered into that state; and the whole character of the marriage relation as constituted by law being such as both she and I entirely and conscientiously disapprove, for this among other reasons, that it confers upon one of the parties to the contract, legal power and control over the person, property, and freedom of action of the other party, independent of her own wishes and will; I, having no means of legally divesting myself of these odious powers (as I most assuredly would do if an engagement to that effect could be made legally binding on me), feel it my duty to put on record a formal protest against the existing law of marriage, in so far as conferring such powers; and a solemn promise never in any case or under any circumstances to use them. And in the event of marriage between Mrs. Taylor and me I declare it to be my will and intention, and the condition of the engagement between us, that she retains in all respects whatever the same absolute freedom of action, and freedom of disposal of herself and of all that does or may at any time belong to her, as if no such marriage had taken place; and I absolutely disclaim and repudiate all pretence to have acquired any *rights* whatever by virtue of such marriage.

J. S. Mill

---

8. Concubine in a harem.
1. At the time Mill wrote this, shortly before his marriage to Harriet Taylor, married women occupied a peculiar position under British law. A woman, upon her marriage, entered into a state called coverture. This meant she was subsumed into the legal personhood of her husband, and could neither sign legal contracts nor own property.

Elizabeth Barrett Browning
1806–1861

Elizabeth Barrett Browning was the most celebrated woman poet of the Victorian era. She was admired by contemporaries as varied as William Wordsworth, Queen Victoria, Edgar Allan Poe (who introduced an American edition of her work), Christina Rossetti, and John Ruskin (who proclaimed *Aurora Leigh* the greatest poem in English). Her popularity was especially remarkable because she interspersed her ardent love lyrics with hard-hitting poems on radical political causes and feminist themes. In the United States, she influenced not only sequestered writers like Emily Dickinson, but also political activists like Susan B. Anthony.

The eldest of eleven children, Elizabeth Barrett grew up in a country manorhouse called Hope End in Hertfordshire. The Barretts were a wealthy family whose fortune derived from a slave plantation in Jamaica. While her submissive mother, Mary Clark, encouraged her to write, it was her protective but authoritarian father, Edward Moulton-Barrett, who dominated her affections and received laudatory poems on his birthdays. From an early age Barrett envisioned herself combining male and female attributes to become "the feminine of Homer." As the critic Dorothy Mermin has pointed out, the ambitious child-poet was already imaginatively inhabiting two gender roles, the imprisoned female muse and the active male quester: "At five I supposed myself a heroine and in my day dreams of bliss I constantly imaged to myself a forlorn damsel in distress rescued by some noble knight."

Barrett took advantage of her family's resources to give herself an exceptional education, unusual for a woman of her day. Her passion for Greek poetry led her to translate Aeschylus's *Prometheus Bound* (1833). Two earlier works also reflected her wide reading: at twelve she wrote a four-book epic, *The Battle of Marathon,* which her father had privately printed, and at twenty she anonymously published a long philosophical poem, *An Essay on Mind, with Other Poems* (1826). But her intellectual development was offset by an illness that broke her health at the age of fifteen. Thereafter, her bold aspirations and mental energy were at odds with her semi-invalid state. Her sense of isolation increased in 1828 when her mother died, and again when declining family fortunes led her father to move the family from the home she loved, first to Sidmouth, Devon, in 1832 and then to London in 1835, where they eventually settled at 50 Wimpole Street.

It was here that Barrett became almost a recluse. Disliking the dirty, foggy city, she hardly left the house, but she corresponded avidly with a circle of literary and public figures. In 1838 chronic lung disease weakened her further; she already had developed what would be a lifelong dependence on morphine as a painkiller. Her doctors insisted that she go to Mediterranean climes, but the farthest her father would allow was Torquay, on the south coast of England. She lived there for three years, returning prostrate with grief after her brother Edward died in a boating accident. For the next several years, her spirits sustained only by her poetry, she worked, slept, and received visitors on a couch in a room sealed against the London air. Often exhausted, she was unable to see the aged Wordsworth when he came to pay his respects.

As she and her small circle of friends were quick to realize, Elizabeth Barrett had become like Tennyson's Lady of Shalott, having no other life but to weave her poetic web in solitude. *The Seraphim and Other Poems* (1838) established her reputation, and the two volumes of *Poems* (1844) consolidated her position as the era's finest "poetess." The latter book included *A Drama of Exile,* a sequel to Milton's *Paradise Lost* in which Eve emerges as a heroine, and also *The Cry of the Children*, condemning child labor in factories. Despite her oppositional politics, the suppleness of her thought and her passionate voice were so highly regarded by critics and public alike that she was mentioned as a candidate for Poet Laureate when Wordsworth died in 1850.

But by then she had utterly transformed her life. In 1845 she began corresponding with Robert Browning—she was nearly forty, and famous; he was thirty-three and his only reputation was for obscurity. Their literary friendship rapidly blossomed into romance, which they had to hide from her father, who had tacitly forbidden his children to marry. After a secret marriage in London in 1846, the couple eloped to Italy, where they settled in Florence at Casa Guidi. There, the fairy tale continued: happily married and living in a warm climate, she recovered much of her health, wrote her best work, gained the love of the Italians with her nationalistic verse, and gave birth to a son, Robert Weidemann Browning ("Pen"), in 1849. She had prophetically written to Browning, in the last letter before their elopement: "I begin to think that none are so bold as the timid, when they are fairly roused."

Her union with Robert Browning was responsible for two works that have since formed the cornerstone of her reputation. The first is their justly famous correspondence. The story of their courtship was widely known, but its intimate details were not revealed until the publication of their letters in 1899. Second, as their relationship developed she wrote a series of love poems to Browning. She finished the last poem two days before their wedding, and the collection was published in 1850, under the deliberately misleading title *Sonnets from the Portuguese*. Among the most significant sonnet sequences since those of Shakespeare and Sidney, these poems revived the form in Victorian England and revised in brilliant new ways what had hitherto been a primarily masculine poetic tradition. Casting the male recipient of her sonnets in the role of sexual object, yet also allowing for his reciprocal passion and poetic drive, Barrett Browning records the interplay of gifted lovers whose desire is inseparable from their quest for verbal mastery.

In her final years Barrett Browning's career continued to flourish. She and her husband enjoyed a wide circle of friends, including Tennyson, Ruskin, Carlyle, Rossetti, and Margaret Fuller. They traveled a great deal, to Rome, Paris, and several times back to London where they were warmly received by both their families—with the exception of her father, who refused to forgive or even see her again. In 1851 she published *Casa Guidi Windows*, which promoted the cause of Italian independence from Austria. *Poems Before Congress* (1860) stirred controversy in England over its volatile and "unwomanly" political views, particularly its scathing attack on American slavery. But her health was failing, and after recurrent illnesses, she died in Florence in her husband's arms. *Last Poems* appeared posthumously in 1862.

Her greatest achievement, however, lies in her verse novel, *Aurora Leigh* (1856), a daring combination of epic, romance, and *bildungsroman*. The first major poem in English in which the heroine, like the author, is a woman writer, *Aurora Leigh* rewrites Wordsworth's *The Prelude* from a female point of view. With its Miltonic echoes, the blank-verse format claims epic importance not only for the growth of the woman poet, but also for a woman's struggle to achieve artistic and economic independence in modern society. The poem blends these themes, moreover, with a witty, Byronic treatment of Victorian manners and social issues, and an emotionally charged love plot that recalls Charlotte Bronte's *Jane Eyre*. The story of how the aspiring poet Aurora Leigh overcomes the prejudices of both a masculine audience and the man she loves, in order to find fame and happiness in Italy, closely mirrors Barrett Browning's own. The poem was an overwhelming success, even though many contemporary readers were scandalized by its radical revision of Victorian ideals of femininity, and its picture of how the two sexes might work together so that each could achieve its fullest human potential. Scorning to measure herself against any but the greatest male authors, Elizabeth Barrett Browning was the first to show English readers the enormous possibilities of a poetic tradition in which women participated on equal terms.

from Sonnets from the Portuguese[1]

1

I thought once how Theocritus had sung
Of the sweet years, the dear and wished-for years,
Who each one in a gracious hand appears
To bear a gift for mortals, old or young:[2]

5 And, as I mused it in his antique tongue,[3]
I saw, in gradual vision through my tears,
The sweet, sad years, the melancholy years,
Those of my own life, who by turns had flung
A shadow across me. Straightway I was 'ware,

10 So weeping, how a mystic Shape did move
Behind me, and drew me backward by the hair;
And a voice said in mastery, while I strove,—
"Guess now who holds thee?"—"Death," I said. But, there,
The silver answer rang,—"Not Death, but Love."

13

And wilt thou have me fashion into speech
The love I bear thee, finding words enough,
And hold the torch out, while the winds are rough,
Between our faces, to cast light on each?—

5 I drop it at thy feet. I cannot teach
My hand to hold my spirit so far off
From myself—me—that I should bring thee proof
In words, of love hid in me out of reach.
Nay, let the silence of my womanhood

10 Commend my woman-love to thy belief,—
Seeing that I stand unwon, however wooed,
And rend the garment of my life, in brief,
By a most dauntless, voiceless fortitude,
Lest one touch of this heart convey its grief.

21

Say over again, and yet once over again,
That thou dost love me. Though the word repeated
Should seem "a cuckoo-song,"[4] as thou dost treat it,
Remember, never to the hill or plain,

---

1. These very personal poems chronicle Elizabeth Barrett's courtship with Robert Browning. She did not show them to him until after they were married, when he pronounced them "the finest sonnets written in any language since Shakespeare's." He overcame her reluctance to publish them by proposing the somewhat cryptic title implying that they are merely translations.

2. In *Idylls* 15, Theocritus, a Greek pastoral poet of the 3rd century B.C., tells how "the dainty-footed Hours" brought Adonis to Aphrodite. The song celebrates the return of spring, the season when Elizabeth Barrett first met Robert Browning.

3. I.e., Greek.

4. Repetitious, like the cuckoo's song.

5   Valley and wood, without her cuckoo-strain
      Comes the fresh Spring in all her green completed.
      Belovèd, I, amid the darkness greeted
      By a doubtful spirit-voice, in that doubt's pain
      Cry, "Speak once more—thou lovest!" Who can fear
10   Too many stars, though each in heaven shall roll,
      Too many flowers, though each shall crown the year?
      Say thou dost love me, love me, love me—toll
      The silver iterance!°—only minding, Dear,   repetition
      To love me also in silence with thy soul.

22

      When our two souls stand up erect and strong,
      Face to face, silent, drawing nigh and nigher,
      Until the lengthening wings break into fire
      At either curvèd point,—what bitter wrong
5   Can the earth do to us, that we should not long
      Be here contented? Think. In mounting higher,
      The angels would press on us and aspire
      To drop some golden orb of perfect song
      Into our deep, dear silence. Let us stay
10   Rather on earth, Belovèd,—where the unfit
      Contrarious moods of men recoil away
      And isolate pure spirits, and permit
      A place to stand and love in for a day,
      With darkness and the death-hour rounding it.

28

      My letters! all dead paper, mute and white!
      And yet they seem alive and quivering
      Against my tremulous hands which loose the string
      And let them drop down on my knee to-night.
5   This said,—he wished to have me in his sight
      Once, as a friend: this fixed a day in spring[5]
      To come and touch my hand . . . a simple thing,
      Yet I wept for it!—this, . . . the paper's light . . .
      Said, *Dear, I love thee*; and I sank and quailed
10   As if God's future thundered on my past.
      This said, *I am thine*—and so its ink has paled
      With lying at my heart that beat too fast.
      And this . . . O Love, thy words have ill availed
      If, what this said, I dared repeat at last!

32

      The first time that the sun rose on thine oath
      To love me, I looked forward to the moon

5. On May 17, 1845, Robert Browning wrote to arrange their first meeting: "I will call at two on Tuesday."

To slacken all those bonds which seemed too soon
And quickly tied to make a lasting troth.
5 Quick-loving hearts, I thought, may quickly loathe;
And, looking on myself, I seemed not one
For such man's love!—more like an out-of-tune
Worn viol, a good singer would be wroth
To spoil his song with, and which, snatched in haste,
10 Is laid down at the first ill-sounding note.
I did not wrong myself so, but I placed
A wrong on *thee*. For perfect strains may float
'Neath master-hands, from instruments defaced,—
And great souls, at one stroke, may do and doat.

38

First time he kissed me, he but only kissed
The fingers of this hand wherewith I write;
And ever since, it grew more clean and white,
Slow to world-greetings, quick with its "Oh, list,"°   listen
5 When the angels speak. A ring of amethyst
I could not wear here, plainer to my sight,
Than that first kiss. The second passed in height
The first, and sought the forehead, and half missed,
Half falling on the hair. O beyond meed!°   deserving
10 That was the chrism[6] of love, which love's own crown,
With sanctifying sweetness, did precede.
The third upon my lips was folded down
In perfect, purple state; since when, indeed,
I have been proud and said, "My love, my own."

43

How do I love thee? Let me count the ways.
I love thee to the depth and breadth and height
My soul can reach, when feeling out of sight
For the ends of Being and ideal Grace.
5 I love thee to the level of everyday's
Most quiet need, by sun and candle-light.
I love thee freely, as men strive for Right;
I love thee purely, as they turn from Praise.
I love thee with the passion put to use
10 In my old griefs, and with my childhood's faith.
I love thee with a love I seemed to lose
With my lost saints,—I love with the breath,
Smiles, tears, of all my life!—and, if God choose,
I shall but love thee better after death.

1845–1847   1850

---

6. Consecrated oil used to anoint during a coronation.
1. Barrett Browning called *Aurora Leigh*, a poem in nine books, a "verse novel." It portrays the struggles of a young poet to find her artistic voice and pursue her vocation despite the obstacles confronting a woman writer.

from **Aurora Leigh**[1]

from *Book 1*

[SELF-PORTRAIT]

Of writing many books there is no end;
And I who have written much in prose and verse
For others' uses, will write now for mine,—
Will write my story for my better self,
As when you paint your portrait for a friend,   5
Who keeps it in a drawer and looks at it
Long after he has ceased to love you, just
To hold together what he was and is.
I, writing thus, am still what men call young;
I have not so far left the coasts of life   10
To travel inward, that I cannot hear
That murmur of the outer Infinite
Which unweaned babies smile at in their sleep
When wondered at for smiling; not so far,
But still I catch my mother at her post   15
Beside the nursery door, with finger up,
"Hush, hush—here's too much noise!" while her sweet eyes
Leap forward, taking part against her word
In the child's riot. Still I sit and feel
My father's slow hand, when she had left us both,   20
Stroke out my childish curls across his knee,
And hear Assunta's daily jest (she knew
He liked it better than a better jest)
Inquire how many golden scudi[2] went
To make such ringlets. O my father's hand,   25
Stroke heavily, heavily the poor hair down,
Draw, press the child's head closer to thy knee!
I'm still too young, too young, to sit alone.
I write. My mother was a Florentine,
Whose rare blue eyes were shut from seeing me   30
When scarcely I was four years old, my life
A poor spark snatched up from a failing lamp
Which went out therefore. She was weak and frail;
She could not bear the joy of giving life,
The mother's rapture slew her. If her kiss   35
Had left a longer weight upon my lips
It might have steadied the uneasy breath,
And reconciled and fraternised my soul
With the new order. As it was, indeed,
I felt a mother-want about the world,   40
And still went seeking, like a bleating lamb
Left out at night in shutting up the fold,—
As restless as a nest-deserted bird
Grown chill through something being away, though what

<hr>

2. Italian coins; Assunta was Aurora's nurse.

45   It knows not. I, Aurora Leigh, was born
To make my father sadder, and myself
Not overjoyous, truly. Women know
The way to rear up children (to be just),
They know a simple, merry, tender knack
50   Of tying sashes, fitting baby-shoes,
And stringing pretty words that make no sense,
And kissing full sense into empty words,
Which things are corals to cut life upon,
Although such trifles: children learn by such,
55   Love's holy earnest in a pretty play
And get not over-early solemnised,
But seeing, as in a rose-bush, Love's Divine
Which burns and hurts not,—not a single bloom,—
Become aware and unafraid of Love.
60   Such good do mothers. Fathers love as well
—Mine did, I know,—but still with heavier brains,
And wills more consciously responsible,
And not as wisely, since less foolishly;
So mothers have God's license to be missed.

65   My father was an austere Englishman,
Who, after a dry lifetime spent at home
In college-learning, law, and parish talk,
Was flooded with a passion unaware,
His whole provisioned and complacent past
70   Drowned out from him that moment. As he stood
In Florence, where he had come to spend a month
And note the secret of Da Vinci's drains,[3]
He musing somewhat absently perhaps
Some English question . . . whether men should pay
75   The unpopular but necessary tax
With left or right hand—in the alien sun
In that great square of the Santissima[4]
There drifted past him (scarcely marked enough
To move his comfortable island scorn)
80   A train of priestly banners, cross and psalm,
The white-veiled rose-crowned maidens holding up
Tall tapers, weighty for such wrists, aslant
To the blue luminous tremor of the air,
And letting drop the white wax as they went
85   To eat the bishop's wafer[5] at the church;
From which long trail of chanting priests and girls,
A face flashed like a cymbal on his face
And shook with silent clangour brain and heart,
Transfiguring him to music. Thus, even thus,
90   He too received his sacramental gift
With eucharistic meanings; for he loved.

3. Leonardo da Vinci (1452–1519) was an architect and engineer, as well as an artist; he designed the aqueduct that supplied Milan's water.

4. The Florentine church of the Santissima Annunziata, or Holy Annunciation.
5. To take Holy Communion.

[HER MOTHER'S PORTRAIT]

And as I grew
In years, I mixed, confused, unconsciously,
Whatever I last read or heard or dreamed,
Abhorrent, admirable, beautiful,
150   Pathetical, or ghastly, or grotesque,
With still that face . . . which did not therefore change,
But kept the mystic level of all forms,
Hates, fears, and admirations, was by turns
Ghost, fiend, and angel, fairy, witch, and sprite,
155   A dauntless Muse who eyes a dreadful Fate,
A loving Psyche who loses sight of Love,[6]
A still Medusa[7] with mild milky brows
All curdled and all clothed upon with snakes
Whose slime falls fast as sweat will; or anon
160   Our Lady of the Passion, stabbed with swords
Where the Babe sucked; or Lamia[8] in her first
Moonlighted pallor, ere she shrunk and blinked
And shuddering wriggled down to the unclean;
Or my own mother, leaving her last smile
165   In her last kiss upon the baby-mouth
My father pushed down on the bed for that,—
Or my dead mother, without smile or kiss,
Buried at Florence. All which images,
Concentred on the picture, glassed themselves
170   Before my meditative childhood, as
The incoherencies of change and death
Are represented fully, mixed and merged,
In the smooth fair mystery of perpetual Life.

[AURORA'S EDUCATION]

Then, land!—then, England! oh, the frosty cliffs[9]
Looked cold upon me. Could I find a home
Among those mean red houses through the fog?
And when I heard my father's language first
255   From alien lips which had no kiss for mine
I wept aloud, then laughed, then wept, then wept,
And some one near me said the child was mad
Through much sea-sickness. The train swept us on:
Was this my father's England? the great isle?
260   The ground seemed cut up from the fellowship
Of verdure, field from field,[1] as man from man;
The skies themselves looked low and positive,
As almost you could touch them with a hand,
And dared to do it they were so far off

---

6. Psyche was beloved of Cupid (or Eros), whom she had never seen, because he always came to her after dark; one night she lit her lamp to look at him as he slept, whereupon he left her.
7. A gorgon, a female monster with serpents for hair, the sight of whom turned people to stone.
8. A monster with the head and upper body of a maiden, and lower body of a serpent.
9. The white chalk cliffs of Dover.
1. English fields are divided by hedgerows.

265 From God's celestial crystals;[2] all things blurred
And dull and vague. Did Shakespeare and his mates
Absorb the light here?—not a hill or stone
With heart to strike a radiant colour up
Or active outline on the indifferent air.

270 I think I see my father's sister stand
Upon the hall-step of her country-house
To give me welcome. She stood straight and calm,
Her somewhat narrow forehead braided tight
As if for taming accidental thoughts
275 From possible pulses;[3] brown hair pricked with gray
By frigid use of life (she was not old,
Although my father's elder by a year),
A nose drawn sharply, yet in delicate lines;
A close mild mouth, a little soured about
280 The ends, through speaking unrequited loves
Or peradventure niggardly half-truths;
Eyes of no colour,—once they might have smiled,
But never, never have forgot themselves
In smiling; cheeks, in which was yet a rose
285 Of perished summers, like a rose in a book,
Kept more for ruth° than pleasure,—if past bloom,   remorse
Past fading also.

           She had lived, we'll say,
A harmless life, she called a virtuous life,
A quiet life, which was not life at all
290 (But that, she had not lived enough to know),
Between the vicar and the country squires,
The lord-lieutenant looking down sometimes
From the empyrean to assure their souls
Against chance vulgarisms, and, in the abyss,
295 The apothecary, looked on once a year
To prove their soundness of humility.
The poor-club exercised her Christian gifts
Of knitting stockings, stitching petticoats,
Because we are of one flesh, after all,
300 And need one flannel° (with a proper sense   petticoat
Of difference in the quality)—and still
The book-club, guarded from your modern trick
Of shaking dangerous questions from the crease,[4]
Preserved her intellectual. She had lived
305 A sort of cage-bird life, born in a cage,
Accounting that to leap from perch to perch
Was act and joy enough for any bird.
Dear heaven, how silly are the things that live
In thickets, and eat berries!

---

2. The stars, or perhaps the crystalline sphere the ancients believed lay beyond them.
3. Pulsations of strong emotion.

4. Books were sold with their pages uncut; one had to cut the folds, or creases, to open the pages and read the book.

I, alas,

310 A wild bird scarcely fledged, was brought to her cage,
And she was there to meet me. Very kind.
Bring the clean water, give out the fresh seed.

She stood upon the steps to welcome me,
Calm, in black garb. I clung about her neck,—
315 Young babes, who catch at every shred of wool
To draw the new light closer, catch and cling
Less blindly. In my ears my father's word
Hummed ignorantly, as the sea in shells,
"Love, love, my child." She, black there with my grief,
320 Might feel my love—she was his sister once—
I clung to her. A moment she seemed moved,
Kissed me with cold lips, suffered me to cling,
And drew me feebly through the hall into
The room she sat in.

There, with some strange spasm

325 Of pain and passion, she wrung loose my hands
Imperiously, and held me at arm's length,
And with two grey-steel naked-bladed eyes
Searched through my face,—ay, stabbed it through and through,
Through brows and cheeks and chin, as if to find
330 A wicked murderer in my innocent face,
If not here, there perhaps. Then, drawing breath,
She struggled for her ordinary calm—
And missed it rather,—told me not to shrink,
As if she had told me not to lie or swear,—
335 "She loved my father and would love me too
As long as I deserved it." Very kind.

I understood her meaning afterward;
She thought to find my mother in my face,
And questioned it for that. For she, my aunt,
340 Had loved my father truly, as she could,
And hated, with the gall of gentle souls,
My Tuscan[5] mother who had fooled away
A wise man from wise courses, a good man
From obvious duties, and, depriving her,
345 His sister, of the household precedence,
Had wronged his tenants, robbed his native land,
And made him mad, alike by life and death,
In love and sorrow. She had pored° for years   *pondered*
What sort of woman could be suitable
350 To her sort of hate, to entertain it with,
And so, her very curiosity
Became hate too, and all the idealism
She ever used in life was used for hate,
Till hate, so nourished, did exceed at last

5. From Tuscany, the region around Florence.

355 The love from which it grew, in strength and heat,
  And wrinkled her smooth conscience with a sense
  Of disputable virtue (say not, sin)
  When Christian doctrine was enforced at church.

  And thus my father's sister was to me
360 My mother's hater. From that day she did
  Her duty to me (I appreciate it
  In her own word as spoken to herself),
  Her duty, in large measure, well pressed out
  But measured always. She was generous, bland,
365 More courteous than was tender, gave me still
  The first place,—as if fearful that God's saints
  Would look down suddenly and say "Herein
  You missed a point, I think, through lack of love."
  Alas, a mother never is afraid
370 Of speaking angerly to any child,
  Since love, she knows, is justified of love.

  And I, I was a good child on the whole,
  A meek and manageable child. Why not?
  I did not live, to have the faults of life:
375 There seemed more true life in my father's grave
  Than in all England. Since *that* threw me off
  Who fain would cleave (his latest will, they say,
  Consigned me to his land), I only thought
  Of lying quiet there where I was thrown
380 Like sea-weed on the rocks, and suffering her
  To prick me to a pattern with her pin,[6]
  Fibre from fibre, delicate leaf from leaf,
  And dry out from my drowned anatomy
  The last sea-salt left in me.

        So it was.
385 I broke the copious curls upon my head
  In braids, because she liked smooth-ordered hair.
  I left off saying my sweet Tuscan words
  Which still at any stirring of the heart
  Came up to float across the English phrase
390 As lilies (*Bene* or *Che che*[7]), because
  She liked my father's child to speak his tongue.
  I learnt the collects and the catechism,
  The creeds, from Athanasius back to Nice,
  The Articles,[8] the Tracts *against* the times[9]
395 (By no means Buonaventure's "Prick of Love"[1]),
  And various popular synopses of

---

6. As in pricking a pattern to embroider.
7. "Good" and "no, indeed" (Italian).
8. The Thirty-nine Articles are the principles of Anglican faith; collects are Anglican prayers.
9. An ironic reference to the High Church movement's

Tracts for the Times, written by Newman, Keble, and Pusey; thus, the aunt is Low Church.
1. Saint Buonaventure (1221–1274) wrote of ecstatic, mystical Christian experiences; he believed in the power of love over the power of reason.

Inhuman doctrines never taught by John,[2]
Because she liked instructed piety.
I learnt my complement of classic French
400   (Kept pure of Balzac and neologism[3])
And German also, since she liked a range
Of liberal education,—tongues, not books.
I learnt a little algebra, a little
Of the mathematics,—brushed with extreme flounce
405   The circle of the sciences, because
She misliked women who are frivolous.
I learnt the royal genealogies
Of Oviedo, the internal laws
Of the Burmese empire,—by how many feet
410   Mount Chimborazo outsoars Teneriffe.
What navigable river joins itself
To Lara, and what census of the year five
Was taken at Klagenfurt,—because she liked
A general insight into useful facts.
415   I learnt much music,—such as would have been
As quite impossible in Johnson's day[4]
As still it might be wished—fine sleights of hand
And unimagined fingering, shuffling off
The hearer's soul through hurricanes of notes
420   To a noisy Tophet;° and I drew . . . costumes   *Hell*
From French engravings, nereids neatly draped
(With smirks of simmering godship): I washed in°   *water-colored*
Landscapes from nature (rather say, washed out).
I danced the polka and Cellarius,
425   Spun glass, stuffed birds, and modelled flowers in wax,
Because she liked accomplishments in girls.
I read a score of books on womanhood
To prove, if women do not think at all,
They may teach thinking (to a maiden aunt
430   Or else the author),—books that boldly assert
Their right of comprehending husband's talk
When not too deep, and even of answering
With pretty "may it please you," or "so it is,"—
Their rapid insight and fine aptitude,
435   Particular worth and general missionariness,
As long as they keep quiet by the fire
And never say "no" when the world says "ay,"
For that is fatal,—their angelic reach
Of virtue, chiefly used to sit and darn,
440   And fatten household sinners,—their, in brief,
Potential faculty in everything
Of abdicating power in it: she owned

---

2. The author of the gospel.
3. Honoré de Balzac (1799–1850), French realist novelist who described things considered unpleasant or immoral, hence unsuitable reading for young ladies. A neologism is

a newly coined word.
4. When informed that a piece of music being played by a young lady was extremely difficult, Samuel Johnson responded, "Would that it had been impossible."

She liked a woman to be womanly,
And English women, she thanked God and sighed
445   (Some people always sigh in thanking God)
Were models to the universe. And last
I learnt cross-stitch, because she did not like
To see me wear the night with empty hands
A-doing nothing. So, my shepherdess
450   Was something after all (the pastoral saints
Be praised for't), leaning lovelorn with pink eyes
To match her shoes, when I mistook the silks;
Her head uncrushed by that round weight of hat
So strangely similar to the tortoise-shell
455   Which slew the tragic poet.[5]

                 By the way,
The works of women are symbolical.
We sew, sew, prick our fingers, dull our sight,
Producing what? A pair of slippers, sir,
To put on when you're weary—or a stool
460   To stumble over and vex you . . . "curse that stool!"
Or else at best, a cushion, where you lean
And sleep, and dream of something we are not
But would be for your sake. Alas, alas!
This hurts most, this—that, after all, we are paid
465   The worth of our work, perhaps.

               In looking down
Those years of education (to return)
I wonder if Brinvilliers suffered more
In the water-torture[6] . . . flood succeeding flood
To drench the incapable throat and split the veins . . .
470   Than I did. Certain of your feebler souls
Go out in such a process; many pine
To a sick, inodorous light; my own endured:
I had relations in the Unseen, and drew
The elemental nutriment and heat
475   From nature, as earth feels the sun at nights,
Or as a babe sucks surely in the dark.
I kept the life thrust on me, on the outside
Of the inner life with all its ample room
For heart and lungs, for will and intellect,
480   Inviolable by conventions. God,
I thank thee for that grace of thine!

               At first
I felt no life which was not patience,—did
The thing she bade me, without heed to a thing
Beyond it, sat in just the chair she placed,
485   With back against the window, to exclude

5. The Greek playwright Aeschylus was supposed to have been killed when an eagle, mistaking his bald head for a stone, dropped a tortoise on it to break the shell.

6. In 1676 Marie Marguerite, Marquise de Brinvilliers, was tortured by having water forced down her throat, then executed.

The sight of the great lime-tree on the lawn,[7]
Which seemed to have come on purpose from the woods
To bring the house a message,—ay, and walked
Demurely in her carpeted low rooms,
490   As if I should not, hearkening my own steps,
Misdoubt I was alive. I read her books,
Was civil to her cousin, Romney Leigh,
Gave ear to her vicar, tea to her visitors,
And heard them whisper, when I changed a cup
495   (I blushed for joy at that),—"The Italian child,
For all her blue eyes and her quiet ways,
Thrives ill in England: she is paler yet
Than when we came the last time; she will die."

[DISCOVERY OF POETRY]

815   The cygnet finds the water, but the man
Is born in ignorance of his element
And feels out blind at first, disorganised
By sin i' the blood,—his spirit-insight dulled
And crossed by his sensations. Presently
820   He feels it quicken in the dark sometimes,
When, mark, be reverent, be obedient,
For such dumb motions of imperfect life
Are oracles of vital Deity
Attesting the Hereafter. Let who says
825   "The soul's a clean white paper," rather say,
A palimpsest,[8] a prophet's holograph
Defiled, erased and covered by a monk's,—
The apocalypse, by a Longus![9] poring on
Which obscene text, we may discern perhaps
830   Some fair, fine trace of what was written once,
Some upstroke of an alpha and omega
Expressing the old scripture.

                    Books, books, books!
I had found the secret of a garret-room
Piled high with cases in my father's name,
835   Piled high, packed large,—where, creeping in and out
Among the giant fossils of my past,
Like some small nimble mouse between the ribs
Of a mastodon, I nibbled here and there
At this or that box, pulling through the gap,
840   In heats of terror, haste, victorious joy,
The first book first. And how I felt it beat
Under my pillow, in the morning's dark,
An hour before the sun would let me read!
My books! At last because the time was ripe,
845   I chanced upon the poets.

7. Cf. Coleridge's *This Lime-Tree Bower My Prison*, page 1639.
8. Parchment where the original writing has been scraped off so it can be reused.

9. I.e., imagine that the words of the apocalyse have been erased and written over by Longus, a Greek writer of romances.

                    As the earth
Plunges in fury, when the internal fires
Have reached and pricked her heart, and, throwing flat
The marts and temples, the triumphal gates
And towers of observation, clears herself
850   To elemental freedom—thus, my soul,
At poetry's divine first finger-touch,
Let go conventions and sprang up surprised,
Convicted of the great eternities
Before two worlds.

              What's this, Aurora Leigh,
855   You write so of the poets, and not laugh?
Those virtuous liars, dreamers after dark,
Exaggerators of the sun and moon,
And soothsayers in a tea-cup?

                  I write so
Of the only truth-tellers now left to God,
860   The only speakers of essential truth,
Opposed to relative, comparative,
And temporal truths; the only holders by
His sun-skirts, through conventional gray glooms;
The only teachers who instruct mankind
865   From just a shadow on a charnel-wall[1]
To find man's veritable stature out
Erect, sublime,—the measure of a man,
And that's the measure of an angel, says
The apostle. Ay, and while your common men
870   Lay telegraphs, gauge railroads, reign, reap, dine,
And dust the flaunty carpets of the world
For kings to walk on, or our president,
The poet suddenly will catch them up
With his voice like a thunder,—"This is soul,
875   This is life, this word is being said in heaven,
Here's God down on us! what are you about?"
How all those workers start amid their work,
Look round, look up, and feel, a moment's space,
That carpet-dusting, though a pretty trade,
880   Is not the imperative labour after all.

from *Book 2*

[WOMAN AND ARTIST]

Times followed one another. Came a morn
I stood upon the brink of twenty years,
And looked before and after, as I stood
Woman and artist,—either incomplete,
5   Both credulous of completion. There I held
The whole creation in my little cup,

---

1. Wall of a building where bodies or bones are deposited.

And smiled with thirsty lips before I drank
"Good health to you and me, sweet neighbor mine,
And all these peoples."

                       I was glad, that day;

10   The June was in me, with its multitudes
Of nightingales all singing in the dark,
And rosebuds reddening where the calyx[1] split.
I felt so young, so strong, so sure of God!
So glad, I could not choose be very wise!

15   And, old at twenty, was inclined to pull
My childhood backward in a childish jest
To see the face of 't once more, and farewell!
In which fantastic mood I bounded forth
At early morning,—would not wait so long

20   As even to snatch my bonnet by the strings,
But, brushing a green trail across the lawn
With my gown in the dew, took will and away
Among the acacias of the shrubberies,
To fly my fancies in the open air

25   And keep my birthday, till my aunt awoke
To stop good dreams. Meanwhile I murmured on
As honeyed bees keep humming to themselves,
"The worthiest poets have remained uncrowned
Till death has bleached their foreheads to the bone;

30   And so with me it must be unless I prove
Unworthy of the grand adversity,
And certainly I would not fail so much.
What, therefore, if I crown myself to-day
In sport, not pride, to learn the feel of it,

35   Before my brows be numbed as Dante's own
To all the tender pricking of such leaves?
Such leaves! what leaves?"

                       I pulled the branches down
To choose from.
             "Not the bay![2] I choose no bay
(The fates deny us if we are overbold),

40   Nor myrtle—which means chiefly love; and love
Is something awful which one dares not touch
So early o' mornings. This verbena strains
The point of passionate fragrance; and hard by,
This guelder-rose, at far too slight a beck

45   Of the wind, will toss about her flower-apples.
Ah—there's my choice,—that ivy on the wall,
That headlong ivy! not a leaf will grow
But thinking of a wreath. Large leaves, smooth leaves,
Serrated like my vines, and half as green.

---

1. The green outer leaves which protect a flowerbud.   2. Laurel; Apollo, the god of poetry, wore a wreath of laurel leaves.

50   I like such ivy, bold to leap a height
'Twas strong to climb; as good to grow on graves
As twist about a thyrsus;[3] pretty too
(And that's not ill) when twisted round a comb."
Thus speaking to myself, half singing it,
55   Because some thoughts are fashioned like a bell
To ring with once being touched, I drew a wreath
Drenched, blinding me with dew, across my brow,
And fastening it behind so, turning faced
. . . My public!—cousin Romney—with a mouth
60   Twice graver than his eyes.

                              I stood there fixed,—
My arms up, like the caryatid,[4] sole
Of some abolished temple, helplessly
Persistent in a gesture which derides
A former purpose. Yet my blush was flame,
65   As if from flax, not stone.

                         "Aurora Leigh,
The earliest of Auroras!"[5]

                         Hand stretched out
I clasped, as shipwrecked men will clasp a hand,
Indifferent to the sort of palm. The tide
Had caught me at my pastime, writing down
70   My foolish name too near upon the sea
Which drowned me with a blush as foolish. "You,
My cousin!"

                   The smile died out in his eyes
And dropped upon his lips, a cold dead weight,
For just a moment, "Here's a book I found!
75   No name writ on it—poems, by the form;
Some Greek upon the margin,—lady's Greek
Without the accents. Read it? Not a word.
I saw at once the thing had witchcraft in't,
Whereof the reading calls up dangerous spirits:
80   I rather bring it to the witch."

                              "My book.
You found it". . .

                         "In the hollow by the stream
That beech leans down into—of which you said
The Oread in it has a Naiad's heart
And pines for waters."[6]
                         "Thank you."
                                   "Thanks to *you*
85   My cousin! that I have seen you not too much

---

3. Ivy-covered staff carried by the Greek god Dionysus.
4. Female figure with upraised arms, used as a supporting architectural column.

5. Aurora, the goddess of the dawn.
6. An Oread is a tree nymph; a Naiad is a water nymph.

Witch, scholar, poet, dreamer, and the rest,
To be a woman also."

     With a glance
The smile rose in his eyes again and touched
The ivy on my forehead, light as air.
90 I answered gravely "Poets needs must be
Or men or women—more's the pity."

        "Ah,
But men, and still less women, happily,
Scarce need be poets. Keep to the green wreath,
Since even dreaming of the stone and bronze
95 Brings headaches, pretty cousin, and defiles
The clean white morning dresses."

       "So you judge!
Because I love the beautiful I must
Love pleasure chiefly, and be overcharged
For ease and whiteness! well, you know the world,
100 And only miss your cousin, 'tis not much.
But learn this; I would rather take my part
With God's Dead, who afford to walk in white
Yet spread His glory, than keep quiet here
And gather up my feet from even a step
105 For fear to soil my gown in so much dust.
I choose to walk at all risks.—Here, if heads
That hold a rhythmic thought, much ache perforce,
For my part I choose headaches,—and to-day's
My birthday."

     "Dear Aurora, choose instead
110 To cure them. You have balsams."

        "I perceive.
The headache is too noble for my sex.
You think the heartache would sound decenter,
Since that's the woman's special, proper ache,
And altogether tolerable, except
115 To a woman."

    [No Female Christ]

      "There it is!—
180 You play beside a death-bed like a child,
Yet measure to yourself a prophet's place
To teach the living. None of all these things
Can women understand. You generalise
Oh, nothing,—not even grief! Your quick-breathed hearts,
185 So sympathetic to the personal pang,
Close on each separate knife-stroke, yielding up
A whole life at each wound, incapable
Of deepening, widening a large lap of life
To hold the world-full woe. The human race
190 To you means, such a child, or such a man,

You saw one morning waiting in the cold,
Beside that gate, perhaps. You gather up
A few such cases, and when strong sometimes
Will write of factories and of slaves, as if
195   Your father were a negro, and your son
A spinner in the mills. All's yours and you,
All, coloured with your blood, or otherwise
Just nothing to you. Why, I call you hard
To general suffering. Here's the world half-blind
200   With intellectual light, half-brutalised
With civilisation, having caught the plague
In silks from Tarsus,[7] shrieking east and west
Along a thousand railroads, mad with pain
And sin too! . . . does one woman of you all
205   (You who weep easily) grow pale to see
This tiger shake his cage?—does one of you
Stand still from dancing, stop from stringing pearls,
And pine and die because of the great sum
Of universal anguish?—Show me a tear
210   Wet as Cordelia's,[8] in eyes bright as yours,
Because the world is mad. You cannot count,
That you should weep for this account, not you!
You weep for what you know. A red-haired child
Sick in a fever, if you touch him once,
215   Though but so little as with a finger-tip,
Will set you weeping; but a million sick . . .
You could as soon weep for the rule of three
Or compound fractions. Therefore, this same world,
Uncomprehended by you, must remain
220   Uninfluenced by you.—Women as you are,
Mere women, personal and passionate,
You give us doating mothers, and perfect wives,
Sublime Madonnas, and enduring saints!
We get no Christ from you,—and verily
225   We shall not get a poet, in my mind."

[AURORA'S REJECTION OF ROMNEY]

There he glowed on me
With all his face and eyes. "No other help?"
345   Said he—"no more than so?"[9]

"What help?" I asked.
"You'd scorn my help,—as Nature's self, you say,
Has scorned to put her music in my mouth
Because a woman's. Do you now turn round

7. I.e., with civilized luxuries come evils, just as the trading ships bringing silks from Tarsus—a wealthy center of
trade in the ancient Middle East—might also have
brought rats that spread the plague.
8. Cordelia weeps when she is reunited with her father
(*King Lear*, 4.7.71); her feelings are entirely personal.
Romney mentions Cordelia to bolster his argument that

women cannot play any role in world affairs because they
are incapable of taking a broad view of human suffering.
9. Romney wants to alleviate the misery of the poor
through social reform. Aurora has offered her approval of
his plans, but he asks if she can offer him another kind of
help—i.e., to be his wife or "helpmate" (line 402 below).

And ask for what a woman cannot give?"

350   "For what she only can, I turn and ask,"
He answered, catching up my hands in his,
And dropping on me from his high-eaved brow
The full weight of his soul,—"I ask for love,
And that, she can; for life in fellowship
355   Through bitter duties—that, I know she can;
For wifehood—will she?"

                "Now," I said, "may God
Be witness 'twixt us two!" and with the word,
Meseemed I floated into a sudden light
Above his stature,—"am I proved too weak
360   To stand alone, yet strong enough to bear
Such leaners on my shoulder? poor to think,
Yet rich enough to sympathise with thought?
Incompetent to sing, as blackbirds can,
Yet competent to love, like HIM?"

                    I paused;
365   Perhaps I darkened, as the lighthouse will
That turns upon the sea. "It's always so.
Anything does for a wife."

            "Aurora, dear,
And dearly honoured,"—he pressed in at once
With eager utterance,—"you translate me ill.
370   I do not contradict my thought of you
Which is most reverent, with another thought
Found less so. If your sex is weak for art
(And I, who said so, did but honour you
By using truth in courtship), it is strong
375   For life and duty. Place your fecund heart
In mine, and let us blossom for the world
That wants love's colour in the grey of time.
My talk, meanwhile, is arid to you, ay,
Since all my talk can only set you where
380   You look down coldly on the arena-heaps
Of headless bodies, shapeless, indistinct!
The Judgment-Angel scarce would find his way
Through such a heap of generalised distress
To the individual man with lips and eyes,
385   Much less Aurora. Ah, my sweet, come down,
And hand in hand we'll go where yours shall touch
These victims, one by one! till, one by one,
The formless, nameless trunk of every man
Shall seem to wear a head with hair you know,
390   And every woman catch your mother's face
To melt you into passion."

             "I am a girl,"
I answered slowly; "you do well to name
My mother's face. Though far too early, alas,

God's hand did interpose 'twixt it and me,
395 I know so much of love as used to shine
In that face and another. Just so much;
No more indeed at all. I have not seen
So much love since, I pray you pardon me,
As answers even to make a marriage with
400 In this cold land of England. What you love
Is not a woman, Romney, but a cause:
You want a helpmate, not a mistress, sir,
A wife to help your ends,—in her no end.
Your cause is noble, your ends excellent,
405 But I, being most unworthy of these and that,
Do otherwise conceive of love. Farewell."

"Farewell, Aurora? you reject me thus?"
He said.

        "Sir, you were married long ago.
You have a wife already whom you love,
410 Your social theory. Bless you both, I say.
For my part, I am scarcely meek enough
To be the handmaid of a lawful spouse.
Do I look a Hagar,[1] think you?"

                        "So you jest."

"Nay, so, I speak in earnest," I replied.
415 "You treat of marriage too much like, at least,
A chief apostle: you would bear with you
A wife . . . a sister . . . shall we speak it out?
A sister of charity."

                "Then, must it be
Indeed farewell? And was I so far wrong
420 In hope and in illusion, when I took
The woman to be nobler than the man,
Yourself the noblest woman, in the use
And comprehension of what love is,—love,
That generates the likeness of itself
425 Through all heroic duties? so far wrong,
In saying bluntly, venturing truth on love,
'Come, human creature, love and work with me,'—
Instead of 'Lady, thou art wondrous fair,
And, where the Graces walk before, the Muse
430 Will follow at the lightning of their eyes,
And where the Muse walks, lovers need to creep:
Turn round and love me, or I die of love.'"

With quiet indignation I broke in.
"You misconceive the question like a man,
435 Who sees a woman as the complement
Of his sex merely. You forget too much
That every creature, female as the male,

1. In Genesis 16, Hagar was the handmaiden of Abraham's lawful wife, Sarah; Hagar bore Abraham a son, Ishmael, when it appeared that Sarah was barren.

Stands single in responsible act and thought
As also in birth and death. Whoever says
440 To a loyal woman, 'Love and work with me,'
Will get fair answers if the work and love,
Being good themselves, are good for her—the best
She was born for. Women of a softer mood,
Surprised by men when scarcely awake to life,
445 Will sometimes only hear the first word, love,
And catch up with it any kind of work,
Indifferent, so that dear love go with it.
I do not blame such women, though, for love,
They pick much oakum;[2] earth's fanatics make
450 Too frequently heaven's saints. But *me* your work
Is not the best for,—nor your love the best,
Nor able to commend the kind of work
For love's sake merely. Ah, you force me, sir,
To be overbold in speaking of myself:
455 I too have my vocation,—work to do,
The heavens and earth have set me since I changed
My father's face for theirs, and, though your world
Were twice as wretched as you represent,
Most serious work, most necessary work
460 As any of the economists'. Reform,
Make trade a Christian possibility,
And individual right no general wrong;
Wipe out earth's furrows of the Thine and Mine,
And leave one green for men to play at bowls,[3]
465 With innings for them all! . . . What then, indeed,
If mortals are not greater by the head
Than any of their prosperities? what then,
Unless the artist keep up open roads
Betwixt the seen and unseen,—bursting through
470 The best of your conventions with his best,
The speakable, imaginable best
God bids him speak, to prove what lies beyond
Both speech and imagination? A starved man
Exceeds a fat beast: we'll not barter, sir,
475 The beautiful for barley.—And, even so,
I hold you will not compass your poor ends
Of barley-feeding and material ease,
Without a poet's individualism
To work your universal. It takes a soul,
480 To move a body: it takes a high-souled man,
To move the masses, even to a cleaner stye:
It takes the ideal, to blow a hair's-breadth off
The dust of the actual.—Ah, your Fouriers[4] failed,
Because not poets enough to understand
485 That life develops from within.—For me,

2. Prisoners and paupers in workhouses were forced to pick oakum (untwist strands of old rope); it was tedious and humble labor.

3. Lawn bowling.
4. François Marie Charles Fourier (1772–1837), a French social theorist who advocated communal property.

Perhaps I am not worthy, as you say,
Of work like this: perhaps a woman's soul
Aspires, and not creates: yet we aspire,
And yet I'll try out your perhaps, sir,
490   And if I fail . . . why, burn me up my straw[5]
Like other false works—I'll not ask for grace;
Your scorn is better, cousin Romney. I
Who love my art, would never wish it lower
To suit my stature. I may love my art.
495   You'll grant that even a woman may love art,
Seeing that to waste true love on anything
Is womanly, past question."

                                        I retain
The very last word which I said that day,
As you the creaking of the door, years past,
500   Which let upon you such disabling news
You ever after have been graver. He,
His eyes, the motions in his silent mouth,
Were fiery points on which my words were caught,
Transfixed for ever in my memory
505   For his sake, not their own. And yet I know
I did not love him . . . nor he me . . . that's sure . . .
And what I said is unrepented of,
As truth is always. Yet . . . a princely man!—
If hard to me, heroic for himself!
510   He bears down on me through the slanting years,
The stronger for the distance. If he had loved,
Ay, loved me, with that retributive face, . . .
I might have been a common woman now
And happier, less known and less left alone,
515   Perhaps a better woman after all,
With chubby children hanging on my neck
To keep me low and wise. Ah me, the vines
That bear such fruit are proud to stoop with it.
The palm stands upright in a realm of sand.
520   And I, who spoke the truth then, stand upright,
Still worthy of having spoken out the truth,
By being content I spoke it though it set
Him there, me here.—O woman's vile remorse,
To hanker after a mere name, a show,
525   A supposition, a potential love!
Does every man who names love in our lives
Become a power for that?

from *Book 3*
[THE WOMAN WRITER IN LONDON]

Why what a pettish, petty thing I grow,—
A mere mere woman, a mere flaccid nerve,

---

5. I.e., destroy my poetry.

A kerchief left out all night in the rain,
Turned soft so,—overtasked and overstrained
40 And overlived in this close London life!
And yet I should be stronger.

                                    Never burn
Your letters, poor Aurora! for they stare
With red seals from the table, saying each,
"Here's something that you know not." Out, alas,
45 'Tis scarcely that the world's more good and wise
Or even straighter and more consequent
Since yesterday at this time—yet, again,
If but one angel spoke from Ararat[1]
I should be very sorry not to hear:
50 So open all the letters! let me read.
Blanche Ord, the writer in the "Lady's Fan,"
Requests my judgment on . . . that, afterwards.
Kate Ward desires the model of my cloak,
And signs "Elisha to you."[2] Pringle Sharpe
55 Presents his work on "Social Conduct," craves
A little money for his pressing debts . . .
From me, who scarce have money for my needs;
Art's fiery chariot which we journey in
Being apt to singe our singing-robes to holes,
60 Although you ask me for my cloak, Kate Ward!
Here's Rudgely knows it,—editor and scribe;
He's "forced to marry where his heart is not,
Because the purse lacks where he lost his heart."
Ah,——lost it because no one picked it up;
65 That's really loss,—(and passable impudence).
My critic Hammond flatters prettily,
And wants another volume like the last.
My critic Belfair wants another book
Entirely different, which will sell (and live?),
70 A striking book, yet not a startling book,
The public blames originalities
(You must not pump spring-water unawares
Upon a gracious public full of nerves):
Good things, not subtle, new yet orthodox,
75 As easy reading as the dog-eared page
That's fingered by said public fifty years,
Since first taught spelling by its grandmother,
And yet a revelation in some sort:
That's hard, my critic Belfair. So—what next?
80 My critic Stokes objects to abstract thoughts;
"Call a man John, a woman Joan," says he,
"And do not prate so of *humanities:*"
Whereat I call my critic simply, Stokes.
My critic Jobson recommends more mirth

---

1. The mountain where Noah's ark rested after the Flood,
and where God spoke to Noah (Genesis 8).
2. When the prophet Elijah was carried to heaven in a
chariot of fire, his cloak fell to earth and was taken up by
his successor Elisha (2 Kings 2.1–15); Kate Ward means
that she wants to copy Aurora's cloak.

85   Because a cheerful genius suits the times,
     And all true poets laugh unquenchably
     Like Shakespeare and the gods. That's very hard.
     The gods may laugh, and Shakespeare; Dante smiled
     With such a needy heart on two pale lips,
90   We cry "Weep rather, Dante." Poems are
     Men, if true poems: and who dares exclaim
     At any man's door, "Here, 'tis understood
     The thunder fell last week and killed a wife
     And scared a sickly husband—what of that?
95   Get up, be merry, shout and clap your hands,
     Because a cheerful genius suits the times—"?
     None says so to the man, and why indeed
     Should any to the poem? A ninth seal;[3]
     The apocalypse is drawing to a close.
100 Ha,—this from Vincent Carrington,—"Dear friend,
     I want good counsel. Will you lend me wings
     To raise me to the subject, in a sketch
     I'll bring to-morrow—may I? at eleven?
     A poet's only born to turn to use:
105 So save you! for the world . . . and Carrington."
     "(Writ after.) Have you heard of Romney Leigh,
     Beyond what's said of him in newspapers,
     His phalansteries[4] there, his speeches here,
     His pamphlets, pleas, and statements, everywhere?
110 He dropped *me* long ago, but no one drops
     A golden apple—though indeed one day
     You hinted that, but jested. Well, at least
     You know Lord Howe who sees him . . . whom he sees
     And *you* see and I hate to see,—for Howe
115 Stands high upon the brink of theories,
     Observes the swimmers and cries 'Very fine,'
     But keeps dry linen equally,—unlike
     That gallant breaster, Romney. Strange it is,
     Such sudden madness seizing a young man
120 To make earth over again,—while I'm content
     To make the pictures. Let me bring the sketch.
     A tiptoe Danae,[5] overbold and hot,
     Both arms a-flame to meet her wishing Jove
     Halfway, and burn him faster down; the face
125 And breasts upturned and straining, the loose locks
     All glowing with the anticipated gold.
     Or here's another on the self-same theme.[6]
     She lies here—flat upon her prison-floor,
     The long hair swathed about her to the heel
130 Like wet seaweed. You dimly see her through
     The glittering haze of that prodigious rain,

3. In Revelation 5.1 there is a book closed with seven seals, the opening of which will herald the Apocalypse. The reference to a ninth seal satirically suggests something more extreme than the Apocalypse itself.
4. The communes advocated by the socialist Fourier.

5. Carrington has sketched Danae, the beloved of Zeus, whom Zeus visited in a shower of gold.
6. I.e., the second picture is also of Danae and the golden shower ("prodigious rain") that is Zeus.

Half blotted out of nature by a love
As heavy as fate. I'll bring you either sketch.
I think, myself, the second indicates
More passion."

135   Surely. Self is put away,
And calm with abdication. She is Jove,
And no more Danae—greater thus. Perhaps
The painter symbolises unaware
Two states of the recipient artist-soul,
140   One, forward, personal, wanting reverence,
Because aspiring only. We'll be calm,
And know that, when indeed our Joves come down,
We all turn stiller than we have ever been.

* * *

Serene and unafraid of solitude,
170   I worked the short days out,—and watched the sun
On lurid morns or monstrous afternoons
(Like some Druidic idol's fiery brass
With fixed unflickering outline of dead heat,
From which the blood of wretches pent inside
175   Seems oozing forth to incarnadine the air[7])
Push out through fog with his dilated disk,
And startle the slant roofs and chimney-pots
With splashes of fierce colour. Or I saw
Fog only, the great tawny weltering fog,
180   Involve the passive city, strangle it
Alive, and draw it off into the void,
Spires, bridges, streets, and squares, as if a sponge
Had wiped out London,—or as noon and night
Had clapped together and utterly struck out
185   The intermediate time, undoing themselves
In the act. Your city poets see such things
Not despicable. Mountains of the south,
When drunk and mad with elemental wines
They rend the seamless mist and stand up bare,
190   Make fewer singers, haply. No one sings,
Descending Sinai: on Parnassus mount[8]
You take a mule to climb and not a muse
Except in fable and figure: forests chant
Their anthems to themselves, and leave you dumb.
195   But sit in London at the day's decline,
And view the city perish in the mist
Like Pharaoh's armaments in the deep Red Sea,[9]
The chariots, horsemen, footmen, all the host,
Sucked down and choked to silence—then, surprised
200   By a sudden sense of vision and of tune,

---

7. It was believed that ancient Celtic druids performed human sacrifices.
8. Sinai is the mountain where God gave the Commandments to Moses; Parnassus is the mountain where the Muses, the Greek goddesses of the arts and of knowledge, dwelled. The idea is that neither biblical nor classical sources can provide poetic inspiration for the modern poet; only the city can do so.
9. In Exodus 14.21–30, God parts the Red Sea so the Israelites can escape from Egypt, but drowns Pharaoh's pursuing armies.

You feel as conquerors though you did not fight,
And you and Israel's other singing girls,
Ay, Miriam[1] with them, sing the song you choose.

from *Book 5*
[EPIC ART AND MODERN LIFE]

The critics say that epics have died out
140 With Agamemnon and the goat-nursed gods;[1]
I'll not believe it. I could never deem,
As Payne Knight[2] did (the mythic mountaineer
Who travelled higher than he was born to live,
And showed sometimes the goitre in his throat[3]
145 Discoursing of an image seen through fog),
That Homer's heroes measured twelve feet high.
They were but men:—his Helen's hair turned grey
Like any plain Miss Smith's who wears a front;[4]
And Hector's infant whimpered at a plume[5]
150 As yours last Friday at a turkey-cock.
All actual heroes are essential men,
And all men possible heroes: every age,
Heroic in proportions, double-faced,
Looks backward and before, expects a morn
155 And claims an epos.°   *epic poem*

          Ay, but every age
Appears to souls who live in't (ask Carlyle[6])
Most unheroic. Ours, for instance, ours:
The thinkers scout it, and the poets abound
Who scorn to touch it with a finger-tip:
160 A pewter age,[7]—mixed metal, silver-washed;
An age of scum, spooned off the richer past,
An age of patches for old gaberdines,°   *overcoats*
An age of mere transition,[8] meaning nought
Except that what succeeds must shame it quite
165 If God please. That's wrong thinking, to my mind,
And wrong thoughts make poor poems.

                    Every age,
Through being beheld too close, is ill-discerned
By those who have not lived past it. We'll suppose
Mount Athos carved, as Alexander schemed,
170 To some colossal statue of a man.[9]

---

1. Miriam, the sister of Moses and Aaron, led the women of Israel in singing to celebrate the drowning of the Egyptian army (Exodus 15.19–21).
1. Agamemnon led the Greeks in the Trojan War, as chronicled in Homer's epic, *The Iliad*; Zeus was nursed by a goat.
2. Richard Payne Knight (1750–1824), a classical scholar who speculated about Homer and the Elgin marbles.
3. A swelling of the throat (caused by lack of iodine in the water at high altitudes), symbolizing the foolishness of Payne Knight's utterances.
4. Hairpiece worn over the forehead; artificial bangs.

5. When the Trojan warrior Hector tried to embrace his infant son before going into battle, the baby was terrified of his father's plumed helmet.
6. In *On Heroes and Hero Worship* (1841) Thomas Carlyle urges a renewal of the idea of the heroic.
7. Inferior to the Golden, the Silver, or even the Bronze Age; Hesiod proposed that history is a constant process of decline.
8. In *The Spirit of the Age* (1831) John Stuart Mill says the present era is "an age of transition."
9. Alexander the Great thought of having Mount Athos carved in the form of a gigantic statue of a conqueror, with a basin in one hand to collect water for the pastures below.

The peasants, gathering brushwood in his ear,
Had guessed as little as the browsing goats
Of form or feature of humanity
Up there,—in fact, had travelled five miles off
175   Or ere the giant image broke on them,
Full human profile, nose and chin distinct,
Mouth, muttering rhythms of silence up the sky
And fed at evening with the blood of suns;
Grand torso,—hand, that flung perpetually
180   The largesse of a silver river down
To all the country pastures. 'Tis even thus
With times we live in,—evermore too great
To be apprehended near.

                    But poets should
Exert a double vision; should have eyes
185   To see near things as comprehensively
As if afar they took their point of sight,
And distant things as intimately deep
As if they touched them. Let us strive for this.
I do distrust the poet who discerns
190   No character or glory in his times,
And trundles back his soul five hundred years,
Past moat and drawbridge, into a castle-court,
To sing—oh, not of lizard or of toad
Alive i' the ditch there,—'twere excusable,
195   But of some black chief, half knight, half sheep-lifter,
Some beauteous dame, half chattel and half queen,
As dead as must be, for the greater part,
The poems made on their chivalric bones;
And that's no wonder: death inherits death.

200   Nay, if there's room for poets in this world
A little overgrown (I think there is),
Their sole work is to represent the age,
Their age, not Charlemagne's,[1]—this live, throbbing age,
That brawls, cheats, maddens, calculates, aspires,
205   And spends more passion, more heroic heat,
Betwixt the mirrors of its drawing-rooms,
Than Roland with his knights at Roncesvalles.[2]
To flinch from modern varnish, coat or flounce,
Cry out for togas and the picturesque,
210   Is fatal,—foolish too. King Arthur's self
Was commonplace to Lady Guenever;
And Camelot to minstrels seemed as flat
As Fleet Street to our poets.[3]

---

1. Charlemagne was king of the Franks (768–814) and emperor of the West, laying the foundation for the Holy Roman Empire.
2. Legendary hero whose defeat at Roncesvalles (in the Spanish Pyrenees) was disastrous for Charlemagne's forces; his exploits are the subject of a medieval epic poem, *Le Chanson de Roland*.
3. I.e., to his wife Guenevere, even the glorious King Arthur was ordinary, and his kingdom was no more a subject for the poets of his own time than Fleet Street—location of London publishers and newspaper offices—is for the poets of the 19th century.

Never flinch,

But still, unscrupulously epic, catch
215   Upon the burning lava of a song
The full-veined, heaving, double-breasted Age:
That, when the next shall come, the men of that
May touch the impress with reverent hand, and say
"Behold,—behold the paps we all have sucked!
220   This bosom seems to beat still, or at least
It sets ours beating: this is living art,
Which thus presents and thus records true life."

1853–1856   1856

PERSPECTIVES

Victorian Ladies and Gentlemen

As Victorian society prospered, social divisions became more fluid, but at the same time class consciousness became more intense. The terms "lady" and "gentleman" had enormous significance, particularly for those aspiring to these ranks, or for those in danger of slipping out of them. Some social distinctions were obvious: regardless of conduct, people born into the aristocracy and landed gentry were indisputably ladies and gentlemen; people who worked with their hands in home, field, or factory were not. The upper and lower boundaries of the middle-class were blurred, however, and everyone was alert to fine gradations. Manners, money, birth, occupation, and leisure time were crucial indicators of social standing, determining not only one's place in society but one's freedom to act, speak, learn, and earn.

Ladies and gentlemen endeavored to conform to the ideology of separate spheres that dominated Victorian thinking about gender. Middle-class women were to preside over the domestic sphere, the home and family, while men entered the fray of the world. Woman's "mission" was to provide a sanctified haven from the rough-and-tumble world of business and politics. Her virtuous passivity, selflessness, and spiritual purity gave her moral authority in the social and domestic realm. The first mass circulation women's periodical, launched in 1852, was called, significantly, *Englishwoman's Domestic Magazine*.

Meanwhile, the world of action and aggression belonged to men: as Ruskin put it in *Sesame and Lilies* (1865): "The man, in his rough work in the open world, must encounter all peril and trial . . . often he must be wounded, or subdued, often misled; and *always* hardened. But he guards the woman from all this; within his house, as ruled by her . . . need enter no danger, no temptation, no cause of error or offense." Tennyson's *The Princess* (1847) gave the polarization of gender roles the aura of timeless law:

> Man for the field and woman for the hearth:
> Man for the sword and for the needle she:
> Man with the head and woman with the heart:
> Man to command and woman to obey:
> All else confusion.

Among middle-class men, the clearest social division was between those who had attended a public school (an elite boarding school) and those who had not. The ideal of gentleman-liness inculcated by these schools became a way for society to remake the upstart middle-classes in the image of the aristocracy. Emphasizing character over intellect, the public schools taught boys how to assimilate the manners and customs of those above them socially, and gave

Father of the Family. "Come, dear; we so seldom go out together now—Can't you take us all to the Play to-night?"

Mistress of House, and M. P. "How you talk, Charles! Don't you see that I am too busy. I have a Committee to-morrow morning, and I have my Speech on the Great Crochet Question to prepare for the evening."

The Parliamentary Female. From *Punch* magazine, 1853.

them a familiarity with Greek, Latin, and school games such as cricket and rugby—hallmarks of an upper-class education. Instilling the values of duty, loyalty, and public service, these schools helped to create a new administrative elite, based more on merit and training than birth, who ran both the Civil Service and the Empire. Sustained by the "old boy" network, in which former schoolmates assisted each other's careers, graduates of places such as Eton, Harrow, Winchester, and Rugby could look forward to positions of influence and affluence.

Although the daughters of some well-to-do families might attend a fashionable boarding school, education was not primarily what determined a woman's claim to be considered a lady. Her position derived from her parents or her husband, and her unproductive leisure was a visible signal of rank. Since aspirations to "refinement" effectively precluded middle-class women from employment, ladies had, as the novelist Dinah Maria Mulock put it in 1858, "literally nothing whatever to do." She complained that "their whole energies are devoted to the massacre of old Time. They prick him to death with crochet and embroidery needles; strum him deaf with piano and harp playing—*not* music; cut him up with morning visitors, or leave his carcass in ten-minute parcels at every 'friend's' house they can think of." In her autobiography, the journalist Harriet Martineau described the expectations in her day: "It was not thought proper for young ladies to study very conspicuously. . . . If ever I shut myself into my own room for an hour of solitude, I knew it was at the risk of being sent for to join the sewing-circle, or to read aloud."

It was a way of life that at once exalted women and paralyzed them. They could not work outside the home; they could not vote; they had no legal rights, even over their own children; they could not attend university or enter the professions. Legally, they were classed with criminals, idiots, and minors. Rejecting women's education, the painter Edward Burne-Jones argued, "The great point is, not that they should understand us, but that they should worship and obey us." Ironically, only economic necessity or illness could liberate a lady from the burden of enforced idleness. When Martineau's family went bankrupt she was enabled to pursue her dream of authorship, for "we had lost our gentility." Similarly, the death of both parents freed Mary Kingsley to travel, and her own recurrent ill-health allowed Isabella Bird to go off in search of a "cure." Both women became prominent travel writers. Florence Nightingale made time for a career by taking to her bed, where only her persistent indisposition released her from the demands of family and social life. Definitions of masculinity and femininity were earnestly contested throughout the period—with increasingly sharp assaults on traditional roles coming from aesthetes and decadents at the end of the century. The following selections illustrate the kinds of arguments and experiences that figured prominently in debates on gender roles in the early and mid-Victorian periods.

◆—◆ Ⲏ◆Ⲏ ◆—◆

Frances Power Cobbe
1822–1904

The education of girls from well-to-do families lacked intellectual challenge, partly because of the belief that the female mind was incapable of serious effort, and partly because the goal was to produce "Ornaments of Society" who would catch husbands. The elaborate and expensive clothes worn by Cobbe and her fellow pupils further reinforced their essentially decorative function. Although Cobbe recalls her teachers' horror at the idea that a woman's education might ever be put to any practical use, she herself became an active philanthropist, reformer, and feminist, who pressed for female suffrage and for women's access to university education and the professions.

from Life of Frances Power Cobbe As Told by Herself
[A FASHIONABLE ENGLISH BOARDING SCHOOL]

When it came to my turn to receive education, it was not in London but in Brighton that the ladies' schools most in estimation were to be found. There were even then (about 1836) not less than a hundred such establishments in the town, but that at No. 32, Brunswick Terrace, of which Miss Runciman and Miss Roberts were mistresses, and which had been founded some time before by a celebrated Miss Poggi, was supposed to be *nec pluribus impar* [equal to the best]. It was, at all events, the most outrageously expensive, the nominal tariff of £120 or £130 per annum representing scarcely a fourth of the charges for "extras" which actually appeared in the bills of many of the pupils. My own, I know, amounted to 1,000 for two years' schooling.[1]

I shall write of this school quite frankly, since the two poor ladies, well-meaning but very unwise, to whom it belonged have been dead for nearly thirty years, and it can hurt nobody to record my conviction that a better system than theirs could scarcely have been devised had it been designed to attain the maximum of cost and labour and the minimum of solid results. It was the typical Higher Education of the period, carried out to the extreme of expenditure and high pressure.

---

1. Compare this figure to the 20 pounds per year that Charlotte Brontë was earning in 1841 as a private governess.

Profane persons were apt to describe our school as a Convent, and to refer to the back door of our garden, whence we issued on our dismal diurnal[2] walks, as the "postern." If we in any degree resembled nuns, however, it was assuredly not those of either a Contemplative or Silent Order. The din of our large double schoolrooms was something frightful. Sitting in either of them, four pianos might be heard going at once in rooms above and around us, while at numerous tables scattered about the rooms there were girls reading aloud to the governesses and reciting lessons in English, French, German, and Italian. This hideous clatter continued the entire day till we went to bed at night, there being no time whatever allowed for recreation, unless the dreary hour of walking with our teachers (when we recited our verbs), could so be described by a fantastic imagination. In the midst of the uproar we were obliged to write our exercises, to compose our themes, and to commit to memory whole pages of prose. On Saturday afternoons, instead of play, there was a terrible ordeal generally known as the "Judgment Day." The two school-mistresses sat side by side, solemn and stern, at the head of the long table. Behind them sat all the governesses as Assessors. On the table were the books wherein our evil deeds of the week were recorded; and round the room against the wall, seated on stools of penitential discomfort, we sat, five-and-twenty "damosels," anything but "Blessed,"[3] expecting our sentences according to our ill-deserts. It must be explained that the fiendish ingenuity of some teacher had invented for our torment a system of imaginary "cards," which we were supposed to "lose" (though we never gained any) whenever we had not finished all our various lessons and practisings every night before bed-time, or whenever we had been given the mark for "stooping," or had been impertinent, or had been "turned" in our lessons, or had been marked "P" by the music master, or had been convicted of "disorder" (e.g., having our long shoe-strings untied), or, lastly, had told lies! Any one crime in this heterogeneous list entailed the same penalty, namely, the sentence, "You have lost your card, Miss So-and-so, for such and such a thing;" and when Saturday came round, if three cards had been lost in the week, the law wreaked its justice on the unhappy sinner's head! Her confession having been wrung from her at the awful judgment-seat above described, and the books having been consulted, she was solemnly scolded and told to sit in the corner for the rest of the evening! Anything more ridiculous than the scene which followed can hardly be conceived. I have seen (after a week in which a sort of feminine barring-out had taken place) no less than nine young ladies obliged to sit for hours in the angles of the three rooms, like naughty babies, with their faces to the wall; half of them being quite of marriageable age, and all dressed, as was de rigueur [the rule] with us every day, in full evening attire of silk or muslin, with gloves and kid slippers. Naturally, Saturday evenings, instead of affording some relief to the incessant overstrain of the week, were looked upon with terror as the worst time of all. Those who escaped the fell destiny of the corner were allowed, if they chose, to write to their parents, but our letters were perforce committed at night to the schoolmistress to seal, and were not as may be imagined, exactly the natural outpouring of our sentiments as regarded those ladies and their school.

Our household was a large one. It consisted of the two schoolmistresses and joint proprietors, of the sister of one of them and another English governess; of a French, an Italian, and a German lady teacher; of a considerable staff of respectable servants; and

2. Daily.

3. An allusion to Dante Gabriel Rossetti's poem, *The Blessed Damozel.*

finally of twenty-five or twenty-six pupils, varying in age from nine to nineteen. All the pupils were daughters of men of some standing, mostly country gentlemen, members of Parliament, and offshoots of the peerage. There were several heiresses amongst us, and one girl whom we all liked and recognised as the beauty of the school, the daughter of Horace Smith, author of *Rejected Addresses*. On the whole, looking back after the long interval, it seems to me that the young creatures there assembled were full of capabilities for widely extended usefulness and influence. Many were decidedly clever and nearly all were well disposed. There was very little malice or any other vicious ideas or feelings, and no worldliness at all amongst us. * * *

But all this fine human material was deplorably wasted. Nobody dreamed that any one of us could in later life be more or less than an "Ornament of Society." That a pupil in that school should ever become an artist, or authoress, would have been looked upon by both Miss Runciman and Miss Roberts as a deplorable dereliction. Not that which was good in itself or useful to the community, or even that which would be delightful to ourselves, but that which would make us admired in society, was the *raison d'être* [reason for being] of each acquirement. Everything was taught us in the inverse ratio of its true importance. At the bottom of the scale were Morals and Religion, and at the top were Music and Dancing; miserably poor music, too, of the Italian school then in vogue, and generally performed in a showy and tasteless manner on harp or piano. I can recall an amusing instance in which the order of precedence above described was naïvely betrayed by one of our schoolmistresses when she was admonishing one of the girls who had been detected in a lie. "Don't you know, you naughty girl," said Miss R. impressively, before the whole school: "don't you know we had *almost* rather find you have a P—" (the mark of Pretty Well) "in your music, than tell such falsehoods?"

It mattered nothing whether we had any "music in our souls" or any voices in our throats, equally we were driven through the dreary course of practising daily for a couple of hours under a German teacher, and then receiving lessons twice or three times a week from a music master (Griesbach by name) and a singing master. Many of us, myself in particular, in addition to these had a harp master, a Frenchman named Labarre, who gave us lessons at a guinea apiece, while we could only play with one hand at a time. Lastly there were a few young ladies who took instructions in the new instruments, the concertina and the accordion!

The waste of money involved in all this, the piles of useless music, and songs never to be sung, for which our parents had to pay, and the loss of priceless time for ourselves, were truly deplorable; and the result of course in many cases (as in my own) complete failure. One day I said to the good little German teacher, who nourished a hopeless attachment for Schiller's Marquis Posa,[4] and was altogether a sympathetic person, "My dear Fraulein, I mean to practise this piece of Beethoven's till I conquer it." "My dear," responded the honest Fraulein, "you do practice that piece for seex hours a day, and you do live till you are seexty, at the end you will *not* play it!" Yet so hopeless a pupil was compelled to learn for years, not only the piano, but the harp and singing!

Next to music in importance in our curriculum came dancing. The famous old Madame Michaud and her husband both attended us constantly, and we danced to their direction in our large play-room (*lucus a non lucendo*[5]), till we had learned not only all the dances in use in England in that ante-polka epoch, but almost every

---

4. In Friedrich von Schiller's play *Don Carlos* (1787), Posa is a self-sacrificing advocate of religious tolerance and democratic rule.

5. An ironic Latin phrase for naming something after what it lacks; Cobbe means that there was no play to be found in that playroom.

national dance in Europe, the Minuet, the Gavotte, the Cachucha, the Bolero, the Mazurka, and the Tarantella. To see the stout old lady in her heavy green velvet dress, with furbelow[6] a foot deep of sable, going through the latter cheerful performance for our ensample, was a sight not to be forgotten. Beside the dancing we had "calisthenic" lessons every week from a "Capitaine" Somebody, who put us through manifold exercises with poles and dumbbells. How much better a few good country scrambles would have been than all these calisthenics it is needless to say, but our dismal walks were confined to parading the esplanade[7] and neighbouring terraces. Our parties never exceeded six, a governess being one of the number, and we looked down from an immeasurable height of superiority on the processions of twenty and thirty girls belonging to other schools. The governess who accompanied us had enough to do with her small party, for it was her duty to utilise these brief hours of bodily exercise by hearing us repeat our French, Italian or German verbs, according to her own nationality.

Next to Music and Dancing and Deportment, came Drawing, but that was not a sufficiently *voyant* [remarkable] accomplishment, and no great attention was paid to it; the instruction also being of a second-rate kind, except that it included lessons in perspective which have been useful to me ever since. Then followed Modern Languages. No Greek or Latin were heard of at the school, but French, Italian and German were chattered all day long, our tongues being only set at liberty at six o'clock to speak English. *Such* French, such Italian, and such German as we actually spoke may be more easily imagined than described. We had bad "Marks" for speaking wrong languages, *e.g.*, French when we were bound to speak Italian or German, and a dreadful mark for bad French, which was transferred from one to another all day long, and was a fertile source of tears and quarrels, involving as it did a heavy lesson out of Noel et Chapsal's Grammar on the last holder at night. We also read in each language every day to the French, Italian and German ladies, recited lessons to them, and wrote exercises for the respective masters who attended every week. * * *

Naturally after (a very long way after) foreign languages came the study of English. We had a writing and arithmetic master (whom we unanimously abhorred and despised, though one and all of us grievously needed his instructions) and an "English master," who taught us to write "themes," and to whom I, for one, feel that I owe, perhaps, more than to any other teacher in that school, few as were the hours which we were permitted to waste on so insignificant an art as composition in our native tongue! * * *

Lastly, as I have said, in point of importance, came our religious instruction. Our well-meaning schoolmistresses thought it was obligatory on them to teach us something of the kind, but, being very obviously altogether worldly women themselves, they were puzzled how to carry out their intentions. They marched us to church every Sunday when it did not rain, and they made us on Sunday mornings repeat the Collect and Catechism; but beyond these exercises of body and mind, it was hard for them to see what to do for our spiritual welfare. One Ash Wednesday, I remember, they provided us with a dish of salt-fish, and when this was removed to make room for the roast mutton, they addressed us in a short discourse, setting forth the merits of fasting, and ending by the remark that they left us free to take meat or not as we pleased, but that they hoped we should fast; "it would be good for our souls AND OUR FIGURES!"

Each morning we were bound publicly to repeat a text out of certain little books, called *Daily Bread*, left in our bedrooms, and always scanned in frantic haste while

6. Showy fringe.   7. A public promenade.

"doing-up" our hair at the glass, or gabbled aloud by one damsel so occupied while her room-fellow (there were never more than two in each bed-chamber) was splashing about behind the screen in her bath. Down, when the prayer-bell rang, both were obliged to hurry and breathlessly to await the chance of being called on first to repeat the text of the day, the penalty for oblivion being the loss of a "card." Then came a chapter of the Bible, read verse by verse amongst us, and then our books were shut and a solemn question was asked. On one occasion I remember it was: "What have you just been reading, Miss S—?" Miss S—(now a lady of high rank and fashion, whose small wits had been wool-gathering) peeped surreptitiously into her Bible again, and then responded with just confidence, "The First Epistle, Ma'am, of General Peter."[8]

It is almost needless to add, in concluding these reminiscences, that the heterogeneous studies pursued in this helter-skelter fashion were of the smallest possible utility in later life; each acquirement being of the shallowest and most imperfect kind, and all real education worthy of the name having to be begun on our return home, after we had been pronounced "finished."

1894

·——◆◆◆——·

Sarah Stickney Ellis
1799–1872

Author of numerous popular guides to female conduct, including *The Women of England* (1839), *The Daughters of England* (1842), *The Wives of England* (1843), and *The Mothers of England* (1845), Sarah Stickney Ellis advised women to accept their inferiority to men and devote themselves to the happiness and moral elevation of their brothers, husbands, and sons. Idealizing the family home as the center of middle-class English life, Ellis fostered the notion of women's separate domestic sphere. Although she ran a school for girls, Ellis discouraged intellectual ambitions, demanding precisely the sort of self-sacrificing domesticity that Florence Nightingale, and many other talented and capable women, found so intolerably confining.

from The Women of England:
Their Social Duties and Domestic Habits
[THE INFLUENCE OF WOMEN]

It is not to be presumed that women *possess* more power than men; but happily for them, such are their early impressions, associations, and general position in the world, that their moral feelings are less liable to be impaired by the pecuniary objects which too often constitute the chief end of man, and which, even under the limitations of better principle, necessarily engage a large portion of his thoughts. There are many humble-minded women, not remarkable for any particular intellectual endowments, who yet possess so clear a sense of the right and wrong of individual actions, as to be of essential service in aiding the judgments of their husbands, brothers, or sons, in those intricate affairs in which it is sometimes difficult to dissever worldly wisdom from religious duty.

* * * And surely they now need more than ever all the assistance which Providence has kindly provided, to win them away from this warfare, to remind them that they are hastening on towards a world into which none of the treasures they are amassing can be admitted; and, next to those holier influences which operate

---

8. Instead of *The First Epistle General of Peter.*

through the medium of revelation, or through the mysterious instrumentality of Divine love, I have little hesitation in saying, that the society of woman in her highest moral capacity, is best calculated to effect this purpose.

How often has man returned to his home with a mind confused by the many voices, which in the mart, the exchange, or the public assembly, have addressed themselves to his inborn selfishness, or his worldly pride; and while his integrity was shaken, and his resolution gave way beneath the pressure of apparent necessity, or the insidious pretences of expediency, he has stood corrected before the clear eye of woman, as it looked directly to the naked truth, and detected the lurking evil of the specious act he was about to commit. Nay, so potent may have become this secret influence, that he may have borne it about with him like a kind of second conscience, for mental reference, and spiritual counsel, in moments of trial; and when the snares of the world were around him, and temptations from within and without have bribed over the witness in his own bosom, he has thought of the humble monitress who sat alone, guarding the fireside comforts of his distant home; and the remembrance of her character, clothed in moral beauty, has scattered the clouds before his mental vision, and sent him back to that beloved home, a wiser and a better man.

The women of England, possessing the grand privilege of being better instructed than those of any other country, in the minutiae of domestic comfort, have obtained a degree of importance in society far beyond what their unobtrusive virtues would appear to claim. The long-established customs of their country have placed in their hands the high and holy duty of cherishing and protecting the minor morals of life, from whence springs all that is elevated in purpose, and glorious in action. The sphere of their direct personal influence is central, and consequently small; but its extreme operations are as widely extended as the range of human feeling. They may be less striking in society than some of the women of other countries, and may feel themselves, on brilliant and stirring occasions, as simple, rude, and unsophisticated in the popular science of excitement; but as far as the noble daring of Britain has sent forth her adventurous sons, and that is to every point of danger on the habitable globe, they have borne along with them a generosity, a disinterestedness, and a moral courage, derived in no small measure from the female influence of their native country.

It is a fact well worthy of our most serious attention, and one which bears immediately upon the subject under consideration, that the present state of our national affairs is such as to indicate that the influence of woman in counteracting the growing evils of society is about to be more needed than ever. ✳ ✳ ✳

Will an increase of intellectual attainments, or a higher style of accomplishments, effect this purpose? Will the common-place frivolities of morning calls, or an interminable range of superficial reading, enable them to assist their brothers, their husbands, or their sons in becoming happier and better men?—No: let the aspect of society be what it may, man is a social being, and beneath the hard surface he puts on, to fit him for the wear and tear of every day, he has a heart as true to the kindly affections of our nature, as that of woman—as true, though not as suddenly awakened to every pressing call. He has therefore need of all her sisterly services—and under the pressure of the present times, he needs them more than ever—to foster in his nature, and establish in his character that higher tone of feeling, without which he can enjoy nothing beyond a kind of animal existence. ✳ ✳ ✳

In order to ascertain what kind of education is most effective in making woman what she ought to be, the best method is to inquire into the character, station, and peculiar duties of woman throughout the largest portion of her earthly career; and then ask, for what she is most valued, admired, and beloved?

In answer to this, I have little hesitation in saying,—For her disinterested kindness. Look at all the heroines, whether of romance or reality—at all the female characters that are held up to universal admiration—at all who have gone down to honoured graves, amongst the tears and the lamentations of their survivors. Have these been the learned, the accomplished women; the women who could speak many languages, who could solve problems, and elucidate systems of philosophy? No: or if they have, they have also been women who were dignified with the majesty of moral greatness— women who regarded not themselves, their own feebleness, or their own susceptibility of pain, but who, endued with an almost super-human energy, could trample under foot every impediment that intervened between them and the accomplishment of some great object upon which their hopes were fixed, while that object was wholly unconnected with their own personal exaltation or enjoyment, and related only to some beloved object, whose suffering was their sorrow, whose good their gain. * * *

Never yet, however, was woman great, because she had great acquirements; nor can she ever be great in herself—personally, and without instrumentality—as an object, not an agent. * * *

Let us single out from any particular seminary a child who has been there from the years of ten to fifteen, and reckon, if it can be reckoned, the pains that have been spent in making that child a proficient in Latin. Have the same pains been spent in making her disinterestedly kind? And yet what man is there in existence who would not rather his wife should be free from selfishness, than be able to read Virgil without the use of a dictionary. * * *

Taking into consideration the various excellencies and peculiarities of woman, I am inclined to think that the sphere which of all others admits of the highest development of her character, is the chamber of sickness; and how frequently and mournfully familiar are the scenes in which she is thus called to act and feel, let the private history of every family declare.

There is but a very small proportion of the daughters of farmers, manufacturers, and tradespeople, in England, who are ever called upon for their Latin, their Italian, or even for their French; but all women in this sphere of life are liable to be called upon to visit and care for the sick; and if in the hour of weakness and of suffering, they prove to be unacquainted with any probable means of alleviation, and wholly ignorant of the most judicious and suitable mode of offering relief and consolation, they are indeed deficient in one of the highest attainments in the way of usefulness, to which a woman can aspire. * * *

Women have the choice of many means of bringing their principles into exercise, and of obtaining influence, both in their own domestic sphere, and in society at large. Amongst the most important of these is *conversation*, an engine so powerful upon the minds and characters of mankind in general, that beauty fades before it, and wealth in comparison is but as leaden coin. If match-making were indeed the great object of human life, I should scarcely dare to make this assertion, since few men choose women for their conversation, where wealth or beauty are to be had. * * *

* * * But if she has no intellectual hold upon her husband's heart, she must inevitably become that most helpless and pitiable of earthly objects—a slighted wife.

Conversation, understood in its proper character, as distinct from mere talk, might rescue her from this. Not conversation upon books, if her husband happens to be a fox-hunter; nor upon fox-hunting, if he is a book-worm; but exactly that kind of conversation which is best adapted to his tastes and habits, yet at the same time capable of leading him a little out of both into a wider field of observation, and subjects he may never have derived amusement from before, simply from the fact of their never having been presented to his notice.—How pleasantly the evening hours may be made to pass, when a woman who really can converse, will thus beguile the time. But, on the other hand, how wretched is the portion of that man who dreads the dulness of his own fireside! who sees the clog of his existence ever seated there—the same, in the deadening influence she has upon his spirits to-day, as yesterday, to-morrow, and the next day, and the next!

1839

━━✦≡✦━━

Charlotte Brontë
1816–1855

To be a governess or schoolteacher was one of the very few professions open to a middle-class woman, but it was not an enviable life. Rarely was the governess treated as an equal by her employers, even though she was expected to be a "lady." Poorly paid and often rudely treated, she could be fired at a moment's notice, for there was an abundance of needy single women eager to take her place. Charlotte Brontë's novel *Jane Eyre* (1847) portrayed the social isolation of a governess, who is ridiculed to her face by visiting ladies. Brontë's own experiences were unhappy, as this letter to her sister reveals. In another letter, Brontë wrote that it was better to be "a housemaid or kitchen girl, rather than a baited, trampled, desolate, distracted governess."

from Letter to Emily Brontë[1]
[The Horrors of Governessing]

STONEGAPPE, June 8th, 1839

* * * I have striven hard to be pleased with my new situation. The country, the house, and the grounds are, as I have said, divine. But, alack-a-day! there is such a thing as seeing all beautiful around you—pleasant woods, winding white paths, green lawns, and blue sunshiny sky—and not having a free moment or a free thought left to enjoy them in. The children are constantly with me, and more riotous, perverse, unmanageable cubs never grew. As for correcting them, I soon quickly found that was entirely out of the question: they are to do as they like. A complaint to Mrs Sidgwick brings only black looks upon oneself, and unjust, partial excuses to screen the children. I have tried that plan once. It succeeded so notably that I shall try it no more. I said in my last letter that Mrs Sidgwick did not know me. I now begin to find that she does not intend to know me, that she cares nothing in the world about me except to contrive how the greatest possible quantity of labour may be squeezed out of me, and to that end she overwhelms me with oceans of needlework, yards of cambric to hem, muslin nightcaps to make, and, above all things, dolls to dress. I do not think she likes me at all, because I can't help being shy in such an entirely novel scene, surrounded as I have hitherto been by strange and constantly changing faces. I used to think I should like to be in the stir of grand

---

1. Text taken from *The Brontës: Their Lives, Friendships and Correspondence,* vol. 1 (1933, rpt. 1980).

Richard Redgrave. *The Poor Teacher*, 1844. Narrative painting was enormously popular with the Victorians, who delighted in "reading" the story in symbolic visual details and drawing a moral from it. Here Redgrave, whose sisters were governesses, draws attention to his subject's social and emotional isolation. Dressed in mourning, the solitary governess sits indoors while her gaily-clad pupils skip rope in the sunlight, apparently indifferent to the bad news contained in her black-bordered letter. She has been playing "Home Sweet Home" on the piano. With copy books still to correct, she is about to consume her supper, a meager slice of bread and a tiny cup of tea. Contemporary observers speculated that she was an orphan, whose pallor revealed that she was already wasting away from illness and overwork.

folks' society but I have had enough of it—it is dreary work to look on and listen. I see now more clearly than I have ever done before that a private governess has no existence, is not considered as a living and rational being except as connected with the wearisome duties she has to fulfil. While she is teaching the children, working for them, amusing them, it is all right. If she steals a moment for herself she is a nuisance. Nevertheless, Mrs Sidgwick is universally considered an amiable woman. Her manners are fussily affable. She talks a great deal, but as it seems to me not much to the purpose. Perhaps I may like her better after a while. At present I have no call to her. Mr Sidgwick is in my opinion a hundred times better—less profession, less bustling condescension, but a far kinder heart. It is very seldom that he speaks to me, but when he does I always feel happier and more settled for some minutes after. He never asks me to wipe the children's smutty noses or tie their shoes or fetch their pinafores or set them a chair. * * *

Anne Brontë
1820–1849

Like her older sisters, Charlotte and Emily, Anne Brontë tried to earn her living as a governess. All of them were made miserable by the constant drudgery and humiliations, and by being cut off, as governesses usually were, from family and friends. Her autobiographical novel *Agnes Grey* (1847) dramatizes Anne Brontë's own experience of working as a governess. Initially, she had looked forward to the job: "How delightful it would be to be a governess!" says Agnes: "To go out into the world; to enter into a new life; to act for myself; to exercise my unused faculties." But Agnes had not yet realized the drawbacks of a governess's anomalous social status: caught between disrespectful children and contemptuous parents, she was made grimly conscious of her dependent position.

from Agnes Grey
[THE GOVERNESS TORMENTED BY HER CHARGES]

I returned, however, with unabated vigour to my work—a more arduous task than any one can imagine, who has not felt something like the misery of being charged with the care and direction of a set of mischievous turbulent rebels, whom his utmost exertions cannot bind to their duty; while, at the same time, he is responsible for their conduct to a higher power, who exacts from him what cannot be achieved without the aid of the superior's more potent authority: which, either from indolence, or the fear of becoming unpopular with the said rebellious gang, the latter refuses to give. I can conceive few situations more harassing than that wherein, however you may long for success, however you may labour to fulfil your duty, your efforts are baffled and set at nought by those beneath you, and unjustly censured and misjudged by those above. * * *

I particularly remember one wild, snowy afternoon, soon after my return in January; the children had all come up from dinner, loudly declaring that they meant "to be naughty"; and they had well kept their resolution, though I had talked myself hoarse, and wearied every muscle in my throat, in the vain attempt to reason them out of it. I had got Tom pinned up in a corner, whence, I told him, he should not escape till he had done his appointed task. Meantime, Fanny had possessed herself of my work-bag, and was rifling its contents—and spitting into it besides. I told her to let it alone, but to no purpose, of course.

"Burn it, Fanny!" cried Tom; and *this* command she hastened to obey. I sprang to snatch it from the fire, and Tom darted to the door.

"Mary Ann, throw her desk[1] out of the window!" cried he: and my precious desk, containing my letters and papers, my small amount of cash, and all my valuables, was about to be precipitated from the three-story window. I flew to rescue it. Meanwhile Tom had left the room, and was rushing down the stairs, followed by Fanny. Having secured my desk, I ran to catch them, and Mary Ann came scampering after. All three escaped me, and ran out of the house into the garden, where they plunged about in the snow, shouting and screaming in exultant glee.

What must I do? If I followed them, I should probably be unable to capture one, and only drive them farther away; if I did not, how was I to get them in? and what would their parents think of me, if they saw or heard the children rioting, hatless, bonnetless, gloveless, and bootless, in the deep, soft snow?

---

1. Portable box for writing materials and letters, sometimes with a sloping surface for writing on.

While I stood in this perplexity, just without the door, trying by grim looks and angry words, to awe them into subjection, I heard a voice behind me, in harshly piercing tones, exclaiming,—

"Miss Grey! Is it possible? What, in the devil's name, can you be thinking about?"

"I can't get them in, sir," said I, turning round, and beholding Mr Bloomfield, with his hair on end, and his pale blue eyes bolting from their sockets.

"But I INSIST upon their being got in!" cried he, approaching nearer, and looking perfectly ferocious.

"Then, sir, you must call them yourself, if you please, for they won't listen to me," I replied, stepping back.

"Come in with you, you filthy brats! or I'll horsewhip you, every one!" roared he; and the children instantly obeyed. "There, you see! they come at the first word!"

"Yes, when *you* speak."

"And it's very strange, that when you've the care of 'em, you've no better control over 'em than that!—Now, there they are, gone upstairs with their nasty snowy feet! Do go after 'em and see them made decent, for Heaven's sake!"

That gentleman's mother was then staying in the house; and, as I ascended the stairs and passed the drawing-room door, I had the satisfaction of hearing the old lady declaiming aloud to her daughter-in-law to this effect (for I could only distinguish the most emphatic words)—

"Gracious Heavens!—never in all my life!—!—get their death as sure as—! Do you think, my dear, she's a *proper person?* Take my word for it—"

I heard no more, but that sufficed.

1847

+·━◆━·+

John Henry Cardinal Newman
1801–1890

The ideal of gentlemanliness was central to the Victorians' notion of themselves, yet for a society in flux it was a concept increasingly difficult to pin down. What exactly *was* a gentleman? In most people's minds, property, birth, courage, and athleticism were essential ingredients. And, of course, a gentleman was assumed to be a Christian. But the theologian and philosopher of education Newman distinguished between the two: in a series of lectures about the purposes of a liberal education he said that while the gentleman has "a cultivated intellect, a delicate taste, a candid, equitable, dispassionate mind, a noble and courteous bearing in the conduct of life . . . they are no guarantee for sanctity or even for conscientiousness; they may attach to the man of the world, to the profligate, to the heartless." Thus for Newman, who was both, a gentleman is not necessarily a Christian: one may have character and education, but not faith. He subtly suggests the vanity behind the gentleman's courtesy; gentility and virtue are not necessarily the same thing.

from The Idea of a University
[A DEFINITION OF A GENTLEMAN]

Hence it is that it is almost a definition of a gentleman to say he is one who never inflicts pain. This description is both refined and, as far as it goes, accurate. He is mainly occupied in merely removing the obstacles which hinder the free and unembarrassed action of those about him; and he concurs with their movements rather than takes the initiative himself. His benefits may be considered as parallel to what are called comforts or conveniences in arrangements of a personal nature: like an easy chair or a good fire, which do their part in dispelling cold and fatigue, though nature provides both means of rest and animal heat without them. The true gentleman in like manner carefully avoids whatever may cause a jar or a jolt in the minds of those with whom he is cast;—all clashing of opinion, or collision of feeling, all restraint, or suspicion, or gloom, or resentment; his great concern being to make every one at their ease and at home. He has his eyes on all his company; he is tender towards the bashful, gentle towards the distant, and merciful towards the absurd; he can recollect to whom he is speaking; he guards against unseasonable allusions, or topics which may irritate; he is seldom prominent in conversation, and never wearisome. He makes light of favours while he does them, and seems to be receiving when he is conferring. He never speaks of himself except when compelled, never defends himself by a mere retort, he has no ears for slander or gossip, is scrupulous in imputing motives to those who interfere with him, and interprets every thing for the best. He is never mean or little in his disputes, never takes unfair advantage, never mistakes personalities or sharp sayings for arguments, or insinuates evil which he dare not say out. From a longsighted prudence, he observes the maxim of the ancient sage, that we should ever conduct ourselves towards our enemy as if he were one day to be our friend. He has too much good sense to be affronted at insults, he is too well employed to remember injuries, and too indolent to bear malice. He is patient, forbearing, and resigned, on philosophical principles; he submits to pain, because it is inevitable, to bereavement, because it is irreparable, and to death, because it is his destiny. If he engages in controversy of any kind, his disciplined intellect preserves him from the blundering discourtesy of better, perhaps, but less educated minds; who, like blunt weapons, tear and hack instead of cutting clean, who mistake the point in argument, waste their strength on trifles, misconceive their adversary, and leave the question more involved than they find it. He may be right or wrong in his opinion, but he is too clear-headed to be unjust; he is as simple as he is forcible, and as brief as he is decisive. Nowhere shall we find greater candour, consideration, indulgence: he throws himself into the minds of his opponents, he accounts for their mistakes. He knows the weakness of human reason as well as its strength, its province and its limits. If he be an unbeliever, he will be too profound and large-minded to ridicule religion or to act against it; he is too wise to be a dogmatist or fanatic in his infidelity. He respects piety and devotion; he even supports institutions as venerable, beautiful, or useful, to which he does not assent; he honours the ministers of religion, and it contents him to decline its mysteries without assailing or denouncing them. He is a friend of religious toleration, and that, not only because his philosophy has taught him to look on all forms of faith with an impartial eye, but also from the gentleness and effeminacy of feeling, which is the attendant on civilization.

1852

━━ ❧❦❧ ━━

Isabella Beeton
1836–1865

The home was a near-sacred institution in Victorian England, and when Mrs. Beeton published her book of advice on household management it became a bestseller second only to the Bible. In over a thousand pages of small print, she instructed women on matters ranging from the supervision of servants to the care of the sick, from meal planning to proper conduct during a social call. Mrs. Beeton's portrait of the mistress of the house reflects a complex, somewhat contradictory, sense of a woman's role: she is at once "the commander of an army"—with the housekeeper as her "second in command"—and a lady of leisure, enjoying "the pleasures of literature" and "the innocent delights of the garden." Yet, like a child, she needs to be scolded to rise early and be punctual. Although Mrs. Beeton was just twenty-four, she was respected as an oracle in the domestic sphere; her cookbook is still used today. She died in childbirth at twenty-eight.

from The Book of Household Management

I must frankly own, that if I had known, beforehand, that this book would have cost me the labour which it has, I should never have been courageous enough to commence it. What moved me, in the first instance, to attempt a work like this, was the discomfort and suffering which I had seen brought upon men and women by household mismanagement. I have always thought that there is no more fruitful source of family discontent than a housewife's badly-cooked dinners and untidy ways. Men are now so well served out of doors,—at their clubs, well-ordered taverns, and dining-houses, that in order to compete with the attractions of these places, a mistress must be thoroughly acquainted with the theory and practice of cookery, as well as be perfectly conversant with all the other arts of making and keeping a comfortable home. * * *

As with the Commander of an Army, or the leader of any enterprise, so is it with the mistress of a house. Her spirit will be seen through the whole establishment; and just in proportion as she performs her duties intelligently and thoroughly, so will her domestics follow in her path. Of all those acquirements, which more particularly belong to the feminine character, there are none which take a higher rank, in our estimation, than such as enter into a knowledge of household duties; for on these are perpetually dependent the happiness, comfort, and well-being of a family. * * *

Early Rising is one of the most Essential Qualities which enter into good Household Management, as it is not only the parent of health, but of innumerable other advantages. Indeed, when a mistress is an early riser, it is almost certain that her house will be orderly and well-managed. On the contrary, if she remain in bed till a late hour, then the domestics, who, as we have before observed, invariably partake somewhat of their mistress's character, will surely become sluggards. * * *

Friendships should not be hastily formed, nor the heart given, at once, to every new-comer. There are ladies who uniformly smile at, and approve everything and everybody, and who possess neither the courage to reprehend vice, nor the generous warmth to defend virtue. The friendship of such persons is without attachment, and their love without affection or even preference. * * *

Hospitality is a most Excellent Virtue; but care must be taken that the love of company, for its own sake, does not become a prevailing passion; for then the habit is no longer hospitality, but dissipation. * * * With respect to the continuance of friendships * * * it may be found necessary, in some cases, for a mistress to relinquish, on assuming the responsibility of a house-hold, many of those commenced in the earlier part of her life. * * *

In Conversation, Trifling Occurrences, such as small disappointments, petty annoyances, and other every-day incidents, should never be mentioned to your friends. The extreme injudiciousness of repeating these will be at once apparent, when we reflect on the unsatisfactory discussions which they too frequently occasion, and on the load of advice which they are the cause of being tendered, and which is, too often, of a kind neither to be useful nor agreeable. * * * If the mistress be a wife, never let an account of her husband's failings pass her lips. * * *

After Breakfast is over, it will be well for the mistress to make a round of the kitchen and other offices, to see that all are in order, and that the morning's work has been properly performed by the various domestics. The orders for the day should then be given, and any questions which the domestics desire to ask, respecting their several departments, should be answered, and any special articles they may require, handed to them from the store-closet. * * *

After this General Superintendence of her servants, the mistress, if a mother of a young family, may devote herself to the instruction of some of its younger members, or to the examination of the state of their wardrobe, leaving the later portion of the morning for reading, or for some amusing recreation. * * *

Unless the means of the mistress be very circumscribed, and she be obliged to devote a great deal of her time to the making of her children's clothes, and other economical pursuits, it is right that she should give some time to the pleasures of literature, the innocent delights of the garden, and to the improvement of any special abilities for music, painting, and other elegant arts, which she may, happily, possess. * * *

After Luncheon, Morning Calls and Visits may be made and received. These may be divided under three heads: those of ceremony, friendship, and congratulation or condolence. Visits of ceremony, or courtesy, which occasionally merge into those of friendship, are to be paid under various circumstances. Thus, they are uniformly required after dining at a friend's house, or after a ball, picnic, or any other party. These visits should be short, a stay of from fifteen to twenty minutes being quite sufficient. A lady paying a visit may remove her boa or neckerchief; but neither her shawl nor bonnet.

When other visitors are announced, it is well to retire as soon as possible, taking care to let it appear that their arrival is not the cause. When they are quietly seated, and the bustle of their entrance is over, rise from your chair, taking a kind leave of the hostess, and bowing politely to the guests. Should you call at an inconvenient time, not having ascertained the luncheon hour, or from any other inadvertence, retire as soon as possible, without, however, showing that you feel yourself an intruder. It is not difficult for any well-bred or even good-tempered person, to know what to say on such an occasion, and, on politely withdrawing, a promise can be made to call again, if the lady you have called on, appear really disappointed.

In Paying Visits of Friendship, it will not be so necessary to be guided by etiquette as in paying visits of ceremony; and if a lady be pressed by her friend to remove her shawl and bonnet, it can be done if it will not interfere with her subsequent arrangements. * * * During these visits, the manners should be easy and cheerful, and the subjects of conversation such as may be readily terminated. Serious discussions or arguments are to be altogether avoided.

1861

Queen Victoria
1819–1901

Queen Victoria, who ruled from 1837 to 1901, was the most prominent woman of the age, and during her reign the monarchy came to symbolize the farflung power of the British empire. Although she was a capable woman who wielded genuine political influence, she felt uncomfortably thrust into greatness, and often deplored the contradictions of her position. A firm believer in the notion that men and women should occupy separate spheres, the queen regarded campaigns for women's rights as "dangerous and unchristian and unnatural." The mother of nine children, Victoria was revered as the embodiment of domestic propriety, but her views on maternity were decidedly unsentimental. Her letters to her eldest daughter lament the sufferings of pregnancy, and in the 1850s Queen Victoria pioneered the use of chloroform in childbirth, thus making anesthesia acceptable for other women.

Letters and Journal Entries on the Position of Women
Journal[1]

20 June 1837

I was awoke at 6 o'clock by Mamma,[2] who told me that the Archbishop of Canterbury and Lord Conyngham were here, and wished to see me. I got out of bed and went into my sitting-room (only in my dressing-gown), and alone, and saw them. Lord Conyngham then acquainted me that my poor Uncle, the King, was no more, and had expired at 12 minutes p. 2 this morning, and consequently that I am Queen. Lord Conyngham knelt down and kissed my hand, at the same time delivering to me the official announcement of the poor King's demise. The Archbishop then told me that the Queen[3] was desirous that he should come and tell me the details of the last moments of my poor, good Uncle; he said that he had directed his mind to religion and had died in a perfectly happy, quiet state of mind, and was quite prepared for his death. He added that the King's sufferings at the last were not very great but that there was a good deal of uneasiness. Lord Conyngham, who I charged to express my feelings of condolence and sorrow to the poor Queen, returned directly to Windsor. I then went to my room and dressed.

Since it has pleased Providence to place me in this station, I shall do my utmost to fulfil my duty towards my country; I am very young and perhaps in many, though not in all things, inexperienced, but I am sure, that very few have more real good will and more real desire to do what is fit and right than I have. * * *

To Princess Frederick William[4]

24 March 1858

That you should feel shy sometimes I can easily understand. I do so very often to this hour. But being married gives one one's position which nothing else can. Think however what it was for me, a girl of 18 all alone, not brought up at court as you were—but very humbly at Kensington Palace—with trials and difficulties, to receive and be everywhere the first! No, no one knows what a life of difficulties mine was—and is! How thankful I am that none of you, please God! ever will have that anomalous and trying position. Now do enter into this in your letters, you so seldom do that, except to answer a question.

Now to reply to your observation that you find a married woman has much more liberty than an unmarried one; in one sense of the word she has,—but what I meant was—in a physical point of view—and if you have hereafter (as I had constantly for the first 2 years of my marriage)—aches—and sufferings and miseries and plagues—which you must struggle against—and enjoyments etc. to give up—constant precautions to take, you will feel the yoke of a married woman! Without that—certainly it is unbounded happiness—if one has a husband one worships! It is a foretaste of heaven. And you have a husband who adores you, and is, I perceive, ready to meet every wish and desire of your's. I had 9 times for 8 months[5] to bear with those above-named enemies and real misery (besides many duties) and I own it tried me sorely; one feels so pinned down—one's wings clipped—in fact, at the best (and few were or

---

1. From *Queen Victoria in Her Letters and Journals*, ed. Christopher Hibbert (1985).
2. Victoria's mother was the widow of Edward, Duke of Kent, the fourth son of George III. Since Edward died when Victoria was an infant, she was brought up by her mother. She had just turned eighteen when she became queen on the death of her uncle, King William IV.
3. Adelaide, the widow of William IV.

4. This and the following letters on marriage and childbirth are from *Dearest Child: Letters between Queen Victoria and the Princess Royal, 1858–1861*, ed. Roger Fulford (1964). On January 25, 1858, at the age of seventeen, Victoria's eldest daughter had married Prince Frederick [Fritz], later Crown Prince of Prussia. Her mother wrote her frequent letters, full of maternal advice.
5. Victoria alludes to her nine pregnancies.

Edwin Landseer. *Windsor Castle in Modern Times*, 1841–1845, showing Queen Victoria and Prince Albert at home with their eldest child Princess Victoria.

are better than I was) only half oneself—particularly the first and second time. This I call the "shadow side" as much as being torn away from one's loved home, parents and brothers and sisters. And therefore—I think our sex a most unenviable one.

26 May 1858

The horrid news contained in Fritz's letter to Papa [that the Princess was pregnant] upset us dreadfully. The more so as I feel certain almost it will all end in nothing.

15 June 1858

What you say of the pride of giving life to an immortal soul is very fine, dear, but I own I cannot enter into that; I think much more of our being like a cow or a dog at such moments; when our poor nature becomes so very animal and unecstatic—but for you, dear, if you are sensible and reasonable not in ecstasy nor spending your day with nurses and wet nurses, which is the ruin of many a refined and intellectual young lady, without adding to her real maternal duties, a child will be a great resource. Above all, dear, do remember never to lose the modesty of a young girl towards others (without being prude); though you are married don't become a matron at once to whom everything can be said, and who minds saying nothing herself—I remained particular to a degree (indeed feel so now) and often feel shocked at the confidences of other married ladies. I fear abroad they are very indelicate about these things.

29 January 1859

God be praised for all his mercies, and for bringing you safely through this awful time![6] Our joy, our gratitude knows no bounds.

My precious darling, you suffered much more that I ever did—and how I wish I could have lightened them for you! Poor dear Fritz—how he will have suffered for you! I think and feel much for him; the dear little boy if I could but see him for one minute, give you one kiss. It is hard, very hard. But we are so happy, so grateful! ∗ ∗ ∗ You will and must feel so thankful all is over! But don't be alarmed for the future, it never can be so bad again!

20 April 1859

I really think I shall never let your sisters marry—certainly not to be so constantly away and see so little of their parents—as till now, you have done, contrary to all that I was originally promised and told. I am so glad to see that you so entirely enter into all my feelings as a mother. Yes, dearest, it is an awful moment to have to give one's innocent child up to a man, be he ever so kind and good—and to think of all that she must go through! I can't say what I suffered, what I felt—what struggles I had to go through—(indeed I have not quite got over it yet) and that last night when we took you to your room, and you cried so much, I said to Papa as we came back "after all, it is like taking a poor lamb to be sacrificed." You now know—what I meant, dear. I know that God has willed it so and that these are the trials which we poor women must go through; no father, no man can feel this! Papa never would enter into it all! As in fact he seldom can in my very violent feelings. It really makes me shudder when I look around at all your sweet, happy, unconscious sisters—and think that I must give them up too—one by one!! Our dear Alice [who was 15], has seen and heard more (of course not what no one ever can know before they marry and before they have had children) than you did, from your marriage—and quite enough to give her a horror rather of marrying.

4 May 1859

Abstractedly, I have no *tendre* for them [babies] till they have become a little human; an ugly baby is a very nasty object—and the prettiest is frightful when undressed—till about four months; in short as long as they have their big body and little limbs and that terrible frog-like action. But from four months, they become prettier and prettier. And I repeat it—your child would delight me at any age.

15 June 1859

Now I must scold you a wee bit for an observation which really seems at variance with your own expressions. You say "how glad" Ada [the Queen's niece] "must be" at being again in that most charming situation, which you yourself very frequently told me last year was so wretched. How can anyone, who has not been married above two years and three quarters, (like Ada) rejoice at being a third time in that condition? I positively think those ladies who are always *enceinte* quite disgusting; it is more like a rabbit or guinea-pig than anything else and really it is not very nice.

16 May 1860

All marriage is such a lottery—the happiness is always an exchange—though it may be a very happy one—still the poor woman is bodily and morally the husband's slave. That always sticks in my throat. When I think of a merry, happy, free young

---

6. After a difficult and dangerous labor, Victoria's daughter had given birth on January 27, 1859; her son was the future Kaiser Wilhelm II, who led Germany against England in the First World War.

girl—and look at the ailing, aching state a young wife generally is doomed to—which you can't deny is the penalty of marriage.

17 November 1860

My beloved child, these lines are to wish you heartily and warmly joy of your 20th birthday—an important age—though married nearly three years and with two children it seems but of little consequence. Still to bid adieu to one's "teens" is a serious thing!

18 December 1861

What is to become of us all?[7] Of the unhappy country, of Europe, of all? For you all, the loss of such a father is totally irreparable! I will do all I can to follow out all his wishes—to live for you all and for my duties. But how I, who leant on him for all and everything—without whom I did nothing, moved not a finger, arranged not a print or photograph, didn't put on a gown or bonnet if he didn't approve it shall be able to go on, to live, to move, to help myself in difficult moments? How I shall long to ask his advice! Oh! it is too, too weary! The day—the night (above all the night) is too sad and weary. The days never pass! I try to feel and think that I am living on with him, and that his pure and perfect spirit is guiding and leading me and inspiring me!

Sweet little Beatrice comes to lie in my bed every morning which is a comfort. I long so to cling to and clasp a loving being. Oh! how I admired Papa! How in love I was with him! How everything about him was beautiful and precious in my eyes! Oh! how, how I miss all, all! Oh! Oh! the bitterness of this—of this woe!

To William Gladstone[8]

6 May 1870

The circumstances respecting the Bill to give women the same position as men with respect to Parliamentary franchise gives her an opportunity to observe that she had for some time past wished to call Mr Gladstone's attention to the mad & utterly demoralizing movement of the present day to place women in the same position as to professions—as *men*;—& amongst others, in the *Medical Line*.

* * * And she is *most* anxious that it should be known how she not only disapproves but *abhors* the attempts to destroy all propriety & womanly feeling which will inevitably be the result of what has been proposed. The Queen is a woman herself—& knows what an anomaly her *own* position is:—but that can be reconciled with reason & propriety tho' it is a terribly difficult & trying one. But to tear away all the barriers which surround a woman, & to propose that they should study with *men*—things which could not be named before them—certainly not *in a mixed* audience—would be to introduce a total disregard of what must be considered as belonging to the rules & principles of morality.

The Queen feels so strongly upon this dangerous & unchristian & unnatural *cry* & movement of "woman's rights,"—in which she knows Mr Gladstone *agrees*, (as he sent her that excellent Pamphlet by Lady) that she is most anxious that Mr Glad-stone & others should take some steps to check this alarming danger & to make whatever use they can of her name. * * *

---

7. Victoria was grief-stricken at the death of her husband, Prince Albert, on December 14, 1861; after his death she mourned him obsessively, going into virtual seclusion for many years. Beatrice was her ninth child, born in 1857. This letter is from *Queen Victoria in Her Letters and Journals*, ed. Christopher Hibbert (1985).

8. Gladstone (1809–1898) was the prime minister in four Liberal governments (1868–1874, 1880–1885, 1886, 1892–1894). This letter is from *The Queen and Mr. Gladstone* (1933) by Philip Guedalla. The Queen refers to the recurrence of the proposal to give women the vote, first presented to the House of Commons in 1866 by J. S. Mill.

Let woman be what God intended; a helpmate for a man—but with totally different duties & vocations.

To Sir Theodore Martin[9]

29 May 1870

The Queen is most anxious to enlist every one who can speak or write to join in checking this mad, wicked folly of "Woman's Rights," with all its attendant horrors, on which her poor feeble sex is bent, forgetting every sense of womanly feeling and propriety. Lady— ought to get a *good whipping.*

It is a subject which makes the Queen so furious that she cannot contain herself. God created men and women different—then let them remain each in their own position. Tennyson has some beautiful lines on the difference of men and women in *The Princess.*[1] Woman would become the most hateful, heartless, and disgusting of human beings were she allowed to unsex herself; and where would be the protection which man was intended to give the weaker sex? The Queen is sure that Mrs Martin agrees with her.

Charles Kingsley
1819–1875

Charles Kingsley was a hearty country clergyman and prolific writer whose sermons praised physical prowess and manly pursuits such as riding, hunting, and fishing. He was a vigorous Protestant, suspicious of celibacy and of what he considered the feminine monasticism of Catholicism: an injudicious remark of his about the dishonesty of the Catholic clergy prompted Newman's *Apologia Pro Vita Sua.* Kingsley is so often paired with Thomas Hughes, author of *Tom Brown's School Days,* that he has been called "the most famous Brown in the Victorian period;" although he didn't go to Rugby, he embodied the spirit of its headmaster Dr. Arnold. "Muscular Christianity" was originally a term of mocking disparagement for boisterous assertions of bodily strength and energy as the foundation of a pure moral life. But the blending of Christianity with manliness was part of an emerging middle-class identity that strove toward an ideal of public service: both Hughes and Kingsley embraced Christian socialism, a movement to respond to the injustices of industrialism.

from Letters and Memories
[MUSCULAR CHRISTIANITY]

[From a letter to his fiancée, Frances Grenfell:]

There has always seemed to me something impious in the neglect of personal health, strength, and beauty, which the religious, and sometimes clergymen of this day affect. It is very often a mere form of laziness. . . . I could not do half the little good I do do here, if it were not for that strength and activity which some consider coarse and degrading. Do not be afraid of my overworking myself. If I stop, I go down. I must work. . . . How merciful God has been in turning all the strength and hardihood I gained in snipe shooting and hunting, and rowing, and jack-fishing in those magnificent fens[1] to His work! While I was following my own fancies, He was preparing me for His work. . . . Is it not an awful proof that matter is not necessarily evil, that we shall be clothed in bodies even in our

---

9. This letter is from *Queen Victoria As I Knew Her* (1908) by Sir Theodore Martin, a lawyer and man of letters.
1. See *The Princess* (page 1927): "For woman is not undevelopt man, / But diverse: could we make her as

the man, / Sweet Love were slain: his dearest bond is this, / Not like to like, but like in difference."
1. Low marshy areas.

perfect state? Think of that! . . . It seems all so harmonious to me. It is all so full of God, that I see no inconsistency in making my sermons while I am cutting wood; and no "bizarrerie" in talking one moment to one man about the points of a horse, and the next moment to another about the mercy of God to sinners. I try to catch men by their leading ideas, and so draw them off insensibly to my leading idea. And so I find—shall I tell you? that God is really permitting me to do His work—I find that dissent is decreasing; people are coming to church who never went anywhere before; that I am loved and respected— or rather that God's ministry, which has been here deservedly despised, alas! is beginning to be respected; and above all, that the young wild fellows who are considered as hopeless by most men, because most men are what they call "spoony Methodists," *i.e.*, effeminate ascetics—dare not gainsay, but rather look up to a man who they see is their superior, if he chose to exert his power, in physical as well as intellectual skill. * * *

1842   1877

[From a letter to the Reverend F. D. Maurice:]

I do feel very deeply the truth which John Mill has set forth in a one-sided way in his new book on Liberty[2] * * * about the past morality of Christendom having taken a somewhat abject tone, and requiring, as a complement, the old Pagan virtues, which our forefathers learnt from Plutarch's Lives, and of which the memory still lingers in our classical education. I do not believe, of course, that the want really exists: but that it was created, principally by the celibate misanthropy of the patristic and mediaeval church. But I have to preach the divineness of the whole manhood, and am content to be called a Muscular Christian, or any other impertinent name, by men who little dream of the weakness of character, sickness of body, and misery of mind, by which I have bought what little I know of the human heart.

1857   1877

* · ⚓ · *

Sir Henry Newbolt
1862–1938

Newbolt's rousing patriotic poems make explicit the link between public school games and the romantic ideology of empire. Schoolboy sports were not merely about keeping fit; with their emphasis on manliness, mettle, and pluck, they were preparing the upper classes to regard imperialism as a grand adventure. School loyalty merged with national patriotism. Games fostered the notion that wars were won by team spirit, holding up the side, and never quitting. Young English officers carried this schoolboy code into combat: they saw war itself as a "great game," and battlefields as playing fields. Their letters from the front during World War I described the action in the language of sports. One officer actually dribbled a soccer ball as he led his men to their deaths in the battle of the Somme.

Vitaï Lampada[1]

There's a breathless hush in the Close[2] to-night—
    Ten to make and the match to win—
A bumping pitch and a blinding light,
    An hour to play and the last man in.
5   And it's not for the sake of a ribboned coat,

---

2. *On Liberty* (1859); see page 1845.
1. The Torch of Life; a reference to a relay race, described in Lucretius's *De Rerum Natura*, where runners hand off a

flaming torch.
2. The playing fields at a public school.

Or the selfish hope of a season's fame,
But his Captain's hand on his shoulder smote—
"Play up! play up! and play the game!"

The sand of the desert is sodden red,—
10   Red with the wreck of a square that broke;—
The Gatling's[3] jammed and the Colonel dead,
    And the regiment blind with dust and smoke.
The river of death has brimmed his banks,
    And England's far, and Honour a name,
15 But the voice of a schoolboy rallies the ranks:
    "Play up! play up! and play the game!"

This is the word that year by year,
    While in her place the School is set,
Every one of her sons must hear,
20   And none that hears it dare forget.
This they all with a joyful mind
    Bear through life like a torch in flame,
And falling fling to the host behind—
    "Play up! play up! and play the game!"

1897

[END OF PERSPECTIVES: VICTORIAN LADIES AND GENTLEMEN]

Alfred, Lord Tennyson
1809–1892

"There, that is the first money you have ever earned by your poetry, and, take my word for it, it will be the last." These were the words of Tennyson's crusty grandfather, as he doled out ten shillings for the teenager's ode on the death of his grandmother. The pen proved mightier than the prediction, however, as Tennyson went on to become the most celebrated poet of the age. His books sold tens of thousands of copies; the Queen and Parliament named him Poet Laureate, then Lord, and finally Baron Tennyson; his annual income surpassed ten thousand pounds a year; and he was widely regarded as something more than a poet—a prophet, a sage, and an infallible moneymaker. A New York publisher once offered him a thousand pounds for any three-stanza poem he cared to write.

    It is often said that Tennyson's greatness lay in eloquently presenting the anxieties and aspirations of his era. In poems such as *Ulysses, In Memoriam,* and *Idylls of the King,* he expressed the energy, resolve, faith, and idealism of an industrious society that was nonetheless racked by deep doubts about its materialism, the truth of the Bible, and the possibility of achieving a truly Christian society. But Tennyson was not just a mouthpiece for his age: in the early and mid-Victorian period Tennyson was one of its most progressive voices, espousing views that were all the more daring for a shy and sensitive man struggling to realize his dream of becoming "a *popular* poet." His assertion in *The Princess* (1847) that "the woman's cause is man's" anticipates Mill's *The Subjection of Women* by more than twenty years; in the course of writing *In Memoriam* (1850) he lucidly formulated some of the main principles of evolutionary theory well before Darwin's *Origin of Species* (1859); he called public attention to the industri-

---

3. An early form of machine gun.

alized misery and revolutionary anger of the poor during the 1840s while the contemporaneous works of Marx and Engels were virtually unknown; and in *Locksley Hall* (1842) he evoked the technological promise of the future as compellingly as any science fiction writer.

One key to Tennyson's poetic success was his prosaic devotion to the Victorian gospel of hard work. He labored patiently, in poverty and without recognition, to overcome his troubled background. Born in Somersby, Lincolnshire, Tennyson was the third surviving son in a close-knit but emotionally unstable family of eleven children, two of whom suffered lifelong mental illness, while two more were addicted to drugs and alcohol. The poet's father, George, was an awkward, tormented man whose ill temper was aggravated into alcoholism and violence when he was disinherited in favor of his younger brother, and then forced to accept a position as village rector. It seems that the entire family was prone to epilepsy. Well into maturity, Alfred was haunted by fear of "the black blood of the Tennysons."

Tennyson's grim childhood was brightened by his mother's warmth and affection, his father's extensive library, and both parents' love of poetry. The rectory was surrounded by large gardens and open countryside, and as a child Tennyson composed nature poetry in the manner of James Thomson's *Seasons*. Early years at a brutally strict grammar school, followed by intensive tutoring from his erudite father, gave Tennyson a solid grounding in Greek, Latin, English, and modern languages by the time he went to Cambridge University in 1827. He had already mastered the styles of poets ranging from Horace and Virgil to Shakespeare, Milton, Scott, and Byron, and earlier that year he published his first book, *Poems by Two Brothers*. It was written with his brother Charles, with whom he used to exchange lines on their country walks, shouting them out across the hedges. The habit of building poems around a series of sonorous individual lines would remain with Tennyson all his life.

At Cambridge the timid country boy began gradually to assume the artistic persona that would be revered throughout the empire. Tall, ruggedly handsome, and with a faraway look in his eyes that was actually due to myopia, Tennyson fit everyone's idea of how a poet should look. He distinguished himself by the quality of his talk, his humorous storytelling, and his acting ability. In 1829 he received the Chancellor's Medal for *Timbuctoo*, the first poem in blank verse ever to win. The same year he and his best friend Arthur Henry Hallam joined "The Apostles," a select group of undergraduates who met to discuss social, philosophical, and literary issues. Members became lifelong friends, and their admiration of his early work helped convince the reticent Tennyson to publish *Poems, Chiefly Lyrical* in 1830. The book received mixed reviews.

In 1831 his father died, and Tennyson had to return home without a degree. Yet Tennyson persevered, issuing in 1832 a new volume, *Poems*. This time, the reviews were actively hostile. Tennyson's morale was sustained only by the visits to Somersby of Hallam, who by now was engaged to Tennyson's sister Emily. Then in 1833 Hallam died suddenly of a cerebral hemorrhage while on a trip to Vienna, and Tennyson's life changed forever.

Within a week of hearing the news, Tennyson began work on his greatest poem, though he did not know then that the brief lyric passages of love, loss, and doubt that he composed to assuage his grief would eventually become *In Memoriam*, an epic meditation on mortality, evolution, and the hard-won consolations of inner faith. He was already proficient, like his early hero Byron, in turning his own private misery into virtuoso evocations of emotionally charged landscapes. As John Stuart Mill wrote in 1835, Tennyson excelled in "the power of *creating* scenery, in keeping with some state of human feeling, so fitted to it as to be the embodied symbol of it, and to summon up the state of feeling itself, with a force not to be surpassed by anything but reality." Quoting *Mariana* as an example, Mill concluded that "words surely never created a more vivid feeling of physical and spiritual dreariness."

Outwardly Tennyson was calm, actively reading, writing, and socializing, but in his poetry he pictured himself as a weeping widower who mourned "a loss forever new." In 1842 he reluctantly published a two-volume edition of *Poems*, improving earlier works and introducing new ones, most notably *Ulysses* and *Morte d'Arthur*. Although his reputation was now rising, the poet was at a low ebb. He was so poor and hampered by responsibilities to his unraveling family that he was forced to postpone indefinitely his marriage to Emily Sellwood, to whom he had become engaged in 1838.

At this point Tennyson lost all his money in a scheme for carving wood by machinery. His friends feared he was on the verge of suicide. Here, as at other dark times in his life, he relied on sheer willpower to follow the advice he once offered to a depressed friend: "Just go grimly on." Eventually travel, hydropathic cures, new acquaintances, and improving finances assuaged his melancholia. Publication of *The Princess* in 1847 finally gave him the popular notice he had long sought.

But it was not until 1850 that Tennyson triumphed in life and art. In May, after seventeen years' brooding, he published *In Memoriam* to great acclaim; on June 13 he married Emily; and by the end of June one reviewer was calling him "the greatest living poet." The sentiment was timely, since Wordsworth had died in April, and by November Tennyson was named Poet Laureate. In 1852 his first son, Hallam, was born, and in 1853 the Tennysons moved to a neo-Gothic country estate called Farringford on the Isle of Wight.

His experimental "monodrama" *Maud* (1855) sold well though it baffled the critics, one of whom remarked that there was one vowel too many, no matter which, in the title. But the combined sales of his works enabled him to buy Farringford, where he could work in peace amid wreaths of tobacco smoke, adored by Emily and protected from his fans by a large staff. There he entertained great personages of the day, from Prince Albert and Garibaldi to his neighbor Julia Margaret Cameron, who badgered him into photographic immortality. Henceforth, whenever he visited London, he was sought after in society and mobbed by admirers.

The stability of his new life enabled Tennyson to pursue many longer projects, including the best-selling narrative poem *Enoch Arden* (1864) and several successful plays. Most of his energies were taken up, however, with the great work of his later life, *Idylls of the King*. A trip to Wales helped fuel his interest in Arthurian legends, and he published groups of *Idylls* in 1859 and 1869. As with *In Memoriam* and *Maud*, the poet gradually felt his way, as he composed the parts, toward a larger design for the whole. All the while he held before him the image of "my lost Arthur," until recollections of his actual friend Arthur Hallam blended with

Max Beerbohm. *Tennyson Reading "In Memoriam" to his Sovereign.*

the two literary Arthurs of *In Memoriam* and *Idylls of the King*. He rounded out his tale to an epic twelve books, not producing a final version until 1888, just a few years before his death.

In the *Idylls* as in much of his earlier poetry, Tennyson is a poet of deferment. His most memorable characters—Mariana, the Lotos Eaters, Ulysses, Tithonus, and the speakers of *In Memoriam* and *Maud*, among them—long for reunions and releases that are ever yet to come, as distant as the return of King Arthur from Avalon. In old age Tennyson remembered of his youth that even before he could read, "the words 'far, far away' always had a strange charm for me."

After Tennyson's death in 1892 and his burial with great pomp in Westminster Abbey, his reputation suffered a decline that lasted till the end of the Modernist period around 1945. But Tennyson's lyric genius was admired by poets as various as the Pre-Raphaelites and Whitman, Poe and Hopkins. Auden and Eliot were in rare agreement that he had "the finest ear of any English poet since Milton." Critics continue to dispute whether the sense of Tennyson's poetry is equal to its magnificent sound, but any close reading of his work will reveal Tennyson's deep ambivalence about the world of which he gradually became both oracle and icon. Often beneath his harmonies we hear echoes of his favorite childhood sound, "voices crying in the wind." As Eliot observed, Tennyson was "the most instinctive rebel against the society in which he was the most perfect conformist."

The Kraken[1]

Below the thunders of the upper deep;
Far, far beneath in the abysmal sea,
His ancient, dreamless, uninvaded sleep
The Kraken sleepeth: faintest sunlights flee
5   About his shadowy sides: above him swell
Huge sponges of millennial growth and height;
And far away into the sickly light,
From many a wondrous grot° and secret cell   *grotto, cave*
Unnumber'd and enormous polypi°   *octopuses*
10   Winnow with giant arms the slumbering green.
There hath he lain for ages and will lie
Battening upon huge seaworms in his sleep,
Until the latter fire[2] shall heat the deep;
Then once by man and angels to be seen,
15   In roaring he shall rise and on the surface die.

1830

Mariana

"Mariana in the moated grange."[1]

Measure for Measure

With blackest moss the flower-plots
    Were thickly crusted, one and all:
The rusted nails fell from the knots
    That held the pear to the gable-wall.
5   The broken sheds look'd sad and strange:
    Unlifted was the clinking latch;
    Weeded and worn the ancient thatch
Upon the lonely moated grange.
    She only said, "My life is dreary,

---

1. Giant mythical sea monster.
2. The fire of Judgement Day, which will consume the world.
1. The *moated grange* was no particular grange, but one which rose to the music of Shakespeare's words: "There, at the moated grange, resides this dejected Mariana" (*Measure for Measure* Act 3. Sc. 1) [Tennyson's note]. In Shakespeare's play, Angelo refuses to marry Mariana after her brother and her dowry are lost in a shipwreck.

10   He cometh not," she said;
    She said, "I am aweary, aweary,
        I would that I were dead!"

Her tears fell with the dews at even;
    Her tears fell ere the dews were dried;
15   She could not look on the sweet heaven.
    Either at morn or eventide.
After the flitting of the bats,
    When thickest dark did trance° the sky,   *traverse*
    She drew her casement-curtain by,
20   And glanced athwart the glooming flats.
    She only said, "The night is dreary,
        He cometh not," she said;
    She said, "I am aweary, aweary,
        I would that I were dead!"

25   Upon the middle of the night,
    Waking she heard the night-fowl crow:
The cock sung out an hour ere light:
    From the dark fen the oxen's low
Came to her: without hope of change,
30   In sleep she seem'd to walk forlorn,
    Till cold winds woke the gray-eyed morn
About the lonely moated grange.
    She only said, "The day is dreary,
        He cometh not," she said;
35   She said, "I am aweary, aweary,
        I would that I were dead!"

About a stone-cast from the wall
    A sluice with blacken'd waters slept,
And o'er it many, round and small,
40   The cluster'd marish-mosses[2] crept.
Hard by a poplar shook alway,
    All silver-green with gnarled bark:
For leagues no other tree did mark
The level waste, the rounding gray.
45   She only said, "My life is dreary,
        He cometh not," she said;
    She said, "I am aweary, aweary,
        I would that I were dead!"

And ever when the moon was low,
50   And the shrill winds were up and away,
In the white curtain, to and fro,
    She saw the gusty shadow sway.
But when the moon was very low,
    And wild winds bound within their cell,[3]
55   The shadow of the poplar fell
Upon her bed, across her brow.

---

2. The little marsh-moss lumps that float on the surface
of water [Tennyson's note].

3. The cave of Aeolus, god of the winds.

She only said, "The night is dreary,
    He cometh not," she said;
She said, "I am aweary, aweary,
60   I would that I were dead!"

All day within the dreamy house,
    The doors upon their hinges creak'd;
The blue fly sung in the pane; the mouse
    Behind the mouldering wainscot shriek'd,
65 Or from the crevice peer'd about.
    Old faces glimmer'd thro' the doors,
    Old footsteps trod the upper floors,
Old voices called her from without.
    She only said, "My life is dreary,
70   He cometh not," she said;
    She said, "I am aweary, aweary,
        I would that I were dead!"

The sparrow's chirrup on the roof,
    The slow clock ticking, and the sound
75 Which to the wooing wind aloof
    The poplar made, did all confound
Her sense; but most she loathed the hour
    When the thick-moted sunbeam lay
    Athwart the chambers, and the day
80 Was sloping toward his western bower.
    Then, said she, "I am very dreary,
        He will not come," she said;
    She wept, "I am aweary, aweary,
        Oh God, that I were dead!"

1830

The Lady of Shalott[1]

Part 1

On either side the river lie
Long fields of barley and of rye,
That clothe the wold° and meet the sky;   *rolling uplands*
And thro' the field the road runs by
5   To many-tower'd Camelot;
And up and down the people go,
Gazing where the lilies blow°   *bloom*
Round an island there below,
        The island of Shalott.

10 Willows whiten, aspens quiver,
Little breezes dusk and shiver
Thro' the wave that runs for ever
By the island in the river
        Flowing down to Camelot.

---

1. The Lady of Shalott is evidently the Elaine of the *Morte d'Arthur*, but I do not think that I had ever heard of the latter when I wrote the former [Tennyson's note]. In Malory, Elaine dies of grief for love of Lancelot, but the curse, the weaving, and the mirror are all Tennyson's inventions.

William Holman Hunt, *The Lady of Shalott*, from the Moxon edition of Tennyson's poems, 1857. This edition was a high point in Victorian book illustration, including drawings by Rossetti and Millais as well as Hunt. Tennyson, however, complained about this illustration because it depicts the lady entangled in the threads of her tapestry, making her unable to leave the loom, as she does in his poem. Hunt responded: "I had only half a page on which to convey the impression of weird fate, whereas you use about fifteen pages to give expression to the complete idea."

15   Four gray walls, and four gray towers,
        Overlook a space of flowers,
        And the silent isle imbowers
                The Lady of Shalott.

        By the margin, willow-veil'd,
20   Slide the heavy barges trail'd
        By slow horses; and unhail'd
        The shallop° flitteth silken-sail'd   *small boat*
                Skimming down to Camelot:
        But who hath seen her wave her hand?
25   Or at the casement seen her stand?
        Or is she known in all the land,
                The Lady of Shalott?

        Only reapers, reaping early
        In among the bearded barley,
30   Hear a song that echoes cheerly
        From the river winding clearly,
                Down to tower'd Camelot:
        And by the moon the reaper weary,
        Piling sheaves in uplands airy,
35   Listening, whispers "'Tis the fairy
                Lady of Shalott.'"

Part 2

There she weaves by night and day
A magic web with colours gay.
She has heard a whisper say,
40   A curse is on her if she stay
        To look down to Camelot.
She knows not what the curse may be,
And so she weaveth steadily,
And little other care hath she,
45   The Lady of Shalott.

And moving thro' a mirror clear[2]
That hangs before her all the year,
Shadows of the world appear.
There she sees the highway near
50   Winding down to Camelot:
There the river eddy whirls,
And there the surly village-churls,°   *peasants*
And the red cloaks of market girls,
        Pass onward from Shalott.

55   Sometimes a troop of damsels glad,
An abbot on an ambling pad,°   *horse*
Sometimes a curly shepherd-lad,
Or long-hair'd page in crimson clad,
        Goes by to tower'd Camelot;
60   And sometimes thro' the mirror blue
The knights come riding two and two:
She hath no loyal knight and true,
        The Lady of Shalott.

But in her web she still delights
65   To weave the mirror's magic sights,
For often thro' the silent nights
A funeral, with plumes and lights
        And music, went to Camelot:
Or when the moon was overhead,
70   Came two young lovers lately wed;
"I am half sick of shadows," said
        The Lady of Shalott.

Part 3

A bow-shot from her bower-eaves,
He rode between the barley-sheaves,
75   The sun came dazzling thro' the leaves,
And flamed upon the brazen greaves°   *leg armor*
        Of bold Sir Lancelot.[3]

2. Working from the back of their tapestries, weavers placed mirrors on the other side to see the effect of their work.

3. The greatest of King Arthur's knights, Lancelot was in love with Queen Guinevere.

A red-cross knight for ever kneel'd
To a lady in his shield,⁴
80   That sparkled on the yellow field,
      Beside remote Shalott.

The gemmy bridle glitter'd free,
Like to some branch of stars we see
Hung in the golden Galaxy.
85   The bridle bells rang merrily
      As he rode down to Camelot:
And from his blazon'd baldric° slung   *ornamented belt*
A mighty silver bugle hung,
And as he rode his armour rung,
90   Beside remote Shalott.

All in the blue unclouded weather
Thick-jewell'd shone the saddle-leather,
The helmet and the helmet-feather
Burn'd like one burning flame together,
95   As he rode down to Camelot.
As often thro' the purple night,
Below the starry clusters bright,
Some bearded meteor, trailing light,
      Moves over still Shalott.

100   His broad clear brow in sunlight glow'd;
On burnish'd hooves his war-horse trode;
From underneath his helmet flow'd
His coal-black curls as on he rode,
      As he rode down to Camelot.
105   From the bank and from the river
He flash'd into the crystal mirror,
"Tirra lirra," by the river
      Sang Sir Lancelot.

She left the web, she left the loom,
110   She made three paces thro' the room,
She saw the water-lily bloom,
She saw the helmet and the plume,
      She look'd down to Camelot.
Out flew the web and floated wide;
115   The mirror crack'd from side to side;
"The curse is come upon me," cried
      The Lady of Shalott.

Part 4

In the stormy east-wind straining,
The pale yellow woods were waning,
160   The broad stream in his banks complaining,

4. Lancelot's shield depicts the Red Cross Knight—a character in Spenser's *Faerie Queene* who champions holiness—kneeling in homage to his lady.

Heavily the low sky raining
    Over tower'd Camelot;
Down she came and found a boat
Beneath a willow left afloat,
125 And round about the prow she wrote
    The Lady of Shalott.

And down the river's dim expanse
Like some bold seër in a trance,
Seeing all his own mischance—
130 With a glassy countenance
    Did she look to Camelot.
And at the closing of the day
She loosed the chain, and down she lay;
The broad stream bore her far away,
135   The Lady of Shalott.

Lying, robed in snowy white
That loosely flew to left and right—
The leaves upon her falling light—
Thro' the noises of the night
140   She floated down to Camelot:
And as the boat-head wound along
The willowy hills and fields among,
They heard her singing her last song,
    The Lady of Shalott.

145 Heard a carol, mournful, holy,
Chanted loudly, chanted lowly,
Till her blood was frozen slowly,
And her eyes were darken'd wholly,
    Turn'd to tower'd Camelot.
150 For ere she reach'd upon the tide
The first house by the water-side,
Singing in her song she died,
    The Lady of Shalott.

Under tower and balcony,
155 By garden-wall and gallery,
A gleaming shape she floated by,
Dead-pale between the houses high,
    Silent into Camelot.
Out upon the wharfs they came;
160 Knight and burgher, lord and dame,
And round the prow they read her name,
    The Lady of Shalott.

Who is this? and what is here?
And in the lighted palace near
165 Died the sound of royal cheer;
And they cross'd themselves for fear,
    All the knights at Camelot:
But Lancelot mused a little space;

He said, "She has a lovely face;
170   God in his mercy lend her grace,
      The Lady of Shalott."

1832, 1842

The Lotos-Eaters[1]

"Courage!" he[2] said, and pointed toward the land,
"This mounting wave will roll us shoreward soon."
In the afternoon they came unto a land[3]
In which it seemed always afternoon.
5   All round the coast the languid air did swoon,
Breathing like one that hath a weary dream.
Full-faced above the valley stood the moon;
And like a downward smoke, the slender stream[4]
Along the cliff to fall and pause and fall did seem.

10   A land of streams! some, like a downward smoke,
Slow-dropping veils of thinnest lawn,[5] did go;
And some thro' wavering lights and shadows broke,
Rolling a slumbrous sheet of foam below.
They saw the gleaming river seaward flow
15   From the inner land: far off, three mountain-tops,
Three silent pinnacles of aged snow,
Stood sunset-flush'd: and, dew'd with showery drops,
Up-clomb the shadowy pine above the woven copse.

The charmèd sunset linger'd low adown
20   In the red West: thro' mountain clefts the dale
Was seen far inland, and the yellow down°   *upland plain*
Border'd with palm, and many a winding vale
And meadow, set with slender galingale;°   *an aromatic herb*
A land where all things always seem'd the same!
25   And round about the keel with faces pale,
Dark faces pale against that rosy flame,
The mild-eyed melancholy Lotos-eaters came.

Branches they bore of that enchanted stem,
Laden with flower and fruit, whereof they gave
30   To each, but whoso did receive of them,
And taste, to him the gushing of the wave
Far far away did seem to mourn and rave
On alien shores; and if his fellow spake,
His voice was thin, as voices from the grave;
35   And deep-asleep he seem'd, yet all awake,
And music in his ears his beating heart did make.

---

1. In Homer's *Odyssey*, book 9, Odysseus (Ulysses) and his men, returning home from the Trojan War, are tempted to stay forever in the land of the Lotus-eaters. Anyone who ate the sweet fruit of the lotus would lose all desire to return home.
2. Odysseus.
3. "The strand" was, I think, my first reading, but the no rhyme of "land" and "land" was lazier [Tennyson's note].
4. Taken from the waterfall at Gavarnie, in the Pyrenees, when I was 20 or 21 [Tennyson's note].
5. Sheer linen fabric, used in theaters to suggest a waterfall.

They sat them down upon the yellow sand,
Between the sun and moon upon the shore;
And sweet it was to dream of Fatherland,
40 Of child, and wife, and slave; but evermore
Most weary seem'd the sea, weary the oar,
Weary the wandering fields of barren foam.
Then some one said, "We will return no more;"
And all at once they sang, "Our island home[6]
45 Is far beyond the wave; we will no longer roam."

Choric Song[7]

1

There is sweet music here that softer falls
Than petals from blown roses on the grass,
Or night-dews on still waters between walls
Of shadowy granite, in a gleaming pass;
50 Music that gentlier on the spirit lies,
Than tir'd eyelids upon tir'd eyes;[8]
Music that brings sweet sleep down from the blissful skies.
Here are cool mosses deep,
And thro' the moss the ivies creep,
55 And in the stream the long-leaved flowers weep,
And from the craggy ledge the poppy hangs in sleep.

2

Why are we weigh'd upon with heaviness,
And utterly consumed with sharp distress,
While all things else have rest from weariness?
60 All things have rest: why should we toil alone,
We only toil, who are the first of things,
And make perpetual moan,
Still from one sorrow to another thrown:
Nor ever fold our wings,
65 And cease from wanderings,
Nor steep our brows in slumber's holy balm;
Nor harken what the inner spirit sings,
"There is no joy but calm!"
Why should we only toil, the roof and crown of things?

3

70 Lo! in the middle of the wood,
The folded leaf is woo'd from out the bud
With winds upon the branch, and there
Grows green and broad, and takes no care,
Sun-steep'd at noon, and in the moon
75 Nightly dew-fed; and turning yellow
Falls, and floats adown the air.
Lo! sweeten'd with the summer light,

---

6. Ithaca, off the west coast of Greece.
7. What follows is sung by Odysseus's men.
8. I printed, contrary to my custom, "tir'd," not "tired,"
for fear that readers might pronounce the word "tired"

[Tennyson's note]. Tennyson wished to make "the word
neither monosyllable or disyllabic, but a dreamy child of
the two."

The full-juiced apple, waxing over-mellow,
Drops in a silent autumn night.
80   All its allotted length of days,
The flower ripens in its place,
Ripens and fades, and falls, and hath no toil,
Fast-rooted in the fruitful soil.

4

Hateful is the dark-blue sky,
85   Vaulted o'er the dark-blue sea.
Death is the end of life; ah, why
Should life all labour be?
Let us alone. Time driveth onward fast,
And in a little while our lips are dumb.
90   Let us alone. What is it that will last?
All things are taken from us, and become
Portions and parcels of the dreadful Past.
Let us alone. What pleasure can we have
To war with evil? Is there any peace
95   In ever climbing up the climbing wave?
All things have rest, and ripen toward the grave
In silence; ripen, fall and cease:
Give us long rest or death, dark death, or dreamful ease.

5

How sweet it were, hearing the downward stream,
100   With half-shut eyes ever to seem
Falling asleep in a half-dream!
To dream and dream, like yonder amber light,
Which will not leave the myrrh-bush on the height;
To hear each other's whisper'd speech;
105   Eating the Lotos day by day,
To watch the crisping ripples on the beach,
And tender curving lines of creamy spray;
To lend our hearts and spirits wholly
To the influence of mild-minded melancholy;
110   To muse and brood and live again in memory,
With those old faces of our infancy
Heap'd over with a mound of grass,
Two handfuls of white dust, shut in an urn of brass!

6

Dear is the memory of our wedded lives,
115   And dear the last embraces of our wives
And their warm tears: but all hath suffer'd change:
For surely now our household hearths are cold:
Our sons inherit us: our looks are strange:
And we should come like ghosts to trouble joy.
120   Or else the island princes[9] over-bold
Have eat our substance, and the minstrel sings
Before them of the ten years' war in Troy,[1]

9. The suitors of Penelope, Odysseus's wife and presumed
widow.

1. The Trojan War, from which Odysseus and his men
are returning.

And our great deeds, as half-forgotten things.
Is there confusion in the little isle?
125   Let what is broken so remain.
The Gods are hard to reconcile:
'Tis hard to settle order once again.
There *is* confusion worse than death,
Trouble on trouble, pain on pain,
130   Long labour unto aged breath,
Sore task to hearts worn out by many wars
And eyes grown dim with gazing on the pilot-stars.

7

But, propt on beds of amaranth and moly,[2]
How sweet (while warm airs lull us, blowing lowly)
135   With half-dropt eyelid still,
Beneath a heaven dark and holy,
To watch the long bright river drawing slowly
His waters from the purple hill—
To hear the dewy echoes calling
140   From cave to cave thro' the thick-twined vine—
To watch the emerald-colour'd water falling
Thro' many a wov'n acanthus-wreath[3] divine!
Only to hear and see the far-off sparkling brine,
Only to hear were sweet, stretch'd out beneath the pine.

8

145   The Lotos blooms below the barren peak:
The Lotos blows by every winding creek:
All day the wind breathes low with mellower tone:
Thro' every hollow cave and alley lone
Round and round the spicy downs the yellow Lotos-dust is blown.
150   We have had enough of action, and of motion we,
Roll'd to starboard, roll'd to larboard, when the surge was seething free,
Where the wallowing monster spouted his foam-fountains in the sea.
Let us swear an oath, and keep it with an equal mind,
In the hollow Lotos-land to live and lie reclined
155   On the hills like Gods together, careless of mankind.
For they lie beside their nectar, and the bolts[4] are hurl'd
Far below them in the valleys, and the clouds are lightly curl'd
Round their golden houses, girdled with the gleaming world:
Where they smile in secret, looking over wasted lands,
160   Blight and famine, plague and earthquake, roaring deeps and fiery sands,
Clanging fights, and flaming towns, and sinking ships, and praying hands.
But they smile, they find a music centred in a doleful song
Steaming up, a lamentation and an ancient tale of wrong,
Like a tale of little meaning tho' the words are strong;
165   Chanted from an ill-used race of men that cleave the soil,
Sow the seed, and reap the harvest with enduring toil,

---

2. *Amaranth*, the immortal flower of legend; *moly*, the sacred herb of mystical power, used as a charm by Odysseus against Circe [Tennyson's note].
3. The plant seen in the capitals of Corinthian pillars [Tennyson's note].
4. Nectar is the food of the gods, and thunderbolts their weapons.

Storing yearly little dues of wheat, and wine and oil;
Till they perish and they suffer—some, 'tis whisper'd—down in hell
Suffer endless anguish, others in Elysian[5] valleys dwell,
170 Resting weary limbs at last on beds of asphodel.[6]
Surely, surely, slumber is more sweet than toil, the shore
Than labour in the deep mid-ocean, wind and wave and oar;
Oh rest ye, brother mariners, we will not wander more.

1832, 1842

Ulysses[1]

It little profits that an idle king,
By this still hearth, among these barren crags,
Match'd with an aged wife, I mete and dole
Unequal laws unto a savage race,
5   That hoard, and sleep, and feed, and know not me.

I cannot rest from travel: I will drink
Life to the lees: all times I have enjoy'd
Greatly, have suffer'd greatly, both with those
That loved me, and alone; on shore, and when
10   Thro' scudding drifts the rainy Hyades[2]
Vext the dim sea: I am become a name;
For always roaming with a hungry heart
Much have I seen and known; cities of men
And manners, climates, councils, governments,
15   Myself not least, but honour'd of them all;
And drunk delight of battle with my peers,
Far on the ringing plains of windy Troy.
I am a part of all that I have met;
Yet all experience is an arch wherethro'
20   Gleams that untravell'd world, whose margin fades
For ever and for ever when I move.
How dull it is to pause, to make an end,
To rust unburnish'd, not to shine in use!
As tho' to breathe were life. Life piled on life
25   Were all too little, and of one to me
Little remains: but every hour is saved
From that eternal silence, something more,
A bringer of new things; and vile it were

5. Paradisical; Elysium was the part of the underworld where the blessed dwelled after death.
6. Flowering plant of the lily family, said to grow in the Elysian fields.
1. The poem was written soon after Arthur Hallam's death, and it gives the feeling about the need of going further and braving the struggle of life perhaps more simply than anything in In Memoriam [Tennyson's note]. In Homer's Odyssey, Ulysses returns home to Ithaca, after ten years of wandering following the fall of Troy, and slays the suitors who have been harassing his wife Pene-

lope. "My father," wrote Tennyson's son, "takes up the story of further wanderings at the end of the Odyssey. Ulysses has lived in Ithaca for a long while before the craving for fresh travel seizes him. The comrades he addresses are of the same heroic mould as his old comrades." Dante also has Ulysses set off on another voyage, this time westward through the Strait of Gibraltar (Inferno 26).
2. The Hyades were a constellation of seven stars whose rising was believed to bring rain.

For some three suns to store and hoard myself,
30   And this gray spirit yearning in desire
To follow knowledge like a sinking star,
Beyond the utmost bound of human thought.

This is my son, mine own Telemachus,
To whom I leave the sceptre and the isle—
35   Well-loved of me, discerning to fulfil
This labour, by slow prudence to make mild
A rugged people, and thro' soft degrees
Subdue them to the useful and the good.
Most blameless is he, centred in the sphere
40   Of common duties, decent not to fail
In offices of tenderness, and pay
Meet adoration to my household gods,
When I am gone. He works his work, I mine.

There lies the port; the vessel puffs her sail:
45   There gloom the dark broad seas. My mariners,
Souls that have toil'd, and wrought, and thought with me—
That ever with a frolic welcome took
The thunder and the sunshine, and opposed
Free hearts, free foreheads—you and I are old;
50   Old age hath yet his honour and his toil;
Death closes all: but something ere the end,
Some work of noble note, may yet be done,
Not unbecoming men that strove with Gods.
The lights begin to twinkle from the rocks:
55   The long day wanes: the slow moon climbs: the deep
Moans round with many voices. Come, my friends,
'Tis not too late to seek a newer world.
Push off, and sitting well in order smite
The sounding furrows; for my purpose holds
60   To sail beyond the sunset, and the baths
Of all the western stars,[3] until I die.
It may be that the gulfs will wash us down:
It may be we shall touch the Happy Isles,[4]
And see the great Achilles, whom we knew.
65   Tho' much is taken, much abides; and tho'
We are not now that strength which in old days
Moved earth and heaven; that which we are, we are;
One equal temper of heroic hearts,
Made weak by time and fate, but strong in will
70   To strive, to seek, to find, and not to yield.

1833   1842

---

3. The Greeks believed that the flat earth was encircled by an ocean into which the stars dipped at times.
4. The Islands of the Blessed were a land of perpetual summer thought to lie in the western ocean beyond the Pillars of Hercules (the Straits of Gibraltar). Great heros—such as Achilles, the Greek warrior who killed the Trojan prince, Hector—were sent by the gods to live there as immortals.

Break, Break, Break[1]

Break, break, break,
    On thy cold gray stones, O Sea!
And I would that my tongue could utter
    The thoughts that arise in me.

5   O well for the fisherman's boy,
    That he shouts with his sister at play!
    O well for the sailor lad,
    That he sings in his boat on the bay!

    And the stately ships go on
10   To their haven under the hill;
But O for the touch of a vanish'd hand,
    And the sound of a voice that is still!

Break, break, break
    At the foot of thy crags, O Sea!
15   But the tender grace of a day that is dead
    Will never come back to me.

1834   1842

The Epic [Morte d'Arthur][1]

At Francis Allen's on the Christmas-eve,—
The game of forfeits[2] done—the girls all kiss'd
Beneath the sacred bush° and past away—   *mistletoe*
The parson Holmes, the poet Everard Hall,
5   The host, and I sat round the wassail-bowl,°   *punch bowl*
Then half-way ebb'd: and there we held a talk,
How all the old honour had from Christmas gone,
Or gone, or dwindled down to some odd games
In some odd nooks like this; till I, tired out
10   With cutting eights that day upon the pond,
Where, three times slipping from the outer edge,
I bump'd the ice into three several stars,
Fell in a doze; and half-awake I heard
The parson taking wide and wider sweeps,
15   Now harping on the church-commissioners,[3]
Now hawking at Geology and schism;[4]
Until I woke, and found him settled down
Upon the general decay of faith
Right thro' the world, "at home was little left,

1. Inspired by the death of the poet's friend, Arthur Hallam. Cf. *In Memoriam*, page 1928.
1. One of Tennyson's lifelong projects was an epic poem about King Arthur, which ultimately became the *Idylls of the King*. The last poem in the sequence, describing the death of Arthur, was actually written first: it was begun in 1833, when Arthur Hallam died, and was called *Morte d'Arthur*. Tennyson framed the poem with *The Epic*, a description of contemporary (i.e., 19th century) Christ-mas Eve festivities, during which the poet—here called Everard Hall—was encouraged to read *Morte d'Arthur* aloud.
2. A party game where players have to forfeit an item, then redeem it by performing a silly task.
3. In 1835 the government set up a system of commissioners to oversee the finances of the Anglican Church.
4. A reference to current scientific and religious controversies.

20   And none abroad: there was no anchor, none,
        To hold by." Francis, laughing, clapt his hand
        On Everard's shoulder, with "I hold by him."
        "And I," quoth Everard, "by the wassail-bowl."
        "Why yes," I said, "we knew your gift that way
25   At college: but another which you had,
        I mean of verse (for so we held it then),
        What came of that?" "You know," said Frank, "he burnt
        His epic, his King Arthur, some twelve books"—
        And then to me demanding why? "Oh, sir,
30   He thought that nothing new was said, or else
        Something so said 'twas nothing—that a truth
        Looks freshest in the fashion of the day;
        God knows: he has a mint of reasons: ask.
        It pleased *me* well enough." "Nay, nay," said Hall,
35   "Why take the style of those heroic times?
        For nature brings not back the Mastodon,
        Nor we those times; and why should any man
        Remodel models? these twelve books of mine
        Were faint Homeric echoes,[5] nothing-worth,
40   Mere chaff and draff, much better burnt." "But I,"
        Said Francis, "pick'd the eleventh from this hearth
        And have it: keep a thing, its use will come.
        I hoard it as a sugar-plum for Holmes."
        He laugh'd, and I, tho' sleepy, like a horse
45   That hears the corn-bin open, prick'd my ears;
        For I remember'd Everard's college fame
        When we were Freshmen: then at my request
        He brought it; and the poet little urged,
        But with some prelude of disparagement,
50   Read, mouthing out his hollow oes and aes,
        Deep-chested music, and to this result.[6]

                    * * *

        Here ended Hall, and our last light, that long
325   Had wink'd and threaten'd darkness, flared and fell:
        At which the Parson, sent to sleep with sound,
        And waked with silence, grunted "Good!" but we
        Sat rapt: it was the tone with which he read—
        Perhaps some modern touches here and there
330   Redeem'd it from the charge of nothingness—
        Or else we loved the man, and prized his work;
        I know not: but we sitting, as I said,
        The cock crew loud; as at that time of year
        The lusty bird takes every hour for dawn:
335   Then Francis, muttering, like a man ill-used,
        "There now—that's nothing!" drew a little back,

---

5. I.e., Hall claims his poems merely echoed the great epics of Homer. He may have been fishing for a compliment: when the poet Walter Savage Landor read Tennyson's *Morte d'Arthur* in manuscript, he declared "it is more Homeric than any poem of our time, and rivals some of the noblest parts of the Odyssey."

6. At this point Hall reads aloud *Morte d'Arthur*; mortally wounded, Arthur is carried away on a barge to the blessed isle of Avalon, from which it is prophesied that he will one day return to rule again.

And drove his heel into the smoulder'd log,
That sent a blast of sparkles up the flue:
And so to bed; where yet in sleep I seem'd
340 To sail with Arthur under looming shores,
Point after point; till on to dawn, when dreams
Begin to feel the truth and stir of day,
To me, methought, who waited with a crowd,
There came a bark that, blowing forward, bore
345 King Arthur, like a modern gentleman
Of stateliest port;° and all the people cried,   *bearing*
"Arthur is come again: he cannot die."[7]
Then those that stood upon the hills behind
Repeated—"Come again, and thrice as fair;"
350 And, further inland, voices echo'd—"Come
With all good things, and war shall be no more."
At this a hundred bells began to peal,
That with the sound I woke, and heard indeed
The clear church-bells ring in the Christmas-morn.

1833–1838   1842

FROM **THE PRINCESS**[1]

Tears, Idle Tears[2]

Tears, idle tears, I know not what they mean,
Tears from the depth of some divine despair
Rise in the heart, and gather to the eyes,
In looking on the happy Autumn-fields,
5 And thinking of the days that are no more.

Fresh as the first beam glittering on a sail,
That brings our friends up from the underworld,
Sad as the last which reddens over one
That sinks with all we love below the verge;
10 So sad, so fresh, the days that are no more.

Ah, sad and strange as in dark summer dawns
The earliest pipe of half-awaken'd birds
To dying ears, when unto dying eyes
The casement° slowly grows a glimmering square;   *window*
15 So sad, so strange, the days that are no more.

Dear as remember'd kisses after death,
And sweet as those by hopeless fancy feign'd
On lips that are for others; deep as love,

---

7. There is a legend that King Arthur will return once
more to lead his people.
1. *The Princess* (1847) is a long narrative poem, set in a
fairy-tale realm, about the effort to found a women's college. (The first British institution for the higher education of women, Queen's College, London, opened the
next year.) The story is interspersed with brief "songs" or
lyrics—some of them added later—whose musicality and

depth of emotion soon won them admiration as independent works of art.
2. This song came to me on the yellowing autumn-tide at
Tintern Abbey, full for me of its bygone memories [Ten-
nyson's note]. The poet would remember not only
Wordsworth's poem *Tintern Abbey* (page 1529), but also
his dead friend Hallam, buried not far away.

20   Deep as first love, and wild with all regret;
        O Death in Life, the days that are no more.

["The Woman's Cause Is Man's"]¹

        "Blame not thyself too much," I said, "nor blame
240   Too much the sons of men and barbarous laws;
        These were the rough ways of the world till now.
        Henceforth thou hast a helper, me, that know
        The woman's cause is man's: they rise or sink
        Together, dwarf'd or godlike, bond or free:
245   For she that out of Lethe² scales with man
        The shining steps of Nature, shares with man
        His nights, his days, moves with him to one goal,
        Stays all the fair young planet in her hands³—
        If she be small, slight-natured, miserable,
250   How shall men grow? but work no more alone!
        Our place is much: as far as in us lies
        We two will serve them both in aiding her—
        Will clear away the parasitic forms
        That seem to keep her up but drag her down—
255   Will leave her space to burgeon out of all
        Within her—let her make herself her own
        To give or keep, to live and learn and be
        All that not harms distinctive womanhood.
        For woman is not undevelopt man,
260   But diverse: could we make her as the man,
        Sweet Love were slain: his dearest bond is this,
        Not like to like, but like in difference.
        Yet in the long years liker must they grow;
        The man be more of woman, she of man;
265   He gain in sweetness and in moral height,
        Nor lose the wrestling thews° that throw the world;   *muscles*
        She mental breadth, nor fail in childward care,
        Nor lose the childlike in the larger mind;
        Till at the last she set herself to man,
270   Like perfect music unto noble words;
        And so these twain, upon the skirts of Time,
        Sit side by side, full-summ'd in all their powers,
        Dispensing harvest, sowing the To-be,
        Self-reverent each and reverencing each,

1. Princess Ida, the heroine of *The Princess*, founds a women's college, and swears she will never marry. But through various exploits—including masquerading as a woman to attend her college—Prince Florian convinces her that her feminist experiment is futile. She turns her college into a hospital and agrees to marry him. In this, his concluding speech (from Book 7), Florian envisions a future in which men and women will be more alike, and the relations between them will be improved.

2. The waters of forgetfulness, here implying a new beginning.

3. Hallam Tennyson notes: "Cf. Ross Wallace's lines:

'The hand that rocks the cradle is the hand that rules the world.' My father felt that woman must train herself more earnestly than heretofore to do the large work that lies before her, even though she may not be destined to be wife or mother, cultivating her understanding not her memory only, her imagination in its highest phases, her inborn spirituality and her sympathy with all that is pure, noble and beautiful, rather than mere social accomplishments; and that then and then only will she further the progress of humanity, then and then only men will continue to hold her in reverence."

275   Distinct in individualities,
         But like each other ev'n as those who love.
         Then comes the statelier Eden back to men:
         Then reign the world's great bridals, chaste and calm:
         Then springs the crowning race of humankind.
280   May these things be!"
                              Sighing she spoke "I fear
         They will not."
                              "Dear, but let us type them now
         In our own lives, and this proud watchword rest
         Of equal; seeing either sex alone
         Is half itself, and in true marriage lies
285   Nor equal, nor unequal: each fulfils
         Defect in each, and always thought in thought,
         Purpose in purpose, will in will, they grow,
         The single pure and perfect animal,
         The two-cell'd heart beating, with one full stroke,
290   Life."
                   And again sighing she spoke: "A dream
         That once was mine! what woman taught you this?"
1839–1847   1847

In Memoriam A. H. H.

When Tennyson was twenty-four, his closest friend Arthur Henry Hallam died suddenly in Vienna. Regarded by all who knew him as the most promising intellect of his generation, Hallam had been Tennyson's confidante, best critic, and strongest supporter. It was Hallam who encouraged Tennyson to publish, helped him get his work through the press, and sustained him amidst criticism, self-doubt, and family crises. His perceptive review of the early poems remains among the best essays ever written on Tennyson. The poet learned of Hallam's death on October 1, 1833, and soon began composing short lyrics exploring the dark questions raised by so devastating an event. "I did not write them with any view of weaving them into a whole," Tennyson later said, "or for publication, until I found I had written so many."

The 131 sections of In Memoriam, produced over sixteen years, constitute a new type of elegy, what T. S. Eliot called "the concentrated diary" of a man confessing his love, sorrow, and doubts about the immortality of the soul. Tennyson drew on many sources, ranging from Greek pastoral elegy and Horace's Odes, to the sonnet sequences of Petrarch and Shakespeare. As in traditional elegy, the death of a friend blights joy in all living things, until the poet asserts his omnipresence in nature. But Tennyson expands his personal loss into the potential death of the human species, questioning the direction of evolution, science's challenges to Christian belief, and the ultimate destiny of the human spirit. The result is an intensely private autobiography of grief that nonetheless registers the troubled spiritual condition of Victorian England.

Presented as a broken narrative of the poet's fitful progress from despair to solace, In Memoriam covers a three-year period, from the death of Hallam in the autumn of 1833 to the spring of 1836. Sections 9–15 describe the return of Hallam's body to England by sea; section 19, its burial. The structural heart of the poem is the succession of three Christmases (sections 28–30, 78, 104–106), whose celebration of Christian rebirth gradually rings less hollow, more convincing. The poet's acceptance of his loss also deepens over the three springs that follow (sections 39, 86, and 115); the timeless renewal of nature eventually reawakens the poet to life. Yet for many readers, the bleak evidence of blindly predatory Nature at the poem's emotional nadir (sections 54, 55, and 56) nearly overshadows the brighter hopes of later sections.

As Eliot remarked, *In Memoriam* triumphs not "because of the quality of its faith, but because of the quality of its doubt."

The form of the poem is justly famous. At the time he was writing Tennyson mistakenly thought he had created a new stanza—iambic tetrameter quatrains, rhyming *abba*—unaware that Sidney and Jonson had preceded him. But Tennyson's brilliant, sustained use of the quatrains was so well adapted to his material that the form has come to be called "the *In Memoriam* stanza." The first line-ending lingers in the memory while the central couplet pushes other sounds to the fore, then the rhyme is completed across that divide just as the stanza ends. This aural pattern of separation and completion parallels the intellectual and emotional progress of the poem: sound and substance combine in a verbal embrace of Tennyson's loss.

from **In Memoriam A. H. H.**

Obiit MDCCCXXXIII[1]

1

I held it truth, with him who sings
   To one clear harp in divers tones,[2]
   That men may rise on stepping-stones
Of their dead selves to higher things.

5   But who shall so forecast the years
   And find in loss a gain to match?
   Or reach a hand thro' time to catch
The far-off interest of tears?[3]

Let Love clasp Grief lest both be drown'd,
10   Let darkness keep her raven gloss:
   Ah, sweeter to be drunk with loss,
To dance with death, to beat the ground,

Than that the victor Hours should scorn
   The long result of love, and boast,
15   "Behold the man that loved and lost,
But all he was is overworn."

2

Old Yew, which graspest at the stones
   That name the under-lying dead,
   Thy fibres net the dreamless head,
Thy roots are wrapt about the bones.

5   The seasons bring the flower again,
   And bring the firstling to the flock;
   And in the dusk of thee, the clock
Beats out the little lives of men.

O not for thee the glow, the bloom,
10   Who changest not in any gale,
   Nor branding summer suns avail

---

1. Died 1833.
2. Goethe, according to Tennyson.

3 The good that grows for us out of grief [Tennyson's note].

To touch thy thousand years of gloom:[4]

And gazing on thee, sullen tree,
  Sick° for thy stubborn hardihood,   *envious*
15   I seem to fail from out my blood
And grow incorporate into thee.
                    * * *
                     5
I sometimes hold it half a sin
  To put in words the grief I feel;
  For words, like Nature, half reveal
And half conceal the Soul within.

5   But, for the unquiet heart and brain,
  A use in measured language lies;
  The sad mechanic exercise,
Like dull narcotics, numbing pain.

In words, like weeds,° I'll wrap me o'er,   *mourning clothes*
10   Like coarsest clothes against the cold:
  But that large grief which these enfold
Is given in outline and no more.
                    * * *
                     7
Dark house, by which once more I stand
  Here in the long unlovely street,[5]
  Doors, where my heart was used to beat
So quickly, waiting for a hand,

5   A hand that can be clasp'd no more—
  Behold me, for I cannot sleep,
  And like a guilty thing I creep
At earliest morning to the door.

He is not here;[6] but far away
10   The noise of life begins again,
  And ghastly thro' the drizzling rain
On the bald street breaks the blank day.
                    * * *
                     9
Fair ship, that from the Italian shore
  Sailest the placid ocean-plains
  With my lost Arthur's loved remains,
Spread thy full wings, and waft him o'er.

5   So draw him home to those that mourn
  In vain; a favourable speed
  Ruffle thy mirror'd mast, and lead
Thro' prosperous floods his holy urn.

All night no ruder air perplex
10   Thy sliding keel, till Phosphor,[7] bright

---

4. Hallam Tennyson says: "No autumn tints ever change the green gloom of the yew."
5. Hallam's house at 67 Wimpole Street in London.
6. "He is not here, but is risen," said the angel at Jesus' tomb (Luke 24.6).
7. The morning star.

As our pure love, thro' early light
Shall glimmer on the dewy decks.

Sphere all your lights around, above;
   Sleep, gentle heavens, before the prow;
15   Sleep, gentle winds, as he sleeps now,
My friend, the brother of my love;

My Arthur, whom I shall not see
   Till all my widow'd race be run;
   Dear as the mother to the son,
20 More than my brothers are to me.
           * * *

         14

If one should bring me this report,
   That thou° hadst touch'd the land to-day,   *the ship*
   And I went down unto the quay,
And found thee lying in the port;

5 And standing, muffled round with woe,
   Should see thy passengers in rank
   Come stepping lightly down the plank,
And beckoning unto those they know;

And if along with these should come
10   The man I held as half-divine;
   Should strike a sudden hand in mine,
And ask a thousand things of home;

And I should tell him all my pain,
   And how my life had droop'd of late,
15   And he should sorrow o'er my state
And marvel what possess'd my brain;

And I perceived no touch of change,
   No hint of death in all his frame,
   But found him all in all the same,
20 I should not feel it to be strange.
           * * *

         19

The Danube to the Severn[8] gave
   The darken'd heart that beat no more;
   They laid him by the pleasant shore,
And in the hearing of the wave.

5 There twice a day the Severn fills;
   The salt sea-water passes by,
   And hushes half the babbling Wye,[9]
And makes a silence in the hills.

The Wye is hush'd nor moved along,
10   And hush'd my deepest grief of all,

---

8. Arthur Hallam died in Vienna, which is on the Danube, and was buried at Clevedon, near the Severn River in southwest England.

9. Taken from my own observation—the rapids of the Wye are stilled by the incoming sea [Tennyson's note]. The Wye is a tributary of the Severn, a tidal river.

When fill'd with tears that cannot fall,
I brim with sorrow drowning song.

The tide flows down, the wave again
 Is vocal in its wooded walls;
15 My deeper anguish also falls,
And I can speak a little then.

    * * *

    27

I envy not in any moods
 The captive void of noble rage,
 The linnet° born within the cage,   *finch*
That never knew the summer woods:

5 I envy not the beast that takes
 His license in the field of time,
 Unfetter'd by the sense of crime,
To whom a conscience never wakes;

Nor, what may count itself as blest,
10 The heart that never plighted troth
 But stagnates in the weeds of sloth;
Nor any want-begotten rest.[1]

I hold it true, whate'er befall;
 I feel it, when I sorrow most;
15 'Tis better to have loved and lost
Than never to have loved at all.

    28

The time draws near the birth of Christ:[2]
 The moon is hid; the night is still;
 The Christmas bells from hill to hill
Answer each other in the mist.

5 Four voices of four hamlets round,
 From far and near, on mead and moor,
 Swell out and fail, as if a door
Were shut between me and the sound:

Each voice four changes[3] on the wind,
10 That now dilate, and now decrease,
 Peace and goodwill, goodwill and peace,
Peace and goodwill, to all mankind.

This year I slept and woke with pain,
 I almost wish'd no more to wake,
15 And that my hold on life would break
Before I heard those bells again:

But they my troubled spirit rule,
 For they controll'd me when a boy;
 They bring me sorrow touch'd with joy,

---

1. Peace of mind owing to lack or "want" of having made commitments.

2. The first Christmas after Hallam's death.
3. Arrangements of church bell ringing.

20   The merry merry bells of Yule.
                        * * *
                        30
            With trembling fingers did we weave
                The holly round the Christmas hearth;
                A rainy cloud possess'd the earth,
            And sadly fell our Christmas-eve.

5   At our old pastimes in the hall
                We gambol'd, making vain pretence
                Of gladness, with an awful sense
            Of one mute Shadow watching all.

            We paused: the winds were in the beech:
10   We heard them sweep the winter land;
                And in a circle hand-in-hand
            Sat silent, looking each at each.

            Then echo-like our voices rang;
                We sung, tho' every eye was dim,
15   A merry song we sang with him
            Last year: impetuously we sang:

            We ceased: a gentler feeling crept
                Upon us: surely rest is meet:°   *fitting*
                "They rest," we said, "their sleep is sweet,"
20   And silence follow'd, and we wept.

            Our voices took a higher range;
                Once more we sang: "They do not die
                Nor lose their mortal sympathy,
            Nor change to us, although they change;

25   "Rapt° from the fickle and the frail   *carried away*
                With gather'd power, yet the same,
                Pierces the keen seraphic flame
            From orb° to orb, from veil to veil."   *star*

            Rise, happy morn, rise, holy morn,
30   Draw forth the cheerful day from night:
                O Father, touch the east, and light
            The light that shone when Hope was born.
                        * * *
                        39
            Old warder⁴ of these buried bones,
                And answering now my random stroke
                With fruitful cloud and living smoke,⁵
            Dark yew, that graspest at the stones

5   And dippest toward the dreamless head,
                To thee too comes the golden hour

---

4. The yew tree that stands by Hallam's grave.   5. The yew, when flowering, in a wind or if struck sends
                                                   up its pollen like smoke [Tennyson's note].

When flower is feeling after flower;
But Sorrow—fixt upon the dead,

And darkening the dark graves of men,—
    What whisper'd from her lying lips?
    Thy gloom is kindled at the tips,[6]
And passes into gloom again.

        * * *

50

Be near me when my light is low,
    When the blood creeps, and the nerves prick
    And tingle; and the heart is sick,
And all the wheels of Being slow.

Be near me when the sensuous frame
    Is rack'd with pangs that conquer trust;
    And Time, a maniac scattering dust,
And Life, a Fury slinging flame.[7]

Be near me when my faith is dry,
    And men the flies of latter spring,
    That lay their eggs, and sting and sing
And weave their petty cells and die.

Be near me when I fade away,
    To point the term of human strife,
    And on the low dark verge of life
The twilight of eternal day.

        * * *

54

Oh yet we trust that somehow good
    Will be the final goal of ill,
    To pangs of nature, sins of will,
Defects of doubt, and taints of blood;

That nothing walks with aimless feet;
    That not one life shall be destroy'd,
    Or cast as rubbish to the void,
When God hath made the pile complete;

That not a worm is cloven in vain;
    That not a moth with vain desire
    Is shrivell'd in a fruitless fire,
Or but subserves another's gain.

Behold, we know not anything;
    I can but trust that good shall fall
    At last—far off—at last, to all,
And every winter change to spring.

So runs my dream: but what am I?
    An infant crying in the night:

---

6. The tips of the yew branches are in flower.   7. The Furies—avengers of crime—carry torches.

An infant crying for the light:
20   And with no language but a cry.

55

The wish, that of the living whole
    No life may fail beyond the grave,
    Derives it not from what we have
The likest God within the soul?[8]

5   Are God and Nature then at strife,
    That Nature lends such evil dreams?
    So careful of the type[9] she seems,
So careless of the single life;

That I, considering everywhere
10   Her secret meaning in her deeds,
    And finding that of fifty seeds
She often brings but one to bear,

I falter where I firmly trod,
    And falling with my weight of cares
15   Upon the great world's altar-stairs
That slope thro' darkness up to God,

I stretch lame hands of faith, and grope,
    And gather dust and chaff, and call
    To what I feel is Lord of all,
20   And faintly trust the larger hope.[1]

56

"So careful of the type?" but no.
    From scarpèd[2] cliff and quarried stone
    She° cries, "A thousand types are gone: *Nature*
I care for nothing, all shall go."

5   "Thou makest thine appeal to me:
    I bring to life, I bring to death:
    The spirit does but mean the breath:
I know no more." And he, shall he,

Man, her last work, who seem'd so fair,
10   Such splendid purpose in his eyes,
    Who roll'd the psalm to wintry skies,
Who built him fanes° of fruitless prayer,   *temples*

Who trusted God was love indeed
    And love Creation's final law—
15   Tho' Nature, red in tooth and claw
With ravine, shriek'd against his creed—

Who loved, who suffer'd countless ills,
    Who battled for the True, the Just,

---

8. The inner consciousness—the divine in man [Tennyson's note].
9. Species; i.e., Nature ensures the preservation of the species, but is indifferent to the fate of the individual.
1. Hallam Tennyson notes: "My father means by 'the larger hope' that the whole human race would through, perhaps, ages of suffering, be at length purified and saved."
2. Steep cut-away cliffs with the strata exposed.

  Be blown about the desert dust,
20 Or seal'd° within the iron hills?[3]   *fossilized*

  No more? A monster then, a dream,
   A discord. Dragons of the prime,
   That tare° each other in their slime,   *tore*
  Were mellow music match'd° with him.   *compared*

25 O life as futile, then, as frail!
   O for thy voice to soothe and bless!
   What hope of answer, or redress?
  Behind the veil, behind the veil.

       * * *

       67
  When on my bed the moonlight falls,
   I know that in thy place of rest
   By that broad water of the west,[4]
  There comes a glory on the walls;

5 Thy marble bright in dark appears,
   As slowly steals a silver flame
   Along the letters of thy name,
  And o'er the number of thy years.

  The mystic glory swims away;
10 From off my bed the moonlight dies;
   And closing eaves of wearied eyes
  I sleep till dusk is dipt in gray:

  And then I know the mist is drawn
   A lucid veil from coast to coast,
15 And in the dark church like a ghost
  Thy tablet glimmers to the dawn.

       * * *

       78
  Again at Christmas[5] did we weave
   The holly round the Christmas hearth;
   The silent snow possess'd the earth,
  And calmly fell our Christmas-eve:

5 The yule-clog° sparkled keen with frost,   *log*
   No wing of wind the region swept,
   But over all things brooding slept
  The quiet sense of something lost.

  As in the winters left behind,
10 Again our ancient games had place,
   The mimic picture's breathing grace,[6]
  And dance and song and hoodman-blind.° *blindman's bluff*

  Who show'd a token of distress?
   No single tear, no mark of pain:

3. The geologic monsters of the early ages [Tennyson's note].
4. The Severn, near which Hallam was buried at Clevedon.
5. The second Christmas after Hallam's death.
6. Tableaux-vivants, an entertainment in which performers reenact a well-known work of art or historical event.

15   O sorrow, then can sorrow wane?
    O grief, can grief be changed to less?

    O last regret, regret can die!
       No—mixt with all this mystic frame,
       Her° deep relations are the same,   *sorrow's*
20   But with long use her tears are dry.
           * * *

          86
    Sweet after showers, ambrosial air,
       That rollest from the gorgeous gloom
       Of evening over brake and bloom
    And meadow, slowly breathing bare

5   The round of space, and rapt below
       Thro' all the dewy-tassell'd wood,
       And shadowing down the hornèd flood[7]
    In ripples, fan my brows and blow

    The fever from my cheek, and sigh
10   The full new life that feeds thy breath
       Throughout my frame, till Doubt and Death,
    Ill brethren, let the fancy fly

    From belt to belt of crimson seas
       On leagues of odour streaming far,
15   To where in yonder orient star
    A hundred spirits whisper "Peace."
          * * *

          95
    By night we linger'd on the lawn,
       For underfoot the herb was dry;
       And genial warmth; and o'er the sky
    The silvery haze of summer drawn;

5   And calm that let the tapers burn
       Unwavering: not a cricket chirr'd:
       The brook alone far-off was heard,
    And on the board the fluttering urn:[8]

    And bats went round in fragrant skies,
10   And wheel'd or lit the filmy shapes°   *moths*
       That haunt the dusk, with ermine capes
    And woolly breasts and beaded eyes;

    While now we sang old songs that peal'd
       From knoll to knoll, where, couch'd at ease,
15   The white kine° glimmer'd, and the trees   *cows*
    Laid their dark arms about the field.

    But when those others, one by one,
       Withdrew themselves from me and night,
       And in the house light after light

---

7. Between two promontories [Tennyson's note].   8. Hot-water urn for making tea or coffee, heated by a
fluttering flame.

20   Went out, and I was all alone,

A hunger seized my heart; I read
   Of that glad year which once had been,
   In those fall'n leaves which kept their green,
The noble letters of the dead:

25   And strangely on the silence broke
   The silent-speaking words, and strange
   Was love's dumb cry defying change
To test his worth; and strangely spoke

The faith, the vigour, bold to dwell
30   On doubts that drive the coward back,
   And keen thro' wordy snares to track
Suggestion to her inmost cell.

So word by word, and line by line,
   The dead man touch'd me from the past.
35   And all at once it seem'd at last
The living soul[9] was flash'd on mine,

And mine in this was wound, and whirl'd
   About empyreal heights of thought,
   And came on that which is, and caught
40   The deep pulsations of the world,

Aeonian music[1] measuring out
   The steps of Time—the shocks of Chance—
   The blows of Death. At length my trance
Was cancell'd, stricken thro' with doubt.[2]

45   Vague words! but ah, how hard to frame
   In matter-moulded forms of speech,
   Or ev'n for intellect to reach
Thro' memory that which I became:

Till now the doubtful dusk reveal'd
50   The knolls once more where, couch'd at ease,
   The white kine glimmer'd, and the trees
Laid their dark arms about the field:

And suck'd from out the distant gloom
   A breeze began to tremble o'er
55   The large leaves of the sycamore,
And fluctuate all the still perfume,

And gathering freshlier overhead,
   Rock'd the full-foliaged elms, and swung
   The heavy-folded rose, and flung
60   The lilies to and fro, and said

9. "His living soul" in the first edition; the next line originally read "And mine in his was wound." Tennyson said that the first version "troubled me, as perhaps giving a wrong impression."

1. The music of the aeons.
2. The trance came to an end in a moment of critical doubt, but the doubt was dispelled by the glory of the dawn of the "boundless day" [Tennyson's note].

"The dawn, the dawn," and died away;
    And East and West, without a breath,
    Mixt their dim lights, like life and death,
To broaden into boundless day.
* * *
104

The time draws near the birth of Christ;[3]
    The moon is hid, the night is still;
    A single church below the hill
Is pealing, folded in the mist.

5   A single peal of bells below,
    That wakens at this hour of rest
    A single murmur in the breast,
That these are not the bells I know.

Like strangers' voices here they sound,
10   In lands where not a memory strays,
    Nor landmark breathes of other days,
But all is new unhallow'd ground.
* * *
106

Ring out, wild bells, to the wild sky,
    The flying cloud, the frosty light:
    The year is dying in the night;
Ring out, wild bells, and let him die.

5   Ring out the old, ring in the new,
    Ring, happy bells, across the snow:
    The year is going, let him go;
Ring out the false, ring in the true.

Ring out the grief that saps the mind,
10   For those that here we see no more;
    Ring out the feud of rich and poor,
Ring in redress to all mankind.

Ring out a slowly dying cause,
    And ancient forms of party strife;
15   Ring in the nobler modes of life,
With sweeter manners, purer laws.

Ring out the want, the care, the sin,
    The faithless coldness of the times;
    Ring out, ring out my mournful rhymes,
20   But ring the fuller minstrel in.

Ring out false pride in place and blood,
    The civic slander and the spite;
    Ring in the love of truth and right,
Ring in the common love of good.

25   Ring out old shapes of foul disease;
    Ring out the narrowing lust of gold;

3. It is now the third Christmas since Hallam's death.

Ring out the thousand wars of old,
Ring in the thousand years of peace.

Ring in the valiant man and free,
30   The larger heart, the kindlier hand;
Ring out the darkness of the land,
Ring in the Christ that is to be.

* * *

115

Now fades the last long streak of snow,
Now burgeons every maze of quick[4]
About the flowering squares, and thick
By ashen roots the violets blow.

5   Now rings the woodland loud and long,
The distance takes a lovelier hue,
And drown'd in yonder living blue
The lark becomes a sightless song.

Now dance the lights on lawn and lea,
10   The flocks are whiter down the vale,
And milkier every milky sail
On winding stream or distant sea;

Where now the seamew pipes, or dives
In yonder greening gleam, and fly
15   The happy birds, that change their sky
To build and brood; that live their lives

From land to land; and in my breast
Spring wakens too; and my regret
Becomes an April violet,
20   And buds and blossoms like the rest.

* * *

118

Contemplate all this work of Time,
The giant labouring in his youth;
Nor dream of human love and truth,
As dying Nature's earth and lime;

5   But trust that those we call the dead
Are breathers of an ampler day
For ever nobler ends. They° say,   scientists
The solid earth whereon we tread

In tracts of fluent heat began,
10   And grew to seeming-random forms,
The seeming prey of cyclic storms,
Till at the last arose the man;

Who throve and branch'd from clime to clime,
The herald of a higher race,
15   And of himself in higher place,
If so he type[5] this work of time

4. Hawthorn hedges are budding; the "flowering squares"   5. Typifies or prefigures.
in the next line are fields.

Within himself, from more to more;
   Or, crown'd with attributes of woe
   Like glories, move his course, and show
20   That life is not as idle ore,

But iron dug from central gloom,
   And heated hot with burning fears,
   And dipt in baths of hissing tears,
And batter'd with the shocks of doom

25   To shape and use. Arise and fly
   The reeling Faun, the sensual feast;
   Move upward, working out the beast,
And let the ape and tiger die.

119

Doors, where my heart was used to beat
   So quickly, not as one that weeps
   I come once more;[6] the city sleeps;
I smell the meadow in the street;

5   I hear a chirp of birds; I see
   Betwixt the black fronts long-withdrawn
   A light-blue lane of early dawn,
And think of early days and thee,

And bless thee, for thy lips are bland,
10   And bright the friendship of thine eye;
   And in my thoughts with scarce a sigh
I take the pressure of thine hand.

120

I trust I have not wasted breath:
   I think we are not wholly brain,
   Magnetic mockeries;° not in vain,   *automatons*
Like Paul with beasts,[7] I fought with Death;

5   Not only cunning casts in clay:
   Let Science prove we are, and then
   What matters Science unto men,
At least to me? I would not stay.

Let him, the wiser man who springs
10   Hereafter, up from childhood shape
   His action like the greater ape,[8]
But I was *born* to other things.

* * *

123

There rolls the deep where grew the tree.
   O earth, what changes hast thou seen!
   There where the long street roars, hath been
The stillness of the central sea.

---

6. Tennyson has returned to Hallam's house in London; see Section 7, page 1930.
7. Saint Paul said: "If after the manner of men I have fought with beasts at Ephesus, what advantageth it me, if the dead rise not" (1 Corinthians 15.32).
8. Spoken ironically against mere materialism, not against evolution [Tennyson's note].

5   The hills are shadows, and they flow
        From form to form, and nothing stands;
        They melt like mist, the solid lands,
    Like clouds they shape themselves and go.

    But in my spirit will I dwell,
10   And dream my dream, and hold it true;
        For tho' my lips may breathe adieu,
    I cannot think the thing farewell.

124

    That which we dare invoke to bless;
        Our dearest faith; our ghastliest doubt;
        He, They, One, All; within, without;
    The Power in darkness whom we guess;

5   I found Him not in world or sun,
        Or eagle's wing, or insect's eye;[9]
        Nor thro' the questions men may try,
    The petty cobwebs we have spun:

    If e'er when faith had fall'n asleep,
10   I heard a voice "believe no more"
        And heard an ever-breaking shore
    That tumbled in the Godless deep;

    A warmth within the breast would melt
        The freezing reason's colder part,
15   And like a man in wrath the heart
    Stood up and answer'd "I have felt."

    No, like a child in doubt and fear:
        But that blind clamour made me wise;
        Then was I as a child that cries,
20   But, crying, knows his father near;

    And what I am beheld again
        What is, and no man understands;
        And out of darkness came the hands
    That reach thro' nature, moulding men.

* * *

130

    Thy voice is on the rolling air;
        I hear thee where the waters run;
        Thou standest in the rising sun,
    And in the setting thou art fair.

5   What art thou then? I cannot guess;
        But tho' I seem in star and flower
        To feel thee some diffusive power,
    I do not therefore love thee less:

    My love involves the love before;
10   My love is vaster passion now;

---

9. Tennyson rejects the argument that God's existence can be inferred from Nature—i.e., that the design of the universe is so orderly and complex that there must have been a designer.

Tho' mix'd with God and Nature thou,
   I seem to love thee more and more.

Far off thou art, but ever nigh;
   I have thee still, and I rejoice;
15   I prosper, circled with thy voice;
I shall not lose thee tho' I die.

131

O living will[1] that shalt endure
   When all that seems shall suffer shock,
   Rise in the spiritual rock,[2]
Flow thro' our deeds and make them pure,

5   That we may lift from out of dust
   A voice as unto him that hears,
   A cry above the conquer'd years
To one that with us works, and trust,

With faith that comes of self-control,
10   The truths that never can be proved
   Until we close with all we loved,
And all we flow from, soul in soul.

            * * *

Crossing the Bar[1]

Sunset and evening star,
   And one clear call for me!
And may there be no moaning of the bar,[2]
   When I put out to sea,

5   But such a tide as moving seems asleep,
   Too full for sound and foam,
When that which drew from out the boundless deep
   Turns again home.

Twilight and evening bell,
10   And after that the dark!
And may there be no sadness of farewell,
   When I embark;

For tho' from out our bourne° of Time and Place   *boundary*
   The flood may bear me far,
15   I hope to see my Pilot face to face[3]
   When I have crost the bar.

1889   1889

---

1. That which we know as Free-will in man [Tennyson's note].

2. "And did all drink the same spiritual drink: for they drank of that spiritual Rock that followed them: and that Rock was Christ" (1 Corinthians 10.4).

1. Tennyson instructed that this poem should appear at the end of every collection of his work, though it was not in fact the last poem he wrote. The poem, he said "came in a moment" while he was crossing the Solent to return home to Farringford on the Isle of Wight.

2. The sandbank that forms at the mouth of a harbor. The "moaning" may be the sound of the river and the sea meeting.

3. The pilot has been on board all the while, but in the dark I have not seen him [Tennyson's note]. Cf. 1 Corinthians 13.12: "For now we see through a glass, darkly; but then face to face: now I know in part; but then shall I know even as also I am known."

—+— ⚏❖⚏ —+—

Charles Darwin
1809–1882

Charles Darwin's five-year excursion on the *Beagle* has become the stuff of legend. No voyage since that of Columbus has had such a profound impact on the world. Darwin's ideas concerning evolution and natural selection brought about a revolution in human thought; they radically transformed our sense of our place in the universe. Yet the *Voyage of the Beagle* is a modestly written account of the meticulous observations of a young naturalist, as interested in ordinary beetles and coral formations as in the weirdly monstrous creatures he saw on the Galapagos Islands.

Nothing in Darwin's youth suggested a great man in the making. His father once warned him, "You care for nothing but shooting, dogs, and rat-catching, and you will be a disgrace to yourself and all your family." Darwin's father was a prosperous doctor, and he sent his son to Edinburgh University for two years to study medicine, but Darwin detested the subject, and neglected his studies. Casting about for an occupation for this unpromising son, his father proposed the undemanding career of a country clergyman. Darwin agreed, and spent the next three years at Cambridge where, according to his autobiography, he did little except collect beetles.

Although he considered his formal education a complete waste, Darwin was busy educating himself in natural history. The turning point in his life was an invitation to become the ship's naturalist on the H.M.S. *Beagle*'s surveying expedition. Knowing the ship would be away for years, Darwin's father initially refused permission to accept. At a time when the word "scientist" did not even exist, he could not see how such an undertaking could lead to any respectable profession. But he left a loophole, telling his son, "If you can find any man of common sense, who advises you to go, I will give my consent." Fortunately, Darwin's uncle supported the idea, and in 1831 the *Beagle* sailed for South America with the twenty-two-year-old Darwin aboard.

Darwin had to put up with cramped quarters, seasickness, and the captain's volatile temper, but he accomplished an extraordinary amount of work. He collected specimens, filled eighteen notebooks with scientific observations, and spent long periods ashore studying plants and animals, fossils, and indigenous cultures. He also kept a diary that eventually became the basis of *The Voyage of the Beagle* (1839, rev. 1845), one of the great classics of travel literature. Out of these investigations, particularly in the volcanic Galapagos Islands off the coast of South America, grew the theory of evolution.

Yet it is a myth that Darwin had a sudden insight concerning the origin of species while examining the strange tortoises, lizards, and finches in the Galapagos. Though he had read with interest the evolutionary speculations of his grandfather, Erasmus Darwin, he had remained a creationist: during the voyage he continued to believe that species were fixed forever at the moment of their creation, as described in the Bible. Only back in England, working through his huge volume of notes, did he become convinced of the mutability of species.

Within a few months of his return home in 1836, Darwin had accepted evolution as the explanation for the natural phenomena he had observed. But he was in no hurry to publish his findings. In fact, twenty years went by before he learned in 1858 that a young naturalist, Alfred Russel Wallace, had arrived independently at the theory of natural selection. A joint paper of their findings was presented to the Linnaean Society, and Darwin at long last rushed to compile and publish *On the Origin of Species by Means of Natural Selection* (1859). Darwin realized that most living organisms produce far more offspring than can survive: not every acorn becomes an oak. Certain genetically favored individuals have a competitive edge in the struggle for life. Nature thus ensures the "survival of the fittest," and eventually their descendants evolve into new and better adapted species.

The book created an immediate sensation. The original edition sold out the day it was published. Darwin was not the first to propose a theory of evolution, but he was the first to offer a persuasive account of the means by which evolution works. Geologists such as Charles Lyell had already shown that the earth was immensely older than six thousand years, the traditional estimate based on biblical chronology. In further undermining the biblical account of creation, Darwin shook the faith of his contemporaries.

Darwin was not eager to offend people, nor did he enjoy controversy. Thus in *The Origin of Species* he tactfully avoided any discussion of human origins, although he was already confident that evolution applied to human beings as well. In *The Descent of Man* (1871) he finally made his position clear: man is an animal. Darwin's ideas were profoundly unsettling. No longer sure of belonging to an ordered world overseen by a beneficent Creator, many people felt they had been set adrift in an indifferent cosmos. Tennyson's memorable phrase, "Nature, red in tooth and claw," expressed the Victorians' collective horror at Darwin's vision of nature as a cruel and violent battlefield.

Darwin's theories were earthshaking, but his private life was not. When the *Beagle* voyage ended, he debated the pros and cons of marriage, telling himself that a wife would provide "an object to be beloved and played with—better than a dog anyhow." Despite these unromantic musings, his marriage to his cousin Emma Wedgwood was long and happy. They settled down in a country house and had many children. For the rest of his life Darwin suffered from mysterious illnesses; they prevented his going into society, but they did not stop him working and writing. He never traveled again.

from The Voyage of the Beagle
from Chapter 10. Tierra Del Fuego[1]

December 17th, 1832.—Having now finished with Patagonia[2] and the Falkland Islands, I will describe our first arrival in Tierra del Fuego. A little after noon we doubled Cape St. Diego, and entered the famous strait of Le Maire. We kept close to the Fuegian shore, but the outline of the rugged, inhospitable Staten-land was visible amidst the clouds. In the afternoon we anchored in the Bay of Good Success. While entering we were saluted in a manner becoming the inhabitants of this savage land. A group of Fuegians partly concealed by the entangled forest, were perched on a wild point overhanging the sea; and as we passed by, they sprang up and waving their tattered cloaks sent forth a loud and sonorous shout. The savages followed the ship, and just before dark we saw their fire, and again heard their wild cry. The harbour consists of a fine piece of water half surrounded by low rounded mountains of clay-slate, which are covered to the water's edge by one dense gloomy forest. A single glance at the landscape was sufficient to show me how widely different it was from any thing I had ever beheld. At night it blew a gale of wind, and heavy squalls from the mountains swept past us. It would have been a bad time out at sea, and we, as well as others, may call this Good Success Bay.

In the morning the Captain sent a party to communicate with the Fuegians. When we came within hail, one of the four natives who were present advanced to receive us, and began to shout most vehemently, wishing to direct us where to land. When we were on shore the party looked rather alarmed, but continued talking and making gestures with great rapidity. It was without exception the most curious and interesting spectacle I ever beheld: I could not have believed how wide was the difference between savage and civilized man: it is greater than between a wild and

---

1. A group of islands off the southern tip of South America.   2. The southernmost region of South America.

Thomas Landseer, after a drawing by C. Martens. *A Fuegian at Portrait Cove*, 1839. This illustration appeared in the *Narrative of the Surveying Voyages of His Majesty's Ships Adventure and Beagle, between the Years 1826 and 1836* (1839); Darwin's part of this report became *The Voyage of the Beagle*.

domesticated animal, inasmuch as in man there is a greater power of improvement. The chief spokesman was old, and appeared to be the head of the family; the three others were powerful young men, about six feet high. The women and children had been sent away. These Fuegians are a very different race from the stunted, miserable wretches farther westward; and they seem closely allied to the famous Patagonians of the Strait of Magellan. Their only garment consists of a mantle made of guanaco[3] skin, with the wool outside; this they wear just thrown over their shoulders, leaving their persons as often exposed as covered. Their skin is of a dirty copper red colour.

The old man had a fillet[4] of white feathers tied round his head, which partly confined his black, coarse, and entangled hair. His face was crossed by two broad transverse bars; one, painted bright red, reached from ear to ear and included the upper lip; the other, white like chalk, extended above and parallel to the first, so that even his eyelids were thus coloured. The other two men were ornamented by streaks of black powder, made of charcoal. The party altogether closely resembled the devils which come on the stage in plays like Der Freischutz.[5]

---

3. A South American mammal with fawn-colored fur.
4. A headband.
5. An 1817 opera by Carl Maria von Weber (1786–1826),

first performed in London in 1824. The story concerns Max, a forester who nearly sells his soul to the devil.

Their very attitudes were abject, and the expression of their countenances distrustful, surprised, and startled. After we had presented them with some scarlet cloth, which they immediately tied round their necks, they became good friends. This was shown by the old man patting our breasts, and making a chuckling kind of noise, as people do when feeding chickens. I walked with the old man, and this demonstration of friendship was repeated several times; it was concluded by three hard slaps, which were given me on the breast and back at the same time. He then bared his bosom for me to return the compliment, which being done, he seemed highly pleased. The language of these people, according to our notions, scarcely deserves to be called articulate. Captain Cook has compared it to a man clearing his throat, but certainly no European ever cleared his throat with so many hoarse, guttural, and clicking sounds.

They are excellent mimics: as often as we coughed or yawned, or made any odd motion, they immediately imitated us. Some of our party began to squint and look awry; but one of the young Fuegians (whose whole face was painted black, excepting a white band across his eyes) succeeded in making far more hideous grimaces. They could repeat with perfect correctness each word in any sentence we addressed them, and they remembered such words for some time. Yet we Europeans all know how difficult it is to distinguish apart the sounds in a foreign language. Which of us, for instance, could follow an American Indian through a sentence of more than three words? All savages appear to possess, to an uncommon degree, this power of mimicry. I was told, almost in the same words, of the same ludicrous habit among the Caffres:[6] the Australians, likewise, have long been notorious for being able to imitate and describe the gait of any man, so that he may be recognized. How can this faculty be explained? is it a consequence of the more practised habits of perception and keener senses, common to all men in a savage state, as compared with those long civilized?

When a song was struck up by our party, I thought the Fuegians would have fallen down with astonishment. With equal surprise they viewed our dancing; but one of the young men, when asked, had no objection to a little waltzing. Little accustomed to Europeans as they appeared to be, yet they knew and dreaded our fire-arms; nothing would tempt them to take a gun in their hands. They begged for knives, calling them by the Spanish word "cuchilla." They explained also what they wanted, by acting as if they had a piece of blubber in their mouth, and then pretending to cut instead of tear it.

I have not as yet noticed the Fuegians whom we had on board. During the former voyage of the *Adventure* and *Beagle* in 1826 to 1830, Captain Fitz Roy[7] seized on a party of natives, as hostages for the loss of a boat, which had been stolen, to the great jeopardy of a party employed on the survey; and some of these natives, as well as a child whom he bought for a pearl-button, he took with him to England, determining to educate them and instruct them in religion at his own expense. To settle these natives in their own country, was one chief inducement to Captain Fitz Roy to undertake our present voyage; and before the Admiralty had resolved to send out this expedition, Captain Fitz Roy had generously chartered a vessel, and would himself have taken them back. The natives were accompanied by a missionary, R. Matthews; of whom and of the natives, Captain Fitz Roy has published a full and excellent account. Two men, one of whom died in England of the smallpox, a boy and a little girl, were originally taken; and we had now on board, York Minster, Jemmy Button (whose name expresses his purchase-money), and Fuegia Basket. York Minster was a

6. Kaffirs are a Bantu-speaking African people.
7. Robert Fitz Roy (1805–1865) was the captain of the

Beagle; he and Darwin had a sometimes difficult relationship.

full-grown, short, thick, powerful man: his disposition was reserved, taciturn, morose, and when excited violently passionate; his affections were very strong towards a few friends on board; his intellect good. Jemmy Button was a universal favourite, but likewise passionate; the expression of his face at once showed his nice disposition. He was merry and often laughed, and was remarkably sympathetic with any one in pain: when the water was rough, I was often a little seasick, and he used to come to me and say in a plaintive voice, "Poor, poor fellow!" but the notion, after his aquatic life, of a man being sea-sick, was too ludicrous, and he was generally obliged to turn on one side to hide a smile or laugh, and then he would repeat his "Poor, poor fellow!" He was of a patriotic disposition; and he liked to praise his own tribe and country, in which he truly said there were "plenty of trees," and he abused all the other tribes: he stoutly declared that there was no Devil in his land. Jemmy was short, thick, and fat, but vain of his personal appearance; he used to wear gloves, his hair was neatly cut, and he was distressed if his well-polished shoes were dirtied. He was fond of admiring himself in a looking-glass; and a merry-faced little Indian boy from the Rio Negro, whom we had for some months on board, soon perceived this, and used to mock him: Jemmy, who was always rather jealous of the attention paid to this little boy, did not at all like this, and used to say, with rather a contemptuous twist of his head, "Too much skylark." It seems yet wonderful to me, when I think over all his many good qualities, that he should have been of the same race, and doubtless partaken of the same character, with the miserable, degraded savages whom we first met here. Lastly, Fuegia Basket was a nice, modest, reserved young girl, with a rather pleasing but sometimes sullen expression, and very quick in learning anything, especially languages. This she showed in picking up some Portuguese and Spanish, when left on shore for only a short time at Rio de Janeiro and Monte Video, and in her knowledge of English. York Minster was very jealous of any attention paid to her; for it was clear he determined to marry her as soon as they were settled on shore. * * *

December 25th, 1832.— * * * While going one day on shore near Wollaston Island, we pulled alongside a canoe with six Fuegians. These were the most abject and miserable creatures I anywhere beheld. On the east coast the natives, as we have seen, have guanaco cloaks, and on the west, they possess seal-skins. Amongst these central tribes the men generally have an otter-skin, or some small scrap about as large as a pocket-handkerchief, which is barely sufficient to cover their backs as low down as their loins. It is laced across the breast by strings, and according as the wind blows, it is shifted from side to side. But these Fuegians in the canoe were quite naked, and even one full-grown woman was absolutely so. It was raining heavily, and the fresh water, together with the spray, trickled down her body. In another harbour not far distant, a woman, who was suckling a recently-born child, came one day alongside the vessel, and remained there out of mere curiosity, whilst the sleet fell and thawed on her naked bosom, and on the skin of her naked baby! These poor wretches were stunted in their growth, their hideous faces bedaubed with white paint, their skins filthy and greasy, their hair entangled, their voices discordant, and their gestures violent. Viewing such men, one can hardly make oneself believe that they are fellow-creatures, and inhabitants of the same world. It is a common subject of conjecture what pleasure in life some of the lower animals can enjoy: how much more reasonably the same question may be asked with respect to these barbarians! At night, five or six human beings, naked and scarcely protected from the wind and rain of this tempestuous climate, sleep on the wet ground coiled up like animals. Whenever it is low water, winter or summer, night or day, they must rise to pick shellfish from the rocks; and the women either dive to collect sea-eggs, or sit patiently in their canoes, and with a baited hairline without any hook, jerk out little fish. If a seal is killed, or the floating carcass of a putrid whale discovered, it is a feast; and such miserable food is assisted by a few tasteless berries and fungi. * * *

The different tribes have no government or chief; yet each is surrounded by other hostile tribes, speaking different dialects, and separated from each other only by a deserted border or neutral territory: the cause of their warfare appears to be the means of subsistence. Their country is a broken mass of wild rocks, lofty hills, and useless forests: and these are viewed through mists and endless storms. The habitable land is reduced to the stones on the beach; in search of food they are compelled unceasingly to wander from spot to spot, and so steep is the coast, that they can only move about in their wretched canoes. They cannot know the feeling of having a home, and still less that of domestic affection; for the husband is to the wife a brutal master to a laborious slave. Was a more horrid deed ever perpetrated, than that witnessed on the west coast by Byron, who saw a wretched mother pick up her bleeding dying infant-boy, whom her husband had mercilessly dashed on the stones for dropping a basket of sea-eggs! How little can the higher powers of the mind be brought into play: what is there for imagination to picture, for reason to compare, for judgment to decide upon? to knock a limpet from the rock does not require even cunning, that lowest power of the mind. Their skill in some respects may be compared to the instinct of animals; for it is not improved by experience: the canoe, their most ingenious work, poor as it is, has remained the same, as we know from Drake, for the last two hundred and fifty years.

Whilst beholding these savages, one asks, whence have they come? What could have tempted, or what change compelled a tribe of men, to leave the fine regions of the north, to travel down the Cordillera[8] or backbone of America, to invent and build canoes, which are not used by the tribes of Chile, Peru, and Brazil, and then to enter on one of the most inhospitable countries within the limits of the globe? Although such reflections must at first seize on the mind, yet we may feel sure that they are partly erroneous. There is no reason to believe that the Fuegians decrease in number; therefore we must suppose that they enjoy a sufficient share of happiness, of whatever kind it may be, to render life worth having. Nature by making habit omnipotent, and its effects hereditary, has fitted the Fuegian to the climate and the productions of his miserable country. * * *

January 15th, 1833.—The *Beagle* anchored in Goeree Roads. Captain Fitz Roy having resolved to settle the Fuegians, according to their wishes, in Ponsonby Sound, four boats were equipped to carry them there through the Beagle Channel. * * *

February 6th.— * * * It was quite melancholy leaving the three Fuegians with their savage countrymen; but it was a great comfort that they had no personal fears. York, being a powerful resolute man, was pretty sure to get on well, together with his wife Fuegia. Poor Jemmy looked rather disconsolate, and would then, I have little doubt, have been glad to have returned with us. His own brother had stolen many things from him; and as he remarked, "what fashion call that?" He abused his countrymen, "all bad men, no sabe (know) nothing," and, though I never heard him swear before, "damned fools." Our three Fuegians, though they had been only three years with civilized men, would, I am sure, have been glad to have retained their new habits; but this was obviously impossible. I fear it is more than doubtful, whether their visit will have been of any use to them. * * *

8. Andean mountain range.

On the 5th of March, we anchored in the cove at Woollya, but we saw not a soul there. We were alarmed at this, for the natives in Ponsonby Sound showed by gestures, that there had been fighting; and we afterwards heard that the dreaded Oens men had made a descent. Soon a canoe, with a little flag flying, was seen approaching, with one of the men in it washing the paint off his face. This man was poor Jemmy,—now a thin haggard savage, with long disordered hair, and naked, except a bit of a blanket round his waist. We did not recognize him till he was close to us; for he was ashamed of himself, and turned his back to the ship. We had left him plump, fat, clean, and well dressed;—I never saw so complete and grievous a change. As soon however as he was clothed, and the first flurry was over, things wore a good appearance. He dined with Captain Fitz Roy, and ate his dinner as tidily as formerly. He told us he had "too much" (meaning enough) to eat, that he was not cold, that his relations were very good people, and that he did not wish to go back to England: in the evening we found out the cause of this great change in Jemmy's feelings, in the arrival of his young and nice-looking wife. With his usual good feeling, he brought two beautiful otter-skins for two of his best friends, and some spear-heads and arrows made with his own hands for the Captain. He said he had built a canoe for himself, and he boasted that he could talk a little of his own language! But it is a most singular fact, that he appears to have taught all his tribe some English: an old man spontaneously announced "Jemmy Button's wife." Jemmy had lost all his property. He told us that York Minster had built a large canoe, and with his wife Fuegia, had several months since gone to his own country, and had taken farewell by an act of consummate villainy; he persuaded Jemmy and his mother to come with him, and then on the way deserted them by night, stealing every article of their property.

Jemmy went to sleep on shore, and in the morning returned, and remained on board till the ship got under weigh, which frightened his wife, who continued crying violently till he got into his canoe. He returned loaded with valuable property. Every soul on board was heartily sorry to shake hands with him for the last time. I do not now doubt that he will be as happy as, perhaps happier than, if he had never left his own country. Every one must sincerely hope that Captain Fitz Roy's noble hope may be fulfilled, of being rewarded for the many generous sacrifices which he made for these Fuegians, by some shipwrecked sailor being protected by the descendants of Jemmy Button and his tribe! When Jemmy reached the shore, he lighted a signal fire, and the smoke curled up, bidding us a last and long farewell, as the ship stood on her course into the open sea.

from *Chapter 17. Galapagos Archipelago*[1]

In the morning (17th)[2] we landed on Chatham Island, which, like the others, rises with a tame and rounded outline, broken here and there by scattered hillocks, the remains of former craters. Nothing could be less inviting than the first appearance. A broken field of black basaltic lava, thrown into the most rugged waves, and crossed by great fissures, is every where covered by stunted, sunburnt brushwood, which shows little signs of life. The dry and parched surface, being heated by the noonday sun, gave to the air a close and sultry feeling, like that from a stove: we fancied even that the bushes smelt unpleasantly. Although I diligently tried to collect as many plants

1. A group of islands located 400 miles off the coast of   2. Of September, 1835.
Ecuador.

as possible, I succeeded in getting very few; and such wretched-looking little weeds would have better become an arctic than an equatorial Flora. The brushwood appears, from a short distance, as leafless as our trees during winter; and it was some time before I discovered that not only almost every plant was now in full leaf, but that the greater number were in flower. * * *

The *Beagle* sailed round Chatham Island, and anchored in several bays. One night I slept on shore on a part of the island, where black truncated cones were extraordinarily numerous: from one small eminence I counted sixty of them, all surmounted by craters more or less perfect. The greater number consisted merely of a ring of red scoriae[3] or slags, cemented together: and their height above the plain of lava was not more than from fifty to a hundred feet: none had been very lately active. The entire surface of this part of the island seems to have been permeated, like a sieve, by the subterranean vapours: here and there the lava, whilst soft, has been blown into great bubbles; and in other parts, the tops of caverns similarly formed have fallen in, leaving circular pits with steep sides. From the regular form of the many craters, they gave to the country an artificial appearance, which vividly reminded me of those parts of Staffordshire, where the great iron-foundries are most numerous. The day was glowing hot, and the scrambling over the rough surface and through the intricate thickets, was very fatiguing; but I was well repaid by the strange Cyclopean[4] scene. As I was walking along I met two large tortoises, each of which must have weighed at least two hundred pounds: one was eating a piece of cactus, and as I approached, it stared at me and slowly stalked away; the other gave a deep hiss, and drew in its head. These huge reptiles, surrounded by the black lava, the leafless shrubs, and large cacti, seemed to my fancy like some antediluvian[5] animals. The few dull-coloured birds cared no more for me, than they did for the great tortoises. * * *

The natural history of these islands is eminently curious, and well deserves attention. Most of the organic productions are aboriginal creations, found nowhere else; there is even a difference between the inhabitants of the different islands; yet all show a marked relationship with those of America, though separated from that continent by an open space of ocean, between 500 and 600 miles in width. The archipelago is a little world within itself, or rather a satellite attached to America, whence it has derived a few stray colonists, and has received the general character of its indigenous productions. Considering the small size of these islands, we feel the more astonished at the number of their aboriginal beings, and at their confined range. Seeing every height crowned with its crater, and the boundaries of most of the lava-streams still distinct, we are led to believe that within a period, geologically recent, the unbroken ocean was here spread out. Hence, both in space and time, we seem to be brought somewhat near to that great fact—that mystery of mysteries—the first appearance of new beings on this earth. * * *

The tortoises, when purposely moving towards any point, travel by night and day, and arrive at their journey's end much sooner than would be expected. The inhabitants, from observing marked individuals, consider that they travel a distance of about eight miles in two or three days. One large tortoise, which I watched, walked at the rate of sixty yards in ten minutes, that is 360 yards in the hour, or four miles a day,—allowing a little time for it to eat on the road. During the breeding season, when the male and female are together, the male utters a hoarse roar or bellowing, which, it is said, can be heard at the distance of more than a hundred yards. The

---

3. Lava.
4. Darwin may mean that the landscape is savage and wild,

like that inhabited by the Cyclopes in Homer's *Odyssey*.
5. Ancient; literally, before the Flood.

female never uses her voice, and the male only at these times; so that when the people hear this noise, they know that the two are together. They were at this time (October) laying their eggs. The female, where the soil is sandy, deposits them together, and covers them up with sand; but where the ground is rocky she drops them indiscriminately in any hole: Mr. Bynoe[6] found seven placed in a fissure. The egg is white and spherical; one which I measured was seven inches and three-eighths in circumference, and therefore larger than a hen's egg. The young tortoises, as soon as they are hatched, fall a prey in great numbers to the carrion-feeding buzzard. The old ones seem generally to die from accidents, as from falling down precipices: at least, several of the inhabitants told me, that they had never found one dead without some evident cause.

The inhabitants believe that these animals are absolutely deaf; certainly they do not overhear a person walking close behind them. I was always amused when overtaking one of these great monsters, as it was quietly pacing along, to see how suddenly, the instant I passed, it would draw in its head and legs, and uttering a deep hiss fall to the ground with a heavy sound, as if struck dead. I frequently got on their backs, and then giving a few raps on the hinder part of their shells, they would rise up and walk away;— but I found it very difficult to keep my balance. The flesh of this animal is largely employed, both fresh and salted; and a beautifully clear oil is prepared from the fat. * * *

There can be little doubt that this tortoise is an aboriginal inhabitant of the Galapagos; for it is found on all, or nearly all, the islands, even on some of the smaller ones where there is no water; had it been an imported species, this would hardly have been the case in a group which has been so little frequented. * * *

I have not as yet noticed by far the most remarkable feature in the natural history of this archipelago; it is, that the different islands to a considerable extent are inhabited by a different set of beings. My attention was first called to this fact by the Vice-Governor, Mr. Lawson, declaring that the tortoises differed from the different islands, and that he could with certainty tell from which island any one was brought. I did not for some time pay sufficient attention to this statement, and I had already partially mingled together the collections from two of the islands. I never dreamed that islands, about fifty or sixty miles apart, and most of them in sight of each other, formed of precisely the same rocks, placed under a quite similar climate, rising to a nearly equal height, would have been differently tenanted; but we shall soon see that this is the case. It is the fate of most voyagers, no sooner to discover what is most interesting in any locality, than they are hurried from it; but I ought, perhaps, to be thankful that I obtained sufficient material to establish this most remarkable fact in the distribution of organic beings. * * *

If we now turn to the Flora, we shall find the aboriginal plants of the different islands wonderfully different. * * *

Hence we have the truly wonderful fact, that in James Island, of the thirty-eight Galapageian plants, or those found in no other part of the world, thirty are exclusively confined to this one island; and in Albemarle Island, of the twenty-six aboriginal Galapageian plants, twenty-two are confined to this one island, that is, only four are at present known to grow in the other islands of the archipelago; and so on. * * *

The only light which I can throw on this remarkable difference in the inhabitants of the different islands, is, that very strong currents of the sea running in a westerly and W.N.W. direction must separate, as far as transportal by the sea is concerned, the southern islands from the northern ones; and between these northern islands a strong N.W.

6. Naval surgeon aboard the *Beagle*.

current was observed, which must effectually separate James and Albemarle Islands. As the archipelago is free to a most remarkable degree from gales of wind, neither the birds, insects, nor lighter seeds, would be blown from island to island. And lastly, the profound depth of the ocean between the islands, and their apparently recent (in a geological sense) volcanic origin, render it highly unlikely that they were ever united; and this, probably, is a far more important consideration than any other, with respect to the geographical distribution of their inhabitants. Reviewing the facts here given, one is astonished at the amount of creative force, if such an expression may be used, displayed on these small, barren, and rocky islands; and still more so, at its diverse yet analogous action on points so near each other. I have said that the Galapagos Archipelago might be called a satellite attached to America, but it should rather be called a group of satellites, physically similar, organically distinct, yet intimately related to each other, and all related in a marked, though much lesser degree, to the great American continent.

1839, 1845

from On the Origin of Species by Means of Natural Selection
or
The Preservation of Favoured Races in the Struggle for Life
from Chapter 3. Struggle for Existence

Before entering on the subject of this chapter, I must make a few preliminary remarks, to show how the struggle for existence bears on Natural Selection. * * * The mere existence of individual variability and of some few well-marked varieties, though necessary as the foundation for the work, helps us but little in understanding how species arise in nature. How have all those exquisite adaptations of one part of the organisation to another part, and to the conditions of life, and of one distinct organic being to another being, been perfected? We see these beautiful co-adaptations most plainly in the woodpecker and missletoe; and only a little less plainly in the humblest parasite which clings to the hairs of a quadruped or feathers of a bird; in the structure of the beetle which dives through the water; in the plumed seed which is wafted by the gentlest breeze; in short, we see beautiful adaptations everywhere and in every part of the organic world.

Again, it may be asked, how is it that varieties which I have called incipient species, become ultimately converted into good and distinct species, which in most cases obviously differ from each other far more than do the varieties of the same species? How do those groups of species, which constitute what are called distinct genera,[1] and which differ from each other more than do the species of the same genus, arise? All these results, as we shall more fully see in the next chapter, follow inevitably from the struggle for life. Owing to this struggle for life, any variation, however slight and from whatever cause proceeding, if it be in any degree profitable to an individual of any species, in its infinitely complex relations to other organic beings and to external nature, will tend to the preservation of that individual, and will generally be inherited by its offspring. The offspring, also, will thus have a better chance of surviving, for, of the many individuals of any species which are periodically born, but a small number can survive. I have called this principle, by which each slight variation, if useful, is preserved, by the term of Natural Selection, in order to mark its relation to man's power of selection. We have seen that man by selection can certainly produce great results, and can adapt organic beings to his own uses,

---

1. Plural of genus, a class of species with common characteristics.

through the accumulation of slight but useful variations, given to him by the hand of Nature. But Natural Selection, as we shall hereafter see, is a power incessantly ready for action, and is as immeasurably superior to man's feeble efforts, as the works of Nature are to those of Art.

We will now discuss in a little more detail the struggle for existence. * * * Nothing is easier than to admit in words the truth of the universal struggle for life, or more difficult—at least I have found it so—than constantly to bear this conclusion in mind. Yet unless it be thoroughly engrained in the mind, I am convinced that the whole economy of nature, with every fact on distribution, rarity, abundance, extinction, and variation, will be dimly seen or quite misunderstood. We behold the face of nature bright with gladness, we often see superabundance of food; we do not see, or we forget, that the birds which are idly singing round us mostly live on insects or seeds, and are thus constantly destroying life; or we forget how largely these songsters, or their eggs, or their nestlings, are destroyed by birds and beasts of prey; we do not always bear in mind, that though food may be now superabundant, it is not so at all seasons of each recurring year.

I should premise that I use the term Struggle for Existence in a large and metaphorical sense, including dependence of one being on another, and including (which is more important) not only the life of the individual, but success in leaving progeny. Two canine animals in a time of dearth, may be truly said to struggle with each other which shall get food and live. But a plant on the edge of a desert is said to struggle for life against the drought, though more properly it should be said to be dependent on the moisture. A plant which annually produces a thousand seeds, of which on an average only one comes to maturity, may be more truly said to struggle with the plants of the same and other kinds which already clothe the ground. The missletoe is dependent on the apple and a few other trees, but can only in a far-fetched sense be said to struggle with these trees, for if too many of these parasites grow on the same tree, it will languish and die. But several seedling missletoes, growing close together on the same branch, may more truly be said to struggle with each other. As the missletoe is disseminated by birds, its existence depends on birds; and it may metaphorically be said to struggle with other fruit-bearing plants, in order to tempt birds to devour and thus disseminate its seeds rather than those of other plants. In these several senses, which pass into each other, I use for convenience sake the general term of struggle for existence.

A struggle for existence inevitably follows from the high rate at which all organic beings tend to increase. Every being, which during its natural lifetime produces several eggs or seeds, must suffer destruction during some period of its life, and during some season or occasional year, otherwise, on the principle of geometrical increase, its numbers would quickly become so inordinately great that no country could support the product. Hence, as more individuals are produced than can possibly survive, there must in every case be a struggle for existence, either one individual with another of the same species, or with the individuals of distinct species or with the physical conditions of life. It is the doctrine of Malthus[2] applied with manifold force to the whole animal and vegetable kingdoms; for in this case there can be no artificial increase of food, and no prudential restraint from marriage. Although some species may be now increasing, more or less rapidly, in numbers, all cannot do so, for the world would not hold them.

---

2. In his *Essay on the Principle of Population* (1803), English economist Thomas Malthus argued that unchecked population growth would threaten the food supply; he proposed "moral restraint" as a partial solution.

There is no exception to the rule that every organic being naturally increases at so high a rate, that if not destroyed, the earth would soon be covered by the progeny of a single pair. Even slow-breeding man has doubled in twenty-five years, and at this rate, in a few thousand years, there would literally not be standing room for his progeny. * * *

In looking at Nature, it is most necessary to keep the foregoing considerations always in mind—never to forget that every single organic being around us may be said to be striving to the utmost to increase in numbers; that each lives by a struggle at some period of its life; that heavy destruction inevitably falls either on the young or old, during each generation or at recurrent intervals. Lighten any check, mitigate the destruction ever so little, and the number of the species will almost instantaneously increase to any amount. The face of Nature may be compared to a yielding surface, with ten thousand sharp wedges packed close together and driven inwards by incessant blows, sometimes one wedge being struck, and then another with greater force. * * *

The amount of food for each species of course gives the extreme limit to which each can increase; but very frequently it is not the obtaining food, but the serving as prey to other animals, which determines the average numbers of a species. Thus, there seems to be little doubt that the stock of partridges, grouse, and hares on any large estate depends chiefly on the destruction of vermin. If not one head of game were shot during the next twenty years in England, and, at the same time, if no vermin were destroyed, there would, in all probability, be less game than at present, although hundreds of thousands of game animals are now annually killed. On the other hand, in some cases, as with the elephant and rhinoceros, none are destroyed by beasts of prey: even the tiger in India most rarely dares to attack a young elephant protected by its dam.

Climate plays an important part in determining the average numbers of a species, and periodical seasons of extreme cold or drought, I believe to be the most effective of all checks. I estimated that the winter of 1854–55 destroyed four-fifths of the birds in my own grounds; and this is a tremendous destruction, when we remember that ten per cent. is an extraordinarily severe mortality from epidemics with man. The action of climate seems at first sight to be quite independent of the struggle for existence; but in so far as climate chiefly acts in reducing food, it brings on the most severe struggle between the individuals, whether of the same or of distinct species, which subsist on the same kind of food. Even when climate, for instance extreme cold, acts directly, it will be the least vigorous, or those which have got least food through the advancing winter, which will suffer most. When we travel from south to north, or from a damp region to a dry, we invariably see some species gradually getting rarer and rarer, and finally disappearing; and the change of climate being conspicuous, we are tempted to attribute the whole effect to its direct action. But this is a very false view: we forget that each species, even where it most abounds, is constantly suffering enormous destruction at some period of its life, from enemies or from competitors for the same place and food; and if these enemies or competitors be in the least degree favoured by any slight change of climate, they will increase in numbers, and, as each area is already fully stocked with inhabitants, the other species will decrease. * * *

That climate acts in main part indirectly by favouring other species, we may clearly see in the prodigious number of plants in our gardens which can perfectly well endure our climate, but which never become naturalised, for they cannot compete with our native plants, nor resist destruction by our native animals. * * *

*** Battle within battle must ever be recurring with varying success; and yet in the long-run the forces are so nicely balanced, that the face of nature remains uniform for long periods of time, though assuredly the merest trifle would often give the victory to one organic being over another. Nevertheless so profound is our ignorance, and so high our presumption, that we marvel when we hear of the extinction of an organic being; and as we do not see the cause, we invoke cataclysms to desolate the world, or invent laws on the duration of the forms of life! ***

As species of the same genus have usually, though by no means invariably, some similarity in habits and constitution, and always in structure, the struggle will generally be more severe between species of the same genus, when they come into competition with each other, than between species of distinct genera. We see this in the recent extension over parts of the United States of one species of swallow having caused the decrease of another species. The recent increase of the missel-thrush in parts of Scotland has caused the decrease of the song-thrush. How frequently we hear of one species of rat taking the place of another species under the most different climates! In Russia the small Asiatic cockroach has everywhere driven before it its great congener.[3] One species of charlock[4] will supplant another, and so in other cases. We can dimly see why the competition should be most severe between allied forms, which fill nearly the same place in the economy of nature; but probably in no one case could we precisely say why one species has been victorious over another in the great battle of life.

A corollary of the highest importance may be deduced from the foregoing remarks, namely, that the structure of every organic being is related, in the most essential yet often hidden manner, to that of all other organic beings, with which it comes into competition for food or residence, or from which it has to escape, or on which it preys. This is obvious in the structure of the teeth and talons of the tiger; and in that of the legs and claws of the parasite which clings to the hair on the tiger's body. But in the beautifully plumed seed of the dandelion, and in the flattened and fringed legs of the water-beetle, the relation seems at first confined to the elements of air and water. Yet the advantage of plumed seeds no doubt stands in the closest relation to the land being already thickly clothed by other plants; so that the seeds may be widely distributed and fall on unoccupied ground. In the water-beetle, the structure of its legs, so well adapted for diving, allows it to compete with other aquatic insects, to hunt for its own prey, and to escape serving as prey to other animals.

The store of nutriment laid up within the seeds of many plants seems at first sight to have no sort of relation to other plants. But from the strong growth of young plants produced from such seeds (as peas and beans), when sown in the midst of long grass, I suspect that the chief use of the nutriment in the seed is to favour the growth of the young seedling, whilst struggling with other plants growing vigorously all around.

Look at a plant in the midst of its range, why does it not double or quadruple its numbers? We know that it can perfectly well withstand a little more heat or cold, dampness or dryness, for elsewhere it ranges into slightly hotter or colder, damper or drier districts. In this case we can clearly see that if we wished in imagination to give the plant the power of increasing in number, we should have to give it some advantage over its competitors, or over the animals which preyed on it. On the confines of its geographical range, a change of constitution with respect to climate would clearly be an advantage to our plant; but we have reason to believe that only a few plants or

---

3. A member of the same genus.   4. Wild mustard.

animals range so far, that they are destroyed by the rigour of the climate alone. Not until we reach the extreme confines of life, in the arctic regions or on the borders of an utter desert, will competition cease. The land may be extremely cold or dry, yet there will be competition between some few species, or between the individuals of the same species, for the warmest or dampest spots.

Hence, also, we can see that when a plant or animal is placed in a new country amongst new competitors, though the climate may be exactly the same as in its former home, yet the conditions of its life will generally be changed in an essential manner. If we wished to increase its average numbers in its new home, we should have to modify it in a different way to what we should have done in its native country; for we should have to give it some advantage over a different set of competitors or enemies.

It is good thus to try in our imagination to give any form some advantage over another. Probably in no single instance should we know what to do, so as to succeed. It will convince us of our ignorance on the mutual relations of all organic beings; a conviction as necessary, as it seems to be difficult to acquire. All that we can do, is to keep steadily in mind that each organic being is striving to increase at a geometrical ratio; that each at some period of its life, during some season of the year, during each generation or at intervals, has to struggle for life, and to suffer great destruction. When we reflect on this struggle, we may console ourselves with the full belief, that the war of nature is not incessant, that no fear is felt, that death is generally prompt, and that the vigorous, the healthy, and the happy survive and multiply.

1859

❈❖❈

Robert Browning
1812–1889

Throughout his life Robert Browning was something of an enigma, a Byronic dandy sporting lemon-yellow gloves and gorgeous waistcoats, who loved dining out and yet kept both his private life and poetic practice out of the conversation. He longed for public recognition but would not make his work more accessible by stepping from behind his elaborate artistic masks. Unable to reconcile the hearty dinner guest with the experimental poet, Henry James concluded that Browning lived equally on both sides of an inner wall which "contained an invisible door through which, working the lock at will, he could swiftly pass." Although Browning sometimes suggested that he was a mere ventriloquist or puppeteer, the genius with which he impersonated other voices extended the range and complexity of English poetry in bold new directions. More than any other nineteenth-century figure, Browning shaped the poetry of the twentieth, influencing British and American poets from Hardy and Yeats to Eliot, Pound, Frost, Lowell, and Stevens.

Browning's early years were quiet, even sheltered. He was born in Camberwell, a rural suburb south of London, and with the exception of a year spent at London University, he lived at home with his parents and sister until the age of thirty-four. His father was an official in the Bank of England, and his mother a pious Nonconformist, both of whom encouraged their son in his passion for poetry, painting, and music. The chief source of his education was extensive, haphazard reading in his father's vast private library. Brought up to be a gentleman, Browning received lessons in dancing, fencing, boxing, drawing, and music, as well as Greek and Latin. His doting parents denied him nothing: when, at fourteen, he expressed an interest in the poetry of Shelley—whose works were unavailable because of his atheism—Browning's devout mother took him to London to find an out-of-print copy.

Uncertain what his genuine calling was, Browning considered and rejected careers in art, music, law, and business. A turning point came in October 1832, when he saw the aging Edmund Kean play Richard III. Stunned by the power of a performance in which the brilliant but weary actor alternately electrified and embarrassed the audience as he struggled to dominate his role, Browning found dramatic confirmation of his evolving theory that all personality was staged and variable. Taking Shakespeare as a model, he envisioned himself as performer, playwright, and stage manager of his own artistic world. That night he conceived a grand plan to "assume I know not how many different characters" in order to write poems, operas, novels, and speeches under different names so that "the world was never to guess" that Robert Browning had been the author.

It is a fascinating literary mystery why Browning should have wanted simultaneously to conceal his own identity and yet dazzle the world by impersonating other people—especially since the authors he most admired (Byron, Keats, and particularly Shelley) spoke so personally. In 1833, Browning began his career anonymously with a long romantic poem, *Pauline*, in which he took an indirect approach, speaking through a narrator who confided: "I will tell / My state, as though 'twere none of mine." *Pauline* failed to sell a single copy, but the book found its way to John Stuart Mill, who commented that the poet possessed "a more intense and morbid self-consciousness than I ever knew in any sane being."

In the next decade Browning produced a string of introspective plays and experimental dramatic poems, including *Paracelsus* (1835), *Strafford* (1837), *Sordello* (1840), and *Pippa Passes* (1841). The notorious difficulty of these unpopular works gave Browning a reputation for obscurity that he labored for the rest of his life to overcome. But by the early 1840s he had discovered where his talent lay: applying to lyric poetry his theatrical instincts and his aversion to self-revelation, he found he could produce startling new effects. Henceforth he would present his audience with a cast of aberrant personalities, each starring in his or her own miniplay. In language adapted to their insecurities and obsessions, Browning's characters unwittingly reveal their own, often shocking secrets—but only if readers make the effort to follow the uncanny logic of their contorted confessions.

In the advertisement for his breakthrough book, *Dramatic Lyrics* (1842), Browning offered the disclaimer that, though the poems are "lyric in expression," they are the "utterances of so many imaginary persons, not mine." These imaginary persons range from the Greek goddess Artemis to lovers in a Venetian gondola, from a medieval damsel in distress to a Spanish monk so consumed by hatred that his soliloquy begins with a growl: "Gr-r-r." The sheer physicality of Browning's words, the thick-textured lines, the aggressive consonant clusters that seem to mock Tennyson's liquid vowels, the staccato lines and convoluted syntax that convey the twistings of tongue and mind struggling to express themselves—all are trademarks of Browning's style. As Gerard Manley Hopkins said, Browning talks like "a man bouncing up from table with his mouth full of bread and cheese and saying that he meant to stand no blasted nonsense."

Browning did not invent the poetic form known as the dramatic monologue—it is used in such classics as Marvell's *To His Coy Mistress* and Tennyson's *Ulysses*—but he brought the form to new levels of complexity. He usually situates his speakers in specific historical places and periods. Sometimes they are well-known figures from the past, such as the Italian painters Andrea del Sarto and Fra Lippo Lippi, or literary characters, such as Caliban and Childe Roland. Browning catches them at a moment of great emotional intensity as they attempt to explain why they think and act as they do. In these passionate outbursts, they reveal their characters as much by idiomatic language, patterns of imagery, speech rhythms, and unintended ironies as by what they actually say.

Browning induces his readers to sympathize—even identify—with speakers of dubious morality and intentions. His gallery of rogues includes a duke who may have murdered his wife, a painter who savors his own cuckoldry, and a dying bishop who recalls with gusto the fleshly delights he has enjoyed. As the critic Robert Langbaum has pointed out, "the utter outrageousness" of such behavior "makes condemnation the least interesting response." Just as Satan becomes the most intriguing figure in *Paradise Lost,* so Browning's narrators elicit a reluctant fascination. Alternating between admiration and revulsion, and compelled by the intricacies of human motivation to suspend judgment, the reader struggles to come to terms with these disclosures.

This theatrical world of passionate utterance spilled over into reality in 1845, when Browning became the coauthor and hero of his own romantic drama. On January 10, he wrote a fan letter to the famous poet Elizabeth Barrett, whom he had never seen. He was thirty-three, she nearly forty, and her poetry was far better known than his. "I love your verses with all my heart," he wrote boldly, "—and I love you too." Her reply was encouraging, and thus began the century's most celebrated literary correspondence. She was an invalid suffering from tuberculosis, and they did not meet until May. But when Browning entered her darkened room, he fell instantly in love with the frail, fiery woman lying on her couch swathed in shawls and blankets. For more than a year and half they kept the nature of their relationship secret, to circumvent the wrath of her tyrannical father, who had permitted none of his children to marry. Finally, Browning decided they must break free: they were married secretly during a morning walk, in September 1846, and eloped to Italy, where they eventually settled in Florence.

Though their marriage was rhapsodic, Browning was frustrated with his art. Preoccupied with his wife, her work, their son "Pen" (born in 1849), and the charms of Florence, the usually prolific Browning wrote only one poem in the first three years of marriage, and published just two books in the fifteen years they lived together. Though she acknowledged his genius, Elizabeth joined with her husband's friends in urging him to write "in the most directest and most impressive way, the mask thrown off." Unable or unwilling to do so, Browning gloomily found that he had acquired a further mask that he had not sought: that of "Mrs. Browning's husband."

Hoping finally to make his name with a wider public, Browning channeled his energies into a new project, fifty monologues published in 1855 as *Men and Women.* These animated self-portraits by artists, lovers, questors, skeptics, and impostors form a dazzling picture gallery containing many of Browning's greatest poems, including *Love Among the Ruins, Fra Lippo Lippi,* and *Childe Roland.* The plural title of *Men and Women* insists on the variability of human experience, and the centrality of sexual difference to every individual's self-definition. But the book was poorly received at the time, except by the Pre-Raphaelites, and was soon overshadowed by the tumultuous acclaim bestowed on Elizabeth Barrett Browning's *Aurora Leigh* in 1856. Dejected by his readers' failure to make the effort to comprehend his art, Browning complained to his friend John Ruskin: "I cannot begin writing poetry till my imaginary reader has conceded licenses to me. . . . You would have me paint it all plain out, which can't be; but by various artifices I try to make shift with touches and bits of outlines which *succeed* if they bear the conception from me to you. You ought, I think, to keep pace with the thought."

Elizabeth Barrett Browning died suddenly in 1861 in Florence. "My life is fixed and sure now," the devastated widower wrote to his sister, "I shall live out the remainder in her direct influence." Browning returned to England with his son and settled down to a steady rhythm of writing and dining out. But with renewed vigor he resumed his demanding experiments with dramatic lyrics, more determined than ever to pursue the indirect forms of expression that the reading public had resisted.

The result was his second masterpiece, *The Ring and the Book,* a novel in verse published in four monthly installments, between 1868 and 1869. The poem reimagines a sensational seventeenth-century Roman murder trial. In extended monologues the various participants tell their versions of the story. We hear the pleas of the dying young bride Pompilia, her cruel husband Guido, her priest and would-be rescuer Caponsacchi, and then the rationale of the Pope, who decides the case. In this sordid tale of marital abuse and dubious justice, Browning explores the relativity of human understanding, the rights of women, and the role of religious belief in determining earthly action. The success of *The Ring and the Book,* together with the increasing popularity of his earlier work, meant that in the 1870s and 1880s Browning was finally recognized as sharing with Tennyson the title of the era's leading poet. He was especially amused and gratified by the adulation of the Browning Societies that sprang up in England and around the world during his later years. When asked if he objected to the amateurish enthusiasm of the clubs that met to discuss his philosophy of life, he replied: "Object to it? No, I like it! . . . I have waited forty years for it, and now—I like it!" In the United States, where Browning mania hit hardest, brown clothing, curtains, and tableware became the rage, and his works were excerpted on railroad timetables. Mark Twain even gave a series of readings of which he boasted: "I can read Browning so Browning himself can understand it."

Browning's last book, *Asolando*, was published to wide acclaim the day he died at his son's home in Venice. Shortly before his death, Browning read aloud from the book's *Epilogue* the stanza that described his dogged determination to keep on striving in a world of limitation and imperfection: "One who never turned his back but marched breast forward, / Never doubted clouds would break." Ultimately, this confidence underlies the bold relativity and deep skepticism that animate Browning's work. Like Hopkins, Browning insists that all of nature, even human nature, bespeaks some part of an unknowable absolute. Thus everything becomes material for poetry, the dirty, deformed, and despicable no less than the beautiful, pure, and radiantly good. As Browning says in *Fra Lippo Lippi*, "This world's no blot for us, / Nor blank; it means intensely, and means good: / To find its meaning is my meat and drink."

Porphyria's Lover[1]

The rain set early in to-night,
    The sullen wind was soon awake,
It tore the elm-tops down for spite,
    And did its worst to vex the lake:
5   I listened with heart fit to break.
When glided in Porphyria; straight
    She shut the cold out and the storm,
And kneeled and made the cheerless grate
    Blaze up, and all the cottage warm;
10   Which done, she rose, and from her form
Withdrew the dripping cloak and shawl,
    And laid her soiled gloves by, untied
Her hat and let the damp hair fall,
    And, last, she sat down by my side
15   And called me. When no voice replied,
She put my arm about her waist,
    And made her smooth white shoulder bare,
And all her yellow hair displaced,
    And, stooping, made my cheek lie there,
20   And spread, o'er all, her yellow hair,
Murmuring how she loved me—she
    Too weak, for all her heart's endeavour,
To set its struggling passion free
    From pride, and vainer ties dissever,
25   And give herself to me for ever.
But passion sometimes would prevail,

---

1. The poem was originally published with another of Browning's dramatic monologues, *Johannes Agricola in Meditation*, under the general title of *Madhouse Cells*.

Nor could to-night's gay feast restrain

A sudden thought of one so pale

For love of her, and all in vain:

30   So, she was come through wind and rain.

Be sure I looked up at her eyes

Happy and proud; at last I knew

Porphyria worshipped me; surprise

Made my heart swell, and still it grew

35   While I debated what to do.

That moment she was mine, mine, fair,

Perfectly pure and good: I found

A thing to do, and all her hair

In one long yellow string I wound

40   Three times her little throat around,

And strangled her. No pain felt she;

I am quite sure she felt no pain.

As a shut bud that holds a bee,

I warily oped her lids: again

45   Laughed the blue eyes without a stain.

And I untightened next the tress

About her neck; her cheek once more

Blushed bright beneath my burning kiss:

I propped her head up as before,

50   Only, this time my shoulder bore

Her head, which droops upon it still:

The smiling rosy little head,

So glad it has its utmost will,

That all it scorned at once is fled,

55   And I, its love, am gained instead!

Porphyria's love: she guessed not how

Her darling one wish would be heard.

And thus we sit together now,

And all night long we have not stirred,

60   And yet God has not said a word!

c. 1835

1836, 1842

My Last Duchess[1]

Ferrara

That's my last Duchess painted on the wall,

Looking as if she were alive. I call

That piece a wonder, now: Frà Pandolf's[2] hands

Worked busily a day, and there she stands.

5   Will't please you sit and look at her? I said

"Frà Pandolf" by design, for never read

Strangers like you that pictured countenance,

The depth and passion of its earnest glance,

---

1. The speaker is modeled on Alfonso II, Duke of Ferrara, who married the fourteen-year-old Lucrezia de Medici in 1558. When she died three years later, poisoning was suspected. In 1565 the Duke married the daughter of Ferdinand I, Count of Tyrol.

2. Brother Pandolf, the imaginary painter of the duchess's portrait.

But to myself they turned (since none puts by
10 The curtain I have drawn for you, but I)
And seemed as they would ask me, if they durst,
How such a glance came there; so, not the first
Are you to turn and ask thus. Sir, 'twas not
Her husband's presence only, called that spot
15 Of joy into the Duchess' cheek: perhaps
Frà Pandolf chanced to say "Her mantle laps
Over my lady's wrist too much," or "Paint
Must never hope to reproduce the faint
Half-flush that dies along her throat:" such stuff
20 Was courtesy, she thought, and cause enough
For calling up that spot of joy. She had
A heart—how shall I say?—too soon made glad,
Too easily impressed; she liked whate'er
She looked on, and her looks went everywhere.
25 Sir, 'twas all one! My favour at her breast,
The dropping of the daylight in the West,
The bough of cherries some officious fool
Broke in the orchard for her, the white mule
She rode with round the terrace—all and each
30 Would draw from her alike the approving speech,
Or blush, at least. She thanked men,—good! but thanked
Somehow—I know not how—as if she ranked
My gift of a nine-hundred-years-old name
With anybody's gift. Who'd stoop to blame
35 This sort of trifling? Even had you skill
In speech—(which I have not)—to make your will
Quite clear to such an one, and say, "Just this
Or that in you disgusts me; here you miss,
Or there exceed the mark"—and if she let
40 Herself be lessoned so, nor plainly set
Her wits to yours, forsooth, and made excuse,
—E'en then would be some stooping; and I choose
Never to stoop. Oh sir, she smiled, no doubt,
Whene'er I passed her, but who passed without
45 Much the same smile? This grew; I gave commands;
Then all smiles stopped together. There she stands
As if alive. Will't please you rise? We'll meet
The company below, then. I repeat,
The Count your master's known munificence
50 Is ample warrant that no just pretence
Of mine for dowry will be disallowed;
Though his fair daughter's self, as I avowed
At starting, is my object.[3] Nay, we'll go
Together down, sir. Notice Neptune, though,
55 Taming a sea-horse, thought a rarity,
Which Claus of Innsbruck cast in bronze for me!

1842   1842

---

3. Only now does the reader learn that the duke is conducting negotiations for his second marriage and has been addressing the envoy of his bride-to-be's father.

The Bishop Orders His Tomb at Saint Praxed's Church[1]

Rome, 15——

Vanity, saith the preacher, vanity![2]
Draw round my bed: is Anselm keeping back?
Nephews—sons mine[3] . . . ah God, I know not! Well—
She, men would have to be your mother once,
Old Gandolf envied me, so fair she was!   5
What's done is done, and she is dead beside,
Dead long ago, and I am Bishop since,
And as she died so must we die ourselves,
And thence ye may perceive the world's a dream.
Life, how and what is it? As here I lie   10
In this state-chamber, dying by degrees,
Hours and long hours in the dead night, I ask
"Do I live, am I dead?" Peace, peace seems all.
Saint Praxed's ever was the church for peace;
And so, about this tomb of mine. I fought   15
With tooth and nail to save my niche, ye know:
—Old Gandolf cozened me,° despite my care;   *cheated*
Shrewd was that snatch from out the corner South
He graced his carrion with, God curse the same!
Yet still my niche is not so cramped but thence   20
One sees the pulpit o' the epistle-side,[4]
And somewhat of the choir, those silent seats,
And up into the aery dome where live
The angels, and a sunbeam's sure to lurk:
And I shall fill my slab of basalt there,   25
And 'neath my tabernacle[5] take my rest,
With those nine columns round me, two and two,
The odd one at my feet where Anselm stands:
Peach-blossom marble all, the rare, the ripe
As fresh-poured red wine of a mighty pulse.[6]   30
—Old Gandolf with his paltry onion-stone,°   *cheap marble*
Put me where I may look at him! True peach,
Rosy and flawless: how I earned the prize!
Draw close: that conflagration of my church
—What then? So much was saved if aught were missed!   35
My sons, ye would not be my death? Go dig
The white-grape vineyard where the oil-press stood,
Drop water gently till the surface sink,
And if ye find . . . Ah God, I know not, I! . . .

1. John Ruskin admired Browning's portrait of a dying bishop's obsession with ordering a sumptuous tomb: "I know of no other piece of modern English, prose or poetry, in which there is so much told, as in these lines, of the Renaissance spirit—its worldliness, inconsistency, pride, hypocrisy, ignorance of itself, love of art, of luxury, and of good Latin. It is nearly all that I have said of the central Renaissance in thirty pages of the *Stones of Venice*, put into as many lines, Browning's also being the antecedent work" (*Modern Painters*, vol. 4, ch. 20, sec. 34).

2. "Vanity of vanities, saith the Preacher, vanity of vanities; all is vanity" (Ecclesiastes 1.2).
3. The supposedly celibate clergy could not marry but sometimes took mistresses; the Bishop euphemistically calls his illegitimate sons "nephews."
4. The right side, as one faces the altar, from which the Epistles of the New Testament are read.
5. Stone canopy beneath which the sculpted effigy of the bishop will repose on his tomb.
6. The pulpy mash of grapes from which strong wine could be made.

40   Bedded in store of rotten fig-leaves soft,
      And corded up in a tight olive-frail,°   *basket*
      Some lump, ah God, of *lapis lazuli*,[7]
      Big as a Jew's head cut off at the nape,
      Blue as a vein o'er the Madonna's breast . . .
45   Sons, all have I bequeathed you, villas, all,
      That brave Frascati[8] villa with its bath,
      So, let the blue lump poise between my knees,
      Like God the Father's globe on both his hands
      Ye worship in the Jesu Church so gay,
50   For Gandolf shall not choose but see and burst!
      Swift as a weaver's shuttle fleet our years:[9]
      Man goeth to the grave, and where is he?
      Did I say basalt for my slab, sons? Black—
      'Twas ever antique-black I meant! How else
55   Shall ye contrast my frieze° to come beneath?   *sculpted band*
      The bas-relief in bronze ye promised me,
      Those Pans and Nymphs ye wot of, and perchance
      Some tripod, thyrsus, with a vase or so,
      The Saviour at his sermon on the mount,
60   Saint Praxed in a glory, and one Pan
      Ready to twitch the Nymph's last garment off,
      And Moses with the tables[1] . . . but I know
      Ye mark me not! What do they whisper thee,
      Child of my bowels, Anselm? Ah, ye hope
65   To revel down my villas while I gasp
      Bricked o'er with beggar's mouldy travertine°   *limestone*
      Which Gandolf from his tomb-top chuckles at!
      Nay, boys, ye love me—all of jasper, then!
      'Tis jasper ye stand pledged to, lest I grieve.
70   My bath must needs be left behind, alas!
      One block, pure green as a pistachio-nut,
      There's plenty jasper somewhere in the world—
      And have I not Saint Praxed's ear to pray
      Horses for ye, and brown Greek manuscripts,
75   And mistresses with great smooth marbly limbs?
      —That's if ye carve my epitaph aright,
      Choice Latin, picked phrase, Tully's every word,
      No gaudy ware like Gandolf's second line—
      Tully, my masters? Ulpian serves his need![2]
80   And then how I shall lie through centuries,
      And hear the blessed mutter of the mass,
      And see God made and eaten all day long,[3]
      And feel the steady candle-flame, and taste

7. A semiprecious bright blue stone.
8. A resort near Rome.
9. Job 7.6: "My days are swifter than a weaver's shuttle and are spent without hope." The next line alludes to Job 7.9 and 14.10.
1. The bronze bas-relief sculptures will mingle pagan and Christian scenes, the goatlike lecherous Pan next to Moses receiving the Ten Commandments. In *Contrasts*

(1841) A. W. Pugin criticized such juxtapositions, which were typical of the Renaissance.
2. Domitius Ulpianus (A.D. 170–228) was considered inferior to Marcus Tullius Cicero (106–43 B.C.), regarded during the Renaissance as the greatest Latin prose stylist.
3. According to the doctrine of transubstantiation, the bread and wine of Holy Communion become the body and blood of Christ.

Good strong thick stupefying incense-smoke!
85 For as I lie here, hours of the dead night,
Dying in state and by such slow degrees,
I fold my arms as if they clasped a crook,
And stretch my feet forth straight as stone can point,
And let the bedclothes, for a mortcloth, drop
90 Into great laps and folds of sculptor's-work:[4]
And as yon tapers dwindle, and strange thoughts
Grow, with a certain humming in my ears,
About the life before I lived this life,
And this life too, popes, cardinals and priests,
95 Saint Praxed at his sermon on the mount,[5]
Your tall pale mother with her talking eyes,
And new-found agate urns as fresh as day,
And marble's language, Latin pure, discreet,
—Aha, ELUCESCEBAT[6] quoth our friend?
100 No Tully, said I, Ulpian at the best!
Evil and brief hath been my pilgrimage.[7]
All *lapis*, all, sons! Else I give the Pope
My villas! Will ye ever eat my heart?
Ever your eyes were as a lizard's quick,
105 They glitter like your mother's for my soul,
Or ye would heighten my impoverished frieze,
Piece out its starved design, and fill my vase
With grapes, and add a vizor and a Term,[8]
And to the tripod ye would tie a lynx
110 That in his struggle throws the thyrsus down,
To comfort me on my entablature°   *platform*
Whereon I am to lie till I must ask
"Do I live, am I dead?" There, leave me, there!
For ye have stabbed me with ingratitude
115 To death—ye wish it—God, ye wish it! Stone—
Gritstone, a-crumble![9] Clammy squares which sweat
As if the corpse they keep were oozing through—
And no more *lapis* to delight the world!
Well go! I bless ye. Fewer tapers there,
120 But in a row: and, going, turn your backs
—Ay, like departing altar-ministrants,
And leave me in my church, the church for peace,
That I may watch at leisure if he leers—
Old Gandolf, at me, from his onion-stone,
125 As still he envied me, so fair she was!

1844   1845

---

4. As he lies in bed, the bishop positions himself like a carved effigy lying on a tomb, holding his ceremonial staff and draping his bedsheets like a "mortcloth" over a corpse.
5. Jesus gave the sermon on the mount, not St. Praxed (who was a woman); the bishop's mind is getting confused.
6. Gandolf's epitaph: "He was illustrious." The bishop disapproves of the verb form; Cicero would have written *elucebat*.

7. Cf. Genesis 47.9, where Jacob says: "The days of the years of my pilgrimage are an hundred and thirty years: few and evil have the days of the years of my life been."
8. The vizor of a helmet is sometimes represented in sculpture; the bishop suggests that his sons might also add a statue of Terminus, the Roman god of boundaries.
9. He fears they might use crumbly sandstone after all.

Love Among the Ruins[1]

1

Where the quiet-coloured end of evening smiles,
      Miles and miles
On the solitary pastures where our sheep
      Half-asleep
5 Tinkle homeward thro' the twilight, stray or stop
      As they crop—
Was the site once of a city great and gay,
      (So they say)
Of our country's very capital, its prince
10   Ages since
Held his court in, gathered councils, wielding far
      Peace or war.

2

Now,—the country does not even boast a tree
      As you see,
15 To distinguish slopes of verdure, certain rills
      From the hills
Intersect and give a name to, (else they run
      Into one)
Where the domed and daring palace shot its spires
20   Up like fires
O'er the hundred-gated circuit of a wall
      Bounding all,
Made of marble, men might march on nor be pressed
      Twelve abreast.

3

25 And such plenty and perfection, see, of grass
      Never was!
Such a carpet as, this summer-time, o'erspreads
      And embeds
Every vestige of the city, guessed alone,
30   Stock or stone—
Where a multitude of men breathed joy and woe
      Long ago;
Lust of glory pricked their hearts up, dread of shame
      Struck them tame;
35 And that glory and that shame alike, the gold
      Bought and sold.

4

Now,—the single little turret that remains
      On the plains,
By the caper° overrooted, by the gourd   *shrub*
40   Overscored,

---

1. The poem's scenery suggests the Roman Campagna but may also allude to archaeological excavations at Babylon, Nineveh, and Egyptian Thebes. Browning invented this stanza form.

While the patching houseleek's head of blossom winks
    Through the chinks—
Marks the basement whence a tower in ancient time
    Sprang sublime,
45   And a burning ring, all round, the chariots traced
    As they raced,
And the monarch and his minions and his dames
    Viewed the games.

5

And I know, while thus the quiet-coloured eve
50   Smiles to leave
To their folding, all our many-tinkling fleece
    In such peace,
And the slopes and rills in undistinguished grey
    Melt away—
55   That a girl with eager eyes and yellow hair
    Waits me there
In the turret whence the charioteers caught soul
    For the goal,
When the king looked, where she looks now, breathless, dumb
60   Till I come.

6

But he looked upon the city, every side,
    Far and wide,
All the mountains topped with temples, all the glades'
    Colonnades,
65   All the causeys,° bridges, aqueducts,—and then,   *causeways*
    All the men!
When I do come, she will speak not, she will stand,
    Either hand
On my shoulder, give her eyes the first embrace
70   Of my face,
Ere we rush, ere we extinguish sight and speech
    Each on each.

7

In one year they sent a million fighters forth
    South and North,
75   And they built their gods a brazen pillar high
    As the sky,
Yet reserved a thousand chariots in full force—
    Gold, of course.
Oh heart! oh blood that freezes, blood that burns!
80   Earth's returns
For whole centuries of folly, noise and sin!
    Shut them in,
With their triumphs and their glories and the rest!
    Love is best.

c. 1852   1855

"Childe Roland to the Dark Tower Came"[1]

(See Edgar's Song in "Lear")[2]

1

My first thought was, he lied in every word,
That hoary cripple, with malicious eye
Askance to watch the working of his lie
On mine, and mouth scarce able to afford
Suppression of the glee, that pursed and scored
Its edge, at one more victim gained thereby.

2

What else should he be set for, with his staff?
What, save to waylay with his lies, ensnare
All travellers who might find him posted there,
And ask the road? I guessed what skull-like laugh
Would break, what crutch 'gin write my epitaph
For pastime in the dusty thoroughfare,

3

If at his counsel I should turn aside
Into that ominous tract which, all agree,
Hides the Dark Tower. Yet acquiescingly
I did turn as he pointed: neither pride
Nor hope rekindling at the end descried,
So much as gladness that some end might be.

4

For, what with my whole world-wide wandering,
What with my search drawn out thro' years, my hope
Dwindled into a ghost not fit to cope
With that obstreperous joy success would bring,—
I hardly tried now to rebuke the spring
My heart made, finding failure in its scope.

5

As when a sick man very near to death
Seems dead indeed, and feels begin and end
The tears and takes the farewell of each friend,
And hears one bid the other go, draw breath
Freelier outside, ("since all is o'er," he saith,
"And the blow fallen no grieving can amend;")

6

While some discuss if near the other graves
Be room enough for this, and when a day
Suits best for carrying the corpse away,
With care about the banners, scarves and staves:

1. Roland was a hero of Charlemagne legends, and a "childe" was a young candidate for knighthood. Although critics have proposed many different interpretations of Roland's strange, nightmarish quest, Browning himself said only that the poem "came upon me as a kind of dream. I had to write it, then and there, and I finished it the same day, I believe. But it was simply that I had to do it. I did not know then what I meant beyond that, and I'm sure I don't know now. But I am very fond of it."
2. In Shakespeare's *King Lear*, Edgar, disguised as the mad beggar Poor Tom, sings: "Child Rowland to the dark tower came; / His word was still, 'Fie, foh and fum, / I smell the blood of a British man'" (3.4.181–83).

35   And still the man hears all, and only craves
          He may not shame such tender love and stay.

                              7

     Thus, I had so long suffered in this quest,
          Heard failure prophesied so oft, been writ
          So many times among "The Band"—to wit,
40   The knights who to the Dark Tower's search addressed
     Their steps—that just to fail as they, seemed best,
          And all the doubt was now—should I be fit?

                              8

     So, quiet as despair, I turned from him,
          That hateful cripple, out of his highway
45   Into the path he pointed. All the day
     Had been a dreary one at best, and dim
     Was settling to its close, yet shot one grim
          Red leer to see the plain catch its estray.°   *stray animal*

                              9

     For mark! no sooner was I fairly found
50   Pledged to the plain, after a pace or two,
          Than, pausing to throw backward a last view
     O'er the safe road, 'twas gone; grey plain all round:
     Nothing but plain to the horizon's bound.
          I might go on; nought else remained to do.

                              10

55   So, on I went. I think I never saw
          Such starved ignoble nature; nothing throve:
          For flowers—as well expect a cedar grove!
     But cockle, spurge,° according to their law   *weeds*
     Might propagate their kind, with none to awe,
60   You'd think; a burr had been a treasure-trove.

                              11

     No! penury, inertness and grimace,
          In some strange sort, were the land's portion. "See
          Or shut your eyes," said Nature peevishly,
     "It nothing skills: I cannot help my case:
65   'Tis the Last Judgment's fire must cure this place,
          Calcine° its clods and set my prisoners free."   *burn to ashes*

                              12

     If there pushed any ragged thistle-stalk
          Above its mates, the head was chopped; the bents°   *coarse grasses*
          Were jealous else. What made those holes and rents
70   In the dock's° harsh swarth leaves, bruised as to baulk   *weed*
     All hope of greenness? 'tis a brute must walk
          Pashing° their life out, with a brute's intents.   *crushing*

                              13

     As for the grass, it grew as scant as hair
          In leprosy; thin dry blades pricked the mud
75   Which underneath looked kneaded up with blood.
     One stiff blind horse, his every bone a-stare,
     Stood stupefied, however he came there:
          Thrust out past service from the devil's stud!

14

Alive? he might be dead for aught I know,
80   With that red gaunt and colloped neck a-strain,
        And shut eyes underneath the rusty mane;
Seldom went such grotesqueness with such woe;
I never saw a brute I hated so;
        He must be wicked to deserve such pain.

15

85   I shut my eyes and turned them on my heart.
        As a man calls for wine before he fights,
        I asked one draught of earlier, happier sights,
Ere fitly I could hope to play my part.
Think first, fight afterwards—the soldier's art:
90   One taste of the old time sets all to rights.

16

Not it! I fancied Cuthbert's reddening face
        Beneath its garniture of curly gold,
        Dear fellow, till I almost felt him fold
An arm in mine to fix me to the place,
95   That way he used. Alas, one night's disgrace!
        Out went my heart's new fire and left it cold.

17

Giles then, the soul of honour—there he stands
        Frank as ten years ago when knighted first.
        What honest man should dare (he said) he durst.
100 Good—but the scene shifts—faugh! what hangman-hands
Pin to his breast a parchment? His own bands
        Read it. Poor traitor, spit upon and curst!

18

Better this present than a past like that;
        Back therefore to my darkening path again!
105   No sound, no sight as far as eye could strain.
Will the night send a howlet° or a bat?   *owl*
I asked: when something on the dismal flat
        Came to arrest my thoughts and change their train.

19

A sudden little river crossed my path
110   As unexpected as a serpent comes.
        No sluggish tide congenial to the glooms;
This, as it frothed by, might have been a bath
For the fiend's glowing hoof—to see the wrath
        Of its black eddy bespate with flakes and spumes.

20

115 So petty yet so spiteful! All along,
        Low scrubby alders kneeled down over it;
        Drenched willows flung them headlong in a fit
Of mute despair, a suicidal throng:
The river which had done them all the wrong,
120   Whate'er that was, rolled by, deterred no whit.

21

Which, while I forded,—good saints, how I feared
        To set my foot upon a dead man's cheek,

Each step, or feel the spear I thrust to seek
   For hollows, tangled in his hair or beard!
125   —It may have been a water-rat I speared,
      But, ugh! it sounded like a baby's shriek.

22

Glad was I when I reached the other bank.
   Now for a better country. Vain presage!
   Who were the strugglers, what war did they wage,
130   Whose savage trample thus could pad° the dank   *tread*
Soil to a plash? Toads in a poisoned tank,
   Or wild cats in a red-hot iron cage—

23

The fight must so have seemed in that fell cirque.°   *terrible arena*
   What penned them there, with all the plain to choose?
135   No foot-print leading to that horrid mews,
None out of it. Mad brewage set to work
   Their brains, no doubt, like galley-slaves the Turk
     Pits for his pastime, Christians against Jews.

24

And more than that—a furlong on—why, there!
140   What bad use was that engine for, that wheel,
     Or brake, not wheel—that harrow fit to reel
Men's bodies out like silk? with all the air
   Of Tophet's° tool, on earth left unaware,   *hell's*
     Or brought to sharpen its rusty teeth of steel.

25

145   Then came a bit of stubbed ground, once a wood,
     Next a marsh, it would seem, and now mere earth
     Desperate and done with; (so a fool finds mirth,
Makes a thing and then mars it, till his mood
   Changes and off he goes!) within a rood°—   *quarter of an acre*
150   Bog, clay and rubble, sand and stark black dearth.

26

Now blotches rankling, coloured gay and grim,
   Now patches where some leanness of the soil's
   Broke into moss or substances like boils;
Then came some palsied oak, a cleft in him
155   Like a distorted mouth that splits its rim
     Gaping at death, and dies while it recoils.

27

And just as far as ever from the end!
   Nought in the distance but the evening, nought
   To point my footstep further! At the thought,
160   A great black bird, Apollyon's[3] bosom-friend,
Sailed past, nor beat his wide wing dragon-penned°   *pinioned*
   That brushed my cap—perchance the guide I sought.

28

For, looking up, aware I somehow grew,
   'Spite of the dusk, the plain had given place

---

3. Devil mentioned in Revelation 9.11 and in Bunyan's *Pilgrim's Progress*.

165   All round to mountains—with such name to grace
       Mere ugly heights and heaps now stolen in view.
       How thus they had surprised me,—solve it, you!
          How to get from them was no clearer case.

29

       Yet half I seemed to recognize some trick
170   Of mischief happened to me, God knows when—
       In a bad dream perhaps. Here ended, then,
       Progress this way. When, in the very nick
       Of giving up, one time more, came a click
          As when a trap shuts—you're inside the den!

30

175   Burningly it came on me all at once,
          This was the place! those two hills on the right,
          Crouched like two bulls locked horn in horn in fight;
       While to the left, a tall scalped mountain . . . Dunce,
       Dotard, a-dozing at the very nonce,°   moment
180   After a life spent training for the sight!

31

       What in the midst lay but the Tower itself?
          The round squat turret, blind as the fool's heart,[4]
          Built of brown stone, without a counterpart
       In the whole world. The tempest's mocking elf
185   Points to the shipman thus the unseen shelf
          He strikes on, only when the timbers start.

32

       Not see? because of night perhaps?—why, day
          Came back again for that! before it left,
          The dying sunset kindled through a cleft:
190   The hills, like giants at a hunting, lay,
       Chin upon hand, to see the game at bay,—
          "Now stab and end the creature—to the heft!"°   hilt

33

       Not hear? when noise was everywhere! it tolled
          Increasing like a bell. Names in my ears
195   Of all the lost adventurers my peers,—
       How such a one was strong, and such was bold,
       And such was fortunate, yet each of old
          Lost, lost! one moment knelled the woe of years.

34

       There they stood, ranged along the hill-sides, met
200   To view the last of me, a living frame
          For one more picture! in a sheet of flame
       I saw them and I knew them all. And yet
       Dauntless the slug-horn[5] to my lips I set,
          And blew. "Childe Roland to the Dark Tower came."

c. 1852   1855

---

4. "The fool hath said in his heart, There is no God"   5. Scottish word for slogan, or battle-cry, though Brown-
(Psalm 14.1).   ing seems to mean "trumpet."

Fra Lippo Lippi[1]

I am poor brother Lippo, by your leave!
You need not clap your torches to my face.
Zooks, what's to blame? you think you see a monk!
What, 'tis past midnight, and you go the rounds,
5   And here you catch me at an alley's end
Where sportive ladies leave their doors ajar?
The Carmine's my cloister:[2] hunt it up,
Do,—harry out, if you must show your zeal,
Whatever rat, there, haps on his wrong hole,
10   And nip each softling of a wee white mouse,
Weke, weke, that's crept to keep him company!
Aha, you know your betters! Then, you'll take
Your hand away that's fiddling on my throat,
And please to know me likewise. Who am I?
15   Why, one, sir, who is lodging with a friend
Three streets off—he's a certain . . . how d'ye call?
Master—a . . . Cosimo of the Medici,[3]
I' the house that caps the corner. Boh! you were best!
Remember and tell me, the day you're hanged,
20   How you affected such a gullet's-gripe![4]
But you, sir,[5] it concerns you that your knaves
Pick up a manner nor discredit you:
Zooks, are we pilchards,° that they sweep the streets   *sardines*
And count fair prize what comes into their net?
25   He's Judas to a tittle, that man is![6]
Just such a face! Why, sir, you make amends:
Lord, I'm not angry! Bid your hangdogs go
Drink out this quarter-florin to the health
Of the munificent House that harbours me
30   (And many more beside, lads! more beside!)
And all's come square again. I'd like his face—
His, elbowing on his comrade in the door
With the pike and lantern,—for the slave that holds
John Baptist's head a-dangle by the hair
35   With one hand ("Look you, now," as who should say)
And his weapon in the other, yet unwiped!
It's not your chance to have a bit of chalk,
A wood-coal or the like? or you should see!
Yes, I'm the painter, since you style me so.
40   What, brother Lippo's doings, up and down,
You know them and they take you? like enough!
I saw the proper twinkle in your eye—
'Tell you, I liked your looks at very first.
Let's sit and set things straight now, hip to haunch.

1. Filippo Lippi (1406–1469) was an early Renaissance painter and monk whose life is described in Giorgio Vasari's *The Lives of the Painters* (1550, 1568); Fra means brother.
2. Santa Maria del Carmine, a Carmelite monastery in Florence.
3. Cosimo de' Medici (1389–1464), a banker and ruler of Florence, was Lippi's patron.
4. How you choked me by the throat.
5. Lippi now addresses the leader of the watchmen.
6. One of the watchmen is the spitting image of Judas.

45   Here's spring come, and the nights one makes up bands
    To roam the town and sing out carnival,[7]
    And I've been three weeks shut within my mew,
    A-painting for the great man, saints and saints
    And saints again. I could not paint all night—
50   Ouf! I leaned out of window for fresh air.
    There came a hurry of feet and little feet,
    A sweep of lute-strings, laughs, and whiffs of song,—
    Flower o' the broom,
    Take away love, and our earth is a tomb!
55   *Flower o' the quince,*
    I let Lisa go, and what good in life since?
    Flower o' the thyme[8]—and so on. Round they went.
    Scarce had they turned the corner when a titter
    Like the skipping of rabbits by moonlight,—three slim shapes,
60   And a face that looked up . . . zooks, sir, flesh and blood,
    That's all I'm made of! Into shreds it went,
    Curtain and counterpane and coverlet,
    All the bed-furniture—a dozen knots,
    There was a ladder! Down I let myself,
65   Hands and feet, scrambling somehow, and so dropped,
    And after them. I came up with the fun
    Hard by Saint Laurence,[9] hail fellow, well met,—
    Flower o' the rose,
    If I've been merry, what matter who knows?
70   And so as I was stealing back again
    To get to bed and have a bit of sleep
    Ere I rise up to-morrow and go work
    On Jerome[1] knocking at his poor old breast
    With his great round stone to subdue the flesh,
75   You snap me of the sudden. Ah, I see!
    Though your eye twinkles still, you shake your head—
    Mine's shaved[2]—a monk, you say—the sting's in that!
    If Master Cosimo announced himself,
    Mum's the word naturally; but a monk!
80   Come, what am I a beast for? tell us, now!
    I was a baby when my mother died
    And father died and left me in the street.
    I starved there, God knows how, a year or two
    On fig-skins, melon-parings, rinds and shucks,
85   Refuse and rubbish. One fine frosty day,
    My stomach being empty as your hat,
    The wind doubled me up and down I went.
    Old Aunt Lapaccia trussed me with one hand,
    (Its fellow was a stinger as I knew)
90   And so along the wall, over the bridge,
    By the straight cut to the convent. Six words there,

---

7. A season of festivities before Lent.
8. The "flower songs" Lippi sings are called *stornelli,*
three-line Tuscan folk songs.
9. The Church of San Lorenzo.

1. The pleasure-loving Lippi is painting the chaste and
ascetic St. Jerome.
2. The tonsure, or partially shaved head, was the emblem
of the monk.

While I stood munching my first bread that month:
"So, boy, you're minded," quoth the good fat father
Wiping his own mouth, 'twas refection-time,°—   *mealtime*
95   "To quit this very miserable world?
Will you renounce" . . . "the mouthful of bread?" thought I;
By no means! Brief, they made a monk of me;
I did renounce the world, its pride and greed,
Palace, farm, villa, shop and banking-house,
100   Trash, such as these poor devils of Medici
Have given their hearts to—all at eight years old.
Well, sir, I found in time, you may be sure,
'Twas not for nothing—the good bellyful,
The warm serge and the rope that goes all round,
105   And day-long blessed idleness beside!
"Let's see what the urchin's fit for"—that came next.
Not overmuch their way, I must confess.
Such a to-do! They tried me with their books:
Lord, they'd have taught me Latin in pure waste!
110   *Flower o' the clove,*
All the Latin I construe is, "amo," I love!
But, mind you, when a boy starves in the streets
Eight years together, as my fortune was,
Watching folk's faces to know who will fling
115   The bit of half-stripped grape-bunch he desires,
And who will curse or kick him for his pains,—
Which gentleman processional and fine,
Holding a candle to the Sacrament,
Will wink and let him lift a plate and catch
120   The droppings of the wax to sell again,
Or holla for the Eight[3] and have him whipped,—
How say I?—nay, which dog bites, which lets drop
His bone from the heap of offal in the street,—
Why, soul and sense of him grow sharp alike,
125   He learns the look of things, and none the less
For admonition from the hunger-pinch.
I had a store of such remarks, be sure,
Which, after I found leisure, turned to use.
I drew men's faces on my copy-books,
130   Scrawled them within the antiphonary's marge,[4]
Joined legs and arms to the long music-notes,
Found eyes and nose and chin for A's and B's,
And made a string of pictures of the world
Betwixt the ins and outs of verb and noun,
135   On the wall, the bench, the door. The monks looked black.
"Nay," quoth the Prior, "turn him out, d' ye say?
In no wise. Lose a crow and catch a lark.
What if at last we get our man of parts,
We Carmelites, like those Camaldolese
140   And Preaching Friars, to do our church up fine

---

3. Send for the magistrates of Florence.   4. The margin of his hymn book.

And put the front on it that ought to be!"[5]
And hereupon he bade me daub away.
Thank you! my head being crammed, the walls a blank,
Never was such prompt disemburdening.

145   First, every sort of monk, the black and white,
I drew them, fat and lean: then, folk at church,
From good old gossips waiting to confess
Their cribs° of barrel-droppings, candle-ends,—   *small thefts*
To the breathless fellow at the altar-foot,

150   Fresh from his murder,[6] safe and sitting there
With the little children round him in a row
Of admiration, half for his beard and half
For that white anger of his victim's son
Shaking a fist at him with one fierce arm,

155   Signing himself[7] with the other because of Christ
(Whose sad face on the cross sees only this
After the passion° of a thousand years)   *suffering*
Till some poor girl, her apron o'er her head,
(Which the intense eyes looked through) came at eve

160   On tiptoe, said a word, dropped in a loaf,
Her pair of earrings and a bunch of flowers
(The brute took growling), prayed, and so was gone.
I painted all, then cried "'Tis ask and have;
Choose, for more's ready!"—laid the ladder flat,

165   And showed my covered bit of cloister-wall
The monks closed in a circle and praised loud
Till checked, taught what to see and not to see,
Being simple bodies,—"That's the very man!
Look at the boy who stoops to pat the dog!

170   That woman's like the Prior's niece[8] who comes
To care about his asthma: it's the life!"
But there my triumph's straw-fire flared and funked;°   *smoked*
Their betters took their turn to see and say:
The Prior and the learned pulled a face

175   And stopped all that in no time. "How? what's here?
Quite from the mark of painting, bless us all!
Faces, arms, legs and bodies like the true
As much as pea and pea! it's devil's-game!
Your business is not to catch men with show,

180   With homage to the perishable clay,
But lift them over it, ignore it all,
Make them forget there's such a thing as flesh.
Your business is to paint the souls of men—
Man's soul, and it's a fire, smoke . . . no, it's not . . .

185   It's vapour done up like a new-born babe—
(In that shape when you die it leaves your mouth)

---

5. The Prior, or head of the monastery, wants to outdo
rival orders of monks by having Lippi paint the church
splendidly.
6. Criminals could take refuge in the church because it
was a sanctuary where civil law had no power.
7. Making the sign of the cross.
8. Probably a euphemism for the Prior's mistress.

It's . . . well, what matters talking, it's the soul!
Give us no more of body than shows soul!
Here's Giotto,[9] with his Saint a-praising God,
190 That sets us praising,—why not stop with him?
Why put all thoughts of praise out of our head
With wonder at lines, colours, and what not?
Paint the soul, never mind the legs and arms!
Rub all out, try at it a second time.
195 Oh, that white smallish female with the breasts,
She's just my niece . . . Herodias, I would say,—
Who went and danced and got men's heads cut off![1]
Have it all out!" Now, is this sense, I ask?
A fine way to paint soul, by painting body
200 So ill, the eye can't stop there, must go further
And can't fare worse! Thus, yellow does for white
When what you put for yellow's simply black,
And any sort of meaning looks intense
When all beside itself means and looks nought.
205 Why can't a painter lift each foot in turn,
Left foot and right foot, go a double step,
Make his flesh liker and his soul more like,
Both in their order? Take the prettiest face,
The Prior's niece . . . patron-saint—is it so pretty
210 You can't discover if it means hope, fear,
Sorrow or joy? won't beauty go with these?
Suppose I've made her eyes all right and blue,
Can't I take breath and try to add life's flash,
And then add soul and heighten them threefold?
215 Or say there's beauty with no soul at all—
(I never saw it—put the case the same—)
If you get simple beauty and nought else,
You get about the best thing God invents:
That's somewhat: and you'll find the soul you have missed,
220 Within yourself, when you return him thanks.
"Rub all out!" Well, well, there's my life, in short,
And so the thing has gone on ever since.
I'm grown a man no doubt, I've broken bounds:
You should not take a fellow eight years old
225 And make him swear to never kiss the girls.
I'm my own master, paint now as I please—
Having a friend, you see, in the Corner-house!°   *Medici palace*
Lord, it's fast holding by the rings in front—
Those great rings serve more purposes than just
230 To plant a flag in, or tie up a horse!
And yet the old schooling sticks, the old grave eyes
Are peeping o'er my shoulder as I work,
The heads shake still—"It's art's decline, my son!

9. Giotto di Bondone (c. 1266–1337), late-medieval Florentine artist and architect.
1. The gospel of Matthew tells how Herod's niece Salomé

danced before him and requested as a reward the head of
John the Baptist (14.6–8). According to Vasari, however,
it was Salomé's mother, Herodias, who danced.

You're not of the true painters, great and old;

235 Brother Angelico's the man, you'll find;
Brother Lorenzo stands his single peer:[2]
Fag° on at flesh, you'll never make the third!"   struggle
Flower o' the pine,
You keep your mistr . . . manners, and I'll stick to mine!

240 I'm not the third, then: bless us, they must know!
Don't you think they're the likeliest to know,
They with their Latin? So, I swallow my rage,
Clench my teeth, suck my lips in tight, and paint
To please them—sometimes do and sometimes don't;

245 For, doing most, there's pretty sure to come
A turn, some warm eve finds me at my saints—
A laugh, a cry, the business of the world—
(*Flower o' the peach,*
Death for us all, and his own life for each!)

250 And my whole soul revolves, the cup runs over,
The world and life's too big to pass for a dream,
And I do these wild things in sheer despite,
And play the fooleries you catch me at,
In pure rage! The old mill-horse, out at grass

255 After hard years, throws up his stiff heels so,
Although the miller does not preach to him
The only good of grass is to make chaff.°   straw
What would men have? Do they like grass or no—
May they or mayn't they? all I want's the thing

260 Settled for ever one way. As it is,
You tell too many lies and hurt yourself:
You don't like what you only like too much,
You do like what, if given you at your word,
You find abundantly detestable.

265 For me, I think I speak as I was taught;
I always see the garden and God there
A-making man's wife: and, my lesson learned,
The value and significance of flesh,
I can't unlearn ten minutes afterwards.

270   You understand me: I'm a beast, I know.
But see, now—why, I see as certainly
As that the morning-star's about to shine,
What will hap some day. We've a youngster here
Comes to our convent, studies what I do,

275 Slouches and stares and lets no atom drop:
His name is Guidi—he'll not mind the monks—
They call him Hulking Tom,[3] he lets them talk—
He picks my practice up—he'll paint apace,
I hope so—though I never live so long,

---

2. Fra Angelico (1387–1455) and Lorenzo Monaco (1370–1425) were important painters in the traditional formalist style.
3. Tommaso Guidi (1401–1428), called Masaccio ("Sloppy Tom"), was probably Lippi's teacher, but Browning casts him as his pupil. Both painters revolted against the highly stylized conventions of medieval art in favor of increased realism.

280   I know what's sure to follow. You be judge!
      You speak no Latin more than I, belike,
      However, you're my man, you've seen the world
      —The beauty and the wonder and the power,
      The shapes of things, their colours, lights and shades,
285   Changes, surprises,—and God made it all!
      —For what? Do you feel thankful, ay or no,
      For this fair town's face, yonder river's line,
      The mountain round it and the sky above,
      Much more the figures of man, woman, child,
290   These are the frame to? What's it all about?
      To be passed over, despised? or dwelt upon,
      Wondered at? oh, this last of course!—you say.
      But why not do as well as say,—paint these
      Just as they are, careless what comes of it?
295   God's works—paint anyone, and count it crime
      To let a truth slip. Don't object, "His works
      Are here already; nature is complete:
      Suppose you reproduce her—(which you can't)
      There's no advantage! you must beat her, then."
300   For, don't you mark? we're made so that we love
      First when we see them painted, things we have passed
      Perhaps a hundred times nor cared to see;
      And so they are better, painted—better to us,
      Which is the same thing. Art was given for that;
305   God uses us to help each other so,
      Lending our minds out. Have you noticed, now,
      Your cullion's hanging face?[4] A bit of chalk,
      And trust me but you should, though! How much more,
      If I drew higher things with the same truth!
310   That were to take the Prior's pulpit-place,
      Interpret God to all of you! Oh, oh,
      It makes me mad to see what men shall do
      And we in our graves! This world's no blot for us,
      Nor blank; it means intensely, and means good:
315   To find its meaning is my meat and drink.
      "Ay, but you don't so instigate to prayer!"
      Strikes in the Prior: "when your meaning's plain
      It does not say to folk—remember matins,°   *morning prayers*
      Or, mind you fast next Friday!" Why, for this
320   What need of art at all? A skull and bones,
      Two bits of stick nailed crosswise, or, what's best,
      A bell to chime the hour with, does as well.
      I painted a Saint Laurence six months since
      At Prato, splashed the fresco in fine style:
325   "How looks my painting, now the scaffold's down?"
      I ask a brother: "Hugely," he returns—
      Already not one phiz° of your three slaves   *face*

---

4. That rascal's drooping face (or perhaps "born to be hanged"—cf. line 19).

Who turn the Deacon off his toasted side,[5]
But's scratched and prodded to our heart's content,
330   The pious people have so eased their own
With coming to say prayers there in a rage:
We get on fast to see the bricks beneath.
Expect another job this time next year,
For pity and religion grow i' the crowd—
335   Your painting serves its purpose!" Hang the fools!

        —That is—you'll not mistake an idle word
Spoke in a huff by a poor monk, God wot,
Tasting the air this spicy night which turns
The unaccustomed head like Chianti wine!
340   Oh, the church knows! don't misreport me, now!
It's natural a poor monk out of bounds
Should have his apt word to excuse himself:
And hearken how I plot to make amends.
I have bethought me: I shall paint a piece
345   . . . There's for you! Give me six months, then go, see
Something in Sant' Ambrogio's![6] Bless the nuns!
They want a cast o' my office. I shall paint
God in the midst, Madonna and her babe,
Ringed by a bowery flowery angel-brood,
350   Lilies and vestments and white faces, sweet
As puff on puff of grated orris-root
When ladies crowd to Church at midsummer.
And then i' the front, of course a saint or two—
Saint John, because he saves the Florentines,
355   Saint Ambrose, who puts down in black and white
The convent's friends and gives them a long day,
And Job, I must have him there past mistake,
The man of Uz (and Us without the z,
Painters who need his patience). Well, all these
360   Secured at their devotion, up shall come
Out of a corner when you least expect,
As one by a dark stair into a great light,
Music and talking, who but Lippo! I!—
Mazed, motionless and moonstruck—I'm the man!
365   Back I shrink—what is this I see and hear?
I, caught up with my monk's-things by mistake,
My old serge gown and rope that goes all round,
I, in this presence, this pure company!
Where's a hole, where's a corner for escape?
370   Then steps a sweet angelic slip of a thing
Forward, puts out a soft palm—"Not so fast!"
—Addresses the celestial presence, "nay—
He made you and devised you, after all,
Though he's none of you! Could Saint John there draw—

5. St. Laurence, a deacon who was martyred by being roasted, is reputed to have asked to be turned over, as he was done on one side.

6. Lippi's *Coronation of the Virgin* was painted for the church of Sant' Ambrogio's convent in Florence.

375   His camel-hair[7] make up a painting-brush?
      We come to brother Lippo for all that,
      Iste perfecit opus!"[8] So, all smile—
      I shuffle sideways with my blushing face
      Under the cover of a hundred wings
380   Thrown like a spread of kirtles° when you're gay   *skirts*
      And play hot cockles,[9] all the doors being shut,
      Till, wholly unexpected, in there pops
      The hothead husband! Thus I scuttle off
      To some safe bench behind, not letting go
385   The palm of her, the little lily thing
      That spoke the good word for me in the nick,
      Like the Prior's niece . . . Saint Lucy, I would say.[1]
      And so all's saved for me, and for the church
      A pretty picture gained. Go, six months hence!
390   Your hand, sir, and good-bye: no lights, no lights!
      The street's hushed, and I know my own way back,
      Don't fear me! There's the grey beginning. Zooks!

1853   1855

Andrea Del Sarto[1]

(called "The Faultless Painter")

      But do not let us quarrel any more,
      No, my Lucrezia; bear with me for once:
      Sit down and all shall happen as you wish.
      You turn your face, but does it bring your heart?
5   I'll work then for your friend's friend, never fear,
      Treat his own subject after his own way,
      Fix his own time, accept too his own price,
      And shut the money into this small hand
      When next it takes mine. Will it? tenderly?
10   Oh, I'll content him,—but to-morrow, Love!
      I often am much wearier than you think,
      This evening more than usual, and it seems
      As if—forgive now—should you let me sit
      Here by the window with your hand in mine
15   And look a half-hour forth on Fiesole,[2]
      Both of one mind, as married people use,
      Quietly, quietly the evening through,
      I might get up to-morrow to my work

---

7. "And John was clothed with camel's hair, and with a girdle of a skin about his loins; and he did eat locusts and wild honey" (Mark 1.6). John the Baptist is the patron saint of Florence.

8. "This man made the work." These words appear beside a figure in the painting, who was assumed to be a self-portrait of Lippi. (It is actually the patron who ordered the painting.)

9. A blindfolded game, here a euphemism for sex.

1. Lippi will paint the Prior's "niece" as the virgin martyr Lucy, whom he has imagined interceding on his behalf with "the celestial presence" (lines 370–377).

1. Browning's depiction of Andrea del Sarto (1486–1531), a technically gifted Florentine Renaissance painter who never quite lived up to his early promise, is based in part on Giorgio Vasari's *The Lives of the Painters* (1550, 1568). Vasari, who had been Andrea's pupil, considered that "had his spirit been as bold as his judgment was profound, he would doubtless have been unequaled. But a timidity of spirit and a yielding simple nature prevented him from exhibiting a burning ardour and dash that, joined to his other qualities, would have made him divine."

2. A suburb of Florence.

Cheerful and fresh as ever. Let us try.
20   To-morrow, how you shall be glad for this!
Your soft hand is a woman of itself,
And mine the man's bared breast she curls inside.
Don't count the time lost, neither; you must serve
For each of the five pictures we require:
25   It saves a model. So! keep looking so—
My serpentining beauty, rounds on rounds!
—How could you ever prick those perfect ears,
Even to put the pearl there! oh, so sweet—
My face, my moon, my everybody's moon,
30   Which everybody looks on and calls his,
And, I suppose, is looked on by in turn,
While she looks—no one's: very dear, no less.
You smile? why, there's my picture ready made,
There's what we painters call our harmony!
35   A common greyness silvers everything,[3]—
All in a twilight, you and I alike
—You, at the point of your first pride in me
(That's gone you know),—but I, at every point;
My youth, my hope, my art, being all toned down
40   To yonder sober pleasant Fiesole.
There's the bell clinking from the chapel-top;
That length of convent-wall across the way
Holds the trees safer, huddled more inside;
The last monk leaves the garden; days decrease,
45   And autumn grows, autumn in everything.
Eh? the whole seems to fall into a shape
As if I saw alike my work and self
And all that I was born to be and do,
A twilight-piece. Love, we are in God's hand.
50   How strange now, looks the life he makes us lead;
So free we seem, so fettered fast we are!
I feel he laid the fetter: let it lie!
This chamber for example—turn your head—
All that's behind us! You don't understand
55   Nor care to understand about my art,
But you can hear at least when people speak:
And that cartoon,° the second from the door   *drawing*
—It is the thing, Love! so such things should be—
Behold Madonna!—I am bold to say.
60   I can do with my pencil what I know,
What I see, what at bottom of my heart
I wish for, if I ever wish so deep—
Do easily, too—what I say, perfectly,
I do not boast, perhaps: yourself are judge,
65   Who listened to the Legate's[4] talk last week,

3. The grey tones of Andrea del Sarto's paintings were regarded in Browning's day as characteristic of his art (rather than the effect of fading and aging); the unusually muted rhythms of this poem attempt to convey the same qualities of restraint and understatement.
4. A representative of the Pope.

And just as much they used to say in France.
At any rate 'tis easy, all of it!
No sketches first, no studies, that's long past:
I do what many dream of, all their lives,
70   —Dream? strive to do, and agonize to do,
And fail in doing. I could count twenty such
On twice your fingers, and not leave this town,
Who strive—you don't know how the others strive
To paint a little thing like that you smeared
75   Carelessly passing with your robes afloat,—
Yet do much less, so much less, Someone[5] says,
(I know his name, no matter)—so much less!
Well, less is more, Lucrezia: I am judged.
There burns a truer light of God in them,
80   In their vexed beating stuffed and stopped-up brain,
Heart, or whate'er else, than goes on to prompt
This low-pulsed forthright craftsman's hand of mine.
Their works drop groundward, but themselves, I know,
Reach many a time a heaven that's shut to me,
85   Enter and take their place there sure enough,
Though they come back and cannot tell the world.
My works are nearer heaven, but I sit here.
The sudden blood of these men! at a word—
Praise them, it boils, or blame them, it boils too.
90   I, painting from myself and to myself,
Know what I do, am unmoved by men's blame
Or their praise either. Somebody remarks
Morello's[6] outline there is wrongly traced,
His hue mistaken; what of that? or else,
95   Rightly traced and well ordered; what of that?
Speak as they please, what does the mountain care?
Ah, but a man's reach should exceed his grasp,
Or what's a heaven for? All is silver-grey
Placid and perfect with my art: the worse!
100   I know both what I want and what might gain,
And yet how profitless to know, to sigh
"Had I been two, another and myself,
Our head would have o'erlooked the world!" No doubt.
Yonder's a work now, of that famous youth
105   The Urbinate who died five years ago.[7]
('Tis copied, George Vasari sent it me.)
Well, I can fancy how he did it all,
Pouring his soul, with kings and popes to see,
Reaching, that heaven might so replenish him,
110   Above and through his art—for it gives way;
That arm is wrongly put—and there again—
A fault to pardon in the drawing's lines,

5. Probably Michelangelo.
6. A mountain near Florence.
7. Raphael (1483–1520) was born in Urbino. Thus the
poem is set in 1525 (when, far from being in autumnal
decline, Andrea was at the height of his powers).

Its body, so to speak: its soul is right,
He means right—that, a child may understand.
115   Still, what an arm! and I could alter it:
But all the play, the insight and the stretch—
Out of me, out of me! And wherefore out?
Had you enjoined them on me, given me soul,
We might have risen to Rafael, I and you!
120   Nay, Love, you did give all I asked, I think—
More than I merit, yes, by many times.
But had you—oh, with the same perfect brow,
And perfect eyes, and more than perfect mouth,
And the low voice my soul hears, as a bird
125   The fowler's pipe, and follows to the snare—
Had you, with these the same, but brought a mind!
Some women do so. Had the mouth there urged
"God and the glory! never care for gain.
The present by the future, what is that?
130   Live for fame, side by side with Agnolo![8]
Rafael is waiting: up to God, all three!"
I might have done it for you. So it seems:
Perhaps not. All is as God over-rules.
Beside, incentives come from the soul's self;
135   The rest avail not. Why do I need you?
What wife had Rafael, or has Agnolo?
In this world, who can do a thing, will not;
And who would do it, cannot, I perceive:
Yet the will's somewhat—somewhat, too, the power—
140   And thus we half-men struggle. At the end,
God, I conclude, compensates, punishes.
'Tis safer for me, if the award be strict,
That I am something underrated here,
Poor this long while, despised, to speak the truth.
145   I dared not, do you know, leave home all day,
For fear of chancing on the Paris lords.[9]
The best is when they pass and look aside;
But they speak sometimes; I must bear it all.
Well may they speak! That Francis, that first time,
150   And that long festal year at Fontainebleau!
I surely then could sometimes leave the ground,
Put on the glory, Rafael's daily wear,
In that humane great monarch's golden look,—
One finger in his beard or twisted curl
155   Over his mouth's good mark that made the smile,
One arm about my shoulder, round my neck,
The jingle of his gold chain in my ear,
I painting proudly with his breath on me,

---

8. Michelangelo (Michel Agnolo Buonarroti), Italian painter (1475–1564).
9. In 1518 Andrea was invited to Fontainebleau by the French king, Francis I, who became his patron. Rumor had it that when he left the court to return to Italy, the king entrusted him with funds, which he spent on a house for Lucrezia. Now he is ashamed to face the scorn of visiting French nobles.

All his court round him, seeing with his eyes,
160 Such frank French eyes, and such a fire of souls
Profuse, my hand kept plying by those hearts,—
And, best of all, this, this, this face beyond,
This in the background, waiting on my work,
To crown the issue with a last reward!
165 A good time, was it not, my kingly days?
And had you not grown restless . . . but I know—
'Tis done and past; 'twas right, my instinct said;
Too live the life grew, golden and not grey,
And I'm the weak-eyed bat no sun should tempt
170 Out of the grange whose four walls make his world.
How could it end in any other way?
You called me, and I came home to your heart.
The triumph was—to reach and stay there; since
I reached it ere the triumph, what is lost?
175 Let my hands frame your face in your hair's gold,
You beautiful Lucrezia that are mine!
"Rafael did this, Andrea painted that;
The Roman's[1] is the better when you pray,
But still the other's Virgin was his wife—"
180 Men will excuse me. I am glad to judge
Both pictures in your presence; clearer grows
My better fortune, I resolve to think.
For, do you know, Lucrezia, as God lives,
Said one day Agnolo, his very self,
185 To Rafael . . . I have known it all these years . . .
(When the young man was flaming out his thoughts
Upon a palace-wall for Rome to see,
Too lifted up in heart because of it)
"Friend, there's a certain sorry little scrub[2]
190 Goes up and down our Florence, none cares how,
Who, were he set to plan and execute
As you are, pricked on by your popes and kings,
Would bring the sweat into that brow of yours!"
To Rafael's!—And indeed the arm is wrong.
195 I hardly dare . . . yet, only you to see,
Give the chalk here—quick, thus the line should go!
Ay, but the soul! he's Rafael! rub it out!
Still, all I care for, if he spoke the truth,
(What he? why, who but Michel Agnolo?
200 Do you forget already words like those?)[3]
If really there was such a chance, so lost,—
Is, whether you're—not grateful—but more pleased.
Well, let me think so. And you smile indeed!
This hour has been an hour! Another smile?
205 If you would sit thus by me every night
I should work better, do you comprehend?

---

1. Raphael worked in Rome after 1509.
2. I.e., Andrea, who is boasting to Lucrezia that

Michelangelo once praised his abilities to Raphael.
3. Lucrezia, bored, has lost the thread of Andrea's story.

I mean that I should earn more, give you more.
See, it is settled dusk now; there's a star;
Morello's gone, the watch-lights show the wall,
210   The cue-owls[4] speak the name we call them by.
Come from the window, love,—come in, at last,
Inside the melancholy little house
We built to be so gay with. God is just.
King Francis may forgive me: oft at nights
215   When I look up from painting, eyes tired out,
The walls become illumined, brick from brick
Distinct, instead of mortar, fierce bright gold,
That gold of his I did cement them with!
Let us but love each other. Must you go?
220   That Cousin here again?[5] he waits outside?
Must see you—you, and not with me? Those loans?
More gaming debts to pay? you smiled for that?
Well, let smiles buy me! have you more to spend?
While hand and eye and something of a heart
225   Are left me, work's my ware, and what's it worth?
I'll pay my fancy. Only let me sit
The grey remainder of the evening out,
Idle, you call it, and muse perfectly
How I could paint, were I but back in France,
230   One picture, just one more—the Virgin's face,
Not yours this time! I want you at my side
To hear them—that is, Michel Agnolo—
Judge all I do and tell you of its worth.
Will you? To-morrow, satisfy your friend.
235   I take the subjects for his corridor,
Finish the portrait out of hand—there, there,
And throw him in another thing or two
If he demurs; the whole should prove enough
To pay for this same Cousin's freak. Beside,
240   What's better and what's all I care about,
Get you the thirteen scudi° for the ruff!   coins
Love, does that please you? Ah, but what does he,
The Cousin! what does he to please you more?

      I am grown peaceful as old age to-night.
245   I regret little, I would change still less.
Since there my past life lies, why alter it?
The very wrong to Francis!—it is true
I took his coin, was tempted and complied,
And built this house and sinned, and all is said.
250   My father and my mother died of want.[6]
Well, had I riches of my own? you see
How one gets rich! Let each one bear his lot.
They were born poor, lived poor, and poor they died:
And I have laboured somewhat in my time

---

4. Owls whose cry sounds like the Italian word *ciù*.
5. Lucrezia's lover, whose gambling debts Andrea has already agreed to pay (lines 5–10).

6. Vasari claimed that Andrea abandoned his aged parents and spent his money on Lucrezia and her family.

255   And not been paid profusely. Some good son
      Paint my two hundred pictures—let him try!
      No doubt, there's something strikes a balance. Yes,
      You loved me quite enough, it seems to-night.
      This must suffice me here. What would one have?
260   In heaven, perhaps, new chances, one more chance—
      Four great walls in the New Jerusalem,[7]
      Meted° on each side by the angel's reed,   *measured*
      For Leonard,[8] Rafael, Agnolo and me
      To cover—the three first without a wife,
265   While I have mine! So—still they overcome
      Because there's still Lucrezia,—as I choose.

      Again the Cousin's whistle! Go, my Love.

c. 1853   1855

Elizabeth Gaskell
1810–1865

During the 1880s and 1890s, short stories enjoyed a golden age in Britain. H. G. Wells said that "People talked about them tremendously, compared them, and ranked them. That was the thing that mattered." Yet short stories had been popular in America and Europe for decades before they caught on in Britain. Previously, the public's appetite for fiction had been sated by novels, which often appeared serially in the leading periodicals. Although many novelists, including Charles Dickens, George Eliot, Anthony Trollope, and Wilkie Collins, occasionally tried their hand at short fiction, three-decker novels were far more profitable—and far more prestigious. Where the novel might be regarded as "serious," stories smacked of the sensational. Henry James observed that "the little story is but scantily relished in England, where readers take their fiction rather by the volume than by the page." Not until late in the century did writers such as Rudyard Kipling and Arthur Conan Doyle build their careers on short stories, and only then did the genre gain the status of a distinct artistic form.

    The growing visibility of short stories was fueled by innovations in the printing process that allowed low-cost mass-circulation periodicals to flourish; Somerset Maugham later argued that "the rich abundance of short stories during the nineteenth century was directly occasioned by the opportunity which the periodicals afforded." Thanks in part to the rage for Sherlock Holmes, *The Strand* sold half-a-million copies a month during the 1890s. Literary magazines were often shaped by the taste and vision of the founding editor; *Household Words,* for example—where Elizabeth Gaskell first published *Cranford*—bore the characteristic stamp of its creator, Charles Dickens.

    The narrator of *Cranford* speaks of having "vibrated all my life" between the rural setting of Cranford and a nearby commercial city. The same was true of Elizabeth Gaskell, who grew up in the small town of Knutsford, but went to live in the industrial city of Manchester after her marriage to a Unitarian minister in 1832. She grappled with the changes wrought by industrialism in novels of social protest, including *Mary Barton* (1848), *Ruth* (1853), and *North and South* (1855). Even in the idyllic village of Cranford, the "obnoxious" new railroad impinges dramatically. The middle-aged spinsters with their out-of-date clothes and manners are only dimly aware of the

---

7. Cf. Revelation 21. 10–21.
8. Leonardo da Vinci (1452–1519), third in the trio of

great Italian Renaissance artists whom del Sarto has failed to equal.

bustling modern world; they linger on as representatives of a bygone era. The story is set in the 1830s, when Dickens's lively comic novel *Pickwick Papers* was hot off the presses, the epitome of modern literature; the Cranford ladies' preference for the stately prose of the eighteenth-century Dr. Johnson humorously dramatizes a society in transition. The young narrator records their eccentricities fondly, but with a subtle sense of the absurd. Yet despite their faintly ridiculous obsession with gentility and "elegant economy," the women of Cranford retain the humanity, compassion, and moral integrity conspicuously lacking in the industrial world.

Our Society at Cranford[1]

In the first place, Cranford is in possession of the Amazons;[2] all the holders of houses above a certain rent are women. If a married couple come to settle in the town, somehow the gentleman disappears; he is either fairly frightened to death by being the only man in the Cranford evening parties, or he is accounted for by being with his regiment, his ship, or closely engaged in business all the week in the great neighbouring commercial town of Drumble,[3] distant only twenty miles on a railroad. In short, whatever does become of the gentlemen, they are not at Cranford. What could they do if they were there? The surgeon has his round of thirty miles, and sleeps at Cranford; but every man cannot be a surgeon. For keeping the trim gardens full of choice flowers without a weed to speck them; for frightening away little boys who look wistfully at the said flowers through the railings; for rushing out at the geese that occasionally venture into the gardens if the gates are left open; for deciding all questions of literature and politics without troubling themselves with unnecessary reasons or arguments; for obtaining clear and correct knowledge of everybody's affairs in the parish; for keeping their neat maid-servants in admirable order; for kindness (somewhat dictatorial) to the poor, and real tender good offices to each other whenever they are in distress, the ladies of Cranford are quite sufficient. "A man," as one of them observed to me once, "is *so* in the way in the house!" Although the ladies of Cranford know all each other's proceedings, they are exceedingly indifferent to each other's opinions. Indeed, as each has her own individuality, not to say eccentricity, pretty strongly developed, nothing is so easy as verbal retaliation; but, somehow, good-will reigns among them to a considerable degree.

The Cranford ladies have only an occasional little quarrel, spirited out in a few peppery words and angry jerks of the head; just enough to prevent the even tenor of their lives from becoming too flat. Their dress is very independent of fashion; as they observe, "What does it signify how we dress here at Cranford, where everybody knows us?" And if they go from home, their reason is equally cogent, "What does it signify how we dress here, where nobody knows us?" The materials of their clothes are, in general, good and plain, and most of them are nearly as scrupulous as Miss Tyler, of cleanly memory;[4] but I will answer for it, the last gigot, the last tight and scanty petticoat in wear in England, was seen in Cranford—and seen without a smile.[5]

I can testify to a magnificent family red silk umbrella, under which a gentle little spinster, left alone of many brothers and sisters, used to patter to church on rainy days. Have you any red silk umbrellas in London? We had a tradition of the first that

1. First published as a self-contained story in December 1851 in *Household Words,* a periodical edited by Charles Dickens. Although Gaskell later said that "I never meant to write more," Dickens persuaded her to continue the story in subsequent issues. In 1853 the collected sketches appeared in book form as *Cranford.*
2. In Greek legend, the Amazons were fierce warriors who formed an all-female state.

3. Manchester.
4. The aunt of Robert Southey (1774–1843)—Poet Laureate at the time when *Cranford* takes place—was famous for her passion for cleanliness.
5. By the mid-1830s, the old-fashioned leg-of-mutton sleeve and straight skirt had given way to the hooped skirt.

had ever been seen in Cranford; and the little boys mobbed it, and called it "a stick in petticoats." It might have been the very red silk one I have described, held by a strong father over a troop of little ones; the poor little lady—the survivor of all—could scarcely carry it.

Then there were rules and regulations for visiting and calls; and they were announced to any young people who might be staying in the town, with all the solemnity with which the old Manx laws were read once a year on the Tinwald Mount.[6]

"Our friends have sent to inquire how you are after your journey to-night, my dear" (fifteen miles in a gentleman's carriage); "they will give you some rest to-morrow, but the next day, I have no doubt, they will call; so be at liberty after twelve—from twelve to three are our calling hours."

Then, after they had called—

"It is the third day; I dare say your mamma has told you, my dear, never to let more than three days elapse between receiving a call and returning it; and also, that you are never to stay longer than a quarter of an hour."

"But am I to look at my watch? How am I to find out when a quarter of an hour has passed?"

"You must keep thinking about the time, my dear, and not allow yourself to forget it in conversation."

As everybody had this rule in their minds, whether they received or paid a call, of course no absorbing subject was ever spoken about. We kept ourselves to short sentences of small talk, and were punctual to our time.

I imagine that a few of the gentlefolks of Cranford were poor, and had some difficulty in making both ends meet; but they were like the Spartans,[7] and concealed their smart under a smiling face. We none of us spoke of money, because that subject savoured of commerce and trade, and though some might be poor, we were all aristocratic. The Cranfordians had that kindly *esprit de corps* which made them overlook all deficiencies in success when some among them tried to conceal their poverty. When Mrs Forrester, for instance, gave a party in her baby-house of a dwelling, and the little maiden disturbed the ladies on the sofa by a request that she might get the tea-tray out from underneath, every one took this novel proceeding as the most natural thing in the world, and talked on about household forms and ceremonies as if we all believed that our hostess had a regular servants' hall, second table, with housekeeper and steward, instead of the one little charity-school maiden,[8] whose short ruddy arms could never have been strong enough to carry the tray upstairs, if she had not been assisted in private by her mistress, who now sat in state, pretending not to know what cakes were sent up, though she knew, and we knew, and she knew that we knew, and we knew that she knew that we knew, she had been busy all the morning making tea-bread and sponge-cakes.

There were one or two consequences arising from this general but unacknowledged poverty, and this very much acknowledged gentility, which were not amiss, and which might be introduced into many circles of society to their great improvement. For instance, the inhabitants of Cranford kept early hours, and clattered home in their pattens,[9] under the guidance of a lantern-bearer, about nine o'clock at night; and the whole town was abed and asleep by half-past ten. Moreover, it was considered

---

6. The population of the Isle of Man customarily assembled once a year on Tynwald Hill to hear the new laws read aloud.
7. The Spartans of ancient Greece were known for their courage and self-control in the face of hardship.

8. Charity schools trained poor children for domestic work; that one such pupil formed Mrs. Forrester's entire domestic staff indicates her meager standard of living.
9. Wooden platform shoes to protect one's shoes from mud.

"vulgar" (a tremendous word in Cranford) to give anything expensive, in the way of eatable or drinkable, at the evening entertainments. Wafer bread-and-butter and sponge-biscuits were all that the Honourable Mrs Jamieson gave; and she was sister-in-law to the late Earl of Glenmire, although she did practise such "elegant economy."

"Elegant economy!" How naturally one falls back into the phraseology of Cranford! There, economy was always "elegant," and money-spending always "vulgar and ostentatious;" a sort of sour-grapeism which made us very peaceful and satisfied. I never shall forget the dismay felt when a certain Captain Brown came to live at Cranford, and openly spoke about his being poor—not in a whisper to an intimate friend, the doors and windows being previously closed, but in the public street! in a loud military voice! alleging his poverty as a reason for not taking a particular house. The ladies of Cranford were already rather moaning over the invasion of their territories by a man and a gentleman. He was a half-pay captain,[1] and had obtained some situation on a neighbouring railroad, which had been vehemently petitioned against by the little town;[2] and if, in addition to his masculine gender, and his connection with the obnoxious railroad, he was so brazen as to talk of being poor—why, then, indeed, he must be sent to Coventry.[3] Death was as true and as common as poverty; yet people never spoke about that, loud out in the streets. It was a word not to be mentioned to ears polite. We had tacitly agreed to ignore that any with whom we associated on terms of visiting equality could ever be prevented by poverty from doing anything that they wished. If we walked to or from a party, it was because the night was *so* fine, or the air *so* refreshing, not because sedan-chairs were expensive.[4] If we wore prints, instead of summer silks, it was because we preferred a washing material; and so on, till we blinded ourselves to the vulgar fact that we were, all of us, people of very moderate means. Of course, then, we did not know what to make of a man who could speak of poverty as if it was not a disgrace. Yet, somehow, Captain Brown made himself respected in Cranford, and was called upon, in spite of all resolutions to the contrary. I was surprised to hear his opinions quoted as authority at a visit which I paid to Cranford about a year after he had settled in the town. My own friends had been among the bitterest opponents of any proposal to visit the Captain and his daughters, only twelve months before; and now he was even admitted in the tabooed hours before twelve. True, it was to discover the cause of a smoking chimney, before the fire was lighted; but still Captain Brown walked upstairs, nothing daunted, spoke in a voice too large for the room, and joked quite in the way of a tame man about the house. He had been blind to all the small slights, and omissions of trivial ceremonies, with which he had been received. He had been friendly, though the Cranford ladies had been cool; he had answered small sarcastic compliments in good faith; and with his manly frankness had overpowered all the shrinking which met him as a man who was not ashamed to be poor. And, at last, his excellent masculine common sense, and his facility in devising expedients to overcome domestic dilemmas, had gained him an extraordinary place as authority among the Cranford ladies. He himself went on in his course, as unaware of his popularity as he had been of the reverse; and I am sure he was startled one day when he found his advice so highly esteemed as to make some counsel which he had given in jest to be taken in sober, serious earnest.

It was on this subject: An old lady had an Alderney cow, which she looked upon as a daughter. You could not pay the short quarter of an hour call without being told

---

1. A retired officer who stayed on reserve at half pay.
2. The railroads were new, and still looked on with suspicion by many country-dwellers.

3. Ostracized.
4. Enclosed chairs carried by servants; more common in the eighteenth century.

of the wonderful milk or wonderful intelligence of this animal. The whole town knew and kindly regarded Miss Betsy Barker's Alderney; therefore great was the sympathy and regret when, in an unguarded moment, the poor cow tumbled into a lime-pit.[5] She moaned so loudly that she was soon heard and rescued; but meanwhile the poor beast had lost most of her hair, and came out looking naked, cold, and miserable, in a bare skin. Everybody pitied the animal, though a few could not restrain their smiles at her droll appearance. Miss Betsy Barker absolutely cried with sorrow and dismay; and it was said she thought of trying a bath of oil. This remedy, perhaps, was recommended by some one of the number whose advice she asked; but the proposal, if ever it was made, was knocked on the head by Captain Brown's decided "Get her a flannel waistcoat and flannel drawers, ma'am, if you wish to keep her alive. But my advice is, kill the poor creature at once."

Miss Betsy Barker dried her eyes, and thanked the Captain heartily; she set to work, and by-and-by all the town turned out to see the Alderney meekly going to her pasture, clad in dark grey flannel. I have watched her myself many a time. Do you ever see cows dressed in grey flannel in London?

Captain Brown had taken a small house on the outskirts of the town, where he lived with his two daughters. He must have been upwards of sixty at the time of the first visit I paid to Cranford after I had left it as a residence. But he had a wiry, well-trained, elastic figure, a stiff military throw-back of his head, and a springing step, which made him appear much younger than he was. His eldest daughter looked almost as old as himself, and betrayed the fact that his real was more than his apparent age. Miss Brown must have been forty; she had a sickly, pained, careworn expression on her face, and looked as if the gaiety of youth had long faded out of sight. Even when young she must have been plain and hard featured. Miss Jessie Brown was ten years younger than her sister, and twenty shades prettier. Her face was round and dimpled. Miss Jenkyns once said, in a passion against Captain Brown (the cause of which I will tell you presently), "that she thought it was time for Miss Jessie to leave off her dimples, and not always to be trying to look like a child." It was true there was something child-like in her face; and there will be, I think, till she dies, though she should live to a hundred. Her eyes were large blue wondering eyes, looking straight at you; her nose was unformed and snub, and her lips were red and dewy; she wore her hair, too, in little rows of curls, which heightened this appearance. I do not know whether she was pretty or not; but I liked her face, and so did everybody, and I do not think she could help her dimples. She had something of her father's jauntiness of gait and manner; and any female observer might detect a slight difference in the attire of the two sisters—that of Miss Jessie being about two pounds per annum more expensive than Miss Brown's. Two pounds was a large sum in Captain Brown's annual disbursements.

Such was the impression made upon me by the Brown family when I first saw them all together in Cranford Church. The Captain I had met before—on the occasion of the smoky chimney, which he had cured by some simple alteration in the flue. In church, he held his double eye-glass to his eyes during the Morning Hymn, and then lifted up his head erect and sang out loud and joyfully. He made the responses louder than the clerk—an old man with a piping feeble voice, who, I think, felt aggrieved at the Captain's sonorous bass, and quavered higher and higher in consequence.

On coming out of church, the brisk Captain paid the most gallant attention to his two daughters. He nodded and smiled to his acquaintances; but he shook hands with none until he had helped Miss Brown to unfurl her umbrella, had relieved her of

5. A pit in which tanners dress skins with lime to remove the hair.

her prayer-book, and had waited patiently till she, with trembling nervous hands, had taken up her gown to walk through the wet roads.

I wondered what the Cranford ladies did with Captain Brown at their parties. We had often rejoiced, in former days, that there was no gentleman to be attended to, and to find conversation for, at the card-parties. We had congratulated ourselves upon the snugness of the evenings; and, in our love for gentility, and distaste of mankind, we had almost persuaded ourselves that to be a man was to be "vulgar"; so that when I found my friend and hostess, Miss Jenkyns, was going to have a party in my honour, and that Captain and the Miss Browns were invited, I wondered much what would be the course of the evening. Card-tables, with green baize tops, were set out by daylight, just as usual; it was the third week in November, so the evenings closed in about four. Candles, and clean packs of cards were arranged on each table. The fire was made up; the neat maid-servant had received her last directions; and there we stood, dressed in our best, each with a candle-lighter in our hands, ready to dart at the candles as soon as the first knock came. Parties in Cranford were solemn festivities, making the ladies feel gravely elated as they sat together in their best dresses. As soon as three had arrived, we sat down to "Preference," I being the unlucky fourth.[6] The next four comers were put down immediately to another table; and presently the tea-trays, which I had seen set out in the store-room as I passed in the morning, were placed each on the middle of a card-table. The china was delicate egg-shell; the old-fashioned silver glittered with polishing; but the eatables were of the slightest description. While the trays were yet on the tables, Captain and the Miss Browns came in; and I could see that, somehow or other, the Captain was a favourite with all the ladies present. Ruffled brows were smoothed, sharp voices lowered at his approach. Miss Brown looked ill, and depressed almost to gloom. Miss Jessie smiled as usual, and seemed nearly as popular as her father. He immediately and quietly assumed the man's place in the room; attended to every one's wants, lessened the pretty maid-servant's labour by waiting on empty cups and bread-and-butterless ladies; and yet did it all in so easy and dignified a manner, and so much as if it were a matter of course for the strong to attend to the weak, that he was a true man throughout. He played for threepenny points with as grave an interest as if they had been pounds; and yet, in all his attention to strangers, he had an eye on his suffering daughter—for suffering I was sure she was, though to many eyes she might only appear to be irritable. Miss Jessie could not play cards: but she talked to the sitters-out, who, before her coming, had been rather inclined to be cross. She sang, too, to an old cracked piano, which I think had been a spinet[7] in its youth. Miss Jessie sang "Jock of Hazeldean"[8] a little out of tune; but we were none of us musical, though Miss Jenkyns beat time, out of time, by way of appearing to be so.

It was very good of Miss Jenkyns to do this; for I had seen that, a little before, she had been a good deal annoyed by Miss Jessie Brown's unguarded admission (à propos of Shetland wool) that she had an uncle, her mother's brother, who was a shopkeeper in Edinburgh. Miss Jenkyns tried to drown this confession by a terrible cough—for the Honourable Mrs Jamieson was sitting at the card-table nearest Miss Jessie, and what would she say or think if she found out she was in the same room with a shopkeeper's niece! But Miss Jessie Brown (who had no tact, as we all agreed the next morning) would repeat the information, and assure Miss Pole she could easily get her the identical Shetland wool required, "through my uncle, who has the

---

6. "Unlucky" because only three people can play this card game at once; the dealer has to sit out.
7. An earlier keyboard instrument, popular before the

invention of the piano.
8. A ballad written in 1816 by Sir Walter Scott.

best assortment of Shetland goods of any one in Edinbro'." It was to take the taste of this out of our mouths, and the sound of this out of our ears, that Miss Jenkyns proposed music; so I say again, it was very good of her to beat time to the song.

When the trays re-appeared with biscuits and wine, punctually at a quarter to nine, there was conversation, comparing of cards, and talking over tricks; but by-and-by Captain Brown sported a bit of literature.

"Have you seen any numbers of 'The Pickwick Papers'?" said he. (They were then publishing in parts.)[9] "Capital thing!"

Now Miss Jenkyns was daughter of a deceased rector of Cranford; and, on the strength of a number of manuscript sermons, and a pretty good library of divinity, considered herself literary, and looked upon any conversation about books as a challenge to her. So she answered and said, "Yes, she had seen them; indeed, she might say she had read them."

"And what do you think of them?" exclaimed Captain Brown. "Aren't they famously good?"

So urged, Miss Jenkyns could not but speak.

"I must say, I don't think they are by any means equal to Dr Johnson.[1] Still, perhaps, the author is young. Let him persevere, and who knows what he may become if he will take the great Doctor for his model?" This was evidently too much for Captain Brown to take placidly; and I saw the words on the tip of his tongue before Miss Jenkyns had finished her sentence.

"It is quite a different sort of thing, my dear madam," he began.

"I am quite aware of that," returned she. "And I make allowances, Captain Brown."

"Just allow me to read you a scene out of this month's number," pleaded he. "I had it only this morning, and I don't think the company can have read it yet."

"As you please," said she, settling herself with an air of resignation. He read the account of the "swarry" which Sam Weller gave at Bath.[2] Some of us laughed heartily. I did not dare, because I was staying in the house. Miss Jenkyns sat in patient gravity. When it was ended, she turned to me, and said with mild dignity—

"Fetch me 'Rasselas,'[3] my dear, out of the bookroom."

When I brought it to her, she turned to Captain Brown—

"Now allow me to read you a scene, and then the present company can judge between your favourite, Mr Boz, and Dr Johnson."

She read one of the conversations between Rasselas and Imlac, in a high-pitched majestic voice: and when she had ended, she said, "I imagine I am now justified in my preference of Dr Johnson as a writer of fiction." The Captain screwed his lips up, and drummed on the table, but he did not speak. She thought she would give a finishing blow or two.

"I consider it vulgar, and below the dignity of literature, to publish in numbers."

"How was the *Rambler*[4] published, ma'am?" asked Captain Brown in a low voice, which I think Miss Jenkyns could not have heard.

9. Dickens published *The Pickwick Papers* serially in 1836 and 1837 under the pseudonym "Boz." Although this form of publication was considered "vulgar," the humorous escapades of Mr. Pickwick were phenomenally successful. When *Cranford* first appeared in Dickens's *Household Words*, he substituted Thomas Hood for himself, to Gaskell's annoyance.

1. Samuel Johnson (1708–1784) wrote more than a hundred years before Dickens; he was noted for his stately, balanced prose.

2. A reference to an episode in *Pickwick Papers* where Mr. Pickwick's servant Sam Weller attends a "soirée" for the footmen at Bath. The quick-witted Sam mocks the pompous servants, but they don't realize it.

3. *Rasselas* is a series of dialogues on moral themes between the prince of Abyssinia and his spiritual mentor, Imlac. Unlike the lively *Pickwick*, it is a serious and slow-paced philosophical work.

4. A periodical started in 1750 by Dr. Johnson and written almost entirely by himself.

"Dr Johnson's style is a model for young beginners. My father recommended it to me when I began to write letters—I have formed my own style upon it; I recommend it to your favourite."

"I should be very sorry for him to exchange his style for any such pompous writing," said Captain Brown.

Miss Jenkyns felt this as a personal affront, in a way of which the Captain had not dreamed. Epistolary writing she and her friends considered as her *forte*. Many a copy of many a letter have I seen written and corrected on the slate, before she "seized the half-hour just previous to post-time to assure" her friends of this or of that; and Dr Johnson was, as she said, her model in these compositions. She drew herself up with dignity, and only replied to Captain Brown's last remark by saying, with marked emphasis on every syllable, "I prefer Dr Johnson to Mr Boz."

It is said—I won't vouch for the fact—that Captain Brown was heard to say, *sotto voce,* "D—n Dr Johnson!" If he did, he was penitent afterwards, as he showed by going to stand near Miss Jenkyns's arm-chair, and endeavouring to beguile her into conversation on some more pleasing subject. But she was inexorable. The next day she made the remark I have mentioned about Miss Jessie's dimples.

2

It was impossible to live a month at Cranford and not know the daily habits of each resident; and long before my visit was ended I knew much concerning the whole Brown trio. There was nothing new to be discovered respecting their poverty; for they had spoken simply and openly about that from the very first. They made no mystery of the necessity for their being economical. All that remained to be discovered was the Captain's infinite kindness of heart, and the various modes in which, unconsciously to himself, he manifested it. Some little anecdotes were talked about for some time after they occurred. As we did not read much, and as all the ladies were pretty well suited with servants, there was a dearth of subjects for conversation. We therefore discussed the circumstance of the Captain taking a poor old woman's dinner out of her hands one very slippery Sunday. He had met her returning from the bakehouse as he came from church, and noticed her precarious footing; and, with the grave dignity with which he did everything, he relieved her of her burden, and steered along the street by her side, carrying her baked mutton and potatoes safely home.[5] This was thought very eccentric; and it was rather expected that he would pay a round of calls, on the Monday morning, to explain and apologise to the Cranford sense of propriety: but he did no such thing: and then it was decided that he was ashamed, and was keeping out of sight. In a kindly pity for him, we began to say, "After all, the Sunday morning's occurrence showed great goodness of heart," and it was resolved that he should be comforted on his next appearance amongst us; but, lo! he came down upon us, untouched by any sense of shame, speaking loud and bass as ever, his head thrown back, his wig as jaunty and well-curled as usual, and we were obliged to conclude he had forgotten all about Sunday.

Miss Pole and Miss Jessie Brown had set up a kind of intimacy on the strength of the Shetland wool and the new knitting stitches; so it happened that when I went to visit Miss Pole I saw more of the Browns than I had done while staying with Miss

---

5. Poor people often brought their meals to cook in the ovens of baker's shops on Sundays and holidays.

Jenkyns, who had never got over what she called Captain Brown's disparaging remarks upon Dr Johnson as a writer of light and agreeable fiction. I found that Miss Brown was seriously ill of some lingering, incurable complaint, the pain occasioned by which gave the uneasy expression to her face that I had taken for unmitigated crossness. Cross, too, she was at times, when the nervous irritability occasioned by her disease became past endurance. Miss Jessie bore with her at these times, even more patiently than she did with the bitter self-upbraidings by which they were invariably succeeded. Miss Brown used to accuse herself, not merely of hasty and irritable temper, but also of being the cause why her father and sister were obliged to pinch, in order to allow her the small luxuries which were necessaries in her condition. She would so fain have made sacrifices for them, and have lightened their cares, that the original generosity of her disposition added acerbity to her temper. All this was borne by Miss Jessie and her father with more than placidity—with absolute tenderness. I forgave Miss Jessie her singing out of tune, and her juvenility of dress, when I saw her at home. I came to perceive that Captain Brown's dark Brutus wig and padded coat[6] (alas! too often threadbare) were remnants of the military smartness of his youth, which he now wore unconsciously. He was a man of infinite resources, gained in his barrack experience. As he confessed, no one could black his boots to please him except himself; but, indeed, he was not above saving the little maid-servant's labours in every way—knowing, most likely, that his daughter's illness made the place a hard one.

He endeavoured to make peace with Miss Jenkyns soon after the memorable dispute I have named, by a present of a wooden fire-shovel (his own making), having heard her say how much the grating of an iron one annoyed her. She received the present with cool gratitude, and thanked him formally. When he was gone, she bade me put it away in the lumber-room; feeling, probably, that no present from a man who preferred Mr Boz to Dr Johnson could be less jarring than an iron fire-shovel.

Such was the state of things when I left Cranford and went to Drumble. I had, however, several correspondents, who kept me *au fait* as to the proceedings of the dear little town. There was Miss Pole, who was becoming as much absorbed in crochet as she had been once in knitting, and the burden of whose letter was something like, "But don't you forget the white worsted at Flint's" of the old song; for at the end of every sentence of news came a fresh direction as to some crochet commission which I was to execute for her. Miss Matilda Jenkyns (who did not mind being called Miss Matty, when Miss Jenkyns was not by) wrote nice, kind, rambling letters, now and then venturing into an opinion of her own; but suddenly pulling herself up, and either begging me not to name what she had said, as Deborah thought differently, and *she* knew, or else putting in a postscript to the effect that, since writing the above, she had been talking over the subject with Deborah, and was quite convinced that, &c.—(here probably followed a recantation of every opinion she had given in the letter). Then came Miss Jenkyns—Debōrah, as she liked Miss Matty to call her, her father having once said that the Hebrew name ought to be so pronounced. I secretly think she took the Hebrew prophetess for a model in character; and, indeed, she was not unlike the stern prophetess[7] in some ways, making allowance, of course, for modern customs and difference in dress. Miss Jenkyns wore a cravat, and a little bonnet like a jockey-cap, and altogether had the appearance of a strong-minded

6. A short, curly hairstyle popular during the French Revolution; padded coats were fashionable in the early 19th century.

7. Deborah was one of the leaders of Israel (Judges 4–5).

woman; although she would have despised the modern idea of women being equal to men. Equal, indeed! she knew they were superior. But to return to her letters. Everything in them was stately and grand like herself. I have been looking them over (dear Miss Jenkyns, how I honoured her!), and I will give an extract, more especially because it relates to our friend Captain Brown:—

"The Honourable Mrs Jamieson has only just quitted me; and, in the course of conversation, she communicated to me the intelligence that she had yesterday received a call from her revered husband's quondam[8] friend, Lord Mauleverer. You will not easily conjecture what brought his lordship within the precincts of our little town. It was to see Captain Brown, with whom, it appears, his lordship was acquainted in the 'plumed wars,' and who had the privilege of averting destruction from his lordship's head when some great peril was impending over it, off the misnomered Cape of Good Hope. You know our friend the Honourable Mrs Jamieson's deficiency in the spirit of innocent curiosity; and you will therefore not be so much surprised when I tell you she was quite unable to disclose to me the exact nature of the peril in question. I was anxious, I confess, to ascertain in what manner Captain Brown, with his limited establishment, could receive so distinguished a guest; and I discovered that his lordship retired to rest, and, let us hope, to refreshing slumbers, at the Angel Hotel; but shared the Brunonian[9] meals during the two days that he honoured Cranford with his august presence. Mrs Johnson, our civil butcher's wife, informs me that Miss Jessie purchased a leg of lamb; but, besides this, I can hear of no preparation whatever to give a suitable reception to so distinguished a visitor. Perhaps they entertained him with 'the feast of reason and the flow of soul;'[1] and to us, who are acquainted with Captain Brown's sad want of relish for 'the pure wells of English undefiled,'[2] it may be matter for congratulation that he has had the opportunity of improving his taste by holding converse with an elegant and refined member of the British aristocracy. But from some mundane failings who is altogether free?"

Miss Pole and Miss Matty wrote to me by the same post. Such a piece of news as Lord Mauleverer's visit was not to be lost on the Cranford letter-writers: they made the most of it. Miss Matty humbly apologised for writing at the same time as her sister, who was so much more capable than she to describe the honour done to Cranford; but in spite of a little bad spelling, Miss Matty's account gave me the best idea of the commotion occasioned by his lordship's visit, after it had occurred; for, except the people at the Angel, the Browns, Mrs Jamieson, and a little lad his lordship had sworn at for driving a dirty hoop against the aristocratic legs, I could not hear of any one with whom his lordship had held conversation.

My next visit to Cranford was in the summer. There had been neither births, deaths, nor marriages since I was there last. Everybody lived in the same house, and wore pretty nearly the same well-preserved, old-fashioned clothes. The greatest event was, that Miss Jenkynses had purchased a new carpet for the drawing-room. Oh, the busy work Miss Matty and I had in chasing the sunbeams, as they fell in an afternoon right down on this carpet through the blindless window! We spread news-

---

8. Former.
9. A pretentious, Latinized version of Brown, part of Miss Jenkyns's unintentionally comic imitation of the style of Dr. Johnson.

1. Alexander Pope, *Imitations of Horace*, Satire 1, Book 2.128 (1733).
2. Edmund Spenser, *The Faerie Queene*, 4.2.32 (1596); the reference is to Chaucer.

papers over the places, and sat down to our book or our work; and, lo! in a quarter of an hour the sun had moved, and was blazing away on a fresh spot; and down again we went on our knees to alter the position of the newspapers. We were very busy, too, one whole morning, before Miss Jenkyns gave her party, in following her directions, and in cutting out and stitching together pieces of newspaper so as to form little paths to every chair set for the expected visitors, lest their shoes might dirty or defile the purity of the carpet. Do you make paper paths for every guest to walk upon in London?

Captain Brown and Miss Jenkyns were not very cordial to each other. The literary dispute, of which I had seen the beginning, was a "raw," the slightest touch on which made them wince. It was the only difference of opinion they had ever had; but that difference was enough. Miss Jenkyns could not refrain from talking *at* Captain Brown; and, though he did not reply, he drummed with his fingers, which action she felt and resented as very disparaging to Dr Johnson. He was rather ostentatious in his preference of the writings of Mr Boz; would walk through the streets so absorbed in them that he all but ran against Miss Jenkyns; and though his apologies were earnest and sincere, and though he did not, in fact, do more than startle her and himself, she owned to me she had rather he had knocked her down, if he had only been reading a higher style of literature. The poor, brave Captain! he looked older, and more worn, and his clothes were very threadbare. But he seemed as bright and cheerful as ever, unless he was asked about his daughter's health.

"She suffers a great deal, and she must suffer more: we do what we can to alleviate her pain;—God's will be done!" He took off his hat at these last words. I found, from Miss Matty, that everything had been done, in fact. A medical man, of high repute in that country neighbourhood, had been sent for, and every injunction he had given was attended to, regardless of expense. Miss Matty was sure they denied themselves many things in order to make the invalid comfortable; but they never spoke about it; and as for Miss Jessie!—"I really think she's an angel," said poor Miss Matty, quite overcome. "To see her way of bearing with Miss Brown's crossness, and the bright face she puts on after she's been sitting up a whole night and scolded above half of it, is quite beautiful. Yet she looks as neat and as ready to welcome the Captain at breakfast-time as if she had been asleep in the Queen's bed all night. My dear! you could never laugh at her prim little curls or her pink bows again if you saw her as I have done." I could only feel very penitent, and greet Miss Jessie with double respect when I met her next. She looked faded and pinched; and her lips began to quiver, as if she was very weak, when she spoke of her sister. But she brightened, and sent back the tears that were glittering in her pretty eyes, as she said—

"But, to be sure, what a town Cranford is for kindness! I don't suppose any one has a better dinner than usual cooked but the best part of all comes in a little covered basin for my sister. The poor people will leave their earliest vegetables at our door for her. They speak short and gruff, as if they were ashamed of it; but I am sure it often goes to my heart to see their thoughtfulness." The tears now came back and overflowed; but after a minute or two she began to scold herself, and ended by going away the same cheerful Miss Jessie as ever.

"But why does not this Lord Mauleverer do something for the man who saved his life?" said I.

"Why, you see, unless Captain Brown has some reason for it, he never speaks about being poor; and he walked along by his lordship looking as happy and cheerful as a prince; and as they never called attention to their dinner by apologies, and as Miss Brown was better that day, and all seemed bright, I dare say his lordship never knew how much care there was in the background. He did send game in the winter pretty often, but now he is gone abroad."

I had often occasion to notice the use that was made of fragments and small opportunities in Cranford; the rose-leaves that were gathered ere they fell to make into a potpourri for some one who had no garden; the little bundles of lavender flowers sent to strew the drawers of some town-dweller, or to burn in the chamber of some invalid. Things that many would despise, and actions which it seemed scarcely worth while to perform, were all attended to in Cranford. Miss Jenkyns stuck an apple full of cloves, to be heated and smell pleasantly in Miss Brown's room; and as she put in each clove she uttered a Johnsonian sentence. Indeed, she never could think of the Browns without talking Johnson; and, as they were seldom absent from her thoughts just then, I heard many a rolling, three-piled sentence.

Captain Brown called one day to thank Miss Jenkyns for many little kindnesses, which I did not know until then that she had rendered. He had suddenly become like an old man; his deep bass voice had a quavering in it, his eyes looked dim, and the lines on his face were deep. He did not—could not—speak cheerfully of his daughter's state, but he talked with manly, pious resignation, and not much. Twice over he said, "What Jessie has been to us, God only knows!" and after the second time, he got up hastily, shook hands all round without speaking, and left the room.

That afternoon we perceived little groups in the street, all listening with faces aghast to some tale or other. Miss Jenkyns wondered what could be the matter for some time before she took the undignified step of sending Jenny out to inquire.

Jenny came back with a white face of terror. "Oh, ma'am! oh, Miss Jenkyns, ma'am! Captain Brown is killed by them nasty cruel railroads!" and she burst into tears. She, along with many others, had experienced the poor Captain's kindness.

"How?—where—where? Good God! Jenny, don't waste time in crying, but tell us something." Miss Matty rushed out into the street at once, and collared the man who was telling the tale.

"Come in—come to my sister at once, Miss Jenkyns, the rector's daughter. Oh, man, man! say it is not true," she cried, as she brought the affrighted carter, sleeking down his hair, into the drawing-room, where he stood with his wet boots on the new carpet, and no one regarded it.

"Please, mum, it is true. I seed it myself," and he shuddered at the recollection. "The Captain was a-reading some new book as he was deep in, a-waiting for the down train; and there was a little lass as wanted to come to its mammy, and gave its sister the slip, and came toddling across the line. And he looked up sudden, at the sound of the train coming, and seed the child, and he darted on the line and cotched it up, and his foot slipped, and the train came over him in no time. O Lord, Lord! Mum, it's quite true—and they've come over to tell his daughters. The child's safe, though, with only a bang on its shoulder as he threw it to its mammy. Poor Captain would be glad of that, mum, wouldn't he? God bless him!" The great rough carter puckered up his manly face, and turned away to hide his tears. I turned to Miss Jenkyns. She looked very ill, as if she were going to faint, and signed to me to open the window.

"Matilda, bring me my bonnet. I must go to those girls. God pardon me, if ever I have spoken contemptuously to the Captain!"

Miss Jenkyns arrayed herself to go out, telling Miss Matilda to give the man a glass of wine. While she was away, Miss Matty and I huddled over the fire, talking in a low and awestruck voice. I know we cried quietly all the time.

Miss Jenkyns came home in a silent mood, and we durst not ask her many questions. She told us that Miss Jessie had fainted, and that she and Miss Pole had had some difficulty in bringing her round; but that, as soon as she recovered, she begged one of them to go and sit with her sister.

"Mr Hoggins says she cannot live many days, and she shall be spared this shock," said Miss Jessie, shivering with feelings to which she dared not give way.

"But how can you manage, my dear?" asked Miss Jenkyns; "you cannot bear up, she must see your tears."

"God will help me—I will not give way—she was asleep when the news came; she may be asleep yet. She would be so utterly miserable, not merely at my father's death, but to think of what would become of me; she is so good to me." She looked up earnestly in their faces with her soft true eyes, and Miss Pole told Miss Jenkyns afterwards she could hardly bear it, knowing, as she did, how Miss Brown treated her sister.

However, it was settled according to Miss Jessie's wish. Miss Brown was to be told her father had been summoned to take a short journey on railway business. They had managed it in some way—Miss Jenkyns could not exactly say how. Miss Pole was to stop with Miss Jessie. Mrs Jamieson had sent to inquire. And this was all we heard that night; and a sorrowful night it was. The next day a full account of the fatal accident was in the county paper which Miss Jenkyns took in. Her eyes were very weak, she said, and she asked me to read it. When I came to the "gallant gentleman was deeply engaged in the perusal of a number of 'Pickwick,' which he had just received," Miss Jenkyns shook her head long and solemnly, and then sighed out, "Poor, dear, infatuated man!"

The corpse was to be taken from the station to the parish church, there to be interred. Miss Jessie had set her heart on following it to the grave; and no dissuasives could alter her resolve. Her restraint upon herself made her almost obstinate; she resisted all Miss Pole's entreaties and Miss Jenkyns's advice. At last Miss Jenkyns gave up the point; and after a silence, which I feared portended some deep displeasure against Miss Jessie, Miss Jenkyns said she should accompany the latter to the funeral.

"It is not fit for you to go alone. It would be against both propriety and humanity were I to allow it."

Miss Jessie seemed as if she did not half like this arrangement; but her obstinacy, if she had any, had been exhausted in her determination to go to the interment. She longed, poor thing, I have no doubt, to cry alone over the grave of the dear father to whom she had been all in all, and to give way, for one little half-hour, uninterrupted by sympathy and unobserved by friendship. But it was not to be. That afternoon Miss Jenkyns sent out for a yard of black crape, and employed herself busily in trimming the little black silk bonnet I have spoken about. When it was finished she put it on, and looked at us for approbation—admiration she despised. I was full of sorrow, but, by one of those whimsical thoughts which come unbidden into our heads, in times of deepest grief, I no sooner saw the bonnet than I was reminded of a helmet; and in that hybrid bonnet, half helmet, half jockey-cap, did Miss Jenkyns attend Captain Brown's funeral, and, I believe, supported Miss Jessie with a tender, indulgent firmness which was invaluable, allowing her to weep her passionate fill before they left.

Miss Pole, Miss Matty, and I, meanwhile attended to Miss Brown: and hard work we found it to relieve her querulous and never-ending complaints. But if we were so weary and dispirited, what must Miss Jessie have been! Yet she came back almost calm, as if she had gained a new strength. She put off her mourning dress, and came in, looking pale and gentle, thanking us each with a soft long pressure of the hand. She could even smile—a faint, sweet, wintry smile—as if to reassure us of her power to endure; but her look made our eyes fill suddenly with tears, more than if she had cried outright.

It was settled that Miss Pole was to remain with her all the watching livelong night; and that Miss Matty and I were to return in the morning to relieve them, and give Miss Jessie the opportunity for a few hours of sleep. But when the morning came, Miss Jenkyns appeared at the breakfast-table, equipped in her helmet-bonnet, and ordered Miss Matty to stay at home, as she meant to go and help to nurse. She was evidently in a state of great friendly excitement, which she showed by eating her breakfast standing, and scolding the household all round.

No nursing—no energetic strong-minded woman could help Miss Brown now. There was that in the room as we entered which was stronger than us all, and made us shrink into solemn awestruck helplessness. Miss Brown was dying. We hardly knew her voice, it was so devoid of the complaining tone we had always associated with it. Miss Jessie told me afterwards that it, and her face too, were just what they had been formerly, when her mother's death left her the young anxious head of the family, of whom only Miss Jessie survived.

She was conscious of her sister's presence, though not, I think, of ours. We stood a little behind the curtain: Miss Jessie knelt with her face near her sister's, in order to catch the last soft awful whispers.

"Oh, Jessie! Jessie! How selfish I have been! God forgive me for letting you sacrifice yourself for me as you did! I have so loved you—and yet I have thought only of myself. God forgive me!"

"Hush, love! hush!" said Miss Jessie, sobbing.

"And my father! my dear, dear father! I will not complain now, if God will give me strength to be patient. But, oh, Jessie! tell my father how I longed and yearned to see him at last, and to ask his forgiveness. He can never know now how I loved him—oh! if I might but tell him, before I die! What a life of sorrow his has been, and I have done so little to cheer him!"

A light came into Miss Jessie's face. "Would it comfort you, dearest, to think that he does know?—would it comfort you, love, to know that his cares, his sorrows"—Her voice quivered, but she steadied it into calmness—"Mary! he has gone before you to the place where the weary are at rest.[3] He knows now how you loved him."

A strange look, which was not distress, came over Miss Brown's face. She did not speak for some time, but then we saw her lips form the words, rather than heard the sound—"Father, mother, Harry, Archy;"—then, as if it were a new idea throwing a filmy shadow over her darkened mind—"But you will be alone, Jessie!"

Miss Jessie had been feeling this all during the silence, I think; for the tears rolled down her cheeks like rain, at these words, and she could not answer at first. Then she put her hands together tight, and lifted them up, and said—but not to us—

"Though He slay me, yet will I trust in Him."[4]

3. Job 3.17.   4. Job 13.15.

In a few moments more Miss Brown lay calm and still—never to sorrow or murmur more.

After this second funeral, Miss Jenkyns insisted that Miss Jessie should come to stay with her rather than go back to the desolate house, which, in fact, we learned from Miss Jessie, must now be given up, as she had not wherewithal to maintain it. She had something above twenty pounds a year, besides the interest of the money for which the furniture would sell; but she could not live upon that: and so we talked over her qualifications for earning money.

"I can sew neatly," said she, "and I like nursing. I think, too, I could manage a house, if any one would try me as housekeeper; or I would go into a shop, as saleswoman, if they would have patience with me at first."

Miss Jenkyns declared, in an angry voice, that she should do no such thing; and talked to herself about "some people having no idea of their rank as a captain's daughter," nearly an hour afterwards, when she brought Miss Jessie up a basin of delicately-made arrowroot, and stood over her like a dragoon until the last spoonful was finished; then she disappeared. Miss Jessie began to tell me some more of the plans which had suggested themselves to her, and insensibly fell into talking of the days that were past and gone, and interested me so much I neither knew nor heeded how time passed. We were both startled when Miss Jenkyns reappeared, and caught us crying. I was afraid lest she would be displeased, as she often said that crying hindered digestion, and I knew she wanted Miss Jessie to get strong; but, instead, she looked queer and excited, and fidgeted round us without saying anything. At last she spoke.

"I have been so much startled—no, I've not been at all startled—don't mind me, my dear Miss Jessie—I've been very much surprised—in fact, I've had a caller, whom you knew once, my dear Miss Jessie"—

Miss Jessie went very white, then flushed scarlet, and looked eagerly at Miss Jenkyns.

"A gentleman, my dear, who wants to know if you would see him."

"Is it?—it is not"—stammered out Miss Jessie—and got no farther.

"This is his card," said Miss Jenkyns, giving it to Miss Jessie; and while her head was bent over it, Miss Jenkyns went through a series of winks and odd faces to me, and formed her lips into a long sentence, of which, of course, I could not understand a word.

"May he come up?" asked Miss Jenkyns, at last.

"Oh, yes! certainly!" said Miss Jessie, as much as to say, this is your house, you may show any visitor where you like. She took up some knitting of Miss Matty's and began to be very busy, though I could see how she trembled all over.

Miss Jenkyns rang the bell, and told the servant who answered it to show Major Gordon upstairs; and, presently, in walked a tall, fine, frank-looking man of forty or upwards. He shook hands with Miss Jessie; but he could not see her eyes, she kept them so fixed on the ground. Miss Jenkyns asked me if I would come and help her to tie up the preserves in the store-room; and, though Miss Jessie plucked at my gown, and even looked up at me with begging eye, I durst not refuse to go where Miss Jenkyns asked. Instead of tying up preserves in the store-room, however, we went to talk in the dining-room; and there Miss Jenkyns told me what Major Gordon had told her; how he had served in the same regiment with Captain Brown, and had become acquainted with Miss Jessie, then a sweet-looking, blooming girl of eighteen;

how the acquaintance had grown into love on his part, though it had been some years before he had spoken; how, on becoming possessed, through the will of an uncle, of a good estate in Scotland, he had offered and been refused, though with so much agitation and evident distress that he was sure she was not indifferent to him; and how he had discovered that the obstacle was the fell disease which was, even then, too surely threatening her sister. She had mentioned that the surgeons foretold intense suffering; and there was no one but herself to nurse her poor Mary, or cheer and comfort her father during the time of illness. They had had long discussions; and on her refusal to pledge herself to him as his wife when all should be over, he had grown angry, and broken off entirely, and gone abroad, believing that she was a cold-hearted person whom he would do well to forget. He had been travelling in the East, and was on his return home when, at Rome, he saw the account of Captain Brown's death in *Galignani*.[5]

Just then Miss Matty, who had been out all the morning, and had only lately returned to the house, burst in with a face of dismay and outraged propriety.

"Oh, goodness me!" she said. "Deborah, there's a gentleman sitting in the drawing-room with his arm round Miss Jessie's waist!" Miss Matty's eyes looked large with terror.

Miss Jenkyns snubbed her down in an instant.

"The most proper place in the world for his arm to be in. Go away, Matilda, and mind your own business." This from her sister, who had hitherto been a model of feminine decorum, was a blow for poor Miss Matty, and with a double shock she left the room.

The last time I ever saw poor Miss Jenkyns was many years after this. Mrs Gordon had kept up a warm and affectionate intercourse with all at Cranford. Miss Jenkyns, Miss Matty, and Miss Pole had all been to visit her, and returned with wonderful accounts of her house, her husband, her dress, and her looks. For, with happiness, something of her early bloom returned; she had been a year or two younger than we had taken her for. Her eyes were always lovely, and, as Mrs Gordon, her dimples were not out of place. At the time to which I have referred, when I last saw Miss Jenkyns, that lady was old and feeble, and had lost something of her strong mind. Little Flora Gordon was staying with the Misses Jenkyns, and when I came in she was reading aloud to Miss Jenkyns, who lay feeble and changed on the sofa. Flora put down the *Rambler* when I came in.

"Ah!" said Miss Jenkyns, "you find me changed, my dear. I can't see as I used to do. If Flora were not here to read to me, I hardly know how I should get through the day. Did you ever read the *Rambler*? It's a wonderful book—wonderful! and the most improving reading for Flora" (which I dare say it would have been, if she could have read half the words without spelling, and could have understood the meaning of a third), "better than that strange old book, with the queer name, poor Captain Brown was killed for reading—that book by Mr Boz, you know—'Old Poz'; when I was a girl—but that's a long time ago—I acted Lucy in 'Old Poz.'"[6] She babbled on long enough for Flora to get a good long spell at the "Christmas Carol,"[7] which Miss Matty had left on the table.

1851, 1853

5. An English newspaper published in Paris and read by tourists and expatriates.
6. A children's play by Maria Edgeworth (1795); Lucy is the young heroine.
7. Published by Dickens in 1843. The topicality of Dickens's works helps date the events of *Cranford*.

John Ruskin
1819–1900

John Ruskin began his career as the most perceptive English art critic of the nineteenth century. But for Ruskin, art was inextricably linked to the moral temper of the age in which it was produced. Thus he was drawn inevitably from art criticism to social criticism, denouncing ugliness and injustice as aspects of the same spiritual decline. His prodigious output of books on painting, literature, architecture, politics, and society culminated with a beautiful and moving autobiography, *Praeterita*, which means "of things past."

For all the magnificence of his prose and the brilliance of his vision, John Ruskin was a rather peculiar man. He was the only child of middle-class parents who lived in the suburbs near London, and whose dearest wish, he wrote, was "to make an evangelical clergyman of me." Forbidden toys, he passed his time studying the patterns in the nursery carpet and garden leaves, delighting already in the visual pleasures that would engross him all his life. His upbringing was strict, secluded, and overprotected: he was educated at home until his mother accompanied him to Oxford, where she remained for the duration of his studies.

Perhaps because he was so sheltered, Ruskin's love life was a series of disastrous ordeals. As a teenager he suffered a hopeless passion for Adèle Domecq, who was rich, French, and Catholic—unsuitable on every count. Later, a miserable six-year marriage to his cousin Effie Gray was annulled on the grounds of nonconsummation (she then married the Pre-Raphaelite painter John Everett Millais, with whom she had many children). The annulment created a scandal, and the whole episode was so painful that Ruskin omitted any reference to his marriage in *Praeterita*. Finally, he became morbidly obsessed with Rose La Touche, thirty years his junior, and only nine years old when he met her. His tragic relationship with her became a secret thread running through his later work.

Ruskin's intensity of vision was already evident in his first book, *Modern Painters*, in which he declared that "to see clearly is poetry, prophecy, and religion—all in one." Ruskin insisted that the impressionistic canvases of J. M. W. Turner were actually more faithful to nature than the carefully rendered detail of Dutch realists. Reading *Modern Painters*, Charlotte Brontë wrote: "I feel . . . as if I had been walking blindfold—this book seems to give me eyes." Published over seventeen years (1843–1860), the five volumes of *Modern Painters* reflect their author's changing preoccupations: from art and nature in the early volumes to humanism and society in the last one, following an experience of religious "unconversion" in 1858.

From boyhood Ruskin loved to travel on the Continent, and his autobiography relates with deep pleasure the many journeys he took, usually with his parents. Venice aroused him to write what the critic John Rosenberg has called "the most elaborate and eloquent monument to a city in our literature," *The Stones of Venice* (1851–1853). Ruskin's Venice is "a ghost upon the sands of the sea, so weak—so quiet,—so bereft of all but her loveliness." The decline and fall of the Venetian empire serves as a warning to the British, which, "if it forget their example, may be led through prouder eminence to less pitied destruction."

The book's central chapter, *The Nature of Gothic*, became the touchstone for Ruskin's subsequent radical social critique of England. He argues that Gothic workmanship, though rude and imperfect, reflected a culture that respected the individual soul of the workman. Societies which demand machinelike perfection dehumanize the craftsman, turning him into a soulless operative. Ruskin thus mingled his hymn to the beauty of Venice with a scathing indictment of the Industrial Revolution.

Ruskin's later writings became increasingly fragmented as he suffered a long, slow decline into madness. "The doctors said I went mad . . . from overwork," he wrote, but "I went mad because nothing came of my work." Yet from 1871 to 1884 he was able to lecture about art at

Oxford and to produce an impassioned series of open letters to English workmen, entitled *Fors Clavigera*. Many of the letters describe the Guild of St. George, a utopian society Ruskin had founded. Tormented by the brutality and folly he saw everywhere around him, Ruskin chose in his final work to record only "what it gives me joy to remember." In the serene and radiant *Praeterita* (1885–1889), which was to inspire Proust's *Remembrance of Things Past*, Ruskin transcended his apocalyptic fury to produce one of the most enchanting yet poignant autobiographies ever written in English.

from Modern Painters
from Definition of Greatness in Art [1]

Painting, or art generally, as such, with all its technicalities, difficulties, and particular ends, is nothing but a noble and expressive language, invaluable as the vehicle of thought, but by itself nothing. He who has learned what is commonly considered the whole art of painting, that is, the art of representing any natural object faithfully, has as yet only learned the language by which his thoughts are to be expressed. He has done just as much towards being that which we ought to respect as a great painter, as a man who has learnt how to express himself grammatically and melodiously has towards being a great poet. The language is, indeed, more difficult of acquirement in the one case than in the other, and possesses more power of delighting the sense, while it speaks to the intellect; but it is, nevertheless, nothing more than language, and all those excellences which are peculiar to the painter as such, are merely what rhythm, melody, precision, and force are in the words of the orator and the poet, necessary to their greatness, but not the tests of their greatness. It is not by the mode of representing and saying, but by what is represented and said, that the respective greatness either of the painter or the writer is to be finally determined. * * *

If I say that the greatest picture is that which conveys to the mind of the spectator the greatest number of the greatest ideas, I have a definition which will include as subjects of comparison every pleasure which art is capable of conveying. If I were to say, on the contrary, that the best picture was that which most closely imitated nature, I should assume that art could only please by imitating nature; and I should cast out of the pale of criticism those parts of works of art which are not imitative, that is to say, intrinsic beauties of colour and form, and those works of art wholly, which, like the Arabesques of Raffaelle in the Loggias,[2] are not imitative at all. Now, I want a definition of art wide enough to include all its varieties of aim. I do not say, therefore, that the art is greatest which gives most pleasure, because perhaps there is some art whose end is to teach, and not to please. I do not say that the art is greatest which teaches us most, because perhaps there is some art whose end is to please, and not to teach. I do not say that the art is greatest which imitates best, because perhaps there is some art whose end is to create and not to imitate. But I say that the art is greatest which conveys to the mind of the spectator, by any means whatsoever, the greatest number of the greatest ideas; and I call an idea great in proportion as it is received by a higher faculty of the mind, and as it more fully occupies, and in occupying, exercises and exalts, the faculty by which it is received.

1. From vol. 1, part 1, sec. 1, ch. 2.
2. The Italian Renaissance painter Raphael (1483–1520) decorated the Loggia of the Vatican with arabesques, wall paintings of interwoven foliage, animals, and human figures.

If this, then, be the definition of great art, that of a great artist naturally follows. He is the greatest artist who has embodied, in the sum of his works, the greatest number of the greatest ideas.

1843

from *Of Modern Landscape*[1]

We turn our eyes, therefore, as boldly and as quickly as may be, from these serene fields and skies of mediaeval art, to the most characteristic examples of modern landscape. And, I believe, the first thing that will strike us, or that ought to strike us, is their *cloudiness*.

Out of perfect light and motionless air, we find ourselves on a sudden brought under sombre skies, and into drifting wind; and, with fickle sunbeams flashing in our face, or utterly drenched with sweep of rain, we are reduced to track the changes of the shadows on the grass, or watch the rents of twilight through angry cloud. And we find that whereas all the pleasure of the mediaeval was in *stability, definiteness,* and *luminousness,* we are expected to rejoice in darkness, and triumph in mutability; to lay the foundation of happiness in things which momentarily change or fade; and to expect the utmost satisfaction and instruction from what it is impossible to arrest, and difficult to comprehend.

We find, however, together with this general delight in breeze and darkness, much attention to the real form of clouds, and careful drawing of effects of mist; so that the appearance of objects, as seen through it, becomes a subject of science with us; and the faithful representation of that appearance is made of primal importance, under the name of aerial perspective. The aspects of sunset and sunrise, with all their attendant phenomena of cloud and mist, are watchfully delineated; and in ordinary daylight landscape, the sky is considered of so much importance, that a principal mass of foliage, or a whole foreground, is unhesitatingly thrown into shade merely to bring out the form of a white cloud. So that, if a general and characteristic name were needed for modern landscape art, none better could be invented than "the service of clouds."

And this name would, unfortunately, be characteristic of our art in more ways than one. In the last chapter, I said that all the Greeks spoke kindly about the clouds, except Aristophanes;[2] and he, I am sorry to say (since his report is so unfavourable), is the only Greek who had studied them attentively. He tells us, first, that they are "great goddesses to idle men"; then, that they are "mistresses of disputings, and logic, and monstrosities, and noisy chattering"; declares that whoso believes in their divinity must first disbelieve in Jupiter, and place supreme power in the hands of an unknown god "Whirlwind"; and, finally, he displays their influence over the mind of one of their disciples, in his sudden desire "to speak ingeniously concerning smoke."

There is, I fear, an infinite truth in this Aristophanic judgment applied to our modern cloud-worship. Assuredly, much of the love of mystery in our romances, our poetry, our art, and, above all, in our metaphysics, must come under that definition so long ago given by the great Greek, "speaking ingeniously concerning smoke." And much of the instinct, which, partially developed in painting, may be now seen throughout every mode of exertion of mind,—the easily encouraged doubt, easily

---

1. From vol. 3, part 4, ch. 16, para. 1–28. 2. Athenian comic playwright (c. 448–380 B.C.) whose works include *The Clouds*.

excited curiosity, habitual agitation, and delight in the changing and the marvellous, as opposed to the old quiet serenity of social custom and religious faith,—is again deeply defined in those few words, the "dethroning of Jupiter," the "coronation of the whirlwind." * * *

The next thing that will strike us, after this love of clouds, is the love of liberty. Whereas the mediaeval was always shutting himself into castles, and behind fosses,[3] and drawing brickwork neatly, and beds of flowers primly, our painters delight in getting to the open fields and moors, abhor all hedges and moats; never paint anything but free-growing trees, and rivers gliding "at their own sweet will";[4] eschew formality down to the smallest detail; break and displace the brickwork which the mediaeval would have carefully cemented; leave unpruned the thickets he would have delicately trimmed; and, carrying the love of liberty even to license, and the love of wildness even to ruin, take pleasure at last in every aspect of age and desolation which emancipates the objects of nature from the government of men;—on the castle wall displacing its tapestry with ivy, and spreading, through the garden, the bramble for the rose.

Connected with this love of liberty we find a singular manifestation of love of mountains, and see our painters traversing the wildest places of the globe in order to obtain subjects with craggy foregrounds and purple distances. Some few of them remain content with pollards[5] and flat land; but these are always men of third-rate order; and the leading masters, while they do not reject the beauty of the low grounds, reserve their highest powers to paint Alpine peaks or Italian promontories. And it is eminently noticeable, also, that this pleasure in the mountains is never mingled with fear, or tempered by a spirit of meditation, as with the mediaeval; but is always free and fearless, brightly exhilarating, and wholly unreflective; so that the painter feels that his mountain foreground may be more consistently animated by a sportsman than a hermit; and our modern society in general goes to the mountains, not to fast, but to feast, and leaves their glaciers covered with chicken-bones and egg-shells.

Connected with this want of any sense of solemnity in mountain scenery, is a general profanity of temper in regarding all the rest of nature; that is to say, a total absence of faith in the presence of any deity therein. Whereas the mediaeval never painted a cloud, but with the purpose of placing an angel in it; and a Greek never entered a wood without expecting to meet a god in it; we should think the appearance of an angel in the cloud wholly unnatural, and should be seriously surprised by meeting a god anywhere. Our chief ideas about the wood are connected with poaching. We have no belief that the clouds contain more than so many inches of rain or hail, and from our ponds and ditches expect nothing more divine than ducks and watercresses.

Finally: connected with this profanity of temper is a strong tendency to deny the sacred element of colour, and make our boast in blackness. For though occasionally glaring or violent, modern colour is on the whole eminently sombre, tending continually to grey or brown, and by many of our best painters consistently falsified, with a confessed pride in what they call chaste or subdued tints; so that, whereas a mediaeval paints his sky bright blue and his foreground bright green, gilds the towers of his castles, and clothes his figures with purple and white, we paint our sky grey, our fore-

---

3. Moats.
4. Wordsworth, *Composed upon Westminster Bridge, September 3, 1802* (see page 1561).

5. Artificially shaped trees that have been polled or cut back.

ground black, and our foliage brown, and think that enough is sacrificed to the sun in admitting the dangerous brightness of a scarlet cloak or a blue jacket.

These, I believe, are the principal points which would strike us instantly, if we were to be brought suddenly into an exhibition of modern landscapes out of a room filled with mediaeval work. It is evident that there are both evil and good in this change; but how much evil, or how much good, we can only estimate by considering, as in the former divisions of our inquiry, what are the real roots of the habits of mind which have caused them.

At first, it is evident that the title "Dark Ages," given to the mediaeval centuries, is, respecting art, wholly inapplicable. They were, on the contrary, the bright ages; ours are the dark ones. I do not mean metaphysically, but literally. They were the ages of gold; ours are the ages of umber.[6]

This is partly mere mistake in us; we build brown brick walls, and wear brown coats, because we have been blunderingly taught to do so, and go on doing so mechanically. There is, however, also some cause for the change in our own tempers. On the whole, these are much *sadder* ages than the early ones; not sadder in a noble and deep way, but in a dim wearied way,—the way of ennui, and jaded intellect, and uncomfortableness of soul and body. The Middle Ages had their wars and agonies, but also intense delights. Their gold was dashed with blood; but ours is sprinkled with dust. Their life was inwoven with white and purple: ours is one seamless stuff of brown. Not that we are without apparent festivity, but festivity more or less forced, mistaken, embittered, incomplete—not of the heart. How wonderfully, since Shakespere's time, have we lost the power of laughing at bad jests! The very finish of our wit belies our gaiety.

The profoundest reason of this darkness of heart is, I believe, our want of faith. There never yet was a generation of men (savage or civilized) who, taken as a body, so wofully fulfilled the words "having no hope, and without God in the world," as the present civilized European race. A Red Indian or Otaheitan[7] savage has more sense of a divine existence round him, or government over him, than the plurality of refined Londoners and Parisians: and those among us who may in some sense be said to believe, are divided almost without exception into two broad classes, Romanist and Puritan; who, but for the interference of the unbelieving portions of society, would, either of them, reduce the other sect as speedily as possible to ashes. * * * Nearly all our powerful men in this age of the world are unbelievers; the best of them in doubt and misery; the worst in reckless defiance; the plurality, in plodding hesitation, doing, as well as they can, what practical work lies ready to their hands. Most of our scientific men are in this last class: our popular authors either set themselves definitely against all religious form, pleading for simple truth and benevolence, (Thackeray, Dickens,) or give themselves up to bitter and fruitless statement of facts, (De Balzac,) or surface-painting, (Scott,) or careless blasphemy, sad or smiling, (Byron, Beranger). Our earnest poets and deepest thinkers are doubtful and indignant, (Tennyson, Carlyle); one or two, anchored, indeed, but anxious or weeping, (Wordsworth, Mrs Browning); and of these two, the first is not so sure of his anchor, but that now and then it drags with him, even to make him cry out,—

> Great God, I had rather be
> A Pagan suckled in some creed outworn;

6. Brown.   7. Tahitian.

> So might I, standing on this pleasant lea,
> Have glimpses that would make me less forlorn.[8]

In politics, religion is now a name; in art, a hypocrisy or affectation. Over German religious pictures the inscription, "See how Pious I am," can be read at a glance by any clear-sighted person. Over French and English religious pictures the inscription, "See how Impious I am," is equally legible. All sincere and modest art is, among us, profane.

This faithlessness operates among us according to our tempers, producing either sadness or levity, and being the ultimate root alike of our discontents and of our wantonnesses. It is marvellous how full of contradiction it makes us: we are first dull, and seek for wild and lonely places because we have no heart for the garden; presently we recover our spirits, and build an assembly-room among the mountains, because we have no reverence for the desert. I do not know if there be game on Sinai, but I am always expecting to hear of some one's shooting over it.

There is, however, another, and a more innocent root of our delight in wild scenery.

All the Renaissance principles of art tended, as I have before often explained, to the setting Beauty above Truth, and seeking for it always at the expense of truth. And the proper punishment of such pursuit—the punishment which all the laws of the universe rendered inevitable—was, that those who thus pursued beauty should wholly lose sight of beauty. All the thinkers of the age, as we saw previously, declared that it did not exist. The age seconded their efforts, and banished beauty, so far as human effort could succeed in doing so, from the face of the earth, and the form of man. To powder the hair, to patch the cheek, to hoop the body, to buckle the foot, were all part and parcel of the same system which reduced streets to brick walls, and pictures to brown stains. One desert of Ugliness was extended before the eyes of mankind; and their pursuit of the beautiful, so recklessly continued, received unexpected consummation in high-heeled shoes and periwigs—Gower Street, and Gaspar Poussin.[9]

Reaction from this state was inevitable, if any true life was left in the races of mankind; and, accordingly, though still forced, by rule and fashion, to the producing and wearing all that is ugly, men steal out, half-ashamed of themselves for doing so, to the fields and mountains; and, finding among these the colour, and liberty, and variety, and power, which are for ever grateful to them, delight in these to an extent never before known; rejoice in all the wildest shattering of the mountain side, as an opposition to Gower Street, gaze in a rapt manner at sunsets and sunrises, to see there the blue, and gold, and purple, which glow for them no longer on knight's armour or temple porch; and gather with care out of the fields, into their blotted herbaria, the flowers which the five orders of architecture have banished from their doors and casements. * * *

It is not, however, only to existing inanimate nature that our want of beauty in person and dress has driven us. The imagination of it, as it was seen in our ancestors, haunts us continually; and while we yield to the present fashions, or act in accordance with the dullest modern principles of economy and utility, we look fondly back to the manners of the ages of chivalry, and delight in painting, to the fancy, the fashions we pretend to despise, and the splendours we think it wise to abandon. The fur-

---

8. From Wordsworth's sonnet *The World Is Too Much With Us* (see page 1561).
9. Gaspard Poussin (1615–1675) was a French landscape painter; Ruskin thought the plain brick houses of Gower Street in London were the epitome of ugliness.

niture and personages of our romance are sought, when the writer desires to please most easily, in the centuries which we profess to have surpassed in everything; the art which takes us into the present times is considered as both daring and degraded, and while the weakest words please us, and are regarded as poetry, which recall the manners of our forefathers, or of strangers, it is only as familiar and vulgar that we accept the description of our own.

In this we are wholly different from all the races that preceded us. All other nations have regarded their ancestors with reverence as saints or heroes; but have nevertheless thought their own deeds and ways of life the fitting subjects for their arts of painting or of verse. We, on the contrary, regard our ancestors as foolish and wicked, but yet find our chief artistic pleasure in descriptions of their ways of life.

The Greeks and mediaevals honoured, but did not imitate their forefathers; we imitate, but do not honour. * * *

Farther: as the admiration of mankind is found, in our times, to have in great part passed from men to mountains, and from human emotion to natural phenomena, we may anticipate that the great strength of art will also be warped in this direction; with this notable result for us, that whereas the greatest painters or painter of classical and mediaeval periods, being wholly devoted to the representation of humanity, furnished us with but little to examine in landscape, the greatest painters or painter of modern times will in all probability be devoted to landscape principally; and farther, because in representing human emotion words surpass painting, but in representing natural scenery painting surpasses words, we may anticipate also that the painter and poet (for convenience' sake I here use the words in opposition) will somewhat change their relations of rank in illustrating the mind of the age; that the painter will become of more importance, the poet of less; and that the relations between the men who are the types and first-fruits of the age in word and work,— namely, Scott[1] and Turner,—will be, in many curious respects, different from those between Homer and Phidias, or Dante and Giotto.[2] * * *

Then, as touching the kind of work done by these two men, the more I think of it I find this conclusion more impressed upon me,—that the greatest thing a human soul ever does in this world is to *see* something, and tell what it *saw* in a plain way. Hundreds of people can talk for one who can think, but thousands can think for one who can see. To see clearly is poetry, prophecy, and religion,—all in one.

1856

from The Stones of Venice
from The Nature of Gothic [1]

I shall endeavour therefore to give the reader in this chapter an idea, at once broad and definite, of the true nature of *Gothic* architecture, properly so called; not of that of Venice only, but of universal Gothic: for it will be one of the most interesting parts of our subsequent inquiry to find out how far Venetian architecture reached the universal or perfect type of Gothic, and how far it either fell short of it, or assumed foreign and independent forms.

---

1. Sir Walter Scott (1771–1832), Scottish novelist and poet.
2. Homer, ancient Greek epic poet; Phidias, ancient Greek sculptor; Dante Alighieri (1265–1321), Florentine

poet; Giotto (1266?–1337), Florentine painter, architect, and sculptor.
1. From vol. 2, ch. 6.

The principal difficulty in doing this arises from the fact that every building of the Gothic period differs in some important respect from every other; and many include features which, if they occurred in other buildings, would not be considered Gothic at all; so that all we have to reason upon is merely, if I may be allowed so to express it, a greater or less degree of *Gothicness* in each building we examine. And it is this Gothicness,—the character which, according as it is found more or less in a building, makes it more or less Gothic,—of which I want to define the nature. * * * That is to say, pointed arches do not constitute Gothic, nor vaulted roofs, nor flying buttresses, nor grotesque sculptures; but all or some of these things, and many other things with them, when they come together so as to have life. * * *

* * * We shall find that Gothic architecture has external forms and internal elements. Its elements are certain mental tendencies of the builders, legibly expressed in it; as fancifulness, love of variety, love of richness, and such others. Its external forms are pointed arches, vaulted roofs, etc. And unless both the elements and the forms are there, we have no right to call the style Gothic. It is not enough that it has the Form, if it have not also the power and life. It is not enough that it has the Power, if it have not the form. * * *

I believe, then, that the characteristic or moral elements of Gothic are the following, placed in the order of their importance:

1. Savageness.
2. Changefulness.
3. Naturalism.
4. Grotesqueness.
5. Rigidity.
6. Redundance.

These characters are here expressed as belonging to the building; as belonging to the builder, they would be expressed thus:—1. Savageness or Rudeness. 2. Love of Change. 3. Love of Nature. 4. Disturbed Imagination. 5. Obstinacy. 6. Generosity. And I repeat, that the withdrawal of any one, or any two, will not at once destroy the Gothic character of a building, but the removal of a majority of them will. I shall proceed to examine them in their order.

(1.) SAVAGENESS. I am not sure when the word "Gothic" was first generically applied to the architecture of the North; but I presume that, whatever the date of its original usage, it was intended to imply reproach, and express the barbaric character of the nations among whom that architecture arose. * * * It is true, greatly and deeply true, that the architecture of the North is rude and wild; but it is not true, that, for this reason, we are to condemn it, or despise. Far otherwise: I believe it is in this very character that it deserves our profoundest reverence. * * *

There is, I repeat, no degradation, no reproach in this, but all dignity and honourableness: and we should err grievously in refusing either to recognize as an essential character of the existing architecture of the North, or to admit as a desirable character in that which it yet may be, this wildness of thought, and roughness of work; this look of mountain brotherhood between the cathedral and the Alp; this magnificence of sturdy power, put forth only the more energetically because the fine finger-touch was chilled away by the frosty wind, and the eye dimmed by the moor-mist, or blinded by the hail; this out-speaking of the strong spirit of men who may not gather redundant fruitage from the earth, nor bask in dreamy benignity of sunshine, but must break the rock for bread, and cleave the forest for fire, and show, even in what they did for their delight, some of the hard habits of the arm and heart that grew on them as they swung the axe or pressed the plough.

If, however, the savageness of Gothic architecture, merely as an expression of its origin among Northern nations, may be considered, in some sort, a noble character, it possesses a higher nobility still, when considered as an index, not of climate, but of religious principle.

In the 13th and 14th paragraphs of Chapter XXI of the first volume of this work, it was noticed that the systems of architectural ornament, properly so called, might be divided into three:—1. Servile ornament, in which the execution or power of the inferior workman is entirely subjected to the intellect of the higher;—2. Constitutional ornament, in which the executive inferior power is, to a certain point, emancipated and independent, having a will of its own, yet confessing its inferiority and rendering obedience to higher powers;—and 3. Revolutionary ornament, in which no executive inferiority is admitted at all. I must here explain the nature of these divisions at somewhat greater length.

Of Servile ornament, the principal schools are the Greek, Ninevite,[2] and Egyptian; but their servility is of different kinds. The Greek master-workman was far advanced in knowledge and power above the Assyrian or Egyptian. Neither he nor those for whom he worked could endure the appearance of imperfection in anything; and, therefore, what ornament he appointed to be done by those beneath him was composed of mere geometrical forms,—balls, ridges, and perfectly symmetrical foliage,—which could be executed with absolute precision by line and rule, and were as perfect in their way, when completed, as his own figure sculpture. The Assyrian and Egyptian, on the contrary, less cognisant of accurate form in anything, were content to allow their figure sculpture to be executed by inferior workmen, but lowered the method of its treatment to a standard which every workman could reach, and then trained him by discipline so rigid, that there was no chance of his falling beneath the standard appointed. The Greek gave to the lower workman no subject which he could not perfectly execute. The Assyrian gave him subjects which he could only execute imperfectly, but fixed a legal standard for his imperfection. The workman was, in both systems, a slave.

But in the mediaeval, or especially Christian, system of ornament, this slavery is done away with altogether; Christianity having recognized, in small things as well as great, the individual value of every soul. But it not only recognizes its value; it confesses its imperfection, in only bestowing dignity upon the acknowledgment of unworthiness. That admission of lost power and fallen nature, which the Greek or Ninevite felt to be intensely painful, and, as far as might be, altogether refused, the Christian makes daily and hourly, contemplating the fact of it without fear, as tending, in the end, to God's greater glory. Therefore, to every spirit which Christianity summons to her service, her exhortation is: Do what you can, and confess frankly what you are unable to do; neither let your effort be shortened for fear of failure, nor your confession silenced for fear of shame. And it is, perhaps, the principal admirableness of the Gothic schools of architecture, that they thus receive the results of the labour of inferior minds; and out of fragments full of imperfection, and betraying that imperfection in every touch, indulgently raise up a stately and unaccusable whole.

2. Nineveh was an ancient Assyrian city.

But the modern English mind has this much in common with that of the Greek, that it intensely desires, in all things, the utmost completion or perfection compatible with their nature. This is a noble character in the abstract, but becomes ignoble when it causes us to forget the relative dignities of that nature itself, and to prefer the perfectness of the lower nature to the imperfection of the higher; not considering that as, judged by such a rule, all the brute animals would be preferable to man, because more perfect in their functions and kind. * * * And therefore, while in all things that we see or do, we are to desire perfection, and strive for it, we are nevertheless not to set the meaner thing, in its narrow accomplishment, above the nobler thing, in its mighty progress; not to esteem smooth minuteness above shattered majesty; not to prefer mean victory to honourable defeat; not to lower the level of our aim, that we may the more surely enjoy the complacency of success. But, above all, in our dealings with the souls of other men, we are to take care how we check, by severe requirement or narrow caution, efforts which might otherwise lead to a noble issue; and, still more, how we withhold our admiration from great excellencies, because they are mingled with rough faults. Now, in the make and nature of every man, however rude or simple, whom we employ in manual labour, there are some powers for better things; some tardy imagination, torpid capacity of emotion, tottering steps of thought, there are, even at the worst; and in most cases it is all our own fault that they *are* tardy or torpid. But they cannot be strengthened, unless we are content to take them in their feebleness, and unless we prize and honour them in their imperfection above the best and most perfect manual skill. And this is what we have to do with all our labourers; to look for the *thoughtful* part of them, and get that out of them, whatever we lose for it, whatever faults and errors we are obliged to take with it. For the best that is in them cannot manifest itself, but in company with much error. Understand this clearly: You can teach a man to draw a straight line, and to cut one; to strike a curved line, and to carve it; and to copy and carve any number of given lines or forms, with admirable speed and perfect precision; and you find his work perfect of its kind: but if you ask him to think about any of those forms, to consider if he cannot find any better in his own head, he stops; his execution becomes hesitating; he thinks, and ten to one he thinks wrong; ten to one he makes a mistake in the first touch he gives to his work as a thinking being. But you have made a man of him for all that. He was only a machine before, an animated tool.

And observe, you are put to stern choice in this matter. You must either make a tool of the creature, or a man of him. You cannot make both. Men were not intended to work with the accuracy of tools, to be precise and perfect in all their actions. If you will have that precision out of them, and make their fingers measure degrees like cog-wheels, and their arms strike curves like compasses, you must unhumanize them. All the energy of their spirits must be given to make cogs and compasses of themselves. * * *

And now, reader, look round this English room of yours, about which you have been proud so often, because the work of it was so good and strong, and the ornaments of it so finished. Examine again all those accurate mouldings, and perfect polishings, and unerring adjustments of the seasoned wood and tempered steel. Many a time you have exulted over them, and thought how great England was, because her slightest work was done so thoroughly. Alas! if read rightly, these perfectnesses are signs of a slavery in our England a thousand times more bitter and more degrading than that of the scourged African, or helot[3] Greek. Men may be beaten, chained, tor-

---

3. Serf or slave.

mented, yoked like cattle, slaughtered like summer flies, and yet remain in one sense, and the best sense, free. But to smother their souls within them, to blight and hew into rotting pollards[4] the suckling branches of their human intelligence, to make the flesh and skin which, after the worm's work on it, is to see God,[5] into leathern thongs to yoke machinery with,—this is to be slave-masters indeed; and there might be more freedom in England, though her feudal lords' lightest words were worth men's lives, and though the blood of the vexed husbandman dropped in the furrows of her fields, than there is while the animation of her multitudes is sent like fuel to feed the factory smoke, and the strength of them is given daily to be wasted into the fineness of a web, or racked into the exactness of a line.

And, on the other hand, go forth again to gaze upon the old cathedral front, where you have smiled so often at the fantastic ignorance of the old sculptors: examine once more those ugly goblins, and formless monsters, and stern statues, anatomiless and rigid; but do not mock at them, for they are signs of the life and liberty of every workman who struck the stone; a freedom of thought, and rank in scale of being, such as no laws, no charters, no charities can secure; but which it must be the first aim of all Europe at this day to regain for her children.

Let me not be thought to speak wildly or extravagantly. It is verily this degradation of the operative into a machine, which, more than any other evil of the times, is leading the mass of the nations everywhere into vain, incoherent, destructive struggling for a freedom of which they cannot explain the nature to themselves. Their universal outcry against wealth, and against nobility, is not forced from them either by the pressure of famine, or the sting of mortified pride. These do much, and have done much in all ages; but the foundations of society were never yet shaken as they are at this day. It is not that men are ill fed, but that they have no pleasure in the work by which they make their bread, and therefore look to wealth as the only means of pleasure. It is not that men are pained by the scorn of the upper classes, but they cannot endure their own; for they feel that the kind of labour to which they are condemned is verily a degrading one, and makes them less than men. Never had the upper classes so much sympathy with the lower, or charity for them, as they have at this day, and yet never were they so much hated by them: for, of old, the separation between the noble and the poor was merely a wall built by law; now it is a veritable difference in level of standing, a precipice between upper and lower grounds in the field of humanity, and there is pestilential air at the bottom of it. * * *

We have much studied and much perfected, of late, the great civilized invention of the division of labour; only we give it a false name. It is not, truly speaking, the labour that is divided; but the men:—Divided into mere segments of men—broken into small fragments and crumbs of life; so that all the little piece of intelligence that is left in a man is not enough to make a pin, or a nail, but exhausts itself in making the point of a pin or the head of a nail. Now it is a good and desirable thing, truly, to make many pins in a day; but if we could only see with what crystal sand their points were polished,—sand of human soul, much to be magnified before it can be discerned for what it is—we should think there might be some loss in it also. And the great cry that rises from all our manufacturing cities, louder than their furnace blast, is all in very deed for this,—that we manufacture everything there except men; we blanch cotton, and strengthen steel, and refine sugar, and shape pottery; but to brighten, to

---

4. Trees that are artificially shaped by pruning.

5. "And though after my skin worms destroy this body, yet in my flesh shall I see God" (Job 19.26).

strengthen, to refine, or to form a single living spirit, never enters into our estimate of advantages. And all the evil to which that cry is urging our myriads can be met only in one way: not by teaching nor preaching, for to teach them is but to show them their misery, and to preach to them, if we do nothing more than preach, is to mock at it. It can be met only by a right understanding, on the part of all classes, of what kinds of labour are good for men, raising them, and making them happy; by a determined sacrifice of such convenience, or beauty, or cheapness as is to be got only by the degradation of the workman; and by equally determined demand for the products and results of healthy and ennobling labour.

And how, it will be asked, are these products to be recognized, and this demand to be regulated? Easily: by the observance of three broad and simple rules:

1. Never encourage the manufacture of any article not absolutely necessary, in the production of which *Invention* has no share.

2. Never demand an exact finish for its own sake, but only for some practical or noble end.

3. Never encourage imitation or copying of any kind, except for the sake of preserving records of great works.

The second of these principles is the only one which directly rises out of the consideration of our immediate subject; but I shall briefly explain the meaning and extent of the first also, reserving the enforcement of the third for another place.

1. Never encourage the manufacture of anything not necessary, in the production of which invention has no share.

For instance. Glass beads are utterly unnecessary, and there is no design or thought employed in their manufacture. They are formed by first drawing out the glass into rods; these rods are chopped up into fragments of the size of beads by the human hand, and the fragments are then rounded in the furnace. The men who chop up the rods sit at their work all day, their hands vibrating with a perpetual and exquisitely timed palsy, and the beads dropping beneath their vibration like hail. Neither they, nor the men who draw out the rods or fuse the fragments, have the smallest occasion for the use of any single human faculty; and every young lady, therefore, who buys glass beads is engaged in the slave-trade, and in a much more cruel one than that which we have so long been endeavouring to put down.

But glass cups and vessels may become the subjects of exquisite invention; and if in buying these we pay for the invention, that is to say, for the beautiful form, or colour, or engraving, and not for mere finish of execution, we are doing good to humanity. * * *

I shall perhaps press this law farther elsewhere, but our immediate concern is chiefly with the second, namely, never to demand an exact finish, when it does not lead to a noble end. For observe, I have only dwelt upon the rudeness of Gothic, or any other kind of imperfectness, as admirable, where it was impossible to get design or thought without it. If you are to have the thought of a rough and untaught man, you must have it in a rough and untaught way; but from an educated man, who can without effort express his thoughts in an educated way, take the graceful expression, and be thankful. Only *get* the thought, and do not silence the peasant because he cannot speak good grammar, or until you have taught him his grammar. Grammar and refinement are good things, both, only be sure of the better thing first. And thus in art, delicate finish is desirable from the greatest masters, and is always given by them. In some places Michael Angelo, Leonardo, Phidias, Perugino, Turner,[6] all finished with the most exquisite care; and the finish they give always leads to the fuller accomplishment of their noble purposes. But lower men than these cannot finish, for it requires consummate knowledge to finish consummately, and then we must take their thoughts as they are able to give them. So the rule is simple: Always look for invention first, and after that, for such execution as will help the invention, and as the inventor is capable of without painful effort, and *no more*. Above all, demand no refinement of execution where there is no thought, for that is slaves' work, unredeemed. Rather choose rough work than smooth work, so only that the practical purpose be answered, and never imagine there is reason to be proud of anything that may be accomplished by patience and sand-paper.

I shall only give one example, which however will show the reader what I mean, from the manufacture already alluded to, that of glass. Our modern glass is exquisitely clear in its substance, true in its form, accurate in its cutting. We are proud of this. We ought to be ashamed of it. The old Venice glass was muddy, inaccurate in all its forms, and clumsily cut, if at all. And the old Venetian was justly proud of it. For there is this difference between the English and Venetian workman, that the former thinks only of accurately matching his patterns, and getting his curves perfectly true and his edges perfectly sharp, and becomes a mere machine for rounding curves and sharpening edges; while the old Venetian cared not a whit whether his edges were sharp or not, but he invented a new design for every glass that he made, and never moulded a handle or a lip without a new fancy in it. And therefore, though some Venetian glass is ugly and clumsy enough when made by clumsy and uninventive workmen, other Venetian glass is so lovely in its forms that no price is too great for it; and we never see the same form in it twice. Now you cannot have the finish and the varied form too. If the workman is thinking about his edges, he cannot be thinking of his design; if of his design, he cannot think of his edges. Choose whether you will pay for the lovely form or the perfect finish, and choose at the same moment whether you will make the worker a man or a grindstone.

Nay, but the reader interrupts me,—"If the workman can design beautifully, I would not have him kept at the furnace. Let him be taken away and made a gentleman, and have a studio, and design his glass there, and I will have it blown and cut for him by common workmen, and so I will have my design and my finish too."

All ideas of this kind are founded upon two mistaken suppositions: the first, that one man's thoughts can be, or ought to be, executed by another man's hands; the second, that manual labour is a degradation, when it is governed by intellect.

On a large scale, and in work determinable by line and rule, it is indeed both possible and necessary that the thoughts of one man should be carried out by the labour of others; in this sense I have already defined the best architecture to be the expression of the mind of manhood by the hands of childhood. But on a smaller scale, and in a design which cannot be mathematically defined, one man's thoughts can never be expressed by another: and the difference between the spirit of touch of the man who is inventing, and of the man who is obeying directions, is often all the difference between a great and a common work of art. How wide the separation is

6. Michelangelo Buonarroti (1475–1564), Italian painter, sculptor, architect, and poet; Leonardo da Vinci (1452–1519), Italian painter, sculptor, architect, and engineer; Phidias (5th century B.C.), ancient Greek sculptor; Pietro Vannucci Perugino (1446–1523), Italian painter; J. M. W. Turner (1775–1851), English painter.

between original and second-hand execution, I shall endeavour to show elsewhere; it is not so much to our purpose here as to mark the other and more fatal error of despising manual labour when governed by intellect; for it is no less fatal an error to despise it when thus regulated by intellect, than to value it for its own sake. We are always in these days endeavouring to separate the two; we want one man to be always thinking, and another to be always working, and we call one a gentleman, and the other an operative; whereas the workman ought often to be thinking, and the thinker often to be working, and both should be gentlemen, in the best sense. As it is, we make both ungentle, the one envying, the other despising, his brother; and the mass of society is made up of morbid thinkers, and miserable workers. Now it is only by labour that thought can be made healthy, and only by thought that labour can be made happy, and the two cannot be separated with impunity. * * *

I should be led far from the matter in hand, if I were to pursue this interesting subject. Enough, I trust, has been said to show the reader that the rudeness or imperfection which at first rendered the term "Gothic" one of reproach is indeed, when rightly understood, one of the most noble characters of Christian architecture, and not only a noble but an *essential* one. It seems a fantastic paradox, but it is nevertheless a most important truth, that no architecture can be truly noble which is *not* imperfect. And this is easily demonstrable. For since the architect, whom we will suppose capable of doing all in perfection, cannot execute the whole with his own hands, he must either make slaves of his workmen in the old Greek, and present English fashion, and level his work to a slave's capacities, which is to degrade it; or else he must take his workmen as he finds them, and let them show their weaknesses together with their strength, which will involve the Gothic imperfection, but render the whole work as noble as the intellect of the age can make it.

But the principle may be stated more broadly still. I have confined the illustration of it to architecture, but I must not leave it as if true of architecture only. Hitherto I have used the words imperfect and perfect merely to distinguish between work grossly unskilful, and work executed with average precision and science; and I have been pleading that any degree of unskilfulness should be admitted, so only that the labourer's mind had room for expression. But, accurately speaking, no good work whatever can be perfect, and *the demand for perfection is always a sign of a misunderstanding of the ends of art.*

This for two reasons, both based on everlasting laws. The first, that no great man ever stops working till he has reached his point of failure: that is to say, his mind is always far in advance of his powers of execution, and the latter will now and then give way in trying to follow it; besides that he will always give to the inferior portions of his work only such inferior attention as they require; and according to his greatness he becomes so accustomed to the feeling of dissatisfaction with the best he can do, that in moments of lassitude or anger with himself he will not care though the beholder be dissatisfied also. I believe there has only been one man who would not acknowledge this necessity, and strove always to reach perfection, Leonardo; the end of his vain effort being merely that he would take ten years to a picture and leave it unfinished. And therefore, if we are to have great men working at all, or less men doing their best, the work will be imperfect, however beautiful. Of human work none but what is bad can be perfect, in its own bad way.[7]

---

7. The Elgin marbles are supposed by many persons to be "perfect." In the most important portions they indeed approach perfection, but only there. The draperies are unfinished, the hair and wool of the animals are unfinished, and the entire bas-reliefs of the frieze are roughly cut [Ruskin's note]. The Elgin marbles are sculptures (including the Parthenon frieze) which were taken from Athens to England by Lord Elgin at the beginning of the 19th century.

The second reason is, that imperfection is in some sort essential to all that we know of life. It is the sign of life in a mortal body, that is to say, of a state of progress and change. Nothing that lives is, or can be, rigidly perfect; part of it is decaying, part nascent. The foxglove blossom,—a third part bud, a third part past, a third part in full bloom,—is a type of the life of this world. And in all things that live there are certain irregularities and deficiencies which are not only signs of life, but sources of beauty. No human face is exactly the same in its lines on each side, no leaf perfect in its lobes, no branch in its symmetry. All admit irregularity as they imply change; and to banish imperfection is to destroy expression, to check exertion, to paralyze vitality. All things are literally better, lovelier, and more beloved for the imperfections which have been divinely appointed, that the law of human life may be Effort, and the law of human judgment, Mercy.

Accept this then for a universal law, that neither architecture nor any other noble work of man can be good unless it be imperfect; and let us be prepared for the otherwise strange fact, which we shall discern clearly as we approach the period of the Renaissance, that the first cause of the fall of the arts of Europe was a relentless requirement of perfection, incapable alike either of being silenced by veneration for greatness, or softened into forgiveness of simplicity.

Thus far then of the Rudeness or Savageness, which is the first mental element of Gothic architecture. It is an element in many other healthy architectures also, as the Byzantine and Romanesque; but true Gothic cannot exist without it.

1851–1853

Matthew Arnold
1822–1888

"I am glad you like the Gipsy Scholar," Matthew Arnold wrote to a friend in 1853, "—but what does it *do* for you?" No Victorian gave more attention than Arnold to the momentous question of how art should affect an audience, and no writer was ever more tortured by it. For much as he delighted in creating the "pleasing melancholy" of *The Scholar-Gipsy*, one of his greatest poems, Arnold felt that literature must directly address the moral needs of readers, "to *animate* and *ennoble* them." This concern with the practical emotional effects of art, Arnold said simply, is "the basis of my nature—and of my poetics."

But in trying to realize his goal, Arnold became a deeply divided man. Author of the era's most distinctive poems of alienation and doubt, he gave up poetry to work for the public good, passionately defending classic literature as a means of remaking the materialist society he abhorred. As a social critic, he aspired to embody his ideal of a balanced mind, to be a man "who saw life steadily and saw it whole." But as a private individual he viewed himself as a forlorn romantic quester, disenchanted with modernity. Unable to believe in the religion of the past, and unwilling to accept the secular values of the present, he described himself as "wandering between two worlds, one dead, / The other powerless to be born." Arnold is unique among the eminent Victorian writers, admired equally for his heartfelt poetry of disillusionment and for his sophisticated prose aimed at pragmatic social reform.

Matthew Arnold was the oldest son of Dr. Thomas Arnold, headmaster of Rugby School, who had become famous for reshaping the curriculum to instill a healthy respect for Christian values, classical languages, and competitive games. Matthew's mother, Mary Penrose Arnold, encouraged her son to be creative, self-conscious, and alert to the comic or dramatic side of daily events. Nicknamed "Crabby" by his father when he wore leg braces for two years, Arnold adopted a sidelong, crab-like approach to his goal of becoming a poet. A lazy, dilettantish, facetious student, Arnold managed through last-minute heroics to win the top prizes: a scholarship in 1840 to Balliol College, Oxford; the renowned Newdigate Prize for poetry in 1843; and in 1845 a Fellowship at Oriel College.

Throughout his life, Arnold seemed most comfortable outdoors and free of the classroom, whether blasting away at game on the English moors (he was a terrible shot), or hiking in the Alps. He spent his early childhood at Laleham, a village on the Thames, perhaps the source of his frequent river imagery. When he should have been studying at Oxford, he roamed the idyllic countryside surrounding it, hunting, fishing, and composing verses. He once pranced naked on a riverbank after swimming, prompting a rebuke from a passing clergyman. Waving his towel, Arnold replied: "Is it possible that you see anything indelicate in the human form divine?"

In 1847 Arnold became private secretary to the liberal politician Lord Lansdowne, spending most of his time in London, working on his poetry, and arguing about poetry and religion with his best friend, the poet Arthur Hugh Clough. They both agreed on the spiritual bankruptcy of modern life: "These are damned times," Arnold wrote to Clough in 1849; "everything is against one . . . the absence of great natures, the unavoidable contact with millions of small ones . . . our own selves, and the sickening consciousness of our difficulties."

Arnold dealt with these difficulties by casting them in poetic form. His first book of poems, The Strayed Reveller, and Other Poems, by "A," appeared in 1849, followed by Empedocles on Etna, and Other Poems (1852) and Poems (1853). Many other important poems, including Dover Beach, also date from this fertile period, though not published until later, in Poems, Second Series (1855) and New Poems (1867).

Arnold's finest poetry is imbued with a love of the countryside. He spent family vacations in the Lake District, whose beauty and poetic associations made a deep impression on him. His parents were friendly with Wordsworth, who was to become the chief influence on Arnold's poetry; when Wordsworth died he mourned, "who will teach us how to feel?" Like Wordsworth, Arnold evokes memorable landscapes in many of his key works in order to ponder the relation between hidden emotions and external objects, and to explore the themes of lost childhood, nostalgia for the past, and the quest for identity. But Arnold rarely found in nature a means of contact with other people or with a deeper self: "The disease of the present age," he wrote in his journal, "is divorce from oneself."

Arnold felt a growing dissatisfaction with his society and with his own poetry. In a controversial preface to his Poems of 1853, he justified not reprinting his major earlier work, Empedocles on Etna, because he felt that it failed to "inspirit and rejoice" readers and teach them how to live. He went on to condemn poetry that merely presents "a continuous state of mental distress . . . unrelieved by incident, hope, or resistance; in which there is everything to be endured, nothing to be done." In these words he accurately summed up—and dismissed—what was most powerful and moving in his own work.

Provoking a heated debate about the poet's relation to contemporary life, Arnold urged that modern poets should turn from their own troubles to build upon timeless, universal "great actions," such as those found in Sophocles and Aeschylus. The Victorian age, he concluded, was an unlikely source of poetic material, because it was "an age wanting in moral grandeur . . . an age of spiritual discomfort."

Too much a man of his time to be able to follow his own advice, Arnold largely abandoned poetry after the mid-1850s. In 1851, two important events occurred that contributed to this abdication: his marriage to Frances Lucy Wightman and his taking a job as a school inspector to support his family. This turned out to be a grueling position assessing the quality of instruction in government-funded schools for the poor. Initially surmising that the job would do well enough "for the next three or four years," Arnold doggedly kept at it for thirty-five years, traveling constantly throughout Britain and later in Europe. He soon realized the importance of expanding and reforming public education, arguing for the schools' crucial role "in civilizing the next generation of the lower classes, who, as things are going, will have most of the political power of the country in their hands."

Thus the anguished poet transformed himself into an energetic public servant, strenuously trying to remedy with his progressive criticism a society that he privately despaired of as hopelessly materialist. In 1857 Arnold was elected Professor of Poetry at Oxford University. He was the first to lecture in English rather than Latin, and for the next ten years he used the occasion of his public lectures to reach the broadest possible audience, promoting his belief that a careful reading of classic literature produces civilizing and morally sustaining effects. He reworked many of his lectures into books and essays, including *On Translating Homer* (1861) and *On the Modern Element in Literature* (1869). The work begun at Oxford eventually helped establish literature as a cornerstone of university programs in the liberal arts.

In 1865 Arnold published *Essays in Criticism*, which began with his famous essay, *The Function of Criticism at the Present Time*. There he argued that criticism is "a free creative activity," one that may well be the most useful and satisfying activity available to an inquiring mind in a modern, unpoetical era. With examples ranging from high art to tabloid journalism, Arnold revealed how British thought is entangled in class relations and political exigencies; his essay anticipates the scope and methods of modern culture studies. In his most important work of social criticism, *Culture and Anarchy* (1869), Arnold called for "disinterested" analysis free of partisan politics. He deplored English pride in "doing as one likes," and found in the self-serving behavior of all classes an anarchic lack of concern for the public good. Only education, he contended, could unite the antagonistic factions of British society, by teaching respect for beauty and intellect—what Arnold termed the virtues of "sweetness and light."

The mocking irony, Olympian assurance, and lucid, cascading style of these works make them exhilarating—or exasperating—reading. Arnold's high-minded attitudes enraged many of his opponents, and his loftiness of tone led even his friends and family to nickname him "the Emperor." For Arnold, education was a lifelong task, and few measured up to the cosmopolitan, European standards he set. He was particularly savage with anyone he considered guilty of self-interest or fuzzy thinking, and he attacked politicians and bishops by name. Leslie Stephen, Virginia Woolf's father, remarked satirically that "I often wished . . . that I too had a little sweetness and light that I might be able to say such nasty things of my enemies."

In the 1870s, Arnold scandalized many people with his attacks on orthodox religion in *St. Paul and Protestantism* (1870), *Literature and Dogma* (1873), and *God and the Bible* (1875). In *The Study of Poetry* (1880), he went so far as to argue that "most of what now passes for religion and philosophy will be replaced by poetry."

In 1883, weary, in debt, and desperate to retire, Arnold tried to raise money by selecting, with his daughter Nelly, 365 mottoes to create a *Matthew Arnold Birthday Book*. In the same year he went on a money-making lecture tour of the United States, meeting with mixed success. The chief intellectual product of his travel was *Discourses in America* (1885), which contained his essay *Literature and Science*. There, Arnold defended the idea of a liberal arts education founded on ancient and modern literatures against Thomas Huxley's contention in *Science and Culture* (1881) that an education based on the natural sciences would do just as well. Arnold felt that the debate had particular relevance for Americans, whose respect for "the average man" was fraught with "danger to the ideal of a high and rare excellence," best conveyed by a humanistic education. Arnold died suddenly of a heart attack in 1888.

Arnold was not a prophetic critic like Carlyle, nor a visionary poet of social reform like Elizabeth Barrett Browning, nor a moral crusader like Dickens. Instead, Arnold offered thoughtful prescriptions for guiding a changing and increasingly democratic society to a fuller understanding of its problems, and a more effective realization of its goals. As a school inspector he developed a deeper understanding of ineffective institutions and the ignorance of the British public than any other important Victorian author. While few have agreed fully with his pronouncements on literature and society, he has influenced almost every significant English-speaking critic since his time, including T. S. Eliot, F. R. Leavis, Lionel Trilling, and Raymond Williams.

Arnold has remained a literary force to be reckoned with as well. In its honest, introspective, sometimes awkward way, Arnold's poetry speaks unforgettably of the anxieties of his era. Though he saw himself as having "less poetical sentiment than Tennyson, and less intellectual vigor and abundance than Browning," he felt that his more balanced "fusion" of these qualities would continue to assure him an audience. His open approach to his innermost feelings is echoed almost everywhere in modern poetry.

Dover Beach

The sea is calm to-night.
The tide is full, the moon lies fair
Upon the straits; on the French coast the light
Gleams and is gone; the cliffs of England stand,
5   Glimmering and vast, out in the tranquil bay.
Come to the window, sweet is the night-air!
Only, from the long line of spray
Where the sea meets the moon-blanched land,
Listen! you hear the grating roar
10   Of pebbles which the waves draw back, and fling,
At their return, up the high strand,
Begin, and cease, and then again begin,
With tremulous cadence slow, and bring
The eternal note of sadness in.

15   Sophocles long ago
Heard it on the Aegean,[1] and it brought
Into his mind the turbid ebb and flow
Of human misery; we
Find also in the sound a thought,
20   Hearing it by this distant northern sea.

The Sea of Faith
Was once, too, at the full, and round earth's shore
Lay like the folds of a bright girdle° furled.   *sash*
But now I only hear
25   Its melancholy, long, withdrawing roar,
Retreating, to the breath
Of the night-wind, down the vast edges drear
And naked shingles° of the world.   *pebble beaches*

Ah, love, let us be true
30   To one another! for the world, which seems
To lie before us like a land of dreams,
So various, so beautiful, so new,
Hath really neither joy, nor love, nor light,
Nor certitude, nor peace, nor help for pain;
35   And we are here as on a darkling plain
Swept with confused alarms of struggle and flight,
Where ignorant armies clash by night.

c. 1851   1867

1. Sophocles was a 5th century B.C. Greek dramatist; the Aegean Sea lies between Greece and Turkey.

The Buried Life

Light flows our war of mocking words, and yet,
Behold, with tears mine eyes are wet!
I feel a nameless sadness o'er me roll.
Yes, yes, we know that we can jest,
5   We know, we know that we can smile!
But there's a something in this breast,
To which thy light words bring no rest,
And thy gay smiles no anodyne.
Give me thy hand, and hush awhile,
10   And turn those limpid eyes on mine,
And let me read there, love! thy inmost soul.

Alas! is even love too weak
To unlock the heart, and let it speak?
Are even lovers powerless to reveal
15   To one another what indeed they feel?
I knew the mass of men concealed
Their thoughts, for fear that if revealed
They would by other men be met
With blank indifference, or with blame reproved;
20   I knew they lived and moved
Tricked in disguises, alien to the rest
Of men, and alien to themselves—and yet
The same heart beats in every human breast!

But we, my love!—doth a like spell benumb
25   Our hearts, our voices? must we too be dumb?

Ah! well for us, if even we,
Even for a moment, can get free
Our heart, and have our lips unchained;
For that which seals them hath been deep-ordained!

30   Fate, which foresaw
How frivolous a baby man would be—
By what distractions he would be possessed,

How he would pour himself in every strife,
And well-nigh change his own identity—
35   That it might keep from his capricious play
His genuine self, and force him to obey
Even in his own despite his being's law,
Bade through the deep recesses of our breast
The unregarded river of our life
40   Pursue with indiscernible flow its way;
And that we should not see
The buried stream, and seem to be
Eddying at large in blind uncertainty,
Though driving on with it eternally.

45   But often, in the world's most crowded streets,
But often, in the din of strife,
There rises an unspeakable desire
After the knowledge of our buried life;

A thirst to spend our fire and restless force
50 In tracking out our true, original course;
A longing to inquire
Into the mystery of this heart which beats
So wild, so deep in us—to know
Whence our lives come and where they go.
55 And many a man in his own breast then delves,
But deep enough, alas! none ever mines.
And we have been on many thousand lines,
And we have shown, on each, spirit and power;
But hardly have we, for one little hour,
60 Been on our own line, have we been ourselves—
Hardly had skill to utter one of all
The nameless feelings that course through our breast,
But they course on for ever unexpressed.
And long we try in vain to speak and act
65 Our hidden self, and what we say and do
Is eloquent, is well—but 'tis not true!
And then we will no more be racked
With inward striving, and demand
Of all the thousand nothings of the hour
70 Their stupefying power;
Ah yes, and they benumb us at our call!
Yet still, from time to time, vague and forlorn,
From the soul's subterranean depth upborne
As from an infinitely distant land,
75 Come airs, and floating echoes, and convey
A melancholy into all our day.

Only—but this is rare—
When a belovéd hand is laid in ours,
When, jaded with the rush and glare
80 Of the interminable hours,
Our eyes can in another's eyes read clear,
When our world-deafened ear
Is by the tones of a loved voice caressed—
A bolt is shot back somewhere in our breast,
85 And a lost pulse of feeling stirs again.
The eye sinks inward, and the heart lies plain,
And what we mean, we say, and what we would, we know.
A man becomes aware of his life's flow,
And hears its winding murmur; and he sees
90 The meadows where it glides, the sun, the breeze.

And there arrives a lull in the hot race
Wherein he doth for ever chase
That flying and elusive shadow, rest.
An air of coolness plays upon his face,
95 And an unwonted calm pervades his breast.
And then he thinks he knows
The hills where his life rose,
And the sea where it goes.

1852

The Scholar-Gipsy

While at Oxford in the mid-1840s, Arnold read the seventeenth-century tale of a young man who left his studies at the university to join a band of gypsies, intending to master their lore. Fascinated by the story, Arnold imagined the scholar still wandering the hills around Oxford, magically untouched by time and change. The poem Arnold eventually wrote, circa 1853, celebrated his own youth at Oxford, "the *freest* and most delightful part, perhaps, of my life," he told his brother Tom, "when with you and Clough . . . I shook off all the bonds and formalities of the place, and enjoyed the spring of life and that unforgotten Oxfordshire and Berkshire country." Arnold accompanied the poem with a note based on his source, Joseph Glanvill's *Vanity of Dogmatizing* (1661):

> There was very lately a lad in the University of Oxford, who was by his poverty forced to leave his studies there; and at last to join himself to a company of vagabond gipsies. Among these extravagant people, by the insinuating subtilty of his carriage, he quickly got so much of their love and esteem as that they discovered to him their mystery. After he had been a pretty while well exercised in the trade, there chanced to ride by a couple of scholars, who had formerly been of his acquaintance. They quickly spied out their old friend among the gipsies; and he gave them an account of the necessity which drove him to that kind of life, and told them that the people he went with were not such impostors as they were taken for, but that they had a traditional kind of learning among them, and could do wonders by the power of imagination, their fancy binding that of others: that himself had learned much of their art, and when he had compassed the whole secret, he intended, he said, to leave their company, and give the world an account of what he had learned.

The Scholar-Gipsy

Go, for they call you, shepherd, from the hill;
  Go, shepherd, and untie the wattled cotes!¹
    No longer leave thy wistful flock unfed,
  Nor let thy bawling fellows rack their throats,
5   Nor the cropped herbage shoot another head.
        But when the fields are still,
  And the tired men and dogs all gone to rest,
    And only the white sheep are sometimes seen
    Cross and recross the strips of moon-blanched green,
10 Come, shepherd, and again begin the quest!

Here, where the reaper was at work of late—
  In this high field's dark corner, where he leaves
    His coat, his basket, and his earthen cruse,°   *jug*
  And in the sun all morning binds the sheaves,
15   Then here, at noon, comes back his stores to use—
       Here will I sit and wait,
  While to my ear from uplands far away
    The bleating of the folded° flocks is borne,   *penned up*
    With distant cries of reapers in the corn—
20 All the live murmur of a summer's day.

Screened is this nook o'er the high, half-reaped field,
  And here till sun-down, shepherd! will I be.
    Through the thick corn the scarlet poppies peep,

---

1. Fences made of woven sticks, used to pen sheep.

And round green roots and yellowing stalks I see
25   Pale pink convolvulus° in tendrils creep;   *morning glory*
        And air-swept lindens yield
Their scent, and rustle down their perfumed showers
      Of bloom on the bent grass where I am laid,
      And bower me from the August sun with shade;
30   And the eye travels down to Oxford's towers.

And near me on the grass lies Glanvil's book—
      Come, let me read the oft-read tale again!
        The story of the Oxford scholar poor,
      Of pregnant parts° and quick inventive brain,   *bursting with ideas*
35   Who, tired of knocking at preferment's door,
        One summer-morn forsook
His friends, and went to learn the gipsy-lore,
      And roamed the world with that wild brotherhood,
      And came, as most men deemed, to little good,
40   But came to Oxford and his friends no more.

But once, years after, in the country-lanes,
      Two scholars, whom at college erst he knew,
        Met him, and of his way of life enquired;
      Whereat he answered, that the gipsy-crew,
45   His mates, had arts to rule as they desired
        The workings of men's brains,
And they can bind them to what thoughts they will.
      "And I," he said, "the secret of their art,
      When fully learned, will to the world impart;
50   But it needs heaven-sent moments for this skill."

This said, he left them, and returned no more.
      But rumours hung about the country-side,
        That the lost Scholar long was seen to stray,
Seen by rare glimpses, pensive and tongue-tied,
55   In hat of antique shape, and cloak of grey,
        The same the gipsies wore.
Shepherds had met him on the Hurst[2] in spring;
      At some lone alehouse in the Berkshire moors,
      On the warm ingle-bench, the smock-frocked boors[3]
60   Had found him seated at their entering,

But, 'mid their drink and clatter, he would fly.
      And I myself seem half to know thy looks,
        And put the shepherds, wanderer! on thy trace;
And boys who in lone wheatfields scare the rooks
65   I ask if thou hast passed their quiet place;
        Or in my boat I lie
Moored to the cool bank in the summer-heats,
      'Mid wide grass meadows which the sunshine fills,
      And watch the warm, green-muffled Cumner hills,
70   And wonder if thou haunt'st their shy retreats.

---

2. Hill near Oxford; most of the places mentioned are in the countryside around Oxford.   3. Rustic peasants; an ingle-bench is beside the fireplace.

For most, I know, thou lov'st retiréd ground!
　　Thee at the ferry Oxford riders blithe,
　　　　Returning home on summer-nights, have met
　　Crossing the stripling Thames at Bab-lock-hithe,
75　　　Trailing in the cool stream thy fingers wet,
　　　　　As the punt's° rope chops round;　　　　　　　*small boat*
　　And leaning backward in a pensive dream,
　　　　And fostering in thy lap a heap of flowers
　　　　Plucked in shy fields and distant Wychwood bowers,
80　And thine eyes resting on the moonlit stream.

And then they land, and thou art seen no more!
　　Maidens, who from the distant hamlets come
　　　　To dance around the Fyfield elm in May,
　　Oft through the darkening fields have seen thee roam,
85　　　Or cross a stile into the public way.
　　　　　Oft thou hast given them store
　　Of flowers—the frail-leafed, white anemone,
　　　　Dark bluebells drenched with dews of summer eves,
　　　　And purple orchises with spotted leaves—
90　But none hath words she can report of thee.

And, above Godstow Bridge, when hay-time's here
　　In June, and many a scythe in sunshine flames,
　　　　Men who through those wide fields of breezy grass
　　Where black-winged swallows haunt the glittering Thames,
95　　　To bathe in the abandoned lasher pass,[4]
　　　　　Have often passed thee near
　　Sitting upon the river bank o'ergrown;
　　　　Marked thine outlandish garb, thy figure spare,
　　　　Thy dark vague eyes, and soft abstracted air—
100　But, when they came from bathing, thou wast gone!

At some lone homestead in the Cumner hills,
　　Where at her open door the housewife darns,
　　　　Thou hast been seen, or hanging on a gate
　　To watch the threshers in the mossy barns.
105　　　Children, who early range these slopes and late
　　　　　For cresses from the rills,
　　Have known thee eying, all an April-day,
　　　　The springing pastures and the feeding kine;
　　　　And marked thee, when the stars come out and shine,
110　Through the long dewy grass move slow away.

In autumn, on the skirts of Bagley Wood—
　　Where most the gipsies by the turf-edged way
　　　　Pitch their smoked tents, and every bush you see
　　With scarlet patches tagged and shreds of grey,[5]
115　　　Above the forest-ground called Thessaly—
　　　　　The blackbird, picking food,
　　Sees thee, nor stops his meal, nor fears at all;

---

4. Pool where water spilling over a dam collects.　　　5. Gypsies spread their clothes on bushes to dry.

So often has he known thee past him stray,
Rapt, twirling in thy hand a withered spray,
120   And waiting for the spark from heaven to fall.

And once, in winter, on the causeway chill
Where home through flooded fields foot-travellers go,
Have I not passed thee on the wooden bridge,
Wrapped in thy cloak and battling with the snow,
125   Thy face tow'rd Hinksey and its wintry ridge?
And thou hast climbed the hill,
And gained the white brow of the Cumner range;
Turned once to watch, while thick the snowflakes fall,
The line of festal light in Christ-Church hall[6]—
130   Then sought thy straw in some sequestered grange.

But what—I dream! Two hundred years are flown
Since first thy story ran through Oxford halls,
And the grave Glanvil did the tale inscribe
That thou wert wandered from the studious walls
135   To learn strange arts, and join a gipsy-tribe;
And thou from earth art gone
Long since, and in some quiet churchyard laid—
Some country-nook, where o'er thy unknown grave
Tall grasses and white flowering nettles wave,
140   Under a dark, red-fruited yew-tree's shade.

—No, no, thou hast not felt the lapse of hours!
For what wears out the life of mortal men?
'Tis that from change to change their being rolls;
'Tis that repeated shocks, again, again,
145   Exhaust the energy of strongest souls
And numb the elastic powers.
Till having used our nerves with bliss and teen,°   grief
And tired upon a thousand schemes our wit,
To the just-pausing Genius[7] we remit
150   Our worn-out life, and are—what we have been.

Thou hast not lived, why should'st thou perish, so?
Thou hadst *one* aim, *one* business, *one* desire;
Else wert thou long since numbered with the dead!
Else hadst thou spent, like other men, thy fire!
155   The generations of thy peers are fled,
And we ourselves shall go;
But thou possessest an immortal lot,
And we imagine thee exempt from age
And living as thou liv'st on Glanvil's page,
160   Because thou hadst—what we, alas! have not.

For early didst thou leave the world, with powers
Fresh, undiverted to the world without,
Firm to their mark, not spent on other things;
Free from the sick fatigue, the languid doubt,

---

6. The dining hall of Christ Church, an Oxford college.
7. The guardian spirit that the ancients believed accompanied a person through life; here it pauses for only a
moment to receive back the life it has shepherded.

165 Which much to have tried, in much been baffled, brings.
    O life unlike to ours!
  Who fluctuate idly without term or scope,
    Of whom each strives, nor knows for what he strives,
    And each half-lives a hundred different lives;
170   Who wait like thee, but not, like thee, in hope.

Thou waitest for the spark from heaven! and we,
  Light half-believers of our casual creeds,
    Who never deeply felt, nor clearly willed,
    Whose insight never has borne fruit in deeds,
175   Whose vague resolves never have been fulfilled;
    For whom each year we see
  Breeds new beginnings, disappointments new;
    Who hesitate and falter life away,
    And lose to-morrow the ground won to-day—
180   Ah! do not we, wanderer! await it too?

Yes, we await it!—but it still delays,
  And then we suffer! and amongst us one,[8]
    Who most has suffered, takes dejectedly
  His seat upon the intellectual throne;
185   And all his store of sad experience he
    Lays bare of wretched days;
  Tells us his misery's birth and growth and signs,
    And how the dying spark of hope was fed,
    And how the breast was soothed, and how the head,
190   And all his hourly varied anodynes.

This for our wisest! and we others pine,
  And wish the long unhappy dream would end,
    And waive all claim to bliss, and try to bear;
  With close-lipped patience for our only friend,
195   Sad patience, too near neighbour to despair—
    But none has hope like thine!
  Thou through the fields and through the woods dost stray,
    Roaming the country-side, a truant boy,
    Nursing thy project in unclouded joy,
200   And every doubt long blown by time away.

O born in days when wits were fresh and clear,
  And life ran gaily as the sparkling Thames;
    Before this strange disease of modern life,
  With its sick hurry, its divided aims,
205   Its heads o'ertaxed, its palsied hearts, was rife—
    Fly hence, our contact fear!
  Still fly, plunge deeper in the bowering wood!
    Averse, as Dido did with gesture stern
    From her false friend's approach in Hades turn,[9]
210   Wave us away, and keep thy solitude!

---

8. Either Goethe, whom Arnold admired, or Tennyson, whose *In Memoriam* had recently been published.
9. In Virgil's *Aeneid*, Dido, queen of Carthage, kills herself after her lover, Aeneas, deserts her. When they meet in Hades, she turns away sternly.

Still nursing the unconquerable hope,
   Still clutching the inviolable shade,
     With a free, onward impulse brushing through,
By night, the silvered branches of the glade—
215   Far on the forest-skirts, where none pursue,
         On some mild pastoral slope
Emerge, and resting on the moonlit pales
   Freshen thy flowers as in former years
     With dew, or listen with enchanted ears,
220   From the dark dingles,° to the nightingales!   *small wooded valleys*

But fly our paths, our feverish contact fly!
   For strong the infection of our mental strife,
     Which, though it gives no bliss, yet spoils for rest;
And we should win thee from thy own fair life,
225   Like us distracted, and like us unblest.
        Soon, soon thy cheer would die,
Thy hopes grow timorous, and unfixed thy powers,
   And thy clear aims be cross and shifting made;
     And then thy glad perennial youth would fade,
230   Fade, and grow old at last, and die like ours.

Then fly our greetings, fly our speech and smiles!
   —As some grave Tyrian trader,[1] from the sea,
     Descried at sunrise an emerging prow
Lifting the cool-haired creepers stealthily,
235   The fringes of a southward-facing brow
        Among the Aegean isles;
And saw the merry Grecian coaster come,
   Freighted with amber grapes, and Chian wine,
     Green, bursting figs, and tunnies steeped in brine—
240   And knew the intruders on his ancient home,

The young light-hearted masters of the waves—
   And snatched his rudder, and shook out more sail;
     And day and night held on indignantly
O'er the blue Midland waters with the gale,
245   Betwixt the Syrtes[2] and soft Sicily,
        To where the Atlantic raves
Outside the western straits; and unbent sails
   There, where down cloudy cliffs, through sheets of foam,
     Shy traffickers, the dark Iberians come;
250   And on the beach undid his corded bales.[3]

c. 1853   1853

1. From Tyre, capital of ancient Phoenicia, in Northern Africa. The poet urges the solitary scholar to shun modern contacts just as he imagines the Tyrian trader once fled from intrusive Greeks.
2. Shoals off North Africa.
3. The last stanza continues the comparison between the scholar and the Tyrian. According to Herodotus's *History* 4.196, the Carthaginians—who came originally from Tyre—would sail out of the Mediterranean to West Africa, place their bales on the beach, and withdraw to their ships. The timid inhabitants would then set gold by the goods, and withdraw in turn; thus the two sides could do business and never meet. Arnold's "shy traffickers" are not Africans but "dark Iberians" (Spanish or Portuguese). He implies that in them—people reminiscent of the dark-skinned reclusive gypsies who "trade" in the Oxford countryside—the sensitive Tyrian has found others as wary as he is.

from **Culture and Anarchy**[1]

from Sweetness and Light

The disparagers of culture make its motive curiosity; sometimes, indeed, they make its motive mere exclusiveness and vanity. The culture which is supposed to plume itself on a smattering of Greek and Latin is a culture which is begotten by nothing so intellectual as curiosity; it is valued either out of sheer vanity and ignorance or else as an engine of social and class distinction, separating its holder, like a badge or title, from other people who have not got it. No serious man would call this *culture,* or attach any value to it, as culture, at all. To find the real ground for the very different estimate which serious people will set upon culture, we must find some motive for culture in the terms of which may lie a real ambiguity; and such a motive the word *curiosity* gives us.

I have before now pointed out that we English do not, like the foreigners, use this word in a good sense as well as in a bad sense. With us the word is always used in a somewhat disapproving sense. A liberal and intelligent eagerness about the things of the mind may be meant by a foreigner when he speaks of curiosity, but with us the word always conveys a certain notion of frivolous and unedifying activity. In the *Quarterly Review,* some little time ago, was an estimate of the celebrated French critic, M. Sainte-Beuve,[2] and a very inadequate estimate it in my judgment was. And its inadequacy consisted chiefly in this: that in our English way it left out of sight the double sense really involved in the word *curiosity,* thinking enough was said to stamp M. Sainte-Beuve with blame if it was said that he was impelled in his operations as a critic by curiosity, and omitting either to perceive that M. Sainte-Beuve himself, and many other people with him, would consider that this was praiseworthy and not blameworthy, or to point out why it ought really to be accounted worthy of blame and not of praise. For as there is a curiosity about intellectual matters which is futile, and merely a disease, so there is certainly a curiosity,—a desire after the things of the mind simply for their own sakes and for the pleasure of seeing them as they are,— which is, in an intelligent being, natural and laudable. Nay, and the very desire to see things as they are implies a balance and regulation of mind which is not often attained without fruitful effort, and which is the very opposite of the blind and diseased impulse of mind which is what we mean to blame when we blame curiosity. Montesquieu[3] says: "The first motive which ought to impel us to study is the desire to augment the excellence of our nature, and to render an intelligent being yet more intelligent." This is the true ground to assign for the genuine scientific passion, however manifested, and for culture, viewed simply as a fruit of this passion; and it is a worthy ground, even though we let the term *curiosity* stand to describe it.

But there is of culture another view, in which not solely the scientific passion, the sheer desire to see things as they are, natural and proper in an intelligent being,

---

1. Arnold's most important work of social criticism, *Culture and Anarchy* (1869) grew out of his final Oxford lecture in 1867. Deploring English pride in "doing as one likes," Arnold connected the self-serving behavior of all classes to the worst effects of laissez-faire capitalism. He felt that Britain was heading toward anarchy; no one seemed to have any concern for the public good. The best of Western culture, Arnold contended, depends on a balance between the Judeo-Christian emphasis on moral conduct (Hebraism), and the Greek ideal of intellectual and artistic cultivation (Hellenism). But in his view a Puritan "strictness of conscience" was now impeding a classical "spontaneity of consciousness." There was only one way to bridge the gap between privileged "Barbarians" (the aristocracy), intolerant "Philistines" (the middle classes), and the uneducated "Populace" (the working classes): by spreading to all parts of society a Hellenistic respect for beauty and intellect—what Arnold termed "sweetness and light."

2. Charles Augustine Sainte-Beuve (1804–1869), French critic whom Arnold admired.

3. Baron de la Brede et de Montesquieu (1689–1755), French political and legal philosopher.

appears as the ground of it. There is a view in which all the love of our neighbour, the impulses towards action, help, and beneficence, the desire for removing human error, clearing human confusion, and diminishing human misery, the noble aspiration to leave the world better and happier than we found it,—motives eminently such as are called social,—come in as part of the grounds of culture, and the main and pre-eminent part. Culture is then properly described not as having its origin in curiosity, but as having its origin in the love of perfection; it is *a study of perfection*. It moves by the force, not merely or primarily of the scientific passion for pure knowledge, but also of the moral and social passion for doing good. As, in the first view of it, we took for its worthy motto Montesquieu's words: "To render an intelligent being yet more intelligent!" so, in the second view of it, there is no better motto which it can have than these words of Bishop Wilson: "To make reason and the will of God prevail!"[4] * * *

The pursuit of perfection, then, is the pursuit of sweetness and light.[5] He who works for sweetness and light, works to make reason and the will of God prevail. He who works for machinery, he who works for hatred, works only for confusion. Culture looks beyond machinery, culture hates hatred; culture has one great passion, the passion for sweetness and light. It has one even yet greater!—the passion for making them *prevail*. It is not satisfied till we *all* come to a perfect man; it knows that the sweetness and light of the few must be imperfect until the raw and unkindled masses of humanity are touched with sweetness and light. If I have not shrunk from saying that we must work for sweetness and light, so neither have I shrunk from saying that we must have a broad basis, must have sweetness and light for as many as possible. Again and again I have insisted how those are the happy moments of humanity, how those are the marking epochs of a people's life, how those are the flowering times for literature and art and all the creative power of genius, when there is a *national* glow of life and thought, when the whole of society is in the fullest measure permeated by thought, sensible to beauty, intelligent and alive. Only it must be *real* thought and *real* beauty; *real* sweetness and *real* light. Plenty of people will try to give the masses, as they call them, an intellectual food prepared and adapted in the way they think proper for the actual condition of the masses. The ordinary popular literature is an example of this way of working on the masses. Plenty of people will try to indoctrinate the masses with the set of ideas and judgments constituting the creed of their own profession or party. Our religious and political organisations give an example of this way of working on the masses. I condemn neither way; but culture works differently. It does not try to teach down to the level of inferior classes; it does not try to win them for this or that sect of its own, with ready-made judgments and watchwords. It seeks to do away with classes; to make the best that has been thought and known in the world current everywhere; to make all men live in an atmosphere of sweetness and light, where they may use ideas, as it uses them itself, freely,—nourished, and not bound by them.

This is the *social idea*; and the men of culture are the true apostles of equality. The great men of culture are those who have had a passion for diffusing, for making prevail, for carrying from one end of society to the other, the best knowledge, the best

4. Thomas Wilson (1663–1755), Bishop of Sodor and Man. His *Maxims*, though little known, were a favorite of Arnold's.
5. The phrase comes from a fable in Swift's *The Battle of the Books* (1704): the Bee (representing ancient culture) ventures forth to fill its hive with honey and wax for light-giving candles, but the home-bound Spider (representing modern culture) produces from itself only cobwebs and poison. The Bee thus provides "the two noblest of things, which are sweetness and light."

ideas of their time; who have laboured to divest knowledge of all that was harsh, uncouth, difficult, abstract, professional, exclusive; to humanise it, to make it effi-cient outside the clique of the cultivated and learned, yet still remaining the *best* knowledge and thought of the time, and a true source, therefore, of sweetness and light. Such a man was Abelard in the Middle Ages, in spite of all his imperfections;[6] and thence the boundless emotion and enthusiasm which Abelard excited. Such were Lessing and Herder in Germany, at the end of the last century;[7] and their services to Germany were in this way inestimably precious. Generations will pass, and literary monuments will accumulate, and works far more perfect than the works of Lessing and Herder will be produced in Germany; and yet the names of these two men will fill a German with a reverence and enthusiasm such as the names of the most gifted mas-ters will hardly awaken. And why? Because they *humanised* knowledge; because they broadened the basis of life and intelligence; because they worked powerfully to diffuse sweetness and light, to make reason and the will of God prevail. With Saint Augus-tine they said: "Let us not leave thee alone to make in the secret of thy knowledge, as thou didst before the creation of the firmament, the division of light from darkness; let the children of thy spirit, placed in their firmament, make their light shine upon the earth, mark the division of night and day, and announce the revolution of the times; for the old order is passed, and the new arises; the night is spent, the day is come forth; and thou shalt crown the year with thy blessing, when thou shalt send forth labourers into thy harvest sown by other hands than theirs; when thou shalt send forth new labourers to new seed-times, whereof the harvest shall be not yet."[8]

from *Doing as One Likes*

I have been trying to show that culture is, or ought to be, the study and pursuit of per-fection; and that of perfection as pursued by culture, beauty and intelligence, or, in other words, sweetness and light, are the main characters. But hitherto I have been insisting chiefly on beauty, or sweetness, as a character of perfection. To complete rightly my design, it evidently remains to speak also of intelligence, or light, as a character of perfection.

First, however, I ought perhaps to notice that, both here and on the other side of the Atlantic, all sorts of objections are raised against the "religion of culture," as the objectors mockingly call it, which I am supposed to be promulgating. It is said to be a religion proposing parmaceti,[1] or some scented salve or other, as a cure for human miseries; a religion breathing a spirit of cultivated inaction, making its believer refuse to lend a hand at uprooting the definite evils on all sides of us, and filling him with antipathy against the reforms and reformers which try to extirpate them. In general, it is summed up as being not practical, or,—as some critics familiarly put it,—all moonshine. That Alcibiades, the editor of the *Morning Star*,[2] taunts me, as its pro-mulgator, with living out of the world and knowing nothing of life and men. That great austere toiler, the editor of the *Daily Telegraph*, upbraids me,—but kindly, and

6. Peter Abelard (1079–1142), French philosopher and theologian, whose love affair with his student, Héloise, ended tragically.
7. Gotthold Ephraim Lessing (1729–1781), critic and playwright, an important figure in the development of German Naturalism; Johann Gottfried Herder (1744–1803), critic and historian, a proponent of literary and historical relativism.
8. *Confessions* (xiii.18) of St. Augustine (354–430),

Bishop of Hippo, Church father, theologian, and auto-biographer.
1. Spermaceti, derived from the oil of the sperm whale, was used in ointments and cosmetics.
2. A penny paper representing the Radicals' position, of which Arnold disapproved. He ironically compares the paper's puritain editor with the dissolute but brilliant Alcibiades, who led the Athenians during the Pelopon-nesian War.

more in sorrow than in anger,—for trifling with aesthetics and poetical fancies, while he himself, in that arsenal of his in Fleet Street,[3] is bearing the burden and heat of the day. An intelligent American newspaper, the *Nation*, says that it is very easy to sit in one's study and find fault with the course of modern society, but the thing is to propose practical improvements for it. While, finally, Mr Frederic Harrison, in a very good-tempered and witty satire, which makes me quite understand his having apparently achieved such a conquest of my young Prussian friend, Arminius, at last gets moved to an almost stern moral impatience, to behold, as he says, "Death, sin, cruelty stalk among us, filling their maws with innocence and youth," and me, in the midst of the general tribulation, handing out my pouncet-box.[4]

It is impossible that all these remonstrances and reproofs should not affect me, and I shall try my very best, in completing my design and in speaking of light as one of the characters of perfection, and of culture as giving us light, to profit by the objections I have heard and read, and to drive at practice as much as I can, by showing the communications and passages into practical life from the doctrine which I am inculcating.

It is said that a man with my theories of sweetness and light is full of antipathy against the rougher or coarser movements going on around him, that he will not lend a hand to the humble operation of uprooting evil by their means, and that therefore the believers in action grow impatient with him. But what if rough and coarse action, ill-calculated action, action with insufficient light, is, and has for a long time been, our bane? What if our urgent want now is, not to act at any price, but rather to lay in a stock of light for our difficulties? In that case, to refuse to lend a hand to the rougher and coarser movements going on round us, to make the primary need, both for oneself and others, to consist in enlightening ourselves and qualifying ourselves to act less at random, is surely the best and in real truth the most practical line our endeavours can take. So that if I can show what my opponents call rough or coarse action, but what I would rather call random and ill-regulated action,—action with insufficient light, action pursued because we like to be doing something and doing it as we please, and do not like the trouble of thinking and the severe constraint of any kind of rule,—if I can show this to be, at the present moment, a practical mischief and dangerous to us, then I have found a practical use for light in correcting this state of things, and have only to exemplify how, in cases which fall under everybody's observation, it may deal with it.

When I began to speak of culture, I insisted on our bondage to machinery, on our proneness to value machinery as an end in itself, without looking beyond it to the end for which alone, in truth, it is valuable. Freedom, I said, was one of those things which we thus worshipped in itself, without enough regarding the ends for which freedom is to be desired. In our common notions and talk about freedom, we eminently show our idolatry of machinery. Our prevalent notion is,—and I quoted a number of instances to prove it,—that it is a most happy and important thing for a man merely to be able to do as he likes. On what he is to do when he is thus free to do as he likes, we do not lay so much stress. Our familiar praise of the British Constitution under which we live, is that it is a system of checks,—a system which stops

---

3. Location of most British newspaper offices.
4. Frederic Harrison, barrister and supporter of working-class causes, satirized Arnold's ideas in "Culture, A Dialogue" (*Fortnightly*, Nov. 1867). In his article Harrison pretended to discuss social issues with "Arminius," a fic-

tional Prussian whom Arnold had created in *Friendship's Garland* (1866–1871). Harrison compares Arnold to the foppish courtier in *Henry IV, Part 1*, who uses parmaceti salve and a perfume or "pouncet" box (1.3.37,58).

and paralyses any power in interfering with the free action of individuals. To this effect Mr Bright,[5] who loves to walk in the old ways of the Constitution, said forcibly in one of his great speeches, what many other people are every day saying less forcibly, that the central idea of English life and politics is *the assertion of personal liberty*. Evidently this is so; but evidently, also, as feudalism, which with its ideas and habits of subordination was for many centuries silently behind the British Constitution, dies out, and we are left with nothing but our system of checks, and our notion of its being the great right and happiness of an Englishman to do as far as possible what he likes, we are in danger of drifting towards anarchy. We have not the notion, so familiar on the Continent and to antiquity, of *the State*,—the nation in its collective and corporate character, entrusted with stringent powers for the general advantage, and controlling individual wills in the name of an interest wider than that of individuals. We say, what is very true, that this notion is often made instrumental to tyranny; we say that a State is in reality made up of the individuals who compose it, and that every individual is the best judge of his own interests. Our leading class is an aristocracy, and no aristocracy likes the notion of a State-authority greater than itself, with a stringent administrative machinery superseding the decorative inutilities of lord-lieutenancy, deputy-lieutenancy, and the *posse comitatus*,[6] which are all in its own hands. Our middle class, the great representative of trade and Dissent, with its maxims of every man for himself in business, every man for himself in religion, dreads a powerful administration which might somehow interfere with it; and besides, it has its own decorative inutilities of vestrymanship and guardianship, which are to this class what lord-lieutenancy and the county magistracy are to the aristocratic class, and a stringent administration might either take these functions out of its hands, or prevent its exercising them in its own comfortable, independent manner, as at present.

Then as to our working class. This class, pressed constantly by the hard daily compulsion of material wants, is naturally the very centre and stronghold of our national idea, that it is man's ideal right and felicity to do as he likes. I think I have somewhere related how M. Michelet said to me of the people of France, that it was "a nation of barbarians civilised by the conscription."[7] He meant that through their military service the idea of public duty and of discipline was brought to the mind of these masses, in other respects so raw and uncultivated. Our masses are quite as raw and uncultivated as the French; and so far from their having the idea of public duty and of discipline, superior to the individual's self-will, brought to their mind by a universal obligation of military service, such as that of the conscription,—so far from their having this, the very idea of a conscription is so at variance with our English notion of the prime right and blessedness of doing as one likes, that I remember the manager of the Clay Cross works in Derbyshire told me during the Crimean war, when our want of soldiers was much felt and some people were talking of a conscription, that sooner than submit to a conscription the population of that district would flee to the mines, and lead a sort of Robin Hood life under ground.

For a long time, as I have said, the strong feudal habits of subordination and deference continued to tell upon the working class. The modern spirit has now almost

---

5. John Bright (1811–1889), Quaker radical who led the left wing of the Liberal Party under Gladstone.
6. Power of the county (Latin); a "posse" was an outdated method of preserving public order by local authority

rather than by the government.
7. From Arnold's *The Popular Education of France* (1861); Jules Michelet (1798–1874), French historian.

entirely dissolved those habits, and the anarchical tendency of our worship of freedom in and for itself, of our superstitious faith, as I say, in machinery, is becoming
very manifest. More and more, because of this our blind faith in machinery, because
of our want of light to enable us to look beyond machinery to the end for which
machinery is valuable, this and that man, and this and that body of men, all over the
country, are beginning to assert and put in practice an Englishman's right to do what
he likes; his right to march where he likes, meet where he likes, enter where he likes,
hoot as he likes, threaten as he likes, smash as he likes. All this, I say, tends to anarchy; and though a number of excellent people, and particularly my friends of the Liberal or progressive party, as they call themselves, are kind enough to reassure us by
saying that these are trifles, that a few transient outbreaks of rowdyism signify nothing, that our system of liberty is one which itself cures all the evils which it works,
that the educated and intelligent classes stand in overwhelming strength and majestic repose, ready, like our military force in riots, to act at a moment's notice,—yet
one finds that one's Liberal friends generally say this because they have such faith in
themselves and their nostrums,[8] when they shall return, as the public welfare
requires, to place and power. But this faith of theirs one cannot exactly share, when
one has so long had them and their nostrums at work, and sees that they have not
prevented our coming to our present embarrassed condition. And one finds, also,
that the outbreaks of rowdyism tend to become less and less of trifles, to become
more frequent rather than less frequent; and that meanwhile our educated and intelligent classes remain in their majestic repose, and somehow or other, whatever happens, their overwhelming strength, like our military force in riots, never does act.

How, indeed, *should* their overwhelming strength act, when the man who gives
an inflammatory lecture, or breaks down the park railings,[9] or invades a Secretary of
State's office, is only following an Englishman's impulse to do as he likes; and our
own conscience tells us that we ourselves have always regarded this impulse as something primary and sacred? Mr Murphy lectures at Birmingham,[1] and showers on the
Catholic population of that town "words," says the Home Secretary, "only fit to be
addressed to thieves or murderers." What then? Mr Murphy has his own reasons of
several kinds. He suspects the Roman Catholic Church of designs upon Mrs Murphy;
and he says if mayors and magistrates do not care for their wives and daughters, he
does. But, above all, he is doing as he likes; or, in worthier language, asserting his personal liberty. "I will carry out my lectures if they walk over my body as a dead corpse;
and I say to the Mayor of Birmingham that he is my servant while I am in Birmingham, and as my servant he must do his duty and protect me." Touching and beautiful
words, which find a sympathetic chord in every British bosom! The moment it is
plainly put before us that a man is asserting his personal liberty, we are half disarmed;
because we are believers in freedom, and not in some dream of a right reason to
which the assertion of our freedom is to be subordinated. Accordingly, the Secretary
of State had to say that although the lecturer's language was "only fit to be addressed
to thieves or murderers," yet, "I do not think he is to be deprived, I do not think that
anything I have said could justify the inference that he is to be deprived, of the right
of protection in a place built by him for the purpose of these lectures; because the

8. Panaceas, quack medicine.
9. On July 23, 1866, the Reform League organized a mass
meeting in Hyde Park. When they were refused entrance,
the demonstrators broke down the park railings and trampled the flowers. The incident was widely viewed as a

symptom of impending anarchy.
1. In 1867 William Murphy, an anti-Catholic agitator,
delivered a series of lectures in Birmingham that led to
riots.

language was not language which afforded grounds for a criminal prosecution." No, nor to be silenced by Mayor, or Home Secretary, or any administrative authority on earth, simply on their notion of what is discreet and reasonable! This is in perfect consonance with our public opinion, and with our national love for the assertion of personal liberty. * * *

There are many things to be said on behalf of this exclusive attention of ours to liberty, and of the relaxed habits of government which it has engendered. It is very easy to mistake or to exaggerate the sort of anarchy from which we are in danger through them. We are not in danger from Fenianism,[2] fierce and turbulent as it may show itself; for against this our conscience is free enough to let us act resolutely and put forth our overwhelming strength the moment there is any real need for it. In the first place, it never was any part of our creed that the great right and blessedness of an Irishman, or, indeed, of anybody on earth except an Englishman, is to do as he likes; and we can have no scruple at all about abridging, if necessary, a non-Englishman's assertion of personal liberty. The British Constitution, its checks, and its prime virtues, are for Englishmen. We may extend them to others out of love and kindness; but we find no real divine law written on our hearts constraining us so to extend them. And then the difference between an Irish Fenian and an English rough is so immense, and the case, in dealing with the Fenian, so much more clear! He is so evidently desperate and dangerous, a man of a conquered race, a Papist, with centuries of ill-usage to inflame him against us, with an alien religion established in his country by us at his expense, with no admiration of our institutions, no love of our virtues, no talents for our business, no turn for our comfort! Show him our symbolical Truss Manufactory on the finest site in Europe,[3] and tell him that British industrialism and individualism can bring a man to that, and he remains cold! Evidently, if we deal tenderly with a sentimentalist like this, it is out of pure philanthropy.

But with the Hyde Park rioter how different! He is our own flesh and blood; he is a Protestant; he is framed by nature to do as we do, hate what we hate, love what we love; he is capable of feeling the symbolical force of the Truss Manufactory; the question of questions, for him, is a wages question. That beautiful sentence Sir Daniel Gooch[4] quoted to the Swindon workmen, and which I treasure as Mrs Gooch's Golden Rule, or the Divine Injunction "Be ye Perfect" done into British,—the sentence Sir Daniel Gooch's mother repeated to him every morning when he was a boy going to work:—"*Ever remember, my dear Dan, that you should look forward to being some day manager of that concern!*"—this fruitful maxim is perfectly fitted to shine forth in the heart of the Hyde Park rough also, and to be his guiding-star through life. He has no visionary schemes of revolution and transformation, though of course he would like his class to rule, as the aristocratic class like their class to rule, and the middle class theirs. But meanwhile our social machine is a little out of order; there are a good many people in our paradisiacal centres of industrialism and individualism taking the bread out of one another's mouths. The rough has not yet quite found his groove and settled down to his work, and so he is just asserting his personal liberty a little, going where he likes, assembling where he likes, bawling as he likes, hustling as he likes. Just as the rest of us,—as the country squires in the aristocratic class, as the political dissenters in the middle class,—he has no idea of a *State*, of the nation in its collective and corporate character controlling, as government, the free swing of this or that

2. A movement dedicated to the overthrow of British rule in Ireland.
3. Coles' Truss Manufactory occupied a corner of Trafalgar Square, called "the finest site in Europe" by Sir Robert Peel. A truss is a padded belt worn to support an abdominal rupture or hernia.
4. Sir Daniel Gooch (1816–1889), railway engineer and inventor, chairman of the Great Western Railway.

one of its members in the name of the higher reason of all of them, his own as well as that of others. He sees the rich, the aristocratic class, in occupation of the executive government, and so if he is stopped from making Hyde Park a bear-garden or the streets impassable, he says he is being butchered by the aristocracy.

His apparition is somewhat embarrassing, because too many cooks spoil the broth; because, while the aristocratic and middle classes have long been doing as they like with great vigour, he has been too undeveloped and submissive hitherto to join in the game; and now, when he does come, he comes in immense numbers, and is rather raw and rough. But he does not break many laws, or not many at one time; and, as our laws were made for very different circumstances from our present (but always with an eye to Englishmen doing as they like), and as the clear letter of the law must be against our Englishman who does as he likes and not only the spirit of the law and public policy, and as Government must neither have any discretionary power nor act resolutely on its own interpretation of the law if any one disputes it, it is evident our laws give our playful giant, in doing as he likes, considerable advantage. Besides, even if he can be clearly proved to commit an illegality in doing as he likes, there is always the resource of not putting the law in force, or of abolishing it. So he has his way, and if he has his way he is soon satisfied for the time. However, he falls into the habit of taking it oftener and oftener, and at last begins to create by his operations a confusion of which mischievous people can take advantage, and which, at any rate, by troubling the common course of business throughout the country, tends to cause distress, and so to increase the sort of anarchy and social disintegration which had previously commenced. And thus that profound sense of settled order and security, without which a society like ours cannot live and grow at all, sometimes seems to be beginning to threaten us with taking its departure.

Now, if culture, which simply means trying to perfect oneself, and one's mind as part of oneself, brings us light, and if light shows us that there is nothing so very blessed in merely doing as one likes, that the worship of the mere freedom to do as one likes is worship of machinery, that the really blessed thing is to like what right reason ordains, and to follow her authority, then we have got a practical benefit out of culture. We have got a much wanted principle, a principle of authority, to counteract the tendency to anarchy which seems to be threatening us. * * *

Well, then, what if we tried to rise above the idea of class to the idea of the whole community, *the State*, and to find our centre of light and authority there? Every one of us has the idea of country, as a sentiment; hardly any one of us has the idea of *the State*, as a working power. And why? Because we habitually live in our ordinary selves, which do not carry us beyond the ideas and wishes of the class to which we happen to belong. And we are all afraid of giving to the State too much power, because we only conceive of the State as something equivalent to the class in occupation of the executive government, and are afraid of that class abusing power to its own purposes. If we strengthen the State with the aristocratic class in occupation of the executive government, we imagine we are delivering ourselves up captive to the ideas and wishes of our fierce aristocratical baronet; if with the middle class in occupation of the executive government, to those of our truculent middle-class Dissenting minister;[5] if with the working class, to those of its notorious tribune, Mr Bradlaugh.[6] And with much justice; owing to the exaggerated notion which we English, as I have said, entertain of the right and blessedness of the mere doing as one

5. Rev. William Cattle, chairman at William Murphy's anti-Catholic lectures (see page 2034, n. 1).

6. Charles Bradlaugh, radical agitator, eventually the first aetheist Member of Parliament.

likes, of the affirming oneself, and oneself just as it is. People of the aristocratic class want to affirm their ordinary selves, their likings and dislikings; people of the middle class the same, people of the working class the same. By our everyday selves, however, we are separate, personal, at war; we are only safe from one another's tyranny when no one has any power; and this safety, in its turn, cannot save us from anarchy. And when, therefore, anarchy presents itself as a danger to us, we know not where to turn.

But by our *best self* we are united, impersonal, at harmony. We are in no peril from giving authority to this, because it is the truest friend we all of us can have; and when anarchy is a danger to us, to this authority we may turn with sure trust. Well, and this is the very self which culture, or the study of perfection, seeks to develop in us; at the expense of our old untransformed self, taking pleasure only in doing what it likes or is used to do, and exposing us to the risk of clashing with every one else who is doing the same! So that our poor culture, which is flouted as so unpractical, leads us to the very ideas capable of meeting the great want of our present embarrassed times! We want an authority, and we find nothing but jealous classes, checks, and a dead-lock; culture suggests the idea of the State. We find no basis for a firm State-power in our ordinary selves; culture suggests one to us in our *best self*.[7] * * *

from *Hebraism and Hellenism*

This fundamental ground is our preference of doing to thinking. Now this preference is a main element in our nature, and as we study it we find ourselves opening up a number of large questions on every side.

Let me go back for a moment to Bishop Wilson, who says: "First, never go against the best light you have; secondly, take care that your light be not darkness."[1] We show, as a nation, laudable energy and persistence in walking according to the best light we have, but are not quite careful enough, perhaps, to see that our light be not darkness. This is only another version of the old story that energy is our strong point and favourable characteristic, rather than intelligence. But we may give to this idea a more general form still, in which it will have a yet larger range of application. We may regard this energy driving at practice, this paramount sense of the obligation of duty, self-control, and work, this earnestness in going manfully with the best light we have, as one force. And we may regard the intelligence driving at those ideas which are, after all, the basis of right practice, the ardent sense for all the new and changing combinations of them which man's development brings with it, the indomitable impulse to know and adjust them perfectly, as another force. And these two forces we may regard as in some sense rivals,—rivals not by the necessity of their own nature, but as exhibited in man and his history,—and rivals dividing the empire of the world between them. And to give these forces names from the two races of men who have supplied the most signal and splendid manifestations of them, we may call them respectively the forces of Hebraism and Hellenism.[2]

7. Chapter 3, omitted here, explores the class-bound "ordinary selves" that Arnold wishes to transcend: the "Barbarian" aristocracy who value individualism, courage, and athleticism over intellect and sensitivity; the middle-class Philistines who stubbornly resist new ideas; and the dangerously "raw and half-developed" working class he calls simply "the Populace."
1. Quoting Thomas Wilson, *Maxims* (see page 2030, n. 4).

2. In Arnold's view Hebraism (the Judeo-Christian tradition) emphasizes duty, industriousness, and a sense of sin. In contrast, Hellenism (the Greek tradition) values rationality, "clearness of mind," and the quest for perfection. While Arnold emphasizes the importance of both traditions, it is Hellenism that he associates with sweetness and light.

Hebraism and Hellenism,—between these two points of influence moves our world. At one time it feels more powerfully the attraction of one of them, at another time of the other; and it ought to be, though it never is, evenly and happily balanced between them.

The final aim of both Hellenism and Hebraism, as of all great spiritual disciplines, is no doubt the same: man's perfection or salvation. The very language which they both of them use in schooling us to reach this aim is often identical. * * *

Still, they pursue this aim by very different courses. The uppermost idea with Hellenism is to see things as they really are; the uppermost idea with Hebraism is conduct and obedience. Nothing can do away with this ineffaceable difference. The Greek quarrel with the body and its desires is, that they hinder right thinking; the Hebrew quarrel with them is, that they hinder right acting. * * *

* * * Eighteen hundred years ago it was altogether the hour of Hebraism. Primitive Christianity was legitimately and truly the ascendant force in the world at that time, and the way of mankind's progress lay through its full development. Another hour in man's development began in the fifteenth century, and the main road of his progress then lay for a time through Hellenism. Puritanism was no longer the central current of the world's progress, it was a side stream crossing the central current and checking it. The cross and the check may have been necessary and salutary, but that does not do away with the essential difference between the main stream of man's advance and a cross or side stream. For more than two hundred years the main stream of man's advance has moved towards knowing himself and the world, seeing things as they are, spontaneity of consciousness; the main impulse of a great part, and that the strongest part, of our nation has been towards strictness of conscience. They have made the secondary the principal at the wrong moment, and the principal they have at the wrong moment treated as secondary. This contravention of the natural order has produced, as such contravention always must produce, a certain confusion and false movement, of which we are now beginning to feel, in almost every direction, the inconvenience. In all directions our habitual courses of action seem to be losing efficaciousness, credit, and control, both with others and even with ourselves. Everywhere we see the beginnings of confusion, and we want a clue to some sound order and authority. This we can only get by going back upon the actual instincts and forces which rule our life, seeing them as they really are, connecting them with other instincts and forces, and enlarging our whole view and rule of life.

from *Porro Unum Est Necessarium*[1]

The matter here opened is so large, and the trains of thought to which it gives rise are so manifold, that we must be careful to limit ourselves scrupulously to what has a direct bearing upon our actual discussion. We have found that at the bottom of our present unsettled state, so full of the seeds of trouble, lies the notion of its being the prime right and happiness, for each of us, to affirm himself, and his ordinary self; to be doing, and to be doing freely and as he likes. We have found at the bottom of it the disbelief in right reason as a lawful authority. It was easy to show from

---

1. In Luke 10.42 Jesus tells Mary that only "one thing is needful"; he appears to mean faith. According to Arnold, the Puritan middle classes think "the one thing needful" is their own narrow "Hebraic" sense of moral conduct.

our practice and current history that this is so; but it was impossible to show why it is so without taking a somewhat wider sweep and going into things a little more deeply. Why, in fact, should good, well-meaning, energetic, sensible people, like the bulk of our countrymen, come to have such light belief in right reason, and such an exaggerated value for their own independent doing, however crude? The answer is: because of an exclusive and excessive development in them, without due allowance for time, place, and circumstance, of that side of human nature, and that group of human forces, to which we have given the general name of Hebraism. Because they have thought their real and only important homage was owed to a power concerned with their obedience rather than with their intelligence, a power interested in the moral side of their nature almost exclusively. Thus they have been led to regard in themselves, as the one thing needful, *strictness of conscience*, the staunch adherence to some fixed law of doing we have got already, instead of *spontaneity of consciousness*, which tends continually to enlarge our whole law of doing. They have fancied themselves to have in their religion a sufficient basis for the whole of their life fixed and certain for ever, a full law of conduct and a full law of thought, so far as thought is needed, as well; whereas what they really have is a law of conduct, a law of unexampled power for enabling them to war against the law of sin in their members and not to serve it in the lusts thereof. The book which contains this invaluable law they call the Word of God, and attribute to it, as I have said, and as, indeed, is perfectly well known, a reach and sufficiency co-extensive with all the wants of human nature.

This might, no doubt, be so, if humanity were not the composite thing it is, if it had only, or in quite overpowering eminence, a moral side, and the group of instincts and powers which we call moral. But it has besides, and in notable eminence, an intellectual side, and the group of instincts and powers which we call intellectual. No doubt, mankind makes in general its progress in a fashion which gives at one time full swing to one of these groups of instincts, at another time to the other; and man's faculties are so intertwined, that when his moral side, and the current of force which we call Hebraism, is uppermost, this side will manage somehow to provide, or appear to provide, satisfaction for his intellectual needs; and when his intellectual side, and the current of force which we call Hellenism, is uppermost, this again will provide, or appear to provide, satisfaction for men's moral needs. But sooner or later it becomes manifest that when the two sides of humanity proceed in this fashion of alternate preponderance, and not of mutual understanding and balance, the side which is uppermost does not really provide in a satisfactory manner for the needs of the side which is undermost, and a state of confusion is, sooner or later, the result. The Hellenic half of our nature, bearing rule, makes a sort of provision for the Hebrew half, but it turns out to be an inadequate provision; and again the Hebrew half of our nature, bearing rule, makes a sort of provision for the Hellenic half, but this, too, turns out to be an inadequate provision. The true and smooth order of humanity's development is not reached in either way. And therefore, while we willingly admit with the Christian apostle that the world by wisdom,—that is, by the isolated preponderance of its intellectual impulses,—knew not God, or the true order of things, it is yet necessary, also, to set up a sort of converse to this proposition, and to say likewise (what is equally true) that the world by Puritanism knew not God. And it is on this converse of the apostle's proposition that it is particularly needful to insist in our own country just at present.

Here, indeed, is the answer to many criticisms which have been addressed to all that we have said in praise of sweetness and light. Sweetness and light evidently have to do with the bent or side in humanity which we call Hellenic. Greek intelligence has obviously for its essence the instinct for what Plato calls the true, firm, intelligible law of things; the law of light, of seeing things as they are. Even in the natural sciences, where the Greeks had not time and means adequately to apply this instinct, and where we have gone a great deal further than they did, it is this instinct which is the root of the whole matter and the ground of all our success; and this instinct the world has mainly learnt of the Greeks, inasmuch as they are humanity's most signal manifestation of it. Greek art, again, Greek beauty, have their root in the same impulse to see things as they really are, inasmuch as Greek art and beauty rest on fidelity to nature,—the *best* nature,—and on a delicate discrimination of what this best nature is. To say we work for sweetness and light, then, is only another way of saying that we work for Hellenism. But, oh! cry many people, sweetness and light are not enough; you must put strength or energy along with them, and make a kind of trinity of strength, sweetness and light, and then, perhaps, you may do some good. That is to say, we are to join Hebraism, strictness of the moral conscience, and manful walking by the best light we have, together with Hellenism, inculcate both, and rehearse the praises of both.

Or, rather, we may praise both in conjunction, but we must be careful to praise Hebraism most. "Culture," says an acute, though somewhat rigid critic, Mr Sidgwick,[2] "diffuses sweetness and light. I do not undervalue these blessings, but religion gives fire and strength, and the world wants fire and strength even more than sweetness and light." By religion, let me explain, Mr Sidgwick here means particularly that Puritanism on the insufficiency of which I have been commenting and to which he says I am unfair. Now, no doubt, it is possible to be a fanatical partisan of light and the instincts which push us to it, a fanatical enemy of strictness of moral conscience and the instincts which push us to it. A fanaticism of this sort deforms and vulgarises the well-known work, in some respects so remarkable, of the late Mr Buckle.[3] Such a fanaticism carries its own mark with it, in lacking sweetness; and its own penalty, in that, lacking sweetness, it comes in the end to lack light too. And the Greeks,—the great exponents of humanity's bent for sweetness and light united, of its perception that the truth of things must be at the same time beauty,—singularly escaped the fanaticism which we moderns, whether we Hellenise or whether we Hebraise, are so apt to show. They arrived,—though failing, as has been said, to give adequate practical satisfaction to the claims of man's moral side,—at the idea of a comprehensive adjustment of the claims of both the sides in man, the moral as well as the intellectual, of a full estimate of both, and of a reconciliation of both; an idea which is philosophically of the greatest value, and the best of lessons for us moderns. So we ought to have no difficulty in conceding to Mr Sidgwick that manful walking by the best light one has,—fire and strength as he calls it,—has its high value as well as culture, the endeavour to see things in their truth and beauty, the pursuit of sweetness and light. But whether at this or that time, and to this or that

2. Henry Sidgwick, Cambridge philosopher who in 1867 had published a response to *Culture and Its Enemies*, the lecture that became the first chapter of *Culture and Anarchy*.

3. Henry Thomas Buckle, whose *History of Civilisation in England* (1857–1861) attributed historical events to geography.

set of persons, one ought to insist most on the praises of fire and strength, or on the praises of sweetness and light, must depend, one would think, on the circumstances and needs of that particular time and those particular persons. And all that we have been saying, and indeed any glance at the world around us shows that with us, with the most respectable and strongest part of us, the ruling force is now, and long has been, a Puritan force,—the care for fire and strength, strictness of conscience, Hebraism, rather than the care for sweetness and light, spontaneity of consciousness, Hellenism.

Well, then, what is the good of our now rehearsing the praises of fire and strength to ourselves, who dwell too exclusively on them already? When Mr Sidgwick says so broadly, that the world wants fire and strength even more than sweetness and light, is he not carried away by a turn for broad generalisation? does he not forget that the world is not all of one piece, and every piece with the same needs at the same time? It may be true that the Roman world at the beginning of our era, or Leo the Tenth's Court at the time of the Reformation, or French society in the eighteenth century,[4] needed fire and strength even more than sweetness and light. But can it be said that the Barbarians who overran the empire needed fire and strength even more than sweetness and light; or that the Puritans needed them more; or that Mr Murphy, the Birmingham lecturer, and his friends, need them more?

The Puritan's great danger is that he imagines himself in possession of a rule telling him the *unum necessarium*, or one thing needful, and that he then remains satisfied with a very crude conception of what this rule really is and what it tells him, thinks he has now knowledge and henceforth needs only to act, and, in this dangerous state of assurance and self-satisfaction, proceeds to give full swing to a number of the instincts of his ordinary self. Some of the instincts of his ordinary self he has, by the help of his rule of life, conquered; but others which he has not conquered by this help he is so far from perceiving to need subjugation, and to be instincts of an inferior self, that he even fancies it to be his right and duty, in virtue of having conquered a limited part of himself, to give unchecked swing to the remainder. He is, I say, a victim of Hebraism, of the tendency to cultivate strictness of conscience rather than spontaneity of consciousness. And what he wants is a larger conception of human nature, showing him the number of other points at which his nature must come to its best, besides the points which he himself knows and thinks of. There is no *unum necessarium*, or one thing needful, which can free human nature from the obligation of trying to come to its best at all these points. The real *unum necessarium* for us is to come to our best at all points. Instead of our "one thing needful," justifying in us vulgarity, hideousness, ignorance, violence,—our vulgarity, hideousness, ignorance, violence, are really so many touchstones which try our one thing needful, and which prove that in the state, at any rate, in which we ourselves have it, it is not all we want. And as the force which encourages us to stand staunch and fast by the rule and ground we have is Hebraism, so the force which encourages us to go back upon this rule, and to try the very ground on which we appear to stand, is Hellenism,—a turn for giving our consciousness free play and enlarging its range. And what I say is, not that Hellenism is always for everybody more wanted than Hebraism, but that for Mr

---

4. The courts of the Roman emperor Nero (A.D. 54–68), of Pope Leo X (1513–1521), and of Louis XV (1715–1774) were renowned for worldly luxury and excess.

Murphy at this particular moment, and for the great majority of us his fellow-countrymen, it is more wanted. * * *

from *Conclusion*

And so we bring to an end what we had to say in praise of culture, and in evidence of its special utility for the circumstances in which we find ourselves, and the confusion which environs us. Through culture seems to lie our way, not only to perfection, but even to safety. Resolutely refusing to lend a hand to the imperfect operations of our Liberal friends, disregarding their impatience, taunts, and reproaches, firmly bent on trying to find in the intelligible laws of things a firmer and sounder basis for future practice than any which we have at present, and believing this search and discovery to be, for our generation and circumstances, of yet more vital and pressing importance than practice itself, we nevertheless may do more, perhaps, we poor disparaged followers of culture, to make the actual present, and the frame of society in which we live, solid and seaworthy, than all which our bustling politicians can do.

For we have seen how much of our disorders and perplexities is due to the disbelief, among the classes and combinations of men, Barbarian or Philistine, which have hitherto governed our society, in right reason, in a paramount best self; to the inevitable decay and break-up of the organisations by which, asserting and expressing in these organisations their ordinary self only, they have so long ruled us; and to their irresolution, when the society, which their conscience tells them they have made and still manage not with right reason but with their ordinary self, is rudely shaken, in offering resistance to its subverters. But for us,—who believe in right reason, in the duty and possibility of extricating and elevating our best self, in the progress of humanity towards perfection,—for us the framework of society, that theatre on which this august drama has to unroll itself, is sacred; and whoever administers it, and however we may seek to remove them from their tenure of administration, yet, while they administer, we steadily and with undivided heart support them in repressing anarchy and disorder; because without order there can be no society, and without society there can be no human perfection.

And this opinion of the intolerableness of anarchy we can never forsake, however our Liberal friends may think a little rioting, and what they call popular demonstrations, useful sometimes to their own interests and to the interests of the valuable practical operations they have in hand, and however they may preach the right of an Englishman to be left to do as far as possible what he likes, and the duty of his government to indulge him and connive as much as possible and abstain from all harshness of repression. And even when they artfully show us operations which are undoubtedly precious, such as the abolition of the slave-trade, and ask us if, for their sake, foolish and obstinate governments may not wholesomely be frightened by a little disturbance, the good design in view and the difficulty of overcoming opposition to it being considered,—still we say no, and that monster-processions in the streets and forcible irruptions into the parks, even in professed support of this good design, ought to be unflinchingly forbidden and repressed; and that far more is lost than is gained by permitting them. Because a State in which law is authoritative and sovereign, a firm and settled course of public order, is requisite if man is to bring to maturity anything precious and lasting now, or to found anything precious and lasting for the future. * * *

1867–1868; 1869

Christina Rossetti
1830–1894

"Here is a great discovery," Christina Rossetti wrote to her brother Dante Gabriel in 1870, as he tried to advise her about her poetic career: "'Women are not Men,' and you must not expect me to possess a tithe of your capacities, though I humbly—or proudly—lay claim to family-likeness." The remark hints at many sides of Rossetti's complex nature: her modest yet firm manner; the touch of irony in her deference; and the "family-likeness" not only of poetic genius but personal temperament—their parents called them the "two storms" in childhood because they were both difficult, irritable, volatile, and creative. Her declaration signals Rossetti's recognition that as a woman and artist she had had to take a very different path from her more famous brother. She renounced from an early age any pleasures or relationships that did not conform to her strict Anglo-Catholic principles—even to the point of giving up chess because it made her too eager to win. Instead she found poetic fulfillment in haunting lyrics about goblin men and love beyond the grave.

Rossetti was born in London in 1830, the youngest of four precocious children of Gabriele Rossetti, an Italian poet-in-exile, and his English-Italian wife Frances Polidori, whose brother John was Byron's physician and traveling companion. Amid a stream of foreign visitors the bilingual Rossetti children listened to animated discussions of art, music, and revolutionary politics. This atmosphere "made us . . . not a little different from British children," her brother William recalled, "and, when Dante and Christina Rossetti proved, as poetic writers, somewhat devious from the British tradition and the insular mind, we may say, if not 'so much the better,' at any rate, 'no wonder.'"

Like many Victorian women of letters, Christina Rossetti suffered from mysterious maladies that served to protect her time and talent. "I am rejoiced to feel that my health does really unfit me for miscellaneous governessing *en permanence*," she confided to William in 1855. Freed from "the necessity of teaching the small daughters of the neighbouring hairdresser or the neighbouring pork-butcher their p's and q's," she was "anxious to secure any literary pickings which might offer."

Shy, devout, and self-sacrificing, Rossetti nevertheless found time for a literary and social life that included as acquaintances Browning, Ruskin, Swinburne, Lewis Carroll, Edmund Gosse, and the Pre-Raphaelites. She modelled as the Virgin Mary in two of Dante Gabriel's finest paintings, *The Girlhood of Mary Virgin* (1848–1849) and *Ecce Ancilla Domini* (1849–1850). Because of her sex, Christina was denied membership in the Pre-Raphaelite Brotherhood, but she did publish her first poems in their journal *The Germ* in 1850. With the appearance of *Goblin Market and Other Poems* in 1862, she acquired a growing critical and popular following. Hailed by Gosse as the "High Priestess of Pre-Raphaelitism" because of her superb technique and keenness of observation, she won even wider fame as an author of religious poetry, inspiring, among others, Gerard Manley Hopkins.

Admirers of Rossetti's passionate, frustrated love poetry have long puzzled over the scanty details of her romantic life. She rejected two suitors because she found their faith wanting. Early biographers assumed that these broken relationships blighted Rossetti's life, but recently critics have regarded her choice of a single life as an act of artistic self-preservation. For Christina not only witnessed Dante's tormented affairs but also had the opportunity to view passion's consequences in a clinical light during the decade she worked as a volunteer at the Highgate House of Charity for "fallen women."

Though brightened by many touches of humor, Rossetti's writing focuses mostly on religious topics or some combination of themes arising from troubled love, grave illness, and anticipations of death—themes she must have pondered during the extended periods she spent taking care of dying family members at home, beginning with her father and continuing with her sister, her brother Dante, her mother (who was always her closest companion), and two maiden aunts. Despite severe illness in later life, she maintained a strict professionalism toward her career, publishing new work during the 1870s and 1880s, then issuing revised editions until her death in 1894.

A spontaneous writer whose lucidity of phrasing has sometimes caused readers to overlook her emotional and symbolic depths, Rossetti mastered a variety of forms, ranging from hymns and a sonnet-sequence to nursery rhymes and a well-known Christmas carol, *In the Bleak Mid-Winter*. Like Emily Dickinson, whose poems she admired when the first selection was published in 1890, Rossetti displays a quirky independence of vision, mingling the morbid, the whimsical, the cooly ironic. What is today her most famous poem, *Goblin Market*, features the enticements of sensual knowledge. Regarded chiefly as a children's tale in the nineteenth century, the poem has subsequently attracted much critical attention, including analyses of it as a struggle between self and soul, a comment on sex as a capitalist commodity, a parable of feminist solidarity, a lesson about poetry's subversive power, and a lesbian love story. This fable about the danger of desire provides insight into the dualistic world of Victorian fantasy. Magical events permitted writers and readers to enter forbidden realms of violence, temptation, and transformation, yet moralized endings sought to tame even the wildest tales for social and ethical instruction. Something similar may be said of Christina Rossetti's life and art: a stormy nature finds release in the tight formal control of the polished artist.

Song

When I am dead, my dearest,
   Sing no sad songs for me;
Plant thou no roses at my head,
   Nor shady cypress tree:
5 Be the green grass above me
   With showers and dewdrops wet;
And if thou wilt, remember,
   And if thou wilt, forget.

I shall not see the shadows,
10   I shall not feel the rain;
I shall not hear the nightingale
   Sing on, as if in pain:
And dreaming through the twilight
   That doth not rise nor set,
15   Haply° I may remember,   *perhaps*
   And haply may forget.

1848   1862

After Death

The curtains were half drawn, the floor was swept
   And strewn with rushes, rosemary and may[1]
Lay thick upon the bed on which I lay,
Where thro' the lattice ivy-shadows crept.
5   He leaned above me, thinking that I slept
   And could not hear him; but I heard him say:

1. Flowers traditionally associated with death.

"Poor child, poor child:" and as he turned away
Came a deep silence, and I knew he wept.
He did not touch the shroud, or raise the fold
10   That hid my face, or take my hand in his,
            Or ruffle the smooth pillows for my head:
            He did not love me living; but once dead
        He pitied me; and very sweet it is
To know he still is warm tho' I am cold.

1849   1862

In an Artist's Studio

One face looks out from all his canvasses,[1]
    One selfsame figure sits or walks or leans;
    We found her hidden just behind those screens,
That mirror gave back all her loveliness.
5   A queen in opal or in ruby dress,
        A nameless girl in freshest summer greens,
        A saint, an angel;—every canvass means
The same one meaning, neither more nor less.
He feeds upon her face by day and night,
10   And she with true kind eyes looks back on him
Fair as the moon and joyful as the light:
        Not wan with waiting, not with sorrow dim;
Not as she is, but was when hope shone bright;
        Not as she is, but as she fills his dream.

1856   1896

Winter: My Secret

I tell my secret? No indeed, not I:
Perhaps some day, who knows?
But not today; it froze, and blows, and snows,
And you're too curious: fie!
5   You want to hear it? well:
Only, my secret's mine, and I won't tell.

Or, after all, perhaps there's none:
Suppose there is no secret after all,
But only just my fun.
10 Today's a nipping day, a biting day;
In which one wants a shawl,
A veil, a cloak, and other wraps:
I cannot ope to every one who taps,
And let the draughts come whistling thro' my hall;
15 Come bounding and surrounding me,
Come buffeting, astounding me,
Nipping and clipping thro' my wraps and all.

1. Christina's brother William wrote: "The reference is apparently to our brother's studio, and to his constantly repeated heads of the lady whom he afterwards married, Miss Siddal."

I wear my mask for warmth: who ever shows
His nose to Russian snows
20   To be pecked at by every wind that blows?
You would not peck? I thank you for good will,
Believe, but leave that truth untested still.

Spring's an expansive time: yet I don't trust
March with its peck of dust,
25   Nor April with its rainbow-crowned brief showers,
Nor even May, whose flowers
One frost may wither thro' the sunless hours.

Perhaps some languid summer day,
When drowsy birds sing less and less,
30   And golden fruit is ripening to excess,
If there's not too much sun nor too much cloud,
And the warm wind is neither still nor loud,
Perhaps my secret I may say,
Or you may guess.

1857   1862

Goblin Market

Morning and evening
Maids heard the goblins cry:
"Come buy our orchard fruits,
Come buy, come buy:
5   Apples and quinces,
Lemons and oranges,
Plump unpecked cherries,
Melons and raspberries,
Bloom-down-cheeked peaches,
10   Swart°-headed mulberries,   *dark*
Wild free-born cranberries,
Crab-apples, dewberries,
Pine-apples, blackberries,
Apricots, strawberries;—
15   All ripe together
In summer weather,—
Morns that pass by,
Fair eves that fly;
Come buy, come buy:
20   Our grapes fresh from the vine,
Pomegranates full and fine,
Dates and sharp bullaces,
Rare pears and greengages,
Damsons[1] and bilberries,
25   Taste them and try:
Currants and gooseberries,
Bright-fire-like barberries,
Figs to fill your mouth,

---

1. Bullaces, greengages, and damsons are types of plums.

Dante Gabriel Rossetti. Frontispiece to the first edition of Christina Rossetti's *Goblin Market*, 1862.

Citrons from the South,
30   Sweet to tongue and sound to eye;
Come buy, come buy."

Evening by evening
Among the brookside rushes,
Laura bowed her head to hear,
35   Lizzie veiled her blushes:
Crouching close together
In the cooling weather,
With clasping arms and cautioning lips,
With tingling cheeks and finger tips.
40   "Lie close," Laura said,
Pricking up her golden head:
"We must not look at goblin men,
We must not buy their fruits:
Who knows upon what soil they fed
45   Their hungry thirsty roots?"
"Come buy," call the goblins
Hobbling down the glen.
"Oh," cried Lizzie, "Laura, Laura,
You should not peep at goblin men."

50 Lizzie covered up her eyes,
    Covered close lest they should look;
    Laura reared her glossy head,
    And whispered like the restless brook:
    "Look, Lizzie, look, Lizzie,
55 Down the glen tramp little men.
    One hauls a basket,
    One bears a plate,
    One lugs a golden dish
    Of many pounds weight.
60 How fair the vine must grow
    Whose grapes are so luscious;
    How warm the wind must blow
    Thro' those fruit bushes."
    "No," said Lizzie: "No, no, no;
65 Their offers should not charm us,
    Their evil gifts would harm us."
    She thrust a dimpled finger
    In each ear, shut eyes and ran:
    Curious Laura chose to linger
70 Wondering at each merchant man.
    One had a cat's face,
    One whisked a tail,
    One tramped at a rat's pace,
    One crawled like a snail,
75 One like a wombat prowled obtuse and furry,
    One like a ratel[2] tumbled hurry skurry.
    She heard a voice like voice of doves
    Cooing all together:
    They sounded kind and full of loves
80 In the pleasant weather.

    Laura stretched her gleaming neck
    Like a rush-imbedded swan,
    Like a lily from the beck,°   brook
    Like a moonlit poplar branch,
85 Like a vessel at the launch
    When its last restraint is gone.

    Backwards up the mossy glen
    Turned and trooped the goblin men,
    With their shrill repeated cry,
90 "Come buy, come buy."
    When they reached where Laura was
    They stood stock still upon the moss,
    Leering at each other,
    Brother with queer brother;
95 Signalling each other,
    Brother with sly brother.
    One set his basket down,
    One reared his plate;

2. A tropical badgerlike nocturnal animal (pronounced "ray-tell").

One began to weave a crown
100 Of tendrils, leaves and rough nuts brown
(Men sell not such in any town);
One heaved the golden weight
Of dish and fruit to offer her:
"Come buy, come buy," was still their cry.
105 Laura stared but did not stir,
Longed but had no money:
The whisk-tailed merchant bade her taste
In tones as smooth as honey,
The cat-faced purr'd,
110 The rat-paced spoke a word
Of welcome, and the snail-paced even was heard;
One parrot-voiced and jolly
Cried "Pretty Goblin" still for "Pretty Polly;"—
One whistled like a bird.

115 But sweet-tooth Laura spoke in haste:
"Good folk, I have no coin;
To take were to purloin:
I have no copper in my purse,
I have no silver either,
120 And all my gold is on the furze[3]
That shakes in windy weather
Above the rusty heather."
"You have much gold upon your head,"
They answered all together:
125 "Buy from us with a golden curl."
She clipped a precious golden lock,
She dropped a tear more rare than pearl,
Then sucked their fruit globes fair or red:
Sweeter than honey from the rock.
130 Stronger than man-rejoicing wine,
Clearer than water flowed that juice;
She never tasted such before,
How should it cloy with length of use?
She sucked and sucked and sucked the more
135 Fruits which that unknown orchard bore;
She sucked until her lips were sore;
Then flung the emptied rinds away
But gathered up one kernel-stone,
And knew not was it night or day
140 As she turned home alone.

Lizzie met her at the gate
Full of wise upbraidings:
"Dear, you should not stay so late,
Twilight is not good for maidens;
145 Should not loiter in the glen
In the haunts of goblin men.
Do you not remember Jeanie,

3. An evergreen shrub that grows on the heath.

How she met them in the moonlight,
Took their gifts both choice and many,
150   Ate their fruits and wore their flowers
Plucked from bowers
Where summer ripens at all hours?
But ever in the noonlight
She pined and pined away;
155   Sought them by night and day,
Found them no more but dwindled and grew grey;
Then fell with the first snow,
While to this day no grass will grow
Where she lies low:
160   I planted daisies there a year ago
That never blow.
You should not loiter so."
"Nay, hush," said Laura:
"Nay, hush, my sister:
165   I ate and ate my fill,
Yet my mouth waters still;
Tomorrow night I will
Buy more:" and kissed her:
"Have done with sorrow;
170   I'll bring you plums tomorrow
Fresh on their mother twigs,
Cherries worth getting;
You cannot think what figs
My teeth have met in,
175   What melons icy-cold
Piled on a dish of gold
Too huge for me to hold,
What peaches with a velvet nap,
Pellucid° grapes without one seed: *translucent*
180   Odorous indeed must be the mead
Whereon they grow, and pure the wave they drink
With lilies at the brink,
And sugar-sweet their sap."

Golden head by golden head,
185   Like two pigeons in one nest
Folded in each other's wings,
They lay down in their curtained bed:
Like two blossoms on one stem,
Like two flakes of new-fall'n snow,
190   Like two wands of ivory
Tipped with gold for awful° kings.   *awe-inspiring*
Moon and stars gazed in at them,
Wind sang to them lullaby,
Lumbering owls forbore to fly,
195   Not a bat flapped to and fro
Round their rest:
Cheek to cheek and breast to breast
Locked together in one nest.

Early in the morning
200 When the first cock crowed his warning,
Neat like bees, as sweet and busy,
Laura rose with Lizzie:
Fetched in honey, milked the cows,
Aired and set to rights the house,
205 Kneaded cakes of whitest wheat,
Cakes for dainty mouths to eat,
Next churned butter, whipped up cream,
Fed their poultry, sat and sewed;
Talked as modest maidens should:
210 Lizzie with an open heart,
Laura in an absent dream,
One content, one sick in part;
One warbling for the mere bright day's delight,
One longing for the night.

215 At length slow evening came:
They went with pitchers to the reedy brook;
Lizzie most placid in her look,
Laura most like a leaping flame.
They drew the gurgling water from its deep;
220 Lizzie plucked purple and rich golden flags,
Then turning homewards said: "The sunset flushes
Those furthest loftiest crags;
Come, Laura, not another maiden lags,
No wilful squirrel wags,
225 The beasts and birds are fast asleep."
But Laura loitered still among the rushes
And said the bank was steep.

And said the hour was early still,
The dew not fall'n, the wind not chill:
230 Listening ever, but not catching
The customary cry,
"Come buy, come buy,"
With its iterated jingle
Of sugar-baited words:
235 Not for all her watching
Once discerning even one goblin
Racing, whisking, tumbling, hobbling;
Let alone the herds
That used to tramp along the glen,
240 In groups or single,
Of brisk fruit-merchant men.
Till Lizzie urged, "O Laura, come;
I hear the fruit-call but I dare not look:
You should not loiter longer at this brook:
245 Come with me home.
The stars rise, the moon bends her arc,
Each glowworm winks her spark,
Let us get home before the night grows dark:

For clouds may gather
250   Tho' this is summer weather,
Put out the lights and drench us thro';
Then if we lost our way what should we do?"

Laura turned cold as stone
To find her sister heard that cry alone,
255   That goblin cry,
"Come buy our fruits, come buy."
Must she then buy no more such dainty fruit?
Must she no more such succous° pasture find,   *juicy*
Gone deaf and blind?
260   Her tree of life drooped from the root:
She said not one word in her heart's sore ache;
But peering thro' the dimness, nought discerning,
Trudged home, her pitcher dripping all the way;
So crept to bed, and lay
265   Silent till Lizzie slept;
Then sat up in a passionate yearning,
And gnashed her teeth for baulked desire, and wept
As if her heart would break.

Day after day, night after night,
270   Laura kept watch in vain
In sullen silence of exceeding pain.
She never caught again the goblin cry:
"Come buy, come buy;"—
She never spied the goblin men
275   Hawking their fruits along the glen:
But when the noon waxed bright
Her hair grew thin and gray;
She dwindled, as the fair full moon doth turn
To swift decay and burn
280   Her fire away.

One day remembering her kernel-stone
She set it by a wall that faced the south;
Dewed it with tears, hoped for a root,
Watched for a waxing shoot,
285   But there came none;
It never saw the sun,
It never felt the trickling moisture run:
While with sunk eyes and faded mouth
She dreamed of melons, as a traveller sees
290   False waves in desert drouth
With shade of leaf-crowned trees,
And burns the thirstier in the sandful breeze.

She no more swept the house,
Tended the fowls or cows,
295   Fetched honey, kneaded cakes of wheat,
Brought water from the brook:
But sat down listless in the chimney-nook
And would not eat.

Tender Lizzie could not bear
300 To watch her sister's cankerous° care   *festering*
Yet not to share.
She night and morning
Caught the goblins' cry:
"Come buy our orchard fruits,
305 Come buy, come buy:"—
Beside the brook, along the glen,
She heard the tramp of goblin men,
The voice and stir
Poor Laura could not hear;
310 Longed to buy fruit to comfort her,
But feared to pay too dear.
She thought of Jeanie in her grave,
Who should have been a bride;
But who for joys brides hope to have
315 Fell sick and died
In her gay prime,
In earliest Winter time,
With the first glazing rime,
With the first snow-fall of crisp Winter time.

320 Till Laura dwindling
Seemed knocking at Death's door:
Then Lizzie weighed no more
Better and worse;
But put a silver penny in her purse,
325 Kissed Laura, crossed the heath with clumps of furze
At twilight, halted by the brook:
And for the first time in her life
Began to listen and look.

Laughed every goblin
330 When they spied her peeping:
Came towards her hobbling,
Flying, running, leaping,
Puffing and blowing,
Chuckling, clapping, crowing,
335 Clucking and gobbling,
Mopping and mowing,
Full of airs and graces,
Pulling wry faces,
Demure grimaces,
340 Cat-like and rat-like,
Ratel- and wombat-like,
Snail-paced in a hurry,
Parrot-voiced and whistler,
Helter skelter, hurry skurry,
345 Chattering like magpies,
Fluttering like pigeons,
Gliding like fishes,—
Hugged her and kissed her,
Squeezed and caressed her:

350   Stretched up their dishes,
       Panniers, and plates:
       "Look at our apples
       Russet and dun,
       Bob at our cherries,
355   Bite at our peaches,
       Citrons and dates,
       Grapes for the asking,
       Pears red with basking
       Out in the sun,
360   Plums on their twigs;
       Pluck them and suck them,
       Pomegranates, figs."—

       "Good folk," said Lizzie,
       Mindful of Jeanie:
365   "Give me much and many:"—
       Held out her apron,
       Tossed them her penny.
       "Nay, take a seat with us,
       Honour and eat with us,"
370   They answered grinning:
       "Our feast is but beginning.
       Night yet is early,
       Warm and dew-pearly,
       Wakeful and starry:
375   Such fruits as these
       No man can carry;
       Half their bloom would fly,
       Half their dew would dry,
       Half their flavour would pass by.
380   Sit down and feast with us,
       Be welcome guest with us,
       Cheer you and rest with us."—
       "Thank you," said Lizzie: "But one waits
       At home alone for me:
385   So without further parleying,
       If you will not sell me any
       Of your fruits tho' much and many,
       Give me back my silver penny
       I tossed you for a fee."—
390   They began to scratch their pates,
       No longer wagging, purring,
       But visibly demurring,
       Grunting and snarling.
       One called her proud,
395   Cross-grained, uncivil;
       Their tones waxed loud,
       Their looks were evil.
       Lashing their tails
       They trod and hustled her,
400   Elbowed and jostled her,

Clawed with their nails,
Barking, mewing, hissing, mocking,
Tore her gown and soiled her stocking,
Twitched her hair out by the roots,
405   Stamped upon her tender feet,
Held her hands and squeezed their fruits
Against her mouth to make her eat.
White and golden Lizzie stood,
Like a lily in a flood,—
410   Like a rock of blue-veined stone
Lashed by tides obstreperously,—
Like a beacon left alone
In a hoary roaring sea,
Sending up a golden fire,—
415   Like a fruit-crowned orange-tree
White with blossoms honey-sweet
Sore beset by wasp and bee,—
Like a royal virgin town
Topped with gilded dome and spire
420   Close beleaguered by a fleet
Mad to tug her standard down.

One may lead a horse to water,
Twenty cannot make him drink.
Tho' the goblins cuffed and caught her,
425   Coaxed and fought her,
Bullied and besought her,
Scratched her, pinched her black as ink,
Kicked and knocked her,
Mauled and mocked her,
430   Lizzie uttered not a word;
Would not open lip from lip
Lest they should cram a mouthful in:
But laughed in heart to feel the drip
Of juice that syrupped all her face,
435   And lodged in dimples of her chin,
And streaked her neck which quaked like curd.
At last the evil people
Worn out by her resistance
Flung back her penny, kicked their fruit
440   Along whichever road they took,
Not leaving root or stone or shoot;
Some writhed into the ground,
Some dived into the brook
With ring and ripple,
445   Some scudded on the gale without a sound,
Some vanished in the distance.
In a smart, ache, tingle,
Lizzie went her way;
Knew not was it night or day;
450   Sprang up the bank, tore thro' the furze,
Threaded copse and dingle,

And heard her penny jingle
Bouncing in her purse,
Its bounce was music to her ear.
455   She ran and ran
As if she feared some goblin man
Dogged her with gibe or curse
Or something worse:
But not one goblin skurried after,
460   Nor was she pricked by fear;
The kind heart made her windy-paced
That urged her home quite out of breath with haste
And inward laughter.

She cried "Laura," up the garden,
465   "Did you miss me?
Come and kiss me.
Never mind my bruises,
Hug me, kiss me, suck my juices
Squeezed from goblin fruits for you,
470   Goblin pulp and goblin dew.
Eat me, drink me, love me;
Laura, make much of me:
For your sake I have braved the glen
And had to do with goblin merchant men."

475   Laura started from her chair,
Flung her arms up in the air,
Clutched her hair:
"Lizzie, Lizzie, have you tasted
For my sake the fruit forbidden?
480   Must your light like mine be hidden,
Your young life like mine be wasted,
Undone in mine undoing
And ruined in my ruin,
Thirsty, cankered, goblin-ridden?"—
485   She clung about her sister,
Kissed and kissed and kissed her:
Tears once again
Refreshed her shrunken eyes,
Dropping like rain
490   After long sultry drouth;
Shaking with aguish fear, and pain,
She kissed and kissed her with a hungry mouth.

Her lips began to scorch,
That juice was wormwood to her tongue,
495   She loathed the feast:
Writhing as one possessed she leaped and sung,
Rent all her robe, and wrung
Her hands in lamentable haste,
And beat her breast.
500   Her locks streamed like the torch
Borne by a racer at full speed,

Or like the mane of horses in their flight,
Or like an eagle when she stems° the light   *makes headway against*
Straight toward the sun,
505   Or like a caged thing freed,
Or like a flying flag when armies run.

Swift fire spread thro' her veins, knocked at her heart,
Met the fire smouldering there
And overbore its lesser flame;
510   She gorged on bitterness without a name:
Ah! fool, to choose such part
Of soul-consuming care!
Sense failed in the mortal strife:
Like the watch-tower of a town
515   Which an earthquake shatters down,
Like a lightning-stricken mast,
Like a wind-uprooted tree
Spun about,
Like a foam-topped waterspout
520   Cast down headlong in the sea,
She fell at last;
Pleasure past and anguish past,
Is it death or is it life?

Life out of death.
525   That night long Lizzie watched by her,
Counted her pulse's flagging stir,
Felt for her breath,
Held water to her lips, and cooled her face
With tears and fanning leaves:
530   But when the first birds chirped about their eaves,
And early reapers plodded to the place
Of golden sheaves,
And dew-wet grass
Bowed in the morning winds so brisk to pass,
535   And new buds with new day
Opened of cup-like lilies on the stream,
Laura awoke as from a dream,
Laughed in the innocent old way,
Hugged Lizzie but not twice or thrice;
540   Her gleaming locks showed not one thread of grey,
Her breath was sweet as May
And light danced in her eyes.

Days, weeks, months, years
Afterwards, when both were wives
545   With children of their own;
Their mother-hearts beset with fears,
Their lives bound up in tender lives;
Laura would call the little ones
And tell them of her early prime,
550   Those pleasant days long gone
Of not-returning time:

Would talk about the haunted glen,
The wicked, quaint fruit-merchant men,
Their fruits like honey to the throat
555   But poison in the blood;
(Men sell not such in any town:)
Would tell them how her sister stood
In deadly peril to do her good,
And win the fiery antidote:
560   Then joining hands to little hands
Would bid them cling together,
"For there is no friend like a sister
In calm or stormy weather;
To cheer one on the tedious way,
565   To fetch one if one goes astray,
To lift one if one totters down,
To strengthen whilst one stands."

1859   1862

"No, Thank You, John"

I never said I loved you, John:
    Why will you teaze me day by day,
And wax a weariness to think upon
    With always "do" and "pray"?

5   You know I never loved you, John;
    No fault of mine made me your toast:
Why will you haunt me with a face as wan
    As shows an hour-old ghost?

I dare say Meg or Moll would take
10   Pity upon you, if you'd ask:
And pray don't remain single for my sake
    Who can't perform that task.

I have no heart?—Perhaps I have not;
    But then you're mad to take offence
15 That I don't give you what I have not got:
    Use your own common sense.

Let bygones be bygones:
    Don't call me false, who owed not to be true:
I'd rather answer "No" to fifty Johns
20   Than answer "Yes" to you.

Let's mar our pleasant days no more,
    Song-birds of passage, days of youth:
Catch at today, forget the days before:
    I'll wink at your untruth.

25 Let us strike hands as hearty friends;
    No more, no less; and friendship's good:
Only don't keep in view ulterior ends,
    And points not understood

In open treaty. Rise above
   Quibbles and shuffling off and on:
30 Here's friendship for you if you like; but love,—
   No, thank you, John.

1860   1862

Promises Like Pie-Crust[1]

Promise me no promises,
   So will I not promise you;
Keep we both our liberties,
   Never false and never true:
5 Let us hold the die uncast,
   Free to come as free to go;
For I cannot know your past,
   And of mine what can you know?

You, so warm, may once have been
10   Warmer towards another one;
I, so cold, may once have seen
   Sunlight, once have felt the sun:
Who shall show us if it was
   Thus indeed in time of old?
15 Fades the image from the glass
   And the fortune is not told.

If you promised, you might grieve
   For lost liberty again;
If I promised, I believe
20   I should fret to break the chain:
Let us be the friends we were,
   Nothing more but nothing less;
Many thrive on frugal fare
   Who would perish of excess.

1861   1896

Sleeping at Last

Sleeping at last, the trouble & tumult over,
Sleeping at last, the struggle & horror past,
Cold & white out of sight of friend & of lover
Sleeping at last.

5 No more a tired heart downcast or overcast,
No more pangs that wring or shifting fears that hover,
Sleeping at last in a dreamless sleep locked fast.

Fast asleep. Singing birds in their leafy cover
Cannot wake her, nor shake her the gusty blast.
10 Under the purple thyme & the purple clover
Sleeping at last.

c. 1893   1896

---

1. English proverb: "Promises are like pie-crust, made to be broken."

Gerard Manley Hopkins
1844–1889

Hopkins is the most modern of Victorian poets, and the most Victorian of modern poets. His stunningly original poems were, with a few exceptions, not published until 1918, placing him at first glance in the company of Eliot and Pound. But his struggle to maintain religious faith, his respect for conventional verse forms, and his quest to find proof of God's work in nature all mark him as quintessentially Victorian. Hopkins combines a microscopic keenness of vision with a Joycean genius for compound words, new coinages, unexpected rhymes, and startling distortions of syntax. The result is a poetry of modernist intensity and compression, fraught with bold ellipses and daring line breaks, but nonetheless dedicated to describing a world "charged with the grandeur of God." Orthodox and self-denying in matters of religion, Hopkins was also the era's most radical literary rebel.

Hopkins was born into a prosperous, pious Anglican family. After attending school in London, he went in 1863 to study classics at Balliol College, Oxford, where the agnostic aesthete Walter Pater was one of his tutors. At the same time, Hopkins came under the influence of the "Oxford Movement." He read John Henry Newman's account of his gravitation toward Roman Catholicism in *Apologia Pro Vita Sua;* subsequent talks with Newman led to Hopkins's own agonizing conversion to Catholicism in 1866. In 1868 he entered the novitiate of the Society of Jesus and burned almost all his early, Keatsian poems. He called his action the "slaughter of the innocents," and resolved "to write no more, as not belonging to my profession, unless it were by the wish of my superiors."

Seven years of poetic silence ensued, as Hopkins studied for the priesthood. But he was also meditating on his idiosyncratic theories of poetic composition. When five nuns were drowned in a shipwreck in 1875, he was suddenly moved to compose the first poem in his new style, *The Wreck of the Deutschland.* But there was no audience prepared to fathom his highly wrought style. Hopkins offered the work to a Jesuit magazine but, he said, "they dared not print it." He never again tried to publish.

Hopkins was ordained a Jesuit priest in 1877. Joyous, he produced a series of radiant sonnets celebrating the presence of God in nature. But his remaining years tested his faith sorely. Often in ill-health, he labored as a parish priest and teacher throughout Britain, including missionary work in the slums of Liverpool. He suffered physically and spiritually from the "vice and horrors" he found in his dreary urban duties: "It made even life a burden to me," he confessed. Then in 1884 he was appointed Professor of Greek and Latin at the Catholic, newly formed University College in Dublin. Already estranged from his family and the English church, he felt separated from his country, too. "I am in Ireland now," he wrote in a sonnet, "now I am at a third / Remove." Yet even as he despaired of accomplishing work of lasting value, he produced many of his best poems, including the famed "terrible sonnets" that describe his sense of spiritual and poetic sterility. Exhausted by his strenuous duties, Hopkins died in Dublin of typhoid at the age of forty-five.

Although Hopkins read the important nineteenth-century poets with care, he deliberately carved his own way. "The effect of studying masterpieces," he said, "is to make me admire and do otherwise." In his journals Hopkins often sounds like an English Thoreau, finely attuned to every nuance of the natural world. His entries are always searching to grasp the essential particularity of a thing, its inner landscape—what he called "inscape." Elaborating his theory in a letter to Robert Bridges, an Oxford friend who later became poet laureate, Hopkins admitted that "no doubt my poetry errs on the side of oddness. . . . it is the vice of distinctiveness to become queer." But he asserted the absolute importance of such "distinctiveness"— this "design, pattern or what I am in the habit of calling *inscape* is what I above all aim at in poetry." Hopkins needed another term to express the dynamic energy that not only makes the inscape cohere but also projects it outward toward the observer. This force that both unifies an object and arouses the senses of its beholder Hopkins called "instress." Taken together, the terms "inscape" and "instress" convey the organic beauty that for Hopkins speaks of God's presence in nature.

To apply these concepts poetically Hopkins developed a new verse line based on "sprung rhythm." As in Old English poetry or nursery rhymes, each line in sprung rhythm has a fixed number of stresses, but the number and placement of unstressed syllables can vary widely. Many poets had employed individual lines of this type, but Hopkins took the idea of flexible metrics to new heights. He loaded his lines with internal rhyme, alliteration, assonance, and strong Anglo-Saxon words, and drove them forward with crashing consonants and wrenching enjambments. Responding to Bridges's confusion, he explained: "Why do I employ sprung rhythm at all? Because it is the nearest to the rhythm of prose, that is the native and natural rhythm of speech, the least forced, the most rhetorical and emphatic of all possible rhythms." Since Hopkins connected the sight and sound of individual words to the religious intensity with which he viewed objects in nature, the effect is akin to impassioned prayer. "My verse is less to be read than heard," he concluded; "it is oratorical."

In his later poetry a tangle of religious and sexual imagery expresses his sense of thwarted love and meager poetic production. He portrays himself as a sapless tree, or as barren sand: "I am soft sift / In an hourglass." In 1885 he wrote to Bridges in frustration, "if I could but produce work I should not mind its being buried, silenced, and going no further; but it kills me to be time's eunuch and never to beget." Such passages, with their images of sexual impotency, poetic infertility, and self-abnegation, suggest what Bridges called "the naked encounter of sensualism and asceticism" in Hopkins's work.

Despite his disclaimers, Hopkins was preoccupied with his lack of an audience. He once informed Bridges: "You are my public and I hope to convert you." Missionary-like, Hopkins's poetry seeks to "convert" the reader with its ecstatic particularity, its intensity of perception. But he speaks of his efforts as a one-way correspondence to God and his public; his poems are "cries like dead letters sent / To dearest him that lives alas! away." Hopkins could not have known that Bridges, despite his difficulty grasping these "dead letters," would finally publish the poems to great acclaim at the close of World War I. Then, like the works of Emily Dickinson and Vincent Van Gogh, they would suddenly seize a central artistic place in a past that had been unaware of their existence. And yet, Hopkins did recognize that his mingling of sensuality and spirituality allied him with another great proto-modernist. "I always knew in my heart Walt Whitman's mind to be more like my own than any other man's living," he told Bridges. "As he is a great scoundrel this is not a pleasant confession."

God's Grandeur

> The world is charged with the grandeur of God.
>   It will flame out, like shining from shook foil;[1]
>   It gathers to a greatness, like the ooze of oil
> Crushed.[2] Why do men then now not reck° his rod?   *heed*
5   Generations have trod, have trod, have trod;
>   And all is seared with trade; bleared, smeared with toil;
>   And wears man's smudge and shares man's smell: the soil
>   Is bare now, nor can foot feel, being shod.

---

1. I mean foil in its sense of leaf or tinsel. . . . Shaken goldfoil gives off broad glares like sheet lightning and also, and this is true of nothing else, owing to its zigzag dints and creasings and network of small many cornered facets, a sort of fork lightning too [Hopkins's note].
2. Oil made by crushing seeds or olives.

And for° all this, nature is never spent;   *despite*
10   There lives the dearest freshness deep down things;
And though the last lights off the black West went
     Oh, morning, at the brown brink eastward, springs—
Because the Holy Ghost over the bent
     World broods with warm breast and with ah! bright wings.
1877   1895

The Windhover:[1]

To Christ Our Lord

I caught this morning morning's minion,[2] king-
     dom of daylight's dauphin,[3] dapple-dawn-drawn Falcon, in his riding
     Of the rolling level underneath him steady air, and striding
High there, how he rung upon the rein[4] of a wimpling wing
5   In his ecstasy! then off, off forth on swing,
     As a skate's heel sweeps smooth on a bow-bend: the hurl and gliding
     Rebuffed the big wind. My heart in hiding
Stirred for a bird,—the achieve of, the mastery of the thing!

Brute beauty and valour and act, oh, air, pride, plume, here
10   Buckle! AND the fire that breaks from thee then, a billion
Times told lovelier, more dangerous, O my chevalier!

     No wonder of it: shéer plód makes plough down sillion[5]
Shine, and blue-bleak embers, ah my dear,
     Fall, gall[6] themselves, and gash gold-vermilion.
1877   1918

Pied[1] Beauty

Glory be to God for dappled things—
     For skies of couple-colour as a brinded[2] cow;
          For rose-moles all in stipple[3] upon trout that swim;
Fresh-firecoal chestnut-falls;[4] finches' wings;
5   Landscape plotted and pieced—fold, fallow, and plough;[5]
          And áll trádes, their gear and tackle and trim.°   *equipment*

All things counter,[6] original, spare, strange;
     Whatever is fickle, freckled (who knows how?)
          With swift, slow; sweet, sour; adazzle, dim;
10   He fathers-forth whose beauty is past change:
          Praise him.
1877   1918

---

1. Kestrel falcon—a small hawk—that appears to hover in the air.
2. Darling, from the French *mignon*.
3. The dauphin was the heir to the French throne.
4. In falconry, a bird rings when it rises in spirals (like a horse circling at the end of a tether or rein). Wimpling means rippling.
5. The furrows of a plowed field.

6. Break their surfaces.
1. Blotched with different colors.
2. Brindled, having dark patches on a tawny ground.
3. Stippled, painted or drawn with dots instead of lines.
4. Chestnuts as bright as coals [Hopkins's journal].
5. Landscape of differently colored fields, some used as pasture ("fold"), some lying fallow, some plowed.
6. Contrary; "spare" means rare.

Felix Randal

Felix Randal the farrier,[1] O he is dead then? my duty all ended,
Who have watched his mould of man, big-boned and hardy-handsome
Pining, pining, till time when reason rambled in it and some
Fatal four disorders, fleshed there, all contended?

5   Sickness broke him. Impatient he cursed at first, but mended
Being anointed[2] and all; though a heavenlier heart began some
Months earlier, since I had our sweet reprieve and ransom[3]
Tendered to him. Ah well, God rest him all road ever° he offended!   *however*

This seeing the sick endears them to us, us too it endears.
10   My tongue had taught thee comfort, touch had quenched thy tears,
Thy tears that touched my heart, child, Felix, poor Felix Randal;

How far from then forethought of, all thy more boisterous years,
When thou at the random[4] grim forge, powerful amidst peers,
Didst fettle° for the great grey drayhorse his bright and battering sandal! *prepare*

1880   1918

Spring and Fall:
to a young child

Márgarét, are you gríeving
Over Goldengrove unleaving?
Leáves, líke the things of man, you
With your fresh thoughts care for, can you?
5   Áh! ás the heart grows older
It will come to such sights colder
By and by, nor spare a sigh
Though worlds of wanwood leafmeal lie;[1]
And yet you wíll weep and know why.
10   Now no matter, child, the name:
Sórrow's spríngs áre the same.
Nor mouth had, no nor mind, expressed
What heart heard of, ghost° guessed: *spirit*
It ís the blight man was born for,
15   It is Margaret you mourn for.

1880   1918

As Kingfishers Catch Fire

As kingfishers catch fire, dragonflies dráw fláme;
As tumbled over rim in roundy wells
Stones ring; like each tucked° string tells, each hung bell's   *plucked*
Bow swung finds tongue to fling out broad its name;

---

1. Blacksmith.
2. Having received Extreme Unction, the sacrament for the dying.
3. Confession, absolution, and Holy Communion.

4. Built of rough irregular stones.
1. The leaves of pale trees lie scattered; "leafmeal" is derived from "piecemeal."

5   Each mortal thing does one thing and the same:
       Deals out that being indoors each one dwells;
       Selves—goes itself; *myself* it speaks and spells;
       Crying *Whát I dó is me: for that I came.*

       Í say móre: the just man justices;
10   Kéeps gráce; thát keeps all his goings graces;
       Acts in God's eye what in God's eye he is—
       Chríst—for Christ plays in ten thousand places,
       Lovely in limbs, and lovely in eyes not his
       To the Father through the features of men's faces.

1881–1882?   1918

[Carrion Comfort][1]

       Not, I'll not, carrion comfort, Despair, not feast on thee;
       Not untwist—slack they may be—these last strands of man
       In me ór, most weary, cry *I can no more*. I can;
       Can something, hope, wish day come, not choose not to be.
5   But ah, but O thou terrible, why wouldst thou rude on me
       Thy wring-world right foot rock? lay a lionlimb against me? scan
       With darksome devouring eyes my bruisèd bones? and fan,
       O in turns of tempest, me heaped there; me frantic to avoid thee and flee?

           Why? That my chaff might fly; my grain lie, sheer and clear.
10   Nay in all that toil, that coil,[2] since (seems) I kissed the rod,
       Hand rather,[3] my heart lo! lapped strength, stole joy, would laugh, chéer.
       Cheer whom though? the hero whose heaven-handling flung me, fóot tród
       Me? or me that fought him? O which one? is it each one? That night, that year
       Of now done darkness I wretch lay wrestling with (my God!) my God.

1885   1918

No Worst, There Is None

       No worst, there is none. Pitched past pitch of grief,
       More pangs will, schooled at forepangs, wilder wring.
       Comforter, where, where is your comforting?
       Mary, mother of us, where is your relief?
5   My cries heave, herds-long;[1] huddle in a main, a chief
       Woe, world-sorrow; on an age-old anvil wince and sing—
       Then lull, then leave off. Fury had shrieked "No ling-
       ering! Let me be fell:° force° I must be brief."   fierce/perforce

           O the mind, mind has mountains; cliffs of fall
10   Frightful, sheer, no-man-fathomed. Hold them cheap

---

1. The title was added by Robert Bridges. This poem is one of the "terrible sonnets" of 1885, as are the next two.
2. Turmoil.

3. I.e., the hand that holds the rod the speaker has kissed.
1. Like a cry of sheep or cattle repeated successively the length of the herd.

May who ne'er hung there. Nor does long our small
Durance° deal with that steep or deep. Here! creep,   *endurance*
Wretch, under a comfort serves in a whirlwind: all
Life death does end and each day dies with sleep.

1885   1918

I Wake and Feel the Fell of Dark, Not Day

I wake and feel the fell[1] of dark, not day.
What hours, O what black hoürs we have spent
This night! what sights you, heart, saw; ways you went!
And more must, in yet longer light's delay.
5   With witness I speak this. But where I say
Hours I mean years, mean life. And my lament
Is cries countless, cries like dead letters sent
To dearest him that lives alas! away.

     I am gall, I am heartburn. God's most deep decree
10   Bitter would have me taste: my taste was me;
Bones built in me, flesh filled, blood brimmed the curse.
     Selfyeast of spirit a dull dough sours. I see
The lost° are like this, and their scourge to be   *souls in Hell*
As I am mine, their sweating selves; but worse.

1885   1918

Thou Art Indeed Just, Lord

Justus quidem tu es, Domine, si disputem tecum: verumtamen
justa loquar ad te: Quare via impiorum prosperatur? &c.[1]

Thou art indeed just, Lord, if I contend
With thee; but, sir, so what I plead is just.
Why do sinners' ways prosper? and why must
Disappointment all I endeavour end?
5   Wert thou my enemy, O thou my friend,
How wouldst thou worse, I wonder, than thou dost
Defeat, thwart me? Oh, the sots and thralls of lust
Do in spare hours more thrive than I that spend,
Sir, life upon thy cause. See, banks and brakes°   *thickets*
10   Now, leavèd how thick! lacèd they are again
With fretty chervil,° look, and fresh wind shakes   *cow-parsley*
Them; birds build—but not I build; no, but strain,
Time's eunuch, and not breed one work that wakes.
Mine, O thou lord of life, send my roots rain.

1889   1893

---

1. Gall, bitterness; but also a hide or covering; a waste-
land; as an adjective, "fell" means fierce or cruel.

1. The first lines of the poem translate these words from
Jeremiah 12.1.

Oscar Wilde
1854–1900

"He hasn't a single redeeming vice." Oscar Wilde's witticism hardly applied to himself: his character was a quixotic mixture of brilliance and folly. Flamboyant, extravagant, outrageous, the most splendid playwright of the century lived his own life on center stage. Though his flagrant self-promotion irritated many, he was generous and good-natured, unable to imagine that the Victorian morality he satirized would finally bring about his own fall.

Wilde was born in Dublin, and although he spent much of his adult life in England, he never lost the sense of himself as a foreigner. His parents—Irish Protestants, ardent nationalists, and prolific writers—were notable figures in their own right: Sir William Robert Wilde was a famous surgeon, fathered three illegitimate children, and was sued by a former patient who claimed he had drugged and raped her. Lady Wilde, who changed her name from Jane Frances to Speranza Francesca, was a self-dramatizing and unconventional woman whom her son adored.

Wilde was educated in Ireland until 1874 when he won a scholarship to Oxford. Here he began to establish a reputation as an Aesthete and an admirer of Pre-Raphaelite poets such as Swinburne, Rossetti, and William Morris. He was also attracted to the contradictory artistic creeds of both John Ruskin and Walter Pater, Ruskin proclaiming that all good art is moral art, Pater preferring "poetic passion, the desire of beauty, the love of art for art's sake." Wilde dressed ostentatiously, wore his hair long, and decorated his rooms with lilies, a favorite symbol of the Aesthetes. His literary abilities won him both the Newdigate Prize for poetry and a double first (highest honors). But along with these academic awards he was celebrated for a remark which seemed to epitomize aestheticism: "I find it harder and harder every day to live up to my blue china."

Following his triumphs at Oxford, Wilde cast about for a career. His father had died leaving only a small inheritance, and Wilde's attempts to win a university fellowship failed. In London he set about making himself conspicuous, and soon he was the center of the social scene. Few could help being dazzled by his witty conversation. Yet some were skeptical, including an actress who said: "What has he done, this young man, that one meets him everywhere? Oh yes he talks well, but what has he done? He has written nothing, he does not sing or paint or act—he does nothing but talk."

Wilde's talk, however, was glorious, and eventually would find lasting expression in his plays. Meanwhile, he played the dandy, and was satirized by Gilbert and Sullivan in *Patience* (1881) as the most illustrious Aesthete of the day, who had walked "down Piccadilly with a poppy or a lily in his medieval hand." Wilde reacted with good humor, observing that "To have done it was nothing, but to make people think one had done it was a triumph."

In the early 1880s Wilde began to refute the charge that he did nothing but talk. He wrote his first play, called *Vera; or, The Nihilists* (1880), about Russian czars and revolutionaries; the play's portrayal of an assassination attempt made it politically unacceptable, and the production was canceled. He privately published a book of poems in 1881, opening with the sonnet *Hélas!* They were praised by Matthew Arnold and by Swinburne, but elsewhere denounced as immoral.

Wilde's finances received an unexpected boost when the New York production of *Patience* led to an invitation to lecture in the United States. His arrival in New York in 1882 was a media event: he was mobbed by reporters, and his every utterance was quoted or misquoted in both the American and British press. He was reported to have been disappointed in the Atlantic—"It is not so majestic as I expected"—and to have told the customs officers, "I have nothing to declare except my genius." He stayed a full year, earned quite a lot of money, and returned home internationally famous.

Oscar Wilde and Lord Alfred Douglas, 1893.

Wilde followed up his conquest of America with a few months in Paris, where he met many leading painters and writers. Back in London, and short of money once again, his thoughts turned to marriage, and in 1884 he wed Constance Lloyd. She was well-educated and well-off, and at first Wilde enjoyed the new roles of husband and then father to two sons, Cyril and Vyvyan. But he soon found married life a bore. Even during his honeymoon in Paris his thoughts were elsewhere: he became enamored of a book known as the Bible of decadence, *A Rebours* (1884) by Joris-Karl Huysmans. As his biographer Richard Ellmann has put it, this book "summoned him towards an underground life."

Wilde was a celebrity. He spent several years lecturing and reviewing, then entered the most inventive period of his life. Although he would later remark, "I have put only my talent into my works. I have put my genius into my life," the creative work of the early 1890s belies him. He articulated his theories on Art and Nature in two dialogues full of provocative paradoxes, *The Decay of Lying* (1888) and *The Critic as Artist* (1890). Then in his essay *The Soul of Man Under Socialism* (1891) he argued that the final goal of social evolution was joyous individualism. He continued his exploration of the relation of art to life in his only novel, *The Picture of Dorian Gray* (1890), which tells of a promising golden boy fascinated by the seductively amoral ideas of a jaded cynic. Dorian makes a Faustian bargain: his corrupted soul will be mirrored, not in his own face—he remains eternally youthful—but in his portrait. Much influenced by *A Rebours*, *Dorian Gray* achieved instantaneous notoriety, not so much for its aestheticism as for its thinly veiled suggestions of homosexuality.

Lady Windermere's Fan (1891) met with the opposite reception: this sparkling comedy depicting a mother's secret sacrifice for her daughter was an immediate success. Inspired in part by the French symbolist poet, Stéphane Mallarmé, Wilde was also writing—in French—a very different play, *Salomé*, about the fatal perversity of love and desire. To Wilde's indignation, *Salomé* was banned in England. However, in 1894 he published an English translation, with dramatic and daring illustrations by Aubrey Beardsley.

Wilde wrote two more comedies, *A Woman of No Importance* and *An Ideal Husband*, followed by his masterpiece, *The Importance of Being Earnest* (1895). Its philosophy, Wilde said, is "That we should treat all trivial things very seriously, and all the serious things of life with sincere and studied triviality." The triumphant opening night of this delightfully sophisticated farce marked the culmination of Wilde's career.

Then, at the very crest of success, Wilde was brought down by catastrophe. Although homosexuality was a criminal offense in Britain, Wilde had made little effort to conceal his relations with younger men, particularly Lord Alfred Douglas. But if society turned a blind eye, Douglas's father, the Marquess of Queensberry, did not. He hounded his son's lover relentlessly, finally sending Wilde a ludicrously misspelled note calling him a "Somdomite." Egged on by Douglas, Wilde sued for libel. It was a fatal mistake. His private affairs were mercilessly exposed in court, and he lost the case. Wilde himself was then prosecuted for committing indecent acts, convicted, and sentenced to two years at hard labor.

His obsession with the young aristocrat—beautiful, vicious, and volatile—had been ruinous in every sense. Wilde was disgraced and bankrupted. So great was the collective repugnance for him that both of his currently running plays, *An Ideal Husband* and *The Importance of Being Earnest*, were obliged to close. But the nightmare was only beginning: following the public humiliation of the trials was the horror of prison. Confined in a small cell with a bare plank bed, revolting food, and no latrine, he suffered constantly from diarrhea. He was allowed only one twenty-minute visit every three months. No talking was permitted. Dreading that he might lose his sanity, Wilde pleaded in vain for early release.

He gave vent to his sufferings in a long letter to Douglas entitled *De Profundis*. It is a terrible indictment of Douglas's selfish behavior, but more than that it is an autobiography, the anguished confession of a soul coming face to face with itself. Painfully he reviews the events that led to his downfall, finding at last his own salvation in forgiveness: "I don't write this letter to put bitterness into your heart, but to pluck it out of mine. For my own sake I must forgive you." Wilde was allowed to take the letter with him when he left prison, but chose not to have it published until after his death.

Wilde emerged from the degradation of prison a broken and penniless man. He spent the remainder of his life in exile outside Britain. He was never again allowed to see his young sons, and their surname was changed to protect them from scandal. All but a few loyal friends shunned him. The man who had lavished champagne on his friends was reduced to scrounging drinks from strangers who pitied him. He was unable to resume his writing, except for *The Ballad of Reading Gaol* (1898), a long poem based upon his prison experience. He converted to Catholicism on his deathbed, in a Paris hotel, but continued bravely inventing witticisms to the end: "I am dying beyond my means."

Impression du Matin[1]

> The Thames nocturne of blue and gold
> Changed to a harmony in gray:[2]

---

1. Impression of the morning (French). The title evokes the paintings of the French Impressionists, and their attempts to show how light transforms the landscape. The group received its name in 1874 when a critic singled out Monet's *Impression: Sunrise* as representative.
2. The American James McNeill Whistler painted a series of Thames night-scenes, called "nocturnes" (including the famous *Nocturne in Blue and Gold: Old Battersea Bridge*, c. 1875). He entitled some of his daytime scenes "harmonies." His close friendship with Wilde turned into a bitter rivalry by the mid-1880s; Whistler accused Wilde of plagiarizing his ideas.

A barge with ochre-coloured hay
Dropt° from the wharf: and chill and cold   *went downstream*

5 The yellow fog came creeping down
   The bridges, till the houses' walls
   Seemed changed to shadows and St. Paul's
Loomed like a bubble o'er the town.

Then suddenly arose the clang
10   Of waking life; the streets were stirred
   With country wagons: and a bird
Flew to the glistening roofs and sang.

But one pale woman all alone,
   The daylight kissing her wan hair,
15   Loitered beneath the gas lamps' flare,
With lips of flame and heart of stone.

1877   1881

The Harlot's House

We caught the tread of dancing feet,
We loitered down the moonlit street,
And stopped beneath the harlot's house.

Inside, above the din and fray,
5 We heard the loud musicians play
The "Treues Liebes Herz" of Strauss.[1]

Like strange mechanical grotesques,
Making fantastic arabesques,[2]
The shadows raced across the blind.

10 We watched the ghostly dancers spin
To sound of horn and violin,
Like black leaves wheeling in the wind.

Like wire-pulled automatons,
Slim silhouetted skeletons
15 Went sidling through the slow quadrille.[3]

They took each other by the hand,
And danced a stately saraband;
Their laughter echoed thin and shrill.

Sometimes a clockwork puppet pressed
20 A phantom lover to her breast,
Sometimes they seemed to try to sing.

Sometimes a horrible marionette
Came out, and smoked its cigarette
Upon the steps like a live thing.

1. "The Heart of True Love," a waltz by Viennese composer Johann Strauss (1825–1899).
2. "Arabesque" is a term both for a ballet posture and, in
art, for patterns of interlaced lines.
3. Square dance for four couples. The saraband (line 17)
is an old Spanish dance.

25   Then, turning to my love, I said,
     "The dead are dancing with the dead,
     The dust is whirling with the dust."

     But she—she heard the violin,
     And left my side, and entered in:
30   Love passed into the house of Lust.

     Then suddenly the tune went false,
     The dancers wearied of the waltz,
     The shadows ceased to wheel and whirl.

     And down the long and silent street,
35   The dawn, with silver-sandalled feet,
     Crept like a frightened girl.

1885, 1908

Symphony in Yellow[1]

     An omnibus across the bridge
      Crawls like a yellow butterfly,
      And, here and there, a passer-by
     Shows like a little restless midge.

5   Big barges full of yellow hay
      Are moored against the shadowy wharf,
      And, like a yellow silken scarf,
     The thick fog hangs along the quay.

     The yellow leaves begin to fade
10   And flutter from the Temple elms,[2]
      And at my feet the pale green Thames
     Lies like a rod of rippled jade.

1889

from The Decay of Lying[1]
An Observation

A dialogue. Persons: Cyril and Vivian.[2]

SCENE: *The library of a country house in Nottinghamshire.*

CYRIL (*coming in through the open window from the terrace*) My dear Vivian, don't coop yourself up all day in the library. It is a perfectly lovely afternoon. The air is exquisite. There is a mist upon the woods, like the purple bloom upon a plum. Let us go and lie on the grass, and smoke cigarettes, and enjoy Nature.

---

1. The title suggests Whistler's series of paintings that he called "symphonies" in various colors. The Aesthetic vogue for titles that mingle the arts originated with the French poet Théophile Gautier, who in 1852 named a poem *Symphony in White Major*. In the 1880s yellow—the color of sunflowers and paperback French novels—became associated with the Aesthetic movement.
2. The Middle Temple and Inner Temple form part of the Inns of Court; their garden runs down to the River Thames.
1. Published in January 1889 in *The Nineteenth Century*, then revised and reprinted in Wilde's *Intentions* (1891). This essay adopts the form of a Platonic dialogue in order to reconsider Plato's famous assertion in *The Republic* that art is falsehood. Wilde agrees with Plato that the artist tells lies, but instead of finding this morally repugnant, he praises the artist's imaginative victory over nature and mere fact. Questioning Plato's claim that art is a shadowy reflection of real life, Wilde claims that art comes first: "life is the mirror, and art the reality." As he explores the paradoxes of his theory that life imitates art, Wilde seeks to shock his audience into revising its aesthetic values; he wittily subverts the Victorian reverence for nature, sincerity, moral teaching, and artistic verisimilitude.
2. Wilde's two sons, aged three and two at the time Wilde wrote this, were named Cyril and Vyvyan.

VIVIAN Enjoy Nature! I am glad to say that I have entirely lost that faculty. People tell us that Art makes us love Nature more than we loved her before; that it reveals her secrets to us; and that after a careful study of Corot and Constable we see things in her that had escaped our observation. My own experience is that the more we study Art, the less we care for Nature. What Art really reveals to us is Nature's lack of design, her curious crudities, her extraordinary monotony, her absolutely unfinished condition. Nature has good intentions, of course, but, as Aristotle once said, she cannot carry them out.[3] When I look at a landscape I cannot help seeing all its defects. It is fortunate for us, however, that Nature is so imperfect, as otherwise we should have had no art at all. Art is our spirited protest, our gallant attempt to teach Nature her proper place. As for the infinite variety of Nature, that is a pure myth. It is not to be found in Nature herself. It resides in the imagination, or fancy, or cultivated blindness of the man who looks at her.

CYRIL Well, you need not look at the landscape. You can lie on the grass and smoke and talk.

VIVIAN But Nature is so uncomfortable. Grass is hard and lumpy and damp, and full of dreadful black insects. Why, even Morris' poorest workman[4] could make you a more comfortable seat than the whole of Nature can. Nature pales before the furniture of "the street which from Oxford has borrowed its name," as the poet you love so much once vilely phrased it.[5] I don't complain. If Nature had been comfortable, mankind would never have invented architecture, and I prefer houses to the open air. In a house we all feel of the proper proportions. Everything is subordinated to us, fashioned for our use and our pleasure. Egotism itself, which is so necessary to a proper sense of human dignity, is entirely the result of indoor life. Out of doors one becomes abstract and impersonal. One's individuality absolutely leaves one. And then Nature is so indifferent, so unappreciative. Whenever I am walking in the park here, I always feel that I am no more to her than the cattle that browse on the slope, or the burdock that blooms in the ditch. Nothing is more evident than that Nature hates Mind. Thinking is the most unhealthy thing in the world, and people die of it just as they die of any other disease. Fortunately, in England at any rate, thought is not catching. Our splendid physique as a people is entirely due to our national stupidity. I only hope we shall be able to keep this great historic bulwark of our happiness for many years to come; but I am afraid that we are beginning to be over-educated; at least everybody who is incapable of learning has taken to teaching—that is really what our enthusiasm for education has come to. In the meantime, you had better go back to your wearisome uncomfortable Nature, and leave me to correct my proofs.

CYRIL Writing an article! That is not very consistent after what you have just said.

VIVIAN Who wants to be consistent? The dullard and the doctrinaire, the tedious people who carry out their principles to the bitter end of action, to the *reductio ad absurdum* of practice. Not I. Like Emerson, I write over the door of my library the word "Whim."[6] Besides, my article is really a most salutary and valuable warning. If it is attended to, there may be a new Renaissance of Art.

CYRIL What is the subject?

---

3. In the *Poetics* Aristotle suggests that through mimesis or imitation of life, the artist completes nature's work.
4. William Morris employed skilled craftsmen to produce handmade furniture and textiles.
5. The goods sold on Oxford Street in London outshine the products of Wordsworth's beloved Nature. The line

in Wordsworth's *The Power of Music* actually reads: "In the street that from Oxford hath borrowed its name."
6. Ralph Waldo Emerson, the American essayist, wrote in *Self-Reliance* (1841): "I shun father and mother and wife and brother when my genius calls me. I would write on the lintels of the doorpost, *Whim*."

VIVIAN I intend to call it "The Decay of Lying: A Protest."

CYRIL Lying! I should have thought that our politicians kept up that habit.

VIVIAN I assure you that they do not. They never rise beyond the level of misrepresentation, and actually condescend to prove, to discuss, to argue. How different from the temper of the true liar, with his frank, fearless statements, his superb irresponsibility, his healthy, natural disdain of proof of any kind! After all, what is a fine lie? Simply that which is its own evidence. If a man is sufficiently unimaginative to produce evidence in support of a lie, he might just as well speak the truth at once. No, the politicians won't do. Something may, perhaps, be urged on behalf of the Bar. The mantle of the Sophist[7] has fallen on its members. Their feigned ardours and unreal rhetoric are delightful. They can make the worse appear the better cause, as though they were fresh from Leontine schools,[8] and have been known to wrest from reluctant juries triumphant verdicts of acquittal for their clients, even when those clients, as often happens, were clearly and unmistakeably innocent. But they are briefed by the prosaic, and are not ashamed to appeal to precedent. In spite of their endeavours, the truth will out. Newspapers, even, have degenerated. They may now be absolutely relied upon. One feels it as one wades through their columns. It is always the unreadable that occurs. I am afraid that there is not much to be said in favour of either the lawyer or the journalist. Besides, what I am pleading for is Lying in art. Shall I read you what I have written? It might do you a great deal of good.

CYRIL Certainly, if you give me a cigarette. Thanks. By the way, what magazine do you intend it for?

VIVIAN For the *Retrospective Review*.[9] I think I told you that the elect had revived it.

CYRIL Whom do you mean by "the elect"?

VIVIAN Oh, The Tired Hedonists of course.[1] It is a club to which I belong. We are supposed to wear faded roses in our button-holes when we meet, and to have a sort of cult for Domitian.[2] I am afraid you are not eligible. You are too fond of simple pleasures.

CYRIL I should be black-balled on the ground of animal spirits, I suppose?

VIVIAN Probably. Besides, you are a little too old. We don't admit anybody who is of the usual age.

CYRIL Well, I should fancy you are all a good deal bored with each other.

VIVIAN We are. That is one of the objects of the club. Now, if you promise not to interrupt too often, I will read you my article.

CYRIL You will find me all attention.

VIVIAN (*reading in a very clear, musical voice*) "THE DECAY OF LYING: A PROTEST.—One of the chief causes that can be assigned for the curiously commonplace character of most of the literature of our age is undoubtedly the decay of Lying as an art, a science, and a social pleasure. The ancient historians gave us delightful fiction in the form of fact; the modern novelist presents us with dull facts under the guise of fiction. The Blue-Book[3] is rapidly becoming his ideal both for method

---

7. The Sophists were Greek philosophers who taught the art of rhetoric; the word now refers to a deceptive reasoner.

8. Leontini was a Greek colony in Sicily where the sophist and rhetorician Gorgias (c. 483–375 B.C.) was educated.

9. A periodical, published in the 1820s and again in the 1850s that promoted interest in earlier literature. It was not, in fact, revived in the 1890s.

1. Hedonists believe that pleasure is the greatest good in life; a tired hedonist would be one exhausted by pleasure (a parody of Wilde's own image).

2. Emperor of Rome (A.D. 81–96), Domitian was famous for his cruelty.

3. Parliamentary reports. The whole passage is aimed at contemporary Realist and Naturalist novelists, such as George Gissing and Émile Zola, who sought to document everyday life, especially among the poor.

and manner. He has his tedious '*document humain*,'[4] his miserable little '*coin de la création*,' into which he peers with his microscope. He is to be found at the Librairie Nationale, or at the British Museum, shamelessly reading up his subject. He has not even the courage of other people's ideas, but insists on going directly to life for everything, and ultimately, between encyclopaedias and personal experience, he comes to the ground, having drawn his types from the family circle or from the weekly washerwoman, and having acquired an amount of useful information from which never, even in his most meditative moments, can he thoroughly free himself.

    * * * Believe me, my dear Cyril, modernity of form and modernity of subject-matter are entirely and absolutely wrong. We have mistaken the common livery of the age for the vesture of the Muses, and spend our days in the sordid streets and hideous suburbs of our vile cities when we should be out on the hillside with Apollo. Certainly we are a degraded race, and have sold our birthright for a mess of facts.[5]

CYRIL There is something in what you say, and there is no doubt that whatever amusement we may find in reading a purely modern novel, we have rarely any artistic pleasure in re-reading it. And this is perhaps the best rough test of what is literature and what is not. If one cannot enjoy reading a book over and over again, there is no use reading it at all. But what do you say about the return to Life and Nature? This is the panacea that is always being recommended to us.

VIVIAN I will read you what I say on that subject. The passage comes later on in the article, but I may as well give it to you now:—

    "The popular cry of our time is 'Let us return to Life and Nature; they will recreate Art for us, and send the red blood coursing through her veins; they will shoe her feet with swiftness and make her hand strong.' But, alas! we are mistaken in our amiable and well-meaning efforts. Nature is always behind the age. And as for Life, she is the solvent that breaks up Art, the enemy that lays waste her house."

CYRIL What do you mean by saying that Nature is always behind the age?

VIVIAN Well, perhaps that is rather cryptic. What I mean is this. If we take Nature to mean natural simple instinct as opposed to self-conscious culture, the work produced under this influence is always old-fashioned, antiquated, and out of date. One touch of Nature may make the whole world kin, but two touches of Nature will destroy any work of Art. If, on the other hand, we regard Nature as the collection of phenomena external to man, people only discover in her what they bring to her. She has no suggestions of her own. Wordsworth went to the lakes, but he was never a lake poet. He found in stones the sermons he had already hidden there.[6] He went moralizing about the district, but his good work was produced when he returned, not to Nature but to poetry. Poetry gave him "Laodamia," and the fine sonnets, and the great Ode,[7] such as it is. Nature gave him "Martha Ray" and "Peter Bell," and the address to Mr Wilkinson's spade.

---

4. Human document, from the title of an essay by Zola, who wrote in *What I Hate:* "A work of art is a nook of creation ("un coin de la création") seen from the perspective of a temperament."
5. When he was hungry, Esau sold his birthright to his brother Jacob for "a mess of pottage" (Genesis 25.30–34).
6. "And this our life, exempt from public haunt, / Finds tongues in trees, books in the running brooks, / Sermons in stones, and good in every thing" (*As You Like It* 2.1.15–17).
7. Presumably Wordsworth's *Ode: Intimations of Immortality.* Vivian next mentions several distinctly lesser poems.

CYRIL I think that view might be questioned. I am rather inclined to believe in the "impulse from a vernal wood,"[8] though of course the artistic value of such an impulse depends entirely on the kind of temperament that receives it, so that the return to Nature would come to mean simply the advance to a great personality. You would agree with that, I fancy. However, proceed with your article.

VIVIAN (reading) "Art begins with abstract decoration, with purely imaginative and pleasurable work dealing with what is unreal and nonexistent. This is the first stage. Then Life becomes fascinated with this new wonder, and asks to be admitted into the charmed circle. Art takes life as part of her rough material, recreates it, and refashions it in fresh forms, is absolutely indifferent to fact, invents, imagines, dreams, and keeps between herself and reality the impenetrable barrier of beautiful style, of decorative or ideal treatment. The third stage is when Life gets the upper hand, and drives Art out into the wilderness. This is the true decadence, and it is from this that we are now suffering.

"Take the case of the English drama. At first in the hands of the monks Dramatic Art was abstract, decorative, and mythological. Then she enlisted Life in her service, and using some of life's external forms, she created an entirely new race of beings, whose sorrows were more terrible than any sorrow man has ever felt, whose joys were keener than lover's joys, who had the rage of the Titans[9] and the calm of the gods, who had monstrous and marvellous sins, monstrous and marvellous virtues. To them she gave a language different from that of actual use, a language full of resonant music and sweet rhythm, made stately by solemn cadence, or made delicate by fanciful rhyme, jewelled with wonderful words, and enriched with lofty diction. She clothed her children in strange raiment and gave them masks, and at her bidding the antique world rose from its marble tomb. A new Caesar stalked through the streets of risen Rome, and with purple sail and flute-led oars another Cleopatra passed up the river to Antioch.[1] Old myth and legend and dream took shape and substance. History was entirely re-written, and there was hardly one of the dramatists who did not recognize that the object of Art is not simple truth but complex beauty. In this they were perfectly right. Art itself is really a form of exaggeration; and selection, which is the very spirit of art, is nothing more than an intensified mode of over-emphasis.

"But Life soon shattered the perfection of the form. Even in Shakespeare we can see the beginning of the end. It shows itself by the gradual breaking up of the blank-verse in the later plays, by the predominance given to prose, and by the over-importance assigned to characterization. The passages in Shakespeare—and they are many—where the language is uncouth, vulgar, exaggerated, fantastic, obscene even, are entirely due to Life calling for an echo of her own voice, and rejecting the intervention of beautiful style, through which alone should Life be suffered to find expression. Shakespeare is not by any means a flawless artist. He is too fond of going directly to life, and borrowing life's natural utterance. He forgets that when Art surrenders her imaginative medium she surrenders everything. Goethe says, somewhere—

In der Beschränkung zeigt sich erst der Meister,[2]

---

8. "One impulse from a vernal wood / May teach you more of man / Of moral evil and of good / Than all the sages can." From Wordsworth's *The Tables Turned.*
9. Mythological giants who were overthrown by the gods.

1. References to Shakespeare's *Julius Caesar* and *Antony and Cleopatra.*
2. From *Nature and Art* by Johann Wolfgang von Goethe (1749–1832).

"'It is in working within limits that the master reveals himself,' and the limitation, the very condition of any art is style. However, we need not linger any longer over Shakespeare's realism. *The Tempest* is the most perfect of palinodes.[3] All that we desired to point out was, that the magnificent work of the Elizabethan and Jacobean artists contained within itself the seeds of its own dissolution, and that, if it drew some of its strength from using life as rough material, it drew all its weakness from using life as an artistic method. As the inevitable result of this substitution of an imitative for a creative medium, this surrender of an imaginative form, we have the modern English melodrama. The characters in these plays talk on the stage exactly as they would talk off it; they have neither aspirations nor aspirates; they are taken directly from life and reproduce its vulgarity down to the smallest detail; they present the gait, manner, costume, and accent of real people; they would pass unnoticed in a third-class railway carriage. And yet how wearisome the plays are! They do not succeed in producing even that impression of reality at which they aim, and which is their only reason for existing. As a method, realism is a complete failure.

"What is true about the drama and the novel is no less true about those arts that we call the decorative arts. The whole history of these arts in Europe is the record of the struggle between Orientalism, with its frank rejection of imitation, its love of artistic convention, its dislike to the actual representation of any object in Nature, and our own imitative spirit. Wherever the former has been paramount, as in Byzantium, Sicily, and Spain, by actual contact, or in the rest of Europe by the influence of the Crusades, we have had beautiful and imaginative work in which the visible things of life are transmuted into artistic conventions, and the things that Life has not are invented and fashioned for her delight. But wherever we have returned to Life and Nature, our work has always become vulgar, common, and uninteresting. Modern tapestry, with its aërial effects, its elaborate perspective, its broad expanses of waste sky, its faithful and laborious realism, has no beauty whatsoever. The pictorial glass of Germany is absolutely detestable. We are beginning to weave possible carpets in England, but only because we have returned to the method and spirit of the East. Our rugs and carpets of twenty years ago, with their solemn depressing truths, their inane worship of Nature, their sordid reproductions of visible objects, have become, even to the Philistine,[4] a source of laughter. A cultured Mahomedan once remarked to us, "You Christians are so occupied in misinterpreting the fourth commandment that you have never thought of making an artistic application of the second."[5] He was perfectly right, and the whole truth of the matter is this: The proper school to learn art in is not Life but Art."

✻ ✻ ✻ Facts are not merely finding a footing-place in history, but they are usurping the domain of Fancy, and have invaded the kingdom of Romance. Their chilling touch is over everything. They are vulgarizing mankind. The crude commercialism of America, its materializing spirit, its indifference to the poetical side of things, and its lack of imagination and of high unattainable ideals, are entirely due to that country having adopted for its national hero a man, who according to his

---

3. A retraction or recantation.
4. In *Culture and Anarchy* (1869) Matthew Arnold used this term to refer to the materialistic and uncultured middle classes.
5. The Fourth Commandment is "Remember the Sabbath day, to keep it holy"; the Second is "Thou shalt not

make unto thee any graven image, or any likeness of any thing that is in heaven above, or that is in the earth beneath, or that is in the water underneath the earth" (Exodus 20.4–5). Islamic art is traditionally decorative rather than imitative, in observance of the second commandment.

own confession, was incapable of telling a lie, and it is not too much to say that the story of George Washington and the cherry-tree has done more harm, and in a shorter space of time, than any other moral tale in the whole of literature."

CYRIL My dear boy!

VIVIAN I assure you it is the case, and the amusing part of the whole thing is that the story of the cherry-tree is an absolute myth. However, you must not think that I am too despondent about the artistic future either of America or of our own country. Listen to this:—

"That some change will take place before this century has drawn to its close we have no doubt whatsoever. Bored by the tedious and improving conversation of those who have neither the wit to exaggerate nor the genius to romance, tired of the intelligent person whose reminiscences are always based upon memory, whose statements are invariably limited by probability, and who is at any time liable to be corroborated by the merest Philistine who happens to be present, Society sooner or later must return to its lost leader, the cultured and fascinating liar. Who he was who first, without ever having gone out to the rude chase, told the wondering cavemen at sunset how he had dragged the Megatherium[6] from the purple darkness of its jasper cave, or slain the Mammoth in single combat and brought back its gilded tusks, we cannot tell, and not one of our modern anthropologists, for all their much-boasted science, has had the ordinary courage to tell us. Whatever was his name or race, he certainly was the true founder of social intercourse. For the aim of the liar is simply to charm, to delight, to give pleasure. He is the very basis of civilized society, and without him a dinner party, even at the mansions of the great, is as dull as a lecture at the Royal Society, or a debate at the Incorporated Authors, or one of Mr Burnand's farcical comedies.[7]

"Nor will he be welcomed by society alone. Art, breaking from the prison-house of realism, will run to greet him, and will kiss his false, beautiful lips, knowing that he alone is in possession of the great secret of all her manifestations, the secret that Truth is entirely and absolutely a matter of style; while Life—poor, probable, uninteresting human life—tired of repeating herself for the benefit of Mr Herbert Spencer,[8] scientific historians, and the compilers of statistics in general, will follow meekly after him, and try to reproduce, in her own simple and untutored way, some of the marvels of which he talks. * * *

* * * All that I desire to point out is the general principle that Life imitates Art far more than Art imitates Life, and I feel sure that if you think seriously about it you will find that it is true. Life holds the mirror up to Art, and either reproduces some strange type imagined by painter or sculptor, or realizes in fact what has been dreamed in fiction. Scientifically speaking, the basis of life—the energy of life, as Aristotle would call it[9]—is simply the desire for expression, and Art is always presenting various forms through which this expression can be attained. Life seizes on them and uses them, even if they be to her own hurt. Young men have committed suicide because Rolla did so, have died by their own hand because by his own hand Werther died.[1] Think of what we owe to the imitation of Christ, of what we owe to the imitation of Caesar.

---

6. Large extinct animal.
7. Frances Cowley Burnand (1836–1917), editor of *Punch* and popular dramatist.
8. English philosopher and theorist of evolution (1820–1903).

9. In his *Physics*, Aristotle equates nature with energy.
1. Rolla is the Byronic hero of *Rolla* (1833), by the French poet Alfred de Musset; Werther is the romantic hero of Goethe's *The Sorrows of Young Werther* (1774).

CYRIL The theory is certainly a very curious one, but to make it complete you must show that Nature, no less than Life, is an imitation of Art. Are you prepared to prove that?

VIVIAN My dear fellow, I am prepared to prove anything.

CYRIL Nature follows the landscape painter then, and takes her effects from him?

VIVIAN Certainly. Where, if not from the Impressionists,[2] do we get those wonderful brown fogs that come creeping down our streets, blurring the gas-lamps and changing the houses into monstrous shadows? To whom, if not to them and their master, do we owe the lovely silver mists that brood over our river, and turn to faint forms of fading grace curved bridge and swaying barge? The extraordinary change that has taken place in the climate of London during the last ten years is entirely due to this particular school of Art. You smile. Consider the matter from a scientific or a metaphysical point of view, and you will find that I am right. For what is Nature? Nature is no great mother who has borne us. She is our creation. It is in our brain that she quickens to life. Things are because we see them, and what we see, and how we see it, depends on the Arts that have influenced us. To look at a thing is very different from seeing a thing. One does not see anything until one sees its beauty. Then, and then only, does it come into existence. At present, people see fogs, not because there are fogs, but because poets and painters have taught them the mysterious loveliness of such effects. There may have been fogs for centuries in London. I dare say there were. But no one saw them, and so we do not know anything about them. They did not exist till Art had invented them. Now, it must be admitted, fogs are carried to excess. They have become the mere mannerism of a clique, and the exaggerated realism of their method gives dull people bronchitis. Where the cultured catch an effect, the uncultured catch cold. And so, let us be humane, and invite Art to turn her wonderful eyes elsewhere. She has done so already, indeed. That white quivering sunlight that one sees now in France, with its strange blotches of mauve, and its restless violet shadows, is her latest fancy, and, on the whole, Nature reproduces it quite admirably. Where she used to give us Corots and Daubignys, she gives us now exquisite Monets and entrancing Pisaros.[3] Indeed there are moments, rare, it is true, but still to be observed from time to time, when Nature becomes absolutely modern. Of course she is not always to be relied upon. The fact is that she is in this unfortunate position. Art creates an incomparable and unique effect, and, having done so, passes on to other things. Nature, upon the other hand, forgetting that imitation can be made the sincerest form of insult, keeps on repeating this effect until we all become absolutely wearied of it. Nobody of any real culture, for instance, ever talks nowadays about the beauty of a sunset. Sunsets are quite old-fashioned. They belong to the time when Turner was the last note in art.[4] To admire them is a distinct sign of provincialism of temperament. Upon the other hand they go on. Yesterday evening Mrs Arundel insisted on my going to the window, and looking at the glorious sky, as she called it. Of course I had to look at it. She is one of those absurdly pretty Philistines, to whom one can deny nothing. And what was it? It

---

2. French Impressionist painters such as Monet, Renoir, and Pissarro sought to capture the interplay of light, atmosphere, and the elements, but it was Whistler (probably the "master" alluded to in the next sentence) who discovered London fogs, barges, and misty bridges as artistic subjects.

3. Earlier in the century, Corot and Daubigny had paint-

ed muted landscapes; Wilde's contemporaries Claude Monet and Camille Pissarro produced bright, Impressionist canvasses.

4. The atmospheric landscape paintings of J. M. W. Turner (1775–1851) were much admired by Ruskin in *Modern Painters* (1843–1860).

was simply a very second-rate Turner, a Turner of a bad period, with all the painter's worst faults exaggerated and over-emphasized. * * * But have I proved my theory to your satisfaction?

CYRIL You have proved it to my dissatisfaction, which is better. But even admitting this strange imitative instinct in Life and Nature, surely you would acknowledge that Art expresses the temper of its age, the spirit of its time, the moral and social conditions that surround it, and under whose influence it is produced.

VIVIAN Certainly not! Art never expresses anything but itself. * * * Remote from reality, and with her eyes turned away from the shadows of the cave,[5] Art reveals her own perfection, and the wondering crowd that watches the opening of the marvellous, many-petalled rose fancies that it is its own history that is being told to it, its own spirit that is finding expression in a new form. But it is not so. The highest art rejects the burden of the human spirit, and gains more from a new medium or a fresh material than she does from any enthusiasm for art, or from any lofty passion, or from any great awakening of the human consciousness. She develops purely on her own lines. She is not symbolic of any age. It is the ages that are her symbols. * * *

CYRIL I quite agree with you there. The spirit of an age may be best expressed in the abstract ideal arts, for the spirit itself is abstract and ideal. Upon the other hand, for the visible aspect of an age, for its look, as the phrase goes, we must of course go to the arts of imitation.

VIVIAN I don't think so. After all, what the imitative arts really give us are merely the various styles of particular artists, or of certain schools of artists. Surely you don't imagine that the people of the Middle Ages bore any resemblance at all to the figures on mediaeval stained glass, or in mediaeval stone and wood carving, or on mediaeval metal-work, or tapestries, or illuminated MSS.[6] They were probably very ordinary-looking people, with nothing grotesque, or remarkable, or fantastic in their appearance. The Middle Ages, as we know them in art, are simply a definite form of style, and there is no reason at all why an artist with this style should not be produced in the nineteenth century. No great artist ever sees things as they really are. If he did, he would cease to be an artist. Take an example from our own day. I know that you are fond of Japanese things. Now, do you really imagine that the Japanese people, as they are presented to us in art, have any existence? If you do, you have never understood Japanese art at all. The Japanese people are the deliberate self-conscious creation of certain individual artists. If you set a picture by Hokusai, or Hokkei,[7] or any of the great native painters, beside a real Japanese gentleman or lady, you will see that there is not the slightest resemblance between them. The actual people who live in Japan are not unlike the general run of English people; that is to say, they are extremely commonplace, and have nothing curious or extraordinary about them. In fact the whole of Japan is a pure invention. There is no such country, there are no such people. * * *

CYRIL But modern portraits by English painters, what of them? Surely they are like the people they pretend to represent?

VIVIAN Quite so. They are so like them that a hundred years from now no one will believe in them. The only portraits in which one believes are portraits where

---

5. In the *Republic*, Plato suggests that reality is to the absolute what shadows in a cave are to the objects which cast the shadows—i.e., dim and imperfect indications.

6. Manuscripts.

7. Katsushika Hokusai (1760–1849) and Hokkei (1780–1850), Japanese artists.

there is very little of the sitter, and a very great deal of the artist. Holbein's drawings of the men and women of his time impress us with a sense of their absolute reality. But this is simply because Holbein compelled life to accept his conditions, to restrain itself within his limitations, to reproduce his type, and to appear as he wished it to appear. It is style that makes us believe in a thing—nothing but style. Most of our modern portrait painters are doomed to absolute oblivion. They never paint what they see. They paint what the public sees, and the public never sees anything.

CYRIL Well, after that I think I should like to hear the end of your article.

VIVIAN With pleasure. Whether it will do any good I really cannot say. Ours is certainly the dullest and most prosaic century possible. * * * However, I must read the end of my article:—

"What we have to do, what at any rate it is our duty to do, is to revive this old art of Lying. Much of course may be done, in the way of educating the public, by amateurs in the domestic circle, at literary lunches, and at afternoon teas. * * * A short primer, 'When to Lie and How,' if brought out in an attractive and not too expensive a form, would no doubt command a large sale, and would prove of real practical service to many earnest and deep-thinking people. Lying for the sake of the improvement of the young, which is the basis of home education, still lingers amongst us, and its advantages are so admirably set forth in the early books of Plato's *Republic*[8] that it is unnecessary to dwell upon them here. It is a mode of lying for which all good mothers have peculiar capabilities, but it is capable of still further development, and has been sadly overlooked by the School Board. Lying for the sake of a monthly salary is of course well known in Fleet Street, and the profession of a political leader-writer is not without its advantages. But it is said to be a somewhat dull occupation, and it certainly does not lead to much beyond a kind of ostentatious obscurity. The only form of lying that is absolutely beyond reproach is Lying for its own sake, and the highest development of this is, as we have already pointed out, Lying in Art. Just as those who do not love Plato more than Truth cannot pass beyond the threshold of the Academe,[9] so those who do not love Beauty more than Truth never know the inmost shrine of Art. The solid stolid British intellect lies in the desert sands like the Sphinx in Flaubert's marvellous tale,[1] and fantasy, *La Chimère*, dances round it, and calls to it with her false, flute-toned voice. It may not hear her now, but surely some day, when we are all bored to death with the commonplace character of modern fiction, it will hearken to her and try to borrow her wings.

"And when that day dawns, or sunset reddens, how joyous we shall all be! Facts will be regarded as discreditable, Truth will be found mourning over her fetters, and Romance, with her temper of wonder, will return to the land. The very aspect of the world will change to our startled eyes. Out of the sea will rise Behemoth and Leviathan,[2] and sail round the high-pooped galleys, as they do on

8. In Books 2 and 3, which discuss the education of the future Guardians of the ideal republic, Plato advocates suppressing stories that evoke the terror of death, or that portray the gods as undignified or immoral.
9. A gibe at Plato's coercive method of teaching. Wilde reverses Aristotle's remark, "Plato is dear to me, but dearer still is truth." Plato's school in Athens was called the Academy because he taught his students in an olive grove dedicated to the hero Academus.

1. *The Temptation of Saint Anthony* (1874) by French novelist Gustave Flaubert.
2. The hippopotamus and the whale in the Book of Job. The rest of the paragraph refers to fabulous mythical animals: the phoenix was a legendary bird that immolated itself on a pyre, then rose regenerated from the ashes; the basilisk was a reptile whose breath and glance were fatal; the hippogriff was part gryphon and part horse.

the delightful maps of those ages when books on geography were actually readable. Dragons will wander about the waste places, and the phoenix will soar from her nest of fire into the air. We shall lay our hands upon the basilisk, and see the jewel in the toad's head. Champing his gilded oats, the Hippogriff will stand in our stalls, and over our heads will float the Blue Bird singing of beautiful and impossible things, of things that are lovely and that never happen, of things that are not and that should be. But before this comes to pass we must cultivate the lost art of Lying."

CYRIL Then we must certainly cultivate it at once. But in order to avoid making any error I want you to tell me briefly the doctrines of the new aesthetics.

VIVIAN Briefly, then, they are these. Art never expresses anything but itself. It has an independent life, just as Thought has, and develops purely on its own lines. It is not necessarily realistic in an age of realism, nor spiritual in an age of faith. So far from being the creation of its time, it is usually in direct opposition to it, and the only history that it preserves for us is the history of its own progress. Sometimes it returns upon its footsteps, and revives some antique form, as happened in the archaistic movement of late Greek Art, and in the pre-Raphaelite movement of our own day. At other times it entirely anticipates its age, and produces in one century work that it takes another century to understand, to appreciate, and to enjoy. In no case does it reproduce its age. To pass from the art of a time to the time itself is the great mistake that all historians commit.

The second doctrine is this. All bad art comes from returning to Life and Nature, and elevating them into ideals. Life and Nature may sometimes be used as part of Art's rough material, but before they are of any real service to art they must be translated into artistic conventions. The moment Art surrenders its imaginative medium it surrenders everything. As a method Realism is a complete failure, and the two things that every artist should avoid are modernity of form and modernity of subject-matter. To us, who live in the nineteenth century, any century is a suitable subject for art except our own. The only beautiful things are the things that do not concern us. It is, to have the pleasure of quoting myself, exactly because Hecuba is nothing to us that her sorrows are so suitable a motive for a tragedy.[3] Besides, it is only the modern that ever becomes old-fashioned. M. Zola sits down to give us a picture of the Second Empire.[4] Who cares for the Second Empire now? It is out of date. Life goes faster than Realism, but Romanticism is always in front of Life.

The third doctrine is that Life imitates Art far more than Art imitates Life. This results not merely from Life's imitative instinct, but from the fact that the self-conscious aim of Life is to find expression, and that Art offers it certain beautiful forms through which it may realize that energy. It is a theory that has never been put forward before, but it is extremely fruitful, and throws an entirely new light upon the history of Art.

It follows, as a corollary from this, that external Nature also imitates Art. The only effects that she can show us are effects that we have already seen through poetry, or in paintings. This is the secret of Nature's charm, as well as the explanation of Nature's weakness.

---

3. Hecuba, queen of Troy, lost her sons and her husband when the Greeks defeated Troy. Wilde alludes to a scene in *Hamlet* where an actor recites a speech about her suffering and Hamlet asks himself, "What's Hecuba to him, or he to Hecuba, / That he should weep for her?" (2.2.559–60).

4. In France, the period from 1852 to 1870.

The final revelation is that Lying, the telling of beautiful untrue things, is the proper aim of Art. But of this I think I have spoken at sufficient length. And now let us go out on the terrace, where "droops the milk-white peacock like a ghost,"[5] while the evening star "washes the dusk with silver."[6] At twilight nature becomes a wonderfully suggestive effect, and is not without loveliness, though perhaps its chief use is to illustrate quotations from the poets. Come! We have talked long enough.

1889, 1891

from The Soul of Man Under Socialism[1]

The chief advantage that would result from the establishment of Socialism is, undoubtedly, the fact that Socialism would relieve us from that sordid necessity of living for others which, in the present condition of things, presses so hardly upon almost everybody. In fact, scarcely anyone at all escapes.

Now and then, in the course of the century, a great man of science, like Darwin; a great poet, like Keats; a fine critical spirit, like M. Renan;[2] a supreme artist, like Flaubert, has been able to isolate himself, to keep himself out of reach of the clamorous claims of others, to stand "under the shelter of the wall," as Plato puts it, and so to realise the perfection of what was in him, to his own incomparable gain, and to the incomparable and lasting gain of the whole world. These, however, are exceptions. The majority of people spoil their lives by an unhealthy and exaggerated altruism—are forced, indeed, so to spoil them. They find themselves surrounded by hideous poverty, by hideous ugliness, by hideous starvation. It is inevitable that they should be strongly moved by all this. The emotions of man are stirred more quickly than man's intelligence; and, as I pointed out some time ago in an article on the function of criticism,[3] it is much more easy to have sympathy with suffering than it is to have sympathy with thought. Accordingly, with admirable though misdirected intentions, they very seriously and very sentimentally set themselves to the task of remedying the evils that they see. But their remedies do not cure the disease: they merely prolong it. Indeed, their remedies are part of the disease.

They try to solve the problem of poverty, for instance, by keeping the poor alive; or, in the case of a very advanced school, by amusing the poor.

But this is not a solution: it is an aggravation of the difficulty. *The proper aim is to try and reconstruct society on such a basis that poverty will be impossible.* And the altruistic virtues have really prevented the carrying out of this aim. Just as the worst slave-owners were those who were kind to their slaves, and so prevented the horror of the system being realised by those who suffered from it, and understood by those who contemplated it, so, in the present state of things in England, the people who do most harm are the people who try to do most good; and at last we have had the spectacle of men who have really studied the problem and know the life—educated men

---

5. From Tennyson's *The Princess* (1847).

6. From Blake's *To the Evening Star* (1783).

1. Published in *The Fortnightly Review* in 1891, this essay had an important underground life during the next few decades; translated into many languages, it was also secretly printed and circulated in Tzarist Russia. In the 1880s and 1890s, socialism, which advocates collective ownership of property and the means of production, emerged as a strong nationwide movement in Britain, bolstered by trade unionism and such intellectual and feminist groups as the Fabian Society and the Ethical Socialists. Wilde had no formal connection to socialist groups, but was sympathetic to many of their concerns, and apparently wrote this essay after attending a meeting where Bernard Shaw was the chief speaker. Wilde's essay is remarkable in its claim that socialism—usually said to put the needs of society ahead of personal interests—will lead to the fulfillment of the individual. He wrote elsewhere: "to make men Socialists is nothing, but to make Socialism human is a great thing."

2. Ernest Renan, French scholar and essayist, author of *La Vie de Jésus* (1863; English trans. 1888).

3. Wilde's essay *The Critic as Artist* (1890) challenged Matthew Arnold's *The Function of Criticism at the Present Time* (1864) by arguing that good criticism is "creative and independent" and "more creative than creation" because it is further removed from life than the work of the writer or artist.

who live in the East-end[4]—coming forward and imploring the community to restrain its altruistic impulses of charity, benevolence, and the like. They do so on the ground that such charity degrades and demoralizes. They are perfectly right. Charity creates a multitude of sins.

There is also this to be said. It is immoral to use private property in order to alleviate the horrible evils that result from the institution of private property. It is both immoral and unfair.

Under Socialism all this will, of course, be altered. There will be no people living in fetid dens and fetid rags, and bringing up unhealthy, hunger-pinched children in the midst of impossible and absolutely repulsive surroundings. The security of society will not depend, as it does now, on the state of the weather. If a frost comes we shall not have a hundred thousand men out of work, tramping about the streets in a state of disgusting misery, or whining to their neighbours for alms, or crowding round the doors of loathsome shelters to try and secure a hunch of bread and a night's unclean lodging. Each member of the society will share in the general prosperity and happiness of the society, and if a frost comes no one will practically be anything the worse.

Upon the other hand, *Socialism itself will be of value simply because it will lead to Individualism.*

Socialism, Communism, or whatever one chooses to call it, by converting private property into public wealth, and substituting cooperation for competition, will restore society to its proper condition of a thoroughly healthy organism, and insure the material well-being of each member of the community. It will, in fact, give Life its proper basis and its proper environment. But for the full development of Life to its highest mode of perfection, something more is needed. What is needed is Individualism. If the Socialism is Authoritarian; if there are Governments armed with economic power as they are now with political power; if, in a word, we are to have Industrial Tyrannies, then the last state of man will be worse than the first. At present, in consequence of the existence of private property, a great many people are enabled to develop a certain very limited amount of Individualism. They are either under no necessity to work for their living, or are enabled to choose the sphere of activity that is really congenial to them, and gives them pleasure. These are the poets, the philosophers, the men of science, the men of culture—in a word, the real men, the men who have realised themselves, and in whom all Humanity gains a partial realisation. Upon the other hand, there are a great many people who, having no private property of their own, and being always on the brink of sheer starvation, are compelled to do the work of beasts of burden, to do work that is quite uncongenial to them, and to which they are forced by the peremptory, unreasonable, degrading Tyranny of want. These are the poor, and amongst them there is no grace of manner, or charm of speech, or civilization, or culture, or refinement in pleasures, or joy of life. From their collective force Humanity gains much in material prosperity. But it is only the material result that it gains, and the man who is poor is in himself absolutely of no importance. He is merely the infinitesimal atom of a force that, so far from regarding him, crushes him: indeed, prefers him crushed, as in that case he is far more obedient.

Of course, it might be said that the Individualism generated under conditions of private property is not always, or even as a rule, of a fine or wonderful type, and that the poor, if they have not culture and charm, have still many virtues. Both these statements would be quite true. The possession of private property is very often extremely demoralising, and that is, of course, one of the reasons why Socialism wants to get rid

4. The poorest section of Victorian London.

of the institution. In fact, property is really a nuisance. Some years ago people went about the country saying that property has duties. They said it so often and so tediously that, at last, the church has begun to say it. One hears it now from every pulpit. It is perfectly true. Property not merely has duties, but has so many duties that its possession to any large extent is a bore. It involves endless claims upon one, endless attention to business, endless bother. If property had simply pleasures, we could stand it; but its duties make it unbearable. In the interest of the rich we must get rid of it. The virtues of the poor may be readily admitted, and are much to be regretted. * * *

Misery and poverty are so absolutely degrading, and exercise such a paralysing effect over the nature of men, that no class is ever really conscious of its own suffering. They have to be told of it by other people, and they often entirely disbelieve them. What is said by great employers of labour against agitators is unquestionably true. Agitators are a set of interfering, meddling people, who come down to some perfectly contented class of the community, and sow the seeds of discontent amongst them. That is the reason why agitators are so absolutely necessary. Without them, in our incomplete state, there would be no advance towards civilization. Slavery was put down in America, not in consequence of any action on the part of the slaves, or even any express desire on their part that they should be free. It was put down entirely through the grossly illegal conduct of certain agitators in Boston and elsewhere, who were not slaves themselves, nor owners of slaves, nor had anything to do with the question really. It was, undoubtedly, the Abolitionists who set the torch alight, who began the whole thing. And it is curious to note that from the slaves themselves they received, not merely very little assistance, but hardly any sympathy even; and when at the close of the war the slaves found themselves free, found themselves indeed so absolutely free that they were free to starve, many of them bitterly regretted the new state of things. To the thinker, the most tragic fact in the whole of the French Revolution is not that Marie Antoinette was killed for being a queen, but that the starved peasant of the Vendée voluntarily went out to die for the hideous cause of feudalism.[5]

It is clear, then, that no Authoritarian Socialism will do. For while under the present system a very large number of people can lead lives of a certain amount of freedom and expression and happiness, under an industrial-barrack system, or a system of economic tyranny, nobody would be able to have any such freedom at all. It is to be regretted that a portion of our community should be practically in slavery, but to propose to solve the problem by enslaving the entire community is childish. Every man must be left quite free to choose his own work. No form of compulsion must be exercised over him. * * *

Now as the State is not to govern, it may be asked what the State is to do. The State is to be a voluntary association that will organize labour, and be the manufacturer and distributor of necessary commodities. *The State is to make what is useful. The individual is to make what is beautiful.* And as I have mentioned the word labour, I cannot help saying that a great deal of nonsense is being written and talked nowadays about the dignity of manual labour. There is nothing necessarily dignified about manual labour at all, and most of it is absolutely degrading. It is mentally and morally injurious to man to do anything in which he does not find pleasure, and many forms of labour are quite pleasureless activities, and should be regarded as such. To sweep a slushy crossing for eight hours on a day when the east wind is blowing is a

5. Marie Antoinette, Queen of France, was beheaded in 1793 during the French Revolution; the Vendée was a center of counterrevolutionary activity.

disgusting occupation. To sweep it with mental, moral, or physical dignity seems to me to be impossible. To sweep it with joy would be appalling. Man is made for something better than disturbing dirt. All work of that kind should be done by a machine.

And I have no doubt that it will be so. Up to the present, man has been, to a certain extent, the slave of machinery, and there is something tragic in the fact that as soon as man had invented a machine to do his work he began to starve. This, however, is, of course, the result of our property system and our system of competition. One man owns a machine which does the work of five hundred men. Five hundred men are, in consequence, thrown out of employment, and having no work to do, become hungry and take to thieving. The one man secures the produce of the machine and keeps it, and has five hundred times as much as he should have, and probably, which is of much more importance, a great deal more than he really wants. Were that machine the property of all, every one would benefit by it. It would be an immense advantage to the community. All unintellectual labour, all monotonous, dull labour, all labour that deals with dreadful things, and involves unpleasant conditions, must be done by machinery. Machinery must work for us in coal mines, and do all sanitary services, and be the stoker of steamers, and clean the streets, and run messages on wet days, and do anything that is tedious or distressing. *At present machinery competes against man. Under proper conditions machinery will serve man.* There is no doubt at all that this is the future of machinery, and just as trees grow while the country gentleman is asleep, so while Humanity will be amusing itself, or enjoying cultivated leisure—which, and not labour, is the aim of man—or making beautiful things, or reading beautiful things, or simply contemplating the world with admiration and delight, machinery will be doing all the necessary and unpleasant work. The fact is, that civilization requires slaves. The Greeks were quite right there. Unless there are slaves to do the ugly, horrible, uninteresting work, culture and contemplation become almost impossible. Human slavery is wrong, insecure, and demoralising. On mechanical slavery, on the slavery of the machine, the future of the world depends. And when scientific men are no longer called upon to go down to a depressing East-end and distribute bad cocoa and worse blankets to starving people, they will have delightful leisure in which to devise wonderful and marvellous things for their own joy and the joy of everyone else. There will be great storages of force for every city, and for every house if required, and this force man will convert into heat, light, or motion, according to his needs. Is this Utopian?[6] A map of the world that does not include Utopia is not worth even glancing at, for it leaves out the one country at which Humanity is always landing. And when Humanity lands there, it looks out, and, seeing a better country, sets sail. Progress is the realisation of Utopias. * * *

It is to be noted also that Individualism does not come to man with any sickly cant about duty, which merely means doing what other people want because they want it; or any hideous cant about self-sacrifice, which is merely a survival of savage mutilation. *In fact, it does not come to man with any claims upon him at all. It comes naturally and inevitably out of man.* It is the point to which all development tends. It is the differentiation to which all organisms grow. It is the perfection that is inherent in every mode of life, and towards which every mode of life quickens. And so Individualism exercises no compulsion over man. On the contrary it says to man that he should suffer no compulsion to be exercised over him. It does not try to force people to be good. It knows that people are good when they are let alone. Man will develop

---

6. I.e., impossibly idealistic. In *Utopia* (1516) Sir Thomas More described an imaginary island of that name as having a perfect social and political system.

Individualism out of himself. Man is now so developing Individualism. To ask whether Individualism is practical is like asking whether Evolution is practical. *Evolution is the law of life, and there is no evolution except towards Individualism.* ✱ ✱ ✱

✱ ✱ ✱ Man has sought to live intensely, fully, perfectly. When he can do so without exercising restraint on others, or suffering it ever, and his activities are all pleasurable to him, he will be saner, healthier, more civilized, more himself. Pleasure is Nature's test, her sign of approval. When man is happy, he is in harmony with himself and his environment. The new Individualism, for whose service Socialism, whether it wills it or not, is working, will be perfect harmony. It will be what the Greeks sought for, but could not, except in Thought, realise completely, because they had slaves, and fed them; it will be what the Renaissance sought for, but could not realise completely except in Art, because they had slaves, and starved them. It will be complete, and through it each man will attain to his perfection. The new Individualism is the new Hellenism.[7]

1891

Preface to *The Picture of Dorian Gray*[1]

The artist is the creator of beautiful things.

To reveal art and conceal the artist is art's aim.

The critic is he who can translate into another manner or a new material his impression of beautiful things.

The highest as the lowest form of criticism is a mode of autobiography.

Those who find ugly meanings in beautiful things are corrupt without being charming. This is a fault.

Those who find beautiful meanings in beautiful things are the cultivated. For these there is hope.

They are the elect to whom beautiful things mean only Beauty.

There is no such thing as a moral or an immoral book.

Books are well written, or badly written. That is all.

The nineteenth century dislike of Realism is the rage of Caliban[2] seeing his own face in a glass.

The nineteenth century dislike of Romanticism is the rage of Caliban not seeing his own face in a glass.

The moral life of man forms part of the subject-matter of the artist, but the morality of art consists in the perfect use of an imperfect medium.

No artist desires to prove anything. Even things that are true can be proved.

No artist has ethical sympathies. An ethical sympathy in an artist is an unpardonable mannerism of style.

No artist is ever morbid. The artist can express everything.

Thought and language are to the artist instruments of an art.

Vice and virtue are to the artist materials for an art.

---

7. I.e., it embodies the ideals of ancient Greece, including a respect for the life of the mind and the love of beautiful things. Also an allusion to Matthew Arnold's argument in *Culture and Anarchy* (see page 2037) that a Hellenic cultivation of these values is what British society most desperately needs.

1. When Wilde's novel *Dorian Gray* first appeared in *Lippincott's Monthly Magazine* in July 1890, it scandalized readers with its portrayal of a cruelly hedonistic young man who remains unblemished by his crimes while his portrait ages hideously. Responding to his critics' charges

that the novel fostered immoral ideas, Wilde published the preface separately in *The Fortnightly Review* in March 1891. He then added it to the revised novel when it came out in book form a month later. In its defiant tone and "art for art's sake" insistence that literature has no moral content, Wilde's preface echoes Théophile Gautier's preface to *Mademoiselle de Maupin* (1835), a founding text of the Aesthetic movement.

2. In Shakespeare's *The Tempest*, the "monster" Caliban is the offspring of the witch Sycorax and is a native of Prospero's island.

From the point of view of form, the type of all the arts is the art of the musician. From the point of view of feeling, the actor's craft is the type.

All art is at once surface and symbol.

Those who go beneath the surface do so at their peril.

Those who read the symbol do so at their peril.

It is the spectator, and not life, that art really mirrors.

Diversity of opinion about a work of art shows that the work is new, complex, and vital.

When critics disagree the artist is in accord with himself.

We can forgive a man for making a useful thing as long as he does not admire it. The only excuse for making a useless thing is that one admires it intensely.

All art is quite useless.

Oscar Wilde

The Importance of Being Earnest

Wilde's last play, *The Importance of Being Earnest*, is one of the great comedies in the English language. Fast-paced and sparkling, the play opened on February 14, 1895, to widespread acclaim. But it was forced to close less than three months later, amidst the scandal surrounding Wilde's trials for sodomy in April 1895. Eventually, however, the play's reputation was firmly established, and Wilde's witty masterpiece took its place in an Anglo-Irish tradition of classic comedies that includes Goldsmith's *She Stoops to Conquer*, Sheridan's *The Rivals*, and Synge's *Playboy of the Western World*. The title alludes to the Victorian obsession with earnestness as both character trait and moral ideal. The play's philosophy, Wilde claimed, was that "We should treat all the trivial things of life seriously, and all the serious things of life with sincere and studied triviality." In the dandified world of this drama, paying scrupulous attention to surfaces is an act of the deepest sincerity.

Wilde drafted the play in four acts, then at the request of the producer revised it to a tauter three-act version that has become the standard text for performance and reading. Formally, *The Importance of Being Earnest* shows the clever construction and neat resolution popular in nineteenth-century British and French drama. But it also fulfills the classical definition of comedy as beginning in error and confusion, and ending in knowledge, recognition, and self-discovery. Questioning social hierarchies based on birth, the plot turns on the mysteries of social and personal identity: "Would you kindly inform me who I am?" asks Jack Worthing at the play's climactic moment.

To explore the fictions of personality, Wilde meticulously sketches the trivialities that constitute social ritual and class distinction. From cucumber sandwiches at the start of the play to champagne and muffins in Act 3, the way Wilde's well-bred sophisticates consume food and drink becomes evidence of their character, emotional state, and social status. While the rigid conventions of this world apparently force young men like Jack and Algy to live double lives, they freely exploit their fictive selves as events dictate. Yet they are easily stage-managed by the women they love. Gwendolen and Cecily, who are more preoccupied with writing in their diaries than with the events they record in them, deploy their self-conscious sexual innocence to make life and love conform to the conventions of literature. *The Importance of Being Earnest* presents life as an aesthetic spectacle, in which the careful observation of outward form is the truest path toward an ironic authenticity and self-fulfillment.

"If I were asked of myself as a dramatist," Wilde mused, "I would say that my unique position was that I had taken the Drama, the most objective form known to art, and made it as personal a mode of expression as the Lyric or the Sonnet, while enlarging the characterization of the stage." Wilde refashioned the late-Victorian theater in his own image through the self-conscious brilliance of his language and the outrageousness of his comic invention. He delighted in artifice and exaggeration for their own sake. As he argued in *The Decay of Lying*, art is not an imitation of life but a more aesthetically satisfying restructuring of it. With droll wordplay, paradox, and ridiculous coincidence casting existential dilemmas into comic relief, *The Importance of Being Earnest* anticipates the modern Theater of the Absurd; it heralds the profound slapstick of Pirandello, Ionesco, Beckett, and Stoppard.

The Importance of Being Earnest
A Trivial Comedy for Serious People
FIRST ACT

SCENE: *Morning-room in Algernon's flat in Half Moon Street.*[1] *The room is luxuriously and artistically furnished. The sound of a piano is heard in the adjoining room.*

[*Lane is arranging afternoon tea on the table, and after the music has ceased, Algernon enters.*]

ALGERNON Did you hear what I was playing, Lane?

LANE I didn't think it polite to listen, sir.

ALGERNON I'm sorry for that, for your sake. I don't play accurately—anyone can play accurately—but I play with wonderful expression. As far as the piano is concerned, sentiment is my forte. I keep science for Life.

LANE Yes, sir.

ALGERNON And, speaking of the science of Life, have you got the cucumber sandwiches cut for Lady Bracknell?

LANE Yes, sir. [*Hands them on a salver.*]

ALGERNON [*inspects them, takes two, and sits down on the sofa*] Oh! . . . by the way, Lane, I see from your book that on Thursday night, when Lord Shoreham and Mr Worthing were dining with me, eight bottles of champagne are entered as having been consumed.

LANE Yes, sir; eight bottles and a pint.

ALGERNON Why is it that at a bachelor's establishment the servants invariably drink the champagne? I ask merely for information.

LANE I attribute it to the superior quality of the wine, sir. I have often observed that in married households the champagne is rarely of a first-rate brand.

ALGERNON Good Heavens! Is marriage so demoralizing as that?

LANE I believe it *is* a very pleasant state, sir. I have had very little experience of it myself up to the present. I have only been married once. That was in consequence of a misunderstanding between myself and a young person.

ALGERNON [*languidly*] I don't know that I am much interested in your family life, Lane.

LANE No, sir; it is not a very interesting subject. I never think of it myself.

ALGERNON Very natural, I am sure. That will do, Lane, thank you.

LANE Thank you, sir. [*Lane goes out.*]

ALGERNON Lane's views on marriage seem somewhat lax. Really, if the lower orders don't set us a good example, what on earth is the use of them? They seem, as a class, to have absolutely no sense of moral responsibility.

---

1. A fashionable address in the West End of London.

[*Enter Lane.*]

LANE Mr Ernest Worthing.

[*Enter Jack. Lane goes out.*]

ALGERNON How are you, my dear Ernest? What brings you up to town?

JACK Oh, pleasure, pleasure! What else should bring one anywhere? Eating as usual, I see, Algy!

ALGERNON [*stiffly*] I believe it is customary in good society to take some slight refreshment at five o'clock. Where have you been since last Thursday?

JACK [*sitting down on the sofa*] In the country.

ALGERNON What on earth do you do there?

JACK [*pulling off his gloves*] When one is in town one amuses oneself. When one is in the country one amuses other people. It is excessively boring.

ALGERNON And who are the people you amuse?

JACK [*airily*] Oh, neighbours, neighbours.

ALGERNON Got nice neighbours in your part of Shropshire?[2]

JACK Perfectly horrid! Never speak to one of them.

ALGERNON How immensely you must amuse them! [*Goes over and takes sandwich.*] By the way, Shropshire is your county, is it not?

JACK Eh? Shropshire? Yes, of course. Hallo! Why all these cups? Why cucumber sandwiches? Why such reckless extravagance in one so young? Who is coming to tea?

ALGERNON Oh! merely Aunt Augusta and Gwendolen.

JACK How perfectly delightful!

ALGERNON Yes, that is all very well; but I am afraid Aunt Augusta won't quite approve of your being here.

JACK May I ask why?

ALGERNON My dear fellow, the way you flirt with Gwendolen is perfectly disgraceful. It is almost as bad as the way Gwendolen flirts with you.

JACK I am in love with Gwendolen. I have come up to town expressly to propose to her.

ALGERNON I thought you had come up for pleasure? . . . I call that business.

JACK How utterly unromantic you are!

ALGERNON I really don't see anything romantic in proposing. It is very romantic to be in love. But there is nothing romantic about a definite proposal. Why, one may be accepted. One usually is, I believe. Then the excitement is all over. The very essence of romance is uncertainty. If I ever get married, I'll certainly try to forget the fact.

JACK I have no doubt about that, dear Algy. The Divorce Court was specially invented for people whose memories are so curiously constituted.

ALGERNON Oh! there is no use speculating on that subject. Divorces are made in Heaven—[*Jack puts out his hand to take a sandwich. Algernon at once interferes.*] Please don't touch the cucumber sandwiches. They are ordered specially for Aunt Augusta. [*Takes one and eats it.*]

JACK Well, you have been eating them all the time.

ALGERNON That is quite a different matter. She is my aunt. [*Takes plate from below.*] Have some bread and butter. The bread and butter is for Gwendolen. Gwendolen is devoted to bread and butter.

JACK [*advancing to table and helping himself*] And very good bread and butter it is too.

2. Worthing's estate is actually in Hertfordshire, which is a long way from Shropshire.

ALGERNON Well, my dear fellow, you need not eat as if you were going to eat it all. You behave as if you were married to her already. You are not married to her already, and I don't think you ever will be.

JACK Why on earth do you say that?

ALGERNON Well, in the first place girls never marry the men they flirt with. Girls don't think it right.

JACK Oh, that is nonsense!

ALGERNON It isn't. It is a great truth. It accounts for the extraordinary number of bachelors that one sees all over the place. In the second place, I don't give my consent.

JACK Your consent!

ALGERNON My dear fellow, Gwendolen is my first cousin. And before I allow you to marry her, you will have to clear up the whole question of Cecily. [Rings bell.]

JACK Cecily! What on earth do you mean? What do you mean, Algy, by Cecily? I don't know anyone of the name of Cecily.

      [Enter Lane.]

ALGERNON Bring me that cigarette case Mr Worthing left in the smoking-room the last time he dined here.

LANE Yes, sir. [Lane goes out.]

JACK Do you mean to say you have had my cigarette case all this time? I wish to goodness you had let me know. I have been writing frantic letters to Scotland Yard[3] about it. I was very nearly offering a large reward.

ALGERNON Well, I wish you would offer one. I happen to be more than usually hard up.

JACK There is no good offering a large reward now that the thing is found.

      [Enter Lane with the cigarette case on a salver. Algernon takes it at once. Lane goes out.]

ALGERNON I think that is rather mean of you, Ernest, I must say. [Opens case and examines it.] However, it makes no matter, for, now that I look at the inscription inside, I find that the thing isn't yours after all.

JACK Of course it's mine. [Moving to him.] You have seen me with it a hundred times, and you have no right whatsoever to read what is written inside. It is a very ungentlemanly thing to read a private cigarette case.

ALGERNON Oh! it is absurd to have a hard-and-fast rule about what one should read and what one shouldn't. More than half of modern culture depends on what one shouldn't read.

JACK I am quite aware of the fact, and I don't propose to discuss modern culture. It isn't the sort of thing one should talk of in private. I simply want my cigarette case back.

ALGERNON Yes; but this isn't your cigarette case. This cigarette case is a present from someone of the name of Cecily, and you said you didn't know anyone of that name.

JACK Well, if you want to know, Cecily happens to be my aunt.

ALGERNON Your aunt!

JACK Yes. Charming old lady she is, too. Lives at Tunbridge Wells.[4] Just give it back to me, Algy.

ALGERNON [retreating to back of sofa] But why does she call herself little Cecily if she is your aunt and lives at Tunbridge Wells? [Reading.] "From little Cecily with her fondest love."

---

3. London police headquarters.   4. A fashionable resort.

JACK [*moving to sofa and kneeling upon it*] My dear fellow, what on earth is there in that? Some aunts are tall, some aunts are not tall. That is a matter that surely an aunt may be allowed to decide for herself. You seem to think that every aunt should be exactly like your aunt! That is absurd! For Heaven's sake give me back my cigarette case. [*Follows Algernon round the room.*]

ALGERNON Yes. But why does your aunt call you her uncle? "From little Cecily, with her fondest love to her dear Uncle Jack." There is no objection, I admit, to an aunt being a small aunt, but why an aunt, no matter what her size may be, should call her own nephew her uncle, I can't quite make out. Besides, your name isn't Jack at all; it is Ernest.

JACK It isn't Ernest; it's Jack.

ALGERNON You have always told me it was Ernest. I have introduced you to every-one as Ernest. You answer to the name of Ernest. You look as if your name was Ernest. You are the most earnest looking person I ever saw in my life. It is perfect-ly absurd your saying that your name isn't Ernest. It's on your cards. Here is one of them. [*Taking it from case.*] "Mr Ernest Worthing, B. 4, The Albany." I'll keep this as a proof that your name is Ernest if ever you attempt to deny it to me, or to Gwendolen, or to anyone else. [*Puts the card in his pocket.*]

JACK Well, my name is Ernest in town and Jack in the country, and the cigarette case was given to me in the country.

ALGERNON Yes, but that does not account for the fact that your small Aunt Cecily, who lives at Tunbridge Wells, calls you her dear uncle. Come, old boy, you had much better have the thing out at once.

JACK My dear Algy, you talk exactly as if you were a dentist. It is very vulgar to talk like a dentist when one isn't a dentist. It produces a false impression.

ALGERNON Well, that is exactly what dentists always do. Now, go on! Tell me the whole thing. I may mention that I have always suspected you of being a confirmed and secret Bunburyist, and I am quite sure of it now.

JACK Bunburyist? What on earth do you mean by a Bunburyist?

ALGERNON I'll reveal to you the meaning of that incomparable expression as soon as you are kind enough to inform me why you are Ernest in town and Jack in the country.

JACK Well, produce my cigarette case first.

ALGERNON Here it is. [*Hands cigarette case.*] Now produce your explanation, and pray make it improbable. [*Sits on sofa.*]

JACK My dear fellow, there is nothing improbable about my explanation at all. In fact it's perfectly ordinary. Old Mr Thomas Cardew, who adopted me when I was a little boy, made me in his will guardian to his granddaughter, Miss Cecily Cardew. Cecily who addresses me as her uncle from motives of respect that you could not possibly appreciate, lives at my place in the country under the charge of her admirable governess, Miss Prism.

ALGERNON Where is that place in the country, by the way?

JACK That is nothing to you, dear boy. You are not going to be invited. . . . I may tell you candidly that the place is not in Shropshire.

ALGERNON I suspected that, my dear fellow! I have Bunburyed all over Shropshire on two separate occasions. Now, go on. Why are you Ernest in town and Jack in the country?

JACK My dear Algy, I don't know whether you will be able to understand my real motives. You are hardly serious enough. When one is placed in the position of guardian, one has to adopt a very high moral tone on all subjects. It's one's duty to do so. And as a high moral tone can hardly be said to conduce very much to either one's health or one's happiness, in order to get up to town I have always pretended to have a younger brother of the name of Ernest, who lives in the Albany, and gets into the most dreadful scrapes. That, my dear Algy, is the whole truth pure and simple.

ALGERNON The truth is rarely pure and never simple. Modern life would be very tedious if it were either, and modern literature a complete impossibility!

JACK That wouldn't be at all a bad thing.

ALGERNON Literary criticism is not your forte, my dear fellow. Don't try it. You should leave that to people who haven't been at a University. They do it so well in the daily papers. What you really are is a Bunburyist. I was quite right in saying you were a Bunburyist. You are one of the most advanced Bunburyists I know.

JACK What on earth do you mean?

ALGERNON You have invented a very useful younger brother called Ernest, in order that you may be able to come up to town as often as you like. I have invented an invaluable permanent invalid called Bunbury, in order that I may be able to go down into the country whenever I choose. Bunbury is perfectly invaluable. If it wasn't for Bunbury's extraordinary bad health, for instance, I wouldn't be able to dine with you at Willis's[5] tonight, for I have been really engaged[6] to Aunt Augusta for more than a week.

JACK I haven't asked you to dine with me anywhere tonight.

ALGERNON I know. You are absurdly careless about sending out invitations. It is very foolish of you. Nothing annoys people so much as not receiving invitations.

JACK You had much better dine with your Aunt Augusta.

ALGERNON I haven't the smallest intention of doing anything of the kind. To begin with, I dined there on Monday, and once a week is quite enough to dine with one's own relations. In the second place, whenever I do dine there I am always treated as a member of the family, and sent down[7] with either no woman at all, or two. In the third place, I know perfectly well whom she will place me next to, tonight. She will place me next Mary Farquhar, who always flirts with her own husband across the dinner-table. That is not very pleasant. Indeed, it is not even decent . . . and that sort of thing is enormously on the increase. The amount of women in London who flirt with their own husbands is perfectly scandalous. It looks so bad. It is simply washing one's clean linen in public. Besides, now that I know you to be a confirmed Bunburyist I naturally want to talk to you about Bunburying. I want to tell you the rules.

JACK I'm not a Bunburyist at all. If Gwendolen accepts me, I am going to kill my brother, indeed I think I'll kill him in any case. Cecily is a little too much interested in him. It is rather a bore. So I am going to get rid of Ernest. And I strongly advise you to do the same with Mr . . . with your invalid friend who has the absurd name.

ALGERNON Nothing will induce me to part with Bunbury, and if you ever get married, which seems to me extremely problematic, you will be very glad to know Bunbury. A man who marries without knowing Bunbury has a very tedious time of it.

JACK That is nonsense. If I marry a charming girl like Gwendolen, and she is the only girl I ever saw in my life that I would marry, I certainly won't want to know Bunbury.

5. An expensive London restaurant.
6. I.e., pledged to attend her dinner party.

7. Sent in to the dining room as someone's escort.

ALGERNON Then your wife will. You don't seem to realize, that in married life three is company and two is none.

JACK [*sententiously*] That, my dear young friend, is the theory that the corrupt French Drama[8] has been propounding for the last fifty years.

ALGERNON Yes; and that the happy English home has proved in half the time.

JACK For heaven's sake, don't try to be cynical. It's perfectly easy to be cynical.

ALGERNON My dear fellow, it isn't easy to be anything nowadays. There's such a lot of beastly competition about. [*The sound of an electric bell is heard.*] Ah! that must be Aunt Augusta. Only relatives, or creditors, ever ring in that Wagnerian manner.[9] Now, if I get her out of the way for ten minutes, so that you can have an opportunity for proposing to Gwendolen, may I dine with you tonight at Willis's?

JACK I suppose so, if you want to.

ALGERNON Yes, but you must be serious about it. I hate people who are not serious about meals. It is so shallow of them.

[*Enter Lane.*]

LANE Lady Bracknell and Miss Fairfax.

[*Algernon goes forward to meet them. Enter Lady Bracknell and Gwendolen.*]

LADY BRACKNELL Good afternoon, dear Algernon, I hope you are behaving very well.

ALGERNON I'm feeling very well, Aunt Augusta.

LADY BRACKNELL That's not quite the same thing. In fact the two things rarely go together. [*Sees Jack and bows to him with icy coldness.*]

ALGERNON [*to Gwendolen*] Dear me, you are smart![1]

GWENDOLEN I am always smart! Aren't I, Mr Worthing?

JACK You're quite perfect, Miss Fairfax.

GWENDOLEN Oh! I hope I am not that. It would leave no room for developments, and I intend to develop in many directions. [*Gwendolen and Jack sit down together in the corner.*]

LADY BRACKNELL I'm sorry if we are a little late, Algernon, but I was obliged to call on dear Lady Harbury. I hadn't been there since her poor husband's death. I never saw a woman so altered; she looks quite twenty years younger. And now I'll have a cup of tea, and one of those nice cucumber sandwiches you promised me.

ALGERNON Certainly, Aunt Augusta. [*Goes over to tea-table.*]

LADY BRACKNELL Won't you come and sit here, Gwendolen?

GWENDOLEN Thanks, mamma, I'm quite comfortable where I am.

ALGERNON [*picking up empty plate in horror*] Good heavens! Lane! Why are there no cucumber sandwiches? I ordered them specially.

LANE [*gravely*] There were no cucumbers in the market this morning, sir. I went down twice.

ALGERNON No cucumbers!

LANE No, sir. Not even for ready money.

ALGERNON That will do, Lane, thank you.

LANE Thank you, sir. [*Goes out.*]

ALGERNON I am greatly distressed, Aunt Augusta, about there being no cucumbers, not even for ready money.

LADY BRACKNELL It really makes no matter, Algernon. I had some crumpets with Lady Harbury, who seems to me to be living entirely for pleasure now.

---

8. Late 19th-century French plays frequently focused on marital infidelity.
9. I.e., loud and dramatic, like the grand operas of

Richard Wagner (1813–1883).
1. Chic.

ALGERNON I hear her hair has turned quite gold from grief.

LADY BRACKNELL It certainly has changed its colour. From what cause I, of course, cannot say. [*Algernon crosses and hands tea.*] Thank you. I've quite a treat for you tonight, Algernon. I am going to send you down with Mary Farquhar. She is such a nice woman, and so attentive to her husband. It's delightful to watch them.

ALGERNON I am afraid, Aunt Augusta, I shall have to give up the pleasure of dining with you tonight after all.

LADY BRACKNELL [*frowning*] I hope not, Algernon. It would put my table completely out. Your uncle would have to dine upstairs. Fortunately he is accustomed to that.

ALGERNON It is a great bore, and, I need hardly say, a terrible disappointment to me, but the fact is I have just had a telegram to say that my poor friend Bunbury is very ill again. [*Exchanges glances with Jack.*] They seem to think I should be with him.

LADY BRACKNELL It is very strange. This Mr Bunbury seems to suffer from curiously bad health.

ALGERNON Yes; poor Bunbury is a dreadful invalid.

LADY BRACKNELL Well, I must say, Algernon, that I think it is high time that Mr Bunbury made up his mind whether he was going to live or to die. This shilly-shallying with the question is absurd. Nor do I in any way approve of the modern sympathy with invalids. I consider it morbid. Illness of any kind is hardly a thing to be encouraged in others. Health is the primary duty of life. I am always telling that to your poor uncle, but he never seems to take much notice . . . as far as any improvement in his ailments goes. I should be much obliged if you would ask Mr Bunbury, from me, to be kind enough not to have a relapse on Saturday, for I rely on you to arrange my music for me. It is my last reception, and one wants something that will encourage conversation, particularly at the end of the season[2] when everyone has practically said whatever they had to say, which, in most cases, was probably not much.

ALGERNON I'll speak to Bunbury, Aunt Augusta, if he is still conscious, and I think I can promise you he'll be all right by Saturday. Of course the music is a great difficulty. You see, if one plays good music, people don't listen, and if one plays bad music people don't talk. But I'll run over the programme I've drawn out, if you will kindly come into the next room for a moment.

LADY BRACKNELL Thank you, Algernon. It is very thoughtful of you. [*Rising, and following Algernon.*] I'm sure the programme will be delightful, after a few expurgations. French songs I cannot possibly allow. People always seem to think that they are improper, and either look shocked, which is vulgar, or laugh, which is worse. But German sounds a thoroughly respectable language, and indeed, I believe is so. Gwendolen, you will accompany me.

GWENDOLEN Certainly, mamma.

[*Lady Bracknell and Algernon go into the music-room, Gwendolen remains behind.*]

JACK Charming day it has been, Miss Fairfax.

GWENDOLEN Pray don't talk to me about the weather, Mr Worthing. Whenever people talk to me about the weather, I always feel quite certain that they mean something else. And that makes me so nervous.

JACK I do mean something else.

GWENDOLEN I thought so. In fact, I am never wrong.

---

2. Fashionable people left their country estates to spend the social season in London; it began in late spring and lasted through July.

JACK And I would like to be allowed to take advantage of Lady Bracknell's temporary absence . . .

GWENDOLEN I would certainly advise you to do so. Mamma has a way of coming back suddenly into a room that I have often had to speak to her about.

JACK [*nervously*] Miss Fairfax, ever since I met you I have admired you more than any girl . . . I have ever met since . . . I met you.

GWENDOLEN Yes, I am quite aware of the fact. And I often wish that in public, at any rate, you had been more demonstrative. For me you have always had an irresistible fascination. Even before I met you I was far from indifferent to you. [*Jack looks at her in amazement.*] We live, as I hope you know, Mr Worthing, in an age of ideals. The fact is constantly mentioned in the more expensive monthly magazines, and has reached the provincial pulpits I am told: and my ideal has always been to love some one of the name of Ernest. There is something in that name that inspires absolute confidence. The moment Algernon first mentioned to me that he had a friend called Ernest, I knew I was destined to love you.

JACK You really love me, Gwendolen?

GWENDOLEN Passionately!

JACK Darling! You don't know how happy you've made me.

GWENDOLEN My own Ernest!

JACK But you don't really mean to say that you couldn't love me if my name wasn't Ernest?

GWENDOLEN But your name is Ernest.

JACK Yes, I know it is. But supposing it was something else? Do you mean to say you couldn't love me then?

GWENDOLEN [*glibly*] Ah! that is clearly a metaphysical speculation, and like most metaphysical speculations has very little reference at all to the actual facts of real life, as we know them.

JACK Personally, darling, to speak quite candidly, I don't much care about the name of Ernest . . . I don't think the name suits me at all.

GWENDOLEN It suits you perfectly. It is a divine name. It has a music of its own. It produces vibrations.

JACK Well, really, Gwendolen, I must say that I think there are lots of other much nicer names. I think Jack, for instance, a charming name.

GWENDOLEN Jack? . . . No, there is very little music in the name Jack, if any at all, indeed. It does not thrill. It produces absolutely no vibrations . . . I have known several Jacks, and they all, without exception, were more than usually plain. Besides, Jack is a notorious domesticity for John! And I pity any woman who is married to a man called John. She would probably never be allowed to know the entrancing pleasure of a single moment's solitude. The only really safe name is Ernest.

JACK Gwendolen, I must get christened at once—I mean we must get married at once. There is no time to be lost.

GWENDOLEN Married, Mr Worthing?[3]

JACK [*astounded*] Well . . . surely. You know that I love you, and you led me to believe, Miss Fairfax, that you were not absolutely indifferent to me.

GWENDOLEN I adore you. But you haven't proposed to me yet. Nothing has been said at all about marriage. The subject has not even been touched on.

JACK Well . . . may I propose to you now?

---

3. Gwendolen reverts to using Jack's last name when she is reminded that he has not yet formally proposed.

GWENDOLEN I think it would be an admirable opportunity. And to spare you any possible disappointment, Mr Worthing, I think it only fair to tell you quite frankly beforehand that I am fully determined to accept you.

JACK Gwendolen!

GWENDOLEN Yes, Mr Worthing, what have you got to say to me?

JACK You know what I have got to say to you.

GWENDOLEN Yes, but you don't say it.

JACK Gwendolen, will you marry me? [Goes on his knees.]

GWENDOLEN Of course I will, darling. How long you have been about it! I am afraid you have had very little experience in how to propose.

JACK My own one, I have never loved anyone in the world but you.

GWENDOLEN Yes, but men often propose for practice. I know my brother Gerald does. All my girl-friends tell me so. What wonderfully blue eyes you have, Ernest! They are quite, quite, blue. I hope you will always look at me just like that, especially when there are other people present.

   [Enter Lady Bracknell.]

LADY BRACKNELL Mr Worthing! Rise, sir, from this semi-recumbent posture. It is most indecorous.

GWENDOLEN Mamma! [He tries to rise; she restrains him.] I must beg you to retire. This is no place for you. Besides, Mr Worthing has not quite finished yet.

LADY BRACKNELL Finished what, may I ask?

GWENDOLEN I am engaged to Mr Worthing, mamma. [They rise together.]

LADY BRACKNELL Pardon me, you are not engaged to anyone. When you do become engaged to some one, I, or your father, should his health permit him, will inform you of the fact. An engagement should come on a young girl as a surprise, pleasant or unpleasant, as the case may be. It is hardly a matter that she could be allowed to arrange for herself. . . . And now I have a few questions to put to you, Mr Worthing. While I am making these inquiries, you, Gwendolen, will wait for me below in the carriage.

GWENDOLEN [reproachfully] Mamma!

LADY BRACKNELL In the carriage, Gwendolen! [Gwendolen goes to the door. She and Jack blow kisses to each other behind Lady Bracknell's back. Lady Bracknell looks vaguely about as if she could not understand what the noise was. Finally turns round.] Gwendolen, the carriage!

GWENDOLEN Yes, mamma. [Goes out, looking back at Jack.]

LADY BRACKNELL [sitting down] You can take a seat, Mr Worthing.
   [Looking in her pocket for note-book and pencil.]

JACK Thank you, Lady Bracknell, I prefer standing.

LADY BRACKNELL [pencil and note-book in hand] I feel bound to tell you that you are not down on my list of eligible young men, although I have the same list as the dear Duchess of Bolton has. We work together, in fact. However, I am quite ready to enter your name, should your answers be what a really affectionate mother requires. Do you smoke?

JACK Well, yes, I must admit I smoke.

LADY BRACKNELL I am glad to hear it. A man should always have an occupation of some kind. There are far too many idle men in London as it is. How old are you?

JACK Twenty-nine.

LADY BRACKNELL A very good age to be married at. I have always been of opinion that a man who desires to get married should know either everything or nothing. Which do you know?

JACK [*after some hesitation*] I know nothing, Lady Bracknell.

LADY BRACKNELL I am pleased to hear it. I do not approve of anything that tampers with natural ignorance. Ignorance is like a delicate exotic fruit; touch it and the bloom is gone. The whole theory of modern education is radically unsound. Fortunately in England, at any rate, education produces no effect whatsoever. If it did, it would prove a serious danger to the upper classes, and probably lead to acts of violence in Grosvenor Square.[4] What is your income?

JACK Between seven and eight thousand a year.

LADY BRACKNELL [*makes a note in her book*] In land, or in investments?

JACK In investments, chiefly.

LADY BRACKNELL That is satisfactory. What between the duties expected of one during one's lifetime, and the duties exacted from one after one's death,[5] land has ceased to be either a profit or a pleasure. It gives one position, and prevents one from keeping it up. That's all that can be said about land.

JACK I have a country house with some land, of course, attached to it, about fifteen hundred acres, I believe; but I don't depend on that for my real income. In fact, as far as I can make out, the poachers are the only people who make anything out of it.

LADY BRACKNELL A country house! How many bedrooms? Well, that point can be cleared up afterwards. You have a town house, I hope? A girl with a simple, unspoiled nature, like Gwendolen, could hardly be expected to reside in the country.

JACK Well, I own a house in Belgrave Square,[6] but it is let by the year to Lady Bloxham. Of course, I can get it back whenever I like, at six months' notice.

LADY BRACKNELL Lady Bloxham? I don't know her.

JACK Oh, she goes about very little. She is a lady considerably advanced in years.

LADY BRACKNELL Ah, nowadays that is no guarantee of respectability of character. What number in Belgrave Square?

JACK 149.

LADY BRACKNELL [*shaking her head*] The unfashionable side. I thought there was something. However, that could easily be altered.

JACK Do you mean the fashion, or the side?

LADY BRACKNELL [*sternly*] Both, if necessary, I presume. What are your politics?

JACK Well, I am afraid I really have none. I am a Liberal Unionist.[7]

LADY BRACKNELL Oh, they count as Tories. They dine with us. Or come in the evening, at any rate. Now to minor matters. Are your parents living?

JACK I have lost both my parents.

LADY BRACKNELL Both? To lose one parent may be regarded as a misfortune—to lose *both* seems like carelessness. Who was your father? He was evidently a man of some wealth. Was he born in what the Radical papers call the purple of commerce, or did he rise from the ranks of the aristocracy?

JACK I am afraid I really don't know. The fact is, Lady Bracknell, I said I had lost my parents. It would be nearer the truth to say that my parents seem to have lost me . . . I don't actually know who I am by birth. I was . . . well, I was found.

LADY BRACKNELL Found!

JACK The late Mr Thomas Cardew, an old gentleman of a very charitable and kindly disposition, found me, and gave me the name of Worthing, because he happened to have a first-class ticket for Worthing in his pocket at the time. Worthing is a place in Sussex. It is a seaside resort.

---

4. A fashionable area in the West End of London.
5. "Death duties" are inheritance taxes.
6. A fashionable West End address in Belgravia.

7. In 1886 Liberal Unionists joined the Conservatives (the "Tories") in voting against the Liberal Prime Minister Gladstone's bill supporting Home Rule for Ireland.

LADY BRACKNELL Where did the charitable gentleman who had a first-class ticket for this seaside resort find you?

JACK [*gravely*] In a hand-bag.

LADY BRACKNELL A hand-bag?

JACK [*very seriously*] Yes, Lady Bracknell. I was in a hand-bag—a somewhat large, black leather hand-bag, with handles to it—an ordinary hand-bag in fact.

LADY BRACKNELL In what locality did this Mr James, or Thomas, Cardew come across this ordinary hand-bag?

JACK In the cloak-room at Victoria Station. It was given to him in mistake for his own.

LADY BRACKNELL The cloak-room at Victoria Station?

JACK Yes. The Brighton line.

LADY BRACKNELL The line is immaterial. Mr Worthing, I confess I feel somewhat bewildered by what you have just told me. To be born, or at any rate bred, in a hand-bag, whether it had handles or not, seems to me to display a contempt for the ordinary decencies of family life that reminds one of the worst excesses of the French Revolution. And I presume you know what that unfortunate movement led to? As for the particular locality in which the hand-bag was found, a cloak-room at a railway station might serve to conceal a social indiscretion—has probably, indeed, been used for that purpose before now—but it could hardly be regarded as an assured basis for a recognized position in good society.

JACK May I ask you then what you would advise me to do? I need hardly say I would do anything in the world to ensure Gwendolen's happiness.

LADY BRACKNELL I would strongly advise you, Mr Worthing, to try and acquire some relations as soon as possible, and to make a definite effort to produce at any rate one parent, of either sex, before the season is quite over.

JACK Well, I don't see how I could possibly manage to do that. I can produce the hand-bag at any moment. It is in my dressing-room at home. I really think that should satisfy you, Lady Bracknell.

LADY BRACKNELL Me, sir! What has it to do with me? You can hardly imagine that I and Lord Bracknell would dream of allowing our only daughter—a girl brought up with the utmost care—to marry into a cloak-room, and form an alliance with a parcel? Good morning, Mr Worthing!

[*Lady Bracknell sweeps out in majestic indignation.*]

JACK Good morning! [*Algernon, from the other room, strikes up the Wedding March. Jack looks perfectly furious, and goes to the door.*] For goodness' sake don't play that ghastly tune, Algy! How idiotic you are!

[*The music stops, and Algernon enters cheerily.*]

ALGERNON Didn't it go off all right, old boy? You don't mean to say Gwendolen refused you? I know it is a way she has. She is always refusing people. I think it is most ill-natured of her.

JACK Oh, Gwendolen is as right as a trivet.[8] As far as she is concerned, we are engaged. Her mother is perfectly unbearable. Never met such a Gorgon[9] . . . I don't really know what a Gorgon is like, but I am quite sure that Lady Bracknell is one. In any case, she is a monster, without being a myth, which is rather unfair . . . I beg your pardon, Algy, I suppose I shouldn't talk about your own aunt in that way before you.

ALGERNON My dear boy, I love hearing my relations abused. It is the only thing

---

8. Reliable and steady, like a stand used to hold a pot over the fire.

9. A mythical female monster with snakes for hair.

that makes me put up with them at all. Relations are simply a tedious pack of people, who haven't got the remotest knowledge of how to live, nor the smallest instinct about when to die.

JACK Oh, that is nonsense!

ALGERNON It isn't!

JACK Well, I won't argue about the matter. You always want to argue about things.

ALGERNON That is exactly what things were originally made for.

JACK Upon my word, if I thought that, I'd shoot myself . . . [*A pause.*] You don't think there is any chance of Gwendolen becoming like her mother in about a hundred and fifty years, do you Algy?

ALGERNON All women become like their mothers. That is their tragedy. No man does. That's his.

JACK Is that clever?

ALGERNON It is perfectly phrased! and quite as true as any observation in civilized life should be.

JACK I am sick to death of cleverness. Everybody is clever nowadays. You can't go anywhere without meeting clever people. The thing has become an absolute public nuisance. I wish to goodness we had a few fools left.

ALGERNON We have.

JACK I should extremely like to meet them. What do they talk about?

ALGERNON The fools? Oh! about the clever people, of course.

JACK What fools!

ALGERNON By the way, did you tell Gwendolen the truth about your being Ernest in town, and Jack in the country?

JACK [*in a very patronizing manner*] My dear fellow, the truth isn't quite the sort of thing one tells to a nice sweet refined girl. What extraordinary ideas you have about the way to behave to a woman!

ALGERNON The only way to behave to a woman is to make love to her,[1] if she is pretty, and to someone else if she is plain.

JACK Oh, that is nonsense.

ALGERNON What about your brother? What about the profligate Ernest?

JACK Oh, before the end of the week I shall have got rid of him. I'll say he died in Paris of apoplexy. Lots of people die of apoplexy, quite suddenly, don't they?

ALGERNON Yes, but it's hereditary, my dear fellow. It's a sort of thing that runs in families. You had much better say a severe chill.

JACK You are sure a severe chill isn't hereditary, or anything of that kind?

ALGERNON Of course it isn't!

JACK Very well, then. My poor brother Ernest is carried off suddenly in Paris, by a severe chill. That gets rid of him.

ALGERNON But I thought you said that . . . Miss Cardew was a little too much interested in your poor brother Ernest? Won't she feel his loss a good deal?

JACK Oh, that is all right. Cecily is not a silly romantic girl, I am glad to say. She has got a capital appetite, goes long walks, and pays no attention at all to her lessons.

ALGERNON I would rather like to see Cecily.

JACK I will take very good care you never do. She is excessively pretty, and she is only just eighteen.

---

1. I.e., to flirt with or court her.

ALGERNON Have you told Gwendolen yet that you have an excessively pretty ward who is only just eighteen?

JACK Oh! one doesn't blurt these things out to people. Cecily and Gwendolen are perfectly certain to be extremely great friends. I'll bet you anything you like that half an hour after they have met, they will be calling each other sister.

ALGERNON Women only do that when they have called each other a lot of other things first. Now, my dear boy, if we want to get a good table at Willis's, we really must go and dress. Do you know it is nearly seven?

JACK [irritably] Oh! it always is nearly seven.

ALGERNON Well, I'm hungry.

JACK I never knew you when you weren't. . . .

ALGERNON What shall we do after dinner? Go to a theatre?

JACK Oh no! I loathe listening.

ALGERNON Well, let us go to the Club?

JACK Oh, no! I hate talking.

ALGERNON Well, we might trot round to the Empire[2] at ten?

JACK Oh, no! I can't bear looking at things. It is so silly.

ALGERNON Well, what shall we do?

JACK Nothing!

ALGERNON It is awfully hard work doing nothing. However, I don't mind hard work where there is no definite object of any kind.

    [Enter Lane.]

LANE Miss Fairfax.

    [Enter Gwendolen. Lane goes out.]

ALGERNON Gwendolen, upon my word!

GWENDOLEN Algy, kindly turn your back. I have something very particular to say to Mr Worthing.

ALGERNON Really, Gwendolen, I don't think I can allow this at all.

GWENDOLEN Algy, you always adopt a strictly immoral attitude towards life. You are not quite old enough to do that.

    [Algernon retires to the fireplace.]

JACK My own darling!

GWENDOLEN Ernest, we may never be married. From the expression on mamma's face I fear we never shall. Few parents nowadays pay any regard to what their children say to them. The old-fashioned respect for the young is fast dying out. Whatever influence I ever had over mamma, I lost at the age of three. But although she may prevent us from becoming man and wife, and I may marry someone else, and marry often, nothing that she can possibly do can alter my eternal devotion to you.

JACK Dear Gwendolen!

GWENDOLEN The story of your romantic origin, as related to me by mamma, with unpleasing comments, has naturally stirred the deeper fibres of my nature. Your Christian name has an irresistible fascination. The simplicity of your character makes you exquisitely incomprehensible to me. Your town address at the Albany I have. What is your address in the country?

JACK The Manor House, Woolton, Hertfordshire.

    [Algernon, who has been carefully listening, smiles to himself, and writes the address on his shirt-cuff. Then picks up the Railway Guide.]

---

2. A popular music hall.

GWENDOLEN There is a good postal service, I suppose? It may be necessary to do something desperate. That of course will require serious consideration. I will communicate with you daily.

JACK My own one!

GWENDOLEN How long do you remain in town?

JACK Till Monday.

GWENDOLEN Good! Algy, you may turn round now.

ALGERNON Thanks, I've turned round already.

GWENDOLEN You may also ring the bell.

JACK You will let me see you to your carriage, my own darling?

GWENDOLEN Certainly.

JACK [to Lane, who now enters] I will see Miss Fairfax out.

LANE Yes, sir. [Jack and Gwendolen go off.]

[Lane presents several letters on a salver to Algernon. It is to be surmised that they are bills, as Algernon, after looking at the envelopes, tears them up.]

ALGERNON A glass of sherry, Lane.

LANE Yes, sir.

ALGERNON Tomorrow, Lane, I'm going Bunburying.

LANE Yes, sir.

ALGERNON I shall probably not be back till Monday. You can put up my dress clothes, my smoking jacket, and all the Bunbury suits . . .

LANE Yes, sir. [Handing sherry.]

ALGERNON I hope tomorrow will be a fine day, Lane.

LANE It never is, sir.

ALGERNON Lane, you're a perfect pessimist.

LANE I do my best to give satisfaction, sir.

[Enter Jack. Lane goes off.]

JACK There's a sensible, intellectual girl! the only girl I ever cared for in my life. [Algernon is laughing immoderately.] What on earth are you so amused at?

ALGERNON Oh, I'm a little anxious about poor Bunbury, that is all.

JACK If you don't take care, your friend Bunbury will get you into a serious scrape some day.

ALGERNON I love scrapes. They are the only things that are never serious.

JACK Oh, that's nonsense, Algy. You never talk anything but nonsense.

ALGERNON Nobody ever does.

[Jack looks indignantly at him, and leaves the room. Algernon lights a cigarette, reads his shirt-cuff, and smiles.]   ACT DROP

SECOND ACT

SCENE: Garden at the Manor House. A flight of gray stone steps leads up to the house. The garden, an old-fashioned one, full of roses. Time of year, July. Basket chairs, and a table covered with books, are set under a large yew tree.

[Miss Prism discovered seated at the table. Cecily is at the back watering flowers.]

MISS PRISM [calling] Cecily, Cecily! Surely such a utilitarian occupation as the watering of flowers is rather Moulton's duty than yours? Especially at a moment when intellectual pleasures await you. Your German grammar is on the table. Pray open it at page fifteen. We will repeat yesterday's lesson.

CECILY [*coming over very slowly*] But I don't like German. It isn't at all a becoming language. I know perfectly well that I look quite plain after my German lesson.

MISS PRISM Child, you know how anxious your guardian is that you should improve yourself in every way. He laid particular stress on your German, as he was leaving for town yesterday. Indeed, he always lays stress on your German when he is leaving for town.

CECILY Dear Uncle Jack is so very serious! Sometimes he is so serious that I think he cannot be quite well.

MISS PRISM [*drawing herself up*] Your guardian enjoys the best of health, and his gravity of demeanour is especially to be commended in one so comparatively young as he is. I know no one who has a higher sense of duty and responsibility.

CECILY I suppose that is why he often looks a little bored when we three are together.

MISS PRISM Cecily! I am surprised at you. Mr Worthing has many troubles in his life. Idle merriment and triviality would be out of place in his conversation. You must remember his constant anxiety about that unfortunate young man his brother.

CECILY I wish Uncle Jack would allow that unfortunate young man, his brother, to come down here sometimes. We might have a good influence over him, Miss Prism. I am sure you certainly would. You know German, and geology, and things of that kind influence a man very much. [*Cecily begins to write in her diary.*]

MISS PRISM [*shaking her head*] I do not think that even I could produce any effect on a character that according to his own brother's admission is irretrievably weak and vacillating. Indeed I am not sure that I would desire to reclaim him. I am not in favour of this modern mania for turning bad people into good people at a moment's notice. As a man sows so let him reap.[3] You must put away your diary, Cecily. I really don't see why you should keep a diary at all.

CECILY I keep a diary in order to enter the wonderful secrets of my life. If I didn't write them down I should probably forget all about them.

MISS PRISM Memory, my dear Cecily, is the diary that we all carry about with us.

CECILY Yes, but it usually chronicles the things that have never happened, and couldn't possibly have happened. I believe that Memory is responsible for nearly all the three-volume novels that Mudie sends us.[4]

MISS PRISM Do not speak slightly of the three-volume novel, Cecily. I wrote one myself in earlier days.

CECILY Did you really, Miss Prism? How wonderfully clever you are! I hope it did not end happily? I don't like novels that end happily. They depress me so much.

MISS PRISM The good ended happily, and the bad unhappily. That is what Fiction means.

CECILY I suppose so. But it seems very unfair. And was your novel ever published?

MISS PRISM Alas! no. The manuscript unfortunately was abandoned. I use the word in the sense of lost or mislaid. To your work, child, these speculations are profitless.

CECILY [*smiling*] But I see dear Dr Chasuble coming up through the garden.

MISS PRISM [*rising and advancing*] Dr Chasuble! This is indeed a pleasure.

[*Enter Canon Chasuble.*][5]

CHASUBLE And how are we this morning? Miss Prism, you are, I trust, well?

---

3. "Be not deceived; God is not mocked: for whatsoever a man soweth, that shall he also reap" (Galatians 6.7).
4. Mudie's Select Library lent novels to subscribers for a

fee; at the time of this play, both Mudie's and the three-volume novel were becoming outmoded.
5. A canon is a cathedral clergyman; a chasuble is a vestment.

CECILY Miss Prism has just been complaining of a slight headache. I think it would do her so much good to have a short stroll with you in the Park, Dr Chasuble.

MISS PRISM Cecily, have not mentioned anything about a headache.

CECILY No, dear Miss Prism, I know that, but I felt instinctively that you had a headache. Indeed I was thinking about that, and not about my German lesson, when the Rector came in.

CHASUBLE I hope Cecily, you are not inattentive.

CECILY Oh, I am afraid I am.

CHASUBLE That is strange. Were I fortunate enough to be Miss Prism's pupil, I would hang upon her lips. [Miss Prism glares.] I spoke metaphorically.—My metaphor was drawn from bees. Ahem! Mr Worthing I suppose, has not returned from town yet?

MISS PRISM We do not expect him till Monday afternoon.

CHASUBLE Ah yes, he usually likes to spend his Sunday in London. He is not one of those whose sole aim is enjoyment, as, by all accounts, that unfortunate young man his brother seems to be. But I must not disturb Egeria[6] and her pupil any longer.

MISS PRISM Egeria? My name is Laetitia, Doctor.

CHASUBLE [bowing] A classical allusion merely, drawn from the Pagan authors. I shall see you both no doubt at Evensong?[7]

MISS PRISM I think, dear Doctor, I will have a stroll with you. I find I have a headache after all, and a walk might do it good.

CHASUBLE With pleasure, Miss Prism, with pleasure. We might go as far as the schools and back.

MISS PRISM That would be delightful. Cecily, you will read your Political Economy in my absence. The chapter on the Fall of the Rupee you may omit.[8] It is somewhat too sensational. Even these metallic problems have their melodramatic side. [Goes down the garden with Dr Chasuble.]

CECILY [picks up books and throws them back on table] Horrid Political Economy! Horrid Geography! Horrid, horrid German!

[Enter Merriman with a card on a salver.]

MERRIMAN Mr Ernest Worthing has just driven over from the station. He has brought his luggage with him.

CECILY [takes the card and reads it] "Mr Ernest Worthing, B.4 The Albany, W." Uncle Jack's brother! Did you tell him Mr Worthing was in town?

MERRIMAN Yes, Miss. He seemed very much disappointed. I mentioned that you and Miss Prism were in the garden. He said he was anxious to speak to you privately for a moment.

CECILY Ask Mr Ernest Worthing to come here. I suppose you had better talk to the housekeeper about a room for him.

MERRIMAN Yes, Miss. [Merriman goes off.]

CECILY I have never met any really wicked person before. I feel rather frightened. I am so afraid he will look just like everyone else.

[Enter Algernon, very gay and debonair.]

He does!

---

6. Roman goddess of fountains; her name was used for a woman who instructed other women.
7. Evening church services.

8. The declining value of the Indian rupee would hurt British civil servants in India, who were paid in rupees.

ALGERNON [*raising his hat*] You are my little cousin Cecily, I'm sure.

CECILY You are under some strange mistake. I am not little. In fact, I believe I am more than usually tall for my age. [*Algernon is rather taken aback.*] But I am your cousin Cecily. You, I see from your card, are Uncle Jack's brother, my cousin Ernest, my wicked cousin Ernest.

ALGERNON Oh! I am not really wicked at all, cousin Cecily. You mustn't think that I am wicked.

CECILY If you are not, then you have certainly been deceiving us all in a very inexcusable manner. I hope you have not been leading a double life, pretending to be wicked and being really good all the time. That would be hypocrisy.

ALGERNON [*looks at her in amazement*] Oh! Of course I have been rather reckless.

CECILY I am glad to hear it.

ALGERNON In fact, now you mention the subject, I have been very bad in my own small way.

CECILY I don't think you should be so proud of that, although I am sure it must have been very pleasant.

ALGERNON It is much pleasanter being here with you.

CECILY I can't understand how you are here at all. Uncle Jack won't be back till Monday afternoon.

ALGERNON That is a great disappointment. I am obliged to go up by the first train on Monday morning. I have a business appointment that I am anxious . . . to miss.

CECILY Couldn't you miss it anywhere but in London?

ALGERNON No: the appointment is in London.

CECILY Well, I know, of course, how important it is not to keep a business engagement, if one wants to retain any sense of the beauty of life, but still I think you had better wait till Uncle Jack arrives. I know he wants to speak to you about your emigrating.

ALGERNON About my what?

CECILY Your emigrating. He has gone up to buy your outfit.

ALGERNON I certainly wouldn't let Jack buy my outfit. He has no taste in neckties at all.

CECILY I don't think you will require neckties. Uncle Jack is sending you to Australia.[9]

ALGERNON Australia! I'd sooner die.

CECILY Well, he said at dinner on Wednesday night, that you would have to choose between this world, the next world, and Australia.

ALGERNON Oh, well! The accounts I have received of Australia and the next world, are not particularly encouraging. This world is good enough for me, cousin Cecily.

CECILY Yes, but are you good enough for it?

ALGERNON I'm afraid I'm not that. That is why I want you to reform me. You might make that your mission, if you don't mind, cousin Cecily.

CECILY I'm afraid I've no time, this afternoon.

ALGERNON Well, would you mind my reforming myself this afternoon?

CECILY It is rather Quixotic[1] of you. But I think you should try.

ALGERNON I will. I feel better already.

CECILY You are looking a little worse.

ALGERNON That is because I am hungry.

---

9. Australia was no longer a penal colony, but it was still a place where families sent their ne'er-do-well sons.

1. Hopelessly idealistic, like Don Quixote.

CECILY How thoughtless of me. I should have remembered that when one is going to lead an entirely new life, one requires regular and wholesome meals. Won't you come in?

ALGERNON Thank you. Might I have a buttonhole[2] first? I never have any appetite unless I have a buttonhole first.

CECILY A Maréchal Niel?[3] [*Picks up scissors.*]

ALGERNON No, I'd sooner have a pink rose.

CECILY Why? [*Cuts a flower.*]

ALGERNON Because you are like a pink rose, Cousin Cecily.

CECILY I don't think it can be right for you to talk to me like that. Miss Prism never says such things to me.

ALGERNON Then Miss Prism is a short-sighted old lady. [*Cecily puts the rose in his buttonhole.*] You are the prettiest girl I ever saw.

CECILY Miss Prism says that all good looks are a snare.

ALGERNON They are a snare that every sensible man would like to be caught in.

CECILY Oh! I don't think I would care to catch a sensible man. I shouldn't know what to talk to him about.

[*They pass into the house. Miss Prism and Dr Chasuble return.*]

MISS PRISM You are too much alone, dear Dr Chasuble. You should get married. A misanthrope I can understand—a womanthrope, never!

CHASUBLE [*with a scholar's shudder*][4] Believe me, I do not deserve so neologistic a phrase. The precept as well as the practice of the Primitive Church was distinctly against matrimony.[5]

MISS PRISM [*sententiously*] That is obviously the reason why the Primitive Church has not lasted up to the present day. And you do not seem to realize, dear Doctor, that by persistently remaining single, a man converts himself into a permanent public temptation. Men should be more careful; this very celibacy leads weaker vessels astray.

CHASUBLE But is a man not equally attractive when married?

MISS PRISM No married man is ever attractive except to his wife.

CHASUBLE And often, I've been told, not even to her.

MISS PRISM That depends on the intellectual sympathies of the woman. Maturity can always be depended on. Ripeness can be trusted. Young women are green. [*Dr Chasuble starts.*] I spoke horticulturally. My metaphor was drawn from fruits. But where is Cecily?

CHASUBLE Perhaps she followed us to the schools.

[*Enter Jack slowly from the back of the garden. He is dressed in the deepest mourning, with crape hat-band and black gloves.*]

MISS PRISM Mr Worthing!

CHASUBLE Mr Worthing?

MISS PRISM This is indeed a surprise. We did not look for you till Monday afternoon.

JACK [*shakes Miss Prism's hand in a tragic manner*] I have returned sooner than I expected. Dr Chasuble, I hope you are well?

---

2. A flower to wear in his lapel.
3. A yellow rose.
4. He shudders because Miss Prism has mangled the language by coining a word, "womanthrope," to describe someone who dislikes women, instead of using the correct term, "misogynist." A neologism is a newly invented word.
5. Protestant clergy are allowed to marry, but as a High Church Anglican, Chasuble is interested in preserving the rituals and practices of the early Catholic church.

CHASUBLE Dear Mr Worthing, I trust this garb of woe does not betoken some terrible calamity?

JACK My brother.

MISS PRISM More shameful debts and extravagance?

CHASUBLE Still leading his life of pleasure?

JACK [*shaking his head*] Dead!

CHASUBLE Your brother Ernest dead?

JACK Quite dead.

MISS PRISM What a lesson for him! I trust he will profit by it.

CHASUBLE Mr Worthing, I offer you my sincere condolence. You have at least the consolation of knowing that you were always the most generous and forgiving of brothers.

JACK Poor Ernest! He had many faults, but it is a sad, sad blow.

CHASUBLE Very sad indeed. Were you with him at the end?

JACK No. He died abroad; in Paris, in fact. I had a telegram last night from the manager of the Grand Hotel.

CHASUBLE Was the cause of death mentioned?

JACK A severe chill, it seems.

MISS PRISM As a man sows, so shall he reap.

CHASUBLE [*raising his hand*] Charity, dear Miss Prism, charity! None of us are perfect. I myself am peculiarly susceptible to draughts. Will the interment take place here?

JACK No. He seemed to have expressed a desire to be buried in Paris.

CHASUBLE In Paris! [*Shakes his head.*] I fear that hardly points to any very serious state of mind at the last. You would no doubt wish me to make some slight allusion to this tragic domestic affliction next Sunday. [*Jack presses his hand convulsively.*] My sermon on the meaning of the manna in the wilderness[6] can be adapted to almost any occasion, joyful, or, as in the present case, distressing. [*All sigh.*] I have preached it at harvest celebrations, christenings, confirmations, on days of humiliation and festal days. The last time I delivered it was in the Cathedral, as a charity sermon on behalf of the Society for the Prevention of Discontent among the Upper Orders. The Bishop, who was present, was much struck by some of the analogies I drew.

JACK Ah! that reminds me, you mentioned christenings I think, Dr Chasuble? I suppose you know how to christen all right? [*Dr Chasuble looks astounded.*] I mean, of course, you are continually christening, aren't you?

MISS PRISM It is, I regret to say, one of the Rector's most constant duties in this parish. I have often spoken to the poorer classes on the subject. But they don't seem to know what thrift is.

CHASUBLE But is there any particular infant in whom you are interested, Mr Worthing? Your brother was, I believe, unmarried, was he not?

JACK Oh, yes.

MISS PRISM [*bitterly*] People who live entirely for pleasure usually are.

JACK But it is not for any child, dear Doctor. I am very fond of children. No! the fact is, I would like to be christened myself, this afternoon, if you have nothing better to do.

CHASUBLE But surely, Mr Worthing, you have been christened already?

6. Cf. Exodus 16.

JACK I don't remember anything about it.

CHASUBLE But have you any grave doubts on the subject?

JACK I certainly intend to have. Of course I don't know if the thing would bother you in any way, or if you think I am a little too old now.

CHASUBLE Not at all. The sprinkling, and, indeed, the immersion of adults is a perfectly canonical practice.

JACK Immersion!

CHASUBLE You need have no apprehensions. Sprinkling is all that is necessary, or indeed I think advisable. Our weather is so changeable. At what hour would you wish the ceremony performed?

JACK Oh, I might trot round about five if that would suit you.

CHASUBLE Perfectly, perfectly! In fact I have two similar ceremonies to perform at that time. A case of twins that occurred recently in one of the outlying cottages on your own estate. Poor Jenkins the carter, a most hard-working man.

JACK Oh! I don't see much fun in being christened along with other babies. It would be childish. Would half-past five do?

CHASUBLE Admirably! Admirably! [*Takes out watch.*] And now, dear Mr Worthing, I will not intrude any longer into a house of sorrow. I would merely beg you not to be too much bowed down by grief. What seem to us bitter trials are often blessings in disguise.

MISS PRISM This seems to me a blessing of an extremely obvious kind.

[*Enter Cecily from the house.*]

CECILY Uncle Jack! Oh, I am pleased to see you back. But what horrid clothes you have got on! Do go and change them.

MISS PRISM Cecily!

CHASUBLE My child! my child!

[*Cecily goes towards Jack; he kisses her brow in a melancholy manner.*]

CECILY What is the matter, Uncle Jack? Do look happy! You look as if you had toothache, and I have got such a surprise for you. Who do you think is in the dining-room? Your brother!

JACK Who?

CECILY Your brother Ernest. He arrived about half an hour ago.

JACK What nonsense! I haven't got a brother.

CECILY Oh, don't say that. However badly he may have behaved to you in the past he is still your brother. You couldn't be so heartless as to disown him. I'll tell him to come out. And you will shake hands with him, won't you, Uncle Jack? [*Runs back into the house.*]

CHASUBLE These are very joyful tidings.

MISS PRISM After we had all been resigned to his loss, his sudden return seems to me peculiarly distressing.

JACK My brother is in the dining-room? I don't know what it all means. I think it is perfectly absurd.

[*Enter Algernon and Cecily hand in hand. They come slowly up to Jack.*]

JACK Good heavens! [*Motions Algernon away.*]

ALGERNON Brother John, I have come down from town to tell you that I am very sorry for all the trouble I have given you, and that I intend to lead a better life in the future.

[*Jack glares at him and does not take his hand.*]

CECILY Uncle Jack, you are not going to refuse your own brother's hand?

JACK Nothing will induce me to take his hand. I think his coming down here disgraceful. He knows perfectly well why.

CECILY Uncle Jack, do be nice. There is some good in everyone. Ernest has just been telling me about his poor invalid friend Mr Bunbury whom he goes to visit so often. And surely there must be much good in one who is kind to an invalid, and leaves the pleasures of London to sit by a bed of pain.

JACK Oh! he has been talking about Bunbury has he?

CECILY Yes, he has told me all about poor Mr Bunbury, and his terrible state of health.

JACK Bunbury! Well, I won't have him talk to you about Bunbury or about anything else. It is enough to drive one perfectly frantic.

ALGERNON Of course I admit that the faults were all on my side. But I must say that I think that Brother John's coldness to me is peculiarly painful. I expected a more enthusiastic welcome, especially considering it is the first time I have come here.

CECILY Uncle Jack, if you don't shake hands with Ernest I will never forgive you.

JACK Never forgive me?

CECILY Never, never, never!

JACK Well, this is the last time I shall ever do it. [*Shakes hands with Algernon and glares*.]

CHASUBLE It's pleasant, is it not, to see so perfect a reconciliation? I think we might leave the two brothers together.

MISS PRISM Cecily, you will come with us.

CECILY Certainly, Miss Prism. My little task of reconciliation is over.

CHASUBLE You have done a beautiful action today, dear child.

MISS PRISM We must not be premature in our judgements.

CECILY I feel very happy. [*They all go off*.]

JACK You young scoundrel, Algy, you must get out of this place as soon as possible. I don't allow any Bunburying here.
   [*Enter Merriman*.]

MERRIMAN I have put Mr Ernest's things in the room next to yours, sir. I suppose that is all right?

JACK What?

MERRIMAN Mr Ernest's luggage, sir. I have unpacked it and put it in the room next to your own.

JACK His luggage?

MERRIMAN Yes, sir. Three portmanteaus, a dressing-case, two hat-boxes, and a large luncheon-basket.

ALGERNON I am afraid I can't stay more than a week this time.

JACK Merriman, order the dog-cart[7] at once. Mr Ernest has been suddenly called back to town.

MERRIMAN Yes, sir. [*Goes back into the house*.]

ALGERNON What a fearful liar you are, Jack. I have not been called back to town at all.

JACK Yes, you have.

ALGERNON I haven't heard anyone call me.

JACK Your duty as a gentleman calls you back.

ALGERNON My duty as a gentleman has never interfered with my pleasures in the smallest degree.

JACK I can quite understand that.

---

7. A horse-drawn cart with seats, and a box for hunting dogs.

ALGERNON Well, Cecily is a darling.

JACK You are not to talk of Miss Cardew like that. I don't like it.

ALGERNON Well, I don't like your clothes. You look perfectly ridiculous in them. Why on earth don't you go up and change? It is perfectly childish to be in deep mourning for a man who is actually staying for a whole week with you in your house as a guest. I call it grotesque.

JACK You are certainly not staying with me for a whole week as a guest or anything else. You have got to leave . . . by the four-five train.

ALGERNON I certainly won't leave you so long as you are in mourning. It would be most unfriendly. If I were in mourning you would stay with me, I suppose. I should think it very unkind if you didn't.

JACK Well, will you go if I change my clothes?

ALGERNON Yes, if you are not too long. I never saw anybody take so long to dress, and with such little result.

JACK Well, at any rate, that is better than being always over-dressed as you are.

ALGERNON If I am occasionally a little over-dressed, I make up for it by being always immensely over-educated.

JACK Your vanity is ridiculous, your conduct an outrage, and your presence in my garden utterly absurd. However, you have got to catch the four-five, and I hope you will have a pleasant journey back to town. This Bunburying, as you call it, has not been a great success for you. [*Goes into the house.*]

ALGERNON I think it has been a great success. I'm in love with Cecily, and that is everything.
    [*Enter Cecily at the back of the garden. She picks up the can and begins to water the flowers.*]
But I must see her before I go, and make arrangements for another Bunbury. Ah, there she is.

CECILY Oh, I merely came back to water the roses. I thought you were with Uncle Jack.

ALGERNON He's gone to order the dog-cart for me.

CECILY Oh, is he going to take you for a nice drive?

ALGERNON He's going to send me away.

CECILY Then have we got to part?

ALGERNON I am afraid so. It's a painful parting.

CECILY It is always painful to part from people whom one has known for a very brief space of time. The absence of old friends one can endure with equanimity. But even a momentary separation from anyone to whom one has just been introduced is almost unbearable.

ALGERNON Thank you.
    [*Enter Merriman.*]

MERRIMAN The dog-cart is at the door, sir.
    [*Algernon looks appealingly at Cecily.*]

CECILY It can wait, Merriman . . . for . . . five minutes.

MERRIMAN Yes, Miss. [*Exit Merriman.*]

ALGERNON I hope, Cecily, I shall not offend you if I state quite frankly and open-ly that you seem to me to be in every way the visible personification of absolute perfection.

CECILY I think your frankness does you great credit, Ernest. If you will allow me I will copy your remarks into my diary. [*Goes over to table and begins writing in diary.*]

ALGERNON Do you really keep a diary? I'd give anything to look at it. May I?

CECILY Oh no. [*Puts her hand over it.*] You see, it is simply a very young girl's record of her own thoughts and impressions, and consequently meant for publication. When it appears in volume form I hope you will order a copy. But pray, Ernest, don't stop. I delight in taking down from dictation. I have reached "absolute perfection." You can go on. I am quite ready for more.

ALGERNON [*somewhat taken aback*] Ahem! Ahem!

CECILY Oh, don't cough, Ernest. When one is dictating one should speak fluently and not cough. Besides, I don't know how to spell a cough. [*Writes as Algernon speaks.*]

ALGERNON [*speaking very rapidly*] Cecily, ever since I first looked upon your wonderful and incomparable beauty, I have dared to love you wildly, passionately, devotedly, hopelessly.

CECILY I don't think that you should tell me that you love me wildly, passionately, devotedly, hopelessly. Hopelessly doesn't seem to make much sense, does it?

ALGERNON Cecily!

   [*Enter Merriman.*]

MERRIMAN The dog-cart is waiting, sir.

ALGERNON Tell it to come round next week, at the same hour.

MERRIMAN [*looks at Cecily, who makes no sign*] Yes, sir. [*Merriman retires.*]

CECILY Uncle Jack would be very much annoyed if he knew you were staying on till next week, at the same hour.

ALGERNON Oh, I don't care about Jack. I don't care for anybody in the whole world but you. I love you, Cecily. You will marry me, won't you?

CECILY You silly boy! Of course. Why, we have been engaged for the last three months.

ALGERNON For the last three months?

CECILY Yes, it will be exactly three months on Thursday.

ALGERNON But how did we become engaged?

CECILY Well, ever since dear Uncle Jack first confessed to us that he had a younger brother who was very wicked and bad, you of course have formed the chief topic of conversation between myself and Miss Prism. And of course a man who is much talked about is always very attractive. One feels there must be something in him after all. I daresay it was foolish of me, but I fell in love with you, Ernest.

ALGERNON Darling! And when was the engagement actually settled?

CECILY On the 14th of February last. Worn out by your entire ignorance of my existence, I determined to end the matter one way or the other, and after a long struggle with myself I accepted you under this dear old tree here. The next day I bought this little ring in your name, and this is the little bangle with the true lovers' knot I promised you always to wear.

ALGERNON Did I give you this? It's very pretty, isn't it?

CECILY Yes, you've wonderfully good taste, Ernest. It's the excuse I've always given for your leading such a bad life. And this is the box in which I keep all your dear letters. [*Kneels at table, opens box, and produces letters tied up with blue ribbon.*]

ALGERNON My letters! But my own sweet Cecily, I have never written you any letters.

CECILY You need hardly remind me of that, Ernest. I remember only too well that I was forced to write your letters for you. I wrote always three times a week, and sometimes oftener.

ALGERNON Oh, do let me read them, Cecily?

CECILY Oh, I couldn't possibly. They would make you far too conceited. [*Replaces box.*] The three you wrote me after I had broken off the engagement are so beautiful, and so badly spelled, that even now I can hardly read them without crying a little.

ALGERNON But was our engagement ever broken off?

CECILY Of course it was. On the 22nd of last March. You can see the entry if you like. [*Shows diary.*] "Today I broke off my engagement with Ernest. I feel it is better to do so. The weather still continues charming."

ALGERNON But why on earth did you break it off? What had I done? I had done nothing at all. Cecily, I am very much hurt indeed to hear you broke it off. Particularly when the weather was so charming.

CECILY It would hardly have been a really serious engagement if it hadn't been broken off at least once. But I forgave you before the week was out.

ALGERNON [*crossing to her, and kneeling*] What a perfect angel you are, Cecily.

CECILY You dear romantic boy. [*He kisses her, she puts her fingers through his hair.*] I hope your hair curls naturally, does it?

ALGERNON Yes, darling, with a little help from others.

CECILY I am so glad.

ALGERNON You'll never break off our engagement again, Cecily?

CECILY I don't think I could break it off now that I have actually met you. Besides, of course, there is the question of your name.

ALGERNON Yes, of course. [*Nervously.*]

CECILY You must not laugh at me, darling, but it had always been a girlish dream of mine to love some one whose name was Ernest. [*Algernon rises, Cecily also.*] There is something in that name that seems to inspire absolute confidence. I pity any poor married woman whose husband is not called Ernest.

ALGERNON But, my dear child, do you mean to say you could not love me if I had some other name?

CECILY But what name?

ALGERNON Oh, any name you like—Algernon—for instance . . .

CECILY But I don't like the name of Algernon.

ALGERNON Well, my own dear, sweet, loving little darling, I really can't see why you should object to the name of Algernon. It is not at all a bad name. In fact, it is rather an aristocratic name. Half of the chaps who get into the Bankruptcy Court are called Algernon. But seriously, Cecily . . . [*moving to her*] . . . if my name was Algy, couldn't you love me?

CECILY [*rising*] I might respect you, Ernest, I might admire your character, but I fear that I should not be able to give you my undivided attention.

ALGERNON Ahem! Cecily! [*Picking up hat.*] Your Rector here is, I suppose, thoroughly experienced in the practice of all the rites and ceremonials of the Church?

CECILY Oh yes. Dr Chasuble is a most learned man. He has never written a single book, so you can imagine how much he knows.

ALGERNON I must see him at once on a most important christening—I mean on most important business.

CECILY Oh!

ALGERNON I shan't be away more than half an hour.

CECILY Considering that we have been engaged since February the 14th, and that I only met you today for the first time, I think it is rather hard that you should leave me for so long a period as half an hour. Couldn't you make it twenty minutes?

ALGERNON I'll be back in no time. [*Kisses her and rushes down the garden.*]

CECILY What an impetuous boy he is! I like his hair so much. I must enter his proposal in my diary.

[*Enter Merriman.*]

MERRIMAN A Miss Fairfax has just called to see Mr Worthing. On very important business Miss Fairfax states.

CECILY Isn't Mr Worthing in his library?

MERRIMAN Mr Worthing went over in the direction of the Rectory some time ago.

CECILY Pray ask the lady to come out here; Mr Worthing is sure to be back soon. And you can bring tea.

MERRIMAN Yes, Miss. [Goes out.]

CECILY Miss Fairfax! I suppose one of the many good elderly women who are associated with Uncle Jack in some of his philanthropic work in London. I don't quite like women who are interested in philanthropic work. I think it is so forward of them.

    [Enter Merriman.]

MERRIMAN Miss Fairfax.

    [Enter Gwendolen. Exit Merriman.]

CECILY [advancing to meet her] Pray let me introduce myself to you. My name is Cecily Cardew.

GWENDOLEN Cecily Cardew? [Moving to her and shaking hands.] What a very sweet name! Something tells me that we are going to be great friends. I like you already more than I can say. My first impressions of people are never wrong.

CECILY How nice of you to like me so much after we have known each other such a comparatively short time. Pray sit down.

GWENDOLEN [still standing up] I may call you Cecily, may I not?

CECILY With pleasure!

GWENDOLEN And you will always call me Gwendolen, won't you?

CECILY If you wish.

GWENDOLEN Then that is all quite settled, is it not?

CECILY I hope so.

    [A pause. They both sit down together.]

GWENDOLEN Perhaps this might be a favourable opportunity for my mentioning who I am. My father is Lord Bracknell. You have never heard of papa, I suppose?

CECILY I don't think so.

GWENDOLEN Outside the family circle, papa, I am glad to say, is entirely unknown. I think that is quite as it should be. The home seems to me to be the proper sphere for the man. And certainly once a man begins to neglect his domestic duties he becomes painfully effeminate, does he not? And I don't like that. It makes men so very attractive. Cecily, mamma, whose views on education are remarkably strict, has brought me up to be extremely short-sighted; it is part of her system; so do you mind my looking at you through my glasses?

CECILY Oh! not at all, Gwendolen. I am very fond of being looked at.

GWENDOLEN [after examining Cecily carefully through a lorgnette] You are here on a short visit I suppose.

CECILY Oh no! I live here.

GWENDOLEN [severely] Really? Your mother, no doubt, or some female relative of advanced years, resides here also?

CECILY Oh no! I have no mother, nor, in fact, any relations.

GWENDOLEN Indeed?

CECILY My dear guardian, with the assistance of Miss Prism, has the arduous task of looking after me.

GWENDOLEN Your guardian?

CECILY Yes, I am Mr Worthing's ward.

GWENDOLEN Oh! It is strange he never mentioned to me that he had a ward. How secretive of him! He grows more interesting hourly. I am not sure, however, that the news inspires me with feelings of unmixed delight. [*Rising and going to her.*] I am very fond of you, Cecily; I have liked you ever since I met you! But I am bound to state that now that I know that you are Mr Worthing's ward, I cannot help expressing a wish you were—well just a little older than you seem to be—and not quite so very alluring in appearance. In fact, if I may speak candidly—

CECILY Pray do! I think that whenever one has anything unpleasant to say, one should always be quite candid.

GWENDOLEN Well, to speak with perfect candour, Cecily, I wish that you were fully forty-two, and more than usually plain for your age. Ernest has a strong upright nature. He is the very soul of truth and honour. Disloyalty would be as impossible to him as deception. But even men of the noblest possible moral character are extremely susceptible to the influence of the physical charms of others. Modern, no less than Ancient History, supplies us with many most painful examples of what I refer to. If it were not so, indeed, History would be quite unreadable.

CECILY I beg your pardon, Gwendolen, did you say Ernest?

GWENDOLEN Yes.

CECILY Oh, but it is not Mr Ernest Worthing who is my guardian. It is his brother—his elder brother.

GWENDOLEN [*sitting down again*] Ernest never mentioned to me that he had a brother.

CECILY I am sorry to say they have not been on good terms for a long time.

GWENDOLEN Ah! that accounts for it. And now that I think of it I have never heard any man mention his brother. The subject seems distasteful to most men. Cecily, you have lifted a load from my mind. I was growing almost anxious. It would have been terrible if any cloud had come across a friendship like ours, would it not? Of course you are quite, quite sure that it is not Mr Ernest Worthing who is your guardian?

CECILY Quite sure. [*A pause.*] In fact, I am going to be his.

GWENDOLEN [*enquiringly*] I beg your pardon?

CECILY [*rather shy and confidingly*] Dearest Gwendolen, there is no reason why I should make a secret of it to you. Our little county newspaper is sure to chronicle the fact next week. Mr Ernest Worthing and I are engaged to be married.

GWENDOLEN [*quite politely, rising*] My darling Cecily, I think there must be some slight error. Mr Ernest Worthing is engaged to me. The announcement will appear in the "Morning Post" on Saturday at the latest.

CECILY [*very politely, rising*] I am afraid you must be under some misconception. Ernest proposed to me exactly ten minutes ago. [*Shows diary.*]

GWENDOLEN [*examines diary through her lorgnette carefully*] It is certainly very curious, for he asked me to be his wife yesterday afternoon at 5.30. If you would care to verify the incident, pray do so. [*Produces diary of her own.*] I never travel without my diary. One should always have something sensational to read in the train. I am so sorry, dear Cecily, if it is any disappointment to you, but I am afraid I have the prior claim.

CECILY It would distress me more than I can tell you, dear Gwendolen, if it caused you any mental or physical anguish, but I feel bound to point out that since Ernest proposed to you he clearly has changed his mind.

GWENDOLEN [*meditatively*] If the poor fellow has been entrapped into any foolish promise I shall consider it my duty to rescue him at once, and with a firm hand.

CECILY [*thoughtfully and sadly*] Whatever unfortunate entanglement my dear boy may have got into, I will never reproach him with it after we are married.

GWENDOLEN Do you allude to me, Miss Cardew, as an entanglement? You are presumptuous. On an occasion of this kind it becomes more than a moral duty to speak one's mind. It becomes a pleasure.

CECILY Do you suggest, Miss Fairfax, that I entrapped Ernest into an engagement? How dare you? This is no time for wearing the shallow mask of manners. When I see a spade I call it a spade.

GWENDOLEN [*satirically*] I am glad to say that I have never seen a spade. It is obvious that our social spheres have been widely different.

[*Enter Merriman, followed by the footman. He carries a salver, table cloth, and plate stand. Cecily is about to retort. The presence of the servants exercises a restraining influence, under which both girls chafe.*]

MERRIMAN Shall I lay tea here as usual, Miss?

CECILY [*sternly, in a calm voice*] Yes, as usual.

[*Merriman begins to clear table and lay cloth. A long pause. Cecily and Gwendolen glare at each other.*]

GWENDOLEN Are there many interesting walks in the vicinity, Miss Cardew?

CECILY Oh! yes! a great many. From the top of one of the hills quite close one can see five counties.

GWENDOLEN Five counties! I don't think I should like that. I hate crowds.

CECILY [*sweetly*] I suppose that is why you live in town?

[*Gwendolen bites her lip, and beats her foot nervously with her parasol.*]

GWENDOLEN [*looking round*] Quite a well-kept garden this is, Miss Cardew.

CECILY So glad you like it, Miss Fairfax.

GWENDOLEN I had no idea there were any flowers in the country.

CECILY Oh, flowers are as common here, Miss Fairfax, as people are in London.

GWENDOLEN Personally, I cannot understand how anybody manages to exist in the country, if anybody who is anybody does. The country always bores me to death.

CECILY Ah! This is what the newspapers call agricultural depression,[8] is it not? I believe the aristocracy are suffering very much from it just at present. It is almost an epidemic amongst them, I have been told. May I offer you some tea, Miss Fairfax?

GWENDOLEN [*with elaborate politeness*] Thank you. [*Aside.*] Detestable girl! But I require tea!

CECILY [*sweetly*] Sugar?

GWENDOLEN [*superciliously*] No, thank you. Sugar is not fashionable any more.

[*Cecily looks angrily at her, takes up the tongs and puts four lumps of sugar into the cup.*]

CECILY [*severely*] Cake or bread and butter?

GWENDOLEN [*in a bored manner*] Bread and butter, please. Cake is rarely seen at the best houses nowadays.

CECILY [*cuts a very large slice of cake, and puts it on the tray*] Hand that to Miss Fairfax.

---

8. A pun on the word "depression"; beginning in the 1870s, British agriculture had been in a slump, causing losses and hardship among landowners.

[*Merriman does so, and goes out with footman. Gwendolen drinks the tea and makes a grimace. Puts down cup at once, reaches out her hand to the bread and butter, looks at it, and finds it is cake. Rises in indignation.*]

GWENDOLEN You have filled my tea with lumps of sugar, and though I asked most distinctly for bread and butter, you have given me cake. I am known for the gentleness of my disposition, and the extraordinary sweetness of my nature, but I warn you, Miss Cardew, you may go too far.

CECILY [*rising*] To save my poor, innocent, trusting boy from the machinations of any other girl there are no lengths to which I would not go.

GWENDOLEN From the moment I saw you I distrusted you. I felt that you were false and deceitful. I am never deceived in such matters. My first impressions of people are invariably right.

CECILY It seems to me, Miss Fairfax, that I am trespassing on your valuable time. No doubt you have many other calls of a similar character to make in the neighbourhood.

[*Enter Jack.*]

GWENDOLEN [*catching sight of him*] Ernest! My own Ernest!

JACK Gwendolen! Darling! [*Offers to kiss her.*]

GWENDOLEN [*drawing back*] A moment! May I ask if you are engaged to be married to this young lady? [*Points to Cecily.*]

JACK [*laughing*] To dear little Cecily! Of course not! What could have put such an idea into your pretty little head?

GWENDOLEN Thank you. You may! [*Offers her cheek.*]

CECILY [*very sweetly*] I knew there must be some misunderstanding, Miss Fairfax. The gentleman whose arm is at present round your waist is my dear guardian, Mr John Worthing.

GWENDOLEN I beg your pardon?

CECILY This is Uncle Jack.

GWENDOLEN [*receding*] Jack! Oh!

[*Enter Algernon.*]

CECILY Here is Ernest.

ALGERNON [*goes straight over to Cecily without noticing anyone else*] My own love! [*Offers to kiss her.*]

CECILY [*drawing back*] A moment, Ernest! May I ask you—are you engaged to be married to this young lady?

ALGERNON [*looking round*] To what young lady? Good heavens! Gwendolen!

CECILY Yes, to good heavens, Gwendolen, I mean to Gwendolen.

ALGERNON [*laughing*] Of course not! What could have put such an idea into your pretty little head?

CECILY Thank you. [*Presenting her cheek to be kissed.*] You may.

[*Algernon kisses her.*]

GWENDOLEN I felt there was some slight error, Miss Cardew. The gentleman who is now embracing you is my cousin, Mr Algernon Moncrieff.

CECILY [*breaking away from Algernon*] Algernon Moncrieff! Oh!

[*The two girls move towards each other and put their arms round each other's waists as if for protection.*]

CECILY Are you called Algernon?

ALGERNON I cannot deny it.

CECILY Oh!

GWENDOLEN Is your name really John?

JACK [*standing rather proudly*] I could deny it if I liked. I could deny anything if I liked. But my name certainly is John. It has been John for years.

CECILY [*to Gwendolen*] A gross deception has been practised on both of us.

GWENDOLEN My poor wounded Cecily!

CECILY My sweet wronged Gwendolen!

GWENDOLEN [*slowly and seriously*] You will call me sister, will you not?
   [*They embrace. Jack and Algernon groan and walk up and down.*]

CECILY [*rather brightly*] There is just one question I would like to be allowed to ask my guardian.

GWENDOLEN An admirable idea! Mr Worthing, there is just one question I would like to be permitted to put to you. Where is your brother Ernest? We are both engaged to be married to your brother Ernest, so it is a matter of some importance to us to know where your brother Ernest is at present.

JACK [*slowly and hesitatingly*] Gwendolen—Cecily—It is very painful for me to be forced to speak the truth. It is the first time in my life that I have ever been reduced to such a painful position, and I am really quite inexperienced in doing anything of the kind. However I will tell you quite frankly that I have no brother Ernest. I have no brother at all. I never had a brother in my life, and I certainly have not the smallest intention of ever having one in the future.

CECILY [*surprised*] No brother at all?

JACK [*cheerily*] None!

GWENDOLEN [*severely*] Had you never a brother of any kind?

JACK [*pleasantly*] Never. Not even of any kind.

GWENDOLEN I am afraid it is quite clear, Cecily, that neither of us is engaged to be married to anyone.

CECILY It is not a very pleasant position for a young girl suddenly to find herself in. Is it?

GWENDOLEN Let us go into the house. They will hardly venture to come after us there.

CECILY No, men are so cowardly, aren't they?
   [*They retire into the house with scornful looks.*]

JACK This ghastly state of things is what you call Bunburying, I suppose?

ALGERNON Yes, and a perfectly wonderful Bunbury it is. The most wonderful Bunbury I have ever had in my life.

JACK Well, you've no right whatsoever to Bunbury here.

ALGERNON That is absurd. One has a right to Bunbury anywhere one chooses. Every serious Bunburyist knows that.

JACK Serious Bunburyist! Good heavens!

ALGERNON Well, one must be serious about something, if one wants to have any amusement in life. I happen to be serious about Bunburying. What on earth you are serious about I haven't got the remotest idea. About everything, I should fancy. You have such an absolutely trivial nature.

JACK Well, the only small satisfaction I have in the whole of this wretched business is that your friend Bunbury is quite exploded. You won't be able to run down to the country quite so often as you used to do, dear Algy. And a very good thing too.

ALGERNON Your brother is a little off colour, isn't he, dear Jack? You won't be able to disappear to London quite so frequently as your wicked custom was. And not a bad thing either.

JACK As for your conduct towards Miss Cardew, I must say that your taking in a sweet, simple, innocent girl like that is quite inexcusable. To say nothing of the fact that she is my ward.

ALGERNON I can see no possible defence at all for your deceiving a brilliant, clever, thoroughly experienced young lady like Miss Fairfax. To say nothing of the fact that she is my cousin.

JACK I wanted to be engaged to Gwendolen, that is all. I love her.

ALGERNON Well, I simply wanted to be engaged to Cecily. I adore her.

JACK There is certainly no chance of your marrying Miss Cardew.

ALGERNON I don't think there is much likelihood, Jack, of you and Miss Fairfax being united.

JACK Well, that is no business of yours.

ALGERNON If it was my business, I wouldn't talk about it. [*Begins to eat muffins.*] It is very vulgar to talk about one's business. Only people like stockbrokers do that, and then merely at dinner parties.

JACK How you can sit there, calmly eating muffins when we are in this horrible trouble, I can't make out. You seem to me to be perfectly heartless.

ALGERNON Well, I can't eat muffins in an agitated manner. The butter would probably get on my cuffs. One should always eat muffins quite calmly. It is the only way to eat them.

JACK I say it's perfectly heartless your eating muffins at all, under the circumstances.

ALGERNON When I am in trouble, eating is the only thing that consoles me. Indeed, when I am in really great trouble, as anyone who knows me intimately will tell you, I refuse everything except food and drink. At the present moment I am eating muffins because I am unhappy. Besides, I am particularly fond of muffins. [*Rising.*]

JACK [*rising*] Well, that is no reason why you should eat them all in that greedy way. [*Takes muffins from Algernon.*]

ALGERNON [*offering tea-cake*] I wish you would have tea-cake instead. I don't like tea-cake.

JACK Good heavens! I suppose a man may eat his own muffins in his own garden.

ALGERNON But you have just said it was perfectly heartless to eat muffins.

JACK I said it was perfectly heartless of you, under the circumstances. That is a very different thing.

ALGERNON That may be. But the muffins are the same. [*He seizes the muffin-dish from Jack.*]

JACK Algy, I wish to goodness you would go.

ALGERNON You can't possibly ask me to go without having some dinner. It's absurd. I never go without my dinner. No one ever does, except vegetarians and people like that. Besides I have just made arrangements with Dr Chasuble to be christened at a quarter to six under the name of Ernest.

JACK My dear fellow, the sooner you give up that nonsense the better. I made arrangements this morning with Dr Chasuble to be christened myself at 5.30, and I naturally will take the name of Ernest. Gwendolen would wish it. We can't both be christened Ernest. It's absurd. Besides, I have a perfect right to be christened if I like. There is no evidence at all that I ever have been christened by anybody. I should think it extremely probable I never was, and so does Dr Chasuble. It is entirely different in your case. You have been christened already.

ALGERNON Yes, but I have not been christened for years.

JACK Yes, but you have been christened. That is the important thing.

ALGERNON Quite so. So I know my constitution can stand it. If you are not quite sure about your ever having been christened, I must say I think it rather dangerous your venturing on it now. It might make you very unwell. You can hardly have forgotten that someone very closely connected with you was very nearly carried off this week in Paris by a severe chill.

JACK Yes, but you said yourself that a severe chill was not hereditary.

ALGERNON It usen't to be, I know—but I daresay it is now. Science is always making wonderful improvements in things.

JACK [picking up the muffin-dish] Oh, that is nonsense; you are always talking nonsense.

ALGERNON Jack, you are at the muffins again! I wish you wouldn't. There are only two left. [Takes them.] I told you I was particularly fond of muffins.

JACK But I hate tea-cake.

ALGERNON Why on earth then do you allow tea-cake to be served up for your guests? What ideas you have of hospitality!

JACK Algernon! I have already told you to go. I don't want you here. Why don't you go!

ALGERNON I haven't quite finished my tea yet! and there is still one muffin left.

[Jack groans, and sinks into a chair. Algernon still continues eating.]   ACT DROP

THIRD ACT

SCENE: Morning-room⁹ at the Manor House.

[Gwendolen and Cecily are at the window, looking out into the garden.]

GWENDOLEN The fact that they did not follow us at once into the house, as anyone else would have done, seems to me to show that they have some sense of shame left.

CECILY They have been eating muffins. That looks like repentance.

GWENDOLEN [after a pause] They don't seem to notice us at all. Couldn't you cough?

CECILY But I haven't got a cough.

GWENDOLEN They're looking at us. What effrontery!

CECILY They're approaching. That's very forward of them.

GWENDOLEN Let us preserve a dignified silence.

CECILY Certainly. It's the only thing to do now.

[Enter Jack followed by Algernon. They whistle some dreadful popular air from a British Opera.]¹

GWENDOLEN This dignified silence seems to produce an unpleasant effect.

CECILY A most distasteful one.

GWENDOLEN But we will not be the first to speak.

CECILY Certainly not.

GWENDOLEN Mr Worthing, I have something very particular to ask you. Much depends on your reply.

CECILY Gwendolen, your common sense is invaluable. Mr Moncrieff, kindly answer me the following question. Why did you pretend to be my guardian's brother?

ALGERNON In order that I might have an opportunity of meeting you.

9. An informal room for receiving morning calls from friends (afternoon visitors were received in the formal drawing room).

1. Probably a reference to Gilbert and Sullivan, who had made fun of Wilde and the Aesthetic movement in *Patience* (1881); see page 2144.

CECILY [to Gwendolen] That certainly seems a satisfactory explanation, does it not?

GWENDOLEN Yes, dear, if you can believe him.

CECILY I don't. But that does not affect the wonderful beauty of his answer.

GWENDOLEN True. In matters of grave importance, style, not sincerity is the vital thing. Mr Worthing, what explanation can you offer to me for pretending to have a brother? Was it in order that you might have an opportunity of coming up to town to see me as often as possible?

JACK Can you doubt it, Miss Fairfax?

GWENDOLEN I have the gravest doubts upon the subject. But I intend to crush them. This is not the moment for German scepticism.[2] [Moving to Cecily.] Their explanations appear to be quite satisfactory, especially Mr Worthing's. That seems to me to have the stamp of truth upon it.

CECILY I am more than content with what Mr Moncrieff said. His voice alone inspires one with absolute credulity.

GWENDOLEN Then you think we should forgive them?

CECILY Yes. I mean no.

GWENDOLEN True! I had forgotten. There are principles at stake that one cannot surrender. Which of us should tell them? The task is not a pleasant one.

CECILY Could we not both speak at the same time?

GWENDOLEN An excellent idea! I nearly always speak at the same time as other people. Will you take the time from me?

CECILY Certainly.

[Gwendolen beats time with uplifted finger.]

GWENDOLEN and CECILY [speaking together] Your Christian names are still an insuperable barrier. That is all!

JACK and ALGERNON [speaking together] Our Christian names! Is that all? But we are going to be christened this afternoon.

GWENDOLEN [to Jack] For my sake you are prepared to do this terrible thing?

JACK I am.

CECILY [to Algernon] To please me you are ready to face this fearful ordeal?

ALGERNON I am!

GWENDOLEN How absurd to talk of the equality of the sexes! Where questions of self-sacrifice are concerned, men are infinitely beyond us.

JACK We are. [Clasps hands with Algernon.]

CECILY They have moments of physical courage of which we women know absolutely nothing.

GWENDOLEN [to Jack] Darling!

ALGERNON [to Cecily] Darling! [They fall into each other's arms.]

[Enter Merriman. When he enters he coughs loudly, seeing the situation.]

MERRIMAN Ahem! Ahem! Lady Bracknell!

JACK Good heavens!

[Enter Lady Bracknell. The couples separate in alarm.] [Exit Merriman.]

LADY BRACKNELL Gwendolen! What does this mean?

GWENDOLEN Merely that I am engaged to be married to Mr Worthing, mamma.

LADY BRACKNELL Come here. Sit down. Sit down immediately. Hesitation of any kind is a sign of mental decay in the young, of physical weakness in the old. [Turns to Jack.] Apprised, sir, of my daughter's sudden flight by her trusty maid,

---

2. Many 19th-century German scholars were skeptical in their treatment of religious texts.

whose confidence I purchased by means of a small coin, I followed her at once by a luggage train. Her unhappy father is, I am glad to say, under the impression that she is attending a more than usually lengthy lecture by the University Extension Scheme on the Influence of a permanent income on Thought. I do not propose to undeceive him. Indeed I have never undeceived him on any question. I would consider it wrong. But of course, you will clearly understand that all communication between yourself and my daughter must cease immediately from this moment. On this point, as indeed on all points, I am firm.

JACK I am engaged to be married to Gwendolen, Lady Bracknell!

LADY BRACKNELL You are nothing of the kind, sir. And now, as regards Algernon! . . . Algernon!

ALGERNON Yes, Aunt Augusta.

LADY BRACKNELL May I ask if it is in this house that your invalid friend Mr Bunbury resides?

ALGERNON [stammering] Oh! No! Bunbury doesn't live here. Bunbury is somewhere else at present. In fact, Bunbury is dead.

LADY BRACKNELL Dead! When did Mr Bunbury die? His death must have been extremely sudden.

ALGERNON [airily] Oh! I killed Bunbury this afternoon. I mean poor Bunbury died this afternoon.

LADY BRACKNELL What did he die of?

ALGERNON Bunbury? Oh, he was quite exploded.

LADY BRACKNELL Exploded! Was he the victim of a revolutionary outrage?[3] I was not aware that Mr Bunbury was interested in social legislation. If so, he is well punished for his morbidity.

ALGERNON My dear Aunt Augusta, I mean he was found out! The doctors found out that Bunbury could not live, that is what I mean—so Bunbury died.

LADY BRACKNELL He seems to have had great confidence in the opinion of his physicians. I am glad, however, that he made up his mind at the last to some definite course of action, and acted under proper medical advice. And now that we have finally got rid of this Mr Bunbury, may I ask, Mr Worthing, who is that young person whose hand my nephew Algernon is now holding in what seems to me a peculiarly unnecessary manner?

JACK That lady is Miss Cecily Cardew, my ward.

[Lady Bracknell bows coldly to Cecily.]

ALGERNON I am engaged to be married to Cecily, Aunt Augusta.

LADY BRACKNELL I beg your pardon?

CECILY Mr Moncrieff and I are engaged to be married, Lady Bracknell.

LADY BRACKNELL [with a shiver, crossing to the sofa and sitting down] I do not know whether there is anything peculiarly exciting in the air of this particular part of Hertfordshire, but the number of engagements that go on seems to me considerably above the proper average that statistics have laid down for our guidance. I think some preliminary enquiry on my part would not be out of place. Mr Worthing, is Miss Cardew at all connected with any of the larger railway stations in London? I merely desire information. Until yesterday I had no idea that there were any families or persons whose origins was a Terminus.[4]

---

3. Anarchy and political assassination were much in the news; Wilde's earliest drama, *Vera, or the Nihilists* (1881), dealt with the subject.

4. A railway station at the end of the line.

[*Jack looks perfectly furious, but restrains himself.*]

JACK [*in a clear, cold voice*] Miss Cardew is the granddaughter of the late Mr Thomas Cardew of 149, Belgrave Square, S.W.; Gervase Park, Dorking, Surrey; and the Sporran, Fifeshire, N.B.[5]

LADY BRACKNELL That sounds not unsatisfactory. Three addresses always inspire confidence, even in tradesmen. But what proof have I of their authenticity?

JACK I have carefully preserved the Court Guides[6] of the period. They are open to your inspection, Lady Bracknell.

LADY BRACKNELL [*grimly*] I have known strange errors in that publication.

JACK Miss Cardew's family solicitors are Messrs Markby, Markby, and Markby.

LADY BRACKNELL Markby, Markby, and Markby? A firm of the very highest position in their profession. Indeed I am told that one of the Mr Markbys is occasionally to be seen at dinner parties. So far I am satisfied.

JACK [*very irritably*] How extremely kind of you, Lady Bracknell! I have also in my possession, you will be pleased to hear, certificates of Miss Cardew's birth, baptism, whooping cough, registration, vaccination, confirmation, and the measles; both the German and the English variety.

LADY BRACKNELL Ah! A life crowded with incident, I see; though perhaps somewhat too exciting for a young girl. I am not myself in favour of premature experiences. [*Rises, looks at her watch.*] Gwendolen! the time approaches for our departure. We have not a moment to lose. As a matter of form, Mr Worthing, I had better ask you if Miss Cardew has any little fortune?

JACK Oh! about a hundred and thirty thousand pounds in the Funds.[7] That is all. Goodbye, Lady Bracknell. So pleased to have seen you.

LADY BRACKNELL [*sitting down again*] A moment, Mr Worthing. A hundred and thirty thousand pounds! And in the Funds! Miss Cardew seems to me a most attractive young lady, now that I look at her. Few girls of the present day have any really solid qualities, any of the qualities that last, and improve with time. We live, I regret to say, in an age of surfaces. [*To Cecily.*] Come over here, dear. [*Cecily goes across.*] Pretty child! your dress is sadly simple, and your hair seems almost as Nature might have left it. But we can soon alter all that. A thoroughly experienced French maid produces a really marvellous result in a very brief space of time. I remember recommending one to young Lady Lancing, and after three months her own husband did not know her.

JACK [*aside*] And after six months nobody knew her.

LADY BRACKNELL [*glares at Jack for a few moments. Then bends, with a practised smile, to Cecily.*] Kindly turn round, sweet child. [*Cecily turns completely round.*] No, the side view is what I want. [*Cecily presents her profile.*] Yes, quite as I expected. There are distinct social possibilities in your profile. The two weak points in our age are its want of principle and its want of profile. The chin a little higher, dear. Style largely depends on the way the chin is worn. They are worn very high, just at present. Algernon!

ALGERNON Yes, Aunt Augusta!

LADY BRACKNELL There are distinct social possibilities in Miss Cardew's profile.

ALGERNON Cecily is the sweetest, dearest, prettiest girl in the whole world. And I don't care twopence about social possibilities.

---

5. North Britain, i.e., Scotland.
6. Annual publications listing the names and London addresses of the upper classes.

7. The Consolidated Funds, reliable interest-bearing government bonds.

LADY BRACKNELL Never speak disrespectfully of Society, Algernon. Only people who can't get into it do that. [*To Cecily.*] Dear child, of course you know that Algernon has nothing but his debts to depend upon. But I do not approve of mercenary marriages. When I married Lord Bracknell I had no fortune of any kind. But I never dreamed for a moment of allowing that to stand in my way. Well, I suppose I must give my consent.

ALGERNON Thank you, Aunt Augusta.

LADY BRACKNELL Cecily, you may kiss me!

CECILY [*kisses her*] Thank you, Lady Bracknell.

LADY BRACKNELL You may also address me as Aunt Augusta for the future.

CECILY Thank you, Aunt Augusta.

LADY BRACKNELL The marriage, I think, had better take place quite soon.

ALGERNON Thank you, Aunt Augusta.

CECILY Thank you, Aunt Augusta.

LADY BRACKNELL To speak frankly, I am not in favour of long engagements. They give people the opportunity of finding out each other's character before marriage, which I think is never advisable.

JACK I beg your pardon for interrupting you, Lady Bracknell, but this engagement is quite out of the question. I am Miss Cardew's guardian, and she cannot marry without my consent until she comes of age. That consent I absolutely decline to give.

LADY BRACKNELL Upon what grounds may I ask? Algernon is an extremely, I may almost say an ostentatiously, eligible young man. He has nothing, but he looks everything. What more can one desire?

JACK It pains me very much to have to speak frankly to you, Lady Bracknell, about your nephew, but the fact is that I do not approve at all of his moral character. I suspect him of being untruthful.

[*Algernon and Cecily look at him in indignant amazement.*]

LADY BRACKNELL Untruthful! My nephew Algernon? Impossible! He is an Oxonian.[8]

JACK I fear there can be no possible doubt about the matter. This afternoon, during my temporary absence in London on an important question of romance, he obtained admission to my house by means of the false pretence of being my brother. Under an assumed name he drank, I've just been informed by my butler, an entire pint bottle of my Perrier-Jouet, Brut, '89; a wine I was specially reserving for myself. Continuing his disgraceful deception, he succeeded in the course of the afternoon in alienating the affections of my only ward. He subsequently stayed to tea, and devoured every single muffin. And what makes his conduct all the more heartless is, that he was perfectly well aware from the first that I have no brother, that I never had a brother, and that I don't intend to have a brother, not even of any kind. I distinctly told him so myself yesterday afternoon.

LADY BRACKNELL Ahem! Mr Worthing, after careful consideration I have decided entirely to overlook my nephew's conduct to you.

JACK That is very generous of you, Lady Bracknell. My own decision, however, is unalterable. I decline to give my consent.

LADY BRACKNELL [*to Cecily*] Come here, sweet child. [*Cecily goes over.*] How old are you, dear?

8. I.e., he attended Oxford University.

CECILY Well, I am really only eighteen, but I always admit to twenty when I go to evening parties.

LADY BRACKNELL You are perfectly right in making some slight alteration. Indeed, no woman should ever be quite accurate about her age. It looks so calculating. . . . [*In a meditative manner*.] Eighteen, but admitting to twenty at evening parties. Well, it will not be very long before you are of age and free from the restraints of tutelage. So I don't think your guardian's consent is, after all, a matter of any importance.

JACK Pray excuse me, Lady Bracknell, for interrupting you again, but it is only fair to tell you that according to the terms of her grandfather's will Miss Cardew does not come legally of age till she is thirty-five.

LADY BRACKNELL That does not seem to me to be a grave objection. Thirty-five is a very attractive age. London society is full of women of the very highest birth who have, of their own free choice, remained thirty-five for years. Lady Dumbleton is an instance in point. To my own knowledge she has been thirty-five ever since she arrived at the age of forty, which was many years ago now. I see no reason why our dear Cecily should not be even still more attractive at the age you mention than she is at present. There will be a large accumulation of property.

CECILY Algy, could you wait for me till I was thirty-five?

ALGERNON Of course I could, Cecily. You know I could.

CECILY Yes, I felt it instinctively, but I couldn't wait all that time. I hate waiting even five minutes for anybody. It always makes me rather cross. I am not punctual myself, I know, but I do like punctuality in others, and waiting, even to be married, is quite out of the question.

ALGERNON Then what is to be done, Cecily?

CECILY I don't know, Mr Moncrieff.

LADY BRACKNELL My dear Mr Worthing, as Miss Cardew states positively that she cannot wait till she is thirty-five—a remark which I am bound to say seems to me to show a somewhat impatient nature—I would beg of you to reconsider your decision.

JACK But my dear Lady Bracknell, the matter is entirely in your own hands. The moment you consent to my marriage with Gwendolen, I will most gladly allow your nephew to form an alliance with my ward.

LADY BRACKNELL [*rising and drawing herself up*] You must be quite aware that what you propose is out of the question.

JACK Then a passionate celibacy is all that any of us can look forward to.

LADY BRACKNELL That is not the destiny I propose for Gwendolen. Algernon, of course, can choose for himself. [*Pulls out her watch*.] Come, dear; [*Gwendolen rises*.] we have already missed five, if not six, trains. To miss any more might expose us to comment on the platform.

[*Enter Dr Chasuble*.]

CHASUBLE Everything is quite ready for the christenings.

LADY BRACKNELL The christenings, sir! Is not that somewhat premature?

CHASUBLE [*looking rather puzzled, and pointing to Jack and Algernon*] Both these gentlemen have expressed a desire for immediate baptism.

LADY BRACKNELL At their age? The idea is grotesque and irreligious! Algernon, I forbid you to be baptized. I will not hear of such excesses. Lord Bracknell would be highly displeased if he learned that that was the way in which you wasted your time and money.

CHASUBLE Am I to understand then that there are to be no christenings at all this afternoon?

JACK I don't think that, as things are now, it would be of much practical value to either of us, Dr Chasuble.

CHASUBLE I am grieved to hear such sentiments from you, Mr Worthing. They savour of the heretical views of the Anabaptists,[9] views that I have completely refuted in four of my unpublished sermons. However, as your present mood seems to be one peculiarly secular, I will return to the church at once. Indeed, I have just been informed by the pew-opener[1] that for the last hour and a half Miss Prism has been waiting for me in the vestry.

LADY BRACKNELL [*starting*] Miss Prism! Did I hear you mention a Miss Prism?

CHASUBLE Yes, Lady Bracknell. I am on my way to join her.

LADY BRACKNELL Pray allow me to detain you for a moment. This matter may prove to be one of vital importance to Lord Bracknell and myself. Is this Miss Prism a female of repellent aspect, remotely connected with education?

CHASUBLE [*somewhat indignantly*] She is the most cultivated of ladies, and the very picture of respectability.

LADY BRACKNELL It is obviously the same person. May I ask what position she holds in your household?

CHASUBLE [*severely*] I am a celibate, madam.

JACK [*interposing*] Miss Prism, Lady Bracknell, has been for the last three years Miss Cardew's esteemed governess and valued companion.

LADY BRACKNELL In spite of what I hear of her, I must see her at once. Let her be sent for.

CHASUBLE [*looking off*] She approaches; she is nigh.

[*Enter Miss Prism hurriedly.*]

MISS PRISM I was told you expected me in the vestry, dear Canon. I have been waiting for you there for an hour and three quarters. [*Catches sight of Lady Bracknell who has fixed her with a stony glare. Miss Prism grows pale and quails. She looks anxiously round as if desirous to escape.*]

LADY BRACKNELL [*in a severe, judicial voice*] Prism! [*Miss Prism bows her head in shame.*] Come here, Prism! [*Miss Prism approaches in a humble manner.*] Prism! Where is that baby? [*General consternation. The Canon starts back in horror. Algernon and Jack pretend to be anxious to shield Cecily and Gwendolen from hearing the details of a terrible public scandal.*] Twenty-eight years ago, Prism, you left Lord Bracknell's house, Number 104, Upper Grosvenor Street, in charge of a perambulator that contained a baby, of the male sex. You never returned. A few weeks later, through the elaborate investigations of the Metropolitan police, the perambulator was discovered at midnight, standing by itself in a remote corner of Bayswater.[2] It contained the manuscript of a three-volume novel of more than usually revolting sentimentality. [*Miss Prism starts in involuntary indignation.*] But the baby was not there! [*Everyone looks at Miss Prism.*] Prism! Where is that baby? [*A pause.*]

MISS PRISM Lady Bracknell, I admit with shame that I do not know. I only wish I did. The plain facts of the case are these. On the morning of the day you mention, a day that is for ever branded on my memory, I prepared as usual to take the baby out in its perambulator. I had also with me a somewhat old, but capacious hand-

---

9. A 16th-century Protestant sect that believed in adult baptism.
1. Usher.

2. An area in the West End of London, near Kensington Gardens.

bag in which I had intended to place the manuscript of a work of fiction that I had written during my few unoccupied hours. In a moment of mental abstraction, for which I never can forgive myself, I deposited the manuscript in the bassinette, and placed the baby in the hand-bag.

JACK [who has been listening attentively] But where did you deposit the hand-bag?

MISS PRISM Do not ask me, Mr Worthing.

JACK Miss Prism, this is a matter of no small importance to me. I insist on knowing where you deposited the hand-bag that contained that infant.

MISS PRISM I left it in the cloak-room of one of the larger railway stations in London.

JACK What railway station?

MISS PRISM [quite crushed] Victoria. The Brighton line. [Sinks into a chair.]

JACK I must retire to my room for a moment. Gwendolen, wait here for me.

GWENDOLEN If you are not too long, I will wait here for you all my life.

[Exit Jack in great excitement.]

CHASUBLE What do you think this means, Lady Bracknell?

LADY BRACKNELL I dare not even suspect, Dr Chasuble. I need hardly tell you that in families of high position strange coincidences are not supposed to occur. They are hardly considered the thing.

[Noises heard overhead as if someone was throwing trunks about. Everyone looks up.]

CECILY Uncle Jack seems strangely agitated.

CHASUBLE Your guardian has a very emotional nature.

LADY BRACKNELL This noise is extremely unpleasant. It sounds as if he was having an argument. I dislike arguments of any kind. They are always vulgar, and often convincing.

CHASUBLE [looking up] It has stopped now. [The noise is redoubled.]

LADY BRACKNELL I wish he would arrive at some conclusion.

GWENDOLEN This suspense is terrible. I hope it will last.

[Enter Jack with a hand-bag of black leather in his hand.]

JACK [rushing over to Miss Prism] Is this the hand-bag, Miss Prism? Examine it carefully before you speak. The happiness of more than one life depends on your answer.

MISS PRISM [calmly] It seems to be mine. Yes, here is the injury it received through the upsetting of a Gower Street omnibus in younger and happier days. Here is the stain on the lining caused by the explosion of a temperance beverage, an incident that occurred at Leamington. And here, on the lock, are my initials. I had forgotten that in an extravagant mood I had had them placed there. The bag is undoubtedly mine. I am delighted to have it so unexpectedly restored to me. It has been a great inconvenience being without it all these years.

JACK [in a pathetic voice] Miss Prism, more is restored to you than this hand-bag. I was the baby you placed in it.

MISS PRISM [amazed] You?

JACK [embracing her] Yes . . . mother!

MISS PRISM [recoiling in indignant astonishment] Mr Worthing! I am unmarried!

JACK Unmarried! I do not deny that is a serious blow. But after all, who has the right to cast a stone against one who has suffered?[3] Cannot repentance wipe out an act of folly? Why should there be one law for men, and another for women? Mother, I forgive you. [Tries to embrace her again.]

---

3. Jesus saves a woman who is about to be stoned for committing adultery, saying "He that is without sin among you, let him first cast a stone at her" (John 8.7).

MISS PRISM [*still more indignant*] Mr Worthing, there is some error. [*Pointing to Lady Bracknell.*] There is the lady who can tell you who you really are.

JACK [*after a pause*] Lady Bracknell, I hate to seem inquisitive, but would you kindly inform me who I am?

LADY BRACKNELL I am afraid that the news I have to give you will not altogether please you. You are the son of my poor sister, Mrs Moncrieff, and consequently Algernon's elder brother.

JACK Algy's elder brother! Then I have a brother after all. I knew I had a brother! I always said I had a brother! Cecily—how could you have ever doubted that I had a brother. [*Seizes hold of Algernon.*] Dr Chasuble, my unfortunate brother. Miss Prism, my unfortunate brother. Gwendolen, my unfortunate brother. Algy, you young scoundrel, you will have to treat me with more respect in the future. You have never behaved to me like a brother in all your life.

ALGERNON Well, not till today, old boy, I admit. I did my best, however, though I was out of practice. [*Shakes hands.*]

GWENDOLEN [*to Jack*] My own! But what own are you? What is your Christian name, now that you have become someone else?

JACK Good heavens! . . . I had quite forgotten that point. Your decision on the subject of my name is irrevocable, I suppose?

GWENDOLEN I never change, except in my affections.

CECILY What a noble nature you have, Gwendolen!

JACK Then the question had better be cleared up at once. Aunt Augusta, a moment. At the time when Miss Prism left me in the hand-bag, had I been christened already?

LADY BRACKNELL Every luxury that money could buy, including christening, had been lavished on you by your fond and doting parents.

JACK Then I was christened! That is settled. Now, what name was I given? Let me know the worst.

LADY BRACKNELL Being the eldest son you were naturally christened after your father.

JACK [*irritably*] Yes, but what was my father's Christian name?

LADY BRACKNELL [*meditatively*] I cannot at the present moment recall what the General's Christian name was. But I have no doubt he had one. He was eccentric, I admit. But only in later years. And that was the result of the Indian climate, and marriage, and indigestion, and other things of that kind.

JACK Algy! Can't you recollect what our father's Christian name was?

ALGERNON My dear boy, we were never even on speaking terms. He died before I was a year old.

JACK His name would appear in the Army Lists of the period, I suppose, Aunt Augusta?

LADY BRACKNELL The General was essentially a man of peace, except in his domestic life. But I have no doubt his name would appear in any military directory.

JACK The Army Lists of the last forty years are here. These delightful records should have been my constant study. [*Rushes to bookcase and tears the books out.*] M. Generals . . . Mallam, Maxbohm,[4] Magley, what ghastly names they have—Markby, Migsby, Mobbs, Moncrieff! Lieutenant 1840, Captain, Lieutenant-Colonel, Colonel, General 1869, Christian names, Ernest John. [*Puts book very quietly down and speaks quite calmly.*] I always told you, Gwendolen, my name was Ernest, didn't I? Well, it is Ernest after all. I mean it naturally is Ernest.

---

4. A pun on the name of Wilde's friend Max Beerbohm.

LADY BRACKNELL Yes, I remember now that the General was called Ernest. I knew I had some particular reason for disliking the name.

GWENDOLEN Ernest! My own Ernest! I felt from the first that you could have no other name!

JACK Gwendolen, it is a terrible thing for a man to find out suddenly that all his life he has been speaking nothing but the truth. Can you forgive me?

GWENDOLEN I can. For I feel that you are sure to change.

JACK My own one!

CHASUBLE [to Miss Prism] Laetitia! [Embraces her.]

MISS PRISM [enthusiastically] Frederick! At last!

ALGERNON Cecily! [Embraces her.] At last!

JACK Gwendolen! [Embraces her.] At last!

LADY BRACKNELL My nephew, you seem to be displaying signs of triviality.

JACK On the contrary, Aunt Augusta, I've now realized for the first time in my life the vital Importance of Being Earnest.

TABLEAU

CURTAIN

1894, performed 1895

1899

Aphorisms[1]

On arriving in America: I have nothing to declare except my genius.

F. Harris, *Oscar Wilde*

We have really everything in common with America nowadays, except, of course, language.

The Canterville Ghost

A poet can survive everything but a misprint.

The Children of the Poets

Meredith is a prose Browning, and so is Browning. He used poetry as a medium for writing in prose.

The Critic as Artist

Anybody can make history. Only a great man can write it.

Ibid.

The one duty we owe to history is to rewrite it.

Ibid.

A little sincerity is a dangerous thing, and a great deal of it is absolutely fatal.

Ibid.

There is only one thing in the world worse than being talked about, and that is not being talked about.

The Picture of Dorian Gray

---

1. Wilde's aphorisms often cleverly invert a cliché in order to produce a seeming paradox; they are perhaps his most characteristic form of expression in his conversation and writing alike. Wilde kept track of his favorite maxims, sometimes revising them in later works. In addition to the epigrammatic preface to *Dorian Gray*, he published two selections: *A Few Maxims for the Instruction of the Over-Educated* appeared anonymously in the *Saturday Review* in November 1894; *Phrases and Philosophies for the Use of the Young* was published in *The Chameleon* in December 1894.

Being natural is simply a pose, and the most irritating pose I know.

Ibid.

A man cannot be too careful in the choice of his enemies.

Ibid.

American girls are as clever at concealing their parents, as English women are at concealing their past.

Ibid.

Perhaps, after all, America never has been discovered. I myself would say that it had merely been detected.

Ibid.

Women give to men the very gold of their lives. But they invariably want it back in such very small change.

Ibid.

I hate vulgar realism in literature. The man who could call a spade a spade should be compelled to use one. It is the only thing he is fit for.

Ibid.

It is better to be beautiful than to be good. But . . . it is better to be good than to be ugly.

Ibid.

I can resist everything except temptation.

Lady Windermere's Fan

It's most dangerous nowadays for a husband to pay any attention to his wife in public. It always makes people think that he beats her when they're alone.

Ibid.

We are all in the gutter, but some of us are looking at the stars.

Ibid.

In this world there are only two tragedies. One is not getting what one wants, and the other is getting it.

Ibid.

What is a cynic? A man who knows the price of everything and the value of nothing.

Ibid.

Experience is the name everyone gives to their mistakes.

Ibid.

Repentance is quite out of date. And besides, if a woman really repents, she has to go to a bad dressmaker, otherwise no one believes in her.

Ibid.

It is perfectly monstrous the way people go about, nowadays, saying things against one behind one's back that are absolutely and entirely true.

A Woman of No Importance

The youth of America is their oldest tradition. It has been going on now for three hundred years.

Ibid.

The English country gentleman galloping after a fox—the unspeakable in full pursuit of the uneatable.

Ibid.

Twenty years of romance make a woman look like a ruin; but twenty years of marriage make her look like a public building.

Ibid.

One should never trust a woman who tells one her real age. A woman who would tell one that, would tell one anything.

Ibid.

The first duty in life is to be as artificial as possible. What the second duty is no one has as yet discovered.

Phrases and Philosophies for the Use of the Young

To love oneself is the beginning of a lifelong romance.

Ibid.

My wallpaper and I are fighting a duel to the death. One or the other of us has to go.

Richard Ellmann, *Oscar Wilde*

from De Profundis[1]

[January–March 1897]   H.M. Prison, Reading

Dear Bosie, After long and fruitless waiting I have determined to write to you myself, as much for your sake as for mine, as I would not like to think that I had passed through two long years of imprisonment without ever having received a single line from you, or any news or message even, except such as gave me pain.

Our ill-fated and most lamentable friendship has ended in ruin and public infamy for me, yet the memory of our ancient affection is often with me, and the thought that loathing, bitterness and contempt should for ever take that place in my heart once held by love is very sad to me: and you yourself will, I think, feel in your heart that to write to me as I lie in the loneliness of prison-life is better than to publish my letters without my permission or to dedicate poems to me unasked, though the world will know nothing of whatever words of grief or passion, of remorse or indifference you may choose to send as your answer or your appeal.

I have no doubt that in this letter in which I have to write of your life and of mine, of the past and of the future, of sweet things changed to bitterness and of bitter things that may be turned into joy, there will be much that will wound your vanity to the quick. If it prove so, read the letter over and over again till it kills your vanity. If you find in it something of which you feel that you are unjustly accused, remember that one should be thankful that there is any fault of which one can be unjustly

---

1. "Out of the depths" [have I cried unto thee, O Lord] (Latin), the first words of Psalm 130. While imprisoned in Reading Gaol, Wilde was allowed pen and paper only to write letters. He thus composed a meditation on his life in the form of a long letter to Lord Alfred Douglas (nicknamed Bosie), written from January to March 1897. Wilde referred to the text as "Epistola: In Carcere et Vinculis" (Letter: In Prison and in Chains). When he was released, he gave the manuscript to his friend, Robert Ross ("Robbie"), who entitled it *De Profundis* and published an abridged version—omitting all mention of Douglas—in 1905, after Wilde's death. In 1949, when Douglas had died, Wilde's son Vyvyan published a fuller text, based on an unreliable typescript supplied by Ross. Only in 1962, when scholars were allowed to consult the original manuscript—given by Ross to the British Museum—did a complete version finally appear.

accused. If there be in it one single passage that brings tears to your eyes, weep as we weep in prison where the day no less than the night is set apart for tears. It is the only thing that can save you. If you go complaining to your mother, as you did with reference to the scorn of you I displayed in my letter to Robbie, so that she may flatter and soothe you back into self-complacency or conceit, you will be completely lost. If you find one false excuse for yourself, you will soon find a hundred, and be just what you were before. Do you still say, as you said to Robbie in your answer, that I "*attribute unworthy motives*" to you? Ah! you had no motives in life. You had appetites merely. A motive is an intellectual aim. That you were "*very young*" when our friendship began? Your defect was not that you knew so little about life, but that you knew so much. The morning dawn of boyhood with its delicate bloom, its clear pure light, its joy of innocence and expectation you had left far behind. With very swift and running feet you had passed from Romance to Realism. The gutter and the things that live in it had begun to fascinate you. That was the origin of the trouble in which you sought my aid, and I, so unwisely according to the wisdom of this world, out of pity and kindness gave it to you. You must read this letter right through, though each word may become to you as the fire or knife of the surgeon that makes the delicate flesh burn or bleed. Remember that the fool in the eyes of the gods and the fool in the eyes of man are very different. One who is entirely ignorant of the modes of Art in its revolution or the moods of thought in its progress, of the pomp of the Latin line or the richer music of the vowelled Greek, of Tuscan sculpture or Elizabethan song may yet be full of the very sweetest wisdom. The real fool, such as the gods mock or mar, is he who does not know himself. I was such a one too long. You have been such a one too long. Be so no more. Do not be afraid. The supreme vice is shallowness. Everything that is realised is right. Remember also that whatever is misery to you to read, is still greater misery to me to set down. To you the Unseen Powers have been very good. They have permitted you to see the strange and tragic shapes of Life as one sees shadows in a crystal. The head of Medusa that turns living men to stone,[2] you have been allowed to look at in a mirror merely. You yourself have walked free among the flowers. From me the beautiful world of colour and motion has been taken away.

I will begin by telling you that I blame myself terribly. As I sit here in this dark cell in convict clothes, a disgraced and ruined man, I blame myself. In the perturbed and fitful nights of anguish, in the long monotonous days of pain, it is myself I blame. I blame myself for allowing an unintellectual friendship, a friendship whose primary aim was not the creation and contemplation of beautiful things, to entirely dominate my life. From the very first there was too wide a gap between us. You had been idle at your school, worse than idle at your university. You did not realise that an artist, and especially such an artist as I am, one, that is to say, the quality of whose work depends on the intensification of personality, requires for the development of his art the companionship of ideas, and intellectual atmosphere, quiet, peace, and solitude. You admired my work when it was finished: you enjoyed the brilliant successes of my first nights, and the brilliant banquets that followed them: you were proud, and quite naturally so, of being the intimate friend of an artist so distinguished: but you could not understand the conditions requisite for the production of artistic work. I am not speaking in phrases of rhetorical exaggeration but in terms of absolute truth to actual fact when I remind you that during the whole time we were together I never wrote

---

2. Medusa was a snake-haired monster, so horrifying that anyone who looked at her turned to stone.

one single line. Whether at Torquay, Goring, London, Florence or elsewhere, my life, as long as you were by my side, was entirely sterile and uncreative. And with but few intervals you were, I regret to say, by my side always. * * *

You send me a very nice poem, of the undergraduate school of verse, for my approval: I reply by a letter of fantastic literary conceits:[3] I compare you to Hylas, or Hyacinth, Jonquil or Narcisse,[4] or someone whom the great god of Poetry favoured, and honoured with his love. The letter is like a passage from one of Shakespeare's sonnets, transposed to a minor key. It can only be understood by those who have read the *Symposium* of Plato, or caught the spirit of a certain grave mood made beautiful for us in Greek marbles. It was, let me say frankly, the sort of letter I would, in a happy if wilful moment, have written to any graceful young man of either University who had sent me a poem of his own making, certain that he would have sufficient wit or culture to interpret rightly its fantastic phrases. Look at the history of that letter! It passes from you into the hands of a loathsome companion: from him to a gang of blackmailers: copies of it are sent about London to my friends, and to the manager of the theatre where my work is being performed: every construction but the right one is put on it: Society is thrilled with the absurd rumours that I have had to pay a huge sum of money for having written an infamous letter to you: this forms the basis of your father's worst attack: I produce the original letter myself in Court to show what it really is: it is denounced by your father's Counsel as a revolting and insidious attempt to corrupt Innocence: ultimately it forms part of a criminal charge: the Crown takes it up: the Judge sums up on it with little learning and much morality: I go to prison for it at last. That is the result of writing you a charming letter. * * *

Other miserable men, when they are thrown into prison, if they are robbed of the beauty of the world, are at least safe, in some measure, from the world's most deadly slings, most awful arrows. They can hide in the darkness of their cells, and of their very disgrace make a mode of sanctuary. The world, having had its will, goes its way, and they are left to suffer undisturbed. With me it has been different. Sorrow after sorrow has come beating at the prison doors in search of me. They have opened the gates wide and let them in. Hardly, if at all, have my friends been suffered to see me. But my enemies have had full access to me always. Twice in my public appearances at the Bankruptcy Court, twice again in my public transferences from one prison to another, have I been shown under conditions of unspeakable humiliation to the gaze and mockery of men. The messenger of Death has brought me his tidings and gone his way,[5] and in entire solitude, and isolated from all that could give me comfort, or suggest relief, I have had to bear the intolerable burden of misery and remorse that the memory of my mother placed upon me, and places on me still. Hardly has that wound been dulled, not healed, by time, when violent and bitter and harsh letters come to me from my wife through her solicitor. I am, at once, taunted and threatened with poverty. That I can bear. I can school myself to worse than that. But my two

---

3. Wilde's letter, praising Douglas's poem, *In Praise of Shame*, was eventually read aloud at his trial:
  My own Boy,
    Your sonnet is quite lovely, and it is a marvel that those red rose-leaf lips of yours should have been made no less for the music of song than for madness of kisses. Your slim gilt soul walks between passion and poetry. I know Hyacinthus, whom Apollo loved so madly, was you in Greek days.

Why are you alone in London, and when do you go to Salisbury? Do go there to cool your hands in the grey twilight of Gothic things, and come here whenever you like. It is a lovely place—it only lacks you; but go to Salisbury first.
  Always, with undying love,
                                        Yours, Oscar

4. Beautiful young men whom Apollo loved.
5. Wilde's mother died while he was in prison.

children are taken from me by legal procedure.[6] That is and always will remain to me a source of infinite distress, of infinite pain, of grief without end or limit. That the law should decide, and take upon itself to decide, that I am one unfit to be with my own children is something quite horrible to me. The disgrace of prison is as nothing compared to it. I envy the other men who tread the yard along with me. I am sure that their children wait for them, look for their coming, will be sweet to them.

The poor are wiser, more charitable, more kind, more sensitive than we are. In their eyes prison is a tragedy in a man's life, a misfortune, a casualty, something that calls for sympathy in others. They speak of one who is in prison as of one who is *"in trouble"* simply. It is the phrase they always use, and the expression has the perfect wisdom of Love in it. With people of our rank it is different. With us prison makes a man a pariah. I, and such as I am, have hardly any right to air and sun. Our presence taints the pleasures of others. We are unwelcome when we reappear. To revisit the glimpses of the moon is not for us.[7] Our very children are taken away. Those lovely links with humanity are broken. We are doomed to be solitary, while our sons still live. We are denied the one thing that might heal us and help us, that might bring balm to the bruised heart, and peace to the soul in pain.

And to all this has been added the hard, small fact that by your actions and by your silence, by what you have done and by what you have left undone,[8] you have made every day of my long imprisonment still more difficult for me to live through. The very bread and water of prison fare you have by your conduct changed. You have rendered the one bitter and the other brackish to me. The sorrow you should have shared you have doubled, the pain you should have sought to lighten you have quickened to anguish. I have no doubt that you did not mean to do so. I know that you did not mean to do so. It was simply that "one really fatal defect of your character, your entire lack of imagination."

And the end of it all is that I have got to forgive you. I must do so. I don't write this letter to put bitterness into your heart, but to pluck it out of mine. For my own sake I must forgive you. One cannot always keep an adder in one's breast to feed on one, nor rise up every night to sow thorns in the garden of one's soul. It will not be difficult at all for me to do so, if you help me a little. Whatever you did to me in old days I always readily forgave. It did you no good then. Only one whose life is without stain of any kind can forgive sins. But now when I sit in humiliation and disgrace it is different. My forgiveness should mean a great deal to you now. Some day you will realise it. Whether you do so early or late, soon or not at all, my way is clear before me. I cannot allow you to go through life bearing in your heart the burden of having ruined a man like me. The thought might make you callously indifferent, or morbidly sad. I must take the burden from you and put it on my own shoulders.

I must say to myself that neither you nor your father, multiplied a thousand times over, could possibly have ruined a man like me: that I ruined myself: and that nobody, great or small, can be ruined except by his own hand. I am quite ready to do so. I am trying to do so, though you may not think it at the present moment. If I have brought this pitiless indictment against you, think what an indictment I bring without pity against myself. Terrible as what you did to me was, what I did to myself was far more terrible still.

I was a man who stood in symbolic relations to the art and culture of my age. I had realised this for myself at the very dawn of my manhood, and had forced my age

---

6. In February 1897 Constance Wilde petitioned for custody of their children, Cyril and Vyvyan, whom Wilde never saw again. Their surname was changed to Holland.

7. Cf. *Hamlet* 1.4.51–53.
8. The Anglican rite of confession asks forgiveness "for what we have done and for what we have left undone."

to realise it afterwards. Few men hold such a position in their own lifetime and have it so acknowledged. It is usually discerned, if discerned at all, by the historian, or the critic, long after both the man and his age have passed away. With me it was different. I felt it myself, and made others feel it. Byron was a symbolic figure, but his relations were to the passion of his age and its weariness of passion. Mine were to something more noble, more permanent, of more vital issue, of larger scope.

The gods had given me almost everything. I had genius, a distinguished name, high social position, brilliancy, intellectual daring: I made art a philosophy, and philosophy an art: I altered the minds of men and the colours of things: there was nothing I said or did that did not make people wonder: I took the drama, the most objective form known to art, and made it as personal a mode of expression as the lyric or the sonnet, at the same time that I widened its range and enriched its characterisation: drama, novel, poem in rhyme, poem in prose, subtle or fantastic dialogue, whatever I touched I made beautiful in a new mode of beauty: to truth itself I gave what is false no less than what is true as its rightful province, and showed that the false and the true are merely forms of intellectual existence. I treated Art as the supreme reality, and life as a mere mode of fiction: I awoke the imagination of my century so that it created myth and legend around me: I summed up all systems in a phrase, and all existence in an epigram.

Along with these things, I had things that were different. I let myself be lured into long spells of senseless and sensual ease. I amused myself with being a *flâneur* [idle stroller], a dandy, a man of fashion. I surrounded myself with the smaller natures and the meaner minds. I became the spendthrift of my own genius, and to waste an eternal youth gave me a curious joy. Tired of being on the heights I deliberately went to the depths in the search for new sensations. What the paradox was to me in the sphere of thought, perversity became to me in the sphere of passion. Desire, at the end, was a malady, or a madness, or both. I grew careless of the lives of others. I took pleasure where it pleased me and passed on. I forgot that every little action of the common day makes or unmakes character, and that therefore what one has done in the secret chamber one has some day to cry aloud on the housetops. I ceased to be Lord over myself. I was no longer the Captain of my Soul, and did not know it. I allowed you to dominate me, and your father to frighten me. I ended in horrible disgrace. There is only one thing for me now, absolute Humility: just as there is only one thing for you, absolute Humility also. You had better come down into the dust and learn it beside me.

I have lain in prison for nearly two years. Out of my nature has come wild despair; an abandonment to grief that was piteous even to look at: terrible and impotent rage: bitterness and scorn: anguish that wept aloud: misery that could find no voice: sorrow that was dumb. I have passed through every possible mood of suffering. Better than Wordsworth himself I know what Wordsworth meant when he said:

> Suffering is permanent, obscure, and dark
> And has the nature of Infinity.[9]

But while there were times when I rejoiced in the idea that my sufferings were to be endless, I could not bear them to be without meaning. Now I find hidden away in my nature something that tells me that nothing in the whole world is meaningless, and suffering least of all. That something hidden away in my nature, like a treasure in a field, is Humility.

It is the last thing left in me, and the best: the ultimate discovery at which I have arrived: the starting-point for a fresh development. It has come to me right out of myself, so I know that it has come at the proper time. It could not have come before, nor later. Had anyone told me of it, I would have rejected it. Had it been brought to

9. From *The Borderers*, Act 3.

me, I would have refused it. As I found it, I want to keep it. I must do so. It is the one thing that has in it the elements of life, of a new life, a *Vita Nuova*[1] for me. Of all things it is the strangest. One cannot give it away, and another may not give it to one. One cannot acquire it, except by surrendering everything that one has. It is only when one has lost all things, that one knows that one possesses it.

Now that I realise that it is in me, I see quite clearly what I have got to do, what, in fact, I must do. And when I use such a phrase as that, I need not tell you that I am not alluding to any external sanction or command. I admit none. I am far more of an individualist than I ever was. Nothing seems to me of the smallest value except what one gets out of oneself. My nature is seeking a fresh mode of self-realisation. That is all I am concerned with. And the first thing that I have got to do is to free myself from any possible bitterness of feeling against you.

I am completely penniless, and absolutely homeless. Yet there are worse things in the world than that. I am quite candid when I tell you that rather than go out from this prison with bitterness in my heart against you or against the world I would gladly and readily beg my bread from door to door. If I got nothing at the house of the rich, I would get something at the house of the poor. Those who have much are often greedy. Those who have little always share. I would not a bit mind sleeping in the cool grass in summer, and when winter came on sheltering myself by the warm close-thatched rick, or under the penthouse of a great barn, provided I had love in my heart. The external things of life seem to me now of no importance at all. You can see to what intensity of individualism I have arrived, or am arriving rather, for the journey is long, and "where I walk there are thorns."[2]

Of course I know that to ask for alms on the highway is not to be my lot, and that if ever I lie in the cool grass at night-time it will be to write sonnets to the Moon. When I go out of prison, Robbie will be waiting for me on the other side of the big iron-studded gate, and he is the symbol not merely of his own affection, but of the affection of many others besides. I believe I am to have enough to live on for about eighteen months at any rate, so that, if I may not write beautiful books, I may at least read beautiful books, and what joy can be greater? After that, I hope to be able to recreate my creative faculty. But were things different: had I not a friend left in the world: were there not a single house open to me even in pity: had I to accept the wallet and ragged cloak of sheer penury: still as long as I remained free from all resentment, hardness, and scorn, I would be able to face life with much more calm and confidence than I would were my body in purple and fine linen, and the soul within it sick with hate. And I shall really have no difficulty in forgiving you. But to make it a pleasure for me you must feel that you want it. When you really want it you will find it waiting for you.

I need not say that my task does not end there. It would be comparatively easy if it did. There is much more before me. I have hills far steeper to climb, valleys much darker to pass through. And I have to get it all out of myself. Neither Religion, Morality, nor Reason can help me at all.

Morality does not help me. I am a born antinomian.[3] I am one of those who are made for exceptions, not for laws. But while I see that there is nothing wrong in what one does, I see that there is something wrong in what one becomes. It is well to have learned that.

Religion does not help me. The faith that others give to what is unseen, I give to what one can touch, and look at. My Gods dwell in temples made with hands, and within the circle of actual experience is my creed made perfect and complete: too

---

1. New life (Italian); Dante's book of this name was one of the few books Wilde was able to have sent to him in prison.

2. From Wilde's play, *A Woman of No Importance*, Act 4.
3. A person who rejects conventional morality.

complete it may be, for like many or all of those who have placed their Heaven in this earth, I have found in it not merely the beauty of Heaven, but the horror of Hell also. When I think about Religion at all, I feel as if I would like to found an order for those who cannot believe: the Confraternity of the Fatherless one might call it, where on an altar, on which no taper burned, a priest, in whose heart peace had no dwelling, might celebrate with unblessed bread and a chalice empty of wine. Everything to be true must become a religion. And agnosticism should have its ritual no less than faith. It has sown its martyrs, it should reap its saints, and praise God daily for having hidden Himself from man. But whether it be faith or agnosticism, it must be nothing external to me. Its symbols must be of my own creating. Only that is spiritual which makes its own form. If I may not find its secret within myself, I shall never find it. If I have not got it already, it will never come to me.

Reason does not help me. It tells me that the laws under which I am convicted are wrong and unjust laws, and the system under which I have suffered a wrong and unjust system. But, somehow, I have got to make both of these things just and right to me. And exactly as in Art one is only concerned with what a particular thing is at a particular moment to oneself, so it is also in the ethical evolution of one's character. I have got to make everything that has happened to me good for me. The plank-bed, the loathsome food, the hard ropes shredded into oakum[4] till one's fingertips grow dull with pain, the menial offices with which each day begins and finishes, the harsh orders that routine seems to necessitate, the dreadful dress that makes sorrow grotesque to look at, the silence, the solitude, the shame—each and all of these things I have to transform into a spiritual experience. There is not a single degradation of the body which I must not try and make into a spiritualising of the soul.

I want to get to the point when I shall be able to say, quite simply and without affectation, that the two great turning-points of my life were when my father sent me to Oxford, and when society sent me to prison. I will not say that it is the best thing that could have happened to me, for that phrase would savour of too great bitterness towards myself. I would sooner say, or hear it said of me, that I was so typical a child of my age that in my perversity, and for that perversity's sake, I turned the good things of my life to evil, and the evil things of my life to good. What is said, however, by myself or by others matters little. The important thing, the thing that lies before me, the thing that I have to do, or be for the brief remainder of my days one maimed, marred, and incomplete, is to absorb into my nature all that has been done to me, to make it part of me, to accept it without complaint, fear, or reluctance. The supreme vice is shallowness. Whatever is realised is right.

When first I was put into prison some people advised me to try and forget who I was. It was ruinous advice. It is only by realising what I am that I have found comfort of any kind. Now I am advised by others to try on my release to forget that I have ever been in a prison at all. I know that would be equally fatal. It would mean that I would be always haunted by an intolerable sense of disgrace, and that those things that are meant as much for me as for anyone else—the beauty of the sun and the moon, the pageant of the seasons, the music of daybreak and the silence of great nights, the rain falling through the leaves, or the dew creeping over the grass and making it silver—would all be tainted for me, and lose their healing power and their power of communicating joy. To reject one's own experiences is to arrest one's own development. To deny one's own experiences is to put a lie into the lips of one's own life. It is no less than a denial of the Soul.

---

4. Prisoners were often forced to pick oakum—i.e., to shred used ropes into fibers.

H. Montgomery Hyde: from The Trials of Oscar Wilde[1]

[THE FIRST TRIAL]

Queensberry's leading counsel[2] rose from his place in the front row of barristers' seats in the Old Bailey courtroom to begin his cross-examination of the prosecutor. As he faced his old college classmate in the witness box, the two figures on whom every eye in court was now fixed presented a striking contrast. There was Wilde, dressed in the height of fashion, a flower in the buttonhole of his frock coat, and exuding an air of easy confidence; opposite him stood Carson, tall, saturnine, and with the most determined expression on his lantern-jawed countenance. * * *

The opening question immediately revealed the cross-examiner's skill. * * *

"You stated that your age was thirty-nine. I think you are over forty. You were born on the 16th of October 1854?" Carson emphasized the point by holding up a copy of the witness's birth certificate.

Wilde appeared momentarily disconcerted, but he quickly recovered his composure. "I have no wish to pose as being young," he replied sweetly. "You have my certificate and that settles the matter."

"But," Carson persisted, "being born in 1854 makes you more than forty?"

"Ah! Very well," Wilde agreed with a sigh, as if to congratulate his opponent on a remarkable feat of mathematics.

It was a small point that Carson had scored in this duel of wits, but not without considerable importance. At the very outset Wilde had been detected in a stupid lie, the effect of which was not lost upon the jury, particularly when Carson followed it up by contrasting Wilde's true age with that of Lord Alfred Douglas,[3] with whom Wilde admitted to having stayed at many places, including hotels, both in England and on the Continent. Furthermore, it appeared that Douglas had also contributed to The Chameleon,[4] namely two poems. Wilde was asked about these poems, which he admitted that he had seen. "I thought them exceedingly beautiful poems," he added. "One was 'In Praise of Shame' and the other 'Two Loves.'"[5]

"These loves," Carson asked, with a note of distaste in his voice. "They were two boys?"

"Yes."

"One boy calls his love 'true love,' and the other boy calls his love 'shame'?"

"Yes."

"Did you think they made any improper suggestion?"

"No, none whatever."

Carson passed on to "The Priest and the Acolyte," which Wilde admitted that he had read.

1. After Lord Alfred Douglas's father, the Marquess of Queensberry, accused Wilde of sodomy, Wilde brought suit for libel. Wilde lost his case, and was in turn prosecuted, in two subsequent criminal trials, for committing indecent acts. He was found guilty and sentenced to two years in prison with hard labor. The three trials took place in 1895, in the Old Bailey in London, and were the focus of immense public curiosity; the sensational story was followed daily in almost every London newspaper. The following excerpts are from H. Montgomery Hyde's The Trials of Oscar Wilde (1948); it should be noted that since no authoritative transcripts of the court proceedings exist, his book is a reconstruction of events based on contemporary press reports and personal reminiscences.

2. Edward Carson, a renowned barrister, had been a classmate of Wilde's at Trinity College, Dublin. He successfully defended Queensberry against Wilde's charge of libel in the first trial.
3. Douglas was twenty-four years old; Wilde was forty.
4. Edited by Jack Bloxam, an Oxford undergraduate, The Chameleon was a literary magazine with a homoerotic tone; it appeared only once, in 1894. Bloxam was the author of The Priest and the Acolyte. At Douglas's request, Wilde had submitted some of his aphorisms to the magazine, and his legal opponents sought to make Wilde appear guilty by association with the allegedly immoral contributions of Douglas and Bloxam.
5. The latter poem appears on page 2159.

"You have no doubt whatever that that was an improper story?"

"From the literary point of view it was highly improper. It is impossible for a man of literature to judge it otherwise; by literature, meaning treatment, selection of subject, and the like. I thought the treatment rotten and the subject rotten."

"You are of opinion, I believe, that there is no such thing as an immoral book?"

"Yes."

"May I take it that you think 'The Priest and the Acolyte' was not immoral?"

"It was worse. It was badly written."[6]

"Was not the story that of a priest who fell in love with a boy who served him at the altar, and was discovered by the rector in the priest's room, and a scandal arose?"

"I have read it only once, last November, and nothing will induce me to read it again. I don't care for it. It doesn't interest me."

"Do you think the story blasphemous?"

"I think it violated every artistic canon of beauty."

"That is not an answer."

"It is the only one I can give."

"I want to see the position you pose in."

"I do not think you should say that."

"I have said nothing out of the way. I wish to know whether you thought the story blasphemous."

"The story filled me with disgust. The end was wrong."

"Answer the question, sir," Carson rapped out sharply. "Did you or did you not consider the story blasphemous?"

"I thought it disgusting."

Professing himself satisfied with this reply, Carson turned to a particular incident in the story. "You know that when the priest in the story administers poison to the boy, he uses the words of the sacrament of the Church of England?"

"That I entirely forgot."

"Do you consider that blasphemous?"

"I think it is horrible. 'Blasphemous' is not a word of mine." When Carson put the passage in question to him and asked whether he approved of the words used by the author, Wilde repeated his previous opinion: "I think them disgusting, perfect twaddle."

"I think you will admit that anyone who would approve of such a story would pose as guilty of improper practices?"

"I do not think so in the person of another contributor to the magazine. It would show very bad literary taste. Anyhow I strongly objected to the whole story. . . . Of course, I am aware that *The Chameleon* may have circulated among the undergraduates of Oxford. But I do not believe that any book or work of art ever had any effect whatever on morality."

"Am I right in saying that you do not consider the effect in creating morality or immorality?"

"Certainly, I do not."

"So far as your works are concerned, you pose as not being concerned about morality or immorality?"

"I do not know whether you use the word 'pose' in any particular sense."

"Is it a favourite word of your own?"

6. Wilde is paraphrasing his preface to *The Picture of Dorian Grey* (see page 2085).

"Is it? I have no pose in this matter. In writing a play or a book, I am concerned entirely with literature—that is, with art. I aim not at doing good or evil, but in trying to make a thing that will have some quality of beauty." * * *

Carson now turned to *The Picture of Dorian Gray*[7] * * *

"'There is no such thing as a moral or an immoral book. Books are well written or badly written.' That expresses your view?"

"My view on art, yes."

"Then I take it, no matter how immoral a book may be, if it is well written, it is, in your opinion, a good book?"

"Yes, if it were well written so as to produce a sense of beauty, which is the highest sense of which a human being can be capable. If it were badly written, it would produce a sense of disgust."

"Then a well-written book putting forward perverted moral views may be a good book?"

"No work of art ever puts forward views. Views belong to people who are not artists."

"A perverted novel might be a good book?" Carson persisted.

"I don't know what you mean by a 'perverted' novel," Wilde answered crisply.

This gave Carson the opening he sought. "Then I will suggest *Dorian Gray* is open to the interpretation of being such a novel?"

Wilde brushed aside the suggestion with contempt. "That could only be to brutes and illiterates," he said. "The views of Philistines on art are unaccountable."

"An illiterate person reading *Dorian Gray* might consider it such a novel?"

"The views of illiterates on art are unaccountable. I am concerned only with my own view of art. I don't care twopence what other people think of it."

"The majority of persons come under your definition of Philistines and illiterates?"

"I have found wonderful exceptions."

"Do you think that the majority of people live up to the position you are giving us?"

"I am afraid they are not cultivated enough."

"Not cultivated enough to draw the distinction between a good book and a bad book?" The note of sarcasm in Carson's voice was unmistakable.

"Certainly not," Wilde replied blandly.

"The affection and love of the artist of *Dorian Gray* might lead an ordinary individual to believe that it might have a certain tendency?"

"I have no knowledge of the views of ordinary individuals."

"You did not prevent the ordinary individual from buying your book?"

"I have never discouraged him!" * * *

Having covered Wilde's published writings, Carson passed on to the allegedly compromising letters Wilde had written to Lord Alfred Douglas. * * *

"Why should a man of your age address a boy nearly twenty years younger as 'My own Boy'?"[8]

"I was fond of him. I have always been fond of him."

"Do you adore him?"

"No, but I have always liked him." Wilde then went on to elaborate upon the letter. "I think it is a beautiful letter. It is a poem. I was not writing an ordinary letter. You might as well cross-examine me as to whether *King Lear* or a sonnet of Shakespeare was proper."

"Apart from art, Mr Wilde?"

"I cannot answer apart from art."

---

7. Wilde's novel describes the passion felt by an artist, Basil Hallward, for a beautiful young man, Dorian Gray, whose portrait he paints.

8. For the text of this letter, a response to Douglas's poem *In Praise of Shame*, see page 2130, n. 3.

"Suppose a man who was not an artist had written this letter, would you say it was a proper letter?"

"A man who was not an artist could not have written that letter."

"Why?"

"Because nobody but an artist could write it. He certainly could not write the language unless he were a man of letters."

"I can suggest, for the sake of your reputation, that there is nothing very wonderful in this 'red rose-leaf lips of yours'?"

"A great deal depends on the way it is read."

"'Your slim gilt soul walks between passion and poetry,'" Carson continued. "Is that a beautiful phrase?"

"Not as you read it, Mr Carson. You read it very badly."

It was now Carson's turn to be nettled. "I do not profess to be an artist," he exclaimed, "and when I hear you give evidence, I am glad I am not."

These words immediately brought Sir Edward Clarke[9] to his feet. "I don't think my learned friend should talk like that," he observed. Then, turning towards his client in the witness box, he added: "Pray do not criticize my learned friend's reading again."

This clash caused a buzz of excitement in the courtroom. When it had died down, Carson went on with his cross-examination, indicating the document he was holding in his hand. "Is not that an exceptional letter?"

"It is unique, I should say." Wilde's answer produced loud laughter in court, which was still largely on the side of the witness.

"Was that the ordinary way in which you carried on your correspondence?"

"No. But I have often written to Lord Alfred Douglas, though I never wrote to another young man in the same way."

"Have you often written letters in the same style as this?"

"I don't repeat myself in style."

Carson held out another sheet of paper. "Here is another letter which I believe you also wrote to Lord Alfred Douglas. Will you read it?"

Wilde refused this invitation. "I don't see why I should," he said.

"Then I will," retorted Carson.

Savoy Hotel
Victoria Embankment
London

Dearest of all Boys,

Your letter was delightful, red and yellow wine to me; but I am sad and out of sorts. Bosie, you must not make scenes with me. They kill me, they wreck the loveliness of life. I cannot see you, so Greek and gracious, distorted with passion. I cannot listen to your curved lips saying hideous things to me. I would sooner—than have you bitter unjust, hating. . . .

I must see you soon. You are the divine thing I want, the thing of grace and beauty; but I don't know how to do it. Shall I come to Salisbury? My bill here is £49 for a week. I have also got a new sitting-room. . . .

Why are you not here, my dear, my wonderful boy? I fear I must leave—no money, no credit, and a heart of lead.

Your own
OSCAR

9. Clarke was Wilde's attorney in all three trials.

"Is that an ordinary letter?" Carson asked, when he had finished reading it.

"Everything I wrote is extraordinary," Wilde answered with a show of impatience. "I do not pose as being ordinary, great heavens! Ask me any question you like about it."

Carson had only one question to ask about this letter, but its effect was deadly. "Is it the kind of letter a man writes to another?"

[THE SECOND TRIAL]

"During 1893 and 1894 you were a great deal in the company of Lord Alfred Douglas?"

"Oh, yes."

"Did he read that poem to you?"[1]

"Yes."

"You can perhaps understand that such verses as these would not be acceptable to the reader with an ordinary balanced mind?"

"I am not prepared to say," Wilde answered. "It appears to me to be a question of taste, temperament, and individuality. I should say that one man's poetry is another man's poison!"

"I daresay!" commented Gill[2] dryly, when the laughter had subsided. "The next poem is one described as 'Two Loves.' * * * Was that poem explained to you?"

"I think that is clear."

"There is no question as to what it means?"

"Most certainly not."

"Is it not clear that the love described relates to natural love and unnatural love?"

"No."

"What is the 'Love that dare not speak its name'?"[3] Gill now asked.

"'The love that dare not speak its name' in this century is such a great affection of an elder for a younger man as there was between David and Jonathan, such as Plato made the very basis of his philosophy, and such as you find in the sonnets of Michelangelo and Shakespeare.[4] It is that deep, spiritual affection that is as pure as it is perfect. It dictates and pervades great works of art like those of Shakespeare and Michelangelo, and those two letters of mine, such as they are. It is in this century misunderstood, so much misunderstood that it may be described as the 'Love that dare not speak its name,' and on account of it I am placed where I am now. It is beautiful, it is fine, it is the noblest form of affection. There is nothing unnatural about it. It is intellectual, and it repeatedly exists between an elder and a younger man, when the elder has intellect, and the younger man has all the joy, hope, and glamour of life before him. That it should be so, the world does not understand. The world mocks at it and sometimes puts one in the pillory for it."

Wilde's words produced a spontaneous outburst of applause from the public gallery, mingled with some hisses, which moved the judge to say he would have the Court cleared if there were any further manifestation of feeling.

---

1. Douglas's sonnet *In Praise of Shame*.
2. Charles Gill was counsel for the prosecution during the second and third trial.
3. Cf. *Two Loves,* line 74, page 2160.
4. King David of Israel, and Jonathan, the son of King Saul, were inseparable friends. On Jonathan's death, David declared that "your love to me was wonderful, passing the love of women" (2 Samuel 1.26). Plato argued that the passion of an older man for a younger one could be translated into a contemplation of the ideal and the universal. Both Shakespeare and Michelangelo wrote sonnets that can be read as describing platonic and/or erotic love between men.

Aestheticism, Decadence, and the *Fin de Siècle*

"I belong to the Beardsley period," Max Beerbohm remarked audaciously in 1894, when he and Aubrey Beardsley were both just twenty-two. Time has proved him correct. The late-Victorian period, the age of Beardsley and Wilde, Kipling and Conan Doyle, has indeed come to be seen as a distinctive era in which the aesthetic and moral values of the nineteenth century were twisted or transmuted into the revolutionary forces of modernism, in a blaze of daring new styles, attitudes, and modes of behavior.

By the early 1880s most of the major mid-Victorian writers had died or were well past their prime. As the Empire reached its peak, Britain's self-confidence eroded under the strain of maintaining its military might and economic supremacy against competition from the United States and Germany. About 1890, the general sense of fatigue and anxiety found expression in the French phrase *fin de siècle*—the "end of the age." The term suggested that Victorian values and energies had become exhausted, and that an unsettling, amoral, post-Darwinian world was emerging in which contradictory impulses vied for attention: exquisite delicacy in poetry and brutal realism in fiction, effete dandyism among some men and hearty imperialism among others, socialism and Catholicism. The proliferation of women in the workforce ran headlong into the diagnosis of inherent female debility by medical authorities. Meanwhile, discussion clubs formed where both sexes openly debated the merits of marriage and free love. It was the era of the Manly Woman and the Womanly Man, the moment when sexology was invented and words like "homosexual," "lesbian," and—belatedly—"heterosexual" were coined to regulate the mysteries of sexual identity.

Partly in flight from the devastated industrial landscape, partly in rebellion against middle-class mores and artistic norms, Aesthetes like Walter Pater, Wilde, Whistler, Beardsley, and Arthur Symons sought to create a pure art of flawless formal design, divorced from moral concerns but open to hitherto unexplored subject matter—the often artificial beauties of cosmetics, music halls, gaslit faces, or city streets seen through mist and rain. By the 1870s, critics were giving the labels "impressionist" and "aesthetic" to paintings by Whistler and Dante Gabriel Rossetti, and to poems by Rossetti, Algernon Swinburne, and William Morris. With the help of flamboyant personalities such as Whistler and Wilde, Aestheticism became known in the 1880s as an entire way of life, involving flowing dress for both men and women, medieval- or Japanese-style home furnishings, and ostentatious worship of the beautiful in all the arts. There was even a distinctive Aesthetic vocabulary: "Constantly yearning for the intense," said one observer, "the language of the Aesthetes is tinged with somewhat exaggerated metaphor, and their adjectives are usually superlative—as supreme, consummate, utter, quite too preciously sublime."

Though its excesses were easy to mock, Aestheticism took hold so forcefully because its various strands had been developing, abroad and at home, for several generations. In 1873 Tennyson complained with some reason that Aesthetes lived on "poisonous honey stolen from France." Swinburne was clearly influenced by the French poets Théophile Gautier and Charles Baudelaire when he declared in 1866: "Art for art's sake first of all," explaining that "her business is not to do good on other grounds, but to be good on her own." Yet Tennyson himself was a pivotal figure for the Aesthetes and their immediate predecessors, the Pre-Raphaelites; both groups were inspired by his medievalism and sonorous morbidity.

Aestheticism often shaded over into Decadence, a term that was confusingly applied not only to the deliberately mannered works of the late Victorians, but also to the scandalous or effeminate conduct of their creators. By the 1890s the word had become a vague and fashionable label of both moral censure and avant-garde respect. The naturalist fiction of George Gissing and Émile Zola was called decadent because of its tawdry subject matter and amoral attitudes; Wilde on the other hand claimed that decadent pleasures alone made life worth living. Depending on one's point of view, "decadent" could describe, with praise or blame, a dissipated

THE SIX-MARK TEA-POT.

Æsthetic Bridegroom. "It is quite consummate, is it not?"
Intense Bride. "It is, indeed! Oh, Algernon, let us live up to it!"

George Du Maurier. *The Six-Mark Tea-Pot*. From *Punch* magazine, 1880. Born in Paris, Du Maurier shuttled between London and Paris, and studies in art and science, until he settled on a career as a magazine illustrator, joining the staff of *Punch* in 1864. His wittily captioned cartoons of Aesthetes fixed the movement in the public imagination. Having established his reputation as a keen satirist of cultural trends, he achieved international fame with his novel *Trilby* (1894), which was based on his days with Whistler as an art student in Paris.

young man like Wilde's Dorian Gray, or a vigorous freethinking feminist like the heroine of Grant Allen's *The Woman Who Did* (1895). In most cases the word suggested an ultra-refined sophistication of taste allied with moral perversity; and many feared that decadent ideas and behavior heralded social collapse and apocalyptic change for Western culture. Max Nordau's 1895 bestseller *Degeneration* portrayed decadence as evidence of "a twilight mood" in Europe; "degeneration and hysteria," he felt, were "the convulsions and spasms of exhaustion" in Western civilization. Delighting in this anxiety, Wilde told Yeats that Pater's *Renaissance* "is the very flower of decadence; the last trumpet should have sounded the moment it was written."

Together, the *fin de siècle* writers helped free English literature of moral inhibition, producing a richly descriptive poetry and prose marked by deep learning, love of London, bold sensuality, spiritual intensity, and a new focus on images rather than events. The concept of Decadence depended on a Christian mentality haunted by notions of sin, forgiveness, and damnation. Dissatisfied with life and art, and tempted by drugs and drinking, opium and absinthe, some writers met early deaths from dissipation or suicide. The quest for absolution led many, including Beardsley and Wilde, to convert to Catholicism.

While they strove for a refined art purified of morality and narrative content, Aesthetes and Decadents made it clear that art had a definitely sexual if often elusive essence. Though "consummate" was a favorite word, much of their work expressed a frustrated longing for a fleeting taste of forbidden fruits. Often both male and female writers envisioned women as dangerous idols, worshipped at first as chaste images of noble art but finally revealed as seductive vampires who sap masculine energy with insatiable desire.

As the critic Elaine Showalter points out, "The decadent or aesthete was the masculine counterpart to the New Woman," lauded by feminist fiction writers of the 1890s. More prevalent in art than life, these two literary figures spurred fears of a sexual revolution and cast doubt on Britain's ability to procreate future generations of Empire-rulers. The anxiety over the blurring of gender boundaries helps explain the strange conflux of misogynist, homoerotic, androgynous, utopianly healthy, and luridly diseased discourses of sexuality that surfaced at this time—culminating in Bram Stoker's *Dracula* (1897), which portrayed the New Woman as an insatiable sexual vampire poised to destroy British manhood. Even a radical advocate of socialist free love, Karl Marx's daughter Eleanor, denounced "the effeminate man and the masculine woman" as horrifyingly unnatural. With slight exaggeration, Max Beerbohm alluded to "that amalgamation of the sexes which is one of the chief planks in the decadent platform."

The heyday of Aestheticism and Decadence came to an end with the trials of Oscar Wilde. When Wilde was arrested for sodomy in 1895, newspapers reported that he carried the notorious decadent magazine, *The Yellow Book*, with him to jail (it was actually a yellow-backed French novel). Mobs stoned the publisher's office; Beardsley, its editor, was fired; the magazine failed. A savage conservative backlash suddenly ended the vogue of the bold New Woman and the languid Aesthete. But it was in the "degenerate" turmoil of the *fin de siècle* that modernism got its start: James, Yeats, Bennett, Wells, Shaw, Ford, and Conrad all published in *The Yellow Book* or its short-lived successor, *The Savoy*. Though the Aesthetic creed seemed like an underground current to many during the Victorian period, by the turn of the century belief in the autonomy of the artist was on the brink of becoming modernism's main stream.

━◆━ ≍◆≍ ━◆━

Aubrey Beardsley
1872–1898

"Awfully Weirdly" *Punch* called him. But his bizarre renderings of warped passion and sexual tension made Aubrey Beardsley the most important English artist of the 1890s. As the controversial illustrator and editor of *The Yellow Book* (1894–1895) and *The Savoy* (1896)—the most notorious magazines of the 1890s—Beardsley put his stamp on the Decadent movement; he gave an instantly recognizable visual style to the amorphous perversity of the era. His use of sinuous lines and distorted floral motifs make him a key figure in the history of Art Nouveau, and in fact it was Beardsley who introduced the term to the British public.

Born in Brighton, Beardsley was working as a clerk in an insurance office, studying art at night, when he received encouragement from the famous Pre-Raphaelite painter Edward Burne-Jones. Stylizing Burne-Jones's already elongated figures, Beardsley met his first success with brooding pen-and-ink drawings for a new edition of Malory's *Morte D'Arthur* (1893–1894). He achieved notoriety, however, with his cool, cruel, bizarrely erotic illustrations of Wilde's *Salomé* (1894). Falling out with Wilde during the project, Beardsley not only mocked Wilde in the drawings but refused to ask him to contribute to *The Yellow Book*. Wilde in turn denounced both Beardsley and the magazine—with ironic results: the public associated Wilde with the scandalous contents of the journal, and when Wilde went to jail Beardsley was fired because he had once worked with Wilde. Beardsley then coedited *The Savoy* with Arthur

Symons, did fanciful drawings on Wagnerian themes, and illustrated an edition of Pope's *The Rape of the Lock* (1896). But his health was deteriorating rapidly. He converted to Catholicism before he died of tuberculosis at the age of twenty-five.

Made for mechanical reproduction, Beardsley's work is the most striking example of the revitalization of book art in the 1890s. His emphasis on overall design makes each page stand on its own; instead of shading, his black-and-white style dramatically relies on virtuoso curves, creepy details, and open space to suggest volume, distance, and psychological insight. His visual genius almost always responds to a literary text, and books themselves figure prominently in his work. The grotesque sexuality, autoeroticism and necrophilia of his illustrations carry over into his own stories and poems, such as the unnerving *The Ballad of a Barber*, who murders a princess while dressing her hair. Noting that Beardsley always worked indoors by candlelight and without models, the critic Holbrook Jackson remarked that he was "the most literary of all modern artists; his drawings are never the outcome of observation—they are always the outcome of thought."

Reproduced here is *"J'ai baisé ta bouche, Iokanaan,"* an illustration for *Salomé*, 1893. Wilde wrote his play in French, but its production on the English stage (starring Sarah Bernhardt) was banned because of its depiction of biblical characters. Beardsley's outrageous illustrations for the English translation (1894) instantly made the book a decadent *cause célèbre* and a classic of Art Nouveau design. Beardsley depicts the play's climactic scene, in which Salomé, who has demanded John the Baptist's head as a reward for her dancing, kisses the dead lips of the prophet who had scorned her love.

✦ ⇥✦⇤ ✦

W. S. Gilbert
1836–1911

William Schwenk Gilbert is best known for his lengthy partnership with the composer Arthur Sullivan. Together they wrote fourteen light operas from 1871 to 1896, immensely popular entertainments that continue to be performed throughout the world today. Known as the "Savoy Operas" because they debuted at the Savoy Theatre built by Richard D'Oyly Carte expressly for their production, Gilbert and Sullivan's works include *H.M.S. Pinafore* (1878), *The Pirates of Penzance* (1879), and *The Mikado* (1885). Typically, these comic operettas poke gentle fun at British institutions such as the law, Parliament, and the navy, while also mocking Victorian obsessions with topics such as social hierarchy or orphanhood. Although Gilbert's satirical librettos perfectly complement Sullivan's sprightly scores, they can be read on their own as nimble evocations of Victorian foibles and follies. *Patience* spoofed Aestheticism just as it reached the public consciousness in the early 1880s; in the process the opera helped to articulate and spread the ideas it mocked. A composite caricature of Whistler and Wilde, the "ultra-poetical, super-aesthetical" Bunthorne is made to confess that his exquisite refinement is just a pose meant to attract the ladies.

If You're Anxious for to Shine in the High Aesthetic Line

> Am I alone,
>   And unobserved? I am!
> Then let me own
>   I'm an aesthetic sham!
> This air severe
>   Is but a mere
>   Veneer!

5

This cynic smile
Is but a wile
10   Of guile!
This costume chaste
Is but good taste
                    Misplaced!
Let me confess!
15   A languid love for lilies does *not* blight me!
Lank limbs and haggard cheeks do *not* delight me!
I do *not* care for dirty greens
By any means.
I do *not* long for all one sees
20   That's Japanese.
I am *not* fond of uttering platitudes
    In stained-glass attitudes.
In short, my mediaevalism's affectation,
Born of a morbid love of admiration![1]

Song

25   If you're anxious for to shine in the high aesthetic line as a man of culture rare,
You must get up all the germs of the transcendental terms,[2] and plant them
    everywhere.
You must lie upon the daisies and discourse in novel phrases of your com-
    plicated state of mind,
The meaning doesn't matter if it's only idle chatter of a transcendental kind.
                    And every one will say,
30   As you walk your mystic way,
"If this young man expresses himself in terms too deep for *me*,
Why, what a very singularly deep young man this deep young man must be!"

Be eloquent in praise of the very dull old days which have long since
    passed away,
And convince 'em, if you can, that the reign of good Queen Anne[3] was
    Culture's palmiest day.
35   Of course you will pooh-pooh whatever's fresh and new, and declare it's
    crude and mean,
For Art stopped short in the cultivated court of the Empress Josephine.[4]
                    And every one will say,
                    As you walk your mystic way,
"If that's not good enough for him which is good enough for *me*,
40   Why, what a very cultivated kind of youth this kind of youth must be!"

1. Stereotypical Aesthetic behavior, combining traits of
Dante Gabriel Rossetti, Whistler, and Wilde, particularly
as they were spoofed by the cartoonist George Du Maurier. Lilies and languid yet soul-tormented lovers figure in
the work of Rossetti, as do medieval subjects and stained
glass; Whistler's paintings featuring Japanese props and
perspective helped create a vogue for Japanese art, dress,
and decoration; Wilde's elaborate clothing and ostentatious worship of beauty were said to be merely attention-
getting poses.

2. Transcendental philosophy values individual visionary
understanding over objective, materialist apprehension of
the world. *The Germ* (1850) was a short-lived Pre-
Raphaelite journal that sought to promote a more spiritual art and poetry in Britain.
3. Queen of Great Britain from 1702–1714; the simplicity
of the era's neoclassical architecture and design found
favor with Aesthetes tired of Victorian ornateness.
4. Wife of Napoleon Bonaparte and empress of France
1804–1809.

Then a sentimental passion of a vegetable fashion must excite your languid
    spleen,[5]
An attachment *à la* Plato for a bashful young potato, or a not-too-French
    French bean!
Though the Philistines may jostle, you will rank as an apostle in the high
    aesthetic band,
If you walk down Piccadilly[6] with a poppy or a lily in your mediaeval hand.
45   And every one will say,
                As you walk your flowery way,
"If he's content with a vegetable love which would certainly not suit *me*,
Why, what a most particularly pure young man this pure young man must be!"

                                    1881

James Abbott McNeill Whistler
1834–1903

An American artist who settled in London in the early 1860s, Whistler provided much of the intellectual energy that inspired the Aesthetic Movement in the 1880s. He studied art in Paris, where he became friends with Gustav Courbet and Henri Fantin-Latour, absorbed the aesthetic doctrine of Théophile Gautier and Charles Baudelaire, and later came to know and influence Claude Monet and the poet Stéphane Mallarmé. Although Whistler never fully abandoned a representational style, he insisted that viewers accept a painting as an arrangement of lines and colors on a flat canvas. "I care nothing for the past, present, or future of the black figure," he said about a shadowy human outline in one of his paintings; "it was placed there because black was wanted at that spot."

    Whistler's *Nocturne in Black and Gold: The Falling Rocket* (1875) earned the ire of Ruskin, who declared that he was an impudent coxcomb who was "flinging a pot of paint in the public's face." Whistler sued Ruskin for libel, and the ensuing trial of 1878 marked a turning point in English art and taste. Whistler won, and the Ruskinian notion of art as a social and moral force yielded ground to Whistler's concept of art as an expression of the artist's subjective vision, something beyond common comprehension.

    Whistler delivered the following lecture in London on February 20, 1885, to an invitation-only audience that included journalists, artists, writers, and society figures. He chose to deliver his "Ten O'Clock" lecture at 10 P.M. so that his fashionable audience would not have to rush dinner. It is the era's clearest manifesto of art for art's sake, setting the artist above and beyond his moment in history. The lecture and its fastidious presentation brought to a larger audience the essentials of Whistler's artistic platform: the attention-getting declaration of artistic independence, the sarcastic dismissals of other theories, and the aggressively elitist public posture that made him "The Master" for other Aesthetes. Mallarmé translated the essay into French in 1888; Whistler himself published it in English in 1890, in *The Gentle Art of Making Enemies*. Struck by one of Whistler's witticisms, Oscar Wilde once confessed that he wished *he* had uttered it himself. Whistler replied dryly, "You will, Oscar, you will."

---

5. I. e., shake you out of your melancholy. The Aesthetes supposedly cherished an idealized, platonic love of such flowering "vegetable" entities as poppies and lilies; here Gilbert applies the concept literally.

6. A fashionable thoroughfare in London. Wilde, whose passion for lilies was well known, is said to have done this.

from **Mr. Whistler's "Ten O'Clock"**

LADIES AND GENTLEMEN:

* * * Art is upon the Town!—to be chucked under the chin by the passing gallant—to be enticed within the gates of the householder—to be coaxed into company, as a proof of culture and refinement.

If familiarity can breed contempt, certainly Art—or what is currently taken for it—has been brought to its lowest stage of intimacy.

The people have been harassed with Art in every guise, and vexed with many methods as to its endurance. They have been told how they shall love Art, and live with it. Their homes have been invaded, their walls covered with paper, their very dress taken to task—until, roused at last, bewildered and filled with the doubts and discomforts of senseless suggestion, they resent such intrusion, and cast forth the false prophets, who have brought the very name of the beautiful into disrepute, and derision upon themselves.

Alas! ladies and gentlemen, Art has been maligned. She has naught in common with such practices. She is a goddess of dainty thought—reticent of habit, abjuring all obtrusiveness, purposing in no way to better others.

She is, withal, selfishly occupied with her own perfection only—having no desire to teach—seeking and finding the beautiful in all conditions and in all times, as did her high priest Rembrandt, when he saw picturesque grandeur and noble dignity in the Jews' quarter of Amsterdam, and lamented not that its inhabitants were not Greeks.[1]

As did Tintoret and Paul Veronese,[2] among the Venetians, while not halting to change the brocaded silks for the classic draperies of Athens.

As did, at the Court of Philip, Velasquez, whose Infantas, clad in inaesthetic hoops, are, as works of Art, of the same quality as the Elgin marbles.[3]

No reformers were these great men—no improvers of the way of others! Their productions alone were their occupation, and, filled with the poetry of their science, they required not to alter their surroundings—for, as the laws of their Art were revealed to them they saw, in the development of their work, that real beauty which, to them, was as much a matter of certainty and triumph as is to the astronomer the verification of the result, foreseen with the light given to him alone. In all this, their world was completely severed from that of their fellow-creatures with whom sentiment is mistaken for poetry; and for whom there is no perfect work that shall not be explained by the benefit conferred upon themselves.

Humanity takes the place of Art, and God's creations are excused by their usefulness. Beauty is confounded with virtue, and, before a work of Art, it is asked: "What good shall it do?"

Hence it is that nobility of action, in this life, is hopelessly linked with the merit of the work that portrays it; and thus the people have acquired the habit of looking, as who should say, not *at* a picture, but *through* it, at some human fact, that shall, or

---

1. Rembrandt (1606–1669) was an important influence on Whistler. The Dutch artist painted many contemporary subjects and even used the costume of his day when portraying classical subjects, as in *Aristotle Contemplating the Bust of Homer*.
2. Tintoretto and Paolo Veronese, Italian Renaissance painters.
3. Diego Rodrigo de Silva y Velasquez (1599–1660), painter at the court of Philip IV of Spain. The Infantas were daughters of the monarch; in their hooped skirts they seemed no less artistic to Whistler than classical Greek statuary.

shall not, from a social point of view, better their mental or moral state. So we have come to hear of the painting that elevates, and of the duty of the painter—of the picture that is full of thought, and of the panel that merely decorates.

A favourite faith, dear to those who teach, is that certain periods were especially artistic, and that nations, readily named, were notably lovers of Art.

So we are told that the Greeks were, as a people, worshippers of the beautiful, and that in the fifteenth century Art was engrained in the multitude.

That the great masters lived in common understanding with their patrons—that the early Italians were artists—all—and that the demand for the lovely thing produced it.

That we, of to-day, in gross contrast to this Arcadian[4] purity, call for the ungainly, and obtain the ugly. * * *

Listen! There never was an artistic period.

There never was an Art-loving nation.

In the beginning, man went forth each day—some to do battle, some to the chase; others, again, to dig and to delve in the field—all that they might gain and live, or lose and die. Until there was found among them one, differing from the rest, whose pursuits attracted him not, and so he stayed by the tents with the women, and traced strange devices with a burnt stick upon a gourd.

This man, who took no joy in the ways of his brethren—who cared not for conquest, and fretted in the field—this designer of quaint patterns—this deviser of the beautiful—who perceived in Nature about him curious curvings, as faces are seen in the fire—this dreamer apart, was the first artist.

And when, from the field and from afar, there came back the people, they took the gourd—and drank from out of it.

And presently there came to this man another—and, in time, others—of like nature, chosen by the Gods—and so they worked together; and soon they fashioned, from the moistened earth, forms resembling the gourd. And with the power of creation, the heirloom of the artist, presently they went beyond the slovenly suggestion of Nature, and the first vase was born, in beautiful proportion. * * *

And centuries passed in this using, and the world was flooded with all that was beautiful, until there arose a new class, who discovered the cheap, and foresaw fortune in the facture of the sham.

Then sprang into existence the tawdry, the common, the gewgaw.

The taste of the tradesman supplanted the science of the artist, and what was born of the million went back to them, and charmed them, for it was after their own heart; and the great and the small, the statesman and the slave, took to themselves the abomination that was tendered, and preferred it—and have lived with it ever since!

And the artist's occupation was gone, and the manufacturer and the huckster took his place.

And now the heroes filled from the jugs and drank from the bowls—with understanding—noting the glare of their new bravery, and taking pride in its worth.

And the people—this time—had much to say in the matter—and all were satisfied. And Birmingham and Manchester[5] arose in their might—and Art was relegated to the curiosity shop.

Nature contains the elements, in colour and form, of all pictures, as the keyboard contains the notes of all music.

---

4. Simple, rustic.   5. Large manufacturing towns.

But the artist is born to pick, and choose, and group with science, these elements, that the result may be beautiful—as the musician gathers his notes, and forms his chords, until he bring forth from chaos glorious harmony.

To say to the painter, that Nature is to be taken as she is, is to say to the player, that he may sit on the piano.

That Nature is always right, is an assertion, artistically, as untrue, as it is one whose truth is universally taken for granted. Nature is very rarely right, to such an extent even, that it might almost be said that Nature is usually wrong: that is to say, the condition of things that shall bring about the perfection of harmony worthy a picture is rare, and not common at all.

This would seem, to even the most intelligent, a doctrine almost blasphemous. So incorporated with our education has the supposed aphorism become, that its belief is held to be part of our moral being, and the words themselves have, in our ear, the ring of religion. Still, seldom does Nature succeed in producing a picture.

The sun blares, the wind blows from the east, the sky is bereft of cloud, and without, all is of iron. The windows of the Crystal Palace[6] are seen from all points of London. The holiday-maker rejoices in the glorious day, and the painter turns aside to shut his eyes.

How little this is understood, and how dutifully the casual in Nature is accepted as sublime, may be gathered from the unlimited admiration daily produced by a very foolish sunset.

The dignity of the snow-capped mountain is lost in distinctness, but the joy of the tourist is to recognise the traveller on the top. The desire to see, for the sake of seeing, is, with the mass, alone the one to be gratified, hence the delight in detail.

And when the evening mist clothes the riverside with poetry, as with a veil, and the poor buildings lose themselves in the dim sky, and the tall chimneys become campanili,[7] and the warehouses are palaces in the night, and the whole city hangs in the heavens, and fairy-land is before us—then the wayfarer hastens home; the working man and the cultured one, the wise man and the one of pleasure, cease to understand, as they have ceased to see, and Nature, who, for once, has sung in tune, sings her exquisite song to the artist alone, her son and her master—her son in that he loves her, her master in that he knows her.

To him her secrets are unfolded, to him her lessons have become gradually clear. He looks at her flower, not with the enlarging lens, that he may gather facts for the botanist, but with the light of the one who sees in her choice selection of brilliant tones and delicate tints, suggestions of future harmonies.

He does not confine himself to purposeless copying, without thought, each blade of grass, as commended by the inconsequent, but, in the long curve of the narrow leaf, corrected by the straight tall stem, he learns how grace is wedded to dignity, how strength enhances sweetness, that elegance shall be the result. * * *

Why this lifting of the brow in deprecation of the present—this pathos in reference to the past?

If Art be rare to-day, it was seldom heretofore.

It is false, this teaching of decay.

---

6. Built in Hyde Park, London, to house the Great Exhibition of 1851, the Crystal Palace was three times the size of St. Paul's Cathedral. Resembling a gigantic greenhouse, it was the world's first building of this size to be constructed of metal and glass, and was considered one of the wonders of the age. In 1855 it was re-erected in Sydenham, Southeast London.
7. Italian bell towers.

The master stands in no relation to the moment at which he occurs—a monument of isolation—hinting at sadness—having no part in the progress of his fellow men.

He is also no more the product of civilisation than is the scientific truth asserted dependent upon the wisdom of a period. The assertion itself requires the *man* to make it. The truth was from the beginning.

So Art is limited to the infinite, and beginning there cannot progress. * * *

False again, the fabled link between the grandeur of Art and the glories and virtues of the State, for Art feeds not upon nations, and peoples may be wiped from the face of the earth, but Art *is*.

It is indeed high time that we cast aside the weary weight of responsibility and co-partnership, and know that, in no way, do our virtues minister to its worth, in no way do our vices impede its triumph!

How irksome! how hopeless! how superhuman the self-imposed task of the nation! How sublimely vain the belief that it shall live nobly or art perish.

Let us reassure ourselves, at our own option is our virtue. Art we in no way affect.

A whimsical goddess, and a capricious, her strong sense of joy tolerates no dulness, and, live we never so spotlessly, still may she turn her back upon us.

As, from time immemorial, she has done upon the Swiss in their mountains.

What more worthy people! Whose every Alpine gap yawns with tradition, and is stocked with noble story; yet, the perverse and scornful one will none of it, and the sons of patriots are left with the clock that turns the mill, and the sudden cuckoo, with difficulty restrained in its box!

For this was Tell a hero! For this did Gessler die![8]

Art, the cruel jade,[9] cares not, and hardens her heart, and hies her off to the East, to find, among the opium-eaters of Nankin,[1] a favourite with whom she lingers fondly—caressing his blue porcelain, and painting his coy maidens, and marking his plates with her six marks of choice—indifferent in her companionship with him, to all save the virtue of his refinement!

He it is who calls her—he who holds her!

And again to the West, that her next lover may bring together the Gallery at Madrid, and show to the world how the Master towers above all;[2] and in their intimacy they revel, he and she, in this knowledge; and he knows the happiness untasted by other mortal.

She is proud of her comrade, and promises that in after-years, others shall pass that way, and understand.

So in all time does this superb one cast about for the man worthy her love—and Art seeks the Artist alone. * * *

Therefore have we cause to be merry!—and to cast away all care—resolved that all is well—as it ever was—and that it is not meet that we should be cried at, and urged to take measures!

Enough have we endured of dulness! Surely are we weary of weeping, and our tears have been cozened from us falsely, for they have called out woe! when there was no grief—and, alas! where all is fair!

---

8. William Tell was a legendary 14th-century Swiss hero whose defiance of Gessler, an Austrian bailiff, led to his well-known punishment: shooting an apple off his son's head. In revenge, Tell killed Gessler and led a revolt to liberate his country from Austrian control.
9. Disreputable woman.

1. The Chinese city of Nanjing.
2. Philip II of Spain created the Prado Gallery in Madrid; its collection was substantially enlarged by Philip IV. The Prado contains many works by "the Master" Velasquez, whose art greatly influenced Whistler.

We have then but to wait—until, with the mark of the Gods upon him—there come among us again the chosen—who shall continue what has gone before. Satisfied that, even were he never to appear, the story of the beautiful is already complete—hewn in the marbles of the Parthenon—and broidered, with the birds, upon the fan of Hokusai—at the foot of Fusiyama.[3]

1885   1890

"Michael Field"

Katharine Bradley
1846–1914

and

Edith Cooper
1862–1913

"I have found a new poet," announced Robert Browning to a hushed dinner party in 1885. He had actually found two poets, both women. "Michael Field" was the pseudonym of Katharine Bradley and her niece Edith Cooper; they were hailed as "the double-headed nightingale" by admirers. Their long collaboration produced twenty-seven poetic dramas on historical themes, and eight volumes of lyric poetry. Their work was praised by Meredith, Swinburne, and Wilde; but the general public was unaware that in lauding "Mr. Field," they were speaking of an aunt who esteemed William Michael Rossetti (Dante and Christina's brother) and a niece nicknamed "Field." Bradley had helped rear Cooper, the child of her invalid sister. In 1878 they moved to Bristol, where they both attended University College, living together from then on in a close emotional and sexual relationship. Commenting on the fabled intimacy of Robert and Elizabeth Barrett Browning, Bradley noted in her diary *"we are closer married."* Having independent means, they spent their time reading, writing, and visiting galleries; they dressed and decorated their rooms in Aesthetic style, and their journals record their acute impressions of the many artists and writers they met. In 1907 both converted to Catholicism, apparently because of the death of their dog Whym Chow, a Dionysian presence who not only inspired a volume of love poems but also killed Kipling's pet rabbit during a visit.

"We have many things to say," they wrote to Browning, "that the world will not tolerate from a woman's lips. . . . We cannot be stifled in drawing-room conventionalities." Their first joint volume of poems, *Long Ago* (1889), dared to complete Sappho's fragments in modern lyrics that highlighted the lesbian nature of the Greek poems. In a poem they proclaimed they would remain "Poets and lovers evermore . . . Indifferent to heaven and hell." Despite the passionate paganism of their early career, they condemned what they saw as the depravity of Zola and Beardsley, and withdrew one of their poems from *The Yellow Book*. "From decadence, Good Lord deliver us!" they exclaimed in a diary entry in 1891. Their poetry is notable for its subtle music and technical improvisation, as well as their sympathetic rendering of the femme-fatale imagery common at the time. Exploring the nature of womanhood was both a personal mission and an artistic ideal: "We hold ourselves bound in life and in literature," Bradley wrote in her diary, "to reveal . . . the beauty of the high feminine standard of *the ought to be.*"

---

3. Katsushika Hokusai (1760–1849), Japanese artist; Fujiyama or Mount Fuji, the highest mountain in Japan, and a frequent subject in Hokusai's works.

La Gioconda[1]
Leonardo Da Vinci
THE LOUVRE

Historic, side-long, implicating eyes;
A smile of velvet's lustre on the cheek;
Calm lips the smile leads upward; hand that lies
Glowing and soft, the patience in its rest
5   Of cruelty that waits and doth not seek
For prey; a dusky forehead and a breast
Where twilight touches ripeness amorously:
Behind her, crystal rocks, a sea and skies
Of evanescent blue on cloud and creek;
10   Landscape that shines suppressive of its zest
For those vicissitudes by which men die.

                                      1892

A Pen-Drawing of Leda[1]
Sodoma[2]
THE GRAND DUKE'S PALACE AT WEIMAR

'Tis Leda lovely, wild and free,
Drawing her gracious Swan down through the grass to see
    Certain round eggs without a speck:
One hand plunged in the reeds and one dinting the downy neck,
5   Although his hectoring bill
       Gapes toward her tresses,
She draws the fondled creature to her will.

    She joys to bend in the live light
Her glistening body toward her love, how much more bright!
10   Though on her breast the sunshine lies
And spreads its affluence on the wide curves of her waist and thighs,
      To her meek, smitten gaze
      Where her hand presses
The Swan's white neck sink Heaven's concentred rays.

                                        1892

"A Girl"

A girl,
    Her soul a deep-wave pearl
Dim, lucent of all lovely mysteries;
    A face flowered for heart's ease,
5   A brow's grace soft as seas

1. Leonardo's painting (c. 1503), also known as the *Mona Lisa*, hangs in the Louvre in Paris. The authors would have known Walter Pater's famous description of it in *The Renaissance*. This and the following poem appeared in their collection *Sight and Song* (1892), which sought "to translate into verse what the lines and colours of certain chosen pictures sing in themselves."

1. In Greek myth Zeus took the form of a swan to have sex with Leda, a mortal; she subsequently gave birth to Helen of Troy. Compare this view of Leda to Yeats's poem *Leda and the Swan*, page 2337.
2. Nickname of the Sienese artist Giovanni Antonio Bazzi (1477–1549).

> Seen through faint forest-trees:
>   A mouth, the lips apart,
> Like aspen-leaflets trembling in the breeze
>   From her tempestuous heart.
> 10 Such: and our souls so knit,
>   I leave a page half-writ—
>   The work begun
> Will be to heaven's conception done,
>   If she come to it.

1893

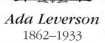

Ada Leverson
1862–1933

"You can't have got up, you must have sat up," said Oscar Wilde to his exquisitely dressed friend Ada Leverson when he was released from prison at an early hour. "How marvellous of you to know exactly the right hat to wear at seven o'clock in the morning to meet a friend who has been away!" Always perfectly attired, Leverson was a witty socialite whose genius for friendship and droll sense of humor put her at the center of *fin de siècle* literary life. Her friends wondered how someone so rich and beautiful could be indifferent to jewelry: "But it lasts so long," she said. Henry James was so struck by her remarks about his books that he called her the "incarnation" of the novelist's dream, "the Gentle Reader." Later she herself became a successful comic novelist, her best works being reissued as *The Little Ottleys* (1962). She wrote in bed, in a confusion of cigarettes, papers, and oranges. To escape parental control she married Ernest Leverson when she was only 19, he 31. She soon regretted it but arranged to carry on quiet romances while he gambled or visited his mistress. The Leversons were united, however, in their emotional and financial support of Wilde after his troubles began; they sheltered Wilde secretly between his trials.

It was Wilde who gave her the lasting nickname of "Sphinx" after she published a parody of his poem by that title in *Punch*. Leverson delighted in deflating Wilde's ego: when Wilde boasted that an Apache had become so devoted to him in Paris that he accompanied him everywhere with a knife in one hand, she replied, "I'm sure he had a fork in the other." She enjoyed exchanging wires with Wilde, claiming that she intended to edit *The Collected Telegrams of Oscar Wilde*. Her short story *Suggestion* was published in *The Yellow Book*, along with her portrait by Walter Sickert, in April, 1895, the month when Wilde was arrested. From its provocative opening line to its immorally moral ending, *Suggestion* skewers Victorian patriarchy and double standards, even as it spoofs the New Woman, Aesthetes, and Wildean affectation. A parody of decadent gender confusion that appeared in *Punch* later that month may well have been aimed at Ada Leverson:

> Woman was woman, man was man,
> When Adam delved and Eve span.
> Now he can't dig and she won't spin
> Unless 'tis tales all slang and sin!

Suggestion

If Lady Winthrop had not spoken of me as "that intolerable, effeminate boy," she might have had some chance of marrying my father. She was a middle-aged widow; prosaic, fond of domineering, and an alarmingly excellent housekeeper; the serious work of her life was paying visits; in her lighter moments she collected autographs. She was highly suitable and altogether insupportable; and this unfortunate remark about me was, as people say, the last straw. Some encouragement from father Lady Winthrop must, I think, have received; for she took to calling at odd hours, asking my sister Marjorie sudden abrupt questions, and being generally impossible. A tradition existed that her advice was of use to our father in his household, and when, last year, he married his daughter's school-friend, a beautiful girl of twenty, it surprised every one except Marjorie and myself.

The whole thing was done, in fact, by suggestion. I shall never forget that summer evening when father first realised, with regard to Laura Egerton, the possible. He was giving a little dinner of eighteen people. *Through a mistake of Marjorie's* (my idea) Lady Winthrop did not receive her invitation till the very last minute. Of course she accepted—we knew she would—but unknowing that it was a dinner party, she came without putting on evening-dress.

Nothing could be more trying to the average woman than such a *contretemps*; and Lady Winthrop was not one to rise, sublimely, and laughing, above the situation. I can see her now, in a plaid blouse and a vile temper, displaying herself, mentally and physically, to the utmost disadvantage, while Marjorie apologised the whole evening, in pale blue crêpe-de-chine; and Laura, in yellow, with mauve orchids, sat—an adorable contrast—on my father's other side, with a slightly conscious air that was perfectly fascinating. It is quite extraordinary what trifles have their little effect in these matters. I had sent Laura the orchids, anonymously; I could not help it if she chose to think they were from my father. Also, I had hinted of his secret affection for her, and lent her Verlaine.[1] I said I had found it in his study, turned down at her favourite page. Laura has, like myself, the artistic temperament; she is cultured, rather romantic, and in search of the *au-delà* [the transcendent]. My father has at times—never to me—rather charming manners; also he is still handsome, with that look of having suffered that comes from enjoying oneself too much. That evening his really sham melancholy and apparently hollow gaiety were delightful for a son to witness, and appealed evidently to her heart. Yes, strange as it may seem, while the world said that pretty Miss Egerton married old Carington for his money, she was really in love, or thought herself in love, with our father. Poor girl! She little knew what an irritating, ill-tempered, absent-minded person he is in private life; and at times I have pangs of remorse.

A fortnight after the wedding, father forgot he was married, and began again treating Laura with a sort of *distrait* [absent-minded] gallantry as Marjorie's friend, or else ignoring her altogether. When, from time to time, he remembers she is his wife, he scolds her about the housekeeping in a fitful, perfunctory way, for he does not know that Marjorie does it still. Laura bears the rebukes like an angel; indeed, rather than take the slightest practical trouble she would prefer to listen to the strongest language in my father's vocabulary.

But she is sensitive; and when father, speedily resuming his bachelor manners, recommended his visits to an old friend who lives in one of the little houses opposite the Oratory,[2] she seemed quite vexed. Father is horribly careless, and Laura found a letter. They had a rather serious explanation, and for a little time after, Laura seemed depressed. She soon tried to rouse herself, and is at times cheerful enough with Mar-

---

1. French decadent poet (1844—1896) whose subtle musicality was much admired by English Aesthetes.
2. The Brompton Oratory, in West London, is a Roman

Catholic church where Cardinal Newman and other leading clerics preached.

jorie and myself, but I fear she has had a disillusion. They never quarrel now, and I think we all three dislike father about equally, though Laura never owns it, and is gracefully attentive to him in a gentle, filial sort of way.

We are fond of going to parties—not father—and Laura is a very nice chaperone for Marjorie. They are both perfectly devoted to me. "Cecil knows everything," they are always saying, and they do nothing—not even choosing a hat—without asking my advice.

Since I left Eton I am supposed to be reading with a tutor,[3] but as a matter of fact I have plenty of leisure; and am very glad to be of use to the girls, of whom I'm, by the way, quite proud. They are rather a sweet contrast; Marjorie has the sort of fresh rosy prettiness you see in the park and on the river. She is tall, and slim as a punt-pole,[4] and if she were not very careful how she dresses, she would look like a drawing by Pilotelle in the *Lady's Pictorial*.[5] She is practical and lively, she rides and drives and dances; skates, and goes to some mysterious haunt called *The Stores*,[6] and is, in her own way, quite a modern English type.

Laura has that exotic beauty so much admired by Philistines; dreamy dark eyes, and a wonderful white complexion. She loves music and poetry and pictures and admiration in a lofty sort of way; she has a morbid fondness for mental gymnastics, and a dislike to physical exertion, and never takes any exercise except waving her hair. Sometimes she looks bored, and I have heard her sigh.

"Cissy," Marjorie said, coming one day into my study, "I want to speak to you about Laura."

"Do you have pangs of conscience too?" I asked, lighting a cigarette.

"Dear, we took a great responsibility. Poor girl! Oh, couldn't we make Papa more—"

"Impossible," I said; "no one has any influence with him. He can't bear even me, though if he had a shade of decency he would dash away an unbidden tear every time I look at him with my mother's blue eyes."

My poor mother was a great beauty, and I am supposed to be her living image.

"Laura has no object in life," said Marjorie. "I have, all girls have, I suppose. By the way, Cissy, I am quite sure Charlie Winthrop is serious."

"How sweet of him! I am so glad. I got father off my hands last season."

"Must I really marry him, Cissy? He bores me."

"What has that to do with it? Certainly you must. You are not a beauty, and I doubt your ever having a better chance."

Marjorie rose and looked at herself in the long pier-glass that stands opposite my writing-table. I could not resist the temptation to go and stand beside her.

"I am just the style that is admired now," said Marjorie, dispassionately.

"So am I," I said reflectively. "But *you* will soon be out of date."

Every one says I am strangely like my mother. Her face was of that pure and perfect oval one so seldom sees, with delicate features, rosebud mouth, and soft flaxen hair. A blondness without insipidity, for the dark-blue eyes are fringed with dark lashes, and from their languorous depths looks out a soft mockery. I have a curious ideal devotion to my mother; she died when I was quite young—only two months old—and I often spend hours thinking of her, as I gaze at myself in the mirror.

---

3. In preparation for attending Oxford or Cambridge.
4. A long, thin pole used to propel a punt, a flat-bottomed boat.
5. Georges Labadie Pilotell (1844–1918), French illustrator and caricaturist.

6. Large department stores, relatively new at the time. In her athleticism and up-to-date practicality, Marjorie is a version of the New Woman—as opposed to Laura's languid Aestheticism.

"Do come down from the clouds," said Marjorie impatiently, for I had sunk into a reverie. "I came to ask you to think of something to amuse Laura—to interest her."

"We ought to make it up to her in some way. Haven't you tried anything?"

"Only palmistry; and Mrs. Wilkinson prophesied her all that she detests, and depressed her dreadfully."

"What do you think she really needs most?" I asked.

Our eyes met.

"Really, Cissy, you're too disgraceful," said Marjorie. There was a pause.

"And so I'm to accept Charlie?"

"What man do you like better?" I asked.

"I don't know what you mean," said Marjorie, colouring.

"I thought Adrian Grant would have been more sympathetic to Laura than to you. I have just had a note from him, asking me to tea at his studio to-day." I threw it to her. "He says I'm to bring you both. Would that amuse Laura?"

"Oh," cried Marjorie, enchanted, "of course we'll go. I wonder what he thinks of me," she added wistfully.

"He didn't say. He is going to send Laura his verses, 'Hearts-ease and Heliotrope.'"[7]

She sighed. Then she said, "Father was complaining again to-day of your laziness."

"I, lazy! Why, I've been swinging the censer in Laura's boudoir because she wants to encourage the religious temperament, and I've designed your dress for the Clives' fancy ball."

"Where's the design?"

"In my head. You're not to wear white; Miss Clive must wear white."

"I wonder you don't marry her," said Marjorie, "you admire her so much."

"I never marry. Besides, I know she's pretty, but that furtive Slade-school[8] manner of hers gets on my nerves. You don't know how dreadfully I suffer from my nerves."

She lingered a little, asking me what I advised her to choose for a birthday present for herself—an American organ, a black poodle, or an *édition de luxe* of Browning. I advised the last, as being least noisy. Then I told her I felt sure that in spite of her admiration for Adrian, she was far too good natured to interfere with Laura's prospects. She said I was incorrigible, and left the room with a smile of resignation.

And I returned to my reading. On my last birthday—I was seventeen—my father—who has his gleams of dry humour—gave me *Robinson Crusoe!* I prefer Pierre Loti,[9] and intend to have an onyx-paved bath-room, with soft apricot-coloured light shimmering through the blue-lined green curtains in my chambers, as soon as I get Margery married, and Laura more—settled down.

I met Adrian Grant first at a luncheon party at the Clives. I seemed to amuse him; he came to see me, and became at once obviously enamoured of my step-mother. He is rather an impressionable impressionist, and a delightful creature, tall and graceful and beautiful, and altogether most interesting. Every one admits he's fascinating; he is very popular and very much disliked. He is by way of being a painter; he has a little money of his own—enough for his telegrams, but not enough for his buttonholes—and nothing could be more incongruous than the idea of his marrying. I

---

7. Hearts-ease is a pansy; heliotrope is a plant with fragrant purple flowers; the title is typical of 1890s preciousness.

8. The Slade School of Art in London, founded 1871, had become more fashionable than the Royal Academy,

whose teaching was regarded as dry and stuffy.

9. Pen name of French impressionist novelist Julien Viaud (1850–1923) who was drawn to exotic civilizations and landscapes.

have never seen Marjorie so much attracted. But she is a good loyal girl, and will accept Charlie Winthrop, who is a dear person, good-natured and ridiculously rich— just the sort of man for a brother-in-law. It will annoy my old enemy Lady Winthrop—he is her nephew, and she wants him to marry that little Miss Clive. Dorothy Clive has her failings, but she could not—to do her justice—be happy with Charlie Winthrop.

Adrian's gorgeous studio gives one the complex impression of being at once the calm retreat of a mediaeval saint and the luxurious abode of a modern Pagan. One feels that everything could be done there, everything from praying to flirting—everything except painting. The tea-party amused me, I was pretending to listen to a brown person who was talking absurd worn-out literary clichés—as that the New Humour is not funny, or that Bourget understood women,[1] when I overheard this fragment of conversation.

"But don't you like Society?" Adrian was saying.

"I get rather tired of it. People are so much alike. They all say the same things," said Laura.

"Of course they all say the same things to *you*," murmured Adrian, as he affected to point out a rather curious old silver crucifix.

"That," said Laura, "is one of the things they say."

About three weeks later I found myself dining alone with Adrian Grant, at one of the two restaurants in London. (The cooking is better at the other, this one is the more becoming.) I had lilies-of-the-valley in my button-hole, Adrian was wearing a red carnation. Several people glanced at us. Of course he is very well known in Society. Also, I was looking rather nice, and I could not help hoping, while Adrian gazed rather absently over my head, that the shaded candles were staining to a richer rose the waking wonder of my face.

Adrian was charming of course, but he seemed worried and a little preoccupied, and drank a good deal of champagne.

Towards the end of dinner, he said—almost abruptly for him—"Carington."

"Cecil," I interrupted. He smiled.

"Cissy . . . it seems an odd thing to say to you, but though you are so young, I think you know everything. I am sure you know everything. You know about me. I am in love. I am quite miserable. What on earth am I to do!" He drank more champagne. "Tell me," he said, "what to do." For a few minutes, while we listened to that interminable hackneyed *Intermezzo*, I reflected; asking myself by what strange phases I had risen to the extraordinary position of giving advice to Adrian on such a subject?

Laura was not happy with our father. From a selfish motive, Marjorie and I had practically arranged that monstrous marriage. That very day he had been disagreeable, asking me with a clumsy sarcasm to raise his allowance, so that he could afford my favourite cigarettes. If Adrian were free, Marjorie might refuse Charlie Winthrop. I don't want her to refuse him. Adrian has treated me as a friend. I like him—I like him enormously. I am quite devoted to him. And how can I rid myself of the feeling of responsibility, the sense that I owe some compensation to poor beautiful Laura?

We spoke of various matters. Just before we left the table, I said, with what seemed, but was not, irrelevance, "Dear Adrian, Mrs. Carington———"

---

1. The "New Humor" is coined on the model of other 1890s trends, such as the New Woman, the New Journalism, and the New Drama; the French author Paul Bourget (1852–1935) wrote psychological novels.

"Go on, Cissy."

"She is one of those who must be appealed to, at first, by her imagination. She married our father because she thought he was lonely and misunderstood."

"*I* am lonely and misunderstood," said Adrian, his eyes flashing with delight.

"Ah, not twice! She doesn't like that now."

I finished my coffee slowly, and then I said,

"Go to the Clives' fancy-ball as Tristan."[2]

Adrian pressed my hand. . . .

At the door of the restaurant we parted, and I drove home through the cool April night, wondering, wondering. Suddenly I thought of my mother—my beautiful sainted mother, who would have loved me, I am convinced, had she lived, with an extraordinary devotion. What would she have said to all this? What would she have thought? I know not why, but a mad reaction seized me. I felt recklessly conscientious. My father! After all, he was my father. I was possessed by passionate scruples. If I went back now to Adrian—if I went back and implored him, supplicated him never to see Laura again!

I felt I could persuade him. I have sufficient personal magnetism to do that, if I make up my mind. After one glance in the looking-glass, I put up my stick and stopped the hansom. I had taken a resolution. I told the man to drive to Adrian's rooms.

He turned round with a sharp jerk. In another second a brougham[3] passed us—a swift little brougham that I knew. It slackened—it stopped—we passed it—I saw my father. He was getting out at one of the little houses opposite the Brompton Oratory.

"Turn round again," I shouted to the cabman. And he drove me straight home.

1895

✦ ═╪═ ✦

Lord Alfred Douglas
1870–1945

Lord Alfred Douglas embodied the new sexual freedom of the early 1890s, both in his life and in his polished verses on erotic themes. He was the son of the pugnacious Marquess of Queensberry, who had established the rules of boxing, but who violated almost every social code in his public antagonism toward his son. In 1891, while Douglas was still an undergraduate at Oxford, Lionel Johnson introduced him to Oscar Wilde, who encouraged both his affections and his writing. Their tempestuous relationship lasted until Wilde's death in 1900, despite Queensberry's constant efforts to disgrace them both. During Wilde's trials, provoked largely by the desire of father and son to injure each other, Douglas stayed safely in France, at Wilde's request. Their reunion after Wilde's imprisonment was marked by mutual recrimination; Wilde addressed to Douglas the bitter accusations detailed in *De Profundis*, and Douglas contended that he alone among Wilde's friends had remained true. In 1902 Douglas surprised everyone by secretly marrying the poet Olive Custance, whom he had met the year before. The marriage ended in 1913, by which time Douglas had converted to Catholicism and renounced his earlier homosexual activity. In his later life Douglas wrote much about his relationship with Wilde, including *Oscar Wilde and Myself* (1914) and *Oscar Wilde: A Summing Up* (1940). Like his father, he took pleasure in attacking the integrity of other people, and in 1923–1924 spent six months in prison for criminally libeling Winston Churchill.

---

2. A fancy dress ball is a costume ball; Tristan was a legendary knight in love with Isolde, his king's wife.

3. A one-horse closed carriage.

Douglas's early career coincided with the period of sexual openness and homosexual activism that occurred between 1885 and 1895. The term "homosexuality" was invented in 1869, and entered English just as Parliament criminalized all homosexual activity in 1885; medical theories of homosexual "degeneration" soon followed. Yet this climate also inspired resistance among authors who lauded the spiritual and emotional rewards of same-sex relationships. Douglas, by contrast, explored the dangerous pleasures of all kinds of sexuality: he translated Wilde's *Salomé* (1894) from French to English, and his own *Impression de Nuit: London* combines the aesthetic preference for urban artifice with the decadent penchant for monstrously appetitive female bodies. He also made two contributions—*In Praise of Shame* and *Two Loves*—to *The Chameleon* (1894), an Oxford magazine with a distinctly homoerotic slant. The prosecution read both poems at Wilde's second trial in an effort to make Wilde appear guilty by association. Already outraged by the exposure of male prostitution in the Cleveland Street Scandal of 1889, the jury and the public found confirmation in Douglas's poetry that a new threat to the nation had arisen, the "deviant" or "invert."

Two Loves

I dreamed I stood upon a little hill,
And at my feet there lay a ground that seemed
Like a waste garden, flowering at its will
With buds and blossoms. There were pools that dreamed
5 Black and unruffled; there were white lilies
A few, and crocuses, and violets,
Purple or pale, snake-like fritillaries[1]
Scarce seen for the rank grass, and through green nets
Blue eyes of shy pervenche[2] winked in the sun.
10 And there were curious flowers, before unknown,
Flowers that were stained with moonlight, or with shades
Of Nature's wilful moods; and here a one
That had drunk in the transitory tone
Of one brief moment in a sunset; blades
15 Of grass that in an hundred springs had been
Slowly but exquisitely nurtured by the stars,
And watered with the scented dew long cupped
In lilies, that for rays of sun had seen
Only God's glory, for never a sunrise mars
20 The luminous air of Heaven. Beyond, abrupt,
A grey stone wall, o'ergrown with velvet moss,
Uprose; and gazing I stood long, all mazed
To see a place so strange, so sweet, so fair.
And as I stood and marvelled, lo! across
25 The garden came a youth; one hand he raised
To shield him from the sun, his wind-tossed hair
Was twined with flowers, and in his hand he bore
A purple bunch of bursting grapes, his eyes
Were clear as crystal, naked all was he,
30 White as the snow on pathless mountains frore,°   frozen
Red were his lips as red wine-spilth that dyes
A marble floor, his brow chalcedony.°   quartz

---

1. A flower similar to the lily.   2. Periwinkle, a small blue flower.

And he came near me, with his lips uncurled
And kind, and caught my hand and kissed my mouth,
35   And gave me grapes to eat, and said, "Sweet friend,
     Come, I will show thee shadows of the world
And images of life. See from the South
Comes the pale pageant that hath never an end."
     And lo! within the garden of my dream
40   I saw two walking on a shining plain
     Of golden light. The one did joyous seem
And fair and blooming, and a sweet refrain
     Came from his lips; he sang of pretty maids
And joyous love of comely girl and boy;
45   His eyes were bright, and 'mid the dancing blades
Of golden grass his feet did trip for joy;
     And in his hands he held an ivory lute
With strings of gold that were as maidens' hair,
     And sang with voice as tuneful as a flute,
50   And round his neck three chains of roses were.
     But he that was his comrade walked aside;
He was full sad and sweet, and his large eyes
     Were strange with wondrous brightness, staring wide
With gazing; and he sighed with many sighs
55   That moved me, and his cheeks were wan and white
Like pallid lilies, and his lips were red
     Like poppies, and his hands he clenchèd tight
And yet again unclenchèd, and his head
     Was wreathed with moon-flowers[3] pale as lips of death.
60   A purple robe he wore, o'erwrought in gold
     With the device of a great snake, whose breath
Was like curved flame: which when I did behold
     I fell a-weeping, and I cried, "Sweet youth,
Tell me why, sad and sighing, thou dost rove
65   These pleasant realms? I pray thee, speak me sooth,
What is thy name?" He said, "My name is Love."
     Then straight the first did turn himself to me
And cried: "He lieth, for his name is Shame,
     But I am Love, and I was wont to be
70   Alone in this fair garden, till he came
     Unasked by night; I am true Love, I fill
The hearts of boy and girl with mutual flame."
     Then sighing, said the other: "Have thy will,
I am the love that dare not speak its name."

                                                 1894

Impression de Nuit[1]

London

See what a mass of gems the city wears
Upon her broad live bosom! row on row

---

3. A fragrant morning glory.   1. Impression of the night.

Rubies and emeralds and amethysts glow.
See! that huge circle like a necklace, stares
5   With thousands of bold eyes to heaven, and dares
The golden stars to dim the lamps below,
And in the mirror of the mire I know
The moon has left her image unawares.

That's the great town at night: I see her breasts,
10   Pricked out with lamps they stand like huge black towers.
I think they move! I hear her panting breath.
And that's her head where the tiara rests.
And in her brain, through lanes as dark as death,
Men creep like thoughts . . . The lamps are like pale flowers.

1894

+—◄◆►—+

Olive Custance
(Lady Alfred Douglas)
1874–1944

In April 1895, *Punch* published a satiric poem by an "Angry Old Buffer" concerned about the masculine New Woman and the effeminate Decadent:

> . . . a new fear my bosom vexes;
> To-morrow there may be *no* sexes!
> Unless, as end to all pother,
> Each one in fact becomes the other.

Olive Custance contributed notably to the era's uncertainty about gender roles and the nature of romantic love. Coming from a well-to-do upper-class background, she fell in love at sixteen with the decadent poet John Gray, who was Oscar Wilde's lover at the time. Nothing came of this infatuation but poetry; by the age of twenty she was known in fashionable society as a beautiful young poet, friend to Aubrey Beardsley and contributor to the daring *Yellow Book* magazine. She called her first book *Opals* (1897), after the semi-precious stones that are said to bring the wearer bad luck; she liked to be called "Opal" herself, and sometimes "Wild Olive." Her poetry, like the long letters she wrote to friends, is remarkable for its intensity and emotional candor.

In 1901 she received a passionate fan letter from Natalie Clifford Barney, an American poet and heiress living in Paris. Custance replied with a daring poem:

> For I would dance to make you smile, and sing
> Of those who with some sweet mad sin have played,
> And how Love walks with delicate feet afraid
> 'Twixt maid and maid.

During their brief, stormy relationship, evoked in the poem *The White Witch*, Barney introduced Custance to the lesbian literary scene in Paris. By the time they traveled to Venice together in 1902, however, Custance was already in love with Wilde's friend Lord Alfred Douglas, to whom *she* had sent a fan letter in 1901. His imagined resemblance to a Roman statue inspired several poems, including the decadent classic, *Statues*, which revises the gender terms of the Pygmalion myth. Jilting an earl to whom she had just become engaged, Custance secretly married Douglas in March 1902. By the time the marriage ended in 1913, partially due to

Douglas's conversion to Catholicism, Custance had stopped writing. After a reconciliation in 1932, they lived apart but saw each other almost every day until her death. Douglas wrote in his autobiography that "the very thing she loved in me was that which I was always trying to suppress and keep under: I mean the feminine part."

The Masquerade[1]

Masked dancers in the Dance of life
We move sedately . . . wearily together,
Afraid to show a sign of inward strife,
We hold our souls in tether.

5   We dance with proud and smiling lips,
With frank appealing eyes, with shy hands clinging.
We sing, and few will question if there slips
A sob into our singing.

Each has a certain step to learn;
10   Our prisoned feet move staidly in set paces,
And to and fro we pass, since life is stern,
Patiently, with masked faces.

Yet some there are who will not dance,
They sit apart most sorrowful and splendid,
15   But all the rest trip on as in a trance,
Until the Dance is ended.

1902

Statues

I have loved statues . . . spangled dawns have seen
Me bowed before their beauty . . . when the green
And silver world of Spring wears radiantly
The morning rainbows of an opal sky . . .
5   And I have chanted curious madrigals[1]
To charm their coldness, twined for coronals[2]
Blossoming branches, thinking thus to change
Their still contempt for mortal love, their bright
Proud scorn to something delicate and strange,
10   More sweet, more marvellous, than mere delight!

I have loved statues—passionately prone
My body worshipped the white form of stone!
And like a flower that lifts its chalice up
Towards the light—my soul became a cup
15   That over-brimming with enchanted wine
Of ecstasy—was raised to the divine
Indifferent lips of some young silent God
Standing aloof from all our tears and strife,

1. Cf. Wilde's *The Harlot's House*, page 2069.
1. Love poems, often sung by several unaccompanied voices.
2. Wreathlike crowns.

Tranced in the paradise of dreams, he trod
20   In the untroubled summer of his life!

I have loved statues . . . and at night the cold
Mysterious moon behind a mask of gold—
Or veiled in silver veils—has seen my pride
Utterly broken—seen the dream denied
25   For which I pleaded—heedless that for me
The miracle of joy could never be . . .
As in old legends beautiful and strange,
When bright gods loved fair mortals born to die,
And the frail daughters of despair and change
30   Become the brides of immortality?

c. 1902   1905

The White Witch

Her body is a dancing joy, a delicate delight,
Her hair a silver glamour in a net of golden light.

Her face is like the faces that a dreamer sometimes meets,
A face that Leonardo would have followed through the streets.

5   Her eyelids are like clouds that spread white wings across blue skies,
Like shadows in still water are the sorrows in her eyes.

How flower-like are the smiling lips so many have desired,
Curled lips that love's long kisses have left a little tired.

c. 1901   1902

Tom Phillips. Illustration to Canto 10 of Dante's *Inferno*, 1983.

The Twentieth Century

BURYING VICTORIA

Writing in 1928, Virginia Woolf described the cultural atmosphere of the Victorian era in the following way:

> Damp now began to make its way into every house. . . . The damp struck within. Men felt the chill in their hearts; the damp in their minds. . . . The life of the average woman was a succession of childbirths. She married at nineteen and had fifteen or eighteen children by the time she was thirty; for twins abounded. Thus the British Empire came into existence; and thus—for there is no stopping damp; it gets into inkpots as it gets into the wood-work—sentences swelled, adjectives multiplied, lyrics became epics, and little trifles that had been essays a column long were now encyclopedias in ten or twenty volumes.

Woolf of course exaggerates here for her own effect; yet this passage does capture nicely the stereotypical view of the Victorians that flourished during the modern period—and helped make it possible. Ezra Pound, for instance, called the later nineteenth century "a rather blurry, messy sort of period, a rather sentimentalistic, mannerish sort of period." Whether accurate or not, polemical descriptions like these served the rhetorical purposes of writers at the start of the new century as they attempted to stake out their terrain and to forge a literature and a perspective of their own.

The opening decade of the new century was a time of transition. Woolf later suggested, her tongue perhaps in her cheek, that as a result of a Post-Impressionist exhibition of paintings in London, "on or about December, 1910, human character changed." Almost no one, however, seems to have maintained that anything changed very decisively on the morning of 1 January 1900. Queen Victoria, at that time on the throne for nearly sixty-five years and in mourning for Prince Albert for almost forty, lived and ruled on into the following year; the subsequent reign of Edward VII (1901–1910) differed only slightly from that of his mother in many respects, the entire nation mourning the loss of their queen as she had the loss of her husband. But Woolf, in a 1924 essay, saw a gulf between herself and the Edwardians: Edwardian novelists, she writes, "established conventions which do their business; and that business is not our business." Edward VII himself, in fact, was clearly not a Victorian. He had a reputation as a playboy and implicitly rebelled against the conventions that his mother had upheld. During his reign, the mannered decadence of the 1890s modulated into a revived social realism seen in ambitious novels like Joseph Conrad's *Nostromo* and H. G. Wells's darkly comic masterpiece *Tono-Bungay*, while poets like Yeats and Hardy produced major poems probing the relations of self, society, and history. Writers in general considered themselves to be voices of a nation taking stock of its place in the world in a new century. They saw their times as marked by accelerating social and technological change and by the burden of a worldwide empire, which achieved its greatest extent in the years between 1900 and 1914—encompassing as much as a quarter of the world's population and dominating world trade through a global network of ports.

This period of consolidation and reflection abruptly came to an end four years into the reign of George V, with the start of World War I in August 1914; the relatively tranquil prewar years of George's early reign were quickly memorialized, and nostalgized, in the wake of the war's disruption to the traditionally English way of life. This first Georgian period was abruptly elevated into a cultural "golden age" by the British public and British publishers, a process that was typified by the pastoral poetry gathered by Edward Marsh in his hugely popular series of five anthologies called *Georgian Poetry*, the first of which was published in 1912. As a consequence of Marsh's skill as a tastemaker, this brief period before the war is frequently known as the Georgian period in British literature, though George V himself remained on the throne until 1936, when the distant rumble of World War II was to be heard by those with ears to hear.

The quarter century from 1914 until the start of the war in 1939 is now conventionally known as the modernist period. To be modern was, in one respect, to rebel openly and loudly against one's philosophical and artistic inheritance, in much the same way that the Romantic writers of the late eighteenth and early nineteenth centuries had sought to distinguish themselves from their Augustan forebears. This gesture—the way in which a new artistic movement seeks to define itself through caricature of the movement(s) that gave it birth—is a recurrent feature in literary history, but it took on a particular urgency and energy among the modernists, who advanced the view summarized in Pound's bold slogan, "Make It New." A great modernist monument to this anti-Victorian sentiment was Lytton Strachey's elegantly ironic *Eminent Victorians* (1918), whose probing biographical portraits punctured a series of Victorian pieties. Much of the playwright Bernard Shaw's writing is animated by anti-Victorian animus as well, taking the theatrical wit of Oscar Wilde and turning it against specific targets. Exaggerated though it was, the ritualized slaughter performed by modernists like Woolf, Strachey, and Shaw seems to have achieved a clearing of the literary and artistic terrain that formed a necessary prelude to further innovation. The modernists' "Victorians" were oversimplified, sometimes straw figures, but the battle that was waged against them was real indeed, and the principles of modernism were forged and refined in the process.

THE FOUNDATIONS OF MODERN SKEPTICISM

The best Victorian writers had not been afraid to ask difficult, unsettling questions. Tennyson's restless skepticism in *In Memoriam*, for example, exemplifies the spirit of Victorian inquiry. But the conclusion of that poem foresees an ongoing progress toward future perfection, guided by "One God, one law, one element, / And one far-off divine event, / To which the whole creation moves." Tennyson himself doubted that such unities could be embodied in the present; twentieth-century writers found increasing fragmentation around them and became more and more suspicious of narratives of historical progress and of social unity. In 1832 Tennyson made a representative man of Ulysses—the wanderer who, though his journey be long and convoluted, ultimately finds his way back to Ithaca, his faithful wife waiting. In Tennyson's poem, however, Ulysses decides to leave once again:

> It little profits that an idle king,
> By this still hearth, among these barren crags,
> Match'd with an aged wife, I mete and dole

> Unequal laws to a savage race,
> That hoard, and sleep, and feed, and know not me.

Leopold Bloom, the modern Odysseus in Joyce's novel *Ulysses* (1922), experiences a heightened version of Ulysses' dilemma: his wife has not remained faithful to begin with, and he has nowhere else but home to go to at the novel's end. In the modern period the quest for certainty associated with the Victorian exploration of values has vanished; modern explorations are undertaken with absolutely no confidence as to the results that will be discovered, still less that a public exists who could understand the writers' discoveries. For that reason Thomas Hardy's ruthless skepticism now seems quintessentially modern. This new attitude is quite clear in Ford Madox Ford's *The Good Soldier* (1915), the first installment of which was published in the inaugural issue of Wyndham Lewis's violently modern magazine *Blast*. John Dowell, the narrator/protagonist of Ford's novel, worries for 250 pages about his sense that the "givens" of civil society seem to have been knocked out from under him, and that he has been left to create values and meaning on his own. Struggling to extract the moral of the story he tells us—the story of his wife's long-standing affair with his best friend, and their consequent deaths—Dowell can only conclude: "I don't know. And there is nothing to guide us. And if everything is so nebulous about a matter so elementary as the morals of sex, what is there to guide us in the more subtle morality of all other personal contacts, associations, and activities? Or are we meant to act on impulse alone? It is all a darkness." In Conrad's *Heart of Darkness*, the narrator Charlie Marlow suffers from a similar moral vertigo. When, at the novella's close, he resolves to perform an action he finds deeply repugnant—to tell a lie—he worries that his willful violation of the moral order will provoke an immediate act of divine retribution. None, however, is forthcoming: "It seemed to me that the house would collapse before I could escape, that the heavens would fall upon my head. But nothing happened. The heavens do not fall for such a trifle." In works like these, a voyage is undertaken into a vast, unknown, dark expanse. Those few who come out alive have seen too much ever to be the same.

Similar perceptions underlie modern humor. The Theater of the Absurd that flourished in the 1950s and 1960s, in the work of playwrights like Samuel Beckett and Harold Pinter, had roots in Wilde and Shaw and their comic explorations of the arbitrary conventionality of long-held social values. Throughout the twentieth century, writers devoted themselves to unfolding many varieties of irony—from the severe ironies of Conrad and Yeats to the more tender ironies of Woolf and Auden, to the farcical absurdities of Tom Stoppard and Joe Orton. Joyce described his mixture of high and low comedy as "jocoserious"; asked the meaning of his dense book *Finnegans Wake*, he replied, "It's meant to make you laugh."

Whether seen in comic or tragic light, the sense of a loss of moorings was pervasive. Following the rapid social and intellectual changes of the previous century, the early twentieth century suffered its share of further concussions tending to heighten modern uncertainty. It was even becoming harder to understand the grounds of uncertainty itself. The critiques of Marx and Darwin had derived new messages from bodies of evidence available in principle to all literate citizens; the most important paradigm shifts of the early twentieth century, on the other hand, occurred in the fields of philosophy, psychology, and physics, and often rested on evidence invisible to the average citizen. The German philosopher Friedrich Nietzsche (1844–1900) was, as his dates suggest, wholly a nineteenth-century man, yet his ideas had their most profound impact in the twentieth century. Nietzsche described his lifelong philosophical project as "the revaluation of all values"; in his 1882 treatise *The Joyful Science*, he went so far as to assert that "God is dead." This deliberately provocative statement came as the culmination of a long and complicated argument, and did not mean simply that Nietzsche was an atheist (though he was). Nietzsche was suggesting that traditional religion had been discredited by advances in the natural and physical sciences, and as transcendent standards of truth disappeared, so logically must all moral and ethical systems depending on some faith for their force. It was from this base that Nietzsche created the idea of the *Übermensch*, the "superman" who because of his intellectual and moral superiority to others must not be bound by social conventions. Conrad's tragic figure Kurtz and Shaw's comic antihero Undershaft represent two very different takes on this idea, building on Nietzsche's interest in showing how all values are "constructed" rather than given—at some level arbitrary, all truths being merely opinions or superstitions.

The new psychology, whose earliest stirrings are to be found in the last decades of the nineteenth century, came of age at the turn of the twentieth. Sigmund Freud's *The Interpretation of Dreams* (1900) and *Psychopathology of Everyday Life* (1901) together illustrate in an especially vivid way his evolving theories about the influence of the unconscious mind, and past (especially childhood) experience, on our daily lives. The whole of Freud's work was translated into English by James Strachey (Lytton's brother), and was published in conjunction with the Hogarth Press, owned and run by Leonard and Virginia Woolf; for this reason, among others, the Freudian revolution was felt early, and strongly, among the London intelligentsia. The new psychology in general, and the theories of Freud in particular, were frequently distorted and misunderstood by the larger public, over whom they exercised a real fascination; among the artistic community Freud provoked a wide range of response, from the enthusiastic adoption of his theories by the Surrealists (a movement founded in Paris in 1924 by André Breton) to nervous rejection by writers like Joyce. This response is complicated, in part, by the fact that Freud himself took an interest in artistic and creative processes, and presumed to explain to writers the psychopathology at the heart of their own genius; as the Freudian literary critic Lionel Trilling succinctly put it, "the poet is a poet by reason of his sickness as well as by reason of his power." As Freud's supporter W. H. Auden wrote in his elegy *In Memory of Sigmund Freud* (1939): "If often he was wrong and at times absurd, / To us he is no more a person / Now but a whole climate of opinion / Under whom we conduct our different lives."

A further intellectual shock wave was the revolution in physics that was spearheaded by Albert Einstein's *Special Theory of Relativity* (1905). In both this theory (dealing with motion) and later in the General Theory of Relativity (dealing with gravity), Einstein shook the traditional understanding of the universe and our relationship to it; the certainty and predictability of the Newtonian description of the universe had been undone. The "uncertainty" of Einstein's universe was seemingly reinforced by developments in quantum physics, such as the work of Niels Bohr (who won the Nobel Prize in physics in 1922) and Werner Heisenberg, author of the famous "Uncertainty Principle" and the principle of complementarity, which together assert that the movement of subatomic particles can only be predicted by probability and not measured, as the very act of measurement alters their behavior. Ironically enough, the true import of these ideas is not, as the truism has it, that "everything is relative"—in fact, Einstein says almost the exact opposite. In Einstein's vision of the world, *nothing* is relative: everything is absolute, and absolutely fixed—except for us, fallible and limited observers, who have no secure standpoint from which "to see the thing as in itself it really is," to quote Matthew Arnold's 1867 formulation of the critic's goal. The only way to experience the truth, it would seem, would be to find what T. S. Eliot called "the still point of the turning world," an "unmoved mover" outside the flux and change of our day-to-day world. Einstein himself never really rejected the idea of transcendent truth; he once said to an interviewer that to him, the idea of our universe without a Creator was inconceivable. In this case, however, the popular fiction has been more influential than the facts, and the work of Einstein, Heisenberg, and Bohr has been used to support the widespread sense that, as Sean O'Casey's character Captain Jack Boyle puts it in *Juno and the Paycock* (1924), "the whole worl's in a state o' chassis!"

The philosophical and moral upheavals of these years were given added force by the profound shock of World War I—"The Great War," as it came to be known. The British entered the conflict against Germany partly in order to preserve their influence in Europe and their dominance around the globe, and partly out of altruistic notions of gallantry and fair play—to aid their weaker allies against German aggression. The conflict was supposed to take a few weeks; it lasted four grueling years and cost hundreds of thousands of British lives. Notions of British invincibility, honor, even of the viability of civilization all weakened over the years of vicious trench warfare in France. The progress of technology, which had raised Victorian standards of living, now led to a mechanization of warfare that produced horrific numbers of deaths—as many as a million soldiers died in the single protracted battle of the Somme in 1916. As poets discovered as they served in the trenches, and as the people back home came to learn, modernity had arrived with a vengeance.

REVOLUTIONS OF STYLE

The end of the war was accompanied by a sense of physical and moral exhaustion. To be modern has been defined as a persistent sense of having arrived on the stage of history after history has finished. The critic Perry Meisel, for instance, describes modernism as "a structure of compensation, a way of adjusting to the paradox of belatedness." Behind Ezra Pound's struggle to reinvent poetry lay a nagging suspicion that there was nothing new left to make or say, and Pound claimed that the very slogan "Make It New" was taken off the bathtub of an ancient Chinese emperor. As T. S. Eliot explains in his essay *Tradition and the Practice of Poetry*, "The perpetual task of poetry is to *make all things new*. Not necessarily to make new things. . . . It is always partly a revolution, or a reaction, from the work of the previous generation."

That revolution was carried out both on the level of subject matter and often on the level of style as well. Some important early twentieth-century fiction writers, like John Galsworthy, Arnold Bennett, H. G. Wells, and George Moore, felt no real need to depart from inherited narrative models, and hewed more or less to a realist or naturalist line, carrying on from the French naturalists like Emile Zola and the Norwegian dramatist Henrik Ibsen. But for those writers we now call modernist, these conventions came to seem too limiting and lifeless. The modern writer was faced with an enormous, Nietzschean task: to create new and appropriate values for modern culture, and a style appropriate to those values. As a consequence, there is often a probing, nervous quality in the modernist explorations of ultimate questions. This quality can be seen at the very start of the century in Conrad's *Heart of Darkness*, a novel about psychological depth and social disintegration that simultaneously implicates its readers in the moral ambiguities of its events. These ambiguities, moreover, are

Soldiers of the 9th Cameronians division prepare to go "over the top" during a daylight raid near Arras, France, 24 March 1917. During such an offensive, troops would make their way quickly across the contested territory between the opposing armies' trenches—the area known as No Man's Land—and attempt to take control of an enemy trench in order to conduct bombing raids and gain whatever intelligence might be found in the abandoned foxholes. The pace of this warfare—where a week's progress might be measured in yards, rather than miles—was, according to troops on both sides, the most salient feature of trench warfare. The human costs included diseases caused by standing water (like infamous "trench foot") and emotional disorders caused by the stress of waiting and constant shelling ("shell shock").

reflected in the very presentation of the narrative itself. In the modern novel, we are no longer allowed to watch from a safe distance while our protagonists mature and change through their trials; instead, we are made to undergo those trials ourselves, through the machinations of the narrative. This technique had already been employed in the nineteenth century, as for instance in the dramatic monologues of Robert Browning; but this narrative of process becomes pervasive in modernist texts, where the uncertainties of the form, the waverings and unpredictability of the narrative, mirror similar qualities in the mind of the narrator or protagonist. Often the reader is drawn into the story's crisis by a heightened use of the technique of plunging the narrative suddenly *in medias res:* "There was no hope for him this time: it was the third stroke" (Joyce, *The Sisters*); "A sudden blow:" (Yeats, *Leda and the Swan*); "'Yes, of course, if it's fine tomorrow,' said Mrs. Ramsay" (Woolf, *To the Lighthouse*). The customary preliminary information—the sort of dossier about the characters that we expect—isn't given; the reader is put in the position of a detective who has to sort all this information out unaided. This narrative decontextualization reaches its culmination in the theater of Beckett and Pinter, who typically withhold any and all background information about characters. "Confusion," Samuel Beckett told an interviewer in 1956, "is all around us and our only chance now is to let it in. The only chance of renovation is to open our eyes and see the mess. It is not a mess you can make sense of."

Early in the century, a number of poets began to dispense with the frames of reference provided by conventional poetic forms. The first real Anglo-American poetic movement of the century was Imagism, a reaction against the expansive wordiness of Victorian poetry like Tennyson's *Idylls of the King* or Browning's *The Ring and the Book*. Imagists like Pound and H. D. wrote short, spare poems embodying a revelatory image or moment. The most memorable Imagist poems have the concentrated impact of a haiku. But the form leaves little scope for narrative development; that path seems to have been opened by a rediscovery of the seventeenth-century metaphysical poets, notably by T. S. Eliot. The techniques of metaphysical poets like John Donne suggested to Eliot a means for expanding the technical repertory of Imagist poetry, which he used to good effect in poems like *The Love Song of J. Alfred Prufrock*, which opens with a thoroughly modernized metaphysical conceit: "Let us go then, you and I, / when the evening is spread out against the sky / Like a patient etherized upon a table."

One strategy for making literature new was to make it difficult; this notion was, in part, a response to the huge proliferation of popular entertainments during the early twentieth century, a proliferation that both disturbed and intrigued many artists, writers, and cultural critics. In such a context, "difficult" literature (such as the densely allusive poetry of Eliot, or the multilayered prose of Joyce) was seen to be of greater artistic merit than the products of an easily consumable mass culture—even as both Eliot and Joyce drew on popular culture and diction as they reshaped the norms of their literary art. Thus, while one of the primary targets of modernist renovation was Victorian literary manners, another was the complacent taste and sensibility of a large, and growing, middle class. Artists had been declaring the need to shock the bourgeoisie since time immemorial; Matthew Arnold worried publicly, and at length, about the dilution of a natural aristocracy of taste by the pseudoculture of newly educated British philistines, at the same time that he campaigned for greatly expanded public education. The Education Act of 1870 resulted in the explosive growth of elementary education, which meant that the reading class grew exponentially. Within the art world, the most obvious result of this anxiety was the "art for art's sake" movement associated with Walter Pater that began in the 1870s. Art was becoming its own material—as, for instance, in French artist Marcel Duchamp's mustache on the Mona Lisa.

In some ways modernist art and literature turned inward, becoming cannibalistic and self-referential. This is demonstrated well in Joyce's novel *A Portrait of the Artist as a Young Man,* whose protagonist is autobiographical in genesis yet critical in intent; the way Joyce accomplishes this is by moving Stephen Dedalus, his artist-protagonist, through various prose poses—writing now like Gustave Flaubert, now like Cardinal Newman, now like Pater. Stephen can only mimic—not create—a style; such is the situation of the modern writer, Joyce suggests, and his novel *Ulysses* dramatizes this by adopting a kaleidoscopic array of styles in its eighteen chapters. It thus becomes increasingly difficult to think of "style" as the achievement of an individual, and more and more it becomes the culmination of a cultural, national, ethnic project or history. As the French critic Roland Barthes has written, the text in the modern period becomes a "multidimensional space in which a variety of writings, none of them original, blend and clash," "a tissue of quotations drawn from innumerable centres of culture"—an apt and dramatic description of modernist texts like Eliot's *The Waste Land*, Joyce's *Ulysses*, and Pound's *Cantos*. To be textual is, during this period, to be intertextual and interdisciplinary as well.

The stylistic experimentation of modernist writers was fueled by the era's technological advances. From the mid-nineteenth century on, Britain had prided itself on its industrial strength and leadership; with the electrification of Britain at the turn of the century, however, the Industrial Revolution was gradually overtaken by a technological revolution. If the sinking of the Titanic on her maiden voyage in 1912 stands as a symbol of the vulnerability of progress—a sort of watery funeral for traditional British industry—the first transatlantic flight in 1919 pointed toward the future. Advances in photographic technology made documentary photographs a part of daily life and brought a heightened visual dimension to political campaigns and to advertising; the advent of quick and inexpensive newspaper photographs put vivid images of the carnage of World War I on Britain's breakfast tables. The texture and pace of daily life changed in the early years of the century to such a degree that average men and women were comfortable referring to themselves by that hopelessly awkward designation, "modern" (from the Latin *modo*, "just now"). And clearly, the London inhabited by the denizens of Eliot's *Waste Land* is a profoundly different place from the London of Dickens. Eliot portrays a woman who works in an office, composes letters on a typewriter, talks to clients on the telephone, plays records on the phonograph at her flat after having casual sex with a co-worker, and eats her evening meal from tins.

The advent of technology had far-reaching effects on the writing of the period. Beckett, famously, imagined a tape recorder before he had ever seen one in order to make possible the memory play of his *Krapp's Last Tape* (1959); more generally, the technology of the transistor radio, and government sponsorship of radio and television by the British Broadcasting Corporation, made possible wholly new literary genres. Beckett and Dylan Thomas were among the first to take advantage of the new media, writing plays for radio and then for television. A generation earlier, Joyce made use of early art film strategies in his "Circe" episode of *Ulysses*. In the most advanced writing of the modernist period we find an increasing sense that the technologies of print affect the text itself. Pound's *Cantos* were composed, not just transcribed, on a typewriter, and cannot be imagined in their current form composed with pen and ink; Joyce plays with the typographic conventions of newspaper headlines in the "Aeolus" chapter of *Ulysses* to create an ironic running commentary on the action. A crucial scene in Joyce's *Finnegans Wake* features a television broadcast (which was not available commercially when the novel was published), blending with a nuclear explosion (also several years before the fact). The scene culminates in "the abnihilisation of the etym"—both a destruction of atom/Adam/etym and its recovery *from* ("ab") nothingness.

MODERNISM AND THE MODERN CITY

Paralleling the new social and artistic opportunities of the twentieth century was a kind of anomie or alienation created by the rush towards industrialization. Vast numbers of human figures remained undifferentiated and the mass-manufactured hats and clothing worn by British industrial workers served only to heighten the monotony of their daily routines. Newspapers eagerly published photographs of thousands of sooty-faced miners. The members of the workforce, which Marx had called "alienated labor," were seen to be estranged not just from their work but from one another as well, as they themselves became mass products. This situation is dramatized especially vividly in the silent films of the period—from the dystopian vision of Fritz Lang's *Metropolis* (1926) to the more comic vision presented by the British-American Charlie Chaplin in *Modern Times* (1936). The sense of major cities being overrun by crowds of nameless human locusts recurs in the poetry of the period:

> A crowd flowed over London Bridge, so many,
> I had not thought death had undone so many.
> Sighs, short and infrequent, were exhaled,
> And each man fixed his eyes before his feet.
>
> (Eliot, *The Waste Land*)

> I have met them at close of day
> Coming with vivid faces
> From counter or desk among grey
> Eighteenth-century houses.
>
> (Yeats, *Easter 1916*)

The Victorian concern over huge numbers of urban poor was seconded by a fear of large numbers of restive urban lower-middle class workers and their families.

The critic Hugh Kenner has described modernism as both metropolitan and also international in character. While the bulk of Victorian British literary production is associated in some way or another with London, writing in the modern period is spread not just throughout England but throughout the Empire (and later the Commonwealth). To this day, London still serves as a spiritual and economic center of British writing, and many of the best British writers, regardless of their provenance, come to London at some point in their career. Modernist literary production was further stimulated by close cross-pollination between writers and other artists in other nations, and much of the most important writing in the modern "British" canon was undertaken in cities as far-flung as Dublin, Paris, Zurich, New York, and Johannesburg. Conversely, much of the important literature written in Britain itself during the twentieth century was produced by immigrants from abroad, from the Polish Joseph Conrad and the American Henry James at the start of the century to V. S. Naipaul, Salman Rushdie, and Hanif Kureishi in recent decades. As a result, the distinctions between "British" and "American" writing often blurred in this period of easy and relatively inexpensive transatlantic travel. Henry James based novels like *The American* and *Portrait of a Lady* on the adventures of Americans living in Europe; James himself was an American who lived most of the last thirty-five years of his life in London, and was naturalized as a British citizen three months before his death. T. S. Eliot moved to London in 1915 and lived there until his death in 1965, becoming a British subject, a communicant of the Church of England, and being knighted along the way. The great comic writer P. G. Wodehouse commuted back and forth across the Atlantic in the 1920s and 1930s as his plays and musical comedies were staged in New York and London. In many ways, New York and London had never been so close. This artistic diaspora has inevitably resulted in a richer, more complex and urbane literature.

PLOTTING THE SELF

The Freudian revolution grew from and reinforced an intense interest in the workings of the individual psyche, and modernists like Woolf and Joyce devoted themselves to capturing the mind's modulations. Both Woolf and Joyce employed versions of what came to be known as the "stream-of-consciousness" technique, in which fragmentary thoughts gradually build up a portrayal of characters' perceptions and of their unstated concerns. Consider this passage from the "interior monologue" of Joyce's protagonist Leopold Bloom, as he prepares a saucer of milk for his cat:

> They call them stupid. They understand what we say better than we understand them. She understands all she wants to. Vindictive too. Wonder what I look like to her. Height of a tower? No, she can jump me. . . . Cruel. Her nature. Curious mice never squeal. Seem to like it.

On the surface, Bloom's staccato thoughts reflect on the cat; at the same time, he identifies the cat with his unfaithful wife Molly, and—without admitting it to himself—he reflects on the cat's foreign psyche as a way of coming to terms with Molly's needs and desires. The development of stream-of-consciousness narrative grows out of a sense that the self is not "natural" or "given" but a construction—specifically a social construction—and that, consequently, traditional methods for depicting character no longer suffice. We are all the products of our own past and we are also, powerfully, products of larger social forces that shape the stories we tell about ourselves, and which others tell about us.

In the Victorian novel, plot crises were typically resolved in some definitive way, such as by a marriage or a change in the financial status of the protagonist. In the modern novel, lasting resolutions growing out of a common vision are few and far between. Walter Pater had counseled his readers, at the conclusion of *The Renaissance*, that "to burn always with a hard, gemlike flame, to maintain this ecstasy" was "success in life"; in the modern period, everyone wants that ecstasy, but no one is sure quite what it looks like amid the ruthless individualism of modern life. "We live as we dream, alone," Conrad's narrator Marlow mutters despondently; "Only connect," the epigraph to E. M. Forster's *Howards End* (1910) implores. On the eve of the London Blitz, however, the characters in Woolf's *Between the Acts* (still the most powerful British novel of World War II) are united only as they sing the refrain, "Dispersed are we." The texts of the modern period, bookended as they are by two world wars, represent a real, agonized meditation on how modern individuals can become united as community again. Woolf herself was skeptical of the possibility and her last novel remains unfinished—or finished only by her husband Leonard—because she took her own life before she could complete it. In the novels of Woolf and Joyce, and in the poetry of Yeats and Auden, community is the glimpsed prospect, the promised land: seen as a possibility but never realized, or embodied precariously in a gesture, a moment, a metaphor, and above all in art itself.

After the modernist high-water mark of the 1920s, the atmosphere darkened amid the international financial depression of the 1930s triggered by the U.S. stock market crash of 1929. The decade saw the growth of British Marxism and widespread labor agitation. The decade also witnessed the international growth of fascism and totalitarianism; writers like Shaw, Wyndham Lewis, Eliot, Yeats, Pound, and Lawrence for a time saw the order and stability promised by authoritarian governments as the only antidote to the "mere anarchy" Yeats decries in his poem *The Second Coming*. In the late thirties, however, intellectual sentiment turned increasingly against the fascist movements being led in Germany by Hitler, in Italy by Mussolini and in Spain by Franco. During Spain's brutal civil war (1936–1939), many writers supported the democratic Republicans against the ultimately victorious fascist General Franco. Meanwhile a series of weak British governments did little to oppose

Hitler's increasing belligerence and extremism; the failure to stand up for democratic principles, coupled with worldwide economic depression, led many young intellectuals and artists to became Leftists.

Compared to the stylistic experiments of the previous two decades, British writing of the 1930s sometimes looks rather flat, neutral. This can be attributed in part to the disillusionment that followed World War I, and the very real sense throughout the thirties that things were building up to another war, that art had become something of an irrelevancy. The German cultural critic Theodor Adorno was to write after the war, "no poetry after Auschwitz"; writers of the thirties seem to have had this sense well in advance of Auschwitz. Yeats admired the character in Auguste de Villiers de L'Isle-Adam's drama *Axël* who said, "As for living, we let the servants do that for us"; the young writers of the thirties, however, were concerned that (in Auden's phrase) "poetry makes nothing happen," and were committed to the idea that it must.

THE RETURN OF THE REPRESSED

Modern British literature is characterized by the increasing presence of women's voices, working-class voices, and voices expressing varied ethnic, religious, and sexual perspectives which, whether methodically or inadvertently, had often been excluded from the British literary tradition. The writings of an author like Woolf made England think hard about who she really was, as did, in another sense, the writings of the former colonial administrator George Orwell. In the modern period, Britain begins to deal in a fully conscious way with its human rights problems—most significantly, its treatment of women and the diverse ethnic groups of its colonial possessions.

The gradual enfranchisement and political and economic liberation of British women in the early years of the twentieth century comprised a fundamental social change; the novelist D. H. Lawrence, a rather equivocal friend of the women's movement, called it "perhaps the greatest revolution of modern times." The Women's Property Act—passed in 1882, the year of Woolf's birth—for the first time allowed married women to own property. Decades of sometimes violent suffragist agitation led finally to full voting rights for women in 1928 and to the gradual opening up of opportunities in higher education and the professions.

The quick pace of these changes naturally made many men uneasy. In their monumental three-volume study *No Man's Land: The Place of the Woman Writer in the Twentieth Century*, critics Sandra Gilbert and Susan Gubar suggest that this "war between the sexes" was one of the primary driving forces behind the modernist literary movement. Having emphasized the revolutionary force of the women's movement, Lawrence goes on to warn that the movement, "is even going beyond, and becoming a tyranny of woman, of the individual woman in the house, and of the feminine ideas and ideals in the world." In a half-serious essay titled *Cocksure Women and Hensure Men*, Lawrence complained of women "more cocky, in their assurance, than the cock himself. . . . It is really out of scheme, it is not in relation to the rest of things. . . . They find, so often, that instead of having laid an egg, they have laid a vote, or an empty ink-bottle, or some other absolutely unhatchable object, which means nothing to them." On the level of literary principles, a masculinist emphasis can be seen in Ezra Pound's insistence that modern poetry should "move against poppy-cock," "be harder and saner . . . 'nearer the bone' . . . as much like granite as it can be."

Other writers, male and female, supported women's rights; almost all writers sought to rebel against Victorian sexual norms and gender roles. Joyce battled with censors beginning in 1906, and his *Ulysses* was put on trial in New York on obscenity charges in 1933 (and cleared of those charges in the same week that the United States repealed Prohibition). Defending his sexual and scatological scenes, Joyce put the modernists' case for frankness this way: "The modern writer has other problems facing him, problems which are more intimate and unusual. We prefer to search in the corners for what has been hidden, and moods, atmospheres and intimate relationships are the modern writers' theme. . . . The modern theme is the subterranean forces, those hidden tides which govern everything and run humanity counter to the apparent flood: those poisonous subtleties which envelop the soul, the ascending fumes of sex." In defense of his "dirty" book *Lady Chatterley's Lover* (1928), whose full text was banned as obscene until 1960, Lawrence wrote: "In spite of all antagonism, I put forth this novel as an honest, healthy book, necessary for us today. . . . We are today, as human beings, evolved and cultured far beyond the taboos which are inherent in our culture. . . . The mind has an old groveling fear of the body and the body's potencies. It is the mind we have to liberate, to civilize on these points." In a rich irony, Joyce and Lawrence hated one another's writing: Joyce insisted on calling Lawrence's best-known novel "Lady Chatterbox's Lover," for he felt the characters talked too much. He dismissed the novel as "a piece of propaganda in favour of something which, outside of D. H. L.'s country at any rate, makes all the propaganda for itself." Lawrence, for his part, thought the last chapter of *Ulysses* (Molly Bloom's famous soliloquy) "the dirtiest, most indecent, obscene thing ever written."

Sexuality of all stripes was on trial. The lesbian writer Radclyffe Hall was tried for obscenity in 1928 for her novel *The Well of Loneliness*—whose most obscene sentence is, "That night they were not divided." The trial became a public spectacle, and was a rallying point for writers like Woolf and E. M. Forster, who spoke valiantly in favor of Hall's right to explore her subject, which was primarily the loneliness, rather than the fleshly joys, of same-sex love. Forster's overtly homosexual writings, including his novel *Maurice*, were not published until after his death in 1970. Woolf was somewhat more open in her novel *Orlando* (1928), whose protagonist changes sex from male to female. In Joyce's *Ulysses*, Leopold Bloom fantasizes about becoming a "new womanly man" and dreams of being chastised by a dominatrix who appears first as Bella and then as Bello Cohen. It was not only sexual taboos that were challenged in the writing of the period; in practice there began to be a loosening of the strict gender and sexual roles, which had been reinforced by the homophobia resulting from Oscar Wilde's trial for homosexual offenses in 1895. Gay, lesbian, and bisexual writers like Forster, Woolf, Hall, Stein, Natalie Barney, Djuna Barnes, H. D., Ronald Firbank, and Carl Van Vechten pushed the comfort level of the British reading public; even the "healthy" version of sexuality celebrated by D. H. Lawrence in his greatest novel *Women in Love* begins to suggest that heterosexuality and homosexuality are boundaries, not immutable categories.

The growing independence of the individual subject began to be matched by drives for independence among imperial subjects as well. In "John Bull's other island," as Bernard Shaw called Ireland in his play of that title, agitations for independence grew widespread from the late nineteenth century onward, culminating in the Easter Rising of 1916 and the 1922 partitioning of Ireland, when the Irish Republic became an independent nation while Northern Ireland remained part of Great Britain. No match for England militarily, the Irish used words as their chief weapon in the struggle for independence. Yeats and Joyce, among other writers, reflected on this war of words in such important works as Yeats's *Easter 1916* and Joyce's *Ivy Day in the Committee Room* and the "Aeolus" chapter from *Ulysses*.

The liberation of Britain's overseas colonial holdings began in the early decades of the century and gathered momentum thereafter. The history of Great Britain in the twentieth century is, in some ways, the story of the centrifugal forces that have largely stripped Britain of its colonial possessions. Britain suffered humiliating losses in the Boer War (1899–1902), fought by the British to take possession of the Boer Republic of South Africa. Half a million British troops were unable to win outright victory over eighty thousand Boers; finally the British adopted a scorched-earth policy that entailed massive arrests and the deaths of thousands of captives in unsanitary camps. This debilitating and unsavory conquest marked the low point of British imperialism, and public disgust led to a reaction against empire itself. Independence movements sprang up in colonies around the world, most notably in India, Britain's largest colony, "the jewel in the crown" of Queen Victoria, where Mohandas Gandhi's Congress Party struggled through nonviolent resistance to force Britain to grant its independence.

WORLD WAR II AND ITS AFTERMATH

The year 1939 and the start of World War II closed the modernist era. It was the year that saw the publication of Joyce's *Finnegans Wake*, which the critic Ihab Hassan calls a "monstrous prophecy" of postmodernity. The seminal modernist careers of Joyce, Woolf, Yeats, Ford, and Freud all came to an end—as did the social and political order of the previous decades. Throughout the late thirties, the government had engaged in futile efforts at diplomacy as Hitler expanded German control in central Europe. Prime Minister Neville Chamberlain finally denounced Hitler when the Germans invaded Czechoslovakia early in 1939; on September 1, Germany invaded Poland, and within days Britain declared war. In contrast to the "Great War," this conflict began with few illusions—but with the knowledge that Britain was facing an implacable and better-armed enemy. Unlike the Great War, fought on foreign soil, the new war hit home directly; during "the Blitz" from July 1940 through 1941, the German Luftwaffe carried out massive bombing raids on London and many other targets around Britain.

During these years, Winston Churchill emerged as a pivotal figure both strategically and morally. First as commander in chief of the navy, and starting in May 1940 as prime minister, he directed British military operations while rallying popular support through stirring speeches and radio addresses. The war had profound effects throughout British society, as almost every man—and many women—between the ages of 14 and 64 came to be involved in the war effort, in conditions that weakened old divisions of region and class and that provided the impetus for new levels of government involvement in social planning. At the war's end in September of 1945, Britain emerged victorious, in concert with its allies. In contrast with the United States, though, Britain had suffered enormous civilian casualties and crushing economic losses, both within Great Britain and throughout its far-flung colonies. As much as a quarter of Britain's national wealth had been consumed by the war. The great city of London had undergone horrific bombing during the the Blitz, whose attacks left the face of this world capital as scarred as had the Great Fire three centuries before. Although morally and socially triumphant in its defeat of Nazism and fascism, Britain was left shattered economically and exhausted spiritually. Its people had come through the war gallantly, only to face grim conditions at home and political unrest throughout the empire.

London during the Blitz, seen from the north transept of St. Paul's Cathedral.

The global effort of that war, whose battles were fought not only in Europe but in Africa, Asia, Latin America, the Middle East, and the Pacific, had forced Britain to draw massively on its colonies for raw materials, money, and soldiers. Since the resistance to the British empire had begun long before World War II, the drafting of millions of already restive colonial subjects into the armed forces intensified the tensions and the conflicts running beneath the surface of the empire. One of the most important political phenomena of the twentieth century was about to hit a depleted Britain with a vengeance: the decolonization of most of the conquered globe in the great wave of independence movements that swept the world after 1945. One by one, with greater and lesser degrees of violence and agony, colonies slipped out of Britain's imperial net. From the independence of India (1947) to the independence struggles of Kenya, Nigeria, Zaire, Palestine, Egypt, and many others, Britain experienced the accelerated loss of the largest empire in Western history. Retaining only a handful of Caribbean, Latin American, and Pacific Rim possessions, the empire had radically shrunk. India, Pakistan, Canada, Australia, and a few other countries adopted commonwealth status, remaining commercially linked but becoming essentially independent politically. The empire on which the sun never set was fast becoming largely confined to England, Scotland, Wales, and Northern Ireland—an ongoing area of tension and conflict to the present day.

   The dizzying pace of decolonization after the war put Britain in a paradoxically modern position ahead of many other Western countries: the unquestioned ability, and the rarely questioned right, of Western societies to dominate the globe had finally encountered decisive opposition. Within fifty years Britain found itself transformed from the dominant global power into a relatively small and, for a time, impoverished island nation, no longer a dictator of the world's history, but merely part of it. This dislocation was profoundly registered in British culture, and British writers strove to assess these losses—and to define the new possibilities for a freer and more open society that might emerge from the wreckage of empire.

A new generation of writers took on the task of evaluating English culture and the tradition of English literature itself from inside. John of Gaunt's beautiful paean to "this sceptered isle, this England," in Shakespeare's *Henry IV* had to be rewritten now: what was "this England" to be? In the absence of its colonial possessions, and in the general misery of shortages and rationing after the war, there was suddenly a sharp new scrutiny of British society. Its class-bound hierarchies appeared in an even harsher light, and its failures at home, in addition to its failure as an empire abroad, became the source of profound self-examination. Rage and anger accompanied this process of self-awareness, and a generation of literary artists dubbed the "angry young men" arose to meet the failures head-on, often in realist drama so faithful to its shabby subjects it was called "kitchen sink" drama, after the cold-water flat settings where the characters played out their rage. Playwrights such as John Osborne (as in the aptly titled *Look Back in Anger*) and novelists such as Anthony Burgess (*A Clockwork Orange*) angrily or satirically probed the discrepancy between England's glorious past and its seemingly squalid present.

A sense of diminishment in the world's eyes led to a passionate critique of British institutions, particularly its class structure, even where the literature produced was conservative in its looking backward. The extraordinary poet Philip Larkin might be seen as a key figure in this generation of writers. Larkin was a librarian in a rural town for most of his adult life. His poetry takes on the sardonic voice of the disenfranchised and the dispossessed—speaking not for the poor or the downtrodden but instead articulating the sense of loss and fury of middle and upper-class England, bereft of its historical prestige, impoverished by modern culture. He sings of nature, home, and country in a voice that is lacerating and self-mocking. Larkin's often jazzy and colloquial poetic diction, and his effective use of Anglo-Saxon expletives—he brought "fuck" into the opening of a major poem—offered a rebarbative retort to pastoral poetry. Larkin also wrote several notable novels at this time, among them *A Girl in Winter,* which explores from a surprisingly feminine and even feminist point of view the struggles of an emigré to Britain who must conceal the traumas her family experienced during the war, in order to "fit in" with a blithe and cavalier aristocratic British family. Larkin's artistry joins that of a host of other postwar writers, mostly male, who write from the center of an England now put off-kilter by the wrenching changes after the war.

Profound historical changes were to continue after the war with the commencement of the Cold War, in which the new world superpowers, the United States and the former Soviet Union, became locked in an intense battle for ideological, political, and economic dominance. Human beings now possessed the technological means to destroy the planet and its inhabitants, and these weapons of destruction were amassed by two societies with sharply conflicting goals. Britain along with Western Europe unequivocally aligned itself on the side of the United States, joining in the long fight against communism and Soviet socialism. While not itself a superpower, Britain had to shape its own social goals in light of the Cold War raging around it. A supremely eloquent voice in the articulation of what was at stake was that of the British writer George Orwell, known for his lucid essays on politics and language. Immediately after the war Orwell crafted *1984*, an enduring parable of Cold War culture. This book envisions a future society in the year 1984 when the infamous "Big

Brother" is watching everyone. That tale of a society of totalitarian surveillance was a thinly veiled allegory of the possibilities inherent not only in a Soviet takeover but even in Western societies and their implicit tendencies toward control and bureaucracy. It may be that Orwell was able to be prophetic about the cultural touchstones of the next several decades because as a British writer he wrote from an oblique angle: the colonial relationship of Britain to the United States had become reversed, with Britain almost becoming an outpost of the United States in terms of its Cold War dominance, reminiscent of Britain's dominance of the fate of the American colonies in the centuries leading up to the American Revolution. It is sometimes possible to see more clearly from a position outside the exact center—and Britain was, in this sense, no longer the center of English-speaking Western civilization. Strangely enough, that ex-centricity granted its literary writers a certain kind of insight.

The British novel after World War II made a retreat from modernist experimentalism. One explanation for a return to the realism that Woolf had so passionately argued against comes, paradoxically, from feminism of the very sort Woolf espouses in *A Room of One's Own* and *Three Guineas*. For as women began to write in large numbers, the novel with characters and a plot became a kind of room these writers needed to make their own. A host of important women writers emerged who revived the novel—which had been declared dead by the French, at least, around 1950—by using its traditions to incorporate their experiences as women, "making it new" not by formal experiments, but by opening that familiar, even a little shabby, room to new voices and new stories. Among the practitioners of this "feminist realism"— although some of them would vehemently deny the label "feminist"—are Jean Rhys, Doris Lessing, Margaret Drabble, A. S. Byatt, Muriel Spark, Iris Murdoch, Nadine Gordimer, and Buchi Emecheta. In every case these are writers who ring changes on ostensibly traditional forms.

Within England a host of dramatic luminaries gave vital energy to the British stage after 1945. While John Osborne created realist dramas of rage and dispossession, Harold Pinter emphasized the careful chiseling of language, bringing out the full ambiguity hidden in seemingly innocuous social conversation. In his meteoric but short dramatic career the playwright Joe Orton took a reverse tack to that of Pinterian ordinary language, and returned to the example of Oscar Wilde. Using a wildly baroque vocabulary and an epigrammatic wit, Orton brought an explicit gay drama and gay sensibility to the postwar theater, in works like *Loot*, which revolves around a seductive lower-class character who wreaks sexual havoc with all the inhabitants of a country estate, male and female, young and old. To very different comic effect, the Czech immigrant Tom Stoppard employs a brilliant rhetorical surface in his plays, which are often modernist puzzle boxes in their annihilation of the rules of time and space.

The most innovative of all British dramatists of the twentieth century after World War I was indubitably the Irishman Samuel Beckett. Living in a form of self-imposed exile in France, and a further self-imposed exile within the French language, Beckett moved from being the writer of mordant novels (*Molloy*; *Malone Dies*) to becoming an extraordinary dramatist. He often wrote his plays first in French, later translating them into English, so that English was their "secondary" language, leading to multiple puns in both English and French. Beckett's contribution to dramatic form, for which he received the Nobel Prize, is nonetheless a creation within British literature. Beckett sculpted his plays out of silence, paring down lines of dialogue until their short sentences and sometimes single words reverberate with the unspoken. Samuel Beckett, more than any other dramatist in English, found the pockets of silence in English speech, and made those silences speak. His characters do not inhabit a real place, like England, for example, but instead occupy an abstract space of human existence, where the human predicaments of longing and desire for redemption, the failures of understanding, and the bafflement of death are experienced in their purest form.

THE SIXTIES AND BEYOND

The impoverishment of the fifties abated in the sixties, at least for the middle class, as British banking and finance reinvigorated the economy. "Swinging London" became a household phrase, as British urban culture set the pace in music, fashion, and style. The Carnaby Street mode of dress and fashion mavens like Mary Quant, Jean Muir, and Zandra Rhodes were copied all over the world, worn by Jean Shrimpton and Twiggy, who were among the first supermodels. British film came out of a postwar slump and movies like *Morgan* and *Georgy Girl* had huge audiences at home and in the United States. A delirious excitement invested British popular culture, and London became a hub of the new once more. The critique of British society mounted by Joe Orton's work found its double in the youth culture of "Mods" and "Rockers." Asked which he was, the Beatles' drummer Ringo Starr claimed to synthesize both: "I'm a mocker."

Amid the cultural ferment of the sixties and seventies, successive British governments struggled with intractable problems of inflation and unemployment, punctuated by frequent strikes by Britain's powerful unions, and rising violence in Northern Ireland. The generally pro-union government of Harold Wilson (1964–1970) was followed by the Conservative government of Edward Heath, who put new stress on private enterprise. A major shift away from the "welfare state," however, came only at the end of the decade, when Heath was succeeded by the formidable Margaret Thatcher, the prime minister of Britain for a record twelve years. The daughter of a lower middle-class family, Thatcher vaulted into politics when that was an exceptionally rare opportunity not only for a woman, but for a person whose father was a shop-keeper. Trained as a chemist, Thatcher worked long and hard for the (Tory) Conservative Party, even as Britain was ruled by a succession of Labour and Socialist governments. When her chance came to lead England as its Tory prime minister, Thatcher and her political and ideological colleagues began a governmental revolution by adopting free-market policies similar to those identified with the Ronald Reagan school of U.S. Republicanism. Thatcher set about dismantling as much of the welfare state of postwar modern Britain as she could—and that was a considerable amount.

Margaret Thatcher had an enormous impact on British identity, as well as on British society. Among the very small number of women worldwide who have ever wielded such substantial political power—Golda Meir and Indira Gandhi come to mind as others—Thatcher's polished good looks, her extreme toughness, and her uncompromising political dictates combined to produce a caricature of her as the domineering English governness, laying down the rules of what would be good for Britain's unruly citizens. Thatcher's economic policies emphasized productivity as never before; under her rule, an entrepreneurial culture began to flourish at the expense of once-sacred British social entitlements, in education, health care, and civic subsidy of the arts and culture. Margaret Thatcher's most breathtaking quota-

The Beatles landing at Heathrow Airport, 29 October 1963.

tion, and the one summing up her philosophy of government, was uttered in response to complaints about what was happening to the fabric of British society and, especially, to its poor, elderly, immigrants, and the mass numbers of the unemployed. "There is no such thing as society," she declared. What she meant was that government had no role to play in creating a unitary, egalitarian society. The forces of the unleashed free market, and the will of private individuals, would replace any notion of a social contract or social compact between and among British citizens. There was irony, of course, in Thatcher's seeming to turn her back on members of her own class and those below it, and despite the power and immense reputation she acquired worldwide, there was always scathing and vocal opposition to her within Britain, as she privatized the universities and abolished tenure, made inroads on the National Health Service, dissolved city councils and established poll taxes. Prime Minister Thatcher declared and fought Britain's last imperial war of modern times, against Argentina over the control of the Falkland Islands, and she was fierce opponent of nationalist sentiment among the Scottish and the Welsh, a firm upholder of Britain's right to control Northern Ireland in perpetuity, and strongly against the move toward joining the European Community. Thatcher became an icon in Britain, as well as its longest-governing Prime Minister: an icon for her certainty, confidence, and her personification of the huge changes she brought about. Though she provoked sharp opposition, her brilliance and energy were never in question, nor was her international influence.

Equally large changes have occurred in the last several years of the twentieth century, however, changes sweeping enough to have diminished Margaret Thatcher's iconic stature, and to have partially reversed the social revolution she began. The historian Simon Schama points out, in an essay analyzing the British reaction to the death of Princess Diana in 1997, that the Thatcher era was simultaneous with the early Diana years. "For, by the time Charles Philip Arthur George and Diana Frances stepped out of the nave of Saint Paul's Cathedral into the sunlight and the cheers of millions, it was Margaret Thatcher who had annexed the idea of a revolutionized "new" Britain within her steely grip. This was to be a Britain in which the worst thing was not, as Diana would later say, 'to feel unloved' but to be unproductive." At the turn of the century, though, the Labour Party has reclaimed countrol of the country, changing course economically and emphasizing the very social contract Thatcher had set aside. Britain is an increasingly pivotal member of the European Community alliance, and its own internal divisions have come productively to the fore. Diana's vision of the need for society to take account for all those who are "unloved" within it can be said to have prevailed over the views of the now-titled Baroness Thatcher, productive in her retirement as a writer and political pundit, although in many ways now a prophet without honor—in the sense of followers—in her own land.

Surprisingly, the twentieth century is ending in much the same way as did the nineteenth century for Britain, with a nationwide debate on home rule. In 1886 and again in 1893 the eminent British prime minister William Gladstone fought for the establishment of a separte Irish parliament—thus the term "home rule"—to allow the Irish colony, with its differing religion of Roman Catholicism and its unique Gaelic culture, to have control over its own internal affairs. Gladstone and his Liberal Party formed an alliance with the Irish National Party's members of Parliament, who were led by the great Charles Steward Parnell, a Protestant Irishman known as "the uncrowned king of Ireland." Parnell's political fall due to an extramarital scandal removed a key player in Gladstone's strategy, and his final attempt in 1893 at voting in home rule failed. This failure led to the Irish revolution, the Irish Civil War, and the continuing violence within Northern Ireland, the six counties still belonging to Britain and occupied by their army.

Britain's new prime minister, Anthony Blair, was elected in 1997 from the Labour Party, breaking the Conservative Party's eighteen-year hold on the position, for twelve years of which the redoubtable Margaret Thatcher ruled, followed by her chosen successor, the rather low-key John Major. One of Blair's main campaign promises was bringing home rule to both Scotland and Wales, regions of Britain with their own language and dialect, their own cultural mores, and a long history of armed conflict with England. The referendum on the Scottish parliament, with the power to raise and lower income taxes within Scotland, and a considerable budget to operate as Scotland chooses, for its schools, health, housing and transport, overwhelmingly passed the popular vote, and is likely to be a reality by 1999; Wales has voted as well for the creation of a Welsh assembly with many of the same powers and responsibilities. While the Republic of Ireland is now a nation in its own right, Tony Blair's commitment to the peace talks in Northern Ireland, and to the inclusion of Sinn Fein in those talks, has also provided the first stirrings of political momentum in resolving the century-old conflict between Northern Irish Protestants who largely wish to remain attached to Britain, and the Northern Irish Catholics who have fought for the autonomy of this part of Ireland.

LANGUAGE AND IDENTITY

Complicated questions of language and identity have increasingly come to dominate the most recent phase of twentieth-century British literature. A great paradox of the British postwar period, in its time of imperial shrinkage, involves the fate of the English language. Britain may have been "kicked out" of many of its former colonies as a governing presence, but English was rarely shown the door at the same time. For economic and cultural reasons English as a global language became even more widely dispersed and dominant after World War II. Of course, the spread of U.S. interests has played a role in the hegemony of English. However, the old contours of the British empire continue to shape much of the production of English literature today. In this way, the former British empire has become part of the fabric of British literature. V. S. Naipaul, for example, has long resided in England, but he was born to Indian parents in Trinidad, where the British had deployed Indian labor. His writing is as much in dialog with the British literary tradition, and an extension of it, as that of any native-born British author.

Salman Rushdie, who is of Pakistani parentage, is another intriguing example of this process of crossing the increasingly porous boundaries of Britishness, as well as a cautionary tale of how powerful literature can be. Rushdie's novels are part of British literature at its modernist best, drawing on the entire English literary tradition, yet informed by a cosmopolitan and a non-Western literary tradition as well. Eight years after he achieved great acclaim for his novel *Midnight's Children* (1980), a book that adapted the "magic realism" of Latin American fiction to the history of Indian independence, Rushdie published *The Satanic Verses*. This novel recounts a magical mystery tour of sorts, the arrival of two South Asian refugees to modern London: one a film star from Bombay, the other a kind of trickster figure. Embedded in this complex tale of migration and identity is a brief dream sequence satirizing the prophet Mohammed. In response to this tiny dream-within-a-dream passage, the Iranian theocratic government delivered a *fatwa*—an edict sentencing Rushdie to death in absentia for treachery to the religion of Islam. Rushdie did not write the book in Arabic, nor did he write it for a Muslim audience, but that was irrelevant to the clerics who pronounced sentence on him before millions of devout adherents. From that time, Rushdie has been forced to live in a form of self-imposed house arrest, guarded by the British government. In an ironic twist, British literature itself has become his prison house of language, his internal exile. It is this tradition that "protects" him as a great writer, and, because of its porous literary borders, is responsible for his predicament. These issues and more underlie his striking story *Chekhov and Zulu*.

In recent years British literature has been infused with new life both from foreign-born writers and from new voices bubbling up from within the British Isles, in the shape of Welsh, Scottish, and Irish literary prose and poetry. The Nobel Prize–winning Irish poet Seamus Heaney is a kind of internal outsider, since, as he has written, he does not consider himself to be part of "British" literature as ordinarily defined, while he nonetheless writes English poetry deeply influenced by English poets from Milton to Wordsworth to Eliot. Some writers have deliberately taken themselves out of British literature for political and literary reasons, using the strongest means possible: they have decided to write in a language other than English. For example, the Kenyan writer Ngugi wa-Thiongo, educated by British missionaries and then at a British university, whose first memorized poem was Wordsworth's *Daffodils*, now writes in the Kikuyu language, and translates his work into English. The Irish poet Nuala Ní Dhomhnaill has made a similar decision: she writes and publishes her poetry first in Irish, and only later translates it into English as a "second" language.

In recent years British writing has been invigorated from "below," as well as from "outside": there has been a profusion of working-class or lower-middle-class novelists, poets, and screenwriters, many of whom adopt the dialect or argot of lower-class Welsh, Scottish, and Irish English. When James Kelman won the Booker Prize for the best novel published in England in 1994, there was widespread outrage: the working-class, expletive-laced speech of his Scottish protagonist was deemed unliterary by many, or at least unreadable and not in conformity with what was revered as the Queen's English. Poetry too has become a vehicle for a range of literary experiments, linking music and film to rhymed and unrhymed, and often performed, verse, connecting the popular and the literary. This upsurge of vivacious and often provocative writing is primarily the work of younger writers, and in many instances the novels are almost immediately being turned into films with international audiences.

In the past hundred years British literature has seen upheavals of aesthetic form, of geographic location, and of linguistic content. What is no longer in question, oddly enough, despite the current age of cyberspace and interactive media, is whether literature itself will survive. As Mark Twain once commented dryly after reading his own obituary in the newspaper: "The reports of my death are greatly exaggerated." The reports of literature's inevitable eclipse at the hands of media and mass culture have, it seems, been greatly exaggerated too. At this moment, British literary creativity is fed from many streams, welling up unpredictably, located in unexpected places. British literature has not merely survived; it remains a vital index of contemporary social and cultural life, and a crucial indication of the shape of things to come.

Joseph Conrad

1857–1924

One of the ironies of twentieth-century British literature is that many of its greatest writers were not conventionally "British." In the case of Joseph Conrad, arguably the first modern British writer, the irony is even more extreme, because Conrad was born a Pole, and learned English only when he was in his twenties. The transformation of Josef Konrad Nalecz Korzeniowski into "Joseph Conrad" is as fascinating and mysterious a story as the transforming journeys at the heart of his fiction.

Joseph Conrad was a lifelong exile from a country that no longer existed on the map of Europe as a separate country. At the time of Conrad's birth in 1857, Poland was divided between Russia and the Austro-Hungarian empire. His parents, Apollo and Eva, were Polish patriots, and after an uprising against Russia in 1863, the family was exiled to a village in the far north of Russia. Eva died when Josef was seven years old; Apollo when he was twelve. Apollo had been both a political activist and a man of letters, a poet and a translator of French and English literature into Polish. In a sense, by becoming a British novelist writing in English, Conrad was carrying on a project of translation begun by his father, a translation across cultures and literatures as well as languages. Hidden within Conrad's poetic and impressionistic literary language is a secret language—Polish—and a secret history of exile from his homeland.

After Conrad's parents died, he was raised by a cosmopolitan uncle, Tadeusz Bobrowski, who was also imbued with patriotic political leanings and a deep love of literature. Josef was sent to school in Cracow, Poland, where he was bored and restless. His uncle then sent him to Switzerland with a private tutor; they argued constantly for a year, and the tutor resigned. Not quite seventeen years old, Conrad proceeded to Marseilles and joined the French merchant navy. He spent twenty years as a sailor and as a ship's captain, spending four years sailing under the French flag, and then sixteen years with British trading ships. In 1894 Josef Korzeniowski completed his transformation into the writer Joseph Conrad by changing his name and settling in England to become a full-time writer.

By the end of the nineteenth century, the nationalistic wars that had led to a divided Poland had been followed by another historical phenomenon: the dividing-up of the globe by the nations of Europe as these powers consolidated empires. The oceans were crucial pathways in these struggles, not simply vast, watery landscapes outside of history. The seafaring Conrad, who had wanted to leave the frustrations of school behind him and see the world, became intimately involved in the everyday business of the making of empires, playing a minor role behind the scenes of the major political forces of the age. Merchant ships of the kind he served on traced the routes of trade and commerce, which now had become the routes of colonization and political conquest as well. As he came to realize he was an eyewitness to modern history in the making, Joseph Conrad discovered his abiding subject as a writer.

Conrad's voyages during this twenty-year odyssey took him East and West, to Indonesia and the Philippines, to Venezuela, the West Indies, and Africa. Working all the while, he watched as bit by bit the patchwork quilt of empire was put together. Wishing to avoid conscription in the French navy when he came of age, in 1878 Conrad joined the British merchant navy. The British empire had become the most extensive and mighty of any imperial power, and in his capacity as seaman Conrad worked in the main ports of call of the empire upon which the sun supposedly never set. He adopted British citizenship in 1886; after his uncle Tadeusz's death in 1894, Conrad made the final decision to become a writer, and to write in English rather than in French. At the age of thirty-seven, Joseph Conrad was newly born.

As a British writer, Conrad was a sort of ventriloquist. On the surface, he was as English as any other writer in his circle: he married an Englishwoman, Jessie George, and became a recognized part of British literary life, forming friendships with other major writers like Henry James and Ford Madox Ford, and achieving great popularity with the British reading public. A stranger from an exotically foreign place, by British standards, a newcomer to the English language, he nonetheless spoke through an English "voice" he created. From his distanced perspective, he was able to make English do things it had not done in the past for native writers of English. Language in Conrad's writing is always a bit off kilter, reading as if it had been translated instead of being, as it was, originally written in English. His prose has a hallucinatory effect, and a poetic intensity linked to his approaching the words of the English language afresh. The most famous of Conrad's narrators is the character Marlow, who appears in several of his major works as an elusive commentator on the action. His Englishness is as real as it can be, for an imitation. Marlow is perhaps even more British than the British, lapsing often into British slang like "By Jove!" as if to authenticate the reality of Conrad's vision of the British world. Through narrative voices like that of Marlow, Conrad can tell stories that may appear to be familiar and ordinary but are in fact anything but that. If modernist writers succeed in making us doubt that we can truly be at home in the world, Conrad can be said to have been the first writer to convey this homelessness in English.

There is another paradox at the heart of Joseph Conrad's work. His writing straddles the nineteenth and the twentieth centuries, with the five major works he wrote in the years before 1900—*Almayer's Folly*, *The Nigger of the "Narcissus,"* *Heart of Darkness*, *Lord Jim*, and *Typhoon*—thought of by many critics as more modernist and experimental than later novels he wrote in the twentieth century—*Nostromo*, *The Secret Agent*, *Under Western Eyes*, *Chance*, and *Victory*. The critic Ian Watt claims that the "intense experimentation which began in 1896 and ended in 1900" resulted from Conrad's concentration in those five earlier works on his own personal experience, a personal experience of travel, exile, and solitude that was a radical premonition of the conditions of modernity. Works like *Heart of Darkness*, written during Queen Victoria's reign, for Watt present "the obdurate incompatibility of the self and the world in which it exists." In book after book, he sets a lone individual into confrontation with the complexities of the modern world, whether the world be that of European imperialism, or political anarchism, or the secret world of spies, or the world of political revolution. His heroes and (much less often) heroines have to find their bearings as society crumbles around them, and Conrad usually depicts them at a moment of choice, when they have to act on their lonely knowledge without any guarantee that they have chosen rightly.

A reliance on personal experience might seem to be a recipe for a straightforward, realist style, but Conrad's prose throughout his work is complex and symbolic, relying on images that are spun into complicated and ambiguous webs of symbolism. What stands out prominently in Conrad's style is its visual nature, the emphasis on making the reader "see." Critcs of Conrad's writing early on seized on the strikingly visual aspect of his effects, and his friend and fellow modernist writer Ford Madox Ford wrote an essay in 1913, *On Impressionism*, which put Conrad in a newly invented camp of impressionist writers. Conrad never fully agreed with this description of his style, nor did he have any special fondness for impressionist painting or the works of its greatest practitioners, Manet and Cézanne. Nonetheless, his own preface to *The Nigger of the "Narcissus"* describes all successful art as based on "an impression conveyed through the senses," and in each of his first five books narrators recount what they have *seen*. The narrator goes back over an experience in retelling it to an audience, an experience whose significance is not necessarily clear even to the narrator but whose meaning is revealed through the accumulation of imagistic details. The powers of sight are directly related to the powers of insight, or self-knowledge. A famous passage from *Heart of Darkness* explains the storytelling technique of the narrator Marlow, but also explains a philosophical conviction at the core of Conrad's writing: "The yarns of seamen have a direct simplicity, the whole meaning of which lies within the shell of a cracked nut. But Marlow was not typical (if his propensity to spin yarns be excepted), and to him the meaning of an episode was not inside like a kernel but outside, enveloping the tale which brought it out only as a glow brings out a haze, in the likeness of one of these misty halos that are sometimes made visible by the spectral illumination of moonshine." Events cast a visual glow and haze where meaning can be found only in the most subtle shades and ambiguous highlights of language. The reader must participate in the gradual, and partial, process of accumulating meaning.

Heart of Darkness is a work at the heart of modern British literature. First published serially in *Blackwood's Magazine* in 1899, it was reprinted as a complete work along with a companion novella, *Youth*, in 1902, and writers have returned to it again and again, in the form of quotations and allusions and imitations of its style; its story has been rewritten by each successive generation, in novels, films like *Apocalypse Now*, and even rock lyrics. Almost mythic in resonance, *Heart of Darkness* itself is structured around a mythical core—that is, the hero's quest. The journey or quest motif pervades world literature and English literature alike, from the *Odyssey* and the *Epic of Gilgamesh* to Dante's *Divine Comedy*, Bunyan's *Pilgrim's Progress*, and Byron's *Childe Harold*. *Heart of Darkness* condenses in its pages an epic range of theme and experience, both the social themes of empire and cultural clash, and the personal theme of the hero's quest for self-discovery.

As with all his early work, Conrad based *Heart of Darkness* on his own experience, in this case a trip he took up the Congo River in 1890 in order to become captain of a small steamship. The trip was an unusual one even by Conrad's standards, as he had been sailing the major oceans of the world on large ships. Conrad had reasons for choosing the assignment, however; he had been fascinated by maps since boyhood, and the blank space on the continent of Africa represented by the then-unexplored interior impelled him on. He was curious to see for himself the scandalous imperial practices of the Belgian King Leopold II in the Congo, who possessed what he called the Congo Free State (now Zaire) as his own private property, draining it of raw materials like ivory, while claiming to be suppressing savagery and spreading European civilization. After traveling two hundred miles upriver to Kinshasa to join his ship, however, he found it was undergoing repairs. He traveled as a passenger on a trip to Stanley Falls, to bring back an ailing company agent, Georges Klein, who died on the return trip to Kinshasa. These events provided the germ of Conrad's novella, which transformed Klein ("Little," in German) into the uncanny figure of Kurtz.

A diary Conrad kept during his journey (excerpted as a Companion Reading following *Heart of Darkness*) records his dawning awareness that King Leopold's policy in the Congo was nothing other than slave labor, ultimately causing the deaths of more than a million Africans. Initially an observer, Conrad became a passionately informed partisan, and made known his findings in the form of journalism and essays in the attempt to halt the King's genocidal policies. *Heart of Darkness* records these evils, and the ravages of Belgian colonialism on the African tribal societies it encountered and uprooted. Scholars of African history have shown how accurate his descriptions are, from the bit of white thread worn around the neck of a certain tribal group, to the construction of the railroad to Kinshasa and its devastating human impact. Conrad never names the Congo, nor the places and landmarks his character Marlow visits, yet he himself later called the book a "Kodak," or a snapshot, of the Congo.

The location is left unnamed in part because Conrad wishes to show that the heart of this darkness can shift on its axis. Marlow is telling the tale to several anonymous Englishmen as they sail the Thames on their yacht. Under the Roman empire, Britain had itself been thought of as a savage wilderness, a dark continent. The journey upriver, as Marlow points out, has been a reverse journey as well, a journey back from Africa to the darkness that lies at the heart of an England that claims to be civilizing those whom it is merely conquering. The seemingly clear-cut boundaries of light and dark, black and white, have blurred and even reversed themselves, and the nested narrative of the story itself challenges our understanding and even our sense of self. In this narrative, as in Conrad's other works, we are confronted with the tragic irony that human knowledge always comes too late.

Preface to *The Nigger of the "Narcissus"*[1]

A work that aspires, however humbly, to the condition of art should carry its justification in every line. And art itself may be defined as a single-minded attempt to render the highest kind of justice to the visible universe, by bringing to light the truth, manifold and one, underlying its every aspect. It is an attempt to find in its forms, in its colours, in its light, in its shadows, in the aspects of matter, and in the facts of life what of each is fundamental, what is enduring and essential—their one illuminating and convincing quality—the very truth of their existence. The artist, then, like the thinker or the scientist, seeks the truth and makes his appeal. Impressed by the aspect of the world the thinker plunges into ideas, the scientist into facts—whence, presently, emerging they make their appeal to those qualities of our being that fit us best for the hazardous enterprise of living. They speak authoritatively to our common sense, to our intelligence, to our desire of peace, or to our desire of unrest; not seldom to our prejudices, sometimes to our fears, often to our egoism—but always to our credulity. And their words are heard with reverence, for their concern is with weighty matters: with the cultivation of our minds and the proper care of our bodies, with the attainment of our ambitions, with the perfection of the means and the glorification of our precious aims.

It is otherwise with the artist.

Confronted by the same enigmatical spectacle the artist descends within himself, and in that lonely region of stress and strife, if he be deserving and fortunate, he finds the terms of his appeal. His appeal is made to our less obvious capacities: to that part of our nature which, because of the warlike conditions of existence, is necessarily kept out of sight within the more resisting and hard qualities—like the vulnerable body within a steel armour. His appeal is less loud, more profound, less distinct, more stirring—and sooner forgotten. Yet its effect endures for ever. The changing wisdom of successive generations discards ideas, questions facts, demolishes theories. But the artist appeals to that part of our being which is not dependent on wisdom; to that in us which is a gift and not an acquisition—and, therefore, more permanently enduring. He speaks to our capacity for delight and wonder, to the sense of mystery surrounding our lives; to our sense of pity, and beauty, and pain; to the latent feeling of fellowship with all creation—and to the subtle but invincible conviction of solidarity that knits together the loneliness of innumerable hearts, to the solidarity in dreams, in joy, in sorrow, in aspirations, in illusions, in hope, in fear, which binds men to each other, which binds together all humanity—the dead to the living and the living to the unborn.

It is only some such train of thought, or rather of feeling, that can in a measure explain the aim of the attempt, made in the tale which follows, to present an unrestful episode in the obscure lives of a few individuals out of all the disregarded multitude of the bewildered, the simple, and the voiceless. For, if any part of truth dwells in the belief confessed above, it becomes evident that there is not a place of splendour or a dark corner of the earth that does not deserve, if only a passing glance of wonder and pity. The motive, then, may be held to justify the matter of the work; but this preface, which is simply an avowal of endeavour, cannot end here—for the avowal is not yet complete.

---

1. Conrad's novella *The Nigger of the "Narcissus"* deals with the tragic death of a black seaman aboard a merchant ship named the *Narcissus*; Conrad had served as first mate on a ship of that name in the Indian Ocean in 1883. He published the novella in *The New Review* in 1897, then added this preface when it came out in book form in 1898.

Fiction—if it at all aspires to be art—appeals to temperament. And in truth it must be, like painting, like music, like all art, the appeal of one temperament to all the other innumerable temperaments whose subtle and resistless power endows passing events with their true meaning, and creates the moral, the emotional atmosphere of the place and time. Such an appeal to be effective must be an impression conveyed through the senses; and, in fact, it cannot be made in any other way, because temperament, whether individual or collective, is not amenable to persuasion. All art, therefore, appeals primarily to the senses, and the artistic aim when expressing itself in written words must also make its appeal through the senses, if its high desire is to reach the secret spring of responsive emotions. It must strenuously aspire to the plasticity of sculpture, to the colour of painting, and to the magic suggestiveness of music—which is the art of arts. And it is only through complete, unswerving devotion to the perfect blending of form and substance; it is only through an unremitting never-discouraged care for the shape and ring of sentences that an approach can be made to plasticity, to colour, and that the light of magic suggestiveness may be brought to play for an evanescent instant over the commonplace surface of words: of the old, old words, worn thin, defaced by ages of careless usage.

The sincere endeavour to accomplish that creative task, to go as far on that road as his strength will carry him, to go undeterred by faltering, weariness, or reproach, is the only valid justification for the worker in prose. And if his conscience is clear, his answer to those who, in the fullness of a wisdom which looks for immediate profit, demand specifically to be edified, consoled, amused; who demand to be promptly improved, or encouraged, or frightened, or shocked, or charmed, must run thus: My task which I am trying to achieve is, by the power of the written word to make you hear, to make you feel—it is, before all, to make you see. That—and no more, and it is everything. If I succeed, you shall find there according to your deserts: encouragement, consolation, fear, charm—all you demand—and, perhaps, also that glimpse of truth for which you have forgotten to ask.

To snatch in a moment of courage, from the remorseless rush of time, a passing phase of life, is only the beginning of the task. The task approached in tenderness and faith is to hold up unquestioningly, without choice and without fear, the rescued fragment before all eyes in the light of a sincere mood. It is to show its vibration, its colour, its form; and through its movement, its form, and its colour, reveal the substance of its truth—disclose its inspiring secret: the stress and passion within the core of each convincing moment. In a single-minded attempt of that kind, if one be deserving and fortunate, one may perchance attain to such clearness of sincerity that at last the presented vision of regret or pity, of terror or mirth, shall awaken in the hearts of the beholders that feeling of unavoidable solidarity; of the solidarity in mysterious origin, in toil, in joy, in hope, in uncertain fate, which binds men to each other and all mankind to the visible world.

It is evident that he who, rightly or wrongly, holds by the convictions expressed above cannot be faithful to any one of the temporary formulas of his craft. The enduring part of them—the truth which each only imperfectly veils—should abide with him as the most precious of his possessions, but they all: Realism, Romanticism, Naturalism, even the unofficial sentimentalism (which, like the poor, is exceedingly difficult to get rid of), all these gods must, after a short period of fellowship, abandon him—even on the very threshold of the temple—to the stammerings of his conscience and to the outspoken consciousness of the difficulties of his work. In that uneasy solitude the supreme cry of Art for Art itself, loses the exciting ring of its apparent immorality. It sounds far off. It has ceased to be a cry, and is heard only as a whisper, often incomprehensible, but at times and faintly encouraging.

Sometimes, stretched at ease in the shade of a roadside tree, we watch the motions of a labourer in a distant field, and after a time, begin to wonder languidly as to what the fellow may be at. We watch the movements of his body, the waving of his arms, we see him bend down, stand up, hesitate, begin again. It may add to the charm of an idle hour to be told the purpose of his exertions. If we know he is trying to lift a stone, to dig a ditch, to uproot a stump, we look with a more real interest at his efforts; we are disposed to condone the jar of his agitation upon the restfulness of the landscape; and even, if in a brotherly frame of mind, we may bring ourselves to forgive his failure. We understood his object, and, after all, the fellow has tried, and perhaps he had not the strength—and perhaps he had not the knowledge. We forgive, go on our way—and forget.

And so it is with the workman of art. Art is long and life is short, and success is very far off. And thus, doubtful of strength to travel so far, we talk a little about the aim—the aim of art, which, like life itself, is inspiring, difficult—obscured by mists. It is not in the clear logic of a triumphant conclusion; it is not in the unveiling of one of those heartless secrets which are called the Laws of Nature. It is not less great, but only more difficult.

To arrest, for the space of a breath, the hands busy about the work of the earth, and compel men entranced by the sight of distant goals to glance for a moment at the surrounding vision of form and colour, of sunshine and shadows; to make them pause for a look, for a sigh, for a smile—such is the aim, difficult and evanescent, and reserved only for a very few to achieve. But sometimes, by the deserving and the fortunate, even that task is accomplished. And when it is accomplished—behold!—all the truth of life is there: a moment of vision, a sigh, a smile—and the return to an eternal rest.

Heart of Darkness

1

The *Nellie*, a cruising yawl,[1] swung to her anchor without a flutter of the sails, and was at rest. The flood had made, the wind was nearly calm, and being bound down the river, the only thing for it was to come to and wait for the turn of the tide.

The sea-reach of the Thames stretched before us like the beginning of an interminable waterway. In the offing the sea and the sky were welded together without a joint, and in the luminous space the tanned sails of the barges drifting up with the tide seemed to stand still in red clusters of canvas sharply peaked, with gleams of varnished sprits. A haze rested on the low shores that ran out to sea in vanishing flatness. The air was dark above Gravesend, and farther back still seemed condensed into a mournful gloom, brooding motionless over the biggest, and the greatest, town on earth.[2]

The Director of Companies was our captain and our host. We four affectionately watched his back as he stood in the bows looking to seaward. On the whole river there was nothing that looked half so nautical. He resembled a pilot, which to a seaman is trustworthiness personified. It was difficult to realise his work was not out there in the luminous estuary, but behind him, within the brooding gloom.

---

1. A two-masted ship.   2. London. Gravesend is the last major town on the Thames estuary, from which the river joins the North Sea.

Between us there was, as I have already said somewhere, the bond of the sea. Besides holding our hearts together through long periods of separation, it had the effect of making us tolerant of each other's yarns—and even convictions. The Lawyer—the best of old fellows—had, because of his many years and many virtues, the only cushion on deck, and was lying on the only rug. The Accountant had brought out already a box of dominoes, and was toying architecturally with the bones. Marlow sat cross-legged right aft, leaning against the mizzen-mast.[3] He had sunken cheeks, a yellow complexion, a straight back, an ascetic aspect, and, with his arms dropped, the palms of hands outwards, resembled an idol. The Director, satisfied the anchor had good hold, made his way aft and sat down amongst us. We exchanged a few words lazily. Afterwards there was silence on board the yacht. For some reason or other we did not begin that game of dominoes. We felt meditative, and fit for nothing but placid staring. The day was ending in a serenity of still and exquisite brilliance. The water shone pacifically; the sky, without a speck, was a benign immensity of unstained light; the very mist on the Essex marshes was like a gauzy and radiant fabric, hung from the wooded rises inland, and draping the low shores in diaphanous folds. Only the gloom to the west, brooding over the upper reaches, became more sombre every minute, as if angered by the approach of the sun.

And at last, in its curved and imperceptible fall, the sun sank low, and from glowing white changed to a dull red without rays and without heat, as if about to go out suddenly, stricken to death by the touch of that gloom brooding over a crowd of men.

Forthwith a change came over the waters, and the serenity became less brilliant but more profound. The old river in its broad reach rested unruffled at the decline of day, after ages of good service done to the race that peopled its banks, spread out in the tranquil dignity of a waterway leading to the uttermost ends of the earth. We looked at the venerable stream not in the vivid flush of a short day that comes and departs for ever, but in the august light of abiding memories. And indeed nothing is easier for a man who has, as the phrase goes, "followed the sea" with reverence and affection, than to evoke the great spirit of the past upon the lower reaches of the Thames. The tidal current runs to and fro in its unceasing service, crowded with memories of men and ships it has borne to the rest of home or to the battles of the sea. It had known and served all the men of whom the nation is proud, from Sir Francis Drake to Sir John Franklin, knights all, titled and untitled—the great knights-errant of the sea.[4] It had borne all the ships whose names are like jewels flashing in the night of time, from the *Golden Hind* returning with her round flanks full of treasure, to be visited by the Queen's Highness and thus pass out of the gigantic tale, to the *Erebus* and *Terror*, bound on other conquests—and that never returned. It had known the ships and the men. They had sailed from Deptford, from Greenwich, from Erith—the adventurers and the settlers; kings' ships and the ships of men on 'Change; captains, admirals, the dark "interlopers" of the Eastern trade, and the commissioned "generals" of East India fleets.[5] Hunters for gold or pursuers of fame, they all had gone out on that stream, bearing the sword, and often the torch, messengers

3. A secondary mast at the stern of the ship.

4. Sir Francis Drake (1540–1596) was captain of *The Golden Hind* in the service of Queen Elizabeth I; his reputation came from the successful raids he mounted against Spanish ships returning laden with gold from the New World (South America). In 1845 Sir John Franklin led an expedition in the *Erebus* and *Terror* in search of the Northwest Passage (to the Pacific); all perished.

5. Deptford, Greenwich, and Erith lie on the Thames between London and Gravesend; "men on 'Change" are brokers on the Stock Exchange; the East India Company, a commercial and trading concern, became *de facto* ruler of large tracts of India in the 18th and 19th centuries.

of the might within the land, bearers of a spark from the sacred fire. What greatness had not floated on the ebb of that river into the mystery of an unknown earth! . . . The dreams of men, the seed of commonwealths, the germs of empires.

The sun set; the dusk fell on the stream, and lights began to appear along the shore. The Chapman lighthouse, a three-legged thing erect on a mudflat, shone strongly. Lights of ships moved in the fairway—a great stir of lights going up and going down. And farther west on the upper reaches the place of the monstrous town was still marked ominously on the sky, a brooding gloom in sunshine, a lurid glare under the stars.

"And this also," said Marlow suddenly, "has been one of the dark places of the earth."

He was the only man of us who still "followed the sea." The worst that could be said of him was that he did not represent his class. He was a seaman, but he was a wanderer too, while most seamen lead, if one may so express it, a sedentary life. Their minds are of the stay-at-home order, and their home is always with them—the ship; and so is their country—the sea. One ship is very much like another, and the sea is always the same. In the immutability of their surroundings the foreign shores, the foreign faces, the changing immensity of life, glide past, veiled not by a sense of mystery but by a slightly disdainful ignorance; for there is nothing mysterious to a seaman unless it be the sea itself, which is the mistress of his existence and as inscrutable as Destiny. For the rest, after his hours of work, a casual stroll or a casual spree on shore suffices to unfold for him the secret of a whole continent, and generally he finds the secret not worth knowing. The yarns of seamen have a direct simplicity, the whole meaning of which lies within the shell of a cracked nut. But Marlow was not typical (if his propensity to spin yarns be excepted), and to him the meaning of an episode was not inside like a kernel but outside, enveloping the tale which brought it out only as a glow brings out a haze, in the likeness of one of these misty halos that sometimes are made visible by the spectral illumination of moonshine.

His remark did not seem at all surprising. It was just like Marlow. It was accepted in silence. No one took the trouble to grunt even; and presently he said, very slow,—

"I was thinking of very old times, when the Romans first came here, nineteen hundred years ago[6]—the other day. . . . Light came out of this river since—you say Knights? Yes; but it is like a running blaze on a plain, like a flash of lightning in the clouds. We live in the flicker—may it last as long as the old earth keeps rolling! But darkness was here yesterday. Imagine the feelings of a commander of a fine—what d'ye call 'em?—trireme in the Mediterranean, ordered suddenly to the north; run overland across the Gauls in a hurry;[7] put in charge of one of these craft the legionaries,—a wonderful lot of handy men they must have been too—used to build, apparently by the hundred, in a month or two, if we may believe what we read. Imagine him here—the very end of the world, a sea the colour of lead, a sky the colour of smoke, a kind of ship about as rigid as a concertina—and going up this river with stores, or orders, or what you like. Sandbanks, marshes, forests, savages,—precious little to eat fit for a civilised man, nothing but Thames water to drink. No Falernian wine here, no going ashore. Here and there a military camp lost in a wilderness, like a needle in a bundle of hay—cold, fog, tempests, disease, exile, and death,—death skulking in the air, in the water, in the bush. They must have been dying like flies

---

6. A Roman force under Julius Caesar landed in Britain in 55 B.C., but it was not until A.D. 43 that the Emperor Claudius decided to conquer the island.
7. A *trireme* is an ancient warship, propelled by oarsmen;
the Gauls were the pre-Roman tribes who occupied present-day France; they were subdued by Julius Caesar between 58–50 B.C.

here. Oh yes—he did it. Did it very well, too, no doubt, and without thinking much about it either, except afterwards to brag of what he had gone through in his time, perhaps. They were men enough to face the darkness. And perhaps he was cheered by keeping his eye on a chance of promotion to the fleet at Ravenna by-and-by, if he had good friends in Rome and survived the awful climate. Or think of a decent young citizen in a toga—perhaps too much dice, you know—coming out here in the train of some prefect, or tax-gatherer, or trader even, to mend his fortunes. Land in a swamp, march through the woods, and in some inland post feel the savagery, the utter savagery, had closed round him,—all that mysterious life of the wilderness that stirs in the forest, in the jungles, in the hearts of wild men. There's no initiation either into such mysteries. He has to live in the midst of the incomprehensible, which is also detestable. And it has a fascination, too, that goes to work upon him. The fascination of the abomination—you know. Imagine the growing regrets, the longing to escape, the powerless disgust, the surrender, the hate."

He paused.

"Mind," he began again, lifting one arm from the elbow, the palm of the hand outwards, so that, with his legs folded before him, he had the pose of a Buddha preaching in European clothes and without a lotus-flower—"Mind, none of us would feel exactly like this. What saves us is efficiency—the devotion to efficiency. But these chaps were not much account, really. They were no colonists; their administration was merely a squeeze, and nothing more, I suspect. They were conquerors, and for that you want only brute force—nothing to boast of, when you have it, since your strength is just an accident arising from the weakness of others. They grabbed what they could get for the sake of what was to be got. It was just robbery with violence, aggravated murder on a great scale, and men going at it blind—as is very proper for those who tackle a darkness. The conquest of the earth, which mostly means the taking it away from those who have a different complexion or slightly flatter noses than ourselves, is not a pretty thing when you look into it too much. What redeems it is the idea only. An idea at the back of it; not a sentimental pretence but an idea; and an unselfish belief in the idea—something you can set up, and bow down before, and offer a sacrifice to . . . ."

He broke off. Flames glided in the river, small green flames, red flames, white flames, pursuing, overtaking, joining, crossing each other—then separating slowly or hastily. The traffic of the great city went on in the deepening night upon the sleepless river. We looked on, waiting patiently—there was nothing else to do till the end of the flood; but it was only after a long silence, when he said, in a hesitating voice, "I suppose you fellows remember I did once turn fresh-water sailor for a bit," that we knew we were fated, before the ebb began to run, to hear about one of Marlow's inconclusive experiences.

"I don't want to bother you much with what happened to me personally," he began, showing in this remark the weakness of many tellers of tales who seem so often unaware of what their audience would best like to hear; "yet to understand the effect of it on me you ought to know how I got out there, what I saw, how I went up that river to the place where I first met the poor chap. It was the farthest point of navigation and the culminating point of my experience. It seemed somehow to throw a kind of light on everything about me—and into my thoughts. It was sombre enough too—and pitiful—not extraordinary in any way—not very clear either. No, not very clear. And yet it seemed to throw a kind of light.

"I had then, as you remember, just returned to London after a lot of Indian Ocean, Pacific, China Seas—a regular dose of the East—six years or so, and I was loafing about, hindering you fellows in your work and invading your homes, just as though I had got a heavenly mission to civilise you. It was very fine for a time, but after a bit I did get tired of resting. Then I began to look for a ship—I should think the hardest work on earth. But the ships wouldn't even look at me. And I got tired of that game too.

"Now when I was a little chap I had a passion for maps. I would look for hours at South America, or Africa, or Australia, and lose myself in all the glories of exploration. At that time there were many blank spaces on the earth, and when I saw one that looked particularly inviting on a map (but they all look that) I would put my finger on it and say, When I grow up I will go there. The North Pole was one of these places, I remember. Well, I haven't been there yet, and shall not try now. The glamour's off. Other places were scattered about the Equator, and in every sort of latitude all over the two hemispheres. I have been in some of them, and . . . well, we won't talk about that. But there was one yet—the biggest, the most blank, so to speak— that I had a hankering after.

"True, by this time it was not a blank space any more. It had got filled since my boyhood with rivers and lakes and names. It had ceased to be a blank space of delightful mystery—a white patch for a boy to dream gloriously over. It had become a place of darkness. But there was in it one river especially, a mighty big river, that you could see on the map, resembling an immense snake uncoiled, with its head in the sea, its body at rest curving afar over a vast country, and its tail lost in the depths of the land. And as I looked at the map of it in a shop-window, it fascinated me as a snake would a bird—a silly little bird. Then I remembered there was a big concern, a Company for trade on that river. Dash it all! I thought to myself, they can't trade without using some kind of craft on that lot of fresh water—steamboats! Why shouldn't I try to get charge of one. I went on along Fleet Street, but could not shake off the idea. The snake had charmed me.

"You understand it was a Continental concern, that Trading Society; but I have a lot of relations living on the Continent, because it's cheap and not so nasty as it looks, they say.

"I am sorry to own I began to worry them. This was already a fresh departure for me. I was not used to get things that way, you know. I always went my own road and on my own legs where I had a mind to go. I wouldn't have believed it of myself; but, then—you see—I felt somehow I must get there by hook or by crook. So I worried them. The men said 'My dear fellow,' and did nothing. Then—would you believe it?—I tried the women. I, Charlie Marlow, set the women to work—to get a job. Heavens! Well, you see, the notion drove me. I had an aunt, a dear enthusiastic soul. She wrote: 'It will be delightful. I am ready to do anything, anything for you. It is a glorious idea. I know the wife of a very high personage in the Administration, and also a man who has lots of influence with,' &c., &c. She was determined to make no end of fuss to get me appointed skipper of a river steamboat, if such was my fancy.

"I got my appointment—of course; and I got it very quick. It appears the Company had received news that one of their captains had been killed in a scuffle with the natives. This was my chance, and it made me the more anxious to go. It was only months and months afterwards, when I made the attempt to recover what was left of the body, that I heard the original quarrel arose from a misunderstanding about some hens. Yes, two black hens. Fresleven—that was the fellow's name, a Dane—thought himself wronged somehow in the bargain, so he went ashore and started to hammer the chief of the village with a stick. Oh, it didn't surprise me in the least to hear this, and at the same time to be told that Fresleven was the gentlest, quietest creature that ever walked on two legs. No doubt he was; but he had been a couple of years already out there engaged in the noble cause, you know, and he probably felt the need at last of asserting his self-respect in some way. Therefore he whacked the old nigger mercilessly, while a big crowd of his people watched him, thunderstruck, till some man,—I was told the chief's son,—in desperation at hearing the old chap yell, made a tentative jab with a spear at the white man—and of course it went quite easy between the shoulder-blades. Then the whole population cleared into the forest, expecting all kinds of calamities to happen, while, on the other hand, the steamer Fresleven commanded left also in a bad panic, in charge of the engineer, I believe. Afterwards nobody seemed to trouble much about Fresleven's remains, till I got out and stepped into his shoes. I couldn't let it rest, though; but when an opportunity offered at last to meet my predecessor, the grass growing through his ribs was tall enough to hide his bones. They were all there. The supernatural being had not been touched after he fell. And the village was deserted, the huts gaped black, rotting, all askew within the fallen enclosures. A calamity had come to it, sure enough. The people had vanished. Mad terror had scattered them, men, women, and children, through the bush, and they had never returned. What became of the hens I don't know either. I should think the cause of progress got them, anyhow. However, through this glorious affair I got my appointment, before I had fairly begun to hope for it.

"I flew around like mad to get ready, and before forty-eight hours I was crossing the Channel to show myself to my employers, and sign the contract. In a very few hours I arrived in a city that always makes me think of a whited sepulchre.[8] Prejudice no doubt. I had no difficulty in finding the Company's offices. It was the biggest thing in the town, and everybody I met was full of it. They were going to run an oversea empire, and make no end of coin by trade.

"A narrow and deserted street in deep shadow, high houses, innumerable windows with venetian blinds, a dead silence, grass sprouting between the stones, imposing carriage archways right and left, immense double doors standing ponderously ajar. I slipped through one of these cracks, went up a swept and ungarnished staircase, as arid as a desert, and opened the first door I came to. Two women, one fat and the other slim, sat on straw-bottomed chairs, knitting black wool. The slim one got up and walked straight at me—still knitting with downcast eyes—and only just as I began to think of getting out of her way, as you would for a somnambulist, stood still, and looked up. Her dress was as plain as an umbrella-cover, and she turned round without a word and preceded me into a waiting-room. I gave my name, and looked about. Deal table in the middle, plain chairs all round the walls, on one end a large shining map, marked with all the colours of a rainbow. There was a vast amount of red—good to see at any time, because one knows that some real work is done in there, a deuce of a lot of blue, a little green, smears of orange, and, on the East Coast, a purple patch, to show where the jolly pioneers of progress drink the jolly lager-beer.[9] However, I wasn't going into any of these. I was going into the yellow. Dead in the centre. And the river was there—fascinating—deadly—like a snake. Ough! A door opened, a white-haired secretarial head, but wearing a compassionate expression, appeared, and a skinny forefinger beckoned me into the sanctuary. Its light was dim, and a heavy writing-desk squatted in the middle. From behind that structure

8. Brussels was the headquarters of the Société Anonyme Belge pour le Commerce du Haut-Congo (Belgian Corporation for Trade in the Upper Congo), with which Conrad obtained his post through the influence of his aunt, Marguerite Poradowska.

9. British territories were traditionally marked in red on colonial maps; lager was originally a continental beer, not much drunk in England.

came out an impression of pale plumpness in a frock-coat. The great man himself. He was five feet six, I should judge, and had his grip on the handle-end of ever so many millions. He shook hands, I fancy, murmured vaguely, was satisfied with my French. *Bon voyage*.

"In about forty-five seconds I found myself again in the waiting-room with the compassionate secretary, who, full of desolation and sympathy, made me sign some document. I believe I undertook amongst other things not to disclose any trade secrets. Well, I am not going to.

"I began to feel slightly uneasy. You know I am not used to such ceremonies, and there was something ominous in the atmosphere. It was just as though I had been let into some conspiracy—I don't know—something not quite right; and I was glad to get out. In the outer room the two women knitted black wool feverishly. People were arriving, and the younger one was walking back and forth introducing them. The old one sat on her chair. Her flat cloth slippers were propped up on a foot-warmer, and a cat reposed on her lap. She wore a starched white affair on her head, had a wart on one cheek, and silver-rimmed spectacles hung on the tip of her nose. She glanced at me above the glasses. The swift and indifferent placidity of that look troubled me. Two youths with foolish and cheery countenances were being piloted over, and she threw at them the same quick glance of unconcerned wisdom. She seemed to know all about them and about me too. An eerie feeling came over me. She seemed uncanny and fateful. Often far away there I thought of these two, guarding the door of Darkness, knitting black wool as for a warm pall, one introducing, introducing continuously to the unknown, the other scrutinising the cheery and foolish faces with unconcerned old eyes. *Ave!* Old knitter of black wool. *Morituri te salutant.*[1] Not many of those she looked at ever saw her again—not half, by a long way.

"There was yet a visit to the doctor. 'A simple formality,' assured me the secretary, with an air of taking an immense part in all my sorrows. Accordingly a young chap wearing his hat over the left eyebrow, some clerk I suppose,—there must have been clerks in the business, though the house was as still as a house in a city of the dead,—came from somewhere upstairs, and led me forth. He was shabby and careless, with ink-stains on the sleeves of his jacket, and his cravat was large and billowy, under a chin shaped like the toe of an old boot. It was a little too early for the doctor, so I proposed a drink, and thereupon he developed a vein of joviality. As we sat over our vermouths he glorified the Company's business, and by-and-by I expressed casually my surprise at him not going out there. He became very cool and collected all at once. 'I am not such a fool as I look, quoth Plato to his disciples,' he said sententiously, emptied his glass with great resolution, and we rose.

"The old doctor felt my pulse, evidently thinking of something else the while. 'Good, good for there,' he mumbled, and then with a certain eagerness asked me whether I would let him measure my head. Rather surprised, I said Yes, when he produced a thing like calipers and got the dimensions back and front and every way, taking notes carefully. He was an unshaven little man in a threadbare coat like a gaberdine, with his feet in slippers, and I thought him a harmless fool. 'I always ask leave, in the interests of science, to measure the crania of those going out there,' he said. 'And when they come back too?' I asked. 'Oh, I never see them,' he remarked; 'and moreover, the changes take place inside, you know.' He smiled, as if at some quiet joke. 'So you are going out there. Famous. Interesting too.' He gave me a searching glance, and made another note. 'Ever any madness in your family?' he asked, in a

---

1. Hail! . . . Those who are about to die salute you!—traditional cry of Roman gladiators.

matter-of-fact tone. I felt very annoyed. 'Is that question in the interests of science too?' 'It would be,' he said, without taking notice of my irritation, 'interesting for science to watch the mental changes of individuals, on the spot, but . . .' 'Are you an alienist?'[2] I interrupted. 'Every doctor should be—a little,' answered that original, imperturbably. 'I have a little theory which you Messieurs who go out there must help me to prove. This is my share in the advantages my country shall reap from the possession of such a magnificent dependency. The mere wealth I leave to others. Pardon my questions, but you are the first Englishman coming under my observation . . .' I hastened to assure him I was not in the least typical. 'If I were,' said I, 'I wouldn't be talking like this with you.' 'What you say is rather profound, and probably erroneous,' he said, with a laugh. 'Avoid irritation more than exposure to the sun. Adieu. How do you English say, eh? Good-bye. Ah! Good-bye. Adieu. In the tropics one must before everything keep calm.' . . . He lifted a warning forefinger. . . . '*Du calme, du calme. Adieu.*'

"One thing more remained to do—say good-bye to my excellent aunt. I found her triumphant. I had a cup of tea—the last decent cup of tea for many days—and in a room that most soothingly looked just as you would expect a lady's drawing-room to look, we had a long quiet chat by the fireside. In the course of these confidences it became quite plain to me I had been represented to the wife of the high dignitary, and goodness knows to how many more people besides, as an exceptional and gifted creature—a piece of good fortune for the Company—a man you don't get hold of every day. Good heavens! and I was going to take charge of a twopenny-half-penny river-steamboat with a penny whistle attached! It appeared, however, I was also one of the Workers, with a capital—you know. Something like an emissary of light, something like a lower sort of apostle. There had been a lot of such rot let loose in print and talk just about that time, and the excellent woman, living right in the rush of all that humbug, got carried off her feet. She talked about 'weaning those ignorant millions from their horrid ways,' till, upon my word, she made me quite uncomfortable. I ventured to hint that the Company was run for profit.

"'You forget, dear Charlie, that the labourer is worthy of his hire,' she said, brightly.[3] It's queer how out of touch with truth women are. They live in a world of their own, and there had never been anything like it, and never can be. It is too beautiful altogether, and if they were to set it up it would go to pieces before the first sunset. Some confounded fact we men have been living contentedly with ever since the day of creation would start up and knock the whole thing over.

"After this I got embraced, told to wear flannel, be sure to write often, and so on—and I left. In the street—I don't know why—a queer feeling came to me that I was an impostor. Odd thing that I, who used to clear out for any part of the world at twenty-four hours' notice, with less thought than most men give to the crossing of a street, had a moment—I won't say of hesitation, but of startled pause, before this commonplace affair. The best way I can explain it to you is by saying that, for a second or two, I felt as though, instead of going to the centre of a continent, I were about to set off for the centre of the earth.

"I left in a French steamer, and she called in every blamed port they have out there, for, as far as I could see, the sole purpose of landing soldiers and custom-house officers. I watched the coast. Watching a coast as it slips by the ship is like thinking about an enigma. There it is before you—smiling, frowning, inviting, grand, mean, insipid, or savage, and always mute with an air of whispering, Come and find out.

2. A psychologist.   3. 1 Timothy 5.18.

This one was almost featureless, as if still in the making, with an aspect of monotonous grimness. The edge of a colossal jungle, so dark-green as to be almost black, fringed with white surf, ran straight, like a ruled line, far, far away along a blue sea whose glitter was blurred by a creeping mist. The sun was fierce, the land seemed to glisten and drip with steam. Here and there greyish-whitish specks showed up, clustered inside the white surf, with a flag flying above them perhaps—settlements some centuries old, and still no bigger than pin-heads on the untouched expanse of their background. We pounded along, stopped, landed soldiers; went on, landed custom-house clerks to levy toll in what looked like a Godforsaken wilderness, with a tin shed and a flag-pole lost in it; landed more soldiers—to take care of the custom-house clerks, presumably. Some, I heard, got drowned in the surf; but whether they did or not, nobody seemed particularly to care. They were just flung out there, and on we went. Every day the coast looked the same, as though we had not moved; but we passed various places—trading places—with names like Gran' Bassam, Little Popo,[4] names that seemed to belong to some sordid farce acted in front of a sinister back-cloth. The idleness of a passenger, my isolation amongst all these men with whom I had no point of contact, the oily and languid sea, the uniform sombreness of the coast, seemed to keep me away from the truth of things, within the toil of a mournful and senseless delusion. The voice of the surf heard now and then was a positive pleasure, like the speech of a brother. It was something natural, that had its reason, that had a meaning. Now and then a boat from the shore gave one a momentary contact with reality. It was paddled by black fellows. You could see from afar the white of their eyeballs glistening. They shouted, sang; their bodies streamed with perspiration; they had faces like grotesque masks—these chaps; but they had bone, muscle, a wild vitality, an intense energy of movement, that was as natural and true as the surf along their coast. They wanted no excuse for being there. They were a great comfort to look at. For a time I would feel I belonged still to a world of straightforward facts; but the feeling would not last long. Something would turn up to scare it away. Once, I remember, we came upon a man-of-war anchored off the coast. There wasn't even a shed there, and she was shelling the bush. It appears the French had one of their wars going on thereabouts. Her ensign dropped limp like a rag; the muzzles of the long eight-inch guns stuck out all over the low hull; the greasy, slimy swell swung her up lazily and let her down, swaying her thin masts. In the empty immensity of earth, sky, and water, there she was, incomprehensible, firing into a continent. Pop, would go one of the eight-inch guns; a small flame would dart and vanish, a little white smoke would disappear, a tiny projectile would give a feeble screech—and nothing happened. Nothing could happen. There was a touch of insanity in the proceeding, a sense of lugubrious drollery in the sight; and it was not dissipated by somebody on board assuring me earnestly there was a camp of natives—he called them enemies!—hidden out of sight somewhere.

"We gave her letters (I heard the men in that lonely ship were dying of fever at the rate of three a day) and went on. We called at some more places with farcical names, where the merry dance of death and trade goes on in a still and earthy atmosphere as of an overheated catacomb;[5] all along the formless coast bordered by danger-

4. Grand Bassam and Grand Popo are the names of ports where Conrad's ship called on its way to the Congo.
5. In a letter in May 1890 Conrad wrote: "What makes me rather uneasy is the information that 60 per cent. of our Company's employés return to Europe before they have completed even six months' service. Fever and dysentery! There are others who are sent home in a hurry at the end of a year, so that they shouldn't die in the Congo." According to a 1907 report, 150 out of every 2,000 native Congolese laborers died each month while in company employ; "All along the [railroad] track one would see corpses."

ous surf, as if Nature herself had tried to ward off intruders; in and out of rivers, streams of death in life, whose banks were rotting into mud, whose waters, thickened into slime, invaded the contorted mangroves, that seemed to writhe at us in the extremity of an impotent despair. Nowhere did we stop long enough to get a particularised impression, but the general sense of vague and oppressive wonder grew upon me. It was like a weary pilgrimage amongst hints for nightmares.

"It was upward of thirty days before I saw the mouth of the big river. We anchored off the seat of the government. But my work would not begin till some two hundred miles farther on. So as soon as I could I made a start for a place thirty miles higher up.

"I had my passage on a little sea-going steamer. Her captain was a Swede, and knowing me for a seaman, invited me on the bridge. He was a young man, lean, fair, and morose, with lanky hair and a shuffling gait. As we left the miserable little wharf, he tossed his head contemptuously at the shore. 'Been living there?' he asked. I said, 'Yes.' 'Fine lot these government chaps—are they not?' he went on, speaking English with great precision and considerable bitterness. 'It is funny what some people will do for a few francs a month. I wonder what becomes of that kind when it goes up country?' I said to him I expected to see that soon. 'So-o-o!' he exclaimed. He shuffled athwart, keeping one eye ahead vigilantly. 'Don't be too sure,' he continued. 'The other day I took up a man who hanged himself on the road. He was a Swede, too.' 'Hanged himself! Why, in God's name?' I cried. He kept on looking out watchfully. 'Who knows? The sun too much for him, or the country perhaps.'

"At last we opened a reach. A rocky cliff appeared, mounds of turned-up earth by the shore, houses on a hill, others, with iron roofs, amongst a waste of excavations, or hanging to the declivity. A continuous noise of the rapids above hovered over this scene of inhabited devastation. A lot of people, mostly black and naked, moved about like ants. A jetty projected into the river. A blinding sunlight drowned all this at times in a sudden recrudescence of glare. 'There's your Company's station,' said the Swede, pointing to three wooden barrack-like structures on the rocky slope. 'I will send your things up. Four boxes did you say? So. Farewell.'

"I came upon a boiler wallowing in the grass, then found a path leading up the hill. It turned aside for the boulders, and also for an undersized railway-truck lying there on its back with its wheels in the air. One was off. The thing looked as dead as the carcass of some animal. I came upon more pieces of decaying machinery, a stack of rusty rails. To the left a clump of trees made a shady spot, where dark things seemed to stir feebly. I blinked, the path was steep. A horn tooted to the right, and I saw the black people run. A heavy and dull detonation shook the ground, a puff of smoke came out of the cliff, and that was all. No change appeared on the face of the rock. They were building a railway. The cliff was not in the way or anything; but this objectless blasting was all the work going on.

"A slight clinking behind me made me turn my head. Six black men advanced in a file, toiling up the path. They walked erect and slow, balancing small baskets full of earth on their heads, and the clink kept time with their footsteps. Black rags were wound round their loins, and the short ends behind wagged to and fro like tails. I could see every rib, the joints of their limbs were like knots in a rope; each had an iron collar on his neck, and all were connected together with a chain whose bights swung between them, rhythmically clinking. Another report from the cliff made me think suddenly of that ship of war I had seen firing into a continent. It was the same kind of ominous voice; but these men could by no stretch of imagination be called enemies. They were called criminals, and the outraged law, like the bursting shells, had come to them, an insoluble mystery from over the sea. All their meagre breasts panted together, the violently dilated nostrils quivered, the eyes stared stonily up-hill. They passed me within six inches, without a glance, with that complete, death-like indifference of unhappy savages. Behind this raw matter one of the reclaimed, the product of the new forces at work, strolled despondently, carrying a rifle by its middle. He had a uniform jacket with one button off, and seeing a white man on the path, hoisted his weapon to his shoulder with alacrity. This was simple prudence, white men being so much alike at a distance that he could not tell who I might be. He was speedily reassured, and with a large, white, rascally grin, and a glance at his charge, seemed to take me into partnership in his exalted trust. After all, I also was a part of the great cause of these high and just proceedings.

"Instead of going up, I turned and descended to the left. My idea was to let that chain-gang get out of sight before I climbed the hill. You know I am not particularly tender; I've had to strike and to fend off. I've had to resist and to attack sometimes—that's only one way of resisting—without counting the exact cost, according to the demands of such sort of life as I had blundered into. I've seen the devil of violence, and the devil of greed, and the devil of hot desire; but, by all the stars! these were strong, lusty, red-eyed devils, that swayed and drove men—men, I tell you. But as I stood on this hillside, I foresaw that in the blinding sunshine of that land I would become acquainted with a flabby, pretending, weak-eyed devil of a rapacious and pitiless folly. How insidious he could be, too, I was only to find out several months later and a thousand miles farther. For a moment I stood appalled, as though by a warning. Finally I descended the hill, obliquely, towards the trees I had seen.

"I avoided a vast artificial hole somebody had been digging on the slope, the purpose of which I found it impossible to divine. It wasn't a quarry or a sandpit, anyhow. It was just a hole. It might have been connected with the philanthropic desire of giving the criminals something to do. I don't know. Then I nearly fell into a very narrow ravine, almost no more than a scar in the hillside. I discovered that a lot of imported drainage-pipes for the settlement had been tumbled in there. There wasn't one that was not broken. It was a wanton smash-up. At last I got under the trees. My purpose was to stroll into the shade for a moment; but no sooner within than it seemed to me I had stepped into the gloomy circle of some Inferno. The rapids were near, and an uninterrupted, uniform, headlong, rushing noise filled the mournful stillness of the grove, where not a breath stirred, not a leaf moved, with a mysterious sound—as though the tearing pace of the launched earth had suddenly become audible.

"Black shapes crouched, lay, sat between the trees, leaning against the trunks, clinging to the earth, half coming out, half effaced within the dim light, in all the attitudes of pain, abandonment, and despair. Another mine on the cliff went off, fol-lowed by a slight shudder of the soil under my feet. The work was going on. The work! And this was the place where some of the helpers had withdrawn to die.

"They were dying slowly—it was very clear. They were not enemies, they were not criminals, they were nothing earthly now,—nothing but black shadows of disease and starvation, lying confusedly in the greenish gloom. Brought from all the recesses of the coast in all the legality of time contracts, lost in uncongenial surroundings, fed on unfamiliar food, they sickened, became inefficient, and were then allowed to crawl away and rest. These moribund shapes were free as air—and nearly as thin. I began to distinguish the gleam of eyes under the trees. Then, glancing down, I saw a face near my hand. The black bones reclined at full length with one shoulder against the tree, and slowly the eyelids rose and the sunken eyes looked up at me, enormous and vacant, a kind of blind, white flicker in the depths of the orbs, which died out slowly. The man seemed young—almost a boy—but you know with them it's hard to tell. I found nothing else to do but to offer him one of my good Swede's ship's biscuits I had in my pocket. The fingers closed slowly on it and held—there was no other movement and no other glance. He had tied a bit of white worsted round his neck—Why? Where did he get it? Was it a badge—an ornament—a charm—a propitiatory act? Was there any idea at all connected with it? It looked startling round his black neck, this bit of white thread from beyond the seas.

"Near the same tree two more bundles of acute angles sat with their legs drawn up. One, with his chin propped on his knees, stared at nothing, in an intolerable and appalling manner: his brother phantom rested its forehead, as if overcome with a great weariness; and all about others were scattered in every pose of contorted collapse, as in some picture of a massacre or a pestilence. While I stood horror-struck, one of these creatures rose to his hands and knees, and went off on all-fours towards the river to drink. He lapped out of his hand, then sat up in the sunlight, crossing his shins in front of him, and after a time let his woolly head fall on his breastbone.

"I didn't want any more loitering in the shade, and I made haste towards the station. When near the buildings I met a white man, in such an unexpected elegance of get-up that in the first moment I took him for a sort of vision. I saw a high starched collar, white cuffs, a light alpaca jacket, snowy trousers, a clear silk necktie, and varnished boots. No hat. Hair parted, brushed, oiled, under a green-lined parasol held in a big white hand. He was amazing, and had a penholder behind his ear.

"I shook hands with this miracle, and I learned he was the Company's chief accountant, and that all the book-keeping was done at this station. He had come out for a moment, he said, 'to get a breath of fresh air.' The expression sounded wonderfully odd, with its suggestion of sedentary desk-life. I wouldn't have mentioned the fellow to you at all, only it was from his lips that I first heard the name of the man who is so indissolubly connected with the memories of that time. Moreover, I respected the fellow. Yes; I respected his collars, his vast cuffs, his brushed hair. His appearance was certainly that of a hairdresser's dummy; but in the great demoralisation of the land he kept up his appearance. That's backbone. His starched collars and got-up shirt-fronts were achievements of character. He had been out nearly three years; and, later on, I could not help asking him how he managed to sport such linen. He had just the faintest blush, and said modestly, 'I've been teaching one of the native women about the station. It was difficult. She had a distaste for the work.' Thus this man had verily accomplished something. And he was devoted to his books, which were in apple-pie order.

"Everything else in the station was in a muddle,—heads, things, buildings. Strings of dusty niggers with splay feet arrived and departed; a stream of manufactured goods, rubbishy cottons, beads, and brass-wire set into the depths of darkness, and in return came a precious trickle of ivory.

"I had to wait in the station for ten days—an eternity. I lived in a hut in the yard, but to be out of the chaos I would sometimes get into the accountant's office. It was built of horizontal planks, and so badly put together that, as he bent over his high desk, he was barred from neck to heels with narrow strips of sunlight. There was no need to open the big shutter to see. It was hot there too; big flies buzzed fiendishly, and did not sting, but stabbed. I sat generally on the floor, while, of faultless appearance (and even slightly scented), perching on a high stool, he wrote, he wrote. Sometimes he stood up for exercise. When a truckle-bed with a sick man (some invalided agent from up-country) was put in there, he exhibited a gentle annoyance. 'The groans of this sick person,' he said, 'distract my attention. And without that it is extremely difficult to guard against clerical errors in this climate.'

"One day he remarked, without lifting his head, 'In the interior you will no doubt meet Mr Kurtz.' On my asking who Mr Kurtz was, he said he was a first-class agent; and seeing my disappointment at this information, he added slowly, laying down his pen, 'He is a very remarkable person.' Further questions elicited from him that Mr Kurtz was at present in charge of a trading-post, a very important one, in the true ivory-country, at 'the very bottom of there. Sends in as much ivory as all the others put together . . .' He began to write again. The sick man was too ill to groan. The flies buzzed in a great peace.

"Suddenly there was a growing murmur of voices and a great tramping of feet. A caravan had come in. A violent babble of uncouth sounds burst out on the other side of the planks. All the carriers were speaking together, and in the midst of the uproar the lamentable voice of the chief agent was heard 'giving it up' tearfully for the twentieth time that day. . . . He rose slowly. 'What a frightful row,' he said. He crossed the room gently to look at the sick man, and returning, said to me, 'He does not hear.' 'What! Dead?' I asked, startled. 'No, not yet,' he answered, with great composure. Then, alluding with a toss of the head to the tumult in the station-yard, 'When one has got to make correct entries, one comes to hate those savages—hate them to the death.' He remained thoughtful for a moment. 'When you see Mr Kurtz,' he went on, 'tell him from me that everything here'—he glanced at the desk—'is very satisfactory. I don't like to write to him—with those messengers of ours you never know who may get hold of your letter—at that Central Station.' He stared at me for a moment with his mild, bulging eyes. 'Oh, he will go far, very far,' he began again. 'He will be a somebody in the Administration before long. They, above—the Council in Europe, you know—mean him to be.'

"He turned to his work. The noise outside had ceased, and presently in going out I stopped at the door. In the steady buzz of flies the homeward-bound agent was lying flushed and insensible; the other, bent over his books, was making correct entries of perfectly correct transactions; and fifty feet below the doorstep I could see the still tree-tops of the grove of death.

"Next day I left that station at last, with a caravan of sixty men, for a two-hundred-mile tramp.

"No use telling you much about that. Paths, paths, everywhere; a stamped-in network of paths spreading over the empty land, through long grass, through burnt grass, through thickets, down and up chilly ravines, up and down stony hills ablaze with heat; and a solitude, a solitude, nobody, not a hut. The population had cleared out a long time ago. Well, if a lot of mysterious niggers armed with all kinds of fearful weapons suddenly took to travelling on the road between Deal[6] and Gravesend, catching the yokels right and left to carry heavy loads for them, I fancy every farm and cottage thereabouts would get empty very soon. Only here the dwellings were gone too. Still, I passed through several abandoned villages. There's something pathetically childish in the ruins of grass walls. Day after day, with the stamp and shuffle of sixty pair of bare feet behind me, each pair under a 60-lb. load. Camp, cook, sleep, strike camp, march. Now and then a carrier dead in harness, at rest in the long grass near the path, with an empty water-gourd and his long staff lying by his

6. An English port.

side. A great silence around and above. Perhaps on some quiet night the tremor of far-off drums, sinking, swelling, a tremor vast, faint; a sound weird, appealing, suggestive, and wild—and perhaps with as profound a meaning as the sound of bells in a Christian country. Once a white man in an unbuttoned uniform, camping on the path with an armed escort of lank Zanzibaris,[7] very hospitable and festive—not to say drunk. Was looking after the upkeep of the road, he declared. Can't say I saw any road or any upkeep, unless the body of a middle-aged negro, with a bullet-hole in the forehead, upon which I absolutely stumbled three miles farther on, may be considered as a permanent improvement. I had a white companion too, not a bad chap, but rather too fleshy and with the exasperating habit of fainting on the hot hillsides, miles away from the least bit of shade and water. Annoying, you know, to hold your own coat like a parasol over a man's head while he is coming-to. I couldn't help asking him once what he meant by coming there at all. 'To make money, of course. What do you think?' he said, scornfully. Then he got fever, and had to be carried in a hammock slung under a pole. As he weighed sixteen stone I had no end of rows with the carriers. They jibbed, ran away, sneaked off with their loads in the night—quite a mutiny. So, one evening, I made a speech in English with gestures, not one of which was lost to the sixty pairs of eyes before me, and the next morning I started the hammock off in front all right. An hour afterwards I came upon the whole concern wrecked in a bush—man, hammock, groans, blankets, horrors. The heavy pole had skinned his poor nose. He was very anxious for me to kill somebody, but there wasn't the shadow of a carrier near. I remembered the old doctor,—'It would be interesting for science to watch the mental changes of individuals, on the spot.' I felt I was becoming scientifically interesting. However, all that is to no purpose. On the fifteenth day I came in sight of the big river again, and hobbled into the Central Station. It was on a back water surrounded by scrub and forest, with a pretty border of smelly mud on one side, and on the three others enclosed by a crazy fence of rushes. A neglected gap was all the gate it had, and the first glance at the place was enough to let you see the flabby devil was running that show. White men with long staves in their hands appeared languidly from amongst the buildings, strolling up to take a look at me, and then retired out of sight somewhere. One of them, a stout, excitable chap with black moustaches, informed me with great volubility and many digressions, as soon as I told him who I was, that my steamer was at the bottom of the river. I was thunderstruck. What, how, why? Oh, it was 'all right.' The 'manager himself' was there. All quite correct. 'Everybody had behaved splendidly! splendidly!'—'You must,' he said in agitation, 'go and see the general manager at once. He is waiting!'

"I did not see the real significance of that wreck at once. I fancy I see it now, but I am not sure—not at all. Certainly the affair was too stupid—when I think of it—to be altogether natural. Still. . . . But at the moment it presented itself simply as a confounded nuisance. The steamer was sunk. They had started two days before in a sudden hurry up the river with the manager on board, in charge of some volunteer skipper, and before they had been out three hours they tore the bottom out of her on stones, and she sank near the south bank. I asked myself what I was to do there, now my boat was lost. As a matter of fact, I had plenty to do in fishing my command out of the river. I had to set about it the very next day. That, and the repairs when I brought the pieces to the station, took some months.

---

7. Africans from Zanzibar, in East Africa; they were widely used as mercenaries.

"My first interview with the manager was curious. He did not ask me to sit down after my twenty-mile walk that morning. He was commonplace in complexion, in feature, in manners, and in voice. He was of middle size and of ordinary build. His eyes, of the usual blue, were perhaps remarkably cold, and he certainly could make his glance fall on one as trenchant and heavy as an axe. But even at these times the rest of his person seemed to disclaim the intention. Otherwise there was only an indefinable, faint expression of his lips, something stealthy—a smile—not a smile—I remember it, but I can't explain. It was unconscious, this smile was, though just after he had said something it got intensified for an instant. It came at the end of his speeches like a seal applied on the words to make the meaning of the commonest phrase appear absolutely inscrutable. He was a common trader, from his youth up employed in these parts—nothing more. He was obeyed, yet he inspired neither love nor fear, nor even respect. He inspired uneasiness. That was it! Uneasiness. Not a definite mistrust—just uneasiness—nothing more. You have no idea how effective such a . . . a . . . faculty can be. He had no genius for organising, for initiative, or for order even. That was evident in such things as the deplorable state of the station. He had no learning, and no intelligence. His position had come to him—why? Perhaps because he was never ill . . . He had served three terms of three years out there . . . Because triumphant health in the general rout of constitutions is a kind of power in itself. When he went home on leave he rioted on a large scale—pompously. Jack ashore—with a difference—in externals only. This one could gather from his casual talk. He originated nothing, he could keep the routine going—that's all. But he was great. He was great by this little thing that it was impossible to tell what could control such a man. He never gave that secret away. Perhaps there was nothing within him. Such a suspicion made one pause—for out there there were no external checks. Once when various tropical diseases had laid low almost every 'agent' in the station, he was heard to say, 'Men who come out here should have no entrails.' He sealed the utterance with that smile of his, as though it had been a door opening into a darkness he had in his keeping. You fancied you had seen things—but the seal was on. When annoyed at meal-times by the constant quarrels of the white men about precedence, he ordered an immense round table to be made, for which a special house had to be built. This was the station's mess-room. Where he sat was the first place—the rest were nowhere. One felt this to be his unalterable conviction. He was neither civil nor uncivil. He was quiet. He allowed his 'boy'—an overfed young negro from the coast—to treat the white men, under his very eyes, with provoking insolence.

"He began to speak as soon as he saw me. I had been very long on the road. He could not wait. Had to start without me. The up-river stations had to be relieved. There had been so many delays already that he did not know who was dead and who was alive, and how they got on—and so on, and so on. He paid no attention to my explanations, and, playing with a stick of sealing-wax, repeated several times that the situation was 'very grave, very grave.' There were rumours that a very important station was in jeopardy, and its chief, Mr Kurtz, was ill. Hoped it was not true. Mr Kurtz was . . . I felt weary and irritable. Hang Kurtz, I thought. I interrupted him by saying I had heard of Mr Kurtz on the coast. 'Ah! So they talk of him down there,' he murmured to himself. Then he began again, assuring me Mr Kurtz was the best agent he had, an exceptional man, of the greatest importance to the Company; therefore I could understand his anxiety. He was, he said, 'very, very uneasy.' Certainly he fidgeted on his chair a good deal, exclaimed, 'Ah, Mr Kurtz!' broke the stick of sealing-wax and seemed dumbfounded by the accident. Next thing he wanted to know 'how long it would take to' . . . I interrupted him again. Being hungry, you know, and kept on my feet too, I was getting savage. 'How can I tell?' I said. 'I haven't even seen the wreck yet—some months, no doubt.' All this talk seemed to me so futile. 'Some months,' he said. 'Well, let us say three months before we can make a start. Yes. That ought to do the affair.' I flung out of his hut (he lived all alone in a clay hut with a sort of verandah) muttering to myself my opinion of him. He was a chattering idiot. Afterwards I took it back when it was borne in upon me startlingly with what extreme nicety he had estimated the time requisite for the 'affair.'

"I went to work the next day, turning, so to speak, my back on that station. In that way only it seemed to me I could keep my hold on the redeeming facts of life. Still, one must look about sometimes; and then I saw this station, these men strolling aimlessly about in the sunshine of the yard. I asked myself sometimes what it all meant. They wandered here and there with their absurd long staves in their hands, like a lot of faithless pilgrims bewitched inside a rotten fence. The word 'ivory' rang in the air, was whispered, was sighed. You would think they were praying to it. A taint of imbecile rapacity blew through it all, like a whiff from some corpse. By Jove! I've never seen anything so unreal in my life. And outside, the silent wilderness surrounding this cleared speck on the earth struck me as something great and invincible, like evil or truth, waiting patiently for the passing away of this fantastic invasion.

"Oh, those months! Well, never mind. Various things happened. One evening a grass shed full of calico, cotton prints, beads, and I don't know what else, burst into a blaze so suddenly that you would have thought the earth had opened to let an avenging fire consume all that trash. I was smoking my pipe quietly by my dismantled steamer, and saw them all cutting capers in the light, with their arms lifted high, when the stout man with moustaches came tearing down to the river, a tin pail in his hand, assured me that everybody was 'behaving splendidly, splendidly,' dipped about a quart of water and tore back again. I noticed there was a hole in the bottom of his pail.

"I strolled up. There was no hurry. You see the thing had gone off like a box of matches. It had been hopeless from the very first. The flame had leaped high, driven everybody back, lighted up everything—and collapsed. The shed was already a heap of embers glowing fiercely. A nigger was being beaten near by. They said he had caused the fire in some way; be that as it may, he was screeching most horribly. I saw him, later on, for several days, sitting in a bit of shade looking very sick and trying to recover himself: afterwards he arose and went out—and the wilderness without a sound took him into its bosom again. As I approached the glow from the dark I found myself at the back of two men, talking. I heard the name of Kurtz pronounced, then the words, 'take advantage of this unfortunate accident.' One of the men was the manager. I wished him a good evening. 'Did you ever see anything like it—eh? it is incredible,' he said, and walked off. The other man remained. He was a first-class agent, young, gentlemanly, a bit reserved, with a forked little beard and a hooked nose. He was stand-offish with the other agents, and they on their side said he was the manager's spy upon them. As to me, I had hardly ever spoken to him before. We got into talk, and by-and-by we strolled away from the hissing ruins. Then he asked me to his room, which was in the main building of the station. He struck a match, and I perceived that this young aristocrat had not only a silver-mounted dressing-case but also a whole candle all to himself. Just at that time the manager was the only man supposed to have any right to candles. Native mats covered the clay walls; a collection of spears, assegais,[8] shields, knives was hung up in trophies. The business intrusted to this fellow was the making of bricks—so I had been informed; but there wasn't a fragment of a brick anywhere in the station, and he had been there more than a year—waiting. It seems he could not make bricks without something, I don't know what—straw maybe. Anyway, it could not be found there, and as it was not likely to be sent from Europe, it did not appear clear to me what he was waiting for. An act of special creation perhaps. However, they were all waiting—all the sixteen or twenty pilgrims of them—for something; and upon my word it did not seem an uncongenial occupation, from the way they took it, though the only thing that ever came to them was disease—as far as I could see. They beguiled the time by backbiting and intriguing against each other in a foolish kind of way. There was an air of plotting about that station, but nothing came of it, of course. It was as unreal as everything else—as the philanthropic pretence of the whole concern, as their talk, as their government, as their show of work. The only real feeling was a desire to get appointed to a trading-post where ivory was to be had, so that they could earn percentages. They intrigued and slandered and hated each other only on that account,—but as to effectually lifting a little finger—oh, no. By heavens! there is something after all in the world allowing one man to steal a horse while another must not look at a halter. Steal a horse straight out. Very well. He has done it. Perhaps he can ride. But there is a way of looking at a halter that would provoke the most charitable of saints into a kick.

"I had no idea why he wanted to be sociable, but as we chatted in there it suddenly occurred to me the fellow was trying to get at something—in fact, pumping me. He alluded constantly to Europe, to the people I was supposed to know there—putting leading questions as to my acquaintances in the sepulchral city, and so on. His little eyes glittered like mica discs—with curiosity,—though he tried to keep up a bit of superciliousness. At first I was astonished, but very soon I became awfully curious to see what he would find out from me. I couldn't possibly imagine what I had in me to make it worth his while. It was very pretty to see how he baffled himself, for in truth my body was full of chills, and my head had nothing in it but that wretched steamboat business. It was evident he took me for a perfectly shameless prevaricator. At last he got angry, and, to conceal a movement of furious annoyance, he yawned. I rose. Then I noticed a small sketch in oils, on a panel, representing a woman, draped and blind-folded, carrying a lighted torch. The background was sombre—almost black. The movement of the woman was stately, and the effect of the torchlight on the face was sinister.

"It arrested me, and he stood by civilly, holding a half-pint champagne bottle (medical comforts) with the candle stuck in it. To my question he said Mr Kurtz had painted this—in this very station more than a year ago—while waiting for means to go to his trading-post. 'Tell me, pray,' said I, 'who is this Mr Kurtz?'

"'The chief of the Inner Station,' he answered in a short tone, looking away. 'Much obliged,' I said, laughing. 'And you are the brickmaker of the Central Station. Every one knows that.' He was silent for a while. 'He is a prodigy,' he said at last. 'He is an emissary of pity, and science, and progress, and devil knows what else. We want,' he began to declaim suddenly, 'for the guidance of the cause intrusted to us by Europe, so to speak, higher intelligence, wide sympathies, a singleness of purpose.'

8. Spears.

'Who says that?' I asked. 'Lots of them,' he replied. 'Some even write that; and so *he* comes here, a special being, as you ought to know.' 'Why ought I to know?' I interrupted, really surprised. He paid no attention. 'Yes. To-day he is chief of the best station, next year he will be assistant-manager, two years more and . . . but I daresay you know what he will be in two years' time. You are of the new gang—the gang of virtue. The same people who sent him specially also recommended you. Oh, don't say no. I've my own eyes to trust.' Light dawned upon me. My dear aunt's influential acquaintances were producing an unexpected effect upon that young man. I nearly burst into a laugh. 'Do you read the Company's confidential correspondence?' I asked. He hadn't a word to say. It was great fun. 'When Mr Kurtz,' I continued severely, 'is General Manager, you won't have the opportunity.'

"He blew the candle out suddenly, and we went outside. The moon had risen. Black figures strolled about listlessly, pouring water on the glow, whence proceeded a sound of hissing; steam ascended in the moonlight; the beaten nigger groaned somewhere. 'What a row the brute makes!' said the indefatigable man with the moustaches, appearing near us. 'Serve him right. Transgression—punishment—bang! Pitiless, pitiless. That's the only way. This will prevent all conflagrations for the future. I was just telling the manager . . .' He noticed my companion, and became crestfallen all at once. 'Not in bed yet,' he said, with a kind of servile heartiness; 'it's so natural. Ha! Danger—agitation.' He vanished. I went on to the river-side, and the other followed me. I heard a scathing murmur at my ear, 'Heap of muffs—go to.' The pilgrims could be seen in knots gesticulating, discussing. Several had still their staves in their hands. I verily believe they took these sticks to bed with them. Beyond the fence the forest stood up spectrally in the moonlight, and through the dim stir, through the faint sounds of that lamentable courtyard, the silence of the land went home to one's very heart,—its mystery, its greatness, the amazing reality of its concealed life. The hurt nigger moaned feebly somewhere near by, and then fetched a deep sigh that made me mend my pace away from there. I felt a hand introducing itself under my arm. 'My dear sir,' said the fellow, 'I don't want to be misunderstood, and especially by you, who will see Mr Kurtz long before I can have that pleasure. I wouldn't like him to get a false idea of my disposition. . . . '

"I let him run on, this papier-mâché Mephistopheles, and it seemed to me that if I tried I could poke my forefinger through him, and would find nothing inside but a little loose dirt, maybe. He, don't you see, had been planning to be assistant-manager by-and-by under the present man, and I could see that the coming of that Kurtz had upset them both not a little. He talked precipitately, and I did not try to stop him. I had my shoulders against the wreck of my steamer, hauled up on the slope like a carcass of some big river animal. The smell of mud, of primeval mud, by Jove! was in my nostrils, the high stillness of primeval forest was before my eyes; there were shiny patches on the black creek. The moon had spread over everything a thin layer of silver—over the rank grass, over the mud, upon the wall of matted vegetation standing higher than the wall of a temple, over the great river I could see through a sombre gap glittering, glittering, as it flowed broadly by without a murmur. All this was great, expectant, mute, while the man jabbered about himself. I wondered whether the stillness on the face of the immensity looking at us two were meant as an appeal or as a menace. What were we who had strayed in here? Could we handle that dumb thing, or would it handle us? I felt how big, how confoundedly big, was that thing that couldn't talk, and perhaps was deaf as well. What was in there? I could see a little ivory coming out from there, and I had heard Mr Kurtz was in there. I had heard

enough about it too—God knows! Yet somehow it didn't bring any image with it—
no more than if I had been told an angel or a fiend was in there. I believed it in the
same way one of you might believe there are inhabitants in the planet Mars. I knew
once a Scotch sailmaker who was certain, dead sure, there were people in Mars. If
you asked him for some idea how they looked and behaved, he would get shy and
mutter something about 'walking on all-fours.' If you as much as smiled, he would—
though a man of sixty—offer to fight you. I would not have gone so far as to fight for
Kurtz, but I went for him near enough to a lie. You know I hate, detest, and can't
bear a lie, not because I am straighter than the rest of us, but simply because it appals
me. There is a taint of death, a flavour of mortality in lies,—which is exactly what I
hate and detest in the world—what I want to forget. It makes me miserable and sick,
like biting something rotten would do. Temperament, I suppose. Well, I went near
enough to it by letting the young fool there believe anything he liked to imagine as
to my influence in Europe. I became in an instant as much of a pretence as the rest of
the bewitched pilgrims. This simply because I had a notion it somehow would be of
help to that Kurtz whom at the time I did not see—you understand. He was just a
word for me. I did not see the man in the name any more than you do. Do you see
him? Do you see the story? Do you see anything? It seems to me I am trying to tell you
a dream—making a vain attempt, because no relation of a dream can convey the
dream-sensation, that commingling of absurdity, surprise, and bewilderment in a
tremor of struggling revolt, that notion of being captured by the incredible which is
of the very essence of dreams. . . ."

He was silent for a while.

". . . No, it is impossible; it is impossible to convey the life-sensation of any given
epoch of one's existence,—that which makes its truth, its meaning—its subtle and
penetrating essence. It is impossible. We live, as we dream—alone. . . ."

He paused again as if reflecting, then added—

"Of course in this you fellows see more than I could then. You see me, whom you
know. . . ."

It had become so pitch dark that we listeners could hardly see one another. For a
long time already he, sitting apart, had been no more to us than a voice. There was
not a word from anybody. The others might have been asleep, but I was awake. I listened, I listened on the watch for the sentence, for the word, that would give me the
clue to the faint uneasiness inspired by this narrative that seemed to shape itself
without human lips in the heavy night-air of the river.

". . . Yes—I let him run on," Marlow began again, "and think what he pleased
about the powers that were behind me. I did! And there was nothing behind me!
There was nothing but that wretched, old, mangled steamboat I was leaning against,
while he talked fluently about 'the necessity for every man to get on.' 'And when one
comes out here, you conceive, it is not to gaze at the moon.' Mr Kurtz was a 'universal genius,' but even a genius would find it easier to work with 'adequate tools—intelligent men.' He did not make bricks—why, there was a physical impossibility in the
way—as I was well aware; and if he did secretarial work for the manager, it was
because 'no sensible man rejects wantonly the confidence of his superiors.' Did I see
it? I saw it. What more did I want? What I really wanted was rivets, by heaven! Rivets. To get on with the work—to stop the hole. Rivets I wanted. There were cases of
them down at the coast—cases—piled up—burst—split! You kicked a loose rivet at
every second step in that station yard on the hillside. Rivets had rolled into the grove
of death. You could fill your pockets with rivets for the trouble of stooping down—

and there wasn't one rivet to be found where it was wanted. We had plates that would do, but nothing to fasten them with. And every week the messenger, a lone negro, letter-bag on shoulder and staff in hand, left our station for the coast. And several times a week a coast caravan came in with trade goods,—ghastly glazed calico that made you shudder only to look at it, glass beads value about a penny a quart, confounded spotted cotton handkerchiefs. And no rivets. Three carriers could have brought all that was wanted to set that steamboat afloat.

"He was becoming confidential now, but I fancy my unresponsive attitude must have exasperated him at last, for he judged it necessary to inform me he feared neither God nor devil, let alone any mere man. I said I could see that very well, but what I wanted was a certain quantity of rivets—and rivets were what really Mr Kurtz wanted, if he had only known it. Now letters went to the coast every week. . . . 'My dear sir,' he cried, 'I write from dictation.' I demanded rivets. There was a way—for an intelligent man. He changed his manner; became very cold, and suddenly began to talk about a hippopotamus; wondered whether sleeping on board the steamer (I stuck to my salvage night and day) I wasn't disturbed. There was an old hippo that had the bad habit of getting out on the bank and roaming at night over the station grounds. The pilgrims used to turn out in a body and empty every rifle they could lay hands on at him. Some even had sat up o' nights for him. All this energy was wasted, though. 'That animal has a charmed life,' he said; 'but you can say this only of brutes in this country. No man—you apprehend me?—no man here bears a charmed life.' He stood there for a moment in the moonlight with his delicate hooked nose set a little askew, and his mica eyes glittering without a wink, then, with a curt Good night, he strode off. I could see he was disturbed and considerably puzzled, which made me feel more hopeful than I had been for days. It was a great comfort to turn from that chap to my influential friend, the battered, twisted, ruined, tin-pot steamboat. I clambered on board. She rang under my feet like an empty Huntley & Palmer[9] biscuit-tin kicked along a gutter; she was nothing so solid in make, and rather less pretty in shape, but I had expended enough hard work on her to make me love her. No influential friend would have served me better. She had given me a chance to come out a bit—to find out what I could do. No, I don't like work. I had rather laze about and think of all the fine things that can be done. I don't like work—no man does—but I like what is in the work,—the chance to find yourself. Your own reality—for yourself, not for others—what no other man can ever know. They can only see the mere show, and never can tell what it really means.

"I was not surprised to see somebody sitting aft, on the deck, with his legs dangling over the mud. You see I rather chummed with the few mechanics there were in that station, whom the other pilgrims naturally despised—on account of their imperfect manners, I suppose. This was the foreman—a boiler-maker by trade—a good worker. He was a lank, bony, yellow-faced man, with big intense eyes. His aspect was worried, and his head was as bald as the palm of my hand; but his hair in falling seemed to have stuck to his chin, and had prospered in the new locality, for his beard hung down to his waist. He was a widower with six young children (he had left them in charge of a sister of his to come out there), and the passion of his life was pigeon-flying. He was an enthusiast and a connoisseur. He would rave about pigeons. After work hours he used sometimes to come over from his hut for a talk about his children and his pigeons; at work, when he had to crawl in the mud under the bottom of the

9. A brand of English cookies.

steamboat, he would tie up that beard of his in a kind of white serviette[1] he brought for the purpose. It had loops to go over his ears. In the evening he could be seen squatted on the bank rinsing that wrapper in the creek with great care, then spreading it solemnly on a bush to dry.

"I slapped him on the back and shouted 'We shall have rivets!' He scrambled to his feet exclaiming 'No! Rivets!' as though he couldn't believe his ears. Then in a low voice, 'You . . . eh?' I don't know why we behaved like lunatics. I put my finger to the side of my nose and nodded mysteriously. 'Good for you!' he cried, snapped his fingers above his head, lifting one foot. I tried a jig. We capered on the iron deck. A frightful clatter came out of that hulk, and the virgin forest on the other bank of the creek sent it back in a thundering roll upon the sleeping station. It must have made some of the pilgrims sit up in their hovels. A dark figure obscured the lighted doorway of the manager's hut, vanished, then, a second or so after, the doorway itself vanished too. We stopped, and the silence driven away by the stamping of our feet flowed back again from the recesses of the land. The great wall of vegetation, an exuberant and entangled mass of trunks, branches, leaves, boughs, festoons, motionless in the moonlight, was like a rioting invasion of soundless life, a rolling wave of plants, piled up, crested, ready to topple over the creek, to sweep every little man of us out of his little existence. And it moved not. A deadened burst of mighty splashes and snorts reached us from afar, as though an ichthyosaurus had been taking a bath of glitter in the great river. 'After all,' said the boiler-maker in a reasonable tone, 'why shouldn't we get the rivets?' Why not, indeed! I did not know of any reason why we shouldn't. 'They'll come in three weeks,' I said, confidently.

"But they didn't. Instead of rivets there came an invasion, an infliction, a visitation. It came in sections during the next three weeks, each section headed by a donkey carrying a white man in new clothes and tan shoes, bowing from that elevation right and left to the impressed pilgrims. A quarrelsome band of footsore sulky niggers trod on the heels of the donkey; a lot of tents, camp-stools, tin boxes, white cases, brown bales would be shot down in the courtyard, and the air of mystery would deepen a little over the muddle of the station. Five such instalments came, with their absurd air of disorderly flight with the loot of innumerable outfit shops and provision stores, that, one would think, they were lugging, after a raid, into the wilderness for equitable division. It was an inextricable mess of things decent in themselves but that human folly made look like the spoils of thieving.

"This devoted band called itself the Eldorado Exploring Expedition,[2] and I believe they were sworn to secrecy. Their talk, however, was the talk of sordid buccaneers: it was reckless without hardihood, greedy without audacity, and cruel without courage; there was not an atom of foresight or of serious intention in the whole batch of them, and they did not seem aware these things are wanted for the work of the world. To tear treasure out of the bowels of the land was their desire, with no more moral purpose at the back of it than there is in burglars breaking into a safe. Who paid the expenses of the noble enterprise I don't know; but the uncle of our manager was leader of that lot.

"In exterior he resembled a butcher in a poor neighbourhood, and his eyes had a look of sleepy cunning. He carried his fat paunch with ostentation on his short legs, and during the time his gang infested the station spoke to no one but his nephew. You could see these two roaming about all day long with their heads close together in an everlasting confab.

---

1. Napkin.
2. Eldorado, legendary land of gold in South America and

the object of many fruitless 16th-century Spanish expeditions.

"I had given up worrying myself about the rivets. One's capacity for that kind of folly is more limited than you would suppose. I said Hang!—and let things slide. I had plenty of time for meditation, and now and then I would give some thought to Kurtz. I wasn't very interested in him. No. Still, I was curious to see whether this man, who had come out equipped with moral ideas of some sort, would climb to the top after all, and how he would set about his work when there."

2

"One evening as I was lying flat on the deck of my steamboat, I heard voices approaching—and there were the nephew and the uncle strolling along the bank. I laid my head on my arm again, and had nearly lost myself in a doze, when somebody said in my ear, as it were: 'I am as harmless as a little child, but I don't like to be dictated to. Am I the manager—or am I not? I was ordered to send him there. It's incredible.' . . . I became aware that the two were standing on the shore alongside the forepart of the steamboat, just below my head. I did not move; it did not occur to me to move: I was sleepy. 'It is unpleasant,' grunted the uncle. 'He has asked the Administration to be sent there,' said the other, 'with the idea of showing what he could do; and I was instructed accordingly. Look at the influence that man must have. Is it not frightful?' They both agreed it was frightful, then made several bizarre remarks: 'Make rain and fine weather—one man—the Council—by the nose'—bits of absurd sentences that got the better of my drowsiness, so that I had pretty near the whole of my wits about me when the uncle said, 'The climate may do away with this difficulty for you. Is he alone there?' 'Yes,' answered the manager; 'he sent his assistant down the river with a note to me in these terms: "Clear this poor devil out of the country, and don't bother sending more of that sort. I had rather be alone than have the kind of men you can dispose of with me." It was more than a year ago. Can you imagine such impudence?' 'Anything since then?' asked the other, hoarsely. 'Ivory,' jerked the nephew; 'lots of it—prime sort—lots—most annoying, from him.' 'And with that?' questioned the heavy rumble. 'Invoice,' was the reply fired out, so to speak. Then silence. They had been talking about Kurtz.

"I was broad awake by this time, but, lying perfectly at ease, remained still, having no inducement to change my position. 'How did that ivory come all this way?' growled the elder man, who seemed very vexed. The other explained that it had come with a fleet of canoes in charge of an English half-caste clerk Kurtz had with him; that Kurtz had apparently intended to return himself, the station being by that time bare of goods and stores, but after coming three hundred miles, had suddenly decided to go back, which he started to do alone in a small dug-out with four paddlers, leaving the half-caste to continue down the river with the ivory. The two fellows there seemed astounded at anybody attempting such a thing. They were at a loss for an adequate motive. As to me, I seemed to see Kurtz for the first time. It was a distinct glimpse: the dug-out, four paddling savages, and the lone white man turning his back suddenly on the headquarters, on relief, on thoughts of home—perhaps; setting his face towards the depths of the wilderness, towards his empty and desolate station. I did not know the motive. Perhaps he was just simply a fine fellow who stuck to his work for its own sake. His name, you understand, had not been pronounced once. He was 'that man.' The half-caste, who, as far as I could see, had conducted a difficult trip with great prudence and pluck, was invariably alluded to as 'that scoundrel.' The 'scoundrel' had reported that the 'man' had been very ill—had recovered imperfectly.

. . . The two below me moved away then a few paces, and strolled back and forth at some little distance. I heard: 'Military post—doctor—two hundred miles—quite alone now—unavoidable delays—nine months—no news—strange rumours.' They approached again, just as the manager was saying, 'No one, as far as I know, unless a species of wandering trader—a pestilential fellow, snapping ivory from the natives.' Who was it they were talking about now? I gathered in snatches that this was some man supposed to be in Kurtz's district, and of whom the manager did not approve. 'We will not be free from unfair competition till one of these fellows is hanged for an example,' he said. 'Certainly,' grunted the other; 'get him hanged! Why not? Anything—anything can be done in this country. That's what I say; nobody here, you understand, *here*, can endanger your position. And why? You stand the climate—you outlast them all. The danger is in Europe; but there before I left I took care to—' They moved off and whispered, then their voices rose again. 'The extraordinary series of delays is not my fault. I did my possible.' The fat man sighed, 'Very sad.' 'And the pestiferous absurdity of his talk,' continued the other; 'he bothered me enough when he was here. "Each station should be like a beacon on the road towards better things, a centre for trade of course, but also for humanising, improving, instructing." Conceive you—that ass! And he wants to be manager! No, it's—' Here he got choked by excessive indignation, and I lifted my head the least bit. I was surprised to see how near they were—right under me. I could have spat upon their hats. They were looking on the ground, absorbed in thought. The manager was switching his leg with a slender twig: his sagacious relative lifted his head. 'You have been well since you came out this time?' he asked. The other gave a start. 'Who? I? Oh! Like a charm—like a charm. But the rest—oh, my goodness! All sick. They die so quick, too, that I haven't the time to send them out of the country—it's incredible!' 'H'm. Just so,' grunted the uncle. 'Ah! my boy, trust to this—I say, trust to this.' I saw him extend his short flipper of an arm for a gesture that took in the forest, the creek, the mud, the river,—seemed to beckon with a dishonouring flourish before the sunlit face of the land a treacherous appeal to the lurking death, to the hidden evil, to the profound darkness of its heart. It was so startling that I leaped to my feet and looked back at the edge of the forest, as though I had expected an answer of some sort to that black display of confidence. You know the foolish notions that come to one sometimes. The high stillness confronted these two figures with its ominous patience, waiting for the passing away of a fantastic invasion.

"They swore aloud together—out of sheer fright, I believe—then, pretending not to know anything of my existence, turned back to the station. The sun was low; and leaning forward side by side, they seemed to be tugging painfully uphill their two ridiculous shadows of unequal length, that trailed behind them slowly over the tall grass without bending a single blade.

"In a few days the Eldorado Expedition went into the patient wilderness, that closed upon it as the sea closes over a diver. Long afterwards the news came that all the donkeys were dead. I know nothing as to the fate of the less valuable animals. They, no doubt, like the rest of us, found what they deserved. I did not inquire. I was then rather excited at the prospect of meeting Kurtz very soon. When I say very soon I mean it comparatively. It was just two months from the day we left the creek when we came to the bank below Kurtz's station.

"Going up that river was like travelling back to the earliest beginnings of the world, when vegetation rioted on the earth and the big trees were kings. An empty stream, a great silence, an impenetrable forest. The air was warm, thick, heavy, slug-

gish. There was no joy in the brilliance of sunshine. The long stretches of the waterway ran on, deserted, into the gloom of overshadowed distances. On silvery sandbanks hippos and alligators sunned themselves side by side. The broadening waters
flowed through a mob of wooded islands; you lost your way on that river as you would
in a desert, and butted all day long against shoals, trying to find the channel, till you
thought yourself bewitched and cut off for ever from everything you had known
once—somewhere—far away—in another existence perhaps. There were moments
when one's past came back to one, as it will sometimes when you have not a moment
to spare to yourself; but it came in the shape of an unrestful and noisy dream, remembered with wonder amongst the overwhelming realities of this strange world of
plants, and water, and silence. And this stillness of life did not in the least resemble a
peace. It was the stillness of an implacable force brooding over an inscrutable intention. It looked at you with a vengeful aspect. I got used to it afterwards; I did not see it
any more; I had no time. I had to keep guessing at the channel; I had to discern, mostly by inspiration, the signs of hidden banks; I watched for sunken stones; I was learning to clap my teeth smartly before my heart flew out, when I shaved by a fluke some
infernal sly old snag that would have ripped the life out of the tin-pot steamboat and
drowned all the pilgrims; I had to keep a look-out for the signs of dead wood we could
cut up in the night for next day's steaming. When you have to attend to things of that
sort, to the mere incidents of the surface, the reality—the reality, I tell you—fades.
The inner truth is hidden—luckily, luckily. But I felt it all the same; I felt often its
mysterious stillness watching me at my monkey tricks, just as it watches you fellows
performing on your respective tight-ropes for—what is it? half-a-crown a tumble—"

"Try to be civil, Marlow," growled a voice, and I knew there was at least one listener awake besides myself.

"I beg your pardon. I forgot the heartache which makes up the rest of the price.
And indeed what does the price matter, if the trick be well done? You do your tricks
very well. And I didn't do badly either, since I managed not to sink that steamboat
on my first trip. It's a wonder to me yet. Imagine a blindfolded man set to drive a van
over a bad road. I sweated and shivered over that business considerably, I can tell
you. After all, for a seaman, to scrape the bottom of the thing that's supposed to float
all the time under his care is the unpardonable sin. No one may know of it, but you
never forget the thump—eh? A blow on the very heart. You remember it, you dream
of it, you wake up at night and think of it—years after—and go hot and cold all over.
I don't pretend to say that steamboat floated all the time. More than once she had to
wade for a bit, with twenty cannibals splashing around and pushing. We had enlisted
some of these chaps on the way for a crew. Fine fellows—cannibals—in their place.
They were men one could work with, and I am grateful to them. And, after all, they
did not eat each other before my face: they had brought along a provision of hippo-
meat which went rotten, and made the mystery of the wilderness stink in my nostrils.
Phoo! I can sniff it now. I had the manager on board and three or four pilgrims with
their staves—all complete. Sometimes we came upon a station close by the bank,
clinging to the skirts of the unknown, and the white men rushing out of a tumble-
down hovel, with great gestures of joy and surprise and welcome, seemed very
strange,—had the appearance of being held there captive by a spell. The word 'ivory'
would ring in the air for a while—and on we went again into the silence, along empty reaches, round the still bends, between the high walls of our winding way, reverberating in hollow claps the ponderous beat of the stern-wheel. Trees, trees, millions
of trees, massive, immense, running up high; and at their foot, hugging the bank

against the stream, crept the little begrimed steamboat, like a sluggish beetle crawling on the floor of a lofty portico. It made you feel very small, very lost, and yet it was not altogether depressing that feeling. After all, if you were small, the grimy beetle crawled on—which was just what you wanted it to do. Where the pilgrims imagined it crawled to I don't know. To some place where they expected to get something, I bet! For me it crawled towards Kurtz—exclusively; but when the steam-pipes started leaking we crawled very slow. The reaches opened before us and closed behind, as if the forest had stepped leisurely across the water to bar the way for our return. We penetrated deeper and deeper into the heart of darkness. It was very quiet there. At night sometimes the roll of drums behind the curtain of trees would run up the river and remain sustained faintly, as if hovering in the air high over our heads, till the first break of day. Whether it meant war, peace, or prayer we could not tell. The dawns were heralded by the descent of a chill stillness; the woodcutters slept, their fires burned low; the snapping of a twig would make you start. We were wanderers on a prehistoric earth, on an earth that wore the aspect of an unknown planet. We could have fancied ourselves the first of men taking possession of an accursed inheritance, to be subdued at the cost of profound anguish and of excessive toil. But suddenly, as we struggled round a bend, there would be a glimpse of rush walls, of peaked grass-roofs, a burst of yells, a whirl of black limbs, a mass of hands clapping, of feet stamping, of bodies swaying, of eyes rolling, under the droop of heavy and motionless foliage. The steamer toiled along slowly on the edge of a black and incomprehensible frenzy. The prehistoric man was cursing us, praying to us, welcoming us—who could tell? We were cut off from the comprehension of our surroundings; we glided past like phantoms, wondering and secretly appalled, as sane men would be before an enthusiastic outbreak in a madhouse. We could not understand, because we were too far and could not remember, because we were travelling in the night of first ages, of those ages that are gone, leaving hardly a sign—and no memories.

"The earth seemed unearthly. We are accustomed to look upon the shackled form of a conquered monster, but there—there you could look at a thing monstrous and free. It was unearthly, and the men were—No, they were not inhuman. Well, you know, that was the worst of it—this suspicion of their not being inhuman. It would come slowly to one. They howled, and leaped, and spun, and made horrid faces; but what thrilled you was just the thought of their humanity—like yours—the thought of your remote kinship with this wild and passionate uproar. Ugly. Yes, it was ugly enough; but if you were man enough you would admit to yourself that there was in you just the faintest trace of a response to the terrible frankness of that noise, a dim suspicion of there being a meaning in it which you—you so remote from the night of first ages—could comprehend. And why not? The mind of man is capable of anything—because everything is in it, all the past as well as all the future. What was there after all? Joy, fear, sorrow, devotion, valour, rage—who can tell?—but truth—truth stripped of its cloak of time. Let the fool gape and shudder—the man knows, and can look on without a wink. But he must at least be as much of a man as these on the shore. He must meet that truth with his own true stuff—with his own inborn strength. Principles? Principles won't do. Acquisitions, clothes, pretty rags—rags that would fly off at the first good shake. No; you want a deliberate belief. An appeal to me in this fiendish row—is there? Very well; I hear; I admit, but I have a voice too, and for good or evil mine is the speech that cannot be silenced. Of course, a fool, what with sheer fright and fine sentiments, is always safe. Who's that grunting? You wonder I didn't go ashore for a howl and a dance? Well, no—I didn't. Fine sentiments, you say? Fine sentiments be hanged! I had no time. I had to mess about with white-lead and strips of woollen blanket helping to put bandages on those leaky steam-pipes—I tell you. I had to watch the steering, and circumvent those snags, and get the tin-pot along by hook or by crook. There was surface-truth enough in these things to save a wiser man. And between whiles I had to look after the savage who was fireman. He was an improved specimen; he could fire up a vertical boiler. He was there below me, and, upon my word, to look at him was as edifying as seeing a dog in a parody of breeches and a feather hat, walking on his hind-legs. A few months of training had done for that really fine chap. He squinted at the steam-gauge and at the water-gauge with an evident effort of intrepidity—and he had filed teeth too, the poor devil, and the wool of his pate shaved into queer patterns, and three ornamental scars on each of his cheeks. He ought to have been clapping his hands and stamping his feet on the bank, instead of which he was hard at work, a thrall to strange witch-craft, full of improving knowledge. He was useful because he had been instructed; and what he knew was this—that should the water in that transparent thing disap-pear, the evil spirit inside the boiler would get angry through the greatness of his thirst, and take a terrible vengeance. So he sweated and fired up and watched the glass fearfully (with an impromptu charm, made of rags, tied to his arm, and a piece of polished bone, as big as a watch, stuck flatways through his lower lip), while the wooded banks slipped past us slowly, the short noise was left behind, the inter-minable miles of silence—and we crept on, towards Kurtz. But the snags were thick, the water was treacherous and shallow, the boiler seemed indeed to have a sulky dev-il in it, and thus neither that fireman nor I had any time to peer into our creepy thoughts.

"Some fifty miles below the Inner Station we came upon a hut of reeds, an inclined and melancholy pole, with the unrecognisable tatters of what had been a flag of some sort flying from it, and a neatly stacked wood-pile. This was unexpected. We came to the bank, and on the stack of firewood found a flat piece of board with some faded pencil-writing on it. When deciphered it said: 'Wood for you. Hurry up. Approach cautiously.' There was a signature, but it was illegible—not Kurtz—a much longer word. Hurry up. Where? Up the river? 'Approach cautiously.' We had not done so. But the warning could not have been meant for the place where it could be only found after approach. Something was wrong above. But what—and how much? That was the question. We commented adversely upon the imbecility of that tele-graphic style. The bush around said nothing, and would not let us look very far, either. A torn curtain of red twill hung in the doorway of the hut, and flapped sadly in our faces. The dwelling was dismantled; but we could see a white man had lived there not very long ago. There remained a rude table—a plank on two posts; a heap of rubbish reposed in a dark corner, and by the door I picked up a book. It had lost its covers, and the pages had been thumbed into a state of extremely dirty softness; but the back had been lovingly stitched afresh with white cotton thread, which looked clean yet. It was an extraordinary find. Its title was, 'An Inquiry into some Points of Seamanship,' by a man Tower, Towson—some such name—Master in his Majesty's Navy. The matter looked dreary reading enough, with illustrative diagrams and repulsive tables of figures, and the copy was sixty years old. I handled this amazing antiquity with the greatest possible tenderness, lest it should dissolve in my hands. Within, Towson or Towser was inquiring earnestly into the breaking strain of ships' chains and tackle, and other such matters. Not a very enthralling book; but at the first glance you could see there a singleness of intention, an honest concern for the right way of going to work, which made these humble pages, thought out so many years ago, luminous with another than a professional light. The simple old sailor, with his talk of chains and purchases, made me forget the jungle and the pilgrims in a delicious sensation of having come upon something unmistakably real. Such a book being there was wonderful enough; but still more astounding were the notes pencilled in the margin, and plainly referring to the text. I couldn't believe my eyes! They were in cipher! Yes, it looked like cipher. Fancy a man lugging with him a book of that description into this nowhere and studying it—and making notes—in cipher at that! It was an extravagant mystery.

"I had been dimly aware for some time of a worrying noise, and when I lifted my eyes I saw the wood-pile was gone, and the manager, aided by all the pilgrims, was shouting at me from the river-side. I slipped the book into my pocket. I assure you to leave off reading was like tearing myself away from the shelter of an old and solid friendship.

"I started the lame engine ahead. 'It must be this miserable trader—this intruder,' exclaimed the manager, looking back malevolently at the place we had left. 'He must be English,' I said. 'It will not save him from getting into trouble if he is not careful,' muttered the manager darkly. I observed with assumed innocence that no man was safe from trouble in this world.

"The current was more rapid now, the steamer seemed at her last gasp, the stern-wheel flopped languidly, and I caught myself listening on tiptoe for the next beat of the float, for in sober truth I expected the wretched thing to give up every moment. It was like watching the last flickers of a life. But still we crawled. Sometimes I would pick out a tree a little way ahead to measure our progress towards Kurtz by, but I lost it invariably before we got abreast. To keep the eyes so long on one thing was too much for human patience. The manager displayed a beautiful resignation. I fretted and fumed and took to arguing with myself whether or no I would talk openly with Kurtz; but before I could come to any conclusion it occurred to me that my speech or my silence, indeed any action of mine, would be a mere futility. What did it matter what any one knew or ignored? What did it matter who was manager? One gets sometimes such a flash of insight. The essentials of this affair lay deep under the surface, beyond my reach, and beyond my power of meddling.

"Towards the evening of the second day we judged ourselves about eight miles from Kurtz's station. I wanted to push on; but the manager looked grave, and told me the navigation up there was so dangerous that it would be advisable, the sun being very low already, to wait where we were till next morning. Moreover, he pointed out that if the warning to approach cautiously were to be followed, we must approach in daylight—not at dusk, or in the dark. This was sensible enough. Eight miles meant nearly three hours' steaming for us, and I could also see suspicious ripples at the upper end of the reach. Nevertheless, I was annoyed beyond expression at the delay, and most unreasonably too, since one night more could not matter much after so many months. As we had plenty of wood, and caution was the word, I brought up in the middle of the stream. The reach was narrow, straight, with high sides like a railway cutting. The dusk came gliding into it long before the sun had set. The current ran smooth and swift, but a dumb immobility sat on the banks. The living trees, lashed together by the creepers and every living bush of the undergrowth, might have been changed into stone, even to the slenderest twig, to the lightest leaf. It was not sleep—it seemed unnatural, like a state of trance. Not the faintest sound of any kind could be heard. You looked on amazed, and began to suspect yourself of being deaf—

then the night came suddenly, and struck you blind as well. About three in the morning some large fish leaped, and the loud splash made me jump as though a gun had been fired. When the sun rose there was a white fog, very warm and clammy, and more blinding than the night. It did not shift or drive; it was just there, standing all round you like something solid. At eight or nine, perhaps, it lifted as a shutter lifts. We had a glimpse of the towering multitude of trees, of the immense matted jungle, with the blazing little ball of the sun hanging over it—all perfectly still—and then the white shutter came down again, smoothly, as if sliding in greased grooves. I ordered the chain, which we had begun to heave in, to be paid out again. Before it stopped running with a muffled rattle, a cry, a very loud cry, as of infinite desolation, soared slowly in the opaque air. It ceased. A complaining clamour, modulated in savage discords, filled our ears. The sheer unexpectedness of it made my hair stir under my cap. I don't know how it struck the others: to me it seemed as though the mist itself had screamed, so suddenly, and apparently from all sides at once, did this tumultuous and mournful uproar arise. It culminated in a hurried outbreak of almost intolerably excessive shrieking, which stopped short, leaving us stiffened in a variety of silly attitudes, and obstinately listening to the nearly as appalling and excessive silence. 'Good God! What is the meaning—?' stammered at my elbow one of the pilgrims,—a little fat man, with sandy hair and red whiskers, who wore side-spring boots, and pink pyjamas tucked into his socks. Two others remained open-mouthed a whole minute, then dashed into the little cabin, to rush out incontinently and stand darting scared glances, with Winchesters at 'ready' in their hands. What we could see was just the steamer we were on, her outlines blurred as though she had been on the point of dissolving, and a misty strip of water, perhaps two feet broad, around her—and that was all. The rest of the world was nowhere, as far as our eyes and ears were concerned. Just nowhere. Gone, disappeared; swept off without leaving a whisper or a shadow behind.

"I went forward, and ordered the chain to be hauled in short, so as to be ready to trip the anchor and move the steamboat at once if necessary. 'Will they attack?' whispered an awed voice. 'We will all be butchered in this fog,' murmured another. The faces twitched with the strain, the hands trembled slightly, the eyes forgot to wink. It was very curious to see the contrast of expressions of the white men and of the black fellows of our crew, who were as much strangers to that part of the river as we, though their homes were only eight hundred miles away. The whites, of course greatly discomposed, had besides a curious look of being painfully shocked by such an outrageous row. The others had an alert, naturally interested expression; but their faces were essentially quiet, even those of the one or two who grinned as they hauled at the chain. Several exchanged short, grunting phrases, which seemed to settle the matter to their satisfaction. Their headman, a young, broad-chested black, severely draped in dark-blue fringed cloths, with fierce nostrils and his hair all done up artfully in oily ringlets, stood near me. 'Aha!' I said, just for good fellowship's sake. 'Catch 'im,' he snapped, with a bloodshot widening of his eyes and a flash of sharp teeth—'catch 'im. Give 'im to us.' 'To you, eh?' I asked; 'what would you do with them?' 'Eat 'im!' he said, curtly, and, leaning his elbow on the rail, looked out into the fog in a dignified and profoundly pensive attitude. I would no doubt have been properly horrified, had it not occurred to me that he and his chaps must be very hungry: that they must have been growing increasingly hungry for at least this month past. They had been engaged for six months (I don't think a single one of them had any clear idea of time, as we at the end of countless ages have. They still belonged to the beginnings of time—had no inherited experience to teach them, as it were), and of course, as long as there was a piece of paper written over in accordance with some farcical law or other made down the river, it didn't enter anybody's head to trouble how they would live. Certainly they had brought with them some rotten hippo-meat, which couldn't have lasted very long, anyway, even if the pilgrims hadn't, in the midst of a shocking hullabaloo, thrown a considerable quantity of it overboard. It looked like a high-handed proceeding; but it was really a case of legitimate self-defence. You can't breathe dead hippo waking, sleeping, and eating, and at the same time keep your precarious grip on existence. Besides that, they had given them every week three pieces of brass wire, each about nine inches long; and the theory was they were to buy their provisions with that currency in river-side villages. You can see how *that* worked. There were either no villages, or the people were hostile, or the director, who like the rest of us fed out of tins, with an occasional old he-goat thrown in, didn't want to stop the steamer for some more or less recondite reason. So, unless they swallowed the wire itself, or made loops of it to snare the fishes with, I don't see what good their extravagant salary could be to them. I must say it was paid with a regularity worthy of a large and honourable trading company. For the rest, the only thing to eat—though it didn't look eatable in the least—I saw in their possession was a few lumps of some stuff like half-cooked dough, of a dirty lavender colour, they kept wrapped in leaves, and now and then swallowed a piece of, but so small that it seemed done more for the looks of the thing than for any serious purpose of sustenance. Why in the name of all the gnawing devils of hunger they didn't go for us—they were thirty to five—and have a good tuck-in for once, amazes me now when I think of it. They were big powerful men, with not much capacity to weigh the consequences, with courage, with strength, even yet, though their skins were no longer glossy and their muscles no longer hard. And I saw that something restraining, one of those human secrets that baffle probability, had come into play there. I looked at them with a swift quickening of interest—not because it occurred to me I might be eaten by them before very long, though I own to you that just then I perceived—in a new light, as it were—how unwholesome the pilgrims looked, and I hoped, yes, I positively hoped, that my aspect was not so—what shall I say?—so—unappetising: a touch of fantastic vanity which fitted well with the dream-sensation that pervaded all my days at that time. Perhaps I had a little fever too. One can't live with one's finger everlastingly on one's pulse. I had often 'a little fever,' or a little touch of other things—the playful paw-strokes of the wilderness, the preliminary trifling before the more serious onslaught which came in due course. Yes; I looked at them as you would on any human being, with a curiosity of their impulses, motives, capacities, weaknesses, when brought to the test of an inexorable physical necessity. Restraint! What possible restraint? Was it superstition, disgust, patience, fear—or some kind of primitive honour? No fear can stand up to hunger, no patience can wear it out, disgust simply does not exist where hunger is; and as to superstition, beliefs, and what you may call principles, they are less than chaff in a breeze. Don't you know the devilry of lingering starvation, its exasperating torment, its black thoughts, its sombre and brooding ferocity? Well, I do. It takes a man all his inborn strength to fight hunger properly. It's really easier to face bereavement, dishonour, and the perdition of one's soul—than this kind of prolonged hunger. Sad, but true. And these chaps too had no earthly reason for any kind of scruple. Restraint! I would just as soon have expected restraint from a hyena prowling amongst the corpses of a battlefield. But there was the fact facing me—the fact dazzling, to be seen, like the foam on the depths of the sea, like a ripple on an unfathomable enigma, a mystery greater—when I thought of it—than the curious, inexplicable note of desperate grief in this savage clamour that had swept by us on the river-bank, behind the blind whiteness of the fog.

"Two pilgrims were quarrelling in hurried whispers as to which bank. 'Left.' 'No, no; how can you? Right, right, of course.' 'It is very serious,' said the manager's voice behind me; 'I would be desolated if anything should happen to Mr Kurtz before we came up.' I looked at him, and had not the slightest doubt he was sincere. He was just the kind of man who would wish to preserve appearances. That was his restraint. But when he muttered something about going on at once, I did not even take the trouble to answer him. I knew, and he knew, that it was impossible. Were we to let go our hold of the bottom, we would be absolutely in the air—in space. We wouldn't be able to tell where we were going to—whether up or down stream, or across—till we fetched against one bank or the other,—and then we wouldn't know at first which it was. Of course I made no move. I had no mind for a smash-up. You couldn't imagine a more deadly place for a shipwreck. Whether drowned at once or not, we were sure to perish speedily in one way or another. 'I authorise you to take all the risks,' he said, after a short silence. 'I refuse to take any,' I said shortly; which was just the answer he expected, though its tone might have surprised him. 'Well, I must defer to your judgment. You are captain,' he said, with marked civility. I turned my shoulder to him in sign of my appreciation, and looked into the fog. How long would it last? It was the most hopeless look-out. The approach to this Kurtz grubbing for ivory in the wretched bush was beset by as many dangers as though he had been an enchanted princess sleeping in a fabulous castle. 'Will they attack, do you think?' asked the manager, in a confidential tone.

"I did not think they would attack, for several obvious reasons. The thick fog was one. If they left the bank in their canoes they would get lost in it, as we would be if we attempted to move. Still, I had also judged the jungle of both banks quite impenetrable—and yet eyes were in it, eyes that had seen us. The river-side bushes were certainly very thick; but the undergrowth behind was evidently penetrable. However, during the short lift I had seen no canoes anywhere in the reach—certainly not abreast of the steamer. But what made the idea of attack inconceivable to me was the nature of the noise—of the cries we had heard. They had not the fierce character boding of immediate hostile intention. Unexpected, wild, and violent as they had been, they had given me an irresistible impression of sorrow. The glimpse of the steamboat had for some reason filled those savages with unrestrained grief. The danger, if any, I expounded, was from our proximity to a great human passion let loose. Even extreme grief may ultimately vent itself in violence—but more generally takes the form of apathy. . . .

"You should have seen the pilgrims stare! They had no heart to grin, or even to revile me; but I believe they thought me gone mad—with fright, maybe. I delivered a regular lecture. My dear boys, it was no good bothering. Keep a look-out? Well, you may guess I watched the fog for the signs of lifting as a cat watches a mouse; but for anything else our eyes were of no more use to us than if we had been buried miles deep in a heap of cotton-wool. It felt like it too—choking, warm, stifling. Besides, all I said, though it sounded extravagant, was absolutely true to fact. What we afterwards alluded to as an attack was really an attempt at repulse. The action was very far from being aggressive—it was not even defensive, in the usual sense: it was undertaken under the stress of desperation, and in its essence was purely protective.

"It developed itself, I should say, two hours after the fog lifted, and its commencement was at a spot, roughly speaking, about a mile and a half below Kurtz's station. We had just floundered and flopped round a bend, when I saw an islet, a mere grassy hummock of bright green, in the middle of the stream. It was the only thing of the kind; but as we opened the reach more, I perceived it was the head of a long sandbank, or rather of a chain of shallow patches stretching down the middle of the river. They were discoloured, just awash, and the whole lot was seen just under the water, exactly as a man's backbone is seen running down the middle of his back under the skin. Now, as far as I did see, I could go to the right or to the left of this. I didn't know either channel, of course. The banks looked pretty well alike, the depth appeared the same; but as I had been informed the station was on the west side, I naturally headed for the western passage.

"No sooner had we fairly entered it than I became aware it was much narrower than I had supposed. To the left of us there was the long uninterrupted shoal, and to the right a high, steep bank heavily overgrown with bushes. Above the bush the trees stood in serried ranks. The twigs overhung the current thickly, and from distance to distance a large limb of some tree projected rigidly over the stream. It was then well on in the afternoon, the face of the forest was gloomy, and a broad strip of shadow had already fallen on the water. In this shadow we steamed up—very slowly, as you may imagine. I sheered her well inshore—the water being deepest near the bank, as the sounding-pole informed me.

"One of my hungry and forbearing friends was sounding in the bows just below me. This steamboat was exactly like a decked scow.[3] On the deck there were two little teak-wood houses, with doors and windows. The boiler was in the fore-end, and the machinery right astern. Over the whole there was a light roof, supported on stanchions. The funnel projected through that roof, and in front of the funnel a small cabin built of light planks served for a pilot-house. It contained a couch, two camp-stools, a loaded Martini-Henry[4] leaning in one corner, a tiny table, and the steering-wheel. It had a wide door in front and a broad shutter at each side. All these were always thrown open, of course. I spent my days perched up there on the extreme fore-end of that roof, before the door. At night I slept, or tried to, on the couch. An athletic black belonging to some coast tribe, and educated by my poor predecessor, was the helmsman. He sported a pair of brass earrings, wore a blue cloth wrapper from the waist to the ankles, and thought all the world of himself. He was the most unstable kind of fool I had ever seen. He steered with no end of a swagger while you were by; but if he lost sight of you, he became instantly the prey of an abject funk, and would let that cripple of a steamboat get the upper hand of him in a minute.

"I was looking down at the sounding-pole, and feeling much annoyed to see at each try a little more of it stick out of that river, when I saw my poleman give up the business suddenly, and stretch himself flat on the deck, without even taking the trouble to haul his pole in. He kept hold on it though, and it trailed in the water. At the same time the fireman, whom I could also see below me, sat down abruptly before his furnace and ducked his head. I was amazed. Then I had to look at the river mighty quick, because there was a snag in the fairway. Sticks, little sticks, were flying about—thick: they were whizzing before my nose, dropping below me, striking behind me against my pilot-house. All this time the river, the shore, the woods, were very quiet—perfectly quiet. I could only hear the heavy splashing thump of the stern-wheel and the patter of these things. We cleared the snag clumsily. Arrows, by Jove!

3. A flat-bottomed boat.   4. A rifle.

We were being shot at! I stepped in quickly to close the shutter on the landside. That fool-helmsman, his hands on the spokes, was lifting his knees high, stamping his feet, champing his mouth, like a reined-in horse. Confound him! And we were staggering within ten feet of the bank. I had to lean right out to swing the heavy shutter, and I saw a face amongst the leaves on the level with my own, looking at me very fierce and steady; and then suddenly, as though a veil had been removed from my eyes, I made out, deep in the tangled gloom, naked breasts, arms, legs, glaring eyes,—the bush was swarming with human limbs in movement, glistening, of bronze colour. The twigs shook, swayed, and rustled, the arrows flew out of them, and then the shutter came to. 'Steer her straight,' I said to the helmsman. He held his head rigid, face forward; but his eyes rolled, he kept on lifting and setting down his feet gently, his mouth foamed a little. 'Keep quiet!' I said in a fury. I might just as well have ordered a tree not to sway in the wind. I darted out. Below me there was a great scuffle of feet on the iron deck; confused exclamations; a voice screamed, 'Can you turn back?' I caught sight of a V-shaped ripple on the water ahead. What? Another snag! A fusillade burst out under my feet. The pilgrims had opened with their Winchesters, and were simply squirting lead into that bush. A deuce of a lot of smoke came up and drove slowly forward. I swore at it. Now I couldn't see the ripple or the snag either. I stood in the doorway, peering, and the arrows came in swarms. They might have been poisoned, but they looked as though they wouldn't kill a cat. The bush began to howl. Our wood-cutters raised a warlike whoop; the report of a rifle just at my back deafened me. I glanced over my shoulder, and the pilot-house was yet full of noise and smoke when I made a dash at the wheel. The fool-nigger had dropped everything, to throw the shutter open and let off that Martini-Henry. He stood before the wide opening, glaring, and I yelled at him to come back, while I straightened the sudden twist out of that steamboat. There was no room to turn even if I had wanted to, the snag was somewhere very near ahead in that confounded smoke, there was no time to lose, so I just crowded her into the bank—right into the bank, where I knew the water was deep.

"We tore slowly along the overhanging bushes in a whirl of broken twigs and flying leaves. The fusillade below stopped short, as I had foreseen it would when the squirts got empty. I threw my head back to a glinting whizz that traversed the pilot-house, in at one shutter-hole and out at the other. Looking past that mad helmsman, who was shaking the empty rifle and yelling at the shore, I saw vague forms of men running bent double, leaping, gliding, distinct, incomplete, evanescent. Something big appeared in the air before the shutter, the rifle went overboard, and the man stepped back swiftly, looked at me over his shoulder in an extraordinary, profound, familiar manner, and fell upon my feet. The side of his head hit the wheel twice, and the end of what appeared a long cane clattered round and knocked over a little camp-stool. It looked as though after wrenching that thing from somebody ashore he had lost his balance in the effort. The thin smoke had blown away, we were clear of the snag, and looking ahead I could see that in another hundred yards or so I would be free to sheer off, away from the bank; but my feet felt so very warm and wet that I had to look down. The man had rolled on his back and stared straight up at me; both his hands clutched that cane. It was the shaft of a spear that, either thrown or lunged through the opening, had caught him in the side just below the ribs; the blade had gone in out of sight, after making a frightful gash; my shoes were full; a pool of blood lay very still, gleaming dark-red under the wheel; his eyes shone with an amazing lustre. The fusillade burst out again. He looked at me anxiously, gripping the spear like something precious, with an air of being afraid I would try to take it away from him. I had to make an effort to free my eyes from his gaze and attend to the steering. With one hand I felt above my head for the line of the steam-whistle, and jerked out screech after screech hurriedly. The tumult of angry and warlike yells was checked instantly, and then from the depths of the woods went out such a tremulous and prolonged wail of mournful fear and utter despair as may be imagined to follow the flight of the last hope from the earth. There was a great commotion in the bush; the shower of arrows stopped, a few dropping shots rang out sharply—then silence, in which the languid beat of the stern-wheel came plainly to my ears. I put the helm hard astarboard at the moment when the pilgrim in pink pyjamas, very hot and agitated, appeared in the doorway. 'The manager sends me—' he began in an official tone, and stopped short. 'Good God!' he said, glaring at the wounded man.

"We two whites stood over him, and his lustrous and inquiring glance enveloped us both. I declare it looked as though he would presently put to us some question in an understandable language; but he died without uttering a sound, without moving a limb, without twitching a muscle. Only in the very last moment, as though in response to some sign we could not see, to some whisper we could not hear, he frowned heavily, and that frown gave to his black death-mask an inconceivably sombre, brooding, and menacing expression. The lustre of inquiring glance faded swiftly into vacant glassiness. 'Can you steer?' I asked the agent eagerly. He looked very dubious; but I made a grab at his arm, and he understood at once I meant him to steer whether or no. To tell you the truth, I was morbidly anxious to change my shoes and socks. 'He is dead,' murmured the fellow, immensely impressed. 'No doubt about it,' said I, tugging like mad at the shoelaces. 'And, by the way, I suppose Mr Kurtz is dead as well by this time.'

"For the moment that was the dominant thought. There was a sense of extreme disappointment, as though I had found out I had been striving after something altogether without a substance. I couldn't have been more disgusted if I had travelled all this way for the sole purpose of talking with Mr Kurtz. Talking with . . . I flung one shoe overboard, and became aware that that was exactly what I had been looking forward to—a talk with Kurtz. I made the strange discovery that I had never imagined him as doing, you know, but as discoursing. I didn't say to myself, 'Now I will never see him,' or 'Now I will never shake him by the hand,' but, 'Now I will never hear him.' The man presented himself as a voice. Not of course that I did not connect him with some sort of action. Hadn't I been told in all the tones of jealousy and admiration that he had collected, bartered, swindled, or stolen more ivory than all the other agents together. That was not the point. The point was in his being a gifted creature, and that of all his gifts the one that stood out pre-eminently, that carried with it a sense of real presence, was his ability to talk, his words—the gift of expression, the bewildering, the illuminating, the most exalted and the most contemptible, the pulsating stream of light, or the deceitful flow from the heart of an impenetrable darkness.

"The other shoe went flying unto the devil-god of that river. I thought, By Jove! it's all over. We are too late; he has vanished—the gift has vanished, by means of some spear, arrow, or club. I will never hear that chap speak after all,—and my sorrow had a startling extravagance of emotion, even such as I had noticed in the howling sorrow of these savages in the bush. I couldn't have felt more of lonely desolation somehow, had I been robbed of a belief or had missed my destiny in life. . . . Why do you sigh in this beastly way, somebody? Absurd? Well, absurd. Good Lord! mustn't a man ever—Here, give me some tobacco." . . .

There was a pause of profound stillness, then a match flared, and Marlow's lean face appeared, worn, hollow, with downward folds and dropped eyelids, with an aspect of concentrated attention; and as he took vigorous draws at his pipe, it seemed to retreat and advance out of the night in the regular flicker of the tiny flame. The match went out.

"Absurd!" he cried. "This is the worst of trying to tell . . . Here you all are, each moored with two good addresses, like a hulk with two anchors, a butcher round one corner, a policeman round another, excellent appetites, and temperature normal— you hear—normal from year's end to year's end. And you say, Absurd! Absurd be— exploded! Absurd! My dear boys, what can you expect from a man who out of sheer nervousness had just flung overboard a pair of new shoes? Now I think of it, it is amazing I did not shed tears. I am, upon the whole, proud of my fortitude. I was cut to the quick at the idea of having lost the inestimable privilege of listening to the gifted Kurtz. Of course I was wrong. The privilege was waiting for me. Oh yes, I heard more than enough. And I was right, too. A voice. He was very little more than a voice. And I heard—him—it—this voice—other voices—all of them were so little more than voices—and the memory of that time itself lingers around me, impalpable, like a dying vibration of one immense jabber, silly, atrocious, sordid, savage, or simply mean, without any kind of sense. Voices, voices—even the girl herself—now—"

He was silent for a long time.

"I laid the ghost of his gifts at last with a lie," he began suddenly. "Girl! What? Did I mention a girl? Oh, she is out of it—completely. They—the women I mean— are out of it—should be out of it. We must help them to stay in that beautiful world of their own, lest ours gets worse. Oh, she had to be out of it. You should have heard the disinterred body of Mr Kurtz saying, "My Intended." You would have perceived directly then how completely she was out of it. And the lofty frontal bone of Mr Kurtz! They say the hair goes on growing sometimes, but this—ah—specimen was impressively bald. The wilderness had patted him on the head, and, behold, it was like a ball—an ivory ball; it had caressed him, and—lo!—he had withered; it had taken him, loved him, embraced him, got into his veins, consumed his flesh, and sealed his soul to its own by the inconceivable ceremonies of some devilish initia- tion. He was its spoiled and pampered favourite. Ivory? I should think so. Heaps of it, stacks of it. The old mud shanty was bursting with it. You would think there was not a single tusk left either above or below the ground in the whole country. 'Mostly fos- sil,' the manager had remarked disparagingly. It was no more fossil than I am; but they call it fossil when it is dug up. It appears these niggers do bury the tusks some- times—but evidently they couldn't bury this parcel deep enough to save the gifted Mr Kurtz from his fate. We filled the steamboat with it, and had to pile a lot on the deck. Thus he could see and enjoy as long as he could see, because the appreciation of this favour had remained with him to the last. You should have heard him say, 'My ivory.' Oh yes, I heard him. 'My Intended, my ivory, my station, my river, my—' everything belonged to him. It made me hold my breath in expectation of hearing the wilderness burst into a prodigious peal of laughter that would shake the fixed stars in their places. Everything belonged to him—but that was a trifle. The thing was to know what he belonged to, how many powers of darkness claimed him for their own. That was the reflection that made you creepy all over. It was impossible—it was not good for one either—trying to imagine. He had taken a high seat amongst the devils of the land—I mean literally. You can't understand. How could you?—with solid pavement under your feet, surrounded by kind neighbours ready to cheer you or to fall on you, stepping delicately between the butcher and the policeman, in the holy terror of scandal and gallows and lunatic asylums—how can you imagine what particular region of the first ages a man's untrammelled feet may take him into by the way of solitude—utter solitude without a policeman—by the way of silence—utter silence, where no warning voice of a kind neighbour can be heard whispering of public opinion? These little things make all the great difference. When they are gone you must fall back upon your own innate strength, upon your own capacity for faithfulness. Of course you may be too much of a fool to go wrong—too dull even to know you are being assaulted by the powers of darkness. I take it, no fool ever made a bargain for his soul with the devil: the fool is too much of a fool, or the devil too much of a devil—I don't know which. Or you may be such a thunderingly exalted creature as to be altogether deaf and blind to anything but heavenly sights and sounds. Then the earth for you is only a standing place—and whether to be like this is your loss or your gain I won't pretend to say. But most of us are neither one nor the other. The earth for us is a place to live in, where we must put up with sights, with sounds, with smells too, by Jove!—breathe dead hippo, so to speak, and not be contaminated. And there, don't you see? your strength comes in, the faith in your ability for the digging of unostentatious holes to bury the stuff in—your power of devotion, not to yourself, but to an obscure, back-breaking business. And that's difficult enough. Mind, I am not trying to excuse or even explain—I am trying to account to myself for—for—Mr Kurtz—for the shade of Mr Kurtz. This initiated wraith from the back of Nowhere honoured me with its amazing confidence before it vanished altogether. This was because it could speak English to me. The original Kurtz had been educated partly in England, and—as he was good enough to say himself—his sympathies were in the right place. His mother was half-English, his father was half-French. All Europe contributed to the making of Kurtz; and by-and-by I learned that, most appropriately, the International Society for the Suppression of Savage Customs had intrusted him with the making of a report, for its future guidance. And he had written it too. I've seen it. I've read it. It was eloquent, vibrating with eloquence, but too high-strung, I think. Seventeen pages of close writing he had found time for! But this must have been before his—let us say—nerves went wrong, and caused him to preside at certain midnight dances ending with unspeakable rites, which—as far as I reluctantly gathered from what I heard at various times—were offered up to him—do you understand?— to Mr Kurtz himself. But it was a beautiful piece of writing. The opening paragraph, however, in the light of later information, strikes me now as ominous. He began with the argument that we whites, from the point of development we had arrived at, 'must necessarily appear to them [savages] in the nature of supernatural beings—we approach them with the might as of a deity,' and so on, and so on. 'By the simple exercise of our will we can exert a power for good practically unbounded,' &c., &c. From that point he soared and took me with him. The peroration was magnificent, though difficult to remember, you know. It gave me the notion of an exotic Immensity ruled by an august Benevolence. It made me tingle with enthusiasm. This was the unbounded power of eloquence—of words—of burning noble words. There were no practical hints to interrupt the magic current of phrases, unless a kind of note at the foot of the last page, scrawled evidently much later, in an unsteady hand, may be regarded as the exposition of a method. It was very simple, and at the end of that moving appeal to every altruistic sentiment it blazed at you, luminous and terrifying, like a flash of lightning in a serene sky: 'Exterminate all the brutes!' The curious part was that he had apparently forgotten all about that valuable postscriptum, because, later on, when he in a sense came to himself, he repeatedly entreated me to take good care of 'my pamphlet' (he called it), as it was sure to have in the future a good influence upon his career. I had full information about all these things, and, besides, as it turned out, I was to have the care of his memory. I've done enough for it to give me the indisputable right to lay it, if I choose, for an everlasting rest in the dust-bin of progress, amongst all the sweepings and, figuratively speaking, all the dead cats of civilisation. But then, you see, I can't choose. He won't be forgotten. Whatever he was, he was not common. He had the power to charm or frighten rudimentary souls into an aggravated witch-dance in his honour; he could also fill the small souls of the pilgrims with bitter misgivings: he had one devoted friend at least, and he had conquered one soul in the world that was neither rudimentary nor tainted with self-seeking. No; I can't forget him, though I am not prepared to affirm the fellow was exactly worth the life we lost in getting to him. I missed my late helmsman awfully,—I missed him even while his body was still lying in the pilot-house. Perhaps you will think it passing strange this regret for a savage who was no more account than a grain of sand in a black Sahara. Well, don't you see, he had done something, he had steered; for months I had him at my back—a help—an instrument. It was a kind of partnership. He steered for me—I had to look after him, I worried about his deficiencies, and thus a subtle bond had been created, of which I only became aware when it was suddenly broken. And the intimate profundity of that look he gave me when he received his hurt remains to this day in my memory—like a claim of distant kinship affirmed in a supreme moment.

"Poor fool! If he had only left that shutter alone. He had no restraint, no restraint—just like Kurtz—a tree swayed by the wind. As soon as I had put on a dry pair of slippers, I dragged him out, after first jerking the spear out of his side, which operation I confess I performed with my eyes shut tight. His heels leaped together over the little doorstep; his shoulders were pressed to my breast; I hugged him from behind desperately. Oh! he was heavy, heavy; heavier than any man on earth, I should imagine. Then without more ado I tipped him overboard. The current snatched him as though he had been a wisp of grass, and I saw the body roll over twice before I lost sight of it for ever. All the pilgrims and the manager were then congregated on the awning-deck about the pilot-house, chattering at each other like a flock of excited magpies, and there was a scandalised murmur at my heartless promptitude. What they wanted to keep that body hanging about for I can't guess. Embalm it, maybe. But I had also heard another, and a very ominous, murmur on the deck below. My friends the woodcutters were likewise scandalised, and with a better show of reason—though I admit that the reason itself was quite inadmissible. Oh, quite! I had made up my mind that if my late helmsman was to be eaten, the fishes alone should have him. He had been a very second-rate helmsman while alive, but now he was dead he might have become a first-class temptation, and possibly cause some startling trouble. Besides, I was anxious to take the wheel, the man in pink pyjamas showing himself a hopeless duffer at the business.

"This I did directly the simple funeral was over. We were going half-speed, keeping right in the middle of the stream, and I listened to the talk about me. They had given up Kurtz, they had given up the station; Kurtz was dead, and the station had been burnt—and so on—and so on. The red-haired pilgrim was beside himself with the thought that at least this poor Kurtz had been properly revenged. 'Say! We must have made a glorious slaughter of them in the bush. Eh? What do you think? Say?' He positively danced, the bloodthirsty little gingery beggar. And he had nearly fainted when he saw the wounded man! I could not help saying, 'You made a glorious lot of smoke, anyhow.' I had seen, from the way the tops of the bushes rustled and flew, that almost all the shots had gone too high. You can't hit anything unless you take aim and fire from the shoulder; but these chaps fired from the hip with their eyes shut. The retreat, I maintained—and I was right—was caused by the screeching of the steam-whistle. Upon this they forgot Kurtz, and began to howl at me with indignant protests.

"The manager stood by the wheel murmuring confidentially about the necessity of getting well away down the river before dark at all events, when I saw in the distance a clearing on the river-side and the outlines of some sort of building. 'What's this?' I asked. He clapped his hands in wonder. 'The station!' he cried. I edged in at once, still going half-speed.

"Through my glasses I saw the slope of a hill interspersed with rare trees and perfectly free from undergrowth. A long decaying building on the summit was half buried in the high grass; the large holes in the peaked roof gaped black from afar; the jungle and the woods made a background. There was no enclosure or fence of any kind; but there had been one apparently, for near the house half-a-dozen slim posts remained in a row, roughly trimmed, and with their upper ends ornamented with round carved balls. The rails, or whatever there had been between, had disappeared. Of course the forest surrounded all that. The river-bank was clear, and on the water-side I saw a white man under a hat like a cart-wheel beckoning persistently with his whole arm. Examining the edge of the forest above and below, I was almost certain I could see movements—human forms gliding here and there. I steamed past prudently, then stopped the engines and let her drift down. The man on the shore began to shout, urging us to land. 'We have been attacked,' screamed the manager. 'I know—I know. It's all right,' yelled back the other, as cheerful as you please. 'Come along. It's all right. I am glad.'

"His aspect reminded me of something I had seen—something funny I had seen somewhere. As I manoeuvred to get alongside, I was asking myself, 'What does this fellow look like?' Suddenly I got it. He looked like a harlequin. His clothes had been made of some stuff that was brown holland[5] probably, but it was covered with patches all over, with bright patches, blue, red, and yellow,—patches on the back, patches on front, patches on elbows, on knees; coloured binding round his jacket, scarlet edging at the bottom of his trousers; and the sunshine made him look extremely gay and wonderfully neat withal, because you could see how beautifully all this patching had been done. A beardless, boyish face, very fair, no features to speak of, nose peeling, little blue eyes, smiles and frowns chasing each other over that open countenance like sunshine and shadow on a wind-swept plain. 'Look out, captain!' he cried; 'there's a snag lodged in here last night.' What! Another snag? I confess I swore shamefully. I had nearly holed my cripple, to finish off that charming trip. The harlequin on the bank turned his little pug nose up to me. 'You English?' he asked, all smiles. 'Are you?' I shouted from the wheel. The smiles vanished, and he shook his head as if sorry for my disappointment. Then he brightened up. 'Never mind!' he cried encouragingly. 'Are we in time?' I asked. 'He is up there,' he replied, with a toss of the head up the hill, and becoming gloomy all of a sudden. His face was like the autumn sky, overcast one moment and bright the next.

5. A smooth linen fabric.

"When the manager, escorted by the pilgrims, all of them armed to the teeth, had gone to the house, this chap came on board. 'I say, I don't like this. These natives are in the bush,' I said. He assured me earnestly it was all right. 'They are simple people,' he added; 'well, I am glad you came. It took me all my time to keep them off.' 'But you said it was all right,' I cried. 'Oh, they meant no harm,' he said; and as I stared he corrected himself, 'Not exactly.' Then vivaciously, 'My faith, your pilot-house wants a clean-up!' In the next breath he advised me to keep enough steam on the boiler to blow the whistle in case of any trouble. 'One good screech will do more for you than all your rifles. They are simple people,' he repeated. He rattled away at such a rate he quite overwhelmed me. He seemed to be trying to make up for lots of silence, and actually hinted, laughing, that such was the case. 'Don't you talk with Mr Kurtz?' I said. 'You don't talk with that man—you listen to him,' he exclaimed with severe exaltation. 'But now—' He waved his arm, and in the twinkling of an eye was in the uttermost depths of despondency. In a moment he came up again with a jump, possessed himself of both my hands, shook them continuously, while he gabbled: 'Brother sailor . . . honour . . . pleasure . . . delight . . . introduce myself . . . Russian . . . son of an arch-priest . . . Government of Tambov[6] . . . What? Tobacco! English tobacco; the excellent English tobacco! Now, that's brotherly. Smoke? Where's a sailor that does not smoke?'

"The pipe soothed him, and gradually I made out he had run away from school, had gone to sea in a Russian ship; ran away again; served some time in English ships; was now reconciled with the arch-priest. He made a point of that. 'But when one is young one must see things, gather experience, ideas; enlarge the mind.' 'Here!' I interrupted. 'You can never tell! Here I have met Mr Kurtz,' he said, youthfully solemn and reproachful. I held my tongue after that. It appears he had persuaded a Dutch trading-house on the coast to fit him out with stores and goods, and had started for the interior with a light heart, and no more idea of what would happen to him than a baby. He had been wandering about that river for nearly two years alone, cut off from everybody and everything. 'I am not so young as I look. I am twenty-five,' he said. 'At first old Van Shuyten would tell me to go to the devil,' he narrated with keen enjoyment; 'but I stuck to him, and talked and talked, till at last he got afraid I would talk the hind-leg off his favorite dog, so he gave me some cheap things and a few guns, and told me he hoped he would never see my face again. Good old Dutchman, Van Shuyten. I sent him one small lot of ivory a year ago, so that he can't call me a little thief when I get back. I hope he got it. And for the rest, I don't care. I had some wood stacked for you. That was my old house. Did you see?'

"I gave him Towson's book. He made as though he would kiss me, but restrained himself. 'The only book I had left, and I thought I had lost it,' he said, looking at it ecstatically. 'So many accidents happen to a man going about alone, you know. Canoes get upset sometimes—and sometimes you've got to clear out so quick when the people get angry.' He thumbed the pages. 'You made notes in Russian?' I asked. He nodded. 'I thought they were written in cipher,' I said. He laughed, then became serious. 'I had lots of trouble to keep these people off,' he said. 'Did they want to kill you?' I asked. 'Oh no!' he cried, and checked himself. 'Why did they attack us?' I pursued. He hesitated, then said shamefacedly, 'They don't want him to go.' 'Don't

---

6. A province of Western Russia.

they?' I said, curiously. He nodded a nod full of mystery and wisdom. 'I tell you,' he cried, 'this man has enlarged my mind.' He opened his arms wide, staring at me with his little blue eyes that were perfectly round."

3

"I looked at him, lost in astonishment. There he was before me, in motley, as though he had absconded from a troupe of mimes, enthusiastic, fabulous. His very existence was improbable, inexplicable, and altogether bewildering. He was an insoluble problem. It was inconceivable how he had existed, how he had succeeded in getting so far, how he had managed to remain—why he did not instantly disappear. 'I went a little farther,' he said, 'then still a little farther—till I had gone so far that I don't know how I'll ever get back. Never mind. Plenty time. I can manage. You take Kurtz away quick—quick—I tell you.' The glamour of youth enveloped his particoloured rags, his destitution, his loneliness, the essential desolation of his futile wanderings. For months—for years—his life hadn't been worth a day's purchase; and there he was gallantly, thoughtlessly alive, to all appearance indestructible solely by the virtue of his few years and of his unreflecting audacity. I was seduced into something like admiration—like envy. Glamour urged him on, glamour kept him unscathed. He surely wanted nothing from the wilderness but space to breathe in and to push on through. His need was to exist, and to move onwards at the greatest possible risk, and with a maximum of privation. If the absolutely pure, uncalculating, unpractical spirit of adventure had ever ruled a human being, it ruled this be-patched youth. I almost envied him the possession of this modest and clear flame. It seemed to have consumed all thought of self so completely, that, even while he was talking to you, you forgot that it was he—the man before your eyes—who had gone through these things. I did not envy him his devotion to Kurtz, though. He had not meditated over it. It came to him, and he accepted it with a sort of eager fatalism. I must say that to me it appeared about the most dangerous thing in every way he had come upon so far.

"They had come together unavoidably, like two ships becalmed near each other, and lay rubbing sides at last. I suppose Kurtz wanted an audience, because on a certain occasion, when encamped in the forest, they had talked all night, or more probably Kurtz had talked. 'We talked of everything,' he said, quite transported at the recollection. 'I forgot there was such a thing as sleep. The night did not seem to last an hour. Everything! Everything! . . . Of love too.' 'Ah, he talked to you of love!' I said, much amused. 'It isn't what you think,' he cried, almost passionately. 'It was in general. He made me see things—things.'

"He threw his arms up. We were on deck at the time, and the headman of my wood-cutters, lounging near by, turned upon him his heavy and glittering eyes. I looked around, and I don't know why, but I assure you that never, never before, did this land, this river, this jungle, the very arch of this blazing sky, appear to me so hopeless and so dark, so impenetrable to human thought, so pitiless to human weakness. 'And, ever since, you have been with him, of course?' I said.

"On the contrary. It appears their intercourse had been very much broken by various causes. He had, as he informed me proudly, managed to nurse Kurtz through two illnesses (he alluded to it as you would to some risky feat), but as a rule Kurtz wandered alone, far in the depths of the forest. 'Very often coming to this station, I had to wait days and days before he would turn up,' he said. 'Ah, it was worth waiting for!—sometimes.' 'What was he doing? exploring or what?' I asked. 'Oh yes, of course'; he had discovered lots of villages, a lake too—he did not know exactly in what direction; it was dangerous to inquire too much—but mostly his expeditions had been for ivory. 'But he had no goods to trade with by that time,' I objected. 'There's a good lot of cartridges left even yet,' he answered, looking away. 'To speak plainly, he raided the country,' I said. He nodded. 'Not alone, surely!' He muttered something about the villages round that lake. 'Kurtz got the tribe to follow him, did he?' I suggested. He fidgeted a little. 'They adored him,' he said. The tone of these words was so extraordinary that I looked at him searchingly. It was curious to see his mingled eagerness and reluctance to speak of Kurtz. The man filled his life, occupied his thoughts, swayed his emotions. 'What can you expect?' he burst out; 'he came to them with thunder and lightning, you know—and they had never seen anything like it—and very terrible. He could be very terrible. You can't judge Mr Kurtz as you would an ordinary man. No, no, no! Now—just to give you an idea—I don't mind telling you, he wanted to shoot me too one day—but I don't judge him.' 'Shoot you!' I cried. 'What for?' 'Well, I had a small lot of ivory the chief of that village near my house gave me. You see I used to shoot game for them. Well, he wanted it, and wouldn't hear reason. He declared he would shoot me unless I gave him the ivory and then cleared out of the country, because he could do so, and had a fancy for it, and there was nothing on earth to prevent him killing whom he jolly well pleased. And it was true too. I gave him the ivory. What did I care! But I didn't clear out. No, no. I couldn't leave him. I had to be careful, of course, till we got friendly again for a time. He had his second illness then. Afterwards I had to keep out of the way; but I didn't mind. He was living for the most part in those villages on the lake. When he came down to the river, sometimes he would take to me, and sometimes it was better for me to be careful. This man suffered too much. He hated all this, and somehow he couldn't get away. When I had a chance I begged him to try and leave while there was time; I offered to go back with him. And he would say yes, and then he would remain; go off on another ivory hunt; disappear for weeks; forget himself amongst these people—forget himself—you know.' 'Why! he's mad,' I said. He protested indignantly. Mr Kurtz couldn't be mad. If I had heard him talk, only two days ago, I wouldn't dare hint at such a thing. . . . I had taken up my binoculars while we talked, and was looking at the shore, sweeping the limit of the forest at each side and at the back of the house. The consciousness of there being people in that bush, so silent, so quiet—as silent and quiet as the ruined house on the hill—made me uneasy. There was no sign on the face of nature of this amazing tale that was not so much told as suggested to me in desolate exclamations, completed by shrugs, in interrupted phrases, in hints ending in deep sighs. The woods were unmoved, like a mask—heavy, like the closed door of a prison—they looked with their air of hidden knowledge, of patient expectation, of unapproachable silence. The Russian was explaining to me that it was only lately that Mr Kurtz had come down to the river, bringing along with him all the fighting men of that lake tribe. He had been absent for several months— getting himself adored, I suppose—and had come down unexpectedly, with the intention to all appearance of making a raid either across the river or down stream. Evidently the appetite for more ivory had got the better of the—what shall I say?— less material aspirations. However, he had got much worse suddenly. 'I heard he was lying helpless, and so I came up—took my chance,' said the Russian. 'Oh, he is bad, very bad.' I directed my glass to the house. There were no signs of life, but there was the ruined roof, the long mud wall peeping above the grass, with three little square window-holes, no two of the same size; all this brought within reach of my hand, as it were. And then I made a brusque movement, and one of the remaining posts of that vanished fence leaped up in the field of my glass. You remember I told you I had been struck at the distance by certain attempts at ornamentation, rather remarkable in the ruinous aspect of the place. Now I had suddenly a nearer view, and its first result was to make me throw my head back as if before a blow. Then I went carefully from post to post with my glass, and I saw my mistake. These round knobs were not ornamental but symbolic; they were expressive and puzzling, striking and disturbing—food for thought and also for the vultures if there had been any looking down from the sky; but at all events for such ants as were industrious enough to ascend the pole. They would have been even more impressive, those heads on the stakes, if their faces had not been turned to the house. Only one, the first I had made out, was facing my way. I was not so shocked as you may think. The start back I had given was really nothing but a movement of surprise. I had expected to see a knob of wood there, you know. I returned deliberately to the first I had seen—and there it was, black, dried, sunken, with closed eyelids,—a head that seemed to sleep at the top of that pole, and, with the shrunken dry lips showing a narrow white line of the teeth, was smiling too, smiling continuously at some endless and jocose dream of that eternal slumber.

"I am not disclosing any trade secrets. In fact the manager said afterwards that Mr Kurtz's methods had ruined the district. I have no opinion on that point, but I want you clearly to understand that there was nothing exactly profitable in these heads being there. They only showed that Mr Kurtz lacked restraint in the gratification of his various lusts, that there was something wanting in him—some small matter which, when the pressing need arose, could not be found under his magnificent eloquence. Whether he knew of this deficiency himself I can't say. I think the knowledge came to him at last—only at the very last. But the wilderness had found him out early, and had taken on him a terrible vengeance for the fantastic invasion. I think it had whispered to him things about himself which he did not know, things of which he had no conception till he took counsel with this great solitude—and the whisper had proved irresistibly fascinating. It echoed loudly within him because he was hollow at the core. . . . I put down the glass, and the head that had appeared near enough to be spoken to seemed at once to have leaped away from me into inaccessible distance.

"The admirer of Mr Kurtz was a bit crestfallen. In a hurried, indistinct voice he began to assure me he had not dared to take these—say, symbols—down. He was not afraid of the natives; they would not stir till Mr Kurtz gave the word. His ascendancy was extraordinary. The camps of these people surrounded the place, and the chiefs came every day to see him. They would crawl . . . 'I don't want to know anything of the ceremonies used when approaching Mr Kurtz,' I shouted. Curious, this feeling that came over me that such details would be more intolerable than those heads drying on the stakes under Mr Kurtz's windows. After all, that was only a savage sight, while I seemed at one bound to have been transported into some lightless region of subtle horrors, where pure, uncomplicated savagery was a positive relief, being something that had a right to exist—obviously—in the sunshine. The young man looked at me with surprise. I suppose it did not occur to him Mr Kurtz was no idol of mine. He forgot I hadn't heard any of these splendid monologues on, what was it? on love, justice, conduct of life—or what not. If it had come to crawling before Mr Kurtz, he crawled as much as the veriest savage of them all. I had no idea of the conditions, he said: these heads were the heads of rebels. I shocked him excessively by laughing. Rebels! What would be the next definition I was to hear? There had been enemies, criminals, workers—and these were rebels. Those rebellious heads looked very subdued to me on their sticks. 'You don't know how such a life tries a man like Kurtz,' cried Kurtz's last disciple. 'Well, and you?' I said. 'I! I! I am a simple man. I have no great thoughts. I want nothing from anybody. How can you compare me to . . . ?' His feelings were too much for speech, and suddenly he broke down. 'I don't understand,' he groaned. 'I've been doing my best to keep him alive, and that's enough. I had no hand in all this. I have no abilities. There hasn't been a drop of medicine or a mouthful of invalid food for months here. He was shamefully abandoned. A man like this, with such ideas. Shamefully! Shamefully! I—I—haven't slept for the last ten nights . . . .'

"His voice lost itself in the calm of the evening. The long shadows of the forest had slipped down-hill while we talked, had gone far beyond the ruined hovel, beyond the symbolic row of stakes. All this was in the gloom, while we down there were yet in the sunshine, and the stretch of the river abreast of the clearing glittered in a still and dazzling splendour, with a murky and overshadowed bend above and below. Not a living soul was seen on the shore. The bushes did not rustle.

"Suddenly round the corner of the house a group of men appeared, as though they had come up from the ground. They waded waist-deep in the grass, in a compact body, bearing an improvised stretcher in their midst. Instantly, in the emptiness of the landscape, a cry arose whose shrillness pierced the still air like a sharp arrow flying straight to the very heart of the land; and, as if by enchantment, streams of human beings—of naked human beings—with spears in their hands, with bows, with shields, with wild glances and savage movements, were poured into the clearing by the dark-faced and pensive forest. The bushes shook, the grass swayed for a time, and then everything stood still in attentive immobility.

"'Now, if he does not say the right thing to them we are all done for,' said the Russian at my elbow. The knot of men with the stretcher had stopped too, half-way to the steamer, as if petrified. I saw the man on the stretcher sit up, lank and with an uplifted arm, above the shoulders of the bearers. 'Let us hope that the man who can talk so well of love in general will find some particular reason to spare us this time,' I said. I resented bitterly the absurd danger of our situation, as if to be at the mercy of that atrocious phantom had been a dishonouring necessity. I could not hear a sound, but through my glasses I saw the thin arm extended commandingly, the lower jaw moving, the eyes of that apparition shining darkly far in its bony head that nodded with grotesque jerks. Kurtz—Kurtz—that means 'short' in German—don't it? Well, the name was as true as everything else in his life—and death. He looked at least seven feet long. His covering had fallen off, and his body emerged from it pitiful and appalling as from a winding-sheet. I could see the cage of his ribs all astir, the bones of his arm waving. It was as though an animated image of death carved out of old ivory had been shaking its hand with menaces at a motionless crowd of men made of dark and glittering bronze. I saw him open his mouth wide—it gave him a weirdly voracious aspect, as though he had wanted to swallow all the air, all the earth, all the men before him. A deep voice reached me faintly. He must have been shouting. He fell back suddenly. The stretcher shook as the bearers staggered forward again, and almost at the same time I noticed that the crowd of savages was vanishing without any perceptible movement of retreat, as if the forest that had ejected these beings so suddenly had drawn them in again as the breath is drawn in a long aspiration.

"Some of the pilgrims behind the stretcher carried his arms—two shot-guns, a heavy rifle, and a light revolver-carbine—the thunderbolts of that pitiful Jupiter. The manager bent over him murmuring as he walked beside his head. They laid him down in one of the little cabins—just a room for a bed-place and a camp-stool or two, you know. We had brought his belated correspondence, and a lot of torn envelopes and open letters littered his bed. His hand roamed feebly amongst these papers. I was struck by the fire of his eyes and the composed languor of his expression. It was not so much the exhaustion of disease. He did not seem in pain. This shadow looked satiated and calm, as though for the moment it had had its fill of all the emotions.

"He rustled one of the letters, and looking straight in my face said, 'I am glad.' Somebody had been writing to him about me. These special recommendations were turning up again. The volume of tone he emitted without effort, almost without the trouble of moving his lips, amazed me. A voice! a voice! It was grave, profound, vibrating, while the man did not seem capable of a whisper. However, he had enough strength in him—factitious no doubt—to very nearly make an end of us, as you shall hear directly.

"The manager appeared silently in the doorway; I stepped out at once and he drew the curtain after me. The Russian, eyed curiously by the pilgrims, was staring at the shore. I followed the direction of his glance.

"Dark human shapes could be made out in the distance, flitting indistinctly against the gloomy border of the forest, and near the river two bronze figures, leaning on tall spears, stood in the sunlight under fantastic head-dresses of spotted skins, warlike and still in statuesque repose. And from right to left along the lighted shore moved a wild and gorgeous apparition of a woman.

"She walked with measured steps, draped in striped and fringed cloths, treading the earth proudly, with a slight jingle and flash of barbarous ornaments. She carried her head high; her hair was done in the shape of a helmet; she had brass leggings to the knee, brass wire gauntlets to the elbow, a crimson spot on her tawny cheek, innumerable necklaces of glass beads on her neck; bizarre things, charms, gifts of witchmen, that hung about her, glittered and trembled at every step. She must have had the value of several elephant tusks upon her. She was savage and superb, wild-eyed and magnificent; there was something ominous and stately in her deliberate progress. And in the hush that had fallen suddenly upon the whole sorrowful land, the immense wilderness, the colossal body of the fecund and mysterious life seemed to look at her, pensive, as though it had been looking at the image of its own tenebrous and passionate soul.

"She came abreast of the steamer, stood still, and faced us. Her long shadow fell to the water's edge. Her face had a tragic and fierce aspect of wild sorrow and of dumb pain mingled with the fear of some struggling, half-shaped resolve. She stood looking at us without a stir, and like the wilderness itself, with an air of brooding over an inscrutable purpose. A whole minute passed, and then she made a step forward. There was a low jingle, a glint of yellow metal, a sway of fringed draperies, and she stopped as if her heart had failed her. The young fellow by my side growled. The pilgrims murmured at my back. She looked at us all as if her life had depended upon the unswerving steadiness of her glance. Suddenly she opened her bared arms and threw them up rigid above her head, as though in an uncontrollable desire to touch the sky, and at the same time the swift shadows darted out on the earth, swept around on the river, gathering the steamer in a shadowy embrace. A formidable silence hung over the scene.

"She turned away slowly, walked on, following the bank, and passed into the bushes to the left. Once only her eyes gleamed back at us in the dusk of the thickets before she disappeared.

"'If she had offered to come aboard I really think I would have tried to shoot her,' said the man of patches, nervously. 'I had been risking my life every day for the last fortnight to keep her out of the house. She got in one day and kicked up a row about those miserable rags I picked up in the storeroom to mend my clothes with. I wasn't decent. At least it must have been that, for she talked like a fury to Kurtz for an hour, pointing at me now and then. I don't understand the dialect of this tribe. Luckily for me, I fancy Kurtz felt too ill that day to care, or there would have been mischief. I don't understand. . . . No—it's too much for me. Ah, well, it's all over now.'

"At this moment I heard Kurtz's deep voice behind the curtain, 'Save me!—save the ivory, you mean. Don't tell me. Save *me!* Why, I've had to save you. You are interrupting my plans now. Sick! Sick! Not so sick as you would like to believe. Never mind. I'll carry my ideas out yet—I will return. I'll show you what can be done. You with your little peddling notions—you are interfering with me. I will return. I . . .'

"The manager came out. He did me the honour to take me under the arm and lead me aside. 'He is very low, very low,' he said. He considered it necessary to sigh, but neglected to be consistently sorrowful. 'We have done all we could for him— haven't we? But there is no disguising the fact, Mr Kurtz has done more harm than good to the Company. He did not see the time was not ripe for vigorous action. Cautiously, cautiously—that's my principle. We must be cautious yet. The district is closed to us for a time. Deplorable! Upon the whole, the trade will suffer. I don't deny there is a remarkable quantity of ivory—mostly fossil. We must save it, at all events—but look how precarious the position is—and why? Because the method is unsound.' 'Do you,' said I, looking at the shore, 'call it "unsound method"?' 'Without doubt,' he exclaimed, hotly. 'Don't you?' . . . 'No method at all,' I murmured after a while. 'Exactly,' he exulted. 'I anticipated this. Shows a complete want of judgment. It is my duty to point it out in the proper quarter.' 'Oh,' said I, 'that fellow—what's his name?—the brickmaker, will make a readable report for you.' He appeared confounded for a moment. It seemed to me I had never breathed an atmosphere so vile, and I turned mentally to Kurtz for relief—positively for relief. 'Nevertheless, I think Mr Kurtz is a remarkable man,' I said with emphasis. He started, dropped on me a cold heavy glance, said very quietly, 'He was,' and turned his back on me. My hour of favour was over; I found myself lumped along with Kurtz as a partisan of methods for which the time was not ripe: I was unsound! Ah! but it was something to have at least a choice of nightmares.

"I had turned to the wilderness really, not to Mr Kurtz, who, I was ready to admit, was as good as buried. And for a moment it seemed to me as if I also were buried in a vast grave full of unspeakable secrets. I felt an intolerable weight oppressing my breast, the smell of the damp earth, the unseen presence of victorious corruption, the darkness of an impenetrable night. . . . The Russian tapped me on the shoulder. I heard him mumbling and stammering something about 'brother seaman—couldn't conceal—knowledge of matters that would affect Mr Kurtz's reputation.' I waited. For him evidently Mr Kurtz was not in his grave; I suspect that for him Mr Kurtz was one of the immortals. 'Well!' said I at last, 'speak out. As it happens, I am Mr Kurtz's friend—in a way.'

"He stated with a good deal of formality that had we not been 'of the same profession,' he would have kept the matter to himself without regard to consequences. He suspected 'there was an active ill-will towards him on the part of these white men that—' 'You are right,' I said, remembering a certain conversation I had overheard. 'The manager thinks you ought to be hanged.' He showed a concern at this intelligence which amused me at first. 'I had better get out of the way quietly,' he said, earnestly. 'I can do no more for Kurtz now, and they would soon find some excuse. What's to stop them? There's a military post three hundred miles from here.' 'Well, upon my word,' said I, 'perhaps you had better go if you have any friends amongst the savages near by.' 'Plenty,' he said. 'They are simple people—and I want nothing, you know.' He stood biting his lip, then: 'I don't want any harm to happen to these whites here, but of course I was thinking of Mr Kurtz's reputation—but you are a brother seaman and—' 'All right,' said I, after a time. 'Mr Kurtz's reputation is safe with me.' I did not know how truly I spoke.

"He informed me, lowering his voice, that it was Kurtz who had ordered the attack to be made on the steamer. 'He hated sometimes the idea of being taken away—and then again . . . But I don't understand these matters. I am a simple man. He thought it would scare you away—that you would give it up, thinking him dead. I could not stop him. Oh, I had an awful time of it this last month.' 'Very well,' I said. 'He is all right now.' 'Ye-e-es,' he muttered, not very convinced apparently. 'Thanks,' said I; 'I shall keep my eyes open.' 'But quiet—eh?' he urged, anxiously. 'It would be awful for his reputation if anybody here—' I promised a complete discretion with great gravity. 'I have a canoe and three black fellows waiting not very far. I am off. Could you give me a few Martini-Henry cartridges?' I could, and did, with proper secrecy. He helped himself, with a wink at me, to a handful of my tobacco. 'Between sailors—you know—good English tobacco.' At the door of the pilot-house he turned round—'I say, haven't you a pair of shoes you could spare?' He raised one leg. 'Look.' The soles were tied with knotted strings sandal-wise under his bare feet. I rooted out an old pair, at which he looked with admiration before tucking it under his left arm. One of his pockets (bright red) was bulging with cartridges, from the other (dark blue) peeped 'Towson's Inquiry,' &c., &c. He seemed to think himself excellently well equipped for a renewed encounter with the wilderness. 'Ah! I'll never, never meet such a man again. You ought to have heard him recite poetry—his own too it was, he told me. Poetry!' He rolled his eyes at the recollection of these delights. 'Oh, he enlarged my mind!' 'Good-bye,' said I. He shook hands and vanished in the night. Sometimes I ask myself whether I had ever really seen him—whether it was possible to meet such a phenomenon! . . .

"When I woke up shortly after midnight his warning came to my mind with its hint of danger that seemed, in the starred darkness, real enough to make me get up for the purpose of having a look round. On the hill a big fire burned, illuminating fitfully a crooked corner of the station-house. One of the agents with a picket of a few of our blacks, armed for the purpose, was keeping guard over the ivory; but deep within the forest, red gleams that wavered, that seemed to sink and rise from the ground amongst confused columnar shapes of intense blackness, showed the exact position of the camp where Mr Kurtz's adorers were keeping their uneasy vigil. The monotonous beating of a big drum filled the air with muffled shocks and a lingering vibration. A steady droning sound of many men chanting each to himself some weird incantation came out from the black, flat wall of the woods as the humming of bees comes out of a hive, and had a strange narcotic effect upon my half-awake senses. I believe I dozed off leaning over the rail, till an abrupt burst of yells, an overwhelming outbreak of a pent-up and mysterious frenzy, woke me up in a bewildered wonder. It was cut short all at once, and the low droning went on with an effect of audible and soothing silence. I glanced casually into the little cabin. A light was burning within, but Mr Kurtz was not there.

"I think I would have raised an outcry if I had believed my eyes. But I didn't believe them at first—the thing seemed so impossible. The fact is, I was completely unnerved by a sheer blank fright, pure abstract terror, unconnected with any distinct shape of physical danger. What made this emotion so overpowering was—how shall I define it?—the moral shock I received, as if something altogether monstrous, intolerable to thought and odious to the soul, had been thrust upon me unexpectedly. This lasted of course the merest fraction of a second, and then the usual sense of common-place, deadly danger, the possibility of a sudden onslaught and massacre, or some-thing of the kind, which I saw impending, was positively welcome and composing. It pacified me, in fact, so much, that I did not raise an alarm.

"There was an agent buttoned up inside an ulster[7] and sleeping on a chair on deck within three feet of me. The yells had not awakened him; he snored very slightly; I left him to his slumbers and leaped ashore. I did not betray Mr Kurtz—it was ordered I should never betray him—it was written I should be loyal to the nightmare of my choice. I was anxious to deal with this shadow by myself alone,—and to this day I don't know why I was so jealous of sharing with any one the peculiar blackness of that experience.

"As soon as I got on the bank I saw a trail—a broad trail through the grass. I remember the exultation with which I said to myself, 'He can't walk—he is crawling on all-fours—I've got him.' The grass was wet with dew. I strode rapidly with clenched fists. I fancy I had some vague notion of falling upon him and giving him a drubbing. I don't know. I had some imbecile thoughts. The knitting old woman with the cat obtruded herself upon my memory as a most improper person to be sitting at the other end of such an affair. I saw a row of pilgrims squirting lead in the air out of Winchesters held to the hip. I thought I would never get back to the steamer, and imagined myself living alone and unarmed in the woods to an advanced age. Such silly things—you know. And I remember I confounded the beat of the drum with the beating of my heart, and was pleased at its calm regularity.

"I kept to the track though—then stopped to listen. The night was very clear: a dark blue space, sparkling with dew and starlight, in which black things stood very still. I thought I could see a kind of motion ahead of me. I was strangely cocksure of everything that night. I actually left the track and ran in a wide semicircle (I verily believe chuck-ling to myself) so as to get in front of that stir, of that motion I had seen—if indeed I had seen anything. I was circumventing Kurtz as though it had been a boyish game.

"I came upon him, and, if he had not heard me coming, I would have fallen over him too, but he got up in time. He rose, unsteady, long, pale, indistinct, like a vapour exhaled by the earth, and swayed slightly, misty and silent before me; while at my back the fires loomed between the trees, and the murmur of many voices issued from the forest. I had cut him off cleverly; but when actually confronting him I seemed to come to my senses, I saw the danger in its right proportion. It was by no means over yet. Suppose he began to shout? Though he could hardly stand, there was still plenty of vigour in his voice. 'Go away—hide yourself,' he said, in that profound tone. It was very awful. I glanced back. We were within thirty yards from the nearest fire. A black figure stood up, strode on long black legs, waving long black arms, across the glow. It had horns—antelope horns, I think—on its head. Some sorcerer, some witch-man, no doubt: it looked fiend-like enough. 'Do you know what you are doing?' I whispered. 'Perfectly,' he answered, raising his voice for that single word: it sounded to me far off and yet loud, like a hail through a speaking-trumpet. If he makes a row we are lost, I thought to myself. This clearly was not a case for fisticuffs, even apart from the very natural aversion I had to beat that Shadow—this wandering and tormented thing. 'You will be lost,' I said—'utterly lost.' One gets sometimes such a flash of inspiration, you know. I did say the right thing, though indeed he could not have been more irre-trievably lost than he was at this very moment, when the foundations of our intimacy were being laid—to endure—to endure—even to the end—even beyond.

7. Long overcoat.

"'I had immense plans,' he muttered irresolutely. 'Yes,' said I; 'but if you try to shout I'll smash your head with—' there was not a stick or a stone near. 'I will throttle you for good,' I corrected myself. 'I was on the threshold of great things,' he pleaded, in a voice of longing, with a wistfulness of tone that made my blood run cold. 'And now for this stupid scoundrel—' 'Your success in Europe is assured in any case,' I affirmed, steadily. I did not want to have the throttling of him, you understand—and indeed it would have been very little use for any practical purpose. I tried to break the spell—the heavy, mute spell of the wilderness—that seemed to draw him to its pitiless breast by the awakening of forgotten and brutal instincts, by the memory of gratified and monstrous passions. This alone, I was convinced, had driven him out to the edge of the forest, to the bush, towards the gleam of fires, the throb of drums, the drone of weird incantations; this alone had beguiled his unlawful soul beyond the bounds of permitted aspirations. And, don't you see, the terror of the position was not in being knocked on the head—though I had a very lively sense of that danger too—but in this, that I had to deal with a being to whom I could not appeal in the name of anything high or low. I had, even like the niggers, to invoke him—himself—his own exalted and incredible degradation. There was nothing either above or below him, and I knew it. He had kicked himself loose of the earth. Confound the man! he had kicked the very earth to pieces. He was alone, and I before him did not know whether I stood on the ground or floated in the air. I've been telling you what we said—repeating the phrases we pronounced,—but what's the good? They were common everyday words,—the familiar, vague sounds exchanged on every waking day of life. But what of that? They had behind them, to my mind, the terrific suggestiveness of words heard in dreams, of phrases spoken in nightmares. Soul! If anybody had ever struggled with a soul, I am the man. And I wasn't arguing with a lunatic either. Believe me or not, his intelligence was perfectly clear—concentrated, it is true, upon himself with horrible intensity, yet clear; and therein was my only chance—barring, of course, the killing him there and then, which wasn't so good, on account of unavoidable noise. But his soul was mad. Being alone in the wilderness, it had looked within itself, and, by heavens! I tell you, it had gone mad. I had—for my sins, I suppose—to go through the ordeal of looking into it myself. No eloquence could have been so withering to one's belief in mankind as his final burst of sincerity. He struggled with himself, too. I saw it,—I heard it. I saw the inconceivable mystery of a soul that knew no restraint, no faith, and no fear, yet struggling blindly with itself. I kept my head pretty well; but when I had him at last stretched on the couch, I wiped my forehead, while my legs shook under me as though I had carried half a ton on my back down that hill. And yet I had only supported him, his bony arm clasped round my neck—and he was not much heavier than a child.

"When next day we left at noon, the crowd, of whose presence behind the curtain of trees I had been acutely conscious all the time, flowed out of the woods again, filled the clearing, covered the slope with a mass of naked, breathing, quivering, bronze bodies. I steamed up a bit, then swung down-stream, and two thousand eyes followed the evolutions of the splashing, thumping, fierce river-demon beating the water with its terrible tail and breathing black smoke into the air. In front of the first rank, along the river, three men, plastered with bright red earth from head to foot, strutted to and fro restlessly. When we came abreast again, they faced the river, stamped their feet, nodded their horned heads, swayed their scarlet bodies; they shook towards the fierce river-demon a bunch of black feathers, a mangy skin with a pendent tail—something that looked like a dried gourd; they shouted periodically together strings of amazing words that resembled no sounds of human language; and the deep murmurs of the crowd, interrupted suddenly, were like the responses of some satanic litany.

"We had carried Kurtz into the pilot-house: there was more air there. Lying on the couch, he stared through the open shutter. There was an eddy in the mass of human bodies, and the woman with helmeted head and tawny cheeks rushed out to the very brink of the stream. She put out her hands, shouted something, and all that wild mob took up the shout in a roaring chorus of articulated, rapid, breathless utterance.

"'Do you understand this?' I asked.

"He kept on looking out past me with fiery, longing eyes, with a mingled expression of wistfulness and hate. He made no answer, but I saw a smile, a smile of indefinable meaning, appear on his colourless lips that a moment after twitched convulsively. 'Do I not?' he said slowly, gasping, as if the words had been torn out of him by a supernatural power.

"I pulled the string of the whistle, and I did this because I saw the pilgrims on deck getting out their rifles with an air of anticipating a jolly lark. At the sudden screech there was a movement of abject terror through that wedged mass of bodies. 'Don't! don't! you frighten them away,' cried some one on deck disconsolately. I pulled the string time after time. They broke and ran, they leaped, they crouched, they swerved, they dodged the flying terror of the sound. The three red chaps had fallen flat, face down on the shore, as though they had been shot dead. Only the barbarous and superb woman did not so much as flinch, and stretched tragically her bare arms after us over the sombre and glittering river.

"And then that imbecile crowd down on the deck started their little fun, and I could see nothing more for smoke.

"The brown current ran swiftly out of the heart of darkness, bearing us down towards the sea with twice the speed of our upward progress; and Kurtz's life was running swiftly too, ebbing, ebbing out of his heart into the sea of inexorable time. The manager was very placid, he had no vital anxieties now, he took us both in with a comprehensive and satisfied glance: the 'affair' had come off as well as could be wished. I saw the time approaching when I would be left alone of the party of 'unsound method.' The pilgrims looked upon me with disfavour. I was, so to speak, numbered with the dead. It is strange how I accepted this unforeseen partnership, this choice of nightmares forced upon me in the tenebrous land invaded by these mean and greedy phantoms.

"Kurtz discoursed. A voice! a voice! It rang deep to the very last. It survived his strength to hide in the magnificent folds of eloquence the barren darkness of his heart. Oh, he struggled! he struggled! The wastes of his weary brain were haunted by shadowy images now—images of wealth and fame revolving obsequiously round his unextinguishable gift of noble and lofty expression. My Intended, my station, my career, my ideas—these were the subjects for the occasional utterances of elevated sentiments. The shade of the original Kurtz frequented the bedside of the hollow sham, whose fate it was to be buried presently in the mould of primeval earth. But both the diabolic love and the unearthly hate of the mysteries it had penetrated fought for the possession of that soul satiated with primitive emotions, avid of lying fame, of sham distinction, of all the appearances of success and power.

"Sometimes he was contemptibly childish. He desired to have kings meet him at railway-stations on his return from some ghastly Nowhere, where he intended to accomplish great things. 'You show them you have in you something that is really profitable, and then there will be no limits to the recognition of your ability,' he would say. 'Of course you must take care of the motives—right motives—always.' The long reaches that were like one and the same reach, monotonous bends that were exactly alike, slipped past the steamer with their multitude of secular[8] trees looking patiently after this grimy fragment of another world, the forerunner of change, of conquest, of trade, of massacres, of blessings. I looked ahead—piloting. 'Close the shutter,' said Kurtz suddenly one day; 'I can't bear to look at this.' I did so. There was a silence. 'Oh, but I will wring your heart yet!' he cried at the invisible wilderness.

"We broke down—as I had expected—and had to lie up for repairs at the head of an island. This delay was the first thing that shook Kurtz's confidence. One morning he gave me a packet of papers and a photograph,—the lot tied together with a shoe-string. 'Keep this for me,' he said. 'This noxious fool' (meaning the manager) 'is capable of prying into my boxes when I am not looking.' In the afternoon I saw him. He was lying on his back with closed eyes, and I withdrew quietly, but I heard him mutter, 'Live rightly, die, die . . .' I listened. There was nothing more. Was he rehearsing some speech in his sleep, or was it a fragment of a phrase from some newspaper article? He had been writing for the papers and meant to do so again, 'for the furthering of my ideas. It's a duty.'

"His was an impenetrable darkness. I looked at him as you peer down at a man who is lying at the bottom of a precipice where the sun never shines. But I had not much time to give him, because I was helping the engine-driver to take to pieces the leaky cylinders, to straighten a bent connecting-rod, and in other such matters. I lived in an infernal mess of rust, filings, nuts, bolts, spanners, hammers, ratchet-drills—things I abominate, because I don't get on with them. I tended the little forge we fortunately had aboard; I toiled wearily in a wretched scrap-heap—unless I had the shakes too bad to stand.

"One evening coming in with a candle I was startled to hear him say a little tremulously, 'I am lying here in the dark waiting for death.' The light was within a foot of his eyes. I forced myself to murmur, 'Oh, nonsense!' and stood over him as if transfixed.

"Anything approaching the change that came over his features I have never seen before, and hope never to see again. Oh, I wasn't touched. I was fascinated. It was as though a veil had been rent. I saw on that ivory face the expression of sombre pride, of ruthless power, of craven terror—of an intense and hopeless despair. Did he live his life again in every detail of desire, temptation, and surrender during that supreme moment of complete knowledge? He cried in a whisper at some image, at some vision,—he cried out twice, a cry that was no more than a breath—

"'The horror! The horror!'

"I blew the candle out and left the cabin. The pilgrims were dining in the mess-room, and I took my place opposite the manager, who lifted his eyes to give me a questioning glance, which I successfully ignored. He leaned back, serene, with that peculiar smile of his sealing the unexpressed depths of his meanness. A continuous shower of small flies streamed upon the lamp, upon the cloth, upon our hands and faces. Suddenly the manager's boy put his insolent black head in the doorway, and said in a tone of scathing contempt—

"'Mistah Kurtz—he dead.'

8. Ancient.

"All the pilgrims rushed out to see. I remained, and went on with my dinner. I believe I was considered brutally callous. However, I did not eat much. There was a lamp in there—light, don't you know—and outside it was so beastly, beastly dark. I went no more near the remarkable man who had pronounced a judgment upon the adventures of his soul on this earth. The voice was gone. What else had been there? But I am of course aware that next day the pilgrims buried something in a muddy hole.

"And then they very nearly buried me.

"However, as you see, I did not go to join Kurtz there and then. I did not. I remained to dream the nightmare out to the end, and to show my loyalty to Kurtz once more. Destiny. My destiny! Droll thing life is—that mysterious arrangement of merciless logic for a futile purpose. The most you can hope from it is some knowledge of yourself—that comes too late—a crop of unextinguishable regrets. I have wrestled with death. It is the most unexciting contest you can imagine. It takes place in an impalpable greyness, with nothing underfoot, with nothing around, without spectators, without clamour, without glory, without the great desire of victory, without the great fear of defeat, in a sickly atmosphere of tepid scepticism, without much belief in your own right, and still less in that of your adversary. If such is the form of ultimate wisdom, then life is a greater riddle than some of us think it to be. I was within a hair's-breadth of the last opportunity for pronouncement, and I found with humiliation that probably I would have nothing to say. This is the reason why I affirm that Kurtz was a remarkable man. He had something to say. He said it. Since I had peeped over the edge myself, I understand better the meaning of his stare, that could not see the flame of the candle, but was wide enough to embrace the whole universe, piercing enough to penetrate all the hearts that beat in the darkness. He had summed up—he had judged. 'The horror!' He was a remarkable man. After all, this was the expression of some sort of belief; it had candour, it had conviction, it had a vibrating note of revolt in its whisper, it had the appalling face of a glimpsed truth—the strange commingling of desire and hate. And it is not my own extremity I remember best—a vision of greyness without form filled with physical pain, and a careless contempt for the evanescence of all things—even of this pain itself. No! It is his extremity that I seem to have lived through. True, he had made that last stride, he had stepped over the edge, while I had been permitted to draw back my hesitating foot. And perhaps in this is the whole difference; perhaps all the wisdom, and all truth, and all sincerity, are just compressed into that inappreciable moment of time in which we step over the threshold of the invisible. Perhaps! I like to think my summing-up would not have been a word of careless contempt. Better his cry—much better. It was an affirmation, a moral victory paid for by innumerable defeats, by abominable terrors, by abominable satisfactions. But it was a victory! That is why I have remained loyal to Kurtz to the last, and even beyond, when a long time after I heard once more, not his own voice, but the echo of his magnificent eloquence thrown to me from a soul as translucently pure as a cliff of crystal.

"No, they did not bury me, though there is a period of time which I remember mistily, with a shuddering wonder, like a passage through some inconceivable world that had no hope in it and no desire. I found myself back in the sepulchral city resenting the sight of people hurrying through the streets to filch a little money from each other, to devour their infamous cookery, to gulp their unwholesome beer, to dream their insignificant and silly dreams. They trespassed upon my thoughts. They were intruders whose knowledge of life was to me an irritating pretence, because I felt so sure they could not possibly know the things I knew. Their bearing, which was simply the bearing of commonplace individuals going about their business in the assurance of perfect safety, was offensive to me like the outrageous flauntings of folly in the face of a danger it is unable to comprehend. I had no particular desire to enlighten them, but I had some difficulty in restraining myself from laughing in their faces, so full of stupid importance. I daresay I was not very well at that time. I tottered about the streets—there were various affairs to settle—grinning bitterly at perfectly respectable persons. I admit my behaviour was inexcusable, but then my temperature was seldom normal in these days. My dear aunt's endeavours to 'nurse up my strength' seemed altogether beside the mark. It was not my strength that wanted nursing, it was my imagination that wanted soothing. I kept the bundle of papers given me by Kurtz, not knowing exactly what to do with it. His mother had died lately, watched over, as I was told, by his Intended. A clean-shaved man, with an official manner and wearing gold-rimmed spectacles, called on me one day and made inquiries, at first circuitous, afterwards suavely pressing, about what he was pleased to denominate certain 'documents.' I was not surprised, because I had had two rows with the manager on the subject out there. I had refused to give up the smallest scrap out of that package, and I took the same attitude with the spectacled man. He became darkly menacing at last, and with much heat argued that the Company had the right to every bit of information about its 'territories.' And, said he, 'Mr Kurtz's knowledge of unexplored regions must have been necessarily extensive and peculiar—owing to his great abilities and to the deplorable circumstances in which he had been placed: therefore—' I assured him Mr Kurtz's knowledge, however extensive, did not bear upon the problems of commerce or administration. He invoked then the name of science. 'It would be an incalculable loss if,' &c., &c. I offered him the report on the 'Suppression of Savage Customs,' with the postscriptum torn off. He took it up eagerly, but ended by sniffing at it with an air of contempt. 'This is not what we had a right to expect,' he remarked. 'Expect nothing else,' I said. 'There are only private letters.' He withdrew upon some threat of legal proceedings, and I saw him no more; but another fellow, calling himself Kurtz's cousin, appeared two days later, and was anxious to hear all the details about his dear relative's last moments. Incidentally he gave me to understand that Kurtz had been essentially a great musician. 'There was the making of an immense success,' said the man, who was an organist, I believe, with lank grey hair flowing over a greasy coat-collar. I had no reason to doubt his statement; and to this day I am unable to say what was Kurtz's profession, whether he ever had any—which was the greatest of his talents. I had taken him for a painter who wrote for the papers, or else for a journalist who could paint—but even the cousin (who took snuff during the interview) could not tell me what he had been—exactly. He was a universal genius—on that point I agreed with the old chap, who thereupon blew his nose noisily into a large cotton handkerchief and withdrew in senile agitation, bearing off some family letters and memoranda without importance. Ultimately a journalist anxious to know something of the fate of his 'dear colleague' turned up. This visitor informed me Kurtz's proper sphere ought to have been politics 'on the popular side.' He had furry straight eyebrows, bristly hair cropped short, an eye-glass on a broad ribbon, and, becoming expansive, confessed his opinion that Kurtz really couldn't write a bit—'but heavens! how that man could talk! He electrified large meetings. He had faith—don't you see?—he had the faith. He could get himself to believe anything—anything. He would have been a splendid leader of an extreme party.' 'What party?' I asked. 'Any party,' answered the other. 'He was an—an—extremist.' Did I not think so? I assented. Did I know, he asked, with a sudden flash of curiosity, 'what it was that had induced him to go out there?' 'Yes,' said I, and forthwith handed him the famous Report for publication, if he thought fit. He glanced through it hurriedly, mumbling all the time, judged 'it would do,' and took himself off with this plunder.

"Thus I was left at last with a slim packet of letters and the girl's portrait. She struck me as beautiful—I mean she had a beautiful expression. I know that the sunlight can be made to lie too, yet one felt that no manipulation of light and pose could have conveyed the delicate shade of truthfulness upon those features. She seemed ready to listen without mental reservation, without suspicion, without a thought for herself. I concluded I would go and give her back her portrait and those letters myself. Curiosity? Yes; and also some other feeling perhaps. All that had been Kurtz's had passed out of my hands: his soul, his body, his station, his plans, his ivory, his career. There remained only his memory and his Intended—and I wanted to give that up too to the past, in a way,—to surrender personally all that remained of him with me to that oblivion which is the last word of our common fate. I don't defend myself. I had no clear perception of what it was I really wanted. Perhaps it was an impulse of unconscious loyalty, or the fulfilment of one of those ironic necessities that lurk in the facts of human existence. I don't know. I can't tell. But I went.

"I thought his memory was like the other memories of the dead that accumulate in every man's life,—a vague impress on the brain of shadows that had fallen on it in their swift and final passage; but before the high and ponderous door, between the tall houses of a street as still and decorous as a well-kept alley in a cemetery, I had a vision of him on the stretcher, opening his mouth voraciously, as if to devour all the earth with all its mankind. He lived then before me; he lived as much as he had ever lived—a shadow insatiable of splendid appearances, of frightful realities; a shadow darker than the shadow of the night, and draped nobly in the folds of a gorgeous eloquence. The vision seemed to enter the house with me—the stretcher, the phantombearers, the wild crowd of obedient worshippers, the gloom of the forests, the glitter of the reach between the murky bends, the beat of the drum, regular and muffled like the beating of a heart—the heart of a conquering darkness. It was a moment of triumph for the wilderness, an invading and vengeful rush which, it seemed to me, I would have to keep back alone for the salvation of another soul. And the memory of what I had heard him say afar there, with the horned shapes stirring at my back, in the glow of fires, within the patient woods, those broken phrases came back to me, were heard again in their ominous and terrifying simplicity. I remembered his abject pleading, his abject threats, the colossal scale of his vile desires, the meanness, the torment, the tempestuous anguish of his soul. And later on I seemed to see his collected languid manner, when he said one day, 'This lot of ivory now is really mine. The Company did not pay for it. I collected it myself at a very great personal risk. I am afraid they will try to claim it as theirs though. H'm. It is a difficult case. What do you think I ought to do—resist? Eh? I want no more than justice.' . . . He wanted no more than justice—no more than justice. I rang the bell before a mahogany door on the first floor, and while I waited he seemed to stare at me out of the glassy panel—stare with that wide and immense stare embracing, condemning, loathing all the universe. I seemed to hear the whispered cry, 'The horror! The horror!'

"The dusk was falling. I had to wait in a lofty drawing-room with three long windows from floor to ceiling that were like three luminous and bedraped columns. The bent gilt legs and backs of the furniture shone in indistinct curves. The tall marble fireplace had a cold and monumental whiteness. A grand piano stood massively in a corner, with dark gleams on the flat surfaces like a sombre and polished sarcophagus. A high door opened—closed. I rose.

"She came forward, all in black, with a pale head, floating towards me in the dusk. She was in mourning. It was more than a year since his death, more than a year since the news came; she seemed as though she would remember and mourn for ever. She took both my hands in hers and murmured, 'I had heard you were coming.' I noticed she was not very young—I mean not girlish. She had a mature capacity for fidelity, for belief, for suffering. The room seemed to have grown darker, as if all the sad light of the cloudy evening had taken refuge on her forehead. This fair hair, this pale visage, this pure brow, seemed surrounded by an ashy halo from which the dark eyes looked out at me. Their glance was guileless, profound, confident, and trustful. She carried her sorrowful head as though she were proud of that sorrow, as though she would say, I—I alone know how to mourn for him as he deserves. But while we were still shaking hands, such a look of awful desolation came upon her face that I perceived she was one of those creatures that are not the playthings of Time. For her he had died only yesterday. And, by Jove! the impression was so powerful that for me too he seemed to have died only yesterday—nay, this very minute. I saw her and him in the same instant of time—his death and her sorrow—I saw her sorrow in the very moment of his death. Do you understand? I saw them together—I heard them together. She had said, with a deep catch of the breath, 'I have survived'; while my strained ears seemed to hear distinctly, mingled with her tone of despairing regret, the summing-up whisper of his eternal condemnation. I asked myself what I was doing there, with a sensation of panic in my heart as though I had blundered into a place of cruel and absurd mysteries not fit for a human being to behold. She motioned me to a chair. We sat down. I laid the packet gently on the little table, and she put her hand over it. . . . 'You knew him well,' she murmured, after a moment of mourning silence.

"'Intimacy grows quickly out there,' I said. 'I knew him as well as it is possible for one man to know another.'

"'And you admired him,' she said. 'It was impossible to know him and not to admire him. Was it?'

"'He was a remarkable man,' I said, unsteadily. Then before the appealing fixity of her gaze, that seemed to watch for more words on my lips, I went on, 'It was impossible not to—'

"'Love him,' she finished eagerly, silencing me into an appalled dumbness. 'How true! how true! But when you think that no one knew him so well as I! I had all his noble confidence. I knew him best.'

"'You knew him best,' I repeated. And perhaps she did. But with every word spoken the room was growing darker, and only her forehead, smooth and white, remained illumined by the unextinguishable light of belief and love.

"'You were his friend,' she went on. 'His friend,' she repeated, a little louder. 'You must have been, if he had given you this, and sent you to me. I feel I can speak to you—and oh! I must speak. I want you—you who have heard his last words—to know I have been worthy of him. . . . It is not pride. . . . Yes! I am proud to know I understood him better than any one on earth—he told me so himself. And since his mother died I have had no one—no one—to—to—'

"I listened. The darkness deepened. I was not even sure whether he had given me the right bundle. I rather suspect he wanted me to take care of another batch of his papers which, after his death, I saw the manager examining under the lamp. And the girl talked, easing her pain in the certitude of my sympathy; she talked as thirsty men drink. I had heard that her engagement with Kurtz had been disapproved by her people. He wasn't rich enough or something. And indeed I don't know whether he had not been a pauper all his life. He had given me some reason to infer that it was his impatience of comparative poverty that drove him out there.

"'. . . Who was not his friend who had heard him speak once?' she was saying. 'He drew men towards him by what was best in them.' She looked at me with intensity. 'It is the gift of the great,' she went on, and the sound of her low voice seemed to have the accompaniment of all the other sounds, full of mystery, desolation, and sorrow, I had ever heard—the ripple of the river, the soughing of the trees swayed by the wind, the murmurs of wild crowds, the faint ring of incomprehensible words cried from afar, the whisper of a voice speaking from beyond the threshold of an eternal darkness. 'But you have heard him! You know!' she cried.

"'Yes, I know,' I said with something like despair in my heart, but bowing my head before the faith that was in her, before that great and saving illusion that shone with an unearthly glow in the darkness, in the triumphant darkness from which I could not have defended her—from which I could not even defend myself.

"'What a loss to me—to us!'—she corrected herself with beautiful generosity; then added in a murmur, 'To the world.' By the last gleams of twilight I could see the glitter of her eyes, full of tears—of tears that would not fall.

"'I have been very happy—very fortunate—very proud,' she went on. 'Too fortunate. Too happy for a little while. And now I am unhappy for—for life.'

"She stood up; her fair hair seemed to catch all the remaining light in a glimmer of gold. I rose too.

"'And of all this,' she went on, mournfully, 'of all his promise, and of all his greatness, of his generous mind, of his noble heart, nothing remains—nothing but a memory. You and I—'

"'We shall always remember him,' I said, hastily.

"'No!' she cried. 'It is impossible that all this should be lost—that such a life should be sacrificed to leave nothing—but sorrow. You know what vast plans he had. I knew of them too—I could not perhaps understand,—but others knew of them. Something must remain. His words, at least, have not died.'

"'His words will remain,' I said.

"'And his example,' she whispered to herself. 'Men looked up to him,—his goodness shone in every act. His example—'

"'True,' I said; 'his example too. Yes, his example. I forgot that.'

"'But I do not. I cannot—I cannot believe—not yet. I cannot believe that I shall never see him again, that nobody will see him again, never, never, never.'

"She put out her arms as if after a retreating figure, stretching them black and with clasped pale hands across the fading and narrow sheen of the window. Never see him! I saw him clearly enough then. I shall see this eloquent phantom as long as I live, and I shall see her too, a tragic and familiar Shade, resembling in this gesture another one, tragic also, and bedecked with powerless charms, stretching bare brown arms over the glitter of the infernal stream, the stream of darkness. She said suddenly very low, 'He died as he lived.'

"'His end,' said I, with dull anger stirring in me, 'was in every way worthy of his life.'

"'And I was not with him,' she murmured. My anger subsided before a feeling of infinite pity.

"'Everything that could be done—' I mumbled.

"'Ah, but I believed in him more than any one on earth—more than his own mother, more than—himself. He needed me! Me! I would have treasured every sigh, every word, every sign, every glance.'

"I felt like a chill grip on my chest. 'Don't,' I said, in a muffled voice.

"'Forgive me. I—I—have mourned so long in silence—in silence. . . . You were with him—to the last? I think of his loneliness. Nobody near to understand him as I would have understood. Perhaps no one to hear. . . .'

"'To the very end,' I said, shakily. 'I heard his very last words. . . .' I stopped in a fright.

"'Repeat them,' she said in a heart-broken tone. 'I want—I want—something—something—to—to live with.'

"I was on the point of crying at her, 'Don't you hear them?' The dusk was repeating them in a persistent whisper all around us, in a whisper that seemed to swell menacingly like the first whisper of a rising wind. 'The horror! the horror!'

"'His last word—to live with,' she murmured. 'Don't you understand I loved him—I loved him—I loved him!'

"I pulled myself together and spoke slowly.

"'The last word he pronounced was—your name.'

"I heard a light sigh, and then my heart stood still, stopped dead short by an exulting and terrible cry, by the cry of inconceivable triumph and of unspeakable pain. 'I knew it—I was sure!' . . . She knew. She was sure. I heard her weeping; she had hidden her face in her hands. It seemed to me that the house would collapse before I could escape, that the heavens would fall upon my head. But nothing happened. The heavens do not fall for such a trifle. Would they have fallen, I wonder, if I had rendered Kurtz that justice which was his due? Hadn't he said he wanted only justice? But I couldn't. I could not tell her. It would have been too dark—too dark altogether. . . ."

Marlow ceased, and sat apart, indistinct and silent, in the pose of a meditating Buddha. Nobody moved for a time. "We have lost the first of the ebb," said the Director, suddenly. I raised my head. The offing was barred by a black bank of clouds, and the tranquil waterway leading to the uttermost ends of the earth flowed sombre under an overcast sky—seemed to lead into the heart of an immense darkness.

COMPANION READINGS

Joseph Conrad: from *Congo Diary*

Arrived at Matadi[1] on the 13th of June, 1890.

Mr Gosse, chief of the station (O.K.) retaining us for some reason of his own.

Made the acquaintance of Mr Roger Casement,[2] which I should consider as a great pleasure under any circumstances and now it becomes a positive piece of luck.

Thinks, speaks well, most intelligent and very sympathetic.

Feel considerably in doubt about the future. Think just now that my life amongst the people (white) around here cannot be very comfortable. Intend avoid acquaintances as much as possible. * * *

---

1. Colonial station near the mouth of the Congo River. Conrad arrived there on his way to take up his command of a steamship upriver at Kinshasa.
2. Casement (1864–1916) and Conrad were employed at the time by the same company. Casement later served as British consul in various parts of Africa, and was the author of a report on the Congo (1904) that did much to make public the terrible conditions there. He was knighted in 1912. In 1916 he was executed by the British for his part in the Easter Rebellion in Ireland.

24th. Gosse and R.C. gone with a large lot of ivory down to Boma. On G.['s] return to start to up the river. Have been myself busy packing ivory in casks. Idiotic employment. Health good up to now. * * *

Prominent characteristic of the social life here: people speaking ill of each other.

* * *

Friday, 4th July.

Left camp at 6h a.m. after a very unpleasant night. Marching across a chain of hills and then in a maze of hills. At 8:15 opened out into an undulating plain. Took bearings of a break in the chain of mountains on the other side. * * *

Saw another dead body lying by the path in an attitude of meditative repose.

In the evening three women of whom one albino passed our camp. Horrid chalky white with pink blotches. Red eyes. Red hair. Features very Negroid and ugly. Mosquitos. At night when the moon rose heard shouts and drumming in distant villages. Passed a bad night.

Saturday, 5th July. go.

Left at 6:15. Morning cool, even cold and very damp. Sky densely overcast. Gentle breeze from NE. Road through a narrow plain up to R. Kwilu. Swift-flowing and deep, 50 yds. wide. Passed in canoes. After[war]ds up and down very steep hills intersected by deep ravines. Main chain of heights running mostly NW-SE or W and E at times. Stopped at Manyamba. Camp[in]g place bad—in hollow—water very indifferent. Tent set at 10:15.

Section of today's road. NNE Distance 12 m. [a drawing]

Today fell into a muddy puddle. Beastly. The fault of the man that carried me. After camp[in]g went to a small stream, bathed and washed clothes. Getting jolly well sick of this fun.

Tomorrow expect a long march to get to Nsona, 2 days from Manyanga. No sunshine today.

* * *

Saturday, 26th.

Left very early. Road ascending all the time. Passed villages. Country seems thickly inhabited. At 11h arrived at large market place. Left at noon and camped at 1h p.m.

[section of the day's march with notes]

a camp—a white man died here—market—govt. post—mount—crocodile pond—Mafiesa. * * *

Sunday, 27th.

Left at 8h am. Sent luggage carriers straight on to Luasi and went ourselves round by the Mission of Sutili.

Hospitable reception by Mrs Comber. All the missio[naries] absent.

The looks of the whole establishment eminently civilized and very refreshing to see after the lots of tumble-down hovels in which the State and Company agents are content to live—fine buildings. Position on a hill. Rather breezy.

Left at 3h pm. At the first heavy ascent met Mr Davis, miss[ionary] returning from a preaching trip. Rev. Bentley away in the South with his wife. * * *

Tuesday, 29th.

Left camp at 7h after a good night's rest. Continuous ascent; rather easy at first. Crossed wooded ravines and the river Lunzadi by a very decent bridge.

At 9h met Mr Louette escorting a sick agent of the Comp[an]y back to Matadi. Looking very well. Bad news from up the river. All the steamers disabled. One wrecked. Country wooded. At 10:30 camped at Inkissi. * * *

Today did not set the tent but put up in Gov[ernmen]t shimbek.³ Zanzibari in charge—very obliging. Met ripe pineapple for the first time. On the road today passed a skeleton tied up to a post. Also white man's grave—no name. Heap of stones in the form of a cross.

Health good now.

Wednesday, 30th.

Left at 6 a.m. intending to camp at Kinfumu. Two hours' sharp walk brought me to Nsona na Nsefe. Market. ½ hour after, Harou arrived very ill with billious [sic] attack and fever. Laid him down in Gov[ernmen]t shimbek. Dose of Ipeca.⁴ Vomiting bile in enormous quantities. At 11h gave him 1 gramme of quinine and lots of hot tea. Hot fit ending in heavy perspiration. At 2 p.m. put him in hammock and started for Kinfumu. Row with carriers all the way. Harou suffering much through the jerks of the hammock. Camped at a small stream.

At 4h Harou better. Fever gone. * * *

Up till noon, sky clouded and strong NW wind very chilling. From 1h pm to 4h pm sky clear and very hot day. Expect lots of bother with carriers tomorrow. Had them all called and made a speech which they did not understand. They promise good behaviour. * * *

Friday, 1st of August 1890.

* * * Row between the carriers and a man stating himself in Gov[ernmen]t employ, about a mat. Blows with sticks raining hard. Stopped it. Chief came with a youth about 13 suffering from gunshot wound in the head. Bullet entered about an inch above the right eyebrow and came out a little inside. The roots of the hair, fairly in the middle of the brow in a line with the bridge of the nose. Bone not damaged apparently. Gave him a little glycerine to put on the wound made by the bullet on coming out. Harou not very well. Mosquitos. Frogs. Beastly. Glad to see the end of this stupid tramp. Feel rather seedy. Sun rose red. Very hot day. Wind S[ou]th.

Sir Henry Morton Stanley: from *Address to the Manchester Chamber of Commerce*¹

There is not one manufacturer here present who could not tell me if he had the opportunity how much he personally suffered through the slackness of trade; and I dare say that you have all some vague idea that if things remain as they are the future of the cotton manufacture is not very brilliant. New inventions are continually cropping up, so that your power of producing, if stimulated, is almost incalculable; but new markets for the sale of your products are not of rapid growth, and as other nations, by prohibitive tariffs, are bent upon fostering native manufacturers to the

---

3. A group of huts.
4. A medicine.
1. The journalist and adventurer Henry Morton Stanley wrote an account of his exploits in Africa in his bestseller *Through the Dark Continent* (1878). He delivered this address to the textile manufacturers of Manchester in

1886, seeking their support for the commercial exploitation of the Congo. This speech gives a striking example of the outlook—and rhetoric—of the people who created the conditions Conrad encountered when he went to the Congo in 1890.

exclusion of your own, such markets as are now open to you are likely to be taken away from you in course of time. Well, then, I come to you with at least one market where there are at present, perhaps, 6,250,000 yards of cheap cottons sold every year on the Congo banks and in the Congo markets.[2]

I was interested the other day in making a curious calculation, which was, supposing that all the inhabitants of the Congo basin were simply to have one Sunday dress each, how many yards of Manchester cloth would be required; and the amazing number was 320,000,000 yards, just for one Sunday dress! (Cheers.) Proceeding still further with these figures I found that two Sunday dresses and four everyday dresses would in one year amount to 3,840,000,000 yards, which at 2d. [two pence] per yard would be of the value of £16,000,000. The more I pondered upon these things I discovered that I could not limit these stores of cotton cloth to day dresses. I would have to provide for night dresses also—(laughter)—and these would consume 160,000,000 yards. (Cheers.) Then the grave cloths came into mind, and, as a poor lunatic, who burned Bolobo Station,[3] destroyed 30,000 yards of cloth in order that he should not be cheated out of a respectable burial, I really feared for a time that the millions would get beyond measurable calculation. However, putting such accidents aside, I estimate that, if my figures of population are approximately correct, 2,000,000 die every year, and to bury these decently, and according to the custom of those who possess cloth, 16,000,000 yards will be required, while the 40,000 chiefs will require an average of 100 yards each, or 4,000,000 yards. I regarded these figures with great satisfaction, and I was about to close my remarks upon the millions of yards of cloth that Manchester would perhaps be required to produce when I discovered that I had neglected to provide for the family wardrobe or currency chest, for you must know that in the Lower Congo there is scarcely a family that has not a cloth fund of about a dozen pieces of about 24 yards each. This is a very important institution, otherwise how are the family necessities to be provided for? How are the fathers and mothers of families to go to market to buy greens, bread, oil, ground nuts, chickens, fish, and goats, and how is the petty trade to be conducted? How is ivory to be purchased, the gums, rubber, dye powders, gunpowder, copper slugs, guns, trinkets, knives, and swords to be bought without a supply of cloth? Now, 8,000,000 families at 300 yards each will require 2,400,000,000. (Cheers.) You all know how perishable such currency must be; but if you sum up these several millions of yards, and value all of them at the average price of 2d. per yard, you will find that it will be possible for Manchester to create a trade—in the course of time—in cottons in the Congo basin amounting in value to about £26,000,000 annually. (Loud cheers.) I have said nothing about Rochdale savelist, or your own superior prints, your gorgeous handkerchiefs, with their variegated patterns, your checks and striped cloths, your ticking and twills.[4] I must satisfy myself with suggesting them; your own imaginations will no doubt carry you to the limbo of immeasurable and incalculable millions. (Laughter and cheers.)

2. The Congo Free State (later Zaire), a vast area of central Africa around the Congo River, was formally brought under the ownership of Leopold II of Belgium and other investors in the International Association of the Congo by the Berlin West Africa Conference of 1884–1885. Stanley's expeditions there (from 1876) had been financed by Leopold, and from 1879 Stanley had set up trading stations along the river to facilitate the exploitation of the area's natural resources.

3. The London *Times* carried frequent reports of disturbances in the Congo at this time; in March 1884, for example, Congolese attacks on foreign trading establishments at Nokki in the Lower Congo had caused the Europeans to "declare war against the natives."

4. Savelist is cheap fabric; ticking is a strong cotton or linen fabric; twill is a kind of textile weave.

Now, if your sympathy for yourselves and the fate of Manchester has been excited sufficiently, your next natural question would be as follows: We acknowledge, sir, that you have contrived by an artful array of imposing millions to excite our attention, at least, to this field; but we beg to ask you what Manchester is to do in order that we may begin realising this sale of untold millions of yards of cotton cloth? I answer that the first thing to do is for you to ask the British Government to send a cruiser to the mouth of the Congo to keep watch and ward over that river until the European nations have agreed among themselves as to what shall be done with the river, lest one of these days you will hear that it is too late. (Hear, hear.) Secondly, to study whether, seeing that it will never do to permit Portugal to assume sovereignty over that river[5]—and England publicly disclaims any wish to possess that river for herself—it would not be as well to allow the International Association to act as guardians of international right to free trade and free entrance and exit into and out of the river. (Hear, hear.) The main point, remember, always is a guarantee that the lower river shall be free, that, however the Upper Congo may be developed, no Power, inspired by cupidity, shall seize upon the mouth of the river and build custom houses. (Hear, hear.) The Lower Congo in the future will only be valuable because down its waters will have to be floated the produce of the rich basin above to the ocean steamships. It will always have a fair trade of its own, but it bears no proportion to the almost limitless trade that the Upper Congo could furnish. If the Association could be assured that the road from Europe to Vivi[6] was for ever free, the first steps to realise the sale of those countless millions of yards of cotton cloth would be taken. Over six millions of yards are now used annually; but we have no means of absorbing more, owing to the difficulties of transport. Every man capable and willing to carry a load is employed. When human power was discovered to be not further available we tested animal power and discovered it to be feebler and more costly than the other; and we have come to the conclusion that steam power must now assist us or we remain in statu quo [as things now stand]. But before having recourse to this steam power, and building the iron road along which your bales of cotton fabrics may roll on to the absorbing markets of the Upper Congo unceasingly, the Association pauses to ask you, and the peoples of other English cities, such as London, Liverpool, Glasgow, Birmingham, Leeds, Preston, Sheffield, who profess to understand the importance of the work we have been doing, and the absorbing power of those markets we have reached, what help you will render us, for your own sakes, to make those markets accessible? (Hear, hear.) The Association will not build that railway to the Upper Congo, nor invest one piece of sterling gold in it, unless they are assured they will not be robbed of it, and the Lower Congo will be placed under some flag that shall be a guarantee to all the world that its waters and banks are absolutely free. (Cheers.)

You will agree with me, I am sure, that trade ought to expand and commerce grow, and if we can coax it into mature growth in this Congo basin that it would be a praiseworthy achievement, honoured by men and gods; for out of this trade, this intercourse caused by peaceful barter, proceed all those blessings which you and I enjoy. The more trade thrives, the more benefits to mankind are multipled, and nearer to gods do men become. (Hear, hear.) The builders of railroads through wilder-

---

5. The mouth of the Congo River had been discovered by the Portuguese in 1482.

6. A town on the Upper Congo river; from 1882 Stanley had been arguing that a railway should be built between the Lower and Upper Congo to facilitate the exploitation of the interior. It was completed in 1898.

nesses generally require large concessions of lands; but the proposed builders of this railway to connect the Lower with the Upper Congo do not ask for any landed concessions; but they ask for a concession of authority over the Lower Congo in order that the beneficent policy which directs the civilising work on the Upper Congo may be extended to the Lower River, and that the mode of government and action may be uniform throughout. The beneficent policy referred to is explained in the treaty made and concluded with the United States Government.[7] That treaty says: "That with the object of enabling civilisation and commerce to penetrate into Equatorial Africa the Free States of the Congo have resolved to levy no customs duties whatever. The Free States also guarantee to all men who establish themselves in their territories the right of purchasing, selling, or leasing any land and buildings, of creating factories and of trade on the sole condition that they conform to the law. The International Association of the Congo is prepared to enter into engagements with other nations who desire to secure the free admission of their products on the same terms as those agreed upon with the United States."

Here you have in brief the whole policy. I might end here, satisfied with having reminded you of these facts, which probably you had forgotten. Obedience to the laws—that is, laws drawn for protection of all—is the common law of all civilised communities, without which men would soon become demoralised. Can anybody object to that condition? Probably many of you here recollect reading those interesting letters from the Congo which were written by an English clerk in charge of an English factory. They ended with the cry of "Let us alone." In few words he meant to say, "We are doing very well as we are, we do not wish to be protected, and least of all taxed—therefore, let us alone. Our customers, the natives, are satisfied with us. The native chiefs are friendly and in accord with us; the disturbances, if any occur, are local; they are not general, and they right themselves quickly enough, for the trader cannot exist here if he is not just and kind in his dealings. The obstreperous and violent white is left to himself and ruin. Therefore, let us alone." Most heartily do I echo this cry; but unfortunately the European nations will not heed this cry; they think that some mode of government is necessary to curb those inclined to be refractory, and if there is at present a necessity to exhibit judicial power and to restrict evil-minded and ill-conditioned whites, as the Congo basin becomes more and more populated this necessity will be still more apparent. At the same time, if power appears on the Congo with an arbitrary and unfeeling front—with a disposition to tax and levy burdensome tariffs just as trade begins to be established—the outlook for enterprise becomes dismal and dark indeed.[8] (Hear, hear.) * * *

No part of Africa, look where I might, appeared so promising to me as this neglected tenth part of the continent. I have often fancied myself—when I had nothing to do better than dream—gazing from some lofty height, and looking down upon this square compact patch of 800,000,000 acres, with its 80,000 native towns, its population of 40,000,000 souls, its 17,000 miles of river waters, and its 30,000 square miles of lakes, all lying torpid, lifeless, inert, soaked in brutishness and bestiality, and I have never yet descended from that airy perch in the empyrean and

7. The United States was the first country to recognize the right of the International Association to govern the Congo territories in April 1884.

8. The right of the International Association to govern the Congo was eventually ended in 1908, following widespread protests against the regime's brutality.

touched earth but I have felt a purpose glow in me to strive to do something to awaken it into life and movement, and I have sometimes half fancied that the face of aged Livingstone,[9] vague and indistinct as it were, shone through the warm, hazy atmosphere, with a benignant smile encouraging me in my purpose. * * *

Yet, though examined from every point of view, a study of the Upper Congo and its capabilities produces these exciting arrays of figures and possibilities, I would not pay a two-shilling piece for it all so long as it remains as it is. It will absorb easily the revenue of the wealthiest nation in Europe without any return. I would personally one hundred times over prefer a snug little freehold in a suburb of Manchester to being the owner of the 1,300,000 English square miles of the Congo basin if it is to remain as inaccessible as it is to-day, or if it is to be blocked by that fearful tariff-loving nation, the Portuguese. (Hear, hear.) But if I were assured that the Lower Congo would remain free, and the flag of the Association guaranteed its freedom, I would if I were able build that railway myself—build it solid and strong—and connect the Lower Congo with the Upper Congo, perfectly satisfied that I should be followed by the traders and colonists of all nations. * * * The Portuguese have had nearly 400 years given them to demonstrate to the world what they could do with the river whose mouth they discovered, and they have been proved to be incapable to do any good with it, and now civilisation is inclined to say to them, "Stand off from this broad highway into the regions beyond—(cheers); let others who are not paralytic strive to do what they can with it to bring it within the number of accessible markets. There are 40,000,000 of naked people beyond that gateway, and the cotton spinners of Manchester are waiting to clothe them. Rochdale and Preston women are waiting for the word to weave them warm blue and crimson savelist. Birmingham foundries are glowing with the red metal that shall presently be made into ironwork in every fashion and shape for them, and the trinkets that shall adorn those dusky bosoms; and the ministers of Christ are zealous to bring them, the poor benighted heathen, into the Christian fold." (Cheers.)

Mr JACOB BRIGHT, M.P., who was received with loud cheers, said: I have listened with extreme interest to one of the ablest, one of the most eloquent addresses which have ever been delivered in this city—(cheers); and I have heard with uncommon pleasure the views of a man whose ability, whose splendid force of character, whose remarkable heroism, have given him a world-wide reputation. (Cheers.) * * *

Mr GRAFTON, M.P., moved:—

> That the best thanks of this meeting be and are hereby given to Mr H. M. Stanley for his address to the members of the Chamber, and for the interesting information conveyed by him respecting the Congo and prospects of international trade on the West Coast and interior of Africa.

He remarked that Mr Stanley's name was already enrolled in the pages of history, and would be handed down to posterity with the names of the greatest benefactors of our species, such as Columbus, who had opened out the pathways of the world. Long might Mr Stanley be spared to witness the benefit of his arduous and beneficent labours. (Cheers.)

---

9. David Livingstone (1813–1873), Scottish explorer and missionary. His expeditions into central Africa, in search of the source of the Nile River, were heavily publicized; when Livingstone "disappeared" in the course of what proved to be his last expedition, Stanley, then a correspondent for the *New York Herald*, was sent to find him. The two men met on the banks of Lake Tanganyika in East Africa in 1871; Stanley published an account of their meeting in *How I Found Livingstone* (1872).

Gang of Four: We Live As We Dream, Alone[1]

Everybody is in too many pieces
No man's land surrounds our desires
To crack the shell we mix with others
Some lie in the arms of lovers

The city is the place to be
With no money you go crazy
I need an occupation
You have to pay for satisfaction

We live as we dream, alone
To crack this shell we mix with others
Some flirt with fascism
Some lie in the arms of lovers

We live as we dream, alone
(repeat)

Everybody is in too many pieces
No man's land surrounds me
Without money we'll all go crazy

Man and woman need to work
It helps to define ourselves
We were not born in isolation
But sometimes it seems that way

We live as we dream, alone
(repeat)

We live as we dream, alone
The space between our work and its product
Some fall into fatalism
As if it started out this way

We live as we dream, alone
(repeat)

We live as we dream, alone
We were not born in isolation
But sometimes it seems that way
The space between our work and its product
As if it must always be this way

With our money we'll . . .

---

1. In 1976 the Sex Pistols set off the British punk revolution with their first single, "Anarchy in the U.K." The Gang of Four is one of many bands that arose during the early years of punk, when a wide range of musical possibilities seemed open to anyone with a guitar. The Gang of Four's music combines the assaultive sound of punk bands with an infectious dance sensibility—lacing this unlikely hybrid with neo-Marxist lyrics about consumerism and labor. "We Live As We Dream, Alone," from their 1982 album *Songs of the Free*, takes a famous line from *Heart of Darkness* and makes it the cry of alienated labor, thereby reframing Conrad's message for a nation dominated by the conservative policies of Thatcherism.

Thomas Hardy
1840–1928

Thomas Hardy led a double life: one of the great Victorian novelists, he abandoned fiction in 1896 and reinvented himself as a poet. In a series of volumes published from 1898 through the early decades of the twentieth century, Hardy emerged as one of the most compelling voices in modern poetry. How should this strangely bifurcated literary career be read? There are continuities as well as divergences between Hardy's fiction and his poetry, and the shifts in his work provide a telling instance of the interwoven links and discontinuities between the Victorian era and the new modernism of the twentieth century.

Hardy was born and reared in the village of Higher Bockhampton, Stinsford, in the rural county of Dorset in southern England. He left home in his early twenties and worked as a church architect in London for five years, then returned to the family home in 1867; he continued to accept architectural commissions while trying his hand at fiction and poetry. In early poems such as *Hap* and *Neutral Tones* Hardy revealed his abiding sense of a universe ruled by a blind or hostile fate, a world whose landscapes are etched with traces of the fleeting stories of their inhabitants. He was not able to find a publisher for such works, and he largely stopped writing poetry, but his first novel, *Desperate Remedies,* was published in 1871. By 1874 he was earning a steady income from his writing and was able to marry Emma Lavinia Gifford, the sister-in-law of a rector whose church he had been restoring. He produced twenty novels within a twenty-five year period, achieving fame, popularity, and no little controversy for the provocative and dark worlds he created. In *Far from the Madding Crowd, The Return of the Native, Tess of the d'Urbervilles,* and *Jude the Obscure,* Hardy transformed the realist novel of manners into tragic accounts of the industrialization of rural Britain, the bankruptcy of religious faith, and irreconcilable tensions between social classes and between men and women. Though he had become a master of characterization and plot, in his later novels Hardy grew increasingly preoccupied with fundamentally lyrical questions of interiority, subjective perception, and personal voice. After the sexual frankness of *Jude the Obscure* provoked shocked reviews—the Bishop of Wakefield went so far as to burn the book—Hardy decided to abandon his prose writing altogether and to mine his chosen territory with the tools of a poet.

He began by recreating in poetry the landscape of his fiction. Hardy's first poetry collection, published when he was fifty-eight, was *Wessex Poems* (1898), its title referring to the imaginary countryside that he had created in his novels, loosely based on regions in the south of England but named for a long-vanished medieval kingdom. Hardy's "Wessex" was a place whose towns and roads and forests and fields were breathed into life by the novelist. The Wessex novels were published with maps of the territory, and the landmarks were to remain constant throughout the disparate books. The region took such a hold on readers' imaginations that a Wessex tourist industry emerged, one which is still in place today. Hardy was as painstaking in giving the precise (although imaginary) coordinates of a village pathway as he was in tracing the path of a character's destiny.

Many of Hardy's poems take root in this same creative landscape, now viewed by an intensely self-aware speaker who retraces his personal history, himself "tracked by phantoms having weird detective ways," as he says in *Wessex Heights*. Burning logs, a photograph, a diminishing figure on a train platform, a deer at a window all provide "moments of vision" (the title of one of his collections) that foreshadow the modernist "epiphanies" of Joyce and Woolf. Like the major modernists, Hardy explored the workings of memory, of perception, and of individual vision. In other poems, he focused on contemporary events, most notably in a series of poems written during World War I, unsparing in their presentation both of the necessity of waging the conflict and of its horrifying waste.

In his poetry as in his prose, Hardy's modern themes are typically set in a rural landscape with ancient roots. A constant feature of the Wessex novels involves characters setting off on one of the myriad footpaths connecting obscure villages and solitary cottages with one another. Hardy invented his own geography for Wessex, but the footpaths really existed and were the most important trails carved into the landscape by travelers over many years. Called "ley lines" in folk culture, such footpaths are thought to gather their energy over time, as hundreds of people gradually wear down a shared path and leave traces of themselves in the form of memory and tradition. Hardy's poems move between personal, historical, and natural levels of experience, but it is the landscape above all that conveys the power of these events.

Hardy embodied his moments of vision in poems that recall old oral and religious forms of verse, especially those of ballads and hymns. Like Wordsworth, Burns, and Kipling, Hardy was fascinated by the power of popular verse forms to convey deep truths in seemingly simple meters and diction; like his predecessors, Hardy brought his traditional forms to life by subtle modulations of their elements. The lines of Hardy's poetry are measured with extreme care and precision—not in any way approaching "free verse." As W. H. Auden wrote of Hardy's poetry: "No English poet, not even Donne or Browning, employed so many and so complicated stanza forms. Anyone who imitates his style will learn at least one thing, how to make words fit into a complicated structure." With architectural care, Hardy built up his words into complicated structures, lines, and stanzas following well-used poetic paths. With its compelling mixture of tradition and modernity, stoic calm and deep emotional intensity, Hardy's poetry has become a touchstone for modern poets writing in English, from Ezra Pound, who said he "needed no other poet," to Philip Larkin, Seamus Heaney, and Derek Walcott. "Auden worshiped his honesty, Eliot disliked his heresy," the critic Irving Howe has commented; "but Hardy prepared the ground for both."

Hardy mined his native landscape, and his own memory, until his death, composing many of his best poems in his seventies and eighties. He had built a house on the outskirts of Dorchester in 1885, and he lived there for the rest of his life, with his wife Emma until her death in 1912, and subsequently with his secretary, Florence Dugdale, whom he married in 1914. When he died, his body was buried in Westminster Abbey; but his heart, as he had directed, was buried in the grave of his wife Emma, next to his father's grave, in the Stinsford churchyard.

Hap°   *chance*

If but some vengeful god would call to me
From up the sky, and laugh: "Thou suffering thing,
Know that thy sorrow is my ecstasy,
That thy love's loss is my hate's profiting!"

5   Then would I bear it, clench myself, and die,
Steeled by the sense of ire unmerited;
Half-eased in that a Powerfuller than I
Had willed and meted° me the tears I shed.   *given*

But not so. How arrives it joy lies slain,
10   And why unblooms the best hope ever sown?
—Crass Casualty obstructs the sun and rain,
And dicing° Time for gladness casts a moan. . . .   *gambling*
These purblind° Doomsters had as readily strown   *half-blind*
Blisses about my pilgrimage as pain.

1866   1898

Neutral Tones

We stood by a pond that winter day,
And the sun was white, as though chidden° of God,   rebuked
And a few leaves lay on the starving sod;
   —They had fallen from an ash, and were gray.

5   Your eyes on me were as eyes that rove
Over tedious riddles of years ago;
And some words played between us to and fro
   On which lost the more by our love.

The smile on your mouth was the deadest thing
10   Alive enough to have strength to die;
And a grin of bitterness swept thereby
   Like an ominous bird a-wing . . . .

Since then, keen lessons that love deceives,
And wrings with wrong, have shaped to me
15   Your face, and the God-curst sun, and a tree,
   And a pond edged with grayish leaves.

1867   1898

Wessex Heights

There are some heights in Wessex,[1] shaped as if by a kindly hand
For thinking, dreaming, dying on, and at crises when I stand,
Say, on Ingpen Beacon eastward, or on Wylls-Neck westwardly,
I seem where I was before my birth, and after death may be.

5   In the lowlands I have no comrade, not even the lone man's friend—
Her who suffereth long and is kind;[2] accepts what he is too weak to mend:
Down there they are dubious and askance; there nobody thinks as I,
But mind-chains do not clank where one's next neighbour is the sky.

In the towns I am tracked by phantoms having weird detective ways—
10   Shadows of beings who fellowed with myself of earlier days:
They hang about at places, and they say harsh heavy things—
Men with a wintry sneer, and women with tart disparagings.

Down there I seem to be false to myself, my simple self that was,
And is not now, and I see him watching, wondering what crass cause
15   Can have merged him into such a strange continuator as this,
Who yet has something in common with himself, my chrysalis.

I cannot go to the great grey Plain; there's a figure against the moon,
Nobody sees it but I, and it makes my breast beat out of tune;
I cannot go to the tall-spired town, being barred by the forms now passed
20   For everybody but me, in whose long vision they stand there fast.

---

1. An imaginary county in southwest England that forms the setting for Hardy's writings; the place names that follow are in "Wessex."

2. Cf. Corinthians 13.4: "Charity suffereth long, and is kind."

There's a ghost at Yell'ham Bottom chiding loud at the fall of the night,
There's a ghost in Froom-side Vale, thin-lipped and vague, in a shroud
    of white,
There is one in the railway train whenever I do not want it near,
I see its profile against the pane, saying what I would not hear.

25   As for one rare fair woman, I am now but a thought of hers,
I enter her mind and another thought succeeds me that she prefers,
Yet my love for her in its fulness she herself even did not know;
Well, time cures hearts of tenderness, and now I can let her go.

So I am found on Ingpen Beacon, or on Wylls-Neck to the west,
30   Or else on homely Bulbarrow, or little Pilsdon Crest,
Where men have never cared to haunt, nor women have walked with me,
And ghosts then keep their distance; and I know some liberty.

1898

The Darkling Thrush[1]

I leant upon a coppice° gate   *wood*
    When Frost was spectre-gray,
And Winter's dregs made desolate
    The weakening eye of day.
5   The tangled bine-stems° scored the sky   *stems of bushes*
    Like strings of broken lyres,
And all mankind that haunted nigh
    Had sought their household fires.

The land's sharp features seemed to be
10   The Century's corpse outleant[2],
His crypt the cloudy canopy,
    The wind his death-lament.
The ancient pulse of germ° and birth   *seed*
    Was shrunken hard and dry,
15   And every spirit upon earth
    Seemed fervourless as I.

At once a voice arose among
    The bleak twigs overhead
In a full-hearted evensong
20   Of joy illimited;
An aged thrush, frail, gaunt, and small,
    In blast-beruffled plume,
Had chosen thus to fling his soul
    Upon the growing gloom.

25   So little cause for carolings
    Of such ecstatic sound
Was written on terrestrial things
    Afar or nigh around,
That I could think there trembled through

---

1. The poem was published on 31 December 1900.   2. As if leaning out from a coffin.

30   His happy good-night air
        Some blessed Hope, whereof he knew
            And I was unaware.

On the Departure Platform

We kissed at the barrier; and passing through
She left me, and moment by moment got
Smaller and smaller, until to my view
        She was but a spot;

5   A wee white spot of muslin fluff
    That down the diminishing platform bore
    Through hustling crowds of gentle and rough
            To the carriage door.

    Under the lamplight's fitful glowers,
10 Behind dark groups from far and near,
    Whose interests were apart from ours,
            She would disappear,

    Then show again, till I ceased to see
    That flexible form, that nebulous white;
15 And she who was more than my life to me
            Had vanished quite . . . .

    We have penned new plans since that fair fond day,
    And in season she will appear again—
    Perhaps in the same soft white array—
20   But never as then!

    —"And why, young man, must eternally fly
    A joy you'll repeat, if you love her well?"
    —O friend, nought happens twice thus; why,
            I cannot tell!

1909

The Convergence of the Twain
(Lines on the loss of the "Titanic")[1]

1
        In a solitude of the sea
        Deep from human vanity,
And the Pride of Life that planned her, stilly couches she.

2
        Steel chambers, late the pyres
5   Of her salamandrine° fires,   *white-hot*
Cold currents thrid°, and turn to rhythmic tidal lyres.   *thread*

3
        Over the mirrors meant
        To glass the opulent
The sea-worm crawls—grotesque, slimed, dumb, indifferent.

1. The largest ocean-liner of its day, the supposedly unsinkable *Titanic* sank on 15 April 1912 on its maiden voyage after colliding with an iceberg; two thirds of its 2,200 passengers died.

4

10   Jewels in joy designed
               To ravish the sensuous mind
Lie lightless, all their sparkles bleared and black and blind.

5

            Dim moon-eyed fishes near
              Gaze at the gilded gear
15   And query: "What does this vaingloriousness down here?" . . .

6

           Well: while was fashioning
             This creature of cleaving wing,
The Immanent Will that stirs and urges everything

7

           Prepared a sinister mate
20   For her—so gaily great—
A Shape of Ice, for the time far and dissociate.[2]

8

           And as the smart ship grew
            In stature, grace, and hue,
In shadowy silent distance grew the Iceberg too.

9

25   Alien they seemed to be:
            No mortal eye could see
The intimate welding of their later history,

10

           Or sign that they were bent
            By paths coincident
30   On being anon twin halves of one august event,

11

           Till the Spinner of the Years
            Said "Now!" And each one hears,
And consummation comes, and jars two hemispheres.

1912   1912

Channel Firing[1]

That night your great guns, unawares,
Shook all our coffins as we lay,
And broke the chancel window-squares,
We thought it was the Judgment-day

5   And sat upright. While drearisome
Arose the howl of wakened hounds:
The mouse let fall the altar-crumb,
The worms drew back into the mounds,
The glebe° cow drooled. Till God called, "No;   *field*
10   It's gunnery practice out at sea
Just as before you went below;
The world is as it used to be:

---

2. According to Hardy, the Immanent Will is that which secretly guides events.

1. The poem refers to military exercises in the English Channel prior to World War 1.

"All nations striving strong to make
Red war yet redder. Mad as hatters
15 They do no more for Christés sake
Than you who are helpless in such matters.

"That this is not the judgment-hour
For some of them's a blessed thing,
For if it were they'd have to scour
20 Hell's floor for so much threatening . . . .

"Ha, ha. It will be warmer when
I blow the trumpet (if indeed
I ever do; for you are men,
And rest eternal sorely need)."

25 So down we lay again. "I wonder,
Will the world ever saner be,"
Said one, "than when He sent us under
In our indifferent century!"

And many a skeleton shook his head.
30 "Instead of preaching forty year,"
My neighbour Parson Thirdly said,
"I wish I had stuck to pipes and beer."

Again the guns disturbed the hour,
Roaring their readiness to avenge,
35 As far inland as Stourton Tower,
And Camelot, and starlit Stonehenge.[2]

April 1914   1914

In Time of "The Breaking of Nations"[1]

1

Only a man harrowing clods
    In a slow silent walk
With an old horse that stumbles and nods
    Half asleep as they stalk.

2

5   Only thin smoke without flame
    From the heaps of couch-grass;
Yet this will go onward the same
    Though Dynasties pass.

3

Yonder a maid and her wight°   man
10   Come whispering by:
War's annals will cloud into night
    Ere their story die.

1915   1916

---

2. The town of Stour Head, which Hardy calls Stourton, is in the county of Dorset. According to legend, Camelot was the site of King Arthur's court; Stonehenge is a prehistoric site in southwest England.

1. Cf. Jeremiah 51.20: "Thou art my battle axe and weapons of war: for with thee will I break in pieces the nations, and with thee will I destroy kingdoms."

I Looked Up from My Writing

I looked up from my writing,
    And gave a start to see,
As if rapt in my inditing,
    The moon's full gaze on me.

5 Her meditative misty head
    Was spectral in its air,
And I involuntarily said,
    "What are you doing there?"

"Oh, I've been scanning pond and hole
10   And waterway hereabout
For the body of one with a sunken soul
    Who has put his life-light out.

"Did you hear his frenzied tattle?
    It was sorrow for his son
15 Who is slain in brutish battle,
    Though he has injured none.

"And now I am curious to look
    Into the blinkered mind
Of one who wants to write a book
20   In a world of such a kind."

Her temper overwrought me,
    And I edged to shun her view,
For I felt assured she thought me
    One who should drown him too.

1917

"And There Was a Great Calm"[1]
(On the Signing of the Armistice, 11 Nov. 1918)[2]

1

There had been years of Passion—scorching, cold,
And much Despair, and Anger heaving high,
Care whitely watching, Sorrows manifold,
Among the young, among the weak and old,
5 And the pensive Spirit of Pity whispered, "Why?"

2

Men had not paused to answer. Foes distraught
Pierced the thinned peoples in a brute-like blindness,
Philosophies that sages long had taught,
And Selflessness, were as an unknown thought,
10 And "Hell!" and "Shell!" were yapped at Lovingkindness.

3

The feeble folk at home had grown full-used
To "dug-outs," "snipers," "'Huns,'"[3] from the war-adept

---

1. A phrase from Mark 4.39, after Jesus has calmed a storm at sea.
2. The armistice ending World War I was signed by Ger-

many and the Allies on this date.
3. Slang for "Germans" during the war.

In the mornings heard, and at evetides perused;
To day-dreamt men in millions, when they mused—
15   To nightmare-men in millions when they slept.

4

Waking to wish existence timeless, null,
Sirius[4] they watched above where armies fell;
He seemed to check his flapping when, in the lull
Of night a boom came thencewise, like the dull
20   Plunge of a stone dropped into some deep well.

5

So, when old hopes that earth was bettering slowly
Were dead and damned, there sounded "War is done!"
One morrow. Said the bereft, and meek, and lowly,
"Will men some day be given to grace? yea, wholly,
25   And in good sooth,° as our dreams used to run?"   truth

6

Breathless they paused. Out there men raised their glance
To where had stood those poplars lank and lopped,
As they had raised it through the four years' dance
Of Death in the now familiar flats of France;
30   And murmured, "Strange, this! How? All firing stopped?"

7

Aye; all was hushed. The about-to-fire fired not,
The aimed-at moved away in trance-lipped song.
One checkless regiment slung a clinching shot
And turned. The Spirit of Irony smirked out, "What?
35   Spoil peradventures° woven of Rage and Wrong?"   perhaps

8

Thenceforth no flying fires inflamed the gray,
No hurtlings shook the dewdrop from the thorn,
No moan perplexed the mute bird on the spray;
Worn horses mused: "We are not whipped to-day;"
40   No weft-winged engines° blurred the moon's thin horn.   early airplanes

9

Calm fell. From Heaven distilled a clemency;
There was peace on earth, and silence in the sky;
Some could, some could not, shake off misery:
The Sinister Spirit sneered: "It had to be!"
45   And again the Spirit of Pity whispered, "Why?"
1918   1919, 1922

Logs on the Hearth
A Memory of a Sister[1]

The fire advances along the log
    Of the tree we felled,
Which bloomed and bore striped apples by the peck°   basketful
    Till its last hour of bearing knelled.

---

4. The brightest star in the night sky.   1. Hardy's sister Mary died in November 1915.

5   The fork that first my hand would reach
          And then my foot
In climbings upward inch by inch, lies now
    Sawn, sapless, darkening with soot.

       Where the bark chars is where, one year,
10   It was pruned, and bled—
Then overgrew the wound. But now, at last,
    Its growings all have stagnated.

       My fellow-climber rises dim
          From her chilly grave—
15 Just as she was, her foot near mine on the bending limb,
    Laughing, her young brown hand awave.

1915   1917

Afterwards

When the Present has latched its postern° behind my tremulous stay,   *gate*
    And the May month flaps its glad green leaves like wings,
Delicate-filmed as new-spun silk, will the neighbours say,
    "He was a man who used to notice such things"?

5 If it be in the dusk when, like an eyelid's soundless blink,
    The dewfall-hawk comes crossing the shades to alight
Upon the wind-warped upland thorn, a gazer may think,
    "To him this must have been a familiar sight."

If I pass during some nocturnal blackness, mothy and warm,
10   When the hedgehog travels furtively over the lawn,
One may say, "He strove that such innocent creatures should come to no harm,
    But he could do little for them; and now he is gone."

If, when hearing that I have been stilled at last, they stand at the door,
    Watching the full-starred heavens that winter sees,
15 Will this thought rise on those who will meet my face no more,
    "He was one who had an eye for such mysteries"?

And will any say when my bell of quittance is heard in the gloom,
    And a crossing breeze cuts a pause in its outrollings,
Till they rise again, as they were a new bell's boom,
20   "He hears it not now, but used to notice such things"?

                                          1917

Epitaph

I never cared for Life: Life cared for me,
And hence I owed it some fidelity.
It now says, "Cease; at length thou hast learnt to grind
Sufficient toll for an unwilling mind,
And I dismiss thee—not without regard
That thou didst ask no ill-advised reward,
Nor sought in me much more than thou couldst find."

                                        1922

The Great War: Confronting the Modern

The multiplying technological, artistic, and social changes at the turn of the twentieth century impressed that generation's artists as a rupture with the past. And no event so graphically suggested that human history had "changed, changed utterly," as World War I—"the Great War."

Great Britain, like its enemy Germany, entered the war with idealistic aims. Prime Minister H. H. Asquith put the justice of the British case this way in a speech to the House of Commons on 7 August 1914: "I do not think any nation ever entered into a great conflict—and this is one of the greatest that history will ever know—with a clearer conscience or stronger conviction that it is fighting not for aggression, not for the maintenance of its own selfish ends, but in defence of principles the maintenance of which is vital to the civilization of the world." But cynicism set in quickly—first among ground troops on the Western Front, dug into trenches and watching "progress" that could be measured in yards per day. Soon the British public became disillusioned with the war effort, partly as a result of technological advances in the news media. Daily papers in England carried photographs from the front, and while editorial policy generally supported the British government and printed heroic images of the fighting, this sanitized version of the war was largely offset by the long published lists of casualties; during the four years and three months that Britain was involved in the war, more than a million British troops—an average of fifteen hundred per day—were killed in action.

The war's lasting legacy was a sense of bitterly rebuffed idealism, bringing with it a suspicion of progress, technology, government, bureaucracy, nationalism, and conventional morality—themes probed in new ways by the period's writers. Just as the war had involved radically new strategies and new technologies, writers intensified their search for new forms and modes of expression as they and their compatriots found themselves in the midst of a conflict unlike anything previously known in the annals of history.

━━━◆━━━

Blast

Wyndham Lewis (1884–1957), founder of the provocative arts magazine *Blast*, was often at odds with his sometime co-conspirator Ezra Pound: indeed both men were usually at odds with most of their friends. But they did agree on one thing: that the writers of Edwardian and Georgian England had failed to throw off the deadening literary mannerisms of the previous century. "As for the nineteenth century," Pound wrote, "with all respects to its achievements, I think we shall look back upon it as a rather blurry, messy sort of a period, a rather sentimental-istic, mannerish sort of a period."

Some violent corrective was needed. The name of Lewis's magazine was intended to suggest an explosive charge that would blow away tired literary and social conventions. It was a calculated assault on good taste, both in its contents and, more immediately, in its form: an oversized, bright pink cover with the single word *BLAST* splashed diagonally across it. Lewis carefully oversaw the details of typography; visually and rhetorically, *Blast* is indebted to the polemical style of the Italian artist F. T. Marinetti (1876–1944), the founder of Italian futurism. Marinetti's vivid manifestos for futurism celebrated a modern aesthetic of speed, technology, and power. Lewis in turn founded a movement he called Vorticism, and *Blast* bore the subtitle *The Review of the Great English Vortex*.

The definition of *vorticism* was left intentionally hazy; as canny an observer as the Vorticist painter William Roberts, one of the signatories of the manifesto, claimed that Vorticism was first and foremost "a slogan." In 1915 Lewis defined it this way: "By Vorticism we mean (a) ACTIVITY as opposed to the tasteful PASSIVITY of Picasso; (b) SIGNIFICANCE as opposed to the

Wyndham Lewis. *The Creditors* (design for *Timon of Athens*). 1912–1913.

dull or anecdotal character to which the Naturalist is condemned; (c) ESSENTIAL MOVEMENT and ACTIVITY (such as the energy of a mind) as opposed to the imitative cinematography, the fuss and hysterics of the Futurists."

In its disorienting layout of typography, the *Vorticist Manifesto* is as much a visual as a literary statement, reflecting the multiple and always skewed interest of its primary author, Lewis. Born on a yacht off the coast of Nova Scotia, he had moved to London with his mother when his parents separated in 1893. A precocious painter, he won a scholarship to the progressive Slade School of Art at age sixteen, but moved to Paris before completing his studies. He returned to London in 1909 and began a career as a painter and writer. During the War, he served both as an artillery officer and as a commissioned war artist. He also wrote an experimental novel, *Tarr* (1918), and went on to produce a range of works in the dozen years thereafter, including pro-fascist political theory in *The Art of Being Ruled* (1926) and more general cultural criticism in *Time and Western Man* (1927), in which he attacked the modern cult of subjectivity. During the thirties, he became increasingly unpopular in London, first as a result of a satirical novel, *The Apes of God,* which lampooned figures in the literary and art world and their patrons; following two libel actions against him, publishers became wary of taking on his works. Lewis and his wife spent the years of World War II living in poverty in America and Canada; after the war, he returned to England, where he became an art critic for the British Broadcasting Corporation. He continued to draw, paint, and write memoirs, satirical stories, and an allegorical fantasy in several volumes.

Along with the *Vorticist Manifesto*, the first issue of *Blast* included poetry by Pound, fiction by Ford Madox Ford and Rebecca West, a play by Lewis, and illustrations by Lewis and others. The timing of the first issue couldn't have been worse: after delays caused by typesetting difficulties, *Blast* went on sale in London on June 20, 1914; World War I began just a few weeks later. While Lewis and his confederates had declared war on conventional artistic and literary taste with their "puce monster"—an advertisement for the first issue announced the "END OF THE CHRISTIAN ERA"—they were usurped by a much more pressing conflict. As Lewis later wrote, "In 1914 I produced a huge review called *Blast,* which for the most part I wrote myself. That was my first public appearance. Immediately the War broke out and put an end to all that." Lewis brought out a second issue in July 1915, attempting to fend off charges of irrelevancy with a special "War Number" that included T. S. Eliot's "Preludes" and "Rhapsody on a Windy Night" and a manifesto from the sculptor Henri Gaudier-Brzeska, "written from the trenches," which concludes poignantly with an obituary for Gaudier, "Mort pour la Patrie" (died for the fatherland). But by this time, *Blast* itself was for all intents and purposes dead; its second issue was its last. Short-lived though it was, however, *Blast* was remarkably important in clearing the way for the new art of modernism.

VORTICIST MANIFESTO
LONG LIVE THE VORTEX!

Long live the great art vortex sprung up in the centre of this town!

We stand for the Reality of the Present—not for the sentimental Future, or the sacripant[1] Past.

We want to leave Nature and Men alone.

We do not want to make people wear Futurist Patches, or fuss men to take to pink and sky-blue trousers.

We are not their wives or tailors.

The only way Humanity can help artists is to remain independent and work unconsciously.

WE NEED THE UNCONSCIOUSNESS OF HUMANITY—their stupidity, animalism and dreams.

We believe in no perfectibility except our own.

Intrinsic beauty is in the Interpreter and Seer, not in the object or content.[2]

We do not want to change the appearance of the world, because we are not Naturalists, Impressionists or Futurists (the latest form of Impressionism), and do not depend on the appearance of the world for our art.

WE ONLY WANT THE WORLD TO LIVE, and to feel its crude energy flowing through us.

It may be said that great artists in England are always revolutionary, just as in France any really fine artist had a strong traditional vein.

Blast sets out to be an avenue for all those vivid and violent ideas that could reach the Public in no other way.

Blast will be popular, essentially. It will not appeal to any particular class, but to the fundamental and popular instincts in every class and description of people, **TO THE INDIVIDUAL.** The moment a man feels or realizes himself as an artist, he ceases to belong to any milieu or time. Blast is created for this timeless, fundamental Artist that exists in everybody.

---

1. Boasting of valor.
2. Although the Vorticists go on to differentiate themselves from the Impressionists, this statement is very close
to the impressionism articulated by Walter Pater in *The Renaissance* (1873).

The Man in the Street and the Gentleman are equally ignored.

Popular art does not mean the art of the poor people, as it is usually supposed to. It means the art of the individuals.

Education (art education and general education) tends to destroy the creative instinct. Therefore it is in times when education has been non-existent that art chiefly flourished.

But it is nothing to do with "the People."

It is a mere accident that that is the most favourable time for the individual to appear.

To make the rich of the community shed their education skin, to destroy politeness, standardization and academic, that is civilized, vision, is the task we have set ourselves.

We want to make in England not a popular art, not a revival of lost folk art, or a romantic fostering of such unactual conditions, but to make individuals, wherever found.

We will convert the King if possible.

A VORTICIST KING! WHY NOT?

DO YOU THINK LLOYD GEORGE[3] HAS THE VORTEX IN HIM?

MAY WE HOPE FOR ART FROM LADY MOND?[4]

We are against the glorification of "the People," as we are against snobbery. It is not necessary to be an outcast bohemian, to be unkempt or poor, any more than it is necessary to be rich or handsome, to be an artist. Art is nothing to do with the coat you wear. A top-hat can well hold the Sixtine.[5] A cheap cap could hide the image of Kephren.

AUTOMOBILISM (Marinetteism) bores us. We don't want to go about making a hullo-bulloo about motor cars, anymore than about knives and forks, elephants or gas-pipes.

Elephants are **VERY BIG.** Motor cars go quickly.

Wilde gushed twenty years ago about the beauty of machinery. Gissing,[6] in his romantic delight with modern lodging houses was futurist in this sense.

The futurist is a sensational and sentimental mixture of the aesthete of 1890 and the realist of 1870.

The "Poor" are detestable animals! They are only picturesque and amusing for the sentimentalist or the romantic! The "Rich" are bores without a single exception, *en tant que riches* [so far as they are rich]!

We want those simple and great people found everywhere.

Blast presents an art of Individuals.

MANIFESTO.

1

BLAST First (from politeness) ENGLAND
CURSE ITS CLIMATE FOR ITS SINS AND INFECTIONS
DISMAL SYMBOL, SET round our bodies,
of effeminate lout within.

---

3. David Lloyd George, British statesman, and Prime Minister 1916–1922.
4. A leader of fashionable London society.

5. The Sistine Chapel in the Vatican.
6. George Gissing (1857–1903), naturalist novelist.

VICTORIAN VAMPIRE, the LONDON cloud sucks
the TOWN'S heart.

A 1000 MILE LONG, 2 KILOMETER Deep

BODY OF WATER even, is pushed against us
from the Floridas, TO MAKE US MILD.
OFFICIOUS MOUNTAINS keep back DRASTIC WINDS

SO MUCH VAST MACHINERY TO PRODUCE

THE CURATE of "Eltham"
BRITANNIC AESTHETE
WILD NATURE CRANK
DOMESTICATED POLICEMAN
LONDON COLISEUM
SOCIALIST-PLAYWRIGHT
DALY'S MUSICAL COMEDY
GAIETY CHORUS GIRL
TONKS[7]

CURSE

the flabby sky that can manufacture no snow, but can only drop the sea on us in a drizzle like a poem by Mr. Robert Bridges.[8]

CURSE

the lazy air that cannot stiffen the back of the **SERPENTINE,** or put Aquatic steel half way down the **MANCHESTER CANAL.**

———

But ten years ago we saw distinctly both snow and ice here.

May some vulgarly inventive, but useful person, arise, and restore to us the necessary **BLIZZARDS.**

LET US ONCE MORE WEAR THE ERMINE
OF THE NORTH.

WE BELIEVE IN THE EXISTENCE OF THIS USEFUL LITTLE CHEMIST IN OUR MIDST!

---

7. Henry Tonks, a teacher at the Slade School of Art (where Lewis and other Vorticists studied) who resisted as "contamination" such modern innovations as Post-Impressionism and Cubism.
8. Poet Laureate from 1913 until his death in 1930, noted for his technical skill and high moral tone.

2
OH BLAST FRANCE

pig plagiarism
BELLY
SLIPPERS
POODLE TEMPER
BAD MUSIC

SENTIMENTAL GALLIC GUSH
SENSATIONALISM
FUSSINESS.

PARISIAN PAROCHIALISM.

Complacent young man, so much respect for Papa and his son!—Oh!— Papa is wonderful: but all papas are!

BLAST

APERITIFS (Pernots, Amers picon)
Bad change
Naively seductive Houri salon-
    picture Cocottes
Slouching blue porters (can carry
    a pantechnicon)
Stupidly rapacious people at
    every step
Economy maniacs
Bouillon Kub (for being a bad pun)

PARIS.

Clap-trap Heaven of amative
    German professor.
Ubiquitous lines of silly little trees.
Arcs de Triomphe.
Imperturbable, endless prettiness.
Large empty cliques, higher up.
Bad air for the individual.

BLAST
MECCA OF THE AMERICAN

because it is not other side of Suez Canal, instead of an afternoon's ride from London.

3
CURSE

WITH EXPLETIVE OF WHIRLWIND
THE BRITANNIC AESTHETE

CREAM OF THE SNOBBISH EARTH
ROSE OF SHARON OF GOD-PRIG
 OF SIMIAN VANITY
SNEAK AND SWOT OF THE SCHOOL-ROOM
IMBERB (or Berbed when in Belsize)-PEDANT

PRACTICAL JOKER
DANDY
CURATE

BLAST all products of phlegmatic cold
Life of LOOKER-ON.
CURSE

SNOBBERY
(disease of feminity)
FEAR OF RIDICULE
(arch vice of inactive, sleepy)
PLAY
STYLISM
SINS AND PLAGUES
of this LYMPHATIC finished
(we admit in every sense
finished)
VEGETABLE HUMANITY.

4
BLAST

THE SPECIALIST
"PROFESSIONAL"
"GOOD WORKMAN"
"GROVE-MAN"
ONE ORGAN MAN

BLAST THE

AMATEUR
SCIOLAST
ART-PIMP
JOURNALIST
SELF MAN
NO-ORGAN MAN

5
BLAST HUMOUR

Quack ENGLISH drug for stupidity and sleepiness.
Arch enemy of REAL, conventionalizing like

> gunshot, freezing supple
> REAL in ferocious chemistry
> of laughter.

BLAST SPORT
HUMOUR'S FIRST COUSIN AND ACCOMPLICE.

> Impossibility for Englishman to be grave and
>   keep his end up, psychologically.
> Impossible for him to use Humour as well
>   and be persistently grave.
> Alas! necessity for big doll's show in front
>   of mouth.
> Visitation of Heaven on
>   English Miss
>   gums, canines of **FIXED GRIN**
> Death's head symbol of Anti-Life.

CURSE those who will hang over this
Manifesto with SILLY CANINES exposed.

6
BLAST
years 1837 to 1900

Curse abysmal inexcusable middle-class (also Aristocracy and
Proletariat).

BLAST

pasty shadow cast by gigantic BOEHM[9]
(Imagined at introduction of BOURGEOIS VICTORIAN
VISTAS).
WRING THE NECK OF all sick inventions born in that pro-
gressive white wake.

---

9. Joseph Edgar Boehm (1834–1890), sculptor for Queen Victoria.

BLAST   their weeping whiskers—hirsute
RHETORIC of EUNUCH and STYLIST—
SENTIMENTAL HYGIENICS
ROUSSEAUISMS (wild Nature cranks)
FRATERNIZING WITH MONKEYS
DIABOLICS—raptures and roses
of the erotic bookshelves
culminating in
PURGATORY OF PUTNEY.[1]

CHAOS OF ENOCH ARDENS[2]

| laughing Jennys[3]
| Ladies with Pains
| good-for-nothing Guineveres.

SNOBBISH BORROVIAN running after
GIPSY KINGS and ESPADAS[4]
bowing the knee to
wild Mother Nature,
her feminine contours,
Unimaginative insult to
MAN.

DAMN

all those to-day who have taken on that Rotten Menagerie, and still crack
their whips and tumble in Piccadilly Circus, as though London were a
provincial town.

WE WHISPER IN YOUR EAR A GREAT SECRET.

LONDON IS <u>NOT</u> A PROVINCIAL TOWN.

We will allow Wonder Zoos. But we do not want the
GLOOMY VICTORIAN CIRCUS in
Piccadilly Circus.

IT IS PICCADILLY'S CIRCUS!

NOT MEANT FOR MENAGERIES trundling
out of Sixties DICKENSIAN CLOWNS,
CORELLI[5] LADY RIDERS, TROUPS
OF PERFORMING GIPSIES (who
complain besides that 1/6 a night
does not pay fare back to Clapham).

---

1. A middle-class suburb of London.
2. *Enoch Arden* (1864), a sentimental narrative poem by Tennyson.
3. From Dante Gabriel Rossetti's popular poem *Jenny* (1870), again disliked for its sentimentality.

4. Refers to the contemporary popularity of the gypsy romances of George Borrow, such as *The Zincali* (1841).
5. Marie Corelli, pseud. of Mary Mackay (1855–1924), author of best-selling religious novels and romances.

BLAST[6]

The Post Office   Frank Brangwyn   Robertson Nicol
Rev. Pennyfeather   Galloway Kyle
(Bells)   (Cluster of Grapes)
Bishop of London and all his posterity
Galsworthy   Dean Inge   Croce   Matthews
Rev Meyer   Seymour Hicks
Lionel Cust   C. B. Fry   Bergson Abdul Bahai
Hawtrey   Edward Elgar   Sardlea
Filson Young   Marie Corelli   Geddes
Codliver Oil   St. Loe Strachey   Lyceum Club
Rhabindraneth Tagore   Lord Glenconner of Glen
Weiniger   Norman Angel   Ad. Mahon
Mr. and Mrs. Dearmer   Beecham   Ella
A. C. Benson   (Pills, Opera, Thomas)   Sydney Webb
British Academy   Messrs. Chapell
Countess of Warwick   George Edwards
Willie Ferraro   Captain Cook   R. J. Campbell
Clan Thesiger   Martin Harvey   William Archer
George Grossmith   R. H. Benson
Annie Besant   Chenil   Clan Meynell
Father Vaughan   Joseph Holbrooke   Clan Strachey

1

BLESS ENGLAND!

BLESS ENGLAND

FOR ITS SHIPS

which switchback on Blue, Green and
Red **SEAS** all around the **PINK
EARTH-BALL,**

BIG BETS ON EACH.

BLESS ALL SEAFARERS.

THEY exchange not one LAND for another, but one ELEMENT for
ANOTHER. The MORE against the LESS ABSTRACT.

---

6. The list of those blasted by the Vorticists falls, according
to the critic William Wees, into seven categories:
(1) members of the (literary and cultural) Establishment
(e.g., William Archer, drama critic of the *Nation*);
(2) people who represented popular or snobbish fads (e.g.,
Sir Abdul Baha Bahai, leader of the Bahai faith); (3) high-
minded popular writers, (e.g., Marie Corelli); (4) mediocre
but popular figures (e.g., the poet Ella Wheeler Wilcox);
(5) fuzzy-minded reformers and idealists (e.g., Sidney
Webb, a leader of the Fabian Socialist organization); (6)
"popular figures whom the Vorticists just didn't like" (e.g.,
C. B. Fry, a cricket player); and (7) "blasting just for the
fun of it . . . or blasting that grew from special circumstances and private reasons known only to insiders" (e.g.,
the Post Office and Cod Liver Oil). See William C. Wees,
Vorticism and the English Avant-Garde (1972), pp. 217–227.

BLESS the vast planetary abstraction of the **OCEAN.**

————————

BLESS THE ARABS OF THE **ATLANTIC.**
THIS ISLAND MUST BE CONTRASTED WITH THE BLEAK WAVES.

————————

BLESS ALL PORTS.

PORTS, RESTLESS MACHINES of

scooped out basins
heavy insect dredgers
monotonous cranes
stations
lighthouses, blazing
   through the frosty
   starlight, cutting the
   storm like a cake
beaks of infant boats,
   side by side,
heavy chaos of
   wharves,
steep walls of
   factories
womanly town

BLESS these **MACHINES** that work the little boats across
clean liquid space, in beelines.

BLESS the great **PORTS**

HULL
LIVERPOOL
LONDON
NEWCASTLE-ON-TYNE
BRISTOL
GLASGOW

BLESS ENGLAND,

Industrial Island machine, pyramidal workshop,
its apex at Shetland, discharging itself on the sea.

BLESS

cold
magnanimous
delicate
gauche
fanciful
stupid

ENGLISHMEN.

2
BLESS the HAIRDRESSER.

He attacks Mother Nature for a small fee.
Hourly he ploughs heads for sixpence,
Scours chins and lips for threepence.
He makes systematic mercenary war on this
WILDNESS.
He trims aimless and retrograde growths
into CLEAN ARCHED SHAPES and
ANGULAR PLOTS.

BLESS this HESSIAN (or SILESIAN) **EXPERT**[7]
correcting the grotesque anachronisms
of our physique.

3
BLESS ENGLISH HUMOUR

It is the great barbarous weapon of
the genius among races.
The wild MOUNTAIN RAILWAY from IDEA
to IDEA, in the ancient Fair of LIFE.

BLESS **SWIFT**   for his solemn bleak
wisdom of laughter.

SHAKESPEARE   for his bitter Northern
Rhetoric of humour.

BLESS ALL ENGLISH EYES
that grow crows-feet with their
FANCY and ENERGY.

BLESS this hysterical WALL built round
the EGO.

BLESS the solitude of LAUGHTER.

BLESS the separating, ungregarious
BRITISH GRIN.

4
BLESS FRANCE

for its BUSHELS of VITALITY
to the square inch.

---

7. From German industrial regions.

HOME OF MANNERS (the Best, the WORST and interesting mixtures).

MASTERLY PORNOGRAPHY (great enemy of progress).

COMBATIVENESS

GREAT HUMAN SCEPTICS

DEPTHS OF ELEGANCE

FEMALE QUALITIES

FEMALES

BALLADS of its PREHISTORIC APACHE

Superb hardness and hardiesse of its

Voyou° type, rebellious adolescent.   raffish

Modesty and humanity of many there.

GREAT FLOOD OF LIFE pouring out

of wound of **1797**.[8]

Also bitterer stream from **1870**.[9]

STAYING POWER, like a cat.

BLESS[1]

Bridget   Berrwolf   Bearline   Cranmer Byng
Frieder Graham   The Pope   Maria de Tomaso
Captain Kemp   Munroe   Gaby   Jenkins
R. B. Cuningham Grahame   Barker
(not his brother)   (John and Granville)
Mrs. Wil Finnimore   Madame Strindberg   Carson
Salvation Army   Lord Howard de Walden
Capt. Craig   Charlotte Corday   Cromwell
Mrs. Duval   Mary Robertson   Lillie Lenton
Frank Rutter   Castor Oil   James Joyce
Leveridge   Lydia Yavorska   Preb. Carlyle   Jenny
Mon. le compte de Gabulis   Smithers   Dick Burge
33 Church Street   Sievier   Gertie Millar
Norman Wallis   Miss Fowler   Sir Joseph Lyons
Martin Wolff   Watt   Mrs. Hepburn
Alfree   Tommy   Captain Kendell   Young Ahearn
Wilfred Walter   Kate Lechmere   Henry Newbolt
Lady Aberconway   Frank Harris   Hamel
Gilbert Canaan   Sir James Mathew Barry
Mrs. Belloc Lowdnes   W. L. George   Rayner
George Robey   George Mozart   Harry Weldon

8. The rise of Napoleon Bonaparte.
9. Beginning of Franco-Prussian War and end of the Second Empire, led by Napoleon Bonaparte's nephew Napoleon III.
1. This list of the blessed falls, according to William Wees, into four categories: (1) "some of the blessings, like most of the blasts, seemed designed to affront respectable public opinion" (e.g., the Pope and the Salvation Army); (2) "working class entertainments such as boxing and music halls"; (3) "a few selected representatives of the fine arts" (e.g., James Joyce); and (4) "friends of the Vorticists or of the avant-garde in general" (e.g., Frank Rutter and P. J. Konody, two sympathetic art critics).

Chaliapine   George Hirst   Graham White
Hucks   Salmet   Shirley Kellogg   Bandsman Rice
Petty Officer Curran   Applegarth   Konody
Colin Bell   Lewis Hind   LEFRANC
Hubert   Commercial Process Co.

MANIFESTO.

I.

1. Beyond Action and Reaction we would establish ourselves.
2. We start from opposite statements of a chosen world. Set up violent structure of adolescent clearness between two extremes.
3. We discharge ourselves on both sides.
4. We fight first on one side, then on the other, but always for the SAME cause, which is neither side or both sides and ours.
5. Mercenaries were always the best troops.
6. We are Primitive Mercenaries in the Modern World.
7. Our Cause is NO-MAN'S.
8. We set Humour at Humour's throat.
   Stir up Civil War among peaceful apes.
9. We only want Humour if it has fought like Tragedy.
10. We only want Tragedy if it can clench its side-muscles like hands on its belly, and bring to the surface a laugh like a bomb.

II.

1. We hear from America and the Continent all sorts of disagreeable things about England: "the unmusical, anti-artistic, unphilosophic country."
2. We quite agree.
3. Luxury, sport, the famous English "Humour," the thrilling ascendancy and idée fixe of Class, producing the most intense snobbery in the World; heavy stagnant pools of Saxon blood, incapable of anything but the song of a frog, in home-counties:—these phenomena give England a peculiar distinction in the wrong sense, among the nations.
4. This is why England produces such good artists from time to time.
5. This is also the reason why a movement towards art and imagination could burst up here, from this lump of compressed life, with more force than anywhere else.
6. To believe that it is necessary for or conducive to art, to "improve" life, for instance—make architecture, dress, ornament, in "better taste," is absurd.
7. The Art-instinct is permanently primitive.
8. In a chaos of imperfection, discord, etc., it finds the same stimulus as in Nature.
9. The artist of the modern movement is a savage (in no sense an "advanced," perfected, democratic, Futurist individual of Mr. Marinetti's limited imagination): this enormous, jangling, journalistic, fairy desert of modern life serves him as Nature did more technically primitive man.

[10] As the steppes and the rigours of the Russian winter, when the peasant has to lie for weeks in his hut, produces that extraordinary acuity of feeling and intelligence we associate with the Slav; so England is just now the most favourable country for the appearance of a great art.

III.

[1] We have made it quite clear that there is nothing Chauvinistic or picturesquely patriotic about our contentions.

[2] But there is violent boredom with that feeble Europeanism, abasement of the miserable "intellectual" before anything coming from Paris, Cosmopolitan sentimentality, which prevails in so many quarters.

[3] Just as we believe that an Art must be organic with its Time,
So we insist that what is actual and vital for the South, is ineffectual and unactual in the North.

[4] Fairies have disappeared from Ireland (despite foolish attempts to revive them)[2] and the bull-ring languishes in Spain.

[5] But mysticism on the one hand, gladiatorial instincts, blood and asceticism on the other, will be always actual, and springs of Creation for these two peoples.

[6] The English Character is based on the Sea.

[7] The particular qualities and characteristics that the sea always engenders in men are those that are, among the many diagnostics of our race, the most fundamentally English.

[8] That unexpected universality as well, found in the completest English artists, is due to this.

IV.

[1] We assert that the art for these climates, then, must be a northern flower.

[2] And we have implied what we believe should be the specific nature of the art destined to grow up in this country, and models of whose flue decorate the pages of this magazine.

[3] It is not a question of the characterless material climate around us.
Were that so the complication of the Jungle, dramatic Tropic growth, the vastness of American trees, would not be for us.

[4] But our industries, and the Will that determined, face to face with its needs, the direction of the modern world, has reared up steel trees where the green ones were lacking; has exploded in useful growths, and found wilder intricacies than those of Nature.

V.

[1] We bring clearly forward the following points, before further defining the character of this necessary native art.

---

2. The Celtic Revival was a nostalgic movement in Irish arts and letters.

2   At the freest and most vigorous period of ENGLAND'S history, her literature, then chief Art, was in many ways identical with that of France.

3   Chaucer was very much cousin of Villon[3] as an artist.

4   Shakespeare and Montaigne[4] formed one literature.

5   But Shakespeare reflected in his imagination a mysticism, madness and delicacy
peculiar to the North, and brought equal quantities of Comic and Tragic
together.

6   Humour is a phenomenon caused by sudden pouring of culture into Barbary.[5]

7   It is intelligence electrified by flood of Naivety.

8   It is Chaos invading Concept and bursting it like nitrogen.

9   It is the Individual masquerading as Humanity like a child in clothes too big for him.

10   Tragic Humour is the birthright of the North.

11   Any great Northern Art will partake of this insidious and volcanic chaos.

12   No great ENGLISH Art need be ashamed to share some glory with France,
tomorrow it may be with Germany, where the Elizabethans did before it.

13   But it will never be French, any more than Shakespeare was, the most catholic
and subtle Englishman.

VI.

1   The Modern World is due almost entirely to Anglo-Saxon genius,—its appearance and its spirit.

2   Machinery, trains, steam-ships, all that distinguishes externally our time, came
far more from here than anywhere else.

3   In dress, manners, mechanical inventions, LIFE, that is, ENGLAND, has influenced Europe in the same way that France has in Art.

4   But busy with this LIFE-EFFORT, she has been the last to become conscious
of the Art that is an organism of this new Order and Will of Man.

5   Machinery is the greatest Earth-medium: incidentally it sweeps away the doctrines of a narrow and pedantic Realism at one stroke.

6   By mechanical inventiveness, too, just as Englishmen have spread themselves all
over the Earth, they have brought all the hemispheres about them in their
original island.

7   It cannot be said that the complication of the Jungle, dramatic tropic growths,
the vastness of American trees, is not for us.

8   For, in the forms of machinery, Factories, new and vaster buildings, bridges and
works, we have all that, naturally, around us.

VII.

1   Once this consciousness towards the new possibilities of expression in present life has come, however, it will be more the legitimate property of Englishmen than of any other people in Europe.

2   It should also, as it is by origin theirs, inspire them more forcibly and directly.

---

3. François Villon (1431–1463?), French poet.
4. Michel de Montaigne (1533–1592), French essayist.

5. An old name for the western part of North Africa; possibly used here to mean "barbarity."

| 3 | They are the inventors of this bareness and hardness, and should be the great enemies of Romance. |

3   They are the inventors of this bareness and hardness, and should be the great enemies of Romance.

4   The Romance peoples will always be, at bottom, its defenders.

5   The Latins are at present, for instance, in their "discovery" of sport, their Futuristic gush over machines, aeroplanes, etc., the most romantic and sentimental "moderns" to be found.

6   It is only the second-rate people in France or Italy who are thorough revolutionaries.

7   In England, on the other hand, there Is no vulgarity in revolt.

8   Or, rather, there is no revolt, it is the normal state.

9   So often rebels of the North and the South are diametrically opposed species.

10   The nearest thing in England to a great traditional French artist, is a great revolutionary English one.

Signatures for Manifesto[6]

R. Aldington
Arbuthnot
L. Atkinson
Gaudier Brzeska
J. Dismorr
C. Hamilton
E. Pound
W. Roberts
H. Sanders
E. Wadsworth
Wyndham Lewis

Rebecca West: Indissoluble Matrimony

Rebecca West (1892–1983) is increasingly appreciated as a writer of fiction, literary criticism, political commentary, and biography, as well as one of the most important journalists of the century. Born Cicely Fairfield in Ireland, she was educated in Edinburgh after her father died when she was ten years old. She became an actress in London, taking the stage name "Rebecca West" from a heroine she had played in Ibsen's drama *Rosmersholm*. By the time she was twenty, she was becoming active in left-wing journalism and in agitation for women's rights. In 1914, when she wrote *Indissoluble Matrimony*, she was involved in a love affair with the free-thinking but married novelist H. G. Wells, with whom she had a son; at the same time, she was working on a critical biography of Henry James. She went on to write searching and sometimes critical essays on male modernists like Joyce, Eliot, and Lawrence, and perceptive essays on Virginia Woolf and Katherine Mansfield. Throughout her life, she wrote both novels and political journalism, notably a major study of Balkan politics and culture, *Black Lamb*

6. The signatories to the manifesto are Richard Aldington, English writer and man of letters; Malcolm Arbuthnot, professional photographer; Lawrence Atkinson, Vorticist artist; Henri Gaudier-Brzeska, Vorticist sculptor and contributor to *Blast* who was killed in the trenches in World War I and whose obituary was included in *Blast II*; Jessica Dismoor, artist whose illustrations were included in *Blast*; Cuthbert Hamilton, avant-garde artist; Ezra Pound; William Roberts, painter; Helen Saunders, Vorticist designer; Edward Wadsworth, Vorticist painter; and Wyndham Lewis.

and Grey Falcon (1942), and a series of brilliant reports on the Nuremberg trials of Nazi war criminals at the end of World War II, collected as *A Train of Powder* (1955). She was made Dame Commander of the British Empire in 1959. Like her political writing, her fiction is notable for its irreverent probing of modernity's fault lines. Though never an orthodox feminist, West demonstrated a keen insight into the psychology of women and men, and portrayed the straitened thinking that made feminism's ultimate victory anything but a foregone conclusion.

Indissoluble Matrimony

When George Silverton opened the front door he found that the house was not empty for all its darkness. The spitting noise of the striking of damp matches and mild, growling exclamations of annoyance told him that his wife was trying to light the dining-room gas. He went in and with some short, hostile sound of greeting lit a match and brought brightness into the little room. Then, irritated by his own folly in bringing private papers into his wife's presence, he stuffed the letters he had brought from the office deep into the pockets of his overcoat. He looked at her suspiciously, but she had not seen them, being busy in unwinding her orange motor-veil. His eyes remained on her face to brood a little sourly on her moving loveliness, which he had not been sure of finding: for she was one of those women who create an illusion alternately of extreme beauty and extreme ugliness. Under her curious dress, designed in some pitifully cheap and worthless stuff by a successful mood of her indiscreet taste—she had black blood in her—her long body seemed pulsing with some exaltation. The blood was coursing violently under her luminous yellow skin, and her lids, dusky with fatigue, drooped contentedly over her great humid black eyes. Perpetually she raised her hand to the mass of black hair that was coiled on her thick golden neck, and stroked it with secretive enjoyment, as a cat licks its fur. And her large mouth smiled frankly, but abstractedly, at some digested pleasure.

There was a time when George would have looked on this riot of excited loveliness with suspicion. But now he knew it was almost certainly caused by some trifle—a long walk through stinging weather, the report of a Socialist victory at a by-election, or the intoxication of a waltz refrain floating from the municipal band-stand across the flats of the local recreation ground. And even if it had been caused by some amorous interlude he would not have greatly cared. In the ten years since their marriage he had lost the quality which would have made him resentful. He now believed that quality to be purely physical. Unless one was in good condition and responsive to the messages sent out by the flesh Evadne could hardly concern one. He turned the bitter thought over in his heart and stung himself by deliberately gazing unmoved upon her beautiful joyful body.

"Let's have supper now!" she said rather greedily.

He looked at the table and saw she had set it before she went out. As usual she had been in an improvident hurry: it was carelessly done. Besides, what an absurd supper to set before a hungry solicitor's clerk! In the centre, obviously intended as the principal dish, was a bowl of plums, softly red, soaked with the sun, glowing like jewels in the downward stream of the incandescent light. Besides them was a great yellow melon, its sleek sides fluted with rich growth, and a honey-comb glistening on a willow-pattern dish. The only sensible food to be seen was a plate of tongue laid at his place.

"I can't sit down to supper without washing my hands!"

While he splashed in the bathroom upstairs he heard her pull in a chair to the table and sit down to her supper. It annoyed him. There was no ritual about it. While he was eating the tongue she would be crushing honey on new bread, or stripping a plum of its purple skin and holding the golden globe up to the gas to see the light filter through. The meal would pass in silence. She would innocently take his dumbness for a sign of abstraction and forbear to babble. He would find the words choked on his lips by the weight of dullness that always oppressed him in her presence. Then, just about the time when he was beginning to feel able to formulate his obscure grievances against her, she would rise from the table without a word and run upstairs to her work, humming in that uncanny, negro way of hers.

And so it was. She ate with an appalling catholicity of taste, with a nice child's love of sweet foods, and occasionally she broke into that hoarse beautiful croon. Every now and then she looked at him with too obvious speculations as to whether his silence was due to weariness or uncertain temper. Timidly she cut him an enormous slice of the melon, which he did not want. Then she rose abruptly and flung herself into the rocking chair on the hearth. She clasped her hands behind her head and strained backwards so that the muslin stretched over her strong breasts. She sang softly to the ceiling.

There was something about the fantastic figure that made him feel as though they were not properly married.

"Evadne?"

"'S?"

"What have you been up to this evening?"

"I was at Milly Stafordale's."

He was silent again. That name brought up the memory of his courting days. It was under the benign eyes of blonde, plebeian Milly that he had wooed the distracting creature in the rocking chair.

Ten years before, when he was twenty-five, his firm had been reduced to hysteria over the estates of an extraordinarily stupid old woman, named Mrs. Mary Ellerker. Her stupidity, grappling with the complexity of the sources of the vast income which rushed in spate from the properties of four deceased husbands, demanded oceans of explanations even over her weekly rents. Silverton alone in the office, by reason of a certain natural incapacity for excitement, could deal calmly with this marvel of imbecility. He alone could endure to sit with patience in the black-panelled drawing-room amidst the jungle of shiny mahogany furniture and talk to a mass of darkness, who rested heavily in the window-seat and now and then made an idiotic remark in a bright, hearty voice. But it shook even him. Mrs. Mary Ellerker was obscene. Yet she was perfectly sane and, although of that remarkable plainness noticeable in most oft-married women, in good enough physical condition. She merely presented the loathsome spectacle of an ignorant mind, contorted by the artificial idiocy of coquetry, lack of responsibility, and hatred of discipline, stripped naked by old age. That was the real horror of her. One feared to think how many women were really like Mrs. Ellerker under their armour of physical perfection or social grace. For this reason he turned eyes of hate on Mrs. Ellerker's pretty little companion, Milly Stafordale, who smiled at him over her embroidery with wintry northern brightness. When she was old she too would be obscene.

This horror obsessed him. Never before had he feared anything. He had never lived more than half-an-hour from a police station, and, as he had by some chance missed the melancholy clairvoyance of adolescence, he had never conceived of any horror with which the police could not deal. This disgust of women revealed to him that the world is a place of subtle perils. He began to fear marriage as he feared death. The thought of intimacy with some lovely, desirable and necessary wife turned him sick as he sat at his lunch. The secret obscenity of women! He talked darkly of it to his friends. He wondered why the Church did not provide a service for the absolution of men after marriage. Wife desertion seemed to him a beautiful return of the tainted body to cleanliness.

On his fifth visit to Mrs. Ellerker he could not begin his business at once. One of Milly Stafordale's friends had come in to sing to the old lady. She stood by the piano against the light, so that he saw her washed with darkness. Amazed, of tropical fruit. And before he had time to apprehend the sleepy wonder of her beauty, she had begun to sing. Now he knew that her voice was a purely physical attribute, built in her as she lay in her mother's womb, and no index of her spiritual values. But then, as it welled up from the thick golden throat and clung to her lips, it seemed a sublime achievement of the soul. It was smouldering contralto such as only those of black blood can possess. As she sang her great black eyes lay on him with the innocent shamelessness of a young animal, and he remembered hopefully that he was good looking. Suddenly she stood in silence, playing with her heavy black plait. Mrs. Ellerker broke into silly thanks. The girl's mother, who had been playing the accompaniment, rose and stood rolling up her music. Silverton, sick with excitement, was introduced to them. He noticed that the mother was a little darker than the conventions permit. Their name was Hannan—Mrs. Arthur Hannan and Evadne. They moved lithely and quietly out of the room, the girl's eyes still lingering on his face.

The thought of her splendour and the rolling echoes of her voice disturbed him all night. Next day, going to his office, he travelled with her on the horse-car that bound his suburb to Petrick. One of the horses fell lame, and she had time to tell him that she was studying at a commercial college. He quivered with distress. All the time he had a dizzy illusion that she was nestling up against him. They parted shyly. During the next few days they met constantly. He began to go and see them in the evening at their home—a mean flat crowded with cheap glories of bead curtains and Oriental hangings that set off the women's alien beauty. Mrs. Hannan was a widow and they lived alone, in a wonderful silence. He talked more than he had ever done in his whole life before. He took a dislike to the widow, she was consumed with fiery subterranean passions, no fit guardian for the tender girl.

Now he could imagine with what silent rapture Evadne had watched his agitation. Almost from the first she had meant to marry him. He was physically attractive, though not strong. His intellect was gently stimulating like a mild white wine. And it was time she married. She was ripe for adult things. This was the real wound in his soul. He had tasted of a divine thing created in his time for dreams out of her rich beauty, her loneliness, her romantic poverty, her immaculate youth. He had known love. And Evadne had never known anything more than a magnificent physical adventure which she had secured at the right time as she would have engaged a cab to take her to the station in time for the cheapest excursion train. It was a quick way to light-hearted living. With loathing he remembered how in the days of their engagement she used to gaze purely into his blinking eyes and with her unashamed kisses incite him to extravagant embraces. Now he cursed her for having obtained his spiritual revolution on false pretences. Only for a little time had he had his illusion, for their marriage was hastened by Mrs. Hannan's sudden death. After three months of savage mourning Evadne flung herself into marriage, and her excited candour had enlightened him very soon.

That marriage had lasted ten years. And to Evadne their relationship was just the same as ever. Her vitality needed him as it needed the fruit on the table before him. He shook with wrath and a sense of outraged decency.

"O George!" She was yawning widely.

"What's the matter?" he said without interest.

"It's so beastly dull."

"I can't help that, can I?"

"No." She smiled placidly at him. "We're a couple of dull dogs, aren't we? I wish we had children."

After a minute she suggested, apparently as an alternative amusement, "Perhaps the post hasn't passed."

As she spoke there was a rat-tat and the slither of a letter under the door. Evadne picked herself up and ran out into the lobby. After a second or two, during which she made irritating inarticulate exclamations, she came in reading the letter and stroking her bust with a gesture of satisfaction.

"They want me to speak at Longton's meeting on the nineteenth," she purred.

"Longton? What's he up to?"

Stephen Longton was the owner of the biggest iron works in Petrick, a man whose refusal to adopt the livery of busy oafishness thought proper to commercial men aroused the gravest suspicions.

"He's standing as Socialist candidate for the town council."

". . . Socialist!" he muttered.

He set his jaw. That was a side of Evadne he considered as little as possible. He had never been able to assimilate the fact that Evadne had, two years after their marriage, passed through his own orthodox Radicalism[1] to a passionate Socialism, and that after reading enormously of economics she had begun to write for the Socialist press and to speak successfully at meetings. In the jaundiced recesses of his mind he took it for granted that her work would have the lax fibre of her character: that it would be infected with her Oriental crudities. Although once or twice he had been congratulated on her brilliance, he mistrusted this phase of her activity as a caper of the sensualist. His eyes blazed on her and found the depraved, over-sexed creature, looking milder than a gazelle, holding out a hand-bill to him.

"They've taken it for granted!"

He saw her name—his name—

MRS. EVADNE SILVERTON.[2]

It was at first the blaze of stout scarlet letters on the dazzling white ground that made him blink. Then he was convulsed with rage.

"Georgie dear!"

She stepped forward and caught his weak body to her bosom. He wrenched himself away. Spiritual nausea made him determined to be a better man than her.

"A pair of you! You and Longton—!" he snarled scornfully. Then, seeing her startled face, he controlled himself.

"I thought it would please you," said Evadne, a little waspishly.

"You mustn't have anything to do with Longton," he stormed.

A change passed over her. She became ugly. Her face was heavy with intellect, her lips coarse with power. He was at arms with a Socialist lead. Much he would have preferred the bland sensualist again.

---

1. An extreme form of Liberalism, still comfortably within the continuum of British democratic politics; Socialism, which Evadne has embraced, advocates the abolition of the current system and is thus too extreme for George's bourgeois attitudes.

2. Evadne would have been addressed in polite society as "Mrs. George Silverton"; George reads this breach of decorum as one more sign that his wife is out of control. Leopold Bloom, the protagonist of James Joyce's *Ulysses*, makes a similar observation when his wife Molly receives a letter from her lover addressed to "Mrs. Marion Bloom."

"Why?"

"Because—his lips stuck together like blotting-paper—he's not the sort of man my wife should—should—"

With movements which terrified him by their rough energy, she folded up the bills and put them back in the envelope.

"George. I suppose you mean that he's a bad man." He nodded.

"I know quite well that the girl who used to be his typist is his mistress." She spoke it sweetly, as if reasoning with an old fool. "But she's got consumption. She'll be dead in six months. In fact, I think it's rather nice of him. To look after her and all that."

"My God!" He leapt to his feet, extending a shaking forefinger. As she turned to him, the smile dying on her lips, his excited weakness wrapped him in a paramnesic illusion:[3] it seemed to him that he had been through all this before—a long, long time ago. "My God, you talk like a woman off the streets!"

Evadne's lips lifted over her strong teeth. With clever cruelty she fixed his eyes with hers, well knowing that he longed to fall forward and bury his head on the table in a transport of hysterical sobs. After a moment of this torture she turned away, herself distressed by a desire to cry.

"How can you say such dreadful, dreadful things!" she protested, chokingly.

He sat down again. His eyes looked little and red, but they blazed on her. "I wonder if you are," he said softly.

"Are what?" she asked petulantly, a tear rolling down her nose.

"You know," he answered, nodding.

"George, George, George!" she cried.

"You've always been keen on kissing and making love, haven't you, my precious? At first you startled me, you did! I didn't know women were like that." From that morass he suddenly stepped on to a high peak of terror. Amazed to find himself sincere, he cried—"I don't believe good women are!"

"Georgie, how can you be so silly!" exclaimed Evadne shrilly. "You know quite well I've been as true to you as any woman could be." She sought his eyes with a liquid glance of reproach. He averted his gaze, sickened at having put himself in the wrong. For even while he degraded his tongue his pure soul fainted with loathing of her fleshliness.

"I—I'm sorry."

Too wily to forgive him at once, she showed him a lowering profile with downcast lids. Of course, he knew it was a fraud: an imputation against her chastity was no more poignant than a reflection on the cleanliness of her nails—rude and spiteful, but that was all. But for a time they kept up the deception, while she cleared the table in a steely silence.

"Evadne, I'm sorry. I'm tired." His throat was dry. He could not bear the discord of a row added to the horror of their companionship. "Evadne, do forgive me—I don't know what I meant by—"

"That's all right, silly!" she said suddenly and bent over the table to kiss him. Her brow was smooth. It was evident from her splendid expression that she was preoccupied. Then she finished clearing up the dishes and took them into the kitchen. While she was out of the room he rose from his seat and sat down in the armchair by the fire, setting his bull-dog pipe alight. For a very short time he was free of her

3. A condition in which fact and fiction become confused.

voluptuous presence. But she ran back soon, having put the kettle on and changed her blouse for a loose dressing-jacket, and sat down on the arm of his chair. Once or twice she bent and kissed his brow, but for the most part she lay back with his head drawn to her bosom, rocking herself rhythmically. Silverton, a little disgusted by their contact, sat quite motionless and passed into a doze. He revolved in his mind the incidents of his day's routine and remembered a snub from a superior. So he opened his eyes and tried to think of something else. It was then that he became conscious that the rhythm of Evadne's movement was not regular. It was broken as though she rocked in time to music. Music? His sense of hearing crept up to hear if there was any sound of music in the breaths she was emitting rather heavily every now and then. At first he could hear nothing. Then it struck him that each breath was a muttered phrase. He stiffened, and hatred flamed through his veins. The words came clearly through her lips. . . . "The present system of wage-slavery. . . ."

"Evadne!" He sprang to his feet. "You're preparing your speech!"

She did not move. "I am," she said.

"Damn it, you shan't speak!"

"Damn it, I will!"

"Evadne, you shan't speak! If you do I swear to God above I'll turn you out into the streets—." She rose and came towards him. She looked black and dangerous. She trod softly like a cat with her head down. In spite of himself, his tongue licked his lips in fear and he cowered a moment before he picked up a knife from the table. For a space she looked down on him and the sharp blade.

"You idiot, can't you hear the kettle's boiling over?"

He shrank back, letting the knife fall on the floor. For three minutes he stood there controlling his breath and trying to still his heart. Then he followed her into the kitchen. She was making a noise with a basinful of dishes.

"Stop that row."

She turned round with a dripping dish-cloth in her hand and pondered whether to throw it at him. But she was tired and wanted peace: so that she could finish the rough draft of her speech. So she stood waiting.

"Did you understand what I said then? If you don't promise me here and now—"

She flung her arms upwards with a cry and dashed past him. He made to run after her upstairs, but stumbled on the threshold of the lobby and sat with his ankle twisted under him, shaking with rage. In a second she ran downstairs again, clothed in a big cloak with black bundle clutched to her breast. For the first time in their married life she was seized with a convulsion of sobs. She dashed out of the front door and banged it with such passion that a glass pane shivered to fragments behind her.

"What's this? What's this?" he cried stupidly, standing up. He perceived with an insane certainty that she was going out to meet some unknown lover. "I'll come and tell him what a slut you are!" he shouted after her and stumbled to the door. It was jammed now and he had to drag at it.

The night was flooded with the yellow moonshine of midsummer: it seemed to drip from the lacquered leaves of the shrubs in the front garden. In its soft clarity he could see her plainly, although she was now two hundred yards away. She was hastening to the north end of Sumatra Crescent, an end that curled up the hill like a silly kitten's tail and stopped abruptly in green fields. So he knew that she was going to the young man who had just bought the Georgian Manor, whose elm-trees crowned the hill. Oh, how he hated her! Yet he must follow her, or else she would cover up her adulteries so that he could not take his legal revenge. So he began to run—silently, for he wore his carpet slippers. He was only a hundred yards behind her when she slipped through a gap in the hedge to tread a field-path. She still walked with pride, for though she was town-bred, night in the open seemed not at all fearful to her. As he shuffled in pursuit his carpet slippers were engulfed in a shining pool of mud: he raised one with a squelch, the other was left. This seemed the last humiliation. He kicked the other one off his feet and padded on in his socks, snuffling in anticipation of a cold. Then physical pain sent him back to the puddle to pluck out the slippers; it was a dirty job. His heart battered his breast as he saw that Evadne had gained the furthest hedge and was crossing the stile into the lane that ran up to the Manor gates.

"Go on, you beast!" he muttered, "Go on, go on!" After a scamper he climbed the stile and thrust his lean neck beyond a mass of wilted hawthorn bloom that crumbled into vagrant petals at his touch.

The lane mounted yellow as cheese to where the moon lay on his iron tracery of the Manor gates. Evadne was not there. Hardly believing his eyes he hobbled over into the lane and looked in the other direction. There he saw her disappearing round the bend of the road. Gathering himself up to a run, he tried to think out his bearings. He had seldom passed this way, and like most people without strong primitive instincts he had no sense of orientation. With difficulty he remembered that after a mile's mazy wanderings between high hedges this lane sloped suddenly to the bowl of heather overhung by the moorlands, in which lay the Petrick reservoirs, two untamed lakes.

"Eh! she's going to meet him by the water!" he cursed to himself. He remembered the withered ash tree, seared by lightning to its root, that stood by the road at the bare frontier of the moor. "May God strike her like that," he prayed," "as she fouls the other man's lips with her kisses. O God! let me strangle her. Or bury a knife deep in her breast." Suddenly he broke into a lolloping run. "O my Lord, I'll be able to divorce her. I'll be free. Free to live alone. To do my day's work and sleep my night's sleep without her. I'll get a job somewhere else and forget her. I'll bring her to the dogs. No clean man or woman in Petrick will look at her now. They won't have her to speak at that meeting now!" His throat swelled with joy, he leapt high in the air.

"I'll lie about her. If I can prove that she's wrong with this man they'll believe me if I say she's a bad woman and drinks. I'll make her name a joke. And then—"

He flung wide his arms in ecstasy: the left struck against stone. More pain than he had thought his body could hold convulsed him, so that he sank on the ground hugging his aching arm. He looked backwards as he writhed and saw that the hedge had stopped; above him was the great stone wall of the county asylum. The question broke on him—was there any lunatic in its confines so slavered with madness as he himself? Nothing but madness could have accounted for the torrent of ugly words, the sea of uglier thoughts that was now a part of him. "O God, me to turn like this!" he cried, rolling over full-length on the grassy bank by the roadside. That the infidelity of his wife, a thing that should have brought out the stern manliness of his true nature, should have discovered him as lecherous-lipped as any pot-house[4] lounger, was the most infamous accident of his married life. The sense of sin descended on him so that his tears flowed hot and bitterly. "Have I gone to the Unitarian chapel every Sunday morning and to the Ethical Society every evening for nothing?" his

---

4. Tavern.

spirit asked itself in its travail. "All those Browning lectures for nothing. . . ."5 He said the Lord's Prayer several times and lay for a minute quietly crying. The relaxation of his muscles brought him a sense of rest which seemed forgiveness falling from God. The tears dried on his cheeks. His calmer consciousness heard the sound of rushing waters mingled with the beating of blood in his ears. He got up and scrambled round the turn of the road that brought him to the withered ash-tree.

He walked forward on the parched heatherland to the mound whose scarred sides, heaped with boulders, tufted with mountain grasses, shone before him in the moonlight. He scrambled up to it hurriedly and hoisted himself from ledge to ledge till he fell on his knees with a squeal of pain. His ankle was caught in a crevice of the rock. Gulping down his agony at this final physical humiliation he heaved himself upright and raced on to the summit, and found himself before the Devil's Cauldron, filled to the brim with yellow moonshine and the fiery play of summer lightning. The rugged crags opposite him were a low barricade against the stars to which the mound where he stood shot forward like a bridge. To the left of this the long Lisbech pond lay like a trailing serpent; its silver scales glittered as the wind swept down from the vaster moorlands to the east. To the right under a steep drop of twenty feet was the Whimsey pond, more sinister, shaped in an unnatural oval, sheltered from the wind by the high ridge so that the undisturbed moonlight lay across it like a sharp-edged sword.

He looked about for some sign of Evadne. She could not be on the land by the margin of the lakes, for the light blazed so strongly that each reed could be clearly seen like a black dagger stabbing the silver. He looked down Lisbech and saw far east a knot of red and green and orange lights. Perhaps for some devilish purpose Evadne had sought Lisbech railway station. But his volcanic mind had preserved one grain of sense that assured him that, subtle as Evadne's villainy might be, it would not lead her to walk five miles out of her way to a terminus which she could have reached in fifteen minutes by taking a train from the station down the road. She must be under cover somewhere here. He went down the gentle slope that fell from the top of the ridge to Lisbech pond in a disorder of rough heather, unhappy patches of cultivated grass, and coppices of silver birch, fringed with flaming broom that seemed faintly tarnished in the moonlight. At the bottom was a roughly hewn path which he followed in hot aimless hurry. In a little he approached a riot of falling waters. There was a slice ten feet broad carved out of the ridge, and to this narrow channel of black shining rock the floods of Lisbech leapt some feet and raced through to Whimsey. The noise beat him back. The gap was spanned by a gaunt thing of paint-blistered iron, on which he stood dizzily and noticed how the wide step that ran on each side of the channel through to the other pond was smeared with sinister green slime. Now his physical distress reminded him of Evadne, whom he had almost forgotten in contemplation of these lonely waters. The idea of her had been present but obscured, as sometimes toothache may cease active torture. His blood lust set him on and he staggered forward with covered ears. Even as he went something caught his eye in a thicket high up on the slope near the crags. Against the slender pride of some silver birches stood a gnarled hawthorn tree, its branches flattened under the stern moorland winds so that it grew squat like an opened umbrella. In its dark shadows, faintly illumined by a few boughs of withered blossom, there moved a strange bluish light. Even while he did not know what it was it made his flesh stir.

5. George's activities—Unitarian church, Ethical Society, Browning Society—suggest that he participated in public exercises of a high moral nature without giving himself over to traditional religious faith, which he would have seen as "irrational" and "unmanly."

The light emerged. It was the moonlight reflected from Evadne's body. She was clad in a black bathing dress, and her arms and legs and the broad streak of flesh laid bare by a rent down the back shone brilliantly white, so that she seemed like a grotesquely patterned wild animal as she ran down to the lake. Whirling her arms above her head she trampled down into the water and struck out strongly. Her movements were full of brisk delight and she swam quickly. The moonlight made her the centre of a little feathery blur of black and silver, with a comet's tail trailing in her wake.

Nothing in all his married life had ever staggered Silverton so much as this. He had imagined his wife's adultery so strongly that it had come to be. It was now as real as their marriage; more real than their courtship. So this seemed to be the last crime of the adulteress. She had dragged him over those squelching fields and these rough moors and changed him from a man of irritations, but no passions, into a cold designer of murderous treacheries, so that he might witness a swimming exhibition! For a minute he was stunned. Then he sprang down to the rushy edge and ran along in the direction of her course, crying—"Evadne! Evadne!" She did not hear him. At last he achieved a chest note and shouted—"Evadne! come here!" The black and silver feather shivered in mid-water. She turned immediately and swam back to shore. He suspected sullenness in her slowness, but was glad of it, for after the shock of this extraordinary incident he wanted to go to sleep. Drowsiness lay on him like lead. He shook himself like a dog and wrenched off his linen collar, winking at the bright moon to keep himself awake. As she came quite near he was exasperated by the happy, snorting breaths she drew, and strolled a pace or two up the bank. To his enragement the face she lifted as she waded to dry land was placid, and she scrambled gaily up the bank to his side.

"O George, why did you come!" she exclaimed quite affectionately, laying a damp hand on his shoulder.

"O damn it, what does this mean!" he cried, committing a horrid tenor squeak. "What are you doing?"

"Why. George," she said," "I came here for a bathe."

He stared into her face and could make nothing of it. It was only sweet surfaces of flesh, soft radiances of eye and lip, a lovely lie of comeliness. He forgot this present grievance in a cold search for the source of her peculiar hatefulness. Under this sick gaze she pouted and turned away with a peevish gesture. He made no sign and stood silent, watching her saunter to that gaunt iron bridge. The roar of the little waterfall did not disturb her splendid nerves and she drooped sensuously over the hand-rail, sniffing up the sweet night smell; too evidently trying to abase him to another apology.

A mosquito whirred into his face. He killed it viciously and strode off towards his wife, who showed by a common little toss of the head that she was conscious of his coming.

"Look here, Evadne!" he panted. "What did you come here for? Tell me the truth and I promise I'll not—I'll not—"

"Not WHAT, George?"

"O please, please tell me the truth, do Evadne!" he cried pitifully.

"But, dear, what is there to carry on about so? You went on so queerly about my meeting that my head felt fit to split, and I thought the long walk and the dip would do me good." She broke off, amazed at the wave of horror that passed over his face.

His heart sank. From the loose-lipped hurry in the telling of her story, from the bigness of her eyes and the lack of subtlety in her voice, he knew that this was the truth. Here was no adulteress whom he could accuse in the law courts and condemn into the street, no resourceful sinner whose merry crimes he could discover. Here was merely his good wife, the faithful attendant of his hearth, relentless wrecker of his soul.

She came towards him as a cat approaches a displeased master, and hovered about him on the stone coping of the noisy sluice.

"Indeed!" he found himself saying sarcastically. "Indeed!"

"Yes, George Silverton, indeed!" she burst out, a little frightened. "And why shouldn't I? I used to come here often enough on summer nights with poor Mamma—"

"Yes!" he shouted. It was exactly the sort of thing that would appeal to that weird half-black woman from the back of beyond. "Mamma!" he cried tauntingly, "Mamma!"

There was a flash of silence between them before Evadne, clutching her breast and balancing herself dangerously on her heels on the stone coping, broke into gentle shrieks. "You dare talk of my Mamma, my poor Mamma, and she cold in her grave! I haven't been happy since she died and I married you, you silly little misery, you!" Then the rage was suddenly wiped off her brain by the perception of a crisis.

The trickle of silence overflowed into a lake, over which their spirits flew, looking at each other's reflection in the calm waters: in the hurry of their flight they had never before seen each other. They stood facing one another with dropped heads, quietly thinking.

The strong passion which filled them threatened to disintegrate their souls as a magnetic current decomposes the electrolyte, so they fought to organise their sensations. They tried to arrange themselves and their lives for comprehension, but beyond sudden lyric visions of old incidents of hatefulness—such as a smarting quarrel of six years ago as to whether Evadne had or had not cheated the railway company out of one and eightpence on an excursion ticket—the past was intangible. It trailed behind this intense event as the pale hair trails behind the burning comet. They were pre-occupied with the moment. Quite often George had found a mean pleasure in the thought that by never giving Evadne a child he had cheated her out of one form of experience, and now he paid the price for this unnatural pride of sterility. For now the spiritual offspring of their intercourse came to birth. A sublime loathing was between them. For a little time it was a huge perilous horror, but afterwards, like men aboard a ship whose masts seek the sky through steep waves, they found a drunken pride in the adventure. This was the very absolute of hatred. It cheapened the memory of the fantasias of irritation and ill-will they had performed in the less boring moments of their marriage, and they felt dazed, as amateurs who had found themselves creating a masterpiece. For the first time they were possessed by a supreme emotion and they felt a glad desire to strip away restraint and express it nakedly. It was ecstasy; they felt tall and full of blood.

Like people who, bewitched by Christ, see the whole earth as the breathing body of God, so they saw the universe as the substance and the symbol of their hatred. The stars trembled overhead with wrath. A wind from behind the angry crags set the moonlight on Lisbech quivering with rage, and the squat hawthorn-tree creaked slowly like the irritation of a dull little man. The dry moors, parched with harsh anger, waited thirstily and, sending out the murmur of rustling mountain grass and the cry of wakening fowl, seemed to huddle closer to the lake. But this sense of the earth's sympathy slipped away from them and they loathed all matter as the dull wrapping of their flame-like passion. At their wishing matter fell away and they saw sarcastic visions. He saw her as a toad squatting on the clean earth, obscuring the stars and pressing down its hot moist body on the cheerful fields. She felt his long boneless body coiled round the roots of the lovely tree of life. They shivered fastidiously. With an uplifting sense of responsibility they realised that they must kill each other.

A bird rose over their heads with a leaping flight that made it seem as though its black body was bouncing against the bright sky. The foolish noise and motion precipitated their thoughts. They were broken into a new conception of life. They perceived that God is war and his creatures are meant to fight. When dogs walk through the world cats must climb trees. The virgin must snare the wanton, the fine lover must put the prude to the sword. The gross man of action walks, spurred on the bloodless bodies of the men of thought, who lie quiet and cunningly do not tell him where his grossness leads him. The flesh must smother the spirit, the spirit must set the flesh on fire and watch it burn. And those who were gentle by nature and shrank from the ordained brutality were betrayers of their kind, surrendering the earth to the seed of their enemies. In this war there is no discharge. If they succumbed to peace now, the rest of their lives would be dishonourable, like the exile of a rebel who has begged his life as the reward of cowardice. It was their first experience of religious passion, and they abandoned themselves to it so that their immediate personal qualities fell away from them. Neither his weakness nor her prudence stood in the way of the event.

They measured each other with the eye. To her he was a spidery thing against the velvet blackness and hard silver surfaces of the pond. The light soaked her bathing dress so that she seemed, against the jagged shadows of the rock cutting, as though she were clad in a garment of dark polished mail. Her knees were bent so clearly, her toes gripped the coping so strongly. He understood very clearly that if he did not kill her instantly she would drop him easily into the deep riot of waters. Yet for a space he could not move, but stood expecting a degrading death. Indeed, he gave her time to kill him. But she was without power too, and struggled weakly with a hallucination. The quarrel in Sumatra Crescent with its suggestion of vast and unmentionable antagonisms; her swift race through the moon-drenched countryside, all crepitant with night noises: the swimming in the wine-like lake: their isolation on the moor, which was expressedly hostile to them, as nature always is to lonely man: and this stark contest face to face, with their resentments heaped between them like a pile of naked swords—these things were so strange that her civilised self shrank back appalled. There entered into her the primitive woman who is the curse of all women: a creature of the most utter femaleness, useless, save for childbirth, with no strong brain to make her physical weakness a light accident, abjectly and corruptingly afraid of man. A squaw, she dared not strike her lord.

The illusion passed like a moment of faintness and left her enraged at having forgotten her superiority even for an instant. In the material world she had a thousand times been defeated into making prudent reservations and practising unnatural docilities. But in the world of thought she had maintained unfalteringly her masterfulness in spite of the strong yearning of her temperament towards voluptuous surrenders. That was her virtue. Its violation whipped her to action and she would have killed him at once, had not his moment come a second before hers. Sweating horribly, he had dropped his head forward on his chest: his eyes fell on her feet and marked the plebeian moulding of her ankle, which rose thickly over a crease of flesh from the heel to the calf. The woman was coarse in grain and pattern.

He had no instinct for honourable attack, so he found himself striking her in the stomach. She reeled from pain, not because his strength overcame hers. For the first time her eyes looked into his candidly open, unveiled by languor or lust: their hard brightness told him how she despised him for that unwarlike blow. He cried out as he realised that this was another of her despicable victories and that the whole burden of the crime now lay on him, for he had begun it. But the rage was stopped on his lips as her arms, flung wildly out as she fell backwards, caught him about the waist with abominable justness of eye and evil intention. So they fell body to body into the quarrelling waters.

The feathery confusion had looked so soft, yet it seemed the solid rock they struck. The breath shot out of him and suffocation warmly stuffed his ears and nose. Then the rock cleft and he was swallowed by a brawling blackness in which whirled a vortex that flung him again and again on a sharp thing that burned his shoulder. All about him fought the waters, and they cut his flesh like knives. His pain was past belief. Though God might be war, he desired peace in his time, and he yearned for another God—a child's God, an immense arm coming down from the hills and lifting him to a kindly bosom. Soon his body would burst for breath, his agony would smash in his breast bone. So great was his pain that his consciousness was strained to apprehend it, as a too tightly stretched canvas splits and rips.

Suddenly the air was sweet on his mouth. The starlight seemed as hearty as a cheer. The world was still there, the world in which he had lived, so he must be safe. His own weakness and loveableness induced enjoyable tears, and there was a delicious moment of abandonment to comfortable whining before he realised that the water would not kindly buoy him up for long, and that even now a hostile current clasped his waist. He braced his flaccid body against the sucking blackness and flung his head back so that the water should not bubble so hungrily against the cords of his throat. Above him the slime of the rock was sticky with moonbeams, and the leprous light brought to his mind a newspaper paragraph, read years ago, which told him that the dawn had discovered floating in some oily Mersey dock, under walls as infected with wet growth as this, a corpse whose blood-encrusted finger-tips were deeply cleft. On the instant his own finger-tips seemed hot with blood and deeply cleft from clawing at the impregnable rock. He screamed gaspingly and beat his hands through the strangling flood. Action, which he had always loathed and dreaded, had broken the hard mould of his self-possession, and the dry dust of his character was blown hither and thither by fear. But one sharp fragment of intelligence which survived this detrition of his personality perceived that a certain gleam on the rock about a foot above the water was not the cold putrescence of the slime, but certainly the hard and merry light of a moon-ray striking on solid metal. His left hand clutched upwards at it, and he swung from a rounded projection. It was, his touch told him, a leaden ring hanging obliquely from the rock, to which his memory could visualise precisely in some past drier time when Lisbech sent no flood to Whimsey, a waterman mooring a boat strewn with pale-bellied perch. And behind the stooping waterman he remembered a flight of narrow steps that led up a buttress to a stone shelf that ran through the cutting. Unquestionably he was safe. He swung in a happy rhythm from the ring, his limp body trailing like a caterpillar through the stream to the foot of the steps, while he gasped in strength. A part of him was in agony, for his arm was nearly dragged out of its socket and a part of him was embarrassed because his hysteria shook him with a deep rumbling chuckle that sounded as though he meditated on some unseemly joke; the whole was pervaded by a twilight atmosphere of unenthusiastic gratitude for his rescue, like the quietly cheerful tone of a Sunday evening sacred concert. After a minute's deep breathing he hauled himself up by the other hand and prepared to swing himself on to the steps.

But first, to shake off the wet worsted rags, once his socks, that now stuck uncomfortably between his toes, he splashed his feet outwards to midstream. A certain porpoise-like surface met his left foot. Fear dappled his face with goose flesh. Without turning his head he knew what it was. It was Evadne's fat flesh rising on each side of her deep-furrowed spine through the rent in her bathing dress.

Once more hatred marched through his soul like a king: compelling service by his godhead and, like all gods, a little hated for his harsh lieu[6] on his worshipper. He saw his wife as the curtain of flesh between him and celibacy, and solitude and all those delicate abstentions from life which his soul desired. He saw her as the invisible worm destroying the rose of the world with her dark secret love.[7] Now he knelt on the lowest stone step watching her wet seal-smooth head bobbing nearer on the waters. As her strong arms, covered with little dark points where her thick hairs were clotted with moisture, stretched out towards safety he bent forward and laid his hands on her head. He held her face under water. Scornfully he noticed the bubbles that rose to the surface from her protesting mouth and nostrils, and the foam raised by her arms and her thick ankles. To the end the creature persisted in turmoil, in movement, in action. . . .

She dropped like a stone. His hands, with nothing to resist them, slapped the water foolishly and he nearly overbalanced forward into the stream. He rose to his feet very stiffly. "I must be a very strong man," he said, as he slowly climbed the steps. "I must be a very strong man," he repeated, a little louder, as with a hot and painful rigidity of the joints he stretched himself out at full length along the stone shelf. Weakness closed him in like a lead coffin. For a little time the wetness of his clothes persisted in being felt: then the sensation oozed out of him and his body fell out of knowledge. There was neither pain nor joy nor any other reckless ploughing of the brain by nerves. He knew unconsciousness, or rather the fullest consciousness he had ever known. For the world became nothingness, and nothingness which is free from the yeasty nuisance of matter and the ugliness of generation was the law of his being. He was absorbed into vacuity, the untamed substance of the universe, round which he conceived passion and thought to circle as straws caught up by the wind. He saw God and lived.

In Heaven a thousand years are a day. And this little corner of time in which he found happiness shrank to a nut-shell as he opened his eyes again. This peace was hardly printed on his heart, yet the brightness of the night was blurred by the dawn. With the grunting carefulness of a man drunk with fatigue, he crawled along the stone shelf to the iron bridge, where he stood with his back to the roaring sluice and rested. All things seemed different now and happier. Like most timid people he disliked the night, and the commonplace hand which the dawn laid on the scene seemed to him a sanctification. The dimmed moon sank to her setting behind the crags. The jewel lights of Lisbech railway station were weak, cheerful twinklings. A steaming bluish milk of morning mist had been spilt on the hard silver surface of the lake, and the reeds no longer stabbed it like little daggers, but seemed a feathery fringe, like the pampas grass in the front garden in Sumatra Crescent. The black crags became brownish, and the mist disguised the sternness of the moor. This weakening of effects was exactly what he had always thought the extinction of Evadne would bring the world. He smiled happily at the moon.

Yet he was moved to sudden angry speech. "If I had my time over again," he said, "I wouldn't touch her with the tongs." For the cold he had known all along he would catch had settled in his head, and his handkerchief was wet through.

---

6. Discipline.   7. A reference to William Blake's poem *The Sick Rose;* see page 1405.

He leaned over the bridge and looked along Lisbech and thought of Evadne. For the first time for many years he saw her image without spirits, and wondered without indignation why she had so often looked like the cat about to steal the cream. What was the cream? And did she ever steal it? Now he would never know. He thought of her very generously and sighed over the perversity of fate in letting so much comeliness.

"If she had married a butcher or a veterinary surgeon she might have been happy," he said, and shook his head at the glassy black water that slid under the bridge to that boiling sluice.

A gust of ague[8] reminded him that wet clothes clung to his fevered body and that he ought to change as quickly as possible, or expect to be laid up for weeks. He turned along the path that led back across the moor to the withered ash tree, and was learning the torture of bare feet on gravel when he cried out to himself: "I shall be hanged for killing my wife." It did not come as a trumpet-call, for he was one of those people who never quite hear what is said to them, and this deafishness extended in him to emotional things. It stole on him clamly, like a fog closing on a city. When he first felt hemmed in by this certainty he looked over his shoulder to the crags, remembering tales of how Jacobite fugitives had hidden on the moors for many weeks. There lay at least another day of freedom. But he was the kind of man who always goes home. He stumbled on, not very unhappy, except for his feet. Like many people of weak temperament he did not fear death. Indeed, it had a peculiar appeal to him; for while it was important, exciting, it did not, like most important and exciting things try to create action. He allowed his imagination the vanity of painting pictures. He saw himself standing in their bedroom, plotting this last event, with the white sheet and the high lights of the mahongany wardrobe shining ghostly at him through the darkness. He saw himself raising a thin hand to the gas bracket and turning on the tap. He saw himself staggering to their bed while death crept in at his nostrils. He saw his corpse lying in full daylight, and for the first time knew himself certainly, unquestionably dignified.

He threw back his chest in pride: but at that moment the path stopped and he found himself staggering down the mound of heatherland and boulders with bleeding feet. Always he had suffered from sore feet, which had not exactly disgusted but, worse still, disappointed Evadne. A certain wistfulness she had always evinced when she found herself the superior animal had enraged and humiliated him many times. He felt that sting him now, and flung himself down the mound cursing. When he stumbled up to the withered ash tree he hated her so much that it seemed as though she were alive again, and a sharp wind blowing down from the moor terrified him like her touch.

He rested there. Leaning against the stripped grey trunk, he smiled up at the sky, which was now so touched to ineffectiveness by the dawn that it looked like a tent of faded silk. There was the peace of weakness in him, which he took to be spiritual, because it had no apparent physical justification: but he lost it as his dripping clothes chilled his tired flesh. His discomfort reminded him that the phantasmic night was passing from him. Daylight threatened him: the daylight in which for so many years he had worked in the solicitor's office and been snubbed and ignored. "'The garish day,'" he murmured disgustedly, quoting the blasphemy of some hymn writer. He wanted his death to happen in this phantasmic night.

8. Fever.

So he limped his way along the road. The birds had not yet begun to sing, but the rustling noises of the night had ceased. The silent highway was consecrated to his proud progress. He staggered happily like a tired child returning from a lovely birthday walk: his death in the little bedroom, which for the first time he would have to himself, was a culminating treat to be gloated over like the promise of a favourite pudding for supper. As he walked he brooded dozingly on large and swelling thoughts. Like all people of weak passions and enterprise he loved to think of Napoleon, and in the shadow of the great asylum wall he strutted a few steps of his advance from murder to suicide, with arms crossed on his breast and thin legs trying to strut massively. He was so happy. He wished that a military band went before him, and pretended that the high hedges were solemn lines of men, stricken in awe to silence as their king rode out to some nobly self-chosen doom. Vast he seemed to himself, and magnificent like music, and solemn like the Sphinx. He had saved the earth from corruption by killing Evadne, for whom he now felt the unremorseful pity a conqueror might bestow on a devastated empire. He might have grieved that his victory brought him death, but with immense pride he found that the occasion was exactly described by a text. "He saved others, Himself He could not save."[9] He had missed the stile in the field above Sumatra Crescent and had to go back and hunt for it in the hedge. So quickly had his satisfaction borne him home.

The field had the fantastic air that jerry-builders[1] give to land poised on the knife-edge of town and country, so that he walked in romance to his very door. The unmarred grass sloped to a stone-hedge of towers of loose brick, trenches and mounds of shining clay, and the fine intentful spires of the scaffolding round the last unfinished house. And he looked down on Petrick. Though to the actual eye it was but a confusion of dark distances through the twilight, a breaking of velvety perspectives, he saw more intensely than ever before its squalid walls and squalid homes where mean men and mean women enlaced their unwholesome lives. Yet he did not shrink from entering for his great experience: as Christ did not shrink from being born in a stable. He swaggered with humility over the trodden mud of the field and the new white flags of Sumatra Crescent. Down the road before him there passed a dim figure, who paused at each lamp post and raised a long wand to behead the yellow gas-flowers that were now wilting before the dawn: a ghostly herald preparing the world to be his deathbed. The Crescent curved in quiet darkness, save for one house, where blazed a gas-lit room with undrawn blinds. The brightness had the startling quality of a scream. He looked in almost anxiously as he passed, and met the blank eyes of a man in evening clothes who stood by the window shaking a medicine. His face was like a wax mask softened by heat: the features were blurred with the suffering which comes from the spectacle of suffering. His eyes lay unshiftingly on George's face as he went by and he went on shaking the bottle. It seemed as though he would never stop.

In the hour of his grandeur George was not forgetful of the griefs of the little human people, but interceded with God for the sake of this stranger. Everything was beautiful, beautiful, beautiful.

His own little house looked solemn as a temple. He leaned against the lamppost at the gate and stared at its empty windows and neat bricks. The disorder of the shattered pane of glass could be overlooked by considering a sign that this house was a holy place: like the Passover blood on the lintel. The propriety of the evenly drawn

---

9. These are the words of the priests and elders mocking   1. Low-wage, slipshod workers.
Jesus at his crucifixion; Matthew 27.42.

blind pleased him enormously. He had always known that this was how the great tragic things of the world had accomplished themselves: quietly. Evadne's raging activity belonged to trivial or annoying things like spring-cleaning or thunderstorms. Well, the house belonged to him now. He opened the gate and went up the asphalt path, sourly noticing that Evadne had as usual left out the lawn-mower, though it might very easily have rained, with the wind coming up as it was. A stray cat that had been sleeping in the tuft of pampas grass in the middle of the lawn was roused by his coming, and fled insolently close to his legs. He hated all wild homeless things, and bent for a stone to throw at it. But instead his fingers touched a slug, which reminded him of the feeling of Evadne's flesh through the slit in her bathing dress. And suddenly the garden was possessed by her presence: she seemed to amble there as she had so often done, sowing seeds unwisely and tormenting the last days of an ailing geranium by insane transplantation, exclaiming absurdly over such mere weeds as morning glory. He caught the very clucking of her voice. . . . The front door opened at his touch.

The little lobby with its closed doors seemed stuffed with expectant silence. He realised that he had come to the theatre of his great adventure. Then panic seized him. Because this was the home where he and she had lived together so horribly he doubted whether he could do this splendid momentous thing, for here he had always been a poor thing with the habit of failure. His heart beat in him more quickly than his raw feet could pad up the oil-clothed stairs. Behind the deal door at the end of the passage was death. Nothingness! It would escape him, even the idea of it would escape him if he did not go to it at once. When he burst at last into its presence he felt so victorious that he sank back against the door waiting for death to come to him without turning on the gas. He was so happy. His death was coming true.

But Evadne lay on his deathbed. She slept there soundly, with her head flung back on the pillows so that her eyes and brow seemed small in shadow, and her mouth and jaw huge above her thick throat in the light. Her wet hair straggled across the pillow on to a broken cane chair covered with her tumbled clothes. Her breast, silvered with sweat, shone in the ray of the street lamp that had always disturbed their nights. The counterpane rose enormously over her hips in rolls of glazed linen. Out of mere innocent sleep her sensuality was distilling a most drunken pleasure.

Not for one moment did he think this a phantasmic appearance. Evadne was not the sort of woman to have a ghost.

Still leaning against the door, he tried to think it all out: but his thoughts came brokenly, because the dawnlight flowing in at the window confused him by its pale glare and that lax figure on the bed held his attention. It must have been that when he laid his murderous hands on her head she had simply dropped below the surface and swum a few strokes under water as any expert swimmer can. Probably he had never even put her into danger, for she was a great lusty creature and the weir was a little place. He had imagined the wonder and peril of the battle as he had imagined his victory. He sneezed exhaustingly, and from his physical distress realised how absurd it was ever to have thought that he had killed her. Bodies like his do not kill bodies like hers.

Now his soul was naked and lonely as though the walls of his body had fallen in at death, and the grossness of Evadne's sleep made him suffer more unlovely a destitution than any old beggarwoman squatting by the roadside in the rain. He had thought he had had what every man most desires: one night of power over a woman for the business of murder or love. But it had been a lie. Nothing beautiful had ever happened to him. He would have wept, but the hatred he had learnt on the moors obstructed all tears in his throat. At least this night had given him passion enough to put an end to it all.

Quietly he went to the window and drew down the sash. There was no fireplace, so that sealed the room. Then he crept over to the gas bracket and raised his thin hand, as he had imagined in his hour of vain glory by the lake.

He had forgotten Evadne's thrifty habit of turning off the gas at the main to prevent leakage when she went to bed.

He was beaten. He undressed and got into bed: as he had done every night for ten years, and as he would do every night until he died. Still sleeping, Evadne caressed him with warm arms.

Ezra Pound: The New Cake of Soap *and* Salutation the Third

Ezra Loomis Pound (1885–1972) was one of the most important, and most controversial, poets of the twentieth century. Born in Idaho and raised outside of Philadelphia, he wrote poetry and studied literature and half a dozen languages in college and during two years of a Ph.D. program at the University of Pennsylvania. He left graduate school in 1907 to become a professor of Romance languages at Wabash Presbyterian College in Indiana. Pound's academic career lasted one semester, at which point he traveled to Spain and Italy before settling in London. He took on literary London in 1908 with a breathtaking amount of enthusiasm, energy, and old-fashioned American optimism; before long he had made influential friends like Yeats, the poet/philosopher T. E. Hulme, and the novelist Ford Madox Ford. He published three volumes of poetry in the two years 1909–1910, and began a series of posts editing poetry and arts magazines, becoming increasingly influential as an arbiter and theorist of experimental literature and art. He was one of the first to champion the writing of such young unknowns as D. H. Lawrence, T. S. Eliot, and James Joyce. In 1912–1914, he led the "Imagist" movement in poetry, which emphasized direct, spare language, in poems often based on moments of vision. His slogan "Make It New" became a rallying-cry for many writers of his time; so pervasive was his influence that the critic Hugh Kenner has labeled these years "The Pound Era."

In Pound's own work, the use of brief, imagistic lyrics coexisted with a tendency toward sprawling works of poetic, cultural, historical, and economic commentary, sometimes taking the form of books of cultural or economic theory, sometimes in radio broadcasts, and often in poetic form. His multi-year and multi-sectioned poem *The Cantos*, begun in 1915, ranging widely across European and world history and culture, was often written while Pound was involving himself in his own century's greatest conflicts. He developed an admiration for the Italian fascist leader Mussolini, and spent World War II in Rome, where he made hundreds of radio broadcasts denouncing the Allies and the Jewish bankers whom he believed were underwriting opposition to Fascism. Captured by American forces at the end of the war, he was imprisoned outside Pisa as a war criminal. There, he translated Confucius and wrote a notable section of the Cantos, *The Pisan Cantos*. He was then sent back to the United States, but was found mentally unfit for trial for treason; he was confined for twelve years in an insane asylum in Washington, D.C. Finally he was released in 1958; he returned to Italy, where he lived, largely in silence, until his death in 1972.

The New Cake of Soap

Lo, how it gleams and glistens in the sun
Like the cheek of a Chesterton[1]

Salutation the Third

Let us deride the smugness of "The Times":
GUFFAW!
    So much the gagged reviewers,
It will pay them when the worms are wriggling in their vitals;
5   These were they who objected to newness,
HERE are their TOMB-STONES.
    They supported the gag and the ring:
A little black BOX contains them.
    SO shall you be also,
10   You slut-bellied obstructionist,
    You sworn foe to free speech and good letters,
You fungus, you continuous gangrene.

Come, let us on with the new deal,
    Let us be done with Jews and Jobbery,[1]
15   Let us SPIT upon those who fawn on the JEWS for their money,
Let us out to the pastures.

PERHAPS I will die at thirty,
Perhaps you will have the pleasure of defiling my pauper's grave,
I wish you JOY, I proffer you ALL my assistance.
20   It has been your HABIT for long to do away with true poets,
You either drive them mad,[2] or else you blink at their suicides,
Or else you condone their drugs, and talk of insanity and genius,
BUT I will not go mad to please you.
    I will not FLATTER you with an early death.
25   OH, NO! I will stick it out,
    I will feel your hates wriggling about my feet,
And I will laugh at you and mock you,
And I will offer you consolations in irony,
    O fools, detesters of Beauty.

30   I have seen many who go about with supplications,
    Afraid to say how they hate you.
    HERE is the taste of my BOOT,
        CARESS it, lick off the BLACKING.

1. G. K. Chesterton (1874–1936), popular essayist and fiction writer. Pound disliked him both for his popularity, and because he was reported to have said "If a thing is worth doing, it's worth doing badly."

1. Pound's anti-Semitism was deep-seated and lifelong; some of his *Cantos* were censored on first publication because of their ugly portrayals of the Jews, who Pound believed to be responsible for international economic instability. When he revised the poem for inclusion in the 1926 edition of his collection *Personae*, Pound changed these lines to read: "Let us be done with panders and jobbery, / Let us spit upon those who pat the big-bellies for profit." Jobbery: Corruption in the conduct of public affairs.

2. Pound may intend a reference here to the savage review of Keats's *Endymion* that appeared in the *Quarterly Review* and was believed to have caused, or at least hastened, Keats's death; Shelley refers to this incident in "Adonais."

Rupert Brooke
1887–1915

Rupert Brooke was the first of Britain's "war poets," and the last poem he completed during his short lifetime—*The Soldier*—is alone enough to guarantee his lasting place in modern poetry.

Brooke rose with extraordinary speed to the center of the British literary establishment. While an undergraduate, he worked with the *Cambridge Review* and came into contact with such influential writers as Henry James, W. B. Yeats, Virginia Woolf, and Lytton Strachey, and the editor and publisher Edward Marsh. In 1912, after the publication of his first volume of poetry, Brooke suffered a nervous breakdown; after a short recovery period, he spent most of the next three years traveling. World War I began shortly after he returned to England in the spring of 1914; Brooke enlisted immediately and was commissioned on a ship that sailed to Antwerp, Belgium, where Brooke saw no action through early 1915. During this lull, Brooke wrote the war sonnets for which he is best remembered today. While his ship was sailing to Gallipoli, Brooke died of blood poisoning, before seeing combat duty.

It is nearly impossible, even at this late date, to separate Brooke the myth from Brooke the poet; he was something of a national hero even before his death, thanks to the popular reception of his volume of war sonnets, *Nineteen Fourteen*. In Brooke's writings about the war, the irony of early poems like *Heaven* ("And in that Heaven of all their wish, / There shall be no more land, say fish") falls away. These patriotic poems—and most especially *The Soldier*, in which Brooke seemed to have foreseen his own death—meshed perfectly with the temperament of the British people as the nation entered into war. When *The Soldier* was read aloud at Saint Paul's Cathedral in London on Easter Sunday, 1915, Brooke the man—whom Yeats called "the handsomest man in England"—was permanently immortalized as the symbol of English pride.

The Soldier

If I should die, think only this of me:
    That there's some corner of a foreign field
That is forever England. There shall be
    In that rich earth a richer dust concealed;
5 A dust whom England bore, shaped, made aware,
    Gave, once, her flowers to love, her ways to roam,
A body of England's, breathing English air,
    Washed by the rivers, blest by suns of home.

And think, this heart, all evil shed away,
10   A pulse in the Eternal mind, no less
      Gives somewhere back the thoughts by England given,
Her sights and sounds; dreams happy as her day;
    And laughter, learnt of friends; and gentleness,
      In hearts at peace, under an English heaven.

Siegfried Sassoon
1886–1967

It is tempting to describe a poet like Siegfried Sassoon by emphasizing his differences from the hugely popular Rupert Brooke. Sassoon was born to a wealthy Jewish family, who made their fortune in India; he lived a life of ease before the war, writing slight Georgian poetry and hunting foxes. World War I suddenly and unequivocally changed all that. Sassoon served with the Royal Welsh Fusiliers, and before the end of 1915 saw action in France; he helped a wounded soldier to safety during heavy fire, for which he was awarded a Military Cross. After being wounded himself, Sassoon refused to return to battle; from his hospital bed, he wrote an open letter to the war department suggesting that the war was being unnecessarily prolonged, and as a result, he narrowly avoided a court-martial. Owing to the intervention of his fellow soldier the poet Robert Graves, he was instead committed to a hospital and treated for "shell-shock." He returned to the front in 1919, and was wounded a second time.

Where the war poetry of Brooke is patriotic to the point of sentimentality, Sassoon's verse is characterized by an unrelentingly realistic portrayal of the horrors of modern warfare. And where Brooke's poetry was eagerly welcomed by an anxious public, Sassoon's was largely rejected as either unpatriotic or unnecessarily grotesque. After the war, he lived in seclusion in the country, writing memoirs and poetry—though rarely with the shock value of his early war poems.

Glory of Women

You love us when we're heroes, home on leave,
Or wounded in a mentionable place.
You worship decorations; you believe
That chivalry redeems the war's disgrace.
5   You make us shells. You listen with delight,
By tales of dirt and danger fondly thrilled.
You crown our distant ardours while we fight,
And mourn our laurelled memories when we're killed.
You can't believe that British troops "retire"
10   When hell's last horror breaks them, and they run,
Trampling the terrible corpses—blind with blood.
    O German mother dreaming by the fire,
While you are knitting socks to send your son
His face is trodden deeper in the mud.

Craiglockhart,[1] 1917

Everyone Sang

Everyone suddenly burst out singing;
And I was filled with such delight
As prisoned birds must find in freedom,
Winging wildly across the white
5   Orchards and dark-green fields; on—on—and out of sight.
Everyone's voice was suddenly lifted;
And beauty came like the setting sun:
My heart was shaken with tears; and horror
Drifted away . . . O, but Everyone
10   Was a bird; and the song was wordless; the singing will never be done.

April 1919

---

1. A hospital near Edinburgh, Scotland, where Sassoon (along with Wilfred Owen) was treated for shell shock.

Wilfred Owen
1893–1918

The poet C. Day Lewis wrote that Owen's poems were "certainly the finest written by any English poet of the First War." In his small body of poems Owen manages to combine his friend Siegfried Sassoon's outrage at the horror of the war with a formal and technical skill reminiscent of his idols Keats and Shelley. Sassoon himself characterized their differences as poets this way: "My trench-sketches were like rockets, sent up to illuminate the darkness. . . . It was Owen who revealed how, out of realistic horror and scorn, poetry might be made."

Owen grew up on the Welsh border in Shropshire, the landscape A. E. Housman was to celebrate in his poetry. After finishing technical school, Owen spent two years in training with an evangelical Church of England vicar, trying to decide whether to pursue formal training as a clergyman. As a result of his experiences, Owen became dissatisfied with the institutional church's response to the poverty and suffering of England's least privileged citizens. In October 1915 he enlisted with the Artists' Rifles, and on 29 December 1916, he left for France as a lieutenant with the Lancashire Fusiliers.

Owen quickly became disillusioned with the war; as a result of almost unimaginable privations, which included being blown into the air while he slept in a foxhole, Owen suffered a breakdown, and was sent to the Craiglockhart War Hospital in Edinburgh. Owen composed nearly all of his poetry in the fourteen months of his rehabilitation, between August 1917 and September 1918; though hard to imagine, it is quite possible that if he had not been sent back to Great Britain to recover from his "shell shock," we might now know nothing of his poetry. While at Craiglockhart he met Sassoon and found his true voice and mode; he published his first poems on war themes anonymously in the hospital's magazine, which he edited. In September 1918 Owen returned to the battlefields of France; he was killed in action at Sambre Canal on November 4, 1918, one week before the Armistice. Dylan Thomas called Owen "one of the four most profound influences upon the poets who came after him"—the others being Hopkins, Yeats, and Eliot.

Anthem for Doomed Youth

What passing-bells for these who die as cattle?
    Only the monstrous anger of the guns.
    Only the stuttering rifles' rapid rattle
Can patter out their hasty orisons.°   *prayers*
5 No mockeries now for them; no prayers nor bells,
    Nor any voice of mourning save the choirs,—
The shrill, demented choirs of wailing shells;
    And bugles calling for them from sad shires.

What candles may be held to speed them all?
10   Not in the hands of boys, but in their eyes
Shall shine the holy glimmers of good-byes.
    The pallor of girls' brows shall be their pall;[1]
Their flowers the tenderness of patient minds,
And each slow dusk a drawing-down of blinds.

---

1. The cloth draped over a coffin.

Strange Meeting

It seemed that out of battle I escaped
Down some profound dull tunnel, long since scooped
Through granites which titanic wars had groined.°   *joined together*
Yet also there encumbered sleepers groaned,
5   Too fast in thought or death to be bestirred.
Then, as I probed them, one sprang up, and stared
With piteous recognition in fixed eyes,
Lifting distressful hands as if to bless.
And by his smile, I knew that sullen hall,
10   By his dead smile I knew we stood in Hell.
With a thousand pains that vision's face was grained;
Yet no blood reached there from the upper ground,
And no guns thumped, or down the flues made moan.
"Strange friend," I said, "here is no cause to mourn."
15   "None," said that other, "save the undone years,
The hopelessness. Whatever hope is yours,
Was my life also; I went hunting wild
After the wildest beauty in the world,
Which lies not calm in eyes, or braided hair,
20   But mocks the steady running of the hour,
And if it grieves, grieves richlier than here.
For of my glee might many men have laughed,
And of my weeping something had been left,
Which must die now. I mean the truth untold,
25   The pity of war, the pity war distilled.
Now men will go content with what we spoiled,
Or, discontent, boil bloody, and be spilled.
They will be swift with swiftness of the tigress.
None will break ranks, though nations trek from progress.
30   Courage was mine, and I had mystery,
Wisdom was mine, and I had mastery:
To miss the march of this retreating world
Into vain citadels that are not walled.
Then, when much blood had clogged their chariot-wheels,
35   I would go up and wash them from sweet wells,
Even with truths that lie too deep for taint.
I would have poured my spirit without stint
But not through wounds; not on the cess of war.
Foreheads of men have bled where no wounds were.
40   I am the enemy you killed, my friend.
I knew you in this dark: for so you frowned
Yesterday through me as you jabbed and killed.
I parried; but my hands were loath and cold.
Let us sleep now. . . ."

Dulce Et Decorum Est[1]

Bent double, like old beggars under sacks,
Knock-kneed, coughing like hags, we cursed through sludge,

---

1. From the *Odes* of the Roman satirist Horace (65–8 B.C.): Dulce et decorum est pro patria mori [sweet and fitting it is to die for your fatherland].

Till on the haunting flares we turned our backs
And towards our distant rest began to trudge.
5 Men marched asleep. Many had lost their boots
But limped on, blood-shod. All went lame; all blind;
Drunk with fatigue; deaf even to the hoots
Of tired, outstripped Five-Nines[2] that dropped behind.

Gas! Gas! Quick, boys!—An ecstasy of fumbling,
10 Fitting the clumsy helmets just in time;
But someone still was yelling out and stumbling
And flound'ring like a man in fire or lime[3] . . .
Dim, through the misty panes and thick green light,
As under a green sea, I saw him drowning.

15 In all my dreams, before my helpless sight,
He plunges at me, guttering, choking, drowning.

If in some smothering dreams you too could pace
Behind the wagon that we flung him in,
And watch the white eyes writhing in his face,
20 His hanging face, like a devil's sick of sin;
If you could hear, at every jolt, the blood
Come gargling from the froth-corrupted lungs,
Obscene as cancer, bitter as the cud
Of vile, incurable sores on innocent tongues,—
25 My friend, you would not tell with such high zest
To children ardent for some desperate glory,
The old Lie: Dulce et decorum est
Pro patria mori.

Isaac Rosenberg
1890–1918

World War I was the spur that goaded some poets, like Wilfred Owen, into the writing of poetry; for Isaac Rosenberg the war was simply the catalyst for a more vivid and powerful verse. Rosenberg began writing poetry on Jewish themes when he was just fifteen; he had published two volumes of poems and a verse play, *Moses*, by the time he joined the army in 1916. Rosenberg's experience of the war was, in important ways, different from the other poets represented here. To begin with, he was the son of Lithuanian Jewish immigrants who had settled in the East End, London's Jewish ghetto. As a child, Rosenberg lived with severe poverty; he was forced to leave school at fourteen to help support his family. He went to war not as an officer, but as a private; as the critic Irving Howe writes, "No glamorous fatality hangs over Rosenberg's head: he was just a clumsy, stuttering Jewish doughboy." He was killed while on patrol outside the trenches—a private's dangerous assignment.

His experiences on the Western Front seem to have provided him with the perfect canvas for his essentially religious art. Siegfried Sassoon, alluding to Rosenberg's training as an artist at the Slade School, later described his poems as "scriptural and sculptural": "His experiments were a strenuous effort for impassioned expression; his imagination had a sinewy and muscular aliveness; often he saw things in terms of sculpture, but he did not carve or chisel; he *modeled*

---

2. Artillery shells used by the Germans.

3. Calcium oxide, a powerfully caustic alkali used, among other purposes, for cleaning the flesh off the bones of corpses.

words with fierce energy and aspiration." His less-than-genteel background also made Rosenberg impatient with the patriotic sentiments of a poet like Rupert Brooke, for whose "begloried sonnets" he had nothing but contempt. In the poetry of Rosenberg, by contrast—according to Sassoon—"words and images obey him, instead of leading him into over-elaboration." Interest in Rosenberg's poetry has recently been revived by critics interested in his use of Jewish themes; the critic Harold Bloom, for instance, calls Rosenberg "an English poet with a Jewish difference," and suggests that he is "the best Jewish poet writing in English that our century has given us."

Break of Day in the Trenches

The darkness crumbles away—
It is the same old druid[1] Time as ever.
Only a live thing leaps my hand—
A queer sardonic rat—
5   As I pull the parapet's poppy
To stick behind my ear.
Droll rat, they would shoot you if they knew
Your cosmopolitan sympathies.
Now you have touched this English hand
10   You will do the same to a German—
Soon, no doubt, if it be your pleasure
To cross the sleeping green between.
It seems you inwardly grin as you pass
Strong eyes, fine limbs, haughty athletes
15   Less chanced than you for life,
Bonds to the whims of murder,
Sprawled in the bowels of the earth,
The torn fields of France.
What do you see in our eyes
20   At the shrieking iron and flame
Hurled through still heavens?
What quaver—what heart aghast?
Poppies whose roots are in man's veins
Drop, and are ever dropping;
25   But mine in my ear is safe,
Just a little white with the dust.

1916   1922

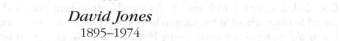

David Jones
1895–1974

David Jones's long narrative poem *In Parenthesis* is arguably the great literary text of World War I. While other poets have more vividly recreated the horrors of the war, and prose chroniclers like Robert Graves have analyzed more precisely the futility and banality of trench warfare, Jones's "writing"—the only generic label he was willing to assign *In Parenthesis*—combines the resources of both poetry and prose, and brings to bear a historical, religious, and

---

1. Member of an ancient Celtic religion.

mythical framework through which to understand the war. In Jones's text the Great War is revealed to be just the most recent battle in the great war that is human history.

Jones was born near London to an English mother and Welsh father; his father impressed upon him the richness of his Welsh heritage. After leaving grammar school, Jones enrolled in art school; when war broke out, however, he was quick to enlist, and joined the Royal Welch Fusiliers as an infantryman in January 1915. He served on the Western Front until March 1918, having been wounded at the battle of the Somme in June 1916; he remarked later that the war "had a permanent effect upon me and has affected my work in all sorts of ways." After the war, Jones went to Ditchling Common, a Catholic artists' guild run by the writer and sculptor Eric Gill. Jones was attracted to Gill's regimen of work and prayer; he converted to Roman Catholicism in 1921 and soon joined the guild, where he lived and worked until 1933.

Jones did not begin to write *In Parenthesis* until 1928. The poem tells the story of Private John Ball, from his embarkation from England in December 1915 to the battle of the Somme. The text modulates from straightforward narrative to a kind of prose poetry to stretches of pure poetry, incorporating echoes and allusions of texts, from the Welsh epic *The Mabinogion* to the medieval battle epic *Y Gododdin* to Malory's *Morte d'Arthur* to Shakespeare's history plays to Eliot's *The Waste Land*—as well as drawing from "subliterary" sources such as soldier's slang. *In Parenthesis* is difficult and allusive, as are many other monumental works of modernist literature, like Joyce's *Ulysses* and *Finnegans Wake*, Pound's *Cantos*, and Eliot's *The Waste Land*. While this difficulty has sometimes kept away the readers Jones deserves, the critic Thomas Dilworth calls *In Parenthesis* "the only authentic and successful epic poem in the language since *Paradise Lost*."

In Parenthesis differs from other war poetry in argument as well as form; the poem is not simply a protest against the war but rather an attempt to place the war into a world-historical context. As the critic Samuel Rees writes, it "is not a poem either to provoke or to end a war . . . except as it adds to the accumulation of testimony to the stupidities and brutality of history that each age must learn from or, more likely, ignore." In the writing he produced after *In Parenthesis* Jones continued to be concerned with contemporary society's loss of interest in the past, and with the depersonalizing effects of technology; his other great poem, *The Anathemata*, was judged by W. H. Auden to be "probably the finest long poem in English in this century."

from In Parenthesis[1]
Part 1. The Many Men So Beautiful[2]

'49 Wyatt, 01549 Wyatt.
Coming sergeant.
Pick 'em up, pick 'em up—I'll stalk within yer chamber.
Private Leg . . . sick.
Private Ball . . . absent.
'01 Ball, '01 Ball, Ball of No. 1.
Where's Ball, 2501 Ball—you corporal,
Ball of your section.
Movement round and about the Commanding Officer.
Bugler, will you sound "Orderly Sergeants."

1. In his preface, Jones writes: "This writing is called 'In Parenthesis' because I have written it in a kind of space between—I don't know between quite what—but as you turn aside to do something; and because for us amateur soldiers (and especially for the writer, who was not only an amateur, but grotesquely incompetent, a knocker-over of piles, a parade's despair) the war itself was a parenthe-sis—how glad we thought we were to step outside its brackets at the end of '18—and also because our curious type of existence here is altogether in parenthesis."
2. Coleridge, *Ancient Mariner*, part iv, verse 4 [Jones's note]. "The many men, so beautiful! / And they all dead did lie: / And a thousand thousand slimy things / Lived on; and so did I."

David Jones. Etching
of World War I soldier
(frontispiece to *In
Parenthesis*). 1937.

A hurrying of feet from three companies converging on the little group apart
where on horses sit the central command. But from "B" Company there is no such
darting out. The Orderly Sergeant of "B" is licking the stub end of his lead pencil; it
divides a little his fairish moist moustache.

Heavily jolting and sideway jostling, the noise of liquid shaken in a small vessel
by a regular jogging movement, a certain clinking ending in a shuffling of the feet
sidelong—all clear and distinct in that silence peculiar to parade grounds and to
refectories. The silence of a high order, full of peril in the breaking of it, like the
coming on parade of John Ball.

He settles between numbers 4 and 5 of the rear rank. It is as ineffectual as the
ostrich in her sand. Captain Gwynn does not turn or move or give any sign.

Have that man's name taken if you please, Mr. Jenkins.

Take that man's name, Sergeant Snell.

Take his name, corporal.

Take his name take his number—charge him—late on parade—the Battalion
being paraded for overseas—warn him for Company Office.

Have you got his name Corporal Quilter.

Temporary unpaid Lance-Corporal Aneirin Merddyn Lewis had somewhere in his Welsh depths a remembrance of the nature of man, of how a lance-corporal's stripe is but held vicariously and from on high, is of one texture with an eternal economy. He brings in a manner, baptism, and metaphysical order to the bankruptcy of the occasion.

'01 Ball is it—there was a man in Bethesda late for the last bloody judgment.

Corporal Quilter on the other hand knew nothing of these things.

Private Ball's pack, ill adjusted and without form, hangs more heavily on his shoulder blades, a sense of ill-usage pervades him. He withdraws within himself to soothe himself—the inequity of those in high places is forgotten. From where he stood heavily, irksomely at ease, he could see, half-left between 7 and 8 of the front rank, the profile of Mr. Jenkins and the elegant cut of his war-time rig and his flax head held front; like San Romano's[3] foreground squire, unhelmeted; but we don't have lances now nor banners nor trumpets. It pains the lips to think of bugles—and did they blow Defaulters[4] on the Uccello horns.

He put his right hand behind him to ease his pack, his cold knuckles find something metallic and colder.

No mess-tin cover.

Shining sanded mess-tin giving back the cold early light. *Improperly dressed, the Battalion being paraded for overseas.* His imaginings as to the precise relationship of this general indictment from the book to his own naked mess-tin were with suddenness and most imperatively impinged upon, as when an animal hunted, stopping in some ill-chosen covert to consider the wickedness of man, is started into fresh effort by the cry and breath of dogs dangerously and newly near. For the chief huntsman is winding his horn, the officer commanding is calling his Battalion by name—whose own the sheep are.

55th Battalion!

Fifty-fifth Bat-tal-i-on

'talion!!

From "D" to "A" his eyes knew that parade. He detected no movement. They were properly at ease.

Reverberation of that sudden command broke hollowly upon the emptied huts behind "D" Company's rear platoons. They had only in them the rolled mattresses, the neatly piled bed-boards and the empty tea-buckets of the orderly-men, emptied of their last gun-fire.[5]

Stirrups taut and pressing upward in the midst of his saddle he continues the ritual words by virtue of which a regiment is moved in column of route:

. . . the Battalion will move in column of fours to the right—"A" Company— "A" Company leading.

Words lost, yet given continuity by that thinner command from in front of No. 1. Itself to be wholly swallowed up by the concerted movement of arms in which the spoken word effected what it signified.

"A" Company came to the slope, their files of four turn right. The complex of command and heel-iron turned confuse the morning air. The rigid structure of their lines knows a swift mobility, patterns differently for those sharp successive cries.

---

3. Cf. painting, "Rout of San Romano." Paolo Uccello (Nat. Gal.) [Jones's note].
4. Soldiers convicted by a court-martial.

5. Tea served to troops before first parade. Rouse parade [Jones's note].

Mr. P. D. I. Jenkins who is twenty years old has now to do his business:
No. 7 Platoon—number seven.
number seven—right—by the right.
How they sway in the swing round for all this multiplicity of gear.
Keept'y'r dressing.
Sergeant Snell did his bit.
Corporal Quilter intones:
Dress to the right—no—other right.
Keep those slopes.
Keep those sections of four.
Pick those knees up.
Throw those chests out.
Hold those heads up.
Stop that talking.
Keep those chins in.
Left left lef'—lef' righ' lef'—you Private Ball it's you I'v got me glad-eye on.

So they came outside the camp. The liturgy of a regiment departing has been sung.
Empty wet parade ground. A campwarden, some unfit men and other details loiter,
dribble away, shuffle off like men whose ship has sailed.

The long hutment lines stand. Not a soul. It rains harder: torn felt lifts to the
wind above Hut 10, Headquarter Company; urinal concrete echoes for a solitary
whistler. Corrugated iron empty—no one. Chill gust slams the vacant canteen door.

Miss Veronica Best who runs the hut for the bun-wallahs[6] stretches on her palliasse,[7]
she's sleepy, she can hear the band: We've got too many buns—and all those wads[8]—
you knew they were going—why did you order them—they won't be in after rouse-
parade even—they've gone.

Know they've gone—shut up—Jocks from Bardown move in Monday. Violet
turns to sleep again.

Horses' tails are rather good—and the way this one springs from her groomed flanks.
He turns slightly in his saddle.
You may march at ease.
No one said march easy Private Ball, you're bleedin' quick at some things ain't yer.

The Squire from the Rout of San Romano smokes Melachrino No. 9.
The men may march easy and smoke, Sergeant Snell.

Some like tight belts and some like loose belts—trussed-up pockets—cigarettes in
ammunition pouches—rifle-bolts, webbing, buckles and rain—gotta light mate—
give us a match chum. How cold the morning is and blue, and how mysterious in
cupped hands glow the match-lights of a concourse of men, moving so early in the
morning.

The body of the high figure in front of the head of the column seemed to change
his position however so slightly. It rains on the transparent talc of his map-case.

The Major's horse rubs noses with the horse of the superior officer. Their docked
manes brush each, as two friends would meet. The dark horse snorts a little for the
pulling at her bridle rein.

---

6. Person pertaining to: e.g. staff-wallah; person addicted
to: e.g. bun-wallah [Jones's note].

7. Straw mattress.
8. Canteen sandwiches [Jones's note].

In "D" Company round the bend of the road in the half-light is movement, like a train shunting, when the forward coaches buffer the rear coaches back. The halt was unexpected. How heavy and how top-heavy is all this martial panoply and how the ground seems to press upward to afflict the feet.

The bastard's lost his way already.

Various messages are passed.

Some lean on their rifles as aged men do on sticks in stage-plays. Some lean back with the muzzle of the rifle supporting the pack in the position of gentlewomen at field sports, but not with so great assurance.

It's cold when you stop marching with all this weight and icy down the back.

Battalion cyclists pass the length of the column. There is fresh stir in "A" Company.

Keep your column distance.

The regular rhythm of the march has re-established itself.

The rain increases with the light and the weight increases with the rain. In all that long column in brand-new overseas boots weeping blisters stick to the hard wool of grey government socks.

I'm bleedin' cripple already Corporal, confides a limping child.

Kipt' that step there.

Keep that proper distance.

Keept' y'r siction o' four—can't fall out me little darlin'.

Corporal Quilter subsides, he too retreats within himself, he has his private thoughts also.

It's a proper massacre of the innocents in a manner of speaking, no so-called seven ages o' man only this bastard military age.

Keep that step there.

Keep that section distance.

Hand us thet gas-pipe young Saunders—let's see you shape—you too, little Benjamin—hang him about like a goddam Chris'us tree—use his ample shoulders for an armoury-rack—it is his part to succour the lambs of the flock.

With some slackening of the rain the band had wiped their instruments. Broken catches on the wind-gust came shrilly back:

Of Hector and Lysander and such great names as these—the march proper to them.[9]

So they went most of that day and it rained with increasing vigour until night-fall. In the middle afternoon the outer parts of the town of embarkation were reached. They halted for a brief while; adjusted puttees,[1] straightened caps, fastened undone buttons, tightened rifle-slings and attended each one to his own bedraggled and irregular condition. The band recommenced playing; and at the attention and in excellent step they passed through the suburbs, the town's centre, and so towards the docks. The people of that town did not acclaim them, nor stop about their business—for it was late in the second year.[2]

By some effort of a corporate will the soldierly bearing of the text books maintained itself through the town, but with a realisation of the considerable distance yet to be covered through miles of dock, their frailty reasserted itself—which slackening called for fresh effort from the Quilters and the Snells, but at this stage with a more persuasive intonation, with almost motherly concern.

---

9. *The British Grenadiers* is the ceremonial march of all Grenadier and Fusilier Regiments [Jones's note].

1. Leggings.

2. That is to say in December 1915 [Jones's note].

Out of step and with a depressing raggedness of movement and rankling of tempers they covered another mile between dismal sheds, high and tarred. Here funnels and mastheads could be seen. Here the influence of the sea and of the tackle and ways of its people fell upon them. They revived somewhat, and for a while. Yet still these interminable ways between—these incessant halts at junctions. Once they about-turned. Embarkation officers, staff people of all kinds and people who looked as though they were in the Navy but who were not, consulted with the Battalion Commander. A few more halts, more passing of messages,—a further intensifying of their fatigue. The platoons of the leading company unexpectedly wheel. The spacious shed is open at either end, windy and comfortless. Multifarious accoutrements, metal and cloth and leather sink with the perspiring bodies to the concrete floor.

Certain less fortunate men were detailed for guard, John Ball amongst them. The others lay, where they first sank down, wet with rain and sweat. They smoked; they got very cold. They were given tins of bully beef and ration biscuits for the first time, and felt like real expeditionary soldiers. Sometime between midnight and 2 a.m. they were paraded. Slowly, and with every sort of hitch, platoon upon platoon formed single file and moved toward an invisible gangway. Each separate man found his own feet stepping in the darkness on an inclined plane, the smell and taste of salt and machinery, the texture of rope, and the glimmer of shielded light about him.

So without sound of farewell or acclamation, shrouded in a dense windy darkness, they set toward France. They stood close on deck and beneath deck, each man upholstered in his life-belt. From time to time a seaman would push between them about some duty belonging to his trade.

Under a high-slung arc-light whose cold clarity well displayed all their sea weariness, their long cramped-upness and fatigue, they stumblingly and one by one trickled from the ship on to French land. German prisoners in green tunics, made greener by the light, heavily unloading timber at a line of trucks—it still rained, and a bitter wind in from the sea.

A young man, comfortable in a short fleece jacket, stood smoking, immediately beneath the centre of the arc—he gave orders in a pleasant voice, that measured the leisure of his circumstances and of his class. Men move to left and right within the orbit of the light, and away into the half darkness, undefined, beyond it.

"B" Company were conducted by a guide, through back ways between high shuttered buildings, to horse-stalls, where they slept. In the morning, they were given Field Service postcards—and sitting in the straw they crossed out what did not apply, and sent them to their mothers, to their sweethearts.

Toward evening on the same day they entrained in cattle trucks; and on the third day, which was a Sunday, sunny and cold, and French women in deep black were hurrying across flat land—they descended from their grimy, littered, limb restricting, slatted vehicles, and stretched and shivered at a siding. You feel exposed and apprehensive in this new world.

from *Part 7. The Five Unmistakable Marks*[3]

At the gate of the wood you try a last adjustment, but slung so, it's an impediment, it's of detriment to your hopes, you had best be rid of it—the sagging web-

---

3. Printed here is the conclusion to the chapter, which closes *In Parenthesis*. The chapter's title comes from Lewis Carroll's narrative poem *The Hunting of the Snark*, which concerns a voyage in search of the Snark; "warranted, genuine Snarks" can be identified by "five unmistakable marks." The poem ends with the death of the explorer who discovers the Snark.

bing and all and what's left of your two fifty—but it were wise to hold on to your mask.

You're clumsy in your feebleness, you implicate your tin-hat rim with the slack sling of it.
Let it lie for the dews to rust it, or ought you to decently cover the working parts.
Its dark barrel, where you leave it under the oak, reflects the solemn star that rises urgently from Cliff Trench.
It's a beautiful doll for us
it's the Last Reputable Arm.
But leave it—under the oak.
leave it for a Cook's tourist to the Devastated Areas[4] and crawl as far as you can and wait for the bearers.

Mrs. Willy Hartington has learned to draw sheets and so has Miss Melpomené;[5] and on the south lawns,
men walk in red white and blue
under the cedars
and by every green tree
and beside comfortable waters.
But why dont the bastards come—
Bearers!—stret-cher bear-errs!
or do they divide the spoils at the Aid-Post.[6]
But how many men do you suppose could bear away a third of us: drag just a little further—he yet may counter-attack.

Lie still under the oak
next to the Jerry
and Sergeant Jerry Coke.
The feet of the reserves going up tread level with your forehead; and no word for you; they whisper one with another; pass on, inward;
these latest succours:
green Kimmerii[7] to bear up the war.

Oeth and Annoeth's hosts they were
who in that night grew
younger men
younger striplings.[8]

The geste says this and the man who was on the field . . . and who wrote the book . . . the man who does not know this has not understood anything.[9]

---

4. This may appear to be an anachronism, but I remember in 1917 discussing with a friend the possibilities of tourist activity if peace ever came. I remember we went into details and wondered if the inexploded projectile lying near us would go up under a holiday-maker, and how people would stand to be photographed on our parapets. I recall feeling very angry about this, as you do if you think of strangers ever occupying a house you live in, and which has, for you, particular associations [Jones's note].
5. Greek muse of tragedy.
6. The R.A.M.C. was suspected by disgruntled men of the fighting units of purloining articles from the kit of the wounded and the dead. Their regimental initials were commonly interpreted: "Rob All My Comrades" [Jones's note].
7. In Homer, the Kimmerioi were a race who lived in eternal darkness, "on whom the sun never looks."
8. Cf. Englyn 30 of the *Englynion y Beddeu*, "The Stanzas of the Graves." See Rhys, *Origin of the Englyn, Y Cymmrodor*, vol. xviii. Oeth and Annoeth's hosts occur in Welsh tradition as a mysterious body of troops that seem to have some affinity with the Legions. They were said to "fight as well in the covert as in the open." Cf. *The Iolo MSS* [Jones's note].
9. Cf. Chanson de Roland, lines 2095–8:

Co dit la geste e cil qui el camp fut,
[Li ber Gilie por qui Deus fait vertuz]
E fist la chartre [el muster de Loum].
Ki tant ne set, ne l'ad prod entendut.

I have used Mr. Rene Hague's translation [Jones's note].

Speeches on Irish Independence

Through the eight centuries of British rule in Ireland, Irish nationalist sentiment remained strong, though it was often forced underground. Ireland had gained a hundred members in the British Parliament when the United Kingdom was formed in 1801, yet on crucial issues they were regularly outvoted by the English majority. As Ireland gradually recovered from the effects of the famine of the 1840s, nationalist agitation increased, only inflamed by English attempts at repression. In 1870 the Home Rule League was formed, to press for legislative independence. In 1877 the League elected as its parliamentary leader a bold young nationalist named Charles Stewart Parnell (1846–1891), who came to dominate the movement for the ensuing dozen years; his tragic fall from power in 1889 shocked both his supporters and his detractors. For Yeats and Joyce especially, Parnell was proof of their suspicion that, as Joyce's character Stephen Dedalus was to put it, Ireland is "the old sow that eats her farrow."

Parnell assembled a powerful coalition in Parliament, bringing other business to a halt until Irish issues were considered. After years of negotiation, the Liberal prime minister Gladstone agreed to introduce a Home Rule bill in 1886. The bill was defeated, but passage was believed to be just a matter of time. Parnell's fortunes were quickly to turn, however. On Christmas Eve, 1889, Captain William O'Shea, a moderate Home Rule member, brought a divorce action against his wife Katherine ("Kitty"), and named Parnell as respondent. Parnell had been conducting an affair with Kitty O'Shea since 1880; some suggest that Captain O'Shea had long known this, and brought the action at this point for political gain. As a result of the divorce, the Irish parliamentary party removed Parnell from the leadership, and the Catholic hierarchy in Ireland turned against him, declaring him unfit for public office; a large portion of the Irish people abandoned him as well. Others, especially in Dublin, remained fiercely loyal to Parnell; but he was a broken man, and died just a few months after his marriage to Kitty O'Shea in June 1891.

The ensuing years were marked by token reforms and by division in Ireland, between ardent nationalists, moderate reformers, and Protestants who opposed weakened ties to England. The Irish republic can be dated from the Easter Rising in 1916 which, though unsuccessful, started the movement toward Irish independence which resulted six years later in the founding of the Irish Free State. After the failure of a third Home Rule bill in 1914, the Irish Republican Brotherhood stepped up their activities and began planning for a large-scale revolutionary uprising. In the spring of 1916 the Irish statesman Sir Roger Casement traveled to Germany to raise support for the planned uprising, but he managed only to obtain some obsolete firearms and was arrested on his return to Ireland. Three days later, on Easter Monday, April 24, a small force of about a thousand rebels seized the General Post Office and other city buildings, and declared a provisional Republican government, in a stirring proclamation read on the Post Office steps by Padriac Pearce, the planned president. W. B. Yeats vividly evokes that historical moment, and its transformation into nationalist mythology, in his poem *Easter 1916*. Street fighting continued for about a week, until Pearse and other leaders were forced to surrender. The execution of these leaders helped to rally support for the Republican cause among the Irish people and contributed to the founding of the Irish Republican Army (IRA) in 1919. Guided by the brilliant tactician Michael Collins, the IRA harrassed British troops and kept them from crushing the nationalist resistance.

As a result of this ongoing state of virtual civil war, the British government was ultimately forced to pass the Government of Ireland Act in 1920, dividing Ireland into two self-governing areas, Northern Ireland and Southern Ireland. Historically, the south has been primarily Catholic (currently more than 90 percent), and the north Protestant (about 65 percent); all twentieth-century political divisions of Ireland have been made with the awareness of these religious and cultural differences. At the close of 1921, the Anglo-Irish Treaty laid the groundwork for Ireland's twenty-six southern counties to establish an Irish Free State, the Republic of

Ireland; the six counties of Northern Ireland would retain their status as a member of the United Kingdom. Michael Collins, who negotiated the 1921 treaty, was ambushed and killed in 1922 by opponents of Irish partition. This division of the island remains in effect today, although recurrent terrorist violence of the IRA has been directed at winning independence as well for Northern Ireland. Thus while Ireland and England are still somewhat uneasy neighbors, 1922 marks the incomplete realization of a 750-year-old dream—in the words of a popular ballad, the dream that Ireland might be "a nation once again."

Charles Stewart Parnell
At Limerick

I firmly believe that, bad as are the prospects of this country, out of that we will obtain good for Ireland. * * * It is the duty of the Irish tenant farmers to combine amongst themselves and ask for a reduction of rent, and if they get no reduction where a reduction is necessary, then I say that it is the duty of the tenant to pay no rent until he gets it. And if they combined in that way, if they stood together, and if being refused a reasonable and just reduction, they kept a firm grip of their homesteads, I can tell them that no power on earth could prevail against the hundreds of thousands of the tenant farmers of this country. Do not fear. You are not to be exterminated as you were in 1847,[1] and take my word for it it will not be attempted. You should ask for concessions that are just. Ask for them in a proper manner, and good landlords will give these conditions. But for the men who had always shown themselves regardless of right and justice in their dealings with these questions, I say it is necessary for you to maintain a firm and determined attitude. If you maintain that attitude victory must be yours. If when a farm was tenantless, owing to any cause, you refuse to take it, and the present most foolish competition amongst farmers came to an end, as undoubtedly it now must, these men who are forgetful of reason and of common sense must come to reconsider their position. I believe that the land of a country ought to be owned by the people of the country. And I think we should centre our exertions upon attaining that end. * * * When we have the people of this country prosperous, self-reliant, and confident of the future, we will have an Irish nation which will be able to hold its own amongst the nations of the world. We will have a country which will be able to speak with the enemy in the gate—we will have a people who will understand their rights, and, knowing those rights, will be resolved to maintain them. We must all have this without injustice to any individual.

Before the House of Commons[1]

* * * I can assure the House that it is not my belief that anything I can say, or wish to say at this time, will have the slightest effect on the public opinion of the House, or upon the public opinion of this country. I have been accustomed during my political life to rely upon the public opinion of those whom I have desired to help, and with whose aid I have worked for the cause of prosperity and freedom in Ireland: and the utmost that I desire to do in the very few words which I shall address to this House, is

1. After the failure of the potato crops in 1845 and 1846, and English refusal to suspend rent payments of Irish tenant farmers, 1847 was perhaps the year of most extreme suffering and starvation. During the years of the Potato Famine, the Irish population plummeted, through starvation, disease, and emigration, from about 8.5 million in 1845 to 6.6 million in 1851. This national tragedy forms the backdrop for Parnell's remarks (31 August 1879) to the tenant farmers of Limerick, who seemed to be facing an agricultural crisis of similar magnitude.

1. Delivered 23 February 1883.

to make my position clear to the Irish people at home and abroad from the unjust aspersions which have been cast upon me by a man[2] who ought to be ashamed to devote his high ability to the task of traducing[3] them. I don't wish to reply to the questions of the right hon. gentleman. I consider he has no right to question me, standing as he does in a position very little better than an informer with regard to the secrets of the men with whom he was associated, and he has not even the pretext of that remarkable informer whose proceedings we have lately heard of.[4] He had not even the pretext of that miserable man that he was attempting to save his own life. No, sir: other motives of less importance seem to have weighed with the right hon. gentleman in the extraordinary course which he has adopted on the present occasion of going out of his way to collect together a series of extracts, perhaps nine or ten in number, out of a number of speeches—many hundreds and thousands—delivered during the Land League movement[5] by other people and not by me, upon which to found an accusation against me for what has been said and done by others. * * * The right hon. gentleman has asked me to defend myself. Sir, I have nothing to defend myself for. The right hon. gentleman has confessed that he attempted to obtain a declaration or public promise from me which would have the effect of discrediting me with the Irish people. He has admitted that he failed in that attempt, and failing in that attempt, he lost his own reputation. He boasted last night that he had deposed me from some imaginary position which he was pleased to assign to me; but, at least, I have this consolation—that he also deposed himself. * * * I have taken very little part in Irish politics since my release from Kilmainham.[6] I expressed my reason for that upon the passing of the Crimes Act.[7] I said that, in my judgment, the Crimes Act would result in such a state of affairs that between the Government and secret societies it would be impossible for constitutional agitation to exist in Ireland. I believe so still. * * * It would have been far better if you were going to pass an Act of this kind and to administer an Act of this kind as you are going to administer it, and as you are obliged to administer it—up to the hilt—that it should be done by the seasoned politician who is now in disgrace. Call him back to his post! Send him to help Lord Spencer[8] in his congenial work of the gallows in Ireland! Send him to look after the Secret Inquisitions of Dublin Castle! Send him to superintend the payment of blood money! Send him to distribute the taxes which an unfortunate and starving peasantry have to pay for crimes not committed by them! All this would be congenial work. We invite you to man your ranks, and send your ablest and best men. Push forward the task of misgoverning Ireland! For my part I am confident as to the future of Ireland. Although her horizon may appear at this moment clouded, I believe that our people will survive the present oppression as we have survived many and worse ones. And although our progress may be slow it will be sure, and the time will come when this House and the people of this country will admit once again that they have been mistaken; that they have been deceived by those who ought to be ashamed of deceiving them; that they have been led astray as to the method of governing a noble, a

---

2. William Edward Forster, chief secretary for Ireland, had attacked Parnell at the beginning of the 1883 session.
3. Slandering.
4. James Carey (1845–1883), one of the Invincibles (an Irish nationalist group who killed the Irish chief secretary and undersecretary in Dublin's Phoenix Park in May 1882). After his arrest, he turned informer but was killed by another of the Invincibles while the British government attempted to transport him to safety in South Africa.

5. A division of the Home Rule Confederation, founded in 1879 by Michael Davitt and led by Parnell, that fought for the tenant farmers' security of tenure, fair rents on property, and their freedom to sell their property.
6. A jail in Dublin where Parnell was held between October 1881 and May 1882, after a series of popular speeches to the Irish people couched in violent language.
7. A coercion act against Irish agitation passed in 1881.
8. John Poyntz, fifth Earl of Spencer; Lord Lieutenant of Ireland for a second term (1882–1885).

generous, and an impulsive people; that they will reject their present leaders who are conducting them into the terrible course, which, I am sorry to say, the Government appears to be determined to enter; that they will reject these guides and leaders with just as much determination as they rejected the services of the right hon. gentleman the member of Bradford.[9]

At Portsmouth, After the Defeat of Mr. Gladstone's Home Rule Bill[1]

It is, I believe, about the first time I have had the honour of addressing a mainly English audience. And I have been induced to do so now because I rely greatly upon the spirit of fair play among the English masses, and because the issues for my country are so great and so vital at the present moment—the issues which underlie this present struggle—that the Irishman who remains silent when it might be possible to do something to help his country would be more unworthy than tongue could describe. * * * I have, in my career as a member of Parliament, never wittingly injured the cause of the English working man. I have done something to show my sympathy for the masses of the people of this country. * * * Some years ago it was my privilege to strike with English members a successful blow in favour of the abolition of flogging in the army and navy. We were met then by the very same arguments as we are met with today, and from the same class of persons. It was said by the late Lord Beaconsfield[2] that the integrity of the British Empire would be endangered if flogging were abolished, and he called a great meeting at one of the Ministerial offices in London, a great meeting of his supporters both in the Lords and Commons, for the purpose of exhorting them to stand shoulder to shoulder in defence of the British Empire against the abolition of flogging in the army. * * * I have shown you that in some respects the Irish settlement proposed by Mr Gladstone does not give a Parliament, a Legislature with the powers possessed by Grattan's Parliament;[3] but I have shown you on the other hand that as regards our own exclusively domestic business it gives larger powers, more important powers, more valuable powers for Ireland itself than was possessed by Grattan's, and therefore we think that this settlement proposed by Mr Gladstone will prove a more durable settlement than the restitution of the Grattan Parliament or the Repeal of the Union would prove. * * * Imperial unity does not require or necessitate unity of Parliaments. Will you carry that away with you and remember it, because it is the keystone of our whole proceedings. * * * I should say that Ireland would justly deserve to lose her privilege if she passed laws oppressive of the minority. * * * So far as coercion was concerned it has not brought you any nearer to the end of the Irish question. * * * One great fault in English coercion has been that no matter what your intentions have been when you have commenced coercion, you have never discriminated between political agitators and breakers of the law. * * * Lord Carnarvon[4] will not deny that he was as strong a Home Ruler as I was last August, and that when he went over to Ireland he became stronger and stronger every day he lived in that country. There is another thing he has not denied: he has not denied that he sought an interview with me in order to speak to me and consult with me about a Constitution for Ireland.[5] * * * Untold is the guilt of that man who,

9. I.e., William Edward Forster.

1. The first Home Rule bill, which would have given Ireland a "wide measure of autonomy"; Parnell gave this speech (25 June 1886), shortly after the bill's defeat.

2. Benjamin Disraeli, Prime Minister of England in 1868, and from 1874 to 1880.

3. Henry Grattan was leader of the movement that gave Ireland legislative independence in 1782.

4. Lord lieutenant of Ireland from 1885 to 1886 and member of the British Parliament.

5. Parnell and Carnarvon met on 1 August 1885, and discussed Irish Home Rule and an Irish Constitution.

for party purposes, does not take advantage of the spirit which is abroad amongst the English to put the hand of the Irish into that of the English to close the strife of centuries—a strife that has been of no advantage to the people of either country; a strife that has only been for the benefit of the money-grabbing landlords; a strife that has impeded popular progress in England as well as in Ireland, and that must continue to impede it; a strife which is fanned for the purpose of cheating you out of your rights, and to divert the energies of the newly enfranchised masses of Great Britain from the redress of their grievances to the odious task of oppressing and keeping down the small sister country.

Speech Delivered in Committee Room No. 15[1]

The men whose ability is now so conspicuously exercised as that of Mr. Healy and Mr. Sexton, will have to bear their responsibility for this. * * * Why did you encourage me to come forward and maintain my leadership in the face of the world if you were not going to stand by me? * * * I want to ask you before you vote my deposition to be sure you are getting value for it. * * * I know what Mr. Gladstone will do for you; I know what Mr. Morley[2] will do for you; and I know there is not a single one of the lot to be trusted unless you trust yourselves. Be to your own selves true and hence it follows, as the day the night, thou can'st not be false to any man.[3] * * * If I am to leave you tonight I should like to leave you in security. I should like, and it is not an unfair thing for me to ask, that I should come within sight of the Promised Land; that I should come with you, having come so far, if not to the end of this course, that I should at least come with you as far as you will allow and permit me to come with you, at least until it is absolutely sure that Ireland and I can go no further.

Proclamation of the Irish Republic
Poblacht na h Eireann[1]
THE PROVISIONAL GOVERNMENT OF THE IRISH REPUBLIC
TO
THE PEOPLE OF IRELAND

Irishmen and Irishwomen:

In the name of God and of the dead generations from which she receives her old tradition of nationhood, Ireland, through us, summons her children to her flag and strikes for her freedom.

Having organised and trained her manhood through her secret revolutionary organisation, the Irish Republican Brotherhood, and through her open miltary organisations, the Irish Volunteers and the Irish Citizen Army, having patiently perfected her discipline, having resolutely waited for the right moment to reveal itself, she now seizes that moment, and, supported by her exiled children in America and by gallant allies in Europe, but relying in the first on her own strength, she strikes in full confidence of victory.

---

1. Office of Parnell's party in Dublin. Parnell spoke to the party leadership on 6 December 1890 following a motion by Timothy Healy and Thomas Sexton to depose him as their leader in Parliament. Healy had been a Member of Parliament allied with Parnell's legislative agenda; Sexton had also supported Parnell in Parliament. In the wake of Parnell's involvement with the O'Shea divorce case, however, both abandoned Parnell and withdrew their support for his policies—an act of treachery which inspired James Joyce's first literary production, at age 8, a poem titled "Et Tu, Healy?"

2. John Morley (1838–1923), twice Chief Secretary for Ireland.

3. A paraphrase of lines from Polonius's speech in *Hamlet*, 1.3.78–80.

1. *Irish Republic*, in the Irish language.

We declare the right of the people of Ireland to the ownership of Ireland, and to the unfettered control of Irish destinies, to be sovereign and indefeasible. The long usurpation of that right by a foreign people and government has not extinguished the right, nor can it ever be extinguished except by the destruction of the Irish people. In every generation the Irish have asserted their right to National freedom and sovereignty; six times during the past three hundred years they have asserted it in arms. Standing on that fundamental right and again asserting it in arms in the face of the world, we hereby proclaim the Irish Republic as a Sovereign Independent State, and we pledge our lives and the lives of our comrades-in-arms to the cause of its freedom, of its welfare, and of its exaltation among the nations.

The Irish Republic is entitled to, and hereby claims, the allegiance of every Irishman and Irishwoman. The Republic guarantees religious and civil liberty, equal rights and equal opportunities to all its citizens, and declares its resolve to pursue the happiness and prosperity of the whole nation and of all its parts, cherishing all the children of the nation equally, and oblivious of the differences carefully fostered by an alien government, which have divided a minority from the majority in the past.

Until our arms have brought the opportune moment for the establishment of a permanent National Government, representative of the whole people of Ireland and elected by the suffrages of all her men and women,[2] the Provisional Government, hereby constituted, will administer the civil and military affairs of the Republic in trust for the people.

We place the cause of the Irish Republic under the protection of the Most High God, Whose blessing we invoke upon our arms, and we pray that no one who serves that cause will dishonor it by cowardice, inhumanity, or rapine. In this supreme hour the Irish nation must, by its valour and discipline and by the readiness of its children to sacrifice themselves for the common good, prove itself worthy of the august destiny to which it is called.

Signed on Behalf of the Provisional Government,
THOMAS J. CLARKE,
SEAN MACDIARMADA,
THOMAS MACDONAGH,
P. H. PEARSE,
EAMONN CEANNT,
JAMES CONNOLLY,
JOSEPH PLUNKETT.

Easter 1916

Padraic Pearse
Kilmainham Prison[1]

The following is the substance of what I said when asked today by the President of the Court-Martial at Richmond Barracks whether I had anything to say in my defence:

I desire, in the first place, to repeat what I have already said in letters to General Maxwell and Brigadier General Lowe.[2] My object in agreeing to an uncondi-

2. This call for women's suffrage in the Irish Republic predates full British women's suffrage by 12 years, and American women's suffrage by four years.
1. 2 May 1916. Pearse had been arrested on 29 April 1916,

ending the street fighting that had begun when he read the Proclamation of the Irish Republic on April 16. Pearse was executed at the conclusion of this military trial.
2. Leaders of the British troops during the Easter Rising.

tional surrender was to prevent the further slaughter of the civil population of Dublin and to save the lives of our gallant fellows, who, having made for six days a stand unparalleled in military history, were now surrounded, and in the case of those under the immediate command of H.Q., without food. I fully understand now, as then, that my own life is forfeit to British law, and I shall die very cheerfully if I can think that the British Government, as it has already shown itself strong, will now show itself magnanimous enough to accept my single life in forfeiture and to give a general amnesty to the brave men and boys who have fought at my bidding.[3]

In the second place, I wish it to be understood that any admissions I make here are to be taken as involving myself alone. They do not involve and must not be used against anyone who acted with me, not even those who may have set their names to documents with me. (The Court assented to this.)

I admit that I was Commandant-General Commanding-in-Chief of the forces of the Irish Republic which have been acting against you for the past week, and that I was President of the Provisional Government. I stand over all my acts and words done or spoken, in these capacities. When I was a child of ten I went on my bare knees by my bedside one night and promised God that I should devote my life to an effort to free my country. I have kept the promise. I have helped to organize, to arm, to train, and to discipline my fellow-countrymen to the sole end that, when the time came, they might fight for Irish freedom. The time, as it seemed to me, did come, and we went into the fight. I am glad we did, we seem to have lost, but we have not lost. To refuse to fight would have been to lose, to fight is to win; we have kept faith with the past, and handed on a tradition to the future. I repudiate the assertion of the prosecutor that I sought to aid and abet England's enemy. Germany is no more to me than England is. I asked and accepted German aid in the shape of arms and an expeditionary force, we neither asked for nor accepted German gold, nor had any traffic with Germany but what I state. My object was to win Irish freedom. We struck the first blow ourselves, but I should have been glad of an ally's aid.

I assume that I am speaking to Englishmen who value their freedom and who profess to be fighting for the freedom of Belgium and Serbia;[4] believe that we too love freedom and desire it. To us it is more desirable than anything in the world. If you strike us down now we shall rise again and renew the fight, you cannot conquer Ireland, you cannot extinguish the Irish passion for freedom; if our deed has not been sufficient to win freedom then our children will win it by a better deed.

Michael Collins
The Substance of Freedom[1]

*** We gather here today to uphold and to expound the Treaty. It was not our intention to hold any meetings until the issue was definitely before the electorate.

---

3. This was not to be the case; in addition to Pearse, several other conspirators were executed by the British.
4. In World War I.
1. The text is compiled from reports of audience members for Collins's speech at a public meeting on 5 March 1922. The "treaty" in question is the Anglo-Irish Treaty establishing 26 of Ireland's 32 counties as the Irish Free State and setting up a parliamentary government in Ireland. The treaty was opposed by Eamon de Valera, a surviving leader of the Easter Rising and leader of Sinn Féin, the Irish Republican organization whose Irish name means "Ourselves Alone." Though he was imprisoned by the newly formed Free State for his refusal to sign the treaty, he later went on to serve as both Prime Minister and President of Ireland.

But as a campaign has been begun in the country by Mr. de Valera and his followers we cannot afford to wait longer.

Mr de Valera's campaign is spoken of as a campaign against the Treaty. It is not really that.

The Irish people have already ratified the Treaty through their elected representatives. And the people of Ireland will stand by that ratification. The weekly paper of our opponents, which they call *The Republic of Ireland*, admits that ratification. Document No. 2[2] lapsed with the approval by the Dáil of the Treaty, they said in a leading article in the issue of February 21st; and in the issue of February 28th it is said "alternative documents are no longer in question."

No, it is not a campaign against the Treaty.

Nothing would disconcert Mr. de Valera and his followers more than the wrecking of the Treaty, than the loss of what has been secured by the Treaty.

It is a campaign, not against the Treaty, but against the Free State. And not only against the Free State, but still more against those who stand for the Free State. "Please God we will win," said Mr. de Valera last Sunday at Ennis, "and then there will be an end to the Free State." And if there were an end to the Free State, what then? What is the object of our opponents? I will tell you what it is.

In the same leading article of February 28th (in *The Republic of Ireland*) they say: "The Republican position is clear," and "We stand against the Treaty for the maintenance of the Republic."

The maintenance of the Republic [exclaimed Mr. Collins]. That is very curious. Because in the previous week's issue we were told by a member of the Dáil Cabinet that before the Truce of July last[3] it had become plain that it was physically impossible to secure Ireland's ideal of a completely isolated Republic in the immediate future, otherwise than by driving the overwhelmingly superior British forces out of the country. * * *

I will tell you what has happened since.

The Treaty has been brought back. It has brought and is bringing such freedom to Ireland in the transference to us of all governmental powers, but, above all, in the departure of the British armed forces, that it has become safe, and simple, and easy, and courageous to stand now for what was surrendered in July, because the British armed forces were still here.

We could not beat the British out by force, so the Republican ideal was surrendered. But when we have beaten them out by the Treaty the Republican ideal, which was surrendered in July, is restored.

The object of Mr de Valera and his party emerges. They are stealing our clothes.

We have beaten out the British by means of the Treaty. While damning the Treaty, and us with it, they are taking advantage of the evacuation which the Treaty secures.

After the surrender of the Republican ideal in July we were sent over to make a Treaty with England.

Some of us were sent very much against our wishes. That is well-known to our opponents. Everyone knew then, and it is idle and dishonest to deny now, that in the event of a settlement some postponement of the realisation of our full national sentiment would have to be agreed to.

---

2. A document proposing an alternative arrangement, put forward by a private session of the Dáil Éireann (Irish Parliament) in December 1921.

3. A 1921 truce that led to negotiations and the Anglo-Irish Treaty.

We were not strong enough to realise the full Republican ideal. In addition, we must remember that there is a strong minority in our country up in the North-East that does not yet share our national views, but has to be reckoned with. In view of these things I claim that we brought back the fullest measure of freedom obtainable—the solid substance of independence.

We signed the Treaty believing it gave us such freedom. Our opponents make use of the advantage of the Treaty while they vilify it and us. The position gained by the Treaty provides them with a jumping off ground. After dropping the Republic while the British were still here, they shout bravely for it now from the safe foothold provided for them by means of the Treaty.

It is a mean campaign.

We were left with the Herculean labour and the heavy responsibility of taking over a Government. This would be a colossal task for the most experienced men of any nation. And we are young and not experienced. While we are thus engaged our former comrades go about the country talking. They tell the people to think of their own strength and the weakness of the enemy. Yes! and what is it that has made us strong and the enemy weak in the last few months? Yes, the enemy becomes weaker every day as his numbers grow less. And as they grow less, louder and louder do our opponents shout for the Republic which they surrendered in July last.

What has made the enemy weaker? The enemy that was then too strong for us? Is it the division in our ranks, which is Mr. de Valera's achievement, and which is already threatening a suspension of the evacuation? Or is it the Treaty which is our achievement?

Mr de Valera, in Limerick last Sunday, compared Ireland to a party that had set out to cross a desert, and they had come to a green spot, he said, and there were some who came along to tell them to lie down and stay there, and be satisfied and not go on.

Yes, we had come by means of the Treaty to a green oasis, the last in the long weary desert over which the Irish nation has been travelling. Oases are the resting-places of the desert, and unless the traveller finds them and refreshes himself he never reaches his destination.

Ireland has been brought to the last one, beyond which there is but a little and an easy stretch to go. The nation has earned the right to rest for a little while we renew our strength, and restore somewhat our earlier vigour.

But there are some amongst us who, while they take full advantage of the oasis—only a fool or a madman would fail to do that—complain of those who have led them to it. They find fault with it. They do nothing to help. They are poisoning the wells, wanting now to hurry on, seeing the road ahead short and straight, wanting the glory for themselves of leading the Irish nation over it, while unwilling to fill and shoulder the pack.

We are getting the British armed forces out of Ireland. Because of that evacuation our opponents are strong enough and brave enough now to say: "They are traitors who got you this. We are men of principle. We stand for the Republic"—that Republic which it was physically impossible to secure until the traitors had betrayed you.

Have we betrayed you? * * *

The arrangement in regard to North-East Ulster is not ideal. But then the position in North-East Ulster is not ideal.

If the Free State is established, however, union is certain. Forces of persuasion and pressure are embodied in the Treaty which will bring the North-East into a united Ireland. If they join us they can have control in their own area. If they stay outside Ireland, then they can only have their own corner, and cannot, and will not, have the counties and areas which belong to Ireland and to the Irish people, according to the wishes of the inhabitants.

Then upon the area remaining outside will fall the burdens and restrictions of the 1920 Partition Act.[4] These disabilities cannot be removed without our consent. If the North-East does not come in, then they are deciding upon bankruptcy for themselves and, remember, this is not our wish but their own.

We must not, however, take a gloomy view of this situation, for, with the British gone, the incentive to partition is gone; but the evacuation is held up by our own disunion—if the Free State is threatened, as long as there is any hope of seeing it destroyed, the North-East will remain apart. Partition will remain.

Destroy the Free State, and you perpetuate Partition. You destroy all hopes of union.

It is best to speak out plainly.

Destroy the Free State now and you destroy more even than the hope, the certainty of union. You destroy our hopes of national freedom, all realisation in our generation of the democratic right of the people of Ireland to rule themselves without interference from any outside power. * * *

But the aim of all of us can be for unity and independence. In public matters it must be realised that we cannot get all each one wants. We have to agree to get what is essential.

We have to agree to sink individual differences or only to work for them on legitimate lines which do not undermine and destroy the basis on which all rests and which alone makes it possible for us all, as Irishmen and women, to pursue our own aims freely in Ireland, namely, the union and independence of the nation as a whole.

We must be Irish first and last, and must be Republicans or Document Two-ites, or Free Staters, only within the limits which leave Ireland strong, united and free.

Would any other form of freedom which was obtainable now, which would have been acquiesced in by so large a body of our countrymen, have fulfilled the objects of Sinn Féin better, have put us in such a strong position to secure any that are yet unfulfilled?

We claim that the solid substance of freedom has been won, and that full powers are in the hands of the nation to mould its own life, quite as full for that purpose as if we had already our freedom in the Republican form.

Any difficulties will not be of our own making. There is no enemy nor any foreign Government here any longer to hinder us. Will we not take the fruits of victory, or do we mean to let them decay in our hands, while we wrangle as to whether they are ripe or whether they have exactly the bloom and shape we dreamed of before they had ripened?

No freedom when realised has quite the glory dreamed of by the captive.

[END OF SPEECHES ON IRISH INDEPENDENCE]

---

4. The act that divided Ireland politically into Northern Ireland (Ulster) and the Republic of Ireland.

William Butler Yeats
1865–1939

Beginning his career as a poet during the languid 1880s and 1890s, Yeats fought, as Ezra Pound said of T. S. Eliot, to modernize himself on his own. At a time when Irish poetry seemed to be in danger of ossifying into a sentimental, self-indulgent luxury, Yeats instead forged a verse that would serve as an exacting instrument of introspection and national inquiry. As a consequence, all modern Irish writing—most clearly poetry, but prose, drama, and literary nonfiction as well—is directly in his debt.

Yeats was born in the Dublin suburb of Sandymount, but his spiritual home, the land of his mother Susan Pollexfen and her people, was the countryside of County Sligo. His father, John Butler Yeats, was an amateur philosopher, an insolvent painter, and a refugee from the legal profession; his grandfather and great-grandfather were both clergymen of the Church of Ireland. Through his mother's family, Yeats traced a close connection with the countryside of Ireland, and the myths and legends of the Irish people. Both parents belonged to the Anglo-Irish Protestant ascendancy, a heritage Yeats remained fiercely proud of all his life; but the success of his poetry, in part, lay in his ability to reconcile the British literary tradition with the native materials of the Irish Catholic tradition.

As he tells it in his autobiography, Yeats's childhood was not a happy one; in 1915 he wrote: "I remember little of childhood but its pain." His father, though a talented painter, lacked the ability to turn his gifts to profit; he would linger over a single portrait for months and sometimes years, revising ceaselessly. When Yeats was three, his father moved his family to London in order to put himself to school as a painter; their existence, though intellectually and artistically rich and stimulating, was quite straitened financially. The young Yeats found London sterile and joyless; fortunately for his imagination, and his future poetry, portions of each year were spent in the Sligo countryside, where Yeats spent time gathering the local folklore and taking long, wide-ranging walks and pony rides. The family remained in London until 1875, and had four more children (though one brother died in childhood). All his surviving siblings were to remain important to Yeats in his artistic life: his brother Jack B. Yeats became an important Irish painter, and his sisters Lily and Lolly together founded the Dun Emer Press, later called the Cuala Press, which published limited-edition volumes of some of Yeats's poetry.

In 1880 the family returned permanently to Ireland, settling first in Howth, in Dublin Bay; the city of Dublin, with its largely unsung history and tradition, fueled Yeats's imagination in a way that London never had. When the time for college came, Yeats was judged unlikely to pass Trinity College's entrance exams, and he was sent instead to the Metropolitan School of Art, apparently in preparation to follow in his father's footsteps. His true gift, it soon appeared, was not for drawing and painting but for poetry. He steeped himself in the Romantic poets, especially Shelley and Keats, as well as the English poet of Irish residence Edmund Spenser. His first poems were published in the *Dublin University Review* in March 1885.

Yeats's early work is self-evidently apprentice work; it draws heavily on the late-Romantic, pre-Raphaelite ambience so important in the painting of his father and his father's colleagues. He also began to take an active interest in the various mystical movements that were then finding a foothold in Dublin and London, and with friends formed a Hermetic Society in Dublin as an antidote to the humanist rationalism to which his father was so passionately attached. At the same time—almost as a self-administered antidote to the teachings of mystics like the Brahmin teacher Mohini Chatterji—Yeats began to attend the meetings of several Dublin political and debating societies, and became increasingly interested in the nationalist artistic revival that would become known as the Irish Renaissance or Celtic Revival. Unlike most of his debating society comrades, Yeats imagined this political and cultural renaissance as resulting from a marriage of Blakean opposites: "I had noticed that Irish Catholics among whom had been born so many political martyrs had not the good taste, the household courtesy and decency of the Protestant Ireland I had known, yet Protestant Ireland seemed to think of nothing but getting on in the world. I thought we might bring the halves together if we had a national literature that made Ireland beautiful in the memory, and yet had been freed from provincialism by an exacting criticism, a European pose."

The Yeats family moved back to London in 1887; finances were difficult as ever, and Yeats contributed to the family's upkeep by editing two anthologies, *Poems and Ballads of Young Ireland* (1888) and *Fairy and Folk Tales of the Irish Peasantry* (1888). His own first collection of poems, *The Wanderings of Oisin and Other Poems*, was published in the following year; the poems are resolutely romantic, Yeats himself describing his manner at the time as "in all things Pre-Raphaelite." The poems were well received, but the praise of one reader in particular caught Yeats's attention. The statuesque beauty Maud Gonne appeared at Yeats's door with an introduction from the Irish revolutionary John O'Leary, and declared that the title poem had brought her to tears. It was a fateful meeting; throughout five decades Yeats continued to write to Gonne, for Gonne—the critic M. L. Rosenthal has suggested that "virtually every poem celebrating a woman's beauty or addressing a beloved woman has to do with her." Rosenthal might have added, every poem decrying the sacrifice of life to politics, including *No Second Troy, Easter 1916, A Prayer for My Daughter*, and others, all of which lament Gonne's increasing political fanaticism. This fanaticism, which Gonne considered simply patriotism, made impossible the spiritual and emotional consummation that Yeats so fervently desired. He proposed marriage, but she declined, marrying instead an Irish soldier who would later be executed for his role in the Easter Rising of 1916. Yeats is, among his other distinctions, a great poet of unrequited love.

The 1890s in London were heady times for a young poet. Yeats became even more active in his studies of the occult, studying with the charismatic Theosophist Madame Blavatsky and attending meetings of the Order of the Golden Dawn, a Christian cabalist society. The practical upshot of these activities for his later poetry was a confirmed belief in a storehouse of all human experience and knowledge, which he called variously the *Spiritus Mundi* and *Anima Mundi*, invoked in later poems like *The Second Coming* (1920). In 1891 Yeats, together with Ernest Rhys, founded the Rhymers' Club, which brought him into almost nightly contact with such important literary figures as Lionel Johnson, Ernest Dowson, Arthur Symons, and Oscar Wilde; during this same period, he established the Irish Literary Society in London, and the National Literary Society in Dublin. Clearly, something of a program for modern Irish poetry was beginning to emerge, even if Yeats himself wasn't yet quite ready to write it. Yeats also spent the years from 1887 to 1891 studying the writings of that most mystic of English poets, William Blake; working with his father's friend Edwin Ellis, he produced an edition of and extended commentary on Blake's prophetic writings. Summing up the lesson of Blake's writings, Yeats wrote: "I had learned from Blake to hate all abstractions."

Romantic abstraction was easier to abjure in principle than in practice; Yeats's poetry of the 1890s still hankers after what one of his dramatis personae would later call "the loveliness that has long faded from the world." As one critic has written, "'Early Yeats was the best poetry in English in late Victorian times; but they were bad times." Yeats began the process of throwing off the false manners of his pre-Raphaelite upbringing with his play *The Countess Cathleen*, first performed by the Abbey Theatre, funded by subscriptions collected by his good friend Lady Augusta Gregory. Yeats's play, like Synge's *Playboy of the Western World* years later on that same stage, offended Irish sensibilities; in it, Cathleen sells her soul in order to protect Irish peasants from starvation. Yeats's volume *The Wind Among the Reeds* (1899) closes out the 1890s quite conveniently; it is ethereal, beautiful, and mannered. With this volume, Yeats's early phase comes to a close.

The early years of the twentieth century found Yeats concentrating his energies on the writing of poetic dramas, including, *The Pot of Broth* (1902) and *On Baile's Strand* (1904), for his fledgling Irish National Theatre. In 1903, the small Dun Emer Press published his volume of poems *In the Seven Woods*. These poems, including *Adam's Curse*, show Yeats working in a more spare idiom, the cadences and rhythms closer to those of actual speech—a consequence, some have argued, of his years writing for the stage. New poems published in *The Green Helmet and Other Poems* (1910) display Yeats as an increasingly mature and confident poet; his treatment of Maud Gonne in *No Second Troy*, for instance, shows a tragic acceptance of the fact that he will never have her, nor master her indomitable spirit. In *A Coat*, the poem that closes the 1914 collection *Responsibilities*, Yeats writes of the embroidered cloak he had fashioned for himself in his early poems, whose vanity is now brought home to him by the gaudiness of his imitators. He resolves, in the volume's closing lines, to set his cloak aside, "For there's more enterprise / In walking naked." This sense was strengthened by his close work, during the winter of 1912–1913, with Ezra Pound, in a cottage in rural Sussex. Both studied the stripped-down Japanese Noh drama and the Orientalist Ernest Fennollosa's work on the Chinese ideogram, and both men no doubt reinforced one another's increasing desire for a poetry that would be, in Pound's phrase, "closer to the bone."

The Easter Rising of 1916 took Yeats by surprise; he was in England at the time and complained of not having been informed in advance. A number of the rebel leaders were personal friends; he writes their names into Irish literature in *Easter 1916*, an excruciatingly honest, and ambivalent, exploration of the nature of heroism and nationalism. Yeats's mixed feelings about the revolution derived in part from a concern that some of his early writings, like the nationalist *The Countess Cathleen*, might have contributed to the slaughter that followed in the wake of Easter 1916; as he wrote many years later, he couldn't help but wonder, "Did that play of mine send out / Certain men the English shot?"

The intricacies of Yeats's emotional and romantic life would require an essay of their own. His first marriage proposal to Maud Gonne in 1891, politely refused, set a pattern that was to remain in place for many years; though a number of poems try to reason through the affair, Yeats remained tragically attracted to this woman who did not return his affection, and multiple proposals were turned down as routinely as the first. He would have done as well, he was to write years later, to profess his love "to a statue in a museum." In the summer of 1917 things reached such a pass that Yeats proposed to Maud Gonne's adopted daughter Iseult; here, again, he was refused. Then, hastily, in October 1917 he married a longtime friend Georgiana ("George") Hyde-Lees. For all the tragicomedy leading up to the marriage, Yeats could not have chosen better; George was intelligent and sympathetic, and she brought the additional gift of an interest in mysticism and a facility in automatic writing that Yeats was soon to take full advantage of. Since early childhood, Yeats had heard voices speaking to him, and when he was twenty-one a voice commanded him "Hammer your thoughts into unity"; this charge had weighed on his mind for years, and his various experiments in mysticism and esoteric religions were intended to discover the system wherein his thoughts might be made to cohere.

With George, Yeats finally created that system on his own; its fullest exposition is found in *A Vision* (1928), though elements of it turn up in his poems beginning as early as *No Second Troy*. The system is complicated enough to fill out over 300 pages in the revised (1937) edition; at the heart of the system, though, is a simple diagram of two interpenetrating cones, oriented horizontally, such that the tip of each cone establishes the center of the base of the opposite cone. These two cones describe the paths of two turning gyres, or spirals, representing two alternating antithetical ages which make up human history. Yeats saw history as composed of cycles of approximately 2,000 years; his apocalyptic poem *The Second Coming*, for instance, describes the anxiety caused by the recognition that the 2,000 years of Christian (in Yeats's terms, "primary") values were about to be succeeded by an antithetical age—the "rough beast" of a time characterized by values and beliefs in every way hostile to those of the Christian era. For Yeats, however, as for William Blake, this vacillation and tension between contraries was not to be regretted; Blake taught that "without Contraries is no progression," and Yeats, that "all the gains of man come from conflict with the opposite of his true being."

Yeats's greatest phase begins with the poems of *Michael Robartes and the Dancer* (1921). His mytho-historical system informs a number of the poems written in the 1920s and after; it explains, for instance, why Yeats saw the brutal rape of Leda by Zeus in the form of a swan as a precursor of the traditional Christian iconography of the Virgin Mary "visited" by God the Father in the form of a dove. A logical corollary of Yeats's belief in historical recurrence was the philosophy, articulated best in his late poem *Lapis Lazuli*, of tragic joy: "All things fall and are built again, / And those that build them again are gay." In a letter inspired by the gift of lapis lazuli that the poem celebrates, Yeats wrote to a friend: "To me the supreme aim is an act of faith or reason to make one rejoice in the midst of tragedy." The influence of the writing of Nietzsche, whom Yeats had been reading, is apparent in these formulations.

While continuing to push at the boundaries of modern literature and modern poetry, Yeats also enjoyed the role of statesman. In the fall of 1922, Yeats was made a senator of the new Irish Free State; in 1923 he was awarded the Nobel Prize for literature, the first Irish writer ever to receive the award. The 1930s also saw Yeats flirt briefly with fascism, as did other writers like Pound and Wyndham Lewis. Yeats's belief in the importance of an aristocracy, and his disappointment over the excesses of revolutionary zeal demonstrated in the Irish civil war, for a time during the 1930s made the fascist program of the Irish Blueshirt movement look attractive. He composed *Three Songs to the Same Tune* as rallying songs for the Blueshirts, but the poems were too recherché for any such use. He soon became disillusioned with the party.

Yeats continued to write major poetry almost until his death; his growing ill health seems only to have made his poetry stronger and more defiant, as evidenced in such sinuous and clearsighted poems as *Lapis Lazuli* and the bawdy Crazy Jane poems. In the work published as *Last Poems* (1939), Yeats most satisfactorily put into practice what he had much earlier discovered in theory: that he must, as he wrote in *The Circus Animals' Desertion*, return for his poetry to "the foul rag-and-bone shop of the heart." After a long period of heart trouble, Yeats died on 28 January 1939; he was buried in Roquebrune, France, where he and George had been spending the winter. In 1948 he was reinterred, as he had wished, in Drumcliff churchyard near Sligo, where his grandfather and great-grandfather had served as rectors. Again according to his wishes, his epitaph is that which he wrote for himself in *Under Ben Bulben*:

> Cast a cold eye
> On life, on death.
> Horseman, pass by!

The Lake Isle of Innisfree[1]

> I will arise and go now, and go to Innisfree,
> And a small cabin build there, of clay and wattles° made: woven twigs
> Nine bean-rows will I have there, a hive for the honey-bee,
> And live alone in the bee-loud glade.
>
> 5   And I shall have some peace there, for peace comes dropping slow,
> Dropping from the veils of the morning to where the cricket sings;
> There midnight's all a glimmer, and noon a purple glow,
> And evening full of the linnet's° wings.   song bird

---

1. A small island in Lough Gill outside the town of Sligo, near the border with Northern Ireland.

I will arise and go now, for always night and day
10   I hear lake water lapping with low sounds by the shore;
While I stand on the roadway, or on the pavements grey,
I hear it in the deep heart's core.
1890   1890

Who Goes with Fergus?[1]

Who will go drive with Fergus now,
And pierce the deep wood's woven shade,
And dance upon the level shore?
Young man, lift up your russet brow,
5   And lift your tender eyelids, maid,
And brood on hopes and fear no more.
And no more turn aside and brood
Upon love's bitter mystery;
For Fergus rules the brazen° cars,   brass
10   And rules the shadows of the wood,
And the white breast of the dim sea
And all dishevelled wandering stars.

                                                                                          1893

No Second Troy[1]

Why should I blame her that she filled my days
With misery, or that she would of late
Have taught to ignorant men most violent ways,
Or hurled the little streets upon the great,
5   Had they but courage equal to desire?
What could have made her peaceful with a mind
That nobleness made simple as a fire,
With beauty like a tightened bow, a kind
That is not natural in an age like this,
10   Being high and solitary and most stern?
Why, what could she have done, being what she is?
Was there another Troy for her to burn?
1908   1910

The Wild Swans at Coole[1]

The trees are in their autumn beauty,
The woodland paths are dry,
Under the October twilight the water
Mirrors a still sky;
5   Upon the brimming water among the stones
Are nine-and-fifty swans.

The nineteenth autumn has come upon me
Since I first made my count;

---

1. The poem is a lyric from the second scene of Yeats's play *The Countess Cathleen*. Fergus was an ancient Irish king who gave up his throne to feast, fight, and hunt.
1. Yeats here compares Maud Gonne to Helen of Troy;

the Trojan War began from two kings' rivalry over Helen.
1. Coole Park was the name of the estate of Yeats's patron Lady Gregory in Galway.

I saw, before I had well finished,
10   All suddenly mount
And scatter wheeling in great broken rings
Upon their clamorous wings.

I have looked upon those brilliant creatures,
And now my heart is sore.
15   All's changed since I, hearing at twilight,
The first time on this shore,
The bell-beat of their wings above my head,
Trod with a lighter tread.

Unwearied still, lover by lover,
20   They paddle in the cold
Companionable streams or climb the air;
Their hearts have not grown old;
Passion or conquest, wander where they will,
Attend upon them still.

25   But now they drift on the still water,
Mysterious, beautiful;
Among what rushes will they build,
By what lake's edge or pool
Delight men's eyes when I awake some day
30   To find they have flown away?

1916   1917

Easter 1916[1]

I have met them at close of day
Coming with vivid faces
From counter or desk among grey
Eighteenth-century houses.
5   I have passed with a nod of the head
Or polite meaningless words,
Or have lingered awhile and said
Polite meaningless words,
And thought before I had done
10   Of a mocking tale or a gibe°   *taunt*
To please a companion
Around the fire at the club,
Being certain that they and I
But lived where motley° is worn: *jester's outfit*
15   All changed, changed utterly:
A terrible beauty is born.

That woman's days were spent
In ignorant good-will,
Her nights in argument
20   Until her voice grew shrill.[2]

1. The Irish Republic was declared on Easter Monday
1916.
2. Countess Markiewicz, née Constance Gore-Booth,

played a prominent part in the Easter Rising and was sentenced to be executed; her sentence was later reduced to
imprisonment.

What voice more sweet than hers
When, young and beautiful,
She rode to harriers?°   *hunting dogs*
This man[3] had kept a school
25   And rode our wingèd horse;
This other[4] his helper and friend
Was coming into his force;
He might have won fame in the end,
So sensitive his nature seemed,
30   So daring and sweet his thought.
This other man[5] I had dreamed
A drunken, vainglorious lout.
He had done most bitter wrong
To some who are near my heart,
35   Yet I number him in the song;
He, too, has resigned his part
In the casual comedy;
He, too, has been changed in his turn,
Transformed utterly:
40   A terrible beauty is born.

Hearts with one purpose alone
Through summer and winter seem
Enchanted to a stone
To trouble the living stream.
45   The horse that comes from the road,
The rider, the birds that range
From cloud to tumbling cloud,
Minute by minute they change;
A shadow of cloud on the stream
50   Changes minute by minute;
A horse-hoof slides on the brim,
And a horse plashes within it;
The long-legged moor-hens dive,
And hens to moor-cocks call;
55   Minute by minute they live:
The stone's in the midst of all.

Too long a sacrifice
Can make a stone of the heart.
O when may it suffice?
60   That is Heaven's part, our part
To murmur name upon name,
As a mother names her child
When sleep at last has come
On limbs that had run wild.
65   What is it but nightfall?
No, no, not night but death;
Was it needless death after all?

3. Padraic Pearse.
4. Thomas MacDonagh, poet executed for his role in the
rebellion.

5. Major John MacBride, briefly married to Maud Gonne,
was also executed.

For England may keep faith
For all that is done and said.
70 We know their dream; enough
To know they dreamed and are dead;
And what if excess of love
Bewildered them till they died?
I write it out in a verse—
75 MacDonagh and MacBride
And Connolly[6] and Pearse
Now and in time to be,
Wherever green is worn,
Are changed, changed utterly:
80 A terrible beauty is born.

1916   1916

The Second Coming[1]

Turning and turning in the widening gyre°   *circle or spiral*
The falcon cannot hear the falconer;
Things fall apart; the centre cannot hold;
Mere anarchy is loosed upon the world,
5   The blood-dimmed tide is loosed, and everywhere
The ceremony of innocence is drowned;
The best lack all conviction, while the worst
Are full of passionate intensity.

Surely some revelation is at hand;
10   Surely the Second Coming is at hand.
The Second Coming! Hardly are those words out
When a vast image out of *Spiritus Mundi*[2]
Troubles my sight: somewhere in sands of the desert
A shape with lion body and the head of a man,
15   A gaze blank and pitiless as the sun,
Is moving its slow thighs, while all about it
Reel shadows of the indignant desert birds.
The darkness drops again; but now I know
That twenty centuries of stony sleep
20   Were vexed to nightmare by a rocking cradle,
And what rough beast, its hour come round at last,
Slouches towards Bethlehem to be born?

1919   1921

A Prayer for My Daughter

Once more the storm is howling, and half hid
Under this cradle-hood and coverlid
My child sleeps on. There is no obstacle

---

6. James Connolly, Marxist commander-in-chief of the
Easter rebels; also executed.
1. Traditionally, the return of Christ to earth on Judgment Day.

2. A storehouse of images and symbols common to all
humankind; similar to Carl Jung's notion of the collective unconscious.

But Gregory's wood and one bare hill
5   Whereby the haystack- and roof-levelling wind,
Bred on the Atlantic, can be stayed;
And for an hour I have walked and prayed
Because of the great gloom that is in my mind.

I have walked and prayed for this young child an hour
10   And heard the sea-wind scream upon the tower,
And under the arches of the bridge, and scream
In the elms above the flooded stream;
Imagining in excited reverie
That the future years had come,
15   Dancing to a frenzied drum,
Out of the murderous innocence of the sea.

May she be granted beauty and yet not
Beauty to make a stranger's eye distraught,
Or hers before a looking-glass, for such,
20   Being made beautiful overmuch,
Consider beauty a sufficient end,
Lose natural kindness and maybe
The heart-revealing intimacy
That chooses right, and never find a friend.

25   Helen[1] being chosen found life flat and dull
And later had much trouble from a fool,
While that great Queen,[2] that rose out of the spray,
Being fatherless could have her way
Yet chose a bandy-leggèd smith[3] for man.
30   It's certain that fine women eat
A crazy salad with their meat
Whereby the Horn of Plenty is undone.

In courtesy I'd have her chiefly learned;
Hearts are not had as a gift but hearts are earned
35   By those that are not entirely beautiful;
Yet many, that have played the fool
For beauty's very self, has charm made wise,
And many a poor man that has roved,
Loved and thought himself beloved,
40   From a glad kindness cannot take his eyes.

May she become a flourishing hidden tree
That all her thoughts may like the linnet° be,   *song bird*
And have no business but dispensing round
Their magnanimities of sound,
45   Nor but in merriment begin a chase,
Nor but in merriment a quarrel.
O may she live like some green laurel
Rooted in one dear perpetual place.

---

1. Helen of Troy, who left her husband Menelaus for
Paris.
2. Aphrodite, Greek goddess of love, born from the sea.

3. Aphrodite's husband Hephaestus, the god of fire, was
lame.

My mind, because the minds that I have loved,
50   The sort of beauty that I have approved,
Prosper but little, has dried up of late,
Yet knows that to be choked with hate
May well be of all evil chances chief.
If there's no hatred in a mind
55   Assault and battery of the wind
Can never tear the linnet from the leaf.

An intellectual hatred is the worst,
So let her think opinions are accursed.
Have I not seen the loveliest woman born
60   Out of the mouth of Plenty's horn,
Because of her opinionated mind
Barter that horn and every good
By quiet natures understood
For an old bellows full of angry wind?

65   Considering that, all hatred driven hence,
The soul recovers radical innocence
And learns at last that it is self-delighting,
Self-appeasing, self-affrighting,
And that its own sweet will is Heaven's will;
70   She can, though every face should scowl
And every windy quarter howl
Or every bellows burst, be happy still.

And may her bridegroom bring her to a house
Where all's accustomed, ceremonious;
75   For arrogance and hatred are the wares
Peddled in the thoroughfares.
How but in custom and in ceremony
Are innocence and beauty born?
Ceremony's a name for the rich horn,
80   And custom for the spreading laurel tree.

June 1919   1919

Sailing to Byzantium[1]

1

That is no country for old men. The young
In one another's arms, birds in the trees,
—Those dying generations—at their song,
The salmon-falls, the mackerel-crowded seas,
5   Fish, flesh, or fowl, commend all summer long
Whatever is begotten, born, and dies.
Caught in that sensual music all neglect
Monuments of unageing intellect.

2

An aged man is but a paltry thing,
10   A tattered coat upon a stick, unless

---

1. Constantinople, now called Istanbul, capital of the Byzantine Empire and the holy city of Eastern Christianity.

Soul clap its hands and sing, and louder sing
For every tatter in its mortal dress,
Nor is there singing school but studying
Monuments of its own magnificence;
15   And therefore I have sailed the seas and come
To the holy city of Byzantium.

3

O sages standing in God's holy fire
As in the gold mosaic of a wall,
Come from the holy fire, perne° in a gyre,   *spin*
20   And be the singing-masters of my soul.
Consume my heart away; sick with desire
And fastened to a dying animal
It knows not what it is; and gather me
Into the artifice of eternity.

4

25   Once out of nature I shall never take
My bodily form from any natural thing,
But such a form as Grecian goldsmiths make
Of hammered gold and gold enamelling
To keep a drowsy Emperor awake;—
30   Or set upon a golden bough to sing
To lords and ladies of Byzantium
Of what is past, or passing, or to come.

1926   1927

Meditations in Time of Civil War

1. Ancestral Houses

Surely among a rich man's flowering lawns,
Amid the rustle of his planted hills,
Life overflows without ambitious pains;
And rains down life until the basin spills,
5   And mounts more dizzy high the more it rains
As though to choose whatever shape it wills
And never stoop to a mechanical
Or servile shape, at others' beck and call.

Mere dreams, mere dreams! Yet Homer had not sung
10   Had he not found it certain beyond dreams
That out of life's own self-delight had sprung
The abounding glittering jet; though now it seems
As if some marvellous empty sea-shell flung
Out of the obscure dark of the rich streams,
15   And not a fountain, were the symbol which
Shadows the inherited glory of the rich.

Some violent bitter man, some powerful man
Called architect and artist in, that they,
Bitter and violent men, might rear in stone
20   The sweetness that all longed for night and day,
The gentleness none there had ever known;

But when the master's buried mice can play,
And maybe the great-grandson of that house,
For all its bronze and marble, 's but a mouse.

25   O what if gardens where the peacock strays
With delicate feet upon old terraces,
Or else all Juno[1] from an urn displays
Before the indifferent garden deities;
O what if levelled lawns and gravelled ways
30   Where slippered Contemplation finds his ease
And Childhood a delight for every sense,
But take our greatness with our violence?
What if the glory of escutcheoned° doors,   *shield-shaped*
And buildings that a haughtier age designed,
35   The pacing to and fro on polished floors
Amid great chambers and long galleries, lined
With famous portraits of our ancestors;
What if those things the greatest of mankind
Consider most to magnify, or to bless,
40   But take our greatness with our bitterness?

2. My House

An ancient bridge, and a more ancient tower,
A farmhouse that is sheltered by its wall,
An acre of stony ground,
Where the symbolic rose can break in flower,
5   Old ragged elms, old thorns innumerable,
The sound of the rain or sound
Of every wind that blows;
The stilted water-hen
Crossing stream again
10   Scared by the splashing of a dozen cows;

A winding stair, a chamber arched with stone,
A grey stone fireplace with an open hearth,
A candle and written page.
Il Penseroso's Platonist[2] toiled on
15   In some like chamber, shadowing forth
How the daemonic rage
Imagined everything.
Benighted travellers
From markets and from fairs
20   Have seen his midnight candle glimmering.

Two men have founded here. A man-at-arms
Gathered a score of horse and spent his days
In this tumultuous spot,
Where through long wars and sudden night alarms
25   His dwindling score and he seemed castaways

---

1. Roman Goddess of marriage and patroness of women; the peacock was sacred to her as a symbol of immortality.

2. Follower of the idealist philosophy of Plato, in Milton's poem *Il Penseroso* ("The Contemplative").

Forgetting and forgot;
And I, that after me
My bodily heirs may find,
To exalt a lonely mind,
30   Befitting emblems of adversity.

3. My Table

Two heavy trestles, and a board
Where Sato's[3] gift, a changeless sword,
By pen and paper lies,
That it may moralise
5   My days out of their aimlessness.
A bit of an embroidered dress
Covers its wooden sheath.
Chaucer had not drawn breath
When it was forged. In Sato's house,
10   Curved like new moon, moon-luminous,
It lay five hundred years.
Yet if no change appears
No moon; only an aching heart
Conceives a changeless work of art.
15   Our learned men have urged
That when and where 'twas forged
A marvellous accomplishment,
In painting or in pottery, went
From father unto son
20   And through the centuries ran
And seemed unchanging like the sword.
Soul's beauty being most adored,
Men and their business took
The soul's unchanging look;
25   For the most rich inheritor,
Knowing that none could pass Heaven's door
That loved inferior art,
Had such an aching heart
That he, although a country's talk
30   For silken clothes and stately walk,
Had waking wits; it seemed
Juno's peacock screamed.

4. My Descendants

Having inherited a vigorous mind
From my old fathers, I must nourish dreams
And leave a woman and a man behind
As vigorous of mind, and yet it seems
5   Life scarce can cast a fragrance on the wind,
Scarce spread a glory to the morning beams,

3. Junzo Sato, Japanese consul who presented Yeats with an ancestral ceremonial sword.

But the torn petals strew the garden plot;
And there's but common greenness after that.

10 And what if my descendants lose the flower
Through natural declension of the soul,
Through too much business with the passing hour,
Through too much play, or marriage with a fool?
May this laborious stair and this stark tower
15 Become a roofless ruin that the owl
May build in the cracked masonry and cry
Her desolation to the desolate sky.

The Primum Mobile[4] that fashioned us
Has made the very owls in circles move;
And I, that count myself most prosperous,
20 Seeing that love and friendship are enough,
For an old neighbour's friendship chose the house
And decked and altered it for a girl's love,
And know whatever flourish and decline
These stones remain their monument and mine.

5. The Road at My Door

An affable Irregular,[5]
A heavily-built Falstaffian[6] man,
Comes cracking jokes of civil war
As though to die by gunshot were
5 The finest play under the sun.

A brown Lieutenant and his men,
Half dressed in national uniform,
Stand at my door, and I complain
Of the foul weather, hail and rain,
10 A pear tree broken by the storm.

I count those feathered balls of soot
The moor-hen guides upon the stream,
To silence the envy in my thought;
And turn towards my chamber, caught
15 In the cold snows of a dream.

6. The Stare's Nest by My Window

The bees build in the crevices
Of loosening masonry, and there
The mother birds bring grubs and flies.
My wall is loosening; honey-bees,
5 Come build in the empty house of the stare.°   *starling*

---

4. Prime mover (Latin); part of the Ptolemaic system that
described the revolution of the heavens around the earth.
5. A member of the Irish Republican Army (IRA), which
opposed any cooperation with British power and started
the civil war.
6. Robust, bawdy, witty; after Sir John Falstaff, comic
character in Shakespeare's *The Merry Wives of Windsor*
and *Henry IV*.

We are closed in, and the key is turned
On our uncertainty; somewhere
A man is killed, or a house burned,
Yet no clear fact to be discerned:
10   Come build in the empty house of the stare.

A barricade of stone or of wood;
Some fourteen days of civil war;
Last night they trundled down the road
That dead young soldier in his blood:
15   Come build in the empty house of the stare.

We had fed the heart on fantasies,
The heart's grown brutal from the fare;
More substance in our enmities
Than in our love; O honey-bees,
20   Come build in the empty house of the stare.

7. I See Phantoms of Hatred
and of the Heart's Fullness
and of the Coming Emptiness

I climb to the tower-top and lean upon broken stone,
A mist that is like blown snow is sweeping over all,
Valley, river, and elms, under the light of a moon
That seems unlike itself, that seems unchangeable,
5   A glittering sword out of the east. A puff of wind
And those white glimmering fragments of the mist sweep by.
Frenzies bewilder, reveries perturb the mind;
Monstrous familiar images swim to the mind's eye.

"Vengeance upon the murderers," the cry goes up,
10   "Vengeance for Jacques Molay."[7] In cloud-pale rags, or in lace,
The rage-driven, rage-tormented, and rage-hungry troop,
Trooper belabouring trooper, biting at arm or at face,
Plunges towards nothing, arms and fingers spreading wide
For the embrace of nothing; and I, my wits astray
15   Because of all that senseless tumult, all but cried
For vengeance on the murderers of Jacques Molay.

Their legs long, delicate and slender, aquamarine their eyes,
Magical unicorns bear ladies on their backs.
The ladies close their musing eyes. No prophecies,
20   Remembered out of Babylonian almanacs,
Have closed the ladies' eyes, their minds are but a pool
Where even longing drowns under its own excess;
Nothing but stillness can remain when hearts are full
Of their own sweetness, bodies of their loveliness.

25   The cloud-pale unicorns, the eyes of aquamarine,
The quivering half-closed eyelids, the rags of cloud or of lace,

---

7. Jacques de Molay, Grand Master of the Knights Templar who was burned as a witch in 1314.

Or eyes that rage has brightened, arms it has made lean,
Give place to an indifferent multitude, give place
To brazen hawks. Nor self-delighting reverie,
30   Nor hate of what's to come, nor pity for what's gone,
Nothing but grip of claw, and the eye's complacency,
The innumerable clanging wings that have put out the moon.

I turn away and shut the door, and on the stair
Wonder how many times I could have proved my worth
35   In something that all others understand or share;
But O! ambitious heart, had such a proof drawn forth
A company of friends, a conscience set at ease,
It had but made us pine the more. The abstract joy,
The half-read wisdom of daemonic images,
40   Suffice the ageing man as once the growing boy.

1921   1928

Leda and the Swan[1]

A sudden blow: the great wings beating still
Above the staggering girl, her thighs caressed
By the dark webs, her nape caught in his bill,
He holds her helpless breast upon his breast.

5   How can those terrified vague fingers push
The feathered glory from her loosening thighs?
And how can body, laid in that white rush,
But feel the strange heart beating where it lies?

A shudder in the loins engenders there
10   The broken wall, the burning roof and tower
And Agamemnon[2] dead.
                        Being so caught up,
So mastered by the brute blood of the air,
Did she put on his knowledge with his power
Before the indifferent beak could let her drop?

1923   1924

Among School Children

1

I walk through the long schoolroom questioning;
A kind old nun in a white hood replies;
The children learn to cipher and to sing,
To study reading-books and history,
5   To cut and sew, be neat in everything
In the best modern way—the children's eyes
In momentary wonder stare upon
A sixty-year-old smiling public man.

1. In Greek mythology, Zeus came to Leda in the form of a swan and raped her; Helen of Troy and Clytemnestra were their offspring.
2. Brother of Menelaus, husband of Helen. When she was abducted by Paris, Agamemnon fought to rescue her. He was murdered by his wife Clytemnestra on his return home.

2

I dream of a Ledaean[1] body, bent
10   Above a sinking fire, a tale that she
Told of a harsh reproof, or trivial event
That changed some childish day to tragedy—
Told, and it seemed that our two natures blent
Into a sphere from youthful sympathy,
15   Or else, to alter Plato's parable,
Into the yolk and white of the one shell.[2]

3

And thinking of that fit of grief or rage
I look upon one child or t'other there
And wonder if she stood so at that age—
20   For even daughters of the swan can share
Something of every paddler's heritage—
And had that colour upon cheek or hair,
And thereupon my heart is driven wild:
She stands before me as a living child.

4

25   Her present image floats into the mind—
Did Quattrocento[3] finger fashion it
Hollow of cheek as though it drank the wind
And took a mess of shadows for its meat?
And I though never of Ledaean kind
30   Had pretty plumage once—enough of that,
Better to smile on all that smile, and show
There is a comfortable kind of old scarecrow.

5

What youthful mother, a shape upon her lap
Honey of generation had betrayed,
35   And that must sleep, shriek, struggle to escape
As recollection or the drug decide,
Would think her son, did she but see that shape
With sixty or more winters on its head,
A compensation for the pang of his birth,
40   Or the uncertainty of his setting forth?

6

Plato thought nature but a spume° that plays   *froth*
Upon a ghostly paradigm of things;
Soldier Aristotle played the taws[4]
Upon the bottom of a king of kings;
45   World-famous golden-thighed Pythagoras[5]
Fingered upon a fiddle-stick or strings
What a star sang and careless Muses heard:
Old clothes upon old sticks to scare a bird.

7

Both nuns and mothers worship images,
50   But those the candles light are not as those

1. Of Leda, the mother of Helen of Troy.
2. According to Plato's parable in the *Symposium*, male and female were once the two halves of a single body; it was subsequently cut in half like a hard-boiled egg.
3. Fifteenth-century artists of Italy's Renaissance.
4. A leather strap, used to spin a top.
5. A 6th-century B.C. Greek philosopher who developed a mathematical basis for the universe and music.

That animate a mother's reveries,
But keep a marble or a bronze repose.
And yet they too break hearts—O Presences
That passion, piety or affection knows,
55   And that all heavenly glory symbolise—
O self-born mockers of man's enterprise;

8

Labour is blossoming or dancing where
The body is not bruised to pleasure soul,
Nor beauty born out of its own despair,
60   Nor blear-eyed wisdom out of midnight oil.
O chestnut tree, great rooted blossomer,
Are you the leaf, the blossom or the bole?
O body swayed to music, O brightening glance,
How can we know the dancer from the dance?

1926   1927

Byzantium

The unpurged images of day recede;
The Emperor's drunken soldiery are abed;
Night resonance recedes, night-walkers' song
After great cathedral gong;
5   A starlit or a moonlit dome disdains
All that man is,
All mere complexities,
The fury and the mire of human veins.

Before me floats an image, man or shade,
10   Shade more than man, more image than a shade;
For Hades' bobbin° bound in mummy-cloth   *spool*
May unwind the winding path;
A mouth that has no moisture and no breath
Breathless mouths may summon;
15   I hail the superhuman;
I call it death-in-life and life-in-death.

Miracle, bird or golden handiwork,
More miracle than bird or handiwork,
Planted on the starlit golden bough,
20   Can like the cocks of Hades crow,
Or, by the moon embittered, scorn aloud
In glory of changeless metal
Common bird or petal
And all complexities of mire or blood.

25   At midnight on the Emperor's pavement flit
Flames that no faggot° feeds, nor steel has lit,   *bundle of sticks*
Nor storm disturbs, flames begotten of flame,
Where blood-begotten spirits come
And all complexities of fury leave,
30   Dying into a dance,
An agony of trance,
An agony of flame that cannot singe a sleeve.

Astraddle on the dolphin's mire and blood,
Spirit after spirit! The smithies break the flood,
35   The golden smithies of the Emperor!
Marbles of the dancing floor
Break bitter furies of complexity,
Those images that yet
Fresh images beget,
40   That dolphin-torn, that gong-tormented sea.

1930   1932

Crazy Jane Talks with the Bishop

I met the Bishop on the road
And much said he and I.
"Those breasts are flat and fallen now
Those veins must soon be dry;
5   Live in a heavenly mansion,
Not in some foul sty."

"Fair and foul are near of kin,
And fair needs foul," I cried.
"My friends are gone, but that's a truth
10   Nor grave nor bed denied,
Learned in bodily lowliness
And in the heart's pride.

"A woman can be proud and stiff
When on love intent;
15   But Love has pitched his mansion in
The place of excrement;
For nothing can be sole or whole
That has not been rent."

1931   1932

Lapis Lazuli[1]
(FOR HARRY CLIFTON[2])

I have heard that hysterical women say
They are sick of the palette and fiddle-bow,
Of poets that are always gay,
For everybody knows or else should know
5   That if nothing drastic is done
Aeroplane and Zeppelin will come out,
Pitch like King Billy bomb-balls[3] in
Until the town lie beaten flat.

All perform their tragic play,
10   There struts Hamlet, there is Lear,
That's Ophelia, that Cordelia;[4]
Yet they, should the last scene be there,
The great stage curtain about to drop,
If worthy their prominent part in the play,

---

1. A rich blue mineral producing the pigment ultramarine; used by the ancients for decoration.
2. A friend who gave Yeats a carving in lapis lazuli on his birthday.

3. German bombs; "King Billy" is a nickname for Kaiser Wilhelm II.
4. Characters from *Hamlet* and *King Lear*.

15 Do not break up their lines to weep.
 They know that Hamlet and Lear are gay;
 Gaiety transfiguring all that dread.
 All men have aimed at, found and lost;
 Black out; Heaven blazing into the head:
20 Tragedy wrought to its uttermost.
 Though Hamlet rambles and Lear rages,
 And all the drop scenes drop at once
 Upon a hundred thousand stages,
 It cannot grow by an inch or an ounce.

25 On their own feet they came, or on shipboard,
 Camel-back, horse-back, ass-back, mule-back,
 Old civilisations put to the sword.
 Then they and their wisdom went to rack:
 No handiwork of Callimachus[5]
30 Who handled marble as if it were bronze,
 Made draperies that seemed to rise
 When sea-wind swept the corner, stands;
 His long lamp chimney shaped like the stem
 Of a slender palm, stood but a day;
35 All things fall and are built again
 And those that build them again are gay.

 Two Chinamen, behind them a third,
 Are carved in Lapis Lazuli,
 Over them flies a long-legged bird
40 A symbol of longevity;
 The third, doubtless a serving-man,
 Carries a musical instrument.

 Every discolouration of the stone,
 Every accidental crack or dent
45 Seems a water-course or an avalanche,
 Or lofty slope where it still snows
 Though doubtless plum or cherry-branch
 Sweetens the little half-way house
 Those Chinamen climb towards, and I
50 Delight to imagine them seated there;
 There, on the mountain and the sky,
 On all the tragic scene they stare.
 One asks for mournful melodies;
 Accomplished fingers begin to play.
55 Their eyes mid many wrinkles, their eyes,
 Their ancient, glittering eyes, are gay.

1936   1938

The Circus Animals' Desertion

1

 I sought a theme and sought for it in vain,
 I sought it daily for six weeks or so.
 Maybe at last being but a broken man

---

5. Greek poet, grammarian, critic, and sculptor (c. 310–c. 240 B.C.).

I must be satisfied with my heart, although
5   Winter and summer till old age began
My circus animals were all on show,
Those stilted boys, that burnished chariot,
Lion and woman and the Lord knows what.

2

What can I but enumerate old themes,
10   First that sea-rider Oisin[1] led by the nose
Through three enchanted islands, allegorical dreams,
Vain gaiety, vain battle, vain repose,
Themes of the embittered heart, or so it seems,
That might adorn old songs or courtly shows;
15   But what cared I that set him on to ride,
I, starved for the bosom of his fairy bride.

And then a counter-truth filled out its play,
"The Countess Cathleen"[2] was the name I gave it,
She, pity-crazed, had given her soul away
20   But masterful Heaven had intervened to save it.
I thought my dear must her own soul destroy
So did fanaticism and hate enslave it,
And this brought forth a dream and soon enough
This dream itself had all my thought and love.

25   And when the Fool and Blind Man stole the bread
Cuchulain[3] fought the ungovernable sea;
Heart mysteries there, and yet when all is said
It was the dream itself enchanted me:
Character isolated by a deed
30   To engross the present and dominate memory.
Players and painted stage took all my love
And not those things that they were emblems of.

3

Those masterful images because complete
Grew in pure mind but out of what began?
35   A mound of refuse or the sweepings of a street,
Old kettles, old bottles, and a broken can,
Old iron, old bones, old rags, that raving slut
Who keeps the till. Now that my ladder's gone
I must lie down where all the ladders start
40   In the foul rag and bone shop of the heart.

1939

Under Ben Bulben[1]

1

Swear by what the Sages spoke
Round the Mareotic Lake[2]

---

1. Mythical Irish poet-warrior, son of the great Finn, who crossed the sea on an enchanted horse; hero of Yeats's early narrative poem *The Wanderings of Oisin*.
2. Yeats's play *The Countess Cathleen* (1899) tells the traditional story of Kathleen ni Houlihan, allegorical symbol of Ireland.
3. Hero of the medieval Irish epic *The Tain*, who single-handedly defended Ulster.
1. A mountain in County Sligo.
2. An ancient region south of Alexandria, Egypt, known as a center of Neoplatonism.

That the Witch of Atlas[3] knew,
Spoke and set the cocks a-crow.

5   Swear by those horsemen, by those women
Complexion and form prove superhuman,
That pale, long-visaged company
That airs an immortality
Completeness of their passions won;
10   Now they ride the wintry dawn
Where Ben Bulben sets the scene.

Here's the gist of what they mean.

2

Many times man lives and dies
Between his two eternities,
15   That of race and that of soul,
And ancient Ireland knew it all.
Whether man dies in his bed
Or the rifle knocks him dead,
A brief parting from those dear
20   Is the worst man has to fear.
Though grave-diggers' toil is long,
Sharp their spades, their muscle strong,
They but thrust their buried men
Back in the human mind again.

3

25   You that Mitchel's prayer have heard,
"Send war in our time, O Lord!"[4]
Know that when all words are said
And a man is fighting mad,
Something drops from eyes long blind,
30   He completes his partial mind,
For an instant stands at ease,
Laughs aloud, his heart at peace.
Even the wisest man grows tense
With some sort of violence
35   Before he can accomplish fate,
Know his work or choose his mate.

4

Poet and sculptor do the work,
Nor let the modish painter shirk
What his great forefathers did,
40   Bring the soul of man to God,
Make him fill the cradles right.

Measurement began our might:
Forms a stark Egyptian[5] thought,
Forms that gentler Phidias wrought.
45   Michael Angelo left a proof
On the Sistine Chapel roof,
Where but half-awakened Adam

---

3. *The Witch of Atlas* is the title of a poem by Percy Shelley.
4. John Mitchel, revolutionary patriot, wrote "Give us war in our time, O Lord!" while in prison.

5. Plotinus, 3rd-century A.D. Egyptian-born philosopher, founder of Neoplatonism.

Can disturb globe-trotting Madam
Till her bowels are in heat,
50   Proof that there's a purpose set
Before the secret working mind:
Profane perfection of mankind.

Quattrocento[6] put in paint
On backgrounds for a God or Saint
55   Gardens where a soul's at ease;
Where everything that meets the eye,
Flowers and grass and cloudless sky
Resemble forms that are, or seem
When sleepers wake and yet still dream,
60   And when it's vanished still declare,
With only bed and bedstead there,
That Heavens had opened.
                                    Gyres run on;
When that greater dream had gone
Calvert and Wilson, Blake and Claude,[7]
65   Prepared a rest for the people of God,
Palmer's phrase,[8] but after that
Confusion fell upon our thought.

5

Irish poets learn your trade,
Sing whatever is well made,
70   Scorn the sort now growing up
All out of shape from toe to top,
Their unremembering hearts and heads
Base-born products of base beds.
Sing the peasantry, and then
75   Hard-riding country gentlemen,
The holiness of monks, and after
Porter-drinkers' randy° laughter;   lusty
Sing the lords and ladies gay
That were beaten into the clay
80   Through seven heroic centuries;[9]
Cast your mind on other days
That we in coming days may be
Still the indomitable Irishry.

6

Under bare Ben Bulben's head
85   In Drumcliff[1] churchyard Yeats is laid.
An ancestor was rector there
Long years ago; a church stands near,
By the road an ancient cross.
No marble, no conventional phrase,

---

6. Fifteenth-century artists of Italy's Renaissance.
7. Edward Calvert (1799–1883), English painter and engraver, disciple of Blake; Richard Wilson (1714–1782), British landscape painter; Claude Lorrain (1600–1682), French landscape painter.
8. Samuel Palmer (1805–1881), English painter of visionary landscapes and admirer of Blake.
9. I.e., the seven centuries since the conquest of Ireland by Henry II.
1. A village lying on the slopes of Ben Bulben, where Yeats was buried.

90   On limestone quarried near the spot
      By his command these words are cut:

          Cast a cold eye
          On life, on death.
          Horseman, pass by!

1938   1939

━━◆━━

James Joyce
1882–1941

James Joyce was one of the great innovators who brought the novel into the modern era. As T. S. Eliot put it, Joyce made "the modern world possible for art." The poet Edith Sitwell wrote that by the turn of the century, "language had become, not so much an abused medium, as a dead and outworn thing, in which there was no living muscular system. Then came the rebirth of the medium, and this was effected, as far as actual vocabularies were concerned, very largely by such prose writers as Mr. James Joyce and Miss Gertrude Stein." Joyce objected to this flaccidity, citing examples in the work of George Moore, the most important Irish novelist of the first decade of the twentieth; Moore's novel *The Untilled Field*, Joyce complained to his brother Stanislaus, was "damned stupid," "dull and flat" and "ill written." In a comment that would have pleased Joyce, one critic writing in 1929 declared that Joyce had by that date "conclusively reduced all the pretensions of the realistic novel to absurdity."

James Augustus Aloysius Joyce was born in Rathgar, a middle-class suburb of Dublin; though he was to leave Ireland more or less permanently at age twenty-two, Ireland generally, and "Dear Dirty Dublin" specifically, were never far from his mind and writing. He was the eldest surviving son in a large family consisting, according to his father, of "sixteen or seventeen children." His father, John Stanislaus Joyce, born and raised in Cork, was a tax collector and sometime Parnellite political employee; his mother was Mary Jane Joyce, née Murray. There is no better imaginative guide to the twists and turns of Joyce's family fortunes, and their effect on the young writer, than his first novel, *A Portrait of the Artist as a Young Man*; the life of Joyce's autobiographical hero Stephen Dedalus closely follows Joyce's own. The novel brings young Stephen from his earliest memories, through his Catholic schooling at Clongowes Wood College and Belvedere College, up to his graduation from University College, Dublin, and departure for Paris. Like Stephen, Joyce in these years first considered entering the priesthood, then began regarding Catholicism with increasing skepticism and irony, coming to view religion, family, and nation as three kinds of net or trap. One of the most important events of the early part of Joyce's life was the betrayal and subsequent death of "the uncrowned king of Ireland," Charles Stewart Parnell, the political leader who was working hard to make Home Rule for Ireland a reality; his demise, after his adulterous affair with Kitty O'Shea was discovered, was remembered by Joyce in his first poem, *Et Tu, Healy*—which he wrote at the age of eight—and in a haunting story, *Ivy Day in the Committee Room*. Joyce moved to Paris after graduation in 1902 and began medical studies, but he soon had to return to Dublin, as his mother was dying. Joyce gave up the idea of a medical career, which his father could not afford to finance in any event; he briefly tried teaching school, and sought to define himself as a writer.

Like Dedalus, the young Joyce first concentrated on writing poetry. The majority of his early poems were collected in the volume *Chamber Music* (1907); both the strength and weakness of the poems is suggested by the praise of Arthur Symons, who in his review in the *Nation* described the lyrics as "tiny, evanescent things." Poetry was ultimately to prove a dead end for Joyce; though he brought out one more volume of thirteen poems during his lifetime (*Pomes*

Penyeach, 1927), and wrote one forgettable play (*Exiles*, 1918), prose fiction is the primary area in which Joyce's influence continues to be felt.

The year 1904 proved to be an absolute watershed in Joyce's development as a writer. In January 1904—indeed, perhaps in the single day 7 January 1904—Joyce wrote an impressionistic prose sketch which would ultimately serve as the manifesto for his first novel. From this beginning, Joyce shaped his novel, which was to have been called *Stephen Hero*; and though he worked on it steadily for more than three years, and the manuscript grew to almost a thousand pages, the novel was not coming together in quite the way Joyce had hoped. Hence in the fall of 1907, he began cutting and radically reshaping the material into what would become *A Portrait of the Artist as a Young Man*, one of the finest examples of the *Künstlerroman* (novel of artistic growth) in English; H. G. Wells called it "by far the most living and convincing picture that exists of an Irish Catholic upbringing."

June 16, 1904, in particular is a crucial day in the Joycean calendar, for it is "Bloomsday"—the day on which the events narrated in *Ulysses* take place—and according to legend, it is the day that Nora Barnacle first agreed to go out walking with Joyce. Joyce's father thought Nora's maiden name a good omen, suggesting that she would "stick to him," and indeed she did; without the benefit of marriage, she agreed to accompany him four months later on his artistic exile to the Continent, and though they were not legally married until 1931, she proved a faithful and devoted partner, a small spot of stability amidst the chaos of Joyce's life. They settled for several years in Trieste, Italy, where Joyce taught English at a Berlitz school and where their two children, Giorgio and Lucia, were born. Joyce returned briefly to Ireland in 1909, seeking unsuccessfully to get work published and to start a movie theater; after another brief visit in 1912, he never returned. He spent most of World War I in Zurich, then moved to Paris, where he eked out an existence with the help of several benefactors as his reputation began to grow.

He had begun his first book in June or July 1904, invited by the Irish man of letters "A.E." (George Russell) to submit a short story to his paper *The Irish Homestead*. Joyce began writing the series of fifteen stories that would be published in 1914 as *Dubliners*. In letters to London publisher Grant Richards about his conception for the short stories, Joyce wrote that he planned the volume to be a chapter of Ireland's "moral history" and that in writing it he had "taken the first step towards the spiritual liberation of my country." Richards, however, objected to the stark realism—or sordidness—of several scenes, and pressed Joyce to eliminate vulgarisms; Joyce refused. Finally, desperate to have the book published, Joyce wrote to Richards: "I seriously believe that you will retard the course of civilisation in Ireland by preventing the Irish people from having one good look at themselves in my nicely polished looking-glass."

During this period, Joyce also experimented with a form of short prose sketch that he called the "epiphany." An epiphany, as it is defined in *Stephen Hero*, is "a sudden spiritual manifestation, whether in the vulgarity of speech or of gesture or in a memorable phase of the mind itself." It consequently falls to the artist to "record these epiphanies with extreme care, seeing that they themselves are the most delicate and evanescent of moments." One benefit of Joyce's experimentation with prose epiphanies is that the searching realism and psychological richness of the stories in *Dubliners* are conveyed with a lucid economy of phrasing—what Joyce called "a style of scrupulous meanness"—and by a similar penchant for understatement on the level of plot. The stories often seem to "stop," rather than end; time and again, Joyce withholds the tidy conclusion that conventional fiction had trained readers to expect. In story after story, characters betray what Joyce termed their "paralysis"—a paralysis of the will that prevents them from breaking out of deadening habit. The final story of the collection, *The Dead*—written after the volume had ostensibly been completed, and comprising a broader scope and larger cast of characters than the other stories—is Joyce's finest work of short fiction, and justly praised as one of the great stories of our time; it was filmed, quite sensitively and beautifully, by director John Huston, the last film project before his death.

A second decisive year for Joyce was 1914. Having completed *Dubliners*, Joyce seems never to have thought seriously about writing short fiction again; and throughout the period he was writing his stories, he continued to work on *A Portrait*. As was the case with *Dubliners*, negotiations for the publication of *A Portrait* were extremely difficult; despite its dazzling language, few editors could get beyond the opening pages, with their references to bedwetting and their use of crude slang. Even though the novel had been published serially in *The Egoist* beginning in 1914, and was praised by influential writers like W. B. Yeats, H. G. Wells, and Ezra Pound, the book was rejected by every publisher in London to whom Joyce offered it, before finally being accepted by B. W. Huebsch in New York, and published in December 1916.

With both his stories and his first novel between hard covers, Joyce was finally able to concentrate his energies on the one novel for which, more than any other, he will be remembered—*Ulysses*; that work, too, had begun in 1914. The novel is structured, loosely, on eighteen episodes from Homer's *Odyssey*; Leopold Bloom, advertising salesman, is a modern-day Ulysses, the streets of Dublin his Aegean Sea, and Molly Bloom his (unfaithful) Penelope. Stephen Dedalus, stuck teaching school and estranged from his real father, is an unwitting Telemachus (Ulysses' son) in search of a father. Critics have disagreed over the years as to how seriously readers should take these Homeric parallels; Eliot understood them to be of the utmost importance—"a way of controlling, of ordering, of giving a shape and a significance to the immense panorama of futility and anarchy which is contemporary history"—while the equally supportive Pound suggested that the parallel structure was merely "the remains of a medieval allegorical culture; it matters little, it is a question of cooking, which does not restrict the action, nor inconvenience it, nor harm the realism, nor the contemporaneity of the action."

Concomitant with the Homeric structure, Joyce sought to give each of his eighteen chapters its own style. Chapter 12, focusing on Bloom's encounter with Dublin's Cyclops, called "the Citizen," is written in a style of "gigantism"—full of mock-epic epithets and catalogues, playfully suggestive of the style of ancient Celtic myth and legend. Chapter 13, which parallels Odysseus's encounter with Nausicäa, is written in the exaggerated style of Victorian women's magazines and sentimental fiction, a style which Joyce characterized as "a namby-pamby jammy marmalady drawersy (alto-là!) style with effects of incense, mariolatry, masturbation, stewed cockles, painter's palette, chitchat, circumlocutions, etc etc." While realist writers sought constantly to flush artifice from their writing, to arrive finally at a style which would be value-neutral, Joyce takes the English language on a voyage in the opposite direction; each chapter, as he wrote to his patron Harriet Shaw Weaver, left behind it "a burnt-up field." It would be difficult to overestimate the influence that *Ulysses* has had on modern writing; Eliot's candid response to the novel, reported in a letter to Joyce, was "I have nothing but admiration; in fact, I wish, for my own sake, that I had not read it."

Other people wanted to make sure that no one else would read it. *Ulysses* was promptly banned as obscene, in Ireland, England, and many other countries. Copies were smuggled into the United States, where a pirated edition was published, paying Joyce no royalties. Finally in 1933, in a landmark decision, a federal judge found that the book's frank language and sexual discussions were fully justified artistically—though he allowed that "*Ulysses* is a rather strong draught to ask some sensitive, though normal, persons to take."

In 1923, with *Ulysses* published, Joyce suddenly reinvented himself and his writing once again, and turned his attention to the writing of the novel that would occupy him almost until his death—*Finnegans Wake*. If *Ulysses* attacks the novel form at the level of style, *Finnegans Wake* targets the very structures of the English language, using a neologismic amalgam of more than a dozen modern and ancient languages—a hybrid that devotees call "Wakese"; when questioned as to the wisdom of such a strategy, Joyce replied that *Ulysses* had proved English to be inadequate. "I'd like a language," he told his friend Stefan Zweig, "which is above all languages, a language to which all will do service. I cannot express myself in English without enclosing myself in a tradition."

On 13 January 1941, Joyce died of a perforated ulcer; his illness and death almost certainly owed something to an adult life of rather heavy drinking. Though his oeuvre consists largely of one volume of short stories and three novels, his importance for students of modern literature is extraordinary. As Richard Ellmann writes at the opening of his magisterial biography, "We are still learning to be James Joyce's contemporaries, to understand our interpreter."

from DUBLINERS

Clay

The matron had given her leave to go out as soon as the women's tea was over and Maria looked forward to her evening out. The kitchen was spick and span: the cook said you could see yourself in the big copper boilers. The fire was nice and bright and on one of the side-tables were four very big barmbracks.[1] These barmbracks seemed uncut; but if you went closer you would see that they had been cut into long thick even slices and were ready to be handed round at tea. Maria had cut them herself.

Maria was a very, very small person indeed but she had a very long nose and a very long chin. She talked a little through her nose, always soothingly: *Yes, my dear,* and *No, my dear.* She was always sent for when the women quarrelled over their tubs and always succeeded in making peace. One day the matron had said to her:

—Maria, you are a veritable peace-maker!

And the sub-matron and two of the Board ladies[2] had heard the compliment. And Ginger Mooney was always saying what she wouldn't do to the dummy[3] who had charge of the irons if it wasn't for Maria. Everyone was so fond of Maria.

The women would have their tea at six o'clock and she would be able to get away before seven. From Ballsbridge to the Pillar, twenty minutes; from the Pillar to Drumcondra, twenty minutes; and twenty minutes to buy the things. She would be there before eight. She took out her purse with the silver clasps and read again the words *A Present from Belfast.* She was very fond of that purse because Joe had brought it to her five years before when he and Alphy had gone to Belfast on a Whit-Monday[4] trip. In the purse were two half-crowns and some coppers. She would have five shillings clear after paying tram fare. What a nice evening they would have, all the children singing! Only she hoped that Joe wouldn't come in drunk. He was so different when he took any drink.

Often he had wanted her to go and live with them; but she would have felt herself in the way (though Joe's wife was ever so nice with her) and she had become accustomed to the life of the laundry. Joe was a good fellow. She had nursed him and Alphy too; and Joe used often say:

—Mamma is mamma but Maria is my proper mother.

After the break-up at home the boys had got her that position in the *Dublin by Lamplight* laundry,[5] and she liked it. She used to have such a bad opinion of Protestants but now she thought they were very nice people, a little quiet and serious, but still very nice people to live with. Then she had her plants in the conservatory and she liked looking after them. She had lovely ferns and wax-plants and, whenever anyone came to visit her, she always gave the visitor one or two slips from her con-

1. Speckled cakes or currant buns.
2. Members of the governing board of the Dublin by Lamplight Laundry.
3. Slang for a mute person.
4. Holiday following Whitsunday, the seventh Sunday after Easter.

5. Joyce's invented benevolent society, run by Protestant women, "saves" Dublin's prostitutes from a life on the streets by giving them honest work in a laundry. Maria works for the laundry but appears not to be a reformed prostitute herself.

servatory. There was one thing she didn't like and that was the tracts[6] on the walls; but the matron was such a nice person to deal with, so genteel.

When the cook told her everything was ready she went into the women's room and began to pull the big bell. In a few minutes the women began to come in by twos and threes, wiping their steaming hands in their petticoats and pulling down the sleeves of their blouses over their red steaming arms. They settled down before their huge mugs which the cook and the dummy filled up with hot tea, already mixed with milk and sugar in huge tin cans. Maria superintended the distribution of the barmbrack and saw that every woman got her four slices. There was a great deal of laughing and joking during the meal. Lizzie Fleming said Maria was sure to get the ring and, though Fleming had said that for so many Hallow Eves, Maria had to laugh and say she didn't want any ring or man either; and when she laughed her grey-green eyes sparkled with disappointed shyness and the tip of her nose nearly met the tip of her chin. Then Ginger Mooney lifted up her mug of tea and proposed Maria's health while all the other women clattered with their mugs on the table, and said she was sorry she hadn't a sup of porter[7] to drink it in. And Maria laughed again till the tip of her nose nearly met the tip of her chin and till her minute body nearly shook itself asunder because she knew that Mooney meant well though, of course, she had the notions of a common woman.

But wasn't Maria glad when the women had finished their tea and the cook and the dummy had begun to clear away the tea-things! She went into her little bedroom and, remembering that the next morning was a mass morning, changed the hand of the alarm from seven to six. Then she took off her working skirt and her house-boots and laid her best skirt out on the bed and her tiny dress-boots beside the foot of the bed. She changed her blouse too and, as she stood before the mirror, she thought of how she used to dress for mass on Sunday morning when she was a young girl; and she looked with quaint affection at the diminutive body which she had so often adorned. In spite of its years she found it a nice tidy little body.

When she got outside the streets were shining with rain and she was glad of her old brown raincloak. The tram was full and she had to sit on the little stool at the end of the car, facing all the people, with her toes barely touching the floor. She arranged in her mind all she was going to do and thought how much better it was to be independent and to have your own money in your pocket. She hoped they would have a nice evening. She was sure they would but she could not help thinking what a pity it was Alphy and Joe were not speaking. They were always falling out now but when they were boys together they used to be the best of friends: but such was life.

She got out of her tram at the Pillar and ferreted her way quickly among the crowds. She went into Downes's cakeshop but the shop was so full of people that it was a long time before she could get herself attended to. She bought a dozen of mixed penny cakes, and at last came out of the shop laden with a big bag. Then she thought what else would she buy: she wanted to buy something really nice. They would be sure to have plenty of apples and nuts. It was hard to know what to buy and all she could think of was cake. She decided to buy some plumcake but Downes's plumcake had not enough almond icing on top of it so she went over to a shop in Henry Street. Here she was a long time in suiting herself and the stylish young lady behind the counter, who was evidently a little annoyed by her, asked her was it wedding-cake she wanted to buy. That made Maria blush and smile at the young lady; but the young lady took it all very seriously and finally cut a thick slice of plumcake, parcelled it up and said:

6. Evangelical religious texts.   7. A heavy, dark brown ale.

—Two-and-four, please.

She thought she would have to stand in the Drumcondra tram because none of the young men seemed to notice her but an elderly gentleman made room for her. He was a stout gentleman and he wore a brown hard hat; he had a square red face and a greyish moustache. Maria thought he was a colonel-looking gentleman and she reflected how much more polite he was than the young men who simply stared straight before them. The gentleman began to chat with her about Hallow Eve and the rainy weather. He supposed the bag was full of good things for the little ones and said it was only right that the youngsters should enjoy themselves while they were young. Maria agreed with him and favoured him with demure nods and hems. He was very nice with her, and when she was getting out at the Canal Bridge she thanked him and bowed, and he bowed to her and raised his hat and smiled agreeably; and while she was going up along the terrace, bending her tiny head under the rain, she thought how easy it was to know a gentleman even when he has a drop taken.

Everybody said: O, here's Maria! when she came to Joe's house. Joe was there, having come home from business, and all the children had their Sunday dresses on. There were two big girls in from next door and games were going on. Maria gave the bag of cakes to the eldest boy, Alphy, to divide and Mrs Donnelly said it was too good of her to bring such a big bag of cakes and made all the children say:

—Thanks, Maria.

But Maria said she had brought something special for papa and mamma, something they would be sure to like, and she began to look for her plumcake. She tried in Downes's bag and then in the pockets of her raincloak and then on the hallstand but nowhere could she find it. Then she asked all the children had any of them eaten it—by mistake, of course—but the children all said no and looked as if they did not like to eat cakes if they were to be accused of stealing. Everybody had a solution for the mystery and Mrs Donnelly said it was plain that Maria had left it behind her in the tram. Maria, remembering how confused the gentleman with the greyish moustache had made her, coloured with shame and vexation and disappointment. At the thought of the failure of her little surprise and of the two and fourpence she had thrown away for nothing she nearly cried outright.

But Joe said it didn't matter and made her sit down by the fire. He was very nice with her. He told her all that went on in his office, repeating for her a smart answer which he had made to the manager. Maria did not understand why Joe laughed so much over the answer he had made but she said that the manager must have been a very overbearing person to deal with. Joe said he wasn't so bad when you knew how to take him, that he was a decent sort so long as you didn't rub him the wrong way. Mrs Donnelly played the piano for the children and they danced and sang. Then the two next-door girls handed round the nuts. Nobody could find the nutcrackers and Joe was nearly getting cross over it and asked how did they expect Maria to crack nuts without a nutcracker. But Maria said she didn't like nuts and that they weren't to bother about her. Then Joe asked would she take a bottle of stout[8] and Mrs Donnelly said there was port wine too in the house if she would prefer that. Maria said she would rather they didn't ask her to take anything: but Joe insisted.

So Maria let him have his way and they sat by the fire talking over old times and Maria thought she would put in a good word for Alphy. But Joe cried that God might strike him stone dead if ever he spoke a word to his brother again and Maria said she

8. An extra-strength ale.

was sorry she had mentioned the matter. Mrs Donnelly told her husband it was a great shame for him to speak that way of his own flesh and blood but Joe said that Alphy was no brother of his and there was nearly being a row[9] on the head of it. But Joe said he would not lose his temper on account of the night it was and asked his wife to open some more stout. The two next-door girls had arranged some Hallow Eve games[1] and soon everything was merry again. Maria was delighted to see the children so merry and Joe and his wife in such good spirits. The next-door girls put some saucers on the table and then led the children up to the table, blindfold. One got the prayer-book and the other three got the water; and when one of the next-door girls got the ring Mrs Donnelly shook her finger at the blushing girl as much as to say: *O, I know all about it!* They insisted then on blindfolding Maria and leading her up to the table to see what she would get; and, while they were putting on the bandage, Maria laughed and laughed again till the tip of her nose nearly met the tip of her chin.

They led her up to the table amid laughing and joking and she put her hand out in the air as she was told to do. She moved her hand about here and there in the air and descended on one of the saucers. She felt a soft wet substance with her fingers and was surprised that nobody spoke or took off her bandage. There was a pause for a few seconds; and then a great deal of scuffling and whispering. Somebody said something about the garden, and at last Mrs Donnelly said something very cross to one of the next-door girls and told her to throw it out at once: that was no play. Maria understood that it was wrong that time and so she had to do it over again: and this time she got the prayer-book.

After that Mrs Donnelly played Miss McCloud's Reel for the children and Joe made Maria take a glass of wine. Soon they were all quite merry again and Mrs Donnelly said Maria would enter a convent before the year was out because she had got the prayer-book. Maria had never seen Joe so nice to her as he was that night, so full of pleasant talk and reminiscences. She said they were all very good to her.

At last the children grew tired and sleepy and Joe asked Maria would she not sing some little song before she went, one of the old songs. Mrs Donnelly said *Do, please, Maria!* and so Maria had to get up and stand beside the piano. Mrs Donnelly bade the children be quiet and listen to Maria's song. Then she played the prelude and said *Now, Maria!* and Maria, blushing very much, began to sing in a tiny quavering voice. She sang *I Dreamt that I Dwelt,*[2] and when she came to the second verse she sang again:

> *I dreamt that I dwelt in marble halls*
> > *With vassals and serfs at my side*
> *And of all who assembled within those walls*
> > *That I was the hope and the pride.*
> *I had riches too great to count, could boast*
> > *Of a high ancestral name,*
> *But I also dreamt, which pleased me most,*
> > *That you loved me still the same.*

---

9. Argument.
1. The primary game that Maria and the girls play is a traditional Irish Halloween game. In its original version, a blindfolded girl would be led to three plates, and would choose one. Choosing the plate with a ring meant that she would soon marry; water meant she would emigrate (probably to America); and soil, or clay, meant she would soon die. In modern times, a prayer book was substituted for this unsavory third option, suggesting that the girl would enter a convent.
2. Aria from Act 2 of *The Bohemian Girl.*

But no one tried to show her her mistake;[3] and when she had ended her song Joe was very much moved. He said that there was no time like the long ago and no music for him like poor old Balfe, whatever other people might say; and his eyes filled up so much with tears that he could not find what he was looking for and in the end he had to ask his wife to tell him where the corkscrew was.

Ivy Day in the Committee Room[1]

Old Jack raked the cinders together with a piece of cardboard and spread them judiciously over the whitening dome of coals. When the dome was thinly covered his face lapsed into darkness but, as he set himself to fan the fire again, his crouching shadow ascended the opposite wall and his face slowly re-emerged into light. It was an old man's face, very bony and hairy. The moist blue eyes blinked at the fire and the moist mouth fell open at times, munching once or twice mechanically when it closed. When the cinders had caught he laid the piece of cardboard against the wall, sighed and said:

—That's better now, Mr O'Connor.

Mr O'Connor, a grey-haired young man, whose face was disfigured by many blotches and pimples, had just brought the tobacco for a cigarette into a shapely cylinder but when spoken to he undid his handiwork meditatively. Then he began to roll the tobacco again meditatively and after a moment's thought decided to lick the paper.

—Did Mr Tierney say when he'd be back? he asked in a husky falsetto.

—He didn't say.

Mr O'Connor put his cigarette into his mouth and began to search his pockets. He took out a pack of thin paste-board cards.

—I'll get you a match, said the old man.

—Never mind, this'll do, said Mr O'Connor.

He selected one of the cards and read what was printed on it:

Municipal Elections

ROYAL EXCHANGE WARD[2]

Mr Richard J. Tierney, P.L.G.,[3] respectfully
solicits the favour of your vote
and influence at the coming election
in the Royal Exchange Ward

Mr O'Connor had been engaged by Mr Tierney's agent to canvass one part of the ward but, as the weather was inclement and his boots let in the wet, he spent a great part of the day sitting by the fire in the Committee Room in Wicklow Street with Jack, the old caretaker. They had been sitting thus since the short day had grown dark. It was the sixth of October, dismal and cold out of doors.

---

3. Maria repeats the first verse rather than singing the second.
1. On October 6—the anniversary of Parnell's death—it was customary among his followers to wear a sprig of ivy in his honor; Committee Room No. 15 was the scene of Parnell's emotional final speech as leader of the Irish par-

liamentary party (see page 2316). Parnell's betrayal and demise form the backdrop of the story; the other personages are fictional.
2. A political ward near the center of Dublin.
3. Poor Law Guardian, elected to oversee the local relief rolls.

Mr O'Connor tore a strip off the card and, lighting it, lit his cigarette. As he did so the flame lit up a leaf of dark glossy ivy in the lapel of his coat. The old man watched him attentively and then, taking up the piece of cardboard again, began to fan the fire slowly while his companion smoked.

—Ah, yes, he said, continuing, it's hard to know what way to bring up children. Now who'd think he'd turn out like that! I sent him to the Christian Brothers[4] and I done what I could for him, and there he goes boosing about. I tried to make him someway decent.

He replaced the cardboard wearily.

—Only I'm an old man now I'd change his tune for him. I'd take the stick to his back and beat him while I could stand over him—as I done many a time before. The mother, you know, she cocks him up with this and that. . . .

—That's what ruins children, said Mr O'Connor.

—To be sure it is, said the old man. And little thanks you get for it, only impudence. He takes th'upper hand of me whenever he sees I've a sup taken. What's the world coming to when sons speaks that way of their father?

—What age is he? said Mr O'Connor.

—Nineteen, said the old man.

—Why don't you put him to something?[5]

—Sure, amn't I never done at the drunken bowsy ever since he left school? *I won't keep you,* I says. *You must get a job for yourself.* But, sure, it's worse whenever he gets a job; he drinks it all.

Mr O'Connor shook his head in sympathy, and the old man fell silent, gazing into the fire. Someone opened the door of the room and called out:

—Hello! Is this a Freemason's[6] meeting?

—Who's that? said the old man.

—What are you doing in the dark? asked a voice.

—Is that you, Hynes? asked Mr O'Connor.

—Yes. What are you doing in the dark? said Mr Hynes, advancing into the light of the fire.

He was a tall slender young man with a light brown moustache. Imminent little drops of rain hung at the brim of his hat and the collar of his jacket-coat was turned up.

—Well, Mat, he said to Mr O'Connor, how goes it?

Mr O'Connor shook his head. The old man left the hearth and, after stumbling about the room returned with two candlesticks which he thrust one after the other into the fire and carried to the table. A denuded room came into view and the fire lost all its cheerful colour. The walls of the room were bare except for a copy of an election address. In the middle of the room was a small table on which papers were heaped.

Mr Hynes leaned against the mantelpiece and asked:

—Has he paid you yet?

—Not yet, said Mr O'Connor. I hope to God he'll not leave us in the lurch to-night.

Mr Hynes laughed.

—O, he'll pay you. Never fear, he said.

—I hope he'll look smart about it if he means business, said Mr O'Connor.

---

4. The Irish Christian Brothers, a conservative Catholic order, operate a number of day schools throughout Ireland.

5. I.e., get him a job.
6. A worldwide secret, fraternal order.

—What do you think, Jack? said Mr Hynes satirically to the old man.

The old man returned to his seat by the fire, saying:

—It isn't but he has it, anyway. Not like the other tinker.[7]

—What other tinker? said Mr Hynes.

—Colgan, said the old man scornfully.

—Is it because Colgan's a working-man you say that? What's the difference between a good honest bricklayer and a publican[8]—eh? Hasn't the working-man as good a right to be in the Corporation[9] as anyone else—ay, and a better right than those shoneens[1] that are always hat in hand before any fellow with a handle to his name? Isn't that so, Mat? said Mr. Hynes, addressing Mr O'Connor.

—I think you're right, said Mr O'Connor.

—One man is a plain honest man with no hunker-sliding[2] about him. He goes in to represent the labour classes. This fellow you're working for only wants to get some job or other.

—Of course, the working-classes should be represented, said the old man.

—The working-man, said Mr Hynes, gets all kicks and no halfpence. But it's labour produces everything. The working-man is not looking for fat jobs for his sons and nephews and cousins. The working-man is not going to drag the honour of Dublin in the mud to please a German monarch.[3]

—How's that? said the old man.

—Don't you know they want to present an address of welcome to Edward Rex if he comes here next year? What do we want kowtowing to a foreign king?

—Our man won't vote for the address, said Mr O'Connor. He goes in on the Nationalist ticket.

—Won't he? said Mr Hynes. Wait till you see whether he will or not. I know him. Is it Tricky Dicky Tierney?

—By God! perhaps you're right, Joe, said Mr O'Connor. Anyway, I wish he'd turn up with the spondulics.[4]

The three men fell silent. The old man began to rake more cinders together. Mr Hynes took off his hat, shook it and then turned down the collar of his coat, displaying, as he did so, an ivy leaf in the lapel.

—If this man was alive, he said, pointing to the leaf, we'd have no talk of an address of welcome.

—That's true, said Mr O'Connor.

—Musha, God be with them times! said the old man. There was some life in it then.

The room was silent again. Then a bustling little man with a snuffling nose and very cold ears pushed in the door. He walked over quickly to the fire, rubbing his hands as if he intended to produce a spark from them.

—No money, boys, he said.

—Sit down here, Mr Henchy, said the old man, offering him his chair.

—O, don't stir, Jack, don't stir, said Mr Henchy.

He nodded curtly to Mr Hynes and sat down on the chair which the old man vacated.

—Did you serve Aungier Street? he asked Mr O'Connor.

7. A gypsy or beggar; a general term of abuse.
8. Bar keeper.
9. The Dublin civil service.
1. Good-for-nothings.
2. Laziness.

3. In July 1903, Edward VII of England, who was related to the German monarch, visited Dublin; the Dublin Corporation refused to make an address of welcome.
4. Money.

—Yes, said Mr O'Connor, beginning to search his pockets for memoranda.

—Did you call on Grimes?

—I did.

—Well? How does he stand?

—He wouldn't promise. He said: *I won't tell anyone what way I'm going to vote.* But I think he'll be all right.

—Why so?

—He asked me who the nominators were; and I told him. I mentioned Father Burke's name. I think it'll be all right.

Mr Henchy began to snuffle and to rub his hands over the fire at a terrific speed. Then he said:

—For the love of God, Jack, bring us a bit of coal. There must be some left.

The old man went out of the room.

—It's no go, said Mr Henchy, shaking his head. I asked the little shoeboy, but he said: *O, now, Mr Henchy, when I see the work going on properly I won't forget you, you may be sure.* Mean little tinker! 'Usha, how could he be anything else?

—What did I tell you, Mat? said Mr Hynes. Tricky Dicky Tierney.

—O, he's as tricky as they make 'em, said Mr Henchy. He hasn't got those little pigs' eyes for nothing. Blast his soul! Couldn't he pay up like a man instead of: *O, now, Mr Henchy, I must speak to Mr Fanning. . . . I've spent a lot of money?* Mean little shoeboy of hell! I suppose he forgets the time his little old father kept the hand-me-down shop in Mary's Lane.

—But is that a fact? asked Mr O'Connor.

—God, yes, said Mr Henchy. Did you never hear that? And the men used to go in on Sunday morning before the houses were open to buy a waistcoat or a trousers—moya! But Tricky Dicky's little old father always had a tricky little black bottle up in a corner. Do you mind now? That's that. That's where he first saw the light.

The old man returned with a few lumps of coal which he placed here and there on the fire.

—That's a nice how-do-you-do, said Mr O'Connor. How does he expect us to work for him if he won't stump up?

—I can't help it, said Mr Henchy. I expect to find the bailiffs in the hall when I go home.

Mr Hynes laughed and, shoving himself away from the mantelpiece with the aid of his shoulders, made ready to leave.

—It'll be all right when King Eddie comes, he said. Well, boys, I'm off for the present. See you later. 'Bye, 'bye.

He went out of the room slowly. Neither Mr Henchy nor the old man said anything but, just as the door was closing, Mr O'Connor who had been staring moodily into the fire, called out suddenly:

—'Bye, Joe.

Mr Henchy waited a few moments and then nodded in the direction of the door.

—Tell me, he said across the fire, what brings our friend in here? What does he want?

—'Usha, poor Joe! said Mr O'Connor, throwing the end of his cigarette into the fire, he's hard up like the rest of us.

Mr Henchy snuffled vigorously and spat so copiously that he nearly put out the fire which uttered a hissing protest.

—To tell you my private and candid opinion, he said, I think he's a man from the other camp. He's a spy of Colgan's if you ask me. *Just go round and try and find out how they're getting on. They won't suspect you.* Do you twig?[5]

—Ah, poor Joe is a decent skin, said Mr O'Connor.

—His father was a decent respectable man, Mr Henchy admitted: Poor old Larry Hynes! Many a good turn he did in his day! But I'm greatly afraid our friend is not nineteen carat. Damn it, I can understand a fellow being hard up but what I can't understand is a fellow sponging. Couldn't he have some spark of manhood about him?

—He doesn't get a warm welcome from me when he comes, said the old man. Let him work for his own side and not come spying around here.

—I don't know, said Mr O'Connor dubiously, as he took out cigarette-papers and tobacco. I think Joe Hynes is a straight man. He's a clever chap, too, with the pen. Do you remember that thing he wrote . . . ?

—Some of these hillsiders and fenians[6] are a bit too clever if you ask me, said Mr Henchy. Do you know what my private and candid opinion is about some of those little jokers? I believe half of them are in the pay of the Castle.[7]

—There's no knowing, said the old man.

—O, but I know it for a fact, said Mr Henchy. They're Castle hacks. . . . I don't say Hynes. . . . No, damn it, I think he's a stroke above that. . . . But there's a certain little nobleman with a cock-eye—you know the patriot I'm alluding to?

Mr O'Connor nodded.

—There's a lineal descendant of Major Sirr[8] for you if you like! O, the heart's blood of a patriot! That's a fellow now that'd sell his country for fourpence—ay—and go down on his bended knees and thank the Almighty Christ he had a country to sell.

There was a knock at the door.

—Come in! said Mr Henchy.

A person resembling a poor clergyman or a poor actor appeared in the doorway. His black clothes were tightly buttoned on his short body and it was impossible to say whether he wore a clergyman's collar or a layman's because the collar of his shabby frock-coat, the uncovered buttons of which reflected the candlelight, was turned up about his neck. He wore a round hat of hard black felt. His face, shining with raindrops, had the appearance of damp yellow cheese save where two rosy spots indicated the cheekbones. He opened his very long mouth suddenly to express disappointment and at the same time opened wide his very bright blue eyes to express pleasure and surprise.

—O, Father Keon! said Mr Henchy, jumping up from his chair. Is that you? Come in!

—O, no, no, no! said Father Keon quickly, pursing his lips as if he were addressing a child.

—Won't you come in and sit down?

—No, no, no! said Father Keon, speaking in a discreet indulgent velvety voice. Don't let me disturb you now! I'm just looking for Mr Fanning. . . .

—He's round at the *Black Eagle*, said Mr Henchy. But won't you come in and sit down a minute?

---

5. Do you get it?

6. The Fenians, also known as Hillside men, were a secret organization trying to overthrow English government in Ireland.

7. Dublin Castle, headquarters of the English government in Dublin.

8. Henry Charles Sirr, chief of Dublin police who worked with the English in putting down the rebellion of 1798.

—No, no, thank you. It was just a little business matter, said Father Keon. Thank you, indeed.

He retreated from the doorway and Mr Henchy, seizing one of the candlesticks, went to the door to light him downstairs.

—O, don't trouble, I beg!

—No, but the stairs is so dark.

—No, no, I can see. . . . Thank you, indeed.

—Are you right now?

—All right, thanks. . . . Thanks.

Mr Henchy returned with the candlestick and put it on the table. He sat down again at the fire. There was silence for a few moments.

—Tell me, John, said Mr O'Connor, lighting his cigarette with another pasteboard card.

—Hm?

—What is he exactly?

—Ask me an easier one, said Mr Henchy.

—Fanning and himself seem to me very thick. They're often in Kavanagh's together. Is he a priest at all?

—'Mmmyes, I believe so. . . . I think he's what you call a black sheep. We haven't many of them, thank God! but we have a few. . . . He's an unfortunate man of some kind. . . .

—And how does he knock it out?[9] asked Mr O'Connor.

—That's another mystery.

—Is he attached to any chapel or church or institution or—

—No, said Mr Henchy. I think he's travelling on his own account. . . . God forgive me, he added, I thought he was the dozen of stout.

—Is there any chance of a drink itself? asked Mr O'Connor.

—I'm dry too, said the old man.

—I asked that little shoeboy three times, said Mr Henchy, would he send up a dozen of stout. I asked him again now but he was leaning on the counter in his shirtsleeves having a deep goster[1] with Alderman Cowley.

—Why didn't you remind him? said Mr O'Connor.

—Well, I couldn't go over while he was talking to Alderman Cowley. I just waited till I caught his eye, and said: *About that little matter I was speaking to you about.* . . . *That'll be all right, Mr H.,* he said. Yerra, sure the little hop-o'-my-thumb has forgotten all about it.

—There's some deal on in that quarter, said Mr O'Connor thoughtfully. I saw the three of them hard at it yesterday at Suffolk Street corner.

—I think I know the little game they're at, said Mr Henchy. You must owe the City Fathers money nowadays if you want to be made Lord Mayor. Then they'll make you Lord Mayor. By God! I'm thinking seriously of becoming a City Father myself. What do you think? Would I do for the job?

Mr O'Connor laughed.

—So far as owing money goes. . . .

—Driving out of the Mansion House, said Mr Henchy, in all my vermin,[2] with Jack here standing up behind me in a powdered wig—eh?

---

9. How does he make a living?
1. Gossip session.

2. A pun on the *ermine* trimming the robes of the Lord Mayor.

—And make me your private secretary, John.

—Yes. And I'll make Father Keon my private chaplain. We'll have a family party.

—Faith, Mr Henchy, said the old man, you'd keep up better style than some of them. I was talking one day to old Keegan, the porter. *And how do you like your new master, Pat?* says I to him. *You haven't much entertaining now,* says I. *Entertaining!* says he. *He'd live on the smell of an oil-rag.* And do you know what he told me? Now, I declare to God, I didn't believe him.

—What? said Mr Henchy and Mr O'Connor.

—He told me: *What do you think of a Lord Mayor of Dublin sending out for a pound of chops for his dinner? How's that for high living?* says he. *Wisha! wisha,* says I. *A pound of chops,* says he, *coming into the Mansion House. Wisha!* says I, *what kind of people is going at all now?*

At this point there was a knock at the door, and a boy put in his head.

—What is it? said the old man.

—From the *Black Eagle,* said the boy, walking in sideways and depositing a basket on the floor with a noise of shaken bottles.

The old man helped the boy to transfer the bottles from the basket to the table and counted the full tally. After the transfer the boy put his basket on his arm and asked:

—Any bottles?

—What bottles? said the old man.

—Won't you let us drink them first? said Mr Henchy.

—I was told to ask for bottles.

—Come back to-morrow, said the old man.

—Here, boy! said Mr Henchy, will you run over to O'Farrell's and ask him to lend us a corkscrew—for Mr Henchy, say. Tell him we won't keep it a minute. Leave the basket there.

The boy went out and Mr Henchy began to rub his hands cheerfully, saying:

—Ah, well, he's not so bad after all. He's as good as his word, anyhow.

—There's no tumblers, said the old man.

—O, don't let that trouble you, Jack, said Mr Henchy. Many's the good man before now drank out of the bottle.

—Anyway, it's better than nothing, said Mr O'Connor.

—He's not a bad sort, said Mr Henchy, only Fanning has such a loan of him. He means well, you know, in his own tinpot[3] way.

The boy came back with the corkscrew. The old man opened three bottles and was handing back the corkscrew when Mr Henchy said to the boy:

—Would you like a drink, boy?

—If you please, sir, said the boy.

The old man opened another bottle grudgingly, and handed it to the boy.

—What age are you? he asked.

—Seventeen, said the boy.

As the old man said nothing further the boy took the bottle, said: *Here's my best respects, sir* to Mr Henchy, drank the contents, put the bottle back on the table and wiped his mouth with his sleeve. Then he took up the corkscrew and went out of the door sideways, muttering some form of salutation.

—That's the way it begins, said the old man.

---

3. Cheapskate.

—The thin edge of the wedge, said Mr Henchy.

The old man distributed the three bottles which he had opened and the men drank from them simultaneously. After having drunk each placed his bottle on the mantel-piece within hand's reach and drew in a long breath of satisfaction.

—Well, I did a good day's work to-day, said Mr Henchy, after a pause.

—That so, John?

—Yes. I got him one or two sure things in Dawson Street, Crofton and myself. Between ourselves, you know, Crofton (he's a decent chap, of course), but he's not worth a damn as a canvasser. He hasn't a word to throw to a dog. He stands and looks at the people while I do the talking.

Here two men entered the room. One of them was a very fat man, whose blue serge clothes seemed to be in danger of falling from his sloping figure. He had a big face which resembled a young ox's face in expression, staring blue eyes and a grizzled moustache. The other man, who was much younger and frailer, had a thin clean-shaven face. He wore a very high double collar and a wide-brimmed bowler hat.

—Hello, Crofton! said Mr Henchy to the fat man. Talk of the devil. . . .

—Where did the boose come from? asked the young man. Did the cow calve?

—O, of course, Lyons spots the drink first thing! said Mr O'Connor, laughing.

—Is that the way you chaps canvass, said Mr Lyons, and Crofton and I out in the cold and rain looking for votes?

—Why, blast your soul, said Mr Henchy, I'd get more votes in five minutes than you two'd get in a week.

—Open two bottles of stout, Jack, said Mr O'Connor.

—How can I? said the old man, when there's no corkscrew?

—Wait now, wait now! said Mr Henchy, getting up quickly. Did you ever see this little trick?

He took two bottles from the table and, carrying them to the fire, put them on the hob.[4] Then he sat down again by the fire and took another drink from his bottle. Mr Lyons sat on the edge of the table, pushed his hat towards the nape of his neck and began to swing his legs.

—Which is my bottle? he asked.

—This lad, said Mr Henchy.

Mr Crofton sat down on a box and looked fixedly at the other bottle on the hob. He was silent for two reasons. The first reason, sufficient in itself, was that he had nothing to say; the second reason was that he considered his companions beneath him. He had been a canvasser for Wilkins, the Conservative,[5] but when the Conservatives had withdrawn their man and, choosing the lesser of two evils, given their support to the Nationalist candidate, he had been engaged to work for Mr Tierney.

In a few minutes an apologetic *Pok!* was heard as the cork flew out of Mr Lyons' bottle. Mr Lyons jumped off the table, went to the fire, took his bottle and carried it back to the table.

—I was just telling them, Crofton, said Mr Henchy, that we got a good few votes to-day.

—Who did you get? asked Mr Lyons.

---

4. Ledge at the back of a fireplace.
5. In this context, a Conservative candidate is one who supports English rule in Ireland, a Nationalist one who opposes it.

—Well, I got Parkes for one, and I got Atkinson for two, and I got Ward of Dawson Street. Fine old chap he is, too—regular old toff,[6] old Conservative! *But isn't your candidate a Nationalist?* said he. *He's a respectable man,* said I. *He's in favour of whatever will benefit this country. He's a big ratepayer,*[7] I said. *He has extensive house property in the city and three places of business and isn't it to his own advantage to keep down the rates? He's a prominent and respected citizen,* said I, *and a Poor Law Guardian, and he doesn't belong to any party, good, bad, or indifferent.* That's the way to talk to 'em.

—And what about the address to the King? said Mr Lyons, after drinking and smacking his lips.

—Listen to me, said Mr Henchy. What we want in this country, as I said to old Ward, is capital. The King's coming here will mean an influx of money into this country. The citizens of Dublin will benefit by it. Look at all the factories down by the quays there, idle! Look at all the money there is in the country if we only worked the old industries, the mills, the shipbuilding yards and factories. It's capital we want.

—But look here, John, said Mr O'Connor. Why should we welcome the King of England? Didn't Parnell himself . . .

—Parnell, said Mr Henchy, is dead. Now, here's the way I look at it. Here's this chap come to the throne after his old mother keeping him out of it till the man was grey. He's a man of the world, and he means well by us. He's a jolly fine decent fellow, if you ask me, and no damn nonsense about him. He just says to himself: *The old one never went to see these wild Irish. By Christ, I'll go myself and see what they're like.* And are we going to insult the man when he comes over here on a friendly visit? Eh? Isn't that right, Crofton?

Mr Crofton nodded his head.

—But after all now, said Mr Lyons argumentatively, King Edward's life, you know, is not the very . . . [8]

—Let bygones be bygones, said Mr Henchy. I admire the man personally. He's just an ordinary knockabout like you and me. He's fond of his glass of grog and he's a bit of a rake, perhaps, and he's a good sportsman. Damn it, can't we Irish play fair?

—That's all very fine, said Mr Lyons. But look at the case of Parnell now.

—In the name of God, said Mr Henchy, where's the analogy between the two cases?

—What I mean, said Mr Lyons, is we have our ideals. Why, now, would we welcome a man like that? Do you think now after what he did Parnell was a fit man to lead us? And why, then, would we do it for Edward the Seventh?

—This is Parnell's anniversary, said Mr O'Connor, and don't let us stir up any bad blood. We all respect him now that he's dead and gone—even the Conservatives, he added, turning to Mr Crofton.

Pok! The tardy cork flew out of Mr Crofton's bottle. Mr Crofton got up from his box and went to the fire. As he returned with his capture he said in a deep voice:

—Our side of the house respects him because he was a gentleman.

—Right you are, Crofton! said Mr Henchy fiercely. He was the only man that could keep that bag of cats in order. *Down, ye dogs! Lie down, ye curs!* That's the way he treated them. Come in, Joe! Come in! he called out, catching sight of Mr Hynes in the doorway.

Mr Hynes came in slowly.

—Open another bottle of stout, Jack, said Mr Henchy. O, I forgot there's no corkscrew! Here, show me one here and I'll put it at the fire.

---

6. Gentleman.
7. Taxpayer.

8. Edward VII's behavior had been somewhat notorious before he became king.

The old man handed him another bottle and he placed it on the hob.

—Sit down, Joe, said Mr O'Connor, we're just talking about the Chief.

—Ay, ay! said Mr Henchy.

Mr Hynes sat on the side of the table near Mr Lyons but said nothing.

—There's one of them, anyhow, said Mr Henchy, that didn't renege him. By God, I'll say for you, Joe! No, by God, you stuck to him like a man!

—O, Joe, said Mr O'Connor suddenly. Give us that thing you wrote—do you remember? Have you got it on you?

—O, ay! said Mr Henchy. Give us that. Did you ever hear that, Crofton? Listen to this now: splendid thing.

—Go on, said Mr O'Connor. Fire away, Joe.

Mr Hynes did not seem to remember at once the piece to which they were alluding but, after reflecting a while, he said:

—O, that thing is it. . . . Sure, that's old now.

—Out with it, man! said Mr O'Connor.

—'Sh, 'sh, said Mr Henchy. Now, Joe!

Mr Hynes hesitated a little longer. Then amid the silence he took off his hat, laid it on the table and stood up. He seemed to be rehearsing the piece in his mind. After a rather long pause he announced:

The Death of Parnell
6TH OCTOBER 1891

He cleared his throat once or twice and then began to recite:

> He is dead. Our Uncrowned King is dead.
>   O, Erin,[9] mourn with grief and woe
> For he lies dead whom the fell gang
>   Of modern hypocrites laid low.
>
> He lies slain by the coward hounds
>   He raised to glory from the mire;
> And Erin's hopes and Erin's dreams
>   Perish upon her monarch's pyre.
>
> In palace, cabin or in cot
>   The Irish heart where'er it be
> Is bowed with woe—for he is gone
>   Who would have wrought her destiny.
>
> He would have had his Erin famed,
>   The green flag gloriously unfurled,
> Her statesmen, bards and warriors raised
>   Before the nations of the World.
>
> He dreamed (alas, 'twas but a dream!)
>   Of Liberty: but as he strove
> To clutch that idol, treachery
>   Sundered him from the thing he loved.
>
> Shame on the coward caitiff[1] hands
>   That smote their Lord or with a kiss

---

9. A poetic name for Ireland.   1. Despicable.

> Betrayed him to the rabble-rout
>   Of fawning priests—no friends of his.
>
> May everlasting shame consume
>   The memory of those who tried
> To befoul and smear th' exalted name
>   Of one who spurned them in his pride.
>
> He fell as fall the mighty ones,
>   Nobly undaunted to the last,
> And death has now united him
>   With Erin's heroes of the past.
>
> No sound of strife disturb his sleep!
>   Calmly he rests: no human pain
> Or high ambition spurs him now
>   The peaks of glory to attain.
>
> They had their way: they laid him low.
>   But Erin, list, his spirit may
> Rise, like the Phoenix from the flames,
>   When breaks the dawning of the day,
>
> The day that brings us Freedom's reign.
>   And on that day may Erin well
> Pledge in the cup she lifts to Joy
>   One grief—the memory of Parnell.

Mr Hynes sat down again on the table. When he had finished his recitation there was a silence and then a burst of clapping: even Mr Lyons clapped. The applause continued for a little time. When it had ceased all the auditors drank from their bottles in silence.

Pok! The cork flew out of Mr Hynes' bottle, but Mr Hynes remained sitting, flushed and bareheaded on the table. He did not seem to have heard the invitation.

—Good man, Joe! said Mr O'Connor, taking out his cigarette papers and pouch the better to hide his emotion.

—What do you think of that, Crofton? cried Mr Henchy. Isn't that fine? What?

Mr Crofton said that it was a very fine piece of writing.

The Dead

Lily, the caretaker's daughter, was literally run off her feet. Hardly had she brought one gentleman into the little pantry behind the office on the ground floor and helped him off with his overcoat than the wheezy hall-door bell clanged again and she had to scamper along the bare hallway to let in another guest. It was well for her she had not to attend to the ladies also. But Miss Kate and Miss Julia had thought of that and had converted the bathroom upstairs into a ladies' dressing-room. Miss Kate and Miss Julia were there, gossiping and laughing and fussing, walking after each other to the head of the stairs, peering down over the banisters and calling down to Lily to ask her who had come.

It was always a great affair, the Misses Morkan's annual dance. Everybody who knew them came to it, members of the family, old friends of the family, the members of Julia's choir, any of Kate's pupils that were grown up enough and even some of

Mary Jane's pupils too. Never once had it fallen flat. For years and years it had gone off in splendid style as long as anyone could remember; ever since Kate and Julia, after the death of their brother Pat, had left the house in Stoney Batter[1] and taken Mary Jane, their only niece, to live with them in the dark gaunt house on Usher's Island,[2] the upper part of which they had rented from Mr Fulham, the cornfactor on the ground floor. That was a good thirty years ago if it was a day. Mary Jane, who was then a little girl in short clothes, was now the main prop of the household for she had the organ in Haddington Road.[3] She had been through the Academy[4] and gave a pupils' concert every year in the upper room of the Antient Concert Rooms. Many of her pupils belonged to better-class families on the Kingstown and Dalkey line.[5] Old as they were, her aunts also did their share. Julia, though she was quite grey, was still the leading soprano in Adam and Eve's,[6] and Kate, being too feeble to go about much, gave music lessons to beginners on the old square piano in the back room. Lily, the caretaker's daughter, did housemaid's work for them. Though their life was modest they believed in eating well; the best of everything: diamond-bone sirloins, three-shilling tea and the best bottled stout.[7] But Lily seldom made a mistake in the orders so that she got on well with her three mistresses. They were fussy, that was all. But the only thing they would not stand was back answers.

Of course they had good reason to be fussy on such a night. And then it was long after ten o'clock and yet there was no sign of Gabriel and his wife. Besides they were dreadfully afraid that Freddy Malins might turn up screwed.[8] They would not wish for worlds that any of Mary Jane's pupils should see him under the influence; and when he was like that it was sometimes very hard to manage him. Freddy Malins always came late but they wondered what could be keeping Gabriel: and that was what brought them every two minutes to the banisters to ask Lily had Gabriel or Freddy come.

—O, Mr Conroy, said Lily to Gabriel when she opened the door for him, Miss Kate and Miss Julia thought you were never coming. Good-night, Mrs Conroy.

—I'll engage[9] they did, said Gabriel, but they forget that my wife here takes three mortal hours to dress herself.

He stood on the mat, scraping the snow from his goloshes, while Lily led his wife to the foot of the stairs and called out:

—Miss Kate, here's Mrs Conroy.

Kate and Julia came toddling down the dark stairs at once. Both of them kissed Gabriel's wife, said she must be perished alive and asked was Gabriel with her.

—Here I am as right as the mail, Aunt Kate! Go on up. I'll follow, called out Gabriel from the dark.

He continued scraping his feet vigorously while the three women went upstairs, laughing, to the ladies' dressing-room. A light fringe of snow lay like a cape on the shoulders of his overcoat and like toecaps on the toes of his goloshes; and, as the buttons of his overcoat slipped with a squeaking noise through the snow-stiffened frieze, a cold fragrant air from out-of-doors escaped from crevices and folds.

—Is it snowing again, Mr Conroy? asked Lily.

---

1. A district in northwest Dublin.
2. Two adjoining quays on the south side of the River Liffey.
3. Played the organ in a church on the Haddington Road.
4. Royal Academy of Music.
5. The train line connecting Dublin to the affluent suburbs south of the city.
6. A Dublin church.
7. An extra-strength ale.
8. Drunk.
9. Wager.

She had preceded him into the pantry to help him off with his overcoat. Gabriel smiled at the three syllables she had given his surname and glanced at her. She was a slim, growing girl, pale in complexion and with hay-coloured hair. The gas in the pantry made her look still paler. Gabriel had known her when she was a child and used to sit on the lowest step nursing a rag doll.

—Yes, Lily, he answered, and I think we're in for a night of it.

He looked up at the pantry ceiling, which was shaking with the stamping and shuffling of feet on the floor above, listened for a moment to the piano and then glanced at the girl, who was folding his overcoat carefully at the end of a shelf.

—Tell me, Lily, he said in a friendly tone, do you still go to school?

—O no, sir, she answered. I'm done schooling this year and more.

—O, then, said Gabriel gaily, I suppose we'll be going to your wedding one of these fine days with your young man, eh?

The girl glanced back at him over her shoulder and said with great bitterness:

—The men that is now is only all palaver[1] and what they can get out of you.

Gabriel coloured as if he felt he had made a mistake and, without looking at her, kicked off his goloshes and flicked actively with his muffler at his patent-leather shoes.

He was a stout tallish young man. The high colour of his cheeks pushed upwards even to his forehead where it scattered itself in a few formless patches of pale red; and on his hairless face there scintillated restlessly the polished lenses and the bright gilt rims of the glasses which screened his delicate and restless eyes. His glossy black hair was parted in the middle and brushed in a long curve behind his ears where it curled slightly beneath the groove left by his hat.

When he had flicked lustre into his shoes he stood up and pulled his waistcoat down more tightly on his plump body. Then he took a coin rapidly from his pocket.

—O Lily, he said, thrusting it into her hands, it's Christmas-time, isn't it? Just ... here's a little. . . .

He walked rapidly towards the door.

—O no, sir! cried the girl, following him. Really, sir, I wouldn't take it.

—Christmas-time! Christmas-time! said Gabriel, almost trotting to the stairs and waving his hand to her in deprecation.

The girl, seeing that he had gained the stairs, called out after him:

—Well, thank you, sir.

He waited outside the drawing-room door until the waltz should finish, listening to the skirts that swept against it and to the shuffling of feet. He was still discomposed by the girl's bitter and sudden retort. It had cast a gloom over him which he tried to dispel by arranging his cuffs and the bows of his tie. Then he took from his waistcoat pocket a little paper and glanced at the headings he had made for his speech. He was undecided about the lines from Robert Browning for he feared they would be above the heads of his hearers. Some quotation that they could recognise from Shakespeare or from the Melodies[2] would be better. The indelicate clacking of the men's heels and the shuffling of their soles reminded him that their grade of culture differed from his. He would only make himself ridiculous by quoting poetry to them which they could not understand. They would think that he was airing his superior education. He would fail with them just as he had failed with the girl in the pantry. He had taken up a wrong tone. His whole speech was a mistake from first to last, an utter failure.

---

1. Empty talk.

2. Thomas Moore's *Irish Melodies*, a perennial favorite volume of poetry.

Just then his aunts and his wife came out of the ladies' dressing-room. His aunts were two small plainly dressed old women. Aunt Julia was an inch or so taller. Her hair, drawn low over the tops of her ears, was grey; and grey also, with darker shadows, was her large flaccid face. Though she was stout in build and stood erect her slow eyes and parted lips gave her the appearance of a woman who did not know where she was or where she was going. Aunt Kate was more vivacious. Her face, healthier than her sister's, was all puckers and creases, like a shrivelled red apple, and her hair, braided in the same old-fashioned way, had not lost its ripe nut colour.

They both kissed Gabriel frankly. He was their favourite nephew, the son of their dead elder sister, Ellen, who had married T.J. Conroy of the Port and Docks.

—Gretta tells me you're not going to take a cab back to Monkstown[3] to-night, Gabriel, said Aunt Kate.

—No, said Gabriel, turning to his wife, we had quite enough of that last year, hadn't we. Don't you remember, Aunt Kate, what a cold Gretta got out of it? Cab windows rattling all the way, and the east wind blowing in after we passed Merrion. Very jolly it was. Gretta caught a dreadful cold.

Aunt Kate frowned severely and nodded her head at every word.

—Quite right, Gabriel, quite right, she said. You can't be too careful.

—But as for Gretta there, said Gabriel, she'd walk home in the snow if she were let.

Mrs Conroy laughed.

—Don't mind him, Aunt Kate, she said. He's really an awful bother, what with green shades for Tom's eyes at night and making him do the dumb-bells, and forcing Eva to eat the stirabout.[4] The poor child! And she simply hates the sight of it! . . . O, but you'll never guess what he makes me wear now!

She broke out into a peal of laughter and glanced at her husband, whose admiring and happy eyes had been wandering from her dress to her face and hair. The two aunts laughed heartily too, for Gabriel's solicitude was a standing joke with them.

—Goloshes! said Mrs Conroy. That's the latest. Whenever it's wet underfoot I must put on my goloshes. Tonight even he wanted me to put them on, but I wouldn't. The next thing he'll buy me will be a diving suit.

Gabriel laughed nervously and patted his tie reassuringly while Aunt Kate nearly doubled herself, so heartily did she enjoy the joke. The smile soon faded from Aunt Julia's face and her mirthless eyes were directed towards her nephew's face. After a pause she asked:

—And what are goloshes, Gabriel?

—Goloshes, Julia! exclaimed her sister. Goodness me, don't you know what goloshes are? You wear them over your . . . over your boots, Gretta, isn't it?

—Yes, said Mrs Conroy. Guttapercha[5] things. We both have a pair now. Gabriel says everyone wears them on the continent.

—O, on the continent, murmured Aunt Julia, nodding her head slowly.

Gabriel knitted his brows and said, as if he were slightly angered:

—It's nothing very wonderful but Gretta thinks it very funny because she says the word reminds her of Christy Minstrels.[6]

—But tell me, Gabriel, said Aunt Kate, with brisk tact. Of course, you've seen about the room. Gretta was saying . . .

—O, the room is all right, replied Gabriel. I've taken one in the Gresham.[7]

---

3. An elegant suburb south of Dublin.
4. Porridge.
5. Rubberized fabric.

6. A 19th-century minstrel show.
7. The most elegant hotel in Dublin.

—To be sure, said Aunt Kate, by far the best thing to do. And the children, Gretta, you're not anxious about them?

—O, for one night, said Mrs Conroy. Besides, Bessie will look after them.

—To be sure, said Aunt Kate again. What a comfort it is to have a girl like that, one you can depend on! There's that Lily, I'm sure I don't know what has come over her lately. She's not the girl she was at all.

Gabriel was about to ask his aunt some questions on this point but she broke off suddenly to gaze after her sister who had wandered down the stairs and was craning her neck over the banisters.

—Now, I ask you, she said, almost testily, where is Julia going? Julia! Julia! Where are you going?

Julia, who had gone halfway down one flight, came back and announced blandly:

—Here's Freddy.

At the same moment a clapping of hands and a final flourish of the pianist told that the waltz had ended. The drawing-room door was opened from within and some couples came out. Aunt Kate drew Gabriel aside hurriedly and whispered into his ear:

—Slip down, Gabriel, like a good fellow and see if he's all right, and don't let him up if he's screwed. I'm sure he's screwed. I'm sure he is.

Gabriel went to the stairs and listened over the banisters. He could hear two persons talking in the pantry. Then he recognised Freddy Malins' laugh. He went down the stairs noisily.

—It's such a relief, said Aunt Kate to Mrs Conroy, that Gabriel is here. I always feel easier in my mind when he's here. . . . Julia, there's Miss Daly and Miss Power will take some refreshment. Thanks for your beautiful waltz, Miss Daly. It made lovely time.

A tall wizen-faced man, with a stiff grizzled moustache and swarthy skin, who was passing out with his partner said:

—And may we have some refreshment, too, Miss Morkan?

—Julia, said Aunt Kate summarily, and here's Mr Browne and Miss Furlong. Take them in, Julia, with Miss Daly and Miss Power.

—I'm the man for the ladies, said Mr Browne, pursing his lips until his moustache bristled and smiling in all his wrinkles. You know, Miss Morkan, the reason they are so fond of me is—

He did not finish his sentence, but, seeing that Aunt Kate was out of earshot, at once led the three young ladies into the back room. The middle of the room was occupied by two square tables placed end to end, and on these Aunt Julia and the caretaker were straightening and smoothing a large cloth. On the sideboard were arrayed dishes and plates, and glasses and bundles of knives and forks and spoons. The top of the closed square piano served also as a sideboard for viands[8] and sweets. At a smaller sideboard in one corner two young men were standing, drinking hop-bitters.[9]

Mr Browne led his charges thither and invited them all, in jest, to some ladies' punch, hot, strong and sweet. As they said they never took anything strong he opened three bottles of lemonade for them. Then he asked one of the young men to move aside, and, taking hold of the decanter, filled out for himself a goodly measure of whisky. The young men eyed him respectfully while he took a trial sip.

—God help me, he said, smiling, it's the doctor's orders.

His wizened face broke into a broader smile, and the three young ladies laughed in musical echo to his pleasantry, swaying their bodies to and fro, with nervous jerks of their shoulders. The boldest said:

---

8. Meats.   9. Dry ale.

—O, now, Mr Browne, I'm sure the doctor never ordered anything of the kind.

Mr Browne took another sip of his whisky and said, with sidling mimicry:

—Well, you see, I'm like the famous Mrs Cassidy, who is reported to have said: *Now, Mary Grimes, if I don't take it, make me take it, for I feel I want it.*

His hot face had leaned forward a little too confidentially and he had assumed a very low Dublin accent so that the young ladies, with one instinct, received his speech in silence. Miss Furlong, who was one of Mary Jane's pupils, asked Miss Daly what was the name of the pretty waltz she had played; and Mr Browne, seeing that he was ignored, turned promptly to the two young men who were more appreciative.

A red-faced young woman, dressed in pansy, came into the room, excitedly clapping her hands and crying:

—Quadrilles![1] Quadrilles!

Close on her heels came Aunt Kate, crying:

—Two gentlemen and three ladies, Mary Jane!

—O, here's Mr Bergin and Mr Kerrigan, said Mary Jane. Mr Kerrigan, will you take Miss Power? Miss Furlong, may I get you a partner, Mr Bergin. O, that'll just do now.

—Three ladies, Mary Jane, said Aunt Kate.

The two young gentlemen asked the ladies if they might have the pleasure, and Mary Jane turned to Miss Daly.

—O, Miss Daly, you're really awfully good, after playing for the last two dances, but really we're so short of ladies to-night.

—I don't mind in the least, Miss Morkan.

—But I've a nice partner for you, Mr Bartell D'Arcy, the tenor. I'll get him to sing later on. All Dublin is raving about him.

—Lovely voice, lovely voice! said Aunt Kate.

As the piano had twice begun the prelude to the first figure Mary Jane led her recruits quickly from the room. They had hardly gone when Aunt Julia wandered slowly into the room, looking behind her at something.

—What is the matter, Julia? asked Aunt Kate anxiously. Who is it?

Julia, who was carrying in a column of table-napkins, turned to her sister and said, simply, as if the question had surprised her:

—It's only Freddy, Kate, and Gabriel with him.

In fact right behind her Gabriel could be seen piloting Freddy Malins across the landing. The latter, a young man of about forty, was of Gabriel's size and build, with very round shoulders. His face was fleshy and pallid, touched with colour only at the thick hanging lobes of his ears and at the wide wings of his nose. He had coarse features, a blunt nose, a convex and receding brow, tumid and protruded lips. His heavy-lidded eyes and the disorder of his scanty hair made him look sleepy. He was laughing heartily in a high key at a story which he had been telling Gabriel on the stairs and at the same time rubbing the knuckles of his left fist backwards and forwards into his left eye.

—Good-evening, Freddy, said Aunt Julia.

Freddy Malins bade the Misses Morkan good-evening in what seemed an off-hand fashion by reason of the habitual catch in his voice and then, seeing that Mr Browne was grinning at him from the sideboard, crossed the room on rather shaky legs and began to repeat in an undertone the story he had just told to Gabriel.

—He's not so bad, is he? said Aunt Kate to Gabriel.

Gabriel's brows were dark but he raised them quickly and answered:

—O no, hardly noticeable.

1. A French square dance.

—Now, isn't he a terrible fellow! she said. And his poor mother made him take the pledge on New Year's Eve. But come on, Gabriel, into the drawing-room.

Before leaving the room with Gabriel she signalled to Mr Browne by frowning and shaking her forefinger in warning to and fro. Mr Browne nodded in answer and, when she had gone, said to Freddy Malins:

—Now, then, Teddy, I'm going to fill you out a good glass of lemonade just to buck you up.

Freddy Malins, who was nearing the climax of his story, waved the offer aside impatiently but Mr Browne, having first called Freddy Malins' attention to a disarray in his dress, filled out and handed him a full glass of lemonade. Freddy Malins' left hand accepted the glass mechanically, his right hand being engaged in the mechanical readjustment of his dress. Mr Browne, whose face was once more wrinkling with mirth, poured out for himself a glass of whisky while Freddy Malins exploded, before he had well reached the climax of his story, in a kink of high-pitched bronchitic laughter and, setting down his untasted and overflowing glass, began to rub the knuckles of his left fist backwards and forwards into his left eye, repeating words of his last phrase as well as his fit of laughter would allow him.

Gabriel could not listen while Mary Jane was playing her Academy piece, full of runs and difficult passages, to the hushed drawing-room. He liked music but the piece she was playing had no melody for him and he doubted whether it had any melody for the other listeners, though they had begged Mary Jane to play something. Four young men, who had come from the refreshment-room to stand in the door-way at the sound of the piano, had gone away quietly in couples after a few minutes. The only persons who seemed to follow the music were Mary Jane herself, her hands racing along the key-board or lifted from it at the pauses like those of a priestess in momentary imprecation, and Aunt Kate standing at her elbow to turn the page.

Gabriel's eyes, irritated by the floor, which glittered with beeswax under the heavy chandelier, wandered to the wall above the piano. A picture of the balcony scene in *Romeo and Juliet* hung there and beside it was a picture of the two murdered princes[2] in the Tower which Aunt Julia had worked in red, blue and brown wools when she was a girl. Probably in the school they had gone to as girls that kind of work had been taught, for one year his mother had worked for him as a birthday present a waistcoat of purple tabinet,[3] with little foxes' heads upon it, lined with brown satin and having round mulberry buttons. It was strange that his mother had had no musical talent though Aunt Kate used to call her the brains carrier of the Morkan family. Both she and Julia had always seemed a little proud of their serious and matronly sister. Her photograph stood before the pierglass.[4] She held an open book on her knees and was pointing out something in it to Constantine who, dressed in a man-o'-war suit, lay at her feet. It was she who had chosen the names for her sons for she was very sensible of the dignity of family life. Thanks to her, Constantine was now senior curate in Balbriggan[5] and, thanks to her, Gabriel himself had taken his degree in the Royal University.[6] A shadow passed over his face as he remembered her sullen opposition to his marriage. Some slighting phrases she had used still rankled in his memory; she had once spoken of Gretta as being country cute and that was not true of Gretta at all. It was Gretta who had nursed her during all her last long illness in their house at Monkstown.

---

2. The young sons of Edward IV, murdered in the Tower of London by order of their uncle, Edward III.
3. Silk and wool fabric.

4. A large high mirror.
5. Seaport 19 miles southeast of Dublin.
6. The Royal University of Ireland, established in 1882.

He knew that Mary Jane must be near the end of her piece for she was playing again the opening melody with runs of scales after every bar and while he waited for the end the resentment died down in his heart. The piece ended with a trill of octaves in the treble and a final deep octave in the bass. Great applause greeted Mary Jane as, blushing and rolling up her music nervously, she escaped from the room. The most vigorous clapping came from the four young men in the doorway who had gone away to the refreshment-room at the beginning of the piece but had come back when the piano had stopped.

Lancers[7] were arranged. Gabriel found himself partnered with Miss Ivors. She was a frank-mannered talkative young lady, with a freckled face and prominent brown eyes. She did not wear a low-cut bodice and the large brooch which was fixed in the front of her collar bore on it an Irish device.

When they had taken their places she said abruptly:

—I have a crow to pluck with you.

—With me? said Gabriel.

She nodded her head gravely.

—What is it? asked Gabriel, smiling at her solemn manner.

—Who is G. C.? answered Miss Ivors, turning her eyes upon him.

Gabriel coloured and was about to knit his brows, as if he did not understand, when she said bluntly:

—O, innocent Amy! I have found out that you write for *The Daily Express*.[8] Now, aren't you ashamed of yourself?

—Why should I be ashamed of myself? asked Gabriel, blinking his eyes and trying to smile.

—Well, I'm ashamed of you, said Miss Ivors frankly. To say you'd write for a rag like that. I didn't think you were a West Briton.[9]

A look of perplexity appeared on Gabriel's face. It was true that he wrote a literary column every Wednesday in *The Daily Express*, for which he was paid fifteen shillings. But that did not make him a West Briton surely. The books he received for review were almost more welcome than the paltry cheque. He loved to feel the covers and turn over the pages of newly printed books. Nearly every day when his teaching in the college was ended he used to wander down the quays to the second-hand booksellers, to Hickey's on Bachelor's Walk, to Webb's or Massey's on Aston's Quay, or to O'Clohissey's in the by-street. He did not know how to meet her charge. He wanted to say that literature was above politics. But they were friends of many years' standing and their careers had been parallel, first at the University and then as teachers: he could not risk a grandiose phrase with her. He continued blinking his eyes and trying to smile and murmured lamely that he saw nothing political in writing reviews of books.

When their turn to cross had come he was still perplexed and inattentive. Miss Ivors promptly took his hand in a warm grasp and said in a soft friendly tone:

—Of course, I was only joking. Come, we cross now.

When they were together again she spoke of the University question[1] and Gabriel felt more at ease. A friend of hers had shown her his review of Browning's poems. That was how she had found out the secret: but she liked the review immensely. Then she said suddenly:

---

7. A type of quadrille for 8 or 16 people.
8. A conservative paper opposed to the struggle for Irish independence.
9. Disparaging term for people wishing to identify Ireland as British.

1. Ireland's oldest most and prestigious university, Trinity College, was open only to Protestants; the "University question" involved, in part, the provision of quality university education to Catholics.

—O, Mr Conroy, will you come for an excursion to the Aran Isles[2] this summer? We're going to stay there a whole month. It will be splendid out in the Atlantic. You ought to come. Mr Clancy is coming, and Mr Kilkelly and Kathleen Kearney. It would be splendid for Gretta too if she'd come. She's from Connacht,[3] isn't she?

—Her people are, said Gabriel shortly.

—But you will come, won't you? said Miss Ivors, laying her warm hand eagerly on his arm.

—The fact is, said Gabriel, I have already arranged to go—

—Go where? asked Miss Ivors.

—Well, you know, every year I go for a cycling tour with some fellows and so—

—But where? asked Miss Ivors.

—Well, we usually go to France or Belgium or perhaps Germany, said Gabriel awkwardly.

—And why do you go to France and Belgium, said Miss Ivors, instead of visiting your own land?

—Well, said Gabriel, it's partly to keep in touch with the languages and partly for a change.

—And haven't you your own language to keep in touch with—Irish? asked Miss Ivors.

—Well, said Gabriel, if it comes to that, you know, Irish is not my language.

Their neighbours had turned to listen to the cross-examination. Gabriel glanced right and left nervously and tried to keep his good humour under the ordeal which was making a blush invade his forehead.

—And haven't you your own land to visit, continued Miss Ivors, that you know nothing of, your own people, and your own country?

—O, to tell you the truth, retorted Gabriel suddenly, I'm sick of my own country, sick of it!

—Why? asked Miss Ivors.

Gabriel did not answer for his retort had heated him.

—Why? repeated Miss Ivors.

They had to go visiting together and, as he had not answered her, Miss Ivors said warmly:

—Of course, you've no answer.

Gabriel tried to cover his agitation by taking part in the dance with great energy. He avoided her eyes for he had seen a sour expression on her face. But when they met in the long chain he was surprised to feel his hand firmly pressed. She looked at him from under her brows for a moment quizzically until he smiled. Then, just as the chain was about to start again, she stood on tiptoe and whispered into his ear:

—West Briton!

When the lancers were over Gabriel went away to a remote corner of the room where Freddy Malins' mother was sitting. She was a stout feeble old woman with white hair. Her voice had a catch in it like her son's and she stuttered slightly. She had been told that Freddy had come and that he was nearly all right. Gabriel asked her whether she had had a good crossing. She lived with her married daughter in Glasgow and came to Dublin on a visit once a year. She answered placidly that she had had a beautiful crossing and that the captain had been most attentive to her. She

---

2. Islands off the west coast of Ireland where the people still retained their traditional culture and spoke Irish.

3. A province on the west coast of Ireland.

spoke also of the beautiful house her daughter kept in Glasgow, and of all the nice friends they had there. While her tongue rambled on Gabriel tried to banish from his mind all memory of the unpleasant incident with Miss Ivors. Of course the girl or woman, or whatever she was, was an enthusiast but there was a time for all things. Perhaps he ought not to have answered her like that. But she had no right to call him a West Briton before people, even in joke. She had tried to make him ridiculous before people, heckling him and staring at him with her rabbit's eyes.

He saw his wife making her way towards him through the waltzing couples. When she reached him she said into his ear:

—Gabriel, Aunt Kate wants to know won't you carve the goose as usual. Miss Daly will carve the ham and I'll do the pudding.

—All right, said Gabriel.

—She's sending in the younger ones first as soon as this waltz is over so that we'll have the table to ourselves.

—Were you dancing? asked Gabriel.

—Of course I was. Didn't you see me? What words had you with Molly Ivors?

—No words. Why? Did she say so?

—Something like that. I'm trying to get that Mr D'Arcy to sing. He's full of conceit, I think.

—There were no words, said Gabriel moodily, only she wanted me to go for a trip to the west of Ireland and I said I wouldn't.

His wife clasped her hands excitedly and gave a little jump.

—O, do go, Gabriel, she cried. I'd love to see Galway again.

—You can go if you like, said Gabriel coldly.

She looked at him for a moment, then turned to Mrs Malins and said:

—There's a nice husband for you, Mrs Malins.

While she was threading her way back across the room Mrs Malins, without adverting to the interruption, went on to tell Gabriel what beautiful places there were in Scotland and beautiful scenery. Her son-in-law brought them every year to the lakes and they used to go fishing. Her son-in-law was a splendid fisher. One day he caught a fish, a beautiful big big fish, and the man in the hotel boiled it for their dinner.

Gabriel hardly heard what she said. Now that supper was coming near he began to think again about his speech and about the quotation. When he saw Freddy Malins coming across the room to visit his mother Gabriel left the chair free for him and retired into the embrasure of the window. The room had already cleared and from the back room came the clatter of plates and knives. Those who still remained in the drawing-room seemed tired of dancing and were conversing quietly in little groups. Gabriel's warm trembling fingers tapped the cold pane of the window. How cool it must be outside! How pleasant it would be to walk out alone, first along by the river and then through the park! The snow would be lying on the branches of the trees and forming a bright cap on the top of the Wellington Monument.[4] How much more pleasant it would be there than at the supper-table!

He ran over the headings of his speech: Irish hospitality, sad memories, the Three Graces, Paris, the quotation from Browning. He repeated to himself a phrase he had written in his review: *One feels that one is listening to a thought-tormented music.* Miss Ivors had praised the review. Was she sincere? Had she really any life of her own

---

4. A monument to the Duke of Wellington, an Irish-born English military hero, located in Phoenix Park, Dublin's major public park.

behind all her propagandism? There had never been any ill-feeling between them until that night. It unnerved him to think that she would be at the supper-table, looking up at him while he spoke with her critical quizzing eyes. Perhaps she would not be sorry to see him fail in his speech. An idea came into his mind and gave him courage. He would say, alluding to Aunt Kate and Aunt Julia: *Ladies and Gentlemen, the generation which is now on the wane among us may have had its faults but for my part I think it had certain qualities of hospitality, of humour, of humanity, which the new and very serious and hypereducated generation that is growing up around us seems to me to lack.* Very good: that was one for Miss Ivors. What did he care that his aunts were only two ignorant old women?

A murmur in the room attracted his attention. Mr Browne was advancing from the door, gallantly escorting Aunt Julia, who leaned upon his arm, smiling and hanging her head. An irregular musketry of applause escorted her also as far as the piano and then, as Mary Jane seated herself on the stool, and Aunt Julia, no longer smiling, half turned so as to pitch her voice fairly into the room, gradually ceased. Gabriel recognised the prelude. It was that of an old song of Aunt Julia's—*Arrayed for the Bridal*.[5] Her voice, strong and clear in tone, attacked with great spirit the runs which embellish the air and though she sang very rapidly she did not miss even the smallest of the grace notes. To follow the voice, without looking at the singer's face, was to feel and share the excitement of swift and secure flight. Gabriel applauded loudly with all the others at the close of the song and loud applause was borne in from the invisible supper-table. It sounded so genuine that a little colour struggled into Aunt Julia's face as she bent to replace in the music-stand the old leather-bound song-book that had her initials on the cover. Freddy Malins, who had listened with his head perched sideways to hear her better, was still applauding when everyone else had ceased and talking animatedly to his mother who nodded her head gravely and slowly in acquiescence. At last, when he could clap no more, he stood up suddenly and hurried across the room to Aunt Julia whose hand he seized and held in both his hands, shaking it when words failed him or the catch in his voice proved too much for him.

—I was just telling my mother, he said, I never heard you sing so well, never. No, I never heard your voice so good as it is to-night. Now! Would you believe that now? That's the truth. Upon my word and honour that's the truth. I never heard your voice sound so fresh and so . . . so clear and fresh, never.

Aunt Julia smiled broadly and murmured something about compliments as she released her hand from his grasp. Mr Browne extended his open hand towards her and said to those who were near him in the manner of a showman introducing a prodigy to an audience:

—Miss Julia Morkan, my latest discovery!

He was laughing very heartily at this himself when Freddy Malins turned to him and said:

—Well, Browne, if you're serious you might make a worse discovery. All I can say is I never heard her sing half so well as long as I am coming here. And that's the honest truth.

—Neither did I, said Mr. Browne. I think her voice has greatly improved.

Aunt Julia shrugged her shoulders and said with meek pride:

—Thirty years ago I hadn't a bad voice as voices go.

5. A popular but challenging song set to music from Bellini's opera *I Puritani* (1835).

—I often told Julia, said Aunt Kate emphatically, that she was simply thrown away in that choir. But she never would be said by me.

She turned as if to appeal to the good sense of the others against a refractory child while Aunt Julia gazed in front of her, a vague smile of reminiscence playing on her face.

—No, continued Aunt Kate, she wouldn't be said or led by anyone, slaving there in that choir night and day, night and day. Six o'clock on Christmas morning! And all for what?

—Well, isn't it for the honour of God, Aunt Kate? asked Mary Jane, twisting round on the piano-stool and smiling.

Aunt Kate turned fiercely on her niece and said:

—I know all about the honour of God, Mary Jane, but I think it's not at all honourable for the pope to turn out the women out of the choirs that have slaved there all their lives and put little whipper-snappers of boys over their heads. I suppose it is for the good of the Church if the pope does it. But it's not just, Mary Jane, and it's not right.

She had worked herself into a passion and would have continued in defence of her sister for it was a sore subject with her but Mary Jane, seeing that all the dancers had come back, intervened pacifically:

—Now, Aunt Kate, you're giving scandal to Mr Browne who is of the other persuasion.

Aunt Kate turned to Mr Browne, who was grinning at this allusion to his religion, and said hastily:

—O, I don't question the pope's being right. I'm only a stupid old woman and I wouldn't presume to do such a thing. But there's such a thing as common everyday politeness and gratitude. And if I were in Julia's place I'd tell that Father Healy straight up to his face . . .

—And besides, Aunt Kate, said Mary Jane, we really are all hungry and when we are hungry we are all very quarrelsome.

—And when we are thirsty we are also quarrelsome, added Mr Browne.

—So that we had better go to supper, said Mary Jane, and finish the discussion afterwards.

On the landing outside the drawing-room Gabriel found his wife and Mary Jane trying to persuade Miss Ivors to stay for supper. But Miss Ivors, who had put on her hat and was buttoning her cloak, would not stay. She did not feel in the least hungry and she had already overstayed her time.

—But only for ten minutes, Molly, said Mrs Conroy. That won't delay you.

—To take a pick itself, said Mary Jane, after all your dancing.

—I really couldn't, said Miss Ivors.

—I am afraid you didn't enjoy yourself at all, said Mary Jane hopelessly.

—Ever so much, I assure you, said Miss Ivors, but you really must let me run off now.

—But how can you get home? asked Mrs Conroy.

—O, it's only two steps up the quay.

Gabriel hesitated a moment and said:

—If you will allow me, Miss Ivors, I'll see you home if you really are obliged to go.

But Miss Ivors broke away from them.

—I won't hear of it, she cried. For goodness sake go in to your suppers and don't mind me. I'm quite well able to take care of myself.

—Well, you're the comical girl, Molly, said Mrs Conroy frankly.

—*Beannacht libh*,[6] cried Miss Ivors, with a laugh, as she ran down the staircase.

Mary Jane gazed after her, a moody puzzled expression on her face, while Mrs Conroy leaned over the banisters to listen for the hall-door. Gabriel asked himself was he the cause of her abrupt departure. But she did not seem to be in ill humour: she had gone away laughing. He stared blankly down the staircase.

At that moment Aunt Kate came toddling out of the supper-room, almost wringing her hands in despair.

—Where is Gabriel? she cried. Where on earth is Gabriel? There's everyone waiting in there, stage to let, and nobody to carve the goose!

—Here I am, Aunt Kate! cried Gabriel, with sudden animation, ready to carve a flock of geese, if necessary.

A fat brown goose lay at one end of the table and at the other end, on a bed of creased paper strewn with sprigs of parsley, lay a great ham, stripped of its outer skin and peppered over with crust crumbs, a neat paper frill round its shin and beside this was a round of spiced beef. Between these rival ends ran parallel lines of side-dishes: two little minsters of jelly, red and yellow; a shallow dish full of blocks of blancmange and red jam, a large green leaf-shaped dish with a stalk-shaped handle, on which lay bunches of purple raisins and peeled almonds, a companion dish on which lay a solid rectangle of Smyrna figs, a dish of custard topped with grated nutmeg, a small bowl full of chocolates and sweets wrapped in gold and silver papers and a glass vase in which stood some tall celery stalks. In the centre of the table there stood, as sentries to a fruit-stand which upheld a pyramid of oranges and American apples, two squat old-fashioned decanters of cut glass, one containing port and the other dark sherry. On the closed square piano a pudding in a huge yellow dish lay in waiting and behind it were three squads of bottles of stout and ale and minerals, drawn up according to the colours of their uniforms, the first two black, with brown and red labels, the third and smallest squad white, with transverse green sashes.

Gabriel took his seat boldly at the head of the table and, having looked to the edge of the carver, plunged his fork firmly into the goose. He felt quite at ease now for he was an expert carver and liked nothing better than to find himself at the head of a well-laden table.

—Miss Furlong, what shall I send you? he asked. A wing or a slice of the breast?

—Just a small slice of the breast.

—Miss Higgins, what for you?

—O, anything at all, Mr Conroy.

While Gabriel and Miss Daly exchanged plates of goose and plates of ham and spiced beef Lily went from guest to guest with a dish of hot floury potatoes wrapped in a white napkin. This was Mary Jane's idea and she had also suggested apple sauce for the goose but Aunt Kate had said that plain roast goose without apple sauce had always been good enough for her and she hoped she might never eat worse. Mary Jane waited on her pupils and saw that they got the best slices and Aunt Kate and Aunt Julia opened and carried across from the piano bottles of stout and ale for the gentlemen and bottles of minerals for the ladies. There was a great deal of confusion and laughter and noise, the noise of orders and counter-orders, of knives and forks, of corks and glass-stoppers. Gabriel began to carve second helpings as soon as he had finished the first round without serving himself. Everyone protested loudly so that he

6. Farewell (Irish).

compromised by taking a long draught of stout for he had found the carving hot work. Mary Jane settled down quietly to her supper but Aunt Kate and Aunt Julia were still toddling round the table, walking on each other's heels, getting in each other's way and giving each other unheeded orders. Mr Browne begged of them to sit down and eat their suppers and so did Gabriel but they said there was time enough so that, at last, Freddy Malins stood up and, capturing Aunt Kate, plumped her down on her chair amid general laughter.

When everyone had been well served Gabriel said, smiling:

—Now, if anyone wants a little more of what vulgar people call stuffing let him or her speak.

A chorus of voices invited him to begin his own supper and Lily came forward with three potatoes which she had reserved for him.

—Very well, said Gabriel amiably, as he took another preparatory draught, kindly forget my existence, ladies and gentlemen, for a few minutes.

He set to his supper and took no part in the conversation with which the table covered Lily's removal of the plates. The subject of talk was the opera company which was then at the Theatre Royal. Mr Bartell D'Arcy, the tenor, a dark-complexioned young man with a smart moustache, praised very highly the leading contralto of the company but Miss Furlong thought she had a rather vulgar style of production. Freddy Malins said there was a negro chieftain singing in the second part of the Gaiety pantomime who had one of the finest tenor voices he had ever heard.

—Have you heard him? he asked Mr Bartell D'Arcy across the table.

—No, answered Mr Bartell D'Arcy carelessly.

—Because, Freddy Malins explained, now I'd be curious to hear your opinion of him. I think he has a grand voice.

—It takes Teddy to find out the really good things, said Mr Browne familiarly to the table.

—And why couldn't he have a voice too? asked Freddy Malins sharply. Is it because he's only a black?

Nobody answered this question and Mary Jane led the table back to the legitimate opera. One of her pupils had given her a pass for *Mignon*. Of course it was very fine, she said, but it made her think of poor Georgina Burns. Mr Browne could go back farther still, to the old Italian companies that used to come to Dublin—Tietjens, Ilma de Murzka, Campanini, the great Trebelli, Giuglini, Ravelli, Aramburo.[7] Those were the days, he said, when there was something like singing to be heard in Dublin. He told too of how the top gallery of the old Royal used to be packed night after night, of how one night an Italian tenor had sung five encores to *Let Me Like a Soldier Fall*, introducing a high C every time, and of how the gallery boys would sometimes in their enthusiasm unyoke the horses from the carriage of some great *prima donna* and pull her themselves through the streets to her hotel. Why did they never play the grand old operas now, he asked, *Dinorah*, *Lucrezia Borgia?* Because they could not get the voices to sing them: that was why.

—O, well, said Mr Bartell D'Arcy, I presume there are as good singers to-day as there were then.

—Where are they? asked Mr Browne defiantly.

—In London, Paris, Milan, said Mr Bartell D'Arcy warmly. I suppose Caruso,[8] for example, is quite as good, if not better than any of the men you have mentioned.

---

7. Famous 19th-century operatic singers.   8. Enrico Caruso (1874–1921), a famous tenor.

—Maybe so, said Mr Browne. But I may tell you I doubt it strongly.

—O, I'd give anything to hear Caruso sing, said Mary Jane.

—For me, said Aunt Kate, who had been picking a bone, there was only one tenor. To please me, I mean. But I suppose none of you ever heard of him.

—Who was he, Miss Morkan? asked Mr Bartell D'Arcy politely.

—His name, said Aunt Kate, was Parkinson. I heard him when he was in his prime and I think he had then the purest tenor voice that was ever put into a man's throat.

—Strange, said Mr Bartell D'Arcy. I never even heard of him.

—Yes, yes, Miss Morkan is right, said Mr Browne. I remember hearing of old Parkinson but he's too far back for me.

—A beautiful pure sweet mellow English tenor, said Aunt Kate with enthusiasm.

Gabriel having finished, the huge pudding was transferred to the table. The clatter of forks and spoons began again. Gabriel's wife served out spoonfuls of the pudding and passed the plates down the table. Midway down they were held up by Mary Jane, who replenished them with raspberry or orange jelly or with blancmange and jam. The pudding was of Aunt Julia's making and she received praises for it from all quarters. She herself said that it was not quite brown enough.

—Well, I hope, Miss Morkan, said Mr Browne, that I'm brown enough for you because, you know, I'm all brown.

All the gentlemen, except Gabriel, ate some of the pudding out of compliment to Aunt Julia. As Gabriel never ate sweets the celery had been left for him. Freddy Malins also took a stalk of celery and ate it with his pudding. He had been told that celery was a capital thing for the blood and he was just then under doctor's care. Mrs Malins, who had been silent all through the supper, said that her son was going down to Mount Melleray[9] in a week or so. The table then spoke to Mount Melleray, how bracing the air was down there, how hospitable the monks were and how they never asked for a penny-piece from their guests.

—And do you mean to say, asked Mr Browne incredulously, that a chap can go down there and put up there as if it were a hotel and live on the fat of the land and then come away without paying a farthing?

—O, most people give some donation to the monastery when they leave, said Mary Jane.

—I wish we had an institution like that in our Church, said Mr Browne candidly.

He was astonished to hear that the monks never spoke, got up at two in the morning and slept in their coffins. He asked what they did it for.

—That's the rule of the order, said Aunt Kate firmly.

—Yes, but why? asked Mr Browne.

Aunt Kate repeated that it was the rule, that was all. Mr Browne still seemed not to understand. Freddy Malins explained to him, as best he could, that the monks were trying to make up for the sins committed by all the sinners in the outside world. The explanation was not very clear for Mr Browne grinned and said:

—I like that idea very much but wouldn't a comfortable spring bed do them as well as a coffin?

—The coffin, said Mary Jane, is to remind them of their last end.

As the subject had grown lugubrious it was buried in a silence of the table during which Mrs Malins could be heard saying to her neighbour in an indistinct undertone:

—They are very good men, the monks, very pious men.

---

9. Site of a Trappist monastery in the south of Ireland.

The raisins and almonds and figs and apples and oranges and chocolates and sweets were now passed about the table and Aunt Julia invited all the guests to have either port or sherry. At first Mr Bartell D'Arcy refused to take either but one of his neighbours nudged him and whispered something to him upon which he allowed his glass to be filled. Gradually as the last glasses were being filled the conversation ceased. A pause followed, broken only by the noise of the wine and by unsettlings of chairs. The Misses Morkan, all three, looked down at the tablecloth. Someone coughed once or twice and then a few gentlemen patted the table gently as a signal for silence. The silence came and Gabriel pushed back his chair and stood up.

The patting at once grew louder in encouragement and then ceased altogether. Gabriel leaned his ten trembling fingers on the tablecloth and smiled nervously at the company. Meeting a row of upturned faces he raised his eyes to the chandelier. The piano was playing a waltz tune and he could hear the skirts sweeping against the drawing-room door. People, perhaps, were standing in the snow on the quay outside, gazing up at the lighted windows and listening to the waltz music. The air was pure there. In the distance lay the park where the trees were weighted with snow. The Wellington Monument wore a gleaming cap of snow that flashed westward over the white field of Fifteen Acres.[1]

He began:

—Ladies and Gentlemen.

—It has fallen to my lot this evening, as in years past, to perform a very pleasing task but a task for which I am afraid my poor powers as a speaker are all too inadequate.

—No, no! said Mr Browne.

—But, however that may be, I can only ask you tonight to take the will for the deed and to lend me your attention for a few moments while I endeavour to express to you in words what my feelings are on this occasion.

—Ladies and Gentlemen. It is not the first time that we have gathered together under this hospitable roof, around this hospitable board. It is not the first time that we have been the recipients—or perhaps, I had better say, the victims—of the hospitality of certain good ladies.

He made a circle in the air with his arm and paused. Everyone laughed or smiled at Aunt Kate and Aunt Julia and Mary Jane who all turned crimson with pleasure. Gabriel went on more boldly:

—I feel more strongly with every recurring year that our country has no tradition which does it so much honour and which it should guard so jealously as that of its hospitality. It is a tradition that is unique as far as my experience goes (and I have visited not a few places abroad) among the modern nations. Some would say, perhaps, that with us it is rather a failing than anything to be boasted of. But granted even that, it is, to my mind, a princely failing, and one that I trust will long be cultivated among us. Of one thing, at least, I am sure. As long as this one roof shelters the good ladies aforesaid—and I wish from my heart it may do so for many and many a long year to come—the tradition of genuine warm-hearted courteous Irish hospitality, which our forefathers have handed down to us and which we in turn must hand down to our descendants, is still alive among us.

A hearty murmur of assent ran round the table. It shot through Gabriel's mind that Miss Ivors was not there and that she had gone away discourteously: and he said with confidence in himself:

1. A section of Phoenix Park.

—Ladies and Gentlemen.

—A new generation is growing up in our midst, a generation actuated by new ideas and new principles. It is serious and enthusiastic for these new ideas and its enthusiasm, even when it is misdirected, is, I believe, in the main sincere. But we are living in a sceptical and, if I may use the phrase, a thought-tormented age: and sometimes I fear that this new generation, educated or hypereducated as it is, will lack those qualities of humanity, of hospitality, of kindly humour which belonged to an older day. Listening to-night to the names of all those great singers of the past it seemed to me, I must confess, that we were living in a less spacious age. Those days might, without exaggeration, be called spacious days: and if they are gone beyond recall let us hope, at least, that in gatherings such as this we shall still speak of them with pride and affection, still cherish in our hearts the memory of those dead and gone great ones whose fame the world will not willingly let die.

—Hear, hear! said Mr Browne loudly.

—But yet, continued Gabriel, his voice falling into a softer inflection, there are always in gatherings such as this sadder thoughts that will recur to our minds: thoughts of the past, of youth, of changes, of absent faces that we miss here to-night. Our path through life is strewn with many such sad memories: and were we to brood upon them always we could not find the heart to go on bravely with our work among the living. We have all of us living duties and living affections which claim, and rightly claim, our strenuous endeavours.

—Therefore, I will not linger on the past. I will not let any gloomy moralising intrude upon us here to-night. Here we are gathered together for a brief moment from the bustle and rush of our everyday routine. We are met here as friends, in the spirit of good-fellowship, as colleagues, also to a certain extent, in the true spirit of camaraderie, and as the guests of—what shall I call them?—the Three Graces[2] of the Dublin musical world.

The table burst into applause and laughter at this sally. Aunt Julia vainly asked each of her neighbors in turn to tell her what Gabriel had said.

—He says we are the Three Graces, Aunt Julia, said Mary Jane.

Aunt Julia did not understand but she looked up, smiling, at Gabriel, who continued in the same vein:

—Ladies and Gentlemen.

—I will not attempt to play to-night the part that Paris[3] played on another occasion. I will not attempt to choose between them. The task would be an invidious one and one beyond my poor powers. For when I view them in turn, whether it be our chief hostess herself, whose good heart, whose too good heart, has become a byword with all who know her, or her sister, who seems to be gifted with perennial youth and whose singing must have been a surprise and a revelation to us all to-night, or, last but not least, when I consider our youngest hostess, talented, cheerful, hard-working and the best of nieces, I confess, Ladies and Gentlemen, that I do not know to which of them I should award the prize.

Gabriel glanced down at his aunts and, seeing the large smile on Aunt Julia's face and the tears which had risen to Aunt Kate's eyes, hastened to his close. He raised his glass of port gallantly, while every member of the company fingered a glass expectantly, and said loudly:

2. Companions to the Muses in Greek mythology.
3. Paris was the judge of a divine beauty contest in which

Hera, Athena, and Aphrodite competed; his selection of Aphrodite was, indirectly, the cause of the Trojan war.

—Let us toast them all three together. Let us drink to their health, wealth, long life, happiness and prosperity and may they long continue to hold the proud and self-won position which they hold in their profession and the position of honour and affection which they hold in our hearts.

All the guests stood up, glass in hand, and, turning towards the three seated ladies, sang in unison, with Mr Browne as leader:

> *For they are jolly gay fellows,*
> *For they are jolly gay fellows,*
> *For they are jolly gay fellows,*
> *Which nobody can deny.*

Aunt Kate was making frank use of her handkerchief and even Aunt Julia seemed moved. Freddy Malins beat time with his pudding-fork and the singers turned towards one another, as if in melodious conference, while they sang, with emphasis:

> *Unless he tells a lie,*
> *Unless he tells a lie.*

Then, turning once more towards their hostesses, they sang:

> *For they are jolly gay fellows,*
> *For they are jolly gay fellows,*
> *For they are jolly gay fellows,*
> *Which nobody can deny.*

The acclamation which followed was taken up beyond the door of the supper-room by many of the other guests and renewed time after time, Freddy Malins acting as officer with his fork on high.

The piercing morning air came into the hall where they were standing so that Aunt Kate said:

—Close the door, somebody. Mrs Malins will get her death of cold.

—Browne is out there, Aunt Kate, said Mary Jane.

—Browne is everywhere, said Aunt Kate, lowering her voice.

Mary Jane laughed at her tone.

—Really, she said archly, he is very attentive.

—He has been laid on here like the gas, said Aunt Kate in the same tone, all during the Christmas.

She laughed herself this time good-humouredly and then added quickly:

—But tell him to come in, Mary Jane, and close the door. I hope to goodness he didn't hear me.

At that moment the hall-door was opened and Mr Browne came in from the doorstep, laughing as if his heart would break. He was dressed in a long green over-coat with mock astrakhan cuffs and collar and wore on his head an oval fur cap. He pointed down the snow-covered quay from where the sound of shrill prolonged whistling was borne in.

—Teddy will have all the cabs in Dublin out, he said.

Gabriel advanced from the little pantry behind the office, struggling into his overcoat and looking round the hall, said:

—Gretta not down yet?

—She's getting on her things, Gabriel, said Aunt Kate.

—Who's playing up there? asked Gabriel.

—Nobody. They're all gone.

—O no, Aunt Kate, said Mary Jane. Bartell D'Arcy and Miss O'Callaghan aren't gone yet.

—Someone is strumming at the piano, anyhow, said Gabriel.

Mary Jane glanced at Gabriel and Mr Browne and said with a shiver:

—It makes me feel cold to look at you two gentlemen muffled up like that. I wouldn't like to face your journey home at this hour.

—I'd like nothing better this minute, said Mr Browne stoutly, than a rattling fine walk in the country or a fast drive with a good spanking goer between the shafts.

—We used to have a very good horse and trap at home, said Aunt Julia sadly.

—The never-to-be-forgotten Johnny, said Mary Jane, laughing.

Aunt Kate and Gabriel laughed too.

—Why, what was wonderful about Johnny? asked Mr Browne.

—The late lamented Patrick Morkan, our grandfather, that is, explained Gabriel, commonly known in his later years as the old gentleman, was a glue-boiler.

—O, now, Gabriel, said Aunt Kate, laughing, he had a starch mill.

—Well, glue or starch, said Gabriel, the old gentleman had a horse by the name of Johnny. And Johnny used to work in the old gentleman's mill, walking round and round in order to drive the mill. That was all very well; but now comes the tragic part about Johnny. One fine day the old gentleman thought he'd like to drive out with the quality to a military review in the park.

—The Lord have mercy on his soul, said Aunt Kate compassionately.

—Amen, said Gabriel. So the old gentleman, as I said, harnessed Johnny and put on his very best tall hat and his very best stock collar and drove out in grand style from his ancestral mansion somewhere near Back Lane, I think.

Everyone laughed, even Mrs Malins, at Gabriel's manner and Aunt Kate said:

—O now, Gabriel, he didn't live in Back Lane, really. Only the mill was there.

—Out from the mansion of his forefathers, continued Gabriel, he drove with Johnny. And everything went on beautifully until Johnny came in sight of King Billy's statue:[4] and whether he fell in love with the horse King Billy sits on or whether he thought he was back again in the mill, anyhow he began to walk round the statue.

Gabriel paced in a circle round the hall in his goloshes amid the laughter of the others.

—Round and round he went, said Gabriel, and the old gentleman, who was a very pompous old gentleman, was highly indignant. *Go on, sir! What do you mean, sir! Johnny! Johnny! Most extraordinary conduct! Can't understand the horse!*

The peals of laughter which followed Gabriel's imitation of the incident were interrupted by a resounding knock at the hall-door. Mary Jane ran to open it and let in Freddy Malins. Freddy Malins, with his hat well back on his head and his shoulders humped with cold, was puffing and steaming after his exertions.

—I could only get one cab, he said.

—O, we'll find another along the quay, said Gabriel.

—Yes, said Aunt Kate. Better not keep Mrs Malins standing in the draught.

Mrs Malins was helped down the front steps by her son and Mr Browne and, after many manoeuvres, hoisted into the cab. Freddy Malins clambered in after her and spent a long time settling her on the seat, Mr Browne helping him with advice.

4. Statue of William of Orange, who defeated the Irish Catholic forces in the Battle of the Boyne in 1690, which stood in College Green in front of Trinity College in the heart of Dublin. It was seen as a symbol of British imperial oppression.

At last she was settled comfortably and Freddy Malins invited Mr Browne into the cab. There was a good deal of confused talk, and then Mr Browne got into the cab. The cabman settled his rug over his knees, and bent down for the address. The confusion grew greater and the cabman was directed differently by Freddy Malins and Mr Browne, each of whom had his head out through a window of the cab. The difficulty was to know where to drop Mr Browne along the route and Aunt Kate, Aunt Julia and Mary Jane helped the discussion from the doorstep with cross-directions and contradictions and abundance of laughter. As for Freddy Malins he was speechless with laughter. He popped his head in and out of the window every moment, to the great danger of his hat, and told his mother how the discussion was progressing till at last Mr Browne shouted to the bewildered cabman above the din of everybody's laughter:

—Do you know Trinity College?

—Yes, sir, said the cabman.

—Well, drive bang up against Trinity College gates, said Mr Browne, and then we'll tell you where to go. You understand now?

—Yes, sir, said the cabman.

—Make like a bird for Trinity College.

—Right, sir, cried the cabman.

The horse was whipped up and the cab rattled off along the quay amid a chorus of laughter and adieus.

Gabriel had not gone to the door with the others. He was in a dark part of the hall gazing up the staircase, a woman was standing near the top of the first flight, in the shadow also. He could not see her face but he could see the terracotta and salmonpink panels of her skirt which the shadow made appear black and white. It was his wife. She was leaning on the banisters, listening to something. Gabriel was surprised at her stillness and strained his ear to listen also. But he could hear little save the noise of laughter and dispute on the front steps, a few chords struck on the piano and a few notes of a man's voice singing.

He stood still in the gloom of the hall, trying to catch the air that the voice was singing and gazing up at his wife. There was grace and mystery in her attitude as if she were a symbol of something. He asked himself what is a woman standing on the stairs in the shadow, listening to distant music, a symbol of. If he were a painter he would paint her in that attitude. Her blue felt hat would show off the bronze of her hair against the darkness and the dark panels of her skirt would show off the light ones. *Distant Music* he would call the picture if he were a painter.

The hall-door was closed; and Aunt Kate, Aunt Julia and Mary Jane came down the hall, still laughing.

—Well, isn't Freddy terrible? said Mary Jane. He's really terrible.

Gabriel said nothing but pointed up the stairs towards where his wife was standing. Now that the hall-door was closed the voice and the piano could be heard more clearly. Gabriel held up his hand for them to be silent. The song seemed to be in the old Irish tonality and the singer seemed uncertain both of his words and of his voice. The voice, made plaintive by distance and by the singer's hoarseness, faintly illuminated the cadence of the air with words expressing grief:

> O, the rain falls on my heavy locks
> And the dew wets my skin,
> My babe lies cold . . .

—O, exclaimed Mary Jane. It's Bartell D'Arcy singing and he wouldn't sing all the night. O, I'll get him to sing a song before he goes.

—O do, Mary Jane, said Aunt Kate.

Mary Jane brushed past the others and ran to the staircase but before she reached it the singing stopped and the piano was closed abruptly.

—O, what a pity! she cried. Is he coming down, Gretta?

Gabriel heard his wife answer yes and saw her come down towards them. A few steps behind her were Mr Bartell D'Arcy and Miss O'Callaghan.

—O, Mr D'Arcy, cried Mary Jane, it's downright mean of you to break off like that when we were all in raptures listening to you.

—I have been at him all the evening, said Miss O'Callaghan, and Mrs Conroy too and he told us he had a dreadful cold and couldn't sing.

—O, Mr D'Arcy, said Aunt Kate, now that was a great fib to tell.

—Can't you see that I'm as hoarse as a crow? said Mr D'Arcy roughly.

He went into the pantry hastily and put on his overcoat. The others, taken aback by his rude speech, could find nothing to say. Aunt Kate wrinkled her brows and made signs to the others to drop the subject. Mr D'Arcy stood swathing his neck carefully and frowning.

—It's the weather, said Aunt Julia, after a pause.

—Yes, everybody has colds, said Aunt Kate readily, everybody.

—They say, said Mary Jane, we haven't had snow like it for thirty years; and I read this morning in the newspapers that the snow is general all over Ireland.

—I love the look of snow, said Aunt Julia sadly.

—So do I, said Miss O'Callaghan. I think Christmas is never really Christmas unless we have the snow on the ground.

—But poor Mr D'Arcy doesn't like the snow, said Aunt Kate, smiling.

Mr D'Arcy came from the pantry, full swathed and buttoned, and in a repentant tone told them the history of his cold. Everyone gave him advice and said it was a great pity and urged him to be very careful of his throat in the night air. Gabriel watched his wife who did not join in the conversation. She was standing right under the dusty fanlight and the flame of the gas lit up the rich bronze of her hair which he had seen her drying at the fire a few days before. She was in the same attitude and seemed unaware of the talk about her. At last she turned towards them and Gabriel saw that there was colour on her cheeks and that her eyes were shining. A sudden tide of joy went leaping out of his heart.

—Mr D'Arcy, she said, what is the name of that song you were singing?

—It's called The Lass of Aughrim, said Mr D'Arcy, but I couldn't remember it properly. Why? Do you know it?

—The Lass of Aughrim, she repeated. I couldn't think of the name.

—It's a very nice air, said Mary Jane. I'm sorry you were not in voice to-night.

—Now, Mary Jane, said Aunt Kate, don't annoy Mr D'Arcy. I won't have him annoyed.

Seeing that all were ready to start she shepherded them to the door where good-night was said:

—Well, good-night, Aunt Kate, and thanks for the pleasant evening.

—Good-night, Gabriel. Good-night, Gretta!

—Good-night, Aunt Kate, and thanks ever so much. Good-night, Aunt Julia.

—O, good-night, Gretta, I didn't see you.

—Good-night, Mr D'Arcy. Good-night, Miss O'Callaghan.

—Good-night, Miss Morkan.

—Good-night, again.

—Good-night, all. Safe home.

—Good-night. Good-night.

The morning was still dark. A dull yellow light brooded over the houses and the river; and the sky seemed to be descending. It was slushy underfoot; and only streaks and patches of snow lay on the roofs, on the parapets of the quay and on the area railings. The lamps were still burning redly in the murky air and, across the river, the palace of the Four Courts[5] stood out menacingly against the heavy sky.

She was walking on before him with Mr Bartell D'Arcy, her shoes in a brown parcel tucked under one arm and her hands holding her skirt up from the slush. She had no longer any grace of attitude but Gabriel's eyes were still bright with happiness. The blood went bounding along his veins; and the thoughts went rioting through his brain, proud, joyful, tender, valorous.

She was walking on before him so lightly and so erect that he longed to run after her noiselessly, catch her by the shoulders and say something foolish and affectionate into her ear. She seemed to him so frail that he longed to defend her against something and then to be alone with her. Moments of their secret life together burst like stars upon his memory. A heliotrope envelope was lying beside his breakfast-cup and he was caressing it with his hand. Birds were twittering in the ivy and the sunny web of the curtain was shimmering along the floor: he could not eat for happiness. They were standing on the crowded platform and he was placing a ticket inside the warm palm of her glove. He was standing with her in the cold, looking in through a grated window at a man making bottles in a roaring furnace. It was very cold. Her face, fragrant in the cold air, was quite close to his; and suddenly she called out to the man at the furnace:

—Is the fire hot, sir?

But the man could not hear her with the noise of the furnace. It was just as well. He might have answered rudely.

A wave of yet more tender joy escaped from his heart and went coursing in warm flood along his arteries. Like the tender fires of stars moments of their life together, that no one knew of or would ever know of, broke upon and illumined his memory. He longed to recall to her those moments, to make her forget the years of their dull existence together and remember only their moments of ecstasy. For the years, he felt, had not quenched his soul or hers. Their children, his writing, her household cares had not quenched all their souls' tender fire. In one letter that he had written to her then he had said: *Why is it that words like these seem to me so dull and cold? Is it because there is no word tender enough to be your name?*

Like distant music these words that he had written years before were borne towards him from the past. He longed to be alone with her. When the others had gone away, when he and she were in their room in the hotel, then they would be alone together. He would call her softly:

—Gretta!

Perhaps she would not hear at once: she would be undressing. Then something in his voice would strike her. She would turn and look at him. . . .

At the corner of Winetavern Street they met a cab. He was glad of its rattling noise as it saved him from conversation. She was looking out of the window and seemed tired. The others spoke only a few words, pointing out some building or

5. The Irish law courts.

street. The horse galloped along wearily under the murky morning sky, dragging his old rattling box after his heels, and Gabriel was again in a cab with her, galloping to catch the boat, galloping to their honeymoon.

As the cab drove across O'Connell Bridge Miss O'Callaghan said:

—They say you never cross O'Connell Bridge without seeing a white horse.

—I see a white man this time, said Gabriel.

—Where? asked Mr Bartell D'Arcy.

Gabriel pointed to the statue, on which lay patches of snow. Then he nodded familiarly to it and waved his hand.

—Good-night, Dan,[6] he said gaily.

When the cab drew up before the hotel Gabriel jumped out and, in spite of Mr Bartell D'Arcy's protest, paid the driver. He gave the man a shilling over his fare. The man saluted and said:

—A prosperous New Year to you, sir.

—The same to you, said Gabriel cordially.

She leaned for a moment on his arm in getting out of the cab and while standing at the curbstone, bidding the others good-night. She leaned lightly on his arm, as lightly as when she had danced with him a few hours before. He had felt proud and happy then, happy that she was his, proud of her grace and wifely carriage. But now, after the kindling again of so many memories, the first touch of her body, musical and strange and perfumed, sent through him a keen pang of lust. Under cover of her silence he pressed her arm closely to his side; and, as they stood at the hotel door, he felt that they had escaped from their lives and duties, escaped from home and friends and run away together with wild and radiant hearts to a new adventure.

An old man was dozing in a great hooded chair in the hall. He lit a candle in the office and went before them to the stairs. They followed him in silence, their feet falling in soft thuds on the thickly carpeted stairs. She mounted the stairs behind the porter, her head bowed in the ascent, her frail shoulders curved as with a burden, her skirt girt tightly about her. He could have flung his arms about her hips and held her still for his arms were trembling with desire to seize her and only the stress of his nails against the palms of his hands held the wild impulse of his body in check. The porter halted on the stairs to settle his guttering candle. They halted too on the steps below him. In the silence Gabriel could hear the falling of the molten wax into the tray and the thumping of his own heart against his ribs.

The porter led them along a corridor and opened a door. Then he set his unstable candle down on a toilet-table and asked at what hour they were to be called in the morning.

—Eight, said Gabriel.

The porter pointed to the tap of the electric-light and began a muttered apology but Gabriel cut him short.

—We don't want any light. We have light enough from the street. And I say, he added, pointing to the candle, you might remove that handsome article, like a good man.

The porter took up his candle again, but slowly for he was surprised by such a novel idea. Then he mumbled good-night and went out. Gabriel shot the lock to.

6. A statue of Daniel O'Connell, 19th-century nationalist leader, stands at the south end of Sackville Street (now called O'Connell Street).

A ghostly light from the street lamp lay in a long shaft from one window to the door. Gabriel threw his overcoat and hat on a couch and crossed the room towards the window. He looked down into the street in order that his emotion might calm a little. Then he turned and leaned against a chest of drawers with his back to the light. She had taken off her hat and cloak and was standing before a large swinging mirror, unhooking her waist. Gabriel paused for a few moments, watching her, and then said:

—Gretta!

She turned away from the mirror slowly and walked along the shaft of light towards him. Her face looked so serious and weary that the words would not pass Gabriel's lips. No, it was not the moment yet.

—You looked tired, he said.

—I am a little, she answered.

—You don't feel ill or weak?

—No, tired: that's all.

She went on to the window and stood there, looking out. Gabriel waited again and then, fearing that diffidence was about to conquer him, he said abruptly:

—By the way, Gretta!

—What is it?

—You know that poor fellow Malins? he said quickly.

—Yes. What about him?

—Well, poor fellow, he's a decent sort of chap after all, continued Gabriel in a false voice. He gave me back that sovereign I lent him and I didn't expect it really. It's a pity he wouldn't keep away from that Browne, because he's not a bad fellow at heart.

He was trembling now with annoyance. Why did she seem so abstracted? He did not know how he could begin. Was she annoyed, too, about something? If she would only turn to him or come to him of her own accord! To take her as she was would be brutal. No, he must see some ardour in her eyes first. He longed to be master of her strange mood.

—When did you lend him the pound? she asked, after a pause.

Gabriel strove to restrain himself from breaking out into brutal language about the sottish Malins and his pound. He longed to cry to her from his soul, to crush her body against his, to overmaster her. But he said:

—O, at Christmas, when he opened that little Christmas-card shop in Henry Street.

He was in such a fever of rage and desire that he did not hear her come from the window. She stood before him for an instant, looking at him strangely. Then, suddenly raising herself on tiptoe and resting her hands lightly on his shoulders, she kissed him.

—You are a very generous person, Gabriel, she said.

Gabriel, trembling with delight at her sudden kiss and at the quaintness of her phrase, put his hands on her hair and began smoothing it back, scarcely touching it with his fingers. The washing had made it fine and brilliant. His heart was brimming over with happiness. Just when he was wishing for it she had come to him of her own accord. Perhaps her thoughts had been running with his. Perhaps she had felt the impetuous desire that was in him and then the yielding mood had come upon her. Now that she had fallen to him so easily he wondered why he had been so diffident.

He stood, holding her head between his hands. Then, slipping one arm swiftly about her body and drawing her towards him, he said softly:

—Gretta dear, what are you thinking about?

She did not answer nor yield wholly to his arm. He said again, softly:

—Tell me what it is, Gretta. I think I know what is the matter. Do I know?

She did not answer at once. Then she said in an outburst of tears:

—O, I am thinking about that song, *The Lass of Aughrim*.

She broke loose from him and ran to the bed and, throwing her arms across the bed-rail, hid her face. Gabriel stood stock-still for a moment in astonishment and then followed her. As he passed in the way of the cheval-glass he caught sight of himself in full length, his broad, well-filled shirt-front, the face whose expression always puzzled him when he saw it in a mirror and his glimmering gilt-rimmed eyeglasses. He halted a few paces from her and said:

—What about the song? Why does that make you cry?

She raised her head from her arms and dried her eyes with the back of her hand like a child. A kinder note than he had intended went into his voice.

—Why, Gretta? he asked.

—I am thinking about a person long ago who used to sing that song.

—And who was the person long ago? asked Gabriel, smiling.

—It was a person I used to know in Galway when I was living with my grandmother, she said.

The smile passed away from Gabriel's face. A dull anger began to gather again at the back of his mind and the dull fires of his lust began to glow angrily in his veins.

—Someone you were in love with? he asked ironically.

—It was a young boy I used to know, she answered, named Michael Furey. He used to sing that song, *The Lass of Aughrim*. He was very delicate.

Gabriel was silent. He did not wish her to think that he was interested in this delicate boy.

—I can see him so plainly, she said after a moment. Such eyes as he had: big dark eyes! And such an expression in them—an expression!

—O then, you were in love with him? said Gabriel.

—I used to go out walking with him, she said, when I was in Galway.

A thought flew across Gabriel's mind.

—Perhaps that was why you wanted to go to Galway with that Ivors girl? he said coldly.

She looked at him and asked in surprise:

—What for?

Her eyes made Gabriel feel awkward. He shrugged his shoulders and said:

—How do I know? To see him perhaps.

She looked away from him along the shaft of light towards the window in silence.

—He is dead, she said at length. He died when he was only seventeen. Isn't it a terrible thing to die so young as that?

—What was he? asked Gabriel, still ironically.

—He was in the gasworks, she said.

Gabriel felt humiliated by the failure of his irony and by the evocation of this figure from the dead, a boy in the gasworks. While he had been full of memories of their secret life together, full of tenderness and joy and desire, she had been comparing him in her mind with another. A shameful consciousness of his own person assailed him. He saw himself as a ludicrous figure, acting as a pennyboy[7] for his aunts,

---

7. Errand boy.

a nervous well-meaning sentimentalist, orating to vulgarians and idealising his own clownish lusts, the pitiable fatuous fellow he had caught a glimpse of in the mirror. Instinctively he turned his back more to the light lest she might see the shame that burned upon his forehead.

He tried to keep up his tone of cold interrogation but his voice when he spoke was humble and indifferent.

—I suppose you were in love with this Michael Furey, Gretta, he said.

—I was great with him at that time, she said.

Her voice was veiled and sad. Gabriel, feeling now how vain it would be to try to lead her whither he had purposed, caressed one of her hands and said, also sadly:

—And what did he die of so young, Gretta? Consumption, was it?

—I think he died for me, she answered.[8]

A vague terror seized Gabriel at this answer as if, at that hour when he had hoped to triumph, some impalpable and vindictive being was coming against him, gathering forces against him in its vague world. But he shook himself free of it with an effort of reason and continued to caress her hand. He did not question her again for he felt that she would tell him of herself. Her hand was warm and moist: it did not respond to his touch but he continued to caress it just as he had caressed her first letter to him that spring morning.

—It was in the winter, she said, about the beginning of the winter when I was going to leave my grandmother's and come up here to the convent. And he was ill at the time in his lodgings in Galway and wouldn't be let out and his people in Oughterard[9] were written to. He was in decline, they said, or something like that. I never knew rightly.

She paused for a moment and sighed.

—Poor fellow, she said. He was very fond of me and he was such a gentle boy. We used to go out together, walking, you know, Gabriel, like the way they do in the country. He was going to study singing only for his health. He had a very good voice, poor Michael Furey.

—Well; and then? asked Gabriel.

—And then when it came to the time for me to leave Galway and come up to the convent he was much worse and I wouldn't be let see him so I wrote a letter saying I was going up to Dublin and would be back in the summer and hoping he would be better then.

She paused for a moment to get her voice under control and then went on:

—Then the night before I left I was in my grandmother's house in Nuns' Island, packing up, and I heard gravel thrown up against the window. The window was so wet I couldn't see so I ran downstairs as I was and slipped out the back into the garden and there was the poor fellow at the end of the garden, shivering.

—And did you not tell him to go back? asked Gabriel.

—I implored him to go home at once and told him he would get his death in the rain. But he said he did not want to live. I can see his eyes as well as well! He was standing at the end of the wall where there was a tree.

—And did he go home? asked Gabriel.

---

8. Gretta here echoes the words of Yeats's Cathleen ni Houlihan: "Singing I am about a man I knew one time, yellow-haired Donough that was hanged in Galway. . . . He died for love of me: many a man has died for love of me." The play was first performed in Dublin on 2 April 1902.

9. A small village in Western Ireland.

—Yes, he went home. And when I was only a week in the convent he died and he was buried in Oughterard where his people came from. O, the day I heard that, that he was dead!

She stopped, choking with sobs, and, overcome by emotion, flung herself face downward on the bed, sobbing in the quilt. Gabriel held her hand for a moment longer, irresolutely, and then, shy of intruding on her grief, let it fall gently and walked quietly to the window.

She was fast asleep.

Gabriel, leaning on his elbow, looked for a few moments unresentfully on her tangled hair and half-open mouth, listening to her deep-drawn breath. So she had had that romance in her life: a man had died for her sake. It hardly pained him now to think how poor a part he, her husband, had played in her life. He watched her while she slept as though he and she had never lived together as man and wife. His curious eyes rested long upon her face and on her hair: and, as he thought of what she must have been then, in that time of her first girlish beauty, a strange friendly pity for her entered his soul. He did not like to say even to himself that her face was no longer beautiful but he knew that it was no longer the face for which Michael Furey had braved death.

Perhaps she had not told him all the story. His eyes moved to the chair over which she had thrown some of her clothes. A petticoat string dangled to the floor. One boot stood upright, its limp upper fallen down: the fellow of it lay upon its side. He wondered at his riot of emotions of an hour before. From what had it proceeded? From his aunt's supper, from his own foolish speech, from the wine and dancing, the merry-making when saying good-night in the hall, the pleasure of the walk along the river in the snow. Poor Aunt Julia! She, too, would soon be a shade with the shade of Patrick Morkan and his horse. He had caught that haggard look upon her face for a moment when she was singing *Arrayed for the Bridal*. Soon, perhaps, he would be sitting in that same drawing-room, dressed in black, his silk hat on his knees. The blinds would be drawn down and Aunt Kate would be sitting beside him, crying and blowing her nose and telling him how Julia had died. He would cast about in his mind for some words that might console her, and would find only lame and useless ones. Yes, yes: that would happen very soon.

The air of the room chilled his shoulders. He stretched himself cautiously along under the sheets and lay down beside his wife. One by one they were all becoming shades. Better pass boldly into that other world, in the full glory of some passion, than fade and wither dismally with age. He thought of how she who lay beside him had locked in her heart for so many years that image of her lover's eyes when he had told her that he did not wish to live.

Generous tears filled Gabriel's eyes. He had never felt like that himself towards any woman but he knew that such a feeling must be love. The tears gathered more thickly in his eyes and in the partial darkness he imagined he saw the form of a young man standing under a dripping tree. Other forms were near. His soul had approached that region where dwell the vast hosts of the dead. He was conscious of, but could not apprehend, their wayward and flickering existence. His own identity was fading out into a grey impalpable world: the solid world itself which these dead had one time reared and lived in was dissolving and dwindling.

A few light taps upon the pane made him turn to the window. It had begun to snow again. He watched sleepily the flakes, silver and dark, falling obliquely against the lamplight. The time had come for him to set out on his journey westward. Yes, the newspapers were right: snow was general all over Ireland. It was falling on every part of the dark central plain, on the treeless hills, falling softly upon the Bog of Allen and, farther westward, softly falling into the dark mutinous Shannon waves.[1] It was falling, too, upon every part of the lonely churchyard on the hill where Michael Furey lay buried. It lay thickly drifted on the crooked crosses and headstones, on the spears of the little gate, on the barren thorns. His soul swooned slowly as he heard the snow falling faintly through the universe and faintly falling, like the descent of their last end, upon all the living and the dead.

Ulysses

Ulysses boldly announced that modern literature had set itself new tasks and devised new means to "make it new." In his review of the novel, T. S. Eliot wrote that Joyce had discovered "a way of controlling, of ordering, of giving a shape and a significance to the panorama of futility and anarchy which is contemporary history. . . . It is, I seriously believe, a step toward making the modern world possible for art . . . ." The technique with which Joyce shaped his materials Eliot called (at Joyce's suggestion) the mythical method—using ancient myth to suggest "a continuous parallel between contemporaneity and antiquity." Joyce's purposes in using myth—in the case of *Ulysses,* a series of parallels to Homer's *Odyssey*—are open to debate; but he was quite frank about the fact that each of the novel's eighteen chapters was modeled, however loosely, on one of Odysseus's adventures. Thus Leopold Bloom, the novel's advertising-salesman protagonist, is in some sense a modern-day Odysseus; rather than finding his way back from Troy and the Trojan Wars, he simply navigates his way through a very full day in Dublin on June 16, 1904. This day, however, has its perils. Bloom, a Jew, is set upon by anti-Semites, threatened with violence, and driven from the pub where he drinks; much later, in Dublin's red-light district, he rescues a very drunk young poet, Stephen Dedalus, from arrest, and takes him back to his home for a cup of cocoa and conversation. Foremost among Bloom's tests on this particular day, however, is his knowledge that his wife Molly will consummate an affair with the brash, egotistical tenor Blazes Boylan—an affair which, owing to his own shortcomings as a husband, Bloom is unwilling to stop.

The chapter given here is the pivotal seventh chapter, in which the realism of the earlier chapters begins to be invaded by other modes of observation and narration. Set in the offices of the *Freeman's Journal* where Bloom works, the chapter takes on a parodoxically reportorial perspective, complete with headlines. Chapter 7 is usually called the "Aeolus" chapter, after its parallel episode in the *Odyssey.* In Book 10, having escaped the Cyclops, Odysseus reaches an island ruled by Aeolus, lord of the winds. Aeolus offers to help Odysseus by trapping all ill winds in a bag which Odysseus then takes with him on his ship; when they are within sight of home, however, Odysseus falls asleep and his crew, curious and jealous about what their captain might have stowed in the bag, open it, releasing the winds and driving the crew back to Aeolia. Joyce builds into his chapter myraid references to wind and air in many forms—from arias to belches, and from conversational shooting the breeze to rhetorical hot air. As Bloom tries to do his job, forget about Molly's plans, and find acceptance among co-workers who will always see him as an outsider, he narrowly misses meeting up with Stephen Dedalus. Stephen has come to the newspaper to deliver a letter on hoof and mouth disease, written by the headmaster of the school where he is teaching. This far from exalted errand only increases Stephen's unease as he negotiates the provincial literary and journalistic world of Dublin, looking for ways to free himself, and capture Dublin, in his art.

---

1. Where Ireland's longest river, the Shannon, empties into the sea.

Photo of Sackville Street (now O'Connell Street), Dublin, with view of Nelson's Pillar.

from **Ulysses**

[Chapter 7. Aeolus]

IN THE HEART OF THE HIBERNIAN METROPOLIS

Before Nelson's pillar trams slowed, shunted, changed trolley, started for Blackrock, Kingstown and Dalkey, Clonskea, Rathgar and Terenure, Palmerston Park and upper Rathmines, Sandymount Green, Rathmines, Ringsend, and Sandymount Tower, Harold's Cross.[1] The hoarse Dublin United Tramway Company's timekeeper bawled them off:

— Rathgar and Terenure!

— Come on, Sandymount Green!

Right and left parallel clanging ringing a doubledecker and a singledeck moved from their railheads, swerved to the down line, glided parallel.

— Start, Palmerston Park!

THE WEARER OF THE CROWN

Under the porch of the general post office shoeblacks called and polished. Parked in North Prince's street His Majesty's vermilion mailcars, bearing on their sides the royal initials, E. R.,[2] received loudly flung sacks of letters, postcards, lettercards, parcels, insured and paid, for local, provincial, British and overseas delivery.

---

1. The names of various tramlines going out from Nelson's Pillar in central Dublin.

2. Edward Rex (Edward VII of England).

GENTLEMEN OF THE PRESS

Grossbooted draymen rolled barrels dullthudding out of Prince's stores and bumped them up on the brewery float. On the brewery float bumped dullthudding barrels rolled by grossbooted draymen out of Prince's stores.

—There it is, Red Murray said. Alexander Keyes.

—Just cut it out, will you? Mr Bloom said, and I'll take it round to the *Telegraph* office.

The door of Ruttledge's office creaked again. Davy Stephens, minute in a large capecoat, a small felt hat crowning his ringlets, passed out with a roll of papers under his cape, a king's courier.

Red Murray's long shears sliced out the advertisement from the newspaper in four clean strokes. Scissors and paste.

—I'll go through the printingworks, Mr Bloom said, taking the cut square.

—Of course, if he wants a par,[3] Red Murray said earnestly, a pen behind his ear, we can do him one.

—Right, Mr Bloom said with a nod. I'll rub that in.

We.

WILLIAM BRAYDEN, ESQUIRE, OF OAKLANDS, SANDYMOUNT

Red Murray touched Mr Bloom's arm with the shears and whispered:

—Brayden.[4]

Mr Bloom turned and saw the liveried porter raise his lettered cap as a stately figure entered between the newsboards of the *Weekly Freeman and National Press* and the *Freeman's Journal and National Press*. Dullthudding Guinness's barrels. It passed stately up the staircase steered by an umbrella, a solemn beardframed face. The broadcloth back ascended each step: back. All his brains are in the nape of his neck, Simon Dedalus says. Welts of flesh behind on him. Fat folds of neck, fat, neck, fat, neck.

—Don't you think his face is like Our Saviour? Red Murray whispered.

The door of Ruttledge's office whispered: ee: cree. They always build one door opposite another for the wind to. Way in. Way out.

Our Saviour: beardframed oval face: talking in the dusk. Mary, Martha. Steered by an umbrella sword to the footlights: Mario the tenor.[5]

—Or like Mario, Mr Bloom said.

—Yes, Red Murray agreed. But Mario was said to be the picture of Our Saviour.

Jesus Mario with rougy cheeks, doublet and spindle legs. Hand on his heart. In *Martha*.[6]

> Co-ome thou lost one,
> Co-ome thou dear one

THE CROZIER[7] AND THE PEN

—His grace phoned down twice this morning, Red Murray said gravely.

They watched the knees, legs, boots vanish. Neck.

---

3. A paragraph.
4. Irish barrister (1865–1933) and editor of the *Freeman's Journal*.
5. Giovanni Matteo (1810–1883), known onstage as "Mario."
6. Light opera (1847) by Friedrich von Flotow.
7. Bishop's staff.

A telegram boy stepped in nimbly, threw an envelope on the counter and stepped off posthaste with a word:

—*Freeman!*

Mr Bloom said slowly:

—Well, he is one of our saviours also.

A meek smile accompanied him as he lifted the counterflap, as he passed in through a sidedoor and along the warm dark stairs and passage, along the now reverberating boards. But will he save the circulation? Thumping, thumping.

He pushed in the glass swingdoor and entered, stepping over strewn packing paper. Through a lane of clanking drums he made his way towards Nannetti's reading closet.[8]

Hynes here too: account of the funeral probably. Thumping thump.

WITH UNFEIGNED REGRET IT IS WE ANNOUNCE THE DISSOLUTION OF A MOST RESPECTED DUBLIN BURGESS

This morning the remains of the late Mr Patrick Dignam. Machines. Smash a man to atoms if they got him caught. Rule the world today. His machineries are pegging away too. Like these, got out of hand: fermenting. Working away, tearing away. And that old grey rat tearing to get in.

HOW A GREAT DAILY ORGAN IS TURNED OUT

Mr Bloom halted behind the foreman's spare body, admiring a glossy crown.

Strange he never saw his real country. Ireland my country. Member for College green. He boomed that workaday worker tack for all it was worth. It's the ads and side features sell a weekly not the stale news in the official gazette. Queen Anne is dead. Published by authority in the year one thousand and. Demesne situate in the townland of Rosenallis, barony of Tinnahinch. To all whom it may concern schedule pursuant to statute showing return of number of mules and jennets exported from Ballina. Nature notes. Cartoons. Phil Blake's weekly Pat and Bull story. Uncle Toby's page for tiny tots. Country bumpkin's queries. Dear Mr Editor, what is a good cure for flatulence? I'd like that part. Learn a lot teaching others. The personal note. M. A. P.[9] Mainly all pictures. Shapely bathers on golden strand. World's biggest balloon. Double marriage of sisters celebrated. Two bridegrooms laughing heartily at each other. Cuprani too, printer. More Irish than the Irish.

The machines clanked in threefour time. Thump, thump, thump. Now if he got paralysed there and no one knew how to stop them they'd clank on and on the same, print it over and over and up and back. Monkeydoodle the whole thing. Want a cool head.

—Well, get it into the evening edition, councillor, Hynes said.

Soon be calling him my lord mayor. Long John is backing him, they say.

The foreman, without answering, scribbled press on a corner of the sheet and made a sign to a typesetter. He handed the sheet silently over the dirty glass screen.

—Right: thanks, Hynes said moving off.

Mr Bloom stood in his way.

---

8. Joseph Patrick Nannetti (1851–1915), Irish-Italian printer and politician, a Dublin Member of Parliament.

9. *Mainly About People,* a weekly paper.

—If you want to draw the cashier is just going to lunch, he said, pointing backward with his thumb.

—Did you? Hynes asked.

—Mm, Mr Bloom said. Look sharp and you'll catch him.

—Thanks, old man, Hynes said. I'll tap him too.

He hurried on eagerly towards the *Freeman's Journal*.

Three bob I lent him in Meagher's. Three weeks. Third hint.

WE SEE THE CANVASSER AT WORK

Mr Bloom laid his cutting on Mr Nannetti's desk.

—Excuse me, councillor, he said. This ad, you see. Keyes, you remember.

Mr Nannetti considered the cutting a while and nodded.

—He wants it in for July, Mr Bloom said.

The foreman moved his pencil towards it.

—But wait, Mr Bloom said. He wants it changed. Keyes, you see. He wants two keys at the top.

Hell of a racket they make. He doesn't hear it. Nannan. Iron nerves. Maybe he understands what I.

The foreman turned round to hear patiently and, lifting an elbow, began to scratch slowly in the armpit of his alpaca jacket.

—Like that, Mr Bloom said, crossing his forefingers at the top.

Let him take that in first.

Mr Bloom, glancing sideways up from the cross he had made, saw the foreman's sallow face, think he has a touch of jaundice, and beyond the obedient reels feeding in huge webs of paper. Clank it. Clank it. Miles of it unreeled. What becomes of it after? O, wrap up meat, parcels: various uses, thousand and one things.

Slipping his words deftly into the pauses of the clanking he drew swiftly on the scarred woodwork.

HOUSE OF KEY(E)S

—Like that, see. Two crossed keys here. A circle. Then here the name Alexander Keyes, tea, wine and spirit merchant. So on.

Better not teach him his own business.

—You know yourself, councillor, just what he wants. Then round the top in leaded: the house of keys. You see? Do you think that's a good idea?

The foreman moved his scratching hand to his lower ribs and scratched there quietly.

—The idea, Mr Bloom said, is the house of keys. You know, councillor, the Manx parliament. Innuendo of home rule.[1] Tourists, you know, from the isle of Man. Catches the eye, you see. Can you do that?

I could ask him perhaps about how to pronounce that *voglio*.[2] But then if he didn't know only make it awkward for him. Better not.

1. The House of Keyes is the lower house of the Isle of Man Parliament. The Isle of Man enjoyed Home Rule, which Parnell was trying to win for Ireland.

2. In Mozart's opera *Don Giovanni*, Don Giovanni tries to seduce a peasant girl, Zerlina, on her wedding day. Tempted, Zerlina sings *"voglio e non vorrei"* ("I want to

and I wouldn't like to"). Bloom's wife Molly is rehearsing this song; Bloom worries both that Molly may be mispronouncing the word (the g of *voglio* is silent) and, more importantly, that the line may accurately represent her willingness to enter into an affair with her eager suitor Blazes Boylan.

—We can do that, the foreman said. Have you the design?

—I can get it, Mr Bloom said. It was in a Kilkenny paper. He has a house there too. I'll just run out and ask him. Well, you can do that and just a little par calling attention. You know the usual. Highclass licensed premises. Longfelt want. So on.

The foreman thought for an instant.

—We can do that, he said. Let him give us a three months' renewal.

A typesetter brought him a limp galleypage. He began to check it silently. Mr Bloom stood by, hearing the loud throbs of cranks, watching the silent typesetters at their cases.

ORTHOGRAPHICAL

Want to be sure of his spelling. Proof fever. Martin Cunningham forgot to give us his spellingbee conundrum this morning. It is amusing to view the unpar one ar alleled embarra two ars is it? double ess ment of a harassed pedlar while gauging au the symmetry with a y of a peeled pear under a cemetery wall. Silly, isn't it? Cemetery put in of course on account of the symmetry.

I could have said when he clapped on his topper. Thank you. I ought to have said something about an old hat or something. No, I could have said. Looks as good as new now. See his phiz[3] then.

Sllt. The nethermost deck of the first machine jogged forward its flyboard with sllt the first batch of quirefolded papers. Sllt. Almost human the way it sllt to call attention. Doing its level best to speak. That door too sllt creaking, asking to be shut. Everything speaks in its own way. Sllt.

NOTED CHURCHMAN AN OCCASIONAL CONTRIBUTOR

The foreman handed back the galleypage suddenly, saying:

—Wait. Where's the archbishop's letter? It's to be repeated in the *Telegraph*. Where's what's his name?

He looked about him round his loud unanswering machines.

—Monks, sir? a voice asked from the castingbox.

—Ay. Where's Monks?

—Monks!

Mr Bloom took up his cutting. Time to get out.

—Then I'll get the design, Mr Nannetti, he said, and you'll give it a good place I know.

—Monks!

—Yes, sir.

Three months' renewal. Want to get some wind off my chest first. Try it anyhow. Rub in August: good idea: horseshow month. Ballsbridge. Tourists over for the show.[4]

A DAYFATHER

He walked on through the caseroom, passing an old man, bowed, spectacled, aproned. Old Monks, the dayfather. Queer lot of stuff he must have put through his hands in his time: obituary notices, pubs' ads, speeches, divorce suits, found drowned.

3. Physiognomy; face.
4. An important horse show is held every August in the Royal Dublin Society's showgrounds in the suburb of Ballsbridge.

Nearing the end of his tether now. Sober serious man with a bit in the savingsbank I'd say. Wife a good cook and washer. Daughter working the machine in the parlour. Plain Jane, no damn nonsense.

AND IT WAS THE FEAST OF THE PASSOVER

He stayed in his walk to watch a typesetter neatly distributing type. Reads it backwards first. Quickly he does it. Must require some practice that. mangiD kcirtaP. Poor papa with his hagadah book, reading backwards with his finger to me. Pessach.[5] Next year in Jerusalem. Dear, O dear! All that long business about that brought us out of the land of Egypt and into the house of bondage *alleluia*.[6] *Shema Israel Adonai Elohenu.* No, that's the other.[7] Then the twelve brothers, Jacob's sons. And then the lamb and the cat and the dog and the stick and the water and the butcher and then the angel of death kills the butcher and he kills the ox and the dog kills the cat.[8] Sounds a bit silly till you come to look into it well. Justice it means but it's everybody eating everyone else. That's what life is after all. How quickly he does that job. Practice makes perfect. Seems to see with his fingers.

Mr Bloom passed on out of the clanking noises through the gallery on to the landing. Now am I going to tram it out all the way and then catch him out perhaps. Better phone him up first. Number? Same as Citron's house. Twentyeight. Twentyeight double four.

ONLY ONCE MORE THAT SOAP[9]

He went down the house staircase. Who the deuce scrawled all over those walls with matches? Looks as if they did it for a bet. Heavy greasy smell there always is in those works. Lukewarm glue in Thom's next door when I was there.

He took out his handkerchief to dab his nose. Citronlemon? Ah, the soap I put there. Lose it out of that pocket. Putting back his handkerchief he took out the soap and stowed it away, buttoned, into the hip pocket of his trousers.

What perfume does your wife use? I could go home still: tram: something I forgot. Just to see before dressing. No. Here. No.[1]

A sudden screech of laughter came from the *Evening Telegraph* office. Know who that is. What's up? Pop in a minute to phone. Ned Lambert it is.

He entered softly.

ERIN, GREEN GEM OF THE SILVER SEA

—The ghost walks, professor MacHugh murmured softly, biscuitfully to the dusty windowpane.

Mr Dedalus, staring from the empty fireplace at Ned Lambert's quizzing face, asked of it sourly:

---

5. Passover; "Next year in Jerusalem" is the final phrase in the Passover night home ceremony when families read the *haggadah* ("story") of the exodus of the Israelites from Egypt (Exodus 12).

6. The Bible actually says "out of Egypt, *from* the house of bondage" (Exodus 13.14).

7. "Hear, O Israel, the Lord our God" (Deuteronomy 6.4)—a daily prayer, not part of the Passover ceremony.

8. Recalling the "Chad Gadya" (One Lamb), a Passover song.

9. Bloom purchased a lemon-scented cake of soap in the "Lotus Eaters" episode (ch. 5); it fits awkwardly in his trousers pocket, and thus intrudes into the narrative from time to time.

1. Bloom considers rushing home and heading off the imminent affair between Molly and Blazes Boylan; his own postal "affair" with Martha Clifford (the sentence "What perfume does your wife use?" is remembered from one of her letters) puts the idea in his head.

—Agonising Christ, wouldn't it give you a heartburn on your arse?

Ned Lambert, seated on the table, read on:

—*Or again, note the meanderings of some purling rill as it babbles on its way, fanned by gentlest zephyrs tho' quarrelling with the stony obstacles, to the tumbling waters of Neptune's blue domain, mid mossy banks, played on by the glorious sunlight or 'neath the shadows cast o'er its pensive bosom by the overarching leafage of the giants of the forest.* What about that, Simon? he asked over the fringe of his newspaper. How's that for high?

—Changing his drink, Mr Dedalus said.

Ned Lambert, laughing, struck the newspaper on his knees, repeating:

—*The pensive bosom and the overarsing leafage.* O boys! O, boys!

—And Xenophon looked upon Marathon, Mr Dedalus said, looking again on the fireplace and to the window, and Marathon looked on the sea.[2]

—That will do, professor MacHugh cried from the window. I don't want to hear any more of the stuff.

He ate off the crescent of water biscuit he had been nibbling and, hungered, made ready to nibble the biscuit in his other hand.

High falutin stuff. Bladderbags. Ned Lambert is taking a day off I see. Rather upsets a man's day a funeral does. He has influence they say. Old Chatterton, the vicechancellor is his granduncle or his greatgranduncle. Close on ninety they say. Subleader for his death written this long time perhaps. Living to spite them. Might go first himself. Johnny, make room for your uncle. The right honourable Hedges Eyre Chatterton. Daresay he writes him an odd shaky cheque or two on gale days. Windfall when he kicks out. Alleluia.

—Just another spasm, Ned Lambert said.

—What is it? Mr Bloom asked.

—A recently discovered fragment of Cicero's[3] Professor MacHugh answered with pomp of tone. *Our lovely land.*

SHORT BUT TO THE POINT

—Whose land? Mr Bloom said simply.

—Most pertinent question, the professor said between his chews. With an accent on the whose.

—Dan Dawson's land, Mr Dedalus said.

—Is it his speech last night? Mr Bloom asked.

Ned Lambert nodded.

—But listen to this, he said.

The doorknob hit Mr Bloom in the small of the back as the door was pushed in.

—Excuse me, J. J. O'Molloy said, entering.

Mr Bloom moved nimbly aside.

—I beg yours, he said.

—Good day, Jack.

—Come in. Come in.

—Good day.

—How are you, Dedalus?

2. Quoting "The Isles of Greece," a poem by Byron included in *Don Juan*, Canto III.

3. Roman rhetorician and statesman (106–43 B.C.).

—Well. And yourself?

J. J. O'Molloy shook his head.

SAD

Cleverest fellow at the junior bar he used to be. Decline poor chap. That hectic flush spells finis for a man. Touch and go with him. What's in the wind, I wonder. Money worry.

—*Or again if we but climb the serried mountain peaks.*

—You're looking extra.

—Is the editor to be seen? J. J. O'Molloy asked, looking towards the inner door.

—Very much so, professor MacHugh said. To be seen and heard. He's in his sanctum with Lenehan.

J. J. O'Molloy strolled to the sloping desk and began to turn back the pink pages of the file.

Practice dwindling. A mighthavebeen. Losing heart. Gambling. Debts of honour. Reaping the whirlwind. Used to get good retainers from D. and T. Fitzgerald. Their wigs to show the grey matter. Brains on their sleeve like the statue in Glasnevin.[4] Believe he does some literary work for the *Express* with Gabriel Conroy.[5] Wellread fellow. Myles Crawford began on the *Independent*. Funny the way those newspaper men veer about when they get wind of a new opening. Weathercocks. Hot and cold in the same breath. Wouldn't know which to believe. One story good till you hear the next. Go for one another baldheaded in the papers and then all blows over. Hailfellow well met the next moment.

—Ah, listen to this for God' sake, Ned Lambert pleaded. *Or again if we but climb the serried mountain peaks* . . .

—Bombast! the professor broke in testily. Enough of the inflated windbag!

—*Peaks*, Ned Lambert went on, *towering high on high, to bathe our souls, as it were* . . .

—Bathe his lips, Mr Dedalus said. Blessed and eternal God! Yes? Is he taking anything for it?

—*As 'twere, in the peerless panorama of Ireland's portfolio, unmatched, despite their wellpraised prototypes in other vaunted prize regions for very beauty, of bosky grove and undulating plain and luscious pastureland of vernal green, steeped in the transcendent translucent glow of our mild mysterious Irish twilight* . . .

—The moon, professor MacHugh said. He forgot Hamlet.

HIS NATIVE DORIC[6]

—*That mantles the vista far and wide and wait till the glowing orb of the moon shine forth to irradiate her silver effulgence* . . . .

—O! Mr Dedalus cried, giving vent to a hopeless groan, shite and onions! That'll do, Ned. Life is too short.

He took off his silk hat and, blowing out impatiently his bushy moustache, welshcombed his hair with raking fingers.

---

4. Site of the large Catholic cemetery in Dublin, where much of the "Hades" episode (ch. 6) takes place.
5. Character in Joyce's story *The Dead*.

6. Rustic dialect, named after the early, simple Doric style in Greece.

Ned Lambert tossed the newspaper aside, chuckling with delight. An instant after a hoarse bark of laughter burst over professor MacHugh's unshaven blackspectacled face.

—Doughy Daw! he cried.

WHAT WETHERUP SAID

All very fine to jeer at it now in cold print but it goes down like hot cake that stuff. He was in the bakery line too wasn't he? Why they call him Doughy Daw. Feathered his nest well anyhow. Daughter engaged to that chap in the inland revenue office with the motor. Hooked that nicely. Entertainments. Open house. Big blow out. Wetherup always said that. Get a grip of them by the stomach.

The inner door was opened violently and a scarlet beaked face, crested by a comb of feathery hair, thrust itself in. The bold blue eyes stared about them and the harsh voice asked:

—What is it?

—And here comes the sham squire himself,[7] professor MacHugh said grandly.

—Getououthat, you bloody old pedagogue! the editor said in recognition.

—Come, Ned, Mr Dedalus said, putting on his hat. I must get a drink after that.

—Drink! the editor cried. No drinks served before mass.

—Quite right too, Mr Dedalus said, going out. Come on, Ned.

Ned Lambert sidled down from the table. The editor's blue eyes roved towards Mr Bloom's face, shadowed by a smile.

—Will you join us, Myles? Ned Lambert asked.

MEMORABLE BATTLES RECALLED

—North Cork militia! the editor cried, striding to the mantelpiece. We won every time! North Cork and Spanish officers![8]

—Where was that, Myles? Ned Lambert asked with a reflective glance at his toecaps.

—In Ohio! the editor shouted.

—So it was, begad, Ned Lambert agreed.

Passing out he whispered to J. J. O'Molloy:

—Incipient jigs.[9] Sad case.

—Ohio! the editor crowed in high treble from his uplifted scarlet face. My Ohio!

—A perfect cretic![1] the professor said. Long, short and long.

O, HARP EOLIAN![2]

He took a reel of dental floss from his waistcoat pocket and, breaking off a piece, twanged it smartly between two and two of his resonant unwashed teeth.

—Bingbang, bangbang.

Mr Bloom, seeing the coast clear, made for the inner door.

---

7. Pretending to identify the editor with a disreputable predecessor, Francis Higgins (1746–1802), who had seduced a woman by pretending to be a country squire.
8. This nonsensical piece of rhetoric invokes the North Cork Militia, which was involved in the failed Rebellion of 1798 and lost every battle it was involved in.
9. Probably the tremors caused by abrupt withdrawal from heavy alcohol use.

1. A poetic foot, made up of one short syllable between two long syllables.
2. The aeolian harp, popular as a symbol among the Romantic poets, is strung so as to allow the passing winds to "play" it. The harp is the national emblem of Ireland.

—Just a moment, Mr Crawford, he said. I just want to phone about an ad.

He went in.

—What about that leader this evening? professor MacHugh asked, coming to the editor and laying a firm hand on his shoulder.

—That'll be all right, Myles Crawford said more calmly. Never you fret. Hello, Jack. That's all right.

—Good day, Myles, J. J. O'Molloy said, letting the pages he held slip limply back on the file. Is that Canada swindle case on today?

The telephone whirred inside.

—Twentyeight . . . No, twenty . . . Double four . . . Yes.

SPOT THE WINNER

Lenehan came out of the inner office with *Sport's* tissues.

—Who wants a dead cert for the Gold cup? he asked. Sceptre with O. Madden up.[3]

He tossed the tissues on to the table.

Screams of newsboys barefoot in the hall rushed near and the door was flung open.

—Hush, Lenehan said. I hear feetstoops.

Professor MacHugh strode across the room and seized the cringing urchin by the collar as the others scampered out of the hall and down the steps. The tissues rustled up in the draught, floated softly in the air blue scrawls and under the table came to earth.

—It wasn't me, sir. It was the big fellow shoved me, sir.

—Throw him out and shut the door, the editor said. There's a hurricane blowing.

Lenehan began to paw the tissues up from the floor, grunting as he stooped twice.

—Waiting for the racing special, sir, the newsboy said. It was Pat Farrell shoved me, sir.

He pointed to two faces peering in round the doorframe.

—Him, sir.

—Out of this with you, professor MacHugh said gruffly.

He hustled the boy out and banged the door to.

J. J. O'Molloy turned the files cracklingly over, murmuring, seeking:

—Continued on page six, column four.

—Yes . . . *Evening Telegraph* here, Mr Bloom phoned from the inner office. Is the boss . . . ? Yes, *Telegraph* . . . To where? . . . Aha! Which auction rooms? . . . Aha! I see . . . Right. I'll catch him.

A COLLISION ENSUES

The bell whirred again as he rang off. He came in quickly and bumped against Lenehan who was struggling up with the second tissue.

—*Pardon, monsieur*, Lenehan said, clutching him for an instant and making a grimace.

—My fault, Mr Bloom said, suffering his grip. Are you hurt? I'm in a hurry.

—Knee, Lenehan said.

---

3. A complicated subplot throughout the novel: Lenehan, looking up horse racing information, asks Bloom (in ch. 6) if he can have a look at Bloom's newspaper. Bloom tells him to take it, for he was just about to "throw it away." Since there's a longshot running in the Gold Cup race at Ascot called Throwaway, Lenehan thinks Bloom is trying to pass him insider information, and wagers a large sum on the horse, who does not win.

He made a comic face and whined, rubbing his knee:

—The accumulation of the *anno Domini.*

—Sorry, Mr Bloom said.

He went to the door and, holding it ajar, paused. J. J. O'Molloy slapped the heavy pages over. The noise of two shrill voices, a mouthorgan, echoed in the bare hallway from the newsboys squatted on the doorsteps:

> *We are the boys of Wexford*
> *Who fought with heart and hand.*[4]

EXIT BLOOM

—I'm just running round to Bachelor's walk, Mr Bloom said, about this ad of Keyes's. Want to fix it up. They tell me he's round there in Dillon's.

He looked indecisively for a moment at their faces. The editor who, leaning against the mantelshelf, had propped his head on his hand, suddenly stretched forth an arm amply.

—Begone! he said. The world is before you.[5]

—Back in no time, Mr Bloom said, hurrying out.

J. J. O'Molloy took the tissues from Lenehan's hand and read them, blowing them apart gently, without comment.

—He'll get that advertisement, the professor said, staring through his black-rimmed spectacles over the crossblind. Look at the young scamps after him.

—Show. Where? Lenehan cried, running to the window.

A STREET CORTEGE

Both smiled over the crossblind at the file of capering newsboys in Mr Bloom's wake, the last zigzagging white on the breeze a mocking kite, a tail of white bowknots.

—Look at the young guttersnipe behind him hue and cry, Lenehan said, and you'll kick. O, my rib risible! Taking off his flat spaugs and the walk.[6] Small nines. Steal upon larks.

He began to mazurka[7] in swift caricature across the floor on sliding feet past the fireplace to J. J. O'Molloy who placed the tissues in his receiving hands.

—What's that? Myles Crawford said with a start. Where are the other two gone?

—Who? the professor said, turning. They're gone round to the Oval for a drink. Paddy Hooper is there with Jack Hall. Came over last night.

—Come on then, Myles Crawford said. Where's my hat?

He walked jerkily into the office behind, parting the vent of his jacket, jingling his keys in his back pocket. They jingled then in the air and against the wood as he locked his desk drawer.

—He's pretty well on, professor MacHugh said in a low voice.

—Seems to be, J. J. O'Molloy said, taking out a cigarette case in murmuring meditation, but it is not always as it seems. Who has the most matches?

---

4. From a ballad, *The Boys of Wexford,* by R. Dwyer Joyce (1830–1883) about the rebellion of 1798—whose heroes turned to drink in later years.
5. The editor here echoes the close of Milton's *Paradise*

Lost, as Adam and Eve leave Eden (12.846).
6. I.e., imitating Bloom's big feet and manner of walking.
7. A lively Polish dance.

THE CALUMET OF PEACE[8]

He offered a cigarette to the professor and took one himself. Lenehan promptly struck a match for them and lit their cigarettes in turn. J. J. O'Molloy opened his case again and offered it.

—*Thanky vous*, Lenehan said, helping himself.

The editor came from the inner office, a straw hat awry on his brow. He declaimed in song, pointing sternly at professor MacHugh:

> 'Twas rank and fame that tempted thee,
> 'Twas empire charmed thy heart.[9]

The professor grinned, locking his long lips.

—Eh? You bloody old Roman empire? Myles Crawford said.

He took a cigarette from the open case. Lenehan, lighting it for him with quick grace, said:

—Silence for my brandnew riddle!

—*Imperium romanum*, J. J. O'Molloy said gently. It sounds nobler than British or Brixton. The word reminds one somehow of fat in the fire.

Myles Crawford blew his first puff violently towards the ceiling.

—That's it, he said. We are the fat. You and I are the fat in the fire. We haven't got the chance of a snowball in hell.

THE GRANDEUR THAT WAS ROME

—Wait a moment, professor MacHugh said, raising two quiet claws. We mustn't be led away by words, by sounds of words. We think of Rome, imperial, imperious, imperative.

He extended elocutionary arms from frayed stained shirtcuffs, pausing:

—What was their civilisation? Vast, I allow: but vile. *Cloacae:* sewers. The jews in the wilderness and on the mountaintop said: *It is meet to be here. Let us build an altar to Jehovah.* The Roman, like the Englishman who follows in his footsteps, brought to every new shore on which he set his foot (on our shore he never set it) only his cloacal obsession. He gazed about him in his toga and he said: *It is meet to be here. Let us construct a watercloset.*[1]

—Which they accordingly did do, Lenehan said. Our old ancient ancestors, as we read in the first chapter of Guinness's,[2] were partial to the running stream.

—They were nature's gentlemen, J. J. O'Molloy murmured. But we have also Roman law.

—And Pontius Pilate is its prophet, professor MacHugh responded.

—Do you know that story about chief baron Palles? J. J. O'Molloy asked. It was at the royal university dinner. Everything was going swimmingly . . .

—First my riddle, Lenehan said. Are you ready?

Mr O'Madden Burke, tall in copious grey of Donegal tweed, came in from the hallway. Stephen Dedalus, behind him, uncovered as he entered.

---

8. The "peace pipe" of Native Americans.
9. Aria from the opera *The Rose of Castille* (1857), by Irish composer Michael William Balfe.
1. Toilet. The claim of an English "cloacal obsession" ironically reverses a charge made against Joyce himself by the English writer H. G. Wells, who had reviewed *A Portrait of the Artist* in 1917, in the (aptly titled) magazine *Nation*. Wells wrote, "Mr. Joyce has a cloacal obsession. He would bring back into the general picture of life aspects which modern drainage and modern decorum have taken out of ordinary intercourse and conversation."
2. A pun on Genesis, the first book of the Bible, and Guinness, producers of stout and lager in Dublin.

—*Entrez, mes enfants!*[3] Lenehan cried.

—I escort a suppliant, Mr O'Madden Burke said melodiously. Youth led by Experience visits Notoriety.

—How do you do? the editor said, holding out a hand. Come in. Your governor is just gone.

? ? ?

Lenehan said to all:

—Silence! What opera resembles a railway line? Reflect, ponder, excogitate, reply.

Stephen handed over the typed sheets, pointing to the title and signature.

—Who? the editor asked.

Bit torn off.

—Mr Garrett Deasy, Stephen said.

—That old pelters, the editor said. Who tore it? Was he short taken?[4]

> *On swift sail flaming*
> *From storm and south*
> *He comes, pale vampire,*
> *Mouth to my mouth.*

—Good day, Stephen, the professor said, coming to peer over their shoulders. Foot and mouth? Are you turned . . . ?

Bullockbefriending bard.[5]

SHINDY IN WELLKNOWN RESTAURANT

—Good day, sir, Stephen answered, blushing. The letter is not mine. Mr Garrett Deasy asked me to . . .

—O, I know him, Myles Crawford said, and knew his wife too. The bloodiest old tartar God ever made. By Jesus, she had the foot and mouth disease and no mistake! The night she threw the soup in the waiter's face in the Star and Garter. Oho!

A woman brought sin into the world. For Helen, the runaway wife of Menelaus, ten years the Greeks. O'Rourke, prince of Breffni.

—Is he a widower? Stephen asked.

—Ay, a grass one,[6] Myles Crawford said, his eye running down the typescript. Emperor's horses. Habsburg. An Irishman saved his life on the ramparts of Vienna. Don't you forget! Maximilian Karl O'Donnell, graf von Tirconnel in Ireland. Sent his heir over to make the king an Austrian fieldmarshal now. Going to be trouble there one day. Wild geese.[7] O yes, every time. Don't you forget that!

—The moot point is did he forget it, J. J. O'Molloy said quietly, turning a horseshoe paperweight. Saving princes is a thank you job.

3. Enter, my children!

4. Stephen had agreed to take a letter to the editor from his employer, a schoolmaster named Garrett Deasy, and to try to place it with one of the Dublin newspapers. A piece is missing because Stephen later had an idea for a poem while walking on the beach but had nothing to write on; the editor playfully suggests that a small bit has been torn off for use as toilet tissue. The italicized lines are the poetry Stephen composed on the torn-off paper, an adaptation of a Gaelic poem translated by the nationalist poet Douglas Hyde in *Love Songs of Connacht* (1893): "He came from the South; / His breast to my bosom, / His mouth to my mouth."

5. The mock-Homeric epithet suggests that in helping Deasy place his letter about cattle disease, Stephen has become a poet ("bard") who has befriended the cattle ("bullocks").

6. A grass widower is a man separated from his wife.

7. Irish expatriates.

Professor MacHugh turned on him.

—And if not? he said.

—I'll tell you how it was, Myles Crawford began. A Hungarian it was one day . . .

LOST CAUSES
NOBLE MARQUESS MENTIONED

—We were always loyal to lost causes, the professor said. Success for us is the death of the intellect and of the imagination. We were never loyal to the successful. We serve them. I teach the blatant Latin language. I speak the tongue of a race the acme of whose mentality is the maxim: time is money. Material domination. *Dominus!* Lord! Where is the spirituality? Lord Jesus! Lord Salisbury. A sofa in a westend club. But the Greek!

KYRIE ELEISON![8]

A smile of light brightened his darkrimmed eyes, lengthened his long lips.

—The Greek! he said again. *Kyrios!* Shining word! The vowels the Semite and the Saxon know not. *Kyrie!* The radiance of the intellect. I ought to profess Greek, the language of the mind. *Kyrie eleison!* The closetmaker and the cloacamaker will never be lords of our spirit. We are liege subjects of the catholic chivalry of Europe that foundered at Trafalgar and of the empire of the spirit, not an *imperium*, that went under with the Athenian fleets at Aegospotami. Yes, yes. They went under. Pyrrhus, misled by an oracle, made a last attempt to retrieve the fortunes of Greece.[9] Loyal to a lost cause.

He strode away from them towards the window.

—They went forth to battle, Mr O'Madden Burke said greyly, but they always fell.

—Boohoo! Lenehan wept with a little noise. Owing to a brick received in the latter half of the *matinée*. Poor, poor, poor Pyrrhus!

He whispered then near Stephen's ear:

LENEHAN'S LIMERICK

—There's a ponderous pundit MacHugh
Who wears goggles of ebony hue.
As he mostly sees double
To wear them why trouble?
I can't see the Joe Miller. Can you?

In mourning for Sallust,[1] Mulligan says. Whose mother is beastly dead. Myles Crawford crammed the sheets into a sidepocket.

—That'll be all right, he said. I'll read the rest after. That'll be all right. Lenehan extended his hands in protest.

—But my riddle! he said. What opera is like a railway line?

—Opera? Mr O'Madden Burke's sphinx face reriddled.

8. Lord have mercy [upon us] (Greek). A formal part of the Mass.
9. The Greek general Pyrrhus (318–272 B.C.) was led to believe, in a dream, that he would triumph over the Spartans, but he was defeated.
1. Roman historian and senator (86–34 B.C.), known for political corruption. The idea of mourning reminds Stephen of a remark made by his friend Malachi ("Buck") Mulligan, about which the two had argued that morning: when Stephen had visited Mulligan at his aunt's house Mulligan had described Stephen as "Dedalus, whose mother is beastly dead."

Lenehan announced gladly:

—*The Rose of Castille*. See the wheeze? Rows of cast steel. Gee!

He poked Mr O'Madden Burke mildly in the spleen. Mr O'Madden Burke fell back with grace on his umbrella, feigning a gasp.

—Help! he sighed. I feel a strong weakness.

Lenehan, rising to tiptoe, fanned his face rapidly with the rustling tissues.

The professor, returning by way of the files, swept his hand across Stephen's and Mr O'Madden Burke's loose ties.

—Paris, past and present, he said. You look like communards.[2]

—Like fellows who had blown up the Bastile, J. J. O'Molloy said in quiet mockery. Or was it you shot the lord lieutenant of Finland between you? You look as though you had done the deed. General Bobrikoff.

—We were only thinking about it, Stephen said.

OMNIUM GATHERUM[3]

—All the talents, Myles Crawford said. Law, the classics . . .

—The turf, Lenehan put in.

—Literature, the press.

—If Bloom were here, the professor said. The gentle art of advertisement.

—And Madam Bloom, Mr O'Madden Burke added. The vocal muse. Dublin's prime favorite.

Lenehan gave a loud cough.

—Ahem! he said very softly. O, for a fresh of breath air! I caught a cold in the park. The gate was open.

"YOU CAN DO IT!"

The editor laid a nervous hand on Stephen's shoulder.

—I want you to write something for me, he said. Something with a bite in it. You can do it. I see it in your face. *In the lexicon of youth* . . .

See it in your face. See it in your eye. Lazy idle little schemer.[4]

—Foot and mouth disease! the editor cried in scornful invective. Great nationalist meeting in Borris-in-Ossory. All balls! Bulldosing the public! Give them something with a bite in it. Put us all into it, damn its soul. Father, Son and Holy Ghost and Jakes M'Carthy.

—We can all supply mental pabulum, Mr O'Madden Burke said.

Stephen raised his eyes to the bold unheeding stare.

—He wants you for the pressgang, J. J. O'Molloy said.

THE GREAT GALLAHER

—You can do it, Myles Crawford repeated, clenching his hand in emphasis. Wait a minute. We'll paralyse Europe as Ignatius Gallaher used to say when he was on the shaughraun,[5] doing billiardmarking in the Clarence. Gallaher, that was a pressman

2. Members of the left-wing Commune of Paris, who controlled Paris for three months in 1871.

3. Mock-Latin for hodgepodge.

4. Professor MacHugh's innocent remark, "I see it in your face," unfortunately reminds Stephen of the language of one of the priests at his parochial school, who accused Stephen of breaking his glasses intentionally in order to get out of work. (*A Portrait of the Artist*, I.iv.)

5. Wandering (Gaelic).

for you. That was a pen. You know how he made his mark? I'll tell you. That was the smartest piece of journalism ever known. That was in eightyone, sixth of May, time of the invincibles, murder in the Phoenix park, before you were born, I suppose. I'll show you.

He pushed past them to the files.

—Look at here, he said turning. The *New York World* cabled for a special. Remember that time?

Professor MacHugh nodded.

—*New York World*, the editor said, excitedly pushing back his straw hat. Where it took place. Tim Kelly, or Kavanagh I mean, Joe Brady and the rest of them. Where Skin-the-Goat drove the car. Whole route, see?

—Skin-the-Goat, Mr O'Madden Burke said. Fitzharris. He has that cabman's shelter, they say, down there at Butt bridge. Holohan told me. You know Holohan?

—Hop and carry one, is it? Myles Crawford said.

—And poor Gumley is down there too, so he told me, minding stones for the corporation. A night watchman.

Stephen turned in surprise.

—Gumley? he said. You don't say so? A friend of my father's, is he?

—Never mind Gumley, Myles Crawford cried angrily. Let Gumley mind the stones, see they don't run away. Look at here. What did Ignatius Gallaher do? I'll tell you. Inspiration of genius. Cabled right away. Have you *Weekly Freeman* of 17 March? Right. Have you got that?

He flung back pages of the files and stuck his finger on a point.

—Take page four, advertisement for Bransome's coffee, let us say. Have you got that? Right.

The telephone whirred.

A DISTANT VOICE

—I'll answer it, the professor said going.

—B is parkgate. Good.

His finger leaped and struck point after point, vibrating.

—T is viceregal lodge. C is where murder took place. K is Knockmaroon gate.

The loose flesh of his neck shook like a cock's wattles. An illstarched dicky jutted up and with a rude gesture he thrust it back into his waistcoat.

—Hello? *Evening Telegraph* here . . . Hello? . . . Who's there? . . . Yes . . . Yes . . . Yes . . .

—F to P is the route Skin-the-Goat drove the car for an alibi. Inchicore, Roundtown, Windy Arbour, Palmerston Park, Ranelagh. F. A. B. P. Got that? X is Davy's publichouse in upper Leeson street.

The professor came to the inner door.

—Bloom is at the telephone, he said.

—Tell him go to hell, the editor said promptly. X is Burke's publichouse, see?

CLEVER, VERY

—Clever, Lenehan said. Very.

—Gave it to them on a hot plate, Myles Crawford said, the whole bloody history.

Nightmare from which you will never awake.[6]

—I saw it, the editor said proudly. I was present, Dick Adams, the besthearted bloody Corkman the Lord ever put the breath of life in, and myself.

Lenehan bowed to a shape of air, announcing:

—Madam, I'm Adam. And Able was I ere I saw Elba.

—History! Myles Crawford cried. The Old Woman of Prince's street was there first. There was weeping and gnashing of teeth over that. Out of an advertisement. Gregor Grey made the design for it. That gave him the leg up. Then Paddy Hooper worked Tay Pay who took him on to the *Star*. Now he's got in with Blumenfeld. That's press. That's talent. Pyatt! He was all their daddies!

—The father of scare journalism, Lenehan confirmed, and the brother-in-law of Chris Callinan.

—Hello? . . . Are you there? . . . Yes, he's here still. Come across yourself.

—Where do you find a pressman like that now, eh? the editor cried.

He flung the pages down.

—Clamn dever, Lenehan said to Mr O'Madden Burke.

—Very smart, Mr O'Madden Burke said.

Professor MacHugh came from the inner office.

—Talking about the invincibles, he said, did you see that some hawkers were up before the recorder . . .

—O yes, J. J. O'Molloy said eagerly. Lady Dudley was walking home through the park to see all the trees that were blown down by that cyclone last year and thought she'd buy a view of Dublin. And it turned out to be a commemoration post-card of Joe Brady or Number One or Skin-the-Goat. Right outside the viceregal lodge, imagine!

—They're only in the hook and eye department, Myles Crawford said. Psha! Press and the bar! Where have you a man now at the bar like those fellows, like Whiteside, like Isaac Butt, like silvertongued O'Hagan?[7] Eh? Ah, bloody nonsense! Only in the halfpenny place.

His mouth continued to twitch unspeaking in nervous curls of disdain.

Would anyone wish that mouth for her kiss? How do you know? Why did you write it then?

RHYMES AND REASONS

Mouth, south. Is the mouth south someway? Or the south a mouth? Must be some. South, pout, out, shout, drouth. Rhymes: two men dressed the same, looking the same, two by two.

> . . . . *la tua pace*
> . . . . *che parlar ti piace*
> *mentre che il vento, come fa, si tace.*[8]

6. In the course of a tortured discussion with Mr. Deasy about British and Irish politics and history in chapter 2, Stephen had exclaimed, "History is a nightmare from which I am trying to awake."

7. James Whiteside (1804–1876), Isaac Butt (1813–1879), and Thomas O'Hagan (1812–1885) were Irish barristers and orators.

8. From Canto 5 of Dante's *Inferno*; the speakers are adulterous lovers, Francesca and Paolo, who tell Dante: "Were the world's King our friend . . . we would entreat Him for thy peace, . . . and speak as thou shalt please, While the winds cease to howl, as now they cease" (lines 92, 94, 96).

He saw them three by three, approaching girls, in green, in rose, in russet, entwining, *per l'aer perso*[9] in mauve, in purple, *quella pacifica oriafiamma,*[1] in gold of oriflamme, *di rimirar fè più ardenti.*[2] But I old men, penitent, leadenfooted, underdarkneath the night: mouth south: tomb womb.

—Speak up for yourself, Mr O'Madden Burke said.

SUFFICIENT FOR THE DAY . . .

J. J. O'Molloy, smiling palely, took up the gage.

—My dear Myles, he said, flinging his cigarette aside, you put a false construction on my words. I hold no brief, as at present advised, for the third profession *qua* profession but your Cork legs are running away with you. Why not bring in Henry Grattan and Flood and Demosthenes and Edmund Burke?[3] Ignatius Gallaher we all know and his Chapelizod boss, Harmsworth of the farthing press, and his American cousin of the Bowery gutter sheet not to mention *Paddy Kelly's Budget, Pue's Occurrences* and our watchful friend *The Skibbereen Eagle.* Why bring in a master of forensic eloquence like Whiteside? Sufficient for the day is the newspaper thereof.[4]

LINKS WITH BYGONE DAYS OF YORE

—Grattan and Flood wrote for this very paper, the editor cried in his face. Irish volunteers. Where are you now? Established 1763. Dr Lucas. Who have you now like John Philpot Curran? Psha!

—Well, J. J. O'Molloy said, Bushe K. C., for example.

—Bushe? the editor said. Well, yes. Bushe, yes. He has a strain of it in his blood. Kendal Bushe or I mean Seymour Bushe.

—He would have been on the bench long ago, the professor said, only for . . . But no matter.

J. J. O'Molloy turned to Stephen and said quietly and slowly:

—One of the most polished periods I think I ever listened to in my life fell from the lips of Seymour Bushe. It was in that case of fratricide, the Childs murder case. Bushe defended him.

> *And in the porches of mine ear did pour.*[5]

By the way how did he find that out? He died in his sleep. Or the other story, beast with two backs?[6]

—What was that? the professor asked.

ITALIA, MAGISTRA ARTIUM

—He spoke on the law of evidence, J. J. O'Molloy said, of Roman justice as contrasted with the earlier Mosaic code, the *lex talionis.* And he cited the Moses of Michelangelo in the Vatican.

---

9. Through the black air.
1. That peaceful gold flame.
2. More ardent to look again. From Dante's *Inferno* and *Paradiso.*
3. Irish statesmen Henry Grattan (1746–1820) and Henry Flood (1732–1791), as well as the Irish-born Edmund Burke (1729–1797), were among the greatest orators of their day. Demosthenes (c. 384–322 B.C.) is traditionally

considered the greatest of Greek orators.
4. Revising Jesus's saying, "Sufficient for the day is the evil thereof" (Matthew 6.34).
5. This is Hamlet's father's description of his poisoning by his brother Claudius, in *Hamlet* (1.5.62–63). "And in the porches of my ears did pour / The leperous distillment."
6. Again from Shakespeare—this time, *Othello;* the phrase means sexual intercourse.

—Ha.

—A few wellchosen words, Lenehan prefaced. Silence!

Pause. J. J. O'Molloy took out his cigarettecase.

False lull. Something quite ordinary.

Messenger took out his match box thoughtfully and lit his cigar.

I have often thought since on looking back over that strange time that it was that small act, trivial in itself, that striking of that match, that determined the whole aftercourse of both our lives.

A POLISHED PERIOD

J. J. O'Molloy resumed, moulding his words:

—He said of it: *that stony effigy in frozen music, horned and terrible, of the human form divine, that eternal symbol of wisdom and of prophecy which, if aught that the imagination or the hand of sculptor has wrought in marble of soultransfigured and of soultransfiguring deserves to live, deserves to live.*

His slim hand with a wave graced echo and fall.

—Fine! Myles Crawford said at once.

—The divine afflatus, Mr O'Madden Burke said.

—You like it? J. J. O'Molloy asked Stephen.

Stephen, his blood wooed by grace of language and gesture, blushed. He took a cigarette from the case. J. J. O'Molloy offered his case to Myles Crawford. Lenehan lit their cigarettes as before and took his trophy, saying:

—Muchibus thankibus.

A MAN OF HIGH MORALE

—Professor Magennis was speaking to me about you, J. J. O'Molloy said to Stephen. What do you think really of that hermetic crowd, the opal hush poets: A. E. the master mystic? That Blavatsky woman started it.[7] She was a nice old bag of tricks. A. E. has been telling some yankee interviewer that you came to him in the small hours of the morning to ask him about planes of consciousness. Magennis thinks you must have been pulling A. E.'s leg. He is a man of the very highest morale, Magennis.

Speaking about me. What did he say? What did he say? What did he say about me? Don't ask.

—No, thanks, professor MacHugh said, waving the cigarette case aside. Wait a moment. Let me say one thing. The finest display of oratory I ever heard was a speech made by John F. Taylor[8] at the college historical society. Mr Justice Fitzgibbon, the present lord justice of appeal, had spoken and the paper under debate was an essay (new for those days), advocating the revival of the Irish tongue.

He turned towards Myles Crawford and said:

—You know Gerald Fitzgibbon. Then you can imagine the style of his discourse.

—He is sitting with Tim Healy, J. J. O'Molloy said, rumour has it, on the Trinity college estates commission.

—He is sitting with a sweet thing in a child's frock, Myles Crawford said. Go on. Well?

---

7. Refers generally to the interest in mysticism, and specifically the Theosophy of Madame Blavatsky (1831–1891), who stressed the fellowship of all humanity and the transmigration of souls. Her disciple A.E. (pseud.

of George Russell, 1867–1935) was a minor Irish poet and mystic, and friend of W. B. Yeats.

8. John F. Taylor (c. 1850–1902), Irish barrister and journalist. Taylor did make this speech on 24 October 1901.

—It was the speech, mark you, the professor said, of a finished orator, full of courteous haughtiness and pouring in chastened diction I will not say the vials of his wrath but pouring the proud man's contumely upon the new movement. It was then a new movement. We were weak, therefore worthless.

He closed his long thin lips an instant but, eager to be on, raised an outspanned hand to his spectacles and, with trembling thumb and ringfinger touching lightly the black rims, steadied them to a new focus.

IMPROMPTU

In ferial tone he addressed J. J. O'Molloy:

—Taylor had come there, you must know, from a sickbed. That he had prepared his speech I do not believe for there was not even one shorthandwriter in the hall. His dark lean face had a growth of shaggy beard round it. He wore a loose white silk neckcloth and altogether he looked (though he was not) a dying man.

His gaze turned at once but slowly from J. J. O'Molloy's towards Stephen's face and then bent at once to the ground, seeking. His unglazed linen collar appeared behind his bent head, soiled by his withering hair. Still seeking, he said:

—When Fitzgibbon's speech had ended John F. Taylor rose to reply. Briefly, as well as I can bring them to mind, his words were these.

He raised his head firmly. His eyes bethought themselves once more. Witless shellfish swam in the gross lenses to and fro, seeking outlet.

He began:

—*Mr chairman, ladies and gentlemen: Great was my admiration in listening to the remarks addressed to the youth of Ireland a moment since by my learned friend. It seemed to me that I had been transported into a country far away from this country, into an age remote from this age, that I stood in ancient Egypt and that I was listening to the speech of some highpriest of that land addressed to the youthful Moses.*

His listeners held their cigarettes poised to hear, their smokes ascending in frail stalks that flowered with his speech. *And let our crooked smokes.* Noble words coming. Look out. Could you try your hand at it yourself?

—*And it seemed to me that I heard the voice of that Egyptian highpriest raised in a tone of like haughtiness and like pride. I heard his words and their meaning was revealed to me.*

FROM THE FATHERS

It was revealed to me that those things are good which yet are corrupted which neither if they were supremely good nor unless they were good, could be corrupted. Ah, curse you! That's saint Augustine.

—*Why will you jews not accept our culture, our religion and our language? You are a tribe of nomad herdsmen: we are a mighty people. You have no cities nor no wealth: our cities are hives of humanity and our galleys, trireme and quadrireme, laden with all manner merchandise furrow the waters of the known globe. You have but emerged from primitive conditions: we have a literature, a priesthood, an agelong history and a polity.*

Nile.

Child, man, effigy.

By the Nilebank the babemaries kneel, cradle of bulrushes: a man supple in combat: stonehorned, stonebearded, heart of stone.

—You pray to a local and obscure idol: our temples, majestic and mysterious, are the abodes of Isis and Osiris, of Horus and Ammon Ra. Yours serfdom, awe and humbleness: ours thunder and the seas. Israel is weak and few are her children: Egypt is an host and terrible are her arms. Vagrants and daylabourers are you called: the world trembles at our name.

A dumb belch of hunger cleft his speech. He lifted his voice above it boldly:

—But, ladies and gentlemen, had the youthful Moses listened to and accepted that view of life, had he bowed his head and bowed his will and bowed his spirit before that arrogant admonition he would never have brought the chosen people out of their house of bondage nor followed the pillar of the cloud by day. He would never have spoken with the Eternal amid lightnings on Sinai's mountaintop nor ever have come down with the light of inspiration shining in his countenance and bearing in his arms the tables of the law, graven in the language of the outlaw.

He ceased and looked at them, enjoying a silence.

OMINOUS—FOR HIM!

J. J. O'Molloy said not without regret:

—And yet he died without having entered the land of promise.

—A sudden–at–the–moment–though–from–lingering–illness–often–previously–expectorated–demise, Lenehan added. And with a great future behind him.

The troop of bare feet was heard rushing along the hallway and pattering up the staircase.

—That is oratory, the professor said uncontradicted.

Gone with the wind. Hosts at Mullaghmast and Tara of the kings. Miles of ears of porches. The tribune's words howled and scattered to the four winds. A people sheltered within his voice. Dead noise. Akasic records of all that ever anywhere wherever was.[9] Love and laud him: me no more.

I have money.

—Gentlemen, Stephen said. As the next motion on the agenda paper may I suggest that the house do now adjourn?

—You take my breath away. It is not perchance a French compliment? Mr O'Madden Burke asked. 'Tis the hour, methinks, when the winejug, metaphorically speaking, is most grateful in Ye ancient hostelry.

—That it be and hereby is resolutely resolved. All who are in favour say ay, Lenehan announced. The contrary no. I declare it carried. To which particular boosingshed . . . ? My casting vote is: Mooney's!

He led the way, admonishing:

—We will sternly refuse to partake of strong waters, will we not? Yes, we will not. By no manner of means.

Mr O'Madden Burke, following close, said with an ally's lunge of his umbrella:

—Lay on, Macduff![1]

—Chip of the old block! the editor cried, slapping Stephen on the shoulder. Let us go. Where are those blasted keys?

He fumbled in his pocket pulling out the crushed typesheets.

---

9. Parody of the language of Theosophy.

1. These are Macbeth's words when he discovers that Macduff is to be his executioner (*Macbeth*, 5.8.33).

—Foot and mouth. I know. That'll be all right. That'll go in. Where are they? That's all right.

He thrust the sheets back and went into the inner office.

LET US HOPE

J. J. O'Molloy, about to follow him in, said quietly to Stephen:

—I hope you will live to see it published. Myles, one moment.

He went into the inner office, closing the door behind him.

—Come along, Stephen, the professor said. That is fine, isn't it? It has the prophetic vision. *Fuit Ilium!*[2] The sack of windy Troy. Kingdoms of this world. The masters of the Mediterranean are fellaheen today.

The first newsboy came pattering down the stairs at their heels and rushed out into the street, yelling:

—Racing special!

Dublin. I have much, much to learn.

They turned to the left along Abbey street.

—I have a vision too, Stephen said.

—Yes? the professor said, skipping to get into step. Crawford will follow.

Another newsboy shot past them, yelling as he ran:

—Racing special!

DEAR DIRTY DUBLIN

Dubliners.

—Two Dublin vestals, Stephen said, elderly and pious, have lived fifty and fiftythree years in Fumbally's lane.

—Where is that? the professor asked.

—Off Blackpitts, Stephen said.

Damp night reeking of hungry dough. Against the wall. Face glistering tallow under her fustian shawl. Frantic hearts. Akasic records. Quicker, darlint!

On now. Dare it. Let there be life.

—They want to see the views of Dublin from the top of Nelson's pillar. They save up three and tenpence in a red tin letterbox moneybox. They shake out the threepenny bits and sixpences and coax out the pennies with the blade of a knife. Two and three in silver and one and seven in coppers. They put on their bonnets and best clothes and take their umbrellas for fear it may come on to rain.

—Wise virgins, professor MacHugh said.[3]

LIFE ON THE RAW

—They buy one and fourpenceworth of brawn[4] and four slices of panloaf at the north city diningrooms in Marlborough street from Miss Kate Collins, proprietress. . . . They purchase four and twenty ripe plums from a girl at the foot of Nelson's pillar to take off the thirst of the brawn. They give two threepenny bits to the gentleman at

---

2. Troy is no more; from Virgil's *Aeneid* 3.325.
3. In Matthew 25.1–13, Jesus tells the parable of the wise

and foolish virgins.
4. Cold, jellied meatloaf.

the turnstile and begin to waddle slowly up the winding staircase, grunting, encouraging each other, afraid of the dark, panting, one asking the other have you the brawn, praising God and the Blessed Virgin, threatening to come down, peeping at the airslits. Glory be to God. They had no idea it was that high.

Their names are Anne Kearns and Florence MacCabe. Anne Kearns has the lumbago for which she rubs on Lourdes water given her by a lady who got a bottleful from a passionist father. Florence MacCabe takes a crubeen and a bottle of double X[5] for supper every Saturday.

—Antithesis, the professor said nodding twice. Vestal virgins. I can see them. What's keeping our friend?

He turned.

A bevy of scampering newsboys rushed down the steps, scampering in all directions, yelling, their white papers fluttering. Hard after them Myles Crawford appeared on the steps, his hat aureoling his scarlet face, talking with J. J. O'Molloy.

—Come along, the professor cried, waving his arm.

He set off again to walk by Stephen's side.

—Yes, he said. I see them.

RETURN OF BLOOM

Mr Bloom, breathless, caught in a whirl of wild newsboys near the offices of the *Irish Catholic* and *Dublin Penny Journal*, called:

—Mr Crawford! A moment!

—*Telegraph*! Racing special!

—What is it? Myles Crawford said, falling back a pace.

A newsboy cried in Mr Bloom's face:

—Terrible tragedy in Rathmines! A child bit by a bellows!

INTERVIEW WITH THE EDITOR

—Just this ad, Mr Bloom said, pushing through towards the steps, puffing, and taking the cutting from his pocket. I spoke with Mr Keyes just now. He'll give a renewal for two months, he says. After he'll see. But he wants a par to call attention in the *Telegraph* too, the Saturday pink. And he wants it copied if it's not too late I told councillor Nannetti from the *Kilkenny People*. I can have access to it in the national library. House of keys, don't you see? His name is Keyes. It's a play on the name. But he practically promised he'd give the renewal. But he wants just a little puff. What will I tell him, Mr Crawford?

K. M. A.

—Will you tell him he can kiss my arse? Myles Crawford said throwing out his arm for emphasis. Tell him that straight from the stable.

A bit nervy. Look out for squalls. All off for a drink. Arm in arm. Lenehan's yachting cap on the cadge beyond. Usual blarney. Wonder is that young Dedalus the moving spirit. Has a good pair of boots on him today. Last time I saw him he had his heels on view. Been walking in muck somewhere. Careless chap. What was he doing in Irishtown?[6]

---

5. A pig's foot and a bottle of beer.
6. During the funeral procession, Bloom and the other members of the funeral party saw Stephen walking along the beach at Sandymount, near Irishtown.

—Well, Mr Bloom said, his eyes returning, if I can get the design I suppose it's worth a short par. He'd give the ad I think. I'll tell him . . .

K. M. R. I. A

—He can kiss my royal Irish arse, Myles Crawford cried loudly over his shoulder. Any time he likes, tell him.

While Mr Bloom stood weighing the point and about to smile he strode on jerkily.

RAISING THE WIND

—*Nulla bona*,[7] Jack, he said, raising his hand to his chin. I'm up to here. I've been through the hoop myself. I was looking for a fellow to back a bill for me no later than last week. You must take the will for the deed. Sorry, Jack. With a heart and a half if I could raise the wind anyhow.

J. J. O'Molloy pulled a long face and walked on silently. They caught up on the others and walked abreast.

—When they have eaten the brawn and the bread and wiped their twenty fingers in the paper the bread was wrapped in, they go nearer to the railings.

—Something for you, the professor explained to Myles Crawford. Two old Dublin women on the top of Nelson's pillar.

SOME COLUMN!—THAT'S WHAT WADDLER ONE SAID

—That's new, Myles Crawford said. That's copy. Out for the waxies' Dargle. Two old trickies, what?

—But they are afraid the pillar will fall, Stephen went on. They see the roofs and argue about where the different churches are: Rathmines' blue dome, Adam and Eve's, saint Laurence O'Toole's. But it makes them giddy to look so they pull up their skirts . . .

THOSE SLIGHTLY RAMBUNCTIOUS FEMALES

—Easy all, Myles Crawford said. No poetic licence. We're in the archdiocese here.

—And settle down on their striped petticoats, peering up at the statue of the onehandled adulterer.[8]

—Onehandled adulterer! the professor cried. I like that. I see the idea. I see what you mean.

DAMES DONATE DUBLIN'S CITS
SPEEDPILLS VELOCITOUS AEROLITHS, BELIEF

—It gives them a crick in their necks, Stephen said, and they are too tired to look up or down or to speak. They put the bag of plums between them and eat the plums out of it, one after another, wiping off with their handkerchiefs the plumjuice that dribbles out of their mouths and spitting the plumstones slowly out between the railings.

He gave a sudden loud young laugh as a close. Lenehan and Mr O'Madden Burke, hearing, turned, beckoned and led on across towards Mooney's.

—Finished? Myles Crawford said. So long as they do no worse.

---

7. "No goods": i.e., no money to lend.
8. Admiral Lord Nelson (1758–1805) was one-armed after a battlefield injury and was involved in a widely publicized extramarital affair.

SOPHIST WALLOPS HAUGHTY HELEN SQUARE ON PROBOSCIS.
SPARTANS GNASH MOLARS.
ITHACANS VOW PEN IS CHAMP.

—You remind me of Antisthenes, the professor said, a disciple of Gorgias, the sophist. It is said of him that none could tell if he were bitterer against others or against himself. He was the son of a noble and a bondwoman. And he wrote a book in which he took away the palm of beauty from Argive Helen and handed it to poor Penelope.

Poor Penelope. Penelope Rich.[9]

They made ready to cross O'Connell street.

HELLO THERE, CENTRAL!

At various points along the eight lines tramcars with motionless trolleys stood in their tracks, bound for or from Rathmines, Rathfarnham, Kingstown, Blackrock and Dalkey, Sandymount Green, Ringsend and Sandymount Tower, Donnybrook, Palmerston Park and Upper Rathmines, all still, becalmed in short circuit. Hackney cars, cabs, delivery waggons, mailvans, private broughams, aerated mineral water floats with rattling crates of bottles, rattled, rolled, horsedrawn, rapidly.

WHAT?—AND LIKEWISE—WHERE?

—But what do you call it? Myles Crawford asked. Where did they get the plums?

VIRGILIAN, SAYS PEDAGOGUE.
SOPHOMORE PLUMPS FOR OLD MAN MOSES.

—Call it, wait, the professor said, opening his long lips wide to reflect. Call it, let me see. Call it: *Deus nobis haec otia fecit.*[1]

—No, Stephen said, I call it *A Pisgah Sight of Palestine or The Parable of The Plums.*[2]

—I see, the professor said.

He laughed richly.

—I see, he said again with new pleasure. Moses and the promised land. We gave him that idea, he added to J. J. O'Molloy.

HORATIO IS CYNOSURE[3] THIS FAIR JUNE DAY

J. J. O'Molloy sent a weary sidelong glance towards the statue and held his peace.

—I see, the professor said.

He halted on sir John Gray's pavement island and peered aloft at Nelson through the meshes of his wry smile.

DIMINISHED DIGITS PROVE TOO TITILLATING
FOR FRISKY FRUMPS. ANNE WIMBLES, FLO
WANGLES-YET CAN YOU BLAME THEM?

—Onehandled adulterer, he said smiling grimly. That tickles me I must say.

—Tickled the old ones too, Myles Crawford said, if the God Almighty's truth was known.

---

9. Adulterous noblewoman (1562–1607), the lovely "Stella" of Sir Philip Sidney's *Astrophel and Stella* (1591).
1. God has made this peace for us (Latin; from Virgil, *Eclogues* 1:6).

2. Moses was granted a view of Israel from the top of Mount Pisgah, without being allowed to enter in before his death; see Deuteronomy 34.1–5.
3. The center of attention.

T. S. Eliot

1888–1965

T. S. Eliot was one of the dominant forces in English-language poetry of the twentieth century. When the entire body of Eliot's writing and influence is taken into account—not only his relatively modest poetic and dramatic production, but his literary criticism, his religious and cultural criticism, his editorial work at the British publishing house Faber and Faber, his influence on younger poets coming up in his wake, and quite simply his *presence* as a literary and cultural icon—no one looms larger. As one of those younger poets, Karl Shapiro, has written: "Eliot is untouchable; he is Modern Literature incarnate and an institution unto himself." Eliot's obituary in *Life* magazine declared that "Our age beyond any doubt has been, and will continue to be, the Age of Eliot."

Thomas Stearns Eliot was born in Saint Louis, Missouri. The roots of Eliot's family tree go deep into American, and specifically New England, soil. His ancestor Andrew Eliot was one of the original settlers of the Massachusetts Bay Colony, emigrating from East Coker, in Somerset, England, in the mid-seventeenth century; he later became one of the jurors who tried the Salem "witches." The Eliots became a distinguished New England family; the Eliot family tree includes a president of Harvard University and three U.S. Presidents (John Adams, John Quincy Adams, and Rutherford B. Hayes). In 1834 the Reverend William Greenleaf Eliot, the poet's grandfather, graduated from Harvard and moved to Saint Louis, where he established the city's first Unitarian church; he went on to found Washington University, and became its chancellor in 1872. It was into this family environment—redolent of New England, New England religion (Unitarianism), and New England educational tradition (Harvard)—that Eliot was born in 1888. And yet in a 1960 essay, Eliot wrote "My urban imagery was that of Saint Louis, upon which that of Paris and London had been superimposed." The sights and sounds of Saint Louis impressed themselves deeply on Eliot's young imagination, especially the looming figure of the Mississippi River (which he was to call "a strong brown god" in *The Dry Salvages*).

From age ten Eliot attended Smith Academy in Saint Louis—also founded by his grandfather—and spent his last year of secondary school at the Milton Academy in Milton, Massachusetts, in preparation for his entrance into Harvard in 1906. Eliot went on to take his A.B. (1909) and M.A. (1910) degrees from Harvard and largely completed a Ph.D. in philosophy from Harvard, first spending a relatively unstructured year in Paris, attending lectures at the Sorbonne and hearing Henri Bergson lecture at the Collège de France. He wrote a doctoral dissertation on the neo-idealist philosopher F. H. Bradley in 1916, which was accepted by the philosophy department at Harvard, but he never returned to Cambridge to defend the dissertation and take the degree. Eliot's year in Paris was crucial in many ways; in addition to breathing in the vital Parisian intellectual and artistic scene, he soaked up the writing of late-nineteenth-century French poets like Jules Laforgue, Tristan Corbière, and Charles Baudelaire.

Eliot's poems are deeply indebted both to French and to British poets. The poem with which Eliot broke onto the modern poetry scene was *The Love Song of J. Alfred Prufrock*, composed between 1910 and 1911. In a strikingly new and jarring idiom, the poem builds on the dramatic monologues of Robert Browning, breaking up the unified voice at the center of Browning's experiments with startling juxtapositions and transitions, and adding the violent and disturbing imagery of the French symbolist poets. The resulting poem is a heavily ironic "love song" in which neither lover nor beloved exists with any solidity outside the straitjacket of "a formulated phrase"; Prufrock, like modern European humanity whom he represents, is unable to penetrate the thick husk of habit, custom, and cliché to arrive at something substantial.

Eliot, and the poem, came to the notice of modern literature impresario Ezra Pound; in 1915 Pound saw to it that *Prufrock* was published in Harriet Monroe's influential *Poetry* magazine, as well as in his own *Catholic Anthology*, which brought Eliot to the notice of the (largely hostile) British literary establishment in the person of reviewers like the *Quarterly Review's* Arthur Waugh. Eliot wrote three other great poems in this early period, *Portrait of a Lady*, *Preludes*, and *Rhapsody on a Windy Night*. Like *Prufrock*, the poems deal unflinchingly with loneliness, alienation, isolation; while isolation is hardly a new theme for poetry, Eliot suggests in a particularly modernist form in these poems that our isolation from others derives from, and tragically mirrors, our isolation from ourselves. This internalized alienation was also one of the themes of Eliot's early and influential review essay *The Metaphysical Poets* (1921); in that piece, he suggested that English poetry had suffered through a long drought, dating from about the time of Milton, caused by what Eliot termed a "dissociation of sensibility." At the time of the metaphysical poets (in the seventeenth century), a poet, or any sensitive thinker, was a unified whole; "A thought to Donne," Eliot writes, "was an experience; it modified his sensibility. . . . the ordinary man's experience is chaotic, irregular, fragmentary." That chaotic consciousness seemed to Eliot especially pronounced in the early decades of the twentieth century; though not sanguine of easy solutions, he did believe that modern poets, writing a poetry that would synthesize the seemingly unrelated sensations and experiences of modern men and women, might show a way out of "the immense panorama of futility and anarchy which is contemporary history," as he wrote in 1923 in a review of Joyce's *Ulysses*.

A collection of Eliot's early poems was published in 1917 as *Prufrock and Other Observations* by the Egoist Press, through the offices of Pound. For the remainder of the decade, however, Eliot's poetic output was small; feeling himself at a creative cul de sac, he wrote a few poems in French in 1917, including *Dans le Restaurant* which later appeared, trimmed and translated, as a part of *The Waste Land*. On Pound's suggestion, Eliot set himself, as a formal exercise, to write several poems modeled on the quatrains of Théophile Gautier. Arguably the most significant and influential of Eliot's early writings, however, were his many critical essays and book reviews; between 1916 and 1921 he wrote nearly a hundred essays and reviews, many of which were published in 1920 as *The Sacred Wood*. Critics still disagree as to whether Eliot's poetry or critical prose has been the more influential; the most important of Eliot's critical precepts, such as the "impersonality" of poetry and the inherent difficulty of modern writing, have entered wholesale into the way that modern literature is studied and taught. Eliot's critical principles, complemented and extended by academics such as I. A. Richards, make up the foundation of what came to be known as the New Criticism, a major mode of reading that emphasizes close attention to verbal textures and to poetic ironies, paradoxes, and tensions between disparate elements—all prominent features of Eliot's own poetry.

Eliot lived in modest circumstances for several years, working as a schoolteacher and then a bank clerk between 1916 and 1922. He then edited an increasingly influential quarterly, *The Criterion* (1922–1939), and became an editor at Faber and Faber, a post he retained until his death. His reputation as a poet was confirmed in 1922 with *The Waste Land*, the epochal work that remains Eliot's best-known and most influential poem; Pound called it "about enough . . . to make the rest of us shut up shop." More than any other text of the century, *The Waste Land* forcibly changed the idiom that contemporary poetry must adopt if it were to remain contemporary. Perhaps the poem's most impressive formal achievement, created in no small part through Ezra Pound's judicious editorial work, is its careful balance between structure and chaos, unity and fragmentation; this poise is created in the poem in equal parts by the mythical structures Eliot used to undergird the contemporary action and the pedantic footnotes he added to the poem, after its periodical publication in the *Dial*, to call the reader's attention to those structures. *The Waste Land*—like *Ulysses*, *Finnegans Wake*, Pound's *Cantos*, and a number of other important texts—looks unified largely because we readers look for it to be unified.

Such a style of reading is one of the great triumphs of modernism, and one Eliot was instrumental in teaching to readers and teachers alike.

The Waste Land is justly celebrated for giving voice to the nearly universal pessimism and alienation of the early decades of the twentieth century Europe—though Eliot maintained to the end that he was not a spokesperson for his generation or for anything else, and that the poem was "only the relief of a personal and wholly insignificant grouse against life; it is just a piece of rhythmical grumbling." Owing to the development of recording technology, to "give voice" in this case is not merely a metaphor, for Eliot's recording of *The Waste Land*, in what Virginia Woolf called Eliot's "sepulchral voice," has been tremendously influential on two generations of poets and students. Eliot's critical principle of "impersonality," however, has sometimes served to obscure how very personal, on one level, the poem is. The poem was completed during Eliot's convalescence at a sanatorium in Margate, England ("On Margate Sands. / I can connect / Nothing with nothing," the speaker despairs in section 3, "The Fire Sermon") and in Lausanne, Switzerland; the speaker, like the poet, is reduced to shoring the fragments of a disappearing civilization against his ruin. The poem also bears painful testimony to the increasingly desperate state of Eliot's wife Vivien Haigh-Wood, whom he had married in 1915; she suffered terribly from what was at the time called "nervousness," and had finally to be institutionalized in 1938. Whole stretches of one-sided "dialogue" from the "A Game of Chess" section would seem to have been taken verbatim from the couple's private conversations: "My nerves are very bad to-night. Yes, bad. Stay with me. / Speak to me. Why do you never speak? Speak." On the draft of the poem, Pound wrote "photography" alongside this passage. *The Waste Land* remains one of the century's most incisive and insightful texts regarding the breakdown of social, communal, cultural, and personal relationships.

In 1930 Eliot's next important poem, the introspective and confessional *Ash Wednesday*, was published; in the time since the publication of *The Waste Land*, however, Eliot's personal belief system had undergone a sea change. In June 1927 he was baptized into the Anglican church; five months later, he was naturalized as a British citizen. In his 1928 monograph *For Lancelot Andrewes*, Eliot declared himself to be "classicist in literature, royalist in politics, and Anglo-Catholic in religion." His poem *Journey of the Magi*, published as a pamphlet a month after his baptism, addresses the journey Eliot himself had made through death to a rebirth—precisely the rebirth which, in the opening lines of *The Waste Land*, seems an impossibility.

The 1930s also saw Eliot's entry into the theater, with three poetic dramas: *The Rock* (1934), *Murder in the Cathedral* (1935), and *The Family Reunion* (1939). In his later years, these highbrow dramas were complemented with a handful of more popular social dramas, *The Cocktail Party* (1950), *The Confidential Clerk* (1954), and *The Elder Statesman* (1959). Though celebrated by critics at the time for their innovative use of verse and their willingness to wrestle with both modern problems and universal themes, the plays have slipped in popularity in recent years. Nevertheless, as fate would have it, Eliot is the posthumous librettist of one of the most successful musicals in the history of British and American theater: his playful children's book *Old Possum's Book of Practical Cats* (1939), light verse written for the enjoyment of his godchildren, was transformed by Andrew Lloyd Webber in 1980 into the smash-hit musical *Cats*.

Eliot's final poetic achievement—and, for many, his greatest—is the set of four poems published together in 1943 as *Four Quartets*. Eliot believed them to be the best of his writing; "The *Four Quartets*: I rest on those," he told an interviewer in 1959. Eliot's last years were brightened by increasing public accolades, including the Nobel Prize for literature in 1948; he became a very popular speaker on the public lecture circuit, attracting an audience of 15,000, for instance, at a lecture at the University of Minnesota in 1956, later published as *The Frontiers of Criticism*. These public appearances largely took the place of creative writing after 1960. In January 1947 Vivien Eliot died in an institution; a decade later, he married Esme Valery Fletcher, and enjoyed a fulfilling companionate marriage until his death in January 1965. Like Hardy and Yeats, Eliot expressed his wish to be buried in his ancestors' parish church, in his case at East Coker, the home of his ancestor Andrew Eliot; thus, in his death and burial, the opening of his poem *East Coker* is literalized: "In my beginning is my end."

The Love Song of J. Alfred Prufrock

> *S'io credessi che mia risposta fosse*
> *a persona che mai tornasse al mondo,*
> *questa fiamma staria senza più scosse.*
> *Ma per ciò che giammai di questo fondo*
> *non tornò vivo alcun, s'i'odo il vero,*
> *senza tema d'infamia ti rispondo.*[1]

    Let us go then, you and I,
When the evening is spread out against the sky
Like a patient etherised upon a table;
Let us go, through certain half-deserted streets,
5   The muttering retreats
Of restless nights in one-night cheap hotels
And sawdust restaurants with oyster-shells:
Streets that follow like a tedious argument
Of insidious intent
10   To lead you to an overwhelming question . . .
Oh, do not ask, "What is it?"
Let us go and make our visit.

In the room the women come and go
Talking of Michelangelo.

15   The yellow fog that rubs its back upon the window-panes,
The yellow smoke that rubs its muzzle on the window-panes,
Licked its tongue into the corners of the evening,
Lingered upon the pools that stand in drains,
Let fall upon its back the soot that falls from chimneys,
20   Slipped by the terrace, made a sudden leap,
And seeing that it was a soft October night,
Curled once about the house, and fell asleep.

And indeed there will be time
For the yellow smoke that slides along the street
25   Rubbing its back upon the window-panes;
There will be time, there will be time
To prepare a face to meet the faces that you meet;
There will be time to murder and create,
And time for all the works and days of hands

---

1. From Dante's *Inferno* (27.61–66). Dante asks one of the damned souls for its name, and it replies: "If I thought my answer were for one who could return to the world, I would not reply, but as none ever did return alive from this depth, without fear of infamy I answer thee."

30   That lift and drop a question on your plate;
      Time for you and time for me,
      And time yet for a hundred indecisions,
      And for a hundred visions and revisions,
      Before the taking of a toast and tea.

35   In the room the women come and go
      Talking of Michelangelo.

      And indeed there will be time
      To wonder, "Do I dare?" and, "Do I dare?"
      Time to turn back and descend the stair,
40   With a bald spot in the middle of my hair—
      (They will say: "How his hair is growing thin!")
      My morning coat, my collar mounting firmly to the chin,
      My necktie rich and modest, but asserted by a simple pin—
      (They will say: "But how his arms and legs are thin!")
45   Do I dare
      Disturb the universe?
      In a minute there is time
      For decisions and revisions which a minute will reverse.

      For I have known them all already, known them all—
50   Have known the evenings, mornings, afternoons,
      I have measured out my life with coffee spoons;
      I know the voices dying with a dying fall
      Beneath the music from a farther room.
          So how should I presume?

55   And I have known the eyes already, known them all—
      The eyes that fix you in a formulated phrase,
      And when I am formulated, sprawling on a pin,
      When I am pinned and wriggling on the wall,
      Then how should I begin
60   To spit out all the butt-ends of my days and ways?
          And how should I presume?

      And I have known the arms already, known them all—
      Arms that are braceleted and white and bare
      (But in the lamplight, downed with light brown hair!)
65   Is it perfume from a dress
      That makes me so digress?
      Arms that lie along a table, or wrap about a shawl.
          And should I then presume?
          And how should I begin?
                        . . .
70   Shall I say, I have gone at dusk through narrow streets
      And watched the smoke that rises from the pipes
      Of lonely men in shirt-sleeves, leaning out of windows? . . .

      I should have been a pair of ragged claws
      Scuttling across the floors of silent seas.
                        . . .

75 And the afternoon, the evening, sleeps so peacefully!
    Smoothed by long fingers,
    Asleep . . . tired . . . or it malingers,
    Stretched on the floor, here beside you and me.
    Should I, after tea and cakes and ices,
80 Have the strength to force the moment to its crisis?
    But though I have wept and fasted, wept and prayed,
    Though I have seen my head (grown slightly bald) brought
        in upon a platter,[2]
    I am no prophet—and here's no great matter;
    I have seen the moment of my greatness flicker,
85 And I have seen the eternal Footman hold my coat, and snicker,
    And in short, I was afraid.

    And would it have been worth it, after all,
    After the cups, the marmalade, the tea,
    Among the porcelain, among some talk of you and me,
90 Would it have been worth while,
    To have bitten off the matter with a smile,
    To have squeezed the universe into a ball
    To roll it towards some overwhelming question,
    To say: "I am Lazarus, come from the dead,
95 Come back to tell you all, I shall tell you all"[3]—
    If one, settling a pillow by her head,
        Should say: "That is not what I meant at all.
        That is not it, at all."

    And would it have been worth it, after all,
100 Would it have been worth while,
    After the sunsets and the dooryards and the sprinkled streets,
    After the novels, after the teacups, after the skirts that trail
        along the floor—
    And this, and so much more?—
    It is impossible to say just what I mean!
105 But as if a magic lantern[4] threw the nerves in patterns on a
        screen:
    Would it have been worth while
    If one, settling a pillow or throwing off a shawl,
    And turning toward the window, should say:
        "That is not it at all,
110   That is not what I meant, at all."
                                    . . .

    No! I am not Prince Hamlet, nor was meant to be;
    Am an attendant lord, one that will do
    To swell a progress, start a scene or two,
    Advise the prince; no doubt, an easy tool,
115 Deferential, glad to be of use,
    Politic, cautious, and meticulous;

2. Cf. Matthew 14. John the Baptist was beheaded by Herod and his head was brought to his wife, Herodias, on a platter.
3. Cf. John 11. Jesus raised Lazarus from the grave after he had been dead four days.
4. A device that employs a candle to project images, rather like a slide projector.

Full of high sentence, but a bit obtuse;
At times, indeed, almost ridiculous—
Almost, at times, the Fool.

120   I grow old . . . I grow old . . .
I shall wear the bottoms of my trousers rolled.

Shall I part my hair behind? Do I dare to eat a peach?
I shall wear white flannel trousers, and walk upon the beach.
I have heard the mermaids singing, each to each.

125   I do not think that they will sing to me.

I have seen them riding seaward on the waves
Combing the white hair of the waves blown back
When the wind blows the water white and black.

We have lingered in the chambers of the sea
130   By sea-girls wreathed with seaweed red and brown
Till human voices wake us, and we drown.

COMPANION READINGS

Arthur Waugh:[1] [Cleverness and the New Poetry]

Cleverness is, indeed, the pitfall of the New Poetry. There is no question about the ingenuity with which its varying moods are exploited, its elaborate symbolism evolved, and its sudden, disconcerting effect exploded upon the imagination. Swift, brilliant images break into the field of vision, scatter like rockets, and leave a trail of flying fire behind. But the general impression is momentary; there are moods and emotions, but no steady current of ideas behind them. Further, in their determination to surprise and even to puzzle at all costs these young poets are continually forgetting that the first essence of poetry is beauty; and that, however much you may have observed the world around you, it is impossible to translate your observation into poetry, without the intervention of the spirit of beauty, controlling the vision, and reanimating the idea.

The temptations of cleverness may be insistent, but its risks are equally great: how great indeed will, perhaps, be best indicated by the example of the "Catholic Anthology," which apparently represents the very newest of all the new poetic movements of the day. This strange little volume bears upon its cover a geometrical device, suggesting that the material within holds the same relation to the art of poetry as the work of the Cubist school hold to the art of painting and design. The product of the volume is mainly American in origin, only one or two of the contributors being of indisputably English birth. But it appears here under the auspices of a house associated with some of the best poetry of the younger generation, and is prefaced by a short lyric by Mr W. B. Yeats, in which that honoured representative of a very different school of inspiration makes bitter fun of scholars and critics, who

Edit and annotate the lines
That young men, tossing on their beds,
Rhymed out in love's despair
To flatter beauty's ignorant ear.

---

1. Influential publisher, editor and critic (1866–1943); father of novelist Evelyn Waugh. The *Catholic Anthology* (1914), which Waugh attacks in this review from the *Quarterly Review* (London), was edited by Ezra Pound and included Eliot's *The Love Song of J. Alfred Prufrock* and printed W. B. Yeats's *The Scholars* as a preface.

The reader will not have penetrated far beyond this warning notice before he finds himself in the very stronghold of literary rebellion, if not of anarchy. Mr Orrick Johns may be allowed to speak for his colleagues, as well as for himself:

> This is the song of youth,
> This is the cause of myself;
> I knew my father well and he was a fool,
> Therefore will I have my own foot in the path before I take a step;
> I will go only into new lands,
> And I will walk on no plank-walks.
> The horses of my family are wind-broken,
> And the dogs are old,
> And the guns rust;
> I will make me a new bow from an ash-tree,
> And cut up the homestead into arrows.

And Mr Ezra Pound takes up the parable in turn, in the same wooden prose, cut into battens:

> Come, my songs, let us express our baser passions.
> Let us express our envy for the man with a steady job and no worry about the future.
> You are very idle, my songs,
> I fear you will come to a bad end.
> You stand about the streets. You loiter at the corners and bus-stops,
> You do next to nothing at all.
> You do not even express our inner nobility,
> You will come to a very bad end.
> And I? I have gone half cracked.[2]

It is not for his audience to contradict the poet, who for once may be allowed to pronounce his own literary epitaph. But this, it is to be noted, is the "poetry" that was to say nothing that might not be said "actually in life—under emotion,"[3] the sort of emotion that settles down into the banality of a premature decrepitude:

> I grow old. . . . I grow old . . .
> I shall wear the bottoms of my trousers rolled.
> Shall I part my hair behind? Do I dare to eat a peach?
> I shall wear white flannel trousers, and walk upon the beach.
> I have heard the mermaids singing, each to each.
> I do not think that they will sing to me.

Here, surely, is the reduction to absurdity of that school of literary license which, beginning with the declaration "I knew my father well and he was a fool" naturally proceeds to the convenient assumption that everything which seemed wise and true to the father must inevitably be false and foolish to the son. Yet if the fruits of emancipation are to be recognised in the unmetrical, incoherent banalities of these literary "Cubists," the state of Poetry is indeed threatened with anarchy which will end in something worse even than "red ruin and the breaking up of laws." From such a catastrophe the humour, commonsense, and artistic judgment of the best of the new "Georgians" will assuredly save their generation; nevertheless, a hint of warning may not be altogether out of place. It was a classic custom in the family hall, when the

---

2. From Pound's *Further Instructions*.

3. Waugh here paraphrases Wordsworth's prescription in the Preface to *Lyrical Ballads*.

feast was at its height, to display a drunken slave among the sons of the household, to the end that they, being ashamed at the ignominious folly of his gesticulations, might determine never to be tempted into such a pitiable condition themselves. The custom had its advantages; for the wisdom of the younger generation was found to be fostered more surely by a single example than by a world of homily and precept.

Ezra Pound: Drunken Helots and Mr. Eliot[1]

Genius has I know not what peculiar property, its manifestations are various, but however diverse and dissimilar they may be, they have at least one property in common. It makes no difference in what art, in what mode, whether the most conservative, or the most ribald-revolutionary, or the most diffident; if in any land, or upon any floating deck over the ocean, or upon some newly contrapted craft in the aether, genius manifests itself, at once some elderly gentleman has a flux of bile from his liver; at once from the throne or the easy Cowperian[2] sofa, or from the gutter, or from the oeconomical press room there bursts a torrent of elderly words, splenetic, irrelevant, they form themselves instinctively into large phrases denouncing the inordinate product.

This peculiar kind of *rabbia* [madness] might almost be taken as the test of a work of art, mere talent seems incapable of exciting it. "You can't fool me, sir, you're a scoundrel," bawls the testy old gentleman.

Fortunately the days when "that very fiery particle" could be crushed out by the "Quarterly" are over, but it interests me, as an archaeologist, to note that the firm which no longer produces Byron, but rather memoirs, letters of the late Queen, etc., is still running a review, and that this review is still where it was in 1812, or whatever the year was; and that, not having an uneducated Keats to condemn, a certain Mr. Waugh is scolding about Mr. Eliot.[3]

All I can find out, by asking questions concerning Mr. Waugh, is that he is "a very old chap," "a reviewer." From internal evidence we deduce that he is, like the rest of his generation of English *gens-de-lettres* [men of letters], ignorant of Laforgue; of De Régnier's "Odelettes," of his French contemporaries generally, of De Gourmont's "Litanies," of Tristan Corbière, Laurent Tailhade.[4] This is by no means surprising. We are used to it from his "b'ilin'."[5]

However, he outdoes himself, he calls Mr. Eliot a "drunken helot." So called they Anacreon[6] in the days of his predecessors, but from the context in the "Quarterly" article I judge that Mr. Waugh does not intend the phrase as a compliment, he is – trying to be abusive, and moreover, he in his limited way has succeeded.

Let us sample the works of the last "Drunken Helot." I shall call my next anthology "Drunken Helots" if I can find a dozen poems written half so well as the following:

[Quotes *Conversation Galante*]

Our helot has a marvellous neatness. There is a comparable finesse in Laforgue's "Votre âme est affaire d'oculiste," but hardly in English verse.

---

1. Pound replied to Waugh's review in the *Egoist*, June 1917. A "helot" is a serf or slave.
2. After 18th-century poet William Cowper.
3. As in *Salutation the Third* (page 2298), Pound invokes the savage review of Keats that appeared in the *Quarterly Review* and was believed by his friends to have hastened Keats's death.
4. A series of French writers and texts that Pound admired. Jules Laforgue (1860–1887) was a French poet who helped develop free verse; he was an important influence on Eliot's early poetry. Henri de Régnier (1864–1936) was a French symbolist poet; Remy de Gourmont (1858–1915) was an influential French poet, novelist, essayist, publisher, and literary critic; Tristan Corbière, pseudonym for Édouard Joachim Corbière (1854–1919), was a French poet who worked with common speech and slang; and Laurent Tailhade (1854–1919) was a satiric French poet.
5. Byline, identifying the author of a newspaper article.
6. Greek writer of love poems and drinking songs.

Let us reconsider this drunkenness:

[Quotes *La Figlia Che Piange*]

And since when have helots taken to reading Dante and Marlowe? Since when have helots made a new music, a new refinement, a new method of turning old phrases into new by their aptness? However the "Quarterly," the century old, the venerable, the praeclarus,[7] the voice of Gehova[8] and Co., Sinai and 51A Albemarle Street, London, W. 1, has pronounced this author a helot. They are all for an aristocracy made up of, possibly, Tennyson, Southey and Wordsworth, the flunkey, the dull and the duller. Let us sup with the helots. Or perhaps the good Waugh is a wag,[9] perhaps he hears with the haspirate[1] and wishes to pun on Mr. Heliot's name: a bright bit of syzygy.[2]

I confess his type of mind puzzles me, there is no telling what he is up to.

I do not wish to misjudge him, this theory may be the correct one. You never can tell when old gentlemen grow facetious. He does not mention Mr. Eliot's name; he merely takes his lines and abuses them. The artful dodger,[3] he didn't (*sotto voce*[4]) "he didn't want 'people' to know that Mr. Eliot was a poet".

The poem he chooses for malediction is the title poem, "Prufrock." It is too long to quote entire.

[Quotes portion of *Prufrock*]

Let us leave the silly old Waugh. Mr. Eliot has made an advance on Browning. He has also made his dramatis personae contemporary and convincing. He has been an individual in his poems. I have read the contents of this book over and over, and with continued joy in the freshness, the humanity, the deep quiet culture. "I have tried to write of a few things that really have moved me" is so far as I know, the sum of Mr. Eliot's "poetic theory." His practice has been a distinctive cadence, a personal modus of arrangement, remote origins in Elizabethan English and in the modern French masters, neither origin being sufficiently apparent to affect the personal quality. It is writing without pretence. Mr. Eliot at once takes rank with the five or six living poets whose English one can read with enjoyment.

The "Egoist" has published the best prose writer of my generation. It follows its publication of Joyce by the publication of a "new" poet who is at least unsurpassed by any of his contemporaries, either of his own age or his elders.

It is perhaps "unenglish" to praise a poet whom one can read with enjoyment. Carlyle's generation wanted "improving" literature, Smile's "Self-Help"[5] and the rest of it. Mr. Waugh dates back to that generation, the virus is in his blood, he can't help it. The exactitude of the younger generation gets on his nerves, and so on and so on. He will "fall into line in time" like the rest of the bread-and-butter reviewers. Intelligent people will read "J. Alfred Prufrock"; they will wait with some eagerness for Mr. Eliot's further inspirations. It is 7.30 p.m. I have had nothing alcoholic to-day, nor yet yesterday. I said the same sort of thing about James Joyce's prose over two years ago. I am now basking in the echoes. Only a half-caste rag for the propaga-

---

7. Preeminent.
8. Jehovah.
9. Joker.
1. To aspirate is to add the "h" sound to the begining of a word: thus Eliot becomes "Hel[i]ot."
2. Any two related things (either similar or opposite).

3. The Artful Dodger is the name of Fagan's favorite pickpocket in Dickens's *Oliver Twist*.
4. In a low voice.
5. Samuel Smiles's *Self-Help* (1859) preached the Victorian gospel of self-improvement.

tion of garden suburbs, and a local gazette in Rochester, N.Y., U.S.A., are left whining in opposition. * * *

However, let us leave these bickerings, this stench of the printing-press, weekly and quarterly, let us return to the gardens of the Muses,

> Till human voices wake us and we drown,

as Eliot has written in conclusion to the poem which the "Quarterly" calls the *reductio ad absurdum:*[6]

> I have seen them riding seaward on the waves
> Combing the white hair of the waves blown back
> When the wind blows the water white and black.
>
> We have lingered in the chambers of the sea
> By sea-girls wreathed with seaweed red and brown
> Till human voices wake us, and we drown.

The poetic mind leaps the gulf from the exterior world, the trivialities of Mr. Prufrock, diffident, ridiculous, in the drawing-room, Mr. Apollinax's laughter "submarine and profound" transports him from the desiccated new-statesmanly atmosphere of Professor Canning-Cheetah's. Mr. Eliot's melody rushes out like the thought of Fragilion "among the birch-trees."[7] Mr. Waugh is my bitten macaroon at this festival.

The Waste Land

Like Conrad's *Heart of Darkness*—from which Eliot had originally planned to take his epigraph, "The horror! the horror!"—*The Waste Land* has become part of the symbolic landscape of twentieth-century Western culture; the text, like Conrad's, has been appropriated by commentators high and low, left and right, as an especially apt description of the psychosocial and interpersonal malaise of modern Europeans. Late in 1921 Eliot, who was suffering under a number of pressures both personal and artistic, took three months' leave from his job at Lloyd's Bank and went for a "rest cure" at a clinic in Lausanne, Switzerland. On his way he passed through Paris and showed the manuscript of the poem—really manuscripts of a number of fragments, whose interrelationship Eliot was trying to work out—to Ezra Pound; Pound and Eliot went through the poem again as Eliot returned to London in January 1922. Pound's editorial work was considerable, as the facsimile edition of the draft reveals; Pound said that he performed the poem's "caesarian operation," and Eliot dedicated *The Waste Land* to Pound—*il miglior fabbro* ("the better craftsman," a phrase from Dante).

The most obvious feature of *The Waste Land* is its difficulty. Eliot was perhaps the first poet and literary critic to argue that such "difficulty" was not just a necessary evil but in fact a constitutive element of poetry that would come to terms with the modern world. In his review of a volume of metaphysical poetry, Eliot implicitly links the complex poetry of Donne and Marvell with the task of the modern poet: "We can only say that it appears likely that poets in our civilization, as it exists at present, must be *difficult*. Our civilization comprehends great variety and complexity, and this variety and complexity, playing upon a refined sensibility, must produce various and complex results." In the case of *The Waste Land*, the difficulty lies primarily in the poem's dense tissue of quotations from and allusions to other texts; as Eliot's

6. Reduction to absurdity (Latin), the rhetorical technique of pushing the consequences of an idea to the point where it looks ridiculous.
7. The names and images in this sentence not taken from

Prufrock are from another of Eliot's early poems, *Mr. Apollinax*. The poem ends with the lines, "Of dowager Mrs. Phlaccus, and Professor and Mrs. Cheetah / I remember a slice of lemon, and a bitten macaroon."

own footnotes to the poem demonstrate, the poem draws its strength, and achieves a kind of universality, by making implicit and explicit reference to texts as widely different as Ovid's *Metamorphoses* and a World War I Australian marching song.

Beyond the density of the poem's quotations and allusions, Eliot hoped to suggest the possibilty of an order beneath the chaos. In his review of Joyce's *Ulysses* (published in November 1923) Eliot was to describe the "mythical method," deploying allusions to classical mythology to suggest an implicit (and recurring) order beneath contemporary history; and while his use of myth was not so methodical as Joyce's, his use of vegetation myth and romance structures points outside the world of the poem to "another world," where the brokenness of the waste land might be healed. At the time of writing the poem, however, Eliot could not see clearly where that healing might come from.

The Waste Land[1]

"Nam Sibyllam quidem Cumis ego ipse oculis meis vidi in ampulla pendere, et cum illi pueri dicerent: Σίβυλλα τί θέλεις; respondebat illa: ἀποθανεῖν θέλω."[2]

FOR EZRA POUND
il miglior fabbro.

I. THE BURIAL OF THE DEAD

April is the cruellest month, breeding
Lilacs out of the dead land, mixing
Memory and desire, stirring
Dull roots with spring rain.
5   Winter kept us warm, covering
Earth in forgetful snow, feeding
A little life with dried tubers.
Summer surprised us, coming over the Starnbergersee[3]
With a shower of rain; we stopped in the colonnade,
10   And went on in sunlight, into the Hofgarten[4],
And drank coffee, and talked for an hour.
Bin gar keine Russin, stamm' aus Litauen, echt deutsch.[5]
And when we were children, staying at the arch-duke's,
My cousin's, he took me out on a sled,
15   And I was frightened. He said, Marie,
Marie, hold on tight. And down we went.

---

1. Not only the title, but the plan and a good deal of the incidental symbolism of the poem were suggested by Miss Jessie L. Weston's book on the Grail legend: *From Ritual to Romance* (Cambridge). Indeed, so deeply am I indebted, Miss Weston's book will elucidate the difficulties of the poem much better than my notes can do; and I recommend it (apart from the great interest of the book itself) to any who think such elucidation of the poem worth the trouble. To another work of anthropology I am indebted in general, one which has influenced our generation profoundly; I mean *The Golden Bough*; I have used especially the two volumes *Adonis, Attis, Osiris*. Anyone who is acquainted with these works will immediately recognize in the poem certain references to vegetation ceremonies [Eliot's note]. Sir James Frazer (1854–1941) brought out the twelve volumes of *The Golden Bough*, a vast work of anthropology and comparative mythology and religion, between 1890 and 1915, with a supplement published in 1936.

2. From the *Satyricon* of Petronius (first century A.D.). "For once I myself saw with my own eyes the Sybil at Cumae hanging in a cage, and when the boys said to her, 'Sybil, what do you want?' she replied, 'I want to die.'" The Sybil was granted anything she wished by Apollo, if only she would be his; she made the mistake of asking for everlasting life, without asking for eternal youth.

3. A lake near Munich.

4. A public park in Munich, with a zoo and cafés.

5. "I'm not a Russian at all; I come from Lithuania, a true German."

In the mountains, there you feel free.
I read, much of the night, and go south in the winter.

What are the roots that clutch, what branches grow
20   Out of this stony rubbish? Son of man,[6]
You cannot say, or guess, for you know only
A heap of broken images, where the sun beats,
And the dead tree gives no shelter, the cricket no relief,[7]
And the dry stone no sound of water. Only
25   There is shadow under this red rock,
(Come in under the shadow of this red rock),
And I will show you something different from either
Your shadow at morning striding behind you
Or your shadow at evening rising to meet you;
30   I will show you fear in a handful of dust.
            Frisch weht der Wind
            Der Heimat zu
            Mein Irisch Kind,
            Wo weilest du?[8]
35   "You gave me hyacinths first a year ago;
They called me the hyacinth girl."
—Yet when we came back, late, from the hyacinth garden,
Your arms full, and your hair wet, I could not
Speak, and my eyes failed, I was neither
40   Living nor dead, and I knew nothing,
Looking into the heart of light, the silence.
Oed' und leer das Meer.[9]

Madame Sosostris, famous clairvoyante,
Had a bad cold, nevertheless
45   Is known to be the wisest woman in Europe,
With a wicked pack of cards.[1] Here, said she,
Is your card, the drowned Phoenician Sailor,
(Those are pearls that were his eyes.[2] Look!)
Here is Belladonna, the Lady of the Rocks,
50   The lady of situations.
Here is the man with three staves, and here the Wheel,

---

6. Cf. Ezekiel 2.7 [Eliot's note]. Ezekiel 2.8 reads: "But thou, son of man, hear what I say unto thee; Be not thou rebellious like that rebellious house: open thy mouth, and eat that I give thee."

7. Cf. Ecclesiastes 12.5 [Eliot's note]. "They shall be afraid of that which is high, and fears shall be in the way, and the almond tree shall flourish, and the grasshopper shall be a burden, and desire shall fail."

8. V. *Tristan and Isolde*, i, verses 5–8 [Eliot's note]. In Wagner's opera, Tristan sings this about Isolde, the woman he is leaving behind as he sails for home: "Fresh blows the wind to the homeland; my Irish child, where are you waiting?"

9. Id. iii, verse 24 [Eliot's note]. Tristan is dying and waiting for Isolde to come to him, but a shepherd, whom Tristan has hired to keep watch for her ship, reports only "Desolate and empty the sea."

1. I am not familiar with the exact constitution of the Tarot pack of cards, from which I have obviously departed to suit my own convenience. The Hanged Man, a member of the traditional pack, fits my purpose in two ways: because he is associated in my mind with the Hanged God of Frazer, and because I associated him with the hooded figure in the passage of the disciples to Emmaus in Part V. The Phoenician Sailor and the Merchant appear later; also the "crowds of people," and Death by Water is executed in Part IV. The Man with Three Staves (an authentic member of the Tarot pack) I associate, quite arbitrarily, with the Fisher King Himself [Eliot's note].

2. From Ariel's song, in Shakespeare's *The Tempest*: "Full fathom five thy father lies; / Of his bones are coral made; / Those are pearls that were his eyes: / Nothing of him that doth fade, / But doth suffer a sea-change" (1.2.399–403).

And here is the one-eyed merchant, and this card,
Which is blank, is something he carries on his back,
Which I am forbidden to see. I do not find
55   The Hanged Man.[3] Fear death by water.
I see crowds of people, walking round in a ring.
Thank you. If you see dear Mrs. Equitone,
Tell her I bring the horoscope myself:
One must be so careful these days.

60   Unreal City,[4]
Under the brown fog of a winter dawn,
A crowd flowed over London Bridge, so many,
I had not thought death had undone so many.[5]
Sighs, short and infrequent, were exhaled,[6]
65   And each man fixed his eyes before his feet.
Flowed up the hill and down King William Street,
To where Saint Mary Woolnoth kept the hours
With a dead sound on the final stroke of nine.[7]
There I saw one I knew, and stopped him, crying: "Stetson!
70   You who were with me in the ships at Mylae![8]
That corpse you planted last year in your garden,
Has it begun to sprout? Will it bloom this year?
Or has the sudden frost disturbed its bed?
O keep the Dog far hence, that's friend to men,[9]
75   Or with his nails he'll dig it up again!
You! hypocrite lecteur!—mon semblable,—mon frère!"[1]

II. A GAME OF CHESS[2]

The Chair she sat in, like a burnished throne,[3]
Glowed on the marble, where the glass
Held up by standards wrought with fruited vines
80   From which a golden Cupidon peeped out
(Another hid his eyes behind his wing)
Doubled the flames of sevenbranched candelabra
Reflecting light upon the table as
The glitter of her jewels rose to meet it,
85   From satin cases poured in rich profusion.
In vials of ivory and coloured glass
Unstoppered, lurked her strange synthetic perfumes,

3. The tarot card that depicts a man hanging by one foot from a cross.
4. Cf. Baudelaire: "Fourmillante cité, cité pleine de rêves, / Où le spectre en plein jour raccroche le passant" [Eliot's note].
5. Cf. *Inferno*, iii.55–7: "si lunga tratta / di gente, ch'io non avrei mai creduto / che morte tanta n'avesse disfatta" [Eliot's note]. "Such an endless train, / Of people, it never would have entered in my head / There were so many men whom death had slain."
6. Cf. *Inferno*, iv. 25–7: "Quivi, secondo che per ascoltare, / non avea pianto, ma' che di sospiri, / che l'aura eterna facevan tremare" [Eliot's note]. "We heard no

loud complaint, no crying there, / No sound of grief except the sound of sighing / Quivering forever through the eternal air."
7. A phenomenon which I have often noticed [Eliot's note].
8. The Battle of Mylae (260 B.C.) in the First Punic War.
9. Cf. the Dirge in Webster's *White Devil* [Eliot's note].
1. V. Baudelaire, Preface to *Fleurs du Mal* [Eliot's note]. "Hypocrite reader—my double—my brother!"
2. Cf. Thomas Middleton's drama *A Game at Chess* (1625), a political satire.
3. Cf. *Antony and Cleopatra*, II. ii. 190 [Eliot's note].

Unguent, powdered, or liquid—troubled, confused
And drowned the sense in odours; stirred by the air
90   That freshened from the window, these ascended
In fattening the prolonged candle-flames,
Flung their smoke into the laquearia,[4]
Stirring the pattern on the coffered ceiling.
Huge sea-wood fed with copper
95   Burned green and orange, framed by the coloured stone,
In which sad light a carvèd dolphin swam.
Above the antique mantel was displayed
As though a window gave upon the sylvan scene[5]
The change of Philomel, by the barbarous king[6]
100   So rudely forced; yet there the nightingale[7]
Filled all the desert with inviolable voice
And still she cried, and still the world pursues,
"Jug Jug" to dirty ears.
And other withered stumps of time
105   Were told upon the walls; staring forms
Leaned out, leaning, hushing the room enclosed.
Footsteps shuffled on the stair.
Under the firelight, under the brush, her hair
Spread out in fiery points
110   Glowed into words, then would be savagely still.

"My nerves are bad to-night. Yes, bad. Stay with me.
Speak to me. Why do you never speak. Speak.
       What are you thinking of? What thinking? What?
I never know what you are thinking. Think."

115   I think we are in rats' alley[8]
Where the dead men lost their bones.

"What is that noise?"
                          The wind under the door.[9]
"What is that noise now? What is the wind doing?"
120   Nothing again nothing.

                                              "Do
"You know nothing? Do you see nothing? Do you remember
Nothing?"
       I remember
125   Those are pearls that were his eyes.

---

4. "Laquearia. V. *Aeneid,* I.726: "dependent lychni laque-
aribus aureis / incensi, et noctem flammis funalia vin-
cunt." [Eliot's note]. "Burning lamps hang from the gold-
panelled ceiling / And torches dispel the night with their
flames"; a *laquearia* is a panelled ceiling. The passage from
Virgil's *Aeneid* describes the banquet given by Dido for
her lover Aeneas.
5. "Sylvan scene. V. Milton, *Paradise Lost,* iv. 140 [Eliot's
note]. "And over head up grew / Insuperable height of
loftiest shade, / Cedar, and Pine, and Fir, and branching
Palm, / A Silvan Scene, and as the ranks ascend / Shade
above shade, a woody Theatre / Of stateliest view" The

passage describes the Garden of Eden, as seen through
Satan's eyes.
6. V. Ovid, *Metamorphoses,* vi, Philomela [Eliot's note].
Philomela was raped by King Tereus, her sister's husband,
and was then changed into a nightingale.
7. Cf. Part III, 1. 204 [Eliot's note].
8. Cf. Part III, 1. 195 [Eliot's note].
9. Cf. Webster: "Is the wind in that door still?" [Eliot's
note]. From John Webster's *The Devil's Law Case,*
3.2.162. The doctor asks this question when he discovers
that a "murder victim" is still breathing.

"Are you alive, or not? Is there nothing in your head?"[1]

But

O O O O that Shakespeherian Rag—[2]
It's so elegant
130   So intelligent
"What shall I do now? What shall I do?"
"I shall rush out as I am, and walk the street
With my hair down, so. What shall we do tomorrow?
What shall we ever do?"

135   The hot water at ten.
And if it rains, a closed car at four.
And we shall play a game of chess,
Pressing lidless eyes and waiting for a knock upon the
        door.[3]
When Lil's husband got demobbed,° I said—   *demobilized*
140   I didn't mince my words, I said to her myself,
HURRY UP PLEASE ITS TIME[4]
Now Albert's coming back, make yourself a bit smart.
He'll want to know what you done with that money he gave you
To get yourself some teeth. He did, I was there.
145   You have them all out, Lil, and get a nice set,
He said, I swear, I can't bear to look at you.
And no more can't I, I said, and think of poor Albert,
He's been in the army four years, he wants a good time,
And if you don't give it him, there's others will, I said.
150   Oh is there, she said. Something o' that, I said.
Then I'll know who to thank, she said, and give me a straight look.
HURRY UP PLEASE ITS TIME
If you don't like it you can get on with it, I said.
Others can pick and choose if you can't.
155   But if Albert makes off, it won't be for lack of telling.
You ought to be ashamed, I said, to look so antique.
(And her only thirty-one.)
I can't help it, she said, pulling a long face,
It's them pills I took, to bring it off, she said.
160   (She's had five already, and nearly died of young George.)
The chemist[5] said it would be all right, but I've never been the same.
You *are* a proper fool, I said.
Well, if Albert won't leave you alone, there it is, I said,
What you get married for if you don't want children?
165   HURRY UP PLEASE ITS TIME
Well, that Sunday Albert was home, they had a hot gammon,°   *ham*
And they asked me in to dinner, to get the beauty of it hot—
HURRY UP PLEASE ITS TIME
HURRY UP PLEASE ITS TIME

---

1. Cf. Part I, l. 37, 48 [Eliot's note].
2. Quoting an American ragtime song featured in Zieg-field's Follies of 1912.
3. Cf. the game of chess in Middleton's *Women beware*

Women [Eliot's note].
4. A British pub-keeper's call for a last round before clos-ing.
5. Pharmacist.

170   Goonight Bill. Goonight Lou. Goonight May. Goonight.
       Ta ta. Goonight. Goonight.
       Good night, ladies, good night, sweet ladies, good night, good night.[6]

III. The Fire Sermon

       The river's tent is broken; the last fingers of leaf
       Clutch and sink into the wet bank. The wind
175   Crosses the brown land, unheard. The nymphs are departed.
       Sweet Thames, run softly, till I end my song.[7]
       The river bears no empty bottles, sandwich papers,
       Silk handkerchiefs, cardboard boxes, cigarette ends
       Or other testimony of summer nights. The nymphs are departed.
180   And their friends, the loitering heirs of City directors;
       Departed, have left no addresses.
       By the waters of Leman[8] I sat down and wept . . .
       Sweet Thames, run softly till I end my song,
       Sweet Thames, run softly, for I speak not loud or long.
185   But at my back in a cold blast I hear
       The rattle of the bones, and chuckle spread from ear to ear.

       A rat crept softly through the vegetation
       Dragging its slimy belly on the bank
       While I was fishing in the dull canal
190   On a winter evening round behind the gashouse
       Musing upon the king my brother's wreck
       And on the king my father's death before him.[9]
       White bodies naked on the low damp ground
       And bones cast in a little low dry garret,
195   Rattled by the rat's foot only, year to year.
       But at my back from time to time I hear[1]
       The sound of horns and motors, which shall bring[2]
       Sweeney to Mrs. Porter in the spring.
       O the moon shone bright on Mrs. Porter[3]
200   And on her daughter
       They wash their feet in soda water
       Et O ces voix d'enfants, chantant dans la coupole![4]

       Twit twit twit
       Jug jug jug jug jug jug

---

6. Ophelia speaks these words in Shakespeare's *Hamlet*, and they are understood by the King as certain evidence of her insanity: "Good night ladies, good night. Sweet ladies, good night, good night" (4.5.72–73).

7. V. Spenser, *Prothalamion* [Eliot's note]; Spenser's poem (1596) celebrates the double marriage of Lady Elizabeth and Lady Katherine Somerset.

8. Lake Geneva. The line echoes Psalm 137, in which, exiled in Babylon, the Hebrew poets are too full of grief to sing.

9. Cf. *The Tempest*, I. ii [Eliot's note].

1. Cf. Marvell, *To His Coy Mistress* [Eliot's note]. "But at my back I always hear / Time's wingéd chariot hurrying near."

2. Cf. Day, *Parliament of Bees*: "When of the sudden, lis-

tening, you shall hear, / A noise of horns and hunting, which shall bring / Actaeon to Diana in the spring, / Where all shall see her naked skin . . ." [Eliot's note].

3. I do not know the origin of the ballad from which these are taken: it was reported to me from Sydney, Australia [Eliot's note]. Sung by Australian soldiers in World War I: "O the moon shone bright on Mrs. Porter / And on the daughter / Of Mrs. Porter / They wash their feet in soda water / And so they oughter / To keep them clean."

4. V. Verlaine, *Parsifal* [Eliot's note]. "And O those children's voices singing in the dome." Paul Verlaine's sonnet describes Parsifal, who keeps himself pure in hopes of seeing the holy grail, and has his feet washed before entering the castle.

205   So rudely forc'd.
           Tereu

           Unreal City
           Under the brown fog of a winter noon
           Mr. Eugenides, the Smyrna[5] merchant
210   Unshaven, with a pocket full of currants
           C.i.f.[6] London: documents at sight,
           Asked me in demotic° French   *vulgar*
           To luncheon at the Cannon Street Hotel[7]
           Followed by a weekend at the Metropole.[8]

215   At the violet hour, when the eyes and back
           Turn upward from the desk, when the human engine waits
           Like a taxi throbbing waiting,
           I Tiresias,[9] though blind, throbbing between two lives,
           Old man with wrinkled female breasts, can see
220   At the violet hour, the evening hour that strives
           Homeward, and brings the sailor home from sea,[1]
           The typist home at teatime, clears her breakfast, lights
           Her stove, and lays out food in tins.
           Out of the window perilously spread
225   Her drying combinations touched by the sun's last rays,
           On the divan are piled (at night her bed)
           Stockings, slippers, camisoles, and stays.
           I Tiresias, old man with wrinkled dugs
           Perceived the scene, and foretold the rest—
230   I too awaited the expected guest.

5. Seaport in western Turkey.
6. The currants were quoted at a price "carriage and insurance free to London"; and the Bill of Lading, etc., were to be handed to the buyer upon payment of the sight draft [Eliot's note].
7. A Hotel in London near the train station used for travel to and from continental Europe.
8. An upscale seaside resort hotel in Brighton.
9. Tiresias, although a mere spectator and not indeed a "character," is yet the most important personage in the poem, uniting all the rest. Just as the one-eyed merchant, seller of currants, melts into the Phoenician Sailor, and the latter is not wholly distinct from Ferdinand Prince of Naples, so all the women are one woman, and the two sexes meet in Tiresias. What Tiresias *sees*, in fact, is the substance of the poem. The whole passage from Ovid is of great anthropological interest: ". . . Cum Iunone iocos et 'maior vestra profecto est / Quam, quae contingit maribus,' dixisse, 'voluptas.' / Illa negat; placuit quae sit sententia docti / Quaerere Tiresiae: venus huic erat utraque nota. / Nam duo magnorum viridi coeuntia silva / Corpora serpentum baculi violaverat ictu / Deque viro factus, mirabile, femina septem / Egerat autumnos; octavo rursus eosdem / Vidit et 'est vestrae si tanta potentia plagae,' / Dixit 'ut auctoris sortem in contraria mutet, / Nunc quoque vos feriam!' percussis anguibus isdem / Forma prior rediit genetivaque venit imago. / Arbiter hic igitur sumptus de lite iocosa / Dicta Iovis firmat; gravius Saturnia iusto / Nec pro materia fertur doluisse suique / Iudicis aeterna damnavit lumina nocte, / At pater omnipotens (neque enim licet inrita cuiquam / Facta dei fecisse deo) pro lumine adempto / Scire futura dedit poenamque levavit honore" [Eliot's note]. This passage from Ovid's *Metamorphosis* describes Tiresias's sex change: "[The story goes that once Jove, having drunk a great deal,] jested with Juno. He said, 'Your pleasure in love is really greater than that enjoyed by men.' She denied it; so they decided to seek the opinion of the wise Tiresias, for he knew both aspects of love. For once, with a blow of his staff, he had committed violence on two huge snakes as they copulated in the green forest; and—wonderful to tell—was turned from a man into a woman and thus spent seven years. In the eighth year he saw the same snakes again and said: 'If a blow struck at you is so powerful that it changes the sex of the giver, I will now strike at you again.' With these words he struck the snakes, and his former shape was restored to him and he became as he had been born. So he was appointed arbitrator in the playful quarrel, and supported Jove's statement. It is said that Saturnia [i.e., Juno] was quite disproportionately upset, and condemned the arbitrator to perpetual blindness. But the almighty father (for no god may undo what has been done by another god), in return for the sight that was taken away, gave him the power to know the future and so lightened the penalty paid by the honor."
1. This may not appear as exact as Sappho's lines but I had in mind the "longshore" or "dory" fisherman, who returns at nightfall [Eliot's note]. "Hesperus, thou bringst home all things bright morning scattered: thou bringst the sheep, the goat, the child to the mother."

He, the young man carbuncular,° arrives,   *pimply*
A small house agent's clerk, with one bold stare,
One of the low on whom assurance sits
As a silk hat on a Bradford[2] millionaire.
235   The time is now propitious, as he guesses,
The meal is ended, she is bored and tired,
Endeavours to engage her in caresses
Which still are unreproved, if undesired.
Flushed and decided, he assaults at once;
240   Exploring hands encounter no defence;
His vanity requires no response,
And makes a welcome of indifference.
(And I Tiresias have foresuffered all
Enacted on this same divan or bed;
245   I who have sat by Thebes below the wall
And walked among the lowest of the dead.)
Bestows one final patronising kiss,
And gropes his way, finding the stairs unlit . . .

She turns and looks a moment in the glass,
250   Hardly aware of her departed lover;
Her brain allows one half-formed thought to pass:
"Well now that's done: and I'm glad it's over."
When lovely woman stoops to folly and[3]
Paces about her room again, alone,
255   She smoothes her hair with automatic hand,
And puts a record on the gramophone.

"This music crept by me upon the waters"[4]
And along the Strand, up Queen Victoria Street.
O City city, I can sometimes hear
260   Beside a public bar in Lower Thames Street,
The pleasant whining of a mandoline
And a clatter and a chatter from within
Where fishmen lounge at noon: where the walls
Of Magnus Martyr[5] hold
265   Inexplicable splendour of Ionian white and gold.

The river sweats[6]
Oil and tar
The barges drift
With the turning tide

2. An industrial town in Yorkshire; many of its residents became wealthy during World War I.
3. V. Goldsmith, the song in *The Vicar of Wakefield* [Eliot's note]. Oliver Goldsmith's character Olivia, on returning to the place where she was seduced, sings, "When lovely woman stoops to folly / And finds too late that men betray / What charm can soothe her melancholy, / What art can wash her guilt away? / The only art her guilt to cover, / To hide her shame from every eye, / To give repentance to her lover / And wring his bosom— is to die."

4. V. *The Tempest*, as above [Eliot's note].
5. The interior of St. Magnus Martyr is to my mind one of the finest among Wren's interiors. See *The Proposed Demolition of Nineteen City Churches* (P.S. King & Son, Ltd.) [Eliot's note].
6. The Song of the (three) Thames-daughters begins here. From line 292 to 306 inclusive they speak in turn. V. *Götterdämmerung*, III.I: the Rhine-daughters [Eliot's note]. In Richard Wagner's opera, *Twilight of the Gods*, the Rhine maidens, when their gold is stolen, lament that the beauty of the river is gone.

270   Red sails
      Wide
      To leeward, swing on the heavy spar.
      The barges wash
      Drifting logs
275   Down Greenwich reach
      Past the Isle of Dogs.[7]
              Weialala leia
              Wallala leialala

      Elizabeth and Leicester[8]
280   Beating oars
      The stern was formed
      A gilded shell
      Red and gold
      The brisk swell
285   Rippled both shores
      Southwest wind
      Carried down stream
      The peal of bells
      White towers
290   Weialala leia
              Wallala leialala

      "Trams and dusty trees.
      Highbury bore me. Richmond and Kew[9]
      Undid me. By Richmond I raised my knees
295   Supine on the floor of a narrow canoe."

      "My feet are at Moorgate,[1] and my heart
      Under my feet. After the event
      He wept. He promised 'a new start.'
      I made no comment. What should I resent?"

300   "On Margate Sands.[2]
      I can connect
      Nothing with nothing.
      The broken fingernails of dirty hands.
      My people humble people who expect
305   Nothing."
              la la

---

7. Greenwich is a borough on the south bank of the River Thames; the Isle of Dogs is a peninsula in East London formed by a sharp bend in the Thames called Greenwich Reach.
8. V. Froude, *Elizabeth*, vol. I, Ch. iv, letter of De Quadra to Philip of Spain: "In the afternoon we were in a barge, watching the games on the river. (The Queen) was alone with Lord Robert and myself on the poop, when they began to talk nonsense, and went so far that Lord Robert at last said, as I was on the spot there was no reason why they should not be married if the queen pleased" [Eliot's note].
9. "Cf. *Purgatorio*, V. 133: "Ricorditi di me, che son la Pia; / Siena mi fe', disfecemi Maremma." [Eliot's note]. "Remember me, that I am called Piety; / Sienna made me and Maremma undid me." Highbury, Richmond, and Kew are suburbs of London near the Thames.
1. A slum in East London.
2. A seaside resort in the Thames estuary.

To Carthage then I came[3]

Burning burning burning burning[4]
O Lord Thou pluckest me out[5]
310   O Lord Thou pluckest

burning

IV. DEATH BY WATER

Phlebas the Phoenician, a fortnight dead,
Forgot the cry of gulls, and the deep sea swell
And the profit and loss.
315   A current under sea
Picked his bones in whispers. As he rose and fell
He passed the stages of his age and youth
Entering the whirlpool.
                         Gentile or Jew
320   O you who turn the wheel and look to windward,
Consider Phlebas, who was once handsome and tall as you.

V. WHAT THE THUNDER SAID[6]

After the torchlight red on sweaty faces
After the frosty silence in the gardens
After the agony in stony places
325   The shouting and the crying
Prison and palace and reverberation
Of thunder of spring over distant mountains
He who was living is now dead
We who were living are now dying
330   With a little patience

Here is no water but only rock
Rock and no water and the sandy road
The road winding above among the mountains
Which are mountains of rock without water
335   If there were water we should stop and drink
Amongst the rock one cannot stop or think
Sweat is dry and feet are in the sand
If there were only water amongst the rock
Dead mountain mouth of carious° teeth that cannot spit   *rotting*
340   Here one can neither stand nor lie nor sit

3. V. St. Augustine's *Confessions*: "to Carthage then I came, where a cauldron of unholy loves sang all about mine ears" [Eliot's note].
4. The complete text of the Buddha's Fire Sermon (which corresponds in importance to the Sermon on the Mount) from which these words are taken, will be found translated in the late Henry Clarke Warren's *Buddhism in Translation* (Harvard Oriental Series). Mr. Warren was one of the great pioneers of Buddhist studies in the Occident [Eliot's note].

5. From St. Augustine's *Confessions* again. The collocation of these two representatives of eastern and western asceticism, as the culmination of this part of the poem, is not an accident [Eliot's note]. Augustine writes: "I entangle my steps with these outward beauties, but thou pluckest me out, O Lord, Thou pluckest me out."
6. In the first part of Part V three themes are employed: the journey to Emmaus, the approach to the Chapel Perilous (see Miss Weston's book), and the present decay of eastern Europe [Eliot's note].

There is not even silence in the mountains
But dry sterile thunder without rain
There is not even solitude in the mountains
But red sullen faces sneer and snarl
345 From doors of mudcracked houses
                                    If there were water
And no rock
If there were rock
And also water
350 And water
A spring
A pool among the rock
If there were the sound of water only
Not the cicada
355 And dry grass singing
But sound of water over a rock
Where the hermit-thrush sings in the pine trees
Drip drop drip drop drop drop drop[7]
But there is no water

360 Who is the third who walks always beside you?
When I count, there are only you and I together[8]
But when I look ahead up the white road
There is always another one walking beside you
Gliding wrapt in a brown mantle, hooded
365 I do not know whether a man or a woman
—But who is that on the other side of you?

What is that sound high in the air[9]
Murmur of maternal lamentation
Who are those hooded hordes swarming
370 Over endless plains, stumbling in cracked earth
Ringed by the flat horizon only
What is the city over the mountains
Cracks and reforms and bursts in the violet air
Falling towers
375 Jerusalem Athens Alexandria

---

7. This is *Turdus aonalaschkae pallasii*, the hermit-thrush which I have heard in Quebec County. Chapman says (*Handbook of Birds of Eastern North America*) "it is most at home in secluded woodland and thickety retreats. . . . Its notes are not remarkable for variety or volume, but in purity and sweetness of tone and exquisite modulation they are unequalled." Its "water-dripping song" is justly celebrated [Eliot's note].

8. The following lines were stimulated by the account of one of the Antarctic expeditions (I forget which, but I think one of Shackleton's): it was related that the party of explorers, at the extremity of their strength, had the constant delusion that there was one more member than could actually be counted [Eliot's note]. There seems also to be an echo of the account of Jesus meeting his disciples on the road to Emmaus: "Jesus himself drew near, and went with them. But their eyes were holden that they should not know him" (Luke 24.13–16).

9. Cf. Hermann Hesse, *Blick ins Chaos:* "Schon ist halb Europa, schon ist zumindest der halbe Osten Europas auf dem Wege zum Chaos, fährt betrunken im heiligen Wahn am Abgrund entlang und singt dazu, singt betrunken und hymnisch wie Dmitri Karamasoff sang. Ueber diese Lieder lacht der Bürger beleidigt, der Heilige und Seher hört sie mit Tränen" [Eliot's note]. "Already half of Europe, already at least half of Eastern Europe, on the way to chaos, drives drunk in sacred infatuation along the edge of the precipice, singing drunkenly, as though singing hymns, as Dmitri Karamazov sang. The offended bourgeois laughs at the songs; the saint and the seer hear them with tears."

Vienna London
Unreal

A woman drew her long black hair out tight
And fiddled whisper music on those strings
380   And bats with baby faces in the violet light
Whistled, and beat their wings
And crawled head downward down a blackened wall
And upside down in air were towers
Tolling reminiscent bells, that kept the hours
385   And voices singing out of empty cisterns and exhausted wells

In this decayed hole among the mountains
In the faint moonlight, the grass is singing
Over the tumbled graves, about the chapel
There is the empty chapel, only the wind's home.
390   It has no windows, and the door swings,
Dry bones can harm no one.
Only a cock stood on the rooftree
Co co rico co co rico
In a flash of lightning. Then a damp gust
395   Bringing rain

Ganga[1] was sunken, and the limp leaves
Waited for rain, while the black clouds
Gathered far distant, over Himavant.[2]
The jungle crouched, humped in silence.
400   Then spoke the thunder
DA
Datta: what have we given?[3]
My friend, blood shaking my heart
The awful daring of a moment's surrender
405   Which an age of prudence can never retract
By this, and this only, we have existed
Which is not to be found in our obituaries
Or in memories draped by the beneficent spider[4]
Or under seals broken by the lean solicitor
410   In our empty rooms
DA
Dayadhvam: I have heard the key[5]
Turn in the door once and turn once only

---

1. The river Ganges.
2. The Himalayas.
3. "Datta, dayadhvam, damyata" (Give, sympathize, control). The fable of the meaning of the Thunder is found in the Brihadaranyaka—Upanishad, 5, I. A translation is found in Deussen's Sechzig Upanishads des Vada, p. 489 [Eliot's note]. "That very thing is repented even today by the heavenly voice, in the form of thunder, in the form of thunder as 'Da,' 'Da,' 'Da,'. . . . Therefore one should practice these three things: self-control, alms-giving, and compassion."
4. Cf. Webster, The White Devil, v. vi: ". . . they'll remarry / Ere the worm pierce your winding-sheet, ere the spider / make a thin curtain for your epitaphs" [Eliot's note].

5. Cf. Inferno, xxxiii. 46: "ed io sentii chiavar l'uscio di sotto / all'orrible torre." Also F. H. Bradley, Appearance and Reality, p. 346: "My external sensations are no less private to myself than are my thoughts or my feelings. In either case my experience falls within my own circle, a circle closed on the outside; and, with all its elements alike, every sphere is opaque to the others which surround it. . . . In brief, regarded as an existence which appears in a soul, the whole world for each is peculiar and private to that soul." [Eliot's note]. In the passage from the Inferno, Ugolino tells Dante of his imprisonment and starvation until he became so desperate that he ate his children: "And I heard below me the door of the horrible tower being locked."

We think of the key, each in his prison
415   Thinking of the key, each confirms a prison
        Only at nightfall, aethereal rumours
        Revive for a moment a broken Coriolanus[6]
        DA
        Damyata: The boat responded
420   Gaily, to the hand expert with sail and oar
        The sea was calm, your heart would have responded
        Gaily, when invited, beating obedient
        To controlling hands

        I sat upon the shore
425   Fishing, with the arid plain behind me[7]
        Shall I at least set my lands in order?
        London Bridge is falling down falling down falling down
        Poi s'ascose nel foco che gli affina[8]
        Quando fiam uti chelidon—O swallow swallow[9]
430   *Le Prince d'Aquitaine à la tour abolie*[1]
        These fragments I have shored against my ruins
        Why then Ile fit you. Hieronymo's mad againe.[2]
        Datta. Dayadhvam. Damyata.
        Shantih   shantih   shantih[3]

Journey of the Magi[1]

        "A cold coming we had of it,
        Just the worst time of the year
        For a journey, and such a long journey:
        The ways deep and the weather sharp,
5   The very dead of winter."
        And the camels galled, sore-footed, refractory,
        Lying down in the melting snow.
        There were times we regretted
        The summer palaces on slopes, the terraces,
10   And the silken girls bringing sherbet.
        Then the camel men cursing and grumbling
        And running away, and wanting their liquor and women,
        And the night-fires going out, and the lack of shelters,

6. In Shakespeare's play of the same name, Coriolanus is a Roman general who is exiled and later leads the enemy in an attack against the Romans.
7. V. Weston, *From Ritual to Romance*; chapter on the Fisher King [Eliot's note].
8. V. *Purgatorio*, xxvi.148: "Ara vos prec per aquella valor / que vos condus al som de l'escalina, / sovegna vos a temps de ma dolor." / Poi s'ascose nel foco che gli affina" [Eliot's note]. In this passage, the poet Arnaut Daniel speaks to Dante: "Now I pray you, by the goodness that guides you to the top of this staircase, be mindful in time of my suffering."
9. V. *Pervigilium Veneris*. Cf. Philomela in Parts II and III [Eliot's note]. Philomel asks, "When shall I be a swallow?"
1. V. Gerard de Nerval, Sonnet *El Desdichado* [Eliot's

note]. "The Prince of Aquitane in the ruined tower."
2. V. Kyd's *Spanish Tragedy* [Eliot's note]. The subtitle of Kyd's play is, "Hieronymo's Mad Againe." His son having been murdered, Hieronymo is asked to compose a court play, to which he responds "Why then Ile fit you"; his son's murder is revenged in the course of the play.
3. Shantih. Repeated as here, a formal ending to an Upanishad. "The Peace which passeth understanding" is a feeble translation of the content of this word [Eliot's note]. The Upanishads are poetic commentaries on the Hindu Scriptures.
1. The narrative of the poem is based upon the tradition of the three wise men who journeyed to Bethlehem to worship the infant Christ; cf. Matthew 2.1–12.

And the cities hostile and the towns unfriendly
15   And the villages dirty and charging high prices:
A hard time we had of it.
At the end we preferred to travel all night,
Sleeping in snatches,
With the voices singing in our ears, saying
20   That this was all folly.

Then at dawn we came down to a temperate valley,
Wet, below the snow line, smelling of vegetation,
With a running stream and a water-mill beating the darkness
And three trees on the low sky.
25   And an old white horse galloped away in the meadow.
Then we came to a tavern with vine-leaves over the lintel,
Six hands at an open door dicing for pieces of silver,
And feet kicking the empty wine-skins.
But there was no information, and so we continued
30   And arrived at evening, not a moment too soon
Finding the place; it was (you may say) satisfactory.

All this was a long time ago, I remember,
And I would do it again, but set down
This set down
35   This: were we led all that way for
Birth or Death? There was a Birth, certainly,
We had evidence and no doubt. I had seen birth and death,
But had thought they were different; this Birth was
Hard and bitter agony for us, like Death, our death.
40   We returned to our places, these Kingdoms,
But no longer at ease here, in the old dispensation,
With an alien people clutching their gods.
I should be glad of another death.

1927

Tradition and the Individual Talent

1

In English writing we seldom speak of tradition, though we occasionally apply its name in deploring its absence. We cannot refer to "the tradition" or to "a tradition"; at most, we employ the adjective in saying that the poetry of So-and-so is "tradition-al" or even "too traditional." Seldom, perhaps, does the word appear except in a phrase of censure. If otherwise, it is vaguely approbative,[1] with the implication, as to the work approved, of some pleasing archaeological reconstruction. You can hardly make the word agreeable to English ears without this comfortable reference to the reassuring science of archaeology.

Certainly the word is not likely to appear in our appreciations of living or dead writers. Every nation, every race, has not only its own creative, but its own critical turn of mind; and is even more oblivious of the shortcomings and limitations of its critical habits than of those of its creative genius. We know, or think we know,

---

1. Approving.

from the enormous mass of critical writing that has appeared in the French language the critical method or habit of the French; we only conclude (we are such unconscious people) that the French are "more critical" than we, and sometimes even plume ourselves a little with the fact, as if the French were the less spontaneous. Perhaps they are; but we might remind ourselves that criticism is as inevitable as breathing, and that we should be none the worse for articulating what passes in our minds when we read a book and feel an emotion about it, for criticizing our own minds in their work of criticism. One of the facts that might come to light in this process is our tendency to insist, when we praise a poet, upon those aspects of his work in which he least resembles any one else. In these aspects or parts of his work we pretend to find what is individual, what is the peculiar essence of the man. We dwell with satisfaction upon the poet's difference from his predecessors, especially his immediate predecessors; we endeavour to find something that can be isolated in order to be enjoyed. Whereas if we approach a poet without this prejudice we shall often find that not only the best, but the most individual parts of his work may be those in which the dead poets, his ancestors, assert their immortality most vigorously. And I do not mean the impressionable period of adolescence, but the period of full maturity.

Yet if the only form of tradition, of handing down, consisted in following the ways of the immediate generation before us in a blind or timid adherence to its successes, "tradition" should positively be discouraged. We have seen many such simple currents soon lost in the sand; and novelty is better than repetition. Tradition is a matter of much wider significance. It cannot be inherited, and if you want it you must obtain it by great labour. It involves, in the first place, the historical sense, which we may call nearly indispensable to any one who would continue to be a poet beyond his twenty-fifth year; and the historical sense involves a perception, not only of the pastness of the past, but of its presence; the historical sense compels a man to write not merely with his own generation in his bones, but with a feeling that the whole of the literature of Europe from Homer and within it the whole of the literature of his own country has a simultaneous existence and composes a simultaneous order. This historical sense, which is a sense of the timeless as well as of the temporal and of the timeless and of the temporal together, is what makes a writer traditional. And it is at the same time what makes a writer most acutely conscious of his place in time, of his own contemporaneity.

No poet, no artist of any art, has his complete meaning alone. His significance, his appreciation is the appreciation of his relation to the dead poets and artists. You cannot value him alone; you must set him, for contrast and comparison, among the dead. I mean this as a principle of aesthetic, not merely historical, criticism. The necessity that he shall conform, that he shall cohere, is not onesided; what happens when a new work of art is created is something that happens simultaneously to all the works of art which preceded it. The existing monuments form an ideal order among themselves, which is modified by the introduction of the new (the really new) work of art among them. The existing order is complete before the new work arrives; for order to persist after the supervention[2] of novelty, the whole existing order must be, if ever so slightly, altered; and so the relations, proportions, values of each work of art toward the whole are readjusted; and this is conformity between the old and the new. Whoever has approved this idea of order, of the form of European, of English litera-

---

2. The appearance of something additional.

ture will not find it preposterous that the past should be altered by the present as much as the present is directed by the past. And the poet who is aware of this will be aware of great difficulties and responsibilities.

In a peculiar sense he will be aware also that he must inevitably be judged by the standards of the past. I say judged, not amputated, by them; not judged to be as good as, or worse or better than, the dead; and certainly not judged by the canons of dead critics. It is a judgment, a comparison, in which two things are measured by each other. To conform merely would be for the new work not really to conform at all; it would not be new, and would therefore not be a work of art. And we do not quite say that the new is more valuable because it fits in; but its fitting in is a test of its value— a test, it is true, which can only be slowly and cautiously applied, for we are none of us infallible judges of conformity. We say: it appears to conform, and is perhaps individual, or it appears individual, and may conform; but we are hardly likely to find that it is one and not the other.

To proceed to a more intelligible exposition of the relation of the poet to the past: he can neither take the past as a lump, an indiscriminate bolus,[3] nor can he form himself wholly on one or two private admirations, nor can he form himself wholly upon one preferred period. The first course is inadmissible, the second is an important experience of youth, and the third is a pleasant and highly desirable supplement. The poet must be very conscious of the main current, which does not at all flow invariably through the most distinguished reputations. He must be quite aware of the obvious fact that art never improves, but that the material of art is never quite the same. He must be aware that the mind of Europe—the mind of his own country—a mind which he learns in time to be much more important than his own private mind—is a mind which changes, and that this change is a development which abandons nothing *en route*, which does not superannuate either Shakespeare, or Homer, or the rock drawing of the Magdalenian draughtsmen.[4] That this development, refinement perhaps, complication certainly, is not, from the point of view of the artist, any improvement. Perhaps not even an improvement from the point of view of the psychologist or not to the extent which we imagine; perhaps only in the end based upon a complication in economics and machinery. But the difference between the present and the past is that the conscious present is an awareness of the past in a way and to an extent which the past's awareness of itself cannot show.

Some one said: "The dead writers are remote from us because we *know* so much more than they did." Precisely, and they are that which we know.

I am alive to a usual objection to what is clearly part of my programme for the *métier* of poetry. The objection is that the doctrine requires a ridiculous amount of erudition (pedantry), a claim which can be rejected by appeal to the lives of poets in any pantheon. It will even be affirmed that much learning deadens or perverts poetic sensibility. While, however, we persist in believing that a poet ought to know as much as will not encroach upon his necessary receptivity and necessary laziness, it is not desirable to confine knowledge to whatever can be put into a useful shape for examinations, drawing-rooms, or the still more pretentious modes of publicity. Some can absorb knowledge, the more tardy must sweat for it. Shakespeare acquired more essential history from Plutarch than most men could from the whole British Museum. What is to be

---

3. A lump; a mass of chewed food.

4. Drawings of hunting scenes, rendered in caves in France and Spain, c. 13,000–10,000 B.C.

insisted upon is that the poet must develop or procure the consciousness of the past and that he should continue to develop this consciousness throughout his career.

What happens is a continual surrender of himself as he is at the moment to something which is more valuable. The progress of an artist is a continual self-sacrifice, a continual extinction of personality.

There remains to define this process of depersonalization and its relation to the sense of tradition. It is in this depersonalization that art may be said to approach the condition of science. I, therefore, invite you to consider, as a suggestive analogy, the action which takes place when a bit of finely filiated[5] platinum is introduced into a chamber containing oxygen and sulphur dioxide.

2

Honest criticism and sensitive appreciation are directed not upon the poet but upon the poetry. If we attend to the confused cries of the newspaper critics and the *susurrus* [buzzing] of popular repetition that follows, we shall hear the names of poets in great numbers; if we seek not Blue-book[6] knowledge but the enjoyment of poetry, and ask for a poem, we shall seldom find it. I have tried to point out the importance of the relation of the poem to other poems by other authors, and suggested the conception of poetry as a living whole of all the poetry that has ever been written. The other aspect of this Impersonal theory of poetry is the relation of the poem to its author. And I hinted, by an analogy, that the mind of the mature poet differs from that of the immature one not precisely in any valuation of "personality," not being necessarily more interesting, or having "more to say," but rather by being a more finely perfected medium in which special, or very varied, feelings are at liberty to enter into new combinations.

The analogy was that of the catalyst. When the two gases previously mentioned are mixed in the presence of a filament of platinum, they form sulphurous acid. This combination takes place only if the platinum is present; nevertheless the newly formed acid contains no trace of platinum, and the platinum itself is apparently unaffected; has remained inert, neutral, and unchanged. The mind of the poet is the shred of platinum. It may partly or exclusively operate upon the experience of the man himself; but, the more perfect the artist, the more completely separate in him will be the man who suffers and the mind which creates; the more perfectly will the mind digest and transmute the passions which are its material.

The experience, you will notice, the elements which enter the presence of the transforming catalyst, are of two kinds: emotions and feelings. The effect of a work of art upon the person who enjoys it is an experience different in kind from any experience not of art. It may be formed out of one emotion, or may be a combination of several; and various feelings, inhering for the writer in particular words or phrases or images, may be added to compose the final result. Or great poetry may be made without the direct use of any emotion whatever: composed out of feelings solely. Canto XV of the *Inferno* (Brunetto Latini) is a working up of the emotion evident in the situation; but the effect, though single as that of any work of art, is obtained by considerable complexity of detail. The last quatrain gives an image, a feeling attaching to an image, which "came," which did not develop simply out of what precedes, but which was probably in suspension in the poet's mind until the proper combination arrived for it to add itself to.[7] The poet's mind is in fact a receptacle for seizing and

---

5. Eliot apparently means "made into filaments."
6. Official government publication.
7. He [Brunetto Latini] turned then, and he seemed, / across that plain, like one of those who run / for the green cloth at Verona; and of those, / more like the one who wins, than those who lose (*Inferno*, 15.119–122).

storing up numberless feelings, phrases, images, which remain there until all the particles which can unite to form a new compound are present together.

If you compare several representative passages of the greatest poetry you see how great is the variety of types of combination, and also how completely any semi-ethical criterion of "sublimity" misses the mark. For it is not the "greatness," the intensity, of the emotions, the components, but the intensity of the artistic process, the pressure, so to speak, under which the fusion takes place, that counts. The episode of Paolo and Francesca employs a definite emotion, but the intensity of the poetry is something quite different from whatever intensity in the supposed experience it may give the impression of. It is no more intense, furthermore, than Canto XXVI, the voyage of Ulysses, which has not the direct dependence upon an emotion.[8] Great variety is possible in the process of transmutation of emotion: the murder of Agamemnon,[9] or the agony of Othello, gives an artistic effect apparently closer to a possible original than the scenes from Dante. In the *Agamemnon*, the artistic emotion approximates to the emotion of an actual spectator; in *Othello* to the emotion of the protagonist himself. But the difference between art and the event is always absolute; the combination which is the murder of Agamemnon is probably as complex as that which is the voyage of Ulysses. In either case there has been a fusion of elements. The ode of Keats contains a number of feelings which have nothing particular to do with the nightingale, but which the nightingale, partly, perhaps, because of its attractive name, and partly because of its reputation, served to bring together.

The point of view which I am struggling to attack is perhaps related to the metaphysical theory of the substantial unity of the soul: for my meaning is, that the poet has, not a "personality" to express, but a particular medium, which is only a medium and not a personality, in which impressions and experiences combine in peculiar and unexpected ways. Impressions and experiences which are important for the man may take no place in the poetry, and those which become important in the poetry may play quite a negligible part in the man, the personality.

I will quote a passage which is unfamiliar enough to be regarded with fresh attention in the light—or darkness—of these observations:

> And now methinks I could e'en chide myself
> For doating on her beauty, though her death
> Shall be revenged after no common action.
> Does the silkworm expend her yellow labours
> For thee? For thee does she undo herself?
> Are lordships sold to maintain ladyships
> For the poor benefit of a bewildering minute?
> Why does yon fellow falsify highways,
> And put his life between the judge's lips,
> To refine such a thing—keeps horse and men
> To beat their valours for her? . . . [1]

In this passage (as is evident if it is taken in its context) there is a combination of positive and negative emotions: an intensely strong attraction toward beauty and an equal-

---

8. Dante's *Inferno*, Canto 5, tells the story of the lovers Paolo and Francesca; Canto 26 tells of the suffering of Ulysses in hell.
9. In Aeschylus's drama *Agamemnon*, Clytemnestra kills her husband Agamemnon for having sacrificed her daughter, Iphigenia, to the goddess Artemis.

1. From Cyril Tourneur's *The Revenger's Tragedy* (1607), 3.4; the speaker is addressing the skull of his former beloved, murdered after she refused to respond to an evil duke's advances. The revenger will make up the skull to look alive, putting poison on its lips; the evil Duke then dies when he kisses this supposed maiden in a dusky garden.

ly intense fascination by the ugliness which is contrasted with it and which destroys it. This balance of contrasted emotion is in the dramatic situation to which the speech is pertinent, but that situation alone is inadequate to it. This is, so to speak, the structural emotion, provided by the drama. But the whole effect, the dominant tone, is due to the fact that a number of floating feelings, having an affinity to this emotion by no means superficially evident, have combined with it to give us a new art emotion.

It is not in his personal emotions, the emotions provoked by particular events in his life, that the poet is in any way remarkable or interesting. His particular emotions may be simple, or crude, or flat. The emotion in his poetry will be a very complex thing, but not with the complexity of the emotions of people who have very complex or unusual emotions in life. One error, in fact, of eccentricity in poetry is to seek for new human emotions to express; and in this search for novelty in the wrong place it discovers the perverse. The business of the poet is not to find new emotions, but to use the ordinary ones and, in working them up into poetry, to express feelings which are not in actual emotions at all. And emotions which he has never experienced will serve his turn as well as those familiar to him. Consequently, we must believe that "emotion recollected in tranquillity"[2] is an inexact formula. For it is neither emotion, nor recollection, nor, without distortion of meaning, tranquillity. It is a concentration, and a new thing resulting from the concentration, of a very great number of experiences which to the practical and active person would not seem to be experiences at all; it is a concentration which does not happen consciously or of deliberation. These experiences are not "recollected," and they finally unite in an atmosphere which is "tranquil" only in that it is a passive attending upon the event. Of course this is not quite the whole story. There is a great deal, in the writing of poetry, which must be conscious and deliberate. In fact, the bad poet is usually unconscious where he ought to be conscious, and conscious where he ought to be unconscious. Both errors tend to make him "personal." Poetry is not a turning loose of emotion, but an escape from emotion; it is not the expression of personality, but an escape from personality. But, of course, only those who have personality and emotions know what it means to want to escape from these things.

3

ὁ δὲ νοῦς ἴσως θειότερον τι καὶ ἀπαθές ἐστιν.[3]

This essay proposes to halt at the frontier of metaphysics or mysticism, and confine itself to such practical conclusions as can be applied by the responsible person interested in poetry. To divert interest from the poet to the poetry is a laudable aim: for it would conduce to a juster estimation of actual poetry, good and bad. There are many people who appreciate the expression of sincere emotion in verse, and there is a smaller number of people who can appreciate technical excellence. But very few know when there is an expression of *significant* emotion, emotion which has its life in the poem and not in the history of the poet. The emotion of art is impersonal. And the poet cannot reach this impersonality without surrendering himself wholly to the work to be done. And he is not likely to know what is to be done unless he lives in what is not merely the present, but the present moment of the past, unless he is conscious, not of what is dead, but of what is already living.

---

2. This is Wordsworth's famous description of poetry in the Preface to *Lyrical Ballads*; see page 1538.

3. The mind is doubtless something more divine and unimpressionable (From Aristotle's *De Anima* [*On the Soul*]).

Virginia Woolf

1882–1941

Virginia Woolf is the foremost woman writer of the twentieth century, writing in any language; within British literature, Woolf is in the company of James Joyce, T. S. Eliot, William Butler Yeats and few others as a major author, of whatever gender. To take account of the transformations in modern English literature—in language, in style, and in substance—requires reckoning with Virginia Woolf, one of the chief architects of literary modernism. By 1962 Edward Albee could sardonically title a play *Who's Afraid of Virginia Woolf?*, knowing that her name would signify the greatness of modern literature. Woolf wrote luminous and intricate novels, two pivotal books on sexual politics, society, and war, several volumes of short stories and collected essays, reviews and pamphlets, and thirty volumes of a remarkable diary. Woolf was a woman of letters in an almost old-fashioned sense, one of the century's subtlest observers of social and psychic life, and a hauntingly beautiful prose writer.

Woolf's writing career began in childhood but was officially launched in 1915 with the publication of her first novel, *The Voyage Out*, when she was thirty-three. *The Voyage Out* was an emblematic beginning for her public career as a novelist, with its title suggesting the need to venture forth, to make a voyage into the world and out of the imprisonments of life and language. This novel paid special homage to *Heart of Darkness*, Joseph Conrad's story of a voyage through Africa that uncovers the heart of Europe's imperial encounter with the African continent and its exploited people. The theme resonated for Woolf throughout her books, because she too concentrated on the costs—both social and personal—of attempting to gain freedom. With the exception of *Orlando* (1928), a playful and flamboyant novel with a few scenes set in Turkey and Russia, Woolf was never again to set a novel outside the geographical confines of England. Voyaging out had become a matter of voyaging within. Woolf does not turn away from the larger world; she sets that larger world and its history squarely in England.

Woolf's own roots went deep in Victorian literary culture. She was born in 1882 into a privileged and illustrious British professional family with connections to the world of letters on both sides. She was the third child of the marriage of Leslie Stephen and Julia Duckworth, both of whom had been widowed; Leslie Stephen had married a daughter of the novelist William Thackeray, and Julia had been the wife of a publisher, and was connected to a long line of judges, teachers, and magistrates. Woolf's father, eventually to become Sir Leslie, was a prominent editor and a striving philosopher, who was appointed president of the London Library. His fame was to come not from his philosophical work but from his massive *Dictionary of National Biography*, a book that placed, and ranked, the leading figures of British national life for many centuries. Woolf's *Orlando*, with its subtitle: *A Biography*, spoofed the entire enterprise of the biography of great men by having *her* great man, Orlando, unexpectedly turn into a woman halfway through the novel.

Woolf grew up as an intensely literary child, surrounded by her father's project of arbitrating the greatness of the (mostly) men of letters she nonetheless sought to emulate. Her mother Julia was a famed beauty, whose magical grace was captured in the photographs of her equally famous relative, the photographer Julia Margaret Cameron. Woolf was to provide a haunting portrait of both her mother and father in her novel *To the Lighthouse* (1927), where the beautiful and consummately maternal Mrs. Ramsay ministers to her irascible and intellectually tormented philosopher husband, Mr. Ramsay, until her sudden death deprives the family and its circle of friends of their ballast in life. Julia Stephen's premature death in 1895 had cast just such a pall over her own family, especially over thirteen-year-old Virginia, who had a mental breakdown. Breakdowns would recur at intervals throughout her life.

The death-haunted life characteristic of the Victorian family was Virginia Woolf's own experience. Two years after Julia died, Woolf's beloved half-sister and mother substitute, Stel-

Virginia Woolf and T. S. Eliot.

la Duckworth, died in childbirth at the age of twenty-seven. Woolf was also to lose her difficult but immensely loved father in 1904 (not so coincidentally, the same year Virginia was to
publish her first essay and review), and her brother Thoby died of typhoid contracted on a trip
to Greece with her in 1906. The novel *Jacob's Room* (1922) deals with a young man named
Jacob and his college room, as perceived by his sister after his death in World War I. The items
in Jacob's room are cloaked in memory and live in the consciousness of the sister as far more
than precious objects—memory infuses them with shared life. The dead return again and again
in Woolf's imagination and in her imaginative work; her development of the "moment of consciousness" in her writing, her novels' concentration on the binding powers of memory, and
her invocation of the spreading, intertwining branches of human relations persisting even after
death, may be the effect of her painful tutelage in loss.

    As an upper-class woman, Woolf and her sisters were not given a formal education, while
Thoby and Adrian both went to fine schools and ultimately to university. The sense of having
been deliberately shut out of education by virtue of her sex, was to inflect all of Woolf's writing and thinking. Education is a pervasive issue in her novels, and an enormous issue in her
essays on social and political life, *A Room of One's Own* (1929) and *Three Guineas* (1938).
Woolf became an autodidact, steeping herself in English literature, history, political theory,
and art history, but she never lost the keen anguish nor the self-doubt occasioned by the closed
doors of the academy to women. Education became for Woolf perhaps the key to transforming
the role and the perception of women in society, and writing became her own mode of entry
into the public world.

In 1912, Virginia Stephens married Leonard Woolf, like herself a member of the Bloomsbury group, but unlike her in being a Jew and coming from a commercial and far less illustrious family. Leonard Woolf was an "outsider" in anti-Semitic Britain no less than Virginia, who as a great woman writer was equally outside the norm. An accomplished writer in his own right, a political theorist and an activist in socialist issues and in anti-imperialist causes, Leonard Woolf devoted himself to Virginia and to her writing career. They established and ran the Hogarth Press together, an imprint that was to publish all of Virginia's books, as well as many important works of poetry, prose, and criticism from others. Virginia Woolf's erotic and emotional ties to women, and, in particular, her romance with Vita Sackville-West, while not necessarily explicit sexual—no one seems to know for a certainty—were indubitably of the greatest importance to her life. Despite this, she placed Leonard Woolf and their marriage at the center of her being, and their rich and complex partnership weathered Virginia's numerous mental breakdowns. When she felt another episode of depression overtaking her in 1941, it was partly her reluctance to subject Leonard to what she saw as the burden of her madness which tragically led her to drown herself in the river near their home and their beloved press.

Woolf's themes and techniques are all seen in the two stories included here. *Mrs Dalloway in Bond Street* (1923) is a story that became the germ of Woolf's great novel *Mrs Dalloway* (1925). For this story she returned to a character she had created in *The Voyage Out*, where Clarissa Dalloway appeared as the wife of Richard Dalloway, a diplomat. In recounting Clarissa Dalloway's excursion to fashionable Bond Street for a pair of gloves, Woolf uses a "stream of consciousness" technique that places the reader inside Clarissa's mind, showing how the modulations of thoughts can turn the simplest events into occasions for reflection on a host of themes: the changes wrought by the passage of time; the persisting effects of the First World War; the complex relations between men and women, middle-class people and servants, modern literature and its predecessors. This story is followed by *The Lady in the Looking-Glass: A Reflection* (1929), whose major characters are the lady of the title—and her drawing-room. "Examine for a moment an ordinary mind on an ordinary day," Woolf wrote in an essay on *Modern Fiction* in 1925:

> The mind receives a myriad impressions—trivial, fantastic, evanescent, or engraved with the sharpness of steel. From all sides they come, an incessant shower of innumerable atoms; and, as they fall, as they shape themselves into the life of Monday or Tuesday, the accent falls differently from of old; the moment of importance came not here but there; so that, if a writer were a free man and not a slave, if he could write what he chose, not what he must, if he could base his work upon his own feeling and not upon convention, there would be no plot, no comedy, no tragedy, no love interest or catastrophe in the accepted style, and perhaps not a single button sewn on as the Bond Street tailors would have it.

Woolf's stories are written out of her own painfully won freedom of observation; the passages that follow from *A Room of One's Own* and *Three Guineas* meditate on the ways in which society and even human character would have to change in order for such freedom to spread.

Mrs Dalloway in Bond Street

Mrs Dalloway said she would buy the gloves herself. Big Ben was striking as she stepped out into the street. It was eleven o'clock and the unused hour was fresh as if issued to children on a beach. But there was something solemn in the deliberate swing of the repeated strokes; something stirring in the murmur of wheels and the shuffle of footsteps.

No doubt they were not all bound on errands of happiness. There is much more to be said about us than that we walk the streets of Westminster.[1] Big Ben too is nothing but steel rods consumed by rust were it not for the care of H.M's Office of Works. Only for Mrs Dalloway the moment was complete; for Mrs Dalloway June was fresh. A happy childhood—and it was not to his daughters only that Justin Parry had seemed a fine fellow (weak of course on the Bench); flowers at evening, smoke rising; the caw of rooks falling from ever so high, down down through the October air— there is nothing to take the place of childhood. A leaf of mint brings it back: or a cup with a blue ring.

Poor little wretches, she sighed, and pressed forward. Oh, right under the horses' noses, you little demon! and there she was left on the kerb stretching her hand out, while Jimmy Dawes grinned on the further side.

A charming woman, posed, eager, strangely white-haired for her pink cheeks, so Scope Purvis, C.B., saw her as he hurried to his office. She stiffened a little, waiting for Durtnall's van to pass. Big Ben struck the tenth; struck the eleventh stroke. The leaden circles dissolved in the air. Pride held her erect, inheriting, handing on, acquainted with discipline and with suffering. How people suffered, how they suffered, she thought, thinking of Mrs Foxcroft at the Embassy last night decked with jewels, eating her heart out, because that nice boy was dead, and now the old Manor House (Durtnall's van passed) must go to a cousin.

"Good morning to you," said Hugh Whitbread raising his hat rather extravagantly by the china shop, for they had known each other as children. "Where are you off to?"

"I love walking in London," said Mrs Dalloway. "Really it's better than walking in the country!"

"We've just come up," said Hugh Whitbread. "Unfortunately to see doctors."

"Milly?" said Mrs Dalloway, instantly compassionate.

"Out of sorts," said Hugh Whitbread. "That sort of thing. Dick all right?"

"First rate!" said Clarissa.

Of course, she thought, walking on, Milly is about my age—fifty—fifty-two. So it is probably *that*. Hugh's manner had said so, said it perfectly—dear old Hugh, thought Mrs Dalloway, remembering with amusement, with gratitude, with emotion, how shy, like a brother—one would rather die than speak to one's brother—Hugh had always been, when he was at Oxford, and came over, and perhaps one of them (drat the thing!) couldn't ride. How then could women sit in Parliament? How could they do things with men? For there is this extraordinarily deep instinct, something inside one; you can't get over it; it's no use trying; and men like Hugh respect it without our saying it, which is what one loves, thought Clarissa, in dear old Hugh.

She had passed through the Admiralty Arch and saw at the end of the empty road with its thin trees Victoria's white mound, Victoria's billowing motherliness, amplitude and homeliness, always ridiculous, yet how sublime thought Mrs Dalloway, remembering Kensington Gardens and the old lady in horn spectacles and being told by Nanny to stop dead still and bow to the Queen. The flag flew above the Palace. The King and Queen were back then. Dick had met her at lunch the other day—a thoroughly nice woman. It matters so much to the poor, thought Clarissa, and to the soldiers. A man in bronze stood heroically on a pedestal with a gun on her

---

1. District of central London, including the Houses of Parliament (with their famous clock tower "Big Ben"); it is also a fashionable residential area.

View of Regent Street, London, 1927.

left hand side—the South African war. It matters, thought Mrs Dalloway walking towards Buckingham Palace. There it stood four-square, in the broad sunshine, uncompromising, plain. But it was character she thought; something inborn in the race; what Indians respected. The Queen went to hospitals, opened bazaars—the Queen of England, thought Clarissa, looking at the Palace. Already at this hour a motor car passed out at the gates; soldiers saluted; the gates were shut. And Clarissa, crossing the road, entered the Park, holding herself upright.

June had drawn out every leaf on the trees. The mothers of Westminster with mottled breasts gave suck to their young. Quite respectable girls lay stretched on the grass. An elderly man, stooping very stiffly, picked up a crumpled paper, spread it out flat and flung it away. How horrible! Last night at the Embassy Sir Dighton had said, "If I want a fellow to hold my horse, I have only to put up my hand." But the religious question is far more serious than the economic, Sir Dighton had said, which she thought extraordinarily interesting, from a man like Sir Dighton. "Oh, the country will never know what it has lost," he had said, talking, of his own accord, about dear Jack Stewart.

She mounted the little hill lightly. The air stirred with energy. Messages were passing from the Fleet to the Admiralty. Piccadilly and Arlington Street and the Mall seemed to chafe the very air in the Park and lift its leaves hotly, brilliantly, upon waves of that divine vitality which Clarissa loved. To ride; to dance; she had adored all that. Or going on long walks in the country, talking, about books, what to do with one's life, for young people were amazingly priggish—oh, the things one had said! But one had conviction. Middle age is the devil. People like Jack'll never know that, she thought; for he never once thought of death, never, they said, knew he was dying. And now can never mourn—how did it go?—a head grown grey. . . . From the contagion of the world's slow stain. . . . Have drunk their cup a round or two before. . . . From the contagion of the world's slow stain![2] She held herself upright.

But how Jack would have shouted! Quoting Shelley, in Piccadilly! "You want a pin," he would have said. He hated frumps. "My God Clarissa! My God Clarissa!"—she could hear him now at the Devonshire House party, about poor Sylvia Hunt in her amber necklace and that dowdy old silk. Clarissa held herself upright for she had spoken aloud and now she was in Piccadilly, passing the house with the slender green columns, and the balconies; passing club windows full of newspapers; passing old Lady Burdett Coutt's house where the glazed white parrot used to hang; and Devonshire House, without its gilt leopards; and Claridge's, where she must remember Dick wanted her to leave a card on Mrs Jepson or she would be gone. Rich Americans can be very charming. There was St James's Palace; like a child's game with bricks; and now—she had passed Bond Street—she was by Hatchard's book shop. The stream was endless—endless—endless. Lords, Ascot, Hurlingham[3]—what was it? What a duck, she thought, looking at the frontispiece of some book of memoirs spread wide in the bow window, Sir Joshua perhaps or Romney; arch, bright, demure; the sort of girl—like her own Elizabeth—the only *real* sort of girl. And there was that absurd book, *Soapy Sponge*, which Jum used to quote by the yard; and Shakespeare's Sonnets. She knew them by heart. Phil and she had argued all day about the Dark Lady, and Dick had said straight out at dinner that night that he had never heard of her. Really, she had married him for that! He had never read Shakespeare! There must be some little cheap book she could buy for Milly—*Cranford*[4] of course! Was there ever anything so enchanting as the cow in petticoats? If only people had that sort of humour, that sort of self-respect now, thought Clarissa, for she remembered the broad pages; the sentences ending; the characters—how one talked about them as if they were real. For all the great things one must go to the past, she thought. From the contagion of the world's slow stain. . . . Fear no more the heat o' the sun. . . . And now can never mourn, can never mourn, she repeated, her eyes straying over the window; for it ran in her head; the test of great poetry; the moderns had never written anything one wanted to read about death, she thought; and turned.

Omnibuses joined motor cars; motor cars vans; vans taxicabs; taxicabs motor cars—here was an open motor car with a girl, alone. Up till four, her feet tingling, I know, thought Clarissa, for the girl looked washed out, half asleep, in the corner of the car after the dance. And another car came; and another. No! No! No! Clarissa smiled good-naturedly. The fat lady had taken every sort of trouble, but diamonds! orchids! at this hour of the morning! No! No! No! The excellent policeman would, when the time came, hold up his hand. Another motor car passed. How utterly unattractive! Why should a girl of that age paint black round her eyes? And a young man with a girl, at this hour, when the country—The admirable policeman raised his hand and Clarissa acknowledging his sway, taking her time, crossed, walked towards Bond Street; saw the narrow crooked street, the yellow banners; the thick notched telegraph wires stretched across the sky.

<hr/>

2. From *Adonais* (stanza 40), Percy Shelley's elegy on the early death of Keats.
3. Locations of fashionable sporting events (cricket, horse racing, and polo).
4. Popular novel by Elizabeth Gaskell (1810–1865); see page 1987.

A hundred years ago her great-great-grandfather, Seymour Parry, who ran away with Conway's daughter, had walked down Bond Street. Down Bond Street the Parrys had walked for a hundred years, and might have met the Dalloways (Leighs on the mother's side) going up. Her father got his clothes from Hill's. There was a roll of cloth in the window, and here just one jar on a black table, incredibly expensive; like the thick pink salmon on the ice block at the fishmonger's. The jewels were exquisite—pink and orange stars, paste, Spanish, she thought, and chains of old gold; starry buckles, little brooches which had been worn on sea-green satin by ladies with high head-dresses. But no looking! One must economise. She must go on past the picture dealer's where one of the odd French pictures hung, as if people had thrown confetti—pink and blue—for a joke. If you had lived with pictures (and it's the same with books and music) thought Clarissa, passing the Aeolian Hall, you can't be taken in by a joke.

The river of Bond Street was clogged. There, like a queen at a tournament, raised, regal, was Lady Bexborough. She sat in her carriage, upright, alone, looking through her glasses. The white glove was loose at her wrist. She was in black, quite shabby, yet, thought Clarissa, how extraordinarily it tells, breeding, self-respect, never saying a word too much or letting people gossip; an astonishing friend; no one can pick a hole in her after all these years, and now, there she is, thought Clarissa, passing the Countess who waited powdered, perfectly still, and Clarissa would have given anything to be like that, the mistress of Clarefield, talking politics, like a man. But she never goes anywhere, thought Clarissa, and it's quite useless to ask her, and the carriage went on and Lady Bexborough was borne past like a queen at a tournament, though she had nothing to live for and the old man is failing and they say she is sick of it all, thought Clarissa and the tears actually rose to her eyes as she entered the shop.

"Good morning," said Clarissa in her charming voice. "Gloves," she said with her exquisite friendliness and putting her bag on the counter began, very slowly, to undo the buttons. "White gloves," she said. "Above the elbow," and she looked straight into the shopwoman's face—but this was not the girl she remembered? She looked quite old. "These really don't fit," said Clarissa. The shop-girl looked at them. "Madame wears bracelets?" Clarissa spread out her fingers. "Perhaps it's my rings," And the girl took the grey gloves with her to the end of the counter.

Yes, thought Clarissa, it's the girl I remember, she's twenty years older. . . . There was only one other customer, sitting sideways at the counter, her elbow poised, her bare hand drooping vacant; like a figure on a Japanese fan, thought Clarissa, too vacant perhaps, yet some men would adore her. The lady shook her head sadly. Again the gloves were too large. She turned round the glass. "Above the wrist," she reproached the grey-headed woman, who looked and agreed.

They waited; a clock ticked; Bond Street hummed, dulled, distant; the woman went away holding gloves. "Above the wrist," said the lady, mournfully, raising her voice. And she would have to order chairs, ices, flowers, and cloak-room tickets, thought Clarissa. The people she didn't want would come; the others wouldn't. She would stand by the door. They sold stockings—silk stockings. A lady is known by her gloves and her shoes, old Uncle William used to say. And through the hanging silk stockings, quivering silver she looked at the lady, sloping shouldered, her hand drooping, her bag slipping, her eyes vacantly on the floor. It would be intolerable if dowdy women came to her party! Would one have liked Keats if he had worn red socks? Oh, at last—she drew into the counter and it flashed into her mind:

"Do you remember before the war you had gloves with pearl buttons?"

"French gloves, Madame?"

"Yes, they were French," said Clarissa. The other lady rose very sadly and took her bag, and looked at the gloves on the counter. But they were all too large—always too large at the wrist.

"With pearl buttons," said the shop-girl, who looked ever so much older. She split the lengths of tissue paper apart on the counter. With pearl buttons, thought Clarissa, perfectly simple—how French!

"Madame's hands are so slender," said the shop-girl, drawing the glove firmly, smoothly, down over her rings. And Clarissa looked at her arm in the looking-glass. The glove hardly came to the elbow. Were there others half an inch longer? Still it seemed tiresome to bother her—perhaps the one day in the month, thought Clarissa, when it's an agony to stand. "Oh, don't bother," she said. But the gloves were brought.

"Don't you get fearfully tired," she said in her charming voice, "standing? When d'you get your holiday?"

"In September, Madame, when we're not so busy."

When we're in the country thought Clarissa. Or shooting. She has a fortnight at Brighton. In some stuffy lodging. The landlady takes the sugar. Nothing would be easier than to send her to Mrs Lumley's right in the country (and it was on the tip of her tongue). But then she remembered how on their honeymoon Dick had shown her the folly of giving impulsively. It was much more important, he said, to get trade with China. Of course he was right. And she could feel the girl wouldn't like to be given things. There she was in her place. So was Dick. Selling gloves was her job. She had her own sorrows quite separate, "and now can never mourn, can never mourn," the words ran in her head, "From the contagion of the world's slow stain," thought Clarissa holding her arm stiff, for there are moments when it seems utterly futile (the glove was drawn off leaving her arm flecked with powder)—simply one doesn't believe, thought Clarissa, any more in God.

The traffic suddenly roared; the silk stockings brightened. A customer came in.

"White gloves," she said, with some ring in her voice that Clarissa remembered.

It used, thought Clarissa, to be so simple. Down, down through the air came the caw of the rooks. When Sylvia died, hundreds of years ago, the yew hedges looked so lovely with the diamond webs in the mist before early church. But if Dick were to die to-morrow? As for believing in God—no, she would let the children choose, but for herself, like Lady Bexborough, who opened the bazaar, they say, with the telegram in her hand—Roden, her favourite, killed—she would go on. But why, if one doesn't believe? For the sake of others, she thought taking the glove in her hand. The girl would be much more unhappy if she didn't believe.

"Thirty shillings," said the shop-woman. "No, pardon me Madame, thirty-five. The French gloves are more."

For one doesn't live for oneself, thought Clarissa.

And then the other customer took a glove, tugged it, and it split.

"There!" she exclaimed.

"A fault of the skin," said the grey-headed woman hurriedly. "Sometimes a drop of acid in tanning. Try this pair, Madame."

"But it's an awful swindle to ask two pound ten!"

Clarissa looked at the lady; the lady looked at Clarissa.

"Gloves have never been quite so reliable since the war," said the shop-girl, apologising, to Clarissa.

But where had she seen the other lady?—elderly, with a frill under her chin; wearing a black ribbon for gold eyeglasses; sensual, clever, like a Sargent drawing. How one can tell from a voice when people are in the habit, thought Clarissa, of making other people—"It's a shade too tight," she said—obey. The shop-woman went off again. Clarissa was left waiting. Fear no more she repeated, playing her finger on the counter. Fear no more the heat o' the sun. Fear no more she repeated. There were little brown spots on her arm. And the girl crawled like a snail. Thou thy wordly task hast done. Thousands of young men had died that things might go on. At last! Half an inch above the elbow; pearl buttons; five and a quarter. My dear slowcoach, thought Clarissa, do you think I can sit here the whole morning? Now you'll take twenty-five minutes to bring me my change!

There was a violent explosion in the street outside. The shop-women cowered behind the counters. But Clarissa, sitting very upright, smiled at the other lady. "Miss Anstruther!" she exclaimed.

The Lady in the Looking-Glass: A Reflection[1]

People should not leave looking-glasses hanging in their rooms any more than they should leave open cheque books or letters confessing some hideous crime. One could not help looking, that summer afternoon, in the long glass that hung outside in the hall. Chance had so arranged it. From the depths of the sofa in the drawing-room one could see reflected in the Italian glass not only the marble-topped table opposite, but a stretch of the garden beyond. One could see a long grass path leading between banks of tall flowers until, slicing off an angle, the gold rim cut it off.

The house was empty, and one felt, since one was the only person in the drawing-room, like one of those naturalists who, covered with grass and leaves, lie watching the shyest animals—badgers, otters, kingfishers—moving about freely, themselves unseen. The room that afternoon was full of such shy creatures, lights and shadows, curtains blowing, petals falling—things that never happen, so it seems, if someone is looking. The quiet old country room with its rugs and stone chimney pieces, its sunken book-cases and red and gold lacquer cabinets, was full of such nocturnal creatures. They came pirouetting across the floor, stepping delicately with high-lifted feet and spread tails and pecking allusive beaks as if they had been cranes or flocks of elegant flamingoes whose pink was faded, or peacocks whose trains were veined with silver. And there were obscure flushes and darkenings too, as if a cuttlefish had suddenly suffused the air with purple; and the room had its passions and rages and envies and sorrows coming over it and clouding it, like a human being. Nothing stayed the same for two seconds together.

But, outside, the looking-glass reflected the hall table, the sunflowers, the garden path so accurately and so fixedly that they seemed held there in their reality unescapably. It was a strange contrast—all changing here, all stillness there. One could not help looking from one to the other. Meanwhile, since all the doors and windows were open in the heat, there was a perpetual sighing and ceasing sound, the voice of the transient and the perishing, it seemed, coming and going like human breath, while in the looking-glass things had ceased to breathe and lay still in the trance of immortality.

Half an hour ago the mistress of the house, Isabella Tyson, had gone down the grass path in her thin summer dress, carrying a basket, and had vanished, sliced off by

1. Published in *Harper's Magazine*, December 1929.

the gilt rim of the looking-glass. She had gone presumably into the lower garden to pick flowers; or as it seemed more natural to suppose, to pick something light and fantastic and leafy and trailing, traveller's joy, or one of those elegant sprays of convolvulus that twine round ugly walls and burst here and there into white and violet blossoms. She suggested the fantastic and the tremulous convolvulus rather than the upright aster, the starched zinnia, or her own burning roses alight like lamps on the straight posts of their rose trees. The comparison showed how very little, after all these years, one knew about her; for it is impossible that any woman of flesh and blood of fifty-five or sixty should be really a wreath or a tendril. Such comparisons are worse than idle and superficial—they are cruel even, for they come like the convolvulus itself trembling between one's eyes and the truth. There must be truth; there must be a wall. Yet it was strange that after knowing her all these years one could not say what the truth about Isabella was; one still made up phrases like this about convolvulus and traveller's joy. As for facts, it was a fact that she was a spinster; that she was rich; that she had bought this house and collected with her own hands—often in the most obscure corners of the world and at great risk from poisonous stings and Oriental diseases—the rugs, the chairs, the cabinets which now lived their nocturnal life before one's eyes. Sometimes it seemed as if they knew more about her than we, who sat on them, wrote at them, and trod on them so carefully, were allowed to know. In each of these cabinets were many little drawers, and each almost certainly held letters, tied with bows of ribbon, sprinkled with sticks of lavender or rose leaves. For it was another fact—if facts were what one wanted—that Isabella had known many people, had had many friends; and thus if one had the audacity to open a drawer and read her letters, one would find the traces of many agitations, of appointments to meet, of upbraidings for not having met, long letters of intimacy and affection, violent letters of jealousy and reproach, terrible final words of parting—for all those interviews and assignations had led to nothing—that is, she had never married, and yet, judging from the mask-like indifference of her face, she had gone through twenty times more of passion and experience than those whose loves are trumpeted forth for all the world to hear. Under the stress of thinking about Isabella, her room became more shadowy and symbolic; the corners seemed darker, the legs of chairs and tables more spindly and hieroglyphic.

Suddenly these reflections were ended violently and yet without a sound. A large black form loomed into the looking-glass; blotted out everything, strewed the table with a packet of marble tablets veined with pink and grey, and was gone. But the picture was entirely altered. For the moment it was unrecognisable and irrational and entirely out of focus. One could not relate these tablets to any human purpose. And then by degrees some logical process set to work on them and began ordering and arranging them and bringing them into the fold of common experience. One realised at last that they were merely letters. The man had brought the post.

There they lay on the marble-topped table, all dripping with light and colour at first and crude and unabsorbed. And then it was strange to see how they were drawn in and arranged and composed and made part of the picture and granted that stillness and immortality which the looking-glass conferred. They lay there invested with a new reality and significance and with a greater heaviness, too, as if it would have needed a chisel to dislodge them from the table. And, whether it was fancy or not, they seemed to have become not merely a handful of casual letters but to be tablets graven with eternal truth—if one could read them, one would know everything there was to be known about Isabella, yes, and about life, too. The pages inside those marble-looking envelopes must be cut deep and scored thick with meaning. Isabella would come in, and take them, one by one, very slowly, and open them, and read them carefully word by word, and then with a profound sigh of comprehension, as if she had seen to the bottom of everything, she would tear the envelopes to little bits and tie the letters together and lock the cabinet drawer in her determination to conceal what she did not wish to be known.

The thought served as a challenge. Isabella did not wish to be known—but she should no longer escape. It was absurd, it was monstrous. If she concealed so much and knew so much one must prize her open with the first tool that came to hand—the imagination. One must fix one's mind upon her at that very moment. One must fasten her down there. One must refuse to be put off any longer with sayings and doings such as the moment brought forth—with dinners and visits and polite conversations. One must put oneself in her shoes. If one took the phrase literally, it was easy to see the shoes in which she stood, down in the lower garden, at this moment. They were very narrow and long and fashionable—they were made of the softest and most flexible leather. Like everything she wore, they were exquisite. And she would be standing under the high hedge in the lower part of the garden, raising the scissors that were tied to her waist to cut some dead flower, some overgrown branch. The sun would beat down on her face, into her eyes; but no, at the critical moment a veil of cloud covered the sun, making the expression of her eyes doubtful—was it mocking or tender, brilliant or dull? One could only see the indeterminate outline of her rather faded, fine face looking at the sky. She was thinking, perhaps, that she must order a new net for the strawberries; that she must send flowers to Johnson's widow; that it was time she drove over to see the Hippesleys in their new house. Those were the things she talked about at dinner certainly. But one was tired of the things that she talked about at dinner. It was her profounder state of being that one wanted to catch and turn to words, the state that is to the mind what breathing is to the body, what one calls happiness or unhappiness. At the mention of those words it became obvious, surely, that she must be happy. She was rich; she was distinguished; she had many friends; she travelled—she bought rugs in Turkey and blue pots in Persia. Avenues of pleasure radiated this way and that from where she stood with her scissors raised to cut the trembling branches while the lacy clouds veiled her face.

Here with a quick movement of her scissors she snipped the spray of traveller's joy and it fell to the ground. As it fell, surely some light came in too, surely one could penetrate a little farther into her being. Her mind then was filled with tenderness and regret. . . . To cut an overgrown branch saddened her because it had once lived, and life was dear to her. Yes, and at the same time the fall of the branch would suggest to her how she must die herself and all the futility and evanescence of things. And then again quickly catching this thought up, with her instant good sense, she thought life had treated her well; even if fall she must, it was to lie on the earth and moulder sweetly into the roots of violets. So she stood thinking. Without making any thought precise—for she was one of those reticent people whose minds hold their thoughts enmeshed in clouds of silence—she was filled with thoughts. Her mind was like her room, in which lights advanced and retreated, came pirouetting and stepping delicately, spread their tails, pecked their way; and then her whole being was suffused, like the room again, with a cloud of some profound knowledge, some unspoken regret, and then she was full of locked drawers, stuffed with letters, like her cabinets. To talk of "prizing her open" as if she were an oyster, to use any but the finest and subtlest and most pliable tools upon her was impious and absurd. One must imagine—here was she in the looking-glass. It made one start.

She was so far off at first that one could not see her clearly. She came lingering and pausing, here straightening a rose, there lifting a pink to smell it, but she never stopped; and all the time she became larger and larger in the looking-glass, more and more completely the person into whose mind one had been trying to penetrate. One verified her by degrees—fitted the qualities one had discovered into this visible body. There were her grey-green dress, and her long shoes, her basket, and something sparkling at her throat. She came so gradually that she did not seem to derange the pattern in the glass, but only to bring in some new element which gently moved and altered the other objects as if asking them, courteously, to make room for her. And the letters and the table and the grass walk and the sunflowers which had been waiting in the looking-glass separated and opened out so that she might be received among them. At last there she was, in the hall. She stopped dead. She stood by the table. She stood perfectly still. At once the looking-glass began to pour over her a light that seemed to fix her; that seemed like some acid to bite off the unessential and superficial and to leave only the truth. It was an enthralling spectacle. Everything dropped from her—clouds, dress, basket, diamond—all that one had called the creeper and convolvulus. Here was the hard wall beneath. Here was the woman herself. She stood naked in that pitiless light. And, there was nothing. Isabella was perfectly empty. She had no thoughts. She had no friends. She cared for nobody. As for her letters, they were all bills. Look, as she stood there, old and angular, veined and lined, with her high nose and her wrinkled neck, she did not even trouble to open them.

People should not leave looking-glasses hanging in their rooms.

A Room of One's Own

A Room of One's Own is difficult to categorize—it is a long essay, a non-fiction novella, a political pamphlet, and a philosophical discourse all in one. Its effects have not been so difficult to categorize—Virginia Woolf's idiosyncratic text has been recognized as a classic from the time of its publication in 1929. The book was a departure from Woolf's output until then; she was a major literary figure, having already published such key novels as *Jacob's Room, Mrs Dalloway, To the Lighthouse*, and *Orlando,* and she was an established essayist with a formidable reputation as an arbiter of the literary tradition. One way of characterizing this book is to see that it represents Woolf's scrutiny of her own position as a woman writer, a self-examination of her public position that inevitably became a political document. The focus is not on Woolf's life or her work per se, but rather on the social and psychological conditions that would make such a life generally possible. The book creates a microcosm of such possibility in the "room" of its title; the book itself is a room within which its author contemplates and analyzes the dimensions of social space for women. Woolf recognizes that seemingly neutral social space, the room of cultural agency just as the room of writing, is in truth a gendered space. She directs her political inquiry toward the making and remaking of such rooms.

    A Room of One's Own comes from established traditions of writing as well. It draws on the conversational tone and novelistic insight of the literary essay as perfected in the nineteenth century by such writers as Charles Lamb—whose *Oxford in the Vacation* was certainly in Woolf's mind when she wrote the opening chapter of her essay. At the same time, Woolf's book joins a lineage of feminist political philosophy, whose most eloquent exponent prior to Woolf herself was Mary Wollstonecraft, who joined the rhetorical ranks of Rousseau and John Stuart Mill with the publication of *A Vindication of the Rights of Woman*, her passionately reasoned exhortation for the equal and universal human rights of women. (Selections from Wollstonecraft's *Vindication* can be found on page 1471.) The century and a half since Wollstonecraft had produced a rich history of feminist agitation and feminist thought. Virginia Woolf draws on this less-known tradition, invoking nineteenth-century figures from the women's movement like Emily Davies,

Josephine Butler, and Octavia Hill. She also places her deliberations in the context of the suffragist movement and its fraught history in Britain. Virginia Woolf was strongly engaged in the
debates of the suffrage movement, and its divisions over radical action or more conciliatory political approaches. Much of Woolf's long essay is devoted to demonstrating the subversive quality of
occupying the blank page, and wielding the printed word.

As politically motivated as *A Room of One's Own* is, it is equally a literary text. Woolf
draws on all the intricacies of literary tropes and figures to mount her argument for women's
education, women's equality, women's social presence. Not the least of her strategies is her
manipulation of the rhetoric of address—in other words, the audience implied by the language
of a text. Woolf creates an ironic space, or room, in which she is a playfully ambiguous speaker
addressing an uncertain audience: women at the colleges where she has been invited to speak,
but also men and women alike who will read her printed text. By doing so, she keeps an ironic
tension in play, holding at bay her anger at being censored or silenced by male readers by creating a sense of privacy and secrecy among women. This underscores Woolf's primary argument,
the need for autonomy and self-determination. Her modest proposal, although faintly ironic, is
also eminently pragmatic—the room of one's own that is her metaphor for the college classroom or the blank canvas or the book's page is at the same time the actual room, paid for and
unintruded upon by domestic worries or social codes, whose possession permits a woman to find
out who she may be.

from A Room of One's Own
Chapter 1

But, you may say, we asked you to speak about women and fiction—what has that got
to do with a room of one's own?[1] I will try to explain. When you asked me to speak
about women and fiction I sat down on the banks of a river and began to wonder
what the words meant. They might mean simply a few remarks about Fanny Burney;
a few more about Jane Austen; a tribute to the Brontës and a sketch of Haworth Parsonage under snow; some witticisms if possible about Miss Mitford; a respectful allusion to George Eliot; a reference to Mrs Gaskell and one would have done.[2] But at
second sight the words seemed not so simple. The title women and fiction might
mean, and you may have meant it to mean, women and what they are like; or it
might mean women and the fiction that they write; or it might mean women and the
fiction that is written about them; or it might mean that somehow all three are inextricably mixed together and you want me to consider them in that light. But when I
began to consider the subject in this last way, which seemed the most interesting, I
soon saw that it had one fatal drawback. I should never be able to come to a conclusion. I should never be able to fulfil what is, I understand, the first duty of a lecturer—to hand you after an hour's discourse a nugget of pure truth to wrap up between
the pages of your notebooks and keep on the mantelpiece for ever. All I could do was
to offer you an opinion upon one minor point—a woman must have money and a
room of her own if she is to write fiction; and that, as you will see, leaves the great
problem of the true nature of woman and the true nature of fiction unsolved. I have
shirked the duty of coming to a conclusion upon these two questions—women and
fiction remain, so far as I am concerned, unsolved problems. But in order to make
some amends I am going to do what I can to show you how I arrived at this opinion
about the room and the money. I am going to develop in your presence as fully and

---

1. Woolf delivered her essay in a shorter version to meetings first at two women's colleges, Newnham and Girton

College, Cambridge University, in October 1928.
2. Important 19th-century novelists.

freely as I can the train of thought which led me to think this. Perhaps if I lay bare the ideas, the prejudices, that lie behind this statement you will find that they have some bearing upon women and some upon fiction. At any rate, when a subject is highly controversial—and any question about sex is that—one cannot hope to tell the truth. One can only show how one came to hold whatever opinion one does hold. One can only give one's audience the chance of drawing their own conclusions as they observe the limitations, the prejudices, the idiosyncrasies of the speaker. Fiction here is likely to contain more truth than fact. Therefore I propose, making use of all the liberties and licences of a novelist, to tell you the story of the two days that preceded my coming here—how, bowed down by the weight of the subject which you have laid upon my shoulders, I pondered it, and made it work in and out of my daily life. I need not say that what I am about to describe has no existence; Oxbridge is an invention; so is Fernham;[3] "I" is only a convenient term for somebody who has no real being. Lies will flow from my lips, but there may perhaps be some truth mixed up with them; it is for you to seek out this truth and to decide whether any part of it is worth keeping. If not, you will of course throw the whole of it into the wastepaper basket and forget all about it.

Here then was I (call me Mary Beton, Mary Seton, Mary Carmichael[4] or by any name you please—it is not a matter of any importance) sitting on the banks of a river a week or two ago in fine October weather, lost in thought. That collar I have spoken of, women and fiction, the need of coming to some conclusion on a subject that raises all sorts of prejudices and passions, bowed my head to the ground. To the right and left bushes of some sort, golden and crimson, glowed with the colour, even it seemed burnt with the heat, of fire. On the further bank the willows wept in perpetual lamentation, their hair about their shoulders. The river reflected whatever it chose of sky and bridge and burning tree, and when the undergraduate had oared his boat through the reflections they closed again, completely, as if he had never been. There one might have sat the clock round lost in thought. Thought—to call it by a prouder name than it deserved—had let its line down into the stream. It swayed, minute after minute, hither and thither among the reflections and the weeds, letting the water lift it and sink it, until—you know the little tug—the sudden conglomeration of an idea at the end of one's line: and then the cautious hauling of it in, and the careful laying of it out? Alas, laid on the grass how small, how insignificant this thought of mine looked; the sort of fish that a good fisherman puts back into the water so that it may grow fatter and be one day worth cooking and eating. I will not trouble you with that thought now, though if you look carefully you may find it for yourselves in the course of what I am going to say.

But however small it was, it had, nevertheless, the mysterious property of its kind—put back into the mind, it became at once very exciting, and important; and as it darted and sank, and flashed hither and thither, set up such a wash and tumult of ideas that it was impossible to sit still. It was thus that I found myself walking with extreme rapidity across a grass plot. Instantly a man's figure rose to intercept me. Nor did I at first understand that the gesticulations of a curious-looking object, in a cutaway coat and evening shirt, were aimed at me. His face expressed horror and indig-

---

3. "Oxbridge" was in fact the common slang term for Oxford and Cambridge universities. "Fernham" suggests Newnham College.
4. Three of the four Marys who by tradition were atten-

dants to Mary, Queen of Scots (executed in 1567), and who figure in many Scottish ballads; the fourth was Mary Hamilton.

nation. Instinct rather than reason came to my help; he was a Beadle; I was a woman. This was the turf; there was the path. Only the Fellows and Scholars are allowed here; the gravel is the place for me.[5] Such thoughts were the work of a moment. As I regained the path the arms of the Beadle sank, his face assumed its usual repose, and though turf is better walking than gravel, no very great harm was done. The only charge I could bring against the Fellows and Scholars of whatever the college might happen to be was that in protection of their turf, which has been rolled for 300 years in succession, they had sent my little fish into hiding.

What idea it had been that had sent me so audaciously trespassing I could not now remember. The spirit of peace descended like a cloud from heaven, for if the spirit of peace dwells anywhere, it is in the courts and quadrangles of Oxbridge on a fine October morning. Strolling through those colleges past those ancient halls the roughness of the present seemed smoothed away; the body seemed contained in a miraculous glass cabinet through which no sound could penetrate, and the mind, freed from any contact with facts (unless one trespassed on the turf again), was at liberty to settle down upon whatever meditation was in harmony with the moment. As chance would have it, some stray memory of some old essay about revisiting Oxbridge in the long vacation brought Charles Lamb to mind—Saint Charles, said Thackeray,[6] putting a letter of Lamb's to his forehead. Indeed, among all the dead (I give you my thoughts as they came to me), Lamb is one of the most congenial; one to whom one would have liked to say, Tell me then how you wrote your essays? For his essays are superior even to Max Beerbohm's, I thought, with all their perfection, because of that wild flash of imagination, that lightning crack of genius in the middle of them which leaves them flawed and imperfect, but starred with poetry. Lamb then came to Oxbridge perhaps a hundred years ago. Certainly he wrote an essay—the name escapes me—about the manuscript of one of Milton's poems which he saw here.[7] It was *Lycidas* perhaps, and Lamb wrote how it shocked him to think it possible that any word in *Lycidas* could have been different from what it is. To think of Milton changing the words in that poem seemed to him a sort of sacrilege. This led me to remember what I could of *Lycidas* and to amuse myself with guessing which word it could have been that Milton had altered, and why. It then occurred to me that the very manuscript itself which Lamb had looked at was only a few hundred yards away, so that one could follow Lamb's footsteps across the quadrangle to that famous library where the treasure is kept. Moreover, I recollected, as I put this plan into execution, it is in this famous library that the manuscript of Thackeray's *Esmond* is also preserved. The critics often say that *Esmond* is Thackeray's most perfect novel. But the affectation of the style, with its imitation of the eighteenth century, hampers one, so far as I remember; unless indeed the eighteenth-century style was natural to Thackeray—a fact that one might prove by looking at the manuscript and seeing whether the alterations were for the benefit of the style or of the sense. But then one would have to decide what is style and what is meaning, a question which—but here I was actually at the door which leads into the library itself. I must have opened it, for instantly there issued, like a guardian angel barring the way with a flutter of black gown

5. A beadle is a disciplinary officer. The fellows of Oxbridge colleges typically tutor the undergraduates, who are divided into scholars and commoners. The commoners form the majority of the student body.
6. William Makepeace Thackeray (1811–1863), novelist and journalist, Woolf's father's first father-in-law.

7. Lamb's *Oxford in the Vacation*—describing the locales Lamb himself was too poor to attend in term time. The manuscript of Milton's elegy *Lycidas* (1638) is in the Wren Library of Trinity College, Cambridge, together with that of Thackeray's novel *The History of Henry Esmond* (1852).

instead of white wings, a deprecating, silvery, kindly gentleman, who regretted in a low voice as he waved me back that ladies are only admitted to the library if accompanied by a Fellow of the College or furnished with a letter of introduction.

That a famous library has been cursed by a woman is a matter of complete indifference to a famous library. Venerable and calm, with all its treasures safe locked within its breast, it sleeps complacently and will, so far as I am concerned, so sleep for ever. Never will I wake those echoes, never will I ask for that hospitality again, I vowed as I descended the steps in anger. Still an hour remained before luncheon, and what was one to do? Stroll on the meadows? sit by the river? Certainly it was a lovely autumn morning; the leaves were fluttering red to the ground; there was no great hardship in doing either. But the sound of music reached my ear. Some service or celebration was going forward. The organ complained magnificently as I passed the chapel door. Even the sorrow of Christianity sounded in that serene air more like the recollection of sorrow than sorrow itself; even the groanings of the ancient organ seemed lapped in peace. I had no wish to enter had I the right, and this time the verger might have stopped me, demanding perhaps my baptismal certificate, or a letter of introduction from the Dean. But the outside of these magnificent buildings is often as beautiful as the inside. Moreover, it was amusing enough to watch the congregation assembling, coming in and going out again, busying themselves at the door of the chapel like bees at the mouth of a hive. Many were in cap and gown; some had tufts of fur on their shoulders; others were wheeled in bath-chairs; others, though not past middle age, seemed creased and crushed into shapes so singular that one was reminded of those giant crabs and crayfish who heave with difficulty across the sand of an aquarium. As I leant against the wall the University indeed seemed a sanctuary in which are preserved rare types which would soon be obsolete if left to fight for existence on the pavement of the Strand.[8] Old stories of old deans and old dons came back to mind, but before I had summoned up courage to whistle—it used to be said that at the sound of a whistle old Professor ———— instantly broke into a gallop—the venerable congregation had gone inside. The outside of the chapel remained. As you know, its high domes and pinnacles can be seen, like a sailing-ship always voyaging never arriving, lit up at night and visible for miles, far away across the hills. Once, presumably, this quadrangle with its smooth lawns, its massive buildings, and the chapel itself was marsh too, where the grasses waved and the swine rootled. Teams of horses and oxen, I thought, must have hauled the stone in wagons from far countries, and then with infinite labour the grey blocks in whose shade I was now standing were poised in order one on top of another, and then the painters brought their glass for the windows, and the masons were busy for centuries up on that roof with putty and cement, spade and trowel. Every Saturday somebody must have poured gold and silver out of a leathern purse into their ancient fists, for they had their beer and skittles presumably of an evening. An unending stream of gold and silver, I thought, must have flowed into this court perpetually to keep the stones coming and the masons working; to level, to ditch, to dig and to drain. But it was then the age of faith, and money was poured liberally to set these stones on a deep foundation, and when the stones were raised, still more money was poured in from the coffers of kings and queens and great nobles to ensure that hymns should be sung here and scholars taught. Lands were granted; tithes were paid. And when the age of faith was over and the age of reason had come, still the same flow of gold and silver went on; fellowships

8. A thoroughfare in central London.

were founded; lectureships endowed; only the gold and silver flowed now, not from the coffers of the king, but from the chests of merchants and manufacturers, from the purses of men who had made, say, a fortune from industry, and returned, in their wills, a bounteous share of it to endow more chairs, more lectureships, more fellowships in the university where they had learnt their craft. Hence the libraries and laboratories; the observatories; the splendid equipment of costly and delicate instruments which now stands on glass shelves, where centuries ago the grasses waved and the swine rootled. Certainly, as I strolled round the court, the foundation of gold and silver seemed deep enough; the pavement laid solidly over the wild grasses. Men with trays on their heads went busily from staircase to staircase. Gaudy blossoms flowered in window-boxes. The strains of the gramophone blared out from the rooms within. It was impossible not to reflect—the reflection whatever it may have been was cut short. The clock struck. It was time to find one's way to luncheon.

It is a curious fact that novelists have a way of making us believe that luncheon parties are invariably memorable for something very witty that was said, or for something very wise that was done. But they seldom spare a word for what was eaten. It is part of the novelist's convention not to mention soup and salmon and ducklings, as if soup and salmon and ducklings were of no importance whatsoever, as if nobody ever smoked a cigar or drank a glass of wine. Here, however, I shall take the liberty to defy that convention and to tell you that the lunch on this occasion began with soles, sunk in a deep dish, over which the college cook had spread a counterpane of the whitest cream, save that it was branded here and there with brown spots like the spots on the flanks of a doe. After that came the partridges, but if this suggests a couple of bald, brown birds on a plate you are mistaken. The partridges, many and various, came with all their retinue of sauces and salads, the sharp and the sweet, each in its order; their potatoes, thin as coins but not so hard; their sprouts, foliated as rosebuds but more succulent. And no sooner had the roast and its retinue been done with than the silent serving-man, the Beadle himself perhaps in a milder manifestation, set before us, wreathed in napkins, a confection which rose all sugar from the waves. To call it pudding and so relate it to rice and tapioca would be an insult. Meanwhile the wineglasses had flushed yellow and flushed crimson; had been emptied; had been filled. And thus by degrees was lit, halfway down the spine, which is the seat of the soul, not that hard little electric light which we call brilliance, as it pops in and out upon our lips, but the more profound, subtle and subterranean glow, which is the rich yellow flame of rational intercourse. No need to hurry. No need to sparkle. No need to be anybody but oneself. We are all going to heaven and Vandyck[9] is of the company—in other words, how good life seemed, how sweet its rewards, how trivial this grudge or that grievance, how admirable friendship and the society of one's kind, as, lighting a good cigarette, one sunk among the cushions in the window-seat.

If by good luck there had been an ash-tray handy, if one had not knocked the ash out of the window in default, if things had been a little different from what they were, one would not have seen, presumably, a cat without a tail. The sight of that abrupt and truncated animal padding softly across the quadrangle changed by some fluke of the subconscious intelligence the emotional light for me. It was as if some one had let fall a shade. Perhaps the excellent hock was relinquishing its hold. Certainly, as I watched the Manx cat pause in the middle of the lawn as if it too questioned the universe, something seemed lacking, something seemed different. But what was lacking,

9. Sir Anthony Van Dyck, prominent 17-century society painter.

what was different, I asked myself, listening to the talk. And to answer that question I had to think myself out of the room, back into the past, before the war indeed,[1] and to set before my eyes the model of another luncheon party held in rooms not very far distant from these; but different. Everything was different. Meanwhile the talk went on among the guests, who were many and young, some of this sex, some of that; it went on swimmingly, it went on agreeably, freely, amusingly. And as it went on I set it against the background of that other talk, and as I matched the two together I had no doubt that one was the descendant, the legitimate heir of the other. Nothing was changed; nothing was different save only—here I listened with all my ears not entirely to what was being said, but to the murmur or current behind it. Yes, that was it—the change was there. Before the war at a luncheon party like this people would have said precisely the same things but they would have sounded different, because in those days they were accompanied by a sort of humming noise, not articulate, but musical, exciting, which changed the value of the words themselves. Could one set that humming noise to words? Perhaps with the help of the poets one could. A book lay beside me and, opening it, I turned casually enough to Tennyson. And here I found Tennyson was singing:

> There has fallen a splendid tear
>   From the passion-flower at the gate.
> She is coming, my dove, my dear;
>   She is coming, my life, my fate;
> The red rose cries, "She is near, she is near";
>   And the white rose weeps, "She is late";
> The larkspur listens, "I hear, I hear";
>   And the lily whispers, "I wait."[2]

Was that what men hummed at luncheon parties before the war? And the women?

> My heart is like a singing bird
>   Whose nest is in a water'd shoot;
> My heart is like an apple tree
>   Whose boughs are bent with thick-set fruit;
> My heart is like a rainbow shell
>   That paddles in a halcyon sea;
> My heart is gladder than all these
>   Because my love is come to me.[3]

Was that what women hummed at luncheon parties before the war?

There was something so ludicrous in thinking of people humming such things even under their breath at luncheon parties before the war that I burst out laughing, and had to explain my laughter by pointing at the Manx cat, who did look a little absurd, poor beast, without a tail, in the middle of the lawn. Was he really born so, or had he lost his tail in an accident? The tailless cat, though some are said to exist in the Isle of Man, is rarer than one thinks. It is a queer animal, quaint rather than beautiful. It is strange what a difference a tail makes—you know the sort of things one says as a lunch party breaks up and people are finding their coats and hats.

This one, thanks to the hospitality of the host, had lasted far into the afternoon. The beautiful October day was fading and the leaves were falling from the trees in the avenue as I walked through it. Gate after gate seemed to close with gentle finali-

---

1. World War I.
2. From Tennyson's *Maud* (1855), lines 908–915.

3. The first stanza of Christina Rossetti's poem *A Birthday* (1857).

ty behind me. Innumerable beadles were fitting innumerable keys into well-oiled locks; the treasure-house was being made secure for another night. After the avenue one comes out upon a road—I forget its name—which leads you, if you take the right turning, along to Fernham.[4] But there was plenty of time. Dinner was not till half-past seven. One could almost do without dinner after such a luncheon. It is strange how a scrap of poetry works in the mind and makes the legs move in time to it along the road. Those words—

> There has fallen a splendid tear
>   From the passion-flower at the gate.
> She is coming, my dove, my dear—

sang in my blood as I stepped quickly along towards Headingley. And then, switching off into the other measure, I sang, where the waters are churned up by the weir:

> My heart is like a singing bird
>   Whose nest is in a water'd shoot;
> My heart is like an apple tree—

What poets, I cried aloud, as one does in the dusk, what poets they were!

In a sort of jealousy, I suppose, for our own age, silly and absurd though these comparisons are, I went on to wonder if honestly one could name two living poets now as great as Tennyson and Christina Rossetti were then. Obviously it is impossible, I thought, looking into those foaming waters, to compare them. The very reason why the poetry excites one to such abandonment, such rapture, is that it celebrates some feeling that one used to have (at luncheon parties before the war perhaps), so that one responds easily, familiarly, without troubling to check the feeling, or to compare it with any that one has now. But the living poets express a feeling that is actually being made and torn out of us at the moment. One does not recognize it in the first place; often for some reason one fears it; one watches it with keenness and compares it jealously and suspiciously with the old feeling that one knew. Hence the difficulty of modern poetry; and it is because of this difficulty that one cannot remember more than two consecutive lines of any good modern poet. For this reason—that my memory failed me—the argument flagged for want of material. But why, I continued, moving on towards Headingley, have we stopped humming under our breath at luncheon parties? Why has Alfred ceased to sing

> She is coming, my dove, my dear?

Why has Christina ceased to respond

> My heart is gladder than all these
> Because my love is come to me?

Shall we lay the blame on the war? When the guns fired in August 1914, did the faces of men and women show so plain in each other's eyes that romance was killed? Certainly it was a shock (to women in particular with their illusions about education, and so on) to see the faces of our rulers in the light of the shell-fire. So ugly they looked—German, English, French—so stupid. But lay the blame where one will, on whom one will, the illusion which inspired Tennyson and Christina Rossetti to sing so passionately about the coming of their loves is far rarer now than then. One has

---

4. Both Girton and Newnham Colleges, established only in the late 19th century, are outside the old university area of Cambridge.

only to read, to look, to listen, to remember. But why say "blame"? Why, if it was an illusion, not praise the catastrophe, whatever it was, that destroyed illusion and put truth in its place? For truth . . . those dots mark the spot where, in search of truth, I missed the turning up to Fernham. Yes indeed, which was truth and which was illusion, I asked myself. What was the truth about these houses, for example, dim and festive now with their red windows in the dusk, but raw and red and squalid, with their sweets and their boot-laces, at nine o'clock in the morning? And the willows and the river and the gardens that run down to the river, vague now with the mist stealing over them, but gold and red in the sunlight—which was the truth, which was the illusion about them? I spare you the twists and turns of my cogitations, for no conclusion was found on the road to Headingley, and I ask you to suppose that I soon found out my mistake about the turning and retraced my steps to Fernham.

As I have said already that it was an October day, I dare not forfeit your respect and imperil the fair name of fiction by changing the season and describing lilacs hanging over garden walls, crocuses, tulips and other flowers of spring. Fiction must stick to facts, and the truer the facts the better the fiction—so we are told. Therefore it was still autumn and the leaves were still yellow and falling, if anything, a little faster than before, because it was now evening (seven twenty-three to be precise) and a breeze (from the south-west to be exact) had risen. But for all that there was something odd at work:

> My heart is like a singing bird
>   Whose nest is in a water'd shoot;
> My heart is like an apple tree
>   Whose boughs are bent with thick-set fruit—

perhaps the words of Christina Rossetti were partly responsible for the folly of the fancy—it was nothing of course but a fancy—that the lilac was shaking its flowers over the garden walls, and the brimstone butterflies were scudding hither and thither, and the dust of the pollen was in the air. A wind blew, from what quarter I know not, but it lifted the half-grown leaves so that there was a flash of silver grey in the air. It was the time between the lights when colours undergo their intensification and purples and golds burn in window-panes like the beat of an excitable heart; when for some reason the beauty of the world revealed and yet soon to perish (here I pushed into the garden, for, unwisely, the door was left open and no beadles seemed about), the beauty of the world which is so soon to perish, has two edges, one of laughter, one of anguish, cutting the heart asunder. The gardens of Fernham lay before me in the spring twilight, wild and open, and in the long grass, sprinkled and carelessly flung, were daffodils and bluebells, not orderly perhaps at the best of times, and now wind-blown and waving as they tugged at their roots. The windows of the building, curved like ships' windows among generous waves of red brick, changed from lemon to silver under the flight of the quick spring clouds. Somebody was in a hammock, somebody, but in this light they were phantoms only, half guessed, half seen, raced across the grass—would no one stop her?—and then on the terrace, as if popping out to breathe the air, to glance at the garden, came a bent figure, formidable yet humble, with her great forehead and her shabby dress—could it be the famous scholar, could it be J——— H——— herself?[5] All was dim, yet intense too, as if the scarf which the dusk had flung over the garden were torn asunder by star or sword—the flash of some terrible reality leaping, as its way is, out of the heart of the spring. For youth———

---

5. Jane Harrison, a famous classical scholar.

Here was my soup. Dinner was being served in the great dining-hall. Far from being spring it was in fact an evening in October. Everybody was assembled in the big dining-room. Dinner was ready. Here was the soup. It was a plain gravy soup. There was nothing to stir the fancy in that. One could have seen through the transparent liquid any pattern that there might have been on the plate itself. But there was no pattern. The plate was plain. Next came beef with its attendant greens and potatoes—a homely trinity, suggesting the rumps of cattle in a muddy market, and sprouts curled and yellowed at the edge, and bargaining and cheapening, and women with string bags on Monday morning. There was no reason to complain of human nature's daily food, seeing that the supply was sufficient and coal-miners doubtless were sitting down to less. Prunes and custard followed. And if any one complains that prunes, even when mitigated by custard, are an uncharitable vegetable (fruit they are not), stringy as a miser's heart and exuding a fluid such as might run in misers' veins who have denied themselves wine and warmth for eighty years and yet not given to the poor, he should reflect that there are people whose charity embraces even the prune. Biscuits and cheese came next, and here the water-jug was liberally passed round, for it is the nature of biscuits to be dry, and these were biscuits to the core. That was all. The meal was over. Everybody scraped their chairs back; the swing-doors swung violently to and fro; soon the hall was emptied of every sign of food and made ready no doubt for breakfast next morning. Down corridors and up staircases the youth of England went banging and singing. And was it for a guest, a stranger (for I had no more right here in Fernham than in Trinity or Somerville or Girton or Newnham or Christchurch),[6] to say, "The dinner was not good," or to say (we were now, Mary Seton and I, in her sitting-room), "Could we not have dined up here alone?" for if I had said anything of the kind I should have been prying and searching into the secret economies of a house which to the stranger wears so fine a front of gaiety and courage. No, one could say nothing of the sort. Indeed, conversation for a moment flagged. The human frame being what it is, heart, body and brain all mixed together, and not contained in separate compartments as they will be no doubt in another million years, a good dinner is of great importance to good talk. One cannot think well, love well, sleep well, if one has not dined well. The lamp in the spine does not light on beef and prunes. We are all *probably* going to heaven, and Vandyck is, we *hope*, to meet us round the next corner—that is the dubious and qualifying state of mind that beef and prunes at the end of the day's work breed between them. Happily my friend, who taught science, had a cupboard where there was a squat bottle and little glasses—(but there should have been sole and partridge to begin with)—so that we were able to draw up to the fire and repair some of the damages of the day's living. In a minute or so we were slipping freely in and out among all those objects of curiosity and interest which form in the mind in the absence of a particular person, and are naturally to be discussed on coming together again—how somebody has married, another has not; one thinks this, another that; one has improved out of all knowledge, the other most amazingly gone to the bad—with all those speculations upon human nature and the character of the amazing world we live in which spring naturally from such beginnings. While these things were being said, however, I became shamefacedly aware of a current setting in of its own accord and carrying everything forward to an end of its own. One might be talking of Spain or Portugal, of book or racehorse, but

6. Trinity, Girton, and Newnham are colleges of Cambridge University; Somerville and Christchurch are at Oxford.

the real interest of whatever was said was none of those things, but a scene of masons on a high roof some five centuries ago. Kings and nobles brought treasure in huge sacks and poured it under the earth. This scene was for ever coming alive in my mind and placing itself by another of lean cows and a muddy market and withered greens and the stringy hearts of old men—these two pictures, disjointed and disconnected and nonsensical as they were, were for ever coming together and combating each other and had me entirely at their mercy. The best course, unless the whole talk was to be distorted, was to expose what was in my mind to the air, when with good luck it would fade and crumble like the head of the dead king when they opened the coffin at Windsor. Briefly, then, I told Miss Seton about the masons who had been all those years on the roof of the chapel, and about the kings and queens and nobles bearing sacks of gold and silver on their shoulders, which they shovelled into the earth; and then how the great financial magnates of our own time came and laid cheques and bonds, I suppose, where the others had laid ingots and rough lumps of gold. All that lies beneath the colleges down there, I said; but this college, where we are now sitting, what lies beneath its gallant red brick and the wild unkempt grasses of the garden? What force is behind the plain china off which we dined, and (here it popped out of my mouth before I could stop it) the beef, the custard and the prunes?

Well, said Mary Seton, about the year 1860—Oh, but you know the story, she said, bored, I suppose, by the recital. And she told me—rooms were hired. Committees met. Envelopes were addressed. Circulars were drawn up. Meetings were held; letters were read out; so-and-so has promised so much; on the contrary, Mr ——— won't give a penny. The *Saturday Review* has been very rude. How can we raise a fund to pay for offices? Shall we hold a bazaar? Can't we find a pretty girl to sit in the front row? Let us look up what John Stuart Mill said on the subject.[7] Can any one persuade the editor of the ——— to print a letter? Can we get Lady ——— to sign it? Lady ——— is out of town. That was the way it was done, presumably, sixty years ago, and it was a prodigious effort, and a great deal of time was spent on it. And it was only after a long struggle and with the utmost difficulty that they got thirty thousand pounds together.[8] So obviously we cannot have wine and partridges and servants carrying tin dishes on their heads, she said. We cannot have sofas and separate rooms. "The amenities," she said, quoting from some book or other, "will have to wait."[9]

At the thought of all those women working year after year and finding it hard to get two thousand pounds together, and as much as they could do to get thirty thousand pounds, we burst out in scorn at the reprehensible poverty of our sex. What had our mothers been doing then that they had no wealth to leave us? Powdering their noses? Looking in at shop windows? Flaunting in the sun at Monte Carlo? There were some photographs on the mantel-piece. Mary's mother—if that was her picture—may have been a wastrel in her spare time (she had thirteen children by a minister of the church), but if so her gay and dissipated life had left too few traces of its pleasures on her face. She was a homely body; an old lady in a plaid shawl which was fastened

7. In 1869 Mill published his essay *The Subjection of Women*, which argued forcefully for women's suffrage and their right to equality with men.
8. "We are told that we ought to ask for £30,000 at least ... It is not a large sum, considering that there is to be but one college of this sort for Great Britain, Ireland and the Colonies, and considering how easy it is to raise immense sums for boys' schools. But considering how few people really wish women to be educated, it is a good deal."—Lady Stephen, *Life of Miss Emily Davies* [Woolf's note].
9. Every penny which could be scraped together was set aside for building, and the amenities had to be postponed.—R. Strachey, *The Cause* [Woolf's note].

by a large cameo; and she sat in a basket-chair, encouraging a spaniel to look at the camera, with the amused, yet strained expression of one who is sure that the dog will move directly the bulb is pressed. Now if she had gone into business; had become a manufacturer of artificial silk or a magnate on the Stock Exchange; if she had left two or three hundred thousand pounds to Fernham, we could have been sitting at our ease tonight and the subject of our talk might have been archaeology, botany, anthropology, physics, the nature of the atom, mathematics, astronomy, relativity, geography. If only Mrs Seton and her mother and her mother before her had learnt the great art of making money and had left their money, like their fathers and their grandfathers before them, to found fellowships and lectureships and prizes and scholarships appropriated to the use of their own sex, we might have dined very tolerably up here alone off a bird and a bottle of wine; we might have looked forward without undue confidence to a pleasant and honourable lifetime spent in the shelter of one of the liberally endowed professions. We might have been exploring or writing; mooning about the venerable places of the earth; sitting contemplative on the steps of the Parthenon, or going at ten to an office and coming home comfortably at half-past four to write a little poetry. Only, if Mrs Seton and her like had gone into business at the age of fifteen, there would have been—that was the snag in the argument—no Mary. What, I asked, did Mary think of that? There between the curtains was the October night, calm and lovely, with a star or two caught in the yellowing trees. Was she ready to resign her share of it and her memories (for they had been a happy family, though a large one) of games and quarrels up in Scotland, which she is never tired of praising for the fineness of its air and the quality of its cakes, in order that Fernham might have been endowed with fifty thousand pounds or so by a stroke of the pen? For, to endow a college would necessitate the suppression of families altogether. Making a fortune and bearing thirteen children—no human being could stand it. Consider the facts, we said. First there are nine months before the baby is born. Then the baby is born. Then there are three or four months spent in feeding the baby. After the baby is fed there are certainly five years spent in playing with the baby. You cannot, it seems, let children run about the streets. People who have seen them running wild in Russia say that the sight is not a pleasant one. People say, too, that human nature takes its shape in the years between one and five. If Mrs Seton, I said, had been making money, what sort of memories would you have had of games and quarrels? What would you have known of Scotland, and its fine air and cakes and all the rest of it? But it is useless to ask these questions, because you would never have come into existence at all. Moreover, it is equally useless to ask what might have happened if Mrs Seton and her mother and her mother before her had amassed great wealth and laid it under the foundations of college and library, because, in the first place, to earn money was impossible for them, and in the second, had it been possible, the law denied them the right to possess what money they earned. It is only for the last forty-eight years that Mrs Seton has had a penny of her own. For all the centuries before that it would have been her husband's property—a thought which, perhaps, may have had its share in keeping Mrs Seton and her mothers off the Stock Exchange.[1] Every penny I earn, they may have said, will be taken from me and disposed of

1. The late 19th century saw the passage of legislation designed to improve the legal status of women. In 1870 the Married Women's Property Act allowed women to retain £200 of their own earnings (which previously had automatically become the property of her husband); in 1884 a further act gave married women the same rights over property as unmarried women, and allowed them to carry on trades or businesses using their property.

according to my husband's wisdom—perhaps to found a scholarship or to endow a fellowship in Balliol or Kings,[2] so that to earn money, even if I could earn money, is not a matter that interests me very greatly. I had better leave it to my husband.

At any rate, whether or not the blame rested on the old lady who was looking at the spaniel, there could be no doubt that for some reason or other our mothers had mismanaged their affairs very gravely. Not a penny could be spared for "amenities"; for partridges and wine, beadles and turf, books and cigars, libraries and leisure. To raise bare walls out of the bare earth was the utmost they could do.

So we talked standing at the window and looking, as so many thousands look every night, down on the domes and towers of the famous city beneath us. It was very beautiful, very mysterious in the autumn moonlight. The old stone looked very white and venerable. One thought of all the books that were assembled down there; of the pictures of old prelates and worthies hanging in the panelled rooms; of the painted windows that would be throwing strange globes and crescents on the pavement; of the tablets and memorials and inscriptions; of the fountains and the grass; of the quiet rooms looking across the quiet quadrangles. And (pardon me the thought) I thought, too, of the admirable smoke and drink and the deep armchairs and the pleasant carpets: of the urbanity, the geniality, the dignity which are the offspring of luxury and privacy and space. Certainly our mothers had not provided us with anything comparable to all this—our mothers who found it difficult to scrape together thirty thousand pounds, our mothers who bore thirteen children to ministers of religion at St Andrews.

So I went back to my inn, and as I walked through the dark streets I pondered this and that, as one does at the end of the day's work. I pondered why it was that Mrs Seton had no money to leave us; and what effect poverty has on the mind; and what effect wealth has on the mind; and I thought of the queer old gentlemen I had seen that morning with tufts of fur upon their shoulders; and I remembered how if one whistled one of them ran; and I thought of the organ booming in the chapel and of the shut doors of the library; and I thought how unpleasant it is to be locked out; and I thought how it is worse perhaps to be locked in; and, thinking of the safety and prosperity of the one sex and of the poverty and insecurity of the other and of the effect of tradition and of the lack of tradition upon the mind of a writer, I thought at last that it was time to roll up the crumpled skin of the day, with its arguments and its impressions and its anger and its laughter, and cast it into the hedge. A thousand stars were flashing across the blue wastes of the sky. One seemed alone with an inscrutable society. All human beings were laid asleep—prone, horizontal, dumb. Nobody seemed stirring in the streets of Oxbridge. Even the door of the hotel sprang open at the touch of an invisible hand—not a boots was sitting up to light me to bed, it was so late.

from *Chapter 3*

It would have been impossible, completely and entirely, for any woman to have written the plays of Shakespeare in the age of Shakespeare. Let me imagine, since facts are so hard to come by, what would have happened had Shakespeare had a wonderfully gifted sister, called Judith, let us say. Shakespeare himself went, very probably— his mother was an heiress—to the grammar school, where he may have learnt

---

2. Balliol is a college of Oxford University; King's is at Cambridge.

Latin—Ovid, Virgil, and Horace—and the elements of grammar and logic. He was, it is well known, a wild boy who poached rabbits, perhaps shot a deer, and had, rather sooner than he should have done, to marry a woman in the neighbourhood, who bore him a child rather quicker than was right. That escapade sent him to seek his fortune in London. He had, it seemed, a taste for the theatre; he began by holding horses at the stage door. Very soon he got work in the theatre, became a successful actor, and lived at the hub of the universe, meeting everybody, knowing everybody, practising his art on the boards, exercising his wits in the streets, and even getting access to the palace of the queen. Meanwhile his extraordinarily gifted sister, let us suppose, remained at home. She was as adventurous, as imaginative, as agog to see the world as he was. But she was not sent to school. She had no chance of learning grammar and logic, let alone of reading Horace and Virgil. She picked up a book now and then, one of her brother's perhaps, and read a few pages. But then her parents came in and told her to mend the stockings or mind the stew and not moon about with books and papers. They would have spoken sharply but kindly, for they were substantial people who knew the conditions of life for a woman and loved their daughter—indeed, more likely than not she was the apple of her father's eye. Perhaps she scribbled some pages up in an apple loft on the sly, but was careful to hide them or set fire to them. Soon, however, before she was out of her teens, she was to be betrothed to the son of a neighbouring wool-stapler. She cried out that marriage was hateful to her, and for that she was severely beaten by her father. Then he ceased to scold her. He begged her instead not to hurt him, not to shame him in this matter of her marriage. He would give her a chain of beads or a fine petticoat, he said; and there were tears in his eyes. How could she disobey him? How could she break his heart? The force of her own gift alone drove her to it. She made up a small parcel of her belongings, let herself down by a rope one summer's night and took the road to London. She was not seventeen. The birds that sang in the hedge were not more musical than she was. She had the quickest fancy, a gift like her brother's, for the tune of words. Like him, she had a taste for the theatre. She stood at the stage door; she wanted to act, she said. Men laughed in her face. The manager—a fat, loose-lipped man—guffawed. He bellowed something about poodles dancing and women acting—no woman, he said, could possibly be an actress. He hinted—you can imagine what. She could get no training in her craft. Could she even seek her dinner in a tavern or roam the streets at midnight? Yet her genius was for fiction and lusted to feed abundantly upon the lives of men and women and the study of their ways. At last—for she was very young, oddly like Shakespeare the poet in her face, with the same grey eyes and rounded brows—at last Nick Greene the actor-manager took pity on her; she found herself with child by that gentleman and so—who shall measure the heat and violence of the poet's heart when caught and tangled in a woman's body?—killed herself one winter's night and lies buried at some cross-roads where the omnibuses now stop outside the Elephant and Castle.[3]

   That, more or less, is how the story would run, I think, if a woman in Shakespeare's day had had Shakespeare's genius. But for my part, I agree with the deceased bishop, if such he was—it is unthinkable that any woman in Shakespeare's day should have had Shakespeare's genius. For genius like Shakespeare's is not born among labouring, uneducated, servile people. It was not born in England among the Saxons and the Britons. It is not born today among the working classes. How, then,

3. A tavern on the outskirts of South London.

could it have been born among women whose work began, according to Professor Trevelyan,[4] almost before they were out of the nursery, who were forced to it by their parents and held to it by all the power of law and custom? Yet genius of a sort must have existed among women as it must have existed among the working classes. Now and again an Emily Brontë or a Robert Burns blazes out and proves its presence. But certainly it never got itself on to paper. When, however, one reads of a witch being ducked, of a woman possessed by devils, of a wise woman selling herbs, or even of a very remarkable man who had a mother, then I think we are on the track of a lost novelist, a suppressed poet, of some mute and inglorious Jane Austen, some Emily Brontë who dashed her brains out on the moor or mopped and mowed about the highways crazed with the torture that her gift had put her to. Indeed, I would venture to guess that Anon, who wrote so many poems without signing them, was often a woman. It was a woman Edward Fitzgerald,[5] I think, suggested who made the ballads and the folk-songs, crooning them to her children, beguiling her spinning with them, or the length of the winter's night.

This may be true or it may be false—who can say?—but what is true in it, so it seemed to me, reviewing the story of Shakespeare's sister as I had made it, is that any woman born with a great gift in the sixteenth century would certainly have gone crazed, shot herself, or ended her days in some lonely cottage outside the village, half witch, half wizard, feared and mocked at. For it needs little skill in psychology to be sure that a highly gifted girl who had tried to use her gift for poetry would have been so thwarted and hindered by other people, so tortured and pulled asunder by her own contrary instincts, that she must have lost her health and sanity to a certainty. No girl could have walked to London and stood at a stage door and forced her way into the presence of actor-managers without doing herself a violence and suffering an anguish which may have been irrational—for chastity may be a fetish invented by certain societies for unknown reasons—but were none the less inevitable. Chastity had then, it has even now, a religious importance in a woman's life, and has so wrapped itself round with nerves and instincts that to cut it free and bring it to the light of day demands courage of the rarest. To have lived a free life in London in the sixteenth century would have meant for a woman who was poet and playwright a nervous stress and dilemma which might well have killed her. Had she survived, whatever she had written would have been twisted and deformed, issuing from a strained and morbid imagination. And undoubtedly, I thought, looking at the shelf where there are no plays by women, her work would have gone unsigned. That refuge she would have sought certainly. It was the relic of the sense of chastity that dictated anonymity to women even so late as the nineteenth century. Currer Bell, George Eliot, George Sand,[6] all the victims of inner strife as their writings prove, sought ineffectively to veil themselves by using the name of a man. Thus they did homage to the convention, which if not implanted by the other sex was liberally encouraged by them (the chief glory of a woman is not to be talked of, said Pericles, himself a much-talked-of man), that publicity in women is detestable.[7] Anonymity runs in their blood. The desire to be veiled still possesses them. They are not even now as concerned about the health of their fame as men are, and, speaking generally, will pass a

---

4. George Trevelyan (1876–1962), historian.
5. Poet and translator (1809–1883).
6. Currer Bell, pen name of Charlotte Brontë; George Eliot, pen name of Mary Ann Evans; George Sand, pen name of Amandine Aurore Lucille Dupin (1804–1876).

7. The Athenian statesman Pericles was reported by the historian Thucydides to have said, "That woman is most praiseworthy whose name is least bandied about on men's lips, whether for praise or dispraise."

tombstone or a signpost without feeling an irresistible desire to cut their names on it, as Alf, Bert or Chas. must do in obedience to their instinct, which murmurs if it sees a fine woman go by, or even a dog, Ce chien est à moi [that dog is mine]. And, of course, it may not be a dog, I thought, remembering Parliament Square, the Sieges Allee[8] and other avenues; it may be a piece of land or a man with curly black hair. It is one of the great advantages of being a woman that one can pass even a very fine negress without wishing to make an Englishwoman of her.

That woman, then, who was born with a gift of poetry in the sixteenth century, was an unhappy woman, a woman at strife against herself. All the conditions of her life, all her own instincts, were hostile to the state of mind which is needed to set free whatever is in the brain. * * * There would always have been that assertion—you cannot do this, you are incapable of doing that—to protest against, to overcome. Probably for a novelist this germ is no longer of much effect; for there have been women novelists of merit. But for painters it must still have some sting in it; and for musicians, I imagine, is even now active and poisonous in the extreme. The woman composer stands where the actress stood in the time of Shakespeare. Nick Greene, I thought, remembering the story I had made about Shakespeare's sister, said that a woman acting put him in mind of a dog dancing. Johnson repeated the phrase two hundred years later of women preaching.[9] And here, I said, opening a book about music, we have the very words used again in this year of grace, 1928, of women who try to write music. "Of Mlle. Germaine Tailleferre one can only repeat Dr. Johnson's dictum concerning a woman preacher, transposed into terms of music. 'Sir, a woman's composing is like a dog's walking on his hind legs. It is not done well, but you are surprised to find it done at all.'"[1] So accurately does history repeat itself.

Thus, I concluded, shutting Mr Oscar Browning's life and pushing away the rest, it is fairly evident that even in the nineteenth century a woman was not encouraged to be an artist. On the contrary, she was snubbed, slapped, lectured and exhorted. Her mind must have been strained and her vitality lowered by the need of opposing this, of disproving that. For here again we come within range of that very interesting and obscure masculine complex which has had so much influence upon the woman's movement; that deep-seated desire, not so much that *she* shall be inferior as that *he* shall be superior, which plants him wherever one looks, not only in front of the arts, but barring the way to politics too, even when the risk to himself seems infinitesimal and the suppliant humble and devoted. Even Lady Bessborough, I remembered, with all her passion for politics, must humbly bow herself and write to Lord Granville Leveson-Gower:[2] ". . . notwithstanding all my violence in politics and talking so much on that subject, I perfectly agree with you that no woman has any business to meddle with that or any other serious business, farther than giving her opinion (if she is ask'd)." And so she goes on to spend her enthusiasm where it meets with no obstacle whatsoever upon that immensely important subject, Lord Granville's maiden speech in the House of Commons. The spectacle is certainly a strange one, I thought. The history of men's opposition to women's emancipation is more interesting perhaps than the story of that emancipation itself. An amusing book might be made of it if some young student at Girton or Newnham would collect examples and deduce a theory— but she would need thick gloves on her hands, and bars to protect her of solid gold.

8. Victory Road, a thoroughfare in Berlin.
9. Samuel Johnson (1709–1784), poet and man of letters.
1. A *Survey of Contemporary Music*, Cecil Gray, p. 246

[Woolf's note].
2. Lady Bessborough (1761–1821), correspondent of the British statesman Lord Granville.

But what is amusing now, I recollected, shutting Lady Bessborough, had to be taken in desperate earnest once. Opinions that one now pastes in a book labelled cock-a-doodle-dum and keeps for reading to select audiences on summer nights once drew tears, I can assure you. Among your grandmothers and great-grandmothers there were many that wept their eyes out. Florence Nightingale shrieked aloud in her agony.[3] Moreover, it is all very well for you, who have got yourselves to college and enjoy sitting-rooms—or is it only bed-sitting-rooms?—of your own to say that genius should disregard such opinions; that genius should be above caring what is said of it. Unfortunately, it is precisely the men or women of genius who mind most what is said of them. Remember Keats. Remember the words he had cut on his tombstone. Think of Tennyson; think—but I need hardly multiply instances of the undeniable, if very unfortunate, fact that it is the nature of the artist to mind excessively what is said about him. Literature is strewn with the wreckage of men who have minded beyond reason the opinions of others.

And this susceptibility of theirs is doubly unfortunate, I thought, returning again to my original enquiry into what state of mind is most propitious for creative work, because the mind of an artist, in order to achieve the prodigious effort of freeing whole and entire the work that is in him, must be incandescent, like Shakespeare's mind, I conjectured, looking at the book which lay open at *Antony and Cleopatra*. There must be no obstacle in it, no foreign matter unconsumed.

For though we say that we know nothing about Shakespeare's state of mind, even as we say that, we are saying something about Shakespeare's state of mind. The reason perhaps why we know so little of Shakespeare—compared with Donne or Ben Jonson or Milton—is that his grudges and spites and antipathies are hidden from us. We are not held up by some "revelation" which reminds us of the writer. All desire to protest, to preach, to proclaim an injury, to pay off a score, to make the world the witness of some hardship or grievance was fired out of him and consumed. Therefore his poetry flows from him free and unimpeded. If ever a human being got his work expressed completely, it was Shakespeare. If ever a mind was incandescent, unimpeded, I thought, turning again to the bookcase, it was Shakespeare's mind.

from *Chapter 4*

The extreme activity of mind which showed itself in the later eighteenth century among women—the talking, and the meeting, the writing of essays on Shakespeare, the translating of the classics—was founded on the solid fact that women could make money by writing. Money dignifies what is frivolous if unpaid for. It might still be well to sneer at "blue stockings with an itch for scribbling," but it could not be denied that they could put money in their purses. Thus, towards the end of the eighteenth century a change came about which, if I were rewriting history, I should describe more fully and think of greater importance than the Crusades or the Wars of the Roses. The middle-class woman began to write. For if *Pride and Prejudice* matters, and *Middlemarch* and *Villette* and *Wuthering Heights* matter,[4] then it matters far more than I can prove in an hour's discourse that women generally, and not merely the lonely aristocrat shut up in her country house among her folios and her flatterers, took to writing. Without those forerunners, Jane Austen and the Brontës and George Eliot

3. See *Cassandra*, by Florence Nightingale, printed in *The Cause*, by R. Strachey [Woolf's note].
4. *Pride and Prejudice* (1813), a novel by Jane Austen; *Middlemarch* (1871–1872) by George Eliot; *Villette* (1853) by Charlotte Brontë; *Wuthering Heights* (1847) by Emily Brontë.

could no more have written than Shakespeare could have written without Marlowe, or Marlowe without Chaucer, or Chaucer without those forgotten poets who paved the ways and tamed the natural savagery of the tongue. For masterpieces are not single and solitary births; they are the outcome of many years of thinking in common, of thinking by the body of the people, so that the experience of the mass is behind the single voice. Jane Austen should have laid a wreath upon the grave of Fanny Burney, and George Eliot done homage to the robust shade of Eliza Carter—the valiant old woman who tied a bell to her bedstead in order that she might wake early and learn Greek. All women together ought to let flowers fall upon the tomb of Aphra Behn[5] which is, most scandalously but rather appropriately, in Westminster Abbey, for it was she who earned them the right to speak their minds. It is she—shady and amorous as she was—who makes it not quite fantastic for me to say to you tonight: Earn five hundred a year by your wits.

Here, then, one had reached the early nineteenth century. And here, for the first time, I found several shelves given up entirely to the works of women. But why, I could not help asking, as I ran my eyes over them, were they, with very few exceptions, all novels? The original impulse was to poetry. The "supreme head of song" was a poetess. Both in France and in England the women poets precede the women novelists. Moreover, I thought, looking at the four famous names, what had George Eliot in common with Emily Brontë? Did not Charlotte Brontë fail entirely to understand Jane Austen? Save for the possibly relevant fact that not one of them had a child, four more incongruous characters could not have met together in a room—so much so that it is tempting to invent a meeting and a dialogue between them. Yet by some strange force they were all compelled, when they wrote, to write novels. Had it something to do with being born of the middle class, I asked; and with the fact, which Miss Emily Davies a little later was so strikingly to demonstrate,[6] that the middle-class family in the early nineteenth century was possessed only of a single sitting-room between them? If a woman wrote, she would have to write in the common sitting-room. And, as Miss Nightingale was so vehemently to complain,—"women never have an half hour . . . that they can call their own"—she was always interrupted. Still it would be easier to write prose and fiction there than to write poetry or a play. Less concentration is required. Jane Austen wrote like that to the end of her days. "How she was able to effect all this," her nephew writes in his Memoir, "is surprising, for she had no separate study to repair to, and most of the work must have been done in the general sitting-room, subject to all kinds of casual interruptions. She was careful that her occupation should not be suspected by servants or visitors or any persons beyond her own family party."[7] Jane Austen hid her manuscripts or covered them with a piece of blotting-paper. Then, again, all the literary training that a woman had in the early nineteenth century was training in the observation of character, in the analysis of emotion. Her sensibility had been educated for centuries by the influences of the common sitting-room. People's feelings were impressed on her; personal relations were always before her eyes. Therefore, when the middle-class woman took to writing, she naturally wrote novels, even though, as seems evident enough, two of the four famous women here named were

5. A dramatist and the first English woman to earn a living by writing (1640–1689). Westminster Abbey, in central London, is the burial place of many of the English kings and queens, as well as of famous poets and statesmen.
6. (Sarah) Emily Davies was prominent in the movement to secure university education for women in the 19th century and was chief founder of Girton College, Cambridge (1873).
7. *Memoir of Jane Austen*, by her nephew, James Edward Austen-Leigh [Woolf's note].

not by nature novelists. Emily Brontë should have written poetic plays; the overflow of George Eliot's capacious mind should have spread itself when the creative impulse was spent upon history or biography. They wrote novels, however; one may even go further, I said, taking *Pride and Prejudice* from the shelf, and say that they wrote good novels. Without boasting or giving pain to the opposite sex, one may say that *Pride and Prejudice* is a good book. At any rate, one would not have been ashamed to have been caught in the act of writing *Pride and Prejudice*. Yet Jane Austen was glad that a hinge creaked, so that she might hide her manuscript before any one came in. To Jane Austen there was something discreditable in writing *Pride and Prejudice*. And, I wondered, would *Pride and Prejudice* have been a better novel if Jane Austen had not thought it necessary to hide her manuscript from visitors? I read a page or two to see; but I could not find any signs that her circumstances had harmed her work in the slightest. That, perhaps, was the chief miracle about it. Here was a woman about the year 1800 writing without hate, without bitterness, without fear, without protest, without preaching. That was how Shakespeare wrote, I thought, looking at *Antony and Cleopatra;* and when people compare Shakespeare and Jane Austen, they may mean that the minds of both had consumed all impediments; and for that reason we do not know Jane Austen and we do not know Shakespeare, and for that reason Jane Austen pervades every word that she wrote, and so does Shakespeare. If Jane Austen suffered in any way from her circumstances it was in the narrowness of life that was imposed upon her. It was impossible for a woman to go about alone. She never travelled; she never drove through London in an omnibus or had luncheon in a shop by herself. But perhaps it was the nature of Jane Austen not to want what she had not. Her gift and her circumstances matched each other completely. But I doubt whether that was true of Charlotte Brontë, I said, opening *Jane Eyre* and laying it beside *Pride and Prejudice*.[8]

I opened it at chapter twelve and my eye was caught by the phrase, "Anybody may blame me who likes." What were they blaming Charlotte Brontë for, I wondered? And I read how Jane Eyre used to go up on to the roof when Mrs Fairfax was making jellies and looked over the fields at the distant view. And then she longed—and it was for this that they blamed her—that "then I longed for a power of vision which might overpass that limit; which might reach the busy world, towns, regions full of life I had heard of but never seen: that then I desired more of practical experience than I possessed; more of intercourse with my kind, of acquaintance with variety of character than was here within my reach. I valued what was good in Mrs Fairfax, and what was good in Adèle; but I believed in the existence of other and more vivid kinds of goodness, and what I believed in I wished to behold.

"Who blames me? Many, no doubt, and I shall be called discontented. I could not help it: the restlessness was in my nature; it agitated me to pain sometimes. . . .

"It is vain to say human beings ought to be satisfied with tranquillity: they must have action; and they will make it if they cannot find it. Millions are condemned to a stiller doom than mine, and millions are in silent revolt against their lot. Nobody knows how many rebellions ferment in the masses of life which people earth.

8. Woolf goes on to describe parts of the plot of *Jane Eyre;* Jane Eyre, a penniless orphan, having suffered greatly during her schooling, takes up the post of governess to Adele, the daughter of Mr. Rochester, a man of strange moods. Rochester falls in love with Jane, who agrees to marry him; however this is prevented by Rochester's mad wife—whom Rochester has locked in the attic, concealing her existence from Jane—who tears Jane's wedding veil on the eve of the marriage. Rochester at first tells Jane that Grace Poole, a servant, had been responsible for this and other strange events, including the uncanny laughter occasionally heard in the house.

Women are supposed to be very calm generally: but women feel just as men feel; they need exercise for their faculties and a field for their efforts as much as their brothers do; they suffer from too rigid a restraint, too absolute a stagnation, precisely as men would suffer; and it is narrow-minded in their more privileged fellow-creatures to say that they ought to confine themselves to making puddings and knitting stockings, to playing on the piano and embroidering bags. It is thoughtless to condemn them, or laugh at them, if they seek to do more or learn more than custom has pronounced necessary for their sex.

"When thus alone I not unfrequently heard Grace Poole's laugh. . . ."

That is an awkward break, I thought. It is upsetting to come upon Grace Poole all of a sudden. The continuity is disturbed. One might say, I continued, laying the book down beside *Pride and Prejudice*, that the woman who wrote those pages had more genius in her than Jane Austen; but if one reads them over and marks that jerk in them, that indignation, one sees that she will never get her genius expressed whole and entire. Her books will be deformed and twisted. She will write in a rage where she should write calmly. She will write foolishly where she should write wisely. She will write of herself where she should write of her characters. She is at war with her lot. How could she help but die young, cramped and thwarted?

One could not but play for a moment with the thought of what might have happened if Charlotte Brontë had possessed say three hundred a year—but the foolish woman sold the copyright of her novels outright for fifteen hundred pounds; had somehow possessed more knowledge of the busy world, and towns and regions full of life; more practical experience, and intercourse with her kind and acquaintance with a variety of character. In those words she puts her finger exactly not only upon her own defects as a novelist but upon those of her sex at that time. She knew, no one better, how enormously her genius would have profited if it had not spent itself in solitary visions over distant fields; if experience and intercourse and travel had been granted her. But they were not granted; they were withheld; and we must accept the fact that all those good novels, *Villette, Emma, Wuthering Heights, Middlemarch*, were written by women without more experience of life than could enter the house of a respectable clergyman; written too in the common sitting-room of that respectable house and by women so poor that they could not afford to buy more than a few quires of paper at a time upon which to write *Wuthering Heights* or *Jane Eyre*. One of them, it is true, George Eliot, escaped after much tribulation, but only to a secluded villa in St John's Wood. And there she settled down in the shadow of the world's disapproval.[9] "I wish it to be understood," she wrote, "that I should never invite any one to come and see me who did not ask for the invitation"; for was she not living in sin with a married man and might not the sight of her damage the chastity of Mrs Smith or whoever it might be that chanced to call? One must submit to the social convention, and be "cut off from what is called the world." At the same time, on the other side of Europe, there was a young man living freely with this gipsy or with that great lady; going to the wars; picking up unhindered and uncensored all that varied experience of human life which served him so splendidly later when he came to write his books. Had Tolstoi lived at the Priory in seclusion with a married lady "cut off from what is called the world," however edifying the moral lesson, he could scarcely, I thought, have written *War and Peace*. * * *

---

9. Following a strictly religious childhood, the novelist George Eliot lost her faith and eloped with G. H. Lewes, a married man, with whom she lived for the rest of his life; her family never forgave her.

* * * I do not want, and I am sure that you do not want me, to broach that very dismal subject, the future of fiction, so that I will only pause here one moment to draw your attention to the great part which must be played in that future so far as women are concerned by physical conditions. The book has somehow to be adapted to the body, and at a venture one would say that women's books should be shorter, more concentrated, than those of men, and framed so that they do not need long hours of steady and uninterrupted work. For interruptions there will always be. Again, the nerves that feed the brain would seem to differ in men and women, and if you are going to make them work their best and hardest, you must find out what treatment suits them—whether these hours of lectures, for instance, which the monks devised, presumably, hundreds of years ago, suit them—what alternations of work and rest they need, interpreting rest not as doing nothing but as doing something but something that is different; and what should that difference be? All this should be discussed and discovered; all this is part of the question of women and fiction. And yet, I continued, approaching the bookcase again, where shall I find that elaborate study of the psychology of women by a woman? If through their incapacity to play football women are not going to be allowed to practise medicine——

Happily my thoughts were now given another turn.

from *Chapter 6*

Next day the light of the October morning was falling in dusty shafts through the uncurtained windows, and the hum of traffic rose from the street. London then was winding itself up again; the factory was astir; the machines were beginning. It was tempting, after all this reading, to look out of the window and see what London was doing on the morning of the twenty-sixth of October 1928. And what was London doing? Nobody, it seemed, was reading *Antony and Cleopatra*. London was wholly indifferent, it appeared, to Shakespeare's plays. Nobody cared a straw—and I do not blame them—for the future of fiction, the death of poetry or the development by the average woman of a prose style completely expressive of her mind. If opinions upon any of these matters had been chalked on the pavement, nobody would have stooped to read them. The nonchalance of the hurrying feet would have rubbed them out in half an hour. Here came an errand-boy; here a woman with a dog on a lead. The fascination of the London street is that no two people are ever alike; each seems bound on some private affair of his own. There were the business-like, with their little bags; there were the drifters rattling sticks upon area railings; there were affable characters to whom the streets serve for clubroom, hailing men in carts and giving information without being asked for it. Also there were funerals to which men, thus suddenly reminded of the passing of their own bodies, lifted their hats. And then a very distinguished gentleman came slowly down a doorstep and paused to avoid collision with a bustling lady who had, by some means or other, acquired a splendid fur coat and a bunch of Parma violets. They all seemed separate, self-absorbed, on business of their own.

At this moment, as so often happens in London, there was a complete lull and suspension of traffic. Nothing came down the street; nobody passed. A single leaf detached itself from the plane tree at the end of the street, and in that pause and suspension fell. Somehow it was like a signal falling, a signal pointing to a force in things which one had overlooked. It seemed to point to a river, which flowed past, invisibly, round the corner, down the street, and took people and eddied them along, as the stream at Oxbridge had taken the undergraduate in his boat and the dead leaves.

Now it was bringing from one side of the street to the other diagonally a girl in patent leather boots, and then a young man in a maroon overcoat; it was also bringing a taxi-cab; and it brought all three together at a point directly beneath my window; where the taxi stopped; and the girl and the young man stopped; and they got into the taxi; and then the cab glided off as if it were swept on by the current elsewhere.

The sight was ordinary enough; what was strange was the rhythmical order with which my imagination had invested it; and the fact that the ordinary sight of two people getting into a cab had the power to communicate something of their own seeming satisfaction. The sight of two people coming down the street and meeting at the corner seems to ease the mind of some strain, I thought, watching the taxi turn and make off. Perhaps to think, as I had been thinking these two days, of one sex as distinct from the other is an effort. It interferes with the unity of the mind. Now that effort had ceased and that unity had been restored by seeing two people come together and get into a taxi-cab. The mind is certainly a very mysterious organ, I reflected, drawing my head in from the window, about which nothing whatever is known, though we depend upon it so completely. Why do I feel that there are severances and oppositions in the mind, as there are strains from obvious causes on the body? What does one mean by "the unity of the mind," I pondered, for clearly the mind has so great a power of concentrating at any point at any moment that it seems to have no single state of being. It can separate itself from the people in the street, for example, and think of itself as apart from them, at an upper window looking down on them. Or it can think with other people spontaneously, as, for instance, in a crowd waiting to hear some piece of news read out. It can think back through its fathers or through its mothers, as I have said that a woman writing thinks back through her mothers. Again if one is a woman one is often surprised by a sudden splitting off of consciousness, say in walking down Whitehall,[1] when from being the natural inheritor of that civilisation, she becomes, on the contrary, outside of it, alien and critical. Clearly the mind is always altering its focus, and bringing the world into different perspectives. But some of these states of mind seem, even if adopted spontaneously, to be less comfortable than others. In order to keep oneself continuing in them one is unconsciously holding something back, and gradually the repression becomes an effort. But there may be some state of mind in which one could continue without effort because nothing is required to be held back. And this perhaps, I thought, coming in from the window, is one of them. For certainly when I saw the couple get into the taxi-cab the mind felt as if, after being divided, it had come together again in a natural fusion. The obvious reason would be that it is natural for the sexes to co-operate. One has a profound, if irrational, instinct in favour of the theory that the union of man and woman makes for the greatest satisfaction, the most complete happiness. But the sight of the two people getting into the taxi and the satisfaction it gave me made me also ask whether there are two sexes in the mind corresponding to the two sexes in the body, and whether they also require to be united in order to get complete satisfaction and happiness. And I went on amateurishly to sketch a plan of the soul so that in each of us two powers preside, one male, one female; and in the man's brain, the man predominates over the woman, and in the woman's brain, the woman predominates over the man. The normal and comfortable state of being is that when the two live in harmony together, spiritually co-operating. If one is a man, still the woman part of the brain must have effect; and a woman also must have intercourse

1. A main thoroughfare in central London and site of government offices.

with the man in her. Coleridge perhaps meant this when he said that a great mind is androgynous.[2] It is when this fusion takes place that the mind is fully fertilised and uses all its faculties. Perhaps a mind that is purely masculine cannot create, any more than a mind that is purely feminine, I thought. * * *

* * * One must turn back to Shakespeare then, for Shakespeare was androgynous; and so was Keats and Sterne and Cowper and Lamb and Coleridge. Shelley perhaps was sexless. Milton and Ben Jonson had a dash too much of the male in them. So had Wordsworth and Tolstoi. In our time Proust was wholly androgynous, if not perhaps a little too much of a woman. But that failing is too rare for one to complain of it, since without some mixture of the kind the intellect seems to predominate and the other faculties of the mind harden and become barren. However, I consoled myself with the reflection that this is perhaps a passing phase; much of what I have said in obedience to my promise to give you the course of my thoughts will seem out of date; much of what flames in my eyes will seem dubious to you who have not yet come of age.

Even so, the very first sentence that I would write here, I said, crossing over to the writing-table and taking up the page headed Women and Fiction, is that it is fatal for any one who writes to think of their sex. It is fatal to be a man or woman pure and simple; one must be woman-manly or man-womanly. It is fatal for a woman to lay the least stress on any grievance; to plead even with justice any cause; in any way to speak consciously as a woman. And fatal is no figure of speech; for anything written with that conscious bias is doomed to death. It ceases to be fertilised. Brilliant and effective, powerful and masterly, as it may appear for a day or two, it must wither at nightfall; it cannot grow in the minds of others. Some collaboration has to take place in the mind between the woman and the man before the act of creation can be accomplished. Some marriage of opposites has to be consummated. The whole of the mind must lie wide open if we are to get the sense that the writer is communicating his experience with perfect fullness. There must be freedom and there must be peace. Not a wheel must grate, not a light glimmer. The curtains must be close drawn. The writer, I thought, once his experience is over, must lie back and let his mind celebrate its nuptials in darkness. He must not look or question what is being done. Rather, he must pluck the petals from a rose or watch the swans float calmly down the river. And I saw again the current which took the boat and the undergraduate and the dead leaves; and the taxi took the man and the woman, I thought, seeing them come together across the street, and the current swept them away, I thought, hearing far off the roar of London's traffic, into that tremendous stream.

Here, then, Mary Beton ceases to speak. She has told you how she reached the conclusion—the prosaic conclusion—that it is necessary to have five hundred a year and a room with a lock on the door if you are to write fiction or poetry. She has tried to lay bare the thoughts and impressions that led her to think this. She has asked you to follow her flying into the arms of a Beadle, lunching here, dining there, drawing pictures in the British Museum, taking books from the shelf, looking out of the window. While she has been doing all these things, you no doubt have been observing her failings and foibles and deciding what effect they have had on her opinions. You have been contradicting her and making whatever additions and deductions seem good to you. That is all as it should be, for in a question like this

---

2. The poet Samuel Taylor Coleridge made the remark in September 1832—"a great mind must be androgynous"—and it was duly recorded in his Table Talk.

truth is only to be had by laying together many varieties of error. And I will end now in my own person by anticipating two criticisms, so obvious that you can hardly fail to make them.

No opinion has been expressed, you may say, upon the comparative merits of the sexes even as writers. That was done purposely, because, even if the time had come for such a valuation—and it is far more important at the moment to know how much money women had and how many rooms than to theorise about their capacities—even if the time had come I do not believe that gifts, whether of mind or character, can be weighed like sugar and butter, not even in Cambridge, where they are so adept at putting people into classes and fixing caps on their heads and letters after their names. I do not believe that even the Table of Precedency which you will find in Whitaker's *Almanac*[3] represents a final order of values, or that there is any sound reason to suppose that a Commander of the Bath will ultimately walk in to dinner behind a Master in Lunacy. All this pitting of sex against sex, of quality against quality; all this claiming of superiority and imputing of inferiority, belong to the private-school stage of human existence where there are "sides," and it is necessary for one side to beat another side, and of the utmost importance to walk up to a platform and receive from the hands of the Headmaster himself a highly ornamental pot. As people mature they cease to believe in sides or in Headmasters or in highly ornamental pots. At any rate, where books are concerned, it is notoriously difficult to fix labels of merit in such a way that they do not come off. Are not reviews of current literature a perpetual illustration of the difficulty of judgment? "This great book," "this worthless book," the same book is called by both names. Praise and blame alike mean nothing. No, delightful as the pastime of measuring may be, it is the most futile of all occupations, and to submit to the decrees of the measurers the most servile of attitudes. So long as you write what you wish to write, that is all that matters; and whether it matters for ages or only for hours, nobody can say. But to sacrifice a hair of the head of your vision, a shade of its colour, in deference to some Headmaster with a silver pot in his hand or to some professor with a measuring-rod up his sleeve, is the most abject treachery, and the sacrifice of wealth and chastity which used to be said to be the greatest of human disasters, a mere flea-bite in comparison.

Next I think that you may object that in all this I have made too much of the importance of material things. * * *

Intellectual freedom depends upon material things. Poetry depends upon intellectual freedom. And women have always been poor, not for two hundred years merely, but from the beginning of time. Women have had less intellectual freedom than the sons of Athenian slaves. Women, then, have not had a dog's chance of writing poetry. That is why I have laid so much stress on money and a room of one's own. However, thanks to the toils of those obscure women in the past, of whom I wish we knew more, thanks, curiously enough, to two wars, the Crimean which let Florence Nightingale out of her drawing-room, and the European War which opened the doors to the average woman some sixty years later, these evils are in the way to be bettered. Otherwise you would not be here tonight, and your chance of earning five hundred pounds a year, precarious as I am afraid that it still is, would be minute in the extreme. * * *

Here I would stop, but the pressure of convention decrees that every speech must end with a peroration. And a peroration addressed to women should have something,

---

3. A compendium of general information first published in 1868.

you will agree, particularly exalting and ennobling about it. I should implore you to remember your responsibilities, to be higher, more spiritual; I should remind you how much depends upon you, and what an influence you can exert upon the future. But those exhortations can safely, I think, be left to the other sex, who will put them, and indeed have put them, with far greater eloquence than I can compass. When I rummage in my own mind I find no noble sentiments about being companions and equals and influencing the world to higher ends. I find myself saying briefly and prosaically that it is much more important to be oneself than anything else. Do not dream of influencing other people, I would say, if I knew how to make it sound exalted. Think of things in themselves.

And again I am reminded by dipping into newspapers and novels and biographies that when a woman speaks to women she should have something very unpleasant up her sleeve. Women are hard on women. Women dislike women. Women . . . but are you not sick to death of the word? I can assure you that I am. Let us agree, then, that a paper read by a woman to women should end with something particularly disagreeable.

But how does it go? What can I think of? The truth is, I often like women. I like their unconventionality. I like their subtlety. I like their anonymity. I like—but I must not run on in this way. That cupboard there,—you say it holds clean table-napkins only; but what if Sir Archibald Bodkin were concealed among them?[4] Let me then adopt a sterner tone. Have I, in the preceding words, conveyed to you sufficiently the warnings and reprobation of mankind? I have told you the very low opinion in which you were held by Mr Oscar Browning. I have indicated what Napoleon once thought of you and what Mussolini thinks now. Then, in case any of you aspire to fiction, I have copied out for your benefit the advice of the critic about courageously acknowledging the limitations of your sex. I have referred to Professor X and given prominence to his statement that women are intellectually, morally and physically inferior to men. I have handed on all that has come my way without going in search of it, and here is a final warning—from Mr John Langdon Davies.[5] Mr John Langdon Davies warns women "that when children cease to be altogether desirable, women cease to be altogether necessary." I hope you will make a note of it.

How can I further encourage you to go about the business of life? Young women, I would say, and please attend, for the peroration is beginning, you are, in my opinion, disgracefully ignorant. You have never made a discovery of any sort of importance. You have never shaken an empire or led an army into battle. The plays of Shakespeare are not by you, and you have never introduced a barbarous race to the blessings of civilisation. What is your excuse? It is all very well for you to say, pointing to the streets and squares and forests of the globe swarming with black and white and coffee-coloured inhabitants, all busily engaged in traffic and enterprise and love-making, we have had other work on our hands. Without our doing, those seas would be unsailed and those fertile lands a desert. We have borne and bred and washed and taught, perhaps to the age of six or seven years, the one thousand six hundred and twenty-three million human beings who are, according to statistics, at present in existence, and that, allowing that some had help, takes time.

There is truth in what you say—I will not deny it. But at the same time may I remind you that there have been at least two colleges for women in existence in Eng-

---

4. Sir Archibald Bodkin was then Director of Public Prosecutions; his office had been responsible for the 1928 prosecution of Radclyffe Hall's novel *The Well of Loneliness* on a charge of obscenity. It was subsequently banned. Woolf had wanted to give evidence in the book's defense at the trial, but expert witnesses were not allowed by the presiding magistrate.

5. *A Short History of Women*, by John Langford Davies [Woolf's note].

land since the year 1866; that after the year 1880 a married woman was allowed by law to possess her own property; and that in 1919—which is a whole nine years ago—she was given a vote? May I also remind you that the most of the professions have been open to you for close on ten years now? When you reflect upon these immense privileges and the length of time time during which they have been enjoyed, and the fact that there must be at this moment some two thousand women capable of earning over five hundred a year in one way or another, you will agree that the excuse of lack of opportunity, training, encouragement, leisure and money no longer holds good. Moreover, the economists are telling us that Mrs Seton has had too many children. You must, of course, go on bearing children, but, so they say, in twos and threes, not in tens and twelves.

Thus, with some time on your hands and with some book learning in your brains—you have had enough of the other kind, and are sent to college partly, I suspect, to be uneducated—surely you should embark upon another stage of your very long, very laborious and highly obscure career. A thousand pens are ready to suggest what you should do and what effect you will have. My own suggestion is a little fantastic, I admit; I prefer, therefore, to put it in the form of fiction.

I told you in the course of this paper that Shakespeare had a sister; but do not look for her in Sir Sidney Lee's life of the poet. She died young—alas, she never wrote a word. She lies buried where the omnibuses now stop, opposite the Elephant and Castle. Now my belief is that this poet who never wrote a word and was buried at the crossroads still lives. She lives in you and in me, and in many other women who are not here tonight, for they are washing up the dishes and putting the children to bed. But she lives; for great poets do not die; they are continuing presences; they need only the opportunity to walk among us in the flesh. This opportunity, as I think, it is now coming within your power to give her. For my belief is that if we live another century or so—I am talking of the common life which is the real life and not of the little separate lives which we live as individuals—and have five hundred a year each of us and rooms of our own; if we have the habit of freedom and the courage to write exactly what we think; if we escape a little from the common sitting-room and see human beings not always in their relation to each other but in relation to reality; and the sky, too, and the trees or whatever it may be in themselves; if we look past Milton's bogey, for no human being should shut out the view; if we face the fact, for it is a fact, that there is no arm to cling to, but that we go alone and that our relation is to the world of reality and not only to the world of men and women, then the opportunity will come and the dead poet who was Shakespeare's sister will put on the body which she has so often laid down. Drawing her life from the lives of the unknown who were her forerunners, as her brother did before her, she will be born. As for her coming without that preparation, without that effort on our part, without that determination that when she is born again she shall find it possible to live and write her poetry, that we cannot expect, for that would be impossible. But I maintain that she would come if we worked for her, and that so to work, even in poverty and obscurity, is worth while.

Three Guineas

Three Guineas marked Virginia Woolf's return to the genre she had employed in *A Room of One's Own*: the extended political and literary essay with a feminist theme. Like the earlier essay, this text is cast as a response to a request—in this case, a letter from an unnamed man asking her opinions on the prevention of war. Woolf wrote *Three Guineas* in 1938, against the backdrop of impending world war. Her analysis of gender inequality, and the social construction of those conditions of inequality, is intensified in the later work because of the urgency of the imminent war. Woolf uses her critique of sexism to investigate the perpetuation of violence in human history and to argue that the same dominances that bring about female inequality are responsible for the evils of war.

Woolf's argument is anything but simple, and her text anything but a straightforward polemic. Her rhetoric is laced with irony and an almost savage playfulness, in light of the seriousness of the historical moment. The primary metaphor of this work—as of her novel *Orlando* (1928)—is that of costume and dress. Hardly a retreat to a frivolous subject, the emphasis on clothing cloaks Woolf's understanding of the invented nature of social power. In other words, she does not attribute male dominance to biological superiority on the part of men; instead, she investigates the degree to which human hierarchies of gender, of class, and of race are made by human culture and are thus "conventional," just as fashion is. While there is something grotesque about comparing Nazi uniforms to the vestments and robes of the clergy, as Woolf does in the essay, her purpose is to scandalously unveil this truth of culture, and thereby to suggest that dominance can be reversed or transformed.

Woolf uses the lens of sexism to investigate the nature of authority—which is generally male authority in the institutions of modern society. Woolf is not reductive in doing this—she never implies that women are "better" in ethical or other ways, nor that authority is less vile when abused by women, as it occasionally is. She is eager to find the skeleton key to unlock the mystery of brute authority, and to warn against the militarism she saw as a permanent feature of British as well as German society. Woolf does not exempt any national culture or any group from susceptibility to power and its corrupting effects. In this essay, which shocked its audience in a way the more playful *A Room of One's Own* did not, she offers a comparative survey of the institutions of authority, or civil society. The vestments of power, Woolf shows, can be adopted by groups and by entire nations and even civilizations. *Three Guineas* is a clarion call to arms, to the weapons of thought and education as alternatives to the unthinkable horrors of a second world war. Virginia Woolf saw her prophecy of war come true shortly after its publication, and that fatal fact, as much as her own mental illness, was a push toward the suicide that claimed her life in 1941.

from Three Guineas[1]

Three years is a long time to leave a letter unanswered, and your letter has been lying without an answer even longer than that. I had hoped that it would answer itself, or that other people would answer it for me. But there it is with its question—How in your opinion are we to prevent war?—still unanswered.

It is true that many answers have suggested themselves, but none that would not need explanation, and explanations take time. In this case, too, there are reasons why it is particularly difficult to avoid misunderstanding. A whole page could be filled with excuses and apologies; declarations of unfitness, incompetence, lack of knowledge, and experience: and they would be true. But even when they were said there would still remain some difficulties so fundamental that it may well prove impossible for you to understand or for us to explain. But one does not like to leave so remarkable a letter as yours—a letter perhaps unique in the history of human correspondence, since when before has an educated man asked a woman how in her opinion war can be prevented?—unanswered. Therefore let us make the attempt; even if it is doomed to failure.

In the first place let us draw what all letter-writers instinctively draw, a sketch of the person to whom the letter is addressed. Without someone warm and breathing on

---

1. A guinea had been a gold coin worth one pound and one shilling (21 shillings); although no longer in circulation, guineas were used in determining professional fees and luxury items.

the other side of the page, letters are worthless. You, then, who ask the question, are a little grey on the temples; the hair is no longer thick on the top of your head. You have reached the middle years of life not without effort, at the Bar;[2] but on the whole your journey has been prosperous. There is nothing parched, mean or dissatisfied in your expression. And without wishing to flatter you, your prosperity—wife, children, house—has been deserved. You have never sunk into the contented apathy of middle life, for, as your letter from an office in the heart of London shows, instead of turning on your pillow and prodding your pigs, pruning your pear trees—you have a few acres in Norfolk—you are writing letters, attending meetings, presiding over this and that, asking questions, with the sound of the guns in your ears. For the rest, you began your education at one of the great public schools and finished it at the university.

It is now that the first difficulty of communication between us appears. Let us rapidly indicate the reason. We both come of what, in this hybrid age when, though birth is mixed, classes still remain fixed, it is convenient to call the educated class. When we meet in the flesh we speak with the same accent; use knives and forks in the same way; expect maids to cook dinner and wash up after dinner; and can talk during dinner without much difficulty about politics and people; war and peace; barbarism and civilization—all the questions indeed suggested by your letter. Moreover, we both earn our livings. But . . . those three dots mark a precipice, a gulf so deeply cut between us that for three years and more I have been sitting on my side of it wondering whether it is any use to try to speak across it. Let us then ask someone else—it is Mary Kingsley—to speak for us.[3] "I don't know if I ever revealed to you the fact that being allowed to learn German was *all* the paid-for education I ever had. Two thousand pounds was spent on my brother's, I still hope not in vain."[4] Mary Kingsley is not speaking for herself alone; she is speaking, still, for many of the daughters of educated men. And she is not merely speaking for them; she is also pointing to a very important fact about them, a fact that must profoundly influence all that follows: the fact of Arthur's Education Fund. You, who have read *Pendennis*,[5] will remember how the mysterious letters A.E.F. figured in the household ledgers. Ever since the thirteenth century English families have been paying money into that account. From the Pastons[6] to the Pendennises, all educated families from the thirteenth century to the present moment have paid money into that account. It is a voracious receptacle. Where there were many sons to educate it required a great effort on the part of the family to keep it full. For your education was not merely in book-learning; games educated your body; friends taught you more than books or games. Talk with them

2. In Britain, "the Bar" refers collectively to lawyers; to be called to the Bar means to enter the profession.
3. Mary Kingsley traveled extensively in West Africa in the final decade of the 19th century, publishing an account of her expeditions in 1897.
4. *The Life of Mary Kingsley*, by Stephen Gwynn, p. 15. It is difficult to get exact figures of the sums spent on the education of educated men's daughters. About £20 or £30 presumably covered the entire cost of Mary Kingsley's education (b. 1862; d. 1900). A sum of £100 may be taken as about the average in the 19th century and even later. The women thus educated often felt the lack of education very keenly. "I always feel the defects of my education most painfully when I go out," wrote Anne J. Clough, the first Principal of Newnham (*Life of Anne J. Clough*, by B. A Clough, p. 60) . . .
But the educated man's daughter in the 19th century was even more ignorant of life than of books. One reason for that ignorance is suggested by the following quotation: "It was supposed that most men were not 'virtuous', that is, that nearly all would be capable of accosting and annoying—or worse—any unaccompanied young woman whom they met." ("Society and the Season," by Mary, Countess of Lovelace, in *Fifty Years*, 1882–1932, p. 37.) She was therefore confined to a very narrow circle; and her "ignorance and indifference" to anything outside it was excusable. The connection between that ignorance and the 19th-century conception of manhood, which—witness the Victorian hero—made "virtue" and virility incompatible is obvious. In a well-known passage, Thackeray complains of the limitations which virtue and virility between them impose upon his art [Woolf's note].
5. *The History of Pendennis* (1848–1850), a novel by William Makepeace Thackeray.
6. *The Paston Letters* (c. 1420–1504) are a record of the domestic conditions of a well-to-do medieval family.

broadened your outlook and enriched your mind. In the holidays you travelled; acquired a taste for art; a knowledge of foreign politics; and then, before you could earn your own living, your father made you an allowance upon which it was possible for you to live while you learnt the profession which now entitles you to add the letters K.C.[7] to your name. All this came out of Arthur's Education Fund. And to this your sisters, as Mary Kingsley indicates, made their contribution. Not only did their own education, save for such small sums as paid the German teacher, go into it; but many of those luxuries and trimmings which are, after all, an essential part of education—travel, society, solitude, a lodging apart from the family house—they were paid into it too. It was a voracious receptacle, a solid fact—Arthur's Education Fund—a fact so solid indeed that it cast a shadow over the entire landscape. And the result is that though we look at the same things, we see them differently. What is that congregation of buildings there, with a semi-monastic look, with chapels and halls and green playing-fields? To you it is your old school, Eton or Harrow;[8] your old university, Oxford or Cambridge; the source of memories and of traditions innumerable. But to us, who see it through the shadow of Arthur's Education Fund, it is a schoolroom table; an omnibus going to a class; a little woman with a red nose who is not well educated herself but has an invalid mother to support; an allowance of £50 a year with which to buy clothes, give presents and take journeys on coming to maturity. Such is the effect that Arthur's Education Fund has had upon us. So magically does it change the landscape that the noble courts and quadrangles of Oxford and Cambridge often appear to educated men's daughters[9] like petticoats with holes in them, cold legs of mutton, and the boat train starting for abroad while the guard slams the door in their faces.

* * *

Here then is your own letter. In that, as we have seen, after asking for an opinion as to how to prevent war, you go on to suggest certain practical measures by which we can help you to prevent it. These are it appears that we should sign a manifesto, pledging ourselves "to protect culture and intellectual liberty";[1] that we should

---

7. King's Counsel; the title for senior barristers.
8. Prestigious boys' schools.
9. Our ideology is still so inveterately anthropocentric that it has been necessary to coin this clumsy term—educated man's daughter—to describe the class whose fathers have been educated at public schools and universities. Obviously, if the term "bourgeois" fits her brother, it is grossly incorrect to use it of one who differs so profoundly in the two prime characteristics of the bourgeoisie—capital and environment [Woolf's note].
1. It is to be hoped that some methodical person has made a collection of the various manifestoes and questionnaires issued broadcast during the years 1936–7. Private people of no political training were invited to sign appeals asking their own and foreign governments to change their policy; artists were asked to fill up forms stating the proper relation of the artist to the State, to religion, to morality; pledges were required that the writer should use English grammatically and avoid vulgar expressions; and dreamers were invited to analyse their dreams. By way of inducement it was generally proposed to publish the results in the daily or weekly Press. What effect this inquisition has had upon governments it is for the politician to say. Upon literature, since the output of books is unstaunched, and grammar would seem to be neither better nor worse, the effect is problematical. But

the inquisition . . . points, indirectly, to the death of the Siren, that much ridiculed and often upper-class lady who by keeping open house for the aristocracy, plutocracy, intelligentsia, ignorantsia, etc., tried to provide all classes with a talking-ground or scratching-post where they could rub up minds, manners and morals more privately, and perhaps as usefully. The part that the Siren played in promoting culture and intellectual liberty in the 18th century is held by historians to be of some importance. Even in our own day she had her uses. Witness W. B. Yeats—"How often have I wished that he [Synge] might live long enough to enjoy that communion with idle, charming cultivated women which Balzac in one of his dedications calls 'the chief consolation of genius'!" (*Dramatis Personae*, W. B. Yeats, p. 127.) Lady St. Helier who, as Lady Jeune, preserved the 18th-century tradition, informs us, however, that "Plovers' eggs at 2s 6d. apiece, forced strawberries, early asparagus, *petits poussins* . . . are now considered almost a necessity by anyone aspiring to give a good dinner" (1909); and her remark that the reception day was "very fatiguing . . . how exhausted I felt when half-past seven came, and how gladly at eight o'clock I sat down to a peaceful *tête-à-tête* dinner with my husband!" (*Memories of Fifty Years*, by Lady St. Helier, pp. 3, 5, 182) may explain why such houses are shut, why such hostesses are dead, and why

join a certain society, devoted to certain measures whose aim is to preserve peace; and, finally, that we should subscribe to that society which like the others is in need of funds.

First, then, let us consider how we can help you to prevent war by protecting culture and intellectual liberty, since you assure us that there is a connection between those rather abstract words and these very positive photographs—the photographs of dead bodies and ruined houses.

But if it was surprising to be asked for an opinion how to prevent war, it is still more surprising to be asked to help you in the rather abstract terms of your manifesto to protect culture and intellectual liberty. Consider, Sir, in the light of the facts given above, what this request of yours means. It means that in the year 1938 the sons of educated men are asking the daughters to help them to protect culture and intellectual liberty. And why, you may ask, is that so surprising? Suppose that the Duke of Devonshire, in his star and garter,[2] stepped down into the kitchen and said to the maid who was peeling potatoes with a smudge on her cheek: "Stop your potato peeling, Mary, and help me to construe this rather difficult passage in Pindar,"[3] would not Mary be surprised and run screaming to Louisa the cook, "Lawks, Louie, Master must be mad!" That, or something like it, is the cry that rises to our lips when the sons of educated men ask us, their sisters, to protect intellectual liberty and culture. But let us try to translate the kitchenmaid's cry into the language of educated people.

* * * The question which concerns us is what possible help we can give you in protecting culture and intellectual liberty—we who have been shut out from the universities so repeatedly, and are only now admitted so restrictedly; we who have received no paid-for education whatsoever, or so little that we can only read our own tongue and write our own language, we who are, in fact, members not of the intelligentsia but of the ignorantsia? * * * Just as any kitchenmaid would attempt to construe a passage in Pindar if told that her life depended on it, so the daughters of educated men, however little their training qualifies them, must consider what they can do to protect culture and intellectual liberty if by so doing they can help you to prevent war. So let us by all means in our power examine this further method of helping you, and see, before we consider your request that we should join your society, whether we can sign this manifesto in favour of culture and intellectual liberty with some intention of keeping our word.

* * *

* * * What were they working for in the nineteenth century—those queer dead women in their poke bonnets and shawls? The very same cause for which we are working now. "Our claim was no claim of women's rights only;"—it is Josephine Butler[4] who speaks—"it was larger and deeper; it was a claim for the rights of all—all men and women—to the respect in their persons of the great principles of Justice and Equality and Liberty." The words are the same as yours; the claim is the same as yours. The daughters of educated men who were called, to their resentment, "feminists" were in fact the advance guard of your own movement. They were fighting the

---

therefore the intelligentsia, the ignorantsia, the aristocracy, the bureaucracy, the bourgeoisie, etc., are driven (unless somebody will revive that society on an economic basis) to do their talking in public. But in view of the multitude of manifestoes and questionnaires now in circulation it would be foolish to suggest another into the minds and motives of the Inquisitors [Woolf's note].

2. Badges of the Order of the Garter, the highest English Order of Knighthood.
3. Greek poet (c. 522–443 B.C.), famous for his poems celebrating the victors at the ancient Olympic Games.
4. Feminist involved in the movement for educational reform (1828–1906).

same enemy that you are fighting and for the same reasons. They were fighting the tyranny of the patriarchal state as you are fighting the tyranny of the Fascist state. Thus we are merely carrying on the same fight that our mothers and grandmothers fought; their words prove it; your words prove it. But now with your letter before us we have your assurance that you are fighting with us, not against us. That fact is so inspiring that another celebration seems called for. What could be more fitting than to write more dead words, more corrupt words, upon more sheets of paper and burn them—the words, Tyrant, Dictator, for example? But, alas, those words are not yet obsolete. We can still shake out eggs from newspapers; still smell a peculiar and unmistakable odour in the region of Whitehall and Westminster. And abroad the monster has come more openly to the surface. There is no mistaking him there. He has widened his scope. He is interfering now with your liberty; he is dictating how you shall live; he is making distinctions not merely between the sexes, but between the races. You are feeling in your own persons what your mothers felt when they were shut out, when they were shut up, because they were women. Now you are being shut out, you are being shut up, because you are Jews, because you are democrats, because of race, because of religion. It is not a photograph that you look upon any longer; there you go, trapesing along in the procession yourselves. And that makes a difference. The whole iniquity of dictatorship, whether in Oxford or Cambridge, in Whitehall or Downing Street, against Jews or against women, in England, or in Germany, in Italy or in Spain is now apparent to you. But now we are fighting together. The daughters and sons of educated men are fighting side by side. That fact is so inspiring, even if no celebration is yet possible, that if this one guinea could be multiplied a million times all those guineas should be at your service without any other conditions than those that you have imposed upon yourself. Take this one guinea then and use it to assert "the rights of all—all men and women—to the respect in their persons of the great principles of Justice and Equality and Liberty." Put this penny candle in the window of your new society, and may we live to see the day when in the blaze of our common freedom the words tyrant and dictator shall be burnt to ashes, because the words tyrant and dictator shall be obsolete.

That request then for a guinea answered, and the cheque signed, only one further request of yours remains to be considered—it is that we should fill up a form and become members of your society. On the face of it that seems a simple request, easily granted. For what can be simpler than to join the society to which this guinea has just been contributed? On the face of it, how easy, how simple; but in the depths, how difficult, how complicated. . . . What possible doubts, what possible hesitations can those dots stand for? What reason or what emotion can make us hesitate to become members of a society whose aims we approve, to whose funds we have contributed? It may be neither reason nor emotion, but something more profound and fundamental than either. It may be difference. Different we are, as facts have proved, both in sex and in education. And it is from that difference, as we have already said, that our help can come, if help we can, to protect liberty, to prevent war. But if we sign this form which implies a promise to become active members of your society, it would seem that we must lose that difference and therefore sacrifice that help. * * *

* * * Thus, Sir, while we respect you as a private person and prove it by giving you a guinea to spend as you choose, we believe that we can help you most effectively by refusing to join your society; by working for our common ends—justice and equality and liberty for all men and women—outside your society, not within.

But this, you will say, if it means anything, can only mean that you, the daughters of educated men, who have promised us your positive help, refuse to join our society in order that you may make another of your own. And what sort of society do you propose to found outside ours, but in co-operation with it, so that we may both work together for our common ends? That is a question which you have every right to ask, and which we must try to answer in order to justify our refusal to sign the form you send. Let us then draw rapidly in outline the kind of society which the daughters of educated men found and join outside your society but in co-operation with its ends. In the first place, this new society, you will be relieved to learn, would have no honorary treasurer, for it would need no funds. It would have no office, no committee, no secretary; it would call no meetings; it would hold no conferences. If name it must have, it could be called the Outsiders' Society. That is not a resonant name, but it has the advantage that it squares with facts—the facts of history, of law, of biography; even, it may be, with the still hidden facts of our still unknown psychology. It would consist of educated men's daughters working in their own class—how indeed can they work in any other?[5]—and by their own methods for liberty, equality and peace. Their first duty, to which they would bind themselves not by oath, for oaths and ceremonies have no part in a society which must be anonymous and elastic before everything, would be not to fight with arms. This is easy for them to observe, for in fact, as the papers inform us, "the Army Council have no intention of opening recruiting for any women's corps.[6]" The country ensures it. Next they would refuse in the event of war to make munitions or nurse the wounded. Since in the last war both these activities were mainly discharged by the daughters of working men, the pressure upon them here too would be slight, though probably disagreeable. On the other hand the next duty to which they would pledge themselves is one of considerable difficulty, and calls not only for courage and initiative, but for the special knowledge of the educated man's daughter. It is, briefly, not to incite their brothers to fight, or to dissuade them, but to maintain an attitude of complete indifference. But the attitude expressed by the word "indifference" is so complex and of such importance that it needs even here further definition. Indifference in the first place must be given a firm footing upon fact. As it is a fact that she cannot understand what instinct compels him, what glory, what interest, what manly satisfaction fighting provides for him— "without war there would be no outlet for the manly qualities which fighting devel-

---

5. In the 19th century much valuable work was done for the working class by educated men's daughters in the only way that was then open to them. But now that some of them at least have received an expensive education, it is arguable that they can work much more effectively by remaining in their own class and using the methods of that class to improve a class which stands much in need of improvement. If on the other hand the educated (as so often happens) renounce the very qualities which education should have brought—reason, tolerance, knowledge—and play at belonging to the working class and adopting its cause, they merely expose that cause to the ridicule of the educated class and do nothing to improve their own. But the number of books written by the educated about the working class would seem to show that the glamour of the working class and the emotional relief afforded by adopting its cause, are today as irresistible to the middle class as the glamour of the aristocracy was 20 years ago (see A la Recherche du Temps Perdu). Meanwhile it would be interesting to know what the true-born work-

ing man or woman thinks of the playboys and playgirls of the educated class who adopt the working-class cause without sacrificing middle-class capital, or sharing working-class experience. "The average housewife," according to Mrs Murphy, Home Service Director of the British Commercial Gas Association, "washed an acre of dirty dishes, a mile of glass and three miles of clothes and scrubbed five miles of floor yearly." (Daily Telegraph, September 29th, 1937.) For a more detailed account of working-class life, see Life as We Have Known It by Co-operative working women, edited by Margaret Llewelyn Davies. The Life of Joseph Wright also gives a remarkable account of working-class life at first hand and not through pro-proletarian spectacles [Woolf's note].

6. "It was stated yesterday at the War Office that the Army Council have no intention of opening recruiting for any women's corps." (The Times, October 22nd, 1937.) This marks a prime distinction between the sexes. Pacifism is enforced upon women. Men are still allowed liberty of choice [Woolf's note].

ops"—as fighting thus is a sex characteristic which she cannot share, the counterpart some claim of the maternal instinct which he cannot share, so is it an instinct which she cannot judge. The outsider therefore must leave him free to deal with this instinct by himself, because liberty of opinion must be respected, especially when it is based upon an instinct which is as foreign to her as centuries of tradition and education can make it.[7] This is a fundamental and instinctive distinction upon which indifference may be based. But the outsider will make it her duty not merely to base her indifference upon instinct, but upon reason. When he says, as history proves that he has said, and may say again, "I am fighting to protect our country" and thus seeks to rouse her patriotic emotion, she will ask herself, "What does 'our country' mean to me an outsider?" To decide this she will analyse the meaning of patriotism in her own case. She will inform herself of the position of her sex and her class in the past. She will inform herself of the amount of land, wealth and property in the possession of her own sex and class in the present—how much of "England" in fact belongs to her. From the same sources she will inform herself of the legal protection which the law has given her in the past and now gives her. And if he adds that he is fighting to protect her body, she will reflect upon the degree of physical protection that she now enjoys when the words "Air Raid Precaution" are written on blank walls. And if he says that he is fighting to protect England from foreign rule, she will reflect that for her there are no "foreigners," since by law she becomes a foreigner if she marries a foreigner. And she will do her best to make this a fact, not by forced fraternity, but by human sympathy. All these facts will convince her reason (to put it in a nutshell) that her sex and class has very little to thank England for in the past; not much to thank England for in the present; while the security of her person in the future is highly dubious. But probably she will have imbibed, even from the governess, some romantic notion that Englishmen, those fathers and grandfathers whom she sees marching in the picture of history, are "superior" to the men of other countries. This she will consider it her duty to check by comparing French historians with English; German with French; the testimony of the ruled—the Indians or the Irish, say—with the claims made by their rulers. Still some "patriotic" emotion, some ingrained belief in the intellectual superiority of her own country over other countries may remain. Then she will compare English painting with French painting; English music with German music; English literature with Greek literature, for translations abound. When all these comparisons have been faithfully made by the use of reason, the outsider will find herself in possession of very good reasons for her indifference. She will find that she has no good reason to ask her brother to fight on her behalf to protect "our" country. "'Our country,'" she will say, "throughout the greater part of its history has treated me as a slave; it has denied me education or any share in its possessions. 'Our' country still ceases to be mine if I marry a foreigner. 'Our' country denies me the means of protecting myself, forces me to pay others a very large sum annually to protect me, and is so little able, even so, to protect me that Air Raid precautions are written on the wall. Therefore if you insist upon fighting to protect me, or 'our' coun-

7. The following quotation shows, however, that if sanctioned the fighting instinct easily develops. "The eyes deeply sunk into the sockets, the features acute, the amazon keeps herself very straight on the stirrups at the head of her squadron . . . Five English parliamentaries look at this woman with the respectful and a bit restless admiration one feels for a 'fauve' of an unknown species . . . The amazon Amalia rides in fact a magnificent dapple-grey horse, with glossy hair, which flatters like a parade horse . . . This woman who has killed five men—but who feels not sure about the sixth—was for the envoys of the House of Commons an excellent introducer to the Spanish War." (*The Matyrdom of Madrid*, Inedited Witnesses, by Louis Delaprée, pp. 34, 5, 6. Madrid, 1937) [Woolf's note].

try, let it be understood, soberly and rationally between us, that you are fighting to gratify a sex instinct which I cannot share; to procure benefits which I have not shared and probably will not share; but not to gratify my instincts, or to protect myself or my country. For," the outsider will say, "in fact, as a woman, I have no country. As a woman I want no country. As a woman my country is the whole world." And if, when reason has said its say, still some obstinate emotion remains, some love of England dropped into a child's ears by the cawing of rooks in an elm tree, by the splash of waves on a beach, or by English voices murmuring nursery rhymes, this drop of pure, if irrational, emotion she will make serve her to give to England first what she desires of peace and freedom for the whole world.

Such then will be the nature of her "indifference" and from this indifference certain actions must follow. She will bind herself to take no share in patriotic demonstrations; to assent to no form of national self-praise; to make no part of any claque or audience that encourages war; to absent herself from military displays, tournaments, tattoos, prize-givings and all such ceremonies as encourage the desire to impose "our" civilization or "our" dominion upon other people. The psychology of private life, moreover, warrants the belief that this use of indifference by the daughters of educated men would help materially to prevent war. For psychology would seem to show that it is far harder for human beings to take action when other people are indifferent and allow them complete freedom of action, than when their actions are made the centre of excited emotion. The small boy struts and trumpets outside the window: implore him to stop; he goes on; say nothing; he stops. That the daughters of educated men then should give their brothers neither the white feather of cowardice nor the red feather of courage, but no feather at all;[8] that they should shut the bright eyes that rain influence, or let those eyes look elsewhere when war is discussed—that is the duty to which outsiders will train themselves in peace before the threat of death inevitably makes reason powerless.

Such then are some of the methods by which the society, the anonymous and secret Society of Outsiders would help you, Sir, to prevent war and to ensure freedom. * * *

It seems, Sir, as we listen to the voices of the past, as if we were looking at the photograph again, at the picture of dead bodies and ruined houses that the Spanish Government sends us almost weekly.[9] Things repeat themselves it seems. Pictures and voices are the same today as they were 2,000 years ago.

Such then is the conclusion to which our enquiry into the nature of fear has brought us—the fear which forbids freedom in the private house. That fear, small, insignificant and private as it is, is connected with the other fear, the public fear, which is neither small nor insignificant, the fear which has led you to ask us to help you to prevent war. Otherwise we should not be looking at the picture again. But it is not the same picture that caused us at the beginning of this letter to feel the same emotions—you called them "horror and disgust"; we called them horror and disgust. For as this letter has gone on, adding fact to fact, another picture has imposed itself

---

8. During the First World War in Britain patriotic women would hand a white feather to men who seemed to have evaded military service.
9. The Republican Government in Spain was then engaged in a war against Fascist forces intent on seizing power; by 1939 the Fascists had gained control of the country.

upon the foreground. It is the figure of a man; some say, others deny, that he is Man himself,[1] the quintessence of virility, the perfect type of which all the others are imperfect adumbrations. He is a man certainly. His eyes are glazed; his eyes glare. His body, which is braced in an unnatural position, is tightly cased in a uniform. Upon the breast of that uniform are sewn several medals and other mystic symbols. His hand is upon a sword. He is called in German and Italian Führer or Duce; in our own language Tyrant or Dictator. And behind him lie ruined houses and dead bodies—men, women and children. But we have not laid that picture before you in order to excite once more the sterile emotion of hate. On the contrary it is in order to release other emotions such as the human figure, even thus crudely in a coloured photograph, arouses in us who are human beings. For it suggests a connection and for us a very important connection. It suggests that the public and the private worlds are inseparably connected; that the tyrannies and servilities of the one are the tyrannies and servilities of the other. But the human figure even in a photograph suggests other and more complex emotions. It suggests that we cannot dissociate ourselves from that figure but are ourselves that figure. It suggests that we are not passive spectators doomed to unresisting obedience but by our thoughts and actions can ourselves change that figure. A common interest unites us; it is one world, one life. How essential it is that we should realise that unity the dead bodies, the ruined houses prove. For such will be our ruin if you in the immensity of your public abstractions forget the private figure, or if we in the intensity of our private emotions forget the public world. Both houses will be ruined, the public and the private, the material and the spiritual, for they are inseparably connected. But with your letter before us we have reason to hope. For by asking our help you recognise that connection; and by reading your words we are reminded of other connections that lie far deeper than the facts on the surface. Even here, even now your letter tempts us to shut our ears to these little facts, these trivial details, to listen not to the bark of the guns and the bray of the gramophones but to the voices of the poets, answering each other, assuring us of a unity that rubs out divisions as if they were chalk marks only; to discuss with you the capacity of the human spirit to overflow boundaries and make unity out of multiplicity. But that would be to dream—to dream the recurring dream that has haunted the human mind since the beginning of time; the dream of peace, the dream of freedom. But, with the sound of the guns in your ears you have not asked us to dream. You have not asked us what peace is; you have asked us how to prevent war. Let us then leave it to the poets to tell us what the dream is; and fix our eyes upon the photograph again: the fact.

Whatever the verdict of others may be upon the man in uniform—and opinions differ—there is your letter to prove that to you the picture is the picture of evil. And though we look upon that picture from different angles our conclusion is the same as yours—it is evil. We are both determined to do what we can to destroy the evil which that picture represents, you by your methods, we by ours. And since we are different, our help must be different. What ours can be we have tried to show—how

---

1. The nature of manhood and the nature of womanhood are frequently defined by both Italian and German dictators. Both repeatedly insist that it is the nature of man and indeed the essence of manhood to fight . . . It is possible that the Fascist States by revealing to the younger generation at least the need for emancipation from the old conception of virility are doing for the male sex what the Crimean and the European wars did for their sisters. Professor Huxley, however, warns us that "any considerable alteration of the hereditary constitution is an affair of millennia, not of decades." On the other hand, as science also assures us that our life on earth is "an affair of millennia, not of decades," some alteration in the hereditary constitution may be worth attempting [Woolf's note].

imperfectly, how superficially there is no need to say.[2] But as a result the answer to your question must be that we can best help you to prevent war not by repeating your words and following your methods but by finding new words and creating new methods. We can best help you to prevent war not by joining your society but by remaining outside your society but in co-operation with its aim. That aim is the same for us both. It is to assert "the rights of all—all men and women—to the respect in their persons of the great principles of Justice and Equality and Liberty." To elaborate further is unnecessary, for we have every confidence that you interpret those words as we do. And excuses are unnecessary, for we can trust you to make allowances for those deficiencies which we foretold and which this letter has abundantly displayed.

To return then to the form that you have sent and ask us to fill up: for the reasons given we will leave it unsigned. But in order to prove as substantially as possible that our aims are the same as yours, here is the guinea, a free gift, given freely, without any other conditions than you choose to impose upon yourself. It is the third of three guineas; but the three guineas, you will observe, though given to three different treasurers are all given to the same cause, for the causes are the same and inseparable.

Now, since you are pressed for time, let me make an end; apologising three times over to the three of you, first for the length of this letter, second for the smallness of the contribution, and thirdly for writing at all. The blame for that however rests upon you, for this letter would never have been written had you not asked for an answer to your own.

from The Diaries

Saturday 2 January [1915]

This is the kind of day which if it were possible to choose an altogether average sample of our life, I should select. We breakfast; I interview Mrs Le Grys. She complains of the huge Belgian appetites, & their preference for food fried in butter. "They never *give* one anything" she remarked. The Count, taking Xmas dinner with them, insisted, after Pork & Turkey, that he wanted a third meat. Therefore Mrs Le G. hopes that the war will soon be over. If they eat thus in their exile, how must they eat at home, she wonders?[1] After this, L[eonard]. & I both settle down to our scribbling. He finishes his Folk Story review, & I do about 4 pages of poor Effie's story;[2] we lunch; & read the papers, agree that there is no news. I read Guy Mannering upstairs for 20 minutes;[3] & then we take Max [a dog] for a walk. Halfway up to the Bridge, we found ourselves cut off by the river, which rose visibly, with a little ebb & flow, like

---

2. Coleridge however expresses the views and aims of the outsiders with some accuracy in the following passage: "Man must be *free* or to what purpose was he made a Spirit of Reason, and not a Machine of Instinct? Man must *obey*; or wherefore has he a conscience? The powers, which create this difficulty, contain its solution likewise, for *their* service is perfect freedom." . . . To which may be added a quotation from Walt Whitman: "Of Equality—as if it harm'd me, giving others the same chances and rights as myself—as if it were not indispensable to my own rights that others possess the same."

And finally the words of a half-forgotten novelist, George Sand, are worth considering: "All lives are bound up with each other, and any human being who would describe his or her selfhood in isolation, without linking it to that of his or her fellows, would only offer a mystery to be untangled . . . That kind of individuality has by itself neither meaning nor importance. It only takes on any kind of meaning by becoming a part of the general life, by grounding itself together with the individuality of each of my fellows, and through that gesture it becomes a part of history." (*Histoire de ma Vie* [The Story of My Life], by George Sand, pp. 240–1) [Woolf's note, quoting Sand in French].

1. Belgian refugees were housed in English homes following the German invasion of Belgium.

2. Later published as *Night and Day* (1919).

3. *Guy Mannering* (1815), a novel by Sir Walter Scott.

the pulse of a heart. Indeed, the road we had come along was crossed, after 5 minutes, by a stream several inches deep. One of the queer things about the suburbs is that the vilest little red villas are always let, & that not one of them has an open window, or an uncurtained window. I expect that people take a pride in their curtains, & there is great rivalry among neighbours. One house had curtains of yellow silk, striped with lace insertion. The rooms inside must be in semi-darkness; & I suppose rank with the smell of meat & human beings. I believe that being curtained is a mark of respectability—Sophie[4] used to insist upon it. And then I did my marketing. Saturday night is the great buying night; & some counters are besieged by three rows of women. I always choose the empty shops, where I suppose, one pays $\frac{1}{2}$ a lb. more. And then we had tea, & honey & cream; & now L. is typewriting his article; & we shall read all the evening & go to bed.

Monday 21 January [1918]

Here I was interrupted on the verge of a description of London at the meeting of sun set & moon rise. I drove on top of a Bus from Oxford St. to Victoria station, & observed how the passengers were watching the spectacle: the same sense of interest & mute attention shown as in the dress circle before some pageant. A Spring night; blue sky with a smoke mist over the houses. The shops were still lit; but not the lamps, so that there were bars of light all down the streets; & in Bond Street I was at a loss to account for a great chandelier of light at the end of the street; but it proved to be several shop windows jutting out into the road, with lights on different tiers. Then at Hyde Park Corner the search light rays out, across the blue; part of a pageant on a stage where all has been wonderfully muted down. The gentleness of the scene was what impressed me; a twilight view of London. Houses very large & looking stately. Now & then someone, as the moon came into view, remarked upon the chance for an air raid. We escaped though, a cloud rising towards night.

Sunday (Easter) 20 April [1919]

* * * In the idleness which succeeds any long article, & Defoe is the 2nd leader this month, I got out this diary, & read as one always does read one's own writing, with a kind of guilty intensity. I confess that the rough & random style of it, often so ungrammatical, & crying for a word altered, afflicted me somewhat. I am trying to tell whichever self it is that reads this hereafter that I can write very much better; & take no time over this; & forbid her to let the eye of man behold it. And now I may add my little compliment to the effect that it has a slapdash & vigour, & sometimes hits an unexpected bulls eye. But what is more to the point is my belief that the habit of writing thus for my own eye only is good practise. It loosens the ligaments. Never mind the misses & the stumbles. Going at such a pace as I do I must make the most direct & instant shots at my object, & thus have to lay hands on words, choose them, & shoot them with no more pause than is needed to put my pen in the ink. I believe that during the past year I can trace some increase of ease in my professional writing which I attribute to my casual half hours after tea. Moreover there looms ahead of me the shadow of some kind of form which a diary might attain to. I might in the course of time learn what it is that one can make of this loose, drifting material of life; finding another use for it than the use I put it to,

4. A former family cook.

so much more consciously & scrupulously, in fiction. What sort of diary should I like mine to be? Something loose knit, & yet not slovenly, so elastic that it will embrace any thing, solemn, slight or beautiful that comes into my mind. I should like it to resemble some deep old desk, or capacious hold-all, in which one flings a mass of odds & ends without looking them through. I should like to come back, after a year or two, & find that the collection had sorted itself & refined itself & coalesced, as such deposits so mysteriously do, into a mould, transparent enough to reflect the light of our life, & yet steady, tranquil composed with the aloofness of a work of art. The main requisite, I think on re-reading my old volumes, is not to play the part of censor, but to write as the mood comes or of anything whatever; since I was curious to find how I went for things put in haphazard, & found the significance to lie where I never saw it at the time. But looseness quickly becomes slovenly. A little effort is needed to face a character or an incident which needs to be recorded. * * *

Wednesday 7 January [1920]

To begin the year on the last pages of my old book—the few I've not torn off for letter writing—is all upside-down of course; but of a part with the character of the work.

This is our last evening. We sit over the fire waiting for post—the cream of the day, I think. Yet every part of the day here has its merits—even the breakfast without toast. That—however it begins—ends with Pippins; most mornings the sun comes in; we finish in good temper; & I go off to the romantic chamber over grass rough with frost & ground hard as brick. Then Mrs Dedman comes to receive orders—to give them, really, for she has planned our meals to suit her days cooking before she comes. We share her oven. The result is always savoury—stews & mashes & deep many coloured dishes swimming in gravy thick with carrots & onions. Elsie, aged 18, can be spoken to as though she had a head on her shoulders. The house is empty by half past eleven; empty now at five o'clock; we tend our fire, cook coffee, read, I find, luxuriously, peacefully, at length.

But I should not spend my time on an indoor chronicle; unless I lazily shirked the describing of winter down & meadow—the recording of what takes my breath away at every turn. Heres the sun out for example & all the upper twigs of the trees as if dipped in fire; the trunks emerald green; even bark bright tinted, & variable as the skin of a lizard. Then theres Asheham hill smoke misted; the windows of the long train spots of sun; the smoke lying back on the carriages like a rabbits lop ears. The chalk quarry glows pink; & my water meadows lush as June, until you see that the grass is short, & rough as a dogfishes back. But I could go on counting what I've noticed page after page. Every day or nearly I've walked towards a different point & come back with a string of these matchings & marvels. Five minutes from the house one is out in the open, a great pull over Asheham; &, as I say, every direction bears fruit. Once we went over the cornfield & up onto the down—a dim Sunday afternoon—muddy on the road, but dry up above. The long down grass pale, & as we pushed through it, up got a hawk at our feet, seeming to trail near the ground, as if weighted down—attached to something. It let the burden fall, & rose high as we came up. We found the wings of a partridge attached to [a] bleeding stump, for the Hawk had almost done his meal. We saw him go back to find it. Further down the hill side a great white owl "wavy" (for that describes his way of weaving a web round a tree—the plumy soft look of him in the dusk adding truth to the word) "wavy in the dusk," flew behind the hedge as we came past. Village girls were returning, & calling out to friends in doors. So we cross the field & churchyard, find our coke burnt through to red, toast the bread—& the evening comes.

L. has spent most of his time pruning the apple trees, & tying plums to the wall. To do this he wears two jackets, 2 pairs of socks, two pairs of gloves; even so the cold bites through. These last days have been like frozen water, ruffled by the wind into atoms of ice against the cheek; then, in the shelter, forming round you in a still pool. * * *

Wednesday 16 August [1922]

I should be reading Ulysses, & fabricating my case for & against. I have read 200 pages so far—not a third; & have been amused, stimulated, charmed interested by the first 2 or 3 chapters—to the end of the Cemetery scene; & then puzzled, bored, irritated, & disillusioned as by a queasy undergraduate scratching his pimples. And Tom,[5] great Tom, thinks this on a par with War & Peace! An illiterate, underbred book it seems to me: the book of a self taught working man, & we all know how distressing they are, how egotistic, insistent, raw, striking, & ultimately nauseating. When one can have the cooked flesh, why have the raw? But I think if you are anaemic, as Tom is, there is a glory in blood. Being fairly normal myself I am soon ready for the classics again. I may revise this later. I do not compromise my critical sagacity. I plant a stick in the ground to mark page 200. * * *

Wednesday 6 September [1922]

* * * I finished Ulysses, & think it a mis-fire. Genius it has I think; but of the inferior water. The book is diffuse. It is brackish. It is pretentious. It is underbred, not only in the obvious sense, but in the literary sense. A first rate writer, I mean, respects writing too much to be tricky; startling; doing stunts. I'm reminded all the time of some callow board school boy, say like Henry Lamb, full of wits & powers, but so self-conscious & egotistical that he loses his head, becomes extravagant, mannered, uproarious, ill at ease, makes kindly people feel sorry for him, & stern ones merely annoyed; & one hopes he'll grow out of it; but as Joyce is 40 this scarcely seems likely. I have not read it carefully; & only once; & it is very obscure; so no doubt I have scamped the virtue of it more than is fair. I feel that myriads of tiny bullets pepper one & spatter one; but one does not get one deadly wound straight in the face—as from Tolstoy, for instance; but it is entirely absurd to compare him with Tolstoy.

Tuesday 19 June [1923]

I took up this book with a kind of idea that I might say something about my writing—which was prompted by glancing at what K.M. said about *her* writing in the Dove's Nest.[6] But I only glanced. She said a good deal about feeling things deeply: also about being pure, which I wont criticise, though of course I very well could. But now what do I feel about *my* writing?—this book, that is, The Hours,[7] if thats its name? One must write from deep feeling, said Dostoevsky. And do I? Or do I fabricate with words, loving them as I do? No I think not. In this book I have almost too many ideas. I want to give life & death, sanity & insanity; I want to criticise the social system, & to show it

---

5. T. S. Eliot.

6. J. M. Murray wrote an introduction to Katherine Mansfield's *The Dove's Nest and Other Stories* (1923), which quotes extracts from her journal.

7. "The Hours" was an early title for *Mrs Dalloway* (1925).

at work, at its most intense—But here I may be posing. I heard from Ka [Arnold-Forster] this morning that she doesn't like In the Orchard.[8] At once I feel refreshed. I become anonymous, a person who writes for the love of it. She takes away the motive of praise, & lets me feel that without any praise, I should be content to go on. This is what Duncan [Grant] said of his painting the other night. I feel as if I slipped off all my ball dresses & stood naked—which as I remember was a very pleasant thing to do. But to go on. Am I writing The Hours from deep emotion? Of course the mad part tries me so much, makes my mind squint so badly that I can hardly face spending the next weeks at it. Its a question though of these characters. People, like Arnold Bennett, say I cant create, or didn't in J[acob]'s R[oom], characters that survive. My answer is—but I leave that to the Nation:[9] its only the old argument that character is dissipated into shreds now: the old post-Dostoevsky argument. I daresay its true, however, that I haven't that "reality" gift. I insubstantise, wilfully to some extent, distrusting reality—its cheapness. But to get further. Have I the power of conveying the true reality? Or do I write essays about myself? Answer these questions as I may, in the uncomplimentary sense, & still there remains this excitement. To get to the bones, now I'm writing fiction again I feel my force flow straight from me at its fullest. After a dose of criticism I feel that I'm writing sideways, using only an angle of my mind. This is justification; for free use of the faculties means happiness. I'm better company, more of a human being. Nevertheless, I think it most important in this book to go for the central things, even though they dont submit, as they should however, to beautification in language. No, I don't nail my crest to the Murrys, who work in my flesh after the manner of the jigger insect. Its annoying, indeed degrading, to have these bitternesses. Still, think of the 18th Century. But then they were overt, not covert, as now.

I foresee, to return to The Hours, that this is going to be the devil of a struggle. The design is so queer & so masterful. I'm always having to wrench my substance to fit it. The design is certainly original, & interests me hugely. I should like to write away & away at it, very quick and fierce. Needless to say, I cant. In three weeks from today I shall be dried up. * * *

Monday 5 May [1924]

    * * * London is enchanting. I step out upon a tawny coloured magic carpet, it seems, & get carried into beauty without raising a finger. The nights are amazing, with all the white porticoes & broad silent avenues. And people pop in & out, lightly, divertingly like rabbits; & I look down Southampton Row, wet as a seal's back or red & yellow with sunshine, & watch the omnibus going & coming, & hear the old crazy organs. One of these days I will write about London, & how it takes up the private life & carries it on, without any effort. Faces passing lift up my mind; prevent it from settling, as it does in the stillness at Rodmell. * * *

Monday 21 December [1925]

    But no Vita! But Vita for 3 days at Long Barn,[1] from which L[eonard]. & I returned yesterday. These Sapphists *love* women; friendship is never untinged with amorosity. In short, my fears & refrainings, my "impertinence" my usual self-

---

8. *In the Orchard* (1923), an essay by Woolf.
9. In a 1923 review of *Jacob's Room*, the novelist Arnold Bennett had written that "I have seldom read a cleverer book than Virginia Woolf's *Jacob's Room* ... But the characters do not vitally survive in the mind because the author has been obsessed by details of originality and clev-

erness." Woolf's reply, *Mr. Bennett and Mrs. Brown*, mocking Bennett's realist fiction as "thin gruel," appeared in the *Nation and Athenaeum* in December 1923.
1. Country home of Vita Sackville-West and her husband Harold Nicolson.

consciousness in intercourse with people who mayn't want me & so on—were all, as L. said, sheer fudge; &, partly thanks to him (he made me write) I wound up this wounded & stricken year in great style. I like her & being with her, & the splendour—she shines in the grocers shop in Sevenoaks with a candle lit radiance, stalking on legs like beech trees, pink glowing, grape clustered, pearl hung. That is the secret of her glamour, I suppose. Anyhow she found me incredibly dowdy, no woman cared less for personal appearance—no one put on things in the way I did. Yet so beautiful, &c. What is the effect of all this on me? Very mixed. There is her maturity & full breastedness: her being so much in full sail on the high tides, where I am coasting down backwaters; her capacity I mean to take the floor in any company, to represent her country, to visit Chatsworth, to control silver, servants, chow dogs; her motherhood (but she is a little cold & offhand with her boys) her being in short (what I have never been) a real woman. Then there is some voluptuousness about her; the grapes are ripe; & not reflective. No. In brain & insight she is not as highly organised as I am. But then she is aware of this, & so lavishes on me the maternal protection which, for some reason, is what I have always most wished from everyone. What L. gives me, & Nessa [Vanessa Bell] gives me, & Vita, in her more clumsy external way, tries to give me. For of course, mingled with all this glamour, grape clusters & pearl necklaces, there is something loose fitting. How much, for example, shall I really miss her when she is motoring across the desert? I will make a note on that next year. Anyhow, I am very glad that she is coming to tea today, & I shall ask her, whether she minds my dressing so badly? I think she does. I read her poem; which is more compact, better seen & felt than anything yet of hers. * * *

[Saturday 31 July 1926]

My own Brain

Here is a whole nervous breakdown in miniature. We came on Tuesday. Sank into a chair, could scarcely rise; everything insipid; tasteless, colourless. Enormous desire for rest. Wednesday—only wish to be alone in the open air. Air delicious—avoided speech; could not read. Thought of my own power of writing with veneration, as of something incredible, belonging to someone else; never again to be enjoyed by me. Mind a blank. Slept in my chair. Thursday. No pleasure in life whatsoever; but felt perhaps more attuned to existence. Character & idiosyncracy as Virginia Woolf completely sunk out. Humble & modest. Difficulty in thinking what to say. Read automatically, like a cow chewing cud. Slept in chair. Friday. Sense of physical tiredness; but slight activity of the brain. Beginning to take notice. Making one or two plans. No power of phrase making. Difficulty in writing to Lady Colefax. Saturday (today) much clearer & lighter. Thought I could write, but resisted, or found it impossible. A desire to read poetry set in on Friday. This brings back a sense of my own individuality. Read some Dante & Bridges, without troubling to understand, but got pleasure from them. Now I begin to wish to write notes, but not yet novel. But today senses quickening. No "making up" power yet; no desire to cast scenes in my book. Curiosity about literature returning: want to read Dante, Havelock Ellis, & Berlioz autobiography; also to make a looking glass with shell frame. These processes have sometimes been spread over several weeks. * * *

Wednesday 15 September [1926]

A State of Mind

Woke up perhaps at 3. Oh its beginning its coming—the horror—physically like a painful wave swelling about the heart—tossing me up. I'm unhappy unhappy!

Down—God, I wish I were dead. Pause. But why am I feeling this? Let me watch the wave rise. I watch. Vanessa. Children. Failure. Yes; I detect that. Failure failure. (The wave rises). Oh they laughed at my taste in green paint! Wave crashes. I wish I were dead! I've only a few years to live I hope. I cant face this horror any more—(this is the wave spreading out over me).

This goes on; several times, with varieties of horror. Then, at the crisis, instead of the pain remaining intense, it becomes rather vague. I doze. I wake with a start. The wave again! The irrational pain: the sense of failure; generally some specific incident, as for example my taste in green paint, or buying a new dress, or asking Dadie for the week end, tacked on.

At last I say, watching as dispassionately as I can, Now take a pull of yourself. No more of this. I reason. I take a census of happy people & unhappy. I brace myself to shove to throw to batter down. I begin to march blindly forward. I feel obstacles go down. I say it doesn't matter. Nothing matters. I become rigid & straight, & sleep again, & half wake & feel the wave beginning & watch the light whitening & wonder how, this time, breakfast & daylight will overcome it; & then hear L. in the passage & simulate, for myself as well as for him, great cheerfulness; & generally am cheerful, by the time breakfast is over. Does everyone go through this state? Why have I so little control? It is not creditable, nor lovable. It is the cause of much waste & pain in my life.

Saturday 27 October [1928]

Thank God, my long toil at the women's lecture[2] is this moment ended. I am back from speaking at Girton, in floods of rain. Starved but valiant young women— that's my impression. Intelligent eager, poor; & destined to become schoolmistresses in shoals. I blandly told them to drink wine & have a room of their own. Why should all the splendour, all the luxury of life be lavished on the Julians & the Francises, & none on the Phares & the Thomases?[3] There's Julian not much relishing it, perhaps. I fancy sometimes the world changes. I think I see reason spreading. But I should have liked a closer & thicker knowledge of life. I should have liked to deal with real things sometimes. I get such a sense of tingling & vitality from an evenings talk like that; one's angularities & obscurities are smoothed & lit. How little one counts, I think: how little anyone counts; how fast & furious & masterly life is; & how all these thousands are swimming for dear life. I felt elderly & mature. And nobody respected me. They were very eager, egotistical, or rather not much impressed by age & repute. Very little reverence or that sort of thing about. The corridors of Girton are like vaults in some horrid high church cathedral—on & on they go, cold & shiny—with a light burning. High gothic rooms; acres of bright brown wood; here & there a photograph. * * *

Wednesday 23 October [1929]

As it is true—I write only for an hour—then sink back feeling I cannot keep my brain on that spin any more—then typewrite, & am done by 12—I will here sum up my impressions before publishing a Room of One's Own. It is a little ominous that Morgan wont review it.[4] It makes me suspect that there is a shrill feminine tone in it

---

2. The lecture that became A Room of One's Own.
3. Elsie Phare was a student at Newnham College, Cambridge; Margaret Thomas was a student at Girton College. Their invitations had brought Woolf to Cambridge. Julian

Bell, Woolf's nephew, was a student at King's College.
4. He [E. M. Forster] wrote yesterday 3rd Dec. & said he very much liked it [Woolf's note].

which my intimate friends will dislike. I forecast, then, that I shall get no criticism, except of the evasive jocular kind, from Lytton, Roger & Morgan; that the press will be kind & talk of its charm, & sprightiness; also I shall be attacked for a feminist & hinted at for a sapphist; Sibyl will ask me to luncheon; I shall get a good many letters from young women. I am afraid it will not be taken seriously. Mrs Woolf is so accomplished a writer that all she says makes easy reading . . . this very feminine logic . . . a book to be put in the hands of girls. I doubt that I mind very much. The Moths; but I think it is to be waves, is trudging along;[5] & I have that to refer to, if I am damped by the other. It is a trifle, I shall say; so it is, but I wrote it with ardour & conviction.

* * *

Friday 20 May [1938]

Time & again I have meant to write down my expectations, dreads, & so on, waiting the publication on—I think June 2nd—of 3 G[uinea]s—but haven't, because what with living in the solid world of Roger, & then (again this morning) in the airy world of Poyntz Hall I feel extremely little.[6] And dont want to rouse feeling. What I'm afraid of is the taunt Charm & emptiness. The book I wrote with such violent feelings to relieve that immense pressure will not dimple the surface. That is my fear. Also I'm uneasy at taking this role in the public eye—afraid of autobiography in public. But the fears are entirely outbalanced (this is honest) by the immense relief & peace I have gained, & enjoy this moment. Now I am quit of that poison & excitement. Nor is that all. For having spat it out, my mind is made up. I need never recur or repeat. I am an outsider. I can take my way: experiment with my own imagination in my own way. The pack may howl, but it shall never catch me. And even if the pack—reviewers, friends, enemies—pays me no attention or sneers, still I'm free. This is the actual result of that spiritual conversion (I cant bother to get the right words) in the autumn of 1933—or 4—when I rushed through London, buying, I remember, a great magnifying glass, from sheer ecstasy, near Blackfriars: when I gave the man who played the harp half a crown for talking to me about his life in the Tube station. The omens are mixed: L. is less excited than I hoped; Nessa highly ambiguous; Miss Hepworth & Mrs Nicholls say "Women owe a great deal to Mrs Woolf" & I have promised Pippa to supply books. Now for R.'s letters & Monks H—at the moment windy & cold.

Wednesday 14 September [1938]

Things worse today. Rioting in Prague. Sudeten ultimatum. It looks as if Hitler meant to slide sideways into war. Raises riots: will say cant be stopped.[7] This came on the 9.30 wireless last night. This morning more marking time. No one knows. Headachy, partly screw of Roger partly this gloom. So I'm stopping Roger;[8] as we go up to lunch with Bella tomorrow. And whats the private position? So black I cant gather

---

5. "The Moths" was an early title for The Waves (1931).
6. "Poyntz Hall" later became Between the Acts (1941).
7. The German Chancellor Adolf Hitler had been putting pressure on the Czechoslovak government to allow the incorporation of that country's German minority into Germany, even though this would mean the disintegration of Czechoslovakia. A speech Hitler made at Nuremberg had given the signal for the German minority (the "Sudeten Germans") in Czechoslovakia to riot; the Czech government imposed martial law, the immediate revocation of which was then demanded by the German government in Berlin. British Prime Minister Neville Chamberlain flew to meet Hitler, and, fearful of war and in the face of German threats to invade Czechoslovakia, informed the Czechs that Britain and France would not support them against German demands. The Germans soon took over Czechoslovakia.
8. Woolf was working on a biography of her friend, Roger Fry, published in 1940 as Roger Fry: A Biography.

together. Work I suppose. If it is war, then every country joins in: chaos. To oppose this with Roger my only private position. Well thats an absurd little match to strike. But its a hopeless war this—when we know winning means nothing. So we're committed, for the rest of our lives, to public misery. This will be slashed with private too. * * *

Sunday 29 January [1939]

Yes, Barcelona has fallen: Hitler speaks tomorrow; the next dress rehearsal begins: I have seen Marie Stopes, Princesse de Polignac, Philip & Pippin, & Dr Freud in the last 3 days,[9] also had Tom to dinner & to the Stephens' party.

Dr Freud gave me a narcissus. Was sitting in a great library with little statues at a large scrupulously tidy shiny table. We like patients on chairs. A screwed up shrunk very old man: with a monkeys light eyes, paralysed spasmodic movements, inarticulate: but alert. On Hitler. Generation before the poison will be worked out. About his books. Fame? I was infamous rather than famous, didnt make £50 by his first book. Difficult talk. An interview. Daughter & Martin helped. Immense potential, I mean an old fire now flickering. When we left he took up the stand What are *you* going to do? The English—war.

Monday 13 May [1940]

I admit to some content, some closing of a chapter, & peace that comes with it, from posting my proofs today: I admit—because we're in the 3rd day of "the greatest battle in history." It began (here) with the 8 oclock wireless announcing, as I lay half asleep, the invasion of Holland & Belgium. The third day of the Battle of Waterloo. Apple blossom snowing the garden. A bowl lost in the pond. Churchill exhorting all men to stand together. "I have nothing to offer but blood & tears & sweat."[1] These vast formless shapes further circulate. They aren't substances; but they make everything else minute. Duncan saw an air battle over Charleston—a silver pencil & a puff of smoke. Percy has seen the wounded arriving in their boots. So my little moment of peace comes in a yawning hollow. But though L. says he has petrol in the garage for suicide shd. Hitler win, we go on. Its the vastness, & the smallness, that make this possible. So intense are my feelings (about Roger): yet the circumference (the war) seems to make a hoop round them. No, I cant get the odd incongruity of feeling intensely & at the same time knowing that there's no importance in that feeling. Or is there, as I sometimes think, more importance than ever? * * *

Sunday 22 December [1940]

How beautiful they were, those old people—I mean father & mother—how simple, how clear, how untroubled. I have been dipping into old letters & fathers memoirs. He loved her—oh & was so candid & reasonable & transparent—& had such a fastidious delicate mind, educated, & transparent. How serene & gay even their life reads to me: no mud; no whirlpools. And so human—with the children & the little hum & song of the nursery. But if I read as a contemporary I shall lose my childs vision & so must stop. Nothing turbulent; nothing involved: no introspection.

---

9. Sigmund Freud, mortally ill with cancer of the jaw, had fled the Nazis and settled in Hampstead with his daughter Anna.
1. Germany invaded Holland, Belgium, and Luxembourg on 10 May; on the same day Neville Chamberlain resigned as prime minister, and Winston Churchill took office at the head of a coalition government. In seeking support for his administration, Churchill said "I have nothing to offer but blood, toil, tears and sweat"; see page 2522 for this speech.

D. H. Lawrence
1885–1930

D. H. Lawrence's meteoric literary life ended in Venice, Italy, in 1930, where he died at the age of forty-five, far from his birthplace in Nottinghamshire, the coal-mining heart of England. If Lawrence was something of a comet in British literature, arcing across its skies with vibrant energy and controversy while he lived, he was equally visible after his death in the excitement and danger that persisted like a halo around his texts. A formidable poet, an exceptional essayist and literary critic, and a major novelist, Lawrence created works that were pioneering in their defiant eroticism, their outspoken treatment of class politics, and their insistence on seeing British literature as part of world literature in a time of global crisis. Many of his writings were censored and unavailable in England until long after his death, or published in expurgated versions or in private printings. Their frank concentration on sexuality, and on female as well as male desire, continues to make Lawrence's novels provocative and even controversial today.

David Herbert Lawrence was the son of a coal miner. As a primarily self-educated writer who studied and taught at Nottingham University College, instead of Oxford or Cambridge, he was unlike many of his literary peers in being lower-class and outside the privileged literary and social circles they moved in. He essentially invented himself, drawing on the support and encouragement of his mother, and nurturing a clear-eyed and furious analysis of British class structure that pervades many of his novels. The sexual frankness of his work is accompanied by its economic frankness, its willingness to point out all the ways that culture and taste are fashioned by income as much as by ideas. The sense of being an outsider to the gentlemanly world of letters fed Lawrence's need to live and work outside Britain, and he traveled restlessly to Europe and America, to Australia and Mexico. Lawrence is deeply associated with many of the countries and places he lived in; with Italy, above all, in the power of his writing about Italian culture and landscape; with the United States, in classic analysis of American literature, and in works set in New Mexico and San Francisco; with France, Germany, and Switzerland as backdrops for his literary works and their cultural theorizing; with Australia for his commentary on this distant British colony and its indigenous peoples, in novels like *Kangaroo*; with Mexico and the primitivism and exoticism he explored in *The Plumed Serpent* and *Aaron's Rod*.

As peripatetic and as open to experience as Lawrence was, his great writing begins with novels and stories set in England. Some of his early and most exceptional works are, in fact, modernist versions of a central nineteenth-century literary genre, the *bildungsroman*, or the story of a personal education. Lawrence's *Sons and Lovers* (1912) has the autobiographical overtones that often accompany a coming-of-age narrative. Written after the death of his devoted mother Lydia Lawrence in 1910, the book delineates the experience of a young man who was as socially and economically disadvantaged as Lawrence himself, and the almost incestuous love between mother and son that allows him to break free from the crushing life in the mines that might have been his only option, and to follow his deep need for love, imagination, and poetry into the writing of literature. His later novel *The Rainbow* (published in an expurgated version in 1915) is also a *bildungsroman*, but featuring as its protagonist a female character and specifically feminine issues of education and freedom. In a preface to the novel, Lawrence wrote that he insisted on portraying characters that were not the old-fashioned character portraits of the past, relying on "the old stable ego." For Lawrence, people were internally fragmented, not completely self-aware, and above all governed by sexual currents that exceeded their conscious knowledge and control. In this Lawrence was profoundly influenced by Freud's discovery of the prominence and power of the unconscious. All of Lawrence's writing engages with the invisible and largely silent realm of the unconscious, whose wishes and impulses are a kind of dynamic dance running under the surface of the conscious sense of self.

To this dance of the unconscious rhythms of life Lawrence added an abiding fascination with myth. He joined most modernist writers in his interest in showing the persistence of myth in modern culture: Joyce, Woolf, Eliot and Faulkner all structured work around mythic parallels or mythic figures. For Lawrence, myth loomed importantly because it allowed for the discussion of hidden patterns and cycles in human action and human relationships, patterns that are much larger than the individual human being. Our personalities are illusions, Lawrence's fiction claims, because they mask deeper mythic forms. In *The Rainbow,* Lawrence draws his mythic structure from the Bible, and the cycles of birth, death, and rebirth in the story of Noah and the flood, with the rainbow of God's promise starting the cycle of rebirth over and over again.

One of Lawrence's greatest novels is *Women in Love,* a story of two sisters confronting modern life as they move out of their country's orbit and take on independence, sexual freedom, and careers in the world. He began writing it in 1916, during World War I. The war was as shattering to Lawrence as it was to every other British writer; for Lawrence, it was the apotheosis and the logical conclusion of the machine culture he hated for having spoiled England even before the war wreaked its devastation. Lawrence sharply criticized industrial capitalism, but not from the vantage point of an aristocratic worldview that regretted the loss of the landed estates. He thought and wrote as the son of a worker whose life was maimed by industrial toil in the mines, and as a school teacher of the impoverished children of miners and laborers who had lost their self-sufficient way of life on the land. Lawrence did not dream of a return to a golden feudal age, but he did dissect the ravages of industry and the connections between world war, capital, and modernization. *Women in Love* embraces these themes and more, as it turns to Europe and its classical culture to try to find a way out of the cultural impasse and sterility Lawrence saw around him. However, in this novel and others Lawrence writes of a death instinct visible for him in European culture, including its philosophy and art. At times, Lawrence's intense hatred of modernity led him to flirt with fascism, which occasionally seemed to him to promise a way out of the dead end of modern society and its hideous conflagrations in war. In order to rescue the life-affirming capacities of human society Lawrence sought out exotic and foreign cultures, and what he termed "primitive" cultures around the world—ostensibly unspoiled agricultural societies still predicated on myth rather than machine. These exotic alternatives, as Lawrence saw, were hardly utopian either, and most such societies were contaminated by colonization and Western influences. Lawrence did seek a less rationalized and less materialistic perspective in the "primitive" or archaic worlds he explored, and found that these cultures were more open to the life-giving force of sexuality. At once intense and engaging, his travel writing gives a sense of immediacy mingled with deep reflection.

Sexuality is the force in human life that most clearly derives from unconscious fantasies and desires, and on that basis it is at the heart of Lawrence's writing. Lawrence's work was thought shocking because it takes for granted the erotic elements hidden in the family—what Freud had called the "family romance." The alliances and the divisions between family members have an erotic component for Lawrence; in addition, relations to friends and to all others one encounters are sexualized in mysterious ways, often involving a powerful homoerotic current. Much of Lawrence's fiction seems to idealize a sexual state beyond words and beyond conscious understanding, and to depict this Lawrence draws on a beautiful incantatory style, filled with a highly musical repetition and rhythm.

Lawrence's own erotic career is as famous as his writing. The passion and frustrations of his marriage to the formidable Frieda Weekely (born Frieda von Richthofen) remained a hidden presence in all his writing after their marriage in 1914. When they met, Frieda was a married woman with an impressive erotic career behind her; she became a close partner in his political and cultural essay writing, and in his restless travels. They lived in Germany, Italy, and in Taos, New Mexico, among other locales. After his death in Italy, she and her then lover transported Lawrence's ashes back to Taos, and the two built a kind of shrine to Lawrence on the grounds of what had been his home with Frieda. It was in this region that they had explored Hispanic and Indian cultures under the sponsorship of a patron of the avant-garde, Mabel Dodge Luhan. Up until the mid-1980s it was possible to pay a dollar to the manager of the Taos Hotel and be admitted into his office, where numerous paintings by D. H. Lawrence were on display. Lawrence was a fascinating, if not a major, painter; the exhibits of his paintings in England were subject to the same censorship and public outrage as his novels. A viewer of the paintings could read them as an allegory for many of the disquieting themes of his literary work: the majority of them depict a couple, usually male and female, locked in an embrace that is as urgent as it is suffocating; around the edges of these couplings Lawrence painted menacing wolves and dogs, often with teeth bared or fangs dripping with blood, emblematic of the intensity and even the destructiveness of erotic relationships.

In his 1923 essay *Surgery for the Novel—or a Bomb*, Lawrence expresses his impatience with the endlessly refined analyses of modernists like Proust and Joyce. "What is the underlying impulse in us," he asks, "that will provide the motive power for a new state of things, when this democratic-industrial-lovey-dovey-darling-take-me-to-mama state of things is bust? *What next?*"

Lawrence's poetry explores related concerns. Like Thomas Hardy before him, Lawrence was equally gifted in both literary endeavors. Lawrence's poetry emanates from the same image-suffused, musically rhythmic, and tautly modern space as his prose works. Like Lawrence himself, his art desires to move *beyond*—beyond the old stable fictions of the ego in his prose, and beyond the old stable fiction of the lyric voice. In his poetry he accomplishes this by a preternatural immediacy, an intensity of "thereness" that includes what might in the past have seemed to be incoherent elements or fragmentary perspectives. What has been silent, veiled, or unconscious, in personal and in public life, rears up and announces itself in Lawrence's writing, appears on the page and defies silencing.

Piano

Softly, in the dusk, a woman is singing to me;
Taking me back down the vista of years, till I see
A child sitting under the piano, in the boom of the tingling strings
And pressing the small, poised feet of a mother who smiles as she sings.

5   In spite of myself, the insidious mastery of song
Betrays me back, till the heart of me weeps to belong
To the old Sunday evenings at home, with winter outside
And hymns in the cosy parlour, the tinkling piano our guide.

So now it is vain for the singer to burst into clamour
10   With the great black piano appassionato. The glamour
Of childish days is upon me, my manhood is cast
Down in the flood of remembrance, I weep like a child for the past.

1908   1913

Tortoise Shout

I thought he was dumb,
I said he was dumb,
Yet I've heard him cry.
First faint scream,
5   Out of life's unfathomable dawn,
Far off, so far, like a madness, under the horizon's dawning rim,
Far, far off, far scream.

Tortoise *in extremis*.

Why were we crucified into sex?
10 Why were we not left rounded off, and finished in ourselves,
As we began,
As he certainly began, so perfectly alone?

A far, was-it-audible scream,
Or did it sound on the plasm direct?

15 Worse than the cry of the new-born,
A scream,
A yell,
A shout,
A paean,
20 A death-agony,
A birth-cry,
A submission,
All tiny, tiny, far away, reptile under the first dawn.

War-cry, triumph, acute-delight, death-scream reptilian,
25 Why was the veil torn?
The silken shriek of the soul's torn membrane?
The male soul's membrane
Torn with a shriek half music, half horror.

Crucifixion.
30 Male tortoise, cleaving behind the hovel-wall of that dense female,
Mounted and tense, spread-eagle, out-reaching out of the shell
In tortoise-nakedness,
Long neck, and long vulnerable limbs extruded, spread-eagle over her
        house-roof,
And the deep, secret, all-penetrating tail curved beneath her walls,
35 Reaching and gripping tense, more reaching anguish in uttermost tension
Till suddenly, in the spasm of coition, tupping like a jerking leap, and oh!
Opening its clenched face from his outstretched neck
And giving that fragile yell, that scream,
Super-audible,
40 From his pink, cleft, old-man's mouth,
Giving up the ghost,
Or screaming in Pentecost,[1] receiving the ghost.

His scream, and his moment's subsidence,
The moment of eternal silence,
45 Yet unreleased, and after the moment, the sudden, startling jerk of coition,
        and at once
The inexpressible faint yell—
And so on, till the last plasm of my body was melted back
To the primeval rudiments of life, and the secret.

So he tups, and screams
50 Time after time that frail, torn scream

1. The day the Holy Spirit descended on Christ's disciples, which marked the beginning of the Christian church's mission
to the world.

After each jerk, the longish interval,
The tortoise eternity,
Age-long, reptilian persistence,
Heart-throb, slow heart-throb, persistent for the next spasm.

55   I remember, when I was a boy,
I heard the scream of a frog, which was caught with his foot in the mouth
      of an up-starting snake;
I remember when I first heard bull-frogs break into sound in the spring;
I remember hearing a wild goose out of the throat of night
Cry loudly, beyond the lake of waters;
60   I remember the first time, out of a bush in the darkness, a nightingale's
      piercing cries and gurgles startled the depths of my soul;
I remember the scream of a rabbit as I went through a wood at midnight;
I remember the heifer in her heat, blorting and blorting through the hours,
      persistent and irrepressible;
I remember my first terror hearing the howl of weird, amorous cats;
I remember the scream of a terrified, injured horse, the sheet-lightning,
65   And running away from the sound of a woman in labour, something like an
      owl whooing,
And listening inwardly to the first bleat of a lamb,
The first wail of an infant,
And my mother singing to herself,
And the first tenor singing of the passionate throat of a young collier,[2] who
      has long since drunk himself to death,
70   The first elements of foreign speech
On wild dark lips.

And more than all these,
And less than all these,
This last,
75   Strange, faint coition yell
Of the male tortoise at extremity,
Tiny from under the very edge of the farthest far-off horizon of life.

The cross,
The wheel on which our silence first is broken,
80   Sex, which breaks up our integrity, our single inviolability, our deep
      silence,
Tearing a cry from us.

Sex, which breaks us into voice, sets us calling across the deeps, calling,
      calling for the complement,
Singing, and calling, and singing again, being answered, having found.
Torn, to become whole again, after long seeking for what is lost,
85   The same cry from the tortoise as from Christ, the Osiris-cry of
      abandonment,[3]
That which is whole, torn asunder,
That which is in part, finding its whole again throughout the universe.

1921

2. A coal miner.
3. Osiris was a major god of ancient Egypt; he was slain and

fragments of his corpse scattered; these were found and
buried, and Osiris became ruler of the underworld.

Bavarian Gentians

Not every man has gentians in his house
in soft September, at slow, sad Michaelmas.[1]

Bavarian gentians, big and dark, only dark
darkening the day-time, torch-like with the smoking blueness of Pluto's gloom,
5   ribbed and torch-like, with their blaze of darkness spread blue
down flattening into points, flattened under the sweep of white day
torch-flower of the blue-smoking darkness, Pluto's dark-blue daze,[2]
black lamps from the halls of Dis, burning dark blue,
giving off darkness, blue darkness, as Demeter's pale lamps give off light,
10   lead me then, lead the way.

Reach me a gentian, give me a torch!
let me guide myself with the blue, forked torch of this flower
down the darker and darker stairs, where blue is darkened on blueness
even where Persephone goes, just now, from the frosted September
15   to the sightless realm where darkness is awake upon the dark
and Persephone herself is but a voice
or a darkness invisible enfolded in the deeper dark
of the arms Plutonic, and pierced with the passion of dense gloom,
among the splendour of torches of darkness, shedding darkness on the lost
    bride and her groom.

1923, 1929   1932

Surgery for the Novel—or a Bomb

You talk about the future of the baby, little cherub, when he's in the cradle cooing; and it's a romantic, glamorous subject. You also talk, with the parson, about the future of the wicked old grandfather who is at last lying on his death-bed. And there again you have a subject for much vague emotion, chiefly of fear this time.

How do we feel about the novel? Do we bounce with joy thinking of the wonderful novelistic days ahead? Or do we grimly shake our heads and hope the wicked creature will be spared a little longer? Is the novel on his death-bed, old sinner? Or is he just toddling round his cradle, sweet little thing? Let us have another look at him before we decide this rather serious case.

There he is, the monster with many faces, many branches to him, like a tree: the modern novel. And he is almost dual, like Siamese twins. On the one hand, the pale-faced, high-browed, earnest novel, which you have to take seriously; on the other, that smirking, rather plausible hussy, the popular novel.

Let us just for the moment feel the pulses of *Ulysses* and of Miss Dorothy Richardson and M. Marcel Proust, on the earnest side of Briareus;[1] on the other, the throb of *The Sheik* and Mr Zane Grey, and, if you will, Mr Robert Chambers and the

---

1. The feast of St. Michael the Archangel, September 29.
2. Persephone was a daughter of Zeus and Demeter, goddess of agriculture; she was abducted by Hades, king of the Underworld (also known as Pluto or Dis), causing Demeter such sorrow that the land became barren. Zeus commanded Hades to release Persephone, which he did, though she was able to emerge from the Underworld each

spring, returning in the fall to her husband. The story offers an explanation of seasonal change.
1. Briareus aided Zeus in fighting the Titans, here represented by the epic modernist novels of Joyce, Proust, and Dorothy Richardson (author of a 12-volume sequence of novels, *Pilgrimage* (1915–1938), of which *Pointed Roofs* was the first).

rest.[2] Is *Ulysses* in his cradle? Oh, dear! What a grey face! And *Pointed Roofs*, are they a gay little toy for nice little girls? And M. Proust? Alas! You can hear the death-rattle in their throats. They can hear it themselves. They are listening to it with acute interest, trying to discover whether the intervals are minor thirds or major fourths. Which is rather infantile, really.

So there you have the "serious" novel, dying in a very long-drawn-out fourteen-volume death-agony, and absorbedly, childishly interested in the phenomenon. "Did I feel a twinge in my little toe, or didn't I?" asks every character of Mr Joyce or of Miss Richardson or M. Proust. Is my aura a blend of frankincense and orange pekoe and boot-blacking, or is it myrrh and bacon-fat and Shetland tweed? The audience round the death-bed gapes for the answer. And when, in a sepulchral tone, the answer comes at length, after hundreds of pages: "It is none of these, it is abysmal chloro-coryamba-sis,"[3] the audience quivers all over, and murmurs: "That's just how I feel myself."

Which is the dismal, long-drawn-out comedy of the death-bed of the serious novel. It is self-consciousness picked into such fine bits that the bits are most of them invisible, and you have to go by smell. Through thousands and thousands of pages Mr Joyce and Miss Richardson tear themselves to pieces, strip their smallest emotions to the finest threads, till you feel you are sewed inside a wool mattress that is being slowly shaken up, and you are turning to wool along with the rest of the woolliness.

It's awful. And it's childish. It really is childish, after a certain age, to be absorbedly self-conscious. One has to be self-conscious at seventeen: still a little self-conscious at twenty-seven; but if we are going it strong at thirty-seven, then it is a sign of arrested development, nothing else. And if it is still continuing at forty-seven, it is obvious senile precocity.

And there's the serious novel: senile-precocious. Absorbedly, childishly concerned with *what I am*. "I am this, I am that, I am the other. My reactions are such, and such, and such. And, oh, Lord, if I liked to watch myself closely enough, if I liked to analyse my feelings minutely, as I unbutton my gloves, instead of saying crudely I unbuttoned them, then I could go on to a million pages instead of a thousand. In fact, the more I come to think of it, it is gross, it is uncivilized bluntly to say: I unbuttoned my gloves. After all, the absorbing adventure of it! Which button did I begin with?" etc.

The people in the serious novels are so absorbedly concerned with themselves and what they feel and don't feel, and how they react to every mortal button; and their audience as frenziedly absorbed in the application of the author's discoveries to their own reactions: "That's me! That's exactly it! I'm just finding myself in this book!" Why, this is more than death-bed, it is almost post-mortem behaviour.

Some convulsion or cataclysm will have to get this serious novel out of its self-consciousness. The last great war made it worse. What's to be done? Because, poor thing, it's really young yet. The novel has never become fully adult. It has never quite grown to years of discretion. It has always youthfully hoped for the best, and felt rather sorry for itself on the last page. Which is just childish. The childishness has become very long-drawn-out. So very many adolescents who drag their adolescence on into their forties and their fifties and their sixties! There needs some sort of surgical operation, somewhere.

---

2. *The Sheik* (1919) was a lurid best-seller by Edith Maude Hull; Zane Grey (1875–1939), popular American writer of westerns; Robert Chalmers (1865–1933), prolific

American novelist.
3. A word of Lawrence's invention.

Then the popular novels—the *Sheiks* and *Babbitts* and Zane Grey novels. They are just as self-conscious, only they do have more illusions about themselves. The heroines do think they are lovelier, and more fascinating, and purer. The heroes do see themselves more heroic, braver, more chivalrous, more fetching. The mass of the populace "find themselves" in the popular novels. But nowadays it's a funny sort of self they find. A Sheik with a whip up his sleeve, and a heroine with weals on her back, but adored in the end, adored, the whip out of sight, but the weals still faintly visible.

It's a funny sort of self they discover in the popular novels. And the essential moral of *If Winter Comes,* for example, is so shaky. "The gooder you are, the worse it is for you, poor you, oh, poor you. Don't you be so blimey good, it's not good enough." Or *Babbitt:*[4] "Go on, you make your pile, and then pretend you're too good for it. Put it over the rest of the grabbers that way. They're only pleased with themselves when they've made their pile. You go one better."

Always the same sort of baking-powder gas to make you rise: the soda counteracting the cream of tartar, and the tartar counteracted by the soda. Sheik heroines, duly whipped, wildly adored. Babbitts with solid fortunes, weeping from self-pity. Winter-Comes heroes as good as pie, hauled off to jail. *Moral:* Don't be too good, because you'll go to jail for it. *Moral:* Don't feel sorry for yourself till you've made your pile and don't need to feel sorry for yourself. *Moral:* Don't let him adore you till he's whipped you into it. Then you'll be partners in mild crime as well as in holy matrimony.

Which again is childish. Adolescence which *can't* grow up. Got into the self-conscious rut and going crazy, quite crazy in it. Carrying on their adolescence into middle age and old age, like the looney Cleopatra in *Dombey and Son,*[5] murmuring "Rose-coloured curtains" with her dying breath.

The future of the novel? Poor old novel, it's in a rather dirty, messy tight corner. And it's either got to get over the wall or knock a hole through it. In other words, it's got to grow up. Put away childish things like: "Do I love the girl, or don't I?"—"Am I pure and sweet, or am I not?"—"Do I unbutton my right glove first, or my left?"—"Did my mother ruin my life by refusing to drink the cocoa which my bride had boiled for her?" These questions and their answers don't really interest me any more, though the world still goes sawing them over. I simply don't care for any of these things now, though I used to. The purely emotional and self-analytical stunts are played out in me. I'm finished. I'm deaf to the whole band. But I'm neither *blasé* nor cynical, for all that. I'm just interested in something else.

Supposing a bomb were put under the whole scheme of things, what would we be after? What feelings do we want to carry through into the next epoch? What feelings will carry us through? What is the underlying impulse in us that will provide the motive power for a new state of things, when this democratic-industrial-lovey-dovey-darling-take-me-to-mamma state of things is bust?

What next? That's what interests me. "What now?" is no fun any more.

If you wish to look into the past for what-next books, you can go back to the Greek philosophers. Plato's Dialogues are queer little novels. It seems to me it was the greatest pity in the world, when philosophy and fiction got split. They used to be one, right

---

4. *If Winter Comes* (1915), a novel by American author A. S. M. Hutchinson; *Babbitt* (1922) by American author Sinclair Lewis.

5. In Dickens's novel *Dombey and Son* (1847–1948), the second wife of Mr. Dombey is known as "Cleopatra."

from the days of myth. Then they went and parted, like a nagging married couple, with Aristotle and Thomas Aquinas and that beastly Kant.[6] So the novel went sloppy, and philosophy went abstract-dry. The two should come together again—in the novel.

You've got to find a new impulse for new things in mankind, and it's really fatal to find it through abstraction. No, no; philosophy and religion, they've both gone too far on the algebraical tack: Let X stand for sheep and Y for goats: then X minus Y equals Heaven, and X plus Y equals Earth, and Y minus X equals Hell. Thank you! But what coloured shirt does X have on?

The novel has a future. It's got to have the courage to tackle new propositions without using abstractions; it's got to present us with new, really new feelings, a whole line of new emotion, which will get us out of the emotional rut. Instead of snivelling about what is and has been, or inventing new sensations in the old line, it's got to break a way through, like a hole in the wall. And the public will scream and say it is sacrilege: because, of course, when you've been jammed for a long time in a tight corner, and you get really used to its stuffiness and its tightness, till you find it suffocatingly cozy; then, of course, you're horrified when you see a new glaring hole in what was your cosy wall. You're horrified. You back away from the cold stream of fresh air as if it were killing you. But gradually, first one and then another of the sheep filters through the gap, and finds a new world outside.

⊢━◆⊒⊣

W. H. Auden
1907–1973

Wystan Hugh Auden's fantastically wrinkled face is a familiar icon from photographs taken in his later years, showing a fissured map of lines across his features. These photographs, many depicting Auden posing with his ever-present cigarette against a cityscape or airport, reveal part of Auden's continuing allure, which is that he was a witness, in his writing and in his person, to the changing scene of life and letters in the middle decades of the twentieth century. Auden came to embody a British literary Golden Age that lived on after the conditions that had brought it into being had changed utterly. His imperturbable face, looking much older than it was, had a sagelike quality of wisdom and the measurement of time passing: a map of modern experience.

Born in York, England, Auden had a pampered childhood, and was too young to see service in World War I. He was of the post-War generation, a group of gifted poets and writers who sought to replace the terrible losses of the war, its literary as well as its human casualties. Auden attended Christ Church College, Oxford, where his precocious literary career began in 1928 with the private publication of his *Poems*, thirty copies of which were put together by his friend and fellow writer Stephen Spender at Oxford. Auden joined a number of his friends and peers in heading to Berlin; his friend Christopher Isherwood's *I Am a Camera* (later the basis for the musical *Cabaret*) documented the phenomenon of these expatriate British writers spending their youthful careers in a decadent and exciting Berlin. Like many of the rest—though some died fighting fascism in Spain—Auden

---

6. All systematic philosophers who wrote syllogistically; in a letter of 1928, Lawrence included Immanuel Kant in a list of "grand perverts."

returned to England; he became a teacher in Scotland and England while writing feverishly. The cultural ferment of the thirties led Auden in many directions: chiefly, he wrote poetry, but he also became a noted literary critic, and he collaborated with Isherwood and others on plays and screenplays.

Auden's literary and political wanderlust took him to Iceland in 1936, where he wrote *Letters from Iceland* with Louis MacNeice; to Spain, which resulted in much poetry and occasional writing; to China, Japan, and the United States, culminating in the book *On the Frontier*. In 1939 he took an epochal step: he settled in the United States, where he became a citizen in 1946. In this he was a reverse T. S. Eliot—Eliot was an American who became a British citizen and is usually included as a premier writer of British, not American, literature. Auden was an American citizen who is always included in British anthologies, and rarely, if ever, in American collections. Part of Auden's desire to live in America had to do with his need to escape a stifling set of expectations for him that obtained in England—social, literary, and even personal expectations. In 1935, he had married Thomas Mann's daughter Erika, largely to protect her from political persecution in Germany, since Auden was a homosexual and lived for most of his adult life with the poet Chester Kallman, whom he met in 1939.

It was during Auden's teaching and fellowship years in the United States that he began to produce the large oeuvre of his poetry and his criticism. He taught and lectured at many colleges and universities, and read widely, taking a particular interest in the existentialist theology of Søren Kierkegaard. Increasingly impatient with Marxist materialism, Auden found a renewed commitment to Christianity in his later decades. During these years he published such notable milestones as his *Collected Shorter Poems*, *The Age of Anxiety*, and the critical work *The Enchafèd Flood*. In 1958 his definitive *Selected Poetry* was published, followed in 1962 by his magisterial work of criticism, *The Dyer's Hand*. His peripatetic and sometimes difficult teaching life led him to accept an offer from Oxford in 1956, to spend summers in Italy and in Austria, and to make a final move to Oxford and Christ Church College in 1972. However, he died shortly thereafter in 1973, in Austria, where he shared the summer house with Kallman.

The title of one of Auden's major long poems, *The Age of Anxiety*, summons up a reigning motif of Auden's poetic writing. Auden's poetry is edgy, tense, worried, psychoanalytic and yet despondent of the powers of psychoanalysis to allay anxiety. Anxiety is in some ways Auden's muse. This arises from the seriousness with which Auden had gauged the world political situation. Having witnessed the depression, the rise of Nazism, totalitarianism, World War II, the Holocaust, the atomic bomb, and the Cold War, Auden's political realism is tinged inevitably with disillusionment. Modern history is one primary source for Auden's poetry; in poems like *Spain 1937* and *September 1, 1939*, he makes no retreat to purely aesthetic subject matter, or to the past, or to pure experimentation. Auden's is a poetry of waiting rooms, radio broadcasts, armed battalions, and of snatched pleasures treasured all the more for their fleeting magic.

Paradoxically, Auden's moral and political engagements coexist with an anarchic streak, a wry wit, and a love of leisure and play. Auden developed one of the most seductively varied voices in modern poetry, creating an endlessly inventive style that draws at will on Latin elegy, Anglo-Saxon alliterative verse forms, Norse runes and "kennings," technical scientific discourse, and the meters and language of British music hall songs and of American blues singers. All these elements can be present in a single stanza, to sometimes dizzying effect; in other poems, these radically different materials are blended and modulated into a deceptively plain style of great power.

A topic of special concern for Auden was the survival of literary language. How would poetry make claims for its relevance, given that it was now surrounded by so many other voices, from those of mass culture to the exigent rhetoric of war? Auden often compared himself poetically to William Butler Yeats, as another political poet in a time when poetry was seen as largely irrelevant or even antithetical to politics.

Auden's poetry remains a profoundly lyric poetry: that is, it celebrates the singular human voice that sings its lines. It is not surprising that he wrote opera librettos, notably *The Rake's Progress*, which he wrote with Chester Kallman for Igor Stravinsky. Auden was an intellectual inheritor of Freud and Marx—he knew the ways that the self could remain unknown to itself, and the ways that history could relentlessly rush on oblivious of the human lives swept up in its current. Still, the human voice of poetry goes on, even in the age of anxiety, framing its lyric songs. In the late phase of his poetry, Auden had despaired of systems, and returned even more to the meticulous versification he was so well versed in. His poems become almost defiant vehicles of traditional rhyme and meter, lodged in the modern, everyday world, where "in the deserts of the heart," Auden would "let the healing fountain start."

Musée des Beaux Arts[1]

About suffering they were never wrong,
The Old Masters: how well they understood
Its human position; how it takes place
While someone else is eating or opening a window or just walking dully along;
5   How, when the aged are reverently, passionately waiting
For the miraculous birth, there always must be
Children who did not specially want it to happen, skating
On a pond at the edge of the wood:
They never forgot
10 That even the dreadful martyrdom must run its course
Anyhow in a corner, some untidy spot
Where the dogs go on with their doggy life and the torturer's horse
Scratches its innocent behind on a tree.

In Brueghel's *Icarus*, for instance: how everything turns away
15 Quite leisurely from the disaster; the ploughman may
Have heard the splash, the forsaken cry,
But for him it was not an important failure; the sun shone
As it had to on the white legs disappearing into the green
Water; and the expensive delicate ship that must have seen
20 Something amazing, a boy falling out of the sky,
Had somewhere to get to and sailed calmly on.

1938   1940

In Memory of W. B. Yeats
(d. January 1939)

1

He disappeared in the dead of winter:
The brooks were frozen, the air-ports almost deserted,
And snow disfigured the public statues;
The mercury sank in the mouth of the dying day.
5   O all the instruments agree
The day of his death was a dark cold day.

---

1. The Musées Royaux des Beaux-Arts in Brussels contain a collection of paintings by the Flemish painter Pieter Brueghel (1525–1569) that includes *The Fall of Icarus*; Brueghel is famous for his acute observation of ordinary life. A figure from Greek mythology, Icarus had wings of wax and feathers but flew too close to the sun, which melted the wax and caused him to fall into the sea.

Far from his illness
The wolves ran on through the evergreen forests,
The peasant river was untempted by the fashionable quays;
10   By mourning tongues
The death of the poet was kept from his poems.

But for him it was his last afternoon as himself,
An afternoon of nurses and rumours;
The provinces of his body revolted,
15   The squares of his mind were empty,
Silence invaded the suburbs,
The current of his feeling failed: he became his admirers.

Now he is scattered among a hundred cities
And wholly given over to unfamiliar affections;
20   To find his happiness in another kind of wood
And be punished under a foreign code of conscience.
The words of a dead man
Are modified in the guts of the living.

But in the importance and noise of to-morrow
25   When the brokers are roaring like beasts on the floor of the Bourse,[1]
And the poor have the sufferings to which they are fairly accustomed,
And each in the cell of himself is almost convinced of his freedom;
A few thousand will think of this day
As one thinks of a day when one did something slightly unusual.

30   O all the instruments agree
The day of his death was a dark cold day.

2

You were silly like us: your gift survived it all;
The parish of rich women, physical decay,
Yourself; mad Ireland hurt you into poetry.
35   Now Ireland has her madness and her weather still,
For poetry makes nothing happen: it survives
In the valley of its saying where executives
Would never want to tamper; it flows south
From ranches of isolation and the busy griefs,
40   Raw towns that we believe and die in; it survives,
A way of happening, a mouth.

3

Earth, receive an honoured guest;
William Yeats is laid to rest:
Let the Irish vessel lie
Emptied of its poetry.

45   Time that is intolerant
Of the brave and innocent,
And indifferent in a week
To a beautiful physique,

Worships language and forgives
50   Everyone by whom it lives;

1. Stock exchange.

Pardons cowardice, conceit,
Lays its honours at their feet.

Time that with this strange excuse
Pardoned Kipling and his views,
55   And will pardon Paul Claudel,[2]
Pardons him for writing well.

In the nightmare of the dark
All the dogs of Europe bark,
And the living nations wait,
60   Each sequestered in its hate;

Intellectual disgrace
Stares from every human face,
And the seas of pity lie
Locked and frozen in each eye.

65   Follow, poet, follow right
To the bottom of the night,
With your unconstraining voice
Still persuade us to rejoice;

With the farming of a verse
70   Make a vineyard of the curse,
Sing of human unsuccess
In a rapture of distress;

In the deserts of the heart
Let the healing fountain start,
75   In the prison of his days
Teach the free man how to praise.

February 1939   1940

Spain 1937[1]

Yesterday all the past. The language of size
Spreading to China along the trade-routes; the diffusion
          Of the counting-frame and the cromlech;[2]
Yesterday the shadow-reckoning in the sunny climates.
5   Yesterday the assessment of insurance by cards,
The divination of water; yesterday the invention
          Of cart-wheels and clocks, the taming of
Horses; yesterday the bustling world of the navigators.

Yesterday the abolition of fairies and giants;
10   The fortress like a motionless eagle eyeing the valley,
          The chapel built in the forest;
Yesterday the carving of angels and of frightening gargoyles.

---

2. Rudyard Kipling (1865–1936), short-story writer, poet, and novelist remembered for his celebration of British imperialism; Paul Claudel (1868–1955), French poet and diplomat noted for his conservative views.
1. Auden visited Spain between January and March 1937, when the civil war between the Spanish govern-ment and military-backed Fascist insurgents was at its height. Many foreigners (the so-called "International Brigade") went to Spain at this time to aid the republican forces.
2. Prehistoric stone circle.

The trial of heretics among the columns of stone;
Yesterday the theological feuds in the taverns
15   And the miraculous cure at the fountain;
Yesterday the Sabbath of Witches. But today the struggle.

Yesterday the installation of dynamos and turbines;
The construction of railways in the colonial desert;
                 Yesterday the classic lecture
20   On the origin of Mankind. But today the struggle.

Yesterday the belief in the absolute value of Greek;
The fall of the curtain upon the death of a hero;
                 Yesterday the prayer to the sunset,
And the adoration of madmen. But today the struggle.

25   As the poet whispers, startled among the pines
Or, where the loose waterfall sings, compact, or upright
                 On the crag by the leaning tower:
"O my vision. O send me the luck of the sailor."

And the investigator peers through his instruments
30   At the inhuman provinces, the virile bacillus
                 Or enormous Jupiter finished:
"But the lives of my friends. I inquire, I inquire."

And the poor in their fireless lodgings dropping the sheets
Of the evening paper: "Our day is our loss. O show us
35   History the operator, the
Organiser, Time the refreshing river."

And the nations combine each cry, invoking the life
That shapes the individual belly and orders
                 The private nocturnal terror:
40   "Did you not found once the city state of the sponge,

"Raise the vast military empires of the shark
And the tiger, establish the robin's plucky canton?
                 Intervene. O descend as a dove or
A furious papa or a mild engineer: but descend."

45   And the life, if it answers at all, replies from the heart
And the eyes and the lungs, from the shops and squares of the city:
                 "O no, I am not the Mover,
Not today, not to you. To you I'm the

"Yes-man, the bar-companion, the easily-duped:
50   I am whatever you do; I am your vow to be
                 Good, your humorous story;
I am your business voice; I am your marriage.

"What's your proposal? To build the Just City? I will.
I agree. Or is it the suicide pact, the romantic
55   Death? Very well, I accept, for
I am your choice, your decision: yes, I am Spain."

Many have heard it on remote peninsulas,
On sleepy plains, in the aberrant fishermen's islands,

In the corrupt heart of the city;
60   Have heard and migrated like gulls or the seeds of a flower.

They clung like burrs to the long expresses that lurch
Through the unjust lands, through the night, through the alpine tunnel;
     They floated over the oceans;
They walked the passes: they came to present their lives.

65   On that arid square, that fragment nipped off from hot
Africa, soldered so crudely to inventive Europe,
     On that tableland scored by rivers,
Our fever's menacing shapes are precise and alive.

Tomorrow, perhaps, the future: the research on fatigue
70   And the movements of packers; the gradual exploring of all the
     Octaves of radiation;
Tomorrow the enlarging of consciousness by diet and breathing.

Tomorrow the rediscovery of romantic love;
The photographing of ravens; all the fun under
75   Liberty's masterful shadow;
Tomorrow the hour of the pageant-master and the musician.

Tomorrow, for the young, the poets exploding like bombs,
The walks by the lake, the winter of perfect communion;
     Tomorrow the bicycle races
80   Through the suburbs on summer evenings: but today the struggle.

Today the inevitable increase in the chances of death;
The conscious acceptance of guilt in the fact of murder;
     Today the expending of powers
On the flat ephemeral pamphlet and the boring meeting.

85   Today the makeshift consolations; the shared cigarette;
The cards in the candle-lit barn and the scraping concert,
     The masculine jokes; today the
Fumbled and unsatisfactory embrace before hurting.

The stars are dead; the animals will not look:
90   We are left alone with our day, and the time is short and
     History to the defeated
May say Alas but cannot help or pardon.

                                                                1937

Lullaby

Lay your sleeping head, my love,
Human on my faithless arm;
Time and fevers burn away
Individual beauty from
5   Thoughtful children, and the grave
Proves the child ephemeral:
But in my arms till break of day
Let the living creature lie,
Mortal, guilty, but to me
10   The entirely beautiful.

Soul and body have no bounds:
To lovers as they lie upon
Her tolerant enchanted slope
In their ordinary swoon,
15 Grave the vision Venus sends
Of supernatural sympathy,
Universal love and hope;
While an abstract insight wakes
Among the glaciers and the rocks
20 The hermit's carnal ecstasy.

Certainty, fidelity
On the stroke of midnight pass
Like vibrations of a bell
And fashionable madmen raise
25 Their pedantic boring cry:
Every farthing of the cost,
All the dreaded cards foretell,
Shall be paid, but from this night
Not a whisper, not a thought,
30 Not a kiss nor look be lost.

Beauty, midnight, vision dies:
Let the winds of dawn that blow
Softly round your dreaming head
Such a day of welcome show
35 Eye and knocking heart may bless,
Find our mortal world enough;
Noons of dryness find you fed
By the involuntary powers,
Nights of insult let you pass
40 Watched by every human love.
1937   1940

September 1, 1939[1]

I sit in one of the dives
On Fifty-Second Street
Uncertain and afraid
As the clever hopes expire
5 Of a low dishonest decade:
Waves of anger and fear
Circulate over the bright
And darkened lands of the earth,
Obsessing our private lives;
10 The unmentionable odour of death
Offends the September night.

Accurate scholarship can
Unearth the whole offence

---

1. Auden arrived in New York City, where he was to spend World War II and much of the rest of his life, in January 1939. German forces marched into Poland on September 1, 1939; Britain and France declared war on September 3.

15 From Luther[2] until now
That has driven a culture mad,
Find what occurred at Linz,[3]
What huge imago made
A psychopathic god:[4]
20 I and the public know
What all schoolchildren learn,
Those to whom evil is done
Do evil in return.

Exiled Thucydides[5] knew
All that a speech can say
25 About Democracy,
And what dictators do,
The elderly rubbish they talk
To an apathetic grave;
Analysed all in his book,
30 The enlightenment driven away,
The habit-forming pain,
Mismanagement and grief:
We must suffer them all again.

Into this neutral air
35 Where blind skyscrapers use
Their full height to proclaim
The strength of Collective Man,
Each language pours its vain
Competitive excuse:
40 But who can live for long
In an euphoric dream;
Out of the mirror they stare,
Imperialism's face
And the international wrong.

45 Faces along the bar
Cling to their average day:
The lights must never go out,
The music must always play,
All the conventions conspire
50 To make this fort assume
The furniture of home;
Lest we should see where we are,
Lost in a haunted wood,
Children afraid of the night
55 Who have never been happy or good.

---

2. Martin Luther, German religious reformer (1483–1546), whose criticisms of Roman Catholic doctrine sparked the Protestant Reformation in Europe.
3. Linz, Austria, was Adolf Hitler's birthplace.
4. In the psychological terminology developed by C. G. Jung (1875–1961), an *imago* is an idealized mental image of self or others, especially parental figures.
5. Fifth-century Athenian historian and general in the Peloponnesian War between Athens and Sparta (431–404

B.C.). In his famous *History of the Peloponnesian War*, which follows events until 411 B.C., Thucydides records the Athenian statesman Pericles' *Funeral Oration*, given at the end of the first year of the war. In it, Pericles describes the benefits and possible dangers of democratic government as it was then practiced at Athens. Thucydides himself was exiled from Athens in 424 B.C., following a military defeat incurred under his leadership.

The windiest militant trash
Important Persons shout
Is not so crude as our wish:
What mad Nijinsky wrote
60   About Diaghilev
Is true of the normal heart;[6]
For the error bred in the bone
Of each woman and each man
Craves what it cannot have,
65   Not universal love
But to be loved alone.

From the conservative dark
Into the ethical life
The dense commuters come,
70   Repeating their morning vow,
"I *will* be true to the wife,
I'll concentrate more on my work,"
And helpless governors wake
To resume their compulsory game:
75   Who can release them now,
Who can reach the deaf,
Who can speak for the dumb?

All I have is a voice
To undo the folded lie,
80   The romantic lie in the brain
Of the sensual man-in-the-street
And the lie of Authority
Whose buildings grope the sky:
There is no such thing as the State
85   And no one exists alone;
Hunger allows no choice
To the citizen or the police;
We must love one another or die.

Defenceless under the night
90   Our world in stupor lies;
Yet, dotted everywhere,
Ironic points of light
Flash out wherever the Just
Exchange their messages:
95   May I, composed like them
Of Eros and of dust,
Beleaguered by the same
Negation and despair,
Show an affirming flame.

1939   1940

---

6. Vaslav Nijinsky (1890–1950), principal male dancer in the Ballet Russes company under the direction of Sergei Pavlovich Diaghilev (1872–1929). The company revolutionized the world of dance, causing a sensation on its visit to Paris in 1909. Auden borrowed the following lines from Nijinsky's (1937) *Diary*: "Diaghilev does not want universal love, but to be loved alone."

In Praise of Limestone[1]

If it form the one landscape that we, the inconstant ones,
    Are consistently homesick for, this is chiefly
Because it dissolves in water. Mark these rounded slopes
    With their surface fragrance of thyme and, beneath,
5   A secret system of caves and conduits; hear the springs
    That spurt out everywhere with a chuckle,
Each filling a private pool for its fish and carving
    Its own little ravine whose cliffs entertain
The butterfly and the lizard; examine this region
10   Of short distances and definite places:
What could be more like Mother or a fitter background
    For her son, the flirtatious male who lounges
Against a rock in the sunlight, never doubting
    That for all his faults he is loved; whose works are but
15   Extensions of his power to charm? From weathered outcrop
    To hill-top temple, from appearing waters to
Conspicuous fountains, from a wild to a formal vineyard,
    Are ingenious but short steps that a child's wish
To receive more attention than his brothers, whether
20   By pleasing or teasing, can easily take.

Watch, then, the band of rivals as they climb up and down
    Their steep stone gennels[2] in twos and threes, at times
Arm in arm, but never, thank God, in step; or engaged
    On the shady side of a square at midday in
25   Voluble discourse, knowing each other too well to think
    There are any important secrets, unable
To conceive a god whose temper-tantrums are moral
    And not to be pacified by a clever line
Or a good lay: for, accustomed to a stone that responds,
30   They have never had to veil their faces in awe
Of a crater whose blazing fury could not be fixed;
    Adjusted to the local needs of valleys
Where everything can be touched or reached by walking,
    Their eyes have never looked into infinite space
35   Through the lattice-work of a nomad's comb; born lucky,
    Their legs have never encountered the fungi
And insects of the jungle, the monstrous forms and lives
    With which we have nothing, we like to hope, in common.
So, when one of them goes to the bad, the way his mind works
40   Remains comprehensible: to become a pimp
Or deal in fake jewellery or ruin a fine tenor voice
    For effects that bring down the house, could happen to all
But the best and worst of us . . .
                   That is why, I suppose,
    The best and worst never stayed here long but sought
45   Immoderate soils where the beauty was not so external,

---

1. This poem is set in the landscape of Yorkshire, where   2. Channels.
Auden was born.

The light less public and the meaning of life
Something more than a mad camp. "Come!" cried the granite wastes,
    "How evasive is your humour, how accidental
Your kindest kiss, how permanent is death." (Saints-to-be
50   Slipped away sighing.) "Come!" purred the clays and gravels.
"On our plains there is room for armies to drill; rivers
    Wait to be tamed and slaves to construct you a tomb
In the grand manner: soft as the earth is mankind and both
    Need to be altered." (Intendant Caesars rose and
55 Left, slamming the door.) But the really reckless were fetched
    By an older colder voice, the oceanic whisper:
"I am the solitude that asks and promises nothing;
    That is how I shall set you free. There is no love;
There are only the various envies, all of them sad."
60   They were right, my dear, all those voices were right
And still are; this land is not the sweet home that it looks,
    Nor its peace the historical calm of a site
Where something was settled once and for all: A backward
    And dilapidated province, connected
65 To the big busy world by a tunnel, with a certain
    Seedy appeal, is that all it is now? Not quite:
It has a worldly duty which in spite of itself
    It does not neglect, but calls into question
All the Great Powers assume; it disturbs our rights. The poet,
70   Admired for his earnest habit of calling
The sun the sun, his mind Puzzle, is made uneasy
    By these marble statues which so obviously doubt
His antimythological myth; and these gamins,[3]
    Pursuing the scientist down the tiled colonnade
75 With such lively offers, rebuke his concern for Nature's
    Remotest aspects: I, too, am reproached, for what
And how much you know. Not to lose time, not to get caught,
    Not to be left behind, not, please! to resemble
The beasts who repeat themselves, or a thing like water
80 Or stone whose conduct can be predicted, these
Are our Common Prayer, whose greatest comfort is music
    Which can be made anywhere, is invisible,
And does not smell. In so far as we have to look forward
    To death as a fact, no doubt we are right: But if
85 Sins can be forgiven, if bodies rise from the dead,
    These modifications of matter into
Innocent athletes and gesticulating fountains,
    Made solely for pleasure, make a further point:
The blessed will not care what angle they are regarded from,
90   Having nothing to hide. Dear, I know nothing of
Either, but when I try to imagine a faultless love
    Or the life to come, what I hear is the murmur
Of underground streams, what I see is a limestone landscape.

1948   1948

3. Street urchins.

World War II and the End of Empire

World War I had been a catastrophe of unprecedented proportions. Never before in world history had a preponderance of national powers joined together into two warring alliances; never before had the theater of war included such a wide expanse of the globe. But for Great Britain, at least, the war was foreign rather than domestic; as demoralizing and bleak as the fighting was, it was "over there," and never touched the British Isles. World War II would be a very different story.

World War II started, technically, with Hitler's invasion of Poland on September 1, 1939; as is the case with all world-historical conflicts, however, the war's genesis can be traced further back—in this case, back two decades to the peace treaties with which World War I was uneasily concluded. The victors of World War I never quite got what they hoped for, and the defeated nations had their defeat transformed into ritual diplomatic humiliation. Meanwhile, a worldwide economic depression had begun in the United States in 1929 and spread to Europe by the early 1930s, weakening democratic governments and lending a seductive edge to the rhetoric of political extremists. As a result, when Hitler began to rise to power in a beleaguered Germany during the 1930s, his message of empowerment was one that many Germans wanted to hear. Beginning with Poland, Hitler overran Denmark, Luxembourg, the Netherlands, Belgium, and Norway in quick succession, and by June 1940 had conquered even France. Britain was next on Hitler's list, as the major remaining obstacle to the domination of Europe.

Hitler hoped to paralyze and demoralize the British by a devastating series of attacks by air. This drew out to become the ten-month long Battle of Britain, in which the German Luftwaffe (air force) engaged Britain's Royal Air Force in the previously inviolable air space over England's green and pleasant land. The battle brought enormous costs—especially during the eight months of nightly air raids over British metropolitan centers known as the Blitz. The bombing caused great destruction to London, which was bombed every night between September 7 and November 2, 1940; more than 15,000 civilians were killed in London (30,000 nationwide), over half a million left homeless, and important cultural and architectural treasures, such as the House of Commons and Buckingham Palace, were damaged or destroyed. This violation of England's homeland was costly in psychological and emotional terms as well; one poignant register of the broad impact of the air raids can be seen in Virginia Woolf's final novel *Between the Acts*, where the sound of bombs falling on distant London unnerves the residents and guests of Pointz Hall. As Woolf's diaries and letters make clear, the sound of those bombs were also a crucial factor in her decision to take her own life in March 1941.

In May of 1941, Germany finally gave up its attempt to conquer Britain from the air. With the bombing of Pearl Harbor by the Japanese in December 1941, the United States entered the war on the side of the Allies; with their help, Britain was able to mount an offensive against Germany on the European mainland and retake land that had been invaded by Germany. In 1942, Britain and the United States began to plan an invasion across the English Channel. The first attempt, a raid staged at the French port of Dieppe in the summer of 1942, was a disappointing failure. The Allies regrouped, however, and planned the offensive known as D-Day. On June 6, 1944, Allied troops, under the command of General Dwight D. Eisenhower, crossed the channel with 2,700 ships and 176,000 soldiers and overcame German defenses; by the end of the month, about a million Allied troops were on the ground in France, and the tide of the war had turned. In April 1945 Hitler committed suicide; one week later, Germany signed a statement of unconditional surrender, with Japan following suit on September 2.

World War II was over; in some important arenas, however, its influence had just begun to be felt. With such a great proportion of its able-bodied young men going off to war, millions of women in both Britain and the United States took employment outside the home for the first time; that trend, once started, has only gained momentum in the years since. The economic and personal freedom ceded to women during the wartime emergency laid the groundwork for the contemporary women's movement in Great Britain; Margaret Thatcher, Britain's first woman Prime Minister (1979–1990), was a postwar inheritor of Winston Churchill's legacy.

At the same time, the United States and the Soviet Union emerged from the war as the preeminent world powers; Britain, while on the winning side, saw its global prestige in eclipse, and found itself in the midst of an economic crisis. At the height of the war, Britain was devoting 54 percent of its gross national product to the war effort; by the war's end it had expended practically all of its foreign financial resources and was several billion pounds in debt to its wartime allies. In short, Britain was bankrupt. As its colonial possessions increased their protests against British rule, Britain had neither the military nor the economic power to control them; India, which had begun its independence movement during World War I, finally won full independence on August 15, 1947, and Burma and Ceylon (now Sri Lanka) quickly followed suit in early 1948. At about the same time, Britain was forced to withdraw from Palestine, and from all of Egypt except for the Suez Canal; the Canal itself was nationalized by Egypt in the summer of 1956. The 1960s saw increased Irish Republican activity in Northern Ireland, degenerating into armed sectarian violence in 1968; recent years have seen periodic waves of IRA violence in support of independence for Ulster, alternating with largely unsuccessful diplomatic attempts to forge a lasting peace in Northern Ireland. In the spring of 1982 Prime Minister Thatcher sent British troops to liberate the Falkland Islands, a small self-governing British colony off the coast of Argentina, from an Argentinian occupying force; Thatcher won a resounding reelection the following year on the strength of the British success, suggesting that pride in the British Empire, while diminishing in importance, was by no means yet extinct.

━━◆⧗◆━━

Sir Winston Churchill
1874–1965

British historian A. J. P. Taylor has written of a unique paradox of World War II: though it was a time of unprecedented stress and anxiety for the British people, "Great Britain was never so free from political controversy." The reason? Winston Churchill's ability to forge a partnership between himself and the British people. "There have been many great British leaders," Taylor continues; "There has only been one whom everyone recognized as the embodiment of the national will." The pictures of Churchill—watch-chain draped across his waistcoat, cigar drooping from his jowly face (above his bow tie and beneath his homburg), index and middle fingers raised in the V of Victory—is perhaps the most familiar and bouyant icon of Allied victory in the war.

Winston Churchill was born at Blenheim Palace, the ancestral home of his grandfather, the seventh duke of Marlborough; his father, Lord Randolph Churchill, had a distinguished career as a Conservative member of Parliament. Young Winston proved not to be an outstanding scholar, however, and instead of university, was sent to the Royal Military Academy. This military training, and his subsequent combat experience on the Western Front and in the Sudan, was to prove invaluable as he led his country as Prime Minister through the darkest days of World War II. Equally important to Churchill the statesman was his early work as a journalist and essayist; the economist John Kenneth Galbraith suggested that Churchill's power as an orator derived from his "fearsome certainty that he was completely right," a certainty made manifest in "his use of language as a weapon." In Churchill's well-known phrases, like "blood, toil, tears and sweat," a nation at war found its rallying cries.

Winston Churchill, June 1943. Returning to 10 Downing Street after meeting with American president Franklin Roosevelt in Washington, D.C., and visiting Allied armies in North Africa, the Prime Minister flashes his famous "V for Victory" sign to reporters.

Two Speeches Before the House of Commons

["BLOOD, TOIL, TEARS AND SWEAT"][1]

I beg to move,

> That this House welcomes the formation of a Government representing the united and inflexible resolve of the nation to prosecute the war with Germany to a victorious conclusion.

On Friday evening last I received His Majesty's Commission to form a new Administration. It was the evident wish and will of Parliament and the nation that this should be conceived on the broadest possible basis and that it should include all parties, both those who supported the late Government and also the parties of the Opposition. I have completed the most important part of this task. A War Cabinet has been formed of five Members, representing, with the Opposition Liberals, the unity of the nation. The three party Leaders have agreed to serve, either in the War Cabinet or in high executive office. The three Fighting Services have been filled. It

1. Delivered in the House of Commons, 13 May 1940.

was necessary that this should be done in one single day, on account of the extreme urgency and rigour of events. A number of other positions, key positions, were filled yesterday, and I am submitting a further list to His Majesty to-night. I hope to complete the appointment of the principal Ministers during to-morrow. The appointment of the other Ministers usually takes a little longer, but I trust that, when Parliament meets again, this part of my task will be completed, and that the administration will be complete in all respects.

I considered it in the public interest to suggest that the House should be summoned to meet to-day. Mr Speaker agreed, and took the necessary steps, in accordance with the powers conferred upon him by the Resolution of the House. At the end of the proceedings to-day, the Adjournment of the House will be proposed until Tuesday, 21st May, with, of course, provision for earlier meeting, if need be. The business to be considered during that week will be notified to Members at the earliest opportunity. I now invite the House, by the Motion which stands in my name, to record its approval of the steps taken and to declare its confidence in the new Government.

To form an Administration of this scale and complexity is a serious undertaking in itself, but it must be remembered that we are in the preliminary stage of one of the greatest battles in history, that we are in action at many other points in Norway and in Holland, that we have to be prepared in the Mediterranean, that the air battle is continuous and that many preparations, such as have been indicated by my hon. Friend below the Gangway, have to be made here at home. In this crisis I hope I may be pardoned if I do not address the House at any length to-day. I hope that any of my friends and colleagues, or former colleagues, who are affected by the political reconstruction, will make allowance, all allowance, for any lack of ceremony with which it has been necessary to act. I would say to the House, as I said to those who have joined this Government: "I have nothing to offer but blood, toil, tears and sweat."

We have before us an ordeal of the most grievous kind. We have before us many, many long months of struggle and of suffering. You ask, what is our policy? I can say: It is to wage war, by sea, land and air, with all our might and with all the strength that God can give us; to wage war against a monstrous tyranny, never surpassed in the dark, lamentable catalogue of human crime. That is our policy. You ask, what is our aim? I can answer in one word: It is victory, victory at all costs, victory in spite of all terror, victory, however long and hard the road may be; for without victory, there is no survival. Let that be realised; no survival for the British Empire, no survival for all that the British Empire has stood for, no survival for the urge and impulse of the ages, that mankind will move forward towards its goal. But I take up my task with buoyancy and hope. I feel sure that our cause will not be suffered to fail among men. At this time I feel entitled to claim the aid of all, and I say, "Come then, let us go forward together with our united strength."

["WARS ARE NOT WON BY EVACUATIONS"][1]

From the moment that the French defenses at Sedan and on the Meuse[2] were broken at the end of the second week of May, only a rapid retreat to Amiens[3] and the south could have saved the British and French Armies who had entered Belgium at the

---

1. Delivered in the Hosue of Commons 4 June 1940. This speech exemplifies Churchill's ability to rally his people amid the greatest difficulties—here, the disastrous defeat of the British and French armies in April–May 1940. What might have been seen as the humiliation of the British army becomes, in Churchill's stirring account, the heroic achievement of a successful evacuation against all odds.

2. A river flowing through France, Belgium, and the Netherlands.

3. A city located on the Somme River in northern France.

appeal of the Belgian King; but this strategic fact was not immediately realized. The French High Command hoped they would be able to close the gap, and the Armies of the north were under their orders. Moreover, a retirement of this kind would have involved almost certainly the destruction of the fine Belgian Army of over 20 divisions and the abandonment of the whole of Belgium. Therefore, when the force and scope of the German penetration were realized and when a new French Generalissimo,[4] General Weygand, assumed command in place of General Gamelin, an effort was made by the French and British Armies in Belgium to keep on holding the right hand of the Belgians and to give their own right hand to the newly created French Army which was to have advanced across the Somme[5] in great strength to grasp it.

However, the German eruption swept like a sharp scythe around the right and rear of the Armies of the north. Eight or nine armored divisions, each of about four hundred armored vehicles of different kinds, but carefully assorted to be complementary and divisible into small self-contained units, cut off all communications between us and the main French Armies. It severed our own communications for food and ammunition, which ran first to Amiens and afterwards through Abbeville, and it shore its way up the coast to Boulogne and Calais, and almost to Dunkirk.[6] Behind this armored and mechanized onslaught came a number of German divisions in lorries, and behind them again there plodded comparatively slowly the dull brute mass of the ordinary German Army and German people, always so ready to be led to the trampling down in other lands of liberties and comforts which they have never known in their own.

I have said this armored scythe-stroke almost reached Dunkirk—almost but not quite. Boulogne and Calais were the scenes of desperate fighting. The Guards defended Boulogne for a while and were then withdrawn by orders from this country. The Rifle Brigade, the 60th Rifles, and the Queen Victoria's Rifles, with a battalion of British tanks and 1,000 Frenchmen, in all about four thousand strong, defended Calais to the last. The British Brigadier was given an hour to surrender. He spurned the offer, and four days of intense street fighting passed before silence reigned over Calais, which marked the end of a memorable resistance. Only 30 unwounded survivors were brought off by the Navy, and we do not know the fate of their comrades. Their sacrifice, however, was not in vain. At least two armored divisions, which otherwise would have been turned against the British Expeditionary Force, had to be sent to overcome them. They have added another page to the glories of the light divisions, and the time gained enabled the Graveline water lines to be flooded and to be held by the French troops.

Thus it was that the port of Dunkirk was kept open. When it was found impossible for the Armies of the north to reopen their communications to Amiens with the main French Armies, only one choice remained. It seemed, indeed, forlorn. The Belgian, British and French Armies were almost surrounded. Their sole line of retreat was to a single port and to its neighboring beaches. They were pressed on every side by heavy attacks and far outnumbered in the air.

When, a week ago today, I asked the House to fix this afternoon as the occasion for a statement, I feared it would be my hard lot to announce the greatest military disaster in our long history. I thought—and some good judges agreed with me—that perhaps 20,000 or 30,000 men might be re-embarked. But it certainly seemed that

4. Supreme commander of the French forces.
5. A river in northern France.

6. Seaports in northern France.

the whole of the French First Army and the whole of the British Expeditionary Force north of the Amiens-Abbeville gap would be broken up in the open field or else would have to capitulate for lack of food and ammunition. These were the hard and heavy tidings for which I called upon the House and the nation to prepare themselves a week ago. The whole root and core and brain of the British Army, on which and around which we were to build, and are to build, the great British Armies in the later years of the war, seemed about to perish upon the field or to be led into an ignominious and starving capacity.

That was the prospect a week ago. But another blow which might well have proved final was yet to fall upon us. The King of the Belgians[7] had called upon us to come to his aid. Had not this Ruler and his Government severed themselves from the Allies, who rescued their country from extinction in the late war, and had they not sought refuge in what was proved to be a fatal neutrality, the French and British Armies might well at the outset have saved not only Belgium but perhaps even Poland. Yet at the last moment, when Belgium was already invaded, King Leopold called upon us to come to his aid, and even at the last moment we came. He and his brave, efficient Army, nearly half a million strong, guarded our left flank and thus kept open our only line of retreat to the sea. Suddenly, without prior consultation, with the least possible notice, without the advice of his Ministers and upon his own personal act, he sent a plenipotentiary[8] to the German Command, surrendered his Army, and exposed our whole flank and means of retreat.

I asked the House a week ago to suspend its judgment because the facts were not clear, but I do not feel that any reason now exists why we should not form our own opinions upon this pitiful episode. The surrender of the Belgian Army compelled the British at the shortest notice to cover a flank to the sea more than 30 miles in length. Otherwise all would have been cut off, and all would have shared the fate to which King Leopold had condemned the finest Army his country had ever formed. So in doing this and in exposing this flank, as anyone who followed the operations on the map will see, contact was lost between the British and two out of the three corps forming the First French Army, who were still farther from the coast than we were, and it seemed impossible that any large number of Allied troops could reach the coast.

The enemy attacked on all sides with great strength and fierceness, and their main power, the power of their far more numerous Air Force, was thrown into the battle or else concentrated upon Dunkirk and the beaches. Pressing in upon the narrow exit, both from the east and from the west, the enemy began to fire with cannon upon the beaches by which alone the shipping could approach or depart. They sowed magnetic mines in the channels and seas; they sent repeated waves of hostile aircraft, sometimes more than a hundred strong in one formation, to cast their bombs upon the single pier that remained, and upon the sand dunes upon which the troops had their eyes for shelter. Their U-boats, one of which was sunk, and their motor launches took their toll of the vast traffic which now began. For four or five days an intense struggle reigned. All their armored divisions—or what was left of them—together with great masses of infantry and artillery, hurled themselves in vain upon the ever-narrowing, ever-contracting appendix within which the British and French Armies fought.

Meanwhile, the Royal Navy, with the willing help of countless merchant seamen, strained every nerve to embark the British and Allied troops; 220 light warships and 650 other vessels were engaged. They had to operate upon the difficult coast,

---

7. Leopold III (1901–1983).   8. Diplomatic agent.

often in adverse weather, under an almost ceaseless hail of bombs and an increasing concentration of artillery fire. Nor were the seas, as I have said, themselves free from mines and torpedoes. It was in conditions such as these that our men carried on, with little or no rest, for days and nights on end, making trip after trip across the dangerous waters, bringing with them always men whom they had rescued. The numbers they have brought back are the measure of their devotion and their courage. The hospital ships, which brought off many thousands of British and French wounded, being so plainly marked were a special target for Nazi bombs; but the men and women on board them never faltered in their duty.

Meanwhile, the Royal Air Force, which had already been intervening in the battle, so far as its range would allow, from home bases, now used part of its main metropolitan fighter strength, and struck at the German bombers and at the fighters which in large numbers protected them. This struggle was protracted and fierce. Suddenly the scene has cleared, the crash and thunder has for the moment—but only for the moment—died away. A miracle of deliverance, achieved by valor, by perseverance, by perfect discipline, by faultless service, by resource, by skill, by unconquerable fidelity, is manifest to us all. The enemy was hurled back by the retreating British and French troops. He was so roughly handled that he did not hurry their departure seriously. The Royal Air Force engaged the main strength of the German Air Force, and inflicted upon them losses of at least four to one; and the Navy, using nearly 1,000 ships of all kinds, carried over 335,000 men, French and British, out of the jaws of death and shame, to their native land and to the tasks which lie immediately ahead. We must be very careful not to assign to this deliverance the attributes of a victory. Wars are not won by evacuations. But there was a victory inside this deliverance, which should be noted. It was gained by the Air Force. Many of our soldiers coming back have not seen the Air Force at work; they saw only the bombers which escaped its protective attack. They underrate its achievements. I have heard much talk of this; that is why I go out of my way to say this. I will tell you about it.

This was a great trial of strength between the British and German Air Forces. Can you conceive a greater objective for the Germans in the air than to make evacuation from these beaches impossible, and to sink all these ships which were displayed, almost to the extent of thousands? Could there have been an objective of greater military importance and significance for the whole purpose of the war than this? They tried hard, and they were beaten back; they were frustrated in their task. We got the Army away; and they have paid fourfold for any losses which they have inflicted. Very large formations of German aeroplanes—and we know that they are a very brave race—have turned on several occasions from the attack of one-quarter of their number of the Royal Air Force, and have dispersed in different directions. Twelve aeroplanes have been hunted by two. One aeroplane was driven into the water and cast away by the mere charge of a British aeroplane, which had no more ammunition. All of our types—the Hurricane, the Spitfire and the new Defiant—and all our pilots have been vindicated as superior to what they have at present to face.

When we consider how much greater would be our advantage in defending the air above this Island against an overseas attack, I must say that I find in these facts a sure basis upon which practical and reassuring thoughts may rest. I will pay my tribute to these young airmen. The great French Army was very largely, for the time being, cast back and disturbed by the onrush of a few thousands of armored vehicles. May it not also be that the cause of civilization itself will be defended by the skill and devotion of a few thousand airmen? There never has been, I suppose, in all the world, in all the history of war, such an opportunity for youth. The Knights of the Round Table, the Crusaders, all fall back into the past—not only distant but prosaic; these young men, going forth every morn to guard their native land and all that we stand for, holding in their hands these instruments of colossal and shattering power, of whom it may be said that

> Every morn brought forth a noble chance
> And every chance brought forth a noble knight,[9]

deserve our gratitude, as do all the brave men who, in so many ways and on so many occasions, are ready, and continue ready to give life and all for their native land.

I return to the Army. In the long series of very fierce battles, now on this front, now on that, fighting on three fronts at once, battles fought by two or three divisions against an equal or somewhat larger number of the enemy, and fought fiercely on some of the old grounds that so many of us knew so well—in these battles our losses in men have exceeded 30,000 killed, wounded and missing. I take occasion to express the sympathy of the House to all who have suffered bereavement or who are still anxious. The President of the Board of Trade [Sir Andrew Duncan] is not here today. His son has been killed, and many in the House have felt the pangs of affliction in the sharpest form. But I will say this about the missing: We have had a large number of wounded come home safely to this country, but I would say about the missing that there may be very many reported missing who will come back home, some day, in one way or another. In the confusion of this fight it is inevitable that many have been left in positions where honor required no further resistance from them.

Against this loss of over 30,000 men, we can set a far heavier loss certainly inflicted upon the enemy. But our losses in materiel are enormous. We have perhaps lost one-third of the men we lost in the opening days of the battle of 21st March, 1918, but we have lost nearly as many guns—nearly one thousand—and all our transport, all the armored vehicles that were with the Army in the north. This loss will impose a further delay on the expansion of our military strength. That expansion had not been proceeding as far as we had hoped. The best of all we had to give had gone to the British Expeditionary Force, and although they had not the numbers of tanks and some articles of equipment which were desirable, they were a very well and finely equipped Army. They had the first-fruits of all that our industry had to give, and that is gone. And now here is this further delay. How long it will be, how long it will last, depends upon the exertions which we make in this Island. An effort the like of which has never been seen in our records is now being made. Work is proceeding everywhere, night and day, Sundays and week days. Capital and Labor have cast aside their interests, rights, and customs and put them into the common stock. Already the flow of munitions has leaped forward. There is no reason why we should not in a few months overtake the sudden and serious loss that has come upon us, without retarding the development of our general program.

Nevertheless, our thankfulness at the escape of our Army and so many men, whose loved ones have passed through an agonizing week, must not blind us to the fact that what has happened in France and Belgium is a colossal military disaster. The French Army has been weakened, the Belgian Army has been lost, a large part of those fortified lines upon which so much faith had been reposed is gone, many valuable mining districts and factories have passed into the enemy's possession, the whole

---

9. Churchill misquotes slightly Tennyson's poem *Morte d'Arthur*, lines 280–281.

of the Channel ports are in his hands, with all the tragic consequences that follow from that, and we must expect another blow to be struck almost immediately at us or at France. We are told that Herr Hitler has a plan for invading the British Isles. This has often been thought of before. When Napoleon lay at Boulogne for a year with his flat-bottomed boats and his Grand Army, he was told by someone. "There are bitter weeds in England." There are certainly a great many more of them since the British Expeditionary Force returned.

The whole question of home defense against invasion is, of course, powerfully affected by the fact that we have for the time being in this Island incomparably more powerful military forces than we have ever had at any moment in this war or the last. But this will not continue. We shall not be content with a defensive war. We have our duty to our Ally. We have to reconstitute and build up the British Expeditionary Force once again, under its gallant Commander-in-Chief, Lord Gort. All this is in train; but in the interval we must put our defenses in this Island into such a high state of organization that the fewest possible numbers will be required to give effective security and that the largest possible potential of offensive effort may be realized. On this we are now engaged. It will be very convenient, if it be the desire of the House, to enter upon this subject in a secret Session. Not that the government would necessarily be able to reveal in very great detail military secrets, but we like to have our discussions free, without the restraint imposed by the fact that they will be read the next day by the enemy; and the Government would benefit by views freely expressed in all parts of the House by Members with their knowledge of so many different parts of the country. I understand that some request is to be made upon this subject, which will be readily acceded to by His Majesty's Government.

We have found it necessary to take measures of increasing stringency, not only against enemy aliens and suspicious characters of other nationalities, but also against British subjects who may become a danger or a nuisance should the war be transported to the United Kingdom. I know there are a great many people affected by the orders which we have made who are the passionate enemies of Nazi Germany. I am very sorry for them, but we cannot, at the present time and under the present stress, draw all the distinctions which we should like to do. If parachute landings were attempted and fierce fighting attendant upon them followed, these unfortunate people would be far better out of the way, for their own sakes as well as for ours. There is, however, another class, for which I feel not the slightest sympathy. Parliament has given us the powers to put down Fifth Column[1] activities with a strong hand, and we shall use those powers subject to the supervision and correction of the House, without the slightest hesitation until we are satisfied, and more than satisfied, that this malignancy in our midst has been effectively stamped out.

Turning once again, and this time more generally, to the question of invasion, I would observe that there has never been a period in all these long centuries of which we boast when an absolute guarantee against invasion, still less against serious raids, could have been given to our people. In the days of Napoleon the same wind which would have carried his transports across the Channel might have driven away the blockading fleet. There was always the chance, and it is that chance which has excited and befooled the imaginations of many Continental tyrants. Many are the tales that are told. We are assured that novel methods will be adopted, and when we see

---

1. Traitorous: a term coined by a Spanish fascist general in 1936, who attacked Madrid with four columns of troops, and later boasted that he had been aided by a "fifth column" of secret fascist supporters inside the city.

the originality of malice, the ingenuity of aggression, which our enemy displays, we may certainly prepare ourselves for every kind of novel stratagem and every kind of brutal and treacherous maneuver. I think that no idea is so outlandish that it should not be considered and viewed with a searching, but at the same time, I hope, with a steady eye. We must never forget the solid assurances of sea power and those which belong to air power if it can be locally exercised.

I have, myself, full confidence that if all do their duty, if nothing is neglected, and if the best arrangements are made, as they are being made, we shall prove ourselves once again able to defend our Island home, to ride out the storm of war, and to outlive the menace of tyranny, if necessary for years, if necessary alone. At any rate, that is what we are going to try to do. That is the resolve of His Majesty's Government—every man of them. That is the will of Parliament and the nation. The British Empire and the French Republic, linked together in their cause and in their need, will defend to the death their native soil, aiding each other like good comrades to the utmost of their strength. Even though large tracts of Europe and many old and famous States have fallen or may fall into the grip of the Gestapo and all the odious apparatus of Nazi rule, we shall not flag or fail. We shall go on to the end, we shall fight in France, we shall fight on the seas and oceans, we shall fight with growing confidence and growing strength in the air, we shall defend our Island, whatever the cost may be, we shall fight on the beaches, we shall fight on the landing grounds, we shall fight in the fields and in the streets, we shall fight in the hills; we shall never surrender, and even if, which I do not for a moment believe, this Island or a large part of it were subjugated and starving, then our Empire beyond the seas, armed and guarded by the British Fleet, would carry on the struggle, until, in God's good time, the New World, with all its power and might, steps forth to the rescue and the liberation of the old.

Stephen Spender
1909–1995

Stephen Spender was an important member of the group of poets writing in the wake of World War I and in the rising shadow of fascism and the approach of World War II. World War I, Spender said, "knocked the ballroom-floor from under middle-class English life"; his first important volume, *Poems*, was published in 1933—the year that Hitler rose to the chancellorship of the Third Reich. Thus the turn toward politics that characterizes the poetry of Spender and the other young Oxford poets who allied themselves with W. H. Auden—the so-called "Auden Generation"—seems in retrospect not so much a decision as an inevitability. Spender speaks this way, too, about his brief affiliation with communism, suggesting that the embrace of communism by British intellectuals in the 1930s was not a matter of economic theory but of conscience. For Spender, Auden, Cecil Day-Lewis and others, fascism was such an obvious, and obviously powerful, evil that only communism appeared strong enough to keep it at bay.

The complex energies and tensions of the 1930s drew forth from Spender his most idealistic and passionate poetry; he will be remembered primarily for the poetry he wrote in his twenties. Some of the energy of his writing derives from his sense of exclusion from English society; his mixed German-Jewish-English ancestry and his bisexuality led him to find, as he wrote, that "my feeling for the English was at times almost like being in love with an alien race." After World War II, Spender wrote little poetry, but continued to work in literary and cultural criticism. His *Collected Poems* was published in 1985.

Icarus[1]

He will watch the hawk with an indifferent eye
    Or pitifully;
Nor on those eagles that so feared him, now
    Will strain his brow;
5   Weapons men use, stone, sling and strong-thewed° bow   *strong-muscled*
    He will not know.

This aristocrat, superb of all instinct,
    With death close linked
Had paced the enormous cloud, almost had won
10   War on the sun;
Till now, like Icarus mid-ocean-drowned,
    Hands, wings, are found.

                              1929

What I Expected

What I expected, was
Thunder, fighting,
Long struggles with men
And climbing.
5   After continual straining
I should grow strong;
Then the rocks would shake
And I rest long.

What I had not foreseen
10   Was the gradual day
Weakening the will
Leaking the brightness away,
The lack of good to touch,
The fading of body and soul
15   Smoke before wind,
Corrupt, unsubstantial.

The wearing of Time,
And the watching of cripples pass
With limbs shaped like questions
20   In their odd twist,
The pulverous° grief   *dusty*
Melting the bones with pity,
The sick falling from earth—
These, I could not foresee.

25   Expecting always
Some brightness to hold in trust
Some final innocence

---

1. In Greek mythology, Icarus was the son of Daedalus, the inventor. To escape from Crete, Daedalus fashioned wings for his son and himself out of wax. Daedalus warned Icarus not to fly too high, for the heat of the sun would melt the wax wings; but Icarus, intoxicated by the power of flight, ignored his father's warning and plunged to his death in the sea.

Exempt from dust,
That, hanging solid,
30   Would dangle through all
Like the created poem,
Or the faceted crystal.

1933

The Express

After the first powerful plain manifesto
The black statement of pistons, without more fuss
But gliding like a queen, she leaves the station.
Without bowing and with restrained unconcern
5   She passes the houses which humbly crowd outside,
The gasworks, and at last the heavy page
Of death, printed by gravestones in the cemetery.
Beyond the town, there lies the open country
Where, gathering speed, she acquires mystery,
10   The luminous self-possession of ships on ocean.
It is now she begins to sing—at first quite low
Then loud, and at last with a jazzy madness—
The song of her whistle screaming at curves,
Of deafening tunnels, brakes, innumerable bolts.
15   And always light, aerial underneath
Retreats the elate metre of her wheels.
Steaming through metal landscape on her lines,
She plunges new eras of white happiness
Where speed throws up strange shapes, broad curves
20   And parallels clean like trajectories from guns.
At last, further than Edinburgh or Rome,
Beyond the crest of the world, she reaches night
Where only a low stream-line brightness
Of phosphorus, on the tossing hills is white.
25   Ah, like a comet through flame, she moves entranced
Wrapt in her music no bird-song, no, nor bough,
Breaking with honey buds, shall ever equal.

1933

The Pylons

The secret of these hills was stone, and cottages
Of that stone made,
And crumbling roads
That turned on sudden hidden villages.

5   Now over these small hills, they have built the concrete
That trails black wire;
Pylons, those pillars
Bare like nude, giant girls that have no secret.

The valley with its gilt and evening look
10   And the green chestnut

Of customary root,
Are mocked dry like the parched bed of a brook.

But far above and far as sight endures
Like whips of anger
15   With lightning's danger
There runs the quick perspective of the future.

This dwarfs our emerald country by its trek
So tall with prophecy:
Dreaming of cities
20   Where often clouds shall lean their swan-white neck.

1933

Elizabeth Bowen
1899–1973

Elizabeth Bowen was born into a world that was, at the turn of the century, on the verge of disappearing forever: the world of the Anglo-Irish ascendancy, the privileged world of the Protestant "big house" tradition. Bowen's Court, an estate in County Cork, had been in her family since an ancestor in the service of Oliver Cromwell had come to Ireland in 1749; the estate passed out of the family in 1960, when Elizabeth could no longer afford to maintain the property, and it was torn down by its new owner in 1963.

In stark contrast to her proud Anglo-Irish heritage, Bowen's childhood was rootless in the extreme. As a young child, the family's time was split between Bowen's Court, in the country, and Dublin, where her father was a barrister; in 1906, he suffered a nervous breakdown, and Elizabeth moved to London with her mother. Bowen's mother died of cancer in 1912, and Elizabeth was shuttled between various relatives. During World War I, she returned to neutral Ireland, where she worked in a hospital with veterans suffering from "shell shock"; she returned to London in 1918 to attend art school and lived primarily in London for the rest of her life.

Bowen was in London during the Blitz. She again volunteered her services to the victims of war, working for the Ministry of Information as an air-raid warden. She wrote a number of vivid, powerful stories about the ravages of war in London during the Blitz—among them *Mysterious Kôr* (1946), which the American novelist and short-story writer Eudora Welty has called the "most extraordinary story of those she wrote out of her life in wartime London."

Bowen's writing was not confined to short fiction; in addition to her more than eighty short stories, she was the author of ten novels—the most popular of which are *The Death of the Heart* (1938) and *The Heat of the Day* (1949)—as well as a great deal of newspaper and magazine writing and a history of her ancestral home, *Bowen's Court* (1964), published the year after it was demolished.

Mysterious Kôr

Full moonlight drenched the city and searched it; there was not a niche left to stand in. The effect was remorseless: London looked like the moon's capital—shallow, cratered, extinct. It was late, but not yet midnight; now the buses had stopped the polished roads and streets in this region sent for minutes together a ghostly unbroken reflection up. The soaring new flats and the crouching old shops and houses looked equally brittle under the moon, which blazed in windows that looked its way. The futility of the black-out[1] became laughable: from the sky, presumably, you could see

---

1. During the Blitz all lights were ordered concealed or extinguished at night so that enemy planes would have difficulty locating their targets.

every slate in the roofs, every whited kerb, every contour of the naked winter flowerbeds in the park; and the lake, with its shining twists and tree-darkened islands would be a landmark for miles, yes, miles, overhead.

However, the sky, in whose glassiness floated no clouds but only opaque balloons, remained glassy-silent. The Germans no longer came by the full moon. Something more immaterial seemed to threaten, and to be keeping people at home. This day between days, this extra tax, was perhaps more than senses and nerves could bear. People stayed indoors with a fervour that could be felt: the buildings strained with battened-down human life, but not a beam, not a voice, not a note from a radio escaped. Now and then under streets and buildings the earth rumbled: the Underground[2] sounded loudest at this time.

Outside the now gateless gates of the park, the road coming downhill from the north-west turned south and became a street, down whose perspective the traffic lights went through their unmeaning performance of changing colour. From the promontory of pavement outside the gates you saw at once up the road and down the street: from behind where you stood, between the gateposts, appeared the lesser strangeness of grass and water and trees. At this point, at this moment, three French soldiers, directed to a hostel[3] they could not find, stopped singing to listen derisively to the waterbirds wakened up by the moon. Next, two wardens coming off duty emerged from their post and crossed the road diagonally, each with an elbow cupped inside a slung-on tin hat. The wardens turned their faces, mauve in the moonlight, towards the Frenchmen with no expression at all. The two sets of steps died in opposite directions, and, the birds subsiding, nothing was heard or seen until, a little way down the street, a trickle of people came out of the Underground, around the anti-panic brick wall. These all disappeared quickly, in an abashed way, or as though dissolved in the street by some white acid, but for a girl and a soldier who, by their way of walking, seemed to have no destination but each other and to be not quite certain even of that. Blotted into one shadow he tall, she little, these two proceeded towards the park. They looked in, but did not go in; they stood there debating without speaking. Then, as though a command from the street behind them had been received by their synchronized bodies, they faced round to look back the way they had come.

His look up the height of a building made his head drop back, and she saw his eyeballs glitter. She slid her hand from his sleeve, stepped to the edge of the pavement and said: "Mysterious Kôr."

"What is?" he said, not quite collecting himself.

"This is—

> *Mysterious Kôr thy walls forsaken stand,*
> *Thy lonely towers beneath a lonely moon—*

—this is Kôr."[4]

"Why," he said, "it's years since I've thought of that."

She said: "I think of it all the time—

> *Not in the waste beyond the swamps and sand,*
> *The fever-haunted forest and lagoon,*
> *Mysterious Kôr thy walls————*

2. The London subway system.
3. An inn.
4. Kôr is the lost city of H. Rider Haggard's 1887 adventure novel *She*. The central character Ayesha, whose name means *She-who-must-be-obeyed*, is incessantly

described as "mysterious." One of Ayesha's statements—"My empire is of the imagination"—may have had an ironic resonance for Bowen, writing about the condition of England during World War II.

—a completely forsaken city, as high as cliffs and as white as bones, with no histo-ry————"

"But something must once have happened: why had it been forsaken?"

"How could anyone tell you when there's nobody there?"

"Nobody there since how long?"

"Thousands of years."

"In that case, it would have fallen down."

"No, not Kôr," she said with immediate authority. "Kôr's altogether different; it's very strong; there is not a crack in it anywhere for a weed to grow in; the corners of stones and the monuments might have been cut yesterday, and the stairs and arches are built to support themselves."

"You know all about it," he said, looking at her.

"I know, I know all about it."

"What, since you read that book?"

"Oh, I didn't get much from that; I just got the name. I knew that must be the right name; it's like a cry."

"Most like the cry of a crow to me." He reflected, then said: "But the poem begins with 'Not'—'*Not in the waste beyond the swamps and sand*—' And it goes on, as I remember, to prove Kôr's not really anywhere. When even a poem says there's no such place—"

"What it tries to say doesn't matter: I see what it makes me see. Anyhow, that was written some time ago, at that time when they thought they had got every-thing taped, because the whole world had been explored, even the middle of Africa. Every thing and place had been found and marked on some map; so what wasn't marked on any map couldn't be there at all. So *they* thought: that was why he wrote the poem. '*The world is disenchanted*,' it goes on. That was what set me off hating civilization."

"Well, cheer up," he said; "there isn't much of it left."

"Oh, yes, I cheered up some time ago. This war shows we've by no means come to the end. If you can blow whole places out of existence, you can blow whole places into it. I don't see why not. They say we can't say what's come out since the bombing started. By the time we've come to the end, Kôr may be the one city left: the abiding city. I should laugh."

"No, you wouldn't," he said sharply. "*You* wouldn't—at least, I hope not. I hope you don't know what you're saying—does the moon make you funny?"

"Don't be cross about Kôr; please don't, Arthur," she said.

"I thought girls thought about people."

"What, these days?" she said. "Think about people? How can anyone think about people if they've got any heart? I don't know how other girls manage: I always think about Kôr."

"Not about me?" he said. When she did not at once answer, he turned her hand over, in anguish, inside his grasp. "Because I'm not there when you want me—is that my fault?"

"But to think about Kôr *is* to think about you and me."

"In that dead place?"

"No, ours—we'd be alone here."

Tightening his thumb on her palm while he thought this over, he looked behind them, around them, above them—even up at the sky. He said finally: "But we're alone here."

"That was why I said 'Mysterious Kôr.'"

"What, you mean we're there now, that here's there, that now's then? . . . I don't mind," he added, letting out as a laugh the sigh he had been holding in for some time. "You ought to know the place, and for all I could tell you we might be anywhere: I often do have it, this funny feeling, the first minute or two when I've come up out of the Underground. Well, well: join the Army and see the world." He nodded towards the perspective of traffic lights and said, a shade craftily: "What are those, then?"

Having caught the quickest possible breath, she replied: "Inexhaustible gases; they bored through to them and lit them as they came up; by changing colour they show the changing of minutes; in Kôr there is no sort of other time."

"You've got the moon, though: that can't help making months."

"Oh, and the sun, of course; but those two could do what they liked; we should not have to calculate when they'd come or go.'

"We might not have to," he said, 'but I bet I should."

"I should not mind what you did, so long as you never said, 'What next?'"

"I don't know about 'next,' but I do know what we'd do first."

"What, Arthur?"

"Populate Kôr."

She said: "I suppose it would be all right if our children were to marry each other?"

But her voice faded out; she had been reminded that they were homeless on this his first night of leave. They were, that was to say, in London without any hope of any place of their own. Pepita shared a two-roomed flatlet with a girl friend, in a by-street off the Regent's Park Road, and towards this they must make their halfhearted way. Arthur was to have the sitting-room divan, usually occupied by Pepita, while she herself had half of her girl friend's bed. There was really no room for a third, and least of all for a man, in those small rooms packed with furniture and the two girls' belongings: Pepita tried to be grateful for her friend Callie's forbearance—but how could she be, when it had not occurred to Callie that she would do better to be away tonight? She was more slow-witted than narrow-minded—but Pepita felt she owed a kind of ruin to her. Callie, not yet known to be home later than ten, would be now waiting up, in her house-coat, to welcome Arthur. That would mean three-sided chat, drinking cocoa, then turning in: that would be that, and that would be all. That was London, this war—they were lucky to have a roof—London, full enough before the Americans came. Not a place: they would even grudge you sharing a grave—that was what even married couples complained. Whereas in Kôr . . .

In Kôr . . . Like glass, the illusion shattered: a car hummed like a hornet towards them, veered, showed its scarlet tail-light, streaked away up the road. A woman edged round a front door and along the area railings timidly called her cat; meanwhile a clock near, then another set further back in the dazzling distance, set about striking midnight. Pepita, feeling Arthur release her arm with an abruptness that was the inverse of passion, shivered; whereat he asked brusquely: "Cold? Well, which way?—we'd better be getting on."

Callie was no longer waiting up. Hours ago she had set out the three cups and saucers, the tins of cocoa and household milk and, on the gas-ring, brought the kettle to just short of the boil. She had turned open Arthur's bed, the living-room divan, in the neat inviting way she had learnt at home—then, with a modest impulse, replaced the cover. She had, as Pepita foresaw, been wearing her cretonne[5] housecoat, the nearest thing to a hostess gown that she had; she had already brushed her hair for the

5. Cotton fabric with a printed pattern.

night, rebraided it, bound the braids in a coronet round her head. Both lights and the wireless[6] had been on, to make the room both look and sound gay: all alone, she had come to that peak moment at which company should arrive—but so seldom does. From then on she felt welcome beginning to wither in her, a flower of the heart that had bloomed too early. There she had sat like an image, facing the three cold cups, on the edge of the bed to be occupied by an unknown man.

Callie's innocence and her still unsought-out state had brought her to take a proprietary pride in Arthur; this was all the stronger, perhaps, because they had not yet met. Sharing the flat with Pepita, this last year, she had been content with reflecting the heat of love. It was not, surprisingly, that Pepita seemed very happy—there were times when she was palpably on the rack, and this was not what Callie could understand. "Surely you owe it to Arthur," she would then say, "to keep cheerful? So long as you love each other———" Callie's calm brow glowed—one might say that it glowed in place of her friend's; she became the guardian of that ideality which for Pepita was constantly lost to view. It was true, with the sudden prospect of Arthur's leave, things had come nearer to earth: he became a proposition, and she would have been as glad if he could have slept somewhere else. Physically shy, a brotherless virgin, Callie shrank from sharing this flat with a young man. In this flat you could hear everything: what was once a three-windowed Victorian drawing-room had been partitioned, by very thin walls, into kitchenette, living-room, Callie's bedroom. The living-room was in the centre; the two others open off it. What was once the conservatory, half a flight down, was now converted into a draughty bathroom, shared with somebody else on the girl's floor. The flat, for these days, was cheap—even so, it was Callie, earning more than Pepita, who paid the greater part of the rent: it thus became up to her, more or less, to express good will as to Arthur's making a third. "Why, it will be lovely to have him here," Callie said. Pepita accepted the good will without much grace—but then, had she ever much grace to spare?—she was as restlessly secretive, as self-centred, as a little half-grown black cat. Next came a puzzling moment: Pepita seemed to be hinting that Callie should fix herself up somewhere else. "But where would I go?" Callie marvelled when this was at last borne in on her. "You know what London's like now. And, anyway"—here she laughed, but hers was a forehead that coloured as easily as it glowed—"it wouldn't be proper, would it, me going off and leaving just you and Arthur; I don't know what your mother would say to me. No, we may be a little squashed, but we'll make things ever so homey. I shall not mind playing gooseberry, really, dear."

But the hominess by now was evaporating, as Pepita and Arthur still and still did not come. At half-past ten, in obedience to the rule of the house, Callie was obliged to turn off the wireless, whereupon silence out of the stepless street began seeping into the slighted room. Callie recollected the fuel target and turned off her dear little table lamp, gaily painted with spots to make it look like a toadstool, thereby leaving only the hanging light. She laid her hand on the kettle, to find it gone cold again and sigh for the wasted gas if not for her wasted thought. Where are they? Cold crept up her out of the kettle; she went to bed.

Callie's bed lay along the wall under the window: she did not like sleeping so close up under glass, but the clearance that must be left for the opening of door and cupboards made this the only possible place. Now she got in and lay rigidly on the

6. Radio.

bed's inner side, under the hanging hems of the window curtains, training her limbs not to stray to what would be Pepita's half. This sharing of her bed with another body would not be the least of her sacrifice to the lovers' love; tonight would be the first night—or at least, since she was an infant—that Callie had slept with anyone. Child of a sheltered middle-class household, she had kept physical distances all her life. Already repugnance and shyness ran through her limbs; she was preyed upon by some more obscure trouble than the expectation that she might not sleep. As to *that*, Pepita was restless; her tossings on the divan, her broken-off exclamations and blurred pleas had been to be heard, most nights, through the dividing wall.

Callie knew, as though from a vision, that Arthur would sleep soundly, with assurance and majesty. Did they not all say, too, that a soldier sleeps like a log? With awe she pictured, asleep, the face that she had not yet, awake, seen— Arthur's man's eyelids, cheekbones and set mouth turned up to the darkened ceiling. Wanting to savour darkness herself, Callie reached out and put off her bedside lamp.

At once she knew that something was happening—outdoors, in the street, the whole of London, the world. An advance, an extraordinary movement was silently taking place; blue-white beams overflowed from it, silting, dropping round the edges of the muffling black-out curtains. When, starting up, she knocked a fold of the curtain, a beam like a mouse ran across her bed. A searchlight, the most powerful of all time, might have been turned full and steady upon her defended window; finding flaws in the blackout stuff, it made veins and stars. Once gained by this idea of pressure she could not lie down again; she sat tautly, drawn-up knees touching her breasts, and asked herself if there were anything she should do. She parted the curtains, opened them slowly wider, looked out—and was face to face with the moon.

Below the moon, the houses opposite her window blazed back in transparent shadow; and something—was it a coin or a ring?—glittered half-way across the chalk-white street. Light marched in past her face, and she turned to see where it went: out stood the curves and garlands of the great white marble Victorian mantelpiece of that lost drawing-room; out stood, in the photographs turned her way, the thoughts with which her parents had faced the camera, and the humble puzzlement of her two dogs at home. Of silver brocade, just faintly purpled with roses, became her housecoat hanging over the chair. And the moon did more: it exonerated and beautified the lateness of the lovers' return. No wonder, she said herself, no wonder—if this was the world they walked in, if this was whom they were with. Having drunk in the white explanation, Callie lay down again. Her half of the bed was in shadow, but she allowed one hand to lie, blanched, in what would be Pepita's place. She lay and looked at the hand until it was no longer her own.

Callie woke to the sound of Pepita's key in the latch. But no voices? What had happened? Then she heard Arthur's step. She heard his unslung equipment dropped with a weary, dull sound, and the plonk of his tin hat on a wooden chair. "Sssh-sssh!" Pepita exclaimed, "she *might* be asleep!"

Then at last Arthur's voice: "But I thought you said—"

"I'm not asleep; I'm just coming!" Callie called out with rapture, leaping out from her form in shadow into the moonlight, zipping on her enchanted house-coat over her nightdress, kicking her shoes on, and pinning in place, with a trembling firmness, her plaits in their coronet round her head. Between these movements of hers she heard not another sound. Had she only dreamed they were there? Her heart beat: she stepped through the living-room, shutting her door behind her.

Pepita and Arthur stood on the other side of the table; they gave the impression of being lined up. Their faces, at different levels—for Pepita's rough, dark head came only an inch above Arthur's khaki shoulder—were alike in abstention from any kind of expression; as though, spiritually, they both still refused to be here. Their features looked faint, weathered—was this the work of the moon? Pepita said at once: "I suppose we are very late?"

"I don't wonder," Callie said, "on this lovely night."

Arthur had not raised his eyes; he was looking at the three cups. Pepita now suddenly jogged his elbow, saying, "Arthur, wake up; say something; this is Callie—well, Callie, this is Arthur, of course."

"Why, yes of course this is Arthur," returned Callie, whose candid eyes since she entered had not left Arthur's face. Perceiving that Arthur did not know what to do, she advanced round the table to shake hands with him. He looked up, she looked down, for the first time: she rather beheld than felt his red-brown grip on what still seemed her glove of moonlight. "Welcome, Arthur," she said. "I'm so glad to meet you at last. I hope you will be comfortable in the flat."

"It's been kind of you," he said after consideration.

"Please do not feel that," said Callie. "This is Pepita's home, too, and we both hope—don't we, Pepita?—that you'll regard it as yours. Please feel free to do just as you like. I am sorry it is so small."

"Oh, I don't know," Arthur said, as though hypnotized; "it seems a nice little place."

Pepita, meanwhile, glowered and turned away.

Arthur continued to wonder, though he had once been told, how these two unalike girls had come to set up together—Pepita so small, except for her too-big head, compact of childish brusqueness and of unchildish passion, and Callie, so sedate, waxy and tall—an unlit candle. Yes, she was like one of those candles on sale outside a church; there could be something votive even in her demeanour. She was unconscious that her good manners, those of an old fashioned country doctor's daughter, were putting the other two at a disadvantage. He found himself touched by the grave good faith with which Callie was wearing that tartish house-coat, above which her face kept the glaze of sleep; and, as she knelt to relight the gas-ring under the kettle, he marked the strong, delicate arch of one bare foot, disappearing into the arty green shoe. Pepita was now too near him ever again to be seen as he now saw Callie—in a sense, he never *had* seen Pepita for the first time: she had not been, and still sometimes was not, his type. No, he had not thought of her twice; he had not remembered her until he began to remember her with passion. You might say he had not seen Pepita coming: their love had been a collision in the dark.

Callie, determined to get this over, knelt back and said: "Would Arthur like to wash his hands?" When they had heard him stumble down the half-flight of stairs, she said to Pepita: "Yes, I was so glad you had the moon."

"Why?" said Pepita. She added: "There was too much of it."

"You're tired. Arthur looks tired, too."

"How would you know? He's used to marching about. But it's all this having no place to go."

"But, Pepita, you——"

But at this point Arthur came back: from the door he noticed the wireless, and went direct to it. "Nothing much on now, I suppose?" he doubtfully said.

"No; you see it's past midnight; we're off the air. And, anyway, in this house they don't like the wireless late. By the same token," went on Callie, friendly smiling, "I'm afraid I must ask you, Arthur, to take your boots off, unless, of course, you mean to stay sitting down. The people below us——"

Pepita flung off, saying something under her breath, but Arthur, remarking, "No, I don't mind," both sat down and began to take off his boots. Pausing, glancing to left and right at the divan's fresh cotton spread, he said: "It's all right is it, for me to sit on this?"

"That's my bed," said Pepita. "You are to sleep in it."

Callie then made the cocoa, after which they turned in. Preliminary trips to the bathroom having been worked out, Callie was first to retire, shutting the door behind her so that Pepita and Arthur might kiss each other good night. When Pepita joined her, it was without knocking: Pepita stood still in the moon and began to tug off her clothes. Glancing with hate at the bed, she asked: "Which side?"

"I expected you'd like the outside."

"What are you standing about for?"

"I don't really know: as I'm inside I'd better get in first."

"Then why not get in?"

When they had settled rigidly, side by side, Callie asked: "Do you think Arthur's got all he wants?"

Pepita jerked her head up. "We can't sleep in all this moon."

"Why, you don't believe the moon does things, actually?"

"Well, it couldn't hope to make some of us *much* more screwy."

Callie closed the curtains, then said: "What do you mean? And—didn't you hear?—I asked if Arthur's got all he wants."

"That's what I meant—have you got a screw loose, really?"

"Pepita, I won't stay here if you're going to be like this."

"In that case, you had better go in with Arthur."

"What about me?" Arthur loudly said through the wall. "I can hear practically all you girls are saying."

They were both startled—rather that than abashed. Arthur, alone in there, had thrown off the ligatures[7] of his social manner: his voice held the whole authority of his sex—he was impatient, sleepy, and he belonged to no one.

"Sorry," the girls said in unison. Then Pepita laughed soundlessly, making their bed shake, till to stop herself she bit the back of her hand, and this movement made her elbow strike Callie's cheek. "Sorry," she had to whisper. No answer: Pepita fingered her elbow and found, yes, it was quite true, it was wet. "Look, shut up crying, Callie: what have I done?"

Callie rolled right round, in order to press her forehead closely under the window, into the curtains, against the wall. Her weeping continued to be soundless: now and then, unable to reach her handkerchief, she staunched her eyes with a curtain, disturbing slivers of moon. Pepita gave up marvelling, and soon slept: at least there is something in being dog-tired.

A clock struck four as Callie woke up again—but something else had made her open her swollen eyelids. Arthur, stumbling about on his padded feet, could be heard next door attempting to make no noise. Inevitably, he bumped the edge of the table. Callie sat up: by her side Pepita lay like a mummy rolled half over, in forbidding, tenacious sleep. Arthur groaned. Callie caught a breath, climbed lightly over Pepita, felt for her torch[8] on the mantelpiece, stopped to listen again. Arthur groaned again:

---

7. Restrictions.   8. Flashlight.

Callie, with movements soundless as they were certain, opened the door and slipped through to the living-room. "What's the matter?" she whispered. "Are you ill?"

"No; I just got a cigarette. Did I wake you up?"

"But you groaned."

"I'm sorry; I'd no idea."

"But do you often?"

"I've no idea, really, I tell you," Arthur repeated. The air of the room was dense with his presence, overhung by tobacco. He must be sitting on the edge of his bed, wrapped up in his overcoat—she could smell the coat, and each time he pulled on the cigarette his features appeared down there, in the fleeting, dull reddish glow. "Where are you?" he said. "Show a light."

Her nervous touch on her torch, like a reflex to what he said, made it flicker up for a second. "I am just by the door; Pepita's asleep; I'd better go back to bed."

"Listen. Do you two get on each other's nerves?"

"Not till tonight," said Callie, watching the uncertain swoops of the cigarette as he reached across to the ashtray on the edge of the table. Shifting her bare feet patiently, she added: "You don't see us as we usually are."

"She's a girl who shows things in funny ways—I expect she feels bad at our putting you out like this—I know I do. But then we'd got no choice, had we?"

"It is really I who am putting you out," said Callie.

"Well, that can't be helped either, can it? You had the right to stay in your own place. If there'd been more time, we might have gone to the country, though I still don't see where we'd have gone there. It's one harder when you're not married, unless you've got the money. Smoke?"

"No, thank you. Well, if you're all right, I'll go back to bed."

"I'm glad she's asleep—funny the way she sleeps, isn't it? You can't help wondering where she is. You haven't got a boy, have you, just at present?"

"No. I've never had one."

"I'm not sure in one way that you're not better off. I can see there's not so much in it for a girl these days. It makes me feel cruel the way I unsettle her: I don't know how much it's me myself or how much it's something the matter that I can't help. How are any of us to know how things could have been? They forget war's not just only war; it's years out of people's lives that they've never had before and won't have again. Do you think she's fanciful?"

"Who, Pepita?"

"It's enough to make her—tonight was the pay-off. We couldn't get near any movie or any place for sitting; you had to fight into the bars, and she hates the staring in bars, and with all that milling about, every street we went, they kept on knocking her even off my arm. So then we took the tube to that park down there, but the place was as bad as daylight, let alone it was cold. We hadn't the nerve—well, that's nothing to do with you."

"I don't mind."

"Or else you don't understand. So we began to play—we were off in Kôr."

"Core of what?"

"Mysterious Kôr—ghost city."

"Where?"

"You may ask. But I could have sworn she saw it, and from the way she saw it I saw it, too. A game's a game, but what's a hallucination? You begin by laughing, then it gets in you and you can't laugh it off. I tell you, I woke up just now not knowing where I'd been; and I had to get up and feel round this table before I even knew where I was. It wasn't till then that I thought of a cigarette. Now I see why she sleeps like that, if that's where she goes."

"But she is just as often restless; I often hear her."

"Then she doesn't always make it. Perhaps it takes me, in some way—Well, I can't see any harm: when two people have got no place, why not want Kôr, as a start? There are no restrictions on wanting, at any rate."

"But, oh, Arthur, can't wanting want what's human?"

He yawned. "To be human's to be at a dead loss." Stopping yawning, he ground out his cigarette: the china tray skidded at the edge of the table. "Bring that light here a moment—that is, will you? I think I've messed ash all over these sheets of hers."

Callie advanced with the torch alight, but at arm's length: now and then her thumb made the beam wobble. She watched the lit-up inside of Arthur's hand as he brushed the sheet; and once he looked up to see her white-nightgowned figure curving above and away from him, behind the arc of light. "What's that swinging?"

"One of my plaits of hair. Shall I open the window wider?"

"What, to let the smoke out? Go on. And how's your moon?"

"Mine?" Marvelling over this, as the first sign that Arthur remembered that she was Callie, she uncovered the window, pushed up the sash, then after a minute said: "Not so strong."

Indeed, the moon's power over London and the imagination had now declined. The siege of light had relaxed; the search was over; the street had a look of survival and no more. Whatever had glittered there, coin or ring, was now invisible or had gone. To Callie it seemed likely that there would never be such a moon again; and on the whole she felt this was for the best. Feeling air reach in like a tired arm round her body, she dropped the curtains against it and returned to her own room.

Back by her bed, she listened; Pepita's breathing still had the regular sound of sleep. At the other side of the wall the divan creaked as Arthur stretched himself out again. Having felt ahead of her lightly, to make sure her half was empty, Callie climbed over Pepita and got in. A certain amount of warmth had travelled between the sheets from Pepita's flank, and in this Callie extended her sword-cold body: she tried to compose her limbs; even they quivered after Arthur's words in the dark, words to the dark. The loss of her own mysterious expectation, of her love for love, was a small thing beside the war's total of unlived lives. Suddenly Pepita flung out one hand: its back knocked Callie lightly across the face.

Pepita had now turned over and lay with her face up. The hand that had struck Callie must have lain over the other, which grasped the pyjama collar. Her eyes, in the dark, might have been either shut or open, but nothing made her frown more or less steadily: it became certain, after another moment, that Pepita's act of justice had been unconscious. She still lay, as she had lain, in an avid dream, of which Arthur had been the source, of which Arthur was not the end. With him she looked this way, that way, down the wide, void, pure streets, between statues, pillars and shadows, through archways and colonnades. With him she went up the stairs down which nothing but moon came; with him trod the ermine[9] dust of the endless halls, stood on terraces, mounted the extreme tower, looked down on the statued squares, the wide, void, pure streets. He was the password, but not the answer: it was to Kôr's finality that she turned.

9. White.

◄━━ ⚜ ━━►

Salman Rushdie
b. 1947

Born in Bombay on the day India achieved independence from Britain, Rushdie was raised in Pakistan after the partition of the subcontinent. He then settled in England, where he soon became one of the most noted writers about the aftermath of empires. His magisterial novel *Midnight's Children* was awarded not only the prestigious Booker McConnell Prize for the best British novel of 1981 but later the "Booker of Bookers," as the best novel in the first twenty-five years of the prize's history. Like Saleem Sinai, the protagonist and narrator of *Midnight's Children*, Rushdie delights in telling its story, in a mixture of history, fantasy, fable, and sheer stylistic exuberance that has come to be known (through the works of Latin American writers like Gabriel Garcia Marquez) as magic realism. At once an Indian and a British writer, Rushdie enjoys a double status as both insider and outsider that allows him to comment both on the history of his native land and on the contemporary politics of Britain with savage and comic incisiveness.

Unfortunately, most who do not know Rushdie's writing well know his name from the publicity surrounding his 1988 novel *The Satanic Verses;* the novel was judged to be an affront to Islam, and on Valentine's Day in 1989 the late Iranian leader Ayatollah Ruhollah Khomeini issued a *fatwa*, or death threat, against both Rushdie and his publisher, carrying a multimillion dollar bounty. As a result, Rushdie was forced to go underground; for nearly ten years he moved from place to place protected by full-time bodyguards, making but unable to receive phone calls, and generally staying out of the public eye and out of harm's way. Under Islamic law, a *fatwa* can be lifted only by the man who imposed it; since Khomeini died with the *fatwa* still in effect, it technically will remain in effect until Rushdie's death, although subsequent Iranian leaders have suggested that the edict would not be enforced. Rushdie has, very recently, begun to make selective, unadvertised public appearances.

It is both appalling and intriguing that the written word still has this much power. The book that followed *The Satanic Verses* was *Haroun and the Sea of Stories*, a tale often (mistakenly) labeled "juvenile." It is in fact an allegory of the power of language—its power to liberate, and the desperate attempts of what political philosopher Louis Althusser calls the "ideological state apparatus" to silence this free, anarchic speech. The story did indeed begin as a bath-time entertainment for Rushdie's son Zafar; but as the affair over the *Satanic Verses* grew and festered, the story matured into a parable of the responsibility of the artist to speak from the heart and conscience, regardless of the political consequences. Similarly, Rushdie's haunting story *Chekov and Zulu* mixes reality and fantasy, East and West, popular culture and high literary art.

Chekov and Zulu
1

On 4th November, 1984, Zulu disappeared in Birmingham, and India House sent his old schoolfriend Chekov to Wembley[1] to see the wife.

"Adaabarz, Mrs Zulu. Permission to enter?"

"Of course come in, Dipty sahib, why such formality?"

"Sorry to disturb you on a Sunday, Mrs Zulu, but Zulu-tho hasn't been in touch this morning?"

"With me? Since when he contacts me on official trip? Why to hit a telephone call when he is probably enjoying?"

"Whoops, sore point, excuse *me*. Always been the foot-in-it blunderbuss type."

---

1. Birmingham is a city in West Midlands, central England; Wembley is a London suburb.

"At least sit, take tea-shee."

"Fixed the place up damn fine, Mrs Zulu, wah-wah.[2] Tasteful decor, in spades, I must say. So much cut-glass! That bounder Zulu must be getting too much pay, more than yours truly, clever dog."

"No, how is it possible? Acting Dipty's tankha[3] must be far in excess of Security Chief."

"No suspicion intended, ji.[4] Only to say what a bargain-hunter you must be."

"Some problem but there is, na?"

"Beg pardon?"

"Arré,[5] Jaisingh! Where have you been sleeping? Acting Dipty Sahib is thirsting for his tea. And biscuits and jalebis, can you not keep two things in your head? Jump, now, guest is waiting."

"Truly, Mrs Zulu, please go to no trouble."

"No trouble is there, Diptyji, only this chap has become lazy since coming from home. Days off, TV in room, even pay in pounds sterling, he expects all. So far we brought him but no gratitude, what to tell you, noth-*thing*."

"Ah, Jaisingh; why not? Excellent jalebi, Mrs Z. Thanking you."

Assembled on top of the television and on shelf units around it was the missing man's collection of *Star Trek* memorabilia: Captain Kirk and Spock dolls, spaceship models—a Klingon Bird of Prey, a Romulan vessel, a space station, and of course the Starship *Enterprise*. In pride of place were large figurines of two of the series's supporting cast.

"These old Doon School nicknames," Chekov exclaimed heartily. "They stay put like stuck records. Dumpy, Stumpy, Grumpy, Humpy. They take over from our names. As in our case our intrepid cosmonaut aliases."

"I don't like. This 'Mrs Zulu' I am landed with! It sounds like a blackie."

"Wear the name with pride, begum[6] sahib. We're old comrades-in-arms, your husband and I; since boyhood days, perhaps he was good enough to mention? Intrepid diplomauts. Our umpteen-year mission to explore new worlds and new civilisations. See there, our alter egos standing on your TV, the Asiatic-looking Russky and the Chink. Not the leaders, as you'll appreciate, but the ultimate professional servants. 'Course laid in!' 'Hailing frequencies open!' 'Warp factor three!' What would that strutting Captain have been without his top-level staffers? Likewise with the good ship Hindustan.[7] We are servants also, you see, just like your fierce Jaisingh here. Never more important than in a moment like the present sad crisis, when an even keel must be maintained, jalebis must be served and tea poured, no matter what. We do not lead, but we enable. Without us, no course can be laid, no hailing frequency opened. No factors can be warped."

"Is he in difficulties, then, your Zulu? As if it wasn't bad enough, this terrible time."

On the wall behind the TV was a framed photograph of Indira Gandhi,[8] with a garland hung around it. She had been dead since Wednesday. Pictures of her cremation had been on the TV for hours. The flower-petals, the garish, unbearable flames.

"Hard to believe it. Indiraji! Words fail one. She was our mother. Hai, hai! Cut down in her prime."

2. Excellent.
3. Wages.
4. Term of respect added to ends of sentences or words.
5. Exclamation of surprise.

6. High-ranking muslim woman.
7. Persian name for India.
8. Indian prime minister between 1966–1977 and 1980–1984; assassinated in 1984.

"And on radio-TV, such-such stories are coming about Delhi goings-on. So many killings, Dipty Sahib. So many of our decent Sikh[9] people done to death, as if all were guilty for the crimes of one-two badmash guards."

"The Sikh community has always been thought loyal to the nation," Chekov reflected. "Backbone of the Army, to say nothing of the Delhi taxi service. Super-citizens, one might say, seemingly wedded to the national idea. But such ideas are being questioned now, you must admit; there are those who would point to the comb, bangle, dagger et cetera as signs of the enemy within."

"Who would dare say such a thing about us? Such an evil thing."

"I know. I know. But you take Zulu. The ticklish thing is, he's not on any official business that we know of. He's dropped off the map, begum sahib. AWOL[1] ever since the assassination. No contact for two days plus."

"O God."

"There is a view forming back at HQ that he may have been associated with the gang. Who have in all probability long-established links with the community over here."

"O God."

"Naturally I am fighting strenuously against the proponents of this view. But his absence is damning, you must see. We have no fear of these tinpot Khalistan wallahs.[2] But they have a ruthless streak. And with Zulu's inside knowledge and security background . . . They have threatened further attacks, as you know. As you must know. As some would say you must know all too well."

"O God."

"It is possible," Chekov said, eating his jalebi, "that Zulu has boldly gone where no Indian diplonaut has gone before."

The wife wept. "Even the stupid name you could never get right. It was with S. 'Sulu.' So-so many episodes I have been made to see, you think I don't know? Kirk Spock McCoy Scott Uhura Chekov *Sulu*."

"But Zulu is a better name for what some might allege to be a wild man," Chekov said. "For a suspected savage. For a putative traitor. Thank you for excellent tea."

2

In August, Zulu, a shy, burly giant, had met Chekov off the plane from Delhi. Chekov at thirty-three was a small, slim, dapper man in grey flannels, stiff-collared shirt and a double-breasted navy blue blazer with brass buttons. He had bat's-wing eyebrows and a prominent and pugnacious jaw, so that his cultivated tones and habitual soft-spokenness came as something of a surprise, disarming those who had been led by the eyebrows and chin to expect an altogether more aggressive personality. He was a high flyer, with one small embassy already notched up. The Acting Number Two job in London, while strictly temporary, was his latest plum.

"What-ho, Zools! Years, yaar,[3] years," Chekov said, thumping his palm into the other man's chest. "So," he added, "I see you've become a hairy fairy." The young Zulu had been a modern Sikh in the matter of hair—sporting a fine moustache at eighteen, but beardless, with a haircut instead of long tresses wound tightly under a turban. Now, however, he had reverted to tradition.

9. Community in the Punjab whose religion attempts to combine Hindusim and Islam.
1. Absent without leave.

2. Sikh military who call for a separate Sikh state called Khalistan; *wallah* means boy or man.
3. Friend, buddy.

"Hullo, ji," Zulu greeted him cautiously. "So then is it OK to utilise the old modes of address?"

"Utilise away! Wouldn't hear of anything else," Chekov said, handing Zulu his bags and baggage tags. "Spirit of the *Enterprise* and all that jazz."

In his public life the most urbane of men, Chekov when letting his hair down in private enjoyed getting interculturally hot under the collar. Soon after his taking up his new post he sat with Zulu one lunchtime on a bench in Embankment Gardens and jerked his head in the direction of various passers-by.

"Crooks," he said, *sotto voce* [softly].

"Where?" shouted Zulu, leaping athletically to his feet. "Should I pursue?"

Heads turned. Chekov grabbed the hem of Zulu's jacket and pulled him back on to the bench. "Don't be such a hero," he admonished fondly. "I meant all of them, generally; thieves, every last one. God, I love London! Theatre, ballet, opera, restaurants! The Pavilion at Lord's on the Saturday of the Test Match![4] The royal ducks on the royal pond in royal St. James's Park! Decent tailors, a decent mixed grill when you want it, decent magazines to read! I see the remnants of greatness and I don't mind telling you I am impressed. The Athenaeum, Buck House, the lions in Trafalgar Square. *Damn* impressive. I went to a meeting with the junior Minister at the F. & C.O. and realised I was in the old India Office. All that John Company black teak, those tuskers rampant on the old bookcases. Gave me quite a turn. I applaud them for their success: hurrah! But then I look at my own home, and I see that it has been plundered by burglars. I can't deny there is a residue of distress."

"I am sorry to hear of your loss," Zulu said, knitting his brows. "But surely the culpables are not in the vicinity."

"Zulu, Zulu, a figure of speech, my simpleton warrior prince. Their museums are full of our treasures, I meant. Their fortunes and cities, built on the loot they took. So on, so forth. One forgives, of course; that is our national nature. One need not forget."

Zulu pointed at a tramp, sleeping on the next bench in a ragged hat and coat. "Did he steal from us, too?" he asked.

"Never forget," said Chekov, wagging a finger, "that the British working class collaborated for its own gain in the colonial project. Manchester cotton workers, for instance, supported the destruction of our cotton industry. As diplomats we must never draw attention to such facts; but facts, nevertheless, they remain."

"But a beggarman is not in the working class," objected Zulu, reasonably. "Surely this fellow at least is not our oppressor."

"Zulu," Chekov said in exasperation, "don't be so bleddy difficult."

Chekov and Zulu went boating on the Serpentine, and Chekov got back on his hobby-horse. "They have stolen us," he said, reclining boatered and champagned on striped cushions while mighty Zulu rowed. "And now we are stealing ourselves back. It is an Elgin marbles[5] situation."

"You should be more content," said Zulu, shipping oars and gulping cola. "You should be less hungry, less cross. See how much you have! It is enough. Sit back and

4. A group of cricket games played between international all-star teams.
5. A group of sculptures removed from the Acropolis in Athens by Lord Elgin in 1801–1803 and purchased by the British Museum in 1816. Recent opinion polls have suggested that over 90 percent of the British public support the return of the marbles to Greece, though a 1996 resolution in the Parliament was tabled.

enjoy. I have less, and it suffices for me. The sun is shining. The colonial period is a closed book."

"If you don't want that sandwich, hand it over," said Chekov. "With my natural radicalism I should not have been a diplomat. I should have been a terrorist."

"But then we would have been enemies, on opposite sides," protested Zulu, and suddenly there were real tears in his eyes. "Do you care nothing for our friendship? For my responsibilities in life?"

Chekov was abashed. "Quite right, Zools old boy. Too bleddy true. You can't imagine how delighted I was when I learned we would be able to join forces like this in London. Nothing like the friendships of one's boyhood, eh? Nothing in the world can take their place. Now listen, you great lummox, no more of that long face. I won't permit it. Great big chap like you shouldn't look like he's about to blub. Blood brothers, old friend, what do you say? All for one and one for all."

"Blood brothers," said Zulu, smiling a shy smile.

"Onward, then," nodded Chekov, settling back on his cushions. "Impulse power only."

The day Mrs Gandhi was murdered by her Sikh bodyguards, Zulu and Chekov played squash in a private court in St John's Wood. In the locker-room after showering, prematurely-greying Chekov still panted heavily with a towel round his softening waist, reluctant to expose his exhaustion-shrivelled purple penis to view; Zulu stood proudly naked, thick-cocked, tossing his fine head of long black hair, caressing and combing it with womanly sensuality, and at last twisting it swiftly into a knot.

"Too good, Zulu yaar. Fataakh! Fataakh! What shots! Too bleddy good for me."

"You desk-pilots, ji. You lose your edge. Once you were ready for anything."

"Yeah, yeah, I'm over the hill. But you were only one year junior."

"I have led a purer life, ji—action, not words."

"You understand we will have to blacken your name," Chekov said softly.

Zulu turned slowly in Charles Atlas pose in front of a full-length mirror.

"It has to look like a maverick stunt. If anything goes wrong, deniability is essential. Even your wife must not suspect the truth."

Spreading his arms and legs, Zulu made his body a giant X, stretching himself to the limit. Then he came to attention. Chekov sounded a little frayed.

"Zools? What do you say?"

"Is the transporter ready?"

"Come on, yaar, don't arse around."

"Respectfully, Mister Chekov, sir, it's my arse. Now then: is the transporter ready?"

"Transporter ready. Aye."

"Then, energise."

Chekov's memorandum, classified top-secret, eyes-only, and addressed to 'JTK' (James T. Kirk):

> My strong recommendation is that Operation Startrek be aborted. To send a Federation employee of Klingon origin unarmed into a Klingon cell to spy is the crudest form of loyalty test. The operative in question has never shown ideological deviation of any sort and deserves better, even in the present climate of mayhem, hysteria and fear. If he fails to persuade the Klingons of his bona fides [good faith] he can expect to be treated with extreme prejudice. These are not hostage takers.

The entire undertaking is misconceived. The locally settled Klingon population is not the central problem. Even should we succeed, such intelligence as can be gleaned about more important principals back home will no doubt be of dubious accuracy and limited value. We should advise Star Fleet Headquarters to engage urgently with the grievances and aspirations of the Klingon people. Unless these are dealt with fair and square there cannot be a lasting peace.

The reply from JTK:

Your closeness to the relevant individual excuses what is otherwise an explosively communalist document. It is not for you to define the national interest nor to determine what undercover operations are to be undertaken. It is for you to enable such operations to occur and to provide back-up as and when required to do so. As a personal favour to you and in the name of my long friendship with your eminent Papaji I have destroyed your last without keeping a copy and suggest you do the same. Also destroy this.

Chekov asked Zulu to drive him up to Stratford for a performance of *Coriolanus*.[6]

"How many kiddiwinks by now? Three?"

"Four," said Zulu. "All boys."

"By the grace of God. She must be a good woman."

"I have a full heart," said Zulu, with sudden feeling. "A full house, a full belly, a full bed."

"Lucky so and so," said Chekov. "Always were warm-blooded. I, by contrast, am not. Reptiles, certain species of dinosaur, and me. I am in the wife market, by the way, if you know any suitable candidates. Bachelordom being, after a certain point, an obstacle on the career path."

Zulu was driving strangely. In the slow lane of the motorway, as they approached an exit lane, he accelerated towards a hundred miles an hour. Once the exit was behind them, he slowed. Chekov noticed that he varied his speed and lane constantly. "Doesn't the old rattletrap have cruise control?" he asked. "Because, sport, this kind of performance would not do on the bridge of the flagship of the United Federation of Planets."

"Anti-surveillance," said Zulu. "Dry-cleaning." Chekov, alarmed, looked out of the back window.

"Have we been rumbled, then?"

"Nothing to worry about," grinned Zulu. "Better safe than sorry is all. Always anticipate the worst-case scenario."

Chekov settled back in his seat. "You liked toys and games," he said. Zulu had been a crack rifle shot, the school's champion wrestler, and an expert fencer. "Every Speech Day," Zulu said, "I would sit in the hall and clap, while you went up for all the work prizes. English Prize, History Prize, Latin Prize, Form Prize. Clap, clap, clap, term after term, year after year. But on Sports Day I got my cups. And now also I have my area of expertise."

"Quite a reputation you're building up, if what I hear is anything to go by."

There was a silence. England passed by at speed.

"Do you like Tolkien?" Zulu asked.

"I wouldn't have put you down as a big reader," said Chekov, startled. "No offence."

6. Shakespeare's bloodiest tragedy; its themes are civil unrest and revolt.

"J.R.R. Tolkien," said Zulu. "*The Lord of the Rings*."[7]

"Can't say I've read the gentleman. Heard of him, of course. Elves and pixies. Not your sort of thing at all, I'd have thought."

"It is about a war to the finish between Good and Evil," said Zulu intently. "And while this great war is being fought there is one part of the world, the Shire, in which nobody even knows it's going on. The hobbits who live there work and squabble and make merry and they have no fucking clue about the forces that threaten them, and those that save their tiny skins." His face was red with vehemence.

"Meaning me, I suppose," Chekov said.

"I am a soldier in that war," said Zulu. "If you sit in an office you don't have one small idea of what the real world is like. The world of action, ji. The world of deeds, of things that are done and maybe undone too. The world of life and death."

"Only in the worst case," Chekov demurred.

"Do I tell you how to apply your smooth-tongued musca-polish to people's behinds?" stormed Zulu. "Then do not tell me how to ply my trade."

Soldiers going into battle pump themselves up, Chekov knew. This chest-beating was to be expected, it must not be misunderstood. "When will you vamoose?" he quietly asked.

"Chekov ji, you won't see me go."

Stratford approached. "Did you know, ji," Zulu offered, "that the map of Tolkien's Middle-earth fits quite well over central England and Wales? Maybe all fairylands are right here, in our midst."

"You're a deep one, old Zools," said Chekov. "Full of revelations today."

Chekov had a few people over for dinner at his modern-style official residence in a private road in Hampstead: a Very Big Businessman he was wooing, journalists he liked, prominent India-lovers, noted Non-Resident Indians. The policy was business as usual. The dreadful event must not be seen to have derailed the ship of State: whose new captain, Chekov mused, was a former pilot himself. As if a Sulu, a Chekov had been suddenly promoted to the skipper's seat.

Damned difficult doing all this without a lady wife to act as hostess, he grumbled inwardly. The best golden plates with the many-headed lion at the centre, the finest crystal, the menu, the wines. Personnel had been seconded from India House to help him out, but it wasn't the same. The secrets of good evenings, like God, were in the details. Chekov meddled and fretted.

The evening went off well. Over brandy, Chekov even dared to introduce a blacker note. "England has always been a breeding ground for our revolutionists," he said. "What would Pandit Nehru[8] have been without Harrow?[9] Or Gandhiji without his formative experiences here? Even the Pakistan idea was dreamt up by young radicals at college in what we then were asked to think of as the Mother Country. Now that England's status has declined, I suppose it is logical that the quality of the revolutionists she breeds has likewise fallen. The Kashmiris![1] Not a hope in hell. And as for these Khalistan types, let them not think that their evil deed has brought their

---

7. Tolkien's triology (1954–1955), written during and just after World War II, concerns a war for control of Middle Earth, in which men, elves, dwarves, and a few British-like hobbits band together to defeat the evil eastern empire of Sauron.

8. Jawaharlal Nehru, first Prime Minister of the Republic of India (1947–1964), father of Indira Gandhi.
9. An exclusive English preparatory school.
1. Residents of Kashmir, a territory in dispute between India and Pakistan since 1947.

dream a day closer. On the contrary. On the contrary. We will root them out and smash them to—what's the right word?—to *smithereens*."

To his surprise he had begun speaking loudly and had risen to his feet. He sat down hard and laughed. The moment passed.

"The funny thing about this blasted nickname of mine," he said quickly to his dinner-table neighbour, the septuagenarian Very Big Businessman's improbably young and attractive wife, "is that back then we never saw one episode of the TV series. No TV to see it on, you see. The whole thing was just a legend wafting its way from the US and UK to our lovely hill-station of Dehra Dun.

"After a while we got a couple of cheap paperback novelisations and passed them round as if they were naughty books like *Lady C* or some such. Lots of us tried the names on for size but only two of them stuck; probably because they seemed to go together, and the two of us got on pretty well, even though he was younger. A lovely boy. So just like Laurel and Hardy we were Chekov and Zulu."

"Love and marriage," said the woman.

"Beg pardon?"

"*You* know," she said. "Go together like is it milk and porridge. Or a car and garage, that's right. I love old songs. La-la-la-something-brother, you can't have fun without I think it's your mother."[2]

"Yes, now I do recall," said Chekov.

3

Three months later Zulu telephoned his wife.

"O my God where have you vanished are you dead?"

"Listen please my bivi. Listen carefully my wife, my only love."

"Yes. OK. I am calm. Line is bad, but."

"Call Chekov and say condition red."

"Arré! What is wrong with your condition?"

"Please. Condition red."

"Yes. OK. Red."

"Say the Klingons may be smelling things."

"Clingers-on may be smelly things. Means what?"

"My darling, I beg you."

"I have it all right here only. With this pencil I have written it, both."

"Tell him, get Scotty to lock on to my signal and beam me up at once."

"What rubbish! Even now you can't leave off that stupid game."

"Bivi. It is urgent. *Beam me up*."

Chekov dropped everything and drove. He went via the dry-cleaners as instructed; he drove round roundabouts twice, jumped red lights, deliberately took a wrong turning, stopped and turned round, made as many right turns as possible to see if anything followed him across the stream of traffic, and, on the motorway, mimicked Zulu's techniques. When he was as certain as he could be that he was clean, he headed for the rendezvous point. "Roll over Len Deighton," he thought, "and tell le Carré the news."[3]

---

2. She is mangling the lyrics of Sammy Cahn's 1955 song *Love and Marriage*: "Love and marriage, love and marriage / Go together like a horse and carriage / This I tell you brother / You can't have one without the other."

3. Len Deighton and John le Carré are two popular contemporary writers of espionage fiction. The line refers to the popular song lyric, "Roll over, Beethoven."

He turned off the motorway and pulled into a lay-by. A man stepped out of the trees, looking newly bathed and smartly dressed, with a sheepish smile on his face. It was Zulu.

Chekov jumped out of the car and embraced his friend, kissing him on both cheeks. Zulu's bristly beard pricked his lips. "I expected you'd have an arm missing, or blood pouring from a gunshot wound, or some black eyes at least," he said. "Instead here you are dressed for the theatre, minus only an opera cloak and cane."

"Mission accomplished," said Zulu, patting his breast pocket. "All present and correct."

"Then what was that 'condition red' bakvaas?"

"The worst-case scenario," said Zulu, "does not always materialise."

In the car, Chekov scanned the names, places, dates in Zulu's brown envelope. The information was better than anyone had expected. From this anonymous Midlands lay-by a light was shining on certain remote villages and urban back-alleys in Punjab.[4] There would be a round-up, and, for some big badmashes at least, there would no longer be shadows in which to hide.

He gave a little, impressed whistle.

Zulu in the passenger seat inclined his head. "Better move off now," he said. "Don't tempt fate."

They drove south through Middle-earth.

Not long after they came off the motorway, Zulu said, "By the way, I quit."

Chekov stopped the car. The two towers of Wembley Stadium were visible through a gap in the houses to the left.

"What's this? Did those extremists manage to turn your head or what?"

"Chekov, ji, don't be a fool. Who needs extremists when there are the killings in Delhi? Hundreds, maybe thousands. Sikh men scalped and burned alive in front of their families. Boy-children, too."

"We know this."

"Then, ji, we also know who was behind it."

"There is not a shred of evidence," Chekov repeated the policy line.

"There are eyewitnesses and photographs," said Zulu. "We know this."

"There are those who think," said Chekov slowly, "that after Indiraji the Sikhs deserved what they got."

Zulu stiffened.

"You know me better than that, I hope," said Chekov. "Zulu, for God's sake, come on. All our bleddy lives."

"No Congress workers have been indicted," said Zulu. "In spite of all the evidence of complicity. Therefore, I resign. You should quit, too."

"If you have gone so damn radical," cried Chekov, "why hand over these lists at all? Why go only half the bleddy hog?"

"I am a security wallah," said Zulu, opening the car door. "Terrorists of all sorts are my foes. But not, apparently, in certain circumstances, yours."

"Zulu, get in, damn it," Chekov shouted. "Don't you care for your career? A wife and four kiddiwinks to support. What about your old chums? Are you going to turn your back on me?"

But Zulu was already too far away.

---

4. Province divided between India and Pakistan.

Chekov and Zulu never met again. Zulu settled in Bombay and as the demand for private-sector protection increased in that cash-rich boom-town, so his Zulu Shield and Zulu Spear companies prospered and grew. He had three more children, all of them boys, and remains happily married to this day.

As for Chekov, he never did take a wife. In spite of this supposed handicap, however, he did well in his chosen profession. His rapid rise continued. But one day in May 1991 he was, by chance, a member of the entourage accompanying Mr Rajiv Gandhi[5] to the South Indian village of Sriperumbudur, where Rajiv was to address an election rally. Security was lax, intentionally so. In the previous election, Rajivji felt, the demands of security had placed an alienating barrier between himself and the electorate. On this occasion, he decreed, the voters must be allowed to feel close.

After the speeches, the Rajiv group descended from the podium. Chekov, who was just a few feet behind Rajiv, saw a small Tamil[6] woman come forward, smiling. She shook Rajiv's hand and did not let go. Chekov understood what she was smiling about, and the knowledge was so powerful that it stopped time itself.

Because time had stopped, Chekov was able to make a number of private observations. "These Tamil revolutionists are not England-returned," he noted. "So, finally, we have learned to produce the goods at home, and no longer need to import. Bang goes that old dinner-party standby, so to speak." And, less dryly: "The tragedy is not how one dies," he thought. "It is how one has lived."

The scene around him vanished, dissolving in a pool of light, and was replaced by the bridge of the Starship *Enterprise*. All the leading figures were in their appointed places. Zulu sat beside Chekov at the front.

"Shields no longer operative," Zulu was saying. On the main screen, they could see the Klingon Bird of Prey uncloaking, preparing to strike.

"One direct hit and we're done for," cried Dr McCoy. "For God's sake, Jim, get us out of here!"

"Illogical," said First Officer Spock. "The degradation of our dilithium crystal drive means that warp speed is unavailable. At impulse power only, we would make a poor attempt indeed to flee the Bird of Prey. Our only logical course is unconditional surrender."

"Surrender to a Klingon!" shouted McCoy. "Damn it, you cold-blooded, pointy-eared adding-machine, don't you know how they treat their prisoners?"

"Phaser banks completely depleted," said Zulu. "Offensive capability nil."

"Should I attempt to contact the Klingon captain, sir?" Chekov inquired. "They could fire at any moment."

"Thank you, Mr Chekov," said Captain Kirk. "I'm afraid that won't be necessary. On this occasion, the worst-case scenario is the one we are obliged to play out. Hold your position. Steady as she goes."

"The Bird of Prey has fired, sir," said Zulu.

Chekov took Zulu's hand and held it firmly, victoriously, as the speeding balls of deadly light approached.

[END OF PERSPECTIVES: WORLD WAR II AND THE END OF EMPIRE]

---

5. Indian Prime Minister 1984–1989, assassinated in May 1991, son of Indira Gandhi.
6. Member of a people of South India and Sri Lanka. The government of India had been aiding the Sri Lankan government in suppressing violent protests by Tamil separatists in Sri Lanka.

Dylan Thomas
1914–1953

One of the most important facts of Dylan Thomas's biography is his birthplace: Swansea, South Wales. Thomas was Welsh first, English second. Although Wales is entirely contained within the borders of England, it is one of the areas of Gaeltacht, the places where forms of Gaelic language are or have been spoken. The Welsh language is a living and thriving one, and it is visible in Wales in place names, street signs, church music, and a host of other daily manifestations. Thomas uses the words of the English language in making his poems, plays, and stories, but these words are defamiliarized, are made strange, by virtue of their having been laid on top, as it were, of absent Welsh words and phrasings that echo nonetheless through the English lines. A common criticism made about Dylan Thomas's poetry by English critics who were his contemporaries was that the poetry was overly emotional and excessively musical, and that it lacked "rigor." These charges against the poems sound all too familiarly like the complaints against the Gaeltachts and their inhabitants—too emotional, too lyrical, too irrational. The innovative and densely lyrical patterns of Thomas's poetry and his prose style come partially out of his "Welshification" of English, a process that has effects on both the style and the subject matter of his work. In another register, he can be seen as the last of the Romantic poets, writing precocious lyrics infused with an intense sense of self.

Dylan Thomas's earliest volume, *18 Poems*, appeared in 1934 when Thomas was twenty years old, a suite of poems based on the cycle of life, birth, childhood, and death in Swansea. It caused a sensation for the magic of its wordplay and the intensely personal focus of the poems. The book was received ecstatically in Britain, but not so in Wales, whose provincial proprieties Thomas always viewed with a half-affectionate sarcasm. Like James Joyce, Thomas felt the necessity of escape; at the age of twenty-one he moved to the metropolitan center, to London, to pursue his hopes of a literary career. There he worked for the BBC as a writer and a performer on radio broadcasts. The short stories of his collection *Portrait of the Artist as a Young Dog* (1940) wittily recount, in obvious homage and parody of Joyce's *Portrait of the Artist as a Young Man*, the travails of the would-be writer who hopes to break through the barriers of class and nation. He spent the years of World War II in London as well, but as a conscientious objector, not a combatant, and, as a Welshman, to a certain degree as an outsider within. The war was traumatizing for him as for so many others, and Thomas's pacifism and despair led to the superb poetry of his volume *Deaths and Entrances*.

Poetry alone could not pay the bills and allow Thomas and his young family to live in London. After the war he turned to screenplays and to short stories. The haunting radio play *Return Journey* gives a medley of voices encountered by the poet returning to a Swansea inhabited by the ghost of his youthful self. It can be compared to some of Hardy's memory-filled poetic landscapes and to stories like *Ivy Day in the Committee Room* in Joyce's *Dubliners*; it also anticipates the spare, ironic dramas that Samuel Beckett would write in the 1960s and 1970s.

In the late 1940s, Thomas returned to his poetry, this time less as a poet than as a performer or public reader of his own work. His vibrant and sonorous Welsh-accented voice (akin to that of the Welsh actor Richard Burton), melded with the incantatory lyricism of his poetic language, proved to be irresistible to the public, both in England and in the United States. His brilliant poetry readings instigated a new popularity for poetry itself on both sides of the Atlantic, and his captivating talents as a reader and indeed an actor created for him the persona of Dylan Thomas, Bohemian poet, which he wore until his early death in New York City, after an overdose of whiskey following a poetry reading. He was on his way to California to stay with Igor Stravinsky, with whom he planned to write an epic opera.

The great American poet John Berryman described certain recurrent words as the "unmistakable signature" of Dylan Thomas's poetry. Berryman chose a list of forty "key words" in Thomas's work, including among them: blood, sea, ghost, grave, death, light, time, sun, night, wind, love, and rain. Berryman noted the symbolic value Thomas made these seemingly simple words carry across the span of many poems. Thomas's themes were agreed by most critics to be simple and elemental ones—related to the cycles of life, to nature and childhood, to life's meaning. Berryman argued fiercely that while these were simple themes on the surface, what a poem means *is* its imagery, the way its words are put into relation to one another: "A poem that works well demonstrates an insight, and the insight may consist, not in the theme, but in the image-relations or the structure-relations." Thomas himself aimed at using wordplay and fractured syntax to create sound as a "verbal music." The musicality of his poems and his prose is stunningly evident, and rarely more so than in his play *Under Milk Wood*, a kind of oratorio for disembodied voices. In the play, published posthumously in 1954, Thomas gives voice to the inhabitants of the Welsh village of Llaregyub, whose voices weave together the actions of nature and humans on one single rural day. There is no "plot," and the actors simply stand on stage and read, taking on many voices as these ebb and flow musically through them.

Oral speech and song are more important than written language in rural countries and cultures, especially when one's written language is officially discouraged or even forbidden. Social memory is passed on in story and song; tales and jokes and sermons and performances loom larger in the society of a country town than do written artifacts. Dylan Thomas was very much a writer, yet his poetry and prose are written to be heard, to exist in the ear of the listener as much as the eye of the reader. The lush richness of Thomas's poetic voice is a verbal music that passes on a tradition of oral culture and its precious gifts. The spoken or sung word is a word accompanied by breath; breath is related in most cultures, but certainly in those of Wales and Ireland, to the spirit. One collection of Dylan Thomas's poetry and sketches he titled *The World I Breathe*. This title could as easily be *The Word I Breathe*.

The Force That Through the Green Fuse Drives the Flower

The force that through the green fuse drives the flower
Drives my green age; that blasts the roots of trees
Is my destroyer.
And I am dumb to tell the crooked rose
5   My youth is bent by the same wintry fever.

The force that drives the water through the rocks
Drives my red blood; that dries the mouthing streams
Turns mine to wax.
And I am dumb to mouth unto my veins
10   How at the mountain spring the same mouth sucks.

The hand that whirls the water in the pool
Stirs the quicksand; that ropes the blowing wind
Hauls my shroud sail.
And I am dumb to tell the hanging man
15   How of my clay is made the hangman's lime.

The lips of time leech to the fountain head;
Love drips and gathers, but the fallen blood
Shall calm her sores.
And I am dumb to tell a weather's wind
20   How time has ticked a heaven round the stars.

And I am dumb to tell the lover's tomb
How at my sheet goes the same crooked worm.

1933

Do Not Go Gentle into That Good Night

Do not go gentle into that good night,
Old age should burn and rave at close of day;
Rage, rage against the dying of the light.

Though wise men at their end know dark is right,
5   Because their words had forked no lightning they
Do not go gentle into that good night.

Good men, the last wave by, crying how bright
Their frail deeds might have danced in a green bay,
Rage, rage against the dying of the light.

10   Wild men who caught and sang the sun in flight,
And learn, too late, they grieved it on its way,
Do not go gentle into that good night.

Grave men, near death, who see with blinding sight
Blind eyes could blaze like meteors and be gay,
15   Rage, rage against the dying of the light.

And you, my father, there on the sad height,
Curse, bless, me now with your fierce tears, I pray.
Do not go gentle into that good night.
Rage, rage against the dying of the light.

1951

Return Journey[1]

NARRATOR It was a cold white day in High Street, and nothing to stop the wind slicing up from the docks, for where the squat and tall shops had shielded the town from the sea lay their blitzed flat graves marbled with snow and headstoned with fences. Dogs, delicate as cats on water, as though they had gloves on their paws, padded over the vanished buildings. Boys romped, calling high and clear, on top of a levelled chemist's and a shoe-shop, and a little girl, wearing a man's cap, threw a snowball in a chill deserted garden that had once been the Jug and Bottle of the Prince of Wales.[2] The wind cut up the street with a soft sea-noise hanging on its arm, like a hooter in a muffler. I could see the swathed hill stepping up out of the town, which you never could see properly before, and the powdered fields of the roofs of Milton Terrace and Watkin Street and Fullers Row. Fish-frailed, net-bagged, umbrella'd, pixie-capped, fur-shoed, blue-nosed, puce-lipped, blinkered like drayhorses, scarved, mittened, galoshed, wearing everything but the cat's blanket, crushes of shopping-women crunched in the little Lapland of the once grey drab street, blew and queued and yearned for hot tea, as I began my search through Swansea town cold and early on that wicked February morning.[3] I went into the hotel. "Good morning."

---

1. Written in February 1947; broadcast by the BBC May 1947.
2. The name of a public house (pub).

3. Swansea, a city in South Wales on the mouth of the river Tawe, is the second largest city in Wales after Cardiff (the capital).

The hall-porter did not answer. I was just another snowman to him. He did not know that I was looking for someone after fourteen years, and he did not care. He stood and shuddered, staring through the glass of the hotel door at the snowflakes sailing down the sky, like Siberian confetti. The bar was just opening, but already one customer puffed and shook at the counter with a full pint of half-frozen Tawe water in his wrapped-up hand. I said Good morning, and the barmaid, polishing the counter vigorously as though it were a rare and valuable piece of Swansea china, said to her first customer:

BARMAID Seen the film at the Elysium Mr Griffiths there's snow isn't it did you come up on your bicycle our pipes burst Monday . . .

NARRATOR A pint of bitter,[4] please.

BARMAID Proper little lake in the kitchen got to wear your Wellingtons when you boil a egg one and four please[5] . . .

CUSTOMER The cold gets me just here . . .

BARMAID . . . and eightpence change that's your liver Mr Griffiths you been on the cocoa again . . .

NARRATOR I wonder whether you remember a friend of mine? He always used to come to this bar, some years ago. Every morning, about this time.

CUSTOMER Just by here it gets me. I don't know what'd happen if I didn't wear a band . . .

BARMAID What's his name?

NARRATOR Young Thomas.

BARMAID Lots of Thomases come here it's a kind of home from home for Thomases isn't it Mr Griffiths what's he look like?

NARRATOR He'd be about seventeen or eighteen . . .
    (*Slowly*)

BARMAID . . . I was seventeen once . . .

NARRATOR . . . and above medium height. Above medium height for Wales, I mean, he's five foot six and a half. Thick blubber lips; snub nose; curly mouse-brown hair; one front tooth broken after playing a game called Cats and Dogs, in the Mermaid, Mumbles; speaks rather fancy; truculent; plausible; a bit of a shower-off; plus-fours and no breakfast, you know; used to have poems printed in the *Herald of Wales*; there was one about an open-air performance of *Electra* in Mrs Bertie Perkins's garden in Sketty; lived up the Uplands; a bombastic adolescent provincial Bohemian with a thick-knotted artist's tie made out of his sister's scarf, she never knew where it had gone, and a cricket-shirt dyed bottle-green; a gabbing, ambitious, mock-tough, pretentious young man; and mole-y, too.

BARMAID There's words what d'you want to find him for I wouldn't touch him with a barge-pole . . . would you, Mr Griffiths? Mind, you can never tell. I remember a man came here with a monkey. Called for 'alf for himself and a pint for the monkey. And he wasn't Italian at all. Spoke Welsh like a preacher.

NARRATOR The bar was filling up. Snowy business bellies pressed their watch-chains against the counter; black business bowlers, damp and white now as Christmas puddings in their cloths, bobbed in front of the misty mirrors. The voice of commerce rang sternly through the lounge.

FIRST VOICE Cold enough for you?

SECOND VOICE How's your pipes, Mr Lewis?

---

4. British beer.   5. One shilling and 4 pence.

THIRD VOICE Another winter like this'll put paid to me, Mr Evans. I got the 'flu . . .

FIRST VOICE Make it a double . . .

SECOND VOICE Similar . . .

BARMAID Okay, baby . . .

CUSTOMER I seem to remember a chap like you described. There couldn't be two like him let's hope. He used to work as a reporter. Down the Three Lamps I used to see him. Lifting his ikkle elbow.

(*Confidentially*)

NARRATOR What's the Three Lamps like now?

CUSTOMER It isn't like anything. It isn't there. It's nothing mun. You remember Ben Evans's stores? It's right next door to that. Ben Evans isn't there either . . .

(*Fade*)

NARRATOR I went out of the hotel into the snow and walked down High Street, past the flat white wastes where all the shops had been. Eddershaw Furnishers, Curry's Bicycles, Donegal Clothing Company, Doctor Scholl's, Burton Tailors, W. H. Smith, Boots Cash Chemists, Leslie's Stores, Upson's Shoes, Prince of Wales, Tucker's Fish, Stead & Simpson—all the shops bombed and vanished. Past the hole in space where Hodges & Clothiers had been, down Castle Street, past the remembered, invisible shops, Price's Fifty Shilling, and Crouch the Jeweller, Potter Gilmore Gowns, Evans Jeweller, Master's Outfitters, Style and Mantle, Lennard's Boots, True Form, Kardomah, R. E. Jones, Dean's Tailor, David Evans, Gregory Confectioners, Bovega, Burton's, Lloyd's Bank, and nothing. And into Temple Street. There the Three Lamps had stood, old Mac magisterial in his corner. And there the Young Thomas whom I was searching for used to stand at the counter on Friday paynights with Freddie Farr Half Hook, Bill Latham, Cliff Williams, Gareth Hughes, Eric Hughes, Glyn Lowry, a man among men, his hat at a rakish angle, in that snug, smug, select Edwardian holy of best-bitter holies . . .

(*Bar noises in background*)

OLD REPORTER Remember when I took you down the mortuary for the first time, Young Thomas? He'd never seen a corpse before, boys, except old Ron on a Saturday night. "If you want to be a proper newspaperman," I said, "you got to be well known in the right circles. You got to be *persona grata* [acceptable] in the mortuary, see." He went pale green, mun.

FIRST YOUNG REPORTER Look, he's blushing now . . .

OLD REPORTER And when we got there what d'you think? The decorators were in at the mortuary, giving the old home a bit of a re-do like. Up on ladders having a slap at the roof. Young Thomas didn't see 'em, he had his pop eyes glued on the slab, and when one of the painters up the ladder said "Good morning, gents" in a deep voice he upped in the air and out of the place like a ferret. Laugh!

BARMAID (*off*) You've had enough, Mr Roberts. You heard what I said.

(*Noise of a gentle scuffle*)

SECOND YOUNG REPORTER (*casually*) There goes Mr Roberts.

OLD REPORTER Well fair do's they throw you out very genteel in this pub . . .

FIRST YOUNG REPORTER Ever seen Young Thomas covering a soccer match down the Vetch and working it out in tries?

SECOND YOUNG REPORTER And up the Mannesman Hall shouting "Good footwork, sir," and a couple of punch-drunk colliers galumphing about like jumbos.

FIRST YOUNG REPORTER What you been reporting to-day, Young Thomas?

SECOND YOUNG REPORTER Two typewriter Thomas the ace news-dick . . .

OLD REPORTER Let's have a dekko[6] at your note-book. "Called at British Legion: Nothing. Called at Hospital: One broken leg. Auction at the Metropole. Ring Mr Beynon *re* Gymanfa Ganu. Lunch: Pint and pasty at the Singleton with Mrs Giles. Bazaar at Bethesda Chapel. Chimney on fire at Tontine Street. Walters Road Sunday School Outing. Rehearsal of the *Mikado* at Skewen'—all front page stuff . . . (*Fade*)

NARRATOR The voices of fourteen years ago hung silent in the snow and ruin, and in the falling winter morning I walked on through the white havoc'd centre where once a very young man I knew had mucked about as chirpy as a sparrow after the sips and titbits and small change of the town. Near the *Evening Post* building and the fragment of the Castle I stopped a man whose face I thought I recognized from a long time ago. I said: I wonder if you can tell me . . .

PASSER-BY Yes?

NARRATOR He peered out of his blanketing scarves and from under his snowballed Balaclava like an Eskimo with a bad conscience. I said: If you can tell me whether you used to know a chap called Young Thomas. He worked on the Post and used to wear an overcoat sometimes with the check lining inside out so that you could play giant draughts on him. He wore a conscious woodbine,[7] too . . .

PASSER-BY What d'you mean, conscious woodbine?

NARRATOR . . . and a perched pork pie with a peacock feather and he tried to slouch like a newshawk even when he was attending a meeting of the Gorseinon Buffalos[8] . . .

PASSER-BY Oh, *him!* He owes me half a crown. I haven't seen him since the old Kardomah days. He wasn't a reporter then, he'd just left the grammar school.[9] Him and Charlie Fisher—Charlie's got whiskers now—and Tom Warner and Fred Janes, drinking coffee-dashes and arguing the toss.

NARRATOR What about?

PASSER-BY Music and poetry and painting and politics. Einstein and Epstein, Stravinsky and Greta Garbo, death and religion, Picasso and girls . . .

NARRATOR And then?

PASSER-BY Communism, symbolism, Bradman, Braque, the Watch Committee, free love, free beer, murder, Michelangelo, ping-pong, ambition, Sibelius, and girls . . .

NARRATOR Is that all?

PASSER-BY How Dan Jones was going to compose the most prodigious symphony, Fred Janes paint the most miraculously meticulous picture, Charlie Fisher catch the poshest trout, Vernon Watkins and Young Thomas write the most boiling poems, how they would ring the bells of London and paint it like a tart . . .

NARRATOR And after that?

PASSER-BY Oh the hissing of the butt-ends in the drains of the coffee-dashes and the tinkle and the gibble-gabble of the morning young lounge lizards as they talked about Augustus John, Emil Jannings, Carnera, Dracula, Amy Johnson, trial marriage, pocket-money, the Welsh sea, the London stars, King Kong, anarchy, darts, T. S. Eliot, and girls. . . . Duw, it's cold!

---

6. British army slang for "a look" (from the Hindi word *dekho*).
7. A brand of cigarette.
8. A pork-pie hat takes its name from the circular shape of a pork pie; Gorseinon is a town near Swansea, appar-ently with a chapter of the Royal Antediluvian Order of Buffaloes (founded 1822), a men's club.
9. Secondary school, typically educating students of ages 11–18.

NARRATOR And he hurried on, into the dervish snow, without a good morning or good-bye, swaddled in his winter woollens like a man in the island of his deafness, and I felt that perhaps he had never stopped at all to tell me of one more departed stage in the progress of the boy I was pursuing. The Kardomah Café was razed to the snow, the voices of the coffee-drinkers—poets, painters, and musicians in their beginnings—lost in the willynilly flying of the years and the flakes.

    Down College Street I walked then, past the remembered invisible shops, Langley's, Castle Cigar Co., T. B. Brown, Pullar's, Aubrey Jeremiah, Goddard Jones, Richards, Hornes, Marles, Pleasance & Harper, Star Supply, Sidney Heath, Wesley Chapel, and nothing. . . . My search was leading me back, through pub and job and café, to the School.

    (*Fade*) (*School bell*)

SCHOOLMASTER Oh yes, yes, I remember him well,
        though I do not know if I would recognize him now:
        nobody grows any younger, or better,
        and boys grow into much the sort of men one would suppose
        though sometimes the moustaches bewilder
        and one finds it hard to reconcile one's memory of a small
        none-too-clean urchin lying his way unsuccessfully out of his homework
        with a fierce and many-medalled sergeant-major with three children or a
        divorced chartered accountant;
        and it is hard to realize
        that some little tousled rebellious youth whose only claim
        to fame among his contemporaries was his undisputed right
        to the championship of the spitting contest
        is now perhaps one's own bank manager.
        Oh yes, I remember him well, the boy you are searching for:
        he looked like most boys, no better, brighter, or more respectful;
        he cribbed, mitched,[1] spilt ink, rattled his desk and
        garbled his lessons with the worst of them;
        he could smudge, hedge, smirk, wriggle, wince,
        whimper, blarney, badger, blush, deceive, be
        devious, stammer, improvise, assume
        offended dignity or righteous indignation as though to the manner born;[2]
        sullenly and reluctantly he drilled, for some small
        crime, under Sergeant Bird, so wittily nicknamed
        Oiseau,° on Wednesday half-holidays,   *bird*
        appeared regularly in detention classes,
        hid in the cloakroom during algebra,
        was, when a newcomer, thrown into the bushes of the
        Lower Playground by bigger boys,
        and threw newcomers into the bushes of the Lower
        Playground when *he* was a bigger boy;
        he scuffled at prayers,
        he interpolated, smugly, the time-honoured wrong
        irreverent words into the morning hymns,
        he helped to damage the headmaster's rhubarb,
        was thirty-third in trigonometry,
        and, as might be expected, edited the School Magazine

    (*Fade*)

---

1. Stole.   2. As though born into a high station in life.

NARRATOR The Hall is shattered, the echoing corridors charred where he scribbled and smudged and yawned in the long green days, waiting for the bell and the scamper into the Yard: the School on Mount Pleasant Hill has changed its face and its ways. Soon, they say, it may be no longer the School at all he knew and loved when he was a boy up to no good but the beat of his blood: the names are havoc'd from the Hall and the carved initials burned from the broken wood. But the names remain. What names did he know of the dead? Who of the honoured dead did he know such a long time ago? The names of the dead in the living heart and head remain for ever. Of all the dead whom did he know?

   (*Funeral bell*)

VOICE

      Evans, K. J.
      Haines, G. C.
      Roberts, I. L.
      Moxham, J.
      Thomas, H.
      Baines, W.
      Bazzard, F. H.
      Beer, L. J.
      Bucknell, R.
      Tywford, G.
      Vagg, E. A.
      Wright, G.

   (*Fade*)

NARRATOR Then I tacked down the snowblind hill, a cat-o'-nine-gales whipping from the sea, and, white and eiderdowned in the smothering flurry, people padded past me up and down like prowling featherbeds. And I plodded through the ankle-high one cloud that foamed the town, into flat Gower Street, its buildings melted, and along long Helen's Road. Now my search was leading me back to the seashore.

   (*Noise of sea, softly*)

NARRATOR Only two living creatures stood on the promenade, near the cenotaph, facing the tossed crystal sea: a man in a chewed muffler and a ratting cap, and an angry dog of a mixed make. The man dithered in the cold, beat his bare blue hands together, waited for some sign from sea or snow; the dog shouted at the weather, and fixed his bloodshot eyes on Mumbles Head. But when the man and I talked together, the dog piped down and fixed his eyes on me, blaming me for the snow. The man spoke towards the sea. Year in, year out, whatever the weather, once in the daytime, once in the dark, he always came to look at the sea. He knew all the dogs and boys and old men who came to see the sea, who ran or gambolled on the sand or stooped at the edge of the waves as though over a wild, wide, rolling ashcan. He knew the lovers who went to lie in the sandhills, the striding masculine women who roared at their terriers like tiger tamers, the loafing men whose work it was in the world to observe the great employment of the sea. He said:

PROMENADE-MAN Oh yes, yes, I remember him well, but I didn't know what was his name. I don't know the names of none of the sandboys. They don't know mine. About fourteen or fifteen years old, you said, with a little red cap. And he used to play by Vivian's Stream. He used to dawdle in the arches, you said, and lark about on the railway-lines and holler at the old sea. He'd mooch about the dunes and watch the tankers and the tugs and the banana boats come out of the

docks. He was going to run away to sea, he said. I know. On Saturday afternoon
he'd go down to the sea when it was a long way out, and hear the foghorns though
he couldn't see the ships. And on Sunday nights, after chapel, he'd be swaggering
with his pals along the prom, whistling after the girls.

(*Titter*)

GIRL Does your mother know you're out? Go away now. Stop following us.

(*Another girl titters*)

GIRL Don't you say nothing, Hetty, you're only encouraging. No thank *you*, Mr
Cheeky, with your cut-glass accent and your father's trilby![3] I don't want *no* walk
on *no* sands. What d'you say? Ooh listen to him, Het, he's swallowed a dictionary.
No, I don't want to go with nobody up no lane in the moonlight, see, and I'm not
a baby-snatcher neither. I seen you going to school along Terrace Road, Mr Glad-
Eye, with your little satchel and wearing your red cap and all. You seen me wearing my . . . no you never. Hetty, mind your glasses! Hetty Harris, you're as bad as
them. Oh go away and do your homework, see. Cheek! Hetty Harris, don't you let
him! Oooh, there's brazen! Well, just to the end of the prom, if you like. No further, mind . . .

PROMENADE-MAN Oh yes, I knew him well. I've known him by the thousands . . .

NARRATOR Even now, on the frozen foreshore, a high, far cry of boys, all like the
boy I sought, slid on the glass of the streams and snowballed each other and the
sky. Then I went on my way from the sea, up Brynmill Terrace and into Glanbry-
dan Avenue where Bert Trick had kept a grocer's shop and, in the kitchen, threatened the annihilation of the ruling classes over sandwiches and jelly and blancmange.[4] And I came to the shops and houses of the Uplands. Here and around
here it was that the journey had begun of the one I was pursuing through his past.

(*Old piano cinema-music in background*)

FIRST VOICE Here was once the flea-pit picture-house where he whooped for the
scalping Indians with Jack Basset and banged for the rustlers' guns.

NARRATOR Jackie Basset, killed.

THIRD VOICE Here once was Mrs Ferguson's, who sold the best gob-stoppers[5] and
penny packets full of surprises and a sweet kind of glue.

FIRST VOICE In the fields behind Cwmdonkin Drive, the Murrays chased him and
all cats.

SECOND VOICE No fires now where the outlaws' fires burned and the paradisiacal
potatoes roasted in the embers.

THIRD VOICE In the Graig beneath Town Hill he was a lonely killer hunting the
wolves (or rabbits) and the red Sioux tribe (or Mitchell brothers).

(*Fade cinema-music into background of children's voices reciting, in unison, the names
of the counties of Wales*)

FIRST VOICE In Mirador School he learned to read and count. Who made the
worst raffia doilies? Who put water in Joyce's galoshes, every morning prompt as
prompt? In the afternoons, when the children were good, they read aloud from
Struwelpeter.[6] And when they were bad, they sat alone in the empty classroom,
hearing, from above them, the distant, terrible, sad music of the late piano lesson.

(*The children's voices fade. The piano lesson continues in background*)

---

3. With an upper-class accent and an elegant hat.
4. A pudding.
5. A kind of candy.

6. *Struwelpeter* ("Shock-head Peter") by the German
Heinrich Hoffman (1809–1874) was a popular book for
children.

NARRATOR And I went up, through the white Grove, into Cwmdonkin Park, the snow still sailing and the childish, lonely, remembered music fingering on in the suddenly gentle wind. Dusk was folding the Park around, like another, darker snow. Soon the bell would ring for the closing of the gates, though the Park was empty. The park-keeper walked by the reservoir, where swans had glided, on his white rounds. I walked by his side and asked him my questions, up the swathed drives past buried beds and loaded utterly still furred and birdless trees towards the last gate. He said:

PARK-KEEPER Oh yes, yes, I knew him well. He used to climb the reservoir railings and pelt the old swans. Run like a billygoat over the grass you should keep off of. Cut branches off the trees. Carve words on the benches. Pull up moss in the rockery, go snip through the dahlias. Fight in the bandstand. Climb the elms and moon up the top like a owl. Light fires in the bushes. Play on the green bank. Oh yes, I knew him well. I think he was happy all the time. I've known him by the thousands.

NARRATOR We had reached the last gate. Dusk drew around us and the town. I said: What has become of him now?

PARK-KEEPER Dead.

NARRATOR The Park-keeper said:

(*The park bell rings*)

PARK-KEEPER Dead . . . Dead . . . Dead . . . Dead . . . Dead . . . Dead.

Samuel Beckett
1906–1989

On January 5, 1953, *En Attendant Godot* (*Waiting for Godot*) premiered at the Théâtre de Babylone, Paris—and the shape of twentieth-century drama was permanently changed. *Godot* helped to strip the modern stage of everything but its essentials: two characters, seemingly without past or future or worldly possessions, and a spare stage: "A country road. A tree. Evening." Critics would subsequently find in Beckett's bleak stage suggestions of a postnuclear holocaust landscape, as they would in the later *Fin de partie* (*Endgame*, 1957); and for the remainder of his long and productive career, Beckett would continue to explore, with unparalleled honesty and courage, that realm of being that he called in one story *Sans*—"lessness."

April 13, 1906—Good Friday—is the date usually given for Samuel Barclay Beckett's birth, though the birth certificate shows May 13. He was born in the family home of Cooldrinagh in Foxrock, an upper-class Protestant suburb south of Dublin, to William Beckett, surveyor, and Mary (May) Roe, the daughter of a wealthy Kildare family. "You might say I had a happy childhood," Beckett later recalled; "my father did not beat me, nor did my mother run away from home." Beckett attended private academies in Dublin, then in 1920 was enrolled in Portora Royal School in Enniskillen, Northern Ireland, where he excelled more in sports than studies as star bowler on the cricket team, captain of rugby and swimming, and light-heavyweight champion in boxing. In 1923 Beckett entered Trinity College, Dublin, studying modern languages; he also enjoyed the freedom of the city, frequenting the Gate Theatre (for the drama of Pirandello and O'Casey), the music hall, and the movies (especially Charlie Chaplin, Laurel and Hardy, Buster Keaton, and the Marx Brothers). All would prove formative influences on his later drama and fiction.

In 1927 Beckett received his B.A. degree, first in his class in modern languages, and went off on fellowship to France to teach for two years at the École Normale Supérieure in Paris. While in Paris he became a friend of James Joyce, who influenced him profoundly. Besides aiding Joyce in various ways with his work, Beckett wrote an important essay, *Dante . . . Bruno . . . Vico . . . Joyce*, on *Finnegans Wake*—for a volume of critical writing published before the novel itself was completed. With characteristic understatement, Beckett has said that "Paris in the twenties was a good place for a young man to be"; at the same time, learning the craft of writing in Paris under the shadow of fellow Irish expatriate James Joyce would be enough to provoke the anxiety of influence in even the best of writers. However, Beckett's respect and admiration for Joyce were boundless and never wavered. In 1969 Beckett admitted that Joyce had become "an ethical ideal" for him: "Joyce had a moral effect on me. He made me realize artistic integrity."

The term of his fellowship in Paris having run out, Beckett returned to Dublin to assume teaching at Trinity College. That he was ill-suited to this role was immediately apparent to students, colleagues, and Beckett himself. "I saw that in teaching," Beckett later said, "I was talking of something I knew little about, to people who cared nothing about it. So I behaved very badly." The bad behavior to which Beckett refers was his resignation by mail while on spring holidays in Germany during his second year. Beckett returned briefly to Paris, where it became clear that the unwelcome attentions of Joyce's daughter Lucia were straining Beckett's relationship with the elder writer. He returned to the family home for a time in 1933, where he worked on his first published fiction, the Joycean collection of short stories *More Pricks than Kicks*.

The 1930s found Beckett shuttling back and forth between poverty in London and the frustrating comforts of home in Dublin; Paris seemed to him forbidden, owing to the break with Joyce. In spite of his difficult living circumstances, however, and occasional crippling attacks of clinical depression, Beckett managed to complete his first novel, *Murphy*. The manuscript was rejected by forty-one publishers before being accepted by Routledge in 1937. At the end of 1937, Beckett overcame his reluctance and moved back to Paris. From then on, he wrote largely in French. During the early years of World War II, he attempted to write but found it increasingly difficult to maintain the neutrality required of him by his Irish citizenship in light of the German invasion of France. He abandoned that neutrality in October 1940, when he joined one of the earliest French Resistance groups; he helped in Paris with Resistance activities until his group had been penetrated and betrayed, and just in the nick of time he and his lover Suzanne Deschevaux-Dumesnil (the two had met in 1938, and would eventually marry in 1961) were smuggled into Unoccupied France. At the end of the war Beckett returned to Paris, where he was awarded the *Croix de Guerre* and the *Médaille de la Résistance* by the French government.

While hiding from the Germans from 1942 to 1945 in the village of Roussillon in southeast France, Beckett wrote *Watt*, a complex and aridly witty novel that was never to enjoy the attention devoted to Beckett's other fiction. Meanwhile, Beckett continued his experiments with drama. Though it is drama for which Beckett is best known, he always put more stock in his fiction; "I turned to writing plays," he once said dismissively, "to relieve myself of the awful depression the prose led me into."

At an impasse in the writing of what would prove to be his greatest novels, the trilogy *Molloy*, *Malone Dies*, and *The Unnameable* (1951–1953), Beckett took off three months to write *Waiting for Godot*; it took four years to get the play produced. It is easy enough, in retrospect, to understand the producers' reservations: *Godot* breaks with the conventions of the well-made play at just about every turn, even down to its symmetrical, mirror-image two-act structure. The Irish critic Vivian Mercier wittily described *Godot* as a play in which "nothing happens, twice." Beckett's play *Krapp's Last Tape* (1960) uses a tape recorder (which, at the time of writing, Beckett had never seen) as a stage metaphor for the struggle over memory. In this play Beckett went farther than ever in stripping down his action, now involving just a single character. The play is less a monologue, though, than Krapp's dialogue with his past and future selves—and with the machine on which the selves of different years have recorded their fragmentary observations and memories.

After the success of his plays of the fifties and early sixties, Beckett turned to shorter and shorter forms, both in drama and fiction; he produced a number of very powerful, very short plays (*Not I*, 1973; *Footfalls*, 1976; *Rockabye*, 1981) and short, poetic texts that he called by a variety of self-deprecating names ("fizzles," "residua," "texts for nothing"). He sought an intensified power in the increasing economy of his works. In 1969 Beckett was awarded the Nobel Prize for literature, for "a body of work," as the citation declares, "that, in new forms of fiction and the theatre, has transmuted the destitution of modern man into exaltation."

Krapp's Last Tape

A late evening in the future.

Krapp's den.

Front centre a small table, the two drawers of which open towards the audience.

Sitting at the table, facing front, i.e. across from the drawers, a wearish old man: Krapp.

Rusty black narrow trousers too short for him. Rusty black sleeveless waistcoat, four capacious pockets. Heavy silver watch and chain. Grimy white shirt open at neck, no collar. Surprising pair of dirty white boots, size ten at least, very narrow and pointed.

White face. Purple nose. Disordered grey hair. Unshaven.

Very near-sighted (but unspectacled). Hard of hearing.

Cracked voice. Distinctive intonation.

Laborious walk.

On the table a tape-recorder with microphone and a number of cardboard boxes containing reels of recorded tapes.

Table and immediately adjacent area in strong white light. Rest of stage in darkness.

Krapp remains a moment motionless, heaves a great sigh, looks at his watch, fumbles in his pockets, takes out an envelope, puts it back, fumbles, takes out a small bunch of keys, raises it to his eyes, chooses a key, gets up and moves to front of table. He stoops, unlocks first drawer, peers into it, feels about inside it, takes out a reel of tape, peers at it, puts it back, locks drawer, unlocks second drawer, peers into it, feels about inside it, takes out a large banana, peers at it, locks drawer, puts keys back in his pocket. He turns, advances to edge of stage, halts, strokes banana, peels it, drops skin at his feet, puts end of banana in his mouth and remains motionless, staring vacuously before him. Finally he bites off the end, turns aside and begins pacing to and fro at edge of stage, in the light, i.e. not more than four or five paces either way, meditatively eating banana. He treads on skin, slips, nearly falls, recovers himself, stoops and peers at skin and finally pushes it, still stooping, with his foot over edge of stage into pit. He resumes his pacing, finishes banana, returns to table, sits down, remains a moment motionless, heaves a great sigh, takes keys from his pockets, raises them to his eyes, chooses key, gets up and moves to front of table, unlocks second drawer, takes out a second large banana, peers at it, locks drawer, puts back keys in his pocket, turns, advances to edge of stage, halts, strokes banana, peels it, tosses skin into pit, puts end of banana in his mouth and remains motionless, staring vacuously before him. Finally he has an idea, puts banana in his waistcoat pocket, the end emerging, and goes with all the speed he can muster backstage into darkness. Ten seconds. Loud pop of cork. Fifteen seconds. He comes back into light carrying an old ledger and sits down at table. He lays ledger on table, wipes his mouth, wipes his hands on the front of his waistcoat, brings them smartly together and rubs them.

KRAPP [*briskly*] Ah! [*He bends over ledger, turns the pages, finds the entry he wants, reads.*] Box . . . thrree . . . spool . . . five. [*He raises his head and stares front. With relish.*] Spool . . . [*Pause.*] Spooool! [*Happy smile. Pause. He bends over table, starts peering and poking at the boxes.*] Box . . . thrree . . . thrree . . . four . . . two . . . [*with surprise*] nine! good God! . . . seven . . . ah! the little rascal! [*He takes up box, peers at it.*] Box thrree. [*He lays it on table, opens it and peers at spools inside.*] Spool . . . [*he peers at ledger*] . . . five . . . [*he peers at spools*] . . . five . . . five . . . ah! the little scoundrel! [*He takes out a spool, peers at it.*] Spool five. [*He lays it on table, closes box three, puts it back with the others, takes up the spool.*] Box thrree, spool five. [*He bends over the machine, looks up. With relish.*] Spooool! [*Happy smile. He bends, loads spool on machine, rubs his hands.*] Ah! [*He peers at ledger, reads entry at foot of page.*] Mother at rest at last. . . . Hm. . . . The black ball. . . . [*He raises his head, stares blankly front. Puzzled.*] Black ball? . . . [*He peers again at ledger, reads.*] The dark nurse. . . . [*He raises his head, broods, peers again at ledger, reads.*] Slight improvement in bowel condition. . . . Hm. . . . Memorable . . . what? [*He peers closer.*] Equinox, memorable equinox. [*He raises his head, stares blankly front. Puzzled.*] Memorable equinox? . . . [*Pause. He shrugs his shoulders, peers again at ledger, reads.*] Farewell to—[*he turns page*]—love. [*He raises his head, broods, bends over machine, switches on and assumes listening posture, i.e. leaning forward, elbows on table, hand cupping ear towards machine, face front.*]

TAPE [*strong voice, rather pompous, clearly Krapp's at a much earlier time*] Thirty-nine today, sound as a—[*Settling himself more comfortably he knocks one of the boxes off the table, curses, switches off, sweeps boxes and ledger violently to the ground, winds tape back to beginning, switches on, resumes posture.*] Thirty-nine today, sound as a bell, apart from my old weakness, and intellectually I have now every reason to suspect at the . . . [*hesitates*] . . . crest of the wave—or thereabouts. Celebrated the awful occasion, as in recent years, quietly at the Winehouse. Not a soul. Sat before the fire with closed eyes, separating the grain from the husks. Jotted down a few notes, on the back of an envelope. Good to be back in my den, in my old rags. Have just eaten I regret to say three bananas and only with difficulty refrained from a fourth. Fatal things for a man with my condition. [*Vehemently.*] Cut'em out! [*Pause.*] The new light above my table is a great improvement. With all this darkness round me I feel less alone. [*Pause.*] In a way. [*Pause.*] I love to get up and move about in it, then back here to . . . [*hesitates*] . . . me. [*Pause.*] Krapp.

[*Pause.*]

The grain, now what I wonder do I mean by that, I mean . . . [*hesitates*] . . . I suppose I mean those things worth having when all the dust has—when all *my* dust has settled. I close my eyes and try and imagine them.

[*Pause. Krapp closes his eyes briefly.*]

Extraordinary silence this evening, I strain my ears and do not hear a sound. Old Miss McGlome always sings at this hour. But not tonight. Songs of her girlhood, she says. Hard to think of her as a girl. Wonderful woman though. Connaught,[1] I fancy. [*Pause.*] Shall I sing when I am her age, if I ever am? No. [*Pause.*] Did I sing as a boy? No. [*Pause.*] Did I ever sing? No.

[*Pause.*]

Just been listening to an old year, passages at random. I did not check in the book, but it must be at least ten or twelve years ago. At that time I think I was still living on and off with Bianca in Kedar Street. Well out of that, Jesus yes! Hopeless business. [*Pause.*] Not much about her, apart from a tribute to her eyes. Very warm. I suddenly saw them again. [*Pause.*] Incomparable! [*Pause.*] Ah well?

---

1. A province in northwestern Ireland.

[*Pause.*] These old P.M.s are gruesome, but I often find them—[*Krapp switches off, broods, switches on.*]—a help before embarking on a new . . . [*hesitates*] . . . retrospect. Hard to believe I was ever that young whelp. The voice! Jesus! And the aspirations! [*Brief laugh in which Krapp joins.*] And the resolutions! [*Brief laugh in which Krapp joins.*] To drink less, in particular. [*Brief laugh of Krapp alone.*] Statistics. Seventeen hundred hours, out of the preceding eight thousand odd, consumed on licensed premises[2] alone. More than 20 per cent, say 40 per cent of his waking life. [*Pause.*] Plans for a less . . . [*hesitates*] . . . engrossing sexual life. Last illness of his father. Flagging pursuit of happiness. Unattainable laxation.[3] Sneers at what he calls his youth and thanks to God that it's over. [*Pause.*] False ring there. [*Pause.*] Shadows of the opus . . . magnum.[4] Closing with a—[*brief laugh*]— yelp to Providence. [*Prolonged laugh in which Krapp joins.*] What remains of all that misery? A girl in a shabby green coat, on a railway-station platform? No?

[*Pause.*]

    When I look—

[*Krapp switches off, broods, looks at his watch, gets up, goes backstage into darkness. Ten seconds. Pop of cork. Ten seconds. Second cork. Ten seconds. Third cork. Ten seconds. Brief burst of quavering song.*]

KRAPP [*sings*] Now the day is over,
                Night is drawing nigh-igh,
                Shadows—

[*Fit of coughing. He comes back into light, sits down, wipes his mouth, switches on, resumes his listening posture.*]

TAPE —back on the year that is gone, with what I hope is perhaps a glint of the old eye to come, there is of course the house on the canal where mother lay a-dying, in the late autumn, after her long viduity [*Krapp gives a start*] and the—[*Krapp switches off, winds back tape a little, bends his ear closer to machine, switches on*]—a- dying, after her long viduity, and the—

[*Krapp switches off, raises his head, stares blankly before him. His lips move in the syllables of "viduity." No sound. He gets up, goes backstage into darkness, comes back with an enormous dictionary, lays it on table, sits down and looks up the word.*]

KRAPP [*reading from dictionary*] State—or condition—of being—or remaining—a widow—or widower. [*Looks up. Puzzled.*] Being—or remaining? . . . [*Pause. He peers again at dictionary. Reading.*] "Deep weeds of viduity." . . . Also of an animal, especially a bird . . . the vidua or weaver-bird. . . . Black plumage of male. . . . [*He looks up. With relish.*] The vidua-bird!

[*Pause. He closes dictionary, switches on, resumes listening posture.*]

TAPE —bench by the weir from where I could see her window. There I sat, in the biting wind, wishing she were gone. [*Pause.*] Hardly a soul, just a few regulars, nursemaids, infants, old men, dogs. I got to know them quite well—oh by appearance of course I mean! One dark young beauty I recollect particularly, all white and starch, incomparable bosom, with a big black hooded perambulator, most funeral thing. Whenever I looked in her direction she had her eyes on me. And yet when I was bold enough to speak to her—not having been introduced—she threatened to call a policeman. As if I had designs on her virtue! [*Laugh. Pause.*]

---

2. Pubs licensed to sell alcohol.
3. Movement of the bowels.

4. A "magnum opus" is a great work; a magnum is a large wine bottle.

The face she had! The eyes! Like . . . [*hesitates*] . . . chrysolite![5] [*Pause.*] Ah well.
. . . [*Pause.*] I was there when—[*Krapp switches off, broods, switches on again.*]—the
blind went down, one of those dirty brown roller affairs, throwing a ball for a little
white dog as chance would have it. I happened to look up and there it was. All
over and done with, at last. I sat on for a few moments with the ball in my hand
and the dog yelping and pawing at me. [*Pause.*] Moments. Her moments, my
moments. [*Pause.*] The dog's moments. [*Pause.*] In the end I held it out to him and
he took it in his mouth, gently, gently. A small, old, black, hard, solid rubber ball.
[*Pause.*] I shall feel it, in my hand, until my dying day. [*Pause.*] I might have kept
it. [*Pause.*] But I gave it to the dog.
    [*Pause.*]
    Ah well. . . .
    [*Pause.*]
    Spiritually a year of profound gloom and indigence until that memorable night
in March, at the end of the jetty, in the howling wind, never to be forgotten,
when suddenly I saw the whole thing. The vision at last. This I fancy is what I
have chiefly to record this evening, against the day when my work will be done
and perhaps no place left in my memory, warm or cold, for the miracle that . . .
[*hesitates*] . . . for the fire that set it alight. What I suddenly saw then was this, that
the belief I had been going on all my life, namely—[*Krapp switches off impatiently,
winds tape forward, switches on again*]—great granite rocks the foam flying up in the
light of the lighthouse and the wind-gauge spinning like a propeller, clear to me at
last that the dark I have always struggled to keep under is in reality my most—
[*Krapp curses, switches off, winds tape forward, switches on again*]—unshatterable
association until my dissolution of storm and night with the light of the understanding and the fire—[*Krapp curses louder, switches off, winds tape forward, switches on again*]—my face in her breasts and my hand on her. We lay there without
moving. But under us all moved, and moved us, gently, up and down, and from
side to side.
    [*Pause.*]
    Past midnight. Never knew such silence. The earth might be uninhabited.
    [*Pause.*]
    Here I end—
    [*Krapp switches off, winds tape back, switches on again.*]
    —upper lake, with the punt,[6] bathed off the bank, then pushed out into the
stream and drifted. She lay stretched out on the floorboards with her hands under
her head and her eyes closed. Sun blazing down, bit of a breeze, water nice and
lively. I noticed a scratch on her thigh and asked her how she came by it. Picking
gooseberries, she said. I said again I thought it was hopeless and no good going on
and she agreed, without opening her eyes. [*Pause.*] I asked her to look at me and
after a few moments—[*Pause.*]—after a few moments she did, but the eyes just
slits, because of the glare. I bent over her to get them in the shadow and they
opened. [*Pause. Low.*] Let me in. [*Pause.*] We drifted in among the flags[7] and stuck.
The way they went down, sighing, before the stem! [*Pause.*] I lay down across her
with my face in her breasts and my hand on her. We lay there without moving. But
under us all moved, and moved us, gently, up and down, and from side to side.

---

5. Green gemstone.   7. Reeds.
6. A small, flat-bottomed boat.

[*Pause.*]

Past midnight. Never knew—

[*Krapp switches off, broods. Finally he fumbles in his pockets, encounters the banana, takes it out, peers at it, puts it back, fumbles, brings out envelope, fumbles, puts back envelope, looks at his watch, gets up and goes backstage into darkness. Ten seconds. Sound of bottle against glass, then brief siphon. Ten seconds. Bottle against glass alone. Ten seconds. He comes back a little unsteadily into light, goes to front of table, takes out keys, raises them to his eyes, chooses key, unlocks first drawer, peers into it, feels about inside, takes out reel, peers at it, locks drawer, puts keys back in his pocket, goes and sits down, takes reel off machine, lays it on dictionary, loads virgin reel on machine, takes envelope from his pocket, consults back of it, lays it on table, switches on, clears his throat and begins to record.*]

KRAPP Just been listening to that stupid bastard I took myself for thirty years ago, hard to believe I was ever as bad as that. Thank God that's all done with anyway. [*Pause.*] The eyes she had! [*Broods, realizes he is recording silence, switches off, broods. Finally.*] Everything there, everything, all the—[*Realizes this is not being recorded, switches on.*] Everything there, everything on this old muckball, all the light and dark and famine and feasting of . . . [*hesitates*] . . . the ages! [*In a shout.*] Yes! [*Pause.*] Let that go! Jesus! Take his mind off his homework! Jesus! [*Pause. Weary.*] Ah well, maybe he was right. [*Pause.*] Maybe he was right. [*Broods. Realizes. Switches off. Consults envelope.*] Pah! [*Crumples it and throws it away. Broods. Switches on.*] Nothing to say, not a squeak. What's a year now? The sour cud and the iron stool.[8] [*Pause.*] Revelled in the word spool. [*With relish.*] Spoool! Happiest moment of the past half million. [*Pause.*] Seventeen copies sold, of which eleven at trade price to free circulating libraries beyond the seas. Getting known. [*Pause.*] One pound six and something, eight I have little doubt. [*Pause.*] Crawled out once or twice, before the summer was cold. Sat shivering in the park, drowned in dreams and burning to be gone. Not a soul. [*Pause.*] Last fancies. [*Vehemently.*] Keep 'em under! [*Pause.*] Scalded the eyes out of me reading *Effie*[9] again, a page a day, with tears again. Effie. . . . [*Pause.*] Could have been happy with her, up there on the Baltic, and the pines, and the dunes. [*Pause.*] Could I? [*Pause.*] And she? [*Pause.*] Pah! [*Pause.*] Fanny came in a couple of times. Bony old ghost of a whore. Couldn't do much, but I suppose better than a kick in the crutch. The last time wasn't so bad. How do you manage it, she said, at your age? I told her I'd been saving up for her all my life. [*Pause.*] Went to Vespers[1] once, like when I was in short trousers. [*Pause. Sings.*]

> Now the day is over,
> Night is drawing nigh-igh,
> Shadows—[*coughing, then almost inaudible*]—of the evening
> Steal across the sky.

[*Gasping.*] Went to sleep and fell off the pew. [*Pause.*] Sometimes wondered in the night if a last effort mightn't—[*Pause.*] Ah finish your booze now and get to your bed. Go on with this drivel in the morning. Or leave it at that. [*Pause.*] Leave it at that. [*Pause.*] Lie propped up in the dark—and wander. Be again in

---

8. Indigestion and constipation.
9. Theodor Fontane's sentimental novel *Effi Briest* (1895).

1. Evening church service.

the dingle[2] on a Christmas Eve, gathering holly, the red-berried. [*Pause.*] Be again on Croghan[3] on a Sunday morning, in the haze, with the bitch, stop and listen to the bells. [*Pause.*] And so on. [*Pause.*] Be again, be again. [*Pause.*] All that old misery. [*Pause.*] Once wasn't enough for you. [*Pause.*] Lie down across her.

[*Long pause. He suddenly bends over machine, switches off, wrenches off tape, throws it away, puts on the other, winds it forward to the passage he wants, switches on, listens staring front.*]

TAPE —gooseberries, she said. I said again I thought it was hopeless and no good going on and she agreed, without opening her eyes. [*Pause.*] I asked her to look at me and after a few moments—[*Pause.*]—after a few moments she did, but the eyes just slits, because of the glare. I bent over to get them in the shadow and they opened. [*Pause. Low.*] Let me in. [*Pause.*] We drifted in among the flags and stuck. The way they went down, sighing, before the stem! [*Pause.*] I lay down across her with my face in her breasts and my hand on her. We lay there without moving. But under us all moved, and moved us, gently, up and down, and from side to side.

[*Pause. Krapp's lips move. No sound.*]

Past midnight. Never knew such silence. The earth might be uninhabited.

[*Pause.*]

Here I end this reel. Box—[*Pause.*]—three, spool—[*Pause.*]—five. [*Pause.*] Perhaps my best years are gone. When there was a chance of happiness. But I wouldn't want them back. Not with the fire in me now. No, I wouldn't want them back.

[*Krapp motionless staring before him. The tape runs on in silence.*]

CURTAIN

from Texts for Nothing[1]

4

Where would I go, if I could go, who would I be, if I could be, what would I say, if I had a voice, who says this, saying it's me? Answer simply, someone answer simply. It's the same old stranger as ever, for whom alone accusative I exist, in the pit of my inexistence, of his, of ours, there's a simple answer. It's not with thinking he'll find me, but what is he to do, living and bewildered, yes, living, say what he may. Forget me, know me not, yes, that would be the wisest, none better able than he. Why this sudden affability after such desertion, it's easy to understand, that's what he says, but he doesn't understand. I'm not in his head, nowhere in his old body, and yet I'm there, for him I'm there, with him, hence all the confusion. That should have been enough for him, to have found me absent, but it's not, he wants me there, with a form and a world, like him, in spite of him, me who am everything, like him who is nothing. And when he feels me void of existence it's of his he would have me void, and vice versa, mad, mad, he's mad. The truth is he's looking for me to kill me, to have me dead like him, dead like the living. He knows all that, but it's no help his knowing it, I don't know it, I know nothing. He protests he doesn't reason and does nothing but reason, crooked, as if that could improve matters. He thinks words fail

2. Valley.
3. Mountain in County Wicklow in Southeastern Ireland.
1. Having completed his *Molloy* trilogy in 1950, Beckett

wrote this series of short texts between 1950 and 1952 as "an attempt to get out of the attitude of disintegration" established in his trilogy—an attempt, Beckett later said, that failed.

him, he thinks because words fail him he's on his way to my speechlessness, to being speechless with my speechlessness, he would like it to be my fault that words fail him, of course words fail him. He tells his story every five minutes, saying it is not his, there's cleverness for you. He would like it to be my fault that he has no story, of course he has no story, that's no reason for trying to foist one on me. That's how he reasons, wide of the mark, but wide of what mark, answer us that. He has me say things saying it's not me, there's profundity for you, he has me who say nothing say it's not me. All that is truly crass. If at least he would dignify me with the third person, like his other figments, not he, he'll be satisfied with nothing less than me, for his me. When he had me, when he was me, he couldn't get rid of me quick enough, I didn't exist, he couldn't have that, that was no kind of life, of course I didn't exist, any more than he did, of course it was no kind of life, now he has it, his kind of life, let him lose it, if he wants to be in peace, with a bit of luck. His life, what a mine, what a life, he can't have that, you can't fool him, ergo it's not his, it's not him, what a thought, treat him like that, like a vulgar Molloy, a common Malone, those mere mortals, happy mortals, have a heart, land him in that shit, who never stirred, who is none but me, all things considered, and what things, and how considered, he had only to keep out of it. That's how he speaks, this evening, how he has me speak, how he speaks to himself, how I speak, there is only me, this evening, here, on earth, and a voice that makes no sound because it goes towards none, and a head strewn with arms laid down and corpses fighting fresh, and a body, I nearly forgot. This evening, I say this evening, perhaps it's morning. And all these things, what things, all about me, I won't deny them any more, there's no sense in that any more. If it's nature perhaps it's trees and birds, they go together, water and air, so that all may go on, I don't need to know the details, perhaps I'm sitting under a palm. Or it's a room, with furniture, all that's required to make life comfortable, dark, because of the wall outside the window. What am I doing, talking, having my figments talk, it can only be me. Spells of silence too, when I listen, and hear the local sounds, the world sounds, see what an effort I make, to be reasonable. There's my life, why not, it is one, if you like, if you must, I don't say no, this evening. There has to be one, it seems, once there is speech, no need of a story, a story is not compulsory, just a life, that's the mistake I made, one of the mistakes, to have wanted a story for myself, whereas life alone is enough. I'm making progress, it was time, I'll learn to keep my foul mouth shut before I'm done, if nothing foreseen crops up. But he who somehow comes and goes, unaided from place to place, even though nothing happens to him, true, what of him? I stay here, sitting, if I'm sitting, often I feel sitting, sometimes standing, it's one or the other, or lying down, there's another possibility, often I feel lying down, it's one of the three, or kneeling. What counts is to be in the world, the posture is immaterial, so long as one is on earth. To breathe is all that is required, there is no obligation to ramble, or receive company, you may even believe yourself dead on condition you make no bones about it, what more liberal regimen could be imagined, I don't know, I don't imagine. No point under such circumstances in saying I am somewhere else, someone else, such as I am I have all I need to hand, for to do what, I don't know, all I have to do, there I am on my own again at last, what a relief that must be. Yes, there are moments, like this moment, when I seem almost restored to the feasible. Then it goes, all goes, and I'm far again, with a far story again, I wait for me afar for my story to begin, to end, and again this voice cannot be mine. That's where I'd go, if I could go, that's who I'd be, if I could be.

8

Only the words break the silence, all other sounds have ceased. If I were silent I'd hear nothing. But if I were silent the other sounds would start again, those to which the words have made me deaf, or which have really ceased. But I am silent, it sometimes happens, no, never, not one second. I weep too without interruption. It's an unbroken flow of words and tears. With no pause for reflection. But I speak softer, every year a little softer. Perhaps. Slower too, every year a little slower. Perhaps. It is hard for me to judge. If so the pauses would be longer, between the words, the sentences, the sylla-bles, the tears, I confuse them, words and tears, my words are my tears, my eyes my mouth. And I should hear, at every little pause, if it's the silence I say when I say that only the words break it. But nothing of the kind, that's not how it is, it's for ever the same murmur, flowing unbroken, like a single endless word and therefore meaningless, for it's the end gives the meaning to words. What right have you then, no, this time I see what I'm up to and put a stop to it, saying, None, none. But get on with the stupid old threne[2] and ask, ask until you answer, a new question, the most ancient of all, the question were things always so. Well I'm going to tell myself something (if I'm able), pregnant I hope with promise for the future, namely that I begin to have no very clear recollection of how things were before (I was!), and by before I mean elsewhere, time has turned into space and there will be no more time, till I get out of here. Yes, my past has thrown me out, its gates have slammed behind me, or I burrowed my way out alone, to linger a moment free in a dream of days and nights, dreaming of me moving, season after season, towards the last, like the living, till suddenly I was here, all mem-ory gone. Ever since nothing but fantasies and hope of a story for me somehow, of hav-ing come from somewhere and of being able to go back, or on, somehow, some day, or without hope. Without what hope, haven't I just said, of seeing me alive, not merely inside an imaginary head, but a pebble sand to be, under a restless sky, restless on its shore, faint stirs day and night, as if to grow less could help, ever less and less and nev-er quite be gone. No truly, no matter what, I say no matter what, hoping to wear out a voice, to wear out a head, or without hope, without reason, no matter what, without reason. But it will end, a desinence[3] will come, or the breath fail better still, I'll be silence, I'll know I'm silence, no, in the silence you can't know, I'll never know any-thing. But at least get out of here, at least that, no? I don't know. And time begin again, the steps on the earth, the night the fool implores at morning and the morning he begs at evening not to dawn. I don't know, I don't know what all that means, day and night, earth and sky, begging and imploring. And I can desire them? Who says I desire them, the voice, and that I can't desire anything, that looks like a contradic-tion, it may be for all I know. Me, here, if they could open, those little words, open and swallow me up, perhaps that is what has happened. If so let them open again and let me out, in the tumult of light that sealed my eyes, and of men, to try and be one again. Or if I'm guilty let me be forgiven and graciously authorized to expiate, coming and going in passing time, every day a little purer, a little deader. The mistake I make is to try and think, even the way I do, such as I am I shouldn't be able, even the way I do. But whom can I have offended so grievously, to be punished in this inexplicable way, all is inexplicable, space and time, false and inexplicable, suffering and tears, and even the old convulsive cry, It's not me, it can't be me. But am I in pain, whether it's me or not, frankly now, is there pain? Now is here and here there is no frankness, all I say will be false and to begin with not said by me, here I'm a mere ventriloquist's dum-

2. Song of lamentation.   3. Termination.

my, I feel nothing, say nothing, he holds me in his arms and moves my lips with a string, with a fish-hook, no, no need of lips, all is dark, there is no one, what's the matter with my head, I must have left it in Ireland, in a saloon, it must be there still, lying on the bar, it's all it deserved. But that other who is me, blind and deaf and mute, because of whom I'm here, in this black silence, helpless to move or accept this voice as mine, it's as him I must disguise myself till I die, for him in the meantime do my best not to live, in this pseudo-sepulture[4] claiming to be his. Whereas to my certain knowledge I'm dead and kicking above, somewhere in Europe probably, with every plunge and suck of the sky a little more overripe, as yesterday in the pump of the womb. No, to have said so convinces me of the contrary, I never saw the light of day, any more than he, ah if no were content to cut yes's throat and never cut its own. Watch out for the right moment, then not another word, is that the only way to have being and habitat? But I'm here, that much at least is certain, it's in vain I keep on saying it, it remains true. Does it? It's hard for me to judge. Less true and less certain in any case than when I say I'm on earth, come into the world and assured of getting out, that's why I say it, patiently, variously, trying to vary, for you never know, it's perhaps all a question of hitting on the right aggregate. So as to be here no more at last, to have never been here, but all this time above, with a name like a dog to be called up with and distinctive marks to be had up with, the chest expanding and contracting unaided, panting towards the grand apnoea.[5] The right aggregate, but there are four million possible, nay probable, according to Aristotle, who knew everything. But what is this I see, and how, a white stick and an ear-trumpet, where, Place de la République, at pernod[6] time, let me look closer at this, it's perhaps me at last. The trumpet, sailing at ear level, suddenly resembles a steam-whistle, of the kind thanks to which my steamers forge fearfully through the fog. That should fix the period, to the nearest half-century or so. The stick gains ground, tapping with its ferrule[7] the noble bassamento of the United Stores, it must be winter, at least not summer. I can also just discern, with a final effort of will, a bowler hat which seems to my sorrow a sardonic synthesis of all those that never fitted me and, at the other extremity, similarly suspicious, a complete pair of brown boots lacerated and gaping. These insignia, if I may so describe them, advance in concert, as though connected by the traditional human excipient,[8] halt, move on again, confirmed by the vast show windows. The level of the hat, and consequently of the trumpet, hold out some hope for me as a dying dwarf or at least hunchback. The vacancy is tempting, shall I enthrone my infirmities, give them this chance again, my dream infirmities, that they may take flesh and move, deteriorating, round and round this grandiose square which I hope I don't confuse with the Bastille,[9] until they are deemed worthy of the adjacent Père Lachaise[1] or, better still, prematurely relieved trying to cross over, at the hour of night's young thoughts. No, the answer is no. For even as I moved, or when the moment came, affecting beyond all others, to hold out my hand, or hat, without previous song, or any other form of concession to self-respect, at the terrace of a café, or in the mouth of the underground, I would know it was not me, I would know I was here, begging in another dark, another silence, for another alm, that of being or of ceasing, better still, before having been. And the hand old in vain would drop the mite and the old feet shuffle on, towards an even vainer death than no matter whose.

---

4. Tomb.
5. Cessation of breathing.
6. A licorice-flavored liqueur.
7. Metal-capped tip.

8. Glue.
9. Parisian prison destroyed during the French Revolution in 1789.
1. Parisian cemetery.

━━◆━━

Philip Larkin
1922–1985

Philip Larkin's lifetime production of poems was quite small but highly influential; he is best known for his three last volumes, *The Less Deceived* (1955), *The Whitsun Weddings* (1964), and *High Windows* (1974), which together collect fewer than one hundred poems. During his lifetime, however, he fulfilled the role—a role that every society seems to require—of the crotchety traditionalist poet, becoming famous for what the poet and critic Donald Hall has called a "genuine, uncultivated, sincere philistinism."

Born in Coventry, Larkin completed a B.A. and M.A. at Oxford (where he was a friend of the novelist Kingsley Amis), and became a professional librarian, working at the University of Hull from 1955 until his death. After two modestly successful novels (*Jill* and *A Girl in Winter*) and two undistinguished volumes of poetry (*The North Ship* and *XX Poems*), Larkin established himself as a new and important voice in British poetry with his collection *The Less Deceived*. According to most critics, the influence of Thomas Hardy's poetry was decisive; Seamus Heaney writes that the "slips and excesses" of his first two volumes—consisting, primarily, of embarrassing echoes of W. B. Yeats—led Larkin "to seek the antidote of Thomas Hardy."

Larkin was attracted to Hardy's bleak outlook on life, as well as his skilled versification and spare language. Larkin's dark vision remained unremitting as late as *Aubade*, the last poem to be published during his lifetime:

> I work all day, and get half drunk at night.
> Waking at four to soundless dark, I stare.
> In time the curtain-edges will grow light.
> Till then I see what's really always there:
> Unresting death, a whole day nearer now,
> Making all thought impossible but how
> And where and when I shall myself die.

Like the most famous postwar British playwright, Samuel Beckett, the most important postwar British poet was not above having a laugh at his own despair; in an oft-repeated remark, Larkin told an interviewer that "deprivation is for me what daffodils were for Wordsworth."

Larkin is one of the most English of modern British poets; he refused to read "foreign" literature—including most American poetry—or to travel abroad; Hull became the center and circumference of his poetic world. He kept to himself to an extraordinary degree; he never married, nor did he maintain any longstanding intimate relationship. In his obituary for Larkin, Kingsley Amis described him as "a man much driven in upon himself, with increasing deafness from early middle age cruelly emphasizing his seclusion."

Church Going

> Once I am sure there's nothing going on
> I step inside, letting the door thud shut.
> Another church: matting, seats, and stone,
> And little books; sprawlings of flowers, cut
> For Sunday, brownish now; some brass and stuff
> Up at the holy end; the small neat organ;
> And a tense, musty, unignorable silence,
> Brewed God knows how long. Hatless, I take off
> My cycle-clips in awkward reverence,

5

10   Move forward, run my hand around the font.
From where I stand, the roof looks almost new—
Cleaned, or restored? Someone would know: I don't.
Mounting the lectern, I peruse a few
Hectoring large-scale verses, and pronounce
15   "Here endeth" much more loudly than I'd meant.
The echoes snigger briefly. Back at the door
I sign the book, donate an Irish sixpence,
Reflect the place was not worth stopping for.

Yet stop I did: in fact I often do,
20   And always end much at a loss like this,
Wondering what to look for; wondering, too,
When churches fall completely out of use
What we shall turn them into, if we shall keep
A few cathedrals chronically on show,
25   Their parchment, plate and pyx[1] in locked cases,
And let the rest rent-free to rain and sheep.
Shall we avoid them as unlucky places?

Or, after dark, will dubious women come
To make their children touch a particular stone;
30   Pick simples° for a cancer; or on some   *medicinal plants*
Advised night see walking a dead one?
Power of some sort or other will go on
In games, in riddles, seemingly at random;
But superstition, like belief, must die,
35   And what remains when disbelief has gone?
Grass, weedy pavement, brambles, buttress, sky,

A shape less recognisable each week,
A purpose more obscure. I wonder who
Will be the last, the very last, to seek
40   This place for what it was; one of the crew
That tap and jot and know what rood-lofts[2] were?
Some ruin-bibber, randy for antique,
Or Christmas-addict, counting on a whiff
Of gown-and-bands and organ-pipes and myrrh?
45   Or will he be my representative,

Bored, uninformed, knowing the ghostly silt
Dispersed, yet tending to this cross of ground
Through suburb scrub because it held unspilt
So long and equably what since is found
50   Only in separation—marriage, and birth,
And death, and thoughts of these—for which was built
This special shell? For, though I've no idea
What this accoutred frowsty° barn is worth,   *stuffy*
It pleases me to stand in silence here;

55   A serious house on serious earth it is,
In whose blent air all our compulsions meet,

1. The vessel in which the consecrated bread of the eucharist is kept.

2. Loft at the top of a carved wood or stone screen, separating the nave from the chancel of a church.

Are recognised, and robed as destinies.
And that much never can be obsolete,
Since someone will forever be surprising
60   A hunger in himself to be more serious,
And gravitating with it to this ground,
Which, he once heard, was proper to grow wise in,
If only that so many dead lie round.

1954   1955

High Windows

When I see a couple of kids
And guess he's fucking her and she's
Taking pills or wearing a diaphragm,
I know this is paradise

5   Everyone old has dreamed of all their lives—
Bonds and gestures pushed to one side
Like an outdated combine harvester,
And everyone young going down the long slide

To happiness, endlessly. I wonder if
10   Anyone looked at me, forty years back,
And thought, *That'll be the life;*
No God any more, or sweating in the dark

About hell and that, or having to hide
What you think of the priest. He
15   *And his lot will all go down the long slide*
Like free bloody birds. And immediately

Rather than words comes the thought of high windows:
The sun-comprehending glass,
And beyond it, the deep blue air, that shows
20   Nothing, and is nowhere, and is endless.

1967   1974

Talking in Bed

Talking in bed ought to be easiest,
Lying together there goes back so far,
An emblem of two people being honest.

Yet more and more time passes silently.
5   Outside, the wind's incomplete unrest
Builds and disperses clouds about the sky,

And dark towns heap up on the horizon.
None of this cares for us. Nothing shows why
At this unique distance from isolation

10   It becomes still more difficult to find
Words at once true and kind,
Or not untrue and not unkind.

1960   1964

MCMXIV[1]

Those long uneven lines
Standing as patiently
As if they were stretched outside
The Oval or Villa Park,
5   The crowns of hats, the sun
On moustached archaic faces
Grinning as if it were all
An August Bank Holiday lark;

And the shut shops, the bleached
10   Established names on the sunblinds,
The farthings and sovereigns,
And dark-clothed children at play
Called after kings and queens,
The tin advertisements
15   For cocoa and twist, and the pubs
Wide open all day;

And the countryside not caring:
The place-names all hazed over
With flowering grasses, and fields
20   Shadowing Domesday[2] lines
Under wheat's restless silence;
The differently-dressed servants
With tiny rooms in huge houses,
The dust behind limousines;

25   Never such innocence,
Never before or since,
As changed itself to past
Without a word—the men
Leaving the gardens tidy,
30   The thousands of marriages
Lasting a little while longer:
Never such innocence again.

1960   1964

Whose Language?

Though Britain's last major overseas colony, Hong Kong, rejoined China in 1997, at least one important reminder of British rule remains in countries as far-flung as India, South Africa, and New Zealand: the English language itself. Twentieth-century linguists, following on the pioneering work of Benjamin Lee Whorf and Edward Sapir, are nearly unanimous in their belief that languages do not merely serve to describe the world but in fact help to create that world, establishing both a set of possibilities and a set of limits.

---

1. 1914, in the style of a monument to the war dead.   2. The Domesday Book is the medieval record of the extent, value, and ownership of lands in England.

The politics of language thus becomes important for writers, especially writers in colonial and postcolonial cultures. In an episode from Joyce's *A Portrait of the Artist as a Young Man*, the Irish protagonist Stephen Dedalus converses with the English-born Dean of Studies at University College, Dublin, where Stephen is a student. In the course of the conversation it becomes clear that Stephen is already a more supple and cunning user of the English language than his teacher, and yet he feels himself at a disadvantage in having to use the language of the invader; he muses: "The language in which we are speaking is his before it is mine. How different are the words *home, Christ, ale, master*, on his lips and on mine! I cannot speak or write these words without unrest of spirit. His language, so familiar and so foreign, will always be for me an acquired speech. I have not made or accepted its words. My voice holds them at bay. My soul frets in the shadow of his language." The Penal Acts of 1695 and 1696 had made the Irish language illegal in Ireland; after 500 years of trying to subdue the "wild Irish," British lawmakers realized that the Irish natives would never be brought under English rule until their tongues were bound. In his poem *Traditions*, Seamus Heaney meditates on the enduring cost of what he has called elsewhere "the government of the tongue":

> Our guttural muse
> was bulled long ago
> by the alliterative tradition,
> her uvula grows
> vestigial, forgotten.

In much colonial and postcolonial writing, however, the confusion of tongues inflicted by British rule has been seen by the writers of Empire as a positive linguistic resource. Nadine Gordimer in South Africa and James Kelman in Scotland both mix local dialect with standard English to take the measure of reality a far cry from London. Salman Rushdie, explaining his decision to use English rather than his native Hindi, writes: "Those of us who do use English do so in spite of our ambiguity towards it, or perhaps because of that, perhaps because we can find in that linguistic struggle a reflection of other struggles taking place in the real world, struggles between the cultures within ourselves and the influences working upon our societies. To conquer English may be to complete the process of making ourselves free." Thus a great deal of contemporary English-language writing—especially in countries where English was once the language of the conqueror (such as Ireland, Scotland, Wales, South Africa, India, and Kenya)—meditates on the blindnesses and insights inherent in using English. Some writers, like the Irish poet Nuala Ní Dhomhnaill, write in defiance of English; if one's native tongue is a minority language like Irish, this decision necessarily narrows a writer's potential audience. More common is the decision made by Rushdie, and by James Joyce before him: to write English as an "outsider," attesting to an alien's perspective on the majority language.

Seamus Heaney
b. 1939

More prominently than any poet since Yeats, Heaney has put Irish poetry back at the center of British literary studies. His first full-length collection, *Death of a Naturalist* (1966), ushered in a period of renewed interest in Irish poetry generally, and Ulster poetry in particular; the subsequent attention to poets like Derek Mahon, Michael Longley, Medbh McGuckian, and Paul Muldoon owes a great deal to the scope of Heaney's popularity.

As a great number of Heaney's early poems bear poignant witness, he spent his childhood in rural County Derry, Northern Ireland; his family was part of the Catholic minority in Ulster, and his experiences growing up were for that reason somewhat atypical. The critic Irvin Ehrenpreis maps the matrix of Heaney's contradictory position as an Irish poet: "Speech is never simple, in Heaney's conception. He grew up as an Irish Catholic boy in a land governed by Protestants whose tradition is British. He grew up on a farm in his country's northern, industrial region. As a person, therefore, he springs from the old divisions of his nation." His experience was split not only along religious lines, then, but also national and linguistic ones; in some of his early poetry Heaney suggests the split through the paired names—"Mossbawn" (the very English name of his family's fifty-acre farm) and "Anahorish" (Irish *anach fhior uisce*, "place of clear water," where he attended primary school). As a result, Heaney's is a liminal poetry—a "door into the dark"—and Heaney stands in the doorway, with one foot in each world. Heaney makes brilliant use of the linguistic resources of both the traditions he inherited, drawing on the heritage of English Romanticism while also relying heavily on Irish-language assonance in lines like "There were dragon-flies, spotted butterflies, / But best of all was the warm thick slobber / of frogspawn that grew like clotted water / In the shade of the banks" (*Death of a Naturalist*).

When he was twelve, Heaney won a scholarship to a Catholic boarding school in Londonderry (now Derry) then went on to Queen's University, Belfast, which was the center of a vital new poetic movement in the 1960s. He was influenced by poets who were able to transform the local into the universal, especially Ted Hughes and Robert Frost. As an "Ulster poet," it has fallen to Heaney to use his voice and his position to comment on Northern Ireland's sectarian violence; ironically enough, however, his most explicitly "political" poems were published before the flare-up of the Troubles that began in 1969, and his most self-conscious response to Ulster's strife, the volume *North* (1975), uses historical and mythological frameworks to address the current political situation obliquely. The Irish critic Seamus Deane has written, "Heaney is very much in the Irish tradition in that he has learned, more successfully than most, to conceive of his personal experience in terms of his country's history"; for Heaney, as the popular saying has it, the personal is the political, and the political the personal. His most successful poems dealing with Ulster's political and religious situation are probably those treating neolithic bodies found preserved in peat bogs. Heaney was living in Belfast, lecturing at Queen's University, at the inception of the Troubles; as a Catholic, he felt a need to convey the urgency of the situation without falling into the easy Republican—or Unionist, for that matter—rhetoric. It was at this point that Heaney discovered the anthropologist P. V. Glob's *The Bog People* (1969), which documents (with riveting photographs) the discovery of sacrificial victims preserved in bogs for 2,000 years. Heaney intuitively knew that he had found his "objective correlative"—what he has called his "emblems of adversity"—with which to explore the Troubles.

Like Yeats, Heaney has, from the very start, enjoyed both popular and critical acclaim. His poems have a surface simplicity; his early poetry especially relishes the carefully observed detail of rural Irish life. As his luminous essay *Feeling into Words* shows, he has continued over the years to probe his debts to English literary tradition, and his distance from it. He has been the recipient of numerous awards, honors, and literary prizes, including in 1995 the Nobel Prize for literature.

Feeling into Words[1]

I intend to retrace some paths into what William Wordsworth called in *The Prelude* "the hiding places."

> The hiding places of my power
> Seem open; I approach, and then they close;

1. Lecture given at the Royal Society of Literature, October 1974.

> I see by glimpses now; when age comes on,
> May scarcely see at all, and I would give,
> While yet we may, as far as words can give,
> A substance and a life to what I feel:
> I would enshrine the spirit of the past
> For future restoration.

Implicit in those lines is a view of poetry which I think is implicit in the few poems I have written that give me any right to speak: poetry as divination, poetry as revelation of the self to the self, as restoration of the culture to itself; poems as elements of continuity, with the aura and authenticity of archaeological finds, where the buried shard has an importance that is not diminished by the importance of the buried city; poetry as a dig, a dig for finds that end up being plants.

"Digging," in fact, was the name of the first poem I wrote where I thought my feelings had got into words, or to put it more accurately, where I thought my *feel* had got into words. Its rhythms and noises still please me, although there are a couple of lines in it that have more of the theatricality of the gunslinger than the self-absorption of the digger. I wrote it in the summer of 1964, almost two years after I had begun to "dabble in verses." This was the first place where I felt I had done more than make an arrangement of words: I felt that I had let down a shaft into real life. The facts and surfaces of the thing were true, but more important, the excitement that came from naming them gave me a kind of insouciance and a kind of confidence. I didn't care who thought what about it: somehow, it had surprised me by coming out with a stance and an idea that I would stand over:

> The cold smell of potato mould, the squelch and slap
> Of soggy peat, the curt cuts of an edge
> Through living roots awaken in my head.
> But I've no spade to follow men like them.
>
> Between my finger and my thumb
> The squat pen rests.
> I'll dig with it.

As I say, I wrote it down years ago; yet perhaps I should say that I dug it up, because I have come to realize that it was laid down in me years before that even. The pen/spade analogy was the simple heart of the matter and *that* was simply a matter of almost proverbial common sense. As a child on the road to and from school, people used to ask you what class you were in and how many slaps you'd got that day and invariably they ended up with an exhortation to keep studying because "learning's easy carried" and "the pen's lighter than the spade." And the poem does no more than allow that bud of wisdom to exfoliate, although the significant point in this context is that at the time of writing I was not aware of the proverbial structure at the back of my mind. Nor was I aware that the poem was an enactment of yet another digging metaphor that came back to me years later. This was the rhyme we used to chant on the road to school, though, as I have said before, we were not fully aware of what we were dealing with:

> "Are your praties dry
> And are they fit for digging?"
> "Put in your spade and try,"
> Says Dirty-Faced McGuigan.

There digging becomes a sexual metaphor, an emblem of initiation, like putting your hand into the bush or robbing the nest, one of the various natural analogies for uncovering and touching the hidden thing. I now believe that the "Digging" poem had for me the force of an initiation: the confidence I mentioned arose from a sense that perhaps I could do this poetry thing too, and having experienced the excitement and release of it once, I was doomed to look for it again and again.

I don't want to overload "Digging" with too much significance. It is a big coarse-grained navvy[2] of a poem, but it is interesting as an example—and not just as an example of what one reviewer called "mud-caked fingers in Russell Square," for I don't think that the subject-matter has any particular virtue in itself—it is interesting as an example of what we call "finding a voice."

Finding a voice means that you can get your own feeling into your own words and that your words have the feel of you about them; and I believe that it may not even be a metaphor, for a poetic voice is probably very intimately connected with the poet's natural voice, the voice that he hears as the ideal speaker of the lines he is making up.

In his novel *The First Circle*, Solzhenitsyn[3] sets the action in a prison camp on the outskirts of Moscow where the inmates are all highly skilled technicians forced to labour at projects dreamed up by Stalin. The most important of these is an attempt to devise a mechanism to bug a phone. But what is to be special about this particular bugging device is that it will not simply record the voice and the message but that it will identify the essential sound patterns of the speaker's voice; it will discover, in the words of the narrative, "what it is that makes every human voice unique," so that no matter how the speaker disguises his accent or changes his language, the fundamental structure of his voice will be caught. The idea was that a voice is like a fingerprint, possessing a constant and unique signature that can, like a fingerprint, be recorded and employed for identification.

Now one of the purposes of a literary education as I experienced it was to turn the student's ear into a poetic bugging device, so that a piece of verse denuded of name and date could be identified by its diction, tropes and cadences. And this secret policing of English verse was also based on the idea of a style as a signature. But what I wish to suggest is that there is a connection between the core of a poet's speaking voice and the core of his poetic voice, between his original accent and his discovered style. I think that the discovery of a way of writing that is natural and adequate to your sensibility depends on the recovery of that essential quick which Solzhenitzyn's technicians were trying to pin down. This is the absolute register to which your proper music has to be tuned.

How, then, do you find it? In practice, you hear it coming from somebody else, you hear something in another writer's sounds that flows in through your ear and enters the echo-chamber of your head and delights your whole nervous system in such a way that your reaction will be, "Ah, I wish I had said that, in that particular way." This other writer, in fact, has spoken something essential to you, something you recognize instinctively as a true sounding of aspects of yourself and your experience. And your first steps as a writer will be to imitate, consciously or unconsciously, those sounds that flowed in, that in-fluence.

One of the writers who influenced me in this way was Gerard Manley Hopkins. The result of reading Hopkins at school was the desire to write, and when I first put

---

2. Manual laborer.

3. Alexander Solzhenitsyn (1918–), dissident Soviet writer and political activist.

pen to paper at university, what flowed out was what had flowed in, the bumpy allit-
erating music, the reporting sounds and ricochetting consonants typical of Hopkins's
verse. I remember lines from a piece called "October Thought" in which some frail
bucolic images foundered under the chainmail of the pastiche:

> Starling thatch-watches, and sudden swallow
> Straight breaks to mud-nest, home-rest rafter
> Up past dry dust-drunk cobwebs, like laughter
> Ghosting the roof of bog-oak, turf-sod and rods of willow . . .

and then there was "heaven-hue, plum-blue and gorse-pricked with gold" and "a
trickling tinkle of bells well in the fold."

Looking back on it, I believe there was a connection, not obvious at the time
but, on reflection, real enough, between the heavily accented consonantal noise of
Hopkins's poetic voice, and the peculiar regional characteristics of a Northern Ireland accent. The late W. R. Rodgers, another poet much lured by alliteration, said in
his poem "The Character of Ireland" that the people from his (and my) part of the
world were

> an abrupt people
> who like the spiky consonants of speech
> and think the soft ones cissy; who dig
> the k and t in orchestra, detect sin
> in sinfonia, get a kick out of
> tin-cans, fricatives, fornication, staccato talk,
> anything that gives or takes attack
> like Micks, Teagues, tinker's gets, Vatican.

It is true that the Ulster accent is generally a staccato consonantal one. Our tongue
strikes the tangent of the consonant rather more than it rolls the circle of the vowel—
Rodgers also spoke of "the round gift of the gab in southern mouths." It is energetic,
angular, hard-edged, and it may be because of this affinity between my dialect and
Hopkins's oddity that those first verses turned out as they did.

I couldn't say, of course, that I had found a voice but I had found a game. I knew
the thing was only word-play, and I hadn't even the guts to put my name to it. I called
myself *Incertus*, uncertain, a shy soul fretting and all that. I was in love with words
themselves, but had no sense of a poem as a whole structure and no experience of how
the successful achievement of a poem could be a stepping stone in your life. Those
verses were what we might call "trial-pieces," little stiff inept designs in imitation of
the master's fluent interlacing patterns, heavy-handed clues to the whole craft.

I was getting my first sense of crafting words and for one reason or another, words
as bearers of history and mystery began to invite me. Maybe it began very early when
my mother used to recite lists of affixes and suffixes, and Latin roots, with their English meanings, rhymes that formed part of her schooling in the early part of the century. Maybe it began with the exotic listing on the wireless dial: Stuttgart, Leipzig,
Oslo, Hilversum. Maybe it was stirred by the beautiful sprung rhythms of the old
BBC weather forecast: Dogger, Rockall, Malin, Shetland, Faroes, Finisterre; or with
the gorgeous and inane phraseology of the catechism; or with the litany of the
Blessed Virgin that was part of the enforced poetry in our household: Tower of Gold,
Ark of the Covenant, Gate of Heaven, Morning Star, Health of the Sick, Refuge of
Sinners, Comforter of the Afflicted. None of these things were consciously savoured

at the time but I think the fact that I still recall them with ease, and can delight in them as verbal music, means that they were bedding the ear with a kind of linguistic hardcore that could be built on some day.

That was the unconscious bedding, but poetry involves a conscious savouring of words also. This came by way of reading poetry itself, and being required to learn pieces by heart, phrases even, like Keats's, from "Lamia":

> and his vessel now
> Grated the quaystone with her brazen prow,

or Wordsworth's:

> All shod with steel,
> We hiss'd along the polished ice,

or Tennyson's:

> Old yew, which graspest at the stones
>   That name the underlying dead,
>   Thy fibres net the dreamless head,
> Thy roots are wrapped about the bones.

These were picked up in my last years at school, touchstones of sorts, where the language could give you a kind of aural goose-flesh. At the university I was delighted in the first weeks to meet the moody energies of John Webster—"I'll make Italian cut-works in their guts / If ever I return"—and later on to encounter the pointed masonry of Anglo-Saxon verse and to learn about the rich stratifications of the English language itself. Words alone were certain good.[4] I even went so far as to write these "Lines to myself":

> In poetry I wish you would
> Avoid the lilting platitude.
> Give us poems humped and strong,
> Laced tight with thongs of song,
> Poems that explode in silence
> Without forcing, without violence.
> Whose music is strong and clear and good
> Like a saw zooming in seasoned wood.
> You should attempt concrete expression,
> Half-guessing, half-expression.

Ah well. Behind that was "Ars Poetica," MacLeish's and Verlaine's, Eliot's "objective correlative" (half understood) and several critical essays (by myself and others) about "concrete realization." At the university I kept the whole thing at arm's length, read poetry for the noise and wrote about half a dozen pieces for the literary magazine. But nothing happened inside me. No experience. No epiphany.[5] All craft—and not much of that—and no technique.

I think technique is different from craft. Craft is what you can learn from other verse. Craft is the skill of making. It wins competitions in the *Irish Times* or the *New Statesman*. It can be deployed without reference to the feelings or the self. It knows how to keep up a capable verbal athletic display; it can be content to be *vox et praeterea nihil*—all voice and nothing else—but not voice as in "finding a voice."

---

4. Cf. W. B. Yeats, *The Song of the Happy Shepherd:* "For words alone are certain good."

5. A moment of transcendent vision and insight, crucial in the poetics of modernists like Joyce and Woolf.

Learning the craft is learning to turn the windlass at the well of poetry. Usually you begin by dropping the bucket halfway down the shaft and winding up a taking of air. You are miming the real thing until one day the chain draws unexpectedly tight and you have dipped into waters that will continue to entice you back. You'll have broken the skin on the pool of yourself. Your praties will be "fit for digging."

At that point it becomes appropriate to speak of technique rather than craft. Technique, as I would define it, involves not only a poet's way with words, his management of metre, rhythm and verbal texture; it involves also a definition of his stance towards life, a definition of his own reality. It involves the discovery of ways to go out of his normal cognitive bounds and raid the inarticulate: a dynamic alertness that mediates between the origins of feeling in memory and experience and the formal ploys that express these in a work of art. Technique entails the watermarking of your essential patterns of perception, voice and thought into the touch and texture of your lines; it is that whole creative effort of the mind's and body's resources to bring the meaning of experience within the jurisdiction of form. Technique is what turns, in Yeats's phrase, "the bundle of accident and incoherence that sits down to breakfast" into "an idea, something intended, complete."

It is indeed conceivable that a poet could have a real technique and a wobbly craft—I think this was true of Alun Lewis and Patrick Kavanagh—but more often it is a case of a sure enough craft and a failure of technique. And if I were asked for a figure who represents pure technique, I would say a water diviner. You can't learn the craft of dowsing or divining—it is a gift for being in touch with what is there, hidden and real, a gift for mediating between the latent resource and the community that wants it current and released. As Sir Philip Sidney notes in his *Apologie for Poetry*: "Among the Romans a Poet was called *Vates*, which is as much as a Diviner . . ."

The poem was written simply to allay an excitement and to name an experience, and at the same time to give the excitement and the experience a small *perpetuum mobile* in language itself. I quote it here, not for its own technique but for the image of technique contained in it. The diviner resembles the poet in his function of making contact with what lies hidden, and in his ability to make palpable what was sensed or raised.

The Diviner

> Cut from the green hedge a forked hazel stick
> That he held tight by the arms of the V:
> Circling the terrain, hunting the pluck
> Of water, nervous, but professionally
>
> Unfussed. The pluck came sharp as a sting.
> The rod jerked with precise convulsions,
> Spring water suddenly broadcasting
> Through a green hazel its secret stations.
>
> The bystanders would ask to have a try.
> He handed them the rod without a word.
> It lay dead in their grasp till nonchalantly
> He gripped expectant wrists. The hazel stirred.

What I had taken as matter of fact as a youngster became a matter of wonder in memory. When I look at the thing now I am pleased that it ends with a verb, "stirred," the heart of the mystery; and I am glad that "stirred" chimes with "word," bringing the two functions of *vates* into the one sound.

Technique is what allows that first stirring of the mind round a word or an image or a memory to grow towards articulation: articulation not necessarily in terms of argument or explication but in terms of its own potential for harmonious self-reproduction. The seminal excitement has to be granted conditions in which, in Hopkins's words, it "selves, goes itself . . . crying / What I do is me, for that I came." Technique ensures that the first gleam attains its proper effulgence. And I don't just mean a felicity in the choice of words to flesh the theme—that is a problem also but it is not so critical. A poem can survive stylistic blemishes but it cannot survive a still-birth. The crucial action is pre-verbal, to be able to allow the first alertness or come-hither, sensed in a blurred or incomplete way, to dilate and approach as a thought or a theme or a phrase. Robert Frost put it this way: "a poem begins as a lump in the throat, a homesickness, a lovesickness. It finds the thought and the thought finds the words." As far as I am concerned, technique is more vitally and sensitively connected with that first activity where the "lump in the throat" finds "the thought" than with "the thought" finding "the words." That first emergence involves the divining, vatic, oracular function; the second, the making function. To say, as Auden did, that a poem is a "verbal contraption" is to keep one or two tricks up your sleeve.

Traditionally an oracle speaks in riddles, yielding its truths in disguise, offering its insights cunningly. And in the practice of poetry, there is a corresponding occasion of disguise, a protean, chameleon moment when the lump in the throat takes protective colouring in the new element of thought. One of the best documented occasions in the canon of English poetry, as far as this process is concerned, is a poem that survived in spite of its blemish. In fact, the blemish has earned it a peculiar fame:

> High on a mountain's highest ridge,
> Where oft the stormy winter gale
> Cuts like a scythe, while through the clouds
> It sweeps from vale to vale;
> Not five yards from the mountain path,
> This thorn you on your left espy;
> And to the left, three yards beyond,
> You see a little muddy pond
> Of water never dry;
> I've measured it from side to side:
> 'Tis three feet long and two feet wide.

Those two final lines were probably more ridiculed than any other lines in *The Lyrical Ballads* yet Wordsworth maintained "they ought to be liked." That was in 1815, seventeen years after the poem had been composed; but five years later he changed them to "Though but of compass small, and bare / To thirsting suns and parching air." Craft, in more senses than one.

Yet far more important than the revision, for the purposes of this discussion, is Wordsworth's account of the poem's genesis. "The Thorn," he told Isabella Fenwick in 1843,

> arose out of my observing on the ridge of Quantock Hills, on a stormy day, a thorn which I had often passed in calm and bright weather without noticing it. I said to myself, "Cannot I by some invention do as much to make this thorn permanently an impressive object, as the storm has made it to my eyes at this moment?" I began the poem accordingly, and composed it with great rapidity.

The storm, in other words, was nature's technique for granting the thorn-tree its epiphany, awakening in Wordsworth that engendering, heightened state which he describes at the beginning of *The Prelude*—again in relation to the inspiring influence of wind:

> For I, methought, while the sweet breath of Heaven
> Was blowing on my body, felt within
> A corresponding, mild, creative breeze,
> A vital breeze which travell'd gently on
> O'er things which it had made, and is become
> A tempest, a redundant energy
> Vexing its own creation.

This is exactly the kind of mood in which he would have "composed with great rapidity"; the measured recollection of the letter where he makes the poem sound as if it were written to the thesis propounded (retrospectively) in the Preface of 1800— "cannot I by some invention make this thorn permanently an impressive object?"— probably tones down an instinctive, instantaneous recognition into a rational procedure. The technical triumph was to discover a means of allowing his slightly abnormal, slightly numinous vision of the thorn to "deal out its being."

What he did to turn "the bundle of accident and incoherence" of that moment into "something intended, complete" was to find, in Yeats's language, a mask. The poem as we have it is a ballad in which the speaker is a garrulous superstitious man, a sea captain, according to Wordsworth, who connects the thorn with murder and distress. For Wordsworth's own apprehension of the tree, he instinctively recognized, was basically superstitious: it was a standing over, a survival in his own sensibility of a magical way of responding to the natural world, of reading phenomena as signs, occurrences requiring divination. And in order to dramatize this, to transpose the awakened appetites in his consciousness into the satisfactions of a finished thing, he needed his "objective correlative." To make the thorn "permanently an impressive object," images and ideas from different parts of his conscious and unconscious mind were attracted by almost magnetic power. The thorn in its new, wind-tossed aspect had become a field of force.

Into this field were drawn memories of what the ballads call "the cruel mother'" who murders her own baby:

> She leaned her back against a thorn
> All around the loney-o
> And there her little babe was born
> Down by the greenwood side-o

is how a surviving version runs in Ireland. But there have always been variations on this pattern of the woman who kills her baby and buries it. And the ballads are also full of briars and roses and thorns growing out of graves in symbolic token of the life and death of the buried one. So in Wordsworth's imagination the thorn grew into a symbol of tragic, feverish death, and to voice this the ballad mode came naturally; he donned the traditional mask of the tale-teller, legitimately credulous, entering and enacting a convention. The poem itself is a rapid and strange foray where Wordsworth discovered a way of turning the "lump in the throat" into a "thought," discovered a set of images, cadences and sounds that amplified his original visionary excitement into "a redundant energy / Vexing its own creation":

And some had sworn an oath that she
Should be to public justice brought;
And for the little infant's bones
With spades they would have sought.
But then the beauteous hill of moss
Before their eyes began to stir;
And for full fifty yards around
The grass it shook upon the ground.

"The Thorn" is a nicely documented example of feeling getting into words, in ways that paralleled much in my own experience; although I must say that it is hard to discriminate between feeling getting into words and words turning into feeling, and it is only on posthumous occasions like this that the distinction arises. Moreover, it is dangerous for a writer to become too self-conscious about his own processes: to name them too definitively may have the effect of confining them to what is named. A poem always has elements of accident about it, which can be made the subject of inquest afterwards, but there is always a risk in conducting your own inquest: you might begin to believe the coroner in yourself rather than put your trust in the man in you who is capable of the accident. Robert Graves's "Dance of Words" puts this delightfully:

To make them move, you should start from lightning
And not forecast the rhythm: rely on chance
Or so-called chance for its bright emergence
Once lightning interpenetrates the dance.

Grant them their own traditional steps and postures
But see they dance it out again and again
Until only lightning is left to puzzle over—
The choreography plain and the theme plain.

What we are engaged upon here is a way of seeing that turns the lightning into "the visible discharge of electricity between cloud and cloud or between cloud and ground" rather than its own puzzling, brilliant self. There is nearly always an element of the bolt from the blue about a poem's origin.

When I called my second book *Door into the Dark* I intended to gesture towards this idea of poetry as a point of entry into the buried life of the feelings or as a point of exit for it. Words themselves are doors; Janus is to a certain extent their deity, looking back to a ramification of roots and associations and forward to a clarification of sense and meaning. And just as Wordsworth sensed a secret asking for release in the thorn, so in *Door into the Dark* there are a number of poems that arise out of the almost unnameable energies that, for me, hovered over certain bits of language and landscape.

The poem "Undine," for example. It was the dark pool of the sound of the word that first took me: if our auditory imaginations were sufficiently attuned to plumb and sound a vowel, to unite the most primitive and civilized associations, the word "undine" would probably suffice as a poem in itself. *Unda*, a wave, *undine*, a water-woman—a litany of undines would have ebb and flow, water and woman, wave and tide, fulfilment and exhaustion in its very rhythms. But, old two-faced vocable that it is, I discovered a more precise definition once, by accident, in a dictionary. An undine is a water-sprite who has to marry a human being and have a child by him before she can become human. With that definition, the lump in the throat, or rather the thump in the ear, *undine*, became a thought, a field of force that called up other images. One of these was an orphaned memory, without a context, obviously a very early one, of watching a man clearing out an old spongy growth from a drain between two fields, focusing in particular on the way the water, in the cleared-out place, as soon as the shovelfuls of sludge had been removed, the way the water began to run free, rinse itself clean of the soluble mud and make its own little channels and currents. And this image was gathered into a more conscious reading of the myth as being about the liberating, humanizing effect of sexual encounter. Undine was a cold girl who got what the dictionary called a soul through the experience of physical love. So the poem uttered itself out of that nexus—more short-winded than "The Thorn," with less red*undant* energy, but still escaping, I hope, from my incoherence into the voice of the undine herself:

> He slashed the briars, shovelled up grey silt
> To give me right of way in my own drains
> And I ran quick for him, cleaned out my rust.
>
> He halted, saw me finally disrobed,
> Running clear, with apparent unconcern.
> Then he walked by me. I rippled and I churned
>
> Where ditches intersected near the river
> Until he dug a spade deep in my flank
> And took me to him. I swallowed his trench
>
> Gratefully, dispersing myself for love
> Down in his roots, climbing his brassy grain—
> But once he knew my welcome, I alone
>
> Could give him subtle increase and reflection.
> He explored me so completely, each limb
> Lost its cold freedom. Human, warmed to him.

I once said it was a myth about agriculture, about the way water is tamed and humanized when streams become irrigation canals, when water becomes involved with seed. And maybe that is as good an explanation as any. The paraphrasable extensions of a poem can be as protean as possible as long as its elements remain firm. Words can allow you that two-faced approach also. They stand smiling at the audience's way of reading them and winking back at the poet's way of using them.

Behind this, of course, there is a good bit of symbolist theory. Yet in practice, you proceed by your own experience of what it is to write what you consider a successful poem. You survive in your own esteem not by the corroboration of theory but by the trust in certain moments of satisfaction which you know intuitively to be moments of extension. You are confirmed by the visitation of the last poem and threatened by the elusiveness of the next one, and the best moments are those when your mind seems to implode and words and images rush of their own accord into the vortex. Which happened to me once when the line "We have no prairies" drifted into my head at bedtime, and loosened a fall of images that constitute the poem "Bogland," the last one in *Door into the Dark*.

I had been vaguely wishing to write a poem about bogland, chiefly because it is a landscape that has a strange assuaging effect on me, one with associations reaching back into early childhood. We used to hear about bog-butter, butter kept fresh for a great number of years under the peat. Then when I was at school the skeleton of an elk had been taken out of a bog nearby and a few of our neighbours had got their photographs in the paper, peering out across its antlers. So I began to get an idea of bog as the memory of the landscape, or as a landscape that remembered everything that happened in and to it. In fact, if you go round the National Museum in Dublin, you will realize that a great proportion of the most cherished material heritage of Ireland was "found in a bog." Moreover, since memory was the faculty that supplied me with the first quickening of my own poetry, I had a tentative unrealized need to make a congruence between memory and bogland and, for the want of a better word, our national consciousness. And it all released itself after "We have no prairies . . ."—but we have bogs.

At that time I was teaching modern literature in Queen's University, Belfast, and had been reading about the frontier and the west as an important myth in the American consciousness, so I set up—or rather, laid down—the bog as an answering Irish myth. I wrote it quickly the next morning, having slept on my excitement, and revised it on the hoof, from line to line, as it came:

> We have no prairies
> To slice a big sun at evening—
> Everywhere the eye concedes to
> Encroaching horizon,
>
> Is wooed into the cyclops' eye
> Of a tarn. Our unfenced country
> Is bog that keeps crusting
> Between the sights of the sun.
>
> They've taken the skeleton
> Of the great Irish Elk
> Out of the peat, set it up
> An astounding crate full of air.
>
> Butter sunk under
> More than a hundred years
> Was recovered salty and white.
> The ground itself is kind, black butter
>
> Melting and opening underfoot,
> Missing its last definition
> By millions of years.
> They'll never dig coal here,
>
> Only the waterlogged trunks
> Of great firs, soft as pulp.
> Our pioneers keep striking
> Inwards and downwards,
>
> Every layer they strip
> Seems camped on before.
> The bogholes might be Atlantic seepage.
> The wet centre is bottomless.

Again, as in the case of "Digging," the seminal impulse had been unconscious. What generated the poem about memory was something lying beneath the very floor of memory, something I only connected with the poem months after it was written, which was a warning that older people would give us about going into the bog. They were afraid we might fall into the pools in the old workings so they put it about (and we believed them) that *there was no bottom* in the bog-holes. Little did they—or I—know that I would filch it for the last line of a book.

There was also in that book a poem called "Requiem for the Croppies" which was written in 1966 when most poets in Ireland were straining to celebrate the anniversary of the 1916 Rising. That rising was the harvest of seeds sown in 1798, when revolutionary republican ideals and national feeling coalesced in the doctrines of Irish republicanism and in the rebellion of 1798 itself—unsuccessful and savagely put down. The poem was born of and ended with an image of resurrection based on the fact that some time after the rebels were buried in common graves, these graves began to sprout with young barley, growing up from barley corn which the "croppies" had carried in their pockets to eat while on the march. The oblique implication was that the seeds of violent resistance sowed in the Year of Liberty had flowered in what Yeats called "the right rose tree" of 1916. I did not realize at the time that the original heraldic murderous encounter between Protestant yeoman and Catholic rebel was to be initiated again in the summer of 1969, in Belfast, two months after the book was published.

From that moment the problems of poetry moved from being simply a matter of achieving the satisfactory verbal icon to being a search for images and symbols adequate to our predicament. I do not mean liberal lamentation that citizens should feel compelled to murder one another or deploy their different military arms over the matter of nomenclatures such as British or Irish. I do not mean public celebrations or execrations of resistance or atrocity—although there is nothing necessarily unpoetic about such celebration, if one thinks of Yeats's "Easter 1916." I mean that I felt it imperative to discover a field of force in which, without abandoning fidelity to the processes and experience of poetry as I have outlined them, it would be possible to encompass the perspectives of a humane reason and at the same time to grant the religious intensity of the violence its deplorable authenticity and complexity. And when I say religious, I am not thinking simply of the sectarian division. To some extent the enmity can be viewed as a struggle between the cults and devotees of a god and a goddess. There is an indigenous territorial numen, a tutelar of the whole island, call her Mother Ireland, Kathleen Ni Houlihan, the poor old woman, the Shan Van Vocht, whatever; and her sovereignty has been temporarily usurped or infringed by a new male cult whose founding fathers were Cromwell, William of Orange and Edward Carson, and whose godhead is incarnate in a rex or caesar resident in a palace in London. What we have is the tail-end of a struggle in a province between territorial piety and imperial power.

Now I realize that this idiom is remote from the agnostic world of economic interest whose iron hand operates in the velvet glove of "talks between elected representatives," and remote from the political manoeuvres of power-sharing; but it is not remote from the psychology of the Irishmen and Ulstermen who do the killing, and not remote from the bankrupt psychology and mythologies implicit in the terms Irish Catholic and Ulster Protestant. The question, as ever, is "How with this rage shall beauty hold a plea?" And my answer is, by offering "befitting emblems of adversity."

Some of these emblems I found in a book that was published in English translation, appositely, the year the killing started, in 1969. And again appositely, it was entitled *The Bog People*. It was chiefly concerned with preserved bodies of men and women found in the bogs of Jutland, naked, strangled or with their throats cut, disposed under the peat since early Iron Age times. The author, P. V. Glob, argues convincingly that a number of these, and in particular the Tollund Man, whose head is now preserved near Aarhus[6] in the museum at Silkeburg, were ritual sacrifices to the Mother Goddess, the goddess of the ground who needed new bridegrooms each winter to bed with her in her sacred place, in the bog, to ensure the renewal and fertility of the territory in the spring. Taken in relation to the tradition of Irish political martyrdom for that cause whose icon is Kathleen Ni Houlihan, this is more than an archaic barbarous rite: it is an archetypal pattern. And the unforgettable photographs of these victims blended in my mind with photographs of atrocities, past and present, in the long rites of Irish political and religious struggles. When I wrote this poem, I had a completely new sensation, one of fear. It was a vow to go on pilgrimage and I felt as it came to me—and again it came quickly—that unless I was deeply in earnest about what I was saying, I was simply invoking dangers for myself. It is called "The Tollund Man":

I

Some day I will go to Aarhus
To see his peat-brown head,
The mild pods of his eye-lids,
His pointed skin cap.

In the flat country nearby
Where they dug him out,
His last gruel of winter seeds
Caked in his stomach,

Naked except for
The cap, noose and girdle,
I will stand a long time.
Bridegroom to the goddess,

She tightened her torc[7] on him
And opened her fen,[8]
Those dark juices working
Him to a saint's kept body,

Trove of the turfcutters'
Honeycombed workings.
Now his stained face
Reposes at Aarhus.

II

I could risk blasphemy,
Consecrate the cauldron bog
Our holy ground and pray
Him to make germinate

The scattered, ambushed
Flesh of labourers,
Stockinged corpses
Laid out in the farmyards,

6. A county in East Jutland, in Denmark.
7. A twisting or rotating force.
8. Low land covered with shallow water.

Tell-tale skin and teeth
Flecking the sleepers
Of four young brothers, trailed
For miles along the lines.

III

Something of his sad freedom
As he rode the tumbril
Should come to me, driving,
Saying the names

Tollund, Grauballe, Nebelgard,[9]
Watching the pointing hands
Of country people,
Not knowing their tongue.

Out there in Jutland
In the old man-killing parishes
I will feel lost,
Unhappy and at home.

And just how persistent the barbaric attitudes are, not only in the slaughter but in the psyche, I discovered, again when the *frisson* of the poem itself had passed, and indeed after I had fulfilled the vow and gone to Jutland, "the holy blisful martyr for to seek."[1] I read the following in a chapter on "The Religion of the Pagan Celts" by the Celtic scholar, Anne Ross:

> Moving from sanctuaries and shrines . . . we come now to consider the nature of the actual deities. . . . But before going on to look at the nature of some of the individual deities and their cults, one can perhaps bridge the gap as it were by considering a symbol which, in its way, sums up the whole of Celtic pagan religion and is as representative of it as is, for example, the sign of the cross in Christian contexts. This is the symbol of the severed human head; in all its various modes of iconographic representation and verbal presentation, one may find the hard core of Celtic religion. It is indeed . . . a kind of shorthand symbol for the entire religious outlook of the pagan Celts.[2]

My sense of occasion and almost awe as I vowed to go to pray to the Tollund Man and assist at his enshrined head had a longer ancestry than I had at the time realized.

I began by suggesting that my point of view involved poetry as divination, as a restoration of the culture to itself. In Ireland in this century it has involved for Yeats and many others an attempt to define and interpret the present by bringing it into significant relationship with the past, and I believe that effort in our present circumstances has to be urgently renewed. But here we stray from the realm of technique into the realm of tradition; to forge a poem is one thing, to forge the uncreated conscience of the race, as Stephen Dedalus put it,[3] is quite another and places daunting pressures and responsibilities on anyone who would risk the name of poet.

---

9. Locations in Jutland.
1. The goal of the storytelling pilgrims in Chaucer's *Canterbury Tales*.
2. *Pagan Celtic Britain: Studies in Iconography and Tradition*

(1967).
3. The protagonist of Joyce's *A Portrait of the Artist as a Young Man* describes his ambition in these terms at the novel's close.

— ⊱✦⊰ —

Nuala Ní Dhomhnaill
b. 1952

Ní Dhomhnaill was born in a coal mining region in England, to Irish parents; she was sent at the age of five, however, to live with relatives in the Gaeltacht (Irish-speaking area) on the Dingle Peninsula in West Kerry—"dropped into it cold-turkey," she says. She thus grew up bilingual, speaking English in the home, Irish out of it. Ní Dhomhnaill quickly learned that translation always picks up and leaves behind meaning; she tells this story: "I recall as a child someone asking my name in Irish. The question roughly translates as 'Who do you belong to?' Still most fluent in English, I replied, 'I don't belong to anybody. I belong to myself.' That became quite a joke in the village." In some ways, Ní Dhomhnaill's poetic career has been the process of discovering who, and whose, she is—and making those discoveries through the medium of the Irish language; her name itself, pronounced *nu-AH-la ne GOE-ne*, sounds different than it looks to English eyes.

"The individual psyche is a rather puny thing," she has said; "One's interior life dries up without the exchange with tradition." Ní Dhomhnaill's fruitful exchange with the Irish literary tradition has resulted in a poetry rich in the imagery of Irish folklore and mythology, and pregnant with the sense of contradiction and irony that undergirds Irish writing ("We [Celts] are truly comfortable only with ambiguity," she says). Ní Dhomhnaill's poetry in Irish includes the prize-winning volumes *An Dealg Droighin* (1981) and *Féar Suaithinseach* (1984), as well as a selection of poems from her volume *Feis* translated into English by the poet Paul Muldoon. The *Irish Literary Supplement* has called her "the most widely known and acclaimed Gaelic poet of the century"; by continuing to write in Irish, she has helped make it a viable language for modern poetry. Ní Dhomhnaill lives in Dublin and teaches at University College, Cork.

Feeding a Child[1]

From honey-dew of milking
from cloudy heat of beestings
the sun rises up the back
of bare hills,
5   a guinea gold
to put in your hand,
my own.
You drink your fill from my breast
and fall back asleep
10   into a lasting dream
laughter in your face.
What is going through your head
you who are but
a fortnight on earth?

15   Do you know day from night
that the great early ebb
announces spring tide?
That the boats
are on deep ocean,
20   where live the seals and fishes
and the great whales,

---

1. Translated by Michael Hartnett.

and are coming hand over hand
each by seven oars manned?
That your small boats swims
25   óró[2] in the bay
with the flippered peoples
and the small sea-creatures
she slippery-sleek
from stem to bow
30   stirring sea-sand up
sinking sea-foam down.

Of all these things are you
ignorant?
As my breast is explored
35   by your small hand
you grunt with pleasure
smiling and senseless.
I look into your face child
not knowing if you know
40   your herd of cattle
graze in the land of giants
trespassing and thieving
and that soon you will hear
the fee-fie-fo-fum
45   sounding in your ear.

You are my piggy
who went to market
who stayed at home
who got bread and butter
50   who got none.
There's one good bite in you
but hardly two—
I like your flesh
but not the broth thereof.
55   And who are the original patterns
of the heroes and giants
if not you and I?

1986

Parthenogenesis[1]

Once, a lady of the Ó Moores
(married seven years without a child)
swam in the sea in summertime.
She swam well, and the day
5   was fine as Ireland ever saw
not even a puff of wind in the air
all the bay calm, all the sea smooth—
a sheet of glass—supple, she struck out
with strength for the breaking waves

2. Soothing nonsense sound in Irish.

1. Translated by Michael Hartnett. "Parthenogenesis" is
the scientific term for virgin birth.

10   and frisked, elated by the world.
        She ducked beneath the surface and there saw
        what seemed a shadow, like a man's.
        And every twist and turn she made
        the shadow did the same
15   and came close enough to touch.
        Heart jumped and sound stopped in her mouth
        her pulses ran and raced, sides near burst.
        The lower currents with their ice
        pierced her to the bone
20   and the noise of the abyss numbed all her limbs
        then scales grew on her skin . . .
        the lure of the quiet dreamy undersea . . .
        desire to escape to sea and shells . . .
        the seaweed tresses where at last
25   her bones changed into coral
        and time made atolls of her arms,
        pearls of her eyes in deep long sleep,
        at rest in a nest of weed,
        secure as feather beds . . .
30   But stop!
        Her heroic heritage was there,
        she rose with speedy, threshing feet
        and made in desperation for the beach:
        with nimble supple strokes she made the sand.
35   Near death until the day,
        some nine months later
        she gave birth to a boy.
        She and her husband so satisfied,
        so full of love for this new son
40   forgot the shadow in the sea
        and did not see what only the midwife saw—
        stalks of sea-tangle in the boy's hair
        small shellfish and sea-ribbons
        and his two big eyes
45   as blue and limpid as lagoons.
        A poor scholar passing by
        who found lodging for the night
        saw the boy's eyes never closed
        in dark or light and when all the world slept
50   he asked the boy beside the fire
        "Who are your people?" Came the prompt reply
        "Sea People."

        This same tale is told in the West
        but the woman's an Ó Flaherty
55   and tis the same in the South
        where the lady's called Ó Shea:
        this tale is told on every coast.
        But whoever she was I want to say
        that the fear she felt
60   when the sea-shadow followed her

is the same fear that vexed
the young heart of the Virgin
when she heard the angels' sweet bell
and in her womb was made flesh
65   by all accounts
the Son of the Living God.

1986

Why I Choose to Write in Irish, The Corpse That Sits Up and Talks Back[1]

Not so long ago I telephoned my mother about some family matter. "So what are you writing these days?" she asked, more for the sake of conversation than anything else. "Oh, an essay for *The New York Times*," I said, as casually as possible. "What is it about?" she asked. "About what it is like to write in Irish," I replied. There was a good few seconds' pause on the other end of the line; then, "Well, I hope you'll tell them that it is mad." End of conversation. I had got my comeuppance. And from my mother, who was the native speaker of Irish in our family, never having encountered a single word of English until she went to school at the age of 6, and well up in her teens before she realized that the name they had at home for a most useful item was actually two words—"safety pin"—and that they were English. Typical.

But really not so strange. Some time later I was at a reception at the American Embassy in Dublin for two of their writers, Toni Morrison and Richard Wilbur. We stood in line and took our buffet suppers along to the nearest available table. An Irishwoman across from me asked what I did. Before I had time to open my mouth her partner butted in: "Oh, Nuala writes poetry in Irish." And what did I write about? she asked. Again before I had time to reply he did so for me: "She writes poems of love and loss, and I could quote you most of them by heart." This was beginning to get up my nose, and so I attempted simultaneously to deflate him and to go him one better. "Actually," I announced, "I think the only things worth writing about are the biggies: birth, death and the most important thing in between, which is sex." "Oh," his friend said to me archly, "and is there a word for sex in Irish?"

I looked over at the next table, where Toni Morrison was sitting, and I wondered if a black writer in America had to put up with the likes of that, or its equivalent. Here I was in my own country, having to defend the official language of the state from a compatriot who obviously thought it was an accomplishment to be ignorant of it. Typical, and yet maybe not so strange.

Let me explain. Irish (as it is called in the Irish Constitution; to call it Gaelic is not P.C. at the moment, but seen as marginalizing) is the Celtic language spoken by a small minority of native speakers principally found in rural pockets on the western seaboard. These Irish-speaking communities are known as the "Gaeltacht," and are the last remnants of an earlier historical time when the whole island was Irish-speaking, or one huge "Gaeltacht." The number of Irish speakers left in these areas who use the language in most of their daily affairs is a hotly debated point, and varies from 100,000 at the most optimistic estimate to 20,000 at the most conservative. For the sake of a round number let us take it to be 60,000, or about 2 percent of the population of the Republic of Ireland.

---

1. Published in *The New York Times Book Review*, January 1995.

Because of the effort of the Irish Revival movement, and of the teaching of Irish in the school system, however, the language is also spoken with varying degrees of frequency and fluency by a considerably larger number of people who have learned it as a second language. So much so that census figures over the last few decades have consistently indicated that up to one million people, or 30 percent of the population of the Republic, claim to be speakers of Irish. To this can be added the 146,000 people in the Six Counties of Northern Ireland who also are competent in Irish. This figure of one million speakers is, of course, grossly misleading and in no way reflects a widespread use of the language in everyday life. Rather it can be seen as a reflection of general good will toward the language, as a kind of wishful thinking. Nevertheless that good will is important.

The fact that the Irish language, and by extension its literature, has a precarious status in Ireland at the moment is a development in marked contrast to its long and august history. I believe writing in Irish is the oldest continuous literary activity in Western Europe, starting in the fifth century and flourishing in a rich and varied manuscript tradition right down through the Middle Ages. During this time the speakers of any invading language, such as Norse, Anglo-Norman and English, were assimilated, becoming "more Irish than the Irish themselves." But the Battle of Kinsale in 1601, in which the British routed the last independent Irish princes, and the ensuing catastrophes of the turbulent 17th century, including forced population transfers, destroyed the social underpinning of the language. Its decline was much accelerated by the great famine of the mid-19th century; most of the one million who died of starvation and the millions who left on coffin ships for America were Irish speakers. The fact that the fate of emigration stared most of the survivors in the eye further speeded up the language change to English—after all, "What use was Irish to you over in Boston?"

The indigenous high culture became the stuff of the speech of fishermen and small farmers, and this is the language that I learned in West Kerry in the 1950's at the age of 5 in a situation of total immersion, when I was literally and figuratively farmed out to my aunt in the parish of Ventry. Irish is a language of enormous elasticity and emotional sensitivity; of quick and hilarious banter and a welter of references both historical and mythological; it is an instrument of imaginative depth and scope, which has been tempered by the community for generations until it can pick up and sing out every hint of emotional modulation that can occur between people. Many international scholars rhapsodize that this speech of ragged peasants seems always on the point of bursting into poetry. The pedagogical accident that had me learn this language at an early age can only be called a creative one.

The Irish of the Revival, or "book Irish," was something entirely different, and I learned it at school. Although my first literary love affair was with the Munster poets, Aodhagán Ó Rathaille and Eoghan Rua Ó Suilleabháin, and I had learned reams and reams of poetry that wasn't taught at school, when I myself came to write it didn't dawn on me that I could possibly write in Irish. The overriding ethos had got even to me. Writing poetry in Irish somehow didn't seem to be intellectually credible. So my first attempts, elegies on the deaths of Bobby Kennedy and Martin Luther King published in the school magazine, were all in English. They were all right, but even I could see that there was something wrong with them.

Writing Irish poetry in English suddenly seemed a very stupid thing to be doing. So I switched language in mid-poem and wrote the very same poem in Irish, and I could see immediately that it was much better. I sent it in to a competition in *The Irish Times*, where it won a prize, and that was that. I never looked back.

I had chosen my language, or more rightly, perhaps, at some very deep level, the language had chosen me. If there is a level to our being that for want of any other word for it I might call "soul" (and I believe there is), then for some reason that I can never understand, the language that my soul speaks, and the place it comes from, is Irish. At 16 I had made my choice. And that was that. It still is. I have no other.

But if the actual choice to write poetry in Irish was easy, then nothing else about it actually is, especially the hypocritical attitude of the state. On the one hand, Irish is enshrined as a nationalistic token (the ceremonial *cúpla focal*—"few words"—at the beginning and end of speeches by politicians, broadcasters and even airline crews is an example). On the other hand, it would not be an exaggeration to speak of the state's indifference, even downright hostility, to Irish speakers in its failure to provide even the most basic services in Irish for those who wish to go about their everyday business in that language.

"The computer cannot understand Irish" leads the excuses given by the state to refuse to conduct its business in Irish, even in the Gaeltacht areas. Every single service gained by Irish speakers has been fought for bitterly. Thus the "Gaelscoileanna," or Irish schools, have been mostly started by groups of parents, often in the very teeth of fierce opposition from the Department of Education. And the only reason we have a single Irish radio station is that a civil rights group started a pirate station 20 years ago in the West and shamed the Government into establishing this vital service. An Irish television channel is being mooted[2] at present, but I'll believe it when I see it.

You might expect at least the cultural nationalists and our peers writing in English to be on our side. Not so. A recent television documentary film about Thomas Kinsella begins with the writer intoning the fact that history has been recorded in Irish from the fifth century to the 19th. Then there is a pregnant pause. We wait for a mention of the fact that life, experience, sentient consciousness, even history is being recorded in literature in Irish in the present day. We wait in vain. By an antiquarian sleight of hand it is implied that Irish writers in English are now the natural heirs to a millennium and a half of writing in Irish. The subtext of the film is that Irish is dead.

So what does that make me, and the many other writers of the large body of modern literature in Irish? A walking ghost? A linguistic specter?

Mind you, it is invidious of me to single out Thomas Kinsella; this kind of insidious "bad faith" about modern literature in Irish is alive and rampant among many of our fellow writers in English. As my fellow poet in Irish, Biddy Jenkinson, has said, "We have been pushed into an ironic awareness that by our passage we would convenience those who will be uneasy in their Irishness as long as there is a living Gaelic tradition to which they do not belong." Now let them make their peace with the tradition if they wish to, I don't begrudge them a line of it. But I'll be damned if their cultural identity is procured at the expense of my existence, or of that of my language.

I can well see how it suits some people to see Irish-language literature as the last rictus[3] of a dying beast. As far as they are concerned, the sooner the language lies down and dies, the better, so they can cannibalize it with greater equanimity, peddling their "ethnic chic" with nice little translations "from the Irish." Far be it from

2. Debated.   3. Gasp.

them to make the real effort it takes to learn the living language. I dare say they must be taken somewhat aback when the corpse that they have long since consigned to choirs of angels, like a certain Tim Finnegan,[4] sits up and talks back to them.

The fault is not always one-sided. The Gaels (Irish-language writers) often fell prey to what Terence Browne, a literary historian, has called an "atmosphere of national self-righteousness and cultural exclusiveness," and their talent did not always equal the role imposed on them. Nevertheless, long after the emergence of a high standard of literature in Irish with Seán Ó Riordáin, Máirtín Ó Direáin and Máire Mhac an tSaoi in poetry, and Máirtín Ó Cadhain in prose, writing in Irish was conspicuously absent from anthologies in the 1950's and 60's. Even as late as the 70's one of our "greats," Seán Ó Riordáin, could hear on the radio two of his co-writers in English saying how "poetry in Ireland had been quiescent in the 50's," thus consigning to nothingness the great work that he and his fellow poets in Irish had produced during that very decade. After a lifetime devoted to poetry, is it any wonder that he died in considerable grief and bitterness?

As for the cultural nationalists, Irish was never the language of nationalist mobilization. Unlike other small countries where nationalism rose throughout the 19th century, in Ireland it was religion rather than language that mostly colored nationalism. Daniel O'Connell, the Liberator, a native-Irish-speaking Kerryman, used to address his monster mass meetings from the 1820's to the 40's in English, even though this language was not understood by 70 percent of the people he was addressing. Why? Because it was at the reporters over from *The Times* of London and their readers that his words were being primarily directed. It is particularly painful to recall that while nationalism was a major motivator in developing modern literary languages out of such varied tongues as Norwegian, Hungarian, Finnish and Estonian, during that very same period the high literary culture of Irish was being reduced to the language of peasants. By the time the revival began, the damage had already been done, and the language was already in irreversible decline (spoken by only 14.5 percent in 1880). The blatant myopia of the cultural nationalists is still alive and glaringly obvious in the disgraceful underrepresentation of Irish in the recently published three-volume *Field Day Anthology of Irish Writing*.

It should not be surprising, then, that we poets and fiction writers in Irish who are included in the anthology feel as if we are being reduced to being exotic background, like Irish Muzak. Thus the cultural nationalists, without granting Irish the intellectual credibility of rational discourse or the popular base of the oral tradition, enshrine it instead as the repository of their own utopian fantasies; pristine, changeless, "creative," but otherwise practically useless.

How does all this affect me, as a poet writing in Irish? Well, inasmuch as I am human and frail and prone to vanity and clamoring for attention, of course it disturbs me to be misunderstood, misrepresented and finally all but invisible in my own country. I get depressed, I grumble and complain, I stand around in rooms muttering darkly. Still and all, at some very deep and fundamental level it matters not one whit. All I ever wanted was to be left alone so that I could go on writing poetry in Irish. I still remember a time when I had an audience I could count on the fingers of one hand. I was perfectly prepared for that. I still am.

---

4. In the vaudeville song *Tim Finnegan's Wake*, the hero takes a drunken fall and dies. At his wake, however, whiskey is spilled over his body and he comes back to life. James Joyce uses this story as the central structure for *Finnegans Wake*.

But it has been gratifying to reach a broader audience through the medium of translations, especially among the one million who profess some knowledge of Irish. Many of them probably had good Irish when they left school but have had no chance of using it since for want of any functional context where it would make sense to use the language. I particularly like it when my poetry in English translation sends them back to the originals in Irish, and when they then go on to pick up the long-lost threads of the language that is so rightly theirs. I also find it pleasant and vivifying to make an occasional trip abroad and to reach a wider audience by means of dual-language readings and publications.

But my primary audience is those who read my work in Irish only. A print run for a book of poems in Irish is between 1,000 and 1,500 copies. That doesn't sound like much until you realize that that number is considered a decent run by many poets in English in Ireland, or for that matter even in Britain or America, where there's a much larger population.

The very ancientness of the Irish literary tradition is also a great source of strength to me as a writer. This works at two levels, one that is mainly linguistic and prosodic and another that is mainly thematic and inspirational. At the linguistic level, Old Irish, though undoubtedly very difficult, is much closer to Modern Irish than, say, Anglo-Saxon is to Modern English. Anyone like me with a basic primary degree in the language and a bit of practice can make a fair job of reading most of the medieval texts in the original.

Thematically too, the older literature is a godsend, though I am only now slowly beginning to assess its unique possibilities to a modern writer. There are known to be well over 4,000 manuscripts in Ireland and elsewhere of material from Old to Modern Irish. Apart from the great medieval codices, only about 50 other manuscripts date from before 1650. Nevertheless, the vast majority of the manuscripts painstakingly copied down after this time are exemplars of much earlier manuscripts that have since been lost. A lot of this is catalogued in ways that are unsatisfactory for our time.

Many items of enormous psychological and sexual interest, for example, are described with the bias of the last century as "indecent and obscene tales, unsuitable for publication." On many such manuscripts human eye has not set sight since they were so described. In addition, most scholarly attention has been paid to pre-Norman-Conquest material as the repository of the unsullied wellsprings of the native soul (those cultural nationalists again!), with the result that the vast area of post-Conquest material has been unfairly neglected. The main advantage of all this material to me is that it is proof of the survival until even a very late historical date of a distinct *Weltanschauung* [worldview] radically different from the Anglo mentality that has since eclipsed it.

Because of a particular set of circumstances, Irish fell out of history just when the modern mentality was about to take off. So major intellectual changes like the Reformation, the Renaissance, the Enlightenment, Romanticism and Victorian prudery have never occurred in it, as they did in the major European languages.

One consequence is that the attitude to the body enshrined in Irish remains extremely open and uncoy. It is almost impossible to be "rude" or "vulgar" in Irish. The body, with its orifices and excretions, is not treated in a prudish manner but is accepted as *an nádúir,* or "nature," and becomes a source of repartee and laughter rather than anything to be ashamed of. Thus little old ladies of quite impeccable and unimpeachable moral character tell risqué stories with gusto and panache. Is there a word for sex in Irish, indeed! Is there an Eskimo word for snow?

By now I must have spent whole years of my life burrowing in the department of folklore at University College, Dublin, and yet there are still days when my hands shake with emotion holding manuscripts. Again, this material works on me on two levels. First is when I revel in the well-turned phrase or nuance or retrieve a word that may have fallen into disuse. To turn the pages of these manuscripts is to hear the voices of my neighbors and my relatives—all the fathers and grandfathers and uncles come to life again. The second interest is more thematic. This material is genuinely ineffable, like nothing else on earth.

Indeed, there is a drawer in the index entitled "Neacha neamhbeo agus nithe nach bhfuil ann" ("Unalive beings and things that don't exist"). Now I am not the greatest empiricist in the world but this one has even me stumped. Either they exist or they don't exist. But if they don't exist why does the card index about them stretch the length of my arm? Yet that is the whole point of this material and its most enduring charm. Do these beings exist? Well, they do and they don't. You see, they are beings from *an saol eile*, the "otherworld," which in Irish is a concept of such impeccable intellectual rigor and credibility that it is virtually impossible to translate into English, where it all too quickly becomes fey and twee and "fairies-at-the-bottom-of-the-garden."

The way so-called depth psychologists go on about the subconscious nowadays you'd swear they had invented it, or at the very least stumbled on a ghostly and ghastly continent where mankind had never previously set foot. Even the dogs in the street in West Kerry know that the "otherworld" exists, and that to be in and out of it constantly is the most natural thing in the world.

This constant tension between reality and fantasy, according to Jeffrey Gantz, the translator of *Early Irish Myths and Sagas,* is characteristic of all Celtic art, but manifests itself particularly in the literature of Ireland. Mr Gantz believes that it is not accidental to the circumstances of the literary transmission but is rather an innate characteristic, a gift of the Celts. It means that the "otherworld" is not simply an anticipated joyful afterlife; it is also—even primarily—an alternative to reality.

This easy interaction with the imaginary means that you don't have to have a raving psychotic breakdown to enter the "otherworld." The deep sense in the language that something exists beyond the ego-envelope is pleasant and reassuring, but it is also a great source of linguistic and imaginative playfulness, even on the most ordinary and banal of occasions.

Let's say I decide some evening to walk up to my aunt's house in West Kerry. She hears me coming. She knows it is me because she recognizes my step on the cement pavement. Still, as I knock lightly on the door she calls out, "An de bheoaibh nó de mhairbh thu?" ("Are you of the living or of the dead?") Because the possibility exists that you could be either, and depending on which category you belong to, an entirely different protocol would be brought into play. This is all a joke, of course, but a joke that is made possible by the imaginative richness of the language itself.

I am not constructing an essentialist argument here, though I do think that because of different circumstances, mostly historical, the strengths and weaknesses of Irish are different from those of English, and the imaginative possibilities of Irish are, from a poet's perspective, one of its greatest strengths. But this is surely as true of, say, Bengali as it is of Irish. It is what struck me most in the Nobel Prize acceptance speech made by the Yiddish writer Isaac Bashevis Singer. When often asked why he wrote in a dead language, Singer said he was wont to reply that he wrote mostly about ghosts, and that is what ghosts speak, a dead language.

Singer's reply touched a deep chord with his Irish audience. It reminded us that the precariousness of Irish is not an Irish problem alone. According to the linguist Michael Krause in *Language* magazine, minority languages in the English language sphere face a 90 percent extinction rate between now and some time in the next century. Therefore, in these days when a major problem is the growth of an originally Anglo-American, but now genuinely global, pop monoculture that reduces everything to the level of the most stupendous boredom, I would think that the preservation of minority languages like Irish, with their unique and unrepeatable way of looking at the world, would be as important for human beings as the preservation of the remaining tropical rain forests is for biological diversity.

Recently, on a short trip to Kerry with my three daughters, I stayed with my brother and his wife in the old house he is renovating on the eastern end of the Dingle peninsula, under the beetling brow of Cathair Chonroi promontory fort. My brother said he had something special to show us, so one day we trooped up the mountain to Derrymore Glen. Although the area is now totally denuded of any form of growth other than lichens and sphagnum moss, the name itself is a dead giveaway: Derrymore from *Doire Mór* in Irish, meaning "Large Oak Grove."

A more desolate spot you cannot imagine, yet halfway up the glen, in the crook of a hanging valley, intricate and gnarled, looking for all the world like a giant bonsai, was a single survivor, one solitary oak tree. Only the top branches were producing leaves, it was definitely on its last legs and must have been at least 200 to 300 years old. How it had survived the massive human and animal depredation of the countryside that occurred during that time I do not know, but somehow it had.

It was very much a *bile*, a sacred tree, dear to the Celts. A fairy tree. A magic tree. We were all very moved by it. Not a single word escaped us, as we stood in the drizzle. At last Ayse, my 10-year-old, broke the silence. "It would just give you an idea," she said, "of what this place was like when it really was a '*Doire Mór*' and covered with oak trees." I found myself humming the air of *Cill Cais*, that lament for both the great woods of Ireland and the largess of the Gaelic order that they had come to symbolize:

> Cad a dhéanfaimid feasta gan adhmad?
> Tá deireadh na gcoillte ar lár.
> Níl trácht ar Chill Cais ná a theaghlach
> is ní chlingfear a chling go brách.

> What will we do now without wood
> Now that the woods are laid low?
> Cill Cais or its household are not mentioned
> and the sound of its bell is no more.

A week later, back in Dublin, that question is still ringing in the air. I am waiting for the children to get out of school and writing my journal in Irish in a modern shopping mall in a Dublin suburb. Not a single word of Irish in sight on sign or advertisement, nor a single sound of it in earshot. All around me are well-dressed and articulate women. I am intrigued by snatches of animated conversation, yet I am conscious of a sense of overwhelming loss. I think back to the lonely hillside, and to Ayse. This is the answer to the question in the song. This is what we will do without wood.

At some level, it doesn't seem too bad. People are warm and not hungry. They are expressing themselves without difficulty in English. They seem happy. I close my notebook with a snap and set off in the grip of that sudden pang of despair that is always lurking in the ever-widening rents of the linguistic fabric of minority languages. Perhaps my mother is right. Writing in Irish is mad. English is a wonderful language, and it also has the added advantage of being very useful for putting bread on the table. Change is inevitable, and maybe it is part of the natural order of things that some languages should die while others prevail.

And yet, and yet . . . I know this will sound ridiculously romantic and sentimental. Yet not by bread alone. . . . We raise our eyes to the hills. . . . We throw our bread upon the waters.[5] There are mythical precedents. Take for instance Moses' mother, consider her predicament. She had the choice of giving up her son to the Egyptian soldiery, to have him cleft in two before her very eyes, or to send him down the Nile in a basket, a tasty dinner for crocodiles. She took what under the circumstances must have seemed very much like *rogha an dá dhiogha* ("the lesser of two evils") and Exodus and the annals of Jewish history tell the rest of the story, and are the direct results of an action that even as I write is still working out its inexorable destiny. I know it is wrong to compare small things with great, yet my final answer to why I write in Irish is this:

Ceist 'na Teangan

Curirim mo dhóchas ar snámh
i mbáidín´ teangan
faoi mar a leagfá naíonán
i gcliabhán
a bheadh fite fuaite
de dhuilleoga feileastraim
is bitiúman agus pic
bheith cuimilte lena thóin

ansan é a leagadh síos
i measc na ngiolcach
is coigeal na mban sí
le taobh na habhann,
féachaint n'fheadaráis
cá dtabharfaidh an sruth é,
féachaint, dála Mhaoise,
an bhfóirfidh iníon Fharoinn?

The Language Issue

I place my hope on the water
in this little boat
of the language, the way a body might put
an infant

in a basket of intertwined
iris leaves,
its underside proofed
with bitumen and pitch,

---

5. Echoing three biblical affirmations of the need to look beyond immediate material wants (Matthew 4.4, Psalm 121.1, Ecclesiastes 11.1). In the first passage cited, Jesus is fasting in the wilderness and rejects Satan's tempting suggestion that he turn stones into bread: "he answered, 'It is written, "Man shall not live by bread alone, but by every word that proceeds from the mouth of God."'"

then set the whole thing down amidst
the sedge
and bulrushes by the edge
of a river

only to have it borne hither and thither,
not knowing where it might end up;
in the lap, perhaps,
of some Pharaoh's daughter.[6]

— ≠◈≥ —

Nadine Gordimer
b. 1923

Nadine Gordimer was born in South Africa to Jewish emigrant parents from London. Thus her childhood, like those of the children of countless middle-class colonial families, was somewhat complex and contradictory. In an interview, Gordimer offers this explanation: "I think when you're born white in South Africa, you're peeling like an orange. You're sloughing off all the conditioning that you've had since you were a child." In Gordimer's case, that "sloughing off" of white, British prejudices and habits of mind has been thorough; the novelist Paul Theroux, for instance, suggests that "Gordimer's vision of Africa is the most complete one we have, and in time to come, when we want to know everything there is to know about a newly independent black African country, it is to this white South African woman . . . that we will turn."

Since Gordimer published her first collection of short stories in 1949 her writing has been praised for its evenhanded and scrupulously honest treatment of the political terrain of South Africa; and over the years she has become, in the words of one critic, "the literary voice and conscience of her society." Among her gifts are an ear sensitive to the cadences and idiosyncrasies of spoken English, and a gift for social satire in service of a finally moral purpose. The longstanding subject of Gordimer's writing—her great theme—is, as critic Michiko Kakutani describes it, "the consequences of apartheid on the daily lives of men and women, the distortions it produces in relationships among both blacks and whites." In Gordimer's writing, these distortions are always shown rather than explained; her presentation is essentially dramatic, a trait she shares with modern masters of short fiction like Chekhov and Joyce.

Gordimer has been faulted for the emphasis in politics in her writing. Her response to this charge is eloquent: "The real influence of politics on my writing is the influence of politics on people. Their lives, and I believe their very personalities, are changed by the extreme political circumstances one lives under in South Africa. I am dealing with people; here are people who are shaped and changed by politics. In that way my material is profoundly influenced by politics." To date, Gordimer has published more than ten novels, including the celebrated *A Guest of Honour* (1970) and *The Conservationist* (1974; cowinner of the Booker McConnell Prize), and more than a dozen collections of short stories. *Jump and Other Stories*, which includes *What Were You Dreaming?*, was published in 1991, the same year Gordimer was awarded the Nobel Prize for Literature. In this story, the disjunction between black and white South African English is the starting-point for an exploration of blocked communication between races and genders alike.

---

6. As happened with Moses when the Israelites were enslaved in Egypt (Exodus 2). Fearing their growing numbers, Pharaoh had ordered all male Hebrew infants to be drowned in the Nile; Moses's mother instead set him adrift in a reed basket, which was found by the Pharaoh's daughter, who adopted him and raised him as an Egyptian. As an adult, Moses led the Israelites out of Egypt to the Promised Land.

What Were You Dreaming?

I'm standing here by the road long time, yesterday, day before, today. Not the same road but it's the same—hot, hot like today. When they turn off where they're going, I must get out again, wait again. Some of them they just pretend there's nobody there, they don't want to see nobody. Even go a bit faster, *ja*. Then they past, and I'm waiting. I combed my hair; I don't want to look like a *skollie* [ruffian]. Don't smile because they think you being too friendly, you think you good as them. They go and they go. Some's got the baby's napkin hanging over the back window to keep out this sun. Some's not going on holiday with their kids but is alone; all alone in a big car. But they'll never stop, the whites, if they alone. Never. Because these *skollies* and that kind've spoilt it all for us, sticking a gun in the driver's neck, stealing his money, beating him up and taking the car. Even killing him. So it's buggered up for us. No white wants some guy sitting behind his head. And the blacks—when they stop for you, they ask for money. They want you must pay, like for a taxi! The blacks!

But then these whites: they stopping; I'm surprised, because it's only two—empty in the back—and the car it's a beautiful one. The windows are that special glass, you can't see in if you outside, but the woman has hers down and she's calling me over with her finger. She ask me where I'm going and I say the next place because they don't like to have you for too far, so she say get in and lean into the back to move along her stuff that's on the back seat to make room. Then she say, lock the door, just push that button down, we don't want you to fall out, and it's like she's joking with someone she know. The man driving smiles over his shoulder and say something—I can't hear it very well, it's the way he talk English. So anyway I say what's all right to say, yes master, thank you master, I'm going to Warmbad. He ask again, but man, I don't get it—*Ekskuus?* Please? And she chips in—she's a lady with grey hair and he's a young chap—My friend's from England, he's asking if you've been waiting a long time for a lift. So I tell them—A long time? Madam! And because they white, I tell them about the blacks, how when they stop they ask you to pay. This time I understand what the young man's saying, he say, And most whites don't stop? And I'm careful what I say, I tell them about the blacks, how too many people spoil it for us, they robbing and killing, you can't blame white people. Then he ask where I'm from. And she laugh and look round where I'm behind her. I see she know I'm from the Cape, although she ask me. I tell her I'm from the Cape Flats[1] and she say she suppose I'm not born there, though, and she's right, I'm born in Wynberg, right there in Cape Town. So she say, And they moved you out?

Then I catch on what kind of white she is; so I tell her, yes, the government kicked us out from our place, and she say to the young man, You see?

He want to know why I'm not in the place in the Cape Flats, why I'm so far away here. I tell them I'm working in Pietersburg.[2] And he keep on, why? Why? What's my job, everything, and if I don't understand the way he speak, she chips in again all the time and ask me for him. So I tell him, panel beater.[3] And I tell him, the pay is very low in the Cape. And then I begin to tell them lots of things, some things is real and some things I just think of, things that are going to make them like me, maybe they'll take me all the way there to Pietersburg.

I tell them I'm six days on the road. I not going to say I'm sick as well, I been home because I was sick—because *she's* not from overseas, I suss that, she know that old story. I tell them I had to take leave because my mother's got trouble with my brothers and

---

1. A small town near Cape Town.
2. A city in northeastern South Africa.
3. A person who does body work on automobiles.

sisters, we seven in the family and no father. And s'true's God, it seem like what I'm saying. When do you ever see him except he's drunk. And my brother is trouble, trouble, he hangs around with bad people and my other brother doesn't help my mother. And that's no lie, neither, how can he help when he's doing time; but they don't need to know that, they only get scared I'm the same kind like him, if I tell about him, assault and intent to do bodily harm. The sisters are in school and my mother's only got the pension. Ja. I'm working there in Pietersburg and every week, madam, I swear to you, I send my pay for my mother and sisters. So then he say, Why get off here? Don't you want us to take you to Pietersburg? And she say, of course, they going that way.

And I tell them some more. They listening to me so nice, and I'm talking, talking. I talk about the government, because I hear she keep saying to him, telling about this law and that law. I say how it's not fair we had to leave Wynberg and go to the Flats. I tell her we got sicknesses—she say what kind, is it unhealthy there? And I don't have to think what, I just say it's *bad, bad,* and she say to the man, *As I told you.* I tell about the house we had in Wynberg, but it's not my grannie's old house where we was all living together so long, the house I'm telling them about is more the kind of house they'll know, they wouldn't like to go away from, with a tiled bathroom, electric stove, everything. I tell them we spend three thousand rands fixing up that house—my uncle give us the money, that's how we got it. He give us his savings, three thousand rands. (I don't know why I say three; old Uncle Jimmy never have three or two or one in his life. I just say it.) And then we just kicked out. And panel beaters getting low pay there; it's better in Pietersburg.

He say, but I'm far from my home? And I tell her again, because she's white but she's a woman too, with that grey hair she's got grown-up kids—Madam. I send my pay home every week, s'true's God, so's they can eat, there in the Flats. I'm saying, *six days on the road.* While I'm saying it, I'm thinking; then I say, look at me, I got only these clothes, I sold my things on the way, to have something to eat. *Six days on the road.* He's from overseas and she isn't one of those who say you're a liar, doesn't trust you—right away when I got in the car, I notice she doesn't take her stuff over to the front like they usually do in case you pinch something of theirs. Six days on the road, and am I tired, tired! When I get to Pietersburg I must try borrow me a rand to get a taxi there to where I live. He say, Where do you live? Not in town? And she laugh, because he don't know nothing about this place, where whites live and where we must go—but I know they both thinking and I know what they thinking; I know I'm going to get something when I get out, don't need to worry about that. They feeling bad about me, now. Bad. Anyhow it's God's truth that I'm tired, tired, that's true.

They've put up her window and he's pushed a few buttons, now it's like in a supermarket, cool air blowing, and the windows like sunglasses: that sun can't get me here.

The Englishman glances over his shoulder as he drives.

"Taking a nap."

"I'm sure it's needed."

All through the trip he stops for everyone he sees at the roadside. Some are not hitching at all, never expecting to be given a lift anywhere, just walking in the heat outside with an empty plastic can to be filled with water or paraffin or whatever it is they buy in some country store, or standing at some point between departure and destination, small children and bundles linked on either side, baby on back. She hasn't said anything to him. He would only misunderstand if she explained why one doesn't give lifts in this country; and if she pointed out that in spite of this, she doesn't mind him breaking the sensible if unfortunate rule, he might misunderstand that, as well—think she was boasting of her disregard for personal safety weighed in the balance against decent concern for fellow beings.

He persists in making polite conversation with these passengers because he doesn't want to be patronizing; picking them up like so many objects and dropping them off again, silent, smelling of smoke from open cooking fires, sun and sweat, there behind his head. They don't understand his Englishman's English and if he gets an answer at all it's a deaf man's guess at what's called for. Some grin with pleasure and embarrass him by showing it the way they've been taught is acceptable, invoking him as *baas* and *master* when they get out and give thanks. But although he doesn't know it, being too much concerned with those names thrust into his hands like whips whose purpose is repugnant to him, has nothing to do with him, she knows each time that there is a moment of annealment[4] in the air-conditioned hired car belonging to nobody—a moment like that on a no-man's-land bridge in which an accord between warring countries is signed—when there is no calling of names, and all belong in each other's presence. He doesn't feel it because he has no wounds, neither has inflicted, nor will inflict any.

This one standing at the roadside with his transistor radio in a plastic bag was actually thumbing a lift like a townee; his expectation marked him out. And when her companion to whom she was showing the country inevitably pulled up, she read the face at the roadside immediately: the lively, cajoling, performer's eyes, the salmon-pinkish cheeks and nostrils, and as he jogged over smiling, the unselfconscious gap of gum between the canines.

A sleeper is always absent; although present, there on the back seat.

"The way he spoke about black people, wasn't it surprising? I mean—he's black himself."

"Oh no he's not. Couldn't you see the difference? He's a Cape Coloured. From the way he speaks English—couldn't you hear he's not like the Africans you've talked to?"

But of course he hasn't seen, hasn't heard: the fellow is dark enough, to those who don't know the signs by which you're classified, and the melodramatic, long-vowelled English is as difficult to follow if more fluent than the terse, halting responses of blacker people.

"Would he have a white grandmother or even a white father, then?"

She gives him another of the little history lessons she has been supplying along the way. The Malay slaves brought by the Dutch East India Company[5] to their supply station, on the route to India, at the Cape in the seventeenth century; the Khoikhoi who were the indigenous inhabitants of that part of Africa; add Dutch, French, English, German settlers whose back-yard progeniture with these and other blacks began a people who are all the people in the country mingled in one bloodstream. But encounters along the road teach him more than her history lessons, or the political analyses in which they share the same ideological approach although he does not share responsibility for the experience to which the ideology is being applied. She has explained Acts, Proclamations, Amendments. The Group Areas Act, Resettlement Act, Orderly Movement and Settlement of Black Persons Act. She has translated these statute-book euphemisms: people as movable goods. People packed onto trucks along with their stoves and beds while front-end loaders scoop away their homes into rubble. People dumped somewhere else. Always somewhere else. People as the figures, decimal

---

4. Tempering by heating.   5. Occupied South Africa from 1652–1795 while it was a Dutch Cape Colony.

points and multiplying zero-zero-zeros into which individual lives—Black Persons Orderly-Moved, -Effluxed, -Grouped—coagulate and compute. Now he has here in the car the intimate weary odour of a young man to whom these things happen.

"Half his family sick . . . it must be pretty unhealthy, where they've been made to go."

She smiles. "Well, I'm not too sure about that. I had the feeling, some of what he said . . . they're theatrical by nature. You must take it with a pinch of salt."

"You mean about the mother and sisters and so on?"

She's still smiling, she doesn't answer.

"But he couldn't have made up about taking a job so far from home—and the business of sending his wages to his mother? That too?"

He glances at her.

Beside him, she's withdrawn as the other one, sleeping behind him. While he turns his attention back to the road, she is looking at him secretly, as if somewhere in his blue eyes registering the approaching road but fixed on the black faces he is trying to read, somewhere in the lie of his inflamed hand and arm that on their travels have been plunged in the sun as if in boiling water, there is the place through which the worm he needs to be infected with can find a way into him, so that he may host it and become its survivor, himself surviving through being fed on. Become like her. Complicity is the only understanding.

"Oh it's true, it's all true . . . not in the way he's told about it. Truer than the way he told it. All these things happen to them. And other things. Worse. But why burden us? Why try to explain to us? Things so far from what we know, how will they ever explain? How will we react? Stop our ears? Or cover our faces? Open the door and throw him out? They don't know. But sick mothers and brothers gone to the bad— these are the staples of misery, mmh? Think of the function of charity in the class struggles in your own country in the nineteenth century; it's all there in your literature. The lord-of-the-manor's compassionate daughter carrying hot soup to the dying cottager on her father's estate. The "advanced" upper-class woman comforting her cook when the honest drudge's daughter takes to whoring for a living. *Shame*, we say here. Shame. You must've heard it? We think it means, what a pity; we think we are expressing sympathy—for them. *Shame*. I don't know what we're saying about ourselves." She laughs.

"So you think it would at least be true that his family were kicked out of their home, sent away?"

"Why would anyone of them need to make that up? It's an everyday affair."

"What kind of place would they get, where they were moved?"

"Depends. A tent, to begin with. And maybe basic materials to build themselves a shack. Perhaps a one-room prefab. Always a tin toilet set down in the veld,[6] if nothing else. Some industrialist must be making a fortune out of government contracts for those toilets. You build your new life round that toilet. His people are Coloured, so it could be they were sent where there were houses of some sort already built for them; Coloureds usually get something a bit better than blacks are given."

"And the house would be more or less as good as the one they had? People as poor as that—and they'd spent what must seem a fortune to them, fixing it up."

"I don't know what kind of house they had. We're not talking about slum clearance, my dear; we're talking about destroying communities because they're black, and white people want to build houses or factories for whites where blacks live. I told you. We're talking about loading up trucks and carting black people out of sight of whites."

---

6. Plains.

"And even where he's come to work—Pietersburg, whatever-it's-called—he doesn't live in the town."

"Out of sight." She has lost the thought for a moment, watching to make sure the car takes the correct turning. "Out of sight. Like those mothers and grannies and brothers and sisters far away on the Cape Flats."

"I don't think it's possible he actually sends all his pay. I mean how would one eat?"

"Maybe what's left doesn't buy anything he really wants."

Not a sound, not a sigh in sleep behind them. They can go on talking about him as he always has been discussed, there and yet not there.

Her companion is alert to the risk of gullibility. He verifies the facts, smiling, just as he converts, mentally, into pounds and pence any sum spent in foreign coinage. "He didn't sell the radio. When he said he'd sold all his things on the road, he forgot about that."

"When did he say he'd last eaten?"

"Yesterday. He said."

She repeats what she has just been told: "Yesterday." She is looking through the glass that takes the shine of heat off the landscape passing as yesterday passed, time measured by the ticking second hand of moving trees, rows of crops, country-store stoeps,[7] filling stations, spiny crook'd fingers of giant euphorbia.[8] Only the figures by the roadside waiting, standing still.

Personal remarks can't offend someone dead-beat in the back. "How d'you think such a young man comes to be without front teeth?"

She giggles whisperingly and keeps her voice low, anyway. "Well, you may not believe me if I tell you . . ."

"Seems odd . . . I suppose he can't afford to have them replaced."

"It's—how shall I say—a sexual preference. Most usually you see it in their young girls, though. They have their front teeth pulled when they're about seventeen."

She feels his uncertainty, his not wanting to let comprehension lead him to a conclusion embarrassing to an older woman. For her part, she is wondering whether he won't find it distasteful if—at her de-sexed age—she should come out with it: for cock-sucking. "No one thinks the gap spoils a girl's looks, apparently. It's simply a sign she knows how to please. Same significance between men, I suppose ? A form of beauty. So everyone says. We've always been given to understand that's the reason."

"Maybe it's just another sexual myth. There are so many."

She's in agreement. "Black girls. Chinese girls. Jewish girls."

"And black men?"

"Oh my goodness, you bet. But we white ladies don't talk about that, we only dream, you know! Or have nightmares."

They're laughing. When they are quiet, she flexes her shoulders against the seat-back and settles again. The streets of a town are flickering their text across her eyes. "He might have had a car accident. They might have been knocked out in a fight."

They have to wake him because they don't know where he wants to be set down. He is staring at her lined white face (turned to him, calling him gently), stunned for a moment at this evidence that he cannot be anywhere he ought to be; and now he blinks and smiles his empty smile caught on either side by a canine tooth, and gulps and gives himself a shake like someone coming out of water. "Sorry! Sorry! Sorry madam!"

What about, she says, and the young man glances quickly, his blue eyes coming round over his shoulder: "Had a good snooze?"

7. Verandas.   8. An African shrub.

"Ooh I was finished, master, finished, God bless you for the rest you give me. And with an empty stummick, you know, you dreaming so real. I was dreaming, dreaming, I didn't know nothing about I'm in the car!"

It comes from the driver's seat with the voice (a real Englishman's from overseas) of one who is hoping to hear something that will explain everything. "What were you dreaming?"

But there is only hissing, spluttery laughter between the two white pointed teeth. The words gambol. "Ag, nothing, master, nothing, all *non-sunce*—"

The sense is that if pressed, he will produce for them a dream he didn't dream, a dream put together from bloated images on billboards, discarded calendars picked up, scraps of newspapers blown about—but they interrupt, they're asking where he'd like to get off.

"No, anywhere. Here it's all right. Fine. Just there by the corner. I must go look for someone who'll praps give me a rand for the taxi, because I can't walk so far, I haven't eaten nothing since yesterday . . . just here, the master can please stop just here—"

The traffic light is red, anyway, and the car is in the lane nearest the kerb. Her thin, speckled white arm with a skilled flexible hand, but no muscle with which to carry a load of washing or lift a hoe, feels back to release the lock he is fumbling at. "Up, up, pull it up." She has done it for him. "Can't you take a bus?"

"There's no buses Sunday, madam, this place is ve-ery bad for us for transport, I must tell you, we can't get nowhere Sundays, only work-days." He is out, the plastic bag with the radio under his arm, his feet in their stained, multi-striped jogging sneakers drawn neatly together like those of a child awaiting dismissal. "Thank you madam, thank you master, God bless you for what you done."

The confident dextrous hand is moving quickly down in the straw bag bought from a local market somewhere along the route. She brings up a pale blue note (the Englishman recognizes the two-rand denomination of this currency that he has memorized by colour) and turns to pass it, a surreptitious message, through the open door behind her. *Goodbye master madam.* The note disappears delicately as a tit-bit finger-fed. He closes the door, he's keeping up the patter, *goodbye master, goodbye madam,* and she instructs—"No, bang it. Harder. That's it." *Goodbye master, goodbye madam*—but they don't look back at him now, they don't have to see him thinking he must keep waving, keep smiling, in case they should look back.

She is the guide and mentor; she's the one who knows the country. She's the one—she knows that too—who is accountable. She must be the first to speak again. "At least if he's hungry he'll be able to buy a bun or something. And the bars are closed on Sunday."

— ✠ —

Derek Walcott
b. 1930

Over the last five decades, Derek Walcott has articulated the tensions of living between two worlds—the competing claims and traditions of the West Indies, his home, and Europe. A concern with issues of national identity runs throughout Walcott's large body of poetry and drama; his poetry exploits the resources of a European literary tradition in the service of Caribbean themes and concerns. No poet, as T. S. Eliot insisted, can write important poetry without tapping into some cultural or literary tradition; in the poem *Forest of Europe,* Walcott puts the question this way:

What's poetry, if it is worth its salt,
but a phrase men can pass from hand to mouth?
From hand to mouth, across the centuries,
the bread that lasts when systems have decayed.

Walcott was born in Castries, Saint Lucia, an isolated, volcanic island in the West Indies. Saint Lucia is a former British colony, and Walcott's education there was thoroughly British. In the introduction to *Dream on Monkey Mountain and Other Plays* (1970), Walcott writes, "The writers of my generation were natural assimilators. We knew the literature of Empires, Greek, Roman, British, through their essential classics; and both the patois of the street and the language of the classroom hid the elation of discovery." Empire and slavery left their impress on the Walcott family; both of his grandmothers were said to be descended from slaves. Walcott attended University College of the West Indies in Jamaica on a British government scholarship; he completed a degree in English in 1953, and from 1954 until 1957 taught in West Indian schools. In 1958 a Rockefeller Fellowship allowed him to spend a year in New York studying theater; the following year he moved to Trinidad and founded the Little Carib Theatre Workshop. It was in his playwriting that Walcott first accomplished the fusion of native and European elements he sought; his 1958 play *Drums and Colours*, for instance, employs calypso music, mime, and carnival masks to "carnivalize" the smooth surface of European drama, creating a literary form which, while written in English, is uniquely Caribbean in character. *O Babylon!* (1976), his most popular play, focuses on the Rastafarians of Jamaica. He is also a talented painter, and his poems are notable for the vivid clarity of their images.

Walcott has written more than fifteen volumes of poetry as well as a dozen plays. His first important poetry collection was *In a Green Night* (1962), which includes the aptly titled poem *A Far Cry from Africa*. Africa and Britain serve as the double setting for his trenchant portrait of a foreign aid bureaucrat in *The Fortunate Traveller* (1981). Walcott himself has never settled in one place for long, and for many years he has split his time between his home in Trinidad and a teaching post at Boston University. Walcott's poems create a landscape of historical and personal memory, overlaying empires, centuries, continents, and stages of his own life. He developed his themes most expansively in his verse novel *Omeros* (1991), which rewrites Homer's *Iliad* as a Caribbean story, interspersed with scenes of the poet's own life and travels in Boston, London, and Dublin. Walcott was awarded the Nobel Prize for literature in 1992, "for a poetic oeuvre of great luminosity, sustained by a historical vision, the outcome of a multicultural commitment."

The Fortunate Traveller[1]
for Susan Sontag

> And I heard a voice in the midst of the four beasts say,
> A measure of wheat for a penny,
> and three measures of barley for a penny;
> and see thou hurt not the oil and the wine.

—*Revelation* 6.6[2]

I

It was in winter. Steeples, spires
congealed like holy candles. Rotting snow
flaked from Europe's ceiling. A compact man,

---

1. Walcott's title invokes Thomas Nashe's tale *The Unfortunate Traveller* (1594). Susan Sontag (b. 1933) is an American cultural critic and novelist.

2. One of the Four Horsemen of the Apocalypse is decreeing the famine and inflation that accompany wars as the end of the world approaches.

I crossed the canal in a grey overcoat,
5   on one lapel a crimson buttonhole
for the cold ecstasy of the assassin.
In the square coffin manacled to my wrist:
small countries pleaded through the mesh of graphs,
in treble-spaced, Xeroxed forms to the World Bank
10   on which I had scrawled the one word, MERCY;

I sat on a cold bench
under some skeletal lindens.
Two other gentlemen, black skins gone grey
as their identical, belted overcoats,
15   crossed the white river.
They spoke the stilted French
of their dark river,
whose hooked worm, multiplying its pale sickle,
could thin the harvest of the winter streets.
20   "Then we can depend on you to get us those tractors?"
"I gave my word."
"May my country ask you why you are doing this, sir?"
Silence.
"You know if you betray us, you cannot hide?"
25   A tug. Smoke trailing its dark cry.

At the window in Haiti, I remember
a gecko[3] pressed against the hotel glass,
with white palms, concentrating head.
With a child's hands. Mercy, monsieur. Mercy.
30   Famine sighs like a scythe
across the field of statistics and the desert
is a moving mouth. In the hold of this earth
10,000,000 shoreless souls are drifting.
Somalia: 765,000, their skeletons will go under the tidal sand.
35   "We'll meet you in Bristol to conclude the agreement?"
Steeples like tribal lances, through congealing fog
the cries of wounded church bells wrapped in cotton,
grey mist enfolding the conspirator
like a sealed envelope next to its heart.

40   No one will look up now to see the jet
fade like a weevil through a cloud of flour.
One flies first-class, one is so fortunate.
Like a telescope reversed, the traveller's eye
swiftly screws down the individual sorrow
45   to an oval nest of antic numerals,
and the iris, interlocking with this globe,
condenses it to zero, then a cloud.
Beetle-black taxi from Heathrow[4] to my flat.
We are roaches,
50   riddling the state cabinets, entering the dark holes

---

3. A small lizard.   4. London's primary airport.

of power, carapaced in topcoats,
scuttling around columns, signalling for taxis,
with frantic antennae, to other huddles with roaches;
we infect with optimism, and when
55 the cabinets crack, we are the first
to scuttle, radiating separately
back to Geneva, Bonn, Washington, London.

Under the dripping planes of Hampstead Heath,
I read her letter again, watching the drizzle
60 disfigure its pleading like mascara. Margo,
I cannot bear to watch the nations cry.
Then the phone: "We will pay you in Bristol."
Days in fetid bedclothes swallowing cold tea,
the phone stifled by the pillow. The telly
65 a blue storm with soundless snow.
I'd light the gas and see a tiger's tongue.
I was rehearsing the ecstasies of starvation
for what I had to do. *And have not charity.*[5]

I found my pity, desperately researching
70 the origins of history, from reed-built communes
by sacred lakes, turning with the first sprocketed
water-driven wheels. I smelled imagination
among bestial hides by the gleam of fat,
seeking in all races a common ingenuity.
75 I envisaged an Africa flooded with such light
as alchemized the first fields of emmer wheat and barley,
when we savages dyed our pale dead with ochre,
and bordered our temples
with the ceremonial vulva of the conch
80 in the grey epoch of the obsidian adze.
I sowed the Sahara with rippling cereals,
my charity fertilized these aridities.

What was my field? Late sixteenth century.
My field was a dank acre. A Sussex don,
85 I taught the Jacobean anxieties: *The White Devil.*[6]
Flamineo's torch startles the brooding yews.
The drawn end comes in strides. I loved my Duchess,
the white flame of her soul blown out between
the smoking cypresses. Then I saw children pounce
90 on green meat with a rat's ferocity.

I called them up and took the train to Bristol,
my blood the Severn's[7] dregs and silver.
On Severn's estuary the pieces flash,
Iscariot's salary,[8] patron saint of spies.

---

5. "Though I speak with the tongues of men and of angels, and have not charity, I am become as sounding brass, or a tinkling cymbal" (1 Corinthians 13.1).
6. Revenge tragedy (c. 1612) by John Webster.

7. A river running through Wales and England.
8. For betraying Jesus Christ, Judas Iscariot was paid 30 pieces of silver by the Roman authorities.

95   I thought, who cares how many million starve?
        Their rising souls will lighten the world's weight
        and level its gull-glittering waterline;
        we left at sunset down the estuary.

        England recedes. The forked white gull
100   screeches, circling back.
        Even the birds are pulled back by their orbit,
        even mercy has its magnetic field.
                                Back in the cabin,
        I uncap the whisky, the porthole
105   mists with glaucoma. By the time I'm pissed,[9]
        England, England will be
        that pale serrated indigo on the sea-line.
        "You are so fortunate, you get to see the world—"
        Indeed, indeed, sirs, I have seen the world.
110   Spray splashes the portholes and vision blurs.

        Leaning on the hot rail, watching the hot sea,
        I saw them far off, kneeling on hot sand
        in the pious genuflections of the locust,
        as Ponce's armoured knees crush Florida
115   to the funereal fragrance of white lilies.

                                II
        Now I have come to where the phantoms live,
        I have no fear of phantoms, but of the real.
        The Sabbath benedictions of the islands.
        Treble clef of the snail on the scored leaf,
120   the Tantum Ergo[1] of black choristers
        soars through the organ pipes of coconuts.
        Across the dirty beach surpliced with lace,
        they pass a brown lagoon behind the priest,
        pale and unshaven in his frayed soutane,[2]
125   into the concrete church at Canaries;
        as Albert Schweitzer[3] moves to the harmonium
        of morning, and to the pluming chimneys,
        the groundswell lifts Lebensraum, Lebensraum.[4]

        Black faces sprinkled with continual dew—
130   dew on the speckled croton,[5] dew
        on the hard leaf of the knotted plum tree,
        dew on the elephant ears of the dasheen.[6]
        Through Kurtz's teeth, white skull in elephant grass,
        the imperial fiction sings. Sunday
135   wrinkles downriver from the Heart of Darkness.
        The heart of darkness is not Africa.
        The heart of darkness is the core of fire

9. Drunk.
1. A hymn sung after the Blessed Sacrament has been exposed in the mass.
2. Black robe.
3. German physician, missionary, and musician in Africa;
winner of the Nobel Peace Prize in 1952.
4. Space to live in; the term is especially associated with Nazi Germany's territorial expansion.
5. A tropical plant.
6. The taro plant of tropical Asia.

in the white center of the holocaust.
The heart of darkness is the rubber claw
140　selecting a scalpel in antiseptic light,
the hills of children's shoes outside the chimneys,
the tinkling nickel instruments on the white altar;
Jacob, in his last card, sent me these verses:
"Think of a God who doesn't lose His sleep
145　if trees burst into tears or glaciers weep.
So, aping His indifference, I write now,
not Anno Domini: After Dachau."[7]

III

The night maid brings a lamp and draws the blinds.
I stay out on the verandah with the stars.
150　Breakfast congealed to supper on its plate.

There is no sea as restless as my mind.
The promontories snore. They snore like whales.
Cetus, the whale, was Christ.
The ember dies, the sky smokes like an ash heap.
155　Reeds wash their hands of guilt and the lagoon
is stained. Louder, since it rained,
a gauze of sand flies hisses from the marsh.

Since God is dead,[8] and these are not His stars,
but man-lit, sulphurous, sanctuary lamps,
160　it's in the heart of darkness of this earth
that backward tribes keep vigil of His Body,
in deya, lampion,[9] and this bedside lamp.
Keep the news from their blissful ignorance.
Like lice, like lice, the hungry of this earth
165　swarm to the tree of life. If those who starve
like these rain-flies who shed glazed wings in light
grew from sharp shoulder blades their brittle vans
and soared towards that tree, how it would seethe—
ah, Justice! But fires
170　drench them like vermin, quotas
prevent them, and they remain
compassionate fodder for the travel book,
its paragraphs like windows from a train,
for everywhere that earth shows its rib cage
175　and the moon goggles with the eyes of children,
we turn away to read. Rimbaud[1] learned that.
　　　　　　　　　　　Rimbaud, at dusk,
idling his wrist in water past temples
the plumed dates still protect in Roman file,
180　knew that we cared less for one human face
than for the scrolls in Alexandria's ashes,
that the bright water could not dye his hand

---

7. Site of the notorious Nazi concentration camp.
8. So the German philosopher Friedrich Nietzsche declared in his 1882 text *The Gay Science*.
9. A small oil lamp with tinted glass.

1. Arthur Rimbaud (1854–1891), French poet. After abandoning poetry at the age of 20, he travelled in Egypt and the Sudan, later settling in Ethiopia as a trader and arms dealer.

any more than poetry. The dhow's[2] silhouette
moved through the blinding coinage of the river
185   that, endlessly, until we pay one debt,
shrouds, every night, an ordinary secret.

IV

The drawn sword comes in strides.
It stretches for the length of the empty beach;
the fishermen's huts shut their eyes tight.
190   A frisson[3] shakes the palm trees.
and sweats on the traveller's tree.
They've found out my sanctuary. Philippe, last night:
"It had two gentlemen in the village yesterday, sir,
asking for you while you was in town.
195   I tell them you was in town. They send to tell you,
there is no hurry. They will be coming back."

In loaves of cloud, *and have not charity,*
the weevil will make a sahara of Kansas,
the ant shall eat Russia.
200   Their soft teeth shall make, *and have not charity,*
the harvest's desolation,
and the brown globe crack like a begging bowl,
and though you fire oceans of surplus grain,
and have not charity,

205   still, through thin stalks,
the smoking stubble, stalks
grasshopper: third horseman,
the leather-helmed locust.[4]

1981

from **Midsummer**
50

I once gave my daughters, separately, two conch shells
that were dived from the reef, or sold on the beach, I forget.
They use them as doorstops or bookends, but their wet
pink palates are the soundless singing of angels.
5   I once wrote a poem called "The Yellow Cemetery,"
when I was nineteen. Lizzie's age. I'm fifty-three.
These poems I heaved aren't linked to any tradition
like a mossed cairn;[1] each goes down like a stone
to the seabed, settling, but let them, with luck, lie
10   where stones are deep, in the sea's memory.
Let them be, in water, as my father, who did watercolours,
entered his work. He became one of his shadows,

---

2. A sailing vessel used by Arabs.
3. Sudden passing excitement.
4. The locust, eater of crops, is here identified with the

horseman of the Apocalypse quoted in the poem's epigraph.
1. A heap of stones marking a trail.

wavering and faint in the midsummer sunlight.
His name is Warwick Walcott. I sometimes believe
15   that his father, in love or bitter benediction,
named him for Warwickshire.[2] Ironies
are moving. Now, when I rewrite a line,
or sketch on the fast-drying paper the coconut fronds
that he did so faintly, my daughters' hands move in mine.
20   Conches move over the sea-floor. I used to move
my father's grave from the blackened Anglican headstones
in Castries[3] to where I could love both at once—
the sea and his absence. Youth is stronger than fiction.

52

I heard them marching the leaf-wet roads of my head,
the sucked vowels of a syntax trampled to mud,
a division of dictions, one troop black, barefooted,
the other in redcoats bright as their sovereign's blood;
5   their feet scuffled like rain, the bare soles with the shod.
One fought for a queen, the other was chained in her service,
but both, in bitterness, travelled the same road.
Our occupation and the Army of Occupation
are born enemies, but what mortar can size
10   the broken stones of the barracks of Brimstone Hill
to the gaping brick of Belfast? Have we changed sides
to the moustached sergeants and the horsy gentry
because we serve English, like a two-headed sentry
guarding its borders? No language is neutral;
15   the green oak of English is a murmurous cathedral
where some took umbrage,[4] some peace, but every shade, all,
helped widen its shadow. I used to haunt the arches
of the British barracks of Vigie[5]. There were leaves there,
bright, rotting like revers of epaulettes[6], and the stenches
20   of history and piss. Leaves piled like the dropped aitches
of soldiers from rival shires, from the brimstone trenches
of Agincourt to the gas of the Somme.[7] On Poppy Day[8]
our schools bought red paper flowers. They were for Flanders.[9]
I saw Hotspur cursing the smoke through which a popinjay
25   minced from the battle. Those raging commanders
from Thersites to Percy,[1] their rant is our model.
I pinned the poppy to my blazer. It bled like a vowel.

2. Birthplace of Shakespeare. Warwick Walcott, journalist, occasional poet, and printer, died when his son was a young child.
3. Port and capital of Saint Lucia.
4. In two senses: offence, shade.
5. Vigie Beach near Castries, Saint Lucia.
6. Turned-up edges of ornamental shoulder pieces worn on uniforms.
7. French sites of important battles in 1415 and in World War I.
8. Veterans Day.
9. Scene of a disastrous World War I offensive—"the battle of the mud"—in which the British lost 324,000 soldiers.
1. The headstrong Sir Henry Percy (1364–1403) became known as "Hotspur"; he serves as rival to Prince Hal in Shakespeare's *Henry IV*. Thersites accuses Achilles of cowardice in Homer's *Iliad*.

54

The midsummer sea, the hot pitch road, this grass, these shacks that made me,
jungle and razor grass shimmering by the roadside, the edge of art;
wood lice are humming in the sacred wood,
nothing can burn them out, they are in the blood;
their rose mouths, like cherubs, sing of the slow science
of dying—all heads, with, at each ear, a gauzy wing.
Up at Forest Reserve, before branches break into sea,
I looked through the moving, grassed window and thought "pines,"
or conifers of some sort. I thought, they must suffer
in this tropical heat with their child's idea of Russia.
Then suddenly, from their rotting logs, distracting signs
of the faith I betrayed, or the faith that betrayed me—
yellow butterflies rising on the road to Valencia[2]
stuttering "yes" to the resurrection; "yes, yes is our answer,"
the gold-robed Nunc Dimittis[3] of their certain choir.
Where's my child's hymnbook, the poems edged in gold leaf,
the heaven I worship with no faith in heaven,
as the Word turned toward poetry in its grief?
Ah, bread of life, that only love can leaven!
Ah, Joseph, though no man ever dies in his own country,[4]
the grateful grass will grow thick from his heart.

1984

[END OF PERSPECTIVES: WHOSE LANGUAGE?]

---

2. A seaport in Eastern Spain.
3. "Lord, now let thy servant depart in peace," sung at the end of Mass.
4. The line echoes Jesus's comment that no prophet is honored in his own country (Mark 6.4). On one level, Joseph may be Jesus's father, mourning his son's early death. *Midsummer* as a whole is addressed to Walcott's friend Joseph Brodsky, the exiled Russian poet.

BIBLIOGRAPHIES
The Romantics and Their Contemporaries

Bibliographies, General Collections, General Reference • Annual bibliographies are published by the Modern Language Association of America, the Modern Humanities Research Association, the *Keats-Shelley Journal*, *The Romantic Movement*, and *The Year's Work in English Studies*. • Stuart Curran, ed., *The Cambridge Companion to British Romanticism*, 1993. • Frank Jordan, ed., *The English Romantic Poets: A Review of Research and Criticism*, 4th ed. 1985 [covers Blake, W. Wordsworth, Coleridge, Byron, P. B. Shelley, Keats]. • Karl Kroeber and Gene Ruoff, eds., *Romantic Poetry: Recent Revisionary Criticism*, 1993. • Jerome McGann, ed., *The New Oxford Book of Romantic Period Verse*, 1993. • Anne K. Mellor and Richard Matlak, eds., *British Literature 1780–1830*, 1996. • David Perkins, ed., *English Romantic Writers*, 2d ed., 1995. • Duncan Wu, ed., *Romanticism, An Anthology*, 1994. • Duncan Wu, ed., *Romanticism, A Critical Reader*, 1995 [essays on Blake, W. Wordsworth, Coleridge, P. B. Shelley, Byron, Keats, Clare, M. Shelley, Austen]. • Several volumes in the series *Approaches to Teaching World Literature* published by the Modern Language Association are devoted to writers in our period: among others, Blake (ed. Robert Gleckner and Mark Greenberg); Byron (ed. F. W. Shilstone); Coleridge (ed. Richard Matlak); Keats (ed. Walter Evert and Jack Rhodes); Mary Shelley (ed. Stephen Behrendt); Percy Shelley (ed. Spencer Hall); and Wordsworth (ed. Spencer Hall and Jonathan Ramsey).

History and Literary History • M. H. Abrams "English Romanticism: The Spirit of the Age," 1963; repr. in *Romanticism and Consciousness: Essays in Criticism*, ed. Harold Bloom, 1970. • Derek Beales, *From Castlereagh to Gladstone 1815–85*, 1969. • Marilyn Butler, *Romantics, Rebels, and Reactionaries: English Literature and Its Background, 1760–1830*, 1981. • Marilyn Butler, "Romanticism in England," *Romanticism in National Context*, ed. Roy Park and Mikuláš Teich, 1988. • Ian R. Christie *Wars and Revolutions*, New History of England, vol. 7, 1982. • J. C. D. Clark, *English Society 1688–1832*, 1985. • Linda Colley, *Britons: Forging the Nation 1707–1837*, 1992. • M. J. Daunton, *Progress and Poverty: An Economic and Social History of Britain 1700–1850*, 1995. • Lee Erickson, *The Economy of Literary Form: English Literature and the Industrialization of Publishing 1800–1850*, 1996. • Norman Gash, *Aristocracy and People: Britain 1815–1865*, 1979. • Marilyn Gaull, *English Romanticism: The Human Context*, 1988. • Élie Halévy, *A History of the English People in 1815*, trans. 1924, repr. 1987. • Ian Jack, *English Literature, 1815–1832*, 1963. • Jon Klancher, *The Making of English Reading Audiences, 1790–1832*, 1987. • John B. Owen, *The Eighteenth Century 1714–1815*, 1974. • Harold Perkin, *Origins of Modern English Society*, 1969. • Roy Porter, *English Society in the Eighteenth Century*, 1982. • W. L. Renwick, *English Literature, 1789–1815*, 1963. • Alan Richardson, *Literature, Education, and Romanticism*, 1994. • E. P. Thompson, *The Making of the English Working Class*, 1963. • E. P. Thompson, *Customs in Common*, 1991. • R. J. White, *Waterloo to Peterloo*, 1957. • Raymond Williams, *Culture and Society 1780–1950*, 1960. • Raymond Williams, *The Country and The City*, 1973. • Carl Woodring, *Politics in English Romantic Poetry*, 1970.

Contemporary Reception • John O. Hayden, *The Romantic Reviewers 1802–24*, 1969. • Theodore Redpath, ed., *The Young Romantics and Critical Opinion, 1807–1824: Poetry of Byron, Shelley, and Keats as Seen by Their Contemporary Critics*, 1973. • Donald H. Reiman, *The Romantics Reviewed: Contemporary Reviews of British Romantic Writers*, 1972.

Poetic Form, Genres, Literary History • M. H. Abrams, "Structure and Style in the Greater Romantic Lyric," 1965, repr. in *Romanticism and Consciousness*, ed. Harold Bloom 1970. • M. H. Abrams, *Natural Supernaturalism: Tradition and Revolution in Romantic Literature*, 1971. • Harold Bloom, "The Internalization of Quest-romance," 1969, repr. in *Romanticism and Consciousness*, ed. Harold Bloom, 1970. • Harold Bloom, *The Anxiety of Influence: A Theory of Poetry*, 1973. • Douglas Bush, *Mythology and the Romantic Tradition in English Poetry*, 1937. • Stuart Curran, *Poetic Form and British Romanticism*, 1986. • Geoffrey Hartman, *Beyond Formalism*, 1970. • John Hollander, "Romantic Verse Form and the Metrical Contract," 1965, repr. in *Romanticism and Consciousness*, ed. Harold Bloom, 1970. • David Perkins, "The Construction of 'The Romantic Movement' as a Literary Classification," *Nineteenth-Century Literature*, 1990. • Thomas Vogler, *Preludes to Vision: On the Epic Venture in Blake, Wordsworth, Keats, and Hart Crane*, 1971. • Brian Wilkie, *Romantic Poets and Epic Tradition*, 1965. • W. K. Wimsatt, "The Structure of Romantic Nature Imagery," in *The Verbal Icon*, 1954; repr. in *Romanticism and Consciousness*, ed. Harold Bloom, 1970. • Susan J. Wolfson, *The Questioning Presence*, 1986. • Susan J. Wolfson, *Formal Charges, The Shaping of British Romantic Poetry*, 1996.

Theory and Criticism • M. H. Abrams, *The Mirror and the Lamp: Romantic Theory and Critical Tradition*, 1953. • M. H. Abrams, *Natural Supernaturalism*, 1971. • M. H. Abrams, *The Correspondent Breeze: Essays on English Romanticism*, 1984. • John Beer, ed., *Questioning Romanticism*, 1995. • Edward E. Bostetter, *The Romantic Ventriloquists: Wordsworth, Coleridge, Shelley, Keats, Byron*, 1963. • Paul De Man, *The Rhetoric of Romanticism*, 1984. • Paul De Man, "The Rhetoric of Temporality," in his *Blindness and Insight*, 2d ed., 1983. • William H. Galperin, *The Return of the Visible in British Romanticism*, 1993. • Karl Kroeber, *British Romantic Art*, 1986. • Jerome McGann, *The Romantic Ideology: A Critical Investigation*, 1983. • Jerome McGann, *The Poetics of Sensibility: A Revolution in Literary Style*, 1996. • Anne K. Mellor, *English Romantic Irony*, 1980. • David Perkins, *The Quest for Permanence: The Symbolism of Wordsworth, Shelley, and Keats*, 1959. • Tilottama Rajan, *Dark Interpreter: The Discourse of Romanticism*, 1980. • Charles R. Rzepka, *The Self as Mind: Vision and Identity in Wordsworth, Coleridge, and Keats*, 1986. • David Simpson, *Irony and Authority in Romantic Poetry*, 1979. • Stuart M. Sperry, "Towards a Definition of Romantic Irony," in *Romantic and Modern: Revaluations of Literary Tradition*, ed. George Bornstein, 1977. • Earl R. Wasserman, "The English Romantics: The Grounds of Knowledge," *Studies in Romanticism*, 1964.

Gender, Women Writers • Paula Feldman, and Theresa M. Kelley, eds., *Romantic Women Writers: Voices and Countervoices*, 1995. • Diane Long Hoeveler, *Romantic Androgyny: The Women Within*, 1990. • Sonia Hofkosh, "A Woman's Profession: Sexual Difference and the Romance of Authorship," *Studies in Romanticism*, 1993. • Anne K. Mellor, ed., *Romanticism and Feminism*, 1988. • Anne K. Mellor, *Romanticism and Gender*, 1993. • Judith Pascoe, *Romantic Theatricality: Gender, Poetry, and Spectatorship*. 1997. • Marlon Ross, *The Contours of Masculine Desire: Romanticism and the Rise of*

Women's Poetry, 1989. • Irene Tayler and Gina Luria, "Women in British Romantic Literature," in *What Manner of Woman*, ed. Marlene Springer, 1977. • Carol Shiner Wilson and Joel Haefner, eds., *Revisioning Romanticism: British Women Writers, 1776–1837*, 1994. • Jonathan Wordsworth, *The Bright Work Grows: Women Writers of the Romantic Age*, 1997.

Perspectives: The Abolition of Slavery and the Slave Trade • *General Studies* • Roger Anstey, *The Atlantic Slave Trade and British Abolition, 1760–1810*, 1975. • Joan Baum, *Mind-forg'd Manacles: Slavery and the English Romantic Poets*, 1994. • Robin Blackburn, *The Overthrow of Colonial Slavery, 1776–1848*, 1988. • Reginald Coupland, *The British Anti-Slavery Movement*, 1933. • Michael Craton, *Sinews of Empire: A Short History of British Slavery*, 1974. • Michael Craton, James Walvin, and David Wright, eds., *Slavery, Abolition and Emancipation: Black Slaves and the British Empire*, 1976 [an anthology of important documents, including the "Mansfield decision" (Somerset v. Stewart, June 1772), and a succinct history]. • David Brion Davis, *The Problem of Slavery in the Age of Revolution*, 1975. • Eva Dyke, *The Negro in English Romantic Thought*, 1942. • Moira Ferguson, *Subject to Others: British Women Writers and Colonial Slavery, 1670–1834*, 1992 [including a massive bibliography]. • Sonia Hofkosh and Alan Richardson, eds., *Romanticism, Race and Imperial Culture*, 1996. • Edith F. Hurwitz, *Politics and Public Conscience: Slave Emancipation and the Abolitionist Movement in Britain*, 1973. • Margaret Kirkham, *Jane Austen, Feminism and Fiction*, 1983 [on the Mansfield Decision and *Mansfield Park*]. • Frank Joseph Klingberg, *The Anti-Slavery Movement in England: A Study in English Humanitarianism*, 1926. • Gordon K. Lewis, *Slavery, Imperialism, and Freedom Studies in English Radical Thought*, 1978. • Dale H. Porter, *The Abolition of the Slave Trade in England, 1784–1807*, 1970. • James Walvin, *Black and White: The Negro and English Society, 1555–1945*, 1973. • James Walvin, *Slavery and British Society, 1776–1846*, 1982. • James Walvin, *England, Slaves, and Freedom, 1776–1838*, 1986. • Eric Williams, *Capitalism and Slavery*, 1944.

Specific Figures • Reginald Coupland, *Wilberforce: A Narrative*, 1923. • E. L. Griggs, *Thomas Clarkson: The Friend of the Slaves*, 1938. • Edmund Heward, *Lord Mansfield*, 1979. • Robert Isaac and Samuel Wilberforce, *The Life of William Wilberforce*, 1835. • C. L. R. James, *The Black Jacobins: Toussaint L'Ou-*

verture and the San Domingo Rebellion, 1938; repr. 1963. • Oliver M. Warner, *William Wilberforce and His Times*, 1962.

Perspectives: The Rights of Man and the Revolution Controversy • Headnote: Coleridge is quoted from *Table Talk*, 4 January 1823; Wordsworth is quoted from a letter of 30 March 1835. • Simon Bainbridge, *Napoleon and English Romanticism*, 1996. • Marilyn Butler, ed., *Burke, Paine, Godwin, and the Revolution Controversy*, 1984. • Ceri Crossley and Ian Small, eds., *The French Revolution and British Culture*, 1989. • Seamus Deane, *The French Revolution and Enlightenment England 1789–1832*, 1988. • H. T. Dickinson, *British Radicalism and the French Revolution*, 1985. • Clive Emsley, *British Society and the French Wars 1793–1815*, 1979. • Burton R. Friedman, *Fabricating History: English Writers and the French Revolution*, 1988. • Kevin Gilmartin, *Print Politics: The Press and Radical Opposition in Early Nineteenth-Century England*, 1996. • Albert Goodwin, *The Friends of Liberty*, 1979. • E. J. Hobsbawm, *The Age of Revolution 1789–1848*, 1962. • Howard Mumford Jones, *Revolution and Romanticism*, 1974. • Anne K. Mellor, "English Women Writers and the French Revolution," in *Rebel Daughters: Women and the French Revolution*, eds. Sara Melzer and Leslie Rabine, 1992. • Ronald Paulson, *Representations of Revolution, 1789–1820*, 1983. • Mark Philp, ed., *The French Revolution and British Popular Politics*, 1991. • Mark Philp, "Vulgar Conservatism, 1792–1793," *English Historical Review*, 1995. • Esther Schor, *Bearing the Dead: The British Culture of Mourning from the Enlightenment to Victoria*, 1994. • David Simpson, *Romanticism, Nationalism, and the Revolt Against Theory*, 1993. • Olivia Smith, *The Politics of Language 1791–1819*, 1984. • Bruce Woodcock and John Coates. *Combative Styles: Romantic Writing and Ideology*, 1995.

A "Vindication" in Context: The Wollstonecraft Controversy and the Rights of Women • *Textual Reference* • Anna Laetitia Le Breton, *Memoir of Mrs. Barbauld*, 1874 [Barbauld's letter to Edgeworth, 4 September 1804]. •

General Studies • Leonore Davidoff and Catherine Hall, *Family Fortunes: Men and Women of the English Middle Class, 1780–1850*, 1987. • Bridget Hill, *Women, Work, and Sexual Politics in Eighteenth-Century England*, 1989. • Gary Kelly, *Women, Writing, and Revolution, 1790–1827*, 1993. • Anne K. Mellor, *Romanticism and Gender*, 1993. • Mitzi Myers, "Reform or Ruin: 'A Revolution in Female Manners,'"

in *Studies in Eighteenth-Century Culture*, 1982. • Mary Poovey, *The Proper Lady and the Woman Writer*, 1984. • Katharine Rogers, *Feminism in Eighteenth-Century England*, 1982. • For Barbauld, Southey, Blake, and More, see the main entries under their names.

The Anti-Jacobin • *Context* • M. Dorothy George, *English Political Caricature: A Study of Opinion and Propaganda, 1793–1832*, 1959.

Text • Charles Edmonds, ed., *Poetry of the Anti-Jacobin*, 1890.

Joanna Baillie • *Biography and Criticism* • Catherine Burroughs, "English Romantic Women Writers and Theatre Theory: Joanna Baillie's Prefaces to Plays on the Passions," in *Revisioning Romanticism*, ed. Carol Shiner Wilson and Joel Haefner, 1994. • Margaret S. Carhart, *The Life and Work of Joanna Baillie*, 1923. • Julie Carlson, *In the Theatre of Romanticism*, 1994. • Andrea Henderson, "Passion and Fashion in Joanna Baillie's 'Introductory Discourse,'" *PMLA*, 1997. • Jonathan Wordsworth, *The Bright Work Grows: Women Writers of the Romantic Age*, 1997. • Paul Zall, "The Question of Joanna Baillie," *The Wordsworth Circle*, 1982.

Our Texts • *The Dramatic and Poetical Works of Joanna Baillie*, 1853; *Byron's Letters and Journals*, ed. Leslie A. Marchand (1973–82): 6 Sept. 1813 and 2 Apr. 1817; the comparison to Byron from "Celebrated Female Writers: Joanna Baillie," *Blackwood's Edinburgh Magazine*, August 1824.

Anna Laetitia Barbauld • *Biography and Editions* • Lucy Aikin, Memoir in *The Works of Anna Letitia Barbauld*, 1825. • William McCarthy, and Elizabeth Kraft, eds., *The Poems of Anna Letitia Barbauld*, 1994. • Betsy Rodgers, *Georgian Chronicle: Mrs. Barbauld and her Family*, 1958.

Criticism • Isobel Armstrong, "The Gush of the Feminine: How Can We Read Women's Poetry of the Romantic Period?" in *Romantic Women Writers*, eds. Theresa Kelley and Paula Feldman, 1995. • William Keach, "A Regency Prophecy and the End of Anna Barbauld's Career," *Studies in Romanticism*, 1994. • William McCarthy, "'We Hoped the Woman Was Going to Appear': Repression, Desire, and Gender in Anna Letitia Barbauld's Early Poems," in *Romantic Women Writers*, eds. Theresa Kelley and Paula Feldman, 1995. • Marlon B. Ross, "Configurations of Feminine Reform: The Woman Writer and the Tradition of Dissent," in *Revisioning Romanticism*, eds. Carol Shiner Wilson and Joel Haefner, 1994. • Jonathan Wordsworth, *The*

Bright Work Grows: Women Writers of the Romantic Age, 1997.

Our Texts • "The Mouse's Petition," "On a Lady's Writing," and "Washing Day" from *A Selection From the Poems . . . of Anna Letitia Barbauld*, ed. Grace Ellis, 1874; "Inscription for an Ice-House" and "The First Fire" from *The Works of Anna Laetitia Barbauld*, ed. Lucy Aikin, 1825; "To the Poor" and "To a Little Invisible Being" from *The Poems of Anna Laetitia Barbauld*, eds. McCarthy and Kraft, 1994.

William Blake • *Biography* • Peter Ackroyd, *Blake*, 1996. • Alexander Gilchrist, *The Life of William Blake, Pictor Ignotus*, 1863. • Mona Wilson, *The Life of William Blake*, 1927.

Illuminations • Oxford University Press: paperback color-plate editions, with commentary by Geoffrey Keynes, of *The Songs of Innocence and of Experience*, 1967; *The Marriage of Heaven and Hell*, 1975; *Visions of the Daughters of Albion*, 1980; Princeton University Press of the *Songs*, 1991; all plates are reproduced in black and white photographs, with commentary, in David V. Erdman, *The Illuminated Blake*, 1974.

Criticism • Harold Bloom, *The Visionary Company*, 1961, rev. 1971. • Harold Bloom, *Blake's Apocalypse*, 1963, rev. 1970. • Leopold Damrosch, *Symbol and Truth in Blake's Myth*, 1980. • Jackie DiSalvo, *War of the Titans: Blake's Critique of Milton and the Politics of Religion*, 1984. • Morris Eaves, *William Blake's Theory of Art*, 1982. • Morris Eaves, *The Counter-Arts Conspiracy: Art and Industry in the Age of Blake*, 1992. • David V. Erdman, *Blake: Prophet Against Empire*, 1969. • Robert Essick, *William Blake, Printmaker*, 1980. • Robert Essick, *William Blake and the Language of Adam*, 1989. • Michael Ferber, "London' and Its Politics," *ELH*, 1981. • Michael Ferber, *The Poetry of William Blake*, 1981. • Northrop Frye, *Fearful Symmetry*, 1947. • Robert Gleckner, *The Piper and the Bard*, 1959. • Heather Glen, *Vision and Disenchantment: Blake's "Songs" and Wordsworth's "Lyrical Ballads,"* 1983. • Nancy Moore Goslee, "Slavery and Sexual Character: Questioning the Master Trope in *Visions of the Daughters of Albion*," *ELH*, 1990. • Jean H. Hagstrum, *William Blake: Poet and Painter*, 1964. • Zachary Leader, *Reading Blake's Songs*, 1981. • John Mee, *Dangerous Enthusiasm: William Blake and the Culture of Radicalism in the 1790s*, 1992. • W. J. T. Mitchell, *Blake's Composite Art*, 1978. • Martin K. Nurmi, "Fact and Symbol in 'The Chimney Sweeper' of Blake's *Songs of Innocence*," *Bulletin of the New York Public Library*, 1964. • Morton Paley, *Energy and the Imagination: A Study of the Development of Blake's Thought*, 1970. • Mark Schorer, *William Blake: the Politics of Vision*, 1946. • Irene Tayler, "The Woman Scaly" [on *Visions of the Daughters of Albion*], 1973; repr. Norton Critical Edition of *Blake's Poetry and Designs*. • E. P. Thompson, *Witness Against the Beast: William Blake and Moral Law*, 1993. • Joseph Viscomi, *Blake and the Idea of the Book*, 1993. • Thomas Vogler, "'In Vain the Eloquent Tongue': An Un-Reading of *Visions of the Daughters of Albion*," in *Blake and the Argument of Method*, eds. Dan Miller, Mark Bracher, and Donald Ault, 1987.

Our Texts • Edited for this volume with reference to the design of Blake's illuminated plates.

Edmund Burke • *Biographical Studies* • Carl B. Cone, *Burke and the Nature of Politics*, 2 vols., 1957, 1964. • C. B. Macpherson, *Burke*, 1980. • Conor Cruise O'Brien, *The Great Melody: A Thematic Biography and Commented Anthology of Edmund Burke*, 1992.

Criticism and Context • James T. Boulton, *The Language of Politics in the Age of Wilkes and Burke*, 1963. • Alfred Cobban, *Edmund Burke and the Revolt Against the Eighteenth Century*, 1929, repr. 1962. • Tom Furniss, *Edmund Burke's Aesthetic Ideology: Language, Gender, and Political Economy in Revolution*, 1993. • J. G. A. Pocock, "Burke and the Ancient Constitution: A Problem in the History of Ideas," in his *Politics, Language, and Time*, 1971. • J. G. A. Pocock "The Political Economy of Burke's Analysis of the French Revolution," in his *Virtue, Commerce, and History*, 1985.

Our Text • *The Works of Edmund Burke*, 1894.

Robert Burns • *Biographical Studies* • Raymond Bentman, *Robert Burns*, 1987. • David Daiches, *Robert Burns and His World*, 1971. • John Delancey Ferguson, *Pride and Passion: Robert Burns*, 1939. • James Mackay, *A Biography of Robert Burns*, 1992.

Editions • John Delancey Ferguson, ed., *The Letters of Robert Burns*, 2 vols., rev. ed. by G. Ross Roy, 1985. • James Kinsley, ed., *The Poems and Songs of Robert Burns*, 3 vols., 1968.

Criticism • Thomas Crawford, *Burns: A Study of the Poems and Songs*, 1960. • Thomas Crawford, ed., *Robert Burns and Cultural Authority*, 1997. • Leopold Damrosch, "Burns, Blake, and the Recovery of Lyric," *Studies in Romanticism*, 1982. • R. D. S. Jack and Andrew Noble, eds., *The Art of Robert Burns*, 1982. • Donald A. Low, ed., *Critical Essays on*

Robert Burns, 1975. • Carol McGuirk, *Robert Burns and the Sentimental Era*, 1985.

Our Texts • *The Centenary Burns*, eds. Ernest Henley and Thomas F. Henderson, 1896–1897; the second version of "Comin' Thro' the Rye" and "The Fornicator" from *The Merry Muses of Caledonia*, 1799–1800.

George Gordon, Lord Byron • *Biography* • Leslie A. Marchand, *Byron: A Biography*, 3 vols., 1957; abridged and revised in one volume as *Byron: A Portrait*, 1970.

Editions • E. H. Coleridge and R. E. Prothero, eds., *The Works of Lord Byron*, 13 vols., 1898–1904. • Leslie A. Marchand, ed., *Byron's Letters and Journals*, 12 vols., 1973–82. • Jerome J. McGann, ed., *Lord Byron: The Complete Poetical Works*, 7 vols., 1980–93.

Criticism • Bernard Beatty, *Byron's Don Juan*, 1985. • Jerome Christensen, *Lord Byron's Strength: Romantic Writing and Commercial Society*, 1993. • Michael G. Cooke, *The Blind Man Traces the Circle: On the Patterns and Philosophy of Byron's Poetry*, 1969. • Louis Crompton, *Byron and Greek Love*, 1985. • Andrew Elfenbein, *Byron and the Victorians*, 1995. • W. Paul Elledge, *Byron and the Dynamics of Metaphor*, 1968. • W. Paul Elledge, "Parting Shots: Byron Ending *Don Juan I*," *Studies in Romanticism*, 1988. • Caroline Franklin, *Byron's Heroines*, 1992. • Robert F. Gleckner, *Byron and the Ruins of Paradise*, 1967. • Robert F. Gleckner, ed., *Critical Essays on Lord Byron*, 1991. • Peter W. Graham, *Don Juan and Regency England*, 1990. • Sonia Hofkosh, "Women and the Romantic Author: The Example of Byron," in *Romanticism and Feminism*, ed. Anne Mellor, 1988. • M. K. Joseph, *Byron the Poet*, 1964. • Malcolm Kelsall, *Byron's Politics*, 1987. • Alice Levine and Robert N. Keane, eds., *Rereading Byron*, 1993. • Peter J. Manning, *Byron and His Fictions*, 1978. • Peter J. Manning, "*Don Juan* and Byron's Imperceptiveness to the English Word," *Studies in Romanticism*, 1979; repr. in his *Reading Romantics*, 1990. • Peter J. Manning, "*Don Juan* and the Revisionary Self," in *Romantic Revisions*, ed. Robert Brinkley and Keith Hanley, 1992. • Jerome J. McGann, *Fiery Dust: Byron's Poetic Development*, 1968. • Jerome J. McGann, *Don Juan in Context*, 1976. • Jerome J. McGann, "The Book of Byron and the Book of a World," in his *The Beauty of Inflections*, 1988. • Donald H. Reiman, "*Don Juan* in Epic Context," in *Studies in Romanticism*, 1977, repr. in his *Romantic Texts and Contexts*, 1987 • George M. Ridenour, *The Style of Don Juan*, 1960. • Andrew

Rutherford, *Byron: A Critical Study*, 1961. • Frederick W. Shilstone, *Byron and the Myth of Tradition*, 1988. • Peter L. Thorslev, *The Byronic Hero: Types and Prototypes*, 1962.

Our Texts • *The Works of Lord Byron, with his Letters and Journals, and His Life*, by Thomas Moore, 1832–34; *Byron's Letters and Journals*, ed. Leslie A. Marchand, 1973–1982.

John Clare • *Biography* • William J. Howard, *John Clare*, 1981. • Edward Storey, *A Right to Song: The Life of John Clare*, 1982. • J. W. Tibble and Anne Tibble, *John Clare: A Life*, rev. 1972.

Criticism • John Barrell, *The Idea of Landscape and the Sense of Place, 1730–1840: An Approach to the Poetry of John Clare*, 1972. • Hugh Haughton, Adam Phillips, and Geoffrey Summerfield, eds., *John Clare in Context*, 1994. • Elizabeth Helsinger, "Clare and the Place of the Peasant Poet," *Critical Inquiry*, 1987. • James C. McKusick, "'A Language that is Ever Green': The Ecological Vision of John Clare," *University of Toronto Quarterly*, 1991–92. • James C. McKusick, "John Clare and The Tyranny of Grammar," *Studies in Romanticism*, 1994. • Mark Storey, *The Poetry of John Clare: A Critical Introduction*, 1974. • L. J. Swingle, "Stalking the Essential John Clare: Clare in Relation to His Romantic Contemporaries," *Studies in Romanticism*, 1975. • Anne Wallace, "Farming on Foot: Tracking Georgic in Clare and Wordsworth," *Texas Studies in Language and Literature*, 1992.

Our Texts • Eric Robinson and David Powell, eds., *John Clare*, 1984; "Written in November" also from *The Village Minstrel*, 1821.

Samuel Taylor Coleridge • *Biography* • Rosemary Ashton, *The Life of Samuel Taylor Coleridge*, 1996. • Walter Jackson Bate, *Coleridge*, 1968. • Richard Holmes, *Coleridge: Early Visions*, 1990.

Editions • Kathryn Coburn, ed., *The Collected Works of Samuel Taylor Coleridge*, Bollingen Series 75, 1969—. Includes (among others): *Essays on His Times*, ed. David V. Erdman, 3 vols., 1978; *Lectures 1808–19 On Literature*, ed. R. A. Foakes, 2 vols., 1987; *Lay Sermons*, ed. R. J. White, 1972; *Biographia Literaria*, ed. James Engell and Walter Jackson Bate, 2 vols., 1983; *Poetical Works*, ed. J. C. C. Mays, 3 vols. (forthcoming). • E. H. Coleridge, ed., *Complete Poetical Works*, 2 vols., 1912. • Susan Eilenberg, *Strange Power of Speech: Wordsworth, Coleridge, and Literary Possession*, 1992. • R. A. Foakes, ed., *Coleridge on Shakespeare: The Text of the Lectures of 1811–12*, 1971. • E. L. Griggs, ed., *Collected Letters of Samuel Taylor Coleridge*, 6 vols.,

1956–71. • Thomas M. Raysor, ed., *Coleridge's Shakespearian Criticism*, 2 vols., 1960. • Martin Wallen, ed., *Coleridge's Ancient Mariner: An Experimental Edition of Texts and Revisions 1798–1828*, 1993.

Criticism • M. H. Abrams, *The Mirror and the Lamp*, 1953. • J. A. Appleyard, *Coleridge's Philosophy of Literature*, 1965. • John Beer, *Coleridge the Visionary*, 1959. • John Beer, *Coleridge's Poetic Intelligence*, 1977. • Frederick Burwick, ed., *Coleridge's Biographia Literaria: Text and Meaning*, 1989. • Jerome Christensen, *Coleridge's Blessed Machine of Language*, 1981. • George Dekker, *Coleridge and the Literature of Sensibility*, 1978. • Kelvin Everest, *Coleridge's Secret Ministry: The Context of the Conversation Poems*, 1979. • Frances Ferguson, "Coleridge and the Deluded Reader: 'The Rime of the Ancient Mariner,'" *Georgia Review*, 1977. • Norman Fruman, *Coleridge: The Damaged Archangel*, 1971. • Christine Gallant, ed., *Coleridge's Theory of Imagination Today*, 1989. • William H. Galperin, "'Desynonymizing' the Self in Wordsworth and Coleridge," *Studies in Romanticism*, 1987. • Paul Hamilton, *Coleridge's Poetics*, 1984. • Anthony John Harding, *Coleridge and the Inspired Word*, 1985. • Alethea Hayter, *Opium and the Romantic Imagination*, 1968. • William Heath, *Wordsworth and Coleridge: A Study of Their Literary Relations in 1801–02*, 1972. • Patrick Keane, *Coleridge's Submerged Politics: The Ancient Mariner and Robinson Crusoe*, 1994. • John Livingston Lowes, *The Road to Xanadu*, 1927. • Paul Magnuson, *Coleridge's Nightmare Poetry*, 1974. • Paul Magnuson, *Coleridge and Wordsworth: A Lyrical Dialogue*, 1989. • Thomas McFarland, *Coleridge and the Pantheist Tradition*, 1969. • Thomas McFarland, *Romanticism and The Forms of Ruin*, 1981. • Jerome J. McGann, "The Ancient Mariner: The Meaning of Meanings," in his *The Beauty of Inflections*, 1985. • James C. McKusick, *Coleridge's Philosophy of Language*, 1986. • Raimonda Modiano, *Coleridge and the Concept of Nature*, 1985. • Raimonda Modiano, "Word and 'Languageless' Meaning: Limits of Expression in *The Rime of the Ancient Mariner*," *Modern Language Quarterly*, 1977. • John Morrow, *Coleridge's Political Thought: Property, Morality, and the Limits of Traditional Discourse*, 1990. • Roy Park, "Coleridge's Two Voices as a Critic of Wordsworth," *ELH*, 1969. • Reeve Parker, *Coleridge's Meditative Art*, 1975. • Arden Reed, *Romantic Weather*, 1983. • Nicholas Roe, *Wordsworth and Coleridge: The Radical Years*, 1988. • Gene W. Ruoff, *Wordsworth and Coleridge: The Making of the Major Lyrics*, 1802–1804, 1989. • Elizabeth Schneider, *Coleridge, Opium, and Kubla Khan*, 1953. • Max F. Schulz, *The Poetic Voices of Coleridge*, 1963. • Elinor Shaffer, *Coleridge, Kubla Khan, and the Fall of Jerusalem*, 1985. • Karen Swann, "Christabel: The Wandering Mother and the Enigma of Form," *Studies in Romanticism*, 1984. • Karen Swann, "Literary Gentlemen and Lovely Ladies: The Debate on the Character of Christabel," *ELH*, 1985. • Kathleen M. Wheeler, *Sources, Processes, and Methods in Coleridge's Biographia Literaria*, 1980.

Our Texts • *The Complete Works of Samuel Taylor Coleridge*, ed. W. G. T. Shedd, 7 vols., 1853; "The Rime of the Ancyent Marinere" from *Lyrical Ballads*, 1798.

William Cowper • Biography • David Cecil, *The Stricken Deer*, 1929. • M. J. Quinlan, *Cowper: A Critical Life*, 1953. • Charles Ryskamp, *William Cowper of the Inner Temple*, 1959.

Editions • John D. Baird and Charles Ryskamp, eds., *Poems of William Cowper*, 3 vols., 1980. • James King and Charles Ryskamp, eds., *Letters and Prose Writings of William Cowper*, 5 vols., 1979–86.

Criticism • Morris Golden, *In Search of Stability: The Poetry of William Cowper*, 1960. • Vincent Newey, *Cowper's Poetry*, 1982.

Our Texts • *Poems*, 1851.

Olaudah Equiano • William L. Andrews, *To Tell a Free Story: The First Century of Afro-American Autobiography*, 1986. • Angelo Costanzo, *Surprizing Narrative: Olaudah Equiano and the Beginnings of Black Autobiography*, 1987. • Henry L. Gates, Jr., *The Signifying Monkey: A Theory of Afro-American Literary Criticism*, 1988. • Susan M. Marren, "Between Slavery and Freedom: The Transgressive Self in Olaudah Equiano's Autobiography," *PMLA*, 1993. • Geraldine Murphy, "Olaudah Equiano, Accidental Tourist," *Eighteenth-Century Studies*, 1994. • Adam Potkay, "Olaudah Equiano and the Art of Spiritual Autobiography," *Eighteenth-Century Studies*, 1994.)

Our Text • *The Life of Olaudah Equiano*, 1814.

William Godwin • John P. Clarke, *The Philosophical Anarchism of William Godwin*, 1977. • R. G. Grylls, *William Godwin and His World*, 1953. • Don Locke, *A Fantasy of Reason: The Life and Thought of William Godwin*, 1980. • Peter H. Marshall, *William Godwin*, 1984. • E. E. Smith and E. G. Smith, *William Godwin*, 1966. • William St. Clair, *The Godwins and the Shelleys*, 1989.

Our Text • An Enquiry Concerning Political Justice, and its Influence on General Virtue and Happiness, 1793.

Felicia Hemans • *Biography* • Henry F. Chorley, *Memorials of Mrs. Hemans, with Illustrations of Her Literary Character from Her Private Correspondence*, 1836. • [Harriett Mary Hughes {Browne}; later Owen], *Memoir of the Life and Writings of Felicia Hemans: By Her Sister*, 1845. • Peter W. Trinder, *Mrs. Hemans*, 1984.

Criticism • Isobel Armstrong, *Victorian Poetry: Poetry, Poetics and Politics*, 1993. • Norma Clarke, *Ambitious Heights: Writing, Friendship, Love*, 1990. • George Gilfillan, "Female Authors. No. I–Mrs. Hemans," *Tait's Edinburgh Magazine*, 1847. • Anthony John Harding, "Felicia Hemans and the Effacement of Woman," in *Romantic Women Writers*, eds. Theresa Kelley and Paula Feldman, 1995. • Angela Leighton, *Victorian Woman Poets: Writing Against the Heart*, 1993. • Tricia Lootens, "Hemans and Home: Victorianism, Feminine 'Internal Enemies,' and the Domestication of National Identity," *PMLA*, 1994. • Jerome J. McGann, "Literary History, Romanticism, and Felicia Hemans," in *Revisioning Romanticism*, eds. Carol Shiner Wilson and Joel Haefner, 1994. • Anne Mellor, *Romanticism and Gender*, 1993. • Herbert F. Tucker, "House Arrest: The Domestication of English Poetry in the 1820s," *ELH*, 1994. • Susan J. Wolfson, "'Domestic Affections' and 'the Spear of Minerva': Felicia Hemans and the Dilemma of Gender," in *Revisioning Romanticism*, eds. Wilson and Haefner, 1994. • Susan J. Wolfson, "Gendering the Soul," in *Romantic Women Writers*, eds. Kelley and Feldman, 1995. • Jonathan Wordsworth, *The Bright Work Grows: Women Writers of the Romantic Age*, 1997.

Our Texts • "The Wife of Asdrubal" in *Tales, and Historical Scenes*, 1819; "Indian-Woman's Death Song" and "Joan of Arc, in Rheims," in *Records of Woman*, 1828. These volumes are repr. by Garland and Woodstock Presses. Other poems, *Poems of Felicia Hemans*, 1873. An edition, *Felicia Hemans*, eds. S. Wolfson and G. Kelly, is forthcoming in 2000.

Francis Jeffrey • *Biography* • Henry Cockburn, *Life of Lord Jeffrey*, 2 vols., 1852.

Editions • Francis Jeffrey, *Contributions to the Edinburgh Review*, 4 vols., 1844.

Criticism • David Bromwich, "Romantic Poetry and the *Edinburgh* Ordinances," *Yearbook of English Studies*, 1986. • Jerome Christensen, "The Detection of the Romantic Conspiracy in Britain," *South Atlantic Quarterly*, 1996. • John Clive, *Scotch Reviewers: The Edinburgh Review 1802–1815*, 1957. • Philip Flynn, *Francis Jeffrey*, 1978. • Peter F. Morgan, *Literary Critics and Reviewers in Early 19th Century Britain*, 1983. • Mark Schoenfield, "Regulating Standards: The *Edinburgh Review* and the Circulations of Judgement," *The Wordsworth Circle*, 1993. • Kim Wheatley, "Paranoid Politics: The *Quarterly* and *Edinburgh* Reviews," *Prose Studies*, 1992.

Our Texts • *Edinburgh Review*, 1 (October 1802), and 24 (November 1814).

John Keats • *Biography and Reception* • Walter Jackson Bate, *John Keats*, 1963. • George H. Ford, *Keats and the Victorians: A Study of His Influence and Rise to Fame 1821–1895*, 1944. • G. M. Matthews, ed., *Keats: The Critical Heritage*, 1971. • Aileen Ward, *John Keats: The Making of a Poet*, 1963. • Susan J. Wolfson, "Feminizing Keats," in *Critical Essays on John Keats*, ed. Hermione de Almeida, 1990.

Criticism • John Barnard, *John Keats*, 1987. • Walter Jackson Bate, *The Stylistic Development of Keats*, 1945. • John Bayley, "Keats and Reality," *Proceedings of the British Academy*, 1962. • Cleanth Brooks, "Keats's Sylvan Historian: History without Footnotes," in *The Well Wrought Urn: Studies in the Structure of Poetry*, 1947. • Douglas Bush, *John Keats: His Life and Writings*, 1966. • Morris Dickstein, *Keats and His Poetry*, 1971. • Stuart Ende, *Keats and the Sublime*, 1976. • Geoffrey Hartman, "Spectral Symbolism and Authorial Self," in *The Fate of Reading*, 1975. • Wolf Z. Hirst, *John Keats*, 1981. • Margaret Homans, "Keats Reading Women, Women Reading Keats," *Studies in Romanticism*, 1990. • John Jones, *John Keats's Dream of Truth*, 1969. • William Keach, "Cockney Couplets: Keats and the Politics of Style," *Studies in Romanticism*, 1986. • Robert Kern, "Keats and the Problem of Romance," *Philological Quarterly*, 1979. • Marjorie Levinson, *Keats's Life of Allegory*, 1988. • Jerome J. McGann, "Keats and the Historical Method in Literary Criticism," 1979, repr. in *The Beauty of Inflections*, 1985. • Andrew Motion, *Keats*, 1998. • Christopher Ricks, *Keats and Embarrassment*, 1976. • Nicholas Roe, *John Keats and the Culture of Dissent*, 1997. • Stuart M. Sperry, *Keats the Poet*, 1973. • Jack Stillinger, "Imagination and Reality in the Odes" and "The Hoodwinking of Madeline," in *"The Hoodwinking of Madeline" and Other Essays on Keats's Poems*, 1971. • Karen Swann, "Harrassing the Muse," in *Romanticism and Feminism*,

Anne Mellor, ed. 1988. • Helen Vendler, *The Odes of John Keats*, 1983. • Leon Waldoff, *Keats and the Silent Work of Imagination*, 1985. • Daniel P. Watkins, *Keats's Poetry and the Politics of the Imagination*, 1989. • Susan J. Wolfson, "Keats and the Manhood of the Poet," *European Romantic Review*, 1995. • Susan J. Wolfson, *The Questioning Presence: Wordsworth, Keats, and the Interrogative Mode in Romantic Poetry*, 1986.

Our Texts • Poems published in Keats's lifetime are from first editions; posthumous publications are from Houghton's *Poetical Works*, 1891, checked against *The Poems of John Keats*, ed. Jack Stillinger, 1978, the best modern edition. • *The Letters of John Keats, 1814–1821*, ed. Hyder E. Rollins, 1958.

Charles Lamb • Biography • David Cecil, *A Portrait of Charles Lamb*, 1983. • Winifred F. Courtney, *Young Charles Lamb 1775–1802*, 1982. • E. V. Lucas, *Life of Charles Lamb*, rev. ed., 2 vols., 1921.

Editions • E. V. Lucas, ed., *The Works of Charles and Mary Lamb*, 1903–1905. • E. W. Marrs, ed., *The Letters of Charles and Mary Anne Lamb*, 3 vols., 1975—.

Critical Studies • Jane Aaron, *A Double Singleness: Gender and the Writing of Charles and Mary Lamb*, 1991. • George L. Barnett, *Charles Lamb*, 1976. • Robert Frank, *Don't Call Me Gentle Charles!*, 1976. • Richard Haven, "The Romantic Art of Charles Lamb," *ELH*, 1963. • Alison Hickey, "Double Bonds: Charles Lamb's Romantic Collaborations," *ELH*, 1996. • Gerald Monsman, *Confessions of a Prosaic Dreamer: Charles Lamb's Art of Autobiography*, 1984. • John Nabholtz, *"My Reader My Fellow-Labourer": A Study of English Romantic Prose*, 1986. • Roy Park, "Lamb, Shakespeare, and the Stage," *Shakespeare Quarterly*, 1982. • Mark Parker, "'A Piece of Autobiography': Reference in Charles Lamb's Essays," *Auto/Biography Studies*, 1986–1987. • Mark Parker, "Ideology and Editing: The Political Context of the Elia Essays," *Studies in Romanticism*, 1991. • F. V. Randel, *The World of Elia*, 1975.

Our Texts • *The Works of Charles and Mary Lamb*, ed. E. V. Lucas, 1903–1905.

Catherine Macaulay • Criticism • Bridget Hill, *Republican Virago: The Life and Times of Catherine Macaulay*, 1992. • Jonathan Wordsworth, *The Bright Work Grows: Women Writers of the Romantic Age*, 1997.

Our Text • *Letters on Education, With Observations on Religious and Metaphysical Subjects* (1790). Reprinted in *Feminist Controversy in England, 1788–1810*, ed. Gina Luria, 1974; excerpts from letters 4 and 21, and all of letters 22 and 23 are included in *A Vindication of the Rights of Woman*, ed. Carol Poston, 2nd ed. 1988.

Hannah More • Biography • M. G. Jones, *Hannah More*, 1952. • W. Roberts, *Memoirs of the Life and Correspondence of Mrs. Hannah More*, 1834. • Mary Alden Hopkins, *Hannah More and Her Circle*, 1947.

Criticism • Elizabeth Kowaleski-Wallace, *Their Fathers' Daughters: Hannah More, Maria Edgeworth and Patriarchal Complicity*, 1991. • Mitzi Myers, "Hannah More's Tracts for the Times: Social Fiction and Female Ideology," *Fetter'd or Free: British Women Novelists, 1670–1815*, eds. Mary Anne Schofield and Cecelia Macheski, 1986. • Alan Richardson, *Literature, Education, and Romanticism*, 1994. • G. H. Spinney, "Cheap Repository Tracts," in *The Library*, 1939. • Jonathan Wordsworth, *The Bright Work Grows: Women Writers of the Romantic Age*, 1997.

Our Texts • *Village Politics*, 1792; *The Works of Hannah More*, 1830.

Thomas Paine • A. J. Ayer, *Thomas Paine*, 1988. • Eric Foner, *Thomas Paine and Revolutionary America*, 1976. • David F. Hawke, *Thomas Paine*, 1974. • John Keane, *Thomas Paine: A Political Life*, 1995. • Mark Philp, *Paine*, 1989.

Our Text • *The Rights of Man*, 1790.

Mary Prince • Moira Ferguson, ed., *The History of Mary Prince*, 1987. • Moira Ferguson, *Subject to Others: British Women Writers and Colonial Slavery, 1670–1834*, 1992. • Jenny Sharpe, "'Something Akin to Freedom': The Case of Mary Prince," in *Differences*, 1996.

Our Text • *History of Mary Prince*, 1831.

Percy Bysshe Shelley • Biography • Kenneth Neill Cameron, *The Young Shelley*, 1950. • Richard Holmes, *Shelley: The Pursuit*, 1974. • Newman Ivey White, *Shelley*, 1940.

Reception • Mark Kipperman, "Absorbing a Revolution: Shelley Becomes a Romantic, 1889–1903," in *Nineteenth-Century Literature*, 1992. • Sylva Norman, *The Flight of the Skylark*, 1954. • N. I. White, *The Unextinguish'd Hearth*, 1938.

General Criticism • Stephen C. Behrendt, *Shelley and His Audiences*, 1989. • Harold Bloom, *Shelley's Mythmaking*, 1959. • Judith

Chernaik, *The Lyrics of Shelley*, 1972. • Frances Ferguson, "Shelley's *Mont Blanc*: What the Mountain Said," in *Romanticism and Language*, ed. Arden Reed, 1984. • Paul Foot, *Red Shelley*, 1980. • Jerrold Hogle, *Shelley's Process*, 1988. • William C. Keach, *Shelley's Style*, 1984. • Angela Leighton, *Shelley and the Sublime*, 1984. • Donald H. Reiman, *Percy Bysshe Shelley*, 1990. • Michael Henry Scrivener, *Radical Shelley*, 1982. • Stuart Sperry, *Shelley's Major Verse*, 1988. • Earl R. Wasserman, *Shelley: A Critical Reading*, 1981. • Milton Wilson, *Shelley's Later Poetry*, 1959. • Ross G. Woodman, *The Apocalyptic Vision in the Poetry of Shelley*, 1964.

On the Mask of Anarchy • *The Masque of Anarchy, A Poem*, with Preface by Leigh Hunt (1832), facsimile repr. ed. Jonathan Wordsworth, 1990. • Stuart Curran, *Shelley's Annus Mirabilis: The Maturing of an Epic Vision*, 1975. • Thomas R. Edwards, *Imagination and Power: A Study of Poetry on Public Themes*, 1971. • Stephen Goldsmith, *Unbinding Jerusalem: Apocalypse and Romantic Imagination*, 1993. • Donald H. Reiman, "*The Mask of Anarchy*": *A Facsimile Edition, with Scholarly Introductions, Bibliographical Descriptions, and Annotations*, 1985. • E. P. Thompson, *The Making of the English Working Class*, 1964. • Susan Wolfson, *Formal Charges* (1997).

Our Texts • *The Complete Poetical Works of Percy Bysshe Shelley*, ed. William Michael Rossetti, 1881, checked against modern editions; *The Mask of Anarchy* is checked against Reiman's 1985 facsimile edition of the 1819 *The Mask of Anarchy*.

Charlotte Smith • **Biography** • Florence May Anna Hilbish, *Charlotte Smith*, 1941.

Editions • *The Poems of Charlotte Smith*, ed. Stuart Curran, 1993.

Criticism • Bishop C. Hunt, "Wordsworth and Charlotte Smith," *The Wordsworth Circle*, 1970. • Judith Pascoe, "Female Botanists and the Poetry of Charlotte Smith," in *Revisioning Romanticism*, eds. Carol Shiner Wilson and Joel Haefner, 1994.

Our Text • *Elegiac Sonnets*, 5th ed., 1789.

William Thompson and Anna Wheeler • **Text, Biography** • Richard Pankhurst's edition of *Appeal*, 1983; Pankhurst has also written a biography of Thompson, 1954.

Criticism (Wheeler) • Stephen Burke, "Letter from a Pioneer Feminist," *Studies in Labour History*, 1976. • Richard Pankhurst, "Anna Wheeler; A Pioneer Socialist and Feminist," *Philological Quarterly*, 1954.

Helen Maria Williams • M. Ray Adams, "Helen Maria Williams and the French Revolution," *Wordsworth and Coleridge*, ed. Earl Leslie Griggs, 1939. • Mary Favret, "Spectatrice as Spectacle: Helen Maria Williams at Home in the Revolution," *Studies in Romanticism*, 1993. • Mary Favret, *Romantic Correspondence: Women, Politics, and the Fiction of Letters*, 1993. • Chris Jones, "Helen Maria Williams and Radical Sensibility," *Prose Studies*, 1989. • Nicola Watson, *Revolution and the Form of the British Novel, 1790–1825*, 1994.

Our Texts • *Letters from France*, 1790, 1796.

Mary Wollstonecraft • **Biography** • William Godwin, *Memoirs of the Author of a Vindication of the Rights of Woman*, 1798. • Gary Kelly, *Revolutionary Feminism: The Mind and Career of Mary Wollstonecraft*, 1992. • Jennifer Lorch, *Mary Wollstonecraft: The Making of a Radical Feminist*, 1990. • Emily Sunstein, *A Different Face—the Life of Mary Wollstonecraft*, 1975. • Claire Tomalin, *The Life and Death of Mary Wollstonecraft*, 1974.

Criticism Relevant to Vindication of the Rights of Woman • Claudia Johnson, *Equivocal Beings: Politics, Gender, and Sentimentality in the 1790s*, 1995. • Anne K. Mellor, *Romanticism and Gender*, 1993. • Ellen Moers, *Literary Women: The Great Writers*, 1963. • Mary Poovey, *The Proper Lady and the Woman Writer*, 1984. • Timothy J. Reiss, "Revolution in Bounds: Wollstonecraft, Women, and Reason," in *Gender and Theory: Dialogues on Feminist Criticism*, ed. Linda Kauffman, 1989. • Orrin Wang, "The Other Reasons," *Yale Journal of Criticism*, 1991. • Virginia Sapiro, *A Vindication of Political Virtue: The Political Theory of Mary Wollstonecraft*, 1992. • In Carol Poston's edition are included appreciations by George Eliot, 1855; Emma Goldman, c. 1910; and Virginia Woolf, 1932; as well as Ferdinand Lundberg and Marynia Farnham's notorious "Mary Wollstonecraft and the Psychopathology of Feminism," 1947; and helpful essays by (among others) Carolyn W. Kors-meyer, "Reason and Morals in the Early Feminist Movement," 1976; Elissa Guralnick on radical politics in *Rights of Woman*, 1977; R. M. Janes, on the reception of *Rights of Woman*, 1978; and Mitzi Myers, "Reform or Ruin," 1982.

On Vindication of the Rights of Men • Gary Kelly, "Mary Wollstonecraft as Vir Bonus," *English Studies in Canada*, 1979. •

Mitzi Myers, "Politics from the Outside," *Studies in Eighteenth-Century Culture*, 1977.

Our Texts • *A Vindication of the Rights of Men, in a Letter to the Right Honourable Edmund Burke; Occasioned by His "Reflections on the Revolution in France,"* 2nd ed,. 1790; *Vindication of the Rights of Woman*, ed. Carol Poston, 2nd ed., 1988; *Maria or the Wrongs of Woman* from William Godwin's edition in *The Posthumous Works*, 1798; repr. Norton, 1975.

William Wordsworth • Biography and Reference • Stephen Gill, *Wordsworth: A Life*, 1989. • John L. Mahoney, *William Wordsworth: A Poetic Life*, 1997. • Mary Moorman, *William Wordsworth: A Biography*, 2 vols., 1957–1965. • Mark L. Reed, *Wordsworth: The Chronology of the Early Years, 1770–1799*, 1967. • Mark L. Reed, *Wordsworth: The Chronology of the Middle Years, 1800–1815*, 1975. • Duncan Wu, *Wordsworth's Reading 1779–1799*, 1993. • Duncan Wu, *Wordsworth's Reading 1800–1815*, 1995.

Editions • R. L. Brett, and A. R. Jones, eds., *Wordsworth and Coleridge: Lyrical Ballads*, 1968. • Beth Darlington, ed., *The Love Letters of William and Mary Wordsworth*, 1981. • Ernest De Selincourt, ed., *The Letters of William and Dorothy Wordsworth*, 2nd ed. rev.: *Early Years, 1787–1805*, ed. Chester L. Shaver, 1967; *Middle Years, Part 1, 1806–1811*, ed. Mary Moorman, 1969, *Part 2, 1812–1820*, ed Alan G. Hill, 1970; *Later Years, Part 1, 1821–1828*, 1978, *Part 2, 1829–1834*, 1979, *Part 3, 1835–1839*, 1982, and *Part 4, 1840–1853*, 1988, all ed. Alan G. Hill. • Michael Mason, ed., *Lyrical Ballads*, 1992. • W. J. B. Owen and Jane Worthington Smyser, eds., *The Prose Works of William Wordsworth*, 3 vols., 1974. • Stephen Parrish, gen. ed., *The Cornell Wordsworth*, 1975–. This series, based on Wordsworth's earliest texts, thus far includes (among others): *The Prelude, 1798–1799*, ed. Stephen Parrish, 1977; *Poems, in Two Volumes and Other Poems 1800–1807*, ed. Jared Curtis, 1983; *The Fourteen-Book Prelude*, ed. W. J. B. Owen, 1985; *The Thirteen-Book Prelude*, ed. Mark L. Reed, 2 vols., 1991; *Shorter Poems, 1807–1820*, ed. Carl H. Ketcham, 1989; *Lyrical Ballads, and Other Poems, 1797–1800*, ed. James Butler and Karen Green, 1992. • Jonathan Wordsworth, M. H. Abrams, and Stephen Gill, eds., *The Prelude 1799, 1805, 1850*, 1979. • Jonathan Wordsworth and Helen Darbishire, eds., *The Poetical Works of William Wordsworth*, 5 vols., 1940–1949. [Based on Wordsworth's final texts.]

Criticism • Jonathan Arac, "Bounding Lines: The Prelude and Critical Revision," *boundary 2*, 1979. • James Averill, *Wordsworth and the Poetry of Human Suffering*, 1980. • Alan Bewell, *Wordsworth and the Enlightenment*, 1989. • Don Bialostosky, *Making Tales: The Poetics of Wordsworth's Narrative Experiments*, 1988. • James K. Chandler, *Wordsworth's Second Nature: A Study of the Poetry and Politics*, 1984. • David Collings, *Wordsworthian Errancies*, 1994. • Jared Curtis, *Wordsworth's Experiments with Tradition: The Lyric Poems of 1802*, 1971. • Paul De Man, "Time and History in Wordsworth," *Diacritics*, 1987. • David Ellis, *Wordsworth, Freud, and the Spots of Time*, 1985. • Elizabeth Fay, *Becoming Wordsworthian*, 1995. • Frances Ferguson, *Wordsworth: Language as Counter-Spirit*, 1977. • William H. Galperin, *Revision and Authority in Wordsworth*, 1989. • Frederick Garber, *Wordsworth and the Poetry of Encounter*, 1971. • George Gilpin, ed., *Critical Essays on William Wordsworth*, 1990. • Heather Glen, *Vision and Disenchantment: Blake's Songs and Wordsworth's Lyrical Ballads*, 1983. • Alan Grob, *The Philosophic Mind: A Study of Wordsworth's Poetry and Thought 1797–1805*, 1973. • Geoffrey Hartman, *Wordsworth's Poetry 1787–1814*, 1964; repr. rev. 1971. • Geoffrey Hartman, *The Unremarkable Wordsworth*, 1987. • James A. W. Heffernan, *Wordsworth's Theory of Poetry*, 1969. • Mary Jacobus, *Romanticism, Writing, and Sexual Difference: Essays on The Prelude*, 1989. • Mary Jacobus, *Tradition and Experiment in Wordsworth's Lyrical Ballads*, 1976. • Kenneth R. Johnston, *Wordsworth and The Recluse*, 1984. • Kenneth R. Johnston, "The Politics of 'Tintern Abbey,'" *The Wordsworth Circle*, 1983. • Kenneth R. Johnston and Gene W. Ruoff, eds., *The Age of William Wordsworth*, 1987. • John E. Jordan, *Why the Lyrical Ballads?*, 1976. • Theresa M. Kelley, *Wordsworth's Revisionary Aesthetics*, 1988. • J. Douglas Kneale, *Monumental Writing: Aspects of Rhetoric in Wordsworth's Poetry*, 1988. • Marjorie Levinson, *Wordsworth's Great Period Poems*, 1986. • Herbert Lindenberger, *On Wordsworth's Prelude*, 1963. • Alan Liu, *Wordsworth: The Sense of History*, 1989. • Peter J. Manning, *Reading Romantics*, 1990. • Richard J. Onorato, *The Character of the Poet: Wordsworth in The Prelude*, 1971. • Judith W. Page, *Wordsworth and the Cultivation of Women*, 1994. • Stephen M. Parrish, *The Art of the Lyrical Ballads*, 1973. • David Perkins, *The Quest for Permanence: The Symbolism of Wordsworth, Shelley, and Keats*, 1959. • Adela Pinch, "Female Chatter: Gender and Feeling in Wordsworth's Early Poetry," in her *Strange Fits of Passion*, 1996. • Jeffrey C. Robinson, *Radical Literary Education:*

A Classroom Experiment with Wordsworth's 'Ode', 1987. • Paul D. Sheats, *The Making of Wordsworth's Poetry 1785–1798*, 1973. • David Simpson, *Wordsworth and the Figurings of the Real*, 1982. • David Simpson, *Wordsworth's Historical Imagination: The Poetry of Displacement*, 1987. • Gayatri C. Spivak, "Sex and History in *The Prelude* (1805): Books Nine to Thirteen," *Texas Studies in Language and Literature*, 1981. • Keith G. Thomas, *Wordsworth and Philosophy*, 1989. • Douglas B. Wilson, *The Romantic Dream: Wordsworth and the Poetics of the Unconscious*, 1993. • Susan J. Wolfson, *The Questioning Presence*, 1986. • Jonathan Wordsworth, *William Wordsworth: The Borders of Vision*, 1982. • For the relations of Wordsworth and Coleridge, see also the entry under Samuel Taylor Coleridge.

Our Texts • *Lyrical Ballads*, 1798; *Complete Poetical Works*, 1892, 1898, and 1911; *The Thirteen-Book Prelude*, ed. Mark L. Reed; *The Excursion* (1814); letter to Mary Ann Rawson from *The Letters of William and Dorothy Wordsworth*, 2nd ed., *Later Years, Part 2*, ed. Alan G. Hill, 1979.

The Victorian Age

Bibliographies • Brahma Chaudhuri, ed., *Annual Bibliography of Victorian Studies*, 1976–. • Brahma Chaudhuri, ed., *A Comprehensive Bibliography of Victorian Studies, 1970–1984*, 3 vols. • *Modern Language Association International Bibliography*, online. • David Nicholls, *Nineteenth-Century Britain, 1815–1914*. 1978. • *Victorian Poetry*. Annual "Guide to the Year's Work on Victorian Poetry." 1963– • *Studies in English Literature*. Annual review of "Recent Studies in the Nineteenth Century" (autumn issue), 1961–. • *Victorian Studies*. Annual "Victorian Bibliography" (summer issue), 1957–.

Guides to Research • David J. DeLaura, *Victorian Prose: A Guide to Research*, 1973. • Frederic E. Faverty, *The Victorian Poets: A Guide to Research*, 2nd ed., 1968. • Lionel Madden, *How to Find Out About the Victorian Period*, 1970. • Lionel Stevenson, ed. *Victorian Fiction: A Guide to Research*, 1964; supplemented by *Victorian Fiction: A Second Guide to Research*, ed. George H. Ford, 1978.

Cultural and Intellectual Background • Richard D. Altick, *Victorian People and Ideas*, 1973. • Asa Briggs, *Victorian People: A Reassessment of Persons and Themes 1851–67*, 1965. • Asa Briggs, *Victorian Things*, 1988. • Jerome H. Buckley, *The Victorian Temper: A Study in Literary Culture*, 1951. • Jerome H. Buckley, *The Triumph of Time: A Study of the Victorian Concepts of Time, History, Progress, and Decadence*, 1966. • David Cannadine, *The Decline and Fall of the British Aristocracy*. 1990. • A. Dwight Culler, *The Victorian Mirror of History*, 1985. • David J. Delaura, *Hebrew and Hellene in Victorian England: Newman, Arnold, and Pater*, 1969. • Peter Gay, *The Bourgeois Experience: From Victoria to Freud*, 2 vols., 1984–1986. • Robin Gilmour, *The Victorian Period: The Intellectual and Cultural Context of English Literature, 1830–1890*. 1993. • Christopher Herbert, *Culture and Anomie: Ethnographic Imagination in the Nineteenth Century*, 1991. • Thomas William Heyck, *The Transformation of Intellectual Life in Victorian England*, 1982. • Walter E. Houghton, *The Victorian Frame of Mind, 1830–1870*, 1957. • Richard Jenkyns, *The Victorians and Ancient Greece*, 1980. • Steven Marcus, *The Other Victorians: A Study of Sexuality and Pornography in Mid-Nineteenth-Century England*, 1964. • Sally Mitchell, ed., *Victorian Britain: An Encyclopedia*, 1988. • E. Royston Pike, ed., *"Hard Times": Human Documents of the Industrial Revolution*, 1966; *"Golden Times": Human Documents of the Victorian Age*, 1967; *"Busy Times": Human Documents of the Age of the Forsytes*, 1969. • Mary Poovey, *Making a Social Body: British Cultural Formation, 1830–1864*, 1995. • Thomas Richards, *The Commodity Culture of Victorian England: Advertising and Spectacle, 1851–1914*, 1990. • Edward Said, *Orientalism*, 1978. • Richard L. Stein, *Victoria's Year: English Literature and Culture, 1837–1838*, 1987. • George W. Stocking, *Victorian Anthropology*, 1987. • Herbert Sussman, *Victorians and the Machine*, 1968. • Frank M. Turner, *Contesting Cultural Authority: Essays in Victorian Intellectual Life*, 1993. • Basil Willey, *Nineteenth Century Studies*, 1949. • Basil Willey, *More Nineteenth Century Studies*, 1956. • Raymond Williams, *Culture and Society 1780–1950*, 1958. • Janet Wolff and John Seed, eds., *The Culture of Capital: Art, Power and the Nineteenth-Century Middle Class*, 1988. • G. M. Young, *Victorian England: Portrait of an Age*, 1936.

Fiction • Richard D. Altick, *The Presence of the Present: Topics of the Day in the Victorian Novel*, 1991. • Nancy Armstrong, *Desire and Domestic Fiction: A Political History of the Novel*, 1987. • Joseph W. Childers, *Novel Possibilities: Fiction and the Formation of Early Victorian Culture*, 1995. • Peter Garrett, *The Victorian Multiplot Novel*, 1980. • Barbara Hardy, *Forms of Feeling in Victorian Fiction*, 1985. • E. A. Horsman, *The Victorian Novel*, 1991. • George Levine, *The Realistic Imagination: English Fiction from Frankenstein to Lady Chatterley*, 1981. • D. A. Miller, *The Novel and the Police*, 1988. • J. Hillis Miller, *The Form of Victorian Fiction*, 1968. • Ira B. Nadel and William E. Fredeman, eds., *Victorian Novelists Before 1885*, in *Dictionary of Literary Biography*, vol. 21, 1983. • Robert Polhemus, *Erotic Faith: Being in Love from Jane Austen to D. H. Lawrence*, 1990. • Barry Qualls, *The Secular Pilgrims of Victorian Fiction*, 1982. • Elaine Showalter, *A Literature of Their Own: British Women Novelists from Brontë to Lessing*, 1977. • Lionel Stevenson, *The English Novel: A Panorama*, 1960. • Ronald R. Thomas, *Dreams of Authority: Freud and the Fictions of the Unconscious*, 1990.

Gender and Culture • Amanda Anderson, *Tainted Souls and Painted Faces: The Rhetoric of Fallenness in Victorian Culture*, 1993. • Nina Auerbach, *Romantic Imprisonment: Women and Other Glorified Outcasts*, 1985. • Nina Auerbach, *Woman and the Demon: The Life of a Victorian Myth*, 1982. • Francoise Basch, *Relative Creatures: Victorian Women in Society and the Novel*, 1974. • Susan Casteras and Linda H. Peterson, *A Struggle for Fame: Victorian Women Artists and Authors*, 1994. • Lloyd Davis, ed., *Virgin Sexuality and Textuality in Victorian Literature*, 1993. • Richard Dellamora, *Masculine Desire: The Sexual Politics of Victorian Aestheticism*, 1990. • Kristine Ottesen Garrigan, ed., *Victorian Scandals: Representations of Gender and Class*, 1992. • Sandra Gilbert and Susan Gubar, *The Madwoman in the Attic: The Woman Writer and the Nineteenth-Century Literary Imagination*, 1979. • A. James Hammerton, *Cruelty and Companionship: Conflict in Nineteenth-Century Married Life*, 1992. • Kathleen Hickok, *Representations of Women: Nineteenth-Century British Women's Poetry*, 1984. • Margaret Homans, *Bearing the Word: Language and Female Experience in Nineteenth-Century Women's Writing*, 1986. • Dorothy Mermin, *Godiva's Ride: Women of Letters in England, 1830–1880*, 1993. • Ellen Moers, *Literary Women*, 1976. • Deborah Epstein Nord, *Walking the Victorian Streets: Women Representation, and the City*, 1995. • Christopher Parker, ed., *Gender Roles and Sexuality in Victorian Literature*, 1995. • Eve Kosofsky Sedgwick, *Between Men: English Literature and Male Homosocial Desire*, 1985. • Alan Sinfield, *Cultural Politics—Queer Reading*, 1994.

History and Politics • Derek Beales, *From Castlereagh to Gladstone: 1815–1885*, 1970. • Patrick Brantlinger, *The Spirit of Reform: British Literature and Politics, 1832–1867*, 1977. • Asa Briggs, *A Social History of England*, 1983. • Barbara Dennis and David Skilton, eds., *Reform and Intellectual Debate in Victorian England*, 1987. • C. C. Eldridge, *Victorian Imperialism*, 1978. • E. J. Feuchtwanger, *Democracy and Empire: Britain, 1865–1914*, 1985. • Jose Harris, *Private Lives, Public Spirit: A Social History of Great Britain, 1870–1914*, 1993. • Patricia Jalland, *Women, Marriage, and Politics, 1860–1914*, 1987. • Patrick Joyce, *Visions of the People: Industrial England and the Question of Class, 1848–1914*, 1991. • J. P. Parry, *The Rise and Fall of Liberal Government in Victorian Britain*, 1994. • David Thomson, *England in the Nineteenth Century*, 1950. • E. P. Thompson, *The Making of the English Working Class*, 1963. • F. M. L. Thompson, *The Rise of Respectable Society: A Social History of Victorian Britain, 1830–1900*, 1988.

Literature • William E. Buckler, *The Victorian Imagination: Essays in Aesthetic Exploration*, 1980. • Raymond Chapman, *The Sense of the Past in Victorian Literature*, 1986. • J. Hillis Miller, *The Disappearance of God: Five Nineteenth Century Writers*, 1963. • J. Hillis Miller, *Victorian Subjects*, 1990. • David Morse, *High Victorian Culture*, 1993. • John R. Reed, *Victorian Conventions*, 1975 • Ruth Robbins and Julian Wolfreys, eds., *Victorian Identities: Social and Cultural Formations in Nineteenth-Century Literature*, 1996.

Nonfiction Prose • Andrea Broomfield and Sally Mitchell, eds., *Prose by Victorian Women: An Anthology*, 1996. • Jerome H. Buckley, *The Turning Key: Autobiography and the Subjective Impulse since 1800*, 1984. • A. O. J. Cockshut, *The Art of Autobiography in 19th and 20th Century England*, 1984. • Mary Jean Corbett, *Representing Femininity: Middle-Class Subjectivity in Victorian and Edwardian Women's Autobiographies*, 1992. • Avrom Fleishman, *Figures of Autobiography: The Language of Self-Writing in Victorian and Modern England*, 1983. • Regenia Gagnier, *Subjectivities: A History of Self-Representation in Britain, 1832–1920*, 1991. • Heather Henderson, *The Victorian Self: Autobiography and Biblical Narrative*, 1989. • John Holloway, *The Victorian Sage*,

1953. • George P. Landow, ed., *Approaches to Victorian Autobiography*, 1979. • A. L. Le Quesne, *Victorian Thinkers: Carlyle, Ruskin, Arnold, Morris*, 1993. • George Levine and William Madden, eds., *The Art of Victorian Prose*, 1968. • Laura Marcus, *Auto/biographical Discourses: Theory, Criticism, Practice*, 1995. • Thaïs E. Morgan, ed., *Victorian Sages and Cultural Discourse: Renegotiating Gender and Power*, 1991. • Linda Peterson, *Victorian Autobiography: The Tradition of Self-Interpretation*, 1986.

Poetry • Isobel Armstrong, *Victorian Poetry: Poetry, Poetics, and Politics*, 1993. • Douglas Bush, *Mythology and the Romantic Tradition in English Poetry*, 1937. • Carol T. Christ, *The Finer Optic: The Aesthetic of Particularity in Victorian Poetry*, 1975. • Carol T. Christ, *Victorian and Modern Poetics*, 1984. • William E. Fredeman and Ira B. Nadel, eds., *Victorian Poets After 1850*, in *Dictionary of Literary Biography*, vol. 35, 1985. • William E. Fredeman, and Ira B. Nadel, eds., *Victorian Poets Before 1850*, in *Dictionary of Literary Biography*, vol. 32, 1984. • Eric Griffiths, *The Printed Voice of Victorian Poetry*, 1989. • Antony H. Harrison, *Victorian Poets and Romantic Poems: Intertextuality and Ideology*, 1990. • E. D. H. Johnson, *The Alien Vision of Victorian Poetry*, 1952. • Robert Langbaum, *The Poetry of Experience: The Dramatic Monologue in Modern Literary Tradition*, 1957. • Angela Leighton, *Victorian Women Poets: Writing Against the Heart*, 1992. • Angela Leighton, ed., *Victorian Women Poets: A Critical Reader*, 1996. • Angela Leighton and Margaret Reynolds, eds., *Victorian Women Poets: An Anthology*, 1995. • Laurence W. Mazzeno, *Victorian Poetry: An Annotated Bibliography*, 1995. • W. David Shaw, *The Lucid Veil: Poetic Truth in the Victorian Age*, 1987.

Reading and Readership • Richard D. Altick, *The English Common Reader: A Social History of the Mass Reading Public 1800–1900*, 1957. • Richard D. Altick, *Writers, Readers, and Occasions*, 1989. • N. N. Feltes, *Modes of Production of Victorian Novels*, 1986. • Kate Flint, *The Woman Reader, 1837–1914*, 1993. • John O. Jordan and Robert L. Patten, eds., *Literature in the Marketplace: Nineteenth-Century British Publishing and Reading Practices*, 1995. • Judith Kennedy, ed., *Victorian Authors and Their Works: Revision, Motivations, and Modes*, 1991. • Q. D. Leavis, *Fiction and the Reading Public*, 1932. • Joanne Shattock and Michael Wolff, eds., *The Victorian Periodical Press*, 1982. • John Sutherland, *Victorian Fiction: Writers, Publishers, Readers*, 1995. • David Vincent, *Literacy and Popular Culture: England 1750–1914*, 1990.

Theater • Michael R. Booth, ed., *English Plays of the Nineteenth Century*, 5 vols., 1969–1976. • Michael R. Booth, *Theater in The Victorian Age*, 1991. • Michael R. Booth, ed., *The Lights o' London and other Victorian Plays*, 1995. • Tracy C. Davis, *Actresses as Working Women: Their Social Identity in Victorian Culture*, 1991. • Anthony Jenkins, *The Making of Victorian Drama*, 1991. • Joel H. Kaplan and Sheila Stowell, *Theatre and Fashion: Oscar Wilde to the Suffragettes*, 1994.

Visual Arts • Richard Altick, *Paintings from Books: Art and Literature in Britain, 1760–1900*, 1985. • Kenneth Bendiner, *An Introduction to Victorian Painting*, 1985. • Deborah Cherry, *Painting Women: Victorian Women Artists*, 1993. • Carol T. Christ and John O. Jordan, eds., *Victorian Literature and the Victorian Visual Imagination*, 1995. • Linda Dowling, *The Vulgarization of Art: The Victorians and Aesthetic Democracy*, 1996. • William Gaunt, *The Pre-Raphaelite Dream*, 1966. • Helmut Gernsheim, *Julia Margaret Cameron: Her Life and Photographic Work*, 1975. • Heinz K. Henisch, *The Photographic Experience, 1839–1914*, 1994. • U. C. Knoepflmacher and G. B. Tennyson, eds., *Nature and the Victorian Imagination*, 1977. • Jeremy Maas, *Victorian Painters*, 1969. • Jan Marsh, *Pre-Raphaelite Sisterhood*, 1985. • Ira Bruce Nadel and F. S. Schwartzbach, eds., *Victorian Artists and the City*, 1980. • Pamela Gerrish Nunn, *Problem Pictures: Women and Men in Victorian Painting*, 1996. • Leslie Parris, ed., *The Pre-Raphaelites*, 1984. • Graham Reynolds, *Victorian Painting*, 1966; rev. 1987. • Lindsay Smith, *Victorian Photography, Painting, and Poetry: The Enigma of Visibility in Ruskin, Morris and the Pre-Raphaelites*, 1995. • Roy Strong, *And When Did You Last See Your Father?: The Victorian Painter and British History*, 1978. • Julian Treuherz, *Victorian Painting*, 1993. • Mike Weaver, *British Photography in the Nineteenth Century: The Fine Art Tradition*, 1989. • Christopher Wood, *The Pre-Raphaelites*, 1981.

World Wide Web Addresses • *British Poetry 1780–1910: A Hypertext Archive of Scholarly Editions:* etext.lib.virginia.edu/britpo.html • *Northeast Victorian Studies Association:* fmc.utm.edu. nvsa/index.html [Maintains list of other Victorian web sites.] • *Victoria Research Web:* www.indiana.edu/~victoria/ vwcont.html [Lists other Victorian web sites, and online Victorian journals and discussion groups.]. • George Landow's *Victorian Web:* www.stg.brown.edu/ projects/hypertext/landow/victorian/victov.html • *Victorian Women Writers Project:* www.indiana .edu/~letrs/vwwp/.

Perspectives: Aestheticism, Decadence and the Fin de Siècle • **Anthologies** Karl Beckson, ed., *Aesthetes and Decadents of the 1890s: An Anthology of British Poetry and Prose*, 1966; 1981. • Graham Hough and Eric Warner, eds., *Strangeness and Beauty: An Anthology of Aesthetic Criticism, 1840–1910*, 2 vols., 1983. • Ian Small, ed., *The Aesthetes: A Sourcebook*, 1979. • Derek Stanford, ed., *Poets of the 'Nineties: A Biographical Anthology*, 1965. • R. K. R. Thornton, ed., *Poetry of the Nineties*, 1970. • Stanley Weintraub, ed., *The Yellow Book: Quintessence of the Nineties*, 1964.

Criticism • Karl Beckson, *London in the 1890s: A Cultural History*, 1992. • Gene H. Bell-Villada, *Art for Art's Sake and Literary Life: How Politics and Markets Helped Shape the Ideology and Culture of Aestheticism, 1790–1990*, 1996. • G. A. Cevasco, ed., *The 1890s: An Encyclopedia of British Literature, Art, and Culture*, 1993. • Richard Dellamora, *Masculine Desire: The Sexual Politics of Victorian Aestheticism*, 1990. • Linda C. Dowling, *Aestheticism and Decadence: A Selective Annotated Bibliography*, 1977. • Linda C. Dowling, *Hellenism and Homosexuality in Victorian Oxford*, 1994. • Linda C. Dowling, *Language and Decadence in the Victorian Fin de Siècle*, 1986. • Bram Dijkstra, *Idols of Perversity: Fantasies of Feminine Evil in Fin-de-Siècle Culture*, 1986. • Ian Fletcher, ed., *Decadence and the 1890s*, 1979. • Hilary Fraser, *Beauty and Belief: Aesthetics and Religion in Victorian Literature*, 1986. • William Gaunt, *The Aesthetic Adventure*, 1945. • Richard Gilman, *Decadence: The Strange Life of an Epithet*, 1979. • Walter Hamilton, *The Aesthetic Movement in England*, 1882. • Simon Houfe, *Fin de Siècle: The Illustrators of the 'Nineties*, 1992. • Graham Hough, *The Last Romantics*, 1947. • Holbrook Jackson, *The Eighteen Nineties*, 1913. • Sally Ledger and Scott McCracken, eds., *Cultural Politics at the Fin de Siècle*, 1995. • Patricia Marks, *Bicycles, Bangs, and Bloomers: The New Woman in the Popular Press*, 1990. • Linda Merrill, *A Pot of Paint: Aesthetics on Trial in "Whistler v. Ruskin,"* 1992. • John R. Reed, *Decadent Style*, 1985. • Elaine Showalter, *Sexual Anarchy: Gender and Culture at the Fin de Siècle*, 1990. • Chris Snodgrass, *Aubrey Beardsley: Dandy of the Grotesque*, 1995. • Robin Spencer, *The Aesthetic Movement: Theory and Practice*, 1972. • John Stokes, *In the Nineties*, 1989. • John Stokes, ed., *Fin de Siècle/Fin de Globe: Fears and Fantasies of the Late Nineteenth Century*, 1992. • Mikulas Teich and Roy Porter, eds., *Fin de Siècle and its Legacy*, 1990. • R. K. R. Thornton, *The Decadent Dilemma*, 1983.

Our Texts • GILBERT: "If You're Anxious for to Shine" from *The Complete Plays of Gilbert and Sullivan*, 1941; WHISTLER: "Mr. Whistler's 'Ten O'Clock'" from *The Gentle Art of Making Enemies*, 2nd ed., 1892; "MICHAEL FIELD": "La Gioconda" and "A Pen-Drawing of Leda" from *Sight and Song*, 1892; "A Girl" from *Underneath the Bough*, 1893; LEVERSON: "Suggestion" from *The Yellow Book*, April 1895; DOUGLAS: "Two Loves" from *Two Loves and Other Poems*, 1990; "Impression de nuit" from *The Collected Poems of Lord Alfred Douglas*, 1919; CUSTANCE: from *The Selected Poems of Olive Custance*, 1995.

Perspectives: The Industrial Landscape • **Anthologies** • F. P. Donovon, *The Railroad in Literature: A Brief Survey of Railroad Fiction, Poetry, Songs, Biography, Essays, Travel, and Drama in the English Language*, 1940. • E. Royston Pike, *"Hard Times": Human Documents of the Industrial Revolution*, 1966. • Jeremy Warburg, ed., *The Industrial Muse: The Industrial Revolution in English Poetry*, 1958.

Criticism • John Belchem, *Industrialization and the Working Class: The English Experience, 1750–1900*, 1990. • Asa Briggs, *Victorian Cities*, 1963. • D. S. L. Cardwell, *The Norton History of Technology*, 1994. • Alice Chandler, *A Dream of Order: The Medieval Ideal in Nineteenth-Century English Literature*, 1970. • S. G. Checkland, *The Rise of Industrial Society in England, 1815–1885*, 1964. • Kenneth Clark, *The Gothic Revival: An Essay in the History of Taste*, 1928. • Bruce I. Coleman, ed., *The Idea of the City in Nineteenth-Century Britain*, 1973. • H. J. Dyos and Michael Wolff, eds., *The Victorian City: Images and Realities*, 2 vols., 1973. • Frank Ferneyhough, *The History of Railways in Britain*, 1975. • E. J. Hobsbawm, *Industry and Empire*, 1968. • Peter Keating, *The Working Classes in Victorian Fiction*, 1971. • David Levine, *The Making of an Industrial Society*, 1991. • Steven Marcus, *Engels, Manchester, and the Working Class*, 1974. • Ivan Melada, *The Captain of Industry in English Fiction, 1821–1871*, 1970. • Joel Mokyr, ed., *The British Industrial Revolution: An Economic Perspective*, 1993. • Joel Mokyr, ed., *The Economics of the Industrial Revolution*, 1986. • Deborah Epstein Nord, *Walking the Victorian Streets: Women, Representation, and the City*, 1995. • Ivy Pinchbeck, *Women Workers and the Industrial Revolution, 1750–1850*, 1930. • Sonya O. Rose, *Limited Livelihoods: Gender and Class in Nineteenth-Century England*, 1992. • Jack Simmons, *The Victorian Railway*, 1991. • Herbert Sussman, *Victorians and the Machine: The Liter-*

ary Response to Technology, 1968. • E. P. Thompson, The Making of the English Working Class, 1963. • Barrie Stewart Trinder, The Making of the Industrial Landscape, 1982. • Martha Vicinus, The Industrial Muse: A Study of Nineteenth Century Working-Class Literature, 1974. • James Walvin, English Urban Life, 1776–1851, 1984. • Raymond Williams, The Country and the City, 1973. • Edward A. Wrigley, Continuity, Chance and Change: The Character of the Industrial Revolution in England, 1989.

Our Texts • "The Steam Loom Weaver" from Martha Vicinus, The Industrial Muse, 1974; KEMBLE: Record of a Girlhood, vol. 2, 1879; MACAULAY: "A Review of Southey's Colloquies" from Edinburgh Review, Jan. 1830; PARLIAMENTARY PAPERS: from Victorian Women: A Documentary Account of Women's Lives, eds. Hellerstein, Hume, and Offen, 1981; DICKENS: Dombey and Son, Charles Dickens Edition, 1867; Hard Times, 1854; DISRAELI: Sybil from The Works of Benjamin Disraeli, 1904; ENGELS: The Condition of the Working Class in England, 1845, trans. W. O. Henderson and W. H. Chaloner, 1958; MAYHEW: London Labour and the London Poor, vols. 1 and 2, 1861–1862.

Perspectives: Victorian Ladies and Gentlemen

• Anthologies • Susan Groag Bell and Karen M. Offen, Woman, the Family, and Freedom: The Debate in Documents, 2 vols, 1983. • Erna Olafson Hellerstein, Leslie Parker Hume, and Karen M. Offen, eds., Victorian Women: A Documentary Account of Women's Lives, 1981. • Elizabeth K. Helsinger, Robin Lauterbach Sheets, and William Veeder, eds., The Woman Question: Society and Literature in Britain and America, 1837–1883, 3 vols., 1983. • Janet Murray, Strong-Minded Women and Other Lost Voices from Nineteenth-Century England, 1982.

Criticism • James Eli Adams, Dandies and Desert Saints: Styles of Victorian Masculinity, 1995. • Patricia Branca, Silent Sisterhood: Middle-Class Women in the Victorian Home, 1975. • Michael Brander, The Victorian Gentleman, 1975. • Joan N. Burstyn, Victorian Education and the Ideal of Womanhood, 1980. • David Castronovo, The English Gentleman: Images and Ideals in Literature and Society, 1987. • John Chandos, Boys Together: English Public Schools, 1800–1864, 1984. • Leonore Davidoff and Catherine Hall, Family Fortunes: Men and Women of the English Middle Class, 1780–1850, 1987. • Jonathan Gathorne-Hardy, The Public School Phenomenon, 1977. • Robin Gilmour, The Idea of the Gentleman in the Victorian Novel,

1981. • Mark Girouard, The Return to Camelot: Chivalry and the English Gentleman, 1981. • Deborah Gorham, The Victorian Girl and the Feminine Ideal, 1982. • Donald E. Hall, ed., Muscular Christianity: Embodying the Victorian Age, 1994. • Lee Holcombe, Victorian Ladies at Work: Middle-Class Women in England and Wales, 1850–1914, 1973. • Richard Holt, Sport and the British: A Modern History, 1989. • Margaret Homans and Adrienne Munich, eds., Remaking Queen Victoria, 1997. • J. R. de S. Honey, Tom Brown's Universe: The Development of the English Public School in the Nineteenth Century, 1977. • Kathryn Hughes, The Victorian Governess, 1993. • Elizabeth Langland, Nobody's Angels: Middle-Class Women and Domestic Ideology in Victorian Culture, 1995. • Anita Levy, Other Women: The Writing of Class, Race, and Gender, 1832–1898, 1991. • Elizabeth Longford, Eminent Victorian Women, 1981. • J. A. Mangan and James Walvin, eds., Manliness and Masculinity: Middle-Class Masculinity in Britain and America, 1800–1940, 1987. • Philip Mason, The English Gentleman: The Rise and Fall of an Ideal, 1982. • Claudia Nelson and Lynne Vallone, eds., The Girl's Own: Cultural Histories of the Anglo-American Girl, 1830–1915, 1994. • Mary Poovey, Uneven Developments: The Ideological Work of Gender in Mid-Victorian England, 1988. • Sonya O. Rose, Limited Livelihoods: Gender and Class in Nineteenth-Century England, 1992. • Brian Simon and Ian Bradley, eds., The Victorian Public School: Studies in the Development of an Educational Institution, 1975. • Herbert Sussman, Victorian Masculinities: Manhood and Masculine Poetics in Early Victorian Literature and Art, 1995. • Dorothy Thompson, Queen Victoria: The Woman, the Monarchy, and the People, 1990. • Norman Vance, The Sinews of the Spirit: The Ideal of Christian Manliness in Victorian Literature and Religious Thought, 1985. • Martha Vicinus, ed., Suffer and Be Still: Women in the Victorian Age, 1972. • Martha Vicinus, ed., A Widening Sphere: Changing Roles of Victorian Women, 1977.

Our Texts • COBBE: Life of Frances Power Cobbe, 1904; ELLIS: The Women of England, 1839; C. BRONTE: The Brontës: Their Lives, Friendships, and Correspondence, eds. Wise and Symington, Vol. 1, 1933; A. BRONTE: Agnes Grey, 1860; NEWMAN: The Idea of a University, 1873; BEETON: The Book of Household Management, 1861; VICTORIA: see footnotes; KINGSLEY: The Works of Charles Kingsley, vol. 7, 1899; NEWBOLT: "Vitaï Lampada," The Island Race, 1898.

Matthew Arnold • *Editions* • Kenneth Allott, ed., *Arnold: The Complete Poems*, 1965; 2nd ed., Miriam Allott, 1979. • Miriam Allott and R. H. Super, eds., *Matthew Arnold*, 1986 [annotated selection]. • Cecil Y. Lang, ed., *The Letters of Matthew Arnold*, 1996–. • Howard Foster Lowry, ed., *The Letters of Matthew Arnold to Arthur Hugh Clough*, 1968. • R. H. Super, ed., *The Complete Prose Works of Matthew Arnold*, 11 vols., 1960–1977.

Biography • Park Honan, *Matthew Arnold: A Life*, 1981. • Nicholas Murray, *A Life of Matthew Arnold*, 1997.

Criticism • Kenneth Allott, ed., *Matthew Arnold*, 1975. • Ruth Roberts, *Arnold and God*, 1983. • Harold Bloom, ed., *Matthew Arnold*, 1987. • William E. Buckler, *On the Poetry of Matthew Arnold*, 1982. • Douglas Bush, *Matthew Arnold: A Survey of His Poetry and Prose*, 1971. • Joseph Carroll, *The Cultural Theory of Matthew Arnold*, 1982. • Stefan Collini, *Arnold*, 1988. • Dwight Culler, *Imaginative Reason*, 1966. • Carl Dawson and John Pfordresher, eds., *Matthew Arnold, the Poetry: The Critical Heritage*, 1973; and *Matthew Arnold, Prose Writings: The Critical Heritage*, 1979. • T. S. Eliot, "Matthew Arnold," in his *The Use of Poetry and the Use of Criticism*, 1933. • T. S. Eliot, "Arnold and Pater," in his *Selected Essays*, 1932. • R. Giddings, ed., *Matthew Arnold: Between Two Worlds*, 1986. • Leon Gottfried, *Matthew Arnold and the Romantics*, 1983. • D. G. James, *Matthew Arnold and the Decline of English Romanticism*, 1961. • Edward D. H. Johnson, *The Alien Vision of Victorian Poetry*, 1952. • James C. Livingston, *Matthew Arnold and Christianity: His Religious Prose Writings*, 1986. • David G. Riede, *Matthew Arnold and the Betrayal of Language*, 1988. • Alan Roper, *Arnold's Poetic Landscapes*, 1969. • G. Robert Stange, *The Poet as Humanist*, 1967. • Lionel Trilling, *Matthew Arnold*, 1949.

Our Texts • The poems in this anthology are from Allott, *Complete Poems*; our prose selections are from Super, *Complete Prose*.

Elizabeth Barrett Browning • *Editions* • Cora Kaplan, ed., *Aurora Leigh and Other Poems*, 1978. • Philip Kelley and Ronald Hudson, eds., *The Brownings' Correspondence*, 1984–. • Elvan Kintner, ed., *The Letters of Robert Browning and Elizabeth Barrett Browning, 1845–1846*, 2 vols, 1969. • Charlotte Porter and Helen Clarke, eds., *Complete Works*, 6 vols., 1900. • Harriet Waters Preston, ed., *The Complete Poetical Works of Elizabeth Barrett Browning*, 1900; 1974. • Margaret Reynolds, ed., *Aurora Leigh*, 1992; 1996.

Biography • Angela Leighton, *Elizabeth Barrett Browning*, 1986. • Gardner B. Taplin, *The Life of Elizabeth Barrett Browning*, 1957.

Criticism • Warner Barnes, *A Bibliography of Elizabeth Barrett Browning*, 1968. • Kathleen Blake, "Elizabeth Barrett Browning and Wordsworth: The Romantic Poet as a Woman," *Victorian Poetry* 24 (1986). • Helen Cooper, *Elizabeth Barrett Browning, Woman and Artist*, 1988. • Deirdre David, *Intellectual Women and Victorian Patriarchy: Harriet Martineau, Elizabeth Barrett Browning, George Eliot*, 1987. • Sandra M. Gilbert, "From *Patria* to *Matria*: Elizabeth Barrett Browning's Risorgimento." *PMLA* 99 (1984); repr. *Victorian Women Poets*, ed. Angela Leighton, 1996. • Alethea Hayter, *Mrs. Browning: A Poet's Work and Its Setting*, 1962. • Dorothy Mermin, *Elizabeth Barrett Browning: The Origins of a New Poetry*, 1989. • Virginia L. Radley, *Elizabeth Barrett Browning*, 1972. • Dolores Rosenblum, "Face to Face: Elizabeth Barrett Browning's *Aurora Leigh* and Nineteenth-Century Poetry," *Victorian Studies* 26 (1983). • Glennis Stephenson, *Elizabeth Barrett Browning and the Poetry of Love*, 1989. • Marjorie Stone, *Elizabeth Barrett Browning*, 1995. • Virginia Woolf, "*Aurora Leigh*," in *The Second Common Reader*, 1932. • Joyce Zonana, "The Embodied Muse: Elizabeth Barrett Browning's *Aurora Leigh* and Feminist Poetics," *Tulsa Studies in Women's Literature* 8 (1989); repr. in *Victorian Women Poets*, ed. Angela Leighton, 1996.

Our Texts • Charlotte Porter and Helen Clarke, eds., *Complete Works*, 6 vols., 1900.

Robert Browning • *Editions* • *Poetical Works of Robert Browning*, 16 vols., 1888–1889. • Ian Jack, Margaret Smith, and Robert Inglesfield, eds., *The Poetical Works of Robert Browning*, 1983–. • Philip Kelley and Ronald Hudson, eds., *The Brownings' Correspondence*, 1984–. • John Pettigrew and Thomas J. Collins, eds., *The Poems*, 2 vols., 1981.

Biography • William Irvine and Park Honan, *The Book, the Ring, and the Poet*, 1974. • John Maynard, *Browning's Youth*, 1977. • Mrs. Sutherland Orr, *Life and Letters of Robert Browning*, 1891; 1908. • Clyde de L. Ryals, *The Life of Robert Browning: A Critical Biography*, 1993.

Criticism • Isobel Armstrong, ed., *Robert Browning*, 1974. • Walter Bagehot, "Wordsworth, Tennyson, and Browning," in *Literary Studies*, ed. R. H. Hutton, 1895. • Harold

Bloom and Adrienne Munich, eds., *Robert Browning: A Collection of Critical Essays*, 1979. • Joseph Bristow, *Robert Browning*, 1991. • G. K. Chesterton, *Robert Browning*, 1903. • Norman B. Crowell, *A Reader's Guide to Robert Browning*, 1972. • William C. DeVane, *A Browning Handbook*, 1955. • Philip Drew, ed., *Robert Browning: A Collection of Critical Essays*, 1966. • Donald Hair, *Browning's Experiments with Genre*, 1972. • Ian Jack, *Browning's Major Poetry*, 1973. • Roma A. King Jr., *The Bow and the Lyre*, 1957. • Robert Langbaum, *The Poetry of Experience: The Dramatic Monologue in Modern Literary Tradition*, 1957. • Boyd Litzinger and K. L. Knickerbocker, eds., *The Browning Critics*, 1965. • Boyd Litzinger and Donald Smalley, eds., *Browning: The Critical Heritage*, 1970. • Loy Martin, *Browning's Dramatic Monologues and the Post-Romantic Subject*, 1985. • William S. Peterson, *Robert and Elizabeth Barrett Browning: An Annotated Bibliography, 1951–1970*, 1974. • W. O. Raymond, *The Infinite Moment*, 1965. • Herbert F. Tucker, *Browning's Beginnings: The Art of Disclosure*, 1980.

Our Texts • From *Poetical Works of Robert Browning*, 16 vols., 1888–1889.

Thomas Carlyle • *Editions* • C. R. Sanders, K. J. Fielding, Clyde de L. Ryals, et al., eds., *The Collected Letters of Thomas and Jane Welsh Carlyle*, 1970–. • H. D. Traill, ed., *The Works of Thomas Carlyle*, 30 vols., 1896–1899.

Biography • J. A. Froude, *Thomas Carlyle: A History of the First Forty Years of his Life, 1795–1835*, 2 vols., 1882; *Thomas Carlyle: A History of his Life in London, 1834–1881*, 2 vols., 1884. • Fred Kaplan, *Thomas Carlyle: A Biography*, 1983.

Criticism • Ruth Roberts, *The Ancient Dialect: Thomas Carlyle and Comparative Religion*, 1988. • K. J. Fielding and Rodger L. Tarr, eds., *Carlyle Past and Present*, 1976. • Michael Goldberg, *Carlyle and Dickens*, 1972. • John Holloway, *The Victorian Sage*, 1953. • Albert J. LaValley, *Carlyle and the Idea of the Modern*, 1968. • George Levine, *The Boundaries of Fiction: Carlyle, Macaulay, Newman*, 1968. • Emery Neff, *Carlyle and Mill*, 1926. • Barry Qualls, *The Secular Pilgrims of Victorian Fiction*, 1983. • John D. Rosenberg, *Carlyle and the Burden of History*, 1985. • Philip Rosenberg, *The Seventh Hero: Thomas Carlyle and the Theory of Radical Activism*, 1974. • Jules Paul Seigel, ed., *Thomas Carlyle: The Critical Heritage*, 1971. • Rodger Tarr, *Thomas Carlyle: A Descriptive Bibliography*,

1990. • G. B. Tennyson, *"Sartor" Called "Resartus,"* 1965. • G. B. Tennyson, "Thomas Carlyle," in *Victorian Prose: A Guide to Research*, ed. David J. DeLaura, 1973. • Chris Vanden Bossche, *Carlyle and the Search for Authority*, 1991. • Basil Willey, *Nineteenth Century Studies*, 1949.

Our Texts • Texts cited from H. D. Traill.

Charles Darwin • *Editions* • Philip Appleman, ed., *Darwin*, 1970; 2nd ed., 1979. • Nora Barlow, ed., *The Autobiography of Charles Darwin, 1809–1882: With Original Omissions Restored*, 1958. • Paul H. Barrett and R. B. Freeman, eds., *The Works of Charles Darwin*, 29 vols., 1986. • Richard E. Leakey, abridged and introduced, *The Illustrated Origin of Species*, 1979; 1986.

Biography • John Bowlby, *Charles Darwin: A New Life*, 1990. • Francis Darwin, ed., *The Life and Letters of Darwin*, 1887–1888. • Adrian Desmond and James Moore, *Darwin*, 1991.

Criticism • Mea Allan, *Darwin and His Flowers: The Key to Natural Selection*, 1977. • Gillian Beer, *Darwin's Plots: Evolutionary Narrative in Darwin, George Eliot, and Nineteenth-Century Fiction*, 1983. • Peter Brent, *Charles Darwin: "A Man of Enlarged Curiosity,"* 1981. • Sir Gavin De Beer, *Charles Darwin: Evolution by Natural Selection*, 1964. • Loren Eiseley, *Darwin's Century: Evolution and the Men Who Discovered It*, 1958. • Michael T. Ghiselin, *The Triumph of the Darwinian Method*, 1984. • Stephen Jay Gould, *Ever Since Darwin*, 1977. • Stephen Jay Gould, *The Flamingo's Smile*, 1985. • David Kohn, ed., *The Darwinian Heritage*, 1985. • George Levine, *Darwin and the Novelists: Patterns of Science in Victorian Fiction*, 1988. • Jonathan Miller and Borin Van Loon, *Darwin for Beginners*, 1982. • John D. Rosenberg, "Mr. Darwin Collects Himself," in *Nineteenth-Century Lives*, ed. Laurence S. Lockridge et al., 1989. • Robert M. Young, *Darwin's Metaphor: Nature's Place in Victorian Culture*, 1985.

Our Texts • *The Voyage of the Beagle*, 1860, repr. 1962, ed. Leonard Engel; *On the Origin of Species*, 1859, repr. 1968, ed. J. W. Burrow.

Elizabeth Gaskell • W. A. Craik, *Elizabeth Gaskell and the English Provincial Novel*, 1975. • Angus Easson, *Elizabeth Gaskell*, 1979. • Angus Easson, ed., *Elizabeth Gaskell: The Critical Heritage*, 1991. • Rowena Fowler, "Cranford: Cow in Grey Flannel or Lion Couchant?" *SEL* 24 (1984). • Winifred Gérin, *Elizabeth Gaskell*, 1980. • Rae Rosenthal, "Gaskell's Feminist Utopia: The Cranfordians and the Reign of Goodwill," in *Utopian and Science Fiction by Women: Worlds of Difference*, eds. Jane

L. Donawerth and Carol A. Kolmerten, 1994. • Hilary M. Schor, *Scheherezade in the Market Place: Elizabeth Gaskell and the Victorian Novel*, 1992. • Patsy Stoneman, *Elizabeth Gaskell*, 1987. • Jenny Uglow, *Elizabeth Gaskell: A Habit of Stories*, 1993. • Patricia A. Wolfe, "Structure and Movement in *Cranford*," in *Nineteenth-Century Fiction*, vol. 23, 1968. • Terence Wright, *Elizabeth Gaskell: "We are not angels": Realism, Gender, Values*, 1995.

Our Text • *The Works of Mrs. Gaskell*, Knutsford Edition, 8 vols., 1906–1920. Ed. A. W. Ward. 1906–1911.

Gerard Manley Hopkins • *Editions* • Claude C. Abbott, ed., *The Correspondence of Gerard Manley Hopkins and Richard Watson Dixon*, 2 vols., 1935; rev. 1955. • Claude C. Abbott, *Further Letters of Gerard Manley Hopkins*, 1938; 1956. • Claude C. Abbott, *The Letters of Gerard Manley Hopkins to Robert Bridges*, 1935; 1955. • Christopher Devlin, ed., *The Sermons and Devotional Writings of Gerard Manley Hopkins*, 1959. • Humphrey House and Graham Storey, eds., *Journals and Papers*, 1959. • Norman H. MacKenzie, ed., *The Poetical Works of Gerard Manley Hopkins*, 1990. • Catherine Phillips, ed., *Gerard Manley Hopkins*, 1986.

Biography • Robert Bernard Martin, *Gerard Manley Hopkins: A Very Private Life*, 1991. • Norman White, *Hopkins: A Literary Biography*, 1992.

Criticism • Tom Dunne, *Gerard Manley Hopkins: A Comprehensive Bibliography*, 1976 [annual updates in *Hopkins Quarterly*]. • William H. Gardner, G. M. *Hopkins: A Study of Poetic Idiosyncrasy in Relation to Poetic Tradition*, 2 vols., 1944; 1949. • Richard F. Giles, ed., *Hopkins Among the Poets: Studies in Modern Responses to Gerard Manley Hopkins*, 1985. • Daniel Harris, *Inspirations Unbidden: The "Terrible Sonnets" of Gerard Manley Hopkins*, 1982. • Norman H. MacKenzie, *A Reader's Guide to Gerard Manley Hopkins*, 1981. • Paul L. Mariani, *A Commentary on the Complete Poems of Gerard Manley Hopkins*, 1970. • Walter J. Ong, *Hopkins, the Self, and God*, 1986. • Alison Sulloway, *Gerard Manley Hopkins and the Victorian Temper*, 1972.

Our Texts • W. H. Gardner, ed., *Poems of Gerard Manley Hopkins*, 1948; Humphrey House, and Graham Storey, eds., *Journals and Papers*, 1959; Claude C. Abbott, ed., *The Correspondence of Gerard Manley Hopkins and Richard Watson Dixon*, 2 vols., 1935; rev. 1955.

John Stuart Mill • *Editions* • John Robson, et al., eds., *Collected Works*, 33 vols., 1963–1991. •

Ann P. Robson and John M. Robson, eds., *Sexual Equality: Writings by John Stuart Mill, Harriet Taylor Mill, and Helen Taylor*, 1994. • David Spitz, ed., *On Liberty*, Norton critical edition, 1975.

Biography • Alexander Bain, *John Stuart Mill*, 1882; 1969. • Michael St. J. Packe, *The Life of John Stuart Mill*, 1954.

Criticism • Fred Berger, *Happiness, Justice, and Freedom*, 1984. • Janice Carlisle, *John Stuart Mill and the Writing of Character*, 1991. • Maurice Cowling, *Mill and Liberalism*, 1963. • F. W. Garforth, *Educative Democracy: John Stuart Mill on Education in Society*, 1980. • Peter Glassman, *The Evolution of a Genius*, 1985. • John Gray and G. W. Smith, eds., *J. S. Mill: On Liberty in Focus*, 1991. • Joseph Hamburger, *Intellectuals in Politics*, 1985. • Michael Laine, *Bibliography of Writings on John Stuart Mill*, 1982. • Michael Laine, ed., *A Cultivated Mind: Essays on J.S. Mill Presented to John M. Robson*, 1991. • John M. Robson, *The Improvement of Mankind: The Social and Political Thought of J. S. Mill*, 1968. • Alan Ryan, *John Stuart Mill*, 1970. • J. B. Schneewind, ed., *Mill: A Collection of Critical Essays*, 1968. • F. Parvin Sharpless, *The Literary Criticism of John Stuart Mill*, 1967. • Lynn Zastoupil, *John Stuart Mill and India*, 1994.

Our Texts • John Robson et al., eds., *Collected Works*, 33 vols., 1963–1991.

Christina Rossetti • *Editions* • Rebecca W. Crump, ed., *The Complete Poems of Christina Rossetti: A Variorum Edition*, 3 vols., 1979–1990. • William M. Rossetti, ed., *The Poetical Works of Christina Rossetti*, 1904. • Rebecca W. Crump, ed., *The Family Letters of Christina Georgina Rossetti*. 1908; 1968.

Biography • Kathleen Jones, *Learning Not to Be First: The Life of Christina Rossetti*, 1991. • Jan Marsh, *Christina Rossetti: A Writer's Life*, 1995.

Criticism • Georgina Battiscombe, *Christina Rossetti: A Divided Life*, 1981. • Kathleen Blake, *Love and the Woman Question in Victorian Literature*, 1983. • Edna Kotin Charles, *Christina Rossetti: Critical Perspectives, 1862–1982*, 1985. • Rebecca W. Crump, *Christina Rossetti: A Reference Guide*, 1976. • Antony H. Harrison, *Christina Rossetti in Context*, 1988. • Antony H. Harrison, ed., *Victorian Poetry*: special issue on Christina Rossetti, vol. 32, no. 3–4, 1994. • Elizabeth K. Helsinger, "Consumer Power and the Utopia of Desire: Christina Rossetti's Goblin Market." *ELH* 58

(1991). • David A., Kent, ed., *The Achievement of Christina Rossetti*, 1987. • Katherine J. Mayberry, *Christina Rossetti and the Poetry of Discovery*, 1989. • Jerome McGann, "Christina Rossetti's Poems: A New Edition and a Revaluation," *Victorian Studies* 23 (1980). • Jerome McGann, "The Religious Poetry of Christina Rossetti," *Critical Inquiry* 10 (1983). • Dorothy Mermin, "Heroic Sisterhood in *Goblin Market*," *Victorian Poetry* 21 (1983). • Dolores Rosenblum, *Christina Rossetti: The Poetry of Endurance*, 1986. • Sharon Smulders, *Christina Rossetti, Revisited*, 1996. • Virginia Woolf, "I Am Christina Rossetti," in *The Second Common Reader*, 1932.

Our Texts • Rebecca W. Crump, ed., *The Complete Poems of Christina Rossetti: A Variorum Edition*, 3 vols., 1979–1990.

John   Ruskin • *Editions* • Harold Bloom, ed., *The Literary Criticism of John Ruskin*, 1965. • Van Akin Burd, ed., *The Ruskin Family Letters, 1801–1843*, 2 vols., 1973. • E. T. Cook and Alexander Wedderburn, eds., *The Works of John Ruskin*, 39 vols., 1903–1912. • John D. Rosenberg, ed., *The Genius of John Ruskin: Selections from His Writings*, 1963.

Biography • Joan Abse, *John Ruskin: The Passionate Moralist*, 1980. • Timothy Hilton, *John Ruskin: The Early Years, 1819–1859*, 1985. • John Dixon Hunt, *The Wider Sea: A Life of John Ruskin*, 1982.

Criticism • Linda M. Austin, *The Practical Ruskin: Economics and Audience in the Late Work*, 1991. • Michael W. Brooks, *John Ruskin and Victorian Architecture*, 1987. • Susan Casteras et al., *John Ruskin and the Victorian Eye*, 1993. • Raymond Fitch, *The Poison Sky: Myth and Apocalypse in Ruskin*, 1982. • Elizabeth Helsinger, *Ruskin and the Art of the Beholder*, 1982. • Robert Hewison, *John Ruskin: The Argument of the Eye*, 1976. • Robert Hewison, ed., *New Approaches to Ruskin: Thirteen Essays*, 1981. • George P. Landow, *The Aesthetic and Critical Theories of John Ruskin*, 1971. • George P. Landow, *Ruskin*, 1985. • Linda Merrill, *A Pot of Paint: Aesthetics on Trial in Whistler v. Ruskin*, 1992. • John D. Rosenberg, *The Darkening Glass: A Portrait of Ruskin's Genius*, 1961. • J. C. Sherburne, *John Ruskin, or the Ambiguities of Abundance: A Study in Social and Economic Criticism*, 1972.

Our Texts • E. T. Cook and Alexander Wedderburn, eds., *The Works of John Ruskin*, 39 vols., 1903–1912.

Alfred Tennyson • *Editions* • Cecil Y. Lang and Edgar F. Shannon Jr., eds., *The Letters of Alfred, Lord Tennyson*, 3 vols., 1981–1990. • Christopher Ricks, ed., *Poems*, 3 vols., 1987. • Hallam Tennyson, ed., *Works*, 9 vols., 1907–1908.

Biography • Robert B. Martin, *Tennyson: The Unquiet Heart*, 1980. • Hallam Tennyson, *Alfred, Lord Tennyson: A Memoir, by His Son*, 2 vols., 1897.

Criticism • Daniel Albright, *Tennyson: The Muses' Tug-of-War*, 1986. • Kirk K. Beetz, *Tennyson: A Bibliography, 1827–1982*, 1984. • Jerome H. Buckley, *Tennyson: The Growth of a Poet*, 1960. • Philip Collins, ed., *Tennyson: Seven Essays*, 1993. • A. Dwight Culler, *The Poetry of Tennyson*, 1977. • Donald S. Hair, *Tennyson's Language*, 1991. • Arthur H. Hallam, "On Some Characteristics of Modern Poetry, and On the Lyrical Poems of Alfred Tennyson," *Englishman's Magazine* (August 1831). • Gerhard Joseph, *Tennyson and the Text: The Weaver's Shuttle*, 1992. • John D. Jump, ed., *Tennyson: The Critical Heritage*, 1967. • John Killham, ed., *Critical Essays on the Poetry of Tennyson*, 1960. • James R. Kincaid, *Tennyson's Major Poems: The Comic and Ironic Patterns*, 1975. • Sir Harold Nicolson, *Tennyson: Aspects of His Life, Character, and Poetry*, 1923. • Norman Page, ed., *Tennyson: Interviews and Recollections*, 1983. • Timothy Peltason, *Reading In Memoriam*, 1985. • F. E. L. Priestley, *Language and Structure in Tennyson's Poetry*, 1973. • Christopher Ricks, *Tennyson*, 1972. • John D. Rosenberg, *The Fall of Camelot: A Study of Tennyson's "Idylls of the King,"* 1973. • Matthew Rowlinson, *Tennyson's Fixations: Psychoanalysis and the Topics of the Early Poetry*, 1994. • Marion Shaw, *An Annotated Critical Bibliography of Alfred, Lord Tennyson*, 1989. • W. David Shaw, *Tennyson's Style*, 1976. • Alan Sinfield, *Alfred Tennyson*, 1986. • Herbert F. Tucker, *Tennyson and the Doom of Romanticism*, 1988. • Herbert F. Tucker, ed., *Critical Essays on Alfred Lord Tennyson*, 1993. • Paul Turner, *Tennyson*, 1976.

Our Texts • Hallam Tennyson, ed., *Works*, 9 vols., 1907–1908.

Oscar Wilde • *Editions* • Richard Ellmann, ed., *The Artist as Critic: Critical Writings of Oscar Wilde*, 1969. • Rupert Hart-Davis, ed., *Letters*, 1962. • Rupert Hart-Davis, *More Letters*, 1985. • Isobel Murray, ed., *The Complete Shorter Fiction of Oscar Wilde*, 1979. • Isobel Murray, ed.,

The Writings of Oscar Wilde, 1989. • Robert Ross, ed., *First Collected Edition*, 14 vols., 1908.

Biography • Richard Ellmann, *Oscar Wilde*, 1987. • Vyvyan Holland, *Oscar Wilde, a Pictorial Biography*, 1960. • Melissa Knox, *Oscar Wilde: A Long and Lovely Suicide*, 1994.

Criticism • Karl Beckson, ed., *Oscar Wilde: The Critical Heritage*, 1970. • Patricia Flanagan Behrendt, *Oscar Wilde: Eros and Aesthetics*, 1991. • Harold Bloom, ed., *Oscar Wilde: Modern Critical Views*, 1985. • Harold Bloom, ed., *Oscar Wilde's "The Importance of Being Earnest": Modern Critical Interpretations*, 1988. • Ed Cohen, *Talk on the Wilde Side: Toward a Geneology of a Discourse on Male Sexualities*, 1993. • Richard Ellmann, ed., *Oscar Wilde: A Collection of Critical Essays*, 1969. • Regenia Gagnier, ed., *Critical Essays on Oscar Wilde*, 1991. • Regenia Gagnier, *Idylls of the Marketplace: Oscar Wilde and the Victorian Public*, 1986. • Christopher S. Nassaar, *Into the Demon Universe: A Literary Exploration of Oscar Wilde*, 1974. • Kerry Powell, *Oscar Wilde and the Theatre of the 1890s*, 1991. • Peter Raby, *The Importance of Being Earnest: A Reader's Companion*, 1995. • Peter Raby, ed., *The Cambridge Companion to Oscar Wilde*, 1997. • Epifanio San Juan Jr., *The Art of Oscar Wilde*, 1967. • Rodney Shewan, *Oscar Wilde: Art and Egotism*, 1977. • John Stokes, *Oscar Wilde: Myths, Miracles, and Imitations*, 1996.

Our Texts • Poems from *First Collected Edition*, ed. Robert Ross, 1908; "The Soul of Man under Socialism" from *Fortnightly Review* (February 1891); "The Decay of Lying," from the Preface to *The Picture of Dorian Gray*, and "The Importance of Being Earnest" from *The Writings of Oscar Wilde*, ed. Isobel Murray, 1989; "De Profundis" from *The Letters of Oscar Wilde*, ed. Rupert Hart-Davis, 1962.

The Twentieth Century

General Background • Shari Benstock, *Women of the Left Bank: Paris, 1900–1940*, 1986. • Joseph Bristow, *Effeminate England: Homoerotic Writing after 1885*, 1995. • Carol T. Christ, *Victorian and Modern Poetics*, 1984. • Valentine Cunningham, *British Writers of the Thirties*, 1988. • Alistair Davies, ed., *An Annotated Critical Bibliography of Modernism*, 1982. • Marianne DeKoven, *Rich and Strange: Gender, History, Modernism*, 1991. • Kevin J. H. Dettmar, ed., *Rereading the New: A Backward Glance at Modernism*, 1992. • Maud Ellmann, *The Poetics of Impersonality: T. S. Eliot and Ezra Pound*, 1987. • David Gervais, *Literary Englands: Versions of "Englishness" in Modern Writing*, 1993. • Sandra Gilbert and Susan Gubar, *No Man's Land: The Place of the Woman Writer in the Twentieth Century*, 3 vols., 1988–. • John Halperin, *Eminent Georgians: The Lives of King George V, Elizabeth Bowen, St. John Philby, and Nancy Astor*, 1995. • Robert Hogan et al., *Dictionary of Irish Literature*, 1996. • Robert Hughes, *The Shock of the New*, 1981. • Hugh Kenner, *The Pound Era*, 1971. • Michael H. Levenson, *A Genealogy of Modernism: A Study of English Literary Doctrine, 1908–1922*, 1984. • James Longenbach, *Stone Cottage: Pound, Yeats, and Modernism*, 1988. • Perry Meisel, *The Myth of the Modern: A Study in British Literature and Criticism after 1850*, 1987. • Peter Nicholls, *Modernisms: A Literary Guide*, 1995. • Michael North, *The Political Aesthetic of Yeats, Eliot, and Pound*, 1991. • Herbert N. Schneidau, *Waking Giants: The Presence of the Past in Modernism*, 1991. • Sanford Schwartz, *The Matrix of Modernism: Pound, Eliot, and Early Twentieth-Century Thought*, 1985. • Bonnie Kime Scott, ed., *The Gender of Modernism: A Critical Anthology*, 1990. • John L. Somer and Barbara Eck Cooper, *American and British Literature, 1945–1975: An Annotated Bibliography of Contemporary Scholarship*, 1980. • C. K. Stead, *The New Poetic: Yeats to Eliot*, 1964. • C. K. Stead, *Pound, Yeats, Eliot, and the Modernist Movement*, 1986. • George Watson, *British Literature since 1945*, 1991.

Perspectives: The Great War: Confronting the Modern • Allyson Booth, *Postcards from the Trenches: Negotiating the Space between Modernism and the First World War*, 1996. • Paul Fussell, *The Great War and Modern Memory*, 1975. • Dorothy Goldman, ed., *Women and World War I: The Written Response*, 1993. • Klein-Holger, *The First World War in Fiction: A Collection of Critical Essays*, 1976. • John Onions, *English Fiction and Drama of the Great*

War, 1918–1939, 1990. • William C. Wees, *Vorticism and the English Avant-Garde*, 1972.

Perspectives: Whose Language? • Eugene Benson and L. W. Conolly, eds., *Encyclopedia of Post-Colonial Literatures in English*, 1994. • Elleke Boehmer, *Colonial and Postcolonial Literature: Migrant Metaphors*, 1995. • Michael Edward Gorra, *After Empire: Scott, Naipaul, Rushdie*, 1997. • Bruce King, ed., *New National and Post-Colonial Literatures: An Introduction*, 1996. • Judie Newman, *The Ballistic Bard: Postcolonial Fictions*, 1995. • Jonathan White, ed., *Recasting the World: Writing after Colonialism*, 1993.

Perspectives: World War II and the End of Empire • Bill Ashcroft, Gareth Griffiths, and Helen Tiffin, *The Empire Writes Back: Theory and Practice in Post-Colonial Literatures*, 1989. • Bernard Bergonzi, *Wartime and Aftermath: English Literature and its Background, 1939–1960*, 1993. • Patrick Brantlinger, *Rule of Darkness: British Literature and Imperialism, 1830–1914*, 1988. • George Richard Esenwein, *Spain at War: The Spanish Civil War in Context, 1931–1939*, 1995. • Robert Hewison, *Under Siege: Literary Life in London, 1939–1945*, 1977. • Karen R. Lawrence, ed., *Decolonizing Tradition: New Views of Twentieth-Century "British" Literary Canons*, 1992. • David Leavitt, *While England Sleeps* [novel], 1993. • David Lloyd, *Anomalous States: Irish Writing and the Post-Colonial Moment*, 1993. • Robert H. MacDonald, *The Language of Empire: Myths and Metaphors of Popular Imperialism, 1880–1918*, 1994. • David Morgan, *The Battle for Britain: Citizenship and Ideology in the Second World War*, 1993. • John M. Muste, *Say That We Saw Spain Die: Literary Consequences of the Spanish Civil War*, 1966. • Andrew Sinclair, *War Like a Wasp: The Lost Decade of the 'Forties*, 1989. • Hugh Thomas, *The Spanish Civil War*, 1986. • Keith Williams, *British Writers and the Media, 1930–1945*, 1996.

Speeches on Irish Independence • Seamus Deane, *Celtic Revivals: Essays in Modern Irish Literature, 1880–1980*, 1985. • Tom Garvin, *1922, The Birth of Irish Democracy*, 1996. • Michael Hopkinson, *Green against Green: The Irish Civil War*, 1988. • Declan Kiberd, *Inventing Ireland*, 1996. • Julian Moynahan, *Anglo-Irish: The Literary Imagination in a Hyphenated Culture*, 1995.

W. H. Auden • George W. Bahlke, ed., *Critical Essays on W. H. Auden*, 1991. • John G.

Blair, *The Poetic Art of W. H. Auden*, 1965. • Harold Bloom, ed., *W. H. Auden*, 1986. • John R. Boly, *Reading Auden: The Returns of Caliban*, 1991. • Frederick Buell, *W. H. Auden as a Social Poet*, 1973. • John Fuller, *A Reader's Guide to W. H. Auden*, 1970. • John Haffenden, ed., *W. H. Auden: The Critical Heritage*, 1983. • Anthony Hecht, *The Hidden Law: The Poetry of W. H. Auden*, 1993. • Richard Davenport Hines, *Auden*, 1995. • Lucy McDiarmid, *Saving Civilization: Yeats, Eliot, and Auden between the Wars*, 1984. • Lucy McDiarmid, *Auden's Apologies for Poetry*, 1990. • Edward Mendelson, ed., *W. H. Auden: A Tribute*, 1974. • Edward Mendelson, *Early Auden*, 1981. • Charles Osborne, *W. H. Auden: The Life of a Poet*, 1979. • Monroe K. Spears, *The Poetry of W. H. Auden: The Disenchanted Island*, 1963. • George T. Wright, *W. H. Auden*, 1969. • George T. Wright, *W. H. Auden*, 1981.

Samuel Beckett • *Biographies* • Lois Gordon, *The World of Samuel Beckett, 1906–1946*, 1996. • James Knowlson, *Damned to Fame: The Life of Samuel Beckett*, 1996.

Criticism • H. Porter Abbott, *Beckett Writing Beckett: the Author in the Autograph*, 1996. • James Acheson, *Samuel Beckett's Artistic Theory and Practice: Criticism, Drama, and Early Fiction*, 1997. • Richard Begam, *Samuel Beckett and The End of Modernity*, 1996. • Linda Ben-Zvi, *Samuel Beckett*, 1986. • Bob Cochran, *Samuel Beckett: A Study of the Short Fiction*, 1992. • Ruby Cohn, *Back to Beckett*, 1974. • Ruby Cohn, *Just Play: Beckett's Theater*, 1980. • J. E. Dearlove, *Accommodating the Chaos: Samuel Beckett's Nonrelational Art*, 1982. • S. E. Gontarski, ed., *The Beckett Studies Reader*, 1993. • S. E. Gontarski, ed., *On Beckett: Essays and Criticism*, 1986. • Lawrence Graver and Raymond Federman, eds., *Samuel Beckett: The Critical Heritage*, 1979. • Mel Gussow, ed., *Conversations With and About Beckett*, 1996. • Hugh Kenner, *Flaubert, Joyce, and Beckett: The Stoic Comedians*, 1962. • Hugh Kenner, *A Reader's Guide to Samuel Beckett*, 1973. • Hugh Kenner, *Samuel Beckett: A Critical Study*, 1968. • Charles R. Lyons, *Samuel Beckett*, 1990. • Patrick A. McCarthy, ed., *Critical Essays on Samuel Beckett*, 1986. • Vivian Mercier, *Beckett/Beckett*, 1977. • Kristin Morrison, *Canters and Chronicles: The Use of Narrative in the Plays of Samuel Beckett and Harold Pinter*, 1983. • Eoin O'Brien, *The Beckett Country: Samuel Beckett's Ireland*, 1993. • John Piling, ed., *The*

Cambridge Companion to Beckett, 1994. •
Christopher B. Ricks, Beckett's Dying Words:
The Clarendon Lectures, 1990, 1993.

Elizabeth Bowen • Biographies • Elizabeth Bowen,
Bowen's Court and Seven Winters: Memories of
a Dublin Childhood, 1984. • Patricia Craig,
Elizabeth Bowen, 1986.

Criticism • Allan E. Austin, Elizabeth Bowen,
1989. • Andrew Bennett and Nicholas Royle,
Elizabeth Bowen and the Dissolution of the
Novel: Still Lives, 1995. • Harold Bloom, ed.,
Elizabeth Bowen, 1987. • Renée Hoogland,
Elizabeth Bowen: A Reputation in Writing,
1994. • Heather B. Jordan, How Will the Heart
Endure: Elizabeth Bowen and the Landscape of
War, 1992. • Phyllis Lassner, Elizabeth Bowen:
A Study of Short Fiction, 1991.

Rupert Brooke • Biographies • John Lehmann,
Rupert Brooke: His Life and His Legend, 1980.

Criticism • Rupert Brooke, The Letters of Ru-
pert Brooke, ed. Geoffrey Keynes, 1968. •
Adrian Caesar, Taking It Like a Man: Suffering,
Sexuality, and the War Poets: Brooke, Sassoon,
Owen, Graves, 1993. • Paul Delany, The Neo-
Pagans: Rupert Brooke and the Ordeal of Youth,
1987. • Pippa Harris, Song of Love: The Letters
of Rupert Brooke and Noel Oliver, 1991. •
William E. Laskowski, Rupert Brooke, 1994.

Sir Winston Churchill • Biographies • William
Manchester, The Last Lion: Winston Spencer
Churchill Visions of Glory, 1874–1932, 1983. •
William Manchester, The Last Lion: Winston
Spencer Churchill: Alone, 1932–1940, 1989.

Criticism • Winston S. Churchill, Memoirs of
The Second World War, 1990. • Victor Feske,
From Belloc to Churchill: Private Scholars, Public
Culture, and the Crisis of British Liberalism,
1900–1939, 1996. • James Humes, Wit and
Wisdom of Winston Churchill, 1995. • Warren
F. Kimball, Churchill and Roosevelt, the Com-
plete Correspondence, 3 vols, 1984. • Warren F.
Kimball, Forged in War: Roosevelt, Churchill,
and the Second World War, 1997. • Sheila
Lawlor, ed., Churchill and the Politics of War,
1940–1941, 1994. • Keith Robbins, Churchill,
1993. • Manfred Weidhorn, Churchill's Rhetoric
and Political Discourse, 1988.

Michael Collins • Biographies • Tim P. Coogan,
Michael Collins: The Man Who Made Ireland,
1996. • James Mackay, Michael Collins: A Life,
1997.

Criticism • P. S. Beaslai, Michael Collins and the
Making of a New Ireland, 2 vols., 1985. • Eoin

Neeson, The Life and Death of Michael Collins,
1968. • Leon O'Broin, ed., In Great Haste: The
Letters of Michael Collins and Kitty Kiernan, 1996.
• Frank O'Connor, The Big Fellow: Michael
Collins and the Irish Revolution, 1965. • Ulick
O'Connor, Michael Collins and the Troubles: The
Struggle for Irish Freedom, 1912–1922, 1996.

Joseph Conrad • Chinua Achebe, "An Image of
Africa." • John Batchelor, The Life of Joseph
Conrad: A Critical Biography, 1993. • Ted
Billy, ed., Critical Essays on Joseph Conrad,
1987. • Harold Bloom, ed., Joseph Conrad's
"Heart of Darkness," 1987. • Harold Bloom,
ed., Joseph Conrad, 1986. • Harold Bloom,
Marlow, 1992. • Keith Carabine, ed., Joseph
Conrad: Critical Assessments, 4 vols., 1992. •
Avrom Fleishman, Conrad's Politics: Commu-
nity and Anarchy in the Fiction of Joseph Con-
rad, 1967. • Ford Madox Ford, Joseph Conrad:
A Personal Remembrance, 1989. • Christo-
pher L. GoGwilt, The Invention of the West:
Joseph Conrad and the Double-Mapping of Eu-
rope and Empire, 1995. • Albert J. Guerard,
Conrad the Novelist, 1958. • Geoffrey Harp-
ham, One of Us: The Mastery of Joseph Con-
rad, 1996. • Fredric Jameson, The Political
Unconscious: Narrative as a Socially Symbolic
Act, 1981. • Frederick Karl, Joseph Conrad:
The Three Lives: A Biography, 1979. • Freder-
ick R. Karl and Laurence Davies, eds., The
Collected Letters of Joseph Conrad, 1983- . •
Jeffrey Meyers, Joseph Conrad: A Biography,
1991. • Vincent P. Pecora, Self and Form in
Modern Narrative, 1989. • Martin Ray, ed.,
Joseph Conrad: Interviews & Recollections,
1990. • Edward W. Said, Joseph Conrad and
the Fiction of Autobiography, 1966. • Edward
W. Said, The World, the Text, and the Critic,
1983. • Norman Sherry, ed., Conrad: The
Critical Heritage, 1973. • J. H. Stape, ed., The
Cambridge Companion to Joseph Conrad, 1996.
• Bruce Teets, Joseph Conrad: An Annotated
Bibliography, 1990. • Ian Watt, Joseph Con-
rad: A Critical Biography, 1979. • Cedric P.
Watts, A Preface to Conrad, 1993. • Mark A.
Wollaeger, Joseph Conrad and the Fictions of
Skepticism, 1990.

T. S. Eliot • Biographies • Peter Ackroyd, T. S.
Eliot: A Life, 1984. • Lyndall Gordon, Eliot's
Early Years, 1977. • Lyndall Gordon, Eliot's
New Life, 1988.

Criticism • Harold Bloom, ed., T. S. Eliot,
1985. • Harold Bloom, ed., T. S. Eliot's "The
Waste Land," 1986. • Jewel Spears Brooker
and Joseph Bentley, Reading "The Waste

Land": Modernism and the Limits of Interpreta- tion, 1990. • Ronald Bush, T. S. Eliot: The Modernist in History, 1991. • T. S. Eliot, The Letters of T. S. Eliot, ed. Valerie Eliot, 1988–. • T. S. Eliot, "The Waste Land": A Facsimile and Transcript of the Original Drafts Including the Annotations of Ezra Pound, ed. Valerie Eliot, 1971. • Maud Ellmann, The Poetics of Impersonality: T. S. Eliot and Ezra Pound, 1987. • Nancy K. Gish, "The Waste Land": A Poem of Memory and Desire, 1988. • Michael Grant, ed., T. S. Eliot: The Critical Heritage, 1982. • Frank Lentricchia, Modernist Quartet, 1994. • James Longenbach, Modernist Poetics of History: Pound, Eliot, and the Sense of the Past, 1987. • Lucy McDiarmid, Saving Civi- lization: Yeats, Eliot, and Auden Between the Wars, 1984. • Gail McDonald, Learning to Be Modern: Pound, Eliot, and the American Uni- versity, 1993. • Louis Menand, Discovering Modernism: T. S. Eliot and His Context, 1986. • Anthony David Moody, ed., The Cambridge Companion to T. S. Eliot, 1994. • Anthony David Moody, Thomas Stearns Eliot, Poet, 1979. • Jeffrey M. Perl, Skepticism and Modern Enmity: Before and After Eliot, 1989. • Christopher B. Ricks, T. S. Eliot and Prejudice, 1988. • John Paul Riquelme, Harmony of Dis- sonances: T. S. Eliot, Romanticism and Imagina- tion, 1990. • Sanford Schwartz, The Matrix of Modernism: Pound, Eliot, and Early Twentieth- Century Thought, 1985. • Grover Cleveland Smith, The Waste Land, 1983. • Stanley Sul- tan, Eliot, Joyce, and Company, 1987. • Stan- ley Sultan, "Ulysses," "The Waste Land," and Modernism: A Jubilee Study, 1977.

Nadine Gordimer • *Biographies* • Nadine Gordimer, Writing and Being, 1995.

Criticism • Nancy T. Bazin and Marilyn D. Seymour, Conversations with Nadine Gordimer, 1990. • Stephen Clingman, The Novels of Na- dine Gordimer: History from the Inside, 1986. • Andrew V. Ettin, Betrayals of the Body Politic: The Literary Commitments of Nadine Gordimer, 1993. • Dominic Head, Nadine Gordimer, 1995. • Christopher Heywood, Nadine Gordimer, 1983. • Bruce King, ed., The Later Fiction of Na- dine Gordimer, 1993. • Judie Newman, Nadine Gordimer, 1988. • Rowland Smith, ed., Critical Essays on Nadine Gordimer, 1990. • Kathrin Wagner, Rereading Nadine Gordimer, 1994.

Thomas Hardy • Harold Bloom, ed., Thomas Hardy, 1987. • Graham Clarke, ed., Thomas Hardy: Critical Assessments, 4 vols., 1993. • Reginald Gordon Cox, Thomas Hardy: The Critical Heritage, 1970. • Ronald P. Draper, An Annotated Critical Bibliography of Thomas Hardy, 1989. • Simon Gatrell, Hardy, the Creator: A Textual Biography, 1988. • James Gibson, Thomas Hardy: A Literary Life, 1996. • Dale Kramer, Critical Essays on Thomas Hardy: The Novels, 1990. • Robert Lang- baum, Thomas Hardy in Our Time, 1995. • C. Day Lewis, The Lyrical Poetry of Thomas Hardy, 1970. • Perry Meisel, Thomas Hardy: The Return of the Repressed: A Study of the Ma- jor Fiction, 1972. • J. Hillis Miller, Thomas Hardy: Distance and Desire, 1970. • Michael Millgate, ed., Selected Letters, 1990. • Michael Millgate, Thomas Hardy: A Biography, 1982. • Charles P. C. Pettit, ed., New Perspectives on Thomas Hardy, 1994. • Richard L. Purdy and Michael Millgate, eds., The Collected Letters of Thomas Hardy, 1978-88. • Merryn Williams, A Preface to Hardy, 1993. • Paul Zietlow, Mo- ments of Vision: The Poetry of Thomas Hardy, 1974.

Seamus Heaney • *Biographies* • Michael Parker, Seamus Heaney: The Making of the Poet, 1993.

Criticism • Elmer Andrews, The Poetry of Sea- mus Heaney, 1988. • Harold Bloom, ed., Sea- mus Heaney, 1986. • Sidney Burris, ed., The Poetry of Resistance: Seamus Heaney and the Pastoral Tradition, 1990. • Neil Corcoran, Sea- mus Heaney: A Faber Student Guide, 1986. • Tony Curtis, ed., The Art of Seamus Heaney, 1994. • Michael J. Durkan and Rand Brandes, Seamus Heaney: A Reference Guide, 1996. • Thomas C. Foster, Seamus Heaney, 1989. • Robert F. Garratt, Critical Essays on Seamus Heaney, 1995. • Henry Hart, Seamus Heaney, Poet of Contrary Progressions, 1992. • Catherin Malloy and Phyllis Carey, eds., Seamus Heaney: The Shaping Spirit, 1996. • Michael R. Molino, Questioning Tradition, Language, and Myth: The Poetry of Seamus Heaney, 1994. • Blake Morrison, Seamus Heaney, 1982. • Bernard O'Donoghue, Seamus Heaney and the Language of Poetry, 1994.

David Jones • *Biographies* • René Hague, ed., Dai Great-Coat: A Self-Portrait of David Jones in His Letters, 1980.

Criticism • Thomas Dilworth, The Shape of Meaning in the Poetry of David Jones, 1988. • Thomas Dilworth, ed., Inner Necessities: The Letters of David Jones to Desmond Chute, 1984. • René Hague, David Jones, 1975. • Jeremy Hooker, David Jones: An Exploratory Study of the Writings, 1975. • David Jones, David Jones: Letters to Vernon Watkins, ed. Ruth Pryor,

1976. • Jonathan Miles and Derek Shiel, *David Jones: The Maker Unmade*, 1996. • Kathleen Raine, *David Jones, Solitary Perfectionist*, 1974. • Kathleen Staudt, ed., *At the Turn of a Civilization: David Jones and Modern Poetics*, 1993.

James Joyce • **Edition** • *Ulysses*, ed. Hans Walter Gabler, 1984.

Biographies • Richard Ellmann, *James Joyce*, 1982. • Herbert S. Gorman, *James Joyce*, 1948.

Criticism • Derek Attridge, ed., *The Cambridge Companion to James Joyce*, 1990. • Richard Brown, *James Joyce and Sexuality*, 1989. • Frank Budgen, *James Joyce and the Making of "Ulysses,"* 1960. • Kevin J. H. Dettmar, *The Illicit Joyce of Postmodernism: Reading Against the Grain*, 1996. • Enda Duffy, *The Subaltern "Ulysses,"* 1994. • Don Gifford, *Ulysses Annotated: Notes for Joyce's "Ulysses,"* 1988. • Stuart Gilbert, *James Joyce's "Ulysses": A Study*, 1930. • Clive Hart and David Hayman, eds., *James Joyce's "Ulysses": Critical Essays*, 1974. • Hugh Kenner, *Joyce's Voices*, 1978. • Hugh Kenner, *Ulysses*, 1987. • R. B. Kershner, *Joyce, Bakhtin, and Popular Literature: Chronicles of Disorder*, 1989. • Karen Lawrence, *The Odyssey of Style in "Ulysses,"* 1981. • A. Walton Litz, *The Art of James Joyce: Method and Design in "Ulysses" and "Finnegans Wake,"* 1961. • Vicki Mahaffey, *Reauthorizing Joyce*, 1988. • Dominic Manganiello, *Joyce's Politics*, 1980. • E. H. Mikhail, *James Joyce: Interviews and Recollections*, 1990. • Margot Norris, *Joyce's Web: The Social Unraveling of Modernism*, 1992. • Richard Pearce, *The Politics of Narration: James Joyce, William Faulkner, and Virginia Woolf*, 1991. • David Pierce, *James Joyce's Ireland*, 1992. • Arthur Power, *Conversations with James Joyce*, 1974. • Mary T. Reynolds, ed., *James Joyce: A Collection of Critical Essays*, 1993. • Bonnie K. Scott, *Joyce and Feminism*, 1984. • Robert E. Spoo, *James Joyce and the Language of History: Dedalus's Nightmare*, 1994. • Jennifer Wicke, *Advertising Fictions: Literature, Advertising, and Social Reading*, 1988.

Philip Larkin • **Biographies** • Andrew Motion, *Philip Larkin: A Writer's Life*, 1993.

Criticism • James Booth, *Philip Larkin: Writer*, 1992. • Richard Hoffpauir, *The Art of Restraint: English Poetry from Hardy to Larkin*, 1991. • Philip Larkin, *Selected Letters: 1940–1985*, ed. Anthony Thwaite, 1993. • Bruce K. Martin, *Philip Larkin*, 1978. • Janice Rossen, *Philip Larkin: His Life's Work*, 1990. • Dale Salwak, ed., *Philip Larkin: The Man and His Work*, 1988. • Andrew Swarbrick, *Out of Reach: The Poetry of Philip Larkin*, 1995. • Anthony Thwaite, *Larkin at Sixty*, 1982. • David Timms, *Philip Larkin*, 1973.

D. H. Lawrence • James T. Boulton, ed., *The Letters of D. H. Lawrence*, 6 vols., 1979– . • Henry Coombes, *D. H. Lawrence: A Critical Anthology*, 1973. • James C. Cowan, *D. H. Lawrence: An Annotated Bibliography of Writings about Him*, 1982. • Paul Delany, *D. H. Lawrence's Nightmare: The Writer and His Circle in the Years of the Great War*, 1978. • R. P. Draper, *D. H. Lawrence: The Critical Heritage*, 1970. • Sandra Gilbert, *Acts of Attention: The Poems of D. H. Lawrence*, 1972. • Leo Hamalian, *D. H. Lawrence: A Collection of Criticism*, 1973. • Philip Hobsbaum, *A Reader's Guide to D.H. Lawrence*, 1981. • Mark Kinkead-Weekes, *D. H. Lawrence: Triumph to Exile, 1912-1922*, 1996. • Dennis Jackson and Fleda Brown Jackson, eds., *Critical Essays on D.H. Lawrence*, 1988. • Thomas Rice Jackson, *D. H. Lawrence: A Guide to Research*, 1983. • F. R. Leavis, *D. H. Lawrence, Novelist*, 1970. • Henry Miller, *The World of Lawrence: A Passionate Appreciation*, 1980. • Kate Millet, *Sexual Politics*, 1970. • Harry T. Moore, *The Priest of Love: A Life of D. H. Lawrence*, 1974. • Ross C. Murfin, *The Poetry of D. H. Lawrence: Texts and Contexts*, 1983. • Joyce Carol Oates, *The Hostile Sun: The Poetry of D.H. Lawrence*, 1973. • F. B. Pinion, *A D. H. Lawrence Companion: Life, Thought, and Works*, 1979. • Tony Pinkney, *D.H. Lawrence and Modernism*, 1990. • Paul Poplawski, *D. H. Lawrence: A Reference Companion*, 1996. • Peter Preston and Peter Hoare, eds., *D.H. Lawrence in the Modern World*, 1989. • Warren Roberts, *A Bibliography of D. H. Lawrence*, 1982. • Keith Sagar, ed., *A D. H. Lawrence Handbook*, 1982. • Keith M. Sagar, *The Art of D.H. Lawrence*, 1975. • Carol Siegel, *Lawrence among the Women: Wavering Boundaries in Women's Literary Traditions*, 1991. • Stephen Spender, *D. H. Lawrence: Novelist, Poet, Prophet*, 1973. • John Worthen, *D. H. Lawrence: A Literary Life*, 1989.

Nuala Ní Dhomhnaill • M. Louise Cannon, "The Extraordinary Within the Ordinary: The Poetry of Eavan Boland and Nuala Ni Dhomhnaill," *South Atlantic Review* 60 (1995). • Deborah McWilliams Consalvo, "The Lingual Ideal in the Poetry of Nuala Ni Dhomh-naill," *Eire-Ireland: A Journal of Irish Studies,* 30 (1995). • Patricia Boyle Haberstroh, *Women Creating Women: Contemporary Irish Women Poets,* 1996.

Wilfred Owen • *Biographies* • Harold Owen, *Journey from Obscurity; Wilfred Owen, 1893–1918,* 1963–1965. • Jon Stallworthy, *Wilfred Owen,* 1974.

Criticism • Sven Bäckman, *Tradition Transformed: Studies in the Poetry of Wilfred Owen,* 1979. • Adrian Caesar, *Taking It Like a Man: Suffering, Sexuality, and the War Poets: Brooke, Sassoon, Owen, Graves,* 1993. • Desmond Graham, *The Truth of War: Owen, Rosenberg and Blunden,* 1984. • Dominic Hibberd, *Owen the Poet,* 1988. • Douglas Kerr, *Wilfred Owen's Voices: Language and Community,* 1993. • Arthur E. Lane, *An Adequate Response: The War Poetry of Wilfred Owen and Siegfried Sassoon,* 1972. • Stephen MacDonald, *Not About Heroes: The Friendship of Siegfried Sassoon and Wilfred Owen,* 1983. • Wilfred Owen, *Wilfred Owen: Collected Letters,* eds. William H. Owen and John Bell, 1967.

Charles Stewart Parnell • *Biographies* • Robert Kee, *The Laurel and the Ivy: The Story of Charles Stewart Parnell and Irish Nationalism,* 1993. • F. S. L. Lyons, *Charles Stewart Parnell,* 1977.

Criticism • Jules Abels, *The Parnell Tragedy,* 1966. • D. George Boyce and Alan O'Day, eds., *Parnell in Perspective,* 1991. • Noel Kissane, *Parnell: A Documentary History,* 1991. • Emmet Larkin, *The Roman Catholic Church in Ireland and the Fall of Parnell, 1888–1891,* 1979. • F. S. L. Lyons, *The Fall of Parnell, 1890–1891,* 1960. • Conor Cruise O'Brien, *Parnell and His Party, 1880–90,* 1968. • Alan O'Day, *Parnell and the First Home Rule Episode 1884–87,* 1986. • Michael Steinman, *Yeats's Heroic Figures: Wilde, Parnell, Swift, Casement,* 1983.

Padraic Pearse • Ruth Dudley Edwards, *Patrick Pearse: The Triumph of Failure,* 1977. • Sean Farrell Moran, *Patrick Pearse and the Politics of Redemption: The Mind of the Easter Rising, 1916,* 1994. • Padraic Pearse, *The Letters of P. H. Pearse,* ed. Seamus O Buachalla, 1980. • Raymond J. Porter, *P.H. Pearse,* 1973.

Ezra Pound • *Biographies* • Humphrey Carpenter, *A Serious Character: The Life of Ezra Pound,* 1988. • Noel Stock, *The Life of Ezra Pound,* 1970.

Criticism • Harold Bloom, ed., *Ezra Pound,* 1987. • Michael Coyle, *Ezra Pound, Popular Genres, and the Discourse of Culture,* 1995. • Reed Way Dasenbrock, *The Literary Vorticism of Ezra Pound and Wyndham Lewis: Towards the Condition of Painting,* 1985. • Eric Homberger, ed., *Ezra Pound: The Critical Heritage,* 1972. • Hugh Kenner, *The Poetry of Ezra Pound,* 1968. • Hugh Kenner, *The Pound Era,* 1971. • Gail McDonald, *Learning to Be Modern: Pound, Eliot, and the American University,* 1993. • Ezra Pound, *The Letters of Ezra Pound, 1907–1941,* ed. D. D. Paige, 1974. • Ezra Pound, *Pound/Lewis: The Letters of Ezra Pound and Wyndham Lewis,* 1985. • K. K. Ruthven, *A Guide to Ezra Pound's "Personae," 1926,* 1969.

Issac Rosenberg • *Biographies* • Joseph Cohen, *Journey to the Trenches: The Life of Isaac Rosenberg: 1890–1918,* 1975. • Jean Moorcroft Wilson, *Isaac Rosenberg, Poet and Painter: A Biography,* 1975.

Criticism • Desmond Graham, *The Truth of War: Owen, Rosenberg and Blunden,* 1984.

Salman Rushdie • Anouar Abdallah, ed., *For Rushdie: A Collection of Essays by 100 Arabic and Muslim Writers,* 1994. • Fawzia Afzal-Khan, *Cultural Imperialism and the Indo-English Novel: Genre and Ideology in R. K. Narayan, Anita Desai, Kamala Markandaya, and Salman Rushdie,* 1993. • Lisa Appignanesi and Sara Maitland, eds., *The Rushdie File,* 1990. • Timothy Brennan, *Salman Rushdie and the Third World: Myths of the Nation,* 1989. • Catherine Cundy, *Salman Rushdie,* 1997. • Michael Edward Gorra, *After Empire: Scott, Naipaul, Rushdie,* 1997. • James Harrison, *Salman Rushdie,* 1991. • Steve MacDonogh, ed., *The Rushdie Letters: Freedom to Speak, Freedom to Write,* 1993. • Daniel Pipes, *The Rushdie Affair: The Novel, the Ayatollah, and the West,* 1990. • Malise Ruthven, *A Satanic Affair: Salman Rushdie and the Rage of Islam,* 1990.

Siegfried Sassoon • *Biographies* • Sanford V. Sternlicht, *Siegfried Sassoon,* 1993.

Criticism • Adrian Caesar, *Taking It Like a Man: Suffering, Sexuality, and the War Poets: Brooke, Sassoon, Owen, Graves,* 1993. • Felicitas Corrigan, ed., *Siegfried Sassoon: Poet's Pilgrimage,* 1973. • John Hildebidle, "Neither Worthy Nor Capable: The War Memoirs of Graves, Blunden, and Sassoon," in *Modernism Reconsidered,* eds. Robert Kiely and John Hildebidle, 1983. • Arthur E. Lane, *An Adequate Response: The War Poetry of Wilfred Owen* and *Siegfried Sassoon*, 1972. • Stephen Mac-Donald, *Not About Heroes: The Friendship of Siegfried Sassoon and Wilfred Owen*, 1983. • Paul Moeyes, *Siegfried Sassoon, Scorched Glory: A Critical Study*, 1997. • Sigfried Sassoon, *Diaries*, 3 vols., ed. Rupert Hart-Davis, 1981–1985. • Michael Thorpe, *Siegfried Sassoon: A Critical Study*, 1966.

Stephen Spender • *Biographies* • Hugh David, *Stephen Spender: A Portrait with Background*, 1992.

Criticism • Hemant Balvantrao Kulkarni, *Stephen Spender: Poet in Crisis*, 1970. • Michael O'Neill, *Auden, MacNeice, Spender: The Thirties Poetry*, 1992. • Surya Nath Pandey, *Stephen Spender: A Study in Poetic Growth*, 1982. • Stephen Spender, *Journals, 1939–1983*, 1986. • Stephen Spender, *Letters to Christopher: Stephen Spender's Letters to Christopher Isherwood, 1929–1939, with "The Line of the Branch"—Two Thirties Journals*, ed. Lee Bartlett, 1980. • Sanford Sternlicht, *Stephen Spender*, 1992. • A. K. Weatherhead, *Stephen Spender and the Thirties*, 1975.

Dylan Thomas • John Ackerman, *Thomas: His Life and Work*, 1996 • Walford Davies, *Dylan Thomas: New Critical Essays*, 1972. • Paul Ferris, ed., *The Collected Letters*, 1985. • Paul Ferris, *Dylan Thomas*, 1977. • Constantine Fitzgibbon, *Selected Letters of Dylan Thomas*, 1966. • Georg Gaston, ed., *Critical Essays on Dylan Thomas*, 1989. • R. B. Kershner, *Dylan Thomas*, 1976. • Ruskworth M. Kidder, *Dylan Thomas: The Country of the Spirit*, 1973. • Jacob Korg, *Dylan Thomas*, 1992. • William T. Moynihan, *The Craft and Art of Dylan Thomas*, 1966. • Andrew Sinclair, *Dylan Thomas: No Man More Magical*, 1975. • Caitlin Thomas, *Leftover Life to Kill*, 1957. • William York Tindall, *A Reader's Guide to Dylan Thomas*, 1962.

Derek Walcott • William Baer, ed., *Conversations with Derek Walcott*, 1996. • Edward Baugh, *Derek Walcott: Memory as Vision: Another Life*, 1978. • Stewart Brown, ed., *Art of Derek Walcott*, 1991. • Robert D. Hamner, *Derek Walcott*, 1993. • Robert D. Hamner, ed., *Critical Perspectives on Derek Walcott*, 1993. • Bruce King, *Derek Walcott and West Indian Drama: Not Only a Playwright But a Company: The Trinidad Theatre Workshop 1959–1993*, 1995. • Tejumola Olaniyan, *Scars of Conquest—Masks of Resistance: The Invention of Cultural Identities in African, African-American, and Caribbean Drama*, 1995. • Michael Parker and Roger Starkey, eds., *Postcolonial Literatures:*

Achebe, Ngugi, Desai, Walcott, 1995. • Rei Terada, *Derek Walcott's Poetry: American Mimicry*, 1992.

Rebecca West • *Biographies* • Victoria Glendinning, *Rebecca West: A Life*, 1987. • J. R. Hammond, *H. G. Wells and Rebecca West*, 1991.

Criticism • Motley F. Deakin, *Rebecca West*, 1980. • Gordon N. Ray, *H. G. Wells and Rebecca West*, 1974. • Bonnie Kime Scott, *Refiguring Modernism. Vol. I: The Women of 1928. Vol. II: Postmodern Feminist Readings of Woolf, West, and Barnes*, 1995. • Peter Wolfe, *Rebecca West: Artist and Thinker*, 1971.

Virginia Woolf • Anne O. Bell, ed., *A Moment's Liberty: The Shorter Diary*, 1992. • Alison Booth, *Greatness Engendered: George Eliot and Virginia Woolf*, 1992. • Rachel Bowlby, ed., *Virginia Woolf*, 1993. • Thomas C. Caramagno, *The Flight of the Mind: Virginia Woolf's Art and Manic-Depressive Illness*, 1992. • Pamela L. Caughie, *Virginia Woolf and Postmodernism: Literature in Quest and Question of Itself*, 1991. • Mary A. Caws, *Women of Bloomsbury: Virginia, Vanessa and Carrington*, 1991. • Lyndall Gordon, *Virginia Woolf: A Writer's Life*, 1993. • Margaret Homans, ed., *Virginia Woolf: A Collection of Critical Essays (20th Century Views)*, 1992. • Mark Hussey, *Virginia Woolf A to Z: A Comprehensive Reference for Students, Teachers, and Common Readers to Her Life, Work, & Critical Reception*, 1996. • Mitchell A. Leaska, ed., *A Passionate Apprentice: The Early Journals, 1897-1909*, 1992. • Eleanor McNees, ed., *Virginia Woolf: Critical Assessments*, 4 vols., 1994. • Andrew McNeillie, ed., *Essays of Virginia Woolf*, 4 vols. • John Mepham, *Virginia Woolf: A Literary Life*, 1991. • Kathy J. Phillips, *Virginia Woolf Against Empire*, 1994. • Panthea Reid, *Art and Affection: A Life of Virginia Woolf*, 1996. • S. P. Rosenbaum, ed., *Women and Fiction: The Manuscript Versions of "A Room of One's Own,"* 1992. • Bonnie Kime Scott, *Refiguring Modernism*, 2 vols., 1995. • Peter Stansky, *On Or about December 1910: Early Bloomsbury and Its Intimate World*, 1996. • J. H. Stape, *Virginia Woolf: Interviews and Recollections*, 1995. • J. H. Stape, *Congenial Spirits: The Selected Letters of Virginia Woolf*, 1991. • Jeanette Winterson, *Art Objects: Essays on Ecstasy and Effrontery*, 1996. • Alex Zwerdling, *Virginia Woolf and Real Life*, 1987.

William Butler Yeats • *Edition* • *The Poems of W. B. Yeats: A New Edition*, ed. Richard J. Finneran, 1983.

Biographies • Richard Ellmann, *Yeats, the Man and the Masks*, 1948. • R. F. Foster, *W. B. Yeats: A Life*, 1997–.

Criticism • Harold Bloom, *Yeats*, 1970. • Elizabeth B. Cullingford, *Gender and History in Yeats's Love Poetry*, 1993. • Una Mary Ellis-Fermor, *The Irish Dramatic Movement*, 1954. • Richard Ellmann, *Eminent Domain: Yeats among Wilde, Joyce, Pound, Eliot, and Auden*, 1967. • Richard J. Finneran, *Critical Essays on W.B. Yeats*, 1986. • Adrian Frazier, *Behind the Scenes: Yeats, Horniman, and the Struggle for the Abbey Theatre*, 1990. • Maud Gonne, *The Gonne-Yeats Letters 1893–1938*, eds. Anna MacBride White and A. Norman Jeffares, 1993. • A. Norman Jeffares, *A New Commentary on the Poems of W. B. Yeats*, 1984. • A. Norman Jeffares, *W. B. Yeats: The Critical Heritage*, 1977. • A. Norman Jeffares, *W. B. Yeats, Man and Poet*, 1996. • Frank Kermode, *Romantic Image*, 1961. • Louis MacNeice, *The Poetry of W. B. Yeats*, 1941. • Edward Greenway Malins, *A Preface to Yeats*, 1974. • Lucy McDiarmid, *Saving Civilization: Yeats, Eliot, and Auden Between the Wars*, 1984. • E. H. Mikhail, ed., *W. B. Yeats: Interviews and Recollections*, 2 vols, 1977. • David Pierce, *Yeats's Worlds: Ireland, England and the Poetic Imagination*, with photographs by Dan Harper, 1995. • John Quinn, *The Letters of John Quinn to William Butler Yeats*, ed. Alan Himber, with George Mills Harper, 1983. • Jahan Ramazani, *Yeats and the Poetry of Death: Elegy, Self-Elegy, and the Sublime*, 1990. • M. L. Rosenthal, *Running to Paradise: Yeats's Poetic Art*, 1994. • Michael J. Sidnell, *Yeats's Poetry and Poetics*, 1996. • Jon Stallworthy, *Between the Lines: Yeats's Poetry in the Making*, 1963. • William York Tindall, *W. B. Yeats*, 1966. • John Eugene Unterecker, *A Reader's Guide to William Butler Yeats*, 1959. • William Butler Yeats, *Collected Letters of W. B. Yeats*, eds. Warwick Gould, John Kelly, and Dierdre Toomey, 1986–.

CREDITS

ILLUSTRATION CREDITS

Cover: Courtesy of the National Portrait Gallery, London. *Inside back cover:* Map of the world showing the extent of the British Empire in 1886, from an illustrated supplement to *The Graphic,* 24 July 1986. Reproduced with permission of the General Research Division, New York Public Library, Astor, Lenox and Tilden Foundations. *Page 1312:* By courtesy of the National Portrait Gallery, London. *Page 1318:* © Tyne and Wear Museums. *Page 1322:* Copyright © The British Museum. *Page 1326:* The Royal Collection © 1999 Her Majesty Queen Elizabeth II. *Page 1337:* Copyright © The British Museum. *Page 1357:* Copyright © The British Museum. *Page 1388:* Copyright © The British Museum. *Pages 1395–1396:* Reproduced from the Collections of the Library of Congress. *Page 1401:* Reproduced from the Collections of the Library of Congress. *Page 1403:* Reproduced from the Collections of the Library of Congress. *Page 1407:* Reproduced from the Collections of the Library of Congress. *Page 1462:* Reproduced from the Collections of the Library of Congress. *Page 1791:* © Culver Pictures. *Page 1787:* Victoria & Albert Museum, London/Art Resource. *Page 1797:* Harvard College Library/Widener Library. *Page 1800:* © Punch Ltd. *Page 1808:* Science and Society Picture Library. *Page 1841:* General Research Division, The New York Public Library, Astor, Lenox & Tilden Foundations. *Page 1910:* Courtesy of Mrs. Eva Reichman. *Page 1914:* William Holman Hunt, "The Lady of Shallot," Manchester City Art Gallery. *Page 1946:* Rare Book Division, The New York Public Library, Astor, Lenox & Tilden Foundations. *Page 1887:* Radio Times Hulton Picture Library. *Page 1896:* © The Board of the Trustees of the Victoria and Albert Museum/Art Resource, NY. *Page 1903:* The Royal Collection © 1999 Her Majesty Queen Elizabeth. *Page 2047:* General Research Division, The New York Public Library, Astor, Lenox & Tilden Foundations. *Page 2067:* Williams Andrew Clark Memorial, Library, University of California, Los Angeles. *Page 2141:* © Punch Ltd. *Page 2164:* © Tom Phillips. *Page 2170:* Imperial War Museum. *Page 2178:* William Vandivert/Life Magazine: © Time Inc. *Page 2182:* © Apple Corps. Ltd. *Page 2265:* © Wadsworth Atheneum, Hartford; The Ella Gallup Sumner and Mary Catlain Sumner Collection Fund. *Page 2306:* © Trustees of the David Jones Estate/National Museum & Gallery, Cardiff. *Page 2390:* National Library of Ireland. *Page 2446:* © Sylvia Beach Papers. Manuscripts Division. Dept. of Rare Books and Special Collections, Princeton University Library. *Page 2449:* © Hulton Deutsch Collection Limited. *Page 2522:* © UPI/Corbis-Bettman.

INDEX